FAMILIAR QUOTATIONS

FAMILIAR QUOTATIONS

A Collection of Passages, Phrases,
and Proverbs Traced to Their
Sources in Ancient and
Modern Literature

By

JOHN BARTLETT

ELEVENTH EDITION
Revised and Enlarged

CHRISTOPHER MORLEY, *Editor*

LOUELLA D. EVERETT, *Associate Editor*

BOSTON
LITTLE, BROWN AND COMPANY
1938

Published November 1937
Reprinted November 1937

PRINTED IN THE UNITED STATES OF AMERICA
BY H. WOLFF BOOK MFG. CO., NEW YORK

PREFACE TO THE ELEVENTH EDITION

What makes words memorable? It would be useful if we knew, but I doubt we ever shall. The subtle adhesions of adult memory are unintentional and unconscious; that is the true Learning by Heart we were told of in school, when they really meant Learning by Rote. Grown minds have an abated regard for the operations of conscious intelligence. We have found (in many a secret surprise) that the images which sink deepest are often those we scarcely knew, at the time, we were noticing at all. Like a skillful diver they went through the outer film of sense with very little splash.

The mind has a delicate property of surface tension, a retracting and tightening function, which creates a superficial envelope against too easy interruption or dispersion of the precious Me within. Whatever somehow punctures that protection is latent for memory. All we dare say about it is that it satisfies some inner necessity of our own, whether it be John Milton or Eddie Guest. It is most likely to be metrical, because we are so ourselves. Well did the word *incantation*, meaning "speech singable," come to assume the suggestion of witchcraft. One can melodize words for years without stopping to consider how silly they are. Who cares? The magic happens —

> It creeps into your mind, you find it there.
> You are my poem then, for in my heart
> Lovelier than a sonnet, you made rhyme
> And I had memorized you unaware.

The iniquity of oblivion — willfully translating Sir Thomas Browne's phrase to mean the unfairness of man's forgettings — weighs heavy on anthologists. In BARTLETT the problem is at least double: not only to preserve as many as possible of those Household Words which were the original editor's prime search, but to seize also some of the Mindhold Words (even of our own day) which the world hardly yet knows it has absorbed. This is in no sense a collection

[v]

of personal choices. It is foremost a salvage of those words which users of the English tongue have shown evidence not willingly to let die. This involves a debatable proportion of adipose sentiment and mediocre art — certainly not the least valuable part of the work for any student of intellectual coefficients. The Public must love bad verse, it reads so much of it. It is not often that one finds the

> jewel five words long
> That on the stretched forefinger of all **Time**
> Sparkles forever,

or

> All the charm of all the Muses
> Flowering in a lonely word.

One of the pleasures of this re-editing has been that one collaborator, by long experience with inquiries for the affable familiar ghosts of print, knows acutely what readers want; and the other believes himself to know what they ought to want. They have striven for a happy compromise; in the final decisions I must take full responsibility.

So we have here, within evident fallibilities, a viva voce of English confession from Caedmon bashful in the byre down to Nathalia Crane equally bashful at the paper-box factory in Brooklyn. Chronological arrangement sets the whole story in perspective. My own choice would be to read backward, beginning with moods familiar to-day and tracing upstream and uphill to the far woodlands where still tingles the voice of that first cuckoo-singer. When I was a boy in Baltimore I used to hear often of a place called Blue Ridge Summit. I never went there; it would probably disillusion; but what a picture of mystic beauty was in the name! To this day I think of the earliest masters of our tongue as not merely a beginning but also a goal. Chaucer is to me truly a Blue Ridge Summit. No poet was in the least astonished by Professor Einstein's pronouncements about the relativity of Time. We knew it always: here is Chaucer thinking the very thoughts that came to us, so hot and immediate and self-englamoured, to-day of days. It is not we who think, but life that thinks us, and Chaucer seems more modern to me than most radio announcers.

(In fact I'm not at all sure that the present era is "modern" at all.

We seem to be sliding rapidly into medievalism, the Thirty Years' War kind of thing. The poets are the most savage historians. There have been plenty who thought "The world falls asunder, being old," — and ends "Not with a bang but a whimper." — And in this preface, by the way, I'm going to quote whatever comes into my head without always grieving to identify. I've done enough identifying for a lifetime.)

You don't labor in a Pandect like this without perceiving that it's not just a scrapbook of belles-lettres, but also a sort of anthropology; a social history; a diary of the race. Here are the Now It's Got To Be Tolds of a good many generations. What is the quality of permanence that makes it worth while to pack in our scanty baggage, for one more trudging hike forward, the remarks of our predecessors? Man is a sententious animal, splendid in syllables and pompous in afterthought; nothing makes so bewildered an impression on him as the disparity between his words and his behavior. He shrewdly learns not to put too much of what he thinks into writing, lest he be held responsible. Therefore he is the more astonished, touched with delight and compunction, when he observes that what he himself had hidden someone else has uncovered. Having learned so much of the cunning of concealment he is fit to appreciate the joy of exposure. One of the most appealing phases of the entertainment called Literature is a psychological strip-tease.

It would be hard to aver which gives us more pleasure when we find it in print: what we wanted to say, or what we wanted not to say. The most familiar dictum of course is that of Pope —

> Nature to advantage dressed,
> What oft was thought, but ne'er so well expressed.

Our satisfaction lies in that delicate divergence between the words before us and the words we ourselves would have used for the same thought (if we had had the same thought). We must not *quite* have had it; but we must have been troubled by its approach. The happy man lives subconsciously to-day among thoughts that he will render articulate to-morrow. Nothing is more exciting (you can see hints and murmurs of it in all sorts of places) than to watch the world getting ready to think ideas quite different from those it is at the moment openly proclaiming.

[vii]

A book like this can be the bliss of solitude: but solitude is chiefly a bliss when it can be terminated at will. Probably the "quality of permanence" is most often found in those passages that strike through into the central loneliness of the heart, for which it scarcely expected any relief. Rilke, the brilliant young German, once said, "Love consists in this, that two solitudes protect and touch and greet each other." And literature is at its happiest in that function of companionship. It offers us the verification of our own secrets without any possible embarrassment. The same Rilke wrote a book, a very moving one for a few readers, called *The Journal of My Other Self*. I like to think that for some this BARTLETT can be the journal of another self, continuing over some six or seven hundred years. Not just a work of reference, but a work of conference; a nest egg for the mind. I have occasionally imagined the editors as Huck and Tom on the raft, floating down the big river and trying to pull aboard, from so much miscellaneous jetsam, what would be enduringly useful. The shock of accuracy is not the only quality that helps words to live; there is also the shock of surprise. And there is the haphazard contingent of mere chance. The great saying requires wit, occasion, and — good luck. Many such have undoubtedly gone into the record wrongly ascribed. Most of our hodiernal instinctive palavers were already old when Heywood collected them in 1546. As the title page of a famous eighteenth-century volume of erotica put it: *Prostant apud Neminem, sed tamen Ubique.*[1] This can hardly be duly translated; as every lover of language knows, nothing ever can. One can render, but there is always a shrinkage in carrying across. The more volatile the wine, the more ullage.

Still pursuing — just for the joy of speculation — this quiddity of endurance in written thought. The pleasure of self-identification; the delight of ideas shrewdly or beautifully put; and then how about a certain overtone of sincerity? Hard to define but recognizable to intuition. There has been much lamentation lately about the decline of poetry, the unintelligibility of modern verse, a general feeling that (as Roy Campbell said) the young poet is an angry man wearing his liver on his sleeve. Then one evening this spring I listened

---

[1] "For sale by no one, but available everywhere." *Nugae Venales sive Thesaurus Ridendi,* 1720. A good example of this kind of thing in our own time would be Mark Twain's disgraceful — and delightful — *1601.*

to the radio (I don't often) and heard (feeling that significant chilblain on the withers) voices saying something new in a new way. It was Archibald MacLeish's remarkable fable "The Fall of the City"; the first time (I think) that a play in verse, written designedly for that oral medium, had been broadcast. Here was a true poet using a fresh technique with beauty and power, saying things of meaning, adapting all the resources of an ancient skill to the opportunities of to-day. The ear is an unsophistered recipient. Among so vast a listening there must have been many who were not likely to observe the conscious efficacy of the poet's devices, or even his political wit, but they must have felt the thrill of that drama on the clairaudient nerve. I said to myself with delight, Here begins a whole new era for poetic drama. And I shall continue to disregard, as I always have, any grievances about the failure of the arts. True, they are painfully subject to imitative corruptions of mode, but (as the Chinaman said) in due season we are granted the artists we require; and they the emotions they need. The emotion comes first.

Sincerity — passion — the sense that the man has something to say — the old alarm "there's something burning" — these rise above, or make unnecessary, "pretty little tricks of style." How it pleases to hear Sir Walter Raleigh (the modern one, distinguished learner and teacher of letters) confess in a fine sonnet "I never cared for literature as such." He continues: —

> The spondee, dactyl, trochee, anapaest,
> Do not inflame my passions in the least;
> And cultured persons do not please me much. . . .

But there is one kind of writing, he exclaims, that surely blasts our indifference: —

> One book among the rest is dear to me;
> As when a man, having tired himself in deed
> Against the world, and falling back to write,
> Sated with love, or crazed by vanity,
> Or drunk with joy, or maimed by Fortune's spite,
> Sets down his Paternoster and his Creed.

Of these personal outcries, wrung from men and women in the strong twist of life, there are plenty in BARTLETT. There is also more laughter than you might suppose. The English-speaking peoples are considered sombre-minded, but they often have a way of making a joke when no one is listening. They even laugh at themselves, which makes it unanimous. — It often strikes me as odd, by the way, that some of the most amusing books in the world have no reputation for humor. I have seen a roomful of people in the purest mirth over Dr. Johnson's *Lives of the Poets,* which is not commonly thought of as a work of merriment. But, as Swift suggested in the "Voyage of Laputa," extracting sunshine from cucumbers is an unlikely project, and too many of the professionals of letters have the cucumber temperament. The sudden glory that maketh those grimaces called laughter (Hobbes) must always remain rare, though a man who retains any of the impressible gust of childhood can scarcely walk along a city street without at least a twitching cheek. But, taken in print, we are mostly a solemn crowd. As Dr. Johnson said of Pope's grotto, "An Englishman has more frequent need to solicit than exclude the sun." And I think that in this new edition BARTLETT is a little less gloomy than before. But old John Bartlett himself, as his letters show, had his lighter moments. His first edition appeared while he was a bookseller in Cambridge, Massachusetts; and only a creature of humor can survive the difficulties of that exacting trade. Let the others hanker, as Jeremy Taylor said, for "strange flesh and heaps of money and popular noises."

The arts, we were saying, are specially susceptible to changes of fashion. One of the prime values of chronological arrangement is that it's possible to trace the diverse tastes, the prevailing moods, of different epochs; and to see how zigzag are the frontiers between periods which textbooks mark off (for convenience only) so net and clear. Everything has to be said all over again, in its own tone of voice, for each succeeding generation. (And thank goodness: if people realized, for instance, that almost everything conceivably sayable had been said in Montaigne, why should they ever buy another book?) I suppose it is natural for the very young to resent, or reject, the thought that everything has already been said; at any rate a strong instinct bids them listen to it only from some of their own kidney. Take for instance the note of *lacrimae rerum.* About every thirty or forty years some singer is likely to pluck that string with just the touch the human ear craves. Toward 1790 it was Robert Burns. In the 1820's, Byron. About 1860 FitzGerald was adapting the tune from Omar. In the late 90's it was A. E. Housman; in the 20's of our own century, Miss Millay. It will be due again presently, and will be (quite rightly) hailed by its contemporaries as thrillingly new, poignant, unique. In the condensation of BARTLETT the reader has the pleasure of tracing down his own paths of affiliation and literary genealogy; and the rather frequent cross references often show the same thought expressed in different ways, which is the supreme vintage-tasting luxury of the connoisseur. I have smiled a good many times at the remark made by a publisher on the wrapper of a recent book of verse by a young writer. " —— ," they said, "scorns the devices of his poetic elders." As if that were conceivably so of anyone sensitive enough, or grateful enough to our inheritance, to be worth the name of poet. Certainly no one ever undertook the task of editing an anthology without saluting old footprints in joy and reverence, as Chaucer himself did in that exquisite passage at the close of his Troilus. Let me quote a word from the king of critics in our lifetime, the magnificent Saintsbury, who spoke of "the most degrading of intellectual slaveries — that of the exclusive Present." [1]

So much may be said as reassurance for those who might have feared that our good old BARTLETT had too violently Gone Modern. At the same time rather extensive clearances have been made. The job, I have said to myself many times, is really that of sweeping the hearth of literature. A menial service, in one sense, yet also in any civilized household an important one. We serve here, no matter how many the errors of judgment and oversight, as proxy for Posterity. It costs a pang to sweep out some worthy who "flourished" in his time and was a hearty favorite fifty years ago but is plainly no longer necessary. (Humanity can't go on carrying all its baggage forever.) Ancient footnotes that have come downstream through former editions have often been dropped when they seemed pointless: one remembers the man (I forget who) described by Dr. Johnson as having "a rage for saying something when there was nothing to be said." A good many shrill huzzas from the patriots of '76 (especially around Boston) have faded out, and perhaps some allusions to unfamiliar names such as Axel Oxenstiern and Von Münch Bellinghausen. Wordsworth's bleatings when he was fecund rather than facund; lozenges from the original Smith Brothers (of the *Rejected Ad-*

[1] "Trollope Revisited," in his *Collected Essays,* Vol. II.

dresses); lesser bits of Byron, once so fashionable; Robert Pollok, a meteor in his day and confidently consigned to immortality by his epitaph — how much of that sort of thing is still essential to this wallowing world? How about the mysterious "Miss Wrother," to whom Hope "told a flattering tale" but disappointment followed? Sometimes mere chance intervened to prolong someone's foundering clutch on futurity. I was about to throw Letitia Landon overboard when Governor Alfred Landon of Kansas was nominated to the Presidency (in 1936). So I pulled L. E. L. back onto the raft as a small kindness toward keeping the name going. (L. E. L. may yet live longer than that candidacy.) Sometimes an old tidbit was left in with perhaps a little touch of malice, to emphasize the ironies of time — for instance Nat Willis's "On the Death of Harrison," who

ascended Fame's ladder so high:
From the round at the top he has stepped to the sky.

But there are awkward questions to ask one's self. How much of "Aurora Leigh" is still desirable? Who was Thomas Kibble Hervey, and how did he get into BARTLETT X when his exact contemporary Nathaniel Hawthorne didn't? For there were some curious gaps in the Tenth Edition. No Herman Melville, no Emily Dickinson, no O. Henry — most astonishing of all, not a line of William Blake. Even De Quincey and Hazlitt appeared only in footnotes.

The questions we asked ourselves just above are ill to answer; however answered there is sure to be grievance somewhere. In such a job one resigns one's self to being the most reprobated editor in print. Perhaps even, to the observer twenty-three years hence, present oversights will seem as fantastic as those of 1914 do now. Previous editors adhered, almost with pedantry, to the touchstone of *familiarity*. Only phrases or quotations that had gained wide recognition, become hypodermic, were admitted. It becomes then a significant footnote in literary history to observe that in 1914 neither Melville nor Emily Dickinson had gained enough currency to catch the eye of our toastmaster. In the matter of new inclusions this edition is not so stringent: we have tried to make literary power the criterion rather than width and vulgarity of fame.

But the hearth must be swept; the new clean fire is not to be choked by too much debris of the past. Every fire builder knows that a bed of

ashes and used coals helps the fresh blaze, catches the glow and ra-
diates warmth, gives depth and bottom to the flame — up to a point.
But there comes a time to open the chute and rake out old cinders. I
breathe a small secret sigh over some of the vanished authors, and
keep their names to myself. Unless some morbid scholiast compares
the indexes of the Eleventh and Tenth Editions they will never be
missed. And there continues to be joy in those who go bravely on
toward the unknown future by the glory of one great line alone —
for instance John William Burgon, with his "rose-red city, half as
old as Time." As for Axel Oxenstiern and Von Münch Bellinghausen, they deserve a footnoted or marginal immortality for their names
alone, and as far as I can help them toward it I shall. They fascinate
me as the pale anonymous curate (squelched by Dr. Johnson) fascinated Max Beerbohm. See Beerbohm's essay "A Clergyman" — indeed, see all his essays.

The tactful editor does not too intrusively nudge his guests. What
a genial impudence was that of the magazine that used to allot "Reading Time" — so many minutes and seconds — for its customers to
accomplish a given piece. Suppose, in the middle of an article or
story, one actually paused to meditate? If we had to specify any limited duration for this work, I suppose it would have to be twenty-
three years, since that seems to be the established elapse between editions of BARTLETT; 1891 — 1914 — 1937 — we should be ripe for
another about 1960. I observe that longevity has been vouchsafed to
BARTLETT editors. Old J. B. died at eighty-five, and Dr. Dole at
eighty-four. The present editors are hopeful. I like the letter J. B.
wrote to his publisher on June 4, 1891, when correcting proof for the
Ninth Edition. He then described his book as "a middle-aged gentleman of thirty-six years, with the tallow which age brings. . . .
There never was such a repertory before and it can never be super-
seded. You will be troubled at not finding some of your good things,
but what could I do. The sensation of fulness is agreeable, that of
repletion is painful."

We have eased the old gentleman of some spiritual tallow; but the
interesting thing is to see how well the senior matter persists. I have
not used a tape measure on the galley proofs, but with one portentous
exception the order of the leaders in space allotted runs pretty much

as it did. Shakespeare and the King James Bible are far in the lead. After them come Milton and Pope. The excitement is to see that Kipling now stands, in the matter of space conceded, just about abreast of Tennyson and Byron. Then come Dr. Johnson, Wordsworth, Browning, Emerson and Longfellow. This reckoning has not been precisely calculated, but I think no fair-minded observer will deny that it approximates the general human suffrage up to date. And more than our predecessors, we have paid willing homage to the Muse of our own day. How vast a world of doing and saying (and doubting) has come to view since Dr. Dole wrote the Tenth Edition preface in — mark the date — July, 1914. Of the modern short-buskined goddess we have at least been able (with Herrick)

to descrie
The happy dawning of her thigh.

Dr. Dole spoke of himself as Elisha inheriting the mantle of Elijah. The successor of Elisha, one remembers, was Jehu; of whom I only know that they broke a box of oil over his head and he drove (or was driven) furiously.[1]

One does not without a twinge of sentiment say good-by to so long a pastime. I can't help feeling like Old Kaspar in Southey's poem, who sits at his cottage door in the sunset while the grandchildren are playing with the skulls — the skulls of dead authors. The cottage is actual, too: I built myself a pine-wood cabin, as aloofly jungled as a Long Island suburb would permit, to consort with the shade of John Bartlett. And my mind goes back to a bitter wintry day when an unexpected visitor joined me. I went out to the cabin to work, and was startled to see sheets of MS. all over the floor, pictures fallen from the top of the shelves, and a certain 1855 Overholt bottle (long empty, but souvenir of an old literary pilgrimage) toppled over but fortunately undamaged. At first I supposed some human mischief, but picking up Miss Everett's folios of beautiful typescript I saw unmistakable proof that the intruder was a bird. Then, from a shadowy perch just under the roof, he swooped across and gave me a start. It was an owl, a handsome fellow with tall ears and speckled breast. He must have come down the chimney. Flattened warily in the triangle of the rafters he watched me steadily. I whistled at him, tried

[1] II Kings, 9.

to frighten him through the open door, but he only coasted from side to side — coming too near my head for comfort. I had no mind to sit there with him perched above me, so I gathered papers and left him in charge, with the door open for exit.

Was it, or was it not, the shade of J. B. himself, offering suggestions? There was a certain facial resemblance . . . and the 1855 bottle was a coincidence: that was the year of BARTLETT's first publication (also *Leaves of Grass*). And the book he had chosen for most frequent perching was the Webster's Unabridged. At any rate it was suggestive to be visited by the bird of wisdom in person. We have tried to adhere to the admirable motto long used on the publisher's colophon, *Non refert quam multos sed quam bonos habeas*. Though there have been times when the editors felt like the Elizabethans described by Virginia Woolf — "Thought plunged into a sea of words and came up dripping." And I have smiled too at a passage in Melville's preface to *Moby Dick* —

This mere painstaking burrower and grubworm of a poor devil appears to have gone through the long Vaticans and street-stalls of the earth, picking up whatever random allusions he could anyways find in any book whatsoever, sacred or profane.

I have left to the end what is the most urgent to be said. Looking wistfully, from time to time, into important books of consultation, I saw something apropos in Professor Clarke Ansley's preface to the *Columbia Encyclopedia* (1935). "The traditional rule for preparing a reference work is, Find the right woman and do what she says." I cannot sufficiently pay tribute to Miss Louella D. Everett, on whom fell the onerous preliminary spadework, and whose accuracy and patience are beyond the scope of creatures like myself. Miss Everett's ideal vision of an all-embracing treasury was, in some respects, beyond the bounds of physical and editorial possibility, and we had our mutual heartburns over problems of omission. But I used to tell her, and still urge it, that there is need of a companion and quite different kind of volume, which might be called *Not in Bartlett* — for which I suggest a pleasant early-Victorian kind of subtitle: *The Librarian's Godsend*. Miss Everett's devotion to this enterprise can never be fully estimated except by her collaborator. As Browning said of Justinian's Pandects, she made precise

What simply sparkled in men's eyes before,
Twitched in their brow or quivered on their lip,
Waited the speech they called but would not come.

If this book is efficient in arrangement and cross-fertility it is due to her indexophile habits. She is Patience personified and this is her monument. One remembers the story current in the press a few years ago, about a vast new post-office building in Pittsburgh. It was magnificent in every circumstance of Federal grandeur, with classic façade, marble paving, pneumatic chutes, sorting and filing niceties, stamp-moistening tricks, apertures for "Letters in Bulk" and what not. The only thing that was forgotten was a quite ordinary slot where a citizen could mail an everyday letter. The most elaborate lavish of Letters in Bulk is futile if access is difficult for the individual emergency.

The section of Translations — which obviously cannot be exhaustive in a book chiefly devoted to the memorabilia of our own tongue — was first examined by Professor J. D. M. Ford, professor of the French and Spanish Languages at Harvard, who made important suggestions. It was subsequently edited in detail by Mr. Theodore McClintock, who has had large experience in educational publishing and whose knowledge of German has been of much value. Mr. McClintock also copy-edited the whole text from beginning to end. The Index, the most wearisome and certainly the most indispensable feature of BARTLETT, is the work of Miss Beatrice L. Miller.

Correspondents and friends who have helped with suggestions, whether available or not, are gratefully thanked, and necessarily without identification. But no editorial scruple can forgo mention of Mr. Roger L. Scaife, of Little, Brown and Company, who has been this edition's appointed overseer from the beginning. It was he who knew with unerring instinct both when to castigate and when to condole. To renew the image of Jehu, it was Mr. Scaife who, as requirement prompted, either broke the box of oil or drove furiously.

And so to press —

CHRISTOPHER MORLEY.

Roslyn Heights, L. I.
May 22, 1937

PREFACE.

The object of this work is to show, to some extent, the obligations our language owes to various authors for numerous phrases and familiar quotations which have become "household words."

This Collection, originally made without any view of publication, has been considerably enlarged by additions from an English work on a similar plan, and is now sent forth with the hope that it may be found a convenient book of reference.

Though perhaps imperfect in some respects, it is believed to possess the merit of accuracy, as the quotations have been taken from the original sources.

Should this be favorably received, endeavors will be made to make it more worthy of the approbation of the public in a future edition.

Cambridge, May, 1855.

FACSIMILE OF PREFACE TO FIRST EDITION

PREFACE TO THE NINTH EDITION

"Out of the old fieldes cometh al this new corne fro yere to yere,"
And out of the fresh woodes cometh al these new flowres here.

The small thin volume, the first to bear the title of this collection, after passing through eight editions, each enlarged, now culminates in its ninth, — and with it, closes its tentative life.

This extract from the Preface of the fourth edition is applicable to the present one: —

"It is not easy to determine in all cases the degree of familiarity that may belong to phrases and sentences which present themselves for admission; for what is familiar to one class of readers may be quite new to another. Many maxims of the most famous writers of our language, and numberless curious and happy turns from orators and poets, have knocked at the door, and it was hard to deny them. But to admit these simply on their own merits, without assurance that the general reader would readily recognize them as old friends, was aside from the purpose of this collection. Still, it has been thought better to incur the risk of erring on the side of fulness."

With the many additions to the English writers, the present edition contains selections from the French, and from the wit and wisdom of the ancients. A few passages have been admitted without a claim to familiarity, but solely on the ground of coincidence of thought.

I am under great obligations to M. H. Morgan, Ph.D., of Harvard University, for the translation of Marcus Aurelius, and for the translation and selections from the Greek tragic writers. I am indebted to the kindness of Mr. Daniel W. Wilder, of Kansas, for the quotations from Pilpay, with contributions from Diogenes Laertius, Montaigne, Burton, and Pope's Homer; to Dr. William J. Rolfe for quotations from Robert Browning; to Mr. James W. McIntyre for quotations from Coleridge, Shelley, Keats, Mrs. Browning, Robert

[xix]

Browning, and Tennyson. And I have incurred other obligations to friends for here a little and there a little.

It gives me pleasure to acknowledge the great assistance I have received from Mr. A. W. Stevens, the accomplished reader of the University Press, as this work was passing through the press.

In withdrawing from this very agreeable pursuit, I beg to offer my sincere thanks to all who have assisted me either in the way of suggestions or by contributions; and especially to those lovers of this subsidiary literature for their kind appreciation of former editions.

Accepted by scholars as an authoritative book of reference, it has grown with its growth in public estimation with each reissue. Of the last two editions forty thousand copies were printed, apart from the English reprints. The present enlargement of text equals three hundred and fifty pages of the previous edition, and the index is increased with upwards of ten thousand lines.

JOHN BARTLETT

Cambridge, March, 1891

PREFACE TO THE TENTH EDITION

"BARTLETT'S FAMILIAR QUOTATIONS" has long since been accepted as indispensable to every scholar and to every writer; it is a
book for every library and every household. Embodying years of
labor and research on the part of its author, "Familiar Quotations"
passed through nine editions, each enlarged, and attained a sale of
three hundred thousand copies before Mr. Bartlett's death in 1905
at the age of eighty-five. Unrevised for twenty-three years, it has still
remained the best book of the kind, though a considerable body of
apothegms have been knocking for admittance to its classic hall of
fame.

In this new edition the main body of John Bartlett's compilation,
up to the beginning of the nineteenth century, has been left practically unchanged; the chief purpose of the revision has been to
incorporate in the work quotations from those writers whose place
in literature has been achieved since the issue of the Ninth Edition in
1891. The selections from Poe, Whittier, Longfellow, Lowell, and
other "best writers of their day" have been filled out extensively, and
many new authors are represented by passages which have met with
the seal of popular approval and are distinctly worthy of perpetua-
tion. In this way the book has been greatly enriched. The attempt
has been made not to admit anything which John Bartlett's impec-
cable judgment would have rejected. It is not always easy for Elisha
to wear the mantle of Elijah; but it is Elisha's business to carry on
his predecessor's work in the same spirit.

A collection of all possible quotations which would satisfy that
multitudinous race of folk who apply to the almost omniscient editors of "Notes and Queries" columns for aid in tracing the origin of
some favorite quotation, half forgotten, would have to be as big as
the Encyclopedia. In the Tenth Edition of "Familiar Quotations"
the aim has been to maintain the high literary standard set by its

predecessors, and ephemeral quotations will not be found included in its pages. The present editor hopes that a book which has given so much pleasure and proved so useful in the past may still find favor with those interested in the best things in literature.

NATHAN HASKELL DOLE

Boston, July, 1914

INDEX OF AUTHORS

NOTE: Names, not British or American, preceded by the prepositional forms *d', de, du, de la,* and *von,* are listed in order of the names, not in order of the prepositional forms.

The asterisk (*) preceding a name indicates that quotations from that author included as Notes are so numerous that the editors consider it impracticable to give the numbers of all the pages where they occur.

[xxiii]

ANONYMOUS AND COLLECTIVE WORKS AND GROUPS
OF QUOTATIONS

FAMILIAR QUOTATIONS

CAEDMON [1]
[*Floruit* 670]

From the text of Benjamin Thorpe
[1782–1870]

Light was first
Through the Lord's word
Named day:
Beauteous, bright creation!
> *Creation. The First Day*

The fiend with all his comrades
Fell then from heaven above,
Through as long as three nights and
    days,
The angels from heaven into hell;
And them all the Lord transformed to
    devils,
Because they his deed and word
Would not revere.
> *Ibid. The Fall of the Rebel Angels*

THOMAS OF ERCILDOUN
[1220–1297]

Whate'er betide,
Haig shall be Haig of Bemersyde.
> *Quoted by* SIR WALTER SCOTT:
> *Thomas the Rhymer, Part 2,*
> *Minstrelsy of the Scottish*
> *Border*

ANONYMOUS
[*Circa* 1250]

Sumer is icumen in,
  Lhude sing cuccu!
Groweth sed, and bloweth med,

And springth the wude nu —
  Sing cuccu!
> *Cuckoo Song.*[1] *Stanza 1*

GEOFFREY CHAUCER
[1340–1400]

From the text of Walter William
Skeat [1835–1912],[2] *and also the*
Globe Edition [Macmillan, 1907]

Hard is his herte that loveth nought
In May.
> *The Romaunt of the Rose. Line 85*

The tyme, that may not sojourne,
But goth, and never may retourne,
As water that doun renneth ay,
But never drope retourne may.
> *Ibid. Line 381*

As round as appel was his face.
> *Ibid. Line 819*

The more she yaf awey,
The more, y-wis, she hadde alwey.
> *Ibid. Line 1159*

A ful gret fool is he, y-wis,
That bothe riche and nigard is.
> *Ibid. Line 1171*

To rede, and dryve the nyght away.
> *The Book of the Duchesse. Line 49*

Morpheus,
Thou knowest him wel, the god of sleep.
> *Ibid. Line 136*

    I was waked
With smale foules a gret hepe,
That had affrayed me out of slepe.
> *Ibid. Line 294*

The lyf so short, the craft so long to
  lerne,[3]
Th' assay so hard, so sharp the conquering.
> *The Parlement of Foules. Line 1*

---

[1] It is pleasant to remember that the Muse of English Verse was born in a stable. The Venerable Bede in his *Ecclesiastical History* (*Book IV, Chapter 24*) tells the legend of Caedmon, the bashful hostler, who retired to the barn when his turn came to recite. There, in his sleep, he was visited by "a person" who said "Caedmon, sing me something." With those words begins the story of English poetry.

[1] The most ancient English song that appears with the musical notes attached. — THOMAS WARTON [1728–1790]: *History of English Poetry*

[2] *The Complete Works of Geoffrey Chaucer.* Oxford University Press [1933].

[3] Ars longa, vita brevis (Art is long: life is brief). — HIPPOCRATES: *Aphorism I*

For out of olde feldes, as men seith,
Cometh al this newe corn fro yeer to
    yere;
And out of olde bokes, in good feith,
Cometh al this newe science that men
    lere.
> *The Parlement of Foules. Line 22*

The jalous swan, ayens his deth that
singeth.
> *Ibid. Line 342*

Nature, the vicaire of th' almyghty
lorde.
> *Ibid. Line 379*

A fool can noght be stille.
> *Ibid. Line 574*

Now welcom somer, with thy sonne
soft,[1]
That hast this wintres weders over-
shake.
> *Ibid. Line 680*

Flee fro the prees, and dwelle with soth-
fastnesse.
> *Truth. Line 1*

Werk wel thy-self, that other folk canst
rede.
> *Ibid. Line 6*

The wrastling for this worlde axeth a
fal.
> *Ibid. Line 16*

A fool may eek a wys man ofte gyde.
> *Troilus and Criseyde.*
> *Book I, Line 630*

Eek somtyme it is craft to seme flee
Fro thing which in effect men hunte
faste.
> *Ibid. Line 747*

Of harmes two, the lesse is for to chese.[2]
> *Ibid. Book II, Line 470*

Lord, this is an huge rayn!
This were a weder for to slepen inne!
> *Ibid. Book. III, Line 656*

Right as an aspen leef she gan to quake.
> *Ibid. Line 1200*

For of fortunes sharp adversitee
The worst kinde of infortune is this,
A man to have ben in prosperitee,
And it remembren, whan it passed is.
> *Troilus and Criseyde.*
> *Book III, Line 1625*

Oon ere it herde, at the other out it
went.[1]
> *Ibid. Book IV, Line 434*

A wonder last but nyne night never in
toune.[2]
> *Ibid. Line 588*

Thus maketh vertue of necessitee.[3]
> *Ibid. Line 1586*

I am right sory for your hevinesse.
> *Ibid. Book V, Line 140*

He that nought n'assayeth, nought n'a-
cheveth.
> *Ibid. Line 1786*

Go, litel book, go litel myn tragedie.
> *Ibid.*

Farewel my boke, and my devocion!
> *The Legend of Good Women,*
> *Prologue, Line 39*

Of alle the floures in the mede,
Than love I most these floures white
and rede,
Swiche as men callen daysies in our
toun.
> *Ibid. Line 41*

Whan that Aprille with his shoures sote
The droghte of Marche hath perced to
the rote.
> *The Canterbury Tales, Prologue.*
> *Line 1*

---

[1] Went in at the tone eare and out at the
tother. — HEYWOOD: *Proverbes, Part II,
Chap. IX*

[2] This wonder lasted nine daies. — HEY-
WOOD: *Proverbes, Part II, Chap. I*
See Shakespeare, page 70.

[3] Also *The Knightes Tale, Line 3042;* and
The Squieres Tale, Line 593
To make a virtue of necessity. — SHAKE-
SPEARE: *Two Gentlemen of Verona, Act IV.
Sc. 1, L. 62.* MATHEW HENRY: *Comm. on Ps.
XXXVII.* DRYDEN: *Palamon and Arcite*
See Burton, page 125.
In the additions of Hadrianus Julius to the
Adages of Erasmus, he remarks, under the
head of *Necessitatem edere,* that a very famil-
iar proverb was current among his country-
men — "Necessitatem in virtutem commutare"
(To make necessity a virtue).
Laudem virtutis necessitati damus (We give
to necessity the praise of virtue). — QUINTIL-
IAN: *Inst. Orat., I, 8, 14*

---

[1] In a somer sesun, whan softe was the
sonne. — WILLIAM LANGLAND [1330–1400]:
The Vision of Piers Plowman, Prologue

[2] Of two evils the less is alway to be
chosen. — THOMAS À KEMPIS: *Imitation of
Christ, Book III, Chap. XII.* HOOKER: *Polity,
Book V, Chap. LXXXI*
Of two evils I have chose the least. — PRIOR:
Imitation of Horace
E duobus malis minimum eligendum (Of
two evils, the least should be chosen). —
ERASMUS: *Adages.* CICERO: *De Officiis, III, 1*

And smale fowles maken melodye,
That slepen al the night with open yë,
(So priketh hem nature in hir corages):
Than longen folk to goon on pilgrim-
ages.
The Canterbury Tales, Prologue.
Line 9

And of his port as meke as is a mayde.
Ibid. Line 69

He was a verray parfit gentil knight.
Ibid. Line 72

He coude songes make and wel endyte.
Ibid. Line 95

Ful wel she song the service divyne,
Entuned in hir nose ful semely;
And Frensh she spak ful faire and
fetisly,
After the scole of Stratford atte Bowe,
For Frensh of Paris was to hir unknowe.
Ibid. Line 122

Amor vincit omnia.[1]
Ibid. Line 162

His palfrey was as broun as is a berye.
Ibid. Line 207

Therfore, in stede of weping and
preyeres,
Men moot yeve silver to the povre
freres.
Ibid. Line 231

A Clerk ther was of Oxenford also.
Ibid. Line 285

For him was lever have at his beddes
heed
Twenty bokes, clad in blak or reed,
Of Aristotle and his philosophye,
Than robes riche, or fithele, or gay
sautrye,
But al be that he was a philosophre,
Yet hadde he but litel gold in cofre.
Ibid. Line 293

And gladly wolde he lerne, and gladly
teche.
Ibid. Line 308

No-wher so bisy a man as he ther nas,
And yet he semed bisier than he was.
Ibid. Line 321

For he was Epicurus owne sone.
Ibid. Line 336

He was a good felawe.[1]
The Canterbury Tales, Prologue.
Line 395

His studie was but litel on the bible.
Ibid. Line 438

For gold in phisik is a cordial,
Therfore he lovede gold in special.
Ibid. Line 443

This noble ensample to his sheep he
yaf,
That first he wroghte, and afterward
he taughte.
Ibid. Line 496

If gold ruste, what shal iren do?
Ibid. Line 500

But Cristes lore, and his apostles
twelve,
He taughte, and first he folwed it him-
selve.
Ibid. Line 527

And yet he hadde a thombe of gold.[2]
Ibid. Line 563

And whan that he wel dronken hadde
the wyn,
Than wolde he speke no word but
Latyn.
Ibid. Line 637

Who-so shal telle a tale after a man,
He moot reherce, as ny as ever he can,
Everich a word, if it be in his charge,
Al speke he never so rudeliche and
large;
Or elles he moot telle his tale untrewe,
Or feyne thing, or finde wordes new.
Ibid. Line 731

For May wol have no slogardye a-night.
The sesoun priketh every gentil herte,
And maketh him out of his sleep to
sterte.
Ibid. The Knightes Tale. Line 1042

Ech man for himself.
Ibid. Line 1182

May, with alle thy floures and thy
grene,
Wel-come be thou, fair fresshe May.
Ibid. Line 1510

---

[1] Love overcomes all obstacles. — VIRGIL:
Eclogue 10, L. 69

[1] King of good fellows. — SHAKESPEARE:
King Henry V, Act V, Sc. 2, L. 260

[2] In allusion to the proverb, "Every honest
miller has a golden thumb."

That feeld hath eyen, and the wode
hath eres.[1]
> *The Canterbury Tales. The*
> *Knightes Tale. Line 1522*

Now up, now doun, as boket in a welle.
> *Ibid. Line 1533*

Cupido,
Up-on his shuldres winges hadde he
two;
And blind he was, as it is ofte sene;
A bowe he bar and arwes brighte and
kene.
> *Ibid. Line 1963*

Up roos the sonne, and up rose Emelye.
> *Ibid. Line 2273*

Myn be the travaille, and thyn be the
glorie!
> *Ibid. Line 2406*

She was al his chere.
> *Ibid. Line 2683*

What is this world? what asketh man
to have?
Now with his love, now in his colde
grave
Allone, with-outen any companye.
> *Ibid. Line 2777*

This world nis but a thurghfare full of
wo,
And we ben pilgrimes, passing to and
fro;
Deeth is an ende of every worldly sore.
> *Ibid. Line 2847*

Jesu Crist, and sëynt Benedight,
Blesse this hous from every wikked
wight.
> *Ibid. The Milleres Tale. Line 3483*

And broghte of mighty ale a large quart.
> *Ibid. Line 3497*

Yet in our asshen olde is fyr y-reke.[2]
> *Ibid. The Reeve's Prologue.*
> *Line 3882*

The gretteste clerkes been noght the
wysest men.
> *The Canterbury Tales. The Reves*
> *Tale. Line 4054*

Thurgh thikke and thurgh thenne.[1]
> *Ibid. Line 4066*

So was hir joly whistle wel y-wet.
> *Ibid. Line 4155*

At Cristemasse merie may ye daunce.
> *Ibid. The Man of Lawe, Prologue.*
> *Line 126*

For in the sterres, clerer than is glas,
Is writen, god wot, who-so coude it rede,
The deeth of every man.
> *Ibid. Line 194*

Sathan, that ever us waiteth to bigyle.
> *Ibid. Line 582*

Mordre wol out, certein, it wol nat
faille.[2]
> *Ibid. The Prioresses Tale. Line 1766*

This may wel be rym dogerel.
> *Ibid. Melibeus, Prologue. Line 2115*

Ful wys is he that can him-selven
knowe.[3]
> *Ibid. The Monkes Tale. Line 3329*

He was of knighthode and of fredom
flour.
> *Ibid. Line 3832*

For dronkenesse is verray sepulture
Of mannes wit and his discrecioun.
> *Ibid. The Pardoner's Tale.*
> *Line 448*

---

[1] Fieldes have eies and woodes have eares.
— HEYWOOD: *Proverbes, Part II, Chap. V*
Wode has erys, felde has sigt. — *King Edward and the Shepherd, MS.* [*circa* 1300]
Walls have ears. — HAZLITT: *English Proverbs, etc.*, P. 446 [*ed. 1869*]
> Woods have tongues
> As walls have ears.
TENNYSON: *Idylls of the King, Balin and Balan,* L. 522
[2] E'en in our ashes live their wonted fires.
— GRAY: *Elegy, St. 23*

---

[1] Through thicke and thin. — SPENSER: *The Faerie Queene, Book III, Canto I, St. 17.* DRAYTON: *Nymphidiæ.* MIDDLETON: *The Roaring Girl, Act IV, Sc. 2.* KEMP: *Nine Days' Wonder.* BUTLER: *Hudibras, Part I, Canto II, L. 370.* DRYDEN: *Absalom and Achitophel, Part II, L. 414.* POPE: *Dunciad, Book II.* STERNE: *Tristram Shandy, Book II, Chap. 9.* COWPER: *John Gilpin, St. 10*
[2] Also in *The Nonne Preestes Tale,* Lines 4242 and 4247.
Murder will out. — CERVANTES: *Don Quixote, Part I, Book III, Chap. 8*
Murder, though it have no tongue, will speak
With most miraculous organ.
SHAKESPEARE: *Hamlet, Act II, Sc. 2, L. 630*
See also Burton, page 122.
[3] Thales was asked what was very difficult; he said, "To know one's self." — DIOGENES LAERTIUS: *Thales, IX*
Know then thyself, presume not God to scan;
The proper study of mankind is man.
ALEXANDER POPE: *An Essay on Man, Epistle II, L. 1*

Gret swering is a thing abhominable,
And false swering is yet more reprev-
able.

> *The Canterbury Tales, Prologue.*
> *The Pardoner's Tale. Line 631*

Thus walke I, lyk a restelees caityf,
And on the ground, which is my modres
gate,
I knokke with my staf, bothe erly and
late,
And seye, "leve moder, leet me in!"

> *Ibid. Line 728*

In his owene grece I made him frye.[1]

> *Ibid. The Wife of Bath's Prologue.*
> *Line 487*

What thing we may nat lightly have,
Ther-after wol we crye al-day and
crave.

> *Ibid. Line 517*

Greet prees at market maketh dere
ware,
And to greet cheep is holde at litel prys.

> *Ibid. Line 522*

And for to see, and eek for to be seye.[2]

> *Ibid. Line 552*

I holde a mouses herte nat worth a
leek,[3]
That hath but oon hole for to sterte to,
And if that faille, thanne is al y-do.

> *Ibid. Line 572*

Loke who that is most vertuous alway,
Privee and apert, and most entendeth
ay
To do the gentil dedes that he can,

And tak him for the grettest gentil
man.

> *The Canterbury Tales. The Tale*
> *of the Wyf of Bathe. Line 1113*

That he is gentil that doth gentil dedis.[1]

> *Ibid. Line 1170*

The lady of the hous [2] ay stille sat.

> *Ibid. The Somnour's Tale. Line 2200*

For though we slepe or wake, or rome,
or ryde,
Ay fleeth the tyme, it nil no man abyde.

> *Ibid. The Clerkes Tale. Line 118*

Love is noght old as when that it is
newe.

> *Ibid. Line 857*

This flour of wyfly pacience.

> *Ibid. Line 919*

No wedded man so hardy be t'assaille
His wyves pacience, in hope to finde
Grisildes, for in certein he shall faille!

> *Ibid. Line 1180*

It is no childes pley
To take a wyf with-oute avysement.

> *Ibid. The Marchantes Tale.*
> *Line 1530*

Love is blind.

> *Ibid. Line 1598*

My wit is thinne.

> *Ibid. Line 1682*

Ther nis no werkman, what-so-ever he
be,
That may bothe werke wel and hastily; [3]
This wol be doon at leyser parfitly.[4]

> *Ibid. Line 1832*

The Pegasee,
The hors that hadde winges for to flee.

> *Ibid. The Squieres Tale. Line 207*

Therfor bihoveth him a ful long spoon
That shal ete with a feend.[5]

> *Ibid. Line 602*

---

[1] Frieth in her own grease. — HEYWOOD:
Proverbes, Part I, Chap. XI

Melted him in his own grease. — SHAKE-
SPEARE: *Merry Wives of Windsor, Act II,
Sc. 1, L. 69*

[2] To see and to be seen. — BEN JONSON:
Epithalamion, St. III, L. 4. GOLDSMITH: *Citizen of the World, letter 71*

Spectatum veniunt, veniunt spectentur ut
ipsæ (They come to see; they come that they
themselves may be seen). — OVID: *The Art of
Love, I, 99*

[3] Consider the little mouse, how sagacious
an animal it is which never entrusts his life
to one hole only. — PLAUTUS: *Truculentus,
Act IV, Sc. 4*

The mouse that hath but one hole is quickly
taken. — GEORGE HERBERT: *Jacula Prudentum*
The mouse that always trusts to one poor hole
Can never be a mouse of any soul.

POPE: *Paraphrase of the Prologue, L. 298*

[1] Handsome is that handsome does. — OLI-
VER GOLDSMITH: *The Vicar of Wakefield,
Chap. 1*

[2] Are you the lady of the house? — SHAKE-
SPEARE: *Twelfth-Night, Act I, Sc. 5, L. 198*

[3] Haste makes waste. — HEYWOOD: *Proverbes, Part I, Chap. II*

Nothing can be done at once hastily and
prudently. — PUBLIUS SYRUS: *Maxim 357*

[4] Ease and speed in doing a thing do not
give the work lasting solidity or exactness of
beauty. — PLUTARCH: *Life of Pericles*

[5] Hee must have a long spoon, shall eat

Men loven of propre kinde newfangel-
nesse.
The Canterbury Tales. The Squieres
Tale. Line 610
I am lorn with-outen remedye.
Ibid. Line 629
Fy on possessioun
But-if a man be vertuous with-al.
Ibid. The Frankelin to the Squier.
Line 686
Pacience is an heigh vertu certeyn.
Ibid. The Frankeleyns Tale.
Line 773
Servant in love, and lord in mariage.
Ibid. Line 793
Tak this for fynal answer as of me.
Ibid. Line 987
It is agayns the proces of nature.
Ibid. Line 1345
Trouthe is the hyeste thing that men
may kepe.
Ibid. Line 1479
For whan a man hath over-greet a wit,
Ful oft him happeth to misusen it.
Ibid. The Canon Yeoman's Prologue.
Line 648
But al thing which that shyneth as the
gold
Nis nat gold, as that I have herd it
told.[1]
Ibid. The Chanouns Yemannes Tale.
Line 962

---

with the devill. — HEYWOOD: *Proverbes, Part
II, Chap. V*
He must have a long spoon that must eat
with the devil. — SHAKESPEARE: *Comedy of
Errors, Act IV, Sc. 3, L. 64*
[1] Hit is not al gold that glareth. *The Hous
of Fame, I, 272*
Tyrwhitt says this is taken from the *Para-
bolæ of* ALANUS DE INSULIS, who died in
1294, — Non teneas aurum totum quod splen-
det ut aurum (Do not hold everything as
gold which shines like gold).
All is not golde that outward shewith
bright. — LYDGATE: *On the Mutability of
Human Affairs*
Gold all is not that doth golden seem. —
SPENSER: *Faerie Queene, Book II, Canto VIII,
St. 14*
All that glisters is not gold. — SHAKESPEARE:
Merchant of Venice, Act II, Sc. 7, L. 65.
GOOGE: *Eglogs, etc.* [1563]. HERBERT: *Jacula
Prudentum*
All is not gold that glisteneth. — MIDDLE-
TON: *A Fair Quarrel, verse 1*

The firste vertu, sone, if thou wolt lere,
Is to restreyne and kepe wel thy tonge.
*The Canterbury Tales. The
Maunciples Tale. Line 332*
Thing that is seyd, is seyd; and forth
it gooth.
Ibid. Line 355
For the proverbe seith: that manye
smale maken a greet.[1]
Ibid. The Persones Tale. Sect. 21
Litel Lowys my sone, I aperceyve wel
by certeyne evydences thyn abilite to
lerne sciences touching nombres and
proporciouns. . . . Therefore have I
yeven the a suffisant Astrolabie as for
oure orizonte compowned after the lati-
tude of Oxenforde.
A Treatise on the Astrolabe.[2]

JOHN WYCLIFFE
[? –1384]

I believe that in the end the truth will
conquer.
To the Duke of Lancaster [1381]
*(Quoted by J. R. GREEN: A Short
History of the English People.
Chap. 5)*

THOMAS À KEMPIS
[1380–1471]

Be not angry that you cannot make
others as you wish them to be, since you
cannot make yourself as you wish to be.
*Imitation of Christ. Book I,
Chap. 16 (Quoted by DR. JOHN-
SON [1778]: Boswell's Life of
Dr. Johnson, Vol. II, Page 165,
Everyman Edition)*
Man proposes, but God disposes.[3]
Ibid. Chap. 19

All, as they say, that glitters is not gold. —
DRYDEN: *The Hind and the Panther.*
Que tout n'est pas or c'on voit luire (Everything is not gold that one sees shining). —
Li Diz de freire Denise Cordelier [circa 1300]
[1] Many small make a great. — HEYWOOD:
Proverbs, Part I, Chap. XI
[2] Written for his ten-year-old boy — and
while hardly a "Familiar Quotation" it has
sure power to touch the thoughtful mind.
Also quoted by SIR ARTHUR QUILLER-COUCH
in his admirable *Oxford Book of English
Prose* [1925]
[3] This expression is of much greater antiquity. It appears in the *Chronicle of Battel Ab-*

What canst thou see elsewhere which thou canst not see here? Behold the heaven and the earth and all the elements; for of these are all things created.

> *Imitation of Christ. Book I.*
> *Chap. 20*

It is easier not to speak a word at all than to speak more words than we should.

> *Ibid.*

No man ruleth safely but he that is willingly ruled.

> *Ibid.*

And when he is out of sight, quickly also is he out of mind.[1]

> *Ibid. Chap. 23*

Of two evils, the less is alway to be chosen.[2]

> *Ibid. Book III, Chap. 12*

JOHN FORTESCUE
[*Circa* 1395–1476]

Moche Crye and no Wull.[3]

> *De Laudibus Legum Angliae.*
> *Chap. 10*

Comparisons are odious.[4]

> *Ibid. Chap. 19*

---

bey, *P. 27* (Lower's translation), and in *The Vision of Piers Ploughman, Line 13994* ed. 1550. HERBERT: *Jacula Prudentum*
A man's heart deviseth his way; but the Lord directeth his steps. — *Proverbs, XVI, 9*
[1] Out of syght, out of mynd.—GOOGE: *Eglogs.* [1563]
   And out of mind as soon as out of sight.
           LORD BROOKE: *Sonnet LVI.*
   Fer from eze, fer from herte,
   Quoth Hendyng.
      HENDYNG: *Proverbs, MSS* [*circa* 1320]
I do perceive that the old proverbis be not alwaies trew, for I do finde that the absence of my Nath. doth breede in me the more continuall remembrance of him. — *Ann Lady Bacon to Jane Lady Cornwallis* [1613]
On page 19 of *The Private Correspondence of Lady Cornwallis*, Sir Nathaniel Bacon speaks of the owlde proverbe, "Out of sighte, out of mynde."
   Out of sight and out of mind. — ROBERT BROWNING: *The Inn Album, I*
[2] See Chaucer, page 4.
[3] All cry and no wool. — BUTLER: *Hudibras, Pt. I, C. I, L. 852*
[4] CERVANTES: *Don Quixote* (Lockhart's ed.), *Part II, Chap. I.* LYLY: *Euphues* [1580]. MARLOWE: *Lust's Dominion, Act III, Sc. 4.* BURTON: *Anatomy of Melancholy, Part III,*

HENRY VI
[1421–1471]

Kingdoms are but cares,
   State is devoid of stay;
Riches are ready snares,
   And hasten to decay.

> *From* SIR JOHN HARRINGTON'S
> *Nugae Antiquae* (*Quoted in* ED-
> WARD BULWER LYTTON'S *novel,*
> *The Last of the Barons, Book*
> *III, Chap. 5*)

SIR RICHARD HOLLAND
[*Floruit* 1450]

O Douglas, O Douglas!
Tendir and trewe.

> *The Buke of the Howlat.*[1]
> *Stanza XXXI*

JOHN SKELTON
[*Circa* 1460–1529]

There is nothynge that more dyspleaseth God,
Than from theyr children to spare the rod.[2]

> *Magnyfycence. Line 1954*

He ruleth all the roste.[3]

> *Why Come Ye Not to Courte.*
> *Line 198*

Sec. 3. THOMAS HEYWOOD: *A Woman Killed with Kindness* [first ed. in 1607], Act I, Sc. 1. DONNE: *Elegy, VIII.* HERBERT: *Jacula Prudentum.* GRANGE: *Golden Aphrodite*
   Comparisons are odorous. — SHAKESPEARE: *Much Ado about Nothing, Act III, Sc. 5, L. 18*
[1] The allegorical poem of *The Howlat* was composed about the middle of the fifteenth century. The author was a Scottish poet, an adherent of the Douglases. *The Buke of the Howlat*, edited by David Laing, was printed by the Bannatyne Club [1823].
   Do you know the truth now up in heaven,
   Douglas, Douglas, tender and true?
      DINAH MULOCK CRAIK: *Too Late, St. 3*
[2] He that spareth the rod hateth his son. — *Proverbs, XIII, 24*
   They spare the rod and spoyl the child. — RALPH VENNING: *Mysteries and Revelations* (second ed.), *P. 5.* [1649]
   Spare the rod and spoil the child. — BUTLER: *Hudibras, Part II, C. I, L. 843*
[3] Rule the rost. — HEYWOOD: *Proverbes, Part I, Chap. V*
   Her that ruled the rost. — THOMAS HEYWOOD: *History of Women*
   Rules the roast. — JONSON, CHAPMAN, MAR-

In the spight of his teeth.[1]

Colyn Cloute. Line 939

He knew what is what.[2]

Ibid. Line 1106

By hoke ne by croke.[3]

Ibid. Line 1240

The wolfe from the dore.

Ibid. Line 1531

Old proverbe says,
That byrd ys not honest
That fyleth hys owne nest.[4]

Poems against Garnesche

Maide, wydowe, or wyffe.

Philip Sparrow

Stedfast of thought,
Well made, well wrought,
Far may be sought,
Ere you can find
So courteous, so kind,
As merry Margaret,
This midsummer flower,
Gentle as falcon,
Or hawk of the tower.

To Mistress Margaret Hussey

SIR THOMAS MORE [5]
[1478-1535]

The Utopians wonder how any man should be so much taken with the glar-

ing doubtful lustre of a jewel or stone, that can look up to a star, or to the sun himself.

Utopia: Of Jewels and Wealth

They wonder much to hear that gold, which in itself is so useless a thing, should be everywhere so much esteemed, that even men for whom it was made, and by whom it has its value, should yet be thought of less value than it is.

Ibid.

They have no lawyers among them, for they consider them as a sort of people whose profession it is to disguise matters.

Ibid. Of Law and Magistrates

Plato by a goodly similitude declareth, why wise men refraine to medle in the commonwealthe. For when they see the people swarme into the stretes, and daily wet to the skinne with rayne, and yet can not persuade them to goe out of the rayne, they do kepe them selfes within their houses, seeinge they cannot remedye the follye of the people.[1]

Ibid. Concerning the Best State of a Commonwealth

Assist me up, and in coming down I will shift for myself.

Said at the scaffold, on the way to execution

Wait till I put aside my beard, for that never committed treason.

To the headsman on the scaffold

HUGH LATIMER
[1485-1555]

Play the man, Master Ridley; we shall this day light such a candle, by God's grace, in England, as I trust shall never be put out.[2]

Addressed to Nicholas Ridley [1500-1555] as they were being burned alive at Oxford, for her-

---

STON: *Eastward Ho, Act II, Sc. 1.* SHAKESPEARE: *2 Henry VI, Part II, Act I, Sc. 1, L. 110*

His wife "ruled the roast."—WASHINGTON IRVING: *Knickerbocker's History of New York, Book IV, Chap. 4*

Rules the roast. — ROBERT BROWNING: *Mr. Sludge, "the Medium."* Also *The Ring and the Book, VI,* and *Prince Hohenstiel-Schwangau.* ALEXANDER SMITH: *Dreamthorp — Christmas*

[1] In spite of my teeth. — MIDDLETON: *A Trick to Catch the Old One, Act I, Sc. 2.* FIELDING: *Eurydice Hissed*

[2] He knew what's what. — BUTLER: *Hudibras, Pt. I, C. I, L. 149*

[3] In hope her to attaine by hooke or crooke. — SPENSER: *Faerie Queene, Book III, C. I, St. 17*

The spoile of peoples evill gotten good,
The which her sire had scrap't by hooke or crooke.

Ibid. Book V, C. II, St. 27

[4] It is a foule byrd that fyleth his owne nest. — HEYWOOD: *Proverbes, Part II, Chap. V*

[5] Canonized by Pope Pius XI [1935].

[1] In the modern phrase, "not sense enough to come in out of the rain."

[2] I shall light a candle of understanding in thine heart, which shall not be put out. — *2 Esdras, XIV, 25*

esy, October 16, 1555[1] (*Quoted by* J. R. GREEN: *A Short History of the English People, Chap. 7*)

SIR DAVID LYNDSAY
[1490–1555]

They gave me first ane thing they call
  citandum;
Within aucht days I gat but *libellan-*
  dum;
Within ane month I gat *ad opponen-*
  dum;
In ane half year I gat *inter loquendum;*
An syne I gat — how call ye it? — *ad*
  replicandum;
But, I could never ane word yet under-
  stand him.
    The Exactions and Delay of the Law
But or they came half gate. to *con-*
  cludendum,
The fient a plack was left for to defend
  him.
                Ibid.
Thus they postponed me twa year, with
  their train,
Syne, *hodie ad octo,* bade me come
  again.
                Ibid.
Of *pronunciandum* they made we won-
  der fain;
But I gat ne'er my gude grey meir again.
                Ibid.

JOHN HEYWOOD [2]
[1497–1580]

The loss of wealth is loss of dirt,
As sages in all times assert;

The happy man's without a shirt.[1]
      Be Merry Friends
Let the world slide,[2] let the world go;
A fig for care, and a fig for woe!
If I can't pay, why I can owe,
And death makes equal the high and
  low.
                Ibid.
All a green willow is my garland.
      The Green Willow
Haste maketh waste.
    Proverbes. Part I, Chap. II
Beware of, Had I wist.[3]
                Ibid.
Good to be merie and wise.[4]
                Ibid.
Beaten with his owne rod.
                Ibid.
Look ere ye leape.[5]
                Ibid.
He that will not when he may,
When he would he shall have nay.[6]
                Ibid.

[1] This line is the theme of many poems, e. g. SIR WALTER SCOTT: *The Search after Happiness; or, the Quest of Sultaun Solimaun.* JOHN HAY: *The Enchanted Shirt.* EDWIN MARKHAM: *The Shoes of Happiness.* EDGAR A. GUEST: *Envy*
  In a footnote to his poem, Scott says the hint for it came from a novel, *La Camiscia Magica,* by GIAM BATTISTA CASTI. A similar work is *The Seven Wives of Bluebeard,* by ANATOLE FRANCE.

[2] Let the world slide. — *Towneley Mysteries, P. 101* [1420]. SHAKESPEARE: *Taming of the Shrew, induc. 1.* BEAUMONT AND FLETCHER: *Wit without Money, Act V, Sc. 2*

[3] A common exclamation of regret occurring in Spenser, Harrington, and the older writers. An earlier instance of the phrase occurs in the *Towneley Mysteries.*

[4] 'Tis good to be merry and wise. — JONSON, CHAPMAN, MARSTON: *Eastward Ho, Act I, Sc. 1.* BURNS: *Here's a health to them that's awa'*

[5] Look ere thou leap. — *Tottel's Miscellany* [1557] and Tusser's *Five Hundred Points of Good Husbandry, Of Wiving and Thriving* [1573]
  Thou shouldst have looked before thou hadst leapt. — JONSON, CHAPMAN, MARSTON: *Eastward Ho, Act V, Sc. 1*
  Look before you ere you leap. — BUTLER: *Hudibras, Pt. II, C. II, L. 502*

[6] He that will not when he may,
  When he will he shall have nay.
    BURTON: *Anatomy of Melancholy, Pt. III, Sec. 2, Memb. 5, Subsect. 5*

[1] See Latimer and Ridley in the might
  Of Faith stand coupled for a common
  flight!
  WORDSWORTH: *Ecclesiastical Sonnets, Part II, XXXIV, Latimer and Ridley*

[2] The *Proverbes of* JOHN HEYWOOD is the earliest collection of English colloquial sayings. It was first printed in 1546. The title of the edition of 1562 is *John Heywoodes Woorkes. A Dialogue conteyning the number in effect of all the proverbes in the English tounge, compact in a matter concernynge two maner of Maryages,* etc. The selection here given is from the edition of 1874 (a reprint of 1598), edited by JULIAN SHARMAN. See also the *Oxford Dictionary of English Proverbs* compiled by W. G. SMITH [1935].

The fat is in the fire.[1]
> *Proverbes. Part I, Chap. II*

When the sunne shineth, make hay.
> *Ibid.*

When the iron is hot, strike.[2]
> *Ibid.*

The tide tarrieth no man.[3]
> *Ibid.*

Than catch and hold while I may, fast binde, fast finde.[4]
> *Ibid.*

And while I at length debate and beate the bush,
There shall steppe in other men and catch the burdes.[5]
> *Ibid.*

While betweene two stooles my taile goe to the ground.[6]
> *Ibid.*

So many heads so many wits.[7]
> *Ibid.*

He that wold not when he might,
He shall not when he wolda.
> PERCY: *Reliques, The Baffled Knight*

[1] All the fatt's in the fire. — MARSTON: *What You Will* [1607]

[2] You should hammer your iron when it is glowing hot. — PUBLIUS SYRUS: *Maxim 262*
Strike whilst the iron is hot. — RABELAIS: *Book II, Chap. XXXI.* WEBSTER: *Westward Hoe, Tom A'Lincolne.* FARQUHAR: *The Beaux' Stratagem, IV, 1*

[3] Hoist up saile while gale doth last,
Tide and wind stay no man's pleasure.
> ROBERT SOUTHWELL: *St. Peter's Complaint* [1595]
Nae man can tether time or tide. — BURNS: *Tam O'Shanter.*

[4] Fast bind, fast find;
A proverb never stale in thrifty mind.
> SHAKESPEARE: *Merchant of Venice, Act II, Sc. 5, L. 54*
Also in *Jests of Scogin* [1565]

[5] It is this proverb which Henry V is reported to have uttered at the siege of Orleans. "Shall I beat the bush and another take the bird?" said King Henry.

[6] Entre deux arcouns chet cul à terre (Between two stools one sits on the ground. — *Les Proverbes del Vilain, MS. Bodleian* [circa 1303]
S'asseoir entre deux selles le cul à terre (One falls to the ground in trying to sit on two stools). — RABELAIS: *Book I, Chap. II*

[7] As many men, so many minds. — TERENCE: *Phormio, II, 4*
As the saying is, So many heades, so many wittes. — QUEEN ELIZABETH: *Godly Meditacyon of the Christian Sowle* [1548]

Wedding is destiny,
And hanging likewise.[1]
> *Proverbes. Part I, Chap. II*

Happy man, happy dole.[2]
> *Ibid.*

God never sends th' mouth but he sendeth meat.
> *Ibid. Chap. IV*

Like will to like.
> *Ibid.*

A hard beginning maketh a good ending.
> *Ibid.*

When the skie falth we shall have Larkes.[3]
> *Ibid.*

More frayd then hurt.
> *Ibid.*

Feare may force a man to cast beyond the moone.[4]
> *Ibid.*

Nothing is impossible to a willing hart.
> *Ibid.*

The wise man sayth, store is no sore.
> *Ibid. Chap. V*

Let the world wagge,[5] and take mine ease in myne Inne.[6]
> *Ibid.*

So many men so many mindes. — GASCOIGNE: *Glass of Government*

[1] Hanging and wiving go by destiny. — *The Schole-hous for Women* [1541]. SHAKESPEARE: *Merchant of Venice, Act II, Sc. 9, L. 83*
Marriage and hanging go by destiny; matches are made in heaven. — BURTON: *Anatomy of Melancholy, Part III, Sec. 2, Memb. 5, Subsect. 5*

[2] Happy man be his dole. — SHAKESPEARE: *Merry Wives, Act III, Sc. 4, L. 68; Winter's Tale, Act I, Sc. 2, L. 163.* BUTLER: *Hudibras, P. I, C. III, L. 168*

[3] Si les nues tomboyent esperoyt prendre les alouettes (If the clouds fall, one may hope to catch larks). — RABELAIS: *Book I, Chap. XI*

[4] To "cast beyond the moon" is a phrase in frequent use by the old writers. LYLY: *Euphues, P. 78.* THOMAS HEYWOOD: *A Woman Killed with Kindness*

[5] Let the world slide. — SHAKESPEARE: *Taming of the Shrew, Ind. 1, L. 6,* and, Let the world slip, *Ind. 2, L. 146*

[6] Shall I not take mine ease in mine inn? — SHAKESPEARE: *Henry IV, Part I, Act III, Sc. 3, L. 91*

Rule the rost.[1]

> *Proverbes. Part I, Chap. V*

Hold their noses to grinstone.[2]

> *Ibid.*

Better to give then to take.[3]

> *Ibid.*

When all candles bee out, all cats be gray.

> *Ibid.*

No man ought to looke a given horse in the mouth.[4]

> *Ibid.*

I perfectly feele even at my fingers end.[5]

> *Ibid. Chap. VI*

A sleveless errand.[6]

> *Ibid. Chap. VII*

We both be at our wittes end.[7]

> *Ibid. Chap. VIII*

Reckeners without their host must recken twice.

> *Ibid.*

A day after the faire.[8]

> *Ibid.*

Cut my cote after my cloth.[1]

> *Proverbes. Part I, Chap. VIII*

The neer to the church, the further from God.[2]

> *Ibid. Chap. IX*

Now for good lucke, cast an old shooe after me.

> *Ibid.*

Better is to bow then breake.[3]

> *Ibid.*

It hurteth not the toung to give faire words.[4]

> *Ibid.*

Two heads are better then one.

> *Ibid.*

A short horse is soone currid.[5]

> *Ibid. Chap. X*

To tell tales out of schoole.

> *Ibid.*

To hold with the hare and run with the hound.[6]

> *Ibid.*

She is nether fish nor flesh, nor good red herring.[7]

> *Ibid.*

All is well that ends well.[8]

> *Ibid.*

---

[1] See Skelton, page 9. SHAKESPEARE: *Henry VI, Part II, Act I, Sc. I, L. 110.* THOMAS HEYWOOD: *History of Women*

[2] Hold their noses to the grindstone. — MIDDLETON: *Blurt, Master-Constable, Act III, Sc. 3*
See Burton, page 125.

[3] It is more blessed to give than to receive. — *Acts, XX, 35*

[4] This proverb occurs in Rabelais, *Book I, Chap. XI;* in *Vulgaria Stambrigi* [*circa* 1510]; in Butler, *Part I, Canto I, Line 490.* Archbishop Trench says this proverb is certainly as old as Jerome of the fourth century, who, when some found fault with certain writings of his, replied that they were free-will offerings, and that it did not behove to look a gift horse in the mouth.

[5] RABELAIS: *Book IV, Chap. LIV.* At my fingers' ends. — SHAKESPEARE: *Twelfth-Night, Act I, Sc. 3, L. 85*

[6] The origin of the word "sleveless," in the sense of unprofitable, has defied the most careful research. It is frequently found allied to other substantives. Bishop Hall speaks of the "sleveless tale of transubstantiation," and Milton writes of a "sleveless reason." Chaucer uses it in the *Testament of Love.* — SHARMAN
On a sleeveless errand. — SHAKESPEARE: *Troilus and Cressida, Act V, Sc. 4, L. 9*
Sending every one of her children upon some sleeveless errand, as she terms it. JOSEPH ADDISON: *The Spectator, No. 47* [April 24, 1711] (referring to April Fool errands).

[7] At their wit's end. — *Psalm CVII, 27*

[8] THOMAS HEYWOOD: *If you know not me, etc.* [1605]. TARLTON: *Jests* [1611]

---

[1] A relic of the Sumptuary Laws. One of the earliest instances occurs, 1530, in the interlude of *Godly Queene Hester.*

[2] Qui est près de l'église est souvent loin de Dieu (He who is near the Church is often far from God). — *Les Proverbes Communs* [*circa* 1500]

[3] Rather to bowe than breke is profitable; Humylite is a thing commendable.
> *The Morale Proverbs of Cristyne,* translated from the French [1390] by Earl Rivers, and printed by Caxton in 1478

[4] Fair words never hurt the tongue. — JONSON, CHAPMAN, MARSTON: *Eastward Ho, Act IV, Sc. I*

[5] FLETCHER: *Valentinian, Act II, Sc. I*

[6] HUMPHREY ROBERT: *Complaint for Reformation* [1572]. LYLY: *Euphues* [1579] (Arber's reprint), *P. 107*

[7] Neither fish nor flesh, nor good red herring. — SIR H. SHEERES: *Satyr on the Sea Officers.* TOM BROWN: *Æneus Sylvius's Letter.* DRYDEN: *Epilogue to the Duke of Guise*

[8] Si finis bonus est, totum bonum erit (If the end be well, all will be well). — *Gesta Romanorum, Tale LXVII*
SHAKESPEARE: *All's Well that Ends Well, Act IV, Sc. 4, L. 35,* and *Act V, Sc. I, L. 25*

Of a good beginning cometh a good end.[1]

Proverbes. Part I, Chap. X

Shee had seene far in a milstone.[2]

Ibid.

Better late than never.[3]

Ibid.

When the steede is stolne, shut the stable durre.[4]

Ibid.

Pryde will have a fall;
For pryde goeth before and shame commeth after.[5]

Ibid.

She looketh as butter would not melt in her mouth.[6]

Ibid.

The still sowe eats up all the draffe.[7]

Ibid.

Ill weede growth fast.[8]

Ibid.

It is a deere collop
That is cut out of th' owne flesh.[9]

Ibid.

[1] Who that well his warke beginneth,
The rather a good ende he winneth.
GOWER: *Confessio Amantis*
[2] LYLY: *Euphues* (Arber's reprint), *P. 288*
[3] TUSSER: *Five Hundred Points of Good Husbandry, An Habitation Enforced.* BUNYAN: *Pilgrim's Progress.* MATHEW HENRY: *Commentaries, Matthew XXI.* MURPHY: *The School for Guardians*
Potius sero quam nunquam (Rather late than never). — LIVY: *IV, II, 14*
[4] Quant le cheval est emblé dounke ferme fols l'estable (When the horse has been stolen, the fool shuts the stable). — *Les Proverbes del Vilain*
[5] Pride goeth before destruction, and a haughty spirit before a fall. — *Proverbs, XVI, 18*
Pryde goeth before, and shame cometh behynde. — *Treatise of a Gallant* [*circa* 1510]
[6] She looks as if butter would not melt in her mouth. — SWIFT: *Polite Conversation*
[7] 'Tis old, but true, still swine eat all the draff. — SHAKESPEARE: *Merry Wives of Windsor, Act IV, Sc. 2, L. 112*
[8] Ewyl weed ys sone y-growe. — *MS. Harleian* [*circa* 1490]
An ill weed grows apace. — CHAPMAN: *An Humorous Day's Mirth*
Great weeds do grow apace. — SHAKESPEARE: *Richard III, Act II, Sc. 4, L. 13.* BEAUMONT AND FLETCHER: *The Coxcomb, Act IV, Sc. 4*
[9] God knows thou art a collop of my flesh. — SHAKESPEARE: *I Henry VI, Act V, Sc. 4, L. 18*

Beggars should be no choosers.[1]

Proverbes. Part I, Chap. X

Every cocke is proud on his owne dunghill.[2]

Ibid. Chap. XI

The rolling stone never gathereth mosse.[3]

Ibid.

To robbe Peter and pay Poule.[4]

Ibid.

A man may well bring a horse to the water,
But he cannot make him drinke without he will.

Ibid.

Men say, kinde will creepe where it may not goe.[5]

Ibid.

The cat would eate fish, and would not wet her feete.[6]

Ibid.

While the grasse groweth the horse starveth.[7]

Ibid.

[1] Beggars must be no choosers. — BEAUMONT AND FLETCHER: *The Scornful Lady, Act V, Sc. 3*
[2] Þet coc is kene on his owne mixenne. — Þe *Ancren Riwle* [*circa* 1250]
[3] The stone that is rolling can gather no moss. — TUSSER: *Five Hundred Points of Good Husbandry*
A rolling stone gathers no moss. — PUBLIUS SYRUS: *Maxim 524.* GOSSON: *Ephemerides of Phialo.* MARSTON: *The Fawn*
Pierre volage ne queult mousse (A rolling stone gathers no moss). — *De l'hermite qui se désespéra pour le larron que ala en paradis avant que lui* [13th century]
[4] To rob Peter and pay Paul is said to have derived its origin when, in the reign of Edward VI, the lands of St. Peter at Westminster were appropriated to raise money for the repair of St. Paul's in London. Also found in *Wycliffe's Works*, Vol. III, page 174. See Herbert, page 138.
[5] You know that love
Will creep in service when it cannot go.
SHAKESPEARE: *Two Gentlemen of Verona, Act IV, Sc. 2, L. 19*
[6] Shakespeare alludes to this proverb in *Macbeth, Act I, Sc. 7, L. 44:*
Letting I dare not wait upon I would,
Like the poor cat i' the adage.
Cat lufat visch, ac he nele his feth wete. — *MS. Trinity College, Cambridge* [*circa* 1250]
[7] Whylst grass doth grow, oft sterves the seely steede. — WHETSTONE: *Promos and Cassandra* [1578]

Better one byrde in hand than ten in
the wood.[1]
> *Proverbes. Part I, Chap. XI*

Rome was not built in one day.
> *Ibid.*

Yee have many strings to your bowe.[2]
> *Ibid.*

Many small make a great.[3]
> *Ibid.*

Children learne to creepe ere they can
learne to goe.
> *Ibid.*

Better is halfe a lofe than no bread.
> *Ibid.*

Nought venter nought have.[4]
> *Ibid.*

Children and fooles cannot lye.[5]
> *Ibid.*

Set all at sixe and seven.[6]
> *Ibid.*

All is fish that comth to net.[7]
> *Ibid.*

Who is worse shod than the shoemaker's
wife?[8]
> *Ibid.*

While the grass grows —
The proverb is something musty.
> SHAKESPEARE: *Hamlet, Act III, Sc. 2,
> L. 365*

[1] An earlier instance occurs in Heywood, in
his *Dialogue on Wit and Folly* [*circa* 1530].
See Herbert, page 137.
[2] Two strings to his bow. — HOOKER:
Polity, Book V, Chap. LXXX. CHAPMAN:
D'Ambois, Act II, Sc. 3. BUTLER: *Hudibras,
Part III, Canto I, Line 1.* CHURCHILL: *The
Ghost, Book IV.* FIELDING: *Love in Several
Masques, Sc. 13*
[3] See Chaucer, page 8.
[4] Naught venture naught have. — TUSSER:
*Five Hundred Points of Good Husbandry,
October Abstract*
[5] 'Tis an old saw, Children and fooles
speake true. — LYLY: *Endymion*
[6] Set all on sex and seven. — CHAUCER:
Troilus and Criseyde, Book IV, Line 622; also
Towneley Mysteries
At six and seven. — SHAKESPEARE: *Richard
II, Act II, Sc. 2, L. 121*
Things going on at sixes and sevens. —
GOLDSMITH: *The Good-Natur'd Man, Act I*
[7] All's fish they get that cometh to net. —
TUSSER: *Five Hundred Points of Good Hus-
bandry, February Abstract*
Where all is fish that cometh to net. —
GASCOIGNE: *Steele Glas.* [1575]
[8] Him that makes shoes go barefoot him-
self. — BURTON: *Anatomy of Melancholy,
Democritus to the Reader*

One good turne asketh another.
> *Proverbes. Part I, Chap. XI*

By hooke or crooke.[1]
> *Ibid.*

She frieth in her owne grease.[2]
> *Ibid.*

Who waite for dead men shall goe long
barefoote.
> *Ibid.*

I pray thee let me and my fellow have
A haire of the dog that bit us last night.[3]
> *Ibid.*

> But in deede,
A friend is never knowne till a man have
neede.
> *Ibid.*

This wonder (as wonders last) lasted
nine daies.[4]
> *Ibid. Part II, Chap. I*

New brome swepth cleene.[5]
> *Ibid.*

All thing is the woorse for the wearing.
> *Ibid.*

Burnt child fire dredth.[6]
> *Ibid. Chap. II*

All is not Gospell that thou doest
speake.[7]
> *Ibid.*

[1] This phrase derives its origin from the
custom of certain manors where tenants are
authorized to take fire-bote *by hook or by
crook;* that is, so much of the underwood
as may be cut with a crook, and so much of
the loose timber as may be collected from the
boughs by means of a hook. One of the earliest
citations of this proverb occurs in John Wycliffe's *Controversial Tracts* [*circa* 1370]. See
Skelton, page 9. RABELAIS: *Book V, Chap.
XIII.* DU BARTAS: *The Map of Man.* SPENSER:
Faerie Queene, Book III, Canto I, St. 17.
BEAUMONT AND FLETCHER: *Women Pleased,
Act I, Sc. 3*
[2] See Chaucer, page 7.
[3] In old receipt books we find it invariably
advised that an inebriate should drink spar-
ingly in the morning some of the same liquor
which he had drunk to excess over night.
[4] See Chaucer, page 4.
[5] Ah, well I wot that a new broome sweep-
eth cleane. — LYLY: *Euphues* (Arber's reprint), *P. 89*
[6] Brend child fur dredth,
Quoth Hendyng.
> *Proverbs of Hendyng, MSS.*
A burnt child dreadeth the fire. — LYLY:
Euphues (Arber's reprint), *P. 319*
[7] You do not speak gospel. — RABELAIS:
Book I, Chap. XIII

Love me litle, love me long.[1]

Proverbes. Part II, Chap. II

A fooles bolt is soone shot.[2]

Ibid. Chap. III

A woman hath nine lives like a cat.[3]

Ibid. Chap. IV

A peny for your thought.[4]

Ibid.

You stand in your owne light.

Ibid.

Though chaunge be no robbry.

Ibid.

Might have gone further and have fared worse.

Ibid.

The grey mare is the better horse.[5]

Ibid.

Three may keepe counsayle, if two be away.[6]

Ibid. Chap. V

Small pitchers have wyde eares.[7]

Ibid.

Many hands make light warke.

Ibid.

[1] MARLOWE: *Jew of Malta, Act IV, Sc. 6.*
BACON: *Formularies.* See Herrick, page 133.
[2] Sottes bolt is sone shote. — *Proverbs of Hendyng, MSS.*
  A fool's bolt is soon shot. — SHAKESPEARE: *King Henry V, Act III, Sc. 7, L. 137*
[3] It has been the Providence of Nature to give this creature nine lives instead of one. — BIDPAY: *The Greedy and Ambitious Cat, Fable III* [B.C.]
[4] LYLY: *Euphues* (Arber's reprint), *P. 80*
[5] *Pryde and Abuse of Women* [1550]. *The Marriage of True Wit and Science.* BUTLER: *Hudibras, P. II, C. I, L. 698.* FIELDING: *The Grub Street Opera, Act II, Sc. 4.* PRIOR: *Epilogue to Lucius.*
  Lord Macaulay (*History of England, Vol. I, Chap. III*) thinks that this proverb originated in the preference generally given to the gray mares of Flanders over the finest coach-horses of England. Macaulay, however, is writing of the latter half of the seventeenth century, while the proverb was used a century earlier.
[6] Two may keep counsel when the third's away. — SHAKESPEARE: *Titus Andronicus, Act IV, Sc. 2, L. 145*
  Three can hold their peace if two be away. — HERBERT: *Jacula Prudentum*
[7] Pitchers have ears. — SHAKESPEARE: *The Taming of the Shrew, Act IV, Sc. 4, L. 52; Richard III, Act II, Sc. 4, L. 37*
  Little pitchers have wide ears. — HERBERT: *Jacula Prudentum*

The greatest Clerkes be not the wisest men.[1]

Proverbes. Part II, Chap. V

Out of Gods blessing into the warme Sunne.[2]

Ibid.

There is no fire without some smoke.[3]

Ibid.

One swallow maketh not summer.[4]

Ibid.

Fieldes have eies and woods have eares.[5]

Ibid.

A cat may looke on a King.

Ibid.

It is a foule byrd that fyleth his owne nest.[6]

Ibid.

Have yee him on the hip.[7]

Ibid.

Hee must have a long spoone, shall eat with the devill.[8]

Ibid.

It had need to bee
A wylie mouse that should breed in the cats eare.[9]

Ibid.

Leape out of the frying pan into the fyre.[10]

Ibid.

[1] See Chaucer, page 6.
[2] Thou shalt come out of a warme sunne into Gods blessing. — LYLY: *Euphues*
  Thou out of Heaven's benediction comest
  To the warm sun.
      SHAKESPEARE: *King Lear, Act II, Sc. 2, L. 168*
[3] There can no great smoke arise, but there must be some fire. — LYLY: *Euphues* (Arber's reprint), *P. 153*
[4] One swallow prouveth not that summer is neare. — NORTHBROOKE: *Treatise against Dancing* [1577]
[5] See Chaucer, page 6.
[6] See Skelton, page 10.
[7] I have thee on the hip. — SHAKESPEARE: *Merchant of Venice, Act IV, Sc. 1, L. 335; Othello, Act II, Sc. 1, L. 317*
[8] See Chaucer, page 7.
[9] A hardy mouse that is bold to breede
  In cattis eeris.
      Order of Foles [MS. *circa* 1450]
[10] The same in *Don Quixote* (Lockhart's ed.), *Part I, Book III, Chap. IV.* BUNYAN: *Pilgrim's Progress.* FLETCHER: *The Wild-Goose Chase, Act IV, Sc. 3*

Time trieth troth in every doubt.[1]
> *Proverbes. Part II, Chap. V*

Mad as a march hare.[2]
> *Ibid.*

Much water goeth by the mill
That the miller knoweth not of.[3]
> *Ibid.*

He must needes goe whom the devill
doth drive.[4]
> *Ibid. Chap. VII*

Set the cart before the horse.[5]
> *Ibid.*

The moe the merrier.[6]
> *Ibid.*

To th' end of a shot and beginning of a
fray.[7]
> *Ibid.*

It is better to be
An old man's derling than a yong man's
werling.
> *Ibid.*

Be the day never so long,
Evermore at last they ring to evensong.[8]
> *Ibid.*

The moone is made of a greene cheese.[1]
> *Proverbes. Part II, Chap. VII*

I know on which side my bread is but-
tred.
> *Ibid.*

It will not out of the flesh that is bred
in the bone.[2]
> *Ibid. Chap. VIII*

Who is so deafe or so blinde as is hee
That wilfully will neither heare nor
see? [3]
> *Ibid. Chap. IX*

The wrong sow by th' eare.[4]
> *Ibid.*

Went in at the tone eare and out at the
tother.[5]
> *Ibid.*

Love me, love my dog.[6]
> *Ibid.*

An ill winde that bloweth no man to
good.[7]
> *Ibid.*

For when I gave you an inch, you tooke
an ell.[8]
> *Ibid.*

---

[1] Time trieth truth. — *Tottel's Miscellany* [reprint, 1867], *P. 221*

Time tries the troth in everything. — TUS-SER: *Five Hundred Points of Good Husbandry, Author's Epistle, Chap. I*

[2] I saye, thou madde March hare. — SKEL-TON: *Replycation against certayne yong scolers*

[3] More water glideth by the mill Than wots the miller of.
SHAKESPEARE: *Titus Andronicus, Act II, Sc. 1, L. 85*

[4] An earlier instance of this proverb occurs in Heywood's *Johan the Husbande* [1533]. He must needs go whom the devil drives. — SHAKESPEARE: *All's Well that Ends Well, Act I, Sc. 3, L. 32*. CERVANTES: *Don Quixote, Part I, Book IV, Chap. IV*. GOSSON: *Ephemerides of Phialo*. PEELE: *Edward I*

[5] Others set carts before the horses. — RABELAIS: *Book V, Chap. XXII*

I run before my horse to market. — SHAKESPEARE: *King Richard III, Act I, Sc. 1, L. 159*

[6] GASCOIGNE: *Roses* [1575]. Title of a book of epigrams [1608]. BEAUMONT AND FLETCHER: *The Scornful Lady, Act I, Sc. 1; The Sea Voyage, Act I, Sc. 2*

[7] To the latter end of a fray and the beginning of a feast. — SHAKESPEARE: *Henry IV, Part II, Act IV, Sc. 2, L. 86*

[8] Be the day short or never so long, At length it ringeth to even song.
FOXE: *Book of Martyrs, Chap. VII, P. 346* Quoted at the stake by George Tankerfield [1555].

[1] *Jack Jugler, P. 46*. RABELAIS: *Book I, Chap. XI*. BLACKLOCH: *Hatchet of Heresies* [1565]. BUTLER: *Hudibras, Part II, C. III, L. 263*

[2] What is bred in the bone will never come out of the flesh. — BIDPAY: *The Two Fishermen, Fable XIV*

It will never out of the flesh that's bred in the bone. — JONSON: *Every Man in his Humour, Act I, Sc. 1*

[3] None so deaf as those that will not hear. — MATHEW HENRY: *Commentaries, Psalm LVIII*

[4] He has the wrong sow by the ear. — JONSON: *Every Man in his Humour, Act II, Sc. 1*

[5] See Chaucer, page 4.

[6] CHAPMAN: *Widow's Tears* [1612]

A proverb in the time of Saint Bernard was, Qui me amat, amet et canem meum (Who loves me will love my dog also). — *Sermo Primus*

The old Sicilian proverb, Love me, love my dog. — JOSEPH ADDISON: *The Spectator, No. 579* [August 11, 1714]

[7] *Falstaff.* What wind blew you hither, Pistol?

Pistol. Not the ill wind which blows no man to good.
SHAKESPEARE: *Henry IV, Part II, Act V, Sc. 3, L. 87*

[8] Give an inch, he'll take an ell. — WEBSTER: *Sir Thomas Wyatt*

Would yee both eat your cake and have
your cake? [1]

> *Proverbes. Part II, Chap. IX*

Every man for himselfe and God for us
all.[2]

> *Ibid.*

Though he love not to buy the pig in
the poke.[3]

> *Ibid.*

This hitteth the naile on the hed.[4]

> *Ibid. Chap. XI*

Enough is as good as a feast.[5]

> *Ibid.*

SIR THOMAS WYATT
[1503–1542]

Noli me tangere, for Caesar's I am,
And wild to hold, though I seem tame.

> *To Anne Boleyn*

JOHN BRADFORD
[1510–1555]

The familiar story, that, on seeing
evil-doers taken to the place of execution, he was wont to exclaim: "But for
the grace of God there goes John Bradford," is a universal tradition, which has
overcome the lapse of time.[6]

> *Biographical Notice, Parker So-*

[1] Wouldst thou both eat thy cake and have
it? — HERBERT: *The Size*

[2] Every man for himself, his own ends, the
Devil for all. — BURTON: *Anatomy of Melancholy, Part III, Sect. I, Memb. III*

[3] For buying or selling of pig in a poke. —
TUSSER: *Five Hundred Points of Good Husbandry, September Abstract*

[4] You have there hit the nail on the head.
— RABELAIS: *Bk. III, Ch. XXXI*

[5] *Dives and Pauper* [1493]. GASCOIGNE:
Poesies [1575]. POPE: *Horace, Book I, Ep.
VII, L. 24.* FIELDING: *Covent Garden Tragedy, Act V, Sc. I.* BICKERSTAFF: *Love in a Village, Act III, Sc. I*

[6] . . . Quoting an English divine . . . , by
the grace of God I am not what I was. —
WILLIAM G. SCHAUFFLER [1798–1893]: *Autobiography* [1887]

Did not Philip Neri [1515–1595] say to
Philip, as he saw a criminal haled to execu-
tion: There thou goest, Philip, but for the
grace of God! — PATRICK AUGUSTINE SHEE-
HAN [1852–1913]: *Under the Cedars and
Stars* [1903], *Part II, Chap. 20, P. 97*

"I never hear of such a case as this that I
do not think of Baxter's words, and say,

*ciety edition, The Writings of
John Bradford, Page XLIII*
[1853]

RICHARD GRAFTON
[? –1572]

Thirty dayes hath Nouember,
Aprill, June, and September,
February hath xxviii alone,
And all the rest have xxxi.[1]

> *Chronicles of England [1562]*

'There, but for the grace of God, goes Sherlock Holmes'." — SIR ARTHUR CONAN DOYLE
[1859–1930]: *The Boscombe Valley Mystery,
P. 106.* (The reference is to RICHARD BAXTER
[1615–1691], author of *The Saint's Everlasting Rest* and *The Call to the Unconverted.*)

The saying is also attributed to the REV-
EREND JOHN NEWTON [1725–1807], and is
said to be preserved in the epitaph he composed for the cenotaph of the Church of
Saint Mary Woolnoth, London, of which he
was rector.

"I say, Mayor — but for the grace of God,
there go we." — JOHN GALSWORTHY: *A Family Man, Act III*

[1] Junius, Aprilis, Septémq; Nouemq; tri-
cenos,
Vnum plus reliqui, Februs tenet octo vi-
cenos,
At si bissextus fuerit superadditur vnus.
WILLIAM HARRISON: *Description of Britain,*
prefixed to Holinshed's *Chronicle* [1577].

Thirty days hath September,
April, June, and November,
February has twenty-eight alone,
All the rest have thirty-one;
Excepting leap year, — that's the time
When February's days are twenty-nine.

> *The Return from Parnassus*
> *[London, 1606]*

Thirty days hath September,
April, June, and November;
All the rest have thirty-one,
Excepting February alone,
Which hath but twenty-eight, **in fine,**
Till leap year gives it twenty-nine.

> *Common in the New England states*

Fourth, eleventh, ninth, and sixth,
Thirty days to each affix;
Every other thirty-one
Except the second month alone.

> *Common in Chester County, Pennsyl-*
> *vania, among the Friends*

Compare the old Latin-class mnemonic: —
In March, July, October, May,
The Ides are on the fifteenth day,
The Nones the seventh; all other months
besides
Have two days less for Nones and Ides.

SIR THOMAS VAUX
[1510–1556]

Companion none is like
Unto the mind alone;
For many have been harmed by speech,
Through thinking, few or none.
Of a Contented Mind. Stanza 3

RICHARD EDWARDS
[1523–1566]

The fallyng out of faithfull frends
renuyng is of loue.[1]
The Paradise of Dainty Devices

THOMAS TUSSER
[1524–1580]

God sendeth and giveth both mouth and
the meat.[2]
*Five Hundred Points of Good
Husbandry*
Except wind stands as never it stood,
It is an ill wind turns none to good.
*A Description of the Properties
of Wind*
At Christmas play and make good
cheer,
For Christmas comes but once a year.
The Farmer's Daily Diet
Such mistress, such Nan,
Such master, such man.[3]
*Five Hundred Points of Good
Husbandry, April's Abstract*

Who goeth a borrowing
Goeth a sorrowing.
*Five Hundred Points of Good
Husbandry, June's Abstract*
'T is merry in hall
Where beards wag all.[1]
Ibid. August's Abstract
Naught venture naught have.[2]
Ibid. October's Abstract
Dry sun, dry wind;
Safe bind, safe find.[3]
Washing
Hast thou a friend, as heart may wish at
will?
Then use him so, to have his friendship
still.
Wouldst have a friend, wouldst know
what friend is best?
Have God thy friend, who passeth all
the rest.
Posies for a Parlour
To Death we must stoop, be we high,
be we low,
But how, and how suddenly, few be
that know;
What carry we then but a sheet to the
grave,
To cover this carcass, of all that we
have?
Tenants of God's Farmstead

ELIZABETH, QUEEN OF ENGLAND
[1533–1603]

The use of the sea and air is common
to all; neither can a title to the ocean
belong to any people or private persons,
forasmuch as neither nature nor public use and custom permit any possession thereof.
To the Spanish Ambassador [1580]

---

[1] The anger of lovers renews the strength
of love. — PUBLIUS SYRUS: *Maxim 24*
Let the falling out of friends be a renewing
of affection. — LYLY: *Euphues*
The falling out of lovers is the renewing of
love. — BURTON: *Anatomy of Melancholy,
Pt. III, Sect. 2*
Amantium iræ amoris integratio est (The
quarrels of lovers are the renewal of love).
— TERENCE: *Andria, Act III, Sc. 3, L. 23*
[2] God sends meat, and the Devil sends
cooks. — JOHN TAYLOR: *Works, Vol. II, P.
85* [1630]. RAY: *Proverbs.* GARRICK: *Epigram on Goldsmith, Retaliation.*
Persian couplet: —
The holy prophet Zoroaster said,
The Lord who made thy teeth shall give
thee bread.
[3] On the authority of M. Cimber, of the
Bibliothèque Royale, we owe this proverb to
Chevalier Bayard: "Tel maître, tel valet."

[1] Merry swithe it is in halle,
When the beards waveth alle.
Life of Alexander [1312]
This has been wrongly attributed to Adam
Davie. There the line runs, —
Swithe mury hit is in halle,
When burdes waiven alle.
[2] See Heywood, page 15.
[3] See Heywood, page 12. SHAKESPEARE:
Merchant of Venice, Act II, Sc. 5, L. 54

My care is like my shadow in the sun —
Follows me flying — flies when I pursue it.
On the Departure of Alençon
[1582]

Monarchs ought to put to death the
authors and instigators of war, as their
sworn enemies and as dangers to their
states.
To Fénélon

I am no lover of pompous title, but
only desire that my name may be recorded in a line or two, which shall
briefly express my name, my virginity,
the years of my reign, the reformation
of religion under it, and my preservation of peace.
To her ladies, discussing her epitaph

EDWARD DYER
[*Circa* 1540–1607]

My mind to me a kingdom is;
　　Such present joys therein I find,
That it excels all other bliss
　　That earth affords or grows by
　　kind:
Though much I want which most would
　　have,
Yet still my mind forbids to crave.
MS. Rawl. 85, P. 17 [1]

Some have too much, yet still do crave;
I little have, and seek no more:
They are but poor, though much they
　　have,
And I am rich with little store:

[1] There is a very similar but anonymous
copy in the British Museum. Additional MS.
15225, P. 85. And there is an imitation in
J. Sylvester's *Works*, P. 651. — HANNAH:
Courtly Poets
My mind to me a kingdom is;
　　Such perfect joy therein I find,
As far exceeds all earthly bliss
　　That God and Nature hath assigned.
Though much I want that most would have,
Yet still my mind forbids to crave.
　　BYRD: *Psalmes, Sonnets, etc.* [1588]
　　My mind to me an empire is,
　　While grace affordeth health.
　　ROBERT SOUTHWELL [1561–1595]:
Look Home
Mens regnum bona possidet (A good mind
possesses a kingdom). — SENECA: *Thyestes,*
II, 380

They poor, I rich; they beg, I give;
They lack, I have; they pine, I live.
MS. Rawl. 85, P. 17

MARY STUART, QUEEN
OF SCOTS
[1542–1587]

O Master and Maker! my hope is in
　　thee.
My Jesus, dear Saviour! now set my
　　soul free.
From this my hard prison, my spirit up-
　　risen,
　　　　Soars upward to thee.
Thus moaning and groaning, and bend-
　　ing the knee,
I adore, and implore that thou liberate
　　me.[1]
*Prayer written before her execu-
tion, translated by the* REVER-
END JAMES FREEMAN CLARKE
[1810–1888]

BISHOP JOHN STILL
[1543–1608]

I cannot eat but little meat,
　　My stomach is not good;
But sure I think that I can drink
　　With him that wears a hood.
Gammer Gurton's Needle,
Drinking Song, Act V [2]

Now let them drink till they nod and
　　wink,
　　Even as good fellows should do;
They shall not miss to have the bliss
　　Good ale doth bring men to.
Ibid. Stanza 4

Back and side go bare, go bare,
　　Both foot and hand go cold;
But, belly, God send thee good ale
　　enough,
　　Whether it be new or old.
Ibid. Refrain

[1] O Domine Deus, speravi in Te,
　　O care mi Jesu, nunc libera me,
　　In dura catena, in misera poena,
　　　　Desidero Te.
　　Languendo, gemendo, et genuflectendo,
　　Adoro, imploro, ut liberes me!
[2] Stated by Dyce to be from a MS. of older
date than *Gammer Gurton's Needle*. See Skel-
ton's *Works* (Dyce's ed.), *Vol. I, Pp. vii–x,
note*

GILES FLETCHER
[1549–1611]

He is a path, if any be misled;
He is a robe, if any naked be;
If any chance to hunger, he is bread;
If any be a bondman, he is free;
If any be but weak, how strong is he!
To dead men life is he, to sick men,
  health;
To blind men, sight, and to the needy,
  wealth;
A pleasure without loss, a treasure with-
  out stealth.
Excellency of Christ

WILLIAM CAMDEN
[1551–1623]

Betwixt the stirrup and the ground,
Mercy I ask'd; mercy I found.
Remains Concerning Britain [*1605*]

SIR EDWARD COKE
[1552–1634]

The gladsome light of jurisprudence.
First Institute
Reason is the life of the law; nay, the
common law itself is nothing else but
reason. . . . The law, which is perfection of reason.[1]
Ibid.
For a man's house is his castle, *et
domus sua cuique tutissimum refu-
gium.*[2]
Third Institute. Page 162
The house of every one is to him as
his castle and fortress, as well for his
defence against injury and violence as
for his repose.
Semayne's Case. 5 Rep. 91
They (corporations) cannot commit
treason, nor be outlawed nor excommu-
nicate, for they have no souls.
Case of Sutton's Hospital. 10 Rep. 32

[1] Let us consider the reason of the case. For
nothing is law that is not reason. — Sir John
Powell: *Coggs* vs. *Bernard, 2 Ld. Raym.
Rep. P. 911*
[2] One's home is the safest refuge to everyone. — *Pandects, Lib. II, Tit. IV, De in Jus
vocando*

Magna Charta is such a fellow that
he will have no sovereign.
Debate in the Commons
[May 17, 1628]
Six hours in sleep, in law's grave study
  six,
Four spend in prayer, the rest on Na-
  ture fix.[1]
Translation of lines quoted by Coke

SIR WALTER RALEIGH
[1552–1618]

If all the world and love were young,
And truth in every shepherd's tongue,
These pretty pleasures might me move
To live with thee, and be thy love.
*The Nymph's Reply to the Pas-
sionate Shepherd.*[2] *Stanza 1*

Fain would I, but I dare not; I dare,
  and yet I may not;
I may, although I care not, for pleasure
  when I play not.
Fain Would I

Passions are likened best to floods and
  streams:
The shallow murmur, but the deep are
  dumb.[3]
The Silent Lover, Prelude

Silence in love bewrays more woe
Than words, though ne'er so witty:
A beggar that is dumb, you know,
May challenge double pity.
Ibid. Stanza 7

Go, Soul, the body's guest,
  Upon a thankless arrant:
Fear not to touch the best,
  The truth shall be thy warrant:

[1] Seven hours to law, to soothing slumber
    seven;
  Ten to the world allot, and all to heaven.
    Sir William Jones
[2] An answer to Christopher Marlowe's
poem, *The Passionate Shepherd to His Love.*
[3] Altissima quæque flumina minimo sono
labi (The deepest rivers flow with the least
sound). — Q. Curtius, *VII, 4, 13*
  Smooth runs the water where the brook is
deep. — Shakespeare: *Henry VI, Part II,
Act III, Sc. I, L. 53*
  Take heed of still waters, the quick pass
away. — Herbert: *Jacula Prudentum*

Go, since I needs must die,
And give the world the lie.
>   *The Lie. Stanza 1* [1] *(Printed in*
>   *Poetical   Rhapsody   [1608];*
>   *manuscript copy traced to 1593)*

Give me my scallop-shell of quiet,
My staff of faith to walk upon,
My scrip of joy, immortal diet,
My bottle of salvation,
My gown of glory, hope's true gage,
And thus I'll take my pilgrimage.
>   *His Pilgrimage*

Methought I saw the grave where Laura
lay.[2]
>   *Verses to Edmund Spenser*

Cowards [may] fear to die; but courage stout,
Rather than live in snuff, will be put
out.
>   *Remains, Page 258 [ed. 1661],*
>   *On the snuff of a candle the*
>   *night before he died.*

Even such is time, that takes in trust
Our youth, our joys, our all we have,
And pays us but with age and dust;
Who in the dark and silent grave,
When we have wandered all our ways,
Shuts up the story of our days.
But from this earth, this grave, this
dust,
My God shall raise me up, I trust!
>   *Written the night before his*
>   *death; found in his Bible in the*
>   *Gate-house at Westminster*

Shall I, like a hermit, dwell
On a rock or in a cell?
>   *Poem*

If she undervalue me,
What care I how fair she be? [3]
>   *Ibid.*

If she seem not chaste to me,
What care I how chaste she be?
>   *Ibid.*

Fain would I climb, yet fear I to fall.[1]

[History] hath triumphed over time,
which besides it nothing but eternity
hath triumphed over.
>   *Historie of the World, Preface*

O eloquent, just, and mightie Death!
whom none could advise, thou hast per-
swaded; what none hath dared, thou
hast done; and whom all the world
hath flattered, thou only hast cast out
of the world and despised. Thou hast
drawne together all the farre stretchèd
greatnesse, all the pride, crueltie, and
ambition of man, and covered it all
over with these two narrow words, *Hic
jacet!*
>   *Ibid. Book V, Part I*

RICHARD HOOKER
[1553–1600]

Of Law there can be no less acknowledged than that her seat is the bosom of
God, her voice the harmony of the
world. All things in heaven and earth
do her homage, — the very least as feeling her care, and the greatest as not ex-
empted from her power.
>   *Ecclesiastical Polity. Book I*

That to live by one man's will became
the cause of all men's misery.
>   *Ibid.*

GEORGE KEITH, FIFTH
EARL MARISCHAL
[1553–1623]

Thai half said. Quhat say thai? Let
thame say.[2]
>   *Family motto, Mitchell Tower,*
>   *Marischal   College,   Aberdeen,*
>   *Scotland, founded in 1593*

---

[1] This poem is included in the Works of
JOSHUA SYLVESTER [1563–1618], where the
title is *The Soul's Errand*. It has also been at-
tributed to FRANCIS DAVISON [*fl.* 1602].
[2] Methought I saw my late espoused saint.
— MILTON: *Sonnet XXIII*
Methought I saw the footsteps of a throne.
— WORDSWORTH: *Sonnet*
[3] If she be not so to me,
   What care I how fair she be?
GEORGE WITHER: *The Shepherd's Resolution*

[1] Written in a glass window obvious to the
Queen's eye. "Her Majesty, either espying or
being shown it, did under-write, 'If thy heart
fails thee, climb not at all.'" — FULLER:
Worthies of England, Vol. I, P. 419
[2] They say. What say they? Let them say.
— *Motto over the fireplace in George Bernard Shaw's home*

JOHN LYLY
[Circa 1553–1606]

Cupid and my Campaspe play'd
At cards for kisses: Cupid paid.

*Alexander and Campaspe. Act III,
Sc. 5*

How at heaven's gates she claps her
    wings,
The morne not waking til she sings.[1]

Ibid. Act V, Sc. 1

Be valyaunt, but not too venturous.
Let thy attyre bee comely, but not
costly.[2]

Euphues [*1579*] (*Arber's reprint*).
Page 39

Though the Camomill, the more it is
trodden and pressed downe the more it
spreadeth.[3]

Ibid. Page 46

The finest edge is made with the
blunt whetstone.

Ibid. Page 47

I cast before the Moone.[4]

Ibid. Page 78

It seems to me (said she) that you
are in some brown study.[5]

Ibid. Page 80

The soft droppes of rain perce the
hard marble; [6] many strokes overthrow
the tallest oaks.[7]

Ibid. Page 81

---

[1] Hark, hark! the lark at heaven's gate
    sings,
And Phœbus 'gins arise.
    SHAKESPEARE: *Cymbeline, Act II,
        Sc. 3, L. 22*
[2] Costly thy habit as thy purse can buy,
    But not express'd in fancy; rich, not
    gaudy.
SHAKESPEARE: *Hamlet, Act I, Sc. 3, L. 70*
[3] The camomile, the more it is trodden on
the faster it grows. — SHAKESPEARE: *Henry
IV, Part I, Act II, Sc. 4, L. 446*
[4] See Heywood, page 12.
[5] A brown study. — SWIFT: *Polite Conversation*
[6] Water continually dropping will wear
hard rocks hollow. — PLUTARCH: *Of the
Training of Children*
Stillicidi casus lapidem cavat (Continual
dropping wears away a stone). LUCRETIUS:
I, 314
[7] Many strokes, though with a little axe,
    Hew down and fell the hardest-timber'd
    oak.
SHAKESPEARE: *Henry VI, Part III, Act II,
        Sc. 1, L. 54*

He reckoneth without his Hostesse.[1]
Love knoweth no lawes.

Euphues [*1579*] (*Arber's reprint*).
Page 84

Did not Jupiter transforme himselfe
into the shape of Amphitrio to embrace
Alcmæna; into the form of a swan to
enjoy Leda; into a Bull to beguile Io;
into a showre of gold to win Danae? [2]

Ibid. Page 93

Lette me stande to the maine chance.[3]

Ibid. Page 104

I mean not to run with the Hare and
holde with the Hounde.[4]

Ibid. Page 107

It is a world to see.[5]

Ibid. Page 116

There can no great smoke arise, but
there must be some fire.[6]

*Euphues and his Euphœbus.
Page 153*

A clere conscience is a sure carde.[7]

Euphues. Page 207

As lyke as one pease is to another.

Ibid. Page 215

Goe to bed with the Lambe, and rise
with the Larke.[8]

Euphues and his England. Page 229

A comely olde man as busie as a bee.

Ibid. Page 252

Maydens, be they never so foolyshe,
yet beeing fayre they are commonly fortunate.

Ibid. Page 279

---

[1] See Heywood, page 13.
[2] Jupiter himself was turned into a satyr,
a shepherd, a bull, a swan, a golden shower,
and what not for love. — BURTON: *Anatomy
of Melancholy, Pt. III, Sect. II, Memb. I,
Subsect. 1*
[3] The main chance. — SHAKESPEARE: *Henry VI, Part II, Act I, Sc. 1, L. 213.* BUTLER:
Hudibras, Part II, Canto II. DRYDEN: *Persius,
Satire VI*
[4] See Heywood, page 13.
[5] 'Tis a world to see. — SHAKESPEARE:
Taming of the Shrew, Act II, Sc. 1, L. 305
[6] See Heywood, page 16.
[7] This is a sure card. — *Thersytes* [*circa
1550*]
[8] To rise with the lark and go to bed with
the lamb. — BRETON: *Court and Country*
[*1618*], *reprint, page 182*
Rise with the lark, and with the lark to bed.
— HURDIS: *The Village Curate*

Where the streame runneth smoothest, the water is deepest.[1]

Euphues and his England. Page 287

Your eyes are so sharpe that you cannot onely looke through a Milstone, but cleane through the minde.

Ibid. Page 289

I am glad that my Adonis hath a sweete tooth in his head.

Ibid. Page 308

A Rose is sweeter in the budde than full blowne.[2]

Ibid. Page 314

EDMUND SPENSER
[1553?–1599]

From the text of J. C. Smith and E. De Selincourt.[3]

Fierce warres and faithfull loves shall moralize my song.[4]

*The Faerie Queene. Introduction,
Stanza 1*

A Gentle Knight was pricking on the plaine.

Ibid. Book I, Canto 1, Stanza 1

A bold bad man.[5]

Ibid. Stanza 37

Her angels face
As the great eye of heaven shyned bright,
And made a sunshine in the shadie place.

Ibid. Canto 3, Stanza 4

Ay me, how many perils doe enfold
The righteous man, to make him daily fall.[6]

Ibid. Canto 8, Stanza 1

As great a noyse, as when in Cymbrian plaine
An heard of Bulles, whom kindly rage doth sting,
Do for the milkie mothers [7] want complaine,

And fill the fields with troublous bellowing.

*The Faerie Queene. Book I,
Canto 8, Stanza 11*

Is not short paine well borne, that brings long ease,
And layes the soule to sleepe in quiet grave?
Sleepe after toyle, port after stormie seas,
Ease after warre, death after life does greatly please.[1]

Ibid. Canto 9, Stanza 40

O happie earth,
Whereon thy innocent feet doe ever tread.

Ibid. Canto 10, Stanza 9

All for love, and nothing for reward.

Ibid. Book II, Canto 8, Stanza 2

Yet gold all is not, that doth golden seeme.[2]

Ibid. Stanza 14

Through thicke and thin, both over banke and bush.[3]

In hope her to attaine by hooke or crooke.[4]

Ibid. Book III, Canto 1, Stanza 17

Her berth was of the wombe of Morning dew,[5]
And her conception of the joyous Prime.

Ibid. Canto 6, Stanza 3

Roses red and violets blew,
And all the sweetest flowres, that in the forrest grew.

Ibid. Stanza 6

All that in this delightfull Gardin growes,
Should happie be, and have immortall blis.

Ibid. Stanza 41

That Squire of Dames.

Ibid. Canto 8, Stanza 44

How over that same dore was likewise writ,

---

[1] See Raleigh, page 21.

[2] The rose is fairest when 'tis budding new. — SCOTT: *Lady of the Lake, Canto III, St. 1*

[3] Oxford University Press [1932].

[4] And moralized his song. — POPE: *Epistle to Dr. Arbuthnot, Line 340*

[5] This bold bad man. — SHAKESPEARE: *Henry VIII, Act II, Sc. 2, L. 44.* MASSINGER: *A New Way to Pay Old Debts, Act IV, Sc. 2*

[6] Ay me! what perils do environ
The man that meddles with cold iron!
BUTLER: *Hudibras, Pt. I, C. III, L. 1*

[7] Milky Mothers. — POPE: *The Dunciad,*

Book II, L. 247. SCOTT: *The Monastery, Chap. XXVIII*

[1] The last two lines are cut on Joseph Conrad's gravestone at Canterbury, England.

[2] See Chaucer, page 8.

[3] *Ibid.,* page 6.

[4] See Skelton, page 10.

[5] The young men come to thee as dew from the womb of the morning.
Psalm 110, 3; Book of Common Prayer, American Revision [1928]

Be bold, be bold, and every where *Be bold.*[1]

> The Faerie Queene. Book III,
> Canto 11, Stanza 54

Another yron dore, on which was writ,
Be not too bold.

> Ibid.

Dan Chaucer, well of English unde-
fyled,
On Fames eternall beadroll worthie to
be fyled.

> Ibid. Book IV, Canto 2, Stanza 32

For all that nature by her mother wit [2]
Could frame in earth.

> Ibid. Canto 10, Stanza 21

Me seemes the world is runne quite out
of square,
From the first point of his appointed
sourse,
And being once amisse growes daily
wourse and wourse.

> Ibid. Book V, Introduction,
> Stanza 1

For from the golden age,[3] that first was
named,
It's now at earst become a stonie one.

> Ibid. Stanza 2

Ill can he rule the great, that cannot
reach the small.

> Ibid. Canto 2, Stanza 43

Who will not mercie unto others shew,
How can he mercy ever hope to have? [4]

> Ibid. Book VI, Canto 1, Stanza 42

The gentle minde by gentle deeds is
knowne.

---

[1] De l'audace, encore de l'audace, et tou-
jours de l'audace (Boldness, again boldness,
and ever boldness). — DANTON: *Speech in the
Legislative Assembly* [1792]
Write on your doors the saying wise and old,
"Be bold! be bold!" and everywhere — "Be
bold;
Be not too bold!"
  LONGFELLOW: *Morituri Salutamus*
[2] Mother wit. — MARLOWE: *Prologue to
Tamberlaine the Great, Part I.* MIDDLETON:
Your Five Gallants, Act I, Sc. 1. SHAKESPEARE:
Taming of the Shrew, Act II, Sc. 1, L. 258
[3] To excel the golden age. — SHAKESPEARE:
The Tempest, Act II, Sc. 1, L. 175
Time will run back and fetch the Age of
Gold. — MILTON: *On the Morning of Christ's
Nativity*
[4] Blessed are the merciful, for they shall ob-
tain mercy. — *Matthew, V, 7*

For a man by nothing is so well be-
wrayed,
As by his manners.

> The Faerie Queene. Book VI,
> Canto 3, Stanza 1

That here on earth is no sure happiness.

> Ibid. Canto 11, Stanza 1

The ever-whirling wheele
Of *Change,* the which all mortall things
doth sway.

> Ibid. Book VII, Canto 6, Stanza 1

Warres and allarums unto Nations
wide.

> Ibid. Stanza 3

But Times do change and move continually.

> Ibid. Stanza 47

But of all burdens, that a man can
beare,
Moste is, a fooles talke to beare and to
heare.

> The Shepheardes Calender.
> Maye, Line 140

To Kerke the narre, from God more
farre,[1]
Has bene an old sayd sawe.
And he that strives to touch the starre,
Oft stombles at a strawe.

> Ibid. July, Line 97

For deeds doe die, how ever noblie
donne,
And thoughts of men do as themselves
decay,
But wise wordes taught in numbers for
to runne,
Recorded by the Muses, live for ay.

> The Ruines of Time. Line 400

Full little knowest thou that hast not
tride,
What hell it is, in suing long to bide:
To loose good dayes, that might be
better spent;
To wast long nights in pensive discontent;
To speed to-day, to be put back to-
morrow;
To feed on hope, to pine with feare and
sorrow.

> Mother Hubberds Tale. Line 895

To fret thy soule with crosses and with
cares;

---

[1] See Heywood, page 13.

To eate thy heart through comfortlesse
     dispaires; [1]
To fawne, to crowche, to waite, to ride,
     to ronne,
To spend, to give, to want, to be un-
     donne.
Unhappie wight, born to desastrous
     end,
That doth his life in so long tendance
     spend.
       Mother Hubberds Tale. Line 903
Hereby I learned have, not to despise,
What ever thing seemes small in com-
     mon eyes. [2]
Visions of the Worlds Vanitie. Line 69
What more felicitie can fall to creature,
Than to enjoy delight with libertie.
       Muiopotmos: or The Fate of
         the Butterflie. Line 209
I hate the day, because it lendeth light
To see all things, and not my love to
     see.
       Daphnaida. Line 407
A sweet attractive kinde of grace,
A full assurance given by lookes,
Continuall comfort in a face,
The lineaments of Gospell bookes,
    I trowe that countenance cannot lie,
    Whose thoughts are legible in the eie.
       An Elegie, or Friends Passion,
       for his Astrophill (SIR PHILIP
       SIDNEY). *Line 103* [3]
Was never eie, did see that face,
Was never eare, did heare that tong,
Was never minde, did minde his grace,
That ever thought the travell long,
    But eies, and eares, and ev'ry
     thought,
    Were with his sweete perfections
     caught.
       Ibid. Line 109

[1] Eat not thy heart; which forbids to afflict
our souls, and waste them with vexatious
cares. — PLUTARCH: *Of the Training of Children*
           But suffered idleness
    To eat his heart away.
    BRYANT: *Homer's Iliad, Book I, Line 319*
[2] Who hath despised the day of small
things. — ZECHARIAH, *IV, 10*
[3] This elegy was printed anonymously in a
miscellany, *The Phoenix' Next* [1593]. It has
been erroneously ascribed to Mathew Roydon
[1580–1622].

Death slue not him, but he made death
     his ladder to the skies.
       An Epitaph upon Sir Philip Sidney.
                   Line 20
And drizling drops that often doe re-
     dound,
The firmest flint doth in continuance
     weare. [1]
       Amoretti. Sonnet 18
Tell her the joyous time wil not be
     staid
Unlesse she doe him by the forelock
     take. [2]
       Ibid. Sonnet 70
Behold whiles she before the altar
     stands
Hearing the holy priest that to her
     speakes
And blesseth her with his two happy
     hands.
       Epithalamion. Line 223
For of the soule the bodie forme doth
     take:
For soule is forme, and doth the bodie
     make.
       An Hymne in Honour of Beautie.
                   Line 132
For all that faire is, is by nature good; [3]
That is a signe to know the gentle blood.
       Ibid. Line 139
Sweete Themmes runne softly, till I
     end my Song.
       Prothalamion. Refrain
It was the time when rest the gift of
     Gods
Sweetely sliding into the eyes of men,
Doth drowne in the forgetfulnesse of
     slepe,
The carefull travailes of the painefull
     day.
       Sonnet 1
I was promised on a time
To have reason for my rhyme;
From that time unto this season,

[1] See Lyly, page 23.
[2] Take Time by the forelock. — THALES of
Miletus [636–546 B. C.]
[3] The hand that hath made you fair hath
made you good. — SHAKESPEARE: *Measure
for Measure, Act III, Sc. 1, L. 182*

I received nor rhyme nor reason.[1]
> *Lines on his Promised Pension*
> (*Quoted by* THOMAS FULLER *in*
> *Worthies of England* [*1662*],
> *Vol. 2, Page 379*)

FULKE GREVILLE, LORD BROOKE
[1554–1628]

O wearisome condition of humanity!
> *Mustapha. Act V, Sc. 4*

And out of mind as soon as out of sight.[2]
> *Sonnet LVI*

SIR PHILIP SIDNEY
[1554–1586]

Sweet food of sweetly uttered knowledge.
> *Defence of Poesy*

He cometh unto you with a tale which holdeth children from play, and old men from the chimney-corner.
> *Ibid.*

I never heard the old song of Percy and Douglas that I found not my heart moved more than with a trumpet.
> *Ibid.*

High-erected thoughts seated in the heart of courtesy.[3]
> *Arcadia. Book I*

They are never alone that are accompanied with noble thoughts.[4]
> *Ibid.*

---

[1] Rhyme nor reason. — BLANCHET: *Pierre Patelin*, quoted by Tyndale in 1530. *Farce du Vendeur des Lieures*, sixteenth century. PEELE: *Edward I.* SHAKESPEARE: *Merry Wives of Windsor*, Act V, Sc. 5, L. 135; *Comedy of Errors*, Act II, Sc. 2, L. 49; *As You Like It*, Act III, Sc. 2, L. 424

Sir Thomas More advised an author, who had sent him his manuscript to read, "to put it in rhyme." Which being done, Sir Thomas said, "Yea, marry, now it is somewhat, for now it is rhyme; before it was neither rhyme nor reason."

[2] See Thomas à Kempis, page 9.
Out of sight and out of mind. — ROBERT BROWNING: *The Inn Album, Canto I*

[3] Great thoughts come from the heart. — VAUVENARGUES: *Maxim CXXVII*

[4] He never is alone that is accompanied with noble thoughts. — FLETCHER: *Love's Cure, Act III, Sc. 3*

Many-headed multitude.[1]
> *Arcadia. Book II*

My dear, my better half.
> *Ibid. Book III*

"Fool!" said my muse to me, "look in thy heart, and write." [2]
> *Astrophel and Stella*

With how sad steps, O Moon, thou climb'st the skies!
> *Ibid.*

Have I caught my heav'nly jewel.[3]
> *Ibid. Second Song*

My true-love hath my heart, and I have his,
By just exchange one for the other given:
I hold his dear, and mine he cannot miss,
There never was a better bargain driven.
> *The Bargain. Stanza 1*

THOMAS LODGE
[1558?–1625]

Love in my bosom like a bee
Doth suck his sweet.
> *Rosalind*

Her paps are centres of delight,
Her breasts are orbs of heavenly frame.
> *Ibid.*

GEORGE PEELE
[1558–1597]

His golden locks time hath to silver turned;
O time too swift! O swiftness never ceasing!
His youth 'gainst time and age hath ever spurned,
But spurned in vain; youth waneth by encreasing.
> *Polyhymnia. The Aged Man-at-Arms, Stanza 1*

---

[1] Many-headed multitude. — SHAKESPEARE: *Coriolanus*, Act II, Sc. 3, L. 18
This many-headed monster, Multitude. — DANIEL: *History of the Civil War, Book II, St. 13*

[2] Look, then, into thine heart and write. — LONGFELLOW: *Voices of the Night, Prelude*

[3] Quoted by Shakespeare in *Merry Wives of Windsor*, Act III, Sc. 3, L. 45

His helmet now shall make a hive for
bees,
    And lovers' songs be turned to holy
    psalms;
A man-at-arms must now serve on his
knees,
    And feed on prayers, which are old
    age's alms.
        *Polyhymnia. The Aged Man-at-
        Arms, Stanza 2*
My merry, merry, merry roundelay
Concludes with Cupid's curse:
They that do change old love for new,
Pray gods, they change for worse!
        Cupid's Curse

GEORGE CHAPMAN
[1559–1634]

None ever loved but at first sight they
loved.[1]
    The Blind Beggar of Alexandria
An ill weed grows apace.[2]
        An Humorous Day's Mirth
Black is a pearl in a woman's eye.[3]
        Ibid.
Exceeding fair she was not; and yet fair
In that she never studied to be fairer
Than Nature made her.
        All Fools. Act I, Sc. 1
I tell thee Love is Nature's second sun,
Causing a spring of virtues where he
shines.
        Ibid.
Cornelia. What flowers are these?
Gazetta. The pansy this.
Cornelia. Oh, that's for lovers'
    thoughts.[4]
        Ibid. Act II, Sc. 1
Fortune, the great commandress of the
world,
Hath divers ways to advance her fol-
lowers:

[1] Who ever loved that loved not at first
sight? — MARLOWE: *Hero and Leander*
    SHAKESPEARE: *As You Like It, Act III,
Sc. 5, L. 82*
    I saw and loved. — GIBBON: *Memoirs, Vol.
I, P. 106*
    [2] See Heywood, page 14.
    [3] Black men are pearls in beauteous ladies'
eyes. — SHAKESPEARE: *Two Gentlemen of Verona, Act V, Sc. 2, L. 12*
    [4] There is pansies, that's for thoughts. —
SHAKESPEARE: *Hamlet, Act IV, Sc. 5, L. 175*

To some she gives honour without de-
serving,
To other some, deserving without hon-
our.
        All Fools. Act V, Sc. 1
Young men think old men are fools;
but old men know young men are fools.
        Ibid.
For one heat, all know, doth drive out
another,
One passion doth expel another still.[1]
        Monsieur D'Olive. Act V, Sc. 1
To put a girdle round about the world.[2]
        Bussy D'Ambois. Act I, Sc. 1
His deeds inimitable, like the sea
That shuts still as it opes, and leaves no
tracts
Nor prints of precedent for poor men's
facts.
        Ibid.
        So our lives
In acts exemplary, not only win
Ourselves good names, but doth to
others give
Matter for virtuous deeds, by which we
live.[3]
        Ibid.
Who to himself is law no law doth need,
Offends no law, and is a king indeed.
        Ibid. Act II, Sc. 1
Give me a spirit that on this life's rough
sea
Loves t' have his sails fill'd with a lusty
wind,
Even till his sail-yards tremble, his
masts crack,
And his rapt ship run on her side so
low
That she drinks water, and her keel
plows air.
        *Conspiracy of Charles, Duke of
        Byron. Act III, Sc. 1*

[1] One fire burns out another's burning,
    One pain is lessened by another's anguish.
SHAKESPEARE: *Romeo and Juliet, Act I,
        Sc. 2, L. 47*
    [2] I'll put a girdle round about the earth. —
SHAKESPEARE: *Midsummer-Night's Dream,
Act II, Sc. 1, L. 175*
    [3] Lives of great men all remind us
    We can make our lives sublime.
        LONGFELLOW: *A Psalm of Life*

Words writ in waters.[1]
> *Revenge for Honour. Act V, Sc. 2*

They're only truly great who are truly good.[2]
> *Ibid.*

Keep thy shop, and thy shop will keep thee.[3] Light gains make heavy purses. 'Tis good to be merry and wise.[4]
> *Eastward Ho.*[5] *Act I, Sc. 1*

Make ducks and drakes with shillings.
> *Ibid.*

Only a few industrious Scots perhaps, who indeed are dispersed over the face of the whole earth. But as for them, there are no greater friends to Englishmen and England, when they are out on't, in the world, than they are. And for my own part, I would a hundred thousand of them were there [Virginia]; for we are all one countrymen now, ye know, and we should find ten times more comfort of them there than we do here.[6]
> *Ibid. Act III, Sc. 2*

Enough's as good as a feast.[7]
> *Ibid.*

Fair words never hurt the tongue.[8]
> *Ibid. Act IV, Sc. 1*

Let pride go afore, shame will follow after.[9]
> *Ibid.*

I will neither yield to the song of the siren nor the voice of the hyena, the tears of the crocodile [1] nor the howling of the wolf.
> *Eastward Ho. Act V, Sc. 1*

Promise is most given when the least is said.
> *Musæus of Hero and Leander*

SIR JOHN HARRINGTON
[1561–1612]

Treason doth never prosper; what's the reason?
Why, if it prosper, none dare call it treason.[2]
> *Epigrams. Of Treason*

Fortune, men say, doth give too much to many,
But yet she never gave enough to any.
> *Ibid. Of Fortune*

The readers and the hearers like my books,
But yet some writers cannot them digest;
But what care I? for when I make a feast
I would my guests should praise it, not the cooks.
> *Ibid. Of Writers who Carp at Other Men's Books*

ROBERT SOUTHWELL
[1561–1595]

What thought can think, another thought can mend.
> *Look Home*

Let this suffice, by this conceive the rest,
He should, he could, he would, he did the best.
> *Ibid.*

---

[1] All your better deeds shall be in water writ, but this in marble. — BEAUMONT AND FLETCHER: *Philaster, Act V, Sc. 3*
Here lies one whose name was writ in water. — *Keats's own Epitaph*

[2] To be noble we'll be good. — *Winifreda* (Percy's *Reliques*)
'T is only noble to be good. — TENNYSON: *Lady Clara Vere de Vere, Stanza 7*

[3] The same in Franklin's *Poor Richard*

[4] See Heywood, page 11.

[5] By Chapman, Jonson, and Marston.

[6] This is the famous passage that gave offence to James I., and caused the imprisonment of the authors. The leaves containing it were cancelled and reprinted, and it only occurs in a few of the original copies. — RICHARD HERNE SHEPHERD

[7] *Dives and Pauper* [1493]. GASCOIGNE: *Memories* [1575]. FIELDING: *Covent Garden Tragedy, Act II, Sc. 6.* BICKERSTAFF: *Love in a Village, Act III, Sc. 1.* See Heywood, page 18.

[8] See Heywood, page 13.

[9] *Ibid.*, page 14.

[1] These crocodile tears. — BURTON: *Anatomy of Melancholy, Part III, Sect. 2, Memb. 2, Subsect. 4*
She's false, false as the tears of crocodiles — SIR JOHN SUCKLING: *The Sad One, Act IV, Sc. 5*

[2] Prosperum ac felix scelus
Virtus vocatur
(Successful and fortunate crime is called virtue).
> SENECA: *Herc. Furens, II, 250*

Time goes by turns, and chances change
    by course,
From foul to fair, from better hap to
    worse.
           Times Go by Turns
No joy so great but runneth to an end,
No hap so hard but may in time amend.
                    Ibid.
When sun is set the little stars will
    shine.
           Scorn Not the Least
He that high growth on cedars did be-
    stow,
Gave also lowly mushrumps leave to
    grow.
                    Ibid.
May never was the month of love,
For May is full of flowers;
But rather April, wet by kind,
For love is full of showers.
           Love's Servile Lot
All states with others' ruin built
    To ruin run amain.
No chance of Fortune's calms
Can cast my fortune down.
When Fortune smiles, I smile to think
How quickly she will frown.
        I Envy Not Their Hap
As I in hoary winter night stood shiver-
    ing in the snow,
Surprised was I with sudden heat which
    made my heart to glow;
And lifting up a fearful eye to view
    what fire was near
A pretty Babe all burning bright did
    in the air appear.
      *The Burning Babe. (A Christ-
      mas poem praised by* BEN JON-
      SON)

SAMUEL DANIEL
[1562–1619]

And for the few that only lend their ear,
That few is all the world.
      Musophilus [*1599*]. *Stanza 97*
This is the thing that I was born to do.
          Ibid. Stanza 100
And who (in time) knows whither we
    may vent
    The treasure of our tongue? To what
      strange shores
This gain of our best glory shall be sent

T' enrich unknowing nations with
    our stores?
What worlds in the yet unformed Oc-
    cident
May come refin'd with th' accents
    that are ours? [1]
      Musophilus [*1599*]. *Stanza 163*
As that the walls worn thin, permit the
    mind
To look out thorough, and his frailty
    find. [2]
      History of the Civil War. [*1609*].
          Book IV, Stanza 84
    Unless above himself he can
Erect himself, how poor a thing is man!
      To the Countess of Cumberland.
                Stanza 12
Care-charmer Sleep, son of the sable
    Night,
Brother to Death, in silent darkness
    born.
          Sonnet: To Delia
Make me to say when all my griefs are
    gone,
Happy the heart that sighed for such a
    one!
      Sonnet: I Must Not Grieve
Love is a sickness full of woes,
    All remedies refusing.
          Hymen's Triumph

MICHAEL DRAYTON
[1563–1631]

Had in him those brave translunary
    things
That the first poets had.
      (*Said of* MARLOWE) *To Henry
      Reynolds, of Poets and Poesy*
For that fine madness still he did re-
    tain
Which rightly should possess a poet's
    brain.
                    Ibid.

[1] Westward the course of empire takes its
way. — BERKELEY: *On the Prospect of Planting Arts and Learning in America*
[2] The soul's dark cottage, batter'd and de-
    cay'd,
    Lets in new light through chinks that
    Time has made.
    WALLER: *Verses upon his Divine Poesy*

The coast was clear.[1]

Nymphidia

Battles so bravely won
Have ever to the sun
  By fame been raised.

The Ballad of Agincourt. Stanza 4

O, when shall Englishmen
With such acts fill a pen,
Or England breed again
  Such a King Harry?

Ibid. Stanza 15

Since there's no help, come let us kiss
    and part.

Sonnet: Love's Farewell

When faith is kneeling by his bed of
    death,
And innocence is closing up his eyes,
Now if thou wouldst, when all have
    given him over,
From death to life thou might'st him
    yet recover.

Ibid.

CHRISTOPHER MARLOWE
[1564-1593]

Comparisons are odious.[2]

Lust's Dominion. Act III, Sc. 4

I'm armed with more than complete
    steel, —
The justice of my quarrel.[3]

Ibid.

Who ever loved that loved not at first
    sight?[4]

Hero and Leander

Come live with me, and be my love;
And we will all the pleasures prove
That hills and valleys, dales and fields,
Woods or steepy mountain yields.

The Passionate Shepherd to his Love

By shallow rivers, to whose falls[1]
Melodious birds sing madrigals.

The Passionate Shepherd to his Love

And I will make thee beds of roses
And a thousand fragrant posies.[1]

Ibid.

Infinite riches in a little room.

The Jew of Malta. Act I

Excess of wealth is cause of covetous-
    ness.

Ibid.

Now will I show myself to have more
of the serpent than the dove;[2] that is,
more knave than fool.

Ibid. Act II

Love me little, love me long.[3]

Ibid. Act IV

Hell hath no limits, nor is circumscribed
In one self-place; for where we are is
    Hell,
And where Hell is, there must we ever
    be.

Faustus [1616]

When all the world dissolves,
And every creature shall be purified,
All places shall be hell that are not
    heaven.

Ibid.

Was this the face that launch'd a thou-
    sand ships,
And burnt the topless towers of Ilium?[4]
Sweet Helen, make me immortal with a
    kiss!
Her lips suck forth my soul:[5] see,
    where it flies!

Ibid.

---

[1] SOMERVILLE: *The Night-Walker.*
[2] See Fortescue, page 9.
[3] Thrice is he armed that hath his quarrel
    just,
    And he but naked, though locked up in
        steel,
    Whose conscience with injustice is cor-
        rupted.
  SHAKESPEARE: *Henry VI, Part II, Act III,
        Sc. 2, L. 233*
[4] Quoted in Shakespeare's *As You Like It,
Act III, Sc. 5, L. 82*
Compare Chapman, page 28.

[1] To shallow rivers, to whose falls
    Melodious birds sing madrigals;
    There will we make our peds of roses,
    And a thousand fragrant posies.
  SHAKESPEARE: *Merry Wives of Windsor,
        Act III, Sc. 1, L. 17* (Sung by Evans).
[2] Be ye therefore wise as serpents, and
harmless as doves. — *Matthew, X, 16*
[3] See Heywood, page 16.
[4] Was this fair face the cause, quoth she,
    Why the Grecians sacked Troy?
  SHAKESPEARE: *All's Well that Ends Well,
        Act I, Sc. 3, L. 75*
[5]   Once he drew
With one long kiss my whole soul through
My lips.
  TENNYSON: *Fatima, Stanza 3*

O, thou art fairer than the evening air
Clad in the beauty of a thousand stars.
Faustus [*1616*]
Stand still, you ever moving spheres of
heaven,
That time may cease, and midnight
never come.
Ibid.
Cut is the branch that might have
grown full straight,
And burnèd is Apollo's laurel bough,[1]
That sometime grew within this
learnèd man.
Ibid.
Yet should there hover in their restless
heads
One thought, one grace, one wonder, at
the least,
Which into words no virtue can digest.
Tamburlaine the Great, I.
Act 5, Sc. 2
My men, like satyrs grazing on the
lawn,
Shall with their goat feet dance the
antic hay.
Edward II. Act 1, Sc. 1

WILLIAM SHAKESPEARE
[1564–1616]

From the text of W. J. Craig,
M.A.[2]

Now would I give a thousand fur-
longs of sea for an acre of barren
ground.
The Tempest. Act I, Sc. 1, Line 70
I would fain die a dry death.
Ibid. Line 73
What seest thou else
In the dark backward and abysm of
time?
Ibid. Sc. 2, Line 49
I, thus neglecting worldly ends, all ded-
icated
To closeness and the bettering of my
mind.
Ibid. Line 89

[1] O, withered is the garland of the war!
The soldier's pole is fallen.
SHAKESPEARE: *Antony and Cleopatra, Act*
IV, Sc. 13, L. 64
[2] *The Complete Works of Shakespeare.* Ox-
ford University Press.

By telling of it,
Made such a sinner of his memory,
To credit his own lie.
The Tempest. Act I, Sc. 2, Line 99
My library
Was dukedom large enough.
Ibid. Line 109
The very rats
Instinctively have quit it.
Ibid. Line 147
Knowing I lov'd my books, he furnish'd
me
From mine own library with volumes
that
I prize above my dukedom.
Ibid. Line 166
From the still-vexed Bermoothes.
Ibid. Line 229
I will be correspondent to command,
And do my spiriting gently.
Ibid. Line 297
Come unto these yellow sands,
And then take hands:
Courtsied when you have, and kiss'd
The wild waves whist.
Ibid. Line 375
Full fathom five thy father lies;
Of his bones are coral made;
Those are pearls that were his eyes:
Nothing of him that doth fade
But doth suffer a sea-change
Into something rich and strange.[1]
Ibid. Line 394
The fringed curtains of thine eye ad-
vance.
Ibid. Act I, Sc. 2, Line 405
Lest too light winning
Make the prize light.
Ibid. Line 448
He receives comfort like cold porridge.
Ibid. Act II, Sc. 1, Line 10
Gonzalo. Here is everything advanta-
geous to life.
Antonio. True; save means to live.
Ibid. Line 52
The golden age.[2]
Ibid. Line 175
A very ancient and fish-like smell.
Ibid. Sc. 2, Line 27

[1] The last three lines are inscribed on Shelley's gravestone.
[2] See Spenser, page 25.

Misery acquaints a man with strange bedfellows.
The Tempest. Act II, Sc. 2, Line 42

I shall laugh myself to death.
Ibid. Line 167

Ferdinand. Here's my hand.
Miranda. And mine, with my heart in't.
Ibid. Act III, Sc. 1, Line 89

Moon-calf.
Ibid. Sc. 2, Line 25

I am in case to justle a constable.
Ibid. Line 30

Keep a good tongue in your head.
Ibid. Line 41

He that dies pays all debts.
Ibid. Line 143

A kind
Of excellent dumb discourse.
Ibid. Sc. 3, Line 38

Do not give dalliance
Too much rein.
Ibid. Act IV, Sc. 1, Line 51

Our revels now are ended. These our actors,
As I foretold you, were all spirits, and
Are melted into air, into thin air;
And, like the baseless fabric of this vision,
The cloud-capp'd towers, the gorgeous palaces,
The solemn temples, the great globe itself,
Yea, all which it inherit, shall dissolve;
And, like this insubstantial pageant faded,
Leave not a rack behind. We are such stuff
As dreams are made on, and our little life
Is rounded with a sleep.
Ibid. Line 148

With foreheads villanous low.
Ibid. Line 252

Deeper than did ever plummet sound
I'll drown my book.
Ibid. Act V, Sc. 1, Line 56

Where the bee sucks, there suck I;
In a cowslip's bell I lie.
Ibid. Line 88

Merrily, merrily shall I live now,
Under the blossom that hangs on the bough.
The Tempest. Act V, Sc. 1, Line 93

'Tis a chronicle of day by day.
Ibid. Line 163

O brave new world,
That has such people in't!
Ibid. Line 183

Let us not burden our remembrances
With a heaviness that's gone.
Ibid. Line 199

I have been in such a pickle since I saw you last.
Ibid. Line 282

My ending is despair.
Ibid. Epilogue, Line 15

Home-keeping youth have ever homely wits.
*The Two Gentlemen of Verona.
Act I, Sc. 1, Line 2*

I have no other but a woman's reason:
I think him so, because I think him so.
Ibid. Sc. 2, Line 23

They do not love that do not show their love.
Ibid. Line 31

O! they love least that let men know their love.
Ibid. Line 32

Since maids, in modesty, say "No" to that
Which they would have the profferer construe "Ay."
Ibid. Line 53

What is't that you took up so gingerly?
Ibid. Line 68

O! how this spring of love resembleth
The uncertain glory of an April day!
Ibid. Sc. 3, Line 84

O jest unseen, inscrutable, invisible,
As a nose on a man's face,[1] or a weathercock on a steeple.
Ibid. Act II, Sc. 1, Line 145

He makes sweet music with th' enamell'd stones,
Giving a gentle kiss to every sedge
He overtaketh in his pilgrimage.
Ibid. Sc. 7, Line 28

---

[1] As clear and as manifest as the nose in a man's face. — BURTON: *Anatomy of Melancholy, Part III, Sect. 3, Memb. 4, Subsect. 1*

That man that hath a tongue, I say, is
no man,
If with his tongue he cannot win a
woman.
> *The Two Gentlemen of Verona.*
> *Act III, Sc. 1, Line 104*

To make a virtue of necessity.[1]
> *Ibid. Act IV, Sc. 1, Line 62*

Who is Sylvia? what is she?
That all our swains commend her?
> *Ibid. Sc. 2, Line 40*

How use doth breed a habit in a man![2]
> *Ibid. Act V, Sc. 4, Line 1*

I will make a Star-chamber matter of it.
> *The Merry Wives of Windsor.*
> *Act I, Sc. 1, Line 2*

All his successors gone before him
have done 't; and all his ancestors that
come after him may.
> *Ibid. Line 14*

Seven hundred pounds and possibilities
is goot gifts.
> *Ibid. Line 65*

Mine host of the Garter.
> *Ibid. Line 146*

I had rather than forty shillings I
had my Book of Songs and Sonnets
here.
> *Ibid. Line 205*

If there be no great love in the beginning, yet heaven may decrease it
upon better acquaintance, when we are
married and have more occasion to
know one another: I hope, upon familiarity will grow more contempt.[3]
> *Ibid. Line 255*

O base Hungarian wight! wilt thou the
spigot wield?
> *Ibid. Sc. 3, Line 21*

"Convey," the wise it call. "Steal!"
foh! a fico for the phrase!
> *Ibid. Line 30*

I am almost out at heels.
> *Ibid. Line 32*

Thou art the Mars of malcontents.
> *Ibid. Line 111*

Here will be an old abusing of God's
patience and the king's English.
> *The Merry Wives of Windsor.*
> *Act I, Sc. 4, Line 5*

Thereby hangs a tale.[1]
> *Ibid. Line 155*

Dispense with trifles.
> *Ibid. Act II, Sc. 1, Line 47*

We burn daylight.[2]
> *Ibid. Line 54*

There's the humour of it.
> *Ibid. Line 139*

Faith, thou hast some crotchets in thy
head now.
> *Ibid. Line 158*

Why, then the world's mine oyster,
Which I with sword will open.
> *Ibid. Sc. 2, Line 2*

This is the short and the long of it.
> *Ibid. Line 62*

Unless experience be a jewel.
> *Ibid. Line 216*

Like a fair house built on another
man's ground.
> *Ibid. Line 229*

Better three hours too soon than a minute too late.
> *Ibid. Line 332*

We have some salt of our youth in us.
> *Ibid. Sc. 3, Line 50*

I cannot tell what the dickens his name
is.[3]
> *Ibid. Act III, Sc. 2, Line 20*

What a taking was he in, when your
husband asked who was in the basket!
> *Ibid. Sc. 3, Line 190*

O, what a world of vile ill-favour'd
faults
Looks handsome in three hundred
pounds a year!
> *Ibid. Sc. 4, Line 32*

A woman would run through fire and
water for such a kind heart.
> *Ibid. Line 106*

---

[1] See Chaucer, page 4.

[2] Custom is almost second nature. — PLU-
TARCH: *Preservation of Health*

[3] Familiarity breeds contempt. — PUBLIUS
SYRUS: *Maxim 640*

[1] Also in *As You Like It*, Act II, Sc. 7,
L. 26; *The Taming of the Shrew*, Act IV,
Sc. 1, L. 60; *Othello*, Act III, Sc. 1, L. 8;
RABELAIS: *Book V, Chap. 4*

[2] Also in *Romeo and Juliet*, Act I, Sc. 4,
L. 43
Burn daylight. — DRYDEN: *The Maiden
Queen*, Act II, Sc. 1

[3] What the dickens! — THOMAS HEYWOOD:
Edward IV, Act III, Sc. 1

I have a kind of alacrity in sinking.
The Merry Wives of Windsor.
Act III, Sc. 5, Line 13

As good luck would have it.[1]
Ibid. Line 86

The rankest compound of villanous smell that ever offended nostril.
Ibid. Line 95

A man of my kidney.
Ibid. Line 119

So curses all Eve's daughters, of what complexion soever.
Ibid. Act IV, Sc. 2, Line 24

Wives may be merry, and yet honest too.
Ibid. Line 110

There is an old tale goes that Herne the hunter
Sometime a keeper here in Windsor forest,
Doth all the winter-time, at still midnight,
Walk round about an oak, with great ragg'd horns.[2]
Ibid. Sc. 4, Line 29

This is the third time; I hope good luck lies in odd numbers. . . . There is divinity in odd numbers, either in nativity, chance, or death.
Ibid. Act V, Sc. 1, Line 2

Life is a shuttle.
Ibid. Line 25

Cry "mum."
Ibid. Sc. 2, Line 6

Better a little chiding than a great deal of heartbreak.
Ibid. Sc. 3, Line 10

Honi soit qui mal y pense.[3]
Ibid. Sc. 5, Line 75

---

[1] As ill luck would have it. — CERVANTES: *Don Quixote, Pt. I, Bk. I, Ch. II*

[2] There is a tradition that Herne ranged near a tree, known as Herne's Oak, in Windsor Park. The tree was blown down in 1863, when its age was estimated as 650 years. Queen Victoria planted a young oak in its place. The novel, *Windsor Castle*, by WILLIAM HARRISON AINSWORTH [1805–1882] tells of various appearances of Herne.

[3] Shamed be he who thinks evil of it. — Motto of the Order of the Garter, founded by Edward III in 1348

St. George he was for England; St. Dennis was for France;
Sing, *Honi soit qui mal y pense.*

Spirits are not finely touch'd
But to fine issues, nor Nature never lends
The smallest scruple of her excellence
But, like a thrifty goddess, she determines
Herself the glory of a creditor,
Both thanks and use.
Measure for Measure. Act I,
Sc. 1, Line 35

He was ever precise in promise-keeping.
Ibid. Sc. 2, Line 80

Good counsellors lack no clients.
Ibid. Line 115

Who may, in the ambush of my name, strike home.
Ibid. Sc. 3, Line 41

I hold you as a thing ensky'd and sainted.
Ibid. Sc. 4, Line 34

A man whose blood
Is very snow-broth; one who never feels
The wanton stings and motions of the sense.
Ibid. Line 57

He arrests him on it;
And follows close the rigour of the statute,
To make him an example.
Ibid. Line 66

Our doubts are traitors,
And make us lose the good we oft might win
By fearing to attempt.
Ibid. Line 78

The jury, passing on the prisoner's life,
May in the sworn twelve have a thief or two
Guiltier than him they try.
Ibid. Act II, Sc. 1, Line 19

Some rise by sin, and some by virtue fall.
Ibid. Line 38

Great with child, and longing for stewed prunes.
Ibid. Line 94

They are not China dishes, but very good dishes.
Ibid. Line 100

St. George for England, in PERCY: *Reliques of Ancient Poetry, Third Series, Book III*

This will last out a night in Russia,[1]
When nights are longest there.
>   *Measure for Measure. Act II,*
>   *Sc. 1, Line 144*

His face is the worst thing about him.
>   *Ibid. Line 167*

Condemn the fault, and not the actor
of it?
>   *Ibid. Sc. 2, Line 37*

No ceremony that to great ones 'longs,
Not the king's crown, nor the deputed
sword,
The marshal's truncheon, nor the
judge's robe,
Become them with one half so good a
grace
As mercy does.[2]
>   *Ibid. Line 59*

Why, all the souls that were, were forfeit once;
And He that might the vantage best
have took
Found out the remedy. How would you
be,
If He, which is the top of judgment,
should
But judge you as you are?
>   *Ibid. Line 73*

The law hath not been dead, though it
hath slept.
>   *Ibid. Line 90*

O, it is excellent
To have a giant's strength; but it is
tyrannous
To use it like a giant.
>   *Ibid. Line 107*

But man, proud man,
Drest in a little brief authority,
Most ignorant of what he's most as-
sured,
His glassy essence, like an angry ape,
Plays such fantastic tricks before high
heaven
As make the angels weep.
>   *Ibid. Sc. 2, Line 117*

That in the captain's but a choleric
word
Which in the soldier is flat blasphemy.
>   *Ibid. Line 130*

It oft falls out,
To have what we would have, we speak
not what we mean.
>   *Measure for Measure. Act II,*
>   *Sc. 4, Line 118*

I'll tell the world.[1]
>   *Ibid. Line 154*

The miserable have no other medicine,
But only hope.
>   *Ibid. Act III, Sc. 1, Line 2*

A breath thou art,
Servile to all the skyey influences.
>   *Ibid. Line 8*

Palsied eld.
>   *Ibid. Line 36*

The sense of death is most in appre-
hension;
And the poor beetle, that we tread upon,
In corporal sufferance finds a pang as
great
As when a giant dies.
>   *Ibid. Line 76*

The cunning livery of hell.
>   *Ibid. Line 93*

Ay, but to die, and go we know not
where;
To lie in cold obstruction and to rot;
This sensible warm motion to become
A kneaded clod; and the delighted
spirit
To bathe in fiery floods, or to reside
In thrilling region of thick-ribbed ice;
To be imprison'd in the viewless winds,
And blown with restless violence round
about
The pendent world.
>   *Ibid. Line 116*

The weariest and most loathed worldly
life
That age, ache, penury, and imprison-
ment
Can lay on nature, is a paradise
To what we fear of death.
>   *Ibid. Line 127*

I have no superfluous leisure.
>   *Ibid. Line 156*

---

[1] Will burn a Poland winter. — *The Comedy of Errors, Act III, Sc. 2, L. 101*
[2] Compare Portia's words in *The Merchant
of Venice, Act IV, Sc. 4, Lines 184–202*

[1] Let me tell the world. — *King Henry IV,
Part I, Act V, Sc. 2, L. 65*
Ay, tell the world! — BROWNING: *Paracel-
sus, Part II*

The hand that hath made you fair hath made you good.[1]

> *Measure for Measure. Act III,*
> *Sc. 1, Line 182*

Virtue is bold, and goodness never fearful.

> *Ibid. Line 214*

There, at the moated grange, resides this dejected Mariana.[2]

> *Ibid. Line 279*

Pygmalion's images, newly made woman.

> *Ibid. Sc. 2, Line 48*

This news is old enough, yet it is every day's news.

> *Ibid. Line 249*

He who the sword of heaven will bear
Should be as holy as severe.

> *Ibid. Line 283*

O, what may man within him hide,
Though angel on the outward side!

> *Ibid. Line 293*

Take, O take those lips away,
  That so sweetly were forsworn;
And those eyes, the break of day,
  Lights that do mislead the morn:
But my kisses bring again, bring again;
Seals of love, but sealed in vain, sealed in vain.[3]

> *Ibid. Act IV, Sc. 1, Line 1*

Every true man's apparel fits your thief.

> *Ibid. Sc. 2, Line 46*

Death's a great disguiser.

> *Ibid. Line 185*

We would, and we would not.

> *Ibid. Sc. 4, Line 37*

A forted residence 'gainst the tooth of time
And razure of oblivion.

> *Ibid. Act V, Sc. 1, Line 12*

---

[1] See Spenser, page 26.

[2] "Mariana in the moated grange." — The motto used by TENNYSON for the poem *Mariana*.

[3] This song occurs in *Act V, Sc. 2* of BEAUMONT AND FLETCHER'S *Bloody Brother*, with the following additional stanza: —

> Hide, O hide those hills of snow,
>   Which thy frozen bosom bears,
> On whose tops the pinks that grow
>   Are of those that April wears!
> But first set my poor heart free,
> Bound in those icy chains by thee.

Truth is truth
To the end of reckoning.

> *Measure for Measure. Act V,*
> *Sc. 1, Line 45*

Neither maid, widow, nor wife.

> *Ibid. Line 173*

They say best men are moulded out of faults.
And, for the most, become much more the better
For being a little bad.

> *Ibid. Line 440*

What's mine is yours, and what is yours is mine.

> *Ibid. Line 539*

The pleasing punishment that women bear.

> *The Comedy of Errors. Act I,*
> *Sc. 1, Line 46*

We may pity, though not pardon thee.

> *Ibid. Line 97*

To tell sad stories of my own mishaps.

> *Ibid. Line 120*

A wretched soul, bruised with adversity.

> *Ibid. Act II, Sc. 1, Line 34*

Every why hath a wherefore.[1]

> *Ibid. Sc. 2, Line 45*

Neither rhyme nor reason.[2]

> *Ibid. Line 49*

There's a time for all things.[3]

> *Ibid. Line 67*

There's no time for a man to recover his hair that grows bald by nature.

> *Ibid. Line 74*

What he hath scanted men in hair, he hath given them in wit.

> *Ibid. Line 83*

Time himself is bald, and therefore to the world's end will have bald followers.

> *Ibid. Line 109*

Small cheer and great welcome makes a merry feast.

> *Ibid. Act III, Sc. 1, Line 26*

There is something in the wind.

> *Ibid. Line 69*

We'll pluck a crow together.

> *Ibid. Line 83*

---

[1] For every why he had a wherefore. — BUTLER: *Hudibras, Pt. I, C. I, L. 132*

[2] See Spenser, page 26.

[3] To every thing there is a season, and a time to every purpose under the heaven. — *Ecclesiastes, III, 1*

For slander lives upon succession,
For ever housed where it gets possession.
> *The Comedy of Errors.*
> *Act III, Sc. 1, Line 105*

Be not thy tongue thy own shame's orator.
> *Ibid. Sc. 2, Line 10*

Ill deeds are doubled with an evil word.
> *Ibid. Line 20*

A back-friend, a shoulder-clapper.
> *Ibid. Act IV, Sc. 2, Line 37*

Give me your hand and let me feel your
pulse.
> *Ibid. Sc. 4, Line 54*

Unquiet meals make ill digestions.
> *Ibid. Act V, Sc. 1, Line 74*

One Pinch, a hungry lean-faced villain,
A mere anatomy.[1]
> *Ibid. Line 238*

A needy, hollow-eyed, sharp-looking
wretch,
A living-dead man.
> *Ibid. Line 241*

I hope I shall have leisure to make good.
> *Ibid. Line 378*

He hath indeed better bettered expectation.
> *Much Ado about Nothing. Act I,*
> *Sc. 1, Line 16*

How much better is it to weep at joy
than to joy at weeping.
> *Ibid. Line 28*

A very valiant trencher-man.
> *Ibid. Line 52*

There's a skirmish of wit between them.
> *Ibid. Line 64*

He wears his faith but as the fashion of
his hat.
> *Ibid. Line 76*

The gentleman is not in your books.
> *Ibid. Line 79*

What! my dear Lady Disdain! are you
yet living?
> *Ibid. Line 123*

I would my horse had the speed of
your tongue, and so good a continuer.
> *Ibid. Line 151*

Shall I never see a bachelor of three-
score again?
> *Ibid. Line 209*

[1] See Burton, page 123.

Benedick the married man.
> *Much Ado about Nothing.*
> *Act I, Sc. 1, Line 278*

He is of a very melancholy disposition.
> *Ibid. Act II, Sc. 1, Line 6*

I could not endure a husband with
a beard on his face: I had rather lie in
the woollen.
> *Ibid. Line 31*

He that hath a beard is more than a
youth, and he that hath no beard is less
than a man.
> *Ibid. Line 38*

As merry as the day is long.
> *Ibid. Line 52*

I have a good eye, uncle; I can see a
church by daylight.
> *Ibid. Line 86*

Speak low, if you speak love.
> *Ibid. Line 104*

Friendship is constant in all other things
Save in the office and affairs of love:
Therefore, all hearts in love use their
own tongues;
Let every eye negotiate for itself,
And trust no agent.
> *Ibid. Line 184*

Silence is the perfectest herald of
joy: I were but little happy, if I could
say how much.
> *Ibid. Line 319*

It keeps on the windy side of care.[1]
> *Ibid. Line 328*

There was a star danced, and under
that was I born.
> *Ibid. Line 351*

I will tell you my drift.[2]
> *Ibid. Line 406*

He was wont to speak plain and to
the purpose.
> *Ibid. Sc. 3, Line 19*

Her hair shall be of what colour it
please God.
> *Ibid. Line 36*

Sigh no more, ladies, sigh no more,
Men were deceivers ever;
One foot in sea and one on shore;
To one thing constant never.
> *Ibid. Line 65*

[1] The windy side of the law. — *Twelfth-Night, Act III, Sc. 4, L. 183*
[2] We know your drift. — *Coriolanus, Act III, Sc. 3, L. 114*

Sits the wind in that corner?
Much Ado about Nothing.
Act II, Sc. 3, Line 108

Bait the hook well: this fish will bite.
Ibid. Line 121

Happy are they that hear their detractions, and can put them to mending.
Ibid. Line 248

Shall quips and sentences and these paper bullets of the brain awe a man from the career of his humour? No; the world must be peopled. When I said I would die a bachelor, I did not think I should live till I were married.
Ibid. Line 260

The pleasant'st angling is to see the fish
Cut with her golden oars the silver stream,
And greedily devour the treacherous bait.
Ibid. Act III, Sc. 1, Line 26

From the crown of his head to the sole of his foot,[1] he is all mirth.
Ibid. Sc. 2, Line 9

He hath a heart as sound as a bell.
Ibid. Line 12

Every one can master a grief but he that has it.
Ibid. Line 28

Are you good men and true?
Ibid. Sc. 3, Line 1

To be a well-favoured man is the gift of fortune; but to write and read comes by nature.
Ibid. Line 14

You shall comprehend all vagrom men.
Ibid. Line 25

2 Watch. How, if a' will not stand?
Dogberry. Why, then, take no note of him, but let him go; and presently call the rest of the watch together, and thank God you are rid of a knave.
Ibid. Line 28

If they make you not then the better answer, you may say they are not the men you took them for.
Ibid. Line 49

They that touch pitch will be defiled.[1]
Much Ado about Nothing.
Act III, Sc. 3, Line 61

The most peaceable way for you if you do take a thief, is to let him show himself what he is and steal out of your company.
Ibid. Line 62

The fashion wears out more apparel than the man.
Ibid. Line 147

I thank God, I am as honest as any man living, that is an old man and no honester than I.
Ibid. Sc. 5, Line 15

Comparisons are odorous.
Ibid. Line 18

A good old man, sir; he will be talking: as they say, When the age is in, the wit is out.
Ibid. Line 36

O! what men dare do! what men may do! what men daily do, not knowing what they do!
Ibid. Act IV, Sc. 1, Line 19

O! what authority and show of truth
Can cunning sin cover itself withal!
Ibid. Line 35

I have mark'd
A thousand blushing apparitions
To start into her face; a thousand innocent shames
In angel whiteness beat away those blushes.
Ibid. Line 160

For it so falls out
That what we have we prize not to the worth
Whiles we enjoy it, but being lack'd and lost,
Why, then we rack the value; then we find
The virtue that possession would not show us
Whiles it was ours.
Ibid. Line 219

---

[1] From the crown of his head to the sole of the foot. — PLINY: *Natural History, Book VII, Chap. XVII.* BEAUMONT AND FLETCHER: *The Honest Man's Fortune, Act II, Sc. 2.* MIDDLETON: *A Mad World, etc.*

[1] He that toucheth pitch shall be defiled therewith. — *Apocrypha: Ecclesiasticus, XIII, 1*

This pitch, as ancient writers do report, doth defile; so doth the company thou keepest. — *King Henry IV, Part I, Act II, Sc. 4, L. 460*

The idea of her life shall sweetly creep
Into his study of imagination,
And every lovely organ of her life,
Shall come apparell'd in more precious
habit,
More moving-delicate, and full of life
Into the eye and prospect of his soul.
>   *Much Ado about Nothing.*
>   *Act IV, Sc. 1, Line 226*

Masters, it is proved already that you
are little better than false knaves; and
it will go near to be thought so shortly.
>   *Ibid. Sc. 2, Line 23*

Flat burglary as ever was committed.
>   *Ibid. Line 54*

Condemned into everlasting redemption.
>   *Ibid. Line 60*

O that he were here to write me down an
ass!
>   *Ibid. Line 80*

A fellow that hath had losses, and one
that hath two gowns, and every thing
handsome about him.
>   *Ibid. Line 90*

Patch grief with proverbs.
>   *Ibid. Act V, Sc. 1, Line 17*

>   Men
Can counsel and speak comfort to that
grief
Which they themselves not feel.
>   *Ibid. Line 20*

Charm ache with air, and agony with
words.
>   *Ibid. Line 26*

'Tis all men's office to speak patience
To those that wring under the load of
sorrow;
But no man's virtue nor sufficiency
To be so moral when he shall endure
The like himself.
>   *Ibid. Line 27*

For there was never yet philosopher
That could endure the toothache patiently.
>   *Ibid. Line 35*

Some of us will smart for it.
>   *Ibid. Line 108*

What though care killed a cat.[1]
>   *Much Ado about Nothing.*
>   *Act V, Sc. 1, Line 135*

I was not born under a rhyming planet.
>   *Ibid. Sc. 2, Line 40*

Done to death by slanderous tongues.
>   *Ibid. Sc. 3, Line 3*

Make us heirs of all eternity.
>   *Love's Labour's Lost.*
>   *Act I, Sc. 1, Line 7*

The huge army of the world's desires.
>   *Ibid. Line 10*

Or, having sworn too hard-a-keeping
oath,
Study to break it, and not break my
troth.
>   *Ibid. Line 65*

Light seeking light doth light of light
beguile.
>   *Ibid. Line 77*

Small have continual plodders ever won,
Save base authority from others'
books.
These earthly godfathers of heaven's
lights
That give a name to every fixed star,
Have no more profit of their shining
nights
That those that walk and wot not
what they are.
>   *Ibid. Line 86*

At Christmas I no more desire a rose
Than wish a snow in May's new-
fangled mirth;
But like of each thing that in season
grows.
>   *Ibid. Line 105*

A man in all the world's new fashion
planted,
That hath a mint of phrases in his brain.
>   *Ibid. Line 163*

And men sit down to that nourishment which is called supper.
>   *Ibid. Line 237*

That unlettered small-knowing soul.
>   *Ibid. Line 251*

---

[1] Care 'll kill a cat. — BEN JONSON: *Every Man in his Humour, Act I, Sc. 1*
Care will kill a cat. — GEORGE WITHER: *Poem* on *Christmas*

A child of our grandmother Eve, a female; or, for thy more sweet understanding, a woman.
Love's Labour's Lost.
Act I, Sc. 1, Line 263

Affliction may one day smile again; and till then, sit thee down, sorrow!
Ibid. Line 312

The world was very guilty of such a ballad some three ages since; but I think now 'tis not to be found.
Ibid. Sc. 2, Line 117

Devise, wit; write, pen; for I am for whole volumes in folio.
Ibid. Line 194

A man of sovereign parts he is esteem'd;
Well fitted in arts, glorious in arms:
Nothing becomes him ill that he would well.
Ibid. Act II, Sc. 1, Line 44

A merrier man,
Within the limit of becoming mirth,
I never spent an hour's talk withal.
Ibid. Line 66

Delivers in such apt and gracious words
That aged ears play truant at his tales,
And younger hearings are quite ravished;
So sweet and voluble is his discourse.
Ibid. Line 73

Remuneration! O! that's the Latin word for three farthings.
Ibid. Act III, Sc. 1, Line 143

A very beadle to a humorous sigh.
Ibid. Line 185

This senior-junior, giant-dwarf, Dan Cupid;
Regent of love-rhymes, lord of folded arms,
The anointed sovereign of sighs and groans,
Liege of all loiterers and malcontents.
Ibid. Line 190

A buck of the first head.
Ibid. Act IV, Sc. 2, Line 10

He hath not fed of the dainties that are bred in a book; he hath not eat paper, as it were; he hath not drunk ink.
Ibid. Line 25

Many can brook the weather that love not the wind.
Ibid. Line 34

You two are book-men.
Love's Labour's Lost.
Act IV, Sc. 2, Line 35

These are begot in the ventricle of memory, nourished in the womb of pia mater, and delivered upon the mellowing of occasion.
Ibid. Line 70

As upright as the cedar.
Ibid. Sc. 3, Line 89

For where is any author in the world
Teaches such beauty as a woman's eye?
Learning is but an adjunct to ourself.
Ibid. Line 312

It adds a precious seeing to the eye.
Ibid. Line 333

As sweet and musical
As bright Apollo's lute, strung with his hair;
And when Love speaks, the voice of all the gods
Makes heaven drowsy with the harmony.
Ibid. Line 342

From women's eyes this doctrine I derive:
They sparkle still the right Promethean fire;
They are the books, the arts, the academes,
That show, contain, and nourish all the world.
Ibid. Line 350

He draweth out the thread of his verbosity finer than the staple of his argument.
Ibid. Act V, Sc. 1, Line 18

They have been at a great feast of languages, and stolen the scraps.
Ibid. Line 39

In the posteriors of this day, which the rude multitude call the afternoon.
Ibid. Line 96

Let me take you a button-hole lower.
Ibid. Sc. 2, Line 705

The naked truth.
Ibid. Line 715

A jest's prosperity lies in the ear
Of him that hears it, never in the tongue
Of him that makes it.
Ibid. Line 869

When daisies pied and violets blue,
And lady-smocks all silver-white,

And cuckoo-buds of yellow hue
Do paint the meadows with delight,
The cuckoo then, on every tree,
Mocks married men.
> *Love's Labour's Lost.*
> *Act V, Sc. 2, Line 902*

The words of Mercury are harsh after
the songs of Apollo.
> *Ibid. Line 938*

The moon, like to a silver bow
New-bent in heaven.
> *A Midsummer-Night's Dream.*
> *Act I, Sc. 1, Line 9*

But earthlier happy is the rose distill'd
Than that which withering on the virgin
thorn [1]
Grows, lives, and dies in single blessedness.
> *Ibid. Line 76*

For aught that I could ever read,
Could ever hear by tale or history,
The course of true love never did run
smooth.
> *Ibid. Line 132*

Swift as a shadow, short as any dream,
Brief as the lightning in the collied
night,
That, in a spleen, unfolds both heaven
and earth,
And ere a man hath power to say, "Be-
hold!"
The jaws of darkness do devour it up:
So quick bright things come to confu-
sion.
> *Ibid. Line 144*

Love looks not with the eyes, but with
the mind,
And therefore is winged Cupid painted
blind.
> *Ibid. Line 234*

Masters, spread yourselves.
> *Ibid. Sc. 2, Line 16*

This is Ercles' vein.
> *Ibid. Line 43*

I'll speak in a monstrous little voice.
> *Ibid. Line 55*

I am slow of study.
> *Ibid. Line 70*

That would hang us, every mother's
son.
> *A Midsummer-Night's Dream.*
> *Act I, Sc. 2, Line 81*

I will roar you as gently as any sucking dove; I will roar you, as 'twere any
nightingale.
> *Ibid. Line 85*

A proper man, as one shall see in a summer's day.
> *Ibid. Line 89*

The human mortals.
> *Ibid. Act II, Sc. 1, Line 101*

Knows not which is which.
> *Ibid. Line 114*

The rude sea grew civil at her song,
And certain stars shot madly from their
spheres
To hear the sea-maid's music.
> *Ibid. Line 152*

And the imperial votaress passed on,
In maiden meditation, fancy-free.
Yet mark'd I where the bolt of Cupid
fell:
It fell upon a little western flower,
Before milk-white, now purple with
love's wound,
And maidens call it Love-in-idleness.
> *Ibid. Line 163*

I'll put a girdle round about the earth
In forty minutes.[1]
> *Ibid. Line 175*

My heart
Is true as steel.[2]
> *Ibid. Line 196*

It is not night when I do see your face.
> *Ibid. Line 221*

For you in my respect are all the world:
Then how can it be said I am alone.
> *Ibid. Line 224*

We cannot fight for love, as men may
do;
We should be woo'd and were not made
to woo.
> *Ibid. Line 241*

I know a bank whereon the wild thyme
blows.
> *Ibid. Line 249*

---

[1] Maidens withering on the stalk. — WORDS-
WORTH: *Personal Talk, Stanza 1*

[1] See Chapman, page 28.
[2] Trewe as steel. — CHAUCER: *Troilus and
Criseyde, Book V, L. 831.* SHAKESPEARE: *Troilus and Cressida, Act III, Sc. 2, L. 184; Romeo
and Juliet, Act II, Sc. 4, L. 212*

As a surfeit of the sweetest things
The deepest loathing to the stomach
brings.
> *A Midsummer-Night's Dream.*
> *Act II, Sc. 2, Line 137*

A lion among ladies is a most dreadful
thing.
> *Ibid. Act III, Sc. 1, Line 32*

A calendar, a calendar! look in the
almanack; find out moonshine.
> *Ibid. Line 55*

Bless thee, Bottom! bless thee! thou art
translated.
> *Ibid. Line 124*

Lord, what fools these mortals be!
> *Ibid. Sc. 2, Line 115*

So we grew together,
Like to a double cherry, seeming parted,
But yet an union in partition—
Two lovely berries moulded on one
stem.
> *Ibid. Line 208*

Though she be but little, she is fierce.
> *Ibid. Line 325*

I have an exposition of sleep come upon
me.
> *Ibid. Act IV, Sc. 1, Line 44*

I have had a dream, past the wit of
man to say what dream it was.
> *Ibid. Line 211*

The eye of man hath not heard, the
ear of man hath not seen,[1] man's hand is
not able to taste, his tongue to conceive,
nor his heart to report, what my dream
was.
> *Ibid. Line 218*

A paramour is, God bless us! a thing of
naught.
> *Ibid. Sc. 2, Line 14*

Eat no onions nor garlic, for we are to
utter sweet breath.
> *Ibid. Line 44*

The lunatic, the lover, and the poet
Are of imagination all compact:
One sees more devils than vast hell can
hold,
That is, the madman: the lover, all as
frantic,
Sees Helen's beauty in a brow of Egypt:
The poet's eye, in a fine frenzy rolling,

Doth glance from heaven to earth, from
earth to heaven;
And as imagination bodies forth
The forms of things unknown, the poet's
pen
Turns them to shapes, and gives to airy
nothing
A local habitation and a name.
Such tricks hath strong imagination,
That if it would but apprehend some
joy,
It comprehends some bringer of that
joy;
Or in the night, imagining some fear,
How easy is a bush supposed a bear!
> *A Midsummer-Night's Dream.*
> *Act V, Sc. 1, Line 7*

The true beginning of our end.[1]
> *Ibid. Line 111*

The best in this kind are but shadows.
> *Ibid. Line 215*

A very gentle beast, and of a good conscience.
> *Ibid. Line 232*

This passion, and the death of a dear
friend, would go near to make a man
look sad.
> *Ibid. Line 295*

With the help of a surgeon, he might
yet recover.
> *Ibid. Line 318*

The iron tongue of midnight hath told
twelve.
> *Ibid. Line 372*

My ventures are not in one bottom
trusted,
Nor to one place.
> *The Merchant of Venice.*
> *Act I, Sc. 1, Line 42*

Now, by two-headed Janus,
Nature hath framed strange fellows in
her time.
> *Ibid. Line 50*

Though Nestor swear the jest be laugh-
able.
> *Ibid. Line 56*

You have too much respect upon the
world:
They lose it that do buy it with much
care.
> *Ibid. Line 74*

---

[1] Eye hath not seen, nor ear heard. —
1 Corinthians, II, 9

[1] I see the beginning of my end. — MAS-
SINGER: *The Virgin Martyr, Act III, Sc. 3*

I hold the world but as the world, Gratiano, —
A stage, where every man must play a part;
And mine a sad one.

*The Merchant of Venice.
Act I, Sc. 1, Line 77*

Why should a man, whose blood is warm within,
Sit like his grandsire cut in alabaster?

Ibid. Line 83

There are a sort of men whose visages
Do cream and mantle like a standing pond.

Ibid. Line 88

I am Sir Oracle,
And when I ope my lips, let no dog bark!

Ibid. Line 93

I do know of these
That therefore only are reputed wise
For saying nothing.

Ibid. Line 95

Fish not, with this melancholy bait,
For this fool gudgeon, this opinion.

Ibid. Line 101

Gratiano speaks an infinite deal of nothing, more than any man in all Venice. His reasons are as two grains of wheat hid in two bushels of chaff: you shall seek all day ere you find them, and when you have them, they are not worth the search.

Ibid. Line 114

In my school-days, when I had lost one shaft,
I shot his fellow of the selfsame flight
The selfsame way, with more advised watch,
To find the other forth; and by adventuring both,
I oft found both.

Ibid. Line 141

They are as sick that surfeit with too much, as they that starve with nothing.

Ibid. Sc. 2, Line 5

Superfluity comes sooner by white hairs, but competency lives longer.

Ibid. Line 9

If to do were easy as to know what were good to do, chapels had been churches, and poor men's cottages princes' palaces.

*The Merchant of Venice.
Act I, Sc. 2, Line 13*

The brain may devise laws for the blood, but a hot temper leaps o'er a cold decree.

Ibid. Line 19

He doth nothing but talk of his horse.

Ibid. Line 43

God made him, and therefore let him pass for a man.

Ibid. Line 59

When he is best, he is a little worse than a man; and when he is worst, he is little better than a beast.

Ibid. Line 93

I dote on his very absence.

Ibid. Line 118

My meaning in saying he is a good man, is to have you understand me that he is sufficient.

Ibid. Sc. 3, Line 15

Ships are but boards, sailors but men: there be land-rats and water-rats, water-thieves and land-thieves.

Ibid. Line 22

I will buy with you, sell with you, talk with you, walk with you, and so following; but I will not eat with you, drink with you, nor pray with you. What news on the Rialto?

Ibid. Line 36

I will feed fat the ancient grudge I bear him.

He hates our sacred nation; and he rails,
Even there where merchants most do congregate.

Ibid. Line 48

The devil can cite Scripture for his purpose.

Ibid. Line 99

A goodly apple rotten at the heart:
O, what a goodly outside falsehood hath!

Ibid. Line 102

For sufferance is the badge of all our tribe.

Ibid. Line 110

You call me misbeliever, cut-throat dog,
And spet upon my Jewish gaberdine.

Ibid. Line 111

Shall I bend low, and in a bondman's key,
With bated breath and whispering humbleness.
The Merchant of Venice.
Act I, Sc. 3, Line 124
O father Abram! what these Christians are,
Whose own hard dealings teaches them suspect
The thoughts of others!
Ibid. Line 161
Mislike me not for my complexion,
The shadow'd livery of the burnish'd sun.
Ibid. Act II, Sc. 1, Line 1
An honest, exceeding poor man.
Ibid. Line 54
The young gentleman, according to Fates and Destinies and such odd sayings, the Sisters Three and such branches of learning, is indeed deceased; or, as you would say in plain terms, gone to heaven.
Ibid. Sc. 2, Line 66
The very staff of my age, my very prop.
Ibid. Line 71
It is a wise father that knows his own child.
Ibid. Line 83.
Truth will come to light; murder cannot be hid long.[1]
Ibid. Line 86
In the twinkling of an eye.
Ibid. Line 183
And the vile squealing of the wry-necked fife.
Ibid. Sc. 5, Line 30
Who risest from a feast
With that keen appetite that he sits down?
Ibid. Sc. 6, Line 8
All things that are,
Are with more spirit chased than enjoy'd.
Ibid. Line 12
But love is blind, and lovers cannot see
The pretty follies that themselves commit.
Ibid. Line 36

[1] See Chaucer, page 6.

Must I hold a candle to my shames?
The Merchant of Venice.
Act II, Sc. 6, Line 41
A golden mind stoops not to show of dross.
Ibid. Sc. 7, Line 20
All that glisters is not gold.[1]
Ibid. Line 65
Young in limbs, in judgment old.
Ibid. Line 71
Even in the force and road of casualty.
Ibid. Sc. 9, Line 30
Hanging and wiving goes by destiny.[2]
Ibid. Line 83
I am a Jew. Hath not a Jew eyes? Hath not a Jew hands, organs, dimensions, senses, affections, passions?
Ibid. Act III, Sc. 1, Line 62
The villany you teach me I will execute, and it shall go hard, but I will better the instruction.
Ibid. Line 76
I would not have given it for a wilderness of monkeys.
Ibid. Line 130
There's something tells me.
Ibid. Sc. 2, Line 4
Makes a swan-like end,
Fading in music.[3]
Ibid. Line 44
Tell me where is fancy bred,
Or in the heart or in the head?
How begot, how nourished?
Reply, reply.
Ibid. Line 63

[1] See Chaucer, page 8.
[2] See Heywood, page 12. See Burton, page 240.
[3] See Chaucer, page 4.
I will play the swan and die in music. — *Othello, Act V, Sc. 2, L. 245*
I am the cygnet to this pale faint swan, Who chants a doleful hymn to his own death. *King John, Act V, Sc. 7, L. 21*
There, swan-like, let me sing and die. — BYRON: *Don Juan, Canto III, St. 86*
You think that upon the score of foreknowledge and divining I am infinitely inferior to the swans. When they perceive approaching death they sing more merrily than before, because of the joy they have in going to the God they serve. — SOCRATES: In *Phaedo, 77*

In law, what plea so tainted and corrupt
But being season'd with a gracious
    voice,
Obscures the show of evil?
The Merchant of Venice.
Act III, Sc. 2, Line 75

There is no vice so simple but assumes
Some mark of virtue on his outward
    parts.
Ibid. Line 81

Thus ornament is but the guiled shore
To a most dangerous sea.
Ibid. Line 97

The seeming truth which cunning times
    put on
To entrap the wisest.
Ibid. Line 100

An unlesson'd girl, unschool'd, unprac-
    tised;
Happy in this, she is not yet so old
But she may learn.[1]
Ibid. Line 160

Here are a few of the unpleasant'st
    words
That ever blotted paper!
Ibid. Line 252

    The kindest man,
The best-condition'd and unwearied
    spirit
In doing courtesies.
Ibid. Line 293

The sins of the father are to be laid
upon the children.
Ibid. Sc. 5, Line 1

Thus when I shun Scylla, your father, I fall into Charybdis, your
mother.[2]
Ibid. Line 17

Let it serve for table-talk.
Ibid. Line 95

A harmless necessary cat.
Ibid. Act IV, Sc. 1, Line 55

What! wouldst thou have a serpent
    sting thee twice?
Ibid. Line 69

---

[1] It is better to learn late than never. —
PUBLIUS SYRUS: *Maxim 864*

[2] Incidis in Scyllam cupiens vitare Charyb-
dim (One falls into Scylla in seeking to avoid
Charybdis). — PHILIPPE GUALTIER: *Alexan-
dreis, Book V, Line 301 [circa 1300.]*

I am a tainted wether of the flock,
Meetest for death: the weakest kind of
    fruit
Drops earliest to the ground.
The Merchant of Venice.
Act IV, Sc. 1, Line 114

To hold opinion with Pythagoras
That souls of animals infuse themselves
Into the trunks of men.[1]
Ibid. Line 131

I never knew so young a body with so
    old a head.[2]
Ibid. Line 163

The quality of mercy is not strain'd,
It droppeth as the gentle rain from
    heaven
Upon the place beneath. It is twice
    bless'd:
It blesseth him that gives and him that
    takes.
'T is mightiest in the mightiest: it be-
    comes
The throned monarch better than his
    crown;
His sceptre shows the force of temporal
    power,
The attribute to awe and majesty,
Wherein doth sit the dread and fear of
    kings;
But mercy is above this sceptred
    sway,
It is enthroned in the hearts of kings,
It is an attribute to God himself;
And earthly power doth then show lik-
    est God's,
When mercy seasons justice. Therefore,
    Jew,
Though justice be thy plea, consider
    this,
That in the course of justice, none of us
Should see salvation: we do pray for
    mercy;

---

[1] *Clown.* What is the opinion of Pythagoras
concerning wild fowl?
Malvolio. That the soul of our grandam
might haply inhabit a bird.
Twelfth-Night, Act IV, Sc. 2, L. 55

[2] He is young, but, take it from me, a very
staid head. — THOMAS WENTWORTH [1593–
1641], EARL OF STRAFFORD: Letter, commend-
ing the Earl of Ormond to Charles I for
appointment as Councillor. *Gentleman's Magazine,* London, October, 1854, page 328.

And that same prayer doth teach us all
to render
The deeds of mercy.
The Merchant of Venice.
Act IV, Sc. 1, Line 184

To do a great right, do a little wrong.
Ibid. Line 216

A Daniel come to judgment! yea, a
Daniel!
Ibid. Line 223

How much more elder art thou than thy
looks.
Ibid. Line 251

Is it so nominated in the bond?
Ibid. Line 260

'Tis not in the bond.
Ibid. Line 263

Speak me fair in death.
Ibid. Line 276

An upright judge, a learned judge!
Ibid. Line 324

A second Daniel, a Daniel, Jew!
Now, infidel, I have thee on the hip.[1]
Ibid. Line 335

I thank thee, Jew, for teaching me that
word.
Ibid. Line 342

You take my house, when you do take
the prop
That doth sustain my house; you take
my life,
When you do take the means whereby
I live.
Ibid. Line 376

He is well paid that is well satisfied.
Ibid. Line 416

How sweet the moonlight sleeps upon
this bank!
Here we will sit and let the sounds of
music
Creep in our ears: soft stillness and the
night
Become the touches of sweet harmony.
Sit, Jessica. Look how the floor of
heaven
Is thick inlaid with patines of bright
gold:
There's not the smallest orb which
thou behold'st
But in his motion like an angel sings,

[1] See Heywood, page 16.

Still quiring to the young-eyed cheru-
bins.
Such harmony is in immortal souls;
But whilst this muddy vesture of decay
Doth grossly close it in, we cannot hear
it.
The Merchant of Venice.
Act V, Sc. 1, Line 54

I am never merry when I hear sweet
music.
Ibid. Line 69

The man that hath no music in himself,
Nor is not moved with concord of sweet
sounds,
Is fit for treasons, stratagems, and
spoils;
The motions of his spirit are dull as
night,
And his affections dark as Erebus.
Let no such man be trusted.
Ibid. Line 83

How far that little candle throws his
beams!
So shines a good deed in a naughty
world.
Ibid. Line 90

How many things by season season'd
are
To their right praise and true perfection!
Ibid. Line 107

This night, methinks, is but the daylight sick.
Ibid. Line 124

A light wife doth make a heavy husband.
Ibid. Line 130

These blessed candles of the night.
Ibid. Line 220

Fleet the time carelessly, as they did in
the golden world.
As You Like It. Act I, Sc. 1, Line 126

Always the dulness of the fool is the
whetstone of the wits.
Ibid. Sc. 2, Line 59

The little foolery that wise men have
makes a great show.
Ibid. Line 97

Well said: that was laid on with a
trowel.
Ibid. Line 113

In the world I fill up a place, which

may be better supplied when I have made it empty.

As You Like It. Act I, Sc. 2, Line 206

Your heart's desires be with you!

Ibid. Line 214

One out of suits with fortune.

Ibid. Line 263

My pride fell with my fortunes.

Ibid. Line 269

Hereafter, in a better world than this,
I shall desire more love and knowledge
of you.

Ibid. Line 301

Celia. Not a word?
Rosalind. Not one to throw at a dog.

Ibid. Sc. 3, Line 2

O, how full of briers is this working-
day world!

Ibid. Line 12

Beauty provoketh thieves sooner than
gold.

Ibid. Line 113

We 'll have a swashing and a martial
outside,
As many other mannish cowards have.

Ibid. Line 123

Sweet are the uses of adversity;
Which, like the toad, ugly and venom-
ous,
Wears yet a precious jewel in his head;
And this our life, exempt from public
haunt,
Finds tongues in trees, books in the run-
ning brooks,
Sermons in stones, and good in every
thing.

Ibid. Act II, Sc. 1, Line 12

The big round tears
Coursed one another down his innocent
nose
In piteous chase.

Ibid. Line 38

"Poor deer," quoth he, "thou mak'st a
testament
As worldlings do, giving thy sum of
more
To that which had too much."

Ibid. Line 47

Sweep on, you fat and greasy citizens.

Ibid. Line 55

And He that doth the ravens feed,
Yea, providently caters for the sparrow,

Be comfort to my age!

As You Like It. Act II, Sc. 3, Line 43

For in my youth I never did apply
Hot and rebellious liquors in my blood.

Ibid. Line 48

Therefore my age is as a lusty winter,
Frosty, but kindly.

Ibid. Line 52

O, good old man; how well in thee appears
The constant service of the antique
world,
When service sweat for duty, not for
meed!
Thou art not for the fashion of these
times,
Where none will sweat but for promotion.

Ibid. Line 56

I will follow thee
To the last gasp [1] with truth and loyalty.

Ibid. Line 69

Ay, now am I in Arden: the more
fool I. When I was at home I was in a
better place; but travellers must be content.

Ibid. Sc. 4, Line 16

If you remember'st not the slightest
folly
That ever love did make thee run into,
Thou hast not lov'd.

Ibid. Line 34

Thou speakest wiser than thou art ware
of.

Ibid. Line 57

I shall ne'er be 'ware of mine own
wit, till I break my shins against it.

Ibid. Line 59

Under the greenwood tree
Who loves to lie with me.

Ibid. Sc. 5, Line 1

What's that "ducdame"?
'Tis a Greek invocation to call fools
into a circle. [2]

Ibid. Line 58

---

[1] Fight till the last gasp. — *King Henry VI,
Part I, Act I, Sc. 2, L. 127*

[2] Your name, even in life, was, alas! a kind
of *ducdame* to bring people of no very great
sense into your circle. — ANDREW LANG: *Letters to Dead Authors, To Percy Bysshe Shelley*

                        I met a fool i' the forest,
A motley fool.
    As You Like It. Act II, Sc. 7, Line 12
And rail'd on Lady Fortune in good
    terms,
In good set terms.
                  Ibid. Line 16
And then he drew a dial from his poke,
And looking on it with lack-lustre eye,
Says, very wisely, "It is ten o'clock:
Thus we may see," quoth he, "how the
    world wags." [1]
                  Ibid. Line 20
And so from hour to hour we ripe and
    ripe,
And then from hour to hour we rot and
    rot;
And thereby hangs a tale. [2]
                  Ibid. Line 26
My lungs began to crow like chanti-
    cleer,
That fools should be so deep-contem-
    plative;
And I did laugh sans intermission
An hour by his dial.
                  Ibid. Line 30
Motley 's the only wear.
                  Ibid. Line 34
    If ladies be but young and fair,
They have the gift to know it; and in
    his brain,
Which is as dry as the remainder bis-
    cuit
After a voyage, he hath strange places
    cramm'd
With observation, the which he vents
In mangled forms.
                  Ibid. Line 37
             I must have liberty
Withal, as large a charter as the wind,
To blow on whom I please.
                  Ibid. Line 47
The "why" is plain as way to parish
    church.
                  Ibid. Line 52
Under the shade of melancholy boughs,
Lose and neglect the creeping hours of
    time;
If ever you have look'd on better days,

[1] So wags the world. — SCOTT: *Ivanhoe*,
Chap. 37
[2] See Shakespeare, page 34.

If ever been where bells have knoll'd to
    church,
If ever sat at any good man's feast.
             As You Like It. Act II,
                Sc. 7, Line 111
True is it that we have seen better days.
                Ibid. Line 120
           And wiped our eyes
Of drops that sacred pity hath engen-
    der'd.
                Ibid. Line 122
Oppress'd with two weak evils, age and
    hunger.
                Ibid. Line 132
The wide and universal theatre.
                Ibid. Line 137
         All the world 's a stage,
And all the men and women merely
    players. [1]
They have their exits and their en-
    trances;
And one man in his time plays many
    parts,
His acts being seven ages. At first the
    infant,
Mewling and puking in the nurse's
    arms.
And then the whining school-boy, with
    his satchel
And shining morning face, creeping like
    snail
Unwillingly to school. And then the
    lover,
Sighing like furnace, with a woful bal-
    lad
Made to his mistress' eyebrow. Then a
    soldier,
Full of strange oaths, and bearded like
    the pard;
Jealous in honour, sudden and quick in
    quarrel,
Seeking the bubble reputation
Even in the cannon's mouth. And then
    the justice,

[1] The world's a theatre, the earth a stage,
Which God and Nature do with actors fill.
    THOMAS HEYWOOD: *Apology for Actors*
                    [1612]
A noble farce, wherein kings, republics, and
emperors have for so many ages played their
parts, and to which the whole vast universe
serves for a theatre. — MONTAIGNE: *Of the
most Excellent Men*
    See Middleton, page 117.

In fair round belly with good capon
　　lined,
With eyes severe and beard of formal
　　cut,
Full of wise saws and modern in-
　　stances;
And so he plays his part. The sixth age
　　shifts
Into the lean and slipper'd pantaloon,
With spectacles on nose and pouch on
　　side;
His youthful hose, well saved, a world
　　too wide
For his shrunk shank; and his big
　　manly voice,
Turning again toward childish treble,
　　pipes
And whistles in his sound. Last scene of
　　all,
That ends this strange eventful histo-
　　ry,
Is second childishness, and mere obliv-
　　ion,
Sans teeth, sans eyes, sans taste, sans
　　everything.

As You Like It. Act II,
Sc. 7, Line 139

Blow, blow, thou winter wind!
Thou art not so unkind
　　As man's ingratitude.

Ibid. Line 174

These trees shall be my books.

Ibid. Act III, Sc. 2, Line 5

The fair, the chaste, and unexpressive
she.

Ibid. Line 10

It goes much against my stomach.
Hast any philosophy in thee, shepherd?

Ibid. Line 21

He that wants money, means, and
content is without three good friends.

Ibid. Line 25

I am a true labourer: I earn that I
eat, get that I wear, owe no man hate,
envy no man's happiness, glad of other
men's good.

Ibid. Line 78

This is the very false gallop of verses.

Ibid. Line 120

Let us make an honourable retreat.

Ibid. Line 170

With bag and baggage.[1]

As You Like It. Act III,
Sc. 2, Line 171

O, wonderful, wonderful, and most
wonderful wonderful! and yet again
wonderful, and after that out of all
hooping.

Ibid. Line 202

Answer me in one word.

Ibid. Line 238

Do you not know I am a woman?
when I think, I must speak.

Ibid. Line 265

I do desire we may be better strangers.

Ibid. Line 276

Jacques. What stature is she of?
Orlando. Just as high as my heart.

Ibid. Line 286

Time travels in divers paces with
divers persons. I'll tell you who Time
ambles withal, who Time trots withal,
who Time gallops withal, and who he
stands still withal.

Ibid. Line 328

Every one fault seeming monstrous
till his fellow fault came to match it.

Ibid. Line 377

Everything about you demonstrating
a careless desolation.

Ibid. Line 405

Neither rhyme nor reason.[2]

Ibid. Line 424

I would the gods had made thee poetical.

Ibid. Sc. 3, Line 16

The common executioner,
Whose heart the accustom'd sight of
　　death makes hard,
Falls not the axe upon the humbled
　　neck
But first begs pardon.

Ibid. Sc. 5, Line 3

The wounds invisible
That love's keen arrows make.

Ibid. Line 30

Down on your knees,
And thank Heaven, fasting, for a good
　　man's love.

Ibid. Line 57

---

[1] And since "bag and baggage" is a phrase.
— ROBERT BROWNING: *The Inn Album, V*
[2] See Spenser, page 26.

I am falser than vows made in wine.
As You Like It. Act III,
Sc. 5, Line 73

It is a melancholy of mine own, compounded of many simples, extracted from many objects, and indeed the sundry contemplation of my travels, in which my often rumination wraps me in a most humorous sadness.
Ibid. Act IV, Sc. 1, Line 16

I had rather have a fool to make me merry than experience to make me sad.
Ibid. Line 28

I'll warrant him heart-whole.
Ibid. Line 51

Good orators, when they are out, they will spit.
Ibid. Line 77

Men have died from time to time, and worms have eaten them, but not for love.
Ibid. Line 110

Can one desire too much of a good thing? [1]
Ibid. Line 128

For ever and a day.
Ibid. Line 151

Men are April when they woo, December when they wed: maids are May when they are maids, but the sky changes when they are wives.
Ibid. Line 153

My affection hath an unknown bottom, like the bay of Portugal.
Ibid. Line 219

The horn, the horn, the lusty horn
Is not a thing to laugh to scorn.
Ibid. Sc. 2, Line 17

Chewing the food of sweet and bitter fancy.
Ibid. Sc. 3, Line 103

It is meat and drink to me to see a clown.
Ibid. Act V, Sc. 1, Line 11

"So so" is good, very good, very excellent good; and yet it is not; it is but so so.
Ibid. Line 30

The fool doth think he is wise, but the wise man knows himself to be a fool.
Ibid. Line 35

[1] Too much of a good thing. — CERVANTES: *Don Quixote, Pt. I, Book I, Chap. VI*

No sooner met but they looked; no sooner looked but they loved; no sooner loved but they sighed; no sooner sighed but they asked one another the reason; no sooner knew the reason but they sought the remedy.
As You Like It. Act V, Sc. 2, Line 37

How bitter a thing it is to look into happiness through another man's eyes!
Ibid. Line 48

Here comes a pair of very strange beasts, which in all tongues are called fools.
Ibid. Sc. 4, Line 36

An ill-favoured thing, sir, but mine own.[1]
Ibid. Line 60

Rich honesty dwells like a miser, sir, in a poor house; as your pearl in your foul oyster.
Ibid. Line 62

The Retort Courteous; . . . the Quip Modest; . . . the Reply Churlish; . . . the Reproof Valiant; . . . the Countercheck Quarrelsome; . . . the Lie with Circumstance; . . . the Lie Direct.
Ibid. Line 75

Your "If" is the only peacemaker; much virtue in "If."
Ibid. Line 108

Good wine needs no bush.[2]
Ibid. Epilogue, Line 4

What a case am I in.
Ibid. Line 7

Look in the chronicles; we came in with Richard Conqueror.
The Taming of the Shrew.
Induc., Sc. 1, Line 4

Let the world slide.[3]
Ibid. Line 5

I'll not budge an inch.[4]
Ibid. Line 14

[1] My glass is not large, but I drink out of my own. — ALFRED DE MUSSET
[2] You need not hang up the ivy branch over the wine that will sell. — PUBLIUS SYRUS: *Maxim 968*
[3] See Heywood, page 11. BEAUMONT AND FLETCHER: *Wit without Money.*
[4] The same in *King Henry VI, Part III, Act V, Sc. 4, L. 66; Romeo and Juliet, Act III, Sc. 1, L. 60; Hamlet, Act III, Sc. 4, L. 18.*

And if the boy have not a woman's gift
To rain a shower of commanded tears,
An onion will do well for such a shift.
The Taming of the Shrew.
Induc. Sc. 1, Line 124

As Stephen Sly and old John Naps of
Greece,
And Peter Turf and Henry Pimpernell,
And twenty more such names and men
as these
Which never were, nor no man ever
saw.
Ibid. Sc. 2, Line 95

Let the world slip: we shall ne'er be
younger.
Ibid. Line 147

No profit grows where is no pleasure
ta'en;
In brief, sir, study what you most affect.
Ibid. Act I, Sc. 1, Line 39

There's small choice in rotten apples.
Ibid. Line 137

Whom should I knock?
Ibid. Sc. 2, Line 6

To seek their fortunes further than at
home,
Where small experience grows.
Ibid. Line 51

As curst and shrewd
As Socrates' Xanthippe.
Ibid. Line 70

Nothing comes amiss, so money comes
withal.
Ibid. Line 82

Tush, tush! fear boys with bugs.
Ibid. Line 214

And do as adversaries do in law,
Strive mightily, but eat and drink as
friends.
Ibid. Line 281

Old fashions please me best.
Ibid. Act III, Sc. 1, Line 81

Who wooed in haste and means to wed
at leisure.[1]
Ibid. Sc. 2, Line 11

A little pot and soon hot.[2]
Ibid. Act IV, Sc. 1, Line 6

A cold world, Curtis, in every office
but thine; and therefore fire.
The Taming of the Shrew.
Act IV, Sc. 1, Line 37

It was the friar of orders grey,
As he forth walked on his way.[1]
Ibid. Line 148

Sits as one new-risen from a dream.
Ibid. Line 189

To kill a wife with kindness.
Ibid. Line 211

Kindness in women, not their beauteous
looks,
Shall win my love.
Ibid. Sc. 2, Line 41

Our purses shall be proud, our garments
poor:
For 'tis the mind that makes the body
rich.
Ibid. Sc. 3, Line 173

And as the sun breaks through the dark-
est clouds,
So honour peereth in the meanest habit.
Ibid. Line 175

Pitchers have ears.[2]
Ibid. Sc. 4, Line 52

So bedazzled with the sun
That everything I look on seemeth
green.
Ibid. Sc. 5, Line 46

My cake is dough.
Ibid. Act V, Sc. 1, Line 146

He that is giddy thinks the world turns
round.
Ibid. Sc. 2, Line 20

A woman moved is like a fountain
troubled,
Muddy, ill-seeming, thick, bereft of
beauty.
Ibid. Line 143

Such duty as the subject owes the
prince,
Even such a woman oweth to her husband.
Ibid. Line 156

Love all, trust a few,
Do wrong to none: be able for thine
enemy

---

[1] Married in haste, we may repent at leisure.
— CONGREVE: *The Old Bachelor, Act V, Sc. 1*
[2] A little chimney heated hot in a moment.
— H. W. LONGFELLOW: *The Courtship of
Myles Standish*

[1] THOMAS PERCY [1728–1811] composed his
ballad, *The Friar of Orders Grey*, of various
ancient fragments found in Shakespeare's
plays.
[2] See Heywood, page 16.

Rather in power than use, and keep
  thy friend
Under thine own life's key: be check'd
  for silence,
But never tax'd for speech.
All's Well that Ends Well.
Act I, Sc. 1, Line 74

It were all one
That I should love a bright particular
  star
And think to wed it.
Ibid. Line 97

The hind that would be mated by the
  lion
Must die for love.
Ibid. Line 103

Our remedies oft in ourselves do lie,
Which we ascribe to Heaven.
Ibid. Line 235

Service is no heritage.
Ibid. Sc. 3, Line 25

He must needs go that the devil drives.[1]
Ibid. Line 32

My friends were poor, but honest.
Ibid. Line 203

Great floods have flown
From simple sources.
Ibid. Act II, Sc. 1, Line 142

Oft expectation fails, and most oft
  there
Where most it promises.
Ibid. Line 145

The horses of the sun.[2]
Ibid. Line 164

I will show myself highly fed and lowly
  taught.
Ibid. Sc. 2, Line 3

They say miracles are past.
Ibid. Sc. 3, Line 1

All the learned and authentic fellows.
Ibid. Line 14

From lowest place when virtuous things
  proceed,
The place is dignified by the doer's
  deed.
Ibid. Line 132

A young man married is a man that's
  marr'd.
All's Well that Ends Well.
Act II, Sc. 3, Line 315

Make the coming hour o'erflow with
  joy,
And pleasure drown the brim.
Ibid. Sc. 4, Line 48

No legacy is so rich as honesty.
Ibid. Act III, Sc. 5, Line 13

The web of our life is of a mingled
yarn, good and ill together.
Ibid. Act IV, Sc. 3, Line 83

All's well that ends well.[1]
Ibid. Sc. 4, Line 35

I am a man whom Fortune hath cruelly
  scratched.
Ibid. Act V, Sc. 2, Line 28

Whose words all ears took captive.
Ibid. Sc. 3, Line 17

Praising what is lost
Makes the remembrance dear.
Ibid. Line 19

The inaudible and noiseless foot of
  Time.[2]
Ibid. Line 41

Love that comes too late,
Like a remorseful pardon slowly carried.
Ibid. Line 57

All impediments in fancy's course
Are motives of more fancy.
Ibid. Line 216

The bitter past, more welcome is the
  sweet.
Ibid. Line 339

If music be the food of love,[3] play on;
Give me excess of it, that, surfeiting,
The appetite may sicken, and so die.
That strain again! it had a dying fall:
O! it came o'er my ear like the sweet
  sound
That breathes upon a bank of violets,
Stealing and giving odour!
Twelfth-Night. Act I, Sc. 1,
Line 1

---

[1] See Heywood, page 17.
[2] Who drives the horses of the sun
  Shall lord it but a day.
  JOHN VANCE CHENEY [1848-1922]: *The*
  Happiest Heart

[1] Also in *Act V, Sc. 1, Line 25.* See Heywood, page 13.
[2] How noiseless falls the foot of time! —
W. R. SPENCER: *Lines to Lady A. Hamilton*
[3] Is not music the food of love? — R. B.
SHERIDAN: *The Rivals, Act II, Sc. 1*

When my tongue blabs, then let mine
eyes not see.
> *Twelfth-Night. Act I,*
> *Sc. 2, Line 61*

I am sure care's an enemy to life.
> *Ibid. Sc. 3, Line 2*

Let them hang themselves in their own
straps.
> *Ibid. Line 13*

At my fingers' ends.[1]
> *Ibid. Line 85*

I am a great eater of beef, and I believe that does harm to my wit.
> *Ibid. Line 92*

Wherefore are these things hid?
> *Ibid. Line 135*

Is it a world to hide virtues in?
> *Ibid. Line 142*

God give them wisdom that have it;
and those that are fools, let them use
their talents.
> *Ibid. Sc. 4, Line 14*

One draught above heat makes him
a fool, the second mads him, and a third
drowns him.
> *Ibid. Sc. 5, Line 139*

What manner of man?[2]
> *Ibid. Line 162*

We will draw the curtain and show you
the picture.
> *Ibid. Line 252*

'Tis beauty truly blent, whose red and
white
Nature's own sweet and cunning hand
laid on:
Lady, you are the cruell'st she alive
If you will lead these graces to the
grave
And leave the world no copy.
> *Ibid. Line 259*

Holla your name to the reverberate
hills,
And make the babbling gossip of the air
Cry out.
> *Ibid. Line 293*

Journeys end in lovers meeting,
Every wise man's son doth know.
> *Ibid. Act II, Sc. 3, Line 46*

Then come kiss me, sweet and twenty,
Youth's a stuff will not endure.
> *Twelfth-Night. Act II,*
> *Sc. 3, Line 54*

He does it with a better grace, but
I do it more natural.
> *Ibid. Line 91*

Is there no respect of place, persons,
nor time in you?
> *Ibid. Line 100*

Sir Toby. Dost thou think, because
thou art virtuous, there shall be no more
cakes and ale?[1]
Clown. Yes, by Saint Anne, and ginger shall be hot i' the mouth too.
> *Ibid. Line 124*

My purpose is, indeed, a horse of that
colour.
> *Ibid. Line 184*

Sport royal.
> *Ibid. Line 190*

That old and antique song we heard
last night.
> *Ibid. Sc. 4, Line 3*

These most brisk and giddy-paced
times.
> *Ibid. Line 6*

Let still the woman take
An elder than herself: so wears she to
him,
So sways she level in her husband's
heart:
For, boy, however we do praise our-
selves,
Our fancies are more giddy and unfirm,
More longing, wavering, sooner lost and
worn,
Than women's are.
> *Ibid. Line 29*

Then let thy love be younger than thyself,
Or thy affection cannot hold the bent.
> *Ibid. Line 36*

The spinsters and the knitters in the
sun
And the free maids that weave their
thread with bones,
Do use to chant it: it is silly sooth,

---

[1] See Heywood, page 13.
[2] What manner of man is this? — *Mark,*
IV, 41

[1] There are cakes, there is ale —ay, and
ginger
Shall be hot in the mouth, as of old.
ANDREW LANG: *A Remonstrance with the*
Fair, St. 6

And dallies with the innocence of love,
Like the old age.
> *Twelfth-Night. Act II,*
> *Sc. 4, Line 44*

Duke.　　　And what's her history?
Viola. A blank, my lord. She never told her love,
But let concealment, like a worm i' the bud,
Feed on her damask cheek: she pined in thought,
And with a green and yellow melancholy
She sat like patience on a monument,
Smiling at grief.
> *Ibid. Line 112*

I am all the daughters of my father's house,
And all the brothers too.
> *Ibid. Line 122*

I know my place, as I would they should do theirs.
> *Ibid. Sc. 5, Line 61*

Some are born great, some achieve greatness, and some have greatness thrust upon them.
> *Ibid. Line 159*

Foolery, sir, does walk about the orb like the sun; it shines everywhere.
> *Ibid. Act III, Sc. 1, Line 44*

Music from the spheres.[1]
> *Ibid. Line 122*

How apt the poor are to be proud.
> *Ibid. Line 141*

Then westward-ho!
> *Ibid. Line 148*

Oh, what a deal of scorn looks beautiful
In the contempt and anger of his lip!
> *Ibid. Line 159*

Love sought is good, but given unsought, is better.
> *Ibid. Line 170*

You will hang like an icicle on a Dutchman's beard.
> *Ibid. Sc. 2, Line 30*

[1] The music of the spheres. *Pericles, Act V, Sc. 1, L. 231*
We may maintain the music of the spheres.
— Sir Thomas Browne: *Religio Medici, Part II, Sect. 9*

Let there be gall enough in thy ink; though thou write with a goose-pen, no matter.
> *Twelfth-Night. Act III,*
> *Sc. 2, Line 54*

Laugh yourself into stitches.
> *Ibid. Line 75*

I can no other answer make but thanks,
And thanks, and ever thanks.
> *Ibid. Sc. 3, Line 14*

Haply your eye shall light upon some toy
You have desire to purchase.
> *Ibid. Line 44*

I think we do know the sweet Roman hand.
> *Ibid. Sc. 4, Line 31*

This is very midsummer madness.
> *Ibid. Line 62*

Put thyself into the trick of singularity.
> *Ibid. Line 80*

What, man! defy the Devil: consider, he's an enemy to mankind.
> *Ibid. Line 109*

'Tis not for gravity to play at cherry-pit with Satan.
> *Ibid. Line 131*

If this were played upon a stage now, I could condemn it as an improbable fiction.
> *Ibid. Line 142*

More matter for a May morning.
> *Ibid. Line 158*

Still you keep o' the windy side of the law.[1]
> *Ibid. Line 183*

My remembrance is very free and clear from any image of offence done to any man.
> *Ibid. Line 251*

Hob, nob, is his word: give 't or take 't.
> *Ibid. Line 265*

I have heard of some kind of men that put quarrels purposely on others to taste their valour.
> *Ibid. Line 269*

He's a very devil.
> *Ibid. Line 304*

An I thought he had been valiant, and so cunning in fence, I'd have seen

[1] The windy side of care. — *Much Ado About Nothing, Act II, Sc. 1, L. 328*

him damned ere I'd have challenged him.

> *Twelfth-Night. Act III,*
> *Sc. 4, Line 314*

Out of my lean and low ability
I'll lend you something.

> *Ibid. Line 380*

I hate ingratitude more in a man
Than lying, vainness, babbling drunkenness,
Or any taint of vice whose strong corruption
Inhabits our frail blood.

> *Ibid. Line 390*

Out of the jaws of death.[1]

> *Ibid. Line 396*

As the old hermit of Prague, that never saw pen and ink, very wittily said to a niece of King Gorboduc, "That that is, is."

> *Ibid. Act IV, Sc. 2, Line 14*

Thus the whirligig of time brings in his revenges.

> *Ibid. Act V, Sc. 1, Line 388*

For the rain it raineth every day.[2]

> *Ibid. Line 404*

You pay a great deal too dear for what's given freely.

> *The Winter's Tale. Act I, Sc. 1,*
> *Line 18*

One good deed, dying tongueless,
Slaughters a thousand waiting upon that.

> *Ibid. Sc. 2, Line 92*

They say we are
Almost as like as eggs.

> *Ibid. Line 130*

He makes a July's day short as December.

> *Ibid. Line 169*

Black brows, they say,
Become some women best, so that there be not
Too much hair there, but in a semicircle,
Or a half-moon made with a pen.

> *Ibid. Act II, Sc. 1, Line 8*

A sad tale's best for winter.

> *The Winter's Tale. Act II,*
> *Sc. 1, Line 24*

There's some ill planet reigns:
I must be patient till the heavens look
With an aspect more favourable.

> *Ibid. Line 104*

The silence often of pure innocence
Persuades when speaking fails.

> *Ibid. Sc. 2, Line 41*

Not so hot.[1]

> *Ibid. Sc. 3, Line 32*

I am a feather for each wind that blows.

> *Ibid. Line 153*

What's gone and what's past help
Should be past grief.

> *Ibid. Act III, Sc. 2, Line 223*

I am gone for ever. [*Exit, pursued by a bear.*][2]

> *Ibid. Sc. 3, Line 57*

This is fairy gold.

> *Ibid. Line 127*

Then comes in the sweet o' the year.

> *Ibid. Act IV, Sc. 2, Line 3*

A snapper-up of unconsidered trifles.

> *Ibid. Line 26*

A merry heart goes all the day,
Your sad tires in a mile-a.

> *Ibid. Line 135*

There's rosemary and rue; these keep
Seeming and savour all the winter long.

> *Ibid. Sc. 3, Line 74*

The marigold, that goes to bed wi' the sun . . .
They are given to men of middle age.

> *Ibid. Line 105*

Daffodils,
That come before the swallow dares, and take
The winds of March with beauty.

> *Ibid. Line 118*

What you do
Still betters what is done.

> *Ibid. Line 135*

When you do dance, I wish you
A wave o' the sea, that you might ever do

---

[1] Into the jaws of death. — TENNYSON: *The Charge of the Light Brigade, Stanza 3*
In the jaws of death. — DU BARTAS: *Divine Weekes and Workes, Second Week, First Day, Part IV*
[2] Also in *King Lear, Act III, Sc. 2, L. 77*

[1] *King Lear, Act V, Sc. 2, L. 67*
SAMUEL PEPYS: *Diary*, April 26, 1664.
[2] Lightly we follow our cue,
"Exit, pursued by a bear."
ARTHUR GUITERMAN: *The Shakespearean Bear, Envoi*

Nothing but that.
> *The Winter's Tale. Act IV,*
> *Sc. 3, Line 140*

I love a ballad in print, a-life, for then we are sure they are true.
> *Ibid. Line 262*

The self-same sun that shines upon his court
Hides not his visage from our cottage, but
Looks on alike.
> *Ibid. Line 457*

To unpathed waters, undreamed shores.
> *Ibid. Line 580*

Let me have no lying; it becomes none but tradesmen.
> *Ibid. Line 747*

To purge melancholy.
> *Ibid. Line 792*

Stars, stars! And all eyes else dead coals.
> *Ibid. Act V, Sc. 1, Line 67*

Where's Bohemia? [1]
> *Ibid. Line 185*

I was no gentleman born.
> *Ibid. Sc. 2, Line 146*

What fine chisel
Could ever yet cut breath?
> *Ibid. Sc. 3, Line 78*

There's time enough for that.
> *Ibid. Line 128*

Lord of thy presence and no land beside.
> *King John. Act I, Sc. 1, Line 137*

And if his name be George, I'll call him Peter;
For new-made honour doth forget men's names.
> *Ibid. Line 186*

For he is but a bastard to the time
That doth not smack of observation.
> *Ibid. Line 207*

Sweet, sweet, sweet poison for the age's tooth.
> *Ibid. Line 213*

Heaven lay not my transgression to my charge.
> *Ibid. Line 256*

[1] A desert Country near the Sea. — *Act III, Sc. 3*

A hazard of new fortunes.[1]
> *King John. Act II, Sc. 1, Line 71*

For courage mounteth with occasion.
> *Ibid. Line 82*

Saint George, that swing'd the dragon, and e'er since
Sits on his horse back at mine hostess' door.
> *Ibid. Line 288*

He is the half part of a blessed man,
Left to be finished by such a she;
And she a fair divided excellence,
Whose fulness of perfection lies in him.
> *Ibid. Line 437*

Talks as familiarly of roaring lions
As maids of thirteen do of puppy-dogs!
> *Ibid. Line 459*

Zounds! I was never so bethump'd with words,
Since I first call'd my brother's father dad.
> *Ibid. Line 466*

I will instruct my sorrows to be proud;
For grief is proud, and makes his owner stoop.
> *Ibid. Act III, Sc. 1, Line 68*

What hath this day deserved? what hath it done
That it in golden letters should be set
Among the high tides in the calendar?
> *Ibid. Line 84*

Thou ever strong upon the stronger side!
Thou Fortune's champion that dost never fight
But when her humorous ladyship is by
To teach thee safety.
> *Ibid. Line 117*

Thou wear a lion's hide! doff it for shame,
And hang a calf's-skin on those recreant limbs.
> *Ibid. Line 128*

I had a thing to say,
But I will fit it with some better time.
> *Ibid. Sc. 3, Line 25*

[1] Title of a novel [1889] by WILLIAM DEAN HOWELLS, who used Shakespearean quotations in this way probably more often than any other novelist.

O, amiable lovely death! [1]
> *King John. Act III, Sc. 4, Line 25*

Grief fills the room up of my absent
  child,
Lies in his bed, walks up and down with
  me,
Puts on his pretty looks, repeats his
  words,
Remembers me of all his gracious parts,
Stuffs out his vacant garments with his
  form.
> *Ibid. Line 93*

Life is as tedious as a twice-told tale,
Vexing the dull ear of a drowsy man.
> *Ibid. Line 108*

When Fortune means to men most
  good,[2]
She looks upon them with a threatening eye.
> *Ibid. Line 119*

And he that stands upon a slippery
  place
Makes nice of no vile hold to stay him
  up.
> *Ibid. Line 137*

To gild refined gold, to paint the lily,
To throw a perfume on the violet,
To smooth the ice, or add another hue
Unto the rainbow, or with taper-light
To seek the beauteous eye of heaven to
  garnish,
Is wasteful and ridiculous excess.
> *Ibid. Act IV, Sc. 2, Line 11*

And oftentimes excusing of a fault
Doth make the fault the worse by the
  excuse.[3]
> *Ibid. Line 30*

We cannot hold mortality's strong
  hand.
> *Ibid. Line 82*

There is no sure foundation set on
  blood,
No certain life achiev'd by others'
  death.
> *Ibid. Line 104*

Make haste; the better foot before.[1]
> *King John. Act IV, Sc. 2, Line 170*

I saw a smith stand with his hammer,
  thus,
The whilst his iron did on the anvil cool,
With open mouth swallowing a tailor's
  news.
> *Ibid. Line 193*

Another lean unwashed artificer.
> *Ibid. Line 201*

How oft the sight of means to do ill
  deeds
Makes ill deeds done!
> *Ibid. Line 219*

Heaven take my soul, and England
  keep my bones.
> *Ibid. Sc. 3, Line 10*

Mocking the air with colours idly
  spread.
> *Ibid. Act V, Sc. 1, Line 72*

The day shall not be up so soon as I,
To try the fair adventure of to-morrow.
> *Ibid. Sc. 5, Line 21*

'Tis strange that death should sing.
I am the cygnet to this pale faint swan,
Who chants a doleful hymn to his own
  death,[2]
And from the organ-pipe of frailty
  sings
His soul and body to their lasting rest.
> *Ibid. Sc. 7, Line 20*

Now my soul hath elbow-room.
> *Ibid. Line 28*

This England never did, nor never shall,
Lie at the proud foot of a conqueror.
> *Ibid. Line 112*

Come the three corners of the world in
  arms,
And we shall shock them. Nought shall
  make us rue,
If England to itself do rest but true.
> *Ibid. Line 116*

Old John of Gaunt, time-honoured
  Lancaster.
> *King Richard II. Act I, Sc. 1,*
> *Line 1*

Mine honour is my life; both grow in
  one;

---

[1] Lovely and soothing death. — WALT
WHITMAN: *When Lilacs Last in the Dooryard
Bloom'd, Sect. 14*

[2] When fortune flatters, she does it to betray. — PUBLIUS SYRUS: *Maxim 278*

[3] Qui s'excuse, s'accuse (He who excuses
himself accuses himself). — GABRIEL MEU-
RIER: *Trésor des Sentences* [1530–1601]

---

[1] Come on, my lords, the better foot be-
fore. — *Titus Andronicus, Act II, Sc. 3, L. 192*
Put forward your best foot. — ROBERT
BROWNING: *Respectability, St. 3*

[2] See Note 3, page 45.

Take honour from me, and my life is done.
King Richard II. Act I, Sc. 1, Line 182

The daintiest last, to make the end most sweet.
Ibid. Sc. 3, Line 68

Truth hath a quiet breast.
Ibid. Line 96

How long a time lies in one little word!
Ibid. Line 213

Things sweet to taste prove in digestion sour.
Ibid. Line 236

All places that the eye of heaven visits
Are to a wise man ports and happy havens.
Ibid. Line 275

O, who can hold a fire in his hand
By thinking on the frosty Caucasus?
Or cloy the hungry edge of appetite
By bare imagination of a feast?
Or wallow naked in December snow
By thinking on fantastic summer's heat?
O, no! the apprehension of the good
Gives but the greater feeling to the worse.
Ibid. Line 294

The tongues of dying men
Enforce attention like deep harmony.
Ibid. Act II, Sc. 1, Line 5

The setting sun, and music at the close,
As the last taste of sweets, is sweetest last,
Writ in remembrance, more than things long past.
Ibid. Line 12

Small showers last long, but sudden storms are short.
Ibid. Line 35

This royal throne of kings, this sceptred isle,
This earth of majesty, this seat of Mars,
This other Eden, demi-paradise,
This fortress built by Nature for herself
Against infection and the hand of war,
This happy breed of men, this little world,
This precious stone set in the silver sea,
Which serves it in the office of a wall
Or as a moat defensive to a house,

Against the envy of less happier lands,
This blessed plot, this earth, this realm, this England.
King Richard II. Act II, Sc. 1, Line 40

The ripest fruit first falls.
Ibid. Line 154

Your fair discourse hath been as sugar,
Making the hard way sweet and delectable.
Ibid. Sc. 3, Line 6

I count myself in nothing else so happy
As in a soul remembering my good friends.
Ibid. Line 46

Evermore thanks, the exchequer of the poor.
Ibid. Line 65

The caterpillars of the commonwealth,
Which I have sworn to weed and pluck away.
Ibid. Line 166

Things past redress are now with me past care.
Ibid. Line 171

I see thy glory like a shooting star
Fall to the base earth from the firmament.
Ibid. Sc. 4, Line 19

Eating the bitter bread of banishment.
Ibid. Act III, Sc. 1, Line 21

Fires the proud tops of the eastern pines.
Ibid. Sc. 2, Line 42

Not all the water in the rough rude sea
Can wash the balm off from an anointed king.
Ibid. Line 55

O, call back yesterday, bid time return!
Ibid. Line 69

Let's talk of graves, of worms, and epitaphs.
Ibid. Line 145

Let's choose executors and talk of wills.
Ibid. Line 148

And nothing can we call our own but death;
And that small model of the barren earth,
Which serves as paste and cover to our bones.
For God's sake, let us sit upon the ground,

And tell sad stories of the death of kings.

> *King Richard II. Act III,*
> *Sc. 2, Line 152*

Comes at the last, and with a little pin
Bores through his castle wall, and farewell king!

> *Ibid. Line 169*

Men judge by the complexion of the sky
The state and inclination of the day.

> *Ibid. Line 194*

He is come to open
The purple testament of bleeding war.

> *Ibid. Sc. 3, Line 93*

And my large kingdom for a little grave,
A little little grave, an obscure grave.

> *Ibid. Line 153*

The noisome weeds, that without profit suck
The soil's fertility from wholesome flowers.

> *Ibid. Sc. 4, Line 38*

Superfluous branches
We lop away that bearing boughs may live.

> *Ibid. Line 63*

Gave
His body to that pleasant country's earth,
And his pure soul unto his captain Christ,
Under whose colours he had fought so long.

> *Ibid. Act IV, Sc. 1, Line 97*

So Judas did to Christ: but he, in twelve,
Found truth in all but one; I, in twelve thousand, none.

> *Ibid. Line 170*

Some of you with Pilate wash your hands [1]
Showing an outward pity.

> *Ibid. Line 239*

A mockery king of snow.

> *Ibid. Line 260*

Come home with me to supper.

> *Ibid. Line 333*

As in a theatre, the eyes of men,
After a well-graced actor leaves the stage,

[1] Pilate . . . took water, and washed his hands. — *Matthew, XXVII, 24*

Are idly bent on him that enters next,
Thinking his prattle to be tedious.

> *King Richard II. Act V,*
> *Sc. 2, Line 23*

No word like "pardon."

> *Ibid. Sc. 3, Line 118*

As hard to come as for a camel
To thread the postern of a small needle's eye. [1]

> *Ibid. Sc. 5, Line 16*

How sour sweet music is
When time is broke and no proportion kept!
So is it in the music of men's lives.

> *Ibid. Line 42*

So shaken as we are, so wan with care.

> *King Henry IV, Part I. Act I,*
> *Sc. 1, Line 1*

In those holy fields
Over whose acres walked those blessed feet
Which fourteen hundred years ago were nail'd
For our advantage on the bitter cross.

> *Ibid. Line 24*

Here is a dear and true industrious friend.

> *Ibid. Line 62*

Diana's foresters, gentlemen of the shade, minions of the moon.

> *Ibid. Sc. 2, Line 29*

So far as my coin would stretch; and where it would not, I have used my credit.

> *Ibid. Line 61*

Old father antic the law.

> *Ibid. Line 69*

I would to God thou and I knew where a commodity of good names were to be bought.

> *Ibid. Line 92*

Thou hast damnable iteration, and art indeed able to corrupt a saint.

> *Ibid. Line 101*

'Tis my vocation, Hal; 'tis no sin for a man to labour in his vocation.

> *Ibid. Line 116*

[1] It is easier for a camel to go through the eye of a needle, than for a rich man to enter into the kingdom of God. — *Matthew, XIX, 24*

He will give the devil his due.[1]
> *King Henry IV, Part I.*
> *Act I, Sc. 2, Line 132*

There's neither honesty, manhood, nor good fellowship in thee.
> *Ibid. Line 154*

If all the year were playing holidays, To sport would be as tedious as to work.
> *Ibid. Line 226*

You tread upon my patience.
> *Ibid. Sc. 3, Line 4*

That title of respect Which the proud soul ne'er pays but to the proud.
> *Ibid. Line 8*

Fresh as a bridegroom; and his chin new reap'd, Showed like a stubble-land at harvest-home; He was perfumed like a milliner, And 'twixt his finger and his thumb he held A pouncet-box, which ever and anon He gave his nose and took 't away again.
> *Ibid. Line 34*

And as the soldiers bore dead bodies by, He called them untaught knaves, unmannerly, To bring a slovenly unhandsome corse Betwixt the wind and his nobility.
> *Ibid. Line 42*

God save the mark.
> *Ibid. Line 56*

And telling me, the sovereign'st thing on earth Was parmaceti for an inward bruise; And that it was great pity, so it was, This villanous saltpetre should be digg'd Out of the bowels of the harmless earth, Which many a good tall fellow had destroy'd So cowardly; and but for these vile guns, He would himself have been a soldier.
> *Ibid. Line 57*

The blood more stirs To rouse a lion than to start a hare!
> *King Henry IV, Part I.*
> *Act I, Sc. 3, Line 197*

By heaven, methinks it were an easy leap To pluck bright honour from the pale-faced moon, Or dive into the bottom of the deep, Where fathom-line could never touch the ground, And pluck up drowned honour by the locks.
> *Ibid. Line 201*

This house is turned upside down.
> *Ibid. Act II, Sc. 1, Line 11*

What's o'clock?
> *Ibid. Line 36*

I know a trick worth two of that.[1]
> *Ibid. Line 40*

If the rascal have not given me medicines to make me love him, I'll be hanged.
> *Ibid. Sc. 2, Line 20*

It would be argument for a week, laughter for a month, and a good jest for ever.
> *Ibid. Line 104*

Falstaff sweats to death, And lards the lean earth as he walks along.
> *Ibid. Line 119*

Out of this nettle, danger, we pluck this flower, safety.
> *Ibid. Sc. 3, Line 11*

Brain him with his lady's fan.
> *Ibid. Line 26*

A Corinthian, a lad of mettle, a good boy.
> *Ibid. Sc. 4, Line 13*

A plague of all cowards, I say.
> *Ibid. Line 129*

There live not three good men unhanged in England, and one of them is fat and grows old.
> *Ibid. Line 146*

Call you that backing of your friends? A plague upon such backing!
> *Ibid. Line 168*

I have peppered two of them: two

---

[1] Thomas Nash: *Have with you to Saffron Walden.* Dryden: *Epilogue to the Duke of Guise*

[1] We know a trick worth two of that. — W. M. Thackeray: *The Newcomes, Vol. I, Chap. 1*

I am sure I have paid, two rogues in buckram suits. I tell thee what, Hal, if I tell thee a lie, spit in my face; call me horse. Thou knowest my old ward; — here I lay, and thus I bore my point. Four rogues in buckram let drive at me —

King Henry IV, Part I.
Act II, Sc. 4, Line 215

Three misbegotten knaves in Kendal green.

Ibid. Line 249

Give you a reason on compulsion! If reasons were as plentiful as blackberries, I would give no man a reason upon compulsion, I.

Ibid. Line 267

Mark now, how a plain tale shall put you down.

Ibid. Line 285

No more of that, Hal, an thou lovest me!

Ibid. Line 316

What doth gravity out of his bed at midnight?

Ibid. Line 328

A plague of sighing and grief! It blows a man up like a bladder.

Ibid. Line 370

You may buy land now as cheap as stinking mackerel.

Ibid. Line 399

That reverend vice, that grey iniquity, that father ruffian, that vanity in years.

Ibid. Line 505

Banish plump Jack, and banish all the world.

Ibid. Line 534

Play out the play.

Ibid. Line 539

O, monstrous! but one half-pennyworth of bread to this intolerable deal of sack!

Ibid. Line 597

Diseased Nature oftentimes breaks forth
In strange eruptions.

Ibid. Act III, Sc. 1, Line 27

I am not in the roll of common men.

Ibid. Line 43

Glendower. I can call spirits from the vasty deep.

Hotspur. Why, so can I, or so can any man;
But will they come when you do call for them?

King Henry IV, Part I.
Act III, Sc. 1, Line 53

While you live, tell truth and shame the devil! [1]

Ibid. Line 58

I had rather be a kitten and cry mew, Than one of these same metre balladmongers.

Ibid. Line 128

But in the way of bargain, mark ye me, I'll cavil on the ninth part of a hair.

Ibid. Line 138

A deal of skimble-skamble stuff.

Ibid. Line 153

Exceedingly well read.

Ibid. Line 165

Those musicians that shall play to you Hang in the air a thousand leagues from hence. [2]

Ibid. Line 226

A good mouth-filling oath.

Ibid. Line 258

A fellow of no mark nor likelihood.

Ibid. Sc. 2, Line 45

To loathe the taste of sweetness, whereof a little
More than a little is by much too much.

Ibid. Line 72

The end of life cancels all bands.

Ibid. Line 157

An I have not forgotten what the inside of a church is made of, I am a pepper-corn.

Ibid. Sc. 3, Line 8

---

[1] BEAUMONT AND FLETCHER: *Wit without Money, Act IV, Sc. 1.* SWIFT: *Mary the Cookmaid's Letter*
Speak the truth and shame the devil. — RABELAIS: *Works, Author's Prologue to the Fifth Book*
I'd tell the truth, and shame the devil. — JOHNSON: *Boswell's Life of Dr. Johnson* (Everyman edition), Vol. I, page 460
    Truth being truth,
    Tell it and shame the devil.
    BROWNING: *The Ring and the Book, III, The Other Half-Rome*
[2] A good motto for a broadcasting company. Or Walt Whitman: "Broadcast doings of the day and night." [1855 Preface.]

Company, villanous company, hath
been the spoil of me.
*King Henry IV, Part I.
Act III, Sc. 3, Line 10*
Shall I not take mine ease in mine inn? [1]
Ibid. Line 91
Rob me the exchequer.
Ibid. Line 204
How has he the leisure to be sick
In such a justling time?
Ibid. Act IV, Sc. 1, Line 17
This sickness doth infect
The very life-blood of our enterprise.
Ibid. Line 28
That daffed the world aside,
And bid it pass.
Ibid. Line 96
Baited like eagles having lately
bathed. . . .
As full of spirit as the month of May,
And gorgeous as the sun at midsummer.
Ibid. Line 99
The cankers of a calm world and a long
peace.
Ibid. Sc. 2, Line 32
There's but a shirt and a half in all
my company; and the half-shirt is two
napkins tacked together and thrown
over the shoulders like an herald's coat
without sleeves.
Ibid. Line 46
Food for powder, food for powder;
they'll fill a pit as well as better.
Ibid. Line 72
To the latter end of a fray and the be-
ginning of a feast
Fits a dull fighter and a keen guest.[2]
Ibid. Line 86
I could be well content
To entertain the lag-end of my life
With quiet hours.
Ibid. Act V, Sc. 1, Line 23
I would 't were bedtime, Hal, and all
well.
Ibid. Line 126
Honour pricks me on. Yea, but how
if honour prick me off when I come on,
— how then? Can honour set to a leg?
no: or an arm? no: or take away the
grief of a wound? no. Honour hath no
skill in surgery, then? no. What is hon-

[1] See Heywood, page 12.
[2] *Ibid.*, page 17.

our? a word. What is in that word honour; what is that honour? air. A trim
reckoning! Who hath it? he that died o'
Wednesday.[1] Doth he feel it? no. Doth
he hear it? no. It is insensible, then?
yea, to the dead. But will it not live
with the living? no. Why? detraction
will not suffer it. Therefore I'll none of
it. Honour is a mere scutcheon. And so
ends my catechism.
*King Henry IV, Part I.
Act V, Sc. 1, Line 131*
The time of life is short;
To spend that shortness basely were too
long.
Ibid. Sc. 2, Line 81
Two stars keep not their motion in one
sphere.
Ibid. Sc. 4, Line 65
This earth, that bears thee dead,
Bears not alive so stout a gentleman.
Ibid. Line 92
Thy ignominy sleep with thee in the
grave,
But not remember'd in thy epitaph!
Ibid. Line 100
I could have better spared a better man.
Ibid. Line 104
The better part of valour is discretion.[2]
Ibid. Line 120
Full bravely hast thou fleshed
Thy maiden sword.
Ibid. Line 132
Lord, Lord, how this world is given to
lying! I grant you I was down and out
of breath; and so was he. But we rose
both at an instant, and fought a long
hour by Shrewsbury clock.
Ibid. Line 148
I'll purge, and leave sack, and live
cleanly.
Ibid. Line 168
Even such a man, so faint, so spiritless,
So dull, so dead in look, so woe-begone,
Drew Priam's curtain in the dead of
night,

[1] Where 's he that died o' Wednesday? —
E. C. STEDMAN: *Falstaff's Song, St. 1*
[2] It show'd discretion the best part of
valour. — BEAUMONT AND FLETCHER: *A King
and no King, Act II, Sc. 3*

And would have told him half his Troy
was burnt.
King Henry IV, Part II.
Act I, Sc. 1, Line 70
Yet the first bringer of unwelcome news
Hath but a losing office, and his tongue
Sounds ever after as a sullen bell,
Remember'd knolling a departing
friend.
Ibid. Line 100
I am not only witty in myself, but
the cause that wit is in other men.[1]
Ibid. Sc. 2, Line 10
A rascally yea-forsooth knave.
Ibid. Line 40
You lie in your throat if you say I am
any other than an honest man.
Ibid. Line 97
Some smack of age in you, some rel-
ish of the saltness of time.
Ibid. Line 112
It is the disease of not listening, the
malady of not marking, that I am trou-
bled withal.
Ibid. Line 139
We that are in the vaward of our youth.
Ibid. Line 201
For my voice, I have lost it with
hollaing and singing of anthems.
Ibid. Line 215
Pray that our armies join not in a
hot day; for, by the Lord, I take but
two shirts out with me, and I mean not
to sweat extraordinarily.
Ibid. Line 237
It was always yet the trick of our
English nation, if they have a good
thing, to make it too common.
Ibid. Line 244
I were better to be eaten to death
with rust than to be scoured to nothing
with perpetual motion.
Ibid. Line 249
If I do, fillip me with a three-man
beetle.
Ibid. Line 259
Who lined himself with hope,
Eating the air on promise of supply.
Ibid. Sc. 3, Line 27

[1] See Johnson, page 238.

When we mean to build,
We first survey the plot, then draw the
model;
And when we see the figure of the house,
Then must we rate the cost of the erec-
tion.[1]
King Henry IV, Part II.
Act I, Sc. 3, Line 41
A habitation giddy and unsure
Hath he that buildeth on the vulgar
heart.
Ibid. Line 89
Past and to come seem best; things
present worst.
Ibid. Line 108
A poor lone woman.
Ibid. Act II, Sc. 1, Line 37
I'll tickle your catastrophe.
Ibid. Line 68
He hath eaten me out of house and
home.
Ibid. Line 82
Thou didst swear to me upon a parcel-
gilt goblet, sitting in my Dolphin-
chamber, at the round table, by a sea-
coal fire, upon Wednesday in Wheeson
week.
Ibid. Line 96
I do now remember the poor creature,
small beer.[2]
Ibid. Sc. 2, Line 12
Let the end try the man.
Ibid. Line 52
Thus we play the fools with the time,
and the spirits of the wise sit in the
clouds and mock us.
Ibid. Line 155
He was indeed the glass
Wherein the noble youth did dress
themselves.
Ibid. Sc. 3, Line 21
A good heart's worth gold.
Ibid. Sc. 4, Line 34

[1] Which of you, intending to build a tower,
sitteth not down first, and counteth the cost,
whether he have sufficient to finish it? —
Luke, XIV, 28
[2] Doth it not show vilely in me to desire
small beer? — *King Henry IV, Part II, Act II,
Sc. 2, L. 7*
To suckle fools and chronicle small beer. —
Othello, Act II, Sc. 1, L. 160
That questionable superfluity — small beer.
— DOUGLAS JERROLD [1803–1857]: *The Trag-
edy of the Till*

Aggravate your choler.
> *King Henry IV, Part II.*
> *Act II, Sc. 4, Line 174*

Is it not strange that desire should so many years outlive performance?
> *Ibid. Line 283*

Now comes in the sweetest morsel of the night, and we must hence and leave it unpicked.
> *Ibid. Line 401*

O sleep, O gentle sleep,[1]
Nature's soft nurse! how have I frighted thee,
That thou no more wilt weigh my eyelids down
And steep my senses in forgetfulness?
> *Ibid. Act III, Sc. 1, Line 5*

With all appliances and means to boot.
> *Ibid. Line 29*

Uneasy lies the head that wears a crown.
> *Ibid. Line 31*

There is a history in all men's lives.
> *Ibid. Line 80*

How many of mine old acquaintance are dead!
> *Ibid. Sc. 2, Line 37*

Death, as the Psalmist saith, is certain to all; all shall die. How a good yoke of bullocks at Stamford fair?
> *Ibid. Line 41*

Accommodated; that is, when a man is, as they say, accommodated; or when a man is, being, whereby a' may be thought to be accommodated, — which is an excellent thing.
> *Ibid. Line 86*

Most forcible Feeble.
> *Ibid. Line 181*

We have heard the chimes at midnight.
> *Ibid. Line 231*

A man can die but once.
> *Ibid. Line 253*

We are ready to try our fortunes
To the last man.
> *Ibid. Act IV, Sc. 2, Line 43*

---

[1] Sleep, most gentle sleep. — OVID: *Metamorphoses, Book II, L. 624*

I may justly say, with the hook-nosed fellow of Rome,[1] "I came, saw, and overcame."
> *King Henry IV, Part II.*
> *Act IV, Sc. 3, Line 44*

If I had a thousand sons, the first human principle I would teach them should be, to forswear thin potations and to addict themselves to sack.
> *Ibid. Line 133*

Will Fortune never come with both hands full
But write her fair words still in foulest letters?
She either gives a stomach and no food;
Such are the poor, in health; or else a feast
And takes away the stomach.
> *Ibid. Sc. 4, Line 103*

Golden care!
That keep'st the ports of slumber open wide
To many a watchful night!
> *Ibid. Sc. 5, Line 22*

Thy wish was father, Harry, to that thought.
> *Ibid. Line 91*

Commit
The oldest sins the newest kind of ways.
> *Ibid. Line 124*

A joint of mutton, and any pretty little tiny kickshaws, tell William cook.
> *Ibid. Act V, Sc. 1, Line 28*

His cares are now all ended.
> *Ibid. Sc. 2, Line 3*

I hope to see London once ere I die.
> *Ibid. Sc. 3, Line 61*

Falstaff. What wind blew you hither, Pistol?
Pistol. Not the ill wind which blows no man to good.[2]
> *Ibid. Line 87*

A foutra for the world and worldlings base!

I speak of Africa and golden joys.
> *Ibid. Line 100*

---

[1] After he routed Pharnaces Ponticus at the first assault, Caesar wrote thus to his friends: "I came, I saw, I conquered" (Veni, vidi, vici). — PLUTARCH'S *Lives: Cæsar*
[2] See Heywood, page 17.
Ill blows the wind that profits nobody. — *King Henry VI, Part III, Act 2, Sc. 5, L. 55*

Under which king, Bezonian? speak, or die!

> *King Henry IV, Part II.*
> *Act V, Sc. 3, Line 116*

Falstaff. What! is the old king dead?
Pistol. As nail in door.[1]

> *Ibid. Line 123*

How ill white hairs become a fool and jester.

> *Ibid. Sc. 4, Line 53*

O! for a Muse of fire, that would ascend
The brightest heaven of invention!

> *King Henry V. Prologue, Line 1*

Consideration like an angel came,
And whipped the offending Adam out of him.

> *Ibid. Act I, Sc. 1, Line 28*

Hear him debate of commonwealth affairs,
You would say it hath been all in all his study.

> *Ibid. Line 41*

Turn him to any cause of policy,
The Gordian knot of it he will unloose,
Familiar as his garter: that when he speaks,
The air, a chartered libertine, is still.

> *Ibid. Line 45*

Wholesome berries thrive and ripen best
Neighbour'd by fruit of baser quality.

> *Ibid. Line 61*

'Tis ever common
That men are merriest when they are from home.

> *Ibid. Sc. 2, Line 271*

O England! model to thy inward greatness,
Like little body with a mighty heart,
What mightst thou do, that honour would thee do,
Were all thy children kind and natural!

> *Ibid. Act II, Prologue, Line 16*

Even at the turning o' the tide.

> *Ibid. Act II, Sc. 3, Line 13*

---

[1] As dead as a door nail. — WILLIAM LANGLAND: *The Vision of Piers Plowman, Part 2, L. 183*

As dead as a door-nail. — *King Henry VI, Part II, Act 4, Sc. 10, L. 43*

Old Marley was as dead as a door-nail. — CHARLES DICKENS: *A Christmas Carol, Stave One*

His nose was as sharp as a pen, and a' babbled of green fields.

> *King Henry V. Act II, Sc. 3, Line 17*

As cold as any stone.

> *Ibid. Line 26*

Self-love, my liege, is not so vile a sin
As self-neglecting.

> *Ibid. Sc. 4, Line 74*

Once more unto the breach, dear friends, once more;
Or close the wall up with our English dead!
In peace there's nothing so becomes a man
As modest stillness and humility;
But when the blast of war blows in our ears,
Then imitate the action of the tiger:
Stiffen the sinews, summon up the blood.

> *Ibid. Act III, Sc. 1, Line 1*

And sheathed their swords for lack of argument.

> *Ibid. Line 21*

The mettle of your pasture.

> *Ibid. Line 27*

I see you stand like greyhounds in the slips,
Straining upon the start.

> *Ibid. Line 31*

I would give all my fame for a pot of ale and safety.

> *Ibid. Sc. 2, Line 14*

Men of few words are the best men.

> *Ibid. Line 40*

He will maintain his argument as well as any military man in the world.

> *Ibid. Line 89*

I know the disciplines of wars.

> *Ibid. Line 156*

Impious war,
Array'd in flames like to the prince of fiends,
Do, with his smirch'd complexion, all fell feats
Enlink'd to waste and desolation.

> *Ibid. Sc. 3, Line 15*

A man that I love and honour with my soul, and my heart, and my duty, and my life, and my living, and my uttermost power.

> *Ibid. Sc. 6, Line 7*

Giddy Fortune's furious fickle wheel,
That goddess blind,
That stands upon the rolling restless
    stone.
King Henry V. Act III, Sc. 6, Line 28
I thought upon one pair of English legs
Did march three Frenchmen.
Ibid. Line 161
We are in God's hand.
Ibid. Line 181
That island of England breeds very
valiant creatures: their mastiffs are of
unmatchable courage.
Ibid. Sc. 7, Line 155
You may as well say that's a val-
iant flea that dare eat his breakfast on
the lip of a lion.
Ibid. Line 160
The hum of either army stilly sounds,
That the fixed sentinels almost receive
The secret whispers of each other's
    watch;
Fire answers fire, and through their
    paly flames
Each battle sees the other's umbered
    face;
Steed threatens steed, in high and boast-
    ful neighs
Piercing the night's dull ear; and from
    the tents
The armourers, accomplishing the
    knights,
With busy hammers closing rivets up,[1]
Give dreadful note of preparation.
Ibid. Act IV, Prologue, Line 5
There is some soul of goodness in things
    evil,
Would men observingly distil it out.
Ibid. Act IV, Sc. 1, Line 4
When blood is their argument.
Ibid. Line 151
Every subject's duty is the king's;
but every subject's soul is his own.
Ibid. Line 189
Who with a body filled and vacant mind
Gets him to rest, crammed with distress-
    ful bread.
Ibid. Line 289
Winding up days with toil and nights
    with sleep.
Ibid. Line 299

[1] With clink of hammers closing rivets up.
— CIBBER: *Richard III (altered), Act V, Sc. 3*

He is as full of valour as of kindness;
Princely in both.
King Henry V. Act IV, Sc. 3, Line 15
But if it be a sin to covet honour,
I am the most offending soul alive.
Ibid. Line 28
This day is called the feast of Crispian:
He that outlives this day, and comes
    safe home,
Will stand a tip-toe when this day is
    named,
And rouse him at the name of Crispian.
Ibid. Line 40
Then shall our names,
Familiar in his mouth as household
    words,
Harry the King, Bedford and Exeter,
Warwick and Talbot, Salisbury and
    Gloucester, —
Be in their flowing cups freshly remem-
    bered.
Ibid. Line 51
We few, we happy few, we band of
    brothers.
Ibid. Line 60
Those that leave their valiant bones in
    France,
Dying like men, . . .
They shall be fam'd; for there the sun
    shall greet them,
And draw their honours reeking up to
    heaven.
Ibid. Line 98
The saying is true, "The empty ves-
sel makes the greatest sound."
Ibid. Sc. 4, Line 72
There is a river in Macedon, and
there is also moreover a river at Mon-
mouth; . . . and there is salmons in
both.
Ibid. Sc. 7, Line 28
There is occasions and causes why
and wherefore [1] in all things.
Ibid. Act V, Sc. 1, Line 3
By this leek, I will most horribly re-
venge. I eat and eat, I swear.
Ibid. Line 49
All hell shall stir for this.
Ibid. Line 72

[1] Every why hath a wherefore. — *The Comedy of Errors, Act II, Sc. 2, L. 45*
See Samuel Butler, page 142.

A fellow of plain and uncoined constancy.

King Henry V. Act V, Sc. 2, Line 160

My comfort is, that old age, that ill layer-up of beauty, can do no more spoil upon my face.

Ibid. Line 246

If he be not fellow with the best king, thou shalt find the best king of good fellows.[1]

Ibid. Line 259

Hung be the heavens with black, yield day to night!

King Henry VI, Part I. Act I, Sc. 1, Line 1

Fight till the last gasp.[2]

Ibid. Sc. 2, Line 127

Halcyon days.

Ibid. Line 131

Glory is like a circle in the water,
Which never ceaseth to enlarge itself,
Till by broad spreading it disperse to nought.

Ibid. Line 133

The sun with one eye vieweth all the world.

Ibid. Sc. 4, Line 84

Between two hawks, which flies the higher pitch;
Between two dogs, which hath the deeper mouth;
Between two blades, which bears the better temper;
Between two horses, which doth bear him best;
Between two girls, which hath the merriest eye;
I have perhaps, some shallow spirit of judgment;
But in these nice sharp quillets of the law,
Good faith, I am no wiser than a daw.

Ibid. Act II, Sc. 4, Line 12

I'll note you in my book of memory.

Ibid. Line 101

Just death, kind umpire of men's miseries.

Ibid. Sc. 5, Line 29

---

[1] He was a good felawe. — CHAUCER: *The Canterbury Tales, Prologue, L. 395*

[2] To the last gasp. — *As You Like It, Act II, Sc. 3, L. 69*

Fair be all thy hopes,
And prosperous be thy life in peace and war!

King Henry VI, Part I. Act II, Sc. 5, Line 113

Chok'd with ambition of the meaner sort.

Ibid. Line 123

Friendly counsel cuts off many foes.

Ibid. Act III, Sc. 1, Line 184

Delays have dangerous ends.[1]

Ibid. Sc. 2, Line 33

Care is no cure, but rather corrosive,
For things that are not to be remedied.

Ibid. Sc. 3, Line 3

Of all base passions, fear is most accurs'd.

Ibid. Act V, Sc. 2, Line 18

She's beautiful and therefore to be wooed,
She is a woman, therefore to be won.

Ibid. Sc. 3, Line 78

For what is wedlock forced, but a hell,
An age of discord and continual strife?
Whereas the contrary bringeth bliss,
And is a pattern of celestial peace.

Ibid. Sc. 5, Line 62

O Lord! that lends me life,
Lend me a heart replete with thankfulness!

Ibid. Part II. Act I, Sc. 1, Line 19

Whose large style
Agrees not with the leanness of his purse.

Ibid. Line 112

'Tis not my speeches that you do mislike,
But 'tis my presence that doth trouble ye.

Rancour will out.

Ibid. Line 141

Main chance.[2]

Ibid. Line 213

Could I come near your beauty with my nails

---

[1] All delays are dangerous in war. — DRYDEN: *Tyrannic Love, Act I, Sc. 1*

[2] Let me stande to the maine chance. — JOHN LYLY: *Euphues* [1579], *page 104*

Have a care o' th' main chance. — BUTLER: *Hudibras, Part II, Canto II*

Be careful still of the main chance. — DRYDEN: *Persius, Satire VI*

I'd set my ten commandments in your face.
>> *King Henry VI, Part II.*
>> *Act I, Sc. 3, Line 144*

Blessed are the peacemakers on earth.[1]
>> *Ibid. Act II, Sc. 1, Line 34*

God be prais'd, that to believing souls
Gives light in darkness, comfort in despair!
>> *Ibid. Line 66*

God defend the right!
>> *Ibid. Sc. 3, Line 55*

Sometimes hath the brightest day a cloud;
And after summer evermore succeeds
Barren winter, with his wrathful nipping cold:
So cares and joys abound, as seasons fleet.
>> *Ibid. Sc. 4, Line 1*

Now 'tis the spring, and weeds are shallow-rooted;
Suffer them now and they'll o'ergrow the garden.
>> *Ibid. Act III, Sc. 1, Line 31*

Smooth runs the water where the brook is deep.[2]
>> *Ibid. Line 53*

In thy face I see
The map of honour, truth, and loyalty.
>> *Ibid. Line 202*

What stronger breastplate than a heart untainted!
Thrice is he armed that hath his quarrel just,
And he but naked, though locked up in steel,
Whose conscience with injustice is corrupted.[3]
>> *Ibid. Sc. 2, Line 232*

For wheresoe'er thou art in this world's globe.
I'll have an Iris that shall find thee out.
>> *Ibid. Line 406*

He dies, and makes no sign.
>> *Ibid. Sc. 3, Line 29*

---

[1] Blessed are the peacemakers. — *Matthew,*
V, 9
[2] See Raleigh, page 21, and Lyly, page 24.
[3] I'm armed with more than complete steel, —
The justice of my quarrel. —
>> CHRISTOPHER MARLOWE: *Lust's Dominion, Act III, Sc. 4*

Close up his eyes and draw the curtain close;
And let us all to meditation.
>> *King Henry VI, Part II.*
>> *Act III, Sc. 3, Line 32*

The gaudy, blabbing, and remorseful day
Is crept into the bosom of the sea.
>> *Ibid. Act IV, Sc. 1, Line 1*

Small things make base men proud.
>> *Ibid. Line 106*

True nobility is exempt from fear.
>> *Ibid. Line 129*

There shall be in England seven halfpenny loaves sold for a penny; the three-hooped pot shall have ten hoops; and I will make it felony to drink small beer.
>> *Ibid. Sc. 2, Line 73*

The first thing we do, let's kill all the lawyers.
>> *Ibid. Line 86*

Is not this a lamentable thing, that of the skin of an innocent lamb should be made parchment? that parchment, being scribbled o'er, should undo a man?
>> *Ibid. Line 88*

Sir, he made a chimney in my father's house, and the bricks are alive at this day to testify it.
>> *Ibid. Line 160*

Thou hast most traitorously corrupted the youth of the realm in erecting a grammar-school; and whereas, before, our forefathers had no other books but the score and the tally, thou hast caused printing to be used; and, contrary to the king, his crown, and dignity, thou hast built a paper-mill.
>> *Ibid. Sc. 7, Line 35*

Beggars mounted run their horse to death.
>> *Ibid. Part III. Act I, Sc. 4, Line 127*

O tiger's heart wrapp'd in a woman's hide! [1]
>> *Ibid. Line 137*

And many strokes, though with a little axe,

---

[1] ROBERT GREENE in his famous attack on Shakespeare, *A Groats-Worth of Wit* [1592], burlesques this line: "Tyger's hart wrapt in a Player's hide."

Hew down and fell the hardest-timbered oak.

King Henry VI, Part III.
Act II, Sc. 1, Line 54

To weep is to make less the depth of grief.

Ibid. Line 85

The smallest worm will turn, being trodden on.

Ibid. Sc. 2, Line 17

       Didst thou never hear
That things ill got had ever bad success?
And happy always was it for that son
Whose father for his hoarding went to hell?

Ibid. Line 45

Thou setter up and plucker down of kings.[1]

Ibid. Sc. 3, Line 37

And what makes robbers bold but too much lenity?

Ibid. Sc. 6, Line 22

My crown is in my heart, not on my head;
Not deck'd with diamonds and Indian stones,
Nor to be seen: my crown is call'd content;
A crown it is that seldom kings enjoy.

Ibid. Act III, Sc. 1, Line 62

       'Tis a happy thing
To be the father unto many sons.

Ibid. Sc. 2, Line 104

Gloucester. That would be ten days' wonder at the least.
Clarence. That's a day longer than a wonder lasts.[2]

Ibid. Line 113

Like one that stands upon a promontory,
And spies a far-off shore where he would tread,
Wishing his foot were equal with his eye.

Ibid. Line 135

Yield not thy neck
To fortune's yoke, but let thy dauntless mind

[1] Proud setter up and puller down of kings.
— *Act III, Sc. 3, L. 156*
[2] See Chaucer, page 4.

Still ride in triumph over all mischance.

King Henry VI, Part III.
Act III, Sc. 3, Line 16

For how can tyrants safely govern home,
Unless abroad they purchase great alliance?

Ibid. Line 69

Having nothing, nothing can he lose.

Ibid. Line 152

Both of you are birds of self-same feather.

Ibid. Line 161

Hasty marriage seldom proveth well.

Ibid. Act IV, Sc. 1, Line 18

Let us be back'd with God and with the seas
Which he hath given for fence impregnable,
And with their helps only defend ourselves:
In them and in ourselves our safety lies.

Ibid. Line 43

What fates impose, that men must needs abide;
It boots not to resist both wind and tide.

Ibid. Sc. 3, Line 57

'Tis no time to talk.

Ibid. Sc. 5, Line 24

Now join your hands, and with your hands your hearts.

Ibid. Sc. 6, Line 39

For many men that stumble at the threshold
Are well foretold that danger lurks within.

Ibid. Sc. 7, Line 11

A little fire is quickly trodden out;
Which, being suffered, rivers cannot quench.

Ibid. Sc. 8, Line 7

When the lion fawns upon the lamb,
The lamb will never cease to follow him.

Ibid. Line 49

What is pomp, rule, reign, but earth and dust?
And, live we how we can, yet die we must.

Ibid. Act V, Sc. 2, Line 27

Every cloud engenders not a storm.

Ibid. Sc. 3, Line 13

We are advertis'd by our loving friends.
*King Henry VI, Part III.
Act V, Sc. 3, Line 18*

What though the mast be now blown over-board,
The cable broke, the holding anchor lost,
And half our sailors swallow'd in the flood?
Yet lives our pilot still.
Ibid. Sc. 4, Line 3

So part we sadly in this troublous world
To meet with joy in sweet Jerusalem.
Ibid. Sc. 5, Line 7

Men ne'er spend their fury on a child.
Ibid. Line 57

He's sudden if a thing comes in his head.
Ibid. Line 86

Suspicion always haunts the guilty mind;
The thief doth fear each bush an officer.
Ibid. Sc. 6, Line 11

This word "love," which greybeards call divine.
Ibid. Line 81

Mirthful comic shows.
Ibid. Sc. 7, Line 43

Now is the winter of our discontent
Made glorious summer by this sun of York.
*King Richard III. Act I, Sc. 1,
Line 1*

Grim-visaged war hath smoothed his wrinkled front.
Ibid. Line 9

To leave this keen encounter of our wits.
Ibid. Sc. 2, Line 116

His better doth not breathe upon the earth.
Ibid. Line 141

Look, how my ring encompasseth thy finger,
Even so thy breast encloseth my poor heart;
Wear both of them, for both of them are thine.
Ibid. Line 204

Was ever woman in this humour wooed?
Was ever woman in this humour won?
Ibid. Line 229

Framed in the prodigality of nature.
Ibid. Line 245

The world is grown so bad,
That wrens make prey where eagles dare not perch.[1]
*King Richard III. Act I,
Sc. 3, Line 70*

They that stand high have many blasts to shake them.
Ibid. Line 259

And thus I clothe my naked villany
With odd old ends stolen forth of holy writ,
And seem a saint when most I play the devil.
Ibid. Line 336

Talkers are no good doers.
Ibid. Line 351

O, I have passed a miserable night,
So full of ugly sights, of ghastly dreams,
That, as I am a Christian faithful man,
I would not spend another such a night,
Though 'twere to buy a world of happy days.
Ibid. Sc. 4, Line 2

Lord, Lord! methought, what pain it was to drown:
What dreadful noise of waters in mine ears!
What ugly sights of death within mine eyes!
Ibid. Line 21

I pass'd, methought, the melancholy flood,
With that grim ferryman which poets write of,
Unto the kingdom of perpetual night.
Ibid. Line 45

Sorrow breaks seasons and reposing hours,
Makes the night morning, and the noontide night.
Ibid. Line 76

Thou art a widow; yet thou art a mother,
And hast the comfort of thy children left thee.
Ibid. Act II, Sc. 2, Line 55

A parlous boy.
Ibid. Sc. 4, Line 35

---

[1] For fools rush in where angels fear to tread. — POPE: *Essay on Criticism, Part III,
L. 66*

So wise so young, they say, do never
live long.[1]
> *King Richard III. Act III,*
> *Sc. 1, Line 79*

Off with his head! [2]
> *Ibid. Sc. 4, Line 75*

Lives like a drunken sailor on a mast,
Ready with every nod to tumble down.
> *Ibid. Line 98*

Even in the afternoon of her best days.
> *Ibid. Sc. 7, Line 185*

Thou troublest me: I am not in the vein.
> *Ibid. Act IV, Sc. 2, Line 117*

Their lips were four red roses on a stalk.
> *Ibid. Sc. 3, Line 12*

The sons of Edward sleep in Abraham's
bosom.
> *Ibid. Line 38*

Let not the heavens hear these tell-tale
women
Rail on the Lord's anointed.
> *Ibid. Sc. 4, Line 150*

Tetchy and wayward.
> *Ibid. Line 169*

An honest tale speeds best being plainly
told.
> *Ibid. Line 359*

Harp not on that string.
> *Ibid. Line 365*

Thus far into the bowels of the land
Have we marched on without impedi-
ment.
> *Ibid. Act V, Sc. 2, Line 3*

True hope is swift, and flies with swallow's wings;
Kings it makes gods, and meaner creatures kings.
> *Ibid. Line 23*

The king's name is a tower of strength.
> *Ibid. Sc. 3, Line 12*

Give me another horse! bind up my
wounds!
> *Ibid. Line 178*

O coward conscience, how dost thou afflict me!
> *Ibid. Line 180*

My conscience hath a thousand several
tongues,

---

[1] A little too wise, they say, do ne'er live
long. — MIDDLETON: *The Phœnix, Act I, Sc. 1*
[2] Off with his head! so much for Buckingham! — CIBBER: *Richard III (altered), Act
IV, Sc. 3*

And every tongue brings in a several
tale,
And every tale condemns me for a villain.
> *King Richard III. Act V,*
> *Sc. 3, Line 194*

The early village cock
Hath twice done salutation to the morn.
> *Ibid. Line 210*

By the apostle Paul, shadows to-night
Have struck more terror to the soul of
Richard
Than can the substance of ten thousand
soldiers.
> *Ibid. Line 217*

A horse! a horse! my kingdom for a
horse!
> *Ibid. Sc. 4, Line 7*

I have set my life upon a cast,
And I will stand the hazard of the die:
I think there be six Richmonds in the
field.
> *Ibid. Line 9*

Order gave each thing view.
> *King Henry VIII. Act I, Sc. 1,*
> *Line 44*

No man's pie is freed
From his ambitious finger.
> *Ibid. Line 52*

The force of his own merit makes his
way.
> *Ibid. Line 64*

Anger is like
A full-hot horse, who being allow'd his
way,
Self-mettle tires him.
> *Ibid. Line 132*

Heat not a furnace for your foe so hot
That it do singe yourself.
> *Ibid. Line 140*

New customs,
Though they be never so ridiculous,
Nay, let 'em be unmanly, yet are fol-
low'd.
> *Ibid. Sc. 3, Line 2*

The mirror of all courtesy.
> *Ibid. Act II, Sc. 1, Line 53*

This bold bad man.[1]
> *Ibid. Sc. 2, Line 44*

---

[1] See Spenser, page 24.

'Tis better to be lowly born,
And range with humble livers in content,
Than to be perked up in a glistering grief
And wear a golden sorrow.
King Henry VIII. Act II, Sc. 3, Line 19

Orpheus with his lute made trees,
And the mountain-tops that freeze,
Bow themselves when he did sing.
Ibid. Act III, Sc. 1, Line 3

Heaven is above all yet; there sits a judge
That no king can corrupt.
Ibid. Line 99

'Tis well said again;
And 'tis a kind of good deed to say well:
And yet words are no deeds.
Ibid. Sc. 2, Line 153

And then to breakfast with
What appetite you have.
Ibid. Line 203

I have touched the highest point of all my greatness;
And from that full meridian of my glory,
I haste now to my setting: I shall fall
Like a bright exhalation in the evening,
And no man see me more.
Ibid. Line 224

Press not a falling man too far!
Ibid. Line 334

Farewell! a long farewell, to all my greatness!
This is the state of man: to-day he puts forth
The tender leaves of hopes; to-morrow blossoms,
And bears his blushing honours thick upon him;
The third day comes a frost, a killing frost;
And, when he thinks, good easy man, full surely
His greatness is a-ripening, nips his root,
And then he falls, as I do. I have ventured,
Like little wanton boys that swim on bladders,
This many summers in a sea of glory,
But far beyond my depth: my high-blown pride
At length broke under me, and now has left me,
Weary and old with service, to the mercy
Of a rude stream, that must forever hide me.
Vain pomp and glory of this world, I hate ye:
I feel my heart new opened. O! how wretched
Is that poor man that hangs on princes' favours!
There is, betwixt that smile we would aspire to,
That sweet aspect of princes, and their ruin,
More pangs and fears than wars or women have —
And when he falls, he falls like Lucifer,
Never to hope again.
King Henry VIII. Act III, Sc. 2, Line 352

A peace above all earthly dignities,
A still and quiet conscience.
Ibid. Line 380

A load would sink a navy.
Ibid. Line 384

And sleep in dull cold marble.
Ibid. Line 434

Say, Wolsey, that once trod the ways of glory,
And sounded all the depths and shoals of honour,
Found thee a way, out of his wrack, to rise in;
A sure and safe one, though thy master missed it.
Ibid. Line 436

I charge thee, fling away ambition:
By that sin fell the angels.
Ibid. Line 441

Love thyself last: cherish those hearts that hate thee;
Corruption wins not more than honesty.
Still in thy right hand carry gentle peace,
To silence envious tongues: be just, and fear not:
Let all the ends thou aim'st at be thy country's,

Thy God's, and truth's; then if thou
fall'st, O Cromwell,
Thou fall'st a blessed martyr!
King Henry VIII. Act III,
Sc. 2, Line 444
Had I but served my God with half the
zeal [1]
I served my king, he would not in mine
age
Have left me naked to mine enemies.
Ibid. Line 456
A royal train, believe me.
Ibid. Act IV, Sc. 1, Line 37
An old man, broken with the storms of
state,
Is come to lay his weary bones among
ye;
Give him a little earth for charity!
Ibid. Sc. 2, Line 21
He gave his honours to the world again,
His blessed part to heaven, and slept in
peace.
Ibid. Line 29
So may he rest; his faults lie gently on
him!
Ibid. Line 31
He was a man
Of an unbounded stomach.
Ibid. Line 33
Men's evil manners live in brass; their
virtues
We write in water.[2]
Ibid. Line 45
He was a scholar, and a ripe and good
one;

[1] Had I served God as well in every part
As I did serve my king and master still,
My scope had not this season been so short,
Nor would have had the power to do me
ill.
THOMAS CHURCHYARD [1520–1604]:
Death of Morton [written in 1593]
[2] For men use, if they have an evil tourne,
to write it in marble: and whoso doth us a
good tourne we write it in duste. — SIR
THOMAS MORE: *Richard III and his Miserable
End*
All your better deeds
Shall be in water writ, but this in marble.
BEAUMONT AND FLETCHER: *Philaster,*
Act V, Sc. 3
L'injure se grave en métal; et le bienfait
s'escrit en l'onde.
(An injury graves itself in metal, but a bene-
fit writes itself in water.)
JEAN BERTAUT [*circa* 1611]

Exceeding wise, fair-spoken, and per-
suading;
Lofty and sour to them that loved him
not,
But to those men that sought him sweet
as summer.
King Henry VIII. Act IV,
Sc. 2, Line 51
Yet in bestowing, madam,
He was most princely.
Ibid. Line 56
After my death I wish no other herald,
No other speaker of my living actions,
To keep mine honour from corruption,
But such an honest chronicler as Grif-
fith.
Ibid. Line 69
To dance attendance on their lordships'
pleasures.
Ibid. Act V, Sc. 2, Line 30
'Tis a cruelty
To load a falling man.
Ibid. Sc. 3, Line 76
You were ever good at sudden commen-
dations.
Ibid. Line 122
Those about her
From her shall read the perfect ways of
honour.
Ibid. Sc. 5, Line 37
Wherever the bright sun of heaven shall
shine,
His honour and the greatness of his
name
Shall be, and make new nations.
Ibid. Line 51
A most unspotted lily shall she pass
To the ground, and all the world shall
mourn her.
Ibid. Line 62
I have had my labour for my travail.[1]
Troilus and Cressida. Act I,
Sc. 1, Line 73
Men prize the thing ungain'd more than
it is.
Ibid. Sc. 2, Line 313
Take but degree away, untune that
string,

[1] Labour for his pains. — EDWARD MOORE:
The Boy and his Rainbow
Labour for their pains. — CERVANTES: *Don
Quixote, The Author's Preface*

And, hark! what discord follows; each thing meets
In mere oppugnancy.[1]
> *Troilus and Cressida. Act I,*
> *Sc. 3, Line 109*

Appetite, a universal wolf.
> *Ibid. Line 121*

To hear the wooden dialogue.
> *Ibid. Line 155*

The baby figure of the giant mass
Of things to come.
> *Ibid. Line 345*

Modest doubt is call'd
The beacon of the wise, the tent that searches
To the bottom of the worst.
> *Ibid. Act II, Sc. 2, Line 15*

'Tis mad idolatry
To make the service greater than the god.
> *Ibid. Line 56*

The remainder viands
We do not throw in unrespective sink
Because we now are full.
> *Ibid. Line 70*

The elephant hath joints, but none for courtesy: his legs are legs for necessity, not for flexure.
> *Ibid. Sc. 3, Line 114*

He that is proud eats up himself; pride is his own glass, his own trumpet, his own chronicle.
> *Ibid. Line 165*

Light boats sail swift, though greater hulks draw deep.
> *Ibid. Line 280*

Words pay no debts.
> *Ibid. Act III, Sc. 2, Line 56*

To fear the worst oft cures the worse.
> *Ibid. Line 77*

All lovers swear more performance than they are able, and yet reserve an ability that they never perform; vowing more than the perfection of ten, and discharging less than the tenth part of one.
> *Ibid. Line 89*

---

[1] Unless degree is preserved, the first place is safe for no one. — PUBLIUS SYRUS: *Maxim 1042*

For to be wise, and love,
Exceeds man's might; that dwells with gods above.
> *Troilus and Cressida. Act III,*
> *Sc. 2, Line 163*

Time hath, my lord, a wallet at his back,
Wherein he puts alms for oblivion.
> *Ibid. Sc. 3, Line 145*

Welcome ever smiles,
And farewell goes out sighing.
> *Ibid. Line 168*

One touch of nature makes the whole world kin
> *Ibid. Line 175*

And give to dust that is a little gilt
More laud than gilt o'er-dusted.
> *Ibid. Line 178*

And, like a dew-drop from the lion's mane,
Be shook to air.
> *Ibid. Line 225*

My mind is troubled, like a fountain stirr'd;
And I myself see not the bottom of it.
> *Ibid. Line 314*

Be moderate, be moderate.
> *Ibid. Act IV, Sc. 4, Line 1*

As many farewells as be stars in heaven.
> *Ibid. Line 44*

The kiss you take is better than you give.
> *Ibid. Sc. 5, Line 38*

There's language in her eye, her cheek, her lip.
> *Ibid. Line 55*

Daughters of the game.
> *Ibid. Line 63*

The end crowns all,
And that old common arbitrator, Time,
Will one day end it.
> *Ibid. Line 223*

He has not so much brain as ear-wax.
> *Ibid. Act V, Sc. 1, Line 58*

A sleeveless errand.
> *Ibid. Sc. 4, Line 9*

O world! world! world! thus is the poor agent despised.
> *Ibid. Sc. 10, Line 36*

Rubbing the poor itch of your opinion,
Make yourselves scabs.
> *Coriolanus. Act I, Sc. 1, Line 171*

The gods sent not
Corn for the rich men only.
Coriolanus. Act I, Sc. 1,
Line 213

Had I a dozen sons, each in my love
alike and none less dear than thine and
my good Marcius, I had rather eleven
die nobly for their country than one
voluptuously surfeit out of action.
Ibid. Sc. 3, Line 24

All the yarn she spun in Ulysses' absence did but fill Ithaca full of moths.
Ibid. Line 93

Nature teaches beasts to know their
friends.
Ibid. Act II, Sc. 1, Line 6

A cup of hot wine with not a drop of
allaying Tiber in't.[1]
Ibid. Line 52

Bid them wash their faces,
And keep their teeth clean.
Ibid. Sc. 3, Line 65

I thank you for your voices: thank you,
Your most sweet voices.
Ibid. Line 179

The mutable, rank-scented many.
Ibid. Act III, Sc. 1, Line 65

Hear you this Triton of the minnows?
Mark you
His absolute "shall"?
Ibid. Line 88

Enough, with over-measure.
Ibid. Line 139

What is the city but the people?
Ibid. Line 198

His nature is too noble for the world:
He would not flatter Neptune for his
trident,
Or Jove for 's power to thunder.
Ibid. Line 254

That it shall hold companionship in
peace
With honour, as in war.
Ibid. Sc. 2, Line 49

I do love
My country's good with a respect more
tender,

[1] When flowing cups pass swiftly round
With no allaying Thames.
RICHARD LOVELACE: *To Althea from*
Prison, St. 2

More holy, more profound, than mine
own life.
Coriolanus. Act III, Sc. 3,
Line 109

3 Servant. Where dwellest thou?
Coriolanus. Under the canopy.
Ibid. Act IV, Sc. 5, Line 40

You know the very road into his kind-
ness,
And cannot lose your way.
Ibid. Act V, Sc. 1, Line 60

Chaste as the icicle
That's curdied by the frost from purest
snow
And hangs on Dian's temple.
Ibid. Sc. 3, Line 65

Is't possible that so short a time can
alter the condition of a man?
Ibid. Sc. 4, Line 10

They'll give him death by inches.
Ibid. Line 43

Splitting the air with noise.
Ibid. Sc. 5, Line 52

If you have writ your annals true, 'tis
there
That, like an eagle in a dove-cote, I
Flutter'd your Volscians in Corioli:
Alone I did it. Boy!
Ibid. Line 114

Thou hast done a deed whereat valour
will weep.
Ibid. Line 135

He shall have a noble memory.
Ibid. Line 155

Sleep in peace, slain in your country's
wars!
Titus Andronicus. Act I, Sc. 1,
Line 91

Sweet mercy is nobility's true badge.
Ibid. Line 119

In peace and honour rest you here, my
sons;
. . . repose you here in rest,
Secure from worldly chances and mishaps!
Ibid. Line 150

These words are razors to my wounded
heart.
Ibid. Line 314

He lives in fame that died in virtue's
cause.
Ibid. Line 390

These dreary dumps.[1]
> *Titus Andronicus. Act I,*
> *Sc. 1, Line 391*

She is a woman, therefore may be
woo'd;
She is a woman, therefore may be won;
She is Lavinia, therefore must be loved.
What, man! more water glideth by the
mill
Than wots the miller of; [2] and easy it is
Of a cut loaf to steal a shive.
> *Ibid. Act II, Sc. 1, Line 82*

What you cannot as you would achieve,
You must perforce accomplish as you
may.
> *Ibid. Line 106*

How easily murder is discovered!
> *Ibid. Sc. 3, Line 287*

Poor harmless fly.
> *Ibid. Act III, Sc. 2, Line 63*

Two may keep counsel when the third's
away.[3]
> *Ibid. Act IV, Sc. 2, Line 145*

The eagle suffers little birds to sing.
> *Ibid. Sc. 4, Line 82*

A pair of star-cross'd lovers.
> *Romeo and Juliet. Act I, Pro-*
> *logue, Line 6*

The weakest goes to the wall.
> *Romeo and Juliet. Act I, Sc. 1,*
> *Line 17*

Gregory, remember thy swashing blow.
> *Ibid. Line 68*

An hour before the worshipp'd sun
Peered forth the golden window of the
east.
> *Ibid. Line 124*

As is the bud bit with an envious worm,
Ere he can spread his sweet leaves to
the air,
Or dedicate his beauty to the sun.
> *Ibid. Line 156*

Saint-seducing gold.
> *Ibid. Line 220*

He that is strucken blind cannot forget
The precious treasure of his eyesight
lost.
> *Ibid. Line 238*

One fire burns out another's burning,[1]
One pain is lessen'd by another's anguish.
> *Romeo and Juliet. Act I,*
> *Sc. 1, Line 47*

I will make thee think thy swan a crow.
> *Ibid. Line 92*

One fairer than my love! the all-seeing
sun
Ne'er saw her match since first the
world begun.
> *Ibid. Line 97*

That book in many eyes doth share the
glory
That in gold clasps locks in the golden
story.
> *Ibid. Sc. 3, Line 91*

Beetle brows.
> *Ibid. Sc. 4, Line 32*

For I am proverb'd with a grandsire
phrase.
> *Ibid. Line 37*

Benvolio. O! then, I see Queen Mab
hath been with you! . . .
Mercutio. She is the fairies' midwife,
and she comes
In shape no bigger than an agate-stone
On the fore-finger of an alderman,
Drawn with a team of little atomies
Athwart men's noses as they lie asleep.
> *Ibid. Line 53*

True, I talk of dreams,
Which are the children of an idle brain,
Begot of nothing but vain fantasy.
> *Ibid. Line 97*

Toes unplagu'd with corns.
> *Ibid. Sc. 5, Line 21*

For you and I are past our dancing
days.[2]
> *Ibid. Line 35*

It seems she hangs upon the cheek of
night
Like a rich jewel in an Ethiop's ear.
> *Ibid. Line 49*

Too early seen unknown, and known
too late!
> *Ibid. Line 143*

Young Adam Cupid, he that shot so
trim

---

[1] And doleful dumps the mind oppress. —
Romeo and Juliet, Act IV, Sc. 5, L. 130
[2] See Heywood, page 17.
[3] *Ibid.*, page 16.

[1] See Chapman, page 28.
[2] My dancing days are done. — BEAUMONT
AND FLETCHER: *The Scornful Lady, Act V,*
Sc. 3

When King Cophetua loved the beggar maid.

> *Romeo and Juliet. Act II,*
> *Sc. 1, Line 13*

He jests at scars, that never felt a wound.

But, soft! what light through yonder window breaks?

It is the east, and Juliet is the sun.

> *Ibid. Sc. 2, Line 1*

She speaks, yet she says nothing.

> *Ibid. Line 12*

See, how she leans her cheek upon her hand.

O! that I were a glove upon that hand,
That I might touch that cheek.

> *Ibid. Line 23*

O Romeo, Romeo! wherefore art thou Romeo?

> *Ibid. Line 33*

What's in a name? That which we call a rose
By any other name would smell as sweet.

> *Ibid. Line 43*

For stony limits cannot hold love out.

> *Ibid. Line 67*

Alack! there lies more peril in thine eye
Than twenty of their swords.

> *Ibid. Line 71*

At lovers' perjuries,[1]
They say, Jove laughs.

> *Ibid. Line 92*

Romeo. Lady, by yonder blessed moon I swear,
That tips with silver all these fruit-tree tops, —

Juliet. O! swear not by the moon, the inconstant moon,
That monthly changes in her circled orb,
Lest that thy love prove likewise variable.

> *Ibid. Line 107*

The god of my idolatry.

> *Ibid. Line 114*

Too like the lightning, which doth cease to be
Ere one can say it lightens.

> *Ibid. Line 119*

[1] Perjuria ridet amantium Jupiter (Jupiter laughs at the perjuries of lovers). — TIBULLUS, III, 6, 49

This bud of love, by summer's ripening breath,
May prove a beauteous flower when next we meet.

> *Romeo and Juliet. Act II,*
> *Sc. 2, Line 121*

A thousand times good-night!

> *Ibid. Line 154*

Love goes toward love, as schoolboys from their books;
But love from love, toward school with heavy looks.

> *Ibid. Line 156*

How silver-sweet sound lovers' tongues by night,
Like softest music to attending ears!

> *Ibid. Line 165*

Good night, good night! parting is such sweet sorrow,
That I shall say good night till it be morrow.

> *Ibid. Line 184*

O! mickle is the powerful grace that lies
In herbs, plants, stones, and their true qualities:
For nought so vile that on the earth doth live
But to the earth some special good doth give,
Nor aught so good but strain'd from that fair use
Revolts from true birth, stumbling on abuse,
Virtue itself turns vice, being misapplied;
And vice sometime's by action dignified.

> *Ibid. Sc. 3, Line 15*

Care keeps his watch in every old man's eye,
And where care lodges, sleep will never lie.

> *Ibid. Line 35*

Wisely and slow; they stumble that run fast.

> *Ibid. Line 94*

Stabbed with a white wench's black eye.

> *Ibid. Sc. 4, Line 14*

The courageous captain of compliments.

> *Ibid. Line 21*

One, two, and the third in your bosom.

> *Ibid. Line 24*

O flesh, flesh, how art thou fishified!
> *Romeo and Juliet. Act II,*
> *Sc. 4, Line 41*

I am the very pink of courtesy.
> *Ibid. Line 63*

If thy wits run the wild-goose chase, I have done.
> *Ibid. Line 77*

A gentleman, nurse, that loves to hear himself talk, and will speak more in a minute than he will stand to in a month.
> *Ibid. Line 155*

A fool's paradise.[1]
> *Ibid. Line 176*

My man's as true as steel.[2]
> *Ibid. Line 212*

Love's heralds should be thoughts,
Which ten times faster glide than the sun's beams.
> *Ibid. Sc. 5, Line 4*

I wouldst thou hadst my bones, and I thy news.
> *Ibid. Line 27*

The excuse that thou dost make in this delay
Is longer than the tale thou dost excuse.
> *Ibid. Line 33*

These violent delights have violent ends.
> *Ibid. Sc. 6, Line 9*

Too swift arrives as tardy as too slow.
> *Ibid. Line 15*

Here comes the lady: O! so light a foot
Will ne'er wear out the everlasting flint.
> *Ibid. Line 16*

---

[1] The earliest instance of this expression is found in the *Paston Letters* [1462], *No. 457.* Also WILLIAM BULLEIN's *Dialogue, P. 28* [1573]
A fool's paradise. — GILES FLETCHER: *The Sorcerer of Vain Delights, St. 3*
The Paradise of Fools, to few unknown. — MILTON: *Paradise Lost, Book III, L. 496*
Hence the fool's paradise. — ALEXANDER POPE: *The Dunciad, Book III, L. 9*
In this fool's paradise he drank delight. — GEORGE CRABBE: *The Borough, Letter XII, Players*
Used also by Middleton and Fielding.
[2] Trewe as steel. — CHAUCER: *Troilus and Criseyde, Book V, L. 831*
As true as steel. — SHAKESPEARE: *Troilus and Cressida, Act III, Sc. 2, L. 184*

Thy head is as full of quarrels as an egg is full of meat.[1]
> *Romeo and Juliet. Act III,*
> *Sc. 1, Line 23*

A word and a blow.[2]
> *Ibid. Line 44*

A plague o' both your houses!
> *Ibid. Line 96*

Romeo. Courage, man; the hurt cannot be much.
Mercutio. No, 'tis not so deep as a well, nor so wide as a church-door; but 'tis enough, 'twill serve.
> *Ibid. Line 100*

When he shall die,
Take him and cut him out in little stars,
And he will make the face of heaven so fine
That all the world will be in love with night,
And pay no worship to the garish sun.
> *Ibid. Sc. 2, Line 21*

Was ever book containing such vile matter
So fairly bound? O! that deceit should dwell
In such a gorgeous palace.
> *Ibid. Line 83*

They may seize
On the white wonder of dear Juliet's hand,
And steal immortal blessing from her lips,
Who, even in pure and vestal modesty,
Still blush, as thinking their own kisses sin.
> *Ibid. Sc. 3, Line 35*

Adversity's sweet milk, philosophy.
> *Ibid. Line 54*

The lark, the herald of the morn.
> *Ibid. Sc. 5, Line 6*

Night's candles are burnt out, and jocund day
Stands tiptoe on the misty mountain-tops.
> *Ibid. Line 9*

---

[1] It's as full of good-nature as an egg's full of meat. — R. B. SHERIDAN: *A Trip to Scarborough, Act III, Sc. 4*
[2] Word and a blow. — DRYDEN: *Amphitryon, Act I, Sc. 1.* BUNYAN: *Pilgrim's Progress, Part I*

Straining harsh discords and unpleasing
sharps.
                    Romeo and Juliet. Act III,
                                Sc. 5, Line 28
                    All these woes shall serve
For sweet discourses in our time to
come.
                            Ibid. Line 52
Thank me no thankings, nor proud me
no prouds.
                            Ibid. Line 153
In that dim monument where Tybalt
lies.[1]
                            Ibid. Line 203
Past hope, past cure, past help!
                    Ibid. Act IV, Sc. 1, Line 45
Not stepping o'er the bounds of mod-
esty.
                    Ibid. Sc. 2, Line 28
My dismal scene I needs must act alone.
                    Ibid. Sc. 3, Line 19
My bosom's lord sits lightly in his
throne.
                    Ibid. Act V, Sc. 1, Line 3
                    Meagre were his looks,
Sharp misery had worn him to the
bones.
                            Ibid. Line 40
A beggarly account of empty boxes.
                            Ibid. Line 45
Famine is in thy cheeks.
                            Ibid. Line 69
The world is not thy friend nor the
world's law.
                            Ibid. Line 72
Apothecary. My poverty, but not my
will, consents.
Romeo. I pay thy poverty, and not thy
will.
                            Ibid. Line 75
                    The strength
Of twenty men.
                            Ibid. Line 78
One writ with me in sour misfortune's
book.
                    Ibid. Sc. 3, Line 82

Her beauty makes
This vault a feasting presence full of
light.
                    Romeo and Juliet. Act V,
                                Sc. 3, Line 85
How oft when men are at the point of
death
Have they been merry!
                            Ibid. Line 88
                    Beauty's ensign yet
Is crimson in thy lips and in thy cheeks,
And death's pale flag is not advanced
there.
                            Ibid. Line 94
                    Eyes, look your last!
Arms, take your last embrace!
                            Ibid. Line 112
                    O true apothecary!
Thy drugs are quick.
                            Ibid. Line 119
'Tis not enough to help the feeble up,
But to support him after.
                    Timon of Athens. Act I, Sc. 1,
                                Line 108
I call the gods to witness.
                            Ibid. Line 138
Satiety of commendations.
                            Ibid. Line 167
Ceremony was but devis'd at first
To set a gloss on faint deeds, hollow
welcomes,
Recanting goodness, sorry ere 'tis
shown;
But where there is true friendship, there
needs none.
                    Ibid. Sc. 2, Line 15
Here's that which is too weak to be a
sinner,
Honest water, which ne'er left man i'
the mire.[1]
                            Ibid. Line 60
Immortal gods, I crave no pelf;
I pray for no man but myself:
Grant I may never prove so fond,
To trust man on his oath or bond.
                            Ibid. Line 64
Men shut their doors against a setting
sun.
                            Ibid. Line 152

---

[1] In that dim monument where Tybalt lies
I would that we lay sleeping side by side.
ARTHUR DAVISON FICKE: *Sonnet*

[1] Inscribed on the drinking fountain in the
market-square of Stratford-on-Avon.

Every room
Hath blazed with lights and bray'd with
    minstrelsy.
        *Timon of Athens. Act II,
                    Sc. 2, Line 170*
Every man has his fault, and honesty is
    his.
        Ibid. Act III, Sc. 1, Line 30
Policy sits above conscience.
        Ibid. Sc. 2, Line 95
We have seen better days.
        Ibid. Act IV, Sc. 2, Line 27
I am Misanthropos, and hate mankind.
        Ibid. Sc. 3, Line 53
I'll example you with thievery:
The sun's a thief, and with his great
    attraction
Rob's the vast sea; the moon's an ar-
    rant thief,
And her pale fire she snatches from the
    sun;
The sea's a thief, whose liquid surge re-
    solves
The moon into salt tears; the earth's a
    thief,
That feeds and breeds by a composture
    stolen
From general excrement, each thing's
    a thief.
        Ibid. Line 441
Life's uncertain voyage.
        Ibid. Act V, Sc. 1, Line 207
A mender of bad soles . . . a surgeon
    to old shoes.
    Julius Caesar. Act I, Sc. 1, Line 15
As proper men as ever trod upon neat's
    leather.
        Ibid. Line 27
The live-long day.
        Ibid. Line 45
Beware the ides of March.
        Ibid. Sc. 2, Line 18
Well, honour is the subject of my story.
I cannot tell what you and other men
Think of this life; but, for my single
    self,
I had as lief not be as live to be
In awe of such a thing as I myself.
        Ibid. Line 92
        "Darest thou, Cassius, now
Leap in with me into this angry flood,
And swim to yonder point?" Upon the
    word,

Accoutred as I was, I plunged in
And bade him follow.
        Julius Caesar. Act I, Sc. 2, Line 102
Help me, Cassius, or I sink!
        Ibid. Line 111
        Ye gods, it doth amaze me,
A man of such a feeble temper should
So get the start of the majestic world
And bear the palm alone.
        Ibid. Line 128
Why, man, he doth bestride the narrow
    world
Like a Colossus; and we petty men
Walk under his huge legs, and peep
    about
To find ourselves dishonourable graves.
Men at some time are masters of their
    fates:
The fault, dear Brutus, is not in our
    stars,
But in ourselves, that we are underlings.
        Ibid. Line 134
Upon what meat doth this our Caesar
    feed,
That he is grown so great? Age, thou
    art shamed!
Rome, thou hast lost the breed of noble
    bloods!
        Ibid. Line 148
There was a Brutus once that would
    have brook'd
The eternal devil to keep his state in
    Rome
As easily as a king.
        Ibid. Line 158
Let me have men about me that are fat;
Sleek-headed men, and such as sleep o'
    nights.
Yond Cassius has a lean and hungry
    look;
He thinks too much: such men are dan-
    gerous.
        Ibid. Line 191
        He reads much;
He is a great observer, and he looks
Quite through the deeds of men.
        Ibid. Line 200
Seldom he smiles, and smiles in such a
    sort
As if he mock'd himself, and scorn'd his
    spirit

That could be moved to smile at anything.

> *Julius Caesar. Act I,*
> *Sc. 2, Line 204*

But, for my own part, it was Greek to me.

> *Ibid. Line 288*

'Tis a common proof,
That lowliness is young ambition's ladder,
Whereto the climber-upward turns his face;
But when he once attains the upmost round,
He then unto the ladder turns his back,
Looks in the clouds, scorning the base degrees
By which he did ascend.

> *Ibid. Act II, Sc. 1, Line 21*

Between the acting of a dreadful thing
And the first motion, all the interim is
Like a phantasma, or a hideous dream:
The Genius and the mortal instruments
Are then in council; and the state of man,
Like to a little kingdom, suffers then
The nature of an insurrection.

> *Ibid. Line 63*

A dish fit for the gods.

> *Ibid. Line 173*

But when I tell him he hates flatterers,
He says he does, being then most flattered.

> *Ibid. Line 207*

Boy! Lucius! Fast asleep? It is no matter;
Enjoy the honey-heavy dew of slumber:
Thou hast no figures nor no fantasies
Which busy care draws in the brains of men;
Therefore thou sleep'st so sound.

> *Ibid. Line 229*

You are my true and honourable wife,
As dear to me as are the ruddy drops
That visit my sad heart.[1]

> *Ibid. Line 288*

Think you I am no stronger than my sex,
Being so father'd and so husbanded?

> *Ibid. Line 296*

[1] Dear as the ruddy drops that warm my heart. — GRAY: *The Bard, I, 3, L. 12*

Cowards die many times before their deaths;
The valiant never taste of death but once.
Of all the wonders that I yet have heard,
It seems to me most strange that men should fear;
Seeing that death, a necessary end,
Will come when it will come.

> *Julius Caesar. Act II,*
> *Sc. 2, Line 32*

How hard it is for women to keep counsel.

> *Ibid. Sc. 4, Line 9*

But I am constant as the northern star,
Of whose true-fix'd and resting quality
There is no fellow in the firmament.

> *Ibid. Act III, Sc. 1, Line 60*

Et tu, Brute!

> *Ibid. Line 77*

How many ages hence
Shall this our lofty scene be acted o'er,
In states unborn and accents yet unknown!

> *Ibid. Line 111*

The choice and master spirits of this age.

> *Ibid. Line 163*

Though last, not least in love.[1]

> *Ibid. Line 189*

O! pardon me, thou bleeding piece of earth,
That I am meek and gentle with these butchers!
Thou art the ruins of the noblest man
That ever lived in the tide of times.

> *Ibid. Line 254*

Cry "Havoc!" and let slip the dogs of war.

> *Ibid. Line 273*

Romans, countrymen, and lovers! hear me for my cause; and be silent, that you may hear.

> *Ibid. Sc. 2, Line 13*

[1] Though last not least. — SPENSER: *Colin Clouts Come Home Againe, L. 444*
Although our last, not least. — *King Lear, Act I, Sc. 1, L. 85*
The last, not least in honour or applause. — ALEXANDER POPE: *The Dunciad, Book IV, L. 577*

Not that I loved Caesar less, but that I loved Rome more.

Julius Caesar. Act III, Sc. 2, Line 22

If any, speak; for him have I offended. I pause for a reply.

Ibid. Line 36

Friends, Romans, countrymen, lend me your ears;
I come to bury Caesar, not to praise him.
The evil that men do lives after them,
The good is oft interred with their bones.

Ibid. Line 79

For Brutus is an honourable man;
So are they all, all honourable men.

Ibid. Line 88

Ambition should be made of sterner stuff.

Ibid. Line 98

O judgment! thou art fled to brutish beasts,
And men have lost their reason.

Ibid. Line 110

But yesterday the word of Caesar might
Have stood against the world; now lies he there,
And none so poor to do him reverence.

Ibid. Line 124

If you have tears, prepare to shed them now.

Ibid. Line 174

See what a rent the envious Casca made.

Ibid. Line 180

This was the most unkindest cut of all.

Ibid. Line 188

Great Caesar fell.
O! what a fall was there, my countrymen;
Then I, and you, and all of us fell down,
Whilst bloody treason flourish'd over us.

Ibid. Line 194

What private griefs they have, alas! I know not.

Ibid. Line 217

I come not, friends, to steal away your hearts:
I am no orator, as Brutus is;

But, as you know me all, a plain blunt man.

Julius Caesar. Act III, Sc. 2, Line 220

I only speak right on.

Ibid. Line 227

Put a tongue
In every wound of Caesar, that should move
The stones of Rome to rise and mutiny.

Ibid. Line 232

When love begins to sicken and decay,
It useth an enforced ceremony.
There are no tricks in plain and simple faith.

Ibid. Act IV, Sc. 2, Line 20

You yourself
Are much condemn'd to have an itching palm.

Ibid. Sc. 3, Line 9

The foremost man of all this world.

Ibid. Line 22

I had rather be a dog, and bay the moon,
Than such a Roman.

Ibid. Line 27

There is no terror, Cassius, in your threats;
For I am arm'd so strong in honesty
That they pass by me as the idle wind,
Which I respect not.

Ibid. Line 66

A friend should bear his friend's infirmities,
But Brutus makes mine greater than they are.

Ibid. Line 85

All his faults observed,
Set in a note-book, learn'd, and conn'd by rote.

Ibid. Line 96

There is a tide in the affairs of men,
Which, taken at the flood, leads on to fortune;
Omitted, all the voyage of their life
Is bound in shallows and in miseries.

Ibid. Line 217

We must take the current when it serves,
Or lose our ventures.

Ibid. Line 222

The deep of night is crept upon our talk,

And nature must obey necessity.
        Julius Caesar. Act IV,
            Sc. 3, Line 225
Brutus. Then I shall see thee again?
Ghost. Ay, at Philippi.
Brutus. Why, I will see thee at Philippi,
    then.
        Ibid. Line 283
But for your words, they rob the Hybla
    bees,
And leave them honeyless.
        Ibid. Act V, Sc. 1, Line 34
Forever, and forever, farewell, Cassius!
If we do meet again, why, we shall
    smile;
If not, why then, this parting was well
    made.
        Ibid. Line 117
O, that a man might know
The end of this day's business, ere it
    come.
        Ibid. Line 123
The last of all the Romans, fare thee
    well!
        Ibid. Sc. 3, Line 99
This was the noblest Roman of them all.
        Ibid. Sc. 5, Line 68
His life was gentle, and the elements
So mix'd in him that Nature might
    stand up
And say to all the world, "This was a
    man!"
        Ibid. Line 73
1 Witch. When shall we three meet
    again
    In thunder, lightning, or in rain?
2 Witch. When the hurlyburly's done,
    When the battle's lost and won.
        Macbeth. Act I, Sc. 1, Line 1
Sleep shall neither night nor day
Hang upon his pent-house lid.
        Ibid. Sc. 3, Line 19
Dwindle, peak, and pine.
        Ibid. Line 23
If you can look into the seeds of time,
And say which grain will grow and
    which will not.
        Ibid. Line 58
Stands not within the prospect of be-
    lief.
        Ibid. Line 74
The earth hath bubbles, as the water
    has,

And these are of them.
        Macbeth. Act I, Sc. 3, Line 79
        The insane root
That takes the reason prisoner.
        Ibid. Line 84
And oftentimes, to win us to our harm,
The instruments of darkness tell us
    truths,
Win us with honest trifles, to betray 's
In deepest consequence.
        Ibid. Line 123
        Come what come may,
Time and the hour runs through the
    roughest day.
        Ibid. Line 146
        Nothing in his life
Became him like the leaving it; he died
As one that had been studied in his
    death
To throw away the dearest thing he
    owed,
As 'twere a careless trifle.
        Ibid. Sc. 4, Line 7
        There's no art
To find the mind's construction in the
    face:
He was a gentleman on whom I built
An absolute trust.
        Ibid. Line 11
More is thy due than more than all can
    pay.
        Ibid. Line 21
        Yet do I fear thy nature;
It is too full o' the milk of human kind-
    ness.[1]
        Ibid. Sc. 5, Line 17
That no compunctious visitings of na-
    ture
Shake my fell purpose.
        Ibid. Line 46
Your face, my thane, is as a book where
    men
May read strange matters. To beguile
    the time,
Look like the time; bear welcome in
    your eye,
Your hand, your tongue: look like the
    innocent flower,
But be the serpent under 't.
        Ibid. Line 63

[1] The thunder of your words has soured
the milk of human kindness in my heart. —
R. B. SHERIDAN: *The Rivals, Act III, Sc. 4*

This castle hath a pleasant seat; the air
Nimbly and sweetly recommends itself
Unto our gentle senses.

> *Macbeth. Act I, Sc. 6, Line 1*

The heaven's breath
Smells wooingly here: no jutty, frieze,
Buttress, nor coign of vantage, but this
bird
Hath made his pendent bed and procre-
ant cradle:
Where they most breed and haunt, I
have observed
The air is delicate.

> *Ibid. Line 5*

If it were done when 'tis done, then
'twere well
It were done quickly; if the assassina-
tion
Could trammel up the consequence,
and catch
With his surcease success; that but this
blow
Might be the be-all and the end-all here,
But here, upon this bank and shoal of
time,
We'd jump the life to come. But in
these cases
We still have judgment here; that we
but teach
Bloody instructions, which, being
taught, return
To plague the inventor; this even-
handed justice
Commends the ingredients of our poi-
son'd chalice
To our own lips.

> *Ibid. Sc. 7, Line 1*

Besides, this Duncan
Hath borne his faculties so meek, hath
been
So clear in his great office, that his vir-
tues
Will plead like angels, trumpet-tongued
against
The deep damnation of his taking-off;
And pity, like a naked new-born babe,
Striding the blast, or heaven's cheru-
bim, horsed
Upon the sightless couriers of the air,
Shall blow the horrid deed in every eye,
That tears shall drown the wind. I have
no spur
To prick the sides of my intent, but only

Vaulting ambition, which o'erleaps itself
And falls on the other.

> *Macbeth. Act I, Sc. 7, Line 16*

I have bought
Golden opinions from all sorts of people.

> *Ibid. Line 32*

Letting "I dare not" wait upon "I
would,"
Like the poor cat i' the adage.[1]

> *Ibid. Line 44*

I dare do all that may become a man;
Who dares do more is none.

> *Ibid. Line 46*

Nor time nor place
Did then adhere.

> *Ibid. Line 51*

Macbeth. If we should fail, —
Lady Macbeth.   We fail!
But screw your courage to the sticking-
place,
And we'll not fail.

> *Ibid. Line 59*

Memory, the warder of the brain.

> *Ibid. Line 65*

There's husbandry in heaven;
Their candles are all out.

> *Ibid. Act II, Sc. 1, Line 4*

Shut up
In measureless content.

> *Ibid. Line 16*

Is this a dagger which I see before me,
The handle toward my hand? Come, let
me clutch thee:
I have thee not, and yet I see thee still.
Art thou not, fatal vision, sensible
To feeling as to sight? or art thou but
A dagger of the mind, a false creation,
Proceeding from the heat-oppressed
brain?

> *Ibid. Line 33*

Now o'er the one half-world
Nature seems dead.

> *Ibid. Line 49*

Thou sure and firm-set earth,
Hear not my steps, which way they
walk, for fear
Thy very stones prate of my where-
about.

> *Ibid. Line 56*

[1] See Heywood, page 14.

The bell invites me.
Hear it not, Duncan; for it is a knell
That summons thee to heaven or to hell.
Macbeth. Act II, Sc. 1, Line 62

It was the owl that shriek'd, the fatal bellman,
Which gives the stern'st good-night.
Ibid. Sc. 2, Line 4

The attempt and not the deed
Confounds us.
Ibid. Line 12

I had most need of blessing, and "Amen"
Stuck in my throat.
Ibid. Line 33

Methought I heard a voice cry, "Sleep no more!
Macbeth does murder sleep!" the innocent sleep,
Sleep that knits up the ravell'd sleave of care,
The death of each day's life, sore labour's bath,
Balm of hurt minds, great nature's second course,
Chief nourisher in life's feast.
Ibid. Line 36

Infirm of purpose!
Ibid. Line 53

Will all great Neptune's ocean wash this blood
Clean from my hand? No, this my hand will rather
The multitudinous seas incarnadine,
Making the green one red.
Ibid. Line 61

Go the primrose way to the everlasting bonfire.
Ibid. Sc. 3, Line 22

It [drink] provokes the desire, but it takes away the performance.
Ibid. Line 34

The labour we delight in physics pain.
Ibid. Line 56

Tongue nor heart
Cannot conceive nor name thee!
Ibid. Line 70

Confusion now hath made his masterpiece!
Most sacrilegious murder hath broke ope

The Lord's anointed temple, and stole thence
The life o' the building!
Macbeth. Act II, Sc. 3, Line 72

Downy sleep, death's counterfeit.
Ibid. Line 83

The wine of life is drawn, and the mere lees
Is left this vault to brag of.
Ibid. Line 102

Who can be wise, amazed, temperate and furious,
Loyal and neutral, in a moment?
Ibid. Line 115

To show an unfelt sorrow is an office
Which the false man does easy.
Ibid. Line 143

A falcon, towering in her pride of place,
Was by a mousing owl hawk'd at and kill'd.
Ibid. Sc. 4, Line 12

I must become a borrower of the night
For a dark hour or twain.
Ibid. Act III, Sc. 1, Line 27

Let every man be master of his time
Till seven at night.
Ibid. Line 41

Murderer. We are men, my liege.
Macbeth. Ay, in the catalogue ye go for men.
Ibid. Line 91

I am one, my liege,
Whom the vile blows and buffets of the world
Have so incensed that I am reckless what
I do to spite the world.
Ibid. Line 108

So weary with disasters, tugg'd with fortune,
That I would set my life on any chance,
To mend it or be rid on 't.
Ibid. Line 112

Things without all remedy
Should be without regard; what's done is done.
Ibid. Sc. 2, Line 11

We have scotch'd the snake, not kill'd it.
Ibid. Line 13

Duncan is in his grave;
After life's fitful fever he sleeps well;

Treason has done his worst: nor steel,
  nor poison,
Malice domestic, foreign levy, nothing
Can touch him further.
          Macbeth. Act III, Sc. 2, Line 22
In them Nature's copy's not eterne.
                    Ibid. Line 38
Now spurs the lated traveller apace
To gain the timely inn.
                 Ibid. Sc. 3, Line 6
But now I am cabin'd, cribb'd, confined,
  bound in
To saucy doubts and fears.
                 Ibid. Sc. 4, Line 24
Now, good digestion wait on appetite,
And health on both!
                    Ibid. Line 38
Thou canst not say I did it; never shake
Thy gory locks at me.
                    Ibid. Line 50
The air-drawn dagger.
                    Ibid. Line 62
      The times have been
That, when the brains were out, the
  man would die,
And there an end; but now they rise
  again,
With twenty mortal murders on their
  crowns,
And push us from our stools.
                    Ibid. Line 78
I drink to the general joy of the whole
  table.
                    Ibid. Line 89
Thou hast no speculation in those eyes
Which thou dost glare with!
                    Ibid. Line 95
    A thing of custom: 'tis no other;
Only it spoils the pleasure of the time.
                    Ibid. Line 97
      What man dare, I dare:
Approach thou like the rugged Russian
  bear,
The arm'd rhinoceros, or the Hyrcan
  tiger,
Take any shape but that, and my firm
  nerves
Shall never tremble.
                    Ibid. Line 99
      Hence, horrible shadow!
Unreal mockery, hence!
                    Ibid. Line 106

Stand not upon the order of your going,
But go at once.
          Macbeth. Act III, Sc. 4, Line 119
Macbeth.   What is the night?
Lady Macbeth. Almost at odds with
  morning, which is which.
                    Ibid. Line 126
      I am in blood
Stepp'd in so far, that, should I wade
  no more,
Returning were as tedious as go o'er.
                    Ibid. Line 136
          My little spirit, see,
Sits in a foggy cloud, and stays for me.
                 Ibid. Sc. 5, Line 35
Double, double toil and trouble;
Fire burn and cauldron bubble.
          Ibid. Act IV, Sc. 1, Line 10
Eye of newt, and toe of frog,
Wool of bat, and tongue of dog.
                    Ibid. Line 14
By the pricking of my thumbs,
Something wicked this way comes.
      Open, locks,
          Whoever knocks!
                    Ibid. Line 44
How now, you secret, black, and mid-
  night hags!
                    Ibid. Line 48
  I'll make assurance double sure,
And take a bond of fate.
                    Ibid. Line 83
Macbeth shall never vanquish'd be un-
  til
Great Birnam wood to high Dunsinane
  hill
Shall come against him.[1]
                    Ibid. Line 92
Show his eyes, and grieve his heart;
Come like shadows, so depart!
                    Ibid. Line 110
What! will the line stretch out to the
  crack of doom?
                    Ibid. Line 117
The weird sisters.
                    Ibid. Line 136
      When our actions do not,
Our fears do make us traitors.
                 Ibid. Sc. 2, Line 3

[1] Till Birnam wood remove to Dunsinane,
  I cannot taint with fear.
          Act V, Sc. 2, Line 2

Things at the worst will cease, or else
   climb upward
To what they were before.
     Macbeth. Act IV, Sc. 2, Line 24
Angels are bright still, though the
   brightest fell.
     Ibid. Sc. 3, Line 22
Pour the sweet milk of concord into
   hell,
Uproar the universal peace, confound
All unity on earth.
     Ibid. Line 98
Stands Scotland where it did?
     Ibid. Line 164
Give sorrow words; the grief that does
   not speak
Whispers the o'er-fraught heart and
   bids it break.
     Ibid. Line 209
What! all my pretty chickens and their
   dam
At one fell swoop?
     Ibid. Line 218
O! I could play the woman with mine
   eyes
And braggart with my tongue.
     Ibid. Line 229
Out, damned spot! out, I say!
     Ibid. Act V, Sc. 1, Line 38
Fie, my lord, fie! a soldier, and afeard?
     Ibid. Line 40
   Yet who would have thought the old
man to have had so much blood in him?
     Ibid. Line 42
   All the perfumes of Arabia will not
sweeten this little hand.
     Ibid. Line 56
     My way of life
Is fall'n into the sere, the yellow leaf;
And that which should accompany old
   age,
As honour, love, obedience, troops of
   friends,
I must not look to have.
     Ibid. Sc. 3, Line 22
Doctor.   Not so sick, my lord,
As she is troubled with thick-coming
   fancies,
That keep her from her rest.
Macbeth.   Cure her of that:
Canst thou not minister to a mind dis-
   eas'd,

Pluck from the memory a rooted sor-
   row,
Raze out the written troubles of the
   brain,
And with some sweet oblivious antidote
Cleanse the stuff'd bosom of that peril-
   ous stuff
Which weighs upon the heart?
Doctor.   Therein the patient
Must minister to himself.
Macbeth. Throw physic to the dogs:
   I'll none of it.
     Macbeth. Act V, Sc. 3, Line 37
I would applaud thee to the very echo,
That should applaud again.
     Ibid. Line 53
Hang out our banners on the outward
   walls;
The cry is still, "They come"; our
   castle's strength
Will laugh a siege to scorn.
     Ibid. Sc. 5, Line 1
     My fell of hair
Would at a dismal treatise rouse and
   stir
As life were in 't. I have supp'd full with
   horrors.
     Ibid. Line 11
To-morrow, and to-morrow, and to-
   morrow,
Creeps in this petty pace from day to
   day,
To the last syllable of recorded time;
And all our yesterdays have lighted
   fools
The way to dusty death. Out, out, brief
   candle!
Life's but a walking shadow, a poor
   player
That struts and frets his hour upon the
   stage
And then is heard no more: it is a tale
Told by an idiot, full of sound and fury,
Signifying nothing.
     Ibid. Line 19
I 'gin to be aweary of the sun.
     Ibid. Line 49
     Blow, wind! come, wrack!
At least we'll die with harness on our
   back.
     Ibid. Line 51
I bear a charmed life.
     Ibid. Sc. 7, Line 41

And be these juggling fiends no more
believ'd,
That palter with us in a double sense;
That keep the word of promise to our
ear
And break it to our hope.
Macbeth. Act V, Sc. 7, Line 48
Live to be the show and gaze o' the time.
Ibid. Line 53
Lay on, Macduff,
And damn'd be him that first cries,
"Hold, enough!"
Ibid. Line 62
For this relief much thanks; 'tis bitter
cold,
And I am sick at heart.
Hamlet. Act I, Sc. 1, Line 8
Not a mouse stirring.
Ibid. Line 10
But in the gross and scope of my opin-
ion,
This bodes some strange eruption to
our state.
Ibid. Line 68
Whose sore task
Does not divide the Sunday from the
week.
Ibid. Line 75
This sweaty haste
Doth make the night joint-labourer
with the day.
Ibid. Line 77
In the most high and palmy state of
Rome,
A little ere the mightiest Julius fell,
The graves stood tenantless and the
sheeted dead
Did squeal and gibber in the Roman
streets.
Ibid. Line 113
And then it started like a guilty thing
Upon a fearful summons.
Ibid. Line 148
The cock, that is the trumpet of the
morn.
Ibid. Line 150
Whether in sea or fire, in earth or air,
The extravagant and erring spirit hies
To his confine.
Ibid. Line 153
It faded on the crowing of the cock.
Some say that ever 'gainst that season
comes

Wherein our Saviour's birth is cele-
brated,
The bird of dawning singeth all night
long:
And then, they say, no spirit can walk
abroad;
The nights are wholesome; then no
planets strike,
No fairy takes, nor witch hath power to
charm,
So hallow'd and so gracious is the time.
Hamlet. Act I, Sc. 1, Line 157
So have I heard, and do in part believe
it.
But, look, the morn in russet mantle
clad,
Walks o'er the dew of yon high eastern
hill.
Ibid. Line 165
The memory be green.[1]
Ibid. Sc. 2, Line 2
With one auspicious and one dropping
eye,
With mirth in funeral and with dirge
in marriage,
In equal scale weighing delight and
dole.
Ibid. Line 11
A little more than kin, and less than
kind.
Ibid. Line 65
All that live must die,
Passing through nature to eternity.
Ibid. Line 72
Seems, madam! Nay, it is; I know not
"seems."
'Tis not alone my inky cloak, good
mother,
Nor customary suits of solemn black.
Ibid. Line 76
But I have that within which passeth
show;
These but the trappings and the suits
of woe.
Ibid. Line 85
O! that this too too solid flesh would
melt,
Thaw and resolve itself into a dew;
Or that the Everlasting had not fix'd

[1] Keep his memory green. — MOORE: *Oh,
Breathe Not His name*
   Lord, keep my memory green. — CHARLES
DICKENS: *The Haunted Man, last line*

His canon 'gainst self-slaughter! O
    God! O God!
How weary, stale, flat, and unprofitable
Seem to me all the uses of this world.
            Hamlet. Act I, Sc. 2, Line 129
That it should come to this!
                    Ibid. Line 137
Hyperion to a satyr; so loving to my
    mother
That he might not beteem the winds of
    heaven
Visit her face too roughly.
                    Ibid. Line 140
        Why, she would hang on him,
As if increase of appetite had grown
By what it fed on.
                    Ibid. Line 143
·Frailty, thy name is woman!
                    Ibid. Line 146
Like Niobe, all tears.
                    Ibid. Line 149
A beast, that wants discourse of reason.
                    Ibid. Line 150
It is not nor it cannot come to good.
                    Ibid. Line 158
Thrift, thrift, Horatio! the funeral
    baked meats
Did coldly furnish forth the marriage
    tables.
                    Ibid. Line 180
In my mind's eye, Horatio.
                    Ibid. Line 185
He was a man, take him for all in all,
I shall not look upon his like again.
                    Ibid. Line 187
Season your admiration for a while.
                    Ibid. Line 192
In the dead vast and middle of the
    night.
                    Ibid. Line 198
Arm'd at points exactly, cap-a-pe.
                    Ibid. Line 200
        Distill'd
Almost to jelly with the act of fear.
                    Ibid. Line 204
A countenance more in sorrow than in
    anger.
                    Ibid. Line 231
While one with moderate haste might
    tell a hundred.
                    Ibid. Line 237
Hamlet. His beard was grizzled, no?

Horatio. It was, as I have seen it in
    his life,
A sable silver'd.
            Hamlet. Act I, Sc. 2, Line 239
Give it an understanding, but no
    tongue.
                    Ibid. Line 249
Foul play.
                    Ibid. Line 255
The chariest maid is prodigal enough
If she unmask her beauty to the moon:
Virtue itself 'scapes not calumnious
    strokes;
The canker galls the infants of the
    spring
Too oft before their buttons be dis-
    closed,
And in the morn and liquid dew of
    youth
Contagious blastments are most im-
    minent.
                    Ibid. Sc. 3, Line 36
Do not, as some ungracious pastors do,
Show me the steep and thorny way to
    heaven,
Whiles, like a puff'd and reckless liber-
    tine,
Himself the primrose path of dalliance
    treads,[1]
And recks not his own rede.[2]
                    Ibid. Line 47
Give thy thoughts no tongue.
                    Ibid. Line 59
Be thou familiar, but by no means vul-
    gar;
Those friends thou hast, and their adop-
    tion tried,
Grapple them to thy soul with hoops
    of steel.
                    Ibid. Line 61
        Beware
Of entrance to a quarrel, but, being in,
Bear 't that the opposed may beware of
    thee.

[1] See *Macbeth, Act II, Sc. 3, L. 22* (p. 86).
[2] Wel oghte a preest ensample for to yive,
    By his clennesse, how that his sheep shold
    live.
    CHAUCER: *Canterbury Tales, Prologue,
                    L. 504*
    And may you better reck the rede,
    Than ever did the adviser.
    ROBERT BURNS: *Epistle to a Young
                    Friend*

Give every man thy ear, but few thy voice;
Take each man's censure, but reserve thy judgment.
Costly thy habit as thy purse can buy,
But not express'd in fancy; rich, not gaudy;
For the apparel oft proclaims the man.
Hamlet. Act I, Sc. 3, Line 65
Neither a borrower, nor a lender be;
For loan oft loses both itself and friend,
And borrowing dulls the edge of husbandry.
This above all: to thine own self be true,
And it must follow, as the night the day,
Thou canst not then be false to any man.
Ibid. Line 75
Springes to catch woodcocks.
Ibid. Line 115
When the blood burns, how prodigal the soul
Lends the tongue vows.
Ibid. Line 116
Be somewhat scanter of your maiden presence.
Ibid. Line 121
Hamlet. The air bites shrewdly; it is very cold.
Horatio. It is a nipping and an eager air.
Ibid. Sc. 4, Line 1
But to my mind, though I am native here
And to the manner born, — it is a custom
More honoured in the breach than the observance.
Ibid. Line 14
Angels and ministers of grace defend us!
Ibid. Line 39
Be thy intents wicked or charitable,
Thou comest in such a questionable shape
That I will speak to thee.
Ibid. Line 42
Hath oped his ponderous and marble jaws.
Ibid. Line 50
What may this mean,
That thou, dead corse, again in complete steel

Revisit'st thus the glimpses of the moon,
Making night hideous,[1] and we fools of nature
So horridly to shake our disposition
With thoughts beyond the reaches of our souls?
Hamlet. Act I, Sc. 4, Line 51
I do not set my life at a pin's fee.
Ibid. Line 65
My fate cries out,
And makes each petty artery in this body
As hardy as the Nemean lion's nerve.
Ibid. Line 81
Unhand me, gentlemen,
By heaven! I'll make a ghost of him that lets me!
Ibid. Line 84
Something is rotten in the state of Denmark.
Ibid. Line 90
I could a tale unfold whose lightest word
Would harrow up thy soul, freeze thy young blood,
Make thy two eyes, like stars, start from their spheres,
Thy knotted and combined locks to part,
And each particular hair to stand an end,
Like quills upon the fretful porpentine.
Ibid. Sc. 5, Line 15
And duller shouldst thou be than the fat weed
That rots itself in ease on Lethe wharf.
Ibid. Line 32
O my prophetic soul!
My uncle!
Ibid. Line 40
O Hamlet, what a falling-off was there!
Ibid. Line 47
But, soft! methinks I scent the morning air;
Brief let me be. Sleeping within my orchard,
My custom always of the afternoon.
Ibid. Line 58
Cut off even in the blossoms of my sin,
Unhousel'd, disappointed, unaneled,

---

[1] And makes night hideous. — POPE: *The Dunciad, Book III, L. 166*

No reckoning made, but sent to my account
With all my imperfections on my head.
> *Hamlet. Act I, Sc. 5, Line 76*

Leave her to heaven
And to those thorns that in her bosom lodge,
To prick and sting her.
> *Ibid. Line 86*

The glow-worm shows the matin to be near,
And 'gins to pale his uneffectual fire.
> *Ibid. Line 89*

While memory holds a seat
In this distracted globe. Remember thee!
Yea, from the table of my memory
I'll wipe away all trivial fond records.
> *Ibid. Line 96*

Within the book and volume of my brain.
> *Ibid. Line 103*

O villain, villain, smiling, damned villain!
My tables, — meet it is I set it down,
That one may smile, and smile, and be a villain;
At least I'm sure it may be so in Denmark.
> *Ibid. Line 106*

There are more things in heaven and earth, Horatio,
Than are dreamt of in your philosophy.
> *Ibid. Line 166*

Rest, rest, perturbed spirit!
> *Ibid. Line 182*

The time is out of joint; O cursed spite,
That ever I was born to set it right!
> *Ibid. Line 188*

Brevity is the soul of wit.
> *Ibid. Act II, Sc. 2, Line 90*

More matter, with less art.
> *Ibid. Line 95*

That he is mad, 'tis true; 'tis true 'tis pity;
And pity 'tis 'tis true.
> *Ibid. Line 97*

Find out the cause of this effect,
Or rather say, the cause of this defect,
For this effect defective comes by cause.
> *Ibid. Line 101*

Doubt thou the stars are fire;
Doubt that the sun doth move;

Doubt truth to be a liar;
But never doubt I love.
> *Hamlet. Act II, Sc. 2, Line 115*

To be honest, as this world goes, is to be one man picked out of ten thousand.
> *Ibid. Line 179*

Still harping on my daughter.
> *Ibid. Line 190*

Polonius. What do you read, my lord?
Hamlet. Words, words, words.
> *Ibid. Line 195*

They have a plentiful lack of wit.
> *Ibid. Line 204*

Though this be madness, yet there is method in 't.
> *Ibid. Line 211*

There is nothing either good or bad, but thinking makes it so.
> *Ibid. Line 259*

This goodly frame, the earth, seems to me a sterile promontory; this most excellent canopy, the air, look you, this brave o'erhanging firmament, this majestical roof fretted with golden fire, why, it appears no other thing to me than a foul and pestilent congregation of vapours. What a piece of work is a man! how noble in reason! how infinite in faculty! in form and moving how express and admirable! in action how like an angel! in apprehension how like a god!
> *Ibid. Line 317*

Man delights not me; no, nor woman neither.
> *Ibid. Line 330*

There is something in this more than natural, if philosophy could find it out.
> *Ibid. Line 392*

I know a hawk from a handsaw.
> *Ibid. Line 406*

They say an old man is twice a child.
> *Ibid. Line 413*

O Jephthah, judge of Israel, what a treasure hadst thou!
> *Ibid. Line 431*

One fair daughter and no more,
The which he loved passing well.
> *Ibid. Line 435*

Come, give us a taste of your quality.
> *Ibid. Line 460*

The play, I remember, pleased not the million; 'twas caviare to the general.

   Hamlet. Act II, Sc. 2, Line 465

They are the abstracts and brief chronicles of the time: after your death you were better have a bad epitaph than their ill report while you live.

     Ibid. Line 555

Use every man after his desert, and who should 'scape whipping?

     Ibid. Line 561

What's Hecuba to him or he to Hecuba, That he should weep for her?

     Ibid. Line 593

  Unpack my heart with words, And fall a-cursing, like a very drab.

     Ibid. Line 622

   The play's the thing Wherein I'll catch the conscience of the king.

     Ibid. Line 641

   With devotion's visage And pious action we do sugar o'er The devil himself.

   Ibid. Act III, Sc. 1, Line 47

To be, or not to be: that is the question:
Whether 'tis nobler in the mind to suffer
The slings and arrows of outrageous fortune,
Or to take arms against a sea of troubles,
And by opposing end them? To die: to sleep:
No more; and by a sleep to say we end
The heartache and the thousand natural shocks
That flesh is heir to, 'tis a consummation
Devoutly to be wish'd. To die, to sleep;
To sleep: perchance to dream: ay, there's the rub:
For in that sleep of death what dreams may come,
When we have shuffled off this mortal coil,
Must give us pause. There's the respect
That makes calamity of so long life;
For who would bear the whips and scorns of time,

The oppressor's wrong, the proud man's contumely,
The pangs of dispriz'd love, the law's delay,
The insolence of office and the spurns
That patient merit of the unworthy takes,
When he himself might his quietus make
With a bare bodkin? who would fardels bear,
To grunt and sweat under a weary life,
But that the dread of something after death,
The undiscover'd country from whose bourn
No traveller returns, puzzles the will
And makes us rather bear those ills we have
Than fly to others that we know not of?
Thus conscience does make cowards of us all;
And thus the native hue of resolution
Is sicklied o'er with the pale cast of thought,
And enterprises of great pith and moment
With this regard their currents turn awry,
And lose the name of action.

  Hamlet. Act III, Sc. 1, Line 56

   Nymph, in thy orisons Be all my sins remember'd.

     Ibid. Line 89

Rich gifts wax poor when givers prove unkind.

     Ibid. Line 101

  Be thou as chaste as ice, as pure as snow, thou shalt not escape calumny. Get thee to a nunnery, go.

     Ibid. Line 142

I have heard of your paintings too, well enough; God has given you one face, and you make yourselves another.

     Ibid. Line 150

O! what a noble mind is here o'erthrown:
The courtier's, soldier's, scholar's eye, tongue, sword.

     Ibid. Line 159

The glass of fashion and the mould of form,

The observed of all observers!
> *Hamlet. Act III, Sc. 1, Line 162*

Now see that noble and most sovereign
 reason,
Like sweet bells jangled, out of tune and
 harsh.
> *Ibid. Line 166*

O, woe is me,
To have seen what I have seen, see what
 I see!
> *Ibid. Line 169*

Nor do not saw the air too much with
your hand, thus; but use all gently: for
in the very torrent, tempest, and as I
may say the whirlwind of passion, you
must acquire and beget a temperance,
that may give it smoothness. Oh, it offends me to the soul to hear a robustious
periwig-pated fellow tear a passion to
tatters, to very rags, to split the ears of
the groundlings, who for the most part
are capable of nothing but inexplicable
dumb-shows and noise. I would have
such a fellow whipped for o'erdoing
Termagant; it out-herods Herod.
> *Ibid. Sc. 2, Line 4*

Suit the action to the word, the word
to the action; with this special observance, that you o'erstep not the modesty of nature.
> *Ibid. Line 20*

To hold, as 'twere, the mirror up to
 nature.
> *Ibid. Line 25*

To show the very age and body of
the time his form and pressure.
> *Ibid. Line 27*

Though it make the unskilful laugh,
cannot but make the judicious grieve.
> *Ibid. Line 29*

Not to speak it profanely.
> *Ibid. Line 35*

I have thought some of Nature's
journeymen had made men and not
made them well, they imitated humanity so abominably.
> *Ibid. Line 38*

First Player. I hope we have reformed
that indifferently with us, sir.
Hamlet. O, reform it altogether.
> *Ibid. Line 41*

No; let the candied tongue lick absurd
 pomp,

And crook the pregnant hinges of the
 knee
Where thrift may follow fawning.
> *Hamlet. Act III, Sc. 2, Line 65*

A man that fortune's buffets and rewards
Hast ta'en with equal thanks.
> *Ibid. Line 72*

They are not a pipe for fortune's finger
To sound what stop she please. Give me
 that man
That is not passion's slave, and I will
 wear him
In my heart's core, ay, in my heart of
 heart,
As I do thee. Something too much of
 this.
> *Ibid. Line 75*

And my imaginations are as foul
As Vulcan's stithy.
> *Ibid. Line 88*

Nay, then, let the devil wear black,
for I'll have a suit of sables.
> *Ibid. Line 138*

There's hope a great man's memory
may outlive his life half a year.
> *Ibid. Line 141*

This is miching mallecho; it means mischief.
> *Ibid. Line 149*

The lady doth protest too much, methinks.
> *Ibid. Line 242*

Let the galled jade wince, our withers
 are unwrung.
> *Ibid. Line 256*

Why, let the stricken deer [1] go weep,
 The hart ungalled play;
For some must watch, while some must
 sleep:
 So runs the world away.
> *Ibid. Line 287*

Pluck out the heart of my mystery.
> *Ibid. Line 389*

Do you think I am easier to be played
 on than a pipe?
> *Ibid. Line 393*

Hamlet. Do you see yonder cloud
that's almost in shape of a camel?
Polonius. By the mass, and 'tis like
a camel, indeed.

[1] I was a stricken deer. — WILLIAM COW-
PER: *The Task, Book III*

Hamlet. Methinks it is like a weasel.
Polonius. It is backed like a weasel.
Hamlet. Or like a whale?
Polonius. Very like a whale.
> *Hamlet. Act III, Sc. 2, Line 400*

They fool me to the top of my bent.
> *Ibid. Line 408*

By and by is easily said.
> *Ibid. Line 411*

'Tis now the very witching time of night,
When churchyards yawn and hell itself breathes out
Contagion to this world.
> *Ibid. Line 413*

I will speak daggers to her, but use none.
> *Ibid. Line 421*

O! my offence is rank, it smells to heaven;
It hath the primal eldest curse upon 't,
A brother's murder.
> *Ibid. Sc. 3, Line 36*

With all his crimes broad blown, as flush as May.
> *Ibid. Line 81*

My words fly up, my thoughts remain below:
Words without thoughts never to heaven go.
> *Ibid. Line 97*

Dead, for a ducat, dead!
> *Ibid. Sc. 4, Line 23*

And let me wring your heart; for so I shall,
If it be made of penetrable stuff.
> *Ibid. Line 35*

False as dicers' oaths.
> *Ibid. Line 45*

A rhapsody of words.
> *Ibid. Line 48*

> What act
That roars so loud and thunders in the index?
> *Ibid. Line 51*

Look here, upon this picture, and on this,
The counterfeit presentment of two brothers.
See, what a grace was seated on this brow;
Hyperion's curls; the front of Jove himself;

An eye like Mars, to threaten and command,
A station like the herald Mercury
New-lighted on a heaven-kissing hill,
A combination and a form indeed,
Where every god did seem to set his seal,
To give the world assurance of a man.
> *Hamlet. Act III, Sc. 4, Line 53*

> At your age
The hey-day in the blood is tame, it's humble.
> *Ibid. Line 68*

O shame! where is thy blush? Rebellious hell,
If thou canst mutine in a matron's bones,
To flaming youth let virtue be as wax,
And melt in her own fire: proclaim no shame
When the compulsive ardour gives the charge,
Since frost itself as actively doth burn,
And reason panders will.
> *Ibid. Line 82*

A king of shreds and patches.[1]
> *Ibid. Line 102*

> How is 't with you,
That you do bend your eye on vacancy?
> *Ibid. Line 115*

This is the very coinage of your brain:
This bodiless creation ecstasy
Is very cunning in.
> *Ibid. Line 136*

Lay not that flattering unction to your soul.
> *Ibid. Line 145*

Assume a virtue, if you have it not.
> *Ibid. Line 160*

> Refrain to-night,
And that shall lend a kind of easiness
To the next abstinence: the next more easy;
For use almost can change the stamp of nature.
> *Ibid. Line 165*

I must be cruel, only to be kind.
> *Ibid. Line 178*

---

[1] A wandering minstrel I —
A thing of shreds and patches.
WILLIAM SCHWENCK GILBERT:
The Mikado, Act I

For 'tis the sport to have the enginer
Hoist with his own petar.
> *Hamlet. Act III, Sc. 4, Line 206*
>> Diseases desperate grown
By desperate appliance are relieved,
Or not at all.[1]
> *Ibid. Act IV, Sc. 3, Line 9*
A man may fish with the worm that
hath eat of a king, and eat of the fish
that hath fed of that worm.
> *Ibid. Line 29*
Sure, he that made us with such large
> discourse,
Looking before and after, gave us not
That capability and godlike reason
To fust in us unused.
> *Ibid. Line 36*
>> Rightly to be great
Is not to stir without great argument,
But greatly to find quarrel in a straw
When honour's at the stake.
> *Ibid. Line 53*
So full of artless jealousy is guilt,
It spills itself in fearing to be spilt.
> *Ibid. Sc. 5, Line 19*
We know what we are, but know not
> what we may be.
> *Ibid. Line 43*
Come, my coach! Good night, sweet
> ladies; good night.
> *Ibid. Line 72*
When sorrows come, they come not
> single spies,
But in battalions.
> *Ibid. Line 78*
There's such divinity doth hedge a
> king,
That treason can but peep to what it
> would.
> *Ibid. Line 123*
There's rosemary, that's for remem-
brance; . . . and there is pansies,
that's for thoughts.
> *Ibid. Line 174*
You must wear your rue with a dif-
ference. There's a daisy; I would give
you some violets, but they withered.
> *Ibid. Line 181*

---

[1] Extreme remedies are very appropriate
for extreme diseases. — HIPPOCRATES: *Aphorism I*
See Dryden, page 175, and Montaigne,
page 1028.

A very riband in the cap of youth.
> *Hamlet. Act IV, Sc. 7, Line 77*
One woe doth tread upon another's
> heel,
So fast they follow.[1]
> *Ibid. Line 164*
>> Nature her custom holds,
Let shame say what it will.
> *Ibid. Line 188*
1 Clown. Argal, he that is not guilty
of his own death shortens not his own
life.
2 Clown. But is this law?
1 Clown. Ay marry, is 't; crowner's
quest law.
> *Ibid. Act V, Sc. 1, Line 20*
There is no ancient gentlemen but
gardeners . . . they hold up Adam's
profession.[2]
> *Ibid. Line 32*
Cudgel thy brains no more about it.
> *Ibid. Line 61*
Has this fellow no feeling of his busi-
> ness?
> *Ibid. Line 71*
Custom hath made it in him a property
> of easiness.
> *Ibid. Line 73*
The hand of little employment hath the
> daintier sense.
> *Ibid. Line 75*
But age, with his stealing steps,
Hath claw'd me in his clutch.
> *Ibid. Line 77*
A politician, . . . one that would cir-
> cumvent God.
> *Ibid. Line 84*
Why may not that be the skull of a
lawyer? Where be his quiddities now,
his quillets, his cases, his tenures, and
his tricks?
> *Ibid. Line 104*

---

[1] Thus woe succeeds a woe, as wave a wave.
— HERRICK: *Sorrows Succeed*
Woes cluster; rare are solitary woes;
They love a train, they tread each other's heel.
   YOUNG: *Night Thoughts, Night III, L. 63*
And woe succeeds to woe. — POPE: *The
Iliad, Book XVI, L. 139*
[2] Oh, Adam was a gardener, and God who
   made him sees
   That half a proper gardener's work is done
   upon his knees.
RUDYARD KIPLING: *The Glory of the
Garden, St 8*

One that was a woman, sir; but, rest her soul, she's dead.

Hamlet. Act V, Sc. 1, Line 145

How absolute the knave is! we must speak by the card, or equivocation will undo us.

Ibid. Line 147

The age is grown so picked that the toe of the peasant comes so near the heel of the courtier, he galls his kibe.

Ibid. Line 150

Alas, poor Yorick! I knew him, Horatio: a fellow of infinite jest, of most excellent fancy; he hath borne me on his back a thousand times; and now, how abhorred in my imagination it is! my gorge rises at it. Here hung those lips that I have kissed I know not how oft. Where be your gibes now? your gambols? your songs? your flashes of merriment, that were wont to set the table on a roar? Not one now, to mock your own grinning? quite chap-fallen? Now get you to my lady's chamber, and tell her, let her paint an inch thick, to this favour she must come.

Ibid. Line 201

To what base uses we may return, Horatio! Why may not imagination trace the noble dust of Alexander, till he find it stopping a bung-hole?

Ibid. Line 222

'Twere to consider too curiously, to consider so.

Ibid. Line 226

Imperious Caesar, dead and turn'd to clay,
Might stop a hole to keep the wind away.

Ibid. Line 235

Lay her i' the earth;
And from her fair and unpolluted flesh
May violets spring! [1]

Ibid. Line 260

A ministering angel shall my sister be.[2]

Ibid. Line 263

Sweets to the sweet: farewell!

Ibid. Line 265

---

[1] And from his ashes may be made
The violet of his native land.
    TENNYSON: *In Memoriam, XVIII*
[2] A ministering angel thou. — SCOTT: *Marmion, Canto VI, St. 30*

I thought thy bride-bed to have deck'd, sweet maid,
And not have strew'd thy grave.

Hamlet. Act V, Sc. 1, Line 267

Though I am not splenetive and rash,
Yet have I in me something dangerous.

Ibid. Line 283

Forty thousand brothers
Could not, with all their quantity of love,
Make up my sum.

Ibid. Line 291

Nay, an thou'lt mouth,
I'll rant as well as thou.

Ibid. Line 305

Let Hercules himself do what he may,
The cat will mew and dog will have his day.

Ibid. Line 313

There's a divinity that shapes our ends,
Rough-hew them how we will.

Ibid. Sc. 2, Line 10

I once did hold it, as our statists do,
A baseness to write fair.

Ibid. Line 33

It did me yeoman's service.

Ibid. Line 36

Popp'd in between the election and my hopes.

Ibid. Line 65

The bravery of his grief did put me
Into a towering passion.

Ibid. Line 79

What imports the nomination of this gentleman?

Ibid. Line 134

'Tis the breathing time of day with me.

Ibid. Line 181

Winnowed opinions.

Ibid. Line 201

There's a special providence in the fall of a sparrow. If it be now, 'tis not to come; if it be not to come, it will be now; if it be not now, yet it will come: the readiness is all. Since no man has aught of what he leaves, what is 't to leave betimes?

Ibid. Line 232

A hit, a very palpable hit.

Ibid. Line 295

This fell sergeant, death,
Is strict in his arrest.

Ibid. Line 350

Report me and my cause aright.
Hamlet. Act V, Sc. 2, Line 353
I am more an antique Roman than a
Dane.
Ibid. Line 355
Absent thee from felicity awhile.
Ibid. Line 361
The rest is silence.[1]
Ibid. Line 372
Now cracks a noble heart.
Ibid. Line 373
My love's
More richer than my tongue.
King Lear. Act I, Sc. 1, Line 79
Nothing will come of nothing.
Ibid. Line 92
Mend your speech a little,
Lest you may mar your fortunes.
Ibid. Line 96
I want that glib and oily art,
To speak and purpose not.
Ibid. Line 227
A still-soliciting eye, and such a tongue
That I am glad I have not.
Ibid. Line 234
As if we were villains by necessity;
fools by heavenly compulsion.
Ibid. Sc. 2, Line 136
Some villain hath done me wrong.[2]
Ibid. Line 186
That which ordinary men are fit for,
I am qualified in; and the best of me
is diligence.
Ibid. Sc. 4, Line 36
Have more than thou showest,
Speak less than thou knowest.
Ibid. Line 133
A little to disquantity your train.[3]
Ibid. Line 272
Ingratitude, thou marble-hearted fiend!
Ibid. Line 283
How sharper than a serpent's tooth it is
To have a thankless child!
Ibid. Line 312
Striving to better, oft we mar what's
well.
Ibid. Line 371

[1] The rest is silence. — JOHN RUSKIN: *The Crown of Wild Olive, Traffic, Sect. 84*
[2] See page 107.
[3] A line often murmured by Long Island commuters about 5 P.M.

The son and heir of a mongrel bitch.
King Lear. Act. II, Sc. 2, Line 23
I have seen better faces in my time
Than stands on any shoulder that I see
Before me at this instant.
Ibid. Line 99
Fortune, good night, smile once more;
turn thy wheel.
Ibid. Line 180
Hysterica passio! down, thou climbing
sorrow!
Thy element's below.
Ibid. Sc. 4, Line 57
That sir which serves and seeks for
gain,
And follows but for form,
Will pack when it begins to rain,
And leave thee in the storm.
Ibid. Line 79
Nature in you stands on the very verge
Of her confine.
Ibid. Line 149
Necessity's sharp pinch!
Ibid. Line 214
Let not women's weapons, water-
drops,
Stain my man's cheeks!
Ibid. Line 280
Blow, winds, and crack your cheeks!
rage! blow!
Ibid. Act III, Sc. 2, Line 1
I tax not you, you elements, with un-
kindness.
Ibid. Line 16
A poor, infirm, weak, and despised old
man.
Ibid. Line 20
There was never yet fair woman but
she made mouths in a glass.
Ibid. Line 35
I will be the pattern of all patience.
Ibid. Line 37
I am a man
More sinn'd against than sinning.
Ibid. Line 59
Oh! that way madness lies; let me shun
that.
Ibid. Sc. 4, Line 21
Poor naked wretches, wheresoe'er you
are,
That bide the pelting of this pitiless
storm,

How shall your houseless heads and un-
fed sides,
Your looped and windowed raggedness,
defend you
From seasons such as these?
King Lear. Act. III, Sc. 4, Line 28
Take physic, pomp;
Expose thyself to feel what wretches
feel.
Ibid. Line 33
Out-paramoured the Turk.
Ibid. Line 91
'Tis a naughty night to swim in.
Ibid. Line 113
The green mantle of the standing pool.
Ibid. Line 137
But mice and rats and such small deer
Have been Tom's food for seven long
year.
Ibid. Line 142
The prince of darkness is a gentleman.[1]
Ibid. Line 147
Poor Tom's a-cold.
Ibid. Line 151
I'll talk a word with this same learned
Theban.
Ibid. Line 161
Child Rowland to the dark tower came.[2]
His word was still, Fie, foh, and fum,
I smell the blood of a British man.
Ibid. Line 185
The little dogs and all,
Tray, Blanch, and Sweetheart, see, they
bark at me.
Ibid. Sc. 6, Line 65
Mastiff, greyhound, mongrel grim,
Hound or spaniel, brach or lym;
Or bobtail tike or trundle-tail.
Ibid. Line 71
I am tied to the stake, and I must stand
the course.
Ibid. Sc. 7, Line 54

[1] The Prince of Darkness is a gentleman. —
SIR JOHN SUCKLING: *The Goblins, Act III*
The Devil is a gentleman. — SHELLEY: *Peter
Bell the Third, Part II, St. 2*
[2] Child Roland to the dark tower came. —
SCOTT: *The Bridal of Triermain*
Dauntless the slug-horn to my lips I set,
And blew. *"Childe Roland to the Dark
Tower came."*
ROBERT BROWNING: *Childe Roland
to the Dark Tower Came, St. 34*

The lowest and most dejected thing of
fortune.
King Lear. Act IV, Sc. 1, Line 3
The worst is not
So long as we can say, "This is the
worst."
Ibid. Line 27
Sunshine and rain at once; her smiles
and tears.
Ibid. Sc. 3, Line 20
It is the stars,
The stars above us, govern our con-
ditions.
Ibid. Line 34
Our foster-nurse of nature is repose.
Ibid. Sc. 4, Line 12
In nothing am I chang'd
But in my garments.
Ibid. Sc. 6, Line 9
Half way down
Hangs one that gathers samphire,
dreadful trade!
Methinks he seems no bigger than his
head:
The fishermen that walk upon the beach
Appear like mice.
Ibid. Line 15
Nature's above art in that respect.
Ibid. Line 87
Ay, every inch a king.
Ibid. Line 110
Give me an ounce of civet, good
apothecary, to sweeten my imagination.
Ibid. Line 133
A man may see how this world goes
with no eyes. Look with thine ears: see
how yond justice rails upon yon simple
thief. Hark, in thine ear: change places;
and, handy-dandy, which is the justice,
which is the thief?
Ibid. Line 154
Through tatter'd clothes small vices do
appear;
Robes and furr'd gowns hide all.
Ibid. Line 169
Mine enemy's dog,
Though he had bit me, should have
stood that night
Against my fire.
Ibid. Sc. 7, Line 36
Pray you now, forget and forgive.
Ibid. Line 84

Men must endure
Their going hence, even as their com-
ing hither.
    King Lear. Act V, Sc. 2, Line 9
Upon such sacrifices, my Cordelia,
The gods themselves throw incense.
    Ibid. Sc. 3, Line 20
The gods are just, and of our pleasant
    vices
Make instruments to plague us.
    Ibid. Line 172
    Her voice was ever soft,
Gentle, and low, an excellent thing in
    woman.
    Ibid. Line 274
Vex not his ghost: O! let him pass! he
    hates him
That would upon the rack of this tough
    world
Stretch him out longer.
    Ibid. Line 315
That never set a squadron in the field,
Nor the division of a battle knows
More than a spinster.
    Othello. Act I, Sc. 1, Line 22
The bookish theoric.
    Ibid. Line 24
    'Tis the curse of service,
Preferment goes by letter and affection,
And not by old gradation, where each
    second
Stood heir to the first.
    Ibid. Line 35
We cannot all be masters.
    Ibid. Line 43
    I will wear my heart upon my sleeve
For daws to peck at.
    Ibid. Line 64
Trust not your daughters' minds
By what you see them act.
    Ibid. Line 171
The wealthy curled darlings of our na-
tion.
    Ibid. Sc. 2, Line 68
Most potent, grave, and reverend si-
    gniors,
My very noble and approv'd good
    masters.
    Ibid. Sc. 3, Line 76
The very head and front of my offend-
ing
Hath this extent, no more.
    Ibid. Line 80

Rude am I in my speech,
And little bless'd with the soft phrase
    of peace:
For since these arms of mine had seven
    years' pith,
Till now some nine moons wasted, they
    have used
Their dearest action in the tented field.
    Othello. Act I, Sc. 3, Line 81
    Little shall I grace my cause
In speaking for myself. Yet, by your
    gracious patience,
I will a round unvarnish'd tale deliver
Of my whole course of love.
    Ibid. Line 88
Still question'd me the story of my life
From year to year, the battles, sieges,
    fortunes
That I have passed.
    Ibid. Line 129
Wherein I spake of most disastrous
    chances,
Of moving accidents by flood and field,
Of hair-breadth 'scapes i' the imminent
    deadly breach.
    Ibid. Line 134
Hills whose heads touch heaven.
    Ibid. Line 141
And of the Cannibals that each other
    eat,
The Anthropophagi, and men whose
    heads
Do grow beneath their shoulders.
    Ibid. Line 143
    My story being done,
She gave me for my pains a world of
    sighs:
She swore, in faith, 'twas strange, 'twas
    passing strange,
'Twas pitiful, 'twas wondrous pitiful:
She wish'd she had not heard it, yet
    she wish'd
That Heaven had made her such a man;
    she thank'd me,
And bade me, if I had a friend that
    loved her,
I should but teach him how to tell my
    story,
And that would woo her. Upon this hint
    I spake:
She loved me for the dangers I had
    pass'd,
And I loved her that she did pity them.

This only is the witchcraft I have used.
Othello. Act I, Sc. 1, Line 158
I do perceive here a divided duty.
Ibid. Line 181
The robb'd that smiles, steals something from the thief.
Ibid. Line 208
Our bodies are our gardens, to the which our wills are gardeners; . . . either to have it sterile with idleness or manured with industry.
Ibid. Line 324
Put money in thy purse.
Ibid. Line 345
The food that to him now is as luscious as locusts, shall be to him shortly as bitter as coloquintida.
Ibid. Line 354
Framed to make women false.
Ibid. Line 404
One that excels the quirks of blazoning pens.
Ibid. Act II, Sc. 1, Line 63
For I am nothing if not critical.
Ibid. Line 119
I am not merry; but I do beguile
The thing I am, by seeming otherwise.
Ibid. Line 122
She that was ever fair and never proud,
Had tongue at will and yet was never loud.
Ibid. Line 148
Iago. She was a wight, if ever such wight were, ──
Desdemona. To do what?
Iago. To suckle fools and chronicle small beer.
Desdemona. O most lame and impotent conclusion!
Ibid. Line 158
You may relish him more in the soldier than in the scholar.
Ibid. Line 165
Base men being in love have then a nobility in their natures more than is native to them.
Ibid. Line 218
Egregiously an ass.
Ibid. Line 321
I have very poor and unhappy brains for drinking.
Ibid. Sc. 3, Line 34

Potations pottle-deep.
Othello. Act II, Sc. 3, Line 57
King Stephen was a worthy peer,
His breeches cost him but a crown;
He held them sixpence all too dear,
With that he called the tailor lown.[1]
Ibid. Line 93
Silence that dreadful bell! it frights the isle
From her propriety.
Ibid. Line 177
Your name is great
In mouths of wisest censure.
Ibid. Line 194
But men are men; the best sometimes forget.
Ibid. Line 243
Thy honesty and love doth mince this matter.[2]
Ibid. Line 249
Cassio, I love thee;
But never more be officer of mine.
Ibid. Line 250
Iago. What! are you hurt, lieutenant?
Cassio. Ay; past all surgery.
Ibid. Line 261
Reputation, reputation, reputation! Oh! I have lost my reputation. I have lost the immortal part of myself, and what remains is bestial.
Ibid. Line 264
Reputation is an idle and most false imposition; oft got without merit, and lost without deserving.
Ibid. Line 270
O thou invisible spirit of wine! if thou hast no name to be known by, let us call thee devil!
Ibid. Line 285
O God! that men should put an enemy in their mouths to steal away their brains!
Ibid. Line 293

[1] These lines are from an old ballad, Take Thy Old Cloak About Thee, found in PERCY's *Reliques:* ──
King Stephen was a worthy peere,
His breeches cost him but a crowne,
He held them sixpence all too deere;
Therefore he called the taylor Lowne [rascal].
[2] Mince the matter. ── CERVANTES: *Don Quixote, Author's Preface.* WILLIAM KING: *Ulysses and Teresias*

Good wine is a good familiar creature if it be well used.

Othello. Act II, Sc. 3, Line 315

How poor are they that have not patience!

Ibid. Line 379

Excellent wretch! Perdition catch my soul,
But I do love thee! and when I love thee not,
Chaos is come again.[1]

Ibid. Act III, Sc. 3, Line 90

Men should be what they seem.

Ibid. Line 126

Speak to me as to thy thinkings,
As thou dost ruminate, and give thy worst of thoughts
The worst of words.

Ibid. Line 131

Good name in man and woman, dear my lord,
Is the immediate jewel of their souls:
Who steals my purse steals trash; 'tis something, nothing;
'Twas mine, 'tis his, and has been slave to thousands;
But he that filches from me my good name
Robs me of that which not enriches him,
And makes me poor indeed.

Ibid. Line 155

O! beware, my lord, of jealousy;
It is the green-eyed monster which doth mock
The meat it feeds on.

Ibid. Line 165

Poor and content is rich, and rich enough.

Ibid. Line 172

If I do prove her haggard,
Though that her jesses were my dear heart-strings,
I'd whistle her off and let her down the wind,
To prey at fortune.

Ibid. Line 260

[1] For he being dead, with him is beauty slain,
And, beauty dead, black chaos comes again.
Venus and Adonis, L. 1019

I am declined
Into the vale of years.

Othello. Act III, Sc. 3, Line 265

O curse of marriage!
That we can call these delicate creatures ours,
And not their appetites. I had rather be a toad,
And live upon the vapour of a dungeon,
Than keep a corner in the thing I love
For others' uses.

Ibid. Line 268

Trifles light as air
Are to the jealous confirmations strong
As proofs of holy writ.

Ibid. Line 323

Not poppy, nor mandragora,
Nor all the drowsy syrups of the world,
Shall ever medicine thee to that sweet sleep
Which thou ow'dst yesterday.

Ibid. Line 331

I swear 'tis better to be much abused
Than but to know 't a little.

Ibid. Line 337

He that is robb'd, not wanting what is stolen,
Let him not know 't and he's not robb'd at all.

Ibid. Line 343

O! now, for ever
Farewell the tranquil mind; farewell content!
Farewell the plumed troop and the big wars
That make ambition virtue! O, farewell!
Farewell the neighing steed, and the shrill trump,
The spirit-stirring drum, the ear-piercing fife,
The royal banner, and all quality,
Pride, pomp, and circumstance of glorious war!
And, O you mortal engines, whose rude throats
The immortal Jove's dread clamours counterfeit,
Farewell! Othello's occupation's gone!

Ibid. Line 348

Be sure of it; give me the ocular proof.

Ibid. Line 361

No hinge nor loop
To hang a doubt on.
>   *Othello. Act III, Sc. 3, Line 366*
On horror's head horrors accumulate.
>   *Ibid. Line 371*
Take note, take note, O world!
To be direct and honest is not safe.
>   *Ibid. Line 378*
But this denoted a foregone conclusion.
>   *Ibid. Line 429*
Swell, bosom, with thy fraught,
For 'tis of aspics' tongues!
>   *Ibid. Line 450*
Like to the Pontick sea,
Whose icy current and compulsive
course
Ne'er feels retiring ebb, but keeps due
on
To the Propontic and the Hellespont,
Even so my bloody thoughts, with
violent pace,
Shall ne'er look back, ne'er ebb to hum-
ble love,
Till that a capable and wide revenge
Swallow them up.
>   *Ibid. Line 454*
Our new heraldry is hands, not hearts.
>   *Ibid. Sc. 4, Line 48*
Fetch me the handkerchief.
>   *Ibid. Line 89*
To beguile many, and be beguil'd by
one.
>   *Ibid. Act IV, Sc. 1, Line 98*
They laugh that win.
>   *Ibid. Line 123*
But yet the pity of it, Iago! O! Iago,
the pity of it, Iago!
>   *Ibid. Line 205*
I understand a fury in your words,
But not the words.
>   *Ibid. Sc. 2, Line 31*
Steep'd me in poverty to the very lips.
>   *Ibid. Line 49*
But, alas! to make me
A fixed figure for the time of scorn
To point his slow and moving finger at!
>   *Ibid. Line 52*
Patience, thou young and rose-lipp'd
cherubin.
>   *Ibid. Line 62*
O thou weed!
Who art so lovely fair and smell'st so
sweet

That the sense aches at thee, would
thou hadst ne'er been born.
>   *Othello. Act IV, Sc. 2, Line 66*
O Heaven! that such companions
thou'dst unfold,
And put in every honest hand a whip
To lash the rascals naked through the
world.
>   *Ibid. Line 141*
'Tis neither here nor there.
>   *Ibid. Sc. 3, Line 60*
It makes us, or it mars us.
>   *Ibid. Act V, Sc. 1, Line 4*
Every way makes my gain.
>   *Ibid. Line 14*
He hath a daily beauty in his life.
>   *Ibid. Line 19*
This is the night
That either makes me or fordoes me
quite.
>   *Ibid. Line 128*
And smooth as monumental alabaster.
>   *Ibid. Sc. 2, Line 5*
Put out the light, and then put out the
light:
If I quench thee, thou flaming minister,
I can again thy former light restore
Should I repent me; but once put out
thy light,
Thou cunning'st pattern of excelling
nature,
I know not where is that Promethean
heat
That can thy light relume.
>   *Ibid. Line 7*
Curse his better angel from his side,
And fall to reprobation.
>   *Ibid. Line 206*
I have done the state some service, and
they know 't;
No more of that. I pray you, in your
letters,
When you shall these unlucky deeds
relate,
Speak of me as I am; nothing exten-
uate,
Nor set down aught in malice: then,
must you speak
Of one that loved not wisely but too
well;
Of one not easily jealous, but, being
wrought,

Perplex'd in the extreme; of one whose
    hand,
Like the base Indian, threw a pearl
    away
Richer than all his tribe; of one whose
    subdued eyes
Albeit unused to the melting mood,
Drop tears as fast as the Arabian trees
Their medicinal gum.
        Othello. Act V, Sc. 2, Line 338
I took by the throat the circumcised
    dog,
And smote him thus.
        Ibid. Line 354
There's beggary in the love that can
    be reckon'd.
        *Antony and Cleopatra. Act I,
            Sc. 1, Line 15*
In nature's infinite book of secrecy
A little I can read.
        Ibid. Sc. 2, Line 11
        On the sudden
A Roman thought hath struck him.
        Ibid. Line 90
Give me to drink mandragora.
        Ibid. Sc. 5, Line 4
Where's my serpent of old Nile?
        Ibid. Line 25
A morsel for a monarch.
        Ibid. Line 31
        My salad days,
When I was green in judgment.
        Ibid. Line 73
        We, ignorant of ourselves,
Beg often our own harms, which the
    wise powers
Deny us for our good; so find we profit
By losing of our prayers.
        Ibid. Act II, Sc. 1, Line 5
        Epicurean cooks
Sharpen with cloyless sauce his appe-
    tite.
        Ibid. Line 24
You patch'd up your excuses.
        Ibid. Sc. 2, Line 60
The barge she sat in, like a burnish'd
    throne,
Burn'd on the water; the poop was
    beaten gold,
Purple the sails, and so perfumed that
The winds were love-sick with them;
    the oars were silver,

Which to the tune of flutes kept stroke,
    and made
The water which they beat to follow
    faster,
As amorous of their strokes. For her
    own person,
It beggar'd all description.
        *Antony and Cleopatra. Act II,
            Sc. 2, Line 199*
Age cannot wither her, nor custom stale
Her infinite variety.
        Ibid. Line 243
I have not kept my square; but that to
    come
Shall all be done by the rule.
        Ibid. Sc. 3, Line 6
        'Twas merry when
You wager'd on your angling; when
    your diver
Did hang a salt-fish on his hook, which
    he
With fervency drew up.
        Ibid. Sc. 5, Line 15
Though it be honest, it is never good
To bring bad news.
        Ibid. Line 85
Come, thou monarch of the vine,
Plumpy Bacchus with pink eyne!
        Ibid. Sc. 7, Line 120
Who does i' the wars more than his
    captain can
Becomes his captain's captain.
        Ibid. Act III, Sc. 1, Line 21
Celerity is never more admir'd
Than by the negligent.
        Ibid. Sc. 7, Line 7
        He wears the rose
Of youth upon him.
        Ibid. Sc. 11, Line 20
        Men's judgments are
A parcel of their fortunes, and things
    outward
Do draw the inward quality after them,
To suffer all alike.
        Ibid. Line 31
Let's have one other gaudy night.
        Ibid. Line 182
To business that we love we rise be-
    time,
And go to 't with delight.
        Ibid. Act IV, Sc. 4, Line 20

This morning, like the spirit of a youth
That means to be of note, begins betimes.
>> *Antony and Cleopatra. Act IV,*
>> *Sc. 4, Line 26*

I have yet
Room for six scotches more.
>> *Ibid. Sc. 7, Line 9*

The shirt of Nessus is upon me.
>> *Ibid. Sc. 10, Line 56*

Sometimes we see a cloud that's drag-
onish;
A vapour sometime like a bear or lion,
A tower'd citadel, a pendant rock,
A forked mountain, or blue promontory
With trees upon 't.
>> *Ibid. Sc. 12, Line 2*

That which is now a horse, even with
a thought
The rack dislimns, and makes it in-
distinct,
As water is in water.
>> *Ibid. Line 9*

I am dying, Egypt, dying.
>> *Ibid. Sc. 13, Line 18*

There is nothing left remarkable
Beneath the visiting moon.
>> *Ibid. Line 67*

Let's do it after the high Roman fashion.
>> *Ibid. Line 87*

For his bounty,
There was no winter in 't; an autumn
'twas
That grew the more by reaping.
>> *Ibid. Act V, Sc. 2, Line 86*

If there be, or ever were, one such,
It's past the size of dreaming.
>> *Ibid. Line 96*

The bright day is done,
And we are for the dark.
>> *Ibid. Line 192*

Mechanic slaves
With greasy aprons, rules, and hammers.
>> *Ibid. Line 208*

A woman is a dish for the gods.
>> *Ibid. Line 274*

I have
Immortal longings in me.
>> *Ibid. Line 282*

Dost thou not see my baby at my
breast,

That sucks the nurse asleep?
>> *Antony and Cleopatra. Act V,*
>> *Sc. 2, Line 311*

Lest the bargain should catch cold and
starve.
>> *Cymbeline. Act I, Sc. 4, Line 186*

Hath his bellyful of fighting.
>> *Ibid. Act II, Sc. 1, Line 24*

How bravely thou becomest thy bed!
>> *Ibid. Sc. 2, Line 15*

The most patient man in loss, the
most coldest that ever turned up ace.
>> *Ibid. Sc. 3, Line 1*

Hark! hark! the lark at heaven's gate
sings,
And Phœbus 'gins arise,[1]
His steeds to water at those springs
On chaliced flowers that lies;
And winking Mary-buds begin
To ope their golden eyes:
With everything that pretty is,
My lady sweet, arise.
>> *Ibid. Line 22*

As chaste as unsunn'd snow.
>> *Ibid. Sc. 5, Line 13*

A kind of conquest
Caesar made here, but made not here
his brag
Of "came, and saw, and overcame."[2]
>> *Ibid. Act III, Sc. 1, Line 22*

Some griefs are med'cinable.
>> *Ibid. Sc. 2, Line 33*

Prouder than rustling in unpaid-for
silk.
>> *Ibid. Sc. 3, Line 24*

So slippery that
The fear's as bad as falling.
>> *Ibid. Line 48*

The game is up.
>> *Ibid. Line 107*

Slander,
Whose edge is sharper than the sword,
whose tongue
Outvenoms all the worms of Nile,
whose breath
Rides on the posting winds and doth
belie
All corners of the world.
>> *Ibid. Sc. 4, Line 35*

Against self-slaughter
There is a prohibition so divine

---

[1] See Lyly, page 23.
[2] See page 65.

That cravens my weak hand.
Cymbeline. Act III, Sc. 4, Line 78

It is no act of common passage, but
A strain of rareness.
Ibid. Line 94

I have not slept one wink.
Ibid. Line 103

Weariness
Can snore upon the flint when resty
sloth
Finds the down pillow hard.
Ibid. Sc. 6, Line 33

An angel! or, if not,
An earthly paragon!
Ibid. Line 42

Society is no comfort
To one not sociable.
Ibid. Act IV, Sc. 2, Line 12

I wear not
My dagger in my mouth.
Ibid. Line 78

And put
My clouted brogues from off my feet.
Ibid. Line 213

Fear no more the heat o' the sun,
Nor the furious winter's rages;
Thou thy worldly task hast done,
Home art gone, and ta'en thy wages.
Ibid. Line 258

Golden lads and girls all must,
As chimney-sweepers, come to dust.
Ibid. Line 262

Fortune brings in some boats that are
not steer'd.
Ibid. Sc. 3, Line 46

By medicine life may be prolong'd, yet
death
Will seize the doctor too.
Ibid. Act V, Sc. 5, Line 29

As an arrow shot
From a well-experienc'd archer hits the
mark
His eye doth level at.
Pericles. Act I, Sc. 1, Line 163

3 Fisherman. Master, I marvel how
the fishes live in the sea.
1 Fisherman. Why, as men do aland;
the great ones eat up the little ones.[1]
Ibid. Act II, Sc. 1, Line 29

[1] See Algernon Sidney, page 170.

My good will is great, though the gift
small.
Pericles. Act III, Sc. 4, Line 18

Bid me discourse, I will enchant thine
ear.
Venus and Adonis. Line 145

Love is a spirit all compact of fire.
Ibid. Line 149

A red morn, that ever yet betoken'd
Wrack to the seaman, tempest to the
field.
Ibid. Line 453

The owl, night's herald.
Ibid. Line 531

The path is smooth that leadeth on to
danger.
Ibid. Line 788

Love comforteth like sunshine after
rain.
Ibid. Line 799

The text is old, the orator too green.
Ibid. Line 806

Lo! here the gentle lark, weary of rest,
From his moist cabinet mounts up on
high,
And wakes the morning.
Ibid. Line 853

For he being dead, with him is beauty
slain,
And, beauty dead, black chaos comes
again.
Ibid. Line 1019

The grass stoops not, she treads on it so
light.
Ibid. Line 1028

Beauty itself doth of itself persuade
The eyes of men without an orator.
The Rape of Lucrece. Line 29

Those that much covet are with gain so
fond,
For what they have not, that which they
possess
They scatter and unloose it from their
bond,
And so, by hoping more, they have but
less.
Ibid. Line 134

One for all, or all for one we gage.[1]
Ibid. Line 144

[1] All for one, one for all, that is our device.
—ALEXANDRE DUMAS [1802–1870]: *The
Three Musketeers, Chap. 9*

For greatest scandal waits on greatest state.
> *The Rape of Lucrece. Line 1006*

For men have marble, women waxen minds.
> *Ibid. Line 1240*

To see sad sights moves more than hear them told.
> *Ibid. Line 1324*

Lucrece swears he did her wrong.[1]
> *Ibid. Line 1462*

To the onlie begetter.
> *Sonnets, Dedication*

Thou art thy mother's glass, and she in thee
Calls back the lovely April of her prime.
> *Sonnet 3*

And stretched metre of an antique song.
> *Sonnet 17*

Shall I compare thee to a summer's day?
> *Sonnet 18*

But thy eternal summer shall not fade.
> *Ibid.*

The painful warrior famoused for fight,
After a thousand victories, once foil'd,
Is from the books of honour razed quite,
And all the rest forgot for which he toil'd.
> *Sonnet 25*

When in disgrace with fortune and men's eyes
I all alone beweep my outcast state.
> *Sonnet 29*

For thy sweet love remember'd such wealth brings
That then I scorn to change my state with kings.
> *Ibid.*

When to the sessions of sweet silent thought
I summon up remembrance of things past,
I sigh the lack of many a thing I sought,
And with old woes new wail my dear times' waste.
> *Sonnet 30*

While I think on thee, dear friend,
All losses are restor'd and sorrows end.
> *Ibid.*

Full many a glorious morning have I seen.
> *Sonnet 33*

Nimble thought can jump both sea and land.
> *Sonnet 44*

My grief lies onward, and my joy behind.
> *Sonnet 50*

Blunting the fine point of seldom pleasure.
> *Sonnet 52*

Like stones of worth they thinly placed are,
Or captain jewels in the carconet.
> *Ibid.*

The rose looks fair, but fairer we it deem
For that sweet odour which doth in it live.
> *Sonnet 54*

Not marble, nor the gilded monuments
Of princes, shall outlive this powerful rhyme.
> *Sonnet 55*

Like as the waves make towards the pebbled shore,
So do our minutes hasten to their end
> *Sonnet 60*

Ruin hath taught me thus to ruminate.
> *Sonnet 64*

Since brass, nor stone, nor earth, nor boundless sea,
But sad mortality o'ersways their power,
How with this rage shall beauty hold a plea,
Whose action is no stronger than a flower?
> *Sonnet 65*

And art made tongue-tied by authority.
> *Sonnet 66*

And simple truth miscall'd simplicity,
And captive good attending captain ill.
> *Ibid.*

That time of year thou may'st in me behold
When yellow leaves, or none, or few, do hang
Upon those boughs which shake against the cold.

[1] See page 98.

Bare ruin'd choirs, where late the sweet birds sang.

Sonnet 73

Clean starved for a look.

Sonnet 75

Your monument shall be my gentle verse,
Which eyes not yet created shall o'er-read;
And tongues to be your being shall re-hearse,
When all the breathers of this world are dead;
You still shall live — such virtue hath my pen —
Where breath most breathes, — even in the mouths of men.

Sonnet 81

Who is it that says most? which can say more
Than this rich praise, — that you alone are you?

Sonnet 84

Farewell! thou art too dear for my possessing.

Sonnet 87

Do not, when my heart hath 'scap'd this sorrow,
Come in the rearward of a conquer'd woe;
Give not a windy night a rainy morrow,
To linger out a purpos'd overthrow.

Sonnet 90

The summer's flower is to the summer sweet,
Though to itself it only live and die.

Sonnet 94

The hardest knife ill-used doth lose his edge.

Sonnet 95

From you I have been absent in the spring,
When proud-pied April, dress'd in all his trim,
Hath put a spirit of youth in everything.

Sonnet 98

That love is merchandiz'd whose rich esteeming
The owner's tongue doth publish every where.

Sonnet 102

Sweets grown common lose their dear delight.

Sonnet 102

To me, fair friend, you never can be old,
For as you were when first your eye I ey'd
Such seems your beauty still.

Sonnet 104

Still constant is a wondrous excellence.

Sonnet 105

The chronicle of wasted time.

Sonnet 106

And beauty, making beautiful old rhyme.

Ibid.

Peace proclaims olives of endless age.

Sonnet 107

That is my home of love; if I have ranged,
Like him that travels, I return again.

Sonnet 109

Made myself a motley to the view.

Sonnet 110

My nature is subdu'd
To what it works in, like the dyer's hand.

Sonnet 111

Let me not to the marriage of true minds
Admit impediments. Love is not love
Which alters when it alteration finds.

Sonnet 116

And ruin'd love, when it is built anew,
Grows fairer than at first, more strong, far greater.

Sonnet 119

'Tis better to be vile than vile esteem'd,
When not to be receives reproach of being;
And the just pleasure lost, which is so deem'd,
Not by our feeling, but by others' seeing.

Sonnet 121

No, I am that I am, and they that level
At my abuses reckon up their own.

Ibid.

To kiss the tender inward of thy hand.

Sonnet 128

That full star that ushers in the even.

Sonnet 132

So on the tip of his subduing tongue
All kind of arguments and question
    deep,
All replication prompt, and reason
    strong,
For his advantage still did wake and
    sleep:
To make the weeper laugh, the laugher
    weep,
He had the dialect and different skill,
Catching all passions in his craft of will.
    A Lover's Complaint. Line 120

O father! what a hell of witchcraft lies
In the small orb of one particular tear.
    Ibid. Line 288

When my love swears that she is made
    of truth,
I do believe her, though I know she lies.
    The Passionate Pilgrim, I

Love's best habit is a soothing tongue.
    Ibid.

Bad in the best, though excellent in
    neither.
    Ibid. VII

Crabbed age and youth cannot live to-
    gether.
Youth is full of pleasure, age is full of
    care.
    Ibid. XII

When as thine eye hath chose the
    dame. . . .
Plainly say thou lov'st her well,
And set thy person forth to sell.
    *Sonnets to Sundry Notes of
    Music. IV*

The strongest castle, tower, and town,
The golden bullet beats it down.
    Ibid.

Have you not heard it said full oft,
A woman's nay doth stand for naught?
    Ibid.

Cursed be he that moves my bones.
    Shakespeare's Epitaph

FRANCIS BACON
[1561–1626]

I hold every man a debtor to his profession; from the which as men of
course do seek to receive countenance
and profit, so ought they of duty to endeavour themselves by way of amends
to be a help and ornament thereunto.
    Maxims of the Law. Preface

Come home to men's business and
bosoms.
    *Dedication to the Essays
    [Edition 1625]*

No pleasure is comparable to the
standing upon the vantage-ground of
truth.
    Of Truth

Men fear death as children fear to go
in the dark; and as that natural fear in
children is increased with tales, so is the
other.
    Of Death

Revenge is a kind of wild justice,
which the more man's nature runs to,
the more ought law to weed it out.
    Of Revenge

It was a high speech of Seneca (after
the manner of the Stoics), that "The
good things which belong to prosperity
are to be wished, but the good things
that belong to adversity are to be admired."
    Of Adversity

It is yet a higher speech of his than
the other, "It is true greatness to have
in one the frailty of a man and the security of a god."
    Ibid.

Prosperity is the blessing of the Old
Testament; adversity is the blessing of
the New.
    Ibid.

Prosperity is not without many fears
and distastes; and adversity is not without comforts and hopes.
    Ibid.

Virtue is like precious odours,—
most fragrant when they are incensed
or crushed.[1]
    Ibid.

He that hath wife and children hath
given hostages to fortune; for they are

---

[1] As aromatic plants bestow
   No spicy fragrance while they grow;
   But crushed or trodden to the ground,
   Diffuse their balmy sweets around.
     GOLDSMITH: *The Captivity, Act I*
   The good are better made by ill,
   As odours crushed are sweeter still.
     ROGERS: *Jacqueline, Stanza 3*

impediments to great enterprises, either of virtue or mischief.

Of Marriage and Single Life

Wives are young men's mistresses, companions for middle age, and old men's nurses.[1]

Ibid.

The monuments of wit survive the monuments of power.

Essex's Device [1595]

A good name is like a precious ointment; it filleth all around about, and will not easily away; for the odors of ointments are more durable than those of flowers.[2]

Of Praise

Men in great place are thrice servants, — servants of the sovereign or state, servants of fame, and servants of business.

Of Great Place

Mahomet made the people believe that he would call a hill to him, and from the top of it offer up his prayers for the observers of his law. The people assembled. Mahomet called the hill to come to him, again and again; and when the hill stood still he was never a whit abashed, but said, "If the hill will not come to Mahomet, Mahomet will go to the hill."

Of Boldness

The desire of power in excess caused the angels to fall; the desire of knowledge in excess caused man to fall.[3]

Of Goodness

The remedy is worse than the disease.[4]

Of Seditions

I had rather believe all the fables in the legends and the Talmud and the Alcoran, than that this universal frame is without a mind.

Of Atheism

A little philosophy inclineth man's mind to atheism, but depth in philosophy bringeth men's minds about to religion.[1]

Of Atheism

Travel, in the younger sort, is a part of education; in the elder, a part of experience. He that travelleth into a country before he hath some entrance into the language, goeth to school, and not to travel.

Of Travel

Princes are like to heavenly bodies, which cause good or evil times, and which have much veneration but no rest.[2]

Of Empire

Fortune is like the market, where many times, if you can stay a little, the price will fall.

Of Delays

In things that a man would not be seen in himself, it is a point of cunning to borrow the name of the world; as to say, "The world says," or "There is a speech abroad."

Of Cunning

There is a cunning which we in England call "the turning of the cat in the pan"; which is, when that which a man says to another, he lays it as if another had said it to him.

Ibid.

It is a good point of cunning for a man to shape the answer he would have in his own words and propositions, for it makes the other party stick the less.

Ibid.

It hath been an opinion that the French are wiser than they seem, and the Spaniards seem wiser than they are; but howsoever it be between nations,

---

[1] BURTON (quoted): *Anatomy of Melancholy, Part III, Sect. 2, Memb. 5, Subsect. 5*

[2] A good name is better than precious ointment. — *Ecclesiastes, VII, 1*

[3] Pride still is aiming at the blest abodes;
　　Men would be angels, angels would be gods.
　Aspiring to be gods if angels fell,
　Aspiring to be angels men rebel.
　　POPE: *Essay on Man, Ep. I, L. 125*

[4] There are some remedies worse than the disease. — PUBLIUS SYRUS: *Maxim 301*

---

[1] Who are a little wise the best fools be. — DONNE: *Triple Fool*

A little skill in antiquity inclines a man to Popery; but depth in that study brings him about again to our religion. — FULLER: *The Holy State, The True Church Antiquary*

A little learning is a dangerous thing. — POPE: *Essay on Criticism, Part II, L. 15*

[2] Kings are like stars: they rise and set;
　　they have
　The worship of the world, but no repose.
　　SHELLEY: *Hellas*

certainly it is so between man and man.

Of Seeming Wise

There is a wisdom in this beyond the rules of physic. A man's own observation, what he finds good of and what he finds hurt of, is the best physic to preserve health.

Of Regimen of Health

Discretion of speech is more than eloquence; and to speak agreeably to him with whom we deal is more than to speak in good words or in good order.

Of Discourse

Men's thoughts are much according to their inclination,[1] their discourse and speeches according to their learning and infused opinions.

Of Custom and Education

Chiefly the mould of a man's fortune is in his own hands.[2]

Of Fortune

If a man look sharply and attentively, he shall see Fortune; for though she is blind, she is not invisible.[3]

Ibid.

Young men are fitter to invent than to judge, fitter for execution than for counsel, and fitter for new projects than for settled business.

Of Youth and Age

Virtue is like a rich stone, — best plain set.

Of Beauty

There is no excellent beauty that hath not some strangeness in the proportion.

Ibid.

God Almighty first planted a garden.[4]

Of Gardens

And because the breath of flowers is far sweeter in the air (where it comes and goes, like the warbling of music) than in the hand, therefore nothing is more fit for that delight than to know what be the flowers and plants that do best perfume the air.

Of Gardens

It is generally better to deal by speech than by letter.

Of Negotiating

Some books are to be tasted, others to be swallowed, and some few to be chewed and digested.

Of Studies

Reading maketh a full man, conference a ready man, and writing an exact man.

Ibid.

Histories make men wise; poets, witty; the mathematics, subtile; natural philosophy, deep; moral, grave; logic and rhetoric, able to contend.

Ibid.

The greatest vicissitude of things amongst men is the vicissitude of sects and religions.[1]

Of Vicissitude of Things

Books must follow sciences, and not sciences books.

Proposition touching Amendment of Laws

Knowledge is power. — Nam et ipsa scientia potestas est.[2]

Meditationes Sacræ, De Hæresibus

Whence we see spiders, flies, or ants entombed and preserved forever in amber, a more than royal tomb.[3]

Historia Vitæ et Mortis, Sylva Sylvarum, Cent. I. Exper., 100

---

[1] Thy wish was father, Harry, to that thought. — SHAKESPEARE: *King Henry IV, Part II, Act IV, Sc. 5, L. 91*

[2] Every man is the architect of his own fortune. — PSEUDO-SALLUST: *Epist. de Rep. Ordin., I, 2*

His own character is the arbiter of every one's fortune. — PUBLIUS SYRUS: *Maxim 283*

[3] Fortune is painted blind, with a muffler afore her eyes, to signify to you that Fortune is blind. — SHAKESPEARE: *Henry V, Act III, Sc. 6, L. 31*

[4] And the Lord God planted a garden eastward in Eden. — *Genesis, II, 8*

God the first garden made, and the first city Cain.

COWLEY: *The Garden, Essay V*

God made the country, and man made the town.

COWPER: *The Task, Book I, L. 749*

Divina natura dedit agros, ars humana ædificavit urbes (Divine Nature gave the fields, human art built the cities). — VARRO: *De Re Rustica, III, 1*

[1] The vicissitude of things. — STERNE: *Sermon XVI.* GIFFORD: *Contemplation*

[2] A wise man is strong; yea, a man of knowledge increaseth strength. — *Proverbs, XXIV, 5*

Knowledge is more than equivalent to force. — JOHNSON: *Rasselas, Chap. XIII*

[3] The bee enclosed and through the amber shown,

When you wander, as you often delight to do, you wander indeed, and give never such satisfaction as the curious time requires. This is not caused by any natural defect, but first for want of election, when you, having a large and fruitful mind, should not so much labour what to speak as to find what to leave unspoken. Rich soils are often to be weeded.

Letter of Expostulation to Coke

"Antiquitas sæculi juventus mundi." These times are the ancient times, when the world is ancient, and not those which we account ancient *ordine retrogrado,* by a computation backward from ourselves.[1]

Advancement of Learning.
Book I [*1605*]

For the glory of the Creator and the relief of man's estate.

Ibid.

Seems buried in the juice which was his own.
            MARTIAL: *Book IV, 32, VI, 15*
                    (Hay's translation)
I saw a flie within a beade
Of amber cleanly buried.
            HERRICK: *On a Fly buried in Amber*
Pretty! in amber to observe the forms
Of hairs, or straws, or dirt, or grubs, or worms.
POPE: *Epistle to Dr. Arbuthnot, L. 169*
[1] As in the little, so in the great world, reason will tell you that old age or antiquity is to be accounted by the farther distance from the beginning and the nearer approach to the end, — the times wherein we now live being in propriety of speech the most ancient since the world's creation. — GEORGE HAKEWILL: *An Apologie or Declaration of the Power and Providence of God in the Government of the World* [London, 1627]
For as old age is that period of life most remote from infancy, who does not see that old age in this universal man ought not to be sought in the times nearest his birth, but in those most remote from it? — PASCAL: *Preface to the Treatise on Vacuum*
It is worthy of remark that a thought which is often quoted from Francis Bacon occurs in [Giordano] Bruno's "Cena di Cenere," published in 1584: I mean the notion that the later times are more aged than the earlier. — WHEWELL: *Philosophy of the Inductive Sciences, Vol. II, P. 198* [London, 1847]
We are Ancients of the earth,
And in the morning of the times.
TENNYSON: *The Day Dream, L'Envoi*

The sun, which passeth through pollutions and itself remains as pure as before.[1]

Advancement of Learning. Book II

It [Poesy] was ever thought to have some participation of divineness, because it doth raise and erect the mind by submitting the shews of things to the desires of the mind.

Ibid.

Sacred and inspired divinity, the sabaoth and port of all men's labours and peregrinations.

Ibid.

Cleanness of body was ever deemed to proceed from a due reverence to God.[2]

Ibid.

States as great engines move slowly.

Ibid.

The world's a bubble, and the life of man
Less than a span.[3]

The World

[1] The sun, though it passes through dirty places, yet remains as pure as before. — *Advancement of Learning* (ed. Dewey)
The sun, too, shines into cesspools and is not polluted. — DIOGENES LAERTIUS, *Lib. VI, Sect. 63*
Spiritalis enim virtus sacramenti ita est ut lux: etsi per immundos transeat, non inquinatur (The spiritual virtue of a sacrament is like light: although it passes among the impure, it is not polluted). — SAINT AUGUSTINE: *Works, Vol. III, in Johannis Evang., Cap. I, Tr. V, Sect. 15*
The sun shineth upon the dunghill, and is not corrupted. — LYLY: *Euphues* (Arber's reprint), *P. 43*
The sun reflecting upon the mud of strands and shores is unpolluted in his beam. — TAYLOR: *Holy Living, Chap. I, P. 3*
Truth is as impossible to be soiled by any outward touch as the sun-beam. — MILTON: *The Doctrine and Discipline of Divorce*
[2] Cleanliness is indeed next to godliness. — JOHN WESLEY (quoted): *Sermon XCII, On Dress*
According to Dr. A. S. Bettelheim, rabbi, this is found in the Hebrew fathers. He cites Phinehas ben Yair, as follows: "The doctrines of religion are resolved into carefulness; carefulness into vigorousness; vigorousness into guiltlessness; guiltlessness into abstemiousness; abstemiousness into cleanliness; cleanliness into godliness," — literally, next to godliness.
[3] Whose life is a bubble, and in length a span. — BROWNE: *Pastoral II*

Who then to frail mortality shall trust
But limns on water, or but writes in
    dust.
                        The World

What then remains but that we still
    should cry
For being born, and, being born, to
    die? [1]
                        Ibid.

My Lord St. Albans said that Nature
did never put her precious jewels into a
garret four stories high, and therefore
that exceeding tall men had ever very
empty heads. [2]
           Apothegms. No. 17

Like the strawberry wives, that laid
two or three great strawberries at the
mouth of their pot, and all the rest were
little ones. [3]
              Ibid. No. 54

Sir Henry Wotton used to say that
critics are like brushers of noblemen's
clothes.
              Ibid. No. 64

Sir Amice Pawlet, when he saw too
much haste made in any matter, was
wont to say, "Stay a while, that we may
make an end the sooner."
              Ibid. No. 76

Alonso of Aragon was wont to say in
commendation of age, that age appears
to be best in four things, — old wood
best to burn, old wine to drink, old
friends to trust, and old authors to
read. [4]
              Ibid. No. 97

Our life is but a span. — *New England
Primer*

[1] This line frequently occurs in almost exactly the same shape among the minor poems
of the time: "Not to be born, or, being born,
to die." — DRUMMOND: *Poems, P. 44.* BISHOP
KING: *Poems, etc.* [1657], *P. 145*

[2] Tall men are like houses of four stories,
wherein commonly the uppermost room is
worst furnished. — HOWELL (quoted): *Letter
I, Book I, Sect. II* [1621]

Often the cockloft is empty in those whom
Nature hath built many stories high. — FUL-
LER: *Andronicus, Sect. VI, Par. 18, 1*

    Such as take lodgings in a head
    That's to be let unfurnished.
    BUTLER: *Hudibras, Part I, Canto I,
                      L. 161*

[3] The custom is not altogether obsolete.

[4] Is not old wine wholesomest, old pippins
toothsomest, old wood burns brightest, old

Pyrrhus, when his friends congratu-
lated to him his victory over the Romans under Fabricius, but with great
slaughter of his own side, said to them,
"Yes; but if we have such another victory, we are undone." [1]
           Apothegms. No. 193

Cosmus, Duke of Florence, was wont
to say of perfidious friends, that "We
read that we ought to forgive our enemies; but we do not read that we ought
to forgive our friends."
             Ibid. No. 206

Cato said the best way to keep good
acts in memory was to refresh them
with new.
             Ibid. No. 247

I do plainly and ingenuously confess
that I am guilty of corruption, and do
renounce all defense. I beseech your
Lordships to be merciful to a broken
reed. [2]

    *On being charged by Parliament
    with corruption in the exercise
    of his office*

I bequeath my soul to God. . . . My
body to be buried obscurely. For my

---

linen wash whitest? Old soldiers, sweetheart,
are surest, and old lovers are soundest. —
WEBSTER: *Westward Hoe, Act II, Sc. 2*

Old friends are best. King James used to
call for his old shoes; they were easiest for
his feet. — SELDEN: *Table Talk, Friends*

Old wood to burn! Old wine to drink! Old
friends to trust! Old authors to read! — Alonso of Aragon was wont to say in commendation of age, that age appeared to be best in
these four things. — MELCHIOR: *Floresta
Española de Apothegmas o sentencias, etc.,
II, 1, 20*

What find you better or more honourable
than age? Take the preheminence of it in
everything, — in an old friend, in old wine, in
an old pedigree. — SHACKERLEY MARMION:
[1603–1639]: *The Antiquary*

I love everything that's old, — old friends.
old times, old manners, old books, old wine. —
GOLDSMITH: *She Stoops to Conquer, Act I*

Old books, old wine, old Nankin blue. —
AUSTIN DOBSON: *Rondeau, To Richard Watson Gilder*

[1] There are some defeats more triumphant
than victories. — MONTAIGNE: *Of Cannibals,
Chap. XXX*

[2] Thou trustest in the staff of this broken
reed. — *Isaiah, XXXVI, 6*

A bruised reed shall he not break. — *Isaiah,
XLII, 3*

name and memory, I leave it to men's charitable speeches, and to foreign nations, and the next age.

From his Will

SIR HENRY WOTTON
[1568–1639]

Love lodged in a woman's breast
Is but a guest.

A Woman's Heart

How happy is he born and taught,
    That serveth not another's will;
Whose armour is his honest thought,
    And simple truth his utmost skill!

*The Character of a Happy Life.
Stanza 1*

Who God doth late and early pray
    More of his grace than gifts to lend;
And entertains the harmless day
    With a religious book or friend.

Ibid. Stanza 5

Lord of himself, though not of lands;
    And having nothing, yet hath all.[1]

Ibid. Stanza 6

You meaner beauties of the night,
    That poorly satisfy our eyes
More by your number than your light;
    You common people of the skies,—
What are you when the moon [2] shall rise?

*On his Mistress, the Queen of
Bohemia.[3] Stanza 1*

He first deceased; she for a little tried
To live without him, liked it not, and died.

*Upon the Death of Sir Albert
Morton's Wife*

I am but a gatherer and disposer of other men's stuff.[4]

*Preface to the Elements of
Architecture*

Hanging was the worst use a man could be put to.

The Disparity between Buckingham and Essex

An ambassador is an honest man sent to lie abroad for the commonwealth.[1]

Reliquiæ Wottonianæ

The itch of disputing will prove the scab of churches.[2]

A Panegyric to King Charles

SIR JOHN DAVIES
[1569–1626]

What can we know? or what can we discern,
When error chokes the windows of the mind?

*The Vanity of Human Learning.
Stanza 15*

For this the wisest of all moral men
Said he knew nought, but that he nought did know,
And the great mocking-master mock'd not then,
When he said, Truth was buried deep below.[3]

Ibid. Stanza 20

We that acquaint ourselves with ev'ry zone,
And pass both tropics, and behold each pole,
When we come home are to ourselves unknown,
And unacquainted still with our own soul.

Ibid. Stanza 25

I know my soul hath power to know all things,
Yet is she blind and ignorant in all:
I know I'm one of Nature's little kings,

---

[1] As having nothing, and yet possessing all things. — *2 Corinthians, VI, 10*

[2] "Sun" in *Reliquiæ Wottonianæ* [eds. 1651, 1654, 1672, 1685]

[3] This was printed with music as early as 1624, in Est's "Sixth Set of Books," etc., and is found in many MSS. — JOHN HANNAH [1818–1888]: *The Courtly Poets* [1870]

[4] I have here only made a nosegay of culled flowers, and have brought nothing of my own but the thread that ties them together. — MICHEL DE MONTAIGNE: *Of Physiognomy*

[1] In a letter to Velserus [1612] Wotton says, "This merry definition of an ambassador I had chanced to set down at my friend's, Mr. Christopher Fleckamore, in his Album."

[2] He directed the stone over his grave to be inscribed: —
Hic jacet hujus sententiæ primus auctor:
DISPUTANDI PRURITUS ECCLESIARUM SCABIES.
    Nomen alias quære
(Here lies the author of this phrase: "The itch for disputing is the sore of churches." Seek his name elsewhere). — IZAAK WALTON: *Life of Wotton* [1651]

[3] See Diogenes Laertius, page 1014.

Yet to the least and vilest things am
  thrall.
> *The Vanity of Human Learning.*
> *Ibid. Stanza 44*

I know my life's a pain, and but a span;
I know my sense is mock'd in ev'ry
  thing:
And to conclude, I know myself a man,
Which is a proud, and yet a wretched
  thing.
> *Ibid. Stanza 45*

Much like a subtle spider which doth
  sit
In middle of her web, which spreadeth
  wide;
If aught do touch the utmost thread of
  it
She feels it instantly on every side.[1]
> *The Immortality of the Soul*

Wedlock, indeed, hath oft compared
  been
To public feasts, where meet a public
  rout, —
Where they that are without would fain
  go in,
And they that are within would fain
  go out.[2]
> *Contention Betwixt a Wife, etc.*

---

[1] As spiders touch'd, seek their web's in-
most part. — DAVIES: *The Vanity of Human
Learning, St. 37*
Our souls sit close and silently within,
And their own webs from their own entrails
  spin;
And when eyes meet far off, our sense is such
That, spider-like, we feel the tenderest touch.
  DRYDEN: *Mariage à la Mode, Act II, Sc. 1*
The spider's touch, how exquisitely fine!
Feels at each thread, and lives along the line.
  POPE: *An Essay on Man, Epistle I, L. 217*
[2] 'Tis just like a summer bird-cage in a
garden: the birds that are without despair to
get in, and the birds that are within fear they shall
and are in a consumption for fear they shall
never get out. — WEBSTER: *The White Devil,
Act I, Sc. 2*
Le mariage est comme une forteresse as-
siégée; ceux qui sont dehors veulent y entrer,
et ceux qui sont dedans veulent en sortir
(Marriage is like a beleaguered fortress: those
who are outside want to get in, and those inside want to get out). — QUITARD: *Études sur
les Proverbes Français, P. 102*
It happens as with cages: the birds without
despair to get in, and those within despair of
getting out. — MONTAIGNE: *Upon some Verses
of Virgil, Chap. V*
Is not marriage an open question, when it is

MARTYN PARKER
[? –1656]

Ye gentlemen of England
  That live at home at ease,
Ah! little do you think upon
  The dangers of the seas.
> *Song*

When the stormy winds do blow.[1]
> *Ibid.*

THOMAS DEKKER
[1570?–1641]

The reason why fond women love to buy
Adulterate   complexion: here   'tis
  read, —
False colours last after the true be dead.
> *A Description of a Lady by Her
> Lover*

This age thinks better of a gilded fool
Than of a threadbare saint in wisdom's
  school.
> *Old Fortunatus*

              The best of men
That e'er wore earth about him was a
  sufferer;
A soft, meek, patient, humble, tranquil
  spirit,
The first true gentleman that ever
  breathed.[2]
> *The Honest Whore. Part I,
> Act I, Sc. 12*

I was ne'er so thrummed since I was a
  gentleman.[3]
> *Ibid. Act IV, Sc. 2*

---

alleged, from the beginning of the world, that
such as are in the institution wish to get out,
and such as are out wish to get in? — EMER-
SON: *Representative Men: Montaigne*
[1] When the battle rages loud and long,
  And the stormy winds do blow.
    CAMPBELL: *Ye Mariners of England*
[2] Of the offspring of the gentilman Jafeth
come Habraham, Moyses, Aron, and the
profettys; also the Kyng of the right lyne of
Mary, of whom that gentilman Jhesus was
borne. — JULIANA BERNERS: *Heraldic Blazonry* [1486]
[3] I was never so bethump'd with words,
  Since I first call'd my brother's father dad.
    SHAKESPEARE: *King John, Act II,
      Sc. 1, L. 466*

This principle is old, but true as fate, —
Kings may love treason, but the traitor
hate.[1]
> *The Honest Whore. Part I,*
> *Act IV, Sc. 4*

We are ne'er like angels till our passion
dies.
> *Ibid. Part II, Act I, Sc. 2*

Turn over a new leaf.[2]
> *Ibid. Act II, Sc. 1*

To add to golden numbers, golden numbers.
> *Patient Grissell. Act I, Sc. 1*

Honest labour bears a lovely face.
> *Ibid.*

THOMAS MIDDLETON
[1570–1627]

As the case stands.[3]
> *The Old Law. Act II, Sc. 1*

On his last legs.
> *Ibid. Act V, Sc. 1*

Hold their noses to the grindstone.[4]
> *Blurt, Master-Constable.*
> *Act III, Sc. 3*

I smell a rat.[5]
> *Ibid.*

A little too wise, they say, do ne'er live
long.[6]
> *The Phœnix. Act I, Sc. 1*

The better day, the better deed.[7]
> *Ibid. Act III, Sc. 1*

The worst comes to the worst.[8]
> *Ibid.*

'Tis slight, not strength, that gives the
greatest lift.[1]
> *Michaelmas Term. Act IV, Sc. 1*

From thousands of our undone widows
One may derive some wit.[2]
> *A Trick to Catch the Old One.*
> *Act I, Sc. 2*

Ground not upon dreams; you know
they are ever contrary.[3]
> *The Family of Love. Act IV, Sc. 3*

Spick and span new.[4]
> *Ibid.*

A flat case as plain as a pack-staff.[5]
> *Ibid. Act V, Sc. 3*

Have you summoned your wits from
wool-gathering?
> *Ibid.*

As true as I live.
> *Ibid.*

From the crown of our head to the sole
of our foot.[6]
> *A Mad World, my Masters.*
> *Act I, Sc. 3*

That disease
Of which all old men sicken, — avarice.[7]
> *The Roaring Girl. Act I, Sc. 1*

Beat all your feathers as flat down as
pancakes.
> *Ibid.*

---

[1] Cæsar said he loved the treason, but hated the traitor. — PLUTARCH: *Life of Romulus*
[2] Also in THOMAS MIDDLETON: *Anything for a Quiet Life, Act III, Sc. 3*
[3] As the case stands. — MATHEW HENRY: *Commentaries, Psalm CXIX*
[4] Hold their noses to grinstone. — JOHN HEYWOOD: *Proverbes, Part I, Chap. 5*
[5] I smell a rat. — BEN JONSON: *Tale of a Tub, Act IV, Sc. 3.* BUTLER: *Hudibras, Part I, Canto I, L. 281*
I begin to smell a rat. — CERVANTES: *Don Quixote, Book IV, Chap. X*
[6] So wise so young, they say, do never live long. — SHAKESPEARE: *King Richard III, Act III, Sc. 1, L. 79*
[7] The better day, the worse deed. — HENRY: *Commentaries, Genesis III*
[8] Worst comes to the worst. — CERVANTES: *Don Quixote, Part I, Book III, Chap. V.* MARSTON: *The Dutch Courtezan, Act III, Sc. 1*

[1] It is not strength, but art, obtains the prize. — POPE: *The Iliad, Book XXIII, L. 383*
[2] Some undone widow sits upon mine arm. — MASSINGER: *A New Way to Pay Old Debts, Act V, Sc. 1*
[3] The visions of the night do often chance contrary. — APULEIUS: *The Golden Ass, Book IV*
Dhrames always go by contrairies, my dear! — SAMUEL LOVER: *Rory O'More, St. 2*
[4] Spick and span new. — CERVANTES: *Don Quixote, Part II, Chap. 58.* JOHN FORD: *The Lover's Melancholy* [1629], *Act I, Sc. 1.* BUTLER: *Hudibras, Part I, Canto III, L. 399.* GEORGE FARQUHAR: *Preface to his Works*
[5] Plain as a pike-staff. — *Terence in English* [1641]. BUCKINGHAM: *Speech in the House of Lords* [1675]. *Gil Blas* (Smollett's translation), *Book XII, Chap. VIII.* BYROM: *Epistle to a Friend*
[6] From the crown of his head to the sole of his foot, he is all mirth. — SHAKESPEARE: *Much Ado about Nothing, Act III, Sc. 2, L. 9*
[7] So for a good old-gentlemanly vice
I think I must take up with avarice.
BYRON: *Don Juan, Canto I, Stanza 216*

There is no hate lost between us.[1]
> *The Witch. Act IV, Sc. 3*

Black spirits and white, red spirits and gray,
Mingle, mingle, mingle, you that mingle may.[2]
> *Ibid. Act V, Sc. 2*

All is not gold that glisteneth.[3]
> *A Fair Quarrel. Act V, Sc. 1*

As old Chaucer was wont to say, that broad famous English poet.
> *More Dissemblers besides Women.*
> *Act I, Sc. 4*

'Tis a stinger.[4]
> *Ibid. Act III, Sc. 2*

The world's a stage on which all parts are played.[5]
> *A Game of Chess. Act V, Sc. 1*

Anything for a quiet life.
> *Title of play* [1662]

Turn over a new leaf.[6]
> *Anything for a Quiet Life.*
> *Act II, Sc. 3*

My nearest
And dearest enemy.[7]
> *Ibid. Act V, Sc. 1*

This was a good week's labour.
> *Ibid. Sc. 3*

---

[1] There is no love lost between us. — CERVANTES: *Don Quixote, Book IV, Chap. XXIII.* BEN JONSON: *Every Man Out of His Humour, Act II, Sc. 1.* GOLDSMITH: *She Stoops to Conquer, Act IV.* GARRICK: *Correspondence* [1759]. FIELDING: *The Grub Street Opera, Act I, Sc. 4*

[2] These lines are introduced into *Macbeth, Act IV, Sc. 1.* According to Steevens, "the song was, in all probability, a traditional one." Collier says, "Doubtless it does not belong to Middleton more than to Shakespeare." Dyce says, "There seems to be little doubt that 'Macbeth' is of an earlier date than 'The Witch.'"

[3] See Chaucer, page 8.

[4] He 'as had a stinger. — BEAUMONT AND FLETCHER: *Wit without Money, Act IV, Sc. 1*

[5] All the world's a stage. — SHAKESPEARE: *As You Like It, Act II, Sc. 7, L. 139*
See Thomas Heywood, page 129.

[6] *A Health to the Gentlemanly Profession of Servingmen* [1598]. Turn over a new leaf. — DEKKER: *The Honest Whore, Part II, Act I, Sc. 2.* BURKE: *Letter to Mrs. Haviland*

[7] My dearest foe. — SHAKESPEARE: *Hamlet, Act I, Sc. 2, L. 182*

How many honest words have suffered corruption since Chaucer's days!
> *No Wit, no Help, Like a Woman's.*
> *Act II, Sc. 1*

By many a happy accident.[1]
> *Ibid. Sc. 2*

JOHN DONNE
[1573–1631]

I have done one braver thing
  Than all the Worthies did;
And yet a braver thence doth spring,
  Which is, to keep that hid.
> *The Undertaking, Stanza 1*

Stay, O sweet, and do not rise!
The light that shines comes from thine eyes;
The day breaks not: it is my heart,
Because that you and I must part.
> *Daybreak, Stanza 1*

She and comparisons are odious.[2]
> *Elegie VIII, The Comparison*

No spring nor summer beauty hath such grace
As I have seen in one autumnal face.
> *Elegie IX, The Autumnal:*
> *To Lady Magdalen Herbert*
> *(mother of George Herbert)*

The snail, which everywhere doth roam
Carrying his own house still, still is at home,
Follow (for he is easy paced) this snail,
Be thine own palace, or the world's thy jail.
> *Verse Letter to Sir Henry Wotton*

Pictures in our eyes to get
Was all our propagation.
> *The Ecstasy*

Go and catch a falling star,
Get with child a mandrake root.
> *Song*

I long to talk with some old lover's ghost,
Who died before the god of love was born.
> *Love's Deity*

---

[1] A happy accident. — MADAME DE STAËL: *L'Allemagne, Chap. XVI.* CERVANTES: *Don Quixote, Book IV, Part II, Chap. LVII*

[2] See Fortescue, page 9.

His office was indulgently to fit
Actives to passives.
Love's Deity

'Twere profanation of our joys
To tell the laity our love.
A Valediction, Forbidding Mourning

Our two souls, therefore, which are one,
    Though I must go, endure not yet
A breach, but an expansion,
    Like gold to airy thinness beat.
Ibid.

A compassionate turquoise which
    doth tell
By looking pale, the wearer is not well.
An Anatomy of the World

I observe the physician with the same
diligence as he the disease.
Devotions, VI

The flea, though he kill none, he does
all the harm he can.
Ibid. XII

He was the Word, that spake it:
He took the bread and brake it;
And what that Word did make it,
I do believe and take it.[1]
Divine Poems. On the Sacrament

        Her pure and eloquent blood
Spoke in her cheeks, and so distinctly
    wrought
That one might almost say her body
    thought.
Funeral Elegies. On the Death of
Mistress Drury

Who are a little wise the best fools be.[2]
The Triple Fool

Death, be not proud, though some have
    called thee
Mighty and dreadful, for thou art not
    so;
For those whom thou think'st thou dost
    overthrow
Die not, poor Death; nor yet canst thou
    kill me.
Sonnet: Death

One short sleep past, we wake eternally;

And death shall be no more; death, thou
    shalt die.
Sonnet: Death

The Sea is as deepe in a calme, as in a
    storme.
Sermons. Mundus Mare

BEN JONSON [1]
[1573?–1637]

He despises me, I suppose, because I
live in an alley: tell him his soul lives
in an alley.
Of James I. Quoted in Leigh Hunt's
essay, Coaches

The dignity of truth is lost with much
    protesting.
Catiline's Conspiracy. Act III, Sc. 2

It was a mighty while ago.
Every Man in his Humour. Act I,
Sc. 3

Hang sorrow! care'll kill a cat.[2]
Ibid.

As he brews, so shall he drink.
Ibid. Act II, Sc. 1

Get money; still get money, boy,
No matter by what means.[3]
Ibid. Sc. 3

Have paid scot and lot there any time
this eighteen years.
Ibid. Act III, Sc. 3

It must be done like lightning.
Ibid. Act IV, Sc. 5

There shall be no love lost.[4]
Every Man out of his Humour.
Act II, Sc. 1

----

[1] Attributed by many writers to Princess
Elizabeth. It is not in the original edition of
Donne, but first appears in the edition of 1654,
P. 352.
[2] See Bacon, page 110.

----

[1] O rare Ben Jonson! — SIR JOHN YOUNG:
Epitaph. (Which was donne at the charge of
Jack Young, who, walking there when the
grave was covering, gave the fellow 18 pence
to cutt it. — JOHN AUBREY: [1626–1697]
Brief Lives)
[2] What though care killed a cat. — SHAKE-
SPEARE: *Much Ado about Nothing, Act V,
Sc. 1, L. 135*
Hang sorrow! care will kill a cat. — GEORGE
WITHER: *Poem on Christmas*
[3] O cives, cives, quaerenda pecunia primum,
    Virtus post nummos: haec Janus summus
        ab imo
    Perdocet.
    HORACE: *Epistles, Book I, Epistle 1, L. 53*
Get place and wealth, if possible with grace;
If not, by any means get wealth and place.
    Translation by ALEXANDER POPE, *L. 103*
[4] See Middleton, page 117.

Still to be neat, still to be drest,
As you were going to a feast.[1]
> *Epicœne; Or, the Silent Woman.
> Act I, Sc. 1*

Give me a look, give me a face,
That makes simplicity a grace;
Robes loosely flowing, hair as free,
Such sweet neglect more taketh me
Than all the adulteries of art:
They strike mine eyes, but not my
    heart.
> *Ibid.*

Truth is the trial of itself
And needs no other touch,
And purer than the purest gold,
Refine it ne'er so much.
> *On Truth, Stanza 1*

Follow a shadow, it still flies you;
Seem to fly it, it will pursue:
So court a mistress, she denies you;
Let her alone, she will court you.
> *Follow a Shadow, Stanza 1*

That old bald cheater, Time.
> *The Poetaster. Act I, Sc. 1*

The world knows only two, — that's
Rome and I.
> *Sejanus. Act V, Sc. 1*

Preserving the sweetness of proportion and expressing itself beyond expression.
> *The Masque of Hymen*

Underneath this stone doth lie
As much beauty as could die;
Which in life did harbour give
To more virtue than doth live.
> *Epitaph on Elizabeth, L. H.*

Whilst that for which all virtue now is
    sold,
And almost every vice, — almighty
    gold.[2]
> *Epistle to Elizabeth, Countess of
> Rutland*

God wisheth none should wreck on a
strange shelf:
To him man's dearer than to himself.
> *The Forest: To Sir Robert Wroth*

Drink to me only with thine eyes,
And I will pledge with mine;

Or leave a kiss but in the cup
And I'll not look for wine.[1]
> *The Forest: To Celia, Stanza 1*

I sent thee late a rosy wreath,
Not so much honouring thee
As giving it a hope that there
It could not wither'd be.
> *Ibid. Stanza 2*

Have you seen but a bright lily grow,
Before rude hands have touched it?
Have you marked but the fall o' the
    snow
Before the soil hath smutched it?
> *Her Triumph. Stanza 3*

Reader, look,
Not at his picture, but his book.
> *On the Portrait of Shakespeare
> Prefixed to the First Folio [1623]*

Soul of the age!
The applause, delight, the wonder of
    our stage!
My Shakespeare, rise! I will not lodge
    thee by
Chaucer or Spenser, or bid Beaumont
    lie
A little further, to make thee a room.[2]
> *To the Memory of Shakespeare*

Marlowe's mighty line.
> *Ibid.*

Small Latin and less Greek.
> *Ibid.*

He was not of an age but for all time.
> *Ibid.*

Who casts to write a living line, must
    sweat.
> *Ibid.*

For a good poet's made, as well as born.
> *Ibid.*

Sweet Swan of Avon!
> *Ibid.*

Underneath this sable hearse
Lies the subject of all verse, —
Sidney's sister, Pembroke's mother.

---

[1] A translation from Bonnefonius.
[2] The flattering, mighty, nay, almighty
gold. — WOLCOT: *To Kien Long, Ode IV*
    Almighty dollar. — IRVING: *The Creole Vil-
lage*

[1] Drink to me with your eyes alone. . . .
And if you will, take the cup to your lips
and fill it with kisses, and give it so to me. —
PHILOSTRATUS: *Letter XXIV*
[2] Renowned Spenser, lie a thought more nigh
    To learned Chaucer, and rare Beaumont lie
    A little nearer Spenser, to make room
    For Shakespeare in your threefold, fourfold
        tomb.
> WILLIAM BASSE: *On Shakespeare*

Death, ere thou hast slain another,
Learn'd and fair and good as she,
Time shall throw a dart at thee.
*Epitaph on the Countess of
Pembroke* [1]

Let those that merely talk and never
think,
That live in the wild anarchy of drink.[2]
*Underwoods. An Epistle, an-
swering to One that asked to
be sealed of the Tribe of Ben*

Still may syllabes jar with time,
Still may reason war with rhyme,
                    Resting never!
Ibid. Fit of Rhyme against Rhyme

In small proportions we just beauties
see,
And in short measures life may perfect
be.
*Ibid. To the immortal Memory
of Sir Lucius Cary and Sir
Henry Morison, III*

He seemed to me ever by his work
one of the greatest men, and most
worthy of admiration. In his adversity
I ever prayed that God would give him
strength; for greatness he could not
want.
                    Of Francis Bacon

The players have often mentioned it
as an honor to Shakespeare, that in his
writing he never blotted out a line. My
answer hath been, Would he had blotted a thousand.
*Timber, or Discoveries Made
Upon Men and Matter*

I loved the man [Shakespeare] and
do honor his memory, on this side idolatry, as much as any.
                    Ibid.

Greatness of name in the father oft-
times overwhelms the son; they stand
too near one another. The shadow kills

the growth: so much, that we see the
grandchild come more and oftener to
be heir of the first.
*Timber, or Discoveries Made
Upon Men and Matter*

Though the most be players, some
must be spectators.
                    Ibid.

Whom the disease of talking once
possesseth, he can never hold his peace.
Nay, rather than he will not discourse
he will hire men to hear him.
                    Ibid.

RICHARD BARNFIELD
[1574–1627]

As it fell upon a day
In the merry month of May,
Sitting in a pleasant shade
Which a grove of myrtles made.
Address to the Nightingale [1]

King Pandion he is dead.[2]
                    Ibid.

Every one that flatters thee
Is no friend in misery.
Words are easy, like the wind;
Faithful friends are hard to find.
Every man will be thy friend
Whilst thou hast wherewith to spend:
But, if store of crowns be scant,
No man will supply thy want.
                    Ibid.

He that is thy friend indeed,
He will help thee in thy need.
                    Ibid.

JOSEPH HALL, BISHOP
OF NORWICH
[1574–1656]

In bonds of love united, man and wife,
Long, yet too short, they spent a happy
life.
*Elegy on Sir Edward and Lady
Lewkenor*

---

[1] This epitaph is generally ascribed to Ben
Jonson. It appears in the editions of his
works; but in a manuscript collection of
Browne's poems preserved amongst the Lans-
downe MS. No. 777, in the British Museum, it
is ascribed to Browne, and awarded to him by
Sir Egerton Brydges in his edition of Browne's
poems.

[2] They never taste who always drink;
They always talk who never think.
PRIOR: *Upon a Passage in the Scaligerana*

[1] This song, attributed to Shakespeare and
included in his *Sonnets to Sundry Notes of
Music*, is found in BARNFIELD's *Poems in Divers Humours*, published in 1598, while Shakespeare's *Passionate Pilgrim*, etc. appeared in
1599. See *Specimens of Early English Romances in Meter*, by George Ellis [1753–1815],
Vol. 2, P. 316

[2] Used as refrain in a ballade by Don
Marquis.

So little in his purse, so much upon his
  back.
> *Portrait of a Poor Gallant*

'Mongst all these stirs of discontented
  strife,
O, let me lead an academic life;
To know much, and to think for nothing, know
Nothing to have, yet think we have
  enow.
> *Discontent of Men with their
> Condition*

Moderation is the silken string running through the pearl chain of all virtues.
> *Christian Moderation. Introduction*

Death borders upon our birth, and
our cradle stands in the grave.[1]
> *Epistles. Dec. III, Ep. 2*

There is many a rich stone laid up
in the bowels of the earth, many a fair
pearl laid up in the bosom of the sea,
that never was seen, nor never shall be.[2]
> *Contemplations. Book IV, The
> Veil of Moses*

THOMAS CAMPION
[1575?–1620?]

Good thoughts his only friends,
  His wealth a well-spent age,
The earth his sober inn
  And quiet pilgrimage.
> *Integer Vitae, after Horace.
> Stanza 6*

Never love unless you can
Bear with all the faults of man:
Men will sometimes jealous be,
Though but little cause they see;
And hang the head, as discontent,
And speak what straight they will re-
  pent.
> *Never Love. Stanza 1*

There is a garden in her face
  Where roses and white lilies blow;
A heavenly paradise that place,
  Wherein all pleasant fruits do grow;

---

[1] And cradles rock us nearer to the tomb.
  Our birth is nothing but our death begun.
  YOUNG: *Night Thoughts, Night V, L. 718*
[2] Full many a gem of purest ray serene
  The dark, unfathomed caves of ocean bear.
  GRAY: *Elegy, Stanza 14*

There cherries grow that none may buy,
Till Cherry-Ripe themselves do cry.
> *Cherry-Ripe.*[1] *Stanza 1*

Those cherries fairly do enclose
Of orient pearl a double row,
Which when her lovely laughter shows,
  They look like rosebuds fill'd with
  snow.
> *Ibid. Stanza 2*

The summer hath his joys,
  And winter his delights;
Though love and all his pleasures are
  but toys,
  They shorten tedious nights.
> *Winter Nights. Stanza 2*

ROBERT BURTON
[1577–1640]

Naught so sweet as melancholy.[2]
> *Anatomy of Melancholy.*[3] *The
> Author's Abstract*

I would help others, out of a fellow-
  feeling.[4]
> *Ibid. Democritus to the Reader*

They lard their lean books with the
fat of others' works.[5]
> *Ibid.*

We can say nothing but what hath
been said.[6] Our poets steal from Homer.

---

[1] See Robert Herrick, page 133.
[2] See Strode, page 144.
  There's not a string attuned to mirth
  But has its chord in melancholy.
  > HOOD: *Ode to Melancholy*
[3] Burton's 'Anatomy of Melancholy,' he
said, was the only book that ever took him out
of bed two hours sooner than he wished to
rise. — JAMES BOSWELL: *The Life of Dr.
Johnson, Everyman Ed., Vol. I, P. 389*
  If the reader has patience to go through his
volumes, he will be more improved for literary
conversation than by the perusal of any
twenty other works with which I am acquainted. — BYRON: *Works, Vol. I, P. 144*
[4] A fellow-feeling makes one wondrous
kind. — GARRICK: *Prologue on quitting the
stage*
  Non ignara mali, miseris succurrere disco
(Being not unacquainted with woe, I learn
to help the unfortunate). — VIRGIL: *Æneid,
Lib. I, L. 630*
[5] And lards the lean earth as he walks along.
— SHAKESPEARE: *King Henry IV, Part I, Act
II, Sc. 2, L. 120*
[6] Nullum est jam dictum, quod non dictum
sit prius (There is nothing said, which has
not been said before). — TERENCE: *Eunuchus,
Prol., L. 41*

. . . Our story-dressers do as much; he that comes last is commonly best.

Anatomy of Melancholy.
Democritus to the Reader

I say with Didacus Stella, a dwarf standing on the shoulders of a giant may see farther than a giant himself.[1]

Ibid.

It is most true, *stylus virum arguit,* — our style bewrays us.[2]

Ibid.

I had not time to lick it into form, as a bear doth her young ones.[3]

Ibid.

As that great captain, Ziska, would have a drum made of his skin when he was dead, because he thought the very noise of it would put his enemies to flight.

Ibid.

Like the watermen that row one way and look another.[4]

Ibid.

Smile with an intent to do mischief, or cozen him whom he salutes.

Ibid.

Him that makes shoes go barefoot himself.[5]

Ibid.

---

[1] A dwarf on a giant's shoulders sees farther of the two. — HERBERT: *Jacula Prudentum*
A dwarf sees farther than the giant when he has the giant's shoulders to mount on. — COLERIDGE: *The Friend, Sect. I, Essay VIII*
Pigmæi gigantum humeris impositi plusquam ipsi gigantes vident (Pigmies placed on the shoulders of giants see more than the giants themselves). — *Didacus Stella in Lucan, 10, Tom. II*
[2] Le style est l'homme même (The style is the man himself). — COMTE DE BUFFON [1707–1788]: *Discours sur le Style,* on admission to the French Academy [1753]
[3] Arts and sciences are not cast in a mould, but are formed and perfected by degrees, by often handling and polishing, as bears leisurely lick their cubs into form. — MONTAIGNE: *Apology for Raimond Sebond, Book II, Chap. XII*
[4] Like watermen who look astern while they row the boat ahead. — PLUTARCH: *Whether 'twas rightfully said, Live concealed*
Like rowers, who advance backward. — MONTAIGNE: *Of Profit and Honour, Book III, Chap. I*
[5] Who is worse shod than the shoemaker's wife? — HEYWOOD: *Proverbes, Part I, Chap. II*

Rob Peter, and pay Paul.[1]

Anatomy of Melancholy.
Democritus to the Reader

Penny wise, pound foolish.

Ibid.

Women wear the breeches.

Ibid.

Like Æsop's fox, when he had lost his tail, would have all his fellow foxes cut off theirs.[2]

Ibid.

Hannibal, as he had mighty virtues, so had he many vices; he had two distinct persons in him.

Ibid.

Carcasses bleed at the sight of the murderer.[3]

Ibid. Part I, Sect. 1, Memb. 2, Subsect. 5

Every man hath a good and a bad angel attending on him in particular, all his life long.

Ibid. Sect. 2, Memb. 1, Subsect. 2

[Witches] steal young children out of their cradles, *ministerio dæmonum,* and put deformed in their rooms, which we call changelings.

Ibid. Subsect. 3

Can build castles in the air.

Ibid.

That which Pythagoras said to his scholars of old, may be for ever applied to melancholy men, *A fabis abstinete,* eat no beans.[4]

Ibid. Memb. 2, Subsect. 1

Joh. Mayor, in the first book of his "History of Scotland," contends much for the wholesomeness of oaten bread; it was objected to him, then living at Paris, that his countrymen fed on oats and base grain. . . . And yet Wecker out of Galen calls it horse-meat, and fitter juments than men to feed on.[5]

Ibid.

---

[1] To robbe Peter and pay Poule. — HEYWOOD: *Proverbes, Part I, Chap. II*
RABELAIS: *Book I, Chap. II*
[2] Aesop: *Fables, Book V, Fable 5*
[3] See Chaucer, page 6.
[4] There will be no beans in the Almost Perfect State. — DON MARQUIS: *The Almost Perfect State*
[5] Oats, — a grain which is generally given to horses, but in Scotland supports the people.

Cookery is become an art, a noble science; cooks are gentlemen.

Anatomy of Melancholy. Part I,
Sect. 2, Memb. 2, Subsect. 2

As much valour is to be found in feasting as in fighting, and some of our city captains and carpet knights will make this good, and prove it.[1]

Ibid.

No rule is so general, which admits not some exception.

Ibid. Subsect. 3

Idleness is an appendix to nobility.

Ibid. Subsect. 6

Why doth one man's yawning make another yawn?

Ibid. Memb. 3, Subsect. 2

A nightingale dies for shame if another bird sings better.

Ibid. Subsect. 6

They do not live but linger.

Ibid. Subsect. 10

[Diseases] crucify the soul of man, attenuate our bodies, dry them, wither them, shrivel them up like old apples, make them so many anatomies.

Ibid.

[Desire] is a perpetual rack, or horsemill, according to Austin, still going round as in a ring.

Ibid. Subsect. 11

[The rich] are indeed rather possessed by their money than possessors.

Ibid. Subsect. 12

Like a hog, or dog in the manger, he doth only keep it because it shall do nobody else good, hurting himself and others.

Ibid.

Were it not that they are loath to lay out money on a rope, they would be hanged forthwith, and sometimes die to save charges.

Ibid.

A mere madness, to live like a wretch and die rich.

Anatomy of Melancholy. Part I,
Sect. 2, Memb. 3, Subsect. 12

I may not here omit those two main plagues and common dotages of human kind, wine and women, which have infatuated and besotted myriads of people; they go commonly together.

Ibid. Subsect. 13

All our geese are swans.[1]

Ibid. Subsect. 14

Though they [philosophers] write *contemptu gloriæ,* yet as Hieron observes, they will put their names to their books.

Ibid.

They are proud in humility; proud in that they are not proud.[2]

Ibid.

We can make majors and officers every year, but not scholars; kings can invest knights and barons, as Sigismund the emperor confessed.[3]

Ibid. Subsect. 15

Hinc quam sic calamus sævior ense, patet. The pen worse than the sword.[4]

Ibid. Memb. 4, Subsect. 4

Homer himself must beg if he want means, and as by report sometimes he did "go from door to door and sing ballads, with a company of boys about him."[5]

Ibid. Subsect. 6

— SAMUEL JOHNSON: *Dictionary of the English Language*

[1] Carpet knights are men who are by the prince's grace and favour made knights at home. . . . They are called carpet knights because they receive their honours in the court and upon carpets. — GERVASE MARKHAM [1568–1637]: *Booke of Honour* [1625]
Carpet knights. — DU BARTAS [ed. 1621], P. 311

[1] Every man thinks his own geese swans. — DICKENS: *The Cricket on the Hearth, Chirp the Second*

[2]   His favourite sin
     Is pride that apes humility.
          SOUTHEY: *The Devil's Walk*

[3] When Abraham Lincoln heard of the death of a private, he said he was sorry it was not a general: "I could make more of them."

[4] Tant la plume a eu sous le roi d'avantage sur l'épée (So far had the pen under the king the superiority over the sword). — LOUIS DE ROUVROY SAINT SIMON: [1675–1755]: *Mémoires, Vol. III, P. 517 (1702)* [ed. 1856]
The pen is mightier than the sword. — BULWER LYTTON: *Richelieu, Act II, Sc. 2*
Pyrrhus was used to say that Cineas had taken more towns with his words than he with his arms. — PLUTARCH: *Pyrrhus*

[5] Seven wealthy towns contend for Homer dead,

See one promontory (said Socrates of old), one mountain, one sea, one river, and see all.[1]

Anatomy of Melancholy. Part I, Sect. 2, Memb. 4, Subsect. 7

Felix Plater notes of some young physicians, that study to cure diseases, catch them themselves, will be sick, and appropriate all symptoms they find related of others to their own persons.

Ibid. Sect. 3, Memb. 1, Subsect. 2

Aristotle said melancholy men of all others are most witty.

Ibid. Subsect. 3

Like him in Æsop, he whipped his horses withal, and put his shoulder to the wheel.[2]

Ibid. Part II, Sect. 1, Memb. 2

Fabricius finds certain spots and clouds in the sun.

Ibid. Sect. 2, Memb. 3

If the heavens then be penetrable, and no lets, it were not amiss to make wings and fly up; and some new-fangled wits, methinks, should some time or other find out.

Ibid.

Seneca thinks the gods are well pleased when they see great men contending with adversity.

Ibid. Sect. 2, Memb. 1, Subsect. 1

Machiavel says virtue and riches seldom settle on one man.

Ibid. Memb. 2

Almost in every kingdom the most ancient families have been at first princes' bastards; their worthiest captains, best wits, greatest scholars, brav-

est spirits in all our annals, have been base [born].

Anatomy of Melancholy. Part II, Sect. 2, Memb. 2

As he said in Machiavel, *omnes eodem patre nati*, Adam's sons, conceived all and born in sin, etc. "We are by nature all as one, all alike, if you see us naked; let us wear theirs and they our clothes, and what is the difference?"

Ibid.

Set a beggar on horseback and he will ride a gallop.[1]

Ibid.

Christ himself was poor. . . . And as he was himself, so he informed his apostles and disciples, they were all poor, prophets poor, apostles poor.[2]

Ibid. Memb. 3

Who cannot give good counsel? 'Tis cheap, it costs them nothing.

Ibid.

Many things happen between the cup and the lip.[3]

Ibid.

What can't be cured must be endured.

Ibid.

Everything, saith Epictetus, hath two handles, — the one to be held by, the other not.

Ibid.

All places are distant from heaven alike.

Ibid. Memb. 4

How much are we bound to those munificent Ptolemies, bountiful Maecenates, heroical patrons, divine spirits,

---

Through which the living Homer begged his bread.

ANONYMOUS

Great Homer's birthplace seven rival cities claim,
Too mighty such monopoly of Fame.
THOMAS SEWARD [1708-1790]: *On Shakespeare's Monument at Stratford-upon-Avon*
Seven cities warred for Homer being dead;
Who living had no roofe to shrowd his head.
THOMAS HEYWOOD: *Hierarchie of the Blessed Angells*
Seven cities claimed him. — ROBERT BROWNING: *Development*
[1] A blade of grass is always a blade of grass, whether in one country or another. — JOHNSON: *Piozzi, 52*
[2] ÆSOP: *Hercules and the Waggoner*

[1] Beggars mounted run their horse to death. — SHAKESPEARE: *King Henry VI, Part III, Act I, Sc. 4, L. 127*
Set a beggar on horseback, and he'll outride the Devil. — BOHN: *Foreign Proverbs, German*
[2] See Wotton, page 114.
[3] There is many a slip 'twixt the cup and the lip. — HAZLITT: *English Proverbs*
Though men determine, the gods doo dispose; and oft times many things fall out betweene the cup and the lip. — ROBERT GREENE [1560-1592]: *Perimedes the Blacke-Smith [1588]*
See Edward Bulwer Lytton, page 425.

that have provided for us so many well-furnished libraries.

Anatomy of Melancholy. Part II, Sect. 2, Memb. 4

The commonwealth of Venice in their armoury have this inscription: "Happy is that city which in time of peace thinks of war."

Ibid. Memb. 6

Every man, as the saying is, can tame a shrew but he that hath her.

Ibid.

Divers have been relieved [of melancholy] by exonerating themselves to a faithful friend.

Ibid.

Tobacco, divine, rare, superexcellent tobacco, which goes far beyond all the panaceas, potable gold and philosopher's stones, a sovereign remedy to all diseases.

Ibid. Sect. 4, Memb. 2, Subsect. 2

"Let me not live," said Aretine's Antonia, "if I had not rather hear thy discourse than see a play."

Ibid. Part III, Sect. 1, Memb. 1, Subsect. 1

Every schoolboy hath that famous testament of Grunnius Corocotta Porcellus at his fingers' end.

Ibid.

Birds of a feather will gather together.

Ibid. Subsect. 2

And hold one another's noses to the grindstone hard.[1]

Ibid. Memb. 3

Every man for himself, his own ends, the Devil for all.[2]

Ibid.

No cord nor cable can so forcibly draw, or hold so fast, as love can do with a twined thread.[3]

Ibid. Sect. 2, Memb. 1, Subsect. 2

To enlarge or illustrate this power and effect of love is to set a candle in the sun.

Anatomy of Melancholy. Part III, Sect. 2, Memb. 1, Subsect. 2

He is only fantastical that is not in fashion.

Ibid. Memb. 2, Subsect. 3

[Quoting Seneca] Cornelia kept her in talk till her children came from school, "and these," said she, "are my jewels."

Ibid.

To these crocodile tears [1] they will add sobs, fiery sighs, and sorrowful countenance.

Ibid. Subsect. 4

Marriage and hanging go by destiny; matches are made in heaven.[2]

Ibid. Subsect. 5

Diogenes struck the father when the son swore.

Ibid.

Though it rain daggers with their points downward.

Ibid. Memb. 3

Going as if he trod upon eggs.

Ibid.

I light my candle from their torches.

Ibid. Memb. 5, Subsect. 1

England is a paradise for women and hell for horses; Italy a paradise for horses, hell for women, as the diverb goes.

Ibid. Sect. 3, Memb. 1, Subsect. 2

The miller sees not all the water that goes by his mill.[3]

Ibid. Memb. 4, Subsect. 1

As clear and as manifest as the nose in a man's face.[4]

Ibid.

Make a virtue of necessity.[5]

Ibid.

---

[1] See Heywood, page 13, and Middleton, page 116.

[2] See Heywood, page 18.

[3] One hair of a woman can draw more than a hundred pair of oxen. — JAMES HOWELL [1594–1666]: *Letters, Book II, IV* [1621]
She knows her man, and when you rant and swear,
Can draw you to her with a single hair.
DRYDEN: *Persius, Satire V, L. 246*

Beauty draws us with a single hair. —
POPE: *The Rape of the Lock, Canto II, L. 27*
And from that luckless hour my tyrant fair
Has led and turned me by a single hair.
ROBERT BLAND [1779–1825]: *Anthology, P. 20* [ed. 1813]

[1] See Chapman, page 29.

[2] See Heywood, page 12, and Shakespeare, page 45.

[3] See Heywood, page 17.

[4] See Shakespeare, page 33.

[5] See Chaucer, page 4.

Where God hath a temple, the Devil will have a chapel.[1]
*Anatomy of Melancholy. Part III,
    Sect. 4, Memb. 1, Subsect. 1*

If the world will be gulled, let it be gulled.
                                    Ibid. Subsect. 2

For "ignorance is the mother of devotion," as all the world knows.[2]
                                    Ibid.

The fear of some divine and supreme powers keeps men in obedience.[3]
                                    Ibid.

Out of too much learning become mad.
                                    Ibid.

The Devil himself, which is the author of confusion and lies.
                                    Ibid. Subsect. 3

Isocrates adviseth Demonicus, when he came to a strange city, to worship by all means the gods of the place.
                                    Ibid. Subsect. 5

When they are at Rome, they do there as they see done.[4]
                                    Ibid. Memb. 2, Subsect. 1

---

[1] For where God built a church, there the Devil would also build a chapel. — MARTIN LUTHER: *Table Talk, LXVII*
God never had a church but there, men say,
The Devil a chapel hath raised by some wyles.
        WILLIAM DRUMMOND [1585–1649]:
                    Posthumous Poems
No sooner is a temple built to God but the Devil builds a chapel hard by. — HERBERT: *Jacula Prudentum*
Wherever God erects a house of prayer,
The Devil always builds a chapel there.
        DANIEL DEFOE [1661–1731]: *The True-
                    born Englishman, Part I, L. 1*
[2] Ignorance is the mother of devotion. — JEREMY TAYLOR [1613–1667]: *To a Person Newly Converted* [1657]
Your ignorance is the mother of your devotion to me. — DRYDEN: *The Maiden Queen, Act I, Sc. 2*
[3] The fear o' hell's a hangman's whip
To haud the wretch in order.
        BURNS: *Epistle to a Young Friend*
[4] Saint Augustine was in the habit of dining upon Saturday as upon Sunday; but being puzzled with the different practices then prevailing (for they had begun to fast at Rome on Saturday), consulted Saint Ambrose on the subject. Now at Milan they did not fast on Saturday, and the answer of the Milan saint was this: "Quando hic sum, non jejuno Sabbato; quando Romæ sum, jejuno Sab-

One religion is as true as another.
*Anatomy of Melancholy. Part III,
    Sect. 4, Memb. 2, Subsect. 1*

They have cheveril consciences that will stretch.
                                    Ibid. Subsect. 3

THOMAS WARD
[1577–1639]

Where to elect there is but one,
'Tis Hobson's choice, — take that or none.[1]
                    *England's Reformation.
                    Chapter IV, Page 326*

JOHN FLETCHER
[1579–1625]

Man is his own star; and the soul that can
Render an honest and a perfect man
Commands all light, all influence, all fate.
Nothing to him falls early, or too late.
Our acts our angels are, or good or ill,
Our fatal shadows that walk by us still.
        Upon an "Honest Man's Fortune"

Man is his own star; and that soul that can
Be honest is the only perfect man.[2]
                                    Ibid.

---

bato" (When I am here, I do not fast on Saturday; when at Rome, I do fast on Saturday). — *Epistle XXXVI, to Casulanus*
[1] *Thomas Hobson* [1544–1631], of whom Steele wrote in *The Spectator, No. 509* [October 14, 1712]:
Mr. Tobias Hobson, from whom we have the expression, . . . was a carrier, . . . the first in this Island who let out hackney-horses. He lived in Cambridge, and observing that the scholars rid hard, his manner was to keep a large stable of horses, with boots, bridles, and whips. . . . When a man came for an horse, he was led into the stable, where there was great choice, but he obliged him to take the horse which stood next to the stable-door; so that every customer was alike well served according to his chance, and every horse ridden with the same justice. From whence it became a proverb, when what ought to be your election was forced upon you, to say Hobson's Choice.
[2] An honest man's the noblest work of God. — POPE: *Essay on Man, Epistle IV, L. 248.*
BURNS: *The Cotter's Saturday Night*

Weep no more, nor sigh, nor groan,
Sorrow calls no time that's gone;
Violets plucked, the sweetest rain
Makes not fresh nor grow again.[1]
> *The Queen of Corinth. Act III,*
> *Sc. 2*

Hence, all you vain delights,
As short as are the nights
Wherein you spend your folly!
There's naught in this life sweet
But only melancholy.
> *Melancholy* [2]

O woman, perfect woman! what dis-
    traction
Was meant to mankind when thou wast
    made a devil!
> *Monsieur Thomas. Act. III, Sc. 1*

Let us do or die.[3]
> *The Island Princess. Act II, Sc. 4*

Hit the nail on the head.
> *Love's Cure. Act II, Sc. 1*

I find the medicine worse than the
    malady.[4]
> *Ibid. Act III, Sc. 2*

He went away with a flea in 's ear.
> *Ibid. Sc. 3*

Drink to-day, and drown all sorrow;
You shall perhaps not do 't to-morrow.
> *The Bloody Brother. Act II, Sc. 2*

And he that will to bed go sober
Falls with the leaf still in October.[5]
> *Ibid.*

Three merry boys, and three merry
    boys,

---

[1] Weep no more, Lady! weep no more,
    Thy sorrow is in vain;
    For violets plucked, the sweetest showers
    Will ne'er make grow again.
PERCY: *Reliques, The Friar of Orders Gray*
[2] See William Strode, page 144.
[3] Let us do or die. — BURNS: *Bannockburn.*
CAMPBELL: *Gertrude of Wyoming, Part III,*
St. 37
    This expression is a kind of common prop-
erty, being the motto, we believe, of a Scottish
family. — SIR WALTER SCOTT: *Miscellanies,*
Vol. I, P. 153, Review of Gertrude
[4] See Bacon, page 110.
[5] The following well-known catch, or glee,
is formed on this song: —
    He who goes to bed, and goes to bed sober,
    Falls as the leaves do, and dies in October;
    But he who goes to bed, and goes to bed
        mellow,
    Lives as he ought to do, and dies an honest
        fellow.

And three merry boys are we,[1]
As ever did sing in a hempen string
    Under the gallows-tree.
> *The Bloody Brother. Act III, Sc. 2*

Hide, oh, hide those hills of snow
    Which thy frozen bosom bears,
On whose tops the pinks that grow
    Are of those that April wears!
But first set my poor heart free,
Bound in icy chains by thee.[2]
> *Ibid. Act V, Sc. 2*

Something given that way.
> *The Lover's Progress. Act I, Sc. 1*

Deeds, not words.[3]
> *Ibid. Act III, Sc. 4*

JOHN TAYLOR
("THE WATER POET")
[1580–1625]

Laugh and be fat.
> *Title of a tract*

God sends meat, and the Devil sends
cooks.[4]
> *Works, Vol. II, Page 85 [ed. 1630.]*

JOHN WEBSTER
[1580–1625]

Glories, like glow-worms, afar off shine
    bright,
But look'd too near have neither heat
    nor light.[5]
> *Duchess of Malfi. Act IV, Sc. 2*

I know death hath ten thousand sev-
    eral doors
For men to take their exit.[6]
> *Ibid.*

---

[1] Three merry men be we. — PEELE: *Old
Wives' Tale* [1595]. WEBSTER (quoted):
Westward Hoe [1607]
[2] See Shakespeare, page 37.
[3] Deeds, not words. — BUTLER: *Hudibras,
Part I, Canto I, L. 867*
[4] See Tusser, page 19.
[5] Love is like a landscape which doth stand
    Smooth at a distance, rough at hand.
        ROBERT HEGGE [1599–1629]: *On Love*
'Tis distance lends enchantment to the view,
And robes the mountain in its azure hue.
    CAMPBELL: *Pleasures of Hope, Part I, L. 7*
[6] Death hath a thousand doors to let out
life. — PHILIP MASSINGER: *A Very Woman,
Act V, Sc. 4*
Death hath so many doors to let out life.
— BEAUMONT AND FLETCHER: *The Custom of
the Country, Act II, Sc. 2*

Heaven-gates are not so highly arch'd
As princes' palaces; they that enter
    there
Must go upon their knees.
        Duchess of Malfi. Act IV, Sc. 2

Other sins only speak; murder shrieks
    out.[1]
                                Ibid.

'Tis just like a summer bird-cage in
a garden, — the birds that are without despair to get in, and the birds that
are within despair and are in a consumption for fear they shall never get
out.[2]
        The White Devil. Act I, Sc. 2

Condemn you me for that the duke did
    love me?
So may you blame some fair and crystal
    river
For that some melancholic, distracted
    man
Hath drown'd himself in 't.
            Ibid. Act III, Sc. 2

We cease to grieve, cease to be fortune's
    slaves,
Yes, cease to die, by dying.
                Ibid. Sc. 6

Vain the ambition of kings
Who seek by trophies and dead things
To leave a living name behind,
And weave but nets to catch the wind.
        The Devil's Law Case. Song

The chiefest action for a man of great
    spirit
Is never to be out of action.
The soul was never put into the body,
Which has so many rare and curious
    pieces
Of mathematical motion, to stand still.
        Honorable Employment

Is not old wine wholesomest, old
pippins toothsomest, old wood burns
brightest, old linen wash whitest? Old
soldiers, sweetheart, are surest, and old
lovers are soundest.[3]
        Westward Hoe. Act II, Sc. 2

I saw him now going the way of all
flesh.
        Westward Hoe. Act II, Sc. 2

SIR THOMAS OVERBURY
[1581–1613]

Give me, next good, an understanding
    wife,
By nature wise, not learnèd much by
    art;
Some knowledge on her part will, all
    her life,
More scope of conversation impart.
                The Wife

    In part to blame is she,
Which hath without consent been only
    tried:
He comes too near that comes to be de-
    nied.[1]
                                Ibid.

Books are a part of man's prerogative;
In formal ink they thoughts and voices
    hold,
That we to them our solitude may give,
And make time present travel that of
    old.
                                Ibid.

BISHOP RICHARD CORBET
[1582–1635]

Farewell rewards and fairies,
    Good housewives now may say.
        Farewell to the Fairies. Stanza 1

Nor too much wealth nor wit come to
    thee,
So much of either may undo thee.
        To His Son, Vincent Corbet

I wish thee all thy mother's graces,
Thy father's fortunes and his places.
                                Ibid.

PHILIP MASSINGER
[1583–1640]

    To be nobly born
Is now a crime.
        The Roman Actor. Act I, Sc. 1
                            [1629]

The thousand doors that lead to death. —
BROWNE: *Religio Medici, Part I, Sect. XLIV*
[1] See Chaucer, page 6.
[2] See Davies, page 115.
[3] See Bacon, page 113.

[1] In part she is to blame that has been tried:
    He comes too near that comes to be de-
    nied.
LADY MARY WORTLEY MONTAGU [1689–
    1762]: *The Lady's Resolve*

I in mine own house am an emperor [1]
And will defend what's mine.
>> *The Roman Actor. Act I, Sc. 2*

Whose wealth
Arithmetic cannot number.
>> *Ibid. Sc. 3*

This many-headed monster.[2]
>> *Ibid. Act III, Sc. 2*

Grim death.[3]
>> *Ibid. Act IV, Sc. 2*

Good kings are mourned for after life;
but ill,
And such as governed only by their will
And not their reason, unlamented
fall, —
No good man's tear shed at their funeral.
>> *Ibid. Act V, Sc. 2*

Some undone widow sits upon mine
arm,
And takes away the use of it; [4] and my
sword,
Glued to my scabbard with wronged
orphans' tears,
Will not be drawn.
>> *A New Way to Pay Old Debts.*
>> *Act V, Sc. 1 [1632]*

Death hath a thousand doors to let out
life.[5]
>> *A Very Woman. Act V, Sc. 4*

THOMAS HEYWOOD
[? –1649]

The world's a theatre, the earth a stage
Which God and Nature do with actors
fill.[6]
>> *Apology for Actors [1612]*

---

[1] A man's house is his castle. — SIR EDWARD COKE: *Third Institute, P. 162*
[2] Many-headed multitude. — SIR PHILIP SIDNEY: *Arcadia, Book II*
Many-headed monster. — SCOTT: *The Lady of the Lake, Canto V, St. 30*
[3] Grim death, my son and foe. — MILTON: *Paradise Lost, Book II, L. 804*
[4] See Middleton, page 116.
[5] See John Webster, page 127.
[6] All the world's a stage,
And all the men and women merely players.
SHAKESPEARE: *As You Like It, Act II, Sc. 7, L. 139*
The world's a stage on which all parts are

Pack clouds away, and welcome day,
With night we banish sorrow.
>> *Pack Clouds Away, Stanza 1*

I hold he loves me best that calls me
Tom.
>> *Hierarchie of the Blessed Angells*

Seven cities warred for Homer being
dead,
Who living had no roofe to shrowd his
head.[1]
>> *Ibid.*

Fear and amazement beat upon my
heart,
Even as a madman beats upon a drum.[2]
>> *A Woman Killed with Kindness.*
>> *Act IV, Sc. 1*

Her that ruled the rost in the kitchen.[3]
>> *History of Women. Page 286*
>> *[ed. 1624]*

FRANCIS BEAUMONT
[1584–1616]

What things have we seen
Done at the Mermaid! heard words that
have been
So nimble and so full of subtile flame
As if that every one from whence they
came
Had meant to put his whole wit in a
jest,
And resolved to live a fool the rest
Of his dull life.
>> *Letter to Ben Jonson*

Mortality, behold and fear!
What a change of flesh is here!
>> *On the Tombs in Westminster*
>> *Abbey*

Here are sands, ignoble things,
Dropt from the ruined sides of kings.
>> *Ibid.*

It is always good
When a man has two irons in the fire.
>> *The Faithful Friends. Act I, Sc. 2*

---

played. — MIDDLETON: *A Game at Chess, Act V, Sc. 1*
[1] See Burton, page 123. See Browning, page 493.
[2] A madman beating on a drum. — OSCAR WILDE: *Ballad of Reading Gaol*
[3] See Skelton, page 9.

JOHN SELDEN
[1584–1654]

Equity is a roguish thing. For Law we have a measure, know what to trust to; Equity is according to the conscience of him that is Chancellor, and as that is larger or narrower, so is Equity. 'Tis all one as if they should make the standard for the measure we call a "foot" a Chancellor's foot; what an uncertain measure would this be! One Chancellor has a long foot, another a short foot, a third an indifferent foot. 'Tis the same thing in the Chancellor's conscience.

Table Talk. Equity

Old friends are best. King James used to call for his old shoes; they were easiest for his feet.[1]

Ibid. Friends

Humility is a virtue all preach, none practise; and yet everybody is content to hear.

Ibid. Humility

'Tis not the drinking that is to be blamed, but the excess.

Ibid.

Commonly we say a judgment falls upon a man for something in him we cannot abide.

Ibid. Judgments

Ignorance of the law excuses no man; not that all men know the law, but because 'tis an excuse every man will plead, and no man can tell how to refute him.

Ibid. Law

No man is the wiser for his learning.

Ibid. Learning

Wit and wisdom are born with a man.

Ibid.

Few men make themselves masters of the things they write or speak.

Ibid.

Take a straw and throw it up into the air, — you may see by that which way the wind is.

Ibid. Libels

Philosophy is nothing but discretion.

Ibid. Philosophy

[1] See Bacon, page 113.

Marriage is a desperate thing.

Table Talk. Marriage

Thou little thinkest what a little foolery governs the world.[1]

Ibid. Pope

They that govern the most make the least noise.

Ibid. Power

Syllables govern the world.

Ibid.

Never king dropped out of the clouds.

Ibid.

Never tell your resolution beforehand.

Ibid. Wisdom

Wise men say nothing in dangerous times.

Ibid.

Pleasures are all alike, simply considered in themselves. He that takes pleasure to hear sermons enjoys himself as much as he that hears plays.

Ibid. Pleasure

A King is a thing men have made for their own sakes, for quietness' sake. Just as in a Family one man is appointed to buy the meat.

Ibid. Of a King

BEAUMONT AND FLETCHER [2]

Francis Beaumont [1584–1616] and John Fletcher [1579–1625]

All your better deeds
Shall be in water writ, but this in marble.[3]

Philaster. Act V, Sc. 3

Upon my burned body lie lightly, gentle earth.

The Maid's Tragedy. Act I, Sc. 2

[1] Behold, my son, with how little wisdom the world is governed. — Axel Oxenstiern [1583–1654]

[2] Of whose partnership John Aubrey [1626–1697] said: "There was a wonderfull consimility of phansey. They lived together not far from the Play-house, had one wench in the house between them, the same cloathes and cloake, &c."

[3] See Shakespeare, page 74.

Then, my good girls, be more than
 women wise;
At least be more than I was; and be
 sure
You credit any thing the light gives
 life to,
Before a man.
    The Maid's Tragedy. Act II, Sc. 2
A soul as white as heaven.
        Ibid. Act IV, Sc. 1
It shrew'd discretion, the best part of
 valour.[1]
    A King and No King. Act IV, Sc. 3
There is a method in man's wicked-
 ness, —
It grows up by degrees.[2]
        Ibid. Act V, Sc. 4
As cold as cucumbers.
    Cupid's Revenge. Act I, Sc. 1
Calamity is man's true touchstone.[3]
    *Four Plays in One. The Triumph
        of Honour, Sc. 1*
Kiss till the cow comes home.
    Scornful Lady. Act III, Sc. 1
    It would talk, —
    Lord! how it talked!
        Ibid. Act V, Sc. 1
Beggars must be no choosers.
        Ibid. Sc. 3
No better than you should be.[4]
    The Coxcomb. Act IV, Sc. 3
From the crown of the head to the sole
 of the foot.[5]
    *The Honest Man's Fortune.
        Act. II, Sc. 2*
One foot in the grave.[6]
    *The Little French Lawyer.
        Act I, Sc. 1*

Go to grass.
    *The Little French Lawyer.
        Act IV, Sc. 7*
There is no jesting with edge tools.[1]
        Ibid.
Though I say it that should not say it.
    *Wit at Several Weapons. Act II,
        Sc. 2*
I name no parties.[2]
        Ibid. Sc. 3
Whistle, and she'll come to you.[3]
    Wit Without Money. Act IV, Sc. 4
Let the world slide.[4]
        Ibid. Act V, Sc. 2

    The fit's upon me now!
    Come quickly, gentle lady;
    The fit's upon me now.
        Ibid. Sc. 4
He comes not in my books.[5]
        The Widow. Act I, Sc. 1
Death hath so many doors to let out
 life.[6]
    *The Custom of the Country.
        Act II, Sc. 2*
Of all the paths [that] lead to a
 woman's love
Pity's the straightest.[7]
    The Knight of Malta. Act I, Sc. 1
Nothing can cover his high fame but
 heaven;
No pyramids set off his memories,
But the eternal substance of his great-
 ness, —
To which I leave him.
    The False One. Act II, Sc. 1

---

[1] See Shakespeare, page 63.
[2] Nemo repente fuit turpissimus (No man
ever became extremely wicked all at once).
— JUVENAL: *II, 83*
Ainsi que la vertu, le crime a ses degrés (As
virtue has its degrees, so has vice). — RACINE:
Phédre, Act IV, Sc. 2
[3] Ignis aurum probat, miseria fortes viros
(Fire is the test of gold; adversity, of strong
men). — SENECA: *De Providentia, V, 9*
[4] She is no better than she should be. —
HENRY FIELDING: *The Temple Beau, Act IV,
Sc. 3*
[5] See Shakespeare, page 39.
[6] An old doting fool, with one foot already
in the grave. — PLUTARCH: *On the Training
of Children*

[1] It is no jesting with edge tools. — *The
True Tragedy of Richard III* [1594]
[2] The use of "party" in the sense of "person" occurs in the *Book of Common Prayer*,
More's *Utopia*, Shakespeare, Ben Jonson, Fuller, and other old English writers.
[3] Whistle, and I'll come to ye. — BURNS:
Whistle, etc.
[4] See Shakespeare, page 52.
[5] See Shakespeare, page 38.
[6] See Webster, page 127.
[7] Pity's akin to love. — THOMAS SOUTH-
ERNE [1660–1746]: *Oroonoko, Act II, Sc. 1*
[1696]
Pity swells the tide of love. — YOUNG:
Night Thoughts, Night III, L. 107

Thou wilt scarce be a man before thy
    mother.[1]
> *Love's Cure. Act II, Sc. 2*

What's one man's poison, signor,
Is another's meat or drink.[2]
> *Ibid. Act III, Sc. 2*

Primrose, first-born child of Ver,
Merry springtime's harbinger.
> *The Two Noble Kinsmen. Act I,*
> *Sc. 1*

O great corrector of enormous times,
Shaker of o'er-rank states, thou grand
    decider
Of dusty and old titles, that healest with
    blood
The earth when it is sick, and curest
    the world
O' the pleurisy of people!
> *Ibid. Act V, Sc. 1*

JOHN FORD
[1586–1639]

Diamond cut diamond.
> *The Lover's Melancholy. Act I,*
> *Sc. 1 [1629]*

NATHANIEL FIELD
[1587–1633]

Needle in a bottle of hay.
> *A Woman's a Weathercock.*

THOMAS HOBBES
[1588–1679]

Words are wise men's counters,—
they do but reckon by them; but they
are the money of fools.
> *Leviathan. Part I, Chap. IV*

The privilege of absurdity; to which
no living creature is subject but man
only.
> *Ibid. Chap. V*

Sudden glory is the passion which
maketh those grimaces called laughter.
> *Ibid. Chap. VI*

The secret thoughts of a man run
over all things, holy, profane, clean, ob-

scene, grave, and light, without shame
or blame.
> *Leviathan. Part I, Chap. VIII*

As the nature of foul weather lieth
not in a shower or two of rain but in
an inclination thereto of many days together, so the nature of war consisteth
not in actual fighting but in the known
disposition thereto during all the time
there is no assurance to the contrary.
All other time is peace.
> *Ibid. Chap. XIII*

[In a state of nature] No arts, no
letters, no society, and, which is worst
of all, continual fear and danger of
violent death, and the life of man solitary, poor, nasty, brutish, and short.
> *Ibid.*

The praise of ancient authors proceeds not from the reverence of the
dead, but from the competition and mutual envy of the living.
> *Ibid. Review and Conclusion*

Such truth as opposeth no man's
profit nor pleasure is to all men welcome.
> *Ibid.*

GEORGE WITHER
[1588–1667]

Shall I, wasting in despair,
Die because a woman's fair?
Or make pale my cheeks with care,
'Cause another's rosy are?
Be she fairer than the day,
Or the flowery meads in May,
  If she be not so to me,
  What care I how fair she be?
> *The Author's Resolution. Stanza 1*

If she love me, this believe,
I will die, ere she shall grieve.
If she slight me when I woo,
I can scorn and let her go.
  For if she be not for me,
  What care I for whom she be?
> *Ibid. Stanza 5*

Her waist exceeding small,
  The fives did fit her shoe:
But now alas she's left me,
  Falero, lero, loo!
> *I Loved a Lass*

---

[1] But strive still to be a man before your
mother. — COWPER: *Connoisseur, Motto of
No. III*

[2] Quod ali cibus est aliis fiat acre venenum
(What is food to one may be fierce poison to
others). — LUCRETIUS: *IV, 637*

Hang sorrow! care will kill a cat,[1]
And therefore let's be merry.
> *Poem on Christmas*

'Twas I that beat the bush,
The bird to others flew.
> *A Love Sonnet. Stanza 11*

Though I am young, I scorn to flit
On the wings of borrowed wit.
> *The Shepherd's Hunting*

And I oft have heard defended, —
Little said is soonest mended.
> *Ibid.*

WILLIAM BROWNE
[1591–1643]

For her gait, if she be walking;
  Be she sitting, I desire her
For her state's sake; and admire her
  For her wit if she be talking.
> *Song*

Whose life is a bubble, and in length a
span.[2]
> *Britannia's Pastorals. Book I,*
> *Song*

There is no season such delight can
bring,
As summer, autumn, winter, and the
spring.
> *Variety*

ROBERT HERRICK
[1591–1674]

What is a kiss? Why this, as some approve:
The sure, sweet cement, glue, and lime
of love.
> *A Kiss*

Bid me to live, and I will live
  Thy Protestant to be,
Or bid me love, and I will give
  A loving heart to thee.
> *To Anthea. Stanza 1*

Cherry ripe, ripe, ripe, I cry,
Full and fair ones, — come and buy!
If so be you ask me where
They do grow, I answer, there,
Where my Julia's lips do smile, —

---

[1] See Jonson, page 118.
[2] See Bacon, page 112.

There's the land, or cherry-isle.
> *Cherry Ripe* [1]

Some asked me where the rubies grew,
  And nothing I did say;
But with my finger pointed to
  The lips of Julia.
> *The Rock of Rubies, and the*
> *Quarrie of Pearls*

Some asked how pearls did grow, and
  where?
  Then spoke I to my girl
To part her lips, and showed them
  there
  The quarelets of pearl.[2]
> *Ibid.*

A sweet disorder in the dress
Kindles in clothes a wantonness.
> *Delight in Disorder*

A winning wave, deserving note,
In the tempestuous petticoat;
A careless shoe-string, in whose tie
I see a wild civility, —
Do more bewitch me than when art
Is too precise in every part.
> *Ibid.*

You say to me-wards your affection's
  strong;
Pray love me little, so you love me long.[3]
> *Love me Little, Love me Long*

Gather ye rosebuds while ye may,
  Old Time is still a-flying,
And this same flower that smiles to-
  day
To-morrow will be dying.[4]
> *To the Virgins to make much*
> *of Time*

Fair daffadills, we weep to see
  You haste away so soon.
> *To Daffadills*

---

[1] "Cherry ripe" was a familiar street-cry of
the time. Compare THOMAS CAMPION:
> There cherries grow that none may buy
> Till cherry-ripe themselves do cry.

[2] Those cherries fairly do enclose
> Of orient pearl a double row.
> THOMAS CAMPION: *Cherry-Ripe*

[3] See Heywood, page 16, and Marlowe,
page 31.

[4] Let us crown ourselves with rose-buds,
before they be withered. — *Wisdom of Solomon, II, 8*
> Gather the rose of love, whilest yet is time.
— SPENSER: *The Faerie Queene, Book II,*
Canto XII, St. 75

Thus woe succeeds a woe, as wave a
    wave.[1]
> *Sorrows Succeed*

Her pretty feet, like snails, did creep
    A little out, and then,[2]
As if they played at bo-peep,
    Did soon draw in again.
> *To Mistress Susanna Southwell*

Her eyes the glow-worm lend thee,
The shooting-stars attend thee;
    And the elves also,
    Whose little eyes glow
Like the sparks of fire, befriend thee.
> *The Night Piece to Julia*

Thus times do shift, — each thing his
    turn does hold;
New things succeed, as former things
    grow old.
> *Ceremonies for Candlemas Eve*

Out-did the meat, out-did the frolick
    wine.
> *Ode for Ben Jonson*

Attempt the end, and never stand to
    doubt;
Nothing's so hard but search will find
    it out.
> *Seek and Find*

But ne'er the rose without the thorn.
> *The Rose*

Here a little child I stand
Heaving up my either hand.
Cold as paddocks though they be,
Here I lift them up to Thee,
For a benison to fall
On our meat, and on us all.
> *A Child's Grace*

Smell of the lamp.
> *His Farewell to Sack*

Her legs were such Diana shows
When tuckt up she a-hunting goes
With Buskins shortned to descrie
The happy dawning of her thigh.
> *The Vision*

Get up, sweet Slug-a-bed, and see
The Dew bespangling Herbe and Tree.
> *Corinna's Going a-Maying*

[1] See Shakespeare, page 96.
[2] Her feet beneath her petticoat,
    Like little mice, stole in and out.
    SIR JOHN SUCKLING: *Ballad upon a
        Wedding, St. 8*

Wash, dresse, be brief in praying:
Few Beads are best, when once we goe
    a-Maying.
> *Corinna's Going a-Maying*

Whenas in silks my Julia goes,
Then, then (methinks) how sweetly
    flowes
That liquefaction of her clothes.
> *Upon Julia's Clothes*

HENRY KING, BISHOP OF CHICHESTER
[1592–1669]

And that tame Lover who unlocks his
    heart
Unto his mistress, teaching her an art
To plague himself, shows her the secret
    way
How she may tyrannize another day!
> *The Steed that Comes to
        Understand*

Thou art the book, —
The library whereon I look.
> *Exequy on the Death of a
        Beloved Wife*

Then we shall rise
And view ourselves with clearer eyes
In that calm region where no night
Can hide us from each other's sight.
> *Ibid.*

Stay for me there; I will not fail
To meet thee in that hollow vale.
> *Ibid.*

FRANCIS QUARLES
[1592–1644]

Death aims with fouler spite
At fairer marks.[1]
> *Divine Poems [ed. 1669]*

Sweet Phosphor, bring the day!
Light will repay
The wrongs of night;
Sweet Phosphor, bring the day!
> *Emblems. Book I, Emblem 14*

Be wisely worldly, be not worldly wise.
> *Ibid. Book II, Emblem 2*

This house is to be let for life or years;
Her rent is sorrow, and her income
    tears.

[1] Death loves a shining mark, a signal blow.
— YOUNG: *Night Thoughts, Night V, L. 1011*

Cupid, 't has long stood void; her bills
  make known,
She must be dearly let, or let alone.
                    Emblems. Book II,
                    Emblem 10, Ep. 10

The slender debt to Nature's quickly
  paid,[1]
Discharged, perchance, with greater
  ease than made.
                    Ibid. Emblem 13

The next way home's the farthest way
  about.[2]
    Ibid. Book IV, Emblem 2, Ep. 2

It is the lot of man but once to die.
        Ibid. Book V, Emblem 7

And what's a life? — a weary pilgrimage,
Whose glory in one day doth fill the
  stage
With childhood, manhood, and decrepit
  age.
            What is Life? Stanza 1

Let all thy joys be as the month of
  May,
And all thy days be as a marriage day:
Let sorrow, sickness, and a troubled
  mind
Be stranger to thee, let them never find
Thy heart at home.
                    To a Bride

THOMAS RAVENSCROFT
[1592–1635]

Nose, nose, nose, nose!
And who gave thee that jolly red nose?
Sinament and Ginger, Nutmegs and
  Cloves,
And that gave me my jolly red nose.
        Deuteromelia. Song No. 7[3]
                    [1609]

---

[1] To die is a debt we must all of us discharge. — EURIPIDES: *Alcestis, L. 418*
[2] The longest way round is the shortest way
home. — BOHN: *Foreign Proverbs, Italian*
[3] Interpolated in BEAUMONT AND FLETCH-
ER'S *The Knight of the Burning Pestle*, Act I,
Sc. 3. RAVENSCROFT'S *Deuteromelia* was a supplement to his *Pammelia*, which was the earliest collection of rounds, catches, and canons
printed in England.

GEORGE HERBERT
[1593–1632]

To write a verse or two is all the praise
    That I can raise.
                    Praise. Stanza 1

Sweet day, so cool, so calm, so bright,
The bridal of the earth and sky.[1]
                    Virtue. Stanza 1

Sweet spring, full of sweet days and
    roses,
A box where sweets compacted lie.
                    Ibid. Stanza 3

Only a sweet and virtuous soul,
Like seasoned timber, never gives.
                    Ibid. Stanza 4

            Like summer friends,[2]
Flies of estate and sunneshine.
                    The Answer

A servant with this clause
    Makes drudgery divine;
Who sweeps a room, as for Thy laws,
    Makes that and th' action fine.
                    The Elixir. Stanza 5

'You must sit down,' says Love, 'and
    taste my meat.'
    So I did sit and eat.
        Love Bade Me Welcome. Stanza 3

A verse may find him who a sermon
    flies,[3]
And turn delight into a sacrifice.
            The Church Porch. Stanza 1

Drink not the third glass, which thou
    canst not tame,
When once it is within thee.
                    Ibid. Stanza 5

Dare to be true: nothing can need a
    lie;
A fault which needs it most, grows two
    thereby.[4]
                    Ibid. Stanza 13

---

[1] Quoted in IZAAK WALTON'S *The Compleat
Angler*
[2] Summer friends. — GRAY: *Hymn on Adversity*
[3] That many people read a song
    Who will not read a sermon.
        WINTHROP MACKWORTH PRAED [1802–
        1839]: *The Chant of the Brazenhead,
        St. 1*
[4] And he that does one fault at first,
    And lies to hide it, makes it two.
        ISAAC WATTS: *Song XV*

Look to thy mouth: diseases enter there.
> *The Church Porch. Stanza 22*

By all means use sometimes to be alone.
> *Ibid. Stanza 25*

By no means run in debt: take thine own measure.

Who cannot live on twenty pound a year,
Cannot on forty.
> *Ibid. Stanza 30*

Wit's an unruly engine, wildly striking
Sometimes a friend, sometimes the engineer.
> *Ibid. Stanza 41*

Be useful where thou livest.
> *Ibid. Stanza 55*

Sum up at night, what thou hast done by day.
> *Ibid. Stanza 76*

For thirty pence he did my death devise,[1]
Who at three hundred did the ointment prize.[2]
> *The Sacrifice. Stanza 5*

Most things move th' under-jaw, the Crocodile not.[3]
Most things sleep lying, th' Elephant leans or stands.[4]
> *Providence. Stanza 35*

Bibles laid open, millions of surprises.
> *Sinne. Stanza 2*

Religion stands on tiptoe in our land,
Ready to pass to the American strand.
> *The Church Militant*

If goodness lead him not, yet weariness
May toss him to my breast.
> *The Pulley. Stanza 4*

---

[1] For thirty pence our Saviour was sold.
Percy's *Reliques, King John and the Abbot of Canterbury, St. 21*
Still as of old men by themselves are priced —
For thirty pieces Judas sold himself, not Christ.
HESTER H. CHOLMONDELEY [19th century]
[2] Why was not this ointment sold for three hundred pence, and given to the poor? — *John, XII, 4*
[3] The crocodile does not move the lower jaw, but is the only animal that brings down its upper jaw to the under one. — HERODOTUS, *Customs of the Egyptians*
[4] Leans the huge elephant. — JAMES THOMSON: *The Seasons, Summer, L. 725*

The fineness which a hymn or psalm affords
Is, when the soul unto the lines accords.
> *A True Hymn. Stanza 2*

Wouldst thou both eat thy cake and have it?[1]
> *The Size. Stanza 3*

Do well and right, and let the world sink.[2]
> *The Country Parson, Chapter 29*

Man proposeth, God disposeth.[3]
> *Jacula Prudentum* [1640]

Pleasing ware is half sold.
> *Ibid.*

Love, and a cough, cannot be hid.
> *Ibid.*

A dwarf on a giant's shoulder, sees further of the two.[4]
> *Ibid.*

Who is so deaf as he that will not hear?
> *Ibid.*

Praise day at night,[5] and life at the end.
> *Ibid.*

---

[1] Would yee both eat your cake and have your cake? — JOHN HEYWOOD: *Proverbes, Part II, Chap. 9.* ISAAC BICKERSTAFF: *Thomas and Sally*
[2] Ruat cœlum, fiat voluntas tua (Though the sky fall, let Thy will be done). — SIR T. BROWNE: *Religio Medici, Part II, Sect. XI*
Fiat justitia ruat cœlum (Let justice be done though the heavens should fall). — WILLIAM WATSON [1559–1603]: *Ten Quodlibetical Questions Concerning Religion and State* [1601]. WILLIAM PRYNNE [1600–1669]: *Fresh Discovery of Prodigious New Wandering-Blazing Stars* [2d ed., London, 1646]. NATHANIEL WARD [1578–1652]: *Simple Cobbler of Agawam in America* [1647]
Fiat Justitia et ruat Mundus (Let justice be done and let the world perish). — [1552], *P. 25,* Camden Society [1840]. LUCY AIKIN [1781–1864]: *Court and Times of James I, Vol. II, P. 500* [1625].
January 31, 1642, the House of Lords used these words: *Regnet Justitia et ruat Cœlum.* — *Old Parliamentary History, Vol. X, P. 28*
[3] See Thomas à Kempis, page 8.
[4] See Burton, page 122.
[5] Thou shalt not praise the day till night is falling,
However fair its dawn and noon may be;
Ofttimes at eventide come storms appalling,
Setting the lightning and the thunder free.
ANONYMOUS

Deceive not thy physician, confessor, nor lawyer.

Jacula Prudentum [*1640*]

Who would do ill ne'er wants occasion.

Ibid.

A snow year, a rich year.

Ibid.

The fox, when he cannot reach the grapes, says they are not ripe.

Ibid.

Love your neighbour, yet pull not down your hedge.

Ibid.

The mill cannot grind with water that's past.[1]

Ibid.

Good words are worth much, and cost little.

Ibid.

Hell is full of good meanings and wishings.[2]

Ibid.

Whose house is of glass, must not throw stones at another.

Ibid.

By suppers more have been killed than Galen ever cured.

Ibid.

The lion is not so fierce as they paint him.[3]

Ibid.

Go not for every grief to the physician, nor for every quarrel to the lawyer, nor for every thirst to the pot.

Ibid.

The best mirror is an old friend.

Ibid.

Stay till the lame messenger come, if you will know the truth of the thing.

Ibid.

When you are an anvil, hold you still; when you are a hammer, strike your fill.

Jacula Prudentum [*1640*]

He that lies with the dogs, riseth with fleas.

Ibid.

He that is not handsome at twenty, nor strong at thirty, nor rich at forty, nor wise at fifty, will never be handsome, strong, rich, or wise.

Ibid.

The buyer needs a hundred eyes, the seller not one.

Ibid.

My house, my house, though thou art small, thou art to me the Escurial.

Ibid.

Trust not one night's ice.

Ibid.

The back door robs the house.

Ibid.

The wearer knows where the shoe wrings.[1]

Ibid.

For want of a nail the shoe is lost, for want of a shoe the horse is lost, for want of a horse the rider is lost.[2]

Ibid.

Pension never enriched a young man.

Ibid.

One flower makes no garland.

Ibid.

One enemy is too much.

Ibid.

The offender never pardons.[3]

Ibid.

Help thyself, and God will help thee.[4]

Ibid.

A feather in hand is better than a bird in the air.[5]

Ibid.

---

[1] The mill cannot grind
With the water that is past.
SARAH DOUDNEY [1843–1926]: *The Lesson of the Water-Mill* [1864]
The mill will never grind again with water that is past. DANIEL CRAIG McCALLUM [1815–1878]:*The Water-Mill* [1870]
See BURTON E. STEVENSON: *Famous Single Poems* [1923].

[2] Sir, Hell is paved with good intentions. — SAMUEL JOHNSON [1775]: *Boswell's Life of Dr. Johnson,* Everyman ed., *Vol. I, P. 555*

[3] The lion is not so fierce as painted. — FULLER: *Expecting Preferment*

[1] See Plutarch, page 997, and Cervantes, page 1037.

[2] A little neglect may breed mischief: for want of a nail, etc. — BENJAMIN FRANKLIN: *Maxim prefixed to Poor Richard's Almanac* [1757]

[3] They ne'er pardon who have done the wrong. — DRYDEN: *The Conquest of Granada*

[4] God helps those who help themselves. — SIDNEY: *Discourses on Government, Sect. XXIII.* FRANKLIN: *Poor Richard's Almanac*

[5] See Heywood, page 15, Plutarch, page 1005, and Cervantes, page 1037.

Thursday come, and the week is
gone.
Jacula Prudentum [*1640*]
Time is the rider that breaks youth.
Ibid.
You may bring a horse to the river,
but he will drink when and what he
pleaseth.
Ibid.
Before you make a friend, eat a
bushel of salt with him.
Ibid.
Show me a liar, and I will show thee
a thief.
Ibid.
No sooner is a temple built to God,
but the Devil builds a chapel hard by.[1]
Ibid.
One father is more than a hundred
school-masters.
Ibid.
Reason lies between the spur and the
bridle.
Ibid.
One sword keeps another in the
sheath.
Ibid.
God's mill grinds slow, but sure.[2]
Ibid.
Every one thinks his sack heaviest.
Ibid.
It is a poor sport that is not worth
the candle.
Ibid.
Give not Saint Peter so much, to
leave Saint Paul nothing.[3]
Ibid.
He that lends, gives.
Ibid.
Poverty is no sin.
Ibid.
Words are women, deeds are men.[4]
Ibid.

[1] See Burton, page 126.
[2] Though the mills of God grind slowly, yet
they grind exceeding small. — F. von Logau
[1604–1655]: *Retribution* (translated by
Longfellow)
[3] See Heywood, page 14.
[4] Words are men's daughters, but God's sons
are things. — Samuel Madden [1686–1765]:
Boulter's Monument (supposed to have been
inserted by Dr. Johnson in 1745)
See Johnson, page 232.

To a close shorn sheep, God gives wind
by measure.[1]
Jacula Prudentum [*1640*]
None knows the weight of another's
burthen.
Ibid.
One hour's sleep before midnight is
worth three after.
Ibid.
He hath no leisure who useth it not.
Ibid.
Half the world knows not how the
other half lives.
Ibid.
Life is half spent before we know
what it is.
Ibid.
All are presumed good till they are
found in a fault.
Ibid.
Every mile is two in winter.
Ibid.
Pains to get, care to keep, fear to
lose.
Ibid.
The eye is bigger than the belly.
Ibid.
His bark is worse than his bite.
Ibid.
To build castles in Spain.
Jacula Prudentum [*second
edition, 1651*]
Whatsoever was the father of a dis-
ease, an ill diet was the mother.
Ibid.
He that steals an egg will steal an ox.
Ibid.
Those that God loves do not live
long.[2]
Ibid.
Of a pig's tail you can never make a
good shaft.[3]
Ibid.

[1] Dieu mésure le froid à la brebis tondue
(God proportions the wind to the shorn
sheep). — Henri Estienne: *Prémices* [1594]
"God tempers the wind," said Maria, "to
the shorn lamb." Laurence Sterne: *A Sentimental Journey, Maria*
[2] See Byron, page 354, and Wordsworth,
page 302.
[3] You cannot make, my Lord, I fear,
A velvet purse of a sow's ear.
John Wolcot ("Peter Pindar") [1738–
1819]: *Lord B. and His Notions*

The mouse that hath but one hole is quickly taken.[1]

Jacula Prudentum [*second edition, 1651*]

There is an hour wherein a man might be happy all his life could he find it.

Ibid.

Woe be to him who reads but one book.[2]

Ibid.

IZAAK WALTON
[1593–1683]

Of which, if thou be a severe, sour-complexioned man, then I here disallow thee to be a competent judge.

The Compleat Angler. Author's Preface

I have laid aside business, and gone a-fishing.

Ibid.

Angling may be said to be so like the mathematics that it can never be fully learnt.

Ibid.

As no man is born an artist, so no man is born an angler.

Ibid.

I shall stay him no longer than to wish him a rainy evening to read this following discourse; and that if he be an honest angler, the east wind may never blow when he goes a fishing.

Ibid.

As the Italians say, Good company in a journey makes the way to seem shorter.

Ibid. Part I, Chap. I

You can't make a silk purse out of a sow's ear. — JONATHAN SWIFT: *Polite Conversation, Dialogue II*

As certainly as you can make a velvet cap out of a sow's ear. — STERNE: *Tristram Shandy, Book IV*

The proverb says you can't make a silk purse out of a sow's ear. — DICKENS: *David Copperfield, Chap. 30*

[1] See Chaucer, page 7.

[2] When St. Thomas Aquinas was asked in what manner a man might best become learned, he answered, "By reading one book." The *homo unius libri* is indeed proverbially formidable to all conversational figurantes. — SOUTHEY: *The Doctor, P. 164*

I am, sir, a Brother of the Angle.

The Compleat Angler.
Part I, Chap. I

Doubt not but angling will prove to be so pleasant that it will prove to be, like virtue, a reward to itself.[1]

Ibid.

Sir Henry Wotton was a most dear lover and a frequent practiser of the Art of Angling; of which he would say, " 'Twas an employment for his idle time, which was then not idly spent, a rest to his mind, a cheerer of his spirits, a diverter of sadness, a calmer of unquiet thoughts, a moderator of passions, a procurer of contentedness"; and "that it begat habits of peace and patience in those that professed and practised it."

Ibid.

You will find angling to be like the virtue of humility, which has a calmness of spirit and a world of other blessings attending upon it.[2]

Ibid.

I remember that a wise friend of mine did usually say, "That which is everybody's business is nobody's business."

Ibid. Chap. II

An honest Ale-house where we shall find a cleanly room, Lavender in the Windows, and twenty Ballads stuck about the wall.

Ibid.

---

[1] Virtue is her own reward. — DRYDEN: *Tyrannic Love, Act III, Sc. 1*

That virtue is her own reward, is but a cold principle. — SIR THOMAS BROWNE: *Religio Medici, Part I, Sect. XLVII.*

Virtue is to herself the best reward. — HENRY MORE [1614–1687]: *Cupid's Conflict*

Virtue is its own reward. — PRIOR: *Imitations of Horace, Book III, Ode 2.* GAY: *Epistle to Methuen.* JOHN HOME [1722–1808]: *Douglas, Act III, Sc. 1*

Virtue was sufficient of herself for happiness. — DIOGENES LAERTIUS: *Plato, XLII*

Ipsa quidem virtus sibimet pulcherrima merces (Virtue herself is her own fairest reward). — SILIUS ITALICUS [25?–99]: *Punica, Lib. XIII, L. 663*

[2] There is certainly something in angling . . . that tends to produce a gentleness of spirit, and a pure serenity of mind. — WASHINGTON IRVING: *The Sketch-Book, The Angler*

Good company and good discourse are the very sinews of virtue.
> *The Compleat Angler.*
> *Part I, Chap. II*

The Chavender or Chub.
> *Ibid. Chap. III*

An excellent angler, and now with God.
> *Ibid. Chap. IV*

Old-fashioned poetry, but choicely good.
> *Ibid.*

A draught of Red Cow's milk.
> *Ibid.*

No man can lose what he never had.
> *Ibid. Chap. V*

We may say of angling as Dr. Boteler[1] said of strawberries: "Doubtless God could have made a better berry, but doubtless God never did"; and so, if I might be judge, God never did make a more calm, quiet, innocent recreation than angling.
> *Ibid.*

Thus use your frog: put your hook through his mouth and out at his gills, and then with a fine needle and silk sew the upper part of his leg with only one stitch to the arming wire of your hook, or tie the frog's leg above the upper joint to the armed wire; and in so doing use him as though you loved him.
> *Ibid. Chap. VIII*

This dish of meat is too good for any but anglers, or very honest men.
> *Ibid.*

Health is the second blessing that we mortals are capable of, — a blessing that money cannot buy.
> *The Compleat Angler.*
> *Part I, Chap. XXI*

And upon all that are lovers of virtue, and dare trust in his Providence, and be quiet and go a-angling.
> *Ibid.*

I in these flowery meads would be;
These crystal springs should solace me;
To whose harmonious bubbling noise,
I with my angle would rejoice.
> *The Angler's Wish. Stanza 1*

But God, who is able to prevail, wrestled with him; marked him for his own.[1]
> *Life of Donne*

The great secretary of Nature, — Sir Francis Bacon.[2]
> *Life of Herbert*

Oh, the gallant fisher's life!
It is the best of any;
'Tis full of pleasure, void of strife,
And 'tis beloved by many.
> *The Angler (John Chalkhill)* [3]

THOMAS CAREW
[1595–1639]

Ask me no more where Jove bestows,
When June is past, the fading rose.
> *To Celia. Stanza 1*

Ask me no more if East or West
The phoenix builds her spicy nest.
> *Ibid. Stanza 5*

He that loves a rosy cheek,
Or a coral lip admires,
Or from star-like eyes doth seek
Fuel to maintain in his fires; —

---

[1] William Butler [1535–1618], styled by Dr. Thomas Fuller in his *Worthies of England, Suffolk,* the "Aesculapius of our age." He attended Prince Henry [1612]. This praise of the strawberry first appeared in the second edition of *The Angler,* [1655]. Roger Williams, in his *Key into the Language of America,* [1643] *P. 98,* says: "One of the chiefest doctors of England was wont to say, that God could have made, but God never did make, a better berry."

I know one person who is simular enough to think Cambridge the very best spot on the habitable globe. "Doubtless God *could* have made a better, but doubtless he never did." — James Russell Lowell: *On a Certain Condescension in Foreigners*

[1] Melancholy marked him for her own. — Gray: *The Epitaph*

[2] Plato, Aristotle, and Socrates are secretaries of Nature. — James Howell [1594–1666]: *Letters, Book II, Letter XI*

[3] In 1683, the year in which he died, Walton prefixed a preface to a work edited by him: "Thealma and Clearchus, a Pastoral History, in smooth and easy verse; written long since by John Chalkhill Esq., an acquaintant and friend of Edmund Spenser."

Chalkhill, — a name unappropriated, a verbal phantom, a shadow of a shade. Chalkhill is no other than our old piscatory friend incognito. — Thomas Zouch [1737–1815]: *Life of Izaak Walton*

As old Time makes these decay,
So his flames must waste away.
>> *Disdain Returned. Stanza 1*
The firstling of the infant year.
>> *The Primrose*
Then fly betimes, for only they
Conquer Love that run away.
>> *Conquest by Flight*
An untimely grave.[1]
>> *On the Duke of Buckingham*
The magic of a face.
>> *Epitaph on the Lady S——*

JAMES SHIRLEY
[1596–1666]

The glories of our blood and state
  Are shadows, not substantial things;
There is no armour against fate;
  Death lays his icy hand on kings.
>> *Contention of Ajax and Ulysses.*
>> *Scene 3* [*1659*]
The garlands wither on your brow;
Then boast no more your mighty deeds.
>> *Ibid.*
Only the actions of the just
Smell sweet and blossom in their dust.[2]
>> *Ibid.*
Death calls ye to the crowd of common
  men.
>> *Cupid and Death*

OLIVER CROMWELL
[1599–1658]

The State, in choosing men to serve
it, takes no notice of their opinions. If
they be willing faithfully to serve it,
that satisfies.
>> *Before the Battle of Marston*
>> *Moor* [*July 2, 1644*]
A few honest men are better than
numbers. If you choose godly, honest
men to be captains of horse, honest men
will follow them.
>> *Reorganization of the Army*
>> [*1645*]

---

[1] An untimely grave. — NAHUM TATE
[1652–1715] AND NICHOLAS BRADY [1659–
1726]: *Metrical Version of Psalm VII*
[2] The sweet remembrance of the just
Shall flourish when he sleeps in dust.
TATE AND BRADY: *Psalm CXXXII, 6*

I would have been glad to have lived
under my woodside, and to have kept
a flock of sheep, rather than to have
undertaken this government.
>> *To Parliament* [*1658*]
I would be willing to live to be further serviceable to God and His people,
but my work is done! Yet God will be
with His people!
>> [*September 1, 1658, two days*
>> *before his death*]

SAMUEL BUTLER
[1600–1680]

And pulpit, drum ecclesiastick,[1]
Was beat with fist instead of a stick.
>> *Hudibras. Part I, Canto I, Line 11*
We grant, although he had much wit,
He was very shy of using it.
>> *Ibid. Line 45*
Beside, 'tis known he could speak
  Greek
As naturally as pigs squeak;[2]
That Latin was no more difficile
Than to a blackbird 'tis to whistle.
>> *Ibid. Line 51*
He could distinguish and divide
A hair 'twixt south and southwest side.
>> *Ibid. Line 67*
For rhetoric, he could not ope
His mouth, but out there flew a trope.
>> *Ibid. Line 81*
For all a rhetorician's rules
Teach nothing but to name his tools.
>> *Ibid. Line 89*
A Babylonish dialect
Which learned pedants much affect.
>> *Ibid. Line 93*
For he by geometric scale
Could take the size of pots of ale.
>> *Ibid. Line 121*
And wisely tell what hour o' the day
The clock does strike, by algebra.
>> *Ibid. Line 125*

---

[1] This is the first we hear of the "drum ec-
clesiastic" beating up for recruits in worldly
warfare in our country. — WASHINGTON IRV-
ING: *Knickerbocker's History of New York,
Book V, Chap. 7*
[2] He Greek and Latin speaks with greater ease
Than hogs eat acorns, and tame pigeons peas.
LIONEL CRANFIELD, EARL OF MIDDLESEX
[1575–1645]: *Panegyric on Tom
Coriate*

Whatever sceptic could inquire for,
For every why he had a wherefore.[1]
    Hudibras. Part I, Canto I, Line 131
Where entity and quiddity,
The ghosts of defunct bodies, fly.
    Ibid. Line 145
He knew what's what,[2] and that's as
    high
As metaphysic wit can fly.
    Ibid. Line 149
Such as take lodgings in a head
That's to be let unfurnished.[3]
    Ibid. Line 161
'Twas Presbyterian true blue.
    Ibid. Line 191
And prove their doctrine orthodox,
By apostolic blows and knocks.
    Ibid. Line 199
Compound for sins they are inclined to,
By damning those they have no mind
    to.
    Ibid. Line 215
The trenchant blade, Toledo trusty,
For want of fighting was grown rusty,
And ate into itself, for lack
Of somebody to hew and hack.
    Ibid. Line 359
For rhyme the rudder is of verses,
With which, like ships, they steer their
    courses.
    Ibid. Line 463
He ne'er consider'd it, as loth
To look a gift-horse in the mouth.[4]
    Ibid. Line 489
And force them, though it was in spite
Of Nature and their stars, to write.
    Ibid. Line 647
Quoth Hudibras, "I smell a rat![5]
Ralpho, thou dost prevaricate."
    Ibid. Line 821
Or shear swine, all cry and no wool.[6]
    Ibid. Line 852
And bid the devil take the hin'most.[7]
    Ibid. Canto II, Line 633

[1] See Shakespeare, pages 37, 67.
[2] See Skelton, page 10.
[3] See Bacon, page 113.
[4] See Heywood, page 13.
[5] See Middleton, page 116.
[6] See Fortescue, page 9.
[7] Bid the Devil take the slowest. — PRIOR:
On the Taking of Namur
    Deil tak the hindmost. — BURNS: *To a
Haggis*

I'll make the fur
Fly 'bout the ears of the old cur.
    *Hudibras. Part I, Canto III,
        Line 277*
These reasons made his mouth to water.
    Ibid. Line 379
I am not now in fortune's power:
He that is down can fall no lower.[1]
    Ibid. Line 871
Cheer'd up himself with ends of verse
And sayings of philosophers.
    Ibid. Line 1011
But those that write in rhyme still
    make
The one verse for the other's sake;
For one for sense, and one for rhyme,
I think's sufficient at one time.
    Ibid. Part II, Canto I, Line 23
Some have been beaten till they know
What wood a cudgel's of by th' blow;
Some kick'd until they can feel whether
A shoe be Spanish or neat's leather.
    Ibid. Line 221
Quoth she, I've heard old cunning
    stagers
Say fools for arguments use wagers.
    Ibid. Line 297
For what is worth in anything
But so much money as 'twill bring?
    Ibid. Line 465
Love is a boy by poets styl'd;
Then spare the rod and spoil the child.[2]
    Ibid. Line 843
The sun had long since in the lap
Of Thetis taken out his nap,
And, like a lobster boil'd the morn
From black to red began to turn.
    Ibid. Canto II, Line 29
For truth is precious and divine, —
Too rich a pearl for carnal swine.
    Ibid. Line 257
He that imposes an oath makes it,
Not he that for convenience takes it;
Then how can any man be said
To break an oath he never made?
    Ibid. Line 377

    The Devil may take the hindmost. —
SOUTHEY: *The March to Moscow*
[1] He that is down needs fear no fall. —
BUNYAN: *Pilgrim's Progress, Part II*
[2] See Skelton, page 9.

As the ancients
Say wisely, have a care o' th' main
  chance,[1]
And look before you ere you leap; [2]
For as you sow, ye are like to reap.[3]
　　　Hudibras. Part II, Canto II,
　　　　　　　Line 501
Doubtless the pleasure is as great
Of being cheated as to cheat.[4]
　　　　Ibid. Canto III, Line 1
He made an instrument to know
If the moon shine at full or no.
　　　　　Ibid. Line 261
To swallow gudgeons ere they're
  catch'd,
And count their chickens ere they're
  hatch'd.[5]
　　　　　Ibid. Line 923
But Hudibras gave him a twitch
As quick as lightning in the breech,
Just in the place where honour's lodg'd,
As wise philosophers have judg'd;
Because a kick in that part more
Hurts honour than deep wounds before.
　　　　　Ibid. Line 1065
As men of inward light are wont
To turn their optics in upon 't.
　　Ibid. Part III, Canto I, Line 481
What makes all doctrines plain and
  clear?
About two hundred pounds a year.
And that which was prov'd true before
Prove false again? Two hundred more.
　　　　　Ibid. Line 1277
Nick Machiavel had ne'er a trick,
Though he gave his name to our Old
  Nick.[6]
　　　　　Ibid. Line 1313
With crosses, relics, crucifixes,

---

[1] See Lyly, page 23.
See Shakespeare, page 68.
[2] See Heywood, page 11.
[3] Whatsoever a man soweth, that shall he
also reap. — *Galatians, VI, 7*
[4] This couplet is enlarged on by SWIFT in
his *Tale of a Tub,* where he says that the
happiness of life consists in being well deceived.
[5] Many count their chickens before they
are hatched. — CERVANTES: *Don Quixote, Part
II, Chap. 55*
Reckon not on your chickens before they are
hatched. — JEFFERYS TAYLOR: [1792–1853]:
The Milkmaid
[6] See Macaulay, page 397.

Beads, pictures, rosaries, and pixes, —
The tools of working our salvation
By mere mechanic operation.
　　　Hudibras. Part III, Canto I,
　　　　　　　Line 1495
True as the dial to the sun,[1]
Although it be not shin'd upon.
　　　Ibid. Canto II, Line 175
For those that fly may fight again,
Which he can never do that's slain.[2]
　　　Ibid. Canto III, Line 243

---

[1] True as the needle to the pole,
　Or as the dial to the sun.
　　BARTON BOOTH [1681–1733]: *Song*
[2] Sed omissis quidem divinis exhortationibus
illum magis Græcum versiculum secularis
sententiæ sibi adhibent, "Qui fugiebat, rursus
prœliabitur": ut et rursus forsitan fugiat (But
overlooking the divine exhortations, they act
rather upon that Greek verse of worldly
significance, "He who flees will fight again,"
and that perhaps to betake himself again to
flight). — TERTULLIAN: *De Fuga in Persecutione, C. 10*
A corresponding Greek passage is ascribed
to Menander. See *Fragments* (appended to
Aristophanes in Didot's *Bibliothèque des au-
teurs Grecs, P. 91*).
　That same man that runnith awaie
　Maie again fight an other daie.
　　ERASMUS: *Apothegms* [1542], trans-
　　　　　　lated by Udall
　Celuy qui fuit de bonne heure
　Peut combattre derechef
　(He who flies at the right time can fight
　again).
　　　　　Satyre Menippée [1594]
　Qui fuit peut revenir aussi;
　Qui meurt, il n'en est pas ainsi
　(He who flies can also return; but it is not so
　with him who dies).
　　PAUL SCARRON [1610–1660]
　He that fights and runs away
　May turn and fight another day;
　But he that is in battle slain
　Will never rise to fight again.
　　JAMES RAY: *History of the Rebellion*
　　　　　　[1752], *P. 48*
　For he who fights and runs away
　May live to fight another day;
　But he who is in battle slain
　Can never rise and fight again.
　　GOLDSMITH: *The Art of Poetry on a
　　New Plan* [1761], *Vol. II, P. 147*
　But since the man that runs away
　Lives to die another day,
　And cowards' funerals, when they come,
　Are not wept so well at home,
　Therefore, though the best is bad,
　Stand and do the best, my lad.
　　A. E. HOUSMAN: *The Day of Battle*

He that complies against his will
Is of his own opinion still.
Hudibras. Part III, Canto III,
Line 547

And poets by their sufferings grow,[1]
As if there were no more to do,
To make a poet excellent,
But only want and discontent.
Fragments

WILLIAM STRODE
[1602–1645]

There's naught in this life sweet,
If man were wise to see 't,
  But only melancholy;
  O sweetest Melancholy! [2]
  A Song in Praise of Melancholy

Fountain heads and pathless groves,
Places which pale passion loves.
Ibid.

SIR KENELM DIGBY
[1603–1665]

The hot water is to remain upon it
[the tea] no longer than whiles you can
say the Miserere Psalm very leisurely.
The Closet Opened. Tea with Eggs

Before the Deer be killed, he ought
to be hunted and chafed as much as
may be.
Ibid. To Bake Venison

All Matter is indifferent to Form.
Of the Vegetation of Plants

If she [the soul after death] be built
up again to a whole Man, out of the
general Magazine of Matter.
Ibid.

[1]   Most wretched men
Are cradled into poetry by wrong;
They learn in suffering what they teach in
  song.
      SHELLEY: *Julian and Maddalo*
[2] JOHN FLETCHER introduced this song in his
play, *The Nice Valour, Act III, Sc. 3,* and it
has also been attributed to him.
Naught so sweet as melancholy. — BURTON:
Anatomy of Melancholy, Author's Abstract

SIR THOMAS BROWNE
[1605–1682]

Too rashly charged the troops of
error, and remain as trophies unto the
enemies of truth.
Religio Medici. Part I,
Sect. VI [1642]

I love to lose myself in a mystery, to
pursue my Reason to an *O altitudo!*
Ibid. Sect. IX

Rich with the spoils of Nature.[1]
Ibid. Sect. XIII

Nature is the art of God.[2]
Ibid. Sect. XVI

The thousand doors that lead to
death.[3]
Ibid. Sect. XLIV

The heart of man is the place the
Devil dwells in: I feel sometimes a hell
within myself.[4]
Ibid. Sect. LI

There is no road or ready way to
virtue.
Ibid. Sect. LV

It is the common wonder of all men,
how among so many millions of faces
there should be none alike.[5]
Ibid. Part II, Sect. II

That worldly principle, *Charity be-*
gins at home.
Ibid. Sect. V

[1] Rich with the spoils of time. — GRAY:
Elegy, St. 13
[2] The course of Nature is the art of God. —
YOUNG: *Night Thoughts, Night IX, L. 1267*
[3] See John Webster, page 127.
[4] The mind is its own place, and in itself
    Can make a heaven of hell, a hell of
       heaven.
    MILTON: *Paradise Lost, Book I, L. 253*
[5] The human features and countenance, although composed of but some ten parts or
little more, are so fashioned that among so
many thousands of men there are no two
in existence who cannot be distinguished
from one another. — PLINY: *Natural History,*
Book VII, Chap. I
Of a thousand shavers, two do not shave so
much alike as not to be distinguished. —
JOHNSON [1777]: *Boswell's Life, Vol. II,*
P. 120, Everyman ed.
There never were in the world two opinions
alike, no more than two hairs or two grains;
the most universal quality is diversity. —
MONTAIGNE: *Of the Resemblance of Children*
to their Fathers, Book I, Chap. XXXVII

There is music even in the beauty, and the silent note which Cupid strikes, far sweeter than the sound of an instrument; for there is music wherever there is harmony, order, or proportion; and thus far we may maintain the music of the spheres.[1]

Religio Medici. Part II, Sect. IX

Ruat cœlum, fiat voluntas tua.[2]

Ibid. Sect. XI

Sleep is a death; oh, make me try
By sleeping, what it is to die,
And as gently lay my head
On my grave, as now my bed!

Ibid. Sect. XII

This is the dormitive I take to bedward.

Ibid.

Times before you, when even living men were antiquities, — when the living might exceed the dead, and to depart this world could not be properly said to go unto the greater number.[3]

Dedication to Urn-Burial

I look upon you as a gem of the old rock.[4]

Ibid.

Quietly rested under the drums and tramplings of three conquests.

Urn-Burial. Chapter 5

What song the Sirens sang, or what name Achilles assumed when he hid himself among women.

Ibid.

The iniquity of oblivion blindly scattereth her poppy.

Ibid.

Herostratus lives that burnt the temple of Diana; he is almost lost that built it.[5]

Ibid.

[1] See Shakespeare, page 55.
Oh, could you view the melody
Of every grace
And music of her face.
LOVELACE: *Orpheus to Beasts*
[2] See Herbert, page 136.
[3] 'Tis long since Death had the majority. — BLAIR: *The Grave, Part II, L. 449*
[4] Adamas de rupe præstantissimus (A most excellent diamond from the rock).
A chip of the old block. — PRIOR: *Life of Burke*
[5] The aspiring youth that fired the Ephesian dome

Oblivion is not to be hired: the greater part must be content to be as though they had not been.

Urn-Burial. Chapter 5

Man is a noble animal, splendid in ashes and pompous in the grave.

Ibid.

When we desire to confine our words, we commonly say they are spoken under the rose.[1]

Vulgar Errors

An old and gray-headed error.

Ibid.

EDMUND WALLER
[1605–1687]

The yielding marble of her snowy breast.

On a Lady Passing through a Crowd of People

That eagle's fate and mine are one,
Which on the shaft that made him die
Espied a feather of his own,
Wherewith he wont to soar so high.[2]

To a Lady Singing a Song of his Composing

To man, that was in th' evening made,
Stars gave the first delight;
Admiring, in the gloomy shade,
Those little drops of light.

An Apology for Having Loved Before

Outlives in fame the pious fool that raised it.
CIBBER: *Richard III, Act III, Sc. 1*
[1] "Sub rosa."
[2] So in the Libyan fable it is told
That once an eagle, stricken with a dart,
Said, when he saw the fashion of the shaft,
"With our own feathers, not by others' hands,
Are we now smitten."
ÆSCHYLUS: *Fragm. 123* (Plumptre's translation)
So the struck eagle, stretch'd upon the plain,
No more through rolling clouds to soar again,
View'd his own feather on the fatal dart,
And wing'd the shaft that quiver'd in his heart.
BYRON: *English Bards and Scotch Reviewers, L. 826*
Like a young eagle, who has lent his plume
To fledge the shaft by which he meets his doom,
See their own feathers pluck'd to wing the dart
Which rank corruption destines for their heart.
THOMAS MOORE: *Corruption*

A narrow compass! and yet there
Dwelt all that's good, and all that's
fair;
Give me but what this riband bound,
Take all the rest the sun goes round!
On a Girdle. Stanza 3

For all we know
Of what the blessed do above
Is, that they sing, and that they love.
While I Listen to thy Voice

Poets that lasting marble seek
Must come in Latin or in Greek.
Of English Verse

Under the tropic is our language spoke,
And part of Flanders hath receiv'd our
yoke.
*Upon the Death of the Lord
Protector*

Go, lovely rose!
Tell her that wastes her time and me
That now she knows,
When I resemble her to thee,
How sweet and fair she seems to be.
Go, Lovely Rose. Stanza 1

How small a part of time they share
That are so wondrous sweet and fair!
Ibid. Stanza 4

Illustrious acts high raptures do infuse,
And every conqueror creates a muse.
Panegyric on Cromwell

In such green palaces the first kings
reign'd,
Slept in their shades, and angels entertain'd;
With such old counsellors they did advise,
And by frequenting sacred groves grew
wise.
On St. James's Park

And keeps the palace of the soul.[1]
Of Tea

Poets lose half the praise they should
have got,
Could it be known what they discreetly
blot.
*Upon Roscommon's Translation
of Horace, De Arte Poetica*

The soul's dark cottage, batter'd and
decay'd,

[1] The dome of thought, the palace of the
soul. — BYRON: *Childe Harold, Canto II, St. 6*

Lets in new light through chinks that
Time has made.[1]
Stronger by weakness, wiser men be-
come
As they draw near to their eternal
home:
Leaving the old, both worlds at once
they view
That stand upon the threshold of the
new.
On the Divine Poems

SIR WILLIAM DAVENANT
[1606–1668]

The lark now leaves his wat'ry nest
And, climbing, shakes his dewy wings.
Who Look for Day. Stanza 1

For angling-rod he took a sturdy oake;[2]
For line, a cable that in storm ne'er
broke;
His hooke was such as heads the end
of pole
To pluck down house ere fire consumes
it whole;
The hook was baited with a dragon's
tale,—
And then on rock he stood to bob for
whale.
*Britannia Triumphans. Page 15
[1637]*

The assembled souls of all that men
held wise.
*Gondibert. Book II, Canto V,
Stanza 37 [1651]*

[1] See Daniel, page 30.
To vanish in the chinks that Time has
made. — ROGERS: *Pæstum*
[2] For angling rod he took a sturdy oak;
For line, a cable that in storm ne'er
broke; . . .
His hook was baited with a dragon's tail, —
And then on rock he stood to bob for whale.
From *The Mock Romance,* a rhapsody
attached to *The Loves of Hero and
Leander,* published in London in the
years 1653 and 1677. CHAMBERS'S
Book of Days, Vol. I, P. 173. DANIEL:
Rural Sports, Supplement, P. 57
His angle-rod made of a sturdy oak;
His line, a cable which in storms ne'er broke;
His hook he baited with a dragon's tail, —
And sat upon a rock, and bobb'd for whale.
WILLIAM KING [1663–1712]: *Upon a
Giant's Angling* (In CHALMERS'S *British
Poets* ascribed to King)

Since knowledge is but sorrow's spy,
It is not safe to know.[1]

> *The Just Italian. Act V, Sc. 1*

How much pleasure they lose (and even the pleasures of heroic poesy are not unprofitable) who take away the liberty of a poet, and fetter his feet in the shackles of a historian.

> *Prefatory Letter to Thomas Hobbes (Quoted in Biographia Literaria by* S. T. COLERIDGE, *Chapter 22)*

I shall ask leave to desist, when I am interrupted by so great an experiment as dying.

> *His apology, in illness, for not having finished Gondibert*

THOMAS FULLER
[1608–1661]

Drawing near her death, she sent most pious thoughts as harbingers to heaven; and her soul saw a glimpse of happiness through the chinks of her sickness-broken body.

> *Life of Monica*

He was one of a lean body and visage, as if his eager soul, biting for anger at the clog of his body, desired to fret a passage through it.[2]

> *Life of the Duke of Alva*

She commandeth her husband, in any equal matter, by constant obeying him.

> *Holy and Profane State. The Good Wife*

He knows little who will tell his wife all he knows.

> *Ibid. The Good Husband*

One that will not plead that cause wherein his tongue must be confuted by his conscience.

> *Ibid. The Good Advocate*

---

[1] From ignorance our comfort flows. —
PRIOR: *To the Hon. Charles Montague*
　　Where ignorance is bliss,
　　'Tis folly to be wise.
　　　　GRAY: *Eton College, St. 10*
[2] A fiery soul, which, working out its way,
Fretted the pygmy-body to decay,
And o'er-inform'd the tenement of clay.
　　DRYDEN: *Absalom and Achitophel,
Part I, L. 156*

Who durst be so bold with a few crooked boards nailed together, a stick standing upright, and a rag tied to it, to adventure into the ocean?

> *Holy and Profane State.
> The Good Sea-Captain*

To smell to a turf of fresh earth is wholesome for the body; no less are thoughts of mortality cordial to the soul.

> *Ibid. The Virtuous Lady*

The lion is not so fierce as painted.[1]

> *Ibid. Of Preferment*

Their heads sometimes so little that there is no room for wit; sometimes so long that there is no wit for so much room.

> *Ibid. Of Natural Fools*

The Pyramids themselves, doting with age, have forgotten the names of their founders.

> *Ibid. Of Tombs*

Learning hath gained most by those books by which the printers have lost.

> *Ibid. Of Books*

Deceive not thy self by overexpecting happiness in the married estate. Remember the nightingales which sing only some months in the spring, but commonly are silent when they have hatched their eggs.

> *Ibid. Of Marriage*

They that marry ancient people, merely in expectation to bury them, hang themselves in hope that one will come and cut the halter.

> *Ibid.*

Fame sometimes hath created something of nothing.

> *Ibid. Fame*

Anger is one of the sinews of the soul; he that wants it hath a maimed mind.

> *Ibid. Of Anger*

Light, God's eldest daughter, is a principal beauty in a building.

> *Ibid. Of Building*

In Building, rather believe any man than an Artificer for matter of charges. Should they tell thee all the cost at the first, it would blast a young Builder in the budding.

> *Ibid.*

---

[1] See Herbert, page 137.

Often the cockloft is empty in those whom Nature hath built many stories high.[1]

> *Andronicus. Sect. VI, Par. 18, 1*

JOHN MILTON
[1608–1674]

Of Man's first disobedience, and the fruit
Of that forbidden tree whose mortal taste
Brought death into the world, and all our woe.

> *Paradise Lost. Book I, Line 1*

Things unattempted yet in prose or rhyme.

> *Ibid. Line 16*

What in me is dark
Illumine, what is low raise and support;
That to the height of this great argument
I may assert eternal Providence,
And justify the ways of God to men.[2]

> *Ibid. Line 22*

As far as angels' ken.

> *Ibid. Line 59*

Where peace
And rest can never dwell, hope never comes
That comes to all.

> *Ibid. Line 65*

What though the field be lost?
All is not lost — th' unconquerable will,
And study of revenge, immortal hate,
And courage never to submit or yield.

> *Ibid. Line 105*

To be weak is miserable,
Doing or suffering.

> *Ibid. Line 157*

And out of good still to find means of evil.

> *Ibid. Line 165*

A mind not to be chang'd by place or time.
The mind is its own place, and in itself

---

[1] See Bacon, page 113.
[2] But vindicate the ways of God to man. —
POPE: *Essay on Man, Epistle I, L. 16*

Can make a heaven of hell, a hell of heaven.[1]

> *Paradise Lost. Book I, Line 253*

Better to reign in hell than serve in heaven.

> *Ibid. Line 263*

Heard so oft
In worst extremes, and on the perilous edge
Of battle.

> *Ibid. Line 275*

His spear, to equal which the tallest pine
Hewn on Norwegian hills to be the mast
Of some great ammiral, were but a wand
He walk'd with, to support uneasy steps
Over the burning marle.

> *Ibid. Line 292*

Thick as autumnal leaves that strow the brooks
In Vallombrosa.

> *Ibid. Line 302*

Awake, arise, or be forever fallen!

> *Ibid. Line 330*

Spirits, when they please,
Can either sex assume, or both.

> *Ibid. Line 423*

When night
Darkens the streets, then wander forth the sons
Of Belial, flown with insolence and wine.

> *Ibid. Line 500*

Th' imperial ensign, which, full high advanc'd,
Shone like a meteor, streaming to the wind.[2]

> *Ibid. Line 536*

Sonorous metal blowing martial sounds:
At which the universal host up sent
A shout that tore hell's concave, and beyond
Frighted the reign of Chaos and old Night.

> *Ibid. Line 540*

---

[1] Which way I fly is Hell; myself am Hell.
— *Book IV, L. 75*
[2] Stream'd like a meteor to the troubled air. — GRAY: *The Bard, I, 2, L. 6*

Anon they move
In perfect phalanx, to the Dorian mood
Of flutes and soft recorders.
Paradise Lost. Book I, Line 549
His form had yet not lost
All her original brightness, nor appear'd
Less than archangel ruin'd, and th' excess
Of glory obscur'd.
Ibid. Line 591
In dim eclipse, disastrous twilight sheds
On half the nations, and with fear of change
Perplexes monarchs.
Ibid. Line 597
Thrice he assay'd, and thrice, in spite of scorn,
Tears, such as angels weep, burst forth.
Ibid. Line 619
Who overcomes
By force hath overcome but half his foe.
Ibid. Line 648
Mammon, the least erected spirit that fell
From heaven; for ev'n in heaven his looks and thoughts
Were always downward bent, admiring more
The riches of heaven's pavement, trodden gold,
Than aught divine or holy else enjoy'd
In vision beatific.
Ibid. Line 679
Let none admire
That riches grow in hell: that soil may best
Deserve the precious bane.
Ibid. Line 690
From morn
To noon he fell, from noon to dewy eve,
A summer's day; and with the setting sun
Dropp'd from the Zenith, like a falling star.
Ibid. Line 742
Fairy elves,
Whose midnight revels, by a forest side
Or fountain, some belated peasant sees,
Or dreams he sees, while overhead the moon

Sits arbitress.
Paradise Lost. Book I, Line 781
High on a throne of royal state, which far
Outshone the wealth of Ormus and of Ind,
Or where the gorgeous East with richest hand
Showers on her kings barbaric pearl and gold,
Satan exalted sat, by merit rais'd
To that bad eminence.
Ibid. Book II, Line 1
The strongest and the fiercest spirit
That fought in heaven, now fiercer by despair.
Ibid. Line 44
Rather than be less,
Car'd not to be at all.
Ibid. Line 47
My sentence is for open war.
Ibid. Line 51
Which, if not victory, is yet revenge.
Ibid. Line 105
But all was false and hollow; though his tongue
Dropp'd manna, and could make the worse appear
The better reason,[1] to perplex and dash
Maturest counsels.
Ibid. Line 112
Th' ethereal mould,
Incapable of stain, would soon expel
Her mischief, and purge off the baser fire,
Victorious. Thus repuls'd, our final hope
Is flat despair.[2]
Ibid. Line 139
For who would lose,
Though full of pain, this intellectual being,
Those thoughts that wander through eternity,
To perish rather, swallow'd up and lost
In the wide womb of uncreated night?
Ibid. Line 146

---

[1] Aristophanes turns Socrates into ridicule . . . as making the worse appear the better reason. — DIOGENES LAERTIUS: *Socrates, V*
[2] Our hap is loss, our hope but sad despair. — SHAKESPEARE: *Henry VI, Part III, Act II, Sc. 3, L. 9*

His red right hand.[1]
Paradise Lost. Book II, Line 174
Unrespited, unpitied, unrepriev'd.
Ibid. Line 185
The never-ending flight
Of future days.
Ibid. Line 221
With grave
Aspect he rose, and in his rising seem'd
A pillar of state; deep on his front engraven
Deliberation sat, and public care;
And princely counsel in his face yet shone,
Majestic though in ruin: sage he stood,
With Atlantean shoulders, fit to bear
The weight of mightiest monarchies; his look
Drew audience and attention still as night
Or summer's noontide air.
Ibid. Line 300
The palpable obscure.
Ibid. Line 406
Long is the way
And hard, that out of hell leads up to light.
Ibid. Line 432
Their rising all at once was as the sound
Of thunder heard remote.
Ibid. Line 476
Others apart sat on a hill retir'd,
In thoughts more elevate, and reason'd high
Of providence, foreknowledge, will, and fate,
Fix'd fate, free-will, foreknowledge absolute;
And found no end, in wand'ring mazes lost.
Ibid. Line 557
Arm th' obdur'd breast
With stubborn patience as with triple steel.
Ibid. Line 568
Far off from these a slow and silent stream,
Lethe the River of Oblivion.
Ibid. Line 582

[1] Rubente dextera. — HORACE: *Ode I, 2, 2,
To Caesar Augustus*

A gulf profound as that Serbonian bog
Betwixt Damiata and Mount Casius old,
Where armies whole have sunk: the parching air
Burns frore, and cold performs th' effect of fire.
Thither by harpy-footed Furies hail'd,
At certain revolutions all the damn'd
Are brought: and feel by turns the bitter change
Of fierce extremes, — extremes by change more fierce;
From beds of raging fire to starve in ice
Their soft ethereal warmth, and there to pine
Immovable, infix'd, and frozen round,
Periods of time; thence hurried back to fire.
Paradise Lost. Book II, Line 592
O'er many a frozen, many a fiery Alp,
Rocks, caves, lakes, fens, bogs, dens, and shades of death.
Ibid. Line 620
Gorgons and Hydras and Chimæras dire.
Ibid. Line 628
The other shape,
If shape it might be call'd that shape had none
Distinguishable in member, joint, or limb;
Or substance might be call'd that shadow seem'd,
For each seem'd either, — black it stood as night,
Fierce as ten furies, terrible as hell,
And shook a dreadful dart; what seem'd his head
The likeness of a kingly crown had on.
Satan was now at hand.
Ibid. Line 666
Whence and what art thou, execrable shape?
Ibid. Line 681
Before mine eyes in opposition sits
Grim Death, my son and foe.
Ibid. Line 803
Hot, cold, moist, and dry, four champions fierce,
Strive here for mast'ry.
Ibid. Line 898

To compare
Great things with small.[1]
Paradise Lost. Book II, Line 921

With ruin upon ruin, rout on rout,
Confusion worse confounded.
Ibid. Line 995

And fast by, hanging in a golden chain,
This pendent world, in bigness as a
star
Of smallest magnitude close by the
moon.
Ibid. Line 1051

Hail, holy light! offspring of heav'n
first-born.
Ibid. Book III, Line 1

The rising world of waters dark and
deep.
Ibid. Line 11

Thus with the year
Seasons return; but not to me returns
Day, or the sweet approach of even or
morn,
Or sight of vernal bloom or summer's
rose,
Or flocks, or herds, or human face di-
vine;
But cloud instead, and ever-during dark
Surrounds me; from the cheerful ways
of men
Cut off, and for the book of knowledge
fair
Presented with a universal blank
Of Nature's works, to me expung'd and
raz'd,
And wisdom at one entrance quite shut
out.
Ibid. Line 40

See golden days, fruitful of golden
deeds,
With joy and love triumphing.
Ibid. Line 337

Dark with excessive bright.
Ibid. Line 380

[1] Compare great things with small. — VIR-
GIL: *Eclogues, I, 24; Georgics, IV, 176.* COW-
LEY: *The Motto.* DRYDEN: *Ovid, Metamor-
phoses, Book I, L. 727.* TICKELL: *Poem on
Hunting.* POPE: *Windsor Forest*
　　To compare
Small things with greatest. — *Paradise Re-
gained, Book IV, L. 563*

Since call'd
The Paradise of Fools,[1] to few un-
known.
Paradise Lost. Book III, Line 495

The hell within him.
Ibid. Book IV, Line 20

Now conscience wakes despair
That slumber'd, — wakes the bitter
memory
Of what he was, what is, and what must
be
Worse.
Ibid. Line 23

At whose sight all the stars
Hide their diminish'd heads.[2]
Ibid. Line 34

A grateful mind
By owing owes not, but still pays, at
once
Indebted and discharg'd.
Ibid. Line 55

Which way shall I fly
Infinite wrath and infinite despair?
Which way I fly is hell; myself am
hell;
And in the lowest deep a lower deep,
Still threat'ning to devour me, opens
wide,
To which the hell I suffer seems a
heaven.
Ibid. Line 73

Ease would recant
Vows made in pain, as violent and void.
Ibid. Book IV, Line 96

So farewell hope, and, with hope, fare-
well fear,
Farewell remorse; all good to me is lost.
Evil, be thou my good.
Ibid. Line 108

Sabean odours from the spicy shore
Of Araby the Blest.
Ibid. Line 162

And on the Tree of Life,
The middle tree and highest there that
grew,
Sat like a cormorant.
Ibid. Line 194

A heaven on earth.
Ibid. Line 208

[1] See Shakespeare, page 79.
[2] Ye little stars! hide your diminished rays.
— POPE: *Moral Essays, Epistle III, L. 282*

Flowers of all hue, and without thorn
  the rose.[1]
> *Paradise Lost. Book IV, Line 256*

For contemplation he and valour
  form'd,
For softness she and sweet attractive
  grace;
He for God only, she for God in him.
> *Ibid. Line 297*

            Implied
Subjection, but requir'd with gentle
  sway,
And by her yielded, by him best re-
  ceiv'd, —
Yielded with coy submission, modest
  pride,
And sweet, reluctant, amorous delay.
> *Ibid. Line 307*

Adam the goodliest man of men since
  born
His sons, the fairest of her daughters
  Eve.
> *Ibid. Line 323*

            And with necessity,
The tyrant's plea,[2] excus'd his devilish
  deeds.
> *Ibid. Line 393*

Imparadis'd in one another's arms.
> *Ibid. Line 506*

            Live while ye may,
Yet happy pair.
> *Ibid. Line 533*

Now came still evening on, and twilight
  gray
Had in her sober livery all things clad.
> *Ibid. Line 598*

            Now glow'd the firmament
With living sapphires; Hesperus, that
  led
The starry host, rode brightest, till the
  moon,
Rising in clouded majesty, at length
Apparent queen, unveil'd her peerless
  light,
And o'er the dark her silver mantle
  threw.
> *Ibid. Line 604*

The timely dew of sleep.
> *Ibid. Line 614*

With thee conversing I forget all time,
All seasons, and their change; all please
  alike.
Sweet is the breath of morn, her rising
  sweet,
With charm of earliest birds; pleasant
  the sun
When first on this delightful land he
  spreads
His orient beams on herb, tree, fruit,
  and flower,
Glist'ring with dew; fragrant the fertile
  earth
After soft showers; and sweet the coming on
Of grateful ev'ning mild, then silent
  night
With this her solemn bird, and this fair
  moon,
And these the gems of heaven, her
  starry train:
> *Paradise Lost. Book IV, Line 639*

Millions of spiritual creatures walk the
  earth
Unseen, both when we wake, and when
  we sleep.
> *Ibid. Line 677*

      In naked beauty more adorn'd,
More lovely, than Pandora.[1]
> *Ibid. Line 713*

            Eas'd the putting off
These troublesome disguises which we
  wear.
> *Ibid. Line 739*

Hail, wedded love, mysterious law, true
  source
Of human offspring.
> *Ibid. Line 750*

Squat like a toad, close at the ear of
  Eve.
> *Ibid. Line 800*

Him thus intent Ithuriel with his spear
Touch'd lightly; for no falsehood can
  endure
Touch of celestial temper.
> *Ibid. Line 810*

Not to know me argues yourselves unknown.
> *Ibid. Line 830*

---

[1] See Herrick, page 134.
[2] Necessity is the argument of tyrants, it is
the creed of slaves. — WILLIAM PITT: *Speech
on the India Bill* [November, 1783]

[1] When unadorned, adorned the most. —
THOMSON: *Autumn, L. 204*

Abash'd the devil stood,
And felt how awful goodness is, and
  saw
Virtue in her shape how lovely.
    Paradise Lost. Book IV, Line 846
All hell broke loose.
        Ibid. Line 918
Like Teneriff or Atlas unremoved.
        Ibid. Line 987
        The starry cope
Of heaven.
        Ibid. Line 992
Now morn, her rosy steps in th' eastern
  clime
Advancing, sow'd the earth with orient
  pearl,
When Adam wak'd, so custom'd; for
  his sleep
Was aery light, from pure digestion
  bred.
        Ibid. Book V, Line 1
Hung over her enamour'd, and beheld
Beauty, which, whether waking or
  asleep,
Shot forth peculiar graces.
        Ibid. Line 13
        My latest found,
Heaven's last, best gift, my ever-new
  delight!
        Ibid. Line 18
        Good, the more
Communicated, more abundant grows.
        Ibid. Line 71
These are thy glorious works, Parent
  of good!
        Ibid. Line 153
A wilderness of sweets.
        Ibid. Line 294
So saying, with despatchful looks in
  haste
She turns, on hospitable thoughts in-
  tent.
        Ibid. Line 331
        Nor jealousy
Was understood, the injur'd lover's hell.
        Ibid. Line 449
The bright consummate flower.
        Ibid. Line 481
Thrones, Dominations, Princedoms,
  Virtues, Powers.
        Ibid. Line 601
They eat, they drink, and in communion
  sweet

Quaff immortality and joy.
    Paradise Lost. Book V, Line 637
Midnight brought on the dusky hour
Friendliest to sleep and silence.
        Ibid. Line 667
Innumerable as the stars of night,
Or stars of morning, dewdrops which
  the sun
Impearls on every leaf and every
  flower.
        Ibid. Line 745
So spake the seraph Abdiel, faithful
  found;
Among the faithless, faithful only he.
        Ibid. Line 896
        Morn,
Wak'd by the circling hours, with rosy
  hand
Unbarr'd the gates of light.
        Ibid. Book VI, Line 2
Servant of God, well done! Well hast
  thou fought
The better fight.
        Ibid. Line 29
        How vain
Against the Omnipotent to rise in arms.
        Ibid. Line 135
        Arms on armour clashing bray'd
Horrible discord, and the madding
  wheels
Of brazen chariots rag'd: dire was the
  noise
Of conflict.
        Ibid. Line 209
Far off his coming shone.
        Ibid. Line 768
        Let it profit thee to have heard,
By terrible example, the reward
Of disobedience.
        Ibid. Line 909
More safe I sing with mortal voice, un-
  chang'd
To hoarse or mute, though fall'n on
  evil days,
On evil days though fall'n, and evil
  tongues.
        Ibid. Book VII, Line 24
        Still govern thou my song,
Urania, and fit audience find, though
  few.
        Ibid. Line 30

Out of one man a race
Of men innumerable.
Paradise Lost. Book VII, Line 155

Heaven open'd wide
Her ever-during gates, harmonious sound,
On golden hinges moving.
Ibid. Line 205

God saw the Light was good;
And light from darkness by the hemisphere
Divided: Light the Day, and Darkness Night,
He named. Thus was the first Day even and morn.
Ibid. Line 249

Endued
With sanctity of reason.
Ibid. Line 507

The breath of life.
Ibid. Line 526

A broad and ample road, whose dust is gold,
And pavement stars, as stars to thee appear
Seen in the galaxy, that milky way
Which nightly as a circling zone thou seest
Powder'd with stars.
Ibid. Line 577

The Angel ended, and in Adam's ear
So charming left his voice that he awhile
Thought him still speaking, still stood fix'd to hear.
Ibid. Book VIII, Line 1

And grace that won who saw to wish her stay.
Ibid. Line 43

To know
That which before us lies in daily life
Is the prime wisdom.
Ibid. Line 192

Liquid lapse of murmuring streams.
Ibid. Line 263

And feel that I am happier than I know.
Ibid. Line 282

Among unequals what society
Can sort, what harmony or true delight?
Ibid. Line 383

Her virtue, and the conscience of her worth,

That would be woo'd, and not unsought be won.
Paradise Lost. Book VIII, Line 502

She what was honour knew,
And with obsequious majesty approv'd
My pleaded reason. To the nuptial bower
I led her blushing like the morn; all heaven
And happy constellations, on that hour
Shed their selectest influence.
Ibid. Line 508

The sum of earthly bliss.
Ibid. Line 522

Accuse not Nature! she hath done her part;
Do thou but thine!
Ibid. Line 561

Oft times nothing profits more
Than self-esteem, grounded on just and right.
Ibid. Line 571

Those graceful acts,
Those thousand decencies that daily flow
From all her words and actions.
Ibid. Line 600

My unpremeditated verse.
Ibid. Book IX, Line 24

Pleas'd me, long choosing and beginning late.
Ibid. Line 26

Unless an age too late, or cold
Climate, or years, damp my intended wing.
Ibid. Line 44

Revenge, at first though sweet,
Bitter ere long back on itself recoils.
Ibid. Line 171

For solitude sometimes is best society,
And short retirement urges sweet return.
Ibid. Line 249

At shut of evening flowers.
Ibid. Line 278

As one who long in populous city pent,
Where houses thick and sewers annoy the air.
Ibid. Line 445

So gloz'd the tempter.
Ibid. Line 549

Led Eve, our credulous mother, to the Tree

Of Prohibition, root of all our woe.
> *Paradise Lost. Book IX, Line 644*
> Left that command
Sole daughter of his voice.[1]
> *Ibid. Line 652*
> His words, replete with guile,
Into her heart too easy entrance won.
> *Ibid. Line 733*
Earth felt the wound, and Nature from
her seat,
Sighing through all her works, gave
signs of woe
That all was lost.
> *Ibid. Line 782*
So dear I love him that with him all
deaths
I could endure, without him live no life.
> *Ibid. Line 832*
> In her face excuse
Came prologue, and apology too
prompt.
> *Ibid. Line 853*
O fairest of Creation, last and best
Of all God's works, creature in whom
excelled
Whatever can to sight or thought be
formed,
Holy, divine, good, amiable, or sweet!
> *Ibid. Line 896*
> Yet I shall temper so
Justice with mercy, as may illustrate
most
Them fully satisfy'd, and thee appease.
> *Ibid. Book X, Line 77*
She gave me of the tree, and I did eat.
> *Ibid. Line 143*
Dust thou art, and shalt to dust return.
> *Ibid. Line 208*
So scented the grim Feature, and up-
turn'd
His nostril wide into the murky air,
Sagacious of his quarry from so far.
> *Ibid. Line 279*
Pandemonium, city and proud seat
Of Lucifer.
> *Ibid. Line 424*
A dismal universal hiss, the sound
Of public scorn.
> *Ibid. Line 508*
Death . . . on his pale horse.
> *Ibid. Line 588*

[1] Stern daughter of the voice of God. —
WORDSWORTH: *Ode to Duty*

> Whatever thing
The scythe of Time mows down.
> *Paradise Lost. Book X, Line 606*
> How gladly would I meet
Mortality, my sentence, and be earth
Insensible! how glad would lay me
down
As in my mother's lap!
> *Ibid. Line 775*
> Morn,
All concerned with out unrest, begins
Her rosy progress smiling.
> *Ibid. Book XI, Line 173*
Must I thus leave thee, Paradise? thus
leave
Thee, native soil? these happy walks
and shades?
> *Ibid. Line 269*
Then purg'd with euphrasy and rue
The visual nerve, for he had much to
see.
> *Ibid. Line 414*
> Moping melancholy,
And moon-struck madness.
> *Ibid. Line 485*
And over them triumphant Death his
dart
Shook, but delay'd to strike, though oft
invok'd.
> *Ibid. Line 491*
The rule of *Not too much.*
> *Ibid. Line 531*
So may'st thou live, till, like ripe fruit,
thou drop
Into thy mother's lap.
> *Ibid. Line 535*
Nor love thy life, nor hate; but what
thou liv'st
Live well; how long or short permit to
Heaven.[1]
> *Ibid. Line 553*
A bevy of fair women.
> *Ibid. Line 582*
> The evening star,
Love's harbinger.
> *Ibid. Line 588*
The brazen throat of war.
> *Ibid. Line 713*
An olive-leaf he brings, pacific sign.
> *Ibid. Line 860*

[1] Summum nec metuas diem, nec optes
(Neither fear nor wish for your last day). —
MARTIAL: *Lib. X, Epigram 47, L. 13*

The world was all before them, where
   to choose
Their place of rest, and Providence
   their guide.
They hand in hand, with wand'ring
   steps and slow,
Through Eden took their solitary way.
      Paradise Lost. Book XII, Line 646
            Most men admire
Virtue who follow not her lore.
      Paradise Regained. Book I, Line 482
            Beauty stands
In the admiration only of weak minds
Led captive.
            Ibid. Book II, Line 220
Rocks whereon greatest men have oft-
   est wreck'd.
            Ibid. Line 228
Of whom to be disprais'd were no small
   praise.
            Ibid. Book III, Line 56
What honour that,
But tedious waste of time, to sit and
   hear
So many hollow compliments and lies,
Outlandish flatteries?
            Ibid. Line 122
Elephants indorsed with towers.
            Ibid. Line 329
Syene, and where the shadow both way
   falls,
Meroë, Nilotic isle.
            Ibid. Book IV, Line 70
Dusk faces with white silken turbants
   wreath'd.
            Ibid. Line 76
      The childhood shows the man,
As morning shows the day.[1]
            Ibid. Line 220
Athens, the eye of Greece, mother of arts
And eloquence.
            Ibid. Line 240
      The olive grove of Academe,
Plato's retirement, where the Attic bird
Trills her thick-warbled notes the sum-
   mer long.
            Ibid. Line 244
Thence to the famous orators repair,
Those ancient whose resistless elo-
   quence
Wielded at will that fierce democratie,

[1] The child is father of the man. — WORDS-
WORTH: *My Heart Leaps Up*

Shook the arsenal, and fulmin'd over
   Greece,
To Macedon, and Artaxerxes' throne.
      Paradise Regained. Book IV,
            Line 267
Socrates . . .
Whom, well inspir'd, the oracle pro-
   nounc'd
Wisest of men.
            Ibid. Line 274
Deep vers'd in books, and shallow in
   himself.
            Ibid. Line 327
As children gath'ring pebbles on the
   shore.
Or, if I would delight my private hours
With music or with poem, where so soon
As in our native language can I find
That solace?
            Ibid. Line 330
      Till morning fair
Came forth with pilgrim steps, in amice
   gray.
            Ibid. Line 426
O loss of sight, of thee I most complain!
      Samson Agonistes. Line 68
O dark, dark, dark, amid the blaze of
   noon,
Irrecoverably dark, total eclipse
Without all hope of day!
            Ibid. Line 80
The sun to me is dark
And silent as the moon,
When she deserts the night,
Hid in her vacant interlunar cave.
            Ibid. Line 86
Ran on embattled armies clad in iron,
And, weaponless himself,
Made arms ridiculous.
            Ibid. Line 129
Just are the ways of God,
And justifiable to men;
Unless there be who think not God at
   all.
            Ibid. Line 293
A grain of manhood.
            Ibid. Line 408
What boots it at one gate to make de-
   fence,
And at another to let in the foe?
            Ibid. Line 560
But who is this, what thing of sea or
   land, —

Female of sex it seems —
That so bedeck'd, ornate, and gay,
Comes this way sailing
Like a stately ship
Of Tarsus, bound for th' isles
Of Javan or Gadire,
With all her bravery on, and tackle
 trim,
Sails fill'd, and streamers waving,
Courted by all the winds that hold them
 play,
An amber scent of odorous perfume
Her harbinger?
　　　Samson Agonistes. Line 710
In argument with men a woman ever
Goes by the worse, whatever be her
 cause.
For want of words, no doubt, or lack
 of breath!
　　　Ibid. Line 903
Fame, if not double-faced, is double-
 mouthed,
And with contrary blast proclaims most
 deeds;
On both his wings, one black, the other
 white,
Bears greatest names in his wild aery
 flight.
　　　Ibid. Line 971
Yet beauty, though injurious, hath
 strange power,
After offence returning, to regain
Love once possess'd.
　　　Ibid. Line 1003
Love-quarrels oft in pleasing concord
 end;
Not wedlock-treachery.
　　　Ibid. Line 1008
Boast not of what thou would'st have
 done, but do
What then thou would'st.
　　　Ibid. Line 1104
He's gone, and who knows how he may
 report
Thy words by adding fuel to the flame?
　　　Ibid. Line 1350
For evil news rides post, while good
 news baits.
　　　Ibid. Line 1538
Suspense in news is torture.
　　　Ibid. Line 1569
Nothing is here for tears, nothing to
 wail

Or knock the breast; no weakness, no
 contempt,
Dispraise, or blame; nothing but well
 and fair,
And what may quiet us in a death so
 noble.
　　　Samson Agonistes. Line 1721
All is best, though we oft doubt
What the unsearchable dispose
Of Highest Wisdom brings about.
　　　Ibid. Line 1745
Calm of mind, all passion spent.
　　　Ibid. Line 1758
Above the smoke and stir of this dim
 spot
Which men call earth.
　　　Comus. Line 5
Bacchus, that first from out the purple
 grape
Crush'd the sweet poison of misusèd
 wine.
　　　Ibid. Line 46
These my sky-robes, spun out of Iris'
 woof.
　　　Ibid. Line 83
The star that bids the shepherd fold.
　　　Ibid. Line 93
Midnight shout and revelry,
Tipsy dance and jollity.
　　　Ibid. Line 103
Ere the blabbing eastern scout,
The nice morn, on th' Indian steep,
From her cabin'd loop-hole peep.
　　　Ibid. Line 138
　　When the gray-hooded Even,
Like a sad votarist in palmer's weed,
Rose from the hindmost wheels of
 Phœbus' wain.
　　　Ibid. Line 188
　　A thousand fantasies
Begin to throng into my memory,
Of calling shapes, and beck'ning shad-
 ows dire,
And airy tongues that syllable men's
 names
On sands and shores and desert wilder-
 nesses.
　　　Ibid. Line 205
Was I deceiv'd, or did a sable cloud
Turn forth her silver lining on the
 night?
　　　Ibid. Line 221

How sweetly did they float upon the
    wings
Of silence, through the empty-vaulted
    night,
At every fall smoothing the raven down
Of darkness till it smil'd!
                    Comus. Line 249

Who, as they sung, would take the
    prison'd soul
And lap it in Elysium.
                    Ibid. Line 256

Such sober certainty of waking bliss.
                    Ibid. Line 263

I took it for a faery vision
Of some gay creatures of the element,
That in the colours of the rainbow live,
And play i' th' plighted clouds.
                    Ibid. Line 298

With thy long levell'd rule of stream-
    ing light.
                    Ibid. Line 340

Virtue could see to do what Virtue
    would
By her own radiant light, though sun
    and moon
Were in the flat sea sunk. And Wisdom's
    self
Oft seeks to sweet retired solitude,
Where, with her best nurse Contempla-
    tion,
She plumes her feathers, and lets grow
    her wings.
                    Ibid. Line 373

              The unsunn'd heaps
Of miser's treasure.
                    Ibid. Line 398

Some say no evil thing that walks by
    night,
In fog or fire, by lake or moorish fen,
Blue meagre hag, or stubborn unlaid
    ghost,
That breaks his magic chains at curfew
    time,
No goblin, or swart faery of the mine,
Hath hurtful power o'er true virginity.
                    Ibid. Line 432

How charming is divine philosophy!
Not harsh and crabbed, as dull fools
    suppose,

But musical as is Apollo's lute,[1]
And a perpetual feast of nectar'd sweets
Where no crude surfeit reigns.
                    Comus. Line 476
Fill'd the air with barbarous disso-
    nance.
                    Ibid. Line 550
              That power
Which erring men call Chance.
                    Ibid. Line 587
          This cordial julep here,
That flames and dances in his crystal
    bounds.
                    Ibid. Line 672
Budge doctors of the Stoic fur.
                    Ibid. Line 707
And live like Nature's bastards, not
    her sons.
                    Ibid. Line 727
It is for homely features to keep
    home, —
They had their name thence; coarse
    complexions
And cheeks of sorry grain will serve to
    ply
The sampler, and to tease the huswife's
    wool.
What need a vermeil-tinctur'd lip for
    that,
Love-darting eyes, or tresses like the
    morn?
                    Ibid. Line 748
Enjoy your dear wit, and gay rhetoric,
That hath so well been taught her daz-
    zling fence.
                    Ibid. Line 790
Sabrina fair,
    Listen where thou art sitting
Under the glassy, cool, translucent
    wave,
    In twisted braids of lilies knitting
The loose train of thy amber-dropping
    hair.
                    Ibid. Line 859
But now my task is smoothly done:
I can fly, or I can run.
                    Ibid. Line 1012

---

[1]   As sweet and musical
As bright Apollo's lute.
    SHAKESPEARE: *Love's Labour's Lost,
            Act IV, Sc. 3, L. 342*

Or, if Virtue feeble were,
Heav'n itself would stoop to her.
Comus. Line 1022

I come to pluck your berries harsh and
crude,
And with forc'd fingers rude
Shatter your leaves before the mellow-
ing year.
Lycidas. Line 3

He knew
Himself to sing, and build the lofty
rhyme.
Ibid. Line 10

Without the meed of some melodious
tear.
Ibid. Line 14

Hence with denial vain, and coy excuse.
Ibid. Line 18

Under the opening eyelids of the morn.
Ibid. Line 26

But oh the heavy change, now thou art
gone,
Now thou art gone and never must return!
Ibid. Line 37

The gadding vine.
Ibid. Line 40

And strictly meditate the thankless
Muse.
Ibid. Line 66

To sport with Amaryllis in the shade,
Or with the tangles of Neæra's hair.
Ibid. Line 68

Fame is the spur that the clear spirit
doth raise [1]
(That last infirmity of noble mind) [2]
To scorn delights, and live laborious
days;
But the fair guerdon when we hope to
find,
And think to burst out into sudden
blaze,

[1] Erant quibus appetentior famæ videretur,
quando etiam sapientibus cupido gloriæ novis-
sima exuitur (Some might consider him as too
fond of fame, for the desire of glory clings
even to the best of men longer than any other
passion) [said of Helvidius Priscus]. — TACI-
TUS: *Historia, IV, 6*

[2] That thirst (for applause), if the last infirmity of noble minds, is also the first infirmity of weak ones; and, on the whole, the
strongest impulsive influence of average humanity. — RUSKIN: *Sesame and Lilies, Of
Kings' Treasuries, 3*

Comes the blind Fury with th' abhorred
shears
And slits the thin-spun life.
Lycidas. Line 70

Fame is no plant that grows on mortal
soil.
Ibid. Line 78

It was that fatal and perfidious bark,
Built in th' eclipse, and rigg'd with
curses dark.
Ibid. Line 100

The Pilot of the Galilean lake;
Two massy keys he bore of metals
twain
(The golden opes, the iron shuts
amain).
Ibid. Line 109

The hungry sheep look up, and are not
fed.
Ibid. Line 123

But that two-handed engine at the
door
Stands ready to smite once, and smite
no more.
Ibid. Line 130

Throw hither all your quaint enamell'd
eyes,
That on the green turf suck the honied
showers,
And purple all the ground with vernal
flowers.
Bring the rathe primrose that forsaken
dies,
The tufted crow-toe, and pale jessa-
mine,
The white pink, and the pansy freaked
with jet,
The glowing violet,
The musk-rose, and the well-attir'd
woodbine,
With cowslips wan that hang the pen-
sive head,
And every flower that sad embroidery
wears.
Ibid. Line 139

So sinks the day-star in the ocean bed,
And yet anon repairs his drooping head,
And tricks his beams, and with new-
spangled ore
Flames in the forehead of the morning
sky.
Ibid. Line 168

He touch'd the tender stops of various quills,
With eager thought warbling his Doric lay.

Lycidas. Line 188

To-morrow to fresh woods, and pastures new.

Ibid. Line 193

Hence, loathed Melancholy,
Of Cerberus and blackest Midnight born.

L'Allegro. Line 1

Haste thee, Nymph, and bring with thee
Jest, and youthful Jollity,
Quips and Cranks and wanton Wiles,
Nods and Becks and wreathèd Smiles.

Ibid. Line 25

Sport, that wrinkled Care derides,
And Laughter holding both his sides.
Come, and trip it, as you go,
On the light fantastic toe.

Ibid. Line 31

The mountain nymph, sweet Liberty.

Ibid. Line 36

And every shepherd tells his tale
Under the hawthorn in the dale.

Ibid. Line 67

Meadows trim, with daisies pied,
Shallow brooks, and rivers wide;
Towers and battlements it sees
Bosom'd high in tufted trees,
Where perhaps some beauty lies,
The cynosure of neighboring eyes.

Ibid. Line 75

Then to the spicy nut-brown ale.

Ibid. Line 100

Tower'd cities please us then,
And the busy hum of men.

Ibid. Line 117

Ladies, whose bright eyes
Rain influence, and judge the prize.

Ibid. Line 121

Such sights as youthful poets dream
On summer eves by haunted stream.
Then to the well-trod stage anon,
If Jonson's learned sock be on,
Or sweetest Shakespeare, Fancy's child,
Warble his native wood-notes wild.

Ibid. Line 129

And ever, against eating cares,
Lap me in soft Lydian airs,

Married to immortal verse,[1]
Such as the meeting soul may pierce,
In notes with many a winding bout
Of linkèd sweetness long drawn out.

L'Allegro. Line 135

Untwisting all the chains that tie
The hidden soul of harmony.

Ibid. Line 143

Vain deluding Joys,
The brood of Folly without father bred!

Il Penseroso. Line 1

The gay motes that people the sunbeams.

Ibid. Line 8

Sober, stedfast, and demure.

Ibid. Line 32

And looks commercing with the skies,
Thy rapt soul sitting in thine eyes.

Ibid. Line 39

Forget thyself to marble.

Ibid. Line 42

And join with thee, calm Peace and Quiet,
Spare Fast, that oft with gods doth diet.

Ibid. Line 45

And add to these retired Leisure,
That in trim gardens takes his pleasure.

Ibid. Line 49

Sweet bird, that shun'st the noise of folly,
Most musical, most melancholy!

Ibid. Line 61

I walk unseen
On the dry smooth-shaven green,
To behold the wandering moon,
Riding near her highest noon,
Like one that had been led astray
Through the heav'n's wide pathless way,
And oft, as if her head she bow'd,
Stooping through a fleecy cloud.

Ibid. Line 65

Where glowing embers through the room
Teach light to counterfeit a gloom.

Ibid. Line 79

Far from all resort of mirth,
Save the cricket on the hearth.

Ibid. Line 81

[1] Wisdom married to immortal verse. — WORDSWORTH: *The Excursion, Book VII*

Sometime let gorgeous Tragedy
In sceptred pall come sweeping by,
Presenting Thebes, or Pelops' line,
Or the tale of Troy divine.

Il Penseroso. Line 97

Or bid the soul of Orpheus sing
Such notes as, warbled to the string,
Drew iron tears down Pluto's cheek.

Ibid. Line 105

Or call up him that left half told
The story of Cambuscan bold.[1]

Ibid. Line 109

Where more is meant than meets the
ear.

Ibid. Line 120

When the gust hath blown his fill,
Ending on the rustling leaves,
With minute-drops from off the eaves.

Ibid. Line 128

Hide me from day's garish eye.

Ibid. Line 141

And storied windows richly dight,
Casting a dim religious light.

Ibid. Line 159

Till old experience do attain
To something like prophetic strain.

Ibid. Line 173

This is the month, and this the happy
morn,
Wherein the Son of Heaven's eternal
King,
Of wedded maid and virgin mother
born,
Our great redemption from above did
bring.

*On the Morning of Christ's Na-
tivity. Stanza 1, Line 1*

No war, or battle's sound
Was heard the world around.

Ibid. Stanza 4, Line 53

Time will run back and fetch the Age
of Gold.[2]

Ibid. Stanza 14, Line 135

The Oracles are dumb;
No voice or hideous hum
Runs through the archèd roof in words
deceiving.

Ibid. Stanza 19, Line 173

From haunted spring and dale
Edg'd with poplar pale

The parting genius is with sighing sent.

*On the Morning of Christ's Na-
tivity. Stanza 20, Line 184*

Peor and Baälim
Forsake their temples dim.

Ibid. Stanza 22, Line 197

The lazy leaden-stepping Hours,
Whose speed is but the heavy plummet's pace.

On Time

All this earthy grossness quit,
Attired with stars we shall for ever sit,
Triumphing over Death, and Chance,
and thee, O Time.

Ibid.

What needs my Shakespeare for his
honour'd bones
The labour of an age in pilèd stones?
Or that his hallow'd relics should be
hid
Under a star-ypointing pyramid?
Dear son of memory, great heir of fame,
What need'st thou such weak witness
of thy name?

On Shakespeare

And so sepúlchred in such pomp dost
lie,
That kings for such a tomb would wish
to die.

Ibid.

Thy liquid notes that close the eye of
day.[1]

Sonnet: To the Nightingale

Time, the subtle thief of youth.

*On His Having Arrived at
the Age of Twenty-three*

As ever in my great Taskmaster's eye.

Ibid.

That old man eloquent.

To the Lady Margaret Ley

That would have made Quintilian stare
and gasp.

*On the Detraction which followed
upon my writing certain Treatises*

License they mean when they cry Liberty;
For who loves that must first be wise
and good.

Ibid. II

---

[1] CHAUCER: *The Squieres Tale*
[2] See Spenser, page 25.

[1] Ye of day. — CHAUCER: *The Legend of
Good Women, Prologue, L. 184*

Peace hath her victories
No less renown'd than war.
To the Lord General Cromwell

Ev'n them who kept thy truth so pure
of old,
When all our fathers worshipp'd stocks
and stones.
On the late Massacre in Piedmont

Thousands at his bidding speed,
And post o'er land and ocean without
rest;
They also serve who only stand and
wait.
On his Blindness

What neat repast shall feast us, light
and choice,
Of Attic taste?
To Mr. Lawrence

In mirth that after no repenting draws.
Sonnet XXI: To Cyriac Skinner

For other things mild Heav'n a time
ordains,
And disapproves that care, though wise
in show,
That with superfluous burden loads the
day,
And, when God sends a cheerful hour,
refrains.
Ibid.

Yet I argue not
Against Heav'n's hand or will, nor bate
a jot
Of heart or hope; but still bear up and
steer
Right onward.
Sonnet XXII

Of which all Europe rings from side
to side.
Ibid.

But oh! as to embrace me she inclin'd,
I wak'd, she fled, and day brought back
my night.
On his Deceased Wife

For such kind of borrowing as this,
if it be not bettered by the borrower,
among good authors is accounted Pla-
giarè.
Iconoclastes, XXIII

Truth is as impossible to be soiled by
any outward touch as the sunbeam.[1]
*Doctrine and Discipline of
Divorce*

[1] See Bacon, page 112.

A poet soaring in the high reason of
his fancies, with his garland and singing robes about him.
*The Reason of Church Govern-
ment. Book II, Introduction*

By labour and intent study (which
I take to be my portion in this life),
joined with the strong propensity of
nature, I might perhaps leave something so written to after times as they
should not willingly let it die.
Ibid.

Beholding the bright countenance of
truth in the quiet and still air of delightful studies.
Ibid.

He who would not be frustrate of his
hope to write well hereafter in laudable
things ought himself to be a true poem.
Apology for Smectymnuus

His words, like so many nimble and
airy servitors, trip about him at command.
Ibid.

Litigious terms, fat contentions, and
flowing fees.
Tractate of Education

Enflamed with the study of learning
and the admiration of virtue; stirred up
with high hopes of living to be brave
men and worthy patriots, dear to God,
and famous to all ages.
Ibid.

Ornate rhetorick taught out of the
rule of Plato. . . . To which poetry
would be made subsequent, or indeed
rather precedent, as being less suttle
and fine, but more simple, sensuous,
and passionate.
Ibid.

In those vernal seasons of the year,
when the air is calm and pleasant, it
were an injury and sullenness against
Nature not to go out and see her riches,
and partake in her rejoicing with
heaven and earth.
Ibid.

Attic tragedies of stateliest and most
regal argument.
Ibid.

As good almost kill a man as kill a
good book: who kills a man kills a
reasonable creature, God's image; but

he who destroys a good book kills reason itself.

Areopagitica

A good book is the precious life-blood of a master-spirit, embalmed and treasured up on purpose to a life beyond life.

Ibid.

I cannot praise a fugitive and cloistered virtue, unexercised and unbreathed, that never sallies out and sees her adversary, but slinks out of the race where that immortal garland is to be run for, not without dust and heat.

Ibid.

Who shall silence all the airs and madrigals that whisper softness in chambers?

Ibid.

Methinks I see in my mind a noble and puissant nation rousing herself like a strong man after sleep, and shaking her invincible locks: methinks I see her as an eagle mewing her mighty youth, and kindling her undazzled eyes at the full midday beam.

Ibid.

Though all the winds of doctrine [1] were let loose to play upon the earth, so Truth be in the field, we do ingloriously, by licensing and prohibiting, to misdoubt her strength. Let her and Falsehood grapple: who ever knew Truth put to the worse in a free and open encounter? [2]

Ibid.

Men of most renowned virtue have sometimes by transgressing most truly kept the law.

Tetrachordon

Such bickerings to recount, met often in these our writers, what more worth is it than to chronicle the wars of kites or crows flocking and fighting in the air?

The History of England. Book IV

[1] *Winds of Doctrine: used as title of a book by* GEORGE SANTAYANA [1913]
[2] *Error of opinion may be tolerated where reason is left free to combat it.* — JEFFERSON: *Inaugural Address* [March 4, 1801]

SIR JOHN SUCKLING
[1609–1642]

Her feet beneath her petticoat
Like little mice, stole in and out,[1]
    As if they feared the light;
But oh, she dances such a way!
No sun upon an Easter-day
    Is half so fine a sight.
        A Ballad upon a Wedding.
            Stanza 8

Her lips were red, and one was thin,
Compared with that was next her chin,
Some bee had stung it newly.
            Ibid. Stanza 11

Why so pale and wan, fond lover?
    Prithee, why so pale?
Will, when looking well can't move her,
    Looking ill prevail?
            Song. Stanza 1

'Tis not the meat, but 'tis the appetite
    Makes eating a delight.
        Of Thee, Kind Boy. Stanza 3

Long graces do
But keep good stomachs off, that would fall to.
            To Lord Lepington

Spare diet is the cause love lasts,
For surfeits sooner kill than fasts.
            Against Absence

Out upon it, I have loved
    Three whole days together;
And am like to love three more,
    If it prove fair weather.
        A Poem with the Answer.
            Stanza 1

'Tis expectation makes a blessing dear,
Heaven were not heaven, if we knew what it were.
        Against Fruition. Stanza 4

Women are the baggage of life: they are
Troublesome, and hinder us in the great march,
And yet we cannot be without 'em.
        The Tragedy of Brennoralt.
            Act I, Sc. 1

Success is a rare paint, hides all the ugliness.
            Ibid.

[1] Her pretty feet, like snails, did creep
    A little out.
        ROBERT HERRICK: *To Mistress Susanna Southwell*

Nipped i' the bud.
> *The Tragedy of Brennoralt.*
> *Act. I, Sc. 1*

Sleep is as nice as woman;
The more I court it, the more it flies me.
> *Ibid. Act II, Sc. 1*

She is pretty to walk with,
And witty to talk with,
And pleasant, too, to think on.
> *Ibid.*

Her face is like the milky way[1] i' the sky, —
A meeting of gentle lights without name.
> *Ibid. Act III, Sc. 1*

Death's no punishment: it is the sense,
The pains and fears afore, that makes a death.
> *Aglaura. Act V, Sc. 1*

But as when an authentic watch is shown,
Each man winds up and rectifies his own,
So in our very judgments.[2]
> *Ibid. Epilogue*

The Prince of Darkness is a gentle-man.[3]
> *The Goblins. Act III*

I' th' very nick of time!
> *Ibid. Act V*

High characters (cries one), and he would see
Things that ne'er were, nor are, nor ne'er will be.[4]
> *Ibid. Epilogue*

---

[1] The milkie way. — GEORGE HERBERT: *Prayer, St. 3*
[2] 'Tis with our judgments as our watches, none Go just alike, yet each believes his own.
POPE: *An Essay on Criticism, Part I, L. 9*
[3] See Shakespeare, page 99.
[4] Whoever thinks a faultless piece to see, Thinks what ne'er was, nor is, nor e'er shall be.
POPE: *An Essay on Criticism, Part II, L. 53*
There's no such thing in Nature, and you'll draw
A faultless monster which the world ne'er saw.
JOHN SHEFFIELD, DUKE OF BUCK-INGHAMSHIRE [1648–1721]: *Essay on Poetry*

WILLIAM CARTWRIGHT
[1611–1643]

St. Francis and St. Benedight,
Bless this house from wicked wight,
From the nightmare and the Goblin
That is hight Good Fellow Robin.
Keep it from all evil spiretes,
Fairies, Wezles, Bats, and Ferrytes
From Curfew Time to the next Prime.
> *A House Blessing*[1]

JAMES GRAHAM,
FIRST MARQUIS OF MONTROSE
[1612–1650]

He either fears his fate too much,
Or his deserts are small,
That dares not put it to the touch
To gain or lose it all.[2]
> *My Dear and Only Love.*
> *Stanza 2*

I'll make thee glorious by my pen,
And famous by my sword.[3]
> *Ibid. Stanza 5*

THOMAS JORDAN
[1612–1685]

Let us drink and be merry, dance, joke, and rejoice,
With claret and sherry, theorbo and voice!
> *Coronemus nos Rosis Antequam*
> *Marcescant.*[4] *Stanza 1*

Fish dinners will make a man spring like a flea.
> *Ibid. Stanza 2*

Though now she be pleasant and sweet to the sense,

---

[1] Matthew, Mark, Luke, and John, The bed be blest that I lye on.
THOMAS ADY: *A Candle in the Dark, P. 58* [London, 1656]
[2] That puts it not unto the touch To win or lose it all.
MARK NAPIER [1798–1879]: *Montrose and the Covenanters, Vol. II, P. 566*
[3] I'll make thee famous by my pen, And glorious by my sword.
SCOTT: *Legend of Montrose, Chap. XV*
[4] One of the songs of Sir Henry Morgan's buccaneers was an adaptation of this poem.

Will be damnable mouldy a hundred
   years hence.
   *Coronemus nos Rosis Antequam
              Marcescant. Stanza 3*
For health, wealth and beauty, wit,
   learning, and sense,
Must all come to nothing a hundred
   years hence.
                Ibid. Stanza 4

RICHARD CRASHAW
[1613–1649]

The conscious water saw its God and
   blushed.[1]
   *Epigrammata Sacra. Aquae in
              Vinum Versae*
Two went to pray? Oh, rather say
One went to brag, the other to pray;
One stands up close and treads on high
Where the other dares not send his eye;
One nearer to God's altar trod,
The other to the altar's God.
   *Two Went up to the Temple to
                          Pray*

   What wilt thou do
To entertain this starry stranger?
         The Shepherds' Hymn
Whoe'er she be,
That not impossible she,
That shall command my heart and me.
   Wishes to his Supposed Mistress
Where'er she lie,
Locked up from mortal eye,
In shady leaves of destiny.
                          Ibid.

Days that need borrow
No part of their good morrow

[1] Nympha pudica Deum vidit et erubuit. —
Quoted by SAMUEL JOHNSON [1778], *Boswell's Life of Dr. Johnson, Vol. II, P. 218,
Everyman ed.* A footnote states that this line
has frequently been attributed to Dryden, but
appeared in Crashaw's *Epigrammata Sacra*
[1634]. Though many writers have translated the epigram, only the last line has survived.
   The bashful stream hath seen its God and
      blushed.
            AARON HILL [1685–1750]
The water hears thy faintest word,
And blushes into wine.
   JOHN SAMUEL BEWLEY MONSELL
[1811–1875]: *Mysterious is Thy
Presence, Lord, St. 1*

From a fore-spent night of sorrow.
   Wishes to his Supposed Mistress
Life that dares send
A challenge to his end,
And when it comes, say, Welcome,
   friend!
                          Ibid.
Sydneian showers
Of sweet discourse, whose powers
Can crown old Winter's head with
   flowers.
                          Ibid.
A happy soul, that all the way
To heaven hath a summer's day.
   *In Praise of Lessius's Rule of
                          Health*
The modest front of this small floor,
Believe me, reader, can say more
Than many a braver marble can, —
"Here lies a truly honest man!"
   Epitaph upon Mr. Ashton

JEREMY TAYLOR
[1613–1667]

I end with a story which I find in the
Jews'[1] Books. When Abraham sat at

[1] In the Latin dedication to the Senate of
Hamburg of a Rabbinical work, *The Rod of
Judah,* the translator, George Genz, gives the
story substantially as found in Jeremy Taylor's *Liberty of Prophesying.* The work of
Genz was published at Amsterdam in 1651,
and the parable was credited to "a most noble
author Sadus." It was afterward found in
the *Bostan,* or *Flower Garden,* of Saadi, the
Persian poet of the twelfth century.
   Henry Home, Lord Kames [1696–1782],
published the *Parable on Persecution* in Volume II of his *Sketches of the History of Man*
in 1774, saying it had been communicated to
him by Benjamin Franklin.
   From Lord Kames' book the parable was
taken for the first English edition of Franklin's
writings, edited by Benjamin Vaughan [1751–
1835], published in London in 1779. Franklin had a copy of the parable bound in his
Bible as an added chapter to the Book of
Genesis.
   The Reverend Sydney Smith read the apologue before the Mayor and Corporation of
Bristol, England, November 5, 1828, and it
is included in Chapter 8 of *A Memoir of the
Reverend Sydney Smith* by his daughter, Lady
Holland, 1855, where it is followed by a letter
from Edward Everett, giving information con-
cerning the parable.
   No. 8 of Edward Everett's *Mount Vernon
Papers,* a series first published in *The New*

his tent-door, according to his custom, waiting to entertain strangers, he espied an old man stooping and leaning on his staffe, weary with age and travelle, coming toward him, who was an hundred years of age; he received him kindly, washed his feet, provided supper, caused him to sit down; but observing that the old man eat and prayed not, nor begged for a blessing on his meat, asked him why he did not worship the God of heaven. The old man told him that he worshiped the fire only, and acknowledged no other God: at which answer Abraham grew so zealously angry, that he thrust the old man out of his tent, and exposed him to all the evils of the night and an unguarded condition. When the old man was gone, God called to him and asked him where the stranger was; he replied, "I thrust him away because he did not worship thee"; God answered him, "I have suffered him these hundred years, although he dishonored me, and couldst thou not endure him one night, when he gave thee no trouble?" Upon this, saith the story, Abraham fetcht him back again, and gave him hospitable entertainment and wise instruction. Go thou and do likewise, and thy charity will be rewarded by the God of Abraham.

The Liberty of Prophesying.
Page 606 [1657]

He that is most knowing hath a capacity to become happy, which a lesse knowing prince or a rich person hath not.

XXVIII Sermons [1651]

We long for perishing meat, and fill our stomachs with corruption; we look after white and red, and the weaker beauties of the night; we are passionate after rings and seals, and enraged at the breaking of a Crystall . . . our hearts are hard and inflexible, having no loves for anything but strange flesh, and heaps of money, and popular noises; and therefore we are a huge way off from the Kingdome of God.

XXV Sermons [1653]

No man ever repented that he arose from the table sober, healthfull, and with his wits about him.

Ibid.

Every man hath in his own life sins enough, in his own minde trouble enough: so that curiositie after the affairs of others cannot be without envy and an evil minde. What is it to me if my Neighbours Grandfather were a Syrian, or his Grandmother illegitimate, or that another is indebted five thousand pounds, or whether his wife be expensive?

Holy Living

Here is no place to sit down in, but you must rise as soon as you are set: for we have gnats in our chambers, and worms in our gardens, and spiders and flies in the palaces of the greatest Kings.

Holy Dying

RICHARD BAXTER
[1615–1691]

I preached as never sure to preach again,
And as a dying man to dying men.
Love Breathing Thanks and
Praise

SIR JOHN DENHAM
[1615–1669]

Though with those streams he [1] no resemblance hold,
Whose foam is amber, and their gravel gold:
His genuine and less guilty wealth t' explore,

York Ledger and brought out in book form in 1860, is devoted to the history of the *Parable on Persecution* and includes the three versions, — those by Jeremy Taylor, Lord Kames, and Benjamin Franklin.

For a happy introduction to Jeremy Taylor's "Atlantic roll of English prose," see Logan Pearsall Smith: *The Golden Grove* [Oxford, 1930].

[1] Viz. the River Thames; described in the same poem as "Thames, the most loved of all the ocean's sons."

Search not his bottom, but survey his
    shore.
        Cooper's Hill.[1] *Line 165* [*1642*]
Oh, could I flow like thee, and make
    thy stream
My great example, as it is my theme!
Though deep, yet clear, though gentle
    yet not dull;
Strong without rage, without o'erflow-
    ing full.
        Ibid. Line 189
I can no more believe old Homer blind,
Than those who say the sun hath never
    shined:
The age wherein he lived was dark,
    but he
Could not want sight who taught the
    world to see.
        Progress of Learning
But whither am I strayed? I need not
    raise
Trophies to thee from other men's dis-
    praise;
Nor is thy fame on lesser ruins built;
Nor needs thy juster title the foul guilt
Of Eastern kings, who, to secure their
    reign,
Must have their brothers, sons, and
    kindred slain.[2]
    On Mr. John Fletcher's Works

SIR ROGER L'ESTRANGE
[1616–1704]

Though this may be play to you,
'Tis death to us.
    Fables from Several Authors.
        Fable 398

ABRAHAM COWLEY
[1618–1667]

What shall I do to be forever known,
And make the age to come my own?
        The Motto

[1] After Edgehill fight, his poem called Cowper's Hill was printed at Oxford in a sort of
browne paper, for then they could gett no
better. — JOHN AUBREY: *Brief Lives*
[2] Poets are sultans, if they had their will;
    For every author would his brother kill.
    ROGER BOYLE, first Earl of Orrery
        [1621–1679]
Should such a man, too fond to rule alone,

His time is forever, everywhere his
    place.
        Friendship in Absence
We spent them not in toys, in lusts, or
    wine,
    But search of deep philosophy,
    Wit, eloquence, and poetry;
Arts which I lov'd, for they, my friend,
    were thine.
        On the Death of Mr. William
        .Harvey
Ye fields of Cambridge, our dear Cam-
    bridge, say
Have ye not seen us walking every day?
        Ibid.
His *faith,* perhaps, in some nice tenets
    might
Be wrong; his *life,* I'm sure, was in the
    right.[1]
        On the Death of Crashaw
The thirsty earth soaks up the rain,
And drinks, and gapes for drink again.
The plants suck in the earth, and are
With constant drinking fresh and fair.
        From Anacreon, II. Drinking
Fill all the glasses there, for why
Should every creature drink but I?
Why, man of morals, tell me why?
        Ibid.
A mighty pain to love it is,
And 'tis a pain that pain to miss;
But of all pains, the greatest pain
It is to love, but love in vain.
        Ibid. VII. Gold
Th' adorning thee with so much art
    Is but a barb'rous skill;
'Tis like the pois'ning of a dart,
    Too apt before to kill.
        The Waiting Maid
Nothing is there to come, and nothing
    past,
But an eternal now does always last.[2]
        Davideis. Book I, Line 25

Bear, like the Turk, no brother near the
    throne.
    POPE: *Prologue to the Satires, L. 197*
[1] For modes of faith let graceless zealots
    fight,
He can't be wrong whose life is in the right.
    POPE: *Essay on Man, Epistle III, L. 305*
[2] One of our poets (which is it?) speaks
of an everlasting now. — SOUTHEY: *The Doctor, Chap. XXV, P. 1*

When Israel was from bondage led,
　Led by the Almighty's hand
　From out of foreign land,
The great sea beheld and fled.
　　　　　Davideis. Book I, Line 41

Let but thy wicked men from out thee
　go,
And all the fools that crowd thee so,
Even thou, who dost thy millions boast,
A village less than Islington wilt grow,
A solitude almost.
　　　　　Of Solitude. VII

The monster London laugh at me.
　　　　　Ibid. XI

The fairest garden in her looks,
And in her mind the wisest books.
　　　　　The Garden. I

God the first garden made, and the first
　city Cain.[1]
　　　　　Ibid. II

Hence, ye profane! I hate ye all,
Both the great vulgar and the small.
　　　　　Horace. Book III, Ode 1

Charm'd with the foolish whistling of a
　name.[2]
　　　　　Virgil, Georgics. Book II, Line 72

Words that weep and tears that speak.[3]
　　　　　The Prophet

We griev'd, we sigh'd, we wept; we
　never blush'd before.
　　　　　Discourse concerning the Government of Oliver Cromwell

Thus would I double my life's fading
　space;
For he that runs it well, runs twice his
　race.[4]
　　　　　*Discourse XI, Of Myself.
　　　　　Stanza XI*

To-morrow let my sun his beams display,
Or in clouds hide them; I have lived
　my day.[5]
　　　　　Ibid.

Well then! I now do plainly see

This busy world and I shall ne'er agree.
　　　　　The Wish

Ah yet, ere I descend to the grave
May I a small house and large garden
　have;
And a few friends, and many books,
　both true,
Both wise, and both delightful too!
　　　　　Ibid.

A mistress moderately fair.
　　　　　Ibid.

RICHARD LOVELACE
[1618–1658]

Oh, could you view the melody
　Of every grace
　And music of her face,[1]
You'd drop a tear;
　Seeing more harmony
　In her bright eye
Than now you hear.
　　　　　Orpheus to Beasts

I could not love thee, dear, so much,
　Lov'd I not honour more.
　　　　　*To Lucasta, on Going to the Wars.
　　　　　Stanza 3*

When flowing cups run swiftly round
With no allaying Thames.[2]
　　　　　To Althea from Prison. Stanza 2

Fishes that tipple in the deep,
　Know no such liberty.
　　　　　Ibid.

Stone walls do not a prison make,[3]
　Nor iron bars a cage;
Minds innocent and quiet take
　That for an hermitage;
If I have freedom in my love,
　And in my soul am free,
Angels alone that soar above
　Enjoy such liberty.
　　　　　Ibid. Stanza 4

---

[1] See Bacon, page 111.
[2] Ravish'd with the whistling of a name. —
POPE: *Essay on Man, Epistle IV, L. 283*
[3] Thoughts that breathe, and words that
burn. — GRAY: *Progress of Poesy, III, 3, 4*
[4] For he lives twice who can at once employ
The present well, and ev'n the past enjoy.
　　POPE: *Imitation of Martial, L. 10*
[5] See Dryden, page 177.

---

[1] See Browne, page 145.
　The mind, the music breathing from her
face. — BYRON: *Bride of Abydos, Canto I,
St. 6*
[2] Not a drop of allaying Tiber in 't. —
SHAKESPEARE: *Coriolanus, Act II, Sc. 2, L. 52*
[3] Stone walls a prisoner make, but not a
slave. — WORDSWORTH: *Humanity*

ANDREW MARVELL
[1620–1678]

Orange bright,
Like golden lamps in a green night.
The Emigrants in Bermudas

And all the way, to guide their chime,
With falling oars they kept the time.[1]
Ibid.

Had we but world enough, and time,
This coyness, lady, were no crime.
To His Coy Mistress

But at my back I always hear
Time's wingèd chariot hurrying near;
And yonder all before us lie
Deserts of vast eternity.
Ibid.

Though we cannot make our sun
Stand still, yet we will make him run.
Ibid.

Annihilating all that's made
To a green thought in a green shade.
The Garden

Casting the body's vest aside,
My soul into the boughs does glide.
Ibid.

The world in all doth but two nations
bear, —
The good, the bad; and these mixed
everywhere.
The Loyal Scot

The inglorious arts of peace.
*Upon Cromwell's return from
Ireland* [1650]

He [2] nothing common did, or mean,
Upon that memorable scene.
Ibid.

So much one man can do,
That does both act and know.
Ibid.

As lines, so loves oblique, may well
Themselves in every angle greet;
But ours, so truly parallel,
Though infinite, can never meet.
The Definition of Love

---

[1] Faintly as tolls the evening chime
Our voices keep tune and our oars keep time.
THOMAS MOORE: *A Canadian Boat
Song*, St. 1

[2] King Charles I.

RALPH VENNING
[1621–1674]

All the beauty of the world, 'tis but
skin deep.[1]
Orthodoxe Paradoxes [*3d ed.,
1650*], *The Triumph of Assurance, Page 41*

They spare the rod, and spoyle the
child.[2]
*Mysteries   and   Revelations,
Page 5*   [1649]

RICHARD RUMBOLD
[1622–1685]

I never could believe that Providence had sent a few men into the
world, ready booted and spurred to
ride, and millions ready saddled and
bridled to be ridden.
On the scaffold [1685], (*Macaulay's History of England,
Chapter 1*)

ALGERNON SIDNEY
[1622–1683]

Manus haec, inimica tyrannis,
Ense petit placidam sub libertate
quietem.[3]
*Life and Memoirs of Algernon
Sidney*

Liars ought to have good memories.[4]
*Discourses on Government.
Chap. 2, Sect. XV* [1698]

---

[1] Many a dangerous temptation comes to
us in fine gay colours that are but skin-deep.
— HENRY: *Commentaries. Genesis, III*

[2] See Skelton, page 9.

[3] This hand, unfriendly to tyrants,
Seeks with the sword placid repose under
liberty.
His father writes to him [August 30, 1660]:
"It is said that the University of Copenhagen
brought their album unto you, desiring you to
write something; and that you did *scribere in
albo* these words." It is said that the first line
is to be found in a patent granted in 1616 by
Camden (Clarencieux). — *Notes and Queries*
[March 10, 1866]
The second line is the motto of the Commonwealth of Massachusetts.

[4] Il faut bonne mémoire, après qu'on a
menti. — PIERRE CORNEILLE: *Le Menteur*
[1642], *Act IV, Sc. 5*
He who has not a good memory should

Men lived like fishes; the great ones devoured the small.[1]

Discourses on Government.
Chap. 2, Sect. XVIII

God helps those who help themselves.[2]
Ibid. Sect. XXIII

It is not necessary to light a candle in the sun.[3]

Ibid.

HENRY VAUGHAN
[1622–1695]

My soul, there is a country
Afar beyond the stars.
Peace. Stanza 1

Search well another world; who studies this,
Travels in clouds, seeks manna, where none is.
The Search

I saw Eternity the other night
Like a great ring of pure and endless light.
The World

The darksome Statesman, hung with weights and woe,
Like a thick midnight fog, moved there so slow. . . .
And clouds of crying witnesses without
Pursued him with one shout.
Ibid.

But felt through all this fleshly dress
Bright shoots of everlastingness.
The Retreat

I see them walking in an air of glory
Whose light doth trample on my days, —
My days, which are at best but dull and hoary,
Mere glimmering and decays.
Departed Friends. Stanza 3

---

never take upon him the trade of lying. —
MONTAIGNE: *Book I, Chap. IX, Of Liars*
[1] See Shakespeare, page 106.
[2] See Herbert, page 137.
Heaven ne'er helps the men who will not act. — SOPHOCLES: *Fragment 288* (Plumptre's translation)
Help thyself, Heaven will help thee. — LA FONTAINE: *Book VI, Fable 18*
[3] Like his that lights a candle to the sun. — FLETCHER: *Letter to Sir Walter Aston*
And hold their farthing candle to the sun. — YOUNG: *Satire VII, L. 56*

Dear, beauteous death, the jewel of the just!
Shining nowhere but in the dark;
What mysteries do lie beyond thy dust,
Could man outlook that mark!
Departed Friends. Stanza 5

Then bless thy secret growth, nor catch
At noise, but thrive unseen and dumb;
Keep clean, bear fruit, earn life, and watch
Till the white-wing'd reapers come!
The Seed Growing Secretly

JOHN PLAYFORD
[1623–1686]

Begone, dull Care! I prithee begone from me!
Begone, dull Care! thou and I shall never agree.
Musical Companion [1687]

WILLIAM WALKER
[1623–1684]

Learn to read slow: all other graces
Will follow in their proper places.[1]
The Art of Reading

GEORGE FOX [2]
[1624–1691]

I used in my dealings the word *verily*, and it was a common saying among people that knew me, if George says *verily* there is no altering him.
Journal

The Lord opened unto me that being bred at Oxford or Cambridge was not enough to fit and qualify men to be ministers of Christ.
Ibid.

My relations were much troubled at me that I would not go with them to hear the priest; for I would get into the orchard or the fields with my Bible by myself.

Ibid.

---

[1] Take time enough; all other graces
Will soon fill up their proper places.
JOHN BYROM [1692–1763]: *Advice to Preach Slow*
[2] The founder of the Society of Friends ("Quakers").

When the Lord sent me forth into the world, He forbade me to put off my hat to any, high or low.

Journal

Justice Bennet of Derby, was the first that called us Quakers, because I bid them tremble at the word of the Lord. This was in the year 1650.

Ibid.

He [Oliver Cromwell] said: 'I see there is a people risen, that I cannot win either with gifts, honours, offices or places; but all other sects and people I can.'

Ibid. [*1654*]

RICHARD FRANCK
[1624–1708]

Art imitates Nature, and necessity is the mother of invention.[1]

Northern Memoirs, edited by Scott [*written in 1658, published in 1694*]

JOHN AUBREY
[1626–1697]

From the Brief Lives, edited by Andrew Clark [*1898*]

He [Thomas Hobbes] walked much and contemplated, and he had in the head of his staffe a pen and ink-horne, carried alwayes a note-booke in his pocket, and as soon as a thought darted, he presently entred it into his booke, or otherwise he might perhaps have lost it.

Ibid. I, 334

He [Hobbes] had read much, but his contemplation was much more than his reading. He was wont to say that

[1] Necessity, mother of invention. — WILLIAM WYCHERLY [1640–1716]: *Love in a Wood* [1671], *Act III, Sc. 3*

Necessity, the mother of invention. — GEORGE FARQUHAR [1678–1707]: *The Twin Rivals* [1702], *Act I*

Magister artis ingenique largitor
Venter

(Hunger is the teacher of the arts and the bestower of invention).

PERSIUS: *Prolog., L. 10*

Sheer necessity, — the proper parent of an art so nearly allied to invention. — R. B. SHERIDAN: *The Critic, Act I, Sc. 2*

if he had read as much as other men, he should have knowne no more than other men.

From the Brief Lives. I, 349

[William Oughtred, mathematician] His wife was a penurious woman, and would not allow him to burne candle after supper, by which means many a good notion is lost.

Ibid. II, 110

Mr. William Shakespear was borne at Stratford upon Avon in the county of Warwick. His father was a butcher, and I have been told heretofore by some of the neighbours, that when he was a boy he exercised his father's trade, but when he killed a calfe he would doe it in a high style and make a speech.

Ben Johnson and he did gather humours of men dayly where ever they came.

Brief Lives. II, 225

JOHN BUNYAN
[1628–1688]

And so I penned
It down, until at last it came to be,
For length and breadth, the bigness which you see.

Pilgrim's Progress. Apology for His Book

Some said, "John, print it"; others said, "Not so."
Some said, "It might do good"; others said, "No."

Ibid.

The name of the slough was Despond.

Ibid. Part I

Every fat must stand upon his bottom.[1]

Ibid.

Dark as pitch.[2]

Ibid.

He came to the house of the Interpreter.

Ibid.

The palace Beautiful.

Ibid.

[1] Every tub must stand upon its bottom. — CHARLES MACKLIN [1697?–1797]: *The Man of the World* [1781], *Act I, Sc. 2*

[2] RAY: *Proverbs*

GAY: *The Shepherd's Week, Wednesday*

The pilgrim they laid in a large upper chamber, whose window opened toward the sun-rising; the name of the chamber was Peace.

Pilgrim's Progress. Part I

I will talk of things heavenly, or things earthly; things moral, or things evangelical; things sacred, or things profane; things past, or things to come; things foreign, or things at home; things more essential, or things circumstantial.

Ibid.

It beareth the name of Vanity Fair, because the town where 'tis kept is lighter than vanity.

Ibid.

A castle called Doubting Castle, the owner whereof was Giant Despair.

Ibid.

They came to the Delectable Mountains.

Ibid.

Some things are of that nature as to make
One's fancy chuckle, while his heart doth ache.

Ibid. The Author's Way of Sending Forth His Second Part of the Pilgrim

A man that could look no way but downwards with a muck-rake in his hand.

Ibid. Part II

He that is down needs fear no fall.[1]

Ibid. The Shepherd Boy's Song

The first string that the musician usually touches is the bass, when he intends to put all in tune. God also plays upon this string first, when he sets the soul in tune for himself.

Ibid.

My sword I give to him that shall succeed me in my pilgrimage, and my courage and skill to him that can get it. My marks and scars I carry with me, to be a witness for me, that I have fought his battles who now will be my rewarder.

Ibid.

[1] He that is down can fall no lower. — SAMUEL BUTLER: *Hudibras, Part I, Canto 3, L. 878*

So he passed over, and all the trumpets sounded for him on the other side.

Pilgrim's Progress. Part II

The captain of all these men of death that came against him to take him away, was the Consumption, for it was that that brought him down to the grave.

The Life and Death of Mr. Badman

SIR WILLIAM TEMPLE
[1628–1699]

Books, like proverbs, receive their chief value from the stamp and esteem of ages through which they have passed.

Ancient and Modern Learning

No clap of thunder in a fair frosty day could more astonish the world than our declaration of war against Holland in 1672.

Memoirs. Vol. II, Page 255

When all is done, human life is, at the greatest and the best, but like a froward child, that must be played with and humoured a little to keep it quiet till it falls asleep, and then the care is over.

Miscellanea. Part II, Of Poetry

WALTER POPE
[1630?–1714]

May I govern my passions with absolute sway,
And grow wiser and better, as strength wears away,
Without gout or stone, by a gentle decay.

The Old Man's Wish

JOHN TILLOTSON
[1630–1694]

If God were not a necessary Being of himself, he might almost seem to be made for the use and benefit of men.[1]

Sermon

[1] If God did not exist, it would be necessary to invent him. — VOLTAIRE: *A l'Auteur du Livre des trois Imposteurs, Épître CXL*

They who are in highest places, and have the most power, have the least liberty, because they are most observed.

Reflections

JOHN DRYDEN
[1631–1700]

Above any Greek or Roman name.[1]

Upon the Death of Lord Hastings.
Line 76

And threat'ning France, plac'd like a painted Jove,
Kept idle thunder in his lifted hand.

Annus Mirabilis. Stanza 39

Whate'er he did was done with so much ease,
In him alone, 'twas natural to please.

Absalom and Achitophel. Part I,
Line 27

A name to all succeeding ages curst.

Ibid. Line 151

A fiery soul, which, working out its way,
Fretted the pygmy-body to decay:
And o'er-inform'd the tenement of clay.[2]

A daring pilot in extremity;
Pleas'd with the danger, when the waves went high
He sought the storms.

Ibid. Line 156

Great wits are sure to madness near allied,
And thin partitions do their bounds divide.[3]

Ibid. Line 163

And all to leave what with his toil he won
To that unfeather'd two-legged thing, a son.

Ibid. Line 169

---

[1] Above all Greek, above all Roman fame. — POPE: *Epistle I, Book II, L. 26*

[2] See Thomas Fuller, page 147.

[3] No excellent soul is exempt from a mixture of madness. — ARISTOTLE: *Problem, Sect. 30*
Nullum magnum ingenium sine mixtura dementiæ (There is no great genius without a tincture of madness). — SENECA: *De Tranquillitate Animi, 15*
What thin partitions sense from thought divide! — POPE: *Essay on Man, Epistle I, L. 226*

Resolv'd to ruin or to rule the state.

Absalom and Achitophel.
Part I, Line 174

And heaven had wanted one immortal song.

Ibid. Line 197

But wild Ambition loves to slide, not stand,
And Fortune's ice prefers to Virtue's land.[1]

Ibid. Line 198

The people's prayer, the glad diviner's theme,
The young men's vision, and the old men's dream![2]

Ibid. Line 238

Behold him setting in his western skies,
The shadows lengthening as the vapours rise.[3]

Ibid. Line 268

Than a successive title long and dark,
Drawn from the mouldy rolls of Noah's ark.

Ibid. Line 301

His courage foes, his friends his truth proclaim.

Ibid. Line 357

Let him give on till he can give no more.

Ibid. Line 389

All empire is no more than power in trust.

Ibid. Line 411

Not only hating David, but the king.

Ibid. Line 512

Who think too little, and who talk too much.[4]

Ibid. Line 534

A man so various, that he seem'd to be
Not one, but all mankind's epitome;
Stiff in opinions, always in the wrong,

---

[1] Greatnesse on Goodnesse loves to slide, not stand,
And leaves, for Fortune's ice, Vertue's ferme land.
RICHARD KNOLLES [1550–1610]: *History of the Turks (under a portrait of Mustapha I)*

[2] Your old men shall dream dreams, your young men shall see visions. — *Joel, II, 28*

[3] Like our shadows,
Our wishes lengthen as our sun declines.
YOUNG: *Night Thoughts, Night V, L. 661*

[4] They always talk who never think. — PRIOR: *Upon a Passage in the Scaligerana*

Was everything by starts, and nothing
    long;
But, in the course of one revolving
    moon
Was chymist, fiddler, statesman, and
    buffoon.[1]
       Absalom and Achitophel.
            Part I, Line 545

So over violent, or over civil,
That every man with him was God or
    Devil.
              Ibid. Line 557

His tribe were God Almighty's gentle-
    men.[2]
              Ibid. Line 645

Large was his wealth, but larger was
    his heart.
              Ibid. Line 826

Him of the western dome, whose
    weighty sense
Flows in fit words and heavenly elo-
    quence.
              Ibid. Line 868

Of ancient race by birth, but nobler yet
In his own worth.
              Ibid. Line 900

Beware the fury of a patient man.[3]
             Ibid. Line 1005

Made still a blund'ring kind of melody;
Spurr'd boldly on, and dashed through
    thick and thin,[4]
Through sense and nonsense, never out
    nor in.
       Ibid. Part II, Line 413

For every inch that is not fool is rogue.
              Ibid. Line 463

Men met each other with erected look,
The steps were higher that they took;

---

[1] Grammaticus, rhetor, geometres, pictor,
    aliptes,
  Augur, schœnobates, medicus, magus, omnia
    novit
(Grammarian, orator, geometrician; painter,
gymnastic teacher, fortune-teller, rope-dancer,
physician, conjurer, — he knew everything).
— JUVENAL: *Satire III, L. 76*

[2] A Christian is God Almighty's gentleman.
— JULIUS CHARLES HARE [1795–1855]:
Guesses at Truth

  A Christian is the highest style of man. —
YOUNG: *Night Thoughts, Night IV, L. 788*

[3] Furor fit læsa sæpius patientia (An overtaxed patience gives way to fierce anger). —
PUBLIUS SYRUS: *Maxim 289*

[4] See Chaucer, page 6.

Friends to congratulate their friends
    made haste,
And long inveterate foes saluted as they
    pass'd.
       Threnodia Augustalis. Line 124

For truth has such a face and such a
    mien,
As to be lov'd needs only to be seen.[1]
       The Hind and the Panther.
             Part I, Line 33

Of all the tyrannies on human kind
The worst is that which persecutes
    the mind.
              Ibid. Line 239

And kind as kings upon their coronation
    day.
              Ibid. Line 271

Too black for heaven, and yet too white
    for hell.
              Ibid. Line 343

And leaves the private conscience for
    the guide.
              Ibid. Line 478

Eternal house, not built with mortal
    hands!
              Ibid. Line 494

Who can believe what varies every day,
Nor ever was, nor will be at a stay?
         Ibid. Part II, Line 36

All have not the gift of martyrdom.
              Ibid. Line 59

That men may err was never yet de-
    nied.[2]
              Ibid. Line 61

All, as they say, that glitters is not
    gold.[3]
              Ibid. Line 215

When the cause goes hard, the guilty
    man
Excepts, and thins his jury all he can.
              Ibid. Line 242

War seldom enters but where wealth
    allures.
              Ibid. Line 706

Jealousy, the jaundice of the soul.
        Ibid. Part III, Line 73

---

[1] Vice is a monster of so frightful mien,
  As to be hated needs but to be seen.
  POPE: *Essay on Man, Epistle II, L. 217*

[2] To err is human. — POPE: *Essay on Criticism, Part II, L. 325*

[3] See Chaucer, page 8.

Let the guiltless person throw the stone.[1]
> *The Hind and the Panther.*
> *Part III, Line 684*

Secret guilt by silence is betrayed.
> *Ibid. Line 763*

Possess your soul with patience.
> *Ibid. Line 839*

For those whom God to ruin has design'd,
He fits for fate, and first destroys their
mind.[2]
> *Ibid. Line 1093*

Desperate cures must be to desperate
ills applied.[3]
> *Ibid. Line 1111*

But Shadwell never deviates into sense.
> *MacFlecknoe. Line 20*

And torture one poor word ten thousand ways.
> *Ibid. Line 208*

Our vows are heard betimes! and
Heaven takes care
To grant, before we can conclude the
prayer:
Preventing angels met it half the way,
And sent us back to praise, who came
to pray.[4]
> *Britannia Rediviva. Line 1*

Genius must be born, and never can be
taught.
> *Epistle to Congreve. Line 60*

Be kind to my remains; and oh defend,

[1] He that is without sin among you, let him
first cast a stone at her. — *John, VIII, 7*

[2] Quos Deus vult perdere prius dementat
(Whom God wishes to destroy he first de-
prives of reason). The author of this saying
is unknown. It has been ascribed to Euripides
by James Boswell in his *Life of Dr. Johnson,*
Everyman ed., II, p. 443.
When Divine power plans evils for a man,
it first injures his mind. — SOPHOCLES: *Anti-
gone*
When falls on man the anger of the gods,
First from his mind they banish understanding.
LYCURGUS
Whom the Gods would destroy they first
make mad. — LONGFELLOW: *The Masque of
Pandora, VI*

[3] See Shakespeare, page 96, and Montaigne,
page 1028.

[4] And fools who came to scoff remain'd to
pray. — GOLDSMITH: *The Deserted Village,*
L. 180

Against your judgment, your departed
friend!
> *Epistle to Congreve. Line 72*

Better to hunt in fields, for health unbought,
Than fee the doctor for a nauseous
draught.
The wise, for cure, on exercise depend;
God never made his work for man to
mend.
> *Epistle to John Dryden of Ches-
> terton. Line 92*

Words, once my stock, are wanting to
commend
So great a poet and so good a friend.
> *Epistle to Peter Antony Mot-
> teux. Line 54*

> Wit will shine
Through the harsh cadence of a rugged
line.
> *To the Memory of Mr. Oldham.*
> *Line 15*

So softly death succeeded life in her,
She did but dream of heaven, and she
was there.
> *Eleonora. Line 315*

Since heaven's eternal year is thine.
> *Elegy on Mrs. Killegrew. Line 15*

O gracious God! how far have we
Profan'd thy heavenly gift of poesy!
> *Ibid. Line 56*

Her wit was more than man, her innocence a child.[1]
> *Ibid. Line 70*

He was exhal'd; his great Creator drew
His spirit, as the sun the morning dew.[2]
> *On the Death of a Very Young*
> *Gentleman*

Three poets, in three distant ages born,
Greece, Italy, and England did adorn.
The first in loftiness of thought sur-
pass'd;
The next, in majesty; in both the last.
The force of Nature could no further
go,

[1] Of manners gentle, of affections mild,
In wit a man; simplicity a child.
POPE: *Epitaph on Gay*

[2] Early, bright, transient, chaste as morning
dew,
She sparkl'd, was exhal'd, and went to
heaven.
YOUNG: *Night Thoughts, Night V, L. 600*

To make a third, she join'd the former
 two.[1]

      Under Mr. Milton's Picture

From harmony, from heavenly har-
 mony,
This universal frame began:
From harmony to harmony
Through all the compass of the notes
 it ran,
The diapason closing full in Man.

     A Song for St. Cecilia's Day.
          Line 11

None but the brave deserves the fair.

     Alexander's Feast. Line 15

With ravish'd ears
The monarch hears;
Assumes the god,
Affects to nod,
And seems to shake the spheres.

         Ibid. Line 37

Bacchus, ever fair and ever young.

         Ibid. Line 54

  Rich the treasure,
  Sweet the pleasure, ——
Sweet is pleasure after pain.

         Ibid. Line 58

Sooth'd with the sound, the king grew
 vain;
Fought all his battles o'er again;
And thrice he routed all his foes, and
 thrice he slew the slain.

         Ibid. Line 66

Fallen from his high estate,
  And welt'ring in his blood;
Deserted, at his utmost need,
By those his former bounty fed,
On the bare earth expos'd he lies,
With not a friend to close his eyes.

         Ibid. Line 78

For pity melts the mind to love.[2]

         Ibid. Line 96

Softly sweet, in Lydian measures,
Soon he sooth'd his soul to pleasures.
War, he sung, his toil and trouble;

Honour but an empty bubble;
  Never ending, still beginning,
Fighting still, and still destroying.
  If all the world be worth thy win-
 ning,
Think, oh think it worth enjoying:
  Lovely Thais sits beside thee,
  Take the good the gods provide thee.

     Alexander's Feast. Line 97

Sigh'd and look'd, and sigh'd again.

         Ibid. Line 120

And, like another Helen, fir'd another
 Troy.

         Ibid. Line 154

Could swell the soul to rage, or kindle
 soft desire.

         Ibid. Line 160

He rais'd a mortal to the skies,
She drew an angel down.

         Ibid. Line 169

A very merry, dancing, drinking,
Laughing, quaffing, and unthinking
 time.

     The Secular Masque. Line 38

The sword within the scabbard keep,
And let mankind agree.

         Ibid. Line 61

Fool, not to know that love endures no
 tie,
And Jove but laughs at lovers' perjury.[1]

     Palamon and Arcite. Book II,
          Line 758

For Art may err, but Nature cannot
 miss.

     The Cock and the Fox. Line 452

Old as I am, for ladies' love unfit,
The power of beauty I remember yet.

     Cymon and Iphigenia. Line 1

He trudg'd along unknowing what he
 sought,
And whistled as he went, for want of
 thought.

         Ibid. Line 84

Love taught him shame; and shame,
 with love at strife,
Soon taught the sweet civilities of life.

         Ibid. Line 133

---

[1] Græcia Mæonidam, jactet sibi Roma Maro-
 nem,
  Anglia Miltonum jactat utrique parem
(Greece boasts her Homer, Rome can Virgil
 claim;
England can either match in Milton's fame).
     SELVAGGI [fl. 1650]: *Ad Joannem*
          Miltonum

[2] See Beaumont and Fletcher, page 131.

[1] Dryden repeats this proverb in *Amphitryon, Act I, Sc. 2*
See Shakespeare, page 78.

JOHN DRYDEN

She hugg'd the offender, and forgave the offence:
Sex to the last.[1]

> *Cymon and Iphigenia. Line 367*

And raw in fields the rude militia swarms,
Mouths without hands; maintain'd at vast expense,
In peace a charge, in war a weak defence;
Stout once a month they march, a blustering band,
And ever but in times of need at hand.

> *Ibid. Line 400*

Of seeming arms to make a short essay,
Then hasten to be drunk, — the business of the day.

> *Ibid. Line 407*

Happy who in his verse can gently steer
From grave to light, from pleasant to severe.[2]

> *The Art of Poetry. Canto I, Line 75*

Happy the man, and happy he alone,
He who can call to-day his own;
He who, secure within, can say,
To-morrow, do thy worst, for I have liv'd to-day.[3]

> *Imitation of Horace. Book III, Ode 29, Line 65*

Not heaven itself upon the past has power;
But what has been, has been, and I have had my hour.

> *Ibid. Line 71*

I can enjoy her while she's kind;
But when she dances in the wind,
And shakes the wings and will not stay,
I puff the prostitute away.

> *Ibid. Line 81*

---

[1] And love the offender, yet detest the offence. — POPE: *Eloisa to Abelard, L. 192*
[2] Heureux qui, dans ses vers, sait d'une voix légère,
Passer du grave au doux, du plaisant au sévère.
  BOILEAU: *L'Art Poétique, Chant I*
Formed by thy converse, happily to steer
From grave to gay, from lively to severe.
  POPE: *Essay on Man, Epistle IV, L. 379*
[3] See Cowley, page 168.
Serenely full, the epicure would say,
Fate cannot harm me; I have dined to-day.
  SYDNEY SMITH: *Recipe for Salad*

And virtue, though in rags, will keep me warm.

> *Imitation of Horace. Book III, Ode 29, Line 87*

Arms and the man I sing, who, forced by fate
And haughty Juno's unrelenting hate.

> *Virgil, Æneid. Line 1*

And new-laid eggs, which Baucis' busy care
Turn'd by a gentle fire and roasted rare.[1]

> *Ovid, Metamorphoses. Book VIII*
> *Baucis and Philemon, Line 97*

Ill habits gather by unseen degrees, —
As brooks make rivers, rivers run to seas.

> *Ibid. Book XV, The Worship of Æsculapius, Line 155*

She knows her man, and when you rant and swear,
Can draw you to her with a single hair.[2]

> *Persius. Satire V, Line 246*

Look round the habitable world: how few
Know their own good, or knowing it, pursue.

> *Juvenal. Satire X*

Our souls sit close and silently within,
And their own web from their own entrails spin;
And when eyes meet far off, our sense is such,
That, spider-like, we feel the tenderest touch.[3]

> *Mariage à la Mode. Act II, Sc. 1*

Thespis, the first professor of our art,
At country wakes sung ballads from a cart.

> *Prologue to Lee's Sophonisba*

Errors, like straws, upon the surface flow;
He who would search for pearls must dive below.

> *All for Love. Prologue*

Men are but children of a larger growth.

> *Ibid. Act IV, Sc. 1*

---

[1] Our scanty mutton scrags on Fridays, and rather more savoury, but grudging, portions of the same flesh, rotten-roasted or rare, on the Tuesdays. — CHARLES LAMB: *Christ's Hospital Five-and-thirty Years Ago*
[2] See Burton, page 125.
[3] See Davies, page 115.

Your ignorance is the mother of your
    devotion to me.[1]
        The Maiden Queen. Act I, Sc. 2
Burn daylight.[2]
        Ibid. Act II, Sc. 1
I am resolved to grow fat, and look
    young till forty.[3]
        Ibid. Act III, Sc. 1
But Shakespeare's magic could not cop-
    ied be;
Within that circle none durst walk but
    he.
        The Tempest. Prologue
I am as free as Nature first made man,
Ere the base laws of servitude began,
When wild in woods the noble savage
    ran.
        The Conquest of Granada.
        Part I, Act I, Sc. 1
Forgiveness to the injured does belong;
But they ne'er pardon who have done
    the wrong.[4]
        Ibid. Part II, Act I, Sc. 2
    What precious drops are those
Which silently each other's track pur-
    sue,
Bright as young diamonds in their in-
    fant dew?
        Ibid. Act III, Sc. 1
Fame then was cheap, and the first
    comer sped;
And they have kept it since by being
    dead.
        Ibid. Epilogue
Death in itself is nothing; but we fear
To be we know not what, we know not
    where.
        Aurengzebe. Act IV, Sc. 1

[1] See Burton, page 126.
[2] See Shakespeare, page 34.
[3] Fat, fair, and forty. — SCOTT: *St. Ronan's Well, Chap. VII*
    Lord —— is going to marry Lady ——,
a fat, fair, and fifty card-playing resident of
the Crescent. — MRS. MELESINA TRENCH
[1768–1827], in a letter [Feb. 18, 1816]
[4] Quos læserunt et oderunt (Whom they
have injured they also hate). — SENECA: *De
Ira, Lib. II, Cap. 33*
    Proprium humani ingenii est odisse quem
læseris (It belongs to human nature to hate
those you have injured). — TACITUS: *Agricola, 42, 15*
    Chi fa ingiuria non perdona mai (He never
pardons those he injures). — *Italian Proverb*

When I consider life, 'tis all a cheat.
Yet fool'd with hope, men favour the
    deceit;
Trust on, and think to-morrow will re-
    pay.
To-morrow's falser than the former
    day;
Lies worse, and while it says we shall be
    blest
With some new joys, cuts off what we
    possest.
Strange cozenage! none would live past
    years again,
Yet all hope pleasure in what yet re-
    main; [1]
And from the dregs of life think to re-
    ceive
What the first sprightly running could
    not give.
        Aurengzebe. Act IV, Sc. 1
'Tis not for nothing that we life pur-
    sue;
It pays our hopes with something still
    that's new.
        Ibid.
All delays are dangerous in war.
        Tyrannic Love. Act I, Sc. 1
Pains of love be sweeter far
Than all other pleasures are.
        Ibid. Act IV, Sc. 1
Whatever is, is in its causes just.[2]
        Œdipus. Act III, Sc. 1
        His hair just grizzled,
As in a green old age.[3]
        Ibid.
Of no distemper, of no blast he died,
But fell like autumn fruit that mellow'd
    long, —
Even wonder'd at, because he dropp'd
    no sooner.
Fate seem'd to wind him up for four-
    score years,
Yet freshly ran he on ten winters more;
Till like a clock worn out with eating
    time,

[1] There are not eight finer lines in Lucretius. — MACAULAY: *History of England,
Chap. XVIII*
[2] Whatever is, is right. — POPE: *Essay on
Man, Epistle I, L. 294*
[3] A green old age unconscious of decays. —
POPE: *The Iliad, Book XXIII, L. 929*

The wheels of weary life at last stood
still.
> *Œdipus. Act IV, Sc. 1*

She, though in full-blown flower of glorious beauty,
Grows cold even in the summer of her
age.
> *Ibid.*

There is a pleasure sure
In being mad which none but madmen
know.[1]
> *The Spanish Friar. Act II, Sc. 1*

Lord of humankind.[2]
> *Ibid.*

Bless the hand that gave the blow.[3]
> *Ibid.*

Second thoughts, they say, are best.[4]
> *Ibid. Sc. 2*

He's a sure card.
> *Ibid.*

As sure as a gun.
> *Ibid. Act III, Sc. 2*

This is the porcelain clay of humankind.[5]
> *Don Sebastian. Act I, Sc. 1*

I have a soul that like an ample shield
Can take in all, and verge enough for
more.[6]
> *Ibid.*

A knock-down argument: 'tis but a
word and a blow.
> *Amphitryon. Act I, Sc. 1*

Whistling to keep myself from being
afraid.[7]
> *Ibid. Act III, Sc. 1*

The true Amphitryon.[8]
> *Ibid. Act IV, Sc. 1*

---

[1] There is a pleasure in poetic pains.
  Which only poets know.
  COWPER: *The Timepiece, L. 285*
[2] Lords of humankind. — GOLDSMITH: *The
Traveller, L. 327*
[3] Adore the hand that gives the blow. —
POMFRET: *Verses to His Friend*
[4] Among mortals second thoughts are the
wisest. — EURIPIDES: *Hippolytus, 438*
[5] The precious porcelain of human clay. —
BYRON: *Don Juan, Canto IV, St. 11*
[6] Give ample room and verge enough. —
GRAY: *The Bard, II, 1*
[7] Whistling aloud to bear his courage up. —
BLAIR: *The Grave, L. 58*
[8] Le véritable Amphitryon
  Est l'Amphitryon où l'on dîne

He [Shakespeare] was the man who
of all Modern, and perhaps Ancient
Poets, had the largest and most comprehensive soul.
> *Essay of Dramatic Poesy* [*1668*]

He needed not the spectacles of
Books to read Nature; he looked in-
wards, and found her there.
> *Ibid.*

[Of Chaucer's *Canterbury Tales*]
Here is God's plenty.[1]
> *Preface to the Fables* [*1699*]

WILLIAM STOUGHTON
[1631–1701]

God sifted a whole nation that he
might send choice grain over into this
wilderness.[2]
> *Election Sermon at Boston*
> [*April 29, 1669*]

BISHOP RICHARD
CUMBERLAND
[1632–1718]

It is better to wear out than to rust out.
> *Quoted by Bishop George Horne*
> [*1730–1792*]: *Sermon on the*
> *Duty of Contending for the*
> *Truth*

SIR CHRISTOPHER WREN
[1632–1723]

Whereas, among labourers and others, that ungodly custom of swearing is
too frequently heard, to the dishonour
of God and contempt of authority; and
to the end that such impiety may be utterly banished from these works, which
are intended for the service of God and
the honour of religion, it is ordered that

(The true Amphitryon is the Amphitryon
where we dine).
  MOLIÈRE: *Amphitryon, Act III, Sc. 5*
[1] Dryden was buried in the same grave with
Chaucer, in Westminster Abbey.
[2] God had sifted three kingdoms to find the
wheat for this planting. — LONGFELLOW:
Courtship of Miles Standish, IV

profane swearing shall be a sufficient crime to dismiss any labourer.
Notice to workmen employed during the building of St. Paul's Cathedral

WENTWORTH DILLON, EARL OF ROSCOMMON
[1633–1685]

Men ever had, and ever will have, leave
To coin new words well suited to the age.
Words are like leaves, some wither ev'ry year,
And ev'ry year a younger race succeeds.
Translation of Horace's Ars Poetica [1680] *Line 73*

For Nature forms, and softens us within,
And writes our fortune's changes in our face.
Ibid. Line 130

The lab'ring mountain scarce brings forth a mouse.
Ibid. Line 168

Old men are only walking hospitals.
Ibid. Line 202

Five acts are the just measure of a play.
Ibid. Line 226

And in one scene no more than three should speak.
Ibid. Line 229

A string may jar in the best master's hand,
And the most skilful archer miss his aim.
Ibid. Line 387

Homer himself hath been observ'd to nod.
Ibid. Line 402

But words once spoke can never be recall'd.[1]
Ibid. Line 438

[1] Thoughts unexpressed may sometimes fall back dead;
But God himself can't kill them when they're said.
WILL CARLETON [1845–1912]: *The First Settler's Story*
Never shall thy spoken word
Be again unsaid, unheard.
ROSE TERRY COOKE [1827–1892]: *Unreturning*
Four things come not back:

'Tis hard to find a man of great estate,
That can distinguish flatterers from friends.
Translation of Horace's Ars Poetica [1680] *Line 478*

True friends appear less mov'd than counterfeit;
As men that truly grieve at funerals
Are not so loud, as those that cry for hire.
Ibid. Line 484

Remember Milo's end,
Wedged in that timber which he strove to rend.
Essay on Translated Verse [1684]. *Line 87*

And choose an author as you choose a friend.
Ibid. Line 96

Immodest words admit of no defence,
For want of decency is want of sense.
Ibid. Line 113

The multitude is always in the wrong.
Ibid. Line 184

My God, my Father, and my Friend,
Do not forsake me in my end.
Translation of Dies Iræ

SAMUEL PEPYS
[1633–1703]

I pray God to keep me from being proud.
Diary.[1] *March 22, 1660*

This morning came home my fine camlet cloak, with gold buttons, and a silk suit, which cost me much money, and I pray God to make me able to pay for it.
Ibid. July 1, 1660

And so to bed.
Ibid. July 22, 1660; December 7, 1660; May 19, 1662; etc.

The spoken word;
The sped arrow;
Time past;
The neglected opportunity.
OMAR IBN AL-HALIF: *Aphorism*

[1] So artless in its vanity,
So fleeting, so eternal,
So packed with "poor Humanity" —
We know as Pepys his Journal.
AUSTIN DOBSON: *Pepys' Diary, St. 6*

I am unwilling to mix my fortune with him that is going down the wind.

Diary. September 6, 1660

I did give ten shillings and no more, though I believe most of the rest did give more, and did believe that I did so too.

Ibid. November 5, 1660

One, by his own confession to me, that can put on two several faces, and look his enemies in the face with as much love as his friends. But, good God! what an age is this, and what a world is this! that a man cannot live without playing the knave and dissimulation.

Ibid. September 1, 1661

Though he be a fool, yet he keeps much company, and will tell all he sees or hears, so a man may understand what the common talk of the town is.

Ibid. September 2, 1661

Besides us and my uncle Fenner's family, there was none of any quality, but poor and rascally people.

Ibid. September 15, 1661

My wife, poor wretch.

Ibid. September 18, 1661;
December 19, 1662; etc.

To the paynter's, and sat and had more of my picture done, but it do not please me, for I fear it will not be like me.

Ibid. December 3, 1661

Thanks be to God, since my leaving drinking of wine, I do find myself much better, and do mind my business better, and do spend less money, and less time lost in idle company.

Ibid. January 26, 1662

Mr. Coventry had already feathered his nest.[1]

Ibid. June 7, 1662

As happy a man as any in the world, for the whole world seems to smile upon me.

Ibid. October 31, 1662

Great talk among people how some of the Fanatiques do say that the end of the world is at hand, and that next Tuesday is to be the day. Against which, whenever it shall be, good God fit us all!

Diary. November 25, 1662

Bought Hudibras again, it being certainly some ill humour to be so against that which all the world cries up to be the example of wit; for which I am resolved once more to read him, and see whether I can find it or no.[1]

Ibid. February 6, 1663

Got my father, brother Tom, and myself together, and I advised my father to good husbandry, and to be living within the compass of £50 a year, and all in such kind words, as not only made both them but myself to weep.

Ibid. May 1, 1663

No high-flyer.

Ibid. May 27, 1663

Troubled to see my wife forced to sit in the back of the coach, though pleased to see her company none but women and one parson.

Ibid. June 15, 1663

Find myself £43 worse than I was the last month . . . chiefly arisen from my layings-out in clothes for myself and wife; viz., for her about £12, and for myself £55.

Ibid. October 31, 1663

Home, and dined, where I found an excellent mastiffe — his name Towser — sent me by a surgeon.

Ibid. February 17, 1664

To the Trinity House, where a very good dinner among the old soakers.

Ibid. February 15, 1665

I am at a loss to know whether it be my hare's foot which is my preservative, or my taking of a pill of turpentine every morning.

Ibid. March 26, 1665

Thus I ended this month with the greatest joy that ever I did any in my life, because I have spent the greatest part of it with abundance of joy, and honour, and pleasant journeys, and

---

[1] How well I feathered my nest. — RABELAIS: *Book II, Chap. 17*

Feather'd well her nest. — DRYDEN: *The Hind and the Panther, Part III, L. 436*

[1] Pepys had bought *Hudibras*, December 26, 1662, but thought it "so silly an abuse of the Presbyter Knight going to the wars" that he sold it the same day.

brave entertainments, and without cost of money.

Diary. July 31, 1665

But Lord! how everybody's looks, and discourse in the street, is of death, and nothing else; and few people going up and down, that the town is like a place distressed and forsaken.[1]

Ibid. August 30, 1665

Saw a wedding in the church; and strange to see what delight we married people have to see these poor fools decoyed into our condition.

Ibid. December 25, 1665

Musick and women I cannot but give way to, whatever my business is.

Ibid. March 9, 1666

The truth is, I do indulge myself a little the more in pleasure, knowing that this is the proper age of my life to do it; and, out of my observation that most men that do thrive in the world do forget to take pleasure during the time that they are getting their estate, but reserve that till they have got one, and then it is too late for them to enjoy it.

Ibid. March 10, 1666

Home, and, being washing-day, dined upon cold meat.

Ibid. April 4, 1666

Anon comes home my wife from Brampton, not looked for till Saturday, which will hinder me of a little pleasure, but I am glad of her coming.

Ibid. April 19, 1666

Musick is the thing of the world that I love most.

Ibid. July 30, 1666

Thus ends this year of publick wonder and mischief to this nation, and, therefore, generally wished by all people to have an end.

Ibid. December 31, 1666

Busy till night, pleasing myself mightily to see what a deal of business goes off a man's hands when he stays by it.

Ibid. January 14, 1667

Did satisfy myself mighty fair in the truth of the saying that the world do not grow old at all, but is in as good

[1] The time of the Great Plague.

condition in all respects as ever it was.

Diary. February 3, 1667

This day I am, by the blessing of God, 34 years old, in very good health and mind's content, and in condition of estate much beyond whatever my friends could expect of a child of their's, this day 34 years. The Lord's name be praised! and may I be thankful for it.

Ibid. February 23, 1667

To church; and with my mourning, very handsome, and new periwigg, make a great show.

Ibid. March 31, 1667

But to think of the clatter they make with his coach, and their own fine cloathes, and yet how meanly they live within doors, and nastily, and borrowing everything of neighbours.

Ibid. April 1, 1667

I have had it much in my thoughts lately that it is not too much for me now, in degree or cost, to keep a coach, but contrarily, that I am almost ashamed to be seen in a hackney.

Ibid. April 21, 1667

Whose red nose makes me ashamed to be seen with him.

Ibid. May 3, 1667

I staid talking below, while my wife dressed herself, which vexed me that she was so long about it.[1]

Ibid. July 14, 1667

Gives me some kind of content to remember how painful it is sometimes to keep money, as well as to get it.

Ibid. October 11, 1667

And there all my Fellow-Officers, and all the world that was within hearing, did congratulate me, and cry my speech as the best thing they ever heard.

Ibid. March 5, 1668

Not to make any more speech, which, while my fame is good, I will avoid, for fear of losing it.

Ibid. March 13, 1668

I find my wife hath something in her gizzard, that only waits an opportunity

[1] In fairness to Mrs. Pepys, it should be added that they were rising at 4 A. M. that warm morning, for a picnic in the country. The account of the day's adventures is so delightful it should be read in full.

of being provoked to bring up; but I will not, for my content-sake, give it.

Diary. June 17, 1668

I by little words find that she hath heard of my going to plays, and carrying people abroad every day, in her absence; and that I cannot but help the storm will break out in a little time.

Ibid. June 18, 1668

In appearance, at least, he being on all occasions glad to be at friendship with me, though we hate one another, and know it on both sides.

Ibid. September 22, 1668

I do hate to be unquiet at home.

Ibid. January 22, 1669

And so I betake myself to that course, which is almost as much as to see myself go into my grave; for which, and all the discomforts that will accompany my being blind, the good God prepare me!

Ibid. May 31, 1669 (final entry)

SIR GEORGE SAVILE, MARQUIS OF HALIFAX
[1633–1695]

Popularity is a crime from the moment it is sought; it is only a virtue where men have it whether they will or no.

Moral Thoughts and Reflections

Misspending a man's time is a kind of self-homicide.

Ibid.

Children and fools want everything, because they want wit to distinguish; there is no stronger evidence of a crazy understanding than the making too large a catalogue of things necessary.

Advice to a Daughter

ROBERT SOUTH
[1634–1716]

Lucid interval.[1]

Sermons. Vol. VIII, Page 403

[1] Lucid interval. — BACON: *Henry VII.* SIDNEY: *On Government, Vol. I, Chap. II, Sect. 24.* FULLER: *A Pisgah Sight of Palestine, Book IV, Chap. II.* PENN: *Some Fruits of Solitude, Preface.* DRYDEN: *MacFlecknoe.* MATHEW HENRY: *Commentaries, Psalm LXXXVIII.*

Speech was given to the ordinary sort of men whereby to communicate their mind; but to wise men, whereby to conceal it.[1]

Sermon [April 30, 1676]

BISHOP THOMAS KEN
[1637–1711]

Teach me to live, that I may dread
The grave as little as my bed.

Morning and Evening Hymn.
Stanza 3

Praise God, from whom all blessings flow!
Praise Him, all creatures here below!
Praise Him above, ye heavenly host!
Praise Father, Son, and Holy Ghost!

Ibid. Stanza 10

SIR CHARLES SEDLEY
[1639–1701]

When change itself can give no more,
'Tis easy to be true.

Reasons for Constancy. Stanza 4

JOHNSON: *Life of Lyttelton.* BURKE: *On the French Revolution*

[1] Speech was made to open man to man, and not to hide him; to promote commerce, and not betray it. — DAVID LLOYD [1635–1692]: *The Statesmen and Favourites of England since the Reformation* [1665, edited by Whitworth], *Vol. I, P. 503*

Men talk only to conceal the mind. — YOUNG: *Love of Fame, Satire II, L. 298*

The true use of speech is not so much to express our wants as to conceal them. — GOLDSMITH: *The Bee, No. 3* [Oct. 20, 1759]

Ils ne se servent de la pensée que pour autoriser leurs injustices, et emploient les paroles que pour déguiser leurs pensées (Men use thought only to justify their wrong doings, and employ speech only to conceal their thoughts). — VOLTAIRE: *Dialogue XIV, Le Chapon et la Poularde* [1766].

When Harel wished to put a joke or witticism into circulation, he was in the habit of connecting it with some celebrated name, on the chance of reclaiming it if it took. Thus he assigned to Talleyrand, in the "Nain Jaune," the phrase, "Speech was given to man to disguise his thoughts." — EDOUARD FOURNIER [1819–1880]: *L'Esprit dans l'Histoire*

SIR EUSTACE PEACHTREE
[*Floruit* 1640]

Among the notionable dictes of antique Rome was the fancy that when men heard thunder on the left the gods had somewhat of special advertisement to impart. Then did the prudent pause and lay down their affaire to study what omen Jove intended.
The Dangers of This Mortall Life

SIR ISAAC NEWTON
[1642–1727]

I do not know what I may appear to the world; but to myself I seem to have been only like a boy playing on the seashore, and diverting myself in now and then finding a smoother pebble or a prettier shell than ordinary, whilst the great ocean of truth lay all undiscovered before me.
Brewster's Memoirs of Newton.
Vol. II, Chap. XXVII

WILLIAM PENN
[1644–1718]

From Fruits of Solitude [*1693*]

A copy of this little book, wrote Robert Louis Stevenson, "I carried in my pocket all about the San Francisco streets, read in street-cars and ferry-boats when I was sick unto death, and found in all times and places a peaceful and sweet companion."

The receipts of cookery are swelled to a volume; but a good stomach excels them all.

Truth often suffers more by the heat of its defenders, than from the arguments of its opposers.

Men are generally more careful of the breed of their horses and dogs than of their children.

It were endless to dispute upon everything that is disputable.

Have a care where there is more sail than ballast.

Passion is a sort of fever in the mind, which ever leaves us weaker than it found us.

The public must and will be served.
Fruits of Solitude

Much reading is an oppression of the mind, and extinguishes the natural candle, which is the reason of so many senseless scholars in the world.
Advice to His Children [*1699*]

HENRY ALDRICH
[1647–1710]

If all be true that I do think,
There are five reasons we should drink:
Good wine — a friend — or being dry —
Or lest we should be by and by —
Or any other reason why.
Five Reasons for Drinking.
From Causae Bibendi,[1] *by John*
Sirmond [*1589–1649*]

JOHN WILMOT, EARL OF ROCHESTER
[1647–1680]

Here lies our sovereign lord the king,
    Whose word no man relies on;
He never says a foolish thing,
    Nor ever does a wise one.
Written on the Bedchamber Door
of Charles II

For pointed satire I would Buckhurst choose,
The best good man with the worst-natured muse.[2]
An Allusion to Horace. Satire X,
Book I

A merry monarch, scandalous and poor.
On the King

The world appears like a great family,
Whose lord, oppressed with pride and poverty,

---

[1] Si bene commemini, causae sunt quinque bibendi:
    Hospitis adventus; praesens sitis atque futura;
    Et vini bonitas, et quaelibet altera causa.
    Ménagiana [1693], compiled by Giles Ménage [1613–1692], French philologist, who attributed the epigram to Sirmond.

[2] Thou best-humour'd man with the worst-humour'd muse! — GOLDSMITH: *Retaliation, Postscript*

(That to the few great bounty he may show)
Is fain to starve the numerous train below.

Like a Great Family

There's not a thing on earth that I can name,
So foolish, and so false, as common fame.

Did E'er This Saucy World

Reason, which fifty times to one does err,
Reason, an ignis fatuus of the mind.

Then Old Age and Experience

Books bear him up a while, and make him try
To swim with bladders of philosophy.

Ibid.

Then Old Age and Experience, hand in hand,
Lead him to death, and make him understand,
After a search so painful and so long,
That all his life he has been in the wrong.

Ibid.

Dead, we become the lumber of the world.

After Death

It is a very good world to live in,
To lend, or to spend, or to give in;
But to beg or to borrow, or to get a man's own,
It is the very worst world that ever was known.[1]

Epigram

JOHN SHEFFIELD, DUKE OF BUCKINGHAMSHIRE
[1648–1721]

Of all those arts in which the wise excel,
Nature's chief masterpiece is writing well.

Essay on Poetry

Read Homer once, and you can read no more;

[1] These four lines are attributed to Rochester, and also to John Bromfield. They were included in a collection of epigrams in 1737. Washington Irving gave them the title, *Lines from an Inn Window* and used them on the flyleaf of the story, *Buckthorne and His Friends* in *Tales of a Traveller*.

For all books else appear so mean, so poor,
Verse will seem prose; but still persist to read,
And Homer will be all the books you need.

Essay on Poetry

And when I feigned an angry look,
Alas! I loved you best.

The Reconcilement

THOMAS OTWAY
[1651–1685]

O woman! lovely woman! Nature made thee
To temper man: we had been brutes without you.

Venice Preserved. Act I, Sc. 1

What mighty ills have not been done by woman!
Who was 't betrayed the Capital? — A woman!
Who lost Mark Antony the world? — A woman!
Who was the cause of a long ten years' war,
And laid at last old Troy in ashes? — Woman!
Destructive, damnable, deceitful woman!

The Orphan. Act III, Sc. 1

Let us embrace, and from this very moment vow an eternal misery together.

Ibid. Act IV, Sc. 2

NAHUM TATE
[1652–1715]
AND
NICHOLAS BRADY
[1659–1726]

Untimely grave.[1]

Psalms. VII

And though he promise to his loss,
He makes his promise good.

Ibid. XV, 5

The sweet remembrance of the just
Shall flourish when he sleeps in dust.

Ibid. CXII, 6

Permit the transports of a British Muse,

[1] An untimely grave. — THOMAS CAREW: *On the Duke of Buckingham*

And pardon raptures that yourselves infuse.

> NAHUM TATE, *as Poet Laureate, to the Parliament* [*1701*]

THOMAS D'URFEY
[1653–1723]

Of ancient modes and former ways
I'll teach you, Sirs, the manner,
In good Queen Bess's golden days,
When I was a Dame of Honor.

> *The Dame of Honor* [*1706*]. *The World Turned Upside Down*

O'er the hills and far away.

> *Pills to Purge Melancholy*

ANDREW FLETCHER OF SALTOUN
[1655–1716]

Give me the making of the songs of a nation, and I care not who makes its laws.[1]

> *Conversation Concerning a Right Regulation of Government for the Common Good of Mankind* [*1703*]

NATHANIEL LEE
[1655–1692]

Then he will talk — good gods! how he will talk![2]

> *Alexander the Great. Act I, Sc. 3*

Vows with so much passion, swears with so much grace,
That 'tis a kind of heaven to be deluded by him.

> *Ibid.*

When Greeks joined Greeks, then was the tug of war.

> *Ibid. Act IV, Sc. 2*

'Tis beauty calls, and glory shows the way.[3]

> *Ibid.*

---

[1] Fletcher's aphorism . . . "Let me make the songs of a people," said he, "and you shall make its laws." — CARLYLE: *Essay on Robert Burns*

[2] See Beaumont and Fletcher, page 131.

[3] "Leads the way" in the stage editions, which contain various interpolations, among them —

Man, false man, smiling, destructive man!

> *Theodosius. Act III, Sc. 2*

JOHN DENNIS
[1657–1734]

A man who could make so vile a pun would not scruple to pick a pocket.

> *The Gentleman's Magazine. Vol. LI, Page 324*

They will not let my play run; and yet they steal my thunder.[1]

JOHN NORRIS
[1657–1711]

How fading are the joys we dote upon!
Like apparitions seen and gone.
But those which soonest take their flight
Are the most exquisite and strong, —
Like angels' visits, short and bright;[2]
Mortality's too weak to bear them long.

> *The Parting*

When after some delays, some dying strife,
The soul stands shivering on the ridge of life;
With what a dreadful curiosity

See the conquering hero comes!
Sound the trumpet, beat the drums! — which was first used by Handel in *Joshua*, and afterwards transferred to *Judas Maccabæus*. The text of both oratorios was written by Dr. Thomas Morell [1703–1784], a clergyman.

[1] Our author, for the advantage of this play ("Appius and Virginia"), had invented a new species of thunder, which was approved of by the actors, and is the very sort that at present is used in the theatre. The tragedy however was coldly received, notwithstanding such assistance, and was acted but a short time. Some nights after, Mr. Dennis, being in the pit at the representation of "Macbeth," heard his own thunder made use of; upon which he rose in a violent passion, and exclaimed, with an oath, that it was his thunder. "See," said he, "how the rascals use me! They will not let my play run, and yet they steal my thunder!" — *Biographia Britannica, Vol. V, P. 103*

[2] Like those of angels, short and far between. — ROBERT BLAIR [1699–1746]: *The Grave* [1743], *L. 588*

Like angel visits, few and far between. — CAMPBELL: *Pleasures of Hope, Part II, L. 378*

Does she launch out into the sea of vast
   eternity.
                                The Meditation

DANIEL DEFOE
[1661–1731]

Wherever God erects a house of prayer,
The Devil always builds a chapel
   there; [1]
And 'twill be found, upon examination,
The latter has the largest congregation.
            The True-Born Englishman.
               Part I, Line 1 [*1701*]

   He bade me observe it, and I should
always find, that the calamities of life
were shared among the upper and lower
part of mankind; but that the middle
station had the fewest disasters.
            Robinson Crusoe. Page 23
                                [*1719*]
   One day, about noon, going towards
my boat, I was exceedingly surprised
with the print of a man's naked foot on
the shore, which was very plain to be
seen on the sand.
                        Ibid. Page 179
   I let him know his name should be
Friday, which was the day I saved his
life.
                        Ibid. Page 234
   I took my man Friday with me.
                                Ibid.

SIR SAMUEL GARTH [2]
[1661–1719]

To die is landing on some silent shore
Where billows never break, nor tem-
   pests roar;
Ere well we feel the friendly stroke, 'tis
   o'er.
            The Dispensary. Canto III,
                        Line 225 [*1699*]
I see the right, and I approve it too,

[1] See Burton, page 126.
[2] Thou hast no faults, or I no faults can
   spy;
   Thou art all beauty, or all blindness I.
CHRISTOPHER CODRINGTON [1668–1710]:
Lines Addressed to Garth on His Dispensary

Condemn the wrong, and yet the wrong
   pursue.[1]
         Ovid, Metamorphoses, VII, 20
         (*translated by Tate and Stone-*
         street, edited by Garth)
For all their luxury was doing good.[2]
               Claremont. Line 149

RICHARD BENTLEY
[1662–1742]

   It is a maxim with me that no man
was ever written out of reputation but
by himself.
      MONK'S *Life of Bentley. Page 90*
   The fortuitous or casual concourse of
atoms.[3]
         Works, Vol. III, Sermon VII,
                  Page 147 [*1692*]

MATHEW HENRY
[1662–1714]

   Many a dangerous temptation comes
to us in fine gay colours that are but
skin-deep.
         Commentaries. Genesis, III
To their own second thoughts.
                        Ibid. Job, VI
He rolls it under his tongue as a sweet
   morsel.
                  Ibid. Psalm XXXVI
Our creature comforts.
                  Ibid. Psalm XXXVII
None so deaf as those that will not
   hear.[4]
               Ibid. Psalm LVIII
They that die by famine die by inches.
               Ibid. Psalm LIX

[1] I know and love the good, yet, ah! the
worst pursue. — PETRARCH: *Sonnet CCXXV,
Canzone XXI, To Laura in Life*
   See Shakespeare, page 44.
[2] And learn the luxury of doing good. —
GOLDSMITH: *The Traveller, L. 22.* CRABBE:
Tales of the Hall, Book III. GRAVES: *The Epicure*
[3] That fortuitous concourse of atoms. —
*Review of Sir Robert Peel's Address, in Quar-
terly Review, Vol. LIII, P. 270* [1835]
   In this article a party was described as a
fortuitous concourse of atoms, — a phrase
supposed to have been used for the first time
many years afterwards by Lord John Russell.
— *Croker Papers, Vol. II, P. 54*
[4] See Heywood, page 17.

To fish in troubled waters.

> *Commentaries. Psalm LX*

Here is bread, which strengthens man's heart, and therefore called the staff of life.[1]

> *Ibid. Psalm CIV*

Hearkners, we say, seldom hear good of themselves.

> *Ibid. Ecclesiastes, VII*

It was a common saying among the Puritans, "Brown bread and the Gospel is good fare."

> *Ibid. Isaiah, XXX*

Blushing is the colour of virtue.[2]

> *Ibid. Jeremiah III*

None so blind as those that will not see.

> *Ibid. Jeremiah, XX*

Not lost, but gone before.[3]

> *Ibid. Matthew, II*

Better late than never.

> *Ibid. Matthew, XXI*

Judas had given them the slip.

> *Ibid. Matthew, XXII*

After a storm comes a calm.

> *Ibid. Acts, IX*

It is good news, worthy of all acceptation; and yet not too good to be true.

> *Ibid. Timothy, I*

It is not fit the public trusts should be lodged in the hands of any, till they are first proved and found fit for the business they are to be entrusted with.[4]

> *Ibid. Timothy, III*

---

[1] Bread is the staff of life. — Swift: *Tale of a Tub*

Corne, which is the staffe of life. — Edward Winslow [1595-1655]: *Good Newes from New England, P. 47* [London, 1624]

The stay and the staff, the whole staff of bread. — *Isaiah, III, 1*

[2] Diogenes once saw a youth blushing, and said: "Courage, my boy, that is the complexion of virtue." — Diogenes Laertius: *Diogenes, VI*

[3] Literally from Seneca: Non amittuntur sed praemittuntur. — *Epistola LXIII, 16*

Not dead, but gone before. — Samuel Rogers: *Human Life* [1819]

[4] To execute laws is a royal office; to execute orders is not to be a king. However, a political executive magistracy, though merely such, is a great trust. — Burke: *On the French Revolution*

When a man assumes a public trust, he should consider himself as public property. — Thomas Jefferson ("Winter in Washington, 1807"), in a conversation with Baron Hum-

---

THOMAS (TOM) BROWN
[1663-1704]

I do not love thee, Doctor Fell,
The reason why I cannot tell;
But this alone I know full well,
I do not love thee, Doctor Fell.[1]

> *Written while a student at*
> *Christ Church, Oxford*

To treat a poor wretch with a bottle of Burgundy, and fill his snuff-box, is like giving a pair of laced ruffles to a man that has never a shirt on his back.[2]

> *Laconics*

In the reign of Charles II. a certain worthy divine at Whitehall thus addressed himself to the auditory at the conclusion of his sermon: "In short, if you don't live up to the precepts of the Gospel, but abandon yourselves to your irregular appetites, you must expect to receive your reward in a certain place which 'tis not good manners to mention here."[3]

> *Ibid.*

---

boldt. See Rayner's *Life of Jefferson, P. 356* [Boston, 1834].

The very essence of a free government consists in considering offices as public trusts, bestowed for the good of the country, and not for the benefit of an individual or a party. — John C. Calhoun: *Speech,* [July 13, 1835]

The phrase, "public office is a public trust," has of late become common property. — Charles Sumner [May 31, 1872]

[1] A slightly different version is found in Brown's *Works,* collected and published in 1707. Dr. John Fell [1625-1686] was Dean of Christ Church and later Bishop of Oxford, and a notable patron of the Oxford University Press. The famous verse is a translation of Martial: —

Non amo te, Sabidi, nec possum dicere quare;

Hoc tantum possum dicere, non amo te.

(I do not love thee, Sabidius, nor can I say why; this only I can say, I do not love thee).

— Martial: *Epigram I, 33*

Je ne vous aime pas, Hylas;
Je n'en saurois dire la cause,
Je sais seulement une chose;
C'est que je ne vous aime pas.

Comte de Bussy Rabutin [1618-1693]

[2] Like sending them ruffles, when wanting a shirt. — Sorbienne [1610-1670]

> Goldsmith: *The Haunch of Venison*

[3] Who never mentions hell to ears polite. — Pope: *Moral Essays, Epistle IV, L. 149*

HENRY CAREY
[1663–1743]

God save our gracious king!
Long live our noble king!
  God save the king!
God Save the King

Namby Pamby's little rhymes,
Little jingle, little rhymes.
Namby Pamby [1] (*Ambrose
        Phillips*)

Aldeborontiphoscophornio!
Where left you Chrononhotonthologos?
Chrononhotonthologos. Act I, Sc. 1

His cogitative faculties immersed
In cogibundity of cogitation.
Ibid.

    Let the singing singers
With vocal voices, most vociferous,
In sweet vociferation out-vociferize
Even sound itself.
Ibid.

To thee, and gentle Rigdom Funnidos,
Our gratulations flow in streams un-
  bounded.
Ibid. Sc. 3

What a monstrous tail our cat has got!
*The Dragon of Wantley.
Act II, Sc. 1*

Of all the girls that are so smart,
  There's none like pretty Sally.
She is the darling of my heart,
  And she lives in our alley.
Sally in Our Alley. Stanza 1

Of all the days that's in the week
  I dearly love but one day,
And that's the day that comes betwixt
  A Saturday and Monday.
Ibid. Stanza 4

WILLIAM WALSH
[1663–1708]

Of all the plagues a lover bears,
  Sure rivals are the worst.
Song

I can endure my own despair,
  But not another's hope.
Ibid.

[1] See Macaulay, page 400.

MATTHEW PRIOR
[1664–1721]

All jargon of the schools.[1]
I Am That I Am, An Ode

Our hopes, like towering falcons, aim
  At objects in an airy height;
The little pleasure of the game
  Is from afar to view the flight.
To the Hon. Charles Montague

Odds life! must one swear to the truth
  of a song?
A Better Answer

Be to her virtues very kind;
Be to her faults a little blind.
An English Padlock

That if weak women went astray,
Their stars were more in fault than
  they.
Hans Carvel

The end must justify the means.
Ibid.

And thought the nation ne'er would
  thrive
Till all the whores were burnt alive.
Paulo Purganti

They never taste who always drink;
They always talk who never think.[2]
Upon a Passage in the Scaligerana

And often took leave, but was loth to
  depart.[3]
The Thief and the Cordelier

Nobles and heralds, by your leave,
  Here lies what once was Matthew
  Prior;

[1] Noisy jargon of the schools. — POMFRET:
Reason
  The sounding jargon of the schools. —
COWPER: *Truth, L. 367*
[2] See Jonson, page 120, and Dryden, page
173.
[3] As men that be lothe to departe do often
take their leff [John Clerk to Wolsey.] —
HENRY ELLIS [1777–1869]: *Letters, Third Series, Vol. I, P. 262*
  "A loth to depart" was the common term
for a song, or a tune played, on taking leave
of friends. TARLTON: *News Out of Purgatory*
[about 1689]. CHAPMAN: *Widow's Tears.*
MIDDLETON: *The Old Law, Act IV, Sc. 1.*
BEAUMONT AND FLETCHER: *Wit at Several
Weapons, Act II, Sc. 2*

The son of Adam and of Eve:
Can Stuart or Nassau claim higher? [1]
Epitaph. Extempore
Lays the rough paths of peevish Nature even,
And opens in each heart a little heaven.
Charity
His noble negligences teach
What others' toils despair to reach.
Alma. Canto II, Line 7
Till their own dreams at length deceive 'em,
And oft repeating, they believe 'em.
Ibid. Canto III, Line 13
Abra was ready ere I called her name;
And though I called another, Abra came.
Solomon on the Vanity of the World. Book II, Line 364
Who breathes must suffer, and who thinks must mourn;
And he alone is bless'd who ne'er was born.
Ibid. Book III, Line 240
A Rechabite poor Will must live,
And drink of Adam's ale.[2]
The Wandering Pilgrim
In public employments industrious and grave,
And alone with his friends, Lord! how merry was he!
For My Own Monument

SIR JOHN VANBRUGH
[1664–1726]
Much of a Muchness.
*The Provoked Husband.
Act I, Sc. 1*

SUSANNAH CENTLIVRE
[1667–1723]
The real Simon Pure.
*A Bold Stroke for a Wife.
Act V, Sc. 1*

[1] The following epitaph was written long before the time of Prior: —
Johnnie Carnegie lais heer.
Descendit of Adam and Eve.
Gif ony con gang hieher,
Ise willing give him leve.
[2] A cup of cold Adam from the next purling stream. — TOM BROWN: *Works, Vol. IV, P. 11*

JOHN POMFRET
[1667–1702]
We bear it calmly, though a ponderous woe,
And still adore the hand that gives the blow.[1]
Verses to His Friend under Affliction
Heaven is not always angry when he strikes,
But most chastises those whom most he likes.
Ibid.

JONATHAN SWIFT
[1667–1745]
So geographers, in Afric maps,
With savage pictures fill their gaps,
And o'er unhabitable downs
Place elephants for want of towns.[2]
On Poetry, a Rhapsody
Hobbes clearly proves that every creature
Lives in a state of war by nature.
Ibid.
So, naturalists observe, a flea
Hath smaller fleas that on him prey;
And these have smaller still to bite 'em;
And so proceed *ad infinitum*.[3]
Ibid.
A college joke to cure the dumps.
Cassinus and Peter
'Tis an old maxim in the schools,
That flattery's the food of fools;

[1] Bless the hand that gave the blow. — DRYDEN: *The Spanish Friar, Act II, Sc. 1*
[2] As geographers, Sosius, crowd into the edges of their maps parts of the world which they do not know about, adding notes in the margin to the effect that beyond this lies nothing but sandy deserts full of wild beasts and unapproachable bogs. — PLUTARCH: *Theseus*
[3] Great fleas have little fleas upon their backs to bite 'em,
And little fleas have lesser fleas, and so *ad infinitum*.
And the great fleas themselves, in turn, have greater fleas to go on;
While these again have greater still, and greater still, and so on.
AUGUSTUS DE MORGAN [1806–1871]: *A Budget of Paradoxes* [1872], P. 377

Yet now and then your men of wit
Will condescend to take a bit.
        Cadenus and Vanessa
Hail fellow, well met.
        My Lady's Lamentation
Conversation is but carving!
Give no more to every guest
Than he's able to digest.
Give him always of the prime,
And but little at a time.
Carve to all but just enough,
Let them neither starve nor stuff,
And that you may have your due,
Let your neighbour carve for you.
        Conversation
Under this window in stormy weather
I marry this man and woman together;
Let none but Him who rules the thun-
  der
Put this man and woman asunder.
        *Marriage Service from His
            Chamber Window*
He [the Emperor] is taller by almost
the breadth of my nail, than any of his
court, which alone is enough to strike
an awe into the beholders.
        *Gulliver's Travels. Part I,
        Chap. II, Voyage to Lilliput*
Big-endians and small-endians.[1]
        Ibid. Chap. IV
It is computed, that eleven thousand
persons have, at several times, suffered
death, rather than submit to break their
eggs at the smaller end.
        Ibid.
And he gave it for his opinion, that
whoever could make two ears of corn, or
two blades of grass, to grow upon a spot
of ground where only one grew before,
would deserve better of mankind, and
do more essential service to his country,
than the whole race of politicians put
together.[2]
        *Ibid. Part II, Chap. VII,
        Voyage to Brobdingnag*

[1] As the political parties of Whig and Tory
are pointed out by the high and low heels of
the Lilliputians (Framecksan and Hameck-
san), those of Papist and Protestant are designated under the Big-endians and Small-endians.
[2] He who makes two blades of grass grow
in place of one renders a service to the State.
— Voltaire: *Letter to M. Moreau* [1765]

He had been eight years upon a project for extracting sunbeams out of cucumbers, which were to be put in phials
hermetically sealed, and let out to warm
the air in raw inclement summers.
        *Gulliver's Travels. Part III,
        Chap. V, Voyage to Laputa*
Seamen have a custom, when they
meet a whale, to fling him out an empty
tub by way of amusement, to divert him
from laying violent hands upon the
ship.[1]
        Tale of a Tub. Preface
Bread is the staff of life.[2]
        Ibid.
Books, the children of the brain.
        Ibid. Sect. I
As boys do sparrows, with flinging salt
upon their tails.
        Ibid. Sect. VII
The two noblest things, which are
sweetness and light.
        Battle of the Books
Censure is the tax a man pays to the
public for being eminent.
        Thoughts on Various Subjects
Every man desires to live long, but
no man would be old.
        Ibid.
If Heaven had looked upon riches to
be a valuable thing, it would not have
given them to such a scoundrel.
        *Letter to Miss Vanhomrigh
        [August 12, 1720]*
Not die here in a rage, like a poisoned
rat in a hole.
        *Letter to Bolingbroke
        [March 21, 1729]*
A penny for your thoughts.[3]
        Polite Conversation, Introduction
The sight of you is good for sore eyes.[4]
        Ibid. Dialogue I

[1] In Sebastian Munster's "Cosmography"
there is a cut of a ship to which a whale was
coming too close for her safety, and of the
sailors throwing a tub to the whale, evidently
to play with. This practice is also mentioned
in an old prose translation of the "Ship of
Fools." — Sir James Mackintosh: *Appendix
to the Life of Sir Thomas More*
[2] See Mathew Henry, page 188.
[3] See Heywood, page 16.
[4] The sight of me *is* good for sore eyes, as
the Scotch say. — Dickens: *David Copperfield, Chap. 28*

'Tis as cheap sitting as standing.
Polite Conversation. Dialogue I

I hate nobody: I am in charity with the world.
Ibid.

I won't quarrel with my bread and butter.
Ibid.

She's no chicken; she's on the wrong side of thirty, if she be a day.
Ibid.

She looks as if butter wou'dn't melt in her mouth.[1]
Ibid.

She wears her clothes as if they were thrown on with a pitchfork.
Ibid.

He was a bold man that first eat an oyster.
Ibid. Dialogue II

That is as well said as if I had said it myself.
Ibid.

You must take the will for the deed.
Ibid.

Fingers were made before forks, and hands before knives.
Ibid.

She has more goodness in her little finger than he has in his whole body.
Ibid.

Lord! I wonder what fool it was that first invented kissing.
Ibid.

They say a carpenter's known by his chips.
Ibid.

The best doctors in the world are Doctor Diet, Doctor Quiet, and Doctor Merryman.[2]
Ibid.

I'll give you leave to call me anything, if you don't call me "spade."
Ibid.

---

[1] See Heywood, page 14.
[2] Use three physicians
First, Dr. Quiet;
Next, Dr. Merryman,
And Dr. Dyet.
Regimen Sanitatis Salernitanum
[edition 1607]

May you live all the days of your life.
Polite Conversation. Dialogue II

I have fed like a farmer: I shall grow as fat as a porpoise.
Ibid.

I always like to begin a journey on Sundays, because I shall have the prayers of the Church to preserve all that travel by land or by water.
Ibid.

I know Sir John will go, though he was sure it would rain cats and dogs.
Ibid.

I thought you and he were hand-in-glove.
Ibid.

There is none so blind as they that won't see.
Ibid. Dialogue III

She watches him as a cat would watch a mouse.
Ibid.

She pays him in his own coin.
Ibid.

There was all the world and his wife.
Ibid.

Only a woman's hair.[1]
Written upon a paper that wrapped a lock of hair, found among Swift's effects

I shall be like that tree, — I shall die at the top.
Sir Walter Scott's *Life of Swift* [2]

Ubi saeva indignatio ulterius cor lacerare nequit:

---

[1] "Only a woman's hair!" We may not guess
If 'twere a mocking sneer or the sharp cry
Of a great heart's o'ermastering agony
That spake in these four words.
James Ashcroft Noble [1844–1896]:
Sonnet, Only a Woman's Hair
[2] When the poem of "Cadenus and Vanessa" was the general topic of conversation, some one said, "Surely that Vanessa must be an extraordinary woman that could inspire the Dean to write so finely upon her." Mrs. Johnson smiled, and answered that "she thought that point not quite so clear; for it was well known the Dean could write finely upon a broomstick." — Johnson: *Life of Swift*

"Where savage indignation can no longer tear his heart."
Inscription on Swift's grave, St. Patrick's, Dublin

UNKNOWN
[*Floruit* 1700?]

Sabina has a thousand charms
  To captivate my heart;
Her lovely eyes are Cupid's arms,
  And every look a dart:
But when the beauteous idiot speaks,
  She cures me of my pain;
Her tongue the servile fetters breaks
  And frees her slave again.
From Amphion Anglicus [*1700*]. *Published in* NORMAN AULT: *Seventeenth Century Lyrics* [*1928*]

WILLIAM CONGREVE
[1670–1729]

Thus grief still treads upon the heels of pleasure;
Married in haste, we may repent at leisure.[1]
  The Old Bachelor. Act V, Sc. 1
Thou liar of the first magnitude.
  Love for Love. Act II, Sc. 2
  [*1695*]
Music hath charms to soothe the savage breast,
To soften rocks, or bend a knotted oak.
  The Mourning Bride. Act I, Sc. 1
  [*1697*]
By magic numbers and persuasive sound.
  Ibid.
Heaven has no rage like love to hatred turned,
Nor hell a fury like a woman scorned.
  Ibid. Act III, Sc. 8
Love's but a frailty of the mind,
When 'tis not with ambition joined:
A sickly flame, which, if not fed, expires,

---

[1] Who wooed in haste and means to repent at leisure. — SHAKESPEARE: *The Taming of the Shrew, Act III, Sc. 2, L. 11*

And feeding, wastes in self-consuming fires.
  The Way of the World. Act III, Sc. 12 [*1700*]
Thou art a Retailer of Phrases, and dost deal in Remnants of Remnants.
  Ibid. Act IV, Sc. 9
If there's delight in love, 'tis when I see
That heart which others bleed for, bleed for me.
  Ibid.
Defer not till to-morrow to be wise,
To-morrow's sun to thee may never rise.
  Letter to Cobham

RICHARD LEVERIDGE
[1670–1758]

When mighty roast beef was the Englishman's food,
It ennobled our hearts, and enriched our blood,
Our soldiers were brave and our courtiers were good.
Oh! the roast beef of old England!
  The Roast Beef of Old England. Stanza 1

COLLEY CIBBER
[1671–1757]

The aspiring youth that fired the Ephesian dome
Outlives in fame the pious fool that rais'd it.[1]
  Richard III (altered). Act III, Sc. 1
As good be out of the world as out of the fashion.
  Love's Last Shift. Act II
We shall find no fiend in hell can match the fury of a disappointed woman.
  Ibid. Act IV
Old houses mended,
Cost little less than new before they're ended.
  The Double Gallant. Prologue
Possession is eleven points in the law.
  Woman's Wit. Act I

---

[1] See Sir Thomas Browne, page 145.

Words are but empty thanks.
Woman's Wit. Act V
This business will never hold water.
She Wou'd and She Wou'd Not.
Act IV
Stolen sweets are best.
The Rival Fools. Act I
The will for the deed.[1]
Ibid. Act III

JOSEPH ADDISON
[1672–1719]

Unbounded courage and compassion join'd,
Tempering each other in the victor's mind,
Alternately proclaim him good and great,
And make the hero and the man complete.
The Campaign [2] [1704]
Line 219
So when an angel, by divine command,
With rising tempests shakes a guilty land
(Such as of late o'er pale Britannia passed); [3]
Calm and serene he drives the furious blast,
And, pleased the Almighty's orders to perform,
Rides in the whirlwind and directs the storm.[4]
Ibid. Line 287
The spacious firmament on high,
With all the blue ethereal sky,
And spangled heavens, a shining frame,
Their great Original proclaim.
Ode [in The Spectator, No. 465,
August 23, 1712]
Soon as the evening shades prevail,
The moon takes up the wondrous tale,
And nightly to the listening earth
Repeats the story of her birth;

[1] See Swift, page 192.
[2] Addison wrote *The Campaign* on commission, in honor of Blenheim.
[3] The reference is to the great tempest of November, 1703, which was the occasion of a parliamentary address and a public fast.
[4] This line is frequently ascribed to Pope, as it is repeated in his *Dunciad, Book III, L. 264.*

While all the stars that round her burn,
And all the planets in their turn,
Confirm the tidings as they roll,
And spread the truth from pole to pole.
Ode [in the Spectator, No. 465,
August 23, 1712]
For ever singing as they shine,
The hand that made us is divine.
Ibid.
Should the whole frame of Nature round him break,
In ruin and confusion hurled,
He, unconcerned, would hear the mighty crack,
And stand secure amidst a falling world.
Horace. Ode III, Book III
The dawn is overcast, the morning lowers,
And heavily in clouds brings on the day,
The great, the important day, big with the fate
Of Cato and of Rome.
Cato.[1] *Act I, Sc. 1 [1713]*
Thy steady temper, Portius,
Can look on guilt, rebellion, fraud, and Caesar,
In the calm lights of mild philosophy.
Ibid.
'Tis not in mortals to command success,
But we'll do more, Sempronius, — we'll deserve it.
Ibid. Sc. 2
Blesses his stars and thinks it luxury.
Ibid. Sc. 4
'T's pride, rank pride, and haughtiness of soul;
I think the Romans call it stoicism.
Ibid.
Were you with these, my prince, you'd soon forget
The pale, unripened beauties of the north.
Ibid.
Beauty soon grows familiar to the lover,
Fades in his eye, and palls upon the sense.

[1] The *Massachusetts Spy* used the following lines from *Cato* as its motto from November 22, 1771 to April 6, 1775, inclusive:
Do thou Great Liberty inspire our Souls —
and make our Lives in thy Possession happy —
Or, our Deaths glorious in thy just Defence.

The virtuous Marcia towers above her sex.

Cato. Act I, Sc. 4

My voice is still for war.
Gods! can a Roman senate long debate
Which of the two to choose, slavery or death?

Ibid. Act II, Sc. 1

The woman that deliberates is lost.

Ibid. Act IV, Sc. 1

Curse on his virtues! they've undone his country.

Ibid. Sc. 4

What pity is it
That we can die but once to save our country! [1]

Ibid.

When vice prevails, and impious men bear sway,
The post of honour is a private station.[2]

Ibid.

It must be so, — Plato, thou reasonest well!
Else whence this pleasing hope, this fond desire,
This longing after immortality?
Or whence this secret dread, and inward horror
Of falling into naught? Why shrinks the soul
Back on herself, and startles at destruction?
'Tis the divinity that stirs within us;
'Tis Heaven itself that points out an hereafter,
And intimates eternity to man.
Eternity! thou pleasing, dreadful thought!

Ibid. Act V, Sc. 1

I'm weary of conjectures, — this must end 'em.
Thus am I doubly armed: my death and life,
My bane and antidote, are both before me:

[1] I only regret that I have but one life to lose for my country. — NATHAN HALE [before his execution, 1775]

[2] Give me, kind Heaven, a private station,
A mind serene for contemplation!
Title and profit I resign;
The post of honour shall be mine.
GAY: *Fables, Part II, The Vulture, the Sparrow, and other Birds*

This in a moment brings me to an end;
But this informs me I shall never die.
The soul, secure in her existence, smiles
At the drawn dagger, and defies its point.
The stars shall fade away, the sun himself
Grow dim with age, and Nature sink in years;
But thou shalt flourish in immortal youth,[1]
Unhurt amidst the war of elements,
The wreck of matter, and the crush of worlds.

Cato. Act V, Sc. 1

Sweet are the slumbers of the virtuous man.

Ibid. Sc. 4

From hence, let fierce contending nations know
What dire effects from civil discord flow.

Ibid.

For wheresoe'er I turn my ravish'd eyes,
Gay gilded scenes and shining prospects rise,
Poetic fields encompass me around,
And still I seem to tread on classic ground.[2]

A Letter from Italy

Round-heads and wooden-shoes are standing jokes.

The Drummer. Prologue, Line 8

I shall endeavour to enliven morality with wit, and to temper wit with morality.

The Spectator. No. 10, March 11, 1711

True happiness is of a retired nature, and an enemy to pomp and noise; it arises, in the first place, from the enjoyment of one's self; and, in the next, from the friendship and conversation of a few select companions.

Ibid. No. 15, March 17, 1711

[1] Smiling always with a never fading serenity of countenance, and flourishing in an immortal youth. — ISAAC BARROW [1630–1677]: *Works, Vol. I, P. 66, Duty of Thanksgiving*

[2] Edmund Malone [1741–1812] states that this was the first time the phrase "classic ground," since so common, was ever used.

In all thy humours, whether grave or
　　mellow,
Thou'rt such a touchy, testy, pleasant
　　fellow;
Hast so much wit, and mirth, and
　　spleen about thee,
There is no living with thee, nor with-
　　out thee.[1]

The Spectator. No. 68,
May 18, 1711

There is not a more unhappy being
than a superannuated idol.

Ibid. No. 73, May 24, 1711

The stage might be made a perpetual source of the most noble and
useful entertainments, were it under
proper regulations.

Ibid. No. 93, June 16, 1711

A man that has a taste of musick,
painting, or architecture, is like one
that has another sense, when compared
with such as have no relish of those
arts.

Ibid.

Of all the diversions of life, there is
none so proper to fill up its empty
spaces as the reading of useful and entertaining authors.

Ibid.

There is not so variable thing in nature as a lady's head-dress.

Ibid. No. 98, June 21, 1711

There is no defence against reproach
but obscurity.

Ibid. No. 101, June 26, 1711

Much may be said on both sides.[2]

Ibid. No. 122, July 20, 1711

Authors have established it as a kind
of rule, that a man ought to be dull
sometimes; as the most severe reader
makes allowances for many rests and
nodding-places in a voluminous writer.

Ibid. No. 124, July 23, 1711

Books are the legacies that a great
genius leaves to mankind, which are
delivered down from generation to gen-

eration, as presents to the posterity of
those who are yet unborn.

The Spectator. No. 166,
September 10, 1711

Good-nature is more agreeable in
conversation than wit, and gives a certain air to the countenance which is
more amiable than beauty.

Ibid. No. 169, September 13, 1711

Were I to prescribe a rule for drinking, it should be formed upon a saying
quoted by Sir William Temple: the first
glass for myself, the second for my
friends, the third for good humour, and
the fourth for mine enemies.

Ibid. No. 195, October 13, 1711

Physick, for the most part, is nothing else but the substitute of exercise
or temperance.

Ibid.

A salamander is a kind of heroine in
chastity, that treads upon fire, and lives
in the midst of flames without being
hurt.

Ibid. No. 198, October 17, 1711

I consider an human soul without
education like marble in the quarry,
which shows none of its inherent beauties till the skill of the polisher fetches
out the colours, makes the surface
shine, and discovers every ornamental
cloud, spot and vein that runs through
the body of it.

Ibid. No. 215, November 6, 1711

I consider time as an immense ocean,
in which many noble authors are entirely swallowed up.

Ibid. No. 223, November 15, 1711

Those marriages generally abound
most with love and constancy that are
preceded by a long courtship.

Ibid. No. 261, December 29, 1711

A true critick ought to dwell rather
upon excellencies than imperfections, to
discover the concealed beauties of a
writer, and communicate to the world
such things as are worth their observation.

Ibid. No. 291, February 2, 1712

Death only closes a man's reputation,
and determines it as good or bad.

Ibid. No. 349, April 10, 1712

---

[1] A translation of MARTIAL, *XII,* 47, who
imitated Ovid, *Amores, III, 11, 39.*

[2] Much may be said on both sides. — FIELD-
ING: *The Covent Garden Tragedy, Act I, Sc. 8*

Mirth is like a flash of lightning, that breaks through a gloom of clouds, and glitters for a moment; cheerfulness keeps up a kind of daylight in the mind, and fills it with a steady and perpetual serenity.

The Spectator. No. 381,
May 17, 1712

Sir Roger made several reflections on the greatness of the British Nation; as, that one Englishman could beat three Frenchmen; that we could never be in danger of Popery so long as we took care of our fleet; that the Thames was the noblest river in Europe . . . with many other honest prejudices which naturally cleave to the heart of a true Englishman.

Ibid. No. 383, May 20, 1712

Could I transport myself with a wish from one country to another, I should choose to pass my winter in Spain, my spring in Italy, my summer in England, and my autumn in France.

Ibid. No. 393, May 31, 1712

The Fraternity of the Henpeck'd.[1]

Ibid. No. 482, September 12, 1712

It is a celebrated thought of Socrates, that if all the misfortunes of mankind were cast into a publick stock, in order to be equally distributed among the whole species, those who now think themselves the most unhappy would prefer the share they are already possessed of.

Ibid. No. 558, June 23, 1714

Perhaps the most eminent Egotist that ever appeared in the world was Montaigne, the author of the celebrated Essays.

Ibid. No. 562, July 2, 1714

A man should always consider how much he has more than he wants, and how much more unhappy he might be than he really is.

Ibid. No. 574, July 30, 1714

We are always doing something for Posterity, but I would fain see Posterity do something for us.

Ibid. No. 587, August 20, 1714

[1] See Byron, page 358.

EDMOND HOYLE [1]
[1672–1769]

When in doubt, win the trick.
Twenty-four Rules for Learners.
Rule 12

SIR RICHARD STEELE
[1672–1729]

Though her mien carries much more invitation than command, to behold her is an immediate check to loose behaviour; to love her was a liberal education.[2]

Tatler. No. 49

Every rich man has usually some sly way of jesting, which would make no great figure were he not a rich man.

The Spectator. No. 2,
March 2, 1711

When you fall into a man's conversation, the first thing you should consider is, whether he has a greater inclination to hear you, or that you should hear him.

Ibid. No. 49, April 26, 1711

Of all the affections which attend human life, the love of glory is the most ardent.

Ibid. No. 139, August 9, 1711

If we would consider how little of this vicissitude of motion and rest, which we call life, is spent with satisfaction, we should be more tender of our friends, than to bring them little sorrows which do not belong to them.

Ibid. No. 143, August 14, 1711

An old gentleman t'other day in discourse with a friend of his, (reflecting upon some adventures they had in youth together) cry'd out, Oh Jack, those were happy days!

Ibid. No. 153, August 25, 1711

Age in a virtuous person, of either sex, carries in it an authority which

[1] Hoyle published [1742] a *Short Treatise on Whist*, which, in subsequent editions, added rules for playing piquet, backgammon, chess, and other games. His *Laws* [1760] ruled whist-playing until 1864. Hence the saying, "according to Hoyle." His book on chess was reissued in 1808.

[2] Lady Elizabeth Hastings [1682–1739]

makes it preferable to all the pleasures of youth.

> *The Spectator. No. 153,*
> *August 25, 1711*

Among all the diseases of the mind there is not one more epidemical or more pernicious than the love of flattery.

> *Ibid. No. 238, December 3, 1711*

Will Honeycomb calls these over-offended ladies the outrageously virtuous.

> *Ibid. No. 266, January 4, 1712*

I beg of you to burn it when you've read it.

> *Ibid. No. 274, January 14, 1712*

That sex which is therefore called fair.

> *Ibid. No. 302, February 15, 1712*

They that live in a trading street are not disturbed at the passage of carts.

> *Ibid. No. 479, September 9, 1712*

A favour well bestowed is almost as great an honour to him who confers it as to him who receives it.

> *Ibid. No. 497, September 30, 1712*

From the Letters to His Wife [1]

I am come to a tavern alone to eat a stake, after which I shall return to the office.

> *October 28, 1707*

I have partly succeeded in my businesse today, and enclose two guineas. Dear Prue, I can't come home to dinner.

> *January 3, 1708*

I was going home two hours ago, but was met by Mr. Griffith, who has kept me ever since. I will come within a pint of wine.

> *Eleven at Night, January 5, 1708*

A little in drink, but at all times yr. faithfull husband.

> *September 27, 1708*

I am busy about the main chance.

> *October 13, 1708*

---

[1] Selected and collated by R. BRIMLEY JOHNSON [1927]. The letters to Prue (his wife) are a classic of matrimonial humors; the perfect wedding present; what O. Henry would have called "A Handbook of Hymen."

If you do not hear of me before three tomorrow afternoon, believe I am too fuddled to take care to observe yr. orders.

> *October 25, 1708*

The finest woman in nature should not detain me an hour from you; but you must sometimes suffer the rivalship of the wisest men.

> *September 17, 1712*

NICHOLAS ROWE
[1673–1718]

As if Misfortune made the throne her seat,
And none could be unhappy but the great.[1]

> *The Fair Penitent. Prologue*

At length the morn and cold indifference came.[2]

> *Ibid. Act I, Sc. 1*

Is this that haughty gallant, gay Lothario?

> *Ibid. Act V, Sc. 1*

ISAAC WATTS
[1674–1748]

Let dogs delight to bark and bite,
  For God hath made them so;
Let bears and lions growl and fight,
  For 'tis their nature too.

> *Divine Songs. XVI*

But, children, you should never let
  Such angry passions rise;
Your little hands were never made
  To tear each other's eyes.

> *Ibid.*

Birds in their little nests agree;
  And 'tis a shameful sight
When children of one family
  Fall out, and chide, and fight.

> *Ibid. XVII*

---

[1] None think the great unhappy, but the great. — YOUNG: *The Love of Fame, Satire 1, L. 238*

[2] But with the morning cool reflection came. — SCOTT: *Chronicles of the Canongate, Chap. IV*

Scott also quotes it in his notes to *The Monastery, Chap. III, note 11;* and with "calm" substituted for "cool" in *The Antiquary, Chap. V;* and with "repentance" for "reflection" in *Rob Roy, Chap. XII.*

How doth the little busy bee
  Improve each shining hour,
And gather honey all the day
  From every opening flower!
                Divine Songs. XX

For Satan finds some mischief still
  For idle hands to do.
                        Ibid.

Hush, my dear, lie still and slumber!
  Holy angels guard thy bed!
Heavenly blessings without number
  Gently falling on thy head.
                A Cradle Hymn

How they served the Lord of Glory
Makes me angry while I sing.
                        Ibid.

'Tis the voice of the sluggard; I heard
  him complain,
"You have wak'd me too soon, I must
  slumber again."
                The Sluggard. Stanza 1

But thanks to my friends for their care
  in my breeding,
Who taught me betimes to love working and reading.
                Ibid. Stanza 5

How proud we are! how fond to shew
Our clothes, and call them rich and
  new!
When the poor sheep and silkworm
  wore
That very clothing long before.
                Against Pride in Clothes.
                        Stanza 3

Lord, in the morning thou shalt hear
My voice ascending high.
                        Psalm V

And while the lamp holds out to burn,
The vilest sinner may return.
        Hymns and Spiritual Songs.
                Book I, Hymn 88

Strange that a harp of thousand strings
Should keep in tune so long!
            Ibid. Book II, Hymn 19

Hark! from the tombs a doleful sound.
                Ibid. Hymn 63

The tall, the wise, the reverend head
Must lie as low as ours.
                        Ibid.

When I can read my title clear
  To mansions in the skies,

I'll bid farewell to every fear,
  And wipe my weeping eyes.
        Hymns and Spiritual Songs.
                Book II, Hymn 65

There is a land of pure delight,
  Where saints immortal reign;
Infinite day excludes the night,
  And pleasures banish pain.
                Ibid. Hymn 66

So, when a raging fever burns,
We shift from side to side by turns;
And 'tis a poor relief we gain
To change the place, but keep the pain.
                Ibid. Hymn 146

Were I so tall to reach the pole,
  Or grasp the ocean with my span,
I must be measured by my soul:
  The mind's the standard of the man.
            Horæ Lyricæ. Book II,
                False Greatness

To God the Father, God the Son,
And God the Spirit, Three in One,
Be honour, praise, and glory given
By all on earth, and all in heaven.
                        Doxology

WILLIAM SOMERVILLE [1]
[1675–1742]

How humble, and how complaisant
Is the proud man reduced to want!
With what a silly, hanging face
He bears his unforeseen disgrace!
                Ready Money

Let all the learned say what they can,
'Tis ready money makes the man.
                        Ibid.

There is something in a face,
An air, and a peculiar grace,
Which boldest painters cannot trace.
                The Lucky Hit

So in each action 'tis success
That gives it all its comeliness.
                        Ibid.

For what is virtue, courage, wit,
In all men, but a lucky hit?
                        Ibid.

So, safe on shore the pensioned sailor
  lies,
And all the malice of the storm defies;

[1] Of whom DR. JOHNSON, in his *Lives of the Poets,* made the famous remark: "He writes very well for a gentleman."

With ease of body blest and peace of
 mind
Pities the restless crew he left behind;
Whilst, in his cell, he meditates alone
On his great voyage to the world un-
 known.
> *The Author, an Old Man, to*
> *His Arm-chair*

JOHN PHILIPS
[1676–1709]

My galligaskins, that have long withstood
The winter's fury, and encroaching
 frosts,
By time subdued (what will not time
 subdue!),
A horrid chasm disclosed.
> *The Splendid Shilling* [*1701*].
> *Line 121*

SIR ROBERT WALPOLE
[1676–1745]

The balance of power.
> *Speech* [*1741*]

Flowery oratory he despised. He ascribed to the interested views of themselves or their relatives the declara-
tions of pretended patriots, of whom he
said, "All those men have their price." [1]
> WILLIAM COXE [*1747–1828*]:
> *Memoirs of Walpole* [*1798*],
> *Vol. IV, P. 369*

Anything but history, for history
must be false.
> *Walpoliana. No. 141*

The gratitude of place-expectants is
a lively sense of future favours. [2]

---

[1] "All men have their price" is commonly
ascribed to Walpole. See Bulwer Lytton, page
425.
 All who prove that each man has his price.
— AKENSIDE: *An Epistle to Curio*
[2] HAZLITT, in his *Wit and Humour*, says,
"This is Walpole's phrase."
 The gratitude of most men is but a secret
desire of receiving greater benefits. — ROCHE-
FOUCAULD: *Maxim 298*

HENRY ST. JOHN,
VISCOUNT BOLINGBROKE
[1678–1751]

I have read somewhere or other, —
in Dionysius of Halicarnassus, I think,
— that history is philosophy teaching
by examples. [1]
> *On the Study and Use of History.*
> *Letter 2*

The dignity of history. [2]
> *Ibid. Letter 5*

It is the modest, not the presumptuous, inquirer who makes a real and safe
progress in the discovery of divine
truths. One follows Nature and Nature's God; that is, he follows God in
his works and in his word. [3]
> *Letter to Mr. Pope*

GEORGE FARQUHAR
[1678–1707]

Like hungry guests, a sitting audience
looks.
> *The Inconstant* [*1702*]. *Prologue*

The prologue is the grace,
Each act, a course, each scene, a different dish.
> *Ibid.*

Necessity, the mother of invention. [4]
> *The Twin Rivals* [*1702*]. *Act I*

Cos. Pray now, what may be that
same bed of honour?

Kite. Oh, a mighty large bed! bigger
by half than the great bed at Ware:
ten thousand people may lie in it together, and never feel one another.
> *The Recruiting Officer* [*1706*].
> *Act I, Sc. 1*

---

[1] The contact with manners then is education; and this Thucydides appears to assert
when he says history is philosophy learned
from examples. — DIONYSIUS OF HALICARNAS-
SUS: *Ars Rhet. XI, 2*
[2] HENRY FIELDING: *Tom Jones, Book XI,
Chap. II.* HORACE WALPOLE: *Advertisement to
Letter to Sir Horace Mann.* MACAULAY: *History of England, Vol. I, Chap. I*
[3] Slave to no sect, who takes no private
 road,
 But looks through Nature up to Nature's
 God.
  POPE: *Essay on Man, Epistle IV, L. 331*
[4] See Richard Franck, page 171.

I believe they talked of me, for they laughed consumedly.
> *The Beaux' Stratagem* [*1707*].
> *Act III, Sc. 1*

'Twas for the good of my country that I should be abroad.[1]
> *Ibid. Sc. 2*

THOMAS PARNELL
[1679–1718]

Still an angel appear to each lover beside,
But still be a woman to you.
> *When Thy Beauty Appears.*
> *Stanza 3*

Remote from man, with God he passed the days;
Prayer all his business, all his pleasure praise.
> *The Hermit. Line 5*

We call it only pretty Fanny's way.
> *An Elegy to an Old Beauty.*
> *Stanza 4*

My days have been so wondrous free
The little birds that fly
With careless ease from tree to tree,
Were but as bless'd as I.
> *Song.[2] Stanza 1*

Let those love now who never loved before;
Let those who always loved, now love the more.
> *Translation of the Pervigilium*
> *Veneris* [3]

[1] Leaving his country for his country's sake. — CHARLES FITZ-GEFFREY [1575–1638]: *The Life and Death of Sir Francis Drake, St. 213* [1596]
True patriots all; for, be it understood,
We left our country for our country's good.
GEORGE BARRINGTON [1755–1804]: *New South Wales, P. 152, Prologue Written for the Opening of the Playhouse at New South Wales, Jan. 16, 1796*
[2] Set to music by Francis Hopkinson; one of the earliest American songs.
[3] Written in the time of Julius Caesar, and by some ascribed to Catullus:
Cras amet qui nunquam amavit;
Quique amavit, cras amet
(Let him love to-morrow who never loved before; and he who has loved, let him love to-morrow).
Love he to-morrow, who loved never;

EDWARD YOUNG
[1683–1765]

Tired nature's sweet restorer, balmy sleep!
> *Night Thoughts. Night I, Line 1*

Night, sable goddess! from her ebon throne,
In rayless majesty, now stretches forth
Her leaden sceptre o'er a slumbering world.
> *Ibid. Line 18*

Creation sleeps! 'Tis as the general pulse
Of life stood still, and Nature made a pause, —
An awful pause! prophetic of her end.
> *Ibid. Line 23*

Poor pensioner on the bounties of an hour.
> *Ibid. Line 67*

Be wise to-day; 'tis madness to defer.[1]
> *Ibid. Line 390*

Procrastination is the thief of time.
> *Ibid. Line 393*

At thirty, man suspects himself a fool;
Knows it at forty, and reforms his plan;
At fifty chides his infamous delay,
Pushes his prudent purpose to resolve;
In all the magnanimity of thought
Resolves, and re-resolves; then dies the same.
> *Ibid. Line 417*

All men think all men mortal but themselves.
> *Ibid. Line 424*

Thy purpose firm is equal to the deed:
Who does the best his circumstance allows
Does well, acts nobly; angels could no more.
> *Ibid. Night II, Line 90*

"I've lost a day!" — the prince who nobly cried,

To-morrow, who hath loved, persever.
Translation by THOMAS STANLEY
[1625–1678]
Love, oh love upon the morrow,
You who never loved before;
And if you have loved in old days,
On the morrow love once more.
Translation by ZECHARIAH CHAFEE, JR.
[b. 1885], in *The Brunonian*, Brown University [1906]
[1] See Congreve, page 193.

Had been an emperor without his crown.[1]

Night Thoughts. Night II, Line 99

Ah, how unjust to Nature and himself
Is thoughtless, thankless, inconsistent man!

Ibid. Line 112

Whose yesterdays look backwards with a smile.

Ibid. Line 334

Thoughts shut up want air,
And spoil, like bales unopen'd to the sun.

Ibid. Line 466

How blessings brighten as they take their flight!

Ibid. Line 602

Heaven's Sovereign saves all beings but himself
That hideous sight, — a naked human heart.

Ibid. Night III, Line 226

Man wants but little, nor that little long.[2]

Ibid. Night IV, Line 118

A Christian is the highest style of man.[3]

Ibid. Line 788

By night an atheist half believes a God.

Ibid. Night V, Line 177

Early, bright, transient, chaste as morning dew,

---

[1] Once at supper, reflecting that he [Emperor Titus] had done nothing for any that day, he broke out into that memorable and justly admired saying, "My friends, I have lost a day!" — SUETONIUS: *Lives of the Twelve Cæsars* (translation by Alexander Thomson)
In the preface to Mr. Nichols's work on autographs, among other albums noticed by him as being in the British Museum is that of David Krieg, with Jacob Bobart's autograph [Dec. 8, 1697] and the verses, —
Virtus sui gloria.
Think that day lost whose descending sun
Views from thy hand no noble action done.
Bobart died in 1719.
Count that day lost whose low descending sun
Views from thy hand no worthy action done.
Staniford: *Art of Reading,* 3d. ed., P. 27
[Boston, 1803]
[2] Man wants but little here below,
Nor wants that little long.
GOLDSMITH: *Edwin and Angelina* [*The Hermit*], St. 8
[3] See Dryden, page 174.

She sparkled, was exhal'd and went to heaven.[1]

Night Thoughts. Night V, Line 600

We see time's furrows on another's brow,
And death intrench'd, preparing his assault;
How few themselves in that just mirror see!

Ibid. Line 627

Like our shadows,
Our wishes lengthen as our sun declines.[2]

Ibid. Line 661

Our birth is nothing but our death begun.[3]

Ibid. Line 719

That life is long which answers life's great end.

Ibid. Line 773

Death loves a shining mark, a signal blow.[4]

Ibid. Line 1011

And all may do what has by man been done.

Ibid. Night VI, Line 606

The man that blushes is not quite a brute.

Ibid. Night VII, Line 496

Too low they build, who build beneath the stars.[5]

Ibid. Night VIII, Line 215

Final Ruin fiercely drives
Her ploughshare o'er creation.[6]

Ibid. Night IX, Line 167

An undevout astronomer is mad.

Ibid. Line 771

The course of Nature is the art of God.[7]

Ibid. Line 1267

The love of praise, howe'er conceal'd by art,
Reigns more or less, and glows in ev'ry heart.

Love of Fame. Satire I, Line 51

---

[1] See Dryden, page 175.
[2] See Dryden, page 173.
[3] See Bishop Joseph Hall, page 121.
[4] See Quarles, page 134.
[5] Inscription on a wall of the Library of Congress, Washington, D. C.
[6] Stern Ruin's ploughshare drives elate
Full on thy bloom.
ROBERT BURNS: *To a Mountain Daisy*
[7] See Sir Thomas Browne, page 144.

Some for renown, on scraps of learning
dote,
And think they grow immortal as they
quote.
Love of Fame. Satire I, Line 89

They that on glorious ancestors enlarge,
Produce their debt instead of their discharge.
Ibid. Line 147

Unlearned men of books assume the
care,
As eunuchs are the guardians of the
fair.
Ibid. Satire II, Line 83

Where Nature's end of language is de-
clin'd,
And men talk only to conceal the mind.
Ibid. Line 207

Be wise with speed;
A fool at forty is a fool indeed.
Ibid. Line 282

For her own breakfast she'll project a
scheme,
Nor take her tea without a stratagem.
Ibid. Satire VI, Line 190

Think naught a trifle, though it small
appear,
Small sands the mountain, moments
make the year.
Ibid. Line 208

One to destroy is murder by the law,
And gibbets keep the lifted hand in
awe;
To murder thousands takes a specious
name,
War's glorious art, and gives immortal
fame.
Ibid. Satire VII, Line 55

How commentators each dark passage
shun,
And hold their farthing candle to the
sun.[1]
Ibid. Line 97

The man that makes a character makes
foes.
To Mr. Pope. Epistle I, Line 28

Their feet through faithless leather met
the dirt,

[1] See Crabbe, page 280.

And oftener chang'd their principles
than shirt.
To Mr. Pope. Epistle I, Line 277

Accept a miracle instead of wit, —
See two dull lines with Stanhope's pen-
cil writ.
*Lines Written with the Diamond
Pencil of Lord Chesterfield* [1]

In records that defy the tooth of time.
The Statesman's Creed

And friend received with thumps upon
the back.[2]
Universal Passion

SIR WILLIAM PULTENEY [3]
[1684–1764]

For twelve honest men have decided
the cause,
Who are judges alike of the facts and
the laws.
The Honest Jury

GEORGE BERKELEY,
BISHOP OF CLOYNE
[1685–1753]

Westward the course of empire takes
its way; [4]
The four first acts already past,
A fifth shall close the drama with the
day:
Time's noblest offspring is the last.
*On the Prospect of Planting
Arts and Learning in Amer-
ica. Stanza 6*

Our youth we can have but to-day,
We may always find time to grow old.
*Can Love Be Controlled by
Advice?* [5]

[Tar water] is of a nature so mild
and benign and proportioned to the

[1] Attributed to Alexander Pope by John
Taylor [1757–1832].

[2] The man that hails you Tom or Jack,
And proves, by thumping on your back.
COWPER: *On Friendship*

[3] One of "the three grand allies," the others
being Stanhope and Walpole. Walpole said
that he feared Pulteney's tongue more than
another man's sword.

[4] See Samuel Daniel, page 30.
Westward the star of empire takes its way.
— JOHN QUINCY ADAMS [1767–1848]: *Ora-
tion at Plymouth* [1802]

[5] In AIKEN: *Vocal Poetry* [London, 1810]

human constitution, as to warm without heating, to cheer but not inebriate.[1]

Siris. Par. 217

He who says there is no such thing as an honest man, you may be sure is himself a knave.

Maxims Concerning Patriotism

Ferments of the worst kind succeed to perfect inaction.

Ibid.

JANE BRERETON
[1685–1740]

The picture placed the busts between
  Adds to the thought much strength;
Wisdom and Wit are little seen,
  But Folly's at full length.

*On Beau Nash's Picture at Full
Length between the Busts of Sir
Isaac Newton and Mr. Pope.*[2]

AARON HILL
[1685–1750]

When Christ at Cana's feast by power
    divine
Inspired cold water with the warmth
    of wine,
"See," cried they, while in redding tide
    it gushed,
"The bashful stream hath seen its God
    and blushed." [3]

Translation from the Latin

First, then, a woman will or won't, depend on 't;
If she will do 't she will; and there's
    an end on 't.
But if she won't, since safe and sound
    your trust is,
Fear is affront, and jealousy injustice.[4]

Zara. Epilogue

---

[1]   Cups
That cheer but not inebriate.
        COWPER: *The Task, Book IV*

[2] In ALEXANDER DYCE [1798–1869]: *Specimens of British Poetesses.* (This epigram is generally ascribed to Chesterfield. See CAMPBELL: *English Poets, note, P. 521.*)

[3] See Crashaw, page 165.

[4] The following lines are copied from the pillar erected on the mount in the Dane John Field, Canterbury: —
Where is the man who has the power and
    skill
To stem the torrent of a woman's will?

Tender-handed stroke a nettle,
  And it stings you for your pains;
Grasp it like a man of mettle,
  And it soft as silk remains.

'Tis the same with common natures:
  Use 'em kindly, they rebel;
But be rough as nutmeg-graters,
  And the rogues obey you well.

*Verses Written on a Window
in Scotland*

SAMUEL MADDEN
[1686–1765]

Some write their wrongs in marble: he
    more just,
Stoop'd down serene and wrote them
    in the dust, —
Trod under foot, the sport of every
    wind,
Swept from the earth and blotted from
    his mind.
There, secret in the grave, he bade
    them lie,
And grieved they could not 'scape the
    Almighty eye.

Boulter's Monument

Words are men's daughters, but God's
    sons are things.[1]

Ibid.

In an orchard there should be enough to eat, enough to lay up, enough to be stolen, and enough to rot upon the ground.

*Quoted by Samuel Johnson
(Boswell's Life of Dr. Johnson,
Vol. II, Page 457, Everyman
edition)*

ALLAN RAMSAY
[1686–1758]

My Peggy is a young thing,
  Just entered in her teens.

Peggy

Farewell to Lochaber, farewell to my
    Jean,

For if she will, she will, you may depend on 't;
And if she won't, she won't; so there's an
    end on 't.

The Examiner [May 31, 1829]

[1] Words are women, deeds are men. —
GEORGE HERBERT: *Jacula Prudentum*
See Johnson, page 232.

Where heartsome wi' thee I hae mony
    days been;
For Lochaber no more, Lochaber no
    more,
We'll maybe return to Lochaber no
    more.
Lochaber No More. Stanza 1

THOMAS TICKELL
[1686–1740]

Just men, by whom impartial laws were
    given;
And saints who taught and led the way
    to heaven.
*On the Death of Mr. Addison.
Line 41*
Nor e'er was to the bowers of bliss con-
    veyed
A fairer spirit or more welcome shade.
Ibid. Line 45
There taught us how to live; and (oh,
    too high
The price for knowledge!) taught us
    how to die.[1]
Ibid. Line 81
The sweetest garland to the sweetest
    maid.
*To a Lady with a Present of
Flowers*
I hear a voice you cannot hear,
    Which says I must not stay;
I see a hand you cannot see,
    Which beckons me away.[2]
Colin and Lucy. Stanza 7

LAURENCE EUSDEN
[1688–1730]

A woman's work, grave sirs, is never
    done.[3]
*At a Cambridge Commencement
[second edition, 1714]*

[1] He who should teach men to die, would
at the same time teach them to live. —MON-
TAIGNE: *Essays, Book I, Chap. 9*
I have taught you, my dear flock, for above
thirty years how to live, and I will show you
in a very short time how to die. — SIR EDWIN
SANDYS [1561–1629]: *Anglorum Speculum,
P. 903*
[2] Scott used this as a heading for Chapter
17 of *Rob Roy.*
[3] Man may work from sun to sun
    But woman's work is never done.
        Traditional version; origin unknown.

JOHN GAY
[1688–1732]

'Twas when the sea was roaring
With hollow blasts of wind,
A damsel lay deploring,
All on a rock reclin'd.
*The What d'ye Call It.
Act II, Sc. 8*
So comes a reckoning when the ban-
    quet's o'er, —
The dreadful reckoning, and men smile
    no more.[1]
Ibid. Sc. 9
'Tis woman that seduces all mankind;
By her we first were taught the whee-
    dling arts.
The Beggar's Opera. Act I, Sc. 1
Over the hills and far away.
Ibid.
If the heart of a man is depress'd with
    cares,
The mist is dispell'd when a woman
    appears.
Ibid. Act II, Sc. 1
The fly that sips treacle is lost in the
    sweets.
Ibid. Sc. 2
How happy could I be with either,
Were t'other dear charmer away!
Ibid.
The charge is prepar'd, the lawyers are
    met,
The judges all ranged, — a terrible
    show!
Ibid. Act III, Sc. 2
All in the Downs the fleet was moor'd.
*Sweet William's Farewell to
Black-eyed Susan*
Adieu, she cried, and waved her lily
    hand.
Ibid.
My lodging is on the cold ground,
    And hard, very hard, is my fare,
But that which grieves me more
    Is the coldness of my dear.
*My Lodging is on the Cold
Ground. Stanza 1*

[1] The time of paying a shot in a tavern
among good fellows, or Pantagruelists, is still
called in France a "quart d'heure de Rabelais,"
— that is, Rabelais's quarter of an hour, when
a man is uneasy or melancholy. — *Life of
Rabelais* (Bohn's edition), *P. 13*

Remote from cities liv'd a swain,
Unvex'd with all the cares of gain;
His head was silver'd o'er with age,
And long experience made him sage.
Fables. Part I, The Shepherd
and the Philosopher

Whence is thy learning? Hath thy toil
O'er books consum'd the midnight oil? [1]
Ibid.

Where yet was ever found a mother
Who'd give her booby for another?
The Mother, the Nurse, and
the Fairy

When we risk no contradiction,
It prompts the tongue to deal in fiction.
The Elephant and the Bookseller

Lest men suspect your tale untrue,
Keep probability in view.
The Painter who Pleased No-
body and Everybody

In ev'ry age and clime we see
Two of a trade can never agree. [2]
The Rat-catcher and Cats

Is there no hope? the sick man said;
The silent doctor shook his head.
The Sick Man and the Angel

While there is life there's hope, he
cried. [3]
Ibid.

Those who in quarrels interpose
Must often wipe a bloody nose.
The Mastiffs

That raven on yon left-hand oak
(Curse on his ill-betiding croak!)
Bodes me no good. [4]
The Farmer's Wife and the Raven

[1] "Midnight oil," — a common phrase, used
by Quarles, Shenstone, Cowper, Lloyd, and
others.
[2] Potter is jealous of potter, and craftsman
of craftsman; and poor man has a grudge
against poor man, and poet against poet. —
HESIOD: *Works and Days, 24*
  Le potier au potier porte envie (The potter
envies the potter). — BOHN: *Handbook of*
Proverbs.
[3] For the living there is hope, but for the
dead there is none. — THEOCRITUS: *Idyl IV, 42*
  Ægroto, dum anima est, spes est (While
the sick man has life, there is hope). — CIC-
ERO: *Epistolarum ad Atticum, IX, 10*
[4] It wasn't for nothing that the raven was
just now croaking on my left hand. — PLAU-
TUS: *Aulularia, Act IV, Sc. 3*

I hate the man who builds his name
On ruins of another's fame.
The Poet and the Rose

The child whom many fathers share
Hath seldom known a father's care.
Fables. Part I, The Hare and
Many Friends

And when a lady's in the case,
You know all other things give place.
Ibid.

Give me, kind Heaven, a private sta-
tion,
A mind serene for contemplation:
Title and profit I resign;
The post of honour shall be mine. [1]
Ibid. Part II, The Vulture, the
Sparrow, and Other Birds

From wine what sudden friendship
springs!
The Squire and His Cur

Life is a jest, and all things show it;
I thought so once, but now I know it.
My Own Epitaph

ALEXANDER POPE [2]
[1688–1744]

Awake, my St. John! leave all meaner
things
To low ambition and the pride of kings.
Let us, since life can little more supply
Than just to look about us, and to die,
Expatiate free o'er all this scene of
man;
A mighty maze! but not without a
plan.
Essay on Man. Epistle I, Line 1

Eye Nature's walks, shoot folly as it
flies,
And catch the manners living as they
rise;
Laugh where we must, be candid where
we can,
But vindicate the ways of God to man.
Ibid. Line 13

[1] When vice prevails, and impious men bear
sway,
  The post of honour is a private station.
    ADDISON: *Cato, Act IV, Sc. 4*
[2] A thousand years may elapse before there
shall appear another man with a power of
versification equal to that of Pope. — DR.
JOHNSON

Say first, of God above or man below,
What can we reason but from what we know?

Essay on Man. Epistle I, Line 17

Heaven from all creatures hides the book of Fate,
All but the page prescrib'd, their present state.

Ibid. Line 77

Pleased to the last, he crops the flowery food,
And licks the hand just raised to shed his blood.

Ibid. Line 83

Who sees with equal eye, as God of all,
A hero perish or a sparrow fall,
Atoms or systems into ruin hurl'd,
And now a bubble burst, and now a world.

Ibid. Line 87

Hope springs eternal in the human breast:
Man never is, but always to be, blest.

Ibid. Line 95

Lo, the poor Indian! whose untutor'd mind
Sees God in clouds, or hears him in the wind;
His soul proud Science never taught to stray
Far as the solar walk or milky way.

Ibid. Line 99

But thinks, admitted to that equal sky,
His faithful dog shall bear him company.

Ibid. Line 111

Seas roll to waft me, suns to light me rise;
My footstool earth, my canopy the skies.[1]

Ibid. Line 139

Die of a rose in aromatic pain.

Ibid. Line 200

The spider's touch, how exquisitely fine,

Feels at each thread, and lives along the line.[1]

Essay on Man. Epistle I, Line 217

Remembrance and reflection how allied!
What thin partitions sense from thought divide![2]

Ibid. Line 225

All are but parts of one stupendous whole,
Whose body Nature is, and God the soul.

Ibid. Line 267

As full, as perfect, in vile man that mourns
As the rapt seraph that adores and burns.
To Him no high, no low, no great, no small;[3]
He fills, he bounds, connects, and equals all!

Ibid. Line 277

All nature is but art, unknown to thee;
All chance, direction, which thou canst not see;
All discord, harmony not understood;
All partial evil, universal good;
And spite of pride, in erring reason's spite,
One truth is clear, Whatever is, is right.[4]

Ibid. Line 289

Know then thyself, presume not God to scan;
The proper study of mankind is man.[5]

Ibid. Epistle II, Line 1

Chaos of thought and passion, all confused;
Still by himself abused or disabused;
Created half to rise, and half to fall;
Great lord of all things, yet a prey to all;

---

[1] All the parts of the universe I have an interest in: the earth serves me to walk upon; the sun to light me; the stars have their influence upon me. — MONTAIGNE: *Apology for Raimond Sebond*

[1] See Sir John Davies, page 115.
[2] See Dryden, page 173.
[3] There is no great and no small. — EMERSON: *Epigraph to History*
[4] See Dryden, page 178.
[5] La vray science et le vray étude de l'homme, c'est l'homme (The true science and the true study of man is man). — PIERRE CHARRON [1541–1603]: *Traité de la Sagesse* [1601], *Book I, Preface*

Trees and fields tell me nothing: men are my teachers. — PLATO: *Phædrus*

Sole judge of truth, in endless error hurled;
The glory, jest, and riddle of the world.
Essay on Man. Epistle II, Line 13
Fix'd like a plant on his peculiar spot,
To draw nutrition, propagate, and rot.
Ibid. Line 63
On life's vast ocean diversely we sail,
Reason the card, but passion is the gale.
Ibid. Line 107
And hence one master-passion in the breast,
Like Aaron's serpent, swallows up the rest.[1]
Ibid. Line 131
The young disease, that must subdue at length,
Grows with his growth, and strengthens with his strength.
Ibid. Line 135
Vice is a monster of so frightful mien,
As to be hated needs but to be seen;
Yet seen too oft, familiar with her face,
We first endure, then pity, then embrace.
Ibid. Line 217
Behold the child, by Nature's kindly law,
Pleased with a rattle, tickled with a straw:
Some livelier plaything gives his youth delight,
A little louder, but as empty quite:
Scarfs, garters, gold, amuse his riper stage,
And beads and prayer-books are the toys of age.
Pleased with this bauble still, as that before,
Till tired he sleeps, and life's poor play is o'er.
Ibid. Line 274
Learn of the little nautilus to sail,
Spread the thin oar, and catch the driving gale.
Ibid. Epistle III, Line 177
For forms of government let fools contest;
Whate'er is best administer'd is best:

[1] For they cast down every man his rod, and they became serpents: but Aaron's rod swallowed up their rods. — Exodus, VII, 12

For modes of faith let graceless zealots fight;
His can't be wrong whose life is in the right.
In faith and hope the world will disagree,
But all mankind's concern is charity.
Essay on Man. Epistle III, Line 303
O happiness! our being's end and aim!
Good, pleasure, ease, content! whate'er thy name:
That something still which prompts the eternal sigh,
For which we bear to live, or dare to die.
Ibid. Epistle IV, Line 1
Reason's whole pleasure, all the joys of sense,
Lie in three words — health, peace, and competence.
Ibid. Line 79
Worth makes the man, and want of it the fellow;
The rest is all but leather or prunella.
Ibid. Line 203
What can ennoble sots or slaves or cowards?
Alas! not all the blood of all the Howards.
Ibid. Line 215
A wit's a feather, and a chief a rod;
An honest man's the noblest work of God.
Ibid. Line 247
One self-approving hour whole years outweighs
Of stupid starers and of loud huzzas:
And more true joy Marcellus exil'd feels
Than Caesar with a senate at his heels.
Ibid. Line 255
If parts allure thee, think how Bacon shin'd,
The wisest, brightest, meanest of mankind!
Or ravish'd with the whistling of a name,
See Cromwell, damn'd to everlasting fame!
Ibid. Line 281
Slave to no sect, who takes no private road,

But looks through Nature up to Nature's God.[1]

Essay on Man. Epistle IV, Line 331

Form'd by thy converse, happily to steer
From grave to gay, from lively to severe.[2]

Ibid. Line 379

Say, shall my little bark attendant sail,
Pursue the triumph and partake the gale?

Ibid. Line 385

Thou wert my guide, philosopher, and friend.[3]

Ibid. Line 390

The fate of all extremes is such:
Men may be read, as well as books, too much.

Moral Essays. Epistle I, Line 9

To observations which ourselves we make,
We grow more partial for th' observer's sake.

Ibid. Line 11

Like following life through creatures you dissect,
You lose it in the moment you detect.

Ibid. Line 29

Not always actions show the man; we find
Who does a kindness is not therefore kind.

Ibid. Line 109

Who combats bravely is not therefore brave,
He dreads a death-bed like the meanest slave
Who reasons wisely is not therefore wise;
His pride in reasoning, not in acting, lies.

Ibid. Line 115

'Tis education forms the common mind:
Just as the twig is bent the tree's inclined.

Ibid. Line 149

Manners with fortunes, humours turn with climes,

Tenets with books, and principles with times.[1]

Moral Essays. Epistle I, Line 172

"Odious! in woollen! 'twould a saint provoke,"
Were the last words that poor Narcissa spoke.

Ibid. Line 246

Give this cheek a little red.

Ibid. Line 251

And you, brave Cobham! to the latest breath
Shall feel your ruling passion strong in death.

Ibid. Line 262

Most women have no characters at all.

Ibid. Epistle II, Line 2

Whether the charmer sinner it or saint it,
If folly grow romantic, I must paint it.

Ibid. Line 15

Choose a firm cloud before it fall, and in it
Catch, ere she change, the Cynthia of this minute.

Ibid. Line 19

Fine by defect, and delicately weak.

Ibid. Line 43

With too much quickness ever to be taught;
With too much thinking to have common thought.

Ibid. Line 97

Men, some to business, some to pleasure take;
But every woman is at heart a rake.

Ibid. Line 215

She who ne'er answers till a husband cools,
Or if she rules him, never shows she rules.

Ibid. Line 261

And mistress of herself though china fall.

Ibid. Line 268

Woman's at best a contradiction still.

Ibid. Line 270

---

[1] See Bolingbroke, page 200.
[2] See Dryden, page 177.
[3] Is this my guide, philosopher, and friend? — POPE: *Epistle I, Book I, L. 177*

[1] Omnia mutantur, nos et mutamur in illis (All things change, and we change with them). — MATTHIAS BORBONIUS: *Deliciæ Poetarum Germanorum, I, 685*

Who shall decide when doctors disagree?
Moral Essays. Epistle III, Line 1
Blest paper-credit! last and best supply!
That lends corruption lighter wings to fly!
Ibid. Line 39
But thousands die without or this or that,
Die, and endow a college or a cat.
Ibid. Line 95
The ruling passion, be it what it will,
The ruling passion conquers reason still.
Ibid. Line 153
Ye little stars! hide your diminish'd rays.[1]
Ibid. Line 282
Who builds a church to God, and not to fame,
Will never mark the marble with his name.
Ibid. Line 285
Where London's column, pointing at the skies,
Like a tall bully, lifts the head and lies.[2]
Ibid. Line 339
Satan now is wiser than of yore,
And tempts by making rich, not making poor.
Ibid. Line 351
Good sense, which only is the gift of Heaven,
And though no science, fairly worth the seven.
Ibid. Epistle IV, Line 43
To rest, the cushion and soft dean invite,
Who never mentions hell to ears polite.[3]
Ibid. Line 149
Statesman, yet friend to truth; of soul sincere,
In action faithful, and in honour clear;
Who broke no promise, serv'd no private end,

Who gain'd no title, and who lost no friend.
Moral Essays. Epistle V,
To Mr. Addison, Line 67
'Tis with our judgments as our watches, none
Go just alike, yet each believes his own.[1]
Essay on Criticism. Part I, Line 9
One science only will one genius fit;
So vast is art, so narrow human wit.
Ibid. Line 60
Be Homer's works your study and delight,
Read them by day, and meditate by night.
Ibid. Line 124
Music resembles poetry; in each
Are nameless graces which no methods teach,
And which a master-hand alone can reach.
Ibid. Line 143
Those oft are stratagems which errors seem,
Nor is it Homer nods, but we that dream.[2]
Ibid. Line 177
Of all the causes which conspire to blind
Man's erring judgment, and misguide the mind,
What the weak head with strongest bias rules,
Is pride, the never-failing vice of fools.
Ibid. Part II, Line 1
A little learning is a dangerous thing;[3]
Drink deep, or taste not the Pierian spring:
There shallow draughts intoxicate the brain,
And drinking largely sobers us again.
Ibid. Line 15
Hills peep o'er hills, and Alps on Alps arise!
Ibid. Line 32
Whoever thinks a faultless piece to see,

---

[1] See Milton, page 151.
[2] Viz. the monument (near London Bridge) built in memory of the great fire of 1666, with an inscription attributing the disaster to a Popish plot.
[3] See Tom Brown, page 188.

[1] See Suckling, page 164.
[2] Quandoque bonus dormitat Homerus (Even the worthy Homer some times nods). — HORACE: *De Arte Poetica, 359*
[3] See Bacon, page 110.

Thinks what ne'er was, nor is, nor e'er shall be.[1]

Essay on Criticism. Part II, Line 53

True wit is Nature to advantage dress'd,
What oft was thought, but ne'er so well express'd.

Ibid. Line 97

Words are like leaves; and where they most abound,
Much fruit of sense beneath is rarely found.

Ibid. Line 109

Such labour'd nothings, in so strange a style,
Amaze th' unlearn'd, and make the learned smile.

Ibid. Line 126

In words, as fashions, the same rule will hold,
Alike fantastic if too new or old:
Be not the first by whom the new are tried,
Nor yet the last to lay the old aside.

Ibid. Line 133

Some to church repair,
Not for the doctrine, but the music there.
These equal syllables alone require,
Though oft the ear the open vowels tire;
While expletives their feeble aid do join,
And ten low words oft creep in one dull line.

Ibid. Line 142

A needless Alexandrine ends the song,
That like a wounded snake, drags its slow length along.

Ibid. Line 156

True ease in writing comes from art, not chance,[1]
As those move easiest who have learn'd to dance.
'Tis not enough no harshness gives offence;
The sound must seem an echo to the sense.

Ibid. Line 162

[1] See Suckling, page 164.
[2] Also in *Epistle II, Book II, L. 178*

Soft is the strain when zephyr gently blows,
And the smooth stream in smoother numbers flows;
But when loud surges lash the sounding shore,
The hoarse rough verse should like the torrent roar.
When Ajax strives some rock's vast weight to throw,
The line, too, labours, and the words move slow:
Not so when swift Camilla scours the plain,
Flies o'er th' unbending corn, and skims along the main.

Essay on Criticism. Part II, Line 166

At ev'ry trifle scorn to take offence.

Ibid. Line 186

Yet let not each gay turn thy rapture move;
For fools admire, but men of sense approve.

Ibid. Line 190

Some judge of authors' names, not works, and then
Nor praise nor blame the writings, but the men.

Ibid. Line 212

But let a lord once own the happy lines,
How the wit brightens! how the style refines!

Ibid. Line 220

Some praise at morning what they blame at night,
But always think the last opinion right.

Ibid. Line 230

Envy will merit as its shade pursue,
But like a shadow proves the substance true.

Ibid. Line 266

To err is human, to forgive divine.[1]

Ibid. Line 325

All seems infected that th' infected spy,
As all looks yellow to the jaundic'd eye.

Ibid. Line 358

[1] See Royall Tyler, page 283.
Then gently scan your brother man,
Still gentler sister woman;
Though they may gang a kennin' wrang,
To step aside is human.
BURNS: *Address to the Unco Guid*
See also C. T. Copeland, page 753.

Men must be taught as if you taught
them not,
And things unknown propos'd as things
forgot.
Essay on Criticism. Part III, Line 15
The bookful blockhead, ignorantly
read,
With loads of learned lumber in his
head.
Ibid. Line 53
For fools rush in where angels fear to
tread.[1]
Ibid. Line 66
What dire offence from amorous causes
springs!
What mighty contests rise from trivial
things!
*The Rape of the Lock. Canto I,
Line 1*
And all Arabia breathes from yonder
box.
Ibid. Line 134
On her white breast a sparkling cross
she wore,
Which Jews might kiss, and infidels
adore.
Ibid. Canto II, Line 7
If to her share some female errors fall,
Look on her face, and you'll forget 'em
all.
Ibid. Line 17
Fair tresses man's imperial race en-
snare,
And beauty draws us with a single
hair.[2]
Ibid. Line 27
Here thou, great Anna! whom three
realms obey,
Dost sometimes counsel take — and
sometimes tea.
Ibid. Canto III, Line 7
At every word a reputation dies.
Ibid. Line 16
The hungry judges soon the sentence
sign,
And wretches hang that jurymen may
dine.
Ibid. Line 21

[1] Wrens make prey where eagles dare not
perch. — SHAKESPEARE: *King Richard III, Act
I, Sc. 3, L. 71*
[2] See Burton, page 125.

Coffee, which makes the politician wise.
*The Rape of the Lock.
Canto III, Line 117*
But when to mischief mortals bend
their will,
How soon they find fit instruments of
ill!
Ibid. Line 125
The meeting points the sacred hair dis-
sever
From the fair head, forever, and for-
ever!
Ibid. Line 153
Steel could the labour of the gods de-
stroy,
And strike to dust th' imperial towers
of Troy; ·
Steel could the works of mortal pride
confound
And hew triumphal arches to the
ground.
Ibid. Line 173
Sir Plume, of amber snuff-box justly
vain,
And the nice conduct of a clouded cane.
Ibid. Canto IV, Line 123
Charms strike the sight, but merit wins
the soul.
Ibid. Canto V, Line 34
"Shut, shut the door, good John!"
fatigued, I said;
"Tie up the knocker! say I'm sick, I'm
dead."
*Epistle to Dr. Arbuthnot, Prologue
to the Satires, Line 1*
Fire in each eye, and papers in each
hand,
They rave, recite, and madden round
the land.
Ibid. Line 5
Is there a parson much bemused in
beer,
A maudlin poetess, a rhyming peer,
A clerk foredoom'd his father's soul to
cross,
Who pens a stanza when he should en-
gross?
Ibid. Line 15
Fired that the house[1] reject him,
" 'Sdeath, I'll print it,
And shame the fools."
Ibid. Line 61

[1] The theatre

No creature smarts so little as a fool.
Epistle to Dr. Arbuthnot, Prologue
to the Satires, Line 84
As yet a child, nor yet a fool to fame,
I lisp'd in numbers, for the numbers
came.
Ibid. Line 127
This long disease, my life.
Ibid. Line 132
Means not, but blunders round about
a meaning;
And he whose fustian's so sublimely
bad,
It is not poetry, but prose run mad.
Ibid. Line 186
Should such a man, too fond to rule
alone,
Bear, like the Turk, no brother near
the throne.[1]
Ibid. Line 197
Damn with faint praise, assent with
civil leer,
And without sneering teach the rest to
sneer;[2]
Willing to wound, and yet afraid to
strike,
Just hint a fault, and hesitate dislike.
Ibid. Line 201
By flatterers besieg'd,
And so obliging that he ne'er oblig'd;
Like Cato, give his little senate laws,[3]
And sit attentive to his own applause.
Ibid. Line 207
Who but must laugh, if such a man
there be?
Who would not weep, if Atticus were
he?
Ibid. Line 213

[1] See Denham, page 167.
[2] When needs he must, yet faintly then he
praises;
Somewhat the deed, much more the means
he raises:
So marreth what he makes, and praising
most, dispraises.
PHINEAS FLETCHER [1582–1650]: *The*
Purple Island [1633], *Canto VII*
Even in the church where boredom is
prolific
I hail thee first, Episcopalian bore:
Who else could serve as social soporific,
And without snoring, teach the rest to snore.
CHRISTOPHER MORLEY: *On a Certain*
Cleric
[3] While Cato gives his little senate laws. —
Prologue to Mr. Addison's Cato, L. 23

Cursed be the verse, how well so e'er
it flow,
That tends to make one worthy man my
foe.
Epistle to Dr. Arbuthnot, Prologue
to the Satires, Line 283
Satire or sense, alas! can Sporus feel?
Who breaks a butterfly upon a wheel?
Ibid. Line 307
Eternal smiles his emptiness betray,
As shallow streams run dimpling all the
way.
Ibid. Line 315
Wit that can creep, and pride that licks
the dust.
Ibid. Line 333
Unlearn'd, he knew no schoolman's
subtle art,
No language but the language of the
heart.
Ibid. Line 398
Me, let the tender office long engage
To rock the cradle of reposing age;
With lenient arts extend a mother's
breath,
Make languor smile, and smooth the
bed of death;
Explore the thought, explain the asking
eye,
And keep awhile one parent from the
sky.
Ibid. Line 408
I cannot sleep a wink.
Satires, Epistles, and Odes of Horace.
Satire I, Book II, Line 12
Satire's my weapon, but I'm too dis-
creet
To run amuck, and tilt at all I meet.
Ibid. Line 69
But touch me, and no minister so sore.
Ibid. Line 76
There St. John mingles with my
friendly bowl,
The feast of reason and the flow of soul.
Ibid. Line 127
For I, who hold sage Homer's rule the
best,
Welcome the coming, speed the going
guest.[1]
Ibid. Satire II, Book II, Line 159

[1] This line is repeated in the translation of
the *Odyssey, Book XV, L. 83*, with "parting"
instead of "going."

I've often wish'd that I had clear,
For life, six hundred pounds a year;
A handsome house to lodge a friend,
A river at my garden's end,
A terrace walk, and half a rood
Of land set out to plant a wood.
Satires, Epistles, and Odes of Horace.
Satire VI, Book II, Line 1
Give me again my hollow tree,
A crust of bread, and liberty.
Ibid. Line 220
A patriot is a fool in ev'ry age.
Epilogue to the Satires. Dialogue I,
Line 41
Laugh then at any but at fools or foes;
These you but anger, and you mend not
those.
Laugh at your friends, and if your
friends are sore,
So much the better, you may laugh the
more.
Ibid. Line 53
Do good by stealth, and blush to find
it fame.
Ibid. Line 136
Never gallop Pegasus to death.
Epistle I. Book I, Line 14
When the brisk minor pants for twenty-
one.
Ibid. Line 38
Not to go back is somewhat to advance.
Ibid. Line 53
He's armed without that's innocent
within.
Ibid. Line 94
Get place and wealth, if possible, with
grace;
If not, by any means get wealth and
place.[1]
Ibid. Line 103
Above all Greek, above all Roman
fame.[2]
Ibid. Book II, Line 26
The mob of gentlemen who wrote with
ease.
Ibid. Line 108
One simile that solitary shines
In the dry desert of a thousand lines.
Ibid. Line 111
Then marble, soften'd into life, grew
warm,

[1] See Ben Jonson, page 118.
[2] See Dryden, page 173.

And yielding metal flow'd to human
form.[1]
Epistle I. Book II, Line 147
Who says in verse what others say in
prose.
Ibid. Line 202
What will a child learn sooner than a
song?
Ibid. Line 205
Ev'n copious Dryden wanted, or forgot,
The last and greatest art — the art to
blot.
Ibid. Line 280
There still remains, to mortify a wit,
The many-headed monster of the pit.[2]
Ibid. Line 304
We poets are (upon a poet's word)
Of all mankind the creatures most ab-
surd:
The season when to come, and when to
go,
To sing, or cease to sing, we never
know.
Ibid. Line 358
Call, if you will, bad rhyming a disease,
It gives men happiness, or leaves them
ease.
Epistle II. Book II, Line 182
The worst of madmen is a saint run
mad.
Epistle VI. Book I, Line 27
Vain was the chief's, the sage's pride!
They had no poet, and they died.
Odes. Book IV, Ode 9, Stanza 4
Nature and Nature's laws lay hid in
night:
God said, Let Newton be! and all was
light.
Epitaph Intended for Sir
Isaac Newton
Whether thou choose Cervantes' seri-
ous air,
Or laugh and shake in Rabelais' easy-
chair.
The Dunciad. Book I, Line 21

[1] The canvas glow'd beyond ev'n Nature
warm;
The pregnant quarry teem'd with human
form.
GOLDSMITH: *The Traveller, L. 137*
[2] See Sidney, page 27.

Poetic Justice, with her lifted scale,
Where in nice balance truth with gold
she weighs,
And solid pudding against empty
praise.
　　　　The Dunciad. Book I, Line 52
While pensive poets painful vigils keep,
Sleepless themselves to give their read-
ers sleep.
　　　　　　　　Ibid. Line 93
Next o'er his books his eyes begin to
roll,
In pleasing memory of all he stole.
　　　　　　　　Ibid. Line 127
Or where the pictures for the page
atone,
And Quarles is sav'd by beauties not his
own.
　　　　　　　　Ibid. Line 139
How index-learning turns no student
pale,
Yet holds the eel of science by the tail.
　　　　　　　　Ibid. Line 279
And gentle Dulness ever loves a joke.
　　　　　　Ibid. Book II, Line 34
A brain of feathers, and a heart of lead.
　　　　　　　　Ibid. Line 44
Another, yet the same.[1]
　　　　　　Ibid. Book III, Line 40
Makes night hideous.[2]
　　　　　　　　Ibid. Line 166
And proud his mistress' order to per-
form,
Rides in the whirlwind and directs the
storm.[3]
　　　　　　　　Ibid. Line 263
A wit with dunces, and a dunce with
wits.[4]
　　　　　Ibid. Book IV, Line 90

The right divine of kings to govern
wrong.
　　　The Dunciad. Book IV, Line 188
　　　　　　　　Stuff the head
With all such reading as was never
read:
For thee explain a thing till all men
doubt it,
And write about it, goddess, and about
it.
　　　　　　　　Ibid. Line 249
To happy convents, bosom'd deep in
vines,
Where slumber abbots purple as their
wines.
　　　　　　　　Ibid. Line 301
Led by my hand, he saunter'd Europe
round,
And gather'd every vice on Christian
ground.
　　　　　　　　Ibid. Line 311
Ev'n Palinurus nodded at the helm.
　　　　　　　　Ibid. Line 614
Religion, blushing, veils her sacred
fires,
And unawares Morality expires.
Nor public flame nor private dares to
shine;
Nor human spark is left, nor glimpse
divine!
Lo! thy dread empire Chaos! is re-
stor'd,
Light dies before thy uncreating word:

[1] Another, yet the same. — TICKELL: *From a Lady in England.* JOHNSON: *Life of Dryden.* DARWIN: *Botanic Garden, Part I, Canto IV, L. 380.* WORDSWORTH: *The Excursion, Book IX.* SCOTT: *The Abbot, Chap. I.* HORACE: *Carmen Saeculare, L. 10* (Aliusque et idem)

[2] See Shakespeare, page 91.

[3] See Addison, page 194.

[4] See Shakespeare, page 68.
This man [Chesterfield], I thought, had been a lord among wits; but I find he is only a wit among lords. — JOHNSON (*Boswell's Life, Vol. I, P. 159, Everyman ed.*)
A fool with judges, amongst fools a judge. — COWPER: *Conversation, L. 298*
Although too much of a soldier among

sovereigns, no one could claim with better right to be a sovereign among soldiers. — WALTER SCOTT: *Life of Napoleon*
He [Steele] was a rake among scholars, and a scholar among rakes. — MACAULAY: *Review of Aikin's Life of Addison*
Temple was a man of the world among men of letters, a man of letters among men of the world. — MACAULAY: *Review of Life and Writings of Sir William Temple*
Greswell in his *Memoirs of Politian* says that Sannazarius himself, inscribing to this lady [Cassandra Marchesia] an edition of his Italian poems, terms her "delle belle eruditissima, delle erudite bellissima" (most learned of the fair; fairest of the learned).
Qui stultis videri eruditi volunt stulti eruditis videntur (Those who wish to appear wise among fools, among the wise seem foolish). — QUINTILIAN, *X, 7, 22*

Thy hand, great Anarch! lets the curtain fall,
And universal darkness buries all.

> *The Dunciad. Book IV, Line 649*

How vast a memory has Love!

> *Sappho to Phaon. Line 52*

Speed the soft intercourse from soul to soul,
And waft a sigh from Indus to the Pole.

> *Eloisa to Abelard. Line 57*

Curse on all laws but those which love has made!
Love, free as air at sight of human ties,
Spreads his light wings, and in a moment flies.

> *Ibid. Line 74*

And love the offender, yet detest the offence.[1]

> *Ibid. Line 192*

How happy is the blameless vestal's lot!
The world forgetting, by the world forgot.

> *Ibid. Line 207*

One thought of thee puts all the pomp to flight,
Priests, tapers, temples, swim before my sight.[2]

> *Ibid. Line 273*

He best can paint them who shall feel them most.

> *Ibid. Line 366 (last line)*

Not chaos-like together crush'd and bruis'd,
But, as the world, harmoniously confus'd:
Where order in variety we see,
And where, though all things differ, all agree.

> *Windsor Forest. Line 13*

Ye Gods! annihilate but space and time,
And make two lovers happy.

> *Martinus Scriblerus on the Art of Sinking in Poetry. Chap. XI*

Nor Fame I slight, nor for her favours call;

---

[1] See Dryden, page 177.
[2] Priests, altars, victims, swam before my sight. — EDMUND SMITH [1672–1710]: *Phœdra and Hippolytus, adapted from Racine, Act I, Sc. 1* [1707]

She comes unlooked for, if she comes at all.

> *The Temple of Fame. Line 513*

Unblemish'd let me live or die unknown;
Oh, grant an honest fame or grant me none!

> *Ibid. Line 523 (last lines)*

I am his Highness'[1] dog at Kew;
Pray tell me, sir, whose dog are you?

> *On the Collar of a Dog*

There, take (says Justice), take ye each a shell:
We thrive at Westminster on fools like you;
'Twas a fat oyster — live in peace, — adieu.[2]

> *Verbatim from Boileau*

Father of all! in every age,
  In every clime adored,
By saint, by savage, and by sage,
  Jehovah, Jove, or Lord!

> *The Universal Prayer. Stanza 1*

And binding Nature fast in fate,
  Left free the human will.

> *Ibid. Stanza 3*

And deal damnation round the land.

> *Ibid. Stanza 7*

Teach me to feel another's woe,
  To hide the fault I see;
That mercy I to others show,
  That mercy show to me.[3]

> *Ibid. Stanza 10*

Happy the man whose wish and care
  A few paternal acres bound.

> *Ode on Solitude. Stanza 1*

Thus let me live, unseen, unknown,
  Thus unlamented let me die;
Steal from the world, and not a stone
  Tell where I lie.

> *Ibid. Stanza 5*

Vital spark of heavenly flame,
Quit, Oh quit, this mortal frame!

> *The Dying Christian to His Soul. Stanza 1*

---

[1] Frederick, Prince of Wales.
[2] "Tenez voilà," dit-elle, "à chacun une écaille,
Des sottises d'autrui nous vivons au Palais;
Messieurs, l'huître étoit bonne. Adieu. Vivez en paix."
> BOILEAU: *Epître II (à M. l'Abbé des Roches)*

[3] See Spenser, page 25.

Is there no bright reversion in the sky
For those who greatly think, or bravely
die?
>*To the Memory of an Unfortunate
Lady. Line 9*

By foreign hands thy dying eyes were
clos'd,
By foreign hands thy decent limbs com-
pos'd,
By foreign hands thy humble grave
adorn'd,
By strangers honoured, and by strangers mourn'd!
>*Ibid. Line 51*

How lov'd, how honour'd once, avails
thee not,
To whom related, or by whom begot;
A heap of dust alone remains of thee:
'Tis all thou art, and all the proud shall
be!
>*Ibid. Line 71*

The saint sustain'd it, but the woman
died.
>*Epitaph on Mrs. Corbet*

Of manners gentle, of affections mild;
In wit a man, simplicity a child.
>*Epitaph on Gay*

Curtain lectures made a restless night.
>*Paraphrases from Chaucer. The
Wife of Bath, Her Prologue,
Line 165*

A glutted market makes provision
cheap.
>*Ibid. Line 262*

To see, be seen, to tell, and gather
tales.[1]
>*Ibid. Line 282*

The wasting moth ne'er spoil'd my best
array;
The cause was this, I wore it every day.
>*Ibid. Line 288*

Whoe'er it be
That tells my faults, I hate him mortally!
>*Ibid. Line 351*

Love seldom haunts the breast where
learning lies,
And Venus sets ere Mercury can rise.
>*Ibid. Line 369*

You beat your pate, and fancy wit will
come;

[1] See Chaucer, page 7.

Knock as you please, there's nobody
at home.
>*Epigram: An Empty House*

For he lives twice who can at once employ
The present well, and ev'n the past enjoy.[1]
>*Imitation of Martial*

Who dare to love their country, and
be poor.
>*On His Grotto at Twickenham*

Party is the madness of many for the
gain of a few.
>*Thoughts on Various Subjects*

I never knew any man in my life
who could not bear another's misfortunes perfectly like a Christian.
>*Ibid.*

A man should never be ashamed to
own he has been in the wrong, which is
but saying, in other words, that he is
wiser to-day than he was yesterday.
>*Ibid.*

It is with narrow-souled people as
with narrow-necked bottles; the less
they have in them the more noise they
make in pouring out.
>*Ibid.*

When men grow virtuous in their old
age, they only make a sacrifice to God
of the devil's leavings.[2]
>*Ibid.*

True disputants are like true sportsmen, their whole delight is in the pursuit.
>*Ibid.*

No literal Translation can be just to
an excellent Original: but it is a great
Mistake to imagine that a rash Paraphrase can make amends for this general Defect.
>*Preface to the Iliad*

[1] Ampliat ætatis spatium sibi vir bonus; hoc
est
Vivere bis vita posse priore frui
(The good man prolongs his life; to be able
to enjoy one's past life is to live twice). —
MARTIAL, X, 237
See Cowley, page 168.
[2] Now their sins are all committed,
Lord, how virtuous they are!
WILHELM BUSCH [1832–1908]: *Die
fromme Helene* (translation by Chris-
topher Morley)

Simplicity is the Mean between Ostentation and Rusticity.

Preface to the Iliad

Achilles' wrath, to Greece the direful
spring
Of woes unnumber'd, heavenly goddess,
sing!

The Iliad of Homer.[1] *Book I,*
Line 1

The distant Trojans never injur'd me.

Ibid. Line 200

Words sweet as honey from his lips distill'd.

Ibid. Line 332

Shakes his ambrosial curls, and gives
the nod, —
The stamp of fate, and sanction of the
god.

Ibid. Line 684

And unextinguish'd laughter shakes the
skies.[2]

Ibid. Line 771

The man who acts the least, upbraids
the most.

Ibid. Book II, Line 311

Thick as autumnal leaves or driving
sand.

Ibid. Line 970

Chiefs, who no more in bloody fights
engage,
But, wise through time, and narrative
with age,
In summer-days like grasshoppers rejoice,
A bloodless race, that send a feeble
voice.

Ibid. Book III, Line 199

She moves a goddess, and she looks a
queen.

Ibid. Line 208

But when he speaks, what elocution
flows!
Soft as the fleeces of descending snows
The copious accents fall, with easy art;
Melting they fall, and sink into the
heart.

Ibid. Line 283

---

[1] A very pretty poem, Mr. Pope, but it's not
Homer. — RICHARD BENTLEY, great classical
scholar
[2] The same line occurs in the translation of
the *Odyssey, Book VIII, L. 366.*

Ajax the great . . .
Himself a host.

The Iliad of Homer. Book III,
Line 293

Wrapt in the cold embraces of the tomb.

Ibid. Line 312

Plough the watery deep.

Ibid. Line 357

And joyful nations join in leagues of
peace.

Ibid. Line 401

The day shall come, the great avenging
day,
Which Troy's proud glories in the dust
shall lay,
When Priam's powers and Priam's self
shall fall,
And one prodigious ruin swallow all.

Ibid. Book IV, Line 196

The first in banquets, but the last in
fight.

Ibid. Line 401

Gods! How the son degenerates from
the sire!

Ibid. Line 451

Not two strong men the enormous
weight could raise, —
Such men as live in these degenerate
days.[1]

Ibid. Book V, Line 371

Whose little body lodg'd a mighty
mind.

Ibid. Line 999

He held his seat; a friend to human
race.
Fast by the road, his ever-open door
Obliged the wealthy, and reliev'd the
poor.[2]

Ibid. Book VI, Line 18

Like leaves on trees the race of man is
found,
Now green in youth, now withering on
the ground:

---

[1] A mass enormous! which in modern days
No two of earth's degenerate sons could
raise.

Book XX, L. 337

[2] Let me live in my house by the side of the
road
And be a friend of man.

SAM WALTER FOSS [1858–1911]: *The
House by the Side of the Road, St. 5*

Another race the following spring supplies:
They fall successive, and successive rise.
> *The Iliad of Homer. Book VI,*
> *Line 181*

Inflaming wine, pernicious to mankind.
> *Ibid. Line 330*

If yet, not lost to all the sense of shame.
> *Ibid. Line 350*

He, from whose lips divine persuasion flows.
> *Ibid. Book VII, Line 143*

Short is my date, but deathless my renown.
> *Ibid. Book IX, Line 535*

Content to follow when we lead the way.
> *Ibid. Book X, Line 141*

He serves me most, who serves his country best.
> *Ibid. Line 201*

Praise from a friend, or censure from a foe,
Are lost on hearers that our merits know.
> *Ibid. Line 293*

The rest were vulgar deaths, unknown to fame.
> *Ibid. Book XI, Line 394*

Without a sign, his sword the brave man draws,
And asks no omen but his country's cause.
> *Ibid. Book XII, Line 283*

A day to fire the brave, and warm the cold,
To gain new glories, or augment the old.
> *Ibid. Line 321*

And seem to walk on wings, and tread in air.
> *Ibid. Book XIII, Line 106*

Not vain the weakest, if their force unite.
> *Ibid. Line 311*

The best of things, beyond their measure, cloy.
> *Ibid. Line 795*

Heroes as great have died, and yet shall fall.
> *Ibid. Book XV, Line 157*

And for our country 'tis a bliss to die.[1]
> *The Iliad of Homer. Book XV,*
> *Line 583*

Like strength is felt from hope, and from despair.
> *Ibid. Line 852*

Two friends, two bodies with one soul inspir'd.[2]
> *Ibid. Book XVI, Line 267*

Sleep and Death, two twins of winged race,
Of matchless swiftness, but of silent pace.
> *Ibid. Line 831*

How vain, without the merit, is the name!
> *Ibid. Book XVII, Line 158*

Achilles absent was Achilles still.
> *Ibid. Book XXII, Line 418*

Forever honour'd, and forever mourn'd.
> *Ibid. Line 422*

Unwept, unhonour'd, uninterr'd he lies![3]
> *Ibid. Line 484*

It is not strength, but art, obtains the prize,[4]
And to be swift is less than to be wise.
'Tis more by art, than force of num'rous strokes.
> *Ibid. Book XXIII, Line 383*

A green old age,[5] unconscious of decays.
> *Ibid. Line 929*

An honest business never blush to tell.
> *The Odyssey of Homer.[6] Book III,*
> *Line 20*

---

[1] Dulce et decorum est pro patria mori (It is sweet and honourable to die for one's country). — HORACE: *Odes, Book III, 2, L. 13*
[2] A friend is one soul abiding in two bodies.
— DIOGENES LAERTIUS: *On Aristotle*
Two souls with but a single thought,
Two hearts that beat as one.
VON MÜNCH BELLINGHAUSEN [1806–1871]: *Ingomar the Barbarian, Act II*
[3] Unwept, unhonoured, and unsung. — SCOTT: *Lay of the Last Minstrel*
Unknelled, uncoffined, and unknown. — BYRON: *Childe Harold, Canto IV, St. 179*
[4] See Middleton, page 116.
[5] See Dryden, page 178.
[6] Pope engaged two friends, ELIJAH FENTON [1683–1730] and WILLIAM BROOME [1689–1745], to translate certain books of *The Odyssey* of Homer for him. The division of the work was: — Pope: Books III, V, VII, IX, XIII, XIV, XVII, XXI, XXII, XXIV,

Urge him with truth to frame his fair
   replies;
And sure he will: for Wisdom never
   lies.
   The Odyssey of Homer. Book III,
                                    Line 25
The lot of man; to suffer and to die.
                         Ibid. Line 117
A faultless body and a blameless mind.
                         Ibid. Line 138
The long historian of my country's
   woes.
                         Ibid. Line 142
When now Aurora, daughter of the
   dawn,
With rosy lustre purpled o'er the lawn.
                       Ibid. Line 516 [1]
Wise to resolve, and patient to perform.
   Ibid. Book IV (Fenton transla-
                       tion), Line 372
The leader, mingling with the vulgar
   host,
Is in the common mass of matter lost.
                         Ibid. Line 397
The people's parent, he protected all.
                         Ibid. Line 921
The big round tear stands trembling in
   her eye.
                         Ibid. Line 936
The windy satisfaction of the tongue.
                        Ibid. Line 1092
No more was seen the human form
   divine. [2]
               Ibid. Book X, Line 278
Oh woman, woman! when to ill thy
   mind
Is bent, all hell contains no fouler
   fiend. [3]
   Ibid. Book XI (Broome transla-
                       tion), Line 531
And what so tedious as a twice-told
   tale. [4]
   Ibid. Book XII (Broome transla-
                       tion), Line 538
He ceas'd; but left so pleasing on their
   ear

His voice, that list'ning still they
   seem'd to hear.
   The Odyssey of Homer. Book XIII,
                                    Line 1
His native home deep imag'd in his
   soul.
                         Ibid. Line 38
The sex is ever to a soldier kind.
               Ibid. Book XIV, Line 246
True friendship's laws are by this rule
   express'd,
Welcome the coming, speed the parting
   guest. [1]
               Ibid. Book XV, Line 83
For too much rest itself becomes a pain.
                         Ibid. Line 429
He knew his lord; he knew, and strove
   to meet;
In vain he strove to crawl and kiss his
   feet;
Yet (all he could) his tail, his ears, his
   eyes
Salute his master, and confess his
   joys. . . .
The dog, whom Fate had granted to
   behold
His lord, when twenty tedious years
   had roll'd,
Takes a last look, and, having seen him,
   dies:
So closed forever faithful Argus' eyes!
               Ibid. Book XVII, Line 359
Unbless'd thy hand, if, in this low dis-
   guise,
Wander, perhaps, some inmate of the
   skies. [2]
                         Ibid. Line 576
Impatient straight to flesh his virgin
   sword.
   Ibid. Book XX (Fenton transla-
                       tion), Line 461
So ends the bloody business of the day.
               Ibid. Book XXII, Line 516
   Blessed is he who expects nothing,
for he shall never be disappointed. [3]
   Letter to Gay [October 6, 1727]

---

and most of X and XV; Fenton: Books I, IV,
XIX, and XX; Broome: Books II, VI, VIII,
XI, XII, XVI, XVIII, XXIII.
   [1] Also *Line 623*
   [2] Human face divine. — MILTON: *Paradise
Lost, Book III, L. 44*
   [3] See Otway, page 185.
   [4] See Shakespeare, page 58.

[1] See Pope, page 213.
[2] Be not forgetful to entertain strangers, for
thereby some have entertained angels unawares. — *Hebrews, XIII, 2*
[3] Pope calls this the eighth beatitude (Roscoe's edition of Pope, *Vol. X, P. 184*).
See Wolcot, page 272.

This is the Jew
That Shakespeare drew.[1]

LEWIS THEOBALD [2]
[1688–1744]

None but himself can be his parallel.[3]
The Double Falsehood

LADY MARY WORTLEY MONTAGU
[1690–1762]

Let this great maxim be my virtue's
guide, —
In part she is to blame that has been
tried:
He comes too near that comes to be de-
nied.
The Lady's Resolve [4]
And we meet, with champagne and a
chicken, at last.[5]
The Lover
Be plain in dress, and sober in your
diet;
In short, my deary, kiss me, and be
quiet.
*A Summary of Lord Lyttelton's
Advice*
Satire should, like a polished razor
keen,

[1] On the 14th of February, 1741, Macklin
established his fame as an actor in the character of Shylock, in the "Merchant of Venice."
. . . Macklin's performance of this character
so forcibly struck a gentleman in the pit that
he, as it were involuntarily, exclaimed, —
"This is the Jew
That Shakespeare drew!"
It has been said that this gentleman was
Mr. Pope, and that he meant his panegyric
on Macklin as a satire against Lord Lans-
downe. — *Biographia Dramatica, Vol. I, Part
II, P. 469*
[2] Editor of Shakespeare, and hero of Pope's
Dunciad.
[3]   Quæris Alcidæ parem?
   Nemo est nisi ipse
(Do you see Alcides' equal? None is, except
himself). — SENECA: *Hercules Furens, I, 1;
84.*
   And but herself admits no parallel. — MAS-
SINGER: *Duke of Milan, Act IV, Sc. 3.*
[4] A fugitive piece, written on a window by
Lady Montagu, after her marriage [1713].
See Overbury, page 128.
[5] What say you to such a supper with such
a woman? — BYRON: *Note to a Second Letter
on Bowles*

Wound with a touch that's scarcely
felt or seen.
*To the Imitator of the First Satire
of Horace. Book II*
But the fruit that can fall without shak-
ing
Indeed is too mellow for me.
The Answer

JOHN BYROM
[1692–1763]

God bless the King, — I mean the
faith's defender!
God bless — no harm in blessing — the
Pretender!
But who pretender is, or who is king, —
God bless us all! — that's quite another
thing.[1]
*Miscellaneous Poems [1773].
To an Officer of the Army, ex-
tempore*
Take time enough: all other graces
Will soon fill up their proper places.[2]
Advice to Preach Slow
Some say, compar'd to Bononcini,
That Mynheer Handel's but a ninny;
Others aver that he to Handel
Is scarcely fit to hold a candle.
Strange all this difference should be
'Twixt Tweedledum and Tweedledee.
*On the Feuds between Handel and
Bononcini* [3]
As clear as a whistle.
Epistle to Lloyd
The point is plain as a pike-staff.[4]
Epistle to a Friend
Bone and Skin, two millers thin,
   Would starve us all, or near it:
But be it known to Skin and Bone
   That Flesh and Blood can't bear it.
Epigram on Two Monopolists

[1] Quoted by SIR WALTER SCOTT in *Redgauntlet, Vol. II, Chap. 1,* Edinburgh edition
[1832].
[2] See Walker, page 170.
[3] Nourse asked me if I had seen the verses
upon Handel and Bononcini, not knowing
that they were mine. — *Byrom's Remains,
Vol. I, P. 173* (Chetham Soc.)
   The last two lines have been attributed
to Swift and Pope (see Scott's edition of
Swift, and Dyce's edition of Pope).
[4] See Middleton, page 116.

Thus adorned, the two heroes, 'twixt
  shoulder and elbow,
Shook hands and went to 't; and the
  word it was bilbow.
> *Upon a Trial of Skill between
> the Great Masters of the Noble
> Science of Defence, Messrs.
> Figg and Sutton*

PHILIP DORMER STANHOPE, EARL OF CHESTERFIELD
[1694–1773]

Whatever is worth doing at all, is
worth doing well.
> *Letters. March 10, 1746*

Do as you would be done by, is the
surest method of pleasing.
> *Ibid. October 16, 1747*

I knew once a very covetous, sordid
fellow,[1] who used to say, "Take care
of the pence, for the pounds will take
care of themselves."
> *Ibid. November 6, 1747*

Sacrifice to the Graces.[2]
> *Ibid. March 9, 1748*

Manners must adorn knowledge, and
smooth its way through the world. Like
a great rough diamond, it may do very
well in a closet by way of curiosity, and
also for its intrinsic value.
> *Ibid. July 1, 1748*

Without some dissimulation no business can be carried on at all.
> *Ibid. May 22, 1749*

Style is the dress of thoughts.
> *Ibid. November 24, 1749*

Religion must still be allowed to be
a collateral security to Virtue.
> *Ibid. January 8, 1750*

Despatch is the soul of business.
> *Ibid. February 5, 1750*

---

[1] William Lowndes [1652–1724], Secretary
of the Treasury in the Reigns of King William, Queen Anne, and King George the First.
He is credited with originating the phrase
"ways and means."

[2] Plato was continually saying to Xeno-
crates, "Sacrifice to the Graces." — DIOGENES
LAERTIUS: *Xenocrates, Book IV, Sect. 2*
  Let us sacrifice to the Muses. — PLUTARCH:
The Banquet of the Seven Wise Men. (A say-
ing of Solon.)

Chapter of accidents.[1]
> *Letters. February 16, 1753*

I assisted at the birth of that most
significant word "flirtation," which
dropped from the most beautiful mouth
in the world.
> *The World. No. 101*

Unlike my subject now shall be my
  song;
It shall be witty, and it sha'n't be long.
> *Impromptu Lines*

The dews of the evening most carefully
  shun, —
Those tears of the sky for the loss of
  the sun.
> *Advice to a Lady in Autumn*

The nation looked upon him as a de-
serter, and he shrunk into insignifi-
cancy and an earldom.
> *Character of Pulteney*

He adorned whatever subject he
either spoke or wrote upon, by the most
splendid eloquence.[2]
> *Character of Bolingbroke*

Women, and young men, are very
apt to tell what secrets they know,
from the vanity of having been trusted.
> *Letters to His Son*

FRANCIS HUTCHESON
[1694–1746]

That action is best which procures
the greatest happiness for the greatest
numbers.[3]
> *Inquiry Concerning Moral Good
> and Evil. Sect. 3* [1720]

---

[1] Chapter of accidents. — BURKE: *Notes
for Speeches* [ed. 1852], *Vol. II, P. 426*
  John Wilkes said that "the Chapter of Accidents is the longest chapter in the book."
— SOUTHEY: *The Doctor, Chap. CXVIII*

[2] Who left scarcely any style of writing untouched,
And touched nothing that he did not adorn.
  JOHNSON: *Epitaph on Goldsmith*
  Il embellit tout ce qu'il touche (He adorns
whatever he touches). — FÉNELON [1651–
1715]: *Lettre sur les Occupations de l'Aca-
démie Française, Sect. IV*

[3] Priestley was the first (unless it was Beccaria) who taught my lips to pronounce this
sacred truth, — that the greatest happiness of
the greatest number is the foundation of

MATTHEW GREEN
[1696–1737]

Fling but a stone, the giant dies.
> *The Spleen. Line 93*

Laugh and be well.
> *Ibid. Line 94*

Life's moving-pictures, well-wrought plays,
To others' grief attention raise.
> *Ibid. Line 131*

Music hath charms,[1] we all may find,
Ingratiate deeply with the mind.
> *Ibid. Line 141*

Happy the man, who, innocent,
Grieves not at ills he can't prevent;
His skiff does with the current glide,
Not puffing pulled against the tide.
> *Ibid. Line 365*

Though pleased to see the dolphins play,
I mind my compass and my way.
> *Ibid. Line 826*

WILLIAM OLDYS
[1696–1761]

Busy, curious, thirsty fly,
Drink with me, and drink as I.
> *On a Fly Drinking out of a Cup*
> *of Ale. Stanza 1*

Three-score summers, when they're gone,
Will appear as short as one.
> *Ibid. Stanza 2*

RICHARD SAVAGE
[1698–1743]

He lives to build, not boast, a generous race;
No tenth transmitter of a foolish face.
> *The Bastard. Line 7*

May see thee now, though late, redeem thy name,

And glorify what else is damn'd to fame.
> *Character of Foster*

WILLIAM WARBURTON, BISHOP OF GLOUCESTER
[1698–1779]

Orthodoxy is my doxy — heterodoxy is another man's doxy.[1]
> *Quoted by* JOSEPH PRIESTLEY
> *[1733–1804]: Memoirs, Vol. I,*
> *Page 572*

JOHN DYER
[1700–1758]

A little rule, a little sway,
A sunbeam in a winter's day,
Is all the proud and mighty have
Between the cradle and the grave.
> *Grongar Hill. Line 89*

Sisyphus, with toil and sweat,
And muscles strain'd, striving to get
Up a steep hill a ponderous stone,
Which near the top recoils, and rolls
impetuous down.[2]
> *Epistle to a Famous Painter.*
> *Line 58*

JAMES THOMSON
[1700–1748]

As those we love decay, we die in part,
String after string is severed from the heart;
Till loosen'd life, at last but breathing clay,
Without one pang is glad to fall away.
> *On the Death of Mr. Aikman.*[3]

---

morals and legislation. — JEREMY BENTHAM [1748–1832]: *Works, Vol. X, P. 142*

The expression is used by CESARE BONENSANO BECCARIA [1735–1794] in the introduction to his *Essay on Crimes and Punishments* [1764].

[1] Music hath charms to soothe the savage breast. — CONGREVE: *The Mourning Bride, Act I, Sc. I*

[1] Priestley relates that, in a debate on the Test Laws, Lord Sandwich said: "I have heard frequent use of the words 'orthodoxy' and 'heterodoxy' but I confess myself at a loss to know precisely what they mean." Bishop Warburton whispered his definition to him.

[2] Optat supremo collocare Sisyphus
In monte saxum: sed vetant leges Jovis.

(Sisyphus endeavors to place the stone on the summit of the mountain, but the decrees of Jove forbid).
> HORACE: *Epodes, XVIII, 68*

[3] William Aikman [1682–1731], portrait painter.

Come, gentle Spring! ethereal Mildness! come.
The Seasons. Spring, Line 1

But who can paint
Like Nature? Can imagination boast,
Amid its gay creation, hues like hers?
Ibid. Line 465

Delightful task! to rear the tender thought,
To teach the young idea how to shoot.
Ibid. Line 1149

An elegant sufficiency, content,
Retirement, rural quiet, friendship, books.
Ibid. Line 1158

The meek-ey'd Morn appears, mother of dews.
Ibid. Summer, Line 47

Falsely luxurious, will not man awake?
Ibid. Line 67

Ships dim-discover'd dropping from the clouds.
Ibid. Line 946

And Mecca saddens at the long delay.
Ibid. Line 979

For many a day, and many a dreadful night,
Incessant lab'ring round the stormy cape.
Ibid. Line 1003

Sigh'd and look'd unutterable things.
Ibid. Line 1188

Who stemm'd the torrent of a downward age.
Ibid. Line 1505

Autumn nodding o'er the yellow plain.
Ibid. Autumn, Line 2

Loveliness
Needs not the foreign aid of ornament,
But is when unadorn'd, adorn'd the most.[1]
Ibid. Line 204

He saw her charming, but he saw not half
The charms her downcast modesty conceal'd.
Ibid. Line 229

For still the world prevail'd, and its dread laugh,

Which scarce the firm philosopher can scorn.
The Seasons. Autumn, Line 233

See, Winter comes to rule the varied year.[1]
Ibid. Winter, Line 1

Cruel as death, and hungry as the grave.
Ibid. Line 393

There studious let me sit,
And hold high converse with the mighty dead.
Ibid. Line 431

The kiss, snatch'd hasty from the sidelong maid.
Ibid. Line 625

These as they change, Almighty Father! these
Are but the varied God. The rolling year
Is full of Thee.
Hymn. Line 1

Shade, unperceiv'd, so softening into shade.
Ibid. Line 25

From seeming evil still educing good.
Ibid. Line 114

Come then, expressive silence, muse His praise.
Ibid. Line 118

A pleasing land of drowsy head it was,
Of dreams that wave before the halfshut eye;
And of gay castles in the clouds that pass,
Forever flushing round a summer sky:
There eke the soft delights that witchingly
Instil a wanton sweetness through the breast,
And the calm pleasures always hover'd nigh;
But whate'er smack'd of noyance or unrest
Was far, far off expell'd from this delicious nest.
The Castle of Indolence. Canto I, Stanza 6

O fair undress, best dress! it checks no vein,

---

[1] See Milton, page 152.

[1] O Winter, ruler of the inverted year.
Cowper: *The Task, Book IV, Winter Evening. L. 34*

But every flowing limb in pleasure drowns,
And heightens ease with grace.
The Castle of Indolence.
Canto I, Stanza 26

Plac'd far amid the melancholy main.
Ibid. Stanza 30

Scoundrel maxim.
Ibid. Stanza 50

A bard here dwelt, more fat than bard beseems.
Ibid. Stanza 68

A little round, fat, oily man of God.
Ibid. Stanza 69

I care not, Fortune, what you me deny:
You cannot rob me of free Nature's grace,
You cannot shut the windows of the sky
Through which Aurora shows her brightening face;
You cannot bar my constant feet to trace
The woods and lawns, by living stream, at eve:
Let health my nerves and finer fibres brace,
And I their toys to the great children leave:
Of fancy, reason, virtue, naught can me bereave.
Ibid. Canto II, Stanza 3

Health is the vital principle of bliss,
And exercise, of health.
Ibid. Stanza 55

Forever, Fortune, wilt thou prove
An unrelenting foe to love;
And when we meet a mutual heart,
Come in between and bid us part?
To Fortune

O Sophonisba! Sophonisba, O! [1]
Sophonisba. Act III, Sc. 2

When Britain first, at Heaven's command,
Arose from out the azure main,
This was the charter of her land,
And guardian angels sung the strain:

Rule, Britannia! Britannia rules the waves!
Britons never shall be slaves.
Alfred. Act II, Sc. 5 [1740]

PHILIP DODDRIDGE
[1702–1751]

Live while you live, the epicure would say,
And seize the pleasures of the present day;
Live while you live, the sacred preacher cries,
And give to God each moment as it flies.
Lord, in my views, let both united be:
I live in pleasure when I live to thee.
Epigram on His Family Arms [1]

Awake, my soul! stretch every nerve,
And press with vigour on;
A heavenly race demands thy zeal,
And an immortal crown.
Zeal and Vigour in the Christian Race. Stanza 1

ROBERT DODSLEY
[1703–1764]

One kind kiss before we part,
Drop a tear and bid adieu;
Though we sever, my fond heart
Till we meet shall pant for you.[2]
The Parting Kiss

No state of life but must to patience bow:
The tradesman must have patience for his bill;
He must have patience who to law will go;
And should he lose his right, more patience still;
Yea, to prevent or heal full many a strife,
How oft, how long must man have patience with his wife.
To Patience

---

[1] The line was altered after the second edition to
"O Sophonisba! I am wholly thine."

[1] A Latin proverb by Junius, — Dum vivimus, vivamus (Let us live while we live). — JOB ORTON [1717–1783]: *Memoirs of Doddridge* [1766]

[2] Ae fond kiss, and then we sever!
Ae farewell, and then for ever!
ROBERT BURNS: *Ae Fond Kiss, St. 1*

JONATHAN EDWARDS
[1703–1758]

Resolved, never to do anything which I should be afraid to do if it were the last hour of my life.
Seventy Resolutions

Intend to live in continual mortification, and never to expect or desire any worldly ease or pleasure.
Diary. 1723

I assert that nothing ever comes to pass without a cause.
The Freedom of the Will [*1754*]

This dictate of common sense.
Ibid.

JOHN WESLEY
[1703–1791]

That execrable sum of all villanies, commonly called the Slave Trade.
Journal. February 12, 1772

Certainly this is a duty, not a sin. "Cleanliness is indeed next to godliness." [1]
Sermon XCIII, On Dress

Though I am always in haste, I am never in a hurry.
Letters. December 10, 1777

Do all the good you can,
By all the means you can,
In all the ways you can,
In all the places you can,
At all the times you can,
To all the people you can,
As long as ever you can.
John Wesley's Rule

SOAME JENYNS
[1704–1787]

Let each fair maid, who fears to be disgraced,
Ever be sure to tie her garters fast,
Lest the loosed string, amidst the public hall,
A wished-for prize to some proud fop should fall.
The Art of Dancing

Ever let my lovely pupils fear

[1] See Bacon, page 112.

To chill their mantling blood with cold small beer:
Destruction lurks within the poisonous dose,
A fatal fever or a pimpled nose.
The Art of Dancing

NATHANIEL COTTON
[1705–1788]

If solid happiness we prize,
Within our breasts this jewel lies,
And they are fools who roam.
The world has nothing to bestow;
From our own selves our joys must flow,
And that dear hut, our home.
The Fireside. Stanza 3

To be resign'd when ills betide,
Patient when favours are deni'd,
And pleas'd with favours given, —
Dear Chloe, this is wisdom's part;
This is that incense of the heart [1]
Whose fragrance smells to heaven.
Ibid. Stanza 11

Yet still we hug the dear deceit.
Content. Vision IV

Hold the fleet angel fast until he bless thee.[2]
To-morrow

BENJAMIN FRANKLIN [3]
[1706–1790]

They that can give up essential liberty to obtain a little temporary safety deserve neither liberty nor safety.[4]
Historical Review of Pennsylvania

[1] The incense of the heart may rise. — John Pierpont [1785–1866]: *Every Place a Temple*

[2] I will not let thee go, except thou bless me. — *Genesis, XXXII, 26*
Like the patriarch's angel hold it fast
Till it gives its blessing.
Whittier: *My Soul and I, St. 34*

[3] Eripuit cœlo fulmen sceptrumque tyrannis (He snatched the lightning from heaven, and the sceptre from tyrants), — a line attributed to Turgot, and inscribed on Houdon's bust of Franklin. Frederick von der Trenck [1726–1794] asserted at his trial [1794] that he was the author of this line.

[4] This sentence was much used in the Revolutionary period. It occurs even so early as November, 1755, in an answer by the Assembly of Pennsylvania to the Governor, and forms the motto of Franklin's "Historical Re-

We are a kind of posterity in respect to them.[1]

Letter to William Strahan [*1745*]

Remember that time is money.

Advice to a Young Tradesman [*1748*]

God helps them that help themselves.

Maxims prefixed to Poor Richard's Almanac [*1757*]

Dost thou love life? Then do not squander time, for that is the stuff life is made of.

Ibid.

Early to bed and early to rise,
Makes a man healthy, wealthy, and wise.[2]

Ibid.

Plough deep while sluggards sleep.

Ibid.

Never leave that till to-morrow which you can do to-day.

Ibid.

Three removes are as bad as a fire.

Ibid.

Little strokes fell great oaks.

Ibid.

A little neglect may breed mischief: for want of a nail the shoe was lost; for want of a shoe the horse was lost; and for want of a horse the rider was lost.

Ibid.

He that goes a borrowing goes a sorrowing.

Ibid.

A man may, if he knows not how to save as he gets, keep his nose to the grindstone.

Ibid.

Vessels large may venture more,
But little boats should keep near shore.

Ibid.

It is hard for an empty sack to stand upright.

Maxims prefixed to Poor Richard's Almanac [*1757*]

Experience keeps a dear school, but fools will learn in no other.

Ibid.

Idleness and pride tax with a heavier hand than kings and parliaments. If we can get rid of the former, we may easily bear the latter.

Letter on the Stamp Act [*July 1, 1765*]

Here Skugg lies snug
As a bug in a rug.[1]

Letter to Miss Georgiana Shipley [*September, 1772*]

There never was a good war or a bad peace.[2]

Letter to Josiah Quincy [*September 11, 1773*]

You and I were long friends: you are now my enemy, and I am yours. B. Franklin.

Letter to William Strahan [*July 5, 1775*]

We must all hang together, or assuredly we shall all hang separately.

At the signing of the Declaration of Independence [*July 4, 1776*]

He has paid dear, very dear, for his whistle.

The Whistle [*November, 1779*]

Here you would know and enjoy what posterity will say of Washington. For a thousand leagues have nearly the same effect with a thousand years.

Letter to Washington [*March 5, 1780*]

Our Constitution is in actual operation; everything appears to promise

---

view," 1759, appearing also in the body of the work. — RICHARD FROTHINGHAM [1812–1880]: *Rise of the Republic of the United States, P. 413*

[1] Byron's European fame is the best earnest of his immortality, for a foreign nation is a kind of contemporaneous posterity. — HORACE BINNEY WALLACE [1817–1856]: *Stanley, or the Recollections of a Man of the World, Vol. II, P. 89*

[2] JOHN CLARKE: *Parœmiolgia* [1639]. My hour is eight o'clock, though it is an

infallible rule, "Sanat, sanctificat, et ditat, surgere mane" (That he may be healthy, happy, and wise, let him rise early). — *A Health to the Gentle Profession of Serving-men* [1598], *P. 121* (reprinted in Roxburghe Library)

[1] Snug as a bug in a rug. — *The Stratford Jubilee, II, 1* [1779]

[2] It hath been said that an unjust peace is to be preferred before a just war. — SAMUEL BUTLER: *Butler's Remains, Speeches in the Rump Parliament*

that it will last; but in this world nothing is certain but death and taxes.

Letter to M. Leroy [1789]

George Washington, Commander of the American armies, who, like Joshua of old, commanded the sun and the moon to stand still, and they obeyed him.

A Toast at a Dinner in Versailles. The British Minister had proposed a toast to George III, in which he likened him to the sun, and the French Minister had toasted Louis XVI, comparing him with the moon.

The next thing most like living one's life over again seems to be a recollection of that life, and to make that recollection as durable as possible by putting it down in writing.

Autobiography. Page 6 (Everyman Edition)

Often I sat up in my room reading the greatest part of the night, when the book was borrowed in the evening and to be returned early in the morning, lest it should be missed or wanted.

Ibid. Page 16

Persons of good sense, I have since observed, seldom fall into disputation, except lawyers, university men, and men of all sorts that have been bred at Edinborough.

Ibid. Page 17

An advantage itinerant preachers have over those who are stationary, the latter cannot well improve their delivery of a sermon by so many rehearsals.

Ibid. Page 129

I shall never ask, never refuse, nor ever resign an office.

Ibid. Page 134

Human felicity is produc'd not so much by great pieces of good fortune that seldom happen, as by little advantages that occur every day.

Ibid. Page 154

When men are employed, they are best contented; for on the days they worked they were good-natured and cheerful, and, with the consciousness of having done a good day's work, they spent the evening jollily; but on our idle days they were mutinous and quarrelsome.

Autobiography. Page 177

8th and lastly. They are so grateful!!

Reasons for Preferring an Elderly Mistress [1] *[1745]*

And God said, Have I not borne with him these hundred ninety and eight years, and nourished him, and clothed him, notwithstanding his rebellion against me: and couldst not thou, that art thyself a sinner, bear with him one night?

An Added Chapter to the Book of Genesis. [2] *Verse 11 [1763]*

The grand leap of the Whale up the Fall of Niagara is esteemed, by all who have seen it, as one of the finest Spectacles in Nature.

To the Editor of a London newspaper [1765], intended to chaff the English for their ignorance of America

I wish the Bald Eagle had not been chosen as the Representative of our Country; he is a Bird of bad moral Character; like those among Men who live by Sharping and Robbing, he is generally poor, and often very lousy.

The Turky is a much more respectable Bird, and withal a true original Native of America.

Letter to Sarah Bache [January 26, 1784]

He [the sun] gives light as soon as he rises.

An Economical Project [3] *[1784]*

HENRY FIELDING
[1707–1754]

All Nature wears one universal grin.

Tom Thumb the Great. Act I, Sc. 1

To-day it is our pleasure to be drunk;

---

[1] Quoted by Dr. A. S. W. Rosenbach, owner of the original MS., in his *The All-Embracing Doctor Franklin* [1932].

[2] Founded on *The Liberty of Prophesying*, by Jeremy Taylor [1657]. See Taylor, page 165.

[3] A letter to the *Journal de Paris* advocating daylight saving.

And this our queen shall be as drunk as we.
Tom Thumb the Great. Act I, Sc. 2

When I'm not thank'd at all, I'm thank'd enough;
I've done my duty, and I've done no more.
Ibid. Sc. 3

Lo, when two dogs are fighting in the streets,
With a third dog one of the two dogs meets;
With angry teeth he bites him to the bone,
And this dog smarts for what that dog has done.[1]
Ibid. Sc. 6

I am as sober as a judge.
Don Quixote in England. Act III, Sc. 14

Much may be said on both sides.
The Covent Garden Tragedy. Act I, Sc. 8

Enough is equal to a feast.
Ibid. Act V, Sc. 1

We must eat to live and live to eat.[2]
The Miser. Act III, Sc. 3

Penny saved is a penny got.
Ibid. Sc. 12

Oh, the roast beef of England,
And old England's roast beef![3]
The Grub Street Opera. Act III, Sc. 2

This story will not go down.
Tumble-down Dick

The dusky night rides down the sky,
And ushers in the morn;
The hounds all join in glorious cry,
The huntsman winds his horn,
And a-hunting we will go.
A-hunting We Will Go. Stanza 1[1]

Can any man have a higher notion of the rule of right and the eternal fitness of things?
The History of Tom Jones. Book IV, Chap. 4

Wisdom, whose lessons have been represented as so hard to learn by those who never were at her school, only teaches us to extend a simple maxim universally known. And this is, not to buy at too dear a price.
Ibid. Book VI, Chap. 3

Distinction without a difference.
Ibid. Chap. 13

Amiable weakness.[2]
Ibid. Book X, Chap. 8

The dignity of history.[3]
Ibid. Book XI, Chap. 2

Nothing more aggravates ill success than the near approach to good.
Ibid. Book XIII, Chap. 2

Hairbreadth missings of happiness look like the insults of Fortune.
Ibid.

Republic of letters.[4]
Ibid. Book XIV, Chap. 1

---

[1] Thus when a barber and a collier fight,
The barber beats the luckless collier —
white;
The dusty collier heaves his ponderous sack,
And big with vengeance beats the barber —
black.
In comes the brick-dust man, with grime o'erspread,
And beats the collier and the barber — red:
Black, red, and white in various clouds are tost,
And in the dust they raise the combatants are lost.
CHRISTOPHER SMART [1722–1770]: *The Trip to Cambridge*
[2] Socrates said, Bad men live that they may eat and drink, whereas good men eat and drink that they may live. — PLUTARCH: *How a Young Man Ought to Hear Poems*
We should eat to live, not live to eat. — MOLIÈRE: *L'Avare, Act III, Sc. 5*
[3] See Richard Leveridge, page 193.

[1] A southerly wind and a cloudy sky
Proclaim a hunting morning;
Before the sun rises we nimbly fly,
Dull sleep and a downy bed scorning.
Hunting Song in *The Sportsmen's Vocal Library* [London, 1811]
It's of three jovial huntsmen, and a-hunting they did go;
And they hunted, and they hollo'd, and they blew their horns also;
Look ye there!
The Three Jovial Huntsmen (old English ballad), *St. 1*
[2] Amiable weaknesses of human nature. — GIBBON: *Decline and Fall of the Roman Empire, Chap. XIV.* Modern Library Giant, Vol. 1, P. 375.
[3] The dignity of history. — BOLINGBROKE: *Letter 5*
[4] Republic of letters. — STERNE: *Tristram Shandy, Book I, Chap. 20.* WASHINGTON IRVING: *Tales of a Traveller, Notoriety*

Illustrious predecessors.[1]
> *Covent Garden Journal*
> [*January 11, 1752*]

Perhaps there is more of Ostentation than of real Utility in ships of this vast and unwieldy Burthen.
> *Journal of a Voyage to Lisbon*

WILLIAM PITT, EARL OF CHATHAM
[1708–1778]

Confidence is a plant of slow growth in an aged bosom.
> *Speech* [*January 14, 1766*]

Where laws ends, tyranny begins.
> *Case of Wilkes. Speech*
> [*January 9, 1770*]

A long train of these practices has at length unwillingly convinced me that there is something behind the throne greater than the King himself.[2]
> *Chatham Correspondence. Speech*
> [*March 2, 1770*]

Reparation for our rights at home, and security against the like future violations.[3]
> *Letter to the Earl of Shelburne*
> [*September 29, 1770*]

You cannot conquer America.
> *Speech* [*November 18, 1777*]

If I were an American, as I am an Englishman, while a foreign troop was landed in my country I never would lay down my arms, — never! never! never!
> *Ibid.*

The poorest man may in his cottage bid defiance to all the force of the Crown. It may be frail; its roof may shake; the wind may blow through it;

the storms may enter, the rain may enter, — but the King of England cannot enter; all his forces dare not cross the threshold of the ruined tenement!
> *Speech on the Excise Bill*

SAMUEL JOHNSON
[1709–1784]

Let observation with extensive view Survey mankind, from China to Peru.[1]
> *Vanity of Human Wishes. Line 1*

Deign on the passing world to turn thine eyes,
And pause a while from learning to be wise.
> *Ibid. Line 157*

There mark what ills the scholar's life assail, —
Toil, envy, want, the patron, and the jail.
> *Ibid. Line 159*

He left the name at which the world grew pale,
To point a moral, or adorn a tale.[2]
> *Ibid. Line 221*

Hides from himself his state, and shuns to know
That life protracted is protracted woe.
> *Ibid. Line 257*

Superfluous lags the veteran on the stage.
> *Ibid. Line 308*

Must helpless man, in ignorance sedate,
Roll darkling down the torrent of his fate?
> *Ibid. Line 345*

Of all the griefs that harass the distrest,
Sure the most bitter is a scornful jest.[3]
> *London. Line 166*

---

[1] Illustrious predecessor. — BURKE: *The Present Discontents*

I tread in the footsteps of illustrious men. . . . In receiving from the people the sacred trust twice confided to my illustrious predecessor [Andrew Jackson]. — MARTIN VAN BUREN [1782–1862]: *Inaugural Address* [March 4, 1837]

[2] Quoted by Lord Mahon [1805–1875], "greater than the throne itself," in his *History of England, Vol. V, P. 258*

[3] Indemnity for the past and security for the future. — RUSSELL: *Memoir of Fox, Vol. III, P. 345, Letter to the Hon. T. Maitland*

[1] All human race, from China to Peru,
Pleasure, howe'er disguised by art, pursue.
> THOMAS WARTON: *Universal Love of Pleasure*

DE QUINCEY (*Works, Vol. X, P. 72*) quotes the criticism of some writer, who contends with some reason that this high-sounding couplet of Dr. Johnson amounts in effect to this: Let observation with extensive observation observe mankind extensively.

[2] Quoted by SIR WALTER SCOTT at the end of *Ivanhoe*.

[3] Nil habet infelix paupertas durius in se,
Quam quod ridiculos homines facit.
> JUVENAL: *Satires, III, 133*
Nothing in poverty so ill is borne

This mournful truth is ev'rywhere con-
fess'd, —
Slow rises worth, by poverty depress'd.[1]
London. Line 176
Call the Betsies, Kates, and Jennies,
All the names that banish care.
One-and-Twenty
In vain the surge's angry shock,
  In vain the drifting sands;
Unharmed, upon the Eternal Rock,
  The Eternal City stands.
The City of God. Stanza 5
Studious to please, yet not ashamed to
fail.
Prologue to the Tragedy of Irene
Each change of many-colour'd life he
drew,
Exhausted worlds, and then imagin'd
new.
*Prologue on the Opening of Drury
Lane Theatre*
And panting Time toil'd after him in
vain.
Ibid.
Declamation roar'd, while Passion
slept.
Ibid.
The wild vicissitudes of taste.
Ibid.
For we that live to please must please
to live.
Ibid.
Catch, then, oh catch the transient
hour;
  Improve each moment as it flies!
Life's a short summer, man a flower;
He dies — alas! how soon he dies!
Winter, An Ode
Officious, innocent, sincere,
Of every friendless name the friend.
*Verses on the Death of Mr. Robert
Levet. Stanza 2*
In misery's darkest cavern known,
  His useful care was ever nigh.[2]
Where hopeless anguish pour'd his
groan,

As its exposing men to grinning scorn.
JOHN OLDHAM [1653–1683]:
translation
[1] Three years later Johnson wrote, "Mere
unassisted merit advances slowly, if — what
is not very common — it advances at all."
[2] Variant, — His ready help was always
nigh.

And lonely want retir'd to die.
*Verses on the Death of Mr. Robert
Levet. Stanza 5*
And sure th' Eternal Master found
  His single talent well employ'd.
Ibid. Stanza 7
Then, with no throbs of fiery pain,[1]
  No cold gradations of decay,
Death broke at once the vital chain,
  And freed his soul the nearest way.
Ibid. Stanza 9
That saw the manners in the face.
Lines on the Death of Hogarth
A Poet, Naturalist, and Historian,
Who left scarcely any style of writing
untouched,
And touched nothing that he did not
adorn.[2]
Epitaph on Goldsmith
How small of all that human hearts
endure,
That part which laws or kings can cause
or cure!
Still to ourselves in every place con-
signed,
Our own felicity we make or find.
*Lines Added to Goldsmith's
Traveller*
From thee, great God, we spring, to
thee we tend, —
Path, motive, guide, original and end.[3]
Motto to The Rambler, No. 7
Curiosity is one of the permanent
and certain characteristics of a vigorous
mind.
The Rambler [*March 12, 1751*]
No place affords a more striking con-
viction of the vanity of human hopes,
than a public library.
Ibid. [*March 23, 1751*]
Parnassus has its flowers of transient
fragrance, as well as its oaks of tower-
ing height, and its laurels of eternal
verdure.
Ibid.

[1] Variant, — Then with no fiery throbbing
pain.
[2] Qui nullum fere scribendi genus
    Non tetigit,
    Nullum quod tetigit non ornavit.
See Chesterfield, page 222.
[3] A translation of Boethius's *De Consolatione Philosophiæ, III, 9, 27.*

Life is surely given us for higher purposes than to gather what our ancestors have wisely thrown away.

> *The Rambler [May 14, 1751]*

It is one of the maxims of the civil law, that definitions are hazardous.

> *Ibid. [May 28, 1751]*

Praise like gold and diamonds owes its value only to its scarcity.

> *Ibid. [June 6, 1751]*

Almost all absurdity of conduct arises from the imitation of those whom we can not resemble.

> *Ibid. [July 2, 1751]*

Ye who listen with credulity to the whispers of fancy, and pursue with eagerness the phantoms of hope; who expect that age will perform the promises of youth, and that the deficiencies of the present day will be supplied by the morrow, — attend to the history of Rasselas, Prince of Abyssinia.

> *Rasselas. Chap. I*

"I fly from pleasure," said the prince, "because pleasure has ceased to please; I am lonely because I am miserable, and am unwilling to cloud with my presence the happiness of others."

> *Ibid. Chap. III*

Ingenious contrivances to facilitate motion, and unite levity with strength.

> *Ibid. Chap. VI, A Dissertation on the Art of Flying*

A man used to vicissitudes is not easily dejected.

> *Ibid. Chap. XII*

Few things are impossible to diligence and skill.

> *Ibid.*

Knowledge is more than equivalent to force.[1]

> *Ibid. Chap. XIII*

I live in the crowd of jollity, not so much to enjoy company as to shun myself.

> *Ibid. Chap. XVI*

Many things difficult to design prove easy to performance.

> *Ibid.*

---

[1] See Bacon, page 111.

The first years of man must make provision for the last.

> *Rasselas. Chap. XVII*

Example is always more efficacious than precept.

> *Ibid. Chap. XXX*

The endearing elegance of female friendship.

> *Ibid. Chap. XLVI*

Words are men's daughters, but God's sons are things.

> *Supposed to have been inserted by Dr. Johnson in Samuel Madden's work, Boulter's Monument [1745]*

I am not so lost in lexicography as to forget that *words are the daughters of earth, and that things are the sons of heaven.*[1]

> *Preface to His Dictionary [1755]*

I dismiss it with frigid tranquillity, having little to fear or hope from censure or from praise.

> *Ibid.*

CLUB — An assembly of good fellows, meeting under certain conditions.

> *Definition in the Dictionary*

ESSAY — A loose sally of the mind; an irregular indigested piece; not a regular and orderly composition.

> *Ibid.*

EXCISE — A hateful tax levied upon commodities, and adjudged not by the common judges of property, but wretches hired by those to whom excise is paid.

> *Ibid.*

GRUBSTREET — The name of a street near Moorsfield, London, much inhabited by writers of small histories, dictionaries, and temporary poems.

> *Ibid.*

OATS — A grain which in England is generally given to horses, but in Scotland supports the people.[2]

> *Ibid.*

---

[1] See Herbert, page 138. See Samuel Madden, page 204.

[2] It was pleasant to me to find, that "Oats," the "food of horses," were so much used as the food of the people in Dr. Johnson's own

PENSION — An allowance made to any one without an equivalent. In England, it is generally understood to mean pay given to a state hireling for treason to his country.
Definition in the Dictionary

PIRATE — A sea robber, any robber; particularly a bookseller who seizes the copies of other men.
Ibid.

Whoever wishes to attain an English style, familiar but not coarse, and elegant but not ostentatious, must give his days and nights to the volumes of Addison.
Life of Addison

To be of no church is dangerous. Religion, of which the rewards are distant, and which is animated only by faith and hope, will glide by degrees out of the mind unless it be invigorated and reimpressed by external ordinances, by stated calls to worship, and the salutary influence of example.
Life of Milton

His death eclipsed the gayety of nations, and impoverished the public stock of harmless pleasure.[1]
Life of Edmund Smith (referring to the death of Garrick)

That man is little to be envied whose patriotism would not gain force upon the plain of Marathon, or whose piety would not grow warmer among the ruins of Iona.
Journey to the Western Islands. Inch Kenneth

He is no wise man that will quit a certainty for an uncertainty.
The Idler. No. 57

What is read twice is commonly better remembered than what is transcribed.
Ibid. No. 74

Boswell. That, Sir, was great fortitude of mind.

---

town. — BOSWELL: *Life of Dr. Johnson, Everyman ed., Vol. I, P. 628*

I own that by my definition of *oats* I meant to vex them [the Scotch]. — *Ibid., Vol. II, P. 434*

[1] Quoted by BOSWELL, *Vol. I, P. 39* and *Vol. II, P. 275.*

Johnson. No, Sir; stark insensibility.
*Boswell's Life of Dr. Johnson.[1]
Vol. I, Page 28*

On clean-shirt-day he went abroad, and paid visits.
Ibid. Page 56

Tom Birch is as brisk as a bee in conversation; but no sooner does he take a pen in his hand, than it becomes a torpedo to him, and benumbs all his faculties.
Ibid. Page 92

I'll come no more behind your scenes, David; for the silk stockings and white bosoms of your actresses excite my amorous propensities.[2]
Ibid. Page 117

Wretched un-idea'd girls.
Ibid. Page 148

Is not a patron, my lord [Chesterfield], one who looks with unconcern on a man struggling for life in the water, and when he has reached ground encumbers him with help? [3]
Ibid. Page 156

Sir, he [Bolingbroke] was a scoundrel and a coward: a scoundrel for charging a blunderbuss against religion and morality; a coward, because he had not resolution to fire it off himself, but left half a crown to a beggarly Scotchman to draw the trigger at his death.
Ibid. Page 160

If a man does not make new acquaintances as he advances through life, he will soon find himself left alone. A man, sir, should keep his friendship in a constant repair.
Ibid. Page 182

Towering in the confidence of twenty-one.[4]
Ibid. Page 197

---

[1] Everyman edition, 2 volumes.
The Life of Johnson is assuredly a great, a very great work. Homer is not more decidedly the first of heroic poets, Shakespeare is not more decidedly the first of dramatists, Demosthenes is not more decidedly the first of orators, than Boswell is the first of biographers. He has no second. — MACAULAY: *Samuel Johnson* [September, 1831]
[2] To David Garrick [1749].
[3] Letter to Chesterfield [Feb. 7, 1755].
[4] Letter to Bennet Langton [Jan. 9, 1758].

Being in a ship is being in a jail, with the chance of being drowned.

Boswell's Life of Dr. Johnson.
Vol. I, Page 215

A short letter to a distant friend is, in my opinion, an insult like that of a slight bow or cursory salutation.[1]

Ibid. Page 223

Nothing is little to him that feels it with great sensibility.[2]

Ibid. Page 230

Bounty always receives part of its value from the manner in which it is bestowed.[3]

Ibid. Page 233

Every man's affairs, however little, are important to himself.[4]

Ibid. Page 235

A man of genius has been seldom ruined but by himself.[5]

Ibid. Page 236

Sir, I think all Christians, whether Papists or Protestants, agree in the essential articles, and that their differences are trivial, and rather political than religious.[6]

Ibid. Page 251

The noblest prospect which a Scotchman ever sees, is the high-road that leads him to England.

Ibid. Page 264

A man ought to read just as inclination leads him; for what he reads as a task will do him little good.[7] A young

[1] Letter to Joseph Baretti [June 10, 1761].
[2] To the same [July 20, 1762].
[3] Letter to the Earl of Bute [July 20, 1762].
[4] To the same [Nov. 3, 1762].
[5] Letter to Joseph Baretti [Dec. 21, 1762].
[6] All denominations of Christians have really little difference in point of doctrine, though they may differ widely in external forms. — *Vol. I, P. 411* [1772]
I do not find that the age or country makes the least difference; no, nor the language the actor spoke, nor the religion which they professed, — whether Arab in the desert, or Frenchman in the Academy. I see that sensible men and conscientious men all over the world were of one religion of well-doing and daring. — EMERSON: *Lectures and Biographical Sketches, The Preacher, P. 215*
See Benjamin Disraeli, page 421.
[7] The book which you read from a sense of duty, or because for any reason you must, does not commonly make friends with you. —

man should read five hours in a day, and so may acquire a great deal of knowledge.

Boswell's Life of Dr. Johnson.
Vol. I, Page 266

If he does really think that there is no distinction between virtue and vice, why, sir, when he leaves our houses let us count our spoons.

Ibid. Page 268

If I accustom a servant to tell a lie for *me,* have I not reason to apprehend that he will tell many lies for *himself?*

Ibid. Page 270

Sir, your levellers wish to level *down* as far as themselves; but they cannot bear levelling *up* to themselves.

Ibid. Page 277

Sherry[1] is dull, naturally dull; but it must have taken him a great deal of pains to become what we now see him. Such an excess of stupidity, sir, is not in Nature.

Ibid. Page 280

Sir, a woman preaching is like a dog's walking on his hind legs. It is not done well; but you are surprised to find it done at all.

Ibid. Page 287

I look upon it, that he who does not mind his belly will hardly mind anything else.

Ibid. Page 290

This was a good dinner enough, to be sure, but it was not a dinner to *ask* a man to.

Ibid. Page 291

Gloomy calm of idle vacancy.[2]

Ibid. Page 294

A very unclubable man.

Ibid. Page 298

He[3] is one of the many who have made themselves *publick,* without making themselves *known.*

Ibid. Page 310

WILLIAM DEAN HOWELLS: *My Literary Passions, Chap. 7*
[1] Thomas Sheridan [1719–1788], actor, lecturer, and author.
[2] Letter to Boswell [Dec. 8, 1763]. See Cowper, page 266.
[3] William Kenrick [1725–1779], a writer who attacked Goldsmith, Garrick, Fielding, Johnson, and Colman.

I cannot see that lectures can do so much good as reading the books from which the lectures are taken.

Boswell's Life of Dr. Johnson.
Vol. I, Page 315

Life is not long, and too much of it must not pass in idle deliberation how it shall be spent.[1]

Ibid. Page 325

Were he not to marry again, it might be concluded that his first wife had given him a disgust to marriage; but by taking a second wife he pays the highest compliment to the first, by showing that she made him so happy as a married man, that he wishes to be so a second time.

Ibid. Page 360

I do not know, sir, that the fellow is an infidel; but if he be an infidel, he is an infidel as a dog is an infidel; that is to say, he has never thought upon the subject.

Ibid. Page 370

It matters not how a man dies, but how he lives.

Ibid. Page 378

That fellow seems to me to possess but one idea, and that is a wrong one.

Ibid. Page 393

The triumph of hope over experience.

Ibid. Page 394

A decent provision for the poor is the true test of civilization.

Ibid. Page 396

A fallible being will fail somewhere.

Ibid. Page 397

Whatever philosophy may determine of material nature, it is certainly true of intellectual nature, that it abhors a vacuum.

Ibid. Page 403

A common prejudice should not be found in one whose trade it is to rectify error.

Ibid. Page 409

Nobody can write the life of a man, but those who have eat and drunk and lived in social intercourse with him.[2]

Ibid. Page 422

The way to make sure of power and influence is by lending money confidentially to your neighbours at a small interest, or perhaps no interest at all, and having their bonds in your possession.

Boswell's Life of Dr. Johnson.
Vol. I, Page 422

I am a great friend to public amusements; for they keep people from vice.

Ibid. Page 424

A cow is a very good animal in the field; but we turn her out of a garden.

Ibid. Page 436

Much may be made of a Scotchman if he be caught young.

Ibid. Page 440

For my part, I'd tell the truth, and shame the devil.[1]

Ibid.

There is nothing, I think, in which the power of art is shown so much as in playing on the fiddle. In all other things we can do something at first.

Ibid. Page 462

The way to spread a work is to sell it at a low price. No man will send to buy a thing that costs even sixpence, without an intention to read it.

Ibid. Page 465

When people find a man of the most distinguished abilities as a writer, their inferior while he is with them, it must be highly gratifying to them.

Ibid. Page 469

An old tutor of a college said to one of his pupils: Read over your compositions, and wherever you meet with a passage which you think is particularly fine, strike it out.[2]

Ibid. Page 470

You are the most unscottified of your countrymen.

Ibid. Page 473

Was ever poet so trusted before? [3]

Ibid. Page 502

---

crimination; and few people who have lived with a man know what to remark about him. —*Vol. I, P. 617*

[1] See Shakespeare, page 62.
[2] See Sydney Smith, page 313.
[3] Of Oliver Goldsmith in a letter to Boswell [July 4, 1774].

[1] Letter to Boswell [Aug. 21, 1766].
[2] They only who live with a man can write his life with any genuine exactness and dis-

Mum, it is a secret.
> *Boswell's Life of Dr. Johnson.*
> *Vol. I, Page 511*

Attack is the reaction. I never think I have hit hard unless it rebounds.
> *Ibid. Page 540*

A man will turn over half a library to make one book.
> *Ibid. Page 545*

Patriotism is the last refuge of a scoundrel.
> *Ibid. Page 547*

Hell is paved with good intentions.[1]
> *Ibid. Page 555*

Knowledge is of two kinds: we know a subject ourselves, or we know where we can find information upon it.
> *Ibid. Page 558*

I never take a nap after dinner but when I have had a bad night; and then the nap takes me.
> *Ibid. Page 589*

In lapidary inscriptions a man is not upon oath.
> *Ibid.*

There is now less flogging in our great schools than formerly, but then less is learned there; so that what the boys get at one end they lose at the other.
> *Ibid.*

There is nothing which has yet been contrived by man by which so much happiness is produced as by a good tavern or inn.[2]
> *Ibid. Page 620*

Questioning is not the mode of conversation among gentlemen.
> *Ibid. Page 635*

A man is very apt to complain of the ingratitude of those who have risen far above him.
> *Ibid. Vol. II, Page 5*

If a man could say nothing against a character but what he can prove, history could not be written.
> *Ibid. Page 13*

No man but a blockhead ever wrote except for money.
> *Boswell's Life of Dr. Johnson.*
> *Vol. II, Page 16*

While grief is fresh, every attempt to divert only irritates.
> *Ibid. Page 21*

We would not be at the trouble to learn a language, if we could have all that is written in it just as well in a translation.
> *Ibid. Page 26*

Life is a progress from want to want, not from enjoyment to enjoyment.
> *Ibid. Page 36*

Life admits not of delays; when pleasure can be had, it is fit to catch it. Every hour takes away part of the things that please us, and perhaps part of our disposition to be pleased.[1]
> *Ibid. Page 98*

In every volume of poems something good may be found.
> *Ibid. Page 117*

When a man is tired of London, he is tired of life; for there is in London all that life can afford.
> *Ibid. Page 131*

He was so generally civil, that nobody thanked him for it.
> *Ibid. Page 134*

To *make* money is to *coin* it; you should say *get* money.
> *Ibid. Page 143*

Everything that enlarges the sphere of human powers, that shows man he can do what he thought he could not do, is valuable.
> *Ibid. Page 168*

Goldsmith, however, was a man, who, whatever he wrote, did it better than any other man could do.
> *Ibid. Page 182*

It is a man's own fault, it is from want of use, if his mind grows torpid in old age.
> *Ibid. Page 183*

Johnson had said that he could repeat a complete chapter of "The Natural History of Iceland," from the Danish of Horrebow, the whole of which

---

[1] See Herbert, page 137.
[2] Whoe'er has travell'd life's dull round,
     Where'er his stages may have been,
   May sigh to think he still has found
     His warmest welcome at an inn.
   WILLIAM SHENSTONE [1714–1763]: *Written on a Window of an Inn at Henley*

---

[1] Letter to Boswell [Sept. 1, 1777].

was exactly (Ch. LXXII. *Concerning snakes*) thus: "There are no snakes to be met with throughout the whole island." [1]

Boswell's Life of Dr. Johnson.
Vol. II, Page 201

As the Spanish proverb says, "He, who would bring home the wealth of the Indies, must carry the wealth of the Indies with him," so it is in travelling, a man must carry knowledge with him if he would bring home knowledge.

Ibid. Page 216

It is amazing how little literature there is in the world.

Ibid. Page 217

It is better to live rich, than to die rich.

Ibid. Page 218

I have known what it was to have a wife, and . . . I have known what it was to lose a wife.

Ibid. Page 219

I would rather be attacked than unnoticed. For the worst thing you can do to an author is to be silent as to his works.

Ibid. Page 257

I remember a passage in Goldsmith's "Vicar of Wakefield," which he was afterwards fool enough to expunge: "I do not love a man who is zealous for nothing."

Ibid. Page 267

Claret is the liquor for boys, port for men; but he who aspires to be a hero must drink brandy.

Ibid. Page 271

Worth seeing? yes; but not worth going to see.

Ibid. Page 291

You see in him vulgar prosperity.

Ibid.

He that outlives a wife whom he has long loved, sees himself disjoined from the only mind that has the same hopes, and fears, and interest; from the only companion with whom he has shared much good and evil; and with whom he could set his mind at liberty, to re-

trace the past or anticipate the future.

Boswell's Life of Dr. Johnson.
Vol. II, Page 298

A Frenchman must be always talking, whether he knows anything of the matter or not; an Englishman is content to say nothing, when he has nothing to say.

Ibid. Page 326

Of Dr. Goldsmith he said, "No man was more foolish when he had not a pen in his hand, or more wise when he had."

Ibid. Page 336

The applause of a single human being is of great consequence.

Ibid. Page 338

Come to me, my dear Bozzy, and let us be as happy as we can. [1]

Ibid. Page 366

The potentiality of growing rich beyond the dreams of avarice. [2]

Ibid. Page 376

Classical quotation is the *parole* of literary men all over the world.

Ibid. Page 386

My friend was of opinion that when a man of rank appeared in that character [as an author], he deserved to have his merits handsomely allowed. [3]

Ibid. Page 393

A jest breaks no bones.

Ibid. Page 405

To let friendship die away by negligence and silence, is certainly not wise. It is voluntarily to throw away one of the greatest comforts of this weary pilgrimage.

Ibid. Page 417

Whatever you have, spend less. [4]

Ibid. Page 427

I never have sought the world; the world was not to seek me. [5]

Ibid. Page 436

---

[1] Chapter XLII is still shorter: "There are no owls of any kind in the whole island."

[1] Letter to Boswell [March 14, 1781].
[2] I am rich beyond the dreams of avarice. — EDWARD MOORE [1712–1757]: *The Gamester, Act II, Sc. 2* [1753]
[3] Usually quoted as "When a nobleman writes a book, he ought to be encouraged."
[4] Letter to Boswell [Dec. 7, 1782].
[5] I have not loved the world, nor the world me. — BYRON: *Childe Harold, Canto III, St. 113*

He is not only dull himself, but the cause of dullness in others.[1]

Boswell's Life of Dr. Johnson.
Vol. II, Page 441

Clear your mind of cant.

Ibid. Page 469

He thought it unnecessary to collect many editions of a book, which were all the same, except as to the paper and print; he would have the original, and all the translations, and all the editions which had any variations in the text.

Ibid. Page 512

Every man should try to collect one book in that manner and present it to a publick library.

Ibid.

You see they'd have fitted him to a T.[2]

Ibid. Page 518

Who drives fat oxen should himself be fat.[3]

Ibid. Page 535

I have found you an argument; I am not obliged to find you an understanding.

Ibid. Page 536

Blown about with every wind of criticism.[4]

Ibid. Page 539

Don't *attitudenize.*

Ibid. Page 541

We now know a method of mounting into the air [balloons], and, I think, are not likely to know more. The vehicles can serve no use till we can guide them; and they can gratify no curiosity till we mount with them to greater heights than we can reach without; till we rise above the tops of the highest mountains, which we have not yet done.

Ibid. Page 566

[1] See Shakespeare, page 64.
[2] We could manage this matter to a T.— STERNE: *Tristram Shandy, Book II, Chap. 5*
You will find it shall echo my speech to a T.—THOMAS MOORE: *Occasional Address for the Opening of the New Theatre of St. Stephen*
[3] A parody on "Who rules o'er freemen should himself be free," from BROOKE'S *Gustavus Vasa, first edition.*
[4] Carried about with every wind of doctrine.—*Ephesians, IV, 14*

I look upon every day to be lost, in which I do not make a new acquaintance.

Boswell's Life of Dr. Johnson.
Vol. II, Page 579

Life is very short, and very uncertain; let us spend it as well as we can.

Ibid. Page 583

God bless you, my dear.

Ibid. Page 609 (His last words)

If the man who turnips cries
Cry not when his father dies,
'Tis a proof that he had rather
Have a turnip than his father.

Johnsoniana. Piozzi, 30

He was a very good hater.

Ibid. 39

The law is the last result of human wisdom acting upon human experience for the benefit of the public.

Ibid. 58

The use of travelling is to regulate imagination by reality, and instead of thinking how things may be, to see them as they are.

Ibid. 154

Dictionaries are like watches; the worst is better than none, and the best cannot be expected to go quite true.

Ibid. 178

Books that you may carry to the fire and hold readily in your hand, are the most useful after all.

Ibid. Hawkins, 197

Round numbers are always false.

Ibid. 235

As with my hat[1] upon my head
I walk'd along the Strand,
I there did meet another man
With his hat in his hand.[2]

Ibid. George Steevens, 310

Abstinence is as easy to me as temperance would be difficult.

Ibid. Hannah More, 467

The limbs will quiver and move after the soul is gone.

Ibid. Northcote, 487

Hawkesworth said of Johnson, "You have a memory that would convict any

[1] Elsewhere found, "I put my hat."
[2] A parody on PERCY'S ballad, *The Hermit of Warkworth.*

author of plagiarism in any court of literature in the world."

Johnsoniana. Kearsley, 600

His conversation does not show the minute-hand, but he strikes the hour very correctly.

Ibid. 604

Hunting was the labour of the savages of North America, but the amusement of the gentlemen of England.

Ibid. 606

I am very fond of the company of ladies. I like their beauty, I like their delicacy, I like their vivacity, and I like their silence.

Ibid. Seward, 617

Tomorrow I purpose to regulate my room.

Prayers and Meditations. 1764

Preserve me from unseasonable and immoderate sleep.

Ibid. 1767

Every man naturally persuades himself that he can keep his resolutions, nor is he convinced of his imbecility but by length of time and frequency of experiment.

Ibid. 1770

This world, where much is to be done and little is to be known.

Ibid. Against Inquisitive and Perplexing Thoughts

Gratitude is a fruit of great cultivation; you do not find it among gross people.

Tour to the Hebrides.
[September 20, 1773]

A fellow that makes no figure in company, and has a mind as narrow as the neck of a vinegar-cruet.

Ibid. [September 30, 1773]

The atrocious crime of being a young man, which the honourable gentleman has with such spirit and decency charged upon me, I shall neither attempt to palliate nor deny; but content myself with wishing that I may be one of those whose follies may cease with their

youth, and not of that number who are ignorant in spite of experience.[1]

Pitt's Reply to Walpole, a Speech
[March 6, 1741]

The hoary Sage replied,
Come, my lad, and drink some beer.

Quoted by MRS. PIOZZI: *Anecdotes*
of Samuel Johnson

Wharton quotes Johnson as saying of Dr. Campbell, "He is the richest author that ever grazed the common of literature."

GEORGE, LORD LYTTELTON
[1709–1773]

For his chaste Muse employ'd her heaven-taught lyre
None but the noblest passions to inspire,
Not one immoral, one corrupted thought,
One line which, dying, he could wish to blot.

Prologue to Thomson's Coriolanus

Women, like princes, find few real friends.

Advice to a Lady

What is your sex's earliest, latest care,
Your heart's supreme ambition? To be fair.

Ibid.

The lover in the husband may be lost.

Ibid.

How much the wife is dearer than the bride.

An Irregular Ode

None without hope e'er lov'd the brightest fair,
But love can hope where reason would despair.

Epigram

Where none admire, 'tis useless to excel;
Where none are beaux, 'tis vain to be a belle.

Soliloquy on a Beauty in the Country

[1] This is the composition of Johnson, founded on some note or statement of the actual speech. Johnson said, "That speech I wrote in a garret, in Exeter Street." — BOSWELL: *Life of Dr. Johnson, 1741*

ALICIA [1] RUTHERFORD COCKBURN
[1712–1794]

I've seen the smiling
Of Fortune beguiling,
I've felt all her favours and found her decay;
Sweet was her blessing,
Kind her caressing:
But now they are fled, are fled far away.
The Flowers of the Forest.
Stanza 1

Thy frown cannot fear me,
Thy smile cannot cheer me —
Since the Flowers o' the Forest are a' wede away.[2]
Ibid. Stanza 4

RICHARD GLOVER
[1712–1785]

As near Porto-Bello lying
On the gently swelling flood,
At midnight with streamers flying
Our triumphant navy rode.
Admiral Hosier's Ghost.[3] Stanza 1
I am Hosier's injur'd ghost.
Ibid. Stanza 4

GEORGE GRENVILLE
[1712–1770]

A wise Government knows how to enforce with temper or to conciliate with dignity.
Speech against the Expulsion of John Wilkes, House of Parliament [1769]

EDWARD MOORE
[1712–1757]

Can't I another's face commend,
And to her virtues be a friend,
But instantly your forehead lowers,

As if *her* merit lessen'd *yours?*
The Farmer, the Spaniel, and the Cat
The maid who modestly conceals
Her beauties, while she hides, reveals;
Give but a glimpse, and fancy draws
Whate'er the Grecian Venus was.
The Spider and the Bee
But from the hoop's bewitching round,
Her very shoe has power to wound.
Ibid.
Time still, as he flies, brings increase to her truth,
And gives to her mind what he steals from her youth.
The Happy Marriage

JOSIAH TUCKER, DEAN OF GLOUCESTER
[1712–1799]

What is true of a shopkeeper is true of a shopkeeping nation.[1]
Tract Against Going to War for the Sake of Trade [1763]

[1] Men who content themselves with the semblance of truth and a display of words talk much of our obligations to Great Britain for protection. Had she a single eye to our advantage? A nation of shopkeepers are [sic] very seldom so disinterested. — From an oration purporting to have been delivered by SAMUEL ADAMS [1722–1803] at the State House in Philadelphia, Aug. 1, 1776. (Philadelphia, printed; London, reprinted for E. Johnson, No. 4 Ludgate Hill, 1776.) W. V. Wells, in his *Life of Adams,* says: "No such American edition has ever been seen, but at least four copies are known of the London issue. A German translation of this oration was printed in 1778, perhaps at Berne; the place of publication is not given."
To found a great empire for the sole purpose of raising up a people of customers may at first sight appear a project fit only for a nation of shopkeepers. It is, however, a project altogether unfit for a nation of shopkeepers; but extremely fit for a nation whose Government is influenced by shopkeepers. — ADAM SMITH [1723–1790]: *Wealth of Nations, Vol. II, Book IV, Chap. 7, Part 3* [1776]
Let Pitt then boast of his victory to his nation of shopkeepers. — BERTRAND BARÈRE [1755–1841]: *Speech* [June 11, 1794]
But it may be said as a rule, that every Englishman in the Duke of Wellington's army paid his way. The remembrance of such a fact surely becomes a nation of shopkeepers.

---

[1] Sometimes given as Alison.
[2] The flowers of the forest are a' wide awae. — JANE ELLIOTT [1727–1805]: *The Flowers of the Forest* (written before Mrs. Cockburn's poem). Also known as *The Lament for Flodden.*
[3] Written on the taking of Porto-Bello from the Spaniards by Admiral Vernon [Nov. 22, 1739]. The ballad is in PERCY'S *Reliques, Series II, Book III.*

LAURENCE STERNE
[1713–1768]

So long as a man rides his hobby-horse peaceably and quietly along the King's highway, and neither compels you or me to get up behind him, — pray, Sir, what have either you or I to do with it?
Tristram Shandy. Book I, Chap. 7

For every ten jokes, thou hast got an hundred enemies.
Ibid. Chap. 12

Whistled up to London, upon a Tom Fool's errand.
Ibid. Chap. 16

'Tis known by the name of perseverance in a good cause, — and of obstinacy in a bad one.
Ibid. Chap. 17

The Republic of letters.[1]
Ibid. Chap. 20

The history of a soldier's wound beguiles the pain of it.
Ibid. Chap. 25

. We could manage this matter to a T.[2]
Ibid. Book II, Chap. 5

Splashing and plunging like a devil thro' thick and thin.[3]
Ibid. Chap. 9

Writing, when properly managed (as you may be sure I think mine is) is but a different name for conversation.
Ibid. Chap. 11

Go, poor devil, get thee gone! Why should I hurt thee? This world surely is wide enough to hold both thee and me. [Uncle Toby to the fly]
Ibid. Chap 12

That's another story,[4] replied my father.
Ibid. Chap. 17

Good — bad — indifferent.[5]
Ibid. Book III, Chap. 2

Great wits jump.
Tristram Shandy.
Book III, Chap. 9

"Our armies swore terribly in Flanders," cried my Uncle Toby, "but nothing to this."
Ibid. Chap. 11

Of all the cants which are canted in this canting world, though the cant of hypocrites may be the worst, the cant of criticism is the most tormenting! [1]
Ibid. Chap. 12

When Ernulphus [2] cursed — no part escaped him.
Ibid.

Angels and ministers of grace defend us.
Ibid. Chap. 20

'Twould be as much as my life was worth.
Ibid.

Before an affliction is digested, consolation ever comes too soon; and after it is digested, it comes too late.
Ibid. Chap. 29

The sweat of a man's brows, and the exudations of a man's brains, are as much a man's own property as the breeches upon his backside.
Ibid. Chap. 34

As certainly as you can make a velvet cap out of a sow's ear.[3]
Ibid. Book IV, Slawkenbergius's Tale

One of the two horns of my dilemma.
Ibid. Chap. 26

The feather put into his cap of having been abroad.
Ibid. Chap. 31

Now or never was the time.
Ibid.

— W. M. THACKERAY [1811–1863]: *Vanity Fair, Vol. I, Chap. 28*

[1] See Fielding, page 229.
[2] See Johnson, page 238.
[3] See Chaucer, page 6.
[4] But that is another story. — KIPLING: *Plain Tales from the Hills, Three and — an Extra*
[5] See Joel Barlow, page 280.

[1] Clear your mind of cant. — JOHNSON: *Boswell's Life of Dr. Johnson, Vol. II, P. 469, Everyman edition*
[2] Ernulph or Arnulph [1040–1124], French Benedictine and Bishop of Rochester.
May all the curses of the good Bishop Ernulphus light on the borrower-and-not-returner or upon the stealer of this book [Sir William Osler's inscription on the fly-leaf of his own copy of his *Textbook on the Principles and Practice of Medicine*]. — HARVEY CUSHING: *Life of Sir William Osler, Vol. I, Chap. 14*
[3] See Herbert, page 138.

The Accusing Spirit, which flew up to heaven's chancery with the oath, blushed as he gave it in; and the Recording Angel, as he wrote it down, dropped a tear upon the word and blotted it out forever.[1]

Tristram Shandy.
Book VI, Chap. 8

A man should know something of his own country, too, before he goes abroad.

Ibid. Book VII, Chap. 2

I am sick as a horse.

Ibid.

Ho! 'tis the time of salads.

Ibid. Chap. 17

"They order," said I, "this matter better in France."

A Sentimental Journey. Page 1

I pity the man who can travel from Dan to Beersheba and cry, " 'Tis all barren!"

Ibid. In the Street, Calais

Tant pis and *tant mieux*,[2] being two of the great hinges in French conversation, a stranger would do well to set himself right in the use of them before he gets to Paris.[3]

Ibid. Montreuil

Hail, ye small, sweet courtesies of life! for smooth do ye make the road of it.

Ibid. The Pulse, Paris

"Disguise thyself as thou wilt, still, Slavery," said I, "still thou art a bitter draught."

Ibid. The Passport, The Hotel at Paris

"God tempers the wind," said Maria, "to the shorn lamb." [4]

Ibid. Maria

---

[1] But sad as angels for the good man's sin,
Weep to record, and blush to give it in.
CAMPBELL: *Pleasures of Hope, Part II, L. 357*

[2] So much the worse; so much the better.

[3] Never go to France
Unless you know the lingo.
THOMAS HOOD: *French and English, St. 1*

[4] Dieu mésure le froid à la brebis tondue (God measures the cold to the shorn lamb).
— HENRI ESTIENNE [1594]: *Prémices, etc., P. 47*

See Herbert, page 138.

The sad vicissitude of things.[1]

Sermon 16, The Character of Shimei

WILLIAM SHENSTONE
[1714–1763]

Whoe'er has travell'd life's dull round,
Where'er his stages may have been,
May sigh to think he still has found
The warmest welcome at an inn.[2]

Written on a Window of an Inn at Henley. Stanza 5

Her cap, far whiter than the driven snow,
Emblems right meet of decency does yield.

The Schoolmistress. Stanza 6

WILLIAM WHITEHEAD
[1715–1785]

With indignation I survey
Such skill and judgment thrown away;
The time profusely squandered there
On vulgar arts beneath thy care,
If well employed at less expense
Had taught thee honour, virtue, sense.

The Youth and the Philosopher

DAVID GARRICK
[1716–1779]

A fellow-feeling makes one wondrous kind.[3]

Prologue on Quitting the Stage in 1776

Let others hail the rising sun:
I bow to that whose course is run.

On the Death of Mr. Pelham

Hearts of oak are our ships,
Gallant tars are our men,
    We always are ready,
    Steady, boys, steady,

---

[1] Revolves the sad vicissitudes of things. — RICHARD GIFFORD [1725–1807]: *Contemplation*

[2] See Johnson, page 236.

[3] ROBERT LEIGHTON [1611–1684], Archbishop of Glasgow, often said that if he were to choose a place to die in, it should be an inn. — *Works, Vol. I, P. 76*

[3] See Burton, page 121.

We'll fight, and we'll conquer again
   and again.
Hearts of Oak

Here lies James Quinn. Deign, reader,
   to be taught,
Whate'er thy strength of body, force
   of thought,
In Nature's happiest mould however
   cast,
To this complexion thou must come at
   last.
Epitaph on Quinn (in MURPHY'S
Life of Garrick. Vol. II, Page 38)

Are these the choice dishes the Doctor
   has sent us?
Is this the great poet whose works so
   content us?
This Goldsmith's fine feast, who has
   written fine books?
Heaven sends us good meat, but the
   Devil sends cooks? [1]
Epigram on Goldsmith's Retaliation
(Ibid., Page 157)

Here lies Nolly Goldsmith, for short-
   ness called Noll,
Who wrote like an angel, and talk'd
   like poor Poll.
Impromptu Epitaph on
Goldsmith

THOMAS GRAY
[1716–1771]

What female heart can gold despise?
What cat's averse to fish?
On the Death of a Favourite Cat.
Stanza 4

A fav'rite has no friend!
Ibid. Stanza 6

Ye distant spires, ye antique towers.
On a Distant Prospect of Eton
College. Stanza 1

Ah, happy hills! ah, pleasing shade!
   Ah, fields beloved in vain!
Where once my careless childhood
   stray'd,
   A stranger yet to pain:
I feel the gales that from ye blow
A momentary bliss bestow.
Ibid. Stanza 2

[1] See Tusser, page 19.

They hear a voice in every wind,
   And snatch a fearful joy.
On a Distant Prospect of Eton
College. Stanza 4

Alas! regardless of their doom,
   The little victims play;
No sense have they of ills to come,
   Nor care beyond to-day.
Ibid. Stanza 6

To each his suff'rings; all are men,
   Condemn'd alike to groan, —
The tender for another's pain,
   Th' unfeeling for his own.

Yet ah! why should they know their
   fate,
Since sorrow never comes too late,
   And happiness too swiftly flies?
   Thought would destroy their para-
   dise.
No more; where ignorance is bliss,
   'Tis folly to be wise. [1]
Ibid. Stanza 10

Daughter of Jove, relentless power,
   Thou tamer of the human breast,
Whose iron scourge and torturing hour
   The bad affright, afflict the best!
Hymn to Adversity. Stanza 1

From Helicon's harmonious springs
A thousand rills their mazy progress
   take.
The Progress of Poesy. I, 1, Line 3

Glance their many-twinkling feet.
Ibid. 3, Line 11

O'er her warm cheek and rising bosom
   move
The bloom of young Desire and purple
   light of Love.
Ibid. Line 16

Or ope the sacred source of sympathetic tears.
Ibid. III, 1, Line 12

He [2] pass'd the flaming bounds of
   place and time:
The living throne, the sapphire-blaze,
Where angels tremble while they gaze,
He saw; but blasted with excess of
   light,
Closed his eyes in endless night.
Ibid. 2, Line 4

[1] See Davenant, page 147.
He that increaseth knowledge increaseth
sorrow. — *Ecclesiastes, I, 18*
[2] Milton.

Bright-eyed Fancy, hov'ring o'er,
Scatters from her pictured urn
Thoughts that breathe and words that
  burn.
> *The Progress of Poesy.*
> *III, 3, Line 2*

Ruin seize thee, ruthless king,
  Confusion on thy banners wait;
Though fann'd by Conquest's crimson
  wing,
  They mock the air with idle state.
> *The Bard. I, 1, Line 1*

Loose his beard, and hoary hair
Stream'd, like a meteor, to the troubled
  air.[1]
> *Ibid. 2, Line 5*

Dear as the light that visits these sad
  eyes,
Dear as the ruddy drops that warm
  my heart.[2]
> *Ibid. 3, Line 12*

Weave the warp, and weave the woof,
  The winding-sheet of Edward's race.
Give ample room and verge enough.[3]
  The characters of hell to trace.
> *Ibid. II, 1, Line 1*

Fair laughs the morn, and soft the
  zephyr blows,
  While proudly riding o'er the azure
    realm,
In gallant trim the gilded vessel goes,
  Youth on the prow, and Pleasure at
    the helm;
Regardless of the sweeping whirlwind's
  sway,
That, hush'd in grim repose, expects
  his evening prey.
> *Ibid. 2, Line 9*

Ye towers of Julius, London's lasting
  shame,
With many a foul and midnight murder fed.
> *Ibid. 3, Line 11*

Visions of glory, spare my aching
  sight;
Ye unborn ages, crowd not on my soul!
> *Ibid. III, 1, Line 11*

And truth severe, by fairy fiction drest.
> *Ibid. 3, Line 3*

[1] See Milton, page 148.
[2] See Shakespeare, page 82.
[3] See Dryden, page 179.

While bright-eyed Science watches
round.
> *Ode for Music. Chorus, Line 3*

The still small voice of gratitude.
> *Ibid. V, Line 8*

Iron sleet of arrowy shower
Hurtles in the darken'd air.
> *The Fatal Sisters. Line 3*

The curfew tolls the knell of parting
  day,
  The lowing herd wind slowly o'er the
    lea,
The ploughman homeward plods his
  weary way,
  And leaves the world to darkness
    and to me.
> *Elegy in a Country Churchyard.*
> *Stanza 1*

Each in his narrow cell forever laid,
  The rude forefathers of the hamlet
    sleep.
> *Ibid. Stanza 4*

Nor grandeur hear with a disdainful
  smile
  The short and simple annals of the
    poor.
> *Ibid. Stanza 8*

The boast of heraldry, the pomp of
  pow'r,
  And all that beauty, all that wealth
    e'er gave,
Await alike the inevitable hour:
  The paths of glory lead but to the
    grave.
> *Ibid. Stanza 9*

Can storied urn, or animated bust
  Back to its mansion call the fleeting
    breath?
Can honour's voice provoke the silent
  dust,
  Or flatt'ry soothe the dull cold ear
    of death?
> *Ibid. Stanza 11*

Hands, that the rod of empire might
  have sway'd,
  Or waked to ecstasy the living lyre.
> *Ibid. Stanza 12*

But Knowledge to their eyes her ample
  page
  Rich with the spoils of time did ne'er
    unroll; [1]

[1] See Sir Thomas Browne, page 144.

Chill penury repress'd their noble rage,
And froze the genial current of the soul.
Elegy in a Country Churchyard.
Stanza 13

Full many a gem of purest ray serene
The dark unfathom'd caves of ocean bear:
Full many a flower is born to blush unseen,
And waste its sweetness on the desert air.[1]
Ibid. Stanza 14

Some village Hampden, that with dauntless breast
The little tyrant of his fields withstood,
Some mute inglorious Milton here may rest,
Some Cromwell guiltless of his country's blood.
Ibid. Stanza 15

Forbade to wade through slaughter to a throne,
And shut the gates of mercy on mankind.
Ibid. Stanza 17

Far from the madding crowd's ignoble strife
Their sober wishes never learn'd to stray;
Along the cool sequester'd vale of life
They kept the noiseless tenor of their way.[2]
Ibid. Stanza 19

Implores the passing tribute of a sigh.
Ibid. Stanza 20

For who, to dumb forgetfulness a prey,
This pleasing anxious being e'er resign'd,
Left the warm precincts of the cheerful day,
Nor cast one longing ling'ring look behind?
Ibid. Stanza 22

E'en from the tomb the voice of nature cries,

E'en in our ashes live their wonted fires.[1]
Elegy in a Country Churchyard.
Stanza 23

One morn I miss'd him on the custom'd hill,
Along the heath, and near his fav'rite tree;
Another came; nor yet beside the rill,
Nor up the lawn, nor at the wood was he.
Ibid. Stanza 28

Here rests his head upon the lap of earth,
A youth to fortune and to fame unknown.
Fair Science frown'd not on his humble birth,
And Melancholy mark'd him for her own.[2]
Ibid. The Epitaph, Stanza 1

Large was his bounty, and his soul sincere,
Heaven did a recompense as largely send:
He gave to mis'ry (all he had) a tear,
He gained from Heav'n ('twas all he wish'd) a friend.
Ibid. Stanza 2

No farther seek his merits to disclose,
Or draw his frailties from their dread abode,
(There they alike in trembling hope repose),
The bosom of his Father and his God.
Ibid. Stanza 3

The hues of bliss more brightly glow,
Chastised by sabler tints of woe.
Ode on the Pleasure Arising from
Vicissitude. Line 45

The meanest floweret of the vale,
The simplest note that swells the gale,
The common sun, the air, the skies,
To him are opening paradise.
Ibid. Line 53

And hie him home, at evening's close,
To sweet repast and calm repose.
Ibid. Line 87

[1] Nor waste their sweetness in the desert air. — CHURCHILL: *Gotham, Book II, L. 20*
[2] Usually quoted "even tenor of their way." See Porteus, page 268.

[1] See Chaucer, page 6.
[2] See Walton, page 140.

The social smile, the sympathetic tear.
Education and Government

When love could teach a monarch to
be wise,
And gospel-light first dawn'd from
Bullen's eyes.
Ibid.

Too poor for a bribe, and too proud to
importune;
He had not the method of making a
fortune.
On His Own Character

Now as the Paradisiacal pleasures
of the Mahometans consist in playing
upon the flute and lying with Houris,
be mine to read eternal new romances
of Marivaux and Crebillon.
*Letters. Third Series, No. IV,
To Mr. West*

HORACE WALPOLE
[1717–1797]

Harry Vane, Pulteney's toad-eater,
Letter to Sir Horace Mann [*1742*]

The world is a comedy to those that
think, a tragedy to those who feel.
Ibid. [*1770*]

A careless song, with a little nonsense in it now and then, does not mis-
become a monarch.[1]
Ibid. [*1774*]

The whole [Scotch] nation hitherto
has been void of wit and humour, and
even incapable of relishing it.[2]
Ibid. [*1778*]

SAMUEL FOOTE
[1720–1777]

He made him a hut, wherein he did put
The carcass of Robinson Crusoe.
O poor Robinson Crusoe!
The Mayor of Garratt. Act I, Sc. 1

Born in a cellar, and living in a garret.[1]
The Author. Act II

Matt Minikin won't set fire to the
Thames though he lives near the
Bridge.
Trip to Calais [*1776*]

So she went into the garden to cut
a cabbage leaf to make an apple pie;
and at the same time a great she-bear,
coming up the street, pops its head into
the shop. "What! no soap?" So he died,
and she very imprudently married the
barber; and there were present the
Picninnies, and the Joblillies, and the
Garyulies, and the Grand Panjandrum
himself, with the little round button at
top, and they all fell to playing the
game of catch as catch can, till the
gunpowder ran out at the heels of their
boots.
*Nonsense written to test the
boasted memory of Charles
Macklin, The Quarterly Review, London* [*September,
1854*], *Page 516. Quoted in
Harry and Lucy, Concluded,
Volume II, by* MARIA EDGE-
WORTH

THOMAS GIBBONS
[1720–1785]

That man may last, but never lives,
Who much receives, but nothing gives;
Whom none can love, whom none can
thank, —
Creation's blot, creation's blank.
When Jesus Dwelt

DENNIS O'KELLY
[1720–1787]

It will be Eclipse first, the rest nowhere.[2]
Declaration at Epsom [*May 3,
1769*] *when the great race-
horse, Eclipse, was to run his
first race. Annals of Sporting,
Volume II, Page 271*

---

[1] A little nonsense now and then
Is relished by the wisest men.
ANONYMOUS

[2] It requires a surgical operation to get a
joke well into a Scotch understanding. —
SYDNEY SMITH: *Lady Holland's Memoir, Vol.
I, Chap. 2*

[1] Born in the garret, in the kitchen bred. —
BYRON: *A Sketch*

[2] He [Boswell] has distanced all his com-
petitors so decidedly that it is not worth while
to place them. Eclipse is first, and the rest
nowhere. — MACAULAY: *Samuel Johnson*
[*September,* 1831]

GEORGE A. STEVENS
[1720–1784]

Cease, rude Boreas, blustering railer!
  List, ye landsmen all, to me;
Messmates, hear a brother sailor
  Sing the dangers of the sea.
                        The Storm

JOHN WOOLMAN
[1720–1772]

On the outside of that part of the ship where the cabin was, I observed sundry sorts of carved work and imagery, and in the cabin some superfluity of workmanship. . . . I felt a scruple with regard to paying my money to defray such expenses.
            Journal. Chapter 11 [1772]

Though the change from day to night is by a motion so gradual as scarcely to be perceived, yet when night is come we behold it very different from the day; and thus as people become wise in their own eyes, and prudent in their own sight, customs rise up from the spirit of this world, and spread by little, and little, till a departure from the simplicity that there is in Christ becomes as distinguishable as light from darkness, to such who are crucified to the world.
      Considerations on the True Harmony of Mankind

Friends in early time refused, on a religious principle, to make or trade in Superfluities; but for want of Faithfulness some gave way, and thus Dimness of Sight came over many.
          On Trading in Superfluities

GILBERT WHITE
[1720–1793]

The tortoise, like other reptiles, has an arbitrary stomach as well as lungs; and can refrain from eating as well as breathing for a great part of the year.
      Natural History of Selborne.
                    April 12, 1772

When one reflects on the state of this strange being, it is a matter of wonder that Providence should bestow such a profusion of days, such a seeming waste of longevity, on a reptile that appears to relish it so little as to squander more than two-thirds of its existence in a joyless stupor, and be lost to all sensation for months together in the profoundest of slumbers.
      Natural History of Selborne.
                    April 21, 1780

WILLIAM COLLINS
[1721–1759]

In numbers warmly pure and sweetly
  strong.
          Ode to Simplicity. Stanza 1

Well may your hearts believe the truths
  I tell:
'Tis virtue makes the bliss, where'er
  we dwell.
      *Oriental Eclogues. I, Selim, or
      The Shepherd's Moral, Line 5*

Curst be the gold and silver which persuade
Weak men to follow far-fatiguing
  trade.
      *Ibid. II, Hassan, or The Camel
              Driver, Line 31*

Now air is hush'd, save where the weak-
  eyed bat,
With short shrill shriek, flits by on
  leathern wing,
  Or where the beetle winds
  His small but sullen horn.
          Ode to Evening. Stanza 3

How sleep the brave, who sink to rest
By all their country's wishes bless'd!
    *Ode Written in the Year 1746.
                    Stanza 1*

By fairy hands their knell is rung;
By forms unseen their dirge is sung.[1]
                Ibid. Stanza 2

When Music, heavenly maid, was
  young,
While yet in early Greece she sung.
          The Passions. Line 1

[1] Variant:
    By hands unseen the knell is rung;
    By fairy forms their dirge is sung.

'Twas sad by fits, by starts 'twas wild.
The Passions. Line 28

In notes by distance made more sweet.
Ibid. Line 60

In hollow murmurs died away.
Ibid. Line 68

O Music, sphere-descended maid,
Friend of Pleasure, Wisdom's aid!
Ibid. Line 95

TOBIAS SMOLLETT
[1721–1771]

Thy spirit, Independence, let me share,
Lord of the lion-heart and eagle-eye,[1]
Thy steps I follow, with my bosom
bare,
Nor heed the storm that howls along
the sky.
Ode to Independence. Strophe 1

Thy fatal shafts unerring move,
I bow before thine altar, Love!
Roderick Random. Chap. XL

Facts are stubborn things.[2]
*Translation of Gil Blas. Book X,
Chap. 1*

CHRISTOPHER SMART
[1722–1770]

O servant of God's holiest charge,
The minister of praise at large.
A Song to David. Stanza 3

Great, valiant, pious, good, and clean,
Sublime, contemplative, serene,
Strong, constant, pleasant, wise!
Ibid. Stanza 4

Strong is the lion — like a coal
His eyeball, — like a bastion's mole
His chest against the foes.
Ibid. Stanza 76

SIR WILLIAM BLACKSTONE
[1723–1780]

The royal navy of England hath ever
been its greatest defence and ornament;

it is its ancient and natural strength, —
the floating bulwark of our island.
*Commentaries. Vol. I, Book I,
Chap. XIII, § 418*

Time whereof the memory of man
runneth not to the contrary.[1]
Ibid. Chap. XVIII, § 472

MRS. GREVILLE [2]
[*Floruit* 1753]

Nor ease, nor peace, that heart can
know,
That like the needle true,
Turns at the touch of joy or woe,
But, turning, trembles too.
*Prayer for Indifference.
Stanza 6*

O! haste to shed the sovereign balm,
My shatter'd nerves new-string;
And for my guest, serenely calm,
The nymph Indifference bring.
Ibid. Stanza 9

JOHN HOME
[1724–1808]

In the first days
Of my distracting grief, I found myself
As women wish to be who love their
lords.
Douglas. Act I, Sc. 1

I'll woo her as the lion woos his brides.
Ibid.

My name is Norval; on the Grampian
hills
My father feeds his flocks; a frugal
swain,
Whose constant cares were to increase
his store,
And keep his only son, myself, at home.
Ibid. Act III, Sc. 1

A rude and boisterous captain of the
sea.
Ibid. Act IV, Sc. 1

Like Douglas conquer, or like Douglas
die.
Ibid. Act V, Sc. 1

---

[1] Quoted by THOMAS CARLYLE in his essay
on Boswell's *Life of Dr. Johnson.*
[2] Facts are stubborn things. — ELLIOT:
Essay on Field Husbandry, P. 35 [1747]

[1] See Emerson, page 413.
[2] The pretty Fanny Macartney. — HORACE
WALPOLE: *Memoirs*

RICHARD GIFFORD
[1725–1807]

Verse sweetens toil, however rude the
   sound;
  She feels no biting pang the while
    she sings;
Nor, as she turns the giddy wheel
    around,[1]
  Revolves the sad vicissitudes of
    things.[2]
                Contemplation

LOGAN, MINGO CHIEF
[1725–1780]

I appeal to any white man to say if
he ever entered Logan's cabin hungry
and he gave him not meat; if ever he
came cold and naked and he clothed
him not?
    *Message to Lord Dunmore,
    Governor of Virginia [Novem-
    ber 11, 1774], in Notes on Vir-
    ginia,* by THOMAS JEFFERSON

WILLIAM MASON
[1725–1797]

The fattest hog in Epicurus' sty.[3]
                Heroic Epistle

OLIVER GOLDSMITH
[1728–1774]

Remote, unfriended, melancholy, slow,
Or by the lazy Scheldt, or wandering
  Po.
        The Traveller. Line 1
Where'er I roam, whatever realms to
   see,
My heart untravell'd fondly turns to
   thee;
Still to my brother turns, with cease-
  less pain,

And drags at each remove a lengthen-
  ing chain.
        The Traveller. Line 7
And learn the luxury of doing good.[1]
        Ibid. Line 22
Such is the patriot's boast, where'er we
  roam,
His first, best country ever is, at home.
        Ibid. Line 73
Where wealth and freedom reign con-
  tentment fails,
And honour sinks where commerce
  long prevails.
        Ibid. Line 91
Man seems the only growth that
  dwindles here.
        Ibid. Line 126
By sports like these are all their cares
  beguil'd,
The sports of children satisfy the child.
        Ibid. Line 153
But winter lingering chills the lap of
  May.
        Ibid. Line 172
Cheerful at morn, he wakes from short
  repose,
Breasts the keen air, and carols as he
  goes.
        Ibid. Line 185
So the loud torrent, and the whirl-
  wind's roar,
But bind him to his native mountains
  more.
        Ibid. Line 217
They please, are pleas'd, they give to
  get esteem,
Till, seeming blest, they grow to what
  they seem.[2]
        Ibid. Line 266
Embosom'd in the deep where Holland
  lies.
Methinks her patient sons before me
  stand,
Where the broad ocean leans against
  the land.
        Ibid. Line 282

---

[1] Thus altered by Johnson, —
  All at her work the village maiden sings,
  Nor, while she turns the giddy wheel around.
[2] See Sterne, page 242.
[3] Me pinguem et nitidum bene curata cute
    vises,
  . . . Epicuri de grege porcum
(You may see me, fat and shining, with well-
cared for hide, — . . . a hog from Epicurus'
herd). — HORACE: *Epistolæ, Lib. I, IV, 15, 16*

[1] CRABBE: *Tales of the Hall, Book III.*
RICHARD GRAVES: *The Epicure.* See Garth,
page 187.
[2] The character of the French.

Pride in their port, defiance in their eye,
I see the lords of humankind pass by.[1]
The Traveller. Line 327

The land of scholars, and the nurse of arms.
Ibid. Line 356

For just experience tells, in every soil,
That those that think must govern those that toil.
Ibid. Line 372

Laws grind the poor, and rich men rule the law.
Ibid. Line 386

Forc'd from their homes, a melancholy train,
To traverse climes beyond the western main;
Where wild Oswego spreads her swamps around,
And Niagara stuns with thundering sound.
Ibid. Line 409

Vain, very vain, my weary search to find
That bliss which only centres in the mind.
Ibid. Line 423

Sweet Auburn! loveliest village of the plain.
The Deserted Village. Line 1

The hawthorn bush, with seats beneath the shade,
For talking age and whispering lovers made.
Ibid. Line 13

The bashful virgin's sidelong looks of love.
Ibid. Line 29

Ill fares the land, to hastening ills a prey,
Where wealth accumulates, and men decay;
Princes and lords may flourish or may fade;
A breath can make them, as a breath has made;[2]

But a bold peasantry, their country's pride,
When once destroy'd, can never be supplied.
The Deserted Village. Line 51

His best companions, innocence and health;
And his best riches, ignorance of wealth.
Ibid. Line 61

How blest is he who crowns in shades like these,
A youth of labour with an age of ease!
Ibid. Line 99

While Resignation gently slopes the way,
And all his prospects brightening to the last,
His heaven commences ere the world be past.
Ibid. Line 110

The watch-dog's voice that bay'd the whispering wind,
And the loud laugh that spoke the vacant mind.
Ibid. Line 121

A man he was to all the country dear,
And passing rich with forty pounds a year.
Ibid. Line 141

Careless their merits or their faults to scan,
His pity gave ere charity began.
Thus to relieve the wretched was his pride,
And even his failings lean'd to Virtue's side.
Ibid. Line 161

And as a bird each fond endearment tries
To tempt its new-fledg'd offspring to the skies,
He tried each art, reprov'd each dull delay,
Allur'd to brighter worlds, and led the way.
Ibid. Line 167

Truth from his lips prevail'd with double sway,

---

[1] See Dryden, page 179.
[2]   C'est un verre qui luit,
Qu'un souffle peut détruire, et qu'un souffle a produit
(It is a shining glass, which a breath may

destroy, and which a breath has produced).
— GILLES DE CAUX [1682–1733], comparing the world to his hour-glass.

And fools, who came to scoff, remain'd
to pray.[1]
The Deserted Village. Line 179
Even children follow'd with endearing
wile,
And pluck'd his gown, to share the good
man's smile.
Ibid. Line 183
As some tall cliff, that lifts its awful
form,
Swells from the vale, and midway
leaves the storm,
Though round its breast the rolling
clouds are spread,
Eternal sunshine settles on its head.
Ibid. Line 189
Well had the boding tremblers learn'd
to trace
The day's disasters in his morning
face;
Full well they laugh'd, with counter-
feited glee,
At all his jokes, for many a joke had
he;
Full well the busy whisper, circling
round,
Convey'd the dismal tidings when he
frown'd.
Yet was he kind; or if severe in aught,
The love he bore to learning was in
fault;
The village all declar'd how much he
knew;
'Twas certain he could write, and
cipher too.
Ibid. Line 199
In arguing too, the parson own'd his
skill,
For e'en though vanquished, he could
argue still;
While words of learned length and
thundering sound
Amaz'd the gazing rustics rang'd
around,
And still they gaz'd, and still the won-
der grew,
That one small head could carry all he
knew.
Ibid. Line 209
Where village statesmen talk'd with
looks profound,

[1] See Dryden, page 175.

And news much older than their ale
went round.
The Deserted Village. Line 223
The whitewash'd wall, the nicely sanded
floor,
The varnish'd clock that click'd be-
hind the door;
The chest contriv'd a double debt to
pay, —
A bed by night, a chest of drawers by
day.[1]
Ibid. Line 227
The twelve good rules, the royal game
of goose.[2]
Ibid. Line 232
To me more dear, congenial to my
heart,
One native charm, than all the gloss
of art.
Ibid. Line 253
And, ev'n while fashion's brightest arts
decoy,
The heart distrusting asks, if this be
joy.
Ibid. Line 263
Her modest looks the cottage might
adorn,
Sweet as the primrose peeps beneath
the thorn.
Ibid. Line 329
Through torrid tracts with fainting
steps they go,
Where wild Altama [3] murmurs to their
woe.
Ibid. Line 344
In all the silent manliness of grief.
Ibid. Line 384
O Luxury! thou curst by Heaven's de-
cree!
Ibid. Line 385
Thou source of all my bliss and all my
woe,

[1] A cap by night, a stocking all the day. —
Description of an Author's Bed-Chamber. See
page 253.
[2] The twelve good rules were ascribed to
King Charles I: 1. Urge no healths. 2. Profane no divine ordinances. 3. Touch no state
matters. 4. Reveal no secrets. 5. Pick no
quarrels. 6. Make no comparisons. 7. Maintain no ill opinions. 8. Keep no bad company.
9. Encourage no vice. 10. Make no long meals.
11. Repeat no grievances. 12. Lay no wagers.
[3] Altamaha River, Georgia.

That found'st me poor at first, and
keep'st me so.
        The Deserted Village. Line 413
Such dainties to them, their health it
might hurt;
It's like sending them ruffles, when
wanting a shirt.[1]
        The Haunch of Venison
That strain once more; it bids remembrance rise.
        The Captivity, An Oratorio.
            Act I
O Memory! thou fond deceiver.
            Ibid.

As aromatic plants bestow
No spicy fragrance while they grow;
But crush'd, or trodden to the ground,
Diffuse their balmy sweets around.[2]
            Ibid.

To the last moment of his breath,
    On hope the wretch relies;
And even the pang preceding death
    Bids expectation rise.[3]
        Ibid. Act II
Hope, like the gleaming taper's light,
    Adorns and cheers our way;[4]
And still, as darker grows the night,
    Emits a brighter ray.
            Ibid.
Our Garrick's a salad; for in him we
see
Oil, vinegar, sugar, and saltness agree!
        Retaliation. Line 11
Who, born for the universe, narrow'd
his mind,
And to party gave up what was meant
for mankind . . .
Who, too deep for his hearers, still went
on refining,
And thought of convincing, while they
thought of dining:
Though equal to all things, for all
things unfit;

---

[1] See Tom Brown, page 188.
[2] See Bacon, page 109.
[3] The wretch condemn'd with life to part
    Still, still on hope relies;
    And every pang that rends the heart
    Bids expectation rise.
            Original MS.
[4] Hope, like the taper's gleamy light,
    Adorns the wretch's way.
            Original MS.

Too nice for a statesman, too proud for
a wit.
        Retaliation. Line 31
His conduct still right, with his argument wrong.
            Ibid. Line 46
A flattering painter, who made it his
care
To draw men as they ought to be, not
as they are.
            Ibid. Line 63
Here lies David Garrick, describe me,
who can,
An abridgment of all that was pleasant
in man.
            Ibid. Line 93
As a wit, if not first, in the very first
line.
            Ibid. Line 96
On the stage he was natural, simple,
affecting;
'Twas only that when he was off he was
acting.
            Ibid. Line 101
He cast off his friends, as a huntsman
his pack,
For he knew when he pleas'd he could
whistle them back.
            Ibid. Line 107
Who pepper'd the highest was surest
to please.
            Ibid. Line 112
When they talk'd of their Raphaels,
Correggios, and stuff,
He shifted his trumpet and only took
snuff.
            Ibid. Line 145
Thou best-humour'd man, with the
worst-humour'd Muse.[1]
            Ibid. Postscript
Good people all, with one accord,
    Lament for Madam Blaize,
Who never wanted a good word —
    From those who spoke her praise.
        Elegy on Mrs. Mary Blaize.[2]
            Stanza 1

---

[1] See Rochester, page 184.
[2] Written in imitation of *Chanson sur le
fameux La Palisse,* which is attributed to
BERNARD DE LA MONNOYE: —
    On dit que dans ses amours
    Il fut caressé des belles,
    Qui le suivirent toujours,

A night-cap deck'd his brows instead
  of bay,
A cap by night, a stocking all the day.[1]
> *Description of an Author's
> Bed-chamber*

This same philosophy is a good horse
in the stable, but an arrant jade on a
journey.[2]
> *The Good-Natur'd Man. Act I*

He calls his extravagance, generosity; and his trusting everybody, universal benevolence.
> *Ibid.*

All his faults were such that one
loves him still the better for them.
> *Ibid.*

Friendship is a disinterested commerce between equals; love, an abject
intercourse between tyrants and slaves.
> *Ibid.*

Silence gives consent.[3]
> *Ibid. Act II*

Measures, not men, have always been
my mark.[4]
> *Ibid.*

I love everything that's old: old
friends, old times, old manners, old
books, old wine.[5]
> *She Stoops to Conquer. Act I*

The very pink of perfection.
> *Ibid.*

Let school-masters puzzle their brain,
  With grammar, and nonsense, and
    learning;
Good liquor, I stoutly maintain,
  Gives *genus* a better discerning.
> *Ibid.*

The genteel thing is the genteel thing
at any time. If so be that a gentleman
bees in a concatenation accordingly.
> *Ibid.*

I'll be with you in the squeezing of a
lemon.
> *She Stoops to Conquer. Act I*

A modest woman, dressed out in all
her finery, is the most tremendous object of the whole creation.
> *Ibid. Act II*

This is Liberty Hall.[1]
> *Ibid.*

They liked the book the better the
more it made them cry.
> *Ibid.*

Ask me no questions, and I'll tell you
no fibs.[2]
> *Ibid. Act III*

There's no love lost between us.[3]
> *Ibid. Act IV*

The very pink of courtesy and circumspection.
> *Ibid.*

I . . . chose my wife, as she did her
wedding-gown, not for a fine glossy
surface, but such qualities as would
wear well.
> *The Vicar of Wakefield. Chap. 1*

We sometimes had those little rubs
which Providence sends to enhance the
value of its favours.
> *Ibid.*

Handsome is that handsome does.[4]
> *Ibid.*

When lovely woman stoops to folly,
  And finds too late that men betray,
What charm can soothe her melancholy?
  What art can wash her guilt away?[5]
> *Ibid. Chap 5, Song, Stanza 1*

The only art her guilt to cover,

Tant qu'il marcha devant elles
(They say that in his love affairs he was petted
by beauties, who always followed him as long
as he walked before them).

[1] See page 251.

[2] Philosophy triumphs easily over past evils
and future evils, but present evils triumph
over it. — ROCHEFOUCAULD: *Maxim 22*

[3] RAY: *Proverbs.* FULLER: *Wise Sentences.*
EURIPIDES: *Iph. Aul., 1142*

[4] Measures, not men. — CHESTERFIELD: *Letters*, March 6, 1742. Not men, but measures.
— BURKE: *Present Discontents*

[5] See Bacon, page 113.

[1] 'Tis a palace of no mortal architect's art,
For Liberty Hall's an American's heart.
    Liberty Hall, St. 6 [Revolutionary
                    War period]

[2] Them that asks no questions isn't told a
lie. — KIPLING: *A Smuggler's Song, St. 6*

[3] See Middleton, page 117.

[4] See Chaucer, page 7.

[5] Lorsqu'une femme, après trop de tendresse,
  D'une homme sent la trahison,
Comment, pour cette si douce foiblesse,
  Peut-elle trouver une guérison?
    SEGUR, an obscure French poet [Paris,
    1719], in *Philadelphia Press* [Feb. 20,
    1889], credited to St. James Gazette.

To hide her shame from every eye,
To give repentance to her lover,
And wring his bosom, is — to die.[1]
The Vicar of Wakefield. Chap. 5,
Song, Stanza 2

I find you want me to furnish you
with argument and intellects too.
Ibid. Chap. 7

Man wants but little here below,
Nor wants that little long.
Ibid. Chap. 8, The Hermit (Edwin
and Angelina), Stanza 8

She was all of a muck of sweat.
Ibid. Chap. 9

They would talk of nothing but high
life, and high-lived company, with
other fashionable topics, such as pictures, taste, Shakespeare, and the musical glasses.[2]
Ibid.

It has been a thousand times observed, and I must observe it once
more, that the hours we pass with
happy prospects in view, are more
pleasing than those crowned with frui-
tion.[3]
Ibid. Chap. 10

A kind and gentle heart he had,
To comfort friends and foes;
The naked every day he clad
When he put on his clothes.
Ibid. Chap. 17, An Elegy on the
Death of a Mad Dog, Stanza 3

And in that town a dog was found,
As many dogs there be,
Both mongrel, puppy, whelp, and
hound,

And curs of low degree.
The Vicar of Wakefield. Chap. 17,
An Elegy on the Death of a
Mad Dog, Stanza 4

The dog, to gain some private ends,
Went mad, and bit the man.
Ibid. Stanza 5

The man recovered of the bite —
The dog it was that died.[1]
Ibid. Stanza 8

To what happy accident [2] is it that
we owe so unexpected a visit?
Ibid. Chap. 19

To what fortuitous concurrence do
we not owe every pleasure and convenience of our lives.
Ibid. Chap. 31

You may all go to pot.
Verses in Reply to an Invitation
to Dinner at Dr. Baker's

For he who fights and runs away
May live to fight another day;
But he who is in battle slain
Can never rise and fight again.[3]
The Art of Poetry on a New
Plan [1761]. Vol. II, Page 147

One writer, for instance, excels at a
plan or a title-page, another works
away the body of the book, and a third
is a dab at an index.[4]
The Bee. No. 1, October 6, 1759

The true use of speech is not so
much to express our wants as to conceal them.[5]
Ibid. No. 3, October 20, 1759

[To Dr. Johnson] If you were to

---

[1] Le seul remède qu'elle peut ressentir,
   La seule revanche pour son tort,
Pour faire trop tard l'amant repentir,
   Helas! trop tard! — est la mort.
                    SEGUR [Paris, 1719]
[2] Chat pleasantly to her of Shakespeare,
also the musical glasses. — SIR ARTHUR WING
PINERO [1855–1934:] *The Notorious Mrs.*
Ebbsmith, Act I
"Shall we talk about Shakespeare?" he
asked sarcastically. "Or the musical glasses?"
— ALDOUS HUXLEY [1894-   ]: *Point Coun-*
ter Point, Chap. 21
[3] An object in possession seldom retains the
same charm that it had in pursuit. — PLINY
THE YOUNGER: *Letters, Book II, Letter*
XV, 1

[1] While Fell was reposing himself in the hay,
A reptile concealed bit his leg as he lay;
But, all venom himself, of the wound he
   made light,
And got well, while the scorpion died of the
   bite.
      GOTTHOLD EPHRAIM LESSING [1729–
      1781]: *Paraphrase of a Greek Epi-*
      gram by Demodocus
[2] See Middleton, page 117.
[3] See Butler, page 143.
[4] There are two things which I am confident
I can do very well: one is an introduction to
any literary work, stating what it is to contain, and how it should be executed in the
most perfect manner. — BOSWELL: *Life of*
Dr. Johnson, 1755. Vol. I, Page 179, Everyman Edition
[5] See South, page 183.

make little fishes talk, they would talk like whales.
> *Boswell's Life of Dr. Johnson. Vol. I, Page 466, Everyman Edition*

I consider an author's literary reputation to be alive only while his name will insure a good price for his copy from the bookseller's.
> *Quoted, Ibid., Page 468*

There is no arguing with Johnson: for if his pistol misses fire, he knocks you down with the butt end of it.
> *Quoted, Ibid., Vol. II, Page 509*

THOMAS PERCY
[1728–1811]

Though only an indifferent poet himself, Bishop Percy is immortal for the "Reliques of Ancient English Poetry," 1765, which collected many of the old ballads and songs. This work has been a feeding-place for poets ever since, and the inspiration of SIR WALTER SCOTT's "Minstrelsy of the Scottish Border."

Everye white will have its blacke,
And everye sweete its sowre.
> *Reliques of Ancient English Poetry. Sir Cauline, Part II, Stanza 1*

Late, late yestreen I saw the new moone
Wi' the auld moone in hir arme.
> *Ibid. Sir Patrick Spence (Spens),[1] Stanza 7*

I think it was never man's destinye
To dye before his day.
> *Ibid. Robin Hood and Guy of Gisborne, Stanza 40*

Have you not heard, these many years ago,
Jephthah was judge of Israel?
He had one only daughter and no mo,
The which he loved passing well;
And, as by lott,

[1] From *Minstrelsy of the Scottish Border.*

God wot,
It so came to pass,
As God's will was.[1]
> *Reliques of Ancient English Poetry. Jephthah, Judge of Israel,[2] Stanza 1*

A Robyn,
Jolly Robyn,
Tell me how thy leman doeth,
And thou shalt know of myn.[3]
> *Ibid. A Robyn Jolly Robyn, Stanza 1*

Where gripinge grefes the hart would wounde
And dolefulle dumps the mynde oppresse,
There musicke with her silver sound
With spede is wont to send redresse.[4]
> *Ibid. A Song to the Lute in Musicke,[5] Stanza 1*

The blinded boy that shootes so trim,
From heaven downe did hie.[6]
> *Ibid. King Cophetua and the Beggar-maid, Stanza 2*

"What is thy name, faire maid?" quoth he.
"Penelophon, O King!" quoth she.[7]
> *Ibid. Stanza 6*

A poore soule sat sighing under a sicamore tree;
O willow, willow, willow!

[1] "As by lot, God wot"; and then you know, "It came to pass, as most like it was."— SHAKESPEARE: *Hamlet, Act II, Sc. 2, L. 444*
[2] *Judges, XI, 34 et seq.*
[3] Clown's song, "Hey Robin, jolly Robin."— SHAKESPEARE: *Twelfth-Night, Act IV, Sc. 2, L. 79*
[4] Quoted in *Romeo and Juliet, Act IV, Sc. 5, Lines 129 and 146.*
[5] The author is thought by Percy to have been Richard Edwards [1523–1566].
[6] Young Adam Cupid, he that shot so trim, When King Cophetua loved the beggar-maid! SHAKESPEARE: *Romeo and Juliet, Act II, Sc. 1, L. 13*
[7] Shakespeare, who alludes to this ballad in *Love's Labour's Lost, Act IV, Sc. 1*, gives Zenelophon as the beggar-maid's name (*L. 67*). The ballad is also referred to in *King Richard the Second, Act V, Sc. 3, L. 80.*
See Tennyson, page 465.

With his hand on his bosom, his head
  on his knee.
> *Reliques of Ancient English Po-*
> *etry. Willow, Willow, Willow,*[1]
> *Stanza 1*

O that beauty should harbour a heart
  that's so hard!
> *Ibid. Stanza 8*

When Arthur first in court began,
  And was approved king,
By force of armes great victorys
  wanne,
  And conquest home did bring.
> *Ibid. Sir Lancelot du Lake,*[2]
> *Stanza 1*

Shall I bid her goe? What, and if I doe?
Shall I bid her goe, and spare not?
O no, no, no, I dare not.[3]
> *Ibid. Corydon's Farewell to*
> *Phillis, Stanza 2*

And this shall be the forfeyture; of
  your owne fleshe a pound.
> *Ibid. Gernutus the Jew of*
> *Venice,*[4] *Couplet 14*

It was a friar of orders gray [5]
Walkt forth to tell his beades.
> *Ibid. The Friar of Orders Gray,*[6]
> *Stanza 1*

And how should I know your true love
  From many another one?
Oh, by his cockle hat, and staff,
  And by his sandal shoone.[7]
> *Ibid. Stanza 3*

O Lady, he is dead and gone!
  Lady, he's dead and gone!
And at his head a green grass turfe,
  And at his heels a stone.[1]
> *Reliques of Ancient English*
> *Poetry. The Friar of Orders*
> *Gray, Stanza 5*

Weep no more, lady, weep no more,
  Thy sorrowe is in vaine;
For violets pluckt, the sweetest show-
  ers
  Will ne'er make grow againe.[2]
> *Ibid. Stanza 12*

Our joys as wingèd dreams doe flye;
  Why then should sorrow last?
Since grief but aggravates thy losse,
  Grieve not for what is past.
> *Ibid. Stanza 13*

Sigh no more, ladies, sigh no more!
  Men were deceivers ever;
One foot in sea and one on shore,
  To one thing constant never.[3]
> *Ibid. Stanza 17*

King Stephen was a worthy peere,
His breeches cost him but a crowne.
> *Ibid. Take Thy Old Coat About*
> *Thee,*[4] *Stanza 7*

Itt's pride that putts this countrye
  downe;
Man, take thine old cloake about thee.
> *Ibid.*

Fight on, my merry men all;
For why, my life is at an end.[5]
> *Ibid. The More Modern Ballad*
> *of Chevy-Chace, Couplet 40*

---

[1] Quoted in *Othello, Act IV, Sc. 3, Lines 41, 49, 51, 56.*
  On a tree by a river a little tom-tit
  Sang "Willow, titwillow, titwillow!"
    WILLIAM SCHWENCK GILBERT: *The Mikado, Act II, Ko-Ko's song*
[2] The subject of this ballad is taken from the ancient romance of *Morte d'Arthur, Chap. 108–110.*
[3] Quoted by Shakespeare in *Twelfth-Night, Act II, Sc. 3, L. 119.*
[4] The story in this ballad is taken from an Italian novel of the fourteenth century, *Peco-rone.* Shakespeare is believed to have taken the episode of Shylock and Antonio in *The Merchant of Venice* from this ballad.
[5] SHAKESPEARE: *The Taming of the Shrew, Act IV, Sc. 1, L. 148.*
[6] Chiefly composed of fragments of old ballads dispersed through Shakespeare's plays, especially those sung by Ophelia in *Hamlet.* An excellent specimen of mosaic-work.
[7] The distinguishing marks of a pilgrim. The chief places of devotion being beyond the

sea, pilgrims put cockle-shells in their hats to denote the intention or performance of their devotion.
[1] Quoted in *Hamlet, Act IV, Sc. 5.*
[2] See Fletcher, page 127.
[3] SHAKESPEARE: *Much Ado About Nothing, Act II, Sc. 3, L. 65.*
[4] This stanza of eight lines is quoted in full in *Othello, Act II, Sc. 3, L. 93.*
[5] "Fight on, my men," Sir Andrew sayes,
  "A little Ime hurt, but yett not slaine;
  Ile but lye downe and bleede awhile,
  And then Ile rise and fight againe."
  Sir Andrew Barton, Part 2, St. 16 (PERCY's
    Reliques, Series II, Book II)
Says Johnnie, "Fight on, my merry men all,
I'm a little wounded, but I am not slain;
I will lay me down for to bleed a while,
Then I'll rise and fight with you again."
  Johnnie Armstrong's Last Good-night,
  St. 18 (DRYDEN's *Miscellanies* [1702])

We'll shine in more substantial hon-
ours,
And to be noble we'll be good.
*Reliques of Ancient English Poetry.
Winifreda,[1] Stanza 2*

And when with envy Time, trans-
ported,
Shall think to rob us of our joys,
You'll in your girls again be courted,
And I'll go wooing in my boys.
Ibid. Stanza 8

Shall never be sayd, the Not-browne
Mayd
Was to her love unkynde.[2]
*Ibid. The Not-Browne Mayd,
Stanza 8*

A fairer ladye there never was seene
Than the blind beggar's daughter of
Bednall-greene.
*Ibid. The Beggar's Daughter of
Bednall-Green,[3] Stanza 33*

When captaines couragious,[4] whom
death cold not daunte,
Did march to the siege of the citty of
Gaunt,
They mustred their souldiers by two
and by three,
And the formost in battle was Mary
Ambree.
Ibid. Mary Ambree,[5] Stanza 1

[1] See Chapman, page 29.
Nobilitas sola est atque unica virtus (Nobility is the one only virtue). — JUVENAL:
Satire VIII, L. 20
"Winifreda" appeared in LEWIS's *Collection*
[1726]
[2] First published in ARNOLD's *Chronicle,* a
miscellany, about 1521.
[3] This very house was built by the blind
beggar of Bednall Green, so much talked of
and sang in ballads. — SAMUEL PEPYS: *Diary,
June 26, 1663*
The ballad was written in the reign of
Elizabeth.
[4] Source of the title of RUDYARD KIPLING's
book, *Captains Courageous.*
[5] This ballad was probably occasioned by
the attempt to regain Ghent, in 1584, when the
Spaniards, commanded by the Prince of Parma, took many fortresses and cities in Flanders and Brabant.
BEN JONSON calls any virago Mary Ambree,
and JOHN FLETCHER mentions Mary Ambree
in *The Scornful Lady* [1616].

Will you hear a Spanish lady,
How shee wooed an English man?
*Reliques of Ancient English
Poetry. The Spanish Lady's
Love,[1] Stanza 1*
Then let Jane Shore with sorrowe sing,
That was belovèd of a king.
Ibid. Jane Shore, Stanza 1
"I'll rest," sayd hee, "but thou shalt
walke";
So doth this wandring Jew
From place to place, but cannot rest
For seeing countries newe.
*Ibid. The Wandering Jew,
Stanza 9*
For thirty pence our Saviour was sold
Amonge the false Jewes, as I have bin
told;
And twenty-nine is the worth of thee,
For I thinke thou art one penny worser
than hee.
*Ibid. King John and the Abbot
of Canterbury, Stanza 21*
But in vayne shee did conjure him
To depart her presence soe;
Having a thousand tongues to allure
him,
And but one to bid him goe.
Ibid. Dulcina,[2] Stanza 2
Glasgerion swore a full great othe,
By oake, and ashe and thorne.
Ibid. Glasgerion,[3] Stanza 19
He that would not when he might,
He shall not when he wolda.[4]
*Ibid. The Baffled Knight,
Stanza 14*
In Scarlet towne, where I was borne,
There was a fair maid dwellin,
Made every youth crye, Wel-awaye!
Her name was Barbara Allen.
*Ibid. Barbara Allen's Cruelty,
Stanza 1*

[1] Founded on the capture of Cadiz by Lord
Essex in 1596.
[2] This song is mentioned as very popular by
IZAAK WALTON in *The Compleat Angler*. It has
been ascribed to Raleigh, on very doubtful
authority.
[3] CHARLES KINGSLEY refers to the oath of
Glasgerion in *Westward Ho, Chap. 2;* and
RUDYARD KIPLING, in *Puck of Pook's Hill*.
CHAUCER refers to the "harper Bret Glas-
curion" in *The House of Fame, Book III,
L. 1208.*
[4] See Heywood, page 11.

No burial this pretty pair
  Of any man receives,
Till Robin Red-breast piously
  Did cover them with leaves.
      *Reliques of Ancient English
      Poetry. The Children in the
          Wood,*[1] *Stanza 16*
Under floods that are deepest,
  Which Neptune obey;
Over rocks that are steepest,
  Love will find out the way.
      *Ibid. Love Will Find Out the
          Way,*[2] *Stanza 1*
For without money, George,
  A man is but a beast:
But bringing money, thou shalt be
  Always my welcome guest.
      Ibid. George Barnwell,[3] *Part II,
          Stanza 25*
And let all women strive to be
As constant as Penelope.
      *Ibid. Constant Penelope,
          Stanza 18*
St. George he was for England; St.
  Dennis was for France;
Sing, *Honi soit qui mal y pense.*[4]
      *Ibid. St. George for England,
          Refrain*
Dark was the night, and wild the storm,
  And loud the torrent's roar;
And loud the sea was heard to dash
  Against the distant shore.
      The Hermit of Warkworth,[5]
          Part I, Stanza 1

THOMAS WARTON
[1728–1790]

All human race, from China to Peru,[6]
Pleasure, howe'er disguis'd by art, pursue.
      Universal Love of Pleasure

Nor rough, nor barren, are the winding ways
Of hoar antiquity, but strewn with flowers.
      *Written on a Blank Leaf of
          Dugdale's Monasticon*
All-powerful Ale! whose sorrow-soothing sweets
Oft I repeat in vacant afternoon.
      A Panegyric on Oxford Ale[1]
With British ale improving British worth.
      Ibid.
Thus too, the matchless bard, whose lay resounds
The Splendid Shilling's praise, in nightly gloom
Of lonesome garret, pined for cheerful ale.[2]
      Ibid.

EDMUND BURKE
[1729–1797]

The writers against religion, whilst they oppose every system, are wisely careful never to set up any of their own.
      Works. Vol. I, Preface, A Vindication of Natural Society

"War," says Machiavel, "ought to be the only study of a prince"; and by a prince he means every sort of state, however constituted. "He ought," says this great political doctor, "to consider peace only as a breathing-time, which gives him leisure to contrive, and furnishes ability to execute military plans." A meditation on the conduct of political societies made old Hobbes imagine that war was the state of nature.
      Ibid.

---

[1] Addison called this ballad one of the darling songs of the common people. It was first published in 1595.

[2] Modernized from an ancient song.

[3] Inspired by GEORGE LILLO's play, *The London Merchant, or the History of George Barnwell,* first acted in 1731.

[4] See Shakespeare, page 35.

[5] Percy's own composition, comprising 213 stanzas.

[6] See Johnson, page 230.

[1] From *The Oxford Sausage* [1764], a famous miscellany of 'varsity rhymes and satires, reprinted in several subsequent editions.

[2] Happy the man who, void of care and strife,
  In silken or in leathern purse retains
  A splendid shilling. He nor hears with pain
  New oysters cried, nor sighs for cheerful ale.
JOHN PHILIPS [1676–1709]: *The Splendid Shilling* [1705]

I am convinced that we have a degree of delight, and that no small one, in the real misfortunes and pains of others.[1]

> *On the Sublime and Beautiful.*
> *Sect. XIV*

Custom reconciles us to everything.

> *Ibid. Sect. XVIII*

There is, however, a limit at which forbearance ceases to be a virtue.

> *Observations on a Late Publication on the Present State of the Nation* [1769]

The wisdom of our ancestors.[2]

> *Ibid. Also in the Discussion on the Traitorous Correspondence Bill* [1793]

Illustrious predecessor.[3]

> *Thoughts on the Cause of the Present Discontents* [*April 23, 1770*]

When bad men combine, the good must associate; else they will fall one by one, an unpitied sacrifice in a contemptible struggle.

> *Ibid.*

Of this stamp is the cant of, Not men, but measures.[4]

> *Ibid.*

So to be patriots as not to forget we are gentlemen.

> *Ibid.*

Public life is a situation of power and energy; he trespasses against his duty who sleeps upon his watch, as well as he that goes over to the enemy.

> *Ibid.*

It ought to be the happiness and glory of a representative to live in the strictest union, the closest correspondence, and the most unreserved communication with his constituents. Their wishes ought to have great weight with him; their opinion high respect; their business unremitted attention. It is his duty to sacrifice his repose, his pleasures, his satisfaction, to theirs; and above all, ever, and in all cases, to prefer their interests to his own.

> *Speech to the Electors of Bristol.*
> [*November 3, 1774*]

Your representative owes you, not his industry only, but his judgment; and he betrays instead of serving you if he sacrifices it to your opinion.

> *Ibid.*

The concessions of the weak are the concessions of fear.

> *Speech on Conciliation with America* [*March 22, 1775*]

There is America, which at this day serves for little more than to amuse you with stories of savage men and uncouth manners, yet shall, before you taste of death, show itself equal to the whole of that commerce which now attracts the envy of the world.

> *Ibid.*

Fiction lags after truth, invention is unfruitful, and imagination cold and barren.

> *Ibid.*

A people who are still, as it were, but in the gristle, and not yet hardened into the bone of manhood.

> *Ibid.*

A wise and salutary neglect.

> *Ibid.*

The religion most prevalent in our northern colonies is a refinement on the principles of resistance: it is the dissidence of dissent, and the protestantism of the Protestant religion.

> *Ibid.*

I do not know the method of drawing up an indictment against an whole people.

> *Ibid.*

The march of the human mind is slow.[1]

> *Ibid.*

---

[1] In the adversity of our best friends we always find something which is not wholly displeasing to us. — ROCHEFOUCAULD: *Reflections, XV*

[2] Lord Brougham says of Bacon, "He it was who first employed the well-known phrase of 'the wisdom of our ancestors.'"
SYDNEY SMITH: *Plymley's Letters, Letter V.*
LORD ELDON: *On Sir Samuel Romilly's Bill* [1815]. CICERO: *De Legibus, II, 2, 3*

[3] See Fielding, page 230.

[4] See Goldsmith, page 253.

---

[1] The march of intellect. — SOUTHEY: *Progress and Prospects of Society, Vol. II, p. 360*

All government, — indeed, every human benefit and enjoyment, every virtue and every prudent act, — is founded on compromise and barter.

Speech on Conciliation with America [*March 22, 1775*]

The worthy gentleman [Mr. Coombe] who has been snatched from us at the moment of the election, and in the middle of the contest, whilst his desires were as warm and his hopes as eager as ours, has feelingly told us what shadows we are, and what shadows we pursue.

Speech at Bristol on Declining the Poll [*September 9, 1780*]

They made and recorded a sort of institute and digest of anarchy, called the Rights of Man.

On the Army Estimates [*February 9, 1790*]

People will not look forward to posterity who never look backward to their ancestors.[1]

Reflections on the Revolution in France [*1790*]

You had that action and counter-action which, in the natural and in the political world, from the reciprocal struggle of discordant powers draws out the harmony of the universe.[2]

Ibid.

It is now sixteen or seventeen years since I saw the Queen of France, then the Dauphiness, at Versailles; and surely never lighted on this orb, which she hardly seemed to touch, a more delightful vision. I saw her just above the horizon, decorating and cheering the elevated sphere she just began to move in, — glittering like the morning star full of life and splendour and joy. . . . Little did I dream that I should have lived to see such disasters fallen upon her in a nation of gallant men, — in a nation of men of honour

and of cavaliers. I thought ten thousand swords must have leaped from their scabbards to avenge even a look that threatened her with insult. But the age of chivalry is gone; that of sophisters, economists, and calculators has succeeded.

Reflections on the Revolution in France [*1790*]

The unbought grace of life, the cheap defence of nations, the nurse of manly sentiment and heroic enterprise is gone.

Ibid.

That chastity of honour which felt a stain like a wound.

Ibid.

Vice itself lost half its evil by losing all its grossness.

Ibid.

Kings will be tyrants from policy, when subjects are rebels from principle.[1]

Ibid.

Learning will be cast into the mire and trodden down under the hoofs of a swinish multitude.

Ibid.

Because half-a-dozen grasshoppers under a fern make the field ring with their importunate chink, whilst thousands of great cattle, reposed beneath the shadow of the British oak, chew the cud and are silent, pray do not imagine that those who make the noise are the only inhabitants of the field; that of course they are many in number; or that, after all, they are other than the little shrivelled, meagre, hopping, though loud and troublesome insects of the hour.

Ibid.

---

[1] The Democratic Party is like a mule — without pride of ancestry or hope of posterity. — IGNATIUS DONNELLY [1831–1901]: *Speech in the Minnesota Legislature*

[2] Quid velit et possit rerum concordia discors (What the discordant harmony of circumstances would and could effect). — HORACE: *Epistle I, 12, 19*

[1] Rebellion to tyrants is obedience to God. —

From an inscription on the cannon near which the ashes of President John Bradshaw were lodged, on the top of a high hill near Martha Bay in Jamaica. — STILES: *History of the Three Judges of King Charles I*

This supposititious epitaph was found among the papers of Mr. Jefferson, and in his handwriting. It was supposed to be one of Dr. Franklin's spirit-stirring inspirations. — RANDALL: *Life of Jefferson, Vol. III, P. 585*

In their nomination to office they will not appoint to the exercise of authority as to a pitiful job, but as to a holy function.
Reflections on the Revolution in France [1790]

The men of England, — the men, I mean, of light and leading in England.
Ibid.

He that wrestles with us strengthens our nerves and sharpens our skill. Our antagonist is our helper.
Ibid.

To execute laws is a royal office; to execute orders is not to be a king. However, a political executive magistracy, though merely such, is a great trust.[1]
Ibid.

You can never plan the future by the past.[2]
Letter to a Member of the National Assembly

The cold neutrality of an impartial judge.
Preface to Brissot's Address

And having looked to Government for bread, on the very first scarcity they will turn and bite the hand that fed them.
Thoughts and Details on Scarcity

All men that are ruined, are ruined on the side of their natural propensities.
Letter I, On a Regicide Peace

Example is the school of mankind, and they will learn at no other.
Ibid.

The people never give up their liberties but under some delusion.
Speech at County Meeting of Bucks [1784]

There never was a bad man that had ability for good service.
Speech in Opening the Impeachment of Warren Hastings [1788, Third Day]

[1] See Mathew Henry, page 188.
[2] I know no way of judging of the future but by the past. — PATRICK HENRY: *Speech in the Virginia Convention* [March, 1775]

Mere parsimony is not economy. . . . Expense, and great expense, may be essential part of true economy.
Letter to a Noble Lord [1796]

Economy is a distributive virtue, and consists not in saving but in selection. Parsimony requires no providence, no sagacity, no powers of combination, no comparison, no judgment.
Ibid.

I would rather sleep in the southern corner of a little country churchyard than in the tomb of the Capulets.
Letter to Matthew Smith

It has all the contortions of the sibyl without the inspiration.[1]
Prior's Life of Burke

He was not merely a chip of the old block, but the old block itself.[2]
On Pitt's First Speech [February 26, 1781]. From Wraxall's Memoirs, First Series, Vol. I, Page 342

WILLIAM GERARD HAMILTON
[1729–1796]

He has made a chasm which not only nothing can fill up, but which nothing has a tendency to fill up. Johnson is dead. — Let us go to the next best: — there is nobody; no man can be said to put you in mind of Johnson.
Quoted in Boswell's Life of Dr. Johnson, Vol. II, Page 611, Everyman Edition

JOHN SCOTT
[1730–1783]

I hate the drum's discordant sound,
Parading round, and round, and round:

[1] When Croft's "Life of Dr. Young" was spoken of as a good imitation of Dr. Johnson's style, "No, no," said he, "it is not a good imitation of Johnson; it has all his pomp without his force; it has all the nodosities of the oak, without its strength; it has all the contortions of the sibyl, without the inspiration." — JAMES PRIOR [1790–1869]: *Life of Burke*
The gloomy companions of a disturbed imagination; the melancholy madness of poetry, without the inspiration. — JUNIUS: *Letter No. VII* [March 3, 1769], *To Sir W. Draper*
[2] See Sir Thomas Browne, page 145.

To me it talks of ravaged plains,
And burning towns, and ruined swains,
And mangled limbs, and dying groans,
And widows' tears, and orphans'
    moans;
And all that Misery's hand bestows
To fill the catalogue of human woes.

*I Hate the Drum's Discordant
    Sound. Stanza 2*

CHARLES CHURCHILL
[1731–1764]

He mouths a sentence as curs mouth a
    bone.

The Rosciad. Line 322

But, spite of all the criticising elves,
Those who would make us feel — must
    feel themselves.[1]

Ibid. Line 961

Like gypsies, lest the stolen brat be
    known,
Defacing first, then claiming for his
    own.[2]

The Apology. Line 232

Apt alliteration's artful aid.

*The Prophecy of Famine.
    Line 86*

There webs were spread of more than
    common size,
And half-starved spiders prey'd on
    half-starved flies.

Ibid. Line 327

With curious art the brain, too finely
    wrought,
Preys on herself, and is destroyed by
    thought.

*Epistle to William Hogarth.
    Line 645*

Men the most infamous are fond of
    fame,
And those who fear not guilt yet start
    at shame.

The Author. Line 233

---

[1]   Si vis me flere, dolendum est
        Primum ipsi tibi
(If you wish me to weep, you yourself must
first feel grief).
    Horace: *Ars Poetica, L. 102*
[2] Steal! to be sure they may; and, egad,
serve your best thoughts as gypsies do stolen
children, — disguise them to make 'em pass
for their own. — Sheridan: *The Critic, Act I,
Sc. 1*

Be England what she will,
With all her faults she is my country
    still.[1]

The Farewell. Line 27

WILLIAM COWPER
[1731–1800]

Happiness depends, as Nature shows,
Less on exterior things than most sup-
    pose.

Table Talk. Line 246

Freedom has a thousand charms to
    show,
That slaves, howe'er contented, never
    know.

Ibid. Line 260

Manner is all in all, whate'er is writ,
The substitute for genius, sense, and
    wit.

Ibid. Line 542

Ages elapsed ere Homer's lamp ap-
    pear'd,
And ages ere the Mantuan swan was
    heard:
To carry nature lengths unknown be-
    fore,
To give a Milton birth, ask'd ages
    more.

Ibid. Line 556

Low ambition and the thirst of praise.[2]

Ibid. Line 591

Made poetry a mere mechanic art.

Ibid. Line 654

Lights of the world, and stars of hu-
    man race.

The Progress of Error. Line 97

How much a dunce that has been sent
    to roam
Excels a dunce that has been kept at
    home!

Ibid. Line 415

---

[1] England, with all thy faults I love thee
        still,
    My country!
    Cowper: *The Task, Book II, The Time-
            piece, L. 206*
Our country! In her intercourse with foreign nations may she always be in the right;
but our country, right or wrong.
    Stephen Decatur [1779–1820]: *Toast
            given at Norfolk,* [April, 1816]
[2] See Pope, page 206.

Just knows, and knows no more, her
    Bible true, —
A truth the brilliant Frenchman never
    knew.
                  Truth. Line 327
The sounding jargon of the schools.[1]
                  Ibid. Line 367
A fool must now and then be right by
    chance.
          Conversation. Line 96
He would not, with a peremptory tone,
Assert the nose upon his face his own.
                  Ibid. Line 121
A moral, sensible, and well-bred man
Will not affront me, — and no other
    can.
                  Ibid. Line 193
Pernicious weed! whose scent the fair
    annoys,
Unfriendly to society's chief joys:
Thy worst effect is banishing for hours
The sex whose presence civilizes ours.
                  Ibid. Line 251
I cannot talk with civet in the room,
A fine puss-gentleman that's all per-
    fume.
                  Ibid. Line 283
The solemn fop; significant and budge;
A fool with judges, amongst fools a
    judge.[2]
                  Ibid. Line 299
His wit invites you by his looks to
    come,
But when you knock, it never is at
    home.[3]
                  Ibid. Line 303
Our wasted oil unprofitably burns,
Like hidden lamps in old sepulchral
    urns.[4]
                  Ibid. Line 357
A business with an income at its heels

[1] See Prior, page 189.
[2] See Pope, page 215.
[3] *Ibid.*, page 217.
[4] That lamp shall burn unquenchably,
    Until the eternal doom shall be.
      Sir Walter Scott: *The Lay of the
      Last Minstrel, Canto II, St.* 17
The story of a lamp which was supposed to
have burned about fifteen hundred years in
the sepulchre of Tullia, the daughter of Cicero,
is told by Pancirollus and others.

Furnishes always oil for its own
    wheels.
             Retirement. Line 615
Absence of occupation is not rest,
A mind quite vacant is a mind dis-
    tress'd.
                  Ibid. Line 623
An idler is a watch that wants both
    hands,
As useless if it goes as if it stands.
                  Ibid. Line 681
Built God a church, and laugh'd His
    word to scorn.
                  Ibid. Line 688
          Philologists, who chase
A panting syllable through time and
    space,
Start it at home, and hunt it in the
    dark
To Gaul, to Greece, and into Noah's
    ark.
                  Ibid. Line 691
I praise the Frenchman,[1] his remark
    was shrewd, —
How sweet, how passing sweet, is soli-
    tude!
But grant me still a friend in my re-
    treat,
Whom I may whisper, Solitude is
    sweet.
                  Ibid. Line 739
Regions Caesar never knew
    Thy posterity shall sway;
Where his eagles never flew,
    None invincible as they!
                  Boadicea
And still to love, though prest with ill,
In wintry age to feel no chill,
With me is to be lovely still,
    My Mary!
             To Mary. Stanza 11
A kick that scarce would move a horse
    May kill a sound divine.
    The Yearly Distress. Stanza 16
I am monarch of all I survey,
    My right there is none to dispute.
    *Verses Supposed to be Written
    by Alexander Selkirk. Stanza 1*
O Solitude! where are the charms
    That sages have seen in thy face?
                  Ibid.

[1] Jean de La Bruyère [1645–1696].

But the sound of the church-going bell
  These valleys and rocks never heard,
Ne'er sigh'd at the sound of a knell,
  Or smiled when a Sabbath appear'd.

> *Verses Supposed to be Written*
> *by Alexander Selkirk. Stanza 4*

How fleet is a glance of the mind!
  Compared with the speed of its
    flight
The tempest itself lags behind,
  And the swift-winged arrows of light.

> *Ibid. Stanza 6*

There goes the parson, O illustrious
    spark!
And there, scarce less illustrious, goes
    the clerk.

> *On Observing Some Names of*
> *Little Note*

But oars alone can ne'er prevail
  To reach the distant coast;
The breath of heaven must swell the
    sail,
  Or all the toil is lost.

> *Human Frailty. Stanza 6*

And the tear that is wiped with a little
    address,
May be follow'd perhaps by a smile.

> *The Rose. Stanza 5*

I shall not ask Jean Jacques Rousseau
If birds confabulate or no.

> *Pairing Time Anticipated*

Misses! the tale that I relate
  This lesson seems to carry, —
Choose not alone a proper mate,
  But proper time to marry.

> *Ibid. Moral*

That though on pleasure she was bent,
  She had a frugal mind.

> *History of John Gilpin. Stanza 8*

A hat not much the worse for wear.

> *Ibid. Stanza 46*

Now let us sing, Long live the king,
  And Gilpin, Long live he;
And when he next doth ride abroad,
  May I be there to see!

> *Ibid. Stanza 63*

The path of sorrow, and that path
    alone,
Leads to the land where sorrow is un-
    known.

> *To an Afflicted Protestant*
> *Lady in France*

God made the country, and man made
    the town.[1]

> *The Task. Book I, The Sofa,*
> *Line 749*

Oh for a lodge in some vast wilder-
    ness,[2]
Some boundless contiguity of shade,
Where rumour of oppression and de-
    ceit,
Of unsuccessful or successful war,
Might never reach me more.

> *Ibid. Book II, The Timepiece,*
> *Line 1*

Mountains interposed
Make enemies of nations, who had else
Like kindred drops been mingled into
    one.

> *Ibid. Line 17*

Slaves cannot breathe in England; if
    their lungs
Receive our air, that moment they are
    free!
They touch our country, and their
    shackles fall.[3]

> *Ibid. Line 40*

Fast-anchor'd isle.

> *Ibid. Line 151*

England, with all thy faults I love thee
    still,
My country![4]

> *Ibid. Line 206*

Presume to lay their hand upon the
    ark[5]

---

[1] See Bacon, page 111.

[2] Oh that I had in the wilderness a lodging-place of wayfaring men! — *Jeremiah, IX, 2*
Oh that the desert were my dwelling-place!
— BYRON: *Childe Harold, Canto IV, St. 177*

[3] Servi peregrini, ut primum Galliæ fines penetraverint eodem momento liberi sunt (Foreign slaves, as soon as they come within the limits of Gaul, that moment they are free). — BODINUS: *Liber I, 5*
Lord Campbell ("Lives of the Chief Justices," vol. ii, p. 418) says that "Lord Mansfield first established the grand doctrine that the air of England is too pure to be breathed by a slave." The words attributed to Lord Mansfield, however, are not found in his judgment. They are in Hargrave's argument, May 14, 1772, where he speaks of England as "a soil whose air is deemed too pure for slaves to breathe in." — LOFFT: *Reports, P. 2*

[4] See Churchill, page 262.

[5] Uzzah put forth his hand to the ark of God, and took hold of it . . . and the anger

Of her magnificent and awful cause.
The Task. Book II, The Time-
piece, Line 231

There is a pleasure in poetic pains
Which only poets know.[1]
Ibid. Line 285

Transforms old print
To zigzag manuscript, and cheats the
eyes
Of gallery critics by a thousand arts.
Ibid. Line 363

Reading what they never wrote,
Just fifteen minutes, huddle up their
work,
And with a well-bred whisper close the
scene!
Ibid. Line 411

Whoe'er was edified, themselves were
not.
Ibid. Line 444

Variety's the very spice of life.
Ibid. Line 606

She that asks
Her dear five hundred friends.
Ibid. Line 642

His head,
Not yet by time completely silver'd
o'er,
Bespoke him past the bounds of freak-
ish youth,
But strong for service still, and un-
impair'd.
Ibid. Line 702

Guilty splendour.
Ibid. Book III, The Garden,
Line 70

I was a stricken deer.[2]
Ibid. Line 108

Great contest follows, and much
learned dust.
Ibid. Line 161

From reveries so airy, from the toil
Of dropping buckets into empty wells,

And growing old in drawing nothing
up.[1]
The Task. Book III, The Garden,
Line 188

Riches have wings,[2] and grandeur is a
dream.
Ibid. Line 265

How various his employments, whom
the world
Calls idle, and who justly in return
Esteems that busy world an idler too!
Ibid. Line 352

Who loves a garden loves a greenhouse
too.
Ibid. Line 566

Now stir the fire, and close the shutters
fast,
Let fall the curtains, wheel the sofa
round,
And while the bubbling and loud-hiss-
ing urn
Throws up a steamy column, and the
cups
That cheer but not inebriate [3] wait on
each,
So let us welcome peaceful evening in.
Ibid. Book IV, The Winter
Evening, Line 36

What is it, but a map of busy life,
Its fluctuations, and its vast concerns?
Ibid. Line 55

'Tis pleasant, through the loopholes of
retreat,
To peep at such a world, to see the stir
Of the great Babel; and not feel the
crowd.
Ibid. Line 88

While fancy, like the finger of a clock,
Runs the great circuit, and is still at
home.
Ibid. Line 118

O Winter, ruler of the inverted year! [4]
Ibid. Line 120

---

of the Lord was kindled against Uzzah. —
2 *Samuel, VI, 6 and 7*
  1 See Dryden, page 179.
  2 Let the stricken deer go weep. — SHAKE-
SPEARE: *Hamlet, Act III, Sc. 2, L. 287*
  Lord David Cecil gave his biography of
Cowper [1930] the title, *The Stricken Deer.*

  1 He has spent all his life in letting down
buckets into empty wells; and he is frittering
away his age in trying to draw them up again.
— *Lady Holland's Memoir of Sydney Smith,*
Vol. I, Chap. 9
  2 Riches certainly make themselves wings.
— *Proverbs, XXIII, 5*
  3 To cheer but not inebriate. — BISHOP
BERKELEY: *Siris* [1744] *Par. 217*
  4 See Thomson, page 224.

With spots quadrangular of diamond
   form,
Ensanguined hearts, clubs typical of
   strife,
And spades, the emblems of untimely
   graves.
> *The Task. Book IV, The Winter
>   Evening, Line 217*

In indolent vacuity of thought.[1]
> *Ibid. Line 297*

It seems the part of wisdom.
> *Ibid. Line 336*

All learned, and all drunk!
> *Ibid. Line 478*

Gloriously drunk, obey the important
   call.
> *Ibid. Line 510*

   Those golden times
And those Arcadian scenes that Maro
   sings,
And Sidney, warbler of poetic prose.
> *Ibid. Line 514*

The Frenchman's darling.[2]
> *Ibid. Line 765*

Silently as a dream the fabric rose;
No sound of hammer or of saw was
   there.[3]
> *Ibid. Book V, The Winter
>   Morning Walk, Line 144*

But war's a game, which, were their
   subjects wise,
Kings would not play at.
> *Ibid. Line 187*

There is in souls a sympathy with
   sounds;
And as the mind is pitch'd the ear is
   pleased
With melting airs or martial, brisk or
   grave;
Some chord in unison with what we
   hear
Is touch'd within us, and the heart
   replies.

[1] Gloomy calm of idle vacancy. — DR.
JOHNSON: *Letter to Boswell* [Dec. 8, 1763]

[2] It was Cowper who gave this now common name to the mignonette.

[3] No hammers fell, no ponderous axes rung,
   Like some tall palm the mystic fabric
   sprung.
   REGINALD HEBER [1783–1826]: *Palestine*
So that there was neither hammer nor axe,
nor any tool of iron heard in the house while
it was in building. — *1 Kings, VI, 7*

How soft the music of those village
   bells
Falling at intervals upon the ear
In cadence sweet!
> *The Task. Book VI, Winter Walk
>   at Noon, Line 1*

   Here the heart
May give a useful lesson to the head,
And Learning wiser grow without his
   books.
> *Ibid. Line 85*

Knowledge is proud that he has learn'd
   so much;
Wisdom is humble that he knows no
   more.
> *Ibid. Line 96*

Some to the fascination of a name,
Surrender judgment hoodwink'd.
> *Ibid. Line 101*

I would not enter on my list of friends,
(Though graced with polish'd manners
   and fine sense,
Yet wanting sensibility), the man
Who needlessly sets foot upon a worm.
> *Ibid. Line 560*

An honest man, close-button'd to the
   chin,
Broadcloth without, and a warm heart
   within.
> *Epistle to Joseph Hill*

Shine by the side of every path we
   tread
With such a lustre, he that runs may
   read.[1]
> *Tirocinium. Line 79*

What peaceful hours I once enjoy'd!
   How sweet their memory still!
But they have left an aching void
   The world can never fill.
> *Walking with God*

God moves in a mysterious way
   His wonders to perform;
He plants his footsteps in the sea
   And rides upon the storm.
> *Light Shining out of Darkness*

Behind a frowning providence
   He hides a shining face.
> *Ibid.*

[1] Write the vision, and make it plain, upon
tables, that he may run that readeth it. —
Habakkuk, II, 2

He that runs may read. — TENNYSON: *The
Flower*

Beware of desperate steps! The darkest day,
Live till to-morrow, will have pass'd
away.
The Needless Alarm. Moral

Oh that those lips had language! Life
has pass'd
With me but roughly since I heard thee
last.
*On the Receipt of My Mother's
Picture*

The man that hails you Tom or Jack,
And proves, by thumping on your
back,[1]
His sense of your great merit,[2]
Is such a friend that one had need
Be very much his friend indeed
To pardon or to bear it.
On Friendship. Stanza 26

Toll for the brave!
The brave that are no more,
All sunk beneath the wave,
Fast by their native shore!
*On the Loss of the Royal George.[3]
Stanza 1*

There is a bird who by his coat,
And by the hoarseness of his note,
Might be supposed a crow.
*The Jackdaw (Translation from
Vincent Bourne).[4] Stanza 1*

He sees that this great roundabout
The world, with all its motley rout,
Church, army, physic, law,
Its customs and its businesses,
Is no concern at all of his,
And says — what says he? — Caw.
Ibid. Stanza 5

For 'tis a truth well known to most,
That whatsoever thing is lost,
We seek it, ere it come to light,
In every cranny but the right.
The Retired Cat

[1] See Young, page 203.
[2] Variant, — How he esteems your merit.
[3] The *Royal George* was an English man-of-war of 108 guns, which suddenly heeled over, under the strain caused by the shifting of her guns, while being refitted at Spithead [August 29, 1782]. The commander, Admiral Kempenfeldt, and 800 of the sailors, marines, and visitors on board, were drowned.
[4] VINCENT BOURNE [1695–1747], a Latin poet. Cowper was one of his pupils at Westminster School, where Bourne was Master.

He that holds fast the golden mean,[1]
And lives contentedly between
The little and the great,
Feels not the wants that pinch the
poor,
Nor plagues that haunt the rich man's
door.
*Translation of Horace. Book II,
Ode X, To Licinius, Stanza 2*

If Fortune fill thy sail
With more than a propitious gale,
Take half thy canvas in.
Ibid. Stanza 6

But strive still to be a man before
your mother.[2]
Connoisseur. Motto of No. III

ERASMUS DARWIN
[1731–1802]

Soon shall thy arm, unconquer'd
steam! afar
Drag the slow barge, or drive the rapid
car;
Or on wide-waving wings expanded
bear
The flying chariot through the field of
air.
*The Botanic Garden. Part I,
Canto I, Line 289*

No radiant pearl which crested For-
tune wears,
No gem that twinkling hangs from
Beauty's ears,
Not the bright stars which Night's
blue arch adorn,
Nor rising suns that gild the vernal
morn,
Shine with such lustre as the tear that
flows
Down Virtue's manly cheek for others'
woes.
Ibid. Part II, Canto III, Line 459

CHARLES LEE
[1731–1782]

Beware that your Northern laurels
do not change to Southern willows.
*To General Horatio Gates
[1728–1806] after surrender of*

[1] Keep the golden mean. — PUBLIUS SYRUS: *Maxim 1072*
[2] See Beaumont and Fletcher, page 132.

Burgoyne at Saratoga [October 17, 1777]. Gates was later defeated by Lord Cornwallis at Camden, South Carolina [August 16, 1780] and was relieved of his command.

BEILBY PORTEUS
[1731–1808]

In sober state,
Through the sequestered vale of rural life,
The venerable patriarch guileless held
The tenor of his way.[1]
Death. Line 108

One murder made a villain,
Millions, a hero. Princes were privileged
To kill, and numbers sanctified the crime.[2]
Ibid. Line 154

War its thousands slays, Peace, its ten thousands.
Ibid. Line 178

Teach him how to live,
And, oh still harder lesson! how to die.[3]
Ibid. Line 316

Love is something so divine,
Description would but make it less;
'Tis what I feel, but can't define,
'Tis what I know, but can't express.
On Love

GEORGE WASHINGTON
[1732–1799]

Labour to keep alive in your breast that little spark of celestial fire, — conscience.
Rule from the copy-book of Washington when a schoolboy

That unmeaning and abominable custom, swearing.
Orders Against Profanity in the Army

Almighty God, we make our earnest prayer that Thou wilt keep the United States in Thy holy protection; that

Thou wilt incline the hearts of the citizens to cultivate a spirit of subordination and obedience to government; to entertain a brotherly affection and love for one another and for their fellow-citizens of the United States at large.
Prayer after Inauguration (from copy in his pew, St. Paul's Chapel, New York)

To be prepared for war is one of the most effectual means of preserving peace.[1]
First Annual Address, to both Houses of Congress [January 8, 1790]

It is our true policy to steer clear of permanent alliances with any portion of the foreign world.
Farewell Address [September 17, 1796]

JOHN ADAMS
[1735–1826]

Yesterday the greatest question was decided which ever was debated in America; and a greater perhaps never was, nor will be, decided among men. A resolution was passed without one dissenting colony, that those United Colonies are, and of right ought to be, free and independent States.
Letter to Mrs. Adams [July 3, 1776]

The second day of July, 1776, will be the most memorable epocha in the history of America. I am apt to believe that it will be celebrated by succeeding generations as the great anniversary festival. It ought to be commemorated as the day of deliverance, by solemn acts of devotion to God Almighty. It ought to be solemnized with pomp and parade, with shows, games, sports, guns, bells, bonfires, and illuminations, from one end of this continent to the

---

[1] See Gray, page 245.
[2] See Young, page 203.
[3] See Tickell, page 205.

[1] Qui desiderat pacem præparet bellum (Who would desire peace should be prepared for war). — VEGETIUS: *Rei Militari 3, Prolog.*
In pace, ut sapiens, aptarit idonea bello (In peace, as a wise man, he should make suitable preparation for war). — HORACE: *Book II Satire II, Line 111*

other, from this time forward for evermore.

Letter to Mrs. Adams
[July 3, 1776]

JAMES BEATTIE
[1735–1803]

Mine be the breezy hill that skirts the down,
Where a green grassy turf is all I crave,
With here and there a violet bestrewn,
Fast by a brook or fountain's murmuring wave;
And many an evening sun shine sweetly on my grave!

The Minstrel. Book II [1774],
Stanza 17

At the close of the day when the hamlet is still,
And mortals the sweets of forgetfulness prove,
When naught but the torrent is heard on the hill,
And naught but the nightingale's song in the grove.

The Hermit

He thought as a sage, though he felt as a man.

Ibid.

ISAAC BICKERSTAFF
[1735–1812?]

There was a jolly miller once lived on the River Dee;
He worked and sung from morn till night, no lark so blithe as he.

Love in a Village. Act I, Sc. 2

And this the burden of his song forever used to be, —
"I care for nobody, no, not I, if nobody cares for me." [1]

Ibid.

[1] Naebody cares for me,
I care for naebody.
ROBERT BURNS: *I Hae a Wife o' My Ain,*
St. 4

I envy none, no, no, not I,
And no one envies me.
CHARLES MACKAY: *The King and the Miller*

JOHN LANGHORNE
[1735–1779]

Cold on Canadian hills or Minden's plain,
Perhaps that parent mourned her soldier slain;
Bent o'er her babe, her eye dissolved in dew,
The big drops mingling with the milk he drew
Gave the sad presage of his future years, —
The child of misery, baptized in tears. [1]

The Country Justice. Part I

WILLIAM JULIUS MICKLE
[1735–1788]

The dews of summer nights did fall,
  The moon (sweet regent of the sky) [2]
Silvered the walls of Cumnor Hall
  And many an oak that grew thereby.

Cumnor Hall. [3] *Stanza 1*

For know, when sickening grief doth prey,
  And tender love's repaid with scorn,
The sweetest beauty will decay:
  What floweret can endure the storm?

Ibid. Stanza 10

For there's nae luck about the house,
  There's nae luck at a';
There's little pleasure in the house
  When our gudeman's awa.

The Mariner's Wife. [4] *Stanza 1*

[1] This allusion to the dead soldier and his widow on the field of battle was made the subject of a print by Bunbury, under which were engraved the pathetic lines of Langhorne. Sir Walter Scott has mentioned that the only time he saw Burns this picture was in the room. Burns shed tears over it; and Scott, then a lad of fifteen, was the only person present who could tell him where the lines were to be found. — LOCKHART: *Life of Scott, Vol. I, Chap. IV*

[2] Jove, thou regent of the skies. — POPE: *The Odyssey, Book II, L. 42*

Now Cynthia, named fair regent of the night. — GAY: *Trivia, Book III.*

And hail their queen, fair regent of the night. — DARWIN: *The Botanic Garden, Part I, Canto II, L. 90*

[3] This ballad is said to have suggested to SIR WALTER SCOTT the writing of *Kenilworth.*

[4] *The Mariner's Wife* is now given "by common consent," says Sarah Tytler, to Jean

Sae true his heart, sae smooth his
  speech,
His breath like caller air;
His very foot has music in 't
As he comes up the stair.
        The Mariner's Wife. Stanza 5

PATRICK HENRY
[1736–1799]

Tarquin and Caesar each had his
Brutus, Charles the First his Cromwell,
and George the Third ["Treason!"
cried the Speaker] — *may profit by
their example*. If *this* be treason, make
the most of it.
        *Speech on the Stamp Act,
        House of Burgesses, Richmond,
        Virginia [May 29, 1765]*

I am not a Virginian, but an American.
        *Speech in First Continental
        Congress, Philadelphia [Oc-
        tober 14, 1774]*

I have but one lamp by which my
feet are guided, and that is the lamp
of experience. I know of no way of
judging of the future but by the past.[1]
        *Speech in Virginia Convention,
        St. John's Episcopal Church,
        Richmond, Virginia [March 23,
        1775]*

We are not weak if we make a
proper use of those means which the
God of Nature has placed in our
power. . . . The battle, sir, is not to
the strong alone;[2] it is to the vigilant,
the active, the brave.
        Ibid.

Is life so dear, or peace so sweet, as
to be purchased at the price of chains
and slavery? Forbid it, Almighty God!
I know not what course others may
take, but as for me, give me liberty, or
give me death!
        *Speech in Virginia Convention,
        St. John's Episcopal Church,
        Richmond, Virginia [March 23,
        1775]*

EDWARD GIBBON
[1737–1794]

The reign of Antoninus is marked by
the rare advantage of furnishing very
few materials for history; which is indeed little more than the register of the
crimes, follies, and misfortunes of
mankind.[1]
        *Decline and Fall of the Roman
        Empire [1776]. Chap. 3. Mod-
        ern Library Giant, Vol. I,
        Page 69*

It has been calculated by the ablest
politicians that no State, without being soon exhausted, can maintain above
the hundredth part of its members in
arms and idleness.
        Ibid. Chap. 5, Page 90

Amiable weaknesses of human nature.[2]
        Ibid. Chap. 14, Page 375

In every deed of mischief he [Adroni-
cus] had a heart to resolve, a head to
contrive, and a hand to execute.[3]
        Ibid. Chap. 48, Vol. II, Page 569

Our sympathy is cold to the relation
of distant misery.
        Ibid. Chap. 49, Page 597

Adam [1710–1765], who published poems by
subscription, later opened a girls' school, and
died in Glasgow poorhouse. The *Dictionary
of National Biography* states that there is
small foundation for crediting the poem to
her. A shorter version of *The Mariner's Wife*,
entitled *There's Nae Luck About the House*,
is in the *Herd Collection of Ancient and Modern Scottish Songs, Heroic Ballads, etc.*

[1] See Burke, page 261.

[2] The race is not to the swift, nor the battle
to the strong. — *Ecclesiastes, IX, 11*

The race is not to the swift, nor the battle
to the strong; but the betting is best that
way. — FRANKLIN P. ADAMS: *The Conning
Tower*

[1] L'histoire n'est que le tableau des crimes
et des malheurs (History is but the record of
crimes and misfortunes). — VOLTAIRE: *L'In-
génu, Chap. X*

[2] See Fielding, page 229 and Sheridan,
page 279.

[3] He [Hampden] had a head to contrive, a
tongue to persuade, and a hand to execute any
mischief. — EDWARD HYDE CLARENDON [1608–
1674]: *History of the Rebellion, Vol. III,
Book 7, Sect. 84*

Heart to conceive, the understanding to direct, or the hand to execute. — JUNIUS: *Letter XXXVII [March 19, 1770]*

The winds and waves are always on the side of the ablest navigators.[1]

> *Decline and Fall of the Roman Empire* [1776]. *Vol. II, Chap. 68, Page 1343*

Vicissitudes of fortune, which spares neither man nor the proudest of his works, which buries empires and cities in a common grave.

> *Ibid. Chap. 71, Page 1438*

All that is human must retrograde if it do not advance.

> *Ibid. Page 1440*

I saw and loved.

> *Memoirs. Vol. I, Page 106*

On the approach of spring I withdrew without reluctance from the noisy and extensive scene of crowds without company, and dissipation without pleasure.

> *Ibid. Page 116*

I was never less alone than when by myself.[2]

> *Ibid. Page 117*

THOMAS PAINE
[1737–1809]

And the final event to himself [Mr. Burke] has been, that, as he rose like a rocket, he fell like the stick.

> *Letter to the Addressers*

These are the times that try men's souls.

> *The American Crisis. No. 1. In Pennsylvania Journal* [December 19, 1776]

What we obtain too cheap, we esteem too lightly; it is dearness only that gives everything its value.

> *Ibid.*

Panics, in some cases, have their uses; they produce as much good as hurt. Their duration is always short; the mind soon grows through them, and acquires a firmer habit than before.

> *The American Crisis. No. 1. In Pennsylvania Journal* [December 19, 1776]

Not a place upon earth might be so happy as America. Her situation is remote from all the wrangling world, and she has nothing to do but to trade with them.

> *Ibid.*

In a chariot of light from the region of day
The Goddess of Liberty came.
Ten thousand celestials directed the way
And hither conducted the dame.
A fair budding branch from the gardens above,
Where millions with millions agree,
She brought in her hand as a pledge of her love,
And the plant she named Liberty Tree.

> *The Liberty Tree. Stanza 1. In Pennsylvania Magazine* [July, 1775]

From the east to the west blow the trumpet to arms!
Through the land let the sound of it flee;
Let the far and the near all unite, with a cheer,
In defence of our Liberty Tree.

> *Ibid. Stanza 4*

War involves in its progress such a train of unforeseen and unsupposed circumstances that no human wisdom can calculate the end. It has but one thing certain, and that is to increase taxes.

> *Prospects on the Rubicon* [1787]

The world is my country,
All mankind are my brethren,[1]
To do good is my religion,
I believe in one God and no more.

> *The Rights of Man. Chap. 5*

The sublime and the ridiculous are often so nearly related, that it is difficult to class them separately. One step above the sublime makes the ridicu-

---

[1] On dit que Dieu est toujours pour les gros bataillons (It is said that God is always on the side of the heaviest battalions). VOLTAIRE: *Letter to M. le Riche* [1770]

[2] Never less alone than when alone. — SAMUEL ROGERS [1763–1855]: *Human Life* [1819]

[1] See William Lloyd Garrison, page 424.

lous, and one step above the ridiculous makes the sublime again.[1]

Age of Reason. Part II, Note

JOHN WOLCOT
("PETER PINDAR")
[1738–1819]

Blessed are those that nought expect,
For they shall not be disappointed.[2]

Ode to Pitt

You cannot make, my Lord, I fear,
A velvet purse of a sow's ear.[3]

Lord B. and His Notions

What rage for fame attends both great and small!
Better be damned than mentioned not at all.

To the Royal Academicians

Care to our coffin adds a nail, no doubt,
And every grin so merry draws one out.

Expostulatory Odes. XV

HESTER LYNCH THRALE
(PIOZZI)
[1739–1821]

The tree of deepest root is found
Least willing still to quit the ground:
'Twas therefore said by ancient sages,
    That love of life increased with years
So much, that in our latter stages,
When pain grows sharp and sickness rages,
    The greatest love of life appears.

Three Warnings

Johnson's conversation was by much too strong for a person accustomed to obsequiousness and flattery; it was mustard in a young child's mouth.

Quoted in Boswell's Life of Dr. Johnson, Vol. II, Page 396, Everyman Edition

---

[1] Probably this is the original of Napoleon's celebrated *mot*, "Du sublime au ridicule il n'y a qu'un pas" (From the sublime to the ridiculous there is but one step).
[2] See Pope, page 220.
[3] See George Herbert, page 138.

DANIEL BLISS
[1740–1806]

God wills us free, man wills us slaves,
I will as God wills, God's will be done.

Epitaph on gravestone of John Jack, "A Native of Africa, who died March 1773, aged about 60 years. Tho' born in a land of slavery he was born free." [1]

JAMES BOSWELL
[1740–1795]

See also under SAMUEL JOHNSON

That favourite subject, Myself.

Letter to Temple [*July 26, 1763*]

Citizen of the world,[2] as I hold myself to be.

Life of Dr. Johnson, Everyman Edition, Page 521 (1775) Vol. I

We cannot tell the precise moment when friendship is formed. As in filling a vessel drop by drop, there is at last a drop which makes it run over; so in a series of kindnesses there is at last one which makes the heart run over.

Ibid. Vol. II, Page 122 (1777)

I think no innocent species of wit or pleasantry should be suppressed; and that a good pun may be admitted among the smaller excellencies of lively conversation.

Ibid. Page 537 (1784)

AUGUSTUS MONTAGUE
TOPLADY
[1740–1778]

Rock of Ages, cleft for me,
Let me hide myself in thee.

Rock of Ages [*1775*]. *Stanza 1*

ANNA LETITIA (AIKEN)
BARBAULD
[1743–1825]

Life! we've been long together
Through pleasant and through cloudy weather;

---

[1] This gravestone is in the Old Hill Burying Ground, Concord, Massachusetts.
[2] See William Lloyd Garrison, page 424.

'Tis hard to part when friends are
    dear, —
Perhaps 'twill cost a sigh, a tear;
Then steal away, give little warning,
    Choose thine own time;
Say not "Good night," but in some
    brighter clime
Bid me "Good morning."
               Life. Stanza 3
So fades a summer cloud away;
  So sinks the gale when storms are
    o'er;
So gently shuts the eye of day;
  So dies a wave along the shore.
      The Death of the Virtuous
This dead of midnight is the noon of
    thought.
  A Summer's Evening Meditation

THOMAS JEFFERSON
[1743–1826]

A lively and lasting sense of filial
duty is more effectually impressed on
the mind of a son or daughter by reading King Lear, than by all the dry volumes of ethics, and divinity, that ever
were written.
    Letter to Robert Skipwith
           [August 3, 1771]

The God who gave us life, gave us
liberty at the same time.
  Summary View of the Rights of
         British America

When, in the course of human events,
it becomes necessary for one people to
dissolve the political bands which have
connected them with another, and to
assume among the powers of the earth
the separate and equal station to which
the laws of nature and of nature's God [1]
entitle them, a decent respect to the
opinions of mankind requires that they
should declare the causes which impel
them to the separation.
    Declaration of Independence

We hold these truths to be self-
evident, — that all men are created
equal; that they are endowed by their
Creator with certain unalienable

[1] See Bolingbroke, page 200.

rights; [1] that among these are life,
liberty, and the pursuit of happiness.
    Declaration of Independence

We mutually pledge to each other
our lives, our fortunes, and our sacred
honour.
                Ibid.

What country before ever existed a
century and a half without a rebellion? . . . The tree of liberty must be
refreshed from time to time with the
blood of patriots and tyrants. It is its
natural manure.
  Letter to William Stevens Smith
         [November 13, 1787]

Error of opinion may be tolerated
where reason is left free to combat it.
    First Inaugural Address
          [March 4, 1801]

Equal and exact justice to all men,
of whatever state or persuasion, religious or political; peace, commerce,
and honest friendship with all nations,
— entangling alliances with none; the
support of the State governments in
all their rights, as the most competent
administrations for our domestic concerns, and the surest bulwarks against
anti-republican tendencies; the preservation of the general government in its
whole constitutional vigour, as the
sheet anchor of our peace at home and
safety abroad; . . . freedom of religion; freedom of the press; freedom
of person under the protection of the
habeas corpus; and trial by juries impartially selected, — these principles
form the bright constellation which has
gone before us, and guided our steps
through an age of revolution and reformation.
                Ibid.

In the full tide of successful experiment.
                Ibid.

Of the various executive abilities, no
one excited more anxious concern than
that of placing the interests of our

[1] All men are born free and equal, and have
certain natural, essential and unalienable
rights. — *Constitution of Massachusetts*
The phrase is frequently misquoted "in-
alienable."

fellow-citizens in the hands of honest men, with understanding sufficient for their stations.[1]

Letter to Elias Shipman and Others of New Haven [*July 12, 1801*]

If a due participation of office is a matter of right, how are vacancies to be obtained? Those by death are few; by resignation, none.[2]

Ibid.

When a man assumes a public trust, he should consider himself as public property.[3]

RAYNER's *Life of Jefferson.*
Page 356

Indeed, I tremble for my country when I reflect that God is just.

Notes on Virginia. Query XVIII,
Manners

WILLIAM PALEY
[1743–1805]

Who can refute a sneer?

Moral Philosophy. Vol. II, Book V,
Chap. 9

ROWLAND HILL
[1744–1833]

Why should the Devil have all the good tunes?

JOSIAH QUINCY
[1744–1775]

Blandishments will not fascinate us, nor will threats of a "halter" intimidate. For, under God, we are determined that wheresoever, whensoever, or howsoever we shall be called to make our exit, we will die free men.

Observations on the Boston Port
Bill [*1774*]

[1] This passage is thus paraphrased by JOHN B. McMASTER in his *History of the People of the United States, Vol. II, P. 586:* "One sentence will undoubtedly be remembered till our republic ceases to exist. 'No duty the Executive had to perform was so trying,' he observed, 'as to put the right man in the right place.'"
[2] Usually quoted, "Few die and none resign."
[3] See Mathew Henry, page 188.

CHARLES DIBDIN
[1745–1814]

There's a sweet little cherub that sits up aloft,
To keep watch for the life of poor Jack.
Poor Jack

Did you ever hear of Captain Wattle?
He was all for love, and a little for the bottle.
Captain Wattle and Miss Roe

Here, a sheer hulk, lies poor Tom Bowling,
The darling of our crew;
No more he'll hear the tempest howling,
For death has broach'd him to.
His form was of the manliest beauty,
His heart was kind and soft;
Faithful below he did his duty,
But now he's gone aloft.
Tom Bowling

For though his body's under hatches,
His soul has gone aloft.
Ibid.

But were it to my fancy given
To rate her charms, I'd call them heaven;
For though a mortal made of clay,
Angels must love Ann Hathaway;
She hath a way so to control,
To rapture the imprisoned soul,
And sweetest heaven on earth display,
That to be heaven Ann hath a way;
She hath a way,
Ann Hathaway, —
To be heaven's self Ann hath a way.
A Love Dittie, in the novel,
Hannah Hewit [*1792*]

Spanking Jack was so comely, so pleasant, so jolly,
Though winds blew great guns, still he'd whistle and sing;
Jack loved his friend, and was true to his Molly,
And if honour gives greatness, was great as a king.
The Sailor's Consolation

WILLIAM PITT
[? –1840]

One night came on a hurricane,
The sea was mountains rolling,
When Barney Buntline turned his quid,

And said to Billy Bowling:
"A strong nor-wester's blowing, Bill;
Hark! don't ye hear it roar, now?
Lord help 'em, how I pities all
Unhappy folks on shore now!"

The Sailor's Consolation.[1] *Stanza 1*

HANNAH MORE
[1745–1833]

To those who know thee not, no words
can paint!
And those who know thee, know all
words are faint!

Sensibility

Since trifles make the sum of human
things,
And half our misery from our foibles
springs.

Ibid.

In men this blunder still you find, —
All think their little set mankind.

Florio and His Friend

Small habits well pursued betimes
May reach the dignity of crimes.

Ibid.

Some phrase that with the public took
Was all he read of any book.

Ibid.

WILLIAM SCOTT, LORD STOWELL
[1745–1836]

A dinner lubricates business.

Quoted in BOSWELL's *Life of Dr. Johnson, London edition [1835], Vol. VIII, Page 67, Note*

The elegant simplicity of the three per cents.[2]

Quoted in CAMPBELL's *Lives of the Lord Chancellors, Vol. X, Chap. 212*

[1] This song, because of a duplication of title, has been ascribed to Charles Dibdin. Sir Harold Boulton, after research, found that William Pitt wrote it. He was Master Attendant at Jamaica Dockyard, and afterward went to Malta, where he died. The song is ascribed to Pitt in CHARLES MACKAY's *Book of Songs* and in the sheet music (A. M. Goodhart, composer) published by Boosey and Company.

[2] The sweet simplicity of the three per cents. — DISRAELI (EARL OF BEACONSFIELD): *Endymion*

JAMES HOOK
[1746–1827]

A little farm well tilled,
A little barn well filled,
A little wife well willed,
   Give me, give me.

The Soldier's Return. Stanza 1

I like the farm well tilled,
And I like the house well filled,
But no wife at all
   Give me, give me.

Ibid. Stanza 3

SIR WILLIAM JONES
[1746–1794]

Than all Bocara's vaunted gold,
Than all the gems of Samarcand.

A Persian Song of Hafiz

Go boldly forth, my simple lay,
Whose accents flow with artless
   ease,
Like orient pearls at random strung.[1]

Ibid.

On parent knees, a naked new-born
   child,
Weeping thou sat'st while all around
   thee smiled;
So live, that sinking in thy last long
   sleep,
Calm thou mayst smile, while all
   around thee weep.

From the Persian

Seven hours to law, to soothing slumber seven,
Ten to the world allot, and all to
   heaven.[2]

Epigram

[1] 'Twas he that ranged the words at random flung,
Pierced the fair pearls and them together strung.
   EDWARD BACKHOUSE EASTWICK
   [1814–1833]: *Anvari Suhaili* (translated from Firdusi)

[2] See Coke, page 21.

CHARLES COTESWORTH PINCKNEY
[1746–1825]

Millions for defence, but not one cent for tribute.[1]
When Ambassador to the French Republic [1796]

JOHN O'KEEFFE
[1747–1833]

A glass is good, and a lass is good,
  And a pipe to smoke in cold weather;
The world is good, and the people are good,
  And we're all good fellows together.
  Sprigs of Laurel. Act II, Sc. 1

And why I'm so plump the reason I tell, —
Who leads a good life is sure to live well.
  Merry Sherwood. A Friar of Orders Gray, Stanza 1

A Rose Tree full in bearing
  Had sweet flowers fair to see;
One rose, without comparing,
  For beauty attracted me.
Though eager once to win it,
  Lovely, blooming, fresh and gay,
I find a canker in it
  And now throw it far away.
  The Poor Soldier [1783]. The Rose Tree (set to an earlier air)

SAMUEL PARR [2]
[1747–1825]

Now that the old lion is dead, every ass thinks he may kick at him.
  While dining with Sir Joshua Reynolds, after the death of Dr. Johnson. Quoted in BOSWELL'S *Life of Dr. Johnson, Vol. II, Page 612, Everyman Edition*

JOHN LOGAN
[1748–1788]

Thou hast no sorrow in thy song,
  No winter in thy year.
  To the Cuckoo

Oh could I fly, I'd fly with thee!
  We'd make with joyful wing
Our annual visit o'er the globe,
  Companions of the spring.
  Ibid.

JONATHAN M. SEWALL
[1748–1808]

No pent-up Utica contracts your powers,
But the whole boundless continent is yours.
  Epilogue to Cato [1]

JOHN EDWIN
[1749–1790]

A man's ingress into the world is naked and bare,
His progress through the world is trouble and care;
And lastly, his egress out of the world, is nobody knows where.
If we do well here, we shall do well there:
I can tell you no more if I preach a whole year.[2]
  The Eccentricities of John Edwin [second edition, London, 1791], Vol. I, Page 74

EDWARD JENNER
[1749–1823]

The hollow winds begin to blow;
The clouds look black, the glass is low;
The soot falls down, the spaniels sleep,
And spiders from their cobwebs peep.
  Forty Signs of Rain

---

[1] Inscribed on the cenotaph in his memory in St. Michael's Church, Charleston, South Carolina. What Pinckney really said was more forcible, — "not *a damned penny* for tribute."
[2] Dr. Parr composed the Latin epitaph for the monument to Dr. Johnson, placed in St. Paul's Cathedral, London, February, 1790.

[1] Written for the Bow Street Theatre, Portsmouth, New Hampshire.
[2] These lines Edwin offers as heads of a "sermon." Longfellow places them in the mouth of the Cobbler of Hagenau, as a "familiar tune." See *The Wayside Inn, Part II, The Student's Tale.*

'Twill surely rain; I see with sorrow
Our jaunt must be put off to-morrow.
Forty Signs of Rain

LADY ANNE BARNARD
(née LINDSAY)
[1750–1825]

When the sheep are in the fauld, and
    the kye's come hame,
And a' the weary warld to rest are gone,
The waes o' my heart fall in showers
    frae my ee,
Unkenn'd by my gudeman, who sleeps
    sound by me.
Auld Robin Gray. Stanza 1
So I will do my best a gude wife to be,
For Auld Robin Gray he is kind to me.
Ibid. Stanza 9

JOHN PHILPOT CURRAN
[1750–1817]

It is the common fate of the indolent
to see their rights become a prey to the
active. The condition upon which God
hath given liberty to man is eternal
vigilance; [1] which condition if he break,
servitude is at once the consequence of
his crime and the punishment of his
guilt.
Speech upon the Right of Election
[1790]

JOHN LOWE
[1750–1798]

The moon had climb'd the highest hill
    Which rises o'er the source of Dee,
And from the eastern summit shed
    Her silver light on tower and tree,
When Mary laid her down to sleep,
    Her thoughts on Sandy far at sea,
When, soft and low, a voice was heard,
    Saying, "Mary, weep no more for
        me!"
Mary's Dream. Stanza 1

[1] Commonly quoted, — Eternal vigilance is
the price of liberty.
There is one safeguard known generally to
the wise, which is an advantage and security
to all, but especially to democracies as against
despots. What is it? Distrust. — DEMOSTHE-
NES: *Philippic 2, Sect. 24*

JOHN TRUMBULL
[1750–1831]

But optics sharp it needs, I ween,
To see what is not to be seen.
McFingal. Canto I, Line 67
But as some muskets so contrive it
As oft to miss the mark they drive at,
And though well aimed at duck or
    plover,
Bear wide, and kick their owners over.
Ibid. Line 93
    As though there were a tie
And obligation to posterity.
We get them, bear them, breed, and
    nurse:
What has posterity done for us?
Ibid. Canto II, Line 121
No man e'er felt the halter draw,
With good opinion of the law.
Ibid. Canto III, Line 489

RICHARD BRINSLEY
SHERIDAN
[1751–1816]

Mrs. Malaprop. Illiterate him, I say,
    quite from your memory.
The Rivals. Act I, Sc. 2
'Tis safest in matrimony to begin with
    a little aversion.
Ibid.
    A circulating library in a town is as
an evergreen tree of diabolical knowl-
edge.
Ibid.
A progeny of learning.
Ibid.
Don't let your simplicity be imposed
    on.
Ibid.
Never say more than is necessary.
Ibid. Act II, Sc. 1
I know you are laughing in your sleeve.
Ibid.
He is the very pine-apple of politeness!
Ibid. Act III, Sc. 3
    If I reprehend anything in this world,
it is the use of my oracular tongue,
and a nice derangement of epitaphs!
Ibid.

As headstrong as an allegory on the banks of the Nile.
The Rivals. Act III, Sc. 3

Too civil by half.[1]
Ibid. Sc. 4

Our ancestors are very good kind of folks; but they are the last people I should choose to have a visiting acquaintance with.
Ibid. Act IV, Sc. 1

No caparisons, miss, if you please. Caparisons don't become a young woman.
Ibid. Sc. 2

We will not anticipate the past; so mind, young people, — our retrospection will be all to the future.
Ibid.

You are not like Cerberus, three gentlemen at once, are you?
Ibid.

The quarrel is a very pretty quarrel as it stands; we should only spoil it by trying to explain it.
Ibid. Sc. 3

You're our envoy; lead the way, and we'll precede.
Ibid. Act V, Sc. 1

There's nothing like being used to a thing.
Ibid. Sc. 3

As there are three of us come on purpose for the game, you won't be so cantankerous as to spoil the party by sitting out.
Ibid.

My valour is certainly going! it is sneaking off! I feel it oozing out, as it were, at the palm of my hands!
Ibid.

I own the soft impeachment.
Ibid.

Love gilds the scene, and women guide the plot.
Ibid. Epilogue

An apothecary should never be out of spirits.
St. Patrick's Day. Act I, Sc. 1

A fluent tongue is the only thing a

---

mother don't like her daughter to resemble her in.
St. Patrick's Day. Act I, Sc. 2

Death's a debt; his mandamus binds all alike — no bail, no demurrer.
Ibid. Act II, Sc. 4

I had rather follow you to your grave than see you owe your life to any but a regular-bred physician.
Ibid.

There is not a passion so strongly rooted in the human heart as envy.
The Critic. Act I, Sc. 1

Steal! to be sure they may; and, egad, serve your best thoughts as gypsies do stolen children, — disfigure them to make 'em pass for their own.[1]
Ibid.

The newspapers! Sir, they are the most villainous, licentious, abominable, infernal — Not that I ever read them! No, I make it a rule never to look into a newspaper.
Ibid.

Egad, I think the interpreter is the hardest to be understood of the two!
Ibid. Sc. 2

A practitioner in panegyric, or, to speak more plainly, a professor of the art of puffing.
Ibid.

Sheer necessity, — the proper parent of an art so nearly allied to invention.[2]
Ibid.

The number of those who undergo the fatigue of judging for themselves is very small indeed.[3]
Ibid.

---

[1] See Churchill, page 262.

[2] See Richard Franck, page 171.

[3] To the vast majority of mankind nothing is more agreeable than to escape the need for mental exertion. . . . To most people nothing is more troublesome than the effort of thinking. — JAMES BRYCE [1838-1922]: *Studies in History and Jurisprudence, Vol. 2, P. 7 and 8, Obedience*

We must view with profound respect the infinite capacity of the human mind to resist the introduction of useful knowledge. — THOMAS RAYNESFORD LOUNSBURY [1838-1915]: Quoted in *The Freshman and His College* [1913], by FRANCIS CUMMINS LOCKWOOD, *P. 44*

---

[1] Also in *The School for Scandal, Act V, Sc. 1.*

No scandal about Queen Elizabeth, I hope?

The Critic. Act II, Sc. 1

Certainly nothing is unnatural that is not physically impossible.

Ibid.

The Spanish fleet thou canst not see — because
— It is not yet in sight.[1]

Ibid.

Though hopeless love finds comfort in despair,
It never can endure a rival's bliss! [2]

Ibid. Act III, Sc. 1

An oyster may be crossed in love.[3]

Ibid.

I ne'er could any lustre see
In eyes that would not look on me;
I ne'er saw nectar on a lip
But where my own did hope to sip.

The Duenna. Act I, Sc. 2

I loved him for himself alone.

Ibid. Sc. 3

I was struck all of a heap.

Ibid. Act II, Sc. 2

A bumper of good liquor
Will end a contest quicker
Than justice, judge, or vicar.[4]

Ibid. Sc. 3

Conscience has no more to do with gallantry than it has with politics.

Ibid. Sc. 4

Tale-bearers are as bad as the tale-makers.

The School for Scandal. Act I, Sc. 1

You shall see them on a beautiful quarto page, where a neat rivulet of text shall meander through a meadow of margin.

Ibid.

You had no taste when you married me.

Ibid. Sc. 2

Here's to the maiden of bashful fifteen;
Here's to the widow of fifty;
Here's to the flaunting, extravagant quean,
And here's to the housewife that's thrifty!
Let the toast pass;
Drink to the lass;
I'll warrant she'll prove an excuse for the glass.

The School for Scandal. Act III, Sc. 3

An unforgiving eye, and a damned disinheriting countenance.

Ibid. Act IV, Sc. 1

Be just before you're generous.

Ibid.

There is no sentiment he has such faith in as that Charity begins at home.[1]

Ibid. Act V, Sc. 1

It was an amiable weakness.[2]

Ibid.

The Right Honorable gentleman is indebted to his memory for his jests, and to his imagination for his facts.

Sheridaniana. Speech in Reply to Mr. Dundas

You write with ease to show your breeding,
But easy writing's curst hard reading.

Clio's Protest. In MOORE's *Life of Sheridan, Vol. I, Page 155*

PHILIP FRENEAU
[1752–1832]

From Susquehanna's utmost springs
Where savage tribes pursue their game,
His blanket tied with yellow strings,
A shepherd of the forest came.

The Indian Student. Stanza 1

In spite of all the learned have said,
I still my old opinion keep;
The posture that we give the dead
Points out the soul's eternal sleep.

*The Indian Burying-Ground.
Stanza 1*

---

[1] From the interpolated tragedy, *The Spanish Armada.*
[2] The same.
[3] The same.
[4] The government of a nation is often decided over a cup of coffee, or the fate of empires changed by an extra bottle of Johannisberg. — GEORGE PAYNE RAINSFORD JAMES [1801–1860]: *Richelieu, Chap. 16*

[1] See Sir Thomas Browne, page 144.
[2] See Fielding, page 229 and Gibbon, page 270.

Then rushed to meet the insulting foe;
They took the spear, but left the
    shield.[1]

> *To the Memory of the Ameri-
> cans who Fell at Eutaw [Sep-
> tember 8, 1781]*

LEONARD McNALLY
[1752–1820]

On Richmond Hill there lived a lass
More bright than May-day morn;
Whose smiles all other maids' surpass,
A rose without a thorn.

> *The Lass of Richmond Hill.*
> *Stanza 1*

ROBERT HAWKER [2]
[1753–1827]

Lord, dismiss us with thy blessing,
Hope, and comfort from above;
Let us each, thy peace possessing,
Triumph in redeeming love.

> *Benediction*

JOEL BARLOW [3]
[1754–1813]

E'en Hasty-Pudding, purest of all food,
May still be bad, indifferent, or good,[4]
As sage experience the short process
    guides,
Or want of skill, or want of care pre-
    sides.

> *Hasty-Pudding*

The laws of husking every wight can
    tell —
And sure no laws he ever keeps so
    well:
For each red ear a general kiss he gains.

> *Ibid.*

GEORGE CRABBE
[1754–1832]

Oh, rather give me commentators plain,
Who with no deep researches vex the
    brain;

Who from the dark and doubtful love
    to run,
And hold their glimmering tapers to
    the sun.[1]

> *The Parish Register. Part I,*
> *Introduction*

In this fool's paradise he drank de-
    light.[2]

> *The Borough. Letter XII, Players*

Books cannot always please, however
    good;
Minds are not ever craving for their
    food.

> *Ibid. Letter XXIV, Schools*

In idle wishes fools supinely stay;
Be there a will, and wisdom finds a way.

> *The Birth of Flattery*

Cut and come again.

> *Tales. VII, The Widow's Tale*

Better to love amiss than nothing to
    have loved.[3]

> *Ibid. XIV, The Struggles of*
> *Conscience*

But 'twas a maxim he had often tried,
That right was right, and there he
    would abide.

> *Ibid. XV, The Squire and the*
> *Priest*

He tried the luxury of doing good.[4]

> *Tales of the Hall. Book III,*
> *Boys at School*

And took for truth the test of ridicule.[5]

> *Ibid. Book VIII, The Sisters*

Time has touched me gently in his race,
And left no odious furrows in my face.

> *Ibid. Book XVII, The Widow*

The ring, so worn as you behold,
So thin, so pale, is yet of gold.

> *A Marriage Ring*

GEORGE BARRINGTON
[1755–1804]

True patriots all; for be it understood

---

[1] When Prussia hurried to the field,
    And snatched the spear, but left the shield.
Scott: *Marmion, Introduction to Canto III*
[2] Not to be confused with Robert Stephen
Hawker [1803–1875].
[3] One of the (so-called) Hartford Wits.
[4] Good — bad — indifferent. — Laurence
Sterne: *Tristram Shandy, Book III, Chap. 2*

[1] See Young, page 203.
[2] See Shakespeare, page 79.
[3] 'Tis better to have loved and lost,
    Than never to have loved at all.
> Tennyson: *In Memoriam, St. 27*
[4] See Goldsmith, page 249.
[5] See Thomas Carlyle, page 377.

We left our country for our country's
good.[1]
> *Prologue Written for the Open-
> ing of the Play-house at New
> South Wales* [*January 16, 1796*]

HENRY LEE
[1756–1818]

To the memory of the Man, first in
war, first in peace, and first in the
hearts of his countrymen.
> *Memoirs of Lee. Eulogy on Wash-
> ington* [*December 26, 1799*] [2]

WILLIAM BLAKE
[1757–1827]

Little lamb, who made thee?
Dost thou know who made thee,
Gave thee life, and bid thee feed
By the streams and o'er the mead?
> *The Lamb. Stanza 1*

Piping down the valleys wild,
  Piping songs of pleasant glee,
On a cloud I saw a child.
> *Songs of Innocence. Introduction*

And I wrote my happy songs
  Every child may joy to hear.
> *Ibid.*

My mother bore me in the southern
wild,
And I am black, but O my soul is white!
> *The Little Black Boy. Stanza 1*

[1] See Farquhar, page 201. According to the
Oxford Companion to English Literature,
"Barrington" was the adopted name of a notorious pickpocket who was transported to
the penal settlement at Botany Bay.

[2] To the memory of the Man, first in war,
first in peace, and first in the hearts of his
fellow-citizens. — *Resolutions Presented to
the United States' House of Representatives,
on the Death of Washington* [December, 1799]
The eulogy was delivered a week later. Marshall, in his *Life of Washington, Vol. V,
P. 767*, says in a note that these resolutions
were prepared by Colonel Henry Lee, who
was then not in his place to read them. General Robert E. Lee, in the life of his father
[1869] prefixed to the Report of his father's
Memoirs of the War of the Revolution, gives
[*P. 5*] the expression "fellow-citizens"; but on
P. 52 he says: "But there is a line, a single line,
in the Works of Lee which would hand him
over to immortality, though he had never
written another: 'First in war, first in peace,
and first in the hearts of his countrymen' will
last while language lasts."

And we are put on earth a little space
  That we may learn to bear the beams
  of love.
> *The Little Black Boy. Stanza 4*

The moon, like a flower
In heaven's high bower,
With silent delight
Sits and smiles on the night.
> *Night. Stanza 1*

Love seeketh not itself to please,
  Nor for itself hath any care,
But for another gives its ease,
  And builds a heaven in hell's despair.
> *The Clod and the Pebble. Stanza 1*

Tiger, tiger, burning bright
In the forests of the night,
What immortal hand or eye
Could frame thy fearful symmetry?
> *The Tiger. Stanza 1*

To see the world in a grain of sand,
  And a heaven in a wild flower;
Hold infinity in the palm of your hand,
  And eternity in an hour.
> *Auguries of Innocence. Stanza 1*

He who doubts from what he sees
Will ne'er believe, do what you please.
If the Sun and Moon should doubt,
They'd immediately go out.
> *Ibid. Stanza 6*

He who bends to himself a Joy
Doth the wingèd life destroy;
But he who kisses the Joy as it flies
Lives in Eternity's sunrise.
> *Eternity*

I was angry with my friend:
I told my wrath, my wrath did end.
I was angry with my foe:
I told it not, my wrath did grow.
> *A Poison Tree. Stanza 1*

He who desires but acts not, breeds
  pestilence.
> *The Marriage of Heaven and Hell*

He who has suffer'd you to impose on
  him, knows you.
> *Ibid.*

A Robin Redbreast in a cage
Puts all heaven in a rage.
> *Proverbs. Line 1*

A dog starved at his master's gate
Predicts the ruin of the state.
> *Ibid. Line 5*

A horse misused upon the road
Calls to heaven for human blood.
                    Proverbs. Line 9
Tools were made, and born were hands,
Every farmer understands.
                    Ibid. Line 83
A truth that's told with bad intent
Beats all the lies you can invent.
                    Ibid. Line 95
Every night and every morn
Some to misery are born;
Every morn and every night
Some are born to sweet delight.
                    Ibid. Line 101
For the tear is an intellectual thing,
And a sigh is the sword of an Angel
        King;
And the bitter groan of a martyr's woe
Is an arrow from the Almighty's bow.
                The Grey Monk. Stanza 10
When I saw that rage was vain
And to sulk would nothing gain,
Turning many a trick and wile
I began to soothe and smile.
                    Infant Sorrow. Stanza 3
The Vision of Christ that thou dost see,
Is my vision's greatest enemy.
Thine is the friend of all Mankind,
Mine speaks in Parables to the blind.
                    The Everlasting Gospel
Seek Love in the pity of others' woe,
    In the gentle relief of another's care,
In the darkness of night and the win-
        ter's snow,
    With the naked and outcast — see
    Love there.
                William Bond. Stanza 13
Never seek to tell thy love.
                    Love's Secret. Stanza 1
The door of Death is made of gold,
That mortal eyes cannot behold.
                Dedication of the Designs for
                BLAIR'S *"Grave." To Queen*
                Charlotte
The Angel that presided at my birth
Said: "Little creature, formed of joy
        and mirth,
Go, love without the help of any thing
        on earth."
                Couplets and Fragments. 15
Great things are done when men and
    mountains meet;

This is not done by jostling in the
    street.
                    Gnomic Verses
The lineaments of gratified desire.
                    Ibid.
The Human Form Divine.[1]
                    The Divine Image
The busy bee has no time for sorrow.
                    Proverbs of Hell
    Think in the morning, act in the
noon, eat in the evening, sleep in the
night.
                    Ibid.
The weak in courage is strong in cunning.
                    Ibid.
Improvement makes straight roads,
but the crooked roads without improve-
ment are roads of genius.
                    Ibid.
Poetry fettered, fetters the human
race. Nations are destroyed or flourish
in proportion as their poetry, painting,
and music are destroyed or flourish.[2]
            Jerusalem. Preface to Chapter 1
A man's worst enemies are those
    Of his own house and family.
        Ibid. Preface to Chapter 2, Stanza 21
I give you the end of a golden string:
    Only wind it into a ball, —
It will lead you in at Heaven's gate,
    Built in Jerusalem's wall.
            Ibid. Preface to Chapter 4
And did those feet in ancient time
    Walk upon England's mountain
        green?
And was the holy Lamb of God
    On England's pleasant pastures seen?
                    Milton
Bring me my bow of burning gold!
    Bring me my arrows of desire!
                    Ibid.

[1] This phrase is used several times by Blake.
See also Pope, page 220.
[2] Vain was the chief's, the sage's pride!
    They had no poet, and they died.
    ALEXANDER POPE: *Odes of Horace, Book IV,*
                    Ode IX, St. 4
They built with bronze and gold and brawn,
    The inner Vision still denied;
Their conquests . . . Ask oblivion! . . .
"They had no poet, and they died."
    DON MARQUIS: *"They Had No Poet . . ."*
                    St. 6

I will not cease from mental fight,
  Nor shall my sword sleep in my
    hand,
Till we have built Jerusalem
  In England's green and pleasant
    land.

Milton

JOHN PHILIP KEMBLE
[1757–1823]

Perhaps it was right to dissemble your
  love,
But — why did you kick me down
  stairs? [1]

The Panel. Act I, Sc. 1

ROYALL TYLER
[1757–1826]

Why should our thoughts to distant
  countries roam,
When each refinement may be found
  at home?

The Contrast. Prologue

We all are mortals, and as mortals err.[2]

Ibid.

This outlandish lingo.

Ibid. Act II, Sc. 2

By the living jingo, you look so top-
ping, I took you for one of the agents
to Congress.

Ibid.

Since General Shays has sneaked off
and given us the bag to hold.

Ibid.

Father and I went to camp,
Along with Captain Goodwin;
And there we saw the men and boys
As thick as hasty pudding,
  Yankee Doodle do.

Ibid. Act III, Sc. 1

I am at the end of my tether.

Ibid.

Every possible display of jocularity,
from an *affettuoso* smile to a *piano* titter, or full chorus *fortissimo* ha, ha, ha!

• *Ibid. Act V, Sc. 1*

---

[1] Altered from BICKERSTAFF'S *'Tis Well 'tis
no Worse*. The lines are also found in DE-
BRETT'S *Asylum for Fugitive Pieces, Vol. I,
P. 15*
[2] To err is human. — POPE: *Essay on Criticism, Part II, L. 325*

JAMES MONROE [1]
[1758–1831]

National honor is national property
of the highest value.

*First Inaugural Address [March 4,
1817]*

The American continents . . . are
henceforth not to be considered as subjects for future colonization by any European powers.

*Annual Message to Congress
[December, 1823] (The Monroe Doctrine)*

We owe it, therefore, to candor, and
to the amicable relations existing between the United States and those powers to declare that we should consider
any attempt on their part to extend
their system to any portion of this
hemisphere as dangerous to our peace
and safety. With the existing colonies
or dependencies of any European power
we . . . shall not interfere. But with
the governments . . . whose independence we have . . . acknowledged, we
could not view any interposition for
the purpose of oppressing them, or controlling, in any other manner, their
destiny, by any European power, in any
other light than as a manifestation of
an unfriendly disposition towards the
United States.

Ibid.

HORATIO NELSON
[1758–1805]

In the battle off Cape St. Vincent,
Nelson gave orders for boarding the
"San Josef," exclaiming "Westminster
Abbey, or victory!"

SOUTHEY'S *Life of Nelson. Vol. I,
Page 93*

---

[1] Monroe's administration was called the
"Era of Good Feeling" (title of an article in
the *Boston Centinel, July 12, 1817*) because
he had practically no opposition, the Federalist party having passed out of existence, and
because the declaration of his "Doctrine" did
much to keep the United States clear of European politics.

England expects every man to do his
duty.[1]
SOUTHEY'S *Life of Nelson.*
Vol. II, Page 131

May the great God, whom I worship,
grant to my country and for the benefit
of Europe in general, a great and glorious victory, and may no misconduct
in anyone tarnish it, and may humanity after the victory be the predominant
feature in the British fleet.
Prayer written in his diary [Octo-
ber 21, 1805]

ROBERT BURNS
[1759–1796]

Auld Nature swears the lovely dears
　Her noblest work she classes, O;
Her 'prentice han' she tried on man,
　And then she made the lasses, O!
　Green Grow the Rashes. Stanza 5
Some books are lies frae end to end.
　Death and Dr. Hornbook. Stanza 1
Some wee short hour ayont the twal.
　Ibid. Stanza 31
The best laid schemes o' mice and men
　Gang aft a-gley;
An' lea'e us nought but grief and pain,
　For promis'd joy.
　To a Mouse. Stanza 7
When chill November's surly blast
　Made fields and forests bare.
　Man Was Made to Mourn. Stanza 1
Man's inhumanity to man
Makes countless thousands mourn.
　Ibid. Stanza 7
Gars auld claes look amaist as weel's
　the new.
　*The Cotter's Saturday Night.
　Stanza 5*
Beneath the milk-white thorn that
　scents the evening gale.
　Ibid. Stanza 9
He wales a portion with judicious care;

And "Let us worship God," he says,
　with solemn air.
　*The Cotter's Saturday Night.
　Stanza 12*
From scenes like these, old Scotia's
　grandeur springs,
　That makes her loved at home, re-
　　vered abroad:
Princes and lords are but the breath
　of kings,
　"An honest man's the noblest work
　　of God."[1]
　Ibid. Stanza 19
For a' that, and a' that,
An' twice as muckle 's a' that.
　The Jolly Beggars
John Barleycorn got up again,
And sore surpris'd them all.
　John Barleycorn. Stanza 3
Life is but a day at most,
Sprung from night,—in darkness lost:
Hope not sunshine ev'ry hour,
Fear not clouds will always lour.
　*Written in Friars Carse Hermitage.
　Stanza 2*
Gie me ae spark o' Nature's fire,
That's a' the learning I desire.
　First Epistle to J. Lapraik. Stanza 13
Gif ye want ae friend that's true,
I'm on your list.
　Ibid. Stanza 15
I winna blaw about mysel,
As ill I like my fauts to tell.
　Ibid. Stanza 16
My worthy friend, ne'er grudge an'
　carp,
Tho' Fortune use you hard an' sharp.
　*Second Epistle to J. Lapraik.
　Stanza 8*
The social, friendly, honest man,
　Whate'er he be,
'Tis he fulfils great Nature's plan,
　And none but he.
　Ibid. Stanza 15
Morality, thou deadly bane,
Thy tens o' thousands thou hast slain!
　A Dedication to Gavin Hamilton
It's hardly in a body's pow'r,
To keep, at times, frae being sour.
　Epistle to Davie. Stanza 2

---

[1] This famous sentence is thus first reported: "Say to the fleet, England confides
that every man will do his duty." Captain
Pasco, Nelson's flag-lieutenant, suggested sub-
stituting "expects" for "confides," which was
adopted. Captain Blackwood, who commanded the *Euryalus,* says that the correction
suggested was from "Nelson expects" to "England expects."

[1] See Fletcher, page 126.

The mair they talk, I'm kend the bet-
ter;
  E'en let them clash.
    A Poet's Welcome to His Love-
      Begotten Daughter. Stanza 2
God knows, I'm no the thing I should
be,
Nor am I even the thing I could be.
    To the Reverend John M'Math,
             Stanza 8
O Life! how pleasant, in thy morning,
Young Fancy's rays the hills adorn-
ing!
Cold-pausing Caution's lesson scorn-
ing,
    We frisk away,
Like schoolboys, at th' expected warn-
ing,
    To joy an' play.
    Epistle to James Smith. Stanza 15
Misled by fancy's meteor ray,
    By passion driven;
But yet the light that led astray
    Was light from heaven.
      The Vision. II, Stanza 18
And, like a passing thought, she fled
  In light away.
        Ibid. Stanza 24
Affliction's sons are brothers in distress;
A brother to relieve, — how exquisite
  the bliss!
    A Winter Night. Stanza 8
His lockèd, lettered, braw brass collar
Showed him the gentleman an' scholar.
    The Twa Dogs. Stanza 3
An' there began a lang digression
About the lords o' the creation.
        Ibid. Stanza 6
Oh wad some power the giftie gie us
To see oursels as others see us!
It wad frae monie a blunder free us,
    An' foolish notion.
      To a Louse. Stanza 8
A dear loved lad, convenience snug,
  A treacherous inclination —
But, let me whisper i' your lug,
  Ye're aiblins nae temptation.
  Address to the Unco Guid. Stanza 6
Then gently scan your brother man,
  Still gentler sister woman;
Though they may gang a kennin
  wrang,

To step aside is human.
  Address to the Unco Guid. Stanza 7
What's done we partly may compute,
  But know not what's resisted.
        Ibid. Stanza 8
Stern Ruin's ploughshare drives elate,
  Full on thy bloom.
    To a Mountain Daisy. Stanza 9
O life! thou art a galling load,
Along a rough, a weary road,
  To wretches such as I!
      Despondency. Stanza 1
Perhaps it may turn out a sang,
Perhaps turn out a sermon.
  Epistle to a Young Friend. Stanza 1
A man may tak a neebor's part,
  Yet hae nae cash to spare him.
        Ibid. Stanza 4
I waive the quantum o' the sin,
  The hazard of concealing;
But, och! it hardens a' within,
  And petrifies the feeling!
        Ibid. Stanza 6
To catch Dame Fortune's golden smile,
  Assiduous wait upon her;
And gather gear by ev'ry wile
  That's justified by honor:
Not for to hide it in a hedge,
  Nor for a train-attendant;
But for the glorious privilege
  Of being independent.
        Ibid. Stanza 7
The fear o' hell's a hangman's whip
  To haud the wretch in order;
But where ye feel your honour grip,
  Let that ay be your border.
        Ibid. Stanza 8
An atheist's laugh's a poor exchange
  For Deity offended!
        Ibid. Stanza 9
And may ye better reck the rede,
  Than ever did the adviser!
        Ibid. Stanza 11
If there's another world, he lives in
  bliss;
If there is none, he made the best of
  this.
    Epitaph on William Muir
Shall I like a fool, quoth he,
For a haughty hizzie die?
She may gae to — France for me! —
Ha, ha, the wooing o't!
    Duncan Gray. Stanza 3

When Nature her great masterpiece
    design'd,
And fram'd her last, best work, the hu-
    man mind,
Her eye intent on all the wondrous
    plan,
She form'd of various stuff the various
    Man.
        To Robert Graham. Stanza 1
Flow gently, sweet Afton, among thy
    green braes;
Flow gently, I'll sing thee a song in thy
    praise.
    Flow Gently, Sweet Afton. Stanza 1
Oh whistle, and I'll come to ye, my lad.[1]
    Whistle, and I'll Come to Ye. Chorus
Naebody cares for me,
I care for naebody.
    I Hae a Wife o' my Ain. Stanza 4
Should auld acquaintance be forgot,
    And never brought to mind?
Should auld acquaintance be forgot,
    And auld lang syne?
        Auld Lang Syne. Stanza 1
We twa hae run about the braes,
    And pou'd the gowans fine.
        Ibid. Stanza 3
We'll tak a cup o' kindness yet
    For auld lang syne!
        Ibid. Stanza 5
To make a happy fireside clime
    To weans and wife,
That's the true pathos and sublime
    Of human life.
    Epistle to Dr. Blacklock. Stanza 9
If there's a hole in a' your coats,
    I rede you tent it;
A chiel's amang you takin' notes,
    And faith he'll prent it.
    On the Late Captain Grose's
    Peregrinations thro' Scotland.
    Stanza 1
John Anderson my jo, John,
    When we were first acquent,
Your locks were like the raven,
    Your bonny brow was brent.
        John Anderson. Stanza 1
This day Time winds th' exhausted
    chain,
To run the twelvemonth's length again.
    New Year's Day, 1791. Stanza 1

[1] See Beaumont and Fletcher, page 131.

The voice of Nature loudly cries,
And many a message from the skies,
That something in us never dies.
    New Year's Day, 1791. Stanza 3
My heart's in the Highlands, my heart
    is not here;
My heart's in the Highlands a-chasing
    the deer.[1]
    My Heart's in the Highlands.
    Chorus
She is a winsome wee thing,
She is a handsome wee thing,
She is a lo'esome wee thing,
This sweet wee wife o' mine.
    My Wife's a Winsome Wee Thing.
    Chorus
The golden hours on angel wings
    Flew o'er me and my dearie;
For dear to me as light and life
    Was my sweet Highland Mary.
        Highland Mary. Stanza 2
But, oh! fell death's untimely frost,
    That nipt my flower sae ear.,.
        Ibid. Stanza 3
It's guid to be merry and wise,
It's guid to be honest and true,
It's guid to support Caledonia's cause
And bide by the buff and the blue.
    Here's a Health to Them that's
        Awa'. Stanza 1
Scots, wha hae wi' Wallace bled,
Scots, wham Bruce has aften led,
Welcome to your gory bed,
    Or to victory!
Now's the day and now's the hour;
See the front o' battle lour.
    Scots, Wha Hae [Bannockburn].
        Stanzas 1 and 2
Liberty's in every blow!
    Let us do, or die.[2]
        Ibid. Stanza 6
In durance vile [3] here must I wake and
    weep,
And all my frowsy couch in sorrow
    steep.
    Epistle from Esopus to Maria

[1] These lines, from an old ballad, entitled
The Strong Walls of Derry, Burns made a
basis for his own beautiful song.
[2] See Fletcher, page 127.
[3] Durance vile. — W. KENRICK [1766]:
Falstaff's Wedding, Act I, Sc. 2. BURKE: *The
Present Discontents*

Oh, my luve is like a red, red rose,
  That's newly sprung in June;
Oh, my luve is like the melodie,
  That's sweetly played in tune.
        A Red, Red Rose. Stanza 1
Contented wi' little, and cantie wi'
  mair.
        Contented wi' Little. Stanza 1
Whare sits our sulky, sullen dame,
Gathering her brows like gathering
  storm,
Nursing her wrath to keep it warm.
        Tam o' Shanter. Stanza 1
Ah, gentle dames! it gars me greet
To think how monie counsels sweet,
How monie lengthened, sage advices,
The husband frae the wife despises.
        Ibid. Stanza 4
His ancient, trusty, drouthy cronie;
Tam lo'ed him like a vera brither, —
They had been fou for weeks thegither.
        Ibid. Stanza 5
The landlady and Tam grew gracious
Wi' secret favours, sweet and precious.
        Ibid.
The landlord's laugh was ready chorus.
        Ibid.
Kings may be blest, but Tam was
  glorious,
O'er a' the ills o' life victorious.
        Ibid. Stanza 6
But pleasures are like poppies spread,
You seize the flower, its bloom is shed;
Or like the snow falls in the river,
A moment white, then melts forever.
        Ibid. Stanza 7
That hour, o' night's black arch the
  keystane.
        Ibid.
Inspiring bold John Barleycorn,
What dangers thou canst make us
  scorn!
        Ibid. Stanza 11
As Tammie glow'red, amazed, and curi-
  ous,
The mirth and fun grew fast and furi-
  ous.
        Ibid. Stanza 13
Her cutty sark,[1] o' Paisley harn,
That while a lassie she had worn,

[1] The famous tea clipper, *Cutty Sark*, designed by Hercules Linton, and built in 1869,
had the story of Tam o' Shanter carved upon

In longitude tho' sorely scanty,
It was her best, and she was vauntie.
        Tam o' Shanter. Stanza 16
But to see her was to love her,
Love but her, and love forever.
        Ae Fond Kiss. Stanza 2
Had we never loved sae kindly,
Had we never loved sae blindly,
Never met — or never parted —
We had ne'er been broken-hearted!
        Ibid.
Ye banks and braes o' bonny Doon,
  How can ye bloom sae fresh and fair?
How can ye chant, ye little birds,
  And I sae weary fu' o' care?
        The Banks o' Doon. Stanza 1
Chords that vibrate sweetest pleasure
Thrill the deepest notes of woe.
  Sensibility How Charming. Stanza 4
The rank is but the guinea's stamp,
The man's the gowd for a' that.
    Is There for Honest Poverty.
        Stanza 1
A prince can mak a belted knight,
  A marquis, duke, and a' that;
But an honest man's aboon his might,
  Guid faith, he mauna fa' that.
        Ibid. Stanza 4
Some hae meat and canna eat,
  And some wad eat that want it;
But we hae meat, and we can eat,
  And sae the Lord be thankit.
        The Selkirk Grace.[1]
It was a' for our rightfu' King
We left fair Scotland's strand.
  It Was a' for Our Rightful King.[2]
        Stanza 1
Now a' is done that men can do,
  And a' is done in vain.
        Ibid. Stanza 2
He turn'd him right and round about
  Upon the Irish shore,
And gae his bridle reins a shake,

her bow and counter. Nannie with flying locks
and scanty chemise was the figurehead.
[1] A note prefacing the verse says: "Allan
Cunningham records that this very characteristic 'Grace before meat' was uttered at the
table of the Earl of Selkirk, while on his tour
through Galloway with his friend Syme in
July, 1793. — William Scott Douglas."
[2] This ballad first appeared in JOHNSON'S
Museum [1796]. Sir Walter Scott was never
tired of hearing it sung.

With adieu for evermore,
    My dear —
And adieu for evermore! [1]
    It Was a' for Our Rightful King.
        Stanza 3

JOHN FERRIAR
[1761–1815]

The princeps copy, clad in blue and gold.
    *Illustrations of Sterne. Biblio-
        mania, Line 6*
Now cheaply bought for thrice their weight in gold.
    Ibid. Line 65
How pure the joy, when first my hands unfold
The small, rare volume, black with tarnished gold!
    Ibid. Line 137

JOANNA BAILLIE
[1762–1851]

Oh, swiftly glides the bonnie boat,
    Just parted from the shore,
And to the fisher's chorus-note
    Soft moves the dipping oar.[2]
        *Oh, Swiftly Glides the Bonnie
            Boat*
The wild-fire dances on the fen,
    The red star sheds its ray;
Uprouse ye then, my merry men!
    It is our op'ning day.
        The Outlaw's Song. Stanza 1
The gowan glitters on the sward,
    The laverock's in the sky,
And Collie on my plaid keeps ward,
    And time is passing by.
        *The Gowan Glitters on the Sward.
            Stanza 1*

[1] Under the impression that this stanza is ancient, Scott has made very free use of it, first in *Rokeby* [1813], and then in *The Monastery* [1816]. In *Rokeby* he thus introduces the verse: —
    He turn'd his charger as he spake,
        Upon the river shore,
    He gave his bridle reins a shake,
        Said, "Adieu for evermore, my love,
        And adieu for evermore."
[2] Our voices keep tune and our oars keep time. — Thomas Moore: *Canadian Boat Song, St. 1*

Oh, who shall lightly say that fame
Is nothing but an empty name,
When but for those, our mighty dead,
All ages past a blank would be.
    The Worth of Fame. Stanza 2
Good-morrow to thy sable beak
And glossy plumage dark and sleek,
Thy crimson moon and azure eye,
Cock of the heath, so wildly shy.
    The Heath-Cock. Stanza 1

ANDREW CHERRY
[1762–1812]

Loud roared the dreadful thunder,
    The rain a deluge showers.
        The Bay of Biscay
As she lay, on that day,
In the bay of Biscay, O!
        Ibid.

GEORGE COLMAN, THE YOUNGER
[1762–1836]

On their own merits modest men are dumb.
    Epilogue to the Heir at Law
And what's impossible can't be,
And never, never comes to pass.
    The Maid of the Moor
Three stories high, long, dull, and old,
As great lords' stories often are.
        Ibid.
        But when ill indeed,
E'en dismissing the doctor don't always succeed.
    Lodgings for Single Gentlemen
When taken,
To be well shaken.
    The Newcastle Apothecary
        O Miss Bailey!
Unfortunate Miss Bailey!
    *Love Laughs at Locksmiths.
        Act II, Song*
'Tis a very fine thing to be father-in-law
To a very magnificent three-tailed Bashaw!
    Blue Beard. Act II, Sc. 5
I had a soul above buttons.
    *Sylvester Daggerwood, or New
        Hay at the Old Market. Sc. 1*

Mynheer Vandunck, though he never
was drunk,
Sipped brandy and water gayly.
Mynheer Vandunck

SAMUEL ROGERS
[1763-1855]

Sweet Memory! wafted by thy gentle
gale,
Oft up the stream of Time I turn my
sail.
The Pleasures of Memory. Part II, I

She was good as she was fair,
None — none on earth above her!
As pure in thought as angels are:
To know her was to love her.[1]
Jacqueline.[2] Stanza 1

The good are better made by ill,
As odours crushed are sweeter still.[3]
Ibid. Stanza 3

A guardian angel o'er his life presiding,
Doubling his pleasures, and his cares
dividing.
Human Life

To fireside happiness, to hours of ease
Blest with that charm, the certainty to
please.
Ibid.

The soul of music slumbers in the shell
Till waked and kindled by the master's
spell;
And feeling hearts, touch them but
rightly, pour
A thousand melodies unheard before!
Ibid.

Then never less alone than when alone.[4]
Ibid.

Those whom he loved so long and sees
no more,

Loved and still loves, — not dead, but
gone before.[1]
Human Life

Mine be a cot beside the hill;
A beehive's hum shall soothe my
ear;
A willowy brook that turns a mill,
With many a fall shall linger near.
A Wish. Stanza 1

That very law which moulds a tear
And bids it trickle from its source, —
That law preserves the earth a sphere,
And guides the planets in their course.
On a Tear. Stanza 6

Go! you may call it madness, folly;
You shall not chase my gloom away!
There's such a charm in melancholy
I would not if I could be gay.
To ——. Stanza 1

There is a glorious city in the sea,
The sea is in the broad, the narrow
streets,
Ebbing and flowing; and the salt sea-
weed
Clings to the marble of her palaces.
Italy. Venice

Lo, a skeleton,
With here and there a pearl, an em-
erald stone,
A golden clasp, clasping a shred of
gold;
All else had perished — save a nuptial
ring,
And a small seal, her mother's legacy,
Engraven with a name, the name of
both, "Ginevra."
Ibid. Ginevra[2] [Modena]

To vanish in the chinks that Time has
made.[3]
Ibid. Pæstum

Ward has no heart, they say, but I
deny it:
He has a heart, and gets his speeches
by it.
Epigram

---

[1] See Burns, page 287.
None knew thee but to love thee. — HAL-
LECK: *On the Death of Joseph Rodman Drake.*
[2] First published in the same volume with
Byron's *Lara* [1813], neither author append-
ing his name to his work.
[3] See Bacon, page 109.
[4] See Gibbon, page 271.
Numquam se minus otiosum esse, quam
quum otiosus, nec minus solum, quam quum
solus esset (He is never less at leisure than
when at leisure, not less alone than when he is
alone). — CICERO: *De Officiis, Liber III, C. 1,*
quoting Publius Scipio

[1] This is literally from SENECA, *Epistola
LXIII,* 16. See Mathew Henry, page 188.
[2] THOMAS HAYNES BAYLY's poem, *The Mistletoe Bough,* relates the same legend of the
bride accidentally imprisoned in a chest on her
wedding night.
[3] See Waller, page 146.

ROBERT HALL
[1764–1831]

His [Burke's] imperial fancy has laid all Nature under tribute, and has collected riches from every scene of the creation and every walk of art.
Apology for the Freedom of the Press

He [Kippis] might be a very clever man by nature for aught I know, but he laid so many books upon his head that his brains could not move.
GREGORY's *Life of Hall*

Call things by their right names. . . . Glass of brandy and water! That is the current but not the appropriate name: ask for a glass of liquid fire and distilled damnation.
Ibid.

THOMAS MORTON
[1764–1838]

What will Mrs. Grundy say? What will Mrs. Grundy think?
Speed the Plough [*1798*]. *Act I, Sc. 1*

Push on, — keep moving.
A Cure for the Heartache. Act II, Sc. 1

Approbation from Sir Hubert Stanley is praise indeed.
Ibid. Act V, Sc. 2

ANN RADCLIFFE
[1764–1823]

Fate sits on these dark battlements and frowns,
And as the portal opens to receive me,
A voice in hollow murmurs through the courts
Tells of a nameless deed.
Motto of her novel, The Mysteries of Udolpho, and presumably of her own composition

HELEN D'ARCY CRANSTOUN (MRS. DUGALD STEWART)
[1765–1838]

I weep not for the silent dead,
Their pains are past, their sorrows o'er.[1]
The Song of Genius

CATHERINE MARIA FANSHAWE
[1765–1834]

'Twas whisper'd in heaven, 'twas mutter'd in hell,
And echo caught faintly the sound as it fell;
On the confines of earth 'twas permitted to rest,
And the depths of the ocean its presence confess'd.
Enigma: The Letter H

MARY LAMB
[1765–1847]

Thou straggler into loving arms,
Young climber-up of knees.
A Child. Stanza 3

SIR JAMES MACKINTOSH
[1765–1832]

Diffused knowledge immortalizes itself.
Vindiciæ Gallicæ

The Commons, faithful to their system, remained in a wise and masterly inactivity.
Ibid.

Disciplined inaction.
Causes of the Revolution of 1688. Chap. VII

The frivolous work of polished idleness.
Dissertation on Ethical Philosophy. Remarks on Thomas Brown

---

[1] Quoted by SIR WALTER SCOTT in *The Talisman, Chap. 26.*

ISAAC DISRAELI
[1766–1848]

They [the early writers] looked with alarm upon the halo of immortality that encircled the printing-press.

Amenities of Literature. Vol. II,
Page 278 [1840]

Whatever is felicitously expressed risks being worse expressed: it is a wretched taste to be gratified with mediocrity when the excellent lies before us.

Curiosities of Literature. On Quotation.

CAROLINA OLIPHANT,
LADY NAIRNE
[1766–1845]

Sweet's the laverock's note and lang,
  Lilting wildly up the glen;
But aye to me he sings ae sang,
  Will ye no come back again?
    Will Ye No Come Back Again?
      Stanza 5

Would you be young again?
So would not I —
One tear to memory given,
  Onward I'd hie.
    Would You Be Young Again?
    [Looking Backward]. Stanza 1

I'm wearin' awa'
  To the land o' the leal.
There's nae sorrow there, John,
There's neither cauld nor care, John,
The day is aye fair
  In the land o' the leal.
    The Land o' the Leal. Stanza 1

Gude nicht, and joy be wi' you a'.
    Gude Nicht.[1]

Oh, we're a' noddin', nid, nid, noddin';
Oh, we're a' noddin' at our house at hame.
    We're a' Noddin'

A penniless lass wi' a lang pedigree.
    The Laird o' Cockpen. Stanza 2

Oh! for ane I'll get better, it's waur
  I'll get ten,

---

[1] SIR ALEXANDER BOSWELL [1775–1822], eldest son of James Boswell, biographer of Dr. Johnson, composed a version of this song.

I was daft to refuse the Laird o' Cockpen.
    The Laird o' Cockpen. Stanza 8

NANCY DENNIS SPROAT
[1766–1826]

Why, Phoebe, are you come so soon?
  Where are your berries, child?
You cannot, sure, have sold them all,
  You had your basket piled.
    The Blackberry Girl.[1] *Stanza 1*

How pleasant is Saturday night,
  When I've tried all the week to be good,
And not spoke a word that was bad,
  And obliged every one that I could.
    Lullabies for Children [1818].
      Saturday Night,[2] *Stanza 1*

To-morrow our holy day comes,
  Which our merciful Father has given,
That we may rest from our work
  And prepare for His beautiful heaven.
    Ibid. Stanza 2

JOHN QUINCY ADAMS
[1767–1848]

Think of your forefathers! Think of your posterity![3]

Speech at Plymouth [December 22, 1802]

In charity to all mankind, bearing no malice or ill-will to any human being, and even compassionating those who hold in bondage their fellow-men, not knowing what they do.[4]

Letter to A. Bronson [July 30, 1838]

My wants are many, and, if told,
  Would muster many a score;

---

[1] From Salem Town's *Third Reader.*
[2] Pierpont's *Reader* [1831].
[3] Et majores vestros et posteros cogitate.
— TACITUS: *Agricola, C. 32, 26*
[4] With malice towards none, with charity for all, with firmness in the right, as God gives us to see the right. — ABRAHAM LINCOLN: *Second Inaugural Address*

And were each wish a mint of gold,
  I still should long for more.
        *The Wants of Man, Stanza 1.
        In The Quincy [Massachu-
        setts] Patriot, September 25,
        1841*

In days of yore, the poet's pen
  From wing of bird was plundered,
Perhaps of goose, but now and then
  From Jove's own eagle sundered.
But now, metallic pens disclose
  Alone the poet's numbers;
In iron inspiration glows,
  Or with the poet slumbers.
                    The Pen

This is the last of earth! I am content.
        *His Last Words [February 21,
                            1848]*

ANDREW JACKSON
[1767–1845]

Our Federal Union: it must be preserved.
        *Toast given on the Jefferson Birth-
            day Celebration [1830]*
  You are uneasy; you never sailed
with *me* before, I see.[1]
    PARTON's *Life of Jackson. Vol. III,
                        Page 493*

DAVID EVERETT
[1769–1813]

You'd scarce expect one of my age
To speak in public on the stage;
And if I chance to fall below
Demosthenes or Cicero,
Don't view me with a critic's eye,
But pass my imperfections by.
Large streams from little fountains
    flow,
Tall oaks from little acorns grow.[2]
        *Lines written for a school dec-
        lamation for Ephraim H. Far-
        rar, aged seven, New Ipswich,
        New Hampshire [1791]*

---

[1] A remark made to an elderly gentleman
who was sailing with Jackson down Chesapeake Bay in an old steamboat, and who exhibited a little fear.
  [2] The lofty oak from a small acorn grows.
— LEWIS DUNCOMBE [1711–1730]: *De Mini-
mis Maxima* (translation)
  Parvis e glandibus quercus. — Latin motto

These thoughts inspire my youthful
    mind
To be the greatest of mankind;
Great, not like Caesar, stained with
    blood,
But only great as I am good.
        *Lines written for a school dec-
            lamation. [1791]*

JOHN HOOKHAM FRERE
[1769–1846]

And don't confound the language of
    the nation
With long-tailed words in *osity* and
    ation.
        *The Monks and the Giants. Canto I,
                            Line 6*
  A sudden thought strikes me, — let
us swear an eternal friendship.[1]
        The Rovers. Act I, Sc. 1
Despair in vain sits brooding over
the putrid eggs of hope.
                    Ibid. Sc. 2
I've often wished that I could write a
    book,
  Such as all English people might pe-
    ruse;
I never should regret the pains it took,
  That's just the sort of fame that I
    should chuse.
        *Prospectus and Specimen of an
        Intended National Work. Proem,
        Stanza 1*
It grieves me much, that names that
    were respected
In former ages, persons of such mark,
And countrymen of ours, should lie
    neglected,
  Just like old portraits, lumbering in
    the dark.
                    Ibid. Stanza 10

ARTHUR WELLESLEY,
DUKE OF WELLINGTON
[1769–1852]

Nothing except a battle lost can be
half so melancholy as a battle won.
                Despatch [1815]

---

[1] See Otway, page 185, and Sydney Smith,
page 313.
  My fair one, let us swear an eternal friendship. — MOLIÈRE: *Le Bourgeois Gentilhomme,
Act IV, Sc. 1*

It is very true that I have said that I considered Napoleon's presence in the field equal to forty thousand men in the balance. This is a very loose way of talking; but the idea is a very different one from that of his presence at a battle being equal to a reinforcement of forty thousand men.

Memoir [1] [*September 18, 1836*]

Circumstances over which I have no control.[2]

I never saw so many shocking bad hats in my life.[3]

Upon seeing the first Reformed Parliament

There is no mistake; there has been no mistake; and there shall be no mistake.

Letter to Mr. Huskisson

I care not one two-penny damn.[4]

The battle of Waterloo was won on the playing fields of Eton.

Attributed to the Duke of Wellington

GEORGE CANNING
[1770–1827]

Weary knife-grinder! little think the proud ones,
Who in their coaches roll along the turnpike-road,
What hard work 'tis crying all day "Knives and
Scissors to grind, oh!"

The Friend of Humanity and the Knife-Grinder. Stanza 2

Story! God bless you! I have none to tell, sir.

The Friend of Humanity and the Knife-Grinder. Stanza 6

I give thee sixpence! I will see thee damned first.

Ibid. Stanza 9

And finds, with keen, discriminating sight,
Black's not so black, — nor white so *very* white.

New Morality

Give me the avowed, the erect, the manly foe,
Bold I can meet, — perhaps may turn his blow!
But of all plagues, good Heaven, thy wrath can send,
Save, save, oh save me from the *candid friend!* [1]

Ibid.

I think of those companions true
Who studied with me at the U--niversity of Göttingen.

Song sung by Rogero in the burlesque play, The Rover. Stanza 1

Here rests, and let no saucy knave
Presume to sneer and laugh,
To learn that mouldering in the grave
Is laid a British Calf.

Epitaph on the Tombstone Erected over the Marquis of Anglesea's Leg, Lost at the Battle of Waterloo. Stanza 1

She saw two legs were lost on him
Who never meant to run.

Ibid. Stanza 9

In matters of commerce the fault of the Dutch
Is offering too little and asking too much.

Dispatch to Sir Charles Bagot, British Minister at The Hague [January 31, 1826]

I called the New World into existence to redress the balance of the Old.

The King's Message [December 12, 1826]

---

[1] PHILIP HENRY STANHOPE [1805–1875]: *Notes of Conversations with Wellington* [1888], *P. 81*

[2] This phrase was first used by the Duke of Wellington in a letter, about 1839 or 1840. — SALA: *Echoes of the Week*, in *London Illustrated News, Aug. 23, 1884.* GREVILLE, *Memoirs, Ch. II* [1823], gives an earlier instance.

[3] SIR WILLIAM FRASER, in *Words on Wellington* [1889], *P. 12*, says this phrase originated with the Duke. CAPTAIN GRONOW, in his *Recollections*, says it originated with the Duke of York, second son of George III, about 1817.

[4] It was the Duke of Wellington who invented this oath, so disproportionate to the greatness of its author. — GEORGE OTTO TREVELYAN: *Life and Letters of Lord Macaulay, Vol. II, P. 221*

[1] "Defend me from my friends; I can defend myself from my enemies." The French *Ana* assign to Maréchal Villars this aphorism when taking leave of Louis XIV.

So down thy hill, romantic Ashbourn,
    glides
The Derby dilly, carrying *three* IN-
SIDES.
> *The Loves of the Triangles.*
> *Line 178*

Here's to the pilot that weathered the
storm!
> *The Pilot that Weathered the*
> *Storm*

JAMES HOGG [1]
[1770–1835]

Blest be the day Kilmeny was born!
Now shall the land of the spirits see,
Now shall it ken what a woman may
be!
> *Kilmeny*

She left this world of sorrow and pain,
And returned to the Land of Thought
again.
> *Ibid.*

Charlie is my darling,
The young Chevalier.
> *Charlie is My Darling. Refrain*

Bird of the wilderness,
Blithesome and cumberless.
> *The Skylark*

Love is like a dizziness,
It winna let a poor body
Gang about his bizziness.
> *Love is Like a Dizziness. Stanza 1*

JOSEPH HOPKINSON
[1770–1842]

Hail, Columbia! happy land!
Hail, ye heroes! heaven-born band!
    Who fought and bled in Freedom's
    cause,
    Who fought and bled in Freedom's
    cause,
And when the storm of war was gone,
Enjoyed the peace your valor won.
    Let independence be our boast,
    Ever mindful what it cost;
    Ever grateful for the prize,
    Let its altar reach the skies!
> *Hail, Columbia.[2] Stanza 1*

[1] The "Ettrick Shepherd."
[2] The musical setting of *Hail, Columbia,*
generally attributed to Philip Phile, was orig-

GEORGE NUGENT
REYNOLDS
[1770–1802]

Every night
The cottage rung,
As they sung:
"Oh! Dulce, dulce domum!" [1]
> *Dulce Domum. Stanza 1*

WILLIAM ROBERT
SPENCER
[1770–1834]

Too late I stayed, — forgive the crime!
    Unheeded flew the hours;
How noiseless falls the foot of time
    That only treads on flowers.
> *Lines to Lady Anne Hamilton.*
> *Stanza 1*

When the black-lettered list to the gods
    was presented,
(The list of what Fate for each mor-
    tal intends,)
At the long string of ills a kind god-
    dess relented,
And slipped in three blessings — wife,
    children, and friends.
> *Wife, Children, and Friends.*
> *Stanza 1*

Oh! where does faithful Gêlert roam,
    The flow'r of all his race?
So true, so brave; a lamb at home,
    A lion in the chase!
> *Beth-Gêlert. Stanza 4*

His gallant hound the wolf had slain,
    To save Llewellyn's heir.
> *Ibid. Stanza 19*

inally *The President's March,* written in 1789
as an inaugural march for George Washington.
In 1798, Joseph Hopkinson was asked by Mr.
Fox, a young actor-singer, to write verses to
the music of the march, to introduce at a
benefit performance. The song was repeated
eight times, and when sung the ninth time,
the audience stood and joined in the chorus.
    At the Republican Festival, in Boston, July
4, 1803, an ode, set to the same music, was
sung, the refrain being:
> By yon orb of living light,
> Swear to guard your native right;
> Sooner let it cease to shine,
> Than your liberties resign.

[1] Sweet, sweet home.

JOHN TOBIN
[1770–1804]

The man that lays his hand upon a
    woman,
Save in the way of kindness, is a wretch
Whom 'twere gross flattery to name a
    coward.
The Honeymoon [1805]. *Act II,*
Sc. 1

            She's adorned
Amply that in her husband's eye looks
    lovely, —
The truest mirror that an honest wife
Can see her beauty in.
Ibid. Act III, Sc. 4

WILLIAM WORDSWORTH [1]
[1770–1850]

Poetry is the breath and finer spirit
of all knowledge; it is the impassioned
expression which is in the countenance
of all Science.
Lyrical Ballads, Second Edition.
Preface

In spite of difference of soil and climate, of language and manners, of laws
and customs, — in spite of things silently gone out of mind, and things
violently destroyed, the Poet binds together by passion and knowledge the
vast empire of human society, as it is
spread over the whole earth, and over
all time.
Ibid.

All men feel something of an honorable bigotry for the objects which have
long continued to please them.
Ibid.

And homeless near a thousand homes I
    stood,
And near a thousand tables pined and
    wanted food.
Guilt and Sorrow. Part II, Stanza 41
        A simple child,
That lightly draws its breath,
And feels its life in every limb,
What should it know of death?
We are Seven. Stanza 1

[1] Coleridge said to Wordsworth (*Memoirs*
by his nephew, *Vol. II, P. 74*), "Since Milton,
I know of no poet with so many *felicities* and
unforgettable lines and stanzas as you."

O Reader! had you in your mind
Such stores as silent thought can bring,
O gentle Reader! you would find
A tale in everything.
Simon Lee. Stanza 9
In that sweet mood when pleasant
    thoughts
Bring sad thoughts to the mind.
Lines Written in Early Spring.
Stanza 1
And 'tis my faith, that every flower
Enjoys the air it breathes.
Ibid. Stanza 3
Nor less I deem that there are Powers
Which of themselves our minds im-
    press;
That we can feed this mind of ours
In a wise passiveness.
Expostulation and Reply. Stanza 6
Up! up! my friend, and quit your
    books;
Or surely you'll grow double:
Up! up! my friend, and clear your
    looks;
Why all this toil and trouble?
The Tables Turned. Stanza 1
Come forth into the light of things,
Let Nature be your teacher.
Ibid. Stanza 4
One impulse from a vernal wood
May teach you more of man,
Of moral evil and of good,
Than all the sages can.
Ibid. Stanza 6
        Sensations sweet,
Felt in the blood, and felt along the
    heart.
Lines Composed a Few Miles
Above Tintern Abbey
That best portion of a good man's
    life, —
His little, nameless, unremembered,
    acts
Of kindness and of love.
Ibid.
        That blessed mood,
In which the burthen of the mystery,
In which the heavy and the weary
    weight
Of all this unintelligible world,
Is lightened.
Ibid.

The sounding cataract
Haunted me like a passion; the tall rock,
The mountain, and the deep and gloomy wood,
Their colours and their forms, were then to me
An appetite; a feeling and a love,
That had no need of a remoter charm,
By thoughts supplied, nor any interest
Unborrowed from the eye.
                Lines Composed a Few Miles
                Above Tintern Abbey
But hearing oftentimes
The still, sad music of humanity.
                                Ibid.
            A sense sublime
Of something far more deeply inter-fused,
Whose dwelling is the light of setting suns,
And the round ocean and the living air,
And the blue sky, and in the mind of man;
A motion and a spirit, that impels
All thinking things, all objects of all thought,
And rolls through all things.
                                Ibid.
Knowing that Nature never did betray
The heart that loved her.
                                Ibid.
Men who can hear the Decalogue and feel
No self-reproach.
                The Old Cumberland Beggar
As in the eye of Nature he has lived,
So in the eye of Nature let him die!
                                Ibid.
Full twenty times was Peter feared,
For once that Peter was respected.
                Peter Bell. Part I, Stanza 3
A primrose by a river's brim
A yellow primrose was to him,
And it was nothing more.
                        Ibid. Stanza 12
The soft blue sky did never melt
Into his heart; he never felt
The witchery of the soft blue sky!
                        Ibid. Stanza 15
On a fair prospect some have looked,
And felt, as I have heard them say,
As if the moving time had been

A thing as steadfast as the scene
On which they gazed themselves away.
                Peter Bell. Part I, Stanza 16
As if the man had fixed his face,
In many a solitary place,
Against the wind and open sky!
                        Ibid. Stanza 26 [1]
One of those heavenly days that can-not die.
                                Nutting
What fond and wayward thoughts will slide
Into a lover's head!
"O mercy!" to myself I cried,
    "If Lucy should be dead!"
        Strange Fits of Passion Have I
                        Known. Stanza 7
She dwelt among the untrodden ways
    Beside the springs of Dove,
A maid whom there were none to praise
    And very few to love.[2]
    Lucy: She Dwelt Among the Un-
            trodden Ways. Stanza 1
A violet by a mossy stone
    Half hidden from the eye! —
Fair as a star, when only one
    Is shining in the sky.
                        Ibid. Stanza 2
She lived unknown, and few could know
    When Lucy ceased to be;
But she is in her grave, and, oh
    The difference to me!
                        Ibid. Stanza 3
The stars of midnight shall be dear
To her; and she shall lean her ear
    In many a secret place

<hr>

[1] The original edition [London, 1819] had the following as the fourth stanza from the end of Part I, which was omitted in all subse-quent editions: —
                Is it a party in a parlour?
Crammed just as they on earth were crammed, —
Some sipping punch, some sipping tea,
But, as you by their faces see,
All silent and all damned.

[2] He lived amidst th' untrodden ways
        To Rydal Lake that lead;
    A bard whom there were none to praise,
        And very few to read.
    Unread his works — his "Milk White Doe"
        With dust is dark and dim;
    It's still in Longmans' shop, and oh!
        The difference to him!
                — *Parody by Hartley Coleridge.*

Where rivulets dance their wayward
   round,
And beauty born of murmuring sound
   Shall pass into her face.
     Lucy: Three Years She Grew in
       Sun and Shower. Stanza 5
May no rude hand deface it,
And its forlorn *hic jacet!*
         Ellen Irwin. Stanza 7
She gave me eyes, she gave me ears;
And humble cares, and delicate fears;
A heart, the fountain of sweet tears;
   And love, and thought, and joy.
     The Sparrow's Nest. Stanza 2
The child is father of the man.[1]
  My Heart Leaps Up When I Behold
The cattle are grazing,
   Their heads never raising;
There are forty feeding like one!
    The Cock Is Crowing. Stanza 1
Sweet childish days, that were as long
As twenty days are now.
    To a Butterfly. Part II, I've
    Watched You Now a Full Half-
    hour, Stanza 2
Often have I sighed to measure
By myself a lonely pleasure,
Sighed to think, I read a book
Only read, perhaps, by me.
    To the Small Celandine. Part II,
        Stanza 4
I thought of Chatterton, the marvel-
   lous boy,
The sleepless soul that perished in his
   pride;
Of him who walked in glory and in
   joy
Following his plough, along the moun-
   tain-side:
By our own spirits are we deified:
We Poets in our youth begin in glad-
   ness;
But thereof come in the end despond-
   ency and madness.
    Resolution and Independence
    [*The Leech Gatherer*]. *Stanza 7*
That heareth not the loud winds when
   they call,
And moveth all together, if it moves at
   all.
         Ibid. Stanza 11

[1] See Milton, page 156.

Choice word and measured phrase,
   above the reach
Of ordinary men.
    Resolution and Independence
    [*The Leech Gatherer*]. *Stanza 14*
And mighty poets in their misery
   dead.
         Ibid. Stanza 17
Ne'er saw I, never felt, a calm so deep!
The river glideth at his own sweet will;
Dear God! the very houses seem
   asleep;
And all that mighty heart is lying still!
    Lines Composed Upon West-
        minster Bridge
The holy time is quiet as a nun
Breathless with adoration.
     It is a Beauteous Evening
Men are we, and must grieve when
   even the shade
Of that which once was great, is passed
   away.
    On the Extinction of the Venetian
       Republic
   Thou hast left behind
Powers that will work for thee; air,
   earth, and skies;
There's not a breathing of the common
   wind
That will forget thee; thou hast great
   allies;
Thy friends are exultations, agonies,
And love, and man's unconquerable
   mind.
      To Toussaint L'Ouverture[1]
One that would peep and botanize
Upon his mother's grave.
    A Poet's Epitaph. Stanza 5
And you must love him, ere to you
He will seem worthy of your love.
         Ibid. Stanza 11
The harvest of a quiet eye.
         Ibid. Stanza 13
Yet sometimes, when the secret cup
Of still and serious thought went
   round,

[1] Sleep calmly in thy dungeon-tomb,
   Beneath Besançon's alien sky,
  Dark Haytien! — for the time shall come,
   Yea, even now is nigh, —
  When, everywhere, thy name shall be
  Redeemed from color's infamy.
    WHITTIER: *Toussaint L'Ouverture*

It seemed as if he drank it up —
He felt with spirit so profound.

> *Matthew. Stanza 7*

The sweetest thing that ever grew
Beside a human door.

> *Lucy Gray. Stanza 2*

A youth to whom was given
So much of earth — so much of heaven.

> *Ruth. Stanza 21*

Something between a hindrance and a
help.

> *Michael*

Drink, pretty creature, drink!

> *The Pet Lamb. Stanza 1*

Plain living and high thinking are no
more: [1]
The homely beauty of the good old
cause
Is gone; our peace, our fearful innocence,
And pure religion breathing household
laws.

> *O Friend! I Know Not Which
> Way I Must Look*

Milton! thou should'st be living at this
hour:
England hath need of thee! . . .
Thy soul was like a star, and dwelt
apart: . . .
So didst thou travel on life's common
way,
In cheerful godliness.

> *London, 1802*

We must be free or die, who speak the
tongue
That Shakespeare spake; the faith and
morals hold
Which Milton held.

> *It Is Not To Be Thought Of*

We meet thee, like a pleasant thought,
When such are wanted.

> *To the Daisy. Part I, Stanza 3*

The poet's darling.

> *Ibid. Stanza 4*

Thou unassuming commonplace
Of Nature.

> *Ibid. Part II, Stanza 1*

Oft on the dappled turf at ease
I sit, and play with similes,

[1] Plain living and high thinking. — R. W.
EMERSON: *Domestic Life*

Loose type of things through all degrees.

> *To the Daisy. Part II, Stanza 2*

Sweet Mercy! to the gates of heaven
This minstrel lead, his sins forgiven;
The rueful conflict, the heart riven
With vain endeavour,
And memory of Earth's bitter leaven
Effaced forever.

> *Thoughts Suggested on the Banks
> of the Nith. Stanza 10*

And stepping westward seemed to be
A kind of heavenly destiny.

> *Stepping Westward. Stanza 2*

For old, unhappy, far-off things,
And battles long ago.

> *The Solitary Reaper. Stanza 3*

Some natural sorrow, loss, or pain,
That has been, and may be again.

> *Ibid.*

The music in my heart I bore
Long after it was heard no more.

> *Ibid. Stanza 4*

Because the good old rule
Sufficeth them, the simple plan,
That they should take, who have the
power,
And they should keep who can.

> *Rob Roy's Grave. Stanza 9*

Yon foaming flood seems motionless as
ice;
Its dizzy turbulence eludes the eye,
Frozen by distance.

> *Address to Kilchurn Castle*

A brotherhood of venerable trees.

> *Sonnet composed at —— Castle*

Let beeves and home-bred kine par-
take
The sweets of Burn-mill meadow;
The swan on still St. Mary's Lake
Float double, swan and shadow!

> *Yarrow Unvisited. Stanza 6*

A remnant of uneasy light.

> *The Matron of Jedborough*

Oh for a single hour of that Dundee
Who on that day the word of onset
gave! [1]

> *Sonnet, in the Pass of Killicranky*

[1] It was on this occasion [the failure in
energy of Lord Mar at the battle of Sheriff-
muir] that Gordon of Glenbucket made the
celebrated exclamation, "Oh for an hour of

O Cuckoo! shall I call thee bird,
Or but a wandering voice?
To the Cuckoo. Stanza 1

She was a phantom of delight
When first she gleamed upon my sight;
A lovely apparition, sent
To be a moment's ornament;
Her eyes as stars of twilight fair,
Like twilight's, too, her dusky hair,
But all things else about her drawn
From May-time and the cheerful dawn.
*She Was a Phantom of Delight.
Stanza 1*

A creature not too bright or good
For human nature's daily food;
For transient sorrows, simple wiles,
Praise, blame, love, kisses, tears, and
smiles.
Ibid. Stanza 2

And now I see with eye serene
The very pulse of the machine.
Ibid. Stanza 3

The reason firm, the temperate will,
Endurance, foresight, strength, and
skill;
A perfect woman, nobly planned,
To warn, to comfort, and command.
Ibid.

I saw a crowd,
A host, of golden daffodils.
*I Wandered Lonely as a Cloud.
Stanza 1*

That inward eye
Which is the bliss of solitude.
Ibid. Stanza 4

Stern Daughter of the Voice of God! [1]
Ode to Duty. Stanza 1

A light to guide, a rod
To check the erring, and reprove.
Ibid.

Thou dost preserve the stars from
wrong;
And the most ancient heavens, through
Thee, are fresh and strong.
Ibid. Stanza 6

Dundee!" — MAHON: *History of England,
Vol. I, P. 184*
Oh for one hour of blind old Dandolo,
The octogenarian chief, Byzantium's conquer-
ing foe!
BYRON: *Childe Harold, Canto IV, St. 12*
[1] See Milton, page 155.

The light that never was, on sea or
land;
The consecration, and the Poet's
dream.
*Suggested by a Picture of Peele
Castle in a Storm. Stanza 4*

Shalt show us how divine a thing
A woman may be made.
*To a Young Lady. Dear Child
of Nature, Stanza 2*

But an old age serene and bright,
And lovely as a Lapland night,
Shall lead thee to thy grave.
Ibid. Stanza 3

Many are our joys
In youth, but oh! what happiness to
live
When every hour brings palpable ac-
cess
Of knowledge, when all knowledge is
delight,
And sorrow is not there!
The Prelude. Book II

Where the statue stood
Of Newton with his prism and silent
face,
The marble index of a mind forever
Voyaging through strange seas of
thought, alone.
Ibid. Book III

There's not a man
That lives who hath not known his god-
like hours.
Ibid.

When from our better selves we have
too long
Been parted by the hurrying world,
and droop,
Sick of its business, of its pleasures
tired,
How gracious, how benign, is Solitude.
Ibid. Book IV

Oh! give us once again the wishing-cap
Of Fortunatus, and the invisible coat
Of Jack the Giant-Killer, Robin Hood,
And Sabra in the forest with St.
George!
The child, whose love is here, at least,
doth reap
One precious gain, that he forgets him-
self.
The Prelude. Book V

'Tis told by one whom stormy waters
threw,
With fellow-sufferers by the shipwreck
spared,
Upon a desert coast, that having
brought
To land a single volume, saved by
chance,
A treatise on Geometry.
The Prelude. Book VI

Multitudes of hours
Pilfered away, by what the Bard who
sang
Of the Enchanter Indolence [1] hath
called
"Good-natured lounging," and behold
a map
Of my collegiate life.
Ibid.

How men lived
Even next-door neighbours, as we say,
yet still
Strangers, not knowing each the other's
name.
Ibid. Book VII
Bliss was it in that dawn to be alive,
But to be young was very heaven!
Ibid. Book XI

There is
One great society alone on earth:
The noble living and the noble dead.
Ibid.
Who is the happy Warrior? Who is he
That every man in arms would wish
to be?
Character of the Happy Warrior
Who, doomed to go in company with
Pain,
And Fear, and Bloodshed, miserable
train!
Turns his necessity to glorious gain.
Ibid.
Controls them and subdues, trans-
mutes, bereaves
Of their bad influence, and their good
receives.
Ibid.
But who, if he be called upon to face
Some awful moment to which Heaven
has joined

[1] THOMSON'S *Castle of Indolence.*

Great issues, good or bad for human-
kind,
Is happy as a lover.
Character of the Happy Warrior
And, through the heat of conflict, keeps
the law
In calmness made, and sees what he
foresaw.
Ibid.
Whom neither shape of danger can dis-
may,
Nor thought of tender happiness be-
tray.
Ibid.
Like, — but oh how different!
Yes, It Was the Mountain Echo
The world is too much with us; late
and soon,
Getting and spending, we lay waste our
powers:
Little we see in Nature that is ours.
The World Is Too Much With Us
Great God! I'd rather be
A Pagan suckled in a creed outworn; [1]
So might I, standing on this pleasant
lea,
Have glimpses that would make me
less forlorn;
Have sight of Proteus rising from the
sea;
Or hear old Triton blow his wreathed
horn.
Ibid.
Where lies the land to which yon Ship
must go? [2]
Fresh as a lark mounting at break of
day,
Festively she puts forth in trim array.
Where Lies the Land
A flock of sheep that leisurely pass by, [3]

[1]   Good Lord! I'd rather be
Quite unacquainted with the A.B.C.
Than write such hopeless rubbish as thy worst.
    JAMES KENNETH STEPHEN [1859–1892]:
                  Sonnet, Wordsworth
[2] Where lies the land to which the ship
      would go?
    Far, far ahead, is all her seamen know.
    ARTHUR HUGH CLOUGH [1819–1861]:
                  Songs of Absence
[3]   An old half-witted sheep
Which bleats articulate monotony,
And indicates that two and one are three.
    JAMES KENNETH STEPHEN: *Sonnet,*
                  Wordsworth

One after one; the sound of rain, and
bees
Murmuring; the fall of rivers, winds
and seas,
Smooth fields, white sheets of water,
and pure sky;
I have thought of all by turns, and yet
do lie
Sleepless!
> *To Sleep. II, A Flock of Sheep*

Blessed barrier between day and day.
> *Ibid.*

Maidens withering on the stalk.[1]
> *Personal Talk. Sonnet 1*

Dreams, books, are each a world; and
books, we know,
Are a substantial world, both pure and
good.
Round these, with tendrils strong as
flesh and blood,
Our pastime and our happiness will
grow.
> *Ibid. Sonnet 3*

The gentle Lady married to the Moor,
And heavenly Una with her milk-white
lamb.
> *Ibid.*

A power is passing from the earth.
> *Lines on the Expected Dissolution of Mr. Fox. Stanza 5*

An unexampled voice of awful memory.
> *On the Death of George III*

Look for the stars, you'll say that there
are none;
Look up a second time, and, one by
one,
You mark them twinkling out with silvery light,
And wonder how they could elude the
sight!
> *Calm Is the Fragrant Air*

The rainbow comes and goes,
And lovely is the rose.
> *Intimations of Immortality.*[2]
> *Stanza 2*

The sunshine is a glorious birth;
But yet I know, where'er I go,

That there hath passed away a glory
from the earth.
> *Intimations of Immortality.*
> *Stanza 2*

Where is it now, the glory and the
dream?
> *Ibid. Stanza 4*

Our birth is but a sleep and a forget-
ting:
The soul that rises with us, our life's
star,
Hath had elsewhere its setting,
And cometh from afar:
Not in entire forgetfulness,
And not in utter nakedness,
But trailing clouds of glory do we
come
From God, who is our home:
Heaven lies about us in our infancy!
> *Ibid. Stanza 5*

At length the man perceives it die
away,
And fade into the light of common day.
> *Ibid.*

As if his whole vocation
Were endless imitation.
> *Ibid. Stanza 7*

Those obstinate questionings
Of sense and outward things,
Fallings from us, vanishings;
Blank misgivings of a creature
Moving about in worlds not realized,
High instincts before which our mortal
nature
Did tremble like a guilty thing sur-
prised.
> *Ibid. Stanza 9*

Truths that wake,
To perish never.
> *Ibid.*

Though inland far we be,
Our souls have sight of that immortal
sea
Which brought us hither.
> *Ibid.*

Though nothing can bring back the
hour
Of splendour in the grass, of glory in
the flower.
> *Ibid. Stanza 10*

In years that bring the philosophic
mind.
> *Ibid.*

---

[1] Withering on the virgin thorn. — SHAKE-
SPEARE: *A Midsummer-Night's Dream, Act I,
Sc. 1, L. 77*
[2] The Ode on Immortality is the high water
mark which the intellect has reached in this
age. — R. W. EMERSON: *English Traits*

The clouds that gather round the set-
ting sun
Do take a sober colouring from an eye
That hath kept watch o'er man's mor-
tality.
Intimations of Immortality.
Stanza 11

To me the meanest flower that blows
can give
Thoughts that do often lie too deep
for tears.
Ibid.

The silence that is in the starry sky,
The sleep that is among the lonely
hills.
*Song at the Feast of Brougham
Castle.*

The monumental pomp of age
Was with this goodly personage;
A stature undepressed in size,
Unbent, which rather seemed to rise,
In open victory o'er the weight
Of seventy years, to loftier height.
The White Doe of Rylstone.
Canto III

A few strong instincts, and a few plain
rules.
*Alas! What Boots the Long
Laborious Quest?*

Strongest minds
Are often those of whom the noisy
world
Hears least.
The Excursion. Book I

The imperfect offices of prayer and
praise.
Ibid.

That mighty orb of song,
The divine Milton.
Ibid.

The good die first,[1]
And they whose hearts are dry as sum-
mer dust
Burn to the socket.
Ibid.

[1] Heaven gives its favourites — early death.
— BYRON: *Childe Harold, Canto IV, St. 102.*
Also *Don Juan, Canto IV, St. 12.*
                    Quem Di diligunt
            Adolescens moritur
(He whom the gods favor dies in youth).
            PLAUTUS: *Bacchides, Act IV, Sc. 7*

Wrongs unredressed, or insults un-
avenged.
The Excursion. Book III

Society became my glittering bride.
Ibid.

There is a luxury in self-dispraise;
And inward self-disparagement affords
To meditative spleen a grateful feast.
Ibid. Book IV

I have seen
A curious child, who dwelt upon a
tract
Of inland ground, applying to his ear
The convolutions of a smooth-lipped
shell,
To which, in silence hushed, his very
soul
Listened intensely; and his counte-
nance soon
Brightened with joy, for from within
were heard
Murmurings, whereby the monitor ex-
pressed
Mysterious union with its native sea.[1]
Ibid.

One in whom persuasion and belief
Had ripened into faith, and faith be-
come
A passionate intuition.
Ibid.

Spires whose "silent finger points to
heaven."[2]
Ibid. Book VI

Ah! what a warning for a thoughtless
man,

[1] But I have sinuous shells of pearly hue . . .
    Shake one, and it awakens; then apply
    Its polisht lips to your attentive ear,
    And it remembers its august abodes,
    And murmurs as the ocean murmurs
        there.
    WALTER SAVAGE LANDOR: *Gebir, Book V*
Upon a mountain height, far from the sea,
    I found a shell,
And to my listening ear the lonely thing
Ever a song of ocean seemed to sing,
    Ever a tale of ocean seemed to tell.
        EUGENE FIELD: *The Wanderer, St. 1*
[2] An instinctive taste teaches men to build
their churches in flat countries with spire
steeples, which, as they cannot be referred to
any other object, point as with silent finger to
the sky and stars. — COLERIDGE: *The Friend,
No. 14*

Could field or grove, could any spot of earth,
Show to his eye an image of the pangs
Which it hath witnessed; render back an echo
Of the sad steps by which it hath been trod!
The Excursion. Book VI

And, when the stream
Which overflowed the soul was passed away,
A consciousness remained that it had left,
Deposited upon the silent shore
Of memory, images and precious thoughts,
That shall not die, and cannot be destroyed.
Ibid. Book VII

Wisdom married to immortal verse.
Ibid.

A man he seems of cheerful yesterdays
And confident to-morrows.
Ibid.

Her bosom heaves and spreads, her stature grows;
And she expects the issue in repose.
Laodamia. Stanza 2

The gods approve
The depth, and not the tumult, of the soul.
Ibid. Stanza 13

Mightier far
Than strength of nerve and sinew, or the sway
Of magic potent over sun and star,
Is Love, though oft to agony distrest,
And though his favorite seat be feeble woman's breast.
Ibid. Stanza 15

Elysian beauty, melancholy grace,
Brought from a pensive though a happy place.
Ibid. Stanza 16

He spake of love, such love as spirits feel
In worlds whose course is equable and pure;
No fears to beat away — no strife to heal, —

The past unsighed for, and the future sure.
Laodamia. Stanza 17

An ampler ether, a diviner air.
Ibid. Stanza 18

But thou that didst appear so fair
To fond imagination,
Dost rival in the light of day
Her delicate creation.
Yarrow Visited. Stanza 6

We bow our heads before Thee, and we laud
And magnify thy name, Almighty God!
But man is thy most awful instrument,
In working out a pure intent.
Ode, Imagination Ne'er Before Content. IV

That kill the bloom before its time;
And blanch, without the owner's crime,
The most resplendent hair.
Lament of Mary Queen of Scots. Stanza 6

The sightless Milton, with his hair
Around his placid temples curled;
And Shakespeare at his side, — a freight,
If clay could think and mind were weight,
For him who bore the world!
The Italian Itinerant. Part I, 1

Meek Nature's evening comment on the shows
That for oblivion take their daily birth
From all the fuming vanities of earth.
Sky-Prospect from the Plain of France

As thou these ashes, little brook, wilt bear
Into the Avon, Avon to the tide
Of Severn, Severn to the narrow seas,
Into main ocean they, this deed accursed
An emblem yields to friends and enemies
How the bold teacher's doctrine, sanctified
By truth, shall spread, throughout the world dispersed.[1]
Ecclesiastical Sonnets. Part II, XVII, To Wickliffe

[1] In obedience to the order of the Council of Constance (1415), the remains of Wickliffe were exhumed and burned to ashes, and these

The feather, whence the pen
Was shaped that traced the lives of
these good men,
Dropped from an angel's wing.[1]

*Ecclesiastical Sonnets. Part III,
V, Walton's Book of Lives*

Give all thou canst; high Heaven re-
jects the lore
Of nicely-calculated less or more.

*Ibid. XLIII, Inside of King's
College Chapel, Cambridge*

Where music dwells
Lingering — and wandering on as loth
to die.

Ibid.

Two voices are there: one is of the
sea,[2]
One of the mountains; each a mighty
voice.

*Thought of a Briton on the
Subjugation of Switzerland*

Or, shipwrecked, kindles on the coast
False fires, that others may be lost.

To the Lady Fleming. Stanza 7

But hushed be every thought that
springs

---

cast into the Swift, a neighbouring brook running hard by; and "thus this brook hath conveyed his ashes into Avon, Avon into Severn,
Severn into the narrow seas, they into the
main ocean. And thus the ashes of Wickliffe
are the emblem of his doctrine, which is now
dispersed all the world over." — FULLER:
Church History, Sect. II, Book IV, Par. 606 [ed.
1641]

What Heraclitus would not laugh, or
what Democritus would not weep? . . . For
though they digged up his body, burned his
bones, and drowned his ashes, yet the word of
God and truth of his doctrine, with the fruit
and success thereof, they could not burn. —
FOXE: *Book of Martyrs, Vol. 1, P. 606* [ed.
1641]

Some prophet of that day said, —
"The Avon to the Severn runs,
The Severn to the sea;
And Wickliffe's dust shall spread abroad
Wide as the waters be."

DANIEL WEBSTER: *Address before the Sons
of New Hampshire* [1849]

[1] The pen wherewith thou dost so heavenly
sing
Made of a quill from an angel's wing.
HENRY CONSTABLE [1562–1613]: *Sonnet*

[2] Two voices are there: one is of the deep.
And one is of an old half-witted sheep.
JAMES KENNETH STEPHEN: *Sonnet, Words-
worth* (See footnote, page 300.)

From out the bitterness of things.

*Elegiac Stanzas, Addressed to
Sir G. H. B. Stanza 7*

Ethereal minstrel! pilgrim of the sky!

To a Skylark. Stanza 1

Type of the wise who soar, but never
roam,
True to the kindred points of heaven
and home.

Ibid. Stanza 2

A Briton, even in love, should be
A subject, not a slave!

*Ere with Cold Beads of Midnight
Dew. Stanza 5*

Scorn not the sonnet. Critic, you have
frowned,
Mindless of its just honours; with this
key
Shakespeare unlocked his heart.[1]

Scorn Not the Sonnet

And, when a damp
Fell round the path of Milton, in his
hand
The thing became a trumpet; whence
he blew
Soul-animating strains, — alas,　too
few!

Ibid.

The bosom-weight, your stubborn gift,
That no philosophy can lift.

Presentiments. Stanza 5

Nature's old felicities.

The Trosachs

Myriads of daisies have shone forth in
flower
Near the lark's nest, and in their natural hour
Have passed away; less happy than
the one
That by the unwilling ploughshare,
died to prove
The tender charm of poetry and love.

*Poems Composed During a Tour
in the Summer of 1833. XXXVII,
Mosgiel*

Small service is true service while it
lasts.
Of humblest friends, bright creature!
scorn not one:

---

[1]　　　　With this same key
Shakespeare unlocked his heart.
ROBERT BROWNING: *House, St. 10*

The daisy, by the shadow that it casts,
Protects the lingering dewdrop from
    the sun.
    To a Child, Written in her Album
Since every mortal power of Coleridge
Was frozen at its marvellous source;
The rapt one, of the godlike forehead,
The heaven-eyed creature sleeps in
    earth:
And Lamb, the frolic and the gentle,
Has vanished from his lonely hearth.
    Extempore Effusion upon the
    Death of James Hogg. Stanzas
    4 and 5
How fast has brother followed brother,
From sunshine to the sunless land!
    Ibid. Stanza 6
Enough if something from our hands
    have power
To live, and act, and serve the future
    hour.
    Sonnet to the River Duddon
We feel that we are greater than we
    know.
    Ibid.
They called thee Merry England in old
    time; [1]
A happy people won for thee that
    name
With envy heard in many a distant
    clime.
    They Called Thee Merry England
Wouldst thou be gathered to Christ's
    chosen flock,
Shun the broad way too easily ex-
    plored,
And let thy path be hewn out of the
    Rock,
The living Rock of God's Eternal
    Word.
    Inscription on a Rock at Rydal
    Mount
How does the meadow-flower its bloom
    unfold?
Because the lovely little flower is free
Down to its root, and, in that freedom,
    bold.
    A Poet! He Hath Put His
    Heart to School

[1] England was merry England, when
Old Christmas brought his sports again.
SIR WALTER SCOTT: *Marmion, Introd.*
    to Canto VI, St. 3

Minds that have nothing to confer
    Find little to perceive.
    Yes, Thou art Fair. Stanza 2

THOMAS DIBDIN
[1771–1841]

Oh, it's a snug little island!
A right little, tight little island.
    The Snug Little Island

JAMES MONTGOMERY
[1771–1854]

To-morrow — oh, 'twill never be,
    If we should live a thousand years!
Our time is all to-day, to-day,
    The same, though changed; and
        while it flies
With still small voice the moments
    say:
    "To-day, to-day, be wise, be wise."
    To-day
Give me the hand that is honest and
    hearty,
Free as the breeze and unshackled by
    party.
    Give Me Thy Hand. Stanza 2
The rose has but a summer reign,
    The daisy never dies.
    The Daisy. Stanza 10
Servant of God! well done; [1]
    Rest from thy loved employ;
The battle fought, the victory won,
    Enter thy Master's joy.
    The Christian Soldier. Stanza 1
"The Press! — What is the Press?" I
    cried;
When thus a wondrous voice replied:
"In me all human knowledge dwells;
    The oracle of oracles,
Past, present, future, I reveal,
    Or in oblivion's silence seal;
What I preserve can perish never,
What I forego is lost forever."
    The Press. Stanza 1
All that philosophers have sought,
Science discovered, genius wrought;
All that reflective memory stores,
Or rich imagination pours;
All that the wit of man conceives,
All that he wishes, hopes, believes;

[1] See Milton, page 153.

All that he loves, or fears, or hates,
All that to heaven and earth relates,
— These are the lessons that I teach
In speaking silence, silent speech.
The Press. Stanza 4

Counts his sure gains, and hurries back
for more.
The West Indies. Part III

Hope against hope, and ask till ye receive.
The World before the Flood.
Canto V, Stanza 10

Joys too exquisite to last,
And yet *more* exquisite when past.
The Little Cloud. Stanza 9

Bliss in possession will not last;
Remembered joys are never past;
At once the fountain, stream, and sea,
They were, they are, they yet shall be.
Ibid. Stanza 10

Friend after friend departs;
Who hath not lost a friend?
There is no union here of hearts
That finds not here an end.
Friends. Stanza 1

Nor sink those stars in empty night:
But hide themselves in heaven's own
light.
Ibid. Stanza 4

'Tis not the whole of life to live,
Nor all of death to die.
The Issues of Life and Death.
Stanza 2

Beyond this vale of tears
There is a life above,
Unmeasured by the flight of years;
And all that life is love.
Ibid. Stanza 3

Who, that hath ever been,
Could bear to be no more?
Yet who would tread again the scene
He trod through life before?
The Falling Leaf. Stanza 7

Here in the body pent,
Absent from Him I roam,
Yet nightly pitch my moving tent
A day's march nearer home.
At Home in Heaven

Prayer is the soul's sincere desire,
Uttered or unexpressed;
The motion of a hidden fire
That trembles in the breast.
What is Prayer? Stanza 1

Prayer is the burden of a sigh,
The falling of a tear;
The upward glancing of an eye,
When none but God is near.
What is Prayer? Stanza 2

ROBERT OWEN
[1771–1858]

All the world is queer save thee and
me, and even thou art a little queer.[1]
On severing business relations
with his partner, William Allen
[1828]

SIR WALTER SCOTT
[1771–1832]

His withered cheek, and tresses gray,
Seem'd to have known a better day.
The Lay of the Last Minstrel.
Introduction

Such is the custom of Branksome Hall.
Ibid. Canto I, Stanza 7

Your mountains shall bend,
And your streams ascend,
Ere Margaret be our foeman's bride!
Ibid. Stanza 18

If thou would'st view fair Melrose
aright,
Go visit it by the pale moonlight.
Ibid. Canto II, Stanza 1

I cannot tell how the truth may be;
I say the tale as 'twas said to me.
Ibid. Stanza 22

In peace, Love tunes the shepherd's
reed;
In war, he mounts the warrior's steed;
In halls, in gay attire is seen;
In hamlets, dances on the green.
Love rules the court, the camp, the
grove,
And men below, and saints above;
For love is heaven, and heaven is love.
Ibid. Canto III, Stanza 2

Her blue eyes sought the west afar,
For lovers love the western star.
Ibid. Stanza 24

---

[1] Priests is queer people, and I don't know
who isn't. — JOHN MILLINGTON SYNGE [1871–
1909]: *The Aran Islands* [Luce ed. 1911],
P. 122

Ne'er
Was flattery lost on poet's ear;
A simple race! they waste their toil
For the vain tribute of a smile.
> *The Lay of the Last Min-*
> *strel. Canto IV, Interlude after*
> *Stanza 35*

Call it not vain: they do not err
Who say, that when the poet dies,
Mute Nature mourns her worshipper,
And celebrates his obsequies.
> *Ibid. Canto V, Stanza 1*

True love's the gift which God has
given
To man alone beneath the heaven:
  It is not fantasy's hot fire,
    Whose wishes, soon as granted,
    fly;
  It liveth not in fierce desire,
    With dead desire it doth not die;
It is the secret sympathy,
The silver link, the silken tie,
Which heart to heart and mind to mind
In body and in soul can bind.
> *Ibid. Stanza 13*

Breathes there the man, with soul so
dead,
Who never to himself hath said,
  This is my own, my native land!
Whose heart hath ne'er within him
  burn'd [1]
As home his footsteps he hath turn'd,
  From wandering on a foreign strand?
If such there breathe, go, mark him
  well;
For him no minstrel raptures swell;
High though his titles, proud his name,
Boundless his wealth as wish can
  claim, —
Despite those titles, power, and pelf,
The wretch, concentred all in self,
Living, shall forfeit fair renown,
And, doubly dying, shall go down
To the vile dust, from whence he
  sprung,
Unwept, unhonour'd, and unsung.[2]
> *Ibid. Canto VI, Stanza 1*

O Caledonia! stern and wild,
Meet nurse for a poetic child!

[1] Did not our heart burn within us while
he talked with us by the way? — *Luke,*
XXIV, 32
[2] See Pope, page 219.

Land of brown heath and shaggy
wood;
Land of the mountain and the flood!
> *The Lay of the Last Minstrel.*
> *Canto VI, Stanza 2*

Stood for his country's glory fast,
And nail'd her colors to the mast!
> *Marmion. Introduction to*
> *Canto I, Stanza 10*

Just at the age 'twixt boy and youth,
When thought is speech, and speech is
truth.
> *Ibid. Introduction to Canto II,*
> *Stanza 4*

When, musing on companions gone,
We doubly feel ourselves alone.
> *Ibid. Stanza 5*

When Prussia hurried to the field,
And snatch'd the spear, but left the
shield.[1]
> *Ibid. Introduction to Canto III,*
> *Stanza 3*

To bring my tribute to his grave: —
'Tis little — but 'tis all I have.
> *Ibid. Introduction to Canto IV,*
> *Stanza 5*

Where's the coward that would not
dare
  To fight for such a land?
> *Ibid. Canto IV, Stanza 30*

Lightly from fair to fair he flew,
And loved to plead, lament, and sue;
Suit lightly won, and short-lived pain,
For monarchs seldom sigh in vain.
> *Ibid. Canto V, Stanza 9*

Young Lochinvar is come out of the
West.
> *Ibid. Stanza 12* [*Lochinvar.*
> *Stanza 1*]

So faithful in love, and so dauntless in
war,
There never was knight like the young
Lochinvar.
> *Ibid.*

With a smile on her lips, and a tear in
her eye.[2]
> *Ibid. Stanza 5*

Heap on more wood! — the wind is
chill;

[1] See Freneau, page 280.
[2] Reproof on her lips, but a smile in her eye.
SAMUEL LOVER: *Rory O'More, St. 1*

But let it whistle as it will,
We'll keep our Christmas merry still.
> *Marmion. Introduction to*
> *Canto VI, Stanza 1*

Still linger, in our northern clime,
Some remnants of the good old time.
> *Ibid. Stanza 4*

And dar'st thou, then,
To beard the lion in his den,
  The Douglas in his hall?
> *Ibid. Canto VI, Stanza 14*

Oh, what a tangled web we weave,
When first we practise to deceive!
> *Ibid. Stanza 17*

O woman! in our hours of ease,
Uncertain, coy, and hard to please,
And variable as the shade
By the light quivering aspen made;
When pain and anguish wring the
  brow,
A ministering angel thou! [1]
> *Ibid. Stanza 30*

"Charge, Chester, charge! on, Stanley,
  on!"
Were the last words of Marmion.
> *Ibid. Stanza 32*

To all, to each, a fair good-night,
And pleasing dreams, and slumbers
  light.
> *Ibid. L'Envoy, To the Reader*

In listening mood she seemed to stand,
The guardian Naiad of the strand.
> *The Lady of the Lake. Canto I,*
> *Stanza 17*

And ne'er did Grecian chisel trace
A Nymph, a Naiad, or a Grace

---

[1] A ministering angel shall my sister be. —
SHAKESPEARE: *Hamlet, Act V, Sc. 1, L. 263*

Scott, writing to Southey in 1810, said: "A witty rogue the other day, who sent me a letter signed Detector, proved me guilty of stealing a passage from one of Vida's Latin poems, which I had never seen or heard of." The passage alleged to be stolen ends with, —
  When pain and anguish wring the brow,
  A ministering angel thou!
which in Vida "ad Eranen," El. ii. v. 21, ran, —
  Cum dolor atque supercilio gravis imminet angor,
  Fungeris angelico sola ministerio.
"It is almost needless to add," says LOCKHART, "there are no such lines." — *Life of Scott, Vol. III, P. 294* (American edition)

Of finer form, or lovelier face.
> *The Lady of the Lake.*
> *Canto I, Stanza 18*

A foot more light, a step more true,
Ne'er from the heath-flower dash'd the
  dew.
> *Ibid.*

On his bold visage middle age
Had slightly press'd its signet sage,
Yet had not quench'd the open truth
And fiery vehemence of youth:
Forward and frolic glee was there,
The will to do, the soul to dare.
> *Ibid. Stanza 21*

Soldier, rest! thy warfare o'er.
> *Ibid. Stanza 31*

Sleep the sleep that knows not breaking,
Morn of toil, nor night of waking.
> *Ibid.*

Hail to the chief who in triumph advances!
> *Ibid. Canto II, Stanza 19*

Some feelings are to mortals given,
With less of earth in them than heaven.
> *Ibid. Stanza 22*

Like the dew on the mountain,
  Like the foam on the river,
Like the bubble on the fountain,
  Thou art gone, and forever!
> *Ibid. Canto III, Stanza 16*
> *[Coronach. Stanza 3]*

Come one, come all! this rock shall fly
From its firm base as soon as I.
> *Ibid. Canto V, Stanza 10*

And the stern joy which warriors feel
In foemen worthy of their steel.
> *Ibid.*

Who o'er the herd would wish to reign,
Fantastic, fickle, fierce, and vain!
Vain as the leaf upon the stream,
And fickle as a changeful dream;
Fantastic as a woman's mood,
And fierce as Frenzy's fever'd blood.
Thou many-headed monster [1] thing,
Oh who would wish to be thy king!
> *Stanza 30*

Where, where was Roderick then!
One blast upon his bugle horn
  Were worth a thousand men!
> *Ibid. Canto VI, Stanza 18*

---

[1] See Massinger, page 129.

Oh, many a shaft at random sent
Finds mark the archer little meant!
And many a word, at random spoken,
May soothe or wound a heart that's
    broken!
          The Lord of the Isles. Canto V,
                              Stanza 18
Randolph, thy wreath has lost a rose.[1]
          Ibid. Canto VI, Stanza 18
There was — and O! how many sor-
    rows crowd
Into these two brief words!
                    Ibid. Conclusion
Where lives the man that has not tried
How mirth can into folly glide,
    And folly into sin!
          The Bridal of Triermain. Canto I,
                              Stanza 21
Long loved, long woo'd, and lately won,
My life's best hope, and now mine
    own.
          Ibid. Introduction to Canto II,
                              Stanza 1
List how she tells, in notes of flame,
"Child Roland to the dark tower
    came." [2]
                      Ibid. Stanza 6
Two sisters by the goal are set,
Cold Disappointment and Regret;
One disenchants the winner's eyes,
And strips of all its worth the prize,
While one augments its gaudy show,
More to enhance the loser's woe.
          Rokeby. Canto I, Stanza 31
Still are the thoughts to memory dear.
                    Ibid. Stanza 33
A mother's pride, a father's joy.
          Ibid. Canto III, Stanza 15
Oh, Brignall banks are wild and fair,
    And Greta woods are green,
And you may gather garlands there
    Would grace a summer's queen.
                    Ibid. Stanza 16
The tear down childhood's cheek that
    flows,
Is like the dewdrop on the rose;

When next the summer breeze comes
    by,
And waves the bush, the flower is dry.
          Rokeby. Canto IV, Stanza 11
Thus aged men, full loth and slow,
The vanities of life forego,
And count their youthful follies o'er,
Till Memory lends her light no more.
          Ibid. Canto V, Stanza 1
No pale gradations quench his ray,
No twilight dews his wrath allay.
          Ibid. Canto VI, Stanza 21
Time will rust the sharpest sword,
Time will consume the strongest cord;
That which moulders hemp and steel,
Mortal arm and nerve must feel.
          Harold the Dauntless. Canto I,
                              Stanza 4
Then strip, lads, and to it, though
    sharp be the weather,
    And if, by mischance, you should
        happen to fall,
There are worse things in life than a
    tumble on heather,
    And life is itself but a game at foot-
        ball.
                      Song.[1] Stanza 5
Vacant heart, and hand, and eye,
Easy live and quiet die.
          Lucy Ashton's Song (in The Bride
              of Lammermoor, Chap. 3).
    Cursed war and racking tax
Have left us scarcely raiment to our
    backs.
          The Search after Happiness.[2]
                              Stanza 16
Paddy had not — a shirt to his back!
                    Ibid. Stanza 22
Come as the winds come, when
    Forests are rended;
Come as the waves come, when
    Navies are stranded.
          Pibroch of Donald Dhu. Stanza 4
A lawyer without history or litera-
ture is a mechanic, a mere working

[1] A rose hath fallen from thy chaplet. —
Halidon Hall, Act II, Sc. 2
    Robert Bruce's censure of Randolph for
permitting an English body of cavalry to pass
his flank on the day preceding the battle of
Bannockburn [June 24, 1314].
[2] See Shakespeare, page 99.

[1] On the lifting of the banner of the House
of Buccleuch at a great football match on
Carterhaugh [December 5, 1815].
[2] JOHN HAY in his poem, *The Enchanted
Shirt,* and EDWIN MARKHAM in *The Shoes of
Happiness,* have the same theme, — a monarch's search for the garment of an absolutely
happy man, and the discovery, when such a
man is found, that he does not possess one.

mason; if he possesses some knowledge of these, he may venture to call himself an architect.

> *Guy Mannering. Chap. 37*

Bluid is thicker than water.[1]

> *Ibid. Chap. 38*

It's no fish ye're buying, it's men's lives.[2]

> *The Antiquary. Chap. 11*

So wags the world.[3]

> *Ivanhoe. Chap. 37*

When Israel, of the Lord belov'd,
Out of the land of bondage came,
Her fathers' God before her mov'd,
An awful guide, in smoke and flame.

> *Ibid. Chap. 39 [Rebecca's Song. Stanza 1]*

Sea of upturned faces.[4]

> *Rob Roy. Chap. 20*

Lochow and the adjacent districts formed the original seat of the Campbells. The expression of "a far cry to Lochow" was proverbial.

> *Ibid. Chap. 29, Note*

There's a gude time coming.[5]

> *Ibid. Chap. 32*

My foot is on my native heath, and my name is MacGregor.

> *Ibid. Chap. 34*

Scared out of his seven senses.[6]

> *Ibid.*

Sound, sound the clarion, fill the fife!
To all the sensual world proclaim,
One crowded hour of glorious life
Is worth an age without a name.[7]

> *Old Mortality. Chap. 34*

The happy combination of fortuitous circumstances.[1]

> *The Monastery. Answer of the Author of Waverley to the Letter of Captain Clutterbuck*

Within that awful volume [2] lies
The mystery of mysteries!

> *The Monastery. Chap. 12*

And better had they ne'er been born,
Who read to doubt, or read to scorn.

> *Ibid.*

When we are handfasted, as we term it, we are man and wife for a year and day; that space gone by, each may choose another mate, or, at their pleasure, may call the priest to marry them for life; and this we call handfasting.[3]

> *Ibid. Chap. 25*

Spur not an unbroken horse; put not your ploughshare too deep into new land.

> *Ibid.*

Meat eaten without either mirth or music is ill of digestion.

> *Ibid.*

I am she, O most bucolic juvenal, under whose charge are placed the milky mothers of the herd.[4]

> *Ibid. Chap. 28*

But with the morning cool reflection came.[5]

> *Chronicles of the Canongate. Chap. 4*

Ah, County Guy, the hour is nigh,
The sun has left the lea.
The orange flower perfumes the bower,
The breeze is on the sea.

> *Quentin Durward. Chap. 4*

---

[1] This is a seventeenth-century proverb, found in RAY's *Collection* and elsewhere.

Blood is thicker, sir, than water, now as then.
　　WALLACE RICE [1859–]: *Blood is Thicker than Water*, St. 9
See Whittier, page 443.

[2] It is not linen you're wearing out,
　　But human creatures' lives.
THOMAS HOOD: *The Song of the Shirt*, St. 4

[3] See Shakespeare, page 49.

[4] DANIEL WEBSTER: *Speech* [Sept. 30, 1842]

[5] There's a good time coming. — CHARLES MACKAY: *The Good Time Coming*

[6] Huzza'd out of my seven senses. — *The Spectator, No. 616, Nov. 5, 1774*

[7] See page 311.

[1] Fearful concatenation of circumstances. — DANIEL WEBSTER: *Argument on the Murder of Captain White* [1830]
Fortuitous combination of circumstances. — DICKENS: *Our Mutual Friend, Vol. II, Chap. VII* (American ed.)

[2] The Bible.

[3] This custom of handfasting actually prevailed in the upland days. It arose partly from the want of priests. While the convents subsisted, monks were detached on regular circuits through the wilder districts, to marry those who had lived in this species of connexion. — ANDREW LANG: *Note* in his edition of *The Monastery*

[4] See Spenser, page 24.

[5] See Rowe, page 198.

But patience, cousin, and shuffle the cards,[1] till our hand is a stronger one.
Quentin Durward. Chap. 8

Too much rest is rust.[2]
The Betrothed. Chap. 13

If you keep a thing seven years, you are sure to find a use for it.
Woodstock. Chap. 28

What can they see in the longest kingly line in Europe, save that it runs back to a successful soldier? [3]
Ibid. Chap. 37

The playbill, which is said to have announced the tragedy of Hamlet, the character of the Prince of Denmark being left out.
The Talisman. Introduction

Rouse the lion from his lair.
Ibid. Heading, Chap. 6

Recollect that the Almighty, who gave the dog to be companion of our pleasures and our toils, hath invested him with a nature noble and incapable of deceit.
Ibid. Chap. 24

Jock, when ye hae naething else to do, ye may be aye sticking in a tree; it will be growing, Jock, when ye're sleeping.[4]
The Heart of Midlothian. Chap. 8

One hour of life, crowded to the full with glorious action, and filled with noble risks, is worth whole years of

those mean observances of paltry decorum.[1]
Count Robert of Paris. Chap. 25

Heaven knows its time; the bullet has its billet.
Ibid.

Fat, fair, and forty.[2]
St. Ronan's Well. Chap. 7

Good wine needs neither bush nor preface
To make it welcome.[3]
Peveril of the Peak. Chap. 4

When I hae a saxpence under my thumb,
Then I get credit in ilka town;
But when I am poor, they bid me gae by,
O, poverty parts good company.
The Abbot. Chap. 7

The jolly old landlord said, "Nothing's to pay."
The Pirate. Chap. 23

Tell that to the marines — the sailors won't believe it.[4]
Redgauntlet. Vol. II, Chap. 7

Although too much of a soldier among sovereigns, no one could claim with better right to be a sovereign among soldiers.[5]
Life of Napoleon

The sun never sets on the immense empire of Charles V.[6]
Ibid. [February, 1807]

---

[1] Patience, and shuffle the cards. — CERVANTES: *Don Quixote, Part II, Chap. 23*
   Cut the fiercest quarrels short
With "Patience, gentlemen, and shuffle."
     W. M. PRAED [1802–1839]: *Quince, St. 5*
Men disappoint me so, I disappoint myself so, yet courage, patience, shuffle the cards.
   MARGARET FULLER OSSOLI [1810–1850]: *Letter to the Reverend W. H. Channing.* Quoted in HIGGINSON'S *biography of Margaret Fuller,* page 112.

[2] German proverb: Rast ich, so rost ich (when I rest, I rust).

[3] Le premier qui fut roi, fut un soldat heureux:
   Qui sert bien son pays, n'a pas besoin d'aïeux
(The first who was king was a successful soldier. He who serves well his country has no need of ancestors). — VOLTAIRE: *Mérope, Act I, Sc. 3*

[4] The words of a Highland laird, while on his death-bed, to his son.

[1] See page 310.
[2] See Dryden, page 178.
[3] Good wine needs no bush. — SHAKESPEARE: *As You Like It, Epilogue*
[4] "Right," quoth Ben, "that will do for the marines." — BYRON: *The Island, Canto II, last line.* A footnote states: " 'That will do for the marines, but the sailors won't believe it,' is an old saying; and one of the few fragments of former jealousies which still survive (in jest only) between these gallant services."
   When they talk about making your fortune all I can say is tell it to the marines. — JOHN GALSWORTHY [1867–1933]: *The Silver Spoon, Part II, Chap. 4*
[5] See Pope, page 215.
[6] A power which has dotted over the surface of the whole globe with her possessions and military posts, whose morning drumbeat, following the sun, and keeping company with the hours, circles the earth with one continuous and unbroken strain of the martial

[Miss Austen] had a talent for describing the involvements and feelings and characters of ordinary life which is to me the most wonderful I ever met with. The Big Bow-wow strain [1] I can do myself like any now going; but the exquisite touch which renders ordinary, commonplace things and characters interesting, from the truth of the description and the sentiment is denied to me.

Journal. March 14, 1826

SYDNEY SMITH
[1771–1845]

It requires a surgical operation to get a joke well into a Scotch understanding.[2]

Lady Holland's Memoir. Vol. I,
Chap. 2

That knuckle-end of England, — that land of Calvin, oat-cakes, and sulphur.

Ibid.

No one minds what Jeffrey says: . . . it is not more than a week ago that I heard him speak disrespectfully of the equator.

Ibid.

We cultivate literature on a little oatmeal.[3]

Ibid.

---

airs of England. — DANIEL WEBSTER: *Speech* [May 7, 1834]

Why should the brave Spanish soldier brag the sun never sets in the Spanish dominions, but ever shineth on one part or other we have conquered for our king? — CAPTAIN JOHN SMITH: *Advertisements for the Unexperienced, &c.* (Mass. Hist. Soc. Coll., Third Series, Vol. III, P. 49)

It may be said of them (the Hollanders) as of the Spaniards, that the sun never sets on their dominions. — GAGE: *New Survey of the West Indies, Epistle Dedicatory* [London, 1648]

[1] He had the most atrocious bow-wow public park manner. — JAMES M. BARRIE [1860–1937]: *What Every Woman Knows, Act 3*

[2] See Walpole, page 246.

[3] Sydney Smith, with reference to the *Edinburgh Review*, says: "The motto I proposed for the 'Review' was 'Tenui musam meditamur avena'; but this was too near the truth to be admitted; so we took our present grave

Preaching has become a by-word for long and dull conversation of any kind; and whoever wishes to imply, in any piece of writing, the absence of everything agreeable and inviting, calls it a sermon.

Lady Holland's Memoir. Vol. I,
Chap. 3

It is always right that a man should be able to render a reason for the faith that is within him.

Ibid.

The sense of sight is indeed the highest bodily privilege, the purest physical pleasure, which man has derived from his Creator.

Ibid.

Avoid shame, but do not seek glory, — nothing so expensive as glory.

Ibid. Chap. 4

It is no part of the duty of a clergyman to preach upon subjects purely political, but it is not therefore his duty to avoid religious subjects which have been distorted into political subjects.

Ibid.

What would have become of us had it pleased Providence to make the weather unchangeable? Think of the state of destitution of the morning callers.

Ibid.

Take short views, hope for the best, and trust in God.

Ibid. Chap. 6

Hope is the belief, more or less strong, that joy will come; desire is the wish it may come. There is no word to designate the remembrance of joys past.

Ibid.

Looked as if she had walked straight out of the ark.

Ibid. Chap. 7

Great men hallow a whole people, and lift up all who live in their time.

Ibid.

The Smiths never had any arms,

---

motto from Publius Syrus, of whom none of us had, I am sure, read a single line."

and have invariably sealed their letters with their thumbs.

*Lady Holland's Memoir. Vol. I,
Chap. 9*

Madam, I have been looking for a person who disliked gravy all my life; let us swear eternal friendship.[1]

Ibid.

Not body enough to cover his mind decently with; his intellect is improperly exposed.

Ibid.

He has spent all his life in letting down empty buckets into empty wells; and he is frittering away his age in trying to draw them up again.[2]

Ibid.

You find people ready enough to do the Samaritan, without the oil and two-pence.

Ibid.

Ah, you flavour everything; you are the vanilla of society.

Ibid.

My living in Yorkshire was so far out of the way, that it was actually twelve miles from a lemon.

Ibid.

As the French say, there are three sexes, — men, women, and clergymen.[3]

Ibid.

To take Macaulay out of literature and society, and put him in the House of Commons, is like taking the chief physician out of London during a pestilence.

Ibid.

Daniel Webster struck me much like a steam-engine in trousers.

Ibid.

"Heat, ma'am!" I said; "it was so dreadful here, that I found there was nothing left for it but to take off my flesh and sit in my bones."

Ibid.

[1] See Frere, page 292.
[2] See Cowper, page 265.
[3] Lord Wharncliffe says, "The well-known sentence, almost a proverb, that 'this world consists of men, women, and Herveys,' was originally Lady Montagu's." — *Montagu Letters, Vol. I, P. 64*

I have gout, asthma, and seven other maladies, but am otherwise very well.

*Lady Holland's Memoir. Vol. I,
Chap. 10*

When you rise in the morning, form a resolution to make the day a happy one to a fellow-creature.

Ibid.

Live always in the best company when you read.

Ibid.

Never give way to melancholy; resist it steadily, for the habit will encroach.

Ibid.

I first gave it a dose of castor-oil, and then I christened it; so now the poor child is ready for either world.

Ibid. Chap. 11

He was a one-book man. Some men have only one book in them; others, a library.

Ibid.

Marriage resembles a pair of shears, so joined that they can not be separated; often moving in opposite directions, yet always punishing anyone who comes between them.[1]

Ibid.

Macaulay is like a book in breeches. . . . He has occasional flashes of silence, that make his conversation perfectly delightful.

Ibid.

Let onion atoms lurk within the bowl And, half suspected, animate the whole.

Ibid. Recipe for Salad

Serenely full, the epicure would say, Fate cannot harm me, — I have dined to-day.[2]

Ibid.

Don't tell me of facts, I never believe facts; you know Canning said nothing was so fallacious as facts, except figures.

Ibid.

What you don't know would make a great book.

Ibid.

In composing, as a general rule, run your pen through every other word you

[1] See Dickens, page 495.
[2] See Dryden, page 177.

have written; you have no idea what vigor it will give your style.[1]

Lady Holland's Memoir. Vol. I, Chap. 11

Thank God for tea! What would the world do without tea? — how did it exist? I am glad I was not born before tea.

Ibid.

That sign of old age, extolling the past at the expense of the present.

Ibid.

We know nothing of to-morrow; our business is to be good and happy today.

Ibid. Chap. 12

Light, dust, contradiction, an absurd remark, the sight of a Dissenter — anything, sets me sneezing; and if I begin sneezing at twelve, I don't leave off till two o'clock, and am heard distinctly in Taunton, when the wind sets that way — a distance of six miles. Turn your mind to this little curse.

To Dr. Holland, about Hay Fever [June, 1835]

Correspondences are like smallclothes before the invention of suspenders; it is impossible to keep them up.

Letter to Mrs. Crowe [January 31, 1841]

If you choose to represent the various parts in life by holes upon a table, of different shapes, — some circular, some triangular, some square, some oblong, — and the persons acting these parts by bits of wood of similar shapes, we shall generally find that the triangular person has got into the square hole, the oblong into the triangular, and a square person has squeezed himself into the round hole. The officer and the office, the doer and the thing done, seldom fit so exactly that we can say they were almost made for each other.[2]

Sketches of Moral Philosophy

The schoolboy whips his taxed top; the beardless youth manages his taxed horse with a taxed bridle on a taxed

[1] See Samuel Johnson, page 235.
[2] Generally accepted as the origin of the phrase "A square peg in a round hole."

road; and the dying Englishman, pouring his medicine, which has paid seven per cent, into a spoon that has paid fifteen per cent, flings himself back upon his chintz bed which has paid twenty-two per cent, and expires in the arms of an apothecary who has paid a license of a hundred pounds for the privilege of putting him to death.

Review of Seybert's Annals of the United States [1820]

In the four quarters of the globe, who reads an American book, or goes to an American play, or looks at an American picture or statue?

Ibid.

Magnificent spectacle of human happiness.

America. In Edinburgh Review, July, 1824

In the midst of this sublime and terrible storm [at Sidmouth], Dame Partington, who lived upon the beach, was seen at the door of her house with mop and pattens, trundling her mop, squeezing out the sea-water, and vigorously pushing away the Atlantic Ocean. The Atlantic was roused; Mrs. Partington's spirit was up. But I need not tell you that the contest was unequal; the Atlantic Ocean beat Mrs. Partington.

Speech at Taunton [1813]

Men who prefer any load of infamy, however great, to any pressure of taxation, however light.

On American Debts

SAMUEL TAYLOR COLERIDGE
[1772–1834]

He holds him with his glittering eye, . . .
And listens like a three years' child.[1]

The Ancient Mariner. Part I, Stanza 4

Red as a rose is she.

Ibid. Stanza 9

[1] WORDSWORTH, in his notes to *We Are Seven*, claims to have written this line.

We were the first that ever burst
Into that silent sea.
>> *The Ancient Mariner.*
>> *Part II, Stanza 5*

As idle as a painted ship
Upon a painted ocean.
>> *Ibid. Stanza 8*

Water, water, everywhere,
Nor any drop to drink.
>> *Ibid. Stanza 9*

Without a breeze, without a tide,
She steadies with upright keel.
>> *Ibid. Part III, Stanza 6*

The nightmare Life-in-Death was she.
>> *Ibid. Stanza 11*

The sun's rim dips, the stars rush out:
At one stride comes the dark;
With far-heard whisper o'er the sea
Off shot the spectre-bark.
>> *Ibid. Stanza 13*

We listen'd and look'd sideways up!
Fear at my heart, as at a cup,
My life-blood seem'd to sip.
>> *Ibid. Stanza 14*

And thou art long, and lank, and
brown,
As is the ribbed sea-sand.[1]
>> *Ibid. Part IV, Stanza 1*

Alone, alone, all, all alone;
Alone on a wide, wide sea.
>> *Ibid. Stanza 3*

The moving moon went up the sky,
And nowhere did abide;
Softly she was going up,
And a star or two beside.
>> *Ibid. Stanza 10*

A spring of love gush'd from my heart,
And I bless'd them unaware.
>> *Ibid. Stanza 14*

Oh sleep! it is a gentle thing,
Beloved from pole to pole.
>> *Ibid. Part V, Stanza 1*

A noise like of a hidden brook
In the leafy month of June,
That to the sleeping woods all night
Singeth a quiet tune.
>> *Ibid. Stanza 17*

Like one that on a lonesome road
Doth walk in fear and dread,
And having once turned round, walks
on,

[1] Coleridge says: "For these lines I am indebted to Mr. Wordsworth."

And turns no more his head;
Because he knows a frightful fiend
Doth close behind him tread.
>> *The Ancient Mariner.*
>> *Part VI, Stanza 10*

Is this the hill? is this the kirk?
Is this mine own countree?
>> *Ibid. Stanza 14*

So lonely 'twas, that God himself
Scarce seemed there to be.
>> *Ibid. Part VII, Stanza 19*

He prayeth well who loveth well
Both man and bird and beast.
>> *Ibid. Stanza 22*

He prayeth best who loveth best
All things both great and small.
>> *Ibid. Stanza 23*

A sadder and a wiser man
He rose the morrow morn.
>> *Ibid. Stanza 25*

And the spring comes slowly up this
way.
>> *Christabel. Part I*

Her gentle limbs did she undress,
And lay down in her loveliness.
>> *Ibid.*

A sight to dream of, not to tell!
>> *Ibid.*

That saints will aid if men will call;
For the blue sky bends over all!
>> *Ibid. Conclusion*

To be wroth with one we love
Doth work like madness in the brain.
>> *Ibid. Part II*

In Xanadu did Kubla Khan
A stately pleasure-dome decree;
Where Alph, the sacred river, ran
Through caverns measureless to man,
Down to a sunless sea.
>> *Kubla Khan*

A savage place! as holy and enchanted
As e'er beneath a waning moon was
haunted
By woman wailing for her demon
lover!
>> *Ibid.*

Ancestral voices prophesying war.
>> *Ibid.*

A damsel with a dulcimer
In a vision once I saw:
It was an Abyssinian maid,

And on her dulcimer she played,
Singing of Mount Abora.
                        Kubla Khan
For he on honey-dew hath fed,
And drunk the milk of Paradise.
                        Ibid.
What is an Epigram? A dwarfish whole,
Its body brevity, and wit its soul.[1]
                        An Epigram
The Eighth Commandment was not
    made for bards.
                The Reproof and Reply
Ere sin could blight or sorrow fade,
    Death came with friendly care;
The opening bud to heaven conveyed,
    And bade it blossom there.
                Epitaph on an Infant
When France in wrath her giant limbs
    up-rear'd.
                    France: An Ode. I.
Yes, while I stood and gazed, my tem-
    ples bare,
And shot my being through earth, sea,
    and air,
Possessing all things with intensest
    love,
O Liberty! my spirit felt thee there.
                        Ibid. V.
Forth from his dark and lonely hiding-
    place
(Portentous sight!) the owlet Atheism,
Sailing on obscene wings athwart the
    noon,
Drops his blue-fring'd lids, and holds
    them close,
And hooting at the glorious sun in
    heaven
Cries out, "Where is it?"
                    Fears in Solitude
And the Devil did grin, for his darling
    sin
    Is pride that apes humility.[2]
            The Devil's Thoughts. Stanza 6

[1] See Shakespeare, page 92.
[2]   His favourite sin
    Is pride that apes humility.
            SOUTHEY: *The Devil's Walk*
ALEXANDER SMITH, in his essay on William
Dunbar, in *Dreamthorp*, says that Dunbar's
satire, *The Devil's Inquest*, probably gave
Coleridge the hint of his poem. Two lines
from Dunbar are:
    The Devil said then, withouten mair,
    "Renounce your God, and cum to me."

All thoughts, all passions, all delights,
Whatever stirs this mortal frame,
    All are but ministers of Love,
    And feed his sacred flame.
                        Love. Stanza 1
Saved from outrage worse than death.
                    Ibid. Stanza 14
Blest hour! it was a luxury — to be!
            *Reflections on Having Left a
                    Place of Retirement*
A charm
For thee, my gentle-hearted Charles,[1]
    to whom
No sound is dissonant which tells of
    life.
            This Lime-tree Bower My Prison
Hast thou a charm to stay the morning
    star
In his steep course?
            Hymn in the Vale of Chamouni
Risest from forth thy silent sea of
    pines.
                        Ibid.
Motionless torrents! silent cataracts!
                        Ibid.
Ye living flowers that skirt the eternal
    frost.
                        Ibid.
Earth, with her thousand voices, praises
    God.
                        Ibid.
Tranquillity! thou better name
Than all the family of Fame.
                Ode to Tranquillity
Aloof with hermit-eye I scan
The present work of present man —
A wild and dream-like trade of blood
    and guile,
Too foolish for a tear, too wicked for a
    smile.
                        Ibid.
The grand old ballad of Sir Patrick
    Spence.[2]
            Dejection, An Ode. Stanza 1
A mother is a mother still,
    The holiest thing alive.
                    The Three Graves
The knight's bones are dust,

[1] Charles Lamb. See Lamb, page 325.
[2] The King sits in Dumferling toune,
    Drinking the blude-reid wine.
    PERCY: *Reliques, Sir Patrick Spence*

And his good sword rust;
His soul is with the saints, I trust.
The Knight's Tomb

How seldom, friend! a good great man
inherits
Honor or wealth, with all his worth and
pains!
It sounds like stories from the land of
spirits
If any man obtains that which he merits,
Or any merit that which he obtains.

.   .   .   .   .   .

Greatness and goodness are not means,
but ends!
Hath he not always treasures, always
friends,
The good great man? Three treasures,
— love, and light,
And calm thoughts, regular as infant's
breath; —
And three firm friends, more sure than
day and night, —
Himself, his Maker, and the angel
Death.
Complaint [*Edition of 1852*]
— The Good Great Man [*Edi-
tion of 1893*]

My eyes make pictures, when they are
shut.
A Day-Dream. Stanza 1

Nought cared this body for wind or
weather,
When youth and I lived in 't together.
Youth and Age. Stanza 1

Flowers are lovely; love is flower-like;
Friendship is a sheltering tree;
Oh the joys that came down shower-
like,
Of friendship, love, and liberty,
Ere I was old!
Ibid. Stanza 2

I have heard of reasons manifold
Why Love must needs be blind,
But this the best of all I hold, —
His eyes are in his mind.[1]
*To a Lady, Offended by a
Sportive Observation*

[1] Love looks not with the eyes, but with
the mind. — SHAKESPEARE: *A Midsummer-
Night's Dream, Act I, Sc. 1, L. 234*

What outward form and feature are
He guesseth but in part;
But what within is good and fair
He seeth with the heart.
*To a Lady, Offended by a
Sportive Observation*

Be that blind bard, who on the Chian
strand,
By those deep sounds possessed with
inward light,
Beheld the Iliad and the Odyssey
Rise to the swelling of the voiceful sea.[1]
Fancy in Nubibus

In many ways doth the full heart reveal
The presence of the love it would con-
ceal.
*Motto to Poems Written in
Later Life*

I counted two-and-seventy stenches,
All well defined, and several stinks.
Cologne

The river Rhine, it is well known,
Doth wash your city of Cologne;
But tell me, nymphs! what power di-
vine
Shall henceforth wash the river Rhine?
Ibid.

Trochee trips from long to short;
From long to long in solemn sort
Slow Spondee stalks.
Metrical Feet

Strongly it bears us along in swelling
and limitless billows;
Nothing before and nothing behind but
the sky and the ocean.
*The Homeric Hexameter
(translated from Schiller)*

In the hexameter rises the fountain's
silvery column,
In the pentameter aye falling in melody
back.
*The Ovidian Elegiac Metre
(from Schiller)*

The intelligible forms of ancient poets,
The fair humanities of old religion,
The power, the beauty, and the majesty
That had their haunts in dale or piny
mountain,

[1] And Iliad and Odyssey
Rose to the music of the sea.
CHRISTIAN STOLBERG [1748–1821]:
Thalatta, P. 132 (From the German)

Or forest by slow stream, or pebbly
    spring,
Or chasms and watery depths, — all
    these have vanished;
They live no longer in the faith of
    reason.
> *Wallenstein. Part I, Piccolo-*
> *mini, Act II, Sc. 4 (translated*
> *from Schiller)*

Clothing the palpable and familiar
With golden exhalations of the dawn.
> *Ibid. Part II, The Death of*
> *Wallenstein, Act V, Sc. 1*

       Often do the spirits
Of great events stride on before the
    events,
And in to-day already walks to-
    morrow.[1]
> *Ibid.*

The happiness of life is made up of
minute fractions — the little soon forgotten charities of a kiss or smile, a
kind look, a heartfelt compliment, and
the countless infinitesimals of pleasurable and genial feeling.
> *The Friend. The Improvisatore*

A dwarf sees farther than the giant
when he has the giant's shoulder to
mount on.[2]
> *Ibid. Sect. I, Essay 8*

An instinctive taste teaches men to
build their churches in flat countries,
with spire steeples, which, as they cannot be referred to any other object,
point as with silent finger to the sky
and star.[3]
> *Ibid. Essay 14*

Not the poem which we have *read,*
but that to which we *return,* with the
greatest pleasure, possesses the genu-

ine power, and claims the name of *es-*
sential poetry.
> *Biographia Literaria. Chap. 1*

Every reform, however necessary,
will by weak minds be carried to an
excess, that itself will need reforming.
> *Ibid.*

Experience informs us that the first
defence of weak minds is to recrimi-
nate.
> *Ibid. Chap. 2*

Through all the works of Chaucer,
there reigns a cheerfulness, a manly hi-
larity, which makes it almost impossible to doubt a correspondent habit of
feeling in the author himself.
> *Ibid.*

Men whose dearest wishes are fixed
on objects wholly out of their own
power, become in all cases more or less
impatient and prone to anger.
> *Ibid.*

Veracity does not consist in *saying,*
but in the intention of *communicating*
truth.
> *Ibid. Chap. 9*

The lamentable difficulty I have always experienced in saying "No."
> *Ibid. Chap. 10*

To have lived in vain must be a painful thought to any man, and especially
so to him who has made literature his
profession.
> *Ibid.*

Never pursue literature as a trade.
> *Ibid. Chap. 11*

The first range of hills that encircles
the scanty vale of human life is the
horizon for the majority of its inhabitants. On *its* ridges the common sun is
born and departs. From *them* the stars
rise, and touching *them,* they vanish.
> *Ibid. Chap. 12*

Good sense is the body of poetic
genius, fancy its drapery, motion its
life, and imagination the soul.
> *Ibid. Chap. 14*

Our myriad-minded Shakespeare.[1]
> *Ibid. Chap. 15*

---

[1] Sed ita a principio inchoatum esse mun-
dum ut certis rebus certa signa præcurrerent
(Thus in the beginning the world was so made
that certain signs come before certain events).
— CICERO: *Divinatione, Liber I, Cap. 52*
    Coming events cast their shadows before. —
CAMPBELL: *Lochiel's Warning*
    Poets are the hierophants of an unappre-
hended inspiration; the mirrors of the gigantic shadows which futurity casts upon the
present. — SHELLEY: *A Defence of Poetry*
[2] See Burton, page 122.
[3] See Wordsworth, page 302.

[1] "A phrase," says Coleridge, "which I have
borrowed from a Greek monk, who applies it
to a patriarch of Constantinople."

Polysyllabic (or what the common people call, *dictionary*) words.

> *Biographia Literaria. Chap. 20*

The infallible test of a blameless style: namely, its untranslatableness in words of the same language, without injury to the meaning.

> *Ibid. Chap. 22*

A poem is not necessarily obscure, because it does not aim to be popular. It is enough if a work be perspicuous to those for whom it is written.

> *Ibid.*

Talk of the devil, and his horns appear, says the proverb.

> *Ibid. Chap. 23*

Reviewers are usually people who would have been poets, historians, biographers, if they could; they have tried their talents at one or the other, and have failed; therefore they turn critics.[1]

> *Lectures on Shakespeare and Milton [1811–1812]. Page 36*

Schiller has the material sublime.

> *Table Talk*

I wish our clever young poets would remember my homely definitions of prose and poetry; that is, prose, — words in their best order; poetry, — the best words in their best order.

> *Ibid.*

That passage is what I call the sublime dashed to pieces by cutting too close with the fiery four-in-hand round the corner of nonsense.

> *Ibid.*

Iago's soliloquy, the motive-hunting of a motiveless malignity — how awful it is!

> *Notes on Some Other Plays of Shakespeare*

Beneath this sod
A poet lies, or that which once seemed he —
Oh, lift a thought in prayer for S.T.C.!

---

[1] Reviewers, with some rare exceptions, are a most stupid and malignant race. As a bankrupt thief turns thief-taker in despair, so an unsuccessful author turns critic. — SHELLEY: *Fragments of Adonais*
You know who critics are? The men who have failed in literature and art. — DISRAELI: *Lothair, Chap. XXXV*

That he, who many a year, with toil of breath,
Found death in life, may here find life in death.

> *Epitaph written for himself*

JOSIAH QUINCY, JR.
[1772–1864]

If this bill [for the admission of Orleans Territory as a State] passes, it is my deliberate opinion that it is virtually a dissolution of the Union; that it will free the States from their moral obligation; and, as it will be the right of all, so it will be the duty of some, definitely to prepare for a separation, — amicably if they can, violently if they must.[1]

> *Abridged Congressional Debates. Vol. IV, Page 327, Jan. 14, 1811*

WILLIAM BARNES RHODES
[1772–1826]

Who dares this pair of boots displace,
Must meet Bombastes face to face.[2]

> *Bombastes Furioso. Act I, Sc. 4*

Bombastes. So have I heard on Afric's burning shore
A hungry lion give a grievous roar;
The grievous roar echoed along the shore.
Artaxaminous. So have I heard on Afric's burning shore
Another lion give a grievous roar;
And the first lion thought the last a bore.

> *Ibid.*

WILLIAM HENRY HARRISON
[1773–1841]

We admit of no government by divine right . . . the only legitimate

---

[1] The gentleman [Mr. Quincy] cannot have forgotten his own sentiment, uttered even on the floor of this House, "Peaceably if we can, forcibly if we must." — HENRY CLAY: *Speech* [Jan. 8, 1813]
[2] Let none but he these arms displace,
Who dares Orlando's fury face.
> CERVANTES: *Don Quixote, Part II, Chap. LXVI*; RAY: *Proverbs*

right to govern is an express grant of power from the governed.

Inaugural Address [*March 4, 1841*]

Never with my consent shall an officer of the people, compensated for his services out of their pockets, become the pliant instrument of the Executive will.

Ibid.

A decent and manly examination of the acts of Government should be not only tolerated, but encouraged.

Ibid.

The delicate duty of devising schemes of revenue should be left where the Constitution has placed it — with the immediate representatives of the people.

Ibid.

If parties in a republic are necessary to secure a degree of vigilance sufficient to keep the public functionaries within the bounds of law and duty, at that point their usefulness ends.

Ibid.

JOHN RANDOLPH
[1773–1833]

The surest way to prevent war is not to fear it.

Speech before Committee of Whole, U. S. House of Representatives [*March 5, 1806*]

So brilliant, yet so corrupt, which, like a rotten mackerel by moonlight, shines and stinks.[1]

Of Henry Clay

SAMUEL JAMES ARNOLD
[1774–1852]

Along the line our signal ran:
"England expects that every man
This day will do his duty." [2]

The Death of Nelson. Stanza 1

[1] Quoted by JOHN MCCONAUGHY in *Who Owns America?*
'Tis vain for present fame to wish.
Our persons first must be forgotten;
For poets are like stinking fish,
They never shine until they're rotten.
MACDONALD CLARKE [1798–1842]:
Epigram

[2] See Nelson, page 284.

ROBERT SOUTHEY
[1774–1843]

"You are old, Father William," the young man cried,
"The few locks which are left you are gray;
You are hale, Father William, a hearty old man, —
Now tell me the reason I pray."

The Old Man's Comforts, and How He Gained Them.[1] *Stanza 1*

"In the days of my youth," Father William replied,
"I remembered that youth could not last;
I thought of the future, whatever I did,
That I never might grieve for the past."

Ibid. Stanza 4

Bishop Hatto fearfully hastened away,
And he crossed the Rhine without delay,
And reached his tower, and barred with care
All the windows, and doors, and loopholes there.

God's Judgment on a Wicked Bishop.[2] *Stanza 12*

[1] Of several parodies of this poem, the one by "Lewis Carroll" is probably better known than the original.
"You are old, father William," the young man said,
"And your hair has become very white;
And yet you incessantly stand on your head —
Do you think, at your age, it is right?"
"LEWIS CARROLL": *You Are Old, Father William, St. 1*
"You are old, Father William, and though one would think
All the veins in your body were dry,
Yet the end of your nose is red as a pink;
I beg your indulgence, but why?"
LEE O. HARRIS AND JAMES WHITCOMB RILEY: *Father William, St. 1*

[2] Hatto, in the time of the great famine of 914, when he saw the poor exceedingly oppressed by famine, assembled a great company of them together into a barn at Kaub and burnt them . . . because he thought the famine would sooner cease if those poor folks were despatched out of the world. . . . But God . . . sent against him a plague of mice . . . and the prelate retreated to a tower in the Rhine . . . but the mice chased him continually . . . and at last he was most miser-

Who is yonder poor maniac, whose
  wildly fixed eyes
  Seem a heart overcharged to express?
She weeps not, yet often and deeply
  she sighs;
She never complains, but her silence
  implies
  The composure of settled distress.
          Mary, the Maid of the Inn.[1]
                    Stanza 1

One dreadful sound could the Rover
  hear,
A sound as if with the Inchcape Bell
The Devil below was ringing his knell.
          The Inchcape Rock.[2] *Stanza 17*

Where Washington hath left
  His awful memory
  A light for after times!
          *Ode Written during the War
              with America* [*1814*]

The march of intellect.[3]
          *Colloquies on the Progress and
          Prospects of Society. Vol. II,
          The Doctor, Chap. Extraordi-
          nary, Page 360*

The laws are with us, and God on
our side.
          *On the Rise and Progress of
          Popular Disaffection* [*1817*].
          Vol. II, Essay VIII, Page 107

Agreed to differ.
                    Life of Wesley.

My days among the dead are passed;
  Around me I behold,
Where'er these casual eyes are cast,
  The mighty minds of old;
My never-failing friends are they,
  With whom I converse night and day.
          Occasional Pieces. The Library

---

ably devoured. — THOMAS CORYAT [1577–
1617]: *Crudities* [1611], *P. 571*
[1] This poem was dramatized by GEORGE
SOANE [1790–1860] as *The Innkeeper's Daughter, or The Smuggler's Fate,* and produced at
the Boston Museum [May 10, 1852].
[2] A rock in the North Sea, off the Firth of
Tay, Scotland, dangerous to navigators because it is covered with every tide. There is a
tradition that a warning bell was fixed on
the rock by the Abbot of Aberbrothok, which
was stolen by a sea pirate, who perished on
the rock a year later. Southey's ballad deals
with this tradition.
[3] See Burke, page 259.

So I told them in rhyme,
For of rhymes I had store.
          The Cataract of Lodore
          Helter-skelter,
          Hurry-scurry.
                    Ibid.

And so never ending, but always descending.
                    Ibid.

And this way the water comes down at
Lodore.
                    Ibid.

"And wherefore do the poor com-
  plain?"
  The rich man asked of me —
"Come walk abroad with me," I said,
  "And I will answer thee."
          The Complaints of the Poor.
                    Stanza 1

From his brimstone bed, at break of
  day,
  A-walking the Devil is gone,
To look at his little snug farm of the
  World,
  And see how his stock went on.
          The Devil's Walk. Stanza 1

How then was the Devil dressed?
O, he was in his Sunday's best;
His coat was red, and his breeches were
  blue,
And there was a hole where his tail
  came through.
                    Ibid. Stanza 3

He passed a cottage with a double
  coach-house, —
  A cottage of gentility;
  And he owned with a grin,
  That his favourite sin
  Is pride that apes humility.[1]
                    Ibid. Stanza 8

          He was always found
Among your ten and twenty pound
  subscribers,
Your benefactors in the newspapers.
His alms were money put to interest
In the other world.
          The Alderman's Funeral

There is not a wife in the west country
But has heard of the well of St. Keyne.
          The Well of St. Keyne. Stanza 1

---

[1] See Coleridge, page 316.

If the husband, of this gifted well
Shall drink before his wife,
A happy man thenceforth is he,
For he shall be master for life.
        The Well of St. Keyne. Stanza 10
As frozen as charity.[1]
            The Soldier's Wife. Stanza 4
"But what good came of it at last?"
Quoth little Peterkin.
"Why, that I cannot tell," said he;
"But 'twas a famous victory."
        The Battle of Blenheim. Stanza 11
Blue, darkly, deeply, beautifully blue.[2]
            Madoc in Wales. Part I, 5
What will not woman, gentle woman
    dare,
When strong affection stirs her spirit
    up?
            Ibid. Part II, 2
How beautiful is night!
A dewy freshness fills the silent air;
No mist obscures, nor cloud, nor speck,
    nor stain,
    Breaks the serene of heaven:
In full-orbed glory yonder moon di-
    vine
    Rolls through the dark blue depths;
    Beneath her steady ray
    The desert circle spreads,
Like the round ocean, girdled with the
    sky.
    How beautiful is night!
        Thalaba. Book I, Stanza 1
And last of all an Admiral came,
A terrible man with a terrible
    name, —
A name which you all know by sight
    very well,
But which no one can speak, and no
    one can spell.
        The March to Moscow. Stanza 8
The Devil may take the hindmost.[3]
            Ibid. Stanza 10
They sin who tell us love can die;
With life all other passions fly,
    All others are but vanity. . . .
    Love is indestructible,

Its holy flame forever burneth;
From heaven it came, to heaven re-
    turneth. . . .
It soweth here with toil and care,
But the harvest-time of love is there.
        The Curse of Kehama. Canto X,
                        Stanza 10
Oh, when a mother meets on high
    The babe she lost in infancy,
Hath she not then for pains and fears,
    The day of woe, the watchful night,
    For all her sorrow, all her tears,
An over-payment of delight?
            Ibid. Stanza 11
Thou hast been called, O sleep! the
    friend of woe;
But 'tis the happy that have called
    thee so.
        Ibid. Canto XV, Stanza 11
The Satanic school.
        Vision of Judgment. Original
                        Preface
Snips and snails and puppy dog tails
And such are little boys made of.
        What All the World is Made of.
Sugar and spice and all things nice.
                        Ibid.

JANE AUSTEN
[1775–1817]

Everything nourishes what is strong
already.
        Pride and Prejudice. Chap. 9
My dear, I have two small favours
to request. First, that you will allow
me the free use of my understanding
on the present occasion; and secondly,
of my room. I shall be glad to have the
library to myself as soon as may be.[1]
            Ibid. Chap. 20
Those who do not complain are never
pitied.
                        Ibid.
Mrs. Bennet was restored to her
usual querulous serenity.
            Ibid. Chap. 42

---

[1] See Hood, page 392.
[2] "Darkly, deeply, beautifully blue,"
    As some one somewhere sings about the
    sky.
        BYRON: *Don Juan, Canto IV, St. 110*
[3] See Butler, page 142.

[1] Rather your room as your company.
    ANONYMOUS: *Marriage of Wit and Wis-
        dom [circa 1570]*

What dreadful hot weather we have! It keeps me in a continual state of inelegance.

Letters to her sister Cassandra.
September 18, 1796

Miss Blachford is agreeable enough. I do not want people to be very agreeable, as it saves me the trouble of liking them a great deal.

Ibid. December 24, 1798

She was highly rouged, and looked rather quietly and contentedly silly than anything else.

Ibid. May 12, 1801

"Only a novel" . . . in short, only some work in which the greatest powers of the mind are displayed, in which the most thorough knowledge of human nature, the happiest delineation of its varieties, are conveyed to the world in the best chosen language.

Northanger Abbey. Chap. 5

CHARLES LAMB
[1775–1834]

The red-letter days, now become, to all intents and purposes, dead-letter days.

Oxford in the Vacation [1]

The human species, according to the best theory I can form of it, is composed of two distinct races, the men who borrow, and the men who lend.[2]

The Two Races of Men

Borrowers of books — those mutilators of collections, spoilers of the symmetry of shelves, and creators of odd volumes.

Ibid.

Of all sound of all bells — (bells, the music nighest bordering upon heaven) — most solemn and touching is the peal which rings out the Old Year.

New Year's Eve

[1] Which, it has been pointed out, was actually written at Cambridge. See E. V. LUCAS: *Lamb and the Universities.*

[2] Compare Max Beerbohm's delightful essay, "Hosts and Guests," in "And Even Now."

A clear fire, a clean hearth, and the rigour of the game.

Mrs. Battle's Opinions on Whist

Sentimentally I am disposed to harmony; but organically I am incapable of a tune.

A Chapter on Ears

Not if I know myself at all.

The Old and New Schoolmaster

Credulity is the man's weakness, but the child's strength.

Witches, and Other Night Fears

Parents do not know what they do when they leave tender babes alone to go to sleep in the dark.

Ibid.

Not many sounds in life, and I include all urban and all rural sounds, exceed in interest a knock at the door.[1]

Valentine's Day

A God-send, as our familiarly pious ancestors termed a benefit received where the benefactor was unknown.

Ibid.

The custom of saying grace at meals had, probably, its origin in the early times of the world, and the hunter-state of man, when dinners were precarious things, and a full meal was something more than a common blessing.

Grace Before Meat

Sassafras wood boiled down to a kind of tea, and tempered with an infusion of milk and sugar, hath to some tastes a delicacy beyond the China luxury.[2]

The Praise of Chimney-Sweepers

A fair sepulchre in the grateful stomach of the judicious epicure.

A Dissertation upon Roast Pig

Presents, I often say, endear absents.

Ibid.

[1] Doorbells are like a magic game,
 Or the grab-bag at a fair —
You never know when you hear one ring
 Who may be waiting there.
          RACHEL FIELD [1894–   ]:
                    Doorbells

[2] Sassafras, oh, sassafras,
 Thou art the stuff for me,
And in the Spring I love to sing,
 Sweet sassafras, of thee!
          EDWARD EGGLESTON [1837–1902]:
                    Sassafras

It argues an insensibility.

A Dissertation upon Roast Pig

Nothing is to me more distasteful than that entire complacency and satisfaction which beam in the countenances of a new-married couple.

The Behaviour of Married People

He has left off reading altogether, to the great improvement of his originality.

Detached Thoughts on Books and Reading

Books think for me.

Ibid.

Books which are no books.

Ibid.

To be strong-backed and neat-bound is the desideratum of a volume. Magnificence comes after.

Ibid.

Newspapers always excite curiosity. No one ever lays one down without a feeling of disappointment.

Ibid.

If there be a regal solitude, it is a sick bed.

The Convalescent

How sickness enlarges the dimensions of a man's self to himself.

Ibid.

Let me caution persons grown old in active business, not lightly, nor without weighing their own resources, to forego their customary employment all at once, for there may be danger in it.

The Superannuated Man

Your absence of mind we have borne, till your presence of body came to be called in question by it.

Amicus Redivivus

A pun is a pistol let off at the ear; not a feather to tickle the intellect.

Popular Fallacies. IX, That the Worst Puns are the Best

A presentation copy . . . is a copy of a book which does not sell, sent you by the author, with his foolish autograph at the beginning of it; for which, if a stranger, he only demands your friendship; if a brother author, he expects from you a book of yours, which does not sell, in return.

Popular Fallacies. XI, That We Must Not Look a Gift-Horse in the Mouth

The growing infirmities of age manifest themselves in nothing more strongly, than in an inveterate dislike of interruption.

Ibid. XII, That Home is Home Though it is Never so Homely

The good things of life are not to be had singly, but come to us with a mixture.

Ibid. XIII, That You Must Love Me and Love My Dog

It has happened not seldom that one work of some author has so transcendently surpassed in execution the rest of his compositions, that the world has agreed to pass a sentence of dismissal upon the latter, and to consign them to total neglect and oblivion.

Eliana. Estimate of Defoe's Secondary Novels

Cannot the heart in the midst of crowds feel frightfully alone?

Ibid.

The greatest pleasure I know is to do a good action by stealth, and to have it found out by accident.

Table Talk. In the Athenaeum [1834]

Reputation said: "If once we sever, Our chance of future meeting is but vain:
Who parts from me, must look to part for ever,
For Reputation lost comes not again."

Love, Death, and Reputation. Stanza 4

Some cry up Haydn, some Mozart,
Just as the whim bites. For my part,
I do not care a farthing candle
For either of them, nor for Handel.

Free Thoughts on Several Eminent Composers

A bird appears a thoughtless thing . . .
No doubt he has his little cares,
And very hard he often fares,
The which so patiently he bears.

Crumbs to the Birds

Gone before
To that unknown and silent shore.
Hester. Stanza 7

I have had playmates, I have had companions,
In my days of childhood, in my joyful school-days.
All, all are gone, the old familiar faces.
Old Familiar Faces

For thy sake, tobacco, I
Would do anything but die.
A Farewell to Tobacco

And half had staggered that stout Stagirite.
Written at Cambridge

Who first invented work, and bound the free
And holiday-rejoicing spirit down . . .
To that dry drudgery at the desk's dead wood?
Work

The economy of Heaven is dark
And wisest clerks have missed the mark.
On an Infant Dying as Soon as Born

I have something more to do than feel.
Letter to Coleridge after the death of Lamb's mother [1796]

The not unpeaceful evening of a day
Made black by morning storms.
Poem-letter to Coleridge [1797]

A good-natured woman, which is as much as you can expect from a friend's wife, whom you got acquainted with a bachelor.
Letter to Hazlitt [1805]

Anything awful makes me laugh. I misbehaved once at a funeral.
Letter to Southey [1815]

Fanny Kelly's divine plain face.
Letter to Mrs. Wordsworth [1818]

I have confessed to you my utter inability to remember in any comprehensive way what I read. I can vehemently applaud, or perversely stickle, at *parts;* but I cannot grasp at a whole.
Letter to Godwin [1803]

For God's sake (I never was more serious) don't make me ridiculous any more by terming me gentle-hearted

in print [1] . . . substitute drunken dog, ragged head, seld-shaven, odd-eyed, stuttering, or any other epithet which truly and properly belongs to the gentleman in question.
To Coleridge [August, 1800]

An archangel a little damaged.
His description of Coleridge

He might have proved a useful adjunct, if not an ornament to society. .
Captain Starkey

Separate from the pleasure of your company, I don't much care if I never see a mountain in my life.
Letter to Wordsworth [1801]

Neat, not gaudy.[2]
Ibid. [1806]

Martin, if dirt was trumps, what hands you would hold!
Lamb's Suppers

I came home for ever!
Letter to Bernard Barton [1825], on leaving his "33 years' desk" at the East India House

WALTER SAVAGE LANDOR
[1775–1864]

Rose Aylmer, whom these wakeful eyes
May weep, but never see,
A night of memories and of sighs
I consecrate to thee.
Rose Aylmer

But I have sinuous shells of pearly hue
Within, and they that lustre have imbibed
In the sun's palace-porch, where when unyoked
His chariot-wheel stands midway in the wave:
Shake one, and it awakens; then apply
Its polisht lips to your attentive ear,
And it remembers its august abodes,
And murmurs as the ocean murmurs there.[3]
Gebir. Book I [1798]

---

[1] See Coleridge, page 316.
[2] Rich, not gaudy. — SHAKESPEARE: *Hamlet*, Act I, Sc. 3, L. 71
[3] See Wordsworth, page 302.

Past are three summers since she first
    beheld
The ocean; all around the child await
Some exclamation of amazement here.
She coldly said, her long-lasht eyes
    abased,
Is this the mighty ocean? is this all?
                        Gebir. Book II
Shakespeare is not our poet, but the
.   world's,[1] —
Therefore on him no speech! And brief
    for thee,
Browning! Since Chaucer was alive
    and hale,
No man hath walk'd along our roads
    with step
So active, so inquiring eye, or tongue
So varied in discourse.
                    To Robert Browning
The Siren waits thee, singing song for
    song.
                        Ibid.
Around the child bend all the three
Sweet Graces — Faith, Hope, Charity.
Around the man bend other faces —
Pride, Envy, Malice, are his Graces.
                    Around the Child
Children are what the mothers are.
No fondest father's fondest care
Can fashion so the infant heart.
                        Children
When we play the fool, how wide
The theatre expands! beside,
How long the audience sits before us!
How many prompters! what a chorus!
                    Plays. Stanza 2
I strove with none, for none was worth
    my strife;
    Nature I loved; and next to Nature,
    Art.
I warm'd both hands against the fire of
    life;
    It sinks, and I am ready to depart.
    Dying Speech of an Old Philosopher
There are no fields of amaranth on
this side of the grave; there are no
voices, O Rhodopè, that are not soon
mute, however tuneful; there is no
name, with whatever emphasis of pas-

sionate love repeated, of which the
echo is not faint at last.
            Imaginary Conversations.
                Aesop and Rhodopè, I

Elegance in prose composition is
mainly this: a just admission of topics
and of words; neither too many nor
too few of either; enough of sweetness
in the sound to induce us to enter and
sit still; enough of illustration and reflection to change the posture of our
minds when they would tire; and
enough of sound matter in the complex
to repay us for our attendance.
    Ibid. Chesterfield and Chatham

Of all failures, to fail in a witticism
is the worst, and the mishap is the
more calamitous in a drawn out and
detailed one.
                        Ibid.

Stand close around, ye Stygian set,
    With Dirce in one boat convey'd!
Or Charon, seeing, may forget
    That he is old, and she a shade.
                        Dirce

'Tis verse that gives
Immortal youth to mortal maids.
                        Verse

JOSEPH BLANCO WHITE
[1775–1841]

Mysterious Night! when our first par-
    ent knew
Thee from report divine, and heard
    thy name,
Did he not tremble for this lovely
    frame,
This glorious canopy of light and blue?
                        Sonnet, Night

Hesperus with the host of heaven came,
And lo! creation widened in man's
    view.
                        Ibid.

Why do we, then, shun Death with anx-
    ious strife?
If Light can thus deceive, wherefore
    not Life?
                        Ibid.

---

[1] Nor sequent centuries could hit
    Orbit and sum of Shakespeare's wit.
        R. W. EMERSON: *Solution*

THOMAS CAMPBELL
[1777–1844]

'Tis distance lends enchantment to the view,
And robes the mountain in its azure hue.[1]
Pleasures of Hope. Part I, Line 7

Hope, for a season, bade the world farewell,
And Freedom shriek'd as Kosciusko fell!
Ibid. Line 381

Who hath not own'd, with rapture-smitten frame,
The power of grace, the magic of a name?
Ibid. Part II, Line 5

The world was sad, the garden was a wild,
And man, the hermit, sigh'd — till woman smiled.
Ibid. Line 37

While Memory watches o'er the sad review
Of joys that faded like the morning dew.
Ibid. Line 45

There shall he love, when genial morn appears,
Like pensive Beauty smiling in her tears.
Ibid. Line 95

And muse on Nature with a poet's eye.
Ibid. Line 98

That gems the starry girdle of the year.
Ibid. Line 194

Melt, and dispel, ye spectre-doubts, that roll
Cimmerian darkness o'er the parting soul!
Ibid. Line 263

O star-eyed Science! hast thou wandered there,

To waft us home the message of despair?
Pleasures of Hope. Part II, Line 325

But, sad as angels for the good man's sin,
Weep to record, and blush to give it in.[1]
Ibid. Line 357

Cease, every joy, to glimmer on my mind,
But leave, oh leave the light of Hope behind!
What though my wingèd hours of bliss have been
Like angel visits, few and far between.[2]
Ibid. Line 375

Oh! once the harp of Innisfail
Was strung full high to notes of gladness;
But yet it often told a tale
Of more prevailing sadness.
O'Connor's Child. Stanza 1

'Tis the sunset of life gives me mystical lore,
And coming events cast their shadows before.[3]
Lochiel's Warning

Shall victor exult, or in death be laid low,
With his back to the field and his feet to the foe,
And leaving in battle no blot on his name,
Look proudly to heaven from the death-bed of fame.
Ibid.

And rustic life and poverty
Grow beautiful beneath his touch.
*Ode to the Memory of Burns.
Stanza 5*

Whose lines are mottoes of the heart,
Whose truths electrify the sage.
Ibid. Stanza 14

Ye mariners of England,
That guard our native seas;
Whose flag has braved, a thousand years,
The battle and the breeze!
Ye Mariners of England. Stanza 1

Britannia needs no bulwarks,
No towers along the steep;

---

[1] See John Webster, page 127.
  The mountains too, at a distance, appear airy masses and smooth, but seen near at hand they are rough. — DIOGENES LAERTIUS: *Pyrrho, IX*

    O distance! thou dear enchanter,
      Still hold in thy magic veil
    The glory of far-off mountains,
      The gleam of the far-off sail.
      CARLOTTA PERRY [1848–1914]: *Distance, the Enchantress, St. 5*

[1] See Sterne, page 242.
[2] See Norris, page 186.
[3] See Coleridge, page 318.

Her march is o'er the mountain waves,
Her home is on the deep.
Ye Mariners of England. Stanza 3

When the battle rages loud and long,
And the stormy winds do blow.
Ibid.

The meteor flag of England
Shall yet terrific burn,
Till danger's troubled night depart,
And the star of peace return.
Ibid. Stanza 4

There was silence deep as death,
And the boldest held his breath,
For a time.
Battle of the Baltic. Stanza 2

The combat deepens. On, ye brave,
Who rush to glory or the grave!
Wave, Munich! all thy banners wave,
And charge with all thy chivalry!
Hohenlinden. Stanza 7

Few, few shall part where many meet!
The snow shall be their winding-sheet
And every turf beneath their feet
Shall be a soldier's sepulchre.
Ibid. Stanza 8

All worldly shapes shall melt in gloom,
The Sun himself must die,
Before this mortal shall assume
Its Immortality!
The Last Man. Stanza 1

I saw the last of human mould
That shall Creation's death behold,
As Adam saw her prime!
Ibid.

There came to the beach a poor exile
of Erin,
The dew on his thin robe was heavy
and chill;
For his country he sigh'd, when at twilight repairing
To wander alone by the wind-beaten
hill.
The Exile of Erin. Stanza 1

On the green banks of Shannon, when
Sheelah was nigh,
No blithe Irish lad was so happy as I;
No harp like my own could so cheerily
play,

And wherever I went was my poor dog
Tray.[1]
The Harper. Stanza 1

Star that bringeth home the bee,
And sett'st the weary labourer free!
Song to the Evening Star. Stanza 1

Oh, how hard it is to find
The one just suited to our mind!
Song. Stanza 1

Triumphal arch, that fill'st the sky
When storms prepare to part,
I ask not proud Philosophy
To teach me what thou art.
To the Rainbow. Stanza 1

To live in hearts we leave behind
Is not to die.
Hallowed Ground. Stanza 6

Oh leave this barren spot to me!
Spare, woodman, spare the beechen
tree![2]
The Beech-Tree's Petition. Stanza 1

Drink ye to her that each loves best!
And if you nurse a flame
That's told but to her mutual breast,
We will not ask her name.
Drink Ye to Her. Stanza 1

A stoic of the woods, — a man without
a tear.
*Gertrude of Wyoming. Part I,
Stanza 23*

HENRY CLAY
[1777–1852]

Sir, the gentleman soils the spot he
stands upon.
*On the proposal to impeach
Thomas Jefferson*

If you wish to avoid foreign collision,
you had better abandon the ocean.
*Speech on the Increase of the
Navy, U. S. House of Representatives [January 22, 1812]*

It would not be thought very just or
wise to arraign the honorable professions of law and physic because the one

[1] Old dog Tray's ever faithful,
Grief cannot drive him away.
STEPHEN COLLINS FOSTER [1826–
1864]: *Old Dog Tray*

[2] Woodman, spare that tree!
Touch not a single bough!
GEORGE POPE MORRIS [1802–1864]:
Woodman, Spare That Tree, St. 1

produces the pettifogger and the other the quack.

> *Speech on the Protection of Home Industry, U. S. House of Representatives [April 26, 1820]*

I have doubtless committed many errors and indiscretions, over which you have thrown the broad mantle of charity. But I can say, and in the presence of my God and of this assembled multitude I do say, that I have honestly served my country — that I have never wronged it — and that, however unprepared I lament that I am to appear in the Divine Presence on other accounts, I invoke the justice of His judgment on my official conduct without the smallest apprehension of His displeasure.

> *Speech at Lexington, Kentucky [1829]*

Government is a trust, and the officers of the government are trustees; and both the trust and the trustees are created for the benefit of the people.

> *Speech at Ashland, Kentucky [March, 1829]*

The arts of power and its minions are the same in all countries and in all ages. It marks its victim; denounces it; and excites the public odium and the public hatred, to conceal its own abuses and encroachments.

> *Speech on the State of the Country, U. S. Senate [March 14, 1834]*

Precedents deliberately established by wise men are entitled to great weight. They are evidence of truth, but *only* evidence. . . . But a solitary precedent . . . which has never been re-examined, can not be conclusive.

> *Speech on Appointments and Removals, U. S. Senate [February 18, 1835]*

I have heard something said about allegiance to the South. I know no South, no North, no East, no West, to which I owe any allegiance.

> *Speech [1848]*

Sir, I would rather be right than be President.

> *Speech [1850], referring to the compromise measures*

General Alexander Smyth, a tedious speaker in Congress, observed: "You, sir, speak for the present generation; but I speak for posterity."

"Yes," said Mr. Clay, "and you seem resolved to speak until the arrival of your audience."

> *Quoted by* EPES SARGENT *in Life of Henry Clay*

HENRY ELLIS
[1777–1869]

To make a mountain of a mole-hill.

> *Original Letters. Second Series, Page 312*

COLONEL VALENTINE BLACKER
[1778–1823]

Put your trust in God, my boys, and keep your powder dry! [1]

> *Oliver's Advice [1834]*

ROBERT EMMET
[1778–1803]

Let there be no inscription upon my tomb; let no man write my epitaph: no man can write my epitaph.

> *Speech on His Trial and Conviction for High Treason [September, 1803]*

WILLIAM HAZLITT
[1778–1830]

One of the pleasantest things in the world is going a journey; but I like to go by myself.

> *On Going a Journey*

---

[1] There is a well-authenticated anecdote of Cromwell. On a certain occasion, when his troops were about to cross a river to attack the enemy, he concluded an address, with these words: "Put your trust in God; but mind to keep your powder dry!" — HAYES: *Ballads of Ireland, Vol. I, P. 191*

The soul of a journey is liberty, perfect liberty, to think, feel, do just as one pleases.

On Going a Journey

Oh! it is great to shake off the trammels of the world and of public opinion — to lose our importunate, tormenting, everlasting personal identity and become the creature of the moment, clear of all ties . . . to be known by no other title than *the Gentleman in the parlour!*

Ibid.

What I mean by living to one's self is living in the world, as in it, not of it. . . . It is to be a silent spectator of the mighty scene of things; . . . to take a thoughtful, anxious interest or curiosity in what is passing in the world, but not to feel the slightest inclination to make or meddle with it.

On Living to One's Self

Even in the common affairs of life, in love, friendship, and marriage, how little security have we when we trust our happiness in the hands of others!

Ibid.

There is not a more mean, stupid, dastardly, pitiful, selfish, spiteful, envious, ungrateful animal than the Public. It is the greatest of cowards, for it is afraid of itself.

Ibid.

When a man is dead, they put money in his coffin, erect monuments to his memory, and celebrate the anniversary of his birthday in set speeches. Would they take any notice of him if he were living? No!

Ibid.

What a sight for sore eyes that would be! [1]

Of Persons One Would Have Seen

Horas non numero nisi serenas [2] — is the motto of a sun-dial near Venice. [3]

---

[1] See Swift, page 191.
[2] I count only the sunny hours.
[3] There stands in the garden of old St. Mark
    A sun-dial quaint and gray.
    WILLIAM CROSWELL DOANE [1832–1913]: *Horas Non Numero*

There is a softness and a harmony in the words and in the thought unparalleled.

On a Sun-Dial

If our hours were all serene, we might probably take almost as little note of them, as the dial does of those that are clouded.

Ibid.

No young man believes he shall ever die.

The Feeling of Immortality in Youth

There is a feeling of Eternity in youth, which makes us amends for everything. To be young is to be as one of the Immortal Gods.

Ibid.

The young are prodigal of life from a superabundance of it; the old are tenacious on the same score, because they have little left, and cannot enjoy even what remains of it.

Ibid.

As we advance in life, we acquire a keener sense of the value of time. Nothing else, indeed, seems of any consequence; and we become misers in this respect.

Ibid.

The only true retirement is that of the heart; the only true leisure is the repose of the passions. To such persons it makes little difference whether they are young or old; and they die as they have lived, with graceful resignation.

Ibid.

If I have not read a book before, it is, to all intents and purposes, new to me, whether it was printed yesterday or three hundred years ago.

On Reading New Books

When I take up a work that I have read before (the oftener the better) I know what I have to expect. The satisfaction is not lessened by being anticipated.

On Reading Old Books

Persons without education certainly do not want either acuteness or strength of mind in what concerns themselves, or in things immediately within their observation; but they have no power of abstraction, no general standard of taste, or scale of opinion. They see their objects always near, and never in the horizon. Hence arises that egotism which has been remarked as the characteristic of self-taught men.

The Round Table. I, 26

It is better to be able neither to read nor write than to be able to do nothing else.

On the Ignorance of the Learned

Men of genius do not excel in any profession because they labour in it, but they labour in it, because they excel.

Characteristics

We are not hypocrites in our sleep.

On Dreams

"The English," says Froissart, "amused themselves sadly after the fashion of their country." They have indeed a way of their own. Their mirth is a relaxation from gravity, a challenge to dull care to be gone; and one is not always clear at first, whether the appeal is successful.

Merry England

Takes up the meanest subjects with the same tenderness that we do an insect's wing, and would not kill a fly.

Lectures on the Comic Writers. Shakespeare

When a person dies who does any one thing better than any one else in the world, it leaves a gap in society.

Table Talk (On the death of John Cavanagh, famous player of "fives," a kind of hand-ball)

HENRY PETER, LORD BROUGHAM
[1779–1868]

Let the soldier be abroad if he will, he can do nothing in this age. There is another personage, — a personage less imposing in the eyes of some, perhaps insignificant. The schoolmaster is abroad,[1] and I trust to him, armed with

[1] At the first meeting of the London Mechanics' Institution, 1825, John Reynolds, head of a school in Clerkenwell, acted as secretary of the meeting. Lord Brougham, who spoke at this meeting, said in the course of his remarks, "Look out, gentlemen, the

his primer, against the soldier in full military array.

Speech, Opening of Parliament [January 29, 1828]

In my mind, he was guilty of no error, he was chargeable with no exaggeration, he was betrayed by his fancy into no metaphor, who once said that all we see about us, kings, lords, and Commons, the whole machinery of the State, all the apparatus of the system, and its varied workings, end in simply bringing twelve good men into a box.

Present State of the Law [February 7, 1828]

Pursuit of knowledge under difficulties.[1]

Death was now armed with a new terror.[2]

THOMAS, LORD DENMAN
[1779–1854]

A delusion, a mockery, and a snare.[3]

O'Connell v. The Queen (in 11 Clark and Finnelly Reports)

The mere repetition of the *Cantilena* of lawyers cannot make it law, unless it can be traced to some competent authority; and if it be irreconcilable, to some clear legal principle.

Ibid.

---

schoolmaster is abroad." The phrase attracted little attention at that time, but when used in a speech three years later, it at once became popular.

[1] The title given by Lord Brougham to a book published in 1830.

[2] Brougham delivered a very warm panegyric upon the ex-Chancellor, and expressed a hope that he would make a good end, although to an expiring Chancellor death was now armed with a new terror. — CAMPBELL: *Lives of the Chancellors, Vol. VII, P. 163*

Lord St. Leonards attributes this phrase to Sir Charles Wetherell, who used it on the occasion referred to by Lord Campbell.

From Edmund Curll's practice of issuing miserable catch-penny lives of every eminent person immediately after his decease, Arbuthnot wittily styled him "one of the new terrors of death." — CARRUTHERS: *Life of Pope (2d ed.), P. 149*

[3] Franklin P. Adams; of a beautiful Spanish woman: "A snare Andalusian."

FRANCIS SCOTT KEY
[1779–1843]

And the star-spangled banner, oh long
  may it wave
O'er the land of the free and the home of
  the brave!
> *The Star-Spangled Banner.*
> *Stanza 2 [September 14, 1814]*

O! thus be it ever when freemen shall
  stand
Between their loved homes and the foe's
  desolation;
Bless'd with victory and peace, may our
  Heaven-rescued land
Praise the Power that hath made and
  preserved us a nation.[1]
> *Ibid. Stanza 4*

Then conquer we must, for our cause
  it is just, —
And this be our motto, — "In God is
  our trust!"
> *Ibid.*

WILLIAM LAMB,
VISCOUNT MELBOURNE
[1779–1848]

I wish that I could be as cocksure of
anything as Tom Macaulay is of everything.
> *Quoted. Attributed also to William
> Windham [1750–1810]*

CLEMENT CLARKE MOORE
[1779–1863]

'Twas the night before Christmas, when
  all through the house
Not a creature was stirring, — not even
  a mouse;[2]
The stockings were hung by the chimney with care,
In hopes that St. Nicholas soon would
  be there.
> *A Visit from St. Nicholas
> [December, 1823]*

"Happy Christmas to all, and to all a
  good-night!"
> *A Visit from St. Nicholas
> [December, 1823]*

HORACE SMITH
[1779–1849]

Thinking is but an idle waste of
  thought,
And nought is everything, and everything is nought.
> *Rejected Addresses. Cui Bono?
> Stanza 8*

In the name of the Prophet — figs.
> *Johnson's Ghost*

And thou hast walked about (how
  strange a story!)
In Thebes's streets three thousand
  years ago,
When the Memnonium was in all its
  glory.
> *Address to the Mummy at Bel-
> zoni's Exhibition.[1] Stanza 1*

Although corruption may our frame
  consume.
The immortal spirit in the skies may
  bloom.
> *Ibid. Stanza 13*

JOSEPH STORY
[1779–1845]

Whene'er you speak, remember every
  cause
Stands not on eloquence, but stands on
  laws;
Pregnant in matter, in expression brief,
Let every sentence stand with bold re-
  lief;
On trifling points not time nor talents
  waste,
A sad offence to learning and to taste;
Nor deal with pompous phrase, nor e'er
  suppose
Poetic flights belong to reasoning prose.
> *Advice to Young Lawyers.
> Stanza 1*

---

[1] It made and preserves us a nation. —
GEORGE POPE MORRIS: *The Flag of Our
Union, St. 1*

[2] Not a mouse stirring. — SHAKESPEARE:
Hamlet, Act I, Sc. 1, L. 10

[1] Giovanni Battista Belzoni [1778–1823],
Italian traveler and explorer, opened the
sepulcher of Seti I, in 1817, and the second
pyramid of Gizeh. He brought the bust of
the "Young Memnon" from Thebes to the
British Museum.

Here shall the Press the People's right
  maintain,
Unaw'd by influence and unbrib'd by
  gain;
Here patriot Truth her glorious precepts
  draw,
Pledg'd to Religion, Liberty, and Law.
  *Motto of the Salem Register
  (In Life of Story, Vol. I, Page 127)*

WILLIAM ELLERY CHANNING
[1780–1842]

The office of government is not to
confer happiness, but to give men opportunity to work out happiness for
themselves.
  *The Life and Character of
  Napoleon Bonaparte*

I see the marks of God in the heavens
and the earth; but how much more in a
liberal intellect, in magnanimity, in unconquerable rectitude, in a philanthropy
which forgives every wrong, and which
never despairs of the cause of Christ
and human virtue: I do and I must
reverence human nature. I bless it for
its kind affections. I honor it for its
achievements in science and art, and
still more for its examples of heroic and
saintly virtue. These are marks of a
divine origin and the pledges of a celestial inheritance; and I thank God that
my own lot is bound up with that of the
human race.
  *Inscription, from his writings, on
  Channing Memorial, Public Garden, Boston*

CHARLES CALEB COLTON
[1780–1832]

Imitation is the sincerest flattery.
  The Lacon

JOHN MARRIOTT
[1780–1825]

In a Devonshire lane, as I tottered
  along,
The other day, much in want of a subject for song,

Thinks I to myself, I have hit on a
  strain —
That marriage is much like a Devonshire lane.
  *How Marriage is Like a Devon-
  shire Lane. Stanza 1*
And the conjugal fence, which forbids
  us to roam,
Looks lovely when decked with the
  comforts of home.
  Ibid. Stanza 6

CHARLES MINER
[1780–1865]

When I see a merchant over-polite
to his customers, begging them to taste
a little brandy and throwing half his
goods on the counter, — thinks I, that
man has an axe to grind.
  Who'll Turn Grindstones [1]

THOMAS MOORE
[1780–1852]

Weep on! and, as thy sorrows flow,
I'll taste the luxury of woe.
  *Anacreontic. Press the Grape,
  Stanza 2*
How shall we rank thee upon glory's
  page?
Thou more than soldier and just less
  than sage!
  To Thomas Hume. Stanza 6
I knew by the smoke, that so gracefully
  curl'd
  Above the green elms, that a cottage
    was near;
And I said, "If there's peace to be found
  in the world,
  A heart that was humble might hope
    for it here!"
  Ballad Stanzas. 1
They made her a grave, too cold and
  damp
  For a soul so warm and true;
And she's gone to the Lake of the Dis-
  mal Swamp,

[1] From *Essays from the Desk of Poor
Robert the Scribe* [Doylestown, Pennsylvania,
1815]. It first appeared in the Wilkes-Barre
Gleaner in 1911.

Where, all night long, by a firefly lamp,
She paddles her white canoe.
*The Lake of the Dismal Swamp.
Stanza 1*

Faintly as tolls the evening chime,
Our voices keep tune and our oars keep
time.[1]
A Canadian Boat-Song. Stanza 1

Row, brothers, row, the stream runs
fast,
The rapids are near, and the daylight's
past.
Ibid.

The minds of some of our statesmen,
like the pupil of the human eye, contract themselves the more, the stronger
light there is shed upon them.
*Preface to Corruption and
Intolerance*

Like a young eagle who has lent his
plume
To fledge the shaft by which he meets
his doom.[2]
Corruption

Young Love may go,
For aught I care,
To Jericho!
When Love is Kind. Stanza 6

A Persian's heaven is easily made:
'Tis but black eyes and lemonade.
Intercepted Letters. VI

There was a little man, and he had a
little soul;
And he said, Little Soul, let us try, try,
try!
*Little Man and Little Soul.
Stanza 1*

Go where glory waits thee![3]
But while fame elates thee,
Oh, still remember me!
*Go Where Glory Waits Thee.
Stanza 1*

Oh, breathe not his name! let it sleep
in the shade,
Where cold and unhonour'd his relics
are laid,
*Oh Breathe Not His Name.
Stanza 1*

And the tear that we shed, though in
secret it rolls,
Shall long keep his memory green in our
souls.[1]
*Oh Breathe Not His Name.
Stanza 2*

The harp that once through Tara's halls
The soul of music shed,
Now hangs as mute on Tara's walls
As if that soul were fled.
So sleeps the pride of former days,
So glory's thrill is o'er;
And hearts that once beat high for
praise
Now feel that pulse no more.
*The Harp That Once Through
Tara's Halls. Stanza 1*

Whose wit in the combat, as gentle as
bright,
Ne'er carried a heart-stain away on its
blade.
*On the Death of Sheridan.
Stanza 11*

Good at a fight, but better at a play;
Godlike in giving, but the devil to pay.
*Life of Sheridan. On a Cast of
Sheridan's Hand*

Fly not yet, — 'tis just the hour,
When pleasure, like the midnight flower
That scorns the eye of vulgar light,
Begins to bloom for sons of night,
And maids who love the moon.
Fly Not Yet. Stanza 1

Oh stay! oh stay!
Joy so seldom weaves a chain
Like this to-night, that oh, 'tis pain
To break its links so soon.
Ibid.

And the heart that is soonest awake to
the flowers
Is always the first to be touch'd by the
thorns.
*Oh, Think Not My Spirits Are
Always as Light. Stanza 1*

Rich and rare were the gems she wore,
And a bright gold ring on her wand
she bore.
*Rich and Rare Were the Gems She
Wore. Stanza 1*

There is not in the wide world a valley
so sweet

---

[1] See Marvell, page 169.
[2] See Waller, page 145.
[3] This goin ware glory waits ye haint one
agreeable feetur. — LOWELL: *The Biglow Papers, First Series, No. 11*

[1] See Shakespeare, page 89.

As that vale in whose bosom the bright
    waters meet.[1]
        The Meeting of the Waters.
            Stanza 1
Come, send round the wine, and leave
    points of belief
To simpleton sages, and reasoning fools.
        Come, Send Round the Wine.
            Stanza 1
Shall I ask the brave soldier, who fights
    by my side
In the cause of mankind, if our creeds
    agree?
Shall I give up the friend I have valued
    and tried,
If he kneel not before the same altar
    with me?
           Ibid. Stanza 2
Beauty lies
    In many eyes,
But Love in yours, my Nora Creina.
      Lesbia Hath a Beaming Eye.
            Stanza 1
So Life's year begins and closes;
    Days though shortening still can
    shine;
What though youth gave love and roses,
    Age still leaves us friends and wine.
      Spring and Autumn. Stanza 1
Ah! little they think who delight in her
    strains,
How the heart of the Minstrel is break-
    ing.
    She is Far from the Land. Stanza 2
No, the heart that has truly lov'd never
    forgets,
    But as truly loves on to the close;
As the sunflower turns on her god, when
    he sets,
    The same look which she turn'd when
    he rose.
    Believe Me, if All Those Endearing
      Young Charms. Stanza 2
The moon looks
    On many brooks,
"The brook can see no moon but this." [2]
    When Gazing on the Moon's Light.
            Stanza 2

[1] The vale of Avoca, County Wicklow, Ireland, where the Avonmore and Avonbeg meet
to form the river Avoca.
[2] This image was suggested by the following
thought, which occurs somewhere in SIR WIL-

And when once the young heart of a
    maiden is stolen,
The maiden herself will steal after
    it soon.
        Ill Omens. Stanza 1
'Tis sweet to think, that, where'er we
    rove,
We are sure to find something bliss-
    ful and dear;
And that when we're far from the lips
    we love,
We've but to make love to the lips
    we are near.
      'Tis Sweet to Think. Stanza 1
Give smiles to those who love you less,
But keep your tears for me.[1]
    When Midst the Gay I Meet.
            Stanza 1
Though wooed by flattering friends,
And fed with fame (if fame it be),
This heart, my own dear mother, bends,
With love's true instinct, back to thee!
      To My Mother. Stanza 2
'Tis believ'd that this harp which I
    wake now for thee
Was a siren of old who sung under the
    sea.
      The Origin of the Harp
But there's nothing half so sweet in life
    As love's young dream.
    Love's Young Dream. Stanza 1
To live with them is far less sweet,
    Than to remember thee.[2]
      I Saw Thy Form. Stanza 3
Eyes of unholy blue.
    By That Lake Whose Gloomy
         Shore. Stanza 2
'Tis the last rose of summer.
    Left blooming alone.
      The Last Rose of Summer.
            Stanza 1
When true hearts lie wither'd
    And fond ones are flown,

LIAM JONES'S *Works:* "The moon looks upon
many night-flowers; the night-flower sees but
one moon."
  [1] Give other friends your lighted face,
    The laughter of the years;
  I come to crave a greater grace —
    Bring me your tears.
      EDWIN MARKHAM: *Your Tears*, St. 1
  [2] In imitation of SHENSTONE's inscription,
"Heu! quanto minus est cum reliquis versari
quam tui meminisse."

Oh, who would inhabit
　This bleak world alone?
　　　　The Last Rose of Summer.
　　　　　　Stanza 3
And the best of all ways
　To lengthen our days
Is to steal a few hours from the night,
　my dear.
　　　The Young May Moon. Stanza 1
You may break, you may shatter the
　vase if you will,
But the scent of the roses will hang
　round it still.
　　　　　　　　Ibid.
No eye to watch, and no tongue to
　wound us,
All earth forgot, and all heaven around
　us.
　　　Come O'er the Sea. Stanza 2
The light that lies [1]
In woman's eyes.
　　　The Time I've Lost in Wooing.
　　　　　　Stanza 1
My only books
　Were woman's looks,
And folly's all they've taught me.
　　　　　　　　Ibid.
I know not, I ask not, if guilt's in that
　heart,
I but know that I love thee, whatever
　thou art.
　　　Come, Rest in This Bosom.
　　　　　　Stanza 2
Oft in the stilly night,
　Ere slumber's chain has bound me,
Fond memory brings the light
　Of other days around me;
　　The smiles, the tears,
　　Of boyhood's years,
The words of love then spoken;
　　The eyes that shone
　　Now dimmed and gone,
The cheerful hearts now broken.
　　Oft in the Stilly Night. Stanza 1
I feel like one,
　Who treads alone
Some banquet-hall deserted,
　Whose lights are fled,

[1] 　　O dreamy eyes,
　They tell sweet lies of Paradise;
　And in those eyes the love-light lies
　And lies — and lies — and lies!
　　ANITA OWEN: *Dreamy Eyes*

Whose garlands dead,
And all but he departed.
　　Oft in the Stilly Night. Stanza 2
Came but for Friendship and took away
　Love.
　　A Temple to Friendship. Stanza 2
As half in shade and half in sun
　This world along its path advances,
May that side the sun's upon
　Be all that e'er shall meet thy
　　glances!
　　Peace Be Around Thee. Stanza 2
If I speak to thee in friendship's name,
　Thou think'st I speak too coldly;
If I mention love's devoted flame,
　Thou say'st I speak too boldly.
　　　How Shall I Woo? Stanza 1
A friendship that like love is warm;
　A love like friendship steady.
　　　　　Ibid. Stanza 3
The bird, let loose in Eastern skies,
　When hastening fondly home,
Ne'er stoops to earth her wing, nor flies
　Where idle warblers roam;
But high she shoots through air and
　light,
　Above all low delay,
Where nothing earthly bounds her
　flight,
　Nor shadow dims her way.
　　　The Bird Let Loose. Stanza 1
This world is all a fleeting show,
　For man's illusion given;
The smiles of joy, the tears of woe,
Deceitful shine, deceitful flow, —
　There's nothing true but Heaven.
　　This World is All a Fleeting Show.
　　　　　　Stanza 1
Sound the loud timbrel o'er Egypt's
　dark sea!
Jehovah has triumph'd, — his people
　are free.
　　　　Sound the Loud Timbrel
As down in the sunless retreats of the
　ocean
　Sweet flowers are springing no mortal
　　can see,
So, deep in my soul the still prayer of
　devotion,
　Unheard by the world, rises silent to
　　Thee.
　　As Down in the Sunless Retreats.
　　　　　　Stanza 1

As still to the star of its worship, though
    clouded,
  The needle points faithfully o'er the
    dim sea,
So, dark as I roam, in this wintry
    world shrouded,
  The hope of my spirit turns trembling
    to Thee.
      As Down in the Sunless Retreats.
                Stanza 2

Ask a woman's advice, and, whate'er
    she advise,
Do the very reverse and you're sure to
    be wise.
    How to Make a Good Politician.
                Stanza 1
  How oft we sigh
When histories charm to think that his-
    tories lie! [1]
              The Sceptic

That best of fame, a rival's praise.
      Rhymes of the Road. XV
Scarce a sail
Is whiskt from England by the gale,
But bears on board some authors, shipt
For foreign shores, all well equipt
With proper book-making machinery,
To sketch the morals, manners, scenery,
Of all such lands as they shall see,
Or not see, as the case may be.
    Thoughts on Patrons. Stanza 3
'Twas nuts to the Father of Lies.
    A Case of Libel. Stanza 16
Oh, call it by some better name,
  For friendship sounds too cold.
    Oh, Call It by Some Better Name.
                Stanza 1
Who has not felt how sadly sweet
  The dream of home, the dream of
    home,
Steals o'er the heart, too soon to fleet,
  When far o'er sea or land we roam?
    The Dream of Home. Stanza 1
When thus the heart is in a vein
Of tender thought, the simplest strain
Can touch it with peculiar power.
    Evenings in Greece. First Evening,
                Stanza 20

[1] On the breast of that huge Mississippi of falsehood called history. — MATTHEW ARNOLD: *Literary Influence of Academies*
  History is a fable agreed upon. — NAPOLEON
  History is bunk. — HENRY FORD (1863–   )

If thou would'st have me sing and play
  As once I play'd and sung,
First take this time-worn lute away,
  And bring one freshly strung.
    If Thou Would'st Have Me Sing
        and Play. Stanza 1
To sigh, yet feel no pain;
  To weep, yet scarce know why;
To sport an hour with Beauty's chain,
  Then throw it idly by.
    M.P., The Blue Stocking. VI
And from the lips of Truth one mighty
    breath
Shall like a whirlwind scatter in its
    breeze
That whole dark pile of human mock-
    eries: —
Then shall the reign of mind commence
    on earth,
And starting fresh as from a second
    birth,
Man in the sunshine of the world's new
    spring
Shall walk transparent like some holy
    thing!
    Lalla Rookh. The Veiled Prophet
        of Khorassan, Part I
The heaven of each is but what each
    desires.
                  Ibid.
This narrow isthmus 'twixt two bound-
    less seas,
The past, the future, — two eternities!
              Ibid. Part II
There's a bower of roses by Bende-
    meer's stream.[1]
                  Ibid.
Like the stained web that whitens in the
    sun,
Grow pure by being purely shone upon.
                  Ibid.
But Faith, fanatic Faith, once wedded
    fast
To some dear falsehood, hugs it to the
    last.
              Ibid. Part III
One morn a Peri at the gate
Of Eden stood disconsolate.
    Ibid. Part IV, Paradise and the Peri

[1] As I recall them the roses bloom again, and the nightingales sing by the calm Bendemeer. — W. M. THACKERAY: *The Newcomes, Chap. 1*

Take all the pleasures of all the spheres
And multiply each through endless
    years, —
One minute of heaven is worth them
    all.
> *Lalla Rookh. The Veiled Prophet
>   of Khorassan, Part IV*

But the trail of the serpent is over them
    all.
> *Ibid.*

Oh! ever thus, from childhood's hour,
    I've seen my fondest hope decay;
I never loved a tree or flower,
    But 'twas the first to fade away.
I never nurs'd a dear gazelle
    To glad me with its soft black eye,
But when it came to know me well
    And love me it was sure to die.[1]
> *Ibid. Part V, The Fire-
>   Worshippers*

Paradise itself were dim
And joyless, if not shared with him!
> *Ibid. Part VI*

Alas! how light a cause may move
Dissension between hearts that love!
Hearts that the world in vain had tried,
And sorrow but more closely tied;
That stood the storm when waves were
    rough
Yet in a sunny hour fall off,
Like ships that have gone down at sea
When heaven was all tranquillity.
> *Ibid. Part VIII, The Light of the
>   Haram*

Like that celestial bird whose nest
    Is found beneath far Eastern skies,
Whose wings though radiant when at
    rest
    Lose all their glory when he flies.[2]
> *Ibid.*

Fly to the desert, fly with me,
Our Arab tents are rude for thee.[3]
> *Ibid.*

---

[1] See Calverley, page 590.

[2] A species of goldfinch, which sings so melodiously that it is called the Celestial Bird. Its wings, when it is perched, appear variegated with beautiful colors, but when it flies they lose all their splendor.

[3] It is thought that the popular song of the 1840s, known as *Ossian's Serenade*, was inspired by the lines of *Fly to the Desert*. See Calder Campbell, page 395.

Humility, that low, sweet root
From which all heavenly virtues shoot.
> *The Loves of the Angels.
>   Third Angel's Story*

EBENEZER ELLIOTT
[1781–1849]

When wilt Thou save the people?
O God of mercy, when?
Not kings and lords, but nations!
Not thrones and crowns, but men!
Flowers of Thy heart, O God are they;
Let them not pass, like weeds, away —
God save the people!
> *Corn Law Rhymes. When Wilt
>   Thou Save the People?, Stanza 1*

What pensioned slave of Attila
    Leads in the rear?
> *Battle Song*

Dark and still, we inly glow,
    Condensed in ire!
> *Ibid.*

ANNA JANE VARDHILL
[1781–1852]

Behold this ruin! 'Twas a skull
Once of ethereal spirit full;
This narrow cell was Life's retreat,
This space was Thought's mysterious
    seat.
> *Lines on a Skeleton. Stanza 1*

THOMAS HART BENTON
[1782–1858]

This new page opened in the book of our public expenditures, and this new departure taken, which leads into the bottomless gulf of civil pensions and family gratuities.
> *Speech, U. S. Senate, against a
>   Grant to President Harrison's
>   Widow [April, 1841]*

JOHN C. CALHOUN
[1782–1850]

Protection and patriotism are reciprocal.
> *Speech, U. S. House of Representa-
>   tives [December 12, 1811]*

The very essence of a free government consists in considering offices as public trusts,[1] bestowed for the good of the country, and not for the benefit of an individual or a party.

Speech [February 13, 1835]

A power has risen up in the government greater than the people themselves, consisting of many and various and powerful interests, combined into one mass, and held together by the cohesive power of the vast surplus in the banks.[2]

Speech [May 27, 1836]

The surrender of life is nothing to sinking down into acknowledgment of inferiority.

*Speech, U. S. Senate
[February 19, 1847]*

SIR CHARLES JAMES NAPIER
[1782–1853]

Peccavi [I have Sind].

*Message to the British War Office
[February 17, 1843] after the surrender of Hyderabad, Province of Sind*

ANN TAYLOR
[1782–1866]

*See also her sister Jane Taylor
[1783–1824]*

Oh, that it were my chief delight
  To do the things I ought!
Then let me try with all my might
  To mind what I am taught.

For a Very Little Child

There's hardly anything so small,
  So trifling or so mean,
That we may never want at all,
  For service unforeseen;
And wilful waste, depend upon 't,
Brings, almost always, woeful want!

The Pin. Stanza 6

'Twas fancied by some, who but slightly
  had seen them,

There was not a pin to be chosen between them.

Jane and Eliza. Stanza 2

One ugly trick has often spoiled
  The sweetest and the best;
Matilda, though a pleasant child,
  One ugly trick possessed,
Which, like a cloud before the skies,
Hid all her better qualities.

Meddlesome Matty. Stanza 1

DANIEL WEBSTER
[1782–1852]

Whatever makes men good Christians, makes them good citizens.

Speech at Plymouth, Massachusetts [December 22, 1820] [1]

We wish that this column, rising towards heaven among the pointed spires of so many temples dedicated to God, may contribute also to produce in all minds a pious feeling of dependence and gratitude. We wish, finally, that the last object to the sight of him who leaves his native shore, and the first to gladden his who revisits it, may be something which shall remind him of the liberty and the glory of his country. Let it rise! let it rise, till it meet the sun in his coming; let the earliest light of the morning gild it, and parting day linger and play on its summit!

Address on Laying the Corner-Stone of the Bunker Hill Monument [June 17, 1825]

Venerable men! you have come down to us from a former generation. Heaven has bounteously lengthened out your lives, that you might behold this joyous day.

Ibid.

Mind is the great lever of all things; human thought is the process by which human ends are ultimately answered.

Ibid.

---

[1] See Mathew Henry, page 188.
[2] From this speech comes the phrase, "Cohesive power of public plunder."

[1] This oration will be read five hundred years hence with as much rapture as it was heard. It ought to be read at the end of every century, and indeed at the end of every year, forever and ever. — JOHN ADAMS: *Letter to Webster* [Dec. 23, 1821]

Knowledge, in truth, is the great sun in the firmament. Life and power are scattered with all its beams.

Address on Laying the Corner-Stone of the Bunker Hill Monument [*June 17, 1825*]

Let our object be our country, our whole country, and nothing but our country.

Ibid.

The staff on which my years should lean
Is broken ere those years come o'er me;
My funeral rites thou shouldst have seen,
But thou art in the tomb before me.

On the Death of His Son, Charles, 1826. Stanza 1

Sink or swim, live or die, survive or perish, I give my hand and my heart to this vote.[1]

Eulogy on Adams and Jefferson, Faneuil Hall, Boston [*August 2, 1826*]

It is my living sentiment, and by the blessing of God it shall be my dying sentiment, — Independence now and Independence forever.[2]

Ibid.

Washington is in the clear upper sky.[3]

Ibid.

He smote the rock of the national resources, and abundant streams of revenue gushed forth. He touched the

dead corpse of Public Credit, and it sprung upon its feet.[1]

Speech on Hamilton [*March 10, 1831*]

One country, one constitution, one destiny.

Speech [*March 15, 1837*]

There are persons who constantly clamor. They complain of oppression, speculation, and pernicious influence of wealth. They cry out loudly against all banks and corporations, and a means by which small capitalists become united in order to produce important and beneficial results. They carry on mad hostility against all established institutions. They would choke the fountain of industry and dry all streams.

Speech, U. S. Senate [*March 12, 1838*]

When tillage begins, other arts follow. The farmers therefore are the founders of human civilization.

Remarks on Agriculture [*January 13, 1840*]

Sea of upturned faces.[2]

Speech [*September 30, 1842*]

America has furnished to the world the character of Washington. And if our American institutions had done nothing else, that alone would have entitled them to the respect of mankind.

Completion of Bunker Hill Monument [*June 17, 1843*]

Thank God! I — I also — am an American!

Ibid.

Justice, sir, is the great interest of man on earth.

On Mr. Justice Story [*September 12, 1845*]

Liberty exists in proportion to wholesome restraint.

Speech at the Charleston Bar Dinner [*May 10, 1847*]

---

[1] Mr. Adams, describing a conversation with Jonathan Sewall in 1774, says: "I answered that the die was now cast; I had passed the Rubicon. Swim or sink, live or die, survive or perish with my country was my unalterable determination." — JOHN ADAMS: *Works, Vol. IV, P. 8*

Live or die, sink or swim. — GEORGE PEELE [1558–1597]: *Edward I* [1584?]

[2] Mr. Webster says of Mr. Adams: "On the day of his death, hearing the noise of bells and cannon, he asked the occasion. On being reminded that it was 'Independent Day,' he replied, 'Independence forever'" — *Webster's Works, Vol. I, P. 150.* BANCROFT: *History of the United States, Vol. VII, P. 65*

[3] We shall be strong to run the race,
And climb the upper sky.
WATTS: *Spiritual Hymns, XXIV*

[1] He it was that first gave to the law the air of a science. He found it a skeleton, and clothed it with life, colour, and complexion; he embraced the cold statue, and by his touch it grew into youth, health, and beauty. — BARRY YELVERTON, LORD AVONMORE [1736–1805]: *On Blackstone*

[2] See Scott, page 310.

The law: It has honored us; may we honor it.

Toast at the Charleston Bar Dinner [May 10, 1847]

I have read their platform, and though I think there are some unsound places in it, I can stand upon it pretty well. But I see nothing in it both new and valuable. "What is valuable is not new, and what is new is not valuable."

Speech at Marshfield, Massachusetts [September 1, 1848]

Labor in this country is independent and proud. It has not to ask the patronage of capital, but capital solicits the aid of labor.

Speech [April 2, 1824]

The gentleman has not seen how to reply to this, otherwise than by supposing me to have advanced the doctrine that a national debt is a national blessing.[1]

Second Speech on Foote's Resolution [January 26, 1830][2]

I shall enter on no encomium upon Massachusetts; she needs none. There she is. Behold her, and judge for yourselves. There is her history; the world knows it by heart. The past, at least, is secure. There is Boston and Concord and Lexington and Bunker Hill; and there they will remain forever.

Ibid.

The people's government, made for the people, made by the people, and answerable to the people.[3]

Ibid.

When my eyes shall be turned to behold for the last time the sun in heaven, may I not see him shining on the broken and dishonored fragments of a once glorious Union; on States dissevered, discordant, belligerent; on a land rent with civil feuds, or drenched, it may be, in fraternal blood.

Second Speech on Foote's Resolution [January 26, 1830]

Liberty and Union, now and forever, one and inseparable.

Ibid.

God grants liberty only to those who love it, and are always ready to guard and defend it.

Speech [June 3, 1834]

On this question of principle, while actual suffering was yet afar off, they [the Colonies] raised their flag against a power to which, for purposes of foreign conquest and subjugation, Rome in the height of her glory is not to be compared, — a power which has dotted over the surface of the whole globe with her possessions and military posts, whose morning drum-beat, following the sun,[1] and keeping company with the hours, circles the earth with one continuous and unbroken strain of the martial airs of England.[2]

Speech [May 7, 1834]

Inconsistencies of opinion, arising from changes of circumstances, are often justifiable.[3]

Speech [July 25 and 27, 1846]

---

[1] A national debt, if it is not excessive, will be to us a national blessing. — ALEXANDER HAMILTON

[2] The resolution introduced into the United States Senate, Dec. 29, 1829, by Samuel Augustus Foote [1780–1846], Senator from Connecticut, which occasioned the famous debate in the Senate between Webster and Senator Robert Young Hayne of South Carolina, was that the Committee on Public Affairs should inquire into the expediency of limiting the sale of public lands for a certain period to those which had already been offered for sale.

[3] Our sovereign, the people. — CHARLES JAMES FOX [1749–1806]: Toast [1798], for which his name was erased from the Privy Council.

When the State of Pennsylvania held its convention to consider the Constitution of

the United States, Judge Wilson said of the introductory clause, "We, the people, do ordain and establish," etc.: "It is not an unmeaning flourish. The expressions declare in a practical manner the principle of this Constitution. It is ordained and established by the people themselves." This was regarded as an authoritative exposition. — *The Nation*

That government of the people, by the people, for the people, shall not perish from the earth. — ABRAHAM LINCOLN: *Speech at Gettysburg* [Nov. 19, 1863]

[1] See Scott, page 311.

[2] The martial airs of England
Encircle still the earth.
    AMELIA BLANFORD EDWARDS [1831–1892]: *The Martial Airs of England*

[3] L'homme absurde est celui qui ne change jamais (The absurd man is he who never

I was born an American; I will live an American; I shall die an American.[1]

Speech [July 17, 1850]

There is no refuge from confession but suicide; and suicide is confession.

Argument on the Murder of Captain White [April 6, 1830]

There is nothing so powerful as truth, — and often nothing so strange.

Ibid.

Fearful concatenation of circumstances.[2]

Works, Vol. VI, Page 88

A sense of duty pursues us ever. It is omnipresent, like the Deity. If we take to ourselves the wings of the morning, and dwell in the uttermost parts of the sea, duty performed or duty violated is still with us, for our happiness or our misery. If we say the darkness shall cover us, in the darkness as in the light our obligations are yet with us.

Ibid. Page 105

I shall defer my visit to Faneuil Hall, the cradle of American liberty, until its doors shall fly open on golden hinges to lovers of Union as well as lovers of liberty.[3]

Letter [April, 1851]

Men hang out their signs indicative of their respective trades: shoemakers hang out a gigantic shoe; jewelers, a monster watch; and the dentist hangs out a gold tooth; but up in the mountains of New Hampshire, God Almighty has hung out a sign to show that there He makes men.

The Old Man of the Mountain

Philosophical argument, especially that drawn from the vastness of the universe, in comparison with the apparent insignificance of this globe, has sometimes shaken my reason for the faith which is in me; but my heart has always assured and reassured me that

the gospel of Jesus Christ must be Divine Reality. The Sermon on the Mount cannot be a mere human production. This belief enters into the very depth of my conscience. The whole history of man proves it.

Epitaph (dictated day before his death) on his tombstone, Marshfield, Massachusetts

I still live.

Last words [October 24, 1852]

PRINCESS AMELIA [1]
[1783–1810]

Unthinking, idle, wild, and young,
I laugh'd and danc'd and talk'd and sung.

Fragment

REGINALD HEBER
[1783–1826]

Failed the bright promise of your early day.

Palestine

No hammers fell, no ponderous axes rung;
Like some tall palm the mystic fabric sprung.[2]
Majestic silence!

Ibid.

Brightest and best of the sons of the morning,
Dawn on our darkness, and lend us thine aid.

Epiphany. Stanza 1

By cool Siloam's shady rill
How sweet the lily grows!

First Sunday after Epiphany. No. II

When Spring unlocks the flowers to paint the laughing soil.

Seventh Sunday after Trinity

Death rides on every passing breeze,
He lurks in every flower.
Each season has its own disease,
Its peril every hour!

At a Funeral. No. I, Stanza 3

---

changes). — Auguste Marseille Barthélemy [1796–1867]: *Ma Justification* [1832]

[1] See Patrick Henry, page 270.

[2] See Scott, page 310.

[3] Webster's reply to the invitation of his friends, who had been refused the use of Faneuil Hall by the Mayor and Aldermen of Boston.

---

[1] Youngest daughter of George III.

[2] Altered in later editions to —
No workman's steel, no ponderous axes rung,
Like some tall palm the noiseless fabric sprung.
See Cowper, page 266.

Thou art gone to the grave; but we will
 not deplore thee,
Though sorrows and darkness encompass the tomb.
     At a Funeral. No. 11

Where, in creation's wide domains,
Can perfect bliss be found?
     Happiness. Stanza 3

The Son of God goes forth to war,
 A kingly crown to gain;
His blood-red banner streams afar,
 Who follows in His train?
  The Son of God Goes Forth to
     War. Stanza 1

From Greenland's icy mountains,
 From India's coral strand,
Where Afric's sunny fountains
 Roll down their golden sand.
    Missionary Hymn. Stanza 1

Though every prospect pleases,
 And only man is vile.
     Ibid. Stanza 2

Thus heavenly hope is all serene,
 But earthly hope, how bright soe'er,
Still fluctuates o'er this changing scene,
 As false and fleeting as 'tis fair.
  On Heavenly Hope and Earthly
       Hope

When hands are linked that dread to
 part,
And heart is met by throbbing heart —
Oh! bitter, bitter is the smart
 Of them that bid farewell!
     Farewell. Stanza 1

WASHINGTON IRVING
[1783–1859]

How convenient it would be to many
of our great men and great families of
doubtful origin, could they have the
privilege of the heroes of yore, who,
whenever their origin was involved in
obscurity, modestly announced themselves descended from a god.
  Knickerbocker's History of New
    York. Book II, Chap. 3

Who ever hears of fat men heading a
riot, or herding together in turbulent
mobs? — no — no, 'tis your lean, hungry men who are continually worrying

society, and setting the whole community by the ears.
  Knickerbocker's History of New
    York. Book III, Chap. 2

Your true dull minds are generally
preferred for public employ, and especially promoted to city honors; your
keen intellects, like razors, being considered too sharp for common service.
       Ibid.

His wife "ruled the roast,"[1] and in
governing the governor, governed the
province, which might thus be said to
be under petticoat government.
    Ibid. Book IV, Chap. 4

The most glorious hero that ever desolated nations might have mouldered
into oblivion among the rubbish of his
own monument, did not some historian
take him into favor, and benevolently
transmit his name to posterity.
    Ibid. Book V, Chap. 1

Whenever a man's friends begin to
compliment him about looking young,
he may be sure that they think he is
growing old.
    Bracebridge Hall. Bachelors

The almighty dollar,[2] that great
object of universal devotion throughout our land, seems to have no genuine
devotees in these peculiar villages.
    Wolfert's Roost. The Creole
       Village

Those calm, sunny seasons in the
commercial world, which are known by
the name of "times of unexampled prosperity."
   Ibid. "A Time of Unexampled
      Prosperity"

The constant interchange of those
thousand little courtesies which imper-
ceptibly sweeten life, has a happy effect
upon the features, and spreads a mellow
evening charm over the wrinkles of old
age.
    Ibid. A Contented Man

There is in every true woman's heart
a spark of heavenly fire, which lies
dormant in the broad daylight of prosperity; but which kindles up, and beams

[1] See Heywood, page 9.
[2] See Jonson, page 119.

and blazes in the dark hour of adversity.

The Sketch-Book. The Wife

Those men are most apt to be obsequious and conciliating abroad, who are under the discipline of shrews at home.

Ibid. Rip Van Winkle

A curtain lecture is worth all the sermons in the world for teaching the virtues of patience and long-suffering.

Ibid.

A sharp tongue is the only edge tool that grows keener with constant use.

Ibid.

That happy age when a man can be idle with impunity.

Ibid.

Language gradually varies, and with it fade away the writings of authors who have flourished their allotted time.

Ibid. The Mutabilities of Literature

There rise authors now and then, who seem proof against the mutability of language, because they have rooted themselves in the unchanging principles of human nature.

Ibid.

His [the author's] renown has been purchased, not by deeds of violence and blood, but by the diligent dispensation of pleasure.

Ibid. Westminster Abbey [The Poets' Corner]

The sorrow for the dead is the only sorrow from which we refuse to be divorced. Every other wound we seek to heal, every other affliction to forget; but this wound we consider it a duty to keep open; this affliction we cherish and brood over in solitude.

Ibid. Rural Funerals

There is certainly something in angling . . . that tends to produce a gentleness of spirit, and a pure serenity of mind.[1]

Ibid. The Angler

"The literary world," said he, "is made up of little confederacies, each looking upon its own members as the lights of the universe; and considering all others as mere transient meteors, doomed soon to fall and be forgotten, while its own luminaries are to shine steadily on to immortality."

Tales of a Traveller. Literary Life

The land of literature is a fairy land to those who view it at a distance, but, like all other landscapes, the charm fades on a nearer approach, and the thorns and briars become visible. The republic of letters [1] is the most factious and discordant of all republics, ancient or modern.

Ibid. Notoriety

[Captain Delaplace [2]] gazed at [Ethan] Allen in bewildered astonishment. "By whose authority do you act?" exclaimed he. "In the name of the great Jehovah, and the Continental Congress!" replied Allen.

Life of Washington. Vol. I, Chap. 38

SELLECK OSBORN
[1783–1826]

"My father's trade! — why, blockhead,
    art thou mad?
My father, sir, did never stoop so low;
He was a Gentleman, I'd have you
    know."
  "Excuse the liberty I take,"
    Modestus said, with archness on
    his brow —
"Pray, why did not your father make
    A Gentleman of you?"

The Modest Retort

JANE TAYLOR
[1783–1824]

*See also her sister Ann Taylor
[1782–1866]*

Though man a thinking being is defined,
Few use the grand prerogative of mind.

[1] See Walton, page 139.

[1] See Fielding, page 229.
[2] Commandant at Fort Ticonderoga, New York, May 10, 1775.

How few think justly of the thinking
   few!
How many never think, who think they
   do!
>   *Essays in Rhyme. On Morals and
>   Manners, Prejudice, Essay I,
>   Stanza 45*

Far from mortal cares retreating,
   Sordid hopes and vain desires,
Here, our willing footsteps meeting,
   Every heart to heaven aspires.
>   *Hymn*

I thank the goodness and the grace
   Which on my birth have smiled,
And made me, in these Christian days,
   A happy Christian child.
>   *A Child's Hymn of Praise.
>   Stanza 1*

Who ran to help me when I fell,
And would some pretty story tell,
Or kiss the place to make it well?
>   My mother.
>   *My Mother. Stanza 6*

One honest John Tompkins, a hedger
   and ditcher,
Although he was poor, did not want to
   be richer;
For all such vain wishes in him were
   prevented
By a fortunate habit of being contented.
>   *Contented John [Honest John
>   Tompkins]. Stanza 1*

The lark is up to greet the sun,
   The bee is on the wing;
The ant its labor has begun,
   The woods with music ring.
>   *The Sun Is Up. Stanza 1*

But success is secure, unless energy
   fails;
And at last he produced the Philosopher's Scales.
>   *The Philosopher's Scales. Stanza 2*

The first thing he weighed was the head
   of Voltaire,
Which retained all the wit that had
   ever been there.
>   *Ibid. Stanza 5*

"Take a seat," said the cow, gently
   waving her hand;
"By no means, dear madam," said he,
   "while you stand."
>   *The Cow and the Ass. Stanza 4*

Twinkle, twinkle, little star,
How I wonder what you are,
Up above the world so high,
Like a diamond in the sky.[1]
>   *The Star [with* ANN TAYLOR*].
>   Stanza 1*

ALLAN CUNNINGHAM
[1784–1842]

A wet sheet and a flowing sea,
   A wind that follows fast,
And fills the white and rustling sail,
   And bends the gallant mast;
And bends the gallant mast, my boys,
   While, like the eagle free,
Away the good ship flies, and leaves
   Old England on the lee.
>   *A Wet Sheet and a Flowing Sea.
>   Stanza 1*

While the hollow oak our palace is,
   Our heritage the sea.
>   *Ibid. Stanza 3*

When looks were fond and words were
   few.
>   *Poet's Bridal-day Song. Stanza 2*

John Grumlie swore by the light o' the
   moon,
And the green leaves on the tree,
That he could do more work in a day
Than his wife could do in three.
>   *John Grumlie (adapted from
>   the old ballad, The Wife of
>   Auchtermuchty).*[2] *Stanza 1*

But henceforth I maun mind the plow,
And ye maun bide at hame.
>   *Ibid. Stanza 6*

The sun rises bright in France,
   And fair sets he;
But he has tint [3] the blythe blink he
   had

---

[1] Scintillate, scintillate, globule vivific,
   Fain would I fathom thy nature specific,
   Loftily poised in ether capacious,
   Strongly resembling a gem carbonaceous.
   — Anonymous Boston version
[2] Another adaptation of the old ballad is
Darby and Joan, by ST. JOHN HONEYWOOD
[1763–1798].—
   When Darby saw the setting sun,
   He swung his scythe and home he run,
   Sat down, drank off his quart, and said:
   "My work is done, I'll go to bed."
[3] Lost.

In my ain countree.
The Sun Rises Bright in France.
Stanza 1
Hame, hame, hame, to my ain coun-
tree.
Hame, Hame, Hame

LEIGH HUNT
[1784–1859]

Abou Ben Adhem (may his tribe in-
crease!)
Awoke one night from a deep dream of
peace.
Abou Ben Adhem
An angel writing in a book of gold.[1]
Ibid.
Write me as one who loves his fellow-
men.
Ibid.
And lo! Ben Adhem's name led all the
rest.
Ibid.
Oh for a seat in some poetic nook,
Just hid with trees and sparkling with
a brook!
Politics and Poetics. Line 72
With spots of sunny openings, and with
nooks
To lie and read in, sloping into brooks.
The Story of Rimini. Canto III,
Line 418
The world was all forgot, the struggle
o'er,
Desperate the joy. — That day they
read no more.
Ibid. Line 607
His lady to remove the toll that makes
the land forlorn,
Will surely ride through Coventry,
naked as she was born.
Godiva. Stanza 1
"No love," quoth he, "but vanity, sets
love a task like that."
The Glove and the Lions.[2]
Stanza 4

---

[1] I am God's messenger, employed to write
Within this book the pious deeds of men.
J. G. SAXE: *Hassan and the Angel*
[2] SCHILLER wrote a poem on the same
theme. In *The Glove*, ROBERT BROWNING
gives a new version of the familiar legend.

Say I'm weary, say I'm sad,
Say that health and wealth have missed
me,
Say I'm growing old, but add,
Jenny kissed me.[1]
Rondeau
Learn the right
Of coining words in the quick mint of
joy.
A Rustic Walk and Dinner. Line 33
Some people say it is a very easy
thing to get up of a cold morning. You
have only, they tell you, to take the
resolution; and the thing is done.
Getting Up on Cold Mornings
Our Old Gentleman, in order to be
exclusively himself, must be either a
widower or a bachelor.
The Old Gentleman
The pocket-book, among other
things, contains a receipt for a cough,
and some verses cut out of an odd sheet
of an old magazine. . . . He intends
this for a commonplace book which he
keeps, consisting of passages in verse
and prose, cut out of newspapers and
magazines, and pasted in columns;
some of them rather gay.
Ibid.
She thinks the young women of the
present day too forward, and the men
not respectful enough; but hopes her
grandchildren will be better; though
she differs with her daughter in several points respecting their management.
The Old Lady
Those who have lost an infant are
never, as it were, without an infant
child. They are the only persons who,
in one sense, retain it always.
Deaths of Little Children
The groundwork of all happiness is
health.
Ibid.
A fireside is a great opiate.
A Few Thoughts on Sleep

---

[1] The "Jenny" was Mrs. Thomas Carlyle,
who kissed Hunt when he brought Carlyle
good news.

The Irish Shilelah, which a friend has well defined to be "a stick with two butt-ends."

Of Sticks

It has been said of ladies when they write letters, that they put their minds in their postscripts — let out the real objects of their writing, as if it were a second thought, or a thing comparatively indifferent.

Anacreon

The only place a new hat can be carried into with safety is a church, for there is plenty of room there.

A Chapter on Hats

The maid-servant, the sailor, and the schoolboy, are the three beings that enjoy a holiday beyond all the rest of the world.

The Maid-Servant

JAMES SHERIDAN KNOWLES
[1784–1862]

A sound so fine, there's nothing lives 'Twixt it and silence.

Virginius. Act V, Sc. 2

THOMAS DE QUINCEY
[1785–1859]

If once a man indulges himself in murder, very soon he comes to think little of robbing; and from robbing he next comes to drinking and Sabbath-breaking, and from that to incivility and procrastination.

On Murder

It is notorious that the memory strengthens as you lay burdens upon it, and becomes trustworthy as you trust it.

Confessions of an English Opium-Eater (Everyman Edition). Page 30

Call for the grandest of all earthly spectacles, what is that? It is the sun going to his rest. Call for the grandest of all human sentiments, what is that? It is that man should forget his anger before he lies down to sleep.

Ibid. Page 86

If in this world there is one misery having no relief, it is the pressure on the heart from the Incommunicable.

Confessions of an English Opium-Eater (Everyman Edition). Page 110

The reception one meets with from the women of a family generally determines the tenor of one's whole entertainment.

Ibid. Page 132

Mails from the North — the East — the West — the South — whence, according to some curious etymologists, comes the magical word NEWS.

Ibid. Page 145

Oxford Street, stony-hearted stepmother, thou that listenest to the sighs of orphans, and drinkest the tears of children.

Ibid. Page 174

The morning was come of a mighty day — a day of crisis and of ultimate hope for human nature, then suffering mysterious eclipse, and labouring in some dread extremity. . . . Some greater interest was at stake, some mightier cause, than ever yet the sword had pleaded, or trumpet had proclaimed.

Ibid. Page 245

Worlds of fine thinking lie buried in that vast abyss [newspapers], never to be disentombed or restored to human admiration.

Reminiscences of the English Lake Poets. Coleridge

Dyspepsy is the ruin of most things: empires, expeditions, and everything else.

Letter to Hessey [1823]

THOMAS LOVE PEACOCK
[1785–1866]

Seamen three! what men be ye?
Gotham's three Wise Men we be.
Whither in your bowl so free?
To rake the moon from out the sea.
The bowl goes trim. The moon doth shine,
And our ballast is old wine.

Three Men of Gotham. Stanza 1

How troublesome is day!
It calls us from our sleep away;
It bids us from our pleasant dreams
    awake,
And sends us forth to keep or break
Our promises to pay.
How Troublesome Is Day

None better knew the feast to sway,
    Or keep mirth's boat in better trim;
For Nature had but little clay
    Like that of which she moulded him.
The meanest guest that graced his board
    Was there the freest of the free,
His bumper toast when Peter poured
    And passed it round with three times
    three.
In His Last Binn Sir Peter Lies.
Stanza 2

A heeltap! a heeltap! I never could
    bear it!
So fill me a bumper, a bumper of
    claret!
Headlong Hall. Chap. 5

Not drunk is he who from the floor
Can rise alone and still drink more;
But drunk is he, who prostrate lies,
Without the power to drink or rise.
The Misfortunes of Elphin
[1829]. Heading, Chap. 3,
translated from the Welsh

The mountain sheep are sweeter,
But the valley sheep are fatter;
We therefore deemed it meeter
To carry off the latter.
Ibid. Chap. 11

OLIVER HAZARD PERRY
[1785–1820]

We have met the enemy, and they are
    ours.
Letter to General Harrison
[dated "United States Brig Ni-
agara. Off the Western Sisters.
Sept. 10, 1813, 4 P. M."]

JOHN PIERPONT
[1785–1866]

A weapon that comes down as still
    As snowflakes fall upon the sod;
But executes a freeman's will,
    As lightning does the will of God;

And from its force nor doors nor locks
Can shield you, — 'tis the ballot-box.
A Word from a Petitioner

The Yankee boy, before he's sent to
    school,
Well knows the mystery of that magic
    tool,
The pocket-knife.
Whittling, A Yankee Portrait.
Stanza 1

HENRY KIRKE WHITE
[1785–1806]

What is this passing scene?
    A peevish April day!
A little sun, a little rain,
And then night sweeps along the plain,
    And all things fade away;
    Man (soon discuss't)
    Yields up his trust,
And all his hopes and fears lie with him
    in the dust.
Ode to Disappointment. Stanza 3

SAMUEL WOODWORTH
[1785–1842]

How dear to this heart are the scenes
    of my childhood,
When fond recollection presents them
    to view.
The Old Oaken Bucket

Then soon with the emblem of truth
    overflowing,
And dripping with coolness, it rose from
    the well.
Ibid.

The old oaken bucket, the iron-bound
    bucket,
The moss-covered bucket, which hung
    in the well.
Ibid.

Pickaxe, shovel, spade, crowbar, hoe,
    and barrow,
Better not invade, Yankees have the
    marrow.
The Patriotic Diggers [1814].
Stanza 1

We'll show him that Kentucky boys
    Are Alligator-horses.
The Hunters of Kentucky.[1] *Stanza 2*

[1] This ballad, having the sub-title, *Half Horse and Half Alligator*, celebrates the par-

So Pakenham he made his brags
　If he in fight was lucky,
He'd have their gals and cotton bags,
　In spite of old Kentucky.
　　The Hunters of Kentucky. Stanza 4

EATON STANNARD BARRETT
[1786–1820]

Not she with trait'rous kiss her Saviour
　stung,
Not she denied him with unholy
　tongue;
She, while apostles shrank, could dan-
　ger brave,
Last at his cross, and earliest at his
　grave.[1]
　　Woman. Part I [1822]

DAVID CROCKETT
[1786–1836]

I leave this rule for others when I'm
　dead,
Be always sure you're right — then go
　ahead.[2]
　　Autobiography [1834]
Don't shoot, colonel, I'll come down:
I know I'm a gone coon.[3]
　　*Story told by Crockett of a treed
　　　　　　　　　raccoon*

---

ticipation of the Kentuckians, under the command of General John Coffee, in the Battle
of New Orleans, January 8, 1815. It was
published as a broadside in Boston, and, in
1826, collected in a volume, *Melodies, Duets,
Trios, Songs, and Ballads*, by JAMES M.
CAMPBELL.

[1] In another edition, the lines read, —
Not she with trait'rous kiss her Master stung,
Not she denied Him with unfaithful tongue;
She, when apostles fled, could danger brave,
Last at His cross, and earliest at His grave.

[2] Crockett's motto in the War of 1812.

[3] The expression, "gone coon," was current
during the Revolutionary War, originating in
the plea of a spy, dressed in raccoon-skins, to
his discoverer, an English rifleman. — *Century
Cyclopedia of Names*

WILLIAM LEARNED MARCY
[1786–1857]

They see nothing wrong in the rule
that to the victors belong the spoils of
the enemy.
　　Speech, U. S. Senate [*January,
　　　　　　　　　1832*]

WINFIELD SCOTT
[1786–1861]

Say to the seceded States, "Wayward
sisters, depart in peace." [1]
　　Letter to W. H. Seward [*March 3,
　　　　　　　　　1861*]

CAROLINE ANNE BOWLES SOUTHEY
[1786–1854]

All day the low-hung clouds have
　dropped
　Their garnered fullness down;
All day that soft gray mist hath
　wrapped
　Hill, valley, grove, and town.
　　An April Day. Stanza 1
Tread softly; bow the head,
　In reverent silence bow;
No passing bell doth toll,
　Yet an immortal soul
　Is passing now.
　　The Pauper's Death-bed. Stanza 1
Come not in terrors clad, to claim
An unresisting prey.
　　To Death
Dashed with a little sweet at best.
　　Ibid.

RICHARD HENRY DANA
[1787–1879]

Of thousands, thou, both sepulchre
　and pall,
Old Ocean!
　　The Little Beach-Bird. Stanza 4

[1] The North would not allow itself to consider seriously of coercing the seceding states;
and there was a party willing to bid them,
with unavailing tears, "Erring sisters, go in
peace," as if the seceding states, being thus
delicately entreated, could not have the heart
to go, even in peace. — WILLIAM DEAN HOW-
ELLS: *Years of My Youth, IV, XI*

A voice within us speaks the startling word,
"Man, thou shalt never die!"

Immortality

Patient endurance of sufferings, bold resistance of power, forgiveness of injuries, hard-tried and faithful friendship, and self-sacrificing love, are seen in beautiful relief over the flat uniformity of life, or stand out in steady and bright grandeur in the midst of the dark deeds of men.

The Man of Ideality

It is an impression, of which we can not rid ourselves if we would, when sitting by the body of a friend, that he has still a consciousness of our presence; that, though he no longer has a concern in the common things of the world, love and thought are still there. The face which we had been familiar with so long, when it was all life and motion, seems only in a state of rest. We know not how to make it real to ourselves that in the body before us there is not a something still alive.

Mother and Son

ELIZA LEE CABOT FOLLEN
[1787–1860]

Dear mother, how pretty
The moon looks to-night!
She was never so cunning before:
Her two little horns
Are so sharp and so bright,
I hope she'll not grow any more.

The New Moon. Stanza 1

BRYAN WALLER PROCTER
("BARRY CORNWALL")
[1787–1874]

We know not alway who are kings by day,
But the king of the night is the bold brown owl.

The Owl. Stanza 3

A thousand miles from land are we,
Tossing about on the roaring sea.

The Stormy Petrel

Humanity's poor sum and story:

Life — Death — and all that is of Glory.

The History of a Life. Stanza 5

The sea! the sea! the open sea!
The blue, the fresh, the ever free!

The Sea. Stanza 1

I'm on the sea! I'm on the sea!
I am where I would ever be,
With the blue above and the blue below,
And silence wheresoe'er I go.

Ibid. Stanza 2

I never was on the dull, tame shore,
But I loved the great sea more and more.

Ibid. Stanza 4

Touch us gently, Time! [1]
Let us glide adown thy stream
Gently, — as we sometimes glide
Through a quiet dream.

A Petition to Time. Stanza 1

Humble voyagers are we,
O'er life's dim, unsounded sea.

Ibid. Stanza 2

EMMA WILLARD
[1787–1870]

Rocked in the cradle of the deep,
I lay me down in peace to sleep.

The Cradle of the Deep

RICHARD HARRIS BARHAM
[1788–1845]

The Lady Jane was tall and slim,
The Lady Jane was fair.

*Ingoldsby Legends. The Knight
and the Lady*

My Lord Tomnoddy got up one day;
It was half after two; he had nothing to do,
So his lordship rang for his cabriolet.

Ibid. The Execution

Right as a trivet.

Ibid. Auto-da-fè

A Franklyn's dogge leped over a style,
And hys name was littel Byngo.
B with a Y, — Y with an N,
N with a G, — G with an O,
They call'd hym littel Byngo!

A Lay of St. Gengulphus

[1] See Crabbe, page 280.

The Devil must be in that little Jack-
daw!
The Jackdaw of Rheims
The Cardinal rose with a dignified look,
He call'd for his candle, his bell, and
his book!
In holy anger, and pious grief,
He solemnly cursed that rascally
thief!
He cursed him at board, he cursed
him in bed;
From the sole of his foot to the
crown of his head;
He cursed him in sleeping, that every
night
He should dream of the devil, and
wake in a fright;
He cursed him in living, he cursed
him in drinking,
He cursed him in coughing, in sneez-
ing, in winking;
He cursed him in sitting, in stand-
ing, in lying;
He cursed him in walking, in riding,
in flying,
He cursed him in living, he cursed
him dying! —
Never was heard such a terrible curse!
But what gave rise to no little
surprise,
Nobody seem'd one penny the worse!
Ibid.
Heedless of grammar, they all cried,
THAT'S HIM!
Ibid.

GEORGE NOEL GORDON, LORD BYRON
[1788–1824]

Farewell! if ever fondest prayer
For other's weal avail'd on high,
Mine will not all be lost in air,
But waft thy name beyond the sky.
*Farewell! If Ever Fondest Prayer.
Stanza 1*
I only know we loved in vain;
I only feel — farewell! farewell!
Ibid. Stanza 2
When we two parted
In silence and tears,

Half broken-hearted,
To sever for years.
When We Two Parted. Stanza 1
Fools are my theme, let satire be my
song.
*English Bards and Scotch Reviewers.
Line 6*
'Tis pleasant, sure, to see one's name
in print;
A book's a book, although there's noth-
in 't.
Ibid. Line 51
With just enough of learning to mis-
quote.
Ibid. Line 66
As soon
Seek roses in December, ice in June;
Hope constancy in wind, or corn in
chaff;
Believe a woman or an epitaph,
Or any other thing that's false, before
You trust in critics.
Ibid. Line 75
So the struck eagle, stretch'd upon the
plain,
No more through rolling clouds to soar
again,
View'd his own feather on the fatal
dart,
And wing'd the shaft that quiver'd in
his heart.[1]
Ibid. Line 826
Yet truth sometimes will lend her
noblest fires,
And decorate the verse herself inspires:
This fact, in virtue's name, let Crabbe
attest, —
Though Nature's sternest painter, yet
the best.
Ibid. Line 839
Maid of Athens, ere we part,
Give, oh give me back my heart!
Maid of Athens. Stanza 1
Near this spot are deposited the re-
mains of one who possessed Beauty
without Vanity, Strength without In-
solence, Courage without Ferocity, and
all the Virtues of Man, without his
Vices. This Praise, which would be un-
meaning Flattery if inscribed over hu-

[1] See Waller, page 145.

man ashes, is but a just tribute to the
Memory of Boatswain, a Dog.

*Inscription on the Monument of a
Newfoundland Dog*

The poor dog, in life the firmest friend,
The first to welcome, foremost to defend.[1]

Ibid.

Vex'd with mirth the drowsy ear of
night.

*Childe Harold's Pilgrimage. Canto I,
Stanza 2*

Had sigh'd to many, though he loved
but one.

Ibid. Stanza 5

If ancient tales say true, nor wrong
these holy men.

Ibid. Stanza 7

Maidens, like moths, are ever caught
by glare,

And Mammon wins his way where
seraphs might despair.

Ibid. Stanza 9

Might shake the saintship of an an-
chorite.

Ibid. Stanza 11

Adieu! adieu! my native shore
Fades o'er the waters blue.

Ibid. Stanza 13

My native land, good night!

Ibid.

In hope to merit heaven by making
earth a hell.

Ibid. Stanza 20

Still from the fount of joy's delicious
springs

Some bitter o'er the flowers its bubbling venom flings.[2]

Ibid. Stanza 82

[1] The one absolutely unselfish friend that
man can have in this selfish world, the one
that never deserts him, the one that never
proves ungrateful or treacherous, is his dog.
A man's dog stands by him in prosperity and
in poverty, in health and in sickness. —
GEORGE GRAHAM VEST [1830–1904]: *Eulogy
on the Dog*, in Johnson County Circuit Court,
Warrensburg, Missouri

[2]   Medio de fonte leporum
    Surgit amari aliquid quod in ipsis floribus
        angat
(In the midst of the fountain of wit there
arises something bitter, which stings in the
very flowers). — LUCRETIUS: *IV, 1133*

War, war is still the cry, — "war even
to the knife!" [1]

*Childe Harold's Pilgrimage. Canto I,
Stanza 86*

Gone, glimmering through the dream
of things that were.

Ibid. Canto II, Stanza 2

The dome of thought, the palace of
the soul.[2]

Ibid. Stanza 6

There was a sound of revelry by night,
And Belgium's capital had gather'd
then

Her beauty and her chivalry, and bright
The lamps shone o'er fair women and
brave men.

A thousand hearts beat happily; and
when

Music arose with its voluptuous swell,
Soft eyes look'd love to eyes which
spake again,

And all went merry as a marriage bell.
But hush! hark! a deep sound strikes
like a rising knell!

Ibid. Canto III, Stanza 21

Did ye not hear it? — No! 'twas but
the wind,

Or the car rattling o'er the stony street.
On with the dance! let joy be uncon-
fined;

No sleep till morn, when Youth and
Pleasure meet

To chase the glowing hours with flying
feet.

Ibid. Stanza 22

And there was mounting in hot haste.

Ibid. Stanza 25

Or whispering, with white lips, "The
foe! They come! they come!"

Ibid.

Like to the apples on the Dead Sea's
shore,

All ashes to the taste.

Ibid. Stanza 34

He who ascends to mountain-tops, shall
find

The loftiest peaks most wrapt in clouds
and snow;

[1] "War even to the knife" was the reply
of Palafox, the governor of Saragossa, when
summoned to surrender by the French, who
besieged that city in 1808.

[2] See Waller, page 146.

He who surpasses or subdues mankind
Must look down on the hate of those
  below.
> *Childe Harold's Pilgrimage.*
> *Canto III, Stanza 45*

All tenantless, save to the crannying
  wind.
> *Ibid. Stanza 47*

History's purchased page to call them
  great.
> *Ibid. Stanza 48*

The castled crag of Drachenfels
Frowns o'er the wide and winding
  Rhine.
> *Ibid. Stanza 55*

To fly from need not be to hate mankind.
> *Ibid. Stanza 69*

By the blue rushing of the arrowy
  Rhone.
> *Ibid. Stanza 71*

I live not in myself, but I become
Portion of that around me:[1] and to me
High mountains are a feeling, but the
  hum
Of human cities torture.
> *Ibid. Stanza 72*

For his mind
Had grown Suspicion's sanctuary.
> *Ibid. Stanza 80*

This quiet sail is as a noiseless wing
To waft me from distraction.
> *Ibid. Stanza 85*

On the ear
Drops the light drip of the suspended
  oar.
> *Ibid. Stanza 86*

All is concentr'd in a life intense,
Where not a beam, nor air, nor leaf is
  lost,
But hath a part of being.
> *Ibid. Stanza 89*

In solitude, where we are least alone.[2]
> *Ibid. Stanza 90*

The sky is changed, — and such a
  change! O night
And storm, and darkness! ye are
  wondrous strong,
Yet lovely in your strength, as is the
  light

[1] I am a part of all that I have met. —
TENNYSON: *Ulysses*
[2] See Gibbon, page 271.

Of a dark eye in woman! Far along,
From peak to peak, the rattling crags
  among,
Leaps the live thunder.
> *Childe Harold's Pilgrimage.*
> *Canto III, Stanza 92*

The morn is up again, the dewy morn,
With breath all incense.[1]
> *Ibid. Stanza 98*

Exhausting thought,
And hiving wisdom with each studious
  year.
> *Ibid. Stanza 107*

Sapping a solemn creed with solemn
  sneer.
> *Ibid.*

Fame is the thirst of youth.
> *Ibid. Stanza 112*

I have not loved the world, nor the
  world me.[2]
> *Ibid. Stanza 113*

I stood
Among them, but not of them; in a
  shroud
Of thoughts which were not their
  thoughts.
> *Ibid.*

I stood in Venice on the Bridge of
  Sighs,
A palace and a prison on each hand.
> *Ibid. Canto IV, Stanza 1*

Where Venice sate in state, throned on
  her hundred isles.
> *Ibid.*

The thorns which I have reap'd are of
  the tree
I planted; they have torn me, and I
  bleed.
I should have known what fruit would
  spring from such a seed.
> *Ibid. Stanza 10*

Oh for one hour of blind old Dandolo,
The octogenarian chief, Byzantium's
  conquering foe![3]
> *Ibid. Stanza 12*

[1] Incense-breathing morn. — GRAY: *Elegy,*
St. 5
[2] Good-bye, proud world; I'm going home.
  Thou art not my friend, and I'm not thine.
  R. W. EMERSON: *Good-bye, Proud World*
  See Johnson, page 237.
[3] See Wordsworth, page 298.

Parting day
Dies like the dolphin, whom each pang
    imbues
With a new colour as it gasps away,
The last still loveliest, till — 'tis gone,
    and all is gray.
        Childe Harold's Pilgrimage.
            Canto IV, Stanza 29
The Ariosto of the North.
        Ibid. Stanza 40
Italia! O Italia! thou who hast
The fatal gift of beauty.[1]
        Ibid. Stanza 42
Fills
The air around with beauty.
        Ibid. Stanza 49
Let these describe the undescribable.
        Ibid. Stanza 53
The starry Galileo, with his woes.
        Ibid. Stanza 54
Ungrateful Florence! Dante sleeps
    afar,
Like Scipio, buried by the upbraiding
    shore.
        Ibid. Stanza 57
The poetry of speech.
        Ibid. Stanza 58
Then farewell Horace, whom I hated
    so,
Not for thy faults, but mine.
        Ibid. Stanza 77
O Rome! my country! city of the soul!
        Ibid. Stanza 78
The Niobe of nations! there she stands.
        Ibid. Stanza 79
I speak not of men's creeds — they
    rest between
Man and his Maker.
        Ibid. Stanza 95
Yet, Freedom! yet thy banner, torn,
    but flying,
Streams like the thunder-storm against
    the wind.
        Ibid. Stanza 98
Heaven gives its favourites — early
    death.[2]
        Ibid. Stanza 102

'Tis but the same rehearsal of the
    past . . .
And History, with all her volumes vast,
Hath but one page.
        Childe Harold's Pilgrimage.
            Canto IV, Stanza 108
Egeria! sweet creation of some heart
Which found no mortal resting-place
    so fair
As thine ideal breast.
        Ibid. Stanza 115
The nympholepsy of some fond des-
    pair.
        Ibid.
Death, the sable smoke where vanishes
    the flame.
        Ibid. Stanza 124
Butcher'd to make a Roman holiday!
        Ibid. Stanza 141
"While stands the Coliseum, Rome
    shall stand;
When falls the Coliseum, Rome shall
    fall;
And when Rome falls — the world."[1]
        Ibid. Stanza 145
Oh! that the desert were my dwelling-
    place,[2]
With one fair spirit for my minister,
That I might all forget the human
    race,
And, hating no one, love but only her!
        Ibid. Stanza 177
There is a pleasure in the pathless
    woods,
There is a rapture on the lonely shore,
There is society, where none intrudes,
By the deep sea, and music in its roar:
I love not man the less, but Nature
    more.
        Ibid. Stanza 178
Roll on, thou deep and dark blue ocean,
    roll!
Ten thousand fleets sweep over thee in
    vain;
Man marks the earth with ruin, — his
    control
Stops with the shore.
        Ibid. Stanza 179

---

[1] A translation of the famous sonnet of
VINCENZO DA FILICAJA [1642–1707]:
    Italia, Italia! O tu cui feo la sorte.
[2] See Herbert, page 138.
See Wordsworth, page 302.

[1] The saying of the ancient pilgrims.
Quoted from Bede by Gibbon: *The Decline
and Fall of the Roman Empire, Chap. LXXI,
Modern Library Giant, Vol. II, P. 1451.*
[2] See Cowper, page 264.

He sinks into thy depths with bubbling
  groan,
Without a grave, unknell'd, uncoffin'd,
  and unknown.[1]
  Childe Harold's Pilgrimage.
  Canto IV, Stanza 179

Time writes no wrinkle on thine azure
  brow —
Such as creation's dawn beheld, thou
  rollest now.[2]
  Ibid. Stanza 182

Thou glorious mirror, where the Al-
  mighty's form
Glasses itself in tempests.
  Ibid. Stanza 183

And I have loved thee, Ocean! and my
  joy
Of youthful sports was on thy breast
  to be
Borne, like thy bubbles, onward; from
  a boy
I wantoned with thy breakers, ...
And trusted to thy billows far and near,
And laid my hand upon thy mane, —
  as I do here.
  Ibid. Stanza 184

Hands promiscuously applied,
Round the slight waist, or down the
  glowing side.
  The Waltz

He who hath bent him o'er the dead,
Ere the first day of death is fled,
The first dark day of nothingness,
The last of danger and distress,
Before decay's effacing fingers
Have swept the lines where beauty
  lingers.
  The Giaour. Line 68

Such is the aspect of this shore;
'Tis Greece, but living Greece no more!
So coldly sweet, so deadly fair,
We start, for soul is wanting there.
  Ibid. Line 90

Shrine of the mighty! can it be
That this is all remains of thee?
  Ibid. Line 106

---

[1] See Pope, page 219.
[2] And thou vast ocean, on whose awful face
Time's iron feet can print no ruin-trace.
  ROBERT MONTGOMERY: *The Omnipresence of the Deity*

For freedom's battle, once begun,
Bequeath'd by bleeding sire to son,
Though baffled oft, is ever won.
  The Giaour. Line 123

And lovelier things have mercy shown
To every failing but their own;
And every woe a tear can claim,
Except an erring sister's shame.
  Ibid. Line 418

The keenest pangs the wretched find
  Are rapture to the dreary void,
The leafless desert of the mind,
  The waste of feelings unemployed.
  Ibid. Line 957

Better to sink beneath the shock
Than moulder piecemeal on the rock.
  Ibid. Line 969

The cold in clime are cold in blood,
Their love can scarce deserve the name.
  Ibid. Line 1099

I die, — but first I have possess'd,
And come what may, I *have been*
  bless'd.
  Ibid. Line 1114

She was a form of life and light
That, seen, became a part of sight,
And rose, where'er I turn'd mine eye,
The morning-star of memory!
  Ibid. Line 1127

Know ye the land where the cypress
  and myrtle
  Are emblems of deeds that are done
  in their clime;
Where the rage of the vulture, the love
  of the turtle,
  Now melt into sorrow, now madden
  to crime? [1]
  The Bride of Abydos. Canto I,
  Stanza 1

Where the virgins are soft as the roses
  they twine,
And all save the spirit of man is divine?
  Ibid.

---

[1] Know'st thou the land where the lemon-
  trees bloom,
  Where the gold orange glows in the deep
  thicket's gloom,
  Where a wind ever soft from the blue
  heaven blows,
  And the groves are of laurel and myrtle
  and rose!
  GOETHE: *Wilhelm Meister's Apprenticeship, Book III, Chap. 1, Heading*

Who hath not proved how feebly words essay
To fix one spark of beauty's heavenly ray?
Who doth not feel, until his failing sight
Faints into dimness with its own delight,
His changing cheek, his sinking heart, confess
The might, the majesty of loveliness?
　　　The Bride of Abydos. Canto I,
　　　　　　　Stanza 6

The light of love, the purity of grace,
The mind, the music breathing from her face,
The heart whose softness harmonized the whole, —
And oh, that eye was in itself a soul!
　　　　　　　　　　　　Ibid.

He makes a solitude, and calls it — peace! [1]
　　　Ibid. Canto II, Stanza 20

Hark! to the hurried question of despair:
"Where is my child?" — an echo answers, "Where?" [2]
　　　　　　Ibid. Stanza 27

The fatal facility of the octosyllabic verse.
　　　The Corsair. Dedication

He left a corsair's name to other times,
Link'd with one virtue, and a thousand crimes. [3]
　　　Ibid. Canto III, Stanza 24

She walks in beauty, like the night
Of cloudless climes and starry skies;
And all that's best of dark and bright
Meet in her aspect and her eyes;
Thus mellow'd to that tender light
Which Heaven to gaudy day denies.
　　　Hebrew Melodies. She Walks in
　　　　　　Beauty, Stanza 1

The Assyrian came down like the wolf on the fold,

And his cohorts were gleaming in purple and gold.
　　　The Destruction of Sennacherib. [1]
　　　　　　　　Stanza 1

Lord of himself, — that heritage of woe!
　　　　　Lara. Canto I, Stanza 2

The hand that kindles cannot quench the flame.
　　　　Ibid. Canto II, Stanza 11

Fare thee well! and if forever,
Still forever, fare thee well.
　　　　Fare Thee Well. Stanza 1

Sighing that Nature form'd but one such man,
And broke the die, in moulding Sheridan. [2]
　　　Monody on the Death of Sheridan.
　　　　　　　　Line 117

O God! it is a fearful thing
To see the human soul take wing
In any shape, in any mood.
　　　The Prisoner of Chillon. Stanza 8

A light broke in upon my brain, —
It was the carol of a bird;
It ceased, and then it came again,
The sweetest song ear ever heard.
　　　　　　Ibid. Stanza 10

I had a dream which was not all a dream.
　　　　　　　　Darkness

My boat is on the shore,
And my bark is on the sea;
But, before I go, Tom Moore,
Here's a double health to thee!
　　　To Thomas Moore. Stanza 1

Here's a sigh to those who love me,
And a smile to those who hate;

---

[1] Solitudinem faciunt, pacem appellant (They make solitude, which they call peace). — TACITUS: *Agricola, C. 30*

[2] I came to the place of my birth, and cried, "The friends of my youth, where are they?" And echo answered, "Where are they?" — *Arabic MS.*

[3] See Burton, page 122.

[1] And it came to pass that night, that the angel of the Lord went out, and smote in the camp of the Assyrians an hundred fourscore and five thousand: and when they arose early in the morning, behold, they were all dead corpses. — *Isaiah, XXXVII, 36. 2 Kings, XIX, 35*

[2] Natura il fece, e poi ruppe la stampa (Nature made him, and then broke the mould). — ARIOSTO: *Orlando Furioso, Canto X, St. 84*

The idea that Nature lost the perfect mould has been a favorite one with all song-writers and poets, and is found in the literature of all European nations. — *Book of English Songs, P. 28*

And, whatever sky's above me,
  Here's a heart for every fate.[1]
        To Thomas Moore. Stanza 2

So we'll go no more a-roving
  So late into the night.
        *Letter to Thomas Moore [Febru-
        ary 26, 1817]*

Mont Blanc is the monarch of moun-
    tains;
  They crowned him long ago
On a throne of rocks, in a robe of
    clouds,
  With a diadem of snow.
        Manfred. Act I, Sc. 1

All farewells should be sudden.
        Sardanapalus. Act V

She was not old, nor young, nor at the
    years
Which certain people call a "certain
    age,"
Which yet the most uncertain age ap-
    pears.
        Beppo. Stanza 22

For most men (till by losing rendered
    sager)
Will back their own opinions by a
    wager.
        Ibid. Stanza 27

His heart was one of those which most
    enamour us, —
Wax to receive, and marble to retain.[2]
        Ibid. Stanza 34

Besides, they always smell of bread
    and butter.
        Ibid. Stanza 39

        That soft bastard Latin,
Which melts like kisses from a female
    mouth.
        Ibid. Stanza 44

One hates an author that's all author.
        Ibid. Stanza 75

O Mirth and Innocence! O milk and
    water!
Ye happy mixtures of more happy
    days.
        Ibid. Stanza 80

---

[1] With a heart for any fate. — LONGFEL-
LOW: *A Psalm of Life*
[2] My heart is wax to be moulded as she
pleases, but enduring as marble to retain. —
CERVANTES: *The Little Gypsy*

By fair exchange, not robbery.[1]
        *The Deformed Transformed. Act I,
        Sc. 1*

    What's drinking?
A mere pause from thinking!
        Ibid. Act III, Sc. 1

He seems
To have seen better days, as who has
    not
Who has seen yesterday?
        Werner. Act I, Sc. 1

The Cincinnatus of the West,
  Whom envy dared not hate,
Bequeathed the name of Washington
  To make man blush there was but
    one! [2]
        Ode to Napoleon Bonaparte. II

And if we do but watch the hour,
There never yet was human power
Which could evade, if unforgiven,
The patient search and vigil long
Of him who treasures up a wrong.
        Mazeppa. Stanza 10

The "good old times" — all times
    when old are good.
        The Age of Bronze. Stanza 1

Whose game was empires and whose
    stakes were thrones,
Whose table earth, whose dice were hu-
    man bones.
        Ibid. Stanza 3

While Franklin's quiet memory climbs
    to heaven,
Calming the lightning which he thence
    had riven,
Or drawing from the no less kindled
    earth
Freedom and peace to that which
    boasts his birth.
        Ibid. Stanza 5

---

[1] Chaunge be no robbry. — HEYWOOD:
Proverbs, Part II, Chap. 4
[2] Washington's a watchword, such as
    ne'er
  Shall sink while there's an echo left to air.
        The Age of Bronze, St. 5
  Washington,
  Whose every battle field is holy ground.
        Don Juan, Canto VIII, St. 5
  George Washington had thanks and
    nought beside,
  Except the all-cloudless glory (which
    few men's is)
  To free his country.
        Ibid. Canto IX, St. 8

How often we forget all time, when
    lone,
Admiring Nature's universal throne,
Her woods, her wilds, her waters, the
    intense
Reply of hers to our intelligence.
    The Island. Canto II, Stanza 16

Sublime tobacco! which from east to
    west
Cheers the tar's labour or the Turk-
    man's rest.[1]
    Ibid. Stanza 19

Divine in hookas, glorious in a pipe
When tipp'd with amber, mellow, rich,
    and ripe;
Like other charmers, wooing the caress
More dazzlingly when daring in full
    dress;
Yet thy true lovers more admire by far
Thy naked beauties — give me a cigar!
    Ibid.

"That will do for the marines." [2]
    Ibid. Stanza 21

My days are in the yellow leaf;
    The flowers and fruits of love are
    gone;
The worm, the canker, and the grief
    Are mine alone!
    On My Thirty-sixth Year. Stanza 2

Brave men were living before Agamem-
    non.[3]
    Don Juan. Canto I, Stanza 5

In virtues nothing earthly could sur-
    pass her,
Save thine "incomparable oil," Macas-
    sar!
    Ibid. Stanza 17

But, oh! ye lords of ladies intellectual,
Inform us truly, — have they not hen-
    peck'd you all? [4]
    Ibid. Stanza 22

[1] Whatever Aristotle, and his worthy cabal,
    may say of it,
    Tobacco is divine, there is nothing to
    equal it.
      THOMAS CORNEILLE [1625–1709]:
      Le Festin de Pierre, Act I, Sc. 1
      [1673]
[2] See Scott, page 311.
[3] Vixere fortes ante Agamemnona
    Multi.
      HORACE: *Book IV, Ode 9, L. 25*
[4] The Fraternity of the Henpeck'd. —
JOSEPH ADDISON: *The Spectator, No. 482,
Sept. 12, 1712*

The languages, especially the dead,
    The sciences, and most of all the
    abstruse,
The arts, at least all such as could be
    said
    To be the most remote from com-
    mon use.
    Don Juan. Canto I, Stanza 40

Her maids were old, and if she took a
    new one,
You might be sure she was a perfect
    fright.
    Ibid. Stanza 48

Her stature tall, — I hate a dumpy
    woman.
    Ibid. Stanza 61

What men call gallantry, and gods
    adultery.
    Ibid. Stanza 63

Christians have burnt each other, quite
    persuaded
That all the Apostles would have done
    as they did.
    Ibid. Stanza 83

And whispering, "I will ne'er consent,"
    — consented.
    Ibid. Stanza 117

'Tis sweet to hear the watch-dog's hon-
    est bark
    Bay deep-mouth'd welcome as we
    draw near home;
'Tis sweet to know there is an eye will
    mark
    Our coming, and look brighter when
    we come.
    Ibid. Stanza 123

Sweet is revenge — especially to
    women.
    Ibid. Stanza 124

And truant husband should return and
    say,
"My dear, I was the first who came
    away."
    Ibid. Stanza 141

Man's love is of man's life a thing
    apart;
'Tis woman's whole existence.
    Ibid. Stanza 194

In my hot youth, when George the
    Third was king.[1]
    Ibid. Stanza 212

[1] Non ego hoc ferrem, callidus juventa,
    Consule Planco

So for a good old-gentlemanly vice
I think I must take up with avarice.[1]

    Don Juan. Canto I, Stanza 216

There's nought, no doubt, so much the
  spirit calms
As rum and true religion.

    Ibid. Canto II, Stanza 34

A solitary shriek, the bubbling cry
Of some strong swimmer in his agony.

    Ibid. Stanza 53

'Tis very certain the desire of life
Prolongs it.

    Ibid. Stanza 64

'Tis said that persons living on annuities
Are longer lived than others.

    Ibid. Stanza 65

    All who joy would win
Must share it, — happiness was born
  a twin.

    Ibid. Stanza 172

Let us have wine and women, mirth and
  laughter,
Sermons and soda-water the day after.[2]

    Ibid. Stanza 178

In her first passion woman loves her
  lover,
In all the others, all she loves is love.[3]

    Ibid. Canto III, Stanza 3

All tragedies are finished by a death,
All comedies are ended by a marriage.

    Ibid. Stanza 9

    He was the mildest manner'd man
That ever scuttled ship or cut a throat.

    Ibid. Stanza 41

Even good men like to make the public stare.

    Ibid. Stanza 81

The isles of Greece, the isles of Greece!
Where burning Sappho loved and
  sung. . . .
Eternal summer gilds them yet,

  (I would not have borne this in my flam-
ing youth while Plancus was consul). —
HORACE: *Book III, Ode 14, Ad Populum
Romanum, St. 7*

[1] See Middleton, page 116.

[2] See Browning, page 495.
It is no time for mirth and laughter,
The cold, gray dawn of the morning after!
  GEORGE ADE: *The Sultan of Sulu, Remorse*

[3] Dans les premières passions les femmes
aiment l'amant, et dans les autres elles aiment
l'amour. — ROCHEFOUCAULD: *Maxim 471*

But all, except their sun, is set.

    Don Juan. Canto III, Stanza 86, 1

The mountains look on Marathon,
  And Marathon looks on the sea;
And musing there an hour alone,
  I dreamed that Greece might still be
  free.

    Ibid. Stanza 86, 3

Earth! render back from out thy breast
A remnant of our Spartan dead!
Of the three hundred grant but three,
To make a new Thermopylæ.

    Ibid. Stanza 86, 7

You have the Pyrrhic dance as yet,
  Where is the Pyrrhic phalanx gone?
Of two such lessons, why forget
  The nobler and the manlier one?
You have the letters Cadmus gave —
Think ye he meant them for a slave?

    Ibid. Stanza 86, 10

Fill high the bowl with Samian wine!

    Ibid. Stanza 86, 11

To think such breasts must suckle
  slaves.

    Ibid. Stanza 86, 15

Place me on Sunium's marble steep,
  Where nothing save the waves and I
May hear our mutual murmurs sweep;
  There, swan-like, let me sing and
  die.[1]

    Ibid. Stanza 86, 16

But words are things, and a small drop
  of ink,
  Falling like dew upon a thought, pro-
    duces
That which makes thousands, perhaps
  millions, think.

    Ibid. Stanza 88

And glory long has made the sages
  smile,
'Tis something, nothing, words, illusion, wind —
Depending more upon the historian's
  style
Than on the name a person leaves
  behind.

    Ibid. Stanza 90

Ah, surely nothing dies but something
  mourns.

    Ibid. Stanza 108

---

[1] See Shakespeare, page 45.

And if I laugh at any mortal thing,
'Tis that I may not weep.[1]
> *Don Juan. Canto IV, Stanza 4*

The precious porcelain of human clay.[2]
> *Ibid. Stanza 11*

"Whom the gods love die young," was
said of yore.[3]
> *Ibid. Stanza 12*

And her face so fair
Stirr'd with her dream, as rose-leaves
with the air.[4]
> *Ibid. Stanza 29*

These two hated with a hate
Found only on the stage.
> *Ibid. Stanza 93*

"Arcades ambo," — *id est*, blackguards
both.
> *Ibid.*

I've stood upon Achilles' tomb,
And heard Troy doubted: time will
doubt of Rome.
> *Ibid. Stanza 101*

There's not a sea the passenger e'er
pukes in,
Turns up more dangerous breakers than
the Euxine.
> *Ibid. Canto V, Stanza 5*

And put himself upon his good behaviour.
> *Ibid. Stanza 47*

That all-softening, overpowering knell,
The tocsin of the soul — the dinner
bell.
> *Ibid. Stanza 49*

The women pardon'd all except her
face.
> *Ibid. Stanza 113*

Heroic, stoic Cato, the sententious,
Who lent his lady to his friend Hor-
tensius.
> *Ibid. Canto VI, Stanza 7*

---

[1] I make haste to laugh at everything, for
fear of being obliged to weep. — PIERRE BEAU-
MARCHAIS [1732–1799]: *The Barber of Se-
ville, Act I, Sc. 2* [1775]

He jested, that he might not weep. — ALEX-
ANDER SMITH: *Dreamthorp, Of Vagabonds.*
(The reference is to Charles Lamb.)

[2] See Dryden, page 179.

[3] See Wordsworth, page 302.

[4]   All her innocent thoughts
Like rose-leaves scatter'd.
    JOHN WILSON ("CHRISTOPHER NORTH")
    [1785–1854]: *On the Death of a Child*
    [1812]

Polygamy may well be held in dread,
Not only as a sin, but as a bore.
> *Don Juan. Canto VI, Stanza 12*

A "strange coincidence," to use a
phrase
By which such things are settled nowadays.
> *Ibid. Stanza 78*

He scratch'd his ear, the infallible resource
To which embarrass'd people have recourse.
> *Ibid. Stanza 100*

'Mongst them were several Englishmen of pith,
Sixteen were called Thompson and
nineteen Smith.
> *Ibid. Canto VII, Stanza 18*

The drying up a single tear has more
Of honest fame than shedding seas of
gore.
> *Ibid. Canto VIII, Stanza 3*

Half-pay for life makes mankind worth
destroying.
> *Ibid. Stanza 14*

Neck or nothing.
> *Ibid. Stanza 45*

Indigestion is — that inward fate
Which makes all Styx through one
small liver flow.
> *Ibid. Canto IX, Stanza 15*

"Gentlemen farmers" — a race worn
out quite.
> *Ibid. Stanza 32*

He said
Little, but to the purpose.
> *Ibid. Stanza 83*

And wrinkles (the damned democrats)
won't flatter.
> *Ibid. Canto X, Stanza 24*

What a delightful thing's a turnpike
road.
> *Ibid. Stanza 78*

When Bishop Berkeley said "there was
no matter,"
And proved it, — 'twas no matter
what he said.[1]
> *Ibid. Canto XI, Stanza 1*

---

[1] What is mind? No matter. What is matter? Never mind. — THOMAS HEWITT KEY
[1799–1875], once Head Master of University College School. Quoted by F. J. Furnivall.

So prime, so swell, so nutty, and so
  knowing.
> *Don Juan. Canto XI, Stanza 19*

'Tis strange the mind, that very fiery
  particle,
Should let itself be snuff'd out by an
  article.
> *Ibid. Stanza 60*

Ready money is Aladdin's lamp.
> *Ibid. Canto XII, Stanza 12*

Cervantes smil'd Spain's chivalry
  away.
> *Ibid. Canto XIII, Stanza 11*

Society is now one polish'd horde,
Formed of two mighty tribes, the *Bores*
  and *Bored.*
> *Ibid. Stanza 95*

All human history attests
That happiness for man, — the hungry
  sinner! —
Since Eve ate apples, much depends on
  dinner.[1]
> *Ibid. Stanza 99*

Death, so called, is a thing which makes
  men weep,
And yet a third of life is passed in
  sleep.
> *Ibid. Canto XIV, Stanza 3*

'Tis strange, but true; for truth is always strange, —
Stranger than fiction.[2]
> *Ibid. Stanza 101*

The Devil hath not, in all his quiver's
  choice,
An arrow for the heart like a sweet
  voice.
> *Ibid. Canto XV, Stanza 13*

A lovely being, scarcely formed or
  moulded,
A rose with all its sweetest leaves yet
  folded.
> *Ibid. Stanza 43*

The antique Persians taught three
  useful things, —

[1] For a man seldom thinks with more
earnestness of anything than he does of his
dinner. — Piozzi: *Anecdotes of Samuel Johnson, P. 149*

[2] Le vrai peut quelquefois n'être pas vrai-
semblable.
(Truth may sometimes be improbable).
  Nicholas Boileau-Despréaux: *L'Art
    Poétique, III, L. 48*

To draw the bow, to ride, and speak
  the truth.[1]
> *Don Juan. Canto XVI, Stanza 1*

Heart ballads of Green Erin or Gray
  Highlands,
That bring Lochaber back to eyes that
  roam
O'er far Atlantic continents or islands.
> *Ibid. Stanza 46*

Friendship is Love without his wings.
> *L'Amitié est l'Amour sans Ailes*

I awoke one morning and found myself famous.
> *Entry in Memoranda after pub-
> lication of first two cantos of
> Childe Harold's Pilgrimage.
> Quoted by* Thomas Moore *in
> his Life of Byron, Chap. 14*

The best of prophets of the future is
  the past.
> *Letter [January 28, 1821]*

What say you to such a supper with
  such a woman? [2]
> *Note to a Letter to Mr. Mur-
> ray on the Reverend W. L.
> Bowles' Strictures on Pope
> [March 25, 1821]*

The world is a bundle of hay,
  Mankind are the asses that pull,
Each tugs in a different way, —
  And the greatest of all is John Bull!
> *Letter to Thomas Moore [June
> 22, 1821]*

SIR WILLIAM HENRY MAULE
[1788–1858]

My lords, we are vertebrate animals,
we are mammalia! My learned friend's
manner would be intolerable in Almighty God to a black beetle.
> *Appeal to the court in a case
> where the opposing counsel,
> Sir Cresswell Cresswell, was
> lofty and offensive in manner.
> Reported by Lord Coleridge*

[1] To ride, shoot straight, and speak the
  truth —
This was the ancient Law of Youth.
Old times are past, old days are done;
But the Law runs true, O little son!
  Charles T. Davis: *For a Little Boy,
    St. 1*

[2] See Lady Montagu, page 221.

WILLIAM MEE
[1788–1862]

She's all my fancy painted her;
She's lovely, she's divine.
Alice Gray

HANNAH FLAGG GOULD
[1789–1865]

Alone I walked the ocean strand;
A pearly shell was in my hand;
I stooped and wrote upon the sand
My name — the year — the day.
A Name on the Sand. Stanza 1

"Now, just to set them a-thinking,
I'll bite this basket of fruit," said he,
"This costly pitcher I'll burst in three;
And the glass of water they've left for
me
Shall 'tchick!' to tell them I'm drink-
ing!"
The Frost. Stanza 4

Wisdom, Power and Goodness meet
In the bounteous field of wheat.
The Wheatfield. Stanza 4

WILLIAM KNOX
[1789–1825]

Oh why should the spirit of mortal be
proud?
Like a fast-flitting meteor, a fast-flying
cloud,
A flash of the lightning, a break of the
wave,
He passes from life to his rest in the
grave.
Songs of Israel [1824]. Mortality,[1]
Stanza 1

'Tis the wink of an eye, 'tis the draught
of a breath,
From the blossom of health to the pale-
ness of death.
Ibid. Stanza 14

The fool hath said: There is no God!
No God! Who lights the morning
sun,

[1] This poem was a favorite of Abraham
Lincoln.

And sends him on his heavenly road,
A far and brilliant course to run?
The Atheist. Stanza 1

CHARLES PHILLIPS
[1789–1859]

Grand, gloomy, and peculiar, he sat
upon the throne a sceptred hermit,
wrapped in the solitude of his own
originality.
The Character of Napoleon

SARAH JOSEPHA HALE
[1790–1879]

Mary had a little lamb,
Its fleece was white as snow,
And everywhere that Mary went
The lamb was sure to go;
He followed her to school one day,
That was against the rule;
It made the children laugh and play
To see a lamb in school.
*Mary's Lamb. In the Juvenile Mis-
cellany [September, 1830]*

"It snows!" cries the school-boy, "Hur-
rah!" and his shout
Is ringing through parlor and hall,
While swift as the wing of a swallow,
he's out,
And his playmates have answered
his call.
It Snows. Stanza 1

FITZ-GREENE HALLECK
[1790–1867]

Strike — till the last armed foe ex-
pires;
Strike — for your altars and your fires;
Strike — for the green graves of your
sires;
God — and your native land!
Marco Bozzaris.[1] *Stanza 3*

Come to the bridal chamber, Death!
Come to the mother, when she feels
For the first time her first-born's
breath;
Come when the blessed seals

[1] A Greek patriot, born about 1788, killed
in a night attack against the Turks, near
Missolonghi, Greece, August 20, 1823.

Which close the pestilence are broke,
And crowded cities wail its stroke;
Come in consumption's ghastly form,
The earthquake's shock, the ocean
    storm;
Come when the heart beats high and
    warm
    With banquet song, and dance, and
        wine,
And thou art terrible: the tear,
The groan, the knell, the pall, the bier,
And all we know, or dream, or fear
    Of agony are thine.
                Marco Bozzaris. Stanza 5
But to the hero, when his sword
    Has won the battle for the free,
Thy voice sounds like a prophet's word,
And in its hollow tones are heard
    The thanks of millions yet to be.
                        Ibid. Stanza 6
One of the few, the immortal names
    That were not born to die.
                        Ibid. Stanza 7
Such graves as his are pilgrim shrines,
    Shrines to no code or creed con-
        fined, —
The Delphian vales, the Palestines,
    The Meccas of the mind.
                    Burns. Stanza 32
Green be the turf above thee,
    Friend of my better days!
None knew thee but to love thee,[1]
    Nor named thee but to praise.
    *On the Death of Joseph Rodman
                            Drake*
There is an evening twilight of the
    heart,
When its wild passion-waves are lulled
    to rest.
                        Twilight
They love their land because it is their
    own,
    And scorn to give aught other rea-
        son why;
Would shake hands with a king upon
    his throne,
    And think it kindness to his Majesty.
                        Connecticut
This bank-note world.
                Alnwick Castle. Stanza 7

[1] See Rogers, page 289.

Lord Stafford mines for coal and salt,
The Duke of Norfolk deals in malt,
    The Douglas in red herrings.
                Alnwick Castle. Stanza 8

SAMUEL GILMAN
[1791–1858]

Fair Harvard! Thy sons to thy Jubilee
    throng,
    And with blessings surrender thee
        o'er,
By these festival rites, from the age
    that is past,
    To the age that is waiting before.
        *Ode, Bicentennial, Harvard Uni-
            versity [September 8, 1836].
            Stanza 1*
Thou wert our parent, the nurse of our
    souls,
    We were moulded to manhood by
        thee,
Till freighted with treasure-thoughts,
    friendships, and hopes,
    Thou didst launch us on Destiny's
        sea.
                        Ibid. Stanza 2

HENRY HART MILMAN
[1791–1868]

And the cold marble leapt to life a
    god.
                The Belvedere Apollo
Too fair to worship, too divine to love.
                        Ibid.
And more than wisdom, more than
    wealth, —
A merry heart that laughs at care.
                The Merry Heart. Stanza 1

LYDIA HUNTLY SIGOURNEY
[1791–1865]

Toll for the queenly boat, wrecked on
    rocky shore!
Sea-weed is in her palace halls; she
    rides the surge no more.
                The Bell of the Atlantic.[1]

[1] The *Atlantic* was wrecked on an island
near New London, Connecticut, in 1846. The
bell, on a portion of the wreck, tolled for
many days until salvaged. It later hung at
the Seamen's Church Institute, South Street,
New York.

Ye say that all have passed away —
  That noble race and brave . . .
But their name is on your waters [1] —
  Ye may not wash it out.
        Indian Names. Stanza 1
Old Massachusetts wears it
  Upon her lordly crown.
        Ibid. Stanza 4
Your mountains build their monu-
    ment,
  Though ye destroy their dust.
        Ibid. Stanza 5
Through the open window's space
Behold, a camel thrust his face.
"My nose is cold," he meekly cried,
"Oh, let me warm it by thy side."
        The Camel's Nose. Stanza 1
To evil habit's earliest wile
Lend neither ear, nor glance, nor
    smile —
Choke the dark fountain ere it flows,
Nor e'en admit the camel's nose.
        Ibid. Stanza 4

CHARLES SPRAGUE
[1791–1875]

Gay, guiltless pair,
What seek ye from the fields of heaven?
Ye have no need of prayer,
Ye have no sins to be forgiven.
        The Winged Worshippers.[2]
           Stanza 1
It is not often thus around
Our old familiar hearth we're found.
Bless, then, the meeting and the spot;
For once be every care forgot;
Let gentle Peace assert her power,
And kind Affection rule the hour.
  We're all — all here.
        The Family Meeting. Stanza 1
Then Shakespeare rose!
Across the trembling strings
His daring hand he flings,
And lo! a new creation glows!
    Ode, Shakespeare Celebration
           [Boston, 1823]

[1] We will give the names of our fearless race
  To each bright river whose course we
    trace.
    FELICIA D. HEMANS: *Song of Emigra-*
                tion
[2] Two swallows that flew into the Chauncy
Place Church, Boston, during a service.

In fields of air, he writes his name,
And treads the chambers of the sky.
        Ode, Art
Yes, social friend, I love thee well,
  In learned doctors' spite;
Thy clouds all other clouds dispel,
  And lap me in delight.
        To My Cigar
Through life's dark road his sordid way
    he wends,
An incarnation of fat dividends.
    Phi Beta Kappa Ode, Curiosity
Here lived and loved another race
of beings. Beneath the same sun that
rolls over your heads the Indian hunter
pursued the panting deer. . . . The
Indian of falcon glance and lion bear-
ing, the theme of the touching ballad,
the hero of the pathetic tale, is gone.
        The American Indian

CHARLES WOLFE
[1791–1823]

Not a drum was heard, not a funeral
    note,
  As his corse to the rampart we hur-
    ried.
    The Burial of Sir John Moore
       at Corunna.[1] *Stanza 1*
But he lay like a warrior taking his
    rest
  With his martial cloak around him.
        Ibid. Stanza 3
Slowly and sadly we laid him down,
  From the field of his fame fresh and
    gory;
We carved not a line, and we raised
    not a stone,
  But we left him alone with his glory.
        Ibid. Stanza 8
If I had thought thou couldst have
    died,
  I might not weep for thee;
But I forgot, when by thy side,
  That thou couldst mortal be.
        To Mary. Stanza 1
Yet there was round thee such a dawn
  Of light ne'er seen before,

[1] First published in the *Newry Telegraph*
[1817].

As fancy never could have drawn,
And never can restore.
To Mary. Stanza 4

Go, forget me! why should sorrow
O'er that brow a shadow fling?
Go, forget me, and to-morrow
Brightly smile and sweetly sing!
Smile, — though I shall not be near
thee;
Sing, — though I shall never hear
thee!
Go, Forget Me!

WILLIAM HOWITT
[1792–1879]

The Wind one morning sprang up from
sleep,
Saying, "Now for a frolic, now for a
leap!
Now for a madcap galloping chase!
I'll make a commotion in every place!"
The Wind in a Frolic

JOHN KEBLE
[1792–1866]

The trivial round, the common task,
Would furnish all we ought to ask.
Morning. Stanza 10

Why should we faint and fear to live
alone,
Since all alone, so Heaven has willed,
we die?
Nor even the tenderest heart, and next
our own,
Knows half the reasons why we
smile and sigh.
The Christian Year. Twenty-fourth Sunday after Trinity

'Tis sweet, as year by year we lose
Friends out of sight, in faith to muse
How grows in Paradise our store.
Burial of the Dead

Abide with me from morn till eve,
For without Thee I cannot live;
Abide with me when night is nigh,
For without Thee I dare not die.
Evening. Stanza 4

JOHN HOWARD PAYNE
[1792–1852]

'Mid pleasures and palaces though we
may roam,
Be it ever so humble, there's no place
like home; [1]
A charm from the skies seems to hallow us there,
Which sought through the world is
ne'er met with elsewhere.

An exile from home splendour dazzles
in vain,
Oh give me my lowly thatched cottage
again;
The birds singing gayly, that came at
my call,
Give me them, and that peace of mind
dearer than all.
Home, Sweet Home.[2] (From the opera Clari, the Maid of Milan)

PERCY BYSSHE SHELLEY
[1792–1822]

With hue like that when some great
painter dips
His pencil in the gloom of earthquake
and eclipse.
The Revolt of Islam. Canto V, Stanza 23

The awful shadow of some unseen
Power
Floats tho' unseen amongst us.
Hymn to Intellectual Beauty. Stanza 1

As long as skies are blue, and fields
are green,
Evening must usher night, night urge
the morrow,
Month follow month with woe, and
year wake year to sorrow.
Adonais. XXI

[1] Home is home, though it be never so
homely. — CLARK: *Parœmiologia, P. 101*
[1639]
[2] See Reynolds, page 294.
The Latin song *Dulce Domum*, words
anonymous, was set to music by John Reading, organist of Winchester Cathedral [1675–
1681] and of Winchester College [1681–
1692]. The refrain of the song is:
Domum, domum, dulce domum,
Dulce, dulce, dulce domum.

I would give
All that I am to be as thou now art!
But I am chained to Time, and can
not thence depart!
Adonais. XXVI

The Pilgrim of Eternity,[1] whose fame
Over his living head like heaven is
bent,
An early but enduring monument,
Came, veiling all the lightnings of his
song
In sorrow.
Ibid. XXX

A pard-like spirit, beautiful and swift.
Ibid. XXXII

In mockery of monumental stone.
Ibid. XXXV

Peace, peace! he is not dead, he doth
not sleep —
He hath awakened from the dream of
life.
Ibid. XXXIX

He has outsoared the shadow of our
night;
Envy and calumny and hate and pain,
And that unrest which men miscall de-
light
Can touch him not and torture not
again;
From the contagion of the world's
slow stain
He is secure, and now can never mourn
A heart grown cold, a head grown gray
in vain.
Ibid. XL

He is made one with Nature: there is
heard
His voice in all her music, from the
moan
Of thunder to the song of night's sweet
bird.
Ibid. XLII

He is a portion of the loveliness
Which once he made more lovely.
Ibid. XLIII

And many more, whose names on
Earth are dark,
But whose transmitted effluence can
not die
So long as fire outlives the parent
spark,

[1] The allusion is to Byron.

Rose, robed in dazzling immortality.
Adonais. XLVI

Life, like a dome of many-coloured
glass,
Stains the white radiance of eternity.
Ibid. LII

The soul of Adonais, like a star,
Beacons from the abode where the
Eternal are.
Ibid. LV

Some say that gleams of a remoter
world
Visit the soul in sleep, — that death is
slumber,
And that its shapes the busy thoughts
outnumber
Of those who wake and live.
Mont Blanc. III

I fall upon the thorns of life! I bleed!
Ode to the West Wind. IV

O, wind,
If Winter comes, can Spring be far be-
hind?
Ibid. V

Chameleons feed on light and air:
Poets' food is love and fame.
An Exhortation. Stanza 1

I bring fresh showers for the thirsting
flowers,
From the seas and the streams.
The Cloud. Stanza 1

That orbèd maiden with white fire
laden,
Whom mortals call the moon.
Ibid. Stanza 4

I am the daughter of Earth and Water,
And the nursling of the Sky;
I pass through the pores of the ocean
and shores,
I change, but I cannot die.
Ibid. Stanza 6

Hail to thee, blithe spirit!
Bird thou never wert.
To a Skylark. Stanza 1

We look before and after,
And pine for what is not;
Our sincerest laughter
With some pain is fraught;
Our sweetest songs are those that tell
of saddest thought.
Ibid. Stanza 18

Teach me half the gladness
That thy brain must know,

Such harmonious madness
From my lips would flow,
The world should listen then, as I am
listening now.
To a Skylark. Stanza 21

Kings are like stars — they rise and
set, they have
The worship of the world, but no repose.[1]
Hellas. Line 195

The moon of Mahomet
Arose, and it shall set;
While, blazoned as on heaven's im-
mortal noon,
The cross leads generations on.
Ibid. Line 221

The world's great age begins anew,
The golden years return,
The earth doth like a snake renew
Her winter weeds outworn.
Ibid. Line 1060

The world is weary of the past,
Oh, might it die or rest at last!
Ibid. Final Chorus

What! alive, and so bold, O earth?
*Written on Hearing the News of
the Death of Napoleon. Stanza 1*

Forms more real than living man,
Nurslings of immortality!
Prometheus Unbound. Act I

Like stars half quencht in mists of silver dew.
Ibid. Act II, Sc. 1

All love is sweet,
Given or returned. Common as light
is love,
And its familiar voice wearies not
ever. . . .
They who inspire it most are fortunate,
As I am now; but those who feel it
most
Are happier still.[2]
Ibid. Sc. 5

Death is the veil which those who live
call life;
They sleep, and it is lifted.
Ibid. Act III, Sc. 3

Good, great and joyous, beautiful and
free;
This is alone Life, Joy, Empire, and
Victory.
*Prometheus Unbound. Act IV,
Closing lines*

Most wretched men
Are cradled into poetry by wrong,
They learn in suffering what they
teach in song.[1]
Julian and Maddalo. Line 544

I could lie down like a tired child,
And weep away the life of care
Which I have borne and yet must bear.
*Stanzas Written in Dejection,
near Naples. Stanza 4*

Jealousy's eyes are green.
Swellfoot the Tyrant. Act II, Sc. 1

Round the decay
Of that colossal wreck, boundless and
bare
The lone and level sands stretch far
away.
Ozymandias

The Devil is a gentleman.[2]
*Peter Bell the Third. Part II,
Stanza 2*

Hell is a city much like London —
A populous and smoky city.
Ibid. Part III, Stanza 1

Teas,
Where small talk dies in agonies.
Ibid. Stanza 12

He had as much imagination
As a pint-pot.
Ibid. Part IV, Stanza 8

Peter was dull — he was at first
Dull — oh so dull — so very dull!
Whether he talked, wrote, or re-
hearsed —
Still with this dulness was he cursed —
Dull — beyond all conception —
dull.
Ibid. Part VII, Stanza 11

A lovely lady, garmented in light
From her own beauty.
The Witch of Atlas. Stanza 5

Music, when soft voices die,
Vibrates in the memory —

---

[1] See Bacon, page 110.
[2] The pleasure of love is in loving. We are much happier in the passion we feel than in that we inspire. — ROCHEFOUCAULD: *Maxim 259*

[1] See Butler, page 144.
[2] See Shakespeare, page 99.

Odours, when sweet violets sicken,
Live within the sense they quicken.
> *To — : Music, When Soft*
> *Voices Die. Stanza 1*

Rarely, rarely, comest thou,
  Spirit of Delight! [1]
> *Song: Rarely, Rarely, Comest*
> *Thou. Stanza 1*

I love tranquil solitude
  And such society
As is quiet, wise, and good.
> *Ibid. Stanza 7*

Sing again, with your dear voice revealing
  A tone
Of some world far from ours,
Where music and moonlight and feeling
  Are one.
> *To Jane: The Keen Stars Were*
> *Twinkling. Stanza 4*

The desire of the moth for the star,
  Of the night for the morrow,
The devotion to something afar
  From the sphere of our sorrow.
> *To — : One Word Is Too Often*
> *Profaned. Stanza 2*

The seed ye sow, another reaps;
The wealth ye find, another keeps;
The robes ye weave, another wears;
The arms ye forge, another bears.
> *Song to the Men of England.*
> *Stanza 5*

Nothing in the world is single,
All things by a law divine
In one spirit meet and mingle.
> *Love's Philosophy. Stanza 1*

I arise from dreams of thee
In the first sweet sleep of night,
When the winds are breathing low,
And the stars are shining bright.
> *The Indian Serenade. Stanza 1*

  The Champak odours pine,
Like sweet thoughts in a dream.
> *Ibid. Stanza 2*

A Sensitive Plant in a garden grew,
And the young winds fed it with silver dew.
> *The Sensitive Plant. I, Stanza 1*

---

[1] Motto of Symphony No. 2 in E-flat, Opus 63, by SIR EDWARD ELGAR [1857–1934].

For love and beauty and delight,
There is no death nor change.
> *The Sensitive Plant.*
> *Conclusion, Stanza 6*

We rest. A dream has power to poison sleep;
We rise. One wandering thought pollutes the day.
> *Mutability. I, Stanza 3*

Man's yesterday may ne'er be like his morrow;
Naught may endure but Mutability.
> *Ibid. Stanza 4*

The flower that smiles to-day
  To-morrow dies;
All that we wish to stay
  Tempts and then flies.
What is this world's delight?
Lightning that mocks the night,
  Brief even as bright.
> *Ibid. II, Stanza 1*

There is no sport in hate when all the rage
Is on one side.
> *Lines to a Reviewer*

The weary Day turned to his rest,
Lingering like an unloved guest.
> *To Night. Stanza 3*

  When the lamp is shattered
The light in the dust lies dead: —
  When the cloud is scattered
The rainbow's glory is shed.
> *When the Lamp Is Shattered.*
> *Stanza 1*

Once, early in the morning,
  Beelzebub arose,
With care his sweet person adorning,
  He put on his Sunday clothes.[1]
> *The Devil's Walk, A Ballad.*
> *Stanza 1*

How wonderful is Death,
Death and his brother Sleep.
> *Queen Mab. 1*

Power, like a desolating pestilence,
Pollutes whate'er it touches; and obedience,
Bane of all genius, virtue, freedom, truth,
Makes slaves of men, and, of the human frame,
A mechanized automaton.
> *Ibid. III*

---

[1] See Southey, page 321.

Heaven's ebon vault,
Studded with stars unutterably bright,
Through which the moon's unclouded
    grandeur rolls,
Seems like a canopy which love had
    spread
To curtain her sleeping world.
                        Queen Mab. IV
Poets are the hierophants of an un-
apprehended inspiration; the mirrors
of the gigantic shadows which futurity
casts upon the present.[1]
                    A Defence of Poetry
Poetry is the record of the best and
happiest moments of the happiest and
best minds.
                                Ibid.
Poets are the unacknowledged legis-
lators of the world.
                                Ibid.

SEBA SMITH ("MAJOR JACK DOWNING")
[1792–1868]

The cold winds swept the mountain-
    height,
    And pathless was the dreary wild,
And 'mid the cheerless hours of night
    A mother wandered with her child:
As through the drifting snows she
    press'd,
The babe was sleeping on her breast.
            The Snow Storm. Stanza 1
'Twas autumn, and the leaves were
    dry,
    And rustled on the ground;
And chilly winds went whistling by
    With low and pensive sound.
        Three Little Graves. Stanza 1

JEFFERYS TAYLOR
[1792–1853]

This moral, I think, may be safely at-
    tached;
Reckon not on your chickens before
    they are hatched.[2]
                The Milkmaid. Moral

[1] See Coleridge, page 318.
[2] See Butler, page 143.

JOHN CLARE
[1793–1864]

I am! yet what I am who cares, or
    knows?
My friends forsake me like a memory
    lost.
            *Written in Northampton
            County Asylum*
The daisy lives, and strikes its little
    root
Into the lap of time: centuries may
    come,
And pass away into the silent tomb,
And still the child, hid in the womb of
    time,
Shall smile and pluck them, when this
    simple rhyme
Shall be forgotten.
                The Daisy's Eternity
With its little brimming eye
    And its yellow rims so pale
    And its crimp and curdled leaf,
Who can pass its beauties by?
                The Primrose Bank
    The world was on thy page
Of victories but a comma.
                    To Napoleon
The wind and clouds, now here, now
    there,
Hold no such strange dominion
As woman's cold, perverted will,
    And soon estranged opinion.
                When Lovers Part
    If life had a second edition, how
I would correct the proofs.[1]
        Quoted by DANIEL BERKELEY
        UPDIKE *in History of the
        Merrymount Press, Introduc-
        tion*

SAMUEL GRISWOLD GOODRICH ("PETER PARLEY")
[1793–1860]

The earth is round, and like a ball
    Seems swinging in the air;
A sky extends around it all,

[1] Compare the epitaph written for himself
(at the age of 22) by Benjamin Franklin:
"Benjamin Franklin, Printer. . . . Will Appear Once More, In a New and More Elegant Edition, Revised and Corrected by the
Author."

And stars are shining there.
Water and land upon the face
Of this round world we see;
The land is man's safe dwelling place,
But ships sail on the sea.
The Earth

FELICIA DOROTHEA
HEMANS
[1793–1835]

The stately homes of England!
    How beautiful they stand,
Amidst their tall ancestral trees,
    O'er all the pleasant land!
        The Homes of England. Stanza 1
The breaking waves dashed high
    On a stern and rock-bound coast,
And the woods, against a stormy sky,
    Their giant branches tossed.
        *The Landing of the Pilgrim
            Fathers. Stanza 1*
A band of exiles moored their bark
On a wild New England shore.
        Ibid. Stanza 2
What sought they thus afar?
    Bright jewels of the mine?
The wealth of seas, the spoils of
        war? —
    They sought a faith's pure shrine.
        Ibid. Stanza 9
Ay, call it holy ground,
    The soil where first they trod!
They have left unstained what there
        they found —
    Freedom to worship God.
        Ibid. Stanza 10
The boy [1] stood on the burning deck,
    Whence all but he had fled; [2]

[1] Giacomo Casabianca, whose father, Louis,
was an officer in the Comte de Grasse's command at the siege of Yorktown. At the battle
of the Nile, in August, 1798, Louis Casabianca
commanded the *Orient,* flagship of Admiral
Brueys, who was killed, Louis then taking
supreme command. The flagship took fire and
blew up, the commander was mortally wounded, and when most of the crew fled, Giacomo
remained aboard, in an effort to help his gallant father.
[2] The first American edition of Mrs. Hemans' *Poems* [1826] gave this line "whence
all but him had fled." English editions and
subsequent American editions seem evenly
divided between "but him" and "but he." The

The flame that lit the battle's wreck
    Shone round him o'er the dead.
        Casabianca. Stanza 1
There came a burst of thunder sound;
    The boy, — oh! where was he?
        Ibid. Stanza 9
Leaves have their time to fall,
And flowers to wither at the north-
        wind's breath,
    And stars to set; — but all,
Thou hast *all* seasons for thine own,
        O Death!
        The Hour of Death. Stanza 1
Come to the sunset tree!
    The day is past and gone;
The woodman's axe lies free,
    And the reaper's work is done.
        Tyrolese Evening Song. Stanza 1
In the busy haunts of men.
        *Tale of the Secret Tribunal.
            Part I*
Oh, call my brother back to me!
    I cannot play alone:
The summer comes with flower and
        bee, —
    Where is my brother gone?
        The Child's First Grief. Stanza 1
I have looked o'er the hills of the
        stormy North,
And the larch has hung all his tassels
        forth.
        The Voice of Spring. Stanza 3
But tell us, thou bird of the solemn
        strain!
    Can those who have loved forget?
We call — and they answer not
        again —
    Do they love — do they love us yet?
        The Messenger Bird
Wave may not foam nor wild wind
        sweep
Where rest not England's Dead.
        England's Dead
'Twas a lovely thought to mark the
        hours
    As they floated in light away,

last edition published while Mrs. Hemans was
still living and presumably approved the contents (Blackwood, Edinburgh, 1829, P. 243),
gives "but he."

By the opening and the folding flowers,
That laugh to the summer's day.
The Dial of Flowers [of Linnaeus]

So moved they calmly to the field,
Thence never to return,
Save bearing back the Spartan shield,
Or on it proudly borne.
The Spartans' March. Stanza 9

The bark that held a prince went down,
The sweeping waves rolled on;
And what was England's glorious crown
To him that wept a son?
He lived — for life may long be borne
Ere sorrow break its chain; —
Why comes not death to those who mourn? —
He never smiled again! [1]
He Never Smiled Again [2]

EDWARD T. TAYLOR ("FATHER TAYLOR") [3]
[1793–1871]

Simon Stone, he spied a boat,
"Oh, here is a boat," cried Simon Stone.
"I've a mind to see if this boat will float,
I'll fish a spell, if I go alone."
Simon Stone (a Ballad of the Disciple, Simon Peter). Stanza 1

WILLIAM CULLEN BRYANT
[1794–1878]

Here the free spirit of mankind, at length,
Throws its last fetters off; and who shall place

---

[1] Prince William, son of King Henry I, perished, in 1120, when the *White Ship* of the royal fleet struck a rock and sank instantly. J. R. GREEN, in *A Short History of the English People,* says: "It was not till the morning that the fatal news reached the King. He fell unconscious to the ground, and rose never to smile again."

[2] D. G. ROSSETTI's ballad, *The White Ship,* deals with the same theme.

[3] CHARLES DICKENS wrote of Father Taylor in *American Notes, Chap. 3* [1842]; and WALT WHITMAN included a three-page sketch about him in *November Boughs.* Father Taylor was known as the "seaman's preacher."

A limit to the giant's unchained strength,
Or curb his swiftness in the forward race?
The Ages. Stanza 33

To him who in the love of Nature holds
Communion with her visible forms, she speaks
A various language.
Thanatopsis

Go forth, under the open sky, and list
To Nature's teachings.
Ibid.

The hills,
Rock-ribbed, and ancient as the sun.
Ibid.

Old ocean's gray and melancholy waste.
Ibid.

All that tread
The globe are but a handful to the tribes
That slumber in its bosom.
Ibid.

So live, that when thy summons comes to join
The innumerable caravan which moves [1]
To that mysterious realm, where each shall take
His chamber in the silent halls of death,
Thou go not, like the quarry-slave at night,
Scourged to his dungeon, but, sustained and soothed

---

[1] The edition of 1821 read, —
The innumerable caravan that moves
To the pale realms of shade, where each shall take.

So live, that when the mighty caravan,
Which halts one night-time in the vale of death,
Shall strike its white tents for the morning march,
Thou shalt mount onward to the Eternal Hills,
Thy foot unwearied, and thy strength renewed,
Like the strong eagle's, for its upward flight.
EDWARD PAYSON WESTON [1819–1879]:
A Vision of Immortality, A Reply to Thanatopsis

By an unfaltering trust, approach thy
  grave,
Like one that wraps the drapery of his
  couch
About him, and lies down to pleasant
  dreams.
                              Thanatopsis

He who, from zone to zone,
Guides through the boundless sky thy
  certain flight,
In the long way that I must tread alone,
Will lead my steps aright.
              To a Waterfowl. Stanza 8

God made his grave, to men unknown,
  Where Moab's rocks a vale infold,
And laid the aged seer alone
  To slumber while the world grows
    old.
  *"No Man Knoweth His Sepul-
          chre."* [1] *Stanza 2*

The stormy March has come at last,
With wind, and cloud, and changing
  skies;
I hear the rushing of the blast,
That through the snowy valley flies.
                    March. Stanza 1

But 'neath yon crimson tree
Lover to listening maid might breathe
  his flame,
Nor mark, within its roseate canopy,
Her blush of maiden shame.
          Autumn Woods. Stanza 9

The groves were God's first temples.
                    A Forest Hymn

Thou com'st from Jersey meadows,
  fresh and green.
            To a Mosquito. Stanza 3

Rogue's Island once — but when the
  rogues were dead,

Rhode Island was the name it took
  instead.[1]
    *A Meditation on Rhode Island
                    Coal. Stanza 1*
The melancholy days are come, the
  saddest of the year,
Of wailing winds, and naked woods,
  and meadows brown and sere.
          *The Death of the Flowers.
                          Stanza 1*
And sighs to find them in the wood and
  by the stream no more.
                    Ibid. Stanza 4
Chained in the market-place he stood,
  A man of giant frame,
Amid the gathering multitude
  That shrunk to hear his name.
          The African Chief. Stanza 1
Loveliest of lovely things are they,
On earth, that soonest pass away.
The rose that lives its little hour
Is prized beyond the sculptured flower.
      *A Scene on the Banks of the
                    Hudson. Stanza 3*
Thou blossom bright with autumn dew,
And colored with the heaven's own
  blue,
That openest when the quiet light
Succeeds the keen and frosty night.
        To the Fringed Gentian. Stanza 1
These are the gardens of the Desert,
  these
The unshorn fields, boundless and
  beautiful,
For which the speech of England has
  no name —
The Prairies.
                          The Prairies
Well knows the fair and friendly moon
  The band that Marion leads —
The glitter of their rifles,
  The scampering of their steeds.
            Song of Marion's [2] *Men.
                          Stanza 4*

---

[1] So Moses the servant of the Lord died
there in the land of Moab, according to the
word of the Lord. And he buried him in a
valley in the Land of Moab, over against
Bethpeor; but no man knoweth of his sepulchre unto this day. — *Deuteronomy, XXXIV,
5, 6*
    And no man knows that sepulchre,
      And no man saw it e'er,
    For the angels of God upturned the sod,
      And laid the dead man there.
        CECIL FRANCES ALEXANDER [1830–
        1895]: *The Burial of Moses, St. 1*

[1] EDWARD EVERETT HALE, in *New England
History in Ballads*, prefaces a ballad, *Roses
Island*, with the suggestion that Rhode Island
was thus named because of the glory of the
rhododendron, blooming in profusion when
Adrian Block landed and gave the island a
name.
[2] Francis Marion [1732–1795], of South
Carolina, a General in the Revolutionary War,
known as the "Swamp Fox."

The praise of those who sleep in earth,
The pleasant memory of their worth,
The hope to meet when life is past,
Shall heal the tortured mind at last.
The Living Lost. Stanza 3

Truth, crushed to earth, shall rise
    again; [1]
The eternal years of God are hers;
But Error, wounded, writhes in pain,
And dies among his worshippers.
The Battle-Field. Stanza 9

How shall I know thee in the sphere
    which keeps
The disembodied spirits of the dead,
When all of thee that time could wither
    sleeps
And perishes among the dust we
    tread?
The Future Life. Stanza 1

Robert of Lincoln is telling his name:
Bob-o'-link, bob-o'-link.
Robert of Lincoln. Stanza 1

Beside a massive gateway built up in
    years gone by,
Upon whose top the clouds in eternal
    shadow lie,
While streams the evening sunshine on
    quiet wood and lea,
I stand and calmly wait till the hinges
    turn for me.
Waiting by the Gate. Stanza 1

I grieve for life's bright promise, just
    shown and then withdrawn.
Ibid. Stanza 7

The fiercest agonies have shortest reign.
Mutation

Tender pauses speak
The overflow of gladness, when words
    are all too weak.
The Damsel of Peru. Stanza 7

Let no maid nor matron grieve,
To see her locks of an unlovely hue,
Frouzy or thin, for liberal art shall
    give
Such piles of curls as Nature never
    knew.
Spring in Town. Stanza 7

Oh mother of a mighty race,
Yet lovely in thy youthful grace!
Oh Mother of a Mighty Race.
Stanza 1

[1] Truth, crushed to earth, burrows out of sight. — J. MISTLETOE

Man foretells afar
The courses of the stars; the very hour
He knows when they shall darken or
    grow bright;
Yet doth the eclipse of Sorrow and of
    Death
Come unforewarned.
An Evening Revery

We plant, upon the sunny lea,
A shadow for the noontide hour,
A shelter from the summer shower,
    When we plant the apple-tree.
The Planting of the Apple-Tree.
Stanza 2

The horrid tale of perjury and strife,
Murder and spoil, which men call his-
    tory.
Earth

Oh, slow to smite and swift to spare,
    Gentle and merciful and just!
Who, in the fear of God, didst bear
    The sword of power, a nation's
    trust!
The Death of Lincoln. Stanza 1

When the blind suppliant in the way,
    By friendly hands to Jesus led,
Prayed to behold the light of day,
    "Receive thy sight," the Saviour
    said.[1]
"Receive Thy Sight." Stanza 1

Lord, who ordainest for mankind
    Benignant toils and tender cares!
We thank Thee for the ties that bind
    The mother to the child she bears.
The Mother's Hymn. Stanza 1

As one who, dwelling in the distant
    fields,
Without a neighbor near him, hides a
    brand
In the dark ashes, keeping carefully
The seeds of fire alive, lest he, per-
    force,
To light his hearth must bring them
    from afar.
Translation of the Odyssey of
Homer. Book V

[1] And Jesus said unto him, Receive thy sight: thy faith hath saved thee. — *Luke,* XVIII, 42

EDWARD EVERETT
[1794–1865]

When I am dead, no pageant train
  Shall waste their sorrows at my bier,
Nor worthless pomp of homage vain
  Stain it with hypocritic tear.
    Alaric the Visigoth. Stanza 1

Ye shall not pile, with servile toil,
  Your monuments upon my breast,
Nor yet within the common soil
  Lay down the wreck of power to
    rest,
Where man can boast that he has trod
On him that was "the scourge of God."
    Ibid. Stanza 2

But ye the mountain-stream shall turn,
  And lay its secret channel bare
And hollow, for your sovereign's urn,
  A resting-place forever there.
    Ibid. Stanza 3

As a work of art, I know few things
more pleasing to the eye, or more capable of affording scope and gratification to a taste for the beautiful, than
a well-situated, well-cultivated farm.
    Address at Buffalo, New York
    [October 9, 1857]

No gilded dome swells from the
lowly roof to catch the morning or evening beam; but the love and gratitude
of united America settle upon it in one
eternal sunshine. From beneath that
humble roof went forth the intrepid
and unselfish warrior, the magistrate
who knew no glory but his country's
good; to that he returned, happiest
when his work was done. There he
lived in noble simplicity, there he died
in glory and peace. While it stands, the
latest generations of the grateful children of America will make this pilgrimage to it as to a shrine; and when it
shall fall, if fall it must, the memory
and the name of Washington shall shed
an eternal glory on the spot.
    Oration on the Character of
    Washington

I am no aristocrat. I do not own a
quadruped larger than a cat, and she
an indifferent mouser; nor any kind of
vehicle, with the exception, possibly, of
a wheelbarrow.
    Mount Vernon Papers. No. 7

The days of palmy prosperity are
not those most favorable to the display
of public virtue or the influence of wise
and good men. In hard, doubtful, unprosperous, and dangerous times, the
disinterested and patriotic find their
way, by a species of public instinct, unopposed, joyfully welcomed, to the
control of affairs.
    Ibid. No. 14

When I contemplate the extent to
which the moral sentiments, the intelligence, the affections of so many millions of people, — sealed up by a sacred charm within the cover of a letter,
— daily circulate through a country, I
am compelled to regard the Post-office,
next to Christianity, as the right arm
of our modern civilization.
    Ibid. No. 27

CAROLINE HOWARD GILMAN
[1794–1888]

You must know I've resolved and
  agreed
My books from my room not to lend,
But you may sit by my fire and read.
    One Good Turn Deserves
    Another. Stanza 2
My bellows I never will lend,
But you may sit at my fire and blow.
    Ibid. Stanza 4

JOHN GIBSON LOCKHART
[1794–1854]

Rise up, rise up, Xarifa! lay your
  golden cushion down;
Rise up! come to the window, and gaze
  with all the town.
    The Bridal of Andalla. Stanza 1
There was crying in Granada when the
  sun was going down;
Some calling on the Trinity — some
  calling on Mahoun.

Here passed away the Koran — there
  in the Cross was borne —
And here was heard the Christian bell
  — and there the Moorish horn.
> *The Flight from Granada.*
> *Stanza 1*

A tower is fallen! a star is set! — Alas,
  alas for Celin.
> *The Lamentation for Celin.*
> *Stanza 1*

Beyond the sphere of Time,
  And sin, and Fate's control,
Serene in changeless prime
  Of body and of soul.
> *Beyond*

MICHAEL MORAN
[1794-1846]

In Egypt's land, contagious to the
  Nile,
King Pharaoh's daughter went to bathe
  in style.
She tuk her dip, then walked unto the
  land,
To dry her royal pelt she ran along the
  strand.
A bulrush tripped her, whereupon she
  saw
A smiling babby in a wad o' straw.
She tuk it up, and said with accents
  mild,
"Tare-and-agers, girls, which av yez
  owns the child?"
> *His parody of his poem, Moses.*
> *Quoted by* W. B. YEATS *in his*
> *essay, The Last Gleeman*

WILLIAM WHEWELL
[1794-1866]

And so no force, however great, can
stretch a cord, however fine, into a
horizontal line which shall be absolutely straight.[1]
> *Elementary Treatise on Me-*
> *chanics* (1st ed.), *The Equili-*
> *brium of Forces on a Point*

[1] Reputed to be an example of unconscious
but perfect rhyme.

JOHN GARDINER CALKINS
BRAINARD
[1795-1828]

Death has shaken out the sands of thy
  glass.
> *Lament for Long Tom*

At the piping of all hands,
When the judgment-signal's spread —
When the islands and the lands
And the seas give up their dead,
And the South and North shall come;
  When the sinner is dismayed,
  And the just man is afraid,
  Then Heaven be thy aid,
    Poor Tom.
> *Ibid.*

Far beneath the tainted foam
That frets above our peaceful home,
We dream in joy and wake in love
Nor know the rage that yells above.[1]
> *The Deep*

I saw two clouds at morning,
  Tinged with the rising sun,
And in the dawn they floated on,
  And mingled into one.
I thought that morning cloud was
  blest,
It moved so sweetly to the West.
> *Epithalamium. Stanza 1*

MARIA GOWEN BROOKS
("MARIA DEL OCCIDENTE")
[1795-1845]

Day in melting purple dying,
Blossoms all around me sighing,
Fragrance from the lilies straying,
Zephyr with my ringlets playing,
Ye but waken my distress:
I am sick of loneliness.
> *Song of Egla. Stanza 1*

THOMAS CARLYLE
[1795-1881]

May blessings be upon the head of
Cadmus or the Phoenicians, or whoever invented books! . . . An art that
carries the voice of man to the extrem-

[1] When winds are raging o'er the upper
ocean. — HARRIET BEECHER STOWE

ities of the earth, and to the latest generations.

Early Letters. To Mr. R. Mitchell

Except by name, Jean Paul Friedrich Richter is little known out of Germany. The only thing connected with him, we think, that has reached this country is his saying, — imported by Madame de Staël, and thankfully pocketed by most newspaper critics, — "Providence has given to the French the empire of the land; to the English that of the sea; to the Germans that of — the air!"

Richter (In Edinburgh Review, June, 1827)

True humour springs not more from the head than from the heart; it is not contempt, its essence is love; it issues not in laughter, but in still smiles, which lie far deeper.

Ibid.

The great law of culture is: Let each become all that he was created capable of being; expand, if possible, to his full growth; resisting all impediments, casting off all foreign, especially all noxious adhesions; and show himself at length in his own shape and stature, be these what they may.

Ibid.

He who would write heroic poems should make his whole life a heroic poem.

Life of Schiller

Literary men are . . . a perpetual priesthood.

State of German Literature [1827]. Fichte

I came hither [Craigenputtoch] solely with the design to simplify my way of life and to secure the independence through which I could be enabled to remain true to myself.

Letter to Goethe [1828]

Fame, we may understand, is no sure test of merit, but only a probability of such.

Goethe (In Edinburgh Review, 1828)

In every man's writings, the character of the writer must lie recorded.

Ibid.

Clever men are good, but they are not the best.

Goethe (In Edinburgh Review, 1828)

We are firm believers in the maxim that, for all right judgment of any man or thing, it is useful, nay essential, to see his good qualities before pronouncing on his bad.

Ibid.

If an individual is really of consequence enough to have his life and character recorded for public remembrance, we have always been of the opinion that the public ought to be made acquainted with all the inward springs and relations of his character.

Burns [1828]

An educated man stands, as it were, in the midst of a boundless arsenal and magazine, filled with all the weapons and engines which man's skill has been able to devise from the earliest time.

Ibid.

How does the poet speak to men, with power, but by being still more a man than they?

Ibid.

A poet without love were a physical and metaphysical impossibility.

Ibid.

His religion, at best, is an anxious wish; — like that of Rabelais, "a great Perhaps." [1]

Ibid.

Aesop's Fly, sitting on the axle of the chariot, has been much laughed at for exclaiming: What a dust I do raise!

On Boswell's Life of Johnson [1832]

Whoso belongs only to his own age, and reverences only its gilt Popinjays or soot-smeared Mumbojumbos, must needs die with it.

Ibid.

There is tolerable travelling on the beaten road, run how it may; only on the new road not yet levelled and paved, and on the old road all broken

---

[1] The grand Perhaps. — ROBERT BROWNING: *Bishop Blougram's Apology*

into ruts and quagmires, is the travelling bad or impracticable.

On Boswell's Life of Johnson.
[1832]

The stupendous Fourth Estate, whose wide world-embracing influences what eye can take in? [1]

Ibid.

Of all outward evils Obscurity is perhaps in itself the least.

Ibid.

Loud clamor is always more or less insane.

Ibid.

All work is as seed sown; it grows and spreads, and sows itself anew.

Ibid.

We have oftener than once endeavoured to attach some meaning to that aphorism, vulgarly imputed to Shaftesbury, which however we can find nowhere in his works, that "ridicule is the test of truth." [2]

Voltaire (In Foreign Review, 1829)

Man makes the circumstances, and spiritually as well as economically is the artificer of his own fortune. . . . Man's circumstances are the element he is appointed to live and work in; . . . so that in another no less genuine

---

[1] The gallery in which the reporters sit has become a fourth estate of the realm. — T. B. MACAULAY: *On Hallam's Constitutional History* [1828]
See pages 380 and 381 for other references by Carlyle to the Fourth Estate.
[2] How comes it to pass, then, that we appear such cowards in reasoning, and are so afraid to stand the test of ridicule? — SHAFTESBURY [1671–1713]: *Characteristics, A Letter concerning Enthusiasm, Sect. 2*
Truth, 'tis supposed, may bear all lights; and one of those principal lights or natural mediums by which things are to be viewed in order to a thorough recognition is ridicule itself. — SHAFTESBURY: *Essay on the Freedom of Wit and Humour, Sect. 1*
'Twas the saying of an ancient sage (Gorgias Leontinus, *apud* Aristotle's "Rhetoric," lib. iii. c. 18), that humour was the only test of gravity, and gravity of humour. For a subject which would not bear raillery was suspicious; and a jest which would not bear a serious examination was certainly false wit. — *Ibid., Sect. 5*
See Crabbe, page 280.

---

sense, it can be said circumstances make the man. [1]

Diderot

There is no heroic poem in the world but is at bottom a biography, the life of a man; also, it may be said, there is no life of a man, faithfully recorded, but is a heroic poem of its sort, rhymed or unrhymed.

Sir Walter Scott (In London and Westminster Review. No. 12, 1838)

There is a great discovery still to be made in Literature, that of paying literary men by the quantity they do not write.

Ibid.

Silence is deep as Eternity; speech is shallow as Time.

Ibid.

No man lives without jostling and being jostled; in all ways he has to elbow himself through the world, giving and receiving offence.

Ibid.

The biographer has this problem set before him: to delineate a likeness of the earthly pilgrimage of a man.

Ibid.

All greatness is unconscious, or it is little and naught.

Ibid.

To the very last, he [Napoleon] had a kind of idea; that, namely, of *la carrière ouverte aux talens*, — the tools to him that can handle them. [2]

Ibid.

Blessed is the healthy nature; it is the coherent, sweetly co-operative, not incoherent, self-distracting, self-destructive one!

Ibid.

The uttered part of a man's life, let us always repeat, bears to the unuttered, unconscious part a small unknown proportion. He himself never knows it, much less do others.

Ibid.

---

[1] See Benjamin Disraeli, page 420.
[2] Carlyle in his essay on Mirabeau [1837] quotes this from a "New England book." This was his *Sartor Resartus*, first published in America.

Ill-health, of body or of mind, is defeat. . . . Health alone is victory. Let all men, if they can manage it, contrive to be healthy!

Sir Walter Scott (*In London and Westminster Review. No. 12, 1838*)

It can be said of him, when he departed he took a Man's life along with him. No sounder piece of British manhood was put together in that eighteenth century of Time.

Ibid.

The lightning-spark of Thought, generated or say rather heaven-kindled, in the solitary mind, awakens its express likeness in another mind, in a thousand other minds, and all blaze up together in combined fire.

Ibid.

Considered as a whole, the Christian religion of late ages has been continually dissipating itself into Metaphysics; and threatens now to disappear, as some rivers do, in deserts of barren sand.

Ibid.

Nothing that was worthy in the past departs; no truth or goodness realized by man ever dies, or can die; but is all still here, and, recognized or not, lives and works through endless changes.

Ibid.

The barrenest of all mortals is the sentimentalist.

Ibid.

Love is ever the beginning of Knowledge, as fire is of light.

Essays. Death of Goethe [*May, 1832*]

Music is well said to be the speech of angels.

Ibid. The Opera

A mystic bond of brotherhood makes all men one.

Ibid. Goethe's Works [*1832*]

Everywhere the human soul stands between a hemisphere of light and another of darkness on the confines of two everlasting hostile empires,— Necessity and Free Will.

Ibid.

Democracy is, by the nature of it, a self-cancelling business; and gives in the long run a net result of zero.

Chartism. Chap. 6, Laissez-Faire

What is Aristocracy? A corporation of the best, of the bravest.

Ibid.

He that works and *does* some Poem, not he that merely *says* one, is worthy of the name of Poet.

Introduction to Cromwell's Letters and Speeches

History is the essence of innumerable biographies.

On History

The Public is an old woman. Let her maunder and mumble.

Journal [*1835*]

It is now almost my sole rule of life to clear myself of cants and formulas, as of poisonous Nessus shirts.

Letter to His Wife [*1835*]

The eye of the intellect "sees in all objects what it brought with it the means of seeing."

Varnhagen von Ense's Memoirs (*In London and Westminster Review, No. 62, 1838*)

There is endless merit in a man's knowing when to have done.

Francia [*1845*]

"A fair day's-wages for a fair day's-work": it is as just a demand as governed men ever made of governing. It is the everlasting right of man.

Past and Present. Book I, Chap. 3

Fire is the best of servants; but what a master! [1]

Ibid. Book II, Chap. 9

All work, even cotton-spinning, is noble; work is alone noble. . . . A life of ease is not for any man, nor for any god.

Ibid. Book III, Chap. 4

Every noble crown is, and on earth will forever be, a crown of thorns.

Ibid. Chap. 7

Even in the meanest sorts of Labor, the whole soul of a man is composed

---

[1] Mammon is like fire: the usefulest of all servants, if the frightfulest of all masters! — *Book IV, Chap. 7*

into a kind of real harmony the instant he sets himself to work.

Past and Present. Book III, Chap. 11

Blessed is he who has found his work; let him ask no other blessedness.

Ibid.

To make some nook of God's Creation a little fruitfuler, better, more worthy of God; to make some human hearts a little wiser, manfuler, happier, — more blessed, less accursed! It is work for a God.

Ibid. Book IV, Chap. 8

Respectable Professors of the Dismal Science.[1]

Latter Day Pamphlets. No. 1 [1850]

A Parliament speaking through reporters to Buncombe and the twenty-seven millions, mostly fools.

Ibid. No. 6

The fine arts once divorcing themselves from *truth* are quite certain to fall mad, if they do not die.

Ibid. No. 8

A healthy hatred of scoundrels.

Ibid. No. 12

Genius . . . which is the transcendent capacity for taking trouble first of all.[2]

Life of Frederick the Great. Book IV, Chap. III

Happy the people whose annals are blank in history-books.[3]

Ibid. Book XVI, Chap. I

[1] Referring to political economy and social science, Carlyle also in his essay on *The Nigger Question* [1849] speaks of "What we might call, by way of Eminence, the Dismal Science."

[2] La génie n'est autre chose qu'une grande aptitude à la patience (Genius is nothing else than a great aptitude for patience). — BUFFON [1707–1788]

This is quoted by MATTHEW ARNOLD in his *Essays in Criticism, A French Coleridge*. There is also a popular proverb: "Genius is patience." DISRAELI, *The Young Duke*: "Patience is a necessary ingredient of genius." LESLIE STEPHEN: "Genius is a capacity for taking trouble." JAN WALÆUS also says: "Genius is an intuitive talent for labor." LORD SYDENHAM [1799–1841] defined genius as a consummate sense of proportion. The more recent version of Carlyle's sentence is "an infinite capacity for taking pains."

[3] MONTESQUIEU: *Aphorism*

No man who has once heartily and wholly laughed can be altogether irreclaimably bad.

Sartor Resartus. Book I, Chap. 4

The man who cannot laugh is not only fit for treasons, stratagems and spoils; but his whole life is already a treason and a stratagem.

Ibid.

He who first shortened the labor of Copyists by device of *Movable Types* was disbanding hired Armies, and cashiering most Kings and Senates, and creating a whole new Democratic world: he had invented the Art of printing.

Ibid. Chap. 5

Be not the slave of Words.

Ibid. Chap. 8

The Philosopher is he to whom the Highest has descended, and the Lowest has mounted up; who is the equal and kindly brother of all.

Ibid. Chap. 10

Wonder is the basis of Worship.

Ibid.

Biography is by nature the most universally profitable, universally pleasant of all things: especially biography of distinguished individuals.

Ibid. Chap. 11

What you see, yet can not see over, is as good as infinite.

Ibid. Book II, Chap. 1

To each is given a certain inward talent, a certain outward environment of Fortune; to each, by wisest combination of these two, a certain maximum of capability.

Ibid. Chap. 4

Sarcasm I now see to be, in general, the language of the Devil; for which reason I have, long since, as good as renounced it.

Ibid.

To consume your own choler, as some chimneys consume their own smoke;[1]

[1] See page 381.

Burn your own smoke and the world will go well.

CHRISTOPHER PEARSE CRANCH [1813–1892]: *Life's Sunny Side, St. 6*

to keep a whole Satanic School spouting, if it must spout, inaudibly, is a negative yet no slight virtue, nor one of the commonest in these times.

Sartor Resartus. Book II, Chap. 6

Alas! the fearful Unbelief is unbelief in yourself.

Ibid. Chap. 7

O thou who art able to write a book, which once in the two centuries or oftener there is a man gifted to do, envy not him whom they name City-builder, and inexpressibly pity him whom they name Conqueror or City-burner. Thou too art a Conqueror and Victor.

Ibid. Chap. 8

Produce! Were it but the pitifulest infinitesimal fraction of a product, produce it in God's name.

Ibid. Chap. 9

As the Swiss inscription says: *Sprechen ist silbern, Schweigen ist golden,* — "Speech is silvern, Silence is golden"; or, as I might rather express it, Speech is of Time, Silence is of Eternity.[1]

Ibid. Book III, Chap. 3

Wouldst thou plant for Eternity, then plant into the deep infinite faculties of man.

Ibid.

Two men I honour, and no third. First, the toilworn craftsman that with earth-made implement laboriously conquers the earth, and makes her man's. . . . A second man I honour, and still more highly: Him who is seen toiling for the spiritually indispensable; not daily bread, but the bread of life.

Ibid. Chap. 4

That there should one man die ignorant who had capacity for knowledge, this I call a tragedy.

Ibid.

In good-breeding, which differs, if at all, from high-breeding, only as it gracefully remembers the rights of others, rather than gracefully insists on its own rights, I discern no special connection with wealth or birth.

Sartor Resartus. Book III, Chap. 6

Trust not the heart of that man for whom old clothes are not venerable.

Ibid.

Does it not stand on record that the English Queen Elizabeth, receiving a deputation of eighteen tailors, addressed them with a "Good morning, gentlemen both!"[1]

Ibid. Chap. 11

No sadder proof can be given by a man of his own littleness than disbelief in great men.

Heroes and Hero-Worship. The Hero as Divinity

The history of the world is but the biography of great men.[2]

Ibid.

We must get rid of Fear.

Ibid.

The greatest of faults, I should say, is to be conscious of none.[3]

Ibid. The Hero as Prophet

A vein of poetry exists in the hearts of all men.

Ibid. The Hero as Poet

The Age of Miracles is forever here!

Ibid. The Hero as Priest

Burke said there were Three Estates in Parliament; but, in the Reporters' Gallery yonder, there sat a Fourth Estate more important far than they all. It is not a figure of speech, or witty saying; it is a literal fact, — very momentous to us in these times.[4]

Ibid. The Hero as a Man of Letters

In books lies the soul of the whole Past Time: the articulate audible voice of the Past, when the body and ma-

---

Consume your own smoke. — BROWNING: *Pacchiarotto,* XXV; Would that he consumed his own smoke. — HERMAN MELVILLE [1819–1891]: Moby Dick, Chap. XCVI; Consume your own smoke with an extra draught of hard work. — SIR WILLIAM OSLER [1849–1919] (in HARVEY CUSHING's *Life of Sir William Osler, Vol. I, P. 619*).

[1] Quoted also in Carlyle's essay on Boswell's *Life of Dr. Johnson.*

[1] Nine tailors make a man. — Old Proverb (the origin of which is said to be nine *tellers* or strokes of the church bell, indicating that the deceased was a man). See *Oxford Dictionary of English Proverbs.*

[2] See Emerson, page 411.

[3] His only fault is that he has none. — PLINY THE YOUNGER: *Book IX, Letter 26*

[4] See page 377.

terial substance of it has altogether vanished like a dream.

Heroes and Hero-Worship.
The Hero as a Man of Letters

All that mankind has done, thought, gained or been: it is lying as in magic preservation in the pages of books.

Ibid.

The true University of these days is a Collection of Books.

Ibid.

The suffering man ought really to consume his own smoke; there is no good in emitting smoke till you have made it into fire.[1]

Ibid.

Adversity is sometimes hard upon a man; but for one man who can stand prosperity, there are a hundred that will stand adversity.

Ibid.

The oak grows silently, in the forest, a thousand years; only in the thousandth year, when the woodman arrives with his axe is there heard an echoing through the solitudes; and the oak announces itself when, with far-sounding crash, it falls.

The French Revolution. Vol. I,
Book II, Chap. 1

No lie you can speak or act but it will come, after longer or shorter circulation, like a bill drawn on Nature's Reality, and be presented there for payment, — with the answer, No effects.

Ibid. Book III, Chap. 1

To a shower of gold most things are penetrable.

Ibid. Chap. 7

"The people may eat grass": [2] hasty words, which fly abroad irrevocable, — and will send back tidings.

Ibid. Chap. 9

O poor mortals, how ye make this earth bitter for each other.

Ibid. Book V, Chap. 5

A Fourth Estate, of able editors,

springs up; increases and multiplies; irrepressible, incalculable.[1]

The French Revolution. Vol. I,
Book VI, Chap. 5

Men that can have communion in nothing else, can sympathetically eat together, can still rise into some glow of brotherhood over food and wine.

Ibid. Book VII, Chap. 2

Battles, in these ages, are transacted by mechanism; with the slightest possible development of human individuality or spontaneity; men now even die, and kill one another, in an artificial manner.

Ibid. Chap. 4

There were certain runaways whom Fritz the Great bullied back into the battle with a: *"R —, wollt ihr ewig leben,* Unprintable Offscouring of Scoundrels, would ye live forever!" [2]

Ibid. Vol. II, Book I, Chap. 4

Flying for life, one does not stickle about the vehicle.

Ibid. Book IV, Chap. 5

Governing persons, were they never so insignificant intrinsically, have for most part plenty of memoir-writers.

Ibid. Vol. III, Book I, Chap. 1

Looking at the Statue of Liberty which stands there, she says bitterly: "O Liberty, what things are done in thy name!" [3]

Ibid. Book V, Chap. 2

Is man's civilization only a wrappage, through which the savage nature of him can still burst, infernal as ever?

Ibid. Chap. 7

"Thou wilt show my head to the people: it is worth showing." [4]

Ibid. Book VI, Chap. 2

So here hath been dawning
    Another blue day:
Think, wilt thou let it
    Slip useless away?

To-day

What is Man? A foolish baby,
    Vainly strives, and fights, and frets.

---

[1] See page 379.
[2] The remark of Foulon, when his finance scheme raised the question: What will the people do?

[1] See Carlyle, page 377.
[2] A similar exclamation was current during the World War.
[3] Madame Roland on the scaffold [Nov. 8, 1793].
[4] Danton's last words [April 5, 1794].

Demanding all, deserving nothing,
One small grave is what he gets.
Cui Bono. Stanza 3

My whinstone house my castle is;
I have my own four walls.
My Own Four Walls

Lord Bacon could as easily have created the planets as he could have written Hamlet.
Remark in discussion

The unspeakable Turk.
In public letter [1877]

GEORGE DARLEY
[1795–1846]

Last night we saw the stars arise,
But clouds soon dimmed the ether blue:
And when we sought each other's eyes
Tears dimmed them too!
Last Night. Stanza 2

A little cross
To tell my loss;
A little bed
To rest my head;
A little tear is all I crave
Under my very little grave.
Robin's Cross. Stanza 1

With nothing more upon it than —
Here lies the Little Friend of Man!
Ibid. Stanza 2

JOSEPH RODMAN DRAKE
[1795–1820]

When Freedom from her mountain-height
Unfurled her standard to the air,
She tore the azure robe of night,
And set the stars of glory there.
She mingled with its gorgeous dyes
The milky baldric of the skies,
And striped its pure, celestial white
With streakings of the morning light.
The American Flag. Stanza 1
(In New York Evening Post,
May 29, 1819)

Flag of the free heart's hope and home!
By angel hands to valour given;
Thy stars have lit the welkin dome,
And all thy hues were born in heaven.

Forever float that standard sheet!
Where breathes the foe but falls before us,
With Freedom's soil beneath our feet,
And Freedom's banner streaming o'er us?
The American Flag. Stanza 5

Go! kneel a worshiper at Nature's shrine!
For you her fields are green, and fair her skies!
For you her rivers flow, her hills arise!
The Culprit Fay. Stanza 14

JOHN KEATS
[1795–1821]

There is not a fiercer hell than the failure in a great object.
Preface to Endymion

A thing of beauty is a joy forever:
Its loveliness increases; it will never
Pass into nothingness.
Endymion. Book I, Line 1

Time, that aged nurse,
Rock'd me to patience.
Ibid. Line 705

A hope beyond the shadow of a dream.
Ibid. Line 857

Pleasure is oft a visitant; but pain
Clings cruelly to us.
Ibid. Line 906

He ne'er is crown'd
With immortality, who fears to follow
Where airy voices lead.
Ibid. Book II, Line 211

'Tis the pest
Of love, that fairest joys give most unrest.
Ibid. Line 365

To sorrow,
I bade good-morrow,
And thought to leave her far away behind;
But cheerly, cheerly,
She loves me dearly;
She is so constant to me, and so kind.
Ibid. Book IV, Line 173

Love in a hut, with water and a crust,
Is — Love, forgive us! — cinders,
  ashes, dust.
                    Lamia. Part II, Line 1
There was an awful rainbow once in
  heaven:
We know her woof, her texture; she is
  given
In the dull catalogue of common
  things.
Philosophy will clip an angel's wings.
                    Ibid. Line 231
St. Agnes' Eve — Ah, bitter chill it
  was!
The owl, for all his feathers, was a-cold.
        The Eve of St. Agnes. Stanza 1
            Music's golden tongue
Flatter'd to tears this aged man and
  poor.
                    Ibid. Stanza 3
The silver, snarling trumpets 'gan to
  chide.
                    Ibid. Stanza 4
Asleep in lap of legends old.
                    Ibid. Stanza 15
Sudden a thought came like a full-
  blown rose,
Flushing his brow.
                    Ibid. Stanza 16
A poor, weak, palsy-stricken, church-
  yard thing.
                    Ibid. Stanza 18
Her rich attire creeps rustling to her
  knees.
                    Ibid. Stanza 26
As though a rose should shut, and be
  a bud again.
                    Ibid. Stanza 27
He play'd an ancient ditty long since
  mute,
In Provence call'd, "La belle dame sans
  mercy."
                    Ibid. Stanza 33
Dance, and Provençal song, and sun-
  burnt mirth!
O for a beaker full of the warm South,
Full of the true, the blushful Hippo-
  crene,
With beaded bubbles winking at the
  brim,
And purple-stainèd mouth.
        Ode to a Nightingale. Stanza 2

I cannot see what flowers are at my
  feet,
Nor what soft incense hangs upon the
  boughs.
        Ode to a Nightingale. Stanza 5
I have been half in love with easeful
  Death,
Call'd him soft names in many a mused
  rhyme.
                    Ibid. Stanza 6
The self-same song that found a path
Through the sad heart of Ruth, when,
  sick for home,
She stood in tears amid the alien corn;
  The same that oft-times hath
Charm'd magic casements, opening on
  the foam
Of perilous seas, in faery lands forlorn.
                    Ibid. Stanza 7
Thou foster-child of Silence and slow
  Time.
        Ode on a Grecian Urn. Stanza 1
Heard melodies are sweet, but those
  unheard
  Are sweeter.
                    Ibid. Stanza 2
For ever wilt thou love, and she be fair!
                    Ibid.
O Attic shape! fair attitude!
                    Ibid. Stanza 5
Beauty is truth, truth beauty, — that
  is all
  Ye know on earth, and all ye need
  to know.
                    Ibid.
  In a drear-nighted December
    Too happy, happy tree
  Thy branches ne'er remember
    Their green felicity.
                    Stanzas
        Hear ye not the hum
Of mighty workings?
    Sonnet 14, Addressed to Haydon
To one who has been long in city pent,
'Tis very sweet to look into the fair
And open face of heaven.
    *Sonnet, To One Who Has Been
            Long in City Pent*
E'en like the passage of an angel's tear
That falls through the clear ether si-
  lently.
                    Ibid.

Much have I travell'd in the realms of
  gold,
    And many goodly states and king-
      doms seen.
      *Sonnet, On First Looking Into
          Chapman's Homer*
Then felt I like some watcher of the
  skies
    When a new planet swims into his
      ken;
Or like stout Cortez when with eagle
  eyes
    He stared at the Pacific and all his
      men
Look'd at each other with a wild sur-
  mise
    Silent, upon a peak in Darien.
                          Ibid.
When I have fears that I may cease to
  be.
          Sonnet, When I Have Fears
Huge cloudy symbols of a high ro-
  mance.
                          Ibid.
Fair creature of an hour!
                          Ibid.
    Life is but a day;
A fragile dewdrop on its perilous way
From a tree's summit.
          Sleep and Poetry. Line 85
Life is the rose's hope while yet un-
  blown.
                  Ibid. Line 90
Too many tears for lovers have been
  shed,
Too many sighs give we to them in fee,
Too much of pity after they are dead,
Too many doleful stories do we see,
Whose matter in bright gold were best
  be read.
      *Isabella [The Pot of Basil].
          Stanza 12*
She wrapp'd it up; and for its tomb did
  choose
A garden-pot, wherein she laid it by,
And cover'd it with mould, and o'er it
  set
Sweet Basil, which her tears kept ever
  wet.
                  Ibid. Stanza 52
Ever let the Fancy roam,
Pleasure never is at home.
                  Fancy. Line 1

Where's the eye, however blue,
Doth not weary? Where's the face
One would meet in every place?
Where's the voice, however soft,
One would hear so very oft?
                  Fancy. Line 72
Souls of Poets dead and gone,
What Elysium have ye known,
Happy field or mossy cavern,
Choicer than the Mermaid Tavern?
      *Lines on the Mermaid Tavern.
                      Line 23*
Bards of Passion and of Mirth,
Ye have left your souls on earth!
Have ye souls in heaven too?
          *Ode (written in a volume of
          Beaumont and Fletcher). Line 1*
Season of mists and mellow fruitful-
  ness,
    Close bosom-friend of the maturing
      sun;
Conspiring with him how to load and
  bless
    With fruit the vines.
              To Autumn. Stanza 1
Their lips touched not, but had not
  bade adieu.
                  Ode to Psyche
    All soft delight
That shadowy thought can win,
A bright torch, and a casement ope at
  night
To let the warm Love in!
                          Ibid.
Emprison her soft hand, and let her
  rave,
And feed deep, deep upon her peerless
  eyes.
          Ode on Melancholy. Stanza 2
Ay, in the very temple of Delight
Veil'd Melancholy has her sovran
  shrine.
                  Ibid. Stanza 3
That large utterance of the early gods!
          Hyperion. Book I, Line 51
Those green-robed senators of mighty
  woods,
Tall oaks, branch-charmed by the
  earnest stars,
Dream, and so dream all night without
  a stir.
                  Ibid. Line 73

Verse, Fame, and Beauty are intense
    indeed,
But Death intenser — Death is Life's
    high meed.
    Sonnet, Why Did I Laugh To-night?
Fame, like a wayward girl, will still be
    coy
To those who woo her with too slavish
    knees.
                 Sonnet on Fame
The day is gone, and all its sweets are
    gone!
  Sweet voice, sweet lips, soft hand,
    and softer breast.
        Sonnet, The Day Is Gone
                   Mortality
Weighs heavily on me like unwilling
    sleep.
  Sonnet, On Seeing the Elgin Marbles
Shed no tear — O shed no tear!
The flower will bloom another year.
Weep no more — O weep no more!
Young buds sleep in the root's white
    core.
                Faery Songs. I
Sweet Hope, ethereal balm upon me
    shed,
And wave thy silver pinions o'er my
    head.
             To Hope. Stanza 1
Disappointment, parent of Despair.
              Ibid. Stanza 3
I stood tip-toe upon a little hill,
The air was cooling, and so very still.
          I Stood Tip-toe. Line 1
Open afresh your round of starry folds,
Ye ardent marigolds!
              Ibid. Line 47
The moon lifting her silver rim
Above a cloud, and with a gradual swim
Coming into the blue with all her light.
           Ibid. Line 113
Nought but a lovely sighing of the
    wind
Along the reedy stream; a half-heard
    strain,
Full of sweet desolation — balmy pain.
           Ibid. Line 160
And no birds sing.
  La Belle Dame Sans Merci. Stanza 1
Bright star, would I were stedfast as
    thou art —

Not in lone splendour hung aloft the
    night
And watching, with eternal lids apart,
Like nature's patient, sleepless Ere-
    mite,
The moving waters at their priestlike
    task
Of pure ablution round earth's hu-
    man shores.
              The Last Sonnet
Pillow'd upon my fair love's ripening
    breast,
To feel for ever its soft fall and swell,
Awake for ever in a sweet unrest.
                  Ibid.
The poetry of earth is never dead.
  Sonnet, On the Grasshopper and
                      Cricket
Four Seasons fill the measure of the
    year;
There are four seasons in the mind of
    man.
    Sonnet, The Human Seasons
Blue! Gentle cousin of the forest-green,
Married to green in all the sweetest
    flowers, —
Forget-me-not, — the   blue   bell, —
    and, that Queen
Of secrecy, the violet.
                 Sonnet, Blue
It keeps eternal whisperings around
  Desolate shores, and with its mighty
    swell
  Gluts twice ten thousand caverns.
            Sonnet, On the Sea
I am certain of nothing but of the
holiness of the heart's affections, and
the truth of Imagination. What the
Imagination seizes as Beauty must be
Truth.
    Letter [November 22, 1817]
Poetry should surprise by a fine ex-
cess, and not by singularity; it should
strike the reader as a wording of his
own highest thoughts, and appear almost a remembrance.
    Letter [February 27, 1818]
A man's life of any worth is a continual Allegory, and very few eyes can
see the Mystery of his life.
    Letter [February 18, 1819]
I have loved the principle of beauty
in all things, and if I had had time I

would have made myself remembered.

Letter [*1820*]

Here lies one whose name was writ in water.[1]

Epitaph for himself

JAMES GATES PERCIVAL
[1795–1856]

Hail to the land whereon we tread,
  Our fondest boast!
The sepulchres of mighty dead,
The truest hearts that ever bled,
Who sleep on glory's brightest bed,
  A fearless host:
No slave is here: — our unchained feet,
Walk freely as the waves that beat
Our coast.

New England

On thy fair bosom, silver lake,
  The wild swan spreads his snowy
    sail,
And round his breast the ripples break,
As down he bears before the gale.

To Seneca Lake. Stanza 1

SIR THOMAS NOON
TALFOURD
[1795–1854]

    'Tis a little thing
To give a cup of water; yet its draught
Of cool refreshment, drained by fev-
  ered lips,
May give a shock of pleasure to the
  frame
More exquisite than when nectarean
  juice
Renews the life of joy in happiest
  hours.

Ion. Act I, Sc. 2

[1] Words writ in waters. — GEORGE CHAP-
MAN: *Revenge for Honour, Act V, Sc. 2*
  Below lies one whose name was traced in
sand. — DAVID GRAY
  Among the many things he has requested of
me to-night, this is the principal, — that on his
gravestone shall be this inscription. — RICH-
ARD MONCKTON MILNES: *Life, Letters, and
Literary Remains of John Keats, Vol. II,
P. 91, Letter to Severn*

Fill the seats of justice
With good men, not so absolute in
  goodness
As to forget what human frailty is.

Ion. Act V

WILLIAM SIDNEY WALKER
[1795–1846]

Too solemn for day, too sweet for night,
Come not in darkness, come not in
  light;
But come in some twilight interim,
When the gloom is soft, and the light
  is dim.

*From the Oxford Book of
English Verse*

ALFRED BUNN
[1796–1860]

I dreamt that I dwelt in marble halls,
With vassals and serfs at my side.

The Bohemian Girl. Act 2, Song

But — I also dreamt, which pleas'd me
  most,
That you loved me still the same.

Ibid.

HARTLEY COLERIDGE
[1796–1849]

Be not afraid to pray; to pray is right.
Pray, if thou canst, with hope, but ever
  pray,
Though hope be weak, or sick with
  long delay.
Pray in the darkness if there be no
  light.

Prayer

The soul of man is larger than the sky,
  Deeper than ocean, or the abysmal
    dark
  Of the unfathomed center.

To Shakespeare

On this hapless earth
There's small sincerity of mirth,
And laughter oft is but an art
To drown the outcry of the heart.

Address to Certain Gold-fishes

She is not fair to outward view
  As many maidens be;
Her loveliness I never knew
  Until she smiled on me:

Oh! then I saw her eye was bright,
A well of love, a spring of light.
                    Song, She Is Not Fair
Her very frowns are fairer far
Than smiles of other maidens are.
                                    Ibid.

THOMAS CHANDLER HALIBURTON ("SAM SLICK")
[1796–1865]

I want you to see Peel, Stanley, Graham, Sheil, Russell, Macaulay, Old Joe, and soon. They are all upper-crust here.[1]
Sam Slick in England.[2] *Chap. XXIV*
Circumstances alter cases.
                    The Old Judge. Chap. XV
We reckon hours and minutes to be dollars and cents.[3]
                            The Clockmaker
We can do without any article of luxury we have never had; but when once obtained, it is not in human natur' to surrender it voluntarily.
                                    Ibid.

HORACE MANN [4]
[1796–1859]

Lost, yesterday, somewhere between sunrise and sunset, two golden hours, each set with sixty diamond minutes. No reward is offered for they are gone forever.
                            Aphorism

[1] Those families, you know, are our upper-crust, — not upper ten thousand. — JAMES FENIMORE COOPER [1789–1851]: *The Ways of the Hour, Chap. VI* [1850]
At present there is no distinction among the upper ten thousand of the city. — N. P. WILLIS: *Necessity for a Promenade Drive*
[2] The "Sam Slick" papers first appeared in a weekly paper in Nova Scotia in 1836.
[3] Remember that time is money. — BENJAMIN FRANKLIN: *Advice to a Young Tradesman* [1748]
[4] American educator. Not to be confused with Sir Horace Mann [1701–1786], the correspondent of Horace Walpole.

WILLIAM AUGUSTUS MUHLENBERG
[1796–1877]

I would not live alway: I ask not to stay
Where storm after storm rises dark o'er the way.
    I Would Not Live Alway. Stanza 2
That heavenly music! what is it I hear?
The notes of the harpers ring sweet in mine ear.
And, see, soft unfolding those portals of gold,
The King all arrayed in his beauty behold!
                        Ibid. Stanza 6

JAMES ROBINSON PLANCHÉ
[1796–1880]

Gentle Zitella, whither away?
Love's ritornella list, while I play.
    The Brigand. Love's Ritornella

WILLIAM HICKLING PRESCOTT
[1796–1859]

The surest test of the civilization of a people — at least, as sure as any — afforded by mechanical art is to be found in their architecture, which presents so noble a field for the display of the grand and the beautiful, and which, at the same time, is so intimately connected with the essential comforts of life.
            The Conquest of Peru. Book I,
                                Chap. 5
Where there is no free agency, there can be no morality. Where there is no temptation, there can be little claim to virtue.[1] Where the routine is rigorously proscribed by law, the law, and not the man, must have the credit of the conduct.
                                    Ibid.

[1] There's many a life of sweet content
Whose virtue is environment.
            WALTER LEARNED [1847–1915]: *On the Fly-Leaf of Manon Lescaut*

Drawing his sword he traced a line with it on the sand from East to West. Then, turning towards the South, "Friends and comrades!" he said, "on that side are toil, hunger, nakedness, the drenching storm, desertion, and death; on this side ease and pleasure. There lies Peru with its riches; here, Panama and its poverty. Choose, each man, what best becomes a brave Castilian. For my part, I go to the South." So saying, he stepped across the line.

The Conquest of Peru.
Book II, Chap. 4

RICHARD RYAN
[1796–1849]

O, saw ye the lass wi' the bonnie blue een?
Her smile is the sweetest that ever was seen,
Her cheek like the rose is, but fresher, I ween,
She's the loveliest lassie that trips on the green.

O, Saw Ye the Lass

JOSEPH AUGUSTINE WADE
[1796–1845]

Meet me by moonlight alone,
   And then I will tell you a tale
Must be told by the moonlight alone,
   In the grove at the end of the vale!
You must promise to come, for I said
   I would show the night-flowers their queen.
Nay, turn not away that sweet head,
   'Tis the loveliest ever was seen.

Meet Me by Moonlight

THOMAS HAYNES BAYLY
[1797–1839]

I'd be a butterfly born in a bower,
   Where roses and lilies and violets meet.

I'd Be a Butterfly. Stanza 1

Those who have wealth must be watchful and wary,
   Power, alas! naught but misery brings!

Ibid. Stanza 2

Oh no! we never mention her, —[1]
   Her name is never heard;
My lips are now forbid to speak
   That once familiar word.

Oh No! We Never Mention Her

We met, — 'twas in a crowd.[2]

We Met

Gayly the troubadour
   Touched his guitar.

Welcome Me Home. Stanza 1

Why don't the men propose, Mamma?
   Why don't the men propose?

Why Don't the Men Propose?

She wore a wreath of roses
   The first night that we met.

She Wore a Wreath

Friends depart, and memory takes them
   To her caverns, pure and deep.

Teach Me to Forget

Tell me the tales that to me were so dear,
   Long, long ago, long, long ago.

Long, Long Ago[3]

The rose that all are praising
   Is not the rose for me.

The Rose That All Are Praising

Oh pilot, 'tis a fearful night!
   There's danger on the deep.

The Pilot

Absence makes the heart grow fonder:[4]
   Isle of Beauty, fare thee well!

Isle of Beauty

Oh, I have roamed o'er many lands,
   And many friends I've met;
Not one fair scene or kindly smile
   Can this fond heart forget.

Oh, Steer My Bark to Erin's Isle

My fond affection thou hast seen,
   Then judge of my regret

[1] Variant: "Oh, no, we never mention him."
[2] Parodied by THOMAS HOOD: "We met, — 'twas in a mob."
[3] A temperance song, sung in the meetings held by John B. Gough, was adapted by MRS. M. LINDSAY BLISS from Bayly's *Long, Long Ago,* and became as popular as the original.
Where are the friends that to me were so dear?
[4] I find that absence still increases love. — CHARLES HOPKINS [1664–1700]: *To C. C.* [1694]
Distance sometimes endears friendship, and absence sweeteneth it. — JAMES HOWELL [1594–1666]: *Familiar Letters, Book I, Sect. 1, No. 6*

To think more happy thou hadst been
  If we had never met.
                    To My Wife
I'm saddest when I sing.[1]
You Think I Have a Merry Heart

SAMUEL LOVER
[1797–1868]

A baby was sleeping,
Its mother was weeping,
For her husband was far on the wild-
  raging sea.
                    The Angel's Whisper

Reproof on her lip, but a smile in her
  eye.
                    Rory O'More. Stanza 1

For dhrames always go by contrairies,
  my dear.
                    Ibid. Stanza 2

"That's eight times to-day that you've
  kissed me before."
"Then here goes another," says he, "to
  make sure,
For there's luck in odd numbers," says
  Rory O'More.[2]
                    Ibid. Stanza 3

As she sat in the low-backed car
The man at the turn-pike bar
Never asked for the toll
But just rubbed his old poll
And looked after the low-backed car.
                    The Low-Backed Car. Stanza 1

Sure my love is all crost
Like a bud in the frost
And there's no use at all in my going
  to bed,
For 'tis dhrames and not slape that
  comes into my head!
                    Molly Carew

And with my advice, faith I wish you'd
  take me.
                    Widow Machree

Sure the shovel and tongs
To each other belongs.
                    Ibid.

---

[1] I am saddest when I sing. — CHARLES FAR-
RAR BROWNE: *Artemus Ward's Lecture*

[2] Also said VIRGIL, *Eclogue VIII, 75:
Numero Deus impare gaudet* (God delights
in an odd number).

WILLIAM MOTHERWELL
[1797–1835]

I've wandered east, I've wandered west,
  Through mony a weary way;
But never, never can forget
  The luve o' life's young day!
                    Jeannie Morrison. Stanza 1

'Twas then we luvit ilk ither weel,
  'Twas then we twa did part:
Sweet time — sad time! twa bairns at
  scule —
Twa bairns and but ae heart.[1]
                    Ibid. Stanza 3

MARY WOLLSTONECRAFT
SHELLEY
[1797–1851]

I beheld the wretch — the miserable
monster whom I had created.
                    Frankenstein. Chap. 5

MACDONALD CLARKE
[1798–1842]

Whilst twilight's curtain spreading far,
Was pinned with a single star.[2]
                    Death in Disguise. Line 227
                    [Boston edition, 1833]

Ha! see where the wild-blazing Grog-
  shop appears,
  As the red waves of wretchedness
    swell;
How it burns on the edge of tempestu-
  ous years —
  The horrible Light-house of Hell!
                    The Rum-hole

---

[1] See Alexander Pope, page 219.

[2] *Variant:* While twilight's curtain gather-
          ing far
      Is pinned with a single diamond
          star

Mrs. L. M. Child says: "He thus describes
the closing day: —
    'Now twilight lets her curtain down,
      And pins it with a star.'"

The moon is a silver pinhead vast
That holds the heavens tent-hangings fast.
          WILLIAM ROUNSEVILLE ALGER [1822–
              1905]: *The Use of the Moon*
When the curtains of night are pinned back
by the stars. — Old song: *I'll Remember You,
Love, in My Prayers*

JOHN ADAMS DIX
[1798–1879]

If any one attempts to haul down the American flag, shoot him on the spot.
An Official Despatch
[January 29, 1861]

ROBERT GILFILLAN
[1798–1850]

There's a hope for every woe,
  And a balm for every pain,[1]
But the first joys of our heart
  Come never back again!
  The Exile's Song. Stanza 4

In the days of langsyne we were happy and free,
Proud lords on the land, and kings on the sea!
To our foes we were fierce, to our friends we were kind,
And where battle raged loudest, you ever did find
The banner of Scotland float high in the wind!
  In the Days o' Langsyne. Stanza 2

THOMAS HOOD
[1798–1845]

There is a silence where hath been no sound,
There is a silence where no sound may be,
In the cold grave — under the deep, deep sea,
Or in wide desert where no life is found.
  Sonnet, Silence

We watched her breathing through the night,
  Her breathing soft and low,
As in her breast the wave of life
  Kept heaving to and fro.
  The Death-Bed. Stanza 1

Our very hopes belied our fears,
  Our fears our hopes belied; —
We thought her dying when she slept,
  And sleeping when she died.
  Ibid. Stanza 3

Never go to France
  Unless you know the lingo,

If you do, like me,
  You will repent, by jingo.
  French and English. Stanza 1

Never, from folly or urbanity,
Praise people thus profusely to their faces,
Till quite in love with their own graces,
They're eaten up by vanity!
  The Turtles. Moral

My life was like a London fog —
What d'ye think of that, my Cat?
What d'ye think of that, my Dog?
  The Bachelor's Dream. Stanza 8

I remember, I remember
The house where I was born,
The little window where the sun
Came peeping in at morn;
He never came a wink too soon
Nor brought too long a day.
  I Remember, I Remember. Stanza 1

I remember, I remember
The fir-trees dark and high;
I used to think their slender tops
Were close against the sky:
It was a childish ignorance,
But now 'tis little joy
To know I'm farther off from heaven
Than when I was a boy.
  Ibid. Stanza 4

She stood breast-high amid the corn,[1]
Clasped by the golden light of morn,
Like the sweetheart of the sun,
Who many a glowing kiss had won.
  Ruth. Stanza 1

Thus she stood amid the stooks,
Praising God with sweetest looks.
  Ibid. Stanza 4

When he's forsaken,
  Withered and shaken,
What can an old man do but die?
  Spring It Is Cheery. Stanza 1

And there is even a happiness
That makes the heart afraid.
  Ode to Melancholy

There's not a string attuned to mirth
But has its chord in melancholy.
  Ibid.

But evil is wrought by want of thought,
As well as want of heart.
  The Lady's Dream. Stanza 16

---

[1] There are balms for all our pain. — R. H.
STODDARD: *The Flight of Youth*

[1] She stood in tears amid the alien corn. —
KEATS: *Ode to a Nightingale*

Oh! would I were dead now,
Or up in my bed now,
To cover my head now,
    And have a good cry!
      A Table of Errata. Stanza 15

Straight down the Crooked Lane,
And all round the Square.
      A Plain Direction. Stanza 1

Be contented. Thou hast got
The most of heaven in thy young lot;
There's sky-blue in thy cup.
      Ode on a Distant Prospect of
            Clapham College

Two stern-faced men set out from Lynn
    through the cold and heavy mist,
And Eugene Aram walked between
    with gyves upon his wrist.
      The Dream of Eugene Aram.
            Stanza 36

No sun — no moon!
No morn — no noon —
No dawn — no dusk — no proper time
    of day —
No sky — no earthly view —
No distance looking blue —
No road — no street — no "t'other
    side the way."
               No
No warmth, no cheerfulness, no health-
    ful ease,
    No comfortable feel in any mem-
      ber —
No shade, no shine, no butterflies, no
    bees,
    No fruits, no flowers, no leaves, no
      birds,
          November!
              Ibid.

Seem'd washing his hands with invis-
    ible soap
In imperceptible water.
      Miss Kilmansegg and Her Pre-
      cious Leg. Her Christening,
      Stanza 10

O bed! O bed! delicious bed!
That heaven upon earth to the weary
    head!
      Ibid. Her Dream, Stanzas 7, 8

He lies like a hedgehog rolled up the
    wrong way,
    Tormenting himself with his prick-
    les.
      Ibid. Stanza 14

There's a double beauty whenever a
    swan
Swims on a lake, with her double
    thereon.[1]
      Miss Kilmansegg and Her Pre-
      cious Leg. Her Honeymoon,
      Stanza 9

Home-made dishes that drive one from
    home.
      Ibid. Her Misery, Stanza 1

Gold! Gold! Gold! Gold!
Bright and yellow, hard and cold.
      Ibid. Her Moral

Spurned by the young, but hugged by
    the old
To the very verge of the churchyard
    mould.
              Ibid.

How widely its agencies vary, —
To save — to ruin — to curse — to
    bless, —
As even its minted coins express,
Now stamped with the image of Good
    Queen Bess,
    And now of a Bloody Mary.
              Ibid.

Another tumble! — that's his precious
    nose!
      Parental Ode to My Infant Son.
            Stanza 3

Boughs are daily rifled
    By the gusty thieves,
And the book of Nature
    Getteth short of leaves.
      The Season. Stanza 2

With fingers weary and worn,
    With eyelids heavy and red,
A woman sat in unwomanly rags
    Plying her needle and thread —
Stitch! stitch! stitch!
      The Song of the Shirt. Stanza 1

O men, with sisters dear!
O men, with mothers and wives!
It is not linen you're wearing out,
    But human creatures' lives![2]
          Ibid. Stanza 4

---

[1] The swan on still St. Mary's lake
  Float double, swan and shadow!
  WORDSWORTH: *Yarrow Unvisited,*
                St. 6
[2] It's no fish ye're buying, it's men's lives. —
SCOTT: *The Antiquary, Chap. 11*

Sewing at once with a double thread,
A shroud as well as a shirt.
The Song of the Shirt. Stanza 4

O God! that bread should be so dear,
And flesh and blood so cheap!
Ibid. Stanza 5

No blessed leisure for love or hope,
But only time for grief.
Ibid. Stanza 10

My tears must stop, for every drop
Hinders needle and thread.
Ibid.

A wife who preaches in her gown,
And lectures in her night-dress.
The Surplice Question. Stanza 2

I saw old Autumn in the misty morn
Stand shadowless like silence, listen-
ing
To silence.
Ode, Autumn. Stanza 1

Peace and rest at length have come
All the day's long toil is past,
And each heart is whispering, "Home,
Home at last."
Home at Last

Ben Battle was a soldier bold,
And used to war's alarms;
But a cannon-ball took off his legs,
So he laid down his arms!
Faithless Nellie Gray. Stanza 1

One more unfortunate,
Weary of breath,
Rashly importunate,
Gone to her death!
The Bridge of Sighs. Stanza 1

Take her up tenderly,
Lift her with care;
Fashioned so slenderly,
Young, and so fair!
Ibid. Stanza 2

Alas for the rarity
Of Christian charity
Under the sun! [1]
Ibid. Stanza 9

No solemn sanctimonious face I pull,
Nor think I'm pious when I'm only
bilious;
Nor study in my sanctum supercilious,

[1] See Southey, page 322.

The organized charity, scrimped and iced,
In the name of a cautious, statistical Christ.
JOHN BOYLE O'REILLY: *In Bohemia, St. 5*

To frame a Sabbath Bill or forge a
Bull.
Ode to Rae Wilson

His death, which happened in his
berth,
At forty-odd befell:
They went and told the sexton, and
The sexton tolled the bell.
Faithless Sally Brown. Stanza 17

That fierce thing
They call a conscience.
Lamia. Scene VII

O'er the earth there comes a bloom;
Sunny light for sullen gloom;
Warm perfume for vapour cold—
I smell the rose above the mould!
Farewell, Life

GEORGE LINLEY
[1798–1865]

Among our ancient mountains,
And from our lovely vales,
Oh, let the prayer re-echo:
"God bless the Prince of Wales!"
*God Bless the Prince of Wales.
Stanza 1*

Above the throne of England
May fortune's star long shine,
And round its sacred bulwarks
The olive branches twine.
Ibid. Stanza 4

Thou art gone from my gaze like a
beautiful dream,
And I seek thee in vain by the meadow
and stream.
Thou Art Gone

Tho' lost to sight, to memory dear
Thou ever wilt remain;
One only hope my heart can cheer,—
The hope to meet again.
Song [1]

[1] This song was written and composed by
Linley for Mr. Augustus Braham, and sung
by him. It is not known when it was written,
— probably about 1830.

Another song, entitled *Though Lost to
Sight, to Memory Dear,* was published in London in 1880, purporting to have been written
by Ruthven Jenkyns in 1703 and published in
the *Magazine for Mariners.* That magazine,
however, never existed, and the composer of
the music acknowledged, in a private letter,
that he copied the words from an American
newspaper. The reputed author, Ruthven Jen-

DAVID MACBETH MOIR
("DELTA")
[1798–1851]

To me, through every season dearest;
In every scene, by day, by night,
Thou, present to my mind appearest
A quenchless star, forever bright;
My solitary sole delight:
Where'er I am, by shore, at sea,
I think of thee.
When Thou at Eve

Were life spun out a thousand years,
It could not match Langsyne.
Langsyne. Stanza 1

ROBERT POLLOK
[1798–1827]

Sorrows remembered sweeten present joy.
The Course of Time. Book I, Line 464

Most wondrous book! bright candle of the Lord!
Star of Eternity! The only star
By which the bark of man could navigate
The sea of life, and gain the coast of bliss
Securely.
Ibid. Book II, Line 270

He touched his harp, and nations heard, entranced,
As some vast river of unfailing source,
Rapid, exhaustless, deep, his numbers flowed,
And opened new fountains in the human heart.
Ibid. Book IV, Line 684

He laid his hand upon "the Ocean's mane," [1]
And played familiar with his hoary locks.
Ibid. Line 689

---

kyns, was living, under another name, in California in 1882.
   Absent or dead, still let a friend be dear. —
ALEXANDER POPE: *Epistle to Robert, Earl of Oxford and Mortimer*
   [1] See Byron, page 355.

HENRY SCOTT RIDDELL
[1798–1870]

Then Scotland's dales and Scotland's vales,
And Scotland's hills for me;
I'll drink a cup to Scotland yet,
Wi' a' the honours three.
Scotland Yet. Stanza 2

AMOS BRONSON ALCOTT
[1799–1888]

Greater is he who is above temptation than he who being tempted overcomes.
Orphic Sayings. No. 12
The true teacher defends his pupils against his own personal influence. He inspires self-distrust. He guides their eyes from himself to the spirit that quickens him. He will have no disciple.
Ibid. The Teacher
Who loves a garden still his Eden keeps,
Perennial pleasures plants, and wholesome harvests reaps.
Tablets. Page 6
Nature is thought immersed in matter.
Ibid. Page 176
I press thee to my heart as Duty's faithful child.
Sonnet to Louisa May Alcott

RUFUS CHOATE
[1799–1859]

The courage of New England was the "courage of Conscience." It did not rise to that insane and awful passion, the love of war for itself.
Address at Ipswich Centennial
[1834]
The final end of Government is not to exert restraint but to do good.
Speech, The Necessity of Compromise in American Politics,
U. S. Senate [July 2, 1841]
There was a state without king or nobles; there was a church without a bishop; [1] there was a people governed

---

[1] The Americans equally detest the pageantry of a king and the supercilious hypocrisy of a bishop. — JUNIUS: *Letter XXXV [Dec.*

by grave magistrates which it had selected, and by equal laws which it had framed.

> *Speech before the New England Society [December 22, 1843]*

We join ourselves to no party that does not carry the flag and keep step to the music of the Union.

> *Letter to the Whig Convention, Worcester [October 1, 1855]*

Its constitution the glittering and sounding generalities [1] of natural right which make up the Declaration of Independence.

> *Letter to the Maine Whig Committee [1856]*

GEORGE DUBOURG
[1799–1882]

A lady help wanted — genteel and refined,
Obliging and cheerful, industrious and kind.

> *Wanted, a Lady Help*

An orphan or destitute lady would find
In return for her services treatment most kind.[2]

> *Ibid.*

19, 1769]. Compare the anonymous poem, *The Puritans' Mistake,* published by Oliver Ditson in 1844: —

Oh, we are weary pilgrims; to this wilderness we bring
A Church without a bishop, a State without a King.

It [Calvinism] established a religion without a prelate, a government without a king. — GEORGE BANCROFT: *History of the United States, Vol. III, Chap. VI*

[1] Six years earlier, Choate gave a lecture in Providence, a review of which, by FRANKLIN J. DICKMAN, appeared in the *Journal* of Dec. 14, 1849. Unless Choate used the words "glittering generalities," and Dickman made reference to them, it would seem as if Dickman must have the credit of inventing the phrase. He wrote: "We fear that the glittering generalities of the speaker have left an impression more delightful than permanent."

[2] This doggerel somehow recalls *The Accomplished Female Friend,* by the Rev. CORNELIUS WHAURR, one stanza of which concludes: —

What lasting joys the man attend
Who has a Polished Female Friend.

MARY HOWITT
[1799–1888]

Old England is our home, and Englishmen are we;
Our tongue is known in every clime, our flag in every sea.

> *Old England Is Our Home*

"Will you walk into my parlour?" said the spider to the fly;
" 'Tis the prettiest little parlour that ever you did spy."

> *The Spider and the Fly*

"Arise, my maiden Mabel,"
Her mother said, "arise!
For the golden sun of midsummer
Is shining in the skies."

> *Mabel on Midsummer Day. Stanza 1*

Little Gretchen, little Gretchen,
Wanders up and down the street.

> *The Little Match Girl.[1] Stanza 1*

God might have bade the earth bring forth
Enough for great and small,
The oak-tree and the cedar-tree,
Without a flower at all.

> *The Use of Flowers. Stanza 1*

GEORGE PAYNE RAINS-FORD JAMES
[1799–1860]

I envy them, those monks of old;
Their books they read, and their beads they told.

> *The Monks of Old*

Thou'rt an ass, Robin, thou'rt an ass,
To think that great men be
More gay than I that lie on the grass
Under the greenwood tree.
I tell thee no, I tell thee no,
The Great are slaves to their gilded show.

> *Richelieu. Chap. 3, Robber's Song, Stanza 1*

The best happiness a woman can boast is that of being most carefully deceived.

> *Ibid. Chap. 4*

---

[1] From the Danish of Hans Christian Andersen [1805–1875].

Turning over a page or two in the book of Nature, I found that the most brilliant actions and the greatest events were generally brought about from the meanest motives and most petty causes.

Richelieu. Chap. 5

Dirty fingers soil no gold.

Ibid.

A single word has sometimes lost or won an empire — even less than a single word, if we may believe the history of Darius's horse, who proclaimed his master emperor without speaking.[1]

Ibid. Chap. 6

A great bad man is worse than one of less talents, for he has the extended capability of doing harm.

Ibid.

Age is the most terrible misfortune that can happen to any man; other evils will mend, this is every day getting worse.

Ibid. Chap. 14

JOHN MOULTRIE
[1799–1874]

"Forget thee?" — If to dream by night
  and muse on thee by day,
If all the worship, deep and wild, a
  poet's heart can pay,
If prayers in absence breathed for thee
  to Heaven's protecting power,
If wingèd thoughts that flit to thee —
  a thousand in an hour,
If busy Fancy blending thee with all
  my future lot —
If this thou call'st forgetting, thou indeed shalt be forgot.

Forget Thee. Stanza 1

[1] The seven candidates for the throne of Persia agreed that he should be king whose horse neighed first. The horse of Darius was the first.

Who found more sweetness in his horse's
  neighing
Than all the Phrygian, Dorian, Lydian playing.

FULKE GREVILLE, LORD BROOKE
[1554–1628]

THOMAS NOEL
[1799–1861]

Rattle his bones over the stones!
He's only a pauper, whom nobody
  owns!

The Pauper's Drive. Stanza 1

By the waters of Life we sat together,
  Hand in hand, in the golden days
Of the beautiful early summer weather,
  When skies were purple and breath
    was praise.

An Old Man's Idyll

MISS WROTHER

Hope tells a flattering tale,
  Delusive, vain, and hollow.
Ah! let not hope prevail,
  Lest disappointment follow.[1]

The Universal Songster. Vol. II,
Page 86

JOSEPH ADDISON ALEXANDER
[1800–1860]

There is a time, we know not when,
  A point we know not where,
That marks the destiny of men,
  For glory or despair.

The Doomed Man. Stanza 1

There is a line, by us unseen,
  That crosses every path;
The hidden boundary between
  God's patience and His wrath.

Ibid. Stanza 2

CALDER CAMPBELL
[*Floruit* 1840]

I'll chase the antelope over the plain,
The tiger's cub I'll bind with a chain,
And the wild gazelle with its silvery
  feet
I'll give thee for a playmate sweet.

Ossian's Serenade.[2] *Refrain*

[1] Hope told a flattering tale,
    That Joy would soon return;
  Ah! naught my sighs avail,
    For Love is doomed to mourn.
  ANONYMOUS, air by Giovanni
  Paisiello [1741–1816]: *Universal Songster, Vol. I, P. 320*

[2] This song was published in *Godey's Lady's Book, Nov., 1840.* The sheet music was

Then come with me in my light canoe,
Where the sea is calm and the sky is
blue.
Ibid. Stanza 2

JULIA CRAWFORD
[1800–1885]

Kathleen mavourneen! the grey dawn
is breaking,
The horn of the hunter is heard on the
hill.
Kathleen Mavourneen. Stanza 1

Hast thou forgotten how soon we must
sever?
Oh! hast thou forgotten this day we
must part?
It may be for years, and it may be forever;
Then why art thou silent, thou voice
of my heart?
Ibid.

We parted in silence, we parted by
night,
On the banks of that lonely river;
Where the fragrant limes their boughs
unite,
We met — and we parted forever!
We Parted in Silence.
Stanza 1

Rest, thou troubled heart,
Within this captive bosom swelling;
Rest, thou troubled heart,
No more of love or glory telling.
Now no more by wrongs or tyrant
power oppressed,
From a thousand woes,
Ah, what sweet repose
Soon will seal these eyes in everlasting
rest.
Pestal's Lay.[1] Rest, Troubled
Heart

---

brought out by Oliver Ditson Company, Boston, in 1850. The song was known as *Ossian's
Serenade,* as it was sung by Ossian E. Dodge,
a popular entertainer of the period. He
achieved fame, or notoriety, when he purchased the first ticket sold for Jenny Lind's
first Boston concert under the auspices of
P. T. Barnum, paying $625 for it.

See Thomas Moore, page 338.

[1] Paul Pestal [1794–1826], a Russian colonel of infantry, is said to have scratched the
words and music of a song on the wall of his

KENELM HENRY DIGBY
[1800–1880]

Island of Saints, still constant, still al-
lied
To the great truths opposed to human
pride;
Island of ruins, towers, cloisters grey,
Whence palmer kings with pontiffs
once did stray
To Rome and Sion, or to kindle fire
Which amid later darkness can inspire
Lands that in fondest memory and
song
Thy pristine glory fearlessly prolong.
Erin

MILLARD FILLMORE
[1800–1874]

Let us remember that revolutions do
not always establish freedom.
Third Annual Address
[December 6, 1852]

It is not strange . . . that such an
exuberance of enterprise should cause
some individuals to mistake change for
progress, and the invasion of the rights
of others for national prowess and
glory.
Ibid.

JOHN WOODCOCK GRAVES
[*Circa* 1800]

Do ye ken John Peel with his coat so
gay?
Do ye ken John Peel at the break of
day?
John Peel. Old Hunting Song
[1832]

---

prison cell while awaiting execution. There
are at least two other versions of his song,
both anonymous:

Yes! it comes at last,
And from a troubled dream awaking,
Death will soon be past,
And brighter worlds around me breaking.
Pestal's Lay, St. 1

Yes! the die is cast!
The turbid dream of life is waning,
The gulf will soon be past,
The soul immortal joy attaining.
In The Silver Bell [a school
songbook, 1864]

'Twas the sound of his horn brought
  me from my bed,
And the cry of his hounds, which he
  oft-times led,
For Peel's view-hallo would waken the
  dead,
Or the fox from his lair in the morning.

> *John Peel. Old Hunting Song*
> *[1832]. Refrain*

JAMES GILBORNE LYONS
[1800–1868]

Now gather all our Saxon bards — let
  harps and hearts be strung,
To celebrate the triumphs of our own
  good Saxon tongue!
For stronger far than hosts that march
  with battle-flags unfurled,
It goes with freedom, thought, and
  truth to rouse and rule the world.

> *The Triumphs of the English*
> *Language*

THOMAS BABINGTON, LORD MACAULAY
[1800–1859]

That is the best government which
desires to make the people happy, and
knows how to make them happy.

> *On Mitford's History of Greece*
> *(In Knight's Quarterly, No-*
> *vember, 1824)*

Free trade, one of the greatest blessings which a government can confer on
a people, is in almost every country unpopular.

> *Ibid.*

Wherever literature consoles sorrow
or assuages pain; wherever it brings
gladness to eyes which fail with wake-
fulness and tears, and ache for the dark
house and the long sleep, — there is
exhibited in its noblest form the immortal influence of Athens.

> *Ibid.*

Out of his surname they have coined
an epithet for a knave, and out of his
Christian name a synonym for the
Devil.[1]

> *On Niccolo de Machiavelli (In*
> *Edinburgh Review, March,*
> *1825)*

Nothing is so useless as a general
maxim.

> *Ibid.*

We hold that the most wonderful and
splendid proof of genius is a great
poem produced in a civilized age.

> *On Milton (In Edinburgh Re-*
> *view, August, 1825)*

Nobles by the right of an earlier
creation, and priests by the imposition
of a mightier hand.

> *Ibid.*

Our academical Pharisees.

> *Ibid.*

The dust and silence of the upper
shelf.

> *Ibid.*

Perhaps no person can be a poet, or
even can enjoy poetry, without a certain unsoundness of mind.

> *Ibid.*

The English Bible, — a book which
if everything else in our language
should perish, would alone suffice to
show the whole extent of its beauty
and power.

> *On John Dryden (In Edin-*
> *burgh Review, January, 1828)*

His imagination resembled the wings
of an ostrich. It enabled him to run,
though not to soar.

> *Ibid.*

A man possessed of splendid talents,
which he often abused, and of a sound
judgment, the admonitions of which he
often neglected; a man who succeeded
only in an inferior department of his
art, but who, in that department, succeeded pre-eminently.

> *Ibid.*

The gallery in which the reporters
sit has become a fourth estate of the
realm.[2]

> *On Hallam's Constitutional*
> *History [September, 1828]*

---

[1] Nick Machiavel had ne'er a trick,
  Though he gave his name to our Old Nick.
  SAMUEL BUTLER: *Hudibras, III, I, 1313*

[2] See Carlyle, pages 377, 380, 381.

Men are never so likely to settle a question rightly as when they discuss it freely.

> Southey's Colloquies [January, 1830]

Nothing is so galling to a people, not broken in from the birth, as a paternal or, in other words, a meddling government, a government which tells them what to read and say and eat and drink and wear.

> Ibid.

I have not the Chancellor's [Brougham] encyclopedic mind. He is indeed a kind of semi-Solomon. He *half* knows everything, from the cedar to the hyssop.[1]

> Letter to Macvey Napier [December 17, 1830]

He had a head which statuaries loved to copy, and a foot the deformity of which the beggars in the streets mimicked.

> On Moore's Life of Lord Byron [June, 1831]

We know no spectacle so ridiculous as the British public in one of its periodical fits of morality.

> Ibid.

From the poetry of Lord Byron they drew a system of ethics compounded of misanthropy and voluptuousness, — a system in which the two great commandments were to hate your neighbour and to love your neighbour's wife.

> Ibid.

What a singular destiny has been that of this remarkable man! — To be regarded in his own age as a classic, and in ours as a companion! To receive from his contemporaries that full homage which men of genius have in general received only from posterity; to be more intimately known to posterity than other men are known to their contemporaries!

> On Boswell's Life of Johnson [September, 1831]

[1] I wish I were as sure of anything as Macaulay is of everything. — WILLIAM WINDHAM [1750–1810]. Attributed also to William Lamb, Viscount Melbourne [1779–1848].

That wonderful book, while it obtains admiration from the most fastidious critics, is loved by those who are too simple to admire it.

> On Bunyan's Pilgrim's Progress [December, 1831]

The conformation of his mind was such that whatever was little seemed to him great, and whatever was great seemed to him little.

> On Horace Walpole [1833]

An acre in Middlesex is better than a principality in Utopia.[1]

> On Lord Bacon

Temple was a man of the world among men of letters, a man of letters among men of the world.[2]

> On Sir William Temple [October, 1838]

She [the Roman Catholic Church] may still exist in undiminished vigour when some traveller from New Zealand shall, in the midst of a vast solitude, take his stand on a broken arch of London Bridge to sketch the ruins of St. Paul's.[3]

> On Ranke's History of the Popes [October, 1840]

[1] Utopia, from the Greek, *no-place*. In Sir Thomas More's political romance, Utopia was an imaginary island, where the laws, the politics, the morals, and the institutions were perfect.

Better fifty years of Europe than a cycle of Cathay. — TENNYSON: *Locksley Hall*, L. 184

[2] See Pope, page 215.

[3] The same image was employed by Macaulay in 1824 in the concluding paragraph of a review of MITFORD'S *Greece*, and he repeated it in his review of MILL'S *Essay on Government* in 1829.

What cities, as great as this, have . . . promised themselves immortality! Posterity can hardly trace the situation of some. The sorrowful traveller wanders over the awful ruins of others. . . . Here stood their citadel, but now grown over with weeds; there their senate-house, but now the haunt of every noxious reptile; temples and theatres stood here, now only an undistinguished heap of ruins. — GOLDSMITH: *The Bee, No. IV* [1759], *A City Night-Piece*

Who knows but that hereafter some traveller like myself will sit down upon the banks of the Seine, the Thames, or the Zuyder Zee, where now, in the tumult of enjoyment, the heart and the eyes are too slow to take in the multitude of sensations? Who knows but he

She [the Catholic Church] thoroughly understands what no other Church has ever understood, how to deal with enthusiasts.

On Ranke's History of the Popes
[October, 1840]

He [Warren Hastings] was a man for whom nature had done much of what the Stoic philosophy pretended. *"Mens aequa in arduis"* [1] is the inscription under his picture in the Government house at Calcutta, and never was there a more appropriate motto.

Letter to Macvey Napier
[January 11, 1841]

The chief-justice was rich, quiet, and infamous.

On Warren Hastings [October, 1841]

In that temple of silence and reconciliation where the enmities of twenty generations lie buried, in the Great Abbey which has during many ages afforded a quiet resting-place to those

---

will sit down solitary amid silent ruins, and weep a people inurned and their greatness changed into an empty name? — CONSTANTIN DE VOLNEY [1757–1820]: *Ruins, Chap. II*

The next Augustan age will dawn on the other side of the Atlantic. There will, perhaps, be a Thucydides at Boston, a Xenophon at New York, in time a Virgil at Mexico, and a Newton at Peru. At last some curious traveller from Lima will visit England, and give a description of the ruins of St. Paul's, like the editions of Balbec and Palmyra. — HORACE WALPOLE: *Letter to Sir Horace Mann [Nov. 24, 1774]*

Where now is Britain? . . .
Even as the savage sits upon the stone
That marks where stood her capitols, and hears
The bittern booming in the weeds, he shrinks
From the dismaying solitude.
HENRY KIRKE WHITE [1785–1806]: *Time*

In the firm expectation that when London shall be a habitation of bitterns, when St. Paul and Westminster Abbey shall stand shapeless and nameless ruins in the midst of an unpeopled marsh, when the piers of Waterloo Bridge shall become the nuclei of islets of reeds and osiers, and cast the jagged shadows of their broken arches on the solitary stream, some Transatlantic commentator will be weighing in the scales of some new and now unimagined system of criticism the respective merits of the Bells and the Fudges and their historians. — SHELLEY: *Dedication to Peter Bell the Third*
[1] An even mind in difficulties.

---

whose minds and bodies have been shattered by the contentions of the Great Hall.

On Warren Hastings [October, 1841]

I shall not be satisfied unless I produce something which shall for a few days supersede the last fashionable novel on the tables of young ladies.

Letter to Macvey Napier
[November 5, 1841]

In order that he might rob a neighbour whom he had promised to defend, black men fought on the coast of Coromandel and red men scalped each other by the great lakes of North America.

On Frederic the Great
[April, 1842]

We hardly know an instance of the strength and weakness of human nature so striking and so grotesque as the character of this haughty, vigilant, resolute, sagacious blue-stocking,[1] half Mithridates and half Trissotin, bearing up against a world in arms, with an ounce of poison in one pocket and a quire of bad verses in the other.

Ibid.

A man who has never looked on Niagara has but a faint idea of a cataract; and he who has not read Barère's Memoirs may be said not to know what it is to lie.

Mémoires de Bertrand Barère
[1843]

Ambrose Phillips . . . who had the honour of bringing into fashion a species of composition which has been

---

[1] About 1748, Benjamin Stillingfleet [1702–1771] was a member of an assembly of men and women meeting to discuss literature, etc. He wore blue stockings. Such was the excellence of his conversation that his absence was felt to be so great a loss that it was said, "We can do nothing without the blue-stockings." Miss Hannah More has admirably described a Blue-stocking Club, in her *Bas Bleu*, a poem in which many of the persons who were most conspicuous there are mentioned.

From a discussion by BOSWELL in his *Life of Dr. Johnson, Vol. II, P. 390,* Everyman ed. Boswell's account is in 1781, but the *Dictionary of National Biography* gives the year as "C. 1748."
See Mrs. Browning, page 430.

called, after his name, Namby Pamby.[1]

Review of Aikin's Life of Addison
[July, 1843]

He [Steele] was a rake among scholars and a scholar among rakes.

Ibid.

The highest proof of virtue is to possess boundless power without abusing it.

Ibid.

There you sit, doing penance for the disingenuousness of years.[2]

Speech, House of Commons
[April 14, 1845]

Your Constitution is all sail and no anchor.

Letter to H. S. Randall, author of a Life of Thomas Jefferson
[May 23, 1857]

Those who compare the age in which their lot has fallen with a golden age which exists only in imagination, may talk of degeneracy and decay; but no man who is correctly informed as to the past, will be disposed to take a morose or desponding view of the present.

History of England. Vol. I,
Chap. 1

I shall cheerfully bear the reproach of having descended below the dignity of history[3] if I can succeed in placing before the English of the nineteenth century a true picture of the life of their ancestors.

Ibid.

The Puritan hated bear-baiting, not because it gave pain to the bear, but because it gave pleasure to the spectators.[4]

Ibid. Chap. 2

There were gentlemen and there were seamen in the navy of Charles II. But the seamen were not gentlemen, and the gentlemen were not seamen.

Ibid. Chap. 3

[1] See Henry Carey, page 189.
[2] Macaulay refers to Sir Robert Peel.
[3] The dignity of history. — BOLINGBROKE: *On the Study and Use of History, Letter V*
[4] Even bear-baiting was esteemed heathenish and unchristian: the sport of it, not the inhumanity, gave offence. — HUME: *History of England, Vol. I, Chap. LXII*

The ambassador [of Russia] and the grandees who accompanied him were so gorgeous that all London crowded to stare at them, and so filthy that nobody dared to touch them. They came to the court balls dropping pearls and vermin.

History of England. Vol. V,
Chap. 23

I met Sir Bulwer Lytton, or Lytton Bulwer. He is anxious about some scheme for some association of literary men. I detest all such associations. I hate the notion of gregarious authors. The less we have to do with each other, the better.

Quoted in GEORGE OTTO TRE-
VELYAN: *Life and Letters of Lord Macaulay. Vol. II,*
Page 245 [Harper, 1877]

Friends, how goes the fight?

The Battle of the Lake Regillus.
Stanza 16

These be the great Twin Brethren
To whom the Dorians pray.

Ibid. Stanza 40

To every man upon this earth
Death cometh soon or late;
And how can man die better
Than facing fearful odds
For the ashes of his fathers,
And the temples of his gods?

Lays of Ancient Rome. Horatius,
Stanza 27

The Romans were like brothers
In the brave days of old.

Ibid. Stanza 32

Those behind cried "Forward!"
And those before cried "Back!"

Ibid. Stanza 50

Oh, Tiber! father Tiber!
To whom the Romans pray,
A Roman's life, a Roman's arms,
Take thou in charge this day.

Ibid. Stanza 59

How well Horatius kept the bridge.

Ibid. Stanza 70

Press where ye see my white plume
shine, amidst the ranks of war,
And be your oriflamme to-day the helmet of Navarre.

Ivry. Line 29

Such night in England ne'er had been,
nor ne'er again shall be.
The Armada. Line 34

Oh! wherefore come ye forth, in triumph from the North,
With your hands, and your feet, and
your raiment all red?
And wherefore doth your rout send
forth a joyous shout?
And whence be the grapes of the
wine-press which ye tread?
The Battle of Naseby. Stanza 1

From a shore no search hath found,
from a gulf no line can sound,
Without rudder or needle we steer;
Above, below, our bark dies the sea-
fowl and the shark,
As we fly by the last Buccaneer.
The Last Buccaneer. Stanza 3

April's ivory moonlight.
The Prophecy of Capys. Stanza 18

The mighty name of Rome.
Ibid. Stanza 31

Soon fades the spell, soon comes the
night;
Say will it not be then the same,
Whether we played the black or white,
Whether we lost or won the game?
Sermon in a Churchyard. Stanza 8

The sweeter sound of woman's praise.
*Lines Written July 30, 1847.
Stanza 20*

Forget all feuds, and shed one English
tear
O'er English dust. A broken heart lies
here.
Epitaph on a Jacobite [1845]

Ye diners-out from whom we guard
our spoons.[1]
Political Georgics

Who never forgot that the end of
Government is the happiness of the
governed.
*Inscription for the Statue of
Lord William Bentinck*

---

[1] I sent these lines to the "Times" about
three years ago. — *Letter* [June 29, 1831]
The louder he talked of his honor, the
faster we counted our spoons. — EMERSON:
Conduct of Life, Worship

LUCIUS O'BRIEN
[? –1841]

To our old Alma Mater, our rock-
bound Highland home,
We'll cast back many a fond regret, as
o'er life's sea we roam,
Until on our last battlefield the lights
of heaven shall glow,
We'll never fail to drink to her and
Benny Havens, oh!
West Point Song[1] *[1838]*

SIR HENRY TAYLOR
[1800–1886]

His food
Was glory, which was poison to his
mind
And peril to his body.
*Philip Van Artevelde. Part I,
Act I, Sc. 5*

The world knows nothing of its greatest men.
Ibid.

An unreflected light did never yet
Dazzle the vision feminine.
Ibid.

He that lacks time to mourn, lacks
time to mend.
Eternity mourns that. 'Tis an ill cure
For life's worst ills, to have no time to
feel them.
Where sorrow's held intrusive and
turned out,
There wisdom will not enter, nor true
power,
Nor aught that dignifies humanity.
Ibid.

We figure to ourselves
The thing we like; and then we build
it up,
As chance will have it, on the rock or
sand, —
For thought is tired of wandering o'er
the world,
And homebound Fancy runs her bark
ashore.
Ibid.

---

[1] Benny Havens had a shop on the academy
grounds. He died in 1877, at the age of 89,
and was buried in Highland Union Cemetery.

Dr. O'Brien was appointed Second Lieutenant, 8th U. S. Infantry, and promoted to
First Lieutenant, December 1, 1839.

Such souls,
Whose sudden visitations daze the
world,
Vanish like lightning, but they leave
behind
A voice that in the distance far away
Wakens the slumbering ages.
*Philip Van Artevelde. Part I,
Act. I, Sc. 5*

RICHARD BETHELL, LORD WESTBURY
[1800–1873]

A solicitor, after hearing Lord Westbury's opinion, ventured to say that he
had turned the matter over in his mind,
and thought that something might be
said on the other side; to which he replied, "Then, sir, you will turn it over
once more in what you are *pleased to
call your mind.*"
Nash: *Life of Lord Westbury.
Vol. II, Page 292*

JANE WELSH CARLYLE (MRS. THOMAS CARLYLE) [1]
[1801–1866]

Medical men all over the world having merely entered into a tacit agreement to call all sorts of maladies people are liable to, in cold weather, by
one name; so that one sort of treatment may serve for all, and their practice be thereby greatly simplified.
*Letter to John Welsh
[March 4, 1837]*

Some new neighbours, that came a
month or two ago, brought with them
an accumulation of all the things to
be guarded against in a London neigh-
bourhood, viz., a pianoforte, a lap-dog,
and a parrot.
*Letter to Mrs. Carlyle [May 6,
1839]*

[1] I have read your glorious letters,
Where you threw aside all fetters,
Spoke your thoughts and mind out freely
In your own delightful style.
Bessie Chandler: *To Mrs. Carlyle,
St. 1* (In *Century Magazine, Nov.,
1883*)

Never does one feel oneself so utterly helpless as in trying to speak
comfort for great bereavement. I will
not try it. Time is the only comforter
for the loss of a mother.
*Letter to Thomas Carlyle
[December 27, 1853]*

If peace and quietness be not in one's
own power, one can always give oneself at least bodily fatigue — no such
bad succedaneum after all.
Journal. October 23, 1855

When one has been threatened with
a great injustice, one accepts a smaller
as a favour.
Ibid. November 21, 1855

Of all God's creatures, man
Alone is poor.
*To a Swallow Building Under
Our Eaves*

GEORGE WASHINGTON CUTTER
[1801–1865]

Harness me down with your iron
bands,
Be sure of your curb and rein:
For I scorn the power of your puny
hands,
As the tempest scorns a chain.
Song of Steam. Stanza 1

JOHN ELLERTON

Now the labourer's task is o'er;
Now the battle day is past;
Now upon the farther shore
Lands the voyager at last.
Father, in Thy gracious keeping
Leave we now Thy servant sleeping.
*Now the Labourer's Task Is
O'er. Stanza 1*

DAVID GLASGOW FARRAGUT
[1801–1870]

Damn the torpedoes! Go ahead!
At Mobile Bay [August 5, 1864]

JOHN HENRY, CARDINAL NEWMAN
[1801–1890]

Time hath a taming hand.
> *Persecution. Stanza 3 [1832]*

Lead, kindly Light, amid the encircling gloom;
Lead thou me on!
The night is dark, and I am far from home;
Lead thou me on!
Keep thou my feet: I do not ask to see
The distant scene; one step enough for me.
> *The Pillar of the Cloud.*
> *Stanza 1 [1833]*

And with the morn, those angel faces smile
Which I have loved long since, and lost awhile.
> *Ibid. Stanza 3*

It is thy very energy of thought
Which keeps thee from thy God.
> *Dream of Gerontius. Part III*

Who lets his feelings run
In soft luxurious flow,
Shrinks when hard service must be done,
And faints at every woe.
> *Flowers Without Fruit*

Living Nature, not dull Art
Shall plan my ways and rule my heart.
> *Nature and Art. Stanza 12*

Mine, the Unseen to display
In the crowded public way,
Where life's busy arts combine
To shut out the Hand Divine.
> *Snapdragon*

Weep not for me;
Be blithe as wont, nor tinge with gloom
The stream of love that circles home,
Light hearts and free!
Joy in the gifts Heaven's bounty lends,
Nor miss my face, dear friends!
I still am near.
> *A Voice from Afar [Knowledge]. Stanza 1*

Growth is the only evidence of life.
> *Dr. Scott, cited by Cardinal Newman*

It is almost a definition of a gentleman to say he is one who never inflicts pain.
> *Idea of a University. The Man of the World*

If he be an unbeliever, he will be too profound and large-minded to ridicule religion or to act against it; he is too wise to be a dogmatist or fanatic in his infidelity. He respects piety and devotion; he even supports institutions as venerable, beautiful, or useful, to which he does not assent; he honours the ministers of religion, and it contents him to decline its mysteries without assailing or denouncing them.
> *Ibid.*

A great memory does not make a philosopher, any more than a dictionary can be called a grammar.
> *Ibid. Knowledge in Relation to Learning*

Ex Umbris et Imaginibus in Veritatem! (From shadows and symbols into the truth.)
> *Epitaph at Edgbaston, composed by himself.*

ALDEN C. SPOONER
[Floruit 1846]

I mused upon the Pilgrim flock
Whose luck it was to land
Upon almost the only rock
Among the Plymouth sand.[1]
> *Old Times and New. Stanza 2*
> *(Written for the New England*
> *Society Festival, New York,*
> *December 22, 1846)*

LYDIA MARIA CHILD
[1802–1880]

Pillars are falling at thy feet,
Fanes quiver in the air,
A prostrate city is thy seat,
And thou alone art there.
> *Marius Amid the Ruins of Carthage*

---

[1] How much better if Plymouth Rock had landed on the Pilgrims. — Modern saying, origin dubious.

Genius hath electric power
  Which earth can never tame,
Bright suns may scorch and dark
    clouds lower,
  Its flash is still the same.
      *Marius Amid the Ruins of
        Carthage*

Over the river and through the wood,
To grandfather's house we'll go;
  The horse knows the way
  To carry the sleigh,
Through the white and drifted snow.
      Thanksgiving Day. Stanza 1

ALBERT GORTON GREENE
[1802–1868]

Old Grimes is dead, that good old man
  We never shall see more;
He used to wear a long black coat
  All buttoned down before.[1]
      Old Grimes. Stanza 1

He had no malice in his mind,
  No ruffles on his shirt.
      Ibid. Stanza 8

His knowledge hid from public gaze,
  He did not bring to view,
Nor made a noise town-meeting days,
  As many people do.
      Ibid. Stanza 10

His worldly goods he never threw
  In trust to fortune's chances.
      Ibid. Stanza 11

Fill every beaker up, my men, pour
    forth the cheering wine:
There's life and strength in every drop,
  — thanksgiving to the vine!
      *The Baron's Last Banquet.
        Stanza 7*

---

[1] John Lee is dead, that good old man, —
    We ne'er shall see him more;
  He used to wear an old drab coat
    All buttoned down before.
  To the memory of John Lee, who died
      May 21, 1823.
  An Inscription in Matherne Churchyard
  Old Abram Brown is dead and gone, —
    You'll never see him more;
  He used to wear a long brown coat
    That buttoned down before.
      HALLIWELL: *Nursery Rhymes of
        England, P. 60*

LETITIA ELIZABETH LANDON
[1802–1838]

As beautiful as woman's blush, —
  As evanescent too.
      Apple Blossoms

Were it not better to forget
Than but remember and regret?
      Despondency

GEORGE POPE MORRIS
[1802–1864]

Woodman, spare that tree!
  Touch not a single bough! [1]
In youth it sheltered me,
  And I'll protect it now.
      *Woodman, Spare That Tree.
        Stanza 1 [1830]*

The iron-armed soldier, the true-
    hearted soldier,
The gallant old soldier of Tippecanoe.[2]
      *Campaign Song for William
        Henry Harrison [1840]*

A song for our banner! The watchword
    recall
  Which gave the Republic her sta-
    tion:
"United we stand, divided we fall!" [3]
  It made and preserves us a nation! [4]
      *The Flag of Our Union.
        Stanza 1*

The union of lakes, the union of lands,
  The union of States none can sever,

---

[1] See Campbell, page 328. — It is interesting
to remember that the elm tree for which Morris pleaded stood just about where is now the
crossing of 98th Street and West End Avenue,
New York. See RIDER'S *Guide to New York
City, P. 346.*
[2] Harrison had distinguished himself in a
victorious battle with Indians, near Tippecanoe River [Indiana], November 7, 1811.
Morris's words, sung to the tune of "The Old
Oaken Bucket," were immensely popular. For
the first time in our land the power of song
was invoked to aid a Presidential candidate.
— BENJAMIN PERLEY POORE [1820–1887]:
Reminiscences, Vol. I, P. 233
[3] Then join hand in hand, brave Americans
all!
  By uniting we stand, by dividing we fall.
      JOHN DICKINSON [1732–1808]:
        The Liberty Song (1768)
[4] See Key, page 332.

The union of hearts, the union of
  hands,
And the flag of our Union forever!
      The Flag of Our Union.
              Refrain

Old Ironsides at anchor lay,
  In the harbor of Mahon;
A dead calm rested on the bay, —
  The waves to sleep had gone;
When little Hal, the captain's son,
  A lad both brave and good,
In sport, up shroud and rigging ran,
  And on the main truck stood!
    The Main Truck, A Leap for
        Life. Stanza 1

The land of the heart is the land of
  the West.
    The West. Stanza 1 (In Lit-
    tell's Magazine, April 5, 1851)

In other countries, when I heard
  The language of my own,
How fondly each familiar word
  Awoke an answering tone.
    I'm With You Once Again.
              Stanza 3

'Tis ever thus, when in life's storm
  Hope's star to man grows dim,
An angel kneels, in woman's form,
  And breathes a prayer for him.
      Pocahontas. Stanza 3

Near the lake where drooped the willow,
      Long time ago!
          Near the Lake

In teaching me the way to live
  It taught me how to die.
      My Mother's Bible.
             Stanza 4

EDWARD COOTE PINKNEY
[1802–1828]

I fill this cup to one made up
  Of loveliness alone,
A woman, of her gentle sex
  The seeming paragon;
To whom the better elements
  And kindly stars have given
A form so fair, that, like the air,
  'Tis less of earth than heaven.
            A Health

Her every tone is music's own,
  Like those of morning birds,
And something more than melody
  Dwells ever in her words.
            A Health

Look out upon the stars, my love,
  And shame them with thine eyes.
          A Serenade

WINTHROP MACKWORTH
PRAED
[1802–1839]

And oh! I shall find how, day by day,
  All thoughts and things look older;
How the laugh of pleasure grows less
  gay,
  And the heart of friendship colder.
    Twenty-eight and Twenty-nine

She was our queen, our rose, our star;
  And then she danced — O Heaven,
  her dancing!
      The Belle of the Ball

I remember, I remember [1]
  How my childhood fleeted by, —
The mirth of its December
  And the warmth of its July.
    I Remember, I Remember

I think, whatever mortals crave,
  With impotent endeavor,
A wreath, a rank, a throne, a grave —
  The world goes round forever;
I think that life is not too long,
  And therefore I determine
That many people read a song
  Who will not read a sermon. [2]
    The Chant of the Brazen Head.
              Stanza 1

His talk was like a stream which runs
  With rapid change from rocks to
  roses,
It slipped from politics to puns;
  It passed from Mahomet to Moses.
      The Vicar. Stanza 5

Events are writ by History's pen:
  Though causes are too much to care
  for: —
Fame talks about the where and when,

---

[1] See Thomas Hood, page 390.
[2] See Herbert, page 135.

While folly asks the why and wherefore.
>   *Epitaph on the Late King of*
>   *the Sandwich Islands. Stanza 4*

There are tones that will haunt us,
though lonely
Our path be o'er mountain or sea;
There are looks that will part from us
only
When memory ceases to be.
>   *Good-Night. Stanza 5*

His partners at the whist-club said
That he was faultless in his dealings.
>   *Quince. Stanza 3*

And cut the fiercest quarrel short
With "Patience, gentlemen, and
shuffle." [1]
>   *Ibid. Stanza 5*

My debts are paid; but Nature's debt
Almost escaped my recollection:
Tom! we shall meet again; and yet
I cannot leave you my direction.
>   *Ibid. Stanza 13*

Dame Fortune is a fickle gipsy,
And always blind, and often tipsy;
Sometimes for years and years to-
gether,
She'll bless you with the sunniest
weather,
Bestowing honour, pudding, pence,
You can't imagine why or whence; —
Then in a moment — Presto, pass! —
Your joys are withered like the grass.
>   *The Haunted Tree*

John Bull was beat at Waterloo!
They'll swear to that in France.
>   *Waterloo*

Of science and logic he chatters,
As fine and as fast as he can;
Though I am no judge of such matters,
I'm sure he's a talented man.
>   *The Talented Man*

MARIAN DIX SULLIVAN
[1802–1860]

Wild roved an Indian girl, bright Al-
farata,
Where sweep the waters of the blue
Juniata.
Swift as an antelope, through the for-
ests going,

[1] See Scott, page 311.

Loose were her jetty locks, in wavy
tresses flowing.
>   *The Blue Juniata* [1850].
>   *Stanza 1*

THOMAS LOVELL BEDDOES
[1803–1849]

The anchor heaves, the ship swings
free,
The sails swell full. To sea, to sea!
>   *Sailor's Song. Stanza 2*

If there were dreams to sell,
  What would you buy? [1]
Some cost a passing-bell;
  Some a light sigh.
>   *Dream-Pedlary*

Tell me how many beads there are
  In a silver chain
  Of evening rain,
Unravell'd from the tumbling main,
And threading the eye of a yellow star:
So many times do I love, again.
>   *Song. Stanza 2*

That divinest hope, which none can
know of
Who have not laid their dearest in the
grave.
>   *Death's Jest Book*

LAMAN BLANCHARD
[1803–1845]

Sooth 'twere a pleasant life to lead,
  With nothing in the world to do
But just to blow a shepherd's reed,
  The silent season thro'
And just to drive a flock to feed, —
  Sheep — quiet, fond and few!
>   *Dolce far Niente. Stanza 1*

Give me to live with Love alone
  And let the world go dine and dress;
For Love hath lowly haunts. . . .
If life's a flower, I choose my own —
'Tis "love in Idleness."
>   *Ibid. Stanza 4*

[1] If there were dreams to sell,
Do I not know full well
  What I would buy?
Hope's dear delusive spell,
It's happy tale to tell,
  Joy's fleeting sigh.
LOUISE CHANDLER MOULTON
[1835–1908]: *If There Were
Dreams to Sell, St. 1*

Pleasures lie thickest where no pleasures seem:
There's not a leaf that falls upon the
ground
But holds some joy of silence or of
sound,
Some sprite begotten of a summer
dream.

Sonnet, Hidden Joys

GEORGE BORROW
[1803–1881]

O England! long, long may it be ere
the sun of thy glory sink beneath the
wave of darkness! Though gloomy and
portentous clouds are now gathering
rapidly around thee, still, still may it
please the Almighty to disperse them,
and to grant thee a futurity longer in
duration and still brighter in renown
than thy past! Or, if thy doom be at
hand, may that doom be a noble one,
and worthy of her who has been styled
the Old Queen of the waters! May thou
sink, if thou dost sink, amidst blood
and flame, with a mighty noise, causing more than one nation to participate
in thy downfall!

The Bible in Spain [1842]

O ye gifted ones, follow your calling,
for, however various your talents may
be, ye can have but one calling capable
of leading ye to eminence and renown;
follow resolutely the one straight path
before you, it is that of your good
angel, let neither obstacles nor temptations induce ye to leave it; bound along
if you can; if not, on hands and knees
follow in it, perish in it, if needful; but
ye need not fear that; no one ever yet
died in the true path of his calling before he had attained the pinnacle.
Turn into other paths, and for a momentary advantage or gratification ye
have sold your inheritance, your immortality. Ye will never be heard of
after death.

Lavengro. Chap. 21 [1851]

Trust not a man's words if you
please, or you may come to very erroneous conclusions; but at all times
place implicit confidence in a man's
countenance in which there is no deceit;

and of necessity there can be none. If
people would but look each other more
in the face, we should have less cause to
complain of the deception of the world;
nothing so easy as physiognomy nor so
useful.

Lavengro. Chap. 22

Translation is at best an echo.

Ibid. Chap. 25

There's night and day, brother, both
sweet things; sun, moon, and stars,
brother, all sweet things; there's likewise a wind on the heath.[1] Life is very
sweet, brother; who would wish to
die?

Ibid.

I have known the time when a pugilistic encounter between two noted
champions was almost considered in
the light of a national affair; when tens
of thousands of individuals, high and
low, meditated and brooded upon it,
the first thing in the morning and the
last at night, until the great event was
decided.

Ibid. Chap. 26

I learnt . . . to fear God, and to
take my own part.

Ibid. Chap. 86

Youth is the only season for enjoyment, and the first twenty-five years
of one's life are worth all the rest of
the longest life of man, even though
those five-and-twenty be spent in penury and contempt, and the rest in the
possession of wealth, honours, respectability.

The Romany Rye. Chap. 30 [1857]

WILLIAM DRIVER
[1803–1886]

I name thee Old Glory.[2]

---

[1] He built life well, the gypsy-man
In those days gone by —
"There's the wind on the heath, brother,
And a quiet sky."
MARGARET WIDDEMER: *Gypsy Wis-
dom, St. 1*

[2] On August 10, 1831, a large American flag
was presented to Captain William Driver of
the brig *Charles Doggett* by a band of women,

RALPH WALDO EMERSON
[1803–1882]

Nor knowest thou what argument
Thy life to thy neighbor's creed has
    lent.
All are needed by each one;
Nothing is fair or good alone.
          Each and All. Stanza 1

I wiped away the weeds and foam,
I fetched my sea-born treasures home;
But the poor, unsightly, noisome things
Had left their beauty on the shore,
With the sun and the sand and the wild
    uproar.
          Ibid. Stanza 3

I like a church; I like a cowl;
I love a prophet of the soul;
And on my heart monastic aisles
Fall like sweet strains or pensive
    smiles;
Yet not for all his faith can see
Would I that cowléd churchman be.
          The Problem. Stanza 1

Not from a vain or shallow thought
His awful Jove young Phidias brought.
          Ibid. Stanza 2

The hand that rounded Peter's dome,
And groined the aisles of Christian
    Rome,
Wrought in a sad sincerity;
Himself from God he could not free;
He builded better than he knew; —
The conscious stone to beauty grew.
          Ibid.

Earth proudly wears the Parthenon
As the best gem upon her zone.
          Ibid. Stanza 3

---

in recognition of his humane service in bringing back the British mutineers of the ship
Bounty from Tahiti to their former home, Pit-
cairn Island. As the flag was hoisted to the
masthead, Captain Driver proclaimed, "I
name thee Old Glory." The flag is now in the
Smithsonian Institution, Washington, D. C.

Who gave you, Old Glory, the name that you
    bear
With such pride everywhere
As you cast yourself free to the rapturous air
And leap out full-length?
    JAMES WHITCOMB RILEY [1849–1916]:
    The Name of Old Glory, St. 1 [1898]

The passive Master lent his hand
To the vast soul that o'er him planned.[1]
          The Problem. Stanza 3

Enclosed
In a tumultuous privacy of storm.
          The Snow-Storm

Life is too short to waste
In critic peep or cynic bark,
Quarrel or reprimand:
'Twill soon be dark;
Up! mind thine own aim, and
God speed the mark!
          To J. W.

There's no rood has not a star above it.
          Musketaquid

All sorts of things and weather
Must be taken in together,
To make up a year
And a Sphere.
      *Fable, The Mountain and the
                Squirrel*

Good-bye, proud world! I'm going
    home;
Thou art not my friend and I'm not
    thine.[2]
          Good-bye. Stanza 1

Oh, when I am safe in my sylvan home,
I tread on the pride of Greece and
    Rome;
And when I am stretched beneath the
    pines
Where the evening star so holy shines,
I laugh at the lore and the pride of
    man,
At the sophist schools, and the learned
    clan;
For what are they all in their high con-
    ceit,
When man in the bush with God may
    meet.[3]
          Ibid. Stanza 4

Let me go where'er I will,
I hear a sky-born music still.
          Fragments

[1] This couplet is inscribed on the boulder
marking Emerson's grave in Sleepy Hollow
Cemetery, Concord, Massachusetts.
[2] See Byron, page 353.
[3] Inscribed on the boulder, a memorial to
Emerson, Schoolmaster's Hill, Franklin Park,
Boston.

But in the mud and scum of things
There alway, alway something sings.
                              Fragments

        If eyes were made for seeing,
Then Beauty is its own excuse for being.[1]
                              The Rhodora

Things are in the saddle,
    And ride mankind.[2]
            *Ode Inscribed to W. H. Chan-
                              ning*

Olympian bards who sung
    Divine ideas below,
Which always find us young,
    And always keep us so.
            The Poet. Ode to Beauty

Heartily know,
When half-gods go,
The gods arrive.
            Give All to Love. Stanza 4

Love not the flower they pluck, and
    know it not,
And all their botany is Latin names.
                              Blight

By the rude bridge that arched the
    flood,
    Their flag to April's breeze un-
    furled,
Here once the embattled farmers
    stood,
    And fired the shot heard round the
    world.[3]
            *Hymn sung at the Completion
            of the Battle Monument, Con-
            cord [April 19, 1836].*
                              Stanza 1

Hast thou named all the birds without
    a gun;[4]

---

[1]   The beautiful seems right,
    By force of beauty.
        E. B. BROWNING: *Aurora Leigh, Book I*
[2] I never could believe that Providence had
sent a few men into the world ready booted
and spurred to ride, and millions ready saddled and bridled to be ridden. — RICHARD
RUMBOLD [1622–1685], colonel of horse regiment, Argyll's expedition to Scotland: *Statement on the scaffold*
[3] No war or battle sound
    Was heard the world around.
        MILTON: *Hymn of Christ's
                              Nativity, L. 31*
[4] To the hunters who hunt for the gunless
    game

Loved the wood-rose, and left it on its
    stalk?
                              Forbearance

And striving to be man, the worm
Mounts through all the spires of form.
                              May-Day

God said, I am tired of kings,
I suffer them no more.
            Boston Hymn [January 1, 1863].
                              Stanza 1

Oh, tenderly the haughty day
    Fills his blue urn with fire.
            Ode, Concord [July 4, 1857].
                              Stanza 1

Go put your creed into your deed,
    Nor speak with double tongue.
                      Ibid. Stanza 5

I think no virtue goes with size.
                              The Titmouse

For well the soul, if stout within,
Can arm impregnably the skin.
                              Ibid.

So nigh is grandeur to our dust,
    So near is God to man,
When Duty whispers low, *Thou must,*
    The youth replies, *I can.*
                      Voluntaries. III

Nor sequent centuries could hit
Orbit and sum of Shakespeare's wit.
                              Solution

Born for success he seemed,
With grace to win, with heart to hold,
With shining gifts that took all eyes.
                              In Memoriam

Nor mourn the unalterable Days
That Genius goes and Folly stays.
                              Ibid.

Fear not, then, thou child infirm,
There's no god dare wrong a worm.
                      Compensation. I

He thought it happier to be dead,
To die for Beauty, than live for bread.
                              Beauty

Wilt thou seal up the avenues of ill?
Pay every debt, as if God wrote the
    bill.
                      "Suum Cuique"

Too busied with the crowded hour to
    fear to live or die.
                              Nature

The streams and the woods belong.
    SAM WALTER FOSS [1858–1911]:
    The Bloodless Sportsman, St. 3

Damsels of Time, the hypocritic Days,
Muffled and dumb like Barefoot der-
   vishes,
And marching single in an endless file,
Bring diadems and fagots in their
   hands.
Days

I, too late,
Under her solemn fillet saw the scorn.
Ibid.

It is time to be old,
To take in sail.
Terminus

Obey the voice at eve obeyed at prime.
Ibid.

Though love repine, and reason chafe,
   There came a voice without reply, —
" 'Tis man's perdition to be safe,
   When for the truth he ought to die."
Sacrifice

For what avail the plough or sail,
Or land or life, if freedom fail?
Boston. Stanza 5

What care though rival cities soar
   Along the stormy coast,
Penn's town, New York, and Balti-
   more,
   If Boston knew the most!
Ibid. Stanza 9

If the red slayer think he slays,
   Or if the slain think he is slain,
They know not well the subtle ways
   I keep, and pass, and turn again.
Brahma

They reckon ill who leave me out;
   When me they fly, I am the wings;
I am the doubter and the doubt,
   And I the hymn the Brahmin sings.
Ibid.

Draw, if thou canst, the mystic line,
Severing rightly his from thine,
Which is human, which divine.
Worship

Nor scour the seas, nor sift mankind,
A poet or a friend to find:
Behold, he watches at the door!
Behold his shadow on the floor!
Saadi

Go where he will, the wise man is at
   home,
His hearth the earth, — his hall the
   azure dome.
Wood-Notes. I, 3

That book is good
Which puts me in a working mood.
Unless to Thought is added Will,
Apollo is an imbecile.
The Poet

In the vaunted works of Art
The master-stroke is Nature's part.[1]
Art

There is no great and no small [2]
   To the Soul that maketh all:
And where it cometh, all things are;
   And it cometh everywhere.
History

I am the owner of the sphere,
Of the seven stars and the solar year,
Of Caesar's hand, and Plato's brain,
Of Lord Christ's heart, and Shake-
   speare's strain.
Ibid.

Ever from one who comes to-morrow
Men wait their good and truth to bor-
   row.
Merlin's Wisdom

The music that can deepest reach,
And cure all ill, is cordial speech.
Ibid.

A day for toil, an hour for sport,
But for a friend is life too short.
Ibid.

Some of your hurts you have cured,
And the sharpest you still have sur-
   vived,
But what torments of grief you en-
   dured
From evils which never arrived!
Borrowing [*From the French*]

He who has a thousand friends has not
   a friend to spare,
And he who has one enemy will meet
   him everywhere.
Translation [3]

A ruddy drop of manly blood
   The surging sea outweighs,

---

[1] Nature paints the best part of a picture, carves the best part of the statue, builds the best part of the house, and speaks the best part of the oration. — *Society and Solitude, Art*

[2] No great, no small. — POPE: *Essay on Man, Epistle I, L. 279*

[3] In his essay, *Considerations by the Way,* Emerson credits this couplet to "an Eastern poet, Ali Ben Abu Taleb," and changes *will* to *shall* in the second line.

The world uncertain comes and goes,
The lover rooted stays.
Friendship

Me too thy nobleness has taught
To master my despair;
The fountains of my hidden life
Are through thy friendship fair.
Ibid.

Time dissipates to shining ether the solid angularity of facts.
History

There is properly no History; only Biography.[1]
Ibid.

Nature is a mutable cloud, which is always and never the same.
Ibid.

A man is a bundle of relations, a knot of roots, whose flower and fruitage is the world.
Ibid.

The virtue in most request is conformity. Self-reliance is its aversion. It loves not realities and creators, but names and customs.
Self-Reliance

Whoso would be a man must be a non-conformist.
Ibid.

A foolish consistency is the hobgoblin of little minds, adored by little statesmen and philosophers and divines.
Ibid.

To be great is to be misunderstood.
Ibid.

An institution is the lengthened shadow of one man.
Ibid.

Nothing can bring you peace but yourself.
Ibid.

Every sweet has its sour; every evil its good.
Compensation

For every thing you have missed, you have gained something else; and for every thing you gain, you lose something.
Ibid.

[1] See Carlyle, page 380.

Everything in Nature contains all the powers of Nature. Everything is made of one hidden stuff.
Compensation

It is as impossible for a man to be cheated by any one but himself, as for a thing to be, and not to be, at the same time.
Ibid.

There is no luck in literary reputation. They who make up the final verdict upon every book are not the partial and noisy readers of the hour when it appears; but a court as of angels, a public not to be bribed, not to be entreated, and not to be overawed, decides upon every man's title to fame.
Spiritual Laws

All mankind love a lover.
Love

No man ever forgot the visitations of that power to his heart and brain, which created all things new; which was the dawn in him of music, poetry, and art.
Ibid.

Thou art to me a delicious torment.
Friendship

Happy is the house that shelters a friend.
Ibid.

A friend is a person with whom I may be sincere. Before him, I may think aloud.
Ibid.

A friend may well be reckoned the masterpiece of Nature.
Ibid.

Two may talk and one may hear, but three cannot take part in a conversation of the most sincere and searching sort.
Ibid.

The only reward of virtue is virtue; the only way to have a friend is to be one.
Ibid.

I do then with my friends as I do with my books. I would have them where I can find them, but I seldom use them.
Ibid.

Do what we can, summer will have its flies. If we walk in the woods, we must feed mosquitoes.

Prudence

In skating over thin ice our safety is our speed.

Ibid.

Heroism feels and never reasons and therefore is always right.

Heroism

Nothing great was ever achieved without enthusiasm.

Circles

Nothing astonishes men so much as common sense and plain dealing.

Art

Nature and Books belong to the eyes that see them.

Experience

No house, though it were the Tuileries, or the Escurial, is good for anything without a master.

Manners

The only gift is a portion of thyself.

Gifts

The less government we have, the better — the fewer laws, and the less confided power.

Politics

Money, which represents the prose of life, and which is hardly spoken of in parlors without an apology, is, in its effects and laws, as beautiful as roses.

Nominalist and Realist

Every man is wanted, and no man is wanted much.

Ibid.

And with Cæsar to take in his hand the army, the empire, and Cleopatra, and say, "All these will I relinquish if you will show me the fountains of the Nile."

New England Reformers

The reward of a thing well done, is to have done it.

Ibid.

Poetry teaches the enormous force of a few words, and, in proportion to the inspiration, checks loquacity.

Parnassus. Preface

There are two classes of poets, — the poets by education and practice, these we respect; and poets by nature, these we love.

Parnassus. Preface

No lover of poetry can spare Chaucer, or should grudge the short study required to command the archaisms of his English, and the skill to read the melody of his verse.[1]

Ibid.

He is great who is what he is from Nature, and who never reminds us of others.

Representative Men. Uses of Great Men

Cecil's saying of Sir Walter Raleigh, "I know that he can toil terribly," is an electric touch.

Ibid.

When nature removes a great man, people explore the horizon for a successor; but none comes, and none will. His class is extinguished with him. In some other and quite different field, the next man will appear.

Ibid.

Every hero becomes a bore at last.

Ibid.

Great geniuses have the shortest biographies.

Ibid. Plato; or, The Philosopher

Keep cool: it will be all one a hundred years hence.

Ibid. Montaigne; or, The Skeptic

Is not marriage an open question, when it is alleged, from the beginning of the world, that such as are in the institution wish to get out, and such as are out wish to get in?[2]

Ibid.

Thought is the property of him who can entertain it, and of him who can adequately place it.

Ibid. Shakespeare; or, The Poet

---

[1] The influence of Chaucer is conspicuous in all our early literature; and, more recently, . . . in the whole society of English writers, a large unacknowledged debt is easily traced. One is charmed with the opulence which feeds so many pensioners. — *Representative Men, Shakespeare*

[2] See Sir John Davies, page 115.

"There shall be no Alps," he said.

Representative Men. Napoleon;
or, The Man of the World

[Napoleon] directed Bourrienne to leave all his letters unopened for three weeks, and then observed with satisfaction how large a part of the correspondence had thus disposed of itself, and no longer required an answer.

Ibid.

Classics which at home are drowsily read have a strange charm in a country inn, or in the transom of a merchant brig.

English Traits

The favorite phrase of their law is "a custom whereof the memory of man runneth not back to the contrary." [1]

Ibid.

The hearing ear is always found close to the speaking tongue.

Ibid. Race

I find the Englishman to be him of all men who stands firmest in his shoes.

Ibid. Manners

A creative economy is the fuel of magnificence.

Ibid. Aristocracy

Coal is a portable climate.

Conduct of Life. Wealth

The world is his, who has money to go over it.

Ibid.

The farmer is covetous of his dollar, and with reason. . . . He knows how many strokes of labor it represents. His bones ache with the day's work that earned it.

Ibid.

Art is a jealous mistress,[2] and, if a man have a genius for painting, poetry, music, architecture, or philosophy, he makes a bad husband, and an ill-provider.

Ibid.

[1] See Blackstone, page 248.
[2] Blackstone's confession of his own original preference for literature, and his perception that the law was "a jealous mistress," who would suffer no rival in his affections. — W. D. Howells: *My Literary Passions, Chap. 19*

One of the benefits of a college education is to show the boy its little avail.

Conduct of Life. Culture

All educated Americans, first or last, go to Europe.

Ibid.

Solitude, the safeguard of mediocrity, is to genius the stern friend.

Ibid.

A man known to us only as a celebrity in politics or in trade, gains largely in our esteem if we discover that he has some intellectual taste or skill.

Ibid.

There is always a best way of doing everything, if it be to boil an egg. Manners are the happy ways of doing things.

Ibid. Behavior

Your manners are always under examination, and by committees little suspected, — a police in citizens' clothes, — but are awarding or denying you very high prizes when you least think of it.

Ibid.

The alleged power to charm down insanity, or ferocity in beasts, is a power behind the eye.

Ibid.

Fine manners need the support of fine manners in others.

Ibid.

The highest compact we can make with our fellow is, — "Let there be truth between us two forevermore."

Ibid.

It is sublime to feel and say of another, I need never meet, or speak, or write to him: we need not reinforce ourselves, or send tokens of remembrance: I rely on him as on myself: if he did thus or thus, I know it was right.

Ibid.

There is no beautifier of complexion, or form, or behavior, like the wish to scatter joy and not pain around us.

Ibid.

We must be as courteous to a man as we are to a picture, which we are willing to give the advantage of a good light.

Ibid.

There is one topic peremptorily forbidden to all well-bred, to all rational mortals, namely, their distempers. If you have not slept, or if you have slept, or if you have headache, or sciatica, or leprosy, or thunder-stroke, I beseech you, by all angels, to hold your peace.

Conduct of Life. Behavior

Shallow men believe in luck.[1]

Ibid. Worship

'Tis a Dutch proverb, that "paint costs nothing," such are its preserving qualities in damp climates.

Ibid. Considerations by the Way

Our chief want in life is somebody who shall make us do what we can.

Ibid.

Make yourself necessary to somebody.

Ibid.

Beauty without grace is the hook without the bait.

Ibid. Beauty

Never read any book that is not a year old.

Ibid. In Praise of Books

I should as soon think of swimming across Charles River, when I wish to go to Boston, as of reading all my books in originals, when I have them rendered for me in my mother tongue.

Ibid.

He who has mastered any law in his private thoughts, is master to that extent of all men whose language he speaks, and of all into whose language his own can be translated.

The American Scholar

Wherever Macdonald sits, there is the head of the table.[2]

Ibid.

If the single man plant himself indomitably on his instincts, and there

abide, the huge world will come round to him.[1]

The American Scholar

Give me health and a day, and I will make the pomp of emperors ridiculous.

*Nature, Addresses and Lectures.
Chap. 3, Beauty*

Men grind and grind in the mill of a truism, and nothing comes out but what was put in. But the moment they desert the tradition for a spontaneous thought, then poetry, wit, hope, virtue, learning, anecdote, all flock to their aid.

Literary Ethics

God may forgive sins, he said, but awkwardness has no forgiveness in heaven or earth.

Society and Solitude

The most advanced nations are always those who navigate the most.

Ibid. Civilization

Hitch your wagon to a star.

Ibid.

The true test of civilization is, not the census, nor the size of cities, nor the crops — no, but the kind of man the country turns out.

Ibid.

Raphael paints wisdom; Handel sings it, Phidias carves it, Shakespeare writes it, Wren builds it, Columbus sails it, Luther preaches it, Washington arms it, Watt mechanizes it.

Ibid. Art

Every genuine work of art has as much reason for being as the earth and the sun.

Ibid.

We boil at different degrees.

Ibid. Eloquence

The ornament of a house is the friends who frequent it.

Ibid. Domestic Life

---

[1] Luck is infatuated with the efficient. *Persian proverb.*

[2] Let me sit wherever I will, that will still be the upper end. — CERVANTES: *Don Quixote, Part II, Chap. 31*

Emerson's sentence is usually quoted with the substitution of "Macgregor" for "Macdonald." When Theodore Parker quoted it, he said "Highlander" in place of "Macdonald."

[1] Everything comes if a man will only wait. — DISRAELI: *Tancred, Book IV, Chap. 8*

Everything comes to him who waits
If he waits in a place that's meet,
But never wait for an uptown car
On the downtown side of the street.

Modern jingle.

We have the newspaper, which does its best to make every square acre of land and sea give an account of itself at your breakfast-table.[1]

Society and Solitude.
Works and Days

Can anybody remember when the times were not hard and money not scarce?

Ibid.

A man builds a fine house; and now he has a master, and a task for life; he is to furnish, watch, show it, and keep it in repair the rest of his days.

Ibid.

We do not count a man's years until he has nothing else to count.

Ibid. Old Age

The establishment of Christianity in the world does not rest on any miracle but the miracle of being the broadest and most humane doctrine.

Miscellanies. Character

Life is not so short but that there is always time enough for courtesy.

Letters and Social Aims. Social Aims

I have heard with admiring submission the experience of the lady who declared that the sense of being well-dressed gives a feeling of inward tranquillity which religion is powerless to bestow.[2]

Ibid.

Do not say things. What you are stands over you the while, and thunders so that I cannot hear what you say to the contrary.

Ibid.

Abraham Lincoln . . . who was at home and welcome with the humblest, and with a spirit and a practical vein in the times of terror that commanded the admiration of the wisest. His heart was as great as the world, but there was no room in it to hold the memory of a wrong.

Greatness

[1] The news! Our morning, noon and evening cry;
Day unto day repeats it till we die.
CHARLES SPRAGUE: *Curiosity*
[2] The lady was Miss Cornelia Frances Forbes [1817–1911] of Milton, Massachusetts.

Next to the originator of a go. tence is the first quoter of it.[1]

Quotation and Origina.

When Shakespeare is charged wit. debts to his authors, Landor replies, "Yet he was more original than his originals. He breathed upon dead bodies and brought them into life."

Ibid.

In fact, it is as difficult to appropriate the thoughts of others as it is to invent.

Ibid.

By necessity, by proclivity, and by delight, we all quote.

Ibid.

Every good poem that I know I recall by its rhythm also. Rhyme is a pretty good measure of the latitude and opulence of a writer. If unskilled, he is at once detected by the poverty of his chimes.

Poetry and Imagination

A good poem goes about the world offering itself to reasonable men, who read it with joy and carry it to their reasonable neighbors.

Morals

Wit makes its own welcome, and levels all distinctions.

The Comic

The perception of the comic is a tie of sympathy with other men.

Ibid.

All thoughts of a turtle are turtles, and of a rabbit, rabbits.

The Natural History of Intellect

What is a weed? A plant whose virtues have not yet been discovered.

Fortune of the Republic

[1] There is not less wit nor less invention in applying rightly a thought one finds in a book, than in being the first author of that thought. Cardinal du Perron has been heard to say that the happy application of a verse of Virgil has deserved a talent. — BAYLE: *Vol. II, P. 779*
Though old the thought and oft exprest,
'Tis his at last who says it best.
LOWELL: *For an Autograph*
He who first praises a book becomingly, is next in merit to the author. — WALTER SAVAGE LANDOR

Great men are they who see that spiritual is stronger than any material force; that thoughts rule the world.

Progress of Culture, Phi Beta Kappa Address [July 18, 1867]

I wish to write such rhymes as shall not suggest a restraint, but contrariwise the wildest freedom.

Journal. June 27, 1839

I trust a good deal to common fame, as we all must. If a man has good corn, or wood, or boards, or pigs to sell, or can make better chairs or knives, crucibles or church organs than anybody else, you will find a broad, hard-beaten road to his house, though it be in the woods.[1]

Journals, edited by Edward Waldo Emerson and Waldo Emerson Forbes [1912], *Vol. 8, P. 528–529, 1855*

[1] The editors appended a footnote: "There has been much inquiry in the newspapers recently as to whether Mr. Emerson wrote a sentence very like the above, which has been attributed to him in print. The editors do not find the latter in his works, but there can be little doubt that it was a memory quotation by some hearer, or quite probably correctly reported from one of his lectures — the same image in differing words."

The West Publishing Company, St. Paul, Minnesota, in an advertisement of the National Reporting System, adapted the Emerson passage to read: "If you write a better book, or preach a better sermon, or build a better mousetrap than your neighbor, the world will make a beaten path to your door."

In *Borrowings,* compiled by MRS. SARAH S. B. YULE and MARY S. KEENE [Dodge Publishing Company, 1889], Mrs. Yule includes the "mousetrap quotation" as written in her notebook, copied from an address heard many years before, this being the first known definite credit to Emerson.

In a Roycroft publication, *The Philistine, July, 1912,* H. T. MORGAN claimed the authorship for Elbert Hubbard [1859–1915], but did not state where and when Mr. Hubbard had printed the "modern proverb," as he termed it. In an earlier Roycroft periodical, *The Fra, May, 1911,* it is said that Mr. Hubbard wrote the "mousetrap" paragraph, and to give it "specific gravity," attributed it to Ralph Waldo Emerson.

A New York shoe store proprietor claimed that Mr. Hubbard wrote the paragraph for his store, and exhibits a framed copy of it.

The *Boston Evening Transcript, Notes and Queries Department, October 14, 1922,* printed

GERALD GRIFFIN
[1803–1840]

A place in thy memory, dearest,
  Is all that I claim;
To pause and look back when thou hearest
  The sound of my name.

A Place in Thy Memory. Stanza 1

When, like the rising day,
  Eileen aroon!
Love sends his early ray,
  Eileen aroon!
What makes his dawning glow
Changeless through joy or woe?
Only the constant know! —
  Eileen aroon!

Eileen Aroon. Stanza 3

On the ocean that hollows the rocks where ye dwell,
A shadowy land has appeared, as they tell;
Men thought it a region of sunshine and rest,
And they called it Hy-Brasail, the isle of the blest.

Hy-Brasail, Isle of the Blest. Stanza 1

ROBERT STEPHEN HAWKER
[1803–1875]

And shall Trelawny die?
Here's twenty thousand Cornish men
Will know the reason why.[1]

The Song of the Western Men. Stanza 1

a compilation of information concerning this famous quotation; and *The Colophon, First Series, XIX,* and *New Series, I, 1,* contains monographs on the subject by BURTON E. STEVENSON.

If a man builds a better mousetrap than his neighbor, the world will not only beat a path to his door, it will make newsreels of him and his wife in beach pajamas, it will discuss his diet and his health, it will publish heart-throb stories of his love life, it will publicize him, analyze him, photograph him, and make his life thoroughly miserable by feeding to the palpitant public intimate details of things that are none of its damned business. — NEWMAN LEVY: [1888–   ] *The Right To Be Let Alone* (In *American Mercury, June, 1935*)

[1] This ballad commemorates the commitment to the Tower of London of Sir Jonathan Trelawny [1650–1721], with six other

RICHARD HENRY HENGIST HORNE
[1803–1884]

'Tis always morning somewhere in the world.[1]
Orion. Book III, Canto II [1843]
A sweet content
Passing all wisdom or its fairest flower.
Ibid.
The wisdom of mankind creeps slowly on,
Subject to every doubt that can retard
Or fling it back upon an earlier time.
Ibid.
Ye rigid Plowmen! Bear in mind
Your labor is for future hours.
Advance! spare not! nor look behind!
Plow deep and straight with all your powers!
The Plow

DOUGLAS JERROLD
[1803–1857]

He is one of those wise philanthropists who in a time of famine would vote for nothing but a supply of toothpicks.
Douglas Jerrold's Wit
Dogmatism is puppyism come to its full growth.
Ibid.
The surest way to hit a woman's heart is to take aim kneeling.
Ibid.
That fellow would vulgarize the day of judgment.
A Comic Author
The best thing I know between France and England is the sea.
The Anglo-French Alliance

The life of the husbandman, — a life fed by the bounty of earth and sweetened by the airs of heaven.
The Husbandman's Life
Some people are so fond of ill-luck that they run half-way to meet it.
Meeting Troubles Half-Way
Earth is here [Australia] so kind, that just tickle her with a hoe and she laughs with a harvest.
A Land of Plenty
The ugliest of trades have their moments of pleasure. Now, if I were a grave-digger, or even a hangman, there are some people I could work for with a great deal of enjoyment.
Ugly Trades
He was so good he would pour rose-water on a toad.
A Charitable Man
As for the brandy, "nothing extenuate"; and the water, put nought in in malice.
Shakespeare Grog
Talk to him of Jacob's ladder, and he would ask the number of the steps.
A Matter-of-fact Man
That questionable superfluity — small beer.[1]
The Tragedy of the Till

JAMES CLARENCE MANGAN
[1803–1849]

I see thee ever in my dreams,
    Karaman!
Thy hundred hills, thy thousand streams,
    Karaman, O Karaman!
As when thy gold-bright morning gleams,
As when the deepening sunset seams
With lines of light thy hills and streams,
    Karaman!
The Karamanian Exile.[2] Stanza 1

---

prelates, in 1688, for refusing to recognize the Declaration of Indulgence issued by King James II. Hawker wrote the ballad in 1825, and it was praised by Sir Walter Scott and Macaulay, under the impression that it was an ancient song. "And shall Trelawny die?" has been a popular phrase throughout Cornwall since the imprisonment of the seven bishops.
[1] 'Tis always morning somewhere. — LONGFELLOW: *Tales of a Wayside Inn, The Birds of Killingworth*

[1] Small beer. — SHAKESPEARE: *King Henry IV, Part II, Act II, Sc. 2, L. 8 and 13; Othello, Act II, Sc. 1, L. 160*
[2] JAMES RYDER RANDALL used this poem as a pattern when writing *Maryland, my Maryland.*

He too had tears for all souls in trouble,
Here and in hell.
The Nameless One. Stanza 14

CHARLES SWAIN
[1803–1874]

Let to-morrow take care of to-
morrow, —
Leave things of the future to fate;
What's the use to anticipate sorrow? —
Life's troubles come never too late!
Imaginary Evils. Stanza 1

Though poor be our purse, and though
narrow our span,
Let us all try to do a good turn when
we can.
Do a Good Turn When You Can

For there's a heart for every one,
If every one could find it!
A Heart for Every One. Stanza 1

Home's not merely four square walls,
Though with pictures hung and
gilded;
Home is where Affection calls, —
Filled with shrines the Heart hath
builded.
Home. Stanza 1

SARAH HELEN POWER
WHITMAN
[1803–1878]

Star of resplendent front! Thy glorious
eye
Shines on me still from out yon clouded
sky.
Arcturus (To Edgar Allan Poe)

Tell him I lingered alone on the shore,
Where we parted, in sorrow, to meet
nevermore;
The night-wind blew cold on my deso-
late heart
But colder those wild words of doom,
— "Ye must part."
Our Island of Dreams

The sweet imperious mouth, whose
haughty valor
Defied all portents of impending doom.
The Portrait [of Poe]

Warm lights are on the sleepy uplands
waning
Beneath soft clouds along the horizon
rolled,

Till the slant sunbeams through the
fringes raining
Bathe all the hills in melancholy gold.
A Still Day in Autumn. Stanza 4

Enchantress of the stormy seas,
Priestess of Night's high mysteries.
Moonrise in May

The summer skies are darkly blue,
The days are still and bright,
And Evening trails her robes of gold
Through the dim halls of Night.[1]
Summer's Call

Raven from the dim dominions
On the Night's Plutonian shore,[2]
Oft I hear thy dusky pinions
Wave and flutter round my door —
See the shadow of thy pinions
Float along the moonlit floor.
The Raven

BENJAMIN DISRAELI,
EARL OF BEACONSFIELD
[1804–1881]

Yes, I am a Jew, and when the ancestors of the right honourable gentleman were brutal savages in an unknown
island, mine were priests in the temple
of Solomon.[3]
*Reply to a taunt by
Daniel O'Connell* [4]

---

[1] I heard the trailing garments of the Night
Sweep through her marble halls.
LONGFELLOW: *Hymn to the Night.
Stanza 1*

[2] Night's Plutonian shore. — POE: *The Raven, St. 8*

[3] You called me a damned Jew. My race
was old when you were all savages. I am
proud to be a Jew.
JOHN GALSWORTHY: *Loyalties, Act II, Sc. 1*
[Quoting a Hungarian friend] We Magyars
are a very old race; we have a civilization of
a thousand years. A thousand years ago, at a
time when your ancestors were savages hunting in the swamps of what is now London,
my ancestors had discovered that a man who
tells the truth is very likely to be disagreeable.
A. EDWARD NEWTON: *Derby Day, Chap. 14*
[4] Disraeli's name shows he is by descent
a Jew. His father became a convert. He is the
better for that in this world, and I hope he
will be the better for it in the next. I have the
happiness of being acquainted with some Jewish families in London, and among them more
accomplished ladies, or more humane, cordial,
high-minded, or better-educated gentlemen I

I will sit down now, but the time will come when you will hear me.[1]
Maiden Speech in the House of Commons [1837]

Free trade is not a principle, it is an expedient.[2]
On Import Duties [April 25, 1843]

The noble lord [3] is the Rupert of debate.[4]
Speech [April, 1844]

The Right Honorable gentleman [5] caught the Whigs bathing and walked away with their clothes.
Speech, House of Commons [February 28, 1845]

A conservative government is an organized hypocrisy.
Speech on Agricultural Interests [March 17, 1845]

A precedent embalms a principle.
Speech on the Expenditures of the Country [February 22, 1848]

Justice is truth in action.
Speech [February 11, 1851]

It is much easier to be critical than to be correct.
Speech [January 24, 1860]

Posterity is a most limited assembly. Those gentlemen who reach posterity are not much more numerous than the planets.
Speech [June 3, 1862]

---

have never met. It will not be supposed, therefore, that when I speak of Disraeli as the descendant of a Jew, that I mean to tarnish him on that account. They were once the chosen people of God. There were miscreants among them, however, also, and it must certainly have been from one of these that Disraeli descended. He possesses just the qualities of the impenitent thief who died upon the Cross, whose name, I verily believe, must have been Disraeli.
DANIEL O'CONNELL [1775–1847]: *Speech*, at trades union meeting in Dublin [1835]
[1] I will be heard! — WILLIAM LLOYD GARRISON: *Salutatory* of his paper, *The Liberator*, January 1, 1831
[2] It is a condition which confronts us, not a theory. — GROVER CLEVELAND: *Annual Message* [1887], referring to the tariff
[3] Lord Stanley.
[4] See Bulwer Lytton, page 425.
[5] Sir Robert Peel.

The characteristic of the present age is craving credulity.
Speech at Oxford Diocesan Conference [November 25, 1864]

What is the question now placed before society with the glib assurance which to me is most astonishing? That question is this: Is man an ape or an angel? [1] I, my lord, I am on the side of the angels. I repudiate with indignation and abhorrence those new fangled theories.
Ibid.

There are rare instances when the sympathy of a nation approaches those tenderer feelings which are generally supposed to be peculiar to the individual and to be the happy privilege of private life; and this is one.
Address, House of Commons [May 1, 1865]

In the character of the victim [Lincoln], and even in the accessories of his last moments, there is something so homely and innocent that it takes the question, as it were, out of all the pomp of history and the ceremonial of diplomacy — it touches the heart of nations and appeals to the domestic sentiment of mankind.
Ibid.

Ignorance never settles a question.
Ibid. [May 14, 1866]

Individualities may form communities, but it is institutions alone that can create a nation.
Speech at Manchester [1866]

However gradual may be the growth of confidence, that credit requires still more time to arrive at maturity.
Speech [November 9, 1867]

The secret of success is constancy to purpose.
Speech [June 24, 1870]

The author who speaks about his own books is almost as bad as a mother who talks about her own children.
Speech [November 19, 1870]

Increased means and increased leisure are the two civilizers of man.
Speech to the Conservatives of Manchester [April 3, 1872]

[1] See C. R. Darwin, page 448.

A university should be a place of light, of liberty, and of learning.
Speech, House of Commons
[March 8, 1873]

The health of the people is really the foundation upon which all their happiness and all their powers as a State depend.
Speech [July 24, 1877]

A sophisticated rhetorician [Gladstone], inebriated with the exuberance of his own verbosity, and gifted with an egotistical imagination that can at all times command an interminable and inconsistent series of arguments to malign an opponent and to glorify himself.
Speech at Riding School, London
[July 27, 1878]

A series of congratulatory regrets.
Lord Hartington's Resolution on the Berlin Treaty [July 30, 1878]

The hare-brained chatter of irresponsible frivolity.
Speech, Guildhall, London
[November 9, 1878]

The microcosm of a public school.
Vivian Grey. Book I, Chap. II
[1826]

I hate definitions.
Ibid. Book II, Chap. VI

Experience is the child of Thought, and Thought is the child of Action. We can not learn men from books.
Ibid. Book V, Chap. I

Variety is the mother of Enjoyment.
Ibid. Chap. IV

There is moderation even in excess.
Ibid. Book VI, Chap. I

I repeat . . . that all power is a trust; that we are accountable for its exercise; that from the people and for the people all springs, and all must exist.[1]
Ibid. Chap. VII

Man is not the creature of circumstances. Circumstances are the creatures of men.[2]
Ibid.

[1] See Webster, page 341, Lincoln, page 456, and Parker, page 477.
[2] See Carlyle, page 377.

The disappointment of manhood succeeds to the delusion of youth: let us hope that the heritage of old age is not despair.
Vivian Grey. Book VIII,
Chap. IV

A dark horse [1] which had never been thought of, and which the careless St. James had never even observed in the list, rushed past the grand stand in sweeping triumph.
The Young Duke. Book I, Chap. V
[1831]

What we anticipate seldom occurs; [2] what we least expected generally happens.
Henrietta Temple. Book II,
Chap. IV [1837]

Nature has given us two ears but only one mouth.
Ibid. Book VI, Chap. XXIV

Youth is a blunder; manhood a struggle; old age a regret.
Coningsby. Book III, Chap. I
[1844]

Property has its duties as well as its rights.[3]
Sybil. Book II, Chap. XI [1845]

Little things affect little minds.
Ibid. Book III, Chap. II

We all of us live too much in a circle.[4]
Ibid. Chap. VII

Mr. Kremlin was distinguished for ignorance; for he had only one idea, and that was wrong.[5]
Ibid. Book IV, Chap. V

[1] A political phrase common in the United States, drawn from racing cant, referring to a little-known competitor who comes to the fore unexpectedly.
[2] What torments of grief you endured
From evils which never arrived.
EMERSON: *Borrowing*
[3] Property has its duties as well as its rights — CAPTAIN THOMAS DRUMMOND [1797-1840], inventor of the Drummond light: *Letter to the Landlords of Tipperary* [May 22, 1838]
[4] The life of man is a self-evolving circle. — EMERSON: *Essays, First Series, Circles*
[5] See Johnson, page 235.

He was fresh and full of faith that "something would turn up." [1]

Tancred. Book III, Chap. VI
[1847]

Everything comes if a man will only wait.[2]

Ibid. Book IV, Chap. VIII

That when a man fell into his anec-dotage, it was a sign for him to retire.

Lothair. Chap. XXVIII [1870]

Every woman should marry — and no man.

Ibid. Chap. XXX

You know who critics are? — the men who have failed in literature and art.[3]

Ibid. Chap. XXXV

"My idea of an agreeable person," said Hugo Bohun, "is a person who agrees with me."

Ibid.

His Christianity was muscular.

Endymion. Chap. XIV [1880]

The Athanasian Creed is the most splendid ecclesiastical lyric ever poured forth by the genius of man.

Ibid. Chap. LII

The world is a wheel, and it will all come round right.

Ibid. Chap. LXX

"As for that," said Waldenshare, "sensible men are all of the same re-ligion." "Pray, what is that?" inquired the Prince. "Sensible men never tell." [4]

Ibid. Chap. LXXXI

The sweet simplicity of the three per cents.[5]

Ibid. Chap. XCVI

---

[1] The perpetual state of Wilkins Micawber in *David Copperfield*. See Dickens, page 496.
[2] See Emerson, page 414.
All things come round to him who will but wait. — LONGFELLOW: *Tales of a Wayside Inn, The Student's Tale* [1862]
[3] See Coleridge, page 319.
[4] See Johnson, page 234.
An anecdote is related of Sir Anthony Ash-ley Cooper [1621–1683], who, in speaking of religion, said, "People differ in their discourse and profession about these matters, but men of sense are really but of one religion." To the inquiry of "What religion?" the Earl said, "Men of sense never tell it." — BURNET: *History of My Own Times, Vol. I, P. 175, note* [ed. 1833].
[5] See Lord Stowell, page 275.

NATHANIEL HAWTHORNE
[1804–1864]

Sleeping or waking, we hear not the airy footsteps of the strange things that almost happen.

Twice-Told Tales. David Swan

The sky, now gloomy as an author's prospects.

Ibid. Sights from a Steeple

Our Creator would never have made such lovely days, and have given us the deep hearts to enjoy them, above and beyond all thought, unless we were meant to be immortal.

Mosses from an Old Manse.
The Old Manse

With that rich perfume of her breath, she blasted the very air.

Ibid. Rappaccini's Daughter

That lack of energy that distin-guishes the occupants of almshouses, and all other human beings who de-pend for subsistence on charity, on monopolized labor, or anything else, but their own independent exertions.

The Scarlet Letter. The Custom-House

Human nature will not flourish, any more than a potato, if it be planted and replanted, for too long a series of generations, in the same worn-out soil.

Ibid.

Neither the front nor the back en-trance of the Custom-House opens on the road to Paradise.

Ibid.

It is a good lesson — though it may often be a hard one — for a man who has dreamed of literary fame, and of making for himself a rank among the world's dignitaries by such means, to step aside out of the narrow circle in which his claims are recognized, and to find how utterly devoid of significance, beyond that circle, is all that he achieves, and all he aims at.

Ibid.

The black flower of civilized society, a prison.

Ibid. Chap. 1

On the breast of her gown, in red cloth, surrounded with an elaborate embroidery and fantastic flourishes of gold-thread, appeared the letter A.

The Scarlet Letter. Chap. 2

She named the infant "Pearl," as being of great price, — purchased with all she had.[1]

Ibid. Chap. 6

It is to the credit of human nature, that, except where its selfishness is brought into play, it loves more readily than it hates.

Ibid. Chap. 13

Let men tremble to win the hand of woman, unless they win along with it the utmost passion of her heart.

Ibid. Chap. 15

No man, for any considerable period, can wear one face to himself, and another to the multitude, without finally getting bewildered as to which may be the true.

Ibid. Chap. 20

Life is made up of marble and mud.

The House of the Seven Gables. Chap. 2

Providence seldom vouchsafes to mortals any more than just that degree of encouragement which suffices to keep them at a reasonably full exertion of their powers.

Ibid. Chap. 3

A stale article, if you dip it in a good, warm, sunny smile, will go off better than a fresh one that you've scowled upon.

Ibid. Chap. 4

Life, within doors, has few pleasanter prospects than a neatly arranged and well-provisioned breakfast-table.

Ibid. Chap. 7

What other dungeon is so dark as one's own heart! What jailer so inexorable as one's self!

Ibid. Chap. 11

There is no greater bugbear than a strong-willed relative, in the circle of his own connections.

Ibid.

Once in every half-century, at longest, a family should be merged into the great, obscure mass of humanity, and forget all about its ancestors.

The House of the Seven Gables. Chap. 12

The world owes all its onward impulses to men ill at ease. The happy man inevitably confines himself within ancient limits.

Ibid. Chap. 20

Of all the events which constitute a person's biography, there is scarcely one . . . to which the world so easily reconciles itself as to his death.

Ibid. Chap. 21

A revolution, or anything that interrupts social order, may afford opportunities for the individual display of eminent virtues; but its effects are pernicious to general morality.

The Snow Image. Old News, Chap. 3

It is a token of healthy and gentle characteristics, when women of high thoughts and accomplishments love to sew; especially as they are never more at home with their own hearts than while so occupied.

The Marble Faun. Chap. 5

Rome? The city of all time, and of all the world!

Ibid. Chap. 12

Every young sculptor seems to think that he must give the world some specimen of indecorous womanhood, and call it Eve, Venus, a Nymph, or any name that may apologize for a lack of decent clothing.

Ibid. Chap. 14

The public, in whose good graces lie the sculptor's or the painter's prospects of success, is infinitely smaller than the public to which literary men make their appeal.

Ibid. Chap. 15

At no time are people so sedulously careful to keep their trifling appointments, attend to their ordinary occupations, and thus put a commonplace aspect on life, as when conscious of some secret that if suspected would make them look monstrous in the general eye.

Ibid. Chap. 20

---

[1] Pearl of great price. — *Matthew, XIII, 46*

Nobody, I think, ought to read poetry, or look at pictures or statues, who cannot find a great deal more in them than the poet or artist has actually expressed.[1]

The Marble Faun. Chap. 41

Caskets! — a vile modern phrase, which compels a person of sense and good taste to shrink more disgustfully than ever before from the idea of being buried at all.

Our Old Home. About Warwick

That odd state of mind wherein we fitfully and teasingly remember some previous scene or incident, of which the one now passing appears to be but the echo and reduplication.

Ibid. Near Oxford

Old soldiers, I know not why, seem to be more accostable than old sailors.

Ibid. Up the Thames

It is not the statesman, the warrior, or the monarch that survives, but the despised poet, whom they may have fed with their crumbs, and to whom they owe all that they now are or have — a name.

Ibid.

Mountains are earth's undecaying monuments.

Sketches from Memory: The Notch of the White Mountains

THOMAS KIBBLE HERVEY
[1804–1859]

The tomb of him who would have made
The world too glad and free.

The Devil's Progress

A love that took an early root,
And had an early doom.

Ibid.

Like ships, that sailed for sunny isles,
But never came to shore.

Ibid.

[1] Every book is written with a constant secret reference to the few intelligent persons whom the writer believes to exist in the million. . . . The artist has always the masters in his eye. — EMERSON: *Progress of Culture*

FRANCIS SYLVESTER MAHONY ("FATHER PROUT")
[1804–1866]

With deep affection
And recollection
I often think of
Those Shandon Bells.

The Bells of Shandon. Stanza 1

The bells of Shandon
That sound so grand on
The pleasant waters
Of the river Lee.

Ibid. Stanza 2

SARAH FLOWER ADAMS
[1805–1848]

Though like the wanderer,
    The sun gone down,
Darkness be over me,
    My rest a stone;
Yet in my dreams I'd be
Nearer, my God, to Thee,
    Nearer to Thee.

Nearer, My God, to Thee. Stanza 2

He sendeth sun, he sendeth shower,
Alike they're needful to the flower;
And joys and tears alike are sent
To give the soul fit nourishment.
As comes to me or cloud or sun,
Father! thy will, not mine, be done.

He Sendeth Sun, He Sendeth Shower

Once have a priest for enemy, good bye
To peace.

Vivia Perpetua. Act III, Sc. II

WILLIAM HARRISON AINSWORTH
[1805–1884]

She must be seen to be appreciated.

Old Saint Paul's. Book I, Chap. 3

HENRY GLASSFORD BELL
[1805–1874]

I looked far back into other years, and lo! in bright array
I saw as in a dream the forms of ages passed away.
It was a stately convent, with its old and lofty walls

And gardens with their broad green
    walks, where soft the footstep falls.
                    Mary, Queen of Scots

The scene was changed. It was a bark
    that slowly held its way
And o'er its lee the coast of France in
    the light of evening lay;
And on its deck a lady sat, who gazed
    with tearful eyes
Upon the fast receding hills that dim
    and distant rise.
                                    Ibid.

The blood of beauty, wealth, and power
    — the heart-blood of a Queen,
The noblest of the Stuart race — the
    fairest earth has seen —
Lapped by a dog! Go think of it in
    silence and alone!
Then weigh against a grain of sand the
    glories of a throne.
                                    Ibid.

WILLIAM LLOYD GARRISON
[1805–1879]

My country is the world; my countrymen are mankind.[1]
    Prospectus of the Public Liberator
                                    [*1830*]

I am in earnest. I will not equivocate;
I will not excuse; I will not retreat a
single inch; and I will be heard![2]
        Salutatory of the Liberator
                    [*January 1, 1831*]

[1] Socrates said he was not an Athenian or a
Greek, but a citizen of the world. — PLU-
TARCH: *On Banishment*
    Diogenes, when asked from what country
he came, replied, "I am a citizen of the world."
— DIOGENES LAERTIUS
    My country is the world, and my religion
is to do good. — THOMAS PAINE: *Rights of
Man, Chap V*
    See Boswell, page 272.
    This famous motto of Garrison's appears in
several different forms. On the first number
of the *Liberator* in 1831, the *my* was changed
to *our*. In the *Prospectus* of Dec. 15, 1837, it
read. Our country is the world; our countrymen are all mankind.
    [2] Inscription on the Garrison monument,
Commonwealth Avenue, Boston.
    The time will come when you will hear
me. — DISRAELI: *Maiden Speech in the House
of Commons* [1837]

I will be as harsh as truth and as
uncompromising as justice.
        The Liberator. Vol. I, No. 1
                                    [*1831*]

The compact which exists between
the North and the South is a covenant
with death and an agreement with hell.[1]
    *Resolution adopted by the Anti-
slavery Society* [*January 27, 1843*]

With reasonable men, I will reason;
with humane men I will plead; but to
tyrants I will give no quarter, nor waste
arguments where they will certainly be
lost.
                Life. Vol. I, Page 188

Since the creation of the world there
has been no tyrant like Intemperance,
and no slaves so cruelly treated as his.
                        Ibid. Page 268

We may be personally defeated, but
our principles never.
                        Ibid. Page 402

Wherever there is a human being, I
see God-given rights inherent in that
being, whatever may be the sex or complexion.
                Ibid. Vol. III, Page 390

The success of any great moral enterprise does not depend upon numbers.
                        Ibid. Page 473

You can not possibly have a broader
basis for any government than that
which includes all the people, with all
their rights in their hands, and with an
equal power to maintain their rights.
                Ibid. Vol. IV, Page 224

'Tis up before the sun, roaming afar,
And in its watches wearies every star.
                        The Free Mind

Though woman never can be man,
    By change of sex and a' that,
To social rights, 'gainst class and clan,
    Her claim is just, for a' that.
    For a' that, and a' that,
    Her Eden slip, and a' that,
In all that makes a living soul
She matches man, for a' that.
        An Autograph [*January 3, 1875*]

[1] We have made a covenant with death, and
with hell are we at agreement. — *Isaiah,
XXVIII, 15*

EDWARD BULWER LYTTON
[1805-1873]

Rank is a great beautifier.
The Lady of Lyons. Act II, Sc. 1
                                    [1838]
Love, like Death,
Levels all ranks,[1] and lays the shep-
    herd's crook
Beside the sceptre.
                    Ibid. Act III, Sc. 2
            Curse away!
And let me tell thee, Beauseant, a wise
    proverb
The Arabs have, — "Curses are like
    young chickens,
And still come home to roost."
                        Ibid. Act V, Sc. 2
    Every man has his price,[2] I will bribe
left and right.
                    Walpole. Act II, Sc. 2
'Tis at sixty man learns how to value
home.
                            Ibid. Sc. 5
        Bear up.
There is many a slip 'twixt the lip and
    the cup.[3]
                            Ibid. Sc. 9
                    You speak
As one who fed on poetry.
            Richelieu. [1839] Act I, Sc. 1
    The mate for beauty
Should be a man, and not a money-
    chest.
                            Ibid. Sc. 2
Great men gain doubly when they
    make foes their friends.
                                Ibid.
Beneath the rule of men entirely great,
The pen is mightier than the sword.[4]
                    Ibid. Act II, Sc. 2

---

[1] Love levels all ranks. — *Walpole, Act II,
Sc. 5*
[2] See Sir Robert Walpole, page 200.
[3] See Burton, page 124.
    "Many's the slip,"
Hath the proverb well said, " 'twixt the cup
    and the lip."
        ROBERT, LORD LYTTON ("Owen Mere-
dith"): *Lucile, Part I, Canto V, Sect. 1*
[4] See Burton, page 123.
    Eloquence a hundred times has turned the
scale of war and peace at will. — EMERSON:
Progress of Culture

    Take away the sword;
States can be saved without it.
            Richelieu. [1839] Act II, Sc. 2
In the lexicon of youth, which fate re-
    serves
For a bright manhood, there is no such
    word
As "fail."
                                Ibid.
Ambition has no risk.
                    Ibid. Act III, Sc. 1
Our glories float between the earth and
    heaven
Like clouds which seem pavilions of the
    sun.
                    Ibid. Act V, Sc. 3
    To what a reed
We bind our destinies, when man we
    love.
            *The Duchess de la Vallière.
                        Act III, Sc. 3*
What's affection, but the power we
give another to torment us?
                Darnley. Act II, Sc. 1
A good cigar is as great a comfort to
a man as a good cry to a woman.
                    Ibid. Act III, Sc. 2
The brilliant chief, irregularly great,
Frank, haughty, rash, — the Rupert of
    debate! [1]
    The New Timon [1847]. Part I
Next cool, and all unconscious of re-
    proach,
Comes the calm "Johnny who upset the
    coach." [2]
                                Ibid.
Alone! — that worn-out word,
So idly spoken, and so coldly heard;
Yet all that poets sing and grief hath
    known
Of hopes laid waste, knells in that word
ALONE!
                            Ibid. Part II
Two lives that once part are as ships
    that divide
    When, moment on moment, there
        rushes between
        The one and the other a sea; — [3]

---

[1] See Disraeli, page 419. The reference is to
Edward, Lord Stanley [1799-1869].
[2] Lord John Russell [1792-1878].
[3] Ships that pass in the night. — LONGFEL-
LOW: *Tales of a Wayside Inn, Part III, The
Theologian's Tale, Elizabeth*

Ah, never can fall from the days that
  have been
A gleam on the years that shall be!
                        A Lament
Memory, no less than hope, owes its
  charm to "the far away." [1]
                        Ibid.

When stars are in the quiet skies,
  Then most I pine for thee;
Bend on me then thy tender eyes,
  As stars look on the sea.
  When Stars Are in the Quiet Skies
A good heart is better than all the
heads in the world.
  The Disowned. Chap. 33 [*1828*]
The easiest person to deceive is one's
own self.
              Ibid. Chap. 42
The magic of the tongue is the most
dangerous of all spells.
  Eugene Aram. Book I, Chap. 7
                        [*1832*]
Fate laughs at probabilities.
              Ibid. Chap. 10
He who has little silver in his pouch
must have the more silk on his tongue.
  The Last of the Barons.
  Book I, Chap. 3 [*1843*]
Happy is the man who hath never
known what it is to taste of fame — to
have it is a purgatory, to want it is a
hell.
      Ibid. Book V, Chap. 1
That should be a warning to you
never again to fall into the error of
the would-be scholar — namely, quote
second-hand.
      My Novel [*1853*]. *Chap. 19*
There are times when the mirth of
others only saddens us, especially the
mirth of children with high spirits, that
jar on our own quiet mood.
      Kenelm Chillingly [*1873*]
The man who smokes, thinks like a
sage and acts like a Samaritan.
      Night and Morning. Chap. 6
The worst part of an eminent man's
conversation is, nine times out of ten,

---

[1] *The Pathos of Distance*—title of book of
essays (1913) by James Huneker [1860–1921].
The phrase is translated from Nietzsche.

to be found in that part which he means
to be clever.
  Caxtonia. Differences Between the
  Urban and Rural Temperament
If the whole be greater than a part,
a whole man must be greater than that
part of him which is found in a book.
      Ibid. Hints on Mental Culture
In science, read, by preference, the
newest works; in literature, the oldest.
The classic literature is always modern.
                        Ibid.
Rhetorically, yes; conscientiously,
no.
      Ibid. Motive Power
In science, address the few, in literature the many. In science, the few must
dictate opinion to the many; in literature, the many, sooner or later, force
their judgment on the few.
      Ibid. Readers and Writers
Doubt the permanent fame of any
work of science which makes immediate reputation with the ignorant multitude; doubt the permanent fame of any
work of imagination which is at once
applauded by a conventional clique that
styles itself "the critical few."
                        Ibid.

PHILIP HENRY STANHOPE, LORD MAHON
[1805–1875]

The island of Sardinia, consisting
chiefly of marshes and mountains, has
from the earliest period to the present
been cursed with a noxious air, an ill-
cultivated soil, and a scanty population.
The convulsions produced by its poisonous plants gave rise to the expression
of sardonic smile, which is as old as
Homer (Odyssey, xx. 302).[1]
      History of England. Vol. 1,
                        Page 287

---

[1] The explanation given by Mahon of the
meaning of "sardonic smile" is to be sure the
traditional one, and was believed in by the
late classical writers. But in the Homeric passage referred to, the word is "sardanion"
(σαρδάνιον), not "sardonion." There is no evidence that Sardinia was known to the composers of what we call Homer. It looks as
though the word was to be connected with the

HERMAN MILLER

Think not the beautiful doings of thy
soul
Shall perish unremembered. They abide
With thee forever; and alone the good
Thou doest nobly, Truth and Love ap-
prove.
Each pure and gentle deed of mercy
brings
An honest recompense, and from it
looms
That sovereign knowledge of thy duty
done —
A joy beyond all dignities of earth.
The Doings of Thy Soul [1]

WILLIAM PITT PALMER
[1805–1884]

I couldn't stand it, sir, at all,
But up and kissed her on the spot!
I know — boo-hoo — I ought to not,
But, somehow, from her looks — boo-
hoo —
I thought she kind o' wished me to!
The Smack in School

ELIZA LEWIS HENING
SCHERMERHORN
[*Floruit* 1840]

Thou are crumbling to the dust, old
pile!
Thou art hastening to thy fall,
And around thee in thy loneliness
Clings the ivy to thy wall.
*Old Blandford Church, Petersburg,
Virginia* [*1840*] [2]

---

verb σαίρω, "show the teeth;" "grin like a
dog;" hence that the "sardonic smile" was a
"grim laugh."—MORRIS HICKEY MORGAN
[1859–1910].
[1] Inscription on the wall above the main entrance of the old Medico-Chirurgical Hospital,
now a part of the Graduate Hospital, University of Pennsylvania, Philadelphia.
[2] This poem was long attributed to Tyrone
Power [1797–1841], Irish comedian, who
toured the United States several times, and
visited Old Blandford Church.

COLONEL SIDNEY SHERMAN
[1805–1873]

Remember the Alamo!
Battle-cry, San Jacinto
[*April 21, 1836*]

WILLIAM ALLEN
[1806–1879]

Fifty-four forty, or fight. [1]

ELIZABETH BARRETT
BROWNING
[1806–1861]

Of all the thoughts of God that are
Borne inward into souls afar,
Along the Psalmist's music deep,
Now tell me if that any is,
For gift or grace, surpassing this:
"He giveth his belovèd — sleep?" [2]
The Sleep. Stanza 1
A child's kiss
Set on thy sighing lips shall make thee
glad;
A poor man served by thee shall make
thee rich;
A sick man helped by thee shall make
thee strong;
Thou shalt be served thyself by every
sense
Of service which thou renderest.
A Drama of Exile. Line 1869
Thou large-brained woman and large-
hearted man.
To George Sand, A Desire
Or from Browning some "Pome-
granate," which, if cut deep down
the middle,

---

[1] The challenge of Senator Allen (of Ohio)
became the slogan of the expansionists who
claimed for the United States the region, now
Oregon, as far north as the southern boundary
of Alaska, latitude 50° 40'. As the campaign
cry of James K. Polk, who was elected President, it is an early example of the popularity
of slogans, such as: "Free soil, free men, free
speech, Frémont" in 1856; "He kept us out of
war" in 1916; "A chicken in every pot, two
cars in every garage" in 1932; "The New
Deal" and "The forgotten man" in the early
days of Franklin D. Roosevelt's presidency.
[2] *Psalm CXXVII, 2*

Shows a heart within blood-tinctured,
of a veined humanity.
Lady Geraldine's Courtship.
Stanza 41

Poets ever fail in reading their own
verses to their worth.
Ibid. Stanza 42

There Shakespeare, on whose forehead
climb
The crowns o' the world; O eyes sub-
lime
With tears and laughters for all time!
A Vision of Poets. Line 298

And Chaucer, with his infantine
Familiar clasp of things divine.
Ibid. Line 388

And Marlowe, Webster, Fletcher, Ben,
Whose fire-hearts sowed our furrows
when
The world was worthy of such men.
Ibid. Line 400

And poor, proud Byron, sad as grave
And salt as life; forlornly brave.
Ibid. Line 412

Life treads on life, and heart on heart;
We press too close in church and mart
To keep a dream or grave apart.
Ibid. Conclusion, Line 820

Knowledge by suffering entereth,
And life is perfected by death.
Ibid. Line 929; also 1005

And I smiled to think God's greatness
flowed around our incomplete-
ness, —
Round our restlessness, His rest.
Rhyme of the Duchess May.
Conclusion, Stanza 11

Do ye hear the children weeping, O my
brothers,
Ere the sorrow comes with years?
The Cry of the Children. Stanza 1

The child's sob in the silence curses
deeper
Than the strong man in his wrath.
Ibid. Stanza 13

Therefore to this dog will I,
Tenderly not scornfully,
Render praise and favor:
With my hand upon his head,
Is my benediction said
Therefore and for ever.
To Flush, My Dog. Stanza 14

The Flushes have their laurels as
well as the Caesars.
Author's note appended to the
foregoing

And lips say "God be pitiful,"
Who ne'er said "God be praised."
The Cry of the Human. Stanza 1

But since he had
The genius to be loved, why let him have
The justice to be honoured in his grave.
Crowned and Buried. Stanza 27

By thunders of white silence.
Hiram Powers's Greek Slave

Unless you can muse in a crowd all day
On the absent face that fixed you;
Unless you can love, as the angels may,
With the breadth of heaven betwixt
you;
Unless you can dream that his faith is
fast,
Through behoving and unbehoving;
Unless you can die when the dream is
past —
Oh, never call it loving!
A Woman's Shortcomings.
Stanza 5

And that dismal cry rose slowly
And sank slowly through the air,
Full of spirit's melancholy
And eternity's despair!
And they heard the words it said —
"Pan is dead — great Pan is dead —
Pan, Pan is dead!" [1]
The Dead Pan. Stanza 26

"Yes," I answered you last night;
"No," this morning, sir, I say:
Colors seen by candle-light
Will not look the same by day. [2]
The Lady's "Yes." Stanza 1

"Guess now who holds thee?" —
"Death," I said. But there
The silver answer rang, — "Not Death,
but Love."
Sonnets from the Portuguese. I

[1] Thamus . . . uttered with a loud voice his
message, "The great Pan is dead." — PLU-
TARCH: *Why the Oracles Cease to Give Answers*

[2] And if I loved you Wednesday,
Well, what is that to you?
I do not love you Thursday —
So much is true.
EDNA ST. VINCENT MILLAY: *Thursday*

Go from me. Yet I feel that I shall stand
Henceforward in thy shadow.
  Sonnets from the Portuguese. VI
  The widest land
Doom takes to part us, leaves thy hand
  in mine
With pulses that beat double. What I do
And what I dream include thee, as the
  wine
Must taste of its own grapes.
  Ibid.
If thou must love me, let it be for
  nought
Except for love's sake only.
  Ibid. XIV
When our two souls stand up erect and
  strong,
Face to face, silent.
  Ibid. XXII
To drop some golden orb of perfect song
Into our deep, dear silence.
  Ibid.
God only, who made us rich, can make
  us poor.
  Ibid. XXIV
How do I love thee? Let me count the
  ways.
  Ibid. XLIII
I shall but love thee better after death.
  Ibid.
  When the dust of death has choked
A great man's voice, the common words
  he said
Turn oracles.
  Casa Guidi Windows. Part I,
  Line 250
She has seen the mystery hid
Under Egypt's pyramid:
By those eyelids pale and close
Now she knows what Rhamses knows.
  Little Mattie. Stanza 2
  But so fair,
She takes the breath of men away
Who gaze upon her unaware.
  Bianca Among the Nightingales.
  Stanza 12
She never found fault with you, never
  implied
Your wrong by her right; and yet men
  at her side
Grew nobler, girls purer, as through the
  whole town

The children were gladder that pulled
  at her gown —
  My Kate.
  My Kate. Stanza 5
We walked too straight for fortune's
  end,
We loved too true to keep a friend;
At last we're tired, my heart and I.
  My Heart and I. Stanza 2
Grief may be joy misunderstood;
Only the Good discerns the good.
  De Profundis. Stanza 21
  Women know
The way to rear up children (to be
  just),
They know a simple, merry, tender
  knack
Of tying sashes, fitting baby-shoes,
And stringing pretty words that make
  no sense.
  Aurora Leigh. Book I, Line 47
God laughs in heaven when any man
Says "Here I'm learned; this I under-
  stand;
In that, I am never caught at fault or
  doubt."
  Ibid. Line 191
  Life, struck sharp on death,
Makes awful lightning.
  Ibid. Line 210
The book-club, guarded from your mod-
  ern trick
Of shaking dangerous questions from
  the crease,
Preserved her intellectual.
  Ibid. Line 302
Alas, a mother never is afraid
Of speaking angerly to any child,
Since love, she knows, is justified of
  love.
  Ibid. Line 369
  We get no good
By being ungenerous, even to a book,
And calculating profits, — so much
  help
By so much reading. It is rather when
We gloriously forget ourselves and
  plunge
Soul-forward, headlong, into a book's
  profound,
Impassioned for its beauty and salt of
  truth —

'Tis then we get the right good from a book.
> *Aurora Leigh. Book I, Line 702*

The beautiful seems right
By force of Beauty, and the feeble wrong
Because of weakness.
> *Ibid. Line 753*

As sings the lark when sucked up out of sight
In vortices of glory and blue air.
> *Ibid. Line 1055*

A woman's always younger than a man
At equal years.
> *Ibid. Book II, Line 329*

Men do not think
Of sons and daughters, when they fall in love.
> *Ibid. Line 608*

Dreams of doing good
To good-for-nothing people.
> *Ibid. Line 645*

I should not dare to call my soul my own.
> *Ibid. Line 786*

God answers sharp and sudden on some prayers,
And thrusts the thing we have prayed for in our face,
A gauntlet with a gift in 't.
> *Ibid. Line 952*

Every wish
Is like a prayer, with God.[1]
> *Ibid. Line 954*

Girls have curious minds
And fain would know the end of everything.
> *Ibid. Line 1194*

I learnt the use
Of the editorial "we" in a review.
> *Ibid. Book III, Line 312*

Is the blue in eyes
As awful as in stockings?[2]
> *Ibid. Line 379*

Pay the income-tax
And break your heart upon 't.
> *Ibid. Line 566*

How many desolate creatures on the earth

[1] Prayer is the soul's sincere desire. — JAMES MONTGOMERY: *What is Prayer?, St. 1*
[2] See Macaulay, page 399.

Have learnt the simple dues of fellowship
And social comfort, in a hospital.
> *Aurora Leigh. Book III, Line 1122*

A good neighbour, even in this,
Is fatal sometimes, — cuts your morning up
To mincemeat of the very smallest talk,
Then helps to sugar her bohea at night
With your reputation.
> *Ibid. Book IV, Line 488*

Good critics who have stamped out poet's hope,
Good statesmen, who pulled ruin on the state,
Good patriots who for a theory risked a cause.
> *Ibid. Line 499*

A little sunburnt by the glare of life.
> *Ibid. Line 1140*

Let no one till his death
Be called unhappy. Measure not the work
Until the day's out and the labor done.
> *Ibid. Book V, Line 76*

Every age
Appears to souls who live in 't (ask Carlyle)
Most unheroic.
> *Ibid. Line 155*

The growing drama has outgrown such toys
Of stimulated stature, face, and speech,
It also peradventure may outgrow
The simulation of the painted scene,
Boards, actors, prompters, gaslight, and costume,
And take for a worthier stage the soul itself,
Its shifting fancies and celestial lights,
With all its grand orchestral silences
To keep the pauses of its rhythmic sounds.
> *Ibid. Line 335*

Men get opinions as boys learn to spell,
By reiteration chiefly.
> *Ibid. Book VI, Line 6*

Surgeons . . .
Spend raptures upon perfect specimens
Of indurated veins, distorted joints,
Or beautiful new cases of curved spine.
> *Ibid. Line 173*

Since when was genius found respectable?
> *Aurora Leigh. Book VI, Line 275*

Earth's crammed with heaven,
And every common bush afire with God; [1]
And only he who sees takes off his shoes —
The rest sit round it and pluck blackberries.
> *Ibid. Book VII, Line 820*

LADY FLORA HASTINGS
[1806–1839]

Get up; for when all things are merry and glad,
Good children should never be lazy and sad;
For God gives us daylight, dear sister, that we
May rejoice like the lark and may work like the bee.
> *Early Rising. A Spring Morning*

CHARLES FENNO HOFFMAN
[1806–1884]

Sparkling and bright in liquid light
  Does the wine our goblets gleam in;
With hue as red as the rosy bed
  Which a bee would choose to dream in.
Then fill to-night, with hearts as light
  To loves as gay and fleeting
As bubbles that swim on the beaker's brim
  And break on the lips while meeting.
> *Sparkling and Bright*

We were not many — we who stood
  Before the iron sleet that day;
Yet many a gallant spirit would
Give half his years, if he but could
  Have been with us at Monterey.
> *Monterey. Stanza 1*

[1] The still small voice in autumn's hush,
  Yon maple wood the burning bush.
  WHITTIER: *The Chapel of the Hermits, St. 16*

WILLIAM GILMORE SIMMS
[1806–1870]

Lithe and long as the serpent train,
  Springing and clinging from tree to tree,
Now darting upward, now down again,
  With a twist and a twirl that are strange to see.
> *The Grape-Vine Swing.[1] Stanza 1*

NATHANIEL PARKER WILLIS
[1806–1867]

The shadows lay along Broadway,
  'Twas near the twilight tide.
> *Unseen Spirits. Stanza 1*

The sin forgiven by Christ in Heaven
By man is cursed alway.
> *Ibid. Stanza 5*

Let us weep, in our darkness, but weep not for him!
Not for him who, departing, leaves millions in tears!
Not for him who has died full of honor and years!
Not for him who ascended Fame's ladder so high:
From the round at the top he has stepped to the sky.
> *The Death of Harrison. Stanza 5*

CHARLES FRANCIS ADAMS
[1807–1886]

It would be superfluous in me to point out to your Lordship that this is war.
> *Despatch to Earl Russell*
> *[September 5, 1863]*

THOMAS HOLLEY CHIVERS
[1807–1858]

Many mellow Cydonian suckets
  Sweet apples, anthosmial, divine,
From the ruby-rimmed beryline buckets
  Star-gemmed, lily-shaped, hyaline;
Like the sweet golden goblet found growing
  On the wild emerald cucumber-tree,

[1] It was on a grapevine swing that man first teetered a little nearer the stars. — CAMERON ROGERS (ed.): *Full and By*

Rich, brilliant, like chrysoprase glow-
ing
Was my beautiful Rosalie Lee.
Rosalie Lee

On the beryl-rimmed rebecs of Ruby
Brought fresh from the hyaline
streams,
She played on the banks of the Yuba
Such songs as she heard in her
dreams.
Lily Adair

Thus she stood on the arabesque bor-
ders
Of the beautiful blossoms that blew
On the banks of the crystalline waters,
Every morn, in the diaphane dew.
The flowers, they were radiant with
glory,
And shed such perfume on the air,
That my soul, now to want them, feels
sorry,
And bleeds for my Lily Adair.
Ibid.

As the diamond is the crystalline
Revelator of the achromatic white light
of Heaven, so is a perfect poem the
crystalline revelation of the Divine
Idea.
Preface to Eonchs of Ruby

In the music of the morns
Blown through the Conchimarian
horns,
Down the dark vistas of the reboantic
Norns,
To the Genius of Eternity
Crying, "Come to me! Come to me!"
The Poet's Vacation

As an egg, when broken, never
Can be mended, but must ever
Be the same crushed egg for ever —
So shall this dark heart of mine!
To Allegra Florence in Heaven

HELEN SELINA SHERIDAN, LADY DUFFERIN
[1807–1867]

I'm very lonely now, Mary,
For the poor make no new friends;
But, oh! they love the better still
The few our Father sends!
Lament of the Irish Emigrant.
Stanza 4

They say there's bread and work for
all,
And the sun shines always there;
But I'll not forget old Ireland,
Were it fifty times as fair.
Lament of the Irish Emigrant.
Stanza 7

JAMES HENRY HAMMOND
[1807–1864]

The very mudsills of society. . . .
We call them slaves. . . . But I will
not characterize that class at the North
with that term; but you have it. It is
there, it is everywhere; it is eternal.
Speech, U. S. Senate
[*March, 1858*]

Cotton is King.[1]
Ibid.

CHARLES JEFFERYS
[1807–1865]

It matters not how dear the spot,
How proud or poor the dome,
Love still retains some deathless chains
That bind the heart to home.
Song of Blanche Alpen. Stanza 3

Oh! if I were Queen of France, or still
better, Pope of Rome,
I'd have no fighting men abroad, no
weeping maids at home;
All should be at peace; or, if kings must
show their might,
Why, let them who make the quarrel be
the only men to fight.
Jeannette and Jeannot. Stanza 4

Why, since the world began, the surest
road to fame
Has been the field where men unknown
might win themselves a name;
And well I know the brightest eyes have
all the brighter shone,
When looking at some warrior bold, returned from battle won.
Jeannot's Answer. Stanza 1

[1] DAVID CHRISTY: *Cotton is King; or, Slavery in the Light of Political Economy* [1855]
Take away *time is money*, and what is left
of England? take away *cotton is king*, and
what is left of America? — VICTOR HUGO: *Les
Misérables, Marius, Book IV, Chap. 4*

Were only kings themselves to fight,
there'd be an end of war.
Jeannot's Answer. Stanza 4

HENRY WADSWORTH LONGFELLOW
[1807-1882]

Look, then, into thine heart, and write! [1]
*Voices of the Night. Prelude,
Stanza 19*

I heard the trailing garments of the Night [2]
Sweep through her marble halls.
Hymn to Night. Stanza 1

Tell me not, in mournful numbers,
Life is but an empty dream!
For the soul is dead that slumbers,
And things are not what they seem. [3]
A Psalm of Life. Stanza 1

Life is real! Life is earnest!
And the grave is not its goal;
Dust thou art, to dust returnest,
Was not spoken of the soul.
Ibid. Stanza 2

Art is long, and Time is fleeting, [4]
And our hearts, though stout and brave,
Still, like muffled drums, are beating
Funeral marches to the grave. [5]
Ibid. Stanza 4

Trust no Future, howe'er pleasant!
Let the dead Past bury its dead!
Act, act in the living present!
Heart within, and God o'erhead!
Ibid. Stanza 6

Lives of great men all remind us
We can make our lives sublime,

And, departing, leave behind us
Footprints on the sands of time.
A Psalm of Life. Stanza 7

Let us, then, be up and doing,
With a heart for any fate; [1]
Still achieving, still pursuing,
Learn to labour and to wait.
Ibid. Stanza 9

There is a Reaper whose name is Death, [2]
And, with his sickle keen,
He reaps the bearded grain at a breath,
And the flowers that grow between.
*The Reaper and the Flowers.
Stanza 1*

Spake full well, in language quaint and olden,
One who dwelleth by the castled Rhine,
When he called the flowers, so blue and golden,
Stars, that in earth's firmament do shine. [3]
Flowers. Stanza 1

The hooded clouds, like friars,
Tell their beads in drops of rain.
*Midnight Mass for the Dying
Year. Stanza 4*

Blue were her eyes as the fairy-flax.
*The Wreck of the Hesperus.
Stanza 2*

Christ save us all from a death like this,
On the reef of Norman's Woe!
Ibid. Stanza 22

If this glass doth fall,
Farewell then, O Luck of Edenhall.
The Luck of Edenhall.[4] Stanza 4

His brow is wet with honest sweat,
He earns whate'er he can,
And looks the whole world in the face,
For he owes not any man.
The Village Blacksmith. Stanza 2

---

[1] See Sir Philip Sidney, page 27.

[2] See Mrs. Whitman, page 418.

[3] Non semper ea sunt quae videntur (Things are not always what they seem). — PHAEDRUS: *Fables, Book IV, Fable 2, L. 5*

[4] The lyf so short, the craft so long to lerne. — CHAUCER: *The Parlement of Foules, L. 1*

Art is long, life is short. — GOETHE: *Wilhelm Meister, VII, 9.* Hippocrates is supposed to have originated this saying, which is better known in Latin: Ars longa, vita brevis est.

Art's long, though time is short. — BROWNING: *The Ring and the Book, IX, Juris Doctor Johannes-Baptista Bottinius*

[5] Our lives are but our marches to the grave. — BEAUMONT AND FLETCHER: *The Humorous Lieutenant, Act III, Sc. 5*

[1] Here's a heart for every fate. — BYRON: *To Thomas Moore, St. 1*

[2] There is a Reaper whose name is death. — ARNIM AND BRENTANO: *Erntelied* (from *Des Knaben Wunderhorn*, ed. 1857, *Vol. I, P. 59*)

[3] Flowerets that shine as blue stars in the green firmament of the earth. — FREDERICK WILHELM CAROVÉ [1789-1852]: *A Story Without an End.* Carové lived in Coblenz on the Rhine.

[4] From the German of UHLAND.

Something attempted, something done,
  Has earned a night's repose.
            The Village Blacksmith. Stanza 7

No one is so accursed by fate,
No one so utterly desolate,
  But some heart, though unknown,
  Responds unto his own.
                  Endymion. Stanza 8

For Time will teach thee soon the truth,
  There are no birds in last year's
  nest! [1]
        It Is Not Always May. Stanza 6

Into each life some rain must fall,
  Some days must be dark and dreary.
            The Rainy Day. Stanza 3

I like that ancient Saxon phrase, which
  calls
The burial-ground God's-Acre!
                  God's-Acre. Stanza 1

Thou hast taught me, Silent River!
  Many a lesson, deep and long;
Thou hast been a generous giver;
  I can give thee but a song.
        To the River Charles. Stanza 3

The prayer of Ajax was for light.[2]
            The Goblet of Life. Stanza 9

Standing with reluctant feet,
Where the brook and river meet,
Womanhood and childhood fleet!
                Maidenhood. Stanza 3

A banner with the strange device,
  Excelsior!
                  Excelsior. Stanza 1

Stars of the summer night!
  Far in yon azure deeps,
Hide, hide your golden light!
  She sleeps.
        The Spanish Student. Act I, Sc. 3,
                              Serenade

[1] En los nidos de antaño
    No hay pajaros hogano
    (In last year's nests
    This year no sparrow rests).
            CERVANTES: *Don Quixote,*
                      Part II, Chap. LXXIV
See FRANÇOIS VILLON:
    Mais où sont les neiges d'antan?
    (Where are the snows of yester year?)
                ROSSETTI'S translation
There is no bird in any last year's nest! —
AUSTIN DOBSON: *The Dying of Tanneguy du
Bois*
[2]   The light of Heaven restore;
    Give me to see, and Ajax asks no more.
    POPE: *The Iliad, Book XVII, L. 730*
More light. — GOETHE'S last words

She floats upon the river of his
  thoughts.[1]
        The Spanish Student. Act II, Sc. 3

Heaven gives almonds
To those who have no teeth. That's nuts
  to crack.
            Ibid. Act III, Sc. 5

Were half the power, that fills the world
  with terror,
  Were half the wealth, bestowed on
  camps and courts,
Given to redeem the human mind from
  error,
  There were no need of arsenals or
  forts.
            The Arsenal at Springfield.
                              Stanza 9

Between the dark and the daylight,
  When the night is beginning to lower,
Comes a pause in the day's occupations,
  That is known as the Children's
  Hour.
        The Children's Hour. Stanza 1

The day is done, and the darkness
  Falls from the wings of Night,
As a feather is wafted downward
  From an eagle in his flight.
            The Day Is Done. Stanza 1

A feeling of sadness and longing
  That is not akin to pain,
And resembles sorrow only
  As the mist resembles the rain.
                  Ibid. Stanza 3

And the night shall be filled with music,
  And the cares, that infest the day,
Shall fold their tents, like the Arabs,
  And as silently steal away.
                  Ibid. Stanza 11

The horologe of Eternity
Sayeth this incessantly, —
"Forever — never!
Never — forever!"
        The Old Clock on the Stairs.
                              Stanza 9

I shot an arrow into the air,
It fell to earth, I knew not where.
        The Arrow and the Song. Stanza 1

[1] The river of his thoughts. — BYRON: *The
Dream, St. 2*

Joy and Temperance and Repose
Slam the door on the doctor's nose.
> *The Best Medicines* [1]

Man-like is it to fall into sin,
Fiend-like is it to dwell therein,
Christ-like is it for sin to grieve,
God-like is it all sin to leave.
> *Sin* [2]

Though the mills of God grind slowly,
  yet they grind exceeding small; [3]
Though with patience He stands waiting, with exactness grinds He all.
> *Retribution* [4]

This is the forest primeval.
> *Evangeline. Prelude*

        Alike were they free from
Fear, that reigns with the tyrant, and
  envy, the vice of republics.
> *Ibid. Part I, 1*

Neither locks had they to their doors,
  nor bars to their windows;
But their dwellings were open as day
  and the hearts of the owners;
There the richest was poor, and the
  poorest lived in abundance.
> *Ibid.*

When she had passed, it seemed like
  the ceasing of exquisite music.
> *Ibid.*

Silently one by one, in the infinite
  meadows of heaven
Blossomed the lovely stars, the forget-
  me-nots of the angels.
> *Ibid. 3*

Talk not of wasted affection! affection
  never was wasted;
If it enrich not the heart of another, its
  waters, returning

[1] From the German of FRIEDRICH VON LO-
GAU [1604–1655].
[2] From the German of FRIEDRICH VON LO-
GAU.
[3] God's mill grinds slow, but sure. — HER-
BERT: *Jacula Prudentum*
'Οψὲ θεοῦ μύλοι ἀλέουσι τὸ λεπτὸν ἄλευρον. —
Oracula Sibylliana, VIII, 14
'Οψὲ θεῶν ἀλέουσι μύλοι, ἀλέουσι δὲ λεπτά. —
LEUTSCH AND SCHNEIDEWIN: *Corpus Parœmi-
ographorum Grœcorum, Vol. I, P. 444*
Sextus Empiricus is the first writer who has
presented the whole of the adage cited by
Plutarch in his treatise *Concerning such whom
God is slow to punish.*
[4] From the German of FRIEDRICH VON
LOGAU.

Back to their springs, like the rain, shall
  fill them full of refreshment:
That which the fountain sends forth
  returns again to the fountain.
> *Evangeline. Part II, 1*

This is the compass-flower,[1] that the
  finger of God has planted
Here in the houseless wild, to direct the
  traveller's journey
Over the sea-like, pathless, limitless
  waste of the desert.
> *Ibid. 4*

We shall sail securely, and safely reach
The Fortunate Isles.[2]
> *The Building of the Ship*

        Sail on, O Ship of State!
Sail on, O Union, strong and great!
Humanity with all its fears,
With all the hopes of future years,
Is hanging breathless on thy fate!
> *Ibid.*

Our hearts, our hopes, are all with thee,
Our hearts, our hopes, our prayers, our
  tears,
Our faith triumphant o'er our fears,
Are all with thee, — are all with thee!
> *Ibid.*

There is no flock, however watched and
  tended,
  But one dead lamb is there!
There is no fireside, howsoe'er de-
  fended,
  But has one vacant chair! [3]
> *Resignation. Stanza 1*

There is no Death! [4] What seems so
  is transition;

[1] Known also as the pilot-weed and polar
plant.
  Look at this delicate plant that lifts its
    head from the meadow;
  See how its leaves all point to the north as
    true as a magnet.
        NELTJE BLANCHAN (DOUBLEDAY)
          [1865–1918]: *Nature's Garden*
[2] You sail and you seek for the Fortunate
    Isles,
  The old Greek Isles of the yellow bird's
    song.
        JOAQUIN MILLER: *The Fortunate Isles*
[3] We shall meet, but we shall miss him,
  There will be one vacant chair.
        HENRY STEVENSON WASHBURN [1813–
          1903]: *The Vacant Chair*
[4] There is no death! The stars go down
  To rise upon some other shore.
        JOHN LUCKEY McCREERY [1835–
          1906]: *There Is no Death*

This life of mortal breath
Is but a suburb of the life elysian,
   Whose portal we call Death.
              Resignation. Stanza 5

Nothing useless is, or low;
   Each thing in its place is best;
And what seems but idle show
   Strengthens and supports the rest.
           The Builders. Stanza 2

In the elder days of Art,
   Builders wrought with greatest care
Each minute and unseen part;
   For the Gods see everywhere.
              Ibid. Stanza 5

God sent his Singers upon earth
With songs of sadness and of mirth.
           The Singers. Stanza 1

But the great Master said, "I see
No best in kind, but in degree;
I gave a various gift to each,
To charm, to strengthen, and to teach."
              Ibid. Stanza 6

All your strength is in your union.
All your danger is in discord;
Therefore be at peace henceforward,
And as brothers live together.
     The Song of Hiawatha. Part I

As unto the bow the cord is,
So unto the man is woman,
Though she bends him, she obeys him,
Though she draws him, yet she follows,
Useless each without the other!
              Ibid. Part X

Oh the long and dreary Winter!
Oh the cold and cruel Winter!
            Ibid. Part XX

If I am not worth the wooing, I surely
   am not worth the winning.
   The Courtship of Miles Standish.
                Part III

"Why don't you speak for yourself,
   John?"
                  Ibid.

God had sifted three kingdoms to find
   the wheat for this planting.[1]
             Ibid. Part IV

He is a little chimney, and heated hot
   in a moment.[2]
             Ibid. Part VI

---

[1] See Stoughton, page 179.
[2] A little pot and soon hot. — SHAKESPEARE:
The Taming of the Shrew, Act IV, Sc. 1, L. 6

Saint Augustine! well hast thou said,
   That of our vices we can frame
A ladder, if we will but tread
   Beneath our feet each deed of shame.[1]
      The Ladder of Saint Augustine.
                 Stanza 1

The heights by great men reached and
   kept
Were not attained by sudden flight,
But they, while their companions slept,
   Were toiling upward in the night.
             Ibid. Stanza 10

All houses wherein men have lived and
   died
Are haunted houses.
       Haunted Houses. Stanza 1

The long mysterious Exodus of death.
   The Jewish Cemetery at Newport.
                 Stanza 1

Pride and humiliation hand in hand
   Walked with them through the world
   where'er they went;
Trampled and beaten were they as the
   sand,
   And yet unshaken as the continent.
             Ibid. Stanza 12

A boy's will is the wind's will,
And the thoughts of youth are long,
   long thoughts.
        My Lost Youth. Stanza 1

Spanish sailors with bearded lips,
And the beauty and mystery of the
   ships,
   And the magic of the sea.
             Ibid. Stanza 3

Whene'er a noble deed is wrought,
Whene'er is spoken a noble thought,
   Our hearts, in glad surprise,
   To higher levels rise.
        Santa Filomena. Stanza 1

A Lady with a Lamp [2] shall stand
In the great history of the land,
   A noble type of good,
Heroic womanhood.
             Ibid. Stanza 10

---

[1] I held it truth, with him who sings
   To one clear harp in divers tones,
   That men may rise on stepping-stones
Of their dead selves to higher things.
      TENNYSON: *In Memoriam, 1*
[2] Florence Nightingale [1820–1910], nurse
at Scutari during the Crimean War [1854–
1856].

And Nature, the old nurse, took
  The child upon her knee,
Saying: "Here is a story-book
  Thy Father has written for thee."
    The Fiftieth Birthday of Agassiz.
        Stanza 2
Ye are better than all the ballads
  That ever were sung or said;
For ye are living poems,
  And all the rest are dead.
        Children. Stanza 9
So it happens with the poets:
  Every province hath its own;
Camaralzaman is famous
  Where Badoura is unknown.
        Vox Populi. Stanza 3
Listen, my children, and you shall hear.
    Tales of a Wayside Inn. Paul
    Revere's Ride, Stanza 1
One if by land, and two if by sea;
And I on the opposite shore will be.
        Ibid. Stanza 2
The fate of a nation was riding that
  night.
        Ibid. Stanza 8
A voice in the darkness, a knock at the
  door,
And a word that shall echo forever-
  more!
        Ibid. Stanza 14
A town that boasts inhabitants like me
Can have no lack of good society.
    Ibid. The Birds of Killingworth,
        Stanza 6
His form was ponderous, and his step
  was slow;
  There never was so wise a man be-
  fore;
He seemed the incarnate "Well, I told
  you so!"
        Ibid. Stanza 9
For after all, the best thing one can do
When it is raining, is to let it rain.
        Ibid. Stanza 26
Moons waxed and waned, the lilacs
  bloomed and died,
In the broad river ebbed and flowed the
  tide,
Ships went to sea, and ships came home
  from sea,
And the slow years sailed by and ceased
  to be.
    Ibid. Lady Wentworth, Stanza 7

A maid of all work, whether coarse or
  fine,
A servant who made service seem di-
  vine! [1]
        Tales of a Wayside Inn.
      Lady Wentworth, Stanza 7
How can I tell the signals and the signs
By which one heart another heart di-
  vines?
How can I tell the many thousand ways
By which it keeps the secret it betrays?
    Ibid. Emma and Eginhard, Stanza 8
Ships that pass in the night, and speak
  each other in passing,
Only a signal shown and a distant voice
  in the darkness;
So on the ocean of life we pass and
  speak one another,[2]
Only a look and a voice; then darkness
  again and a silence.
        Ibid. Elizabeth, IV
The unfinished window in Aladdin's
  tower
Unfinished must remain!
        Hawthorne. Stanza 9
No endeavor is in vain;
Its reward is in the doing,
And the rapture of pursuing
Is the prize the vanquished gain.
      The Wind Over the Chimney.
        Stanza 10
Let nothing disturb thee,
Nothing affright thee;
All things are passing;

---

[1] See Herbert, page 135.
[2] And soon, too soon, we part with pain,
  To sail o'er silent seas again.
    THOMAS MOORE: *Meeting of the Ships*
Two lives that once part are as ships that
  divide.
    EDWARD BULWER LYTTON: *A Lament*
We twain have met like the ships upon the sea.
    ALEXANDER SMITH: *A Life Drama*
As two floating planks meet and part on the
  sea,
O friend! so I met and then parted from thee.
    W. R. ALGER: *The Brief Chance Encounter*
Like as a plank of driftwood, tossed on a
  stormy sea,
Another plank encounters, meets, touches,
  parts again.
    SIR EDWIN ARNOLD: *Driftwood*
As vessels starting from ports thousands of
miles apart pass close to each other in the
naked breadths of the ocean, nay, sometimes
even touch in the dark.
  HOLMES: *Professor at the Breakfast Table*

God never changeth;
Patient endurance
Attaineth to all things;
Who God possesseth
In nothing is wanting;
Alone God sufficeth.
Santa Teresa's Book-Mark [1]

He speaketh not; and yet there lies
A conversation in his eyes.
The Hanging of the Crane. III

"O Caesar, we who are about to die
Salute you!" was the gladiators' cry
In the arena, standing face to face
With death and with the Roman popu-
lace.
Morituri Salutamus. Stanza 1

Let him not boast who puts his armor on
As he who puts it off, the battle done.
Ibid. Stanza 9

Write on your doors the saying wise
and old,
"Be bold! be bold!" and everywhere
— "Be bold;
Be not too bold!" [2]
Ibid. Stanza 10

Better like Hector in the field to die,
Than like a perfumed Paris turn and
fly.
Ibid.

Ye, against whose familiar names not
yet
The fatal asterisk of death is set.
Ibid. Stanza 11

The love of learning, the sequestered
nooks,
And all the sweet serenity of books.
Ibid. Stanza 21

Ah, nothing is too late,
Till the tired heart shall cease to palpi-
tate.
Cato learned Greek at eighty; Sophocles
Wrote his grand Oedipus, and Simonides

[1] From the Spanish of Santa Teresa. 1515–
1582.
[2] See Spenser, page 25.
One would say, he had read the inscription
on the gates of Busyrane, — "Be bold'; and
on the second gate, — "Be bold, be bold, and
evermore be bold": and then again had paused
well at the third gate, — "Be not too bold." —
EMERSON: *Plato; or, the Philosopher*

Bore off the prize of verse from his
compeers,
When each had numbered more than
fourscore years.
Morituri Salutamus. Stanza 22

Chaucer, at Woodstock with the night-
ingales,
At sixty wrote the Canterbury Tales;
Goethe at Weimar, toiling to the last,
Completed Faust when eighty years
were past.
Ibid.

For age is opportunity no less
Than youth itself, though in another
dress,
And as the evening twilight fades away
The sky is filled with stars, invisible
by day.
Ibid. Stanza 24

So when a great man dies,
For years beyond our ken,
The light he leaves behind him lies
Upon the paths of men.
Charles Sumner. Stanza 9

Sweet the memory is to me
Of a land beyond the sea,
Where the waves and mountains meet,
Where, amid her mulberry-trees
Sits Amalfi in the heat.
Amalfi. Stanza 1

The birds, God's poor who cannot wait.
*The Sermon of St. Francis.
Stanza 3*

Be not like a stream that brawls
Loud with shallow waterfalls,
But in quiet self-control
Link together soul and soul.
Songo River. Stanza 11

Nothing that is can pause or stay;
The moon will wax, the moon will wane,
The mist and cloud will turn to rain,
The rain to mist and cloud again,
To-morrow be to-day.
Kéramos

Thine was the prophet's vision, thine
The exaltation, the divine
Insanity of noble minds,
That never falters nor abates,
But labors and endures and waits,
Till all that it foresees it finds,
Or what it can not find creates!
Ibid.

Turn, turn, my wheel! 'Tis nature's plan
The child should grow into the man.
Kéramos

The willow pattern, that we knew
In childhood, with its bridge of blue.
Ibid.

He has singed the beard of the king of Spain.[1]
A Dutch Picture. Stanza 1

She knew the life-long martyrdom,
The weariness, the endless pain
Of waiting for some one to come
Who nevermore would come again.
Vittoria Colonna. Stanza 6

Three Kings came riding from far away,
Melchior and Gaspar and Baltasar;
Three Wise Men out of the East were they,
And they travelled by night and they slept by day,
For their guide was a beautiful, wonderful star.
The Three Kings. Stanza 1

Stay, stay at home, my heart, and rest;
Home-keeping hearts are happiest.
Song. Stanza 1

So Nature deals with us, and takes away
Our playthings one by one, and by the hand
Leads us to rest.
Nature

Not in the clamor of the crowded street,
Not in the shouts and plaudits of the throng,
But in ourselves, are triumph and defeat.
The Poets

Three Silences there are: the first of speech,
The second of desire, the third of thought;
This is the lore a Spanish monk, distraught

With dreams and visions, was the first to teach.
The Three Silences of Molinos [1]

The holiest of all holidays are those
Kept by ourselves in silence and apart;
The secret anniversaries of the heart.
Holidays

His presence haunts this room to-night,
A form of mingled mist and light
From that far coast.
Welcome beneath this roof of mine!
Welcome! this vacant chair is thine,
Dear guest and ghost!
Robert Burns. Stanza 9

Your silent tents of green [2]
We deck with fragrant flowers;
Yours has the suffering been,
The memory shall be ours.
Decoration Day. Stanza 6

Great is the art of beginning, but greater the art is of ending;
Many a poem is marred by a superfluous verse.
Elegiac Verse. Stanza 14

Out of the shadows of night
The world rolls into light;
It is daybreak everywhere.
The Bells of San Blas.[3] *Stanza 11*

Who ne'er his bread in sorrow ate,
Who ne'er the mournful midnight hours
Weeping upon his bed has sate,
He knows you not, ye Heavenly Powers.[4]
Hyperion. Book I, Motto

Alas! it is not till time, with reckless hand, has torn out half the leaves from the Book of Human Life to light the

---

[1] Sir Francis Drake entered the harbour of Cadiz, April 19, 1587, and destroyed shipping to the amount of ten thousand tons lading. To use his own expressive phrase, he had "singed the Spanish king's beard." — CHARLES KNIGHT [1791–1873]: *Pictorial History of England, Vol. III, P. 215*

[1] Miguel Molinos [1640–1696], a Spanish mystic, founder of the Quietists.
[2] The low green tent
Whose curtain never outward swings.
WHITTIER: *Snow-Bound*
The little green tent is a country's shrine where patriots kneel and pray. — WALT MASON: *The Little Green Tents*
[3] The last poem written by Longfellow. It is dated March 15, 1882. He died March 24, 1882.
[4] Wer nie sein Brod mit Thränen ass,
Wer nicht die kummervollen Nächte
Auf seinem Bette weinend sass,
Der kennt euch nicht, ihr himmlischen Mächte.
GOETHE: *Wilhelm Meister's Apprenticeship, Book II, Chap. 13*

fires of passion with from day to day, that man begins to see that the leaves which remain are few in number.

Hyperion. Book IV, Chap. 8

Look not mournfully into the Past. It comes not back again. Wisely improve the Present. It is thine. Go forth to meet the shadowy Future, without fear, and with a manly heart.[1]

Ibid.

Time has laid his hand
Upon my heart, gently, not smiting it,
But as a harper lays his open palm
Upon his harp to deaden its vibrations.

The Golden Legend. IV, The Cloisters

The grave itself is but a covered bridge
Leading from light to light, through a
brief darkness.[2]

Ibid. V, A Covered Bridge at Lucerne

Don't cross the bridge till you come to it,
Is a proverb old, and of excellent wit.

Ibid. VI, The School of Salerno

If we could read the secret history of our enemies, we should find in each man's life sorrow and suffering enough to disarm all hostility.

Driftwood

Music is the universal language of mankind, — poetry their universal pastime and delight.

Outre-Mer

Hold the fleet angel fast until he bless thee.[3]

Kavanagh

Give what you have. To some one, it may be better than you dare to think.

Ibid.

There is no greater sorrow
Than to be mindful of the happy time
In misery.[1]

Inferno. Canto V, Line 121

There was a little girl
Who had a little curl
Right in the middle of her forehead;
And when she was good
She was very, very good,
But when she was bad she was horrid.

There Was a Little Girl[2]

ROBERT MONTGOMERY

[1807–1855]

And thou, vast ocean! on whose awful face
Time's iron feet can print no ruin-trace.[3]

The Omnipresence of the Deity.
Part I

The soul aspiring pants its source to mount,
As streams meander level with their fount.[4]

Ibid.

---

[1]   Nessun maggior dolore
        Che ricordarsi del tempo felice
        Nella miseria.

In omni adversitate fortunæ, infelicissimum genus est infortunii fuisse felicem (In every adversity of fortune, to have been happy is the most unhappy kind of misfortune). — BOETHIUS: *De Consolatione Philosophiæ, II*
        This is truth the poet sings,
That a sorrow's crown of sorrow is remembering happier things.
        TENNYSON: *Locksley Hall, L. 75*
See Chaucer, page 4.

[2] BLANCHE ROOSEVELT TUCKER, in *The Home Life of Henry W. Longfellow* [1882], states that these lines were written by the poet for his children on a day when Edith did not want to have her hair curled.

[3] Time writes no wrinkle on thine azure brow. — BYRON: *Childe Harold's Pilgrimage, Canto IV, St. 182*

[4] We take this to be, on the whole, the worst similitude in the world. In the first place, no stream meanders or can possibly meander level with the fount. In the next place, if streams did meander level with their founts, no two motions can be less like each other than that of meandering level and that of mounting upwards. — MACAULAY: *Review of Montgomery's Poems* (Eleventh Edition), in *Edinburgh Review, April, 1830.*

These lines were omitted in the subsequent edition of the poem.

---

[1] The original inscription on the wall of the chapel of St. Gilgen, a small village in the Austrian Alps, near Salzburg, thus translated by Longfellow, is:

Blicke nicht trauernd in die Vergangenheit,
Sie kommt nicht wieder, nutze weise die
    Gegenwart,
Sie ist dein, der düsteren Zukunft geh ohne
    Furcht mit männlichem Sinne entgegen.

Bayard Taylor's translation duplicates Longfellow's.

[2] See Whittier, page 443.

[3] Quoted from *To-morrow*, by NATHANIEL COTTON [1705–1788].

I will not let thee go, except thou bless me. — *Genesis, XXXII, 26*

RICHARD CHEVENIX TRENCH
[1807–1886]

True servant's title he may wear,
  He only who has not
For his lord's gifts, how rich soe'er,
  His lord himself forgot.
The Spilt Pearls. Stanza 8

Lord, what a change within us one
    short hour
Spent in Thy presence will prevail to
    make!
Prayer

We kneel, how weak! we rise, how full
    of power!
Ibid.

I say to thee, — do thou repeat
To the first man thou mayest meet
In lane, highway, or open street,
That he and we and all men move
Under a canopy of love
As broad as the blue sky above.
The Kingdom of God. Stanzas 1 and 2

To leave unseen so many a glorious
    sight,
  To leave so many lands unvisited,
To leave so many worthiest books un-
    read,
  Unrealized so many visions bright: —
Oh! wretched yet inevitable spite
  Of our brief span.
Here and Hereafter

Make channels for the stream of love
Where they may broadly run,
And love has overflowing streams
To fill them every one.
The Law of Love

Thou hast said that mine my life is,
  Till the water of that cup
I have drained; then bid thy servants
  That spilled water gather up!
Harmosan

Bring another cup, and straightway
  To the noble Persian give:
Drink, I said before, and perish, —
  Now I bid thee drink and live!
Ibid.

JOHN GREENLEAF WHITTIER
[1807–1892]

The Present, the Present is all thou hast
  For thy sure possessing;
Like the patriarch's angel hold it fast
  Till it gives its blessing.[1]
My Soul and I. Stanza 34

Pluck one thread, and the web ye mar;
  Break but one
Of a thousand keys, and the paining
    jar
  Through all will run.
Ibid. Stanza 38

The Night is mother of the Day,
  The Winter of the Spring,
And ever upon old Decay
  The greenest mosses cling.
A Dream of Summer. Stanza 4

Art's perfect forms no moral need,
  And beauty is its own excuse;[2]
But for the dull and flowerless weed
Some healing virtue still must plead.
Songs of Labor. Dedication, Stanza 5

Heap high the farmer's wintry hoard!
Heap high the golden corn!
No richer gift has Autumn poured
  From out her lavish horn!
The Corn-Song. Stanza 1

Speak, Ximena, speak and tell us, who
    has lost, and who has won?
The Angels of Buena Vista. Stanza 6

What calls back the past, like the rich
    pumpkin pie?
The Pumpkin. Stanza 3

And the prayer, which my mouth is
    too full to express,
Swells my heart that thy shadow may
    never be less.
Ibid. Stanza 5

The tissue of the Life to be
  We weave with colors all our own,
And in the field of Destiny
  We reap as we have sown.
Raphael. Stanza 16

God blesses still the generous thought,
  And still the fitting word He speeds,

[1] See Cotton, page 226.
[2] In a footnote, Whittier acknowledges his indebtedness for this line to EMERSON'S *The Rhodora*.

And Truth, at His requiring taught,
He quickens into deeds.
                Channing. Stanza 23

So fallen! so lost! the light withdrawn
Which once he wore!
The glory from his gray hairs gone
For evermore!
                Ichabod. Stanza 1

When faith is lost, when honor dies
The man is dead!
                Ibid. Stanza 8

Through the shadowy lens of even
The eye looks farthest into heaven
On gleams of star and depths of blue
The glaring sunshine never knew!
                All's Well

Yet sometimes glimpses on my sight,
Through present wrong the eternal right;
And, step by step, since time began,
I see the steady gain of man.
                The Chapel of the Hermits. Stanza 11

We lack but open eye and ear
To find the Orient's marvels here;
The still small voice in autumn's hush,
Yon maple wood the burning bush.[1]
                Ibid. Stanza 16

Search thine own heart. What paineth thee
In others in thyself may be.
                Ibid. Stanza 85

The Beauty which old Greece or Rome
Sung, painted, wrought, lies close at home.
                To —, Lines Written after a Summer Day's Excursion. Stanza 7

Give lettered pomp to teeth of Time,
So "Bonnie Doon" but tarry;
Blot out the Epic's stately rhyme,
But spare his "Highland Mary!"
                Burns: On Receiving a Sprig of Heather in Blossom. Stanza 29

We seemed to see our flag unfurled,
Our champion waiting in his place
For the last battle of the world, —
The Armageddon of the race.
                Rantoul. Stanza 6

O for a knight like Bayard,
Without reproach or fear.[1]
                The Hero. Stanza 1

Blessings on thee, little man,
Barefoot boy, with cheek of tan!
                The Barefoot Boy. Stanza 1

Health that mocks the doctor's rules,
Knowledge never learned of schools.
                Ibid. Stanza 2

The age is dull and mean. Men creep,
Not walk.
                Lines Inscribed to Friends under Arrest for Treason Against the Slave Power. Stanza 1

God's ways seem dark, but, soon or late,
They touch the shining hills of day.
                Ibid. Stanza 5

Nature speaks in symbols and in signs.
                To Charles Sumner

We cross the prairie as of old
    The pilgrims crossed the sea,
To make the West, as they the East,
    The homestead of the free!
                The Kansas Emigrants. Stanza 1

Tradition wears a snowy beard, romance is always young.
                Mary Garvin. Stanza 4

Better heresy of doctrine, than heresy of heart.
                Ibid. Stanza 22

For of all sad words of tongue or pen,
The saddest are these: "It might have been!"[2]
                Maud Muller. Stanza 53

Ah, well! for us all some sweet hope lies
Deeply buried from human eyes.
                Ibid. Stanza 54

I know not how, in other lands,
    The changing seasons come and go;
What splendors fall on Syrian sands,
    What purple lights on Alpine snow.
                The Last Walk in Autumn. Stanza 7

I pray the prayer of Plato old:
God make thee beautiful within.
                My Namesake. Stanza 40

---

[1] Every common bush afire with God. —
MRS. BROWNING: *Aurora Leigh, Book VII,
L. 821*

[1] Bayard [1476–1524], "le Chevalier sans peur et sans reproche," a French national hero.

[2] More sad are these we daily see:
    It is, but hadn't ought to be.
    FRANCIS BRET HARTE: *Mrs. Judge Jenkins*

The great eventful Present hides the
Past; but through the din
Of its loud life hints and echoes from
the life behind steal in.
The Garrison of Cape Ann. Stanza 5

And the white magnolia-blossoms star
the twilight of the pines.
Ibid. Stanza 11

Soon or late to all our dwellings come
the spectres of the mind.
Ibid. Stanza 22

True and tender and brave and just,
That man might honor and woman
trust.
*The Prophecy of Samuel Sewall.
Stanza 1*

Old roads winding, as old roads will.
Ibid. Stanza 6

Old Floyd Ireson, for his hard heart,
Tarred and feathered and carried in a
cart
By the women of Marblehead.
Skipper Ireson's Ride. Stanza 1

Round the silver domes of Lucknow,
Moslem mosque and Pagan shrine,
Breathed the air to Britons dearest,
The air of Auld Lang Syne.[1]
The Pipes at Lucknow. Stanza 9

The windows of my soul I throw
Wide open to the sun.
My Psalm. Stanza 2

No longer forward nor behind
I look in hope or fear;
But, grateful, take the good I find,
The best of now and here.
Ibid. Stanza 3

Death seems but a covered way
Which opens into light.[2]
Ibid. Stanza 14

Dead Petra in her hill-tomb sleeps,
Her stones of emptiness remain;
Around her sculptured mystery sweeps
The lonely waste of Edom's plain.[3]
"The Rock" in El Ghor. Stanza 1

[1] It was the pipes of the Highlanders,
And now they played "Auld Lang Syne."
ROBERT TRAILL SPENCE LOWELL [1816–
1891]: *The Relief of Lucknow, September 25, 1857*

[2] See Longfellow, page 440.

[3] A rose-red city, half as old as time.
JOHN WILLIAM BURGON [1813–1888]:
Petra [Newdigate Prize Poem, 1845]

Who never wins can rarely lose,
Who never climbs as rarely falls.
To James T. Fields. Stanza 13

Happy is he who heareth
The signal of his release
In the bells of the Holy City,
The chimes of eternal peace!
The Red River Voyageur. Stanza 10

Perish with him the folly that seeks
through evil good.
Brown of Ossawatomie. Stanza 6

Once more the liberal year laughs out
O'er richer stores than gems or gold;
Once more with harvest-song and shout
Is Nature's bloodless triumph told.
For an Autumn Festival. Stanza 5

Strike, Thou the Master, we Thy keys,
The anthem of the destinies!
The minor of Thy loftier strain,
Our hearts shall breathe the old refrain,
Thy will be done!
Thy Will Be Done. Stanza 7

O Englishmen! — in hope and creed,
In blood and tongue our brothers!
We too are heirs of Runnymede;
And Shakespeare's fame and Crom-
well's deed
Are not alone our mother's.
To Englishmen. Stanza 5

"Thicker than water," [1] in one rill
Through centuries of story
Our Saxon blood has flowed, and still
We share with you its good and ill,
The shadow and the glory.
Ibid. Stanza 6

"Shoot, if you must, this old gray head,
But spare your country's flag," she said.
Barbara Frietchie. Stanza 18

O, rank is good, and gold is fair,
And high and low mate ill;
But love has never known a law
Beyond its own sweet will!
Amy Wentworth

Shut in from all the world without,
We sat the clean-winged hearth about.
Snow-Bound

Melt not in an acid sect
The Christian pearl of charity.
Ibid.

Angel of the backward look.
Ibid.

[1] See Sir Walter Scott, page 310.

Yet Love will dream, and Faith will
    trust,
(Since He who knows our need is just,)
That somehow, somewhere, meet we
    must.
Alas for him who never sees
The stars shine through his cypress-
    trees!
Who, hopeless, lays his dead away,
Nor looks to see the breaking day
Across the mournful marbles play!
                        Snow-Bound

Life is ever lord of Death
And Love can never lose its own.
                                Ibid.

To eat the lotus of the Nile
    And drink the poppies of Cathay.
        The Tent on the Beach. Stanza 4
    The life to be
Is still the unguessed mystery:
Unscaled, unpierced the cloudy walls
    remain,
We beat with dream and wish the
    soundless doors in vain.
    *Ibid. Interlude after The Grave by
                        the Lake*

And so beside the Silent Sea
    I wait the muffled oar.
        The Eternal Goodness. Stanza 19

I know not where His islands lift
    Their fronded palms in air;
I only know I cannot drift
    Beyond His love and care.
                Ibid. Stanza 20

Flowers spring to blossom where she
    walks
    The careful ways of duty;
Our hard, stiff lines of life with her
    Are flowing curves of beauty.[1]
            Among the Hills. Stanza 52

If woman lost us Eden, such
    As she alone restore it.
                Ibid. Stanza 60

Heaven's gate is shut to him who comes
    alone;

[1] Straight is the line of Duty,
    Curved is the line of Beauty,
    Follow the straight line, thou shalt see
    The curved line ever follow thee.
        WILLIAM MACCALL [1812–1888]: *Duty*
See Ellen Sturgis Hooper, page 508.

Save thou a soul, and it shall save thy
    own!
                        The Two Rabbis
And so, I find it well to come
For deeper rest to this still room,
For here the habit of the soul
Feels less the outer world's control.
                        The Meeting
The world that time and sense have
    known
Falls off and leaves us God alone.
                                Ibid.
He lives to learn, in life's hard school,
    How few who pass above him
Lament their triumph and his loss,
    Like her, — because they love him.
            In School-Days. Stanza 11
Let the thick curtain fall;
I better know than all
How little I have gained,
How vast the unattained.
                My Triumph. Stanza 7
Sweeter than any sung
My songs that found no tongue;
Nobler than any fact
My wish that failed of act.
                        Ibid. Stanza 9
Others shall sing the song,
Others shall right the wrong, —
Finish what I begin,
And all I fail of win.
                        Ibid. Stanza 10
God is and all is well.[1]
                My Birthday. Stanza 2
He brings cool dew in his little bill,
    And lets it fall on the souls of sin;
You can see the mark on his red breast
    still
    Of fires that scorch as he drops it in.[2]
                The Robin. Stanza 4
One language held his heart and lip,
    Straight onward to his goal he trod,

[1] God's in his heaven:
    All's right with the world.
        ROBERT BROWNING: *Pippa Passes,
                        Part I*
[2] Far, far away, is a land of woe and darkness, spirits of evil and fire. Day after day a
little bird flies there, bearing in his bill a drop
of water to quench the flame. So near the
burning stream does he fly that his feathers
are scorched by it, and hence he is named
"Bron-rhuddyn" — breast-burned. — Carmar-
thenshire Legend of the Robin

And proved the highest statesmanship
  Obedience to the voice of God.
                Charles Sumner. Stanza 17

With fifty years between you and your
  well-kept wedding vow,
The Golden Age, old friends of mine,
  is not a fable now.
    The Golden Wedding at Longwood.
                Stanza 1

Still, as at Cana's marriage-feast, the
  best wine is the last.[1]
                Ibid. Stanza 2

The holiest task by Heaven decreed,
  An errand all divine,
The burden of our common need
  To render less is thine.
                The Healer.[2] Stanza 4

Touched by a light that hath no name,
  A glory never sung,
Aloft on sky and mountain wall
  Are God's great pictures hung.
    Sunset on the Bearcamp. Stanza 2

Our fathers' God! from out whose hand
The centuries fall like grains of sand.
            Centennial Hymn. Stanza 1

Behold in the bloom of apples
  And the violets in the sward
A hint of the old, lost beauty
  Of the Garden of the Lord!
    The Minister's Daughter. Stanza 7

If any words of mine,
Through right of life divine,
Remain, what matters it
Whose hand the message writ?
            An Autograph. Stanza 5

Whate'er his life's defeatures,
He loved his fellow-creatures.
                Ibid. Stanza 10

Hater of din and riot
He lived in days unquiet;
And, lover of all beauty,
Trod the hard ways of duty.
                Ibid. Stanza 15

---

[1] Thou hast kept the good wine until now.
— *John, II, 10*
[2] A well trained sensible family doctor is
one of the most valuable assets in a community, worth to-day, as in Homer's time,
many another man. . . . Few men live lives
of more devoted self-sacrifice. — SIR WILLIAM
OSLER: *Aequanimitas and Other Addresses,
XIV, Chauvinism in Medicine*

Our first and best! — his ashes lie
Beneath his own Virginian sky.
    The Vow of Washington. Stanza 14

Close to my heart I fold each lovely
  thing
The sweet day yields; and, not dis-
  consolate,
With the calm patience of the woods
  I wait
For leaf and blossom when God gives
  us Spring!
                A Day. Stanza 6

HORATIUS BONAR
[1808–1889]

In the still air the music lies unheard;
  In the rough marble beauty lies unseen;
To wake the music and the beauty
  needs
  The master's touch, the sculptor's
  chisel keen.
        The Master's Touch. Stanza 1

The star is not extinguished when it
  sets
Upon the dull horizon; it but goes
To shine in other skies, then reappear
  In ours, as fresh as when it first
  arose.
            Life from Death. Stanza 1

Calm me, my God, and keep me calm,
  While these hot breezes blow;
Be like the night-dew's cooling balm
  Upon earth's fevered brow.
            Calm Me, My God. Stanza 1

Beyond the smiling and the weeping
  I shall be soon;
Beyond the waking and the sleeping,
Beyond the sowing and the reaping.
            A Little While. Stanza 1

We have no time to sport away the
  hours;
All must be earnest in a world like ours.
                Our One Life. Stanza 1

SALMON PORTLAND CHASE
[1808–1873]

The Constitution, in all its provisions, looks to an indestructible Union
composed of indestructible States.
        Decision in Texas v. White,
                7 Wallace, 725

The only way to resumption is to resume.

Letter to Horace Greeley
[March 17, 1866]

HENRY FOTHERGILL CHORLEY
[1808–1872]

A song to the oak, the brave old oak,
Who hath ruled in the greenwood
long!
The Brave Old Oak. Stanza 1

Then here's to the oak, the brave old
oak,
Who stands in his pride alone!
And still flourish he, a hale green tree,
When a hundred years are gone!
Ibid. Refrain

Go to the dreamless bed
Where grief reposes;
Thy book of toil is read;
The long day closes.
The Long Day Closes. Stanza 3

FRANCES DANA GAGE
[1808–1884]

The home we first knew on this beautiful earth,
The friends of our childhood, the place
of our birth,
In the heart's inner chamber sung always will be,
As the shell ever sings of its home in
the sea! [1]
Home

Wife, mother, nurse, seamstress, cook,
housekeeper, chambermaid, laun-

---

[1] As a sea-shell of the sea
Ever shall I sing of thee.
GEORGE MEREDITH: *Love Within*
the Lover's Breast
Listen thou well, for my shell hath speech.
CHARLES HENRY WEBB: *With a*
Nantucket Shell
One song it sang, —
Sang of the awful mysteries of the tide,
Sang of the misty sea, profound and wide, —
Ever with echoes of the ocean rang.
EUGENE FIELD: *The Wanderer*

---

dress, dairy-woman, and scrub
generally, doing the work of six,
For the sake of being supported.
The Housekeeper's Soliloquy.
Stanza 10

ANDREW JOHNSON
[1808–1875]

We are swinging round the circle.
On the Presidential Reconstruction
Tour [August, 1866]

THOMAS MILLER
[1808–1874]

What though upon his hoary head
Have fallen many a winter's snow?
His wreath is still as green and red
As 'twas a thousand years ago.
For what has he to do with care!
His wassail-bowl and old arm-chair
Are ever standing ready there,
For Christmas comes but once a year.
Christmas Comes but Once a Year

CAROLINE ELIZABETH SHERIDAN NORTON, LADY MAXWELL
[1808–1877]

We have been friends together,
In sunshine and in shade,
Since first beneath the chestnut-tree
In infancy we played.
But coldness dwells within thine heart
A cloud is on thy brow;
We have been friends together,
Shall a light word part us now?
We Have Been Friends. Stanza 1

I am listening for the voices
Which I heard in days of old.
The Lonely Harp

Love not! love not! ye hopeless sons
of clay;
Hope's gayest wreaths are made of
earthly flowers —
Things that are made to fade and fall
away,
Ere they have blossomed for a few
short hours.
Love Not

I need no squire, no page with bended
    knee,
To bear my baby through the wild-
    wood track,
Where Allan Percy used to roam with
    me.
           Allan Percy. Stanza 3
A soldier of the Legion lay dying in
    Algiers;
There was lack of woman's nursing,
    there was dearth of woman's tears.
        Bingen on the Rhine. Stanza 1
Too innocent for coquetry, too fond for
    idle scorning, —
Oh friend! I fear the lightest heart
    makes sometimes heaviest mourn-
    ing.
               Ibid. Stanza 5
Every poet hopes that after-times
Shall set some value on his votive lay.
        To the Duchess of Sutherland
O Twilight! Spirit that dost render
    birth
To dim enchantments; melting heaven
    with earth,
Leaving on craggy hills and running
    streams
A softness like the atmosphere of
    dreams.
            The Winter's Walk
For death and life, in ceaseless strife,
  Beat wild on this world's shore,
And all our calm is in that balm —
  Not lost but gone before.
        Not Lost but Gone Before

GEORGE WASHINGTON
PATTEN
[1808–1882]

Blaze, with your serried columns!
  I will not bend the knee!
The shackles ne'er again shall bind
  The arm which now is free.
    The Seminole's Reply. Stanza 1
I scorn your proffered treaty!
  The paleface I defy,
Revenge is stamped upon my spear,
  And blood my battle-cry!
             Ibid. Stanza 2
I'll taunt ye with my latest breath,
  And fight ye till I die!
             Ibid. Stanza 5

Keep honor, like your sabre, bright,
  Shame coward fear — and then,
If we must perish in the fight,
  Oh! let us die like men.
    Oh, Let Us Die Like Men. Stanza 4
Joys that we've tasted
  May sometimes return,
But the torch when once wasted,
  Ah! how can it burn?
Splendors now clouded,
  Say, when will ye shine?
Broke is the goblet,
  And wasted the wine.
      Joys That We've Tasted. Stanza 1

SAMUEL FRANCIS SMITH
[1808–1895]

My country, 'tis of thee,
Sweet land of liberty,
  Of thee I sing:
Land where my fathers died,
Land of the pilgrims' pride,
From every mountain-side
  Let freedom ring.
               America
Our fathers' God, to thee,
Author of liberty,
  To thee I sing;
Long may our land be bright
With freedom's holy light;
Protect us by thy might,
  Great God, our King!
               Ibid.
Our glorious land to-day,
'Neath Education's sway,
  Soars upward still.
Its halls of learning fair,
Whose bounties all may share,
Behold them everywhere,
  On vale and hill.
      Ibid. (Discarded stanza)

CHARLES TENNYSON-
TURNER
[1808–1879]

The shadow of our travelling earth
Hung on the silver moon.
         Eclipse of the Moon
And while she hid all England with a
  kiss,

Bright over Europe fell her golden hair.
Letty's Globe

The little moulted feathers, saffron-
tipt,

The perches, which his faltering feet
embraced,

All these remain — not even his bath
removed —

But where's the spray and flutter that
we loved?
The Vacant Cage

FREDERICK WILLIAM
THOMAS
[1808–1866]

'Tis said that absence conquers love;
But oh believe it not!
I've tried, alas! its power to prove,
But thou art not forgot.
Absence Conquers Love

PARK BENJAMIN
[1809–1864]

I'm king of the dead — and I make my
throne
On a monument slab of marble cold;
And my scepter of rule is the spade I
hold:
Come they from cottage or come they
from hall,
Mankind are my subjects, all, all, all!
Let them loiter in pleasure or toilfully
spin —
I gather them in, I gather them in! [1]
The Old Sexton

CHARLES ROBERT DARWIN
[1809–1882]

I have called this principle, by which
each slight variation, if useful, is preserved, by the term Natural Selection.
The Origin of Species. Chap. 3

The expression often used by Mr.
Herbert Spencer, of the Survival of the

---

[1] These words came from his lips so thin:
"I gather them in — I gather them in!"
EUGENE FIELD: *The Old Sexton*
(a parody)

Fittest, is more accurate, and is sometimes equally convenient.[1]
The Origin of Species. Chap. 3

We will now discuss in a little more
detail the Struggle for Existence.[2]
Ibid.

Even when we are quite alone, how
often do we think with pleasure or pain
of what others think of us — of their
imagined approbation or disapprobation.
The Descent of Man. Chap. 4

The highest possible stage in moral
culture is when we recognize that we
ought to control our thoughts.
Ibid.

The presence of a body of well-
instructed men, who have not to labor
for their daily bread, is important to a
degree which cannot be overestimated;
as all high intellectual work is carried
on by them, and on such work material
progress of all kinds mainly depends,
not to mention other and higher advantages.
Ibid. Chap. 5

Progress has been much more general
than retrogression.
Ibid.

The Simiadae then branched off into
two great stems, the New World and
Old World monkeys; and from the latter at a remote period, Man, the wonder and the glory of the universe, proceeded.[3]
Ibid. Chap. 6

---

[1] This survival of the fittest which I have
here sought to express in mechanical terms, is
that which Mr. Darwin has called "natural selection, or the preservation of favoured races
in the struggle for life." — HERBERT SPENCER:
Principles of Biology, Indirect Equilibration

[2] The perpetual struggle for room and food.
— MALTHUS: *On Population, Chap. III, P. 48*
[1798]

[3] Pouter, tumbler and fantail are from the
same source;
The racer and hack may be traced to one
horse;
So men were developed from monkeys,
of course,
Which nobody can deny.
LORD CHARLES NEAVES [1800–1876]:
The Origin of Species

See Benjamin Disraeli, page 419.

False facts are highly injurious to the progress of science, for they often endure long; but false views, if supported by some evidence, do little harm, for every one takes a salutary pleasure in proving their falseness.

The Descent of Man. Chap. 21

Physiological experiment on animals is justifiable for real investigation, but not for mere damnable and detestable curiosity.[1]

Letter to E. Ray Lankester

I love fools' experiments. I am always making them.

Remark cited in Life of Darwin

As for a future life, every man must judge for himself between conflicting vague probabilities.

Life and Letters

Believing as I do that man in the distant future will be a far more perfect creature than he now is, it is an intolerable thought that he and all other sentient beings are doomed to complete annihilation after such long-continued slow progress. To those who fully admit the immortality of the human soul, the destruction of our world will not appear so dreadful.

Ibid.

Among the scenes which are deeply impressed on my mind, none exceed in sublimity the primeval forests undefaced by the hand of man. No one can stand in these solitudes unmoved, and not feel that there is more in man than the mere breath of his body.

Journal during the Voyage of H. M. S. Beagle. Chap. 21

[1] The main cause of this unparalleled progress in physiology, pathology, medicine and surgery has been the fruitful application of the experimental method of research, just the same method which has been the great lever of all scientific advance in modern times. — DR. WILLIAM H. WELCH [1850-1934]: *Argument against Antivivisection Bill* (Senate No. 34), Fifty-sixth Congress, First Session, February 21, 1900. Quoted in HARVEY CUSHING: *Life of Sir William Osler, Vol. I, P. 521.*

EDWARD FITZGERALD [1]
[1809-1883]

Whether we wake or we sleep,
Whether we carol or weep,
The Sun with his Planets in chime,
Marketh the going of Time.

Chronomoros

The King in a carriage may ride,
And the Beggar may crawl at his side;
But in the general race,
They are traveling all the same pace.

Ibid.

Mrs. Browning's death was rather a relief to me, I must say; no more Aurora Leighs, thank God!

Letter [July 15, 1861] [2]

The soul indeed is far away,
But we would reverence the clay
In which she made so long a stay.

On the Death of Bernard Barton

I have heard tell of another Poet's saying that he knew of no human outlook so solemn as that from an Infant's Eyes.

Euphranor

'Tis a dull sight
To see the year dying,
When winter winds
Set the yellow wood sighing.

Literary Remains: Old Song, Stanza 1

[1] For translation of *The Rubaiyat* of Omar Khayyám, see Translations.

[2] I chanced upon a new book yesterday;
  I opened it, and where my fingers lay
  'Twixt page and uncut page these words
    I read —
  Some six or seven at most — and learned
    thereby
  That you, Fitzgerald, whom by ear and
    eye
  She never knew, thanked God my wife
    was dead.
  Aye, dead! and were yourself alive, good
    Fitz,
  How to return your thanks would pass
    my wits.
  Kicking you seems the common lot of
    curs,
  While more appropriate greeting lends
    you grace.
  Surely to spit there glorifies your face,
  Spitting with lips once sanctified by hers.
  ROBERT BROWNING in *The Athenaeum*, London, July 13, 1889. Quoted by E. F. BENSON: *As We Were, a Victorian Peep-Show, P. 126*

WILLIAM EWART GLADSTONE
[1809–1898]

To be engaged in opposing wrong affords, under the conditions of our mental constitution, but a slender guarantee for being right.

Time and Place of Homer.
Introduction

Decision by majorities is as much an expedient as lighting by gas.

Speech, House of Commons [*1858*]

The disease of an evil conscience is beyond the practice of all the physicians of all the countries in the world.

Speech, Plumstead [*1878*]

National injustice is the surest road to national downfall.

Ibid.

I have always regarded that Constitution as the most remarkable work known to me in modern times to have been produced by the human intellect, at a single stroke (so to speak), in its application to political affairs.[1]

Letter to the Committee in charge of the celebration of the Centennial Anniversary of the American Constitution [*July 20 1887*]

Selfishness is the greatest curse of the human race.

Speech, Hawarden [*May 28, 1890*]

Tell him, O gracious Lord, if it may be, how much I love him and miss him and long to see him again; and if there be ways in which he may come, vouchsafe him to me as a guide and guard, and grant me a sense of his nearness, in such degree as Thy laws permit.

A Prayer for a Friend Out of Sight

Within the short and narrow bound;
From morn to eventide
In quick, successive train,

---

[1] As the British Constitution is the most subtle organism which has proceeded from progressive history, so the American Constitution is the most wonderful work ever struck off at a given time by the brain and purpose of man. — *Kin Beyond the Sea* (in *The North American Review, September, 1878*)

An infant lived and died
And lived again.

On an Infant Who Was Born, Was Baptized, and Died on the Same Day [*1836*]. *Stanza 12*

Lord, as Thy temple's portals close
Behind the outward-parting throng,
So shut my spirit in repose,
So bind it there, Thy flock among.
The fickle wanderer else will stray
Back to the world's wide parchèd way.

Holy Communion. Stanza 1

OLIVER WENDELL HOLMES [1]
[1809–1894]

Ay, tear her tattered ensign down!
Long has it waved on high,
And many an eye has danced to see
That banner in the sky.

Old Ironsides. Stanza 1

Nail to the mast her holy flag,
Set every threadbare sail,
And give her to the god of storms,
The lightning and the gale!

Ibid. Stanza 3

The mossy marbles rest
On the lips that he has prest
In their bloom —
And the names he loved to hear
Have been carved for many a year
On the tomb.

The Last Leaf. Stanza 4

I know it is a sin
For me to sit and grin
At him here;
But the old three-cornered hat,
And the breeches, and all that,
Are so queer!

Ibid. Stanza 7

And if I should live to be
The last leaf upon the tree
In the spring,
Let them smile, as I do now,
At the old forsaken bough [2]
Where I cling.

Ibid. Stanza 8

---

[1] The most successful combination the world has ever seen, of physician and man of letters. — SIR WILLIAM OSLER. Quoted in HARVEY CUSHING: *Life of Sir William Osler, Vol. I, Chap. 15*

[2] A forsaken bough. — *Isaiah, XVII, 9*

Thou say'st an undisputed thing
 In such a solemn way.
                    To an Insect. Stanza 7
One sad, ungathered rose
On my ancestral tree.
                    My Aunt. Stanza 6
You think they are crusaders, sent
 From some infernal clime,
To pluck the eyes of Sentiment
 And dock the tail of Rhyme,
To crack the voice of Melody
 And break the legs of Time.
        The Music Grinders. Stanza 9
And silence, like a poultice, comes
 To heal the blows of sound.
                    Ibid. Stanza 10
I'm not a chicken; I have seen
Full many a chill September.
        The September Gale. Stanza 1
And since, I never dare to write
 As funny as I can.
        The Height of the Ridiculous.
                        Stanza 8
Little I ask; my wants are few,
 I only wish a hut of stone,
(A *very plain* brownstone will do,)
 That I may call my own.[1]
            Contentment. Stanza 1
When the last reader reads no more.
                    The Last Reader
The freeman, casting with unpurchased
 hand,
The vote that shakes the turret of the
 land.
    Poetry, a Metrical Essay. Proem
Age, like distance, lends a double
 charm.[2]
        A Rhymed Lesson. Urania
And when you stick on conversation's
 burs,
Don't strew your pathway with those
 dreadful *urs*.
                            Ibid.
Be sure your tailor is a man of sense.
                            Ibid.
Wear seemly gloves; not black, nor yet
 to light,
And least of all the pair that once was
 white.
                            Ibid.

[1] See Goldsmith, page 254.
[2] See Campbell, page 327.

Have a good hat; the secret of your
 looks
Lives with the beaver in Canadian
 brooks;
Virtue may flourish in an old cravat,
But man and nature scorn the shock-
 ing hat.[1]
        A Rhymed Lesson. Urania
Learn the sweet magic of a cheerful
 face;
Not always smiling, but at least serene.
                The Morning Visit
There was a young man in Boston town,
 He bought him a stethoscope nice
 and new,
All mounted and finished and polished
 down,
 With an ivory cap and a stopper too.
        The Stethoscope Song. Stanza 1
Now when a doctor's patients are per-
 plexed,
A consultation comes in order next —
You know what that is? In a certain
 place
Meet certain doctors to discuss a case
And other matters, such as weather,
 crops,
Potatoes, pumpkins, lager-beer, and
 hops.
            Rip Van Winkle, M.D.
Wake in our breast the living fires,
The holy faith that warmed our sires;
Thy hand hath made our Nation free;
To die for her is serving Thee.
            Army Hymn. Stanza 2
Thine eye was on the censer,
 And not the hand that bore it.
        Lines by a Clerk. Stanza 5
Where go the poet's lines?
 Answer, ye evening tapers!
Ye auburn locks, ye golden curls,
 Speak from your folded papers!
            The Poet's Lot. Stanza 3
A few can touch the magic string,
 And noisy Fame is proud to win
 them: —
Alas for those that never sing,
 But die with all their music in them!
            The Voiceless. Stanza 1

[1] See page 454.

O hearts that break and give no sign
Save whitening lip and fading
tresses.
The Voiceless. Stanza 3

When darkness gathers over all,
And the last tottering pillars fall,
Take the poor dust thy mercy warms,
And mould it into heavenly forms!
*The Living Temple [Anatomist's
Hymn]. Stanza 7*

We will not speak of years to-night, —
For what have years to bring
But larger floods of love and light,
And sweeter songs to sing?
*At a Birthday Festival [for
James Russell Lowell]. Stanza 1*

And faith that sees the ring of light
Round nature's last eclipse!
Ibid. Stanza 6

The lusty days of long ago,
When you were Bill and I was Joe.
Bill and Joe. Stanza 1

Where are the Marys, and Anns, and
Elizas,
Loving and lovely of yore?
Questions and Answers. Stanza 3

Oh for one hour of youthful joy!
Give back my twentieth spring!
The Old Man Dreams. Stanza 1

Old Time is a liar! We're twenty to-
night!
The Boys. Stanza 1

Where the snow-flakes fall thickest
there's nothing can freeze!
Ibid. Stanza 2

You hear that boy laughing? [1] — You
think he's all fun;
But the angels laugh, too, at the good
he has done;
The children laugh loud as they troop
to his call,
And the poor man that knows him
laughs loudest of all.
Ibid. Stanza 9

One flag, one land, one heart, one hand,
One Nation, evermore!
*Voyage of the Good Ship Union.
Stanza 12*

Good to the heels the well-worn slipper
feels

[1] The Reverend Samuel May, abolitionist.

When the tired player shuffles off the
buskin;
A page of Hood may do a fellow good
After a scolding from Carlyle or
Ruskin.
How Not to Settle It. Stanza 3

Build thee more stately mansions, O
my soul,
As the swift seasons roll!
Leave thy low-vaulted past!
Let each new temple, nobler than the
last,
Shut thee from heaven with a dome
more vast,
Till thou at length art free,
Leaving thine outgrown shell by life's
unresting sea!
The Chambered Nautilus. Stanza 5

One unquestioned text we read,
All doubt beyond, all fear above, —
Nor crackling pile nor cursing creed
Can burn or blot it: God is love. [1]
What We All Think. Stanza 10

When lawyers take what they would
give
And doctors give what they would take.
Latter-day Warnings. Stanza 4

His home! — the Western giant smiles,
And twirls the spotty globe to find
it; —
This little speck, the British Isles?
'Tis but a freckle, — never mind it!
*A Good Time Going (to Charles
Mackay). Stanza 3*

But Memory blushes at the sneer,
And Honor turns with frown defiant,
And Freedom, leaning on her spear,
Laughs louder than the laughing
giant.
Ibid. Stanza 4

Have you heard of the wonderful one-
hoss shay,
That was built in such a logical way
It ran a hundred years to a day?
The Deacon's Masterpiece. Stanza 1

A general flavor of mild decay.
Ibid. Stanza 10

[1] God is love. — *1 John, IV, 8*
God! Thou art love! I build my faith on
that. — ROBERT BROWNING: *Paracelsus, V*

It went to pieces all at once, —
All at once, and nothing first,
Just as bubbles do when they burst.
The Deacon's Masterpiece. Stanza 11

Learn to give
Money to colleges while you live.
Don't be silly and think you'll try
To bother the colleges, when you die,
With codicil this, and codicil that,
That Knowledge may starve while Law
grows fat;
For there never was pitcher that
wouldn't spill,
And there's always a flaw in a donkey's
will.
Parson Turell's Legacy

Our truest steps are human still, —
To walk unswerving were divine.
The Crooked Footpath. Stanza 8

The living fountain overflows
For every flock, for every lamb,
Nor heeds, though angry creeds oppose
With Luther's dike or Calvin's dam.
Robinson of Leyden. Stanza 6

Where we love is home,
Home that our feet may leave, but not
our hearts.
Homesick in Heaven. Stanza 5

And from two things left behind him, —
(Be sure they'll try to find him,)
The tax-bill and assessor, —
Heaven keep the great Professor!
A Farewell to Agassiz

The brightest blade grows dim with
rust,
The fairest meadow white with snow.
Chanson Without Music. Stanza 3

There is no time like the old time, when
you and I were young.[1]
No Time Like the Old Time. Stanza 1

Fame is the scentless sunflower, with
gaudy crown of gold;
But friendship is the breathing rose,
with sweets in every fold.
Ibid. Stanza 3

'Tis like stirring living embers when,
at eighty, one remembers

All the achings and the quaking of "the
times that tried men's souls." [1]
*Grandmother's Story of Bunker-Hill
Battle. Stanza 1*

Trained in the holy art whose lifted
shield
Wards off the darts a never-slumbering
foe,
By hearth and wayside lurking, waits
to throw.[2]
Sonnet, Joseph Warren, M.D.

The style's the man, so books avow;
The style's the woman, anyhow.
*How the Old Horse Won the Bet.
Stanza 2*

I come not here your morning hour to
sadden,
A limping pilgrim, leaning on his
staff, —
I, who have never deemed it sin to
gladden
This vale of sorrows with a wholesome laugh.
The Iron Gate. Stanza 16

I read it in the story-book, that, for to
kiss his dear,
Leander swam the Hellespont, — and
I will swim this here.
*The Ballad of the Oysterman.
Stanza 3*

Lean, hungry, savage, anti-everythings.
A Modest Request. The Speech.

This body in which we journey
across the isthmus between the two
oceans is not a private carriage, but an
omnibus.
The Guardian Angel. Chap. 3

He comes of the Brahmin caste of
New England. This is the harmless, in-
offensive, untitled aristocracy.
The Brahmin Caste of New England [3]

A thought is often original, though
you have uttered it a hundred times.
*The Autocrat of the Breakfast-
Table. I*

Everybody likes and respects self-
made men. It is a great deal better to

---

[1] There are no days like the good old days,
The days when we were youthful!
EUGENE FIELD: *Old Times, Old
Friends, Old Love*

[1] See Thomas Paine, page 271.
[2] Amid an eternal heritage of sorrow and
suffering our work is laid. — SIR WILLIAM OS-
LER: *Aequanimitas* [1906], *XX, The Student
Life.*
[3] In *The Atlantic Monthly, January, 1860.*

be made in that way than not to be made at all.

The Autocrat of the Breakfast-Table. I

Insanity is often the logic of an accurate mind overtaxed.

Ibid.

Put not your trust in money, but put your money in trust.

Ibid. II

Sin has many tools, but a lie is the handle which fits them all.

Ibid. VI

There is that glorious epicurean paradox uttered by my friend the historian,[1] in one of his flashing moments: "Give us the luxuries of life, and we will dispense with its necessaries." To this must certainly be added that other saying of one of the wittiest of men:[2] "Good Americans, when they die, go to Paris."

Ibid.

Boston State-house is the hub of the solar system. You couldn't pry that out of a Boston man, if you had the tire of all creation straightened out for a crowbar.

Ibid.

The axis of the earth sticks out visibly through the centre of each and every town or city.

Ibid.

The world's great men have not commonly been great scholars, nor its great scholars great men.

Ibid.

Knowledge and timber shouldn't be much used till they are seasoned.

Ibid.

The hat is the *ultimum moriens* of respectability.[3]

Ibid. XIII

I firmly believe that if the whole *materia medica* as now used could be sunk to the bottom of the sea, it would be all

the better for mankind — and all the worse for the fishes.[1]

Address, Massachusetts Medical Society [May 30, 1860]

To be seventy years young is sometimes far more cheerful and hopeful than to be forty years old.

On the Seventieth Birthday of Julia Ward Howe [May 27, 1889]

FRANCES ANNE KEMBLE
[1809–1893]

What shall I do with all the days and hours
  That must be counted ere I see thy face?
How shall I charm the interval that lowers
  Between this time and that sweet time of grace?

Absence. Stanza 1

Maids must be wives and mothers to fulfil
The entire and holiest end of woman's being.

Woman's Heart

A sacred burden is this life ye bear:
Look on it, lift it, bear it solemnly,
Stand up and walk beneath it steadfastly.
Fail not for sorrow, falter not for sin,
But onward, upward, till the goal ye win.

Lines addressed to the Young Gentleman leaving the Lenox Academy, Massachusetts

MARK LEMON
[1809–1870]

Oh would I were a boy again,
  When life seemed formed of sunny years,

[1] Stir the mixture well
    Lest it prove inferior,
    Then put half a drop
    Into Lake Superior.

    Every other day
    Take a drop in water,
    You'll be better soon
    Or at least you oughter.
    BISHOP WILLIAM CROSWELL DOANE [1832–1913]: *Lines on Homœopathy*

---

[1] John Lothrop Motley [1814–1877].
Said Scopas of Thessaly, "We rich men count our felicity and happiness to lie in these superfluities, and not in those necessary things." — PLUTARCH: *On the Love of Wealth*
[2] Thomas Gold Appleton [1812–1884]
[3] See Holmes, page 451.

And all the heart then knew of pain
  Was wept away in transient tears!
When every tale Hope whispered then,
  My fancy deemed was only truth.
Oh, would that I could know again,
  The happy visions of my youth.
        Oh Would I Were a Boy Again
Forth we went, a gallant band —
  Youth, Love, Gold and Pleasure.
        Last Song

ABRAHAM LINCOLN
[1809–1865]

If the good people, in their wisdom, shall see fit to keep me in the background, I have been too familiar with disappointments to be very much chagrined.
> *Address, New Salem, Illinois [March 9, 1832]*

I go for all sharing the privileges of the government who assist in bearing its burden.
> *Letter to Editor of the Sangamo Journal, New Salem, Illinois [June 13, 1835]*

There is no grievance that is a fit object of redress by mob law.
> *Address, Young Men's Lyceum, Springfield, Illinois [January 27, 1837]*

Whether or not the world would be vastly benefited by a total and final banishment from it of all intoxicating drinks seems to me not now an open question. Three-fourths of mankind confess the affirmative with their tongues, and, I believe, all the rest acknowledge it in their hearts. Ought any, then, to refuse their aid in doing what good the good of the whole demands?
> *Speech, Washingtonian Temperance Society, Springfield, Illinois [February 22, 1842]*

I believe this government cannot endure permanently half slave and half free.
> *Speech, Republican State Convention, Springfield, Illinois [June 16, 1858]*

Nobody has ever expected me to be president. In my poor, lean lank face nobody has ever seen that any cabbages were sprouting.
> *Second Campaign Speech against Douglas,[1] Springfield, Illinois [July 17, 1858]*

As I would not be a slave, so I would not be a master. This expresses my idea of democracy. Whatever differs from this, to the extent of the difference, is no democracy.
> *Letter [August 1 (?), 1858]*

Let us have faith that right makes might; and in that faith let us to the end, dare to do our duty as we understand it.
> *Address, Cooper Union, New York [February 27, 1860]*

Trusting to Him who can go with me, and remains with you, and be everywhere for good, let us confidently hope that all will yet be well.
> *Farewell Address, Springfield, Illinois [February 11, 1861]*

If we do not make common cause to save the good old ship of the Union on this voyage, nobody will have a chance to pilot her on another voyage.
> *Address, Cleveland, Ohio [February 15, 1861]*

Why should there not be a patient confidence in the ultimate justice of the people? Is there any better or equal hope in the world?
> *First Inaugural Address [March 4, 1861]*

No government proper ever had a provision in its organic law for its own termination.
> *Ibid.*

While the people retain their virtue and vigilance, no administration, by any extreme of wickedness or folly, can very seriously injure the government in the short space of four years.
> *Ibid.*

---

[1] They have seen in his [Douglas's] round, jolly fruitful face, post-offices, land-offices, marshalships and cabinet-appointments, charge-ships and foreign missions, bursting and sprouting out in wonderful exuberance, ready to be laid hold of by their greedy hands. — *Ibid.*

Labor is prior to, and independent of, capital. Capital is only the fruit of labor, and could never have existed if labor had not first existed.

First Annual Message to Congress
[December 3, 1861]

It is difficult to make a man miserable while he feels he is worthy of himself and claims kindred to the great God who made him.

Address on Colonization to a
Deputation of Colored Men
[August 14, 1862]

My paramount object in this struggle is to save the Union, and is not either to save or destroy slavery. If I could save the Union without freeing any slave, I would do it; and if I could do it by freeing all the slaves, I would do it; and if I could save it by freeing some and leaving others alone, I would also do that.

Letter to Horace Greeley
[August 22, 1862]

I shall try to correct errors where shown to be errors, and I shall adopt new views as fast as they shall appear to be true views.

Ibid.

In giving freedom to the slave we assure freedom to the free, — honorable alike in what we give and what we preserve.

Second Annual Message to Congress
[December 1, 1862]

Beware of rashness, but with energy and sleepless vigilance go forward and give us victories.

Letter to Major-General Joseph
Hooker [January 26, 1863]

The Father of Waters [1] again goes unvexed to the sea.

Letter to James C. Conkling
[August 26, 1863]

Among freemen there can be no successful appeal from the ballot to the bullet, and . . . they who take such appeal are sure to lose their case and pay the cost.

Ibid.

[1] Ol' Man River [Mississippi] . . . he keeps on rollin' along. — Song by OSCAR HAMMERSTEIN 2ND., music by JEROME KERN. (1927).

I have endured a great deal of ridicule without much malice; and have received a great deal of kindness, not quite free from ridicule.

Letter to J. H. Hackett
[November 2, 1863]

But, in a larger sense, we cannot dedicate, we cannot consecrate, we cannot hallow this ground. The brave men, living and dead, who struggled here, have consecrated it, far above our poor power to add or to detract. The world will little note nor long remember what we say here, but it can never forget what they did here.

Address, Gettysburg
[November 19, 1863]

It is rather for us to be here dedicated to the great task remaining before us; that from these honored dead we take increased devotion to that cause for which they gave the last full measure of devotion.

Ibid.

That this nation, under God, shall have a new birth of freedom, and that government of the people, by the people, for the people, shall not perish from the earth.[1]

Ibid.

The world has never had a good definition of the word liberty, and the American people, just now, are much in want of one.

Address, Sanitary Fair, Baltimore
[April 18, 1864]

It is no fault in others that the Methodist Church sends more soldiers to the field, more nurses to the hospital, and more prayers to heaven than any. God bless the Methodist Church. Bless all the churches, and blessed be God, who, in this our great trial, giveth us the churches.

To a Methodist Delegation
[May 14, 1864]

I have not permitted myself, gentlemen, to conclude that I am the best man in the country; but I am reminded in this connection of a story of an old Dutch farmer, who remarked to a com-

[1] See Daniel Webster, page 341, and Theodore Parker, page 477.

panion once that it was not best to swap horses when crossing a stream.

Reply to National Union League [June 9, 1864]

Truth is generally the best vindication against slander.

Letter to Secretary Stanton, refusing to dismiss Postmaster-General Montgomery Blair [July 18, 1864]

It has long been a grave question whether any government, not too strong for the liberties of its people, can be strong enough to maintain its existence in great emergencies.

Response to a Serenade [November 10, 1864]

Human nature will not change. In any future great national trial, compared with the men of this, we shall have as weak and as strong, as silly and as wise, as bad and as good.

Ibid.

I pray that our Heavenly Father may assuage the anguish of your bereavement and leave you only the cherished memory of the loved and lost, and the solemn pride that must be yours to have laid so costly a sacrifice upon the altar of freedom.

Letter to Mrs. Bixby, whose five sons were reported killed in battle [November 21, 1864]

The religion that sets men to rebel and fight against their Government, because, as they think, that Government does not sufficiently help some men to eat their bread in the sweat of other men's faces, is not the sort of religion upon which people can get to heaven.

Reply to two women who had pleaded for the release of their husbands [Washington Chronicle, December 7, 1864]

The Almighty has His own purposes.

Second Inaugural Address [March 4, 1865]

Fondly do we hope, fervently do we pray, that this mighty scourge of war may speedily pass away. Yet, if God wills that it continue until all the wealth piled by the bondman's two-hundred and fifty years of unrequited toil shall be sunk, and until every drop of blood drawn with the lash shall be paid by another drawn with the sword, as was said three thousand years ago, so still it must be said, that the judgments of the Lord are true and righteous altogether.

Second Inaugural Address [March 4, 1865]

With malice toward none; with charity for all; with firmness in the right, as God gives us to see the right,[1] let us strive on to finish the work we are in; to bind up the nation's wounds; to care for him who shall have borne the battle, and for his widow and his orphan — to do all which may achieve and cherish a just and lasting peace among ourselves and with all nations.

Ibid.

Men are not flattered by being shown that there has been a difference of purpose between the Almighty and them.

Letter to Thurlow Weed [March 15, 1865]

Important principles may and must be flexible.

Last public address, Washington [April 11, 1865]

If you once forfeit the confidence of your fellow citizens, you can never regain their respect and esteem. It is true that you may fool all the people some of the time; you can even fool some of the people all the time; but you can't fool all of the people all the time.

To a caller at the White House. In ALEXANDER K. McCLURE: *Lincoln's Yarns and Stories, Page 124*

One night he dreamed that he was in a crowd, when someone recognized him as the President, and exclaimed in surprise, "He is a very common-looking man." Whereupon he answered, "Friend, the Lord prefers common-looking people. That is the reason he makes so many of them."

JAMES MORGAN: *Our Presidents, Chap. 6*

[1] See J. Q. Adams, page 291.

If I were to try to read, much less answer, all the attacks made on me, this shop might as well be closed for any other business. I do the very best I know how — the very best I can; and I mean to keep doing so until the end. If the end brings me out all right, what is said against me won't amount to anything. If the end brings me out wrong, ten angels swearing I was right would make no difference.

Conversation at the White House, reported by Frank B. Carpenter

As thin as the homœopathic soup that was made by boiling the shadow of a pigeon that had been starved to death.

Quoted by ALONZO ROTHS-CHILD: *Lincoln, Master of Men, Chap. 3*

Conceited whelp! we laugh at thee,
  Nor mind that not a few
Of pompous, two-legged dogs there be
  Conceited quite as you.

The Bear Hunt (Original manuscript in the J. Pierpont Morgan Library, New York)

I don't s'pose anybody on earth likes gingerbread better'n I do — and gets less'n I do.

Quoted by CARL SANDBURG: *Abraham Lincoln: The Prairie Years, II, 290*

If you call a tail a leg, how many legs has a dog? Five? No; calling a tail a leg don't *make* it a leg.

Traditionally attributed to Lincoln

RICHARD MONCKTON MILNES (LORD HOUGHTON) [1]
[1809–1885]

But on and up, where Nature's heart
Beats strong amid the hills.
  Tragedy of the Lac de Gaube.
    Stanza 2

Great thoughts, great feelings, came to them,
  Like instincts unawares.
    The Men of Old. Stanza 5

A man's best things are nearest him,
  Lie close about his feet.
    Ibid. Stanza 7

I wandered by the brookside,
  I wandered by the mill;
I could not hear the brook flow,
  The noisy wheel was still.
    The Brookside. Stanza 1

The beating of my own heart
Was all the sound I heard.
    Ibid.

The hills of manhood wear a noble face
  When seen from far;
The mist of light from which they take their grace
  Hides what they are.
    Carpe Diem

Oh glory, that we wrestle
  So valiantly with Time!
    The Eld

Heaven was not Heaven if Phaon was not there.
    A Dream of Sappho

A poet's Mistress is a hallowed thing.
    Tempe

Mohammed's truth lay in a holy Book,
  Christ's in a sacred Life.
    Mohammedanism

A fair little girl sat under a tree,
Sewing as long as her eyes could see;
Then smoothed her work, and folded it right,
And said, "Dear work, good-night, good-night."
    Good-Night and Good-Morning.
      Stanza 1

If what shone afar so grand
Turn to nothing in thy hand,
On again! the virtue lies
In the struggle, not the prize.
    The World to the Soul

Heart of the people! Workingmen!
  Marrow and nerve of human powers;
Who on your sturdy backs sustain

---

[1] George Otto Trevelyan referred to Lord Houghton as "he whom men name Baron Houghton, but the gods call Dicky Milnes." Another friend said of him: "Plenty of people will visit you in misfortune, but Milnes is the only one who will visit you in disgrace." — Unidentified newspaper clipping

Through streaming time this world
of ours.
                    Labor. Stanza 1
Thus all must work: with head or
hand,
  For self or others, good or ill;
Life is ordained to bear, like land,
  Some fruit, be fallow as it will.
                    Ibid. Stanza 6
O little fleet that on thy quest divine
Sailest from Palos one bright autumn
    morn,
Say, has old ocean's bosom ever borne
A freight of faith and hope to match
    with thine?
          Columbus and the Mayflower.
                    Stanza 1
They who have steeped their souls in
    prayer
Can every anguish calmly bear.
          The Sayings of Rabia. IV
Lady Moon, Lady Moon, where are
    you roving?
Over the sea.
Lady Moon, Lady Moon, whom are
    you loving?
All that love me!
                    A Child's Song
  The sense of humour is the just bal-
ance of all the faculties of man, the
best security against the pride of
knowledge and the conceits of the
imagination, the strongest inducement
to submit with a wise and pious patience to the vicissitudes of human
existence.
          Memoir of Thomas Hood

ALBERT PIKE
[1809–1891]

The spring has less of brightness,
  Every year;
And the snow a ghastlier whiteness,
  Every year;
Nor do summer flowers quicken,
Nor the autumn fruitage thicken,
As they once did, for they sicken,
  Every year.
          Every Year.[1] Stanza 1

[1] A very similar poem, with the title, *The
Old Bachelor's New Year,* is included in *The
Poetical Works* of CHARLES GRAHAM HALPINE

EDGAR ALLAN POE
[1809–1849]

All that we see or seem
Is but a dream within a dream.
          A Dream within a Dream.
                    Stanza 1
Sound loves to revel in a summer night.
          Al Aaraaf. Part II
Years of love have been forgot
In the hatred of a minute.
                    To ——
The viol, the violet, and the vine.
          The City in the Sea. Stanza 2
From a proud tower in the t⌐wn
Death looks gigantically down.
                    Ibid.
The play is the tragedy, "Man,"
And its Hero the Conqueror Worm.
          Ligeia. The Conqueror Worm,
                    Stanza 5
Vastness! and Age! and Memories of
    Eld!
Silence! and Desolation! and dim
    Night!
          The Coliseum. Stanza 2
This — all this — was in the olden
    Time long ago.
          The Haunted Palace. Stanza 2
Unthought-like thoughts that are the
    souls of thought.
                    To Marie Louise
This maiden she lived with no other
    thought
Than to love and be loved by me.
          Annabel Lee. Stanza 1
I was a child and she was a child,
  In this kingdom by the sea,
But we loved with a love that was more
    than love—
  I and my Annabel Lee—
With a love that the winged seraphs
    of heaven
Coveted her and me.
                    Ibid. Stanza 2
Keeping time, time, time,
  In a sort of Runic rhyme,
To the tintinnabulation that so musi-
    cally wells
  From the bells.
          The Bells. Stanza 1

────

(MILES O'REILLY), compiled and published
after his death, in 1869.

Hear the mellow wedding bells,
    Golden bells!
What a world of happiness their har-
    mony foretells!
    Through the balmy air of night
    How they ring out their delight!
                The Bells. Stanza 2
Thou wast all that to me, love,
    For which my soul did pine—
A green isle in the sea, love,
    A fountain and a shrine,
All wreathed with fairy fruits and flow-
    ers,
    And all the flowers were mine.
            To One in Paradise. Stanza 1
And all my days are trances,
    And all my nightly dreams
Are where thy dark eye glances
    And where thy footstep gleams —
In what ethereal dances,
    By what eternal streams!
                Ibid. Stanza 4
I feel that, in the Heavens above,
    The angels, whispering to one an-
        other,
Can find, among their burning terms
    of love,
    None so devotional as that of
    "Mother."
        To My Mother [Mrs. Clemm]
The fever called "Living"
    Is conquered at last.
                For Annie. Stanza 1
O'er his heart a shadow
    Fell as he found
    No spot of ground
That looked like Eldorado.
                Eldorado. Stanza 2
A dirge for her, the doubly dead in that
    she died so young.
                Lenore. Stanza 1
O, human love! thou spirit given,
On Earth, of all we hope in Heaven!
                Tamerlane. Stanza 15
In Heaven a spirit doth dwell
    "Whose heart-strings are a lute"; [1]
None sing so wildly well
As the angel Israfel.
                Israfel. Stanza 1

[1] And the angel Israfel, whose heart-strings
are a lute, and who has the sweetest voice of
all God's creatures. — *The Koran*

Once upon a midnight dreary, while I
    pondered, weak and weary,
Over many a quaint and curious vol-
    ume of forgotten lore —
While I nodded, nearly napping, sud-
    denly there came a tapping,
As of some one gently rapping.
                The Raven. Stanza 1
Ah, distinctly I remember, it was in the
    bleak December,
And each separate dying ember
    wrought its ghost upon the floor.
                Ibid. Stanza 2
And the silken sad uncertain rustling of
    each purple curtain
Thrilled me — filled me with fantastic
    terrors never felt before.
                Ibid. Stanza 3
Deep into that darkness peering, long
    I stood there, wondering, fearing,
Doubting, dreaming dreams no mortal
    ever dared to dream before.
                Ibid. Stanza 5
Perched upon a bust of Pallas just
    above my chamber door —
    Perched, and sat, and nothing more.
                Ibid. Stanza 7
        Whom unmerciful Disaster
Followed fast and followed faster.
                Ibid. Stanza 11
Take thy beak from out my heart, and
    take thy form from off my door!
    Quoth the Raven, "Nevermore."
                Ibid. Stanza 17
And my soul from out that shadow that
    lies floating on the floor
    Shall be lifted — Nevermore!
                Ibid. Stanza 18
Helen, thy beauty is to me
    Like those Nicæan barks of yore,
That gently, o'er a perfumed sea,
    The weary, wayworn wanderer bore
    To his own native shore.
                To Helen. Stanza 1
To the glory that was Greece,
And the grandeur that was Rome.
                Ibid. Stanza 2
The skies they were ashen and sober;
    The leaves they were crispèd and
        sere —
    The leaves they were withering and
        sere;

It was night in the lonesome October
Of my most immemorial year.
Ulalume. Stanza 1

It was down by the dank tarn of
Auber,
In the ghoul-haunted woodland of
Weir.
Ibid.

Here once, through an alley Titanic,
Of cypress, I roamed with my
soul —
Of cypress, with Psyche, my soul.
Ibid. Stanza 2

And now, as the night was senescent
And star-dials pointed to morn. . . .
At the end of our path a liquescent
And nebulous lustre was born.
Ibid. Stanza 4

Thus I pacified Psyche and kissed her,
And tempted her out of her gloom.
Ibid. Stanza 8

It is with literature as with law or
empire — an established name is an
estate in tenure, or a throne in possession.
*Poems [1831], Introduction,
Letter to Mr. B——*

With me poetry has been not a purpose, but a passion; and the passions
should be held in reverence: they must
not — they can not at will be excited,
with an eye to the paltry compensa-
tions, or the more paltry commendations, of mankind.
Poems [1845], Preface

The object Truth, or the satisfaction
of the intellect, and the object Passion,
or the excitement of the heart, are, although attainable, to a certain extent,
in poetry, far more readily attainable
in prose.
The Philosophy of Composition

I would define, in brief, the Poetry
of words as the Rhythmical Creation of
Beauty. Its sole arbiter is Taste.
The Poetic Principle

Can it be fancied that Deity ever vin-
dictively

Made in his image a mannikin merely
to madden it? [1]
The Rationale of Verse

A Quixotic sense of the honorable —
of the chivalrous.
*Letter to Mrs. Whitman
[October 18, 1848]*

Glitter — and in that one word how
much of all that is detestable do we
express!
Philosophy of Furniture

There is something in the unselfish
and self-sacrificing love of a brute,
which goes directly to the heart of him
who has had frequent occasion to test
the paltry friendship and gossamer
fidelity of mere Man.
The Black Cat

Perverseness is one of the primitive
impulses of the human heart.
Ibid.

There are chords in the hearts of the
most reckless which can not be touched
without emotion. Even with the utterly
lost, to whom life and death are equally
jests, there are matters of which no
jest can be made.
The Masque of the Red Death

The boundaries which divide Life
from Death are at best shadowy and
vague. Who shall say where the one
ends, and where the other begins?
The Premature Burial

The question is not yet settled,
whether madness is or is not the loftiest
intelligence — whether much that is
glorious — whether all that is profound — does not spring from disease
of thought — from moods of mind exalted at the expense of the general intellect.
Eleonora

Those who dream by day are cognizant of many things which escape
those who dream only by night.
Ibid.

---

[1] What! out of senseless Nothing to provoke
A conscious Something to resent the yoke
FITZGERALD: *The Rubáiyát of Omar
Khayyám, 78*

ALFRED, LORD TENNYSON
[1809–1892]

This laurel greener from the brows
Of him that uttered nothing base.
To the Queen. Stanza 2

And statesmen at her council met
  Who knew the seasons when to take
  Occasion by the hand, and make
The bounds of freedom wider yet.
Ibid. Stanza 8

Broad based upon her people's will,
And compassed by the inviolate sea.
Ibid. Stanza 9

For it was in the golden prime
  Of good Haroun Alraschid.
*Recollections of the Arabian
Nights. Stanza 2*

A still small voice spake unto me,
"Thou art so full of misery,
Were it not better not to be?"
The Two Voices. Stanza 1

This truth within thy mind rehearse,
That in a boundless universe
Is boundless better, boundless worse.
Ibid. Stanza 9

Tho' thou wert scattered to the wind,
Yet is there plenty of the kind.[1]
Ibid. Stanza 11

I know that age to age succeeds,
Blowing a noise of tongues and deeds,
A dust of systems and of creeds.
Ibid. Stanza 69

Like glimpses of forgotten dreams.
Ibid. Stanza 127

No life that breathes with human
  breath
Has ever truly longed for death.
Ibid. Stanza 132

'Tis life, whereof our nerves are scant,
Oh life, not death, for which we pant;
More life, and fuller, that I want.
Ibid. Stanza 133

Across the walnuts and the wine.
The Miller's Daughter. Stanza 4

[1] And fear not lest Existence closing *your*
Account, and mine, should know the like
  no more.
The Eternal Sáki from that Bowl has
  pour'd
Millions of Bubbles like us, and will pour.
FITZGERALD: *The Rubáiyát of Omar
Khayyám* [1889], *XLVI*

Dowered with the hate of hate, the
  scorn of scorn,
The love of love.
The Poet. Stanza 1

O love, O fire! once he drew
With one long kiss my whole soul
  through
My lips, as sunlight drinketh dew.[1]
Fatima. Stanza 3

Self-reverence, self-knowledge, self-
  control,
These three alone lead life to sovereign
  power.
Œnone. Stanza 12

I built my soul a lordly pleasure-house,
  Wherein at ease for aye to dwell.
The Palace of Art. Stanza 1

The daughter of a hundred Earls.
*Lady Clara Vere de Vere.
Stanza 1*

A simple maiden in her flower
  Is worth a hundred coats-of-arms.
Ibid. Stanza 2

The lion on your old stone gates
  Is not more cold to you than I.
Ibid. Stanza 3

Her manners had not that repose
  Which stamps the caste of Vere de
  Vere.
Ibid. Stanza 5

From yon blue heavens above us
  bent,
The grand old gardener and his wife [2]
  Smile at the claims of long descent.
Ibid. Stanza 7

Howe'er it be, it seems to me,
  'Tis only noble to be good.[3]
Kind hearts are more than coronets,
  And simple faith than Norman
  blood.
Ibid.

If time be heavy on your hands,
Are there no beggars at your gate,
  Nor any poor about your lands?

[1] See Marlowe, page 31.
[2] This line stands in Moxon's edition of
1842,—
  "The gardener Adam and his wife,"—
and was restored by the author in his edition
of 1873.
[3] See Chapman, page 29.

Oh! teach the orphan-boy to read,
  Or teach the orphan-girl to sew.
        Lady Clara Vere de Vere.
              Stanza 9

You must wake and call me early, call
  me early, mother dear;
To-morrow 'ill be the happiest time of
  all the glad New Year, —
Of all the glad New Year, mother, the
  maddest, merriest day;
For I'm to be Queen o' the May,
  mother, I'm to be Queen o' the
  May.
        The May Queen. Stanza 1

There is sweet music here that softer
  falls
Than petals from blown roses on the
  grass.
    The Lotos-Eaters. Choric Song,
              Stanza 1

Music that gentlier on the spirit lies,
Than tir'd eyelids upon tir'd eyes;
Music that brings sweet sleep down
  from the blissful skies.
                    Ibid.

      Ah, why
Should life all labour be?
            Ibid. Stanza 4

Time driveth onward fast,
And in a little while our lips are dumb.
Let us alone. What is it that will last?
All things are taken from us, and be-
  come
Portions and parcels of the dreadful
  Past.
                    Ibid.

Give us long rest or death, dark death
  or dreamful ease.
                    Ibid.

The spacious times of great Elizabeth.
      A Dream of Fair Women.
              Stanza 2

A daughter of the gods, divinely tall,
  And most divinely fair.
            Ibid. Stanza 22

God gives us love. Something to love
  He lends us; but when love is grown
To ripeness, that on which it throve
Falls off, and love is left alone.
            To J. S. Stanza 4

Sleep sweetly, tender heart, in peace;
  Sleep, holy spirit, blessed soul,

While the stars burn, the moons increase,
  And the great ages onward roll.
            To J. S. Stanza 18

Sleep till the end, true soul and sweet!
  Nothing comes to thee new or
  strange.
Sleep full of rest from head to feet;
  Lie still, dry dust, secure of change.
            Ibid. Stanza 19

The old order changeth, yielding place
  to new; [1]
And God fulfils himself in many ways,
Lest one good custom should corrupt
  the world.
        Morte D'Arthur. Line 408

More things are wrought by prayer
Than this world dreams of. Wherefore,
  let thy voice
Rise like a fountain for me night and
  day.
              Ibid. Line 415

      I am going a long way
With these thou seest — if indeed I
  go —
(For all my mind is clouded with a
  doubt)
To the island-valley of Avilion,
Where falls not hail, or rain, or any
  snow,
Nor ever wind blows loudly; but it
  lies
Deep-meadowed, happy, fair with or-
  chard lawns
And bowery hollows crowned with
  summer sea,
Where I will heal me of my grievous
  wound.
              Ibid. Line 424

My first, last love; the idol of my
  youth,
The darling of my manhood, and, alas!
Now the most blessed memory of mine
  age!
        The Gardener's Daughter

The long mechanic pacings to and fro,
The set gray life, and apathetic end.
              Love and Duty

    Ah! when shall all men's good
Be each man's rule, and universal peace
Lie like a shaft of light across the land,

---

[1] Also in *The Coming of Arthur, L. 508.*

And like a lane of beams athwart the sea,
Thro' all the circle of the golden year?
The Golden Year

Much have I seen and known; cities of men
And manners, climates, councils, governments,
Myself not least, but honour'd of them all;
And drunk delight of battle with my peers,
Far on the ringing plains of windy Troy.
Ulysses

I am a part of all that I have met.[1]
Ibid.

How dull it is to pause, to make an end,
To rust unburnished, not to shine in use,
As tho' to breathe were life!
Ibid.

The deep
Moans round with many voices. Come, my friends,
'Tis not too late to seek a newer world.
Ibid.

It may be we shall touch the Happy Isles,
And see the great Achilles, whom we knew.
Ibid.

To strive, to seek, to find, and not to yield.[2]
Ibid.

Here at the quiet limit of the world.
Tithonus

In the spring a livelier iris changes on the burnished dove;
In the spring a young man's fancy lightly turns to thoughts of love.
Locksley Hall. Line 19

He will hold thee, when his passion shall have spent its novel force,
Something better than his dog, a little dearer than his horse.
Ibid. Line 49

[1] See Byron, page 353.
[2] Inscribed on the memorial cross erected to the memory of Captain Robert Falcon Scott and his men at Hut Point in the Antarctic.

This is truth the poet sings,
That a sorrow's crown of sorrow is remembering happier things.[1]
Locksley Hall. Line 75

Like a dog, he hunts in dreams.
Ibid. Line 79

With a little hoard of maxims preaching down a daughter's heart.
Ibid. Line 94

But the jingling of the guinea helps the hurt that Honour feels.
Ibid. Line 105

For I dipt into the future, far as human eye could see,
Saw the Vision of the world, and all the wonder that would be;
Saw the heavens fill with commerce, argosies of magic sails,
Pilots of the purple twilight, dropping down with costly bales;
Heard the heavens fill with shouting, and there rain'd a ghastly dew
From the nations' airy navies grappling in the central blue.
Ibid. Line 119

Till the war drum throbbed no longer and the battle flags were furled
In the Parliament of Man, the Federation of the world.
Ibid. Line 127

Yet I doubt not through the ages one increasing purpose runs,
And the thoughts of men are widened with the process of the suns.
Ibid. Line 137

Knowledge comes, but wisdom lingers.
Ibid. Line 141

Woman is the lesser man.
Ibid. Line 151

I will take some savage woman, she shall rear my dusky race.
Ibid. Line 168

I the heir of all the ages in the foremost files of time.
Ibid. Line 178

Let the great world spin forever down the ringing grooves of change.
Ibid. Line 182

[1] See Longfellow, page 440.
The remembrance of past happiness adds an insupportable weight to our ills. — VOLTAIRE: *L'Enfant Prodigue, Act III, Sc. 1*

Better fifty years of Europe than a
cycle of Cathay.
Locksley Hall. Line 184

And on her lover's arm she leant,
And round her waist she felt it fold,
And far across the hills they went
In that new world which is the old.
*The Day-Dream. The Departure,
Stanza 1*

And o'er the hills, and far away
Beyond their utmost purple rim,
Beyond the night, across the day,
Thro' all the world she followed him.
Ibid. Stanza 4

We are Ancients of the earth,
And in the morning of the times.
Ibid. L'Envoi, Stanza 1

My strength is as the strength of ten,
Because my heart is pure.
Sir Galahad. Stanza 1

Others' follies teach us not,
Nor much their wisdom teaches;
And most, of sterling worth, is what
Our own experience preaches.
*Will Waterproof's Lyrical Mon-
ologue. Stanza 22*

And wheresoe'r thou move, good luck
Shall fling her old shoe after.
Ibid. Stanza 27

As she fled fast through sun and shade
The happy winds upon her played,
Blowing the ringlet from the braid.
*Sir Launcelot and Queen Guine-
vere. Stanza 5*

Cophetua sware a royal oath;
"This beggar maid shall be my
queen!" [1]
The Beggar Maid. Stanza 2

For now the poet can not die,
Nor leave his music as of old,
But round him ere he scarce be cold
Begins the scandal and the cry.
*To —— , after Reading a Life and
Letters. Stanza 4*

He gave the people of his best:
His worst he kept, his best he gave.
Ibid. Stanza 7

But O for the touch of a vanished
hand,

[1] See Percy, page 255.

And the sound of a voice that is
still!
Break, Break, Break. Stanza 3

But the tender grace of a day that is
dead
Will never come back to me.
Ibid. Stanza 4

Cast all your cares on God; that anchor holds.
Enoch Arden

For men may come and men may go,
But I go on forever.
The Brook

Insipid as the queen upon a card.
Aylmer's Field

Marriages are made in Heaven.
Ibid.

Mastering the lawless science of our
law,
That codeless myriad of precedent,
That wilderness of single instances.
Ibid.

He cursed his credulousness,
And that one unctuous mouth which
lured him, rogue,
To buy strange shares in some Peru-
vian mine.[1]
Sea Dreams

Is it so true that second thoughts are
best? [2]
Ibid.

He that wrongs his friend
Wrongs himself more, and ever bears
about
A silent court of justice in his breast,
Himself the judge and jury, and him-
self
The prisoner at the bar, ever con-
demn'd.
Ibid.

The worst is yet to come.
Ibid.

Veneer'd with sanctimonious theory.
The Princess. Prologue, Line 117

[1] Money invested in a library gives much
better returns than mining stock. — Sir William Osler: *Letter* [Feb. 11, 1908], quoted in
Cushing: *Life of Sir William Osler, Vol. II,
Chap. 28*
[2] Second thoughts, they say, are best. —
Dryden: *The Spanish Friar, Act II, Sc. 2*
Second thoughts are ever wiser. — Euripides: *Hippolytus, Fragment 436*

With prudes for proctors, dowagers for deans,
And sweet girl-graduates in their golden hair.
The Princess. Prologue, Line 141

A rosebud set with little wilful thorns,
And sweet as English air could make her, she.
Ibid. Line 153

A little street half garden and half house.
Ibid. Part I, Line 211

When we fall out with those we love
And kiss again with tears.
Ibid. Part II, Song

Two heads in council, two beside the hearth,
Two in the tangled business of the world,
Two in the liberal offices of life.
Ibid. Line 154

Jewels five-words-long
That on the stretched forefinger of all Time
Sparkle forever.
Ibid. Line 355

Sweet and low,
Wind of the western sea.
Ibid. Part III, Song

The splendour falls on castle walls
And snowy summits old in story.
Ibid. Part IV, Song, Stanza 1

Blow, bugle, blow, set the wild echoes flying,
Blow, bugle; answer, echoes, dying, dying, dying.
Ibid.

The horns of Elfland faintly blowing.
Ibid. Stanza 2

O Love, they die in yon rich sky,
They faint on hill or field or river:
Our echoes roll from soul to soul,
And grow forever and forever.
Ibid. Stanza 3

There sinks the nebulous star we call the sun.
Ibid. Part IV, Line 1

Tears, idle tears, I know not what they mean.
Tears from the depth of some divine despair
Rise in the heart, and gather to the eyes,

In looking on the happy autumn-fields,
And thinking of the days that are no more.
The Princess. Part IV, Song, Stanza 1

Unto dying eyes
The casement slowly grows a glimmering square.
Ibid. Stanza 3

Dear as remembered kisses after death,
And sweet as those by hopeless fancy feigned
On lips that are for others; deep as love,
Deep as first love, and wild with all regret;
Oh death in life, the days that are no more.
Ibid. Stanza 4

Sweet is every sound,
Sweeter thy voice, but every sound is sweet;
Myriads of rivulets hurrying thro' the lawn,
The moan of doves in immemorial elms,
And murmuring of innumerable bees.
Ibid. Part VII, Line 203

Happy he
With such a mother! faith in womankind
Beats with his blood, and trust in all things high
Comes easy to him; and tho' he trip and fall,
He shall not blind his soul with clay.
Ibid. Line 308

Some sense of duty, something of a faith,
Some reverence for the laws ourselves have made,
Some patient force to change them when we will,
Some civic manhood firm against the crowd.
Ibid. Conclusion, Line 54

Rich in saving common-sense,
And, as the greatest only are,
In his simplicity sublime.
Ode on the Death of the Duke of Wellington. Stanza 4

Oh good gray head which all men knew!

> *Ode on the Death of the Duke of Wellington. Stanza 4*

O iron nerve to true occasion true,
O fall'n at length, that tower of strength
Which stood four-square to all the winds that blew.

> *Ibid.*

Not once or twice in our rough island story
The path of duty was the way to glory.[1]

> *Ibid. Stanza 8*

We are not cotton-spinners all.

> *The Third of February, 1852. Stanza 8*

All in the valley of death
Rode the six hundred.

> *The Charge of the Light Brigade. Stanza 1*

Some one had blundered:
Theirs not to make reply,
Theirs not to reason why,
Theirs but to do and die.

> *Ibid. Stanza 2*

Cannon to right of them,
Cannon to left of them,
Cannon in front of them. . . .
Into the jaws of death,[2]
Into the mouth of hell
Rode the six hundred.

> *Ibid. Stanza 3*

That a lie which is half a truth is ever the blackest of lies,
That a lie which is all a lie may be met and fought with outright,
But a lie which is part a truth is a harder matter to fight.

> *The Grandmother. Stanza 8*

Doänt thou marry for munny, but goä wheer munny is!

> *Northern Farmer: New Style. Stanza 5*

Read my little fable:
He that runs may read.[1]
Most can raise the flowers now,
For all have got the seed.

> *The Flower. Stanza 5*

Speak to Him thou for He hears, and Spirit with Spirit can meet —
Closer is He than breathing, and nearer than hands and feet.

> *The Higher Pantheism. Stanza 6*

Flower in the crannied wall,
I pluck you out of the crannies,
I hold you here, root and all, in my hand,
Little flower — but if I could understand
What you are, root and all, and all in all,
I should know what God and man is.

> *Flower in the Crannied Wall*

Dear, near and true — no truer Time himself
Can prove you, tho' he make you evermore
Dearer and nearer, as the rapid of life
Shoots to the fall.

> *A Dedication*

Our little systems have their day.

> *In Memoriam. Prologue, Stanza 5*

Let knowledge grow from more to more.

> *Ibid. Stanza 7*

I held it truth, with him who sings [2]
To one clear harp in divers tones,
That men may rise on stepping-stones
Of their dead selves to higher things.[3]

> *Ibid. Part I, Stanza 1*

I sometimes hold it half a sin
To put in words the grief I feel.

> *Ibid. Part V, Stanza 1*

But, for the unquiet heart and brain
A use in measured language lies;

---

[1] He that runs may read. — COWPER: *Tirocinium, Line 79*

[2] The poet alluded to is Goethe. I know this from Lord Tennyson himself, although he could not identify the passage; and when I submitted to him a small book of mine on his marvellous poem, he wrote, "It is Goethe's creed," on this very passage. — REV. DR. GETTY (Vicar of Ecclesfield, Yorkshire)

[3] See Longfellow, page 436.

---

[1] The paths of glory lead but to the grave. — GRAY: *Elegy Written in a Country Churchyard, St. 9.*

[2] Jaws of death. — SHAKESPEARE: *Twelfth-Night, Act III, Sc. 4, L. 396*

DU BARTAS: *Weekes and Workes, Day I, Part 4.*

The sad mechanic exercise,
Like dull narcotics numbing pain.
> *In Memoriam. Part V, Stanza 2*

Never morning wore
To evening, but some heart did break.
> *Ibid. Part VI, Stanza 2*

And topples round the dreary west
A looming bastion fringed with fire.
> *Ibid. Part XV, Stanza 5*

And from his ashes may be made
The violet of his native land.[1]
> *Ibid. Part XVIII, Stanza 1*

I do but sing because I must,
And pipe but as the linnets sing.[2]
> *Ibid. Part XXI, Stanza 6*

The shadow cloaked from head to foot.
> *Ibid. Part XXIII, Stanza 1*

Who keeps the keys of all the creeds.
> *Ibid. Stanza 2*

And Thought leapt out to wed with Thought
Ere Thought could wed itself with Speech.
> *Ibid. Stanza 4*

And round us all the thicket rang
To many a flute of Arcady.
> *Ibid. Stanza 6*

'Tis better to have loved and lost
Than never to have loved at all.[3]
> *Ibid. Part XXVII. Stanza 4;*
> *Part LXXXV, Stanza 1*

[1] From her fair and unpolluted flesh
May violets spring.
SHAKESPEARE: *Hamlet, Act V, Sc. 1, L. 261*

That every Hyacinth the Garden wears
Dropt in her Lap from some once lovely Head.
FITZGERALD: *The Rubáiyát of Omar Khayyám, XIX*

[2] Ich singe, wie der Vogel singt
Der in den Zweigen wohnet.
GOETHE: *Wilhelm Meister's Apprenticeship, Book II, Chap. 11*

[3] Say what you will, 'tis better to be left
Than never to have loved.
CONGREVE: *The Way of the World, Act II, Sc. 1*

Better to love amiss than nothing to have
loved.
CRABBE: *Tale 14, The Struggles of Conscience*

What voice did on my spirit fall,
Peschiera, when thy bridge I crost?
'Tis better to have fought and lost
Than never to have fought at all.
ARTHUR HUGH CLOUGH: *Peschiera*

Her eyes are homes of silent prayer.
> *In Memoriam. Part XXXII, Stanza 1*

Whose faith has centre everywhere,
Nor cares to fix itself to form.
> *Ibid. Part XXXIII, Stanza 1*

How fares it with the happy dead?
> *Ibid. Part XLIV, Stanza 1*

Short swallow-flights of song, that dip
Their wings in tears, and skim away.
> *Ibid. Part XLVIII, Stanza 4*

Be near me when my light is low.
> *Ibid. Part L, Stanza 1*

Do we indeed desire the dead
Should still be near us at our side?
> *Ibid. Part LI, Stanza 1*

Hold thou the good; define it well;
For fear divine Philosophy
Should push beyond her mark, and be
Procuress to the Lords of Hell.
> *Ibid. Part LIII, Stanza 4*

Oh yet we trust that somehow good
Will be the final goal of ill.
> *Ibid. Part LIV, Stanza 1*

But what am I?
An infant crying in the night:
An infant crying for the light:
And with no language but a cry.
> *Ibid. Stanza 5*

So careful of the type she seems,
So careless of the single life.
> *Ibid. Part LV, Stanza 2*

The great world's altar-stairs,
That slope through darkness up to God.
> *Ibid. Stanza 4*

Who battled for the True, the Just.
> *Ibid. Part LVI, Stanza 5*

The sweetest soul
That ever look'd with human eyes.
> *Ibid. Part LVII, Stanza 3*

Who breaks his birth's invidious bar,
And grasps the skirts of happy chance,
And breasts the blows of circumstance.
> *Ibid. Part LXIV, Stanza 2*

And lives to clutch the golden keys,
To mould a mighty state's decrees,
And shape the whisper of the throne.
> *Ibid. Stanza 3*

Sleep, Death's twin-brother.
> *Ibid. Part LXVIII, Stanza 1*

So many worlds, so much to do,
  So little done, such things to be.[1]
> *In Memoriam. Part LXXIII,*
> *Stanza 1*

Thy leaf has perished in the green,
  And, while we breathe beneath the
    sun,
The world which credits what is done
Is cold to all that might have been.
> *Ibid. Part LXXV, Stanza 4*

O last regret, regret can die!
> *Ibid. Part LXXVIII, Stanza 5*

The little speedwell's darling blue.
> *Ibid. Part LXXXIII, Stanza 2*

God's fingers touch'd him, and he
  slept.
> *Ibid. Part LXXXV, Stanza 5*

There lives more faith in honest doubt,[2]
Believe me, than in half the creeds.
> *Ibid. Part XCVI, Stanza 3*

He seems so near, and yet so far.
> *Ibid. Part XCVII, Stanza 6*

Ring out, wild bells, to the wild sky!
> *Ibid. Part CVI, Stanza 1*

Ring out the old, ring in the new,
Ring, happy bells, across the snow!
> *Ibid. Stanza 2*

Ring in the nobler modes of life
With sweeter manners, purer laws.
> *Ibid. Stanza 4*

Ring out old shapes of foul disease,
  Ring out the narrowing lust of gold;
  Ring out the thousand wars of old,
Ring in the thousand years of peace!
> *Ibid. Stanza 7*

Ring in the valiant man and free,
  The larger heart, the kindlier hand!
  Ring out the darkness of the land,
Ring in the Christ that is to be!
> *Ibid. Stanza 8*

The blind hysterics of the Celt.
> *Ibid. Part CIX, Stanza 4*

And thus he bore without abuse
  The grand old name of gentleman,
  Defamed by every charlatan,
And soiled with all ignoble use.
> *Ibid. Part CXI, Stanza 6*

---

[1] How little I have gained,
  How vast the unattained.
        WHITTIER: *My Triumph, St. 7*
[2] Who never doubted never half believed.
    P. J. BAILEY: *Festus: A Country Town*

Wearing all that weight
Of learning lightly like a flower.
> *In Memoriam. Conclusion,*
> *Stanza 10*

One God, one law, one element,
  And one far-off divine event,
To which the whole creation moves.
> *Ibid. Stanza 36*

Faultily faultless, icily regular, splen-
  didly null.
> *Maud. Part I, II*

That jewelled mass of millinery,
That oiled and curled Assyrian Bull.
> *Ibid. VI, Stanza 6*

One still strong man in a blatant land.
> *Ibid. X, Stanza 5*

Gorgonized me from head to foot,
  With a stony British stare.
> *Ibid. XIII, Stanza 2*

Come into the garden, Maud,
  For the black bat, night, has flown,
Come into the garden, Maud,
  I am here at the gate alone.
> *Ibid. XXII, Stanza 1*

Queen rose of the rosebud garden of
  girls.
> *Ibid. Stanza 9*

She is coming, my own, my sweet;
  Were it ever so airy a tread,
My heart would hear her and beat,
  Were it earth in an earthy bed;
My dust would hear her and beat,
  Had I lain for a century dead.
> *Ibid. Stanza 11*

Ah Christ, that it were possible
  For one short hour to see
The souls we loved, that they might
  tell us
What and where they be.
> *Ibid. Part II, IV, Stanza 3*

Wearing the white flower of a blameless life,
Before a thousand peering littlenesses,
In that fierce light which beats upon a
  throne.
> *Idylls of the King. Dedication,*
> *Line 24*

Large divine and comfortable words.[1]
> *Ibid. The Coming of Arthur,*
> *Line 267*

---

[1] Hear what comfortable words our Saviour
Christ saith unto all who truly turn to him. —
Book of Common Prayer, Holy Communion

Live pure, speak true, right wrong, follow the King —
Else, wherefore born?
*Idylls of the King. Gareth and
Lynette, Line 117*

Eyes of pure women, wholesome stars
of love.
Ibid. Line 367

A damsel of high lineage, and a brow
May-blossom, and a cheek of apple-blossom,
Hawk-eyes; and lightly was her slender nose
Tip-tilted like the petal of a flower.
Ibid. Line 574

Our hoard is little, but our hearts are
great.
*Ibid. Geraint and Enid, I,
Line 352*

For man is man and master of his fate.[1]
Ibid. Line 355

The useful trouble of the rain.
Ibid. II, Line 770

The world will not believe a man repents;
And this wise world of ours is mainly
right.
Ibid. Line 899

The whole wood-world is one full peal
of praise.
Ibid. Balin and Balan, Line 444

Mere white truth in simple nakedness.
Ibid. Line 509

Woods have tongues
As walls have ears.[2]
Ibid. Line 522

As love, if love be perfect, casts out
fear,
So hate, if hate be perfect, casts out
fear.
Ibid. Merlin and Vivien, Line 41

[1] I am the master of my fate:
I am the captain of my soul.
W. E. HENLEY: *To R. T. Hamilton Bruce*
(*Invictus*)
Be the proud captain still of thine own fate.
JAMES BENJAMIN KENYON [1858–1924]:
A Challenge
Dux atque imperator vitae mortalium animus est (The soul is the captain and ruler of the life of mortals). — SALLUST: *Jugurtha,
Chap. 1*
[2] That feeld hath eyen, and the wode hath
eres.
CHAUCER: *The Knightes Tale, L. 1522*

Faith and unfaith can ne'er be equal
powers:
Unfaith in aught is want of faith in all.
*Idylls of the King. Merlin and
Vivien, Line 384*

It is the little rift within the lute,
That by and by will make the music
mute,
And ever widening slowly silence all.
Ibid. Line 386

Blind and naked Ignorance
Delivers brawling judgments, unashamed,
On all things all day long.
Ibid. Line 662

For men at most differ as heaven and
earth,
But women, worst and best, as heaven
and hell.
Ibid. Line 812

I know the Table Round, my friends of
old;
All brave, and many generous, and
some chaste.
Ibid. Line 814

There must be now no passages of love
Betwixt us twain henceforward evermore.
Ibid. Line 911

Elaine, the lily maid of Astolat.
Ibid. Lancelot and Elaine. Line 2

But, friend, to me
He is all fault who hath no fault at all.
For who loves me must have a touch
of earth.
Ibid. Line 132

In me there dwells
No greatness, save it be some far-off
touch
Of greatness to know well I am not
great.
Ibid. Line 447

The shackles of an old love straitened
him,
His honour rooted in dishonour stood,
And faith unfaithful kept him falsely
true.
Ibid. Line 870

Sweet is true love tho' given in vain,
in vain;
And sweet is death who puts an end
to pain.
Ibid. Line 1000

As when we dwell upon a word we
know,
Repeating, till the word we know so
well
Becomes a wonder, and we know not
why,
So dwelt the father on her face, and
thought
"Is this Elaine?"

> *Idylls of the King. Lancelot and
> Elaine. Line 1020*

He makes no friend who never made
a foe.

> *Ibid. Line 1082*

Figs out of thistles.

> *Ibid. The Last Tournament,
> Line 356*

The greater man the greater courtesy.

> *Ibid. Line 628*

The vow that binds too strictly snaps
itself.

> *Ibid. Line 652*

For courtesy wins woman all as well
As valor may.

> *Ibid. Line 702*

For manners are not idle, but the fruit
Of loyal nature and of noble mind.

> *Ibid. Guinevere, Line 333*

To love one maiden only, cleave to her,
And worship her by years of golden
deeds.

> *Ibid. Line 472*

No more subtle master under heaven
Than is the maiden passion for a maid,
Not only to keep down the base in man
But teach high thought, and amiable
words
And courtliness, and the desire of fame
And love of truth, and all that makes
a man.

> *Ibid. Line 475*

To where beyond these voices there is
peace.

> *Ibid. Last line*

I found Him in the shining of the stars,
I mark'd Him in the flowering of His
fields,
But in His ways with men I find Him
not.

> *Ibid. The Passing of Arthur,
> Line 9*

For why is all around us here
As if some lesser god had made the
world,
But had not force to shape it as he
would? [1]

> *Idylls of the King. The Passing
> of Arthur, Line 13*

The golden guess
Is morning-star to the full round of
truth.

> *Columbus*

Cleave ever to the sunnier side of
doubt,
And cling to Faith beyond the forms
of Faith.

> *The Ancient Sage*

The shell must break before the bird
can fly.

> *Ibid.*

All the charm of all the Muses often
flowering in a lonely word.

> *To Virgil*

Slav, Teuton, Kelt, I count them all
My friends and brother souls,
With all the peoples, great and small,
That wheel between the poles.

> *The Charge of the Heavy Brigade.
> Epilogue*

The song that nerves a nation's heart
Is in itself a deed.

> *Ibid.*

That man's the best Cosmopolite
Who loves his native country best.

> *Hands All Round*

Love your enemy, bless your haters,
said the Greatest of the great;
Christian love among the Churches
looked the twin of heathen hate.

> *Locksley Hall Sixty Years After.
> Line 85*

Charm us, orator, till the lion look no
larger than the cat.

> *Ibid. Line 112*

Authors — essayist, atheist, novelist,
realist, rhymester, play your part,

[1] Ah Love! could you and I with Him con-
spire
To grasp this sorry Scheme of Things en-
tire,
Would not we shatter it to bits — and
then
Re-mould it nearer to the Heart's Desire!
FITZGERALD: *The Rubáiyát of Omar
Khayyám, XCIX*

Paint the mortal shame of nature with
   the living hues of art.
                 Locksley Hall Sixty Years After.
                             Line 139

Be patient. Our Playwright may show
In some fifth act what this wild Drama
means.
                             The Play

A mastiff dog
May love a puppy cur for no more
   reason
Than that the twain have been tied up
   together.
                 Queen Mary. Act I, Sc. 4

My lord, you know what Virgil sings—
Woman is various and most mutable.[1]
                 Ibid. Act III, Sc. 6

Come out, my lord, it is a world of
   fools.[2]
                 Ibid. Act IV, Sc. 3

Unalterably and pesteringly fond.
                 Ibid. Act V, Sc. 1

Old men must die, or the world would
   grow mouldy, would only breed
   the past again.
                 Becket. Prologue

Not of the sunlight,
Not of the moonlight,
Not of the starlight!
O young Mariner,
Down to the haven,
Call your companions,
Launch your vessel
And crowd your canvas,
And, ere it vanishes
Over the margin,
After it, follow it,
Follow the Gleam.[3]
                 Merlin and the Gleam. Stanza 10

Sunset and evening star,
   And one clear call for me!

[1] Varium et mutabile semper femina. —
VIRGIL: *Aeneid, IV, 569*
    La donna è mobile. — *Rigoletto, Duke's
Song*
[2] Tous les hommes sont fous. — BOILEAU,
Satire IV
    The twenty-seven millions, mostly fools.
— CARLYLE: *Latter Day Pamphlets, No. 6*
[3] The Gleam . . . signifies in my poem
the higher poetic imagination. — TENNYSON:
Memoir, Vol. II, P. 366

And may there be no moaning of the
   bar,
   When I put out to sea.
                 Crossing the Bar. Stanza 1

But such a tide as moving seems asleep,
   Too full for sound and foam,
When that which drew from out the
   boundless deep
   Turns again home.
                             Ibid. Stanza 2

Twilight and evening bell,
   And after that the dark.
                             Ibid. Stanza 3

I hope to meet my Pilot face to face
   When I have crossed the bar.
                             Ibid. Stanza 4

ROBERT CHARLES WINTHROP
[1809–1894]

Our Country,[1] — whether bounded
by the St. John's and the Sabine, or
however otherwise bounded [2] or described, and be the measurements more
or less, — still our Country, to be
cherished in all our hearts, to be defended by all our hands.
       *Toast at Faneuil Hall [Fourth of
                         July, 1845]*

A star for every State, and a State
for every star.
   Address on Boston Common [1862]

The poor must be wisely visited and
liberally cared for, so that mendicity
shall not be tempted into mendacity,
nor want exasperated into crime.
                 Yorktown Oration [1881]

[1] With all her faults she is my country still.
— CHARLES CHURCHILL [1731–1764]: *The
Farewell, L. 27*
    Our country! In her intercourse with for-
eign nations may she always be in the right;
but our country, right or wrong. — STEPHEN
DECATUR [1779–1820]: Toast, Norfolk, Virginia [April, 1816]
    I hope to find my country in the right:
however, I will stand by her, right or wrong.
— JOHN JORDAN CRITTENDEN [1787–1863]:
On the Mexican War
[2] The United States — bounded on the
north by the Aurora Borealis, on the south by
the precession of the equinoxes, on the east by
the primeval chaos, and on the west by the
Day of Judgment. — JOHN FISKE [1842–
1901]: *Bounding the United States*

Slavery is but half abolished, emancipation is but half completed, while millions of freemen with votes in their hands are left without education. Justice to them, the welfare of the States in which they live, the safety of the whole Republic, the dignity of the elective franchise, — all alike demand that the still remaining bonds of ignorance shall be unloosed and broken, and the minds as well as the bodies of the emancipated go free.

Yorktown Oration [1881]

JAMES ALDRICH
[1810–1856]

Her suffering ended with the day,
  Yet lived she at its close,
And breathed the long, long night away
  In statue-like repose.
A Death-Bed. Stanza 1

But when the sun in all his state
  Illumed the eastern skies,
She passed through Glory's morning-gate,
  And walked in Paradise.[1]
Ibid. Stanza 2

HENRY ALFORD
[1810–1871]

My bark is wafted to the strand
  By breath divine;
And on the helm there rests a hand
  Other than mine.
I Know Not if the Dark or Bright.
Stanza 4

Life is so short, so fast the lone hours fly,
We ought to be together, you and I.
You and I. Stanza 4

DAVID BATES [2]
[1810–1876]

Speak gently; it is better far
  To rule by love than fear.

Speak gently; let no harsh word mar
  The good we may do here.
Speak Gently.[1] Stanza 1

The tooth is out; once more again
  The throbbing, jumping nerves are stilled;
Reader, would you avoid this pain?
  Then have your crumbling teeth well filled.
The Toothache. Stanza 11

PAKENHAM BEATTY
[*Floruit* 1881]

By thine own soul's law learn to live,
And if men thwart thee, take no heed,
And if men hate thee, have no care;
Sing thou thy song, and do thy deed,
Hope thou thy hope, and pray thy prayer.
Self-Reliance. Stanza 1

WILLIAM HENRY CHANNING
[1810–1884]

To live content with small means; to seek elegance rather than luxury, and refinement rather than fashion; to be worthy, not respectable, and wealthy, not rich; to study hard, think quietly, talk gently, act frankly; to listen to stars and birds, to babes and sages, with open heart; to bear all cheerfully, do all bravely, await occasions, hurry never. In a word, to let the spiritual, unbidden and unconscious, grow up through the common. This is to be my symphony.

My Symphony

JAMES FREEMAN CLARKE
[1810–1888]

Beneath the shadow of the Great Protection,
  The soul sits, hushed and calm.
The Shadow. Stanza 2

Nought that He has made, below, above,
  Can part us from His love.
Ibid. Stanza 3

---

[1] Parodied by PHOEBE CARY. See page 557.
[2] A Philadelphian, known as "Old Mortality."

[1] Wrongly attributed to G. W. Langford and others.

Dear friend, whose presence in the house,
Whose gracious word benign,
Could once, at Cana's wedding feast,
Change water into wine,
Come, visit us and when dull work
Grows weary, line on line,
Revive our souls, and let us see
Life's water turned to wine.
Cana

Every inmost aspiration is God's angel undefiled;
And in every "O my Father!" slumbers deep a "Here, my child!" [1]
Prayer Its Own Answer (translated from Jelal-el-Deen). Couplet 8

DANIEL CLEMENT COLESWORTHY
[1810–1893]

Ay, soon upon the stage of life,
Sweet, happy children, you will rise,
To mingle in its care and strife,
Or early find the peaceful skies.
Then be it yours, while you pursue
The golden moments, quick to haste
Some noble work of love to do,
Nor suffer one bright hour to waste.
School is Out

A little word in kindness spoken,
A motion or a tear,
Has often healed the heart that's broken,
And made a friend sincere.
A Little Word. Stanza 1

Then deem it not an idle thing
A pleasant word to speak;
The face you wear — the thoughts you bring —
The heart may heal or break.
Ibid. Stanza 3

[1] Thy love is but a girdle of the love I bear to thee,
And sleeping in thy "Come, O Lord!" there lies "Here, son!" from me.
WILLIAM ROUNSEVILLE ALGER [1822–1905]: *The Contents of Piety*

MARY STANLEY BUNCE DANA
[1810–1883]

I saw the young bride in her beauty and pride,
Bedecked in her snowy array.
Pass Under the Rod. Stanza 1
'Twas the voice of her God:
"I love thee, I love thee — pass under the rod."
Ibid.

SAMUEL DODGE
[*Floruit* 1868]

You may go through this world, but 'twill be very slow
If you listen to all that is said as you go;
You'll be worried and fretted and kept in a stew,
For meddlesome tongues must have something to do,
For people will talk, you know.
People Will Talk. Stanza 1

SIR FRANCIS HASTINGS DOYLE
[1810–1888]

Last night, among his fellow roughs,
He jested, quaffed, and swore;
A drunken private of the Buffs,
Who never looked before.
To-day, beneath the foeman's frown,
He stands in Elgin's place,
Ambassador from Britain's crown,
And type of all her race.
The Private of the Buffs.[1] Stanza 1

[1] Doyle's poem is prefaced by the following news item from the London *Times*, correspondence from China:
Some Seiks, and a private of the Buffs, East Kent Regiment, having remained behind with the grog-carts, fell into the hands of the Chinese. On the next morning they were brought before the authorities, and commanded to perform the kotou. The Seiks obeyed; but Moyse, the English soldier, declaring that he would not prostrate himself before any Chinaman alive, was immediately knocked upon the head, and his body thrown on a dunghill.
In JOHN GALSWORTHY's novel, *Flowering Wilderness*, Wilfrid Desert becomes a Mohammedan in order to save his life when taken prisoner by a band of fanatical Arabs.

Vain, mightiest fleets of iron framed;
  Vain, those all-shattering guns;
Unless proud England keep, untamed,
  The strong heart of her sons.
    The Private of the Buffs. Stanza 5

So we made women with their children
  go,
The oars ply back again, and yet
  again;
Whilst, inch by inch, the drowning
  ship sank low,
  Still, under steadfast men.
    The Loss of the "Birkenhead." [1]
      Stanza 10

Not hopeless, round this calm sepul-
  chral spot,
  A wreath, presaging life, we twine;
If God be love, what sleeps below was
  not
  Without a spark divine.
    Epitaph on a Favourite Dog

ELIZABETH CLEGHORN GASKELL
[1810–1865]

A man is *so* in the way in the house.
    Cranford. Chap. 1

Correspondence, which bears much
the same relation to personal intercourse that the books of dried plants I
sometimes see ("Hortus Siccus," I
think they call the thing) do to the
living and fresh flowers in the lanes
and meadows.
    Ibid. Chap. 3

People talk a great deal about ideal-
izing nowadays, whatever that may
mean.
    Ibid. Chap. 5

One gives people in grief their own
way.
    Ibid. Chap. 6

A little credulity helps one on
through life very smoothly.
    Ibid. Chap. 11

I'll not listen to reason. . . . Reason always means what some one else
has got to say.
    Ibid. Chap. 14

[1] Origin of the Birkenhead Drill, "women
and children first" [Feb. 26, 1852].

JAMES SLOANE GIBBONS
[1810–1892]

We are coming, Father Abraham, three
  hundred thousand more,
From Mississippi's winding stream and
  from New England's shore;
We leave our ploughs and workshops,
  our wives and children dear,
With hearts too full for utterance, with
  but a silent tear.
    Three Hundred Thousand More. [1]
      Stanza 1

ORRIN GOODRICH
[*Floruit* 1855]

A stranger preached last Sunday,
  And crowds of people came
To hear a two-hour sermon
  On a theme I scarce can name.
'Twas all about some heathen,
  Thousands of miles afar,
Who lived in a land of darkness
  Called Borrioboola Gha.
    Borrioboola Gha. [2] *Stanza 1*

Alas, for the cold and hungry
  That met me every day,
While all my tears were given
  To the suffering far away!
    Ibid. Stanza 8

WILLIAM MILLER
[1810–1872]

Wee Willie Winkie rins through the
  toun,
Upstairs and dounstairs, in his nicht-
  goun,
Tirlin' at the window, cryin' at the
  lock,
"Are the weans in their bed? for it's
  nou ten o'clock."
    Willie Winkie

(SARAH) MARGARET FULLER OSSOLI
[1810–1850]

What I mean by the Muse is that
unimpeded clearness of the intuitive

[1] First printed in the *New York Evening
Post* [July 16, 1862].
[2] *Knickerbocker Magazine, Vol. 45* [1855].

powers, which a perfectly truthful adherence to every admonition of the higher instincts would bring to a finely organized human being. . . . Should these faculties have free play, I believe they will open new, deeper and purer sources of joyous inspiration than have yet refreshed the earth.

Woman in the 19th Century
[circa 1832]

It does not follow because many books are written by persons born in America that there exists an American literature. Books which imitate or represent the thoughts and life of Europe do not constitute an American literature. Before such can exist, an original idea must animate this nation and fresh currents of life must call into life fresh thoughts along its shores.

In the New York Tribune [1833]

Truth is the nursing mother of genius. No man can be absolutely true to himself, eschewing cant, compromise, servile imitation, and complaisance, without becoming original for there is in every creature a fountain of life which, if not choked back by stones and other dead rubbish, will create a fresh atmosphere, and bring to life fresh beauty.

Ibid.

When an immortal poet was secure only of a few copyists to circulate his works, there were princes and nobles to patronize literature and the arts. Here is only the public, and the public must learn how to cherish the nobler and rarer plants, and to plant the aloe, able to wait a hundred years for its bloom, or its garden will contain, presently, nothing but potatoes and pot-herbs.

Ibid.

Beware of over-great pleasure in being popular or even beloved. As far as an amiable disposition and powers of entertainment make you so, it is happiness, but if there is one grain of plausibility, it is a poison.

Letter to her brother Arthur
[December 20, 1840]

I myself am more divine than any I see.

Letter to R. W. Emerson
[March 1, 1838]

Put up at the moment of greatest suffering a prayer, not for thy own escape, but for the enfranchisement of some being dear to thee, and the sovereign spirit will accept thy ransom.

Recipe to prevent the cold of January from utterly destroying life [January 30, 1841]

The golden-rod is one of the fairy, magical flowers; it grows not up to seek human love amid the light of day, but to mark to the discerning what wealth lies hid in the secret caves of earth.

Journal. September, 1840

This was one of the rye-bread days, all dull and damp without.

Diary. Quoted by THOMAS
WENTWORTH HIGGINSON: *Life of Margaret Fuller Ossoli, Chap. 7*

For precocity some great price is always demanded sooner or later in life.

Ibid. Chap. 18

Genius will live and thrive without training, but it does not the less reward the watering-pot and pruning-knife.

Ibid.

It does not follow, because the United States print and read more books, magazines, and newspapers than all the rest of the world, that they really have therefore a literature.

Quoted by WALT WHITMAN *in an article on American National Literature*

THEODORE PARKER
[1810–1860]

Truth never yet fell dead in the streets; it has such affinity with the soul of man, the seed however broadcast will catch somewhere and produce its hundredfold.

A Discourse of Matters Pertaining to Religion

Truth stood on one side and Ease on the other; it has often been so.

Ibid.

Man never falls so low that he can see nothing higher than himself.

Essay, A Lesson for the Day

A democracy, — that is a government of all the people, by all the people, for all the people; [1] of course, a government of the principles of eternal justice, the unchanging law of God; for shortness' sake I will call it the idea of Freedom.

The American Idea [2]

All men desire to be immortal.

A Sermon on the Immortal Life
[September 20, 1846]

We look to Thee; Thy truth is still the Light
Which guides the nations, groping on their way,
Stumbling and falling in disastrous night,
Yet hoping ever for the perfect day.

The Way, the Truth, and the Life.
Stanza 2

EDMUND HAMILTON SEARS
[1810–1876]

Calm on the listening ear of night
Come Heaven's melodious strains,
Where wild Judea stretches far
Her silver-mantled plains.

Christmas Song

It came upon the midnight clear,
That glorious song of old.

The Angels' Song

For lo! the days are hastening on,
By prophet-bards foretold,
When with the ever-circling years,
Comes round the age of gold;

[1] See Daniel Webster, page 341, and Lincoln, page 456.

Parker used the same phrase in a speech delivered in Boston [May 31, 1854] and in a sermon in Music Hall, Boston [July 4, 1858]. WILLIAM H. HERNDON visited Boston and on his return to Springfield, Illinois, took with him some of Parker's sermons and addresses. In his *Abraham Lincoln, Vol. 2, P. 65,* Herndon says that Lincoln marked with pencil the portion of the Music Hall address, "Democracy is direct self-government, over all the people, by all the people, for all the people."

[2] Speech at the New England Anti-Slavery Convention, Boston [May 29, 1850].

When Peace shall over all the earth
Its ancient splendors fling
And the whole world send back the song
Which now the angels sing.

The Angels' Song

GEORGE SHARSWOOD
[1810–1883]

It is not uncommon to hear the expression, "The law is a jealous mistress." It is true that this profession, like all others, demands of those who would succeed in it an earnest and entire devotion.[1]

Memoir of William Blackstone,
Blackstone's Commentaries
[1860]

MARTIN FARQUHAR TUPPER
[1810–1889]

A babe in a house is a well-spring of pleasure.

Of Education

Analogy is milk for babes, but abstract truths are strong meat.

Ibid.

God, from a beautiful necessity, is Love.

Of Immortality

Error is a hardy plant: it flourisheth in every soil.

Of Truth in Things False

Wait, thou child of hope, for Time shall teach thee all things.

Of Good in Things Evil

Clamorous pauperism feasteth
While honest Labor, pining, hideth his sharp ribs.

Of Discretion

[1] I have never regretted reading a first volume of Blackstone through, or not going on to the second; his frank declaration that the law was a jealous mistress and would brook no divided love, was upon reflection quite enough for one whose heart was given to a different muse. — WILLIAM DEAN HOWELLS: *Years of My Youth, II, XI*

A similar passage occurs in HOWELLS: *My Literary Passions, Chap. 19.*

Well-timed silence hath more eloquence than speech.

Of Discretion

It is well to lie fallow for a while.

Of Recreation

A good book is the best of friends, the same to-day and for ever.

Of Reading

Who can wrestle against Sleep? — Yet is that giant very gentleness.

Of Beauty

Never give up! — if adversity presses,
    Providence wisely has mingled the cup,
And the best counsel, in all your distresses,
    Is the stout watchword of "Never give up!"

Never Give Up. Stanza 3

Nature's own Nobleman, friendly and frank,
Is a man with his heart in his hand!

Nature's Nobleman. Stanza 1

Hope and be happy that all's for the best!

All's for the Best. Stanza 3

Never go gloomily, man with a mind!
Hope is a better companion than fear.

Cheer Up. Stanza 1

JOHN FRANCIS WALLER
[1810–1894]

Near the city of Sevilla,
    Years and years ago,
Dwelt a lady in a villa,
    Years and years ago.

Magdalena, or the Spanish Duel [1]

JOHN BRIGHT
[1811–1889]

And even if I were alone, if mine were a solitary voice, raised amid the din of arms and the clamours of a venal press, I should have the consolation I

[1] Read her Waller's "Magdalena" —
    She had Magdalena's grace.
    Read her of the Spanish duel,
    Of the brother, courtly, cruel,
    Who between the British wooer
    And the Seville lady came.
    HENRY CUYLER BUNNER [1855–1896]:
        "Magdalena"

have to-night — and which I trust will be mine to the last moment of my existence — the priceless consolation that no word of mine has tended to the squandering of my country's treasure or the spilling of one single drop of my country's blood.

*Speech on the Crimean War,
House of Commons [December
22, 1854]*

The Angel of Death has been abroad throughout the land; you may almost hear the beating of his wing.

*Speech, House of Commons
[February 23, 1855]*

The right honorable gentleman [Robert Lowe, Viscount Sherbrooke] is the first of the new party who has retired into his political cave of Adullam [1] and he has called about him everyone that was in distress and everyone that was discontented.

Speech [March, 1866]

Force is no remedy.

On the Irish Troubles [1880]

Had they [the Tories] been in the wilderness they would have complained of the Ten Commandments.

Remark

ALFRED DOMETT [2]
[1811–1887]

It was the calm and silent night!
    Seven hundred years and fifty-three
Had Rome been growing up to might,
    And now was queen of land and sea.
No sound was heard of clashing wars,
    Peace brooded o'er the hushed domain;

[1] I Samuel, XXII, 1.
    I Chronicles, XI, 15.
[2] An early friend of ROBERT BROWNING and subject of his poem, *Waring:*
    What's become of Waring
    Since he gave us all the slip,
    Chose land-travel or seafaring,
    Boots and chest or staff and scrip,
    Rather than pace up and down
    Any longer London town?
An account of Domett's life and work will be found in the Appendix to the Cambridge Edition of ROBERT BROWNING'S *Complete Poetical Works, Pp. 1019–1020.*

Apollo, Pallas, Jove, and Mars
  Held undisturbed their ancient reign,
  In the solemn midnight,
  Centuries ago.
                 Christmas Hymn

HORACE GREELEY
[1811–1872]

The illusion that times that were
are better than those that are, has
probably pervaded all ages.
        The American Conflict
A widow of doubtful age will marry
almost any sort of a white man.
  Letter to Dr. Rufus Wilmot Griswold
And now, having fully expressed our
conviction that the punishment of
death is one which should sometimes
be inflicted, we may add that we would
have it resorted to as unfrequently as
possible. Nothing, in our view, but cold-
blooded, premeditated, unpalliated
murder, can fully justify it. Let this
continue to be visited with the sternest
penalty.
    The New Yorker [June, 1836]
If, on a full and final review, my life
and practice shall be found unworthy
my principles, let due infamy be heaped
on my memory; but let none be thereby
led to distrust the principles to which
I proved recreant, nor yet the ability
of some to adorn them by a suitable
life and conversation. To unerring time
be all this committed.
    *Statement [1846] quoted on
    the first page of Life of Horace
    Greeley [1855] by* JAMES PAR-
    TON *[1822–1891]*
The best business you can go into
you will find on your father's farm or
in his workshop. If you have no family
or friends to aid you, and no prospect
opened to you there, turn your face to
the great West,[1] and there build up a
home and fortune.
    *To Aspiring Young Men (Ibid.
    Page 414)*

---

[1] See J. B. L. Soule, page 505.

Wisdom is never dear, provided the
article be genuine.
   *Address on Agriculture, Houston,
        Texas [May 23, 1871]*
The Niagara of edifices.
    Of St. Peter's, Rome (PARTON,
              Page 370)
'Twas the voice of the Press — on the
  startled ear breaking
In giant-born prowess, like Pallas of
  old;
'Twas the flash of Intelligence, glori-
  ously waking
A glow on the cheek of the noble and
  bold.
      Ode to the Press. Stanza 2

ROBERT LOWE, VISCOUNT SHERBROOKE
[1811–1892]

Soft lies the turf on those who find their
  rest
Beneath our common mother's ample
  breast,
Unstained by meanness, avarice, or
  pride;
They never cheated, and they never
  lied;
They ne'er intrigued a rival to dispose;
They ran, but never betted on the race;
Content with harmless sport and simple
  food,
Boundless in faith and love and grati-
  tude;
Happy the man, if there be any such —
Of whom his epitaph can say as much.
        A Horse's Epitaph

WENDELL PHILLIPS
[1811–1884]

Revolutions are not made; they
come.
    Speech [January 28, 1852]
What the Puritans gave the world
was not thought, but action.
    Speech [December 21, 1855]
One on God's side is a majority.
    Speech [November 1, 1859]
Every man meets his Waterloo at
last.
                   Ibid.

Revolutions never go backward.
Speech [February 12, 1861]
Some doubt the courage of the
Negro. Go to Haiti and stand on those
fifty thousand graves of the best sol-
diers France ever had, and ask them
what they think of the Negro's sword.
Address on Toussaint L'Ouverture
[1861]
Aristocracy is always cruel.
Ibid.

Take the whole range of imaginative literature, and we are all wholesale
borrowers. In every matter that relates
to invention, to use, or beauty or form,
we are borrowers.
Lecture, The Lost Arts

JANE CROSS SIMPSON
[1811–1886]

Go, when the morning shineth;
Go, when the noon is bright;
Go, when the eve declineth;
Go, in the high of night;
Go with pure mind and feeling,
Fling earthly cares away,
And in thy chamber kneeling,
Do thou in secret pray.
Prayer

HARRIET BEECHER STOWE [1]
[1811–1896]

It lies around us like a cloud,
    A world we do not see;
Yet the sweet closing of an eye
    May bring us there to be.
The Other World. Stanza 1
Let death between us be as naught,
    A dried and vanished stream;
Your joy be the reality —
    Our suffering life the dream!
Ibid. Stanza 10
Still, still with Thee, when purple
    morning breaketh,

When the bird waketh and the shadows
    flee.
Still, Still with Thee. Stanza 1
When winds are raging o'er the upper
    ocean,
    And billows wild contend with angry
        roar,
'Tis said, far down beneath the wild
    commotion,
    That peaceful stillness reigneth,
        evermore.
Hymn. Stanza 1
Far, far beneath, the noise of tempests
    dieth,
    And silver waves chime ever peace-
        fully,
And no rude storm, how fierce soe'er it
    flieth,
    Disturbs the Sabbath of that deeper
        sea.[1]
Ibid. Stanza 2
Eliza made her desperate retreat
across the river just in the dusk of twi-
light. The grey mist of evening, rising
slowly from the river, enveloped her as
she disappeared up the bank, and the
swollen current and floundering masses
of ice presented a hopeless barrier between her and her pursuer.
Uncle Tom's Cabin. Chap. 8
I 'spect I growed. Don't think nobody
never made me.
Ibid. Chap. 20
I's wicked — I is. I's mighty wicked,
anyhow. I can't help it.
Ibid.
Whipping and abuse are like lau-
danum: you have to double the dose as
the sensibilities decline.
Ibid.
Legree, taking up a cow-hide, and
striking Tom a heavy blow across the
cheek, and following up the infliction
by a shower of blows.
Ibid. Chap. 33

CHARLES SUMNER
[1811–1874]

There is the National flag. He must
be cold, indeed, who can look upon its

---

[1] We have seen an American woman write
a novel of which a million copies were sold
in all languages, and which had one merit,
of speaking to the universal heart, and was
read with equal interest to three audiences,
namely, in the parlor, in the kitchen, and in
the nursery of every house. — R. W. EMER-
SON: *Society and Solitude, Success*

[1] See J. G. C. Brainard, page 375, and
F. W. H. Myers, page 667.

folds rippling in the breeze without pride of country. If in a foreign land, the flag is companionship, and country itself, with all its endearments.

Are We a Nation? [*November 19, 1867*]

White is for purity; red, for valor; blue for justice. And altogether, bunting, stripes, stars, and colors, blazing in the sky, make the flag of our country, to be cherished by all our hearts, to be upheld by all our hands.

Ibid.

The phrase, "public office is a public trust," has of late become common property.[1]

Statement [*May 31, 1872*]

WILLIAM MAKEPEACE THACKERAY
[1811–1863]

Although I enter not,
Yet round about the spot
    Ofttimes I hover;
And near the sacred gate,
With longing eyes I wait,
    Expectant of her.
        At the Church Gate [2]

The play is done; the curtain drops,
    Slow falling to the prompter's bell:
A moment yet the actor stops,
    And looks around, to say farewell.
It is an irksome word and task;
    And when he's laughed and said his say,
He shows, as he removes the mask,
    A face that's anything but gay.
        Doctor Birch and His Young Friends. Epilogue, The End of the Play, Stanza 1

Christmas is here:
Winds whistle shrill,
Icy and chill,
Little care we;
Little we fear
Weather without,

[1] See Mathew Henry, page 188.
[2] In *Pendennis, Vol. I, Chap. 31*, the third and fourth lines read:
        Sometimes I hover,
        And at the sacred gate.

Shelter about
The Mahogany Tree.
        The Mahogany Tree. Stanza 1

Though more than half the world was his,
He [1] died without a rood his own;
And borrow'd from his enemies
Six foot of ground to lie upon.
        The Chronicle of the Drum. Part II

Werther had a love for Charlotte
    Such as words could never utter;
Would you know how first he met her?
    She was cutting bread and butter.[2]
        Sorrows of Werther. Stanza 1

Charlotte, having seen his body
    Borne before her on a shutter,
Like a well-conducted person,
    Went on cutting bread and butter.
        Ibid. Stanza 4

Though small was your allowance,
    You saved a little store;
And those who save a little
    Shall get a plenty more.
        The King of Brentford's Testament. Stanza 22

This Bouillabaisse a noble dish is —
    A sort of soup, or broth, or brew.
        The Ballad of Bouillabaisse. Stanza 2

Ho, pretty page, with the dimpled chin,
That never has known the barber's shear,
All your wish is woman to win,
This is the way that boys begin, —
    Wait till you come to Forty Year.
        Rebecca and Rowena. The Age of Wisdom, Stanza 1

Then sing as Martin Luther sang:
"Who loves not wine, woman, and song,
He is a fool his whole life long!"
        The Adventures of Philip. A Credo, Stanza 1

Away from the world and its toils and its cares,

[1] Napoleon Bonaparte. The ballad was written in Paris at the time of the second funeral of Napoleon [1841].
[2] Charlotte held a brown loaf in her hand, and was cutting slices for the little ones all round in proportion to their age and appetite. — GOETHE: *The Sorrows of Werther, June 16th*

I've a snug little kingdom up four pair
of stairs.
The Cane-Bottom'd Chair. Stanza 1
A man — I let the truth out —
Who's had almost every tooth out,
Cannot sing as once he sung,
When he was young as you are young,
When he was young and lutes were
strung,
And love-lamps in the casement hung.
Mrs. Katherine's Lantern. Stanza 6
The rose upon my balcony the morning
air perfuming,
Was leafless all the winter time and
pining for the spring.
*The Rose Upon My Balcony.
Stanza 1*
There lived a sage in days of yore,
And he a handsome pigtail wore;
But wondered much and sorrowed more
Because it hung behind him.
*A Tragic Story (from von Chamisso).
Stanza 1*
In the brave days when I was twenty-
one.
The Garret. Refrain
Always remember to take the door-key.
The Willow-Tree. Stanza 9
As we go on the downhill journey,
the milestones are gravestones, and on
each more and more names are writ-
ten; unless haply you live beyond
man's common age, when friends have
dropped off, and, tottering, and feeble,
and unpitied, you reach the terminus
alone.
*The Roundabout Papers.
On Letts' Diary*
I'm no angel.
Vanity Fair. Vol. I, Chap. 2
This I set down as a positive truth.
A woman with fair opportunities, and
without an absolute hump, may marry
whom she likes.[1]
Ibid. Chap. 4

[1] I should like to see any kind of a man,
distinguishable from a gorilla, that some good
and even pretty woman could not shape a
husband out of. — O. W. HOLMES: *The Professor at the Breakfast Table*
   The whole world is strewn with snares,
traps, gins and pitfalls for the capture of men
by women. — BERNARD SHAW: *Man and Superman, Epistle Dedicatory*

Them's my sentiments.[1]
Vanity Fair. Vol. I, Chap. 21
Everybody in Vanity Fair must have
remarked how well those live who are
comfortably and thoroughly in debt;
how they deny themselves nothing;
how jolly and easy they are in their
minds.
Ibid. Chap. 22
When we say of a gentleman that he
lives elegantly on nothing a year, we
use the word "nothing" to signify something unknown; meaning, simply, that
we don't know how the gentleman in
question defrays the expenses of his
establishment.
Ibid. Chap. 35
Mother is the name for God in the
lips and hearts of little children.
Ibid. Chap. 37
I think I could be a good woman if
I had five thousand a year.[2]
Ibid. Vol. II, Chap. 1
A comfortable career of prosperity,
if it does not make people honest, at
least keeps them so.
Ibid.
By economy and good management,
— by a sparing use of ready money and
by paying scarcely anybody, — people
can manage, for a time at least, to make
a great show with very little means.
Ibid. Chap. 11
Ah! Vanitas Vanitatum! which of us
is happy in this world? Which of us has
his desire? or, having it, is satisfied?
Ibid. Chap. 27
'Tis strange what a man may do and
a woman yet think him an angel.
Henry Esmond. Chap. 7
The book of female logic is blotted
all over with tears, and Justice in their
courts is forever in a passion.
The Virginians. Chap. 4
Heaven does not choose its elect
from among the great and wealthy.
Ibid. Chap. 5
Women like not only to conquer, but
to be conquered. *Ibid.*

[1] Them's my sentiments, tew. — WILL
CARLETON [1845-1912]: *The Schoolmaster's
Guests*
[2] See Huxley, page 563.

George sat down at the harpsichord and played and sang "Malbrook s'en va t'en guerre; Mironton, mironton, mirontaine." [1]

The Virginians. Chap. 8

Next to the very young, I suppose the very old are the most selfish.

Ibid. Chap. 61

'Tis hard with respect to Beauty, that its possessor should not have even a life-enjoyment of it, but be compelled to resign it after, at the most, some forty years' lease.

Ibid. Chap. 73

For a steady self-esteem and indomitable confidence in our own courage, greatness, magnanimity, who can compare with Britons, except their children across the Atlantic?

Ibid. Chap. 89

Through all the doubt and darkness, the danger and long tempest of the war, I think it was only the American leader's [2] indomitable soul that remained entirely steady.

Ibid. Chap. 90

To endure is greater than to dare; to tire out hostile fortune; to be daunted by no difficulty; to keep heart when all have lost it; to go through intrigue spotless; to forego even ambition when the end is gained — who can say this is not greatness?

Ibid. Chap. 92

Remember, it's as easy to marry a rich woman as a poor woman.

Pendennis. Chap. 28

Of the Corporation of the Goose-quill — of the Press, . . . of the fourth estate.[1] . . . There she is — the great engine — she never sleeps. She has her ambassadors in every quarter of the world — her courtiers upon every road. Her officers march along with armies, and her envoys walk into statesmen's cabinets. They are ubiquitous.

Pendennis. Chap. 30

The best way is to make your letters safe. I never wrote a letter in all my life that would commit me, and demmy, sir, I have had some experience of women.

Ibid. Chap. 64

How hard it is to make an Englishman acknowledge that he is happy!

Ibid. Chap. 69

The true pleasure of life is to live with your inferiors.

The Newcomes. Chap. 9

The wicked are wicked, no doubt, and they go astray and they fall, and they come by their deserts; but who can tell the mischief which the very virtuous do?

Ibid. Chap. 20

Just as the last bell struck, a peculiar sweet smile shone over his face, and he lifted up his head a little, and quickly said "Adsum!" and fell back. It was the word we used at school, when names were called; and lo, he, whose heart was as that of a little child, had answered to his name, and stood in the presence of The Master.[2]

Ibid. Chap. 80

Certain opuscules, denominated "Christmas Books," with the ostensible intention of swelling the tide of exhilaration, or other expansive emotions, incident upon the exodus of the old and the inauguration of the new year.

The Kickleburys on the Rhine. Preface to Second Edition

A pedigree reaching as far back as the Deluge.

The Rose and the Ring. Chap. 2

---

[1] Malbrouk has gone to the war —
  Mironton, mironton, mirontaine! —
Malbrouk has gone to war,
  Ah, when will he return?
He will be back at Easter —
  Mironton, mironton, mirontaine! —
He will be back at Easter,
  Or else at Trinity.
This French ballad, sometimes thought to refer to the Duke of Marlborough, is said to have originated at the time of the Crusades. See DAVID GRAHAM ADEE: *The Story of a Song*, in *Harper's Monthly, September, 1895.*
[2] George Washington.

[1] For Carlyle's references to the fourth estate, see pages 377, 380, and 381.
[2] He answered, "I am here."
  R. H. STODDARD: *Adsum (On the Death of Thackeray, December 23-24, 1863)*

Bravery never goes out of fashion.
The Four Georges. George II
Fiction carries a greater amount of truth in solution than the volume which purports to be all true.
The English Humourists. Steele
Harlequin without his mask is known to present a very sober countenance, and was himself, the story goes, the melancholy patient whom the Doctor advised to go and see Harlequin.[1]
Ibid. Swift

ROBERT BROWNING
[1812–1889]

Sun-treader,[2] life and light be thine forever!
Pauline
I am a watcher whose eyes have grown dim
With looking for some star which breaks on him
Altered and worn and weak and full of tears.
Ibid.
For music (which is earnest of a heaven,
Seeing we know emotions strange by it,
Not else to be revealed,) is like a voice,
A low voice calling fancy, as a friend,
To the green woods in the gay summer time.
Ibid.
I go to prove my soul!
I see my way as birds their trackless way.
I shall arrive! what time, what circuit first,
I ask not; but unless God send his hail
Or blinding fire-balls, sleet or stifling snow,
In some time, his good time, I shall arrive:
He guides me and the bird. In his good time!
Paracelsus. Part I
Are there not, dear Michal,
Two points in the adventure of the diver,
One — when, a beggar, he prepares to plunge,

[1] See Lombroso, page 1077.   [2] Shelley.

One — when, a prince, he rises with his pearl?
Festus, I plunge!
Paracelsus. Part I
Ay, tell the world! [1]
Ibid. Part II
Heap logs and let the blaze laugh out!
Ibid. Part III
Respect all such as sing when all alone!
Ibid.
I detest all change,
And most a change in aught I loved long since.[2]
Ibid.
Every joy is gain
And gain is gain, however small.
Ibid. Part IV
Over the sea our galleys went.
Ibid.
The sad rhyme of the men who proudly clung
To their first fault, and withered in their pride.
Ibid.
Jove strikes the Titans down
Not when they set about their mountain-piling
But when another rock would crown the work.
Ibid. Part V
I give the fight up: let there be an end,
A privacy, an obscure nook for me.
I want to be forgotten even by God.
Ibid.
Would you have your songs endure?
Build on the human heart.
Sordello. II
Thoughts may be
Over-poetical for poetry.
Ibid. III
'Twere too absurd to slight
For the hereafter the to-day's delight!
Ibid. VI
Any nose
May ravage with impunity a rose.
Ibid.
Day!
Faster and more fast,

[1] See Shakespeare, page 36.
[2] Which I have loved long since. — CARDINAL NEWMAN: *The Pillar of the Cloud* [*Lead, Kindly Light*]

O'er night's brim, day boils at last.
Pippa Passes. Introduction
Say not "a small event!" Why "small"?
Costs it more pain that this, ye call
A "great event," should come to pass,
Than that?
Ibid.
The year's at the spring
And day's at the morn.
Ibid. Part I
God's in his heaven:
All's right with the world.[1]
Ibid.
One may do whate'er one likes
In Art: the only thing is, to make sure
That one does like it.
Ibid. Part II
Some unsuspected isle in far-off seas.
Ibid.
May's warm slow yellow moonlit summer nights —
Gone are they, but I have them in my soul!
Ibid. Part III
In the morning of the world,
When earth was nigher heaven than now.
Ibid.
June reared that bunch of flowers you carry,
From seeds of April's sowing.
Ibid.
All service ranks the same with God:
With God, whose puppets, best and worst,
Are we; there is no last nor first.
Ibid. Part IV
Great-hearted gentlemen, singing this song.
Cavalier Tunes. I, Marching Along
King Charles, and who'll do him right now?
Ibid. II, Give a Rouse
Boot, saddle, to horse, and away!
Ibid. III, Boot and Saddle
Just for a handful of silver he left us,
Just for a riband to stick in his coat.
The Lost Leader [2]

We shall march prospering, — not thro' his presence;
Songs may inspirit us, — not from his lyre;
Deeds will be done, — while he boasts his quiescence,
Still bidding crouch whom the rest bade aspire.
The Lost Leader
Never glad confident morning again.
Ibid.
And into the midnight we galloped abreast.
How They Brought the Good News from Ghent to Aix. Stanza 1
Round the cape of a sudden came the sea,
And the sun looked over the mountain's rim:
And straight was a path of gold for him,
And the need of a world of men for me.
Parting at Morning
Where the apple reddens
Never pry —
Lest we lose our Edens,
Eve and I.
A Woman's Last Word. Stanza 5
Be a god and hold me
With a charm!
Be a man and fold me
With thine arm!
Ibid. Stanza 6
Teach me, only teach, Love!
As I ought
I will speak thy speech, Love,
Think thy thought.
Ibid. Stanza 7
Just because I was thrice as old
And our paths in the world diverged so wide,
Each was naught to each, must I be told?
We were fellow mortals, naught beside?
Evelyn Hope. Stanza 3
No, indeed! for God above
Is great to grant, as mighty to make,

[1] See O. W. Holmes, page 452.
[2] Written in reference to Wordsworth's abandonment of the Liberal cause, with perhaps a thought of Southey, but it is applicable to any popular apostasy. — ARTHUR

SYMONS: *An Introduction to the Study of Browning* [1906], *P. 77.*

And creates the love to reward the
love;
I claim you still, for my own love's
sake!
       Evelyn Hope. Stanza 4
Dear dead women.
       A Toccata of Galuppi's.[1] *Stanza 15*
This world, and the wrong it does.
       Old Pictures in Florence. Stanza 7
What a man's work comes to! So he
plans it,
Performs it, perfects it, makes amends
For the toiling and moiling, and then,
  sic transit!
       Ibid. Stanza 10
They are perfect — how else? — they
shall never change:
  We are faulty — why not? — we
have time in store.
       Ibid. Stanza 16
What's come to perfection perishes.
Things learned on earth, we shall prac-
tise in heaven:
Works done least rapidly, Art most
cherishes.
       Ibid. Stanza 17
Italy, my Italy!
Queen Mary's saying serves for me—
  (When fortune's malice
  Lost her, Calais):
Open my heart, and you will see
Graved inside of it, "Italy."
       De Gustibus
Oh, to be in England,
Now that April's there.
       Home-Thoughts from Abroad.
          Stanza 1
That's the wise thrush; he sings each
song twice over,
Lest you should think he never could
recapture
The first fine careless rapture!
       Ibid. Stanza 2
God made all the creatures, and gave
them our love and our fear,

To give sign, we and they are his chil-
dren, one family here.
       Saul. VI
How good is man's life, the mere liv-
ing! how fit to employ
All the heart and the soul and the senses
forever in joy!
       Ibid. IX
I have lived, seen God's hand through
a lifetime, and all was for best.
       Ibid.
  God is seen God
In the star, in the stone, in the flesh,
in the soul and the clod.[1]
       Saul. XVII
'Tis not what man Does which exalts
him, but what man Would do!
       Ibid. XVIII
How well I know what I mean to do
When the long dark evenings come.
       By the Fireside. Stanza 1
O woman-country![2] wooed not wed,
  Loved all the more by earth's male-
lands,
Laid to their hearts instead.
       Ibid. Stanza 6
When earth breaks up and heaven ex-
pands,
  How will the change strike me and
you
In the house not made with hands?
       Ibid. Stanza 27
Oh, the little more, and how much it is!
And the little less, and what worlds
away!
       Ibid. Stanza 39
If two lives join, there is oft a scar.
  They are one and one, with a shad-
owy third;
One near one is too far.
       Ibid. Stanza 46
       Only I discern
Infinite passion, and the pain
Of finite hearts that yearn.
       Two in the Campagna. Stanza 12

---

[1] Baldassarre Galuppi, surnamed Buranello
[1706–1785], a Venetian composer.
  He was an immensely prolific composer,
and abounded in melody, tender, pathetic,
brilliant, which in its extreme simplicity and
slightness occasionally rose to the highest
beauty. — VERNON LEE (Violet Paget):
[1856–1935]: *Studies of the Eighteenth Century in Italy* [1880], *P. 101*

---

[1] God sleeps in the stone, breathes in the
plant, moves in the animal, and wakes to
consciousness in the man. — Quoted, as from
the German, by JONATHAN BRIERLEY in
Studies of the Soul, Chap. 1, and as from
the Greek in BENJAMIN RAND's *Modern Classical Philosophers.* It has also been attributed
to Hindu theosophy.
  [2] Italy.

This is a spray the Bird clung to,
Making it blossom with pleasure.
> *Misconceptions. Stanza 1*

Room after room,
I hunt the house through
We inhabit together.
> *Love in a Life. Stanza 1*

Escape me?
Never —
Beloved!
While I am I, and you are you.
> *Life in a Love. Stanza 1*

To dry one's eyes and laugh at a fall,
And baffled, get up and begin again.
> *Ibid. Stanza 2*

Ah, did you once see Shelley plain,
And did he stop and speak to you,
And did you speak to him again?
How strange it seems and new! [1]
> *Memorabilia. I*

There's a woman like a dewdrop, she's
so purer than the purest.
> *A Blot in the 'Scutcheon. Act I,
Sc. 3*

When is man strong until he feels
alone? [2]
> *Colombe's Birthday. Act III*

"You're wounded!" "Nay," the sol-
dier's pride
Touched to the quick, he said:
"I'm killed, Sire!" And his chief be-
side,
Smiling the boy fell dead.
> *Incident of the French Camp.
Stanza 5*

The lie was dead,
And damned, and truth stood up instead.
> *Count Gismond. Stanza 13*

Over my head his arm he flung
Against the world.
> *Ibid. Stanza 19*

Morning, evening, noon and night,
"Praise God!" sang Theocrite.
> *The Boy and the Angel*

[1] And did you once find Browning plain?
And did he really seem quite clear?
And did you read the book again?
How strange it seems and queer.
CHARLES WILLIAM STUBBS [1845–1912]:
Parody
[2] The strongest man on earth is he who
stands most alone. — HENRIK IBSEN: *The
Enemy of the People, Act V*

Just my vengeance complete,
The man sprang to his feet,
Stood erect, caught at God's skirts, and
prayed!
—So, *I* was afraid!
> *Instans Tyrannus. Stanza 7*

When a man's busy, why, leisure
Strikes him as wonderful pleasure:
'Faith, and at leisure once is he?
Straightway he wants to be busy.
> *The Glove.[1] Stanza 1*

Fail I alone, in words and deeds?
Why, all men strive, and who succeeds?
> *The Last Ride Together. Stanza 5*

All labor, yet no less
Bear up beneath their unsuccess.
Look at the end of the work, contrast
The petty done, the undone vast,
This present of theirs with the hopeful
past!
> *Ibid.*

What hand and brain went ever paired?
What heart alike conceived and dared?
What act proved all its thought had
been?
> *Ibid. Stanza 6*

Sing, riding's a joy! For me I ride.
> *Ibid. Stanza 7*

Earth being so good, would heaven
seem best?
> *Ibid. Stanza 9*

Changed not in kind, but in degree.
> *Ibid. Stanza 10*

A thousand guilders! Come, take fifty!
> *The Pied Piper of Hamelin.
Stanza 9*

If we've promised them aught, let us
keep our promise!
> *Ibid. Stanza 15*

When the liquor's out, why clink the
cannikin?
> *The Flight of the Duchess. XVI*

It's a long lane that knows no turnings.
> *Ibid. XVII*

That low man seeks a little thing to do,
Sees it and does it;
This high man, with a great thing to
pursue,
Dies ere he knows it.

[1] Another version of the legend forming
the theme of SCHILLER'S *The Glove* and
LEIGH HUNT'S *The Glove and the Lions.*

That low man goes on adding one to
one,
His hundred's soon hit;
This high man, aiming at a million,
Misses an unit.
That has the world here — should he
need the next.
Let the world mind him!
This throws himself on God, and un-
perplexed
Seeking shall find him.
A Grammarian's Funeral.

The sin I impute to each frustrate ghost
Is — the unlit lamp and the ungirt loin.
The Statue and the Bust.
Stanza 83

And inasmuch as feeling, the East's
gift,
Is quick and transient, — comes, and
lo, is gone —
While Northern thought is slow and
durable.
Luria. Act V

Ah, but a man's reach should exceed
his grasp,
Or what's a heaven for?
Andrea del Sarto.[1]

How I shall lie through centuries,
And hear the blessed mutter of the
mass,
And see God made and eaten all day
long,
And feel the steady candle-flame, and
taste
Good strong thick stupefying incense-
smoke!
*The Bishop Orders His Tomb at
Saint Praxed's Church*

The common problem, yours, mine,
every one's,
Is — not to fancy what were fair in life
Provided it could be, — but, finding
first
What may be, then find how to make it
fair
Up to our means.
Bishop Blougram's Apology[2]

Just when we are safest, there's a sun-
set-touch,
A fancy from a flower-bell, some one's
death,
A chorus-ending from Euripides.
Bishop Blougram's Apology

One wise man's verdict outweighs all
the fools'.
Ibid.

You call for faith:
I show you doubt, to prove that faith
exists.
The more of doubt, the stronger faith,
I say,
If faith o'ercomes doubt.
Ibid.

When the fight begins within himself,
A man's worth something.
Ibid.

The sprinkled isles,
Lily on lily, that o'erlace the sea.
Cleon

And I have written three books on the
soul,
Proving absurd all written hitherto,
And putting us to ignorance again.
Ibid.

Rafael made a century of sonnets.
One Word More. II

Does he paint? he fain would write a
poem, —
Does he write? he fain would paint a
picture.
Ibid. VIII

God be thanked, the meanest of his
creatures
Boasts two soul-sides, one to face the
world with,
One to show a woman when he loves
her!
Ibid. XVII

Oh, their Rafael of the dear Madonnas,
Oh, their Dante of the dread Inferno,
Wrote one song — and in my brain I
sing it,
Drew one angel — borne, see, on my
bosom!
Ibid. XIX

---

[1] The poem is based on the account of
the artist given in VASARI'S *Lives of the Painters.*

[2] It is no secret that Blougram himself is,
in the main, modelled after and meant for
Cardinal Wiseman, who, it is said, was the

writer of a good-humoured review of the
poem in the Catholic Journal, The Rambler
(January, 1856).—ARTHUR SYMONS: *An Introduction to the Study of Browning* [1906],
P. *112.*

Was there naught better than to enjoy?
No feat which, done, would make
time break,
And let us pent-up creatures through
Into eternity, our due?
No forcing earth teach heaven's em-
ploy?
Dîs Aliter Visum. Stanza 24

That out of three sounds he frame, not
a fourth sound, but a star.
Abt Vogler.[1] *Stanza 7*

There shall never be one lost good!
What was, shall live as before;
The evil is null, is naught, is silence
implying sound;
What was good shall be good, with for
evil so much good more;
On the earth the broken arcs; in the
heaven, a perfect round.
Ibid. Stanza 9

The high that proved too high, the heroic for earth too hard,
The passion that left the ground to lose
itself in the sky.
Ibid. Stanza 10

Sorrow is hard to bear, and doubt is
slow to clear,
Each sufferer says his say, his scheme
of the weal and woe:
But God has a few of us whom he whispers in the ear;
The rest may reason and welcome:
'tis we musicians know.
Ibid. Stanza 12

Grow old along with me!
The best is yet to be,
The last of life, for which the first was
made.
Our times are in his hand.
Rabbi Ben Ezra.[2] *Stanza 1*

[1] The Abt or Abbé George Joseph Vogler
was born at Würzburg, Bavaria, in 1749, and
died at Darmstadt in 1824. He was a composer, professor, Kapellmeister, and writer on
music. Weber and Meyerbeer were among his
pupils. He invented a musical instrument, a
type of organ, called an orchestrion.
[2] Rabbi ben Ezra was a universal genius
and wanderer, whose travels brought him as
far as England. — SIR WILLIAM OSLER: *Address,* Jewish Historical Society of England
[April 27, 1914], quoted in CUSHING: *Life of
Sir William Osler, Vol. II, Chap. 34, P. 404*

Then welcome each rebuff
That turns earth's smoothness
rough,
Each sting that bids nor sit nor stand,
but go!
Be our joys three-parts pain!
Strive, and hold cheap the
strain;
Learn, nor account the pang; dare,
never grudge the throe!
Rabbi Ben Ezra. Stanza 6

What I aspired to be,
And was not, comforts me.
Ibid. Stanza 7

Therefore I summon age
To grant youth's heritage.
Ibid. Stanza 13

Thou waitedst age: wait death nor be
afraid!
Ibid. Stanza 19

Look not thou down but up!
Ibid. Stanza 30

Progress, man's distinctive mark alone,
Not God's, and not the beasts': God is,
they are;
Man partly is, and wholly hopes to be.
A Death in the Desert.

The ultimate, angels' law,
Indulging every instinct of the soul
There where law, life, joy, impulse are
one thing!
Ibid.

How sad and bad and mad it was — [1]
But then, how it was sweet!
Confessions. Stanza 9

Fear death? — to feel the fog in my
throat,
The mist in my face.
Prospice

No! let me taste the whole of it, fare
like my peers,
The heroes of old,
Bear the brunt, in a minute pay glad
life's arrears
Of pain, darkness, and cold.
Ibid.

Hold me but safe again within the bond
Of one immortal look.
Eurydice to Orpheus

[1] Villon, our sad bad glad mad brother's
name.
SWINBURNE: *A Ballad of François Villon,
Refrain*

This could but have happened once, —
  And we missed it, lost it forever.
          Youth and Art. Stanza 17
All that I own is a print,
An etching, a mezzotint.
          A Likeness
He never saw, never before to-day,
What was able to take his breath away,
A face to lose youth for, to occupy age
With the dream of, meet death with.[1]
          Ibid.
We find great things are made of little
  things,
And little things go lessening till at last
Comes God behind them.
          Mr. Sludge, "the Medium"
I'm — now the President, now Jenny
  Lind,
Now Emerson, now the Benicia Boy
  —[2]
With all the civilized world a-wonder-
  ing
And worshipping.
          Ibid.
It's wiser being good than bad;
  It's safer being meek than fierce;
It's fitter being sane than mad.
My own hope is, a sun will pierce
The thickest cloud earth ever stretched;
  That, after Last, returns the First,
Though a wide compass round be
    fetched;
    That what began best can't end
      worst,
  Nor what God blessed once, prove
    accurst.
          Apparent Failure. Stanza 7
O Lyric Love, half angel and half bird,
And all a wonder and a wild desire.
          The Ring and the Book. I
Call in law when a neighbor breaks
  your fence,
Cribs from your field, tampers with
  rent or lease,
Touches the purse or pocket, — but
  woos your wife?

[1] A face that a man might die for. — SIR
ARTHUR CONAN DOYLE: *The Adventures of
Sherlock Holmes. A Scandal in Bohemia*
[1892], P. 16.
[2] The Benicia Boy was John C. Heenan, an
American pugilist, of Benicia, Solano County,
California.

No: take the old way trod when men
  were men!
          The Ring and the Book.
          II, Half-Rome
Years make men restless — they needs
  must spy
Some certainty, some sort of end
  assured,
Some sparkle, though from topmost
  beacon-tip,
That warrants life a harbor through
  the haze.
          Ibid. III, The Other Half-Rome
There is but one way to browbeat this
  world,
Dumb-founder doubt, and repay scorn
  in kind, —
To go on trusting, namely, till faith
  move
Mountains.
          Ibid.
"The serpent tempted me and I did
  eat."
So much of paradisal nature, Eve's!
Her daughters ever since prefer to urge
"Adam so starved me I was fain accept
The apple any serpent pushed my
  way."
          Ibid. IV, Tertium Quid
The truth was felt by instinct here,
— Process which serves a world of
  trouble and time.
          Ibid.
Justinian's Pandects only make precise
What simply sparkled in men's eyes
  before,
Twitched in their brow or quivered on
  their lip,
Waited the speech they called but
  would not come.
          Ibid. V, Count Guido Franceschini
'Twas a thief that said the last kind
  word to Christ:
Christ took the kindness and forgave
  the theft.
          Ibid. VI, Giuseppe Caponsacchi
Read the little prayer
To Raphael, proper for us travellers![1]
          Ibid.

[1] Raphael, the archangel, in the guise of a
traveller, accompanied Tobias on his journey.
The account is given in the *Apocrypha:
Tobit, V.*

All human plans and projects come to naught.
> *The Ring and the Book.*
> *VII, Pompilia*

All poetry is difficult to read,
— The sense of it is, anyhow.
> *Ibid.*

No work begun shall ever pause for death!
> *Ibid.*

So, let him wait God's instant men call years;
Meantime hold hard by truth and his great soul,
Do out the duty! Through such souls alone
God stooping shows sufficient of his light
For us i' the dark to rise by.
> *Ibid.*

There's a blessing on the hearth,
A special providence for fatherhood!
> *Ibid. VIII, Dominus Hyacinthus*
> *de Archangelis*

How it disgusts when weakness, false-refined,
Censures the honest rude effective strength, —
When sickly dreamers of the impossible
Decry plain sturdiness which does the feat
With eyes wide open.
> *Ibid. IX, Juris Doctor Johannes-*
> *Baptista Bottinius*

Steep horsehair certain weeks,
In water, there will be produced a snake;
Spontaneous product of the horse.
> *Ibid.*

The curious crime, the fine
Felicity and flower of wickedness.
> *Ibid. X, The Pope*

What I call God,
And fools call Nature.[1]
> *Ibid.*

Why comes temptation, but for man to meet
And master and make crouch beneath his foot,

[1] Some of us call it Autumn,
And others call it God.
WILLIAM HERBERT CARRUTH [1859–1924]:
Each in His Own Tongue, St. 2

And so be pedestaled in triumph?
> *The Ring and the Book.*
> *X, The Pope*

White shall not neutralize the black, nor good
Compensate bad in man, absolve him so:
Life's business being just the terrible choice.
> *Ibid.*

You never know what life means till you die:
Even throughout life, 'tis death that makes life live,
Gives it whatever the significance.
> *Ibid. XI, Guido*

A man in armor is his armor's slave.
> *Herakles*

Life's a little thing!
Such as it is, then, pass life pleasantly
From day to night, nor once grieve all the while.
> *Ibid.*

I recognize
Power passing mine, immeasurable, God.
> *Prince Hohenstiel-Schwangau* [1]

In God's good time,
Which does not always fall on Saturday
When the world looks for wages.[2]
> *Ibid.*

The great mind knows the power of gentleness,
Only tries force, because persuasion fails.
> *Ibid.*

'Tis the great gardener grafts the excellence
On wildings where he will.
> *Ibid.*

'Twas not for every Gawain to gaze upon the Grail!
> *Fifine at the Fair. IV*

[1] Louis Napoleon. The name, Hohenstiel-Schwangau, is formed from Hohenschwangau, one of the castles of the King of Bavaria.
[2] The old Tuscan proverb, "*Iddio non paga sabato*"; "God does not pay Saturdays." — *Life in Letters of William Dean Howells, Vol. II, P. 169, Letter to Mrs. James T. Fields* [Feb. 23, 1903]

No creature's made so mean ·
But that, some way, it boasts, could we
    investigate,
Its supreme worth.
                Fifine at the Fair. XXIX
So absolutely good is truth, truth never
    hurts
The teller.
                Ibid. XXXII
Death reads the title clear —
What each soul for itself conquered
    from out things here.
                Ibid. LV
Clash forth life's common chord,
    whence, list how there ascend
Harmonics far and faint, till our per-
    ception end.
                Ibid. LXII
That far land we dream about,
Where every man is his own architect.
                *Red Cotton Night-Cap Coun-
                    try. II*
Who is a poet needs must apprehend
Alike both speech and thoughts which
    prompt to speak.
Part these, and thought withdraws to
    poetry:
Speech is reported in the newspaper.
                Ibid. IV
A secret's safe
'Twixt you, me, and the gate-post!
                The Inn Album. II
Better have failed in the high aim, as I,
Than vulgarly in the low aim suc-
    ceed, —
As, God be thanked, I do not!
                Ibid. IV
Earth's a mill where we grind and wear
    mufflers:
A whip awaits shirkers and shufflers
Who slacken their pace, sick of lugging
At what don't advance for their tug-
    ging.
                Pacchiarotto. XXI
Things rarely go smooth at Rehearsal.
                Ibid. XXII
No ear! or if ear, so tough-gristled —
He thought that he sung while he whis-
    tled.
                Ibid. XXVI
Have you found your life distasteful?
    My life did and does smack sweet.
Was your youth of pleasure wasteful?

Mine I saved and hold complete.
Do your joys with age diminish?
    When mine fail me, I'll complain.
Must in death your daylight finish?
    My sun sets to rise again.
                At the "Mermaid." Stanza 10

I find earth not gray but rosy,
    Heaven not grim but fair of hue.
Do I stoop? I pluck a posy.
    Do I stand and stare? [1] All's blue.
                Ibid. Stanza 12

"With this same key
Shakespeare unlocked his heart" [2] once
    more!
Did Shakespeare? If so, the less Shake-
    speare he!
                House. Stanza 10

Because a man has shop to mind
    In time and place, since flesh must
        live,
Needs spirit lack all life behind,
    All stray thoughts, fancies fugitive,
    All love except what trade can give?
                Shop. Stanza 20

Save the squadron, honor France, love
    thy wife the Belle Aurore!
                Hervé Riel.[3] Stanza 11

Good, to forgive;
    Best, to forget!
Living, we fret;
    Dying, we live.
                La Saisiaz. Introduction, Stanza 1

Can we love but on condition that the
    thing we love must die?
                Ibid.

Such a starved bank of moss
    Till, that May-morn,

---

[1] What is this life if, full of care,
    We have no time to stand and stare.
                W. H. DAVIES: *Leisure*
[2] The line is quoted from *Scorn not the
Sonnet*, by WORDSWORTH.
[3] The ballad of "Hervé Riel" which has no
rival but Tennyson's "Revenge" among modern sea-ballads, was written at Croisic, 30th
September, 1867, and was published in the
Cornhill Magazine for March, 1871, in order
that the hundred pounds which had been
offered for it might be sent to the Paris
Relief Fund. — ARTHUR SYMONS: *An Introduction to the Study of Browning* [1906],
P. 200

Blue ran the flash across:
Violets were born!
The Two Poets of Croisic.
Introduction, Stanza 1

Sky — what a scowl of cloud
Till, near and far,
Ray on ray split the shroud:
Splendid, a star!
Ibid. Stanza 2

As if true pride
Were not also humble!
In an Album

Wanting is — what?
Summer redundant,
Blueness abundant,
— Where is the blot?
Wanting is — What? [1]

Out of the wreck I rise.[2]
Ixion

Climb the rounds
Of life's long ladder, one by slippery
one.
Jochanan Hakkadosh. Stanza 27

The way of all flesh.[3]
Ibid. Stanza 48

What Youth deemed crystal, Age finds
out was dew
Morn set a-sparkle, but which noon
quick dried.
Ibid. Stanza 101

Never the time and the place
And the loved one all together!
Never the Time and the Place

Help me with knowledge — for Life's
Old — Death's New!
Epitaph on Levi Lincoln Thaxter
[1824–1884] [4]

But little do or can the best of us:
That little is achieved through Lib-
erty.
Why I Am a Liberal

What if the rose-streak of morning
Pale and depart in a passion of tears?
Once to have hoped is no matter for
scorning!
Love once — e'en love's disappoint-
ment endears!
A minute's success pays the failure of
years.
Apollo and the Fates. Stanza 42

Cease from anger at the fates
Which thwart themselves so madly.
Live and learn,[1]
Not first learn and then live.
Parleyings with Certain People.
With Christopher Smart, IX

There is no truer truth obtainable
By Man than comes of music.
Ibid. With Charles Avison, VI

Oh, fancies that might be, oh, facts
that are!
Asolando.[2] Inapprehensiveness

What most moved him was a certain
meal on beans.
Ibid. The Bean-Feast, Stanza 1

That I have appetite, digest, and thrive
— that boon's for me.[3]
Ibid. Stanza 11

Songs, Spring thought perfection,
Summer criticizes:
What in May escaped detection,
August, past surprises,
Notes, and names each blunder.
Ibid. Flute-Music, with an
Accompaniment, Stanza 11

Homer, all the world knows: of his life
Doubtless some facts exist: it's every-
where:
We have not settled, though, his place
of birth:
He begged, for certain, and was blind
beside:
Seven cities claimed him.[4]
Ibid. Development

---

[1] Browning is — what?
Riddle redundant,
Baldness abundant,
Sense, who can spot?
ANONYMOUS, in *Punch, April 21, 1883*
[2] Title of a novel [1912] by BEATRICE HAR-
RADEN.
[3] Title of a novel by SAMUEL BUTLER
[1835–1902]. Also in JOHN WEBSTER: *West-*
ward Hoe! II, 2 (1603).
[4] Carved on the boulder marking Thaxter's
grave at Kittery Point, Maine.

[1] It is good to live and learn. — CERVANTES:
Don Quixote, Part II, Chap. 32
[2] Asolando (a name taken from the invented verb *Asolare*, "to disport in the open
air") was published on the day of Browning's
death. — ARTHUR SYMONS: *An Introduction*
to the Study of Browning [1906], *P. 231*
[3] To eat is human; to digest, divine. —
CHARLES TOWNSEND COPELAND: *Epigram*
[4] See Thomas Heywood, page 129.

One who never turned his back but
    marched breast forward,
Never doubted clouds would break,
Never dreamed, though right were
    worsted, wrong would triumph,
Held we fall to rise, are baffled to fight
    better,
Sleep to wake.
                Asolando. Epilogue, Stanza 3
No, at noonday in the bustle of man's
    work-time
Greet the unseen with a cheer!
                            Ibid. Stanza 4

SAMUEL DICKINSON
BURCHARD
[1812–1891]

We are Republicans, and don't propose to leave our party and identify
ourselves with the party whose ante-
cedents have been Rum, Romanism,
and Rebellion.
        Speaking for a deputation of
        clergymen calling upon James
        G. Blaine, the Republican Pres-
        idential candidate, New York
        [October 29, 1884]

CHARLES DICKENS
[1812–1870]

He had used the word in its Pick-
wickian sense.
            Pickwick Papers. Chap. 1
Did it ever strike you on such a
morning as this that drowning would
be happiness and peace?
                    Ibid. Chap. 5
Be wery careful o' vidders all your
life.
                    Ibid. Chap. 20
The wictim o' connubiality.
                            Ibid.
Despair seldom comes with the first
severe shock of misfortune. A man has
confidence in untried friends, he remembers the many offers of service so
freely made by his boon companions
when he wanted them not; he has hope
— the hope of happy inexperience.
                    Ibid. Chap. 21

I have heerd how many ord'nary
women one vidder's equal to, in pint
o' comin' over you. I think it's five-and-
twenty, but I don't rightly know vether
it a'n't more.
            Pickwick Papers. Chap. 23
As grand a personage as the fastest
walker would find out, between sunrise and sunset, on the twenty-first of
June.
                    Ibid. Chap. 24
Bold Turpin vunce, on Hounslow
    Heath,
His bold mare Bess bestrode.
            Ibid. Chap. 43, Romance
Please, sir, I want some more.
                Oliver Twist. Chap. 2
There are books of which the backs
and covers are by far the best parts.
                    Ibid. Chap. 14
There is something about a roused
woman, especially if she add to all
her other strong passions, the fierce
impulses of recklessness and despair,
which few men like to provoke.
                    Ibid. Chap. 16
There's light enough for wot I've
got to do.
                    Ibid. Chap. 47
"If the law supposes that," said Mr.
Bumble, . . . "the law is a ass, a
idiot."
                    Ibid. Chap. 51
A demd, damp, moist, unpleasant
body!
            Nicholas Nickleby. Chap. 34
He has gone to the demnition bowwows.
                    Ibid. Chap. 64
My life is one demd horrid grind.
                            Ibid.
What is the odds, so long as the
wing of friendship never moults a
feather . . . and the present moment
is the least happiest of our existence.
        The Old Curiosity Shop. Chap. 2
She's the ornament of her sex.
                    Ibid. Chap. 5
In love of home, the love of country
has its rise.
                    Ibid. Chap. 38

That vague kind of penitence which holidays awaken next morning.[1]

The Old Curiosity Shop. Chap. 40

The memory of those who lie below passes away so soon. At first they tend them, morning, noon, and night; they soon begin to come less frequently; from once a day, to once a week; from once a week to once a month; then at long and uncertain intervals; then, not at all.

Ibid. Chap. 54

When Death strikes down the innocent and young, for every fragile form from which he lets the panting spirit free, a hundred virtues rise, in shapes of mercy, charity, and love, to walk the world, and bless it.

Ibid. Chap. 72

Any man may be in good spirits and good temper when he's well dressed. There ain't much credit in that.

Martin Chuzzlewit. Chap. 5

Regrets are the natural property of gray hairs.

Ibid. Chap. 10

Keep up appearances whatever you do.

Ibid. Chap. 11

We are the two halves of a pair of scissors, when apart, Pecksniff, but together we are something.[2]

Ibid.

Buy an annuity cheap, and make your life interesting to yourself and everybody else that watches the speculation.

Ibid. Chap. 18

Leave the bottle on the chimley-piece, and don't ask me to take none, but let me put my lips to it when I am so dispoged.

Ibid. Chap. 19

What we've got to do, is to keep up our spirits, and be neighbourly. We shall come all right in the end, never fear.

Ibid. Chap. 33

A man ain't got no right to be a public man, unless he meets the public views.

Martin Chuzzlewit. Chap. 34

Here are all kinds of employers wanting all sorts of servants, and all sorts of servants wanting all kinds of employers, and they never seem to come together.

Ibid. Chap. 36

Oh Sairey, Sairey, little do we know wot lays afore us!

Ibid. Chap. 40

I don't believe there's no sich a person!

Ibid. Chap. 49

Old Marley was as dead as a doornail.[1] . . . The wisdom of our ancestors is in the simile.

A Christmas Carol. Stave One

Secret, and self-contained, and solitary as an oyster.

Ibid.

I wear the chain I forged in life.

Ibid.

In came Mrs. Fezziwig, one vast substantial smile.

Ibid. Stave Two

As good as gold.

Ibid. Stave Three

"God bless us every one!" said Tiny Tim.

Ibid.

It was always said of him, that he knew how to keep Christmas well.

Ibid. Stave Five

The good old times, the grand old times, the great old times![2]

The Chimes. First Quarter

Facts and Figures! Put 'em down!

Ibid.

The New Year, like an Infant Heir to the whole world, was waited for, with welcomes, presents, and rejoicings.

Ibid. Second Quarter

O let us love our occupations,
Bless the squire and his relations,
Live upon our daily rations,
And always know our proper stations.

Ibid.

---

[1] See Byron, page 359.
[2] See Sydney Smith, Page 313.

[1] See Shakespeare, page 66.
[2] See Holmes, page 453.

Oh the nerves, the nerves; the mysteries of this machine called Man! Oh the little that unhinges it: poor creatures that we are!

The Chimes. Third Quarter

Give us, in mercy, better homes when we're a-lying in our cradles; give us better food when we're a-working for our lives; give us kinder laws to bring us back when we're a-going wrong; and don't set Jail, Jail, Jail afore us, everywhere we turn.

Ibid.

I know that our inheritance is held in store for us by Time. I know there is a sea of Time to rise one day, before which all who wrong us or oppress us will be swept away like leaves. I see it, on the flow!

Ibid. Fourth Quarter

He's tough, ma'am, tough is J. B.; tough and devilish sly.

Dombey and Son. Chap. 7

I want to know what it says. . . . The sea, Floy, what it is that it keeps on saying.[1]

Ibid. Chap. 8

When found, make a note of.

Ibid. Chap. 15

A mind equal to any undertaking that he puts it alongside of.

Ibid. Chap. 23

The bearings of this observation lays in the application on it.

Ibid.

Lord, keep my memory green.[2]

The Haunted Man. Last line

You'll find us rough, Sir, but you'll find us ready.

David Copperfield. Chap. 3

I am a lone lorn creetur . . . and everythink goes contrairy with me.

Ibid.

Barkis is willin'.

Ibid. Chap. 5

That he may be ready — in case of anything turning up.[3]

Ibid. Chap. 12

I never will desert Mr. Micawber.

Ibid.

Annual income twenty pounds, annual expenditure nineteen nineteen six, result happiness. Annual income twenty pounds, annual expenditure twenty pounds ought and six, result misery.

David Copperfield. Chap. 12

It's a mad world. Mad as Bedlam.

Ibid. Chap. 14

"Did he [Mr. Dick] say anything to you about King Charles the First, child?"

"Yes, aunt."

"Ah!" said my aunt, rubbing her nose as if she were a little vexed. "That's his allegorical way of expressing it. He connects his illness with great disturbance and agitation, naturally, and that's the figure, or the simile, or whatever it's called, which he chooses to use. And why shouldn't he, if he thinks proper?"[1]

Ibid.

I'm a very umble person.[2]

Ibid. Chap. 16

The winds you are going to tempt, have wafted thousands upon thousands to fortune, and brought thousands upon thousands happily back.

Ibid.

I only ask for information.

Ibid. Chap. 20

It was as true . . . as turnips is. It was as true . . . as taxes is. And nothing's truer than them.

Ibid. Chap. 21

Ain't I volatile?

Ibid. Chap. 22

Nobody's enemy but his own.

Ibid. Chap. 25

Accidents will occur in the best regulated families.

Ibid. Chap. 28

Ride on! Rough-shod if need be, smooth-shod if that will do, but ride

---

[1] See Joseph Edwards Carpenter, page 500.
[2] See Shakespeare, page 89.
[3] See Disraeli, page 421.

[1] "King Charles's Head" has passed into common use in the English language as a phrase meaning some whimsical obsession. — G. B. STERN: *Monogram*
[2] Not only humble but umble, which I look upon to be the comparative, or, indeed, superlative degree. — ANTHONY TROLLOPE: *Doctor Thorne, Chap. 4*

on! Ride on over all obstacles, and win the race!

David Copperfield. Chap. 28

A long pull, and a strong pull, and a pull altogether.

Ibid. Chap. 30

People can't die, along the coast . . . except when the tide's pretty nigh out. They can't be born, unless it's pretty nigh in — not properly born, till flood. He's going out with the tide.

Ibid.

There wasn't room to swing a cat there.[1]

Ibid. Chap. 35

I ate umble pie with an appetite.

Ibid. Chap. 39

Let sleeping dogs lie.

Ibid.

Skewered through and through with office-pens, and bound hand and foot with red tape.

Ibid. Chap. 43

A man must take the fat with the lean.

Ibid. Chap. 51

Least said, soonest mended.

Ibid. Chap. 52

Trifles make the sum of life.

Ibid. Chap. 53

The seamen said it blew great guns.

Ibid. Chap. 55

Our distinguished guest, the ornament of our town. May he never leave us but to better himself, and may his success among us be such as to render his bettering himself impossible.

Ibid. Chap. 63

So may thy face be by me when I close my life indeed; so may I, when realities are melting from me like the shadows which I now dismiss, still find thee near me, pointing upward!

Ibid. Chap. 64, Closing lines

Not to put too fine a point upon it.

Bleak House. Chap. 32

The dreams of childhood — its airy fables; its graceful, beautiful, humane, impossible adornments of the world beyond: so good to be believed in once,

so good to be remembered when outgrown.

Hard Times. Book II, Chap. 9

One always begins to forgive a place as soon as it's left behind.

Little Dorrit. Book I, Chap. 2

Whatever was required to be done, the Circumlocution Office was beforehand with all the public departments in the art of perceiving HOW NOT TO DO IT.

Ibid. Chap. 10

A person who can't pay, gets another person who can't pay, to guarantee that he can pay.

Ibid. Chap. 23

Papa, potatoes, poultry, prunes, and prism, are all very good words for the lips: especially prunes and prism.

Ibid. Book II, Chap. 5

It is at least as difficult to stay a moral infection as a physical one.

Ibid. Chap. 13

It was the best of times, it was the worst of times, it was the age of wisdom, it was the age of foolishness, it was the epoch of belief, it was the epoch of incredulity, it was the season of Light, it was the season of Darkness, it was the spring of hope, it was the winter of despair.

A Tale of Two Cities. Book I, Chap. 1

A wonderful fact to reflect upon, that every human creature is constituted to be that profound secret and mystery to every other.

Ibid. Chap. 3

The calm that must follow all storms — emblem to humanity of the rest and silence into which the storm called Life must hush at last.

Ibid. Chap. 6

Detestation of the high is the involuntary homage of the low.

Ibid. Book II, Chap. 9

Dead as mutton.

Ibid. Chap. 14

He's as thin as a lath.

Ibid.

The murmuring of many voices, the upturning of many faces, the pressing on of many footsteps in the outskirts of the crowd, so that it swells forward

[1] You can swing a cat here. — JOHN GALSWORTHY: *The Man of Property,* Part I, Chap. 8

in a mass, like one great heave of water, all flashes away. Twenty-three.

A Tale of Two Cities. Book III, Chap. 15

It is a far, far better thing that I do, than I have ever done; it is a far, far better rest that I go to, than I have ever known.

Ibid.

I have known a vast quantity of nonsense talked about bad men not looking you in the face. Don't trust that conventional idea. Dishonesty will stare honesty out of countenance, any day in the week, if there is anything to be got by it.

Hunted Down. Chap. 2

In the little world in which children have their existence, whosoever brings them up, there is nothing so finely perceived and so finely felt, as injustice.

Great Expectations. Chap. 9

Probably every new and eagerly expected garment ever put on since clothes came in, fell a trifle short of the wearer's expectation.

Ibid. Chap. 19

Heaven knows we need never be ashamed of our tears, for they are rain upon the blinding dust of earth, overlying our hard hearts.

Ibid.

Throughout life, our worst weaknesses and meannesses are usually committed for the sake of the people whom we most despise.

Ibid. Chap. 27

The Bigwig family (composed of all the stateliest people thereabouts, and all the noisiest).

Nobody's Story

And I *do* come home at Christmas. We all do, or we all should. We all come home, or ought to come home, for a short holiday — the longer, the better — from the great boarding-school, where we are forever working at our arithmetical slates, to take, and give a rest.

A Christmas Tree

My best of wishes for your merry Christmases and your happy New Years, your long lives and your true prosperities. Worth twenty pound good if they are delivered as I send them. Remember! Here's a final prescription added, "To be taken for life."

Doctor Marigold. Chap. 1

EDWARD LEAR
[1812–1888]

They went to sea in a sieve, they did;
In a sieve they went to sea;
In spite of all their friends could say.

The Jumblies. Stanza 1

Far and few, far and few,
Are the lands where the Jumblies live:
Their heads are green, and their hands are blue
And they went to sea in a sieve.

Ibid.

The Pobble who has no toes
Swam across the Bristol Channel;
But before he set out he wrapped his nose
In a piece of scarlet flannel.

The Pobble Who Has No Toes. Stanza 2

On the top of the Crumpetty Tree
The Quangle Wangle sat,
But his face you could not see,
On account of his Beaver Hat.

The Quangle Wangle's Hat. Stanza 1

On the coast of Coromandel
Where the early pumpkins blow,
In the middle of the woods
Lived the Yonghy-Bonghy-Bò.
Two old chairs, and half a candle,
One old jug without a handle, —
These were all his worldly goods.

The Courtship of the Yonghy-Bonghy-Bò. Stanza 1

The Owl and the Pussy-Cat went to sea
In a beautiful pea-green boat.

The Owl and the Pussy-Cat. Stanza 1

They sailed away, for a year and a day,
To the land where the bong-tree grows.

Ibid. Stanza 2

When awful darkness and silence reign
Over the great Gromboolian plain,

Through the long, long wintry nights.
The Dong with the Luminous Nose. Stanza 1

Who, or why, or which, or *what*,
Is the Akond of Swat?
The Akond of Swat [1] [*September, 1873*]

Does he study the wants of his own dominion?
Or doesn't he care for public opinion?
Ibid.

Some one, or nobody, knows I wot
Who or which or why or what.
Ibid.

There was an old man at a Station,
Who made a promiscuous oration.
Limerick

He made them a book
And with laughter they shook.
Limerick

There was an Old Man with a beard,
Who said: "It is just as I feared!
Two Owls and a Hen,
Four Larks and a Wren
Have all built their nests in my beard."
Limerick

He weareth a runcible hat.
*How Pleasant to Know Mr. Lear.
Stanza 5*

Ere the days of his pilgrimage vanish,
How pleasant to know Mr. Lear!
Ibid. Stanza 8

Ploffskin, Pluffskin, Pelican jee!
We think no Birds so happy as we!
Plumpskin, Ploshkin, Pelican jill!
We think so then, and we thought so still.
The Pelican Chorus.

WILLIAM JAMES LINTON
[1812–1898]

He boasts nor wealth nor high descent, yet he may claim to be
A gentleman to match the best of any pedigree:

His blood hath run in peasant veins through many a noteless year;
Yet, search in every prince's court, you'll rarely find his peer.
For he's one of Nature's Gentlemen, the best of every time.
Nature's Gentleman. Stanza 1

Be patient, O be patient! Put your ear against the earth;
Listen there how noiselessly the germ o' the seed has birth;
How noiselessly and gently it upheaves its little way
Till it parts the scarcely broken ground, and the blade stands up in day.
Patience [1]

NORMAN MACLEOD
[1812–1872]

Courage, brother! do not stumble,
Though thy path be dark as night;
There's a star to guide the humble,
Trust in God and do the Right.
Trust in God. Stanza 1

FRANCES SARGENT OSGOOD
[1812–1850]

Work — for some good, be it ever so slowly;
Cherish some flower, be it ever so lowly;
Labor! — all labor is noble and holy!
Let thy great deeds be thy prayer to thy God!
Laborare est Orare. [2] *Stanza 6*

A whisper woke the air —
A soft, light tone, and low,
Yet barbed with shame and woe.
Calumny. Stanza 1

From ear to lip, from lip to ear,
Until it reached a gentle heart
That throbbed from all the world apart
And that — it broke!
Ibid. Stanza 2

---

[1] The Ahkoond is dead! — GEORGE THOMAS LANIGAN [1845–1886]: *A Threnody, St. 1* [January, 1878]
It borders upon Swat. — G. T. LANIGAN: *Dirge of the Moolla of Kotal, Rival of the Ahkoond of Swat, St. 1*

[1] From LINTON's *Poems of Freedom*. This poem is attributed to R. C. TRENCH in some anthologies.
[2] To labor is to pray. — Motto of BENEDICT [480–543], founder of the Benedictine Order.

WILLIAM EDMONDSTOUNE AYTOUN
[1813–1865]

News of battle! — news of battle!
Hark! 'tis ringing down the street;
And the archways and the pavement
Bear the clang of hurrying feet.
Edinburgh after Flodden.
Stanza 1

The German heart is stout and true,
the German arm is strong,
The German foot goes seldom back
where armed foemen throng;
But never had they faced in field so
stern a charge before,
And never had they felt the sweep of
Scotland's broad claymore.
The Island of the Scots

'Twas I that led the Highland host
through wild Lochaber's snows,
What time the plaided clans came
down to battle with Montrose.
The Execution of Montrose.
Stanza 2

Had I been there with sword in hand,
and fifty Camerons by,
That day through high Dunedin's
streets had pealed the slogan cry.
Ibid. Stanza 6

HENRY WARD BEECHER
[1813–1887]

If there were no religion, if that vast
sphere, out of which glow all the super-
eminent truths of the Bible, was a mere
emptiness and void, yet, methinks, the
very idea of Fatherland, the exceeding
preciousness of the laws and liberties of
a great people, would enkindle such a
high and noble enthusiasm that all
baser feelings would be consumed.
The Dishonest Politician

A thoughtful mind, when it sees a
Nation's flag, sees not the flag only,
but the Nation itself; and whatever
may be its symbols, its insignia, he
reads chiefly in the flag the Government, the principles, the truths, the
history which belongs to the Nation
that sets it forth.
The American Flag

Nothing marks the increasing wealth
of our times and the growth of the public mind toward refinement, more than
the demand for books.
Star Papers. Subtleties of Book
Buyers

Where is human nature so weak as
in the book-store!
Ibid.

No subtle manager or broker ever
saw through a maze of financial embarrassments half so quick as a poor book-
buyer sees his way clear to pay for
what he *must* have.
Ibid.

You cannot forget if you would,
those golden kisses all over the cheeks
of the meadow, queerly called dandelions.
Ibid. A Discourse on Flowers

JOHN WILLIAM BURGON
[1813–1888]

It seems no work of man's creative
hand
By labor wrought as wavering fancy
planned,
But from the rock as if by magic
grown,
Eternal, silent, beautiful, alone!
Petra [1] *[Newdigate Prize Poem,*
1845]

Match me such marvel save in Eastern
clime,
A rose-red city half as old as time.
Ibid.

JOSEPH EDWARDS CARPENTER
[1813–1885]

What are the wild waves saying,[2]
Sister, the whole day long,
That ever amid our playing
I hear but their low, lone song?
What Are the Wild Waves
Saying? Stanza 1

Yes, but the waves seem ever
Singing the same sad thing,

[1] See Whittier, page 443.
[2] See Dickens, page 496.

And vain is my weak endeavor
  To guess what the surges sing.
        What Are the Wild Waves
          Saying? Stanza 3
Yes! but there's something greater
  That speaks to the heart alone:
'Tis the voice of the great Creator
  Dwells in that mighty tone.
          Ibid. Refrain
For her voice lives on the breeze,
  And her spirit comes at will,
In the midnight on the seas,
  Her bright smile haunts me still.
      Her Bright Smile Haunts Me
         Still. Stanza 1

WILLIAM LORENZO CARTER
[1813–1860]

Young Charlotte lived by a mountain-
  side in a wild and lonely spot,
There was no village for miles around
  except her father's cot;
And yet on many a wintry night young
  boys would gather there, —
Her father kept a social board, and she
  was very fair.
        Young [or Fair] Charlotte.[1]
            Stanza 1
"O daughter, dear," her mother said,
  "this blanket round you fold,
'Tis such a dreadful night abroad you
  will catch your death of cold."
         Ibid. Stanza 3
Young ladies, think of this fair girl and
  always dress aright,
And never venture thinly clad on such
  a wintry night.
        Ibid. Last stanza

CHRISTOPHER PEARSE
CRANCH
[1813–1892]

Thought is deeper than all speech,
  Feeling deeper than all thought;

[1] Carter was a Vermont man, but his ballad has become a folk-song of the South and a cowboy song of the West. There is a sketch, *William Carter, the Bensontown Homer*, by Phillips Barry, in the *Journal of American Folk-Lore*, April–June, 1912. The ballad is included in the published collections of Lomax, Spaeth, Cox, Pound, and others.

Souls to souls can never teach
  What unto themselves was taught.
        Thought [Gnosis]. Stanza 1
We are spirits clad in veils;
  Man by man was never seen;
All our deep communing fails
  To remove the shadowy screen.
         Ibid. Stanza 2
We are columns left alone
  Of a temple once complete.
         Ibid. Stanza 3
No night so wild but brings the con-
  stant sun
With love and power untold;
No time so dark but through its woof
  there run
Some blessed threads of gold.
        Oh, Love Supreme
O Light divine! we need no fuller test
  That all is ordered well;
We know enough to trust that all is
  best
Where Love and Wisdom dwell.
         Ibid.

JOHN SULLIVAN DWIGHT
[1813–1893]

Is not true leisure
  One with true toil? [1]
        Rest.[2] *Stanza 1*
Rest is not quitting
  The busy career,
Rest is the fitting
  Of self to its sphere.
        Ibid. Stanza 4
'Tis the brook's motion,
  Clear without strife,
Fleeing to ocean
  After its life.
        Ibid. Stanza 5
'Tis loving and serving
  The Highest and Best!
'Tis onwards! unswerving,
  And that is true rest.
        Ibid. Stanza 7
Work, and thou wilt bless the day
  Ere the toil be done;
They that work not, can not pray,
  Can not feel the sun.

[1] Absence of occupation is not rest.
      Cowper: *Retirement, L. 615*
[2] Wrongly attributed to Goethe.

God is living, working still,
    All things work and move;
Work, or lose the power to will,
    Lose the power to love.
                    Working

JOSEPH HOOKER
[1813–1879]

Well, General, we have not had many
dead cavalrymen lying about lately.
        *Remark to General William
        Woods Averell, of the Cavalry
        [November, 1862]*

JESSE HUTCHINSON, JR. [1]
[1813–1853]

Of all the mighty nations
    In the east or in the west,
O this glorious Yankee nation
    Is the greatest and the best.
We have room for all creation,
    And our banner is unfurled,
Here's a general invitation
    To the people of the world.
        Uncle Sam's Farm. Stanza 1
Uncle Sam is rich enough
    To give us all a farm.
                Ibid. Refrain
Then ho, brothers, ho,
    To California go;
There's plenty of gold in the world
        we're told
On the banks of the Sacramento.
    Ho for California [1849]. Refrain
The gold is thar, most anywhar,
    And they dig it out with an iron bar.
                Ibid. Stanza 3

ELIJAH KELLOGG
[1813–1901]

If ye are men, follow me! Strike
down your guard, gain the mountain
passes, and then do bloody work, as
did your sires at old Thermopylae! Is
Sparta dead? Is the old Grecian spirit
frozen in your brains, that you do
cower like a belabored hound beneath
his master's lash? O comrades, war-

[1] A member of the famous Hutchinson
Family of Singers, of Lynn, Massachusetts,
which toured the country in the 1860s.

riors, Thracians! If we must fight, let
us fight for ourselves. If we must
slaughter, let it be under the clear sky,
by the bright waters, in noble, honorable battle!
        Spartacus to the Gladiators

EPES SARGENT
[1813–1881]

A life on the ocean wave,
    A home on the rolling deep;
Where the scattered waters rave,
    And the winds their revels keep!
Like an eagle caged I pine
    On this dull, unchanging shore:
Oh, give me the flashing brine,
    The spray and the tempest's roar!
            *A Life on the Ocean Wave.
                        Stanza 1*

JONES VERY
[1813–1880]

'Tis all a great show,
    The world that we're in —
None can tell when 'twas finished —
    None saw it begin.
            The World. Stanza 1

HENRY STEVENSON
WASHBURN
[1813–1903]

We shall meet, but we shall miss him,
    There will be one vacant chair;
We shall linger to caress him
    When we breathe our evening
        prayer.[1]
        The Vacant Chair. Stanza 1

THOMAS OSBORNE DAVIS
[1814–1845]

Come in the evening, or come in the
        morning,
Come when you're looked for, or come
        without warning.
                The Welcome. Stanza 1
The starlight of heaven above us shall
    quiver

[1] See Longfellow, page 435.

As our souls flow in one down eternity's
river.
The Welcome. Stanza 3

AUBREY THOMAS DE VERE
[1814–1902]

Count each affliction, whether light or
grave,
God's messenger sent down to thee; do
thou
With courtesy receive him.
Sorrow

Grief should be
Like joy, majestic, equable, sedate,
Confirming, cleansing, raising, making
free;
Strong to consume small troubles; to
commend
Great thoughts, grave thoughts,
thoughts lasting to the end.
Ibid.

Sad is our youth, for it is ever going,
Crumbling away beneath our very
feet;
Sad is our life, for onward it is flowing
In current unperceived, because so
fleet.
Sad Is Our Youth. Stanza 1

Of all great Nature's tones that sweep
Earth's resonant bosom, far or near,
Low-breathed or loudest, shrill or deep,
How few are grasped by mortal ear.
Implicit Faith. Stanza 1

In holy music's golden speech
Remotest notes to notes respond:
Each octave is a world: yet each
Vibrates to worlds its own beyond.
Ibid. Stanza 4

FREDERICK WILLIAM
FABER
[1814–1863]

For right is right, since God is God,
And right the day must win;
To doubt would be disloyalty,
To falter would be sin.
On the Field

The sea, unmated creature, tired and
lone.

Makes on its desolate sands eternal
moan.
The Sorrowful World

O majesty unspeakable and dread!
Wert thou less mighty than Thou
art,
Thou wert, O Lord, too great for our
belief,
Too little for our heart.
The Greatness of God

Hark! Hark! my soul, angelic songs
are swelling
O'er earth's green fields, and ocean's
wave-beat shore;
How sweet the truth those blessed
strains are telling
Of that new life when sin shall be
no more!
Pilgrims of the Night

O Paradise! O Paradise!
Who doth not crave for rest?
Who would not seek the happy land
Where they that love are blest?
Paradise

CHARLES MACKAY
[1814–1889]

Cleon hath a million acres, — ne'er a
one have I;
Cleon dwelleth in a palace, — in a cottage I.
Cleon and I. Stanza 1

But the sunshine aye shall light the
sky,
As round and round we run;
And the truth shall ever come upper-
most,
And justice shall be done.
Eternal Justice. Stanza 4

Men of thought and men of action,
Clear the way!
Clear the Way. Stanza 1

Aid the dawning, tongue and pen;
Aid it, hopes of honest men!
Ibid. Stanza 2

Some love to roam o'er the dark sea's
foam,
Where the shrill winds whistle free.
Some Love to Roam

There's a good time coming, boys! [1]
    A good time coming.
        The Good Time Coming. Stanza 1
Cannon-balls may aid the truth,
    But thought's a weapon stronger;
We'll win our battles by its aid; —
    Wait a little longer.
                                Ibid.

The smallest effort is not lost,
Each wavelet on the ocean tost
    Aids in the ebb-tide or the flow;
Each rain-drop makes some floweret
    blow;
Each struggle lessens human woe.
            The Old and the New
There is no such thing as death.
    In Nature nothing dies.
From each sad remnant of decay
    Some forms of life arise.
    There Is No Such Thing as Death
To every dungeon comes a ray
Of God's interminable day.
        *The Ivy in the Dungeon.
                Stanza 10*
Whenever a rascal strove to pass,
Instead of silver, a coin of brass,
He took his hammer, and said, with a
    frown,
"The coin is spurious, nail it down." [2]
    The Coin Is Spurious. Stanza 1
Old Tubal Cain was a man of might,
In the days when earth was young.
            Tubal Cain. Stanza 1
Not alone for the blade was the bright
    steel made,
And he fashioned the first plowshare. [3]
            Ibid. Stanza 4
To the West! to the West! to the land
    of the free,
Where the mighty Missouri rolls down
    to the sea.
            To the West. Stanza 1
Where the prairies, like seas where the
    billows have rolled,

---

[1] See Scott, page 310.
[2] There was an old custom that all counterfeit coins taken in a shop should be nailed to the counter, door-frame, or any solid woodwork, so that they could not be passed again.
[3] Tubal fashioned the hand-flung spears
    And showed his neighbours peace.
    KIPLING: *Jubal and Tubal Cain, St. 3*

Are broad as the kingdoms and em-
    pires of old.
            To the West. Stanza 2
A traveler through a dusty road
    strewed acorns on the lea,
And one took root and sprouted up,
    and grew into a tree.
            Small Beginnings. Stanza 1
A nameless man, amid a crowd that
    thronged the daily mart,
Let fall a word of Hope and Love, un-
    studied, from the heart;
A whisper on the tumult thrown, — a
    transitory breath, —
It raised a brother from the dust; it
    saved a soul from death.
            Ibid. Stanza 4
Croesus! hast thou riches
    That with mine can vie?
Pope! hast thou dominion
    Absolute as I?
                Day Dreams
Make my coffee strong!
                The Quarrel
The king can drink the best of wine —
    So can I;
And has enough when he would dine —
    So have I;
And can not order rain or shine —
    Nor can I.
Then where's the difference — let me
    see —
Betwixt my lord the king and me?
                Differences
If happy I and wretched he,
Perhaps the king would change with
    me.
                    Ibid.
You have no enemies, you say?
    Alas! my friend, the boast is poor —
He who has mingled in the fray
    Of duty, that the brave endure,
Must have made foes! If you have
    none,
Small is the work that you have done;
You've hit no traitor on the hip;
You've dashed no cup from perjured
    lip;
You've never turned the wrong to
    right —

You've been a coward in the fight! [1]
> Quoted by MARIE CORELLI
> (*Mackay's adopted daughter*)
> in *Free Opinions: The Happy
> Life, Page 369*

THOMAS WESTWOOD
[1814–1888]

Storm upon the mountain, night upon
its throne!
And the little snow-white lamb left
alone — alone!
> *The Pet Lamb. Stanza 1*

MICHAEL WENTWORTH BECK
[1815–1843]

This world is not so bad a world
As some would like to make it;
Though whether good, or whether bad,
Depends on how we take it.
> *The World as It Is. Stanza 1*

RICHARD HENRY DANA
[1815–1882]

Six days shalt thou labor and do all
thou art able,
And on the seventh — holystone the
decks and scrape the cable.
> *Two Years Before the Mast.
> Chap. 3, Philadelphia Cate-
> chism*

Like a true ship, committed to her
element once for all at her Launching,
she perished at sea.
> *Ibid. Twenty-Four Years After
> [1869]*

DANIEL DECATUR EMMET
[1815–1904]

In Dixie land, I'll took my stand,
To lib an' die in Dixie,
Away, away,
Away down South in Dixie.
> *I Wish I Was in Dixie's Land
> [1859]*

[1] From the German of ANASTASIUS GRUEN
(COUNT VON AUERSPERG) [1806–1876].

JOHN BABSONE LANE SOULE
[1815–1891]

Go west, young man. [1]
> *Article in the Terre Haute,
> Indiana, Express [1851]*

ANTHONY TROLLOPE [2]
[1815–1882]

He argued that the principal duty
which a parent owed to a child was to
make him happy.
> *Doctor Thorne. Chap. 3*

In these days a man is nobody unless his biography is kept so far posted
up that it may be ready for the national
breakfast-table on the morning after
his demise.
> *Ibid. Chap. 25*

How I do hate those words, "an excellent marriage." In them is contained
more of wicked worldliness than any
other words one ever hears spoken.
> *The Small House at Allington.
> Chap. 39*

Those who offend us are generally
punished for the offence they give; but
we so frequently miss the satisfaction
of knowing that we are avenged!
> *Ibid. Chap. 50*

She understood how much louder a
cock can crow in its own farmyard than
elsewhere.
> *The Last Chronicle of Barset.
> Vol. I, Chap. 17*

Always remember that when you go
into an attorney's office door, you will
have to pay for it, first or last.
> *Ibid. Chap. 20*

[1] Horace Greeley [1811–1872] was attracted by the expression, and used it in an
editorial in *The New York Tribune.* As the
saying, "Go west, young man, and grow up
with the country," gained popularity, Greeley
printed Soule's article, to show the source of
his inspiration.

Many men have stated that the advice was
given to them by Greeley, among them William S. Verity [1837–1934], who said Greeley
had given it to him in 1859.

[2] I proclaim the fact that Anthony Trollope
has written a greater number of first-class
novels than Dickens or Thackeray or George
Eliot. — A. EDWARD NEWTON: *The Trollope
Society* (1934).

It is a comfortable feeling to know that you stand on your own ground. Land is about the only thing that can't fly away.
> *The Last Chronicle of Barset.*
> *Vol. II, Chap. 58*

It's dogged as does it.
> *Ibid. Chap. 61*

Nothing reopens the springs of love so fully as absence, and no absence so thoroughly as that which must needs be endless.
> *Ibid. Chap. 67*

PHILIP JAMES BAILEY
[1816-1902]

Let each man think himself an act of God,
His mind a thought, his life a breath of God;
And let each try, by great thoughts and good deeds,
To show the most of Heaven he hath in him.
> *Festus. Proem*

Evil and good are God's right hand and left.
> *Ibid.*

Art is man's nature; nature is God's art.
> *Ibid.*

It matters not how long we live, but how.
> *Ibid. Wood and Water*

The world must have great minds, even as great spheres
Or suns, to govern lesser restless minds.
> *Ibid. Water and Wood*

I loved her for that she was beautiful.
> *Ibid.*

Men might be better if we better deemed
Of them. The worst way to improve the world
Is to condemn it.[1]
> *Ibid. A Mountain, Sunrise*

[1] The surest plan to make a Man
Is, think him so.
    J. R. Lowell: *The Biglow Papers,*
    Jonathan to John, St. 9

It is much less what we do
Than what we think, which fits us for the future.
> *Festus. Alcove and Garden*

The first and worst of all frauds is to cheat
Oneself.
> *Ibid. Anywhere*

Who never doubted never half believed.[1]
Where doubt there truth is — 'tis her shadow.
> *Ibid. A Country Town*

We live in deeds, not years; in thoughts, not breaths;
In feelings, not in figures on a dial.
We should count time by heart-throbs. He most lives
Who thinks most — feels the noblest — acts the best.
Life's but a means unto an end; that end
Beginning, mean, and end to all things — God.
> *Ibid.*

Envy's a coal comes hissing hot from hell.
> *Ibid.*

The sole equality on earth is death.
> *Ibid.*

I should like to macadamize the world;
The road to Hell wants mending.
> *Ibid.*

America, half-brother of the world!
With something good and bad of every land.
> *Ibid. The Surface*

Beauty, but skin deep.
> *Ibid. A Village Feast*

Worthy books
Are not companions — they are solitudes:
We lose ourselves in them and all our cares.
> *Ibid.*

Music tells no truths.
> *Ibid.*

Respect is what we owe; love, what we give.
> *Ibid.*

[1] There lives more faith in honest doubt,
Believe me, than in half the creeds.
    Tennyson: *In Memoriam, XCVI, 3*

Who can mistake great thoughts?
They seize upon the mind — arrest,
  and search,
And shake it.
  Festus. A Village Feast
The worst men often give the best ad-
vice.
  Ibid.
Man is a military animal,
Glories in gunpowder, and loves pa-
rade.
  Ibid. A Metropolis
Poets are all who love, who feel great
  truths,
And tell them; and the truth of truths
  is love.
  Ibid. Another and a Better World
The great ancients' writings, beside
  ours,
Look like illuminated manuscripts
Before plain press print.
  Ibid. Home
There is no disappointment we endure
One half so great as that we are to our-
selves.[1]
  Ibid. The Sun
There are some hearts, aloe-like flower
  once, and die.[2]
  *Ibid. A Gathering of Kings and
  People*
It is folly to tell women truth!
They would rather live on lies, so they
  be sweet.
  *The Devil's Advice on Love-
  Making*

DAVID BARKER
[1816–1874]

One night, as old St. Peter slept,
  He left the door of Heaven ajar,
When through, a little angel crept,
  And came down with a falling star.
  My Child's Origin. Stanza 1

[1] Every really able man, if you talk sin-
cerely with him, considers his work, however
much admired, as far short of what it should
be. — R. W. EMERSON: *Immortality*
[2] Have you heard the tale of the aloe plant,
  Away in the sunny clime?
By humble growth of an hundred years
  It reaches its blooming time.
  HENRY HARBAUGH [1817–1867]:
  Through Death to Life

CHARLOTTE BRONTË
[1816–1855]

Life, believe, is not a dream
  So dark as sages say;
Oft a little morning rain
  Foretells a pleasant day.
  Life. Stanza 1
The human heart has hidden treasures,
  In secret kept, in silence sealed; —
The thoughts, the hopes, the dreams,
  the pleasures,
  Whose charms were broken if re-
  vealed.
  Evening Solace. Stanza 1
An abundant shower of curates has
fallen upon the north of England.
  Shirley, Chap. I

FRANCES BROWN
[1816–1864]

Sad losses have ye met,
  But mine is heavier yet,
For a believing heart hath gone from
  me.
  Losses. Stanza 5
The age is weary with work and gold;
  And high hopes wither,[1] and mem-
  ories wane,
On hearths and altars the fires are
  dead;
  But that brave faith hath not lived
  in vain.
  Is It Come? Stanza 6
Oh! those blessed times of old! with
  their chivalry and state;
I love to read their chronicles, which
  such brave deeds relate;
I love to sing their ancient rhymes, to
  hear their legends told —
But, Heaven be thanked! I live not in
  those blessed times of old!
  *Oh! the Pleasant Days of Old.
  Stanza 7*

JOSIAH DEAN CANNING
[1816–1892]

O'er the ruins of home, o'er my heart's
  desolation,

[1] High hopes faint on a warm hearth stone.
  KIPLING: *The Winners, St. 2*

No more shalt thou hear my unblest
      lamentation,
For death's dark encounter I make
      preparation,
He hears the last cry of the wild
      Cherokee.
            The Lament of the Cherokee.[1]
                              Stanza 5

CHARLOTTE CUSHMAN
[1816–1876]

God conceived the world, that was
      poetry;
He formed it, that was sculpture;
He colored it; that was painting;
He peopled it with living beings; that
      was the grand, divine, eternal
      drama.
      *On the Curtain of Ford's Opera
      House, Baltimore, Maryland*

JAMES THOMAS FIELDS
[1816–1881]

How sweet and gracious, even in com-
      mon speech,
Is that fine sense which men call Cour-
      tesy!
                              Courtesy
It transmutes aliens into trusting
      friends,
And gives its owner passport round the
      globe.
                              Ibid.
No wonder skies upon you frown;
You've nailed the horse-shoe upside
      down!
Just turn it round, and soon you'll see
How you and Fortune will agree.
      The Lucky Horse-shoe. Stanza 6
"Paint me as I am," said Cromwell,
      Rough with age and gashed with
      wars;
"Show my visage as you find it, —
      Less than truth my soul abhors."
            On a Portrait of Cromwell.
                              Stanza 1

Oh, to be home again, home again,
      home again![1]
Under the apple-boughs, down by
      the mill!
                        In a Strange Land
Just then, with a wink and a sly normal
      lurch,
The owl, very gravely, got down from
      his perch,
Walked round, and regarded his fault-
      finding critic
(Who thought he was stuffed) with a
      glance analytic.
                        The Owl-Critic
"I'm an owl; you're another. Sir Critic,
      good day!"
And the barber kept on shaving.
                              Ibid.
The skipper stormed, and tore his hair,
      Hauled on his boots and roared to
      Marden,
"Nantucket's sunk, and here we are
      Right over old Marm Hackett's gar-
      den!"
      The Nantucket Skipper. Stanza 10
'Tis a fearful thing in winter
      To be shattered in the blast,
And to hear the rattling trumpet
      Thunder, "Cut away the mast!"
      Ballad of the Tempest. Stanza 2
Is not God upon the ocean,
      Just the same as on the land?[2]
                        Ibid. Stanza 5

ELLEN STURGIS HOOPER[3]
[1816–1841]

I slept and dreamed that life was
      beauty.

---

[1] So it's home again, and home again,
      America for me.
    My heart is turning home again, and
      there I long to be.
    HENRY VAN DYKE: *America for Me, St. 2*
[2] Sir Humphrey Gilbert [1539 ?–1583], on
embarking on his ill-fated voyage homeward,
— "We are as near to Heaven by sea as by
land." — J. R. GREEN: *A Short History of
the English People, Chap. 8*
      "Do not fear! Heaven is as near,"
      He said, "by water as by land!"
    LONGFELLOW: *Sir Humphrey Gilbert, St. 6*
[3] Mrs. Ellen Hooper, wife of Dr. R. W.
Hooper, — a woman of genius, who gave our
literature a classic in the lines beginning, —

[1] This poem has been attributed erroneously to John Howard Payne. It is in Canning's early book, *Harp and Plow,* and a later
book, *Connecticut River Reeds.*

I woke — and found that life was
    duty; [1]
Was my dream, then, a shadowy lie?
Toil on, sad heart, courageously,
And thou shalt find thy dream shall be
A noonday light and truth to thee.
           Beauty and Duty

ROBERT TRAILL SPENCE LOWELL
[1816–1891]

It was the pipes of the Highlanders,
    And now they played "Auld Lang
    Syne."
It came to our men like the voice of
    God,
    And they shouted along the line.
        The Relief of Lucknow, [2]
           September 25, 1857

JOHN GODFREY SAXE
[1816–1887]

There's a castle in Spain, very charm-
    ing to see,
Though built without money or toil;
Of this handsome estate I am owner in
    fee,
    And paramount lord of the soil.
        My Castle in Spain. Stanza 1

There is a saying of the ancient sages:
    No noble human thought,
However buried in the dust of ages,
    Can ever come to naught.
        Spes est Vates. Stanza 1

The saying is wise, though it sounds
    like a jest,
    That "the gods don't allow us to be
    in their debt,"
For though we may think we are spe-
    cially blest,
    We are certain to pay for the favors
    we get!
        The Gifts of the Gods. Stanza 1

When skies are clear, expect the cloud;
    In darkness, wait the coming light;

"I slept, and dreamed that life was beauty."
— Thomas Wentworth Higginson: *Margaret Fuller Ossoli, Chap. 10*

[1] See Whittier, page 444.
[2] *Ibid.,* page 443.

Whatever be thy fate to-day,
    Remember, "This will pass away!" [1]
        The Old Man's Motto. Stanza 6

Of all amusements for the mind,
    From logic down to fishing,
There isn't one that you can find
    So very cheap as "wishing."
        Wishing. Stanza 1

I wish that practising was not
    So different from preaching.
        Ibid. Stanza 4

I'm growing fonder of my staff;
    I'm growing dimmer in the eyes;
I'm growing fainter in my laugh;
    I'm growing deeper in my sighs;
I'm growing careless of my dress;

[1] At the time of his trial in England, Warren Hastings related to his friends an Indian tale which had given him much comfort: A monarch, who suffered many hours of discouragement, urged his courtiers to devise a motto, short enough to be engraved on a ring, which should be suitable alike in prosperity and in adversity. After many suggestions had been rejected, his daughter offered an emerald bearing the inscription in Arabic, "This, too, will pass."

This greatest mortal consolation, which we derive from the transitoriness of all things — from the right of saying, in every conjuncture, — "This, too, will pass away."
    Nathaniel Hawthorne: *The Marble Faun, Chap. 16*

Whate'er thou art, where'er thy footsteps stray,
Heed these wise words: This, too, shall pass away.
    Paul Hamilton Hayne: *This, Too, Shall Pass Away*

Solemn words, and these were they:
"Even this shall pass away."
    Theodore Tilton: *All Things Shall Pass Away*

"Even this will pass away."
    Thomas Bailey Aldrich: Title of sonnet

Lo! characters of glory play
'Mid shades — "This, too, shall pass away."
    Benjamin Davis Winslow [1815–1839]: *This, Too, Shall Pass Away*

Many the maxims sent the king, men say;
The one he chose, "This, too, shall pass away."
    Ella Wheeler Wilcox: *This, Too, Shall Pass Away*

Let these few words their fullest import bear:
"This, too, will pass away."
    Mrs. Lanta Wilson Smith [1856–]: *This, Too, Shall Pass Away*

This, Too, Shall Pass Away.
    Jamie Sexton Holme: Title of poem

I'm growing frugal of my gold;
I'm growing wise; I'm growing —
     yes, —
I'm growing old!
          I'm Growing Old. Stanza 3

For she was rich, and he was poor
     And so it might not be.
          The Way of the World. Stanza 1

Of all the notable things on earth,
The queerest one is pride of birth,
     Among our "fierce Democracie"!
A bridge across a hundred years,
Without a prop to save it from
     sneers, —
Not even a couple of rotten Peers, —
A thing for laughter, fleers, and jeers,
     Is American aristocracy.
          The Proud Miss MacBride.
               Stanza 13

Depend upon it, my snobbish friend,
Your family thread you can't ascend,
Without good reason to apprehend
You may find it waxed at the farther
     end
By some plebeian vocation;
Or, worse than that, your boasted Line
May end in a loop of stronger twine,
     That plagued some worthy relation!
          Ibid. Stanza 15

He takes the strangest liberties, —
     But never takes his leave!
          My Familiar. Stanza 2

A frown is no extinguisher —
     It does not put him out!
          Ibid. Stanza 6

Bless me! this is pleasant
     Riding on the Rail.
          Rhyme of the Rail. Stanza 1

In battle or business, whatever the
     game,
In law or in love, it is ever the same;
In the struggle for power, or the scram-
     ble for pelf,
Let this be your motto, — Rely on
     yourself!
For, whether the prize be a ribbon or
     throne,
The victor is he who can go it alone! [1]
          The Game of Life. Stanza 7

[1] He travels the fastest who travels alone.
          KIPLING: *The Winners*

"Got any boys," the Marshal said
     To a lady from over the Rhine;
And the lady shook her flaxen head,
     And civilly answered, *"Nein!"*
          The Puzzled Census-Taker.
               Stanza 1

I'll find a way, or make it! [1]
          Where There's a Will There's a
               Way. Stanza 2

"God bless the man who first invented
     sleep!"
So Sancho Panza said, and so say I.
          Early Rising. Stanza 1

I like the lad, who when his father
     thought
To clip his morning nap by hackneyed
     phrase
Of vagrant worm by early songster
     caught,
Cried, "Served him right! It's not at all
     surprising;
The worm was punished, Sir, for early
     rising!"
          Ibid. Stanza 8

How goes the Money? — Sure,
I wish the ways were something fewer;
It goes for wages, taxes, debts;
It goes for presents, goes for bets,
For paint, pomade, and eau de rose,
And that's the way the Money goes! [2]
          How the Money Goes. Stanza 3

I know a girl with teeth of pearl,
And shoulders white as snow;
     She lives, — ah! well,
     I must not tell, —
Wouldn't you like to know?
          Wouldn't You Like to Know?
               Stanza 1

It was six men of Indostan
     To learning much inclined,
Who went to see the Elephant
     (Though all of them were blind),

[1] Aut viam inveniam, aut faciam. — Latin motto
[2] Up and down the City Road,
     In and out the Eagle,
     That's the way the money goes —
     Pop goes the weasel!
          Popular song in London [1852–1853]
The Eagle was a music-hall, in which drinks were sold, on the City Road, London. The weasel was a tool used by hatters, often pawned on Saturday night, "pop" being equivalent to "hock".

That each by observation
  Might satisfy his mind.
    The Blind Men and the Elephant.
      Stanza 1
"Whose very charming grounds are
    these?
And — pardon me — be pleased to tell
Who in this splendid house may dwell?"
To which, in Dutch, the puzzled man
Replied what seemed like *"Nick Van
    Stann."* [1]
    The Romance of Nick Van Stann
With sudden anger, Hassan looked
    around,
And saw an angel standing on the
    ground,
With wings of gold, and robe of purest
    white.
"I am God's messenger, employed to
    write
Within this book the pious deeds of
    men;
I have revised thy reckoning: look
    again." [2]
    Hassan and the Angel
"Whose work is this?" Murillo said,
  The while he bent his eager gaze
Upon a sketch (a Virgin's head)
  That filled the painter with amaze. [3]
    Murillo and His Slave. [4] *Stanza 1*
'Tis wise to learn; 'tis God-like to
    create.
    The Library
I asked of Echo, 't other day
  (Whose words are few and often
    funny),
What to a novice she could say
  Of courtship, love, and matrimony?

Quoth Echo, plainly: — "Matter-o'-
    money."
    Echo. Stanza 1
Young ladies! — beware of hasty con-
    nections;
And don't marry suitors of swarthy
    complexions;
For though they may chance to be cap-
    ital fellows,
Depend upon it, they're apt to be jeal-
    ous!
    Othello, the Moor. Moral

MICHAEL JOSEPH BARRY
[1817–1889]

Death is a common friend or foe,
  As different men may hold,
And at his summons each must go,
  The timid and the bold;
But when the spirit, free and warm,
  Deserts it, as it must,
What matter where the lifeless form
  Dissolves again to dust?
    *The Place Where Men Should
      Die.* [1] *Stanza 2*
But whether on the scaffold high
  Or in the battle's van, [2]
The fittest place where man can die
  Is where he dies for man!
    Ibid. Stanza 5

ELIZA COOK
[1817–1889]

There's a magical tie to the land of our
    home,
Which the heart cannot break, though
    the footsteps may roam. [3]
    The Land of My Birth. Stanza 1
Whom do we dub as Gentlemen? The
    knave, the fool, the brute —
If they but own full tithe of gold, and
    wear a courtly suit.
    Nature's Gentleman. Stanza 1

---

[1] "I say, whose house is that there here?"
    "House! *Je vous n'entends pas, Mon-
      sieur.*"
    "What, Nongtongpaw again!" cries John;
    "This fellow is some mighty Don."
        CHARLES DIBDIN [1745–1814]:
          Nongtongpaw
[2] See Leigh Hunt, page 346.
[3] "Who is your master, boy?"
    "You, Señor," said the trembling slave;
    "Nay, who, I mean, instruction gave,
    Before that Virgin's head you drew?"
      SUSAN WILSON: *The Painter of Seville*
[4] The incident related in the poem occurred
about 1630. The slave was Sebastian Gómez.
See DOLORES BACON [1870–1934]: *Pictures
Every Child Should Know. P. 219.*

[1] Printed in *The Dublin Nation, Sept. 28,
1844, Vol. II, P. 809.*
[2] Whether on the scaffold high, or the bat-
      tlefield we die,
    O what matter, when for Erin dear we
      fall!
      TIMOTHY DANIEL SULLIVAN [1827–
          1914]: *God Save Ireland*
[3] See Holmes, page 453.

They hold the rank no king can give,
    no station can disgrace;
Nature puts forth her Gentleman, and
    monarchs must give place.[1]
        Nature's Gentleman. Stanza 6

There's a land that bears a well-known
    name,
    Though it is but a little spot;
I say 'tis first on the scroll of Fame,
    And who shall say it is not?
        The Englishman. Stanza 1

There's a star in the West that shall
    never go down
Till the records of Valour decay;
We must worship its light, though it is
    not our own,
    For liberty burst in its ray.
        There's a Star in the West.[2]
                Stanza 1

I love it, I love it; and who shall dare
To chide me for loving that old arm-
    chair?
        The Old Arm-Chair

How cruelly sweet are the echoes that
    start
When memory plays an old tune on the
    heart!
        Old Dobbin. Stanza 16

Better build schoolrooms for "the boy"
Than cells and gibbets for "the man." [3]
    A Song for the Ragged Schools.
                Stanza 12

"God speed the plough!" be this a
    prayer
To find its echo everywhere.
        God Speed the Plough. Stanza 1

How busy we are on Tom Tidler's
    ground
    Looking for gold and silver.[4]
        Tom Tidler's Ground. Stanza 1

---

[1] See Linton, page 499.
[2] The poem is in praise of George Washington.
[3] Give them a chance — if you stint them
    now, to-morrow you'll have to pay
A larger bill for a darker ill.
    DENIS A. MCCARTHY [1870–1931]:
      Give Them a Place to Play, St. 4
[4] Here we are on Tom Tidler's ground,
picking up gold and silver. — A children's
game

"And why Tom Tidler's ground?" asked
the Traveller.

Whenever you find your heart despair
    Of doing some goodly thing,
Con over this strain, try bravely again,
    And remember the Spider and King.[1]
        Try Again. Stanza 16

JOHN BALLANTINE GOUGH
[1817–1886]

What is a minority? The chosen heroes of this earth have been in a minority. There is not a social, political, or religious privilege that you enjoy to-day that was not bought for you by the blood and tears and patient suffering of the minority. It is the minority that have stood in the van of every moral conflict, and achieved all that is noble in the history of the world.
        What Is a Minority?

Everywhere water is a thing of beauty, gleaming in the dewdrop; singing in the summer rain; shining in the ice-gems till the leaves all seem to turn to living jewels; spreading a golden veil over the setting sun; or a white gauze around the midnight moon.
        A Glass of Water

My old gray mare run up the hill, and as she turned the top, she waved her tail back at me, seemingly to say — fare ye well, brother Watkins.
        Brother Watkins

"Because he scatters halfpence to Tramps
and such-like." — DICKENS: *Christmas Stories, Tom Tiddler's Ground*
[1] Bruce, banned and hunted on his native
    soil,
    With curious eyes surveyed a spider's
      toil;
Six times the little climber strove and
    failed;
Six times the chief before his foe had
    quailed.
"Once more," he cried, "in thine my doom
    I read,
Once more I dare the fight if thou succeed."
'Twas done; the insect's fate he made his
    own;
Once more the battle waged, and gained
    a throne.
CHARLES SPRAGUE [1791–1875]: *Curiosity*

FRANCIS DE HAES JANVIER
[1817–1885]

The woes of thirty millions filled his
   burdened heart with grief,
Embattled hosts on land and sea acknowledged him their chief,
And yet amid the din of war he heard
   the plaintive cry
Of that poor soldier as he lay in prison,
   doomed to die.
   The Sleeping Sentinel.[1] *Stanza 10*

SIR AUSTEN HENRY
LAYARD
[1817–1894]

I have always believed that success
would be the inevitable result if the
two services, the army and the navy,
had fair play, and if we sent the right
man to fill the right place.
   Speech in Parliament [2]
   [January 15, 1855]

TOM TAYLOR
[1817–1880]

You lay a wreath on murdered Lin-
   coln's bier,
   You, who, with mocking pencil,
      wont to trace,
Broad for self-complacent British
   sneer,
   His length of shambling limb, his
      furrowed face.
   *Abraham Lincoln Foully
   Assassinated.*[3] *Stanza 1*

[1] A poem, largely romance, on President
Lincoln's pardoning a Vermont soldier, William Scott, who slept while on guard duty.
President Lincoln did not pardon Scott, according to a paper, *The Element of Romance
in Military History,* by COLONEL GEORGE G.
BENEDICT, read before the Vermont Com-
mandery, Loyal Legion, March 14, 1893.

In 1936 the Vermont Historical Society
published a book on the subject by WALDO
F. GLOVER, presenting various documents in
Scott's case.

There are other versions of the legend, in
both verse and prose, one being *The Soldier's
Reprieve: The Generous Soldier Saved* in
Tiffany's Gems for the Fireside.

[2] Reported in T. C. HANSARD's *Parliamentary Debates, Third Series, Vol. 138, P. 2077.*

[3] Printed in *Punch,* London, May 6, 1865.
(Taylor became editor of *Punch* in 1874.) It
was at a performance of Taylor's play, *Our
American Cousin,* that Lincoln was shot.

Yes: he had lived to shame me from
   my sneer,
   To lame my pencil, and confute my
      pen;
To make me own this hind of Princes
   peer,
   This rail-splitter a true-born king of
      men.
   *Abraham Lincoln Foully
   Assassinated. Stanza 5*

How his quaint wit made home-truth
   seem more true.
   Ibid. Stanza 6

He went about his work — such work
   as few
   Ever had laid on head and heart and
      hand —
As one who knows, where there's a task
   to do,
   Man's honest will must Heaven's
      good grace command.
   Ibid. Stanza 8

The Old World and the New, from sea
   to sea,
   Utter one voice of sympathy and
      shame.
Sore heart, so stopped when it at last
   beat high!
   Sad life, cut short, just as its triumph
      came!
   Ibid. Stanza 17

HENRY DAVID THOREAU
[1817–1862]

My life is like a stroll upon the beach,
   As near the ocean's edge as I can go.
   The Fisher's Boy.[1] *Stanza 1*

I have but few companions on the
   shore, —
   They scorn the strand who sail upon
      the sea;
Yet oft I think the ocean they've sailed
   o'er
   Is deeper down upon the strand to
      me.
   Ibid. Stanza 3

Whate'er we leave to God, God does
   And blesses us.
   Inspiration. Proem

[1] Entitled *The Fisher's Son* in Thoreau's
Journal [1840] and *Upon the Beach* in some
anthologies.

I hear beyond the range of sound,
I see beyond the range of sight,
New earths and skies and seas around,
And in my day the sun doth pale his
light.
Inspiration. Stanza 7
She with one breath attunes the
spheres,
And also my poor human heart.
Ibid. Stanza 15
I am a parcel of vain strivings tied
By a chance bond together.
Sic Vita.[1] *Stanza 1*
Great God, I ask thee for no meaner
pelf
Than that I may not disappoint myself,
That in my action I may soar as high
As I can now discern with this clear
eye.
A Prayer.[2] *Stanza 1*
Any man more right than his neigh-
bors, constitutes a majority of one.
The Duty of Civil Disobedience
I have travelled a good deal in Con-
cord.
Walden. I, Economy
What a man thinks of himself, that
it is which determines, or rather indi-
cates, his fate.
Ibid.
As if you could kill time without
injuring eternity.
Ibid.
Most of the luxuries, and many of
the so-called comforts, of life are not
only not indispensable, but positive hin-
drances to the elevation of mankind.
Ibid.
It is true, I never assisted the sun ma-
terially in his rising; but, doubt not, it
was of the last importance only to be
present at it.
Ibid.
For many years I was self-appointed
inspector of snow-storms and rain-
storms, and did my duty faithfully.
Ibid.
Beware of all enterprises that require
new clothes.
Ibid.

[1] Published [July, 1841] in *The Dial*,
edited by Margaret Fuller.
[2] *The Dial* [July, 1842].

The swiftest traveller is he that goes
afoot.
Walden. I, Economy
The man who goes alone can start to-
day; but he who travels with another
must wait till that other is ready.
Ibid.
There is no odor so bad as that which
arises from goodness tainted.
Ibid. Philanthropy
There are a thousand hacking at the
branches of evil to one who is striking
at the root.
Ibid.
Philanthropy is almost the only vir-
tue which is sufficiently appreciated by
mankind.
Ibid.
To him whose elastic and vigorous
thought keeps pace with the sun, the
day is a perpetual morning.
Ibid. II, What I Lived For
To be awake is to be alive.
Ibid.
I went to the woods because I wished
to live deliberately, to front only the
essential facts of life, and see if I could
not learn what it had to teach, and not,
when I came to die, discover that I had
not lived.
Ibid.
Our life is frittered away by detail.
. . . Simplify, simplify.
Ibid.
Time is but the stream I go a-fishing
in.
Ibid.
Books must be read as deliberately
and reservedly as they were written.
Ibid. III, Reading
The works of the great poets have
never yet been read by mankind, for
only great poets can read them.
Ibid.
I love a broad margin to my life.
Ibid. IV, Sounds
Our horizon is never quite at our
elbows.
Ibid. V, Solitude
I never found the companion that
was so companionable as solitude.
Ibid.

Society is commonly too cheap. We meet at very short intervals, not having had time to acquire any new value for each other.

Walden. V, Solitude

I had three chairs in my house: one for solitude, two for friendship, three for society.

Ibid. VI, Visitors

I was determined to know beans.

Ibid. VII, The Beanfield

If the day and the night are such that you greet them with joy, and life emits a fragrance like flowers and sweet-scented herbs, is more elastic, more starry, more immortal, — that is your success.

Ibid. XI, Higher Laws

There is never an instant's truce between virtue and vice. Goodness is the only investment that never fails.

Ibid.

Every man is the builder of a temple, called his body.

Ibid.

While men believe in the infinite, some ponds will be thought to be bottomless.

Ibid. XVI, The Pond in Winter

Through our own recovered innocence we discern the innocence of our neighbors.

Ibid. XVII, Spring

If one advances confidently in the direction of his dreams, and endeavors to live the life which he has imagined, he will meet with a success unexpected in common hours.

Ibid. XVIII, Conclusion

If a man does not keep pace with his companions,[1] perhaps it is because he hears a different drummer. Let him step to the music which he hears, however measured or far away.

Ibid.

Love your life, poor as it is. You may perhaps have some pleasant, thrilling, glorious hours, even in a poorhouse. The setting sun is reflected from the windows of the almshouse as brightly as from the rich man's abode.

Walden. XVIII, Conclusion

It is life near the bone where it is sweetest.

Ibid.

Rather than love, than money, than fame, give me truth.

Ibid.

Only that day dawns to which we are awake. There is more day to dawn. The sun is but a morning star.

Ibid.

I saw a delicate flower had grown up two feet high between the horses' feet and the wheel track. An inch more to right or left had sealed its fate, or an inch higher. Yet it lived to flourish, and never knew the danger it incurred. It did not borrow trouble, nor invite an evil fate by apprehending it.

Journal. September, 1850

The blue-bird carries the sky on his back.

Ibid. April 3, 1852

The perception of beauty is a moral test.

Ibid. June 21, 1852

The youth gets together his materials to build a bridge to the moon, or, perchance, a palace or temple on the earth, and, at length, the middle-aged man concludes to build a woodshed with them.[1]

Ibid. July 14, 1852

Fire is the most tolerable third party.

Ibid. January 2, 1853

Some circumstantial evidence is very strong, as when you find a trout in the milk.

Ibid. November 11, 1854

That man is the richest whose pleasures are the cheapest.

Ibid. March 11, 1856

---

[1] This reminds the editor of the old cockney story of the infatuated mother who saw her hobbledehoy marching in a company of recruits. "All out of step but Bill!" she exclaimed proudly.

[1] At noon he bounded out for food, and nothing less than roast lion would content him. But by suppertime milk toast would do. — Quoted without provenance in *We Accept With Pleasure*, by BERNARD DE VOTO (1897–   ).

When the playful breeze drops in the pool, it springs to right and left, quick as a kitten playing with dead leaves.[1]
Journal. April 9, 1859

CECIL FRANCES ALEXANDER
[1818–1895]

By Nebo's lonely mountain,
  On this side Jordan's wave,
In a vale in the land of Moab,
  There lies a lonely grave.[2]
      The Burial of Moses. Stanza 1
Noiselessly as the spring-time
  Her crown of verdure weaves,
And all the trees on all the hills
  Open their thousand leaves.
          Ibid. Stanza 3
This was the truest warrior
  That ever buckled sword;
This the most gifted poet
  That ever breathed a word;
And never earth's philosopher
  Traced with his golden pen
On the deathless page, truths half so sage
  As he wrote down for men.
          Ibid. Stanza 7
The roseate hues of early dawn,
  The brightness of the day,
The crimson of the sunset sky,
  How fast they fade away!
      *The Roseate Hues of Early
          Dawn. Stanza 1*
There was no other good enough
  To pay the price of sin;
He only could unlock the gate
  Of heaven and let us in.
    *There Is a Green Hill Far Away.
          Stanza 4*

EMILY BRONTË
[1818–1848]

Sleep not, dream not; this bright day
Will not, cannot last for aye;

[1] See the kitten on the wall,
  Sporting with the leaves that fall.
    WORDSWORTH: *The Kitten and the
              Falling Leaves*
[2] See Bryant, page 372.

Bliss like thine is bought by years
Dark with torment and with tears.
          Sleep Not. Stanza 1
The Bluebell is the sweetest flower
  That waves in summer air:
Its blossoms have the mightiest power
  To soothe my spirit's care.
          The Bluebell. Stanza 1
Love is like the wild rose-briar;
  Friendship like the holly-tree.
The holly is dark when the rose-briar
      blooms,
  But which will bloom most con-
      stantly?
      Love and Friendship. Stanza 1
I'll walk where my own nature would
      be leading —
It vexes me to choose another guide —
Where the grey flocks in ferny glens are
      feeding,
Where the wild wind blows on the
      mountain-side.
          Often Rebuked. Stanza 4
Cold in the earth — and fifteen wild
      Decembers
From those brown hills have melted
      into spring:
Faithful, indeed, is the spirit that re-
      members
After such years of change and suffer-
      ing!
              Remembrance
No coward soul is mine,
  No trembler in the world's storm-
      troubled sphere:
I see Heaven's glories shine,
  And faith shines equal, arming me
      from fear.
          Last Lines. Stanza 1
There is not room for Death.
          Ibid. Stanza 7

BENJAMIN FRANKLIN BUTLER
[1818–1893]

There is no need for me to answer the gentleman from New York. Every negro minstrel just now is singing the answer, and the hand-organs are playing the tune, "Shoo, Fly, Don't Bodder Me." [1]

Debate. House of Representatives

WILLIAM ELLERY CHANNING
[1818–1901]

Habitant of castle gray,
Creeping thing in sober way,
Visible sage mechanician,
Skilfulest arithmetician.

The Spider. [2]

It is not far beyond the village church,
After we pass the wood that skirts the road,
A lake, — the blue-eyed Walden, that doth smile
Most tenderly upon its neighbor pines.

Walden Lake, Concord

Beneath the endless surges of the deep,
Whose green content o'erlaps them evermore,
A host of mariners perpetual sleep,
Too hushed to heed the wild commotion's roar.

Death. Stanza 1

I laugh, for hope hath happy place with me, —
If my bark sinks, 'tis to another sea.

A Poet's Hope

I sing New England, as she lights her fire

In every Prairie's midst; and where the bright
Enchanting stars shine pure through Southern night,
She still is there, the guardian on the tower,
To open for the world a purer hour.

New England

Most joyful let the Poet be;
It is through him that all men see.

The Poet of the Old and New Times

My highway is unfeatured air,
  My consorts are the sleepless stars,
And men my giant arms upbear —
  My arms unstained and free from scars.

The Earth. Stanza 1

A wail in the wind is all I hear;
  A voice of woe for a lover's loss.

Tears in Spring. Lament for Thoreau, Stanza 3

The hills are reared, the seas are scooped in vain
If learning's altar vanish from the plain.

Inscription for the Alcott House, Concord [1]

ARTHUR CLEVELAND COXE
[1818–1896]

I never can see the old churchyard
  But I breathe to God a prayer,
That, sleep as I may in this fevered life,
  I may rest when I slumber there.

St. George's Churchyard, Hempstead, Long Island

WILLIAM MAXWELL EVARTS
[1818–1901]

The pious ones of Plymouth, who, reaching the Rock, first fell upon their

---

[1] In his *Autobiography of Seventy Years,* George Frisbie Hoar [1826–1904] tells of a five-minute debate in the House of Representatives. Samuel Sullivan ("Sunset") Cox [1824–1889], Democratic member from New York, had attacked Butler savagely. In his reply, Butler took no notice of Cox until the close of his argument.

The song, *Shoo Fly, Don't Bodder Me,* was written by Thomas Brigham Bishop, set to music by Frank Campbell, popularized by Billy Reeves, in the late 1860s.

It would get to running through his head, like the "shoo-fly" song which Butler sings in the House.
Charles Dudley Warner: *My Summer in a Garden, Eighth Week*

[2] His first poem, published in *The New England Magazine* [Oct., 1835].

[1] This couplet remains over the mantelpiece in Alcott House, Concord, Massachusetts, just as it was painted by May Alcott. Ellery Channing, the poet, who supplied the motto, was a nephew of the clergyman of the same name.

own knees and then upon the aborigines.[1]

Quoted by HENRY WATTERSON *in The Louisville Courier-Journal* [*July 4, 1913*]

JOHN JAMES ROBERT MANNERS, DUKE OF RUTLAND
[1818–1906]

No: by the names inscribed in History's page,
Names that are England's noblest heritage,
Names that shall live for yet unnumbered years
Shrined in our hearts with Cressy and Poictiers;
Let wealth and commerce, laws and learning die,
But leave us still our old nobility.

England's Trust. Part III, Line 227

JOHN MASON NEALE
[1818–1866]

There must in every cause be some first Martyr
To suffer and to fall;
There must be also those content to barter
Their victory for their all.

Abraham Lincoln. Stanza 1

Jerusalem the golden, with milk and honey blest,
Beneath thy contemplation sink heart and voice oppressed.

Hymn (paraphrased from the Latin of Bernard de Cluny)

Brief life is here our portion.

Hymn

HENRY PETERSON
[1818–1891]

Sing, bird, on green Missouri's plain,
The saddest song of sorrow.

Lyon.[2] Stanza 1

[1] This pun has been attributed to Oliver Wendell Holmes, Bill Nye, and George Frisbie Hoar. See Guiterman, page 815.
[2] General Nathaniel Lyon [1818–1861], killed in battle at Wilson's Creek, Missouri, August 10, 1861.

HENRY WHEELER SHAW ("JOSH BILLINGS")
[1818–1885]

It is better to know nothing than to know what ain't so.[1]

Proverb [1874]

A sekret ceases tew be a sekret if it iz once confided — it iz like a dollar bill, once broken, it iz never a dollar agin.

Affurisms [2]

Love iz like the meazles; we kant have it bad but onst, and the later in life we have it the tuffer it goes with us.

Ibid.

Put an Englishman into the garden of Eden, and he would find fault with the whole blarsted consarn; — put a Yankee in, and he would see where he could alter it to advantage; — put an Irishman in, and he would want tew boss the thing; — put a Dutchman in, and he would proceed tew plant it.

Ibid.

Better make a weak man your enemy than your friend.

Ibid.

I never knu a man trubbled with melankolly, who had plenty to dew, and did it.

Ibid.

Poverty iz the step-mother ov genius.

Ibid.

Manifest destiny iz the science ov going tew bust, or enny other place before yu git thare.

Manifest Destiny

Thare iz such a thing az manifest destiny, but when it occurs it iz like the number ov rings on the rakoon's tale, ov no great consequense only for ornament.

Ibid.

The wheel that squeaks the loudest
Is the one that gets the grease.

The Kicker

[1] Better know nothing than half-know many things. — NIETZSCHE: *Thus Spake Zarathustra, Part IV, 64*
[2] From *Josh Billings: His Sayings.*

ARTHUR HUGH CLOUGH
[1819–1861]

It fortifies my soul to know
That, though I perish, Truth is so:
That, howsoe'er I stray and range,
Whate'er I do, Thou dost not change.
I steadier step when I recall
That, if I slip, Thou dost not fall.
"With Whom Is no Variableness" [1]

Because we can't do all we would,
Does it follow, to do nothing's good?
Dipsychus. Part I, Sc. 4

And almost every one when age,
  Disease, or sorrows strike him,
Inclines to think there is a God,
  Or something very like Him.
Ibid. Sc. 5

This world is very odd we see,
  We do not comprehend it;
But in one fact we all agree,
  God won't, and we can't, mend it.
Ibid. Part II, Sc. 2

How pleasant it is to have money!
Ibid.

  In light things
Prove thou the arms thou long'st to
  glorify,
Nor fear to work up from the lowest
  ranks
Whence come great Nature's Captains.
  And high deeds
Haunt not the fringy edges of the fight
But the pell-mell of men.
Ibid. Sc. 4

Grace is given of God, but knowledge
  is bought in the market.
*The Bothie of Tober-na-Vuolich.
Part IV*

A world where nothing is had for nothing.
Ibid. Part VIII

There is a great Field-Marshal, my
  friend, who arrays our battalions;
Let us to Providence trust, and abide
  and work in our stations.
Ibid. Part IX

Where lies the land to which the ship
  would go?

Far, far ahead, is all her seamen
  know.
Songs of Absence

That out of sight is out of mind [1]
Is true of most we leave behind;
It is not sure, nor can be true,
My own and only love, of you.
Ibid.

How in God's name did Columbus get
  over
  Is a pure wonder to me.
Columbus. Stanza 1

What if wise men had, as far back as
  Ptolemy,
  Judged that the earth, like an orange
  was round,
None of them ever said, Come along,
  follow me,
  Sail to the West, and the East will be
  found.
Ibid. Stanza 3

Say not, the struggle naught availeth,
  The labor and the wounds are vain,
The enemy faints not, nor faileth,
  And as things have been they remain.
*Say Not the Struggle Naught
Availeth. Stanza 1*

For while the tired waves, vainly break-
  ing,
  Seem here no painful inch to gain,
Far back, through creeks and inlets
  making,
  Comes silent, flooding in, the main.
Ibid. Stanza 3

And not by eastern windows only,
  When daylight comes, comes in the
  light;
In front, the sun climbs slow, how
  slowly,
  But westward, look, the land is
  bright.
Ibid. Stanza 4

As ships, becalmed at eve, that lay
  With canvas drooping, side by side,
Two towers of sail, at dawn of day
  Are scarce long leagues apart de-
  scried.
Qua Cursum Ventus. Stanza 1

[1] *James, I, 17.*

[1] See Thomas à Kempis, page 9.

MARIAN EVANS CROSS ("GEORGE ELIOT")
[1819–1880]

'Tis God gives skill,
But not without men's hands: He could
    not make
Antonio Stradivari's violins
Without Antonio.
Stradivarius

O may I join the choir invisible
Of those immortal dead who live again
In minds made better by their presence.
O May I Join the Choir Invisible

May I reach
That purest heaven, be to other souls
The cup of strength in some great
    agony.
Ibid.

Boots and shoes are the greatest
trouble of my life. Everything else one
can turn and turn about, and make old
look like new; but there's no coaxing
boots and shoes to look better than
they are.
Amos Barton. Chap. 2

It's no trifle at her time of life to
part with a doctor who knows her constitution.
Janet's Repentance. Chap. 3

Any coward can fight a battle when
he's sure of winning; but give me the
man who has pluck to fight when he's
sure of losing. That's my way, sir; and
there are many victories worse than a
defeat.
Ibid. Chap. 6

Opposition may become sweet to a
man when he has christened it persecution.
Ibid. Chap. 8

It's but little good you'll do water-
ing last year's crops.
Adam Bede. Chap. 18

He was like a cock who thought the
sun had risen to hear him crow.
Ibid. Chap. 33

We all have a chance of meeting
with some pity, some tenderness, some
charity, when we are dead; it is the
living only who cannot be forgiven.
The Lifted Veil

I've never any pity for conceited
people, because I think they carry their
comfort about with them.[1]
The Mill on the Floss.
Book V, Chap. 4

Below their names it was written:
"In their death they were not di-
vided." [2]
Ibid. Last line of book

Blessed is the man who, having nothing to say, abstains from giving in
words evidence of the fact.
Impressions of Theophrastus Such

Life is too precious to be spent in
this weaving and unweaving of false
impressions, and it is better to live
quietly under some degree of misrepresentation than to attempt to remove it
by the uncertain process of letter-
writing.
Life and Letters.[3] *Letter to*
Mrs. Peter Taylor [June 8, 1856]

The years seem to rush by now, and
I think of death as a fast approaching
end of a journey — [4] double and treble
reason for loving as well as working
while it is day.
Ibid. Letter to Miss Sara Hen-
nell [November 22, 1861]

It seems to me much better to read
a man's own writing than to read what
others say about him, especially when
the man is first-rate and the "others"
are third-rate.
Ibid. To Miss Hennell
[October 28, 1865]

I have the conviction that excessive
literary production is a social offence.
Ibid. Letter to Alexander Main
[September 11, 1871]

To hear of a friend's illness after he

---

[1] There is not enough of love and goodness in the world to throw any of it away
on conceited people.
NIETZSCHE: *Human, All Too Human, 129*
[2] *2 Samuel I, 23.*
[3] Edited [1884] by J. W. CROSS.
[4] I think of death as some delightful journey
    That I shall take when all my tasks are
    done.
ELLA WHEELER WILCOX: *The Journey,*
St. 1

has got well through it, is the least painful way of learning the bad news.

Life and Letters. Letter to John Blackwood [February 21, 1872]

I like not only to be loved, but also to be told that I am loved. I am not sure that you are of the same kind. But the realm of silence is large enough beyond the grave. This is the world of light and speech, and I shall take leave to tell you that you are very dear.

Ibid. Letter to Mrs. Burne-Jones [May 11, 1875]

All biography diminishes in interest when the subject has won celebrity — or some reputation that hardly comes up to a celebrity. But autobiography at least saves a man or woman that the world is curious about from the publication of a string of mistakes called "Memoirs."

Ibid. Letter to Miss Sara Hennell [November 22, 1876]

THOMAS DUNN ENGLISH
[1819–1902]

Don't you remember sweet Alice, Ben Bolt?
  Sweet Alice, whose hair was so brown;
Who wept with delight when you gave her a smile,
  And trembled with fear at your frown!

Ben Bolt [1]

Your eyes were filled with love, Kate Vane;
Ah, would that we were young again!

Kate Vane

Up with three cheers and a tiger!
  Let the flags wave as they come!
Give them the blare of the trumpet!
  Give them the roll of the drum!

The Charge by the Ford. Stanza 11

For one on the ocean of crime long tossed,
Who loves his mother, is not quite lost.

Smiting the Rock

Less good from genius we may find
  Than that from perseverance flowing;
So have good grist at hand to grind,
  And keep the mill a-going.

Keep the Mill a-Going. Stanza 7

Though little dangers they may fear,
When greater dangers men environ
Then women show a front of iron;
And, gentle in their manner, they
Do bold things in a quiet way.

Betty Zane. [1] *Stanza 1*

Not one has lineage prouder than
(Be he poor or rich) the man
Who boasts that in his spotless strain
Mingles the blood of Betty Zane.

Ibid. Stanza 10

JOSIAH GILBERT HOLLAND
[1819–1881]

Heaven is not reached at a single bound;
  But we build the ladder by which we rise
  From the lowly earth to the vaulted skies,
And we mount to its summit round by round. [2]

Gradatim. Stanza 1

Wings for the angels, but feet for men.

Ibid. Stanza 6

Only in dreams is a ladder thrown
  From the weary earth to the sapphire walls;
  But the dreams depart, and the vision falls,
And the sleeper wakes on his pillow of stone.

Ibid. Stanza 7

---

[1] First published in *The New York Mirror*, Sept. 2, 1843. It was set to music, an adaptation of an old German melody, by NELSON KNEASS, and sung in a play, *The Battle of Buena Vista*. In 1894, GEORGE DU MAURIER used the song in his novel, *Trilby*, and it became popular at once.

[1] Fort Henry (now Wheeling, West Virginia) was attacked by Simon Girty and a band of Wyandot Indians, September 27–28, 1777. Betty Zane ran from the blockhouse to the log hut on the hill, and returned with a cask of gunpowder wrapped in her apron. Zanesville, Ohio, is named for the Zane family.

[2] Step after step the ladder is ascended. — HERBERT: *Jacula Prudentum*

He could see naught but vanity in
  beauty,
    And naught but weakness in a fond
    caress,
And pitied men whose views of Christian duty
    Allowed indulgence in such foolish-
    ness.
                        Daniel Gray. Stanza 9

More human, more divine than we —
In truth, half human, half divine
Is woman when good stars agree
To temper with their beams benign
The hour of her nativity.
                        Kathrina

Who can tell what a baby thinks?
                        Cradle Song. Stanza 2

My dear dumb friend, low lying there,
  A willing vassal at my feet —
Glad partner of my home and fare,
  My shadow in the street.
                To My Dog, Blanco. Stanza 1

God give us men! A time like this de-
  mands
  Strong minds, great hearts, true
    faith, and ready hands;
Men whom the lust of office does not
  kill;
  Men whom the spoils of office can-
    not buy;
Men who possess opinions and a will;
  Men who have honor; men who will
    not lie;
Men who can stand before a demagogue
  And damn his treacherous flatteries
    without winking;
Tall men, sun-crowned, who live above
  the fog
  In public duty and in private think-
    ing.
                        The Day's Demand

Hearts, like apples, are hard and sour,
Till crushed by Pain's resistless power.
                Bitter-Sweet. First Episode

Nay, Whittier, thou art not old;
Thy register a lie hath told,
For lives devote to love and truth
Do only multiply their youth.
                Ten Times Seven.[1] *Stanza 3*

[1] Written for Whittier's seventieth birthday, December 17, 1877.

Where shall the baby's dimple be,
Cheek, chin, knuckle or knee?
                *Where Shall the Baby's
                        Dimple Be?*

JULIA WARD HOWE
[1819–1910]

Mine eyes have seen the glory of the
  coming of the Lord;
He is trampling out the vintage where
  the grapes of wrath are stored;
He hath loosed the fateful lightning of
  His terrible, swift sword;
  His truth is marching on.
        *Battle Hymn of the Republic.
                        Stanza 1*

In the beauty of the lilies Christ was
  born across the sea,
With a glory in His bosom that transfigures you and me;
As He died to make men holy, let us die
  to make men free.
                        Ibid. Stanza 5

Weave no more silks, ye Lyons looms,
  To deck our girls for gay delights!
The crimson flower of battle blooms,
  And solemn marches fill the nights.
                        Our Orders

I gave my son a palace
  And a kingdom to control:
The palace of his body,
  The kingdom of his soul.
                        Palace and Kingdom

Don't trouble more to celebrate this
  natal day of mine,
But keep the grasp of fellowship which
  warms us more than wine.
Let us thank the lavish hand that gives
  world beauty to our eyes,
And bless the days that saw us young,
  and years that make us wise.
                        Growing Old

I have made a voyage upon a golden
  river,
  'Neath clouds of opal and of ame-
    thyst;
Along its banks bright shapes were
  moving ever,
  And threatening shadows melted
    into mist.
        Reminiscences [1899]. At the end

CHARLES KINGSLEY
[1819–1875]

O Mary, go and call the cattle home,
And call the cattle home,
And call the cattle home,
Across the sands o' Dee!
The Sands of Dee. Stanza 1

The cruel crawling foam.
Ibid. Stanza 4

Men must work, and women must weep,
And there's little to earn and many to keep,
Though the harbor bar be moaning.
The Three Fishers. Stanza 1

Be good, sweet maid, and let who can be clever;
Do lovely things, not dream them, all day long;
And so make Life, Death, and that vast Forever
One grand sweet song.
A Farewell. Stanza 3

O haud your hands frae inkhorns, though a' the Muses woo;
For critics lie, like saumon fry, to mak' their meals o' you.
The Oubit. Stanza 3

Oh green is the colour of faith and truth,
And rose the colour of love and youth,
And brown of the fruitful clay.
Dartside, 1849

Oh! that we two were Maying.
The Saint's Tragedy. Act II, Sc. 9

Oh! that we two lay sleeping
In our nest in the churchyard sod,
With our limbs at rest on the quiet earth's breast,
And our souls at home with God.
Ibid.

The world goes up and the world goes down,
And the sunshine follows the rain;
And yesterday's sneer and yesterday's frown
Can never come over again.
Dolcino to Margaret

Oh England is a pleasant place for them that's rich and high,

But England is a cruel place for such poor folks as I.
The Last Buccanier. Stanza 1

In the light of fuller day,
Of purer science, holier laws.[1]
On the Death of a Certain Journal.[2] Stanza 5

Young blood must have its course, lad,
And every dog his day.[3]
Water Babies. Song II, Stanza 1

When all the world is old, lad,
And all the trees are brown;
And all the sport is stale, lad,
And all the wheels run down.
Ibid. Stanza 2

God grant you find one face there
You loved when all was young!
Ibid.

I once had a sweet little doll, dears,
The prettiest doll in the world;
Her cheeks were so red and so white, dears,
And her hair was so charmingly curled.
Ibid. Song IV, Stanza 1

So fleet the works of men, back to their earth again;
Ancient and holy things fade like a dream.
Old and New: A Parable. Stanza 1

Do the work that's nearest,
Though it's dull at whiles,
Helping, when you meet them,
Lame dogs over stiles;
See in every hedgerow
Marks of angels' feet,
Epics in each pebble
Underneath our feet.
The Invitation to Tom Hughes

We were crawling slowly along, looking out for Virgin Garda; the first of those numberless isles which Columbus, so goes the tale, discovered on St. Ursula's day, and named them after the saint and her eleven thousand mythical virgins. Unfortunately, English buccaneers have since given to most of them less poetic names. The

[1] See Tennyson, page 469.
[2] *The Christian Socialist.*
[3] Dog will have his day. — SHAKESPEARE: *Hamlet, Act V, Sc. 1, L. 314*

Dutchman's Cap, Broken Jerusalem, The Dead Man's Chest,[1] Rum Island, and so forth, mark a time and race more prosaic.

At Last [1870]. Chap. 1

A lone man's companion, a bachelor's friend, a hungry man's food, a sad man's cordial, a wakeful man's sleep, and a chilly man's fire . . . there's no herb like unto it under the canopy of heaven.

[Tobacco] Westward Ho, Chap. 7

Thank God every morning when you get up that you have something to do that day which must be done, whether you like it or not. Being forced to work, and forced to do your best, will breed in you temperance and self-control, diligence and strength of will, cheerfulness and content, and a hundred virtues which the idle never know.

Letter

To be discontented with the divine discontent, and to be ashamed with the noble shame, is the very germ of the first upgrowth of all virtue.

Health and Education. The Science of Health [1874]

"What is the secret of your life?" asked Mrs. Browning of Charles Kingsley. "Tell me, that I may make mine beautiful, too." He replied: "I had a friend."

Related by WILLIAM CHANNING GANNETT

JAMES RUSSELL LOWELL
[1819–1891]

She doeth little kindnesses
Which most leave undone, or despise.

My Love. Stanza 4

Be noble! and the nobleness that lies
In other men, sleeping, but never dead,
Will rise in majesty to meet thine own.

Sonnet IV

Great Truths are portions of the soul of man;

---

[1] Treasure Island came out of Kingsley's "At Last," where I got the Dead Man's Chest — and that was the seed. — R. L. STEVENSON in a letter to Sidney Colvin

Great souls are portions of Eternity.

Sonnet VI

To win the secrets of a weed's plain heart.

Sonnet XXV

Who speaks the truth stabs Falsehood to the heart.

L'Envoi

His words were simple words enough,
And yet he used them so,
That what in other mouths was rough
In his seemed musical and low.

The Shepherd of King Admetus. Stanza 5

All thoughts that mould the age begin
Deep down within the primitive soul.

An Incident in a Railroad Car. Stanza 13

It may be glorious to write
Thoughts that shall glad the two or three
High souls, like those far stars that come in sight
Once in a century.

Ibid. Stanza 19

No man is born into the world whose work
Is not born with him; there is always work,
And tools to work withal, for those who will;
And blessèd are the horny hands of toil.

A Glance Behind the Curtain

They are slaves who fear to speak
For the fallen and the weak. . . .
They are slaves who dare not be
In the right with two or three.

Stanzas on Freedom. IV

The nurse of full-grown souls is solitude.

Columbus

And I believed the poets; it is they
Who utter wisdom from the central deep,
And, listening to the inner flow of things,
Speak to the age out of eternity.

Ibid.

Once to every man and nation comes the moment to decide,
In the strife of Truth with Falsehood, for the good or evil side.

The Present Crisis. Stanza 5

Truth forever on the scaffold, Wrong
forever on the throne.[1]
   The Present Crisis. Stanza 8

Then to side with Truth is noble when
we share her wretched crust,
Ere her cause bring fame and profit,
and 'tis prosperous to be just;
Then it is the brave man chooses, while
the coward stands aside,
Doubting in his abject spirit, till his
Lord is crucified.
   Ibid. Stanza 11

New occasions teach new duties; Time
makes ancient good uncouth;
They must upward still, and onward,
who would keep abreast of Truth.
   Ibid. Stanza 18

The birch, most shy and ladylike of
trees.
   An Indian-Summer Reverie.
    Stanza 8

Dear common flower, that grow'st beside the way,
Fringing the dusty road with harmless
gold.
   To the Dandelion. Stanza 1

They came three thousand miles, and
died,
To keep the Past upon its throne;
Unheard, beyond the ocean tide,
Their English mother made her moan.[2]
   Graves of Two English Soldiers
   on Concord Battle-ground.
    Stanza 3

Slowly the Bible of the race is writ,
And not on paper leaves nor leaves of
stone;
Each age, each kindred, adds a verse
to it,
Texts of despair or hope, of joy or
moan.
   Bibliolatres. Stanza 6

Thou art not idle: in thy higher sphere
Thy spirit bends itself to loving
tasks,

And strength to perfect what it
dreamed of here
Is all the crown and glory that it
asks.
   Elegy on the Death of
   Dr. Channing. Stanza 12

Not only around our infancy
Doth heaven with all its splendors lie;
Daily, with souls that cringe and plot,
We Sinais climb and know it not.
   The Vision of Sir Launfal.
   Part I, Prelude, Stanza 2

'Tis heaven alone that is given away;
'Tis only God may be had for the ask-
ing.
   Ibid. Stanza 4

And what is so rare as a day in June?
Then, if ever, come perfect days;
Then Heaven tries the earth if it be in
tune,
And over it softly her warm ear lays.
   Ibid. Stanza 5

He gives only the worthless gold
Who gives from a sense of duty.
   Ibid. Part I, Stanza 6

The gift without the giver is bare; [1]
Who gives himself with his alms feeds
three, —
Himself, his hungering neighbor, and
me.
   Ibid. Part II, Stanza 8

Got the ill name of augurs, because
they were bores.
   A Fable for Critics

A weed is no more than a flower in disguise.[2]
   Ibid.

For reading new books is like eating
new bread,
One can bear it at first, but by gradual
steps he
Is brought to death's door of a mental
dyspepsy.
   Ibid.

---

[1] Worth on foot, and rascals in the coach.
  DRYDEN: *Art of Poetry, L. 376*
 Wrong rules the land, and waiting Jus-
tice sleeps.
  J. G. HOLLAND: *The Day's Demand*
[2] Inscribed on the memorial to the two
British soldiers, Concord, Massachusetts.

[1] The only gift is a portion of thyself. —
EMERSON: *Gifts*
 See Walt Whitman, page 535.
[2] And what is a weed? A plant whose vir-
tues have not yet been discovered. — EMER-
SON: *Fortune of the Republic*
 A weed is but an unloved flower!
  ELLA WHEELER WILCOX: *The Weed, St. 1*

A reading-machine, always wound up
    and going,
He mastered whatever was not worth
    - the knowing.
                A Fable for Critics

I've thought very often 'twould be a
    good thing
In all public collections of books, if a
    wing
Were set off by itself, like the seas from
    the dry lands,
Marked *Literature suited to desolate
    islands.*
                        Ibid.

There comes Emerson first, whose rich
    words, every one,
Are like gold nails in temples to hang
    trophies on;
Whose prose is grand verse, while his
    verse, the Lord knows,
Is some of it pr — No, 'tis not even
    prose.[1]
                        Ibid.

And I honor the man who is willing to
    sink
Half his present repute for the freedom
    to think,
And, when he has thought, be his cause
    strong or weak,
Will risk t' other half for the freedom
    to speak.
                        Ibid.

There comes Poe, with his raven, like
    Barnaby Rudge,
Three fifths of him genius and two
    fifths sheer fudge.
                        Ibid.

Nature fits all her children with some-
    thing to do,
He who would write and can't write,
    can surely review.
                        Ibid.

Ez fer war, I call it murder, —
    There you hev it plain an' flat;
I don't want to go no furder
    Than my Testyment fer that. . . .
An' you've gut to git up airly
    Ef you want to take in God.
       *The Biglow Papers. Series I,
                No. 1, Stanza 5*

---

[1] Meredith is only a prose Browning — and
so was Browning. — Impromptu by OSCAR
WILDE.

Laborin' man an' laborin' woman
    Hev one glory an' one shame;
Ev'y thin' thet's done inhuman
    Injers all on 'em the same.
       *The Biglow Papers. Series I,
              No. 1, Stanza 10*

This goin' ware glory waits ye haint
    one agreeable feetur.[1]
            Ibid. No. 2, Stanza 6

Gineral C. is a dreffle smart man:
    He's ben on all sides thet give places
    or pelf;
But consistency still wuz a part of his
    plan, —
    He's ben true to *one* party, — an'
    thet is himself.
           Ibid. No. 3, Stanza 3

We kind o' thought Christ went agin
    war an' pillage.
                 Ibid. Stanza 5

    But John P.
      Robinson, he
Sez they didn't know everythin' down
    in Judee.
                 Ibid. Stanza 8

A marciful Providence fashioned us
    holler
O' purpose thet we might our princi-
    ples swaller.
           Ibid. No. 4, Stanza 2

I should like to shoot
The holl gang, by the gret horn spoon![2]
           Ibid. No. 5, Stanza 2

I du believe with all my soul
    In the gret Press's freedom,[3]
To pint the people to the goal
    An' in the traces lead 'em.
           Ibid. No. 6, Stanza 7

I *don't* believe in princerple,
    But oh I *du* in interest.
                 Ibid. Stanza 9

It ain't my princerples nor men
    My preudunt course is steadied, —
I scent which pays the best, an' then
    Go into it baldheaded.
               Ibid. Stanza 10

---

[1] Go where glory waits thee. — THOMAS
MOORE: Poem of same title
[2] He vow'd by the great horn spoon.
    French Claim, St. 5 (an anonymous
    song of the Revolutionary War pe-
    riod)
[3] See Herbert Clark Hoover, page 830.

Of my merit
On thet pint you yourself may jedge;
All is, I never drink no sperit,
Nor I haint never signed no pledge.
The Biglow Papers. Series I,
No. 7, Stanza 9

Ez to my princerples, I glory
In hevin' nothin' o' the sort.
Ibid. Stanza 10

God makes sech nights, all white and
still,
Fur'z you can look or listen.
Ibid. Series II, The Courtin',
Stanza 1

His heart kep' goin' pity-pat,
But hern went pity-Zekle.
Ibid. Stanza 15

To say why gals acts so or so,
Or don't, 'ould be presumin';
Mebby to mean *yes* an' say *no*
Comes nateral to women.[1]
Ibid. Stanza 18

All kin' o' smily round the lips,
An' teary round the lashes.
Ibid. Stanza 21

My gran'ther's rule was safer 'n 'tis to
crow:
Don't never prophesy — onless ye
know.
Ibid. No. 2

It's 'most enough to make a deacon
swear.
Ibid.

The one thet fust gits mad's most ol-
lers wrong.
Ibid.

Folks never understand the folks they
hate.
Ibid.

Ef you want peace, the thing you've
gut tu du
Is jes' to show you're up to fightin', tu.
Ibid.

Bad work follers ye ez long's ye live.
Ibid.

Don't give up afore the ship goes down.[2]
Ibid.

Our papers don't purtend to print on'y
wut Guv'ment choose,
An' thet insures us all to git the very
best o' noose.
The Biglow Papers. Series II,
No. 3

The thing's a gone coon.[1]
Ibid. No. 4

Facts are contrary 'z mules.[2]
Ibid.

No, never say nothin' without you're
compelled tu,
An' then don't say nothin' thet you can
be held tu.
Ibid. No. 5

Our lives in sleep are some like streams
that glide
'Twixt flesh an' sperrit boundin' on
each side,
Where both shores' shadders kind o'
mix an' mingle
In sunthin' thet ain't jes' like either
single.
Ibid. No. 6, Sunthin' in the
Pastoral Line

Wut's words to them whose faith an'
truth
On War's red techstone rang true
metal,
Who ventered life an' love an' youth
For the gret prize o' death in battle?
Ibid. No. 10, Stanza 17

What public, were they new to-day,
would ever stop to read
The Iliad, the Shanàmeh, or the Nibe-
lungenlied?
Fragments of an Unfinished Poem

Each year to ancient friendships adds
a ring,
As to an oak.
Under the Willows

I thought of a mound in sweet Auburn
Where a little headstone stood;
How the flakes were folding it gently,
As did robins the babes in the wood.[3]
The First Snowfall. Stanza 5

---

[1] See Mrs. Browning, page 428.
[2] Tell the men to fire faster and not to
give up the ship; fight her till she sinks. —
COMMANDER JAMES LAWRENCE, U.S.N. [1781–
1813] on board the *Chesapeake,* June 1, 1813.

[1] See David Crockett, page 349.
[2] See Smollett, page 248.
Facts are stubborn things. — LE SAGE:
Gil Blas, X, 1
[3] See Percy, page 258.

The shell disdained a soul had gained,
The lyre had been discovered.
The Finding of the Lyre.
Stanza 4

Though old the thought and oft ex-
prest,
'Tis his at last who says it best.[1]
For an Autograph. Stanza 1

Not failure, but low aim, is crime.
Ibid. Stanza 5

When I was a beggarly boy,
  And lived in a cellar damp,
I had not a friend nor a toy,
  But I had Aladdin's lamp.
Aladdin. Stanza 1

Granting our wish one of Fate's sad-
dest jokes is![2]
*Two Scenes from the Life of
Blondel.[3] Sc. II, Stanza 2*

For somehow the poor old Earth blunders along,
  Each son of hers adding his mite of
  unfitness,
And, choosing the sure way of coming
out wrong,
  Gets to port as the next generation
  will witness.
Ibid. Stanza 4

What men call treasure and the Gods
call dross.
*Ode Recited at the Harvard
Commemoration, 1865. IV*

Here was a type of the true elder race,
And one of Plutarch's men talked with
us face to face.
Ibid. VI

Safe in the hallowed quiets of the past.
The Cathedral.[4] Stanza 9

---

[1] See Emerson, page 415.
[2] Beware, my lord! Beware lest stern
Heaven hate you enough to hear your
prayers! — ANATOLE FRANCE: *The Crime of
Sylvestre Bonnard, Part II, Chap. 4*
See Oscar Wilde, page 724.
  The fates are not quite obdurate;
    They have a grim, sardonic way
  Of granting men who supplicate
    The things they wanted — yesterday.
      ROSELLE MERCIER MONTGOMERY:
                    The Fates
[3] See Ingelow, page 541.
[4] Chartres.

The one thing finished in this hasty
world.
The Cathedral. Stanza 9

The unmotived herd that only sleep and
feed.[1]
*Under the Old Elm. Part VII,
Stanza 3*

These pearls of thought in Persian gulfs
were bred,
Each softly lucent as a rounded moon;
The diver Omar plucked them from
their bed,
Fitzgerald strung them on an English
thread.
*In a Copy of Omar Khayyàm.
Stanza 1*

The wisest man could ask no more of
Fate
Than to be simple, modest, manly, true,
Safe from the Many, honored by the
Few;
To count as naught in World, or
Church, or State;
But inwardly in secret to be great.
Sonnet, Jeffries Wyman

But life is sweet, though all that makes
it sweet
Lessen like sound of friends' departing
feet;
And Death is beautiful as feet of friend
Coming with welcome at our journey's
end.
*Epistle to George William Curtis,
Postscript.*

For me Fate gave, whate'er she else
denied,
A nature sloping to the southern side;
I thank her for it, though when clouds
arise
Such Natures double-darken gloomy
skies.
Ibid.

Like him who, in the desert's awful
frame,
Notches his cockney initials on the
Sphinx.
*Sonnet on Being Asked for an
Autograph in Venice*

---

[1] What is a man,
  If his chief good and market of his time
  Be but to sleep and feed? a beast, no
  more.
    SHAKESPEARE: *Hamlet, Act IV, Sc. 4, l. 33*

The Maple puts her corals on in May.
The Maple

As brief
As a dragon-fly's repose.
Scherzo. Stanza 3

In life's small things be resolute and great
To keep thy muscle trained: know'st thou when Fate
Thy measure takes, or when she'll say to thee,
"I find thee worthy; do this deed for me"?
Sayings. I

In vain we call old notions fudge,
And bend our conscience to our dealing;
The Ten Commandments will not budge,
And stealing will continue stealing.
Motto of the American Copyright League [November 20, 1885]

As life runs on, the road grows strange
With faces new, and near the end
The milestones into headstones change,
'Neath every one a friend.
Sixty-Eighth Birthday

The story of any one man's real experience finds its startling parallel in that of every one of us.
Spenser

Solitude is as needful to the imagination as society is wholesome for the character.
Dryden

Men have their intellectual ancestry, and the likeness of some one of them is forever unexpectedly flashing out in the features of a descendant, it may be after a gap of several generations. In the parliament of the present every man represents a constituency of the past.
Keats

From the days of the first grandfather, everybody has remembered a golden age behind him!
Carlyle

Notoriety may be achieved in a narrow sphere, but fame demands for its evidence a more distant and prolonged reverberation.
A Great Public Character

A wise scepticism is the first attribute of a good critic.
Shakespeare Once More

Truly there is a tide in the affairs of men, but there is no gulf-stream setting forever in one direction.
New England Two Centuries Ago

There is no better ballast for keeping the mind steady on its keel, and saving it from all risk of crankiness, than business.
Ibid.

Puritanism, believing itself quick with the seed of religious liberty, laid, without knowing it, the egg of democracy.
Ibid.

It was in making education not only common to all, but in some sense compulsory on all, that the destiny of the free republics of America was practically settled.
Ibid.

Talent is that which is in a man's power; genius is that in whose power a man is.
Rousseau and the Sentimentalists

There is no work of genius which has not been the delight of mankind, no word of genius to which the human heart and soul have not sooner or later responded.
Ibid.

Every man feels instinctively that all the beautiful sentiments in the world weigh less than a single lovely action.
Ibid.

It is singular how impatient men are with over-praise of others, how patient with over-praise of themselves; and yet the one does them no injury, while the other may be their ruin.
Literary Remains of the Rev. Homer Wilbur

Things always seem fairer when we look back at them, and it is out of that inaccessible tower of the past that Longing leans and beckons.
A Few Bits of Roman Mosaic

There is nothing so desperately monotonous as the sea, and I no longer wonder at the cruelty of pirates.
Fireside Travels. At Sea

An umbrella is of no avail against a Scotch Mist.

On a Certain Condescension in Foreigners

It is by presence of mind in untried emergencies that the native metal of a man is tested.

Abraham Lincoln [1864]

The soil out of which such men as he are made is good to be born on, good to live on, good to die for and to be buried in.

Garfield

Mishaps are like knives, that either serve us or cut us, as we grasp them by the blade or the handle.

Cambridge Thirty Years Ago

No man, I suspect, ever lived long in the country without being bitten by these meteorological ambitions. He likes to be hotter and colder, to have been more deeply snowed up, to have more trees and larger blown down than his neighbors.

My Garden Acquaintance

As if old age were never kindly as well as frosty; as if it had no reverend graces of its own as good in their way as the noisy impertinence of childhood, the elbowing self-conceit of youth, or the pompous mediocrity of middle life!

A Good Word for Winter

What a sense of security in an old book which Time has criticised for us!

A Library of Old Authors

There is no good in arguing with the inevitable. The only argument available with an east wind is to put on your overcoat.

Democracy and Addresses

Let us be of good cheer, however, remembering that the misfortunes hardest to bear are those which never come.[1]

Ibid.

It is curious how tyrannical the habit of reading is, and what shifts we make to escape thinking.[2] There is no bore

[1] See Emerson, page 410, and Foss, page 733.
[2] See Sheridan, page 278.

we dread being left alone with so much as our own minds.

A Moosehead Journal

There are few brains that would not be better for living on their own fat a little while.

Ibid.

If I were asked what book is better than a cheap book, I should answer that there is one book better than a cheap book, — and that is a book honestly come by.

Before the U. S. Senate Committee on Patents [January 29, 1886]

HERMAN MELVILLE [1]
[1819–1891]

Thou belongest to that hopeless, sallow tribe which no wine of this world will ever warm; and for whom even Pale Sherry would be too rosy-strong; but with whom one sometimes loves to sit, and feel poor-devilish, too; and grow convivial upon tears; and say to them bluntly, with full eyes and empty glasses, and in not altogether unpleasant sadness — Give it up, Sub-Subs! For by how much the more pains ye

[1] May one cry of human distress interpolate here? The editors of BARTLETT confess the complete inadequacy of these few quotations from *Moby Dick*. For that great book there is no substitute; it cannot be represented in excerpts; to attempt that would require (as we have said before) a Moby Dictionary.

"He sank without a ripple of renown" was the fine valediction of RAYMOND M. WEAVER in his *Herman Melville, Mariner and Mystic* (1921). Melville died the same year that John Bartlett completed the Ninth Edition of this work. Neither then, nor in Dole's Tenth Edition (1914) was Melville's name mentioned. It was his centennial in 1919, coming in the general quickening and disgust of After-War, that brought him alive for a new generation. But he is too dense with intuition to be parcelled out in clippings.

"To read *Moby Dick* and absorb it is the crown of one's reading life." — VIOLA MEYNELL, introduction to World's Classics Edition.

We forward the problem to the editor of the Twelfth Edition, which should be due about 1960.

take to please the world, by so much the more shall ye for ever go thankless!

Moby Dick: Preface, the Sub-Sub-Librarian

The Nantucketer, out of sight of land, furls his sails and lays him to his rest, while under his very pillow rush herds of walruses and whales.

Ibid. Chap. 14

A whale ship was my Yale College and my Harvard.

Ibid. Chap. 24

Thou great democratic God! who didst not refuse to the swart convict, Bunyan, the pale poetic pearl; Thou who didst clothe with doubly hammered leaves of finest gold, the stumped and paupered arm of old Cervantes; Thou who didst pick up Andrew Jackson from the pebbles; who didst hurl him upon a warhorse; who didst thunder him higher than a throne!

Ibid. Chap. 26

The starred and stately nights seemed haughty dames in jewelled velvets, nursing at home in lonely pride the memory of their absent conquering Earls, the golden helmeted suns!

Ibid. Chap. 29

The choice hidden handful of the Divine Inert.

Ibid. Chap. 33

Give me a condor's quill! Give me Vesuvius' crater for an inkstand! . . . To produce a mighty book you must choose a mighty theme.

Ibid. Chap. 104

Where lies the final harbour, whence we unmoor no more?

Ibid. Chap. 114

Sailor or landsman, there is some sort of Cape Horn for all. Boys! beware of it; prepare for it in time. Greybeards! thank God it is passed.

White-Jacket. Chap. 26

All dies! and not alone
The aspiring trees and men and grass;
The poets' forms of beauty pass,
And noblest deeds they are undone,
Even truth itself decays, and lo,
From truth's sad ashes pain and falsehood grow.

The Lake

There is no faith, and no stoicism, and no philosophy, that a mortal man can possibly evoke, which will stand the final test in a real impassioned onset of Life and Passion upon him. Faith and philosophy are air, but events are brass.

Pierre

THOMAS WILLIAM PARSONS
[1819–1892]

Sorrow and the scarlet leaf,
  Sad thoughts and sunny weather:
Ah me, this glory and this grief
  Agree not well together!

A Song for September

We have forgot what we have been,
And what we are we little know;
We fancy new events begin,
But all has happened long ago.

Stanzas. I

To larger sight the rim of shadow is the line of light.

Inscription for a sundial at Milton, Massachusetts

JOHN RUSKIN
[1819–1900]

He is the greatest artist who has embodied, in the sum of his works, the greatest number of the greatest ideas.

Modern Painters. Vol. I, Part I, Chap. 2, Sect. 9

The greatest thing a human soul ever does in this world is to *see* something, and tell what it *saw* in a plain way. Hundreds of people can talk for one who can think, but thousands can think for one who can see. To see clearly is poetry, prophecy, and religion, all in one.

Ibid. Vol. III, Part IV, Chap. 16, Sect. 28

In order that people may be happy in their work, these three things are needed: They must be fit for it: They must not do too much of it: And they must have a sense of success in it.

Pre-Raphaelitism

No great intellectual thing was ever done by great effort; a great thing can only be done by a great man, and he does it *without* effort.

Pre-Raphaelitism

It is chiefly by private, not by public, effort that your city must be adorned.

Lectures on Architecture and Painting.[1] *1*

Blue colour is everlastingly appointed by the Deity to be a source of delight.

Ibid.

Whenever men have become skillful architects at all, there has been a tendency in them to build high.

Ibid.

Life being very short, and the quiet hours of it few, we ought to waste none of them in reading valueless books.[2]

Sesame and Lilies. Preface

The greatest efforts of the race have always been traceable to the love of praise, as its greatest catastrophes to the love of pleasure.

Ibid. Of Kings' Treasuries, Sect. 3

At the portières of that silent Faubourg St. Germain, there is but brief question, "Do you deserve to enter? Pass. Do you ask to be the companion of nobles? Make yourself noble, and you shall be. Do you long for the conversation of the wise? Learn to understand it, and you shall hear it. But on other terms? — no. If you will not rise to us, we cannot stoop to you."

Ibid. Sect. 12

There are masked words abroad, I say, which nobody understands, but which everybody uses, and most people will also fight for, live for, or even die for, fancying they mean this, or that, or the other, of things dear to them.

Ibid. Sect. 16

The very cheapness of literature is making even wise people forget that if a book is worth reading, it is worth buying. No book is worth anything which is not worth *much;* nor is it serviceable, until it has been read, and

[1] At Edinburgh, November, 1853.
[2] Life is too short for reading inferior books. — JAMES BRYCE [1838–1922]: *Address at Rutgers College,* Nov. 10, 1911

re-read, and loved, and loved again; and marked, so that you can refer to the passages you want in it.

Sesame and Lilies. Of King's Treasuries, Sect. 32

The power of the press in the hands of highly-educated men, in independent position, and of honest purpose, may indeed become all that it has been hitherto vainly vaunted to be.

Ibid. Sect. 37, Footnote

When men are rightly occupied, their amusement grows out of their work, as the colour-petals out of a fruitful flower.

Ibid. Sect. 39

He only is advancing in life, whose heart is getting softer, whose blood warmer, whose brain quicker, whose spirit is entering into Living peace. And the men who have this life in them are the true lords or kings of the earth — they, and they only.

Ibid. Sect. 42

This is the true nature of home — it is the place of Peace; the shelter, not only from all injury, but from all terror, doubt, and division.

Ibid. Of Queens' Gardens, Sect. 68

Borrowers are nearly always ill-spenders, and it is with lent money that all evil is mainly done, and all unjust war protracted.

The Crown of Wild Olive. Work, Sect. 34

Give a little love to a child, and you get a great deal back.

Ibid. Sect. 49

There's no music in a "rest," Katie, that I know of: but there's the making of music in it.[1] And people are always missing that part of the life-melody.

Ethics of the Dust. Lecture 4, The Crystal Orders

That treacherous phantom which men call Liberty.

Seven Lamps of Architecture. Chap. 7, The Lamp of Obedience, Sect. 1

[1] "There is no music in a rest,
But there is music's making";

Life without industry is guilt, industry without art is brutality.
> *Lectures on Art. III, The Relation of Art to Morals*

Engraving, then, is, in brief terms, the Art of Scratch.
> *Ariadne Florentina. Lecture I*

Wealth, therefore, is "the possession of the valuable by the valiant."
> *Unto This Last. Sect. 64*

There is no Wealth but Life.
> *Ibid. Sect. 77*

That country is the richest which nourishes the greatest number of noble and happy human beings; that man is richest who, having perfected the functions of his own life to the utmost, has also the widest helpful influence, both personal, and by means of his possessions, over the lives of others.
> *Ibid.*

Trust thou thy Love: if she be proud, is she not sweet?
Trust thou thy Love: if she be mute, is she not pure?
Lay thou thy soul full in her hands, low at her feet;
Fail, Sun and Breath! — yet, for thy peace, she shall endure.
> *Trust Thou Thy Love*

WILLIAM WETMORE STORY
[1819–1895]

I sing the hymn of the conquered, who fell in the Battle of Life,[1] —
The hymn of the wounded, the beaten, who died overwhelmed in the strife.
> *A Poet's Portfolio. Io Victis*

The hymn of the low and the humble, the weary, the broken in heart,
Who strove and who failed, acting bravely a silent and desperate part.
> *Ibid.*

For melody is best expressed
By pause and re-awaking.
MARY E. WISEWELL: *Rests*, St. 1 [1872]
[1] It seems to me, when it cannot be help'd, that defeat is great.
WALT WHITMAN: *Leaves of Grass, To a Foil'd European Revolutionaire*

Speak, History! Who are life's victors? Unroll thy long annals and say;
Are they those whom the world calls the victors, who won the success of a day?
The martyrs, or Nero? The Spartans who fell at Thermopylae's tryst,
Or the Persians and Xerxes? Pilate, or Christ?
> *A Poet's Portfolio. Io Victis*

Give me the old enthusiasms back,
Give me the ardent longings that I lack, —
The glorious dreams that fooled me in my youth,
The sweet mirage that lured me on its track, —
And take away the bitter, barren truth.
Ah, yes! Success, I fear, has come too late!
> *Girolamo, Detto il Fiorentino*

Mosquito critics with a poisonous sting.
> *Ibid.*

A picture is not wrought
By hands alone, good Padre, but by thought.
In the interior life it first must start,
And grow to form and colour in the soul;
There once conceived and rounded to a whole,
The rest is but the handicraft of art.
> *Padre Bandelli Proses*

Of every noble work the silent part is best,
Of all expression that which can not be expressed.
> *The Unexpressed*

What looks like swindling with a petty sum,
Is on a grand and speculative scale
Honest enough, so it be large enough.
> *Baron Fisco at Home*

Man is content to know that he is loved,
And tires the constant phrase "I love" to hear;
But woman doubts the instrument is broke
Unless she daily hear the sweet refrain.
> *Ginevra da Siena*

We live as much in all that we have
lost
As what we own.
> *Sonnet, After Long Days of*
> *Dull Perpetual Rain*

All Arts are one, howe'er distributed
they stand;
Verse, tone, shape, color, form, are
fingers on one hand.
> *Couplets. V*

QUEEN VICTORIA
[1819–1901]

We are not amused.
> *Comment, upon seeing an imi-*
> *tation of herself by the Hon-*
> *orable Alexander Grantham*
> *Yorke, Groom-in-Waiting to*
> *the Queen* [1884–1901]

WILLIAM ROSS WALLACE
[1819–1881]

They say that man is mighty, he governs land and sea;
He wields a mighty sceptre o'er lesser
powers that be.
> *The Hand That Rules the World.*
> *Stanza 1*

The hand that rocks the cradle is the
hand that rules the world.
> *Ibid.*

WALT WHITMAN [1]
[1819–1892]

Once fully enslaved, no nation, state,
city of this earth, ever afterward
resumes its liberty.
> *To the States*

I hear America singing, the varied
carols I hear.
> *I Hear America Singing*

Shut not your doors to me proud libraries,
For that which was lacking on all your

[1] In a certain sense, Whitman interpreted
America to Europe; and to America he tried
to interpret the universe. — WILLIAM LYON
PHELPS: *Howells, James, Bryant and Other
Essays* [1924]

well-fill'd shelves, yet needed
most, I bring.
> *Shut Not Your Doors*

I will write the evangel-poem of comrades and of love.
> *Starting from Paumanok. 6*

I say the whole earth and all the
stars in the sky are for religion's sake.
> *Ibid. 7*

None has begun to think how divine
he himself is, and how certain the future is.
> *Ibid.*

I say the real and permanent grandeur of these States must be their religion.
> *Ibid.*

Nothing can happen more beautiful
than death.[1]
> *Ibid. 12*

Whoever you are, to you endless an-
nouncements!
> *Ibid. 14*

I celebrate myself and sing myself,
And what I assume you shall assume.
> *Song of Myself. 1*

I loafe and invite my soul.
> *Ibid.*

Creeds and schools in abeyance.
> *Ibid.*

I have no mockings or arguments; I
witness and wait.
> *Ibid. 4*

It [grass] is the handkerchief of the
Lord.
> *Ibid. 6*

[1] Why fear death? Death is only a beautiful adventure. — CHARLES FROHMAN [1860–
1915]: Last words to a group of friends as
the *Lusitania* was sinking [May 7, 1915].
Report of conversation with Rita Jolivet, a
survivor, in a letter from C. Haddon Chambers to Alfred Hayman [May 18, 1915].

Why should I fear Death's call? Can there
e'er be
In life more beautiful adventure than
To re-embark upon that unknown sea?
> JAMES TERRY WHITE [1845–1920]:
> *Why Fear? St. 1*

"A beautiful adventure" — to be dead;
Or, in long pauses of one's dying breath,
To turn some splendid compliment to
death.
> RICHARD LEGALLIENNE: *Charles Froh-*
> *man, St. 3*

All goes onward and outward, nothing collapses,
And to die is different from what any one supposed, and luckier.
Song of Myself. 6

Whether I come to my own [1] to-day or in ten thousand or ten million years,
I can cheerfully take it now, or with equal cheerfulness I can wait.
Ibid. 20

I hear the violoncello, ('tis the young man's heart's complaint).
Ibid. 26

The orchestra whirls me wider than Uranus flies,
It wrenches such ardors from me I did not know I possess'd them.
Ibid.

I believe a leaf of grass is no less than the journey-work of the stars.
Ibid. 31

And the tree-toad is a chef-d'oeuvre for the highest. . . .
And a mouse is miracle enough to stagger sextillions of infidels.
Ibid.

I think I could turn and live with animals, they are so placid and self-contain'd.
Ibid. 32

Behold, I do not give lectures or a little charity,
When I give I give myself.[2]
Ibid. 40

And when you rise in the morning you will find what I tell you is so.
Ibid.

The clock indicates the moment — but what does eternity indicate?
Ibid. 44

In the faces of men and women I see God.
Ibid. 48

I sound my barbaric yawp over the roofs of the world.
Ibid. 52

[1] Nor time, nor space, nor deep, nor high, Can keep my own away from me.
JOHN BURROUGHS [1837–1931]: *Waiting, St. 6*

[2] See Lowell, page 525.

If any thing is sacred the human body is sacred.
Children of Adam. 8

I hear it was charged against me that I sought to destroy institutions,
But really I am neither for nor against institutions.
I Hear It Was Charged Against Me

When I peruse the conquer'd fame of heroes and the victories of mighty generals, I do not envy the generals.
When I Peruse the Conquer'd Fame

Henceforth I ask not good-fortune, I myself am good-fortune,
Henceforth I whimper no more, postpone no more, need nothing,
Done with indoor complaints, libraries, querulous criticisms,
Strong and content I travel the open road.
Song of the Open Road. 1

A great city is that which has the greatest men and women.
Song of the Broad-Axe. 4

All architecture is what you do to it when you look upon it.
A Song for Occupations. 4

All music is what awakes from you when you are reminded by the instruments.
Ibid.

In this broad earth of ours,
Amid the measureless grossness and the slag,
Enclosed and safe within its central heart,
Nestles the seed perfection.
Song of the Universal. 1

All, all for immortality,
Love like the light silently wrapping all.
Ibid. 4

Through the battle, through defeat, moving yet and never stopping,
Pioneers! O pioneers!
Pioneers! O Pioneers! 13

Youth, large, lusty, loving — Youth, full of grace, force, fascination,
Do you know that Old Age may come

after you, with equal grace, force, fascination?

Youth, Day, Old Age and Night. 1

Out of the cradle endlessly rocking,
Out of the mocking-bird's throat, the musical shuttle.

Out of the Cradle Endlessly Rocking. 1

A pennant universal, subtly waving all time, o'er all brave sailors,
All seas, all ships.

Song for All Seas, All Ships. 2

Roaming in thought over the Universe,
I saw the little that is Good steadily hastening towards immortality,
And the vast that is Evil I saw hastening to merge itself and become lost and dead.[1]

Roaming in Thought After Reading Hegel

Over all the sky — the sky! far, far out of reach, studded, breaking out, the eternal stars.

Bivouac on a Mountain Side

Long, too long America,
Traveling roads all even and peaceful you learn'd from joys and prosperity only,
But now, ah now, to learn from crises of anguish, advancing, grappling with direst fate and recoiling not.

Long, Too Long America

Give me the splendid silent sun, with all his beams full-dazzling!

Give Me the Splendid Silent Sun. 1

Lo, the moon ascending,
Up from the East, the silvery round moon,
Beautiful over the house-tops, ghastly, phantom moon,
Immense and silent moon.

Dirge for Two Veterans. 2

Beautiful that war and all its deeds of carnage must in time be utterly lost,
That the hands of the sisters Death and Night incessantly softly wash

[1] Evil perpetually tends to disappear. — HERBERT SPENCER: *The Evanescence of Evil*

again and ever again, this soiled world.

Reconciliation

When lilacs last in the door-yard bloom'd,
And the great star early droop'd in the western sky in the night,
I mourn'd, and yet shall mourn with ever-returning spring.

When Lilacs Last in the Dooryard Bloom'd. 1

Come lovely and soothing death,
Undulate round the world, serenely arriving, arriving,
In the day, in the night, to all, to each,
Sooner or later, delicate death.

Ibid. 14

Prais'd be the fathomless universe,
For life and joy, and for objects and knowledge curious,
And for love, sweet love — But praise! praise! praise!
For the sure-enwinding arms of cool-enfolding Death.

Ibid.

O Captain! my Captain! our fearful trip is done!
The ship has weather'd every wrack, the prize we sought is won,
The port is near, the bells I hear, the people all exulting.

O Captain! My Captain! 1

The ship is anchor'd safe and sound, its voyage closed and done,
From fearful trip the victor ship comes in with object won.

Ibid. 3

I with mournful tread,
Walk the deck my Captain lies,
Fallen cold and dead.

Ibid.

No more for him life's stormy conflicts,
Nor victory, nor defeat — no more time's dark events,
Charging like ceaseless clouds across the sky.

Hush'd be the Camps To-day. 2

This dust was once the man,
Gentle, plain, just and resolute.

This Dust Was Once the Man

He or she is greatest who contributes the greatest original practical example.

By Blue Ontario's Shore. 13

The whole theory of the universe is directed unerringly to one single individual — namely to You.

Ibid. 15

Not till the sun excludes you do I exclude you.

To a Common Prostitute

Liberty is to be subserved whatever occurs.

To a Foil'd European Revolutionaire. 1

I do not think seventy years is the time of a man or woman, . . . Nor that years will ever stop the existence of me, or any one else.

Who Learns My Lesson Complete?

Joyous we too launch out on trackless seas, Fearless for unknown shores.

Passage to India. 8

My terminus near, The clouds already closing in upon me, The voyage balk'd, the course disputed, lost, I yield my ships to Thee.

Prayer of Columbus. 9

What do you suppose will satisfy the soul, except to walk free and own no superior?

Laws for Creations. 3

To me every hour of the light and dark is a miracle, Every cubic inch of space is a miracle.

Miracles. 2

Whispers of heavenly death murmur'd I hear.

Whispers of Heavenly Death

I was thinking the day most splendid till I saw what the not-day exhibited, I was thinking this globe enough till there sprang out so noiseless around me myriads of other globes.

Night on the Prairies

I swear I think there is nothing but immortality!

To Think of Time. 9

The paths to the house I seek to make, But leave to those to come the house itself.

Thou Mother with Thy Equal Brood. 1

As a strong bird on pinions free, Joyous, the amplest spaces heavenward cleaving, Such be the thought I'd think of thee, America, Such be the recitative I'd bring for thee.

Ibid. 2

Sail, sail thy best, ship of Democracy. Of value is thy freight, 'tis not the Present only, The Past is also stored in thee.

Ibid. 4

This is thy hour O Soul, thy free flight into the wordless, Away from books, away from art, the day erased, the lesson done, Thee fully forth emerging, silent, gazing, pondering the themes thou lovest best, Night, sleep, death and the stars.

A Clear Midnight

Society waits unform'd, and is for a while between things ended and things begun.

Thoughts. 1

Our life is closed, our life begins, The long, long anchorage we leave, The ship is clear at last, she leaps! She swiftly courses from the shore, Joy, shipmate, joy.

Joy, Shipmate, Joy!

Now obey thy cherished secret wish, Embrace thy friends, leave all in order, To port and hawser's tie no more returning, Depart upon thy endless cruise, old Sailor.

Now Finalè to the Shore [1]

I announce the great individual, fluid as Nature, chaste, affectionate, compassionate, fully armed; I announce a life that shall be copious, vehement, spiritual, bold, And I announce an end that shall

[1] To Tennyson.

lightly and joyfully meet its trans-
lation.
So Long!
Camerado, this is no book,
Who touches this touches a man.
Ibid.
The world, the race, the soul — in
space and time the universes,
All bound as is befitting each — all
surely going somewhere.
Going Somewhere
Thanks in old age — thanks ere I go,
For health, the midday sun, the impal-
pable air — for life, mere life,
For precious ever-lingering memories.
Thanks in Old Age
I am the Poem of Earth, said the voice
of the rain,
Eternal I rise impalpable out of the
land and the bottomless sea.
The Voice of the Rain
Have you not learn'd great lessons
from those who reject you, and
brace themselves against you? or
who treat you with contempt, or
dispute the passage with you?
Stronger Lessons
Soon to be lost for aye in the darkness
— loth, O so loth to depart!
Garrulous to the very last.
After the Supper and Talk
No one will ever get at my verses
who insists upon viewing them as a literary performance.
*A Backward Glance O'er
Travel'd Roads*
None of the artists or pictures has
caught the deep, though subtle and indirect expression of this man's face.
There is something else there. One of
the great portrait painters of two or
three centuries ago is needed.
*Specimen Days. Of Lincoln,
August 12, 1863*
I never see that man without feeling
that he is one to become personally attach'd to, for his combination of purest, heartiest tenderness, and native
western form of manliness.
*Ibid. The Inauguration [of
Lincoln] March 4, 1865*
He leaves for America's history and
biography, so far, not only its most

dramatic reminiscence — he leaves, in
my opinion, the greatest, best, most
characteristic, artistic, moral personality.
*Specimen Days. Death of President
Lincoln, April 16, 1865*
The real war will never get in the
books.
Ibid. The Real War, etc.
Tone your wants and tastes down
low enough, and make much of nega-
tives, and of mere daylight and the
skies.
Ibid. An Interregnum Paragraph
After you have exhausted what
there is in business, politics, convivial-
ity, and so on — have found that none
of these finally satisfy, or permanently
wear — what remains? Nature remains.
Ibid. New Themes Entered Upon
Hast Thou, pellucid, in Thy azure
depths, medicine for case like mine?
Ibid. The Sky. October 20, 1876
One is never entirely without the instinct of looking around.
Ibid. One of the Human Kinks
You must not know too much, or be
too precise or scientific about birds and
trees and flowers and water-craft; a
certain free margin, and even vagueness — perhaps ignorance, credulity —
helps your enjoyment of these things.
Ibid. Birds. May 14, 1881
In the civilization of to-day it is undeniable that, over all the arts, literature dominates, serves beyond all.
Democratic Vistas
The main social, political spine-
character of the States will probably
run along the Ohio, Missouri and Mississippi rivers, and west and north of
them, including Canada.
Ibid.
Political democracy, as it exists and
practically works in America, with all
its threatening evils, supplies a training-
school for making first-class men. It is
life's gymnasium, not of good only, but
of all.
Ibid.
It is native personality, and that
alone, that endows a man to stand be-

fore presidents or generals, or in any distinguish'd collection, with *aplomb* — and *not* culture, or any knowledge or intellect whatever.

Democratic Vistas

If the United States haven't grown poets, on any scale of grandeur, it is certain they import, print, and read more poetry than any equal number of people elsewhere — probably more than all the rest of the world combined.

Notes Left Over. Ventures, on an Old Theme

To have great poets, there must be great audiences, too.

Ibid.

No really great song can ever attain full purport till long after the death of its singer — till it has accrued and incorporated the many passions, many joys and sorrows, it has itself aroused.

November Boughs. The Bible as Poetry

The United States themselves are essentially the greatest poem. . . . Here at last is something in the doings of man that corresponds with the broadcast doings of the day and night.

Preface to Leaves of Grass [1855]

The proof of a poet is that his country absorbs him as affectionately as he has absorbed it.

Ibid.

URANIA LOCKE STOUGHTON BAILEY ("JULIA GILL")
[1820–1882]

I want to be an angel,
    And with the angels stand,
A crown upon my forehead,
    A harp within my hand.

I Want to Be an Angel. Stanza 1

WILLIAM COX BENNETT
[1820–1895]

"God wills but ill," the doubter said,
    "Lo, time doth evil only bear;
Give me a sign His love to prove,
    His vaunted goodness to declare!"
The poet pointed where a flower,
    A simple daisy, starred the sod,

And answered, "Proof of love and power
Behold, behold a smile of God!"

A Thought [1]

Man of the Future, what shall be
The life of Earth that you shall see?
What strange new facts the years will show?
What wonders rare your eyes shall know?
To what new realms of marvel, say,
Will conquering science war its way?

To a Boy. Stanza 1

Oh! come you from the Indies, and, soldier, can you tell
Aught of the gallant Ninetieth, and who are safe and well?
O soldier, say my son is safe — for nothing else I care,
And you shall have a mother's thanks — shall have a widow's prayer.

From India. Stanza 1

HENRY HOWARD BROWNELL
[1820–1872]

As vonce I valked by a dismal svamp,
There sot an Old Cove in the dark and damp,
And at everybody as passed that road
A stick or a stone this Old Cove throwed.
And venever he flung his stick or his stone,
He'd set up a song of "Let me alone." [2]

Let Us Alone

A head how sober; a heart how spacious;
    A manner equal with high or low;
Rough but gentle, uncouth but gracious,
    And still inclining to lips of woe.

Abraham Lincoln. Stanza 24

Patient when saddest, calm when sternest,
    Grieved when rigid for justice sake;
Given to jest, yet ever in earnest

---

[1] Nathaniel Hawthorne copied this verse in an autograph album in 1853.

[2] All we ask is to be let alone. — JEFFERSON DAVIS [1808–1889] in his first message to the Confederate Congress [March, 1861]

If aught of right or truth were at
    stake.
        Abraham Lincoln. Stanza 25

ALICE CARY
[1820–1871]

There must be rough, cold weather,
    And winds and rains so wild;
Not all good things together
    Come to us here, my child.
        November

So when some dear joy loses
    Its beauteous summer glow,
Think how the roots of roses
    Are kept alive in the snow.
        Ibid.

Kiss me, though you make believe;
    Kiss me, though I almost know
You are kissing to deceive.
        Make Believe. Stanza 1

My soul is full of whispered song, —
    My blindness is my sight;
The shadows that I feared so long
    Are full of life and light.
        Dying Hymn

Three little bugs in a basket,
    And hardly room for two.
        Three Bugs. Stanza 1

JAMES ORCHARD
HALLIWELL
[1820–1889]

A warke it ys as easie to be done
As tys to saye *Jacke robyson*.[1]
        Archaeological Dictionary
        (*cited from an old play*)

JEAN INGELOW
[1820–1897]

But two are walking apart forever,
    And wave their hands for a mute
        farewell.
        Divided. VI, 5

---

[1] The current phrase, "Before you could
say Jack Robinson," is said to be derived
from a humorous song by Hudson, a tobac-
conist in Shoe Lane, London. He was a professional song-writer and vocalist, who used
to be engaged to sing at supper-rooms and
theatrical houses.

If there be memory in the world to
    come,
  If thought recur to some things si-
      lenced here,
Then shall the deep heart be no longer
    dumb,
  But find expression in that happier
      sphere.
        The Star's Monument. Stanza 1

Play uppe, play uppe, O Boston bells!
Ply all your changes, all your swells,
Play uppe "The Brides of Enderby."
        *High Tide on the Coast of
        Lincolnshire, 1571. Stanza 1*

"Cusha! Cusha! Cusha!" calling,
Ere the early dews were falling.
        Ibid. Stanza 4

Come uppe, Whitefoot! come uppe,
    Lightfoot!
Come uppe, Jetty! rise and follow,
Jetty, to the milking shed.
        Ibid.

A sweeter woman ne'er drew breath
Than my sonne's wife, Elizabeth.
        Ibid. Stanza 11

Man dwells apart, though not alone,
    He walks among his peers unread;
The best of thoughts which he hath
    known
    For lack of listeners are not said.
        Afterthought. Stanza 1

It is a comely fashion to be glad, —
Joy is the grace we say to God.
        Dominion

Many fair tombs in the glorious glooms
    At Westminster they show;
The brave and the great lie there in
    state:
    Winstanley lieth low.
        Winstanley.[1] Stanza 77

Like coral insects multitudinous
The minutes are whereof our life is
    made.
        Work

---

[1] Henry Winstanley [1644–1703] designed
the Eddystone Lighthouse, 1696. While su-
perintending its construction, he was captured by a French privateer in 1697, and
later released. He completed the lighthouse,
but lost his life in a storm which demolished
the structure in 1703.

Blondel, when his lay
Pierced the strong tower, and Richard
answered it.[1]
Wishing

I marked my love by candle-light
Sewing her long white seam.
The Long White Seam. Stanza 1

A land where all the men are stones,
Or all the stones are men.
*A Land That Living Warmth
Disowns*

THEODORE O'HARA
[1820–1867]

On Fame's eternal camping-ground
Their silent tents are spread,
And Glory guards, with solemn round,
The bivouac of the dead.
*The Bivouac of the Dead.[2]
Stanza 1*

Sons of the Dark and Bloody ground,[3]
Ye must not slumber there,
Where stranger steps and tongues re-
sound
Along the heedless air.
Ibid. Stanza 9

MARGARET JUNKIN
PRESTON
[1820–1897]

You have read of the Moslem palace,
The marvelous fane that stands
On the banks of the distant Jumna,
The wonder of all the lands.[4]
For Love's Sake. Stanza 1

[1] There is a tradition that Blondel, a French troubadour, attendant and friend of Richard Cœur de Lion, discovered Richard, imprisoned in the castle of Dürrenstein, by singing beneath the tower window a song which they had composed and to which the king responded.

Blondel were royal himself, if he knew it!
J. R. LOWELL: *Two Scenes from the
Life of Blondel, II, 6*

[2] Written in August, 1847, to commemorate the Americans slain in the battle of Buena Vista, Feb. 22–23, 1847.
[3] Translation of the Indian name, Kentucky.
[4] The Taj Mahal.

If from his home the lad that day
His five small loaves had failed to
take,
Would Christ have wrought — can any
say —
This miracle beside the lake?
A Store of Loaves. Stanza 7

And therefore, I, William Bradford
(by the grace of God to-day,
And the franchise of this good people),
governor of Plymouth, say —
Through virtue of vested power — ye
shall gather with one accord,
And hold in the month of November,
thanksgiving unto the Lord.
*The First Thanksgiving Day,
1622. Stanza 2*

What use for the rope if it be not flung
Till the swimmer's grasp to the rock
has clung?
What Use?

What worth is eulogy's blandest breath,
When whispered in ears that are hushed
in death?
Ibid.

GEORGE FREDERICK ROOT
[1820–1895]

And the hollow eye grows bright,
And the poor heart almost gay,
As we think of seeing home and friends
once more.
Tramp, Tramp, Tramp. Stanza 3

Rally round the flag, boys,
Rally once again,
Shouting the battle-cry of Freedom.
*The Battle-cry of Freedom.
Stanza 1*

SIR WILLIAM HOWARD
RUSSELL
[1820–1907]

The Russians dashed on towards
that thin red-line [1] streak tipped with a
line of steel.
*Correspondence to the London
Times from the Crimea, describ-*

[1] Soon the men of the column began to see that though the scarlet line was slender,

ing the British infantry at Balaclava [October 25, 1854] [1]

WILLIAM TECUMSEH SHERMAN
[1820–1891]

War is cruel and you cannot refine it.
> Reply to the protest of the Atlanta, Georgia, city government on invasion [1864]

Hold the fort! I am coming!
> Signaled to General Corse in Allatoona from the top of Kenesaw [October 5, 1864]

War at best is barbarism.
> Letter to General Steele

I am tired and sick of war. Its glory is all moonshine. It is only those who have neither fired a shot nor heard the shrieks and groans of the wounded who cry aloud for blood, more vengeance, more desolation. War is hell.[2]
> Attributed to an address before the graduating class, Michigan Military Academy [June 19, 1879], in a letter published in The National Tribune, Washington, D. C., November 26, 1914

JOHN TYNDALL
[1820–1893]

It is one of the disadvantages of reading books about natural scenery that they fill the mind with pictures, often exaggerated, often distorted, often blurred, and, even when well drawn, injurious to the freshness of first impressions.
> Fragments of Science. Vol. I, Niagara

It is not my habit of mind to think otherwise than solemnly of the feeling which prompts prayer. It is a power which I should like to see guided, not extinguished — devoted to practicable objects instead of wasted upon air.
> Ibid. Vol. II, Prayer as a Form of Physical Energy

Life is a wave, which in no two consecutive moments of its existence is composed of the same particles.
> Ibid. Vitality

We are truly heirs of all the ages; but as honest men it behooves us to learn the extent of our inheritance, and as brave ones not to whimper if it should prove less than we had supposed.
> Ibid. Matter and Force

The mind of man may be compared to a musical instrument with a certain range of notes, beyond which in both directions we have an infinitude of silence.
> Ibid.

The brightest flashes in the world of thought are incomplete until they have been proved to have their counterparts in the world of fact.
> Ibid. Scientific Materialism

The formation of right habits is essential to your permanent security. They diminish your chance of falling when assailed, and they augment your chance of recovery when overthrown.
> Ibid. An Address to Students

"Two things," said Immanuel Kant, "fill me with awe: the starry heavens, and the sense of moral responsibility in man."
> Ibid. Scientific Use of the Imagination

Believing, as I do, in the continuity of nature, I cannot stop abruptly where

---

it was very rigid and exact. — A. W. KINGLAKE [1809–1891]: Invasion of the Crimea, Vol. III, P. 455

The spruce beauty of the slender red line. —Ibid. (sixth edition), P. 248

It's "Thin red line of 'eroes" when the drums begin to roll.
> KIPLING: Tommy, St. 3

Robert Gibb [1845–1932], Scottish artist, painted The Thin Red Line, which was exhibited at the Royal Scottish Academy Exposition in 1881.

[1] Later included in Russell's book, The British Expedition to the Crimea (revised edition), P. 187.

[2] This is the soldier brave enough to tell
The glory-dazzled world that "war is hell":
Lover of peace, he looks beyond the strife,

And rides through hell to save his country's life.
> HENRY VAN DYKE: The Statue of Sherman by St. Gaudens

our microscopes cease to be of use. Here the vision of the mind authoritatively supplements the vision of the eye. By a necessity engendered and justified by science I cross the boundary of the experimental evidence, and discern in that Matter which we, in our ignorance of its latent powers, and notwithstanding our professed reverence for its Creator, have hitherto covered with opprobrium, the promise and potency of all terrestrial Life.[1]

> *Fragments of Science. Address at Belfast* [*August 19, 1874*]

Accept, if the choice be forced upon you, commotion before stagnation, the breezy leap of the torrent before the fetid stillness of the swamp.

> *Ibid.*

To look at his picture as a whole, a painter requires distance; and to judge of the total scientific achievement of any age, the standpoint of a succeeding age is desirable.

> *Ibid. Science and Man*

It is not given to any man, however endowed, to rise spontaneously into intellectual splendor without the parentage of antecedent thought.

> *Ibid.*

It is as fatal as it is cowardly to blink facts because they are not to our taste.

> *Ibid.*

Charles Darwin, the Abraham of scientific men — a searcher as obedient to the command of truth as was the patriarch to the command of God.

> *Ibid.*

Superstition may be defined as constructive religion which has grown incongruous with intelligence.

> *Ibid.*

Religious feeling is as much a verity as any other part of human consciousness; and against it, on the subjective side, the waves of science beat in vain.

> *Ibid. Professor Virchow and Evolution*

[1] This statement aroused much bitterness, and Tyndall was subjected to lively abuse.

GEORGE LINNAEUS BANKS
[1821–1881]

I live for those who love me,
  Whose hearts are kind and true;
For the Heaven that smiles above me,
  And awaits my spirit too;
For all human ties that bind me,
For the task by God assigned me,
For the bright hopes yet to find me,
  And the good that I can do.

> *What I Live For. Stanza 1*

For the cause that lacks assistance,
For the wrong that needs resistance,
For the future in the distance.

> *Ibid. Stanza 5*

GEORGE SHEPARD BURLEIGH
[1821–1903]

Behold the mansion reared by daedal Jack.
See the malt stored in many a plethoric sack,
In the proud cirque of Ivan's bivouac.
Mark how the rat's felonious fangs invade
The golden stores in John's pavilion laid.

> *The Domicile Erected by John* [1857]

Here walks forlorn the damsel crowned with rue.

> *Ibid.*

That horned brute morose
That tossed the dog that worried the cat that kilt
The rat that ate the malt that lay in the house that Jack built.

> *Ibid.*

SIR RICHARD FRANCIS BURTON
[1821–1890]

Why meet we on the bridge of Time to 'change one greeting and to part?

> *The Kasidah of Haji Abdu El-Yazdi. I, 11*

Why must we meet, why must we part, why must we bear this yoke of MUST,

Without our leave or asked or given,
  by tyrant Fate on victim thrust?
        The Kasidah of Haji Abdu.
                El-Yazdi. I, 13

Friends of my youth, a last adieu!
  haply some day we meet again;
Yet ne'er the selfsame men shall meet;
  the years shall make us other men.
                    Ibid. 16

What endless questions vex the
  thought, of Whence and Whither,
  When and How?
                Ibid. II, 3

How short this Life, how long withal;
  how false its weal, how true its
  woes,
This fever-fit with paroxysms to mark
  its opening and its close.
                Ibid. III, 23

Hardly we learn to wield the blade before the wrist grows stiff and old;
Hardly we learn to ply the pen ere
  Thought and Fancy faint with
  cold.
                Ibid. 32

Life, atom of that Infinite Space that
  stretcheth, 'twixt the Here and
  There.
                Ibid. 36

All Faith is false, all Faith is true:
  Truth is the shattered mirror
  strown
In myriad bits; while each believes
  his little bit the whole to own.
                Ibid. VI, 1

Indeed he knows not how to know who
  knows not also how to un-know.
                Ibid. 18

What men are pleased to call their
  souls was in the hog and dog begun.
                Ibid. VII, 6

Life is a ladder infinite-stepped, that
  hides its rungs from human eyes;
Planted its foot in chaos-gloom, its
  head soars high above the skies.
                Ibid. 7

Our hearts, affections, hopes and fears
  for Life-to-be shall ever crave.
                Ibid. VIII, 5

Mankind a future life must have to
  balance life's unequal lot.
                Ibid. 9

When doctors differ [1] who decides amid
  the milliard-headed throng? [2]
        The Kasidah of Haji Abdu.
                El-Yazdi. VIII, 29

Do what thy manhood bids thee do,
  from none but self expect applause;
He noblest lives and noblest dies who
  makes and keeps his self-made
  laws.
                Ibid. 37

With Ignorance wage eternal war, to
  know thyself for ever strain,[3]
Thine ignorance of thine ignorance is
  thy fiercest foe, thy deadliest bane.
                Ibid. IX, 14

Enough to thee the small still voice [4]
  aye thundering in thine inner ear.
                Ibid. 19

Wend now thy way with brow serene,
  fear not thy humble tale to tell:
The whispers of the Desert-wind; the
  tinkling of the Camel's-bell.[5]
                Ibid. 45

JOSEPH WARREN FABENS
[1821–1875]

I've seen the land of all I love
  Fade in the distance dim;
I've watched above the blighted heart,
  Where once proud hope had been;
But I've never known a sorrow
  That could with that compare,
When off the blue Canaries
  I smoked my last cigar.
        My Last Cigar. Stanza 4

DORA GREENWELL
[1821–1882]

A world of care without,
A world of strife shut out,
A world of love shut in.
        Home. Stanza 2

[1] Who shall decide when doctors disagree?
POPE: *Moral Essays, Epistle III, L. 1*
[2] See Sidney, page 27.
[3] See Chaucer, page 6.
Make it thy business to know thyself,
which is the most difficult lesson in the
world. — CERVANTES: *Don Quixote, Part II,
Book III, Chap. 42*
[4] A still, small voice. — *1 Kings, XIX, 12*
[5] Death rides a camel. — Arabian legend

FREDERICK LOCKER-LAMPSON
[1821–1895]

"Vanitas vanitatum" has rung in the ears
Of gentle and simple for thousands of years;
The wail still is heard, yet its notes never scare
Either simple or gentle from Vanity Fair.

Vanity Fair

This rhyme is the commonplace passion
That glows in a fond woman's heart;
Lay it by in some sacred deposit
For relics, — we all have a few!
Love, some day they'll print it, because it
Was written to you.

A Nice Correspondent. Stanza 7

What an arm — what a waist
For an arm!

To My Grandmother

The world's as ugly, ay, as Sin, —
And almost as delightful.

The Jester's Plea

If you lift a guinea-pig up by the tail
His eyes drop out!

A Garden Lyric. Stanza 5

GEORGE JOHN WHYTE-MELVILLE
[1821–1878]

When you sleep in your cloak there's no lodging to pay.

Boots and Saddles

For everything created
In the bounds of earth and sky
Has such longing to be mated,
It must couple or must die.

Like to Like

Ah, better to love in the lowliest cot
Than pine in a palace alone.

Chastelar

There are men both good and wise who hold that in a future state
Dumb creatures we have cherished here below

Shall give us joyous greeting when we pass the golden gate.

The Place Where the Old Horse Died

In the choice of a horse and a wife, a man must please himself, ignoring the opinion and advice of friends.

Riding Recollections

Education should be as gradual as the moonrise, perceptible not in progress but in result.

Ibid.

Pluck takes us into a difficulty, nerve brings us out of it. Both are comprised in the noble quality we call valor.

Ibid.

MATTHEW ARNOLD
[1822–1888]

One lesson, Nature, let me learn of thee.

Sonnet 1, Quiet Work

Be his
My special thanks, whose even-balanced soul,
From first youth tested up to extreme old age,
Business could not make dull, nor Passion wild:
Who saw life steadily and saw it whole.

Sonnet 2, To a Friend

Others abide our question. Thou art free.
We ask and ask: Thou smilest and art still,
Out-topping knowledge.

Sonnet 3, Shakespeare

The will is free:
Strong is the Soul, and wise, and beautiful:
The seeds of godlike power are in us still:
Gods are we, Bards, Saints, Heroes, if we will.

Sonnet 4, Written in Emerson's Essays

France, famed in all great arts, in none supreme.

Sonnet 10, To a Republican Friend, 1848

To its own impulse every creature stirs:
Live by thy light, and Earth will live
by hers.
Sonnet 11, Religious Isolation
Strew on her roses, roses,
And never a spray of yew.
In quiet she reposes:
Ah! would that I did too.
Requiescat. Stanza 1
Tonight it doth inherit
The vasty Hall of Death.
Ibid. Stanza 4
Ennobling this dull pomp, the life of
kings,
By contemplation of diviner things.
Mycerinus. Stanza 2
From grief, that is but passion;
From mirth, that is but feigning;
From tears, that bring no healing;
From wild and weak complaining;
Thine old strength revealing;
Save, oh, save.
Stagirius
Fate gave, what Chance shall not con-
trol,
His sad lucidity of soul.
Resignation
Yet they, believe me, who await
No gifts from Chance, have conquered
Fate.
Ibid.
Resolve to be thyself: and know, that
he
Who finds himself, loses his misery.
Self-Dependence. Stanza 8
We cannot kindle when we will
The fire that in the heart resides.
Morality. Stanza 1
But tasks in hours of insight will'd
Can be through hours of gloom ful-
fill'd.
Ibid.
With aching hands and bleeding feet
We dig and heap, lay stone on stone;
We bear the burden and the heat
Of the long day, and wish 'twere
done.
Not till the hours of light return
All we have built do we discern.
Ibid. Stanza 2
Calm Soul of all things! make it mine
To feel, amid the city's jar,
That there abides a peace of thine,

Man did not make, and can not mar.
*Lines Written in Kensington
Gardens. Stanza 10*
Eternal Passion,
Eternal Pain!
Philomela
So Tiberius might have sat,
Had Tiberius been a cat.
Poor Matthias
Physician of the Iron Age,
Goethe has done his pilgrimage.
He took the suffering human race,
He read each wound, each weakness
clear —
And struck his finger on the place
And said — Thou ailest here, and here.
Memorial Verses. Stanza 3
Time may restore us in his course
Goethe's sage mind and Byron's force;
But where will Europe's latter hour
Again find Wordsworth's healing
power?
Ibid. Stanza 5
Wandering between two worlds, one
dead,
The other powerless to be born.
*Stanzas from the Grande Char-
treuse. Stanza 15*
The kings of modern thought are
dumb.
Ibid. Stanza 20
Children of men! not that your age
excel
In pride of life the ages of your sires;
But that you too feel deeply, bear fruit
well,
The Friend of man desires.
Progress
Ah, love, let us be true
To one another!
Dover Beach
And we are here as on a darkling
plain
Swept with confused alarms of struggle
and flight,
Where ignorant armies clash by
night.
Ibid.
People who lived here long ago
Did by this stone, it seems, intend
To name for future times to know

The dachs-hound, Geist, their little friend.
>> *Geist's Grave. Stanza 20*

The foot less prompt to meet the morning dew,
The heart less bounding to emotion new,
And hope, once crush'd, less quick to spring again.
>> *Thyrsis. Stanza 14*

We do not what we ought;
>> What we ought not, we do;
And lean upon the thought
>> That Chance will bring us through.
>> *Empedocles on Etna*

Is it so small a thing
To have enjoy'd the sun,
To have lived light in the spring,
To have loved, to have thought, to have done;
To have advanced true friends, and beat down baffling foes?
>> *Ibid.*

The day in its hotness,
The strife with the palm;
The night in its silence,
The stars in their calm.
>> *Ibid. Callicles' Song*

Peace, peace is what I seek, and public calm;
Endless extinction of unhappy hates.
>> *Merope*

With women the heart argues, not the mind.
>> *Ibid.*

This strange disease of modern life.
>> *The Scholar Gypsy. Stanza 21*

Still nursing the unconquerable hope,
>> Still clutching the inviolable shade.
>> *Ibid. Stanza 22*

Most men eddy about
Here and there — eat and drink,
Chatter and love and hate,
Gather and squander, are raised
Aloft, are hurl'd in the dust,
Striving blindly, achieving
Nothing; and then they die.
>> *Rugby Chapel*

Radiant with ardour divine,
Beacons of Hope ye appear!
Languor is not in your heart,

Weakness is not in your word,
Weariness not on your brow.
>> *Rugby Chapel*

What shelter to grow ripe is ours?
>> What leisure to grow wise?
>> *Stanzas in Memory of the Author of "Obermann."* [1] *Stanza 18*

We, in some unknown Power's employ,
>> Move on a rigorous line;
Can neither, when we will, enjoy;
>> Nor, when we will, resign.
>> *Ibid. Stanza 34*

The East bow'd low before the blast
In patient deep disdain;
She let the legions thunder past
And plunged in thought again.
>> *"Obermann" Once More. Stanza 28*

Hath man no second life? *Pitch this one high!*
Sits there no judge in Heaven, our sin to see?
More strictly then the inward judge obey!
Was Christ a man like us? *Oh, let us try*
If we then, too, can be such men as he!
>> *The Better Part*

Let the long contention cease!
Geese are swans, and swans are geese.[2]
>> *The Last Word. Stanza 2*

When the forts of folly fall,
Find thy body by the wall!
>> *Ibid. Stanza 4*

Spare me the whispering, crowded room,
>> The friends who come and gape and go,
The ceremonious air of gloom —
>> All, which makes death a hideous show.
>> *A Wish*

Below the surface stream, shallow and light,
Of what we say and feel — below the stream,

[1] Étienne Pivert de Sénancour, born at Paris [1770], died at St. Cloud [1846], French author, much influenced by Rousseau. His most notable work, *Obermann*, in two volumes, was published in 1804.

[2] See Burton, page 123.

As light, of what we think we feel, there flows
With noiseless current, strong, obscure and deep,
The central stream of what we feel indeed.

Essays. St. Paul and Protestantism [1]

Poetry is simply the most beautiful, impressive and widely effective mode of saying things, and hence its importance.

Ibid. Heinrich Heine

Philistine must have originally meant, in the mind of those who invented the nickname, a strong, dogged, unenlightened opponent of the children of the light.

Ibid.

On the breast of that huge Mississippi of falsehood called history, a foam-bell more or less is of no consequence.[2]

Ibid. Literary Influence of Academies

The pursuit of the perfect, then, is the pursuit of sweetness and light.

Ibid. Culture and Anarchy

There is no better motto which it [culture] can have than these words of Bishop Wilson, "To make reason and the will of God prevail."

Ibid.

Whispering from her towers the last enchantments of the Middle Age . . .

[1] For admission of Arnold's authorship of this interpolated verse, see his *Letters, Vol. II, P. 32, Feb. 21, 1870.*

[2]   The fretful foam
Of vehement actions without scope or term,
Called History.
ARNOLD: *Sonnet to the Duke of Wellington*
With so little knowledge is history w. itten, and thus doth each chattering brook of a "Life" swell with its tribute "that great Mississippi of falsehood," Biography. — ANDREW LANG: *Letters to Dead Authors, To Pierre de Ronsard*
See Thomas Moore, page 337.
History is nothing more than the belief in the senses, the belief in falsehood. — NIETZSCHE: *The Twilight of the Idols, "Reason" in Philosophy, 1*
History never embraces more than a small part of reality.—LA ROCHEFOUCAULD: *Paul Sabatier*

home of lost causes, and forsaken beliefs, and unpopular names, and impossible loyalties!

Essays in Criticism. Oxford

DION BOUCICAULT
[1822–1890]

Then take the shamrock from your hat and cast it on the sod,
It will take root and flourish still, though under foot it's trod.

The Wearing of the Green.[1]
Stanza 2

I have another life I long to meet,
Without which life my life is incomplete,
Oh, sweeter self! Like me, art thou astray?
Trying with all thy heart to find the way
To mine? Straying, like mine, to find the breast
On which alone can weary heart find rest?

Led Astray [*1873*]

MARGARET COURTNEY
[1822–1862]

Be kind to thy father, for when thou wert young,
Who loved thee so fondly as he?
He caught the first accents that fell from thy tongue,
And joined in thy innocent glee.

Be Kind. Stanza 1

MARY BAKER EDDY
[1822–1910]

The prayer that reforms the sinner and heals the sick is an absolute faith that all things are possible to God, — a spiritual understanding of Him, an unselfed love.

Science and Health with Key to the Scriptures. Page 1

The basis of all health, sinlessness, and immortality is the great fact that God is the only Mind; and this Mind

[1] Adapted, from the traditional Irish ballad, for Boucicault's play *Arrah-na-Pogue.* [1865]

must be not merely believed, but it must be understood.

> *Science and Health with Key to the Scriptures. Page 339*

Being is holiness, harmony, immortality. It is already proved that a knowledge of this, even in small degree, will uplift the physical and moral standard of mortals, will increase longevity, will purify and elevate character. Thus progress will finally destroy all error, and bring immortality to light.

> *Ibid. Page 492*

Divine Love always has met and always will meet every human need.

> *Ibid. Page 494*

How would you define Christian Science?

As the law of God, the law of good, interpreting and demonstrating the divine Principle and rule of universal harmony.

> *Rudimental Divine Science. Page 1*

To live and let live, without clamor for distinction or recognition; to wait on divine Love; to write truth first on the tablet of one's own heart, — this is the sanity and perfection of living, and my human ideal.

> *Message to the Mother Church for 1902. Page 2*

To live so as to keep human consciousness in constant relation with the divine, the spiritual, and the eternal, is to individualize infinite power; and this is Christian Science.

> *The First Church of Christ, Scientist, and Miscellany. Page 160*

It matters not what be thy lot,
  So Love doth guide;
For storm or shine, pure peace is thine,
  Whate'er betide.

> *Satisfied. Stanza 1*

Blest Christmas morn, though murky clouds
  Pursue thy way,
Thy light was born where storm enshrouds
  Nor dawn nor day!

> *Christmas Morn. Stanza 1*

Shepherd, show me how to go
  O'er the hillside steep,
How to gather, how to sow,
  How to feed Thy sheep;
I will listen for Thy voice,
  Lest my footsteps stray,
I will follow and rejoice
  All the rugged way.

> *Shepherd, Show Me How to Go. Stanza 1*

O'er waiting harp-strings of the mind
  There sweeps a strain,
Low, sad, and sweet, whose measures bind
  The pow'r of pain.

> *O'er Waiting Harp-strings of the Mind. Stanza 1*

My prayer, some daily good to do
  To Thine, for Thee —
An off'ring pure of Love, whereto
  God leadeth me.

> *Ibid. Stanza 7*

ULYSSES S. GRANT
[1822–1885]

No terms except an unconditional and immediate surrender can be accepted. I propose to move immediately upon your works.

> *To General S. B. Buckner, Fort Donelson [February 16, 1862]*

I propose to fight it out on this line, if it takes all summer.

> *Despatch to Washington, Before Spottsylvania Court House [May 11, 1864]*

Let us have peace.

> *Accepting a Nomination for the Presidency [May 29, 1868]*

I know no method to secure the repeal of bad or obnoxious laws so effective as their stringent execution.

> *Inaugural Address [March 4, 1869]*

Let no guilty man escape, if it can be avoided. No personal considerations should stand in the way of performing a public duty.

> *Indorsement of a Letter relating to the Whiskey Ring [July 29, 1875]*

Leave the matter of religion to the family altar, the church, and the private school, supported entirely by private contributions. Keep the church and the State for ever separate.

Speech at Des Moines, Iowa [1875]

Labor disgraces no man; unfortunately you occasionally find men disgrace labor.

Speech at Midland International Arbitration Union, Birmingham, England [1877]

They [the Pilgrim Fathers] fell upon an ungenial climate, where there were nine months of winter and three months of cold weather and that called out the best energies of the men, and of the women too, to get a mere subsistence out of the soil, with such a climate. In their efforts to do that they cultivated industry and frugality at the same time — which is the real foundation of the greatness of the Pilgrims.

Speech at New England Society Dinner [December 22, 1880]

EDWARD EVERETT HALE
[1822–1909]

To look up and not down,
To look forward and not back,
To look out and not in, and
To lend a hand.[1]

Ten Times One Is Ten [1870]

I am only one,
But still I am one.
I cannot do everything,
But still I can do something;
And because I cannot do everything
I will not refuse to do the something
that I can do.

For the Lend-a-Hand Society

Let the scroll
Fill as it may as years unroll;
But when again she calls her youth
To serve her in the ranks of Truth,
May she find all one heart, one soul —
At home or on some distant shore —
"All present, or accounted for!"

Alma Mater's Roll [For a Harvard dinner, 1875]

[1] Rule of the Harry Wadsworth Club.

Its pink and white are everywhere,
A ray of sun — and all the slope
Laughs with its white and red.
"It is the Mayflower of our hope;
The spring is come."

The Finding of the First Mayflower. Stanza 3

Behind all these men you have to do with, behind officers, and government, and people even, there is the Country Herself, your Country, and . . . you belong to Her as you belong to your own mother. Stand by Her, boy, as you would stand by your mother.

The Man Without a Country

He loved his country as no other man has loved her, but no man deserved less at her hands.

Ibid. Epitaph of Philip Nolan

I taught him four speeches. . . .
1. "Very well, thank you. And you?" This for an answer to casual salutations.
2. "I am very glad you liked it."
3. "There has been so much said, and, on the whole, so well said, that I will not occupy the time."
4. "I agree, in general, with my friend the other side of the room."

My Double and How He Undid Me

It is not necessary to finish your sentences in a crowd, but by a sort of mumble, omitting sibilants and dentals. This, indeed, if your words fail you, answers even in public extempore speech, but better where other talking is going on.

Ibid.

THOMAS HUGHES
[1822–1896]

Throo aal the waarld owld Gaarge would bwoast,
Commend me to merry owld England mwoast;
While vools gwoes prating vur and nigh,
We stwops at whum, my dog and I.

Tom Brown's School-days. Chap. I [1]

[1] The verse is ascribed to "Gaarge Ridler, old west-country yeoman."

Life isn't all beer and skittles; [1] but beer and skittles, or something better of the same sort, must form a good part of every Englishman's education.

Tom Brown's School-days.
Chap. 2

ROBERT LEIGHTON
[1822–1869]

I have a thought that, as we live else-
where,
So will those dear creations of the
brain;
That what I lose unread, I'll find, and
there
Take up my joy again.
Books. Stanza 2

With liberty and endless time to read
The libraries of Heaven!
Ibid. Stanza 3

GEORGE LIPPARD
[1822–1854]

There was tumult in the city,
In the quaint old Quaker town,
And the streets were rife with people
Pacing restless up and down.
Independence Bell. Stanza 1

When a nation's life's at hazard,
We've no time to think of men!
Ibid. Stanza 3

DONALD GRANT MITCHELL ("IK. MARVEL")
[1822–1908]

Ashes follow blaze inevitably as death follows life. Misery treads on the

---

[1] It's a regular holiday to them — all porter and skittles. . . . Down-hearted fellers as can't svig avay at the beer, nor play at skittles neither. — DICKENS: *Pickwick Papers, Chap. 41*
Life is with such all beer and skittles. — C. S. CALVERLEY: *Contentment*
That it should not be all beer and skittles with us, and therefore apt to pall, my cousins and I had to work pretty hard. — GEORGE DU MAURIER: *Peter Ibbetson, P. 47*
And though life's not all beer and skittles,
Yet the sun, on occasion, can shine.
ANDREW LANG: *A Remonstrance with the Fair*

---

heels of joy; anguish rides swift after pleasure.
Reveries of a Bachelor. First Reverie, Part III

Blessed be letters — they are the monitors, they are also the comforters, and they are the only true heart-talkers.
Ibid. Second Reverie

Coquetry whets the appetite; flirta-tion depraves it. Coquetry is the thorn that guards the rose — easily trimmed off when once plucked. Flirtation is like the slime on water-plants, making them hard to handle, and when caught, only to be cherished in slimy waters.
Ibid.

A man without some sort of religion is at best, a poor reprobate, the foot-ball of destiny, with no tie linking him to infinity, and the wondrous eternity that is begun with him; but a woman without it is even worse — a flame without heat, a rainbow without color, a flower without perfume!
Ibid.

JOHN TYLER PETTEE
[1822–1907]

Pray for peace and grace and spiritual
food,
For wisdom and guidance, for all these
are good,
But don't forget the potatoes.
Prayer and Potatoes

EDWARD JOHN PHELPS
[1822–1900]

Waiting for that delusive train
That, always coming, never comes,
Till weary and worn, cold and forlorn,
And paralyzed in every function,
I hope in hell
Their souls may dwell
Who first invented Essex Junction.
Essex Junction. Stanza 1

THOMAS BUCHANAN READ
[1822–1872]

Within his sober realm of leafless trees,
The russet year inhaled the dreamy
air;

Like some tanned reaper in his hour of
    ease,
  When all the fields are lying brown
    and bare.
          The Closing Scene. Stanza 1
My soul to-day
Is far away
Sailing the Vesuvian Bay.
          Drifting. Stanza 1
With dreamful eyes
My spirit lies
Under the walls of Paradise.
          Ibid. Stanza 5
There is the shaded doorway still,
But a stranger's foot has crossed the
    sill.
          The Stranger on the Sill. Stanza 1
The old, old sea, as one in tears,
  Comes murmuring with its foamy
    lips,
And knocking at the vacant piers,
  Calls for its long-lost multitude of
    ships.[1]
          Come, Gentle Trembler,
              Stanza 5
I stood by the open casement
  And looked upon the night,
And saw the westward-going stars
  Pass slowly out of sight.
          The Celestial Army. Stanza 1
Now begins
The housewife's happiest season of the
    year.
The ground, already broken by the
    spade —
The beds, made level by the passing
    rake.
          The New Pastoral. Book V
Boone, the pioneer,
Whose statue, in the eternal niche of
    fame,
Leans on his gleaming rifle; and whose
    name
Is carved so deep in the Kentuckian
    rocks,
It may not be effaced.
          Ibid. Book XXVII
The terrible grumble, and rumble, and
    roar,
Telling the battle was on once more,

---

[1] Misquoted by MARK TWAIN: *Life on the
Mississippi, Chap. 22.*

And Sheridan twenty miles away.
          Sheridan's Ride. Stanza 1
I hate the sin, but I love the sinner.
          What a Word May Do.
              Stanza 1

BERNARD ELLIOTT BEE
[1823–1861]

See, there is Jackson, standing like
a stone-wall.
          Of General T. J. Jackson, at the
              Battle of Bull Run [1] *[July 21,*
              1861]

GEORGE HENRY BOKER
[1823–1890]

"Freedom!" their battle-cry, —
"Freedom! or leave to die!"
          The Black Regiment. Stanza 5
Lay him low, lay him low,
In the clover or the snow!
What cares he? he cannot know.
          Dirge for a Soldier.[2] *Stanza 1*
"Give me but two brigades," said
    Hooker, frowning at fortified
    Lookout.
          Battle of Lookout Mountain.[3]
              Stanza 1
All through the long, long polar day,
  The vessels westward sped;
And wherever the sail of Sir John was
    blown,
  The ice gave way and fled.
          The Ballad of Sir John Frank-
              lin.[4] *Stanza 7*
And there, while thread shall hang to
    thread,
  Oh, let that ensign fly!
The noblest constellation set
  Against the Northern sky.
          The Cumberland.[5] *Stanza 37*

---

[1] Bee was killed in this battle.
[2] General Philip Kearny [1815–1862], killed
near Chantilly, Virginia [Sept. 1, 1862].
[3] Chattanooga, Tennessee [Nov. 24, 1863].
[4] Arctic explorer [1786–1847].
[5] Sunk by the *Merrimac,* off Hampton
Roads, Virginia [March 8, 1862]. Commanded
by Lieutenant George U. Morris, she went
down with all on board and colors flying.
Most of the crew were lost.

I am that blessing which men fly from
— Death.
Countess Laura. Stanza 13
Love is that orbit of the restless soul
Whose circle grazes the confines of
space,
Bounding within the limits of its
race
Utmost extremes.
Sonnet, Love

WILLIAM BRIGHTY RANDS
("MATTHEW BROWNE")
[1823–1880]

Never do to-day what you can
Put off till to-morrow.
Lilliput Levee
Great wide, beautiful, wonderful world,
With the wonderful waters round you
curled,
And the wonderful grass upon your
breast,
World, you are beautifully drest.
The Child's World. Stanza 1
You are more than the earth, though
you are such a dot;
You can love and think, and the earth
cannot!
Ibid. Stanza 5

JULIA A. FLETCHER
CARNEY
[1823–1908]

Little drops of water, little grains of
sand,
Make the mighty ocean and the pleas-
ant land.
So the little moments, humble though
they be,
Make the mighty ages of eternity.
Little Things [1845]
Little deeds of kindness, little words of
love,
Help to make earth happy like the
heaven above.
Ibid.

ROBERT COLLIER
[1823–1912]

Steadily steering, eagerly peering,
Trusting in God, your fathers came,

Pilgrims and strangers, fronting all
dangers,
Cool-headed Saxons, with hearts
aflame.
Saxon Grit. Stanza 7

WILLIAM JOHNSON CORY
[1823–1892]

All beauteous things for which we live
By laws of time and space decay.
But oh, the very reason why
I clasp them, is because they die.
Mimnermus in Church. Stanza 4
Somewhere beneath the sun,
These quivering heart-strings prove it,
Somewhere there must be one
Made for this soul, to move it.
Amaturus
Oh, earlier shall the rosebuds blow,
In after years, those happier years;
And children weep, when we lie low,
Far fewer tears, far softer tears.
A Song. Stanza 1
For waste of scheme and toil we grieve,
For snowflakes on the wave we sigh,
For writings on the sand that leave
Naught for to-morrow's passer-by.
On Livermead Sands. Stanza 1
You come not, as aforetime, to the
headstone every day,
And I, who died, I do not chide be-
cause, my friend, you play;
Only, in playing, think of him who once
was kind and dear,
And, if you see a beauteous thing, just
say, he is not here.
Remember
They told me, Heraclitus, they told me
you were dead;
They brought me bitter news to hear
and bitter tears to shed.
I wept, as I remembered, how often you
and I
Had tired the sun with talking and sent
him down the sky.
And now that thou art lying, my dear
old Carian guest,
A handful of grey ashes, long long ago
at rest,

Still are thy pleasant voices, thy Night-
    ingales,[1] awake,
For Death, he taketh all away, but
    them he cannot take.
        Heraclitus,[2] Paraphrase from
                    Callimachus [3]

BARTHOLOMEW DOWLING
[1823–1863]

We meet 'neath the sounding rafter,
    And the walls around are bare;
As they shout back our peals of laugh-
    ter
It seems that the dead are there.
Then stand to your glasses, steady!
    We drink in our comrades' eyes:
One cup to the dead already —
    Hurrah for the next that dies!
             The Revel.[4] *Stanza 1*

[1] *The Nightingales* was the title of the poems left by Heraclitus.
[2] They told me, Herakleitos, thou wast dead.
    What tears I shed!
As I remembered how we two as one
    Talked down the sun.
Well, Halicarnessian friend, long since
    thou must
    Have turned to dust;
Yet live thy Nightingales, and Hades, who
    Doth all subdue,
Shall never until Time itself shall close
    Lay hand on those.
        Translation by BASIL LANNEAU GILDER-
               SLEEVE [1831–1924]
One told me, Heraclitus, of thy fate;
He brought me tears, he brought me memo-
    ries;
Alas, my Carian friend, how oft, how late,
We twain have talked the sun adown the skies,
And somewhere thou art dust without a date!
But of thy songs death maketh not his prize,
In death's despite, that stealeth all, they wait,
The new year's nightingale that never dies!
        ANDREW LANG [1844–1912]: *Heraclitus*
They tell me, Heraclitus, thou art dead,
And many are the tears for thee I shed,
With memories of those summer nights op-
    prest
When we together talked the sun to rest.
Alas! my guest, my friend! no more art thou;
Long, long ago wert ashes, and yet now
Thy Nightingales live on, I hear them sing,
E'en death spares them, who spares not any-
    thing.
        LILLA CABOT PERRY [1848–1933]:
    translated from Callimachus, *Greek
    Anthology, Book VII, Epigram 80*
[3] ? –A.D. 240.
[4] Commemorating those who died in a great cholera epidemic in India.

There's a mist on the glass congealing,
    'Tis the hurricane's sultry breath;
And thus does the warmth of feeling
    Turn ice in the grasp of Death.
            The Revel. Stanza 6
Who dreads to the dust returning?
    Who shrinks from the sable shore,
Where the high and haughty yearning
    Of the soul can sting no more?
               Ibid. Stanza 7

AUGUSTINE JOSEPH HICKEY DUGANNE
[1823–1884]

"Heimgang!" So the German people
    Whisper when they hear the bell
Tolling from some gray old steeple,
    Death's familiar tale to tell;
When they hear the organ surges
    Swelling out from chapel dome,
And the singers chanting dirges,
    "Heimgang!" Always going home.
            Heimgang. Stanza 1

THOMAS WENTWORTH HIGGINSON
[1823–1911]

To be parochial is to turn away from
the great and look at the little. . . .
To look out of the little world into the
great, that is enlargement; all else is
parochialism.
        *Margaret Fuller Ossoli.
                Chap. 9*

The test of an author is not to be
found merely in the number of his
phrases that pass current in the corner
of newspapers . . . but in the number
of passages that have really taken root
in younger minds.
               Ibid. Chap. 18

When a thought takes one's breath
away, a lesson on grammar seems an
impertinence.
        Preface to EMILY DICKINSON'S
              Poems, First Series
An easy thing, O Power Divine,
To thank Thee for these gifts of Thine,
For summer's sunshine, winter's snow,
For hearts that kindle, thoughts that
    glow;

But when shall I attain to this —
To thank Thee for the things I miss?
>> *The Things I Miss*

Age, I make light of it,
Fear not the sight of it,
Time's but our playmate, whose toys
are divine.
>> *Sixty and Six: A Fountain*
>> *of Youth*

WILLIAM WALSHAM HOW
[1823–1897]

For all the saints who from their labours rest,
Who Thee by faith before the world
confest,
Thy name, O Jesus, be forever blest.
>> *For All the Saints* [*1864*].
>> *Stanza 1*

JOHN KELLS INGRAM
[1823–1907]

Who fears to speak of Ninety-eight?
Who blushes at the name?
When cowards mock the patriot's fate,
Who hangs his head for shame?
>> *The Memory of the Dead.*[1]
>> *Stanza 1*

GEORGE MARTIN LANE
[1823–1897]

The waiter he to him doth call,
And gently whispers — "One Fish-
ball."
The waiter roars it through the hall,
The guests they start at "One Fish-
ball!"
The guest then says, quite ill at ease,
"A piece of bread, sir, if you please."
The waiter roars it through the hall:
"We don't give bread with one Fish-
ball!"
>> *One Fish-ball.*[2] *Couplets 7–10*
>> [*The Drawer, Harper's*
>> *Monthly, July, 1855*]

[1] First published anonymously in *The Dublin Nation, April 1, 1843.*
[2] The author was Professor of Latin at Harvard; in a memoir of him by PROFESSOR MOR-
GAN, it is stated that the embarrassment of the
"lone fish-ball" was an actual experience.
The ballad was translated into Italian by

JAMES MATTHEWS LEGARÉ
[1823–1859]

Go bow thy head in gentle spite,
Thou lily white,
For she who spies thee waving here,
With thee in beauty can compare
As day with night.
>> *To a Lily*

Thou in thy lake dost see
Thyself: so she
Beholds her image in her eyes
Reflected. Thus did Venus rise
From out the sea.
>> *Ibid.*

CAROLINE ATHERTON
BRIGGS MASON
[1823–1890]

Do they miss me at home — do they
miss me?
'Twould be an assurance most dear,
To know that this moment some loved
one
Were saying, "I wish he were here."
>> *Do They Miss Me at Home?*
>> *Stanza 1*

His grave a nation's heart shall be,
His monument a people free!
>> *President Lincoln's Grave*

Whichever way the wind doth blow,
Some heart is glad to have it so;
Then, blow it east, or blow it west,
The wind that blows, that wind is best.
>> *En Voyage. Stanza 1*

When I am old, and oh, how soon
Will life's sweet morning yield to noon,
And noon's broad, fervid, earnest light
Be shaded in the solemn night,
Till, like a story well-nigh told,
Will seem my life — when I am old.
>> *When I Am Old. Stanza 1*

EDWARD HAZEN PARKER
[1823–1896]

Life's race well run,
Life's work well done,

PROFESSOR FRANCIS J. CHILD, who, with
JAMES RUSSELL LOWELL, made a one-act opera, Il Pesceballo, based upon it, which was
produced at Harvard in 1862.
See *The Bibelot, Vol. 17, No. 11,* published
by Thomas Bird Mosher.

Life's victory won,
    Now cometh rest.
        Funeral Ode on James A. Garfield.
            Stanza 1

COVENTRY KERSEY DIGHTON PATMORE
[1823–1896]

The sunshine dreaming upon Salmon's
    height
Is not so sweet and white
As the most heretofore sin-spotted Soul
That darts to its delight
Straight from the absolution of a faith-
    ful fight.
        Peace

Life is not life at all without delight.
        Victory in Defeat

To have nought
Is to have all things without care or
    thought!
        Legem Tuam Dilexi

For want of me the world's course will
    not fail;
When all its work is done, the lie shall
    rot;
The truth is great, and shall prevail
When none cares whether it prevail or
    not.
        Magna est Veritas

None thrives for long upon the happiest
    dream.
        Tired Memory

The flower of olden sanctities.
            1867

Ah, wasteful woman! she who may
    On her sweet self set her own price,
Knowing he cannot choose but pay,
    How has she cheapened Paradise!
How given for nought her priceless gift,
    How spoiled the bread and spilled the
        wine,
Which, spent with due respective thrift,
    Had made brutes men and men
        divine! [1]
        The Angel in the House. Preludes,
            Unthrift

Love wakes men, once a lifetime each;
They lift their heavy lids, and look;

[1] Quoted by JOHN RUSKIN in *Sesame and
Lilies.*

And, lo, what one sweet page can teach
They read with joy, then shut the book.
        The Angel in the House. Canto 8,
            Prelude 2, The Revelation

Love's perfect blossom only blows
    Where noble manners veil defect.
Angels may be familiar; those
    Who err each other must respect.
        Thoughts. V, Courtesy

Be not amazed at life; 'tis still
    The mode of God with his elect
Their hopes exactly to fulfil,
    In times and ways they least expect.
        The Heart's Prophecies

He that but once too nearly hears
The music of forefended spheres,
Is thenceforth lonely.
        He That But Once

If I were dead, you'd sometimes say,
"Poor Child!"
        If I Were Dead

It is not true that Love will do no
    wrong.
        Ibid.

Thou rememberest of what toys
    We made our joys,
How weakly understood,
    Thy great commanded good.
        The Toys

Some who do not consider that
Christianity has proved a failure, do,
nevertheless, hold that it is open to
question whether the race, as a race,
has been much affected by it, and
whether the external and visible evil
and good which have come of it do not
pretty nearly balance one another.
        Christianity and Progress

Atheism in art, as well as in life, has
only to be pressed to its last consequences in order to become ridiculous.
        Emotional Art

The poet, as a rule, should avoid religion altogether as a direct subject.
        Bad Morality Is Bad Art

It is a great consolation to reflect that,
among all the bewildering changes to
which the world is subject, the character of woman cannot be altered.
        Ibid.

A Woman is a foreign land,
    Of which, though there he settle
        young,

A man will ne'er quite understand
The customs, politics, and tongue.
Woman

EDWARD POLLOCK
[1823–1858]

There's something in the parting hour
Will chill the warmest heart,
Yet kindred, comrades, lovers, friends,
Are fated all to part.
The Parting Hour
The one who goes is happier
Than those he leaves behind.
Ibid.

JOHN R. THOMPSON
[1823–1873]

No unresponsive soul had heard
That plaintive note's appealing,
So deeply "Home, Sweet Home" had
stirred
The hidden founts of feeling.
Music in Camp. Stanza 14
Never have I seen Carcassonne.[1]
From the French of GUSTAVE
NADAUD [1820–1893]

PHOEBE CARY
[1824–1874]

I think true love is never blind,
But rather brings an added light,
An inner vision quick to find
The beauties hid from common sight.
True Love. Stanza 1
Give plenty of what is given to you,
And listen to pity's call;
Don't think the little you give is great
And the much you get is small.
A Legend of the North'and. I,
Stanza 8
Sometimes, I think, the things we see
Are shadows of the things to be;
That what we plan we build;
That every hope that hath been crossed,
And every dream we thought was lost,
In heaven shall be fulfilled.
Dreams and Realities.[2] Stanza 7

[1] See Julia C. R. Dorr, page 562.
[2] Her last poem.

I'm done gone, Massa — step on me,
And you can scale the wall!
The Hero of Fort Wagner
And though hard be the task,
"Keep a stiff upper lip."
Keep a Stiff Upper Lip
One sweetly solemn thought
Comes to me o'er and o'er;
I am nearer home to-day
Than I ever have been before.
Nearer Home. Stanza 1
Kate Ketcham on a Winter's night
Went to a party dressed in white.
Kate Ketcham (Parody on
WHITTIER'S *Maud Muller)*
For of all the hard things to bear and
grin,
The hardest is being taken in.
Ibid.
Her washing ended with the day,
Yet lived she at its close,
And passed the long, long night away
In darning ragged hose.
The Wife (Parody on JAMES
ALDRICH'S *A Death-Bed)*[1]
But when the sun in all its state
Illumed the Eastern skies,
She passed about the kitchen grate
And went to making pies.
Ibid.

PHILA HENRIETTA CASE
[*Floruit* 1864]

Oh! why does the wind blow upon me
so wild?
Is it because I'm nobody's child?
Nobody's Child. Stanza 1

ELIZABETH HANNAH
JOCELYN CLEAVELAND
[1824–1911]

I'm bound for heaven and when I'm
there
I shall want my Book of Common
Prayer,
And though I put on a starry crown,
I should feel quite lost without my
gown.
No Sects in Heaven [1860].
Stanza 4

[1] See James Aldrich, page 473.

Side by side, for the way was one,
The toilsome journey of life was done,
And priest and Quaker, and all who
    died,
Came out alike on the other side;
No forms or crosses, or books had they,
No gowns of silk, or suits of gray.
       No Sects in Heaven [*1860*]
               Stanza 23

GEORGE WILLIAM CURTIS
[1824–1892]

I walked beside the evening sea
And dreamed a dream that could not
    be;
The waves that plunged along the
    shore
Said only: "Dreamer, dream no more!"
       Ebb and Flow. Stanza 1
  In that calm Syrian afternoon, memory, a pensive Ruth, went gleaning
the silent fields of childhood and found
the scattered grain still golden and the
morning sunlight fresh and fair.
    The Howadji in Syria. Ave Maria
  While we read history we make history.
       The Call of Freedom
  Every great crisis of human history is
a pass of Thermopylae, and there is always a Leonidas and his three hundred
to die in it, if they can not conquer.
               Ibid.
  Gentlemen, this is the convention of
free speech, and I have been given the
floor. I have only a few words to say to
you, but I shall say them if I stand
here until to-morrow morning.
    At the Republican National
       Convention [*1860*]
  Imagination is as good as many voyages — and how much cheaper.
       Prue and I. Preface
  Every mother who has lost an infant,
has gained a child of immortal youth.
       Ibid. Chap. 3
  I think that to have known one good
old man — one man who, through the
chances and rubs of a long life, has
carried his heart in his hand, like a
palm branch, waving all discords into

peace, helps our faith in God, in ourselves, and in each other, more than
many sermons.
       Prue and I. Chap. 4

Happiness is speechless.
               Ibid.

  It is not observed in history that
families improve with time. It is rather
discovered that the whole matter is like
a comet, of which the brightest part is
the head; and the tail, although long
and luminous, is gradually shaded into
obscurity.
       Ibid. Chap. 6

  The pride of ancestry increases in the
ratio of distance.
               Ibid.

  It is a great pity that men and
women forget that they have been children. Parents are apt to be foreigners
to their sons and daughters. Maturity
is the gate of Paradise which shuts behind us; and our memories are gradually weaned from the glories in which
our nativity was cradled.
       Ibid. Chap. 7

Love is the coldest of critics.
               Ibid.

SYDNEY THOMPSON
DOBELL
[1824–1874]

Children brave and free
Of the great Mother-tongue, and ye
    shall be
Lords of an empire wide as Shakes-
    peare's soul,
Sublime as Milton's immemorial theme,
And rich as Chaucer's speech, and fair
    as Spenser's dream.
       Sonnets on America

AMANDA M. EDMOND
[1824–1862]

Give me three grains of corn, mother,
Only three grains of corn;

It will keep the little life I have
Till the coming of the morn.
Give Me Three Grains of Corn.[1]
Stanza 1

There are rich and proud men there,
    mother,
With wondrous wealth to view,
And the bread they fling to their dogs
    to-night
Would give life to me and you.
Ibid. Stanza 6

CHARLES GODFREY LELAND
[1824–1903]

Hans Breitmann gife a barty —
    Where ish dat barty now?
Hans Breitmann's Party

All goned afay mit de Lager Beer,
    Afay in de Ewigkeit!
Ibid.

Der noble Ritter Hugo
    Von Schwillensanftenstein
Rode out mit shpeer und helmet,
    Und he coom to de panks of de
        Rhine.
Ritter Hugo. Stanza 1

If all the world must see the world
    As the world the world hath seen,
Then it were better for the world
    That the world had never been.
The World and the World

The greatest sharp some day will find
    a sharper wit;
It always makes the devil laugh to see
    a biter bit;
It takes two Spaniards any day to
    come a Yankee o'er — [2]
Even two like Don Alonzo Estabán San
    Salvador.
El Capitan-General. Stanza 12

"A New Year's gift to the world," said
    the Frost,
"Rich lace curtains which nothing
    cost."
Frost Pictures. Stanza 4

[1] Mrs. Edmond learned of the incident related in the poem while visiting in Ireland at the time of the great famine in 1846.

[2] It takes three Jews to cheat a Greek, and three Greeks to cheat an Armenian.
    Levantine Proverb. Used as a chapter heading in Stamboul Nights, by H. G. Dwight.

They saw a Dream of Loveliness descending from the train.
The Masher

The brave deserve the lovely — every
    woman may be won.
Ibid.

GEORGE MACDONALD
[1824–1905]

Alas! how easily things go wrong!
A sigh too much or a kiss too long,
And there follows a mist and a weeping
    rain,
And life is never the same again.
Phantastes. Song

Where did you come from, baby dear?
Out of the everywhere into the here.
At the Back of the North Wind.
Baby, Stanza 1

Where did you get those eyes so blue?
Out of the sky as I came through.
Ibid. Stanza 2

We must do the thing we *must*
    Before the thing we *may;*
We are unfit for any trust
    Till we can and do obey.
Willie's Question

They were all looking for a king
    To slay their foes and lift them high;
Thou cam'st, a little baby thing
    That made a woman cry.
That Holy Thing. Stanza 1

Love is the part, and love is the whole;
    Love is the robe, and love is the pall;
Ruler of heart and brain and soul,
    Love is the lord and the slave of all!
A Lover's Thought of Love.
Stanza 1

The man that feareth, Lord, to doubt,
    In that fear doubteth Thee.
The Disciple

Said the Wind to the Moon, "I will
    blow you out!"
The Wind and the Moon.
Stanza 1

Age is not all decay; it is the ripening, the swelling, of the fresh life within, that withers and bursts the husks.
The Marquess of Lossie

WILLIAM MORLEY PUNSHON
[1824–1881]

There is a beautiful Indian apologue, which says: A man once said to a lump of clay, "What art thou?" The reply was, "I am but a lump of clay, but I was placed beside a rose and I caught its fragrance."

Our Prayers

CHARLES P. SHIRAS
[1824–1854]

Dimes and dollars! dollars and dimes!
An empty pocket's the worst of crimes!
The Popular Credo. Stanza 1

Oh, the debtor is but a shamefaced dog
  With the creditor's name on his collar;
While I am king and you are queen,
  For we owe no man a dollar!
I Owe No Man a Dollar. Stanza 1

WALTER CHALMERS SMITH
[1824–1908]

And all through life I see a cross —
  Where sons of God yield up their breath;
There is no gain except by loss;
  There is no life except by death;
  There is no vision but by faith.
Olrig Grange. Book 6

JOHN WHITTAKER WATSON
[1824–1890]

O the snow, the beautiful snow,
Filling the sky and the earth below.
Over the house-tops, over the street,
Over the heads of the people you meet,
  Dancing,
    Flirting,
  Skimming along,
Beautiful snow, it can do nothing wrong.
Beautiful Snow.[1] Stanza 1

[1] From *Beautiful Snow and Other Poems* [1869].

Once I was fair as the beautiful snow,
With an eye like its crystals, a heart like its glow.
Beautiful Snow. Stanza 5

HENRY DE LAFAYETTE WEBSTER
[1824–1896]

The years creep slowly by, Lorena,
The snow is on the grass again.
Lorena.[1] Stanza 1

'Twas not thy woman's heart that spoke —
Thy heart was always true to me.
A duty stern and pressing broke
The tie that links my soul with thee.
Ibid. Stanza 5

There is a Future, O thank God!
  Of life this is so small a part!
'Tis dust to dust beneath the sod,
  But There — up There — 'tis heart to heart!
Ibid. Stanza 6

ADELINE DUTTON TRAIN WHITNEY
[1824–1906]

God does not send strange flowers every year.
  When the spring winds blow o'er the pleasant places,
  The same dear things lift up the same fair faces,
The violet is here.
A Violet. Stanza 1

So after the death-winter it must be
  God will not put strange signs in heavenly places,
  The old love shall look out from the old faces.
Ibid. Stanza 3

Ah, look thou largely, with lenient eyes,
  On whatso betide thee may creep and cling,
For the possible beauty that underlies
  The passing phase of the meanest thing.
Larvae. Stanza 5

[1] One of the most popular songs of the Civil War period.

The sun of life has crossed the line;
  The summer-shine of lengthened
    light
Faded and failed — till, where I stand,
  'Tis equal day and equal night.
                Equinoctial. Stanza 1

I bow me to the threatening gale:
  I know when that is overpast,
Among the peaceful harvest days
  An Indian Summer comes at last.
                Ibid. Stanza 6

EDWARD HENRY
BICKERSTETH, BISHOP OF
EXETER
[1825–1906]

Give us men! [1]
Men from every rank,
Fresh and free and frank;
Men of thought and reading,
Men of light and leading,
Men of loyal breeding,
The nation's welfare speeding.
                Give Us Men. Stanza 1

Men who when the tempest gathers
Grasp the standard of their fathers
  In the thickest fight;
Men who strike for home and altar,
(Let the coward cringe and falter,)
  God defend the right!
                Ibid. Stanza 3

Our years are like the shadows
  The sunny hills that lie,
Or grasses in the meadows
  That blossom but to die;
A sleep, a dream, a story
  By strangers quickly told,
An unremaining glory
  Of things that soon are old.
                O God, the Rock of Ages. Stanza 2

RICHARD DODDRIDGE
BLACKMORE
[1825–1900]

Women, who are, beyond all doubt,
the mothers of all mischief, also nurse
that babe to sleep when he is too noisy.
                Lorna Doone. Chap. 57

[1] See J. G. Holland, page 522.

In the hour of death, after this life's
    whim,
When the heart beats low, and the eyes
    grow dim,
And pain has exhausted every limb —
The lover of the Lord shall trust in
    Him.
                Dominus Illuminatio Mea.
                        Stanza 1

For even the purest delight may pall,
And power must fail and pride must
    fall,
And the love of the dearest friends
    grow small —
But the glory of the Lord is all in all.
                Ibid. Stanza 4

WILLIAM ALLEN BUTLER
[1825–1902]

We read Virginia's blazoned roll
  Of heroes, and forthwith
Greets us upon the starry scroll
  That homeliest name, — *John
    Smith!*
                Virginia's Virgin. Part I, Stanza 1

No record of her high descent
  There needs, nor memory of her
    name;
Enough that Raphael's colors blent
  To give her features deathless fame.
                The Incognita of Raphael. Stanza 3

Dresses for breakfasts, and dinners,
    and balls;
Dresses to sit in, and stand in, and
    walk in;
Dresses to dance in, and flirt in, and
    talk in;
Dresses in which to do nothing at all;
Dresses for Winter, Spring, Summer,
    and Fall.
                Nothing to Wear.[1]

This same Miss McFlimsey of Madison
    Square,
The last time we met was in utter de-
    spair,
Because she had nothing whatever to
    wear!
                Ibid.

[1] *Harper's Weekly, Feb. 7, 1857.*

OBADIAH MILTON CONOVER
[1825–1884]

Alone I walk the peopled city,
  Where each seems happy with his
    own;
O friends, I ask not for your pity —
  I walk alone.
          Via Solitaria [*1863*]

JULIA CAROLINE RIPLEY DORR
[1825–1913]

Fair the cabin-walls were gleaming in
  the sunbeams' golden glow,
On that lovely April morning, near a
  hundred years ago;
And upon the humble threshold stood
  the young wife, Margery Grey,
With her fearless blue eyes glancing
  down the lonely forest way.
      *Margery Grey, A Legend of
          Vermont.*[1] *Stanza 1*

I can scarce believe the tale
Borne to me on every gale!
You have been to Carcassonne?
Looked its stately towers upon?
      *To One Who Went to Carcas-
          sonne.*[2] *Stanza 1*

How can I cease to pray for thee?
  Somewhere
  In God's great universe thou art to-
    day:
Can He not reach thee with His tender
  care?
  Can He not hear me when for thee I
    pray?
          Somewhere. Stanza 1

Under thy hooded mantle I can see
Thy wavelets of soft hair, like those
  that lie

---

[1] *Our Young Folks, September, 1865.*
[2] Ah, me! I might have died content
    When I had looked on Carcassonne.
      GUSTAVE NADAUD: *Carcassonne, St. 4*
    The towers are grey — not blue and white,
    As looked the far-off Carcassonne.
      GRACE NOLL CROWELL: *Carcassonne
                              Attained*
    Perhaps the goal we still shall gain,
    We're on our way to Carcassonne.
      BERTON BRALEY: *Carcassonne, St. 3*

On a girl's forehead; and thy unlined
  brow,
Pregnant with thought inbreathed, be-
  trayeth not
One of thy secrets saving this alone, —
That thou hast loved and suffered.[1]
          In Rock Creek Cemetery

GEORGE WARD HUNT
[1825–1877]

We don't want to fight, but, by jingo,
  if we do,
We've got the ships, we've got the men,
  we've got the money, too.
We've fought the Bear before, and
  while we're Britons true,
  The Russians shall not have Con-
    stantinople.
              Song [2]

HENRIETTA A. HEATHORN (MRS. THOMAS H.) HUXLEY
[1825–1914]

This day within the Abbey, where of
  old
Our Kings are sepulchred, a king of
  song,

---

[1] The sculpture by Augustus Saint Gaudens
for the grave of Mrs. Henry Adams, Rock
Creek Cemetery, Washington, D. C.

This is not death, nor sorrow, nor sad Hope;
Nor rest that follows strife, but oh, more
  dread!
'Tis Life, for all its agony, serene,
Immortal, and unmournful and content.
      RICHARD WATSON GILDER: *The Saint
                          Gaudens Memorial*
Yes, I have lived! Pass on
And trouble me with questions nevermore —
I suffered. I have won
A solemn peace — my peace forevermore.
Leave me in silence here.
I have no hope, no care,
I know no fear;
For I have borne — but now no longer bear.
      HILDEGARDE HAWTHORNE: *On the Saint
                  Gaudens Work in Rock Creek Cemetery*
[2] Sung by Gilbert Hastings Macdermott
(Farrell) [1845–1901], "the great Macder-
mott," in 1878, and adding the term "by jingo"
to political vocabulary, though it had been
used earlier by Oliver Goldsmith and Thomas
Hood.
    George Jacob Holyoake [1817–1906], a re-
former, used the word "jingo" as a political
designation in a letter published in *The London Daily News, March 13, 1878.*

Browning, among his peers, is laid to rest.

Browning's Funeral, December 31, 1889

Be not afraid, ye waiting hearts that weep,
For God still giveth His belovèd sleep,[1]
And if an endless sleep He wills — so best.[2]

Ibid.

To all the gossip that I hear
I'll give no faith; to what I see
But only half, for it is clear
All that led up is dark to me.

Learn we the larger life to live,
To comprehend is to forgive.

"Tout Comprendre, c'est Tout Pardonner"

THOMAS HENRY HUXLEY
[1825–1895]

I cannot but think that he who finds a certain proportion of pain and evil inseparably woven up in the life of the very worms, will bear his own share with more courage and submission.

On the Educational Value of the National History Sciences [1854]

To a person uninstructed in natural history, his country or seaside stroll is a walk through a gallery filled with wonderful works of art, nine-tenths of which have their faces turned to the wall.

Ibid.

Education is the instruction of the intellect in the laws of Nature, under which name I include not merely things and their forces, but men and their ways; and the fashioning of the affections and of the will into an earnest and loving desire to move in harmony with those laws.

A Liberal Education [1868]

For every man the world is as fresh as it was at the first day, and as full of

untold novelties for him who has the eyes to see them.

A Liberal Education [1868]

It is much better to want a teacher than to want the desire to learn.

Ibid.

Literature is the greatest of all sources of refined pleasure, and one of the great uses of a liberal education is to enable us to enjoy that pleasure.

Ibid.

The rung of a ladder was never meant to rest upon, but only to hold a man's foot long enough to enable him to put the other somewhat higher.

On Medical Education [1870]

There is the greatest practical benefit in making a few failures early in life.

Ibid.

That mysterious independent variable of political calculation, Public Opinion.

Universities, Actual and Ideal [1874]

Veracity is the heart of morality.

Ibid.

Becky Sharp's acute remark that it is not difficult to be virtuous on ten thousand a year[1] has its application to nations; and it is futile to expect a hungry and squalid population to be anything but violent and gross.

Joseph Priestley [1874]

Size is not grandeur, and territory does not make a nation.

On University Education [1876]

The chess-board is the world, the pieces are the phenomena of the universe, the rules of the game are what we call the laws of Nature. The player on the other side is hidden from us. We know that his play is always fair, just, and patient. But also we know, to our cost, that he never overlooks a mistake, or makes the smallest allowance for ignorance.

Lay Sermons

Perhaps the most valuable result of all education is the ability to make yourself do the thing you have to do,

---

[1] He giveth his belovèd — sleep. — MRS. BROWNING: *The Sleep*

[2] These lines were carved on Huxley's tomb by his own request.

[1] See Thackeray, page 482.

when it ought to be done, whether you like it or not; it is the first lesson that ought to be learned; and however early a man's training begins, it is probably the last lesson that he learns thoroughly.

Technical Education [*1877*]

The great end of life is not knowledge but action.

Ibid.

If a little knowledge is dangerous, where is the man who has so much as to be out of danger?

On Elemental Instruction in Physiology [*1877*]

Irrationally held truths may be more harmful than reasoned errors.

The Coming of Age of "The Origin of Species"

It is the customary fate of new truths to begin as heresies and to end as superstitions.

Ibid.

If some great Power would agree to make me always think what is true and do what is right, on condition of being turned into a sort of clock and wound up every morning before I got out of bed, I should instantly close with the offer.

Materialism and Idealism

Logical consequences are the scarecrows of fools and the beacons of wise men.

Animal Automatism

ELIJAH JONES
[? –1869]

How great was Alexander, pa,
    That people call him great?
Was he, like old Goliath, tall?
    His spear a hundredweight?

How Great Was Alexander? Stanza 1

'Twas not his stature made him great,
    But greatness of his name.

Ibid. Stanza 3

JAMES K. JONES
[*Floruit* 1880]

Change the name of Arkansas? Never!

Speech in the United States Senate [1]

FRANCIS TURNER PALGRAVE
[1825–1897]

Their little language the children
    Have, on the knee as they sit;
And only those who love them
    Can find the key to it.

Love's Language. Stanza 1

Time's corrosive dewdrop eats
    The giant warrior to a crust
Of earth in earth and rust in rust.

A Danish Barrow

ADELAIDE ANNE PROCTER
[1825–1864]

One by one the sands are flowing,
    One by one the moments fall;
Some are coming, some are going;
    Do not strive to grasp them all.

One by One. Stanza 1

"What is Life, father?" "A Battle, my child,
    Where the strongest lance may fail,
Where the wariest eyes may be beguiled,
And the stoutest heart may quail."

Life and Death. Stanza 1

Seated one day at the organ,
    I was weary and ill at ease,
And my fingers wandered idly
    Over the noisy keys.

A Lost Chord. Stanza 1

It seemed the harmonious echo
    From our discordant life.

Ibid. Stanza 4

I will not let you say a woman's part
    Must be to give exclusive love alone;
Dearest, although I love you so, my heart

---

[1] After a New England Senator had introduced a bill to change the pronunciation of the last syllable of Arkansas from *saw* to *sas*. (In 1881 the Arkansas Legislature passed a law making *saw* the official pronunciation.)

Answers a thousand claims besides
  your own.
> *A Woman's Answer. Stanza 1*

Heaven is yours at last;
In that one minute's anguish
Your thousand years have passed.[1]
> *The Story of the Faithful Soul.*[2]
> *Stanza 16*

RICHARD HENRY STODDARD
[1825–1903]

Pale in her fading bowers the Summer
  stands,
Like a new Niobe with claspèd hands,
Silent above the flowers, her children
  lost,
Slain by the arrows of the early Frost.
> *Ode*

There are gains for all our losses,
  There are balms for all our pain.
> *The Flight of Youth.*[3] *Stanza 1*

Joy may be a miser,
  But Sorrow's purse is free.
> *Persian Song*

Not what we would, but what we must,
  Makes up the sum of living;
Heaven is both more and less than just
  In taking and in giving.
> *The Country Life. Stanza 1*

The angel came by night
  (Such angels still come down),
And like a winter cloud
  Passed over London town;
Along its lonesome streets,
  Where Want had ceased to weep,
Until it reached a house
  Where a great man lay asleep.
> *Adsum (on the Death of Thack-*
> *eray, December 23–24, 1863)*

He answered, "I am here."[4]
> *Ibid.*

---

[1] The angel answered, "Nay, sad soul, go
  higher!
To be deceived in your true heart's desire
Was bitterer than a thousand years of
  fire!"
JOHN HAY [1838–1905]: *A Woman's Love*
[2] Founded on an old French legend.
[3] See Gilfillan, page 390.
[4] See Thackeray, page 483.

BAYARD TAYLOR
[1825–1878]

Till the sun grows cold,
  And the stars are old,
And the leaves of the Judgment Book
  unfold.
> *Bedouin Song*

They sang of love, and not of fame;
  Forgot was Britain's glory;
Each heart recalled a different name,
  But all sang "Annie Laurie."
> *The Song of the Camp. Stanza 5*

The bravest are the tenderest, —
  The loving are the daring.
> *Ibid. Stanza 11*

Shelved round us lie
  The mummied authors.
> *The Poet's Journal. Third Eve-*
> *ning, Stanza 2*

No sound was heard but the dashing
  Of waves on the sandy bar,
When Pablo of San Diego
  Rode down to the Paso del Mar.
> *The Fight of Paso del Mar.*
> *Stanza 1*

Strike the tent! the sun has risen; not
  a vapor streaks the dawn,
And the frosty prairie brightens to the
  westward, far and wan.
> *The Bison Track. Stanza 1*

The violet loves a sunny bank,
  The cowslip loves the lea;
The scarlet creeper loves the elm,
  But I love — thee.
> *Proposal. Stanza 1*

Little one, come to my knee!
Hark how the rain is pouring
Over the roof, in the pitch-black night,
  And the wind in the woods a-roaring.
> *A Story for a Child [A Night*
> *with a Wolf]. Stanza 1*

Wolves in the forest, and bears in the
  bush,
  And I on my path belated.
> *Ibid. Stanza 3*

For every sentence uttered, a million
  more are dumb:
Men's lives are chains of chances, and
  History their sum.
> *Napoleon at Gotha. Stanza 1*

The world goes round: the sun sets on
  despair,

The morrow makes it hope. Each little life
Thinks the great axle of the universe
Turns on its fate, and finds impertinence
In joy or grief conflicting with its own.
Lars, A Pastoral of Norway.
Book I

The healing of the world
Is in its nameless saints. Each separate star
Seems nothing, but a myriad scattered stars
Break up the Night, and make it beautiful.
Ibid. Book III

Learn to live, and live to learn,
Ignorance like a fire doth burn,
Little tasks make large return.
To My Daughter. Stanza 1

WILLIAM WHITING
[1825–1878]

Eternal Father! strong to save,
Whose arm hath bound the restless wave,
Who bidd'st the mighty ocean deep
Its own appointed limits keep:
O, hear us when we cry to Thee
For those in peril on the sea!
Eternal Father, Strong to Save.
Stanza 1

FREDERICK TEMPLE HAMILTON BLACKWOOD, LORD DUFFERIN
[1826–1902]

In the market-place lay a dead dog.
Of the group gathered around it, one
said: "This carcass is disgusting." Another said, "The sight of it is torment."
Every man spoke in this strain. But
Jesus drew near and said, "Pearls are
not equal in whiteness to his teeth.
Look not on the failures of others and
the merits of thyself; cast thine eye on
thine own fault." [1]
Installation Address as Lord

[1] Then Jesus spake, and dropped on him the saving wreath:

Rector of St. Andrews University [*1891*]

GEORGE W. BUNGAY
[1826–1892]

In rituals and faith excel!
Chimed out the Episcopalian bell.
The Creeds of the Bells. Stanza 2
All is well! is well! is well!
Pealed out the good old Dutch church bell.
Ibid. Stanza 3
O swell! ye rising waters, swell!
Pealed out the clear-toned Baptist bell.
Ibid. Stanza 4
Do well!
Rang out the Unitarian bell.
Ibid. Stanza 5
Salvation's free, we tell! we tell!
Shouted the Methodistic bell.
Ibid. Stanza 6
No hell!
Rang out the Universalist bell.
Ibid. Stanza 7
All hail, ye saints, the chorus swell!
Chimed in the Roman Catholic bell.
Ibid. Stanza 10
Drink from the well!
In rapture rang the Temperance bell.
Ibid. Stanza 11
The merchant who for silk would sell
The cotton woven in,
Something that is not truth will tell,
And think it little sin.
The False and the True. Stanza 4

ROBERT BARRY COFFIN
[1826–1886]

I have ships that went to sea
More than fifty years ago:
None have yet come home to me,
But keep sailing to and fro.
Ships at Sea. Stanza 1

"Even pearls are dark before the whiteness of his teeth."
W. R. ALGER [1822–1905]: *Charity's Eye, St. 4* (translated from NIZAMI [1114–1203], a Persian poet)
"No pearl," said He, "from seas of the south
Is half so white as his pearly teeth."
KATHARINE TYNAN HINKSON [1861–1931]: *An Old Story*

So I never quite despair,
  Nor let hope or courage fail;
And some day when skies are fair,
  Up the bay my ship will sail.
              Ships at Sea. Stanza 4

DINAH MARIA MULOCK CRAIK
[1826–1887]

Two hands upon the breast,
  And labour's done; [1]
Two pale feet crossed in rest,
  The race is won.
              Now and Afterwards
Love that asketh love again
Finds the barter nought but pain;
Love that giveth in full store
Aye receives as much, and more.
              Love that Asketh Love Again
Two to the world for the world's work
  sake,
But each unto each, as in Thy sight,
  one.
              Plighted. Stanza 4
God rest ȳe, merry gentlemen! let
  nothing you dismay,
For Jesus Christ, our Saviour, was
  born on Christmas day.
              A Christmas Carol. Stanza 1
A friend stands at the door;
In either tight-closed hand
Hiding rich gifts, three hundred and
  three-score.
              A Psalm for New Year's Eve.
                           Stanza 1
Could ye come back to me, Douglas,
  Douglas!
In the old likeness that I knew,
I would be so faithful, so loving,
  Douglas,
Douglas, Douglas, tender and true!
              Douglas, Tender and True. [2]
                           Stanza 1
Oh, my son's my son till he gets him a
  wife,
But my daughter's my daughter all her
  life.
              Young and Old

[1] Two hands upon the breast, and labour is
past. — Russian proverb
[2] See Sir Richard Holland, page 9.

Oh, the comfort, the inexpressible
comfort of feeling safe with a person,
having neither to weigh thoughts nor
measure words, but pouring them all
right out, just as they are, chaff and
grain together; certain that a faithful
hand will take and sift them, keep what
is worth keeping, and then with the
breath of kindness blow the rest away.
              A Life for a Life [*1859*].
                           Page 169

STEPHEN COLLINS FOSTER
[1826–1864]

Old dog Tray's ever faithful;
  Grief can not drive him away;
He is gentle, he is kind —
  I'll never, never find
A better friend than old dog Tray!
              Old Dog Tray. [1] *Chorus*
The day goes by like a shadow o'er the
  heart,
  With sorrow where all was delight;
The time has come when the darkies
  have to part:
  Then my old Kentucky home, good
  night!
              My Old Kentucky Home. Stanza 2
Oh! darkies, how my heart grows
  weary,
  Far from the old folks at home.
              The Old Folks at Home. Chorus
'Tis the song, the sigh of the weary,
Hard times, come again no more.
              Hard Times Come Again No More
Where are the hearts once so happy and
  so free?
The children so dear that I held upon
  my knee?
Gone to the shore where my soul has
  longed to go,
I hear their gentle voices calling, "Old
  Black Joe!"
              Old Black Joe. Stanza 3
O, Susanna! O, don't you cry for me,
I've come from Alabama, wid my banjo
  on my knee.
              O, Susanna. Chorus

[1] I had always a friend in my poor dog
Tray.
THOMAS CAMPBELL: *The Harper, St. 3*

Gwine to run all night!
Gwine to run all day!
I'll bet my money on de bobtail nag —
Somebody bet on de bay.
Camptown Races
I dream of Jeanie with the light brown
hair,
Borne like a vapor on the summer
air;
I see her tripping where the bright
streams play,
Happy as the daisies that dance on
her way.
Jeanie with the Light Brown
Hair. Stanza 1
Beautiful dreamer, wake unto me,
Starlight and dewdrop are waiting for
thee;
Sounds of the rude world heard in the
day,
Lulled by the moonlight have all
passed away.
Beautiful Dreamer. Stanza 1

COATES KINNEY
[1826–1904]

What a bliss to press the pillow
Of a cottage-chamber bed
And to listen to the patter
Of the soft rain overhead!
Rain on the Roof. Stanza 1
That subdued, subduing strain
Which is played upon the shingles
By the patter of the rain.
Ibid. Stanza 6

LUCY LARCOM
[1826–1893]

Oh, her heart's adrift, with one
On an endless voyage gone!
Night and morning
Hannah's at the window binding shoes.
Hannah Binding Shoes. Stanza 2
I do not own an inch of land,
But all I see is mine.
A Strip of Blue
If the world seems cold to you,
Kindle fires to warm it!
Three Old Saws
If the world's a wilderness,
Go, build houses in it!
Ibid.

If the world's a vale of tears,
Smile, till rainbows span it!
Three Old Saws
There is light in shadow and shadow in
light,
And black in the blue of the sky.
Black in Blue Sky. Stanza 2
Though Augustine to his mother sailed
long since the death-wave o'er,
Still his word sweeps down the ages like
the surging of the sea:
"Bless Thee, Lord, that we are restless,
till we find our rest in Thee!"
Monica and Augustine. Stanza 16
When for me the silent oar
Parts the Silent River,
And I stand upon the shore
Of the strange Forever,
Shall I miss the loved and known?
Shall I vainly seek mine own?
Across the River

WILLIAM HAINES LYTLE
[1826–1863]

I am dying, Egypt, dying! [1]
Ebbs the crimson life-tide fast,
And the dark Piutonian shadows [2]
Gather on the evening blast.
Antony to Cleopatra. Stanza 1

HORATIO NELSON POWERS
[1826–1890]

A flower unblown; a book unread;
A tree with fruit unharvested;
A path untrod; a house whose rooms
Lack yet the heart's divine perfumes;
A landscape whose wide border lies
In silent shade 'neath silent skies;
A wondrous fountain yet unsealed;
A casket with its gifts concealed —
This is the Year that for you waits
Beyond to-morrow's mystic gates.
The New Year

[1] See Shakespeare, page 105.
[2] Night's Plutonian shore. — E. A. POE:
The Raven
See Joaquin Miller, page 658.

MARY B. C. SLADE
[1826–1882]

Dame Margery said, "Ah! don't you
  know
If last year's blossoms stay,
The next year's blooms will fail to grow
  Till these are broken away?
For this year's lilacs cannot live
  With seeds of last year's spring."
Ma'am Allison learned that she must
  give,
  If she would have a thing.
Lilacs. Stanza 5

ETHEL LYNN BEERS
[1827–1879]

All quiet along the Potomac to-night,
  No sound save the rush of the river,
While soft falls the dew on the face of
  the dead, —
  The picket's off duty forever.
The Picket Guard.[1] *Stanza 6*

The flag's come back to Tennessee.
On the Shores of Tennessee.
Stanza 9

Where are the dear, old-fashioned
  posies,
Quaint in form and bright in hue,
Such as grandma gave her lovers
  When she walked the garden
  through?
Old-Fashioned Flowers. Stanza 1

Will the modern florist's triumph
  Look so fair or smell so sweet?
Ibid. Stanza 9

How many pounds does the baby
  weigh —
  Baby who came a month ago?
How many pounds from the crowning
  curl
  To the rosy point of the restless toe?
Weighing the Baby. Stanza 1

[1] *Harper's Weekly, Sept. 30, 1861.*

EDWARD STUYVESANT
BRAGG
[1827–1912]

They love him most for the enemies
he has made.[1]
Speech seconding the nomina-
tion of Grover Cleveland for
the Presidency, Democratic
National Convention, Chicago
[July 9, 1884]

ANSON GLEASON CHESTER
[1827–1911]

Let us take to our hearts a lesson —
  no lesson can braver be —
From the ways of the tapestry weavers
  on the other side of the sea.
The Tapestry Weavers. Stanza 1

He works on the wrong side evermore,
  but works for the right side ever.
Ibid. Stanza 3

MORTIMER COLLINS
[1827–1876]

Just take a trifling handful, O philos-
  opher!
Of magic matter: give it a slight toss
  over
  The ambient ether — and I don't
  see why
  You shouldn't make a sky.
Sky-Making (To Professor
(Tyndall)

There was an Ape in the days that were
  earlier;
Centuries passed, and his hair became
  curlier;
Centuries more gave a thumb to his
  wrist —
Then he was Man — and a Positivist.
The Positivists

Life and the Universe show spontaneity;
Down with ridiculous notions of Deity!
  Churches and creeds are lost in the
  mists;

[1] An adaptation of Governor Bragg's expression became a Cleveland campaign slogan:
"We love him for the enemies he has made."

Truth must be sought with the Positivists.

The Positivists

Then the oars of Ithaca dip so
  Silently into the sea
That they wake not sad Calypso,
  And the Hero wanders free:
He breasts the ocean-furrows,
  At war with the words of Fate,
And the blue tide's low susurrus
  Comes up to the Ivory Gate.[1]

The Ivory Gate. Stanza 2

A man is as old as he's feeling,
A woman as old as she looks.

How Old Are You?

ROSE TERRY COOKE
[1827–1892]

Yet courage, soul! nor hold thy
    strength in vain,
  In hope o'ercome the steeps God set
    for thee;
For past the Alpine summits of great
    pain,
  Lieth thine Italy.[2]

Beyond. Stanza 4

Ah! cruel records keeps the earth
On her broad bosom sleeping;
Her face is writ with scars of woe,
Her blossoms wet with weeping.
The loveliest spot she hath may be
Some lonely soul's Gethsemane.[3]

A Memory. Stanza 6

Three things never come again. . . .
Never to the bow that bends
Comes the arrow that it sends. . . .
Never comes the chance that passed,
That one moment was its last. . . .
Never shall thy spoken word
Be again unsaid, unheard.

Unreturning

---

[1] And through the iv'ry gate the vision flies.
  Pope: *The Dunciad, Book III, L. 340*
[2] Hannibal, encouraging his men: Quarum
alterum latus Italiae sit.
  Livy: *Ab Urbe Condita Libri, XXI, 30, 5*
[3] All paths that have been or shall be,
  Pass somewhere through Gethsemane.
  Ella Wheeler Wilcox: *Gethsemane, St. 3*

LIZZIE DOTEN
[1827–1913]

John and Peter, and Robert and Paul,
God in His wisdom created them all.

The Chemistry of Character.
Stanza 1

Out of Earth's elements, mingled with
    flame,
Out of Life's compound of glory and
    shame,
Fashioned and shaped by no will of
    their own,
And helplessly into life's history
    thrown.

Ibid. Stanza 2

God of the granite and the rose!
  Soul of the sparrow and the bee!
The mighty tide of being flows
  Through countless channels, Lord,
    to thee.

Reconciliation. Stanza 1

CHARLES B. FAIRBANKS
("AGUECHEEK")
[1827–1859]

I have a profound respect for the sea
as a moral teacher. No man can be
tossed about upon it without feeling
his impotence and insignificance.

My Unknown Chum. A Passage
Across the Atlantic, Page 10

Cleanliness is a great virtue; but
when it is carried to such an extent that
you cannot find your books and papers
which you left carefully arranged on
your table — when it gets to be a monomania with man or woman — it becomes a bore.

Ibid. Antwerp and Brussels,
Page 36

Buildings are the books that everybody unconsciously reads; and if they
are a libel on the laws of architecture,
they will surely vitiate in time the taste
of those who become familiarized to
their deformity.[1]

Ibid. Page 38

---

[1] Architecture is an art for all men to learn,
because all are concerned with it. — Ruskin:
Architecture and Painting [Edinburgh, November, 1853], *Lecture 1*

A book is to me like a hat or coat — a very uncomfortable thing until the newness has been worn off.

My Unknown Chum. Genoa and Florence, Page 56

Art is the surest and safest civilizer. . . . Open your galleries of art to the people, and you confer on them a greater benefit than mere book education; you give them a refinement to which they would otherwise be strangers.

Ibid. Paris, Page 139

Slander, like Death, loves a shining mark.

Ibid. Napoleon the Third, Page 159

Foreign travel ought to soften prejudices, religious or political, and liberalize a man's mind; but how many there are who seem to have travelled for the purpose of getting up their rancour against all that is opposed to their notions.

Ibid. The Philosophy of Foreign Travel, Page 165

Nine-tenths of all the fine things in our literature concerning the charms of country life, have been written, not beneath the shade of over-arching boughs, but within the crowded city's smoke-stained walls.

Ibid. Paris to Boulogne, Page 181

The genuine human boy may, I think, safely be set down as the noblest work of God. . . . There is a generous instinct in boys which is far more trustworthy than those sliding, and unreliable, and deceptive ideas which we call settled principles.

Ibid. Boyhood and Boys, Page 294

The sewing-circle — the Protestant confessional, where each one confesses, not her own sins, but the sins of her neighbors.

Ibid. Memorials of Mrs. Grundy, Page 336

FRANCIS MILES FINCH
[1827–1907]

These in the robings of glory,
Those in the gloom of defeat,

All with the battle-blood gory,
In the dusk of eternity meet:
Under the sod and the dew,
Waiting the judgment-day;
Under the laurel, the Blue,
Under the willow, the Gray.

The Blue and the Gray. Stanza 2

To drum-beat and heart-beat
A soldier marches by;
There is color in his cheek,
There is courage in his eye.

Nathan Hale.[1] Stanza 1

CHARLES ELIOT NORTON
[1827–1908]

It is perhaps the highest distinction of the Greeks that they recognized the indissoluble connection of beauty and goodness.

Fifth Annual Report [1883–84] of the Executive Committee of the Archaeological Institute of America. Page 28

I think that a knowledge of Greek thought and life, and of the arts in which the Greeks expressed their thought and sentiment, essential to high culture. A man may know everything else, but without this knowledge he remains ignorant of the best intellectual and moral achievements of his own race.

Letter to F. A. Tupper [1885][2]

The artistic temperament is not a national trait of the English race. Our complex and exciting civilization has, indeed, developed, especially in America, a sensitiveness of nervous organization which often wears the semblance of the artistic temperament, and shows itself in manual dexterity and refined technical skill. And this tends to make mere workmanship, mere excellence of

---

[1] Nathan Hale [1755–1776], whose last words were: "I only regret that I have but one life to lose for my country."

The tranquil and intrepid soul
Who died for us amid the death-drum's roll.
CHESTER FIRKINS [1882–1915]:
Nathan Hale

[2] In the *Harvard Alumni Bulletin, 1927,* P. 258.

execution, the common test of merit in a work of the fine arts.

A Definition of the Fine Arts [1]

Is there a moral advance at all in proportion to the material? There is a wider diffusion of virtue, morality has become democratic, more men and women are controlled by right principles, but better men and even women than there were two thousand years ago are not easy to find.

Letter to Samuel G. Ward
[August 8, 1900]

The refuge from pessimism is the good men and women at any time existing in the world, — they keep faith and happiness alive.

Letter to Moorfield Storey
[August 29, 1903]

Whatever your occupation may be and however crowded your hours with affairs, do not fail to secure at least a few minutes every day for refreshment of your inner life with a bit of poetry.[2]

Used by a Boston newspaper as a heading for a column of reprinted poems

JOHN TOWNSEND TROWBRIDGE
[1827–1916]

For me the diamond dawns are set
  In rings of beauty,
And all my ways are dewy wet
  With pleasant duty.
Service

Darius was clearly of the opinion
That the air is also man's dominion,
And that, with paddle or fins or pinion,
  We soon or late
  Shall navigate
The azure, as now we sail the sea.
Darius Green and His Flying Machine

Of nothing comes nothing: springs rise not above
  Their source in the far-hidden heart of the mountains:
Whence then have descended the Wisdom and Love

That in man leap to light in intelligent fountains?
The Missing Leaf

Men are polished, through act and speech,
  Each by each,
As pebbles are smoothed on the rolling beach.
A Home Idyl

Over the hill the farm-boy goes,
His shadow lengthens along the land,
A giant staff in a giant hand.
Evening at the Farm. Stanza 1

We are two travelers, Roger and I.
Roger's my dog: — come here, you scamp!
The Vagabonds. Stanza 1

Mark Haley drives along the street,
Perched high upon his wagon-seat;
His sombre face the storm defies,
And thus from morn till eve he cries, —
  "Charco'! Charco'!"
While echo faint and far replies, —
  "Hark, O! Hark, O!"
The Charcoal Man. Stanza 1

We broke the oar and the boat went down,
And so the messenger chanced to drown;
The messenger lost, we lost the town;
And the loss of the town has cost a crown;
And all these things are trifles! [1]
How the King Lost His Crown

If you will observe, it doesn't take
A man of giant mould to make
A giant shadow on the wall;
And he who in our daily sight
Seems but a figure mean and small,
Outlined in Fame's illusive light,
May stalk, a silhouette sublime,
Across the canvas of his time.
Authors' Night

Our days, our deeds, all we achieve or are,
Lay folded in our infancy; the things
  Of good or ill we choose while yet unborn.
Nativity

---

[1] In *The Forum, March, 1889.*
[2] See Oscar Wilde, page 723.

[1] See George Herbert, page 137, and Benjamin Franklin, page 227.

Not in rewards, but in the strength to
  strive,
  The blessing lies.
             Two-score and Ten
I keep some portion of my early gleam;
  Brokenly bright, like moonbeams on
    a river,
It lights my life, a far illusive dream,
  Moves as I move, and leads me on
    forever.
                     Ibid.
The all-enclosing freehold of Content.
                  Guy Vernon
With years a richer life begins,
  The spirit mellows:
Ripe age gives tone to violins,
  Wine, and good fellows.
               Three Worlds
Heroic soul, in homely garb half hid,
  Sincere, sagacious, melancholy,
    quaint,
What he endured, no less than what he
  did,
  Has reared his monument and
    crowned him saint.
             Abraham Lincoln

SEPTIMUS WINNER
("ALICE HAWTHORNE")
[1827–1902]

When the charms of spring awaken,
And the mocking-bird is singing on the
  bough,
I feel like one forsaken,
Since my Hallie is no longer with me
  now.
       Listen to the Mocking-Bird.
                   Stanza 3

WILLIAM ALLINGHAM
[1828–1889]

Up the airy mountain,
  Down the rushy glen,
We daren't go a-hunting
  For fear of little men.
        The Fairies. Stanza 1
Robin's here in coat of brown,
And scarlet breast-knot gay.
      Robin Redbreast. Stanza 1
No funeral gloom, my dears, when I am
  gone,

Corpse-gazings, tears, black raiment,
  graveyard grimness;
Yours still, you mine, remember all the
  best
Of our past moments, and forget the
  rest,
And so, to where I wait, come gently
  on.[1]
    Quoted on Page 388 of William
    Allingham: A Diary, edited
    [1907] by his widow, HELEN
    ALLINGHAM, *and* DOLLIE RAD-
    FORD

ROBERT BARNABAS
BROUGH
[1828–1860]

My Lord Tomnoddy is thirty-four;
The Earl can last but a few years more.
My Lord in the Peers will take his
  place:
Her Majesty's councils his words will
  grace.
Office he'll hold and patronage sway;
Fortunes and lives he will vote away;
And what are his qualifications? —
  ONE!
He's the Earl of Fitzdotterel's eldest
  son.
        My Lord Tomnoddy[2]
Christians were on the earth ere Christ
  was born. . . .
Thousands of years ago men dared to
  die
Loving their enemies — and wondered
  why!
         An Early Christian

ELIZABETH RUNDLE
CHARLES
[1828–1896]

Go make thy garden fair as thou canst,
  Thou workest never alone;
Perchance he whose plot is next to
  thine
  Will see it, and mend his own.
       The Child on the Judgment
               Seat. Stanza 16

---

[1] Found in Ellen Terry's handwriting on
the fly-leaf of *Imitation of Christ* by Thomas
à Kempis, and at first attributed to her.
[2] See Barham, page 350.

To know how to say what others only know how to think is what makes men poets or sages; and to dare to say what others only dare to think makes men martyrs or reformers or both.

Chronicles of the Schönberg-Cotta Family

GERALD MASSEY
[1828–1907]

In this dim world of clouding cares,
  We rarely know, till wildered eyes
  See white wings lessening up the
    skies,
The angels with us unawares.
Babe Cristabel

Where our vanguard camps To-day
Our rear shall march To-morrow.
To-day and To-morrow

Not by appointment do we meet Delight
And Joy; they heed not our expectancy;
But round some corner in the streets of life,
They, on a sudden, clasp us with a smile.
The Bridegroom of Beauty

GEORGE MEREDITH
[1828–1913]

Bury thy sorrows, and they shall rise
As souls to the immortal skies,
And there look down like mothers' eyes.
Sorrows and Joys. Stanza 1

Hearty faith and honest cheer
Welcome in the sweet o' the year.
The Sweet o' the Year

All wisdom's armory this man could wield.
The Sage Enamored

How much we gain who make no claims.
Ibid.

Life is but the pebble sunk;
Deeds, the circle growing!
The Head of Bran the Blest. IV, Stanza 4

Not till the fire is dying in the grate,
Look we for any kinship with the stars.
Oh, wisdom never comes when it is gold,

And the great price we pay for it full worth;
We have it only when we are half earth.
Little avails that coinage to the old!
Modern Love. IV

And if I drink oblivion of a day,
So shorten I the stature of my soul.
Ibid. XII

The actors are, it seems, the usual three:
Husband, and wife, and lover.
Ibid. XXV

How many a thing which we cast to the ground,
When others pick it up becomes a gem! [1]
Ibid. XLI

  In tragic life, Got wot,
No villain need be! Passions spin the plot:
We are betrayed by what is false within.
Ibid. XLIII

Ah, what a dusty answer gets the soul
When hot for certainties in this our life!
Ibid. L

  See ye not, Courtesy
  Is the true Alchemy,
Turning to gold all it touches and tries?
The Song of Courtesy. IV

The old hound wags his shaggy tail,
  And I know what he would say:
It's over the hills we'll bound, old hound,
  Over the hills, and away.
Over the Hills

I've studied men from my topsy-turvy
Close, and, I reckon, rather true.
Some are fine fellows: some, right scurvy:
Most, a dash between the two.
Juggling Jerry. VII

Two of a trade, lass, never agree. [2]
Ibid. IX

---

[1] Once in a golden hour
    I cast to earth a seed.
  Up there came a flower,
    The people said, a weed.
            TENNYSON: *The Flower*
[2] But two of a trade, one always hears, might get in each other's way,

Women are such expensive things.
> *The Beggar's Soliloquy. I*

The mountains Britain boasts are men.
> *The Patriot Engineer. Stanza 14*

Into the breast that gives the rose
Shall I with shuddering fall?
> *The Spirit of Earth in Autumn.*
> *Stanza 11*

Earth knows no desolation.
She smells regeneration
In the moist breath of decay.
> *Ibid. Stanza 14*

Around the ancient track marched, rank
on rank,
The army of unalterable law.
> *Lucifer in Starlight*

Earth has got him whom God gave,
Earth may sing, and earth shall smart!
None of earth shall know his grave.
They that dig with Death depart.
Attila, my Attila.
> *The Nuptials of Attila. Stanza 27*

Full lasting is the song, though he,
The singer, passes.
> *The Thrush in February. Stanza 17*

She whom I love is hard to catch and
conquer,
Hard, but O the glory of the winning
were she won!
> *Love in the Valley. Stanza 2*

Darker grows the valley, more and
more forgetting:
So were it with me if forgetting could
be willed.
Tell the grassy hollow that holds the
bubbling well-spring,
Tell it to forget the source that keeps
it filled.
> *Ibid. Stanza 5*

Love that so desires would fain keep
her changeless;
Fain would fling the net, and fain have
her free.
> *Ibid. Stanza 6*

But O the truth, the truth! the many
eyes
That look on it! the diverse things they
see.
> *A Ballad of Fair Ladies in Revolt.*
> *Stanza 16*

And you might be wanting to sing, God
wot, when I desired to play.
MARGARET WIDDEMER: *Warning, St. 3*

With patient inattention hear him
prate.
> *Bellerophon. Stanza 4*

When we have thrown off this old suit,
So much in need of mending,
To sink among the naked mute,
Is that, think you, our ending?
> *The Question Whither. Stanza 1*

Believe not that all living seed
Must flower above the surface.
> *Ibid.*

We have seen mighty men ballooning
high,
And in another moment bump the
ground.
He falls; and in his measurement is
found
To count some inches o'er the common fry.
> *The Warning*

If that thou hast the gift of strength,
then know
Thy part is to uplift the trodden low;
Else in a giant's grasp until the end
A hopeless wrestler shall thy soul con-
tend.
> *The Burden of Strength*

Who call her Mother and who calls her
Wife
Look on her grave and see not Death
but Life.
> *Epitaph: Marie Meredith*

Our life is but a little holding, lent
To do a mighty labour: we are one
With heaven and the stars when it is
spent
To serve God's aim: else die we with
the sun.
> *The Opera of Camilla*
> *(from Vittoria)*

Thence had he the laugh . . .
Broad as ten thousand beeves
At pasture
> *The Spirit of Shakespeare*

Civil limitation daunts
His utterance never; the nymphs blush,
not he.
> *An Orson of the Muse*
> *[Walt Whitman]*

Cannon his name,
Cannon his voice, he came.
> *Napoleon. I*

For Order's cause he laboured, as in-
    cl:ned
A soldier's training and his Euclid
    mind. . . .
That creature, woman, was the sofa
    soft,
When warriors their dusty armour
    doffed,
And read their manuals for the mak-
    ing truce
With rosy frailties framed to repro-
    duce.
                            Napoleon. IX

Evermore shall tyrant Force
Beget the greater for its overthrow.
                            Ibid. XIII

Seen like some rare treasure-galleon
Hull down, with masts against the
    Western hues.
                            Ibid.

For iron Winter held her firm;
Across her sky he laid his hand;
And bird he starved, he stiffened worm;
A sightless heaven, a shaven land.
                            Tardy Spring

Now the North wind ceases,
The warm South-west awakes,
The heavens are out in fleeces,
And earth's green banner shakes.
                            Ibid.

Days, when the ball of our vision
Had eagles that flew unabashed to sun;
When the grasp on the bow was de-
    cision,
And arrow and hand and eye were one;
When the Pleasures, like waves to a
    swimmer,
Came heaving for rapture ahead! —
Invoke them, they dwindle, they glim-
    mer
As lights over mounds of the dead.
                    Ode to Youth in Memory

Sword of Common Sense! . . .
Bright, nimble of the marrow-nerve
To wield thy double edge, retort
Or hold the deadlier reserve.
                    Ode to the Comic Spirit

A witty woman is a treasure; a witty
beauty is a power.
                Diana of the Crossways. Chap. 1

The well of true wit is truth itself.
                            Ibid.

Ireland gives England her soldiers,
her generals too.
                Diana of the Crossways. Chap. 2

The sun is coming down to earth,
and the fields and the waters shout to
him golden shouts.
                The Ordeal of Richard Feverel.
                            Chap. 19

ARTHUR JOSEPH MUNBY
[1828–1910]

Thou art my own, my darling, and my
    wife;
And when we pass into another life,
Still thou art mine. All this which now
    we see
Is but the childhood of Eternity.
                            Marriage

One may go first, and one remain
    To hail a second call;
But nothing now can make us twain,
    Whatever may befall.
            In Eternum, Domine. Stanza 4

FITZ-JAMES O'BRIEN
[1828–1862]

The enchanted circle of the Upper Ten.[1]
            The Diamond Lens.[2] Chap. 2

It was of a famous vintage, that of
1848, a year when war and wine throve
together.
                            Ibid. Chap. 4

I know a lake where the cool waves
    break
    And softly fall on the silver sand:
And no steps intrude on that solitude,
    No voice, save mine, disturbs the
    strand.
                        Loch Ine. Stanza 1

And so the crew went one by one,
    Some with gladness, and few with
    fear —
Cold and hardship such work had done
    That few seemed frightened when
    death was near.
Thus every soul on board went down —
    Sailor and passenger, little and great;
The last that sank was a man of my
    town,

[1] See Haliburton, page 387.
[2] In *The Atlantic Monthly, January, 1858.*

A capital swimmer — the second mate.
The Second Mate. Stanza 9

DANTE GABRIEL ROSSETTI
[1828–1882]

The blessed damozel leaned out
From the gold bar of Heaven:
Her eyes were deeper than the depth
Of waters stilled at even;
She had three lilies in her hand,
And the stars in her hair were seven.
The Blessed Damozel. Stanza 1

And the souls mounting up to God
Went by her like thin flames.
Ibid. Stanza 7

If God in His wisdom have brought close
The day when I must die,
That day by water or fire or air
My feet shall fall in the destined snare
Wherever my road may lie.
The King's Tragedy. Stanza 50

I have been here before,
But when or how I can not tell;
I know the grass beyond the door,
The sweet keen smell,
The sighing sound, the lights around the shore.
Sudden Light. Stanza 1

Still we say as we go, —
"Strange to think by the way,
Whatever there is to know,
That shall we know one day."
The Cloud Confines. Stanza 1

Gather a shell from the strown beach
And listen at its lips: [1] they sigh
The same desire and mystery,
The echo of the whole sea's speech.
The Sea Limits. Stanza 4

Was it a friend or foe that spread these lies?
Nay, who but infants question in such wise,
'Twas one of my most intimate enemies.
Fragment

This King never smiled again.[2]
The White Ship

[1] See F. D. Gage, page 446.
[2] See F. D. Hemans, page 371.

A Sonnet is a moment's monument, —
Memorial from the Soul's eternity
To one dead deathless hour.
The House of Life. Proem

And though thy soul sail leagues and leagues beyond, —
Still, leagues beyond those leagues, there is more sea.
Ibid. 73, The Choice, III

Look in my face: my name is Might-have-been;
I am also called No-more, Too-late, Farewell.
Ibid. 97, A Superscription

GEORGE WALTER THORNBURY
[1828–1876]

Man's life is but a jest,
A dream, a shadow, bubble, air, a vapor at the best.[1]
The Jester's Sermon

The fool that eats till he is sick must fast till he is well.
Ibid.

Get out the hounds; I'm well to-night, and young again and sound;
I'll have a run once more before they put me underground:
They brought my father home feet first, and it never shall be said
That his son Joe, who rode so straight, died quietly in his bed.
The Death of th' Owd Squire

GEORGE WILLIAM CHILDS
[1829–1894]

Do not keep the alabaster boxes of your love and tenderness sealed up until your friends are dead. Fill their lives with sweetness. Speak approving, cheering words while their ears can hear

[1] Life is a jest, and all things show it;
I thought so once, but now I know it.
JOHN GAY: *My Own Epitaph*
Life is an empty dream. — ROBERT BROWNING: *Paracelsus, II*
Life seems a jest of Fate's contriving.
LOWELL: *Harvard Commemoration Ode, IV*
Life is mostly froth and bubble.
A. L. GORDON: *Ye Wearie Wayfarer*

them, and while their hearts can be thrilled and made happier by them.

A Creed

I would rather have a plain coffin without a flower, a funeral without a eulogy, than a life without the sweetness of love and sympathy. Let us learn to anoint our friends beforehand for their burial. Post-mortem kindness does not cheer the burdened spirit. Flowers on the coffin cast no fragrance backward over the weary way.

Ibid.

ROSCOE CONKLING
[1829–1888]

He will hew to the line of right, let the chips fall where they may.

Speech nominating General Grant for a third term, National Republican Convention, Chicago [June 5, 1880]

CHARLES GRAHAM HALPINE ("MILES O'REILLY")
[1829–1868]

Old pipe, now battered, bruised, and brown,
  With silver spliced and linked together,
With hopes high up and spirits down
I've puffed thee in all kinds of weather.

My Broken Meerschaum. Stanza 1

If Christ again should visit earth,
  A man of toil and care,
Howe'er divine, whate'er his worth,
  How, think you, would he fare?

A Dollar in His Pouch. Stanza 5

And if asked what state he hails from,
  This our sole reply shall be,
"From near Appomattox Court-house,
  With its famous apple-tree."[1]

A Bumper to Grant. Stanza 8

Brain and heart
Alike depart
From him who worships gin or brandy.

Holland Gin. Stanza 3

[1] Quoted by Roscoe Conkling, campaign manager for U. S. Grant, in a speech nominating Grant for the Presidency, Republican Convention [June, 1880]

A paragraph to make one laugh
Should be of ten lines just a half;
A trivial theme — a brilliant stream
Of verbiage, metaphor, and dream.

*General Orders of the Citizen.
Stanza 1*

There's never a bond, old friend, like this, —
We have drunk from the same canteen![1]

The Canteen. Stanza 1

Gayly the *Post* of the plot may make light,
And talk of the "Tooley Street tailors."[2]

*The Night Ride of Ancient Abe.
Stanza 7*

So don't despise the little things
  Which happen daily round us,
For some of them may chance take wings
  To startle and astound us.
Trace back the greatest deed — it springs
From trifles which no poet sings.

*A Little Rhyme of Little Things.
Stanza 5*

The constellation of O'Ryan, ignorantly and falsely spelled Orion.

Subtitle of poem, Irish Astronomy

JOSEPH JEFFERSON
[1829–1905]

Are we to blame for being caterpillars?
Will the same God that doomed us crawl the earth
A prey to every bird that's given birth,
Forgive our captor as he eats and sings,
And damn poor us because we have not wings?

Immortality[3]

[1] But it's lemonade of a watery grade
That they drink from the same canteen.
    EUGENE FIELD: *From the Same Canteen, St. 3*
[2] In the early seventeenth century a petition of protest against some taxation was sent to Parliament, commencing: "We, the People of England." There were nine signers, all discovered to be tailors on Tooley Street, on the south side of the Thames, near London Bridge. Hence, "It comes from the nine tailors of Tooley Street" has come to mean a protest of small importance.
[3] In *The New York Tribune* [1905].

I won't count this time.
Dramatization of Rip Van Winkle

Are we so soon forgot?
                                        Ibid.

God bless the little church around the
    corner.[1]

GUY HUMPHRIES McMASTER
[1829–1887]

In their ragged regimentals,
Stood the old Continentals,
    Yielding not,
While the grenadiers were lunging,
And like hail fell the plunging
    Cannon-shot.
    Carmen Bellicosum.[2] Stanza 1

And the villainous saltpeter
Rang a fierce, discordant meter.
                            Ibid. Stanza 3

JOHN HUGH McNAUGHTON
[1829–1891]

Soon beyond the harbor bar,
Shall my bark be sailing far, —
O'er the world I wander lone,
    Sweet Belle Mahone.
            Belle Mahone. Stanza 1

No stone marks the sod o'er my lad so
    brave and true,
In his lonely grave he sleeps, in his
    faded coat of blue.
    The Faded Coat of Blue. Stanza 5

The epochs in our lives are three:
And here we grope in rifts between
The Is, the Was, the Might Have Been.
                            Onnalinda

[1] Said after the death of George Holland, a well-loved old actor, in December 1870. A certain rector declined to hold the funeral in his church and recommended Jefferson to "A little church around the corner." This was the Church of the Transfiguration, East 29th Street, New York, popularly known ever since by that term of affection. See *The Little Church Around the Corner*, by GEORGE MAC-ADAM (1925).

[2] In the *Knickerbocker Magazine* [1849].

SILAS WEIR MITCHELL [1]
[1829–1914]

Up anchor! Up anchor!
    Set sail and away!
The ventures of dreamland
    Are thine for a day.
                            Dreamland

Death's but one more to-morrow.
        *Of One Who Seemed to Have
                                    Failed*

Ave materna,
Loving and wise,
The light of the ages
Is bright in thy eyes.
        *The University of Pennsylvania.
                                Stanza 1*

When youth as lord of my unchallenged
    fate,[2]
And time seemed but the vassal of my
    will,
I entertained certain guests of state —
The great of older days.
        *On a Boy's First Reading of
                "King Henry V"*

There is no dearer lover of lost hours
            Than I.
I can be idler than the idlest flowers,
            More idly lie.
                            Idleness

Show me his friends and I the man
    shall know;
This wiser turn a larger wisdom lends:
Show me the books he loves and I shall
    know
The man far better than through mor-
    tal friends.
        Books and the Man.[3] Stanza 1

[1] We have to go to other centuries to find a parallel to his career, not, it is true, in professional work — for others have done more — but in the combination of a life devoted to the best interests of science with literary and social distinction.
    WILLIAM OSLER: *Obituary of Dr. Mitchell* in *British Medical Journal*, quoted in CUSHING: *Life of Sir William Osler*, Vol. II, Chap. 34, P. 393.
[2] I am the master of my fate.
    W. E. HENLEY: *To R.T.H.B. [Invictus]*
[3] Read at the farewell dinner given by the Charaka Club to Dr. William Osler [March 4, [1905], quoted in CUSHING: *Life of Sir William Osler, Vol. I, Chap. 24, P. 673.*

Good night! No night is good for me
That does not hold a thought of thee.
Good Night. Stanza 1

I know the night is near at hand.
The mists lie low on hill and bay,
The autumn sheaves are dewless, dry;
But I have had the day.
Vesperal. Stanza 1

The first thing to be done by a biographer in estimating character is to examine the stubs of the victim's cheque-books.

Quoted in CUSHING: *Life of Sir William Osler. Vol. I, Chap. 21, Page 583*

JOSHUA DAVENPORT ROBIN-SON
[1829–1866]

I shall see his toys and his empty chair,
And the horse he used to ride,
And they will speak with a silent speech
Of the little boy that died.
*The Little Boy that Died.
Stanza 3*

CARL SCHURZ
[1829–1906]

Ideals are like stars; you will not succeed in touching them with your hands. But like the seafaring man on the desert of waters, you choose them as your guides, and following them you will reach your destiny.
*Address, Faneuil Hall, Boston
[April 18, 1859]*

You are underrating the President [Lincoln]. I grant that he lacks higher education and his manners are not in accord with European conceptions of the dignity of a chief magistrate. He is a well-developed child of nature and is not skilled in polite phrases and poses. But he is a man of profound feeling, correct and firm principles and incorruptible honesty. His motives are unquestionable, and he possesses to a remarkable degree the characteristic,

God-given trait of this people, sound common sense.
*Letter to Theodore Petrasch
[October, 1864]*

Our country, right or wrong.[1] When right, to be kept right; when wrong, to be put right.
Address in Congress [1872]

HERBERT SPENCER
[1829–1903]

We too often forget that not only is there "a soul of goodness in things evil."[2] but very generally a soul of truth in things erroneous.
First Principles

The fact disclosed by a survey of the past that majorities have been wrong must not blind us to the complementary fact that majorities have usually not been entirely wrong.
Ibid.

Volumes might be written upon the impiety of the pious.
Ibid.

We have unmistakable proof that throughout all past time, there has been a ceaseless devouring of the weak by the strong.
Ibid.

Survival of the fittest.
Ibid.

With a higher moral nature will come a restriction on the multiplication of the inferior.
Ibid.

Architecture, sculpture, painting, music, and poetry, may truly be called the efflorescence of civilized life.
Essays on Education. Education: What Knowledge is of Most Worth?

Every cause produces more than one effect.
Ibid. On Progress: Its Law and Cause

---

[1] See Churchill, page 262.
[2] There is some soul of goodness in things evil,
Would men observingly distil it out.
SHAKESPEARE: *King Henry V,
Act IV, Sc. 1, L. 4*

The tyranny of Mrs. Grundy [1] is worse than any other tyranny we suffer under.

Essays on Education. On Progress: On Manners and Fashion

Old forms of government finally grow so oppressive that they must be thrown off even at the risk of reigns of terror.

Ibid.

Music must take rank as the highest of the fine arts — as the one which, more than any other, ministers to human welfare.

Ibid. On the Origin and Function of Music

Evil perpetually tends to disappear. [2]

The Evanescence of Evil

Morality knows nothing of geographical boundaries or distinctions of race.

Ibid.

No one can be perfectly free till all are free; no one can be perfectly moral till all are moral; no one can be perfectly happy till all are happy.

Ibid.

The Republican form of government is the highest form of government: [3] but because of this it requires the highest type of human nature — a type nowhere at present existing.

The Americans

The ultimate result of shielding men from the effects of folly is to fill the world with fools.

State Tamperings with Money Banks

If a single cell, under appropriate conditions, becomes a man in the space of a few years, there can surely be no difficulty in understanding how, under appropriate conditions, a cell may, in the course of untold millions of years, give origin to the human race. [4]

Principles of Biology

[1] See Morton, page 290.
[2] See Walt Whitman, page 536.
[3] A monarchy is a merchantman, which sails well, but will sometimes strike on a rock and go to the bottom; while a republic is a raft, which would never sink, but then your feet are always in water. — FISHER AMES [1758–1808], quoted by R. W. EMERSON in *Politics*
[4] As nine months go to the shaping an infant ripe for his birth,

HIRAM LADD SPENCER
[1829–1915]

O where will be the birds that sing,
  A hundred years to come?
    A Hundred Years to Come. [1]
        Stanza 1

But other men our lands will till,
And others then our streets will fill,
While other birds will sing as gay,
As bright the sunshine as to-day.
        Ibid. Stanza 3

HENRY TIMROD
[1829–1867]

Spring, with that nameless pathos in the air
Which dwells with all things fair,
Spring, with her golden suns and silver rain,
Is with us once again.
        Spring. Stanza 1

There is no holier spot of ground
Than where defeated valor lies,
By mourning beauty crowned!
        Ode, Decorating the Graves of the Confederate Dead, Magnolia Cemetery, Charleston, South Carolina, 1867. Stanza 5

Most men know love but as a part of life;
They hide it in some corner of the breast,
Even from themselves.
        Sonnet

Spring is a true reconstructionist.
        Spring's Lessons

CHARLES DUDLEY WARNER
[1829–1900]

To own a bit of ground, to scratch it with a hoe, to plant seeds, and watch the renewal of life, — this is the com-

So many a million of ages have gone to the making of man.
TENNYSON: *Maud, Part I, IV, St. 6*
[1] Published anonymously in *The Voice of Freedom,* Brandon, Vermont, of which William Goldsmith Brown [1812–1905], who also wrote verse, was assistant editor. Spencer's poem was therefore attributed to Brown.

monest delight of the race, the most satisfactory thing a man can do.
My Summer in a Garden.
Preliminary

Broad acres are a patent of nobility; and no man but feels more of a man in the world if he have a bit of ground that he can call his own. However small it is on the surface, it is four thousand miles deep; and that is a very handsome property.
Ibid.

What a man needs in gardening is a cast-iron back, with a hinge in it.
Ibid. Third Week

Lettuce is like conversation: it must be fresh and crisp, so sparkling that you scarcely notice the bitter in it.
Ibid. Ninth Week

If you wish to save men from any particular vice, set up a tremendous cry of warning about some other, and they will all give their special efforts to the one to which attention is called.[1]
Ibid. Tenth Week

In this sort of family discussion, "I will say no more" is the most effective thing you can close up with.
Ibid.

There is a good deal of fragmentary conversation going on among the birds, even on the warmest days.
Ibid. Eleventh Week

The plumbers had occasion to make me several visits. Sometimes they would find, upon arrival, that they had forgotten some indispensable tool; and one would go back to the shop, a mile and a half, after it; and his comrade would await his return with the most exemplary patience, and sit down and talk, — always by the hour.
Ibid.

If you do things by the job, you are perpetually driven: the hours are scourges. If you work by the hour, you gently sail on the stream of Time,

which is always bearing you on to the haven of Pay, whether you make any effort, or not.
My Summer in a Garden.
Eleventh Week

The toad, without which no garden would be complete.
Ibid. Thirteenth Week

It is difficult to be emphatic when no one is emphatic on the other side.
Ibid.

True it is that politics makes strange bedfellows.
Ibid. Fifteenth Week

What small potatoes we all are, compared with what we might be!
Ibid.

Public opinion is stronger than the legislature, and nearly as strong as the ten commandments.
Ibid. Sixteenth Week

The thing generally raised on city land is taxes.
Ibid.

CHARLES HAMILTON AÏDÉ
[1830–1906]

I sit beside my lonely fire
  And pray for wisdom yet:
For calmness to remember
  Or courage to forget.
Remember or Forget

Do you recall that night in June
  Upon the Danube River;
We listened to the ländler-tune,
  We watched the moonbeams quiver.
The Danube River

When the morn breaks, and the throstle awakes,
  Remember the maid of the mill.
The Maid of the Mill

When we are parted, let me lie
  In some far corner of thy heart,
Silent, and from the world apart,
Like a forgotten melody.
When We Are Parted

CHARLOTTE ALINGTON BARNARD ("CLARIBEL")
[1830–1869]

By the blue Alsatian mountains dwelt
  a maiden young and fair,

---

[1] When classes are exasperated against each other, the peace of the world is always kept by striking a new note. Instantly the units part, and form in a new order, and those who were opposed are now side by side. — R. W. EMERSON: *Progress of Culture*

Like the careless flowing fountains were
    the ripples of her hair.
           The Blue Alsatian Mountains
I cannot sing the old songs I sang long
    years ago,
For heart and voice would fail me, and
    foolish tears would flow.
           I Cannot Sing the Old Songs [1]
Take back the heart that thou gavest,
    What is my anguish to thee?
Take back the freedom thou cravest,
    Leaving the fetters to me.
               Take Back the Heart [2]
Drink deep of life's fond illusion,
    Gaze on the storm cloud and flee
Swiftly through strife and confusion,
    Leaving the burden to me.
                           Ibid.

JAMES GILLESPIE BLAINE [3]
[1830–1893]

Let us think that his dying eyes read
a mystic meaning which only the rapt
and parting soul may know. Let us believe that in the silence of the receding
world he heard the great waves breaking on the farther shore, and felt already upon his wasted brow the breath
of eternal morning.
       Eulogy on James A. Garfield
                       [1881]

NOAH BROOKS
[1830–1903]

Conductor, when you receive a fare,
Punch in the presence of the passenjare.
A blue trip slip for an eight cent fare,
A buff trip slip for a six cent fare,

---

[1] Yet though I'm full of music
     As choirs of singing birds,
  "I cannot sing the old songs" —
     I do not know the words.
   ROBERT JONES BURDETTE [1844–1914]:
                   Songs Without Words
  See Calverley, page 590.
 [2] This fine old song was revived with great
applause in the Hoboken production of *After
Dark* (BOUCICAULT) 1928–1929. The music is
given in SIGMUND SPAETH: *Read 'Em And
Weep.*
 [3] Plumed knight. — ROBERT G. INGERSOLL:
Speech nominating Blaine for President, Re-
publican National Convention, Cincinnati,
Ohio [1876].

A pink trip slip for a five cent fare,
Punch in the presence of the passenjare.
Punch, brothers, punch with care,
Punch in the presence of the passenjare.
      *Inspired by a notice to conduc-
       tors, posted in New York horse-
       cars* [1]

THOMAS EDWARD BROWN
[1830–1897]

A Garden is a lovesome thing, God wot!
    Rose plot,
    Fringed pool,
    Ferned grot —
    The veriest school
    Of Peace; and yet the fool
Contends that God is not —
Not God! in Gardens! when the eve is
        cool?
Nay, but I have a sign:
'Tis very sure God walks in mine.
                           My Garden

EMILY DICKINSON [2]
[1830–1886]

Success is counted sweetest
By those who ne'er succeed.
       *First Series. Life, I, Success,
                           Stanza 1*
Our share of night to bear,
Our share of morning.
               Ibid. II, Stanza 1
Here a star, and there a star,
Some lose their way.
Here a mist, and there a mist:
Afterwards — day!
                   Ibid. Stanza 2
If I can stop one heart from breaking,
I shall not live in vain;
If I can ease one life the aching,
Or cool one pain,
Or help one fainting robin
Unto his nest again,
I shall not live in vain.
                       Ibid. VI

---

[1] Attributed to Isaac H. Bromley and to
Mark Twain; included by the latter in *A Lit-
erary Nightmare.*
 [2] Centenary Edition of *The Poems of Emily
Dickinson*, published by Little, Brown and
Company, Boston, 1930.

A precious, mouldering pleasure 'tis
To meet an antique book,
In just the dress his century wore.
First Series. Life, X, In a
Library, Stanza 1
The soul selects her own society,
Then shuts the door.
Ibid. XIII, Exclusion, Stanza 1
To fight aloud is very brave,
But gallanter, I know,
Who charge within the bosom
The cavalry of woe.
Ibid. XVI, Stanza 1
I taste a liquor never brewed,
From tankards scooped in pearl.
Ibid. XX, Stanza 1
Inebriate of air am I,
And debauchee of dew,
Reeling, through endless summer days,
From inns of molten blue.
Ibid. Stanza 2
He ate and drank the precious words,
His spirit grew robust;
He knew no more that he was poor,
Nor that his frame was dust.
He danced along the dingy days,
And this bequest of wings
Was but a book. What liberty
A loosened spirit brings.
Ibid. XXI, A Book
Mine by the right of the white election!
Mine by the royal seal!
Ibid. Love, I, Mine, Stanza 1
Alter? When the hills do.
Falter? When the sun
Question if his glory
Be the perfect one.
Ibid. III, Stanza 1
The pedigree of honey
Does not concern the bee;
A clover, any time, to him
Is aristocracy.
Ibid. Nature, V
Some keep the Sabbath going to
church;
I keep it staying at home,
With a bobolink for a chorister,
And an orchard for a dome.
Ibid. A Service of Song, VI,
Stanza 1
These are the days when birds come
back,
A very few, a bird or two,

To take a backward look.
First Series. Nature, XXVII,
Indian Summer, Stanza 1
The morns are meeker than they were,
The nuts are getting brown;
The berry's cheek is plumper,
The rose is out of town.
Ibid. XXVIII, Autumn,
Stanza 1
That short, potential stir
That each can make but once,
That bustle so illustrious
'Tis almost consequence,
Is the *éclat* of death.
Ibid. Time and Eternity, XIII,
The Funeral
I never saw a moor,
I never saw the sea;
Yet I know how the heather looks,
And what a wave must be.
Ibid. XVII, Stanza 1
The sweeping up the heart,
And putting love away
We shall not want to use again
Until eternity.
Ibid. XXII, Stanza 2
Afraid? Of whom am I afraid?
Not death; for who is he?
The porter of my father's lodge
As much abasheth me.
Ibid. XXIV, Stanza 1
Because I could not stop for Death,
He kindly stopped for me;
The carriage held but just ourselves
And Immortality.
Ibid. XXVII, The Chariot,
Stanza 1
If I shouldn't be alive
When the robins come,
Give the one in red cravat
A memorial crumb.
Ibid. XXXVII, Stanza 1
I'm nobody! Who are you?
Are you nobody, too?
Second Series. Life, I, Stanza 1
How dreary to be somebody!
How public, like a frog
To tell your name the livelong day
To an admiring bog!
Ibid. Stanza 2
For each ecstatic instant
We must an anguish pay

In keen and quivering ratio
To the ecstasy.

> *Second Series. Life, XI, Compensation, Stanza 1*

God gave a loaf to every bird,
But just a crumb to me.

> *Ibid. XXVII, Enough, Stanza 1*

Just lost when I was saved!
Just felt the world go by!
Just girt me for the onset with eternity,
When breath blew back,
And on the other side
I heard recede the disappointed tide!

> *Ibid. LVII, Called Back, Stanza 1*

"Going to him! Happy letter! Tell him —
Tell him the page I didn't write;
Tell him I only said the syntax,
And left the verb and pronoun out."

> *Ibid. Love, V, The Letter, Stanza 1*

One of the ones that Midas touched,
Who failed to touch us all,
Was that confiding prodigal,
The blissful oriole.

> *Ibid. Nature, XIII, The Oriole, Stanza 1*

A bird came down the walk:
He did not know I saw;
He bit an angle-worm in halves
And ate the fellow, raw.

> *Ibid. XXIII, In the Garden, Stanza 1*

God made a little gentian;
It tried to be a rose
And failed, and all the summer laughed.

> *Ibid. XLVIII, Fringed Gentian*

Besides the autumn poets sing,
A few prosaic days
A little this side of the snow
And that side of the haze.

> *Ibid. XLIX, November, Stanza 1*

One need not be a chamber to be haunted;
One need not be a house;
The brain has corridors surpassing
Material place.

> *Ibid. Time and Eternity, XXIX, Ghosts, Stanza 1*

A word is dead
When it is said,

Some say.
I say it just
Begins to live
That day.

> *Third Series. Life, VI, A Word*

We never know how high we are
Till we are called to rise;
And then, if we are true to plan,
Our statures touch the skies.

> *Ibid. XIV, Aspiration, Stanza 1*

There is no frigate like a book
To take us lands away,
Nor any coursers like a page
Of prancing poetry.
This traverse may the poorest take
Without oppress of toll:
How frugal is the chariot
That bears a human soul!

> *Ibid. XVI, A Book*

Who has not found the heaven below
Will fail of it above.
God's residence is next to mine,
His furniture is love.

> *Ibid. XVII*

Adrift! A little boat adrift!
And night is coming down!
Will no one guide a little boat
Unto the nearest town?

> *Ibid. Time and Eternity, XLVII, Stanza 1*

Reverse cannot befall that fine Prosperity
Whose sources are interior.

> *The Single Hound. VIII*

Glory is that bright tragic thing,
That for an instant
Means Dominion,
Warms some poor name
That never felt the sun,
Gently replacing
In oblivion.

> *Ibid. XX*

The Soul's superior instants
Occur to her alone.

> *Ibid. XXXIII*

This quiet dust was Gentlemen and Ladies,
And Lads and Girls;
Was laughter and ability and sighing,
And frocks and curls.

> *Ibid. LXXIV*

Eden is that old-fashioned House
We dwell in every day,

Without suspecting our abode
Until we drive away.
The Single Hound. CVI
To see her is a picture,
To hear her is a tune,
To know her an intemperance
As innocent as June.
Further Poems. CXXIX
And this of all my hopes —
This is the silent end;
Bountiful colored my morning rose,
Early and sere its end.
Ibid. CLXIX
A bayonet's contrition
Is nothing to the Dead!
Glory.[1] Stanza 4
If I read a book and it makes my
whole body so cold no fire can ever
warm me, I know that is poetry. If I
feel physically as if the top of my head
were taken off, I know that is poetry.
These are the only ways I know it. Is
there any other way?
*Quoted in Life and Letters of
Emily Dickinson, by* MARTHA
GILBERT DICKINSON BIANCHI

L. VIRGINIA FRENCH
[1830–1881]

When they planted independence, as a
symbol and a sign —
They struck deep soil and planted the
Palmetto and the Pine.
*The Palmetto and the Pine.
Stanza 1*

PAUL HAMILTON HAYNE
[1830–1886]

I see the cloud-born squadrons of the
gale,
Their lines of rain like glittering spears
deprest.
A Storm in the Distance. Stanza 1
The leveled lances of the rain
At earth's half-shielded breast take glit-
tering aim.
Ibid. Stanza 5
Art thou in misery, brother? Then I
pray

[1] In *The Atlantic Monthly, June, 1935*

Be comforted! Thy grief shall pass
away.
Art thou elated? Ah, be not too gay;
Temper thy joy: this, too, shall pass
away.[1]
This, Too, Shall Pass Away
Know you why the robin's breast
Gleameth of a dusky red,
Like the lustre 'mid the stars
Of the potent planet Mars?
'Tis — a monkish myth has said —
Owing to his cordial heart;
For, long since, he took the part
Of those hapless children, sent
Heavenward, for punishment;
And to quench the fierce desire
Bred in them by ruthless fire,
Brought on tiny bill and wing
Water from some earthly spring.[2]
Why the Robin's Breast Is Red [3]

ROBERT MORRIS
[*Floruit* 1880]

We meet upon the Level and we part
upon the Square; [4]
What words sublimely beautiful those
Words Masonic are.
They fall like strains of melody upon
the listening ears,

[1] See J. G. Saxe, page 509.
[2] See Whittier, page 444.
[3] Sweet Robin, I have heard them say
That thou wert there upon the day
That Christ was crowned in cruel scorn,
And bore away one bleeding thorn;
That so the blush upon thy breast
In shameful sorrow was imprest,
And thence thy genial sympathy
With our redeemed humanity.
    WILLIAM CROSWELL DOANE [1832–
        1913]: *Robin Redbreast*
A little bird that warbled near,
  That memorable day,
Flitted around and strove to wrench
  One single thorn away;
The cruel spike impaled his breast,
  And thus, 'tis sweetly said,
The robin wears his silver vest
  In panoplies of red.
    JAMES RYDER RANDALL [1839–1908]:
      Why the Robin's Breast Is Red
[4] We met upon the Level an' we parted on
  the Square,
An' I was Junior Deacon in my Mother-
  Lodge out there!
    RUDYARD KIPLING: *The Mother-Lodge*

As they've sounded Hallelujahs to the
world three thousand years.
> *The Level and the Square.*
> *Stanza 1*

MRS. DAVID PORTER
[*Floruit* 1860]

Thou hast wounded the spirit that
loved thee
And cherish'd thine image for years;
Thou hast taught me at last to forget
thee,
In secret, in silence, and tears.
> *Thou Hast Wounded the Spirit.*
> *Stanza 2*

CHRISTINA GEORGINA ROSSETTI
[1830–1894]

Hope is like a harebell trembling from
its birth,
Love is like a rose the joy of all the
earth,
Faith is like a lily lifted high and white,
Love is like a lovely rose the world's
delight.
Harebells and sweet lilies show a thorn-
less growth,
But the rose with all its thorns excels
them both.
> *Hope Is Like a Harebell*

In life our absent friend is far away:
But death may bring our friend exceeding near.
> *Sonnet 28, Later Life*

My heart is like a singing bird.
> *A Birthday. Stanza 1*

When I am dead, my dearest,
  Sing no sad songs for me;
Plant thou no roses at my head,
  Nor shady cypress tree.
> *Song. Stanza 1*

I shall not see the shadows,
  I shall not feel the rain.
> *Ibid. Stanza 2*

Beyond the sea of death Love lies
For ever, yesterday, to-day.
> *One Day. Stanza 3*

Remember me when I am gone away,
Gone far away into the silent land.
> *Remember*

Better by far you should forget and
  smile
Than that you should remember and
  be sad.
> *Remember*

Does the road wind up-hill all the way?
Yes, to the very end.
> *Up-Hill. Stanza 1*

All earth's full rivers can not fill
The sea, that drinking thirsteth still.
> *By the Sea*

One day in the country
Is worth a month in town.
> *Summer*

Silence more musical than any song.
> *Rest*

Let bygones be bygones.
> *"No, Thank You, John." Stanza 5*

Somewhere or other there must surely
  be
The face not seen, the voice not heard,
The heart that not yet — never yet —
  ah, me!
Made answer to my word.
> *Somewhere or Other. Stanza 1*

ALEXANDER SMITH
[1830–1867]

Some books are drenchèd sands
On which a great soul's wealth lies all
  in heaps,
Like a wrecked argosy.
> *A Life Drama. Sc. 2*

Like a pale martyr in his shirt of fire.
> *Ibid.*

In winter, when the dismal rain
  Comes down in slanting lines,
And Wind, that grand old harper, smote
  His thunder-harp of pines.
> *Ibid.*

A poem round and perfect as a star.
> *Ibid.*

The saddest thing that can befall a soul
Is when it loses faith in God and
  woman.
> *Ibid. Sc. 12*

We twain have met like the ships upon
  the sea,[1]
Who hold an hour's converse, so short,
  so sweet;

[1] See Longfellow, page 437.

One little hour! And then, away they
speed
On lonely paths, through mist and
cloud and foam,
To meet no more.
A Life Drama. Part IV

I loved you, and above my life still
hangs that love intact —
Like a mild consoling rainbow, or a
savage cataract.
Love has saved me, Barbara!
Barbara. Stanza 6

We hear the wail of the remorseful
winds
In their strange penance. And this
wretched orb
Knows not the taste of rest; a maniac
world,
Homeless and sobbing through the deep
she goes.
Unrest and Childhood

The soul of man is like the rolling
world,
One half in day, the other dipt in night;
The one has music and the flying cloud,
The other, silence and the wakeful
stars.
Horton

Each time we love,
We turn a nearer and a broader mark
To that keen archer, Sorrow, and he
strikes.
A Boy's Dream

Time has fallen asleep in the afternoon
sunshine.
Dreamthorp. First Essay

The man who in this world can keep
the whiteness of his soul, is not likely
to lose it in any other.
Ibid.

It is not of so much consequence
what you say, as how you say it. Memorable sentences are memorable on account of some single irradiating word.
Ibid. On the Writing of Essays

The world is not so much in need
of new thoughts as that when thought
grows old and worn with usage it
should, like current coin, be called in,
and, from the mint of genius, reissued
fresh and new.
Ibid.

Death is the ugly fact which Nature
has to hide, and she hides it well.
Dreamthorp. Of Death and the
Fear of Dying

Everything is sweetened by risk.
Ibid.

In life there is nothing more unexpected and surprising than the arrivals
and departures of pleasure. If we find
it in one place to-day, it is vain to seek
it there to-morrow. You can not lay a
trap for it.
Ibid.

A man's real possession is his memory. In nothing else is he rich, in nothing else is he poor.
Ibid.

Scotland had invaded England more
than once, but the blue bonnets never
went over the border [1] so triumphantly
as when they did so in the shape of
songs and ballads.
Ibid. William Dunbar

A large proportion of mankind feel
a quite peculiar interest in famous
writers.
Ibid. Men of Letters

Just consider what a world this would
be if ruled by the best thoughts of men
of letters! Ignorance would die at once,
war would cease, taxation would be
lightened, not only every Frenchman,
but every man in the world, would have
his hen in the pot. [2]
Ibid.

I would rather be remembered by a
song than by a victory. I would rather
build a fine sonnet than have built St.
Paul's.
Ibid.

To be occasionally quoted is the only
fame I care for.
Ibid.

A man gazing on the stars is proverbially at the mercy of the puddles
on the road.
Ibid.

[1] When the Blue Bonnets came over the
Border.
SCOTT: *The Monastery, Chap. 25,*
Border Ballad
[2] A chicken in every pot. — Republican
campaign slogan [1932].

Trifles make up the happiness or the misery of mortal life. The majority of men slip into their graves without having encountered on their way thither any signal catastrophe or exaltation of fortune or feeling.

Dreamthorp. Men of Letters

The skin of the man of letters is peculiarly sensitive to the bite of the critical mosquito; and he lives in a climate in which such mosquitoes swarm. He is seldom stabbed to the heart — he is often killed by pin-pricks.

Ibid.

Every man's road in life is marked by the graves of his personal likings.

Ibid. On the Importance of a Man to Himself

In the wide arena of the world, failure and success are not accidents as we so frequently suppose, but the strictest justice. If you do your fair day's work, you are certain to get your fair day's wage — in praise or pudding, whichever happens to suit your taste.

Ibid.

The great man is the man who does a thing for the first time.

Ibid.

Turn where you will, some fragment of a ballad is sure to meet you. Go into the loneliest places of experience and passion, and you discover that you are walking in human footprints.

Ibid. A Shelf in My Bookcase

How deeply seated in the human heart is the liking for gardens and gardening.

Ibid. Books and Gardens

If you have once planted a tree for other than commercial purposes, — and in that case it is usually done by your orders and by the hands of hirelings, — you have always in it a peculiar interest. You care more for it than you care for all the forests of Norway or America. *You* have planted it, and that is sufficient to make it peculiar amongst the trees of the world.

Ibid.

A man does not plant a tree for himself, he plants it for posterity.

Dreamthorp. Books and Gardens

It is high time, it seems to me, that a moral game-law were passed for the preservation of the wild and vagrant feelings of human nature.

Ibid. On Vagabonds

A good portrait is a kind of biography, and neither painter nor biographer can carry out his task satisfactorily unless he be admitted behind the scenes.

Ibid.

MATTHIAS BARR
[1831–?]

Only a baby small,
    Dropt from the skies;
Small, but how dear to us,
    God knoweth best.

Only a Baby Small

Moon, so round and yellow,
    Looking from on high,
How I love to see you
    Shining in the sky.

Moon, So Round and Yellow

Come, give me your hand, sir, my
    friend and my brother:
    If honest, why sure that's enough.
One hand, if it's true, is as good as another,
    No matter how brawny or rough.

Give Me Your Hand

Though it toil for a living at hedges or
    ditches,
    Or make for its owner a name,
Or fold in its hand all the dainties of
    riches,
    If honest I love it the same.

Ibid.

CHARLES STUART CALVERLEY
[1831–1884]

I have a liking old
For thee, though manifold
Stories, I know, are told,
    Not to thy credit!

Ode to Tobacco. Stanza 2

I sit alone at present, dreaming darkly
        of a Dun.
                                In the Gloaming
I can not sing the old songs now!
        It is not that I deem them low;
'Tis that I can't remember how
                They go.[1]
                                Changed
O my own, my beautiful, my blue-
        eyed!
        To be young once more and bite my
                thumb
At the world and all its cares with you,
        I'd
        Give no inconsiderable sum.
                        First Love. Stanza 7
A clod — a piece of orange peel —
        An end of a cigar —
Once trod on by a Princely heel,
        How beautiful they are![2]
                        Precious Stones. Stanza 6
The farmer's daughter hath soft brown
        hair
        (*Butter and eggs and a pound of
        cheese*)
And I met with a ballad, I can't say
        where,
        That wholly consisted of lines like
        these.
                        *Ballad, after William Morris
                        [The Auld Wife]. Part I,
                        Stanza 6*
And this song is considered a perfect
        gem,
        And as to the meaning, it's what you
        please.
                        Ibid. Part II, Stanza 4
'Twas ever thus from childhood's hour!
        My fondest hopes would not decay:
I never loved a tree or flower
        Which was the first to fade away.[3]
                Disaster, after Moore. Stanza 1
But ah! disasters have their use;
        And life might e'en be too sunshiny.
                                Ibid. Stanza 5
The boundless ineffable prairie;
        The splendor of mountain and lake
With their hues that seem ever to vary;
        The mighty pine forests which shake

[1] See Barnard, page 583.
[2] Misquoted in DU MAURIER: *Trilby*
Part 5.
[3] See Thomas Moore, page 338.

In the wind, and in which the unwary
        May tread on a snake.
                *The Schoolmaster Abroad with
                        His Son. Stanza 7*

O Memory! That which I gave thee
To guard in thy garner yest'reen —
Little deeming thou e'er couldst behave
        thee
Thus basely — hath gone from thee
        clean!
                        Flight. Stanza 1

Mine was a joke for the ages;
        Full of intricate meaning and pith;
A feast for your scholars and sages —
        How it would have rejoiced Sydney
        Smith!
'Tis such thoughts that ennoble a
        mortal;
        And, singling him out from the herd,
Fling wide immortality's portal —
        — But what was the word?
                        Ibid. Stanza 9

As the flight of a bird in the air
Is the flight of a joke.
                        Ibid. Stanza 10

Forever; 'tis a single word!
        Our rude forefathers deemed it two:
Can you imagine so absurd
                A view?
                                Forever

Ere the morn the East has crimsoned,
        When the stars are twinkling there
(As they did in Watts' hymns, and
        Made him wonder what they were)
When the forest-nymphs are beading
        Fern and flower with silvery dew
My infallible proceeding
        Is to wake, and think of you.
                        The 14th of February

JAMES ABRAM GARFIELD
[1831–1881]

Fellow Citizens! Clouds and darkness are round about Him. His pavilion
is dark waters and thick clouds of the
skies. Justice and judgment are the establishment of His throne. Mercy and
truth shall go before His face. Fellow

Citizens! God reigns, and the Government at Washington still lives!

*Address in Wall Street,
New York [April 15, 1865]*

For mere vengeance I would do nothing. This nation is too great to look for mere revenge. But for the security of the future I would do everything.

Ibid.

I am not willing that this discussion should close without mention of the value of a true teacher. Give me a log hut, with only a simple bench, Mark Hopkins [1] on one end and I on the other, and you may have all the buildings, apparatus and libraries without him.

Address to Williams College Alumni, New York [December 28, 1871] [2]

ROWLAND HOWARD
[*Floruit* 1876]

Waste not, want not, is a maxim I would
  teach.
Let your watchword be dispatch, and
  practise what you preach;
Do not let your chances like sunbeams
  pass you by,
For you never miss the water till the
  well runs dry.

You Never Miss the Water [3]

HELEN HUNT JACKSON
("SAXE HOLM")
[1831–1885]

O suns and skies and clouds of June,
  And flowers of June together,
Ye cannot rival for one hour
  October's bright blue weather.

*October's Bright Blue Weather.
Stanza 1*

The lesson of St. Christopher,
  Who spent his strength for others,
And saved his soul by working hard

To help and save his brothers.

*The Parable of St. Christopher.[1]
Stanza 54*

Only a night from old to new,
  Only a sleep from night to morn.
The new is but the old come true,
  Each sunrise sees a new year born.

New Year's Morning. Stanza 3

Find me the men on earth who care
  Enough for faith or creed to-day
To seek a barren wilderness
  For simple liberty to pray.

The Pilgrim Forefathers. Stanza 5

Like a blind spinner in the sun,
  I tread my days;
I know that all the threads will run
  Appointed ways;
I know each day will bring its task,
And, being blind, no more I ask.

Spinning. Stanza 1

On the king's gate the moss grew gray;
  The king came not. They called him
    dead
And made his eldest son one day
  Slave in his father's stead.

Coronation. Stanza 10

Oh, write of me, not "Died in bitter
  pains,"
But "Emigrated to another star!"

Emigravit [2]

Father, I scarcely dare to pray,
  So clear I see, now it is done,
How I have wasted half my day,
  And left my work but just begun.

A Last Prayer. Stanza 1

My body, eh. Friend Death, how now?
  Why all this tedious pomp of writ?
Thou hast reclaimed it sure and slow
  For half a century, bit by bit.

Habeas Corpus.[3] Stanza 1

There is nothing so skilful in its own
defence as imperious pride.

Ramona. Chap. 13

Wounded vanity knows when it is mortally hurt; and limps off the field, piteous, all disguises thrown away. But pride carries its banner to the last.

Ibid.

---

[1] Mark Hopkins [1802–1887], president of Williams College [1836–1872], and president of the American Board of Commissioners for Foreign Missions [1857–1881]. See Guiterman, page 815.

[2] In BURKE A. HINSDALE: *President Garfield and Education* [1882], *P. 43*.

[3] In *Peterson's Magazine*, 1876.

[1] In *St. Nicholas, January, 1876*.

[2] Emigravit is the inscription on the tombstone where he [Dürer] lies;
  Dead he is not, but departed, — for the artist never dies.

  LONGFELLOW: *Nuremberg, St. 13*

[3] Her last poem, left unfinished.

There cannot be found in the animal kingdom a bat, or any other creature, so blind in its own range of circumstance and connection, as the greater majority of human beings are in the bosoms of their families.

Ramona. Chap. 13

That indescribable expression peculiar to people who hope they have not been asleep, but know they have.

Ibid. Chap. 14

EDWARD ROBERT BULWER LYTTON, EARL OF LYTTON ("OWEN MEREDITH")
[1831–1891]

Since we parted yester eve,
I do love thee, love, believe,
Twelve times dearer, twelve hours longer —
One dream deeper, one night stronger,
One sun surer — thus much more
Than I loved thee, love, before.

Since We Parted

Death comes at last to all mankind;
Yet ere I die, I know not where,
I know not how, but I must find
Fair Yoland with the yellow hair.

Fair Yoland with the Yellow Hair. Stanza 13

The heart of a man's like that delicate weed
Which requires to be trampled on, boldly indeed,
Ere it gives forth the fragrance you wish to extract.[1]

Lucile.[2] Part I, Canto 1, IV

A dwarf on a dead giant's shoulders sees more
Than the 'live giant's eyesight availed to explore.[3]

Ibid. Canto 2, III

The man who seeks one thing in life, and but one,
May hope to achieve it before life be done;

[1] See Lyly, page 23.
[2] Lord Lytton, the Viceroy, who still lives in the literary hall of fame as the author of Lucile — a vast, stale Victorian piece of poetry. — WILLIAM E. WOODWARD: *Meet General Grant, Part 4, Chap. 30*
[3] See Burton, page 122.

But he who seeks all things, wherever he goes
Only reaps from the hopes which around him he sows
A harvest of barren regrets.

Lucile. Part I, Canto 2, IV

Let any man once show the world that he feels
Afraid of its bark, and 'twill fly at his heels:
Let him fearlessly face it, 'twill leave him alone:
But 'twill fawn at his feet if he flings it a bone.

Ibid. VII

The Italians have voices like peacocks; the Spanish
Smell, I fancy, of garlic; the Swedish and Danish
Have something too Runic, too rough and unshod, in
Their accent for mouths not descended from Odin;
German gives me a cold in the head, sets me wheezing
And coughing; and Russian is nothing but sneezing.

Ibid. XII

Whene'er I hear French spoken as I approve,
I feel myself quietly falling in love.

Ibid.

We may live without poetry, music and art;
We may live without conscience and live without heart;
We may live without friends; we may live without books;
But civilized man can not live without cooks.
He may live without books, — what is knowledge but grieving?
He may live without hope, — what is hope but deceiving?
He may live without love, — what is passion but pining?
But where is the man that can live without dining?

Ibid. XIX

The world is a nettle; disturb it, it stings:

Grasp it firmly, it stings not.[1]

Lucile. Part I, Canto 3, II

The face the most fair to our vision allowed
Is the face we encounter and lose in the crowd.

The thought that most thrills our existence is one
Which, before we can frame it in language, is gone.

Ibid. Canto 5, I

Having largely invested
Not only where treasure is never molested
By thieves, moth, or rust; but on this earthly ball
Where interest was high, and security small.

Ibid. Canto 6, XX

In Rome, — in the Forum, — there opened one night
A gulf. All the augurs turned pale at the sight.
In this omen the anger of Heaven they read.
Men consulted the gods: then the oracle said: —
"Ever open this gulf shall endure, till at last
That which Rome hath most precious within it be cast."
The Romans threw in their corn and their stuff,
But the gulf yawned as wide. Rome seemed likely enough
To be ruined ere this rent in her heart she could choke.
Then Curtius, revering the oracle, spoke:
"O Quirites! to this Heaven's question has come:
What to Rome is most precious? The manhood of Rome."
He plunged, and the gulf closed.[2]

Ibid. Part II, Canto 1, XVI

[1] See Aaron Hill, page 204.
[2] Marcus Curtius, legendary hero of Rome. In 362 B.C., a chasm having been formed in the Forum by an earthquake, the soothsayers announced that it could be closed only by the sacrifice of Rome's greatest treasure. Marcus Curtius, a noble youth, declared that the state possessed no greater treasure than a brave citizen in arms, and, in full armor, mounted on

There's no weapon that slays
Its victim so surely (if well aimed) as praise.

Lucile. Part II, Canto 1, XX

A wink is as good as a nod to the wise.

Ibid. Canto 2, I

Those true eyes
Too pure and too honest in aught to disguise
The sweet soul shining through them.[1]

Ibid. III

Thought alone is eternal.

Ibid. Canto 5, XV

A nun hath no nation.
Wherever man suffers or woman may soothe,
There her land! there her kindred!

Ibid. Canto 6, XII

Love thou the rose, yet leave it on its stem.

The Wanderer, Prologue, Part I, 19

Oh, moment of sweet peril, perilous sweet!
When woman joins herself to man.

Ibid. 27

I will not cant that commonplace of friends,
Which never yet hath dried one mourner's tears,
Nor say that grief's slow wisdom makes amends
For broken hearts and desolated years.

*The Wanderer in Italy.
A Love-Letter, 29*

I would that this woman's head
Were less golden about the hair:
I would her lips were less red,
And her face less deadly fair.

Ibid. The Vampire, 5

But I am sick of all the din
That's made in praising Verdi,
Who only know a violin
Is not a hurdy-gurdy.

*The Wanderer in France.
"Prensus in Aegaeo"*

his steed, leaped into the chasm, which closed after him.

[1] Ils sont si transparents qu'ils laissent voir votre âme.

THÉOPHILE GAUTIER: *The Two Beautiful Eyes*

Could we find out her heart through
   that velvet and lace!
Can it beat without ruffling her sump-
   tuous dress?
She will show us her shoulder, her
   bosom, her face;
But what the heart's like, we must
   guess.
         The Wanderer in France.
         Madame La Marquise, 12
Of all the operas that Verdi wrote,
The best, to my taste, is the Trova-
   tore.
         Ibid. Aux Italiens, 2
And I think, in the lives of most women
   and men,
There's a moment when all would
   go smooth and even,
If only the dead could find out when
To come back, and be forgiven.
         Ibid. 27
Who knows how sculptor on sculptor
   starved
With the thought in the head by the
   hand uncarved?
And he that spread out in its ample
   repose
That grand, indifferent, godlike brow,
How vainly his own may have ached,
   who knows,
'Twixt the laurel above and the wrinkle
   below?
         The Wanderer in England.
         Babylonia
         The ages roll
Forward; and forward with them draw
   my soul
Into Time's infinite sea.
And to be glad, or sad, I care no more;
But to have done and to have been, be-
   fore
I cease to do and be!
         The Wanderer in Switzerland.
         A Confession and Apology, 9
My life is a torn book. But at the end
A little page, quite fair, is saved, my
   friend,
Where thou didst write thy name.
         The Wanderer in Holland.
         Jacqueline
Nor shall I leave thee wholly. I shall be
An evening thought, — a morning
   dream to thee, —

A silence in thy life when, through the
   night,
The bell strikes, or the sun, with sinking light,
Smites all the empty windows.
         The Wanderer in Holland.
         Jacqueline
Death is no evil, since it comes to all.[1]
         Palingenesis. Epilogue, Part I, 12
Ay, there are some good things in life,
   that fall not away with the rest.
And, of all best things upon earth, I
   hold that a faithful friend is the
   best.
         Last Words
Talk not of genius baffled. Genius is
   master of man.
Genius does what it must, and talent
   does what it can.
         Ibid.
When Richelieu learned that Wallen-
   stein was dead,
His thin face sharpened to an edge. He
   said,
"Soon as the great tree falls, the rabble
   run
To strip him of his branches one by
   one."
         Wallenstein's Death

PHILIP HENRY SHERIDAN
[1831–1888]

The only good Indians I ever saw
were dead.[2]
         Remark at Fort Cobb, Indian
         Territory [January, 1869]

LOUISA MAY ALCOTT
[1832–1888]

A little kingdom I possess,
Where thoughts and feelings dwell;

[1] That must be somehow best that comes
to all.
         C. P. CRANCH: *Life and Death*
[2] Edward Sylvester Ellis [1840–1916] reported that after Custer's fight with Black
Kettle's band of Cheyenne Indians, the Co-
manche Chief Toch-a-way (Turtle Dove)
was presented to General Sheridan. The Indian
said: "Me Toch-a-way, me good Indian." The
General's reply has become a familiar quotation.

And very hard the task I find
  Of governing it well.
        Life, Letters and Journals.
   Chap. 3, My Kingdom,[1] *Stanza 1*
I do not ask for any crown
  But that which all may win;
Nor try to conquer any world
  Except the one within.
          Ibid. Stanza 4
  I had a pleasant time with my mind,
for it was happy.
                Ibid.
  I know what death means, — a lib-
erator for her, a teacher for us.[2]
         Ibid. Chap. 5
  Resolved to take Fate by the throat
and shake a living out of her.
                Ibid.
  Life is my college. May I graduate
well, and earn some honors!
                Ibid.
For such as he there is no death; —
His life the eternal life commands;
Above man's aims his nature rose.
The wisdom of a just content
Made one small spot a continent,
And tuned to poetry Life's prose.[3]
        Life, Letters and Journals.
   Chap. 7, Thoreau's Flute,[4] *Stanza 2*
  My definition [of a philosopher] is
of a man up in a balloon, with his fam-
ily and friends holding the ropes which
confine him to earth and trying to haul
him down.
         Ibid. Chap. 10
To smooth the rough and thorny way
  Where other feet begin to tread;
To feed some hungry soul each day
  With sympathy's sustaining bread.
     Ibid. Chap. 11, My Prayer,
              Stanza 4
  Now I am beginning to live a little,
and feel less like a sick oyster at low
tide.
         Ibid. Chap. 11
A child her wayward pencil drew
  On margins of her book:

---

[1] Written at the age of thirteen years.
[2] Miss Alcott's sister Beth.
[3] The word "tuned" is frequently misprinted
as "turned."
[4] In *The Atlantic Monthly, September,
1863.*

Garlands of flowers, dancing elves,
  Bird, butterfly and brook.
Lessons undone, and play forgot,
  Seeking with hand and heart
The teacher whom she learned to love
  Before she knew 'twas Art.
         Our Madonna.[1] *Stanza 1*
Death, the stern sculptor, with a touch
  No earthly power can stay,
Changes to marble in an hour
  The beautiful, pale clay.
          Ibid. Stanza 6
Philosophers sit in their sylvan hall
And talk of the duties of man,
Of Chaos and Cosmos, Hegel and Kant,
With the Oversoul well in the van;
All on their hobbies they amble away
And a terrible dust they make;
Disciples devout both gaze and adore,
As daily they listen and bake.
          Philosophers[2]

ELIZABETH AKERS ALLEN
[1832–1911]

Backward, turn backward, O Time, in
  your flight,
Make me a child again just for to-
  night!
        Rock Me to Sleep.[3] *Stanza 1*
Backward, flow backward, O tide of
  the years!
I am so weary of toil and of tears —
Toil without recompense, tears all in
  vain —
Take them and give me my childhood
  again!
           Ibid. Stanza 2
Over my heart in the days that have
  flown,
No love like mother-love ever has
  shone;
No other worship abides and endures,

---

[1] May Alcott Neiriker, youngest of the Alcott sisters.
[2] Quoted by MRS. FLORENCE WHITING
BROWN: *Alcott and the Concord School of
Philosophy* [1926], *P. 46.*
[3] Written by Elizabeth Akers in May, 1860,
and sent to *The Saturday Evening Post* under
her pen-name, "Florence Percy." The poem
was published in that periodical on June 9,
1860.

Faithful, unselfish, and patient, like
   yours.
            Rock Me to Sleep. Stanza 4

How much the heart may bear, and yet
   not break!
How much the flesh may suffer and not
   die!
I question much if any pain or ache
Of soul or body brings our end more
   nigh:
Death chooses his own time.
            Endurance. Stanza 1

Behold, we live through all things —
   famine, thirst,
Bereavement, pain; all grief and
   misery,
All woe and sorrow; life inflicts its
   worst
On soul and body — but we can not die,
Though we be sick, and tired, and faint,
   and worn, —
Lo, all things can be borne!
            Ibid. Stanza 5

Unremembered and afar
I watched you as I watched a star,
Through darkness struggling into view,
And loved you better than you knew.
            Left Behind. Stanza 5

And all the pain of lonely days,
   And nights with sleepless sorrow
      wild,
Hides in the quaint and stilted phrase,
   "An amiable child."
            "An Amiable Child." [1] Stanza 15

Let all unselfish spirits heed
The story of Johnny Appleseed.
He had another and prouder name
In far New England, whence he came,
But by this title, and this alone,

---

[1] On the stone marking the grave of St. Clair
Pollock, near Grant's Tomb, on Riverside
Drive, New York, is inscribed: "Erected to
the memory of an amiable child." The boy
died July 15, 1797, at the age of five years.
   At Riverside, on the slow hill-slant,
      Two memoried graves are seen;
   A granite dome is over Grant,
      And over a child the green.
            ANNA CATHERINE MARKHAM:
                  An Amiable Child

Was the kindly wanderer loved and
   known.
            Johnny Appleseed.[1] Stanza 1
Carve not upon a stone when I am dead
   The praises which remorseful mourn-
      ers give
To women's graves — a tardy recom-
      pense —
   But speak them while I live.
            Till Death. Stanza 6

SIR EDWIN ARNOLD
[1832–1904]

He who died at Azan sends
This to comfort all his friends: —
Faithful friends! It lies I know
Pale and white and cold as snow;
And ye say, "Abdallah's dead!"
Weeping at the feet and head.
I can see your falling tears,
I can hear your sighs and prayers;
Yet I smile and whisper this:
I am not the thing you kiss.
Cease your tears and let it lie;
It was mine — it is not I.
            After Death in Arabia
Farewell, friends! Yet not farewell;
Where I am, ye too shall dwell.
I am gone before your face,
A moment's time, a little space.
            Ibid.
Ay! it will come, — the bitter hour! —
   but bringing
   A better love beyond, more subtle-
      sweet;
A higher road to tread, with happier
   singing,
   And no cross-ways to part familiar
      feet!
            The New Lucian
Not a face below the sun
But is precious — unto one!

---

[1] John Chapman [1775–1847].

One pouch with hoarded seed was packed,
From Penn-land cider-presses.
            WILLIAM HENRY VENABLE:
                  Johnny Appleseed, St. 11
Long, long after,
When settlers put up beam and rafter,
They asked of the birds: "Who gave this
   fruit?"
            VACHEL LINDSAY: *Johnny
                  Appleseed, Part III*

Not an eye, however dull,
But seems — somewhere — beautiful.
Facies non Omnibus Una
We are they who will not take
From palace, priest, or code,
A meaner Law than "Brotherhood" —
A lower Lord than God.
*Armageddon: A War Song of
the Future. Stanza 4*
And richer than red gold that dull
bronze seems,
Since it was bought with lavish waste
of worth
Whereto the wealth of Earth's gold-
sanded streams
Were but a lack, and dearth.
*The First Distribution of the
Victoria Cross, 1856. Stanza 4*
Don't poets know
Better than others?
God can't be always everywhere: and,
so,
Invented Mothers.
Mothers. Stanza 6
Somewhere there waiteth in this world
of ours
For one lone soul, another lonely
soul —
Each chasing each through all the
weary hours,
And meeting strangely at one sud-
den goal;
Then blend they — like green leaves
with golden flowers,
Into one beautiful and perfect
whole —
And life's long night is ended, and the
way
Lies open onward to eternal day.[1]
Destiny

[1] A sublime hope cheers ever the faithful
heart, that elsewhere, in other regions of the
universal powers, souls are now acting, endur-
ing and daring, which can love us, and which
we can love.
R. W. EMERSON: *Friendship*
Two shall be born the whole wide world apart
And speak in different tongues and have no
thought
Each of the other's being and no heed.
And these o'er unknown seas to unknown
lands
Shall cross, escaping wreck, defying death;
And all unconsciously shape every act
And bend each wandering step to this one end,

We are the voices of the wandering
wind,
Which moan for rest and rest can never
find;
Lo! as the wind is, so is mortal life,
A moan, a sigh, a sob, a storm, a strife.
The Deva's Song
Never the spirit was born; the spirit
shall cease to be never;
Never was time it was not; End and
Beginning are dreams!
Birthless and deathless and changeless
remaineth the spirit for ever;
Death hath not touched it at all, dead
though the house of it seems.
*The Song Celestial (Translated
from The Bhagavad-Gita)*
The end of birth is death; the end of
death is birth: this is ordained.
Ibid.

WILLIAM CROSWELL DOANE
[1832–1913]

Their Lent is over, and their Easter
won.
Death
There stands in the garden of old St.
Mark
A sun-dial quaint and gray.
"Horas non Numero Nisi Serenas."
Stanza 1
"I number none but the cloudless
hours," [1]
Its motto the live day long.
Ibid. Stanza 2
I am quite sure he thinks that I am
God —
Since he is God on whom each one de-
pends
For life and all things that His bounty
sends —
My dear old dog, most constant of all
friends.
Cluny
He had lived out his life, but not his
love;

That one day out of darkness they shall meet
And read life's meaning in each other's eyes.
SUSAN MARR SPALDING [1841–1908]:
Fate, St. 1

[1] See Hazlitt, page 330.

Daily up steep and weary stair he
  came,
His big heart bursting with the strain,
  to prove
    His loneliness without me.
        In Memory of Cluny,
        May 24–25, 1902

CHARLES LUTWIDGE DODGSON ("LEWIS CARROLL")
[1832–1898]

Alice! a childish story take
  And with a gentle hand
Lay it where childhood's dreams are
  twined
    In Memory's mystic band,
Like pilgrim's withered wreath of flow-
  ers
    Plucked in a far-off land.
     Alice's Adventures in Wonder-
       land. Introduction

"You are old, Father William," the
  young man said,
  "And your hair has become very
    white;
And yet you incessantly stand on your
  head —
  Do you think, at your age, it is
    right?" [1]
         Ibid. Chap. 5

"Really, now you ask me," said
Alice, very much confused, "I don't
think — "
"Then you shouldn't talk," said the
Hatter.
         Ibid. Chap. 7

"Tut, tut, child," said the Duchess.
"Everything's got a moral if only you
can find it."
         Ibid. Chap. 9

Take care of the sense and the sounds
will take care of themselves.
         Ibid.

"Reeling and Writhing, of course, to
begin with," the Mock Turtle replied,
"and the different branches of Arithmetic — Ambition, Distraction, Uglifi-
cation, and Derision."
         Ibid.

Child of the pure, unclouded brow
  And dreaming eyes of wonder!

[1] See Southey, page 320.

Though time be fleet and I and thou
  Are half a life asunder,
Thy loving smile will surely hail
  The love-gift of a fairy-tale.
     Through the Looking-Glass and
      What Alice Found There. In-
      troduction

'Twas brillig, and the slithy toves
  Did gyre and gimble in the wabe;
All mimsy were the borogoves,
  And the mome raths outgrabe.
    Ibid. Chap. 1 (Jabberwocky.
        Stanza 1)

He chortled in his joy.
        Ibid. (Stanza 6)

"The horror of that moment," the
King went on, "I shall never, *never* forget!"
"You will, though," the Queen said,
"if you don't make a memorandum of
it."
         Ibid.

"A slow sort of country," said the
Queen. "Now, *here,* you see, it takes all
the running you can do, to keep in the
same place. If you want to get somewhere else, you must run at least twice
as fast as that!"
         Ibid. Chap. 2

"The time has come," the Walrus said,
  "To talk of many things:
Of shoes — and ships — and sealing-
  wax —
Of cabbages — and kings —
And why the sea is boiling hot —
  And whether pigs have wings."
    Ibid. Chap. 4, The Walrus and
       the Carpenter, Stanza 11

"The rule is, jam to-morrow, and
jam yesterday — but never jam *to-
day.*"
"It *must* come sometimes to 'jam to-
day,'" Alice objected.
"No, it can't," said the Queen. "It's
jam every *other* day: to-day isn't any
other day, you know."
         Ibid. Chap. 5

"When I use a word," Humpty-
Dumpty said, "it means just what I
choose it to mean — neither more nor
less."
         Ibid. Chap. 6

As large as life and twice as natural.
*Through the Looking Glass and
What Alice Found There.
Chap. 7*

He had bought a large map represent-
ing the sea,
Without the least vestige of land:
And the crew were much pleased when
they found it to be
A map they could all understand.
*The Hunting of the Snark.
Fit the Second, Stanza 2*

"What's the good of Mercator's North
Poles and Equators,
Tropics, Zones and Meridian Lines?"
So the Bellman would cry: and the
crew would reply
"They are merely conventional
signs!"
Ibid. Stanza 3

It is this, it is this that oppresses my
soul.
Ibid. Fit the Third, Stanza 11

And my heart is like nothing so much
as a bowl
Brimming over with quivering curds.
Ibid.

You may charge me with murder — or
want of sense —
(We are all of us weak at times):
But the slightest approach to a false
pretence
Was never among my crimes!
Ibid. Fit the Fourth, Stanza 4

And summed it so well that it came to
far more
Than the Witnesses ever had said!
Ibid. Fit the Sixth, Stanza 11

There are certain things — as, a spider,
a ghost,
The income-tax, gout, an umbrella
for three —
That I hate, but the thing that I hate
the most
Is a thing they call the Sea.
A Sea Dirge. Stanza 1

Then, if you'd be impressive,
Remember what I say,
That abstract qualities begin
With capitals alway:

The Good, the True, the Beautiful, —
Those are the things that pay!
*Poeta Fit, non Nascitur.
Stanza 5*

Such epithets, like pepper,
Give zest to what you write;
And, if you strew them sparely,
They whet the appetite:
But if you lay them on too thick,
You spoil the matter quite!
Ibid. Stanza 10

Where Life becomes a Spasm,
And History a Whiz:
If that is not Sensation,
I don't know what it is.
Ibid. Stanza 16

And I said "This is scrumptious!" —
a phrase I had learned from the
Devonshire shrimpers.
*Atalanta in Camden-Town.
Stanza 4*

What *you* call healthy appetite
I feel as Hunger's savage tooth:
And, when no dinner is in sight,
The dinner-bell's a sound of ruth! [1]
Peter and Paul. Stanza 17

BENJAMIN H. HILL
[1832–1882]

He was a foe without hate, a friend
without treachery, a soldier without
cruelty, and a victim without murmuring. He was a public officer without
vices, a private citizen without wrong,
a neighbor without reproach, a Christian without hypocrisy, and a man without guilt. He was Caesar without his
ambition, Frederick without his tyranny, Napoleon without his selfishness,
and Washington without his reward.
Tribute to Robert E. Lee. [2]

---

[1] Noon. As the Texas darky said: "Dinner-
time fur some folks; but just twelve o'clock
fur me!" — IRVIN SHREWSBURY COBB: *Paths
of Glory* [1915], *Chap. 5*
[2] Quoted in *General Lee* by FITZHUGH LEE
and in *Robert E. Lee* by THOMAS NELSON
PAGE.

NORA PERRY
[1832–1896]

Tying her bonnet under her chin,
She tied her raven ringlets in;
But not alone in the silken snare
Did she catch her lovely floating hair,
For, tying her bonnet under her chin,
She tied a young man's heart within.
The Love-Knot. Stanza 1

O, did you see him riding down,
And riding down, while all the town
Came out to see, came out to see,
And all the bells rang mad with glee?
Riding Down. Stanza 1

What silences we keep, year after year,
With those who are most near to us,
and dear! [1]
Too Late. Stanza 1

Some day of days, threading the street
With idle, heedless pace,
Unlooking for such grace,
I shall behold your face!
Some Day of Days. Stanza 1

Who knows the thoughts of a child?
Who Knows? Stanza 1

Gayly and gayly rang the gay music,
The blithe merry music of harp and of
horn,
The mad, merry music, that set us a-
dancing
Till over the midnight came stealing
the morn.
*That Waltz of von Weber's.
Stanza 1*

They sat and combed their beautiful
hair,
Their long, bright tresses, one by
one,
As they laughed and talked in the
chamber there,
After the revel was done.
After the Ball. Stanza 1

[1] Often, the sayings which are dearest to our hearts are least frequent on our lips; and those great ideas which cheer men in their direst struggles are not things which they are likely to inflict by frequent repetition upon those they live with. There is a certain reticence with us as regards anything we deeply love. — SIR ARTHUR HELPS [1813–1875]: *Friends in Council*

THEODORE WATTS-DUNTON
[1832–1914]

Love's old songs shall never die
Yet the new shall suffer proof:
Love's old drink of Yule brew I,
Wassail for new love's behoof.
Christmas at the Mermaid Tavern
A sonnet is a wave of melody.
The Sonnet's Voice

HENRY CLAY WORK
[1832–1884]

At the captain's forequarters they said
he would pass —
They'd train him up well in the in-
fantry class —
So they've grafted him into the
Army.
Grafted into the Army. Stanza 1
So we made a thoroughfare for Free-
dom and her train,
Sixty miles in latitude; three hundred
to the main.
*Marching through Georgia.
Stanza 5*

It mus' be now de kingdom coming,
An' de year ob Jubilo!
Kingdom Coming. Chorus
O don't you know dat
Babylon is fallen,
An' we's gwine to occupy de land?
Babylon Is Fallen. Chorus
Nicodemus, the slave, was of African
birth,
And was bought for a bag full of
gold:
He was reckoned as part of the salt of
the earth,
But he died, years ago, very old.
Wake Nicodemus. Stanza 1
There's a good time coming, it's almost
here,
'Twas a long, long time on the way.
Ibid. Chorus
Father, dear father, come home with
me now,
The clock in the steeple strikes one;
You said you were coming right home
from the shop
As soon as your day's work was done.
Come Home, Father. Stanza 1

My grandfather's clock was too large
  for the shelf,
  So it stood ninety years on the floor.
Grandfather's Clock
But it stopped short — never to go
  again —
  When the old man died.
Ibid.

ISAAC HILL BROMLEY
[1833–1898]

Listen! John A. Logan is the Head
Center, the Hub, the King Pin, the
Main Spring, Mogul and Mugwump [1]
of the final plot by which partisanship
was installed in the Commission.
Editorial in New York Tribune
  [February 16, 1877]
Bring me honey of Hymettus, bring me
  stores of Attic salt;
I am weary of the commonplace, to dul-
  ness call a halt!
These dinner speeches tire me, they are
  tedious, flat, and stale:
From a hundred thousand banquet ta-
  bles comes a melancholy wail,
As a hundred thousand banqueters sit
  up in evening dress
And salute each mouldy chestnut with
  a signal of distress.
Our Chauncey.[2] Stanza 2

RICHARD WATSON DIXON
[1833–1900]

Forth comes the moon, the sweet sur-
  prise of heaven,
And her footfall light
Drops on the multiplied wave.
The Spirit Wooed
I must have love in my degree,
  A human heart, a human hand.
For oh! 'tis better far to share,
  Though life all dark and bitter be,
With human bosoms human care.
The Wanderer

[1] A mugwump is a person educated beyond
his intellect.
  HORACE PORTER [1837–1921] in the
  Cleveland-Blaine campaign [1884].
[2] In praise of Chauncey M. Depew. Read at
the annual dinner of the New York Yale
Alumni Association [Jan. 23, 1891].

There is a soul above the soul of each,
A mightier soul, which yet to each be-
  longs:
There is a sound made of all human
  speech,
And numerous as the concourse of all
  songs.
Humanity

ADAM LINDSAY GORDON
[1833–1870]

Question not, but live and labour
  Till yon goal be won,
Helping every feeble neighbour,
  Seeking help from none;
Life is mostly froth and bubble,
  Two things stand like stone —
Kindness in another's trouble,
  Courage in our own.
Ye Wearie Wayfarer.
Finis Exoptatus, Stanza 8
For good undone and gifts misspent
  and resolutions vain,
  'Tis somewhat late to trouble. This
    I know —
I should live the same life over, if I had
  to live again;
  And the chances are I go where most
    men go.
The Sick Stockrider
A little season of love and laughter,
  Of light and life, and pleasure and
    pain,
And a horror of outer darkness after,
  And dust returneth to dust again.
The Swimmer
In a thousand years we shall all forget
The things that trouble us now.
After the Quarrel
On earth there's little worth a sigh,
  And nothing worth a tear!
To My Sister. Stanza 8
Lay me low, my work is done,
  I am weary. Lay me low.
Valedictory

JOHN JAMES INGALLS
[1833–1900]

The purification of politics is an iridescent dream.
Epigram

Every man is the center of a circle, whose fatal circumference he can not pass.

> *Eulogy on Benjamin Hill, United States Senate [January 23, 1882]*

In the democracy of the dead, all men at last are equal. There is neither rank nor station nor prerogative in the republic of the grave.

> *On the Death of Senator Barnes*

Next in profusion to the divine profusion of water, light and air, those three physical facts which render existence possible, may be reckoned the universal beneficence of grass.

> *Blue Grass*

Grass is the forgiveness of nature — her constant benediction. Fields trampled with battle, saturated with blood, torn with the ruts of the cannon, grow green again with grass, and carnage is forgotten. Forests decay, harvests perish, flowers vanish, but grass is immortal.

> *Ibid.*

It bears no blazonry of bloom to charm the senses with fragrance or splendor, but its homely hue is more enchanting than the lily or the rose. It yields no fruit in earth or air, and yet, should its harvest fail for a single year, famine would depopulate the world.

> *Ibid.*

I knock unbidden once at every gate!
If sleeping, wake; if feasting, rise before
I turn away. It is the hour of fate.

> *Opportunity*

ROBERT GREEN INGERSOLL
[1833–1899]

These heroes are dead. They died for liberty — they died for us. They are at rest. They sleep in the land they made free, under the flag they rendered stainless, under the solemn pines, the sad hemlocks, the tearful willows, the embracing vines. They sleep beneath the shadows of the clouds, careless alike of sunshine or storm, each in the windowless palace of rest. Earth may run red with other wars — they are at peace. In the midst of battles, in the roar of conflict, they found the serenity of death.

> *Vision of War [Speech at Indianapolis, Indiana, September 21, 1876; repeated by request in the Metropolitan Opera House, New York, May 30, 1888]*

Life is a narrow vale between the cold and barren peaks of two eternities. We strive in vain to look beyond the heights. We cry aloud — and the only answer is the echo of our wailing cry. From the voiceless lips of the unreplying dead there comes no word. But in the night of Death Hope sees a star and listening Love can hear the rustling of a wing.

> *At the Grave of his Brother, Ebon Clark Ingersoll [June, 1879] [1]*

He added to the sum of human joy, and were every one to whom he did some loving service to bring a blossom to his grave, he would sleep to-night beneath a wilderness of flowers.

> *Ibid.*

I am the inferior of any man whose rights I trample under foot. Men are not superior by reason of the accidents of race or color. They are superior who have the best heart — the best brain.

> *Liberty*

The superior man is the providence of the inferior. He is eyes for the blind, strength for the weak, and a shield for the defenseless. He stands erect by bending above the fallen. He rises by lifting others.

> *Ibid.*

Every cradle asks us, "Whence?" and every coffin, "Whither?" The poor barbarian, weeping above his dead, can answer these questions as intelligently as the robed priest of the most authentic creed.

> *Address at a Little Boy's Grave*

[1] Read at the service for Luther Burbank [April 14, 1926].

We, too, have our religion, and it is this: Help for the living, hope for the dead.

Address at a Little Boy's Grave

I would rather have been a French peasant and worn wooden shoes. I would rather have lived in a hut with a vine growing over the door and the grapes growing purple in the kisses of the Autumn sun. I would rather have been that poor peasant with my loving wife by my side, knitting as the day died out of the sky, with my children upon my knee and their arms about me. I would rather have been that man and gone down to the tongueless silence of the dreamless dust than to have been that imperial impersonation of force and murder known as Napoleon the Great.

At the Tomb of Napoleon

And will there, some time, be another world? We have our dream. The idea of immortality, that like a sea has ebbed and flowed in the human heart, beating with its countless waves against the sands and rocks of time and fate, was not born of any creed, nor of any book, nor of any religion. It was born of human affection, and it will continue to ebb and flow beneath the mists and clouds of doubt and darkness, as long as love kisses the lips of death.

At the Bier of a Friend

Few rich men own their own property. The property owns them.

Address to the McKinley League, Carnegie Hall, New York [*October 29, 1896*]

An honest God is the noblest work of man.

Epigram

Though Scotland boasts a thousand names,
Of patriot, king and peer,
The noblest, grandest of them all
Was loved and cradled here.

The Birthplace of Burns, Ayr [1]
[*August 19, 1878*]

[1] This poem hangs in the Burns birthplace, Ayr.

And here the world, through all the years,
As long as day returns,
The tribute of its love and tears
Will pay to Robert Burns.

The Birthplace of Burns, Ayr
[*August 19, 1878*]

Justice is the only worship.
Love is the only priest.
Ignorance is the only slavery.
Happiness is the only good.
The time to be happy is now,
The place to be happy is here,
The way to be happy is to make others so.

Creed

Is there beyond the silent night
An endless day?
Is death a door that leads to light?
We cannot say.

Declaration of the Free. Stanza 16

DAVID ROSS LOCKE
("PETROLEUM V. NASBY")
[1833–1888]

The contract 'twixt Hannah, God and me,
Was not for one or twenty years, but for eternity.

Hannah Jane.[1] *Stanza 29*

JULIA HARRIS MAY
[1833–1912]

Slower, sweet June,
Each step more slow;
Linger and loiter as you go.

Slower, Sweet June. Stanza 1

If we could know
Which of us, darling, would be first to go,
Which would be first to breast the swelling tide,
And step alone upon the other side,
If we could know!

If We Could Know. Stanza 1

[1] In *Harper's Monthly, October, 1871.*

EMILY HUNTINGTON MILLER
[1833–1913]

Hang up the baby's stocking;
  Be sure you don't forget
The dear little dimpled darling!
  She ne'er saw Christmas yet.
      Hang Up the Baby's Stocking

SIR LEWIS MORRIS
[1833–1907]

The wind that sighs before the dawn
  Chases the gloom of night,
The curtains of the East are drawn,
  And suddenly — 'tis light.
      Le Vent de l'Esprit. Stanza 1

There shall rise from this confused
    sound of voices
A firmer faith than that our fathers
    knew,
A deep religion which alone rejoices
In worship of the Infinitely True.
      Brotherhood. Stanza 1

Call no faith false which e'er hath
    brought
Relief to any laden life,
Cessation from the pain of thought,
Refreshment 'mid the dust of strife.
      Tolerance. Stanza 1

CHARLES CARROLL SAWYER
[1833– ?]

When this cruel war is over,
Praying that we meet again.
      Weeping, Sad and Lonely (When
        This Cruel War is Over)

EDMUND CLARENCE STEDMAN
[1833–1908]

Prison-mate and dock-yard fellow,
  Blades to Meg and Molly dear,
Off to capture Porto Bello
  Sailed with Morgan the Buccaneer!
      Morgan.[1] Stanza 1

---

[1] The old bold mate of Henry Morgan.
    JOHN MASEFIELD: *Captain Stratton's*
        Fancy

Where's he that died o' Wednesday? [1]
What place on earth hath he?
      Falstaff's Song. Stanza 1

Just where the Treasury's marble front
  Looks over Wall Street's mingled na-
    tions;
Where Jews and Gentiles most are wont
  To throng for trade and last quota-
    tions.
      Pan in Wall Street. Stanza 1

Give me to die unwitting of the day,
And stricken in Life's brave heat, with
    senses clear!
      Sonnet, Mors Benefica

Crops failed; wealth took a flight;
    house, treasure, land,
  Slipped from my hold — thus plenty
    comes and goes.
One friend I had, but he too loosed his
    hand
  (Or was it I?) the year I met with
    Rose.
      The World Well Lost. Stanza 2

Not braver he that leaps the wall
  By level musket-flashes litten,
Than I, who stepped before them all,
  Who longed to see me get the mitten.
      On the Doorstep. Stanza 2

"Oh, anywhere! Forward! 'Tis all the
    same, Colonel:
  You'll find lovely fighting along the
    whole line!"
      Kearny[2] at Seven Pines. Stanza 3

Look on this cast, and know the hand
  That bore a nation in its hold:
From this mute witness understand
  What Lincoln was, — how large of
    mould.
      The Hand of Lincoln. Stanza 1

Give us a man of God's own mould,
  Born to marshal his fellow-men;
One whose fame is not bought and sold
  At the stroke of a politician's pen.
      Wanted — a Man. Stanza 2

Not thou, not thou — 'tis we
Are deaf, are dumb, are blind!
      Helen Keller. Stanza 4

---

[1] See Shakespeare, page 63.
[2] General Philip Kearny [1815–1862].

JULIA LOUISE MATILDA WOODRUFF
("W. M. L. JAY")
[1833–1909]

Out of the strain of the doing,
Into the peace of the done.
Gone

HORATIO ALGER
[1834–1899]

'Twas on Lake Erie's broad expanse,
    One bright midsummer day,
The gallant steamer Ocean Queen
    Swept proudly on her way.
        John Maynard.[1] *Stanza 1*
Three hundred grateful voices rise
    In praise to God that He
Hath saved them from the fearful fire,
    And from the engulfing sea.
        Ibid. Stanza 11

GEORGE ARNOLD
[1834–1865]

"Learn while you're young," he often
    said,
"There is much to enjoy down here be-
    low;
Life for the living, and rest for the
    dead!"
Said the jolly old pedagogue, long ago.
    The Jolly Old Pedagogue. Stanza 2
"The living need charity more than the
    dead."
        Ibid. Stanza 3
"I need so little," he often said,
"And my friends and relatives here be-
    low

[1] John Maynard was a pilot on a steamboat plying between Detroit and Buffalo. The steamer did not carry boats, and one summer afternoon, when proceeding with large quantities of resin and tar on board, it caught fire, seven miles from Buffalo. Passengers and crew crowded the forward part of the ship. John Maynard stayed at the helm and beached the ship, all lives being saved except his own. — JOHN B. GOUGH [1817–1886]: *Sermon*

And, sure's you're born, they all got off
    Afore the smokestacks fell, —
And Bludso's ghost went up alone
    In the smoke of the Prairie Belle.
        JOHN HAY [1838–1905]:
            Jim Bludso, St. 6

Won't litigate over me when I am
    dead."
        The Jolly Old Pedagogue. Stanza 4
I,
Being dry,
Sit, idly sipping here
    My Beer.
        Beer
O, finer far
Than fame, or riches, are
The graceful smoke-wreaths of this free
    cigar!
        Ibid.
Gray distance hid each shining sail,
    By ruthless breezes borne from me;
And lessening, fading, faint, and pale
    My ships went forth to sea.
        Jubilate. Stanza 1

SIR JOHN LUBBOCK, LORD AVEBURY
[1834–1913]

The world would be better and brighter if our teachers would dwell on the Duty of Happiness as well as on the Happiness of Duty, for we ought to be as cheerful as we can, if only because to be happy ourselves is a most effectual contribution to the happiness of others.
        The Pleasures of Life. Page 2
As the sun colors flowers, so does art color life.
        Ibid. Page 177
The idle man does not know what it is to enjoy rest. Hard work, moreover, not only tends to give us rest for the body, but, what is even more important, peace to the mind.
        Ibid. Page 316

SABINE BARING-GOULD
[1834–1924]

Crowns and thrones may perish,
    Kingdoms rise and wane,
But the church of Jesus
    Constant will remain.
        Onward, Christian Soldiers
Now the day is over,
    Night is drawing nigh;

Shadows of the evening
   Steal across the sky.
      Now the Day Is Over. Stanza 1
Comfort every sufferer
   Watching late in pain;
Those who plan some evil,
   From their sin restrain.
                Ibid. Stanza 5

CHARLES FARRAR BROWNE ("ARTEMUS WARD")
[1834–1867]

My pollertics, like my religion, being of an exceedin' accommodatin' character.
                The Crisis
The fack can't be no longer disgised that a Krysis is onto us.
                Ibid.
I am not a politician, and my other habits are good.
      Fourth of July Oration
The prevailin' weakness of most public men is to Slop over. G. Washington never slopt over.
                Ibid.
I can't sing. As a singist I am not a success. I am saddest when I sing. So are those who hear me. They are sadder even than I am.
      Artemus Ward's Lecture
N. B. This is rote Sarcastikul.
     A Visit to Brigham Young
Did you ever have the measels, and if so, how many?
           The Census
I have alreddy given Two cousins to the war, & I stand reddy to sacrifiss my wife's brother ruther 'n not see the rebelyin krusht. And if wuss comes to wuss, I'll shed ev'ry drop of blud my able-bodid relations has got.
      To the Prince of Wales
Why is this thus? What is the reason of this thusness?
        Moses, the Sassy
He is dreadfully married. "He's the most married man I ever saw in my life."
                Ibid.

Let us all be happy and live within our means, even if we have to borrow the money to do it with.
         Natural History
The sun has a right to "set" where it wants to, and so, I may add, has a hen.
      A Morman Romance. IV
They cherish his mem'ry, and them as sell picturs of his birth-place, etc., make it prof'tible cherishin' it.
   At the Tomb of Shakespeare

GEORGE LOUIS PALMELLA BUSSON DU MAURIER
[1834–1896]

He had never heard such music as this, never dreamt such music was possible. He was conscious, while it lasted, that he saw deeper into the beauty, the sadness of things, the very heart of them, and their pathetic evanescence, as with a new inner eye — even into eternity itself, beyond the veil.
        Trilby.[1] Part I
Meat so dressed and sauced and seasoned that you didn't know whether it was beef or mutton — flesh, fowl, or good red herring.[2]
                Ibid.
Lovely female shapes are terrible complicators of the difficulties and dangers of this earthly life, especially for their owner.
                Ibid.
A wave of religious emotion rolled over Little Billee and submerged him; swept him off his little legs, swept him out of his little self, drowned him in a great seething surge of love — love of his kind, love of love, love of life, love of death, love of all that is and ever was and ever will be.
        Ibid. Part III
That is the worst of those dear people who have charm; they are so terrible to do without, when once you

[1] *Trilby* was published serially in *Harper's Monthly*, beginning with the January, 1894 issue.
[2] See Heywood, page 13.

have got accustomed to them and all their ways.

Trilby. Part V

Every single phrase is a string of perfect gems, of purest ray serene,[1] strung together on a loose golden thread.

Ibid. Part VI

She was one of those rarely gifted beings who cannot look or speak or even stir without waking up (and satisfying) some vague longing that lies dormant in the hearts of most of us.

Ibid. Part VII

There can be prayers without words just as well as songs, I suppose.

Ibid. Part VIII

Grief tires more than anything, and brings a deeper slumber.

Ibid.

A little work, a little play,
To keep us going — and so, good-day!

A little warmth, a little light,
Of love's bestowing — and so, good-night! [2]

---

[1] Full many a gem of purest ray serene.
THOMAS GRAY: *Elegy in a Country
Churchyard, St. 14*

[2]   La vie est vaine:
            Un peu d'amour,
            Un peu de haine. . . .
            Et puis — Bonjour!

        La vie est brève:
            Un peu d'espoir,
            Un peu de rêve,
            Et puis — Bon soir!
LEON MONTENAEKEN [1859–   ]:
            Peu de Chose
Ah, brief is Life,
    Love's short sweet way,
With dreamings rife,
    And then — Good-day!

And Life is vain —
    Hope's vague delight,
Grief's transient pain,
    And then — Good-night.
        Translation by LOUISE
        CHANDLER MOULTON

In *The London Daily Express, July 3, 1902,*
a third stanza by Montenaeken was published
with a somewhat imperfect translation:
    La vie est telle
    Que Dieu le fit;

A little fun, to match the sorrow
Of each day's growing — and so, good-morrow!

A little trust that when we die
We reap our sowing! and so — good-by!

Trilby. Part VIII

That aristocratic flavor, so grateful and comforting to scholar and ignoramus alike, which the costly British public-school system (and the British accent) alone can impart to a dead language.

Peter Ibbetson. Page 49

The wretcheder one is, the more one smokes; and the more one smokes, the wretcheder one gets — a vicious circle! [1]

Ibid. Page 135

I do not know if little dogs cause as large griefs when they die as big ones.

Ibid. Page 152

There is an old French air,
A little song of loneliness and grief —
Simple as nature, sweet beyond compare —
And sad — past all belief!

*Ibid. Page 153 (The Chime.
Stanza 1)*

Songs without words are best.

Ibid. Page 162

What matter if it be a fool's paradise? [2] Paradise is paradise, for whoever owns it!

Ibid. Page 265

What matters what anybody thinks? "It will be all the same a hundred years hence." That is the most sensible proverb ever invented.

Ibid. Page 268

        Et telle quelle —
        Elle suffit!

    Life is but such
        As wrought God's will;
    'Tis naught, and still —
        'Tis oft too much!
[1] Bobus, you are in a vicious circle, rounder
than one of your own sausages. — THOMAS
CARLYLE: *Past and Present, Book I, Chap. 5.*
[2] See Shakespeare, page 79.

I have no talent for making new friends, but oh, such a genius for fidelity to old ones!

Peter Ibbetson. Page 276

There is both an impertinence and a lack of taste in any man's laying bare to the public eye — to any eye — the bliss that has come to him through the love of a devoted woman, with whose life his own has been bound up.

Ibid. Page 305

Happiness is like time and space — we make and measure it ourselves; it is a fancy — as big, as little, as you please; just a thing of contrasts and comparisons.

Ibid. Page 399

All will be well for us all, and of such a kind that all who do not sigh for the moon will be well content.

Ibid. Page 415

CHARLES WILLIAM ELIOT
[1834–1926]

Carrier of news and knowledge
Instrument of trade and commerce
Promoter of mutual acquaintance
Among men and nations and hence
Of peace and good will.

Carrier of love and sympathy
Messenger of friendship
Consoler of the lonely
Servant of the scattered family
Enlarger of the public life.

Inscriptions for the East and West Pavilions, Post Office, Washington, D. C.[1]

[1] These inscriptions were edited by Woodrow Wilson, to read:
    Carrier of news and knowledge
    Instrument of trade and
    Promoter of mutual acquaintance
    Of peace and good will
    Among men and nations.

    Messenger of sympathy and love
    Servant of parted friends
    Consoler of the lonely
    Bond of the scattered family
    Enlarger of the common life.

MARY ANNE HEARN
("MARIANNE FARNING-HAM")
[1834–1909]

I cannot tell why there should come to me
    A thought of someone miles and years away.

Unforgotten. Stanza 1

Will any one there, at the beautiful gate,
    Be waiting and watching for me?

*Waiting and Watching for Me.
Stanza 1*

WALTER KITTREDGE
[1834–1905]

We're tenting to-night on the old camp-ground,
    Give us a song to cheer
Our weary hearts, a song of home
    And friends we love so dear.

*Tenting on the Old Camp-ground.
Stanza 1*

WILLIAM MORRIS
[1834–1896]

I know a little garden-close,
Set thick with lily and red rose,
Where I would wander if I might
From dewy morn to dewy night.

*The Life and Death of Jason.
A Garden by the Sea, Stanza 1*

The idle singer of an empty day.

*The Earthly Paradise. An
Apology, Stanza 1*

Dreamer of dreams, born out of my due time,
Why should I strive to set the crooked straight?

Ibid. Stanza 4

Masters, I have to tell a tale of woe,
A tale of folly and of wasted life,
Hope against hope, the bitter dregs of strife,
Ending, where all things end, in death at last.

Ibid. Prologue

Forget six counties overhung with smoke,

Forget the snorting steam and piston
  stroke,
Forget the spreading of the hideous
  town;
Think rather of the pack-horse on the
  down,
And dream of London, small, and white,
  and clean.
            The Earthly Paradise. Prologue
Love is enough, though the world be
  a-waning.
                        Love Is Enough

RODEN BERKELEY WRIOTHESLEY NOEL
[1834–1894]

After battle sleep is best,
  After noise, tranquillity.
                            The Old
The bass eternal of the sea.
                            Beatrice
Ah! what if some unshamed iconoclast
Crumbling old fetish raiments of the
  past,
Rises from dead cerements the Christ
  at last?
What if men take to following where
  He leads,
Weary of mumbling Athanasian creeds?
                        The Red Flag

RICHARD REALF
[1834–1878]

Back of the canvas that throbs, the
  painter is hinted and hidden;
Into the statue that breathes, the soul
  of the sculptor is bidden.
                Indirection. Stanza 3
Back of the sound broods the silence,
  back of the gift stands the giving;
Back of the hand that receives thrill
  the sensitive nerves of receiving.
                    Ibid. Stanza 4
Harms of the world have come unto us,
  Cups of sorrow we yet shall drain;
But we have a secret that doth show us
  Wonderful rainbows in the rain.
            An Old Man's Idyl. Stanza 7
Here, gathered from all places and all
  time,

The waifs of wisdom and of folly meet.
                        In a Scrap-Book

ABRAM JOSEPH RYAN
[1834–1886]

But far on the deep there are billows
That never shall break on the beach;
And I have heard songs in the Silence
That never shall float into speech.
                Song of the Mystic. Stanza 9
I wish I were the little key
That locks Love's Captive in.
            A Child's Wish Before an Altar.
                                Stanza 1
When falls the soldier brave,
Dead at the feet of wrong,
The poet sings and guards his grave
With sentinels of song.
                Sentinel Songs. Stanza 1
Hearts that are great are always lone,
They never will manifest their best;
Their greatest greatness is unknown —
Earth knows a little — God, the rest.
                A Thought. Stanza 3
  A land without ruins is a land with-
out memories — a land without mem-
ories is a land without history.
                A Land Without Ruins.
                                Foreword
  Crowns of roses fade — crowns of
thorns endure. Calvaries and crucifix-
ions take deepest hold of humanity —
the triumphs of might are transient —
they pass and are forgotten — the sufferings of right are graven deepest on
the chronicle of nations.
                                Ibid.

HENRY THOMPSON STANTON
[1834–1898]

Ah, search the wide world wherever
  you can,
There is no open door for the money-
  less man!
                The Moneyless Man. Stanza 1

FRANK RICHARD STOCKTON
[1834–1902]

  He could open either door he pleased.
. . . If he opened the one, there came
out of it a hungry tiger, the fiercest and

most cruel that could be procured, which immediately sprang upon him, and tore him to pieces, as a punishment for his guilt. . . . But if the accused person opened the other door, there came forth from it a lady, the most suitable to his years and station that his Majesty could select among his fair subjects. . . . So I leave it with all of you: Which came out of the opened door — the lady or the tiger?

The Lady or the Tiger?

JAMES THOMSON
[1834–1882]

The wine of Love is music,
    And the feast of Love is song:
And when Love sits down to the banquet,
    Love sits long.

The Vine. Stanza 1

Let my voice ring out and over the earth
    Through all the grief and strife,
With a golden joy in a silver mirth,
    Thank God for life!

Life, Love and You. Stanza 1

Give a man a horse he can ride,
    Give a man a boat he can sail;
And his rank and wealth, his strength and health
    On sea nor shore shall fail.

Gifts. Stanza 1

Give a man a pipe he can smoke,
    Give a man a book he can read:
And his home is bright with a calm delight,
    Though the room be poor indeed.

Ibid. Stanza 2

Singing is sweet, but be sure of this,
Lips only sing when they cannot kiss.

Art

Statues and pictures and verse may be grand,
But they are not the Life for which they stand.

Ibid.

He came to the desert of London town
    Grey miles long.

William Blake. Stanza 1

Be assured; no secret can be told
To any who divined it not before:

None uninitiate by many a presage
Will comprehend the language of the message,
    Although proclaimed aloud for evermore.

The City of Dreadful Night.
Proem.

As I came through the desert thus it was
As I came through the desert. . . .
    But I rode on austere;
    No hope could have no fear.

Ibid. IV

Dateless oblivion and divine repose.

Ibid. XIII

CHARLES HENRY WEBB
("JOHN PAUL")
[1834–1905]

Turn out more ale, turn up the light;
I will not go to bed to-night.
Of all the foes that man should dread
The first and worst one is a bed.

Dum Vivimus Vigilamus.
Stanza 1

Friends I have had both old and young,
And ale we drank and songs we sung:
Enough you know when this is said,
That, one and all, — they died in bed.
    In bed they died and I'll not go
    Where all my friends have perished so.

Ibid.

For I've been born and I've been wed —
All of man's peril comes of bed.

Ibid. Stanza 2

I care not a pin what the world may say
    In regard to the wrong or right;
My money goes as well as my song
    For the dog that keeps out of the fight!

The Outside Dog in the Fight.
Stanza 3

The King and the Pope together
    Have sent a letter to me;
It is signed with a golden sceptre,
    It is sealed with a golden key.

The King wants me out of his eye-
sight;
The Pope wants me out of his See.
                    The King and the Pope.
                              Stanza 1
That 'tis well to be off with the old
love
Before one is on with the new
Has somehow passed into a proverb,[1]
But who follows its teaching may
rue.
                    Proverbum Sap. Stanza 1
Were the proverb not wiser if mended,
And the fickle and wavering told
To be sure that they're on with the new
love
Before being off with the old?
                    Ibid. Stanza 3
Of Christian souls more have been
wrecked on shore
    Than ever were lost at sea.
With a Nantucket Shell. Stanza 3

JAMES McNEILL WHISTLER
[1834–1903]

The rare Few, who, early in Life,
have rid Themselves of the Friendship
of the Many.
            *The Gentle Art of Making
                Enemies. Dedication*
To say of a picture, as is often said
in its praise, that it shows great and
earnest labour, is to say that it is incomplete and unfit for view.
            Ibid. Propositions, 2
Industry in Art is a necessity — not
a virtue — and any evidence of the
same, in the production, is a blemish,
not a quality; a proof, not of achievement, but of absolutely insufficient
work, for work alone will efface the
footsteps of work.
                            Ibid.

---

[1] It's gude to be merry and wise,
    It's gude to be honest and true;
  It's gude to be off with the old love,
    Before you are on with the new.
        ANONYMOUS [1816]. Quoted by AN-
    THONY TROLLOPE in *Barchester Tow-
    ers, Chap. 46.*
  See G. B. Shaw, page 720.

The work of the master reeks not of
the sweat of the brow — suggests no
effort and is finished from the beginning.
            *The Gentle Art of Making
                Enemies. Propositions, 2*

The masterpiece should appear as
the flower to the painter — perfect in
its bud as in its bloom — with no reason
to explain its presence — no mission to
fulfil — a joy to the artist, a delusion
to the philanthropist — a puzzle to the
botanist — an accident of sentiment
and alliteration to the literary man.
                            Ibid.

Art should be independent of all
clap-trap — should stand alone, and
appeal to the artistic sense of eye and
ear, without confounding this with
emotions entirely foreign to it, as devotion, pity, love, patriotism, and the
like. All these have no kind of concern
with it.
                            Ibid.

The imitator is a poor kind of creature. If the man who paints only the
tree, or flower, or other surface he sees
before him were an artist, the king of
artists would be the photographer. It
is for the artist to do something beyond
this: in portrait painting to put on canvas something more than the face the
model wears for that one day; to paint
the man, in short, as well as his features.
                            Ibid.

Nature sings her exquisite song to the
artist alone, her son and her master —
her son in that he loves her, her master
in that he knows her.
            Ibid. Ten O'Clock

Two and two continue to make four,
in spite of the whine of the amateur for
three, or the cry of the critic for five.
            Ibid. Whistler vs. Ruskin [1]

---

[1] In the law-suit for libel [1878]. Ruskin
had written of Whistler's *Nocturne in Black
and Gold,* "I never expected to hear a coxcomb ask two hundred guineas for flinging a
pot of paint in the public's face."

One cannot continually disappoint a Continent
> *The Gentle Art of Making Enemies. (Of a contemplated visit to the U. S.)*

Wilde. I wish I'd said that.

Whistler. You will, Oscar, you will.
> *Traditional Dialogue*

I am not arguing with you — I am telling you.
> *Quoted by* ELIZABETH ROBINS PENNELL *in Art of Whistler*

Why drag in Velasquez?
> *Traditional (quoted by Mrs. Pennell)*

ALFRED AUSTIN
[1835–1913]

So long as Faith with Freedom reigns,
  And loyal Hope survives,
And gracious Charity remains
  To leaven lowly lives;
While there is one untrodden tract
  For intellect or will,
And men are free to think and act,
  Life is worth living still.
> *Is Life Worth Living?* [1]

Why should we lodge in marble or in bronze
Spirits more vast than earth, or sea, or sky?
Wiser the silent worshiper who cons
Their page for Wisdom that will never die.
> *On the Proposal to Erect a Statue to Shakespeare in London*

Gods for themselves are monuments enough.
> *Ibid.*

Kinsmen, hail!
We severed have been too long.
Now let us have done with a worn-out tale —
The tale of an ancient wrong —
And our friendship last long as our love doth, and be stronger than death is strong.
> *To America*

Who say we cherish far-off feud,
  Still nurse the ancient grudges?
Show me the title of this brood
  Of self-appointed judges;

[1] See William James, page 663.

Their name, their race, their nation, clan,
  And we will teach them whether
We do not, as none others can,
  Feel, think and work together.
> *Together*

THOMAS BRIGHAM BISHOP
[1835–1905]

John Brown's body lies a-mouldering in the grave,
His soul goes marching on.
> *John Brown's Body*

Shoo, fly! don't bodder me! I belong to Company G,
  I feel like a morning star.
> *Shoo, Fly.*[1] *Refrain*

MARY EMILY BRADLEY
[1835–1898]

Of all the bonny buds that blow
  In bright or cloudy weather,
Of all the flowers that come and go
  The whole twelve months together,
This little purple pansy brings
Thoughts of the sweetest, saddest things.
> *Heart's Ease. Stanza 1*

PHILLIPS BROOKS
[1835–1893]

O little town of Bethlehem!
  How still we see thee lie;
Above thy deep and dreamless sleep
  The silent stars go by;
Yet in thy dark streets shineth
  The everlasting Light;
The hopes and fears of all the years
  Are met in thee to-night.
> *O Little Town of Bethlehem. Stanza 1*

Everywhere, everywhere, Christmas to-night!
Christmas in lands of the fir-tree and pine,
Christmas in lands of the palm-tree and vine;
Christmas where snow-peaks stand solemn and white,

[1] See B. F. Butler, page 516.

Christmas where corn-fields lie sunny
and bright.
>> *A Christmas Carol. Stanza 1*

Life comes before literature, as the
material always comes before the work.
The hills are full of marble before the
world blooms with statues.
>> *Literature and Life*

Do not pray for easy lives. Pray to
be stronger men! Do not pray for tasks
equal to your powers. Pray for powers
equal to your tasks.
>> *Twenty Sermons. 18, Going up
to Jerusalem*

May I try to tell you again where
your only comfort lies? It is not in forgetting the happy past. People bring
us well-meant but miserable consolation when they tell what time will do
to help our grief. We do not want to
lose our grief, because our grief is
bound up with our love and we could
not cease to mourn without being
robbed of our affections.
>> *Letter to a friend on the death
of his mother [November 19,
1891]*

SAMUEL BUTLER
[1835–1902]

It is far safer to know too little than
too much. People will condemn the one,
though they will resent being called
upon to exert themselves to follow the
other.
>> *The Way of All Flesh.[1] Chap. 5*

Adversity, if a man is set down to it
by degrees, is more supportable with
equanimity by most people than any
great prosperity arrived at in a single
lifetime.
>> *Ibid.*

It is our less conscious thoughts and
our less conscious actions which mainly
mould our lives and the lives of those
who spring from us.
>> *Ibid.*

To me it seems that youth is like
spring, an over-praised season — de-

[1] I saw him now going the way of all flesh.
— JOHN WEBSTER: *Westward Hoe, Act II,
Sc. 2*

lightful if it happen to be a favoured
one, but in practice very rarely favoured and more remarkable, as a general rule, for biting east winds than
genial breezes.
>> *The Way of All Flesh. Chap. 6*

In old age we live under the shadow
of Death, which, like a sword of Da-
mocles, may descend at any moment,
but we have so long found life to be
an affair of being rather frightened than
hurt that we have become like the people who live under Vesuvius, and chance
it without much misgiving.
>> *Ibid.*

A pair of lovers are like sunset and
sunrise: there are such things every day
but we very seldom see them.
>> *Ibid. Chap. 11*

Every man's work, whether it be
literature or music or pictures or architecture or anything else, is always a
portrait of himself, and the more he
tries to conceal himself the more clearly
will his character appear in spite of
him.
>> *Ibid. Chap. 14*

A virtue, to be serviceable, must,
like gold, be alloyed with some commoner but more durable metal.
>> *Ibid. Chap. 19*

One great reason why clergymen's
households are generally unhappy is
because the clergyman is so much at
home and close about the house.
>> *Ibid. Chap. 24*

The best liar is he who makes the
smallest amount of lying go the longest way — who husbands it too carefully to waste it where it can be dis-
pensed with.
>> *Ibid. Chap. 39*

If people would dare to speak to one
another unreservedly, there would be a
good deal less sorrow in the world a
hundred years hence.
>> *Ibid. Chap. 44*

Everyone has a mass of bad work in
him which he will have to work off and
get rid of before he can do better —
and indeed, the more lasting a man's
ultimate good work, the more sure he
is to pass through a time, and perhaps

a very long one, in which there seems very little hope for him at all. We must all sow our spiritual wild oats.

The Way of All Flesh. Chap. 51

It is in the uncompromisingness with which dogma is held and not in the dogma or want of dogma that the danger lies.

Ibid. Chap. 68

When people get it into their heads that they are being specially favoured by the Almighty, they had better as a general rule mind their p's and q's.

Ibid. Chap. 71

An empty house is like a stray dog or a body from which life has departed.[1]

Ibid. Chap. 72

A man's friendships are, like his will, invalidated by marriage — but they are also no less invalidated by the marriage of his friends.

Ibid. Chap. 75

I reckon being ill as one of the great pleasures of life, provided one is not too ill and is not obliged to work till one is better.

Ibid. Chap. 80

A hen is only an egg's way of making another egg.

Life and Habit. Chap. 8

Stowed away in a Montreal lumber
    room
The Discobolus standeth and turneth
    his face to the wall;
Dusty, cobweb-covered, maimed and
    set at naught,
Beauty crieth in an attic and no man
    regardeth.
    O God! O Montreal!

A Psalm of Montreal.[2] Stanza 1

The Discobolus is put here because he
    is vulgar —
He has neither vest nor pants with
    which to cover his limbs;
I, Sir, am a person of most respectable
    connections. —

[1] I suppose I've passed it a hundred times,
    but I always stop for a minute
And look at the house, the tragic house,
    the house with nobody in it.
    JOYCE KILMER: *The House with
        Nobody in It*
[2] In *The London Spectator, May 18, 1878.*

My brother-in-law is haberdasher to
    Mr. Spurgeon.
    O God! O Montreal!

A Psalm of Montreal. Stanza 5

Life is the art of drawing sufficient conclusions from insufficient premises.

Note-Books. Lord, What Is Man?

All progress is based upon a universal innate desire on the part of every organism to live beyond its income.

Ibid.

Though analogy is often misleading, it is the least misleading thing we have.

Ibid. Music, Pictures, and Books

I have gone in for posthumous fame. . . . Posterity will give a man a fair hearing; his own times will not do so if he is attacking vested interests, and I have attacked two powerful sets of vested interests at once — the Church and Science.

Ibid. Homo Unius Libri [1883]

Ideas and opinions, like living organisms, have a normal rate of growth which cannot be either checked or forced beyond a certain point. The more unpopular an opinion is, the more necessary is it that the holder should be somewhat punctilious in his observance of conventionalities generally.

*Ibid. The Art of Propagating
Opinion*

I do not think America is a good place in which to be a genius. A genius can never expect to have a good time anywhere, but America is about the last place in which life will be endurable at all for an inspired writer.

Ibid. Cash and Credit

The Ancient Mariner would not have taken so well if it had been called *The Old Sailor.*

Ibid. Titles and Subjects

The public buys its opinions as it buys its meat, or takes in its milk, on the principle that it is cheaper to do this than to keep a cow. So it is, but the milk is more likely to be watered.

*Ibid. Sequel to "Alps and
Sanctuaries"*

How holy people look when they are sea-sick!

Ibid. The Channel Passage

The man who lets himself be bored is even more contemptible than the bore.[1]

The Fair Haven. Memoir, Chap. 3

O Critics, Cultured Critics!
Who will praise me after I am dead,
Who will see in me both more and less
    than I intended,
But who will swear that whatever it was
    it was all perfectly right;
You will think you are better than the
    people who, when I was alive,
    swore that whatever I did was
    wrong,
And damned my books for me as fast as
    I could write them;
But you will not be better, you will be
    just the same, neither better nor
    worse,
And you will go for some future Butler
    as your fathers have gone for me;
Oh, how I should have hated you!

To Critics and Others

SAMUEL LANGHORNE
CLEMENS
("MARK TWAIN") [2]
[1835–1910]

This is petrified truth.

*A Complaint about Corre-
spondents*

This poor little one-horse town.

The Undertaker's Story

---

[1] See, on this topic, an exquisitely humorous essay by HILAIRE BELLOC, "A Guide to Boring," in his volume *A Conversation with a Cat, etc.* (1931).

[2] I was a fresh, new journalist, and needed a *nom de guerre;* so I confiscated the ancient mariner's discarded one ["Mark Twain"], and have done my best to make it remain what it was in his hands — a sign and symbol and warrant that whatever is found in its company may be gambled on as being the petrified truth. — MARK TWAIN: *Life on the Mississippi, Chap. 50.* (The earlier use of the penname was by Captain Isaiah Sellers, in *The New Orleans Picayune.*)

By American literature in the proper sense we ought to mean literature written in an American way, with an American turn of language and an American cast of thought. The test is that it couldn't have been written anywhere else. — STEPHEN LEACOCK: *Mark Twain as a National Asset*

They spell it Vinci and pronounce it Vinchy; foreigners always spell better than they pronounce.

The Innocents Abroad

He is now fast rising from affluence to poverty.

Henry Ward Beecher's Farm

I'll resk forty dollars that he can outjump any frog in Calaveras county.

The Notorious Jumping Frog

There is no red outside the arteries of an archangel that can compare with it.[1]

*Lotos Club Speech [January 11,
1908]*

A classic is something that everybody wants to have read and nobody wants to read.

The Disappearance of Literature

A powerful agent is the right word. Whenever we come upon one of those intensely right words in a book or a newspaper the resulting effect is physical as well as spiritual, and electrically prompt.

Essay on William Dean Howells

Work consists of whatever a body is *obliged* to do, and Play consists of whatever a body is not obliged to do.

*The Adventures of Tom Sawyer.
Chap. 2*

Pilgrim's Progress, about a man that left his family, it didn't say why. The statement was interesting but tough.

*The Adventures of Huckleberry
Finn. Chap. 17*

But soft you, the fair Ophelia:
Ope not thy ponderous and marble
    jaws,
But get thee to a nunnery — go!

*Ibid. Chap. 21 (The Duke's
version of Hamlet's soliloquy)*

Cauliflower is nothing but cabbage with a college education.

Pudd'nhead Wilson's Calendar

If you pick up a starving dog and make him prosperous, he will not bite you. This is the principal difference between a dog and a man.

Ibid.

---

[1] His scarlet Doctor's gown from Oxford.

It is difference of opinion that makes horse races.

Pudd'nhead Wilson's Calendar

Why is it that we rejoice at a birth and grieve at a funeral? It is because we are not the person involved.

Ibid.

The reports of my death are greatly exaggerated.

Cable from Europe to the Associated Press

Barring that natural expression of villainy which we all have, the man looked honest enough.

A Mysterious Visit

An experienced, industrious, ambitious, and often quite picturesque liar.

My Military Campaign

I will set down a tale as it was told to me by one who had it of his father, which latter had it of *his* father, this last having in like manner had it of *his* father.

The Prince and the Pauper. Foreword

The world and the books are so accustomed to use, and over-use, the word "new" in connection with our country, that we early get and permanently retain the impression that there is nothing old about it.

Life on the Mississippi.[1]
Chap. 1

When I'm playful I use the meridians of longitude and parallels of latitude for a seine, and drag the Atlantic Ocean for whales. I scratch my head with the lightning and purr myself to sleep with the thunder.

Ibid. Chap. 3

The Child of Calamity.

Ibid.

I was gratified to be able to answer promptly, and I did. I said I didn't know.

Ibid. Chap. 6

A limb of Satan.[1]

Life on the Mississippi.
Chap. 8

The first time I ever saw St. Louis I could have bought it for six million dollars, and it was the mistake of my life that I did not do it.

Ibid. Chap. 22

Give an Irishman lager for a month, and he's a dead man. An Irishman is lined with copper, and the beer corrodes it. But whiskey polishes the copper and is the saving of him.

Ibid. Chap. 23

Spread open on the rack, where the plaintive singer had left it, *Ro*-holl on, silver *moo*-hoon, guide the *trav*-el-lerr his *way*.[2]

Ibid. Chap. 38

All the modern inconveniences.

Ibid. Chap. 43

The educated Southerner has no use for an *r*, except at the beginning of a word.

Ibid. Chap. 44

The Northern word "guess" —imported from England, where it used to be common, and now regarded by satirical Englishmen as a Yankee original — is but little used among Southerners. They say "reckon."

Ibid.

War talk by men who have been in a war is always interesting; whereas moon talk by a poet who has not been in the moon is likely to be dull.

Ibid. Chap. 45

It was without a compeer among swindles. It was perfect, it was rounded, symmetrical, complete, colossal.

Ibid. Chap. 52

When I retired from the rebel army in '61 I retired upon Louisiana in good order; at least in good enough order for a person who had not yet learned how

---

[1] If it's your Mississippi in dry time,
  If it's yours, Uncle Sam, when it's wet,
  If it's your Mississippi in fly time,
  In flood time it's your Mississippi yet.
  ANONYMOUS: *Whose is the Mississippi? St. 6*, printed in *The Helena (Arkansas) World* [1913]

[1] Also in *The Prince and the Pauper, Chap. 13.*
[2] Roll on, silver moon, point the traveler his way. — Popular song of the 1840s. The words were old English, and the music by Joseph W. Turner, who later became musical editor of *The Waverly Magazine.*

to retreat according to the rules of war, and had to trust to native genius.

Life on the Mississippi. Chap. 53

Weather is a literary speciality, and no untrained hand can turn out a good article on it.

An American Claimant. Foreword

In Boston they ask, How much does he know? In New York, How much is he worth? In Philadelphia, Who were his parents?

What Paul Blouet [1] Thinks of Us

There's millions in it!

The Gilded Age [2]

There is a sumptuous variety about the New England weather that compels the stranger's admiration — and regret. The weather is always doing something there; always attending strictly to business; always getting up new designs and trying them on people to see how they will go. But it gets through more business in Spring than in any other season. In the Spring I have counted one hundred and thirty-six different kinds of weather inside of twenty-four hours.

New England Weather, Speech at dinner of New England Society, New York [December 22, 1876]

Probable nor'-east to sou'-west winds, varying to the southard and westard and eastard and points between; high and low barometer, sweeping round from place to place; probable areas of rain, snow, hail, and drought, succeeded or preceded by earthquakes with thunder and lightning.

Ibid.

We haven't all had the good fortune to be ladies; we haven't all been generals, or poets, or statesmen; but when the toast works down to the babies, we stand on common ground.

Answering a Toast to the Babies, Banquet in honor of Gen-

eral *U. S. Grant, Palmer House, Chicago [November 14, 1879]*

Among the three or four million cradles now rocking in the land are some which this nation would preserve for ages as sacred things, if we could know which ones they are.

Ibid.

RICHARD GARNETT
[1835–1906]

Man and Woman may only enter Paradise hand in hand. Together, the myth tells us, they left it and together must they return.

De Flagello Myrteo. Preface, XII

Have patience with the jealousies and petulances of actors, for their hour is their eternity.

Ibid. Preface, XV

Evergreens are said to be associated with Death as emblems of immortality, and this is true. But there is another and perhaps a deeper symbol: that all seasons are alike to him, as to them.

Ibid. Preface, XXXI

The three eldest children of Necessity: God, the World, and Love.

Ibid. I

Love is God's essence; Power but his attribute; therefore is his love greater than his power.

Ibid. IV

To become Love, Friendship needs what Morality needs to become Religion — the fire of emotion.

Ibid. LV

Perfect Love casts out Prudery together with Fear.

Ibid. LIX

Joy to forgive and joy to be forgiven Hang level in the balances of Love.

Ibid. LXII

Sleep, if thou wilt, with thy Love's picture or letter under thy pillow, but remember not to leave them there.

Ibid. LXXXVII

When Silence speaks for Love she has much to say.

Ibid. XCIX

Is life worth living? This if thou inquire,

---

[1] "Max O'Rell" [1848–1903], French author and lecturer.

[2] Written in collaboration with CHARLES DUDLEY WARNER.

'Tis probable that thou hast never
  lived,
And palpable that thou hast never
  loved.
> *De Flagello Myrteo. CCVII*

The thought that would delight thy
Love must first have delighted thyself.
> *Ibid. CCXLIII*

Sweet are the words of Love, sweeter
  his thoughts:
Sweetest of all what Love nor says nor
  thinks.
> *Ibid. CCL*

Ascend above the restrictions and
conventions of the World, but not so
high as to lose sight of them.
> *Ibid. CCCXXXIII*

"Let the man that woos to win
Woo with an unhairy chin;"
Thus she said, and as she bid
Each devoted Vizier did.
> *The Fair Circassian. Stanza 3*

SIR ALFRED COMYN LYALL
[1835–1911]

"I think till I'm weary of thinking,"
  Said the sad-eyed Hindu King,
"And I see but shadows around me,
  Illusion in everything."
> *The Hindu King's Reply to the*
> *Missionary*

All the world over, I wonder, in lands
  that I never have trod,
Are the people eternally seeking for the
  signs and the steps of a God?
> *Meditations of a Hindu Prince*
> *and Sceptic*

Is life, then, a dream and delusion, and
  where shall the dreamer awake?
Is the world seen like shadows on water,
  and what if the mirror break?
Shall it pass a camp that is struck, as a
  tent that is gathered and gone
From the sands that were lamplit at
  eve, and at morning are level and
  lone?
> *Ibid.*

JOHN LUCKEY McCREERY
[1835–1906]

There is no death! The stars go down
  To rise upon some other shore,

And bright in heaven's jeweled crown
  They shine for evermore.
> *There Is No Death.*[1] *Stanza 1*

And ever near us, though unseen,
  The dear immortal spirits tread;
For all the boundless universe
  Is Life — there are no dead!
> *Ibid. Stanza 10*

Machines, that equity demands
  Should benefit the human race,
But serve, in heartless owners' hands,
  Competing workmen to displace;
So every great invention means
  Another multi-millionaire,
Whose hirelings — also his machines —
  Subsist on less than prison fare.
> *Decoration Day* [1903]. *Stanza 7*

ADAH ISAACS MENKEN [2]
[1835–1868]

Where is the promise of my years,
  Once written on my brow?
Ere errors, agonies, and fears
Brought with them all that speaks in
  tears,
Ere I had sunk beneath my peers; —
  Where sleeps that promise now?
> *El Suspiro* (*Infelix*)

I stand a wreck on Error's shore,
A spectre not within the door,
A houseless shadow evermore,
  An exile lingering here.
> *Ibid.*

AGNES E. MITCHELL
[*Floruit* 1880]

Klingle, klangle, klingle,
Far down the dusky dingle,
The cows are coming home;
Now sweet and clear, and faint and
  low,
The airy tinklings come and go,
Like chimings from the far-off tower,
Or patterings of an April shower
That makes the daisies grow.
> *When the Cows Come Home.*
> *Stanza 1*

[1] In *Arthur's Home Magazine* (Philadelphia), *July, 1863*.
[2] This is she that was the world's delight.
SWINBURNE: *Laus Veneris, St. 2*

LOUISE CHANDLER MOULTON
[1835–1908]

Bend low, O dusky Night,
  And give my spirit rest,
  Hold me to your deep breast,
And put old cares to flight.
Give back the lost delight
  That once my soul possest,
  When Love was loveliest.
                    To-night

I hied me off to Arcady —
  The month it was the month of May,
  And all along the pleasant way,
The morning birds were mad with glee,
And all the flowers sprang up to see,
As I went on to Arcady.[1]
                The Secret of Arcady

HENRY CODMAN POTTER
[1835–1908]

We have exchanged the Washingtonian dignity for the Jeffersonian simplicity, which was in truth only another name for the Jacksonian vulgarity.

> *Address at the Washington Centennial Service in St. Paul's Chapel, New York [April 30, 1889]*

If there be no nobility of descent, all the more indispensable is it that there should be nobility of ascent, — a character in them that bear rule so fine and high and pure that as men come within the circle of its influence they involuntarily pay homage to that which is the one preeminent distinction, the royalty of virtue.

> *Ibid.*

W. S. RALPH
[*Floruit* 1880]

Unless there's a boy there a-whistling,
  Its music will not be complete.
          Whistling in Heaven. Stanza 1

[1] See H. C. Bunner, page 715.

HARRIET PRESCOTT SPOFFORD
[1835–1921]

The awful phantom of the hungry poor.
          Sonnet, A Winter's Night

Ah, happy world, where all things live
  Creatures of one great law, indeed;
Bound by strong roots, the splendid
    flower, —
  Swept by great seas, the drifting
    seed!
          The Story of the Flower

Dear the people coming home,
  Dear glad faces long away,
Dear the merry cries, and dear
  All the glad and happy play.
Dear the thanks, too, that we give
For all of this, Thanksgiving Day.
          Every Day Thanksgiving Day.
                          Stanza 3

CELIA LAIGHTON THAXTER
[1835–1894]

Sad soul, take comfort, nor forget
That sunrise never failed us yet.
          *The Sunrise Never Failed
              Us Yet. Stanza 4*

I have so loved thee, but cannot, cannot hold thee!
Fading like a dream, the shadows fold
    thee.
Slowly thy perfect beauty fades away,
Good-bye, sweet day.
          Good-bye, Sweet Day. Stanza 1

Already the dandelions
  Are changed into vanishing ghosts.
                          Already

Staunch friends are we, well tried and
    strong,
  The little sandpiper and I.
          The Sandpiper. Stanza 3

From wind to wind, earth has one tale
    to tell;
All other sounds are dulled, and
    drowned, and lost,
  In this one cry, "Farewell."
          Farewell. Stanza 6

THEODORE TILTON
[1835–1907]

I won a noble fame,
But, with a sudden frown,
The people snatched my crown,
And in the mire trod down
    My lofty name.
            Sir Marmaduke's Musings
                [1871]. Stanza 1

So, lest I be inclined
    To render ill for ill —
    Henceforth in me instil,
    O God, a sweet good-will
To all mankind.
                Ibid. Stanza 7

Once in Persia reigned a king,
Who upon his signet ring
Graved a maxim true and wise,
Which, if held before the eyes,
Gave him counsel at a glance
Fit for every change and chance;
Solemn words, and these are they:
"Even this shall pass away." [1]
        Even This Shall Pass Away.
                Stanza 1

    Toll! Roland, toll!
In old St. Bavon's Tower.
At midnight hour
The great Bell Roland spoke,
And all who slept in Ghent awoke.
            The Great Bell Roland [2]

THOMAS BAILEY ALDRICH
[1836–1907]

Somewhere — in desolate wind-swept
        space —
    In   Twilight-land — in   No-man's
        land —
Two hurrying Shapes met face to face,
    And bade each other stand.
                Identity. Stanza 1

"And who are you?" cried one agape,
    Shuddering in the gloaming light.
"I know not," said the second Shape,
    "I only died last night."
                Ibid. Stanza 2

---

[1] See J. G. Saxe, page 509.
[2] This poem was written the day on which
President Lincoln issued his proclamation calling for volunteers, and was distributed to the
first regiments and at public meetings, to stir
patriotism.

So precious life is! Even to the old
    The hours are as a miser's coins!
            Broken Music. Stanza 4

A man should live in a garret aloof,
And have few friends, and go poorly
        clad,
With an old hat stopping a chink in the
        roof,
To keep the Goddess constant and glad.
            The Flight of the Goddess.
                Stanza 1

We knew it would rain, for the poplars
        showed
        The white of their leaves.
                Before the Rain. Stanza 3

You do poets and their song
A grievous wrong,
If your own soul does not bring
To their high imagining
As much beauty as they sing.
            Appreciation. Stanza 2

I would be the Lyric
Ever on the lip,
Rather than the Epic
Memory lets slip.
                Lyrics and Epics

When were December and May known
    to be happy together?
                Thalia. Stanza 4

It has become almost an honor
    Not to be crowned.
                Popularity

Black Tragedy lets slip her grim dis-
        guise
And shows you laughing lips and ro-
        guish eyes;
But when, unmasked, gay Comedy ap-
        pears,
How wan her cheeks are, and what
        heavy tears!
                Masks

Some weep because they part,
And languish broken-hearted,
And others — O my heart! —
Because they never parted.
                The Difference

Sweet courtesy has done its most
If you have made each guest forget
That he himself is not the host.
                Hospitality

'Tis said the seeds wrapped up among
    the balms
And hieroglyphics of Egyptian kings

Hold strange vitality, and, planted,
      grow
After the lapse of thrice a thousand
      years.[1]
> *At the Funeral of a Minor Poet*

My mind lets go a thousand things,
Like dates of wars and deaths of kings.
> *Memory*

The folk who lived in Shakespeare's
      day
And saw that gentle figure pass
By London Bridge, his frequent way —
They little knew what man he was.
> *Guilielmus Rex. Stanza 1*

Enamored architect of airy rhyme,
Build as thou wilt, heed not what each
      man says.
> *Enamored Architect of Airy*
> *Rhyme*

They fail, and they alone, who have not
      striven.
> *Ibid.*

From the dead Danish sculptor let us
      learn
To make Occasion, not to be denied:
Against the sheer precipitous mountain-
      side
Thorwaldsen carved his Lion at Lu-
      cerne.
> *Thorwaldsen*

I vex me not with brooding on the
      years
That were ere I drew breath: why
      should I then
Distrust the darkness that may fall
      again
When life is done?
> *I Vex Me Not*

What is more cheerful, now, in the
fall of the year, than an open-wood-
fire? Do you hear those little chirps
and twitters coming out of that piece
of apple-wood? Those are the ghosts of
the robins and blue-birds that sang
upon the bough when it was in blossom last Spring. In Summer whole
flocks of them come fluttering about

[1] In Cairo, I secured a few grains of wheat
that had slumbered for more than three thousand years in an Egyptian tomb. — WILLIAM
JENNINGS BRYAN: *The Prince of Peace*

the fruit-trees under the window: so I
have singing birds all the year round.
> *Miss Mehitabel's Son*

It was very pleasant to me to get a
letter from you the other day. Perhaps
I should have found it pleasanter if I
had been able to decipher it. I don't
think that I mastered anything beyond
the date (which I knew) and the signature (which I guessed at). There's
a singular and a perpetual charm in a
letter of yours; it never grows old, it
never loses its novelty. . . . Other
letters are read and thrown away and
forgotten, but yours are kept forever
— unread. One of them will last a
reasonable man a lifetime.
> *Letter to Professor Edward*
> *Sylvester Morse*

EDWARD ERNEST BOWEN
[1836–1901]

Forty years on, when afar and asunder
      Parted are those who are singing to-
            day,
When you look back, and forgetfully
            wonder
      What you were like in your work and
            your play;
Then, it may be, there will often come
            o'er you
      Glimpses of notes like the catch of a
            song —
Visions of boyhood shall float them be-
            fore you,
      Echoes of dreamland shall bear them
            along.
> *Forty Years On, Harrow Foot-*
> *ball Song* [1872]

JOSEPH CHAMBERLAIN
[1836–1914]

I never like being hit without striking
      back.
> *Speech on Tariff Reform,*
> *Greenock, Scotland* [Octo-
> *ber 7, 1903*]

London is the clearing-house of the
world.
> *Speech, Guildhall, London*
> [*January 19, 1904*]

The day of small nations has passed
away; the day of Empires has come.
Speech, Birmingham
[May 13, 1904]

JOHN CLIFFORD
[1836–1923]

Last evening I paused beside a blacksmith's door
And heard the anvil ring the vesper
chime.
Hammer and Anvil. Stanza 1

"How many anvils have you had,"
said I,
"To wear and batter all these hammers so?"
"Just one," said he; then said with
twinkling eye,
"The anvil wears the hammers out,
you know."
Ibid. Stanza 2

And so, I thought, the anvil of God's
Word
For ages skeptic blows have beat
upon;
Yet, though the noise of falling blows
was heard,
The anvil is unharmed — the ham-
mers gone.
Ibid. Stanza 3

WILLIAM SCHWENCK GILBERT [1]
[1836–1911]

Of all the ships upon the blue,
No ship contain'd a better crew
Than that of worthy Captain Reece,
Commanding of The Mantelpiece.
Captain Reece. Stanza 1

The Times and Saturday Review
Beguiled the leisure of the crew.
Ibid. Stanza 7

I write the pretty mottoes which you
find inside the crackers.
Ferdinando and Elvira

The Ballyshannon foundered off the
coast of Cariboo,

[1] His foe was folly and his weapon wit. —
Inscription by ANTHONY HOPE HAWKINS on
Gilbert memorial, Victoria Embankment,
London.

And down in fathoms many went the
captain and the crew;
Down went the owners — greedy men
whom hope of gain allured:
Oh, dry the starting tear, for they were
heavily insured.
Etiquette. Stanza 1

These passengers, by reason of their
clinging to a mast,
Upon a desert island were eventually
cast.
They hunted for their meals, as Alexander Selkirk used,
But they couldn't chat together — they
had not been introduced.
Ibid. Stanza 3

Oh, I am a cook and a captain bold
And the mate of the *Nancy* brig,
And a bo'sun tight, and a midshipmite,
And the crew of the captain's gig.
The Yarn of the "Nancy Bell."
Stanza 3

Roll on, thou ball, roll on
Through pathless realms of Space,
Roll on!
To the Terrestrial Globe. Stanza 1

It's true I've got no shirts to wear;
It's true my butcher's bill is due;
It's true my prospects all look blue,
But don't let that unsettle you!
Never *you* mind!
Roll on!   (*It rolls on.*)
Ibid. Stanza 2

As innocent as a new-laid egg.
Engaged. Act I [1877]

Bad language or abuse,
I never, never use,
Whatever the emergency;
Though "Bother it" I may
Occasionally say,
I never never use a big, big D.
H.M.S. Pinafore. Act I,
I Am the Captain

What, never?
Hardly ever.
Ibid.

And so do his sisters, and his cousins,
and his aunts.
Ibid. I Am the Monarch of the Sea

Now landsmen all, whoever you may be,
If you want to rise to the top of the tree
If your soul isn't fettered to an office
stool,

Be careful to be guided by this golden
    rule —
Stick close to your desks and *never go
    to sea,*
And you all may be Rulers of the
    Queen's Navee!
> *H.M.S. Pinafore
> Act I, When I Was a Lad*

Say, why is everything
Either at sixes or at sevens? [1]
> *Ibid. Act II, Fair Moon*

Things are seldom what they seem,
Skim milk masquerades as cream.
> *Ibid. Duet, Buttercup and Captain*

He is an Englishman!
  For he himself has said it,
  And it's greatly to his credit,
That he is an Englishman!
> *Ibid. Boatswain's Song*

For he might have been a Roosian,
A French or Turk or Proosian,
Or perhaps Itali-an.
  But in spite of all temptations
  To belong to other nations,
He remains an Englishman.
> *Ibid.*

I know the Kings of England, and I
    quote the fights historical,
From Marathon to Waterloo, in order
    categorical.
> *The Pirates of Penzance. Act I,
> Major-General's Song*

Ah, take one consideration with an-
    other —
A policeman's lot is not a happy one!
> *Ibid. Act II, Sergeant's Song*

Come, friends, who plough the sea,[2]
  Truce to navigation,
  Take another station;
Let's vary piracee
With a little burglaree.
> *Ibid. Pirates' Chorus*

The enemy of one
The enemy of all is.
> *Patience. Act I, Dragoons' Chorus*

---

[1] See Heywood, page 15.
  Let things go at sixes and sevens. — CER-
VANTES: *Don Quixote, Part I, Book IV,
Chap. 3*
[2] The roystering chorus, "Hail, hail, the
gang's all here," is sung to Sir Arthur Sullivan's music for these lines.

The pluck of Lord Nelson on board of
  the *Victory.*
> *Patience. Act I, Colonel's Song*

Set them to simmer and take off the
  scum,
And a Heavy Dragoon is the residuum!
> *Ibid.*

It's one to a million
That any civilian
My figure and form'll surpass.
> *Ibid. When I First Put This
> Uniform On*

I am not fond of uttering platitudes
In stained-glass attitudes.
> *Ibid. Bunthorne's Song*

If he's content with a vegetable love
  which would certainly not suit *me,*
Why, what a most particularly pure
  young man this pure young man
  must be!
> *Ibid.*

"High diddle diddle"
Will rank as an idyll,
If I pronounce it chaste!
> *Ibid. Duet, Bunthorne and
> Grosvenor*

None shall part us from each other,
  One in life and death are we:
All in all to one another —
  I to thee and thou to me!
Thou the tree and I the flower —
  Thou the idol; I the throng —
Thou the day and I the hour —
  Thou the singer; I the song!
> *Iolanthe. Act I, Duet, Strephon
> and Phyllis*

The Law is the true embodiment
Of everything that's excellent.
It has no kind of fault or flaw,
And I, my Lords, embody the Law.
> *Ibid. Lord Chancellor's Song*

Here's a pretty kettle of fish!
> *Ibid. Act II, Peers' Chorus*

Did nothing in particular
And did it very well.
> *Ibid. Lord Mountararat*

I love my fellow-creatures — I do all
  the good I can —
Yet everybody says I'm such a disagreeable man!
    And I can't think why!
> *Princess Ida. Act I, King Gama's
> Song*

Darwinian Man, though well-behaved,
At best is only a monkey shaved!
> *Princess Ida. Act II,*
> *Psyche's Song*

As some day it may happen that a victim must be found,
  I've got a little list — I've got a little
  list.
Of society offenders who might well be
  under ground,
  And who never would be missed —
  who never would be missed.
> *The Mikado. Act I, KoKo's Song*

The people who eat peppermint and
  puff it in your face.
> *Ibid.*

The idiot who praises, with enthusiastic
  tone,
All centuries but this, and every country but his own.
> *Ibid.*

Here's a pretty state of things!
Here's a pretty how-de-do.
> *Ibid. Duet, Yum Yum and*
> *Nanki-Poo*

My object all sublime
I shall achieve in time —
To let the punishment fit the crime.
> *Ibid. Mikado's Song*

"Is it weakness of intellect, birdie?" I
  cried,
"Or a rather tough worm in your little
  inside?"
With a shake of his poor little head he
  replied,
"Oh, Willow, titwillow, titwillow!"
> *Ibid. Act II, KoKo's Song*

Hail the Bridegroom — hail the Bride!
When the nuptial knot is tied.
> *Ruddigore. Act I, Chorus of*
> *Bridesmaids*

He led his regiment from behind —
He found it less exciting.
> *The Gondoliers. Act I,*
> *Duke of Plaza-Toro*

No soldier in that gallant band
  Hid half as well as he did.
He lay concealed throughout the war,
  And this preserved his gore, O!
> *Ibid.*

Of that there is no manner of doubt —
No probable, possible shadow of
  doubt —

No possible doubt whatever.
> *The Gondoliers. Act I,*
> *Don Alhambra's Song*

Life's a pudding full of plums;
Care's a canker that benumbs,
Wherefore waste our elocution
On impossible solution?
Life's a pleasant institution,
Let us take it as it comes!
> *Ibid. Life's Tangled Skein*

Life's perhaps the only riddle
That we shrink from giving up.
> *Ibid.*

The gratifying feeling that our duty has
  been done.
> *Ibid. Giuseppe's Song*

Go search the world and search the sea,
Then come you home and sing with me
There's no such gold and no such pearl
As a bright and beautiful English girl!
> *Utopia Limited. Act II,*
> *Mr. Goldbury's Song*

Here they come, the couple plighted —
  On life's journey gaily start them.
Soon to be for aye united,
  Till divorce or death shall part them.
> *The Grand Duke. Act I, Chorus*

Old wine is a true panacea
  For ev'ry conceivable ill,
When you cherish the soothing idea
  That somebody else pays the bill!
> *Ibid. Act II, Baroness' Song*

Quixotic is his enterprise and hopeless
  his adventure is,
Who seeks for jocularities that haven't
  yet been said.
The world has joked incessantly for
  over fifty centuries,
And every joke that's possible has long
  ago been made.
> *His Excellency. The Played-Out*
> *Humorist* [*1894*]

Humour is a drug which it's the fashion
  to abuse.
> *Ibid.*

WASHINGTON GLADDEN
[1836–1918]

When the anchors that faith has cast
  Are dragging in the gale,

I am quietly holding fast
　To the things that cannot fail.
Ultima Veritas. Stanza 1
In the darkest night of the year,
　When the stars have all gone out,
That courage is better than fear,
　That faith is truer than doubt.
Ibid. Stanza 4

FRANCES RIDLEY HAVERGAL
[1836–1879]

Silence is no certain token
　That no secret grief is there;
Sorrow which is never spoken
　Is the heaviest load to bear.
Misunderstood. Stanza 15
Seldom can the heart be lonely,
　If it seek a lonelier still;
Self-forgetting, seeking only
　Emptier cups of love to fill.
Ibid. Stanza 16

CHARLES FREDERICK JOHNSON
[1836–1931]

Surely, the ups and downs of this world
　are past calculation.
The Modern Romans
Persian and Arab, and Greek, and Hun,
　and Roman, and Vandal,
Master the world in turn and then dis-
　appear in the darkness,
Leaving a remnant as hewers of wood
　and drawers of water.
Ibid.
Genius finds in our every-day words
The music of the woodland birds,
Discloses hidden beauty furled
In the commonplace stuff of the every-
　day world,
And for her highest vision looks
To the world of men, not the world of
　books.
The Shakespearean Phrase

FITZHUGH LUDLOW
[1836–1870]

When we want, we have for our pains
The promise that if we but wait

Till the want has burnt out of our
　brains,
Every means shall be present to sate;
While we wait for the napkin, the soup
　gets cold,
While the bonnet is trimming, the face
　grows old,
When we've matched our buttons, the
　pattern is sold,
And everything comes too late — too
　late.
Too Late. Stanza 2

SARAH MORGAN BRYANT PIATT
[1836–1919]

My mother says I must not pass
Too near that glass;
She is afraid that I will see
A little witch that looks like me,
With a red mouth to whisper low
The very thing I should not know.
The Witch in the Glass
Other suns will shine as golden,
　Other skies be just as blue;
Other south winds blow as softly,
　Gently drinking up the dew.
To-day. Stanza 1
All the glories of the sunset
　In the sunrise one may see;
That which others call the dawning
　Is the night for you and me.
Ibid. Stanza 3
You did not sing to Shelley such a song
　As Shelley sang to you.
A Word with a Skylark

WILLIAM JEFFREY PROWSE
[1836–1870]

How we laughed as we laboured to-
　gether!
The City of Prague. Stanza 3 [1]
Though the latitude's rather uncertain,
And the longitude likewise is vague,
Still the people I pity who know not the
　City,
The beautiful City of Prague.
Ibid. Stanza 5

---

[1] Stanza 3 is used by Leonard Merrick as a chapter heading in his novel, *Conrad in Quest of His Youth.*

MARY ASHLEY TOWNSEND
[1836–1901]

I believe if I should die
And you should kiss my eyelids when I
    lie
Cold, dead, and dumb to all the world
    contains,
The folded orbs would open at thy
    breath,
And, from its exile in the isles of death,
Life would come gladly back along my
    veins.
Creed. Stanza 1

To every life there comes a time su-
    preme;
One day, one night, one morning, or one
    noon,
One freighted hour, one moment oppor-
    tune,
One rift through which sublime fulfil-
    ments gleam.
Sonnet, Opportunity

WILLIAM HENRY VENABLE
[1836–1918]

Remember Johnny Appleseed,[1]
    All ye who love the apple;
He served his kind by Word and Deed,
    In God's grand greenwood chapel.
Johnny Appleseed. Stanza 25

WILLIAM WINTER
[1836–1917]

Who cares for nothing alone is free, —
Sit down, good fellow, and drink with
    me!
Orgia

Though all the bards of earth were
    dead,
    And all their music passed away,
What Nature wishes should be said
    She'll find the rightful voice to say!
The Golden Silence

There is not anything of human trial
    That ever love deplored or sorrow
    knew,
No glad fulfilment and no sad denial,

[1] See E. A. Allen, page 596.

Beyond the pictured truth that
    Shakespeare drew.
Ashes

On wings of deeds the soul must mount!
    When we are summoned from afar,
Ourselves, and not our words, will
    count —
    Not what we said, but what we are!
George Fawcett Rowe

The golden time of Long Ago.
I. H. Bromley

His love was like the liberal air, —
    Embracing all, to cheer and bless;
And every grief that mortals share
    Found pity in his tenderness.
Ibid.

Fierce for the right, he bore his part
    In strife with many a valiant foe;
But Laughter winged his polished dart,
    And kindness tempered every blow.
Ibid.

Cold the stars are, cold the earth is,
    Everything is grim and cold!
Strange and drear the sound of mirth is
    — Life and I are old.
Age

One other bitter drop to drink,
    And then — no more!
One little pause upon the brink,
    And then — go o'er!
The Rubicon

And, lucid in that second birth,
    I shall discern
What all the sages of the earth
    Have died to learn.
Ibid.

MARY GARDINER
BRAINARD
[1837–1905]

I see not a step before me as I tread on
    another year;
But I've left the Past in God's keeping,
    — the Future His mercy shall
    clear;
And what looks dark in the distance,
    may brighten as I draw near.
Not Knowing. Stanza 2

RICHARD MAURICE BUCKE
[1837–1892]

Only a little while now and we shall be again together and with us those other noble and well-beloved souls gone before. I am sure I shall meet you and them; that you and I shall talk of a thousand things and of that unforgettable day and of all that followed it; and that we shall clearly see that all were parts of an infinite plan which was wholly wise and good.

Cosmic Consciousness. Dedication

SIR FRANCIS COWLEY BURNAND
[1837–1917]

In the very earliest and darkest ages of our ancient earth, before even the Grand Primeval forests could boast the promise of an incipient bud, there existed in the inexhaustible self-inexhausting Possible, innumerable types. . . .

Burlesque philosophical treatise in Happy Thoughts [1866]

JOHN BURROUGHS
[1837–1921]

In sorrow he learned this truth —
One may return to the place of his birth,
He cannot go back to his youth.

The Return. Stanza 3

Serene, I fold my hands and wait,
  Nor care for wind, nor tide, nor sea;
I rave no more 'gainst time or fate,
  For lo! my own shall come to me.

Waiting. Stanza 1 [1862]

Nor time, nor space, nor deep, nor high,
Can keep my own away from me.

Ibid. Stanza 6

I was born with a chronic anxiety about the weather.

Is It Going to Rain?

Literature is an investment of genius which pays dividends to all subsequent times.

Literary Fame

It is always easier to believe than to deny. Our minds are naturally affirmative.

The Light of Day. The Modern Skeptic

Time does not become sacred to us until we have lived it.

The Spell of the Past

Nature teaches more than she preaches. There are no sermons in stones. It is easier to get a spark out of a stone than a moral.

Time and Change. The Gospel of Nature

I go to books and to nature as a bee goes to the flower, for a nectar that I can make into my own honey.

The Summit of the Years

Life is a struggle, but not a warfare.

Ibid.

How far are we from home?

Last words [March 29, 1921], on a train crossing Ohio, homeward bound from California

GROVER CLEVELAND
[1837–1908]

Public officers are the servants and agents of the people, to execute the laws which the people have made.

Letter accepting the nomination for Governor of New York [October, 1882]

Your every voter, as surely as your chief magistrate, exercises a public trust.[1]

Inaugural Address [March 4, 1885]

However plenty silver dollars may become, they will not be distributed as gifts among the people.

First Annual Message [December 8, 1885]

The so-called debtor class . . . are not dishonest because they are in debt.

Ibid.

After an existence of nearly twenty years of almost innocuous desuetude these laws are brought forth.

Message [March 1, 1886]

[1] The familiar saying "Public office is a public trust" seems to have been paraphrased from various campaign speeches by Cleveland in 1884.

When more of the people's sustenance is exacted through the form of taxation than is necessary to meet the just obligations of Government and expenses of its economical administration, such exaction becomes ruthless extortion and a violation of the fundamental principles of a free Government.

> Second Annual Message
> [December, 1886]

It is a condition which confronts us — not a theory.[1]

> Third Annual Message
> [December 6, 1887]

The lessons of paternalism ought to be unlearned and the better lesson taught that while the people should patriotically and cheerfully support their Government, its functions do not include the support of the people.

> Inaugural Address [March 4, 1893]

I have tried so hard to do the right.

> Last Words

MARY KYLE DALLAS
[1837–1897]

Man never quite forgets his very first love,
  Unless she's true.

> After Ten Years. Stanza 4

He'd nothing but his violin,
  I'd nothing but my song;
But we were wed when skies were blue,
  And summer days were long.

> Brave Love

But those who wait for gold or gear,
  For houses or for kine,
Till youth's sweet spring grows brown and sere,
  And love and beauty tine,
Will never know the joy of hearts
  That met without a fear.

> Ibid.

JOHN RICHARD GREEN
[1837–1883]

The words of consecration, "Hoc est corpus," were travestied into a nick-

[1] See Disraeli, page 419.

name for jugglery, as "Hocus-pocus." [1]

> A Short History of the English
> People. Chap. VII, Sect. 1

CLARA B. SAWYER HEATH
[1837–1911]

Four-score! yet softly the years have swept by thee,
  Touching thee lightly with tenderest care;
Sorrow and death they have often brought nigh thee,
  Yet they have left thee but beauty to wear,
Growing old gracefully, graceful and fair.[2]

> Growing Old Gracefully

WILLIAM DEAN HOWELLS [3]
[1837–1920]

We live, but a world has passed away
With the years that perished to make us men.

> The Mulberries

Lord, for the erring thought
Not into evil wrought:
Lord, for the wicked will
Betrayed and baffled still:
For the heart from itself kept,
Our thanksgiving accept.

> Thanksgiving

Though I move with leaden feet,
Light itself is not so fleet;
And before you know me gone
Eternity and I are one.

> Time

[1] The law is a sort of hocus-pocus science. — CHARLES MACKLIN [1690–1797]: Love à la Mode, Act II, Sc. 1

Hocus was an old cunning attorney. — DR. JOHN ARBUTHNOT [1667–1735]: Law is a Bottomless Pit: or, History of John Bull, Chap. 5 [1712]

[2] Let me grow lovely, growing old — So many fine things do.
  KARLE WILSON BAKER: Old Lace, Let Me Grow Lovely

[3] No tribute to his art would be complete without a tribute to the beauty of his character. I never met a better man than Mr. Howells, I never saw one who was more generous, more sincere, more genuine, more essentially noble. — WILLIAM LYON PHELPS: Howells, James, Bryant and Other Essays [1924]

I know his name, I know his note,
  That so with rapture takes my soul;
Like flame the gold beneath his throat,
  His glossy cope is black as coal.
                The Song the Oriole Sings
He who sleeps in continual noise is wak-
  ened by silence.
                          Pordenone. IV
It shall belong hereafter to all who per-
  ceive and enjoy it,
Rather than him who made it.
                                Ibid.
See how to-day's achievement is only
  to-morrow's confusion;
See how possession always cheapens the
  thing that was precious.
                                Ibid.
Yes, death is at the bottom of the cup,
And every one that lives must drink it
  up;
And yet between the sparkle at the top
And the black lees where lurks that bit-
  ter drop,
There swims enough good liquor,
  Heaven knows,
To ease our hearts of all their other
  woes.
                                    If
The first night, when at night I went
  about
Locking the doors and windows every-
  where,
After she died, I seemed to lock her out
In the starred silence and the homeless
  air.
                            Experience
Tossing his mane of snows in wildest
  eddies and tangles,
Lion-like March cometh in, hoarse,
  with tempestuous breath.
                Earliest Spring. Stanza 1
Rapture of life ineffable, perfect — as
  if in the brier,
Leafless there by my door, trembled a
  sense of the rose.
                    Ibid. Stanza 3
  The Bostonian who leaves Boston
ought to be condemned to perpetual
exile.
      The Rise of Silas Lapham. Chap. 5
  The book which you read from a
sense of duty, or because for any reason

you must, does not commonly make
friends with you. It may happen that it
will yield you an unexpected delight,
but this will be in its own unentreated
way and in spite of your good intentions.
          My Literary Passions. Chap. 7
  Does it afflict you to find your books
wearing out? I mean literally. . . .
The mortality of all inanimate things is
terrible to me, but that of books most
of all.
      *Letter to Charles Eliot Norton
      [April 6, 1903] (Life in Letters,
      Vol. II, Page 171)*
  I am not sorry for having wrought in
common, crude material so much; that
is the right American stuff; and perhaps hereafter, when my din is done,
if any one is curious to know what that
noise was, it will be found to have proceeded from a small insect which was
scraping about on the surface of our
life and trying to get into its meaning
for the sake of the other insects larger
or smaller. That is, such has been my
unconscious work; consciously, I was
always, as I still am, trying to fashion
a piece of literature out of the life next
at hand.
      *Letter to Charles Eliot Norton
      [April 26, 1903] (Ibid., Page
      173)*
  Last night, after I got back from my
Balfour tailor, I expressed my surprise
that B. should go to such a simple shop.
"Well, I don't think, sir, Mr. Balfour
cares much for his clothes, sir. Them
distinguished men can't, sir. Their
thoughts soars to 'igher things, sir."
      *Letter to Mrs. Howells [April
      12, 1904], quoting his London
      landlord (Ibid., Page 191)*
  Spain, where most of my boyhood
was past while I was working at case in
my father's printing-office in Northern
Ohio.
      *Letter to Brander Matthews
      [July 22, 1911], referring to his
      love for Don Quixote (Ibid.,
      Page 301)*

HENRY SAMBROOKE LEIGH
[1837–1883]

A tiny paper, tightly rolled
    About some Latakia,
Contains within its magic fold
    A mighty panacea.
         My Three Loves. Stanza 3

In form and feature, face and limb,
    I grew so like my brother,
That folks got taking me for him
    And each for one another.
         The Twins. Stanza 1

And when I died the neighbors came
    And buried brother John.
         Ibid. Stanza 5

My love she is a kitten,
    And my heart's a ball of string.
         My Love and My Heart. Stanza 1

Said I, "What is it makes you bad?
How many apples have you had?"
    She answered, "Only seven!"
         Only Seven (Parody of Wordsworth)

JOHN L. PARKER
[1837–1917]

The little brown button,
The sacred bronze button,
The Grand Army button
He wears on his coat.
         The Little Bronze Button [1]

INNES RANDOLPH
[1837–1887]

I am a good old rebel —
    Yes; that's just what I am —
And for this land of freedom
    I do not give a dam'.
I'm glad I fit agin 'em,
    And I only wish we'd won;
And I don't ax no pardon
    For anything I've done.
         A Good Old Rebel (Unreconstructed). [2] *Stanza 1*

---

[1] The highly prized button, the dearly
    bought button,
  That binds us together in bonds so true.
    SAMUEL C. LAMBERT: *The Little
           Bronze Button*
[2] An adaptation of this ballad became a
popular cowboy song in the Southwest.

I cotch the rheumatism
    A-campin' in the snow,
But I killed a chance of Yankees,
    I'd like to kill some mo'.
         A Good Old Rebel (Unreconstructed). Stanza 4

I won't be reconstructed.
         Ibid. Stanza 6

The *tours de force* of the great Paganini
Have never found favor in Old Virginny.
         A Fish Story

The waves settled placidly over his
    head,
And his last remark was a bubble.
         Ibid.

ALGERNON CHARLES SWINBURNE
[1837–1909]

Lo, this is she that was the world's delight.
         Laus Veneris. Stanza 3

Ah yet would God this flesh of mine
    might be
Where air might wash and long leaves
    cover me,
Where tides of grass break into foam of
    flowers,
Or where the wind's feet shine along the
    sea.
         Ibid. Stanza 14

And lo, between the sundawn and the
    sun,
His day's work and his night's work
    are undone;
And lo, between the nightfall and the
    light,
He is not, and none knoweth of such
    an one.
         Ibid. Stanza 19

O sad kissed mouth, how sorrowful it
    is!
         Ibid. Stanza 79

To have known love, how bitter a
    thing it is.
         Ibid. Stanza 103

There will no man do for your sake, I
    think,
    What I would have done for the
    least word said.

I had wrung life dry for your lips to
    drink,
  Broken it up for your daily bread.
    The Triumph of Time. Stanza 12

I wish we were dead together to-day,
  Lost sight of, hidden away out of
    sight,
Clasped and clothed in the cloven clay,
  Out of the world's way, out of the
    light.
    Ibid. Stanza 15

At the door of life, by the gate of breath,
There are worse things waiting for men
  than death.
    Ibid. Stanza 20

I will go back to the great sweet mother,
  Mother and lover of men, the sea.
    Ibid. Stanza 33

There lived a singer in France of old,
  By the tideless dolorous midland sea.
In a land of sand and ruin and gold
  There shone one woman, and none
    but she.
And finding life for her love's sake fail,
Being fain to see her, he bade set sail,
Touched land, and saw her as life grew
  cold,
  And praised God, seeing; and so died
    he.
    Ibid. Stanza 41

O brother, the gods were good to you.
  Sleep, and be glad while the world en-
    dures.
Be well content as the years wear
    through;
  Give thanks for life, and the loves
    and lures.
    Ibid. Stanza 43

I shall never be friends again with
    roses;
  I shall loathe sweet tunes.
    Ibid. Stanza 45

Marvellous mercies and infinite love.
    Les Noyades. Stanza 1

I am sick of singing; the bays burn deep
    and chafe: I am fain
To rest a little from praise and grievous
    pleasure and pain.
    *Hymn to Proserpine: After the
    Proclamation in Rome of the
    Christian Faith*

Thou hast conquered, O pale Galilean;
  the world has grown grey from thy
    breath;
We have drunken of things Lethean,
  and fed on the fulness of death.
Laurel is green for a season, and love is
    sweet for a day;
But love grows bitter with treason, and
    laurel outlives not May.
Sleep, shall we sleep after all? for the
    world is not sweet in the end;
For the old faiths loosen and fall, the
    new years ruin and rend.
    Hymn to Proserpine: Ibid.

I shall die as my fathers died, and sleep
    as they sleep; even so.
For the glass of the years is brittle
    wherein we gaze for a span.
    Ibid.

For there is no God found stronger than
    death; and death is a sleep.
    Ibid.

If you loved me ever so little,
  I could bear the bonds that gall,
I could dream the bonds were brittle;
  You do not love me at all.
    Satia te Sanguine. Stanza 1

While he lives let a man be glad,
  For none hath joy of his death.
    A Lamentation. I, 4

If love were what the rose is,
  And I were like the leaf,
Our lives would grow together
In sad or singing weather.
    A Match. Stanza 1

If you were April's lady,
  And I were lord in May.
    Ibid. Stanza 5

If you were queen of pleasure,
  And I were king of pain,
We'd hunt down love together,
Pluck out his flying feather,
And teach his feet a measure,
  And find his mouth a rein.
    Ibid. Stanza 6

For in the time we know not of
    Did fate begin
Weaving the web of days that wove
    Your doom, Faustine.
    Faustine. Stanza 24

A love machine
With clockwork joints of supple gold —
No more, Faustine.
Faustine. Stanza 36

Take hand and part with laughter;
  Touch lips and part with tears;
Once more and no more after,
  Whatever comes with years.
Rococo. Stanza 1

Forget that I remember,
  And dream that I forget.
Ibid. Stanza 2

The burden of long living. Thou shalt fear
  Waking, and sleeping mourn upon thy bed;
And say at night "Would God the day were here,"
  And say at dawn "Would God the day were dead." [1]
A Ballad of Burdens. Stanza 4

For life is sweet, but after life is death.
This is the end of every man's desire.
Ibid. L'Envoy

O love, O lover, loose or hold me fast,
I had thee first, whoever have thee last.
Erotion

I shall remember while the light lives yet.
And in the night-time I shall not forget.
Though (as thou wilt) thou leave me ere life leave,
I will not, for thy love I will not, grieve.
Ibid.

O wise among women, and wisest,
  Our Lady of Pain.
Dolores. Stanza 5

Despair the twin-born of devotion.
Ibid. Stanza 14

I have passed from the outermost portal
  To the shrine where a sin is a prayer.
Ibid. Stanza 17

What ailed us, O gods, to desert you
  For creeds that refuse and restrain?
Come down and redeem us from virtue,
  Our Lady of Pain.
Ibid. Stanza 35

[1] In the morning thou shalt say, Would God it were even! and at even thou shalt say, Would God it were morning! for the fear of thine heart wherewith thou shalt fear, and for the sight of thine eyes which thou shalt see. — *Deuteronomy, XXVIII, 27*

Then love was the pearl of his oyster,
  And Venus rose red out of wine.
Dolores. Stanza 39

Time stoops to no man's lure;
  And love, grown faint and fretful,
  With lips but half regretful
  Sighs, and with eyes forgetful
Weeps that no loves endure.
The Garden of Proserpine.
Stanza 10

From too much love of living,
  From hope and fear set free,
We thank with brief thanksgiving
  Whatever gods may be
That no life lives forever;
That dead men rise up never;
That even the weariest river
  Winds somewhere safe to sea.
Ibid. Stanza 11

The sweetest name that ever love
Waxed weary of.
Félise. Stanza 18

Ah that such sweet things should be fleet,
Such fleet things sweet!
Ibid. Stanza 22

Those eyes the greenest of things blue,
  The bluest of things grey.
Ibid. Stanza 24

Eyes colored like a water-flower,
  And deeper than the green sea's glass;
Eyes that remember one sweet hour —
  In vain we swore it should not pass.
Ibid. Stanza 36

Two gifts perforce he has given us yet,
  Though sad things stay and glad things fly;
Two gifts he has given us, to forget
  All glad and sad things that go by,
    And then to die.
Ibid. Stanza 56

We know not whether death be good,
  But life at least it will not be:
Men will stand saddening as we stood,
  Watch the same fields and skies as we
    And the same sea.
Ibid. Stanza 57

Live and let live, as I will do,
  Love and let love, and so will I.
But, sweet, for me no more with you:

Not while I live, not though I die.
    Good-night, good-bye.
                    Félise. Stanza 59

I remember the way we parted,
    The day and the way we met;
You hoped we were both broken-
    hearted
And knew we should both forget.
            An Interlude. Stanza 11

And the best and the worst of this is
    That neither is most to blame,
If you have forgotten my kisses
    And I have forgotten your name.
                Ibid. Stanza 14

By the waters of Babylon we sat down
    and wept,
        Remembering thee.
        Super Flumina Babylonis.
                    Stanza 1

A creed is a rod,
    And a crown is of night;
But this thing is God,
    To be man with thy might,
To grow straight in the strength of thy
    spirit, and to live out thy life as the
    light.
            Hertha. Stanza 15

In the grey beginning of years, in the
    twilight of things that began,
The word of the earth in the ears of
    the world, was it God? was it man?
            Hymn of Man

O strong-winged soul with prophetic
    Lips hot with the bloodbeats of song,
With tremor of heartstrings magnetic,
    With thoughts as thunders in throng.
        To Walt Whitman in America.
                    Stanza 3

Ask nothing more of me, sweet,
    All I can give you I give;
Heart of my heart, were it more,
    More would be laid at your feet:
Love that should help you to live,
    Song that should spur you to soar.
            The Oblation. Stanza 1

Poor splendid wings so frayed and
    soiled and torn!
        A Ballad of François Villon.
                    Stanza 3

Many loves of many a mood and many
    a kind

Fill the life of man, and mould the
    secret mind.
                    Erechtheus

For the shades are about us that hover
    When darkness is half withdrawn,
And the skirts of the dead night cover
    The face of the live new dawn.
                The Last Oracle
Is the sun yet cast out of heaven?
Is the song yet cast out of man?
Life that had song for its leaven
    To quicken the blood that ran.
                    Ibid.
Out of heaven they shall cast not the
    day,
They shall cast not out song from the
    world.
                    Ibid.

In a coign of the cliff between lowland
    and highland,
    At the sea-down's edge between
    windward and lee,
Walled round with rocks as an inland
    island,
    The ghost of a garden fronts the sea.[1]
        The Forsaken Garden. Stanza 1
The year of the rose is brief;
From the first blade blown to the sheaf,
From the thin green leaf to the gold,
It has time to be sweet and grow old.
            The Year of the Rose. Stanza 1
A rain and ruin of roses
    Over the red rose-land.
                Ibid. Stanza 9
When the hounds of spring are on win-
    ter's traces.
        Atalanta in Calydon. Chorus
For winter's rains and ruins are over,
    And all the season of snows and sins;
The days dividing lover and lover,
    The light that loses, the night that
    wins.
                    Ibid.
Before the beginning of years
    There came to the making of man
Time with a gift of tears,
    Grief with a glass that ran.
                    Ibid.

---

[1] On the grass of the cliff, at the edge of the
    steep,
        God planted a garden, a garden of sleep.
    CLEMENT W. SCOTT [1841-1904]: *The
    Garden of Sleep* (Cromer, England)

He weaves, and is clothed with derision;
   Sows, and he shall not reap;
His life is a watch or a vision
   Between a sleep and a sleep.
     Atalanta in Calydon. Chorus

A little while and I shall laugh; and
   then
I shall weep never and laugh not any
   more.
     Ibid.

And through the trumpet of a child of
   Rome
Rang the pure music of the flutes of
   Greece.
     Song for the Centenary
     of Walter Savage Landor.
     Stanza 17

No sweeter thing than children's ways
   and wiles,
   Surely, we say, can gladden eyes and
   ears:
Yet sometimes sweeter than their words
   or smiles
   Are even their tears.
     A Child's Pity. Stanza 1

All the bells of heaven may ring,
All the birds of heaven may sing,
All the wells on earth may spring,
All the winds on earth may bring
   All sweet sounds together.
     A Child's Laughter. Stanza 1

Faith in faith established evermore
Stands a sea-mark in the tides of time.
     A Sea-Mark. Stanza 5

Not with dreams, but with blood and
   with iron,
   Shall a nation be moulded to last.
     A Word for the Country. Stanza 13

Is not Precedent indeed a King of men?
     A Word from the Psalmist. Stanza 4

Stately, kindly, lordly friend
   Condescend
Here to sit by me.
     To a Cat

There is no help for these things;
   none to mend,
And none to mar; not all our songs,
   O friend,
Will make death clear or make life dur-
   able.
     Ave atque Vale: In Memory of
     Charles Baudelaire. Stanza 16

A little soul scarce fledged for earth
Takes wing with heaven again for goal
Even while we hailed as fresh from
   birth
   A little soul.
     A Baby's Death. I, 1

Who knows but on their sleep may rise
Such light as never heaven let through
To lighten earth from Paradise?
     Ibid. IV, 2

A baby's feet, like sea-shells pink,
   Might tempt, should heaven see meet,
An angel's lips to kiss, we think,
   A baby's feet.
     Étude Réaliste. I, 1

The sweetest flowers in all the world —
   A baby's hands.
     Ibid. II, 3

All our past acclaims our future: Shakespeare's voice and Nelson's hand,
Milton's faith and Wordsworth's trust
   in this our chosen and chainless
   land,
Bear as witness: come the world against
   her, England yet shall stand.
     England, An Ode. II, 5

Shelley, lyric lord of England's lordliest
   singers, here first heard
Ring from lips of poets crowned and
   dead the Promethean word
Whence his soul took fire, and power to
   outsoar the sunward-soaring bird.
     Eton, An Ode. III

Body and spirit are twins: God only
   knows which is which.
     The Higher Pantheism in a Nut-
     shell (Imitation of Tennyson).
     Stanza 7

God, whom we see not, is: and God,
   who is not, we see:
Fiddle, we know, is diddle: and diddle,
   we take it, is dee.
     Ibid. Stanza 12

The most BEAUT—iful babbie ever beheld by mortal eyes.
     Quoted by MAX BEERBOHM, *in*
     No. 2, The Pines

It is long since Mr. Carlyle expressed
his opinion that if any poet or other literary creature could really be "killed
off by one critique" or many, the sooner
he was so despatched the better; a sen-

timent in which I for one humbly but heartily concur.

Under the Microscope

A blatant Bassarid of Boston, a rampant Maenad of Massachusetts.

Ibid.

To wipe off the froth of falsehood from the foaming lips of inebriated virtue, when fresh from the sexless orgies of morality and reeling from the delirious riot of religion, may doubtless be a charitable office.

Ibid.

The more congenial page of some tenth-rate poeticule worn out with failure after failure and now squat in his hole like the tailless fox, he is curled up to snarl and whimper beneath the inaccessible vine of song.

Ibid.

The tadpole poet will never grow into anything bigger than a frog; not though in that stage of development he should puff and blow himself till he bursts with windy adulation at the heels of the laureled ox.

Ibid.

FORCEYTHE WILLSON
[1837–1867]

And I heard a Bugle sounding, as from
    some celestial Tower;
And the same mysterious voice said:
    "It is the Eleventh Hour!
Orderly Sergeant — Robert Burton —
    it is the Eleventh Hour!"

The Old Sergeant.[1] *Stanza 9*

HENRY BROOKS ADAMS
[1838–1918]

Accident counts for much in companionship as in marriage.

The Education of Henry Adams.
Chap. 4

[1] In *The Louisville* (Kentucky) *Journal,* Jan. 1, 1863.
Forceythe Willson, whose poem of "The Old Sergeant" Doctor Holmes used to read publicly in the closing year of the civil war, was of a Western altitude of figure, and of an extraordinary beauty of face in an oriental sort. — W. D. HOWELLS: *Literary Friends and Acquaintance, Part VIII, Chap. 8*

Women have, commonly, a very positive moral sense; that which they will, is right; that which they reject, is wrong; and their will, in most cases, ends by settling the moral.

The Education of Henry Adams.
Chap. 6

All experience is an arch, to build upon.[1]

Ibid.

Only on the edge of the grave can man conclude anything.

Ibid.

Although the Senate is much given to admiring in its members a superiority less obvious or quite invisible to outsiders, one Senator seldom proclaims his own inferiority to another, and still more seldom likes to be told of it.

Ibid. Chap. 7

Friends are born, not made.

Ibid.

A friend in power is a friend lost.

Ibid. (Also in Chap. 16)

The effect of power and publicity on all men is the aggravation of self, a sort of tumor that ends by killing the victim's sympathies.

Ibid. Chap. 10

Young men have a passion for regarding their elders as senile.

Ibid. Chap. 11

Knowledge of human nature is the beginning and end of political education.

Ibid. Chap. 12

These questions of taste, of feeling, of inheritance, need no settlement. Everyone carries his own inch-rule of taste, and amuses himself by applying it, triumphantly, wherever he travels.

Ibid.

Intimates are predestined.

Ibid. Chap. 13

His first struggle with a sleeping-car made him doubt the value — to him — of a Pullman civilization.

Ibid. Chap. 16

[1] Yet all experience is an arch wherethrough
Gleams that untraveled world.
TENNYSON: *Ulysses*

Chaos often breeds life, when order breeds habit.

> *The Education of Henry Adams.*
> *Chap. 16*

At best, the renewal of broken relations is a nervous matter.

> *Ibid.*

Sumner's[1] mind had reached the calm of water which receives and reflects images without absorbing them; it contained nothing but itself.

> *Ibid.*

The difference is slight, to the influence of an author, whether he is read by five hundred readers, or by five hundred thousand; if he can select the five hundred, he reaches the five hundred thousand.

> *Ibid. Chap. 17*

The newspaper-man is, more than most men, a double personality; and his person feels best satisfied in its double instincts when writing in one sense and thinking in another.

> *Ibid.*

A teacher affects eternity; he can never tell where his influence stops.

> *Ibid. Chap. 20*

One friend in a lifetime is much; two are many; three are hardly possible. Friendship needs a certain parallelism of life, a community of thought, a rivalry of aim.

> *Ibid.*

What one knows is, in youth, of little moment; they know enough who know how to learn.

> *Ibid. Chap. 21*

He had often noticed that six months' oblivion amounts to newspaper-death, and that resurrection is rare. Nothing is easier, if a man wants it, than rest, profound as the grave.

> *Ibid. Chap. 22*

Morality is a private and costly luxury.

> *Ibid.*

Nothing is more tiresome than a superannuated pedagogue.

> *Ibid. Chap. 23*

[1] Charles Sumner [1811–1874].

The study of history is useful to the historian by teaching him his ignorance of women. . . . The woman who is known only through a man is known wrong.

> *The Education of Henry Adams.*
> *Chap. 23*

He too serves a certain purpose who only stands and cheers.[1]

> *Ibid. Chap. 24*

Practical politics consists in ignoring facts.

> *Ibid.*

Nothing in education is so astonishing as the amount of ignorance it accumulates in the form of inert facts.

> *Ibid. Chap. 25*

Power when wielded by abnormal energy is the most serious of facts.

> *Ibid. Chap. 28*

Those who seek education in the paths of duty are always deceived by the illusion that power in the hands of friends is an advantage to them.

> *Ibid.*

Power is poison. Its effect on Presidents had been always tragic, chiefly as an almost insane excitement at first, and a worse reaction afterwards; but also because no mind is so well balanced as to bear the strain of seizing unlimited force without habit or knowledge of it; and finding it disputed with him by hungry packs of wolves and hounds whose lives depend on snatching the carrion.

> *Ibid.*

A certain chronic irritability — a sort of Bostonitis — which, in its primitive Puritan forms, seemed due to knowing too much of his neighbors and thinking too much of himself.

> *Ibid.*

Modern politics is, at bottom, a struggle not of men but of forces.

> *Ibid.*

We combat obstacles in order to get repose, and, when got, the repose is insupportable.

> *Ibid. Chap. 29*

[1] And if I should lose, let me stand by the road
And cheer as the winners go by!
BERTON BRALEY: *Prayer of a Sportsman*

Simplicity is the most deceitful mistress that ever betrayed man.
> *The Education of Henry Adams.*
> *Chap. 30*

No one means all he says, and yet very few say all they mean, for words are slippery and thought is viscous.
> *Ibid. Chap. 31*

The movement from unity into multiplicity, between 1200 and 1900, was unbroken in sequence, and rapid in acceleration. Prolonged one generation longer, it would require a new social mind.
> *Ibid. Chap. 34*
> *(A Law of Acceleration)*

Even in America, the Indian Summer of life should be a little sunny and a little sad, like the season, and infinite in wealth and depth of tone — but never hustled.
> *Ibid. Chap. 35*

Perhaps some day — say 1938, their centenary — . . . they would find a world that sensitive and timid natures could regard without a shudder.
> *Ibid. Closing words*

JOSEPH ASHBY-STERRY
[1838–1917]

When the glass is at ninety a man is a fool
Who directs not his efforts to try to keep cool.
> *Ninety in the Shade*

Half-hidden in its grassy bed
You'll find that slender silver thread —
The tiny Thames; which, here set free,
Begins its journey to the sea!
> *The Source of the Thames*

The ruddy ripe tomata
  In china bowl of ice,
And grouse worth a sonata
  Undoubtedly are nice.
> *The Riparian Philosopher*

It's much too hot for reason,
  And far too warm for rhyme.
> *Ibid.*

There are people, I'm told — some say there are heaps —
Who speak of the talkative Samuel as Peeps;

And some so precise and pedantic their step is,
Who call the delightful old diarist Pepys;
But those I think right, and I follow their steps,
Ever mention the garrulous gossip as Pepys.
> *Pepys*

JAMES BRYCE [1]
[1838–1922]

The greatest liberty that man has taken with Nature.
> *South America [Of the*
> *Panama Canal]*

What you want [in Washington] is to have a city which every one who comes from Maine, Texas, Florida, Arkansas, or Oregon can admire as being something finer and more beautiful than he had ever dreamed of before; something which makes him even more proud to be an American.
> *The Nation's Capital [2]*

You have never sufficiently foreseen how enormously rich and populous a nation you are going to be.
> *Ibid.*

Medicine, the only profession that labours incessantly to destroy the reason for its own existence.
> *Address at dinner for General*
> *W. C. Gorgas [March 23,*
> *1914]*

To most people nothing is more troublesome than the effort of thinking.
> *Studies in History and Jurisprudence, Vol. 2, Page 7*

GEORGE COOPER
[1838–1927]

October gave a party;
  The leaves by hundreds came:
The ashes, oaks, and maples,
  And those of every name.
> *October's Party. Stanza 1*

[1] Ambassador from Great Britain to the United States, 1906–1913.
[2] In *The National Geographic Magazine,* 1913.

After the shower, the tranquil sun;
  After the snow, the emerald leaves;
Silver stars when the day is done;
  After the harvest, golden sheaves.
                    After. Stanza 1

Brave your storm with firm endeavor,
  Let your vain repinings go!
Hopeful hearts will find forever
  Roses underneath the snow!
            Roses Underneath the Snow.
                           Stanza 1

Sweet Genevieve,
The days may come, the days may go,
But still the hands of memory weave
The blissful dreams of long ago.
                     Sweet Genevieve

GEORGE DEWEY
[1838–1917]

You may fire when ready, Gridley.
          At battle of Manila Bay
                    [May 1, 1898]

I am convinced that the office of the
President is not such a very difficult one
to fill, his duties being mainly to execute the laws of Congress.
    Interview in The New York World,
                     April 4, 1900

MARY ABIGAIL DODGE
("GAIL HAMILTON")
[1838–1896]

Whatever an author puts between
the two covers of his book is public
property; whatever of himself he does
not put there is his private property, as
much as if he had never written a word.
    Country Living and Country
              Thinking. Preface

The moment an audacious head is
lifted one inch above the general level,
pop! goes the unerring rifle of some
biographical sharpshooter, and it is all
over with the unhappy owner.
    Skirmishes and Sketches. The
          New School of Biography

What's virtue in man can't be vice in a
cat.
                        Both Sides

MARY MAPES DODGE
[1838–1905]

Grandma told me all about it,
Told me, so I couldn't doubt it,
How she danced — my Grandma
    danced! —
          Long ago.
              The Minuet. Stanza 1

Whimpy, little Whimpy,
  Cried so much one day,
His grandma couldn't stand it,
  And his mother ran away.
          Little Whimpy. Stanza 1

Whenever a snowflake leaves the sky,
It turns and turns to say "Good-by!
Good-by, dear clouds, so cool and
    gray!"
Then lightly travels on its way.
                        Snowflakes

Life is a mystery as deep as ever death
    can be;
Yet oh, how sweet it is to us, this life
    we live and see!
          The Two Mysteries. Stanza 3

But I believe that God is overhead;
And as life is to the living, so death is to
    the dead.
                   Ibid. Stanza 5

KATE FIELD
[1838–1896]

My faithful cavalier,
At dusk he draweth near,
  To wait outside my wicket.
I hear him draw his bow,
He playeth soft and low,
  My dusky little cricket.
          My Serenade. Stanza 3

They talk about a woman's sphere as
    though it had a limit;
There's not a place in earth or heaven,
There's not a task to mankind given,
There's not a blessing or a woe,
There's not a whispered "yes" or "no,"
There's not a life, or death, or birth,
That has a feather's weight of worth
Without a woman in it.
                    Woman's Sphere

JOHN HAY [1]
[1838–1905]

A keerless man in his talk was Jim,
  And an awkward hand in a row,
He never flunked, and he never lied, —
  I reckon he never knowed how.
Jim Bludso

"I'll hold her nozzle agin the bank
  Till the last galoot's ashore."
Ibid.

And they all had trust in his cussedness,
  And knowed he would keep his word.
Ibid.

He weren't no saint — but at jedgment
  I'd run my chance with Jim,
'Longside of some pious gentlemen
  That wouldn't shook hands with him.
He seen his duty, a dead-sure thing, —
  And went for it thar and then;
And Christ ain't a-going to be too hard
  On a man that died for men.
Ibid.

I don't go much on religion,
  I never ain't had no show;
But I've got a middlin' tight grip, sir,
  On the handful o' things I know.
I don't pan out on the prophets
  And free-will, and that sort of
    thing, —
But I b'lieve in God and the angels
  Ever sence one night last spring.
Little Breeches

And I think that saving a little child,
  And fotching him to his own,
Is a derned sight better business
  Than loafing around The Throne.
Ibid.

He trumped Death's ace for me that
  day,
  And I'm not goin' back on him!
Banty Tim

He was hard on women and rough on
  his friends;
  And he didn't have many, I'll let you
    know.
Golyer

[1] It is strange how the memory of a man may float to posterity on what he would have himself regarded as the most trifling of his works. — SIR WILLIAM OSLER, quoted by HARVEY CUSHING: *Life of Sir William Osler*, Vol. II, Chap. 31, P. 301

But I never seed nothing that could or
  can
Jest get all the good from the heart of a
  man
  Like the hands of a little child.
Golyer

The King will be well if he sleeps one
  night
  In the Shirt of a Happy Man.
The Enchanted Shirt. [1] *Part 1*

"An idle man has so much to do
  That he never has time to be sad."
Ibid. Part 2

"I would do it, God wot," and he roared
  with the fun,
"But I haven't a shirt to my back."
Ibid.

The night comes down, the lights burn
  blue;
And at my door the Pale Horse stands,[2]
To bear me forth to unknown lands.
The Stirrup Cup

Bring me to-night a lotus tied
With thread from a house where none
  has died.[3]
The Law of Death

There stands not by the Ganges' side
A house where none hath ever died.
Ibid.

I know not what this man may be,
Sinner or saint; but as for me,
One thing I know, — that I am he
Who once was blind, and now I see.[4]
Religion and Doctrine

Good Luck is the gayest of all gay girls,
  Long in one place she will not stay,
Back from your brow she strokes the
  curls,
  Kisses you quick and flies away.

[1] See Sir Walter Scott, page 309.
[2] A pale horse: and his name that sat on him was Death. — *Revelation, VI, 8*
[3] "A grain of mustard-seed," the sage replied,
  "Found where none old or young has ever died,
  Will cure the pain you carry in your side."
JOHN WHITE CHADWICK:
Buddha's Lesson
[4] Whether he be a sinner or no, I know not: one thing I know, that, whereas I was blind, now I see. — *John, IX, 25*.

But Madame Bad Luck soberly
　　comes . . .
　And sits by your bed, and brings her
　　knitting.
　　　Good and Bad Luck (After Heine)
There are three species of creatures who
　when they seem coming are going,
When they seem going they come:
　Diplomats, women, and crabs.
　　　　　　　　　　Distichs. II
When you break up housekeeping, you
　learn the extent of your treasures.
　　　　　　　　　　Ibid. IX
Who would succeed in the world should
　be wise in the use of his pronouns.
Utter the You twenty times, where you
　once utter the I.
　　　　　　　　　　Ibid. XIII
True luck consists not in holding the
　best of the cards at the table:
Luckiest he who knows just when to rise
　and go home.
　　　　　　　　　　Ibid. XV
Try not to beat back the current, yet be
　not drowned in its waters;
Speak with the speech of the world,
　think with the thoughts of the few.
　　　　　　　　　　Ibid. XVII

GEORGE WASHINGTON
JOHNSON
[1838–1917]

I wandered to-day to the hill, Maggie,
　To watch the scene below,
The creek and the creaking old mill,
　Maggie,[1]
　As we used to, long ago.
　　　When You and I Were Young,
　　　　　　　Maggie. Stanza 1
To me you're as fair as you were, Mag-
　gie,
　When you and I were young.
　　　　　　　　Ibid. Stanza 3

WILLIAM EDWARD
HARTPOLE LECKY
[1838–1903]

Offspring of an idle hour,
Whence has come thy lasting power?
　　　　　　　　On an Old Song

---

[1] The mill was situated on the bank of
Twenty Mile Creek, Glanford, Ontario, Canada. It is now owned by Henry Ford.

The stately ship is seen no more,
The fragile skiff attains the shore;
And while the great and wise decay,
And all their trophies pass away,
Some sudden thought, some careless
　rhyme,
Still floats above the wrecks of Time.
　　　　　　　　On an Old Song

EMMA A. LENT
[Floruit 1885]

They said, "The Master is coming
　To honor the town to-day,
And none can tell at whose house or
　home
　The Master will choose to stay."
And I thought, while my heart beat
　wildly,
　What if He should come to mine?
How would I strive to entertain
　And honor the Guest divine?
　　　　　The Master Is Coming

GEORGE LEYBOURNE
[? –1884]

He'd fly through the air with the great-
　est of ease,
This handsome young man on the fly-
　ing trapeze;
His movements were graceful, all girls
　he could please,
And my love he purloined away!
　　　The Man on the Flying Trapeze
　　　　　　　　　　[1865]

JOSEPH MALINS [1]
[Floruit 1895]

Better put a strong fence 'round the
　top of the cliff,
　Than an ambulance down in the
　valley.
　　　A Fence or an Ambulance.
　　　　　　　　　Stanza 7

---

[1] Editor of *The Reciter*, an English publication.

JOHN, VISCOUNT MORLEY
[1838–1923]

Evolution is not a force but a process; not a cause but a law.
On Compromise

It is not enough to do good; one must do it the right way.
Ibid.

You have not converted a man because you have silenced him.
Ibid.

The great business of life is to be, to do, to do without, and to depart.
Address on Aphorisms [*1887*]

The gravity and concision of Thucydides are of specially wholesome example in these days of over-coloured and over-voluminous narrative.
Ibid.

Those who would treat politics and morality apart will never understand the one or the other.
Rousseau

You can not demonstrate an emotion or prove an aspiration.
Ibid.

Literature — the most seductive, the most deceiving, the most dangerous of professions.
Burke

No man can climb out beyond the limitations of his own character.
Robespierre

A great interpreter of life ought not himself to need interpretation.
Emerson

The most frightful idea that has ever corroded human nature — the idea of eternal punishment.
Vauvenargues

Where it is a duty to worship the sun it is pretty sure to be a crime to examine the laws of heat.
Voltaire

A man will already be in no mean Paradise if at the hour of sunset a ray of good hope may fall upon him like harmonies of music.
Ibid.

Simplicity of character is no hindrance to subtlety of intellect.
Life of Gladstone

Every man of us has all the centuries in him.
Life of Gladstone

Great economic and social forces flow with a tidal sweep over communities that are only half conscious of that which is befalling them. Wise statesmen are those who foresee what time is thus bringing, and endeavor to shape institutions and to mold men's thought and purpose in accordance with the change that is silently surrounding them.
Life of Richard Cobden.
Closing paragraph

There are some books which cannot be adequately reviewed for twenty or thirty years after they come out.
Recollections. Vol. I, Book 2,
Chap. 8

The proper memory for a politician is one that knows what to remember and what to forget.
Ibid. Vol. II, Book 4, Chap. 2

Men bound to make their watches keep time in two longitudes at once.
Ibid. Book 5, Chap. 1

In my creed, waste of public money is like the sin against the Holy Ghost.
Ibid. Chap. 3

Success depends on three things: who says it, what he says, how he says it; and of these three things, what he says is the least important.
Ibid. Chap. 4

Excess of severity is not the path to order. On the contrary, it is the path to the bomb.
Ibid.

MOSES OWEN
[1838–1878]

Nothing but flags! but simple flags,
Tattered and torn and hanging in rags;
And we walk beneath them with careless tread,
Nor think of the hosts of the mighty dead

Who have marched beneath them in days gone by.

The Returned Maine Battle Flags.[1] Stanza 1

EMILY REBECCA PAGE
[1838–1860]

Where the rocks are gray and the shore is steep,
And the waters below look dark and deep,
Where the rugged pine, in its lonely pride
Leans gloomily over the murky tide; . . .
Where the shadow is heavy the whole day through,
There lies at its moorings the old canoe.

The Old Canoe.[2] Stanza 1

EDNA DEAN PROCTOR
[1838–1923]

The rose may bloom for England,
  The lily for France unfold;
Ireland may honor the shamrock,
  Scotland her thistle bold;
But the shield of the great Republic,
  The glory of the West,
Shall bear a stalk of the tasselled corn —
  The sun's supreme bequest!

Columbia's Emblem

Good-night! and sweetest dreams be thine
  Through all their shining way,
Till darkness goes, and bird and rose
  With rapture greet the day.

Good-Night. Stanza 6

[1] Written on hearing a visitor exclaim, "Nothing but flags!" as she passed through a room in the State Capitol, Augusta, Maine.

[2] Miss Page lived at Bradford, Vermont, on the Connecticut River, where her father was tollkeeper of the bridge.
The authorship of the poem has been ascribed to Thomas J. Worthen, of Little Rock, Arkansas. Earlier the poem had been credited to Albert Pike, who denied that he had either written or claimed the poem.

MARGARET ELIZABETH SANGSTER
[1838–1912]

I know — yet my arms are empty,
  That fondly folded seven,
And the mother heart within me
  Is almost starved for heaven.

Are the Children at Home?

Never yet was a springtime,
  Late though lingered the snow,
That the sap stirred not at the whisper
  Of the southwind, sweet and low;
Never yet was a springtime
  When the buds forgot to blow.

Awakening

A tiny flower, pale and sweet,
  That blooms o'er breath of ice;
And glad are they, on any day,
  Who find the edelweiss.

The Edelweiss. Stanza 1

There's joy in sailing outward —
  Though we leave upon the pier,
With faces grieved and wistful,
  Our very dearest dear.

The Joy of Coming Home. Stanza 1

There's nothing half so pleasant
  As coming home again.

Ibid. Stanza 3

We have careful thought for the stranger,
  And smiles for the sometime guest,
But oft for our own the bitter tone,
  Though we love our own the best.

Our Own. Stanza 3

The tender word forgotten,
  The letter you did not write,
The flower you might have sent, dear,
  Are your haunting ghosts to-night.

At Sunset (The Sin of Omission). Stanza 1

Child of the boundless prairie, son of the virgin soil,
Heir to the bearing of burdens, brother to them that toil;
God and Nature together shaped him to lead in the van,
In the stress of the wildest weather, when the nation needed a man.

Abraham Lincoln. Stanza 1

FREDERICK WHITTAKER
[1838–1917]

Dead! Is it possible? He, the bold
rider;
Custer, our hero, the first in the fight,
Charming the bullets of yore to fly
wider,
Shunning our battle-king's ringlets of
light!
Custer's Last Charge. Stanza 1

HEZEKIAH BUTTERWORTH
[1839–1905]

The bird with the broken pinion
Never soared as high again.
The Bird with a Broken Wing
One taper lights a thousand,
Yet shines as it has shone;
And the humblest light may kindle
A brighter than its own.
The Taper. Stanza 10
Methinks when I stand in life's sunset,
As I stood when we parted at school,
I shall see the bright faces of children
I loved in the village of Yule.
*The Beautiful Village of Yule.
Stanza 9*

FRANCIS PHARCELLUS
CHURCH
[1839–1906]

Virginia, your little friends are wrong.
They have been affected by the skepticism of a skeptical age. They do not believe except they see. They think that
nothing can be which is not compre-
hensible by their little minds. All minds,
Virginia, whether they be men's or children's, are little. In this great universe
of ours man is a mere insect, an ant,
in his intellect, as compared with the
boundless world about him, as measured by the intelligence capable of
grasping the whole of truth and knowledge.
Editorial: Is There a Santa Claus? [1]

[1] First published in *The New York Sun,
Sept. 21, 1897*, in reply to an inquiry from Virginia O'Hanlon. These extracts are included by
permission of *The New York Sun*.

Not believe in Santa Claus? You
might as well not believe in fairies.
Is There a Santa Claus?
No Santa Claus! Thank God, he
lives, and he lives forever. A thousand
years from now, Virginia, nay, ten
times ten thousand years from now, he
will continue to make glad the heart of
childhood.
Ibid.

FRANCIS BRET HARTE [1]
[1839–1902]

The patient stars
Lean from their lattices, content to wait.
All is illusion till the morning bars
Slip from the levels of the Eastern gate.
Night is too young, O friend! day is too
near;
Wait for the day that maketh all things
clear.
Not yet, O friend, not yet!
Cadet Grey. Song, Not Yet.
All is not true,
All is not ever as it seemeth now.
Ibid.
What lieth dark, O love, bright day will
fill;
Wait for thy morning, be it good or ill.
Ibid.
Fades the light,
And afar
Goeth day, cometh night;
And a star
Leadeth all,
Speedeth all
To their rest. [2]
Ibid. Bugle Song

[1] Yon yellow sun melts in the sea;
A sombre ship sweeps silently
Past Alcatraz tow'rd Orient skies —
A mist is rising to the eyes —
Good-bye, Bret Harte, good-night, good-
night.
JOAQUIN MILLER: *Good-Bye, Bret Harte*
[May, 1902], *Stanza 1*
[2] Fading light
Dims the sight,
And the stars gem the sky,
Gleaming bright,
From afar drawing nigh,
Falls the night.
JOSEPH BERG ESENWEIN [1867–   ]:
Taps, St. 1

Love, good-night!
  Must thou go
  When the day
And the light
  Need thee so?
            Cadet Grey. Bugle Song

Bells of the Past, whose long-forgotten
    music
Still fills the wide expanse,
Tingeing the sober twilight of the Pres-
    ent
  With color of romance!
        *The Angelus Heard at the
            Mission Dolores, 1868*

Until points of gravest import yielded
    slowly one by one,
And by Love was consummated what
    Diplomacy begun.
            Concepcion de Arguello

Never a tear bedims the eye
That time and patience will not dry;
Never a lip is curved with pain
That can't be kissed into smiles again.
            The Lost Galleon

And the way to look for a thing is plain,
To go where you lost it, back again.
            Ibid.

Which I wish to remark,
  And my language is plain,
That for ways that are dark
  And for tricks that are vain,
The heathen Chinee is peculiar.
        *Plain Language from Truthful
            James. Stanza 1*

Ah Sin was his name.
            Ibid. Stanza 2

With the smile that was childlike and
    bland.
            Ibid. Stanza 4

We are ruined by Chinese cheap labor.[1]
            Ibid. Stanza 7

But still, when the mists of Doubt pre-
    vail,
And we lie becalmed by the shores of
    Age,
  We hear from the misty troubled
    shore
  The voice of the children gone before,
    Drawing the soul to its anchorage.
    A Greyport Legend. Stanza 6

[1] Not a Chinaman's chance. — This saying
originated when the Californians were opposing the introduction of Chinese labor.

And ever since then, when the clock
    strikes two,
  She walks unbidden from room to
    room,
And the air is filled that she passes
    through
  With a subtle, sad perfume.
        A Newport Romance. Stanza 6

He read aloud wherein the Master
  Had writ of "Little Nell."
            Dickens in Camp. Stanza 4

And on that grave where English oak
    and holly
  And laurel wreaths entwine,
Deem it not all a too presumptuous
    folly,
  This spray of Western pine!
            Ibid. Stanza 10

These things are managed so well in
    France.[1]
            The Tale of a Pony

Brief words, when actions wait, are
    well:
The prompter's hand is on his bell;
The coming heroes, lovers, kings,
Are idly lounging in the wings;
Behind the curtain's mystic fold
The glowing future lies unrolled.
        *Address at opening of the Cali-
            fornia Theatre, San Francisco
            [January 19, 1870]*

What was it the Engines said,
Pilots touching, — head to head
Facing on the single track,
Half a world behind each back?
        *What the Engines Said (Opening
            of the Pacific Railroad)* [2]

I reside at Table Mountain, and my
    name is Truthful James;
I am not up to small deceit, or any sin-
    ful games.
        The Society upon the Stanislaus

He smiled a kind of sickly smile, and
    curled up on the floor

[1] "They order," said I, "this matter better in
France." — LAURENCE STERNE: *A Sentimental
Journey, P. 1*
[2] Drill, ye tarriers, drill,
    And it's work all day
    Without sugar in your tay,
    When you're working for the U.P. Rail-
      way.
        Laborers' song during the construc-
        tion of the Union Pacific Railway

And the subsequent proceedings interested him no more.

The Society upon the Stanislaus

For there be women, fair as she,
Whose verbs and nouns do more agree.

Mrs. Judge Jenkins

Oh, yer's yer good old whiskey,
   Drink it down.

Two Men of Sandy Bar. Act IV

One big vice in a man is apt to keep out a great many smaller ones.

Ibid.

Give me a man that is capable of a devotion to anything, rather than a cold, calculating average of all the virtues!

Ibid.

I'm acquainted with affliction,
Chiefly in the form of fiction,
As 'tis offered up by strangers
   At the consul's open door.

At the Consul's Open Door.[1]

I think I know all fancy
Styles of active mendicancy.

Ibid.

I know the worthy tourist,
Who by accident the purest,
Lost his letters, watch and wallet,
From the cold deck coming o'er.

Ibid.

JAMES PROCTOR KNOTT
[1839–1911]

Duluth! The word fell upon my ear with a peculiar and indescribable charm, like the gentle murmur of a low fountain stealing forth in the midst of roses, or the soft sweet accent of an angel's whisper in the bright, joyous dream of sleeping innocence. 'Twas the name for which my soul had panted for years, as the hart panteth for the waterbrooks.

Speech on the St. Croix and Bayfield Railroad Bill [January 27, 1871]

[1] Written while Harte was a U. S. Consul at Glasgow, after receiving a note of warning from Bristol, England, that an impostor had been pretending to be a destitute American and procuring money from United States consuls.

SIBYL F. PARTRIDGE
(SISTER MARY XAVIER)

Lord, for to-morrow and its needs,
   I do not pray;
Keep me, my God, from stain of sin,
   Just for to-day.

Just for To-day [1877]

WALTER PATER
[1839–1894]

Every intellectual product must be judged from the point of view of the age and the people in which it was produced.

The Renaissance. Mirandola

Its generous belief that nothing which had ever interested the human mind could wholly lose its vitality.

Ibid.

That sweet look of devotion which men have never been able altogether to love, and which still makes the born saint an object almost of suspicion to his earthly brethren.

Ibid. Botticelli

The sunless pleasures of weary people, whose care for external things is slackening.

Ibid. Michelangelo

Hers is the head upon which all "the ends of the world are come," and the eyelids are a little weary. It is a beauty wrought out from within upon the flesh, the deposit, little cell by cell, of strange thoughts and fantastic reveries and exquisite passions.

Ibid. Leonardo da Vinci.
[Monna Lisa]

All art constantly aspires towards the condition of music.

Ibid. Giorgione

A circle which in an age of great troubles, losses, anxieties, can amuse itself with art, poetry, intrigue.

Ibid. Du Bellay

Religions, as they grow by natural laws out of man's life, are modified by whatever modifies his life.

Ibid. Winckelmann

Let us understand by poetry all literary production which attains the power of giving pleasure by its form, as distinct from its matter.

The Renaissance. Winckelmann

What we have to do is to be for ever curiously testing new opinions and courting new impressions.

Ibid. Conclusion

Art comes to you proposing frankly to give nothing but the highest quality to your moments as they pass.

Ibid.

A book, like a person, has its fortunes with one; is lucky or unlucky in the precise moment of its falling in our way, and often by some happy accident counts with us for something more than its independent value.

Marius the Epicurean. Chap. 6

To know when one's self is interested, is the first condition of interesting other people.

Ibid.

Given the hardest terms, supposing our days are indeed but a shadow, even so, we may well adorn and beautify, in scrupulous self-respect, our souls, and whatever our souls touch upon.

Ibid. Chap. 8

Certainly, flowers were pleasant to the eye. Such things had even their sober use, as making the outside of human life superficially attractive, and thereby promoting the first steps towards friendship and social amity.

Ibid. Chap. 12

By the attainment of a true philosophy to attain happiness; or, having missed both, to perish, as one of the vulgar herd.

Ibid. Chap. 24

There is but one road that leads to Corinth.[1]

Ibid.

[1] Non cuivis homini contingit adire Corinthum
(It is not every man's lot to gain Corinth).
HORACE: *Epistles, Book I, XVII, To Scaeva, L. 36*
'Tis not every one who can afford to go to Corinth. — PLUTARCH: *Parallel Lives, Aristophanes*
"There is but one way to Corinth," as of old. —ANDREW LANG: *Letters to Dead Authors, To Lucian of Samosata*

I hardly know wherein philosophy and wine are alike unless it be in this, that the philosophers exchange their ware for money, like the wine-merchants; some of them with a mixture of water or worse, or giving short measure.

Marius the Epicurean. Chap. 24

We need some imaginative stimulus, some not impossible ideal such as may shape vague hope, and transform it into effective desire, to carry us year after year, without disgust, through the routine-work which is so large a part of life.

Ibid. Chap. 25

The aim of a true philosophy must lie, not in futile efforts towards the complete accommodation of man to the circumstances in which he chances to find himself, but in the maintenance of a kind of candid discontent, in the face of the very highest achievement.

Ibid.

Through the survival of their children, happy parents are able to think calmly, and with a very practical affection, of a world in which they are to have no direct share.

Ibid.

JAMES RYDER RANDALL
[1839–1908]

Hark to an exiled son's appeal,
    Maryland, my Maryland!
My Mother State, to thee I kneel.[1]

Maryland, My Maryland. Stanza 2

From hill to hill, from creek to creek,
Potomac calls to Chesapeake,
    Maryland, my Maryland.

Ibid. Stanza 7

Hushed in the alabaster arms of Death
    Our young Marcellus sleeps.

John Pelham

After a little while,
    The birds will serenade in bush and tree,
But not for me;

[1] Randall, a native of Baltimore, was working on *The New Orleans Sunday Delta* when he wrote this song in April, 1861.

On billows duskier than the gloomy
Nile
  My barque must be —
After a little while.
                 After a Little While. Stanza 5
Teach me, my God, to bear my cross
  As Thine was borne;
Teach me to make of every loss
  A crown of thorn.
                 Resurgam
The Robin wears his silver vest
  In panoplies of red.
        Why the Robin's Breast Is Red [1]

SAMUEL JOHN STONE
[1839–1900]

Where did I come from, then? Ah,
  where indeed?
This is a riddle monstrous hard to read.
I have it! Why, of course,
All things are moulded by some plastic
  force
Out of some atoms somewhere up in
  space,
Fortuitously concurrent anyhow —
There, now!
That's plain as is the beak upon my
  face.
        *Soliloquy of a Rationalistic
                       Chicken* [2]
What I can't see, I never will believe in!
                 Ibid.

G. W. BELLAMY

Old Simon, the cellarer, keeps a rare
  store
  Of Malmsey and Malvoisie,
And Cyprus, and who can say how
  many more?
        Simon, the Cellarer. Stanza 1

WILFRID SCAWEN BLUNT
[1840–1922]

He who has once been happy is for aye
  Out of destruction's reach.
                 Sonnet, With Esther
Nor has the world a better thing,
  Though one should search it round,

---

[1] See P. H. Hayne, page 586.
[2] In *Harper's Monthly, Sept., 1875.*

Than thus to live one's own sole king,
  Upon one's own sole ground.
                 The Old Squire. Stanza 14
Ay, this is the famed rock, which Her-
  cules
And Goth and Moor bequeathed us. At
  this door
England stands sentry.
                 Sonnet, Gibraltar

HENRY BURTON
[1840–1930]

Have you had a kindness shown?
  Pass it on.
                 Pass It On. [1] *Stanza 1*
Hold thy lighted lamp on high,
Be a star in someone's sky.
                 Ibid. Stanza 4

HENRY BERNARD
CARPENTER
[1840–1887]

Oh, there are moments in man's mortal
  years
When for an instant that which long
  has lain
Beyond our reach is on a sudden found
In things of smallest compass, and we
  hold
The unbounded shut in one small min-
  ute's space,
And worlds within the hollow of our
  hand, —
A world of music in one word of love,
A world of love in one quick wordless
  look,
A world of thought in one translucent
  phrase,
A world of memory in one mournful
  chord,
A world of sorrow in one little song.
                 Liber Amoris
The time will come when this, our Holy
  Church,
Shall melt away in ever widening walls,
And be for all mankind. And in its
  place
Shall rise another church, whose cove-
  nant word

---

[1] Official poem of the International Sunshine Society.

Shall be the act of love. Not *Credo* then
But *Amo* shall be the watchword
    through its gate.
                    Liber Amoris

LIZZIE YORK CASE
[1840–1911]

There is no unbelief;
Whoever plants a seed beneath the sod
And waits to see it push away the clod,
    He trusts in God.
                    Unbelief. Stanza 1
Whoever says "To-morrow," "The un-
    known,"
"The future," trusts the Power alone
    He dares disown.
                    Ibid. Stanza 5

JOHN WHITE CHADWICK
[1840–1904]

If good men were only better,
    Would the wicked be so bad?
                    A Timely Question. Stanza 1
It singeth low in every heart,
    We hear it each and all, —
A song of those who answer not,
    However we may call.
                    Auld Lang Syne. Stanza 1
They cannot be where God is not,
    On any sea or shore.
                    Ibid. Stanza 3

HENRY AUSTIN DOBSON
[1840–1921]

Once at the Angelus
    (Ere I was dead),
Angels all glorious
    Came to my bed.
                    "Good-Night, Babette!"
I am so old! . . . Good-night, Babette!
                    Ibid.
For lo! the same old myths that made
    The early "stage successes,"
Still "hold the boards," and still are
    played,
    "With new effects and dresses."
                    *The Drama of the Doctor's
                    Window. Prologue, Stanza 6*

I am a Shade: a Shadowe too arte thou:
I marke the Time: saye, Gossip, dost
    thou soe?
                    The Sundial. Stanza 2
He had played for his lordship's levee,
    He had played for her ladyship's
        whim,
Till the poor little head was heavy,
    And the poor little brain would swim.
                    The Child-Musician. Stanza 1
Time goes, you say? Ah no!
Alas, Time stays, *we* go.
                    The Paradox of Time. Stanza 1
O Poet, then, forbear
    The loosely-sandalled verse,
Choose rather thou to wear
    The buskin — strait and terse.
                    *Ars Victrix (Imitated from
                    Théophile Gautier). Stanza 2*
All passes. Art alone
    Enduring stays to us;
The Bust outlasts the throne, —
    The Coin, Tiberius.
                    Ibid. Stanza 8
Paint, chisel, then, or write;
    But, that the work surpass,
With the hard fashion fight, —
    With the resisting mass.
                    Ibid. Stanza 10
The ladies of St. James's!
    They're painted to the eyes;
Their white it stays for ever,
    Their red it never dies:
But Phyllida, my Phyllida!
    Her color comes and goes;
It trembles to a lily, —
    It wavers to a rose.
                    The Ladies of St. James's. Stanza 4
Far better, in some nook unknown,
    To sleep for once — and soundly —
Than still survive in wistful stone,
    Forgotten more profoundly.
                    *To an Unknown Bust in the
                    British Museum. Stanza 6*
Yet would to-day when Courtesy grows
    chill,
And life's fine loyalties are turned to
    jest,
Some fire of thine might burn within us
    still!
Ah, would but one might lay his lance
    in rest,

And charge in earnest . . . were it but
a mill!
Don Quixote

I grant you freely that he sought his
Ends
Not always wisely — but he lov'd his
Friends.
*A Dialogue to the Memory of
Mr. Alexander Pope*

Ye gods! how he talk'd! What a torrent of sound,
His hearers invaded, encompass'd and
— drown'd!
A Postscript to "Retaliation"

He made little fishes talk vastly like
whales.[1]
Ibid.

Read him for Style.
Ibid.

"Not to be tuneless in old age!" [2]
*Henry Wadsworth Longfellow.
Stanza 1*

Rather we count thee one
Who, when his race is run,
Layeth him down,
Calm — through all coming days,
Filled with a nation's praise,
Filled with renown.
Alfred, Lord Tennyson. Stanza 6

Form is the Cage and Sense the Bird.
The Poet twirls them in his Mind,
And wins the Trick with both combined.
The Toyman

He praised the Thing he understood;
'Twere well if every Critic would.
The 'Squire at Vauxhall. Moral 2

What is a Patron? Johnson knew,
And well that lifelike portrait drew.
He is a Patron who looks down
With careless eye on men who drown;
But if they chance to reach the land,
Encumbers them with helping hand.[3]
The Noble Patron

But little lore of loving can any flagon
teach,

[1] See Goldsmith, page 254.
[2] Nec turpem senectam
    Degere, nec cithara carentem
    (That in age I may not drift
    Long years, my lyre forgot!)
    HORACE: *Odes, Book I, XXXI,
    To Apollo, L. 19*
[3] See Johnson, page 233.

For when my tongue is loosèd most,
then most I lose my speech.
*The Maltworm's Madrigal.
Stanza 6*

I intended an Ode,
And it turned to a Sonnet.
Urceus Exit

Love comes back to his vacant dwelling, —
The old, old Love that we knew of
yore!
The Wanderer. Stanza 1

This is the Actor's gift; to share
All moods, all passions, nor to care
One whit for scene, so he without
Can lead men's minds the round-
about,
Stirred as of old those hearers were
When Burbadge played!
When Burbadge Played. Stanza 3

What flaws! what faults! — on every
page,
When *Finis* comes.
When Finis Comes. Stanza 2

O Singer of the field and fold,
Theocritus! Pan's pipe was thine, —
Thine was the happier Age of Gold.
*For a Copy of Theocritus.
Stanza 1*

Life, — 'tis of thee they fable so.
Thou bidd'st us eat, and still denied,
Still fasting, from thy board we go: —
"Where is *thy* feast, O Barmecide?"
*The Ballad of the Barmecide.
Envoy*

Dear Critics, whose verdicts are always
so new! —
One word in your ear. There were Critics before . . .
And the man who plants cabbages imitates, too! [1]
The Ballad of Imitation

In the work-a-day world, — for its
needs and woes,
There is place and enough for the pains
of prose;
But whenever the May-bells clash and
chime,

[1] C'est imiter quelqu'un que de planter des
choux (We are imitating someone even when
planting cabbages). — ALFRED DE MUSSET:
Namouna, Canto 2, St. 9

Then hey! — for the ripple of laughing
rhyme!
The Ballad of Prose and Rhyme.
Envoy

Old books, old wine, old Nankin
blue; —
All things, in short, to which belong
The charm, the grace that Time
makes strong, —
All these I prize, but (*entre nous*)
Old friends are best!
To Richard Watson Gilder.
Stanza 3

So artless in its vanity,
So fleeting, so eternal,
So packed with "poor Humanity" —
We know as Pepys his Journal.
Pepys' Diary. Stanza 6

Fame is a food that dead men eat, —
I have no stomach for such meat.
Fame Is a Food that Dead Men
Eat. Stanza 1

The Press is too much with us: small
and great;
We are undone of chatter and *on dit*,
Report, retort, rejoinder, repartee,
Mole-hill and mare's nest, fiction up-to-
date.
A Pleasant Invective Against
Printing

I shall not see the morning sky;
I shall not hear the night-wind sigh;
I shall be mute, as all men must
In after days!
In After Days

He held his pen in trust
To Art, not serving shame or lust.
Ibid.

WILLIAM CHANNING
GANNETT
[1840–1923]

The poem hangs on the berry bush
When comes the poet's eye;
The street begins to masquerade
When Shakespeare passes by.
The Christ sees white in Judas's heart
And loves His traitor well;
The God, to angel His new heaven,
Explores His lowest hell.
We See as We Are

MRS. C. GILDERSLEEVE
(LONGSTREET)
[*Floruit* 1885]

Mrs. Lofty keeps a carriage,
So do I;
She has dappled grays to draw it,
None have I;
She's no prouder with her coachman
Than am I
With my blue-eyed, laughing baby
Trundling by.
Mrs. Lofty and I. Stanza 1

THOMAS HARDY
[1840–1928]

When false things are brought low,
And swift things have grown slow,
Feigning like froth shall go,
Faith be for aye.
Between Us Now

Whence comes solace? Not from seeing,
What is doing, suffering, being;
Not from noting Life's conditions,
Not from heeding Time's monitions;
But in cleaving to the Dream
And in gazing at the Gleam
Whereby gray things golden seem.[1]
On a Fine Morning

Why doth IT so and so, and ever so,
This viewless, voiceless Turner of the
Wheel?
The Dynasts. Fore Scene,
Spirit of the Pities

A local thing called Christianity.
Ibid. Spirit of the Years, Sc. 6

Aggressive Fancy working spells
Upon a mind o'erwrought.
Ibid. Act I, Sc. 6, Napoleon

Ere systemed suns were globed and lit
The slaughters of the race were writ.
Ibid. Act II, Sc. 5, Semi-chorus

My argument is that War makes rattling good history; but Peace is poor
reading.
Ibid. Spirit Sinister

Like the British Constitution, she
owes her success in practice to her inconsistencies in principle.
The Hand of Ethelberta

[1] No longer a shadow,
But clothed with the Gleam.
TENNYSON: *Merlin and the Gleam, L. 93*

A lover without indiscretion is no lover at all.

The Hand of Ethelberta

That cold accretion called the world, which, so terrible in the mass, is so unformidable, even pitiable, in its units.

Tess of the D'Urbervilles.
Chap. 13

That shabby corner of God's allotment where He lets the nettles grow, and where all unbaptized infants, notorious drunkards, suicides, and others of the conjecturally damned are laid.

Ibid. Chap. 14

The chronic melancholy which is taking hold of the civilized races with the decline of belief in a beneficent power.

Ibid. Chap. 18

The debatable land between predilection and love.

Ibid. Chap. 20

Patience, that blending of moral courage with physical timidity.

Ibid. Chap. 43

"Justice" was done, and the President of the Immortals (in Aeschylean phrase) had ended his sport with Tess.

Ibid. Chap. 59

We have triumphed: this achievement
turns the bane to antidote,
Unsuccesses to success,
Many thought-worn eves and morrows
to a morrow free of thought.

Friends Beyond. Stanza 4

No more need we corn and clothing,
feel of old terrestrial stress;
Chill detraction stirs no sigh;
Fear of death has even bygone us:
death gave all that we possess.

Ibid. Stanza 5

A bird sings the selfsame song,
With never a fault in its flow,
That we listened to here those long
Long years ago.

The Selfsame Song. Stanza 1

I heard a Voice from I knew not
where: —
"The Great Adjustment is taking
place!"

"There Seemed a Strangeness,"
A Phantasy. Stanza 1

And they shall see what is, ere long,
Not through a glass, but face to face;
And Right shall disestablish Wrong.

"There Seemed a Strangeness,"
A Phantasy. Stanza 4

That faiths by which my comrades
stand
Seem fantasies to me,
And mirage-mists their Shining Land,
Is a strange destiny.

The Impercipient at a Cathedral
Service. Stanza 1

He who breathes All's-Well to these
Breathes no All's-Well to me.

Ibid. Stanza 3

Let me enjoy the earth no less
Because the all-enacting Might
That fashioned forth its loveliness
Had other aims than my delight.

Let Me Enjoy. Minor Key,
Stanza 1

There trembled through
His happy good-night air
Some blessed Hope, whereof he knew
And I was unaware.

The Darkling Thrush. By the
Century's Death-Bed, Stanza 4

To see stand weeping by
A woman once embraced, will try
The tension of a man the most austere.

The Contretemps. Stanza 6

One pairing is as good as another
Where all is venture!

Ibid. Stanza 10

You have not known
Men's lives, deaths, toils, and teens;
You are but a heap of stick and stone:
A new house has no sense of the have-
beens.[1]

The Two Houses. Stanza 5

"Yes; quaint and curious war is!
You shoot a fellow down
You'd treat if met where any bar is,
Or help to half-a-crown."

The Man He Killed. Stanza 5

We have lost somewhat, afar and near,
Gentlemen,

---

[1] There's nothing mournful about it; it cannot be sad and lone
For the lack of something within it that it has never known.
Joyce Kilmer: *The House with Nobody in It, St. 5*

The thinning of our ranks each year
Affords a hint we are nigh undone,
That we shall not be ever again
The marked of many, loved of one.
An Ancient to Ancients. Stanza 3
We who met sunrise sanguine-souled,
    Gentlemen,
Are wearing weary. We are old;
These younger press; we feel our rout
Is imminent to Aïdes' den, —
The evening shades are stretching out.
Ibid. Stanza 7
Much is there waits you we have
    missed;
Much lore we leave you worth the
    knowing;
Much, much has lain outside our ken.
Nay, rush not: time serves; we are go-
    ing.
Ibid. Stanza 10
You have dropped your dusty cloak and
    taken your wondrous wings
    To another sphere,
Where no pain is.
"Why Do I?" Stanza 2
A star looks down at me,
And says: "Here I and you
Stand, each in our degree:
What do you mean to do?"
Waiting Both. Stanza 1
We two kept house, the Past and I,
    The Past and I;
I tended while it hovered nigh,
Leaving me never alone.
The Ghost of the Past. Stanza 1
Do you think of me at all,
    Wistful ones?
Do you think of me at all
    As if nigh?
*Dead "Wessex," the Dog, to the
    Household. Stanza 1*
You may hear a jump or trot
On the stair or path or plot;
But I shall cause it not,
    Be not there.
Ibid. Stanza 3
Further and further still
Through the world's vaporous vitiate
    air
His words wing on — as strong words
    will.
*George Meredith, 1828–1909.
    Stanza 6*

Yes, yes; I am old. In me appears
The history of a hundred years.
Empires', kings', captives' births and
    deaths;
Strange faiths and fleeting shibboleths;
Tragedy, comedy, through my pages
Beyond all mummed on any stages;
Cold hearts beat hot, hot hearts beat
    cold,
And I beat on.
*The Newspaper Soliloquizes:
    London Observer, March 14,
    1926*
I traversed a dominion
    Whose spokesmen spake out strong
Their purpose and opinion
    Through pulpit, press, and song.

I saw, in web unbroken
    Its history outwrought
Not as the loud had spoken
    But as the mute had thought.
I Traversed a Dominion

ROSSITER JOHNSON
[1840–1931]

O for a lodge in a garden of cucumbers!
    O for an iceberg or two at control!
O for a vale which at mid-day the dew
    cumbers!
    O for a pleasure trip up to the Pole!
Ninety-nine in the Shade. Stanza 1
Then O for a draught from a cup of
    cold pizen,
    And O for a resting-place in the cold
    grave!
With a bath in the Styx where the thick
    shadow lies on
    And deepens the chill of its dark-
    running wave.
Ibid. Stanza 6

SAMUEL ALROY JONAS
[?–1915]

Representing nothing on God's earth
    now,
    And naught in the waters below it,
As a pledge of a nation that's dead and
    gone,
    Keep it, dear friend, and show it.
*Lines on the Back of a
    Confederate Note*

COSMO MONKHOUSE
[1840–1901]

So we must part, my body, you and I
  Who've spent so many pleasant years
    together.
'Tis sorry work to lose your company
  Who clove to me so close.
                    Any Soul to Any Body

M. T. MORRISON
[*Circa* 1840– ?]

A foolish little maiden bought a foolish
  little bonnet,
With a ribbon and a feather and a bit
  of lace upon it;
And that all the other maidens in the
  little town might know it,
She thought she'd go to meeting the
  next Sunday, just to show it.
    *What the Choir Sang about the
        New Bonnet. Stanza 1*

"Alleluia, Alleluia!" sang the choir
    above her head;
"Hardly knew you, hardly knew you!"
    were the words she thought they
    said.
                    Ibid. Stanza 3

WILLIAM HENRY HARRISON
("ADIRONDACK") MURRAY
[1840–1904]

Ah, friends, dear friends, as years go on
    and heads get gray, how fast the
    guests do go!
Touch hands, touch hands, with those
    that stay.
Strong hands to weak, old hands to
    young, around the Christmas
    board, touch hands.
The false forget, the foe forgive, for
    every guest will go and every fire
    burn low and cabin empty stand.
Forget, forgive, for who may say that
    Christmas day may ever come to
    host or guest again.
Touch hands!
                    John Norton's Vagabond

MINNA PAULL
[*Floruit* 1890]

From an old English parsonage,
  Down by the sea,
There came in the twilight
  A message to me;
Its quaint Saxon legend,
  Deeply engraven,
Hath, as it seems to me,
  Teaching from Heaven;
And through the hours
  The quiet words ring,
Like a low inspiration,
  "Doe ye nexte thynge."
                *"Doe Ye Nexte Thynge."
                        Stanza 1*

ROSSITER WORTHINGTON
RAYMOND
[1840–1918]

In Paestum's ancient fanes I trod,
  And mused on those strange men of
  old,
Whose dark religion could unfold
  So many gods, and yet no God.
            Ramblings in Greece. Stanza 1
  Life is eternal; and love is immortal;
and death is only a horizon; and a
horizon is nothing save the limit of our
sight.
            A Commendatory Prayer

BENJAMIN SCOVILLE
[*Floruit* 1890]

Some day I'll pass by the Great Gates
    of Gold,
And see a man pass through unques-
    tioned and bold.
"A Saint?" I'll ask, and old Peter'll
    reply:
"No, he carries a pass — he's a news-
    paper guy."
            The Newspaper Guy. Stanza 4

SIR HENRY M. STANLEY
[1840–1904]

  Dr. Livingstone, I presume?
    *On meeting Livingstone in Ujiji,
    Central Africa [November 10,
    1871]*

WILLIAM GRAHAM SUMNER
[1840–1910]

The Forgotten Man [1] works and votes — generally he prays — but his chief business in life is to pay. . . . Who and where is the Forgotten Man in this case, who will have to pay for it all?

Essay, The Forgotten Man [1883]

JOHN ADDINGTON SYMONDS
[1840–1893]

No seed shall perish which the soul hath sown.

Sonnet, Versöhnung, A Belief

Gods fade; but God abides and in man's heart
Speaks with the clear unconquerable cry
Of energies and hopes that can not die.

Sonnet, On the Sacro Monte

She smiled, and the shadows departed;
She shone, and the snows were rain;
And he who was frozen-hearted
Bloomed up into love again.

Eyebright

These things shall be, — a loftier race
Than e'er the world hath known shall rise
With flame of freedom in the souls,
And light of knowledge in their eyes.

The Days That Are to Be

KATHARINE KENT CHILD (MRS. EDWARD ASHLEY) WALKER
[1840–1916]

However divinity schools may refuse to "skip" in unison, and may butt and butter each other about the doctrine and origin of human depravity, all will join devoutly in the credo, I believe in the total depravity of inanimate things.[1]

The Total Depravity of Inanimate Things.[2]

There is melancholy pleasure in the knowledge that a great soul has gone mourning before me in the path I am now pursuing. It was only to-day that in glancing over the pages of Victor Hugo's greatest work I chanced upon the following: "Everyone will have noticed with what skill a coin let fall upon the ground runs to hide itself, and what art it has in rendering itself invisible."

Ibid.

Stern necessity, proverbially known as "the mother of invention," and practically the stepmother of ministers' daughters.

Ibid.

The elusiveness of soap, the knottiness of strings, the transitory nature of buttons, the inclination of suspenders to twist and of hooks to forsake their lawful eyes, and cleave only unto the hairs of their hapless owner's head.

Ibid.

HENRY WATTERSON
[1840–1921]

Things have come to a heluva pass
When a man can't cudgel his own jackass.

Reply when rebuked for criticizing the Governor of Kentucky

JOHN WILSON [3]
[? –1889]

O for a Booke and a shadie nooke,
    eyther in-a-doore or out;
With the grene leaves whisp'ring over-
    hede, or the Streete cryes all about.
Where I maie Reade all at my ease,
    both of the Newe and Olde;

---

[1] The forgotten man at the bottom of the economic pyramid. — FRANKLIN DELANO ROOSEVELT: Radio address [April 7, 1932]

[1] Outrage from lifeless things. — MILTON: *Paradise Lost, X, 707*
[2] In *The Atlantic Monthly, Sept., 1864* (Vol. XIV, Pp. 357–364).
[3] A London bookseller, friend of Austin Dobson.

For a jollie goode Booke whereon to
  looke is better to me than Golde.
            *For a Catalogue of Second-
                      hand Books*

MATHILDE BLIND
[1841–1896]

We are so tired; my heart and I.
Of all things here beneath the sky
Only one thing would please us best —
Endless, unfathomable rest.
            Rest. Stanza 1

ROBERT BUCHANAN
[1841–1901]

      Alone at nights,
I read my Bible more and Euclid less.
        An Old Dominie's Story
Beauty and Truth, tho' never found,
  are worthy to be sought.
            To David in Heaven
  I saw the starry Tree
  Eternity
Put forth the blossom Time.
                  Proteus
Full of a sweet indifference.
                  Charmian
I say, the world is lovely,
  And that loveliness is enough.
            Artist and Model
    A race that binds
Its body in chains and calls them Lib-
  erty,
And calls each fresh link Progress.
            Political Mystics.
            Titan and Avatar

CHARLES EDWARD CARRYL
[1841–1920]

The night was thick and hazy
When the *Piccadilly Daisy*
Carried down the crew and Captain in
  the sea;
And I think the water drowned 'em,
For they never, never found 'em,
And I know they didn't come ashore
  with me.
        Robinson Crusoe. Stanza 1

I had that fellow Friday [1]
Just to keep the tavern tidy.
            Robinson Crusoe. Stanza 3
Canary birds feed on sugar and seed,
  Parrots have crackers to crunch;
And as for the poodles, they tell me the
  noodles
Have chicken and cream for their
  lunch.
          But there's never a question
          About my digestion —
Anything does for me!
            The Camel's Complaint.
                      Stanza 1
A capital ship for an ocean trip
  Was the "Walloping Window-blind."
No gale that blew dismayed her crew
  Or troubled the Captain's mind.
The man at the wheel was taught to feel
  Contempt for the wildest blow,
And it often appeared, when the
  weather had cleared,
  That he'd been in his bunk below.
      *Davy and the Goblin, A Nautical
                  Ballad. Stanza 1*

OLIVER WENDELL
HOLMES (JR.)
[1841–1935]

  The riders in a race do not stop short
when they reach the goal. There is a
little finishing canter before coming to
a standstill. There is time to hear the
kind voice of friends and to say to one's
self: "The work is done." But just as
one says that, the answer comes: "The
race is over, but the work never is done
while the power to work remains." The
canter that brings you to a standstill
need not be only coming to rest. It
cannot be, while you still live. For to
live is to function. That is all there is
in living.
      *Radio address on his ninetieth
        birthday [March 8, 1931]*

WILLIAM HENRY HUDSON
[1841–1922]

  When I meet with a falsehood, I care
not who the great persons who proclaim

[1] I took my man Friday with me. — DANIEL
DEFOE: *Robinson Crusoe*

it may be, I do not try to like it or believe it or mimic the fashionable prattle of the world about it.

The Purple Land. Chap. 28

When I hear people say they have not found the world and life so agreeable or interesting as to be in love with it, or that they look with equanimity to its end, I am apt to think they have never been properly alive nor seen with clear vision the world they think so meanly of, or anything in it — not a blade of grass. Only I know that mine is an exceptional case, that the visible world is to me more beautiful and interesting than to most persons, that the delight I experienced in my communings with Nature did not pass away, leaving nothing but a recollection of vanished happiness to intensify a present pain. The happiness was never lost, but owing to that faculty I have spoken of, had a cumulative effect on the mind and was mine again, so that in my worst times, when I was compelled to exist shut out from Nature in London for long periods, sick and poor and friendless, I could yet always feel that it was infinitely better to be than not to be.

Far Away and Long Ago. Chap. 24

SIR RICHARD CLAVER-
HOUSE JEBB
[1841–1905]

At the middle point of the [Greek] stage, some steps — known as "Charon's staircase," because the ghost sometimes comes up by them — lead down into what we should call the pit.

Greek Literature. Page 76

JOHN ALEXANDER JOYCE
[*Floruit* 1885]

You must leave your many millions
And the gay and festive crowd;
Though you roll in royal billions,
There's no pocket in a shroud.

There's No Pocket in a Shroud.
Stanza 1

I shall love you in December
With the love I gave in May!

Question and Answer. Stanza 8

For the sake of the almighty dollar [1]
And whatever else he could gain.

The Sutler

MARY ARTEMISIA
LATHBURY [2]
[1841–1913]

Day is dying in the west;
Heaven is touching earth with rest.

Day Is Dying in the West
[1877]. Stanza 1

Children of yesterday,
    Heirs of to-morrow,
What are you weaving?
    Labor and sorrow?
Look to your looms again,
    Faster and faster
Fly the great shuttles
    Prepared by the Master.
Life's in the loom,
Room for it — room!

Song of Hope. Stanza 1

BREWER MATTOCKS
[1841–1934]

The parish priest
Of Austerity
Climbed up in a high church steeple
To be nearer God,
So that he might hand
His word down to His people.

The Preacher's Mistake. Stanza 1

In his age God said —
"Come down and die!"
And he cried out from the steeple,
"Where art Thou, Lord?"
And the Lord replied,
"Down here among my people."

Ibid. Stanza 5

---

[1] Almighty gold. — BEN JONSON: *Epistle to Elizabeth, Countess of Rutland*
    The almighty dollar. — IRVING: *Bracebridge Hall, The Stout Gentleman*
[2] Miss Lathbury was known as the Chautauqua Laureate.

CINCINNATUS HEINE ("JOAQUIN") [1] MILLER
[1841–1913]

Is it worth while that we jostle a brother
  Bearing his load on the rough road of
    life?
Is it worth while that we jeer at each
    other
  In blackness of heart? — that we
    war to the knife?
  God pity us all in our pitiful strife.
        Is It Worth While? Stanza 1

That man who lives for self alone
Lives for the meanest mortal known.
        Walker in Nicaragua. Chant I,
                Stanza 1

Who harvests what his hand hath sown,
Does more for God, for man, his own —
Dares more than all mad heroes dare.
        Ibid. Stanza 3

I do not question school nor creed
Of Christian, Protestant, or Priest; [2]
I only know that creeds to me
Are but new names for mystery,
That good is good from east to east,
And more I do not know nor need
To know, to love my neighbor well.
        The Tale of the Tall Alcalde

It is not wise to be a poet now,
For, oh, the world it has so modest
    grown
It will not praise a poet to his face,
But waits till he is dead some hundred
    years,

[1] In a paper, *How I Came to be a Writer of Books*, contributed to *Lippincott's Magazine* in 1886, and quoted in STUART P. SHERMAN's introduction to *The Poetical Works of Joaquin Miller* (G. P. Putnam's Sons, 1923), Miller explains the origin of his pen-name. His first writing was a public letter in defense of Joaquin Murietta, the outlaw. A Sacramento newspaper banteringly identified him with the outlaw, and friends continued the banter. The name "Joaquin" clung to him, so Miller accepted it and used it in the title of his first book and thereafter.

[2] Shall I give up the friend I have valued
    and tried,
If he kneel not before the same altar with
    me?
        THOMAS MOORE: *Come, Send
                Round the Wine*

Then uprears marbles cold and stupid
    as itself.
        Bits from Ina, a Drama. Sc. 4

In men whom men condemn as ill
I find so much of goodness still,
In men whom men pronounce divine
I find so much of sin and blot,
I do not dare to draw a line [1]
Between the two, where God has not.
        Byron

Lo! Christ himself chose only twelve,
Yet one of these turned out a thief.
        A Song of the South. Part II,
                Canto 3

Who taught you tender Bible tales
Of honey-lands, of milk and wine?
Of happy, peaceful Palestine?
Of Jordan's holy harvest vales?
Who gave the patient Christ? I say
Who gave your Christian creed? Yea,
    yea,
Who gave your very God to you?
Your Jew! Your Jew! Your hated Jew!
        To Russia. Stanza 3

The bravest battle that ever was
    fought;
  Shall I tell you where and when?
On the maps of the world you will find
    it not;
  It was fought by the mothers of men.
        The Bravest Battle. Stanza 1

Man's books are but man's alphabet,
Beyond and on his lessons lie —
The lessons of the violet,
The large gold letters of the sky.
        The Larger College
        [Man's Books]. Stanza 7

The soul that feeds on books alone —
I count that soul exceeding small
That lives alone by book and creed, —
A soul that has not learned to read.
        Ibid. Stanza 10

Honor and glory forever more
  To this good man gone to rest;

[1] There is so much good in the worst of us,
    And so much bad in the best of us,
    That it hardly behooves any of us
    To talk about the rest of us.
        First printed in *The Marion* (Kansas) *Record*, owned by Governor Edward Wallis Hoch [1849–1925], and assumed to have been written by him.

Peace on the dim Plutonian shore; [1]
Rest in the land of the blest.
Peter Cooper, April, 1883. [2]
Stanza 1

Aye, wisest he is in this whole wide
land,
Of hoarding till bent and gray;
For all you can hold in your cold, dead
hand
Is what you have given away.
Ibid. [3] *Stanza 3*

The biggest dog has been a pup.
William Brown of Oregon.
Stanza 5

Behind him lay the gray Azores,
Behind the Gates of Hercules;
Before him not the ghost of shores,
Before him only shoreless seas.
Columbus. Stanza 1

He gained a world; he gave that world
Its grandest lesson: "On! sail on!"
Ibid. Stanza 5

The Lightning reached a fiery rod,
And on Death's fearful forehead wrote
The autograph of God.
With Love to You and Yours.
Part I, Canto III

KATE PUTNAM OSGOOD
[1841–1910]

The great tears sprang to their meeting
eyes,
For the heart must speak when the
lips are dumb;
And under the silent evening skies
Together they followed the cattle
home.
Driving Home the Cows. [4]
Stanza 12

[1] Night's Plutonian shore. — POE: *The Raven, St. 8*
See Lytle, page 568.
[2] In his autobiography, *My Life and Memories,* JOSEPH I. C. CLARKE [1846–1925] devotes several pages to an account of Miller bringing this poem to the office of *The New York Herald* on the night of Peter Cooper's death in April, 1883.
[3] The world did not want all I had to say of this gentle old man and kept only the three little verses. — MILLER: Comment on the poem
[4] In *Harper's Monthly Magazine, March, 1865.*

EMILY BRUCE ROELOFSON
[1841–1921]

When to the flowers so beautiful
The Father gave a name,
Back came a little blue-eyed one
(All timidly it came);
And standing at its Father's feet
And gazing in His face,
It said, in low and trembling tone,
"Dear God, the name Thou gavest
me,
Alas! I have forgot!"
Kindly the Father looked Him down
And said: "Forget-me-not."
The Origin of the Forget-me-not

MINOT JUDSON SAVAGE
[1841–1918]

Oh, where is the sea? the fishes cried,
As they swam its crystal clearness
through.
Where Is God? Stanza 1

A man's truest monument must be a
man.
The Song of a Man
(Phillips Brooks). Stanza 8

CLEMENT WILLIAM SCOTT
[1841–1904]

Bring, novelist, your notebook! Bring,
dramatist, your pen!
And I'll tell you a simple story of what
women do for men.
It's only a tale of a lifeboat, of the dy-
ing and the dead,
Of the terrible storm and shipwreck
that happened off Mumbles Head!
The Women of Mumbles Head.
Stanza 1

Be this our covenant, apart, alone,
Carve thou this sign upon Love's altar-
stone,
Mizpah! [1]
Mizpah. Stanza 1

[1] Mizpah . . . The Lord watch between thee and me, when we are absent one from another. — *Genesis, XXXI, 49*

KATE BROWNLEE SHERWOOD
[1841–1914]

Washington rode from the bloody fray
  Up to the gun that a woman manned.
"Molly Pitcher, you saved the day,"
  He said, as he gave her a hero's hand.
Molly Pitcher.[1] *Stanza 5*

EDWARD ROWLAND SILL
[1841–1887]

At the punch-bowl's brink
Let the thirsty think
  What they say in Japan:
"First the man takes a drink,
Then the drink takes a drink,
  Then the drink takes the man!"
An Adage from the Orient

I would be satisfied if I might tell,
  Before I go,
That one warm word, — how I have
    loved them well,
  Could they but know.
A Foolish Wish

The light we almost had
Shall make them glad;
The words we waited long
Shall run in music from their voice
  and song.
Field Notes.[2] *XII*

Then came the king's son, wounded,
  sore bestead,
And weaponless, and saw the broken
  sword,
Hilt-buried in the dry and trodden
  sand,
And ran and snatched it, and with
  battle-shout
Lifted afresh he hewed his enemy
  down,
And saved a great cause that heroic day.
Opportunity

No pity, Lord, could change the heart
  From red with wrong to white as
    wool;
The rod must heal the sin: but Lord,
  Be merciful to me, a fool!
The Fool's Prayer

'Tis by our follies that so long
  We hold the earth from heaven away.
Ibid.

The ill-timed truth we might have
  kept —
Who knows how sharp it pierced and
  stung?
The word we had not sense to say —
Who knows how grandly it had rung?
Ibid.

Earth bears no balsam for mistakes;
  Men crown the knave, and scourge
    the tool
That did his will.[1]
Ibid.

What may we take into the vast for-
  ever?
  That marble door
Admits no fruit of all our long endeavor,
No fame-wreathed crown we wore,
  No garnered lore.
The Future

What if some morning, when the stars
  were paling,
  And the dawn whitened, and the East
    was clear,
Strange peace and rest fell on me from
  the presence
Of a benignant Spirit standing near.
A Morning Thought

And what if then, while the still morn-
  ing brightened,
  And freshened in the elm the Sum-
    mer's breath,
Should gravely smile on me the gentle
  angel
  And take my hand and say, "My
    name is Death."
Ibid.

---

[1] Molly Pitcher was the wife of a Revolutionary soldier, and after he had been killed, she took his place at the cannon in the Battle of Monmouth [June 28, 1778].
  Sure, honor's name will aye be richer
  For the bright name of Molly Pitcher.
    LAURA ELIZABETH RICHARDS:
      Molly Pitcher
[2] For the class of 1882, Smith College.

[1] The law locks up both man and woman
  Who steals the goose from off the common,
  But lets the greater felon loose
  Who steals the common from the goose.
  Anonymous. Quoted by EDWARD POTTS CHEYNEY: *Social and Industrial History of England* [1901], *Introduction*

You need not think to palm yourself off as a freakish young zephyr, just born of yonder snow-streak and the sun-warmed rock; you have been roaming this planet ever since its birth. You have whirled in cyclones and danced with the streamers of the aurora; it was you that breathed Job's curses, and the love vows of the first lover that was ever forsworn.

The Mountain Wind,
Sierra Nevadas

GEORGE ALFRED TOWNSEND ("GATH")
[1841–1914]

Here a suffering animal lies,
Faithful, trusty, and true;
If she lives, she lives — if she dies, she dies;
And nothing more can I do.
The Cow and the Bishop

EUGENE FITCH WARE ("IRONQUILL")
[1841–1911]

When back into the alphabet
The critic's satires shall have crumbled,
When into dust his hand is humbled,
One verse of mine may linger yet.
The Rhymes of Ironquill. Preface

In the suds and in the soap,
Worked a woman full of hope;
Working, singing, all alone,
In a sort of undertone:
"With the Savior for a friend,
He will keep me to the end."
The Washerwoman's Song

Human hopes and human creeds
Have their root in human needs.
Ibid.

The charm of a love is its telling, the telling that goes with the giving;
The charm of a deed is its doing; the charm of a life is its living;
The soul of the thing is the thought; the charm of the act is the actor;

The soul of the fact is its truth, and the NOW is its principal factor.
The Now

Man builds no structure which outlives a book.
The Book

Of all the States, but three will live in story:
Old Massachusetts with her Plymouth Rock
And old Virginia with her noble stock,
And sunny Kansas with her woes and glory.
Three States

O Dewey was the morning
Upon the first of May,
And Dewey was the Admiral
Down in Manila Bay;
And Dewey were the Regent's eyes,
"Them" orbs of royal blue!
And Dewey feel discouraged?
I Dew not think we Dew.
In The Topeka (Kansas) Daily
Capital, May 3, 1898

Work brings its own relief;
He who most idle is
Has most of grief.
To-day

No evil deed live oN.
The Palindrome.

No matter how long the river, the river will reach the sea.
The Blizzard

Hour after hour the cards were fairly shuffled
And fairly dealt, but still I got no hand.
Whist

I like the game and want to play;
And through the long, long night will I, unruffled,
Play what I get until the break of day.
Ibid.

I'm ignorant of music, but still, in spite of that,
I always drop a quarter in an organ-grinder's hat.
The Organ-Grinder

The ballads of the people are the bulwarks of the State.
Ibid.

The highest of renown
Are the surest stricken down;
But the stupid and the clown
They remain.
Paresis

The Turks,
  Becoming somewhat sad,
Surrendered every
  Consonant they had.
The Siege of Djklxprwbz

We fixed him up an epitaph,
"Death loves a mining shark."
A Shining Mark

Oft the statesman and the saint
Think they're doing good, but ain't.
Aesop's Fables. No. 17

The days of long-haired poets now are
  o'er;
The short-haired poet seems to have the
  floor.
The Short-Haired Poet. Stanza 3

No town can hope prosperity and trade,
Unless the Press shall vigorously aid.
Ibid. Stanza 63

The farmer works the soil,
The agriculturist works the farmer.
The Kansas Bandit

When a person knows a story that he
  thinks he ought to tell,
If he doesn't get to tell it, why of course
  he don't feel well;
And if no one stops to listen, why of
  course a man will feel
All broke up and dislocated, and uneasy as an eel.
A Romance. Preface.

Human beings are like boilers, and the
  same rules, it would seem,
Have an equal application to affection
  and to steam.
Making love and putting steam on will
  entail the same mishaps —
When you get on too much pressure, all
  is lost by a collapse.
Ibid. Chap. IV

SARAH WILLIAMS
[1841–1868]

Is it so, O Christ in heaven, that the
  highest suffer most?
That the strongest wander farthest and
  most hopelessly are lost?

That the mark of rank in nature is ca-
  pacity for pain,
And the anguish of the singer makes the
  sweetness of the strain?
"I have many things to tell you, but ye
  cannot bear them now."[1]
Is It So, O Christ in Heaven?
Stanza 3

Though my soul may set in darkness, it
  will rise in perfect light,
I have loved the stars too fondly to be
  fearful of the night.
The Old Astronomer. Stanza 4

CHARLES FOLLEN ADAMS
[1842–1918]

I haf von funny leedle poy
  Vot gomes schust to mine knee;
Der queerest schap, der createst rogue,
  As efer you dit see.
He runs, und schumps, und schmashes
    dings
  In all barts off der house:
But vot off dot? He vas mine son,
  Mine leedle Yawcob Strauss.
Yawcob Strauss. Stanza 1

I schtill vill remember dot oldt country
    kitchen
Und dot long-handled dipper, dot hangs
    py der sink.
Dot Long-Handled Dipper.

I vants to gondradict dot shap
  Dot made dis leedle shoke:
"A voman vas der glinging vine,
  Und man der shturdy oak."
Der Oak und der Vine. Stanza 1

AMBROSE BIERCE
[1842–1914 ?]

Whose laws, imperfect and unjust,
  Thy just and perfect purpose serve;
  The needle, howsoe'er it swerve,
Still warranting the sailor's trust.
Invocation

Cynic, perforce, from study of mankind
In the false volume of his single mind,
He damned his fellows for his own un-
  worth,
And, bad himself, thought nothing good
  on earth.

[1] *John, XVI, 12*

He yearned to squander what he lived
    to save
And did not, for he could not, cheat the
    grave.
>   *An Epitaph*

To men a man is but a mind. Who cares
What face he carries or what form he
    wears?
But woman's body is the woman. O
Stay thou, my sweetheart, and do never
    go.
>   *The Devil's Dictionary*

Bore: a person who talks when you wish
    him to listen.
>   *Ibid.*

Garter: an elastic band intended to
    keep a woman from coming out of
    her stockings and desolating the coun-
    try.
>   *Ibid.*

Labor: one of the processes by which A
    acquires property for B.
>   *Ibid.*

Marriage: a community consisting of a
    master, a mistress, and two slaves,
    making in all, two.
>   *Ibid.*

Woman would be more charming if
one could fall into her arms without
falling into her hands.
>   *Epigrams*

You are not permitted to kill a
woman who has injured you, but nothing forbids you to reflect that she is
growing older every minute. You are
avenged 1440 times a day.
>   *Ibid.*

Self-denial is indulgence of a propensity to forego.
>   *Ibid.*

CHARLES MONROE DICKINSON [1]
[1842–1924]

If the days grow dark, if care and pain
Press close and sharp on heart and
    brain,

---

[1] Mr. Dickinson, who was the editor and publisher of *The Binghamton* (New York) *Republican* for many years, suggested and initiated the Associated Press in 1892.

Then lovely pictures still shall bloom
Upon the walls of memory's room.
>   *My Burdens*

When the lessons and tasks are all
    ended,
  And the school for the day is dis-
    missed,
And the little ones gather around me
  To bid me "good-night" and be
    kissed.
>   *The Children.*[1] *Stanza 1*

Within an ancient hollow oak
  That stood beside the road,
Just on the border of a wood,
  An aged Owl abode.
>   *A Sharp Trade. Stanza 1*

WILLIAM JAMES
[1842–1910]

Habit is thus the enormous fly-wheel
of society, its most precious conservative agent. It alone is what keeps us all
within the bounds of ordinance.
>   *Psychology. Chap. 10* [*1892*]

It is well for the world that in most of
us, by the age of thirty, the character
has set like plaster, and will never
soften again.
>   *Ibid.*

There is no more miserable human
being than one in whom nothing is
habitual but indecision.
>   *Ibid.*

No matter how full a reservoir of
maxims one may possess, and no matter
how good one's *sentiments* may be, if
one have not taken advantage of every
concrete opportunity to *act,* one's character may remain entirely unaffected
for the better. With mere good intentions, hell is proverbially paved.[2]
>   *Ibid.*

Keep the faculty of effort alive in you
by a little gratuitous exercise every day.
That is, be systematically ascetic or heroic in little unnecessary points, do

---

[1] This poem is frequently attributed to Charles Dickens, because of the similarity of names.

[2] See Johnson, page 236.

The road to hell is paved with good intentions. — KARL MARX: *Capital,* Modern Library ed. (abridged), *P. 42.*

every day or two something for no other reason than that you would rather not do it, so that when the hour of dire need draws nigh, it may find you not unnerved and untrained to stand the test.

Psychology. Chap. 10 [1892]

The hell to be endured hereafter, of which theology tells, is no worse than the hell we make for ourselves in this world by habitually fashioning our characters in the wrong way.

Ibid.

No state [of mind] once gone can recur and be identical with what it was before.

Ibid. Chap. 11

We are not only gregarious animals, liking to be in sight of our fellows, but we have an innate propensity to get ourselves noticed, and noticed favorably, by our kind. No more fiendish punishment could be devised, were such a thing physically possible, than that one should be turned loose in society and remain absolutely unnoticed by all the members thereof.

Ibid. Chap. 12

In the practical as in the theoretic life, the man whose acquisitions *stick* is the man who is always achieving and advancing, whilst his neighbors, spending most of their time in relearning what they once knew but have forgotten, simply hold their own.

Ibid. Chap. 18

Genius, in truth, means little more than the faculty of perceiving in an unhabitual way.

Ibid. Chap. 20

The great source of terror to infancy is solitude.

Ibid. Chap. 25

The deepest thing in our nature is this dumb region of the heart in which we dwell alone with our willingnesses and our unwillingnesses, our faiths and our fears.

The Will to Believe [1897]

Be not afraid of life. Believe that life *is* worth living, and your belief will help create the fact.[1]

Ibid.

[1] See Alfred Austin, page 612.

The whole drift of my education goes to persuade me that the world of our present consciousness is only one out of many worlds of consciousness that exist.

The Varieties of Religious Experience [1902]. Lecture XX

SIDNEY LANIER
[1842–1881]

The sun is a-wait at the ponderous gate of the West.

The Marshes of Glynn. IV, 3

Ye marshes, how candid and simple and
    nothing-withholding and free
Ye publish yourselves to the sky and
    offer yourselves to the sea!
Tolerant plains, that suffer the sea and
    the rains and the sun,
Ye spread and span like the catholic
    man who hath mightily won
God out of knowledge and good out of
    infinite pain
And sight out of blindness and purity
    out of a stain.

Ibid. 6

As the marsh-hen secretly builds on the
    watery sod,
Behold I will build me a nest on the
    greatness of God:
I will fly in the greatness of God as the
    marsh-hen flies
In the freedom that fills all the space
    'twixt the marsh and the skies:
By so many roots as the marsh-grass
    sends in the sod
I will heartily lay me a-hold on the
    greatness of God:
Oh, like to the greatness of God is the
    greatness within
The range of the marshes, the liberal
    marshes of Glynn.

Ibid. 7

Out of the hills of Habersham,
Down the valleys of Hall.

Song of the Chattahoochee.
Stanza 1

Downward the voices of Duty call —
Downward, to toil and be mixed with
    the main,

The dry fields burn, and the mills are to turn.
Song of the Chattahoochee.
Stanza 5

Death, thou'rt a cordial old and rare:
Look how compounded, with what care!
Time got his wrinkles reaping thee
Sweet herbs from all antiquity.
The Stirrup-Cup. Stanza 1

The incalculable Up-and-Down of Time.
Clover

Life! thou sea-fugue, writ from east to west,
  Love, Love alone can pore
  On thy dissolving score
Of harsh half-phrasings,
  Blotted ere writ,
And double erasings
  Of chords most fit.
The Symphony

Music is Love in search of a word.
Ibid.

Into the woods my Master went,
Clean forspent.
A Ballad of Trees and the Master. Stanza 1

'Twas on a tree they slew Him — last
When out of the woods He came.
Ibid. Stanza 2

Now in the sea's red vintage melts the sun,
  As Egypt's pearl dissolved in rosy wine,
And Cleopatra night drinks all.
Evening Song. Stanza 2

A rainbow span of fifty years,
Painted upon a cloud of tears,
In blue for hopes and red for fears,
  Finds end in a golden hour to-day.
The Golden Wedding of Sterling and Sarah Lanier. Stanza 1

Through seas of dreams and seas of phantasies,
Through seas of solitudes and vacancies,
And through my Self, the deepest of the seas,
  I strive to thee, Nirvâna.
Nirvâna. Stanza 1

My soul is sailing through the sea,
But the Past is heavy and hindereth me.
Barnacles. Stanza 1

T. MACLAGAN
[*Floruit* 1870]

I'm Captain Jinks of the Horse Marines,
I give my horse good corn and beans;
Of course 'tis quite beyond my means,
  Though a Captain in the army.
Captain Jinks. Refrain

ARTHUR MACY
[1842–1904]

Cheers for the sailors that fought on the wave for it,
Cheers for the soldiers that always were brave for it,
Tears for the men that went down to the grave for it,
  Here comes the Flag!
The Flag. Stanza 4

A little cat played on a silver flute,
  And a big cat sat and listened;
The little cat's strains gave the big cat pains,
  And a tear on his eyelids glistened.
The Boston Cats

Sit closer, friends, around the board!
  Death grants us yet a little time.
Now let the cheering cup be poured,
  And welcome song and jest and rhyme;
Enjoy the gifts that fortune sends,
Sit closer, friends.
Sit Closer, Friends: To the Papyrus Club, Boston. Stanza 1

Dear Omar, should you chance to meet
  Our Brother Somewhere in the Gloom,
Pray give to Him a Message Sweet,
  For Brothers in the Tavern Room.
He will not ask who 'tis that sends,
For We were Friends.
Ibid. Stanza 6

DAVID LAW PROUDFIT
("PELEG ARKWRIGHT")
[1842–1897]

A man sat on a rock and sought
  Refreshment from his thumb;
A dinotherium wandered by
  And scared him some.
His name was Smith. The kind of rock

He sat upon was shale.
One feature quite distinguished him —
He had a tail.
Prehistoric Smith

Nature abhors imperfect work
And on it lays her ban;
And all creation must despise
A tailless man.
Ibid.

ANNIE DOUGLAS GREEN ROBINSON ("MARION DOUGLAS")
[1842–1913]

Said old Gentleman Gay, "On a
Thanksgiving Day,
If you want a good time, then give
something away."
A Good Thanksgiving

There was once a pretty chicken, but
his friends were pretty few,
For he thought that there was nothing
in the world but what he knew.
The Ugly Duckling

DEXTER SMITH
[1842–?]

Ring the bell softly, there's crape on
the door.
Ring the Bell Softly

MAY RILEY (MRS. ALBERT) SMITH
[1842–1927]

Strange we never prize the music
Till the sweet-voiced bird has flown,
Strange that we should slight the violets
Till the lovely flowers are gone.
If We Knew [1]

The sweetest face in all the world to me,
Set in a frame of shining golden hair,
With eyes whose language is fidelity:
This is my mother. Is she not most
fair?
Dedication in Cradle and Arm Chair

[1] First published in *The Rochester*, New
York, *Union and Advertiser*, Feb. 23, 1867.

I wonder so that mothers ever fret
At little children clinging to their
gown;
Or that the footprints, when the days
are wet,
Are ever black enough to make them
frown.
Tired Mothers. Stanza 3

Life's sweetest joys are hidden
In unsubstantial things;
An April rain, a fragrance,
A vision of blue wings.
The Treetop Road. Stanza 2

My life's swift river widens to the sea,
The careless babble of the brook is
past;
A few late roses blossom still for me,
But spring is gone, and summer can-
not last.
If I Could Choose. Stanza 6

RUSSELL HERMAN CONWELL
[1843–1925]

I ask not for a larger garden,
But for finer seeds.
My Prayer. Stanza 1

Acres of diamonds.
Title of lecture

HUGH ANTOINE D'ARCY
[1843–1925]

With chalk in hand the vagabond began
To sketch a face that well might buy
the soul of any man.
Then as he placed another lock upon
the shapely head,
With a fearful shriek he leaped and fell
across the picture — dead!
The Face Upon the Floor [1887] [1]

SARAH DOUDNEY
[1843–1926]

The pure, the beautiful, the bright,
That stirred our hearts in youth,
The impulse to a wordless prayer,
The dreams of love and truth,
The longings after something lost,

[1] Often misquoted as "The Face on the Bar-
room Floor."

The spirit's yearning cry,
The strivings after better hopes, —
These things can never die.

Things That Never Die

Listen to the water-mill
Through the livelong day,
How the clicking of its wheel
Wears the hours away. . . .
And a proverb haunts my mind
As a spell is cast —
"The mill cannot grind
With the water that is past."

The Lesson of the Water-Mill [1]
[*1864*]

Oh, the wasted hours of life
That have drifted by!
Oh, the good that might have been,
Lost without a sigh!

Ibid.

Sleep on, beloved, sleep, and take thy rest;
Lay down thy head upon thy Saviour's breast;
We love thee well, but Jesus loves thee best —
Good-night!

Good-Night. [2] *Stanza 1*

EDWARD DOWDEN
[1843–1913]

I said, "I will find God," and forth I went
To seek him in the clearness of the sky,

[1] In 1870, Major-General DANIEL CRAIG McCALLUM [1815–1878] published a book of verse, *The Water-Mill, and Other Poems,* in which the first poem was practically the same as Miss Doudney's, and caused international dispute. His poem contained the following lines:
Oh! listen to the water-mill, through all the live-long day,
As the clicking of the wheel, wears hour by hour away. . . .
The mill will never grind again with water that is past. . . .
Oh! the wasted hours of life, that have swiftly drifted by,
Alas! the good we might have done, all gone without a sigh.

Miss Doudney's poem was first published in 1864. See Burton E. Stevenson: *Famous Single Poems* [1923].

[2] Ira D. Sankey composed music for this poem, and sang it at the funeral of the Reverend Charles H. Spurgeon, Feb., 1892.

But he over me, stood unendurably
Only a pitiless sapphire firmament
Ringing the world — blank splendor.

Sonnet, Seeking God

ANNA E. HAMILTON
[1843–1876]

This learned I from the shadow of a tree,
That to and fro did sway against a wall,
Our shadow selves, our influence, may fall
Where we ourselves can never be.

Influence

ALPHONSO ALVA HOPKINS
[1843–1918]

'Tis the joys the most prized that are fleetest,
And that soonest creep out from the heart,
As perfumes that are richest and sweetest
Are the earliest ones to depart.

Flitting Away

Flitting away, flitting away,
All that we cherished most dear;
There is nothing on earth that will stay,
Roses must die with the year.

Ibid.

HENRY JAMES
[1843–1916]

There are few hours in life more agreeable than the hour dedicated to the ceremony known as afternoon tea.

The Portrait of a Lady. I

At moments she discovered she was grotesquely wrong, and then she treated herself to a week of passionate humility.

Ibid. VI

The time-honored bread-sauce of the happy ending.

Theatricals: Second Series

It's a complex fate, being an American, and one of the responsibilities it entails is fighting against a superstitious valuation of Europe.

Letter, 1872. (Quoted by Van Wyck Brooks: The Pilgrimage of Henry James)

Try to be one of the people on whom nothing is lost.

The Art of Fiction

There are few things more exciting to me than a psychological reason.

Ibid.

The chances and changes, the personal history of any absolute genius, draw us to watch his adventure with curiosity and inquiry, lead us on to win more of his secret and borrow more of his experience (I mean, needless to say, when we are at all critically minded); but there is something in the clear safe arrival of the poetic nature, in a given case, at the point of its free and happy exercise, that provokes, if not the cold impulse to challenge or cross-question it, at least the need of understanding so far as possible how, in a world in which difficulty and disaster are frequent, the most wavering and flickering of all fine flames has escaped extinction.

Preface to Rupert Brooke's Letters from America (1916)

FREDERIC WILLIAM HENRY MYERS
[1843–1901]

Look when the clouds are blowing
   And all the winds are free:
In fury of their going
   They fall upon the sea.
But though the blast is frantic,
   And though the tempest raves,
The deep immense Atlantic
   Is still beneath the waves.

Wind, Moon, and Tides

Christ, I am Christ's, and let the name suffice you;
Aye, for me, too, it greatly hath sufficed.
Lo, with no winning words would I entice you,
Paul hath no honor and no friend but Christ.

Saint Paul

Coldly sublime, intolerably just.

Ibid.

Whoso has felt the Spirit of the Highest
   Cannot confound nor doubt Him nor deny:
Yea, with one voice, O world, though thou deniest,
   Stand thou on that side, for on this am I.

The Inner Light

In no single act or passion can salvation stand; far hence, beyond Orion and Andromeda, the cosmic process works and shall work forever through unbegotten souls.

Human Personality. Chap. X

JOSEPHINE POLLARD
[1843–1892]

Though he has Eden to live in,
   Man cannot be happy alone.

*We Cannot Be Happy Alone.
Stanza 5*

Miss Annabel McCarty
Was invited to a party,
"Your company from four to ten," the invitation said;
And the maiden was delighted
To think she was invited
To sit up till the hour when the big folks went to bed.

The First Party. Stanza 1

She screamed: "I want my supper — and I want to go to bed!"

Ibid. Stanza 7

I knew a man and his name was Horner,
Who used to live in Grumble Corner;
Grumble Corner in Cross Patch Town,
And he never was seen without a frown.

Grumble Corner

And many a discontented mourner
Is spending his days in Grumble Corner;
Sour and sad, whom I long to entreat
To take a house in Thanks-giving Street.

Ibid.

CHARLES WARREN STODDARD
[1843–1909]

And every note of every bell
Sang Gabriel! rang Gabriel!

In the tower that is left the tale to tell
Of Gabriel, the Archangel.
The Bells of San Gabriel

My heart to thy heart,
  My lips to thine,
In the dew of the cornfield
  The blood of the vine.
The last sigh at leaving,
  The word as we part
Is, my lips to thy lips,
  We two, heart to heart.
Lines on a Loving Cup

GEORGE BIRDSEYE
[1844–1919]

The longest day is in June, they say;
  The shortest in December.
They did not come to me that way:
  The shortest I remember
You came a day with me to stay,
  And filled my heart with laughter;
The longest day — you were away —
  The very next day after.
Shortest and Longest [1]

A Hindoo died — a happy thing to do
When twenty years united to a shrew.
The Hindoo's Paradise
  "He has married been,
And so on earth has suffered for all sin."
"Married? 'Tis well; for I've been mar-
  ried twice!"
"Begone! We'll have no fools in Para-
  dise."
Ibid.

ROBERT BRIDGES [2]
[1844–1930]

Beneath the crisp and wintry carpet hid
  A million buds but stay their blos-
    soming;
  And trustful birds have built their
    nests amid
The shuddering boughs, and only wait
    to sing
  Till one soft shower from the south
    shall bid,
And hither tempt the pilgrim steps
    of Spring.
The Growth of Love. Sonnet 6

[1] In *The Century Magazine, June, 1889.*
[2] Appointed Poet Laureate in 1913.

Beauty being the best of all we know
Sums up the unsearchable and secret
  aims
Of nature.
The Growth of Love. Sonnet 8

I live on hope and that I think do all
Who come into this world.
Ibid. Sonnet 63

Behind the western bars
The shrouded day retreats,
And unperceived the stars
Steal to their sovran seats.
The Clouds Have Left the Sky.
Stanza 3

And whiter grows the foam,
The small moon lightens more;
And as I turn me home,
My shadow walks before.
Ibid. Stanza 4

Whither, O splendid ship, thy white
    sails crowding,
  Leaning across the bosom of the ur-
    gent West,
That fearest nor sea rising, nor sky
    clouding,
  Whither away, fair rover, and what
    thy quest?
A Passer-By. Stanza 1

I have loved flowers that fade,
  Within whose magic tents
Rich hues have marriage made
  With sweet unmemoried scents.
I Have Loved Flowers that Fade.
Stanza 1

Ah! little at best can all our hopes avail
    us
  To lift this sorrow, or cheer us, when
    in the dark,
    Unwilling, alone we embark,
And the things we have seen and have
    known and have heard of, fail us.
On a Dead Child. Stanza 7

Gird on thy sword, O man, thy strength
    endue,
In fair desire thine earth-born joy re-
    new.
Live thou thy life beneath the making
    sun
Till Beauty, Truth, and Love in thee
    are one.
A Hymn of Nature. VII, Stanza 1

When first we met we did not guess
That Love would prove so hard a mas-
ter.
Of more than common friendliness
When first we met we did not guess.
Triolet

So sweet love seemed that April morn,
When first we kissed beside the thorn,
So strangely sweet, it was not strange
We thought that love could never
change.
Shorter Poems. Book V, 5

Now learn, love, have, do, be the best;
Each in one thing excel the rest:
Strive; and hold fast this truth of
heaven —
To him that hath shall more be given.
*Ode on the Ninth Jubilee of
Eton College*

My delight and thy delight
Walking, like two angels white,
In the gardens of the night.
New Poems. Number 9

Love, from whom the world begun,
Hath the secret of the sun.
Love can tell, and love alone,
Whence the million stars were strewn,
Why each atom knows its own.
Ibid.

The nightingale
as amorous of his art as of his brooding
mate
practiseth every phrase of his espousal
lay,
and still provoketh envy of the lesser
songsters
with the same notes that woke poetic
eloquence
alike in Sophocles and the sick heart of
Keats.
The Testament of Beauty

Wisdom will repudiate thee, if thou
think to enquire
WHY things are as they are or whence
they came: thy task
is first to learn WHAT IS, and in pur-
suant knowledge
pure intellect will find pure pleasure
and the only ground
for a philosophy conformable to truth.
Ibid.

Sickening thought itself engendereth
corporal pain.
The Testament of Beauty
Our hope is ever livelier than despair,
our joy
livelier and more abiding than our sorrows are.
Ibid.

For what were pleasure if never contemplation gave
a spiritual significance to objects of
sense,
nor in thought's atmosphere poet vision
arose?
Ibid.

Man, in the unsearchable darkness,
knoweth one thing
that as he is, so was he made: and if
the Essence
and characteristic faculty of humanity
is our conscient Reason and our desire
of knowledge,
that was Nature's Purpose in the making of man.
Ibid.

ROBERT JONES BURDETTE
[1844–1914]

I love the man who knows it all,
From east to west, from north to
south,
Who knows all things, both great and
small,
And tells it with his tiresome mouth.
He Knows It All. Stanza 1

Since she went home —
The evening shadows linger longer
here, —
The winter days fill so much of the year,
And even summer winds are chill and
drear.
Since She Went Home. Stanza 1

I would receive my sight; my clouded
eyes
Miss the glad radiance of the morning sun,
The changing tints that glorify the skies
With roseate splendors when the day
is done;
The shadows soft and gray, the pearly
light

Of summer twilight deep'ning into
night.

Bartimeus.[1] *Stanza 1*

There are two days in the week about
which and upon which I never worry.
Two carefree days, kept sacredly free
from fear and apprehension. One of
these days is Yesterday. . . . And the
other day I do not worry about is To-
morrow.

The Golden Day

GEORGE WASHINGTON CABLE
[1844–1925]

There came to port last Sunday night
　The queerest little craft,
Without an inch of rigging on;
　I looked and looked — and laughed!

The New Arrival. Stanza 1

She has no manifest but this,
　No flag floats o'er the water;
She's too new for the British Lloyd's —
　My daughter! O my daughter!

Ibid. Stanza 2

EDWARD CARPENTER
[1844–1929]

So thin a veil divides
Us from such joy, past words,
Walking in daily life — the business of
　the hour, each detail seen to;
Yet carried, rapt away, on what sweet
　floods of other Being:
Swift streams of music flowing, light far
　back through all Creation shining,
Loved faces looking.

So Thin a Veil

Newer ways are ours,
New thoughts, new fancies, and we
　deem our lives
New-fashioned in a mould of vaster
　powers;
But as of old with flesh the spirit strives.

The World-Spirit. Stanza 14

It should be as easy to expel an obnoxious thought from your mind as to
shake a stone out of your shoe.

A Visit to a Gnani. Chap. 3

[1] The blind man said unto him, Lord, that
I might receive my sight. — *Mark, X, 51*

(*Also in From Adam's Peak to
Elephanta*)

Motherhood is, after all, woman's
great and incomparable work.

*Love's Coming-of-Age.
Woman in Freedom*

Each one thinks that the current in
which he lives is the whole ocean.

Ibid. The Free Society

There is nothing that is evil except
because a man has not mastery over it;
and there is no good thing that is not
evil if it have a mastery over a man.

*Towards Democracy. The
Secret of Time and Satan*

When Death comes, breaking into the
circle of our friends, words fail us, our
mental machinery ceases to operate, all
our little stores of wit and wisdom, our
maxims, our mottoes, accumulated
from daily experience, evaporate and
are of no avail. These things do not
seem to touch or illuminate in any effective way the strange vast Presence
whose wings darken the world for us.

*The Drama of Love and Death.
Chap. 1*

Love is an Art, and the greatest of
the Arts.

Ibid. Chap. 4

Nothing is more certain than that
worlds on worlds, and spheres on
spheres, stretch behind and beyond
the actually seen.

Ibid. Chap. 7

Every new movement or manifestation of human activity, when unfamiliar to people's minds, is sure to be mis-
represented and misunderstood.

Ibid. Chap. 8, Note

In Man, the positive content of religion is the instinctive sense — whether
conscious or subconscious — of an inner unity and continuity with the
world around. This is the stuff out of
which religion is made.

*Pagan and Christian Creeds.
Chap. 4*

The first condition of social happiness and prosperity must be the sense
of the Common Life.

Ibid. Chap. 17

There is a presence and an influence in Nature and the Open which expands the mind and causes brigand cares and worries to drop off — whereas in confined places foolish and futile thoughts of all kinds swarm like microbes and cloud and conceal the soul.

Lecture I, The Teaching of the Upanishads. Rest

EDWARD A. CHURCH
[1844-1929]

Friends, whom the softest whistle of my call
  Brought to my side in love that knew no doubt,
Would I not seek to cross the jasper wall
  If haply I might find you there "without"?

Without Are Dogs.[1] Stanza 3

Of all the words the Evangelists record,
To comfort souls perplexèd and distressed,
This ever seems to me divinest, best —
The thought that Peter spoke — "Thou knowest, Lord."

Sonnet, Thou Knowest

Come, holy fire, consume this clay,
  Ashes to ashes now return;
An outworn garment here we lay,
  As on thine Altar, Lord, to burn.

Cremation Hymn. Stanza 1

Not to corruption and the worm
  Our shrinking spirits yield the claim,
But give this well-beloved form
  The cleanly burial of the flame.

Ibid. Stanza 2

From duty's path, however steep, we ask
  For no ill-timed release;
Only — for strength to finish well our task —
  Grant us thy peace!

A Prayer. Stanza 6

Bragging of crests and pedigrees —
And all most noble through and through!
Cadets of Gascony are these
With Carbon de Castel Jaloux.

Gasconade. Stanza 1

[1] Revelation, XXII, 15.

I strike at close of the Envoy.

Ballade of the Duel, Cyrano de Bergerac

INA DONNA COOLBRITH
[1844-1928]

He walks with God upon the hills!
And sees, each morn, the world arise
New-bathed in light of paradise.

The Poet

It must be sweet, O thou my dead, to lie
  With hands that folded are from every task,
Sealed with the seal of that great mystery,
  The lips that nothing answer, nothing ask,
The lifelong struggle ended.

Beside the Dead

MARY AINGE DE VERE ("MADELINE BRIDGES")
[1844-1920]

There are loyal hearts, there are spirits brave,
  There are souls that are pure and true;
Then give to the world the best you have,
  And the best will come back to you.

Life's Mirror. Stanza 1

For life is the mirror of king and slave,
'Tis just what we are and do.

Ibid. Stanza 5

God keep you, dearest, all this lonely night:
  The winds are still,
  The moon drops down behind the western hill;
God keep you, dearest, till the light.

God Keep You. Stanza 1

RICHARD WATSON GILDER
[1844-1909]

Not from the whole wide world I chose thee,
  Sweetheart, light of the land and the sea!
The wide, wide world could not enclose thee,

For thou art the whole wide world
to me.
Song

Through love to light! Oh wonderful
the way
That leads from darkness to the perfect day!
After-song

I am a woman — therefore I may not
Call to him, cry to him,
Fly to him,
Bid him delay not.
A Woman's Thought

How to the singer comes the song?
How to the summer fields
Come flowers? How yields
Darkness to happy morn? How doth
the night
Bring stars?
*How to the Singer Comes the
Song? Stanza 4*

This house that looks to east, to west,
This, dear one, is our home, our rest;
Yonder the stormy sea, and here
The woods that bring the sunset near.
*The Woods that Bring the
Sunset Near. Stanza 3*

What is a sonnet? 'Tis a pearly shell
    That murmurs of the far-off mur-
    muring sea;
    A precious jewel carved most curi-
    ously;
It is a little picture painted well.
The Sonnet

This is the poet's triumph, his high
doom!
After life's stress —
For him the silent, dark, o'ershadowing
tomb
Is shadowless.
And this the miracle and mystery —
In that he gives
His soul away, magnificently free,
By this he lives.
On Reading of a Poet's Death

I count my time by times that I meet
thee;
These are my yesterdays, my morrows,
noons
And nights; these my old moons and
my new moons.
The New Day. Book IV, 6

GERARD MANLEY HOPKINS [1]
[1844–1889]

The world is charged with the grandeur
of God. . . .
There lives the dearest freshness deep
down things.
God's Grandeur

Glory be to God for dappled things —
For skies as couple-colored as a brindled
cow;
For rose-moles all in stipple upon trout
that swim.
Pied Beauty

Elected Silence, sing to me
And beat upon my whorlèd ear,
Pipe me to pastures still and be
The music that I care to hear.
The Habit of Perfection

I say that we are wound
With mercy round and round
As if with air.
Mary Mother of Divine Grace

World-mothering air, air wild,
Wound with thee, in thee isled,
Fold home, fast fold thy child.
Ibid.

Summer ends now; now, barbarous in
beauty, the stooks rise
    Around; up above, what wind-walks!
    what lovely behavior
    Of silk-sack clouds! Has wilder,
    willful-wavier
Meal-drift molded ever and melted
across skies?
Hurrahing in Harvest

I have asked to be
    Where no storms come,
Where the green swell is in the havens
dumb
    And out of the swing of the sea.
Heaven-Haven

I kiss my hand
To the stars, lovely-asunder
Starlight, wafting him out of it; and
Glow, glory in thunder. . . .

[1] He has left us only 90 poems — but so
essential that they will colour and convert the
development of English poetry for many decades to come. — HERBERT READ (1893–   )
in *The Criterion, April, 1931.*

Since though he is under the world's
  splendour and wonder,
His mystery must be instressed,
  stressed;
For I greet him the days I meet him,
  and bless when I understand.
  The Wreck of the Deutschland.
  Stanza 5

To lift up the hands in prayer gives
God glory, but a man with a dungfork
in his hand, a woman with a slop-pail,
give him glory too. He is so great that
all things give him glory if you mean
they should. So then, my brethren, live.
  An Address on St. Ignatius

ANDREW LANG
[1844–1912]

My mind is gay but my soul is melancholy.
  Quoted by Mrs. Lang *in Pref-*
  ace, The Poetical Works of
  Andrew Lang

St. Andrews by the northern sea,
A haunted town it is to me!
A little city, worn and gray,
The gray North Ocean girds it round.
  Almae Matres (St. Andrews,
  1862; Oxford, 1865). Stanza 1

You can cover a great deal of country
in books.
  To the Gentle Reader. Stanza 5

Such is the fate of borrowed books:
  they're lost,
Or not the book returneth, but its
  ghost!
  From Colletet

Here stand my books, line upon line
They reach the roof, and row by row,
They speak of faded tastes of mine,
And things I did, but do not, know.
  Ballade of His Books. Stanza 1

The watches of the night reveal
The books that never can be mine!
  Ballade of the Unattainable.
  Stanza 3

One gift the fairies gave me: (three
They commonly bestowed of yore)
The love of books, the golden key
That opens the enchanted door.
  Ballade of the Bookworm.
  Stanza 2

When others fail him, the wise man
  looks
To the sure companionship of books.
  Old Friends

Prince, you may storm and ban —
Joe Millers *are* a pest,
Suppress me if you can!
I am a Merry Jest!
  Ballade of the Primitive Jest.
  Envoy

Why, why are rhymes so rare to *love?*
  Ballade of Difficult Rhymes

There's a joy without canker or cark,
  There's a pleasure eternally new,
'Tis to gloat on the glaze and the mark
Of china that's ancient and blue.
  Ballade of Blue China. Stanza 1

Here's a pot with a cot in a park
  In a park where the peach-blossoms
  blew;
Where the lovers eloped in the dark,
  Lived, died, and were changed into
  two
Bright birds that eternally flew
Through the boughs of the may, as they
  sang;
'Tis a tale was undoubtedly true
In the reign of the Emperor Hwang.
  Ibid. Stanza 3

We marvel, now we look behind:
Life's more amusing than we thought!
  Ballade of Middle Age. Stanza 1

Prince, 'tis a melancholy lay!
For youth, for life we both regret!
How fair they seem, how far away;
With Aucassin and Nicolete.
  Ballade of Aucassin. Envoy

The windy lights of Autumn flare:
  I watch the moonlit sails go by;
I marvel how men toil and fare,
  The weary business that they ply!
  Their voyaging is vanity,
And fairy gold is all their gain,
  And all the winds of winter cry,
"My Love returns no more again."
  Ballade of Autumn. Stanza 2

I'd leave all the hurry, the noise, and
  the fray,
For a house full of books, and a garden
  of flowers.
  Ballade of True Wisdom. Stanza 3

Sleep, that giv'st what Life denies,
Shadowy bounties and supreme,

Bring the dearest face that flies
Following darkness like a dream!
　　　Ballade of the Dream. Envoy
O bargains in books that they send us,
Ye come through the Ivory Gate!
　　　Ballade of the Real and Ideal.
　　　　　Stanza 2
So gladly, from the songs of modern
　　speech
Men turn, and see the stars, and feel
　　the free
　　　Shrill wind beyond the close of
　　　　heavy flowers;
　　　And, through the music of the
　　　　languid hours,
They hear like ocean on a western
　　beach
　　　The surge and thunder of the Odys-
　　　　sey.
　　　　　Sonnet, The Odyssey
The Angler hath a jolly life
　　Who by the rail runs down,
And leaves his business and his wife,
　　And all the din of town.
The wind down stream is blowing
　　straight,
　　And nowhere cast can he:
Then lo, he doth but sit and wait
　　In kindly company.
　　　The Contented Angler. Stanza 1
When we have cut each other's throats
　　And robbed each other's land;
And turned, and changed, and lost our
　　coats,
　　Till progress is at stand;
When every "programme's" been gone
　　through
This good old world will wake anew!
　　　An Aspiration. Stanza 1
A land where newspapers were dumb
From scandal and from scare.[1]
　　　　　Ibid. Stanza 6

---

[1] In 1895, a New York paper was carrying
a series of comic strips, "Hogan's Alley," by
Richard Felton Outcault [1863–1928]. In
1896, a rival paper engaged the artist to begin
a new series portraying "The Yellow Kid."
The quarrel of the two newspapers over the
right to run the cartoons, together with the
similarity in the manner in which the two
newspapers displayed sensational news, led to
the coining of the term, "Yellow Journalism."
— Condensed from *The New York Sun, May
15, 1898*

Why ladies read what they *do* read
　　Is a thing that no man may explain.
　　　A Remonstrance with the Fair.
　　　　　Stanza 1
From the damp sheiling on the draggled
　　island
Mountains divide you, and no end of
　　seas.
But, though your heart is genuinely
　　Highland,
Still, you're in luck to be away from
　　these! [1]
　　　To Fiona, Parody of Canadian
　　　　　Boat Song
Had cigarettes no ashes,
　　And roses ne'er a thorn,
The big trout would not ever
Escape into the river.
　　　A Highly Valuable Chain of
　　　　　Thoughts. Stanza 2
We meet him first in Homer's verse,
　　The dog by the Aegean seas;
He barks at strangers, ay, and worse,
He bites! We learn, in language terse,
That even Argos has the curse
　　　　Of fleas! [2]
　　　The Friend of Man. Stanza 3

---

[1] From the lone sheiling of the misty island
　　Mountains divide us, and the waste of
　　　seas —
　　Yet still the blood is strong, the heart is
　　　Highland,
　　　And we in dreams behold the Hebrides.
　　　　　Canadian Boat Song, St. 2
This poem appeared in *Noctes Ambrosiana,*
No. 46, in *Blackwood's Magazine, Vol. 26,
P. 400, Sept., 1829.* It is generally credited to
JOHN GALT [1779–1839], but JOHN WILSON
("Christopher North"), who won the first
Newdigate Prize, founded in 1805, has been
suggested as the author. John Gibson Lock-
hart, son-in-law of Sir Walter Scott, noted, on
a copy of the poem in his own handwriting,
that the song had been sent to him by a friend
in Upper Canada. Galt, author of *Annals of
the Parish,* was in Canada in 1824 and 1826.
The poem was likewise found in the handwriting of Hugh Montgomerie [1739–1819],
twelfth Earl of Eglinton, ascribed to a Gaelic
origin.
　　Robert Louis Stevenson misquotes the second stanza of the song in *The Silverado
Squatters,* Chap. 4. Joseph Chamberlain, the
British statesman, gave Stevenson's version in
a speech at Inverness.
[2] There lay the old dog, Argos, full of fleas!
　　THOMAS HOBBES [1588–1679]: *Odyssey*

Who wins his love shall lose her,
  Who loses her shall gain.
                    Lost Love. Stanza 1
In dreams she grows not older
  The lands of dream among;
Though all the world wax colder,
  Though all the songs be sung,
In dreams doth he behold her
  Still fair and kind and young.
                    Ibid. Stanza 4
And, if one Rag of Character they
    spare,
Comes the Biographer, and strips it
    bare!
          *Letters to Dead Authors. Epistle
                    to Mr. Alexander Pope*
'Tis the fault of all art to seem anti-
quated and faded in the eyes of the suc-
ceeding generation.
                    Ibid. To Jane Austen
Contemporary spites do not harm
true genius.
                    Ibid. To M. Chapelain
Perchance for poets dead there is
prepared a place more beautiful than
their dreams.
                    Ibid. To Theocritus
The dusty and stony ways of contemporary criticism.
                    Ibid. To Edgar Allan Poe
About the writers of his own generation a leader of that generation should
hold his peace.
                    Ibid.
Great minds should only criticize the
great who have passed beyond the
reach of eulogy or fault-finding.
                    Ibid.
The eye of each man sees but what
it has the power of seeing.
                    Ibid. To Homer

JAMES HILARY MULLIGAN
[1844–1916]

The moonlight is the softest, in Ken-
    tucky,
Summer days come oftest, in Kentucky,
  Friendship is the strongest,
  Love's fires glow the longest,
  Yet a wrong is always wrongest,
    In Kentucky.
                    In Kentucky. Stanza 1

Songbirds are sweetest, in Kentucky,
Thoroughbreds the fleetest, in Ken-
    tucky;
  The mountains tower proudest,
  Thunder peals the loudest,
  The landscape is the grandest,
  And politics the damnedest,
    In Kentucky.
                    In Kentucky. Stanza 7

JOHN BOYLE O'REILLY
[1844–1890]

Though it lash the shallows that line
    the beach,
  Afar from the great sea-deeps,
There is never a storm whose might can
    reach
  Where the vast leviathan sleeps.
Like a mighty thought in a mighty
    mind
  In the clear cold depths he swims;
Whilst above him the pettiest form of
    his kind
  With a dash o'er the surface skims.
                Prelude to the Amber Whale
They who see the Flying Dutchman
  never, never reach the shore.
                    The Flying Dutchman
Doubt is brother-devil to Despair.
                    Prometheus
The world is large when weary leagues
    two loving hearts divide
But the world is small when your enemy
    is loose on the other side.
                    Distance
The red rose whispers of passion
  And the white rose breathes of love;
O, the red rose is a falcon,
  And the white rose is a dove.
                    A White Rose. Stanza 1
You may grind their souls in the self-
    same mill,
  You may bind them, heart and brow;
But the poet will follow the rainbow
    still,
  And his brother will follow the plow.
                    The Rainbow's Treasure.
                    Stanza 5
There are times when a dream delicious
  Steals into a musing hour,

Like a face with love capricious,
   That peeps from a woodland bower.
               An Old Picture. Stanza 1

You gave me the key to your heart, my
   love;
   Then why do you make me knock?
"Oh, that was yesterday; Saints above,
   Last night I changed the lock!"
               Constancy

First across the gulf we cast
Kite-borne threads, till lines are passed,
And habit builds the bridge at last!
        A Builder's Lesson. Stanza 3

He draws no rein, but he shakes the
   street
With a shout and the ring of the galloping feet;
And this the cry he flings to the wind:
"To the hills for your lives, the flood
   is behind!" [1]
        The Ride of Collins Graves

The wealth of mankind is the wisdom
   they leave.
           Rules of the Road

Be silent and safe — silence never betrays you.
                Ibid.

"I had" is a heartache, "I have" is a
   fountain,
You're worth what you saved, not the
   million you made.
                Ibid.

This truth keep in sight, — every man
   on the planet
Has just as much right as yourself to
   the road.
                Ibid.

The organized charity, scrimped and
   iced,
In the name of a cautious, statistical
   Christ.[2]
          In Bohemia. Stanza 5

Oh, I long for the glow of a kindly
   heart and the grasp of a friendly
   hand!
And I'd rather live in Bohemia than in
   any other land.
          Ibid. Stanza 6

---

[1] The breaking of the dam over Mill River,
Williamsburg, Massachusetts, May 16, 1874.
[2] See Southey, page 322, and Hood, page
392.

Well blest is he who has a dear one
   dead;
A friend he has whose face will never
   change —
A dear communion that will not grow
   strange;
The anchor of a love is death.
          Forever. Stanza 3

ARTHUR WILLIAM EDGAR O'SHAUGHNESSY
[1844–1881]

What man is able to master
And stem the great Fountain of Tears?
        The Fountain of Tears.
                Stanza 8

We are the music-makers,
   And we are the dreamers of dreams,
Wandering by lone sea-breakers,
   And sitting by desolate streams;
World-losers and world-forsakers,
   On whom the pale moon gleams:
Yet we are the movers and shakers
   Of the world forever, it seems.
            Ode. Stanza 1

One man with a dream, at pleasure,
   Shall go forth and conquer a crown;
And three with a new song's measure
   Can trample an empire down.
           Ibid. Stanza 2

For each age is a dream that is dying,
   Or one that is coming to birth.
           Ibid. Stanza 3

MAURICE THOMPSON
[1844–1901]

May one who fought in honor for the
   South
Uncovered stand and sing by Lincoln's
   grave?
          At Lincoln's Grave

A soft Kentucky strain was in his voice,
And the Ohio's deeper boom was there,
With some wild accents of old Wabash
   days,
   And winds of Illinois;
And when he spoke he took us unaware,
With his high courage and unselfish
   ways.
                Ibid.

The sky is like a woman's love,
  The ocean like a man's;
Oh, neither knows, below, above,
  The measure that it spans!
        Love's Horizon. Stanza 1

ELIZABETH STUART PHELPS WARD
[1844–1911]

O tender arms that meet and clasp!
Gather and cherish while ye may.
The morrow knoweth God. Ye know
Your own are yours to-day.
        Gloucester Harbor. Stanza 7
There breaks in every Gloucester wave
A widowed woman's heart.
        Ibid. Stanza 8
There is no vacant chair. To love is
  still
  To have.
        Afterward. Stanza 5
Our souls are like the sparrows
  Imprisoned in the clay;
Bless Him who came to give them
  wings,
Upon a Christmas Day.
        *A Jewish Legend: The Clay
        Sparrows. Stanza 10*

JOHN B. BOGART [1]
[1845–1921]

When a dog bites a man, that is not
news, because it happens so often. But
if a man bites a dog, that is news.
        Quoted by FRANK M. O'BRIEN
        in The Story of The Sun [*1918*]

JOHN HENRY BONER
[1845–1903]

Ah, we fondly cherish
  Faded things
That had better perish.
  Memory clings
To each leaf it saves.
        Gather Leaves and Grasses
Here lived the soul enchanted
  By melody of song;

[1] City Editor of *The Sun*, New York, 1873–1890.

Here dwelt the spirit haunted
  By a demoniac throng.
        Poe's Cottage at Fordham

WILL CARLETON
[1845–1912]

Worm or beetle — drought or tempest
  — on a farmer's land may fall,
Each is loaded full o' ruin, but a mort-
  gage beats 'em all.
        The Tramp's Story
I've watched my duty, straight an'
  true,
  An' tried to do it well;
Part of the time kept heaven in view,
  An' part steered clear of hell.
        *The New Church Doctrine.
        Stanza 2*
My business on the jury's done — the
  quibblin' all is through —
I've watched the lawyers, right and
  left, and give my verdict true.
        Goin' Home To-day. Stanza 1
If there's a heaven upon the earth, a
  fellow knows it when
He's been away from home a week, and
  then gets back again.
        Ibid. Stanza 7
"There is nothing worth the doing that
  it does not pay to try,"
Thought the little black-eyed rebel,
  with a twinkle in her eye.
        *The Little Black-Eyed Rebel.
        Stanza 11*
Boys flying kites haul in their white-
  winged birds;
You can't do that way when you're flying words.
"Careful with fire," is good advice, we
  know:
"Careful with words," is ten times
  doubly so.
Thoughts unexpressed may sometimes
  fall back dead;
But God himself can't kill them when
  they're said.
        The First Settler's Story
Not a log in this buildin' but its memories has got,

And not a nail in this old floor but
    touches a tender spot.
        *Out of the Old House, Nancy.
            Stanza 17*
Fare you well, old house! you're naught
    that can feel or see,
But you seem like a human being — a
    dear old friend to me;
And we never will have a better home,
    if *my* opinion stands,
Until we commence a-keepin' house in
    the house not made with hands.
        Ibid. Stanza 20
    The kind old country doctor
Whom the populace considered with a
    mingled love and dread.
        The Country Doctor. Stanza 1
He has seen old views and patients dis-
    appearing, one by one,
He has learned that Death is master
    both of Science and of Art.
        Ibid. Stanza 3
Them's my sentiments, tew.[1]
        *The Schoolmaster's Guests.
            Canto 3*
If we who have sailed together
    Flit out of each other's view,
The world will sail on, I think,
    Just as it used to do.
        One and Two. Stanza 3
But ships long time together
Can better the tempest weather
    Than any other two.
        Ibid.
Things at home are crossways, and
    Betsey and I are out.
        Betsey and I Are Out. Stanza 1
I have talked with Betsey, and Betsey
    has talked with me,
And so we've agreed together that we
    can't never agree.
        Ibid. Stanza 3
Betsey, like all good women, had a
    temper of her own.
        Ibid. Stanza 4
The more we arg'ed the question the
    more we didn't agree.
        Ibid. Stanza 5
I don't complain of Betsey, or any of
    her acts,

[1] See Thackeray, page 482.

Exceptin' when we've quarreled, and
    told each other facts.
        Betsey and I Are Out. Stanza 18
You see, when we came to division,
    there was things that wouldn't
    divide.
        *Betsey Destroys the Paper.
            Stanza 6*
Now he didn't give you that baby, by
    a hundred thousand mile;
He just think you need some sunshine,
    and he lent him for a while.
        The Funeral. Stanza 6
I'm going away to-day with a hand-
    somer man than you.
        *Gone with a Handsomer Man.
            Stanza 4*
    To appreciate heaven well
'Tis good for a man to have some fif-
    teen minutes of hell.
        Ibid. Stanza 20
Over the hill to the poor-house I'm
    trudgin' my weary way.
        *Over the Hill to the Poor-
            House. Stanza 1*
She had an edication, an' that was good
    for her;
But when she twitted me on mine,
    'twas carryin' things too fur.
        Ibid. Stanza 14

WILLIAM ULICK O'CONNOR CUFFE (LORD DESART)
[1845–1898]

Mother Hubbard, you see, was old:
there being no mention of others, we
may presume she was alone; a widow
— a friendless, old, solitary widow. Yet
did she despair? Did she sit down and
weep, or read a novel, or wring her
hands? No! She went to the cupboard.
    *Mock Sermon: Old Mother
        Hubbard* [1877]

CHARLES FLETCHER DOLE
[1845–1927]

Good Will is the mightiest practical
force in the universe.
    Cleveland Address

The Golden Rule works like gravitation.

Cleveland Address

Democracy is on trial in the world, on a more colossal scale than ever before.

The Spirit of Democracy

EDWARD HARRIGAN
[1845–1911]

The best of luck is always waiting on
  you
If you pick up on the road a horse's
  shoe.

Never Take the Horseshoe from
the Door. Stanza 1

The drums and fifes, how sweetly they
  did play,
As we march'd, march'd, march'd in the
  Mulligan Guard.

The Mulligan Guard [1873]

As I walk the street each friend I meet
Says, "There goes Muldoon. He's a
  solid man."

Muldoon, the Solid Man

DANIEL WEBSTER HOYT
[1845–1936]

If you have a friend worth loving,
  Love him. Yes, and let him know
That you love him, ere life's evening
  Tinge his brow with sunset glow.
Why should good words ne'er be said
Of a friend till he is dead?

A Sermon in Rhyme [1878].
Stanza 1

If you hear a song that thrills you,
  Sung by any child of song,
Praise it. Do not let the singer
  Wait deservèd praises long.
Why should one who thrills your heart
Lack the joy you may impart?

Ibid. Stanza 2

MARGARET THOMSON JANVIER ("MARGARET VANDEGRIFT")
[1845–1913]

You needn't be trying to comfort me —
  I tell you my dolly is dead!

There's no use in saying she isn't, with
  a crack like that in her head.

The Dead Doll. Stanza 1

GEORGE THOMAS LANIGAN
[1845–1886]

What, what, what,
What's the news from Swat?
  Sad news,
  Bad news,
Comes by cable led
Through the Indian Ocean's bed,
Through the Persian Gulf, the Red
Sea and the Med-
Iterranean — he's dead;
The Ahkoond is dead! [1]

A Threnody [January, 1878].
Stanza 1

Alas, unhappy land; ill-fated spot
Kotal — though where or what
On earth Kotal is, the bard has forgot;
Further than this indeed he knoweth
  not —
It borders upon Swat.

Dirge of the Moolla of Kotal,
Rival of the Ahkoond of Swat.
Stanza 1

EUGENE LEE-HAMILTON
[1845–1907]

The hollow sea-shell, which for years
  hath stood
On dusty shelves, when held against the
  ear
Proclaims its stormy parent, and we
  hear
The faint, far murmur of the breaking
  flood.
We hear the sea. [2] The Sea? It is the
  blood
In our own veins, impetuous and near.

Sonnet, Sea-shell Murmurs

---

[1] See Lear, page 499.
Now the Ahkoond of Swat is a vague sort of
  man
Who lives in a country far over the sea;
Pray tell me, good reader, if tell me you can,
  What's the Ahkoond of Swat to you folks
  or to me?
    EUGENE FIELD: *The Ahkoond of Swat*
      [Sept. 19, 1884]
[2] See F. D. Gage, page 446.

It is the pure white diamond Dante
    brought
  To Beatrice; the sapphire Laura
    wore
When Petrarch cut it sparkling out of
    thought;
  The ruby Shakespeare hewed from
    his heart's core;
The dark, deep emerald that Rossetti
    wrought
  For his own soul, to wear for ever-
    more.

What Is a Sonnet?

Things bygone are the only things that
    last:
The present is mere grass, quick-mown
    away;
The past is stone, and stands for ever
    fast.

Roman Baths

GEORGE SAINTSBURY
[1845–1933]

It must be remembered that the
point of honour which decrees that a
man must not under any circumstances
accept money from a woman with
whom he is on certain terms, is of very
modern growth, and is still tempered
by the proviso that he may take as
much as he likes or can get from his
wife.

Preface to FIELDING'S *Tom Jones*

I have myself a great admiration for
nice fine points of honour — I don't
think you can make them too nice or
too fine.

Ibid.

One of the commonest but most uncritical faults of criticism — the refusal
to consider what it is that the author
intended to give us.

Ibid.

Criticism is the endeavor to find, to
know, to love, to recommend, not only
the best, but all the good, that has been
known and thought and written in the
world.

A History of Criticism

It is the first duty of the novelist to
let himself be read — anything else

that he gives you is a bonus, a trimming, a dessert.

History of the English Novel

I have never tried to be in the fashion
for the sake of being in it, and seldom,
I think, to be out of it for the sake of
being out of it. Logic and history have
been the only external guides I have
accepted in temporal things, except
where pure taste has reigned alone.

Notes on a Cellar Book. Preface

When they [wines] were good they
pleased my sense, cheered my spirits,
improved my moral and intellectual
powers, besides enabling me to confer
the same benefits on other people.

Ibid.

Men will try to persuade themselves,
or at least others, that they read poetry
because it is a criticism of life, because
it expresses the doubts and fears and
thoughts and hopes of the time, because it is a substitution for religion,
because it is a relief from serious work,
because and because and because. As a
matter of fact, they (that is to say,
those of them who like it generally)
read it because they like it, because it
communicates an experience of half-
sensual, half-intellectual pleasure to
them.

Corrected Impressions.
Tennyson

R. L. SHARPE

Each is given a bag of tools,
A shapeless mass,
A book of rules;
And each must make,
Ere life is flown,
A stumbling-block
Or a stepping-stone.

Stumbling-Block or Stepping-
Stone. Stanza 2

ARABELLA EUGENIA SMITH
[1845–1916]

If I should die to-night,
My friends would look upon my quiet
    face,
Before they laid it in its resting place,

And deem that death had left it almost fair.

If I Should Die To-night.[1]
Stanza 1

Keep not your kisses for my dead, cold brow;
The way is lonely, let me feel them now.

Ibid. Stanza 4

When dreamless rest is mine, I shall not need
The tenderness for which I long to-night.

Ibid.

CHARLES WILLIAM STUBBS
[1845–1912]

I sat alone with my conscience
In a place where time had ceased,
And we talked of my former living
In the land where the years increased.

*Conscience and Future
Judgment [1876]*

The ghost of forgotten actions
Came floating before my sight,
And things that I thought were dead things
Were alive with a terrible might.

Ibid.

To sit alone with my conscience
Will be judgment enough for me.[2]

Ibid.

JOHN BANISTER TABB
[1845–1909]

When Christ was taken from the rood,
One thorn upon the ground,
Still moistened with the Precious Blood,
An early robin found,

---

[1] First printed in *The Christian Union, June 18, 1873.*
The parody by BEN KING [1857–1894] has become better known than the original. See page 729.
[2] There's just ae thing I cannae bear,
An' that's my conscience.
R. L. STEVENSON: *In Scots, XIV, My Conscience*
Conscience allus welts it to me with a mighty cuttin' rod,
When thar ain't nobody near me, 'ceptin' God.
JAMES BARTON ADAMS: *A Cowboy Alone with His Conscience*

And wove it crosswise in his nest,
Where, lo, it reddened all his breast! [1]

Robin Redbreast

The ghost am I
Of winds that die
Alike on land or sea.

The Fog. Stanza 1

No more the battle or the chase
The phantom tribes pursue,
But each in its accustomed place
The Autumn hails anew;
And still from solemn councils set
On every hill and plain,
The smoke of many a calumet
Ascends to heaven again.

Indian Summer

Before a clock was in the tower
Or e'er a watch was worn,
I knew of night the passing hour
And prophesied the morn;
To man of every age and clime
The oldest chronicler of time.

The Cock

How many an acorn falls to die
For one that makes a tree!
How many a heart must pass me by
For one that cleaves to me!

Compensation. Stanza 1

Out of the dusk a shadow,
Then a spark;
Out of the cloud a silence,
Then a lark;
Out of the heart a rapture,
Then a pain;
Out of the dead, cold ashes,
Life again.

Evolution

A little Boy of heavenly birth,
But far from home to-day,
Comes down to find His ball, the earth,
That sin has cast away.
O comrades, let us one and all
Join in to get Him back His ball!

Out of Bounds

With locks of gold to-day;
To-morrow silver-gray;
Then blossom-bald. Behold,
O man, thy fortune told!

The Dandelion

Why should I stay? Nor seed nor fruit have I,

---

[1] See Hayne, page 586.

But, sprung at once to beauty's perfect
round,
Nor loss nor gain nor change in me is
found, —
A life-complete in death-complete to
die.
> *The Bubble*

Back to the primal gloom
Where life began.
> *Going Blind*

And in the School of Darkness learn
What mean
"The things unseen."
> *Ibid.*

Well, chile, de slip may come to all,
But den de diff'ence foller;
For, if you watch him when he fall,
De jus' man do not *waller*.
> *The Difference. Stanza 2*

ELLEN H. UNDERWOOD
[1845–1930]

The bread that bringeth strength I want
to give,
The water pure that bids the thirsty
live;
I want to help the fainting day by day;
I'm sure I shall not pass again this
way.[1]
> *I Shall Not Pass Again This
> Way. Stanza 1*

JAMES TERRY WHITE
[1845–1920]

And when I face the dark, and must resign
Love's tender, human touch; must dis-
entwine
Its dear, detaining clasp; when fears
depress,
Those mortal fears I cannot quite repress,

[1] I shall pass through this world but once.
— Attributed to Etienne de Grellet [1773–
1855]
  I shall not pass this way again —
  Although it bordered be with flowers.
      Eva Rose York [1858–   ]: *I Shall
            Not Pass This Way Again, St. 1*

For all my faith and trust — O Love
divine,
Hold thou my hands!
> *Hold Thou My Hands. Stanza 3*

If thou of fortune be bereft
And in thy store there be but left
Two loaves, sell one and with the dole
Buy hyacinths to feed thy soul.
> *Not by Bread Alone*[1]

SARAH CHAUNCEY WOOLSEY
("SUSAN COOLIDGE")
[1845–1905]

Every day is a fresh beginning,
Every morn is the world made new.[2]
> *New Every Morning. Stanza 1*

The tasks are done and the tears are
shed.
Yesterday's errors let yesterday cover;
Yesterday's wounds, which smarted and
bled,
Are healed with the healing that night
has shed.
> *Ibid. Stanza 2*

A little rudely sculptured bed,
With the shadowing folds of marble
lace,
And quilt of marble, primly spread,
And folded round a baby's face.
> *The "Cradle Tomb" at
> Westminster*

Men die, but sorrow never dies.
> *Ibid.*

These are weighty secrets, and we must
whisper them.
> *Secrets*

"A commonplace life," we say, and we
sigh;
But why should we sigh as we say?
The commonplace sun in the common-
place sky
Makes up the commonplace day.
> *Commonplace*

And God, who studies each commonplace soul,

[1] In *The Century Magazine, Aug., 1907.*
Adaptation of a Persian theme.
[2] Every step is an end, and every step is a
fresh beginning. — Goethe: *Elective Affini-
ties, Book I, Chap. 10*

Out of commonplace things makes His
beautiful whole.
Commonplace

"MICHAEL FIELD"
(KATHARINE BRADLEY)
[1846–1914]
(EDITH COOPER)
[1862–1913]

The enchanting miracles of change.
Renewal

Come, mete out my loneliness, O wind,
For I would know
How far· the living who must stay be-
hind
Are from the dead who go.
Mete Out My Loneliness

Praying and sighing through the Lon-
don streets
While my heart beats
To do some miracle, when suddenly
At curve of Regent Circus I espy,
Set 'mid a jeweller's trays of spangle-
glitter,
A tiny metal insect-pin, a fly.
This utter trifle for my love I buy,
And thinking of it on her breast
My heart has rest.
A Miracle [1]

Among the hills I trace the path that I
must wend;
I watch, not bidding him farewell, the
sun descend.
Sweet and of their nature vacant are
the days I spend —
Quiet as a plough laid by at the furrow's end.
Old Age

JOSEPH IGNATIUS
CONSTANTINE CLARKE
[1846–1925]

"Here's to the Maine, and I'm sorry for
Spain,"
Said Kelly and Burke and Shea.
The Fighting Race. Stanza 1

"Wherever there's Kellys there's trouble," said Burke.
"Wherever fighting's the game,

[1] Surely the prettiest poem on shopping
in our language. — LOGAN PEARSALL SMITH

Or a spice of danger in grown man's
work,"
Said Kelly, "you'll find my name."
The Fighting Race. Stanza 2

"Oh, the fighting races don't die out,
If they seldom die in bed."
Ibid. Stanza 5

GRANVILLE STANLEY HALL
[1846–1924]

The mother's face and voice are the
first conscious objects as the infant soul
unfolds, and she soon comes to stand in
the very place of God to her child.[1]
Article in Pedagogical Seminary,
June, 1891, Page 199

HAMILTON WRIGHT MABIE
[1846–1916]

The peculiarity of the New England
hermit has not been his desire to get
near to God, but his anxiety to get away
from man.
Backgrounds of Literature.
Emerson and Concord

There will come another era when it
shall be light and man will awaken from
his lofty dreams, and find his dreams
all there, and nothing is gone save his
sleep.
The Awakening

LLOYD MIFFLIN
[1846–1921]

Inscrutable, colossal, and alone.
Sesostris

The affrighted ostrich dare not dust her
wings
Anear this Presence.
Ibid.

RICHARD LEWIS
NETTLESHIP
[1846–1892]

The only strength for me is to be
found in the sense of a personal presence everywhere, it scarcely matters
whether it be called human or divine; a

[1] Mother is the name for God in the lips
and hearts of little children. — THACKERAY:
Vanity Fair, Vol. I, Chap. 37

presence which only makes itself felt at first in this and that particular form and feature.

Lectures and Memories. I, 72

Into this presence we come, not by leaving behind what are usually called earthly things, or by loving them less, but by living more intensely in them, and loving more what is really lovable in them.

Ibid.

It is literally true that this world *is* everything to us, if only we choose to make it so, if only we "live in the present" *because* it is eternity.

Ibid.

ALEXANDER MacGREGOR ROSE
[1846–1898]

Der Kaiser auf der Vaterland
Und Gott on high, all dings gommand,
Ve two, ach, don'd you understandt?
Meinself — und Gott.

Hoch! Der Kaiser (Kaiser & Co.).[1] *Stanza 1*

Gott pulls mit me, und I mit him.

Ibid. Stanza 16

JOHN PETER ALTGELD [2]
[1847–1902]

In writing "Progress and Poverty," he dipped his pen into the tears of the human race, and with celestial clearness wrote down what he conceived to be eternal truths.

Memorial Address on Henry George [1897]

When he died, there was nowhere a soul that cried out: "There is one iron hand less to grind us, one wolf less to tear our flesh," but everywhere a feeling that a friend of the race had gone.

Memorial Address on Henry George [1897]

HENRY AUGUSTIN BEERS
[1847–1926]

He sang one song and died — no more but that;
A single song and carelessly complete.

The Singer of One Song [1]

So through the poets' orchestra, which weaves
One music from a thousand stops and strings,
Pierces the note of that immortal song:
"High over all the lonely bugle grieves." [2]

Ibid.

CHARLES HEBER CLARK ("MAX ADELER")
[1847–1915]

Willie had a purple monkey climbing on a yellow stick,
And when he sucked the paint all off it made him deathly sick.

The Purple Monkey. Stanza 1

We have lost our little Hanner in a very painful manner.

Little Hanner. Stanza 1

JOHN WALLACE ("CAPTAIN JACK") CRAWFORD
[1847–1917]

When a bit of sunshine hits ye,
After passing of a cloud,
When a fit of laughter gits ye
An' yer spine is feelin' proud,
Don't fergit to up and fling it
At a soul that's feelin' blue,
For the minute that ye sling it,
It's a boomerang to you.

The Boomerang

---

[1] The verses were first published in *The Montreal*, Canada, *Herald*, in 1897. They created a stir when recited by Captain Joseph Bullock Coghlan [1844–1908] at a dinner given in his honor at the Union League Club, New York, April 21, 1899. Captain Coghlan (later Rear Admiral) had commanded the United States Cruiser *Raleigh* of Admiral Dewey's squadron, Manila Bay, May 1, 1898.
[2] Eagle forgotten.

VACHEL LINDSAY: *The Eagle That Is Forgotten*

[1] Grenville Mellen [1799–1841].
[2] And high above the fight the lonely bugle grieves!

GRENVILLE MELLEN: *Ode on the Celebration of the Battle of Bunker Hill, June 17, 1825*

EDGAR FAWCETT
[1847–1904]

She remembers so many graves
That no one else will remember.
The Grass. Stanza 3

In some blithe moment, was it Nature's
choice
To dower a scrap of sunset with a
voice?
To an Oriole

Two haggard shapes in robes of mist
For longer years than each will tell,
Joined by a stern gyve, wrist to wrist,
Have roamed the courts of hell.
Their blank eyes know each other
not —
Their cold hearts hate the union
drear;
Yet one poor ghost was Lancelot,
And one was Guinevere.
Lancelot and Guinevere

WALTER LEARNED
[1847–1915]

To you whose temperate pulses flow
With measured beat, serene and slow,
The even tenor of whose way
Is undisturbed by passion's sway,
This tale of wayward love may seem
The record of a fevered dream.
On the Flyleaf of "Manon Lescaut"

A lure more strong, a wish more faint,
Makes one a monster, one a saint.[1]
Ibid.

There's many a life of sweet content
Whose virtue is environment.
Ibid.

O carping world! If there's an age
Where youth and manhood keep
An equal poise, alas! I must
Have passed it in my sleep.
To Critics. Stanza 3

Her lips were so near
That — what else could I do?
An Explanation

This world is a difficult world, indeed,
And people are hard to suit,

[1] If you take temptations into account, who
is to say that he is better than his neighbor?
— THACKERAY: *Vanity Fair, Vol. II, Chap. 1*

And the man who plays on the violin
Is a bore to the man with the flute.
Consolation. Stanza 4

JOHN LOCKE [1]
[1847–1889]

O Ireland, isn't it grand you look —
Like a bride in her rich adornin'?
And with all the pent-up love of my
heart
I bid you the top o' the mornin'!
*The Exile's Return (Dawn on
the Irish Coast). Stanza 1*

JULIA A. MOORE [2]
[1847–1920]

Dear Friends, I write for money,
With a kind heart and hand,
I wish to make no Enemies
Throughout my native land.
Kind friends, now I close my rhyme,
And lay my pen aside,
Between me and my critics
I leave you to decide.
*To My Friends and Critics.
Stanza 6*

Leave off the agony, leave off style,
Unless you've got money by you all the
while.
If you look about you you'll often have
to smile
To see so many poor people putting on
style.
Leave Off the Agony in Style

"Lord Byron" was an Englishman
A poet I believe,
His first works in old England
Was poorly received.
Perhaps it was "Lord Byron's" fault
And perhaps it was not.
His life was full of misfortunes,
Ah, strange was his lot.
*Sketch of Lord Byron's Life.
Stanza 1*

[1] Known as "The Southern Gael."
[2] "The Sweet Singer of Michigan."

MILTON NOBLES
[1847–1924]

The villain still pursued her.
The Phœnix. Act I, Sc. 3 [1875]

JAMES JEFFREY ROCHE
[1847–1908]

A brave endeavor
To do thy duty, whate'er its worth,
Is better than life with love for-
ever ——
And love is the sweetest thing on earth.
Sir Hugo's Choice

The love of man and woman is as fire
To warm, to light, but surely to con-
sume
And self-consuming die . . .
But comrade-love is as a welding blast
Of candid flame and ardent tempera-
ture:
Glowing more fervent, it doth bind
more fast.
My Comrade

What gain is it to the people that a God
laid down His life,
If twenty centuries after, His world be
a world of strife?
For the People. Stanza 4

What matter if king or consul or presi-
dent holds the rein,
If crime and poverty ever be links in the
bondsman's chain?
What careth the burden-bearer that
Liberty packed his load,
If Hunger presseth behind him with a
sharp and ready goad?
Ibid. Stanza 6

The slaves of Pilate have washed his
hands
As white as a king's might be.
Barabbas with wrists unfettered stands,
For the world has made him free.
But Thy palms toil-worn by nails are
torn,
O Christ, on Calvary.
The Way of the World. Stanza 2

For all knew Davy Crockett, blithe and
generous and bold,
And strong and rugged as the quartz
that hides its heart of gold.

His simple creed for word or deed true
as the bullet sped,
And rung the target straight: "Be sure
you're right, then go ahead." [1]
The Men of the Alamo

Yea, the gateway shall be free
Unto all, from sea to sea;
And no fratricidal slaughter
Shall defile its sacred water;
But — the hand that ope'd the gate
shall forever hold the key!
Panama

"No enemies! Can such a grace
To any erring mortal fall?"
A smile lit up the grim old face:
"None, padre, none; I slew them all."
Carvajal the Thorough

I'd rather be handsome than homely;
I'd rather be youthful than old;
If I can't have a bushel of silver
I'll do with a barrel of gold.
Contentment

All loved Art in a seemly way
With an earnest soul and a capital A.
The V-A-S-E

Baby's brain is tired of thinking
On the Wherefore and the Whence;
Baby's precious eyes are blinking
With incipient somnolence.
A Boston Lullaby. Stanza 1

The stranger wrote. I read the scrawl
The sacred page engrossed on;
The name was nought, the place was
all, —
"J. Winthrop Wiggins, Boston."
A Title Clear

ARCHIBALD PHILIP PRIM-
ROSE, EARL OF ROSEBERY
[1847–1929]

Few speeches which have produced
an electrical effect on an audience can
bear the colorless photography of a
printed record.
Life of Pitt

It is beginning to be hinted that we
are a nation of amateurs.
Rectorial Address, Glasgow
[*November 16, 1900*]

[1] See Crockett, page 349.

GEORGE ROBERT SIMS
[1847–1922]

Lor', but women's rum cattle to deal
  with, the first man found that to
  his cost,
And I reckon it's just through a woman
  the last man on earth'll be lost.
           Moll Jarvis o' Morley

O gleaming lamps of London, that gem
  the city's crown,
What fortunes lie within you, O Lights
  of London Town?
    The Lights of London Town.
                Stanza 1

You come here to see how paupers the
  season of Christmas spend;
You come here to watch us feeding, as
  they watch the captured beast.
  Christmas Day in the Workhouse.
                Stanza 8

EDWARD NOYES
WESTCOTT
[1847–1898]

Yes, an' no, an' mebbe, an' mebbe
not.
         David Harum. Chap. 1

Do unto the other feller the way he'd
like to do unto you an' do it fust.
         Ibid. Chap. 20

They say a reasonable number of
fleas is good fer a dog — keeps him
from broodin' over bein' a dog.
         Ibid. Chap. 32

The' ain't nothin' truer in the Bible
'n that sayin' thet them that has gits.
         Ibid. Chap. 35

I've often had to notice that a man'll
sometimes do the foolishest thing or
meanest thing in his hull life after he's
dead.
         Ibid.

ARTHUR JAMES BALFOUR
[1848–1930]

The energies of our system will decay; the glory of the sun will be
dimmed, and the earth, tideless and inert, will no longer tolerate the race
which has for a moment disturbed its

solitude. Man will go down into the pit
and all his thoughts will perish.
    The Foundations of Belief

Biography should be written by an
acute enemy.
    Quoted by S. K. RATCLIFFE *in
    The London Observer, January
    30, 1927*

JOHN VANCE CHENEY
[1848–1922]

Who drives the horses of the sun
  Shall lord it but a day;
Better the lowly deed were done,
  And kept the humble way.
    The Happiest Heart. Stanza 1

The happiest heart that ever beat
  Was in some quiet breast
That found the common daylight sweet,
  And left to Heaven the rest.
         Ibid. Stanza 3

DIGBY MACKWORTH
DOLBEN
[1848–1867]

The world is young to-day:
  Forget the gods are old,
  Forget the years of gold
When all the months were May.
          A Song

Poetry, the hand that wrings,
Bruised albeit at the strings,
Music from the soul of things.
          Core

As fresh as when the first sunrise
Awoke the lark in Paradise.
        The Shrine

W. G. ELMSLIE
[1848–1889]

He held the lamp of Truth that day
So low that none could miss the way;
And yet so high to bring in sight
That picture fair — the World's Great
  Light —
That gazing up — the lamp between —
The hand that held it scarce was seen.
    The Hand That Held It. Stanza 1

WILLIAM DUDLEY FOULKE
[1848–1935]

What makes a city great? [1] Huge piles
    of stone
Heaped heavenward? Vast multitudes
    who dwell
Within wide circling walls?
             The City's Crown
True glory dwells where glorious deeds
    are done,
Where great men rise whose names
    athwart the dusk
Of misty centuries gleam like the sun!
                    Ibid.
So may the city that I love be great
Till every stone shall be articulate.
                    Ibid.

SAMUEL MILLER HAGEMAN
[1848–1905]

Slowly climb the moon-touched moun-
    tains up their stairway to the sky,
Slowly each white cloud ascending,
    seems a soul that passed on high.
       Silence. Stanza 1 [*1876*]
Every sound shall end in silence, but
    the silence never dies.
            Ibid. Stanza 10
Earth is but the frozen echo of the si-
    lent voice of God.
            Ibid. Stanza 19
Every sound that breaks the silence
    only makes it more profound,
Like a crash of deafening thunder in
    the sweet blue stillness drowned;
Let thy soul walk slowly in thee, as a
    saint in heaven unshod,
For to be alone with Silence is to be
    alone with God.
            Ibid. Stanza 23
Somewhere in the far-off silence, I shall
    feel a vanished hand.[2]
            Ibid. Stanza 46

---

[1] Why build these cities glorious
    If man unbuilded goes?
 In vain we build the world, unless
    The builder also grows.
      EDWIN MARKHAM: *Man-Making*
[2] O for the touch of a vanished hand.
    TENNYSON: *Break, Break, Break*

Faith is but an idle canvas, flapping on
    an idle mast,
If it be not found within thee as the
.   work of life at last.
         Silence. Stanza 70
Tamper not with idle rumor, lest the
    truth appear to lie,
Carve thy life to hilted silence, wrong
    shall fall on it, and die:
Tamper not with accusation, harvest
    not what thou hast heard,
Christ stood in the court of Pilate, but
    he answered not a word.
            Ibid. Stanza 74
Creature in Creator meeting, crystal-
    lizing into one,
As stalactite meets stalagmite, standing
    pillared where they run.
            Ibid. Stanza 92

JOEL CHANDLER HARRIS
[1848–1908]

Brer Fox, he lay low.
    Legends of the Old Plantation
Ez soshubble ez a baskit er kittens.
                 Ibid.
Lazy fokes's stummucks don't git
tired.
        Plantation Proverbs
Jay-bird don't rob his own nes'.
                 Ibid.
Licker talks mighty loud w'en it gits
loose from de jug.
                 Ibid.
Hungry rooster don't cackle w'en he
fine a wum.
                 Ibid.
Youk'n hide de fier, but w'at you
gwine do wid de smoke?
                 Ibid.
Dogs don't bite at de front gate.
                 Ibid.
Watch out w'en youer gittin' all you
want. Fattenin' hogs ain't in luck.
                 Ibid.
De place wharbouts you spill de grease,
    Right dar youer boun' ter slide,
An' whar you fine a bunch er ha'r,
    You'll sholy fine de hide.
            Uncle Remus

Bred en bawn in a brier-patch, Brer
Fox.
Uncle Remus
You do de pullin', Sis Cow, en I'll do
de gruntin'.
Ibid.
He diggy, diggy, diggy, but no meat
dar!
Ibid.
W'en ole man Rabbit say 'scoot,' dey
scooted, en w'en ole Miss Rabbit say
'scat,' dey scatted.
Ibid.
Hop light, ladies,
  Oh, Miss Loo!
Oh, swing dat yaller gal!
  Do, boys, do!
Plantation Play Song
How many po' sinners'll be kotched
    out late
En fin' no latch ter de golden gate?
No use fer ter wait twell ter-morrer,
De sun mus'n't set on yo' sorrer, —
Sin's ez sharp ez a bamboo-brier, —
O Lord! fetch de mo'ners up higher!
Negro Revival Hymn. Stanza 1
When you've got a thing to say,
Say it! Don't take half a day.
When your tale's got little in it,
Crowd the whole thing in a minute!
Life is short — a fleeting vapor —
Don't you fill the whole blamed paper
With a tale which, at a pinch,
Could be cornered in an inch!
Boil her down until she simmers,
Polish her until she glimmers.
Advice to Writers for the
Daily Press

RICHARD JEFFERIES
[1848–1887]

Give me fulness of life like to the sea
and the sun; give me fulness of physical
life, mind equal and beyond their fulness; give me a greatness and perfection
of soul higher than all things; give me
my inexpressible desire.
The Story of My Heart. Chap. VI
No thought which I have ever had
has satisfied my soul.
Ibid.
The most extraordinary spectacle is

the vast expenditure of labor and time
wasted in obtaining mere subsistence.
The Story of My Heart. Chap. X
The world works only for today, as
the world worked twelve thousand
years ago, and our children's children
will still have to toil and slave for the
bare necessities of life.
Ibid.
I hope succeeding generations will be
able to be idle. I hope that nine-tenths
of their time will be leisure time; that
they may enjoy their days, and the
earth, and the beauty of this beautiful
world; that they may rest by the sea
and dream; that they may dance and
sing, and eat and drink.
Ibid. Chap. XI
Let me exhort everyone to do their
utmost to think outside and beyond our
present circle of ideas. For every idea
gained is a hundred years of slavery
remitted.
Ibid.

CHARLOTTE AUGUSTA
("CARLOTTA") PERRY
[1848–1914]

If you have gifts and I have none,
If I have shade and you have sun,
'Tis yours with freer hand to give,
'Tis yours with truer grace to live,
Than I, who giftless, sunless, stand
With barren life and hand.
Noblesse Oblige. Stanza 1
The sails we see on the ocean
  Are as white as white can be;
But never one in the harbor,
  As white as the sails at sea.
Distance, the Enchantress.
Stanza 1
It was only a glad "Good morning,"
  As she passed along the way,
But it spread the morning's glory
  Over the livelong day.
Good Morning

LILLA CABOT PERRY
[1848–1933]

Forgive me not! Hate me and I shall
know

Some of Love's fire still burns in your
    breast!
Forgiveness finds its home in hearts
    at rest,
On dead volcanoes only lies the snow.
Forgive Me Not
I turn to you, who have known pain and
    fear
And failure and despair, and in your
    eyes
I read companionship; and though your
    cloak
Be threadbare, half of it is mine.
You are my friend.
A Friend. Stanza 2
Death is Love's friend: it sets a holy
    seal
  On all the past that never can be
    broken;
Its beautifying touch knows to reveal
  On lips long silent eloquence un-
    spoken.
Love's Not Death's Slave.
Stanza 2

EBEN EUGENE REXFORD
[1848–1916]

Love can never more grow old,
Locks may lose their brown and gold,
Cheeks may fade and hollow grow,
But the hearts that love will know
Never winter's frost and chill,
Summer's warmth is in them still.
Silver Threads Among the Gold

WILL HENRY THOMPSON
[1848–   ]

Then at the brief command of Lee
Moved out that matchless infantry,
With Pickett leading grandly down,
To rush against the roaring crown
Of those dread heights of destiny.[1]
The High Tide at Gettysburg.[2]
Stanza 2
The voice that rang through Shiloh's
    woods
And Chickamauga's solitudes,
The fierce South cheering on her sons!
Ibid. Stanza 3

[1] See Cone, page 737.
[2] In *The Century Magazine, July, 1888.*

The brave went down! Without dis-
    grace
They leaped to Ruin's red embrace;
They only heard Fame's thunders wake,
And saw the dazzling sunburst break
In smiles on Glory's bloody face!
The High Tide at Gettysburg.
Stanza 11
Fold up the banners! Smelt the guns!
Love rules. Her gentle purpose runs;
A mighty mother turns in tears
The pages of her battle years,
Lamenting all her fallen sons!
Ibid. Stanza 15

FREDERIC EDWARD
WEATHERLY
[1848–1929]

Playing all my heart remembers,
  Old, old songs from far away;
Golden Junes and bleak Decembers
  Rise around me as I play.
Fiddle and I. Stanza 2
Always the same, Darby, my own,
Always the same to your old wife Joan.
Darby and Joan.[1] *Stanza 1*
The sailor's wife the sailor's star shall
  be.
Nancy Lee
Ah, Lisette! my pretty Lisette!
  Do not listen! do not care!
Lips are laughing, but eyes are wet,
  Hearts are breaking in Vanity Fair.
Lisette
Back to the joyless duties,
  Back to the fruitless tears,
Loving, and yet divided,
  All through the empty years.
Parted. Stanza 1

ROLLIN JOHN WELLS
[1848–1923]

A little more tired at close of day,
A little less anxious to have our way;
A little less ready to scold and blame,
A little more care of a brother's name;
And so we are nearing our journey's
    end,
Where time and eternity meet and
    blend.
Growing Old. Stanza 1

[1] See Cunningham, page 345.

A little more laughter, a few more tears,
And we shall have told our increasing
    years;
The book is closed and the prayers are
    said,
And we are part of the countless dead.
Thrice happy if then some soul can say,
"I live because he has passed my way."
Growing Old. Stanza 5

JAMES LANE ALLEN
[1849–1925]

Good friend, around these hearth-
stones speak no evil word of any creature.
A Kentucky Cardinal

The finest music in the room is that
which streams out to the ear of the
spirit in many an exquisite strain from
the little shelf of books on the opposite
wall. Every volume there is an instrument which some melodist of the mind
created and set vibrating with music.
Ibid.

The birds are moulting. If man could
only moult also — his mind once a year
its errors, his heart once a year its useless passions.
Ibid.

I have yet to encounter that common
myth of weak men, an insurmountable
barrier.
The Choir Invisible. Chap. 3

By degrees the comforting light of
what you may actually do and be in an
imperfect world will shine close to you
and all around you, more and more. It
is this that will lead you never to perfection, but always toward it.
Ibid. Chap. 20

JOSEPH GREEN FRANCIS
[1849–1930]

But the kittens were rude and grabbed
    their food,
And treated the Dolls with jeers;
Which caused their Mother an aching
    heart
And seven or eight large tears.
*A Little Girl Asked Some Kittens
to Tea*

A Tam o' Shanter Dog
And a plaintive piping Frog,
With a Cat whose one extravagance was
    clothes,
Went to see a Bounding Bug
Dance a jig upon a rug,
While a Beetle balanced bottles on his
    nose.
The Book of Cheerful Cats

" 'Tis a perfect picnic day!" the little
    dog did say.
Ibid.

A Raging, Roaring Lion, of a Lamb-
    devouring kind,
Reformed and led a sweet, submissive
    life.
For with face all steeped in smiles
He propelled a Lamb for miles
And he wed a woolly Spinster for a
    wife.
Ibid.

EDMUND GOSSE
[1849–1928]

It is a curious reflection, that the ordinary private person who collects objects of a modest luxury, has nothing
about him so old as his books.
Gossip in a Library

The girls nowadays display a shocking freedom; but they were partly led
into it by the relative laxity of their
mothers, who, in their turn, gave great
anxiety to a still earlier generation.
The Whole Duty of Woman

There never, we suppose, from the
beginning of the world, was a man-
preacher who did not warn the women
of his congregation against the vanity
of fair raiment.
Ibid.

Where are the cities of old time?
The Ballade of Dead Cities

The wizard silence of the hours of dew.
The White Throat

Canst thou not wait for Love one flying
    hour,
O heart of little faith?
Dejection and Delay

The Past is like a funeral gone by,
The Future comes like an unwelcome
   guest.
                        May-Day
I do not hunger for a well-stored mind,
I only wish to live my life, and find
My heart in unison with all mankind.
                Lying in the Grass
To all at length an end!
All sailors to some unseen harbour
   float.
Farewell, mysterious, happy, twilight
   boat.
Farewell, my friend!
                The Vanishing Boat

MARGARET JOHNSTON GRAFFLIN
[1849–1925]

None other can pain me as you, dear,
   can do;
None other can please me or praise me
   as you.
                To My Son. Stanza 1
"Like mother, like son," is the saying
   so true,
The world will judge largely of
   "Mother" by you.
                Ibid. Stanza 2

THOMAS CHALMERS HARBAUGH
[1849–1924]

I've sung the Psalms of David for
   nearly eighty years,
They've been my staff and comfort and
   calmed life's many fears;
I'm sorry I disturb the choir, perhaps
   I'm doing wrong,
But when my heart is filled with praise
   I can't keep back a song.
      Trouble in the "Amen Corner."
                Stanza 15

WILLIAM ERNEST HENLEY
[1849–1903]

The Hospital, grey, quiet, old,
Where Life and Death like friendly
   chafferers meet.
            In Hospital. Enter Patient

Life is (I think) a blunder and a shame.
                In Hospital. Waiting
Far in the stillness a cat
Languishes loudly.
                        Ibid. Vigil
A well-bred silence always at command.
                Ibid. Lady-Probationer
From the winter's gray despair,
From the summer's golden languor,
Death, the lover of Life,
Frees us for ever.
                Ibid. Ave, Caesar
His wise, rare smile is sweet with cer-
   tainties,
And seems in all his patients to compel
Such love and faith as failure cannot
   quell.
                Ibid. "The Chief" (Lister)
Bland as a Jesuit, sober as a hymn.
                Ibid. House-Surgeon
   I know
That in the shade of Fujisan,
What time the cherry-orchards blow,
I loved you once in old Japan.
                Ballade of a Toyokuni
                        Colour-Print
As dust that drives, as straws that blow,
Into the night go one and all.
                Ballade of Dead Actors
Fate's a fiddler, Life's a dance.
            Double Ballade of Life and Fate
Let us break out, and taste the morning
   prime . . .
      Let us be drunk.
                        To F. W.
The ways of Death are soothing and
   serene,
And all the words of Death are grave
   and sweet.
                In Memoriam R. G. C. B.
What is to come we know not. But we
   know
That what has been was good.
                What Is to Come
Out of the night that covers me,
   Black as the Pit from pole to pole,
I thank whatever gods may be
   For my unconquerable soul.
      Echoes. IV, In Memorian R. T.
      Hamilton Bruce ["Invictus"]
Under the bludgeonings of chance
   My head is bloody, but unbowed.
                        Ibid.

It matters not how strait the gate,
How charged with punishments the
scroll,
I am the master of my fate;
I am the captain of my soul.[1]
Echoes. IV, In Memoriam R. T.
Hamilton Bruce ["Invictus"]

Praise the generous gods for giving
In a world of wrath and strife,
With a little time for living,
Unto all the joy of life.
Ibid. VI

We'll go no more a-roving by the light
of the moon.[2]
November glooms are barren beside the
dusk of June.
Ibid. VIII

The nightingale has a lyre of gold,
The lark's is a clarion call,
And the blackbird plays but a boxwood
flute,
But I love him best of all.
Ibid. XVIII, To A. D.

Tired of experience, he turns
To the friendly and comforting breast
Of the old nurse, Death.
Ibid. XXIX, To R. L. S.

A late lark twitters from the quiet skies.
Ibid. XXXV, In Memoriam
Margaritae Sorori

Night with her train of stars
And her great gift of sleep.
Ibid.

So be my passing!
My task accomplished and the long day
done,
My wages taken, and in my heart
Some late lark singing.
Ibid.

Or ever the knightly years were gone
With the old world to the grave,
I was a King in Babylon
And you were a Christian Slave.
Ibid. XXXVII, To W. A.

[1] Dux atque imperator vitae mortalium animus est (The soul is the captain and master of the life of mortals). — SALLUST: *Jugurtha, Chap. I*
Be the proud captain still of thine own fate.
JAMES BENJAMIN KENYON
[1858–1924]: *A Challenge*
[2] So we'll go no more a-roving.
BYRON: *Letter to Thomas Moore*

The Spirit of Wine
Sang in my glass, and I listened
With love to his odorous music,
His flushed and magnificent song.
Echoes. XLI, To R. A. M. S.

These poor Might-Have-Beens,
These fatuous, ineffectual Yesterdays!
To James McNeill Whistler

For Death and Time bring on the prime
Of God's own chosen weather,
And we lie in the peace of the Great
Release
As once in the grass together.
In Memoriam R. L. S.

What have I done for you,
England, my England?
Rhymes and Rhythms. XXV

In the street of By-and-By
Stands the hostelry of Never,
Dream from deed he must dissever
Who his fortune here would try.
In the Street of By-and-By

With what a genius for administration
We rearrange the rumbling universe,
And map the course of man's regeneration
Over a pipe.
Inter Sodales

SARAH ORNE JEWETT
[1849–1909]

A harbor, even if it is a little harbor,
is a good thing, since adventurers come
into it as well as go out, and the life in
it grows strong, because it takes something from the world and has something
to give in return.
Country By-Ways. River
Driftwood

God bless them all who die at sea!
If they must sleep in restless waves,
God make them dream they are ashore,
With grass above their graves.
The Gloucester Mother.[1] Stanza 3

Look bravely up into the sky,
And be content with knowing
That God wished for a buttercup
Just here, where you are growing.
Discontent. Stanza 9

[1] In *McClure's Magazine*, Oct., 1908.

FREDERICK LANGBRIDGE
[1849–1923]

Yield thy poor best, and muse not how
   or why,
Lest one day, seeing all about thee
   spread,
A mighty crowd and marvellously fed,
Thy heart break out into a bitter cry:
"I might have furnished, I, yea, even I,
The two small fishes and the barley
   bread." [1]

   A Cluster of Quiet Thoughts

EMMA LAZARUS
[1849–1887]

Give me your tired, your poor,
Your huddled masses yearning to
   breathe free,
The wretched refuse of your teeming
   shore,
Send these, the homeless, tempest-
   tossed, to me:
I lift my lamp beside the golden door.

   *The New Colossus: Inscription
   for the Statue of Liberty, New
   York harbor*

GRACE DENIO LITCHFIELD
[1849–   ]

We have no dearer word for our
   heart's friend,
For him who journeys to the world's
   far end,
And scars our soul with going; thus we
   say,
As unto him who steps but o'er the
   way —
"Good-by."

   Good-by. Stanza 2

SIR WILLIAM OSLER
[1849–1919]

Speck in cornea, 50¢.
   *Entry in his account-book, first
   fee as a practicing physician.
   From Life of Sir William Osler
   by* HARVEY CUSHING, *Vol. I,
   Chap. 6*

[1] *Luke*, IX, 16.

After all, there is no such literature
as a Dictionary.
   *Life of Sir William Osler.
      Vol. I, Chap. 11*

The desire to take medicine is perhaps the greatest feature which dis-
tinguishes man from animals.
   Ibid. Chap. 14

This is yet the childhood of the world,
and a supine credulity is still the most
charming characteristic of man.
   Ibid.

We are here to add what we can *to*,
not to get what we can *from*, Life. [1]
   Ibid.

To have striven, to have made an effort, to have been true to certain ideals
— this alone is worth the struggle.
   Ibid. Chap. 16

Humanity has but three great enemies: fever, famine and war; of these
by far the greatest, by far the most
terrible, is fever.
   Ibid.

Though a little one, the master-word
[Work] looms large in meaning. It is
the open sesame to every portal, the
great equalizer in the world, the true
philosopher's stone which transmutes
all the base metal of humanity into
gold. [2]
   Ibid. Chap. 22

Things cannot always go your way.
Learn to accept in silence the minor
aggravations, cultivate the gift of taci-
turnity and consume your own smoke [3]
with an extra draught of hard work, so
that those about you may not be an-
noyed with the dust and soot of your
complaints.
   Ibid.

We are here not to get all we can out
of life for ourselves, but to try to make
the lives of others happier.
   Ibid.

Take the sum of human achieve-
ment in action, in science, in art, in lit-

[1] Also in *Doctor and Nurse*, Paper II in
Aequanimitas and Other Addresses.
[2] Lecture, *The Master-Word in Medicine*,
Toronto, Oct. 1, 1903. Paper XVIII in *Aequanimitas.*
[3] See Carlyle, page 379.

erature — subtract the work of the men above forty, and while we should miss great treasures, even priceless treasures, we would practically be where we are to-day. . . . The effective, moving, vitalizing work of the world is done between the ages of twenty-five and forty.[1]

Life of Sir William Osler.
Vol. I, Chap. 24

My second fixed idea is the uselessness of men above sixty years of age, and the incalculable benefit it would be in commercial, political, and in professional life if, as a matter of course, men stopped work at this age.

Ibid.

In that charming novel, "The Fixed Period," [by] Anthony Trollope, . . . the plot hinges upon the admirable scheme of a college into which at sixty men retired for a year of contemplation before a peaceful departure by chloroform. That incalculable benefits might follow such a scheme is apparent to anyone who, like myself, is nearing the limit, and who has made a careful study of the calamities which may befall men during the seventh and eighth decades.[2]

Ibid.

Nothing will sustain you more potently than the power to recognize in your humdrum routine, as perhaps it may be thought, the true poetry of life — the poetry of the commonplace, of the ordinary man, of the plain, toilworn woman, with their loves and their joys, their sorrows and their griefs.

Ibid. (The Student Life)

Lift up one hand to heaven and thank your stars if they have given you the proper sense to enable you to appreciate the inconceivably droll situations in which we catch our fellow creatures.

Ibid.

I have three personal ideals. One, to

[1] Address, *The Fixed Period,* Johns Hopkins University, Baltimore, Feb. 22, 1905.

[2] This valedictory address caused much discussion and misquotation. It was headlined in the press, "Osler Recommends Chloroform at Sixty," and occasioned many columns of letters, caustic cartoons, etc., until to "Oslerize" became a byword.

do the day's work well and not to bother about to-morrow. . . . The second ideal has been to act the Golden Rule, as far as in me lay, toward my professional brethren and toward the patients committed to my care. And the third has been to cultivate such a measure of equanimity as would enable me to bear success with humility, the affection of my friends without pride, and to be ready when the day of sorrow and grief came to meet it with the courage befitting a man.

Life of Sir William Osler. (Farewell
Dinner, May 2, 1905)

Throw all the beer and spirits into the Irish Channel, the English Channel, and the North Sea for a year, and people in England would be infinitely better. It would certainly solve all the problems with which the philanthropists, the physicians, and the politicians have to deal.[1]

Ibid. Vol. II, Chap. 26

No man is really happy or safe without a hobby, and it makes precious little difference what the outside interest may be — botany, beetles or butterflies, roses, tulips or irises; fishing, mountaineering or antiquities — anything will do so long as he straddles a hobby and rides it hard.[2]

Ibid. Chap. 29

Nothing in life is more wonderful than faith — the one great moving force which we can neither weigh in the balance nor test in the crucible.[3]

Ibid. Chap. 30

In the life of a young man the most essential thing for happiness is the gift of friendship.

Ibid. Chap. 31

No bubble is so iridescent or floats longer than that blown by the successful teacher.

Ibid.

[1] Address at Working Men's College, Camden Town, Nov. 17, 1906.
[2] Address, Medical Library Association, Belfast, July 28, 1909.
[3] The Faith That Heals.

The nation's Valhalla [Westminster Abbey].[1]

Life of Sir William Osler.
Vol. II, Chap. 32

It is one of the greatest blessings that so many women are so full of tact. The calamity happens when a woman who has all the other riches of life just lacks that one thing.[2]

Ibid. Chap. 33

It is the prime duty of a woman of this terrestrial world to look well. Neatness is the asepsis of clothes.

Ibid.

The quest for righteousness is Oriental, the quest for knowledge, Occidental.[3]

Ibid. Chap. 34

In science the credit goes to the man who convinces the world, not to the man to whom the idea first occurs.[4]

Ibid. Chap. 38

JAMES WHITCOMB RILEY
[1849–1916]

O'er folded blooms
   On swirls of musk,
The beetle booms adown the glooms
   And bumps along the dusk.

The Beetle. Stanza 7

The ripest peach is highest on the tree.

The Ripest Peach. Stanza 1

An' the Gobble-uns'll git you
   Ef you don't watch out.

Little Orphant Annie. Stanza 1

His Mammy heered him holler, an' his Daddy heered him bawl,
An' when they turn't the kivvers down, he wasn't there at all!

Ibid. Stanza 2

I cannot say, and I will not say
That he is dead. — He is just away!

Away

Heaven holds all for which you sigh —
There! little girl; don't cry!

A Life-Lesson. Stanza 3

[1] See Beaumont, page 129.
[2] Commencement Address, Johns Hopkins Hospital School of Nursing, May 7, 1913.
[3] Address, Jewish Historical Society of England, April 27, 1914.
[4] Address, Royal Society of Medicine, Historical Section, May 15, 1918.

I can see the pink sunbonnet and the little checkered dress
She wore when first I kissed her and she answered the caress
With the written declaration that, "as surely as the vine
Grew 'round the stump," she loved me — that old sweetheart of mine.

An Old Sweetheart of Mine.
Stanza 12

How the grand band-wagon shone with a splendor all its own,
And glittered with a glory that our dreams had never known!

The Circus-Day Parade. Stanza 2

When over the fair fame of friend or foe
   The shadow of disgrace shall fall, instead
Of words of blame, or proof of thus and so,
   Let something good be said.

Let Something Good Be Said.
Stanza 1

Forget not that no fellow-being yet
   May fall so low but love may lift his head.

Ibid. Stanza 2

You think them "out of reach," your dead?
   Nay, by my own dead, I deny
Your "out of reach." — Be comforted:
   'Tis not so far to die.

"Out of Reach." Stanza 1

"God bless us every one!" prayed Tiny Tim.[1]

God Bless Us Every One. Stanza 1

"Well, good-by, Jim:
Take keer of yourse'f!"

The Old Man and Jim. Stanza 1

Fer the world is full of roses, and the roses full of dew,
And the dew is full of heavenly love that drips fer me and you.

Thoughts fer the Discuraged
Farmer. Stanza 5

'Long about knee-deep in June,
'Bout the time strawberries melts
On the vine.

Knee-deep in June. Stanza 1

Oh! the old swimmin'-hole! When I last saw the place,

[1] See Dickens, page 495.

The scene was all changed, like the change in my face.
> *The Old Swimmin'-Hole. Stanza 5*

Work is the least o' my idees
When the green, you know, gits back in the trees!
> *When the Green Gits Back in the Trees. Stanza 1*

O, the Raggedy Man he works fer Pa,
An' he's the goodest man ever you saw!
> *The Raggedy Man. Stanza 1*

There's a boil on his ear and a corn on his chin, —
He calls it a dimple — but dimples stick in.
> *The Man in the Moon. Stanza 3*

A pictur' that no painter has the colorin' to mock —
When the frost is on the punkin and the fodder's in the shock.
> *When the Frost Is on the Punkin.*
> *Stanza 2*

Le's go a-visitin' back to Griggsby's Station —
Back where we ust to be so happy and so pore!
> *Griggsby's Station. Stanza 1*

And thus, borne to me o'er the seas between
Thy land and mine, thy song of certain wing
Circles above me.
> *Reply to Rudyard Kipling.[1]*
> *Stanza 3*

EDWARD BELLAMY [2]
[1850–1898]

If we could have devised an arrangement for providing everybody with music in their homes, perfect in quality, unlimited in quantity, suited to every mood, and beginning and ceasing at will, we should have considered the limit of human felicity already attained.
> *Looking Backward* [*1887*]

Your system was liable to periodical convulsions, overwhelming alike the wise and unwise, the successful cutthroat as well as his victim. I refer to the business crises at intervals of five to ten years, which wrecked the industries of the nation.
> *Ibid.*

AUGUSTINE BIRRELL
[1850–1933]

Libraries are not made; they grow.
> *Obiter Dicta. Book-Buying*

Good as it is to inherit a library, it is better to collect one.
> *Ibid.*

FLORENCE EARLE COATES
[1850–1927]

Far, far the mountain peak from me
Where lone He stands, with look caressing;
I lift my dreaming eyes and see
His hand stretched forth in blessing.
> *The Christ of the Andes.[1] Stanza 1*

The messenger of sure and swift relief,
Welcomed with wailings and reproachful grief;
The friend of those that have no friend but me,
I break all chains, and set all captives free.
> *Death. Stanza 2*

There is always room for beauty: memory
A myriad lovely blossoms may enclose,
But, whatsoe'er hath been, there still must be
Room for another rose.
> *The Poetry of Earth. Stanza 1*

How living are the dead!
Enshrined, but not apart,

---

[1] Your trail runs to the westward,
  And mine to my own place;
There is water between our lodges
And I have not seen your face.
  RUDYARD KIPLING: *To J. W. R., St. 1*

[2] There is at least a fair chance that another fifty years will confirm Edward Bellamy's position as one of the most authentic prophets of our age. — HEYWOOD BROUN [1931]

[1] The statue, The Christ of the Andes, by the Argentine sculptor, Mateo Alonso, commemorates the peaceful settlement of boundary disputes between Chile and Argentina. It was cast in bronze from melted cannon, and dedicated in March, 1904.

How safe within the heart
　　We hold them still — our dead,
　　Whatever else be fled!
　　　　　　　Immortal. Stanza 1

Think not of love as a debt —
　　Due in May [1] or in December.
　　　　　　　Mother-Love. Stanza 1

EUGENE FIELD
[1850–1895]

I feel a sort of yearnin' 'nd a chokin' in
　　my throat
When I think of Red Hoss Mountain
　　'nd of Casey's tabble dote!
　　　　Casey's Table d'Hôte. Stanza 1

He could whip his weight in wildcats.
　　　　Modjesky as Cameel. Stanza 10

Let my temptation be a book,
　　Which I shall purchase, hold, and keep.
　　　　The Bibliomaniac's Prayer.
　　　　　　　　　Stanza 2

No matter what conditions
　　Dyspeptic come to feaze,
The best of all physicians
　　Is Apple-pie and cheese!
　　　　Apple-Pie and Cheese. Stanza 5

A little peach in the orchard grew, —
A little peach of emerald hue;
Warmed by the sun and wet by the dew
　　It grew.
　　　　The Little Peach. Stanza 1

And God had set upon his head a crown
　　uv silver hair
In promise uv the golden crown He
　　meaneth him to wear.

So, uv us boys that met him out'n Den-
　　ver, there wuz none
But fell in love with Dana uv the Noo
　　York Sun.[2]
　　　　Mr. Dana, of the New York Sun.
　　　　　　　　　Stanza 5

You'll need no epitaph but this: "Here
　　sleeps the man who run
That best 'nd brightest paper, the Noo
　　York Sun."
　　　　　　　Ibid. Stanza 9

I like the Anglo-Saxon speech
　　With its direct revealings;

---

[1] "Mother's Day," the second Sunday in
May.
[2] Charles Anderson Dana [1819–1897].

It takes a hold, and seems to reach
　　'Way down into your feelings.
　　　　"Good-by — God Bless You!"
　　　　　　　　　Stanza 1

I'm sure no human heart goes wrong
　　That's told "Good-by — God bless
　　you!"
　　　　　　　Ibid. Stanza 2

Conjectures obtain that for language
　　profane
There is no such place as Flanders.[1]
　　　　　In Flanders. Stanza 5

I never lost a little fish — yes, I am free
　　to say
It always was the biggest fish I caught
　　that got away.
　　　　Our Biggest Fish. Stanza 2

How gracious those dews of solace that
　　over my senses fall
At the clink of the ice in the pitcher the
　　boy brings up the hall!
　　　　The Clink of the Ice. Stanza 1

When one's all right, he's prone to spite
　　The doctor's peaceful mission;
But when he's sick, it's loud and quick
　　He bawls for a physician.[2]
　　　　　Doctors. Stanza 2

We twain
Discussed with buoyant hearts
The various things that appertain
To bibliomaniac arts.
　　　　Dibdin's Ghost. Stanza 2

When I demanded of my friend what
　　viands he preferred,

---

[1] Our armies swore terribly in Flanders. —
STERNE: *Tristram Shandy, Book 3, Chap. 11*
[2] Three faces wears the doctor: when first
　　sought
　　　An Angel's; and a god's the cure half-
　　　　wrought;
　　But when, the cure complete, he seeks his
　　　fee,
　　The Devil looks less terrible than he.
　　　　　　　　　Anonymous

God and the soldier
All men adore
In time of trouble
And no more;
For when war is over
And all things righted,
God is neglected —
The old soldier slighted.
　　　　Lines found on an old stone sentry-
　　　　box in Gibraltar. They have been
　　　　adapted to read "God and the doc-
　　　　tor."

He quoth: "A large cold bottle, and a
  small hot bird!"
  The Bottle and the Bird. Stanza 1
Have you ever heard of the Sugar-Plum
  Tree?
  'Tis a marvel of great renown!
It blooms on the shore of the Lollipop
  sea
  In the garden of Shut-Eye Town.
    The Sugar-Plum Tree. Stanza 1
I pray that, risen from the dead,
  I may in glory stand —
A crown, perhaps, upon my head,
  But a needle in my hand.
    Grandma's Prayer. Stanza 1
Wynken, Blynken, and Nod one night
Sailed off in a wooden shoe —
Sailed on a river of crystal light
  Into a sea of dew.
    Wynken, Blynken, and Nod.
      Stanza 1
The little toy dog is covered with dust,
  But sturdy and stanch he stands;
And the little toy soldier is red with
  rust,
  And his musket moulds in his hands;
Time was when the little toy dog was
  new,
  And the soldier was passing fair;
And that was the time when our Little
  Boy Blue
  Kissed them and put them there
    Little Boy Blue. Stanza 1
The Rock-a-By Lady from Hushaby
  street
  Comes stealing; comes creeping.
    The Rock-a-By Lady. Stanza 1
Have you ever heard the wind go
  "Yoooooo"?
  'Tis a pitiful sound to hear!
It seems to chill you through and
  through
  With a strange and speechless fear.
    The Night Wind. Stanza 1
The Dinkey-Bird goes singing
  In the amfalula tree!
    The Dinkey-Bird. Stanza 1
The gingham dog went "Bow-wow-
  wow!"
And the calico cat replied "Mee-ow!"
The air was littered, an hour or so,
With bits of gingham and calico.
    The Duel. Stanza 2

We all hev our choice, an' you, like the
  rest,
Allow that the dorg which you've got
  is the best;
I wouldn't give much for the boy 'at
  grows up
With no friendship subsistin' 'tween
  him an' a pup!
    The Bench-Legged Fyce.
      Stanza 7
Father calls me William, sister calls me
  Will,
Mother calls me Willie, but the fellers
  call me Bill!
    Jest 'Fore Christmas. Stanza 1
'Most all the time, the whole year
  round, there ain't no flies on me,
But jest 'fore Christmas I'm as good
  as I kin be!
    Ibid.
Shuffle-Shoon and Amber-Locks
Sit together, building blocks;
Shuffle-Shoon is old and gray,
Amber-Locks a little child,
But together at their play
Age and Youth are reconciled.
    Shuffle-Shoon and Amber-Locks.
      Stanza 1
Mother tells me "Happy dreams!" and
  takes away the light,
An' leaves me lyin' all alone an' seein'
  things at night.
    Seein' Things. Stanza 1
Over the hills and far away,
A little boy steals from his morning
  play
And under the blossoming apple-tree
He lies and he dreams of the things
  to be.
    Over the Hills and Far Away.
      Stanza 1
That the troubles of the little boy pur-
  sue the man through life;
That here and there along the course
  wherein we hoped to glide
Some envious hand has sprinkled ashes
  just to spoil our slide!
    Ashes on the Slide. Stanza 5
Strive not to hew your path through
  life — it really doesn't pay;
Be sure the salve of flattery soaps all
  you do and say;

Herein the only royal road to fame and
fortune lies:
Put not your trust in vinegar — mo-
lasses catches flies!
Uncle Eph. Stanza 4
And speechless pride and rapture in-
effable shall fill
The beatific bosom of Penn Yan Bill.
Penn Yan Bill. Stanza 9
The sturdiest peak is Fame's!
And there be many on its very height,
Who strut in pride and vaunt their
empty claims,
While those poor human asses who
delight
To place them there have unremem-
bered names!
Pike's Peak. Stanza 4

JOHN CHEEVER GOODWIN
[1850–1912]

For that elephant ate all night,
And that elephant ate all day;
Do what he could to furnish him food,
The cry was still *more hay.*
Wang: The Man with an Ele-
phant on His Hands [1891]

JANE ELLEN HARRISON
[1850–1928]

Language is as much an art and as
sure a refuge as painting or music or
literature.
Reminiscences of a Student's
Life. Chap. 2
Old age, believe me, is a good and
pleasant time. It is true that you are
gently shouldered off the stage, but
then you are given such a comfortable
front stall as spectator, and, if you have
really played your part, you are more
content to sit down and watch.
Ibid. Conclusion
Life does not cease when you are old,
it only suffers a rich change. You go
on loving, only your love, instead of a
burning, fiery furnace, is the mellow
glow of an autumn sun.
Ibid.

ROSE HENNIKER HEATON

She answered by return of post
The invitation of her host.
She caught the train she said she would,
And changed at junctions as she should.
She brought a light and smallish box
And keys belonging to the locks.
The Perfect Guest
She left no little things behind
Excepting loving thoughts and kind.
Ibid.

HENRY CABOT LODGE
[1850–1924]

New England has a harsh climate, a
barren soil, a rough and stormy coast,
and yet we love it, even with a love
passing that of dwellers in more favored regions.
Address, New England Society
of New York [December 22,
1884]
Of "Americanism" of the right sort
we cannot have too much. Mere vapor-
ing and boasting become a nation as
little as a man. But honest, outspoken
pride and faith in our country are infinitely better and more to be respected
than the cultivated reserve which sets
it down as ill-bred and in bad taste ever
to refer to our country except by way
of deprecation, criticism, or general negation.
Ibid.
Let every man honor and love the
land of his birth and the race from
which he springs and keep their memory green. It is a pious and honorable
duty. But let us have done with Brit-
ish-Americans and Irish-Americans and
German-Americans, and so on, and all
be Americans. . . . If a man is going
to be an American at all let him be so
without any qualifying adjectives; and
if he is going to be something else, let
him drop the word American from his
personal description.[1]
The Day We Celebrate (Fore-
fathers' Day), Address, New
England Society of Brooklyn
[December 21, 1888]

[1] See Theodore Roosevelt, page 734.

There was no hour down to the end when he would not turn aside from everything else to preach the doctrine of Americanism, of the principles and the faith upon which American government rested, and which all true Americans should wear in their heart of hearts. He was a great patriot, a great man; above all, a great American. His country was the ruling, mastering passion of his life from the beginning even unto the end.

Theodore Roosevelt, Address before Congress [February 9, 1919]

PHILIP BOURKE MARSTON
[1850–1887]

A little time for laughter,
    A little time to sing,
    A little time to kiss and cling,
And no more kissing after.
                    After. Stanza 1

ALICE MEYNELL
[1850–1922]

My heart shall be thy garden. Come, my own,
    Into thy garden; thine be happy hours
Among my fairest thoughts, my tallest flowers,
From root to crowning petal thine alone.
                    Sonnet, The Garden
She walks — the lady of my delight —
    A shepherdess of sheep.
Her flocks are thoughts. She keeps them white;
    She guards them from the steep.
                    The Shepherdess. Stanza 1
I must not think of thee; and, tired yet strong,
    I shun the thought that lurks in all delight —
The thought of thee — and in the blue heaven's height
And in the sweetest passage of a song.
                    Sonnet, Renouncement
With the first dream that comes with the first sleep

I run, I run, I am gathered to thy heart.
                    Sonnet, Renouncement
O heavenly colour, London town
    Has blurred it from her skies;
And, hooded in an earthly brown,
    Unheaven'd the city lies.
                    November Blue. Stanza 1
Blue comes to earth, it walks the street,
    It dyes the wide air through;
A mimic sky about their feet,
    The throng go crowned with blue.
                    Ibid. Stanza 2
It is principally for the sake of the leg that a change in the dress of man is so much to be desired. . . . The leg is the best part of the figure . . . and the best leg is the man's. Man should no longer disguise the long lines, the strong forms, in those lengths of piping or tubing that are of all garments the most stupid.[1]
                    Essays. Unstable Equilibrium

LAURA ELIZABETH RICHARDS
[1850–   ]

Great is truth and shall prevail,
Therefore must we weep and wail.
                    The Mameluke and the Hospodar
Every little wave had its nightcap on.
                    A Song for Hal
"Trifles are trifles, but serious matters, They must be seen to," says little Prince Tatters.
                    Prince Tatters. Stanza 3
Ponsonby Perks,
He fought with Turks,
Performing many wonderful works.
                    Nonsense Verses. Stanza 2
The branches of the pencil-tree
    Are pointed every one.
                    Song of the Mother whose Children Are Fond of Drawing. Stanza 2

[1]   In creased and flapping bags,
Dull parallels of cloth from cush to kibe,
Where is your mannish limb? For lack of praise
It atrophies and shrivels.
                    — Shakespeare in Modern Dress
                    (C. M.)

The fairest spot to me,
On the land or on the sea,
Is the charming little cupboard where
the jam-pots grow.
Master Jack's Song

Baby said
When she smelt the rose,
"Oh! what a pity
I've only one nose!"
The Difference. Stanza 1

ROBERT RICHARDSON
[1850–1901]

Warm summer sun, shine friendly
here;
Warm western wind, blow kindly here;
Green sod above, rest light, rest light —
Good-night, Annette! Sweetheart, good-
night.[1]

To Annette

ROBERT LOUIS STEVENSON
[1850–1894]

In winter I get up at night
And dress by yellow candle-light.
In summer, quite the other way,
I have to go to bed by day.
Bed in Summer. Stanza 1

A child should always say what's true
And speak when he is spoken to,
And behave mannerly at table;
At least as far as he is able.
Whole Duty of Children

Dark brown is the river,
Golden is the sand.
It flows along for ever,
With trees on either hand.
Where Go the Boats? Stanza 1

The pleasant land of counterpane.
*The Land of Counterpane.
Stanza 4*

I have a little shadow that goes in and
out with me,

[1] Mark Twain adapted this verse, by an
Australian poet, for the stone marking the
grave of his daughter, Olivia Susan Clemens,
who died August 18, 1896, aged 24 years:
Warm summer sun, shine kindly here;
Warm southern wind, blow softly here;
Green sod above, lie light, lie light —
Good-night, dear heart, good-night, good-
night.

And what can be the use of him is more
than I can see.
My Shadow. Stanza 1

The world is so full of a number of
things,
I'm sure we should all be as happy as
kings.
Happy Thought

The eternal dawn, beyond a doubt,
Shall break on hill and plain,
And put all stars and candles out
Ere we be young again.
To Minnie

All that I could think of, in the darkness and the cold,
Was just that I was leaving home and
my folks were growing old.
Christmas at Sea. Stanza 11

There are men and classes of men
that stand above the common herd: the
soldier, the sailor, and the shepherd not
infrequently; the artist rarely; rarelier
still, the clergyman; the physician almost as a rule. He is the flower (such as
it is) of our civilization.
Underwoods. Dedication

Generosity he has, such as is possible
to those who practise an art, never to
those who drive a trade; discretion,
tested by a hundred secrets; tact, tried
in a thousand embarrassments; and
what are more important, Heraclean
cheerfulness and courage.
Ibid.

Gratitude is but a lame sentiment;
thanks, when they are expressed, are
often more embarrassing than welcome.
Ibid.

Go, little book, and wish to all
Flowers in the garden, meat in the hall,
A bin of wine, a spice of wit,
A house with lawns enclosing it,
A living river by the door,
A nightingale in the sycamore!
Ibid. Envoy

Youth now flees on feathered foot.
Ibid. To Will H. Low [1]

Life is over, life was gay:
We have come the primrose way.
Ibid.

[1] American painter [1853–1932], whose wife
translated Stevenson's fable, *The Strange
Case of Dr. Jekyll and Mr. Hyde,* into French.

Dear Andrew, with the brindled hair [1]
Underwoods. To Andrew Lang

Under the wide and starry sky,
Dig the grave and let me lie.
Glad did I live and gladly die,
  And I laid me down with a will.
              Ibid. Requiem,[2] *Stanza 1*

This be the verse you grave for me:
Here he lies where he longed to be;
Home is the sailor, home from sea,
  And the hunter home from the hill.
              Ibid. Stanza 2

If I have faltered more or less
In my great task of happiness.
              Ibid. The Celestial Surgeon

If beams from happy human eyes
Have moved me not; if morning skies,
Books, and my food, and summer rain
Knocked on my sullen heart in vain: —
Lord, thy most pointed pleasure take
And stab my spirit broad awake.
              Ibid.

Yet, O stricken heart, remember, O remember
  How of human days he lived the better part.
April came to bloom and never dim December
  Breathed its killing chills upon the head or heart.
    Ibid. In Memoriam F. A. Sitwell [3]
              [*1881*]

Let first the onion flourish there,
Rose among roots, the maiden-fair
Wine-scented and poetic soul
Of the capacious salad bowl.
              Ibid. To a Gardener

In the highlands, in the country places,
Where the old plain men have rosy faces,

[1] Dear Louis of the awful cheek!
  Who told you it was right to speak,
  Where all the world might hear and stare,
  Of other fellows' "brindled hair"?
              ANDREW LANG: *To R. L. S.*
[2] As originally written, *Requiem* had as a second stanza:
    Here may the winds about me blow;
    Here the clouds may come and go;
    Here shall be rest for evermo',
      And the heart for aye shall be still.
[3] Lady Colvin's son by her first marriage; he died at the age of eighteen.

And the young fair maidens
Quiet eyes.
              Underwoods. XVI

My body, which my dungeon is,
And yet my parks and palaces.
              Ibid. XXXVII

There are kind hearts still, for friends to fill
  And fools to take and break them;
But the nearest friends are the auldest friends
  And the grave's the place to seek them.
        Ibid. In Scots, XVI, Stanza 3

Wealth I ask not, hope nor love,
  Nor a friend to know me;
All I ask, the heaven above
  And the road below me.
              The Vagabond. Stanza 4

And this shall be for music when no one else is near,
The fine song for singing, the rare song to hear!
        Romance (I Will Make You Brooches). Stanza 3

God, if this were enough,
That I see things bare to the buff.
              If This Were Faith

For all the story-books you read:
For all the pains you comforted:
For all you pitied, all you bore,
In sad and happy days of yore . . .
Take, nurse, the little book you hold!
        To Alison Cunningham from Her Boy

Bright is the ring of words
When the right man rings them.
              Songs of Travel. XV

I have trod the upward and the downward slope;
I have endured and done in days before;
I have longed for all, and bid farewell to hope;
And I have lived and loved and closed the door.
              Ibid. XXII

Be it granted me to behold you again in dying,
  Hills of home!
        Ibid. XLIII, To S. R. Crockett

Trusty, dusky, vivid, true,
With eyes of gold and bramble-dew,

Steel-true and blade-straight
The great artificer made my mate.
To My Wife. Stanza 1

I am in the habit of looking not so much to the nature of a gift as to the spirit in which it is offered.
New Arabian Nights. The Suicide Club

I was a great solitary when I was young.
The Pavilion on the Links

I have played the sedulous ape to Hazlitt, to Lamb, to Wordsworth, to Sir Thomas Browne, to Defoe, to Hawthorne, to Montaigne, to Baudelaire and to Obermann.
A College Magazine

Mankind was never so happily inspired as when it made a cathedral.
An Inland Voyage. Noyon Cathedral

Every man is his own doctor of divinity, in the last resort.
Ibid.

To love is the great Amulet that makes this world a garden.
Travels with a Donkey. The Heart of the Country

The cruellest lies are often told in silence.
Virginibus Puerisque. IV, Truth of Intercourse

Old and young, we are all on our last cruise.
Ibid. Crabbed Age and Youth

Give me the young man who has brains enough to make a fool of himself.
Ibid.

Books are good enough in their own way, but they are a mighty bloodless substitute for life.
Ibid. An Apology for Idlers

Perpetual devotion to what a man calls his business, is only to be sustained by perpetual neglect of many other things.
Ibid.

There is no duty we underrate so much as the duty of being happy.
Ibid.

To travel hopefully is a better thing than to arrive.
Virginibus Puerisque. El Dorado

To be what we are, and to become what we are capable of becoming, is the only end of life.
Familiar Studies of Men and Books

Science carries us into zones of speculation, where there is no habitable city for the mind of man.
Pulvis et Umbra

In the harsh face of life faith can read a bracing gospel.
Ibid.

You cannot run away from a weakness; you must some time fight it out or perish; and if that be so, why not now, and where you stand?
The Amateur Emigrant

Youth is wholly experimental.
A Letter to a Young Gentleman

Fifteen men on the Dead Man's Chest — [1]
Yo-ho-ho, and a bottle of rum! [2]
Drink and the devil had done for the rest —
Yo-ho-ho, and a bottle of rum!
Treasure Island

Doctors is all swabs.
Ibid. Billy Bones, Chap. 3

Many's the long night I've dreamed of cheese — toasted, mostly.
Ibid. Ben Gunn, Chap. 15

There's no music like a little river's. It plays the same tune (and that's the favourite) over and over again, and yet does not weary of it like men fiddlers. It takes the mind out of doors; and though we should be grateful for good houses, there is, after all, no house like God's out-of-doors.
Prince Otto. Chap. 2

I feel very strongly about putting questions; it partakes too much of the style of the day of judgment. You start a question, and it's like starting a stone.

[1] See Charles Kingsley, page 524.
[2] While we shared all by the rule of thumb —
Yo-ho-ho and a bottle of rum!
YOUNG EWING ALLISON [1853–1932]:
Derelict

You sit quietly on the top of a hill; and away the stone goes, starting others.

The Strange Case of Dr. Jekyll and Mr. Hyde

"A Penny Plain and Twopence Coloured."

Memories and Portraits. Essay about Skelt's Juvenile Drama

Let any man speak long enough, he will get believers.

The Master of Ballantrae. Summary of Events

Not every man is so great a coward as he thinks he is — nor yet so good a Christian.

Ibid. Mr. Mackellar's Journey

Am I no a bonny fighter?

Alan Breck. Kidnapped. Chap. 10

If I have at all learned the trade of using words to convey truth and to arouse emotion, you have at last furnished me with a subject.

An Open Letter on Father Damien [1]

The kingdom of heaven is of the childlike, of those who are easy to please, who love and give pleasure.

Across the Plains. A Christmas Sermon

So long as we love we serve; so long as we are loved by others, I would almost say that we are indispensable; and no man is useless while he has a friend.

Lay Morals

To be honest, to be kind — to earn a little and spend a little less, to make upon the whole a family happier for his presence, to renounce when that shall be necessary and not to be embittered, to keep a few friends, but these without capitulation — above all, on the same grim conditions, to keep friends with himself — here is a task for all that a man has of fortitude and delicacy.

A Christmas Sermon

Chiefs! Our road is not built to last a thousand years, yet in a sense it is. When a road is once built, it is a strange thing how it collects traffic, how every year as it goes on, more and more people are found to walk thereon, and others are raised up to repair and perpetuate it, and keep it alive.[1]

Vailima Letters. Address to the Chiefs on the Opening of the Road of Gratitude, October, 1894

Give us grace and strength to forbear and to persevere. Give us courage and gaiety and the quiet mind, spare to us our friends, soften to us our enemies.

Prayer [2]

ROSA HARTWICK THORPE

[1850–   ]

England's sun was slowly setting o'er the hilltops far away,
Filling all the land with beauty at the close of one sad day.

Curfew Must Not Ring To-night. Stanza 1

Long, long years I've rung the curfew from that gloomy, shadowed tower;
Every evening, just at sunset, it has told the twilight hour;
I have done my duty ever, tried to do it just and right,
Now I'm old I will not falter, — Curfew it must ring to-night.

Ibid. Stanza 3

Out she swung — far out; the city seemed a speck of light below,
There 'twixt heaven and earth suspended as the bell swung to and fro.

Ibid. Stanza 7

---

[1] And Molokai's lord of love
And tenderness, and piteous tears
For stricken man!
JOAQUIN MILLER: *With Love to You and Yours, III, 3*

[1] Robert Louis Stevenson was a roadmender. . . . Ay, and with more than his pen. . . . I wonder was he ever so truly great, so entirely the man we know and love, as when he inspired the chiefs to make a highway in the wilderness. Surely no more fitting monument could exist to his memory than the Road of Gratitude, cut, laid, and kept by the pureblood tribe kings of Samoa. — MICHAEL FAIRLESS (Margaret Fairless Barber) [1869–1901]: *The Roadmender, Chap. 5*

[2] On the bronze memorial to Stevenson in St. Giles Cathedral, Edinburgh, Scotland.

SAMUEL VALENTINE COLE
[1851–1925]

Why fret you at your work because
  The deaf world does not hear and
    praise?
Were it so bad, O workman true,
  To work in silence all your days?
           In Silence. Stanza 1

"Hammer away, ye hostile hands,
Your hammers break, God's anvil
    stands." [1]
           Hammer and Anvil

Where'er men go, in heaven, or earth,
  or hell,
They find themselves, and that is all
  they find.
           The Difference

The man who knows and knows he
  knows,[2]
  To him your homage bring;
He wields the power that waits and
  wins,
  And he is rightful king.
      An Old Saw Reset. Stanza 1

He who walked in our common ways,
With the seal of a king on his brow;
Who lived as a man among men his
  days,
And "belongs to the ages" now.[3]
           Lincoln

In April Rome was founded; Shakes-
  peare died;
  The shot whose sound rang out from
    Concord town
  And brought an avalanche of echoes
    down,
Shaking all thrones of tyranny and
  pride,
Was fired in April; Sumter far and
  wide

---

[1] Inscription on a memorial to the Huguenots, Rue de Rivoli, Paris.
[2] He who knows not, and knows not that
    he knows not, is a fool. Shun him.
  He who knows not, and knows that he
    knows not, is simple. Teach him.
  He who knows, and knows not that he
    knows, is asleep. Waken him.
  He who knows, and knows that he knows,
    is wise. Follow him.
           Arabic apothegm
[3] Now he belongs to the ages. — EDWIN M.
STANTON [1814–1869], Secretary of War, at
the deathbed of President Lincoln.

Lifted a voice the years will never
  drown;
'Twas April when they laid the
  martyr's crown
On Lincoln's brow.
           In April

SIR WILLIAM ROBERTSON
NICOLL
[1851–1923]

He is, if we may be allowed the expression, a typical John Bull, and it is
his John Bullism in religion that has
made him so popular with all classes of
the community.
    *Said of the Reverend Charles
    Haddon Spurgeon [1834–1892]*

LOUIS SHREVE OSBORNE
[1851–1912]

Maiden's hair is tumbled,
  And then and there appeared
Cunning little ear-ring
  Caught in student's beard.
      In the Tunnel.[1] Stanza 6

MARIANA GRISWOLD
(MRS. SCHUYLER)
VAN RENSSELAER
[1851–1934]

Sorrow is mine, but there is no more
  dread.
The word has come — On the field of
  battle, dead.
      It Is Well with the Child

BENJAMIN BRECKINRIDGE
WARFIELD
[1851–1921]

"There is a place for everything,
  In earth, or sky, or sea,
Where it may find its proper use,
  And of advantage be,"
    Quoth Augustine, the saint.
    Augustine's Philosophy. Stanza 1

---

[1] In *The Harvard Advocate, Nov. 10, 1871.*

FRANCIS WILLIAM BOURDILLON
[1852–1921]

The night has a thousand eyes,
  And the day but one;
Yet the light of the bright world dies,
  With the dying sun.
Light. Stanza 1

The mind has a thousand eyes,
  And the heart but one;
Yet the light of a whole life dies,
  When love is done.
Ibid. Stanza 2

Upon the valley's lap
  The dewy morning throws
A thousand pearly drops
  To wash a single rose.
So, often in the course
  Of life's few fleeting years,
A single pleasure costs
  The soul a thousand tears.
Upon the Valley's Lap

MOLLIE E. MOORE (MRS. THOMAS E.) DAVIS
[1852–1909]

If thou shouldst bid thy friend farewell,
  But for one night though that farewell should be,
Press thou his hand in thine; how canst thou tell
  How far from thee
Fate, or caprice, may lead his feet
  Ere that to-morrow come? Men have been known
Lightly to turn the corner of a street,[1]
  And days have grown
To months, and months to lagging years,
  Before they looked in loving eyes again.
Counsel [2]

[1] Round the corner of the street
  Who can say what waits for us?
    JAMES WHITCOMB RILEY: *Reach Your Hand to Me*
[2] Frequently attributed to Coventry Patmore.

NATHAN HASKELL DOLE [1]
[1852–1935]

We have no leas, no larks, no rooks,
No swains, no nightingales,
No singing milkmaids (save in books) —
The poet does his best,
It is the rhyme that fails!
Larks and Nightingales. Stanza 6

What other State compares with Maine
  In glorious coasts, where ocean tides
Have for long ages beat in vain
  To storm the coves where safety hides;
Where pillared cliffs like sentries stand
To guard the entries to the land,
  From Kittery to Calais!
•The State of Maine. Stanza 1

ROBERT BONTINE CUNNINGHAME GRAHAM
[1852–1936]

Success, which touches nothing that it does not vulgarize, should be its own reward . . . the odium of success is hard enough to bear, without the added ignominy of popular applause.
Success

The ancient seat of pedantry [Oxford], where they manufacture prigs as fast as butchers in Chicago handle hogs.
With the North-West Wind

Every American child should learn at school the history of the conquest of the West. The names of Kit Carson, of General Custer and of Colonel Cody should be as household words to them. These men as truly helped to form an empire as did the Spanish conquistadores. Nor should Sitting Bull, the Short Wolf, Crazy Horse, and Rain-in-the-Face be forgotten. They too were Americans, and showed the same heroic qualities as did their conquerors.
Letter to Theodore Roosevelt
[*1917*]

[1] Editor of the tenth edition of *Bartlett's Familiar Quotations* (1914).

God forbid that I should go to any heaven in which there are no horses.

Letter to Theodore Roosevelt
[1917]

The rain had cleared and the sun poured down upon us, as in procession, headed by the acolytes and priests, we bore the coffin to the grave. A semi-circle of Scotch firs formed, as it were, a little harbour for him. The breeze blew freshly, south-west by south a little westerly — a good wind, as I thought, to steer up Channel by, and one that he who would no longer feel it on his cheek, looking aloft to see if all the sails were drawing properly, must have been glad to carry when he struck soundings, passing the Wolf Rock or the Smalls after foul weather in the Bay.

Handsomely, as he who lay in it might well have said, they lowered the coffin down. The priest had left his Latin and said a prayer or two in English, and I was glad of it, for English surely was the speech the Master Mariner most loved, and honoured in the loving with new graces of his own.

Harboured [*The burial of*
Joseph Conrad, 1924]

EDWIN MARKHAM

[1852–]

Bowed by the weight of centuries he leans
Upon his hoe and gazes on the ground,
The emptiness of ages in his face,
And on his back the burden of the world.

The Man with the Hoe.[1] *Stanza 1*

O masters, lords and rulers in all lands,
Is this the handiwork you give to God?

Ibid. Stanza 3

Here was a man to hold against the world,
A man to match the mountains[2] and the sea.

Lincoln, the Man of the People.
Stanza 1

[1] Millet's painting.
[2] A man to match his mountains, not to creep

The color of the ground was in him, the red earth,
The smack and tang of elemental things.

Lincoln, the Man of the People.
Stanza 2

So came the Captain with the mighty heart;
And when the judgment thunders split the house,
Wrenching the rafters from their ancient rest,
He held the ridgepole up, and spiked again
The rafters of the Home.

Ibid. Stanza 4

And when he fell in whirlwind, he went down
As when a lordly cedar, green with boughs,
Goes down with a great shout upon the hills,
And leaves a lonesome place against the sky.

Ibid.

Three times I came to your friendly door;
Three times my shadow was on your floor.
I was the beggar with bruisèd feet;
I was the woman you gave to eat;
I was the child on the homeless street.

How the Great Guest Came

He drew a circle that shut me out —
Heretic, rebel, a thing to flout.
But Love and I had the wit to win:
We drew a circle that took him in.

Outwitted

For all your days prepare,
And meet them ever alike:
When you are the anvil, bear —
When you are the hammer, strike.[1]

Preparedness

Dwarfed and abased below them.
　　WHITTIER: *Among the Hills, Prelude*
Bring me men to match my mountains.
　　SAM WALTER FOSS: *The Coming*
　　　　　　　　　　　　American
[1] Stand like an anvil when it is beaten upon.
　　ST. IGNATIUS THEOPHORUS, Bishop of
　　　　　　　　　　　Antioch [A. D. 104]
See George Herbert, page 137.

GEORGE MOORE
[1852–1933]

After all there is but one race — humanity.
>*The Bending of the Bough. Act III*

The difficulty in life is the choice.
>*Act IV*

The wrong way always seems the more reasonable.
>*Ibid.*

A quotation, a chance word heard in an unexpected quarter, puts me on the trail of the book destined to achieve some intellectual advancement in me.
>*Confessions of a Young Man. XII*

A constant and careful invocation of meaning that was a little aside of the common comprehension, and also a sweet depravity of ear for unexpected falls of phrase.
>*Ibid.*

English, Scotchmen, Jews, do well in Ireland — Irishmen never; even the patriot has to leave Ireland to get a hearing.
>*Ave. Overture*

Within the oftentimes bombastic and truculent appearance that I present to the world, trembles a heart shy as a wren in the hedgerow or a mouse along the wainscoting.
>*Ibid. Chap. 2*

My one claim to originality among Irishmen is that I have never made a speech.
>*Ibid. Chap. 4*

Modern painting is uninteresting because there is no innocency left in it.
>*Ibid. Chap. 6*

As the moon is more interested in the earth than in any other thing, there is always some woman more interested in a man's mind than in anything else, who is willing to follow it sentence by sentence.
>*Ibid. Chap. 10*

It is the plain duty of every Irishman to disassociate himself from all memories of Ireland — Ireland being a fatal disease, fatal to Englishmen and doubly fatal to Irishmen.
>*Ibid. Chap. 11*

Death is in such strange contradiction to life that it is no matter for wonder that we recoil from it, and turn to remembrances, and find recompense in perceiving that those we have loved live in our memories as intensely as if they were still before our eyes.
>*Ave. Chap. 13*

A man travels the world over in search of what he needs and returns home to find it.
>*The Brook Kerith. Chap. 11*

My definition of pure poetry, something that the poet creates outside of his own personality.
>*Anthology of Pure Poetry.*
>*Introduction*

HENRY VAN DYKE
[1852–1933]

If all the skies were sunshine,
Our faces would be fain
To feel once more upon them
The cooling plash of rain.
>*If All the Skies. Stanza 1*

Men have dulled their eyes with sin,
And dimmed the light of heaven with doubt,
And built their temple-walls to shut thee in,
And framed their iron creeds to shut thee out.
>*God of the Open Air. Stanza 3*

"Raise the stone, and thou shalt find me; cleave the wood and there am I." [1]
>*The Toiling of Felix. Part I,*
>*Prelude*

This is the gospel of labour, ring it, ye bells of the kirk!
The Lord of Love came down from above, to live with the men who work;
This is the rose that He planted, here in the thorn-curst soil:
Heaven is blest with perfect rest, but the blessing of Earth is toil.
>*Ibid. Envoy, Stanza 5*

Oh, London is a man's town, there's power in the air;

[1] *Oxyrhynchus Logia (Agrapha), the Unwritten Sayings of Jesus, Fifth Logion.*

And Paris is a woman's town, with
flowers in her hair.
"America for Me." Stanza 3
It's home again, and home again, Amer-
ica for me!
I want a ship that's westward bound to
plough the rolling sea,
To the blessèd Land of Room Enough
beyond the ocean bars,
Where the air is full of sunlight and the
flag is full of stars.
Ibid. Stanza 6
This is my work; my blessing, not my
doom;
Of all who live, I am the one by whom
This work can best be done in the right
way.
The Three Best Things. I, Work
Not to the swift, the race:
Not to the strong, the fight: [1]
Not to the righteous, perfect grace:
Not to the wise, the light.
Reliance. Stanza 1
Oh, was I born too soon, my dear, or
were you born too late,
That I am going out the door while you
come in the gate?
Rencontre. Stanza 1
The lintel low enough to keep out pomp
and pride:
The threshold high enough to turn de-
ceit aside.
For the Friends at Hurstmont.
The Door
Self is the only prison that can ever
bind the soul.
The Prison and the Angel
He that planteth a tree is a servant of
God,
He provideth a kindness for many gen-
erations,
And faces that he hath not seen shall
bless him.
The Friendly Trees. Stanza 10
The heavenly hills of Holland —
How wondrously they rise
Above the smooth green pastures
Into the azure skies!

[1] In anguish we uplift
A new unhallowed song:
The race is to the swift;
The battle to the strong.
JOHN DAVIDSON: War-Song, St. 1

With blue and purple hollows,
With peaks of dazzling snow,
Along the far horizon
The clouds are marching slow.
The Heavenly Hills of Holland.
Stanza 1
Individuality is the salt of common
life. You may have to live in a crowd,
but you do not have to live like it, nor
subsist on its food.
The School of Life. Page 33
It is with rivers as it is with people:
the greatest are not always the most
agreeable nor the best to live with.
Little Rivers. Chap. 2
The first day of spring is one thing,
and the first spring day is another. The
difference between them is sometimes
as great as a month.
Fisherman's Luck. Chap. 5

YOUNG EWING ALLISON
[1853–1932]

The mate was fixed by the bos'n's pike,
The bos'n brained with a marlinspike,
And Cookey's throat was marked belike
    It had been gripped
        By fingers ten;
    And there they lay,
        All good dead men,
Like break-o'-day in a boozing ken —
Yo-ho-ho and a bottle of rum! [1]
Derelict, A Reminiscence of
Treasure Island

The very texture of every enduring
work of art must imbed the glowing life
of its own times and the embers of the
past. If it does not cover space as history it must plumb the depths of emo-

[1] See Stevenson, page 704.
Fifteen men on the dead man's chest —
    Yo-ho-ho and a bottle of rum!
Young E. Allison done all the rest —
    Yo-ho-ho and a bottle of rum!
He's sung this song for you and me,
    Jest as it wuz — or it ort to be —
Clean through time and eternity.
    Yo-ho-ho and a bottle of rum!
JAMES WHITCOMB RILEY: To Young
E. Allison
See Y. E. A. and a Bottle of Rum in Buried
Caesars by Vincent Starrett [1923].

tion in an individual to reach the universal perception.

"My Old Kentucky Home"
[Stephen] Foster's songs have been received into the world's choir. His music lives and has become universal, but the name and memory of the man who created it lie dead amidst the singing crowds awaiting resurrection in the world that owes him so much of pleasure and profound solace.

Ibid.

HALL CAINE
[1853–1931]

I reject the monstrous theory that while a man may redeem the past a woman never can.

The Eternal City. Part VI,
Chap. 18

A great outrage on the spirit of Justice breaks down all barriers of race and nationality.

Ibid. Part VII, Chap. 5

FRANK DESPREZ
[1853–1916]

Lasca used to ride
On a mouse-gray mustang close to my
side.

Lasca

And I wonder why I do not care
For the things that are, like the things
that were.
Does half my heart lie buried there,
In Texas, down by the Rio Grande?

Ibid.

EDGAR WATSON HOWE
[1853–1937]

A really busy person never knows how much he weighs.

Country Town Sayings

What people say behind your back is your standing in the community.

Ibid.

There is nothing so well known as that we should not expect something for nothing — but we all do and call it Hope.

Ibid.

ROBERT UNDERWOOD JOHNSON
[1853–1937]

In tears I tossed my coin from Trevi's
edge, —
A coin unsordid as a bond of love, —
And, with the instinct of the homing
dove,
I gave to Rome my rendezvous and
pledge.

Italian Rhapsody. Stanza 18

For lover or nightingale who can wait?
Whenever he cometh he cometh late.

Spring at the Villa Conti

Song's but solace for a day;
Wine's a traitor not to trust;
Love's a kiss and then away;
Time's a peddler deals in dust.

Hearth-Song. Stanza 2

"Gridley," says the Commodore,
"You may fire when ready."

Dewey at Manila. Stanza 12

EMILIE POULSSON
[1853–   ]

"Now put in one thing more; I give you
leave to try."
The mousie chuckled to himself, and
then he softly stole
Right to the stocking's crowded toe,
and gnawed a little hole!

Santa Claus and the Mouse

The essence of Boston, now grown
somewhat rare,
Still lends its aroma to Louisburg
Square.

Louisburg Square. Stanza 1

Books are keys to wisdom's treasure;
Books are gates to lands of pleasure;
Books are paths that upward lead;
Books are friends. Come, let us read.

Inscription for the Children's
Reading Room, Hopkinton,
Massachusetts

CECIL JOHN RHODES
[1853–1902]

I desire to encourage and foster an appreciation of the advantages which will result from the union of the English-speaking peoples throughout the world.

and to encourage in the students from the United States of America an attachment to the country from which they have sprung without I hope withdrawing them or their sympathies from the land of their adoption or birth.

Will, establishing the
Rhodes Scholarships

Educational relations make the strongest tie.

Ibid.

So little done — so much to do.
Last words

IRWIN RUSSELL [1]
[1853–1879]

De man what keeps pullin' de grape-
vine shakes down a few bunches
at leas'.
Precepts at Parting. Stanza 3
You mus' reason with a mule.
Nebuchadnezzar. Stanza 3
You bless us, please sah, eben ef we's
doin' wrong to-night,
Kase den we'll need de blessin' more'n
ef we's doin' right;
An' let de blessin' stay wid us untel we
comes to die
An' goes to keep our Christmas wid dem
sheriffs in de sky.
Christmas Night in the Quarters.
Blessing the Dance
"Dar's gwine to be a overflow," said
Noah, lookin' solemn —
Fur Noah tuk de *Herald*, an' he read
de ribber column —
An' so he sot his hands to wuk a-clarin'
timber-patches,
An' 'lowed he's gwine to build a boat
to beat de steamah *Natchez*.
De Fust Banjo. Stanza 2

MARION COUTHOUY SMITH
[1853–1931]

Go, then, and plant a tree, lovely in sun
and shadow,

---

[1] Among the first — if not the very first — of Southern writers to appreciate the literary possibilities of the negro character. — JOEL CHANDLER HARRIS

Gracious in every kind — maple and
oak and pine.
Peace of the forest glade, wealth of the
fruitful meadow,
Blessings of dew and shade, here-
after shall be thine.
The Planting of a Tree.
Stanza 4

FRANCIS MARION CRAWFORD
[1854–1909]

The sea is Death's garden, and he sows
dead men in the loam,
When the breast of the waters is
ploughed like a field by the gale,
When the ocean is turned up and rent
in long furrows of foam
By the coulter and share of the wind
and the harrow of hail.
The Song of the Sirens.[1]
Stanza 7

JULIAN STEARNS CUTLER
[1854–1930]

A common thing is a grass blade small,
Crushed by the feet that pass,
But all the dwarfs and giants tall,
Working till doomsday shadows fall
Can't make a blade of grass.
Wonderful. Stanza 1
You're only a dog, old fellow; a dog,
and you've had your day;
But never a friend of all my friends has
been truer than you alway.
Roger and I. Stanza 1
Never a heaven shall harbor me, where
they won't let Roger in.[2]
Ibid. Stanza 4

WILLIAM HENRY DRUMMOND
[1854–1907]

De win' can blow lak hurricane
An' s'pose she blow some more,

---

[1] At the close of the novel, *With the Immortals* [1888].
[2] If there is no God for thee
Then there is no God for me.
ANNA HEMPSTEAD BRANCH:
To a Dog, St. 1

You can't get drown on Lac St. Pierre
   So long you stay on shore.
   The Wreck of the "Julie Plante."
                 Stanza 6
Do w'at you lak wit' your old gran-
   'pere
For w'en you're beeg feller he won't be
   dere —
   Leetle Bateese!
       Little Bateese. Stanza 7
To the hut of the peasant, or lordly
   hall,
To the heart of the king, or humblest
   thrall,
Sooner or late, love comes to all.
   The Grand Seigneur. Stanza 1

SIR JAMES GEORGE FRAZER
[1854–   ]

The wine-coloured amethyst received
its name, which means "not drunken,"
because it was supposed to keep the
wearer of it sober.
   The Golden Bough.[1] *Chap. 3*

Dwellers by the sea cannot fail to be
impressed by the sight of its ceaseless
ebb and flow, and are apt, on the principles of that rude philosophy of sympathy and resemblance . . . to trace a
subtle relation, a secret harmony, between its tides and the life of man. . . .
The belief that most deaths happen at
ebb tide is said to be held along the
east coast of England from Northum-
berland to Kent.[2]
                  Ibid.

The heaviest calamity in English
history, the breach with America,
might never have occurred if George
the Third had not been an honest dul-
lard.
                  Ibid.

By religion, then, I understand a
propitiation or conciliation of powers

superior to man which are believed to
direct and control the course of nature
and of human life.
      The Golden Bough. Chap. 4

It is a common. rule with primitive
people not to waken a sleeper, because
his soul is away and might not have
time to get back.
          Ibid. Chap. 18

The awe and dread with which the
untutored savage contemplates his
mother-in-law are amongst the most
familiar facts of anthropology.
                  Ibid.

The world cannot live at the level of
its great men.
          Ibid. Chap. 37

QUINCY KILBY
[1854–1931]

Here in my library I sit,
Amid rare volumes richly bound,
A mine of cleverness and wit,
From authors everywhere renowned.
To-night their words seem flat and
   stale,
Their weakness fills me with disgust,
I want that crude, hard-fisted tale,[1]
Where *seven more redskins bit the dust.*
   "And Seven More Redskins Bit
          the Dust." [2] *Stanza 4*

He who has quickened multitudes to
   mirth,
  Who won their frank applause, their
     hearty laughter,
Has bade a final long farewell to earth,
  And sought the pathway to the
     Grand Hereafter.
   Henry Clay Barnabee [1917]

---

[1] Hugo, Huxley, Darwin, too,
   And twenty score beside,
   They lined his book-shelves while he read
   "Proud Poll, the Pirate's Bride."
     WILBUR DICK NESBIT [1871–1927]:
             Mr. Bluff, St. 1
[2] A line familiar to readers of Western
stories by "Ned Buntline" (EDWARD Z. C.
JUDSON [1822–1886]).

---

[1] Abridged one-volume edition, The Mac-
millan Company [1922].
[2] Just between twelve and one, even at the
turning o' the tide. — SHAKESPEARE: *King
Henry V, Act II, Sc. 3* (Falstaff's death)
See Dickens, page 497.

THOMAS RILEY MARSHALL
[1854–1925]

What this country needs is a good five-cent cigar.[1]

Remark to John Crockett, Chief Clerk of the United States Senate

EVA MARCH TAPPAN
[1854–1930]

We drove the Indians out of the land,
But a dire revenge these redmen planned,
For they fastened a name to every nook,
And every boy with a spelling-book
Will have to toil till his hair turns gray
Before he can spell them the proper way.[2]

On the Cape. Stanza 1

EDITH MATILDA THOMAS
[1854–1925]

I come to the velvet, imperial crowd,
The wine-red, the gold, the crimson, the pied, —
The dahlias that reign by the garden-side.

"Frost To-night." Stanza 2

In my garden of Life with its all-late flowers,
I heed a Voice in the shrinking hours:
"Frost to-night — so clear and dead-still" . . .
Half sad, half proud, my arms I fill.

Ibid. Stanza 4

The god of music dwelleth out of doors.

Music

The love of my life came not
As love unto others is cast;
For mine was a secret wound —
But the wound grew a pearl, at last.

The Deep-Sea Pearl. Stanza 1

And they are with us at Life's farthest reach,
A light when into shadow all else dips,

As, in the stranger's land, their native speech
Returns to dying lips.

The Triumph of Forgotten Things. Stanza 6

WILLARD DUNCAN VANDIVER
[1854–1932]

I come from a State that raises corn and cotton and cockleburs and Democrats, and frothy eloquence neither convinces nor satisfies me. I am from Missouri. You have got to show me.[1]

Speech at a naval banquet in Philadelphia, while a Representative in Congress from Missouri, and a member of the House Committee on Naval Affairs [1899]

WILLIAM COWPER BRANN [2]
[1855–1898]

Boston runs to brains as well as to beans and brown bread. But she is cursed with an army of cranks whom nothing short of a straight-jacket or a swamp-elm club will ever control.

The Iconoclast. Beans and Blood

No man can be a patriot on an empty stomach.

Ibid. Old Glory [July 4, 1893]

It has the subtle flavor of an old pair of sox.

Ibid. Godey's Magazine

The Lydian notes of Andrew Carnegie as he warbles a riant roundelay in praise of poverty, or laments in pathetic spondees the woes of the man with spondulix.

Ibid. Our American Czars

---

[1] What this country needs is a good five-cent nickel. — FRANKLIN P. ADAMS [1932].

[2] See Mrs. Sigourney, page 364.

[1] *Festus:* Angel bosoms know no jealousy.
  Helen: Show me.
          PHILIP JAMES BAILEY: *Festus, A Visit*

[2] Known as "The Iconoclast," from the name of his paper, first published in Austin, Texas, and later in Waco. He was shot by an outraged reader.

Every few years our industrial system gets the jim-jams. Capital flies to cover, factories close and labor goes tramping across the country seeking honest employment and receiving a warm welcome — from militia companies with shotted guns. Cheerful idiots begin to prattle of "over-production," the economic M. D.'s to refurbish all the old remedies, from conjure-bags to communism. They all know exactly what caused the "crisis" and what to do for it; but despite the doctors the patient usually — survives. And the M. D. who succeeds in cramming his pet panacea down its throat claims all the credit for the recovery. We are slowly emerging from the crash of '93, and the cuckoos are cock-sure that a country fairly bursting with wealth was saved from the demnition bowwows by the blessed expedient of going into debt.

Slave or Sovereign
[Speech, August 10, 1895]

GERALD BRENNAN
[*Floruit* 1899]

Th' mem'ry comes like a banshee meself an' me wealth between,
An' I long for a mornin's mornin' in Shanahan's ould shebeen.
Shanahan's Ould Shebeen.[1]
Stanza 4

If you couldn't afford good whiskey, he'd take you on trust for beer.
Ibid. Stanza 5

MARY DOW BRINE

She's somebody's mother, boys, you know,
For all she's aged and poor and slow.
Somebody's Mother

HENRY CUYLER BUNNER
[1855–1896]

Love must kiss that mortal's eyes
Who hopes to see fair Arcady.
The Way to Arcady

[1] Published in *Puck* [1899].

That pitcher of mignonette
Is a garden in heaven set
To the little sick child in the basement.
A Pitcher of Mignonette

Off with your hat as the flag goes by!
And let the heart have its say;
You're man enough for a tear in your eye
That you will not wipe away.
The Old Flag. Stanza 1

It was an old, old, old, old lady,
And a boy that was half-past three;
And the way that they played together
Was beautiful to see.
"One, Two, Three." Stanza 1

What does he plant who plants a tree?
He plants the friend of sun and sky;
He plants the flag of breezes free;
The shaft of beauty towering high.
The Heart of the Tree. Stanza 1

Happy the mortal free and independent,
Master of the mainspring of his own volition!
Look on us with the eye of sweet compassion:
We are Cook's Tourists.
The Wail of the "Personally Conducted." Stanza 6

I have a bookcase, which is what
Many much better men have not.
There are no books inside, for books,
I am afraid, might spoil its looks.
But I've three busts, all second-hand,
Upon the top. You understand
I could not put them underneath —
Shake, Mulleary and Go-ethe.
Shake, Mulleary and Go-ethe.
Stanza 1

I of my landlady am lockèd in
For being short on this sad Saturday,
Nor having shekels of silver wherewith to pay:
She turned and is departed with my key.
Behold the Deeds! Stanza 1

Behold the deeds that are done of Mrs. Jones!
Ibid.

HEINRICH CONRIED
[1855–1909]

These words no Shakespeare wrote,
These words no Byron penned,
Nor poet classical, with fancy free;
It is an honest heart speaks to a precious friend,
And yet it sounds like purest poetry.

Interpolated Song [1]

BETH DAY
[*Circa* 1855]

If you are tempted to reveal
A tale to you someone has told
About another, make it pass,
Before you speak, three gates of gold:
These narrow gates. First, "Is it true?"
Then, "Is it needful?" In your mind
Give truthful answer. And the next
Is last and narrowest, "Is it kind?"
And if to reach your lips at last
It passes through these gateways three,
Then you may tell the tale, nor fear
What the result of speech may be.[2]

Three Gates of Gold

FRANK FRANKFORT MOORE
[1855–1931]

He knew that to offer a man friendship when love is in his heart is like giving a loaf of bread to one who is dying of thirst.

The Jessamy Bride.[3] *Chap. 9*

---

[1] Written, with B. F. Roeder, for the American production of a Viennese opera, *The King's Fool* (*Der Hofnarr*), presented at the Hollis Street Theatre, Boston, March, 1890. The song is not in the German libretto by H. Wittman and J. Bauer.

[2] If your lips would keep from slips,
Five things observe with care:
To whom you speak; of whom you speak;
And how, and when, and where.
  Nursery rhyme quoted by WILLIAM EDWARD NORRIS [1847–1925] in *Thirlby Hall*

[3] This age of ours
But marks your grass-grown headstone now
By Goldsmith's jasmine flowers!
  AUSTIN DOBSON: *On a Picture by Hoppner,* St. 6 (Mrs. Gwyn, Oliver Goldsmith's "Jessamy Bride")

No man of letters is deserving of an eulogy who is scared by a detraction.

The Jessamy Bride. Chap. 16

Happy it is for mankind that Heaven has laid on few men the curse of being poets.

Ibid. Chap. 18

To strike at a serpent that hisses may only cause it to spring.

Ibid. Chap. 19

Destiny has more resources than the most imaginative composer of fiction.

Ibid. Chap. 22

Patchwork should not only be made, it should be used by the blind.

Ibid. Chap. 26

WALTER HINES PAGE
[1855–1918]

There is one thing better than good government, and that is government in which all the people have a part.

Life and Letters. Vol. 3, Page 31

Every letter of declination ought to be written by a skilful man — a diplomatist who can write an unpleasant truth without offence.

A Publisher's Confession [1905]

SIR ARTHUR WING PINERO
[1855–1934]

It is to laugh.

The Amazons

You may dive into many waters, but there is one social Dead Sea.

*The Second Mrs. Tanqueray.
Act I*

From forty to fifty a man is at heart either a stoic or a satyr.

Ibid.

There are two sorts of affection — the love of a woman you respect, and the love for the woman you love.

Ibid. Act II

It is only one step from toleration to forgiveness.

Ibid.

I believe the future is only the past again, entered through another gate.

Ibid. Act IV

I've heard what doctors' consultations consist of. After looking at the pictures you talk about whist.

> *The Notorious Mrs. Ebbsmith.*
> *Act I*

How many "coming men" has one known! Where on earth do they all go to?

> *Ibid.*

There's only one hour in a woman's life. . . . One supreme hour. Her poor life is like the arch of a crescent; so many years lead up to that hour, so many weary years decline from it.

> *Ibid. Act III*

Vanity is the cause of a great deal of virtue in men; the vainest are those who like to be thought respectable.

> *Ibid. Act IV*

OLIVE SCHREINER
("RALPH IRON")
[1855–1920]

It came to pass that after a time the artist was forgotten, but the work lived.

> *Dreams. The Artist's Secret*

At last they came to where Reflection sits, — that strange old woman, who had always one elbow on her knee, and her chin in her hand, and who steals light out of the past to shed it on the future.

> *Ibid. The Lost Joy*

There's something so beautiful in coming on one's very own inmost thoughts in another. In one way it's one of the greatest pleasures one has.

> *Letter to Havelock Ellis*
> *[March 2, 1885]*

A thoughtful life, in which one might read and creep into the hearts of books, as they can only be crept into when the wheels of the daily life are grinding soft and low.

> *From Man to Man. Chap. 1*

If you are an artist, may no love of wealth or fame or admiration and no fear of blame or misunderstanding make you ever paint, with pen or brush, an ideal or a picture of external life otherwise than as you see it.

> *Ibid. Chap. 7*

Man individually and as a race is possible on earth only because, not for weeks or months but for years, love and the guardianship of the strong over the weak has existed.

> *From Man to Man. Chap. 7*

The higher the flame has leaped, the colder and deader the ashes.

> *Ibid. Chap. 8*

WILLIAM SHARP
("FIONA MACLEOD")
[1855–1905]

My heart is a lonely hunter that hunts
on a lonely hill.

> *The Lonely Hunter. Stanza 6*

But sometimes, through the Soul of
Man,
Slow moving o'er his pain,
The moonlight of a perfect peace
Floods heart and brain.

> *The White Peace. Stanza 2*

Across the silent stream
Where the slumber-shadows go,
From the dim blue Hills of Dream
I have heard the west wind blow.

> *From the Hills of Dream. Stanza 1*

I hear the little children of the wind
Crying solitary in lonely places.

> *Little Children of the Wind*

CY WARMAN
[1855–1914]

Every daisy in the dell knows my secret, knows it well,
And yet I dare not tell, sweet Marie.

> *Sweet Marie. Stanza 1*

Oft when I feel my engine swerve,
As o'er strange rails we fare,
I strain my eyes around the curve
For what awaits us there.
When swift and free she carries me
Through yards unknown at night,
I look along the line to see
That all the lamps are white.

> *Will the Lights be White? Stanza 1*

Swift towards life's terminal I trend,
The run seems short to-night;
God only knows what's at the end —
I hope the lamps are white.

> *Ibid. Stanza 3*

ELLA WHEELER WILCOX
[1855–1919]

Talk happiness. The world is sad
  enough
Without your woe. No path is wholly
  rough.
                    Speech. Stanza 1

Talk faith. The world is better off without
Your uttered ignorance and morbid
  doubt.
                    Ibid. Stanza 2

Talk health. The dreary, never-ending
  tale
Of mortal maladies is more than stale;
You cannot charm or interest or please
By harping on that minor chord, dis-
  ease.
Say you are well, or all is well with you,
And God shall hear your words and
  make them true.
                    Ibid. Stanza 3

The two kinds of people on earth that
  I mean
Are the people who lift and the people
  who lean.
                    To Lift or to Lean

It ever has been since time began,
    And ever will be, till time lose breath,
That love is a mood — no more — to
  man,
    And love to woman is life or death.
                    Blind. Stanza 1

Since life is short, we need to make it
    broad;
Since life is brief, we need to make it
    bright;
Then keep the old king's motto well in
    sight,
And let its meaning permeate each day
Whatever comes — "This, too, shall
    pass away." [1]
            This, Too, Shall Pass Away.
                    Stanza 7

It is easy to sit in the sunshine
    And talk to the man in the shade;
It is easy to float in a well-trimmed
    boat,
    And point out the places to wade.
            Practice vs. Preaching. Stanza 1

[1] See J. G. Saxe, page 509.

Laugh, and the world laughs with you;
    Weep, and you weep alone;
For the sad old earth must borrow its
    mirth,
    But has trouble enough of its own.
                    Solitude. Stanza 1

Feast, and your halls are crowded;
    Fast, and the world goes by.
                    Ibid. Stanza 3

So many gods, so many creeds,
    So many paths that wind and wind,
    When just the art of being kind
Is all this sad world needs.
                    The World's Need

No question is ever settled
    Until it is settled right.
            Settle the Question Right

We flatter those we scarcely know,
    We please the fleeting guest,
And deal full many a thoughtless blow
    To those who love us best.
            Life's Scars. Stanza 3

GEORGE EDWARD WOODBERRY
[1855–1930]

O, inexpressible as sweet,
    Love takes my voice away;
I cannot tell thee when we meet
    What most I long to say.
                    Song

Where are the friends that I knew in my
    Maying,
In the days of my youth, in the first of
    my roaming?
We were dear; we were leal; oh, far we
    went straying,
Now never a heart to my heart comes
    homing!
                    Comrades. Stanza 1

FRANCIS M. BELLAMY
[1856–1931]

I pledge allegiance to the flag of the
United States and to the republic for
which it stands, one nation, indivisible,
with liberty and justice for all.
            The Pledge of Allegiance to the
                    Flag [1892]

KENYON COX
[1856–1919]

Work thou for pleasure — paint, or sing, or carve
The thing thou lovest, though the body starve —
Who works for glory misses oft the goal;
Who works for money coins his very soul.
Work for the work's sake, then, and it may be
That these things shall be added unto thee.

Work

SARAH PRATT McLEAN GREENE
[1856–1935]

De massa ob de sheepfol',
Dat guards de sheepfol' bin,
Look out in de gloomerin' meadows
Wha'r de long night rain begin;
So he call to de hirelin' shepa'd —
"Is my sheep, is dey all come in?"

De Sheepfol'. Stanza 1
[Towhead, 1883]

EDWARD SANDFORD MARTIN
[1856–   ]

Within my earthly temple there's a crowd.
There's one of us that's humble; one that's proud.
There's one that's broken-hearted for his sins,
And one who, unrepentant, sits and grins.
There's one who loves his neighbor as himself,
And one who cares for naught but fame and pelf.
From much corroding care would I be free
If once I could determine which is Me.

Mixed

ROBERT EDWIN PEARY
[1856–1920]

We returned from the Pole to Cape Columbia in only sixteen days . . . the exhilaration of success lent wings to our sorely battered feet. But Ootah, the Eskimo, had his own explanation. Said he: "The devil is asleep or having trouble with his wife, or we should never have come back so easily."

The North Pole

LIZETTE WOODWORTH REESE
[1856–1935]

When I consider Life and its few years —
A wisp of fog betwixt us and the sun;
A call to battle, and the battle done
Ere the last echo dies within our ears.

Tears

The burst of music down an unlistening street.

Ibid.

How each hath back what once he stayed to weep;
Homer his sight, David his little lad!

Ibid.

Creeds grow so thick along the way,
Their boughs hide God.

Doubt

Glad that I live am I;
That the sky is blue;
Glad for the country lanes,
And the fall of dew.

A Little Song of Life. Stanza 1

An apple orchard smells like wine;
A succory flower is blue;
Until Grief touched these eyes of mine,
Such things I never knew.

Wise. Stanza 1

GEORGE BERNARD SHAW
[1856–   ]

My method is to take the utmost trouble to find the right thing to say, and then to say it with the utmost levity.

Answers to Nine Questions

We have no more right to consume happiness without producing it than to consume wealth without producing it.

Candida. Act I

A prosperous man of business, who probably never read anything but a newspaper since he left school.

Cashel Byron's Profession. Chap. 5

All this struggling and striving to make the world better is a great mistake; not because it isn't a good thing to improve the world if you know how to do it, but because striving and struggling is the worst way you could set about doing anything.

Ibid. Chap. 6

We don't bother much about dress and manners in England, because, as a nation we don't dress well and we've no manners.

You Never Can Tell. Act I

A family enjoying the unspeakable peace and freedom of being orphans.

Ibid. Act II

The great advantage of a hotel is that it's a refuge from home life.

Ibid.

It's well to be off with the Old Woman before you're on with the New.[1]

The Philanderer. Act II

The fickleness of women I love is only equaled by the infernal constancy of the women who love me.

Ibid.

The test of a man or woman's breeding is how they behave in a quarrel.

Ibid. Act IV

People are always blaming their circumstances for what they are. I don't believe in circumstances. The people who get on in this world are the people who get up and look for the circumstances they want, and, if they can't find them, make them.

Mrs. Warren's Profession. Act II

There are no secrets better kept than the secrets that everybody guesses.

Ibid. Act III

A great devotee of the Gospel of Getting On.

Ibid. Act IV

This is the true joy in life, the being used for a purpose recognized by yourself as a mighty one; the being thor-

oughly worn out before you are thrown on the scrap heap; the being a force of Nature instead of a feverish selfish little clod of ailments and grievances complaining that the world will not devote itself to making you happy.

Man and Superman. Epistle Dedicatory

A lifetime of happiness! No man alive could bear it: it would be hell on earth.

Man and Superman. Act I

The more things a man is ashamed of, the more respectable he is.

Ibid.

You think that you are Ann's suitor: that you are the pursuer and she the pursued; that it is your part to woo, to persuade, to prevail, to overcome. Fool: it is you who are the pursued, the marked-down quarry, the destined prey.

Ibid. Act II

Marry Ann and at the end of a week you'll find no more inspiration in her than in a plate of muffins.

Ibid.

Home life as we understand it is no more natural to us than a cage is natural to a cockatoo.

Getting Married. Preface

In the extreme instances of reaction against convention, female murderers get sheaves of offers of marriage.

Ibid.

When two people are under the influence of the most violent, most insane, most delusive, and most transient of passions, they are required to swear that they will remain in that excited, abnormal, and exhausting condition continuously until death do them part.

Ibid.

A man is like a phonograph with half-a-dozen records. You soon get tired of them all; and yet you have to sit at table whilst he reels them off to every new visitor.

Ibid. (The Play)

In England we always let an institution strain itself until it breaks.

Ibid.

[1] See Charles Henry Webb, page 611.

The whole strength of England lies in the fact that the enormous majority of the English people are snobs.

Getting Married (The Play)

You don't learn to hold your own in the world by standing on guard, but by attacking, and getting well hammered yourself.

Ibid.

Religion is a great force — the only real motive force in the world; but what you fellows don't understand is that you must get at a man through his own religion and not through yours.

Ibid.

The modest cough of a minor poet.

The Dark Lady of the Sonnets

This writing of plays is a great matter, forming as it does the minds and affections of men in such sort that whatsoever they see done in show on the stage, they will presently be doing in earnest in the world, which is but a larger stage.

Ibid.

I like a bit of a mongrel myself, whether it's a man or a dog; they're the best for every day.

Misalliance. Episode I

If parents would only realize how they bore their children!

Ibid.

He's a gentleman: look at his boots.

Pygmalion. Act I

Women upset everything. When you let them into your life, you find that the woman is driving at one thing and you're driving at another.

Ibid. Act II

I have to live for others and not for myself; that's middle class morality.

Ibid. Act V

The great secret, Eliza, is not having bad manners or good manners or any other particular sort of manners, but having the same manner for all human souls: in short, behaving as if you were in Heaven, where there are no third-class carriages, and one soul is as good as another.

Ibid.

Independence? That's middle class blasphemy. We are all dependent on one another, every soul of us on earth.

Pygmalion. Act V

The nauseous sham goodfellowship our democratic public men get up for shop use.

Back to Methuselah. Gospel of the Brothers Barnabas

Life is a disease; and the only difference between one man and another is the stage of the disease at which he lives.

Ibid.

I enjoy convalescence. It is the part that makes the illness worth while.

Ibid.

A nap, my friend, is a brief period of sleep which overtakes superannuated persons when they endeavor to entertain unwelcome visitors or to listen to scientific lectures.

Ibid. Tragedy of an Elderly Gentleman

Everything happens to everybody sooner or later if there is time enough.

Ibid. As Far As Thought Can Reach

Silence is the most perfect expression of scorn.

Ibid.

The worst cliques are those which consist of one man.

Ibid.

The Jews generally give value. They make you pay; but they deliver the goods. In my experience the men who want something for nothing are invariably Christians.

Saint Joan. Scene IV

Kings are not born: they are made by universal hallucination.

The Revolutionist's Handbook

At last I went to Ireland,
'Twas raining cats and dogs:
I found no music in the glens,
Nor purple in the bogs.
And as far as angels' laughter in the
smelly Liffy's tide —
Well, my Irish daddy said it, but the
dear old humbug lied.

Envoi added to a song, My Irish

Daddy, by Miss MAISIE HURL
[*May, 1931*]

Every person who owes his life to civilized society and who has enjoyed since his childhood its very costly protections and advantages should appear at reasonable intervals before a properly qualified jury to justify his existence, which should be summarily and painlessly terminated if he fails to justify it and it develops that he is a positive nuisance and more trouble than he is worth. Nothing less will really make people responsible citizens.

Radio address from London to America [*October 11, 1931*]

You put up in New York Harbor a monstrous idol which you called "Liberty." [1]

Speech, Metropolitan Opera House, [2] *New York* [*April 11, 1933*]

You in America should trust to that volcanic political instinct which I have divined in you.

Ibid.

KATE DOUGLAS WIGGIN
[1856–1923]

My heart is open wide to-night
  For stranger, kith or kin.
I would not bar a single door
  Where Love might enter in.
  The Romance of a Christmas Card

OSCAR FINGAL O'FLAHERTIE WILLS WILDE
[1856–1900]

Tread lightly, she is near
  Under the snow,

[1] "I see," said he, speaking to some American friends, "that you too put up monuments to your great dead!" — Story of a distinguished Frenchman on a visit to the United States during Prohibition; related by RALPH NEVILL: *Paris of To-day* [1924]

[2] Made before the Academy of Political Science, and broadcast by radio.

Speak gently, she can hear
  The daisies grow.
      Requiescat. Stanza 1

Thy name was writ in water [1] — it shall stand:
And tears like mine will keep thy memory green,
As Isabella did her Basil-tree.
      The Grave of Keats

  Think of all
The suns that go to make one speedwell blue!
      Quia Multum Amavi. Stanza 4

These are the letters which Endymion wrote
  To one he loved in secret, and apart.
And now the brawlers of the auction mart
Bargain and bid for each poor blotted note.
      On the Sale by Auction of Keats' Love Letters

Yet each man kills the thing he loves,
  By each let this be heard,
Some do it with a bitter look,
  Some with a flattering word,
The coward does it with a kiss,
  The brave man with a sword!
      The Ballad of Reading Gaol. I, 7

I never saw a man who looked
  With such a wistful eye
Upon that little tent of blue
  Which prisoners call the sky,
And at every wandering cloud that trailed
  Its ravelled fleeces by.
      Ibid. II, 2

For he that lives more lives than one
  More deaths than one must die.
      Ibid. III, 37

All that we know who lie in gaol
  Is that the wall is strong;
And that each day is like a year,
  A year whose days are long.
      Ibid. V, 1

The vilest deeds like poison-weeds
  Bloom well in prison-air:
It is only what is good in Man
  That wastes and withers there:

[1] See Keats, page 386.

Pale Anguish keeps the heavy gate
And the Warder is Despair.
The Ballad of Reading Gaol. V, 5
Down the long and silent street,
The dawn, with silver-sandaled feet,
Crept like a frightened girl.
The Harlot's House
A poet can survive everything but a
misprint.
The Children of the Poets
Most modern calendars mar the
sweet simplicity of our lives by remind-
ing us that each day that passes is the
anniversary of some perfectly uninter-
esting event.
A Poetic Calendar
Though it would be dangerous to
make calendars the basis of Culture, we
should all be much improved if we began each day with a fine passage of
English poetry.[1]
Ibid.
To say "mither" instead of "mother"
seems to many the acme of romance.
Romantic Poems and Ballads
An age that has no criticism is either
an age in which art is immobile, hieratic,
and confined to the reproduction of
formal types, or an age that possesses
no art at all.
The Critic as Artist. Part I
It is through Art, and through Art
only, that we can realize our perfec-
tion; through Art and Art only that we
can shield ourselves from the sordid
perils of actual existence.
Ibid. Part II
As long as war is regarded as wicked,
it will always have its fascination.
When it is looked upon as vulgar, it will
cease to be popular.
Ibid.
There is no sin except stupidity.
Ibid.
Where there is sorrow there is holy
ground.
De Profundis
There is no such thing as a moral or
an immoral book. Books are well writ-
ten, or badly written. That is all.
The Picture of Dorian Gray.
Preface

[1] See Charles Eliot Norton, page 572.

All art is quite useless.
The Picture of Dorian Gray.
Preface
There is only one thing in the world
worse than being talked about, and that
is not being talked about.
Ibid. Chap. 1
Conscience and cowardice are really
the same things.
Ibid.
Laughter is not at all a bad beginning
for a friendship, and it is far the best
ending for one.
Ibid.
The only way to get rid of a tempta-
tion is to yield to it.
Ibid. Chap. 2
He knew the precise psychological
moment [1] when to say nothing.
Ibid.
The only difference between a caprice
and a lifelong passion is that the caprice
lasts a little longer.
Ibid.
Children begin by loving their par-
ents; as they grow older they judge
them; sometimes they forgive them.
Ibid. Chap. 5
Conscience makes egotists of us all.
Ibid. Chap. 8
When a woman marries again it is
because she detested her first husband.
When a man marries again, it is because
he adored his first wife.[2] Women try
their luck; men risk theirs.
Ibid. Chap. 15

[1] In all considerations the psychological mo-
mentum or factor must be allowed to play a
prominent part, for without its co-operation,
there is little to be hoped from the work of
the artillery. — The *Neue Preussische Kreuz-
Zeitung, Dec. 16, 1870,* commenting upon the
siege of Paris.
An error in translation gave us "psychological moment" (i. e., the critical moment). Attributed to German pedantry, the Parisians
ridiculed the phrase, but it speedily became
universal.

Felt the psychologic moment.
KIPLING: *Et Dona Ferentes, St. 4*
[1896]
[2] See Samuel Johnson, page 235.

Over the piano was printed a notice: Please do not shoot the pianist. He is doing his best.

Impressions of America. Leadville

Now-a-days we are all of us so hard up, that the only pleasant things to pay are compliments. They're the only things we *can* pay.

Lady Windermere's Fan. Act I

I can resist everything except temptation.

Ibid.

History is merely gossip.

Ibid. Act III

In this world there are only two tragedies. One is not getting what one wants, and the other is getting it.

Ibid.

What is a cynic? A man who knows the price of everything, and the value of nothing.

Ibid.

Experience is the name everyone gives to his mistakes.

Ibid.

They say that when good Americans die they go to Paris.

A Woman of No Importance. Act I

Nothing spoils a romance so much as a sense of humour in the woman.

Ibid.

Men always want to be a woman's first love. That is their clumsy vanity. We women have a more subtle instinct about things. What we like is to be a man's last romance.

Ibid. Act II

Discontent is the first step in the progress of a man or a nation.

Ibid.

Talk to every woman as if you loved her, and to every man as if he bored you, and at the end of your first season you will have the reputation of possessing the most perfect social tact.

Ibid. Act III

I delight in men over seventy. They always offer one the devotion of a lifetime.

Ibid. Act IV

I have invented an invaluable invalid called Bunbury, in order that I may be able to go down into the country whenever I choose.

The Importance of Being Earnest. Act I

Memory is the diary that we all carry about with us.

Ibid. Act II

No woman should ever be quite accurate about her age. It looks so calculating.

Ibid. Act III

An acquaintance that begins with a compliment is sure to develop into a real friendship.

An Ideal Husband. Act I

Nothing produces such an effect as a good platitude.[1]

Ibid.

Private information is practically the source of every large modern fortune.

Ibid. Act II

When the gods wish to punish us they answer our prayers.[2]

Ibid.

To love oneself is the beginning of a lifelong romance.

Ibid. Act III

As for borrowing Mr. Whistler's ideas about art, the only thoroughly original ideas I have ever heard him express have had reference to his own superiority as a painter over painters greater than himself.

Reply to an attack by James McNeill Whistler, Truth [January 9, 1890]

WOODROW WILSON
[1856–1924]

You deal in the raw material of opinion, and, if my convictions have any validity, opinion ultimately governs the world.

Address to the Associated Press [April 20, 1915]

There is such a thing as a man being too proud to fight.

Address to Foreign-Born Citizens [May 10, 1915]

---

[1] Stroke a platitude until it purrs like an epigram. — DON MARQUIS: *The Sun Dial.*

[2] See James Russell Lowell, page 528.

The things that the flag stands for were created by the experiences of a great people. Everything that it stands for was written by their lives. The flag is the embodiment, not of sentiment, but of history. It represents the experiences made by men and women, the experiences of those who do and live under that flag.

Address [June 14, 1915]

There must be, not a balance of power, but a community of power; not organized rivalries, but an organized common peace.

Address to the Senate [January 22, 1917]

I am seeking only to face realities and to face them without soft concealments.

Ibid.

A little group of willful men, representing no opinion but their own.

Of certain members of the United States Senate [March 4, 1917]

To such a task we dedicate our lives, our fortunes, everything that we are and everything that we have, with the pride of those who know that the day has come when America is privileged to spend her blood and her might for the principles that gave her birth and happiness and the peace which she has treasured. God helping her, she can do no other.

Address to Congress, asking for a declaration of war [April 2, 1917]

The world must be made safe for democracy.

Ibid.

Open covenants of peace, openly arrived at.

Address to Congress [January 8, 1918]

GERTRUDE FRANKLIN ATHERTON
[1857–   ]

Women love the lie that saves their pride, but never an unflattering truth.

The Conqueror. Book III, Chap. 6

To put a tempting face aside when duty demands every faculty, it is a lesson which takes most men longest to learn.

The Conqueror. Book III, Chap. 6

The perfect friendship of two men is the deepest and highest sentiment of which the finite mind is capable; women miss the best in life.

Ibid. Chap. 12

No matter how hard a man may labour, some woman is always in the background of his mind. She is the one reward of virtue.

Ibid. Book IV, Chap. 3

ALICE BROWN
[1857–   ]

Praise not the critic, lest he think
You crave the shelter of his ink;
But pray his halo, when he dies,
May tip the steelyards of the skies.

The Critic

Yet thou, O banqueter on worms,
  Who wilt not let corruption pass! —
Dost search out mildew, mould and
  stain,
  Beneath a magnifying-glass.

The Slanderer

Of this round earth whereon I stand,
I do not own one inch of land; [1]
I shall not lose upon the day
When Gaffer Death drags me away.

Autolycus. Stanza 1

Whip of toil no more shall touch you,
  nor din of turmoil hinder,
Nor fate affright your quiet with his
  grisly mask of doom.
You shall lie by living waters, you shall
  walk with laughing heroes,
You are garnered up in safety in a large
  and lofty room.

On the Death of Louise Imogen Guiney [2]

He holds his spear benignant, sceptrewise,
And strikes out flame from the adoring hills.

Sunrise on Mansfield Mountain

[1] I do not own an inch of land,
  But all I see is mine.
        LUCY LARCOM: *A Strip of Blue*
[2] In *The Atlantic Monthly, March, 1921.*

JOSEPH CONRAD
[1857–1924]

A work that aspires, however humbly, to the condition of art should carry its justification in every line.

The Nigger of the Narcissus.
Preface

But the artist appeals to that part of our being which is not dependent on wisdom; to that in us which is a gift and not an acquisition — and, therefore, more permanently enduring. He speaks to our capacity for delight and wonder, to the sense of mystery surrounding our lives: to our sense of pity, and beauty, and pain.

Ibid.

The ship, a fragment detached from the earth, went on lonely and swift like a small planet.

Ibid. Chap. 2

Goodbye, brothers! You were a good crowd. As good a crowd as ever fisted with wild cries the beating canvas of a heavy foresail; or tossing aloft, invisible in the night, gave back yell for yell to a westerly gale.

Ibid. Chap. 5

She strode like a grenadier, was strong and upright like an obelisk, had a beautiful face, a candid brow, pure eyes, and not a thought of her own in her head.

Tales of Unrest. The Return

What greatness had not floated on the ebb of that river [the Thames] into the mystery of an unknown earth! . . . The dreams of men, the seed of commonwealths, the germs of empires.

Heart of Darkness

Running all over the sea trying to get behind the weather.

Typhoon. Chap. 2

The sea never changes and its works, for all the talk of men, are wrapped in mystery.

Ibid. Falk: A Reminiscence

I have known the sea too long to believe in its respect for decency.

Ibid.

An elemental force is ruthlessly frank.

Typhoon. Falk: A Reminiscence

Efficiency of a practically flawless kind may be reached naturally in the struggle for bread. But there is something beyond — a higher point, a subtle and unmistakable touch of love and pride beyond mere skill; almost an inspiration which gives to all work that finish which is almost art — which *is* art.

The Mirror of the Sea.
The Fine Art

The East Wind, an interloper in the dominions of Westerly Weather, is an impassive-faced tyrant with a sharp poniard held behind his back for a treacherous stab.

Ibid. Rulers of East and West

The autocratic sway of the West Wind, whether forty north or forty south of the equator, is characterized by an open, generous, frank, barbarous recklessness. For he is a great autocrat, and to be a great autocrat you must be a great barbarian.

Ibid.

The air of the New World seems favorable to the art of declamation.

Nostromo. Chap. 6

There are on earth no actors too humble and obscure not to have a gallery; that gallery which envenoms the play by stealthy jeers, counsels of anger, amused comments, or words of perfidious compassion.

Chance. Part II, Chap. 4

What all men are really after is some form, or perhaps only some formula, of peace.

Under Western Eyes. Part 1

A man's real life is that accorded to him in the thoughts of other men by reason of respect or natural love.

Ibid. 1

Let a fool be made serviceable according to his folly.

Ibid. 3

The belief in a supernatural source of evil is not necessary; men alone are quite capable of every wickedness.

Ibid. Part II, 4

Why should a man certain of immortality think of his life at all?

Under Western Eyes. Part II, 4

No woman is an absolute fool. . . . No woman is ever completely deceived.

Ibid. 5

That strange impulse of indiscretion, common to men who lead secret lives, and accounting for the invariable existence of "compromising documents" in all the plots and conspiracies of history.

Ibid. Part III, 1

You can't ignore the importance of a good digestion. The joy of life . . . depends on a sound stomach, whereas a bad digestion inclines one to skepticism, incredulity, breeds black fancies and thoughts of death.

Ibid. 3

All ambitions are lawful except those which climb upward on the miseries or credulities of mankind.

A Personal Record. Preface

The sight of human affairs deserves admiration and pity. And he is not insensible who pays them the undemonstrative tribute of a sigh which is not a sob, and of a smile which is not a grin.

Ibid.

Only in men's imagination does every truth find an effective and undeniable existence. Imagination, not invention, is the supreme master of art as of life.

Ibid. Chap. 1

For Englishmen especially, of all the races of the earth, a task, any task, undertaken in an adventurous spirit acquires the merit of romance.

Ibid. Chap. 5

Only a moment; a moment of strength, of romance, of glamour — of youth! . . . A flick of sunshine upon a strange shore, the time to remember, the time for a sigh, and — goodbye! — Night — Goodbye . . . !

Youth

There is no rest for a messenger till the message is delivered.

The Rescue. Part VI, 8

I am a great foe of favouritism in public life, in private life, and even in the delicate relationship of an author to his works.

Lord Jim. Author's Note

There is a weird power in a spoken word. . . . And a word carries far — very far — deals destruction through time as the bullets go flying through space.

Ibid. Chap. 15

That faculty of beholding at a hint the face of his desire and the shape of his dream, without which the earth would know no lover and no adventurer.

Ibid. Chap. 16

Felicity, felicity — how shall I say it? — is quaffed out of a golden cup in every latitude: the flavour is with you — with you alone, and you can make it as intoxicating as you please.

Ibid.

It is when we try to grapple with another man's intimate need that we perceive how incomprehensible, wavering, and misty are the beings that share with us the sight of the stars and the warmth of the sun.

Ibid.

We wander in our thousands over the face of the earth, the illustrious and the obscure, earning beyond the seas our fame, our money, or only a crust of bread; but it seems to me that for each of us going home must be like going to render an account. We return to face our superiors, our kindred, our friends — those whom we obey, and those whom we love.

Ibid. Chap. 21

You shall judge of a man by his foes as well as by his friends.

Ibid. Chap. 34

Vanity plays lurid tricks with our memory.

Ibid. Chap. 41

Some great men owe most of their greatness to the ability of detecting in those they destine for their tools the exact quality of strength that matters for their work.

Ibid. Chap. 42

In plucking the fruit of memory one runs the risk of spoiling its bloom.

The Arrow of Gold.
Author's Note

Historian of fine consciences.

Notes on Life and Letters.
Henry James, An Appreciation

Most of us, if you will pardon me for betraying the universal secret, have, at some time or other, discovered in ourselves a readiness to stray far, ever so far, on the wrong road.

Ibid. A Happy Wanderer

What humanity needs is not the promise of scientific immortality, but compassionate pity in this life and infinite mercy on the Day of Judgment.

Ibid. The Life Beyond

JOHN DAVIDSON
[1857–1909]

That minister of ministers,
  Imagination, gathers up
The undiscovered Universe,
  Like jewels in a jasper cup.

There Is a Dish to Hold the Sea

My feet are heavy now but on I go,
My head erect beneath the tragic years.

I Felt the World A-spinning

Fame is the breath of power:
What valid work was ever for itself
Wrought solely, be it war, art, statesmanship?

Smith

Our language is too worn, too much abused,
Jaded and over-spurred, wind-broken, lame, —
The hackneyed roadster every bagman mounts.

Ibid.

Dance and sing, we are eternal;
  Let us still be mad with drinking:
'Tis a madness less infernal
  Than the madness caused by thinking.

Song of Bacchantes and Satyrs.
Stanza 1

Nothing is lost that's wrought with tears:

The music that you made below
Is now the music of the spheres.

A Ballad of Heaven. Stanza 26

I leave the righteous God behind;
I go to worship sinful man.

A Ballad of a Nun. Stanza 16

A vagrant bee twanged like an airy lyre
Of one rich-hearted chord.

The Ordeal

The lowliest men would sooner face
A thousand dreadful deaths, than come
Before their loved ones in disgrace.

A Ballad of a Coward. Stanza 12

Some diplomat no doubt
Will launch a heedless word,
And lurking war leap out.

War-Song

And blood in torrents pour
In vain — always in vain,
For war breeds war again.

Ibid.

The hostess of the sky, the moon.

Afternoon. Stanza 1

Do I believe in Heaven and Hell? I do;
We have them here; the world is nothing else.

Dedication to the Generation
Knocking at the Door

Men should no longer degrade themselves under such appellations as Christian, Mohammedan, Agnostic, Monist, etc. Men are the Universe become conscious: the simplest man should consider himself too great to be called after any name.

Fleet Street and Other Poems.[1]
Foreword [1909]

MARGARET WADE DELAND
[1857–   ]

By one great Heart the Universe is stirred:
  By its strong pulse, stars climb the darkening blue;
  It throbs in each fresh sunset's changing hue,

---

[1] Davidson was never seen alive after he left his home to mail the manuscript of this book to his publisher. Six months later his body was found in the English Channel.

And thrills through low sweet song of
every bird.
Life. Stanza 1

Alas! that men must see
Love, before Death!
Else they content might be
With their short breath.
Love and Death

HENRY BLAKE FULLER
[1857–1929]

The martyrdom involved in a fort-
night's entertainment of anybody
whomsoever.
The Chevalier of Pensieri-Vani.
Chap. 10

GEORGE GISSING
[1857–1903]

It is because nations tend to stupidity and baseness that mankind moves
so slowly; it is because individuals have
a capacity for better things that it
moves at all.
The Private Papers of Henry
Ryecroft. I, 16

It is a joy to go through booksellers'
catalogues, ticking here and there a possible purchase.
Ibid. 17

Greater still is the happiness of unpacking volumes which one has bought
without seeing them. . . . The first
glimpse of bindings when the inmost
protective wrapper has been folded
back! The first scent of books! The
first gleam of a gilded title!
Ibid.

The mind which renounces, once and
for ever, a futile hope, has its compensation in ever-growing calm.
Ibid. 20

Education is a thing of which only
the few are capable; teach as you will
only a small percentage will profit by
your most zealous energy.
Ibid. 22

For the man sound in body and serene of mind there is no such thing as
bad weather; every sky has its beauty,
and storms which whip the blood do but
make it pulse more vigorously.
The Private Papers of Henry
Ryecroft. IV, 1

In the days to come, as through all
time that is past, man will lord it over
his fellow, and earth will be stained red
from veins of young and old. That
sweet and sounding name of *patria* becomes an illusion and a curse.
By the Ionian Sea. XVIII

I wished it were mine to wander endlessly amid the silence of the ancient
world, today and all its sounds forgotten.
Ibid.

BENJAMIN FRANKLIN
KING, JR.
[1857–1894]

Old friends are most too home-like now.
They know your age, and when
You got expelled from school, and lots
Of other things.
Like the New Friends Best

Nothing to do but work,
Nothing to eat but food,
Nothing to wear but clothes
To keep one from going nude.
The Pessimist (The Sum of Life).
Stanza 1

Nowhere to go but out,
Nowhere to come but back.
Ibid. Stanza 4

If I should die to-night [1]
And you should come in deepest grief
and woe —
And say: "Here's that ten dollars that
I owe,"
I might arise in my large white cravat
And say, "What's that?"
If I Should Die. Stanza 1

MARY HANNAH KROUT
[1857–1927]

Those who toil bravely are strongest;
The humble and poor become great;
And so from these brown-handed chil-
dren
Shall grow mighty rulers of state.

[1] See Arabella E. Smith, page 681.

The pen of the author and statesman —
The noble and wise of the land —
The sword, and the chisel, and palette
    Shall be held in the little brown hand.
                Little Brown Hands. Stanza 4

AGNES MARY FRANCES ROBINSON
[1857–   ]

To think the face we love shall ever die,
    And be the indifferent earth, and
        know us not!
To think that one of us shall live to cry
On one long buried in a distant spot!
                Etruscan Tombs. I
Let us forget we ever loved each other
        much,
    Let us forget we ever have to part,
Let us forget that any look or touch
    Once let in either to the other's heart.
                Tuscan Cypress. XII
You hail from Dream-land, Dragon-
        fly?
A stranger hither? So am I,
And (sooth to say) I wonder why
        We either of us came!
                To a Dragon-fly
In the cup of life, 'tis true,
Dwells a draught of bitter dew . . .
Yet no other cup I know
Where such radiant waters glow.
                Epilogue

EDGAR SMITH
[1857–1938]

You may tempt the upper classes
With your villainous demi-tasses,
But Heaven will protect the Working
        Girl.
                Heaven Will Protect the
                Working Girl [1]

FRANK LEBBY STANTON
[1857–1927]

Jest a-wearyin' fer you —
All the time a-feelin' blue;

[1] Sung by Marie Dressler [1873–1934] in
Tillie's Nightmare.

Wishin' fer you — wonderin' when
You'll be comin' home again.
                Wearyin' for You. Stanza 1
Sweetes' li'l' feller —
    Everybody knows;
Dunno what ter call 'im,
    But he mighty lak' a rose!
                Sweetes' Li'l' Feller. Stanza 1
Year ain't been the very best;
Purty hard by trouble pressed;
But the rough way leads to rest —
        Here's hopin'!
                Here's Hopin'. Stanza 1
If you strike a thorn or rose,
    Keep a-goin'!
                Keep a-Goin'. Stanza 1
This world that we're a-livin' in
    Is mighty hard to beat;
You get a thorn with every rose,
    But ain't the roses sweet!
                The World

THORSTEIN VEBLEN
[1857–1929]

With the exception of the instinct of
self-preservation, the propensity for
emulation is probably the strongest and
most alert and persistent of the economic motives proper.
        The Theory of the Leisure Class.
                Chap. 5

The dog commends himself to our
favour by affording play to our propensity for mastery, and as he is also an
item of expense, and commonly serves
no industrial purpose, he holds a well-
assured place in men's regard as a thing
of good repute.
                Ibid. Chap 6

The visible imperfections of the hand-
wrought goods, being honorific, are
accounted marks of superiority in point
of beauty, or serviceability, or both.
Hence has arisen that exaltation of the
defective, of which John Ruskin and
William Morris were such eager spokes-
men in their time. . . . The Kelmscott
Press reduced the matter to an absurdity by issuing books for modern use,
edited with the obsolete spelling,

printed in black-letter, and bound in limp vellum fitted with thongs.

The Theory of the Leisure Class.
Chap. 6

The womanliness of woman's apparel resolves itself into the more effective hindrance to useful exertion offered by the garments peculiar to women.

Ibid. Chap. 7

Priestly vestments show, in accentuated form, all the features that have been shown to be evidence of a servile status and a vicarious life.

Ibid.

The walking-stick serves the purpose of an advertisement that the bearer's hands are employed otherwise than in useful effort, and it therefore has utility as an evidence of leisure.

Ibid. Chap. 10

The sporting man's sense of luck and chance is an inarticulate or inchoate animism . . . it implies the possibility of propitiating, or of deceiving and cajoling, or otherwise disturbing the unfolding of propensities resident in the objects which constitute the apparatus and accessories of any game of skill or chance. There are few sporting men who are not in the habit of wearing charms or talismans.

Ibid. Chap. 11

To meet the requirements of the highest economic efficiency under modern conditions, the world process must habitually be apprehended in terms of quantitative, dispassionate force and sequence.

Ibid. Chap. 12

The adoption of the cap and gown is one of the striking atavistic features of modern college life.

Ibid. Chap. 14

The classics have scarcely lost in absolute value as a voucher of scholastic respectability, since for this purpose it is only necessary that the scholar should be able to put in evidence some learning which is conventionally recognized as evidence of wasted time.

Ibid.

As felicitous an instance of futile classicism as can well be found is the conventional spelling of the English language. English orthography satisfies all the requirements of the canons of reputability under the law of conspicuous waste. It is archaic, cumbrous, and ineffective; its acquisition consumes much time and effort; failure to acquire it is easy of detection.

The Theory of the Leisure Class.
Chap. 14

HENRY WILLARD AUSTIN
[1858–1912]

Genius, that power which dazzles mortal eyes,
Is oft but perseverance in disguise.

Perseverance Conquers All

MALTBIE DAVENPORT
BABCOCK
[1858–1901]

Back of the loaf is the snowy flour,
  And back of the flour the mill,
And back of the mill is the wheat and
    the shower,
  And the sun and the Father's will.

"Give Us this Day Our
Daily Bread"

HENRY A. BARNHART
[1858–1934]

A message from home to-day stating that old Bob, deaf and decrepit, but the family pet and pride and protector for fifteen years, had died, halted interest in all else with me save memory of the past; and while he was only a fox terrier dog, no affair of state nor burst of congressional eloquence, nor dream of future glory attracts my attention.

Congressional Record,
April 29, 1912

EDITH NESBIT
(MRS. HUBERT BLAND)
[1858–1924]

Dear Mother, in whose eyes I see
All that I would and cannot be,
Let thy pure light forever shine,

Though dimly, through this life of
mine.
>   *To Our Lady: For a Picture*
>   *by Giovanni Bellini*

The chestnut's proud, and the lilac's
pretty,
The poplar's gentle and tall,
But the plane tree's kind to the poor
dull city —
I love him best of all!
>   *Child's Song in Spring*

JAMES BUCKHAM
("PAUL PASTNOR")
[1858–1908]

King Hassan, well beloved, was wont
to say
When aught went wrong, or any project failed:
"To-morrow, friends, will be another
day!"
And in that faith he slept and so prevailed.
>   *To-morrow. Stanza 1*

WILLISTON FISH
[1858–   ]

A will is a solemn matter, even with
men whose life is given up to business,
and who are by habit mindful of the
future.
>   *A Last Will* [1]

I, Charles Lounsbury, being of sound
and disposing mind and memory [he
lingered on the word memory], do now
make and publish this my last will and
testament, in order, as justly as I may,
to distribute my interests in the world
among succeeding men.
>   *Ibid.*

I leave to children exclusively, but
only for the life of their childhood, all
and every the dandelions of the fields
and the daisies thereof, with the right
to play among them freely.
>   *Ibid.*

And I devise to children the yellow
shores of creeks and the golden sands

[1] In *Harper's Weekly, Sept. 3, 1898,* and repeated by request of many readers, *Dec. 12,
1908.*

beneath the waters thereof, with the
dragon-flies that skim the surface of
said waters.
>   *A Last Will*

To lovers I devise their imaginary
world, with whatever they may need,
as the stars of the sky, the red, red
roses by the wall, the snow of the hawthorn, the sweet strains of music, or
aught else they may desire to figure to
each other the lastingness and beauty
of their love.
>   *Ibid.*

To those who are no longer children,
or youths, or lovers, I leave, too, the
knowledge of what a rare, rare world
it is.
>   *Ibid.*

SAM WALTER FOSS
[1858–1911]

We are waiting for you there — for you,
the man!
Come up from the jostle as soon as
you can;
Come up from the crowd there, for
you are the man,
The man who comes up from the crowd.
>   *The Man from the Crowd.*
>   *Stanza 4*

Bring me men to match my mountains,[1]
Bring me men to match my plains,
Men with empires in their purpose,
And new eras in their brains.
>   *The Coming American. Stanza 1*

The plain man is the basic clod
From which we grow the demigod;
And in the average man is curled
The hero stuff that rules the world.
>   *In Memoriam. Stanza 2*

Strew gladness on the paths of men —
You will not pass this way again.
>   *I Shall Not Pass This Way Again* [2]

A voice came o'er the waters far:
"Just drop your bucket where you are."
And then they dipped and drank their
fill

[1] A man to match his mountains, not to
creep
Dwarfed and abased below them.
>   WHITTIER: *Among the Hills, Prelude*
[2] See Underwood, page 682.

Of water fresh from mead and hill;
And then they knew they sailed upon
The broad mouth of the Amazon.
Drop Your Bucket Where You
Are. Stanza 1

No financial throe volcanic
Ever yet was known to scare it;
Never yet was any panic
Scared the firm of Grin and Barrett.
The Firm of Grin and Barrett.
Stanza 1

A hundred thousand men were led
By one calf near three centuries dead.
They followed still his crooked way,
And lost one hundred years a day;
For thus such reverence is lent
To well-established precedent.
The Calf-Path

A rodless Walton of the brooks,
A bloodless sportsman, I.[1]
The Bloodless Sportsman

There are plenty of fish still left in the
streams
For the angler who has no rod.
Ibid.

The path that leads to a Loaf of Bread
Winds through the Swamps of Toil,
And the path that leads to a Suit of
Clothes
Goes through a flowerless soil,
And the paths that lead to a Loaf of
Bread
And the Suit of Clothes are hard to
tread.
Paths. Stanza 1

Let me live in my house by the side of
the road
Where the race of men go by;
They are good, they are bad, they are
weak, they are strong,
Wise, foolish — so am I.
Then why should I sit in the scorner's
seat,
Or hurl the cynic's ban?
Let me live in my house by the side of
the road
And be a friend of man.
The House by the Side of the
Road.[2] Stanza 5

On the thirty-second day of the thirteenth month of the eighth day of
the week,
On the twenty-fifth hour and the sixty-
first minute, we'll find all things
that we seek.
The Eighth Day of the Week

I say the very things that make the
greatest Stir
An' the most interestin' things, are
things that didn't occur.[1]
Things That Didn't Occur

He had a startling genius, but somehow it didn't emerge;
Always on the evolution of things
that wouldn't evolve;
Always verging toward some climax,
but he never reached the verge;
Always nearing the solution of some
theme he could not solve.
The Inventor[2]

JOHN TROTWOOD MOORE
[1858–1929]

Only the game fish swims up stream.[3]
The Unafraid

I sing softly to myse'f dat good ole
hymn, sung by Moses an' de profets so
long ergo:
"Baptis', Baptis' is my name,
I'm Baptis' till I die.
I've been baptized in de Baptis' church,
Gwin' ter eat all de Baptis' pie!"
Old Mistis. How the Bishop
Broke the Record

He welcomed to his house beside the way
All comers.
HOMER: *Iliad, Book VI*, translated by
WILLIAM CULLEN BRYANT
[1] What torments of grief you endured
From evils which never arrived.
R. W. EMERSON: *Borrowing*
See Lowell, page 530; Waterman, page
750.
[2] Ef you want to be sick of your life,
Jest come and change places with me a
spell — for I'm an inventor's wife.
MRS. E. T. CORBETT: *The Inventor's*
Wife [1883]
[3] See Grantland Rice, page 865.

---

[1] See R. W. Emerson, page 409.
[2] See Alexander Pope, page 218.
And greatly was he loved, for courteously

THEODORE ROOSEVELT
[1858-1919]

I wish to preach, not the doctrine of ignoble ease,[1] but the doctrine of the strenuous life.

Speech before the Hamilton Club, Chicago [April 10, 1899]

Far better it is to dare mighty things, to win glorious triumphs, even though checkered by failure, than to take rank with those poor spirits who neither enjoy much nor suffer much, because they live in the gray twilight that knows not victory nor defeat.

Ibid.

We must remember not to judge any public servant by any one act, and especially should we beware of attacking the men who are merely the occasions and not the causes of disaster.

Ibid.

I am as strong as a bull moose.

Letter to Mark Hanna, 1900

There is a homely adage which runs, "Speak softly and carry a big stick; you will go far." If the American nation will speak softly and yet build and keep at a pitch of the highest training a thoroughly efficient navy, the Monroe Doctrine will go far.

Speech at Minnesota State Fair [September 2, 1901]

A man who is good enough to shed his blood for his country is good enough to be given a square deal afterward. More than that no man is entitled to, and less than that no man shall have.

Speech at Springfield, Illinois [July 4, 1903]

Men with the muck-rake [2] are often indispensable to the well-being of society, but only if they know when to stop raking the muck.

Address, Laying of the Corner Stone, Office Building of House of Representatives, Washington [April 14, 1906]

[1]   Me . . . dulcis alebat
Parthenope, studiis florentem ignobilis otii (Sweet Parthenope [Naples] nourished me flourishing in the studies of ignoble ease). VIRGIL: *Georgics, Book 4, L. 563.*
[2] See John Bunyan, page 172.

Malefactors of great wealth.

Speech at Provincetown, August 20, 1907

Nature-faker.

Everybody's Magazine, September, 1907

We have room for but one language here, and that is the English language, for we intend to see that the crucible turns our people out as Americans, and not as dwellers in a polyglot boarding house.

Letter read at the All American Festival, New York [January 5, 1919]

The lunatic fringe in all reform movements.

Autobiography. Chap. 7

LANGDON SMITH
[1858-1908]

When you were a tadpole and I was
   a fish,
In the Paleozoic time.

Evolution. Stanza 1 [1895]

And that was a million years ago,
In a time that no man knows;
Yet here to-night in the mellow light,
We sit at Delmonico's.

Ibid. Stanza 11

CLARENCE URMY
[1858-1923]

Old songs are best — how sweet to hear
The strains to home and memory dear!
Old books are best — how tale and
   rhyme
Float with us down the stream of time!

Old Songs Are Best

Not what we have, but what we use;
Not what we see, but what we choose —
These are the things that mar or bless
The sum of human happiness.

The Things that Count. Stanza 1

BOOKER TALIAFERRO WASHINGTON
[1858-1915]

No race can prosper till it learns that there is as much dignity in tilling a field as in writing a poem.

Up From Slavery

SIR WILLIAM WATSON
[1858–1935]

April, April,
Laugh thy girlish laughter;
Then, the moment after,
Weep thy girlish tears.
Song

And though circuitous and obscure
The feet of Nemesis how sure!
Europe at the Play

O let me leave the plains behind,
 And let me leave the vales below!
Into the highlands of the mind,
 Into the mountains let me go.
Shakespeare. Stanza 1

Here are the heights, crest beyond
 crest,
With Himalayan dews impearled;
And I will watch from Everest
 The long heave of the surging world.
Ibid. Stanza 3

All the rapturous heart of things
Throbs through his own.
Shelley's Centenary. Stanza 17

Where is the singer whose large notes
 and clear
 Can heal and arm and plenish and
 sustain?
Lo, one with empty music floods the
 ear,
 And one, the heart refreshing, tires
 the brain.
Wordsworth's Grave. V, Stanza 2

But he preserved from chance control
The fortress of his 'stablisht soul;
In all things sought to see the Whole;
 Brooked no disguise;
And set his heart upon the goal,
 Not on the prize.
In Laleham Churchyard.[1]
Stanza 11

What is so sweet and dear
As a prosperous morn in May,
The confident prime of the day,
And the dauntless youth of the year,
When nothing that asks for bliss,
Asking aright, is denied,
And half of the world a bridegroom is,
And half of the world a bride.
Ode in May. Stanza 2

[1] Matthew Arnold's grave.

He[1] hath fared forth, beyond these
 suns and showers.
Lachrymae Musarum. Stanza 2

The seasons change, the winds they
 shift and veer;
The grass of yesteryear
Is dead; the birds depart, the groves
 decay:
Empires dissolve and peoples disap-
 pear:
Song passes not away.
Captains and conquerors leave a little
 dust,
And kings a dubious legend of their
 reign;
The swords of Caesars, they are less
 than rust:
The poet doth remain.
Ibid. Stanza 9

Master who crown'st our immelodious
 days
With flower of perfect speech.
Ibid.

The Poet gathers fruit from every tree,
Yea, grapes from thorns, and figs from
 thistles, he.
Epigram

Love, like a bird, hath perch'd upon a
 spray
 For thee and me to hearken what he
 sings.
Contented, he forgets to fly away;
 But hush! . . . remind not Eros of
 his wings.
Epigram

Too long the gulf betwixt
This man and that man fixt
 Yawns yet unspanned.
Too long, that some may rest,
Tired millions toil unblessed.
A New National Anthem.
Stanza 3

His delicate ears and superfine long
 nose,
With that last triumph, his distin-
 guished tail,
In their collective glory spoke his race
The flower of Collie aristocracy.
A Study in Contrasts. Part I

His friends he loved. His fellest earthly
 foes —

[1] Tennyson.

Cats — I believe he did but feign to
  hate.
My hand will miss the insinuated nose,
  Mine eyes the tail that wagg'd con-
  tempt at Fate.
                              An Epitaph
      I count him wise
Who loves so well Man's noble mem-
  ories
He needs must love Man's nobler hopes
  yet more.
                              To a Friend
Momentous to himself, as I to me,
  Hath each man been that ever
  woman bore;
Once, in a lightning-flash of sympathy,
  I *felt* this truth, an instant, and no
  more.
                              Epigram
Say what thou wilt, the young are
  happy never.
Give me bless'd Age, beyond the fire
  and fever, —
Past the delight that shatters, hope
  that stings,
And eager flutt'ring of life's ignorant
  wings.
                              Epigram
Too avid of earth's bliss, he was of
  those
  Whom Delight flies because they
  give her chase.
Only the odour of her wild hair blows
  Back in their faces hungering for her
  face.
                    Byron the Voluptuary
Strange the world about me lies,
  Never yet familiar grown —
Still disturbs me with surprise,
  Haunts me like a face half known.
                World-Strangeness. Stanza 1
Five-and-thirty black slaves,
  Half-a-hundred white,
All their duty but to sing
  For their Queen's delight.
                    The Key-board. Stanza 1
Hate and mistrust are the children of
  blindness, —
  Could we but see one another, 'twere
  well!
Knowledge is sympathy, charity, kind-
  ness,
  Ignorance only is maker of hell.

Could we but gaze for an hour, for a
  minute,
  Deep in each other's unfaltering
  eyes,
Love were begun — for that look
  would begin it —
  Born in the flash of a mighty sur-
  prise.
                    England to Ireland. Stanza 3
For still the ancient riddles mar
Our joy in man, in leaf, in star.
The Whence and Whither give no rest,
The Wherefore is a hopeless quest.
                    An Epistle to N. A. Stanza 4
And whether, stepping forth, my soul
  shall see
  New prospects, or fall sheer — a
  blinded thing!
There is, O grave, thy hourly victory,
  And there, O death, thy sting.
                The Great Misgiving. Stanza 5
To dress, to call, to dine, to break
  No canon of the social code,
The little laws that lacqueys make,
  The futile decalogue of Mode, —
How many a soul for these things lives,
  With pious passion, grave intent!
While Nature careless-handed gives
  The things that are more excellent.
                    *The Things that Are More
                    Excellent. Stanza 6*
The sense of greatness keeps a nation
  great.
                    Our Eastern Treasure
Yet do the songsmiths
Quit not their forges;
Still on life's anvil
  Forge they the rhyme.
                *England My Mother. Part I,
                              Stanza 5*
Lo, with the ancient
Roots of man's nature,
Twines the eternal
  Passion of song.
                    Ibid. Part II, Stanza 1
Ever Love fans it,
Ever Life feeds it,
Time cannot age it,
  Death cannot slay.
                              Ibid. Stanza 2
Trees in their blooming,
Tides in their flowing,

Stars in their circling,
  Tremble with song.
      England My Mother. Part II,
            Stanza 5

She is not old, she is not young,
The woman with the serpent's tongue.
    The Woman with the Serpent's
            Tongue [1]

Who half makes love to you to-day,
To-morrow gives her guest away.
                    Ibid.

KATHARINE LEE BATES
[1859–1929]

O beautiful for patriot dream
  That sees beyond the years
Thine alabaster cities gleam
  Undimmed by human tears!
America! America!
God shed His grace on thee,
And crown thy good with brotherhood
From sea to shining sea!
    America the Beautiful. Stanza 4

Because the years are few, I must be
    glad;
  Because the silence is so near, I sing;
'Twere ill to quit an inn where I have
    had
  Such bounteous fare nor pay my
    reckoning.
            The Debt. Stanza 1

WILLIAM HERBERT
CARRUTH
[1859–1924]

Some call it Evolution,
  And others call it God.
    Each in His Own Tongue. Stanza 1

A haze on the far horizon,
  The infinite, tender sky,
The ripe, rich tint of the cornfields,
  And the wild geese sailing high —
And all over upland and lowland
  The charm of the golden-rod,

Some of us call it Autumn,
  And others call it God.[1]
    Each in His Own Tongue. Stanza 2

HELEN GRAY CONE
[1859–1934]

Pickett's Virginians were passing
    through;
  Supple as steel and brown as leather,
Rusty and dusty of hat and shoe,
  Wonted to hunger and war and
    weather;
Peerless, fearless, an army's flower!
Sterner soldiers the world saw never,
Marching lightly, that summer hour,
  To death and failure and fame for-
    ever.[2]
        Greencastle Jenny. Stanza 4

Dash the bomb on the dome of
    Paul's, —
Deem ye the fame of the Admiral falls?
Pry the stone from the chancel floor, —
Dream ye that Shakespeare shall live
    no more?
Where is the giant shot that kills
Wordsworth walking the old green
    hills?
        A Chant of Love for England

SIR ARTHUR CONAN DOYLE
[1859–1930]

Come, Watson, come! The game is
afoot.
    The Adventure of the Abbey Grange
To Sherlock Holmes she is always *the*
woman.
            A Scandal in Bohemia
I [Sherlock Holmes] abhor the dull
routine of existence. I crave for mental exaltation.
        The Sign of The Four
Elementary, my dear Watson.
            The Crooked Man
It is a great thing to start life with
a small number of really good books
which are your very own.
    Through the Magic Door [*1908*]
No British autobiography has ever
been frank, and consequently no Brit-

---

[1] Was he a "guest" — who dares to wrong
His hostess in so foul a song?
O poet with the coward's tongue!
  RICHARD LEGALLIENNE: *The Poet with*
        a Coward's Tongue

[1] See Browning, page 491.
[2] See Will Henry Thompson, page 690.

ish autobiography has ever been good. Of all forms of literature it is the one least adapted to the national genius. You could not imagine a British Rousseau, still less a British Benvenuto Cellini.

Through the Magic Door [*1908*]

Several incidents in my life have convinced me of spiritual interposition — of the promptings of some beneficent force outside ourselves, which tries to help us where it can.

Ibid.

The bow was made in England,
Of true wood, of yew wood.
The Song of the Bow. Stanza 1

My life is gliding downward, it speeds swifter to the day
When it shoots the last dark canyon to the Plains of Faraway;
But while its streams are running through the years that are to be,
The mighty voice of Canada will ever call to me.
The Athabasca Trail

The Grenadiers of Austria are proper men and tall;
The Grenadiers of Austria have scaled the city wall;
They have marched from far away
Ere the dawning of the day,
And the morning saw them masters of Cremona.
Cremona. Stanza 1

One favor we entreat,
We were called a little early, and our toilet's not complete.
We've no quarrel with the shirt,
But the breeches wouldn't hurt,
For the evening air is chilly in Cremona.[1]
Ibid. Stanza 20

[1] In the surprise attack on Cremona, Feb. 1, 1702, the Irish Brigade rushed out to resist the invaders, without waiting to dress.

Through the naked battalions the cuirassiers
go; —
But the man, not the dress, makes the soldier,
I trow.
THOMAS OSBORNE DAVIS [1814–1845]:
The Surprise of Cremona, St. 6

ARTHUR WENTWORTH HAMILTON EATON
[1859–1937]

O give me a place in the garden of song,
I would linger and labor there all summer long,
There are corners to care for, stray beds to make bloom,
I ask not for wages, I only seek room
In the garden of song.
The Garden of Song. Stanza 1

Pity the man who has no gift of speech
For those compelling thoughts, that peace and pain,
That press unsought from the remoter reach
Of mind and soul to the near heart and brain.
Compelling Thoughts. Stanza 1

His heart was breaking, breaking,
'Neath loads of care and wrong;
Who blames the man for taking
What life denied so long?
The Suicide.[1] *Stanza 1*

HAVELOCK ELLIS
[1859–   ]

To be a leader of men one must turn one's back on men.
Introduction to J. K. HUYSMANS' *Against the Grain*

The text of the Bible is but a feeble symbol of the Revelation held in the text of Men and Women.
Impressions and Comments

God is an Unutterable Sigh in the Human Heart, said the old German mystic.
Ibid.

[1] There is a justice according to which we may deprive a man of life, but none that permits us to deprive him of death: this is merely cruelty. — NIETZSCHE: *Human, All Too Human, Prevention of Suicide*

When he went blundering back to God,
His songs half written, his work half done,
Who knows what paths his bruised feet trod,
What hills of peace or pain he won?
CHARLES HANSON TOWNE: *Of One Self-Slain, St. 1*

See Charlotte P. S. Gilman, page 754.

Without an element of the obscene there can be no true and deep aesthetic or moral conception of life. . . . It is only the great men who are truly obscene. If they had not dared to be obscene they could never have dared to be great.

Impressions and Comments

The omnipresent process of sex, as it is woven into the whole texture of our man's or woman's body, is the pattern of all the process of our life.

The New Spirit

The Normans who came over to England with William the Conqueror and constituted the proud English nobility were simply a miscellaneous set of adventurers, professional fighting men, of unknown, and no doubt for the most part undistinguished, lineage. William the Conqueror himself was the son of a woman of the people.

The Task of Social Hygiene.
Introduction

If men and women are to understand each other, to enter into each other's nature with mutual sympathy, and to become capable of genuine comradeship, the foundation must be laid in youth.

Ibid. Chap. 1

The larger our great cities grow, the more irresistible becomes the attraction which they exert on the children of the country, who are fascinated by them, as the birds are fascinated by the lighthouse or the moths by the candle.[1]

Ibid. Chap. 5

An urban life saps that calm and stolid strength which is necessary for all great effort and stress, physical or intellectual.

Ibid.

Prosperity and civilization are far from being synonymous terms. The

[1] It is well known that a number of eminent men have been born in London; but, in the course of a somewhat elaborate study of the origins of British men of genius, I have not been able to find that any were genuinely Londoners by descent. — *A Study of British Genius*

working community that is suddenly glutted by an afflux of work and wages is in exactly the same position as the savage who is suddenly enabled to fill himself with a rich mass of decaying blubber. It is prosperity, it is not civilization.

The Task of Social Hygiene.
Chap. 5

There are few among us who have not suffered from too early familiarity with the Bible and the conceptions of religion.

Ibid. Chap. 7

The German feels nothing of that sensitive jealousy with which the French seek to guard private life and the rights of the individual.

Ibid. Chap. 9

The Englishman's reverence for the individual's rights goes beyond the Frenchman's, for in France there is a tendency to subordinate the individual to the family, and in England the interests of the individual predominate.

Ibid.

Holland is one of the traditional lands of freedom; it was the home of independent intellect, of free religion, of autonomous morals, when every other country in Europe was closed to these manifestations of the spirit.

Ibid.

When Charles V retired in weariness from the greatest throne in the world to the solitude of the monastery at Yuste, he occupied his leisure for some weeks in trying to regulate two clocks. It proved very difficult. One day, it is recorded, he turned to his assistant and said: "To think that I attempted to force the reason and conscience of thousands of men into one mould, and I cannot make two clocks agree!"

Ibid.

The extension of trade is a matter of tariffs rather than of war, and in any case the trade of a country with its own acquisitions by conquest is a comparatively insignificant portion of its total trade.

Ibid. Chap. 10

So far as business and money are concerned, a country gains nothing by a successful war, even though that war involves the acquisition of immense new provinces.

> *The Task of Social Hygiene.*
> *Chap. 10*

Conquest brings self-conceit and intolerance, the reckless inflation and dissipation of energies. Defeat brings prudence and concentration; it ennobles and fortifies.

> *Ibid.*

A nation's art-products and its scientific activities are not mere national property; they are international possessions, for the joy and service of the whole world. The nations hold them in trust for humanity.

> *Ibid.*

There has never been any country at every moment so virtuous and so wise that it has not sometimes needed to be saved from itself.

> *Ibid.*

Those persons who are burning to display heroism may rest assured that the course of social evolution will offer them every opportunity.

> *Ibid.*

The immense value of becoming acquainted with a foreign language is that we are thereby led into a new world of tradition and thought and feeling.

> *Ibid. Chap. 11*

While some would claim for the English the supreme poetic literature, there can be no doubt that the French own the supreme prose literature of modern Europe.

> *Ibid.*

The family only represents one aspect, however important an aspect, of a human being's functions and activities. . . . A life is beautiful and ideal, or the reverse, only when we have taken into our consideration the social as well as the family relationship.

> *Little Essays of Love and Virtue.*
> *Chap. 1*

One can know nothing of giving aught that is worthy to give unless one also knows how to take.

> *Little Essays of Love and Virtue.*
> *Chap. 1*

That indeed were a world fit to perish, wherein the moralist had set up the ignoble maxim: Safety first.

> *Ibid. Chap. 2*

The by-product is sometimes more valuable than the product.

> *Ibid. Chap. 3*

It has taken God — or Nature, if we will — unknown millions of years of painful struggle to evolve Man, and to raise the human species above that helpless bondage to reproduction which marks the lower animals.

> *Ibid.*

All civilization has from time to time become a thin crust over a volcano of revolution.

> *Ibid. Chap. 7*

The greatest task before civilization at present is to make machines what they ought to be, the slaves, instead of the masters of men.

> *Ibid.*

The art of dancing stands at the source of all the arts that express themselves first in the human person. The art of building, or architecture, is the beginning of all the arts that lie outside the person; and in the end they unite.

> *The Dance of Life. Chap. 2*

Dancing is the loftiest, the most moving, the most beautiful of the arts, because it is no mere translation or abstraction from life; it is life itself.

> *Ibid.*

The place where optimism most flourishes is the lunatic asylum.

> *Ibid. Chap. 3*

He who would walk sanely amid the opposing perils in the path of life always needs a little optimism; he also needs a little pessimism.

> *Ibid.*

Thinking in its lower grades is comparable to paper money, and in its higher forms it is a kind of poetry.

> *Ibid.*

In philosophy, it is not the attainment of the goal that matters, it is the things that are met with by the way.

The Dance of Life. Chap. 2

Every man of genius sees the world at a different angle from his fellows, and there is his tragedy.

Ibid.

The mathematician has reached the highest rung on the ladder of human thought.

Ibid.

The verse of every young poet, however original he may afterwards grow, usually has plainly written across it the rhythmic signature of some great master. . . . The same thing happens with prose, but the rhythm of the signature is less easy to hear.

Ibid. Chap. 4

The most obviously beautiful things in the world of Nature are birds and flowers and the stones we call precious.

Ibid.

All the conventional rules of the construction of speech may be put aside if a writer is thereby enabled to follow more closely and lucidly the form and process of his thought.

Ibid.

If at some period in the course of civilization we seriously find that our science and our religion are antagonistic, then there must be something wrong either with our science or with our religion.

Ibid. Chap. 5

A man must not swallow more beliefs than he can digest.

Ibid.

The Promised Land always lies on the other side of a wilderness.

Ibid.

What we call "morals" is simply blind obedience to words of command.

Ibid. Chap. 6

There is no occasion for any one who is told that he has written a "moral" book to be unduly elated, or when he is told that his book is "immoral" to be unduly cast down. The significance of these adjectives is strictly limited. Neither the one nor the other can have

more than the faintest effect on the march of the great compact majority of the social army.

The Dance of Life. Chap. 6

The world's greatest thinkers have often been amateurs; for high thinking is the outcome of fine and independent living, and for that a professorial chair offers no special opportunities.

Ibid.

For the artist life is always a discipline, and no discipline can be without pain. That is so even of dancing, which of all the arts is most associated in the popular mind with pleasure. To learn to dance is the most austere of disciplines.

Ibid.

The methods of statistics are so variable and uncertain, so apt to be influenced by circumstance, that it is never possible to be sure that one is operating with figures of equal weight.

Ibid. Chap. 7

The prevalence of suicide, without doubt, is a test of height in civilization; it means that the population is winding up its nervous and intellectual system to the utmost point of tension and that sometimes it snaps.[1]

Ibid.

The more rapidly a civilization progresses, the sooner it dies for another to arise in its place.

Ibid.

The sun and the moon and the stars would have disappeared long ago — as even their infinitely more numerous analogues on the earth beneath are likely to disappear — had they happened to be within the reach of predatory human hands.

Ibid.

Had there been a Lunatic Asylum in the suburbs of Jerusalem, Jesus Christ would infallibly have been shut up in it at the outset of his public career. That interview with Satan on a pinnacle of the Temple would alone have damned him, and everything that happened after could but have confirmed

[1] See Eaton, page 738.

the diagnosis. The whole religious complexion of the modern world is due to the absence from Jerusalem of a Lunatic Asylum.

*Impressions and Comments.
Series III, Page 130*

KENNETH GRAHAME
[1859–1932]

As a rule, indeed, grown-up people are fairly correct on matters of fact; it is in the higher gift of imagination that they are so sadly to seek.

*The Golden Age. The Finding of
the Princess*

A man can stand very much in the cause of love: poverty, aunts, rivals, barriers of every sort, — all these only serve to fan the flame. But personal ridicule is a shaft that reaches the very vitals.

Ibid. "Young Adam Cupid"

The year was in its yellowing time, and the face of Nature a study in old gold.

Ibid. A Harvesting

Those who painfully and with bleeding feet have scaled the crags of mastery over musical instruments have yet their loss in this, — that the wild joy of strumming has become a vanished sense.

Ibid.

I began to like this man. He answered your questions briefly and to the point, and never tried to be funny. I felt I could be confidential with him.

Ibid. The Roman Road

Monkeys, who very sensibly refrain from speech, lest they should be set to earn their livings.

Ibid. "Lusisti Satis"

Grown-up people really ought to be more careful. Among themselves it may seem but a small thing to give their word and take back their word.

The Magic Ring

There is nothing — absolutely nothing — half so much worth doing as simply messing about in boats, . . . or

with boats. . . . In or out of 'em, it doesn't matter.

The Wind in the Willows. Chap. 1

Villagers all, this frosty tide,
Let your doors swing open wide,
Though wind may follow, and snow beside,
Yet draw us in by your fire to bide;
Joy shall be yours in the morning!

Ibid. Chap. 5 (Carol)

ALFRED EDWARD
HOUSMAN
[1859–1936]

Loveliest of trees, the cherry now
Is hung with bloom along the bough.

A Shropshire Lad. II

Now, of my threescore years and ten,
Twenty will not come again,
And take from seventy springs a score,
It only leaves me fifty more.

Ibid.

Clay lies still, but blood's a rover;
    Breath's a ware that will not keep.
Up, lad: when the journey's over
    There'll be time enough to sleep.

Ibid. IV, Reveille

The sun moves always west;
The road one treads to labour
    Will lead one home to rest,
    And that will be the best.

Ibid. VII

If the heats of hate and lust
    In the house of flesh are strong,
Let me mind the house of dust
    Where my sojourn shall be long.

Ibid. XII

When I was one-and-twenty
    I heard a wise man say,
"Give crowns and pounds and guineas
    But not your heart away;
Give pearls away and rubies
    But keep your fancy free."
But I was one-and-twenty,
    No use to talk to me.

Ibid. XIII

"The heart out of the bosom
    Was never given in vain;
'Tis paid with sighs a-plenty
    And sold for endless rue."

And I am two-and-twenty,
  And Oh, 'tis true, 'tis true.
            A Shropshire Lad. XIII

His folly has not fellow
  Beneath the blue of day
That gives to man or woman
  His heart and soul away.
            Ibid. XIV

To-day, the road all runners come,
Shoulder-high, we bring you home,
And set you at your threshold down,
Townsman of a stiller town.
        *Ibid. XIX, To an Athlete
                    Dying Young*

And silence sounds no worse than
    cheers
After earth has stopped the ears.
            Ibid.

That is the land of lost content,
  I see it shining plain,
The happy highways where I went
  And cannot come again.
            Ibid. XL

Oh, 'tis jesting, dancing, drinking
  Spins the heavy world around.
If young hearts were not so clever,
Oh, they would be young for ever:
Think no more; 'tis only thinking
  Lays lads underground.
            Ibid. XLIX

With rue my heart is laden
  For golden friends I had,
For many a rose-lipt maiden
  And many a lightfoot lad.
            Ibid. LIV

By brooks too broad for leaping
  The lightfoot boys are laid.
            Ibid.

And cowards' funerals, when they
    come,
Are not wept so well at home,
Therefore, though the best is bad,
Stand and do the best, my lad.
        Ibid. LVI, The Day of Battle

Why, if 'tis dancing you would be,
There's brisker pipes than poetry.
            Ibid. LXII

Oh many a peer of England brews
Livelier liquor than the Muse,
And malt does more than Milton can
To justify God's ways to man.

Ale, man, ale's the stuff to drink
For fellows whom it hurts to think.
            A Shropshire Lad. LXII

Oh, I have been to Ludlow fair
And left my necktie God knows where,
And carried half way home, or near,
Pints and quarts of Ludlow beer.
            Ibid.

Luck's a chance, but trouble's sure,
I'd face it as a wise man would,
And train for ill and not for good.
            Ibid.

Mithridates, he died old.
            Ibid.

We'll to the woods no more,
The laurels all are cut,[1]
The bowers are bare of bay
That once the Muses wore.
            Last Poems. Foreword

The troubles of our proud and angry
    dust
  Are from eternity, and shall not fail.
Bear them we can, and if we can we
    must.
  Shoulder the sky, my lad, and drink
    your ale.
            Ibid. IX

Could man be drunk for ever
  With liquor, love, or fights,
Lief should I rouse at morning
  And lief lie down of nights.
            Ibid. X

The laws of God, the laws of man,
He may keep that will and can;
Not I: let God and man decree
Laws for themselves and not for me.
            Ibid. XII

And how am I to face the odds
Of man's bedevilment and God's?
I, a stranger and afraid
In a world I never made.
            Ibid.

And then the clock collected in the
    tower
  Its strength, and struck.
        Ibid. XV, Eight O'Clock

These, in the day when heaven was
    falling,

----

[1] Nous n'irons plus au bois, les lauriers sont
coupés (We'll go no longer to the woods, the
laurel trees are clipped).
  Théodore de Banville [1823–1891], based
on an old French folksong, Tiersot collection

The hour when earth's foundations
fled,
Followed their mercenary calling
And took their wages and are dead.
*Last Poems. XXXVII, Epitaph
on an Army of Mercenaries* [1]

Oh stay with company and mirth
And daylight and the air;
Too full already is the grave
Of fellows that were good and brave
And died because they were.
Ibid. XXXVIII

They say my verse is sad: no wonder;
Its narrow measure spans
Tears of eternity, and sorrow,
Not mine, but man's.
More Poems [*1936*]

The thoughts of others
Were light and fleeting,
Of lovers' meeting
Or luck or fame;
Mine were of trouble
And mine were steady,
So I was ready
When trouble came.
Ibid. VI

The rainy Pleiads wester,
Orion plunges prone,
And midnight strikes and hastens,
And I lie down alone.
Ibid. XI

Oh, the pearl seas are yonder,
The gold and amber shore;
Shires where the girls are fonder,
Towns where the pots hold more.
Ibid. XXXIII

Silent hills indenting
The orange band of eve.
Ibid.

We now to peace and darkness
And earth and thee restore
Thy creature that thou madest
And wilt cast forth no more.
Ibid. XLVII, For My Funeral

Good night. Ensured release,
Imperishable peace,
Have these for yours. [2]
While sky and sea and land

And earth's foundations stand
And heaven endures.
More Poems [*1936*]
XLVIII, Alta Quies

I was brought up in the Church of
England and in the High Church party,
which is much the best religion I have
ever come across. But Lemprière's
"Classical Dictionary," read when I
was eight, made me prefer paganism
to Christianity; I abandoned Christianity at thirteen, and became an
atheist at twenty-one.
*Autobiographical note written
for a French translation of his
poems*

I am not a pessimist but a pejorist
(as George Eliot said she was not an
optimist but a meliorist); and that
philosophy is founded on my observation of the world, not on anything so
trivial and irrelevant as personal history. Secondly, I did not begin to write
poetry in earnest until the really emotional part of my life was over; and
my poetry, so far as I could make out,
sprang chiefly from physical causes,
such as a relaxed sore throat during
my most prolific period, the first five
months of 1895.
Ibid.

Good literature continually read for
pleasure must, let us hope, do some
good to the reader: must quicken his
perception though dull, and sharpen
his discrimination though blunt, and
mellow the rawness of his personal opinions.
The Name and Nature of Poetry [1]

Poems very seldom consist of poetry
and nothing else; and pleasure can be
derived also from their other ingredients.
Ibid.

Good religious poetry, whether in
Keble or Dante or Job, is likely to be
most justly appreciated and most dis-
criminatingly relished by the undevout.
Ibid.

---

[1] To the British who made the retreat from
Mons.
[2] These three lines are on a tablet over
Housman's grave in the parish church at
Ludlow (Shropshire).

[1] The Leslie Stephen Lecture, delivered at
Cambridge University, May 9, 1933.

Even when poetry has a meaning, as it usually has, it may be inadvisable to draw it out. . . . Perfect understanding will sometimes almost extinguish pleasure.

The Name and Nature of Poetry

Experience has taught me, when I am shaving of a morning, to keep watch over my thoughts, because, if a line of poetry strays into my memory, my skin bristles so that the razor ceases to act. . . . The seat of this sensation is the pit of the stomach.

Ibid.

I have seldom written poetry unless I was rather out of health, and the experience, though pleasurable, was generally agitating and exhausting.

Ibid.

I can no longer expect to be revisited by the continuous excitement under which in the early months of 1895 I wrote the greater part of my other book [*A Shropshire Lad*].

Last Poems, Preface [*1922*]

ELBERT HUBBARD
[1859–1915]

It is not book learning young men need, nor instruction about this and that, but a stiffening of the vertebrae which will cause them to be loyal to a trust, to act promptly, concentrate their energies, do a thing — "carry a message to Garcia."[1]

A Message to Garcia[2]

The man who is anybody and who does anything is surely going to be criticized, vilified, and misunderstood. This is a part of the penalty for greatness, and every great man understands it; and understands, too, that it is no proof of greatness. The final proof of greatness lies in being able to endure contumely without resentment.

Get Out or Get in Line

If you work for a man, in heaven's name work for him! If he pays you wages that supply you your bread and butter, work for him — speak well of him, think well of him, stand by him and stand by the institution he represents.

Ibid.

JEROME KLAPKA JEROME
[1859–1927]

Let your boat of life be light, packed with only what you need — a homely home and simple pleasures, one or two friends, worth the name, some one to love and some one to love you,[1] a cat, a dog, and a pipe or two, enough to eat and enough to wear, and a little more than enough to drink; for thirst is a dangerous thing.

Three Men in a Boat. Chap. 3

Fox-terriers are born with about four times as much original sin in them as other dogs.

Ibid. Chap. 13

They [bagpipes] appear to be a trying instrument to perform upon. You have to get enough breath for the whole tune before you start.

Ibid. Chap. 14

It is in the circumstantial detail, the embellishing touches of probability, the general air of scrupulous — almost of pedantic — veracity, that the experienced angler is seen.

Ibid. Chap. 17

"Nothing, so it seems to me," said the stranger, "is more beautiful than the love that has weathered the storms of life. . . . The love of the young for the young, that is the beginning of life. But the love of the old for the old, that is the beginning of—of things longer."

*The Passing of the Third Floor
Back*

---

[1] After the declaration of the Spanish-American War, Andrew Summers Rowan, then Lieutenant, United States Bureau of Military Intelligence, was sent to communicate with General Calixto Garcia. He landed in an open boat near Turquino Peak, April 24, 1898, executed the mission, and brought back information regarding the insurgent army.

[2] In *The Philistine, March, 1900.*

[1] Find someone to love . . . and, oh, someone to love you. — SACHA GUITRY: *Deburau,* translated by H. GRANVILLE BARKER

There is a certain satisfaction in feeling you are bearing with heroic resignation the irritating folly of others.
The Passing of the Third Floor Back

Leave-takings are but wasted sadness. Let me pass out quietly.
Ibid.

WILLIAM JAMES LAMPTON
[1859–1917]

Same old slippers,
  Same old rice,
Same old glimpse of
  Paradise.
June Weddings. Stanza 10

Where the corn is full of kernels
And the colonels full of corn.
Kentucky

ALBERT EDWARD LANCASTER
[*Floruit* 1890]

An "unelected infant" sighed out its
  little breath,
And wandered through the darkness
  along the shores of death,
Until the gates of heaven, a-gleam with
  pearl, it spied.
The Unelected Infant. Stanza 1

"Who are you, thus to hallow my unelected brow?"

"Dear child, my name was Calvin, —
  but I see things better now."
Ibid. Stanza 2

EDWIN GORDON LAWRENCE
[1859–   ]

Take these two messengers
With you o'er land or seas
To close and ope the doors:
"Thank you" and "If you please."[1]
Two Messengers. Stanza 1

[1] Hearts, like doors, will ope with ease
  To very, very little keys;
  And don't forget that two of these
  Are "I thank you" and "If you please."
    Nursery Rhyme

CHARLES FLETCHER LUMMIS
[1859–1928]

I am bigger than anything that can happen to me. All these things, sorrow, misfortune, and suffering, are outside my door. I am in the house and I have the key.
Epigram

My cigarette! The amulet
  That charms afar unrest and sorrow,
The magic wand that, far beyond
  To-day, can conjure up to-morrow.
My Cigarette. Stanza 1

ERNEST RHYS
[1859–   ]

Wales England wed; so I was bred.
  'Twas merry London gave me
    breath.
I dreamt of love, and fame: I strove.
But Ireland taught me love was best.
And Irish eyes, and London cries, and
  streams of Wales may tell the rest.
What more than these I asked of Life
  I am content to have from Death.
An Autobiography

WALLACE RICE
[1859–   ]

Ebbs and flows the muddy Pei-Ho by
  the Gulf of Pechili,
  Idly floats beside the stream the
    dragon-flag;
Past the batteries of China, looking
  westward still you see
  Lazy junks along the lazy river lag.
Let the long, long years drip slowly
  on that lost and ancient land,
  Ever dear one scene to hearts of gal-
    lant men;
There's a hand-clasp and a heart-throb,
  there's a word we understand:
  Blood is thicker, sir, than water, now
    as then.
"Blood Is Thicker Than Water."[1]
Stanza 9

[1] See Scott, page 310.
  In 1857, Commodore Josiah Tatnall [1795–1871] went to the rescue of an English ship in trouble in the Pei-Ho River, China,

NORA ARCHIBALD SMITH
[1859–1934]

They'd knock on a tree and would timidly say
To the Spirit who might be within
there that day:
"Fairy fair, Fairy fair, wish thou me
well;
'Gainst evil witcheries weave me a
spell!"
>   *Knocking on Wood. Stanza 3*

An e'en to this day is the practice made
good
When, to ward off disaster, we knock
upon wood.
>   *Ibid. Stanza 4*

SIR CECIL ARTHUR
SPRING-RICE
[1859–1918]

I vow to thee, my country — all earthly
things above —
Entire and whole and perfect, the service of my love.
The love that asks no questions; the
love that stands the test,
That lays upon the altar the dearest
and the best;
The love that never falters, the love
that pays the price,
The love that makes undaunted the
final sacrifice.
>   *I Vow to Thee, My Country* [1]

And there's another country, I've heard
of long ago —
Most dear to them that love her, most
great to them that know —
We may not count her armies; we may
not see her King;
Her fortress is a faithful heart, her
pride is suffering —
And soul by soul and silently her shining bounds increase,
And her ways are ways of gentleness,
and all her paths are peace.
>   *Ibid.*

----

while China was at war with the English and
French.

[1] Written Jan. 12, 1918, on his last night as
British Ambassador in Washington.

CHARLES E. STANTON [1]
[1859–1933]

America has joined forces with the
Allied Powers, and what we have of
blood and treasure are yours. Therefore it is that with loving pride we
drape the colors in tribute of respect
to this citizen of your great republic.
And here and now in the presence of
the illustrious dead we pledge our
hearts and our honor in carrying this
war to a successful issue. Lafayette,
we are here.
>   *Address at the Tomb of Lafayette,*
>   *Picpus Cemetery, Paris [July 4,*
>   *1917]*

JAMES KENNETH STEPHEN
[1859–1892]

Searching an infinite Where,
Probing a bottomless When,
   Dreamfully wandering,
   Ceaselessly pondering,
What is the Wherefore of men.
>   *Lapsus Calami. The Philosopher*
>   *and the Philanthropist, Stanza 1*

If all the harm that women have done
Were put in a bundle and rolled into
one,
   Earth would not hold it,
   The sky could not enfold it,
It could not be lighted nor warmed by
the sun.
>   *Ibid. A Thought, Stanza 1*

An old half-witted sheep
Which bleats articulate monotony,
And indicates that two and one are
three.
>   *Ibid. Sonnet (Parody of Words-*
>   *worth's Two Voices)*

Of sentences that stir my bile,
   Of phrases I detest,
There's one beyond all others vile:
"He did it for the best."
>   *Ibid. The Malefactor's Plea,*
>   *Stanza 1*

----

[1] Nephew of Edwin M. Stanton, Secretary
of War in President Lincoln's Cabinet. He
was chief disbursing officer of the American
Expeditionary Forces in France, and was
deputed by General John J. Pershing to speak
on behalf of the A. E. F. on this occasion.

No cat so sweet a mistress owned;
No mistress owned so sweet a cat.
Lapsus Calami. Elegy on
De Marsay, Stanza 9

Once there was a famous nation
  With a long and glorious past:
Very splendid was its station,
  And its territory vast.
A Political Allegory

To the nation now occurred an
  Opportunity of saying
What they thought about the burden
  Which the government was laying
On their shoulders: and they said it
  In uncompromising terms.
Ibid.

But the nation — mark the moral,
  For its value is untold —
During each successive quarrel
  Grew and prospered as of old.
Ibid.

FRANCIS THOMPSON
[1859–1907]

The fairest things have fleetest end,
  Their scent survives their close:
But the rose's scent is bitterness
  To him that loved the rose.
Daisy. Stanza 10

She went her unremembering way,
  She went and left in me
The pang of all the partings gone,
  And partings yet to be.
Ibid. Stanza 12

Nothing begins, and nothing ends,
  That is not paid with moan;
For we are born in other's pain,
  And perish in our own.
Ibid. Stanza 15

Look for me in the nurseries of
Heaven.[1]
To My Godchild

The innocent moon, that nothing does
  but shine,
Moves all the labouring surges of the
  world.
Sister Songs. Part II

We speak a lesson taught we know not
how,

[1] This line is inscribed on Thompson's tombstone in Kensal Green.

And what it is that from us flows
The hearer better than the utterer
  knows.
Sister Songs. Part II

O Captain of the wars, whence won Ye
  so great scars?
In what fight did Ye smite, and what
  manner was the foe?
Was it on a day of rout they compassed
  Thee about,
Or gat Ye these adornings when Ye
  wrought their overthrow?
The Veteran of Heaven. Stanza 1

I fear to love thee, Sweet, because
Love's the ambassador of loss.
To Olivia

Little Jesus, wast Thou shy
Once, and just so small as I?
And what did it feel like to be
Out of Heaven, and just like me?
Little Jesus

I fled Him, down the nights and down
  the days;
  I fled Him, down the arches of the
  years;
I fled Him, down the labyrinthine ways
  Of my own mind; and in the mist
  of tears
I hid from Him, and under running
  laughter.
The Hound of Heaven

Across the margent of the world I fled,
  And troubled the gold gateways of
  the stars,
  Smiting for shelter on their clangèd
  bars;
  Fretted to dulcet jars
And silvern chatter the pale ports o'
  the moon.
Ibid.

Still with unhurrying chase,
And unperturbèd pace,
Deliberate speed, majestic instancy,
Came on the following Feet,
And a Voice above their beat —
"Naught shelters thee, who wilt not
  shelter Me."
Ibid.

I stand amid the dust o' the mounded
  years —
My mangled youth lies dead beneath
  the heap.

My days have crackled and gone up in
smoke,
Have puffed and burst as sun-starts on
a stream.
The Hound of Heaven

Ever and anon a trumpet sounds
From the hid battlements of Eternity.
Ibid.

All which I took from thee I did but
take,
Not only for thy harms,
But just that thou might'st seek it
in My arms.
All which thy child's mistake
Fancies as lost, I have stored for thee
at home.
Ibid.

There is no expeditious road
To pack and label men for God,
And save them by the barrel-load.
Epilogue, A Judgment in Heaven

Thou canst not stir a flower
Without troubling of a star.
The Mistress of Vision

When thy seeing blindeth thee
To what thy fellow-mortals see;
When their sight to thee is sightless;
Their living, death; their light, most
lightless;
Search no more —
Pass the gates of Luthany, tread the
region Elenore.
Ibid.

From stones and poets you may know,
Nothing so active is, as that which least
seems so.
Contemplation

Happiness is the shadow of things past,
Which fools still take for that which is
to be!
From the Night of Forebeing

O world invisible, we view thee,
O world intangible, we touch thee,
O world unknowable, we know thee.
*The Kingdom of God ("In No
Strange Land"). Stanza 1*

The drift of pinions, would we hearken,
Beats at our own clay-shuttered doors.
Ibid. Stanza 3

The angels keep their ancient places; —
Turn but a stone, and start a wing!

'Tis ye, 'tis your estrangèd faces,
That miss the many-splendoured thing.
*The Kingdom of God.
Stanza 4*

Upon thy so sore loss
Shall shine the traffic of Jacob's ladder
Pitched betwixt Heaven and Charing
Cross.
Ibid. Stanza 5

And lo, Christ walking on the water
Not of Gennesareth, but Thames!
Ibid. Stanza 6

Short arm needs man to reach to
Heaven
So ready is Heaven to stoop to him.
Grace of the Way. Stanza 6

Know you what it is to be a child?
It is to be something very different
from the man of to-day. It is to have
a spirit yet streaming from the waters
of baptism; it is to believe in love, to
believe in loveliness, to believe in belief; it is to be so little that the elves
can reach to whisper in your ear; it is to
turn pumpkins into coaches, and mice
into horses, lowness into loftiness, and
nothing into everything, for each child
has its fairy godmother in its soul.
Shelley [1]

Children's griefs are little, certainly;
but so is the child, so is its endurance,
so is its field of vision, while its nervous
impressionability is keener than ours.
Grief is a matter of relativity; the sorrow should be estimated by its proportion to the sorrower; a gash is as painful to one as an amputation to another.
Ibid.

Few poets were so mated before, and
no poet was so mated afterwards, until
Browning stooped and picked up a fair-
coined soul that lay rusting in a pool
of tears.
Ibid.

The designs of his bright imagination were never etched by the sharp
fumes of necessity.
Ibid.

A poet must to some extent be a
chameleon, and feed on air. But it need

[1] In *The Dublin Review, July, 1908.*

not be the musty breath of the multitude.

Shelley

Mighty meat for little guests, when the heart of Shelley was laid in the cemetery of Caius Cestius!

Ibid.

NIXON WATERMAN
[1859–   ]

We shall do so much in the years to
    come,
But what have we done to-day?
We shall give our gold in a princely
    sum,
But what did we give to-day?

What Have We Done To-day?

No man can feel himself alone
    The while he bravely stands
Between the best friends ever known —
    His two good, honest hands.

Interludes

Though life is made up of mere bubbles,
'Tis better than many aver,
For while we've a whole lot of troubles,
The most of them never occur.[1]

Why Worry?

JANE ADDAMS
[1860–1935]

Private beneficence is totally inadequate to deal with the vast numbers of the city's disinherited.

Twenty Years at Hull House

The common stock of intellectual enjoyment should not be difficult of access because of the economic position of him who would approach it.

Ibid.

JAMES MATTHEW BARRIE
[1860–1937]

The life of every man is a diary in which he means to write one story, and writes another; and his humblest hour is when he compares the volume as it is with what he vowed to make it.

The Little Minister. Chap. 1

---

[1] See Emerson, page 410; Lowell, page 530; Foss, page 733.

The most gladsome thing in the world is that few of us fall very low; the saddest that, with such capabilities, we seldom rise high.

The Little Minister. Chap. 3

If it's heaven for climate, it's hell for company.

Ibid.

It's a weary warld, and nobody bides in't.

Ibid. Chap. 4

Has it ever struck you that the trouts bite best on the Sabbath? God's critters tempting decent men.

Ibid. Chap. 8

We should be slower to think that the man at his worst is the real man, and certain that the better we are ourselves the less likely is he to be at his worst in our company. Every time he talks away his own character before us he is signifying contempt for ours.

Ibid. Chap. 9

You canna expect to be baith grand and comfortable.

Ibid. Chap. 10

A house is never still in darkness to those who listen intently; there is a whispering in distant chambers, an unearthly hand presses the snib of the window, the latch rises. Ghosts were created when the first man woke in the night.

Ibid. Chap. 22

Let no one who loves be called altogether unhappy. Even love unreturned has its rainbow.

Ibid. Chap. 24

Them that has china plates themsels is the maist careful no to break the china plates of others.

Ibid. Chap. 26

The humourist's like a man firin' at a target — he doesna ken whether he hits or no till them at the target tells 'im.

A Window in Thrums. Chap. 5

Those who bring sunshine to the lives of others cannot keep it from themselves.

Ibid. Chap. 18

Though it was really one laugh with a tear in the middle I counted it as two.

Margaret Ogilvy. Chap. 1

So much of what is great in Scotland has sprung from the closeness of the family ties.

Ibid. Chap. 2

We never understand how little we need in this world until we know the loss of it.

Ibid. Chap. 8

In dinner talk it is perhaps allowable to fling on any faggot rather than let the fire go out.

Tommy and Grizel. Chap. 3

Do you believe in fairies?

Peter and Wendy. Chap. 13

Eyes that say you never must, nose that says why don't you? and a mouth that says I rather wish you could: such is the portrait of Mary A —— .

The Little White Bird. Chap. 1

Shall we make a new rule of life from tonight: always to try to be a little kinder than is necessary?

Ibid. Chap. 4

The only ghosts, I believe, who creep into this world, are dead young mothers, returned to see how their children fare. There is no other inducement great enough to bring the departed back.

Ibid.

She was the thing we call romance, which lives in the little hut beyond the blue haze of the pine-woods.

Ibid. Chap. 9

I am in danger, I see, of being included among the whimsical fellows.

Ibid.

Every maid, I say, is for him who can know her. The others had but followed the glamour in which she walked, but I had pierced it and found the woman.

Ibid.

The reason birds can fly and we can't is simply that they have perfect faith, for to have faith is to have wings.

Ibid. Chap. 14

Poets are people who despise money except what you need for today.

Ibid. Chap. 15

When a great man dies — and this was one of the greatest since Shakespeare — the immortals await him at the top of the nearest hill.

George Meredith [1]

When you come to write my epitaph, Charles, let it be in these delicious words, "She had a long twenty-nine." [2]

Rosalind

One's religion is whatever he is most interested in, and yours is Success.

The Twelve-Pound Look

Alick: What *is* charm, exactly, Maggie?

Maggie: Oh, it's — it's a sort of bloom on a woman. If you have it, you don't need to have anything else; and if you don't have it, it doesn't much matter what else you have. Some women, the few, have charm for all; and most have charm for one. But some have charm for none. [3]

What Every Woman Knows. Act I

The tragedy of a man who has found himself out.

Ibid. Act IV

Every man who is high up loves to think that he has done it all himself; and the wife smiles, and lets it go at that.

Ibid.

The greatest glory that has ever come to me was to be swallowed up in London, not knowing a soul, with no means of subsistence, and the fun of

---

[1] In *The Westminster Gazette, May 26, 1909.*

[2] I have never admitted that I am more than twenty-nine, or thirty at the most. Twenty-nine when there are pink shades, thirty when there are not. — OSCAR WILDE: *Lady Windermere's Fan, Act IV*

She had said she was twenty-eight years old when she came, and she was twenty-eight still; and they sometimes speculated as to when she would have another birthday. — OLIVE SCHREINER: *From Man to Man, Chap. 6*

[3] What is charm? It is what the violet has and the camellia has not. — FRANCIS MARION CRAWFORD: *Children of the King, Chap. 5*

"Charm" — which means the power to effect work without employing brute force — is indispensable to women. Charm is a woman's strength just as strength is a man's charm. — HAVELOCK ELLIS: *The Task of Social Hygiene, Chap. 3*

working till the stars went out. To have known any one would have spoilt it. I did not even quite know the language.

Courage, Rectorial Address at St. Andrews [May 3, 1922]

Do you keep to the old topics? King Charles's head;[1] and Bacon wrote Shakespeare, or if he did not he missed the opportunity of his life. Don't forget to speak scornfully of the Victorian age; there will be time for meekness when you try to better it.

Ibid.

Mighty are the Universities of Scotland, and they will prevail. But even in your highest exultations never forget that they are not four, but five. The greatest of them is the poor, proud homes you come out of, which said so long ago: "There shall be education in this land."

Ibid.

For several days after my first book was published I carried it about in my pocket, and took surreptitious peeps at it to make sure that the ink had not faded.

Speech at the Critics' Circle, London [1922]

JOHN COLLINS BOSSIDY
[1860–1928]

And this is good old Boston,
   The home of the bean and the cod,
Where the Lowells talk only to Cabots
And the Cabots talk only to God.[2]

Toast, Midwinter Dinner, Holy Cross Alumni [1910]

---

[1] See Dickens, page 496.
[2] Patterned on the toast given at the twenty-fifth anniversary dinner of the Harvard Class of 1880, by a Western man:
Here's to old Massachusetts,
   The home of the sacred cod,
Where the Adamses vote for Douglas,
   And the Cabots walk with God.

Here's to the town of New Haven,
The home of the Truth and the Light,
   Where God talks to Jones
   In the very same tones
That he uses with Hadley and Dwight.
FREDERICK SCHEETZ JONES [1862–   ]: *A Toast for New Haven: Lux et Veritas,* at a dinner of the Yale Alumni Associ-

HAROLD EDWIN BOULTON
[1859–1935]

Speed, bonnie boat, like a bird on the wing;
   Onward, the sailors cry:
Carry the lad that's born to be King
   Over the sea to Skye.

Skye Boat Song. Stanza 1

PAULINE CARRINGTON RUST BOUVÉ
[1860–1928]

In the land of the Island Kingdom,
   'Mid Shinto temple and shrine,
Where the lights of a thousand altars
   To a thousand false gods shine,
There is carved an odd, quaint lesson,
   Wondrously cut in the wood —
The three wise monkeys of Nikko,
   Who see, speak, hear, but the good!

The Three Wise Monkeys.[1] Stanza 1

WILLIAM JENNINGS BRYAN
[1860–1925]

The humblest citizen of all the land, when clad in the armor of a righteous cause is stronger than all the hosts of Error.

Speech at the National Democratic Convention,[2] Chicago [1896]

---

tion, Waterbury, Connecticut, Feb. 5, 1915
Here's to the town of Hanover,
The home of the "Indian voice,"
   Where God talks to all
   Who will hark to His call —
Words of wisdom, and does it from choice.
CHARLES THEODORE GALLAGHER [1851–1919]: *Dartmouth College Toast*
Here's to New Haven and Boston,
   And the turf that the Puritans trod,
In the rest of mankind little virtue they find,
   But they feel quite chummy with God.
WALTER FOSTER ANGELL [1858–   ]: *Brown University Toast*
[1] Mizaru, Kikazaru, and Iwazaru.
In a temple at Kioto in far-away Japan,
The little Apes of Nikko are sitting, wondrous wise.
FLORENCE BOYCE DAVIS: *The Three Wise Monkeys*
[2] After Bryan made his "cross of gold" speech at the convention, a railroad president offered him the use of a private car for cam-

You shall not press down upon the brow of labor this crown of thorn. You shall not crucify mankind upon a cross of gold.

Speech at the National Democratic Convention [*1896*]

If the Father deigns to touch with divine power the cold and pulseless heart of the buried acorn and to make it burst forth from its prison walls, will He leave neglected in the earth the soul of man made in the image of his Creator?

The Prince of Peace

If matter mute and inanimate, though changed by the forces of Nature into a multitude of forms, can never die, will the spirit of man suffer annihilation when it has paid a brief visit, like a royal guest, to this tenement of clay? No. I am as sure that there is another life as I am that I live to-day.

Ibid.

If this invisible germ of life in the grain of wheat can thus pass unimpaired through three thousand resurrections, I shall not doubt that my soul has power to clothe itself with a new body, suited to its new existence, when this early frame has crumbled into dust.

Ibid.

CHARLES TOWNSEND COPELAND
[1860–   ]

For the common man, the best memorial is some beneficent thing or function that shall bear his name.

Tribute to Nathaniel Southgate Shaler [*July, 1906*]
Copeland Reader

A man is always better than a book.

Ibid.

To blame him were absurd; to pity were profane.

Not "Poor Charles Lamb." Copeland Reader Introduction

Whenever we encounter the typical essayist, he is found to be a tatler, a spectator, a rambler, a lounger, and, in the best sense, a citizen of the world.

Copeland Reader Introduction

Where novelists are concerned, because with lyric poets novelists are the most personal of writers, the question of the best book is likely to be as alluring as it is ultimately futile.

Ibid.

To eat is human; to digest, divine.[1]

Epigram

HAMLIN GARLAND
[1860–   ]

Do you fear the force of the wind,
  The slash of the rain?
Go face them and fight them,
  Be savage again.

Do You Fear the Wind?

The palms of your hands will thicken,
  The skin of your cheek will tan,
You'll go ragged and weary and swarthy,
  But you'll walk like a man!

Ibid.

CHARLOTTE PERKINS STETSON GILMAN
[1860–1935]

Said the little Eohippus,
  "I am going to be a horse!"

Similar Cases

Cried all, "Before such things can come,
You idiotic child,
You must alter Human Nature!"
And they all sat back and smiled.

Ibid.

Said I, in scorn all burning hot,
  In rage and anger high,
"You ignominious idiot!
  Those wings are made to fly!"

A Conservative. Stanza 5

"I do not want to be a fly!
I want to be a worm!"

Ibid. Stanza 6

---

paign travel. Willis John Abbot [1863–1934], present when the offer was made, advised Bryan not to accept, saying: "You are the Great Commoner."

[1] See Pope, page 211 and Robert Browning, page 493.

I ran against a Prejudice
  That quite cut off the view.
            An Obstacle. Stanza 1
I walked directly through him,
  As if he wasn't there.
            Ibid. Stanza 8
There's a whining at the threshold —
There's a scratching at the floor —
To work! To work! In Heaven's name!
  The wolf is at the door!
        The Wolf at the Door. Stanza 6
Shall you complain who feed the world?
Who clothe the world?
Who house the world?
Shall you complain who are the world,
  Of what the world may do?
   As from this hour
    You use your power,
  The world must follow you!
                To Labor. Stanza 1
The people people work with best
  Are sometimes very queer;
The people people own by birth
  Quite shock your first idea.
The people people have for friends
  Your common sense appal,
But the people people marry
  Are the queerest folk of all.
                Queer People
If fifty men did all the work,
  And gave the price to five,
And let those five make all the rules —
You'd say the fifty men were fools,
  Unfit to be alive.
            Five and Fifty. Stanza 1
Below my window goes the cattle train,
  And stands for hours along the river
      park,
Fear, cold, exhaustion, hunger, thirst,
      and pain;
  Dumb brutes we call them — Hark!
            The Cattle Train. Stanza 1
We kill these weary creatures, sore and
      worn,
  And eat them — with our friends.
                Ibid. Stanza 4
Human life consists in mutual serv-
ice. No grief, pain, misfortune, or
"broken heart," is excuse for cutting
off one's life while any power of service
remains. But when all usefulness is
over, when one is assured of an un-
avoidable and imminent death, it is the

simplest of human rights to choose a
quick and easy death in place of a slow
and horrible one.[1]
      Note written before her suicide
            [August 17, 1935]

HENRY LAWSON
[Floruit 1896]

When you wear a cloudy collar and a
    shirt that isn't white,
And you cannot sleep for thinking how
    you'll reach tomorrow night,
You may be a man of sorrows, and on
    speaking terms with Care,
And as yet be unacquainted with the
    Demon of Despair;
But I rather think that nothing heaps
    the trouble on your mind
Like the knowledge that your trousers
    badly need a patch behind.
    When Your Pants Begin to Go.[2]
                        Stanza 1
A man's an awful coward when his
    pants begin to go.
                        Ibid.

MISS L. M. LITTLE
[Floruit 1905]

There will be always one or two who
    hold
Earth's coin of less account than fairy
    gold;
Their treasure, not the spoil of crowds
    and kings,
But the dim beauty at the heart of
    things.
                    Fairy Gold[3]

JAMES BALL NAYLOR
[1860–   ]

King David and King Solomon
  Led merry, merry lives,

[1] Asthma and other annoyances I have tolerated for years; but I cannot put up with
cancer.
      JOHN DAVIDSON: *Fleet Street and Other
                Poems*, Preface [1909]
[2] From *In the Days When the World Was
Wide*, published by Angus & Robertson,
Sydney, Australia, 1896.
[3] Thomas Bird Mosher printed these lines
on the fly-leaf of *A Little Garland of Celtic
Verse* in 1905. He had no biographical infor-

With many, many lady friends
And many, many wives;
But when old age crept over them —
With many, many qualms,
King Solomon wrote the Proverbs
And King David wrote the Psalms.
Ancient Authors

BLISS PERRY
[1860–   ]

The permanent vitality of a work of art does consist in its capacity for stimulating and transmitting pleasure.
A Study of Poetry. Chap. 1
You and I may never see it, but ultimately nothing is so certain as the triumph of the things of the spirit over the gross material forces of American civilization.
A Study of Prose Fiction. Chap. 13
The fact is, we are not a book-reading people. The vast majority of our ninety-odd millions of population have no literary appetites which cannot be supplied by the newspapers, the magazines, and an occasional "best-seller" novel.
The Praise of Folly. Criticism in American Periodicals

CHARLES GEORGE DOUGLAS ROBERTS
[1860–   ]

Comes the lure of green things growing,
Comes the call of waters flowing —
And the wayfarer desire
Moves and wakes and would be going.
Afoot. Stanza 1

HARRY ROMAINE
[*Floruit* 1895]

At the muezzin's call for prayer,
The kneeling faithful thronged the square.
Ad Coelum
The one great God looked down and smiled,
And counted each His loving child;
For Turk and Brahmin, monk and Jew,

mation concerning the author except that she lived in Ireland.

Had reached Him through the gods they knew.
Ad Coelum
The little lonely souls go by,
Seeking their God who lives on high,
With conscious step and hat and all,
As if on Him they meant to call
In some sad ceremonial.
The Sabbath. Stanza 1
The man who idly sits and thinks,
May sow a nobler crop than corn,
For thoughts are seeds of future deeds,
And when God thought — the world was born!
Inaction

CLINTON SCOLLARD
[1860–1932]

Don't you hear the flutes of April calling clear and calling cool
From the crests that front the morning, from the hidden valley pool,
Runes of rapture half forgotten, tunes wherein old passions rule?
The Flutes of April. Stanza 1
So Farmer Johnson shouldered his gun,
And left his scythe in the rain and the sun.
The Scythe Tree.[1] Stanza 2

FRED NEWTON SCOTT
[1860–1931]

I am the hero of this little tale;
I'm Romeo, Romeo.
I am that sadly susceptible male;
I'm Romeo, Romeo.
Scarce did a lover e'er do as I did,
When his best girl to eternity slided;
I took cold poison and I suicided.
I'm Romeo, Romeo.
Glee Club Song. Stanza 2
I am the heroine of this tale of woe.
I'm Juliet, I'm Juliet.
I am the darling that mashed Romeo.
I'm Juliet, I'm Juliet.

[1] Farmer Tyler J. Snyder hung his scythe in the crotch of a tree near Geneva, New York, as he left his hayfield in August, 1862, to answer President Lincoln's call for volunteers. He never returned, and the scythe remains in the tree as a mute memorial.

Locked in a tomb with no pickaxe to
force it,
Gloomy old hole without room to stand
or sit,
I up and stabbed myself right in the
corset.
I'm Juliet, I'm Juliet.
Glee Club Song. Stanza 3

How dear to my heart are the scenes of
Ann Arbor,
The ramshackled sidewalks, the one
lonesome cop,
The beauties of Dutchtown, the fat col-
ored barber,
And e'en the gay widow I took to the
hop,
That tough-hearted widow, that frisky
old widow,
That gay college widow I took to the
hop.
College Days. Stanza 1

FRANK DEMPSTER
SHERMAN
[1860–1916]

Of all the threads of rhyme
Which I have spun,
I shall be glad if Time
Save only one.
His Desire

A land-flower broken from the stem,
And few indeed there be of them
Fitted so perfectly to gem
The blue Atlantic.
Nantucket

Out of the scabbard of the night,
By God's hand drawn,
Flashes his shining sword of light,
And lo, — the dawn!
Dawn

Here in their bright metropolis of
flowers
The banker bees are busy with their
gold.
In a Garden

Hark to the noisy caravans of brown,
Intrepid Sparrows, — Arabs of the air!
City Sparrows

Give me the room whose every nook
Is dedicated to a book.
The Library

. . . Such be the library; and take
This motto of a Latin make
To grace the door through which I
pass:
Hic habitat Felicitas!
The Library

And now, behold him dead, alas!
Where he made joy so long:
A bit of blue amid the grass, —
A tiny, broken song.
A Bird's Elegy

GEORGE MEASON WHICHER
[1860–1937]

How are the mighty withered! You are
now
Become your book, and that (O last
of woes!)
Shrunk to a school-room bogey. Ped-
ants plow
With salt your fields; and there no
harvest grows
Save juiceless weeds of grammar.
Ave Caesar! Stanza 3

Butchered to make the school-girl's exercise!
Ibid.

Two thousand years ago! O god that
gave
The power divine that saved his [1] song
from death. . . .
O save this praise thus shapen by my
breath:
Link deathless to his name one word of
mine — one word!
A Prayer to Apollo

OWEN WISTER
[1860–   ]

When you call me that, *smile!*
The Virginian. Chap. 2 [1902]

RICHARD BURTON
[1861–   ]

From their folded mates they wander
far,
Their ways seem harsh and wild;
They follow the beck of a baleful star,
Their paths are dream-beguiled.
Black Sheep

[1] Horace.

How often in the summer-tide,
His graver business set aside,
Has stripling Will, the thoughtful-
  eyed,
As to the pipe of Pan,
Stepped blithesomely with lover's pride
Across the fields to Anne.
    Across the Fields to Anne. Stanza 1
I sit in mine house at ease,
  Moving nor foot nor hand;
Yet sail through uncharted seas
  And wander from land to land.
            Travel

BLISS CARMAN
[1861–1929]

Have little care that life is brief,
And less that art is long.
Success is in the silences
Though fame is in the song.
    Songs from Vagabondia. Foreword
An open hand, an easy shoe,
And a hope to make the day go through.
            The Joys of the Road
A comrade neither glum nor merry.
            Ibid.
No fidget and no reformer, just
A calm observer of ought and must.
            Ibid.
And two brown arms at the journey's
  end!
            Ibid.
These are the joys of the open road —
For him who travels without a load.
            Ibid.
Make me over, mother April,
When the sap begins to stir!
    Spring Song. Stanza 1
Make me over in the morning
From the rag-bag of the world!
Scraps of dream and duds of daring,
Home-brought stuff from far sea-faring.
            Ibid. Stanza 12
O foolish ones, put by your cares!
Where wants are many, joys are few;
And at the wilding springs of peace
God keeps an open house for you.
    The Mendicants. Stanza 5
Over the shoulders and slopes of the
  dune

I saw the white daisies go down to the
  sea.
            Daisies. Stanza 1
And all of their singing was, "Earth, it
  is well!"
And all of their dancing was, "Life,
  thou art good!"
            Ibid. Stanza 2
The scarlet of the maples can shake me
  like a cry
Of bugles going by.
    A Vagabond Song. Stanza 2
There is something in October sets the
  gypsy blood astir.
            Ibid. Stanza 3
Hack and Hew were the sons of God
In the earlier earth than now;
One at his right hand, one at his left,
To obey as he taught them how.
    Hack and Hew. Stanza 1
Hem and Haw were the sons of sin,
Created to shally and shirk;
Hem lay 'round and Haw looked on
While God did all the work.
    Hem and Haw. Stanza 1
Lord of the far horizons,
  Give us the eyes to see
Over the verge of the sundown
  The beauty that is to be.
    Lord of the Far Horizons. Stanza 1
We are the roadside flowers,
Straying from garden grounds, —
Lovers of idle hours,
Breakers of ordered bounds.
    Roadside Flowers. Stanza 1
Here we came when love was young.
Now that love is old,
Shall we leave the floor unswept
And the hearth acold?
    The Homestead. Stanza 1
Heaven is no larger than Connecticut;
No larger than Fairfield County.
    A Measure of Heaven
There is virtue in the open; there is
  healing out of doors;
The great Physician makes his rounds
  along the forest floors.
    An Open Letter, Christmas, 1920.[1]
            Stanza 4

[1] Written at Lake Placid, New York, while
Carman was a patient there.

I took a day to search for God,
And found Him not. But as I trod
   By rocky ledge, through woods un-
      tamed,
Just where one scarlet lily flamed,
I saw His footprint in the sod.
                    Vestigia. Stanza 1

LOUISE IMOGEN GUINEY
[1861–1920]

He has done with roofs and men,
Open, Time, and let him pass.
                    Ballad of Kenelm
A short life in the saddle, Lord!
Not long life by the fire.
         The Knight Errant. Stanza 2
To fear not sensible failure,
   Nor covet the game at all,
But fighting, fighting, fighting,
   Die, driven against the wall!
                The Kings. Stanza 9
Cowley said it engagingly: *Bene qui
latuit, bene vixit:* he lives well, that has
lain well hidden. The pleasantest con-
dition of life is in incognito.
         *Patrins. On the Delights of an
                             Incognito*
"Isn't there heaven,"
   (She was but seven)
"Isn't there" (sobbing), "for dogs?"
   she said.
                    Davy. Stanza 1
Man is immortal, sage or fool;
Animals end by different rule.
                    Ibid. Stanza 2
Use me in honor; cherish me
As ivy from a sacred tree:
Mine in the winds of war to close
Around the armor of Montrose,
And kiss the death-wound of Dundee.
   The Graham Tartan to a Graham
A passing salute to this world and her
   pitiful beauty.
            The Wild Ride. Stanza 5
We spur to a land of no name, outrac-
   ing the stormwind;
We leap to the infinite dark like sparks
   from the anvil.
                    Ibid. Stanza 7
A certain sesquipedalianism is natural to Americans: witness our press
editorials, our Fourth of July orations,
and the public messages of all our Presidents since Lincoln.
            *In Scribner's Magazine,
                       January, 1911*
Quotations (such as have point and
lack triteness) from the great old authors are an act of filial reverence on
the part of the quoter, and a blessing
to a public grown superficial and external.
                    Ibid.

KATHARINE TYNAN
HINKSON
[1861–1931]

All in the April evening,
   April airs were abroad,
I saw the sheep with their lambs,
   And thought on the Lamb of God.
            Sheep and Lambs. Stanza 6
There's a lark in the noon sky, a thrush
   on the tree,
And a linnet sings wildly across the
   green lea,
And the finches are merry, the cuckoos
   still call,
But where is my Blackbird, the dearest
   of all?
            The Blackbird.[1] *Stanza 1*
The Spring comes slowly up this way,[2]
   Slowly, slowly!
A little nearer every day.
            A New Old Song. Stanza 1
I served Christ Jesus and I bear
   His Cross upon my rough grey back.
Dear Christian people, pray you, spare
   The whip, for Jesus Christ His sake.
            The Ass Speaks.[3] *Stanza 9*
Of all the birds from East to West
   That tuneful are and dear,
I love that farmyard bird the best,
   They call him Chanticleer.
            Chanticleer. Stanza 1

[1] Mrs. Hinkson was called "the blackbird's
poet."
[2] A line from Coleridge's *Christabel, Part I.*
[3] Fools! For I also had my hour;
   One far fierce hour and sweet:
There was a shout about my ears,
   And palms before my feet.
            GILBERT KEITH CHESTERTON:
                    The Donkey, St. 4

God made the country,
  Man made the town.[1]
God clad the country
  In a green gown.
                    The Maker. Stanza 1

Lest Heaven be thronged with grey-
    beards hoary,
  God, who made boys for His delight,
Stoops in a day of grief and glory
  And calls them in, in from the night.
When they come trooping from the war
Our skies have many a young new star.
              Flower of Youth. Stanza 1

JOHN LUTHER LONG
[1861–1927]

  To die with honour when one can no
longer live with honour.[2]
    *Madam Butterfly (inscription on
                    Samurai blade)*

JUSTIN HUNTLY
McCARTHY
[1861–1936]

On level lines of woodwork stand
My books obedient to my hand.
                        My Books
The playwrights mouth, the preachers
    jangle,
  The critics challenge and defend,
And Fiction turns the Muses' mangle —
  Of making books there is no end.
        *A Ballade of Book-Making.
                        Stanza 2*
A simple ballad, to a sylvan air,
Of love that ever finds your face more
    fair;
I could not give you any goodlier thing
        If I were king.
            If I Were King. Stanza 2
Alas for lovers! Pair by pair
  The Wind has blown them all away;

[1] God made the country, and man made
the town.
  COWPER: *The Task, Book I, L. 749*
[2] One should die proudly when it is no
longer possible to live proudly. — NIETZSCHE:
*The Twilight of the Idols, Skirmishes in a
War with the Age, 36,* translated by AN-
THONY M. LUDOVICI

The young and yare, the fond and fair;
  Where are the Snows of Yesterday?
    *A Ballad of Dead Ladies: After
                    Villon. Envoy*

EDWARD MacDOWELL
[1861–1908]

A house of Dreams untold
That looks out over the whispering
    tree-tops
And faces the setting sun.
            House of Dreams [1]

BYRON RUFUS NEWTON
[1861–1938]

Vulgar of manner, overfed,
Overdressed and underbred;
Heartless, Godless, hell's delight,
Rude by day and lewd by night;
Bedwarfed the man, o'ergrown the
    brute,
Ruled by Jew and prostitute;
Purple-robed and pauper-clad,
Raving, rotting, money-mad;
A squirming herd in Mammon's mesh,
A wilderness of human flesh;
Crazed with avarice, lust, and rum,
New York, thy name's Delirium.
            Owed to New York [1906]

SIR WALTER RALEIGH
[1861–1922]

I wish I loved the Human Race;
I wish I loved its silly face;
I wish I liked the way it walks;
I wish I liked the way it talks;
And when I'm introduced to one
I wish I thought *What Jolly Fun!*
    *Wishes of an Elderly Man (Wished
        at a Garden-Party, June, 1914)*
Brief delight, eternal quiet,
How change these for endless riot
Broken by a single rest?
Well you know that sleep is best.
                    My Last Will
Listen; you may be allowed
To hear my laughter from a cloud.
                        Ibid.

[1] Preface to his composition, *From a Log
Cabin,* and inscribed on the memorial tablet
near his grave.

SIR OWEN SEAMAN
[1861–1936]

Whene'er I walk the public ways,
How many poor that lack ablution
Do probe my heart with pensive gaze,
And beg a trivial contribution!
The Bitter Cry of the Great
Unpaid

O hearts of metal pure as finest gold!
O great ensample, where our sons
may trace,
Too proud for tears, their birthright
from of old,
Heirs of the Island Race!
In Memoriam: The Scott Antarctic
Expedition, 1912. Stanza 4

Ye that have faith to look with fearless
eyes
Beyond the tragedy of a world at
strife,
And trust that out of night and death
shall rise
The dawn of ampler life;
Rejoice, whatever anguish rend your
heart,
That God has given you for a price-
less dower,
To live in these great times and have
your part
In Freedom's crowning hour;
That you may tell your sons who see
the light
High in the heavens — their heritage
to take —
"I saw the powers of Darkness put to
flight,
I saw the Morning break."
Between Midnight and Morning [1]

Still where the countless ripples laugh
above
The blue of halcyon seas, long may
you keep
Your course unbroken, buoyed upon a
love
Ten thousand fathoms deep!
In Memoriam. Mark Twain [2]

[1] Written for *The Book of King Albert* of
Belgium.
[2] In *Punch* [1910].

WENDELL PHILLIPS STAFFORD
[1861–   ]

My heart is where the hills fling up
Green garlands to the day.
'Tis where the blue lake brims her cup,
The sparkling rivers play.
My heart is on the mountain still,
Where'er my steps may be,
Vermont, O maiden of the hills,
My heart is there with thee!
Vermont: A Song. Stanza 1

JOHN KENDRICK BANGS
[1862–1922]

Shakespeare was not accounted great
When good Queen Bess ruled Eng-
land's state,
So why should I to-day repine
Because the laurel is not mine?
Consolation. Stanza 1

He does not read at all, yet he doth
hoard
Rich books. In exile on his shelves
they're stored;
And many a volume, sweet and good
and true,
Fails in the work that it was made to
do.
The Bibliomiser

Be sure to keep a mirror always nigh
In some convenient, handy sort of
place,
And now and then look squarely in
thine eye,
And with thyself keep ever face to
face.
Face to Face. Stanza 1

I think mankind by thee would be less
bored
If only thou wert not thine own reward.
A Hint to Virtue

I have no dog, but it must be
Somewhere there's one belongs to me —
A little chap with wagging tail,
And dark brown eyes that never quail.
My Dog. Stanza 1

I never seen a night
So dark there wasn't light

Somewhere about if I took care
To strike a match an' find out where.
My Philosophy. Stanza 5
I love to watch the rooster crow,
He's like so many men I know
Who brag and bluster, rant and shout
And beat their manly breasts, without
The first damn thing to crow about.
The Rooster
To dig and delve in nice clean dirt
Can do a mortal little hurt.
Gardening
"I'm just as big for me," said he,
"As you are big for you!"
The Little Elfman. Stanza 2

ARTHUR CHRISTOPHER BENSON
[1862–1925]

Friend, of my infinite dreams
Little enough endures;
Little howe'er it seems,
It is yours, all yours.
Faith hath a fleeting breath,
Hopes may be frail but fond,
But Love shall be Love till death,
And perhaps beyond.
The Gift
If it be well with him,
If it be well, I say,
I will not try with a childish cry
To draw him thence away:
Only my day is dim,
Only I long for him,
Where is my friend to-day?
My Friend
Thy name is writ in water, ay, 'tis writ
As when the moon, a chill and friendless thing,
Passes and writes her will upon the tide,
And piles the ocean in a moving ring:
And every stagnant bay is brimmed with it,
Each mast-fringed port, each estuary wide.
Keats
Land of Hope and Glory, Mother of the Free,
How shall we extol thee, who are born of thee?

Wider still and wider shall thy bounds
be set;
God, who made thee mighty, make thee
mightier yet.
Land of Hope and Glory. Chorus
Edward Fitzgerald said that he
wished we had more lives of obscure
persons; one wants to know what other
people are thinking and feeling about
it all. . . . If the dullest person in the
world would only put down sincerely
what he or she thought about his or her
life, about work and love, religion and
emotion, it would be a fascinating doc-
ument.
From a College Window

JAMES W. BLAKE
[1862–1935]

East Side, West Side, all around the
town,
The tots sang "Ring-a-rosie," "London
Bridge is falling down";
Boys and girls together, me and Mamie
Rorke,
Tripped the light fantastic on the side-
walks of New York.
The Sidewalks of New York [1]
[*1894*]

CARRIE JACOBS BOND
[1862–   ]

For Memory has painted this perfect
day
With colors that never fade,
And we find at the end of a perfect day
The soul of a friend we've made.
A Perfect Day. Stanza 2

NICHOLAS MURRAY BUTLER
[1862–   ]

An expert is one who knows more and
more about less and less. [2]
*Commencement Address,
Columbia University*

---

[1] The music of the song was composed by
Charles B. Lawlor [1852–1925].
[2] An expert is a person who avoids the
small errors as he sweeps on to the grand
fallacy. — Benjamin Stolberg [1891–   ]

JOHN ARMSTRONG CHALONER
[1862–1935]

Who's loony now?
Message to his brother, Robert Chanler [*December, 1911*]

GOLDSWORTHY LOWES DICKINSON
[1862–1932]

Chinese poetry is of all poetry I know the most human and the least symbolic or romantic. It contemplates life just as it presents itself, without any veil of ideas, any rhetoric or sentiment; it simply clears away the obstruction which habit has built up between us and the beauty of things.
An Essay on the Civilizations of India, China, and Japan. Page 47

Consider the American continent! How simple it is! How broad! How large! How grand in design! A strip of coast, a range of mountains, a plain, a second range, a second strip of coast! That is all! Contrast the complexity of Europe, its lack of symmetry, its variety, irregularity, disorder and caprice! The geography of the two continents already foreshadows the differences in their civilizations.
A Modern Symposium

The United States of America — the greatest potential force, material, moral, and spiritual, in the world.
The Choice Before Us. Chap. 1

To the man who has the religion of peace, the supreme value is love. To the man who has the religion of war, the supreme value is strife.
Ibid. Chap. 3

Government is everywhere to a great extent controlled by powerful minorities, with an interest distinct from that of the mass of the people.
Ibid. Chap. 4

The true way for one civilization to "conquer" another is for it to be so obviously superior in this or that point that others desire to imitate it.
Ibid. Chap. 5

War is not "inevitable," but proceeds from definite and removable causes.
The Choice Before Us. Chap. 9

Nations are quite capable of starving every other side of life — education, sanitation, housing, public health, everything that contributes to life, physical, intellectual, moral, and spiritual, in order to maintain their armaments.
Ibid. Chap. 11

Every kind of discrimination is a protection of the incompetent against the competent, with the result that the motive to become competent is taken away.
Ibid. Chap. 12

What we commonly have in our mind when we speak of religion is a definite set of doctrines, of a more or less metaphysical character, formulated in a creed and supported by an organization distinct from the state.
The Greek View of Life. Chap. 1, Sect. 1

A fundamental, and as many believe, the most essential part of Christianity, is its doctrine of reward and punishment in the world beyond; and a religion which had nothing at all to say about this great enigma we should hardly feel to be a religion at all.
Ibid. Sect. 11

All modern societies aim, to this extent at least, at equality, that their tendency, so far as it is conscious and avowed, is not to separate off a privileged class of citizens, set free by the labour of others to live the perfect life, but rather to distribute impartially to all the burdens and advantages of the state, so that every one shall be at once a labourer for himself and a citizen of the state.
Ibid. Chap. 2, Sect. 12

Dissatisfaction with the world in which we live and determination to realize one that shall be better, are the prevailing characteristics of the modern spirit.
Ibid. Chap. 5

ANNIE JOHNSON FLINT
[1862–1932]

The thrones are rocking to their fall —
It is the twilight of the Kings!
  The Twilight of the Kings [1]
Have you come to the Red Sea place
 in your life,
Where, in spite of all you can do,
There is no way out, there is no way
 back,
There is no other way but through?
  At the Place of the Sea. Stanza 1

NORMAN GALE
[1862–   ]

Here in the country's heart
 Where the grass is green,
Life is the same sweet life
 As it e'er hath been.
  The Country Faith. Stanza 1
God comes down in the rain,
 And the crop grows tall —
This is the country faith,
 And the best of all!
  Ibid. Stanza 3
The cheated stockings lean and long,
The swift-descending petticoat,
The breasts that heave because they
 ran,
The rounded arms, the brilliant limbs,
The pretty necklaces of tan.
  The Shaded Pool
Write: — He had made a finer man
 And left increased renown behind,
If he had only shut his books
 To read the chapters of mankind!
  Last Words. Stanza 10

ELLA HIGGINSON
[1862–   ]

Oh, every year hath its winter,
 And every year hath its rain —

[1] This is the twilight of the kings. Western Europe of the people may be caught in this debacle, but never again. Eastern Europe of the kings will be remade and the name of God shall not give grace to a hundred square miles of broken bodies. If Divinity enters here it comes with a sword to deliver the people from the sword. It is the twilight of the kings. The republic marches east in Europe. — Editorial, *The Chicago Tribune,* *Aug. 2, 1914*

But a day is always coming
 When the birds go north again.
  When the Birds Go North Again.
    Stanza 1
One leaf is for hope, and one is for
 faith,
And one is for love, you know,
And God put another in for luck.
  Four-Leaf Clover. Stanza 2
The low brown hills, the bare brown
 hills
 Of San Francisco Bay.
  The Low Brown Hills. Stanza 1
Forgive you? — Oh, of course, dear,
 A dozen times a week!
We women were created
 Forgiveness but to speak.
  Wearing Out Love. Stanza 1
It's what you do, unthinking,
 That makes the quick tear start;
The tear may be forgotten —
 But the hurt stays in the heart.
  Ibid. Stanza 3

E. PAULINE JOHNSON
("TEKAHIONWAKE")
[1862–1913]

And down these nineteen centuries
 anew
 Comes the hoarse-throated, brutal-
 ized refrain,
"Give us Barabbas, crucify the Jew!"
 Once more a man must bear a na-
 tion's stain.
  "Give Us Barabbas." [1] *Stanza 3*

WALT MASON
[1862–   ]

The little green tents where the soldiers sleep and the sunbeams play and the women weep, are covered with flowers to-day.
  The Little Green Tents

[1] Written after Captain Alfred Dreyfus [1859–1935] was exiled to Devil's Island, 1894.

In all ages the multitude has looked upon Barabbas as a less violent and dangerous disrupter of social laws than the Christ — not this man but Barabbas!
  OLIVE SCHREINER: *From* *Man to Man, Chap. 7*

The statesman throws his shoulders
    back, and straightens out his tie,
And says, "My friends, unless it rains,
    the weather will be dry."
And when this thought into our brains
    has percolated through,
We common people nod our heads and
    loudly cry, "How true!"

                The Statesman

    There's a man in the world who
is never turned down, wherever he
chances to stray; he gets the glad hand
in the populous town, out where the
farmers make hay; he's greeted with
pleasure on deserts of sand, and deep
in the aisles of the woods; wherever he
goes there's the welcoming hand —
he's the Man Who Delivers the Goods.

    The Man Who Delivers the Goods

    Little drops of water poured into the
milk, give the milkman's daughter
lovely gowns of silk. Little grains of
sugar mingled with the sand, make the
grocer's assets swell to beat the band.

                Little Things

    Why taste the wormwood when the
prunes are wholesome, sweet and
cheap? The night is coming on eftsoons
when we lie down to sleep.

                      Why?

SIR HENRY NEWBOLT
[1862–1938]

To set the cause above renown,
    To love the game beyond the prize,
To honor, while you strike him down,
    The foe that comes with fearless
        eyes;
To count the life of battle good
    And dear the land that gave you
        birth,
And dearer yet the brotherhood
    That binds the brave of all the earth.

           Clifton Chapel. Stanza 2

Qui procul hinc, the legend's writ, —
    The frontier-grave is far away —
Qui ante diem periit:
    Sed miles, sed pro patria.[1]

            Ibid. Stanza 4

[1] Who died far away, before his time; but
as a soldier, for his country.

    When the strong command
Obedience is best.

      A Ballad of John Nicholson

And now he saw with lifted eyes
The East like a great chancel rise,
And deep through all his senses drawn,
Received the sacred wine of dawn.

           The Last Word

Like a sun bewitched in alien realms of
    night,
Mellow and yellow and rounded hangs
    the moon.

              Moonset

April's anger is swift to fall,
April's wonder is worth it all.

    The Adventurers. Stanza 8

Beyond the book his teaching sped,
He left on whom he taught the trace
Of kinship with the deathless dead.

             Ionicus

Admirals all, they went their way
    To the haven under the hill.
But they left us a kingdom none can
    take,
    The realm of the circling sea.

           Admirals All

He's sailed in a hundred builds o' boat,
He's fought in a thousand kinds o' coat,
He's the senior flag of all that float,
    And his name's Admiral Death.

          Admiral Death

    Craven spoke,
Spoke as he lived and fought, with a
    captain's pride,
"After you, Pilot": the pilot woke,
Down the ladder he went, and Craven
    died.[1]

    Craven: August 5, 1864. Stanza 6

Sidney thirsting a humbler need to
    slake,
Nelson waiting his turn for the sur-
    geon's hand,
Lucas crushed with chains for a com-
    rade's sake,
Outram coveting right before com-
    mand.

            Ibid. Stanza 8

[1] Caught by the under-death,
  In the drawing of a breath
Down went dauntless Craven,
He and his hundred!

      HENRY HOWARD BROWNELL:
            The Bay Fight

Princes of courtesy, merciful, proud and strong.
Craven: August 5, 1864. Stanza 9

Their fame's on Torres Vedras, their fame's on Vigo Bar,
Far-flashed to Cape St. Vincent; it burns from Trafalgar;
Mark as ye go the beacons that woke the world with light
When down their ancient highway your fathers passed to fight.
The Sailing of the Long-ships

The sand of the desert is sodden red —
  Red with the wreck of a square that broke —
The gatling's jammed, and the colonel dead,
  And the regiment blind with the dust and smoke:
The river of death has brimmed its banks,
  And England's far and honour a name.
Vitai Lampada

This they all with a joyful mind
  Bear through life like a torch in flame,
And, falling, fling to the hosts behind,
  "Play up! play up! and play the game!"
Ibid.

Come, boys, come!
You that mean to fight it out, wake and take your load again,
  Fall in! Fall in! Follow the fife and drum!
The Toy Band

Drake he was a Devon man, an' ruled the Devon seas.
Drake's Drum. Stanza 2

"Take my drum to England, hang et by the shore,
  Strike et when your powder's runnin' low;
If the Dons sight Devon, I'll quit the port o' Heaven,
  An' drum them up the Channel as we drummed them long ago."
Ibid.

England! where the sacred flame
  Burns before the inmost shrine,
Where the lips that love thy name
  Consecrate their hopes and thine,

Where the banners of thy dead
Weave their shadows overhead,
Watch beside thine arms to-night,
Pray that God defend the Right.
The Vigil. Stanza 1

EDEN PHILLPOTTS
[1862–   ]

A sudden wakin', a sudden weepin',
A li'l suckin', a li'l sleepin';
A cheel's full joys an' a cheel's short sorrows,
Wi' a power o' faith in gert to-morrows.
Man's Days. Stanza 1

A li'l dreamin', a li'l dyin':
A li'l lew corner o' airth to lie in.
Ibid. Stanza 3

'Tis here they say the journey ends
  And little doubt it must be so;
But, as I tell my bestest friends,
  I hate to go.
Lament. Stanza 1

By all the agonies of all the past,
By earth's cold dust and ashes at the last,
By her return to the unconscious vast,
Oh, hear!
Litany to Pan. Stanza 7

WILLIAM MARION REEDY
[1862–1920]

Force is good and fire is good and fancy is good in a poet, but if he have not Love then he is as sounding brass and tinkling cymbal. Love is best of all. There is not, nor ever shall be, true song without it.
A Nest of Singing Birds

ROBERT CAMERON ROGERS
[1862–1912]

The hours I spent with thee, dear heart,
  Are as a string of pearls to me;
I count them over, every one apart,
  My rosary, my rosary.
My Rosary

Oh memories that bless — and burn!
  Oh barren gain — and bitter loss!
I kiss each bead and strive at last to learn
  To kiss the cross,

Sweetheart,
To kiss the cross.
My Rosary

Sage-brush to kindle with,
Quaking-asp to glow,
Pine-roots to last until the dawn-winds
blow.
Oh smoke full of fancies,
And dreams gone to smoke,
At the camp-fires dead long ago!
A Ballad of Dead Camp-Fires

Oh master mine, lo I remember thee, —
But I am old and weak and near to
death —
I cannot fawn and leap and be thy dog,
Thy dog of old — I cannot show the
love
That I have kept so long for one ca-
ress, —
But, master, I have not forgotten thee.
The Death of Argus [1]

Visions I no longer see,
And smoke is only smoke to me,
Now I am old.
The Old Smoker

EDITH WHARTON
[1862–1937]

There are two ways of spreading light:
to be
The candle or the mirror that reflects
it.
Vesalius in Zante

Somewhere I read, in an old book whose
name
Is gone from me, I read that when the
days
Of a man are counted, and his business
done,
There comes up the shore at evening,
with the tide,
To the place where he sits, a boat —
And in the boat, from the place where
he sits, he sees,
Dim in the dusk, dim and yet so familiar,
The faces of his friends long dead; and
knows
They come for him, brought in upon
the tide,

[1] See Pope, p. 220.

To take him where men go at set of
day.[1]
*With the Tide: Theodore
Roosevelt*

I was never allowed to read the popular American children's books of my
day because, as my mother said, the
children spoke bad English *without the
author's knowing it.*
A Backward Glance. Chap. 3

My parents and their group, though
they held literature in great esteem,
stood in nervous dread of those who
produced it. Washington Irving, Fitz-
Greene Halleck and William Dana were
the only representatives of the disquiet-
ing art who were deemed uncontami-
nated by it; though Longfellow, they
admitted, if a popular poet, was nevertheless a gentleman. As for Herman
Melville, a cousin of the Van Rens-
selaers, and qualified by birth to figure
in the best society, he was doubtless
excluded from it by his deplorable Bo-
hemianism, for I never heard his name
mentioned, or saw one of his books.
Ibid.

To [Henry] James's intimates, however, these elaborate hesitancies, far
from being an obstacle, were like a cob-
web bridge flung from his mind to
theirs, an invisible passage over which
one knew that silver-footed ironies,
veiled jokes, tiptoe malices, were stealing to explode a huge laugh at one's
feet.
Ibid. Chap. 8

"Summer afternoon — summer afternoon; to me those have always been the
two most beautiful words in the English
language."
(*Said by* HENRY JAMES *to* E. W.)
Ibid. Chap. 10

One day when the Sultan was in his
palace at Damascus a beautiful youth
who was his favourite rushed into his
presence, crying out in great agitation

[1] Whenever a good Haida is about to die
he sees a canoe manned by some of his dead
friends, who come with the tide to bid him
welcome to the spirit land. — SIR JAMES G.
FRAZER: *The Golden Bough* (abridged edition), *Chap. 3*

that he must fly at once to Baghdad, and imploring leave to borrow his Majesty's swiftest horse.

The Sultan asked why he was in such haste to go to Baghdad. "Because," the youth answered, "as I passed through the garden of the Palace just now, Death was standing there, and when he saw me he stretched out his arms as if to threaten me, and I must lose no time in escaping from him."

The young man was given leave to take the Sultan's horse and fly; and when he was gone the Sultan went down indignantly into the garden, and found Death still there. "How dare you make threatening gestures at my favourite?" he cried; but Death, astonished, answered: "I assure your Majesty I did not threaten him. I only threw up my arms in surprise at seeing him here, because I have a tryst with him tonight in Baghdad." [1]

A Backward Glance. Chap. 11

HENRY HOLCOMB BENNETT
[1863–1924]

Hats off!
Along the street there comes
A blare of bugles, a ruffle of drums,
A flash of color beneath the sky:
Hats off!
The flag is passing by.
The Flag Goes By. Stanza 1

GAMALIEL BRADFORD
[1863–1932]

My art is the painting of soul,
So fine, so exacting, so strange:
To blend in one tangible whole
The manifold features of change.
Soul. Stanza 1

My prose is decorous,
Or strips other men,
Discreetly sonorous
On things that have been.
My verse tears the curtain

[1] Story told E. W. by JEAN COCTEAU. The same fable was current many years later under the title *Appointment in Samarra*.

From shuddering me,
Pale, haggard, uncertain,
As souls should not be.
My Art. Stanza 2

I sometimes wish that God were back
In this dark world and wide;
For though some virtues he might lack,
He had his pleasant side.
Exit God

Youth is alive, and once we too were
young,
Dreamed we could make the world
all over new,
Tossed eager projects lightly from the
tongue,
And hoped the hurrying years would
prove them true.
Wellesley at Fifty, 1881–1931

That odd, fantastic ass, Rousseau,
Declared himself unique.
How men persist in doing so,
Puzzles me more than Greek.
Rousseau

The sins that tarnish whore and thief
Beset me every day.
My most ethereal belief
Inhabits common clay.
Ibid.

JOSEPH HAYDEN
[*Floruit* 1896]

There'll be a hot time in the old town
to-night.
A Hot Time in the Old Town [1]
[1896]

OLIVER HERFORD
[1863–1935]

God made Man
Frail as a bubble;
God made Love,
Love made Trouble.
God made the Vine,

[1] Theodore August Metz [1848–1936] composed a march, *A Hot Time in the Old Town To-night,* in 1886 for the McIntyre and Heath minstrel show. In 1896 Joseph Hayden wrote words for the music, and the song was published. It became the favorite rallying song of Theodore Roosevelt's Rough Riders in Cuba, and later was the campaign song of Colonel Roosevelt.

Was it a sin
That Man made Wine
  To drown Trouble in?
A Plea

The Gargoyle often makes his perch
On a cathedral or a church,
Where, mid ecclesiastic style,
He smiles an early-Gothic smile.
The Gargoyle

Children, behold the Chimpanzee:
He sits on the ancestral tree
From which we sprang in ages gone.
The Chimpanzee

It hath been writ that anye manne
May blameless kiss what mayde he
  canne
Nor anyone shall say hym "no"
Beneath the holye mistletoe.
The Enchanted Oak. Stanza 5

Ermined and minked and Persian-
  lambed,
Be-puffed (be-painted, too, alas!)
Be-decked, be-diamonded — be-
  damned!
The women of the better class.
The Women of the Better Class.
Stanza 4

It is not fair to visit all
The blame on Eve, for Adam's fall;
The most Eve did was to display
Contributory negligé.
Eve: Apropos de Rien

O Mongoose, where were you that day
When Mistress Eve was led astray?
If you'd but seen the serpent first,
Our parents would not have been
  cursed.
Child's Natural History.
The Mongoose

JOSEPH P. MacCARTHY
[1863–1934]

You must select the Puritans for
your ancestors. You must have a sheltered youth and be a graduate of Harvard. . . . Eat beans on Saturday
night and fish-balls on Sunday morning. . . . You must be a D.A.R., a
Colonial Dame, an S.A.R. or belong
to the Mayflower Society. . . . You
must read the Atlantic Monthly. . . .
You must make sure in advance that

your obituary appears in the Boston
Transcript. There is nothing else.
To be Happy in New England,
Letter to the Editor of The Chris-
tian Register

ARTHUR MACHEN
[1863–   ]

It was better, he thought, to fail in
attempting exquisite things than to
succeed in the department of the utterly contemptible.
The Hill of Dreams. Chap. 5

CLARENCE OUSLEY
[1863–   ]

When the mint is in the liquor and its
  fragrance on the glass,
It breathes a recollection that can
  never, never pass —
When the South was in the glory of a
  never-ending June,
The strings were on the banjo and the
  fiddle was in tune,
And we reveled in the plenty that we
  thought could never pass
And lingered at the julep in the ever-
  brimming glass.
When the Mint Is in the Liquor.
Stanza 1

SIR ARTHUR THOMAS
QUILLER-COUCH
[1863–   ]

Literature is not an abstract science,
to which exact definitions can be applied. It is an art, the success of which
depends on personal persuasiveness, on
the author's skill to give as on ours to
receive.
Inaugural Lecture at Cambridge
University [1913]

JAMES HARVEY ROBINSON
[1863–1935]

Political campaigns are designedly
made into emotional orgies which endeavor to distract attention from the
real issues involved, and they actually

paralyze what slight powers of cerebration man can normally muster.

The Human Comedy. Chap. 9

With supreme irony, the war to "make the world safe for democracy" [1] ended by leaving democracy more unsafe in the world than at any time since the collapse of the revolutions of 1848.

Ibid.

GEORGE SANTAYANA
[1863–   ]

He carries his English weather in his heart wherever he goes, and it becomes a cool spot in the desert, and a steady and sane oracle amongst all the delirium of mankind.

Soliloquies in England. The British Character

England is the paradise of individuality, eccentricity, heresy, anomalies, hobbies, and humours.

Ibid.

The world is a perpetual caricature of itself; at every moment it is the mockery and the contradiction of what it is pretending to be.

Ibid. Dickens

There is no cure for birth and death save to enjoy the interval.

Ibid. War Shrines

I like to walk about amidst the beautiful things that adorn the world; but private wealth I should decline, or any sort of personal possessions, because they would take away my liberty.

Ibid. The Irony of Liberalism

My atheism, like that of Spinoza, is true piety towards the universe and denies only gods fashioned by men in their own image, to be servants of their human interests.

Ibid. On My Friendly Critics

The human race, in its intellectual life, is organized like the bees: the masculine soul is a worker, sexually atrophied, and essentially dedicated to impersonal and universal arts; the feminine is a queen, infinitely fertile, omnipresent in its brooding industry, but passive and abounding in intuitions

[1] See Woodrow Wilson, page 725.

without method and passions without justice.

The Life of Reason. Vol. 2

Civilisation is perhaps approaching one of those long winters that overtake it from time to time. Romantic Christendom — picturesque, passionate, unhappy episode — may be coming to an end. Such a catastrophe would be no reason for despair.

Character and Opinion in the United States [1922]

American life is a powerful solvent. It seems to neutralise every intellectual element, however tough and alien it may be, and to fuse it in the native good-will, complacency, thoughtlessness, and optimism.

Ibid.

All his life he [the American] jumps into the train after it has started and jumps out before it has stopped; and he never once gets left behind, or breaks a leg.

Ibid.

There is nothing impossible in the existence of the supernatural: its existence seems to me decidedly probable.

The Genteel Tradition at Bay

It is a great advantage for a system of philosophy to be substantially true.

The Unknowable

The young man who has not wept is a savage, and the old man who will not laugh is a fool.

Dialogues in Limbo. III

Beauty is pleasure regarded as the quality of a thing.

The Sense of Beauty. On Nature of Beauty

The infinity which moves us is the sense of multiplicity in uniformity. Accordingly, things which have enough multiplicity, as the lights of a city seen across water, have an effect similar to that of the stars, if less intense; whereas a star, if alone, because the multiplicity is lacking, makes a wholly different impression.

Ibid. On Form

Beauty as we feel it is something indescribable: what it is or what it means can never be said.

> *The Sense of Beauty.*
> *On Expression*

Beauty is a pledge of the possible conformity between the soul and nature, and consequently a ground of faith in the supremacy of the good.

> *Ibid.*

Let a man once overcome his selfish terror at his own finitude, and his finitude is, in one sense, overcome.

> *Introduction to The Ethics of*
> *Spinoza*

Perhaps the only true dignity of man is his capacity to despise himself.

> *Ibid.*

Miracles are propitious accidents, the natural causes of which are too complicated to be readily understood.

> *Ibid.*

The Bible is literature, not dogma.

> *Ibid.*

O World, thou choosest not the better part!
  It is not wisdom to be only wise,
  And on the inward vision close the eyes,
But it is wisdom to believe the heart.

> *O World, Thou Choosest Not*

Columbus found a world, and had no chart,
  Save one that faith deciphered in the skies;
  To trust the soul's invincible surmise
Was all his science and his only art.

> *Ibid.*

Heaven is to be at peace with things;
Come chaos now, and in a whirlwind's rings
Engulf the planets. I have seen the best.

> *Sonnet 49*

Old age, on tiptoe, lays her jeweled hand
Lightly in mine. Come, tread a stately measure,
Most gracious partner, nobly poised and bland.

> *A Minuet on Reaching the Age of*
> *Fifty*

ERNEST LAWRENCE THAYER
[1863–   ]

The outlook wasn't brilliant for the Mudville nine that day.

> *Casey at the Bat.*[1] *Stanza 1*

There was ease in Casey's manner as he stepped into his place,
There was pride in Casey's bearing, and a smile lit Casey's face,
And when, responding to the cheers, he lightly doffed his hat,
No stranger in the crowd could doubt 'twas Casey at the bat.

> *Ibid. Stanza 6*

"Strike one," the umpire said.

> *Ibid. Stanza 8*

From the benches dark with people there went up a muffled roar,
Like the beating of the storm-waves on a stern but distant shore.

> *Ibid. Stanza 9*

With a smile of Christian charity great Casey's visage shone;
He stilled the rising tumult, he bade the game go on.

> *Ibid. Stanza 10*

Oh, somewhere in this favored land the sun is shining bright;
The band is playing somewhere, and somewhere hearts are light,
And somewhere men are laughing and little children shout,
But there is no joy in Mudville, great Casey has struck out.

> *Ibid. Stanza 13*

AMÉLIE RIVES TROUBETZKOY
[1863–   ]

Oh, my laddie, my laddie,
I lo'e your very plaidie,
I lo'e your very bonnet
Wi' the silver buckle on it.

> *My Laddie. Stanza 1*

---

[1] First printed in *The San Francisco Examiner, June 3, 1888.*
  Yet I'd take my chance with fame,
    Calmly let it go at that,
  With the right to sign my name
    Under "Casey at the Bat."
  GRANTLAND RICE: *The Masterpiece*

SIR ROGER CASEMENT
[1864–1916]

All that was beautiful and just,
    All that was pure and sad,
Went in one little, moving plot of dust
    The world called bad.
      In the Streets of Catania. Stanza 1

It is gone from the hill and glen,
    The strong speech of our sires;
It is sunk in the mire and the fen
    Of our nameless desires.
      The Irish Language. Stanza 1

OSCAR W. FIRKINS
[1864–1932]

I should have enjoyed the country [Switzerland] more thoroughly if the poets and romancers had not corrupted my mind with their pestiferous superlatives.
      Letter [August 3, 1913] [1]

My state is contentment *within* despair.
      Letter [December 29, 1922]

The great art includes much that the small art excludes: humor, pain, and evil. Much that is repulsive when alone becomes beautiful in its relation. To find the ennobling relation is the task of life and of art.
      Lecture Notes

A classic is produced by the cooperation of the public with the author. A classic is a work which is fit to enter into permanent relations with a large section of mankind.
      Ibid.

RICHARD HOVEY
[1864–1900]

In all climes we pitch our tents,
    Cronies of the elements,
With the secret lords of birth
    Intimate and free.
      The Wander-lovers. Stanza 2

Comrades, pour the wine to-night
For the parting is with dawn!

[1] These quotations are from *Memoirs and Letters of O. W. Firkins,* University of Minnesota Press, 1934.

Oh, the clink of cups together,
With the daylight coming on!
      Comrades

For 'tis always fair weather
When good fellows get together
With a stein on the table and a good
    song ringing clear.
      A Stein Song. Stanza 1

The guns that spoke at Lexington
    Knew not that God was planning then
The trumpet word of Jefferson
    To bugle forth the rights of men.
      Unmanifest Destiny. Stanza 3

I do not know beneath what sky
    Nor on what seas shall be thy fate:
I only know it shall be high,
    I only know it shall be great.
      Ibid. Stanza 7

Whose furthest footstep never strayed
Beyond the village of his birth
Is but a lodger for the night
In this old wayside inn of earth.
      More Songs from Vagabondia.
      Envoy, Stanza 1

There are worser ills to face
    Than foemen in the fray;
And many a man has fought because —
    He feared to run away.
      The Marriage of Guenevere.
      Act IV, Sc. 3

I have need of the sky,
I have business with the grass;
I will up and get me away where the
    hawk is wheeling
Lone and high,
And the slow clouds go by.
I will get me away to the waters that
    glass
The clouds as they pass.
I will get me away to the woods.
      I Have Need of the Sky

MARK ANTONY DE WOLFE HOWE
[1864–   ]

The village sleeps, a name unknown, till men
    With life-blood stain its soil, and pay the due

That lifts it to eternal fame, — for then
  'Tis grown a Gettysburg or Water-
    loo.
Distinction

Not for the star-crowned heroes, the
    men that conquer and slay,
But a song for those that bore them, the
    mothers braver than they!
With never a blare of trumpets, with
    never a surge of cheers,
They march to the unseen hazard —
    pale, patient volunteers.
The Valiant

When morning broke, and day
  Smiled up across the tide,
Here in the harbor safe she lay,
  Her rescue by her side!
A Birthday Verse. Stanza 2

ROBERT LOVEMAN
[1864–1923]

It is not raining rain to me,
  It's raining daffodils;
In every dimpled drop I see
  Wild flowers on the hills.
April Rain.[1] Stanza 1

A health unto the happy!
  A fig for him who frets! —
It is not raining rain to me,
  It's raining violets.
Ibid. Stanza 4

PAUL ELMER MORE [2]
[1864–1937]

As our private memory is not a
merely passive retention of sensations,
so in literature the critical spirit is at
work as a conscious energy of selection. The function of criticism is far
removed from the surrender to luxurious revery.
Shelburne Essays. Criticism

Great music is a psychical storm,
agitating to fathomless depths the mystery of the past within us. Or we might

---

[1] In *Harper's Magazine, May, 1901.*
[2] To read him is to enter an austere and
elevated realm of ideas and to know a man
who, in the guise of a critic, is authentically
concerned with the first and last things of
human experience. — WALTER LIPPMANN, in
*The Saturday Review of Literature, March
15, 1930*

---

say that it is a prodigious incantation.
There are tones that call up all ghosts
of youth and joy and tenderness; —
there are tones that evoke all phantom
pains of perished passion; — there are
tones that revive all dead sensations of
majesty and might and glory, — all expired exultations, — all forgotten mag-
nanimities. Well may the influence of
music seem inexplicable to the man
who idly dreams that his life began
less than a hundred years ago! He who
has been initiated into the truth knows
that to every ripple of melody, to every billow of harmony, there answers
within him, out of the Sea of Death
and Birth, some eddying immeasurable
of ancient pleasure and pain.
Shelburne Essays. Lafcadio Hearn

All things are fleeting; nothing is our
own, not even this spark of life which
is owed to Death; but Oh, grant that
after our going some interposition of
human memory come between us and
utter obliteration!
Ibid. The Greek Anthology

A. EDWARD NEWTON
[1864–   ]

Young man, get a hobby; preferably
get two, one for indoors and one for
out; get a pair of hobby-horses that
can safely be ridden in opposite directions.
*Amenities of Book-Collecting.
Chap. 1*

I may as well confess that the envy
shown by our fellow collectors when we
display our treasures is not annoying to
us.
Ibid.

Possession is the grave of bliss. No
sooner do we own some great book than
we want another.
Ibid. Chap. 3

Only when a man is safely ensconced
under six feet of earth, with several
tons of enlauding granite upon his
chest, is he in a position to give advice
with any certainty, and then he is silent.
Ibid. Chap. 4

A good resolution is, never to be satisfied with a poor copy of a book at any price; a superlatively fine copy of a good book is always cheap.

This Book-Collecting Game.
Chap. 2

I wish that some one would give a course in how to live. It can't be taught in the colleges: that's perfectly obvious, for college professors don't know any better than the rest of us.

Ibid. Chap. 10

Gilbert White discovered the formula for complete happiness, but he died before making the announcement, leaving it for me to do so. It is to be very busy with the unimportant.

Ibid.

What a delight it is, at the end of a busy day, to throw one's self into an arm chair before a wood fire, and think. No, not think! muse is a better word. I am by no means sure that I've ever thought, and I'm not certain that I wish to; looking about me, I see thinkers, and it does not appear that they are any wiser or better or happier than I.

A Magnificent Farce. Chap. 7

From contemplation one may become wise, but knowledge comes only from study.

Ibid. Chap. 8

I read for pleasure, mark you. In general I like wedding bells at the end of novels. "They married and lived happily ever after" — why not? it has been done.

A Great Victorian

STEPHEN PHILLIPS
[1864–1915]

The moment deep
When we are conscious of the secret dawn,
Amid the darkness that we feel is green.
Marpessa

Thy face remembered is from other worlds,
It has been died for, though I know not when,

It has been sung of, though I know not where.
Marpessa

Women that remember in the night.
Ibid.

The half of music, I have heard men say,
Is to have grieved.
Ibid.

Out of our sadness have we made this world
So beautiful.
Ibid.

The constable with lifted hand
Conducting the orchestral Strand.
The Wife

O to recall!
What to recall?
Not the star in waters red,
Not this:
Laughter of a girl that's dead,
O this!
Lyrics. I Stanza 4

Thou shalt stand
Gazing for ever on the earth, and watch
How fast thy words incarnadine the world!
Christ in Hades

Who shall set a shore to love?
When hath it ever swerved from death, or when
Hath it not burned away all barriers,
Even dearest ties of mother and of son,
Even of brothers?
Paolo and Francesca. Act II, Sc. 1

We two rush
Together through the everlasting years.
Us, then, whose only pain can be to part,
How wilt Thou punish? For what ecstasy
Together to be blown about the globe!
What rapture in perpetual fire to burn
Together!
Ibid. Act IV

JOSEPH BERT SMILEY
[1864–1903]

Thirty years with that tongue so sharp?
Ho! Angel Gabriel! Give him a Harp!
St. Peter at the Gate (Thirty Years with a Shrew). Stanza 13

See that on finest ambrosia he feeds,
He's had about all the Hades he needs;
It isn't just hardly the thing to do
To roast him on earth and the future,
    too.
St. Peter at the Gate
Stanza 14

ISRAEL ZANGWILL
[1864–1926]

In how many lives does Love really
play a dominant part? The average taxpayer is no more capable of a "grand
passion" than of a grand opera.
Romeo and Juliet and Other Love
Stories

JOHN BENNETT
[1865–   ]

God made memory cruel, that men
might know remorse; but the Devil devised forgetfulness, anodyne of regret.
Madame Margot. Page 82

If Life's a lie, and Love's a cheat,
    As I have heard men say,
Then here's a health to fond deceit —
    God bless you, dear, to-day!
God Bless You, Dear, To-day.
Stanza 3

A hundred years from now, dear heart,
    We shall not care at all.
It will not matter then a whit,
    The honey or the gall.
In a Rose Garden. Stanza 1 [1895]

I want men to remember,
    When gray Death sets me free,
I was a man who had many friends,
    And many friends had me.
I Want an Epitaph

But, yet . . . he made a thousand
    friends.
    Yes: and, by God! he kept them.
Ibid.

We are all but fellow-travellers
    Along Life's weary way;
If any man can play the pipes,
    In God's name, let him play.
Year Book, Poetry Society of
South Carolina [1921]

MADISON JULIUS CAWEIN
[1865–1914]

Some reckon time by stars,
    And some by hours;
Some measure days by dreams,
    And some by flowers;
My heart alone records
    My days and hours.
Some Reckon Time by Stars.
Stanza 1

Here is the place where Loveliness keeps
    house,
Between the river and the wooded hills.
Here Is the Place

High as a star, yet lowly as a flower,
    Unknown she takes her unassuming
    place
At Earth's proud masquerade — the
    appointed hour
    Strikes, and, behold, the marvel of
    her face.
Beauty

An old Spanish saying is that "a kiss
without a moustache is like an egg
without salt."
Nature-Notes. Page 119

ROBERT WILLIAM
CHAMBERS
[1865–1933]

Sez Corporal Madden to Private Mc-
    Fadden:
"Yer figger wants padd'n —
Sure, man, ye've no shape!
Behind ye yer shoulders
Stick out like two bowlders;
Yer shins are as thin
As a pair of pen-holders!"
The Recruit. Stanza 3

FRANK MOORE COLBY [1]
[1865–1925]

True satire is not the sneering substance that we know, but satire that includes the satirist.
Essays. Vol. 1

---

[1] He possessed a sense of humor which for
depth, comprehension, and incisiveness is un-
equalled in the whole range of American
criticism. — JOHN ABBOT CLARK

Men will confess to treason, murder, arson, false teeth, or a wig. How many of them will own up to a lack of humor?
Essays. Vol. 1

Nobody can describe a fool to the life, without much patient self-inspection.
Ibid.

Every man ought to be inquisitive through every hour of his great adventure down to the day when he shall no longer cast a shadow in the sun. For if he dies without a question in his heart, what excuse is there for his continuance?
Ibid.

In spite of the large population of this planet, men and women remain to-day the most inaccessible things on it.
Ibid. Vol. 2

A new movement is not a stampede to some new object, but a stampede away from some old person.
Ibid.

The attempt to turn a complex problem of the head into a simple moral question for the heart to answer, is of course a necessary part of all political discussions.
Ibid.

I have found some of the best reasons I ever had for remaining at the bottom simply by looking at the men at the top.
Ibid.

A "new thinker," when studied closely, is merely a man who does not know what other people have thought.
The Margin of Hesitation

Were it not for the presence of the unwashed and the half-educated, the formless, queer and incomplete, the unreasonable and absurd, the infinite shapes of the delightful human tadpole, the horizon would not wear so wide a grin.
Imaginary Obligations

In public we say the race is to the strongest; in private we know that a lopsided man runs the fastest along the little side-hills of success.
Constrained Attitudes

Journalists have always been our most old-fashioned class, being too busy with the news of the day to lay aside the mental habits of fifty years before.
Constrained Attitudes

HOLMAN FRANCIS DAY
[1865–1935]

He pasted a sheet of postage stamps
  from snout clear down to tail,
Put on a quick delivery stamp, and
  sent the cod by mail.
Cure for Homesickness

The purest affection the heart can hold
Is the honest love of a nine-year-old.
That May-basket for Mabel Fry

If ye only knew the backaches in an
  old stun' wall!
An Old Stun' Wall

"LAURENCE HOPE"
(ADELA FLORENCE CORY NICOLSON)
[1865–1904]

Less than the dust, beneath thy Chariot
  wheel,
Less than the rust, that never stained
  thy Sword.
Less Than the Dust. Stanza 1

For this is Wisdom; to love, to live,
To take what Fate, or the Gods, may
  give.
The Teak Forest

To have, — to hold, — and, — in time,
  — let go!
Ibid.

Pale hands I loved beside the Shalimar,
  Where are you now? Who lies beneath your spell?
Whom do you lead on Rapture's road-
  way, far,
  Before you agonize them in farewell?
Kashmiri Song. Stanza 1

Yet I, this little while ere I go hence,
Love very lightly now, in self-defence.
Verse by Taj Mahomed

Men should be judged, not by their tint
  of skin,
  The Gods they serve, the Vintage that they drink,
Nor by the way they fight, or love, or
  sin,

But by the quality of thought they think.
Men Should Be Judged

Often devotion to virtue arises from sated desire.
I Arise and Go Down to the River.
Stanza 6

RUDYARD KIPLING
[1865–1936]

I have eaten your bread and salt.
I have drunk your water and wine.
The deaths ye died I have watched beside
And the lives ye led were mine.
Departmental Ditties. Prelude,
Stanza 1

Who shall doubt "the secret hid
Under Cheops' pyramid"
Was that the contractor did
Cheops out of several millions?
A General Summary. Stanza 4

Little Tin Gods on Wheels.
Public Waste. Stanza 4

Trust me, To-day's Most Indispensables,
Five hundred men can take your place or mine.
The Last Department. Stanza 8

The blush that flies at seventeen
Is fixed at forty-nine.
My Rival. Stanza 2

The toad beneath the harrow knows
Exactly where each tooth-point goes;
The butterfly upon the road
Preaches contentment to that toad.
Pagett, M.P.

Cross that rules the Southern Sky!
Stars that sweep, and turn, and fly,
Hear the Lovers' Litany: —
"Love like ours can never die!"[1]
The Lovers' Litany. Stanza 2

But seamen learnt — what landsmen know —
That neither gifts nor gain

---

[1] The tender motto, writ so fair,
Upon his 'bacco box he views,
Nancy the poet, Love the muse:
"If you loves I as I loves you,
No pair so happy as we two."
CHARLES DIBDIN [1745–1814]:
The Token

Can hold a winking Light o' Love
Or Fancy's flight restrain.
The Ballad of Fisher's Boarding-House. Stanza 9

And a woman is only a woman, but a good cigar is a smoke.
The Betrothed. Stanza 25

The temper of chums, the love of your wife,[1] and a new piano's tune —
Which of the three will you trust at the end of an Indian June?
Certain Maxims of Hafiz. IV

Pleasant the snaffle of Courtship, improving the manners and carriage;
But the colt who is wise will abstain from the terrible thorn-bit of Marriage.
Ibid. XI

If She have spoken a word, remember thy lips are sealed,
And the Brand of the Dog is upon him by whom is the secret revealed.
If She have written a letter, delay not an instant but burn it.
Ibid. XV

If there be trouble to Herward, and a lie of the blackest can clear,
Lie, while thy lips can move or a man is alive to hear.
Ibid.

My Son, if a maiden deny thee and scufflingly bid thee give o'er,
Yet lip meets with lip at the lastward. Get out! She has been there before.
They are pecked on the ear and the chin and the nose who are lacking in lore.
Ibid. XVI

You'll never plumb the Oriental mind,
And if you did, it isn't worth the toil.
One Viceroy Resigns

How can I turn from any fire
On any man's hearthstone?
I know the wonder and desire
That went to build my own!
The Fires. Stanza 7

---

[1] It is as foolish to make experiments upon the constancy of a friend, as upon the chastity of a wife. — DR. SAMUEL JOHNSON: Letter to James Boswell, Sept. 9, 1779

It may be that Fate will give me life
  and leave to row once more —
Set some strong man free for fighting
  as I take awhile his oar.
But to-day I leave the galley. Shall I
  curse her service then?
God be thanked! Whate'er comes after,
  I have lived and toiled with Men!
      The Galley-Slave. Stanza 10

I am sick of endless sunshine, sick of
  blossom-burdened bough.
Give me back the leafless woodlands
  where the winds of Springtime
  range —
Give me back one day in England, for
  it's Spring in England now!
      In Springtime. Stanza 1

They rise to their feet as He passes by,
  gentlemen unafraid.
      Barrack Room Ballads.
      Dedication, Stanza 5

He scarce had need to doff his pride or
  slough the dross of Earth —
E'en as he trod that day to God so
  walked he from his birth,
In simpleness and gentleness and honour and clean mirth.[1]
      Ibid. Stanza 7

Since spoken word Man's Spirit stirred
  Beyond his belly-need,
What is is Thine of fair design
  In Thought and Craft and Deed.
      To the True Romance. Stanza 3

It's like a book, I think, this bloomin'
  world,
Which you can read and care for just
  so long,
But presently you feel that you will die
Unless you get the page you're readin'
  done,
An' turn another — likely not so good;
But what you're after is to turn 'em all.
      Sestina of the Tramp-Royal.
      Stanza 6

And the tunes that mean so much to
  you alone —
Common tunes that make you choke
  and blow your nose,
Vulgar tunes that bring the laugh that
  brings the groan —

[1] Wolcott Balestier [1861–1891], Mrs. Kipling's brother.

I can rip your very heartstrings out
  with those.
      The Song of the Banjo. Stanza 6

"Something hidden. Go and find it. Go
  and look behind the Ranges —
Something lost behind the Ranges.
  Lost and waiting for you. Go!"
      The Explorer. Stanza 2

Anybody might have found it but —
  His Whisper came to Me!
      Ibid. Stanza 18

Who hath desired the Sea? — the sight
  of salt water unbounded —
The heave and the halt and the hurl
  and the crash of the comber wind-
  hounded?
      The Sea and the Hills. Stanza 1

So and no otherwise — hillmen desire
  their Hills!
      Ibid.

Lord, send a man like Robbie Burns to
  sing the Song o' Steam!
      M'Andrew's Hymn

Interdependence absolute, foreseen, ordained, decreed,
To work, ye'll note, at any tilt an' every
  rate o' speed.
      Ibid.

But I ha' lived an' I ha' worked. Be
  thanks to Thee, Most High!
An' I ha' done what I ha' done — judge
  Thou if ill or well.
      Ibid.

Absolute, unvarying rigidity, rigidity!
      The Ship that Found Herself

They copied all they could follow, but
  they couldn't copy my mind.
      The "Mary Gloster"

Overloaded, undermanned, meant to
  founder, we
Euchred God Almighty's storm, bluffed
  the Eternal Sea!
      The Ballad of the "Bolivar."
      Stanza 12

King Solomon drew merchantmen
  Because of his desire
For peacocks, apes, and ivory,
  From Tarshish unto Tyre.[1]
      The Merchantmen. Stanza 1

[1] See Masefield, page 832.

The God of Fair Beginnings
  Hath prospered here my hand —
The cargoes of my lading,
  And the keels of my command.
*   The Song of Diego Valdez.*
*   Stanza 1*

The Liner she's a lady, and if a war
  should come,
The Man-o'-War's 'er 'usband, and 'e'd
  bid 'er stay at home;
But, oh, the little cargo-boats that fill
  with every tide!
'E'd 'ave to up an' fight for them for
  they are England's pride.
*   The Liner She's a Lady. Stanza 5*

And it's time to turn on the old trail,
  our own trail, the out trail,
Pull out, pull out, on the Long Trail —
  the trail that is always new!
*   The Long Trail. Stanza 1*

There be triple ways to take, of the
  eagle or the snake,
  Or the way of a man with a maid; [1]
But the sweetest way to me is a ship's
  upon the sea
  In the heel of the North-East Trade.
*   Ibid. Stanza 4*

We have fed our sea for a thousand
  years
  And she calls us, still unfed,
Though there's never a wave of all her
  waves
  But marks our English dead.
*   The Song of the Dead. II, Stanza 1*

If blood be the price of admiralty,
  Lord God, we ha' paid in full!
*   Ibid.*

Deeper than speech our love, stronger
  than life our tether,
But we do not fall on the neck nor kiss
  when we come together.
*   England's Answer*
  So long as The Blood endures,
I shall know that your good is mine: ye
  shall feel that my strength is
  yours:
In the day of Armageddon, at the last
  great fight of all,
That Our House stand together and
  the pillars do not fall.
*   Ibid.*

[1] See *Proverbs, XXX, 18 and 19.*

Go to your work and be strong, halting
  not in your ways,
Baulking the end half-won for an instant dole of praise.
Stand to your work and be wise — certain of sword and pen,
Who are neither children nor God, but
  men in a world of men!
*   England's Answer*

Ever the wide world over, lass,
  Ever the trail held true,
Over the world and under the world,
  And back at the last to you.
*   The Gipsy Trail. Stanza 2*

The wild hawk to the wind-swept sky,
  The deer to the wholesome wold
And the heart of a man to the heart of
  a maid,
  As it was in the days of old.
*   Ibid. Stanza 11*

Daughter am I in my mother's house;
But mistress in my own.
*   Our Lady of the Snows.[1] Stanza 1*

Enslaved, illogical, elate,
  He greets the embarrassed Gods, nor
  fears
To shake the iron hand of Fate
  Or match with Destiny for beers.
*   An American. Stanza 13*

Buy my English posies!
  Kent and Surrey may —
Violets of the Undercliff
  Wet with Channel spray;
Cowslips from a Devon combe —
  Midland furze afire.
*   The Flowers. Stanza 1*

They change their skies above them,
  But not their hearts that roam.
*   The Native-born. Stanza 2*

Last toast — and your foot on the
  table! —
A health to the Native-born!
*   Ibid. Stanza 11*

There's a Legion that never was 'listed,
  That carries no colours or crest.
*   The Lost Legion. Stanza 1*

Old Days! The wild geese are flighting,
  Head to the storm as they faced it
  before!
For where there are Irish there's loving
  and fighting,

[1] The Dominion of Canada.

And when we stop either, it's Ireland
no more!
The Irish Guards. Stanza 4

And he wrote for them wonderful verses
that swept the land like flame,
Till the fatted souls of the English were
scourged with the thing called
Shame.
The Last of the Light Brigade.
Stanza 8

God gives all men all earth to love,
But since man's heart is small,
Ordains for each one spot shall prove
Belovèd over all.
Sussex. Stanza 12

A fool there was and he made his prayer
(Even as you and I!)
To a rag and a bone and a hank of hair
(We called her the woman who did not
care)
But the fool he called her his lady
fair —
(Even as you and I!)
The Vampire. Stanza 1

Oh, the years we waste and the tears
we waste
And the work of our head and hand
Belong to the woman who did not
know . . .
And did not understand.
Ibid. Stanza 2

When Earth's last picture is painted,
and the tubes are twisted and
dried,
When the oldest colours have faded,
and the youngest critic has died,
We shall rest, and, faith, we shall need
it — lie down for an æon or two,
Till the Master of All Good Workmen
shall put us to work anew.
When Earth's Last Picture Is
Painted. Stanza 1

And only the Master shall praise us,
and only the Master shall blame;
And no one shall work for money, and
no one shall work for fame;
But each for the joy of the working,
and each, in his separate star,
Shall draw the Thing as he sees It for
the God of Things as They Are!
Ibid. Stanza 3

Oh, East is East, and West is West, and
never the twain shall meet,
Till Earth and Sky stand presently at
God's great Judgment Seat.
But there is neither East nor West, Bor-
der, nor Breed, nor Birth,
When two strong men stand face to
face, though they come from the
ends of the earth!
The Ballad of East and West

Send the road is clear before you when
old Spring-fret comes o'er you,
And the Red Gods call for you!
The Feet of the Young Men

Make ye no truce with Adam-zad —
the Bear that walks like a Man!
The Truce of the Bear. Stanza 2

The Goth and the shameless Hun!
The Rowers. Stanza 11

Cock the gun that is not loaded, cook
the frozen dynamite —
But oh, beware my Country, when my
Country grows polite!
Et Dona Ferentes. Stanza 11

A Tinker out of Bedford,
A vagrant oft in quod,
A private under Fairfax,
A minister of God, —
Two hundred years and thirty
Ere Armageddon came
His single hand portrayed it,
And Bunyan was his name!
The Holy War. Stanza 1

Broke to every known mischance, lifted
over all
By the light sane joy of life, the buckler
of the Gaul;
Furious in luxury, merciless in toil.
France [1913]

Strictest judge of her own worth, gentlest of man's mind,
First to face the Truth and last to leave
old Truths behind —
France, beloved of every soul that loves
or serves its kind!
Ibid.

All we have of freedom, all we use or
know —
This our fathers bought for us long and
long ago.
The Old Issue. Stanza 5

Ancient Right unnoticed as the breath
we draw —
Leave to live by no man's leave, underneath the law.
The Old Issue. Stanza 6

We have had a jolly good lesson, and it
serves us jolly well right!
The Lesson [1902]. Stanza 2

We have forty million reasons for failure, but not a single excuse.
Ibid. Stanza 8

With the flannelled fools at the wicket
or the muddied oafs at the goals.
The Islanders [1902]

No doubt but ye are the People — absolute, strong, and wise;
Whatever your heart has desired ye
have not withheld from your eyes.
On your own heads, in your own hands,
the sin and the saving lies!
Ibid.

Creation's cry goes up on high
From age to cheated age:
"Send us the men who do the work
For which they draw the wage!"
The Wage-Slaves. Stanza 3

This is our lot if we live so long and
labour unto the end —
That we outlive the impatient years
and the much too patient friend:
And because we know we have breath
in our mouth and think we have
thoughts in our head,
We shall assume that we are alive,
whereas we are really dead.
The Old Men. Stanza 1

Take up the White Man's burden.
*The White Man's Burden.
Stanza 1*

The tumult and the shouting dies;
The Captains and the Kings depart:
Still stands Thine ancient sacrifice,
An humble and a contrite heart.
Recessional. Stanza 2

Lest we forget — lest we forget! [1]
Ibid.

[1] Best by remembering God, say some,
We keep our high imperial lot.
Fortune, I fear, hath oftenest come
When we forgot — when we forgot.
SIR WILLIAM WATSON:
The Unknown God, St. 10

Lo, all our pomp of yesterday
Is one with Nineveh and Tyre!
Recessional. Stanza 3

But, spite all modern notions, I've
found her first and best —
The only certain packet for the Islands
of the Blest.
The Three-Decker. Stanza 1

One was Admiral of the North from
Solway Firth to Skye,
And one was Lord of the Wessex Coast
and all the lands thereby,
And one was Master of the Thames
from Limehouse to Blackwall,
And he was Chaplain of the Fleet —
the bravest of them all.
*The Rhyme of the Three Captains
[1890]* [1]

The Devil whispered behind the leaves,
"It's pretty, but is it Art?"
The Conundrum of the Workshops

Ah! what avails the classic bent
And what the cultured word,
Against the undoctored incident
That actually occurred?
The Benefactors. Stanza 1

It is not learning, grace nor gear,
Nor easy meat and drink,
But bitter pinch of pain and fear
That makes creation think.
Ibid. Stanza 3

There are nine and sixty ways of con-
structing tribal lays,
And every single one of them is right.
In the Neolithic Age. Stanza 5

You must hack through much deposit
Ere you know for sure who was it
Came to burial with such honour in the
Files
(Only seven seasons back beneath the
Files).
"Very great our loss and grievous —
So our best and brightest leave us,
And it ends the Age of Giants," say
the Files.
The Files

When your Imp of Blind Desire
Bids you set the Thames afire,

[1] William Black, Thomas Hardy, Walter
Besant. The poem is an elaborate satire on the
lack of copyright protection in the United
States at that time.

You'll remember men have done so —
    in the Files.
                  The Files

And the naked soul of Tomlinson grew
    white as a rain-washed bone.
                  Tomlinson

The sin they do by two and two they
    must pay for one by one.
                  Ibid.

Those who have passed to the further
    shore
May be hailed — at a price — on the
    road to En-dor.[1]
          En-Dor. Stanza 2

The female of the species is more
    deadly than the male.
        The Female of the Species.
                  Stanza 1

For as we come and as we go (and
    deadly-soon go we!)
The people, Lord, Thy people, are
    good enough for me!
       A Pilgrim's Way. Stanza 1

And when they bore me overmuch, I
    will not shake mine ears,
Recalling many thousand such whom I
    have bored to tears.
And when they labour to impress, I will
    not doubt nor scoff;
Since I myself have done no less and
    — sometimes pulled it off.
            Ibid. Stanza 3

"Goodbye, Romance" . . . and all un-
    seen
Romance brought up the nine-fifteen.
                  The King

The Sons of Mary seldom bother, for
    they have inherited that good
    part;
But the Sons of Martha favour their
    Mother of the careful soul and the
    troubled heart.[2]
       The Sons of Martha. Stanza 1

It is their care in all the ages to take
    the buffet and cushion the shock.
It is their care that the gear engages; it
    is their care that the switches lock.
            Ibid. Stanza 2

Raise ye the stone or cleave the wood [1]
    to make a path more fair or flat;
Lo, it is black already with blood some
    Son of Martha spilled for that!
Not as a ladder from Earth to Heaven,
    not as a witness to any creed,
But simple service simply given to his
    own kind in their common need.
       The Sons of Martha. Stanza 7

They have cast their burden upon the
    Lord, — and the Lord He lays it
    on Martha's Sons!
            Ibid. Stanza 8

My son was killed while laughing at
    some jest. I would I knew
What it was, and it might serve me in
    a time when jests are few.
       Epitaphs of the War. A Son

They've taken of his buttons off an' cut
    his stripes away,
An' they're hangin' Danny Deever in
    the mornin'.
       Danny Deever. Stanza 5

We aren't no thin red 'eroes.[2]
            Tommy. Stanza 4

Single men in barricks don't grow into
    plaster saints.
                  Ibid.

It's Tommy this, an' Tommy that, an'
    "Chuck 'im out, the brute!"
But it's "Savior of 'is country," when
    the guns begin to shoot.
            Ibid. Stanza 5

So 'ere's *to* you, Fuzzy-Wuzzy, at your
    'ome in the Soudan;
You're a pore benighted 'eathen but a
    first-class fightin' man.
       "Fuzzy-Wuzzy." Stanza 1

'E's all 'ot sand an' ginger when alive,
An' 'e's generally shammin' when 'e's
    dead.
            Ibid. Stanza 4

Though I've belted you and flayed you,
By the livin' Gawd that made you,
You're a better man than I am, Gunga
    Din!
        Gunga Din. Stanza 5

---

[1] Behold there is a woman that hath a familiar spirit at En-dor. — *1 Samuel, XXVIII, 7*
[2] Martha, thou art careful and troubled
about many things. — *Luke, X, 41*

[1] See Henry van Dyke, page 709.
[2] See Russell, page 541.

'Ave you 'eard o' the Widow at Windsor
    With a hairy gold crown on 'er 'ead?
      The Widow at Windsor. Stanza 1

Walk wide o' the Widow at Windsor,
    For 'alf o' Creation she owns:
We 'ave bought 'er the same with the
    sword an' the flame,
    An' we've salted it down with our
      bones!
      Ibid. Stanza 2

On the road to Mandalay,
Where the flyin'-fishes play,
An' the dawn comes up like thunder
    outer China 'crost the Bay!
      Mandalay. Stanza 1

I've a neater, sweeter maiden in a
    cleaner, greener land.
      Ibid. Stanza 5

Ship me somewheres east of Suez,
    where the best is like the worst,
Where there aren't no Ten Command-
    ments an' a man can raise a thirst.
      Ibid. Stanza 6

Back to the Army again, sergeant,
    Back to the Army again.
Out o' the cold an' the rain.
    "Back to the Army Again."
      Refrain

For there isn't a job on the top of the
    earth the beggar don't know, nor
    do.
    "Soldier an' Sailor Too." Stanza 2

'E's a sort of a bloomin' cosmopolouse
    — soldier an' sailor too.
      Ibid.

To stand an' be still to the Birken'ead
    drill [1] is a damn' tough bullet to
    chew.
      Ibid. Stanza 5

I've taken my fun where I've found it.
    The Ladies. Stanza 1

An' I learned about women from 'er.
    Ibid. Refrain

For the Colonel's Lady an' Judy
    O'Grady
Are sisters under their skins!
      Ibid. Stanza 8

We met upon the level an' we parted
    on the Square,

[1] See F. H. Doyle, page 475.

An' I was Junior Deacon in my Mother-
    Lodge out there!
    The Mother-Lodge. Refrain

The backbone of the Army is the Non-
    commissioned Man!
    The 'Eathen. Stanza 18

For to admire an' for to see,
For to be'old this world so wide —
It never done no good to me
But I can't drop it if I tried!
    "For to Admire." Refrain

He's an absent-minded beggar, but he
    heard his country's call,
And his reg'ment didn't need to send
    to find him!
    The Absent-minded Beggar.
      Stanza 3

A kopje is always a kopje,
And a Boojer is always a Boer!
    Two Kopjes. Stanza 2

Boots — boots — boots — boots —
    movin' up and down again!
There's no discharge in the war! [1]
    Boots. Stanza 1

The bachelor may risk 'is 'ide
    To 'elp you when you're downed;
But the married man will wait beside
    Till the ambulance comes round.
    The Married Man. Stanza 5

The married man must sink or swim
    An' — 'e can't afford to sink!
    Ibid. Stanza 7

If England was what England seems,
    An' not the England of our dreams,
But only putty, brass, an' paint,
    'Ow quick we'd drop 'er! But she
    ain't.
    The Return. Refrain

Of all the trees that grow so fair,
    Old England to adorn,
Greater are none beneath the Sun,
    Than Oak, and Ash, and Thorn. [2]
    A Tree Song. Stanza 1

Take of English earth as much
As either hand may rightly clutch.
In the taking of it breathe
Prayer for all who lie beneath.
    A Charm. Stanza 1

[1] There is no discharge in that war. — *Ecclesiastes, VIII, 8*

[2] Glasgerion swore a full great othe,
    By oake, and ashe, and thorne.
    PERCY: *Reliques, Glasgerion, St. 19*

Ride with an idle whip, ride with an
    unused heel,
But, once in a way, there will come a
    day
When the colt must be taught to feel
The lash that falls, and the curb that
    galls, and the sting of the row-
    elled steel.
        *The Conversion of Aurelian
                McGoggin*
If there be good in that I wrought
Thy Hand compelled it, Master, Thine.
      "My New-cut Ashlar." Stanza 2
One stone the more swings into place
In that dread Temple of Thy worth.
It is enough that, through Thy Grace,
I saw nought common on Thy Earth.
              Ibid. Stanza 6
Help me to need no aid from men
That I may help such men as need!
              Ibid. Stanza 7
One man in a thousand, Solomon says,
Will stick more close than a brother.
      The Thousandth Man. Stanza 1
But the Thousandth Man will stand by
    your side
To the gallows-foot — and after!
              Ibid. Stanza 4
Down to Gehenna or up to the Throne,
He travels the fastest who travels alone.
        The Winners. Stanza 1
King over all the children of pride
Is the Press.
           The Press. Stanza 5
The end of the fight is a tombstone
    white with the name of the late de-
    ceased,
And the epitaph drear: "A Fool lies
    here who tried to hustle the East."
        The Naulahka. Chap. 5
"Let us now praise famous men" — [1]
Men of little showing —
For their work continueth,
Broad and deep continueth,
Greater than their knowing.
        A School Song. Stanza 1
When Pack meets with Pack in the
    Jungle, and neither will go from
    the trail,

---

[1] Let us now praise famous men. — *Apocrypha, Ecclesiasticus, XLIV, 1*

Lie down till the leaders have spoken
    — it may be fair words shall pre-
    vail.
      The Law of the Jungle. Stanza 6
Now these are the Laws of the Jungle,
    and many and mighty are they;
But the head and the hoof of the Law
    and the haunch and the hump is
    — Obey!
            Ibid. Refrain
Anything green that grew out of the
    mould
Was an excellent herb to our fathers of
    Old.
      "Our Fathers of Old." Stanza 1
Wonderful little our fathers knew,
Half their remedies cured you dead —
Most of their teaching was quite un-
    true.
              Ibid. Stanza 3
By — they are by with mirth and tears,
Wit or the works of Desire —
Cushioned about on the kindly years
Between the wall and the fire.
      "Our Fathers Also." Stanza 2
Land of our Birth, we pledge to thee
Our love and toil in the years to be.
      The Children's Song. Stanza 1
Teach us Delight in simple things,
And Mirth that has no bitter springs.
              Ibid. Stanza 7
If you can meet with Triumph and
    Disaster
    And treat those two impostors just
    the same.
             If. Stanza 2
If you can talk with crowds and keep
    your virtue,
    Or walk with Kings — nor lose the
    common touch.
             Ibid. Stanza 4
Yours is the Earth and everything that's
    in it,
    And — which is more — you'll be a
    Man, my son!
                Ibid.
And thrones on Shrieking Circumstance
The Sacredly Absurd.
      The Necessitarian. Stanza 3
When the body that lived at your single
    will,
With its whimper of welcome, is stilled
    (how still!)

When the spirit that answered your every mood
Is gone — wherever it goes — for good,
You will discover how much you care,
And will give your heart to a dog to tear.
    The Power of the Dog. Stanza 4

The arrows of our anguish
Fly farther than we guess.
    The Rabbi's Song. Stanza 3

I keep six honest serving-men
  (They taught me all I knew);
Their names are What and Why and When
And How and Where and Who.
    The Elephant's Child. Stanza 1

I'd love to roll to Rio
Some day before I'm old!
    *The Beginning of the Armadilloes.
        Stanza 4*

When the ship goes *wop* (with a wiggle between)
And the steward falls into the soup-tureen. . . .
Why, then you will know (if you haven't guessed)
You're "Fifty North and Forty West!"
    How the Whale Got His Throat

We must go back with Policeman Day —
  Back from the City of Sleep!
    The City of Sleep. Stanza 1

Until thy feet have trod the Road
Advise not wayside folk.
    The Comforters. Stanza 1

Roses red and roses white
Plucked I for my love's delight.
She would none of all my posies —
Bade me gather her blue roses.
    Blue Roses. Stanza 1

Lo, I have wrought in common clay
Rude figures of a rough-hewn race.
    *Soldiers Three. Dedication,
        Stanza 2*

If I were damned of body and soul,
I know whose prayers would make me whole,
    Mother o' mine.
    Mother o' Mine

Them that asks no questions isn't told a lie.
    A Smuggler's Song. Stanza 6

When the robust and Brass-bound Man
  commissioned first for sea
His fragile raft, Poseidon laughed, and
  "Mariner," said he . . .
"You the unhoodwinked wave shall test
  — the immediate gulf condemn —
Except ye owe the Fates a jest, be slow
  to jest with them."
    Poseidon's Law

If once you have paid him the Dane-geld
  You never get rid of the Dane.
    Danegeld. Stanza 4

Far — oh, very far behind,
  So far she cannot call to him,
Comes Tegumai alone to find
  The daughter that was all to him.
    Merrow Down. Stanza 11

Say "we," "us" and "ours" when you're
  talking instead of "you fellows"
  and "I."
    Norman and Saxon. Stanza 6

At Runnymede, at Runnymede,
What say the reeds at Runnymede?
    *The Reeds of Runnymede.
        Stanza 1*

When Crew and Captain understand
  each other to the core,
It takes a gale and more than a gale to
  put their ship ashore.
    Together. Stanza 2

The snow lies thick on Valley Forge,
  The ice on the Delaware,
But the poor dead soldiers of King George
  They neither know nor care.
    *The American Rebellion. II, After,
        Stanza 1*

If you're off to Philadelphia in the morning,
  You mustn't take my stories for a guide.
There's little left, indeed, of the city
  you will read of,
  And all the folk I write about have died.
    Philadelphia. Stanza 1

When 'Omer smote 'is blooming lyre,
He'd 'eard men sing by land an' sea;
An' what he thought 'e might require,
'E went an' took — the same as me!
    *When 'Omer Smote 'is Bloomin'
        Lyre. Stanza 1*

Our England is a garden, and such gardens are not made
By singing: — "Oh, how beautiful!" and sitting in the shade.
The Glory of the Garden. Stanza 5
Oh, Adam was a gardener, and God who made him sees
That half a proper gardener's work is done upon his knees.
Ibid. Stanza 8
Our realm is diminished
With Great-Heart away.
Great-Heart (Theodore Roosevelt). Stanza 1
Zogbaum draws with a pencil,[1]
And I do things with a pen,
And you sit up in a conning tower
Bossing eight hundred men.
Inscription to Robley D. Evans
As I pass through my incarnations in every age and race,
I make my proper prostrations to the gods of the Market Place;
Peering through reverent fingers, I watch them flourish and fall,
And the Gods of the Copybook Maxims, I notice, outlast them all.
The Gods of the Copybook Maxims. Stanza 1
Master, this is Thy Servant.
He is rising eight weeks old.
He is mainly Head and Tummy.
His legs are uncontrolled.
His Apologies [Scottish terrier]
There rise her timeless capitals of empires daily born,
Whose plinths are laid at midnight and whose streets are packed at morn;
And here come tired youths and maids that feign to love or sin
In tones like rusty razor blades to tunes like smitten tin.
Naaman's Song[2]
It takes a great deal of Christianity to wipe out uncivilized Eastern instincts, such as falling in love at first sight.
Plain Tales. Lispeth

[1] Rufus Fairchild Zogbaum [1849–1925], artist and author.
[2] Interpreted as a description of Hollywood, California.

After marriage arrives a reaction, sometimes a big, sometimes a little, one; but it comes sooner or later, and must be tided over by both parties if they desire the rest of their lives to go with the current.
Plain Tales. Three and — an Extra
But that is another story.[1]
Ibid.
This is worth remembering. Speaking to, or crying over, a husband never did any good yet.
Ibid.
A woman's guess is much more accurate than a man's certainty.
Ibid.
The silliest woman can manage a clever man; but it needs a very clever woman to manage a fool!
Ibid.
Never praise a sister to a sister, in the hope of your compliments reaching the proper ears.
Ibid. False Dawn
If you hit a pony over the nose at the outset of your acquaintance, he may not love you, but he will take a deep interest in your movements ever afterwards.
Ibid.
Meddling with another man's folly is always thankless work.
Ibid. The Rescue of Pluffles
Many religious people are deeply suspicious. They seem — for purely religious purposes, of course — to know more about iniquity than the Unregenerate.
Ibid. Watches of the Night
She was as immutable as the Hills. But not quite so green.
Ibid. Venus Annodomini
Youth had been a habit of hers for so long, that she could not part with it.
Ibid.
Every one is more or less mad on one point.[2]
Ibid. On the Strength of a Likeness

[1] See Sterne, page 241.
[2] Semel insanivimus omnes (We have all once been mad). — Latin proverb; attributed to Virgil

Little Friend of All the World.
> *Kim. Chap. 1*

The first proof a man gives of his interest in a woman is by talking to her about his own sweet self. If the woman listens without yawning, he begins to like her. If she flatters the animal's vanity, he ends by adoring her.
> *Under the Deodars. The Education*
> *of Otis Yeere*

He wrapped himself in quotations [1] — as a beggar would enfold himself in the purple of Emperors.
> *Many Inventions. The Finest*
> *Story in the World*

Man that is born of woman is small potatoes and few in a hill.
> *Life's Handicap. The Head of the*
> *District*

I hold by the Ould Church, for she's the mother of them all — ay, an' the father, too. I like her bekase she's most remarkable regimental in her fittings. I may die in Honolulu, Nova Zambra, or Cape Cayenne, but wherever I die, me bein' fwhat I am, an' a priest handy, I go under the same orders an' the same words an' the same unction as tho' the pope himself come down from the dome av St. Peter's to see me off. There's neither high nor low, nor broad nor deep, nor betwixt nor between with her, an' that's what I like.
> *Mine Own People. On Greenhow*
> *Hill*

More men are killed by overwork than the importance of the world justifies.
> *The Phantom 'Rickshaw*

For all we take we must pay, but the price is cruel high.
> *The Courting of Dinah Shadd.*
> *Chap. 1*

Never show a woman that ye care the snap av a finger for her, an' begad she'll come bleatin' to your boot heels.
> *Ibid. Chap. 2*

As the day wears and the impetus of the morning dies away, there will come upon you an overwhelming sense of the uselessness of your toil. This must be striven against.
> *The Judgment of Dungara*

There aren't twelve hundred people in the world who understand pictures. The others pretend and don't care.
> *The Light That Failed. Chap. 7*

"What did the Governor of North Carolina say to the Governor of South Carolina?"

"Excellent notion. It *is* a long time between drinks." [1]
> *Ibid. Chap. 8*

'Tisn't beauty, so to speak, nor good talk necessarily. It's just It.
> *Traffics and Discoveries.*
> *Mrs. Bat'hurst*

He who rebukes the world is rebuked by the world.
> *Second Jungle Book.*
> *The Undertakers*

He had been, as the old law recommends, twenty years a youth, twenty years a fighter, though he had never carried a weapon in his life, and twenty years head of a household.
> *Ibid. Miracle of Purun Bhagat*

Hot and bothered.
> *Independence* [2]

If you have not your own rations you must feed out of your Tribe's hands — with all that that implies.
> *Ibid.*

---

[1] In literature quotation is good only when the writer whom I follow goes my way, and, being better mounted than I, gives me a cast. — R. W. EMERSON: *Quotation and Originality*

[1] Of the several traditions relating to the origin of this remark, the most reasonable one traces it to John Motley Morehead [1796–1866], who was Governor of North Carolina 1841–1845. He was visited by James H. Hammond [1807–1864], who was Governor of South Carolina 1842–1844. They engaged in discussion and argument, and when the latter waxed hot, Governor Morehead was reported by a servant to have exclaimed: "It's a long time between drinks." — Personal letter from John Motley Morehead, Nov. 21, 1934

Do you know what the Governor of South Carolina said to the Governor of North Carolina? It's a long time between drinks, observed that powerful thinker. — R. L. STEVENSON: *The Wrong Box, Chap. 8*

[2] Rectorial Address, St. Andrews, Oct. 10, 1923.

A man may be festooned with the whole haberdashery of success, and go to his grave a castaway.

Independence

Enough work to do, and strength enough to do the work.

A Doctor's Work [1]

That packet of assorted miseries which we call a Ship.

The First Sailor

For what there is of it — for such as it is — and for what it may be worth — will you drink to England and the English?

St. George's Day Dinner, 1920

An imperfectly denatured animal intermittently subject to the unpredictable reactions of an unlocated spiritual area.

Surgeons and The Soul [1923]. (*Definition of man*)

This new ship here, is fitted according to the reported increase of knowledge among mankind. Namely, she is cumbered, end to end, with bells and trumpets and clocks and wires which, it has been told to me, can call Voices out of the air or the waters to con the ship while her crew sleep. But sleep *Thou* lightly, O Nakhoda! [Captain]. It has not yet been told to me that the Sea has ceased to be the Sea.

Foreword to the Publisher [1935]

When your Daemon is in charge, do not try to think consciously. Drift, wait, and obey.

Something of Myself. Chap. 8 (*Posthumous autobiography, 1937*)

LOGAN PEARSALL SMITH
[1865–   ]

I rang the bell as of old; as of old I gazed at the great shining Door and waited. But, alas! that flutter and beat of the wild heart, that delicious Doorstep Terror — it was gone; and with it dear, fantastic, panic-stricken Youth

---

[1] Address, Oct., 1908, at Middlesex Hospital (where Kipling died in 1936).

had rung the bell, flitted around the corner and vanished for ever.

Trivia. On the Doorstep

'For the Pen,' said the Vicar; and in the sententious pause which followed I felt that I would offer any gifts of gold to avert or postpone the solemn, inevitable, and yet, as it seemed to me, perfectly appalling statement that 'the Pen is mightier than the Sword.'

Ibid. In Church

What a bore it is, waking up in the morning always the same person. I wish I were unflinching and emphatic, and had big, bushy eyebrows and a Message for the Age. I wish I were a deep Thinker, or a great Ventriloquist.

Ibid. Green Ivory

Enshrined in a box of white pasteboard I keep upstairs a black ceremonial object: it's my last link with Christendom and grave Custom: only on sacred occasions does it make its appearance, only at some great tribal dance of my race. To pageants of Woe I march with it, or of the hugest Felicity: at great Hallelujahs of Wedlock, or at last Valedictions, I hold it bareheaded as I bow before altars and tombs.

Ibid. The Fetish

But when in modern books, reviews, and thoughtful magazines I read about the Needs of the Age, its Complex Questions, its Dismays, Doubts, and Spiritual Agonies, I feel an impulse to go out and comfort that bewildered Epoch, to wipe away its tears, still its cries, and speak edifying words of Consolation to it.

Ibid. My Mission

And as at night I went past the Abbey, saw its walls towering high and solemn among the Autumn stars, I pictured to myself the white population in the vast darkness of its interior — all that hushed people of Heroes — ; not dead, I would think them, but animated with a still kind of life, and at last, after all their intolerable toils, the sounding tumult of battle, and perilous sea-paths, resting there, tranquil and satisfied and glorious, amid the epitaphs and allegorical figures of their tombs; — those high-piled, trophied, shapeless Abbey tombs, that long ago they toiled for, and laid down their gallant lives to win.

Trivia. The Abbey at Night

There are two things to aim at in life: first, to get what you want; and, after that, to enjoy it. Only the wisest of mankind achieve the second.

Afterthoughts [*1931*]

Happiness is a wine of the rarest vintage, and seems insipid to a vulgar taste.

Ibid.

How awful to reflect that what people say of us is true!

Ibid.

Solvency is entirely a matter of temperament and not of income.

Ibid.

That we should practise what we preach is generally admitted; but anyone who preaches what he and his hearers practise must incur the gravest moral disapprobation.

Ibid.

It is almost always worth while to be cheated; people's little frauds have an interest which more than repays what they cost us.

Ibid.

'Well, for my part,' they say, 'I cannot see the charm of Mrs. Jones.'

'Is it not just conceivable,' I feel inclined to answer, 'that Mrs. Jones hasn't tried to charm you?'

Ibid.

Why are happy people not afraid of Death, while the insatiable and the unhappy so abhor that grim feature?

Ibid.

When they come downstairs from their Ivory Towers, Idealists are apt to walk straight into the gutter.

Ibid.

The indefatigable pursuit of an unattainable Perfection, even though it consist in nothing more than in the pounding of an old piano, is what alone gives a meaning to our life on this unavailing star.

Ibid.

Eat with the Rich, but go to the play with the Poor, who are capable of Joy.

Afterthoughts [*1931*]

We need new friends; some of us are cannibals who have eaten their old friends up: others must have ever-renewed audiences before whom to re-enact an ideal version of their lives.

Ibid.

A best-seller is the gilded tomb of a mediocre talent.

Ibid.

What I like in a good author is not what he says, but what he whispers.

Ibid.

People say that life is the thing, but I prefer reading.

Ibid.

Most of all I envy the octogenarian poet [1] who joined three words — 'Go, lovely Rose' — so happily together, that he left his name to float down through Time on the wings of a phrase and a flower.

Ibid.

Thank heavens, the sun has gone in, and I don't have to go out and enjoy it.

Ibid.

What with its crude awakenings can youth know of the rich returns of awareness to elderly people from their afternoon naps; of their ironic thoughts and long retrospections, and the sweetness they taste of not being dead?

Ibid.

How I should like to distil my disesteem of my contemporaries into prose so perfect that all of them would have to read it!

Ibid.

Unsaleability is almost the hallmark, in modern times, of quality in writing . . . the enormous and half-educated publics of present-day England and America, though welcoming the novels of our famous novelists, have as a rule acclaimed as masterpieces books that were soon forgotten, while ignoring at first all that was exquisite and rare.

Fine Writing

[1] Edmund Waller [1606–1687]. See page 146.

ARTHUR SYMONS
[1865–   ]

And I would have, now love is over,
  An end to all, an end:
I cannot, having been your lover,
  Stoop to become your friend!
                    After Love. Stanza 3
As a perfume doth remain
In the folds where it hath lain,
So the thought of you, remaining
Deeply folded in my brain,
Will not leave me: all things leave me:
You remain.
                    Memory. Stanza 1
Life is a dream in the night, a fear
  among fears,
A naked runner lost in a storm of spears.
        In the Wood of Finvara. Stanza 1
Saint Anthony of Padua, whom I bear
In effigy about me, hear my prayer:
Kind saint who findest what is lost, I
  pray,
Bring back her heart: I lost it yester-
  day.
          *A Prayer to Saint Anthony of
                              Padua*
Out of the eternal bronze and mortal
  breath,
  And to the glory of man, me Rodin
  wrought;
Before the gates of glory and of death
  I bear the burden of the pride of
  thought.
        For Le Penseur of Rodin [1905]
  He knew that the whole mystery of
beauty can never be comprehended by
the crowd, and that while clearness is
a virtue of style, perfect explicitness is
not a necessary virtue.
          *The Symbolist Movement in
          Literature. Gérard de Nerval*
Without charm there can be no fine
literature, as there can be no perfect
flower without fragrance.
          Ibid. Stéphane Mallarmé
  The mystic too full of God to speak
intelligibly to the world.
              Ibid. Arthur Rimbaud
Many excellent writers, very many
painters, and most musicians are so tedious on any subject but their own.
                              Ibid.

  I have ever held that the rod with
which popular fancy invests criticism
is properly the rod of divination: a
hazel-switch for the discovery of buried
treasure, not a birch-twig for the casti-
gation of offenders.
          *An Introduction to the Study of
          Browning. Preface, first edition*

HERBERT TRENCH
[1865–1923]

A circumnavigator of the soul.
                Shakespeare. Stanza 4
Last: if upon the cold green mantling
  sea
  Thou cling, alone with Truth, to the
  last spar —
  Both castaway,
And one must perish — let it not be he
Whom thou art sworn to obey!
                    A Charge. Stanza 4

JOHN E. WOODROW
[? –1905]

The Church should have a tapering
  spire,
To point to realms where sin's forgiven,
And lead men's thoughts from earth to
  heaven.
                    Spire and Tower
  I like a tower,
It speaks of strength, of might, of
  power —
An emblem of the Church's strength
To overcome the world at length.
                              Ibid.

WILLIAM BUTLER YEATS
[1865–   ]

  The land of faery,
Where nobody gets old and godly and
  grave,
Where nobody gets old and crafty and
  wise,
Where nobody gets old and bitter of
  tongue.
              The Land of Heart's Desire
  When we are young
We long to tread a way none trod be-
  fore,

But find the excellent old way through love
And through the care of children to the hour
For bidding Fate and Time and Change good-bye.
The Land of Heart's Desire

I would mould a world of fire and dew
With no one bitter, grave, or over wise,
And nothing marred or old to do you wrong.
Ibid.

Land of Heart's Desire,
Where beauty has no ebb, decay no flood,
But joy is wisdom, Time an endless song.
Ibid.

Have I not seen the loveliest woman born
Out of the mouth of Plenty's horn,
Because of her opinionated mind
Barter that horn and every good
By quiet natures understood
For an old bellows full of angry wind?
A Prayer for My Daughter.
Stanza 8

Though I am old with wandering
Through hollow lands and hilly lands,
I will find out where she has gone,
And kiss her lips and take her hands;
And walk among long dappled grass,
And pluck till time and times are done
The silver apples of the moon,
The golden apples of the sun.
The Song of Wandering Aengus.
Stanza 3

All things uncomely and broken, all things worn out and old,
The cry of a child by the roadway, the creak of a lumbering cart,
The heavy steps of the ploughman, splashing the wintry mould,
Are wronging your image that blossoms a rose in the deeps of my heart.
The Lover Tells of the Rose in His Heart. Stanza 1

The wrong of unshapely things is a wrong too great to be told.
Ibid. Stanza 2

The years like great black oxen tread the world

And God, the herdsman, goads them on behind.
The Countess Cathleen

I find, under the boughs of love and hate,
In all poor foolish things that live a day,
Eternal beauty wandering on her way.
To the Rose upon the Rood of Time

Had I the heavens' embroidered cloths,
Enwrought with gold and silver light.
He Wishes for the Cloths of Heaven

But I, being poor, have only my dreams;
I have spread my dreams under your feet;
Tread softly because you tread on my dreams.
Ibid.

When you are old and gray and full of sleep,
And nodding by the fire, take down this book.
When You Are Old

How many loved your moments of glad grace,
And loved your beauty, with love false or true;
But one man loved the pilgrim soul in you,
And loved the sorrows of your changing face.
Ibid.

She bid me take life easy, as the grass grows on the weirs;
But I was young and foolish, and now am full of tears.
Down by the Salley Gardens

I will arise and go now, and go to Innisfree,
And a small cabin build there, of clay and wattles made;
Nine bean-rows will I have there, a hive for the honey-bee,
And live alone in the bee-loud glade.
The Lake Isle of Innisfree [1]

[1] I had still the ambition, formed in Sligo in my teens, of living in imitation of Thoreau on Innisfree, a little island in Lough Gill, and when walking through Fleet Street very homesick I heard a little tinkle of water and saw a fountain in a shop-window which balanced a little ball upon its jet, and began to

I hear it in the deep heart's core.
The Lake Isle of Innisfree
When I play on my fiddle in Dooney,
Folk dance like a wave of the sea.
The Fiddler of Dooney. Stanza 1
For the good are always the merry,
Save by an evil chance,
And the merry love the fiddle,
And the merry love to dance.
Ibid. Stanza 4
Romantic Ireland's dead and gone,
It's with O'Leary in the grave.
September, 1913. Stanza 1

GEORGE W. YOUNG

The word must be spoken that bids you
depart —
Though the effort to speak it should
shatter my heart —
Though in silence, with blighted affec-
tion, I pine,
Yet the lips that touch liquor must
never touch mine!
The Lips That Touch Liquor.
Stanza 5

GEORGE ADE
[1866–]

Last night at twelve I felt immense,
But now I feel like thirty cents.
The Sultan of Sulu. Remorse
But, R-E-M-O-R-S-E!
The water-wagon is the place for me;
It is no time for mirth and laughter,
The cold, gray dawn of the morning
after! [1]
Ibid.
A good folly is worth what you pay
for it.
Fables in Slang. A Lot for Three
Dollars
In uplifting, get underneath.
Ibid. The Good Fairy
He had been kicked in the Head by
a Mule when young and believed every-
thing he read in the Sunday Papers.
Ibid. The Slim Girl

---

remember lake water. From the sudden remembrance came my poem Innisfree. — *The*
Trembling of the Veil (autobiography)
[1] See Byron, page 359, and Dickens, page
495.

Only the more rugged mortals should
attempt to keep up with current liter-
ature.
Fables in Slang. Didn't Care for
Story-books
Never put off until To-morrow what
should have been Done early in the
Seventies.
Forty Modern Fables. The Third
and Last Call
To insure Peace of Mind ignore the
Rules and Regulations.
Ibid. The Crustacean
If it were not for the Presents, an
Elopement would be Preferable.
Ibid. The General Manager of
the Love Affair
Stay with the Procession or you will
Never Catch up.
Ibid. The Old-Time Pedagogue
The Time to enjoy a European trip
is about Three Weeks after Unpacking.
Ibid. The Hungry Man
The Julep is built in a Tall Vase. It
consists of a Leafy Roof-Garden super-
imposed on a Display of Small Fruit,
the whole underlaid with a Nansen Ice-
Floe.
Ibid. The Brotherhood of States
Draw your Salary before Spending it.
Ibid. The People's Choice
The Man was a Pinhead in a good
many Respects, but he was Wise as a
Serpent.
Ibid. The Wise Piker
For Parlor Use the Vague Generality
is a Life-Saver.
Ibid.

GELETT BURGESS
[1866–]

I'd rather have Fingers than Toes,
I'd rather have Eyes than a Nose;
And as for my Hair
I'm glad it's all there,
I'll be awfully sad when it goes.
Nonsense Verses
He joyed of life's pleasures
All he could find;
Yet richest the treasures
He found in his mind.
Epitaph. Stanza 2

Leave the lady, Willy, let the racket rip,
She is going to fool you, you have lost
    your grip,
Your brain is in a muddle, and your
    heart is in a whirl,
Come along with me, Willy, never mind
    the girl!
          Willy and the Lady. Stanza 1

I never saw a Purple Cow,
  I never hope to see one;
But I can tell you, anyhow,
  I'd rather see than be one.
               The Purple Cow

Ah, yes, I wrote the "Purple Cow" —
  I'm sorry, now, I wrote it!
But I can tell you, anyhow,
  I'll kill you if you quote it.
               Cinq Ans Après

"ETHNA CARBERY"
(MRS. SEUMAS MacMANUS)
[1866–1902]

Blow softly down the valley,
  O wind, and stir the fern
That waves its green fronds over
  The King of Ireland's Cairn.
       The King of Ireland's Cairn.
                    Stanza 1

'Tis well he seeks no tidings —
  His heart would ache to know
That all is changed in Ireland,
  And Tara lieth low.[1]
               Ibid. Stanza 11

EDMUND VANCE COOKE
[1866–1932]

Well, did you hear? Tom Lincoln's wife
  to-day,
The devil's luck for folk as poor as
  they!
Poor Tom! poor Nance!
Poor youngun born without a chance!
      Born Without a Chance. Stanza 1

The Woman tempted me — and tempts
  me still!

---

[1] No more to chiefs and ladies bright
    The harp of Tara swells;
  The chord alone, that breaks at night,
    Its tale of ruin tells.
      THOMAS MOORE: *The Harp that*
        Once thro' Tara's Halls, St. 2

Lord God, I pray You that she ever
  will!
                        Adam

'Tis not the weight of jewel or plate,
  Or the fondle of silk and fur;
'Tis the spirit in which the gift is rich,
  As the gifts of the wise ones were;
And we are not told whose gift was gold
  Or whose was the gift of myrrh.
            The Spirit of the Gift

Oh, a trouble's a ton, or a trouble's an
  ounce,
  Or a trouble is what you make it,
And it isn't the fact that you're hurt
  that counts,
  But only how did you take it.
          How Did You Die? Stanza 1

Now by the rood, as Hamlet says, it
  grieves me sore to say
The stage is not as once it was when
  I was wont to play.
        The Other One Was Booth.
                        Stanza 1

True artists are a rare, rare breed; there
  were but two, forsooth,
In all my time, the stage's prime; and
  the other one was Booth.
                        Ibid.

My pa held me up to the moo-cow-moo,
  So clost I could almost touch,
En' I fed him a couple of times or two,
  En' I wasn't a fraid-cat — much.
         The Moo-Cow-Moo. Stanza 1

RICHARD LE GALLIENNE
[1866–   ]

Yea, howso we dream,
  Or how bravely we do;
The end is the same,
  Be we traitor or true:
    And after the bloom
    And the passion is past,
Death cometh at last.
         An Old Man's Song. Stanza 4

There's too much beauty upon this
  earth
For lonely men to bear.
       A Ballad of Too Much Beauty.
                       Stanza 1

One asked of Regret,
  And I made reply:

To have held the bird,
    And let it fly.
Regret

Canst thou be true across so many
    miles,
    So many days that keep us still apart?
Ah, canst thou live upon remembered
    smiles,
    And ask no warmer comfort for thy
    heart?
Love Platonic. 17

Bear to-day whate'er To-day may
    bring,
'Tis the one way to make To-morrow
    sing.
Ibid. In Her Diary

She's somewhere in the sunlight strong,
    Her tears are in the falling rain,
She calls me in the wind's soft song,
    And with the flowers she comes again.
Song

Shadow and sun — so too our lives are
    made —
Here learn how great the sun, how
    small the shade!
For Sundials

How many friends I loved are gone!
    Death delicately takes the best:
    O Death, be careful of the rest!
I cannot spare another one.
How Many Friends

May is building her house. With apple
    blooms
She is roofing over the glimmering
    rooms.
May Is Building Her House.
Stanza 1

I meant to do my work to-day —
    But a brown bird sang in the apple-
    tree,
And a butterfly flitted across the field,
    And all the leaves were calling me.
Transgression. Stanza 1

Poet of doom, dementia, and death.
For the Birthday of Edgar Allan Poe

Behind the times I know I am,
But what is a tired man to do?
I light my pipe, and read Charles Lamb.
Ballade of the Noisiness of the
Times. Stanza 1

I would make a list against the evil days
Of lovely things to hold in memory.
A Ballade-Catalogue of Lovely
Things. Stanza 1

None else can equal, by the Rood,
Dickens, Dumas, or Walter Scott.
A Bookman's Ballade of "The
Big Three"

Ah London! London! our delight,
Great flower that opens but at night.
A Ballad of London

Leaping alight on either hand
The iron lilies of the Strand.
Ibid.

Yet all the while my Lord I meet
In every London lane and street.[1]
The Second Crucifixion

"Name your favorite writer" should
be one of the first questions in the En-
gagement Catechism.
The Quest of the Golden Girl.
Book II, Chap. 6

Wild oats will get sown some time,
and one of the arts of life is to sow them
at the right time.
Ibid. Book III, Chap. 9

WALTER MALONE
[1866–1915]

They do me wrong who say I come no
    more
When once I knock and fail to find
    you in;
For every day I stand outside your
    door,
    And bid you wake, and rise to fight
    and win.
Opportunity. Stanza 1

And if a lowly singer dries one tear,
    Or soothes one humble human heart
    in pain,
Be sure his homely verse to God is dear,
    And not one stanza has been sung in
    vain.
The Humbler Poets. Stanza 3

---

[1] Mark Symons [1887–1935], an English
artist, chose this couplet as the theme and title
of his controversial painting of Christ preaching in the street to a modern crowd. The
Royal Academy rejected the painting, which
is now in a private collection in New York.

GILBERT MURRAY
[1866–   ]

Romantic plays with happy endings are almost of necessity inferior in artistic value to true tragedies. Not, one would hope, simply because they end happily; happiness in itself is certainly not less beautiful than grief; but because a tragedy in its great moments can generally afford to be sincere, while romantic plays live in an atmosphere of ingenuity and make-believe.

Preface to The Iphigenia in
Tauris of Euripides

The enemy has no definite name, though in a certain degree we all know him. He who puts always the body before the spirit, the dead before the living; who makes things only in order to sell them; who has forgotten that there is such a thing as truth, and measures the world by advertisement or by money; who daily defiles the beauty that surrounds him and makes vulgar the tragedy.

Religio Grammatici [*1918*]

JOHN OXENHAM

Art thou lonely, O my brother?
Share thy little with another!
Stretch a hand to one unfriended,
And thy loneliness is ended.

Lonely Brother

Kneel always when you light a fire!

The Sacrament of Fire

Thank God for sleep!
And, when you cannot sleep,
Still thank Him that you live
To lie awake.

The Sacrament of Sleep

For ears to hear the heavenly harmonies;
For eyes to see the unseen in the seen;
For vision of The Worker in the work;
For hearts to apprehend Thee everywhere; —
    We thank Thee, Lord!

A Little Te Deum of the
Commonplace

JOHN JEROME ROONEY
[1866–1934]

Yea, "writ in water," child of earth and sky,
Sprung from the sod, yet winging from on high:
Untainted, blithe, in beauty's passion strong
And shimmering with the rainbow hues of song!

John Keats

DORA SIGERSON
(MRS. CLEMENT SHORTER)
[1866–1918]

For if thy charity be overstrained
    And would bring slander where it cannot bless,
Give me but silence where good friendship waned,
    Grant me the mercy of forgetfulness.

If You Should Pass. Stanza 5

All night the small feet of the rain
    Within my garden ran,
And gentle fingers tapped the pane
    Until the dawn began.

April. Stanza 1

BERT LESTON TAYLOR
[1866–1921]

Profitless others, and stale and flat —
There are no more books in the world like that.

"Treasure Island." Stanza 2

When quacks with pills political would dope us,
    When politics absorbs the livelong day,
I like to think about the star Canopus,
    So far, so far away!

Canopus. Stanza 1

I meditate on interstellar spaces,
    And smoke a mild seegar.

Ibid. Stanza 4

A star that has no parallax to speak of,
    Conduces to repose.

Ibid. Stanza 5

To free, what I am pleased to call my mind,[1]

---

[1] See Lord Westbury, page 402.

From matters that perplex it and embarrass,
I take a glass, and seek until I find,
Far in the heaven, southward from Polaris,
A wisp of cloud — a nebula by name,
Andromeda provides a starry frame.
Ataraxia. Stanza 1

Hate of the millions who've choked you down,
In country kitchen or house in town,
We love a thousand, we hate but one,
With a hate more hot than the hate of the Gun —
Bread Pudding!
Chant of Hate for Bread Pudding.
Stanza 2

These scoffers, these obstructionists,
These fossils — who are they?
The glad young, mad young futurists
Who prance around to-day.
So Shall It Be. Stanza 6

Everywhere I look I see —
Fact or fiction, life or play,
Still the little game of Three:
B and C in love with A.
Old Stuff. Stanza 3

Consider, friends, this trio —
How little fuss they made.
They didn't curse when it was worse
Than ninety in the shade.
They moved about serenely
Within the furnace bright,
And soon forgot that it was hot,
With "no relief in sight."
A Hot Weather Classic: Shadrach,
Meshach, and Abed-nego. Stanza 4

When my sun of life is low,
When the dewy shadows creep,
Say for me before I go,
"Now I lay me down to sleep."
Sundown. Stanza 1

HERBERT GEORGE WELLS
[1866–   ]

The professional military mind is by necessity an inferior and unimaginative mind; no man of high intellectual quality would willingly imprison his gifts in such a calling.
The Outline of History. Chap. 40
[1920]

The Great War and the Petty Peace.
The Outline of History. Chap. 40
[1920]

Human history is in essence a history of ideas.
Ibid.

Every one of these hundreds of millions of human beings is in some form seeking happiness. . . . Not one is altogether noble nor altogether trustworthy nor altogether consistent; and not one is altogether vile. Not a single one but has at some time wept.
Ibid.

A federation of all humanity, together with a sufficient measure of social justice to ensure health, education, and a rough equality of opportunity, would mean such a release and increase of human energy as to open a new phase in human history.
Ibid. Chap. 41

Our true nationality is mankind.
Ibid.

While the poor little affairs of obscure, industrious men of letters are made the subject of intensive research, the far more romantic, thrilling and illuminating documents about the seekers and makers of great fortunes, are neither gathered nor cherished.
The Work, Wealth and Happiness of Mankind. Chap. 10 [1931]

In England we have come to rely upon a comfortable time-lag of fifty years or a century intervening between the perception that something ought to be done and a serious attempt to do it.
Ibid. Chap. 11

ERNEST DOWSON
[1867–1900]

They are not long, the weeping and the laughter,
Love and desire and hate:
I think they have no portion in us after
We pass the gate.
Vitae Summa Brevis. Stanza 1

I have been faithful to thee, Cynara!
　　in my fashion.
　　　　Non Sum Qualis Eram Bonae
　　　　　　Sub Regno Cynarae [1]
I cried for madder music and for
　　stronger wine.
　　　　　　　　　Ibid.
You would have understood me, had
　　you waited;
　　I could have loved you, dear! as
　　　　well as he:
Had we not been impatient, dear! and
　　fated
　　　　Always to disagree.
　　You Would Have Understood Me.
　　　　　　　　Stanza 1
What is the use of speech? Silence were
　　fitter:
　　Lest we should still be wishing things
　　　　unsaid.
　　　　　　　Ibid. Stanza 2
We have walked in Love's land a little
　　way,
　　We have learnt his lesson a little
　　　　while,
And shall we not part at the end of
　　day,
　　　　With a sigh, a smile?
　　　　　　April Love. Stanza 1
Always I know, how little severs me
From mine heart's country, that is yet
　　so far.
　　　　　Terre Promise. Stanza 2
From troublous sights and sounds set
　　free;
　　In such a twilight hour of breath,
Shall one retrace his life, or see,
　　Through shadows, the true face of
　　　　death?
　　　　Extreme Unction. Stanza 3
When this, our rose, is faded,
　　And these, our days, are done,
In lands profoundly shaded
　　From tempest and from sun;
Ah, once more come together,
　　Shall we forgive the past,
And safe from worldly weather
　　Possess our souls at last?
　　　　Amantium Irae. Stanza 1

---

[1] I am not the man I was under the reign
　　of the good Cynara.
　　HORACE: *Book 4, Ode 1, Ad Venerem*

Before my light goes out forever if God
　　should give me a choice of graces,
I would not reck of length of days, nor
　　crave for things to be;
But cry: "One day of the great lost
　　days, one face of all the faces,
Grant me to see and touch once more
　　and nothing more to see."
　　Impenitentia Ultima. Stanza 1

FINLEY PETER DUNNE ("MR. DOOLEY")
[1867–1936]

Th' dead ar-re always pop'lar. I
knowed a society wanst to vote a mon-
yment to a man an' refuse to help his
fam'ly, all in wan night.
　　　　　　　On Charity
Life'd not be worth livin' if we
didn't keep our inimies.
　　On New Year's Resolutions
No matther whether th' constitution
follows th' flag or not, th' Supreme
Coort follows th' iliction returns.
　　The Supreme Court's Decisions
Ivrything that's worth havin' goes
to th' city; th' counthry takes what's
left.
　　The City as a Summer Resort
I think a lie with a purpose is wan
iv th' worst kind an' th' mos' profit-
able.
　　　　　　　　On Lying
Th' dimmycratic party ain't on
speakin' terms with itsilf.
　　*Mr. Dooley Discusses Party
　　　　　　　　Politics*
Th' raypublican party broke ye, but
now that ye're down we'll not turn a
cold shoulder to ye. Come in an' we'll
keep ye broke.
　　　　　　　　Ibid.
What's fame, afther all, me la-ad?
'Tis as apt to be what some wan writes
on ye'er tombstone.
　　　　　　　　Fame
When ye build yer triumphal arch to
yer conquerin' hero, Hinnissey, build
it out of bricks so the people will have
somethin' convanient to throw at him
as he passes through.
　　　　　　　　Ibid.

Vice . . . is a creature of such hee-jus mien, . . . that the more ye see it th' better ye like it.

> *The Crusade Against Vice*

"D'ye think th' colledges has much to do with th' progress iv th' wurruld?" asked Mr. Hennessy.

"D'ye think," said Mr. Dooley, " 'tis th' mill that makes th' wather run?"

> *Colleges and Degrees*

"Ye know a lot about marriage, but ye niver marrid," said Mr. Hennessy.

"No," said Mr. Dooley. "No, say I, givin' three cheers, I know about marriage th' way an astronomer knows about th' stars."

> *Marriage*

"It's too bad that th' goolden days has passed. Capital still pats labor on th' back, but on'y with an axe. Labor rayfuses to be threated as a friend. It wants to be threated as an inimy. It thinks it gets more that way. They ar-re still a happy fam'ly, but it's more like an English fam'ly. They don't speak."

> *Labor and Capital*

EDWIN FRANCIS EDGETT
[1867–   ]

He may have a message
For the world,
But he is welcome
To no editorial haunts
If he rolls his manuscript.

> *The Manuscript Roller*

JOHN GALSWORTHY
[1867–1933]

Justice is a machine that, when some one has once given it the starting push, rolls on of itself.

> *Justice. Act II*

There is nothing more tragic in life than the utter impossibility of changing what you have done.

> *Ibid.*

You don't know what marriage is. Day after day, year after year. It's no use being sentimental — for people brought up as we are to have different

manners is worse than to have different souls. . . . It's the little things.

> *The Eldest Son. Act II*

You called me a damned Jew. My race was old when you were all savages. I am proud to be a Jew.[1]

> *Loyalties. Act II, Sc. 1*

Public opinion's always in advance of the Law.

> *Windows. Act I*

The value of a sentiment is the amount of sacrifice you are prepared to make for it.

> *Ibid. Act II*

For a man that can't see an inch into human nature, give me a psychological novelist.

> *Ibid.*

Love is no hot-house flower, but a wild plant, born of a wet night, born of an hour of sunshine; sprung from wild seed, blown along the road by a wild wind. A wild plant that, when it blooms by chance within the hedge of our gardens, we call a flower; and when it blooms outside we call a weed; but, flower or weed, whose scent and colour are always wild!

> *The Man of Property. Part II, Chap. 4*

By the cigars they smoke, and the composers they love, ye shall know the texture of men's souls.

> *Indian Summer of a Forsyte. Chap. 1*

A man of action, forced into a state of thought, is unhappy until he can get out of it.

> *Maid in Waiting. Chap. 3*

---

[1] In his *Reminiscences of Sixty Years in the National Metropolis*, BENJAMIN PERLEY POORE [1820–1887] quotes this reply of Senator Judah P. Benjamin [1181–1884] to a Senator of German extraction who taunted him with being a Jew: "The gentleman will please remember that when his half-civilized ancestors were hunting the wild boar in the forests of Silesia, mine were the Princes of the earth." See Disraeli, page 418.

We were running naked and staining ourselves with woad in our woods, when the looms of India and China were producing the delicate fabrics we seek now to imitate. —OLIVE SCHREINER: *From Man to Man, Chap. 7*

Politicians are marvels of energy and principle when they're out of office, but when they get in, they simply run behind the machine.

Maid in Waiting. Chap. 5

There's just one rule for politicians all over the world: Don't say in Power what you say in Opposition; if you do, you only have to carry out what the other fellows have found impossible.

Ibid. Chap. 7

One's eyes are what one is, one's mouth what one becomes.

Flowering Wilderness. Chap. 2

She had that peculiar feeling, experienced by all at times, of having once been someone else, which accounts for so much belief in the transmigration of souls.

Ibid. Chap. 11

The beginnings and endings of all human undertakings are untidy, the building of a house, the writing of a novel, the demolition of a bridge, and, eminently, the finish of a voyage.

Over the River. Chap. 1

He ordered himself a dozen oysters; but, suddenly remembering that the month contained no "r," changed them to a fried sole.[1]

The White Monkey. Part III, Chap. 7

It has often been remarked that the breakfast-tables of people who avow themselves indifferent to what the Press may say of them are garnished by all the newspapers on the morning when there is anything to say.

The Silver Spoon. Part II, Chap. 2

I've seen the moon, with lifted wing,
A white hawk, over cypress tree,

---

[1] Is is unseasonable and unwholesome in all months that have not an *R* in their name to eat an oyster. — WILLIAM BUTLER [1535–1618]: *Dyet's Dry Dinner* [1599]

Let's sing a song of glory to Themistocles O'Shea,
Who ate a dozen oysters on the second day of May.

STODDARD KING [1889–1933]: *The Man Who Dared*

The lover's star, the bloom of spring,
And evening folded on Tennessee.

At Sunset. Stanza 1

I, who exulted in sunshine and laughter,
Dreamed not of dying — death is such waste of me!

Valley of the Shadow

LIONEL JOHNSON [1]
[1867–1902]

The splendid silence clings
Around me: and around
The saddest of all kings
Crowned, and again discrowned.

By the Statue of King Charles at Charing Cross. Stanza 2

Vanquished in life, his death
By beauty made amends.

Ibid. Stanza 8

I know you: solitary griefs,
  Desolate passions, aching hours!
I know you: tremulous beliefs,
  Agonized hopes, and ashen flowers!

The Precept of Silence. Stanza 1

Some players upon plaintive strings
  Publish their wistfulness abroad;
I have not spoken of these things,
  Save to one man, and unto God.

Ibid. Stanza 3

Dear, human books,
With kindly voices, winning looks!
Enchaunt me with your spells of art,
And draw me homeward to your heart.

Oxford Nights

ERNEST FENWICK JOHNSTONE
[1867–1938]

I dreamed that I went to the City of Gold,
  To Heaven resplendent and fair,
And after I entered that beautiful fold
By one in authority there I was told
That not a Vermonter was there.

No Vermonters in Heaven. Stanza 1

---

[1] Inter Poetas Wiccamicos Haud Minimus Habebitur (Among the poets of Wykeham he will be held not least). — Tablet to Johnson in the cloisters of Winchester College.

We give them the best the Kingdom
    provides;
They have everything here that they
    want,
But not a Vermonter in Heaven abides;
A very brief period here he resides,
    Then hikes his way back to Ver-
    mont.
No Vermonters in Heaven.
Stanza 6

W. COMPTON LEITH

What song the Sirens sang? . . .
They sang of all that is above fulfilment and beyond clear vision; of the
immeasurable, the uncontained, the
half-imagined; of that which is touched
but never held, implored but unpos-
sessed. . . . They sang the vileness of
all who live contented upon an alms,
and are at ease in bonds, the slaves
whose servitude is made sweet by
habit.

Sirenica [*1913*]

The third hour after the meridian,
which is the day's autumn, the fatal
hour, unbearably steeped in sorrow.
Many, asked in what hour they have
perceived themselves most desolate
and under Medusa's eyes, would answer: "At this hour, and upon a summer's day."

Ibid.

JUDD MORTIMER LEWIS
[1867–   ]

If you know of a skeleton hidden away
In a closet and guarded and kept from
    the day
In the dark; and whose showing, whose
    sudden display
Would cause grief and sorrow and
    lifelong dismay,
  It's a pretty good plan to forget it.
Forget It. Stanza 2

CHARLES EDWARD
MONTAGUE
[1867–1928]

All authentic affection rests upon
vision . . . the state of mind and
heart which does not merely apprehend evidence but broods excitedly
over some completed and transfigured
image of an apprehended object.
The Right Place. Chap. 8

London on an early autumn afternoon of quiet sunshine, when all the
air is mysterious with a vaporous gold-
dust of illuminated motes and the hum
of the traffic seems to fall pensive and
muted round the big, benign London
policeman
    with uplifted hand
Conducting the orchestral Strand.[1]
Ibid. Chap. 14

A gifted small girl has explained
that pins are a great means of saving
life, "by not swallowing them."
Dramatic Values

Germany lay at our feet, a world's
wonder of downfall, a very Lucifer,
fallen, broken, bereaved beyond all the
retributive griefs which Greek tragedy
shows you afflicting the great who were
insolent, wilful, and proud. But it was
not enough for our small epicures of
revenge. They wanted to twist the enemy's wrists, where he lay bound, and
to run pins into his eyes. And they had
the upper hand of us now. The soldiers could only look on while the
scurvy performance dragged itself out
till the meanest of treaties was signed
at Versailles.
Disenchantment. Chap. 13 [*1922*]

"The freedom of Europe," "The
war to end war," "The overthrow of
militarism," "The cause of civilization" — most people believe so little
now in anything or anyone that they
would find it hard to understand the
simplicity and intensity of faith with
which these phrases were once taken
among our troops, or the certitude felt
by hundreds of thousands of men who
are now dead that if they were killed
their monument would be a new Europe not soured or soiled with the hates
and greeds of the old.
Ibid.

[1] Stephen Phillips, see page 773.

Among the mind's powers is one that comes of itself to many children and artists. It need not be lost, to the end of his days, by anyone who has ever had it. This is the power of taking delight in a thing, or rather in anything, everything, not as a means to some other end, but just because it is what it is, as the lover dotes on whatever may be the traits of the beloved object. A child in the full health of his mind will put his hand flat on the summer turf, feel it, and give a little shiver of private glee at the elastic firmness of the globe.

Disenchantment. Chap. 15

All dullness is in the mind; it comes out thence and diffuses itself over everything round the dull person, and then he terms everything dull, and thinks himself the victim of the impact of dull things. In stupid rich people, in boys and girls deadeningly taught at dead-alive schools, in all disappointed weaklings and in declining nations, this loss of power to shed anything but dullness upon what one sees and hears is common enough.

Ibid.

The paradoxes of conduct begin to twinkle into sight; sugar is good, but there is a time to refrain from taking it though you can; a lie will easily get you out of a scrape, and yet, strangely and beautifully, rapture possesses you when you have taken the scrape and left out the lie.

Ibid.

War hath no fury like a non-combatant.

Ibid.

Burgundy was the winiest wine, the central, essential, and typical wine, the soul and greatest common measure of all the kindly wines of the earth.

Judith

"I was born below par to th' extent of two whiskies."

Fiery Particles

WILLIAM SYDNEY PORTER ("O. HENRY")
[1867–1910]

Hard ye may be in the tumult,
  Red to your battle hilts,
Blow give for blow in the foray,
  Cunningly ride in the tilts;
But when the roaring is ended,
  Tenderly, unbeguiled,
Turn to a woman a woman's
  Heart, and a child's to a child.

The Crucible.[1] *Stanza 1*

Lost, your Excellency. Lost associations and societies. Lost right reverends and wrong reverends of every order. Lost reformers and lawmakers, born with heavenly compassion in your hearts, but with the reverence of money in your souls. And lost thus around us every day.[2]

Elsie in New York

He was outwardly decent and managed to preserve his aquarium, but inside he was impromptu and full of unexpectedness.

The Octopus Marooned

East is East, and West is San Francisco, according to Californians. Californians are a race of people; they are not merely inhabitants of a State. They are the Southerners of the West.

A Municipal Report

Take of London fog 30 parts; malaria 10 parts; gas leaks 20 parts; dewdrops gathered in a brick-yard at sunrise 25 parts; odor of honeysuckle 15 parts. Mix. The mixture will give you an approximate conception of a Nashville drizzle.

Ibid.

Most wonderful of all are words, and how they make friends one with another, being oft associated, until not even obituary notices them do part.

Calloway's Code

---

[1] Verses found among his MSS after his death.

[2] A paraphrase of the closing lines of Chap. 47, *Bleak House*, by Dickens.

If men knew how women pass the time when they are alone, they'd never marry.

> *Memoirs of a Yellow Dog*

Ready to melt in the crucible of her ire a little more gold plating from the wrought steel chains of matrimony.

> *The Pendulum*

He no longer saw a rabble, but his brothers seeking the ideal.

> *Brickdust Row*

She would have made a splendid wife, for crying only made her eyes more bright.

> *No Story*

A man asleep is certainly a sight to make angels weep. Now, a woman asleep you regard as different. No matter how she looks, you know it's better for all hands for her to be that way.

> *The Hiding of Black Bill*

There was too much scenery and fresh air. What I need is a steam-heated flat with no ventilation or exercise.

> *Letter [April 15, 1910]*

Turn up the lights; I don't want to go home in the dark.

> *Last words (quoted in the biography by* C. ALPHONSO SMITH)

GEORGE W. RUSSELL ("AE")
[1867–1935]

Our hearts were drunk with a beauty
Our eyes could never see.

> *The Unknown God*

Twilight, a timid fawn, went glimmering by,
And Night, the dark-blue hunter, followed fast.

> *Refuge*

That blazing galleon the sun,
This dusky coracle I ride,
Both under secret orders sail,
And swim upon the selfsame tide.

> *Mutiny. Stanza 1*

Its edges foamed with amethyst and rose,
Withers once more the old blue flower of day:

There where the ether like a diamond glows,
Its petals fade away.

> *The Great Breath. Stanza 1*

When the breath of twilight blows to flame the misty skies,
All its vaporous sapphire, violet glow and silver gleam,
With their magic flood me through the gateway of the eyes;
I am one with the twilight's dream.

> *By the Margin of the Great Deep.*
> *Stanza 1*

HARRY LEON WILSON
[1867–]

It would never do with us.

> *Ruggles of Red Gap*

I can be pushed just so far.

> *Ibid.*

She'd fight a rattlesnake and give it the first two bites.

> *Ibid.*

MARY HUNTER AUSTIN
[1868–1934]

Whisper of the wind along the sage,
Only wait till I can get the word —
Never was it printed in a page,
Never was it spoken, never heard.

> *Whisper of the Wind*

There are no fairy-folk in our Southwest,
The cactus spines would tear their filmy wings,
There's no dew anywhere for them to drink
And no green grass to make them fairy rings.

> *Western Magic. Stanza 1*

What need has he of clocks who knows
When highest peaks are gilt and rose
Day has begun?

> *Clocks and Calendars. Stanza 1*

At midnight drink no water,
For I have heard said
That on the stroke of midnight
All water goes dead.

> *Dead Water. New Mexico Legend,*
> *Stanza 1*

I arise, facing east,
I am asking toward the light:
I am asking that my day
Shall be beautiful with light.
Morning Prayer

THOMAS WILLIAM HODGSON CROSLAND
[1868–1924]

God's infinite mercy, how that child did
cry,
In spite of bottle, bauble, peppermint,
nurse!
The Baby in the Ward

Unhonoured by his fellows he grew old
And trod the path to hell,
But there were many things he might
have sold
And did not sell.
Epitaph. Stanza 2

CHIDDEN still murmurs,
SLAPPED and RAPPED complain,
HURT, with a thousand tongues,
Whines out his pain.

This is the learning
Unto which we come:
PROPERLY WALLOPED
Is for ever dumb.
Recipe

GEORGE NORMAN DOUGLAS
[1868–   ]

You can tell the ideals of a nation by
its advertisements.
South Wind. Chap. 7

What a pity that Latin, as scholars'
language, for the definition and regis-
tration of ideas, was ever abandoned!
It has the incalculable advantage that
the meanings of words are irrevocably
fixed by authority.
Ibid. Chap. 8

Men have lost sight of distant horizons. Nobody writes for humanity, for
civilization; they write for their country, their sect; to amuse their friends
or annoy their enemies.
Ibid.

No one can expect a majority to be
stirred by motives other than ignoble.
South Wind. Chap. 10

A love-match is generally a failure
and a money-match is always a mistake. The heroes, the saints and sages —
they are those who face the world alone.
Ibid. Chap. 11

No great man is ever born too soon or
too late. When we say that the time is
not ripe for this or that celebrity, we
confess by implication that this very
man, and no other, is required.
Ibid. Chap. 13

Impoverished them to such an extent
that for three consecutive months they
could barely afford the most unnecessary luxuries of life.
Ibid. Chap. 20

Many a man who thinks to found a
home discovers that he has merely
opened a tavern for his friends.
Ibid. Chap. 24

WILLIAM EDWARD BURGHARDT DuBOIS
[1868–   ]

Herein lies the tragedy of the age:
not that men are poor — all men know
something of poverty; not that men are
wicked — who is good? Not that men
are ignorant — what is truth? Nay, but
that men know so little of men.
The Souls of Black Folk [1903]

GRENVILLE KLEISER
[1868–   ]

She gleans how long you wish to stay;
She lets you go without delay.
The Ideal Hostess

She is not difficult to please;
She can be silent as the trees.
She shuns all ostentatious show;
She knows exactly when to go.
The Ideal Guest

HERMAN W. KNICKERBOCKER
[1868–1934]

I believe that when you say one is a "dead game sport" you have reached the climax of human philosophy.

Eulogy at the funeral of Riley Grannan, Rawhide, Nevada [April 3, 1908]

If I had the power to-day by the simple turning of my hand to endow myself with personal immortality, in my infinite ignorance I would refuse to turn my hand. God knows best.

Ibid.

EDWARD VERRALL LUCAS
[1868–1938]

You ask me "why I like him." Nay,
I cannot; nay, I would not, say.
I think it vile to pigeonhole
The pros and cons of a kindred soul.
Friends. Stanza 1

A stamp's a tiny, flimsy thing,
No thicker than a beetle's wing,
And yet 'twill roam the world for you
Exactly where you tell it to.
*The Three-Halfpenny Traveller.
Stanza 1*

When clay has such red mouths to kiss,
  Firm hands to grasp, it is enough:
How can I take it aught amiss
  We are not made of rarer stuff?
Clay. Stanza 3

Has any reader ever found perfect accuracy in the newspaper account of any event of which he himself had inside knowledge?
Of Accuracy

The art of life is to be so well known at a good restaurant that you can pay by cheque.
Over Bemerton's

The art of life is to keep down acquaintances. One's friends one can manage, but one's acquaintances can be the devil.
Ibid.

The noise from good toast should reverberate in the head like the thunder of July.
A Word on Toast

O to hunt books in
The Charing Cross Road!
The Friendly Town

Lamb's great discovery was that he himself was better worth laying bare than obscuring: that his memories, his impressions, his loyalties, his dislikes, his doubts, his beliefs, his prejudices, his enthusiasms, in short, everything that was his, were suitable material for literature. Pope said that the proper study of mankind was man; Lamb amended this to — the proper study of man is himself.
At the Shrine of Saint Charles

WILLIAM TYLER PAGE
[1868–   ]

I believe in the United States of America as a Government of the people, by the people, for the people; whose just powers are derived from the consent of the governed; a democracy in a republic, a sovereign Nation of many sovereign States; a perfect Union one and inseparable; established upon those principles of freedom, equality, justice and humanity for which American patriots sacrificed their lives and fortunes. I therefore believe it is my duty to my country to love it, to support its Constitution, to obey its laws, to respect its flag, and to defend it against all enemies.
The American's Creed.[1]

ROBERT FALCON SCOTT
[1868–1912]

Make the boy interested in natural history if you can; it is better than games; they encourage it at some schools.
Last Message to His Wife

He [Oates] [2] said: "I am just going outside, and may be some time." He went out into the blizzard, and we have not seen him since. . . . We knew that

---

[1] Adopted by the House of Representatives [April 3, 1918].

[2] Lawrence Edward Grace Oates [1880–1912], of the Inniskilling Dragoons, one of Scott's last Antarctic expedition.

poor Oates was walking to his death, but though we tried to dissuade him, we knew that it was the act of a brave man and an English gentleman. We all hope to meet the end with a similar spirit, and assuredly the end is not far.

Diary. March 16, 1912

Had we lived, I should have had a tale to tell of the hardihood, endurance, and courage of my companions which would have stirred the heart of every Englishman. These rough notes and our dead bodies must tell the tale.

Journal. Message to the Public.[1]

ARTHUR FREDERICK SHELDON
[1868–1935]

He profits most who serves best.

Motto for Rotary International

WILLIAM ALLEN WHITE
[1868–   ]

And thus the King of Boyville first set his light little foot upon the soil of an unknown country.

The King of Boyville [1896]

LAURENCE BINYON
[1869–   ]

O World, be nobler, for her sake!
  If she but knew thee what thou art,
What wrongs are borne, what deeds are done
  In thee, beneath thy daily sun,
  Know'st thou not that her tender heart
For pain and very shame would break?
O World, be nobler, for her sake!

O World, Be Nobler

Our speech is spun from the pain
Of thought and heavy with years,
And dyed with an ancient stain
From passion and blood and tears.

One Year Old. Stanza 5

[1] Inscribed on the memorial to Captain Scott and his companions, Waterloo Place, London.

For Mercy, Courage, Kindness, Mirth,
There is no measure upon earth.
Nay, they wither, root and stem,
If an end be set to them.

A Song

They shall grow not old, as we that are
    left grow old:
Age shall not weary them, nor the years
    condemn.
At the going down of the sun and in the
    morning
We will remember them.

For the Fallen. Stanza 4

In the terrible hour of the dawn, when
    the veins are cold,
  They led her forth to the wall.
"I have loved my land," she said, "but
    it is not enough:
  Love requires of me all."

Edith Cavell.[1] *Stanza 5*

J. GORDON COOGLER
[1869–   ]

Alas! for the South, her books have
    grown fewer —
She never was much given to literature.

Purely Original Verse (1897)

From early youth to the frost of age
  Man's days have been a mixture
Of all that constitutes in life
  A dark and gloomy picture.

Ibid.

She died after the beautiful snow had
    melted
  And was buried beneath the slush.

Ibid. In Memorial

My style and my sentiments are MY
  OWN, purely original.

Ibid. Preface

ROBERT HOBART ("BOB") DAVIS
[1869–   ]

I am the printing-press, born of the mother earth. My heart is of steel, my limbs are of iron, and my fingers are of brass.

[1] Have pity on her. — BRAND WHITLOCK [1869–1934]: Letter to Baron von der Lancken, Civil Governor of Brussels

I sing the songs of the world, the oratorios of history, the symphonies of all time.

I am the voice of to-day, the herald of to-morrow. I weave into the warp of the past the woof of the future. I tell the stories of peace and war alike.

I make the human heart beat with passion or tenderness. I stir the pulse of nations, and make brave men do better deeds, and soldiers die. . . .

I am the laughter and tears of the world, and I shall never die until all things return to the immutable dust.

I am the printing-press.

I Am the Printing-Press
[July, 1911]

"MICHAEL FAIRLESS" (MARGARET FAIRLESS BARBER)
[1869–1901]

The people who make no roads are ruled out from intelligent participation in the world's brotherhood.

The Roadmender. I, 5

Necessity can set me helpless on my back, but she cannot keep me there; nor can four walls limit my vision.

Ibid. II, 6

Revelation is always measured by capacity.

Ibid. III, 3

STRICKLAND GILLILAN
[1869–   ]

Make 'em brief, Finnigin!

Finnigin to Flannigan. Stanza 3

Bilin' down his repoort, wuz Finnigin!
An' he writed this here: "*Muster Flannigan —*
Off ag'in, on ag'in,
Gone ag'in. — FINNIGIN.*"

Ibid. Stanza 6

Just stand aside and watch yourself go by;
Think of yourself as "he" instead of "I."

Watch Yourself Go By. Stanza 1

FREDERIC LAWRENCE KNOWLES
[1869–1905]

When navies are forgotten
    And fleets are useless things,
When the dove shall warm her bosom
    Beneath the eagle's wings.

The New Age. Stanza 1

In the conquest which is service,
    In the victory which is peace!

Ibid. Stanza 4

These are the best of him,
Pathos and jest of him;
Earth holds the rest of him.

On a Fly-Leaf of Burns's Songs.
Stanza 1

Each little lyrical
Grave or satirical
Musical miracle!

Ibid. Stanza 3

Helen's lips are drifting dust;
Ilion is consumed with lust;
All the galleons of Greece
Drink the ocean's dreamless peace;
Lost was Solomon's purple show
Restless centuries ago.

Love Triumphant

This body is my house — it is not I:
Triumphant in this faith I live and die.

The Tenant

Our crosses are hewn from different
    trees,
But we all must have our Calvaries.

Golgotha

STEPHEN LEACOCK
[1869–   ]

The classics are only primitive literature. They belong to the same class as primitive machinery and primitive music and primitive medicine.

Homer and Humbug

If I were founding a university I would found first a smoking room; then when I had a little more money in hand I would found a dormitory; then after that, or more probably with it, a decent reading room and a library. After that, if I still had more money that I couldn't use, I would hire a professor and get some textbooks.

Oxford As I See It

EDGAR LEE MASTERS
[1869–   ]

All, all are sleeping on the hill.
Spoon River Anthology. The Hill

Tick, tick, tick, what little iambics,
While Homer and Whitman roared in
the pines.
Ibid. Petit, the Poet.

Out of me unworthy and unknown
The vibrations of deathless music;
"With malice toward none, with charity
for all."
Ibid. Anne Rutledge

I am Anne Rutledge who sleep beneath
these weeds,
Beloved in life of Abraham Lincoln,
Wedded to him, not through union,
But through separation.
Bloom forever, O Republic,
From the dust of my bosom!
Ibid.

WILLIAM VAUGHN MOODY
[1869–1910]

Jill-o'er-the-ground is purple blue,
Blue is the quaker-maid,
The wild geranium holds its dew
Long in the boulder's shade.
Gloucester Moors. Stanza 2

This earth is not the steadfast place
We landsmen build upon;
From deep to deep she varies pace,
And while she comes is gone.
Ibid. Stanza 4

But on, but on does the old earth steer
As if her port she knew.
Ibid. Stanza 5

But thou, vast outbound ship of souls,
What harbor town for thee?
What shapes, when thy arriving tolls,
Shall crowd the banks to see?
Shall all the happy shipmates then
Stand singing brotherly?
Ibid. Stanza 10

Then not to kneel, almost
Seemed like a vulgar boast.
Good Friday. Stanza 9

Gigantic, wilful, young,
Chicago sitteth at the northwest gates,
With restless violent hands and casual
tongue
Moulding her mighty fates.
An Ode in Time of Hesitation.
Stanza 3

The wars we wage
Are noble, and our battles still are won
By justice for us, ere we lift the gage.
We have not sold our loftiest heritage.
The proud republic hath not stooped to
cheat
And scramble in the market-place of
war.
Ibid. Stanza 5

Our fluent men of place and conse-
quence
Fumble and fill their mouths with hol-
low phrase,
Or for the end-all of deep arguments
Intone their dull commercial liturgies.
Ibid. Stanza 7

Blindness we may forgive, but baseness
we will smite.
Ibid. Stanza 9

Praise, and never a whispered hint but
the fight he fought was good;
Never a word that the blood on his
sword was his country's own
heart's-blood.
On a Soldier Fallen in the
Philippines. Stanza 2

And souls are restless, plagued, impa-
tient things,
All dream and unaccountable desire;
Crawling, but pestered with the
thought of wings;
Spreading through every inch of earth's
old mire
Mystical hanker after something
higher.
The Menagerie. Stanza 19

Shrill and high, newsboys cry
The worst of the city's infamy.
In New York. Stanza 4

The roaring street is hung for miles
With fierce electric fire.
Ibid. Stanza 9

Of wounds and sore defeat
I made my battle stay;

Winged sandals for my feet
I wove of my delay.
> *The Fire-Bringer.*
> *Pandora's Song, II*

WILLIAM HENRY OGILVIE
[1869–   ]

Ragged, uncomely, and old and gray,
  A woman walked in a northern town,
And through the crowd as she wound
    her way
  One saw her loiter and then stoop
    down,
  Putting something away in her old
    torn gown.
> *A Royal Heart. Stanza 1*

"It's broken glass,"
She said: "I hae lifted it frae the street
To be oot o' the road o' the bairnies'
    feet!"
> *Ibid. Stanza 3*

The real ones, the right ones, the
    straight ones and the true,
The pukka, peerless sportsmen — their
    numbers are but few;
The men who keep on playing though
    the sun be in eclipse,
The men who go on losing with a laugh
    upon their lips.
> *The True Sportsman*

When the last fence looms up, I am
    ready
  And I hope when the rails of it crack,
There'll be nothing in front but the
    master,
  The huntsman, the fox and the pack.
> *The Last Fence. Stanza 1*

EDWIN ARLINGTON
ROBINSON
[1869–1935]

We cannot know how much we learn
From those who never will return,
Until a flash of unforeseen
Remembrance falls on what has been.
> *Flammonde*

To shake the tree
Of life itself and bring down fruit un-
    heard-of.
> *Ben Jonson Entertains a Man*
> *from Stratford*

I would have rid the earth of him
  Once, in my pride. . . .
I never knew the worth of him
  Until he died.
> *An Old Story*

Life is the game that must be played:
  This truth at least, good friends, we
    know;
So live and laugh, nor be dismayed
  As one by one the phantoms go.
> *Ballade by the Fire. Envoy*

The songs of one who strove to play
  The broken flutes of Arcady.
> *Ballade of Broken Flutes*

There be two men of all mankind
  That I'm forever thinking on:
They chase me everywhere I go, —
  Melchizedek, Ucalegon.
> *Two Men*

Like dead, remembered footsteps on old
  floors.
> *The Pity of the Leaves*

Oh for a poet — for a beacon bright
To rift this changeless glimmer of dead
    gray;
To spirit back the Muses, long astray,
And flush Parnassus with a newer light.
> *Sonnet*

Look at a branch, a bird, a child, a rose,
Or anything God ever made that
    grows, —
Nor let the smallest vision of it slip,
Till you may read, as on Belshazzar's
    wall,
The glory of eternal partnership.
> *Sonnet*

      And thus we die,
Still searching, like poor old astrono-
    mers
Who totter off to bed and go to sleep
To dream of untriangulated stars.
> *Octaves. XI*

Two kinds of gratitude: the sudden
    kind
We feel for what we take, the larger
    kind
We feel for what we give.
> *Captain Craig. Part I*

Friends
To borrow my books and set wet glasses
    on them.
> *Ibid. Part II*

The saddest among kings of earth,
Bowed with a galling crown, this man
Met rancor with a cryptic mirth,
Laconic — and Olympian.
The Master: Lincoln

And have one Titan at a time.
Ibid.

Wearing upon his forehead, with no
fear,
The laurel of approved iniquity.
Uncle Ananias

Miniver loved the Medici,
Albeit he had never seen one;
He would have sinned incessantly
Could he have been one.
Miniver Cheevy

Miniver Cheevy, born too late,
Scratched his head and kept on think-
ing;
Miniver coughed, and called it fate,
And kept on drinking.
Ibid.

Thrall to the gilded ease
Of every day,
Mocker of all degrees
And always gay,
Child of the Cyclades
And of Broadway.
Bon Voyage

Who of us, being what he is,
May scoff at others' ecstasies?
However we may shine to-day,
More-shining ones are on the way.
Atherton's Gambit

The forehead and the little ears
Have gone where Saturn keeps the
years;
The breast where roses could not live
Has done with rising and with falling.
For a Dead Lady

Death, like a friend unseen, shall say to
me
My toil is over and my work begun.
The Three Taverns

If I have loosed
A shaft of language that has flown
sometimes
A little higher than the hearts and
heads
Of nature's minions, it will yet be heard.
Ibid.

I shall have more to say when I am
dead.
John Brown

Like a physician who can do no good,
But knows how soon another would
have his fee
Were he to tell the truth.
Avon's Harvest

Art's long hazard, where no man may
choose
Whether he play to win, or toil to lose.
Caput Mortuum

Love that's wise
Will not say all it means.
Tristram. Part VII

For when a woman is left too much
alone,
Sooner or later she begins to think;
And no man knows what then she may
discover.
Ibid.

There is a little watchman in my heart
Who is always telling me what time it
is.
Ibid. Part VIII

Love must have wings to fly away from
love,
And to fly back again.
Ibid.

I like rivers
Better than oceans, for we see both
sides.
An ocean is forever asking questions
And writing them aloud along the
shore.
Roman Bartholow. Part III

Once in a life, they tell us, and once
only,
So great a thing as a great love may
come —
To crown us, or to mark us with a scar
No craft or custom shall obliterate.
Ibid. Part IV

A thousand golden sheaves were lying
there,
Shining and still, but not for long to
stay —
As if a thousand girls with golden hair
Might rise from where they slept and go
away.
The Sheaves

Of all small things
That have the most infernal power to
grow,
Few may be larger than a few small
words
That may not say themselves and be
forgotten.
Genevieve and Alexandra
Here where the wind is always north-
north-east
And children learn to walk on frozen
toes.
New England

HERBERT SHIPMAN
[1869–1930]

Across the gateway of my heart
I wrote "No Thoroughfare,"
But love came laughing by, and cried:
"I enter everywhere."
No Thoroughfare. Stanza 1

GEORGE STERLING
[1869–1926]

Their hearts, contemptuous of death,
shall dare
His roads between the thunder and
the sun.
The Black Vulture
Thou art the star for which all evening
waits.
Aldebaran at Dusk
Like truant children going home
We turn to thee, the beautiful and best.
The Final Faith
Into a crystal cup the dusky wine
I pour, and, musing at so rich a shrine,
I watch the star that haunts its ruddy
gloom.
A Wine of Wizardry
Let us be just with life. Although it
bear
A thousand thorns for every perfect
rose,
And though the happy day have
mournful close,
Slumber awaits to house the mind from
care.
The Balance

NEWTON BOOTH TARKINGTON
[1869–   ]

Penrod was doing something very unusual and rare, something almost never
accomplished except by coloured people or by a boy in school on a spring
day: he was doing really nothing at all.
He was merely a state of being.
Penrod. Chap. 8

There are two things that will be believed of any man whatsoever, and one
of them is that he has taken to drink.
Ibid. Chap. 10

They were upon their great theme:
"When I get to be a man!" Being human, though boys, they considered
their present estate too commonplace to
be dwelt upon. So, when the old men
gather, they say: "When I was a boy!"
It really is the land of nowadays that
we never discover.
Ibid. Chap. 26

HILAIRE BELLOC
[1870–   ]

The voyage which I was born to
make in the end, and to which my desire
has driven me, is towards a place in
which everything we have known is forgotten, except those things which, as we
knew them, reminded us of an original
joy.
The Harbour in the North

Child, do not throw this book about,
Refrain from the unholy pleasure
Of cutting all the pictures out,
Regard it as your choicest treasure.
A Bad Child's Book of Beasts.
Foreword

Balliol made me, Balliol fed me,
Whatever I had she gave me again:
And the best of Balliol loved and led
me.
God be with you, Balliol men.
To the Balliol Men Still in Africa
[1900]

Oh, he didn't believe in Adam and
Eve —
He put no faith therein;
His doubts began with the fall of man,
And he laughed at original sin.
Song of the Pelagian Heresy

The Tipple's aboard and the night is
young,
The door's ajar and the Barrel is
sprung,
I am singing the best song ever was
sung
And it has a rousing chorus.
West Sussex Drinking Song.
Chorus

A lovely river, all alone,
She lingers in the hills and holds
A hundred little towns of stones,
Forgotten in the western wolds.
The Evenlode

Don poor at Bed and worse at Table,
Don pinched, Don starved, Don miser-
able;
Don stuttering, Don with roving eyes,
Don nervous, Don of crudities. . . .
Don middle-class, Don sycophantic,
Don dull, Don brutish, Don pedantic;
Don hypocritical, Don bad,
Don furtive, Don three-quarters mad;
Don (since a man must make an end),
Don that shall never be my friend.
Lines to a Don

The moon on the one hand, the dawn
on the other:
The moon is my sister, the dawn is my
brother.
The moon on my left and the dawn on
my right.
My brother, good morning: my sister,
good night.
The Early Morning

The great hills of the South Country
They stand along the sea;
And it's there walking in the high
woods
That I could wish to be,
And the men that were boys when I was
a boy
Walking along with me.
The South Country. Stanza 2

If I ever become a rich man,
Or if ever I grow to be old,
I will build a house with deep thatch

To shelter me from the cold,
And there shall the Sussex songs be
sung
And the story of Sussex told.
The South Country. Stanza 9

And the men that were boys when I was
a boy
Shall sit and drink with me.
Ibid. Stanza 10

He does not die that can bequeath
Some influence to the land he knows,
Or dares, persistent, interwreath
Love permanent with the wild hedge-
rows;
He does not die, but still remains
Substantiate with his darling plains.
Duncton Hill. Stanza 1

They say that in the unchanging place,
Where all we loved is always dear,
We meet our mornings face to face
And find at last our twentieth year.
Dedicatory Ode

From quiet homes and first beginning,
Out to the undiscovered ends,
There's nothing worth the wear of win-
ning
But laughter and the love of friends.
Ibid.

For no one, in our long decline,
So dusty, spiteful and divided,
Had quite such pleasant friends as
mine,
Or loved them half as much as I did.
Ibid.

Of Courtesy, it is much less
Than Courage of Heart or Holiness,
Yet in my walks it seems to me
That the Grace of God is in Courtesy.
Courtesy

Drinking when I had a mind to,
Singing when I felt inclined to.
The Path to Rome

Most holy Night, that still dost keep
The keys of all the doors of sleep,
To me when my tired eyelids close
Give thou repose.
The Night. Stanza 1

Do you remember an Inn,
Miranda?
Do you remember an Inn?
And the tedding and the spreading
Of the straw for a bedding,

And the fleas that tease in the High
    Pyrenees,
And the wine that tasted of the tar?
                    Tarantella
  Noting one that brings
With careless step a mist of shadowy
    things:
Laughter and memories, and a few re-
    grets,
Some honour, and a quantity of debts,
A doubt or two of sorts, a trust in God,
And (what will seem to you extremely
    odd)
His father's granfer's father's father's
    name,
Unspoilt, untitled, even spelt the same;
Charon, who twenty thousand times be-
    fore
Has ferried Poets to the ulterior shore,
Will estimate the weight I bear, and
    cry —
"Comrade!"
                    To Dives
I said to Heart, "How goes it?" Heart
    replied:
"Right as a Ribstone Pippin!" But it
    lied.
              The False Heart
When I am dead, I hope it may be said:
"His sins were scarlet, but his books
    were read."
                On His Books

CHARLES T. DAVIS

To ride, shoot straight, and speak the
    truth — [1]
This was the ancient Law of Youth.
Old times are past, old days are done;
But the Law runs true, O little son!
      For a Little Boy. Stanza 1

ANNA BUNSTON DE BARY

O little lark, you need not fly
To seek your Master in the sky,
    He treads our native sod;
Why should you sing aloft, apart?
Sing to the heaven of my heart;
    In me, in me, in me is God!
    *A Basque Peasant Returning
    from Church. Stanza 1*

[1] See Byron, page 361.

LORD ALFRED DOUGLAS
[1870-   ]

I have been profligate of happiness
And reckless of the world's hostility,
The blessèd part has not been given to
    me
Gladly to suffer fools.
                    To Olive
    Trace
Under the common thing the hidden
    grace
And conjure wonder out of emptiness,
Till mean things put on beauty like a
    dress
And all the world was an enchanted
    place.
              The Dead Poet

JAMES STANLEY GILBERT
[? -1906]

Close the door — across the river
    He has gone.
With an abscess on his liver
    He has gone.
Many years of rainy seasons
And malaria's countless treasons
Are among the many reasons
    Why he's gone.
        *Panama Patchwork.
    He Has Gone, Stanza 1*

DENIS ALOYSIUS McCARTHY
[1870-1931]

Proud is the city — she finds a place for
    many a fad to-day,
But she's more than blind if she fails
    to find a place for the boys to
    play! [1]
      *Give Them a Place to Play.
             Stanza 3*
The newspaper poet's a commonplace
    fellow —
The humblest may know what his
    poetry means.
But clearness is treason, and so, for this
    reason,
He never gets into the big magazines.
      The Newspaper Poet. Stanza 1

[1] See Eliza Cook, page 512.

CHARLOTTE MEW
[1870–1928]

What shall we do with this strange
   Summer, meant for you, —
Dear, if we see the Winter through
What shall be done with Spring — ?
To a Child in Death

Bury your heart in some deep green
   hollow
Or hide it up in a kind old tree;
Better still, give it the swallow
When she goes over the sea.
Saturday Market

HECTOR HUGH MUNRO
("SAKI")
[1870–1916]

She took to telling the truth; she said
she was forty-two and five months. It
may have been pleasing to the angels,
but her elder sister was not gratified.
Reginald [1904]

The cook was a good cook, as cooks
go; and as cooks go she went.
Ibid.

Women and elephants never forget
an injury.
Ibid.

I might have been a gold-fish in a
glass bowl for all the privacy I got.
Ibid.

Hating anything in the way of ill-
natured gossip ourselves, we are always
grateful to those who do it for us.
Reginald in Russia

"It was their Silver Wedding; such
lots of silver presents, quite a show."

"We must not grudge them their
show of presents after twenty-five years
of married life; it is the silver lining to
their cloud."
The Unbearable Bassington

Sherard Blaw, the dramatist who had
discovered himself, and who had given
so ungrudgingly of his discovery to the
world.
Ibid.

Confront a child, a puppy, and a kitten with a sudden danger; the child will
turn instinctively for assistance, the
puppy will grovel in abject submission,
the kitten will brace its tiny body for a
frantic resistance.
The Achievement of the Cat

FRANK NORRIS
[1870–1902]

He's the kind of man that gets up a
reputation for being clever and artistic
by running down the very one particular thing that every one likes, and
cracking up some book or picture or
play that no one has ever heard of.
The Pit. Chap. 2

ALICE HEGAN RICE
[1870–   ]

"Was he a church member?" . . .
"Well, no, not exactly," admitted
Mrs. Wiggs, reluctantly. "But he was
what you might say a well-wisher."
Mrs. Wiggs of the Cabbage Patch

CAROLYN WELLS

Youth is a silly, vapid state;
Old age with fears and ills is rife;
This simple boon I beg of Fate —
A thousand years of Middle Life!
My Boon

"A noble theme!" the tyro cried,
   And straightway scribbled off a son-
   net.
"A noble theme," the poet sighed,
   "I am not fit to write upon it."
Humility

I love the Christmas-tide, and yet,
   I notice this, each year I live;
I always like the gifts I get,
   But how I love the gifts I give!
A Thought

He laughs best who laughs last,
   The wiseacres vow;
But I am impatient,
   I want to laugh now.
Delays Are Dangerous. Stanza 1

The books we think we ought to read
   are poky, dull and dry;
The books that we would like to read
   we are ashamed to buy;
The books that people talk about we
   never can recall;

And the books that people give us, Oh,
  they're the worst of all.
                    On Books
They borrow books they will not buy,
  They have no ethics or religions;
I wish some kind Burbankian guy
  Could cross my books with homing
  pigeons.
                Book-Borrowers
I don't believe the half I hear,
  Nor the quarter of what I see!
But I have one faith, sublime and true,
  That nothing can shake or slay;
Each spring I firmly believe anew
  All the seed catalogues say!
                One Firm Faith
The smile that won't come off.
    Winning slogan in a contest

STEPHEN CRANE
[1871–1900]

He had fought like a pagan who de-
fends his religion.
        The Red Badge of Courage.
                    Chap. 17
Within him, as he hurled himself for-
ward, was born a love, a despairing
fondness for this flag which was near
him. It was a creation of beauty and
invulnerability.
            Ibid. Chap. 19
None of them knew the color of the
sky.
            The Open Boat
Presently, God said,
"And what did you do?"
The little blade answered, "Oh, my
  Lord,
Memory is bitter to me,
For, if I did good deeds,
I know not of them."
Then God, in all His splendor,
Arose from His throne.
"O best little blade of grass!" He said.
            The Blades of Grass
A man said to the universe:
  "Sir, I exist!"
"However," replied the universe,
"That fact has not created in me
A sense of obligation."
        War Is Kind. Fragment

THOMAS AUGUSTINE DALY
[1871–   ]

I gotta love for Angela,
  I love Carlotta, too.
I no can marry both o' dem,
  So w'at I gona do?
        Between Two Loves. Stanza 1

Da spreeng ees com'; but oh, da joy
  Eet ees too late!
He was so cold, my leetla boy,
  He no could wait.
            Da Leetla Boy. Stanza 1

When all is still within these walls
And Thy sweet sleep through darkness
  falls
On little hearts that trust in me,
However bitter toil may be,
For length of days, O Lord! on Thee
  My spirit calls.
                The Man's Prayer

Kind Reader, here's a tip for you:
  Go buy, though skinny be your purse
And other books of yours be few,
  "The Oxford Book of English Verse."
    Ballade of the Tempting Book.
                    L'Envoi

Up to the breeze of the morning I fling
  you,
  Blending your folds with the dawn in
  the sky;
There let the people behold you, and
  bring you
  Love and devotion that never shall
  die.
Proudly, agaze at your glory, I stand,
Flag o' my land! flag o' my land!
            Flag o' My Land. Stanza 1

Flo was fond of Ebenezer —
  "Eb," for short, she called her beau.
Talk of tides of love, great Caesar!
  You should see them — Eb and Flo.
            The Tides of Love

Sing clear, O! throstle,
  Thou golden-tongued apostle
And little brown-frocked brother
  Of the loved Assisian!
                To a Thrush

W'at good eesa wife eef she don'ta be
  fat?
                Da Styleesha Wife

Giuseppe, da barber, ees greata for
"mash,"
He gotta da bigga, da blacka moustache,
Good clo'es an' good styla an' playnta
good cash.

Mia Carlotta

I'm Home's heart! Warmth I give and
light,
If you but feed me.
I blossom in the winter night,
When most you need me.

Inscription for a Fireplace

WILLIAM HENRY DAVIES
[1871–   ]

A poor life this if, full of care,
We have no time to stand and stare.

Leisure

They sniffed, poor things, for their
green fields,
They cried so loud I could not sleep:
For fifty thousand shillings down
I would not sail again with sheep.

Sheep. Stanza 5

So every time we passed it by,
Sailing to England's slaughter-house,
Eight ragged sheep-men — tramps and
thieves —
Would stroke that sheep's black nose.

A Child's Pet. Stanza 5

What glorious sunsets have their birth
In Cities fouled by smoke!
This tree — whose roots are in a
drain —
Becomes the greenest Oak!

Love's Rivals

Look, there's a rainbow now!
See how that lovely rainbow throws
Her jewelled arm around
This world, when the rain goes.

The Rainbow. Stanza 2

I turned my head and saw the wind,
Not far from where I stood,
Dragging the corn by her golden hair
Into a dark and lonely wood.

The Villain

I am as certain of my song,
When first it warms the brain,
As woman of her unborn child,
Or wind that carries rain.

The Birth of Song

Nature's real king, to whom the power
was given
To make an inkdrop scent the world
for ever.

Shakespeare

I had Ambition, by which sin
The angels fell;
I climbed and, step by step, O Lord,
Ascended into Hell.

Ambition

There was a battle in her face,
Between a lily and a rose;
My love would have the lily win,
And I the lily lose.

Song

I'll make my Joy a secret thing,
My face shall wear a mask of care;
And those who hunt a Joy to death,
Shall never know what sport is
there!

Hunting Joy. Stanza 3

I see at last our great Lamorna Cove,
Which, danced on by ten thousand silver feet,
Has all those waves that run like little
lambs,
To draw the milk from many a rocky
teat,
Spilt in white gallons all along the
shore.

Lamorna Cove

The mind, with its own eyes and ears,
May for these others have no care;
No matter where this body is,
The mind is free to go elsewhere. . . .
And when I'm passing near St. Paul's,
I see, beyond the dome and crowd,
Twm Barlum, that green pap in Gwent,
With its dark nipple in a cloud.

The Mind's Liberty

Strive not for gold, for greedy fools
Measure themselves by poor men
never;
Their standards still being richer men,
Makes them poor ever.

Songs of Joy. Stanza 3

LADY PAMELA WYNDHAM
GLENCONNER
[1871–1928]

Bitter are the tears of a child:
Sweeten them.

Deep are the thoughts of a child:
    Quiet them.
Sharp is the grief of a child:
    Take it from him.
Soft is the heart of a child:
    Do not harden it.
                                        A Child

ARTHUR GUITERMAN
[1871–   ]

Hail Guest! We ask not what thou art:
If Friend, we greet thee, hand and
    heart;
If Stranger, such no longer be;
If Foe, our love shall conquer thee.
                                    Door Verse

The Antiseptic Baby and the Prophy-
    lactic Pup
Were playing in the garden when the
    Bunny gamboled up;
They looked upon the Creature with a
    loathing undisguised; —
It wasn't Disinfected and it wasn't Ster-
    ilized.
            Strictly Germ-Proof. Stanza 1

The Pilgrims landed, worthy men,
    And saved from wreck on raging seas,
They fell upon their knees, and then
    Upon the Aborigines.[1]
            *The Pilgrims' Thanksgiving
                    Feast. Stanza 1*

The Cat on your hearthstone to this
    day presages,
By solemnly sneezing, the coming of
    rain! [2]
                The First Cat. Stanza 7

Oh, the saddest of sights in a world of
    sin
Is a little lost pup with his tail tucked
    in!
            Little Lost Pup. Stanza 1

He stood with his muzzle thrust out
    through the door
The whole forty days of that terrible
    pour!
Because of which drenching, the Sages
    unfold,

---

[1] See W. M. Evarts, page 517.
[2] While rain depends, the pensive cat gives
    o'er
    Her frolics, and pursues her tail no more.
    JONATHAN SWIFT: *Description of a
                        City Shower*

The Nose of a Healthy Dog always is
    Cold.[1]
                The Dog's Cold Nose

The finest thing in London is the
    Bobby;
Benignant information is his hobby.
            The Lyric Baedeker. London

Drab is the town as a shawl-hooded
    crone,
And dreary and cold with a chill all its
    own.
You ask them for bread and they give
    you a scone,
            In Glasgow.
            Ibid. Glasgow, Stanza 2

For Education is, Making Men;
So is it now, so was it when
Mark Hopkins sat on one end of a log
And James Garfield sat on the other.[2]
                                    Education

Amoebas at the start
    Were not complex;
They tore themselves apart
    And started Sex.
                    Sex. Stanza 1

The three-toed tree-toad
Sings his sweet ode
    To the moon.
                    Nocturne

I breathed a song into the air;
That little song of beauty rare
Is flying still, for all I know,
Around the world by Radio.
                    Radiolatry

They earned a name that lives in song,
    Those woodsmen stout and plucky
Whose hair and rifles both were long —
    The Hunters of Kentucky.[3]
                    The Tall Men

Of all cold words of tongue or pen
The worst are these: "I knew him
    when — "
            Prophets in Their Own Country

---

[1] Most frozen was his honest nose,
    And never could it lose again
    The dampness of that dreadful rain.
        MARGARET EYTINGE: *Why the Dog's
                        Nose Is Cold* [1883]
[2] See James A. Garfield, page 591.
[3] See Woodworth, page 348.

Much have I sorrowed,
  Learning to my cost
That a book that's borrowed
  Is a book that's lost!
      Lament in a Library. Stanza 3

My sword is Strength, my spear is
  Song;
With these upon a stubborn field
I challenge Falsehood, Fear and
  Wrong;
  But Laughter is my shield.
      Re-armed. Stanza 1

Oh, the Brown Missouri Mule has a
  copper-plated throat
And the welkin splits apart when he
  hits an upper note.
      Mule Song. Stanza 1

Lightly we follow our cue,
"Exit, pursued by a bear." [1]
    The Shakespearean Bear. Envoi

Then up he rose, and forth they went
Away from battleground, fortress, tent,
Mountain, wilderness, field and farm,
Death and the General, arm in arm.
  Death and General Putnam.
    Death and General Putnam.
        Stanza 8

RALPH HODGSON
[1871–]

'Twould ring the bells of Heaven
The wildest peal for years,
If Parson lost his senses
And people came to theirs,
And he and they together
Knelt down with angry prayers
For tamed and shabby tigers
And dancing dogs and bears,
And wretched, blind pit ponies,
And little hunted hares.
      The Bells of Heaven

God loves an idle rainbow
No less than labouring seas.
      A Wood Song

I saw with open eyes
Singing birds sweet
Sold in the shops
For the people to eat,

[1] Stage direction, *The Winter's Tale*, Act
III, Sc. 3.

Sold in the shops of
Stupidity Street.
    Stupidity Street. Stanza 1

Time, you old gipsy man,
  Will you not stay,
Put up your caravan
  Just for one day?
    Time, You Old Gipsy Man.
        Stanza 1

Pity him, this dupe of dream,
Leader of the herd again
Only in his daft old brain,
Once again the bull supreme.
      The Bull

Wondering, listening,
Listening, wondering,
Eve with a berry
Half-way to her lips.
      Eve. Stanza 4

Oh, had our simple Eve
Seen through the make-believe!
      Ibid. Stanza 5

I stared into the sky,
As wondering men have always done
Since beauty and the stars were one,
Though none so hard as I.
      The Song of Honor

I heard it all, I heard the whole
Harmonious hymn of being roll
Up through the chapel of my soul
And at the altar die,
And in the awful quiet then
Myself I heard, Amen, Amen,
Amen I heard me cry!
      Ibid.

Reason has moons, but moons not hers
  Lie mirrored on her sea,
Confounding her astronomers,
  But O! delighting me.
      Reason

JAMES WELDON JOHNSON
[1871–1938]

O black and unknown bards of long
  ago,
How came your lips to touch the sacred
  fire?
How, in your darkness, did you come to
  know
The power and beauty of the minstrel's
  lyre?
    O Black and Unknown Bards.
        Stanza 1

Weep not, weep not,
She is not dead;
She's resting in the bosom of Jesus.
Heart-broken husband — weep no
    more;
Grief-stricken son — weep no more;
Left-lonesome daughter — weep no
    more;
She's only just gone home.
> *Go Down Death: A Funeral*
> *Sermon. Stanza 1*

CHARLES RANN KENNEDY
[1871–]

A peculiar kind of fear they call courage.
> *The Terrible Meck*

The meek, the terrible meek, the
fierce agonizing meek, are about to enter into their inheritance.
> *Ibid.*

AGNES LEE
(MRS. OTTO FREER)

Then she gazed down some wilder,
    darker hour,
And said — when Mary questioned,
    knowing not,
"Who art thou, mother of so sweet a
    son?" —
"I am the mother of Iscariot."
> *Motherhood. Stanza 6*

Bed is the boon for me!
It's well to bake and sweep,
But hear the word of old Lizette:
It's better than all to sleep.
> *Old Lizette on Sleep. Stanza 1*

There's nothing, nothing, nothing, I
    say,
That's worth the lying awake!
> *Ibid. Stanza 3*

EDDIE NEWTON AND
T. LAURENCE SEIBERG

Casey Jones! Orders in his hand.
Casey Jones! Mounted to the cabin,
Took his farewell journey to that prom-
    ised land.
> *Casey Jones* [*1900*] (*Adapted*

from verses and melody by
WALLACE SAUNDERS) [1]

HERBERT GEORGE
PONTING
[1871–1935]

On the outside grows the furside, on the
    inside grows the skinside;
So the furside is the outside, and the
    skinside is the inside.
> *The Sleeping Bag* [2]

JOHN MILLINGTON
SYNGE
[1871–1909]

It's in a lonesome place you do have
to be talking with someone, and looking for someone, in the evening of the
day.
> *In the Shadow of the Glen*

What is the price of a thousand
horses against a son where there is one
son only?
> *Riders to the Sea*

Bartley will have a fine coffin out of
the white boards, and a deep grave
surely. What more can we want than
that? No man at all can be living for
ever, and we must be satisfied.
> *Ibid.*

When I was writing "The Shadow of
the Glen" I got more aid than any
learning could have given me from a
chink in the floor of the old Wicklow
house where I was staying, that let me
hear what was being said by the servant
girls in the kitchen.
> *The Playboy of the Western*
> *World. Preface*

---

[1] Of the many versions of this traditional
ballad, the most familiar is printed in CARL
SANDBURG'S *The American Songbag* [1927].
It begins:
Come all you rounders, for I want you to hear
The story of a brave engineer.
Casey Jones was the rounder's name,
On a big eight-wheeler of a mighty fame.
[2] For *The South Polar Times, Midwinter
Day, June 22, 1911,* prepared by the men of
Captain Robert Falcon Scott's last Antarctic
expedition.

Drink a health to the wonders of the western world, the pirates, preachers, poteen-makers, with the jobbing jockies; parching peelers, and the juries fill their stomachs selling judgments of the English law.

The Playboy of the Western World. Act II

May I meet him with one tooth and it aching, and one eye to be seeing seven and seventy divils in the twists of the road, and one old timber leg on him to limp into the scalding grave. There he is now crossing the strands, and that the Lord God would send a high wave to wash him from the world.[1]

Ibid.

Aid me for to win her, and I'll be asking God to stretch a hand to you in the hour of death, and lead you short cuts through the Meadows of Ease, and up the floor of Heaven to the Footstool of the Virgin's Son.

Ibid.

A man who is not afraid of the sea will soon be drowned, he said, for he will be going out on a day he shouldn't. But we do be afraid of the sea, and we do only be drownded now and again.

The Aran Islands. Page 127

There is no language like the Irish for soothing and quieting.

Ibid. Page 180

A translation is no translation, he said, unless it will give you the music of a poem along with the words of it.

Ibid. Page 181

ALBERT EDWARD WIGGAM
[1871–   ]

Intelligence appears to be the thing that enables a man to get along without education. Education appears to be

---

[1] May the grass grow at your door and the fox build his nest on your hearthstone. May the light fade from your eyes, so you never see what you love. May your own blood rise against you, and the sweetest drink you take be the bitterest cup of sorrow. May you die without benefit of clergy; may there be none to shed a tear at your grave, and may the hearthstone of hell be your best bed forever. — Traditional Wexford curse

---

the thing that enables a man to get along without the use of his intelligence.

The New Decalogue of Science

Statesmanship should quickly learn the lesson of biology, as stated by Conklin, that "Wooden legs are not inherited, but wooden heads are."

Ibid.

If your father went crazy from a hit on the head with a brickbat, you do not inherit his cracked brain but only his inability to dodge brickbats.

Ibid.

JULIET WILBOR TOMPKINS
[1871–   ]

The hurrying footsteps came and went,
And the heart beat thick for the great event,
    When the Minister came to tea.[1]

When the Minister Came to Tea.
Stanza 1

MAX BEERBOHM
[1872–   ]

I have known no man of genius who had not to pay, in some affliction or defect either physical or spiritual, for what the gods had given him.

No. 2, The Pines

It seems to be a law of nature that no man ever is loth to sit for his portrait. A man may be old, he may be ugly, he may be burdened with grave responsibilities to the nation, and that nation be at a crisis of its history; but none of these considerations, nor all of them together, will deter him from sitting for his portrait.

Quia Imperfectum

To say that a man is vain means merely that he is pleased with the effect he produces on other people. A conceited man is satisfied with the effect he produces on himself.

Ibid.

---

[1] Pa has shaved as slick as can be, and I'm
    rigged way up in G,
And it's all because we're goin' ter have
    the minister ter tea.
    JOSEPH CROSBY LINCOLN: *When the
        Minister Comes to Tea, St. 1*

Strange, when you come to think of it, that of all the countless folk who have lived before our time on this planet not one is known in history or in legend as having died of laughter.

Laughter

He was fond of quoting those incomparable poets, Homer.

Works

JAMES BONE
[1872–   ]

The mighty fleet of Wren, with their topgallants and mainsails of stone.

The nautical simile leaps to the mind at the sight of Wren's white spires and towers, and it is appropriate, too, to the material in which Wren worked. Portland stone is a marine deposit of the Jurassic period before Britain first at Heaven's command arose from out the azure main. Its beds are full of fossils of marine creatures, cockles, sea-urchins, starfish, and oysters. You can see shell imprints on the freshly cut whitbed stone on the top of the new Bush Building, and you can see 'horses' heads' — as certain shell fossils are called by masons — on the weather-beaten south parapet of St. Paul's. You can see and feel the shells projecting from the plinth of King Charles's statue at Charing Cross. It is a strange thought that the majesty of the capital of this sea-joined empire should come itself from beneath the sea. How could our poets have missed such a theme?

The London Perambulator

The City of Dreadful Height.

Description of New York [1]

CALVIN COOLIDGE
[1872–1933]

Have faith in Massachusetts. In some unimportant detail some other States may surpass her, but in the general results, there is no place on earth where the people secure, in larger measure, the blessings of organized govern-

[1] In *The Manchester Guardian.*

ment, and nowhere can those functions more properly be termed self-government.

Address to the Massachusetts Senate on being elected its president [January 7, 1914]

There is no right to strike against the public safety by anybody, anywhere, any time.

Telegram to Samuel Gompers, President of the American Federation of Labor [September 14, 1919], on the occasion of the Boston police strike

Vermont is a State I love. I could not look upon the peaks of Ascutney, Killington, Mansfield, and Equinox without being moved in a way that no other scene could move me. It was here that I first saw the light of day; here I received my bride; here my dead lie pillowed on the loving breast of our everlasting hills. I love Vermont because of her hills and valleys, her scenery and invigorating climate, but most of all because of her indomitable people. They are a race of pioneers who have almost beggared themselves to serve others. If the spirit of liberty should vanish in other parts of our Union and support of our institutions should languish, it could all be replenished from the generous store held by the people of this brave little State of Vermont.

Address from train platform, Bennington, Vermont [September 21, 1928]

To my friend, in recollection of his son, and my son, who, by the grace of God, have the privilege of being boys throughout Eternity.

Inscription in a friend's book, after the death of Calvin Coolidge, Jr.

JAMES B. DOLLARD
[1872–   ]

I'm sick o' New York City an' the roarin' o' the thrains
That rowl above the blessèd roofs an' undernaith the dhrains;

Wid dust an' smoke an' divilmint I'm
    moidhered head an' brains,
    An' I'm thinkin' o' the skies of ould
    Kilkinny!
*   Ould Kilkinny!*

PAUL LAURENCE DUNBAR
[1872–1906]

Sometimes the sun, unkindly hot,
My garden makes a desert spot;
Sometimes a blight upon the tree
Takes all my fruit away from me;
And then with throes of bitter pain
Rebellious passions rise and swell;
But — life is more than fruit or grain,
And so I sing, and all is well.
*   The Poet and His Song*
Folks ain't got no right to censuah otha
    folks about dey habits;
Him dat giv' de squir'ls de bushtails
    made de bobtails fu' de rabbits.
*   Accountability*
You cain't sta't no notes a-flyin'
    Lak de ones dat rants and rings
From de kitchen to de big woods
    When Malindy sings.
*   When Malindy Sings*
There is a heaven, for ever, day by day,
The upward longing of my soul doth
    tell me so.
There is a hell, I'm quite as sure; for
    pray,
If there were not, where would my
    neighbours go?
*   Theology*
An' you couldn't he'p f'om dancin' ef
    yo' feet was boun' wif twine,
When Angelina Johnson comes a-swing-
    in' down de line.
*   Angelina*
Speak up, Ike, an' 'spress yo'se'f.
*   Encouragement*
Sweetah den de music of a lovesick
    mockin'-bird,
Comin' f'om de gal you loves better den
    yo' kin,
"Howdy, honey, howdy, won't you step
    right in?"
*   "Howdy, Honey, Howdy!"*
Heish yo' mouf, I's only tu'nin' of de
    chillun in de bed.
The Turning of the Babies in the Bed

It's easy 'nough to titter w'en de stew
    is smokin' hot,
But hit's mighty ha'd to giggle w'en
    dey's nuffin' in de pot.
*   Philosophy*

EVA GORE-BOOTH
[1872–1926]

The little waves of Breffny go stumbling
    through my soul.
*   The Little Waves of Breffny.*
*   Stanza 3*

MILDRED HOWELLS
[1872–   ]

Yet close, I feel, there wraps us all
    around
Some mighty force, some mystery pro-
    found,
    And through my doubts and igno-
        rance, I trust
The power that bound with laws the
    moon and tide
And hung the stars in heavenly spaces
    wide,
    Must, by their witness, be both wise
        and just.
*   If This Be All. Stanza 3*
Within a garden once there grew
    A flower that seemed the very pattern
Of all propriety; none knew
    She was at heart a wandering slattern.
*   A Very Wild Flower. Stanza 1*
And so it criticized each flower,
    This supercilious seed;
Until it woke one summer hour,
    And found itself a weed.
*   The Difficult Seed. Stanza 5*

JOHN McCRAE
[1872–1918]

In Flanders fields the poppies blow
Between the crosses, row on row.
*   In Flanders Fields. Stanza 1* [1]
Take up our quarrel with the foe:
To you from failing hands we throw
    The torch; be yours to hold it high.

[1] In London *Punch, Dec. 8, 1915.*

If ye break faith with us who die
We shall not sleep, though poppies grow
   In Flanders fields.
    In Flanders Fields. Stanza 3

JOHN CLAIR MINOT
[1872–]

May the God we trust as a nation
  Throw the light of His peace and
    grace
On a flag with its stripes untarnished,
  And with every star in place.
    The Flag of Fort McHenry.
          Stanza 10

PATRICK F. O'KEEFE
[1872–1934]

Say it with flowers.
    *Slogan for the Society of Amer-
    ican Florists* [1917]

BERTRAND ARTHUR
WILLIAM RUSSELL
[1872–]

It is preoccupation with possession,
more than anything else, that prevents
men from living freely and nobly.
  Principles of Social Reconstruction
Mathematics possesses not only
truth, but supreme beauty — a beauty
cold and austere, like that of sculpture,
without appeal to any part of our
weaker nature, sublimely pure, and capable of a stern perfection such as only
the greatest art can show.
    The Study of Mathematics
Mathematics takes us into the region
of absolute necessity, to which not only
the actual world, but every possible
world, must conform.
              Ibid.

LEONORA SPEYER
[1872–]

Out of my sorrow
I'll build a stair,
And every to-morrow
Will climb to me there

With ashes of yesterday
In its hair.
    Duet: I Sing with Myself.

HENRY NOEL BRAILSFORD
[1873–]

Music is neither secular nor religious.
It can at best suggest the beating of
the pulse, the rhythm of the blood that
accompanies a given order of ideas.
    On Handel's Largo
The musician who tries to rival the
painter by describing external things,
is a magician who has thrown aside his
wand to wield a quarter-staff.
    The Sea in Music

GUY WETMORE CARRYL
[1873–1904]

You call it a waste of time, this taste
  For popular tunes, and yet
Good-bye to care when you whistle the
    air
  Of the song that you can't forget.
    The Organ Man. Stanza 3
How imposing it would be
If pumpkins grew upon a tree!
    The Iconoclast and the Acorn.
          Stanza 1
And in his dim, uncertain sight
Whatever wasn't must be right,
From which it follows he had strong
Convictions that what was, was wrong.
          Ibid. Stanza 2
In every new and smart disease,
From housemaid's knee to heart dis-
    ease,
  She recognized the symptoms as her
    own!
    *How Jack Found That Beans May
    Go Back on a Chap. Stanza 2*

ARTHUR CHAPMAN
[1873–1935]

Out where the handclasp's a little
stronger,

Out where the smile dwells a little
    longer,
  That's where the West begins.
       Out Where the West Begins.[1]
               Stanza 1

Out where the skies are a trifle bluer,
Out where friendship's a little truer.
            Ibid. Stanza 2

Where there's more of singing and less
    of sighing,
Where there's more of giving and less of
    buying,
And a man makes friends without half
    trying.
            Ibid. Stanza 3

Oh, the quickly faded glory
Of the cowboy's brief, brief story!
How the old range beckons vainly in the
    sunshine and the rain!
       The Cow-Puncher's Elegy.
               Stanza 2

Plain duty's a term that is harsh to men
In the country God forgot.
    The Border Riders. Stanza 1

WALTER DE LA MARE
[1873–   ]

Slowly, silently, now the moon
Walks the night in her silver shoon.
               Silver

Couched in his kennel, like a log,
With paws of silver sleeps the dog.
               Ibid.

When all at peace, two friends at ease
    alone
Talk out their hearts; yet still

[1] Up where the north winds blow just a
    little keener,
  Up where the grasses grow just a little
    greener,
  Up where the mountain peaks rise a little
    higher,
  Up where the human kind draws a little
    nigher,
    That's where Vermont comes in.
    CHARLES HIAL DARLING [1859–   ]:
      Where Vermont Comes In

  Down where I fear there's a terrible lot
    o' me,
  Down where some people are hippopot-
    ami,
  In the department of laparotomy,
    That's where the vest begins.
    ARTHUR GUITERMAN: *Vulgar Lines
    for a Distinguished Surgeon, St. 3*

Between the grace notes of
  The voice of love
From each to each
  Trembles a rarer speech,
And with its presence every pause doth
    fill.
               Silence

"World of divine delight," heart whis-
    pereth,
Though all its all lie but 'twixt birth
    and death.
           Divine Delight

Softly along the road of evening,
  In a twilight dim with rose,
Wrinkled with age, and drenched with
    dew,
  Old Nod, the shepherd, goes.
          Nod. Stanza 1

Here lies a most beautiful lady,
Light of step and heart was she.
          An Epitaph

"Is there anybody there?" said the
    Traveller,
  Knocking on the moonlit door;
And his horse in the silence champed
    the grasses
  Of the forest's ferny floor.
         The Listeners

"Tell them that I came, and no one
    answered,
  That I kept my word," he said.
               Ibid.

If I were Lord of Tartary,
  Myself and me alone,
My bed should be of ivory,
  Of beaten gold my throne.
       Tartary. Stanza 1

I saw sweet Poetry turn troubled eyes
On shaggy Science nosing in the grass;
For by that way poor Poetry must pass
On her long pilgrimage to Paradise.
      The Happy Encounter

Look thy last on all things lovely
Every hour. Let no night
Seal thy sense in deathly slumber
Till to delight
Thou have paid thy utmost blessing.
       Farewell. Stanza 3

Here lies, but seven years old, our little
    maid,
Once of the darkness, oh, so sore afraid.
Light of the World — remember that
    small fear,

And when nor moon nor stars do shine
— draw near!
An Epitaph

'Tis the immortal thought
Whose passion still
Makes of the unchanging
The unchangeable.
When the Rose Is Faded.
Stanza 3

No lovelier hills than thine have laid
My tired thoughts to rest:
No peace of lovelier valleys made
Like peace within my breast.
England. Stanza 1

My heart within me faints to roam
In thought even far from thee:
Thine be the grave whereto I come,
And thine my darkness be.
Ibid. Stanza 4

Nay, nay, sweet England, do not
grieve!
Not one of these poor men who died
But did within his soul believe
That death for thee was glorified.
"How Sleep the Brave." Stanza 1

And into Time's enormous nought,
Sweet-fed, will flit away.
Titmouse. Stanza 3

Hi! handsome hunting man,
Fire your little gun.
Bang! Now the animal
Is dead and dumb and done.
Nevermore to peep again, creep again,
leap again,
Eat or sleep or drink again, oh, what
fun!
Hi!

"Chariots of gold," says Timothy;
"Silvery wings," says Elaine;
"A bumpity ride in a wagon of hay
For me," says Jane.
Bunches of Grapes. Stanza 3

Ann, Ann!
Come! quick as you can!
There's a fish that *talks*
In the frying pan.
Alas, Alack

It's a very odd thing —
As odd as can be —
That whatever Miss T. eats
Turns into Miss T.
Miss T.

Who said, "Ay, mum's the word";
Sexton to willow:
Who said, "Green dusk for dreams,
Moss for a pillow"?
Who said, "All Time's delight
Hath she for narrow bed;
Life's troubled bubble broken"? —
That's what I said.
Song of the Mad Prince. Stanza 2

Be not too wildly amorous of the far,
Nor lure thy fantasy to its utmost
scope.
The Imagination's Pride

But what can Miss Emily
Want with a box
So long, narrow, shallow,
And without any locks?
Peeping Tom

At lip, miraculous, life's wine,
At hand, its wondrous bread.
The Sleeper

Never was sweeter seraph hid
Within so small a house —
A tiny, inch-long, eager, ardent
Feathered mouse.
Jenny Wren

Grotesque, irrational, and sans
All law and order known as Man's.
Dreams. Stanza 3

At his absence all elate,
His body's artisans sustain
Their toil in sinew, nerve, and brain:
Nothing recks he: he roves afar,
Past compass, chart, and calendar.
Ibid. Stanza 4

The genius of William Hamilton
Sought the square root of *minus* one;
In vain; till — all thought of it leagues
away —
The problem flowered from a dream one
day.
Ibid. Stanza 25

And Conscience less my mind indicts
For idle days than dreamless nights.
Ibid. Stanza 37

FORD MADOX (HUEFFER) FORD
[1873–   ]

But we who remain shall grow old,
We shall know the cold
Of cheerless

Winter and the rain of Autumn and the
   sting
Of poverty, of love despised and of dis-
   graces,
And mirrors showing stained and aging
   faces,
And the long ranges of comfortless
   years
And the long gamut of human fears —
But for you — it shall be forever
   Spring.
One Day's List

LENA GUILBERT FORD
[*Floruit* 1915]

Keep the home fires burning,
While your hearts are yearning,
Though your lads are far away
They dream of home.
There's a silver lining
Through the dark clouds shining,
Turn the dark clouds inside out,
Till the boys come home.
Keep the Home Fires
Burning [*1915*]

WILLIAM HERSCHELL
[1873–   ]

The Kid has gone to the Colors
   And we don't know what to say;
The Kid we have loved and cuddled
   Stepped out for the Flag to-day.
The Kid Has Gone to the
Colors [*1917*]. *Stanza 1*

What do little girls talk about?
   What is their mystic theme?
Those still too young for puppy love,
   Yet old enough to dream.
What Do Little Girls Talk
About? Stanza 1

Ain't God good to Indiana!
   Folks, a feller never knows
Just how close he is to Eden
   Till, sometime, he ups and goes
Seekin' fairer, greener pastures
   Than he has right here at home.
Ain't God Good to Indiana!
Stanza 1

DANIEL GREGORY MASON
[1873–   ]

The ideal of Independence requires
resistance to the herd spirit now so
widespread, to our workshop of quantity and indifference to quality, to our
unthinking devotion to organization,
standardization, propaganda, and advertising.
Artistic Ideals. Page 3

Art of any profundity can be appreciated only slowly, gradually, in leisurely contemplation.
Ibid. Page 105

JAMES JACKSON MONTAGUE
[1873–   ]

My beagle bit a Kleagle
Of the Ku Klux Klan.
Doomed. Stanza 1

But no one ever is allowed in Sleepy-
   town, unless
He goes to bed in time to take the
   Sleepytown Express!
The Sleepytown Express. Stanza 1

ELIZABETH CUTTER
(MRS. DWIGHT WHITNEY)
MORROW
[1873–   ]

My friend and I have built a wall
   Between us thick and wide:
The stones of it are laid in scorn
   And plastered high with pride.
Wall. Stanza 1

There is no lover like an island shore
   For lingering embrace;
No tryst so faithful as the turning tide
   At its accustomed place.
Islands. Stanza 1

He who has given
A hostage knows
All ways of dying
Terror shows.
Hostage

H. M. TOMLINSON
[1873–   ]

The sea is at its best at London, near
midnight, when you are within the arms

of a capacious chair, before a glowing fire, selecting phases of the voyages you will never make.

The Sea and the Jungle

In the west was a steep range of cloudland rising from the sea, and against it was inclined the flame of a rainbow. The world's noble emblem was aloft. I demanded of the Skipper if he would run up our ensign in reply to it; but he only peered at me curiously.

Ibid.

How many grave speeches, which have surprised, shocked, and directed the nation, have been made by Great Men too soon after a noble dinner, words winged by the Press without an accompanying and explanatory wine list.

Waiting for Daylight

That figure of Nobody in sodden khaki, cumbered with ugly gear, its precious rifle wrapped in rags, no brightness anywhere about it except the light of its eyes, its face seamed with lines which might have been dolorous, which might have been ironic, with the sweat running from under its steel casque, looms now in the memory, huge, statuesque, silent but questioning, like an overshadowing challenge. . . .

What is that figure now? The ghost of what was fair, but was broken, and is lost.

Ibid. The Nobodies [November 11, 1918]

The reader who is illuminated is, in a real sense, the poem.

Between the Lines [1]

Bad and indifferent criticism of books is just as serious as a city's careless drainage.

Ibid.

It has to be a good book which can maintain its value beside the lamp of a ship's berth at midnight — the best time and place in all the world for reading.

South to Cadiz. Sea-Light

[1] Lecture at the Harvard Union, Oct. 14, 1927.

What was created in Concord, though in so airy a fashion, may be standing to America's credit when her vast engine shops are homes for spiders.

The Road to Concord [1931]

MAURICE BARING
[1874–   ]

Because of you we will be glad and gay,
　Remembering you, we will be brave and strong;
And hail the advent of each dangerous day,
　And meet the great adventure with a song.

Julian Grenfell (1888–1915) [1]

And you will speed us onward with a cheer,
　And wave beyond the stars that all is well.

Ibid.

All theories of what a good play is, or how a good play should be written, are futile. A good play is a play which when acted upon the boards makes an audience interested and pleased. A play that fails in this is a bad play.

Have You Anything to Declare?

DAVID WILLIAM BONE
[1874–   ]

"Ah wouldna go in them if ye wass t' gif me thirrty pounss a munss! Coaffins, Ah caall them!"

I thought of a ship staggering hard-pressed to windward of a ledge of cruel rocks, the breakers shrieking for a prey, and the old grey-haired Master of her slapping the rail and shouting, "Up t' it, m' beauty! T' windward, ye bitch!"

"Aye, coaffins," he repeated. "That iss what they are!"

I had no answer — he was a steamboat man, and would not have understood.

The Brassbounder. Chap. 26

[1] Julian Grenfell, Captain in the First Royal Dragoons, wounded near Ypres, March 13, 1915, died at Boulogne, May 26.

We sailors are jealous for our vessels. Abuse us if you will, but have a care for what you may say of our ships. We alone are entitled to call them bitches, wet brutes, stubborn craft, but we will stand for no such liberties from the beach.

Merchantmen-at-Arms

Nobly she has held afloat to the debarking of the last man. There is no further life in her. Evenly, steadily, as we had seen her leave the launching ways at Meadowside, she goes down.[1]

Ibid.

GORDON BOTTOMLEY
[1874-   ]

Many deaths have place in men
  Before they come to die;
Joys must be used and spent, and then
  Abandoned and passed by.

New Year's Eve, 1913

Poetry is founded on the hearts of men:
Though in Nirvana or the Heavenly
    courts
The principle of beauty shall persist,
Its body of poetry, as the body of man,
Is but a terrene form, a terrene use,
That swifter being will not loiter with;
And, when mankind is dead and the
    world cold,
Poetry's immortality will pass.

Atlantis

When you destroy a blade of grass
  You poison England at her roots.

To Iron Founders and Others

Your worship is your furnaces,
  Which, like old idols, lost obscenes,
Have molten bowels; your vision is
  Machines for making more machines.

Ibid.

GILBERT KEITH
CHESTERTON
[1874-1936]

Nothing sublimely artistic has ever arisen out of mere art, any more than anything essentially reasonable has ever arisen out of the pure reason. There

must always be a rich moral soil for any great aesthetic growth.

A Defence of Nonsense

Every great literature has always been allegorical — allegorical of some view of the whole universe.

Ibid.

The whole difference between construction and creation is exactly this: that a thing constructed can only be loved after it is constructed; but a thing created is loved before it exists.

Preface to DICKENS' *Pickwick Papers*

A man knows what style of book he wants to write when he knows nothing else about it.

Ibid.

The book originated in the suggestion of a publisher; as many more good books have done than the arrogance of the man of letters is commonly inclined to admit.

Ibid.

A good joke is the one ultimate and sacred thing which cannot be criticized. Our relations with a good joke are direct and even divine relations.

Ibid.

The world will never starve for wonders; but only for want of wonder.

Inscription on General Motors Building, A Century of Progress Exposition, Chicago

But they that fought for England,
  Following a fallen star,
Alas, alas for England
  They have their graves afar.

Elegy in a Country Churchyard

If I ever go back to Baltimore,
The City of Maryland,
I shall miss again as I missed before
A thousand things of the world in store,
The story standing in every door
That beckons on every hand.

Memory

Like the white lock of Whistler, that lit
    our aimless gloom,
Men showed their own white feather as
    proudly as a plume.

The Man Who Was Thursday. Dedication, to Edmund Clerihew Bentley

---

[1] Sinking of the *Cameronia*, torpedoed in the Mediterranean.

Far out of fish-shaped Paumanok some
cry of cleaner things; [1]
And the Green Carnation withered, as
in forest fires that pass.[2]
The Man Who Was Thursday.
Dedication

Truth out of Tusitala [3] spoke and
pleasure out of pain.
Ibid.

Thieves respect property. They
merely wish the property to become
their property that they may more perfectly respect it.
Ibid.

Mr. Max Beerbohm attempted to
analyze the jokes at which the mob
laughs. He divided them into three sections: jokes about bodily humiliation,
jokes about things alien, such as foreigners, and jokes about bad cheese.
Cockneys and Their Jokes

Art is limitation; the essence of every
picture is the frame.
Orthodoxy. Chap. 3

You can free things from alien or accidental laws, but not from the laws of
their own nature. . . . Do not go
about as a demagogue, encouraging tri-
angles to break out of the prison of
their three sides. If a triangle breaks out
of its three sides, its life comes to a
lamentable end.
Ibid.

The English poor, broken in every revolt, bullied by every fashion, long despoiled of property, and now being
despoiled of liberty, entered history
with a noise of trumpets, and turned
themselves in two years into one of the
iron armies of the world.
A Short History of England
[*1917*]

Don John of Austria is going to the war.
Lepanto

The hidden room in a man's house
where God sits all the year,

[1] Walt Whitman.
[2] Oscar Wilde.
[3] Robert Louis Stevenson.

The secret window whence the world
looks small and very dear.
Lepanto

Cervantes on his galley sets the sword
back in the sheath
(Don John of Austria rides homeward
with a wreath).
And he sees across a weary land a strag-
gling road in Spain,
Up which a lean and foolish knight forever rides in vain.
Ibid.

To an open house in the evening
Home shall men come,
To an older place than Eden
And a taller town than Rome.
The House of Christmas

Burn from my brain and from my
breast
Sloth, and the cowardice that clings,
And stiffness and the soul's arrest:
And feed my brain with better things.
A Ballade of a Book-Reviewer

I think I will not hang myself to-day.
A Ballade of Suicide

St. George he was for England,
And before he killed the dragon
He drank a pint of English ale
Out of an English flagon.
The Englishman

Step softly, under snow or rain,
To find the place where men can
pray;
The way is all so very plain
That we may lose the way.
The Wise Men

And Noah he often said to his wife
when he sat down to dine,
"I don't care where the water goes if
it doesn't get into the wine."
Wine and Water

Before the Roman came to Rye or out
to Severn strode,
The rolling English drunkard made the
rolling English road.
The Rolling English Road

If an angel out of heaven
Brings you other things to drink,
Thank him for his kind attentions,
Go and pour them down the sink.
The Song of Right and Wrong

Tea is like the East he grows in,
A great yellow Mandarin
With urbanity of manner
And unconsciousness of sin.
        The Song of Right and Wrong
And, like all the East he grows in,
He is Poison when he's strong.
                              Ibid.

Cocoa is a cad and coward.
                              Ibid.

Heaven sent us Soda Water
As a torment for our crimes.
                              Ibid.

For the great Gaels of Ireland
    Are the men that God made mad,
For all their wars are merry,
    And all their songs are sad.[1]
        *The Ballad of the White
                    Horse. Book II*
And if ever ye ride in Ireland,
    The jest may yet be said,
There is the land of broken hearts,
    And the land of broken heads.
                    Ibid. Book V
    I also had my hour;
One far fierce hour and sweet:
There was a shout about my ears,
And palms before my feet.[2]
                        The Donkey
The Yankee is a dab at electricity and
        crime,
He tells you how he hustles and it takes
        him quite a time,
I like his hospitality that's cordial and
        frank,
I do not mind his money but I do not
        like his swank.
                A Song of Self-Esteem
The Faith of Tennessee has wafted
        o'er the sea,
The odour of its sanctity — and Golly
        how it stank![3]
                              Ibid.

[1] For the Young Gaels of Ireland
        Are the lads that drive me mad;
    For half their words need footnotes,
        And half their rhymes are bad.
            ARTHUR GUITERMAN: *The Young
                        Celtic Poets*, St. 2
[2] My shoulders were His throne.
            JOHN B. TABB: *The Burthen
                        of the Ass*
[3] The prosecution of John Thomas Scopes
in Dayton, Tennessee, July, 1925, for teach-

ISABEL FISKE CONANT
[1874-   ]

Give me but a tearing,
    A scrap of Beauty's cloth,
Warm from her wearing;
    A song, a shell, a moth,
Still faintly fragrant;
    Her glove, her torn veil,
And I will find vagrant
    Beauty's trail.
            Hound of Beauty. Stanza 1
He who loves an old house
Never loves in vain,
How can an old house
Used to sun and rain,
To lilac and larkspur,
And an elm above,
Ever fail to answer
The heart that gives it love?
                    Old House. Stanza 1
If haloed Christ still walked to-day
And made new saints again,
I'd have for mine, in bright array,
Old Ellen, down the lane.
                    Old Ellen. Stanza 1

CLARENCE DAY
[1874-1935]

A race of civilized beings descended
from the great cats would have been
rich in hermits and solitary thinkers.
The recluse would not have been stig-
matized as peculiar, as he is by us
simians. They would not have been a
credulous people, or easily religious.
False prophets and swindlers would
have found few dupes. And what generals they would have made! what consummate politicians!
                    This Simian World. VI
Curiosity is a valuable trait. It will
make the simians learn many things.
But the curiosity of a simian is as excessive as the toil of an ant. Each
simian will wish to know more than his
head can hold, let alone ever deal with;
and those whose minds are active will
wish to know everything going. It would
stretch a god's skull to accomplish such

ing the theory of evolution in his classroom
at the Central High School.

an ambition, yet simians won't like to think it's beyond their powers. Even small tradesmen and clerks, no matter how thrifty, will be eager to buy costly encyclopedias, or books of all knowledge. Almost every simian family, even the dullest, will think it is due to themselves to keep all knowledge handy.

This Simian World. IX

Simians even believe, many of them, that knowledge is power. Unfortunate dupes of this saying will keep on reading, ambitiously, till they have stunned their native initiative, and made their thoughts weak; and will then wonder dazedly what in the world is the matter, and why the great power they were expecting to gain fails to appear. Again, if they ever forget what they read, they'll be worried. Those who *can* forget — those with fresh eyes who have swept from their minds such facts as the exact month and day that their children were born, or the numbers on houses, or the names (the mere meaningless labels) of the people they meet, — will be urged to go live in sanitariums or see memory doctors!

Ibid.

Huge seas of talk of every sort and kind, in print, speech, and writing, will roll unceasingly, involving an unbelievable waste in labor and time, and sapping the intelligence talk is supposed to upbuild. In a simian civilization, great halls will be erected for lectures, and great throngs will actually pay to go inside at night to hear some self-satisfied talk-maker chatter for hours. Almost any subject will do for a lecture, or talk; yet very few subjects will be counted important enough for the average man to do any *thinking* on them, off by himself.

Ibid. X

It is possible that our race may be an accident, in a meaningless universe, living its brief life uncared-for, on this dark, cooling star: but even so — and all the more — what marvelous creatures we are! What fairy story, what tale from the Arabian Nights of the jinns, is a hundredth part as wonderful as this true fairy story of simians! It is so much more heartening, too, than the tales we invent. A universe capable of giving birth to many such accidents is — blind or not — a good world to live in, a promising universe.

This Simian World. XIX

Father declared he was going to buy a new plot in the cemetery, a plot all for himself. "And I'll buy one on a corner," he added triumphantly, "where I can get out!"

Mother looked at him, startled but admiring, and whispered to me, "I almost believe he could do it."

Life with Father

JAMES WILLIAM FOLEY
[1874–   ]

It does a heap o' good sometimes, to go
        a little slow,
To say a word o' comfort to th' man
        that's stubbed his toe.

Stubbed His Toe. Stanza 2

I take a little bunch of words and set
        'em in a row,
I take a little bit of ink and mark 'em
        down just so.[1]

Technique

THEODOSIA GARRISON
[1874–   ]

I sicken of men's company,
        The crowded tavern's din,
Where all day long with oath and song
        Sit they who entrance win,
So come I out from noise and rout
        To rest in God's Green Inn.

The Green Inn. Stanza 1

ELLEN GLASGOW
[1874–   ]

I have observed with wonder so many intellectual and literary fashions that I have come at last to rely positively

---

[1] Webster has the words, and I
    Pick them up from where they lie,
    Twist and turn them one by one
    And give them places in "The Sun."
    Don Marquis: *On the Ease of Column
                            Writing*

upon one conviction alone. No idea is so antiquated that it was not once modern. No idea is so modern that it will not some day be antiquated. . . . To seize the flying thought before it escapes us is our only touch with reality.
Address to the Modern Language Association [*1936*]

HARRY GRAHAM
[1874–1936]

Though the noblest disposition you inherit,
And your character with piety is pack'd,
All such qualities have very little merit,
Unaccompanied by Tact.
Tact. Stanza 1

HERBERT CLARK HOOVER
[1874–   ]

A great social and economic experiment, noble in motive and far-reaching in purpose.
[*Of National Prohibition.*] *Letter to Senator Borah, February 28, 1928*

We were challenged with a peace-time choice between the American system of rugged individualism and a European philosophy of diametrically opposed doctrines — doctrines of paternalism and state socialism.
Campaign speech, New York [*October 22, 1928*]

Absolute freedom of the press to discuss public questions is a foundation stone of American liberty.[1]
Address, Annual Luncheon of the Associated Press, New York [*April 22, 1929*]

[1] Where dwells the man that dare suppress
The noble freedom of the press?
Sure he who would attempt the thing,
On Haman's gallows ought to swing.
ANONYMOUS: *The Freedom of the Press, St. 1*, in *Freeman's Journal* (*North American Intelligencer*), *June 27, 1787*
See James Russell Lowell, page 526.

No economic equality can survive the working of biological inequality.
The Challenge to Liberty [*1934*]. *Chap. 3*

While I can make no claim for having introduced the term "rugged individualism," I should be proud to have invented it. It has been used by American leaders for over a half-century in eulogy of those God-fearing men and women of honesty whose stamina and character and fearless assertion of rights led them to make their own way in life.
Ibid. Chap. 5

When I comb over these accounts of the New Deal, my sympathy arises for the humble decimal point. His is a pathetic and hectic life, wandering around among regimented ciphers, trying to find some of the old places he used to know.
Address, John Marshall Republican Club, St. Louis, Missouri [*December 16, 1935*]

A good many things go around in the dark besides Santa Claus.
Ibid.

HENRY HERBERT KNIBBS
[1874–   ]

We'll dance a merry saraband from here to drowsy Samarcand;
Along the sea, across the land, the birds are flying South,
And you, my sweet Penelope, out there somewhere you wait for me,
With buds of roses in your hair and kisses on your mouth.
Out There Somewhere

I'm strong for the man who named it, The Valley that God Forgot.
The Valley that God Forgot

Have ye dreamed of the mesa grass starred with the flower of blue;
Morning haze in the mountain-pass, sage in the silver dew?
Last of the Cavaliers

Sage a-shinin' in the sun that's just
   a-breakin' cover;
All around the ranges loomin' high and
   cold and still.
The Far and Lonely Hill
After the coffee things ain't so bad.
That Inside Song
You haven't whipped religion; just a
   man.
The Fighting Parson
Far trails await me; valleys vast and
   still,
   Vistas undreamed-of, cañon-guarded
     streams,
Lowland and range, fair meadow,
   flower-girt hill,
   Forests enchanted, filled with magic
     dreams.
Make Me No Grave
The heart of a dog — and he love a
   man — may never forget or
   change.
The Dog-Star Pup
Roll a rock down when I slide into glory,
And say that I went like a ranger
   should go.
Roll a Rock Down

AMY LOWELL
[1874–1925]

My words are little jars
For you to take and put upon a shelf.
Their shapes are quaint and beautiful,
And they have many pleasant colours
   and lustres
To recommend them.
A Gift
Hung all over with mouse-traps of
   metres, and cages
Of bright-plumaged rhythms, with
   pages and pages
Of colours slit up into streaming confetti.
A Critical Fable [1] (*passage
   describing herself*)
   Hedges of England, peppered with
sloes; hedges of England, rows and rows
of thorn and brier raying out from the
fire where London burns with its steam-
ing lights, throwing a glare on the sky
o' nights. Hedges of England, road after

[1] First published anonymously.

road, lane after lane, and on again to
the sea at the North, to the sea at the
East, blackberry hedges, and man and
beast plod and trot and gallop between
hedges of England, clipped and clean;
beech, and laurel, and hornbeam, and
yew, wheels whirl under, and circle
through, tunnels of green to the sea at
the South; wind-blown hedges to mark
the mouth of Thames or Humber, the
Western rim. Star-point hedges, smooth
and trim.
Hedge Island
I walk down the garden paths,
And all the daffodils
Are blowing, and the bright blue squills.
Patterns
A pattern called a war.
Christ! What are patterns for?
Ibid.
All about us peal the loud, sweet *Te
   Deums* of the Canterbury bells.
Madonna of the Evening Flowers
Heart-leaves of lilac all over New Eng-
   land,[1]
Roots of lilac under all the soil of New
   England,
Lilac in me because I am New England.
Lilacs
The sight of a white church above thin
   trees in a city square
Amazes my eyes as though it were the
   Parthenon.
Meeting-House Hill

JOHN MASEFIELD [2]
[1874–   ]

Not of the princes and prelates with
   periwigged charioteers
Riding triumphantly laurelled to lap
   the fat of the years, —
Rather the scorned — the rejected —
   the men hemmed in with the
   spears.
A Consecration. Stanza 1
Others may sing of the wine and the
   wealth and the mirth,

[1] Stands the lilac-bush tall-growing with
heart-shaped leaves of rich green.
WALT WHITMAN: *When Lilacs Last
in the Dooryard Bloom'd*
[2] Appointed Poet Laureate, 1930.

The portly presence of potentates goodly in girth; —
Mine be the dirt and the dross, the dust and scum of the earth!

A Consecration. Stanza 6

Theirs be the music, the colour, the glory, the gold;
Mine be a handful of ashes, a mouthful of mould.
Of the maimed, of the halt and the blind in the rain and the cold —
Of these shall my songs be fashioned, my tales be told.

Ibid. Stanza 7

I must go down to the seas again, to the lonely sea and the sky,
And all I ask is a tall ship and a star to steer her by.

Sea-Fever. Stanza 1

And all I ask is a merry yarn from a laughing fellow-rover,
And quiet sleep and a sweet dream when the long trick's over.

Ibid. Stanza 3

The schooners and the merry crews are laid away to rest,
A little south the sunset in the Islands of the Blest.

A Ballad of John Silver. Stanza 6

And he who gives a child a treat
Makes joy-bells ring in Heaven's street,
And he who gives a child a home
Builds palaces in Kingdom come.

The Everlasting Mercy

To get the whole world out of bed
And washed, and dressed, and warmed, and fed,
To work, and back to bed again,
Believe me, Saul, costs worlds of pain.

Ibid.

Whatever seems, God doth not slumber
Though he lets pass times without number.
He'll come with trump to call his own,
And this world's way'll be overthrown.

Ibid.

O Christ who holds the open gate,
O Christ who drives the furrow straight,
O Christ, the plough, O Christ, the laughter
Of holy white birds flying after.

Ibid.

The rain that makes things new,
The earth that hides things old.

The Everlasting Mercy

When I am buried, all my thoughts and acts
Will be reduced to lists of dates and facts,
And long before this wandering flesh is rotten
The dates which made me will be all forgotten.

Biography

O Time, bring back those midnights and those friends,
Those glittering moments that a spirit lends.

Ibid.

The days that make us happy make us wise.

Ibid.

Man with his burning soul
Has but an hour of breath
To build a ship of Truth
In which his soul may sail,
Sail on the sea of death,
For death takes toll
Of beauty, courage, youth,
Of all but Truth.

Truth. Stanza 1

Spanish waters, Spanish waters, you are ringing in my ears,
Like a slow sweet piece of music from the grey forgotten years.

Spanish Waters. Stanza 1

In the dark womb where I began
My mother's life made me a man.
Through all the months of human birth
Her beauty fed my common earth.
I cannot see, nor breathe, nor stir,
But through the death of some of her.

C. L. M. Stanza 1

Quinquireme of Nineveh from distant Ophir,
Rowing home to haven in sunny Palestine,
With a cargo of ivory,
And apes and peacocks,[1]
Sandalwood, cedarwood, and sweet white wine.

Cargoes. Stanza 1

[1] Once in three years came the navy of Tharshish, bringing gold, and silver, ivory, and apes and peacocks. — *I Kings, X, 22*
See Kipling, page 777.

But rum alone's the tipple, and the
  heart's delight
  Of the old bold mate of Henry
    Morgan.
    Captain Stratton's Fancy. Stanza 1
So I'm for drinking honestly, and dying
  in my boots.
             Ibid. Stanza 7
Oh London Town's a fine town, and
  London sights are rare,
And London ale is right ale, and brisk's
  the London air.
       London Town. Stanza 1
Laugh and be merry, remember, better
  the world with a song,
Better the world with a blow in the
  teeth of a wrong.
Laugh, for the time is brief, a thread
  the length of a span.
Laugh and be proud to belong to the
  old proud pageant of man.
    Laugh and Be Merry. Stanza 1
I hold that when a person dies
  His soul returns again to earth;
Arrayed in some new flesh-disguise
  Another mother gives him birth.
With sturdier limbs and brighter brain
The old soul takes the roads again.
         A Creed. Stanza 1
And may we find, when ended is the
  page,
Death but a tavern on our pilgrimage.
             The Word
For bitter moments given, bitter pay,
The time for payment comes, early or
  late,
No earthly debtor but accounts to Fate.
    The Widow in the Bye Street.
                Part 2
All the great things of life are swiftly
  done,
Creation, death, and love the double
  gate.
However much we dawdle in the sun
We have to hurry at the touch of Fate;
When Life knocks at the door no one
  can wait,
When Death makes his arrest we have
  to go.
                 Ibid.
Love is a flame to burn out human wills,
Love is a flame to set the will on fire,
Love is a flame to cheat men into mire.

One of the three, we make Love what
  we choose.
    The Widow in the Bye Street.
                Part 2
What good can painting do to anyone?
I don't say never do it; far from that —
No harm in sometimes painting just
  for fun.
Keep it for fun, and stick to what
  you're at.
          Dauber. Part 2
Spit brown, my son, and get a hairy
  breast.
                 Ibid.
All through the windless night the
  clipper rolled
In a great swell with oily gradual
  heaves
Which rolled her down until her time-
  bells tolled,
Clang, and the weltering water moaned
  like beeves.
The thundering rattle of slatting shook
  the sheaves,
Startles of water made the swing ports
  gush.
The sea was moaning and sighing and
  saying "Hush!"
          Ibid. Part 6
Then in the sunset's flush they went
  aloft,
And unbent sails in that most lovely
  hour,
When the light gentles and the wind is
  soft,
And beauty in the heart breaks like a
  flower.
          Ibid. Part 7
What am I, Life? A thing of watery
  salt
Held in cohesion by unresting cells,
Which work they know not why, which
  never halt,
Myself unwitting where their Master
  dwells?
          Sonnets. 14
Is there a great green commonwealth
  of Thought
Which ranks the yearly pageant, and
  decides
How Summer's royal progress shall be
  wrought,

By secret stir which in each plant
abides?
Sonnets. 28

With such dumb loving of the Berkshire loam
As breaks the dumb hearts of the English kind.
August, 1914

If there be any life beyond the grave,
It must be near the men and things we
love.
Ibid.

O beautiful is love and to be free
Is beautiful, and beautiful are friends.
Love, freedom, comrades, surely make
amends
For all these thorns through which we
walk to death.
Enslaved

O beautiful in this living that passes
like the foam,
It is to go with sorrow, yet come with
beauty home.
Ibid.

Perhaps, long since, there was a land
beyond
Westward from death, some city, some
calm place,
Where one could taste God's quiet and
be fond
With the little beauty of a human face.
The Lemmings

Be with me Beauty for the fire is dying,
My dog and I are old, too old for rov-
ing,
Man, whose young passion sets the
spindrift flying
Is soon too lame to march, too cold for
loving.
On Growing Old. Sonnet 1

Bitter it is, indeed, in human Fate
When Life's supreme temptation
comes too late.
The Woman Speaks

Go forth to seek: the quarry never
found
Is still a fever to the questing hound,
The skyline is a promise, not a bound.
The Wanderer of Liverpool

I touch my country's mind, I come to
grips
With half her purpose, thinking of
these ships,

That art untouched by softness, all that
line
Drawn ringing hard to stand the test of
brine. . . .
That art of masts, sail crowded, fit to
break,
Yet stayed to strength and backstayed
into rake. . . .
They mark our passage as a race of
men,
Earth will not see such ships as those
again.
Ships

May shipwreck and collision, fog and
fire,
Rock, shoal and other evils of the sea
Be kept from you; and may the heart's
desire
Of those who speed your launching
come to be.
Launching of the "Queen Mary,"
September 26, 1934. Stanza 7

When Custom presses on the souls
apart,
Who seek a God not worshipped by the
herd,
Forth, to the wilderness, the chosen
start
Content with ruin, having but the
Word.
Lines on the Tercentenary of
Harvard College [1936]

There was a preacher in that little band,
John Harvard, son of one from Strat-
ford town,
Who may have shaken William Shake-
speare's hand. . . .
Would that his human eyes, untimely
dead,
Freed from that quiet where the gen-
erous are,
Might see this scene of living corn
made bread
This Lamp of human hope become a
star.
Ibid.

Commonplace people dislike tragedy,
because they dare not suffer and cannot exult. The truth and rapture of
man are holy things, not lightly to be
scorned. A carelessness of life and
beauty marks the glutton, the idler, and

the fool in their deadly path across history.

The Tragedy of Nan. Preface

Man consists of body, mind, and imagination. His body is faulty, his mind untrustworthy, but his imagination has made him remarkable. In some centuries, his imagination had made life on this planet an intense practice of all the lovelier energies.

Shakespeare and Spiritual Life

There is another way to truth: by the minute examination of facts. That is the way of the scientist: a hard and noble and thankless way. It is not the way of the great poet, the rare unreasonable who comes once in ten generations. He apprehends truth by power: the truth which he apprehends cannot be defined, save by greater power, and there is no greater power.

Ibid.

WILLIAM SOMERSET MAUGHAM
[1874–   ]

Do you know that conversation is one of the greatest pleasures in life? But it wants leisure.

The Trembling of a Leaf. Chap. 3

The tragedy of love is indifference.

Ibid. Chap. 4

The mystic sees the ineffable, and the psycho-pathologist the unspeakable.

The Moon and Sixpence. Chap. 1

I forget who it was that recommended men for their soul's good to do each day two things they disliked: . . . it is a precept that I have followed scrupulously; for every day I have got up and I have gone to bed.

Ibid. Chap. 2

Impropriety is the soul of wit.

Ibid. Chap. 4

Conscience is the guardian in the individual of the rules which the community has evolved for its own preservation.

Ibid. Chap. 14

It is not true that suffering ennobles the character; happiness does that

sometimes, but suffering, for the most part, makes men petty and vindictive.

The Moon and Sixpence. Chap. 17

A woman can forgive a man for the harm he does her, but she can never forgive him for the sacrifices he makes on her account.

Ibid. Chap. 41

He made one laugh sometimes by speaking the truth, but this is a form of humour which gains its force only by its unusualness.

Ibid. Chap. 44

ROSELLE MERCIER MONTGOMERY
[1874–1933]

Companioned years have made them comprehend
The comradeship that lies beyond a kiss.
The young ask much of life — they ask but this,
To fare the road together to its end.

For a Wedding Anniversary

The fates are not quite obdurate;
They have a grim, sardonic way
Of granting men who supplicate
The things they wanted — yesterday.[1]

The Fates

JOSEPHINE PRESTON PEABODY (MRS. LIONEL MARKS)
[1874–1922]

Truly, one thing is sweet
Of things beneath the Sun;
This, that a man should earn his bread and eat
Rejoicing in his work which he hath done.

The Singing Man

[1] See J. R. Lowell, page 528, and Oscar Wilde, page 724.
A voice cried out to you, as to the imprudent Theseus: "Beware, my lord! Beware lest stern Heaven hate you enough to hear your prayers! Often 'tis in wrath that Heaven receives our sacrifices; its gifts are often the punishment of our crimes." — ANATOLE FRANCE: *The Crime of Sylvestre Bonnard*, trans. by LAFCADIO HEARN, *Part II, Chap. 4*

Flooding the waste of this dishonored
Star.
The Singing Man
Cry, from the deep of world-accusing
waves,
With longing more than all since
Light began,
Above the nations, — underneath the
graves, —
"Give back the Singing Man."
Ibid.
The little Road says, Go;
The little House says, Stay;
And oh, it's bonny here at home,
But I must go away.
The House and the Road. Stanza 1

EDWARD HERSEY
RICHARDS
[1874-   ]

A wise old owl sat on an oak,
The more he saw the less he spoke;
The less he spoke the more he heard;
Why aren't we like that wise old bird?
A Wise Old Owl

GERTRUDE STEIN [1]
[1874-   ]

Rose is a rose is a rose is a rose.
Sacred Emily
Pigeons in the grass alas.
Four Saints in Three Acts
Before the Flowers of Friendship Faded
Friendship Faded.
Title
In the United States there is more
space where nobody is than where any-
body is.
This is what makes America what
it is.
*The Geographical History
of America*

[1] There's a notable family called Stein:
There's Gertrude, there's Ep, and there's
Ein.
Gert's writings are punk,
Ep's statues are junk,
And nobody understands Ein.
ANONYMOUS: *Stein Song*
Ep = Jacob Epstein, sculptor.
Ein = Albert Einstein, mathematician.

ARTHUR STRINGER
[1874-   ]

Beauty is not immortal. In a day
Blossom and June and rapture pass
away.
*A Fragile Thing Is Beauty.
Stanza 2*
When my life has enough of love,
And my spirit enough of mirth,
When the ocean no longer beckons me,
When the roadway calls no more,
Oh, on the anvil of Thy wrath,
Remake me, God, that day!
A Wanderer's Litany. Stanza 1
Yea, It, the heart of her who bore
Him as a child, slimed Hell's worn floor.
On Its slow tears he slipped, and fell
On that bruised heart that knew him
well.
And It, ere he rose up to go,
Lay close to him and whispered low,
Whispered tenderly, whispered clear:
"Son of mine, did I hurt you, dear?"
Mother and Son (After Echegaray)

ROBERT GILBERT WELSH
[1874-1924]

His wings are gray and trailing,
Azrael, Angel of Death.
And yet the souls that Azrael brings
Across the dark and cold,
Look up beneath those folded wings,
And find them lined with gold.
Azrael. Stanza 2

H. J. WILLIAMS
[1874-1924]

Good-bye, Piccadilly,
Farewell, Leicester Square,
It's a long, long way to Tipperary,
But my heart's right there!
Tipperary

WILLIAM E. WOODWARD
[1874-   ]

In the queer mess of human destiny
the determining factor is Luck. For every important place in life there are
many men of fairly equal capacities.

Among them Luck decides who shall accomplish the great work, who shall be crowned with laurel, and who shall fall back into obscurity and silence.
George Washington.
Chap. 3, Part 2

The turning points of lives are not the great moments. The real crises are often concealed in occurrences so trivial in appearance that they pass unobserved.
Ibid.

Vanity as an impulse has without doubt been of far more benefit to civilization than modesty has ever been.
Ibid. Chap. 5, Part 1

In the face of opposition he [Charles Sumner] would support his theories with formidable citations from history, law, economics, belles-lettres, anthropology, chemistry and religion. He would quote Spinoza and the Boston Cooking School in the same breath. But he rarely, if ever, cited common sense.
Meet General Grant.
Chap. 25, Part 2

Here is another bead on the string of confusions.
Ibid. Chap. 27, Part 5

JOHN BUCHAN, LORD TWEEDSMUIR
[1875–   ]

In perfect honour, perfect truth,
And gentleness to all mankind,
You trod the golden paths of youth,
Then left the world and youth behind.
Ah, no! 'tis we who fade and fail —
And you, from Time's slow torments free,
Shall pass from strength to strength and scale
The steeps of immortality.
Fratri Dilectissimo, W.H.B.
Stanza 5

LOUISE DRISCOLL
[1875–   ]

Happy New Year! There's always hope, there's promise!

No sorrow ever held a crocus back.
The rigid earth revives, day breaks; to-morrow,
Deliberate, comes down the starry track.
New Year. Stanza 8

There you will find what
Every man needs,
Wild religion
Without any creeds.
Spring Market. Stanza 5

You can't forget a garden
When you have planted seed —
When you have watched the weather
And know a rose's need.
You Can't Forget a Garden

Villon among the birds is he,
A bold, bright rover, bad and free;
Yet not without such loveliness
As makes the curse upon him less.
The Blue Jay. Stanza 1

ELLEN THORNEYCROFT FOWLER
[1875–1929]

The inner half of every cloud
Is bright and shining;
I therefore turn my clouds about,
And always wear them inside out
To show the lining.
The Wisdom of Folly. Stanza 3

ROBERT FROST
[1875–   ]

Something there is that doesn't love a wall.
Mending Wall

My apple trees will never get across
And eat the cones under his pines, I tell him.
He only says, "Good fences make good neighbors."
Ibid.

I'd like to get away from earth awhile
And then come back to it and begin over.
May no fate wilfully misunderstand me
And half grant what I wish and snatch me away
Not to return. Earth's the right place for love:

I don't know where it's likely to go
  better.
Birches
  The nearest friends can go
With anyone to death, comes so far
  short
They might as well not try to go at all.
No, from the time when one is sick to
  death,
One is alone, and he dies more alone.
Friends make pretence of following to
  the grave,
But before one is in it, their minds are
  turned
And making the best of their way back
  to life
And living people, and things they un-
  derstand.
Home Burial
Nothing to look backward to with
  pride,
And nothing to look forward to with
  hope.
The Death of the Hired Man.
"Home is the place where, when you
  have to go there
They have to take you in." "I should
  have called it
Something you somehow haven't to de-
  serve."
Ibid.
As a child misses the unsaid Good-
  night,
And falls asleep with heartache.
The Black Cottage
Most of the change we think we see in
  life
Is due to truths being in and out of
  favour.
Ibid.
I shall be telling this with a sigh
Somewhere ages and ages hence:
Two roads diverged in a wood, and I —
I took the one less travelled by,
And that has made all the difference.
The Road Not Taken
The blue's but a mist from the breath
  of the wind,
A tarnish that goes at a touch of the
  hand.
Blueberries
The best way out is always through.
A Servant to Servants

Pressed into service means pressed out
  of shape.
The Self-Seeker
I have been one acquainted with the
  night.
Acquainted with the Night
I wonder about the trees:
Why do we wish to bear
Forever the noise of these
More than another noise
So close to our dwelling-place?
The Sound of Trees
I met a Californian who would
Talk California — a state so blessed,
He said, in climate none had ever died
  there
A natural death.
New Hampshire. Stanza 3
In the market with a climate.
Ibid.
     Do you know,
Considering the market, there are more
Poems produced than any other thing?
No wonder poets sometimes have to
  seem
So much more business-like than busi-
  ness men.
Their wares are so much harder to get
  rid of.
Ibid. Stanza 17
She's one of the two best states in the
  Union.
Vermont's the other.
Ibid. Stanza 18
Anything I can say about New Hamp-
  shire
Will serve almost as well about Ver-
  mont,
Excepting that they differ in their
  mountains.
The Vermont mountains stretch ex-
  tending straight;
New Hampshire mountains curl up in a
  coil.
Ibid. Stanza 19
The sun was warm but the wind was
  chill.
You know how it is with an April day:
When the sun is out and the wind is
  still,
You're one month on in the middle of
  May.
But if you so much as dare to speak,

A cloud comes over the sunlit arch,
A wind comes off a frozen peak,
And you're two months back in the
    middle of March.
                Two Tramps in Mud Time
Don't join too many gangs. Join few if
    any.
Join the United States and join the
    family —
But not much in between unless a col-
    lege.
                            Build Soil
Why make so much of fragmentary
    blue
In here and there a bird, or butterfly,
Or flower, or wearing-stone, or open
    eye,
When heaven presents in sheets the
    solid hue?
            Fragmentary Blue. Stanza 1
Keep cold, young orchard. Good-bye
    and keep cold.
Dread fifty above more than fifty be-
    low.
                Good-bye and Keep Cold
The woods are lovely, dark and deep.
But I have promises to keep,
And miles to go before I sleep.
            *Stopping by Woods on a
                    Snowy Evening*
Never ask of money spent
Where the spender thinks it went.
Nobody was ever meant
To remember or invent
What he did with every cent.
            The Hardship of Accounting
If, as they say, some dust thrown in my
    eyes
Will keep my talk from getting over-
    wise,
I'm not the one for putting off the proof.
Let it be overwhelming.
                    Dust in the Eyes
No ship of all that under sail or steam
Has gathered people to us more and
    more
But Pilgrim-manned the Mayflower in
    a dream
Has been their anxious convoy in to
    shore.
                        Immigrants
Some say the world will end in fire,
Some say in ice.

From what I've tasted of desire
I hold with those who favor fire.
But if it had to perish twice,
I think I know enough of hate
To say that for destruction ice
Is also great
And would suffice.
                        Fire and Ice

FREDERICK PALMER
LATIMER
[1875–   ]

I wish I were a little rock,
    A-sitting on a hill,
A-doing nothing, all day long,
    But just a-sitting still;
I wouldn't eat, I wouldn't sleep,
    I wouldn't even wash —
I'd sit and sit a thousand years,
    And rest myself, b' Gosh!
                    The Weary Wisher

PERCY MACKAYE
[1875–   ]

Because he never wore his sentient
    heart
For crows and jays to peck, ofttimes to
    such
He seemed a silent fellow, who o'er-
    much
Held from the general gossip-ground
    apart,
Or tersely-spoke, and tart.
                    Uriel. Stanza 11

A man went down to Panama
    Where many a man has died
To slit the sliding mountains
    And lift the eternal tide:
A man stood up in Panama,
    And the mountains stood aside.
                Goethals. Stanza 1

        The lover,
And the young of soul, his friend,
And the artist, follow after
The children in their laughter,
And the daring half discover,
And the happy comprehend.
                    The Sybil

MOIRA O'NEILL
(MRS. N. H. SKRINE)

Youth's for an hour,
Beauty's a flower,
But love is the jewel that wins the
world.
Beauty's a Flower

"If she was tall?" Like a king's own
daughter.
"If she was fair?" Like a mornin' o'
May.
A Broken Song. Stanza 2

Corrymeela an' the blue sky over it.
Corrymeela. Stanza 1

The memory's fairly spoilt on me
Wid mindin' to forget.
"Forgettin'." Stanza 5

RAFAEL SABATINI
[1875–   ]

Born with the gift of laughter and a
sense that the world is mad.[1]
Scaramouche. Chap. 1

RIDGELY TORRENCE
[1875–   ]

God gave them Youth, God gave them
Love, and even God can give no
more.
The House of a Hundred Lights.
The Young Lovers

Of all the languages of earth in which
the human kind confer
The Master Speaker is the Tear: it is
the Great Interpreter.
Ibid. The Conclusion of the
Whole Matter

I was weak as a rained-on bee.
Eye-Witness. The Tramp Sings

It feels like frost was near —
His hair was curly.
The spring was late that year,
But the harvest early.
The Son. Stanza 4

[1] Inscribed on one of the new buildings at
Yale University under the misapprehension
that this sentiment was a translation of some
ancient classic.

EVELYN UNDERHILL
(MRS. STUART MOORE)
[1875–   ]

I come in the little things,
Saith the Lord:
My starry wings
I do forsake,
Love's highway of humility to take.
Immanence. Stanza 3

I shall achieve My Immemorial Plan,
Pass the low lintel of the human heart.
Ibid.

I saw the race fulfil
The spiral of its steep ascent, predes-
tined of the Will.
Yet not unled, but shepherded by one
they may not see —
The one who walked with starry feet
the western road by me!
Uxbridge Road. Stanza 5

THOMAS WALSH
[1875–1928]

A little world — we truly say
While days are young and careless-
hearted;
From clime to clime we speed to-day,
Earth's paths are cleared and ocean's
charted;
But ah, how large a world we stray
When thou and I are parted!
Zither Song

Death sallied forth upon this fateful
day
Through Spain and England for a
mighty prey,
And struck two masters with a single
blow
And laid Cervantes and Will Shakespeare low!
April Twenty-third

HAROLD MacDONALD
ANDERSON
[1876–   ]

Alone?
Is he alone at whose right side rides
Courage, with Skill within the cockpit
and Faith upon the left? Does solitude
surround the brave when Adventure
leads the way and Ambition reads the

dials? Is there no company with him for whom the air is cleft by Daring and the darkness is made light by Emprise?

True, the fragile bodies of his fellows do not weigh down his plane; true, the fretful minds of weaker men are lacking from his crowded cabin; but as his airship keeps her course he holds communion with those rarer spirits that inspire to intrepidity and by their sustaining potency give strength to arm, resource to mind, content to soul.

Alone? With what other companions would that man fly to whom the choice were given?

> "Lindbergh Flies Alone," Editorial, New York Sun, May 21, 1927 [1]

SHERWOOD ANDERSON
[1876–   ]

Everyone in the world is Christ and they are all crucified.
> Winesburg, Ohio. The Philosopher

I am a lover and have not found my thing to love.
> Ibid. Tandy

ANNA HEMPSTEAD BRANCH
[1875–1937]

Order is a lovely thing;
On disarray it lays its wing,
Teaching simplicity to sing.
> The Monk in the Kitchen

Shape, the strong and awful Spirit,
Laid his ancient hand on you.
He waste chaos doth inherit;
He can alter and subdue.
> Ibid.

His screaming stallions maned with whistling wind.
> Nimrod Wars with the Angels

God wove a web of loveliness,
Of clouds and stars and birds,

[1] Included by permission of Mr. Anderson and The Sun.

But made not anything at all
So beautiful as words.
> Songs for My Mother:
> Her Words. Stanza 5

If there is no God for thee
Then there is no God for me.
> To a Dog

WILLA SIBERT CATHER
[1876–   ]

Oh, this is the joy of the rose:
That it blows,
And goes.
> In Rose-Time

Where are the loves that we have loved before
When once we are alone, and shut the door?
> L'Envoi

Fireflies gleam in the damp and mould, —
All that is left of the Caesars' gold.
> The Palatine. Stanza 3

The old West, the old time,
The old wind singing through
The red, red grass a thousand miles,
And, Spanish Johnny, you!
> Spanish Johnny. Stanza 1

A Polack's brat
Joylessly torments a cat. . . .
To hurt and to be hurt; he knows
All he will know on earth, or need to know.
> Street in Packingtown (Chicago)

How smoothly the trains run beyond the Missouri.
> Going Home, Burlington Route

No one can build his security upon the nobleness of another person.
> Alexander's Bridge. Chap. 8

There are only two or three human stories, and they go on repeating themselves as fiercely as if they had never happened before.
> O Pioneers! Part II, Chap. 4

I like trees because they seem more resigned to the way they have to live than other things do.
> Ibid. Chap. 8

Winter lies too long in country towns; hangs on until it is stale and shabby, old and sullen.
> My Ántonia. Book II, Chap. 7

Old men are like that, you know. It makes them feel important to think they're in love with somebody.
> *My Antonia. Book III, Chap. 4*

We all like people who do things, even if we only see their faces on a cigar-box lid.
> *The Song of the Lark.*
> *Part I, Chap. 18*

That irregular and intimate quality of things made entirely by the human hand.
> *Death Comes for the Archbishop.*
> *Book I, Chap. 3*

The Miracles of the Church seem to me to rest not so much upon faces or voices or healing power coming suddenly near to us from afar off, but upon our perceptions being made finer, so that for a moment our eyes can see and our ears can hear what is there about us always.
> *Ibid. Chap. 4*

The universal human yearning for something permanent, enduring, without shadow of change.
> *Ibid. Book III, Chap. 3*

PATRICK REGINALD CHALMERS

Oh, bright as a berry,
  They're red and they're rare,
The setters from Kerry,
  And Cork and Kildare!
> *The Red Dogs*

A year of philatelic fame,
  For — lest my point should miss
    you —
In eighteen forty-seven came
  The first Mauritius issue.
> *Tuppenny Blues: A Tale for*
> *Philatelists. Stanza 3*

"I find," said 'e, "things very much as 'ow I've always found,'
For mostly they goes up and down or else goes round and round."
> *Roundabouts and Swings.*
> *Stanza 2*

What's lost upon the roundabout we pulls up on the swings!
> *Ibid.*

If you'd move to a bygone measure,
  Or shape your heart to an ancient
    mould,
Maroons and schooners and buried
    treasure
  Wrought on a page of gold, —

Then take the book in the dingy binding,
  Still the magic comes, bearded, great,
And swaggering files of sea-thieves
    winding
Back, with their ruffling cut-throat
    gait,
Reclaim an hour when we first went
    finding
  Pieces of Eight — of Eight.
> *"Treasure Island"*

RICHARD BUTLER GLAENZER
[1876–1937]

Indian only in this:
  Your sudden way
Of stealing on us — but to kiss
  With peace, not slay!
> *Indian Summer. Stanza 1*

NORAH MARY HOLLAND (MRS. LIONEL WILLIAM CLAXTON)
[1876–1925]

High up in the courts of Heaven to-day
  A little dog-angel waits:
With the other angels he will not play,
  But he sits alone at the gates.
> *The Little Dog-Angel*

Yet, in that land of shadows, there are
    two
Whose welcome will not fail me,
    though I stray
Bewildered, lost, alone in that dim
    way
'Mid the unfriendly ghosts — my dog
    and you.[1]
> *Two*

[1] See St. John Lucas, page 858.

WALLACE IRWIN
[1876–   ]

It's happy goes as lucky goes
  To Romany in June.
       Upon the Road to Romany.
                Stanza 1

Of all the fish that swim or swish
  In ocean's deep autocracy,
There's none possess such haughtiness
  As the codfish aristocracy.
       Codfish Aristocracy. Stanza 1

"Suppose that this here vessel," says
  the skipper, with a groan,
"Should lose 'er bearin's, run away, and
  bump upon a stone;
Suppose she'd shiver and go down,
  when save ourselves we could-
  n't — "
The mate replies, "O, blow me eyes,
  suppose again she shouldn't."
       The Sorrows of a Skipper.
                Stanza 3

Better than years with Ibsen spent, I
  said,
One Evening with my Friend, Boccac-
  cio.
      Rubáiyát of Omar Khayyám, Jr.
                XXXVI

I ask to know.
    Letters of a Japanese Schoolboy

"GORDON JOHNSTONE"
(JOSEPH SWEENEY)
[1876–1926]

Death's but an open door,
  We move from room to room.
There is one life, no more,
  No dying, and no tomb.
      There Is No Death. Stanza 3

WILLIAM ELLERY LEONARD
[1876–   ]

The shriveled stalks of goldenrod are
  sere,
And crisp and white their flashing old
  racemes.
(. . . forever . . . forever . . . forever . . .)
This is the lonely season of the year,
This is the season of our lonely dreams.

(*O Earth-and-Autumn of the setting
  Sun,*
*She is not by, to know my task is
  done!*)
      Two Lives. Indian Summer
And, ever wistful of the doom to come,
I built her many a fire for love . . . for
  mirth. . . .
(When snows were falling on our oaks
  outside,
Dear, many a winter fire upon the
  hearth) . . .
(. . . farewell . . . farewell . . . farewell
  . . .)
We dare not think too long on those
  who died,
While still so many yet must come to
  birth.
                Ibid.

GRACE FALLOW NORTON
[1876–   ]

I have loved many, the more and the
  few —
I have loved many, that I might love
  you.
    Song of the Sum of All. Stanza 1

TED OLSON

Honor and truth and manhood —
  These are the things that stand,
Though the sneer and jibe of the cynic
  tribe
Are loud through the width of the
  land.
      Things That Endure. Stanza 1
But a lie, whatever the guise it wears,
  Is a lie as it was of yore,
And a truth that has lasted a million
  years
  Is good for a million more.
           Ibid. Stanza 3

FRANK WARD O'MALLEY
[1876–1932]

Life is just one damned thing after
another.[1]
    Quoted in The Literary Digest,
          November 5, 1932

[1] Also attributed to Elbert Hubbard; probably precedes them both.

ABRAHAM S. WOLF ROSENBACH
[1876–   ]

On February 14, 1493, Columbus carefully prepared as complete an account of his marvelous voyage as was possible under the circumstances. He wrote the details of his journey on a stout piece of parchment, wrapped it carefully in a piece of waterproof cloth, then placed it in an iron-bound barrel and threw it into the raging ocean. . . . If I thought there were one chance in a million of finding it I would take my power boat, the *First Folio,* and cruise in the neighborhood of the Azores forever!

(1927) Page 269. Books and Bidders

After love, book collecting is the most exhilarating sport of all.

(1936) Page 106. A Book Hunter's Holiday

Brooklyn has the proud distinction of having had more distinguished bibliophiles than any other city of its size in the world.

Page 126. Ibid.

Lives of great men all remind us
As their pages o'er we turn,
That we're apt to leave behind us
Letters that we ought to burn.

Page 36. Ibid. Quoted by Dr. Rosenbach, *authorship unknown*

ROBERT WILLIAM SERVICE
[1876–   ]

This is the Law of the Yukon, that only
the Strong shall thrive;
That surely the Weak shall perish, and
only the Fit survive.[1]

The Law of the Yukon

Master, I've filled my contract, wrought
in Thy many lands;

---

[1] An obvious echo of Kipling's *The Law of the Jungle:*
Now this is the Law of the Jungle — as old
    and as true as the sky;
And the Wolf that shall keep it may prosper,
    but the Wolf that shall break it must die.

Not by my sins wilt Thou judge me,
but by the work of my hands.
Master, I've done Thy bidding, and the
light is low in the west,
And the long, long shift is over . . .
Master, I've earned it — Rest.

The Song of the Wage-Slave

Back of the bar, in a solo game, sat
Dangerous Dan McGrew,
And watching his luck was his light-o'-
love, the lady that's known as
Lou.

*The Shooting of Dan McGrew.
Stanza 1*

There's a race of men that don't fit in,
A race that can't stay still;
So they break the hearts of kith and kin,
And they roam the world at will.

*The Men That Don't Fit In.
Stanza 1*

Fate has written a tragedy; its name is
"The Human Heart."
The Theatre is the House of Life,
Woman the mummer's part;
The Devil enters the prompter's box
and the play is ready to start.

The Harpy. Stanza 12

God made a heart of gold, of gold,
Shining and sweet and true;
Gave it a home of fairest mould,
Blest it, and called it — You.

Sunshine. VI

I just think that dreams are best,
Just to sit and fancy things;
Give your gold no acid test,
Try not how your silver rings.

Dreams Are Best. Stanza 1

It's easy to cry that you're beaten —
and die;
It's easy to crawfish and crawl;
But to fight and to fight when hope's
out of sight —
Why, that's the best game of them
all!

The Quitter. Stanza 3

A million stars are in the sky;
A million planets plunge and die;
A million million men are sped;
A million million wait ahead.
Each plays his part and has his day —
What ho! the World's all right, I say.

The World's All Right. Stanza 3

They talk o' England's glory and a-
  'oldin' of our trade,
Of Empire and 'igh destiny until we're
  fair flimflammed;
But if it's for the likes o' that that
  bloody war is made,
Then wot I say is: Empire and 'igh
  destiny be damned!
    A Song of the Sandbags. Stanza 5

Ah! the clock is always slow;
It is later than you think.
    It Is Later than You Think.
    Stanza 7

That classic that the world has lost,
The Little Book I Never Wrote.
    My Masterpiece. Stanza 2

I have some friends, some honest
  friends,
And honest friends are few;
My pipe of briar, my open fire,
A book that's not too new.
    I Have Some Friends. Stanza 2

When we, the Workers, all demand:
  "What are we fighting for?" . . .
Then, then we'll end that stupid crime,
  that devil's madness — War.
    Michael

EDGAR WALLACE
[1876–1932]

'E doesn't want no pass;
'E's journeying first-class;
'Is trav'ling rug's a Union Jack, which
  isn't bad at all;
The tune the drummers play
It ain't so very gay,
But a rather slow selection from a piece
  that's known as "Saul."
    Burial of Private Ginger Jones.
    Stanza 6

Oh God of Battles, Lord of Might — a
  sentry in the silent night —
I, 'oo've never prayed
Kneel on the dew-damp sands to say:
Oh, keep me through the coming day!
But, please remember, though I pray,
That I am not afraid.
    The Prayer by Private Edgar
    Wallace, R.A.M.C. Stanza 1

GRACE NOLL
(MRS. NORMAN H.)
CROWELL
[1877–   ]

No day has ever failed me quite:
Before the grayest day is done
I find some misty purple bloom,
Or a late line of crimson sun.
    The Day. Stanza 3

I hold to my heart when the geese are
  flying —
A wavering wedge on the high, bright
  blue —
I tighten my lips to keep from crying:
"Beautiful birds, let me go with you."
    Wild Geese. Stanza 1

GEORGE ALLAN ENGLAND
[1877–1936]

He yawned, and laid his cigaret aside,
And on the baggage-check, grimly
  stamped "Body," wrote
Two simple words. Scrawled words,
  with careless fingers. Just a note
Of this poor shipment's worthlessness.
She who had died,
Two days before, was sunshine, joy,
  and life
To all of us.
    "No Value"

"No Value!" And the world had ceased
  to turn:
And all the gold from here to Babylon
  might burn
To dross, unminded, for we bore our
  dead.
    Ibid.

ANTHONY EUWER
[1877–   ]

As a beauty I'm not a great star.
Others are handsomer far;
  But my face — I don't mind it
  Because I'm behind it;
It's the folks out in front that I jar.
    Limerick [1]

I like a good grouch when I get it,
Sea-deep and dark indigo blue.
    My Grouch. Stanza 1

[1] Often quoted by Woodrow Wilson.

ROSE FYLEMAN
[1877–   ]

The Fairies have never a penny to
spend,
They haven't a thing put by,
But theirs is the dower of bird and of
flower,
And theirs are the earth and the sky.
*The Fairies Have Never a Penny
to Spend. Stanza 1*

And though you be foolish or though
you be wise,
With hair of silver or gold,
You could never be young as the fairies
are,
And never as old.
Ibid. Stanza 2

A fairy went a-marketing —
She bought a little fish;
She put it in a crystal bowl
Upon a golden dish.
*A Fairy Went A-Marketing.
Stanza 1*

Cheerfully adorn the proudest table,
Since yours it is to bear the glorious
label —
"Richest in Vitamines!"
To an Orange. Stanza 4

SIR JAMES HOPWOOD JEANS
[1877–   ]

Hubble[1] estimates that about two
million such nebulae are visible in the
great 100-inch telescope at Mount Wilson, and that the whole universe has
about a thousand million times the volume of that part of space visible in this
telescope. Let us now multiply 1,000
million by 2 million, and the product by
1,000 million. The answer (2×10^{24})
gives some indication of the probable
number of stars in the universe; the
same number of grains of sand spread
over England would make a layer hundreds of yards in depth. Let us reflect
that our earth is one millionth part of
one such grain of sand, and our mun-
dane affairs, our troubles and our
achievements, begin to appear in their

[1] Edwin Powell Hubble [1889–   ], distinguished American astronomer.

correct proportion to the universe as a
whole.
*The Wider Aspects of Cosmog-
ony [1928]*

Observation and theory agree in indicating that the universe is melting
away into radiation. Our position is
that of polar bears on an iceberg that
has broken loose from the icepack surrounding the pole, and is inexorably
melting away as the iceberg drifts to
warmer latitudes and ultimate extinction.
Ibid.

Taking a very gloomy view of the
future of the human race, let us suppose that it can only expect to survive
for two thousand million years longer,
a period about equal to the past age of
the earth. Then, regarded as a being
destined to live for threescore years and
ten, humanity, although it has been
born in a house seventy years old, is itself only three days old.
Ibid.

It does not at present look as though
Nature had designed the universe pri-
marily for life; the normal star and the
normal nebula have nothing to do with
life except making it impossible. Life is
the end of a chain of by-products; it
seems to be the accident, and torrential
deluges of life-destroying radiation the
essential.
Ibid.

DOUGLAS MALLOCH
[1877–   ]

If you can't be a pine on the top of the
hill,
Be a scrub in the valley — but be
The best little scrub by the side of the
rill;
Be a bush if you can't be a tree.
*Be the Best of Whatever You Are.
Stanza 1*

The tree that never had to fight
For sun and sky and air and light;
That stood out in the open plain
And always got its share of rain,

Never became a forest king,
But lived and died a scrubby thing.
Good Timber. Stanza 1

Time brings not death, it brings but
    changes;
  I know he rides, but rides afar,
To-day some other planet ranges
  And camps to-night upon a star
Where all his other comrades are.
  *A Comrade Rides Ahead: To
  the Memory of Emerson Hough
  [1857–1923]. Stanza 1*

JESSIE BELLE RITTENHOUSE
(MRS. CLINTON SCOLLARD)

My debt to you, Belovèd,
  Is one I cannot pay
In any coin of any realm
  On any reckoning day.
Debt

I worked for a menial's hire,
  Only to learn, dismayed,
That any wage I had asked of Life,
  Life would have paid.
My Wage

LEONARD H. ROBBINS
[1877–   ]

Be true while there yet is time.
For this is the cry of a thousand souls
  that down to the Pit have trod —
Who keeps the Truth from the people
  stands in the way of God!
*The Truth and John Billington.
  Stanza 8*

THEODORE GOODRIDGE
ROBERTS
[1877–   ]

The wide seas and the mountains called
  to him
And gray dawn saw his campfires in the
  rain.
A Vagrant's Epitaph. Stanza 1

Change was his mistress, Chance his
  counselor.
The dark pines knew his whistle up the
  trail.

Why tarries he to-day? And yester-
    night
Adventure lit her stars without avail.
A Vagrant's Epitaph. Stanza 4

LAURA SIMMONS
[1877–   ]

What though you hide it in your
    trunk —
  Ere sailing hour has set?
Jammed down beneath your old blue
    serge?
  Don't think you can forget!
The face within that passport book
  Will rise to haunt you yet.
Your Passport Picture

CHARLES HANSON TOWNE
[1877–   ]

Youth, there are countless stories
    spread
  By gentlemen whose hair is gray.
Believe them not, but me instead —
  The 'Nineties were not really gay.
Ballade of Gentle Denial

Does the skylark, singing sweet and
    clear,
Beg the cold world to hear?
*The Quiet Singer
  (Francis Thompson)*

As if upon the breeze,
There came the teeming wonder of his
    words —
A golden troop of birds,
Caged in a little volume made to love.
Ibid.

ARTHUR UPSON
[1877–1908]

My days are phantom days, each one
  The shadow of a hope;
My real life never was begun
Nor any of my real deeds done.
Phantom Life

Late the fond tyrant who misrules our
    land,
Bidding his serfs dig deep in marshes
    old,
Trembled, not knowing wherefore, as
    they drew

From out this swampy bed of ancient
  mould
A shattered torch held in a mighty
  hand.
>   *The Statue of Liberty* (*New*
>   *York Harbour, A.D. 2900*)

All are folded now so peacefully
Within her breast whose glory was their
  dream —
From her own sanguine fields, from isles
  extreme,
From the long tumult of the land and
  sea —
Where lies the steel Potomac's jewelled
  stream
Like the surrendered sword of Memory.
>   *Arlington*

Dig my life deep enough, you must
Find broken friendships round its inner
  wall —
Which once my careless hand let slip
  and fall —
Brave with faint memories, rich in
  rainbow-crust.
>   *Octaves in an Oxford Garden.*
>   *XXV, Roman Glassware Pre-*
>   *served in the Ashmolean*

Wine that was spilt in haste
  Arising in fumes more precious;
Garlands that fell forgot
  Rooting to wondrous bloom;
Youth that would flow to waste
  Pausing in pool-green valleys —
And Passion that lasted not
  Surviving the voiceless Tomb!
>   *After a Dolmetsch Concert.*
>   *Stanza 2*

McLANDBURGH WILSON

From out our crowded calendar
  One day we pluck to give;
It is the day the Dying pause
  To honor those who live.
>   *Memorial Day*

Our hero is a man of peace,
  Preparedness he implores;
His sword within its scabbard sleeps,
  But mercy, how it snores!
>   *Theodore Roosevelt*

LOUIS KAUFMAN
ANSPACHER
[1878–   ]

Marriage is that relation between
man and woman in which the independence is equal, the dependence mutual,
and the obligation reciprocal.
>   *Address, Boston*
>   [*December 30, 1934*]

BERTHA ADAMS BACKUS
[*Floruit* 1911]

Build for yourself a strong-box,
  Fashion each part with care;
When it's strong as your hand can make
  it,
  Put all your troubles there;
Hide there all thought of your failures,
  And each bitter cup that you quaff;
Lock all your heartaches within it,
  Then sit on the lid and laugh.
>   *Then Laugh.*[1] *Stanza 1*

KARLE WILSON
(MRS. THOMAS ELLIS)
BAKER
[1878–   ]

Masters have wrought in prisons,
  At peace in cells of stone:
From their thick walls I fashion
  Windows to light my own.
>   *Prisons*
Brother, the creed would stifle me
  That shelters you.
>   *Creeds. Stanza 2*
Let me grow lovely, growing old—[2]
  So many fine things do:
Laces, and ivory, and gold,
  And silks need not be new.
>   *Old Lace: Let Me Grow Lovely*
To-day I have grown taller from walk-
  ing with the trees.
>   *Good Company*
I love the friendly faces of old sorrows;
I have no secrets that they do not know.
>   *I Love the Friendly Faces.*
>   *Stanza 1*

[1] In *Munsey's Magazine*, Feb., *1911.*
[2] See Heath, page 628.

HENRY SEIDEL CANBY
[1878–   ]

We can put our children on wheels to see the world, but we cannot give them the kind of home that any town provided in the nineties, not at any price.

The Age of Confidence. Chap. 14

Arrogance, pedantry, and dogmatism are the occupational diseases of those who spend their lives directing the intellects of the young.

Alma Mater

Poet who disdained to be just a poet and so fell something short of his powers [Walt Whitman], he belongs now in that Platonic world where republics never realized keep their power to enrich the imagination. . . . He remembered things impossible for us, impossible but intelligible, and which will become unintelligible at our peril.

Classic Americans. Walt Whitman

GEORGE MICHAEL COHAN
[1878–   ]

Hurried and worried until we're buried, and there's no curtain call,
Life's a very funny proposition, after all.

Life's a Funny Proposition

No matter what may happen, whatever may befall,
I only know I'm mighty glad I'm living, that is all.

I'm Mighty Glad I'm Living

You won't do any business, if you haven't got a band:
The folks expect a street parade and uniforms so grand.

You Won't Do Any Business

Always leave them laughing when you say good-bye.

Title of song

GRACE HAZARD CONKLING
[1878–   ]

I have an understanding with the hills
At evening when the slanted radiance fills
Their hollows, and the great winds let them be,

And they are quiet and look down at me.

After Sunset

Invisible beauty has a word so brief
A flower can say it or a shaken leaf,
But few may ever snare it in a song.

Ibid.

To build the trout a crystal stair.

The Whole Duty of Berkshire Brooks

Oh, cut me reeds to blow upon,
Or gather me a star,
But leave the sultry passion-flowers
Growing where they are.

Tampico

He who gives a passion-flower
Always asks it back.

Ibid.

ADELAIDE CRAPSEY
[1878–1914]

These be
Three silent things:
The falling snow . . . the hour
Before the dawn . . . the mouth of one
Just dead.

Cinquain: Triad

EDWARD JOHN MORETON DRAX PLUNKETT, LORD DUNSANY
[1878–   ]

We shall be with you in your distant time,
Shall lean towards you across many a year,
Shall bring you courage with a wayworn rhyme:
We were not wholly here.

To Those That Come After. Stanza 3

A new thing came and they could not see,
A new wind blew and they would not feel it.

In His Own Country. Stanza 1

May you go safe, my friend, across that dizzy way
No wider than a hair, by which your people go

From Earth to Paradise; may you go
    safe to-day
With stars and space above, and time
    and stars below.

> *May You Go Safe: On the
> Death of a Muhammedan
> Friend. Stanza 1*

All who write put me in mind of sailors hastily making rafts upon doomed
ships.

When we break up under the heavy
years and go down into eternity our
thoughts like small lost rafts float on
awhile upon Oblivion's sea. They will
not carry much over those tides, our
names and a phrase or two and little
else. . . .

See now Oblivion shimmering all
around us, its very tranquillity deadlier
than tempest. . . .

There goes the raft that Homer made
for Helen.

> *Fifty-One Tales. The Raft Builders*

WILFRID WILSON GIBSON
[1878–   ]

I did not write; and now I cannot
    write —
    Or, rather, it were useless; no king's
      head
That pence or pounds might purchase
    may secure
    Delivery in the region of the dead —
And all I meant to say remains unsaid.

> *The Unwritten Letter*

One song leads on to another,
One friend to another friend,
So I'll travel along
With a friend and a song —
I'll travel along
Ten thousand strong —
To the end.

> *The Empty Purse. Stanza 1*

All life moving to one measure —
Daily bread.

> *All Life Moving to One Measure*

And as I lingered, lost in divine delight,
My heart thanked God for the goodly
    gift of sight
And all youth's lively senses keen and
    quick —
When suddenly, behind me in the night,

I heard the tapping of a blind man's
    stick.

> *Sight. Stanza 2*

That night when she came home
Her arms were full of blossom.
She'd scarcely left a pot or pan
For me to cook a meal in.

> *Holiday*

Just what it meant to smile and smile
And let my son go cheerily —
My son . . . and wondering all the
    while
What stranger would come back to me.

> *The Return. Stanza 2*

Though now beyond earth's farthest
    hills you fare,
Song-crowned, immortal, sometimes it
    seems to me
That, if I listen very quietly,
Perhaps I'll hear a light foot on the
    stair
And see you, standing with your angel
    air,
Fresh from the uplands of eternity.

> *Rupert Brooke*

When I must breast the stiller sea
That stretches everlastingly
Beneath the starless unknown night,
The darkness round me falling,
May it be given me to hear
Life calling me as crystal-clear —
To glance back once through failing
    light
And answer that sweet calling.

> *The Voice. Stanza 2*

OLIVER ST. JOHN GOGARTY
[1878–   ]

O Boys, the times I've seen!
The things I've done and known!
If you knew where I have been
Or half the joys I've had,
You never would leave me alone;
But pester me to tell,
Swearing to keep it dark,
What . . . but I know quite well:
Every solicitor's clerk
Would break out and go mad;
And all the dogs would bark!

> *O Boys! O Boys!*

No one believes in joys,
And Peace on Earth is a joke,

Which, anyhow, telling destroys;
So better go on with your work:
But Boys! O Boys! O Boys!

        O Boys! O Boys!

Our friends go with us as we go
  Down the long path where Beauty
    wends,
Where all we love foregathers, so
  Why should we fear to join our
    friends?

                Non Dolet

Only the Lion and the Cock,
As Galen says, withstand Love's shock.
So, Dearest, do not think me rude
If I yield now to lassitude,
But sympathize with me. I know
You would not have me roar, or crow.

                After Galen

PERCY ADAMS HUTCHISON
[1878–   ]

Ay, down the years, behold, He rides,
  The lowly Christ, upon an ass;
But conquering? Ten shall heed the
    call,
  A thousand idly watch Him pass.

         The Swordless Christ:
         Vicisti Galilæe. Stanza 1

DONALD ROBERT PERRY
MARQUIS
[1878–1937]

The saddest ones are those that wear
  The jester's motley garb.

        The Tavern of Despair

The world hath just one tale to tell, and
  it is very old,[1]
A little tale — a simple tale — a tale
  that's easy told:
"There was a youth in Babylon who
  greatly loved a maid!"

         News from Babylon

Who storms the moss-grown walls of eld
  And beats some falsehood down
Shall pass the pallid gates of death
  Sans laurel, love, or crown;
For him who fain would teach the world
  The world holds hate in fee —

[1] See Kendall Banning, page 855.

For Socrates, the hemlock cup;
  For Christ, Gethsemane.

                The Wages

No doubt the cherubs earn their wage
  Who wind each ticking star.

                The Rebel

Still mounts the Dream on shining pin-
  ion . . .
  Still broods the dull distrust . . .
Which shall have ultimate dominion,
  Dream, or dust?

             A Little While

A little while with grief and laughter,
  And then the day will close;
The shadows gather . . . what comes
  after
  No man knows.

                   Ibid.

Let us not babble of eternity
Who stand upon this little edge of
  time!
Even old godheads sink in space and
  drown,
Their arks like foundered galleons
  sucked down.

              Transient

Noah an' Jonah an' Cap'n John Smith,
Mariners, travelers, magazines of myth,
Settin' up in Heaven, chewin' and a-
  chawin'
Eatin' their terbaccy, talkin' and a-
  jawin'.

         Noah an' Jonah an'
         Cap'n John Smith [1]

Fill me with sassafras, nurse,
  And juniper juice!
Let me see if I'm still any use!
For I want to be young and to sing
  again,
  Sing again, sing again!
  Middle age is a curse! [2]

             Spring Ode

For I want to hire out as the Skipper
  (Who dodges life's stress and its
    strains)

[1] In *The Sun* (New York), *July 28, 1919.*
[2] Of middle age the best that can be said is
that a middle-aged person has likely learned
how to have a little fun in spite of his troubles. — *The Almost Perfect State*

Of the Trolley, the Toonerville Trolley,
The Trolley that Meets all the
Trains.
The Toonerville Trolley:
To Fontaine Fox

A dollar a line,
The Uplifting stuff brings a dollar a
line!
Yes, Song Is Coming into Its
Own Again

And similar goddamned phrases.
Ballade of Goddamned Phrases [1]

A man has jest naturally got to have
something to cuss around and boss, so's
to keep himself from finding out he
don't amount to nothing.
Danny's Own Story

It's a DEE-vice.
The Old Soak. Act I

Jehovah. Did I ever mention publicly
how Hell got started? I don't think I
ever did. It was this way: I thought
I'd do something nice for a lot of theologians who had, after all, been doing
the best they could, according to their
lights; so I gave them an enormous
tract of Heaven to do what they pleased
with — set it apart for them to inhabit
and administer. I didn't pay any attention to it for a few thousand years, and
when I looked at it again, they'd made
it into Hell.
Chapters for the Orthodox.
Chap. 7

Dreadful things are just as apt to
happen when stupid people control a
situation as when definitely ill-natured
people are in charge.
Ibid. Chap. 8

All religion, all life, all art, all expression come down to this: to the effort of the human soul to break through
its barrier of loneliness, of intolerable
loneliness, and make some contact with
another seeking soul, or with what all
souls seek, which is (by any name)
God.
Ibid. Chap. 11

[1] Inspired by a protest from General Ian
Hamilton, Commander of the Mediterranean
Expeditionary Force [1915], against turning
his cables into hackneyed phrases.

procrastination is the
art of keeping
up with yesterday
archy and mehitabel. certain
maxims of archy. [1] page 43
[1927]

dance mehitabel dance
caper and shake a leg
what little blood is left
will fizz like wine in a keg
Ibid. mehitabel dances with
boreas. page 140

but still her word
is toujours gai
archys life of mehitabel: the
life of mehitabel the cat. page 2
[1933]

i have noticed that when chickens
quit quarrelling over their food they
often find that there is enough for all of
them i wonder if it might not be the
same way with the human race
Ibid. random thoughts by archy.
page 82

nowadays an author owns his stuff
only between air programs
Ibid. archy on the radio. page 108

so unlucky
that he runs into accidents
which started out to happen
to somebody else
Ibid. archy says. page 146

theres life in the old dame yet
Ibid. the retreat from hollywood.
page 155

a suicide is a person who has
considered his own case and decided
that he is worthless and who acts
as his own judge jury and executioner
and he probably knows better
than anyone else whether there is justice
in the verdict [2]
archy does his part. now look at
it. page 7 [1935]

[1] Archy, a cockroach, is unable to use the
shift-key on the typewriter; therefore he
cannot print capital letters and punctuation
marks.
[2] See Eaton, page 738, and Ellis, page
741.

it is a cheering thought to think
that god is on the side of the best digestion [1]

> *archy does his part. the
> big bad wolf. page 11*

there is bound to be a certain amount of
trouble running any country
if you are president the trouble happens
to you
but if you are a tyrant you can arrange
things so
that most of the trouble happens to
other people

> *Ibid. archy's newest deal. page 18*

there is always
a comforting thought
in time of trouble when
it is not our trouble

> *Ibid. comforting thoughts.
> page 149*

too many creatures
both insects and humans
estimate their own value
by the amount of minor irritation
they are able to cause
to greater personalities than themselves

> *Ibid. pride. page 171*

the females of all species are most
dangerous when they appear to retreat

> *Ibid. a farewell. page 252*

Comet, shake out your locks and let
them flare
Across the startled heaven of my soul!
Pluck out the hairpins, Sue, and let her
roll!
Don't be so stingy with your blooming
hair.

> *Sonnets to a Red-Haired Lady. I*

I love you as New Englanders love pie!

> *Ibid. XII*

Their names were . . . Ask oblivion!
"They had no poet, and they died." [2]

> *"They Had No Poet"*

Should chance strike out of me some
human heat,
Leap not at that and think to grasp
my soul!

---

[1] Give me a good digestion, Lord,
And also something to digest.
A Pilgrim's Grace, St. 1 (From a souvenir card given those who visit Chester Cathedral, Cheshire, England)
[2] See Pope, page 214.

I flee new bonds. My self must still retreat
Down devious ways to keep me free
and whole.

> *A Gentleman of Fifty Soliloquizes*

One boob may die, but deathless is
The royal race of hicks —
When Ahab went to Ascalon
They sold him gilded bricks.

> *Boob Ballad*

How often when they find a sage
As sweet as Socrates or Plato
They hand him hemlock for his wage,
Or bake him like a sweet potato!

> *Taking the Longer View*

There will be no beans in the Almost
Perfect State.

> *The Almost Perfect State*

For a territory the size of the United
States five millions of people would be
about right. . . . The human population of the entire world should be kept
well under a hundred millions. . . . If
the world were not so full of people, and
most of them did not have to work so
hard, there would be more time for
them to get out and lie on the grass, and
there would be more grass for them to
lie on.

> *Ibid.*

"You go and find her Husband's name
and other similar facks,"
Says the king to the Execushioner, "and
measure his neck for an ax;
For the turtle doves is singing sweet —
Oh, what the hell, it's Spring!
And just for the sake of argyment, I'll
show 'em who is king."

> *David and Bathsheba
> (As Interpreted by the Old Soak)*

To stroke a platitude until it purrs
like an epigram.

> *The Sun Dial*

Publishing a volume of verse is like
dropping a rose-petal down the Grand
Cañon and waiting for the echo.

> *Ibid.*

Poetry is what Milton saw when he
went blind.

> *Ibid.*

If you make people think they're
thinking, they'll love you. If you really
make them think they'll hate you.
The Sun Dial
An Idea isn't responsible for the peo-
ple who believe in it.
Ibid.
Speed, I bid you, speed the earth
Onward with a shout of mirth,
Fill your eager eyes with light,
Put my face and memory
Out of mind and out of sight.
Nothing I have caused or done,
But this gravestone, meets the sun:
Friends, a great simplicity
Comes at last to you and me.
Lines for a Gravestone

EDWIN MEADE ROBINSON
[1878–   ]

Write me a verse, my old machine —
I lack for an inspiration;
The skies are blue and the trees are
green,
And I long for a long vacation.
The Typewriter's Song. Stanza 1
A start! A thrill! A rattle — and then
It pounds out, swift and hearty —
"Now is the time for all good men
To come to the aid of the party."
Ibid. Stanza 4
Dying and letting die, they call "living
and letting live";
They do not even make mistakes for
live ones to forgive;
Wouldst thou be Nothing? Then, my
son, be a Conservative!
Conservatives

CARL SANDBURG
[1878–   ]

Pile the bodies high at Austerlitz and
Waterloo,
Shovel them under and let me work —
I am the grass; I cover all.
Grass
The fog comes on little cat feet.
Fog
O prairie mother, I am one of your
boys.

I have loved the prairie as a man with
a heart shot full of pain over love.
Prairie
I tell you the past is a bucket of ashes.
Ibid.
The peace of great churches be for you,
Where the players of lofty pipe organs
Practice old lovely fragments, alone.
For You
The peace of great books be for you,
Stains of pressed clover leaves on pages,
Bleach of the light of years held in
leather.
Ibid.
For the gladness here where the sun is
shining at evening on the weeds of
the river,
Our prayer of thanks.
Our Prayer of Thanks
For the laughter of children who tumble
barefooted and bareheaded in the
summer grass.
Ibid.
The republic is a dream.
Nothing happens unless first a dream.
Washington Monument by Night
Death sends a radiogram every day:
When I want you I'll drop in —
and then one day he comes with a
master-key and lets himself in and
says: We'll go now.
Death Snips Proud Men
That sergeant at Belleau Woods,
Walking into the drumfires, calling his
men,
"Come on, you . . . Do you want to
live forever?" [1]
Losers
When Abraham Lincoln was shoveled
into the tombs, he forgot the cop-
perheads and the assassin . . . in
the dust, in the cool tombs.
Cool Tombs
Take any streetful of people buying
clothes and groceries, cheering a
hero or throwing confetti and blowing tin horns . . . tell me if the
lovers are losers . . . tell me if
any get more than the lovers . . .
in the dust . . . in the cool tombs.
Ibid

[1] See Thomas Carlyle, page 381.

Lay me on an anvil, O God.
Beat me and hammer me into a crow-
bar.
Let me pry loose old walls.
Let me lift and loosen old foundations.
Prayers of Steel
I won't take my religion from any man
who never works except with his
mouth and never cherishes any
memory except the face of the
woman on the American silver dol-
lar.
To a Contemporary Bunkshooter
Look out how you use proud words.
When you let proud words go, it is not
easy to call them back.
They wear long boots, hard boots. . . .
Look out how you use proud words.
Primer Lesson
Time is a sandpile we run our fingers in.
Hotel Girl
Hog Butcher for the World,
Tool Maker, Stacker of Wheat,
Player with Railroads and the Nation's
Freight Handler;
Stormy, husky, brawling,
City of the Big Shoulders.
Chicago
I know a Jew fish crier down on Max-
well Street, with a voice like a
north wind blowing over corn
stubble in January. . . .
His face is that of a man terribly glad
to be selling fish.
Fish Crier

LOUIS EDWIN THAYER
[1878–   ]

Here is a toast that I want to give
To a fellow I'll never know;
To the fellow who's going to take my
place
When it's time for me to go.
To My Successor. Stanza 1 [1909]
I fancy when I go to rest some one will
bring to light
Some kindly word or goodly act long
buried out of sight;
But, if it's all the same to you, just give
to me, instead,

The bouquets while I'm living and the
knocking when I'm dead.
Of Post-Mortem Praises. Stanza 1

EDWARD THOMAS
[1878–1917]

Out of the night, two cocks together
crow,
Cleaving the darkness with a silver
blow.
Cock-Crow
The swift with wings and tail as sharp
and narrow
As if the bow had flown off with the ar-
row.
Haymaking
If I should ever by chance grow rich
I'll buy Codham, Cockridden, and
Childerditch,
Roses, Pyrgo, and Lapwater,
And let them all to my elder daughter.
If I Should Ever by Chance

KENDALL BANNING
[1879–   ]

The world has but one song to sing,[1]
And it is ever new;
The first and last of all the songs,
For it is ever true;
A little song, a tender song,
The only song it hath:
"There was a youth of Ascalon
Who loved a girl of Gath."
Once on a Time. Stanza 2

GEORGE SANDS BRYAN
[1879–   ]

"What has upheld you on your way?
What has supported you when faint?
On what have you for strength relied?"
"My vittles," said the dear old saint.
Aunt Phoebe. Stanza 4

JAMES BRANCH CABELL
[1879–   ]

Why is the King of Hearts the only
one that hasn't a moustache?
The Rivet in Grandfather's Neck

[1] See Don Marquis, page 851.

Divers queens who die with Antony
But live a great while first with Julius.
Retractions. V

LEE WILSON DODD
[1879–1933]

You steal green apples from the Tree
Of Life, miscalling greenness pleasure.
To the Younger Generation

Much that I sought, I could not find;
Much that I found, I could not bind;
Much that I bound, I could not free;
Much that I freed returned to me.
Ronde Macabre

Furious Propaganda, with her brand,
Fires the dry prairies of our wide Waste
Land;
Making the Earth, Man's temporal sta-
tion, be
One stinking altar to Publicity.
The Great Enlightenment

JOHN ERSKINE
[1879–   ]

The Moral Obligation to Be Intelligent.
Title of book [1915]

And win, with simple gratitude and
wonder,
Peace in themselves, which is their sole
applause.
At the Front [1918]

EDWARD MORGAN FORSTER
[1879–   ]

The historian must have some conception of how men who are not historians behave.
*Abinger Harvest. Captain Ed-
ward Gibbon*

It is not that the Englishman can't
feel — it is that he is afraid to feel. He
has been taught at his public school
that feeling is bad form. He must not
express great joy or sorrow, or even
open his mouth too wide when he talks
— his pipe might fall out if he did.
Ibid. Notes on English Character

English literature is a flying fish. It
is a sample of the life that goes on day
after day beneath the surface; [1] it is a

[1] Viz. of the English character.

proof that beauty and emotion exist in
the salt, inhospitable sea.
*Abinger Harvest. Notes on
English Character*

How rare, how precious is frivolity!
How few writers can prostitute all their
powers! They are always implying "I
am capable of higher things."
Ibid. Ronald Firbank

NICHOLAS VACHEL LINDSAY
[1879–1931]

Man is a torch, then ashes soon,
May and June, then dead December,
Dead December, then again June.
Who shall end my dream's confusion?
Life is a loom, weaving illusion.
The Chinese Nightingale

They spoke, I think, of perils past.
They spoke, I think, of peace at last.
One thing I remember:
Spring came on forever,
Spring came on forever,
Said the Chinese nightingale.
Ibid.

The flower-fed buffaloes of the spring
In the days of long ago,
Ranged where the locomotives sing
And the prairie flowers lie low.
The Flower-Fed Buffaloes

Then you died on the prairie, and
scorned all disgraces,
O broncho that would not be broken of
dancing.
*The Broncho that Would Not
Be Broken. Stanza 5*

Booth died blind and still by faith he
trod,
Eyes still dazzled by the ways of God.
*General William Booth Enters
into Heaven*

Drabs and vixens in a flash made
whole!
Gone was the weasel-head, the snout,
the jowl; . . .
The banjos rattled, and the tambou-
rines
Jing-jing-jingled in the hands of
Queens!
Ibid.

Record it for the grandson of your
    son —
A city is not builded in a day;
Our little town cannot complete her
    soul
Till countless generations pass away.
        On the Building of Springfield.
                      Stanza 2

A bronzed, lank man! His suit of an-
    cient black,
A famous high top-hat and plain worn
    shawl
Make him the quaint great figure that
    men love,
The prairie-lawyer, master of us all.
        Abraham Lincoln Walks at
            Midnight. Stanza 3

Sleep softly, . . . eagle forgotten, . . .
    under the stone,
Time has its way with you there and
    the clay has its own.
Sleep on, O brave-hearted, O wise man,
    that kindled the flame —
To live in mankind is far more than to
    live in a name,
To live in mankind, far, far more . . .
    than to live in a name.
        The Eagle That Is Forgotten.[1]
                    Stanza 5

I look on the specious electrical light
Blatant, mechanical, crawling and
    white,
Wickedly red or malignantly green
Like the beads of a young Senegambian
    queen.
        A Rhyme About an Electrical
              Advertising Sign

See how the generations pass
Like sand through Heaven's blue hour-
    glass.
                    Shantung

I want live things in their pride to re-
    main.
I will not kill one grasshopper vain
Though he eats a hole in my shirt like
    a door.

[1] John Peter Altgeld [1847–1902], Governor of Illinois [1893–1897], widely criticized
for pardoning, in June, 1893, three anarchists
who were serving terms in prison for their
part in the Haymarket Riot at Chicago,
May 4, 1886. In 1896 and 1900 he supported
W. J. Bryan's candidacy for the Presidency.

I let him out, give him one chance more.
Perhaps, while he gnaws my hat in his
    whim,
Grasshopper lyrics occur to him.
            The Santa Fé Trail

Far away the Rachel-Jane
Not defeated by the horns
Sings amid a hedge of thorns: —
"Love and life,
Eternal youth —
Sweet, sweet, sweet, sweet,
Dew and glory,
Love and truth,
Sweet, sweet, sweet, sweet."
                    Ibid.

We shall see silver ships,
We shall see singing ships,
Valleys of spray today,
Mountains of foam.
We have been long away,
Far from our wonderland.
Here come the ships of love
Taking us home.
        The Lame Boy and the Fairy

The blood-fed captains nod. . . .
Rise, rise,
Take the sick dragons by surprise,
Highly establish
In the name of God,
The United States of Europe, Asia, and
    the World.
          Sew the Flags Together [1]

Fat black bucks in a wine-barrel room,
Barrel-house kings, with feet unstable,
Sagged and reeled and pounded on the
    table,
Pounded on the table,
Beat an empty barrel with the handle
    of a broom,
Hard as they were able,
Boom, boom, Boom,
With a silk umbrella and the handle of
    a broom,
Boomlay, boomlay, boomlay, Boom.
              The Congo. Part I

Then I saw the Congo, creeping through
    the black,
Cutting through the jungle with a
    golden track.
                    Ibid.

[1] Written November, 1918.

Mumbo-Jumbo is dead in the jungle,
Never again will he hoo-doo you.
The Congo. Part III

"I am your slave," said the Jinn.
Aladdin and the Jinn

God give such dawns as when, his venture o'er,
The Sailor looked upon San Salvador.
God lead us past the setting of the sun
To wizard islands, of august surprise;
God make our blunders wise.
Litany of the Heroes. Stanza 16

Come let us forget our ivory-towers,[1]
brothers,
Come let us be bold with our songs.
*Every Soul Is a Circus. Part IV,
The Pontoon Bridge Miracle*

Planting the trees that would march
and train

---

[1] Charles-Augustin Sainte-Beuve [1804–1869] is the first writer known to have likened a poet's retreat to an ivory tower. In his *Pensées d'Août, To M. Villemain*, St. 3, dated October, 1837, he wrote:

Hugo, dur partisan
. . . combattit sous l'armure,
Et tint haut sa bannière au milieu du murmure;
Il la maintient encore; et Vigny, plus secret,
Comme en sa tour d'ivoire, avant midi, rentrait
        (Hugo, strong partisan
. . . fought in armor,
And held high his banner in the midst of the tumult:
He still holds it; and Vigny, more discreet,
As if in his tower of ivory, retired before noon).

The poet, retired in his Tower of Ivory, isolated, according to his desire, from the world of man, resembles, whether he so wishes or not, another solitary figure, the watcher enclosed for months at a time in a lighthouse at the head of a cliff. — JULES DE GAULTIER [1858–   ]: *La Guerre et les Destinées de l'Art*

The ivory tower awakened my desire;
I longed to enclose myself in selfish bliss.
RUBÉN DARIO [1867–1916]: *Portico,
St. 13*

A tower of ivory it is
Beside a shoreless sea;
I look out of my lattices
And the saints appear to me.
WILFRED ROWLAND CHILDE [1890–   ]:
Turris Eburnea, St. 5

On, in his name to the great Pacific,
Like Birnam Wood to Dunsinane,[1]
Johnny Appleseed swept on.[2]
*In Praise of Johnny Appleseed
(1775–1847)*

ST. JOHN LUCAS
[1879–1934]

The curate thinks you have no soul;
I know that he has none.
My Dog

This prayer at least the gods fulfill:
That when I pass the flood and see
Old Charon by the Stygian coast
Take toll of all the shades who land,
Your little, faithful, barking ghost
May leap to lick my phantom hand.[3]
Ibid.

I would resort to any method —
megaphones in the street, sonnets on
the partitions of third-class carriages,
and even the biograph — if by such
base uses I could really arouse an interest in things that are fine.
The Rose-Winged Hours. Preface

HAROLD MONRO
[1879–1932]

How lonely we shall be!
What shall we do,
You without me,
I without you?
Midnight Lamentation

She nestles over the shining rim,
Buries her chin in the creamy sea;
Her tail hangs loose; each drowsy paw
Is doubled under each bending knee.
Milk for the Cat

We are going *Out*. You know the pitch
of the word,
Probing the tone of thought as it comes
through fog
And reaches by devious means (half-smelt, half-heard)
The four-legged brain of a walk-ecstatic
dog.
Dog

---

[1] *Macbeth, Act V, Sc. 5.*
[2] See Allen, page 596.
[3] See Norah Holland, page 842.

PADRAIC H. PEARSE
[1879–1916]

Naked I saw thee,
  O beauty of beauty!
And I blinded my eyes
  For fear I should flinch.
Ideal. Stanza 1

Of wealth or of glory
I shall leave nothing behind me
(I think it, O God, enough!)
But my name in the heart of a child.
To Death. Stanza 2

FELIX RIESENBERG
[1879–   ]

City, lyric city. . . .
City kind to actresses; tolerant of
actors; city of independent handmaid-
ens. City of contraceptions, contrap-
tions, and curses thundered from a
thousand pulpits. City of unfortunate fortune tellers. City entered by
night. . . .
Reporters cover you, yet you are
never covered. . . .
City of carpenters without wood, of
plumbers without mercy. City of uncomfortable comfort stations. City of
clanging radiators, of supine superin-
tendents. City wherein there is no room
to die. . . .
City wrought in flame. City of arguments unending. City of terminals, city
of endings, city of the last attempt. City
wherein no one knows whether he is
coming or going. . . . City of oda-
lisques working in stores, of seraglios
seeking for sultans, of tired old women
scrubbing offices by night. Great glorious patriotic city, giving its canes to
crippled soldiers. Fairy city in those
magic hours of the passing night; the
pause before the dawn. . . .
Dress-suit city, for hire and for
keeps. . . .
City that breathes of things too large
for books, that is too beautiful for poets,
too terrible for drama, too true for
testimony. . . .

City worth visiting, if only for a
week.
East Side, West Side, 1919–1929
The sea has always been a seducer,
a careless lying fellow, not feminine, as
many writers imagine, but strongly
masculine in its allurement. The king
of the sea, with his whiskers of weed
and his trident and dolphins, truly represents the main and gives it character.
The sea, like a great sultan, supports
thousands of ships, his lawful wives.
These he caresses and chastises as the
case may be. This explains the feminine
gender of all proper vessels.
Vignettes of the Sea
Have you ever considered that if
every thumb print is different, perhaps
everything else is different? No two
people are alike. Yet originals, individu-
alists, bright intellects, and the gang
who lead the laughter and point the
way, are alarmed by an idea that we
are becoming standardized.
Endless River
If the ship is troubled with rats, place
a good deal of dry newspaper in the
sail locker for the rats to chew on.
Standard Seamanship

WILL ROGERS [1]
[1879–1935]

All I know is just what I read in the
papers.
Prefatory remark
I never met a man I didn't like.
*Address, Tremont Temple,
Boston [June, 1930]*
There is a lot of difference in pioneer-
ing for gold and pioneering for spinach.
*Last syndicated contribution to
the press, sent from Fairbanks,
Alaska, and published the day
after his death in an airplane
crash [August 15, 1935]*

[1] I worked with gum and grin and lariat
To entertain the proletariat,
And with my Oklahomely wit
I brightened up the earth a bit.
OGDEN NASH [1902–   ]

ROBERT HAVEN SCHAUFFLER
[1879–   ]

At the gate of the West I stand,
On the isle where the nations throng,
We call them "scum o' the earth."
Scum o' the Earth

Newcomers all from the eastern seas,
Help us incarnate dreams like these.
Forget, and forgive, that we did you
    wrong.
Help us to father a nation strong
In the comradeship of an equal birth,
In the wealth of the richest bloods of
    earth.
Ibid.

BESSIE ANDERSON
(MRS. ARTHUR J.) STANLEY
[1879–   ]

He has achieved success who has
lived well, laughed often and loved
much; who has enjoyed the trust of
pure women, the respect of intelligent
men and the love of little children; who
has filled his niche and accomplished his
task; who has left the world better than
he found it, whether by an improved
poppy, a perfect poem, or a rescued
soul; who has never lacked appreciation
of earth's beauty or failed to express it;
who has always looked for the best in
others and given them the best he had;
whose life was an inspiration; whose
memory a benediction.
*Success (prize-winning defini-
tion in a contest conducted by
the Brown Book Magazine, Boston, 1904)*

ROSE PASTOR STOKES
[1879–1933]

Some pray to marry the man they love,
    My prayer will somewhat vary:
I humbly pray to Heaven above
    That I love the man I marry.
My Prayer

SIMEON STRUNSKY
[1879–   ]

If you made a poll of newspaper editors, you might find a great many who
think that war is evil. But if you were
to take a census among pastors of fashionable metropolitan churches —
*Professor Latimer's Progress
[1918]*

We need a vindication of the night,
and especially of night in the city. . . .
The more you think of it the more you
will be persuaded that night is prima-
rily the time of the innocent industries,
and for the most part the primitive industries, employing simple, innocent,
primitive men — slow-speaking truck
farmers, husky red-faced slaughterers in
the abattoirs, solid German bakers, and
milkmen. The milkman alone is enough
to redeem the night from its undeserved
evil reputation. A cartload of pasteur-
ized milk for nurslings at four o'clock in
the morning represents more service to
civilization than a cartful of bullion on
its way from the Sub-treasury to the
vaults of a national bank five hours
later.
Belshazzar Court. Night Life

ROY ATWELL
[1880–   ]

In these days of indigestion
It is oftentimes a question
As to what to eat and what to leave
    alone;
For each microbe and bacillus
Has a different way to kill us,
And in time they always claim us for
    their own.
*Some Little Bug Is Going to
Find You Some Day. Stanza 1*

Some little bug is going to find you
    some day,
Some little bug will creep behind you
    some day,
Ibid. Stanza 3

HENRY HOWARTH BASHFORD
[1880–   ]

As I came down the Highgate Hill
  I met the sun's bravado,
And saw below me, fold on fold,
Grey to pearl and pearl to gold,
This London like a land of old,
  The land of Eldorado.

Romance. Stanza 1

ALBERT JAY COOK

It's Heaven, Hell or Hoboken [1] before
next Christmas Day.
Heaven, Hell or Hoboken [2]

ROBERT BROWNING HAMILTON
[1880–   ]

I walked a mile with Pleasure.
  She chattered all the way,
But left me none the wiser
  For all she had to say.

I walked a mile with Sorrow,
  And ne'er a word said she;
But, oh, the things I learned from her
  When Sorrow walked with me!

Along the Road

ROBERT CORTES HOLLIDAY
[1880–   ]

The best, the most exquisite automobile is a walking-stick; and one of the finest things in life is going a journey with it.

Walking-Stick Papers [1918]

They [women] are too personal for the high enjoyment of going a journey. They must be forever thinking about you or about themselves; with them everything in the world is somehow tangled up in these matters; and when you are with them (you cannot help it, or if you could they would not allow it), you must be forever thinking about them or yourself. Nothing on either side can be seen detached. They cannot rise to that philosophic plane of mind which is the very marrow of going a journey. One reason for this is that they can never escape from the idea of society. You are in their society, they are in yours.

Walking-Stick Papers [1918]

There is not in the press any reading so improving as the "obits" . . . I doubt very much indeed whether any one could read obituaries every day for a year and remain a bad man or woman.

Ibid. The Deceased

We go into the feature headed "Died," a department similar in design to that on the literary page headed "Books Received." We are arranged alphabetically according to the first letter of our surnames. We are set in small type with lines following the name line indented. It is difficult for me to tell with certainty from the printed page but I think we are set without leads.

Ibid.

HELEN KELLER [1]
[1880–   ]

Literature is my Utopia. Here I am not disfranchised. No barrier of the senses shuts me out from the sweet, gracious discourse of my book-friends. They talk to me without embarrassment or awkwardness.

The Story of My Life

At first I was rather unwilling to study Latin grammar. It seemed absurd to waste time analyzing every word I came across — noun, genitive, singular, feminine — when its meaning was quite plain. I thought I might just as well describe my pet in order to know it — order, vertebrate; division, quadruped; class, mammalia; genus, filinus; species, cat; individual, Tabby. But as I got deeper into the subject, I became more interested, and the beauty of the language delighted me. I often amused myself by reading Latin passages, picking up words I understood and trying to

---

[1] Hoboken, New Jersey, was a port of embarkation and return for the American Expeditionary Forces during the World War.
[2] Published in *The Stars and Stripes* during the World War.

[1] Helen Keller has been blind and deaf since infancy.

make sense. I have never ceased to enjoy this pastime.

The Story of My Life

MARY ANTIN

So at last I was going to America! Really, really going, at last! The boundaries burst. The arch of heaven soared. A million suns shone out for every star. The winds rushed in from outer space, roaring in my ears, "America! America!"

The Promised Land

Spirit of all childhood! Forgive me, forgive me, for so lightly betraying a child's dream-secrets. I that smile so scoffingly today at the unsophisticated child that was myself, have I found any nobler thing in life than my own longing to be noble? Would I not rather be consumed by ambitions that can never be realized than live in stupid acceptance of my neighbor's opinion of me? The statue in the public square is less a portrait of a mortal individual than a symbol of the immortal aspiration of humanity.

Ibid.

RUDOLPH CHAMBERS LEHMANN

When eight strong fellows are out to row,
  With a slip of a lad to guide them,
I warrant they'll make the light ship go,
  Though the coach on the launch may chide them,
With his "Six, get on to it! Five, you're late!
Don't hurry the slides, and use your weight!
You're bucketing, Bow; and, as to Four,
The sight of his shoulders makes me sore!"

At Putney. Stanza 1

They have slipped through Barnes; they are round the bend;
  And the chests of the eight are tightening.
"Now spend your strength, if you've strength to spend,

And away with your hands like lightning!
Well rowed!" — and the coach is forced to cheer —
"Now stick to it, all, for the post is near!"
And, lo, they stop at the coxswain's call,
With its message of comfort, "Easy all!"

At Putney. Stanza 4

HENRY LOUIS MENCKEN
[1880–   ]

The virulence of the national appetite for bogus revelation.

A Book of Prefaces. Chap. 1, Sect. 2

To the man with an ear for verbal delicacies — the man who searches painfully for the perfect word, and puts the way of saying a thing above the thing said — there is in writing the constant joy of sudden discovery, of happy accident.

Ibid. Chap. 2, Sect. 2

Poverty is a soft pedal upon all branches of human activity, not excepting the spiritual.

Ibid. Chap. 4, Sect. 3

Formalism is the hall-mark of the national culture.

Ibid. Sect. 6

Time is a great legalizer, even in the field of morals.

Ibid.

All successful newspapers are ceaselessly querulous and bellicose. They never defend anyone or anything if they can help it; if the job is forced upon them, they tackle it by denouncing someone or something else.

Prejudices, First Series. Chap. 13

The great artists of the world are never Puritans, and seldom even ordinarily respectable.

Ibid. Chap. 16

To be in love is merely to be in a state of perceptual anaesthesia — to mistake an ordinary young man for a Greek god or an ordinary young woman for a goddess.

Ibid.

Here, more than anywhere else in the world, the daily panorama of human existence — the unending procession of governmental extortions and chicaneries, of commercial brigandages and throat-slittings, of theological buffooneries, of aesthetic ribaldries, of legal swindles and harlotries — is so inordinately extravagant, so perfectly brought up to the highest conceivable amperage, that only the man who was born with a petrified diaphragm can fail to go to bed every night grinning from ear to ear, and awake every morning with the eager, unflagging expectations of a Sunday-school superintendent touring the Paris peep-shows.

On Being an American [1922]

Human enterprises that, in all other countries, are resigned despairingly to an incurable dulness — things that seem devoid of exhilarating amusement by their very nature — are here lifted to such inordinate buffoonery that contemplating them tears the very midriff from its moorings.

Ibid.

To be happy one must be (*a*) well fed, unhounded by sordid cares, at ease in Zion, (*b*) full of a comfortable feeling of superiority to the masses of one's fellow men, and (*c*) delicately and unceasingly amused according to one's taste. It is my contention that, if this definition be accepted, there is no country in the world wherein a man constituted as I am — a man of my peculiar weakness, vanities, appetites, and aversions — can be so happy as he can be in the United States. Going further, I lay down the doctrine that it is a sheer physical impossibility for such a man to live in the United States and *not* be happy.

Ibid.

All the more pretentious American authors try to write chastely and elegantly; the typical literary product of the country is still a refined essay in the *Atlantic Monthly*, perhaps gently jocose but never rough — by Emerson, so to speak, out of Charles Lamb.

The American Language [1919]

Philadelphia is the most pecksniffian of American cities, and thus probably leads the world.

The American Language [1919]

MENCKEN AND NATHAN
[GEORGE JEAN NATHAN]
[1882–   ]

From the American Credo [1920]

That all one has to do to gather a large crowd in New York is to stand on the curb a few moments and gaze intently at the sky.

That the postmasters in small towns read all the postcards.

That all theater box-office employés are very impolite and hate to sell a prospective patron a ticket.

That all newspaper reporters carry notebooks.

That, when shaving on a railway train, a man invariably cuts himself.

That the jokes in *Punch* are never funny.

That nicotine keeps the teeth in a sound condition.

That the wife of a rich man always wistfully looks back into the past and wishes she had married a poor man.

That the quality of the champagne may be judged by the amount of noise the cork makes when it is popped.

That all French women are very passionate, and will sacrifice everything to love.

That beer is very fattening.

That the cloth used in suits made in England is so good that it never wears out.

That Philadelphia is a very sleepy town.

That if one swallows an ounce of olive oil before going to a banquet, one will not get drunk.

That the worst actress in the company is always the manager's wife.

That milking a cow is an operation demanding a special talent that is possessed only by yokels, and that a person born in a large city can never hope to acquire it.

ALFRED NOYES
[1880–   ]

There was music all about us, we were
    growing quite forgetful
We were only singing seamen from the
    dirt of Londontown.
       Forty Singing Seamen. Stanza 4

There's a magic in the distance, where
    the sea-line meets the sky.
             Ibid. Stanza 9

The music's not immortal, but the world
    has made it sweet.
       The Barrel-Organ. Stanza 1

Go down to Kew in lilac-time, in lilac-
    time, in lilac-time;
  Go down to Kew in lilac-time (it isn't
    far from London!)
And you shall wander hand in hand
    with love in summer's wonder-
    land;
  Go down to Kew in lilac-time (it isn't
    far from London!)
             Ibid. Stanza 5

Ye that follow the vision
  Of the world's weal afar,
Have ye met with derision
  And the red laugh of war?
Yet the thunder shall not hurt you
  Nor the battle storms dismay;
Tho' the sun in heaven desert you
  "Love will find out the way." [1]
      Love Will Find Out the Way

England, my mother,
  Lift to my Western Sweetheart
One full cup of English mead, breathing
  of the May!
Pledge the may-flower in her face that
  you and ah, none other,
    Sent her from the mother-land
    Across the dashing spray.
    America, My Sweetheart. Stanza 1
    (*prologue to the American edition
    of Drake*)

The wind was a torrent of darkness
    among the gusty trees,
The moon was a ghostly galleon tossed
    upon cloudy seas,

---

[1] Under floods which are deepest,
    Which Neptune obey;
  Over rocks that are steepest,
    Love will find out the way.
    PERCY: *Reliques, Love Will Find
          Out the Way*

The road was a ribbon of moonlight
    over the purple moor,
And the highwayman came riding —
    Riding — riding —
The highwayman came riding, up to the
    old inn-door.
       The Highwayman. I, Stanza 1

I'll come to thee by moonlight, though
  hell should bar the way.
            Ibid. Stanza 5

The cymbals crash,
  And the dancers walk,
With long silk stockings
  And arms of chalk.
       A Victory Dance. Stanza 1

God how the dead men
  Grin by the wall,
Watching the fun
  Of the Victory Ball.
            Ibid. Stanza 9

Die to the little hatreds; die to greed;
  Die to the old ignoble selves we knew;
Die to the base contempts of sect and
  creed.
  A Victory Celebration. Sonnet VII

And that's not done by sword, or tongue,
  or pen,
There's but one way. God make us better men.
                Ibid.

Gardener of God, if wild and weak de-
  sires
  Choke the true growth, and rob the
    soul of power,
Use thy sharp knife on wandering shoots
  and briars,
  Cut the weak stem hard back, and let
    it flower.
    The Rose and the Knife [1934]

VILDA SAUVAGE OWENS

If I ever have time for things that
    matter,
If ever I have the smallest chance,
I'm going to live in
Little Broom Gardens,
Moat-by-the-Castle,
Nettlecombe, Hants.
    *If I Ever Have Time for the Things
           That Matter. Stanza 1*

EDMUND LESTER PEARSON
[1880–1937]

The agile bookworm eats, conceal'd
from sight,
Also the prowling mouse abhors the
light,
But be assur'd that Philobiblos knows,
The hellish Cockroach is the chief of
foes.
The Old Librarian's Almanack [1]

Matrimony is no fit Diversion for the
Librarian. The dissipations of Time, the
vain Emptinesses of Amusement, the
general be-pesterment . . . agree to
harass the Librarian and woo him from
his legitimate tasks.
Ibid.

No agreement about books can make
us look upon another man with so
friendly an eye as the discovery that he
belonged to our period, and shared our
special enthusiasms about reading, in
the years that stretched between the
sixth birthday and the sixteenth.
Books in Black or Red

The eccentricities of collectors are as
merry as the cantrips of unicorns on a
grassy plain.
Ibid.

GRANTLAND RICE
[1880–   ]

Where the puddle is shallow, the weak-
fish stay
To drift along with the current's flow:
To take the tide as it moves each day
With the idle ripples that come and
go.
Ballade of the Gamefish
Where the far heights call through the
silver glow,

"Only the gamefish swims up
stream." [1]
Ballade of the Gamefish
Keep coming back for all they've got,
and take it with a grin
When disappointment trips you up or
failure barks your shin;
Keep coming back — and if at last you
lose the game of right
Let those who whipped you know at
least they, too, have had a fight.
Alumnus Football

GILES LYTTON STRACHEY
[1880–1932]

Bertie [2] seemed to display a deep-
seated repugnance to every form of
mental exertion.
Queen Victoria. Chap. 6
In women's hearts he [3] had always
read as in an open book. . . . He realised everything — the interacting com-
plexities of circumstance and character,
the pride of place mingled so inextric-
ably with personal arrogance, the super-
abundant emotionalism, the ingenuous-
ness of outlook, the solid, the laborious
respectability, shot through so incon-
gruously by temperamental cravings for
the coloured and the strange, the singular intellectual limitations, and the mys-
teriously essential female elements im-
pregnating every particle of the whole.
A smile hovered over his impassive features, and he dubbed Victoria "the
Faery."
Ibid. Chap. 8
The inconsistency of the Elizabethans exceeds the limits permitted to man.
Their elements fly off from one another
wildly; we seize them; we struggle hard
to shake them together into a single
compound, and the retort bursts. How
is it possible to give a coherent account

---

[1] An ingenious literary hoax. This "Almanack for the year 1774," purporting to have
been issued by "Jared Bean" in New Haven
in 1773, was published by Mr. Pearson in
1909, and successfully fooled many critics and
bibliophiles — even the late Sir William Osler.
See Pearson's *Books in Black or Red, Chap. 2.*

[1] See John Trotwood Moore, page 733.
Mr. Rice used this line in another poem, *Ex-
panding the Theme.*

Only the gamefish swims upstream,
But the sensible fish swims down.
OGDEN NASH [1902–   ]: *When You
Say That, Smile*
[2] King Edward VII as a child.
[3] Disraeli.

of their subtlety and their *naïveté,* their delicacy and their brutality, their piety and their lust?

> *Elizabeth and Essex. Chap. 2*

Perhaps of all the creations of man language is the most astonishing.

> *Words and Poetry*

RICHARD HENRY TAWNEY
[1880–   ]

The burden of our civilization is not merely, as many suppose, that the product of industry is ill-distributed, or its conduct tyrannical, or its operation interrupted by bitter disagreements. It is that industry itself has come to hold a position of exclusive predominance among human interests, which no single interest, and least of all the provision of the material means of existence, is fit to occupy. Like a hypochondriac who is so absorbed in the processes of his own digestion that he goes to the grave before he has begun to live, industrialized communities neglect the very objects for which it is worth while to acquire riches in their feverish preoccupation with the means by which riches can be acquired.

That obsession by economic issues is as local and transitory as it is repulsive and disturbing. To future generations it will appear as pitiable as the obsession of the seventeenth century by religious quarrels appears today.

> *The Acquisitive Society*

NANCY BYRD TURNER
[1880–   ]

The Bookshop has a thousand books,
All colors, hues, and tinges,
And every cover is a door
That turns on magic hinges.

> *The Bookshop. Stanza 2*

May I have eyes to see
Beauty in this plain room
Where I am called to be.

> *A Prayer for the Kitchen Wall*

Aisne-Marne, Chavignon, St. Mihiel,
Meuse-Argonne — east and west —
The old strange names, familiar now as
heart-beats in each breast,
And keen with memories of those they
left to sleep alone,
Dust to dust in an alien land, yet still
New England's Own.

> *New England's Own.*[1] *Stanza 3*

MARGARET WIDDEMER

I have shut my little sister in from life
and light
(For a rose, for a ribbon, for a wreath
across my hair),
I have made her restless feet still under
the night,
Locked from sweets of summer and from
wild spring air.

> *The Factories. Stanza 1*

The old road to Paradise
Easy it is missed!

> *The Old Road to Paradise.*
> *Stanza 2*

Carnations and my first love! And he
was seventeen,
And I was only twelve years — a stately
gulf between.

> *Carnations. Stanza 1*

Well, if the thing is over, better it is
for me,
The lad was ever a rover, loving and
laughing and free.

> *Mary, Helper of Heartbreak.*
> *Stanza 1*

Mary, helper of heartbreak, send him
to me to-night!

> *Ibid. Stanza 3*

The only work about writing —
It's a very terrible thing —
Is wrapping your stuff and stamping it
And tying it up with string.

> *Confession. Stanza 3*

WILLIAM W. WOOLLCOTT

I am a One Hundred Per-Cent American.

> *Refrain of ironical patriotic anthem*

[1] Commemorating the return of the Yankee Division from France, April 25, 1919.

I am an anti-Darwin intellectual:
The man that says any nice young boy
    or gal
Is a descendant of the ape
Shall never from Hell's fire escape.
    Refrain of ironical patriotic anthem
In art I pull no high-brow stuff,
I know what I like, and that's enough.
            Ibid.

THOMAS R. YBARRA

Oh, the Roman was a rogue,
    He erat was, you bettum;
He ran his automobilus
    And smoked his cigarettum.
He wore a diamond studibus
    And elegant cravattum,
A maxima cum laude shirt,
    And such a stylish hattum.
        Lay of Ancient Rome

LASCELLES ABERCROMBIE
[1881–   ]

But here's the happiest light can lie on
    ground,
Grass sloping under trees
Alive with yellow shine of daffodils!
        Ryton Firs
These, who desired to live, went out to
    death:
Dark underground their golden youth is
    lying.
We live: and there is brightness in our
    breath
They could not know — the splendour
    of their dying.
          Epitaph
No faith can last
That never sings.
        The Stream's Song
The great blue ceremony of the air
Did a new morrow for the earth prepare.
        Mary and the Bramble
    What is all
The world, but an awning scaffolded
    amid
The waste perilous Eternity, to lodge
This Heaven-wander'd princess, wom-
    an's beauty?
          Vashti

FRANKLIN PIERCE ADAMS
("F.P.A.")
[1881–   ]

Christmas is over and Business is Busi-
    ness.
        For the Other 364 Days
"Up, to the office, . . . and so to bed."
    A Ballade of Mr. Samuel Pepys.
          Refrain
"Oh, why do you gaze, my dear, my
    dear,
    And muse on the misty sky?"
"I'm afraid that it isn't going to clear,
    And we won't get the washing dry."
        Sehnsucht. Stanza 5
If, my dear, you seek to slumber,
Count of stars an endless number;
If you still continue wakeful,
Count the drops that make a lakeful;
Then, if vigilance yet above you
Hover, count the times I love you;
And if slumber still repel you,
Count the times I do not tell you.
          Lullaby
I've been from Banff to Painted Post,
    From Harrisburg to Monterey,
    From Cedarhurst to San José;
From Santa Cruz to Valley Forge,
    And yet, on all my witless way,
I've never called a waiter "George."
    A Ballade of Egregiousness.
          Stanza 1
Ruthlessly pricking our gonfalon bub-
    ble,
Making a Giant hit into a double,
Words that are weighty with nothing
    but trouble:
"Tinker to Evers to Chance."
        Baseball's Sad Lexicon
The rich man has his motor-car,
    His country and his town estate.
He smokes a fifty-cent cigar
    And jeers at Fate.
        The Rich Man. Stanza 1
Yet though my lamp burn low and dim,
    Though I must slave for livelihood —
Think you that I would change with
    him?
    You bet I would!
        Ibid. Stanza 3

It is cold, O Thaliarchus, and Soracte's
  crest is white;
There is skating on the Tiber; there is
  No Relief in Sight.
Tell the janitor the radiator's absolutely
  cold. . . .
Let us crack a quart of Sabine; I've a
  case of four-year old.
          The Cold Wave of 32 B. C.
              (*Horace, Odes I, 9*)

The best you get is an even break.
          *Ballade of Schopenhauer's
                    Philosophy*

I shot a poem into the air,
It was reprinted everywhere
From Bangor to the Rocky Range
And always credited to
          — Exchange.
              Frequently

O bards of rhyme and metre free,
My gratitude goes out to ye
For all your deathless lines — ahem!
Let's see now. . . . What *is* one of
  them?
              To a Vers Librist

Of making many books there is no
  end —
So Sancho Panza said, and so say I.
Thou wert my guide, philosopher and
  friend
  When only one is shining in the sky.
          *Lines on and from "Bartlett's
                    Familiar Quotations"*

Go, lovely Rose that lives its little hour!
Go, little booke! and let who will be
  clever!
Roll on! From yonder ivy-mantled
  tower
  The moon and I could keep this up
  forever.
              Ibid.

WITTER BYNNER
[1881–   ]

Name me no names for my disease,
  With uninforming breath;
I tell you I am none of these,
  But homesick unto death.
          *The Patient to the Doctors.
                    Stanza 1*

Sometimes when people pity me,
  I tell them with no rancor
That for what it costs me to be free
  I might have bought an anchor.
              When People Pity Me

You must keep your goal in sight,
Labor toward it day and night,
Then at last arriving there —
You shall be too old to care.
              Wisdom

What's the use of a new-born
  child? [1] . . .
To raise the dead heart? — to set wild
  The fettered hope?
              Poor Richard

The look in your eyes
Was as soft as the underside of soap in a
  soap-dish.
              I Evade

There is a solitude in seeing you,
Followed by your company when you
  are gone.
              Lightning

What is so nameless as beauty,
Which poets, who give it a name,
Are only unnaming forever? —
Content, though it go, that it came.
              Grass-Tops

JOSEPH CAMPBELL
[1881–   ]

As a white candle
In a holy place,
So is the beauty
Of an aged face.
          The Old Woman. Stanza 1

Her thoughts as still
As the waters
Under a ruined mill.
              Ibid. Stanza 3

---

[1] "What is the use of this new invention?"
some one asked Franklin. "What is the use
of a new-born child?" was his reply. — JAMES
PARTON: *The Life and Times of Benjamin
Franklin* [1864], *Vol. 2, Pp. 514–515.* (A footnote states that the anecdote is taken from the
memoirs of Baron de Grimm.)
  The economist of 1855 who asks, Of what
use are the lords? may learn of Franklin, Of
what use is a baby? — R. W. EMERSON: *English Traits*

FRANCIS CARLIN (JAMES FRANCIS CARLIN MacDONNELL)
[1881–   ]

My Love has crossed an Ocean
  O'er which no breezes blow,
And I would it had the motion
  Of but an ebb and flow.
                The Stilly Sea. Stanza 1

My Love is o'er a Water,
  A calm and tideless sea,
And I would that I had taught her
  To come in dreams to me.
                Ibid. Stanza 2

That which is in disorder
  Has neither rule nor rhyme,
Like the stars at Heaven's border
  And the troubled laughter of Time.
                The Ravelled Edge. Stanza 3

ROBERT WILLIAM CHAPMAN
[1881–   ]

A house is infinitely communicative, and tells many things besides the figure of its master's income. There are houses that confess intellectual penury, and houses that reek of enlightenment.
                The Portrait of a Scholar [1920]

All poetry, and all good prose, invite me to utterance. I hope I do not sit muttering in public places; but if I cannot give voice, my ear hearkens to unheard melodies . . . but I believe that most readers are deaf. . . . This conspiracy of silence has much to answer for in the general decay of writing and the false notions of style now commonly entertained.
                Ibid. Reading Aloud

A quotation, like a pun, should come unsought, and then be welcomed only for some propriety or felicity justifying the intrusion.
                Ibid. The Art of Quotation

A collector should not be too careful to be sure of what he buys, or the sporting spirit will atrophy; and he who collects that he may have the best collection, or a better than his friend's, is little more than a miser.
                Ibid. Silver Spoons

When I dine out and find my soup embellished by a notable spoon, as may often happen to those who dine in Colleges or Inns of Court, my manners are seldom proof against temptation. I contrive a furtive scrutiny of the underside.
                The Portrait of a Scholar.
                Silver Spoons

PADRAIC COLUM
[1881–   ]

Oh, to have a little house!
  To own the hearth and stool and all!
                An Old Woman of the Roads.
                Stanza 1

And I am praying God on high,
  And I am praying Him night and day,
For a little house — a house of my
    own —
  Out of the wind's and the rain's way.
                Ibid. Stanza 6

A tune is more lasting than the voice of
    the birds.
A song is more lasting than the riches of
    the world.
                Polonius and the Ballad-Singers

JOHN FREEMAN
[1881–1929]

Who may regret what was, since it has
    made
Himself himself? All that I was I am,
And the old childish joy now lives in
    me
At sight of a green field or a green tree.
                All That I Was I Am

I knew how beauty seen from unseen
    must rise,
  How the body's joy for more than
    body's use was made.
I knew then how the body is the body of
    the mind,
  And how the mind's own fire beneath
    the cool skin played.
                The Body

Knowing that beauty's self rose visible
    in the world
  Over age that darkens, and griefs that
    destroy.
                Ibid.

HELEN GRANVILLE-BARKER

Night and the curtains drawn,
 The household still,
Fate, with appointed strength,
 Hath worked its will.
Night and the Curtains Drawn

Dearest, the whole world ends,
 Ends well — in this —
Night — and the firelit dark,
 Your touch, your kiss.
Ibid.

EDGAR ALBERT GUEST
[1881–   ]

Somebody said that it couldn't be done
 But he with a chuckle replied
That "maybe it couldn't," but he would
 be one
Who wouldn't say so till he'd tried.
It Couldn't Be Done

It takes a heap o' livin' in a house t'
 make it home,
A heap o' sun an' shadder, an' ye sometimes have t' roam
Afore ye really 'preciate the things ye
 lef' behind,
An' hunger fer 'em somehow, with 'em
 allus on yer mind.
Home

How do you tackle your work each day?
 Are you scared of the job you find?
Do you grapple the task that comes your
 way
 With a confident, easy mind?
How Do You Tackle Your Work?

The things that haven't been done be-
 fore,
 Those are the things to try;
Columbus dreamed of an unknown
 shore
 At the rim of the far-flung sky.
*The Things That Haven't Been
Done Before*

I'd rather see a sermon than hear one
 any day;
I'd rather one should walk with me than
 merely tell the way.
Sermons We See

In this bright little package, now isn't
 it odd?

You've a dime's worth of something
 known only to God!
The Package of Seeds

Here is one of God's miracles soon to
 unfold,
Thus for ten cents an ounce is Divinity
 sold!
Ibid.

JOHN EDWARD HAZZARD
[1881–1935]

It worries me to beat the band
To hear folks say our lives is grand;
Wish they'd try some one-night stand.
 Ain't it awful, Mabel!
Ain't It Awful, Mabel!

WILLIAM McFEE
[1881–   ]

To those who live and toil and lowly die,
 Who pass beyond and leave no last-
 ing trace,
To those from whom our queen Pros-
 perity
 Has turned away her fair and fickle
 face.
Casuals of the Sea. Dedication

A trouble is a trouble, and the general idea, in the country, is to treat it
as such, rather than to snatch the
knotted cords from the hand of God and
deal out murderous blows.
Ibid. Book I

It is extraordinary how many emotional storms one may weather in safety
if one is ballasted with ever so little
gold.
Ibid.

The world belongs to the Enthusiast
who keeps cool.
Ibid. Book II

Terrible and sublime thought, that
every moment is supreme for some man
and woman, every hour the apotheosis
of some passion!
Ibid.

Responsibility's like a string we can
only see the middle of. Both ends are
out of sight.
Ibid.

And so, having sailed the seas for many years, having debauched the gifts of God, and the love of women, having avoided with incredible dexterity the esteem of man and the joy of accomplishment, Jan Ostade went out into the void.
Casuals of the Sea. Book III

A certain incomprehensible reticence of soul which is peculiar to the English.
Command. Chap. 6

The alluring yet ineluctable problem of human folly.
Aliens. Preface [1917]

It has become fashionable to blame America for sins that are the common heritage of mankind . . . it is amusing to witness the astonishment and even incredulity of Americans who learn that such outstanding and typical citizens as Edgar Guest, Father Coughlin, Bishop Manning and Aimee McPherson were all born British.
On Living in America

Steam engines are very human. Their very weaknesses are understandable. Steam engines do not flash back and blow your face in. They do not short-circuit and rive your heart with imponderable electric force. They have arms and legs and warm hearts and veins full of warm vapour. Give us steam every time. You know where you are with steam.
A Six-Hour Shift [1917]

High-brow communists affect vast interest in pictures of machinery as art. They discover aesthetic qualities in a photograph of a broken crankshaft or the gear-wheels of a power press. A couple of screws lying on a mirror will send them into toothy ecstasies of appreciation.
More Harbours of Memory. Introduction [1934]

The bourgeois artist who retains his integrity is the only really happy man in the modern world. He is unable to envy anybody because nobody has anything he can use which is not his already.
Ibid.

Most of our nautical fictions seem to be caulked with hokum . . . it is almost impossible to get Americans to view the life of a seafaring man save as a chapter out of Jack London's *Sea Wolf* or some equally virile and odious fiction.
More Harbours of Memory. Romance

JOHN GNEISENAU NEIHARDT
[1881–   ]

Come back and bring the summer in your eyes,
The peace of evening in your quiet ways;
Come back and lead again to Paradise
The errant days!
Come Back. Stanza 1

Let me live out my years in heat of blood!
Let me die drunken with the dreamer's wine!
Let me not see this soul-house built of mud
Go toppling to the dust — a vacant shrine!
Let Me Live Out My Years

Give me high noon — and let it then be night!
Ibid.

And grant me, when I face the grisly Thing,
One haughty cry to pierce the gray Perhaps!
O let me be a tune-swept fiddlestring
That feels the Master Melody — *and snaps!*
Ibid.

Glowing through the gray rack
Breaks the Day —
Like a burning haystack
Twenty farms away!
Break of Day. Stanza 13

STUART PRATT SHERMAN
[1881–1926]

Nine-tenths of our university teachers are more competent to discuss the literature of England than the literature of America.

Introduction [*1923*] *to American Prose Masters by* W. C. BROWNELL

If a choice must be made, the American student should choose to be familiar with the Federalist rather than with the Letters of Junius, with Irving rather than Leigh Hunt, with Emerson rather than Carlyle, with Thoreau rather than Richard Jefferies, with Whitman rather than William Morris, with Mark Twain rather than Oscar Wilde, with Henry James rather than George Moore, and with Theodore Roosevelt rather than Queen Victoria.

Ibid.

The delectable form which intelligence takes in its moments of surplus power — the form of wit.

Ibid.

MARY (MRS. HENRY BERTRAM LAW) WEBB
[1881–1927]

The past is only the present become invisible and mute; and because it is invisible and mute, its memoried glances and its murmurs are infinitely precious. We are to-morrow's past.

Precious Bane.[1] *Foreword*

It made me gladsome to be getting some education, it being like a big window opening.

Ibid. Book I, Chap. 5

Saddle your dreams afore you ride 'em.

Ibid. Chap. 6

If you stop to be kind, you must swerve often from your path.

Ibid. Book II, Chap. 3

When you dwell in a house you mislike, you will look out of window a deal more than those that are content with their dwelling.

Ibid. Book III, Chap. 5

It's the folk that depend on us for this and for the other that we most do miss.

[1]   That soil may best
Deserve the precious bane.
MILTON: *Paradise Lost, Book I, L. 689*

So the mother is more let and hindered lacking the little creatures clinging to her skirt than she is when they be there, for she has no heart for her work.

Precious Bane. Book IV, Chap. 4

BERTON BRALEY
[1882–   ]

Got any river they say isn't crossable?
    Got any mountains that can't be cut through?
We specialize in the wholly impossible,
    Doing things "nobody ever could do."

At Your Service. Stanza 2

Trained by a task that's the biggest in history:
    Who has a job for this Panama Gang?

Ibid. Stanza 3

The grammar has a rule absurd
    Which I would call an outworn myth:
"A preposition is a word
    You mustn't end a sentence with!"

No Rule to be Afraid of. Stanza 1

And so they sailed away, these three,
    Mencken,
        Nathan
            And God.[1]

Three Minus One. Stanza 1

With doubt and dismay you are smitten,
    You think there's no chance for you, son?
Why, the best books haven't been written,
    The best race hasn't been run.

Opportunity. Stanza 1

If with pleasure you are viewing any work a man is doing,
    If you like him or you love him, tell him now.

Do It Now. Stanza 1

Do not wait till life is over and he's underneath the clover,
    For he cannot read his tombstone when he's dead!

Ibid. Stanza 2

[1] I shall name you the fishermen three:
        Wynken,
        Blynken,
        And Nod.
EUGENE FIELD: *Wynken, Blynken, and Nod, St. 3*

If neither cold poverty, famished and
    gaunt,
Nor sickness nor pain
Of body or brain
Can turn you away from the thing that
    you want,
If dogged and grim you besiege and be-
    set it,
You'll get it!
                      Success

Give the boy a dog and you've furnished
    him a playmate
    Always true and faithful as can be.[1]
                 A Gift. Stanza 1

It's seldom any one bestows
    The praise that Father should have
    had,
But — here's the debt that one man
    owes,
    I sing a little song to Dad!
             It's Only Fair. Envoy

Back of the beating hammer
    By which the steel is wrought,
Back of the workshop's clamor
    The seeker may find the Thought.
           The Thinker. Stanza 1

Back of the Job — the Dreamer
    Who's making the dream come true!
             Ibid. Stanza 4

JOHN DRINKWATER
[1882–1937]

This be my pilgrimage and goal,
    Daily to march and find
The secret phrases of the soul,
    The evangels of the mind.
                  Vocation

Great hills that fold above the sea,
    Ecstatic airs and sparkling skies,
Sing out your words to master me,
    Make me immoderately wise.
                Invocation

And not a girl goes walking
    Along the Cotswold lanes
But knows men's eyes in April
    Are quicker than their brains.
             Cotswold Love

---

[1] Dogs are faithful; they will stick to a bone
after everybody has deserted it. — HENRY
WHEELER SHAW ("Josh Billings"): *Animile
Statistix*

O Love, you happy wayfarer,
Be still my fond interpreter,
Of all the glory that can be
As once on starlight Winchelsea,
Finding upon my pilgrim way
A burning bush for every day.
           The Burning Bush

Grant us the will to fashion as we feel,
Grant us the strength to labor as we
    know,
Grant us the purpose, ribbed and edged
    with steel,
    To strike the blow.
           A Prayer. Stanza 9

When the high heart we magnify,
    And the clear vision celebrate,
And worship greatness passing by,
    Ourselves are great.
           Abraham Lincoln

CECILY FOX-SMITH
[1882–   ]

Lord knows it's bitter in an open boat
    to see your shipmates die.
        The Open Boat. Stanza 4

As I went down by Hastings Mill I
    lingered in my going
To smell the smell of piled-up deals and
    feel the salt wind blowing.
        Hastings Mill. Stanza 1

Along the wharves in sailor town a sing-
    ing whisper goes
Of wind among the anchored ships, the
    wind that blows
Off a broad brimming water, where the
    summer day had died
Like a wounded whale a-sounding in
    the sunset tide.
        Sailor Town. Stanza 1

When the long day's tramp is over, when
    the journey's done,
I shall dip down from some hill-top at
    the going down o' the sun,
And turn in at the open door, and lay
    down staff and load,
And wash me clean of the heat o' the
    day, and white dust o' the road.
        Journey's End. Stanza 1

HERMANN HAGEDORN
[1882–   ]

Down the fair-chambered corridor of
  years,
The quiet shutting, one by one, of doors.
Doors

You'll find us kindly on the whole,
  though queer;
Not ever quite so bad as we appear,
And at our maddest not without our
  graces.
  "A Traveler from a Distant Land"

How like the stars are these white,
  nameless faces —
These far innumerable burning coals!
This pale procession out of stellar
  spaces,
This Milky Way of souls!
Each in its own bright nebulae enfurled,
Each face, dear God, a world!
Broadway

HUGH S. JOHNSON
[1882–   ]

There was never a war at arms that
was not merely the extension of a preceding war of commerce grown fiercer
until the weapons of commerce seemed
no longer sufficiently deadly.
  *Radio broadcast for "World
  Peaceways" [1935]*

It is some commercial stake or ambition that makes all wars, and we
haven't got enough commercial stake
or ambition in the whole of Europe to
be worth the life or heart's blood of one
single mother's son.
  Ibid.

THOMAS SAMUEL JONES, JR.
[1882–1932]

Across the fields of yesterday
  He sometimes comes to me,
A little lad just back from play —
  The lad I used to be.
  Sometimes. Stanza 1

I wonder if he hopes to see
  The man I might have been.
  Ibid. Stanza 2

There is an island in the silent sea,
Whose marge the wistful waves lap list-
  lessly —
An isle of rest for those who used to be.
  *The Island [For the painting,
  The Isle of the Dead, by* ARNOLD
  BOECKLIN, *1827–1901* [1]]

JAMES JOYCE
[1882–   ]

Pity is the feeling which arrests the
mind in the presence of whatsoever is
grave and constant in human sufferings
and unites it with the human sufferer.
  *A Portrait of the Artist as a
  Young Man. Chap. 5*

Welcome, O life! I go to encounter
for the millionth time the reality of experience and to forge in the smithy of
my soul the uncreated conscience of my
race. Old father, old artificer, stand me
now and ever in good stead.
  *Ibid. Concluding words of
  Stephen Dedalus* [2]

A man of genius makes no mistakes.
His errors are volitional and are the
portals of discovery.
  *Ulysses. Page 188 [Random
  House edition]* [3]

Let some meinherr from Almany
grope his life long for deephid meanings in the depth of the buckbasket.
  Ibid. Page 202

He [Shakespeare] has hidden his own
name, a fair name, William, in the
plays, a super here, a clown there, as
a painter of old Italy set his face in a

---

[1] One of Boecklin's five versions of this subject was acquired by the Metropolitan Museum of Art, New York, in 1926. It was
painted in 1880.

[2] The reader must never forget the sym-
bolism in the name Dedalus. — HERBERT GOR-
MAN: Introduction to Modern Library edition.

[3] In respect of the recurrent emergence of
the theme of sex in the minds of his characters, it must always be remembered that his
locale was Celtic and his season spring . . .
in many places the effect on the reader is
somewhat emetic, nowhere does it tend to be
an aphrodisiac. "Ulysses" may, therefore, be
admitted into the United States. — Judge
JOHN M. WOOLSEY: decision of U. S. District
Court [Dec. 6, 1933]

dark corner of his canvas. He has revealed it in the sonnets where there is Will in overplus. Like John O'Gaunt his name is dear to him, as dear as the coat of arms he toadied for, on a bend sable a spear or steeled argent, honorificabilitudinitatibus, dearer than his glory of greatest shakescene in the country. What's in a name? That is what we ask ourselves in childhood when we write the name that we are told is ours. A star, a daystar, a firedrake rose at his birth. It shone by day in the heavens alone, brighter than Venus in the night, and by night it shone over delta in Cassiopeia, the recumbent constellation which is the signature of his initial among the stars. His eyes watched it, lowlying on the horizon, eastward of the bear, as he walked by the slumberous summer fields at midnight, returning from Shottery and from her arms.

Ulysses. Page 207

Every life is many days, day after day. We walk through ourselves, meeting robbers, ghosts, giants, old men, young men, wives, widows, brothers-in-love. But always meeting ourselves.

Ibid. Page 210

WINIFRED MARY LETTS
[1882–   ]

I saw the spires of Oxford
  As I was passing by,
The gray spires of Oxford
  Against a pearl-gray sky.
The Spires of Oxford. Stanza 1

God rest you, happy gentlemen,
  Who laid your good lives down. . . .
God bring you to a fairer place
  Than even Oxford town.
Ibid. Stanza 4

That God once loved a garden
We learn in Holy writ.
And seeing gardens in the Spring
I well can credit it.
But if God walks in Dublin,
I think that He'd be seen
Pacing up and down the paths
That lead through Stephen's Green.
Stephen's Green. Stanza 1

I like the people who keep shops,
Busy and cheerful folk with friendly
  faces.
Shops. Stanza 1

To serve us seems their only aim,
Asking our wishes, quick to crave our
  pardon,
And yet I know in each of these shop
  people
There dwells a soul withdrawn from us,
  elusive,
The shop can never know — a secret
  garden.
Ibid. Stanza 4

Then God go with you, priest of God,
For all is well, and shall be well.
What though you tread the roads of
  Hell,
Your Captain these same ways has trod.
Above the anguish and the loss
Still floats the ensign of His Cross.
Chaplain to the Forces

I laugh when I hear thim make it plain
That dogs and men never meet again.
For all their talk, who'd listen to thim,
With the soul in the shining eyes of him?
Would God be wasting a dog like Tim?
Tim, an Irish Terrier. Stanza 4

RICHARD MIDDLETON
[1882–1911]

Servant of the eternal Must
  I lie here, here let me lie,
In the ashes and the dust,
  Dreaming, dreaming pleasantly.
Pagan Epitaph

Why are her eyes so bright, so bright,
  Why do her lips control
The kisses of a summer night
  When I would love her soul?
Any Lover, Any Lass

The Silver Girl she came to me
  When spring was dancing green,
She said "I've come to wait on you
  And keep your cabin clean;
To wash your face and hands and feet
  And keep your forehead cool —
I'll get you into Heaven yet,
  You damned old fool!"
The Silver Girl

ALAN ALEXANDER MILNE
[1882–   ]

Could we have some butter for
The Royal slice of bread?
The King's Breakfast

"Nobody, my darling,
Could call me
A fussy man —
   BUT
I do like a little bit of butter to my
   bread!"
Ibid.

It isn't really
Anywhere!
It's somewhere else
Instead!
Halfway Down. Stanza 2

If I were a bear,
   And a big bear, too,
I shouldn't much care
   If it froze or snew.
Furry Bear

What shall I call my dear little dor-
   mouse?
His eyes are small, but his tail is e-nor-
   mouse.
The Christening

Christopher Robin goes
Hoppity, hoppity,
Hoppity, hoppity, hop.
Whenever I tell him
Politely to stop it, he
Says he can't possibly stop.
Hoppity

James James
Morrison Morrison
Weatherby George Dupree
Took great
Care of his Mother
Though he was only three.
James James
Said to his Mother,
"Mother," he said, said he:
You must never go down to the end of
   the town, if you don't go down with
   me.
Disobedience

FRANKLIN DELANO
ROOSEVELT
[1882–   ]

The forgotten man [1] at the bottom of
the economic pyramid.
Radio address [April 7, 1932]

The only thing we have to fear is
fear itself.
First Inaugural Address
[March 4, 1933]

In the field of world policy I would
dedicate this nation to the policy of the
good neighbor.[2]
Ibid.

For the trust reposed in me I will return the courage and the devotion that
befit the time. I can do no less. We face
the arduous days that lie before us in
the warm courage of national unity;
with the clear consciousness of seeking
old and precious moral values; with the
clean satisfaction that comes from the
stern performance of duty by old and
young alike. We aim at the assurance of
a rounded and permanent national life.
We do not distrust the future of essential democracy.
Ibid.

Continued dependence upon relief in-
duces a spiritual and moral disintegra-
tion fundamentally destructive to the
national fibre. To dole out relief in this

[1] Wealth comes only from production, and
all that the wrangling grabbers, loafers and
jobbers get to deal with comes from somebody's toil and sacrifice. Who, then, is he who
provides it all? The Forgotten Man . . .
delving away in patient industry, supporting
his family, paying his taxes, casting his vote,
supporting the church and the school . . .
but he is the only one for whom there is no
provision in the great scramble and the big
divide. Such is the Forgotten Man. He works,
he votes, generally he prays — but he always
pays. . . . All the burdens fall on him, or on
her, for the Forgotten Man is not seldom a
woman. — WILLIAM GRAHAM SUMNER [1840–
1910], Professor of Political and Social Science
at Yale: *The Forgotten Man* [1883], a speech
[2] I am as desirous of being a good neighbor
as I am of being a bad subject. — HENRY
DAVID THOREAU: *On the Duty of Civil Disobedience* [1848]

way is to administer a narcotic, a subtle destroyer of the human spirit.

> *Message to Congress*
> *[January 4, 1935]*

I hope that calm counsel and constructive leadership will provide the steadying influence and the time necessary for the coming of new and more practical forms of representative government throughout the world wherein privilege will occupy a lesser place and welfare a greater.

> *Ibid.*

Economic royalists.

> *Speech accepting renomination*
> *[June 27, 1936]*

This generation of Americans has a rendezvous with destiny.

> *Ibid.*

We have always known that heedless self-interest was bad morals; we know now that it is bad economics.

> *Second Inaugural Address*
> *[January 20, 1937]*

The change in the moral climate of America.

> *Ibid.*

The test of our progress is not whether we add more to the abundance of those who have much; it is whether we provide enough for those who have too little.

> *Ibid.*

If they can take it, I can.

> *Replying to the suggestion that the inauguration ceremony be held indoors on account of bad weather [January 20, 1937]*

JAMES STEPHENS
[1882–   ]

I hear a sudden cry of pain!
There is a rabbit in a snare.

> *The Snare*

I saw God! Do you doubt it?
Do you dare to doubt it?
I saw the Almighty Man! His hand
Was resting on a mountain! And
He looked upon the World, and all
about it.

> *What Tomas Said in a Pub.*
> *Stanza 1*

Forgive us all our trespasses,
Little creatures, everywhere!

> *Little Things. Stanza 5*

Let the man who has and doesn't give
Break his neck, and cease to live!
Let him who gives without a care
Gather rubies from the air!

> *In the Imperative Mood*

When you walk in a field,
Look down
Lest you tramp
On a daisy's crown!

> *When You Walk. Stanza 1*

God help the horse, and the driver too!
And the people and beasts who have
never a friend!

> *To the Four Courts, Please.*
> *Stanza 3*

In cloud and clod to sing
Of everything and anything.

> *The Pit of Bliss*

Women are wiser than men because they know less and understand more.

> *The Crock of Gold. Chap. 2*

Virtue is the performance of pleasant actions.

> *Ibid. Chap. 10*

Women and birds are able to see without turning their heads, and that is indeed a necessary provision, for they are both surrounded by enemies.

> *The Demi-Gods. Chap. 2*

If a person desires to be a humorist it is necessary that the people around him shall be at least as wise as he is, otherwise his humor will not be comprehended.

> *Ibid. Chap. 27*

Something depressing comes on the mind when it has been too extensively occupied with the female sex.

> *In the Land of Youth. Chap. 28*

VIRGINIA WOOLF [1]
[1882–   ]

Those comfortably padded lunatic asylums which are known, euphemistically, as the stately homes of England.

> *The Common Reader. Lady*
> *Dorothy Nevill*

---

[1] Virginia Woolf is the best living example of that sort of mind which had its innings

Trivial personalities decomposing in the eternity of print.

The Common Reader. The Modern Essay

There is no room for the impurities of literature in an essay.

Ibid.

That complete statement which is literature.

Ibid. How It Strikes a Contemporary

The word-coining genius, as if thought plunged into a sea of words and came up dripping.

Ibid. An Elizabethan Play

MORRIS BISHOP
[1883–　]

After the day is over
　And the passers-by are rare
The lights burn low in the barber-shop
　And the shades are drawn with care
To hide the haughty barbers
　Cutting each other's hair.

The Tales the Barbers Tell

And on the pedestal these words appear:
"My name is Ozymandias, king of kings!
Look on my works, ye Mighty, and despair!"
Also the names of Emory P. Gray,
Mr. and Mrs. Dukes, and Oscar Baer,
Of 17 West 4th Street, Oyster Bay.

Ozymandias Revisited [1]

BADGER CLARK, JR.
[1883–　]

I waste no thought on my neighbor's birth
Or the way he makes his prayer.

---

in letters in the eighteenth century — a mind partly critical, partly philosophical, highly imaginative, incapable of the vaster emotions but so subtle in its emotionalized intellectuality, so polished, that it makes most other contemporary writers appear to be parvenus of the intellect. — MARY M. COLUM in *The New York Herald-Tribune, May 8, 1927*

The talent of this generation which is most certain of survival. — REBECCA WEST: *Ending in Earnest* [1931]

[1] SHELLEY: *Ozymandias of Egypt.*

I grant him a white man's room on earth
If his game is only square.
While he plays it straight I'll call him mate;
If he cheats I drop him flat.

The Westerner. Stanza 3

O Lord, I've never lived where churches grow,
I love creation better as it stood
That day You finished it so long ago,
And looked upon Your work and called it good.

A Cowboy's Prayer. Stanza 1

I thank You, Lord, that I am placed so well,
That You have made my freedom so complete,
That I'm no slave of whistle, clock, or bell,
No weak-eyed prisoner of wall and street.

Ibid. Stanza 2

And guide me on the long, dim trail ahead
That stretches upward toward the Great Divide.

Ibid. Stanza 4

Oh, stranger, tell my pards below
I took a rampin' dream in tow,
And if I never lay him low,
　I'll never turn him loose!

The Glory Trail [also known as High-Chin Bob]

ARTHUR DAVISON FICKE
[1883–　]

When this my mortal course is run
And I withdraw to far retreat
Among the angels, there is one
I hope with all my heart to meet —
That worthy prelate Dr. Donne
Strolling down the Celestial Street.

Soul in Torment. Stanza 1

Put up his spear, his knightly pennon furled,
And died of the unworthiness of the world.

Don Quixote. IV

O great Don Quixote! Let your reckless mood
Still be our light, through midnights of despair —

That we, though knowing all that once
    you knew,
Hopeless and grim, adventure forth with
    you!
      Nocturne in a Library [*Phi Beta*
         Kappa Poem, Harvard, 1925]

I am in love with high far-seeing places
    That look on plains half-sunlight and
      half-storm,
In love with hours when from the cir-
    cling faces
    Veils pass, and laughing fellowship
      glows warm.
    Sonnets of a Portrait-Painter. XIII

No man of elder years than fifty
Should be empowered with lands and
    gold.
It turns them shrewd and over-thrifty,
It makes them cruel and blind and cold.
      Youth and Age. Stanza 1

Old men in impotence can beget
New wars to kill the lusty young.
Young men can sing: old men forget
That any song was ever sung.
        Ibid. Stanza 3

Those great obscure momentous souls
Whom fame does not record,
Whose impulse still our fate controls
With deathless deed or word.
    Immortals in Exile. Stanza 2

. . . the snivelling servant maid
With injured peevish look,
Who on the lagging fire-coals laid
Carlyle's long-labored book.
        Ibid. Stanza 4

. . . The Man from Porlock strode
Whose visit broke the wizard song
Of Kubla Khan's abode.
        Ibid. Stanza 6

Men who perhaps down wells have
    thrown
Plays of Euripides.
        Ibid. Stanza 7

Or sold some budding Shakespeare
    drink,
Or shut in cells some Blake,
Or forced some Shelley to death's brink
For true religion's sake.
        Ibid. Stanza 8

LOUISA FLETCHER

I wish that there were some wonderful
    place
    Called the Land of Beginning Again.
      The Land of Beginning Again.
                Stanza 1

I am the color of audacity,
    Of rhythmic tribal dance, of tropic
      love;
I am that tint released upon the air
    When cymbals kiss, or comets meet
    above.
      Mandarin Red. Stanza 1

KAHLIL GIBRAN
[1883–1931]

Let there be spaces in your together-
ness.
      The Prophet. On Marriage
You are the bows from which your
children as living arrows are sent forth.
      Ibid. On Children
You give but little when you give of
your possessions. It is when you give of
yourself that you truly give.[1]
      Ibid. On Giving
Work is love made visible. And if you
cannot work with love but only with
distaste, it is better that you should
leave your work and sit at the gate of
the temple and take alms of those who
work with joy.
      Ibid. On Work.
The lust for comfort, that stealthy
thing that enters the house a guest, and
then becomes a host, and then a master.
      Ibid. On Houses
The master spirit of the earth shall
not sleep peacefully upon the wind till
the needs of the least of you are satisfied.
      Ibid. On Buying and Selling
When one of you falls down he falls
for those behind him, a caution against
the stumbling stone. Ay, and he falls
for those ahead of him, who though
faster and surer of foot, yet removed
not the stumbling stone.
      Ibid. On Crime and Punishment

[1] The gift without the giver is bare.
    LOWELL: *The Vision of Sir Launfal,*
                Part II, VIII

What is evil but good tortured by its own hunger and thirst.

The Prophet. On Good and Evil

You pray in your distress and in your need; would that you might pray also in the fullness of your joy and in your days of abundance.

Ibid. On Prayer

Beauty is eternity gazing at itself in a mirror.

Ibid. On Beauty

He who wears his morality but as his best garment were better naked.

Ibid. On Religion

What is it to cease breathing, but to free the breath from its restless tides, that it may rise and expand and seek God unencumbered?

Ibid. On Death

I have learned silence from the talkative, toleration from the intolerant, and kindness from the unkind; yet strange, I am ungrateful to those teachers.

Sand and Foam

An exaggeration is a truth that has lost its temper.

Ibid.

Sadness is a wall between two gardens.

Ibid.

We shall never understand one another until we reduce the language to seven words.

Ibid.

HARRY KEMP
[1883–   ]

I pitied him in his blindness;
But can I boast, "I see"?
Perhaps there walks a spirit
Close by, who pities me.

Blind. Stanza 2

Joses, the brother of Jesus, plodded from day to day,
With never a vision within him to glorify his clay;
Joses, the brother of Jesus, was one with the heavy clod,

But Christ was the soul of rapture and soared, like a lark, with God.

Joses, Brother of Jesus.[1] Stanza 1

GEOFFREY ANKETELL STUDDERT-KENNEDY ("WOODBINE WILLIE")[2]
[1883–1929]

When Jesus came to Birmingham, they simply passed Him by,
They never hurt a hair of Him, they only let Him die.

Indifference

HOWARD ARNOLD WALTER
[1883–1918]

I would be true, for there are those who trust me;
I would be pure, for there are those who care;
I would be strong, for there is much to suffer;
I would be brave, for there is much to dare.

My Creed

ANNA WICKHAM (MRS. PATRICK HEPBURN)
[1883–   ]

The true male never yet walked
Who liked to listen when his mate talked.

The Affinity

From a wealth of living I have proved
I must be silent, if I would be loved.

Ibid.

My mind is like a catacomb, where early Christians pray.

Ibid.

Because of the body's hunger are we born,
And by contriving hunger are we fed;
Because of hunger is our work well done,
And so our songs well sung, and things well said.

Sehnsucht

---

[1] Is not his mother called Mary? and his brethren, James, and Joses, and Simon, and Judas? — *Matthew, XIII, 55*

[2] The affectionate nickname given him by the soldiers to whom, while chaplain, he distributed cigarettes in the trenches.

For all the frittered days
That I have spent in shapeless ways,
Give me one perfect thing.
Envoi

LAURA BENÉT
[1884–   ]

Lost in the spiral of his conscience, he
  Detachedly takes rest.
The Snail. Stanza 1

He spoke: she teetered up
  On pink rheumatic feet;
"Go forth, my dove," he said,
  "That we may eat."
Noah's Dove. Stanza 6

JAMES ELROY FLECKER
[1884–1915]

I who am dead a thousand years,
  And wrote this sweet archaic song,
Send you my words for messengers
  The way I shall not pass along.
To a Poet a Thousand Years
Hence. Stanza 1

O friend unseen, unborn, unknown,
  Student of our sweet English tongue,
Read out my words at night, alone:
  I was a poet, I was young.
Ibid. Stanza 5

Since I can never see your face,
  And never shake you by the hand,
I send my soul through time and space
  To greet you. You will understand.
Ibid. Stanza 6

God be thy guide from camp to camp:
  God be thy shade from well to well;
God grant beneath the desert stars thou
  hear the Prophet's camel bell.
Gates of Damascus

Yet is not death the great adventure
  still,
And is it all loss to set ship clean anew,
When heart is young and life an eagle
  poised?
The Burial in England

I am Don Juan, curst from age to age
By priestly tract and sentimental stage:
Branded a villain or believed a fool,
Battered by hatred, seared by ridicule.
Don Juan Declaims

At last they knew that they had died
When they heard music in that land,
And some one there stole forth a hand
To draw a brother to his side.
Tenebris Interlucentem. Stanza 2

The lean and swarthy poet of despair.
Envoy

I have seen old ships sail like swans
  asleep
Beyond the village which men still call
  Tyre.
The Old Ships

That talkative, bald-headed seaman
  came
(Twelve patient comrades sweating at
  the oar)
From Troy's doom-crimson shore,
And with great lies about his wooden
  horse
Set the crew laughing, and forgot his
  course.
Ibid.

My brother and good friend, the Sun.
A Western Voyage

West of these out of seas colder than
  the Hebrides
    I must go
Where the fleet of stars is anchored and
  the young
      Star-captains glow.
The Dying Patriot

We who with songs beguile your pilgrimage
  And swear that Beauty lives though
  lilies die,
We Poets of the proud old lineage
  Who sing to find your hearts, we know
  not why.
The Golden Journey to Samar-
kand. Prologue

When even lovers find their peace at
  last,
  And Earth is but a star, that once had
  shone.
Ibid.

What would ye, ladies? It was ever
  thus;
  Men are unwise and curiously
  planned.
They have their dreams and do not
  think of us.

We make the Golden Journey to
Samarkand.
The Golden Journey to Samar-
kand. Epilogue

Out he goes: the mirror strains to kiss
her darling; out he goes!
Since the flame is out, the water can
but freeze.
The water froze.
The Hammam Name: Poem by
a Turkish Lady. Stanza 6

A ship, an isle, a sickle moon —
With few but with how splendid stars.
A Ship, An Isle, A Sickle Moon

I am emptied of all my dreams:
I only hear Earth turning, only see
Ether's long bankless streams,
And only know I should drown if you
laid not your hand on me.
Stillness. Stanza 3

FANNY HEASLIP LEA
[1884–   ]

It's odd to think we might have been
Sun, moon and stars unto each
other —
Only, I turned down one little street
As you went up another.
Fate. Stanza 5

KEITH PRESTON
[1884–1927]

Imperial Caesar dead and turned to
clay
Estopped a hole to keep the wind away;
The great god Ra whose shrine once
covered acres
Is filler now for cross-word puzzle
makers.
The Destiny That Shapes Our Ends

Love, lay thy phobias to rest,
Inhibit thy taboo!
We twain shall share, forever blest,
A complex built for two.
Love Song, Freudian

Among our literary scenes,
Saddest this sight to me,
The graves of little magazines
That died to make verse free.
The Liberators

He must not laugh at his own wheeze:
A snuff box has no right to sneeze.
The Humorist

RUTH MASON RICE
[1884–1927]

A curve for the shore,
A line for the lea,
A tint for the sky —
Where the sunrise will be;
A stroke for a gull,
A sweep for the main;
The skill to do more,
With the will to refrain.
A Japanese Print

ODELL SHEPARD
[1884–   ]

October in New England,
And I not there to see
The glamour of the goldenrod,
The flame of the maple tree!
Home Thoughts. Stanza 1

SIR JOHN COLLINGS SQUIRE
[1884–   ]

Princess, inscribe beneath my name:
"He never begged, he never sighed,
He took his medicine as it came";
For this the poets lived — and died.
Ballade of the Poetic Life. Envoi

And stared, and saw, and did not under-
stand,
Columbus's doom-burdened caravels
Slant to the shore, and all their seamen
land.
Sonnet

SARA TEASDALE
[1884–1933]

When I am dead and over me bright
April
Shakes out her rain-drenched hair,
Though you should lean above me
broken-hearted,
I shall not care.
I Shall Not Care. Stanza 1

When I can look Life in the eyes,
Grown calm and very coldly wise,

Life will have given me the Truth,
And taken in exchange — my youth.
Wisdom

How many million Aprils came
  Before I ever knew
How white a cherry bough could be,
  A bed of squills, how blue!
Blue Squills. Stanza 1

Strephon's kiss was lost in jest,
  Robin's lost in play,
But the kiss in Colin's eyes
  Haunts me night and day.
The Look. Stanza 2

Let it be forgotten, as a flower is forgotten,
  Forgotten as a fire that once was singing gold,
Let it be forgotten for ever and ever,
  Time is a kind friend, he will make us old.
Let It Be Forgotten. Stanza 1

I must have passed the crest a while ago
  And now I am going down —
Strange to have crossed the crest and not to know,
  But the brambles were always catching the hem of my gown.
The Long Hill. Stanza 1

Never think she loves him wholly,
  Never believe her love is blind,
All his faults are locked securely
  In a closet of her mind.
Appraisal

I make the most of all that comes,
  And the least of all that goes.
The Philosopher. Stanza 4

DAVID HERBERT
LAWRENCE
[1885–1930]

I never saw a wild thing
Sorry for itself.
Self-Pity

When I wish I was rich, then I know I am ill.
Riches

When I read Shakespeare I am struck with wonder

That such trivial people should muse and thunder
In such lovely language.
When I Read Shakespeare. Stanza 1

And Hamlet, how boring, how boring to live with,
So mean and self-conscious, blowing and snoring
His wonderful speeches, full of other folks' whoring!
Ibid. Stanza 3

My mother was a superior soul
  A superior soul was she,
Cut out to play a superior rôle
  In the god-damn bourgeoisie.
Red-Herring. Stanza 2

Tell me a word
That you've often heard
Yet it makes you squint
If you see it in print!
Conundrums. Stanza 1

Tell me what's wrong
With words or with you
That you don't mind the thing
Yet the name is taboo.
Ibid. Stanza 4

Men are free when they are in a living homeland, not when they are straying and breaking away. . . . The most unfree souls go west, and shout of freedom. Men are freest when they are most unconscious of freedom. The shout is a rattling of chains.
Studies in Classic American Literature. Chap. 1

One realm we have never conquered — the pure present. One great mystery of time is terra incognita to us — the instant. The most superb mystery we have hardly recognized — the immediate, instant self. The quick of all time is the instant. The quick of all the universe, of all creation, is the incarnate, carnal self.
New Poems. Preface

It has been a savage enough pilgrimage.
Quoted by CATHERINE CARSWELL *in The Savage Pilgrimage, a biography*

The dead don't die. They look on and help. .

> *Quoted by* CATHERINE CARS-
> WELL *in The Savage Pilgrimage,
> a biography*

RINGGOLD WILMER
LARDNER
[1885–1933]

A good many young writers make the mistake of enclosing a stamped, self-addressed envelope, big enough for the manuscript to come back in. This is too much of a temptation to the editor.

Personally I have found it a good scheme to not even sign my name to the story, and when I have got it sealed up in its envelope and stamped and addressed, I take it to some town where I don't live and mail it from there. The editor has no idea who wrote the story, so how can he send it back? He is in a quandary.

> *How to Write Short Stories*

Mother set facing the front of the train, as it makes her giddy to ride backwards. I set facing her, which does not affect me.

> *The Golden Honeymoon*

Mother pointed out that she had the money.

"Well," I said, "we are in Washington and I could of borrowed from the United States Treasury. I would of pretended I was an Englishman."

> *Ibid.*

SINCLAIR LEWIS
[1885–   ]

Babbitt's spectacles had huge, circular, frameless lenses of the very best glass; the ear-pieces were thin bars of gold. In them he was the modern business man; one who gave orders to clerks and drove a car and played occasional golf and was scholarly in regard to Salesmanship . . . a Solid Citizen.

> *Babbitt. Chap.* 1

A sensational event was changing from the brown suit to the gray the contents of his pockets. He was earnest about these objects. They were of eternal importance, like baseball or the Republican Party. They included a fountain pen and a silver pencil (always lacking a supply of new leads) which belonged in the righthand upper vest pocket. Without them he would have felt naked. On his watch-chain were a gold penknife, silver cigar-cutter, seven keys (the use of two of which he had forgotten), and incidentally a good watch. Depending from the chain was a large, yellowish elk's-tooth — proclamation of his membership in the Brotherly and Protective Order of Elks. Most significant of all was his loose-leaf pocket note-book, that modern and efficient note-book which contained the addresses of people whom he had forgotten, prudent memoranda of postal money-orders which had reached their destinations months ago, stamps which had lost their mucilage, clippings of verses by T. Cholmondeley Frink and of the newspaper editorials from which Babbitt got his opinions and his polysyllables, notes to be sure and do things which he did not intend to do, and one curious inscription — D.S.S.D.M.Y.P. D.F.[1]

> *Babbitt. Chap.* 1

Not only Gopher Prairie, but ten thousand towns from Albany to San Diego . . . not a dozen buildings which suggested that, in the fifty years of Gopher Prairie's existence, the citizens had realized that it was either desirable or possible to make this, their common home, amusing or attractive.

> *Main Street. Chap.* 4

Pastoral visiting:
  No partiality.
  Don't neglect hired girls, be cordial.
  Guard conversation, pleasing manner
    and laugh and maybe one funny
    story but no scandal or crit. of
    others.
  Stay only 15–30 minutes.
  Ask if like to pray with, not insist.

---

[1] Don't Smoke So Damn Much You Poor Damn Fool.

Rem gt opportunities during sickness, sorrow, marriage.

Ask jokingly why husband not oftener to church.

Elmer Gantry. Chap. 8, notes on Practical Theology lectures

Love:
a rainbow
AM & PM star
from cradle to tomb
inspires art etc. music voice of love
slam atheists etc. who not appreciate
love

Ibid. Chap. 10, Elmer's notes for sermon

I can be whatever I will to be; I turn my opened eyes on my Self and possess whatever I desire.

I am God's child, God created all good things including wealth, and I will to inherit it.

I am resolute — I am utterly resolute — I fear no man, whether in offices or elsewhere.

Power is in me, encompassing you to my demands.

Hold fast, O Subconscious, the thought of Prosperity.

In the divine book of achievements my name is written in Gold. I am thus of the world's nobility and now, this moment, I take possession of my kingdom.

Ibid. Chap. 16, Elmer's incantation

Between the Pulitzer Prizes, the American Academy of Arts and Letters and its training-school the National Institute of Arts and Letters, amateur boards of censorship, and the inquisition of earnest literary ladies, every compulsion is put upon writers to become safe, polite, obedient, and sterile. In protest, I declined election to the National Institute of Arts and Letters some years ago, and now I must decline the Pulitzer Prize.

I invite other writers to consider the fact that by accepting the prizes and approval of these vague institutions, we are admitting their authority, publicly confirming them as the final judges of literary excellence, and I inquire whether any prize is worth that subservience.

Letter declining the Pulitzer Prize for his novel, Arrowsmith [1926]

To a true-blue professor of literature in an American university, literature is not something that a plain human being, living today, painfully sits down to produce. No; it is something dead; it is something magically produced by superhuman beings who must, if they are to be regarded as artists at all, have died at least one hundred years before the diabolical invention of the typewriter. To any authentic don, there is something slightly repulsive in the thought that literature could be created by any ordinary human being, still to be seen walking the streets, wearing quite commonplace trousers and coat and looking not so unlike a chauffeur or a farmer. Our American professors like their literature clear and cold and pure and very dead.

The American Fear of Literature, address given at Stockholm, on receiving the Nobel Prize for Literature [December 12, 1930]

WILLIAM ALEXANDER PERCY
[1885–]

I heard a bird at break of day
  Sing from the autumn trees
A song so mystical and calm,
  So full of certainties.

Overtones

EZRA POUND
[1885–]

Sing we for love and idleness,
Naught else is worth the having.

An Immorality

And I would rather have my sweet,
Though rose-leaves die of grieving,
Than do high deeds in Hungary
To pass all men's believing.

Ibid.

They'll no get him a' in a book I think
Though they write it cunningly;
No mouse of the scrolls was the Goodly
    Fere
But aye loved the open sea.
        Ballad of the Goodly Fere,[1]
            Stanza 6

"Ye ha' seen me heal the lame and blind,
And wake the dead," says he.
"Ye shall see one thing to master all:
'Tis how a brave man dies on the tree."
            Ibid. Stanza 8

A master of men was the Goodly Fere,
A mate of the wind and sea.
If they think they ha' slain our Goodly
    Fere
They are fools eternally.
            Ibid. Stanza 13

For God, our God, is a gallant foe that
    playeth behind the veil.
Whom God deigns not to overthrow hath
    need of triple mail.
        Ballad for Gloom. Stanza 7

Winter is icummen in,
Lhude sing Goddamm,
Raineth drop and staineth slop,
And how the wind doth ramm!
        Sing: Goddamm.
            Ancient Music

I beg you, my friendly critics,
Do not set about to procure me an
    audience.
I mate with my free kind upon the crags.
            Tenzone

Go, my songs, to the lonely and the un-
    satisfied,
Go also to the nerve-wracked, go to the
    enslaved-by-convention,
Bear to them my contempt for their op-
    pressors.
            Commission

Lovely thou art, to hold me close and
    kisst,
Now cry the birds out in the meadow
    mist,
Despite the cuckold, do thou as thou
    list,
So swiftly goes the night,
        And day comes on!
            Langue D'Oc. Vergier

[1] Companion.

They will come no more,
The old men with beautiful manners.
            I Vecchii

Real education must ultimately be
limited to men who insist on knowing
the rest is mere sheep-herding.
        A, B, C of Reading. Page 70
            [1934]

It is only after long experience that
most men are able to define a thing in
terms of its own genus, painting as
painting, writing as writing. You can
spot the bad critic when he starts by
discussing the poet and not the poem.
            Ibid. Page 71

There is no reason why the same man
should like the same book at 18 and at
48.
            Ibid. Page 72

Any one who is too lazy to master
the comparatively small glossary necessary to understand Chaucer deserves to
be shut out from the reading of good
books forever.
            Ibid. Page 87

Men do not understand books until
they have had a certain amount of life,
or at any rate no man understands a
deep book, until he has seen and lived
at least part of its contents.
            Ibid. Page 88

WILLIAM LEROY STIDGER
[1885–   ]

I saw God wash the world last night.
    Ah, would He had washed me
As clean of all my dust and dirt
    As that old white birch tree.
        I Saw God Wash the World.
            Stanza 5

LOUIS UNTERMEYER
[1885–   ]

May nothing evil cross this door
And may ill fortune never pry
About these windows; may the roar
And rains go by.
        Prayer for a New House. Stanza 1

And though these shattering walls are
    thin,

May they be strong to keep hate out
  And hold love in.
          Prayer for a New House. Stanza 4

God, if You wish for our love,
  Fling us a handful of stars!
          Caliban in the Coal Mines.
                        Stanza 4

God, though this life is but a wraith,
  Although we know not what we use,
Although we grope with little faith,
  Give me the heart to fight — and
    lose.
          Prayer. Stanza 1

Open my ears to music; let
  Me thrill with Spring's first flutes
    and drums —
But never let me dare forget
  The bitter ballads of the slums.
          Ibid. Stanza 4

God, keep me still unsatisfied.
          Ibid. Stanza 5

Is it a tribute or betrayal when
Turning from all the sweet, accustomed
    ways,
I leave your lips and eyes to see you in
Some other face?
          The Wanderer. Stanza 1

Why has our poetry eschewed
The rapture and response of food?
What hymns are sung, what praises said
For home-made miracles of bread?
          Food and Drink

Proverbial parsnips; muscular cheese.
          Ibid.

Eternity is thrust upon
A bit of earth, a senseless stone.
A grain of dust, a casual clod
Receives the greatest gift of God.
          Irony. Stanza 1

There is no kind of death to kill
The sands that lie so meek and still . . .
But Man is great and strong and wise —
    And so he dies.
          Ibid. Stanza 2

HUMBERT WOLFE
[1885–   ]

All I had, you thought, was given —
  Life and ladies, you were wrong;
In a poet's secret heaven
  There is always one last song.
          Heine's Last Song

Even he is half afraid of,
  Even he but hears in part,
For the stuff that it is made of,
  Ladies, is the poet's heart.
          Heine's Last Song

Who thought of the lilac?
"I," dew said,
"I made up the lilac
out of my head."
          The Lilac. Stanza 1

Like a small grey
coffee-pot
sits the squirrel.
          The Grey Squirrel. Stanza 1

What will they give me, when journey's
    done?
Your own room to be quiet in, Son!
          Journey's End

ZOË AKINS
[1886–   ]

So much do I love wandering,
  So much I love the sea and sky,
That it will be a piteous thing
  In one small grave to lie.
          The Wanderer. Stanza 2

Nothing seems so tragic to one who
is old as the death of one who is young,
and this alone proves that life is a good
thing.
          The Portrait of Tiero

CLIFFORD BAX
[1886–   ]

Count me not with those that whine
    for what is over, —
All that once was good is good for ever-
    more.
          Musician. Stanza 12

All we had of joy endures, a joy within
    us;
All the rest of life is lovelier for those
    years.
          Ibid. Stanza 13

WILLIAM ROSE BENÉT
[1886–   ]

I flung my soul to the air like a falcon
    flying. . . .
  I shall start a heron soon

In the marsh beneath the moon —
A strange white heron rising with silver
    on its wings.
          The Falconer of God. Stanza 1

I beat forever
The fens and the sedges.
The pledge is still the same — for all
    disastrous pledges,
    All hopes resigned!
My soul still flies above me for the
    quarry it shall find.
          Ibid. Stanza 4

You are to me what the bowstring is
    to the shaft,
Speeding my purpose aloft and aflame
    and afar.
          Dedication. Stanza 2

Neither will I put myself forward as
    others may do,
Neither, if you wish me to flatter, will
    I flatter you;
I will look at you grimly, and so you
    will know I am true.
          Eternal Masculine. Stanza 1

Rain, with a silver flail;
    Sun, with a golden ball;
Ocean, wherein the whale
    Swims minnow-small.
          Whale. Stanza 1

"With flanged and battering tail,
    With huge and dark baleen,"
He said, "Let there be Whale
    In the Cold and Green!"
          Ibid. Stanza 3

For the Lord said, "Let Whale Be!"
    And there was Whale!
          Ibid. Stanza 22

Monarch is night
Of all eldest things,
Pain and affright,
Rapturous wings.
          Night. Stanza 3

Times she'll be docile as the gentlest
    thing
That ever blinked in fur or folded wing,
And then, like lightning in the dead of
    night,
Fill with wild, crackling, intermitting
    light
My mind and soul and senses, — and
    next be
Aloof, askance as a dryad in a tree.
    The Woodcutter's Wife. Stanza 2

You cannot slay yourself in me,
Nor I — to all eternity —
Destroy my truest self in you.
All that our ingrate thought would do,
All senseless wounds we give and take,
Are powerless — for the other's sake.
          We Ask No Shield. Stanza 3

O Love, a thousand, thousand voices,
    From night to dawn, from dawn to
        night,
Have cried the passion of their choices
    To orb your name and keep it bright.
          The Name of Love. Stanza 1

In vast infant sagacity brooding.
          Mad Blake

Like a knight in glittering armor,
    Laughter
Stood up at his side.
          The Last Ally

Lay her sword by her,
Her steel of spirit,
Her phantom blade,
Lest the loud liar
In his hell inherit
What her soul made.
          For the Eyes Loved —

Time, the dark whale, spouts blithely
    from his spiracle
A jet of memory that makes glad the
    sun.
          Sonnets to My Father. III

Blue oblivion, largely lit, smiled and
    smiled at me.
          Mid-Ocean

Jesse James was a two-gun man
    (*Roll on, Missouri!*)
    Jesse James: American Myth

In seven states he cut up dadoes.
He's gone with the buffler an' the des-
    peradoes.
          Ibid.

I know some force is mighty, some force
    I cannot reach.
I know that words are said to me that
    are not said with speech.
My heart has learned a lesson that I
    can never teach.
Only this I know, that I am overtaken
By a swifter runner Whose breath is
    never shaken,
That I follow on His pace, and that
    round me, as I waken,

Are the headlands of home and the blue
    sea swinging
And the flowers of the valleys their
    fresh scents flinging
And the prophets and the poets, with
    their singing — with their singing!
                  Man Possessed

Who writes poetry imbibes honey
from the poisoned lips of life.
                 Ibid. Preface

Chilled Martini like Ithuriel's spear
Transfixing all dubiety within,
Oiled by an olive and shred of lemon-
    peel!
                    The Martini

Like flame, like wine, across the still
    lagoon
The colors of the sunset stream.
Spectral in heaven as climbs the frail
    veiled moon,
So climbs my dream.
Out of the heart's eternal torture fire
No flaming Phœnix risen —
Only the naked soul, spent with desire,
Bursts its prison.
        Gaspara Stampa. Stanza 1

The gods returned to earth when Venice
    broke
Like Venus from the dawn-encircled
    sea.
Wide laughed the skies with light when
    Venice woke
Crowned of antiquity,
And like a spoil of gems unmined on
    earth
Art in her glorious mind
Jewelled all Italy for joy's rebirth
To all mankind.
               Ibid. Stanza 9

So let it be, let it be,
Fretting all the day!
What is this or that to me
Who talked it out in Tartary
Centuries away!

Yet a while with love I stroll
Bright streets of air,
Silver precincts few extol,
Mist-blue cities of the soul,
Countries here nor there.
       Smooth-Sliding Mincius.
               Stanzas 5 and 6

One speck within vast star-space lying
Awoke, arose, resumed its clothing,
And crawled another day toward dying.
        Animalcule. Stanza 7

Voice of the forum loud and harsh
Full of frog-rhetoric of the marsh;
Awful percipience whose small eye
Views art through ordure of the sty;
Apocalyptic commonplace
Whose every utterance is base —
Yearlong the nations cry to thee,
God of our gods, Stupidity!
        Hymn to Stupidity

You came to climb,
And you endure —
So turn your face to the rock of Time,
Make one more foothold sure!
      Because You Came to Climb

O there beloved, all loved, forever
As light you are, in light you move;
Pride of the father, tears of the mother,
Silver sister and golden brother —
The glowing mind of all endeavor,
The full irradiancy of love.
     Nebular Hypothesis. Stanza 5

Only madmen seize the story
With coals of fire upon their tongue.
            Ibid. Stanza 13

When at our history men stand
    amazed . . .
Our captains may have grown as quaint
And crazed as any medieval saint.
         Ode for an Epoch

VAN WYCK BROOKS
[1886–   ]

His wife not only edited his works
but edited him.
    The Ordeal of Mark Twain
         [1920]. *Chap. 5*

Read, writers of America, the driven,
disenchanted, anxious faces of your
sensitive countrymen; remember the
splendid parts your confrères have
played in the human drama of other
times and other peoples, and ask yourselves whether the hour has not come
to put away childish things and walk
the stage as poets do.
          Ibid. Chap. 11

Even the Concord ice had bubbles in it. As wood and grass were its only staples, Emerson advised his fellow-townsmen to manufacture school-teachers and make them the best in the world.

The Flowering of New England.
Chap. 13

FRANCES CORNFORD
[1886–   ]

I had a little dog and my dog was very small;
He licked me in the face, and he answered to my call;
Of all the treasures that were mine I loved him most of all.
A Child's Dream. Stanza 1

His body covered thick with hair was very good to smell;
His little stomach underneath was pink as any shell;
And I loved him and honoured him, more than words can tell.
Ibid. Stanza 3

Deep in my heart I thought with pride, "I know a person who has died."
A Recollection

JOYCE KILMER
[1886–1918]

The midnight train is slow and old,
But of it let this thing be told,
To its high honor be it said,
It carries people home to bed.
My cottage lamp shines white and clear.
God bless the train that brought me here.
The Twelve-Forty-Five

I think that I shall never see
A poem lovely as a tree.
Trees [1]

A tree that may in Summer wear
A nest of robins in her hair.
Ibid.

Poems are made by fools like me,
But only God can make a tree.
Ibid.

[1] First published in *Poetry: A Magazine of Verse*, Chicago, *August, 1913.*

The pleasantest sort of poet
Is the poet who's old and wise.
Old Poets

The young poet screams forever
About his sex and his soul.
Ibid.

There is no peace to be taken
With poets who are young,
For they worry about the wars to be fought
And the songs that must be sung.
Ibid.

Her lips' remark was: "Oh, you kid!"
Her soul spoke thus (I know it did):
"O king of realms of endless joy,
My own, my golden grocer's boy."
Servant Girl and Grocer's Boy

Pile laurel wreaths upon his grave
Who did not gain, but was, success.
Martin

A house that has echoed a baby's laugh
and held up his stumbling feet,
Is the saddest sight, when it's left alone,
that ever your eyes could meet.
The House with Nobody in It

Main Street bordered with autumn leaves, it was a pleasant thing.
Main Street

But we who inherit the primal curse,
and labour for our bread,
Have yet, thank God, the gift of Home,
though Eden's gate is barred.
The Snowman in the Yard

For nothing keeps a poet
In his high singing mood
Like unappeasable hunger
For unattainable food.
Apology

It is stern work, it is perilous work, to thrust your hand in the sun
And pull out a spark of immortal flame to warm the hearts of men.
The Proud Poet

Unlock the door this evening
And let your gate swing wide,
Let all who ask for shelter
Come speedily inside.
What if your yard be narrow?
What if your house be small?
There is a Guest is coming
Will glorify it all.
Gates and Doors

In a wood they call the Rouge Bouquet
There is a new-made grave to-day,
Built by never a spade nor pick
Yet covered with earth ten metres thick.
Rouge Bouquet
My shoulders ache beneath my pack
(Lie easier, Cross, upon His back).
Prayer of a Soldier in France

DAVID MORTON
[1886–   ]

Corridors, like windy tulip beds,
Of swaying girls and lifted, tossing
heads.
In a Girls' School
Who walks with Beauty has no need of
fear;
The sun and moon and stars keep pace
with him;
Invisible hands restore the ruined year,
And time, itself, grows beautifully dim.
Who Walks with Beauty

SHAEMAS O'SHEEL
[1886–   ]

They went forth to battle, but they al-
ways fell;
Their eyes were fixed above the sul-
len shields;
Nobly they fought and bravely, but not
well,
And sank heart-wounded by a subtle
spell.
*They Went Forth to Battle but
They Always Fell. Stanza 1*
He whom a dream hath possessed
knoweth no more of doubting,
For mist and the blowing of winds and
the mouthing of words he scorns;
Not the sinuous speech of schools he
hears, but a knightly shouting,
And never comes darkness down, but he
greeteth a million morns.
*He Whom a Dream Hath
Possessed. Stanza 1*
The ruin of worlds that fall he views
from eternal arches,
And rides God's battlefield in a flashing
and golden car.
Ibid. Stanza 4

ELIZABETH MADOX ROBERTS
[1886–   ]

I used to think when I was a young-
one, Jasper, that all the things you read
about or hear came to pass in some
country, all in one country somewheres.
"Oh, Mary go and call the cattle home,"
and "Lady Nancy died like it might be
today," all in one country. . . . A country a far piece off. Off past Tennessee
somewheres. But now I know better
and know how the world is, a little.
The Time of Man

SIEGFRIED SASSOON
[1886–   ]

Soldiers are citizens of death's grey
land,
Drawing no dividend from time's to-
morrows.
In the great hour of destiny they stand,
Each with his feuds, and jealousies, and
sorrows.
Soldiers are sworn to action; they must
win
Some flaming, fatal climax with their
lives.
Soldiers are dreamers; when the guns
begin
They think of firelit homes, clean beds,
and wives.
Dreamers
Have you forgotten yet?
Look down and swear by the slain of
the War that you'll never forget.
Aftermath
Guest of those infinitely privileged ones
Whose lives are padded, petrified, and
pleasant.
*On Reading the War Diary of a
Defunct Ambassador. Stanza 3*
The visionless officialized fatuity
That once kept Europe safe for Per-
petuity.
Ibid. Stanza 6
Religion beats me. I'm amazed at folk
Drinking the gospels in and never
scratching
Their heads for questions.
The Old Huntsman

O Jesus, send me a wound today,
And I'll believe in Your bread and wine,
And get my bloody old sins washed
    white!
        Stand-to: Good Friday Morning [1]
"He's a cheery old card," grunted Harry
    to Jack
As they slogged up to Arras with rifle
    and pack. . . .
But he did for them both by his plan of
    attack.
        The General
In me the cave-man clasps the seer,
And garlanded Apollo goes
Chanting to Abraham's deaf ear.
In me the tiger sniffs the rose.
Look in my heart, kind friends, and
    tremble,
Since there your elements assemble.
        The Heart's Journey. VIII
Who will remember, passing through
    this Gate,
The unheroic Dead who fed the guns?
Who shall absolve the foulness of their
    fate, —
Those doomed, conscripted, unvictori-
    ous ones?
        On Passing the New Menin Gate
"Do you remember the five-thirty
from Paddington? What a dear old
train it was!"
        *Memoirs of a Fox-Hunting Man
        (homesick conversation in the
        trenches during the War)*

VINCENT STARRETT
[1886–   ]

Suicide . . . to the many is the final
proof of insanity, and, therefore, in a
writing man (or a painting man) of
genius.
        Buried Caesars. Two Suicides
    The day before yesterday always has
been a glamor day. The present is sordid and prosaic. Time colors history as
it does a meerschaum pipe.
        *Ibid. Robert Neilson Stephens and
        The Costume Novel*

[1] In 1922 a New Zealand publisher was con-
victed of "blasphemous libel" for republish-
ing this poem in his paper.

Centenary celebrations are posterity's tributes to the favored children of
fame; sometimes they are tardy ac-
knowledgments to genius. Too often
does genius sup late, and sometimes it
does not sup at all.
        *Buried Caesars. "Black Beauty"
        and its Author, Anna Sewell*
    Westminster Abbey is a mausoleum;
the book barrows in Charing Cross
Road are resurrection grounds.
        *The Diamond in the Dust Heap
        [1925]*
    When we are collecting books, we are
collecting happiness.
        *The A B C of First Editions
        [1926]*

JOHN HALL WHEELOCK
[1886–   ]

There is a panther caged within my
    breast,
But what his name there is no breast
    shall know
Save mine, nor what it is that drives
    him so,
Backward and forward, in relentless
    quest.
        The Black Panther
When death has carved me to his stern
    design
And of this self only the shell endures,
If any face look down with love on
    mine,
Beloved, may it be yours.
        Finale. Stanza 1
For, as all flesh must die, so all
Now dust, shall live.
        This Quiet Dust
A bit of God Himself I keep
Between two vigils fallen asleep.
        Ibid.

LEONARD BACON
[1887–   ]

Technique! The very word is like the
    shriek
Of outraged Art. It is the idiot name
Given to effort by those who are too
    weak,

Too weary, or too dull to play the
game.
The mighty have no theory of tech-
nique.
Ph.D's. Sophia Trenton
Interpreting the simplest symbol
wrong,
Missing the gold and treasuring the
tin,
Dwelling upon the trivial so long,
And spinning allegory out so thin
That the line parts, and neither brawn
nor brain
Can splice the mainbrace of the mind
again.
Ibid.

Men have laughed at me, that I jotted
down
What was their only title to renown.
Evening in Great Portland Street
(James Boswell speaks)

Let 'em laugh at my notebooks. It was
much
To have the ears of Midas — and the
touch.
Ibid.

O graven Imagist!
Was it then thou, grey Fancy's strang-
est child?
Sweet Anarch, literary Nihilist
Thick warbling thy jaw-breaking
woodnotes wild?
Was it then thou, delicious egotist?
Well of soft incoherence undefiled!
The Banquet of the Poets

Those who dwell upon ivory towers
Have heads of the same material.
Tower of Ivory

Go forth, my book, and take whatever
pounding
The heavy-fisted destinies prepare.
I know you are not anything astound-
ing,
And, to be quite sincere, I don't much
care.
Get off your overcoat. The gong is
sounding.
The enemy has risen from his chair.
He doesn't look so overwhelming, but
His arm is long. Watch for an upper-
cut.
Ulug Beg. Introduction

RUPERT BROOKE [1]
[1887–1915]

Somewhere, behind Space and Time,
Is wetter water, slimier slime!
Heaven

And in that Heaven of all their wish,
There shall be no more land, say fish.
Ibid.

Unkempt about those hedges blows
An English unofficial rose.
The Old Vicarage, Grantchester
[1912]

Curates, long dust, will come and go
On lissom, clerical, printless toe.
Ibid.

England's the one land, I know,
Where men with Splendid Hearts may
go;
And Cambridgeshire, of all England,
The shire of Men who Understand.
Ibid.

Say, is there Beauty yet to find?
And Certainty? and Quiet kind?
Deep meadows yet, for to forget
The lies, and truths, and pain? . . .
oh! yet
Stands the Church clock at ten to three?
And is there honey still for tea?
Ibid.

Breathless, we flung us on the windy
hill,
Laughed in the sun, and kissed the
lovely grass.
The Hill

And then you suddenly cried, and
turned away.
Ibid.

For what they'd never told me of,
And what I never knew,
It was that all the time, my love,
Love would be merely you.
Song

Spend in pure converse our eternal day;
Think each in each, immediately
wise;
Learn all we lacked before; hear, know,
and say

[1] Among all who have been poets and died
young, it is hard to think of one who, both in
life and death, has so typified the ideal radiance of youth and poetry. — GILBERT MUR-
RAY [1915]

What this tumultuous body now denies;
And feel, who have laid our groping
   hands away;
  And see, no longer blinded by our
    eyes.

Sonnet

I have been so great a lover: filled my
   days
So proudly with the splendor of Love's
   praise. . . .
These I have loved:
  White plates and cups, clean-gleam-
    ing . . .
The cool kindliness of sheets, that soon
Smooth away trouble; and the rough
   male kiss
Of blankets; grainy wood; live hair that
   is
Shining and free; blue-massing clouds;
   the keen
Unpassioned beauty of a great machine;
The benison of hot water; furs to touch;
The good smell of old clothes.

The Great Lover

If I should die, think only this of me:
  That there's some corner of a foreign
   field
That is for ever England.

The Soldier

   This heart, all evil shed away,
A pulse in the eternal mind, no less
Gives somewhere back the thoughts by
   England given.

Ibid.

Now, God be thanked, who has matched
   us with his hour,
And caught our youth, and wakened us
   from sleeping.

Peace

The worst friend and enemy is but
   Death.

Ibid.

Blow out, you bugles, over the rich
   dead!
  There's none of these so lonely and
    poor of old,
  But, dying, has made us rarer gifts
    than gold.

The Dead. I

Honour has come back, as a king, to
   earth,

And paid his subjects with a royal
   wage;
And Nobleness walks in our ways
   again;
And we have come into our heritage.

The Dead. I

ISAAC GOLDBERG
[1887–   ]

Diplomacy is to do and say
The nastiest thing in the nicest way.

The Reflex

JAMES NORMAN HALL
[1887–   ]

The thing that numbs the heart is this:
   That men cannot devise
Some scheme of life to banish fear
   That lurks in most men's eyes.

Fear

Fear of the lack of shelter, food,
   And fire for winter's cold;
Fear of their children's lacking these,
   This in a world so old.

Ibid.

This is my sure, my very firm belief:
That life, to one born whole, is worth
   the living,
Well worth the taking, having, and the
   giving.

A Starry Night at Arué

ROBINSON JEFFERS
[1887–   ]

The gulls, the cloud-calligraphers of
   windy spirals before a storm.

The Cycle

Four pelicans went over the house,
Sculled their worn oars over the court-
   yard:
  I saw that ungainliness
Magnifies the idea of strength.

Pelicans

While this America settles in the mould
   of its vulgarity, heavily thickening
   to empire,
And protest, only a bubble in the molten
   mass, pops and sighs out, and the
   mass hardens. . . .

Shine, Perishing Republic.
Stanza 1

You make haste on decay: not blame-
    worthy; life is good, be it stub-
    bornly long or suddenly
A mortal splendor: meteors are not
    needed less than mountains: shine,
    perishing republic.

But for my children, I would have them
    keep their distance from the thick-
    ening center; corruption
Never has been compulsory, when the
    cities lie at the monster's feet there
    are left the mountains.
                Shine, Perishing Republic.
                Stanzas 3 and 4

All these tidal gatherings, growth and
    decay,
Shining and darkening, are forever
Renewed; and the whole cycle impeni-
    tently
Revolves, and all the past is fu-
    ture: ——
Make it a difficult world . . . for prac-
    tical people.
                Practical People

After all, after all we endured, who has
    grown wise?
We take our mortal momentary hour
With too much gesture, the derisive
    skies
Twinkle against our wrongs, our rights,
    our power.
Look up the night, starlight's a steady-
    ing draught
For nerves at angry tension.
        The Truce and the Peace. 7 [1918]

"Loyal to your highest, sensitive, brave,
Sanguine, some few ways wise, you and
    all men are drawn out of this
    depth
Only to be these things you are, as
    flowers for color, falcons for swift-
    ness,
Mountains for mass and quiet. Each for
    its quality
Is drawn out of this depth. Your tragic
    quality
Required the huge delusion of some ma-
    jor purpose to produce it.
What, that the God of the stars needed
    your help?" He said "This is my
    last

Worst pain, the bitter enlightenment
    that buys peace."
            Woodrow Wilson [1924]
All the arts lose virtue
Against the essential reality
Of creatures going about their business
    among the equally
Earnest elements of nature.
                    Boats in a Fog.
Singing to himself the fool south-border
    couplet
"No tengo tabaco, no tengo papel,
No tengo dinero, God damn it to hell."
                        Tamar. VI
Grass that is made each year equals the
    mountains in her past and future;
Fashionable and momentary things we
    need not see nor speak of.
                        Point Joe
Lend me the stone strength of the past
    and I will lend you
The wings of the future, for I have them.
How dear you will be to me when I too
    grow old, old comrade.
            To the Rock That Will Be a
                        Cornerstone
Divinely superfluous beauty
Rules the games, presides over destinies,
    makes trees grow
And hills tower, waves fall.
The incredible beauty of joy.
            Divinely Superfluous Beauty
The beauty of things was born before
    eyes and sufficient to itself; the
    heart-breaking beauty
Will remain when there is no heart to
    break for it.
                        Credo
The heads of strong old age are beauti-
    ful
Beyond all grace of youth. They have
    strange quiet,
Integrity, health, soundness, to the full
They've dealt with life and been atemp-
    ered by it.
                Promise of Peace

ORRICK JOHNS
[1887–]
There's nothing very beautiful and
    nothing very gay

About the rush of faces in the town by
day,
But a light tan cow in a pale green mead,
That is very beautiful, beautiful indeed.
Little Things

And better is a temple made of bark and
thong
Than a tall stone temple that may stand
too long.
Ibid.

Love is a proud and gentle thing, a better thing to own
Than all of the wide impossible stars
over the heavens blown.
The Door

Yet maybe now there passes here,
In reverential dream, a boy
Whose voice shall rise another year
And rouse the sleeping lords of joy.
Second Avenue

He shall bring back the faded bays,
The Muses to their ancient rule,
The temples to the market-place,
The genius nearer to the fool.
Ibid.

SISTER MARY MADELEVA
[1887–   ]

Death is no foeman, we were born to-
gether;
He dwells between the places of my
breath.
Night vigil at my heart he keeps and
whether
I sleep or no, he never slumbereth.
Knights-Errant

It was a bird first spoke to me at Oxford
Through the white fog a single, tentative word.
I Enter Oxford

Oh! there are bells and there are spires
at Oxford,
Ancient, heart-breaking, wordless,
splendorous things;
Only to me belongs this simple, silver
Welcome on wings.
Ibid.

The day you do not write and silence
follows, to be broken only by my
life's end,

I shall know that you have not forgotten, that now you love me perfectly,
For I shall understand that you are
dead.
The Day No Letter Comes

Two doves I bring;
One broods all day;
One has a broken wing;
One is the prayer I have no words to
say;
One is the song I have no words to sing.
Presentation

HARRY IRVING ("H.I.") PHILLIPS
[1887–   ]

Horse-sense in an atmosphere of
Pomp and glory,
Self-effacement in a generation
Of self-salesmanship,
A Vermont Yankee in
King Ballyhoo's Court!
Calvin Coolidge

EDITH SITWELL
[1887–   ]

Down the horn
Of her ear-trumpet I convey
The news that: "It is Judgment Day!"
"Speak louder; I don't catch, my dear."
I roared: *"It is the Trump we hear!"*
"The *What?*" — "The TRUMP!" . . .
"I shall complain —
Those boy-scouts practising again!"
Solo for Ear-Trumpet

Every hundred years or so it becomes
necessary for a change to take place in
the body of poetry . . . a fresh movement appears and produces a few great
men, and once more the force and vigour die from the results of age; the
movement is carried on by weak and
worthless imitators, and a change becomes necessary again.
Poetry and Criticism [*1926*]

ALEXANDER WOOLLCOTT
[1887–   ]

The attitude of the professional players toward the amateurs is best summed up in a raffish story they delight in telling on all occasions. It begins with a touching picture of an old broken-down tragedian sharing a park bench with a bedraggled and unappetizing street-walker. "Ah, Madame," says the tragedian, *"quelle Ironie! The two oldest professions in the world — ruined by amateurs."*

The Knock at the Stage-Door

Beerbohm Tree said what we have all wanted to say of the extra-women in nearly every throne-room and ball-room and school-room scene since the theater began. "Ladies," said Tree, peering at them plaintively through his monocle, "just a little more virginity, if you don't mind."

Capsule Criticism

ELINOR HOYT WYLIE
[1887–1928]

We shall walk in velvet shoes:
　Wherever we go
Silence will fall like dews
　On white silence below.
We shall walk in the snow.

Velvet Shoes. Stanza 4

Avoid the reeking herd,
　Shun the polluted flock,
Live like that stoic bird
　The eagle of the rock.

The Eagle and the Mole. Stanza 1

If you would keep your soul
　From spotted sight or sound,
Live like the velvet mole;
　Go burrow underground.

Ibid. Stanza 5

She, whose song we loved the best,
　Is voiceless in a sudden night;
On your light limbs, O, Loveliest,
　May the dust be light!

On a Singing Girl. Stanza 2

I was, being human, born alone;
　I am, being woman, hard beset;

I live by squeezing from a stone
　The little nourishment I get.

Let No Charitable Hope. Stanza 2

In masks outrageous and austere
The years go by in single file;
But none has merited my fear,
And none has quite escaped my smile.

Ibid. Stanza 3

Farewell, sweet dust; I was never a
　miser:
　Once, for a minute, I made you mine:
Now you are gone, I am none the wiser,
　But the leaves of the willow are
　bright as wine.

Farewell, Sweet Dust. Stanza 4

I have believed that I prefer to live
Preoccupied by a Platonic mind;
I have believed me obdurate and blind
To those sharp ecstasies the pulses give:
The clever body five times sensitive
I never have discovered to be kind
As the poor soul, deceived and half-
　divined,
Whose hopes are water in a witch's
　sieve.

*Angels and Earthly Creatures.
Sonnet VI*

A subtle spirit has my path attended,
In likeness not a lion but a pard;
And when the arrows flew like hail, and
　hard,
He licked my wounds, and all my
　wounds were mended;
And happy I, who walked so well-
　defended,
With that translucid presence for a
　guard,
Under a sky reversed and evil-starred;
A woman by an archangel befriended.

Ibid. Sonnet IX

If any have a stone to throw
It is not I, ever or now.

The Pebble

Alembics turn to stranger things
Strange things, but never while we live
Shall magic turn this bronze that sings
To singing water in a sieve.

*Bronze Trumpets and Sea Wa-
ter (On Turning Latin into English). Stanza 1*

Pity the prickly star that frightens
  The Christ Child with its shattered
    spear;
Pity the midnight when it lightens;
  Pity me, my dear.
                Pity Me. Stanza 3
The worst and best are both inclined
To snap like vixens at the truth;
But, O, beware the middle mind
That purrs and never shows a tooth!
              Nonsense Rhyme. Stanza 2
  Honied words like bees,
Gilded and sticky, with a little sting.
                     Pretty Words
She'd give the shirt from off her back,
  except that
She doesn't wear a shirt, and most men
  do;
And often and most bitterly she's wept
  that
A starving tramp can't eat a silver shoe,
Or some poor beggar, slightly alcoholic,
Enjoy with Donne a metaphysical
  frolic.
          Portrait in Black Paint. Stanza 2
Farewell, incomparable element,
Whence man arose, where he shall not
  return;
And hail, imperfect urn
Of his last ashes, and his firstborn fruit;
Farewell, the long pursuit,
And all the adventures of his discontent.
                 Hymn to Earth. Stanza 1
Hail, element of earth, receive thy own,
And cherish, at thy charitable breast,
This man, this mongrel beast:
He plows the sand, and, at his hardest
  need,
He sows himself for seed.
                      Ibid. Stanza 6
Receive him as thy lover for an hour
Who will not weary, by a longer stay,
The kind embrace of clay.
                      Ibid. Stanza 7

HEYWOOD CAMPBELL
BROUN
[1888–   ]

"You've got a kiss coming to you.
When you live up as far as 168th Street
you've got to do at least that much for
any fellow that takes you home. . . .

"And say, listen, next month I'm going to move to 242nd Street."
              The Boy Grew Older. Chap. 13
The ability to make love frivolously
is the chief characteristic which distin-
guishes human beings from the beasts.
          It Seems to Me. A Spring Sunday
I saw a money-changer in the neighborhood of the temple late yesterday
afternoon, and it did not seem to me
that he was on his way to catch an outbound train. On the contrary, he was
headed up the steps, cool as a cucumber. "I wonder if the old place has
changed," he remarked as we passed.
          Ibid. "The Worst Is Over" [1933]
"Trees" (if I have the name right) is
one of the most annoying pieces of verse
within my knowledge. The other one is
Kipling's "If," with third place reserved
for Henley's "Invictus."
"Trees" maddens me, because it contains the most insincere line ever written by mortal man. Surely the Kilmer
tongue must have been not far from the
Kilmer cheek when he wrote, "Poems
are made by fools like me."
          Ibid. "Trees," "If," and "Invictus"
It is a good trick when a writer can go
out and set down with accuracy some
living being whom he has observed with
fidelity. He holds the mirror up to Nature.
But that is not the furthest reach of
literature. There are a few who venture
forth and say with divine arrogance: "I
see it this way. Let Nature catch up
with my conception."
Life is a copycat and can be bullied
into following the master artist who
bids it come to heel.
              Ibid. Nature the Copycat
I have known people to stop and buy
an apple on the corner and then walk
away as if they had solved the whole
unemployment problem.
                  Ibid. Chummy Charlie
The Irish are the cry-babies of the
Western world. Even the mildest quip
will set them off into resolutions and
protests.
          Ibid. The Piece That Got Me Fired

ANNE CAMPBELL
(MRS. GEORGE W. STARK)
[1888–   ]

You are the trip I did not take;
You are the pearls I cannot buy;
You are my blue Italian lake;
You are my piece of foreign sky.
To My Child

NORMAN DAVEY
[1888–   ]

By the canal in Flanders I watched a
    barge's prow
Creep slowly past the poplar-trees; and
    there I made a vow
That when these wars are over and I
    am home at last
However much I travel I shall not
    travel fast.

Horses and cars and yachts and planes:
    I've no more use for such:
For in three years of war's alarms I've
    hurried far too much;
And now I dream of something sure, si-
    lent and slow and large;
So when the War is over — why, I
    mean to buy a barge.
By the Canal in Flanders

By Charing Cross in London Town
There runs a road of high renown,
Where antique books are ranged on
    shelves
As dark and dusty as themselves.
And many booklovers have spent
Their substance there with great con-
    tent,
And vexed their wives and filled their
    homes
With faded prints and massive tomes.
The Booklover

THOMAS STEARNS ELIOT
[1888–   ]

April is the cruelest month, breeding
Lilacs out of dead land, mixing
Memory and desire, stirring
Dull roots with spring rain.
The Waste Land

But at my back from time to time I hear
The sound of horns and motors, which
    shall bring
Sweeney to Mrs. Porter in the spring.
O the moon shone bright on Mrs. Porter
And on her daughter
They wash their feet in soda water.
The Waste Land

When lovely woman stoops to folly and
Paces about her room again, alone,
She smooths her hair with automatic
    hand,
And puts a record on the gramophone.
Ibid.

We are the hollow men
We are the stuffed men
Leaning together
Headpiece filled with straw. Alas!
Our dried voices, when
We whisper together
Are quiet and meaningless
As wind in dry grass
Or rats' feet over broken glass
In our dry cellar.
The Hollow Men. I

Eyes I dare not meet in dreams
In death's dream kingdom
These do not appear:
There, the eyes are
Sunlight on a broken column
There, is a tree swinging
And voices are
In the wind's singing
More distant and more solemn
Than a fading star.
Ibid. II

This is the way the world ends
Not with a bang but a whimper.
Ibid. V

Where is the Life we have lost in living?
Where is the wisdom we have lost in
    knowledge?
Where is the knowledge we have lost in
    information?
The cycles of Heaven in twenty cen-
    turies
Bring us farther from God and nearer to
    the Dust.
The Rock

Donne, I suppose, was such another
Who found no substitute for sense.
Whispers of Immortality

Uncorseted, her friendly bust
Gives promise of pneumatic bliss.
Whispers of Immortality

Sweeney shifts from ham to ham
Stirring the water in his bath.
The masters of the subtle schools
Are controversial, polymath.
Sunday Morning Service

Reorganized upon the floor
She yawns and draws a stocking up.
Sweeney Among the Nightingales

The evening is spread out against the
sky
Like a patient etherized upon a table.
The Love Song of J. Alfred Prufrock

Should I, after tea and cakes and ices,
Have the strength to force the moment
to its crisis?
But though I have wept and fasted, wept
and prayed,
Though I have seen my head (grown
slightly bald) brought in upon a
platter,
I am no prophet — and here's no great
matter;
I have seen the moment of my greatness
flicker,
And I have seen the eternal Footman
hold my coat, and snicker,
And in short, I was afraid.
Ibid.

No! I am not Prince Hamlet, nor was
meant to be;
Am an attendant lord, one that will do
To swell a progress, start a scene or two
Advise the prince; no doubt, an easy
tool,
Deferential, glad to be of use,
Politic, cautious, and meticulous;
Full of high sentence, but a bit obtuse;
At times, indeed, almost ridiculous —
Almost, at times, the Fool.
Ibid.

I grow old. . . . I grow old. . . .
I shall wear the bottoms of my trousers
rolled.
Ibid.

The readers of the *Boston Evening
Transcript*
Sway in the wind like a field of ripe corn.
The Boston Evening Transcript

Upon the glazen shelves kept watch
Matthew and Waldo, guardians of the
faith,
The army of unalterable law.
Cousin Nancy

The broad-backed hippopotamus
Rests on his belly in the mud;
Although he seems so firm to us
He is merely flesh and blood.
The Hippopotamus

We have been, let us say, to hear the
latest Pole
Transmit the Preludes, through his hair
and finger-tips.
Portrait of a Lady. I

My smile falls heavily among the bric-
à-brac.
Ibid. III

I am aware of the damp souls of house-
maids
Sprouting despondently at area gates.
Morning at the Window

The new years walk, restoring
Through a bright cloud of tears, the
years, restoring
With a new verse the ancient rhyme.
Redeem
The time. Redeem
The unread vision in the higher dream
While jewelled unicorns draw by the
gilded hearse.
Ash-Wednesday. IV

JULIAN GRENFELL
[1888–1915]

All the bright company of Heaven
Hold him in their high comradeship,
The Dog-star, and the Sisters Seven,
Orion's Belt and sworded hip.
Into Battle. Stanza 3

But Day shall clasp him with strong
hands,
And Night shall fold him in soft
wings.
Ibid. Stanza 10

MOLLY ANDERSON (MRS. FRANK LeROY) HALEY
[1888–   ]

Between the tonics and the beauty-
  creams,
This shabby slowly-turning shelf of
  dreams!
*Loan Library at the Corner
Drug Store*

ALINE (MRS. JOYCE) KILMER
[1888–   ]

I shall not be afraid any more,
  Either by night or day;
What would it profit me to be afraid
  With you away?
I Shall Not Be Afraid. Stanza 1

Deborah danced, when she was two,
As buttercups and daffodils do.
Experience

Smilingly, out of my pain,
I have woven a little song;
You may take it away with you.
I shall not sing it again.
Tour de Force

I'm sorry you are wiser,
  I'm sorry you are taller;
I liked you better foolish,
  And I liked you better smaller.
*For the Birthday of a Middle-
Aged Child. Stanza 1*

My heart shall keep the child I knew,
  When you are really gone from me,
And spend its life remembering you
  As shells remember the lost sea.
Prevision (To a Child). Stanza 4

If I live till my fighting days are done
I must fasten my armour on my eldest
  son.
Against the Wall. Stanza 1

Things have a terrible permanence
  When people die.
Things. Stanza 6

THOMAS EDWARD LAWRENCE [1]
[1888–1935]

I loved you, so I drew these tides of men
  into my hands and wrote my will
  across the sky in stars.
*Seven Pillars of Wisdom.
Dedication*

Arabs could be swung on an idea as
on a cord; for the unpledged allegiance
of their minds made them obedient
servants. None of them would escape
the bond till success had come, and with
it responsibility and duty and engage-
ments. Then the idea was gone and the
work ended — in ruins. Without a creed
they could be taken to the four corners
of the world (but not to heaven) by being shown the riches of earth and the
pleasures of it; but if on the road, led
in this fashion, they met the prophet of
an idea, who had nowhere to lay his
head and who depended for his food on
charity or birds, then they would all
leave their wealth for his inspiration.
Ibid. Chap. 3

There could be no honour in a sure
success, but much might be wrested
from a sure defeat. Omnipotence and
the Infinite were our two worthiest foemen, indeed the only ones for a full man
to meet, they being monsters of his own
spirit's making; and the stoutest enemies were always of the household. In
fighting Omnipotence, honour was
proudly to throw away the poor resources that we had, and dare Him
empty-handed.
Revolt in the Desert. Chap. 19

I grew proud of the enemy [the Ger-
mans] who had killed my brothers.
They were two thousand miles from
home, without hope and without guides,
in conditions mad enough to break the
bravest nerves. Yet their sections held
together in firm rank, sheering through
the wrack of Turk and Arab like ar-
moured ships, high-faced and silent.
When attacked they halted, took position, fired to order. There was no haste,

[1] Changed his name to T. E. Shaw, 1927.

no crying, no hesitation. They were glorious.

Revolt in the Desert. Chap. 34

It came upon me freshly how the secret of uniform was to make a crowd solid, dignified, impersonal: to give it the singleness and tautness of an upstanding man. This death's livery which walled its bearers from ordinary life, was sign that they had sold their wills and bodies to the State: and contracted themselves into a service not the less abject for that its beginning was voluntary. Some of them had obeyed the instinct of lawlessness: some were hungry: others thirsted for glamour, for the supposed colour of a military life: but, of them all, those only received satisfaction who had sought to degrade themselves, for to the peace-eye they were below humanity.

Ibid. Chap. 35

Appearing first in the war news from Arabia as a personage rather more incredible than Prester John, and presently emerging into clear definition as the author of one of the great histories of the world, recording his own conquests at an age at which young company officers are hardly allowed to speak at the mess table.

BERNARD SHAW, in *The New York Evening Post, April 16, 1927*

NEWMAN LEVY
[1888–   ]

In Spain, where the courtly Castilian
   hidalgo twangs lightly each night
   his romantic guitar,
Where the castanets clink on the gay
   piazetta, and strains of fandangoes
   are heard from afar,
There lived, I am told, a bold hussy
   named Carmen, a pampered young
   vamp full of devil and guile.
Cigarette and cigar men were smitten
   with Carmen; from near and from
   far men were caught with her smile.

Opera Guyed. Carmen

But here's our friend José who seizes
   her bridle. A wild homicidal glint
   gleams in his eye.
He's mad and disgusted and cries out,
   "You've busted the heart that once
   trusted you. Wed me or die!"
Though Carmen is frightened at how
   this scene might end, I'm forced to
   admit she is game to the last.
She says to him "Banish the notion and
   vanish. *Vamos!*" which is Spanish
   for "run away fast."
A scream and a struggle! She reels and
   she staggers, for Don José's dagger's plunged deep in her breast.
No more will she flirt in her old way,
   that's certain. So ring down the
   curtain, poor Carmen's at rest.

Opera Guyed. Carmen

EUGENE O'NEILL
[1888–   ]

Dat ole davil, sea.

Anna Christie. Act I

We're all poor nuts and things happen, and we yust get mixed in wrong, that's all.

Ibid. Act IV

For de little stealin' dey gits you in jail soon or late. For de big stealin' dey makes you emperor and puts you in de Hall o' Fame when you croaks. If dey's one thing I learns in ten years on de Pullman cars listenin' to de white quality talk, it's dat same fact.

The Emperor Jones. Sc. 1

The child was diseased at birth, stricken with a hereditary ill that only the most vital men are able to shake off. I mean poverty — the most deadly and prevalent of all diseases.

Fog

He couldn't design a cathedral without it looking like the First Supernatural Bank!

The Great God Brown

Yank. Sure! Lock me up! Put me in a cage! Dat's de on'y answer yuh know. G'wan, lock me up!
Policeman. What you been doin'?
Yank. Enough to gimme life for! I was born, see? Sure, dat's de charge.

Write it in de blotter. I was born, get
me!
The Hairy Ape

Our lives are merely strange dark interludes in the electrical display of God
the Father!

Strange Interlude

JOHN CROWE RANSOM
[1888–   ]

Up once I rose, in a fury of heard-of
things,
To travel the splendid sphere and see
its fame;
But the wars and ships and towns and
the roaring kings
But flashed with the image of her!
and back I came.

Sonnet of a Sure Heart

Hands hold much of heat in little stor-
age.
They Hail the Sunrise

The lazy geese, like a snow cloud
Dripping their snow on the green grass,
Tricking and stopping, sleepy and
proud,
Who cried in goose, Alas.

*Bells for John Whitesides'
Daughter*

Here lies a lady of beauty and high degree.
Of chills and fever she died, of fever and
chills,
The delight of her husband, her aunts,
an infant of three,
And of medicos marvelling sweetly on
her ills.
Here Lies a Lady

Two evils, monstrous either one apart,
Possessed me, and were long and loath
at going:
A cry of Absence, Absence, in the heart,
And in the wood the furious winter
blowing.
Winter Remembered

Do they not hear the burst of bells
Pealing at every step you take?
Are not their eyelids winking too,
Feeling your sudden brightness break?
O, too much glory shut with us,
O, walls too narrow and opaque!

O, come into the night with me
And let me speak, for Jesus' sake!
The Lover

Long, long before men die I sometimes
read
Their stoic backs as plain as graveyard
stones.
The Resurrection

And kept their blue eyes blue to any
weather.
Men

Mouth he remembered: the quaint ori-
fice
From which came heat that flamed
upon the kiss.
The Equilibrists

In Heaven you have heard no marriage
is,
No white flesh tinder to your lecheries,
Your male and female tissue sweetly
shaped
Sublimed away, and furious blood
escaped.
Ibid.

Equilibrists lie here; stranger, tread
light;
Close, but untouching in each other's
sight;
Mouldered the lips and ashy the tall
skull,
Let them lie perilous and beautiful.
Ibid.

He rose and was himself again.
Simply another morning, and simply
Jane.
Morning

God have mercy on the sinner
Who must write with no dinner,
No gravy and no grub,
No pewter and no pub,
No belly and no bowels,
Only consonants and vowels.
Survey of Literature

Athens, a fragile kingdom by the foam,
Assumed the stranger's yoke; but then
behold how meek
Those unbred Caesars grew, who spent
their fruits of Rome
Forever after, trying to be Greek.
Triumph

LEW SARETT
[1888–   ]

God, let me flower as I will!
For I am weary of the chill
Companionship of waxen vines
And hothouse-nurtured columbines.
Let Me Flower as I Will. Stanza 1

Walk softly, March, forbear the bitter
    blow;
Her feet within a trap, her blood upon
    the snow,
The four little foxes saw their mother
    go —
Walk softly.
Four Little Foxes. Stanza 2

ALAN SEEGER
[1888–1916]

Whether I am on the winning or losing side is not the point with me: it is
being on the side where my sympathies
lie that matters, and I am ready to see
it through to the end. Success in life
means doing that thing than which
nothing else conceivable seems more noble or satisfying or remunerative, and
this enviable state I can truly say that
I enjoy, for had I the choice I would be
nowhere else in the world than where I
am.[1]
Letter to his mother [July 3, 1915]

I have a rendezvous with Death [2]
At some disputed barricade,
When Spring comes back with rustling
    shade
And apple-blossoms fill the air.
I Have a Rendezvous with Death

---

[1] I think he would not wish himself any
where but where he is. — SHAKESPEARE: *King
Henry V, Act IV, Sc. 1, L. 125*
[2] We who have walked with Death in
France,
When all the world with death was rife,
Who came through all that devils' dance,
When life was but a circumstance,
A sniper's whim, a bullet's glance,
We have a rendezvous with life!
        HERVEY ALLEN: *We, St. 2*
I have a rendezvous with Life,
When Spring's first heralds hum.
    COUNTEE CULLEN: *I Have a Rendez-
        vous with Life*

When Spring trips north again this year,
And I to my pledged word am true,
I shall not fail that rendezvous.
I Have a Rendezvous with Death

MRS. BERTYE YOUNG WILLIAMS
[1888–   ]

The inn was full. There was no room.[1]
    But certainly I could have done
Something if I had known for whom —
    Ah, that my door should be the one
To shut out Mary and her Son!
*The Bethlehem Innkeeper Speaks.
        Stanza 3*

CONRAD AIKEN
[1889–   ]

Music I heard with you was more than
    music,
And bread I broke with you was more
    than bread.
Music I Heard with You. Stanza 1

It is morning, Senlin says, and in the
    morning
When the light drips through the shut-
    ters like the dew,
I arise, I face the sunrise,
And do the things my fathers learned to
    do.
Stars in the purple dusk above the roof-
    tops
Pale in a saffron mist and seem to die,
And I myself on a swiftly tilting planet
Stand before a glass and tie my tie.
Senlin. Morning Song

One by one in the moonlight there,
Neighing far off on the haunted air,
The unicorns come down to the sea.
Ibid. Evening Song

Rock meeting rock can know love bet-
    ter
Than eyes that stare or lips that touch.
All that we know in love is bitter,
And it is not much.
Annihilation. Stanza 8

When trout swim down Great Ormond
    Street,
And sea-gulls cry above them lightly,

---

[1] There was no room for them in the inn. —
Luke, II, 7

And hawthorns heave cold flagstones
up
To blossom whitely. . . .
> *Priapus and the Pool. III*

Then I shall hold my breath and die,
Swearing I never loved you; no,
"You were not lovely!" I shall cry,
"I never loved you so."
> *Ibid.*

How shall we praise the magnificence of
the dead,
The great man humbled, the haughty
brought to dust?
Is there a horn we should not blow as
proudly
For the meanest of us all, who creeps
his days,
Guarding his heart from blows, to die
obscurely?
> *Tetélestai*

HERVEY ALLEN
[1889–   ]

Christ Jesus, when I come to die
Grant me a clean, sweet, summer sky,
Without the mad wind's panther cry.
Send me a little garden breeze
To gossip in magnolia trees;
For I have heard, these fifty years,
Confessions muttered at my ears,
Till every mumble of the wind
Is like tired voices that have sinned.
> *The Priest and the Pirate: A*
> *Ballad of Theodosia Burr.*[1]
> *Stanza 3*

Grow up as soon as you can. It pays.
The only time you really live fully is
from thirty to sixty. . . . The young
are slaves to dreams; the old servants
of regrets. Only the middle-aged have
all their five senses in the keeping of
their wits.
> *Anthony Adverse. Chap. 31*

What is even a wise book but a blast
from the lungs made visible to the eyes?
> *Ibid.*

[1] Theodosia Burr, daughter of Aaron Burr,
perished at sea while on a voyage from
Charleston, S. C., to New York, in January,
1813. The wreck was plundered by pirates.

Practise what I call a decent mam-
malian philosophy.
> *Anthony Adverse. Chap. 31*

ROBERT CHARLES
BENCHLEY
[1889–   ]

I haven't been abroad in so long that
I almost speak English without an accent.
> *The Old Sea Rover Speaks*

*Enter first Lady-in-Waiting (Flour-
ish,*[1] *Hautboys*[2] *and*[3] *torches).*[4]
> *First Lady-in-Waiting*—What[5] ho![6]
> Where[7] is[8] the[9] music?[10]

NOTES

1. *Flourish:* The stage direction here
is obscure. Clarke claims it should read
"flarish," thus changing the meaning
of the passage to "flarish" (that is,
the King's), but most authorities have
agreed that it should remain "flourish,"
supplying the predicate which is to be
flourished. There was at this time a custom in the countryside of England to
flourish a mop as a signal to the passing vender of berries, signifying that
in that particular household there was a
consumer-demand for berries, and this
may have been meant in this instance.
That Shakespeare was cognizant of this
custom of flourishing the mop for berries is shown in a similar passage in the
second part of King Henry IV, where
he has the Third Page enter and say,
"Flourish." Cf. also Hamlet, IV, 7:4.
> *Of All Things. Shakespeare*
> *Explained*

CHARLES DIVINE
[1889–   ]

I wonder who is haunting the little snug
café,
That place, half restaurant and home,
since we have gone away;
The candled dimness, smoke and talk,
and tables brown and bare —
But no one thinks of tablecloths when
love and laughter's there.
> *At the Lavender Lantern. Stanza 1*

Where hearts were high and fortunes
low, and onions in the stew.
    At the Lavender Lantern. Stanza 3
A crooked street goes past my door, en-
twining love of every land;
It wanders, singing, round the world, to
Askelon and Samarkand.
    The Crooked Street of Dreams.
        Stanza 1

PHILIP GUEDALLA
[1889–]

Biography, like big game hunting, is
one of the recognized forms of sport,
and it is as unfair as only sport can be.
High on some far hill-side of politics or
history the amateur marks down his distant quarry. Follows an intensely distasteful period of furtive approach to
the subject which leads the deer-stalker
up gullies and ravines and the biographer through private letters and
washing-books. The burns grow deeper
and wetter, the letters take a more private and a less publishable turn, until
at last our sportsman, well within range,
turns to his publisher, who carries the
guns, and empties one, two, and (if the
public will stand it) three barrels into
his unprotesting victim: because it is a
cruel truth that the subjects of *Lives*
are rarely themselves alive.
    Supers and Supermen

Whispering from its towers the last
enchantment of the middle-class, the
Foreign Office occupies an eligible central situation between Whitehall and
St. James's Park. The grateful taxpayer
provides it with an abundance of admirable stationery, and it is perhaps the
last place in London where everybody is
a gentleman.
    Ibid.

Because the sporting England of
Queen Victoria could never understand
the unathletic France of President
Thiers, we have all in our time conjured
up delightful visions of legions of little
Frenchmen in flat-brimmed silk hats
going fox-shooting with packs of poodles. No picture of life in Calais was too
ludicrous to be believed in Dover; that
is one of the advantages of being an
Island Race.[1]
    Supers and Supermen

There is no Gibbon but Gibbon, and
Gibbon is his prophet. The solemn
march of his cadences, the majestic impropriety of his innuendo are without
rivals in the respective annals of British
eloquence and British indelicacy.
    Ibid.

The work of Henry James has always seemed divisible by a simple dy-
nastic arrangement into three reigns:
James I, James II, and the Old Pretender.
    Ibid.

An Englishman is a man who lives on
an island in the North Sea governed by
Scotsmen.
    Ibid.

Walker . . . followed with the full
energy of a man born in Nashville, Tennessee, the high calling of a filibuster.
He was the son of an insurance manager, and he became almost mechan-
ically a pirate. . . . Walker filiburst
(if that is the appropriate aorist).
    General Walker

The cheerful clatter of Sir James Barrie's cans as he went round with the
milk of human kindness.
    Some Critics

A somewhat disjointed series of stac-
cato notes which leave one with the misleading impression that Mr. Pound's
shirt-cuffs have been sent to the printer
instead of to the laundress.
    Ibid.

Strange that pre-eminence in Germany has more than once been indi-
cated by an eccentric pattern in the hair
upon the upper lip.
    The Hundred Years

The true history of the United States
is the history of transportation . . . in
which the names of railroad presidents
are more significant than those of Presidents of the United States.
    Ibid.

---

[1] Cf. the immortal headline in the London
Times: TERRIBLE GALE IN THE CHANNEL —
CONTINENT ISOLATED.

His [Du Maurier's] incomparable duchesses drew together like tall galleons in mid-ocean, as the first American heiresses came brightly on the social scene.

The Hundred Years

STODDARD KING
[1889–1933]

A writer owned an Asterisk,
  And kept it in his den,
Where he wrote tales (which had large
      sales)
  Of frail and erring men;
And always, when he reached the point
  Where carping censors lurk,
He called upon the Asterisk
  To do his dirty work.

The Writer and the Asterisk.
Stanza 1

The books I read and the life I lead
  Are sensible, sane and mild.
I like calm hats and I don't wear spats,
  But I want my neckties wild!

The Tie That Blinds

Give me a wild tie, brother,
  One with a cosmic urge!
A tie that will swear and rip and tear
  When it sees my old blue serge.

Ibid.

But since I am not lord of the sun, nor
      yet of the realms below,
Would you care to be told that I have
      two seats for an elegant movie
      show?

A Matter-of-Fact Love Song.
Stanza 1

Of all the pestilences dire,
Including famine, flood, and fire,
By Satan and his imps rehearsed,
The neighbors' children are the worst.

Philosophy for Parents. Stanza 1

KATHERINE MANSFIELD
(MRS. JOHN MIDDLETON
MURRY)
[1889–1923]

Oh, flock of thoughts with their shepherd Fear
Shivering, desolate, out in the cold,
That entered into my heart to fold!

Two Nocturnes. II, Stanza 3

Whenever I prepare for a journey I prepare as though for death. Should I never return, all is in order. This is what life has taught me.

Journal, 1922

I want, by understanding myself, to understand others. I want to be all that I am capable of becoming. . . . This all sounds very strenuous and serious. But now that I have wrestled with it, it's no longer so. I feel happy — deep down. *All is well.*

Ibid. (end of her journal)

WALTER JAMES TURNER
[1889–]

When I was but thirteen or so
  I went into a golden land,
Chimborazo, Cotopaxi
  Took me by the hand.

Romance. Stanza 1

Chimborazo, Cotopaxi
  They had stolen my soul away!

Ibid. Stanza 7

T. P. CAMERON WILSON
[1889–1918]

Stare Sphinx-like into space,
Nor march the chalky floor all tousle-
      haired
  When bright boys mention with a
      cheerful face
That $(a + a)$ is written down a^2.

The Mathematical Master to
His Blackboard

God gives to each man, however beset he may be with the world, a few minutes at least daily, when he is utterly alone. I have read Shelley in a Public Lavatory, and learnt Rupert Brooke's war sonnets by heart while I was doing my morning duty to this body.

Waste Paper Philosophy. IX

WILLIAM BOLITHO
[1890–1930]

When the Poincarés and Ludendorffs have brought a man to death they have not finished with him. They use his body to slay others. The most precious

gain of Nationalism from war and bloodshed (and they have many) is this profiteering in the dead.
Leviathan [*1923*]

The adventurer is within us, and he contests for our favour with the social man we are obliged to be. These two sorts of life are incompatibles; one we hanker after, the other we are obliged to. There is no other conflict so deep and bitter as this, whatever the pious say, for it derives from the very constitutions of human life, which so painfully separate us from all other beings. We, like the eagles, were born to be free. Yet we are obliged, in order to live at all, to make a cage of laws for ourselves and to stand on the perch. We are born as wasteful and unremorseful as tigers; we are obliged to be thrifty, or starve, or freeze. We are born to wander, and cursed to stay and dig.
Twelve Against the Gods [*1929*].
Introduction

He, and the world with him, — for Wilson's adventure was the world's, and one day the world will know it, even the fools — were not the victims of a vulgar trick, unless the dizziness that pulls down climbers from the peak is some cunning of the Alps. We fell there because the height was too great, because he saw all the countries of the world, the bare immensity of the mass of common people which he had worshipped all his life, but never imagined until that day he knew he had them, their lives, and all uncountable, future ages of them in his own two hands. Seeing, a great vertigo leapt on him. Those days have passed more utterly from memory than if a hundred years had gone since then; but a few who lived through them, and stood near where the pedestal of Wilson was standing can remember, vaguely, as if they had read it somewhere, something of the madness, the sheer panic, mixed with exaltation, of the times.
Ibid. Woodrow Wilson

Like Arthur and the legendary Alexander, and many other lesser men, he

[Woodrow Wilson] left, even though defeated, a hope, a promise, that League, which is as it were a symbol of his perished flesh and blood, a fragment torn out of his heart and left with us, to serve for one who will come after in a retaking up of his adventure.
Twelve Against the Gods [*1929*]
Woodrow Wilson

MARCUS COOK CONNELLY
[1890–   ]

Gangway for de Lawd God Jehovah!
The Green Pastures.[1]

God. I'll jest r'ar back an' pass a miracle.
Ibid.

Gabriel. How about cleanin' up de whole mess of 'em and sta'tin all over ag'in wid some new kind of animal?

God. An' admit I'm licked?
Ibid.

Even bein' Gawd ain't a bed of roses.
Ibid.

ALAN PATRICK HERBERT
[1890–   ]

When laughing Ann trips down the street
  The sun comes out as well,
The town is at her twinkling feet,
  The crier rings his bell,
The young men leap like little fish,
  Policemen stand and purr,
While husbands look behind and wish
  That they had married her.
Laughing Ann. Stanza 1

I wish I hadn't broke that dish,
  I wish I was a movie-star,
I wish a lot of things, I wish
  That life was like the movies are;
It May Be Life, But Ain't It Slow?
Stanza 1

    If there's a dish
    For which I wish
  More frequent than the rest,
    If there's a food
    On which I brood
  When starving or depressed,

[1] First produced in 1930. Suggested by Roark Bradford's stories, *Ol' Man Adam an' His Chillun.*

If there's a thing that life can give
Which makes it worth our while to live,
  If there's an end
   On which I'd spend
My last remaining cash,
It's sausage, friend,
It's sausage, friend,
It's sausage, friend, and mash.
    Sausage and Mash. Stanza 1
  When Love is dead,
  Ambition fled,
And Pleasure, lad, and Pash,
  You'll still enjoy
  A sausage, boy,
A sausage, boy, and mash.
      Ibid. Stanza 3
Teetot'lers seem to die the same as others,
So what's the use of knocking off the beer?
    The Ladies' Bar. Refrain
The chameleon's life is confusing,
 He is used to adventure and pain;
But if ever he sat on Aunt Maggie's cretonne,
And noticed what curious colors he'd gone,
I don't think he'd do it again.
    The Chameleon. Stanza 4
The sturgeon belongs to the King,
 And if in some desolate chasm,
You feloniously catch one or two on a string
 You must see that His Majesty has 'em.
     Caviare. Stanza 1
I regard the pub as a valuable institution.
  Letter to the Electors of Oxford University [*1935*] [1]
I shall examine with some suspicion any proposals that may be made for the distribution of the British Empire among foreign countries, whatever their birth-rate, insolence or inefficiency.
      Ibid.
I have no plan for the restoration of world trade: there will be 613 members of the new Parliament, who have.
      Ibid.

[1] Mr. Herbert was elected to the House of Commons, November, 1935, as one of the two representatives of Oxford University.

They tell us that capitalism is doomed: Karl Marx, I believe, made the same announcement 80 years ago. He may still be right: but the old clock ticks on; and it does not help very much to throw stones at it. It would be surprising indeed if our system had survived quite unshaken the unprecedented upheaval of a World War. But it is infinitely adaptable and has not, I think, exhausted its resources.
  Letter to the Electors of Oxford University [*1935*]
We shall not produce equality by turning everything upside-down. My reason, such as it is, reluctantly rebels when I am asked to believe that after thousands of years of not wholly fruitless civilization the best and only way of managing this complicated world has been revealed to my old football captain, Sir Stafford Cripps.
      Ibid.
I know nothing about Agriculture.
      Ibid.
Holy Deadlock.
  Title of novel [*1934*] *satirizing the paradoxes of British divorce law*

SAMUEL HOFFENSTEIN
[1890–]

When trouble drives me into rhyme,
Which is two-thirds of all the time,
What peace a thought like this can give —
Great is the age in which we live!
  Songs to Break the Tedium. III
Oh, how various is the scene
Allowed to Man for his demesne!
  Verses Demonstrating That No Man Can Be Unhappy
You buy some flowers for your table;
You tend them tenderly as you're able;
You fetch them water from hither and thither —
What thanks do you get for it all? They wither.
  Poems in Praise of Practically Nothing. I

When the wind is in the tree,
It makes a noise just like the sea,
As if there were not noise enough
To bother one, without that stuff.
A Garden of Verses for the Little Ones. XIII, The Wind in the Tree

Loyal be to loyal friends;
Make them pay you dividends;
Work, like the industrious bee,
Your friends and foes impartially.
Ibid. XIX, For Little Boys Destined for Big Business

I'd rather listen to a flute
In Gotham, than a band in Butte.
Songs about Life. VIII

The apple grows so bright and high,
And ends its days in apple pie.
Ibid. XXXIII

Of all the birds that sing and fly
Between the housetops and the sky,
The muddy sparrow, mean and small,
I like, by far, the best of all.
Ibid. LIII

I play with the bulls and the bears;
I'm the Bartlett of market quotations.
Songs for an Old-Fashioned Lute. VI

The stars, like measles, fade at last.
The Mimic Muse. V

Babies haven't any hair;
Old men's heads are just as bare; —
Between the cradle and the grave
Lies a haircut and a shave.
Songs of Faith in the Year after Next. VIII

The head that wears a crown may be
Inclined to some anxiety,
But, on the other hand, I know
A derby domes its meed of woe.
Ibid. XVI

Your little voice,
So soft and kind;
Your little soul,
Your little mind!
Love-songs. XIII

The countless cousins of the Czar,
Grand Duke or Duchess, every one,
As multitudinous as are
The spheres (who borrow from the sun).
Invocation. Stanza 15

Blessings love disguise.
Serenades and Songs for a Pent-House Window. III

My soul is dark with stormy riot,
Directly traceable to diet.
Out of the Everywhere into the Here. XIII

Which six of the seven cities that
claimed Homer were liars?
The Moist Land. I

Little by little we subtract
Faith and Fallacy from Fact,
The Illusory from the True,
And starve upon the residue.
Rag-Bag, II. Observation, Stanza 1

To You, oh, Goddess of Efficiency,
Your happy vassals bend the reverent knee,
Save when arthritis, your benighted foe,
Sulks in the bones and sourly mumbles "No!"
Hymn to Science

To all the starry host of Heaven they cried,
But had no radio and of course they died.
Ibid.

Smelling like a municipal budget.
Entr' Acte. VI

The heart's dead
Are never buried.
Summer Day

Though poor he lived among the throng,
And though obscure he died,
With a betrothal-ring of song
He made the world his bride.
To Genius, Dying Young. Stanza 1

Greater than all my songs am I;
Much more have seen, have heard much more —
For who shall fetch in a pitcher of singing
All that lies on the ocean's floor?
Apologia. Stanza 5

THEODORE MAYNARD
[1890–   ]

I know a sheaf of splendid songs by
heart

Which stir the blood or move the soul
    to tears,
Of death or honour or of love's sweet
    smart,
The runes and legends of a thousand
    years;
And some of them go plaintively and
    slow,
And some are jolly like the earth in
    May —
But this is *really* the best song I know:
    I-tiddly-iddly-i-ti-iddly-ay.
       *Ballade of the Best Song in the
          World. Stanza 1*

VIOLA MEYNELL

His kisses touch her marvelling eyes
And wander searching through her
    thinking face;
And though so loved and near she lies
He knows he travels in a distant place.
    A Girl Adoring. Prefatory verses
He does not know how far, how far;
Only she makes him think of some
    strange land.
Beyond the earth his journeys are,
Touching that wild, wild heart and
    thinking hand.
             Ibid. Stanza 5

CHRISTOPHER MORLEY
[1890–   ]

There is no prince or prelate
    I envy — no, not one.
No evil can befall me —
    By God, I have a son!
             Secret Laughter
And of all man's felicities
    The very subtlest one, say I,
Is when for the first time he sees
    His hearthfire smoke against the sky.
    A Hallowe'en Memory. Stanza 5
Heaven is not built of country seats,
But little queer suburban streets.
    To the Little House. Stanza 4
The man who never in his life
Has washed the dishes with his wife
Or polished up the silver plate —
He still is largely celibate.
    Washing the Dishes. Stanza 4

The greatest poem ever known
Is one all poets have outgrown:
The poetry, innate, untold,
Of being only four years old.
             To a Child
One good nocturne
Deserves another,
Said George Sand
When she met Chopin.
             Reciprocation
Now fades the glossy, cherished anthra-
    cite;
The radiators lose their temperature:
How ill avail, on such a frosty night,
    The short and simple flannels of the
    poor.[1]
    *Elegy Written in a Country
               Coal-Bin*
Unhappy lovers always should be
    Frenchmen,
So sweet a tongue for any kind of pain!
          Toulemonde. III
Such color as the curtained bee would
    know
Drowsed in the bedstead of a crimson
    rose,
Such color as the vineyard speck might
    swim
Deepened in the full Burgundian glass,
Such color as the unborn Juliet felt
Nursed in the reddest vein of Shake-
    speare's heart.
                Ibid. V
        Women all
Raiment themselves most brightly for
    the dark
Which is, on information and belief,
Their true dominion.
               Ibid. VI
Know, then, that I consider brown
For ladies' eyes, the only color;
And deem all other orbs in town
(Compared to yours) opaquer, duller.
    To His Brown-Eyed Mistress

[1] Daily she came from Bromley to the City,
    Pink underclothes of crêpe de Chine she
      wore,
  So that in each backyard she viewed with
      pity
  The short and simple flannels of the poor.
       — OLIVER HERFORD? Quoted by
      A. EDWARD NEWTON, in *Derby Day*

I bid you, mock not Eros;
   He knows not doubt or shame,
And, unaware of proverbs,
   The burnt child craves the flame.
Of a Child That Had Fever

With pained surprise
Men learn that poetry's not just the skill
Of words long dead, but actual You's and I's —
And if you have not learned that yet, you will.
Memoranda for a Sonnet Sequence

A human being: an ingenious assembly of portable plumbing.
Human Being. Chap. 11

How great a bonfire the savages of New York kindle for their evening meal!
Ibid. Chap. 33

Prophets were twice stoned — first in anger; then, after their death, with a handsome slab in the graveyard.
Where the Blue Begins. Chap. 11

He is too experienced a parent ever to make positive promises.
Thunder on the Left. Chap. 5

Informal's what women always say they're going to be and never are.
Ibid.

As calmly detached as nurses in a hospital who smile faintly at what the patients say under ether.
Ibid. Chap. 6

If you have to keep reminding yourself of a thing, perhaps it isn't so.
Ibid. Chap. 9

Life is a foreign language: all men mispronounce it.
Ibid. Chap. 14

Poetry comes with anger, hunger and dismay; it does not often visit groups of citizens sitting down to be literary together, and would appal them if it did.
John Mistletoe. 7

April prepares her green traffic light and the world thinks Go.
Ibid. 8

JAMES RORTY
[1890–   ]

There is a peewee bird that cries
"La, sol, me
"La, sol, me" —
He is the only thing that sighs
Beside the western sea.
California Dissonance. Stanza 1

The blue jays chatter, "Tcha! Tcha! Tcha!"
And cheer for California
The real estate men chortle "Whee!"
And tout the loud calliope.
The sky is blue, the land is glad —
The peewee bird alone is sad
And sings in minor key.
Ibid. Stanza 2

It was a shock, I own, to see
Sedition sitting in a tree.
Ibid. Stanza 3

FRANCIS LEDWIDGE
[1891–1917]

Had I a golden pound to spend,
My love should mend and sew no more.
And I would buy her a little quern,
Easy to turn on the kitchen floor.
Had I a Golden Pound. Stanza 1

From its blue vase the rose of evening drops;
Upon the streams its petals float away.
An Evening in England

IRENE RUTHERFORD
McLEOD (MRS. AUBREY
DE SELINCOURT)
[1891–   ]

I'm a lean dog, a keen dog, a wild dog, and lone;
I'm a rough dog, a tough dog, hunting on my own;
I'm a bad dog, a mad dog, teasing silly sheep;
I love to sit and bay the moon, to keep fat souls from sleep.
Lone Dog. Stanza 1

I've hated all that's mean and cold,
All that's dusty, tame, and old,
Comfortable lies in books,
Pallid Virtue's sidelong looks,

Saints who wash their hands too clean,
And walk where only saints have been.
Rebel

HERBERT V. WILEY
[1891–   ]

Stand by to crash.
*Last command to the crew of
the falling U. S. Navy dirigible
Akron [April 4, 1933]*

RICHARD ALDINGTON
[1892–   ]

The moon,
With a rag of gauze about her loins.
Evening

PEARL SYDENSTRICKER
BUCK
(MRS. RICHARD J. WALSH)
[1892–   ]

Be born anywhere, little embryo novelist, but do not be born under the shadow of a great creed, not under the burden of original sin, not under the doom of salvation. Go out and be born among gypsies or thieves or among happy workaday people who live in the sun and do not think about their souls.
Advice to Unborn Novelists

How could an actual person fit into the covers of a book? The book is not a continent, not a definite geographical measure, it cannot contain so huge a thing as an actual full-size person. Any person has to be scaled by eliminations to fit the book world.
Ibid.

STELLA BENSON (MRS. J. C.
O'GORMAN ANDERSON)
[1892–1933]

Call no man foe, but never love a stranger.
Build up no plan, nor any star pursue.
Go forth with crowds; in loneliness is danger.
Thus nothing God can send,

And nothing God can do
Shall pierce your peace, my friend.
To the Unborn. Stanza 3
Oh, bless your blindness, glory in your groping!
Mock at your betters with an upward chin!
And when the moment has gone by for hoping,
Sling your fifth stone, O son of mine, and win.

Grief do I give you, grief and dreadful laughter;
Sackcloth for banner, ashes in your wine.
Go forth, go forth, nor ask me what comes after;
The fifth stone shall not fail you, son of mine.

Go forth, go forth, and slay the Philistine.
*Five Smooth Stones.
Stanzas 12 and 13*
High and miraculous skies bless and astonish my eyes;
All my dead secrets arise, all my dead stories come true.
Here is the Gate to the Sea. Once you unlocked it for me;
Now, since you gave me the key, shall I unlock it for you?
This Is the End
Did Older and Wiser people ever shout and jump with joy in their pyjamas in the moonlight? Did they ever feel just drunk with being young? And were Older and Wiser people's jokes ever funny?
Ibid.
Family jokes, though rightly cursed by strangers, are the bond that keeps most families alive.
Pipers and a Dancer. Chap. 9

ELIZABETH ASQUITH
BIBESCO

I have made a great discovery.
What I love belongs to me. Not the chairs and tables in my house, but the masterpieces of the world.

It is only a question of loving them enough.

Balloons

He is invariably in a hurry. Being in a hurry is one of the tributes he pays to life.

Ibid.

It is sometimes the man who opens the door who is the last to enter the room.

The Fir and the Palm. Chap. 13

You are such a wonderful Baedeker to life. All of the stars are in the right places.

Ibid.

It is never any good dwelling on good-byes. It is not the being together that it prolongs, it is the parting.

Ibid. Chap. 15

ROBERT PETER TRISTRAM COFFIN
[1892–   ]

If men could still be holy anywhere,
  It would be in towers such as these
That line the coasts with lamps and
  warn the ships —
  The holy towers of the silences.

Towers of Silence

A man should choose with careful eye
The things to be remembered by.

The Weather Vane

Life and death upon one tether
And running beautiful together.

Crystal Moment

FRANCIS E. FALKENBURY

As I came down to South Street by the
  soft sea-water,
  I saw long ships, their mast-heads
  ever bowing:
Sweet slender maids in clinging gowns
  of golden,
Curtseying stately in a fashion olden,
Bowing sweetly — each a king's fair
  daughter —
To me, their millionth, millionth lover,
I, the seventh son of the old sea-rover,
As I came down to South Street by the
  myriad moving water.

South Street

JOHN BURDON SANDERSON HALDANE
[1892–   ]

Science is vastly more stimulating to the imagination than are the classics.

Daedalus

ARCHIBALD MacLEISH
[1892–   ]

Sometimes within the brain's old
  ghostly house,
  I hear, far off, at some forgotten door,
A music and an eerie faint carouse,
  And stir of echoes down the creaking
  floor.

Chambers of Imagery. Stanza 1

Beauty is that Medusa's head
Which men go armed to seek and sever.
It is most deadly when most dead,
And dead will stare and sting forever.

Beauty

A poem should not mean
But be.

Ars Poetica

Here, face downward in the sun
To feel how swift, how secretly,
The shadow of the night comes on.

You, Andrew Marvell

There with vast wings across the can-
  celed skies,
There in the sudden blackness, the
  black pall
Of nothing, nothing, nothing — nothing at all.

The End of the World

The world was always yours: you would
  not take it.

Speech to a Crowd

Speaking alone for myself it's the steep
  hill and the
Toppling lift of the young men I am
  toward now —
Waiting for that as the wave for the
  next wave.
Let them go over us all I say with the
  thunder of
What's to be next in the world. It's we
  will be under it!

*"Dover Beach" — A Note to
That Poem*

Christ but this earth goes over to the squall of time!
Hi but she heels to it — rail down: ribs down: rolling
Dakotas under her hull! And the night climbing
Sucking the green from the ferns by these Berkshire boulders!

The Sunset Piece

EDNA ST. VINCENT MILLAY (MRS. EUGEN JAN BOISSEVAIN)
[1892–   ]

And what are you that, missing you,
    I should be kept awake
As many nights as there are days
    With weeping for your sake?

The Philosopher

Death devours all lovely things;
    Lesbia with her sparrow
Shares the darkness, — presently
    Every bed is narrow.

Passer Mortuus Est. Stanza 1

All I could see from where I stood
Was three long mountains and a wood.

Renascence. Line 1

I would I were alive again
To kiss the fingers of the rain,
To drink into my eyes the shine
Of every slanting silver line,
To catch the freshened, fragrant breeze
From drenched and dripping apple-trees.

Ibid. Line 119

I know not how such things can be,
I only know there came to me
A fragrance such as never clings
To aught save happy living things;
A sound as of some joyous elf
Singing sweet songs to please himself,
And, through and over everything,
A sense of glad awakening.

Ibid. Line 143

The world stands out on either side
No wider than the heart is wide;
Above the world is stretched the sky, —
No higher than the soul is high.
The heart can push the sea and land
Farther away on either hand;

The soul can split the sky in two,
And let the face of God shine through.

Renascence. Line 189

She that had no need of me,
Is a little lonely child
Lost in Hell. Persephone,
Take her head upon your knee,
Say to her: "My dear, my dear,
It is not so dreadful here."

A Prayer to Persephone

I know I am but summer to your heart,
And not the full four seasons of the year.

Two Seasons. Sonnet 1

I drank at every vine.
    The last was like the first.
I came upon no wine
    So wonderful as thirst.

Feast. Stanza 1

I only know that summer sang in me
A little while, and in me sings no more.

What Lips My Lips Have Kissed

Euclid alone
Has looked on Beauty bare.[1] Fortunate they
Who, though once only and then but far away,
Have heard her massive sandal set on stone.

Euclid Alone Has Looked on Beauty Bare

My candle burns at both ends;
    It will not last the night;
But, ah, my foes, and, oh, my friends —
    It gives a lovely light.[2]

Figs from Thistles. First Fig

Safe upon the solid rock the ugly houses stand:
Come and see my shining palace built upon the sand!

Ibid. Second Fig

----

[1] Mathematics possesses not only truth, but supreme beauty — a beauty cold and austere, like that of sculpture, without appeal to any part of our weaker nature, yet sublimely pure, and capable of a stern perfection such as only the greatest art can show. — BERTRAND RUSSELL [1872–   ]: *The Principles of Mathematics* [1903]

[2] I burned my candle at both ends,
    And now have neither foes nor friends.
    SAMUEL HOFFENSTEIN: *Songs of Fairly Utter Despair, VIII*

Oh, come again to Astolat!
  I will not ask you to be kind;
And you may go when you will go,
  And I will stay behind.
  Elaine. Stanza 1

Music my rampart, and my only one.
  *On Hearing a Symphony of
                    Beethoven*

Stranger, pause and look;
From the dust of ages
Lift this little book,
Turn the tattered pages,
Read me, do not let me die!
Search the fading letters, finding
Steadfast in the broken binding
All that once was I!
  The Poet and His Book. Stanza 6

Weep him dead and mourn as you may,
  Me, I sing as I must:
Blessed be death, that cuts in marble
  What would have sunk in dust.
  Keen. Stanza 1

Who builds her a house with love for
    timber,
  Builds her a house of foam;
And I'd rather be bride to a lad gone
    down
  Than widow to one safe home.
  Ibid. Stanza 5

Spring rides no horses down the hill,
But comes on foot, a goose girl still.
And all the loveliest things there be
Come simply, so it seems to me.
If ever I said, in grief or pride,
I tired of honest things, I lied.
  The Goose Girl

I'll keep a little tavern
  Below the high hill's crest,
Wherein all gray-eyed people
  May sit them down and rest.
  The Little Tavern. Stanza 1

Aye, 'tis a curious fancy —
  But all the good I know
Was taught me out of two gray eyes
  A long time ago.
  Ibid. Stanza 4

O world, I cannot hold thee close
    enough!
Thy winds, thy wide gray skies!
Thy mists, that roll and rise!

Thy woods, this autumn day, that ache
    and sag
And all but cry with color.
  God's World. Stanza 1

Lord, I do fear
Thou'st made the world too beautiful
    this year.
My soul is all but out of me — let fall
No burning leaf; prithee, let no bird
    call.
  Ibid. Stanza 2

I will be the gladdest thing under the
    sun!
I will touch a hundred flowers and not
    pick one.
  Afternoon on a Hill

And if I loved you Wednesday,
  Well, what is that to you?
I do not love you Thursday —
  So much is true.
  Thursday. Stanza 1

There's little kind and little fair
  Is worth its weight in smoke
To me, that's grown so free from care
  Since my heart broke!
  The Merry Maid. Stanza 2

Love has gone, and left me and the days
    are all alike.
  Eat I must, and sleep I will — and
    would that night were here!
But ah, to lie awake and hear the slow
    hours strike!
  Would that it were day again, with
    twilight near!
  Ashes of Life. Stanza 1

Life goes on forever like the gnawing of
    a mouse.
  Ibid. Stanza 3

Thanks be to God, the world is wide,
  And I am going far from home!
And I forgot in Camelot
  The man I loved in Rome.
  Fugitive. Stanza 1

My heart is warm with the friends I
    make,
  And better friends I'll not be know-
    ing;
Yet there isn't a train I wouldn't take,
  No matter where it's going.
  Travel. Stanza 3

I know some poison I could drink;
  I've often thought I'd taste it;

But Mother bought it for the sink,
  And drinking it would waste it.
      The Cheerful Abstainer. Stanza 3

Men say the winter
  Was bad that year;
Fuel was scarce,
  And food was dear.
A wind with a wolf's head
  Howled about our door.
      The Ballad of the Harp-Weaver.
          Stanzas 13, 14.

I am not resigned to the shutting away
  of loving hearts in the hard ground.
So it is, and so it will be, for so it has
  been, time out of mind:
Into the darkness they go, the wise and
  the lovely. Crowned
With lilies and with laurel they go.
      Dirge Without Music. Stanza 1

Death is our master, — but his seat is
  shaken;
He rides victorious, — but his ranks are
  thinned.
      Not That It Matters

I had a little Sorrow,
  Born of a little Sin.
      The Penitent. Stanza 1

You leave me much against my will.
      To S. M.

Whether or not we find what we are
  seeking
Is idle, biologically speaking.
      Sonnet: I Shall Forget You
          Presently

Breathes but one mortal on the teeming
  globe
Could minister to my soul's or body's
  needs —
Physician minus physic, minus robe;
Confessor minus Latin, minus beads.
Yet should you bid me name him, I am
  dumb;
For though you summon him, he would
  not come.
      Fatal Interview. IV

Love in the open hand, nothing but
  that,
Ungemmed, unhidden, wishing not to
  hurt,
As one should bring you cowslips in a
  hat
Swung from the hand, or apples in her
  skirt,

I bring you, calling out as children do:
"Look what I have! — And these are
  all for you."
      Fatal Interview. XI

ELIZABETH J. COATSWORTH
(MRS. HENRY BESTON)
[1893–   ]

Let it be understood that I am Don
  Juan Gomez!
My saddle cloth is fringed with scalps
  of Indians I have slain,
And when I see a girl and knock upon
  her shutter,
Though it be dawn or dark, I need not
  knock again.
      Announcement. Stanza 2

And when I pray, the saints go hurrying
  to the Virgin,
And cry, "Don Juan is praying, and
  must not pray in vain!"
      Ibid. Stanza 3

Cat, if you go outdoors you must walk
  in the snow.
You will come back with little white
  shoes on your feet,
Little white slippers of snow that have
  heels of sleet.
Stay by the fire, my Cat. Lie still, do
  not go.
      On a Night of Snow

JAMES BRYANT CONANT
[1893–   ]

Behavior which appears superficially
correct but is intrinsically corrupt always irritates those who see below the
surface.
      Baccalaureate Address, Harvard
          College [June 17, 1934]

Slogans are both exciting and comforting, but they are also powerful opi-
ates for the conscience.
      Ibid.

Some of mankind's most terrible misdeeds have been committed under the
spell of certain magic words or phrases.
      Ibid.

DOROTHY FRANCES BLOMFIELD (MRS. GERALD) GURNEY
[–1932]

The kiss of the sun for pardon,
The song of the birds for mirth, —
One is nearer God's heart in a garden
Than anywhere else on earth.[1]
The Lord God Planted a Garden.
Stanza 4

CECILY W. HALLACK

Lord of the pots and pipkins, since I
have no time to be
A saint by doing lovely things and vig-
illing with Thee,
By watching in the twilight dawn, and
storming Heaven's gates,
Make me a saint by getting meals and
washing up the plates!
The Divine Office of the Kitchen.
Stanza 1

ROBERT MALISE BOWYER NICHOLS
[1893–   ]

God, if Thou livest, Thine eye on me
bend,
And stay my grief and bring my pain to
end:
Pain for my lost, the deepest, rarest
friend
Man ever had, whence groweth this
despair.
Plaint of Friendship by Death
Broken. Stanza 1

Beauty is its own reward,
Being a form of Peace.
The Water-Lily. Stanza 2

Was there love once? I have forgotten
her.
Was there grief once? grief yet is mine.
Fulfilment

[1] Inscription at the Bok Singing Tower,
Lake Wales, Florida.
The garden seems the one spot on earth
where history does not assert itself, and, no
doubt, when Nero was fiddling over the blaze
of Rome, there were florists counting the petals of rival roses at Paestum as peacefully and
conscientiously as any gardeners of to-day.
EDMUND GOSSE: *Gossip in a Library,*
Gerard's Herbal

WILFRED OWEN
[1893–1918]

What passing-bells for these who died
as cattle?
Only the monstrous anger of the guns.
Only the stuttering rifles' rapid rattle
Can patter out their hasty orisons.
The Anthem for Doomed Youth

. . . . You would not tell with such
high zest
To children ardent for some desperate
glory,
The old lie: *Dulce et decorum est*
Pro patria mori.
Dulce et Decorum Est

DOROTHY PARKER (MRS. ALAN CAMPBELL)
[1893–   ]

Where's the man could ease a heart
Like a satin gown?
The Satin Dress. Stanza 1

Yet this the need of woman, this her
curse:
To range her little gifts, and give, and
give,
Because the throb of giving's sweet to
bear.
I Know I Have Been Happiest

Four be the things I am wiser to know:
Idleness, sorrow, a friend, and a foe.
Inventory

Four be the things I'd been better
without:
Love, curiosity, freckles, and doubt.
Ibid.

And this is the sum of a lasting lore:
Scratch a lover, and find a foe.
Ballade of a Great Weariness.
Stanza 1

Men seldom make passes
At girls who wear glasses.
News Item

Razors pain you;
Rivers are damp;
Acids stain you;
And drugs cause cramp.
Guns aren't lawful;
Nooses give;

Gas smells awful;
You might as well live.
                              Résumé
Why is it no one ever sent me yet
    One perfect limousine, do you sup-
      pose?
Ah no, it's always just my luck to get
    One perfect rose.
                    One Perfect Rose. Stanza 3
Then if my friendships break and bend,
    There's little need to cry
The while I know that every foe
    Is faithful till I die.
                          The Leal. Stanza 2
He lies below, correct in cypress wood,
And entertains the most exclusive
    worms.
            Epitaph for a Very Rich Man
I never saw a sweeter child —
    The little one, the darling one! —
I mind I told her, when he smiled
    You'd know he was his mother's son.
            The Maid-Servant at the Inn.
                              Stanza 4
It's queer that I should see them so —
    The time they came to Bethlehem
Was more than thirty years ago;
    I've prayed that all is well with them.
                          Ibid. Stanza 5
The man she had was kind and clean
    And well enough for every day,
But, oh, dear friends, you should have
      seen
    The one that got away!
                          The Fisherwoman
There was nothing more fun than a
  man!
                The Little Old Lady in
                      Lavender Silk
Women and elephants never forget.
        Ballade of Unfortunate Mammals.
                              Refrain

HERBERT READ
[1893–   ]

The only literature which is at the
same time vital and popular is the literature of the music-hall.
                Phases of English Poetry
Poetry can never again become a popular art until the poet gives himself

wholly to "the cadence of consenting
feet." [1]
                Phases of English Poetry

DOROTHY L. SAYERS
[1893–   ]

To that still center where the spinning
    world
Sleeps on its axis, to the heart of rest.
            Gaudy Night. Chap. 18, Sonnet
    Death seems to provide the minds of
the Anglo-Saxon race with a greater
fund of innocent amusement than any
other single subject . . . the tale must
be about dead bodies or very wicked
people, preferably both, before the
Tired Business Man can feel really
happy.
            The Third Omnibus of Crime.
                        Introduction

SYLVIA TOWNSEND WARNER
[1893–   ]

John Bird, a laborer, lies here,
Who served the earth for sixty year
With spade and mattock, drill and
      plough;
But never found it kind till now.
                              Epitaph

JOHN VAN ALSTYN WEAVER
[1893–1938]

Don't you ever try to go there —
    It's to dream of, not to find.
Lovely things like that is always
    Mostly in your mind.
                      Legend. Stanza 7
Sure enough, the towers and castles
    Went like lightnin' out of sight —
Nothin' there but filthy Jersey
    On a drizzly night.
                          Ibid. Stanza 9

---

[1] The quotation is from FRANCIS BARTON
GUMMERE [1855–1919]: *The Beginnings of
Poetry.*

WINIFRED WELLES
[1893–   ]

My squirrel with his tail curved up
Like half a silver lyre.
Silver for Midas. Stanza 4

Oh all you safe and smooth of heart
Listen to song from me,
Whose wooden throat was once a part
Of the north side of a tree!
The Violin. Stanza 4

Once, on a cliff, I saw perfection happen.
The full, gold moon was balanced on
the sea
Just as the red sun rested on the moor.
The summer evening ripened and fell
open;
And people walking through that fruit's
rich core
Were suddenly what they were meant
to be.
The Heart of Light

DON BLANDING
[1894–   ]

When I have a house . . . as I some-
time may . . .
I'll suit my fancy in every way.
I'll fill it with things that have caught
my eye
In drifting from Iceland to Molokai.
Vagabond's House. Stanza 1

There are times when only a dog will do
For a friend . . . when you're beaten
sick and blue
And the world's all wrong, for he won't
care
If you break and cry, or grouch and
swear,
For he'll let you know as he licks your
hands
That he's downright sorry . . . and
understands.[1]
Ibid. Stanza 5

And the thought will strike with a swift
sharp pain
That I probably never will build again

This house that I'll have in some far
day.
Well . . . it's just a dream-house anyway.
Vagabond's House. Stanza 21

Hollywood . . . Hollywood . . .
Fabulous Follywood . . .
Celluloid Babylon, glorious, glamorous.
Hollywood. Stanza 1

It's more than just an easy word for
casual good-bye;
It's gayer than a greeting, and it's sadder than a sigh.
Aloha Oe: Its Meaning

It's said a hundred different ways, in
sadness and in joy,
Aloha means "I love you." So I say
"Aloha Oe."
Ibid.

EDWARD ESTLIN
CUMMINGS [1]
[1894–   ]

when the proficient poison of sure sleep
bereaves us of our slow tranquilities

and He without Whose favour nothing
is
(being of men called Love) upward
doth leap
from the mute hugeness of depriving
deep,

with thunder of those hungering wings
of His,

into the lucent and large signories
— i shall not smile beloved; i shall not
weep.
When the Proficient Poison of
Sure Sleep

while in an earthless hour my fond
soul seriously yearns beyond
this fern of sunset frond on frond
opening in a rare
Slowness of gloried air. . . .
Always Before Your Voice

---

[1] In the whole history of the world there is
but one thing that money can not buy — to
wit, the wag of a dog's tail. — HENRY
WHEELER SHAW ("Josh Billings"). Quoted in
KATE SANBORN's *My Literary Zoo* [1896],
P. 69.

[1] "The terror of typesetters, an enigma to
book reviewers, and the special target of all
the world's literary philistines." — Publisher's
note, Modern Library edition of *The Enor-*
mous Room.

nobody, not even the rain, has such
    small hands
             Somewhere I Have Never
                          Travelled

"next to of course god america i
love you land of the pilgrims' and so
    forth oh
say can you see by the dawn's early my
country 'tis of centuries come and go
and are no more what of it we should
    worry
in every language even deafanddumb
thy sons acclaim your glorious name by
    gorry
by jingo by gee by gosh by gum
why talk of beauty what could be more
    beaut-
iful than these heroic happy dead
who rushed like lions to the roaring
    slaughter
they did not stop to think they died
    instead
then shall the voices of liberty be
    mute?"

He spoke. And drank rapidly a glass of
    water.
             Next To Of Course God

KING EDWARD VIII
[1894–   ]

I am better known to most of you as
the Prince of Wales, as the man who
during the war and since has had the
opportunity of getting to know the people of nearly every country of the world
under all conditions and circumstances.
And although I now speak to you as the
King, I am still the same man who has
had the experience, and whose constant
effort will be to continue to promote the
well-being of his fellow men.
    First broadcast to the Empire
    after ascending the throne
    [March 1, 1936]

At long last I am able to say a few
words of my own. I have never wanted
to withhold anything, but until now it
has not been constitutionally possible
for me to speak.

I have found it impossible to carry
the heavy burden of responsibility and
to discharge my duties as King as I
would wish to do without the help and
support of the woman I love.

I now quit altogether public affairs
and I lay down my burden.

It may be some time before I return
to my native land, but I shall always
follow the fortunes of the British race
and empire with profound interest and
if, at any time in the future, I can be
found of service to His Majesty in a
private station I shall not fail.

And now we all have a new King. I
wish him and you, his people, happiness
and prosperity with all my heart.

God bless you all! God save the
King!
    Farewell broadcast after abdication
            [December 11, 1936]

ALDOUS LEONARD HUXLEY
[1894–   ]

It is far easier to write ten passably
effective Sonnets, good enough to take
in the not too inquiring critic, than one
effective advertisement that will take in
a few thousand of the uncritical buying
public.
                On the Margin

There are not enough *bon mots* in
existence to provide any industrious
conversationalist with a new stock for
every social occasion.[1]
    Point Counter Point. Chap. 7

A bad book is as much of a labour to
write as a good one; it comes as sincerely from the author's soul.
            Ibid. Chap. 13

---

[1] What horrors, when it flashed over him
that he had made this fine speech, word for
word, twice over! Yet it was not true, as the
lady might perhaps have fairly inferred, that
he had embellished his conversation with the
Huma daily during that whole interval of
years. — OLIVER WENDELL HOLMES: *The Autocrat of the Breakfast Table, Every Man His
Own Boswell*

There is no substitute for talent. Industry and all the virtues are of no avail.
Point Counter Point. Chap. 13

Parodies and caricatures are the most penetrating of criticisms.
Ibid. Chap. 28

Over her the swan shook slowly free
The folded glory of his wings, and made
A white-walled tent of soft and luminous shade.
Leda

Seated upon the convex mound
Of one vast kidney, Jonah prays
And sings his canticles and hymns,
Making the hollow vault resound
God's goodness and mysterious ways,
Till the great fish spouts music as he swims.
Jonah

Blood of the world, time stanchless flows;
The wound is mortal and is mine.
Seasons

Life is their madness, life that all night long
Bids them to sing and sing, they know not why;
Mad cause and senseless burden of their song;
For life commands, and Life! is all their cry.
The Cicadas. Stanza 5

Clueless we go; but I have heard thy voice,
Divine Unreason! harping in the leaves,
And grieve no more; for wisdom never grieves,
And thou hast taught me wisdom; I rejoice.
Ibid. Stanza 14

A million million spermatozoa,
All of them alive:
Out of their cataclysm but one poor Noah
Dare hope to survive.
And among that billion minus one
Might have chanced to be
Shakespeare, another Newton, a new Donne —
But the One was Me.
Fifth Philosopher's Song

ROBERT NATHAN
[1894–   ]

Love hath no physic for a grief too deep.
A Cedar Box. Sonnet V

Because my grief seems quiet and apart,
Think not for such a reason it is less.
True sorrow makes a silence in the heart,
Joy has its friends, but grief its loneliness.
Ibid. Sonnet VII

So we stand silent, having lost so soon
The best of us, the high and silver flute;
The clearest melody, the happiest tune,
The loveliest voice of all our times is mute.
For Elinor Wylie

Toward men and toward God, she maintained a respectful attitude, lightened by the belief that in a crisis she could deal adequately with either of them.
The Road of Ages. Chap. 2

WESTBROOK PEGLER
[1894–   ]

The Era of Wonderful Nonsense.[1]
Mr. Gump Himself

For the fifth year in succession I have pored over the catalogue of dogs in the show at Madison Square Garden without finding a dog named Rover, Towser, Sport, Spot or Fido.

Who is the man who can call from his back door at night: "Here, Champion Alexander of Clane o' Wind-Holme! Here, Champion Alexander of Clane o' Wind-Holme"?
Here, Rover!

I am a member of the rabble in good standing.
The Lynching Story

After a quiet study of the rules and tools of civilized table warfare your correspondent has decided that the French combine the greatest simplicity with the best results.

[1] Viz. the period of spending and speculation during what used to be called "Coolidge Prosperity," before the depression of (approximately) 1930-1935.

The Frenchman, like the old Scotch golfer, endeavors to do what there is to be done without superfluous weapons or fancy gestures. He sits down, ties his napkin behind his ears, picks up a knife and fork and goes to work with admirable directness. He dunks his bread in the juice of the snail, he chases fragments of steak and gravy with a piece of crust, he licks his fingers, says, "Ah!" and gets fed.

France in One Easy Lesson

The French avoid no hazards, they take food as it comes without false restrictions on style or stance, and they make their victuals holler "Uncle!"

Ibid.

H. PHELPS PUTNAM
[1894–   ]

We have insulted you as Lady Luck.
Hymn to Chance

Hard-boiled, unbroken egg, what can you care
For the enfolded passion of the Rose?
Hasbrouck and the Rose

In Springfield, Massachusetts, I devoured
The mystic, the improbable, the Rose.
Ibid.

MARGARET E. SANGSTER
(MRS. GERRIT VAN DETH)
[1894–   ]

Oh, cakes and friends we should choose with care,
Not always the fanciest cake that's there
Is the best to eat! And the plainest friend
Is sometimes the finest one in the end!
French Pastry. Stanza 3

I think that folk should carry bright umbrellas in the rain,
To smile into the sullen sky and make it glad again.
On a Rainy Day. Stanza 4

GENEVIEVE TAGGARD
[1894–   ]

Try tropic for your balm,
Try storm,
And after storm, calm.
Try snow of heaven, heavy, soft, and slow,
Brilliant and warm.
Nothing will help, and nothing do much harm.
Of the Properties of Nature for Healing an Illness. Stanza 1

Drink iron from rare springs; follow the sun;
Go far
To get the beam of some medicinal star;
Or in your anguish run
The gauntlet of all zones to an ultimate one.
Fever and chill
Punish you still,
Earth has no zone to work against your will.
Ibid. Stanza 2

Terror touches me when I
Dream I am touching a butterfly.
The Enamel Girl

Defiant even now, it tugs and moans
To be untangled from these mother's bones.
With Child. Stanza 3

MARK VAN DOREN
[1894–   ]

Grass nibbling inward
Like green fire.
Former Barn Lot. Stanza 3

The sun
Drew semicircles smooth and high.
A week was seven domes across a desert,
And any afternoon took long to die.
The Difference. Stanza 1

Wit is the only wall
Between us and the dark.
Wit. Stanza 1

Wit is the only breath
That keeps our eyelids warm,
Facing the driven ice
Of an old storm
That blows as ever it has blown
Against imperishable stone.
Ibid. Stanza 2

MARGARET L. FARRAND

A curve in the road and a hillside
Clear-cut against the sky;
A tall tree tossed by the Autumn wind,
And a white cloud riding high;
Ten men went along that road
And all but one passed by.
                The Seeing Eye. Stanza 1
And he put them down on canvas
For the other nine men to buy.
                        Ibid. Stanza 2

ROBERT GRAVES
[1895-   ]

As you are woman, so be lovely:
As you are lovely, so be various,
Merciful as constant, constant as vari-
    ous,
So be mine, as I yours for ever.
                Pygmalion to Galatea
With a fork drive Nature out,
    She will ever yet return.[1]
                        Marigolds
Look: the constant marigold
    Springs again from hidden roots.
Baffled gardener, you behold
    New beginnings and new shoots.
                            Ibid.
Hate is a fear, and fear is rot
    That cankers root and fruit alike:
Fight cleanly then, hate not, fear not,
    Strike with no madness when you
        strike.
                Hate Not, Fear Not
"How is your trade, Aquarius,
This frosty night?"
"Complaints is many and various,
And my feet are cold," says Aquarius.
                Star Talk. Stanza 5
I do not love the Sabbath,
    The soapsuds and the starch,
The troops of solemn people
    Who to Salvation march.
                The Boy Out of Church
Resolved that church and Sabbath
Were never made for man.
                            Ibid.

[1] Naturam expelles furca, tamen usque re-
    curret.
        HORACE: *Epistles, I, 10, 24*

When a dream is born in you
    With a sudden clamorous pain,
When you know the dream is true
    And lovely, with no flaw nor stain,
O then, be careful, or with sudden
        clutch
You'll hurt the delicate thing you prize
    so much.
                A Pinch of Salt. Stanza 1
May the gift of heavenly peace
And glory for all time
Keep the boy Tom who, tending geese,
First made the nursery rhyme.
                A Ballad of Nursery Rhyme.
                            Stanza 6
    A well-chosen anthology is a com-
plete dispensary of medicine for the
more common mental disorders, and
may be used as much for prevention as
cure.[1]
                On English Poetry. XXIX

ROBERT HILLYER
[1895-   ]

As one who bears beneath his neighbor's
        roof
Some thrust that staggers his unready
        wit
And brooding through the night on such
        reproof
Too late conceives the apt reply to it,
So all our life is but an afterthought.
                Sonnet: As One Who Bears
Fate harries us; we answer not a word,
Or answering too late, we waste our
        breath;
Not even a belated quip is heard
From those who bore the final taunt of
        death.
                            Ibid.

LEWIS MUMFORD
[1895-   ]

    People have hesitated to call Whit-
man's poems poetry; it is useless to
deny that they belong to sacred literature.
                The Golden Day. V

[1] The same idea has been admirably pursued in Robert Haven Schauffler's anthology,
*The Poetry Cure: A Pocket Medicine Chest
of Verse* [1925].

The jolly and comfortable bourgeois tradition of the Victorian age, a state of mind composed of felt slippers and warm bellywash.

The Golden Day. VIII

In Whitman and Melville letters again became as racy as the jabber of a waterside saloon; in all of Poe's poetry there is scarcely a line as good as pages of the best of Melville's prose.

Ibid.

E. MERRILL ROOT
[1895–   ]

Quietly I rise again
Over violence or chicane —
Defying from the deeper granite
The skin-diseases of the planet.

Scrub Oak. Stanza 5

Build on waste and desolation
Your green towers of affirmation.

Ibid. Stanza 6

JOHN RODERIGO
DOS PASSOS
[1896–   ]

All along the rails there were faces; in the portholes there were faces. Leeward a stale smell came from the tubby steamer that rode at anchor listed a little to one side with the yellow quarantine flag drooping at the foremast.

"I'd give a million dollars," said the old man resting on his oars, "to know what they come for."

"Just for that pop," said the young man who sat in the stern. "Ain't it the land of opportoonity?"

"One thing I do know," said the old man. "When I was a boy it was wild Irish came in the spring with the first run of shad. . . . Now there ain't no more shad, an them folks, Lord knows where they come from."

"It's the land of opportoonity."

Manhattan Transfer. Dollars

BEN RAY REDMAN
[1896–   ]

"What are you reading? . . . My dear! *not* a detective story!"

The delinquent hung her head. "Yes, it is," she murmured. Then, looking bravely up, she added: "But, you see, I am not reading to retain."

Reading at Random

DIXIE WILLSON

He may look just the same to you,
    And he may be just as fine,
But the next-door dog is the next-door
    dog,
And mine — is — mine!

Next-Door Dog

DOROTHY KEELEY ALDIS
[1897–   ]

Why, when I was told the news,
I felt wings upon my shoes
And gallivanted down the street
Wanting to be indiscreet
And shout to all the world that I
Was about to multiply.

Maternity

JOSEPH AUSLANDER
[1897–   ]

This man is dead.
Everything you can say
Is now quite definitely said:
This man held up his head
And had his day,
Then turned his head a little to one
    way
And slept instead.

Steel

    Spring had come
Like the silver needle-note of a fife,
Like a white plume and a green lance
    and a glittering knife
And a jubilant drum.

Ibid.

BERNARD DE VOTO
[1897–   ]

Much energy has been spent in an effort to determine where the West begins. The definitions of poetry and the luncheon clubs are unsatisfactory: vagueness should not be invoked when a precise answer is possible. The West begins where the average annual rainfall drops below twenty inches. When you reach the line which marks that drop — for convenience, the one hundredth meridian — you have reached the West.

The Plundered Province

Their [the Vermont highlanders'] ancestral religion told them that the world is a battleground whereon mankind is sentenced to defeat — an idea not inappropriate to the granite against which they must make their way. By the granite they have lived on for three centuries, tightening their belts and hanging on, by the sense of what is real. They are the base of the Yankee commonwealth, and America, staring apprehensively through fog that may not lift in this generation, may find their knowledge of hard things more than a little useful.

New England: There She Stands

New England is a finished place. Its destiny is that of Florence or Venice, not Milan, while the American empire careens onward toward its unpredicted end. . . . It is the first American section to be finished, to achieve stability in the conditions of its life. It is the first old civilization, the first permanent civilization in America.

Ibid.

Pessimism is only the name that men of weak nerves give to wisdom.

Mark Twain: The Ink of History

PHOEBE HOFFMAN (MRS. SPENCER BICKERTON)

In the long spring evening's twilight,
    when the sun is setting low,
And the smoke from all the engines
    flushes up, a rosy glow,
Then I come up to the bridge-head,
    watch the lights and net-work
    rails,
Think of when I rode the freighters —

engines spouting steam like
    whales,
D.L.W., Jersey Central, old *Rock
    Island, Pere Marquette,*
Reading coal cars down from Scranton,
    piled with anthracite like jet.
    The Freight Yards. Stanza 1

N. and W., the *Great Northern, Lehigh Valley, B. and O.,*
Like a giant earth-worm twisting,
    slowly 'round the curve they flow.
Caravans of freight move westward,
    bearing eastern goods away —
To come back with hogs and cattle,
    bales of sweet Kentucky hay.
Brakemen walk along the roof-tops,
    lingering for a moment's chat:
There an engineer, while smoking, long
    and eloquently spat.
    Ibid. Stanza 2
*L. and N., D. L. and W., Erie, Reading,
    P.R.R.*
Riding on your sliding roof-tops, that's
    where joy and freedom are.
    Ibid. Stanza 4

BERNICE LESBIA KENYON (MRS. WALTER GILKYSON) [1897–]

Never return in August to what you
    love;
Along the leaves will be rust
And over the hedges dust,
And in the air vague thunder and silence burning . . .
Choose some happier time for your returning.
    Return. Stanza 1

DAVID T. W. McCORD [1897–]

An old man sleeps. The house-fly goes,
Tasting the salt-lick of his nose.
    Salt Lick. Stanza 3
There were two engines: a great
Bull, his iron spouse,
Under the bridge in wait,
Breathing by Westinghouse.[1]
    8:15. Stanza 2

[1] George Westinghouse [1846–1914], inventor of the air-brake.

No sound, no cry: The longest aisle
Shows the deep colon rabbit-flight,
And where he went in pretty style,
As now his tracks go, out of sight.
>> *Tracks in the Snow. Stanza 5*
This bit of marmalade
which I've not ate,
this almost square of toast,
they'll save me yet.
>> *Moment in Marmalade*
By and by
God caught his eye.
>> *Epitaphs. The Waiter.*

THORNTON NIVEN WILDER
[1897–   ]

The whole purport of literature,
which is the notation of the heart. Style
is but the faintly contemptible vessel in
which the bitter liquid is recommended
to the world.
>> *The Bridge of San Luis Rey. II*
For what human ill does not dawn
seem to be an alleviation?
>> *Ibid. III*
We come from a world where we
have known incredible standards of excellence, and we dimly remember beauties which we have not seized again.
. . . The public for which masterpieces
are intended is not on this earth.
>> *Ibid. IV*

STEPHEN VINCENT BENÉT
[1898–   ]

I died in my boots like a pioneer
With the whole wide sky above me.
>> *The Ballad of William Sycamore*
He could fiddle all the bugs off a sweet-
potato-vine.
>> *The Mountain Whippoorwill.*
>> *Stanza 22*
Oh, Georgia booze is mighty fine booze,
The best yuh ever poured yuh,
But it eats the soles right offen yore
shoes,
For Hell's broke loose in Georgia.
>> *Ibid. Stanza 48*
He cleansed and anointed, took fresh
apparel,
And worshiped the Lord in a tuneful
carol.
>> *King David. Part VI, Stanza 5*

Down where the taproots of New Eng-
land trees
Suck bare existence from the broken
stones.
>> *The Golden Corpse. Sonnet 4*
The years have hardier tasks
Than listening to a whisper or a sigh.
They creep among us with a bag of
masks
And fit them to our brows obsequiously.
Some are of iron, to affront the gay,
And some of bronze, to satirize the
brave,
But most are merely a compost of clay
Cut in the sleepy features of a slave.
>> *Ibid. Sonnet 5*
There are sorceries more excellent
Than the first conflagration of the dust,
But none are quite so single in intent
Or unsophisticated with distrust.
The ripened fruit is golden to the core.
But an enchantment fosters it no more.
>> *Ibid. Sonnet 6*
American Muse, whose strong and di-
verse heart
So many men have tried to understand
But only made it smaller with their
art,
Because you are as various as your
land.
>> *John Brown's Body. Invocation*
Thames and all the rivers of the kings
Ran into Mississippi and were drowned.
>> *Ibid.*
Lincoln, six feet one in his stocking feet,
The lank man, knotty and tough as a
hickory rail,
Whose hands were always too big for
white-kid gloves,
Whose wit was a coonskin sack of dry,
tall tales,
Whose weathered face was homely as
a plowed field.
>> *Ibid. Book 2*
Honesty rare as a man without self-
pity,
Kindness as large and plain as a prairie
wind.
>> *Ibid.*
The Union's too big a horse to keep
changing the saddle
Each time it pinches you. As long as
you're sure

The saddle fits, you're bound to put up with the pinches
And not keep fussing the horse.
> *John Brown's Body. Book 2*

The small, dim noises, thousand-fold,
That all old houses and forests hold.
> *Ibid.*

So many letters come to a War Department,
One can hardly bother the clerks to answer them all.
> *Ibid. Book 3*

The ladies remember Butler for fifty years . . .
Make war on the men — the ladies have too-long memories.
> *Ibid. Book 4*

Broad-streeted Richmond. . . .
The trees in the streets are old trees used to living with people,
Family-trees that remember your grandfather's name.
> *Ibid.*

A little galled by Jefferson Davis . . .
He is not from Virginia, we never knew his grandfather.
> *Ibid.*

Whitman, with his sack of tobacco and comfits,
Passing along the terrible, crowded wards,
Listening, writing letters, trying to breathe
Strong life into lead-colored lips.
> *Ibid.*

Stonewall Jackson, wrapped in his beard and his silence.
> *Ibid.*

Comes Traveller and his master [Lee].
. . . Such horses are
The jewels of the horseman's hands and thighs,
They go by the word and hardly need the rein.
They bred such horses in Virginia then,
Horses that were remembered after death
And buried not so far from Christian ground.
> *Ibid.*

A great victor, in defeat as great,
No more, no less, always himself in both.
> *John Brown's Body. Book 4*

The ant finds kingdoms in a foot of ground.
> *Ibid.*

Grant . . .
There is no brilliant lamp in that dogged mind
And no conceit of brilliance to shake the hand,
But hand and mind can use the tools they get.
. . . The quiet, equable, deadly holder-on,
Faded-brown as a cinnamon-bear in Spring.
> *Ibid. Book 6*

"Let us cross the river," he said, "and rest under the shade of the trees." [1]
> *Ibid.*

So, when the crowd gives tongue
And prophets, old or young,
Bawl out their strange despair
Or fall in worship there,
Let them applaud the image or condemn
But keep your distance and your soul from them,
And, if the heart within your breast must burst
Like a cracked crucible and pour its steel
White-hot before the white heat of the wheel,
Strive to recast once more
That attar of the ore
In the strong mold of pain
Till it is whole again,
And while the prophets shudder or adore
Before the flame, hoping it will give ear,
If you at last must have a word to say,
Say neither, in their way,
"It is a deadly magic and accursed,"
Nor "It is blest," but only "It is here."
> *Ibid. Book 8. Conclusion*

---

[1] General "Stonewall" Jackson's last words [May 10, 1863].

It is so they die on the plains, the great,
old buffalo,
The herd-leaders, the beasts with the
kingly eyes,
Innocent, curly-browed,
They sink to the earth like mountains,
hairy and silent,
And their tongues are cut by the hunter.
Oh, singing tongue!
Great tongue of bronze and salt and the
free grasses,
Tongue of America, speaking for the
first time,
Must the hunter have you at last?

Now, face to face, you saw him
And lifted the right arm once, as a pilot
lifts it,
Signalling with the bell,
In the passage at night, on the river
known yet unknown,
— Perhaps to touch his shoulder, per-
haps in pain —
Then the rain fell on the roof and the
twilight darkened
And they said that in death you looked
like a marvelous old, wise child.
Ode to Walt Whitman. I
You're still the giant lode we quarry
For gold, fools' gold and all the earthy
metals,
The matchless mine.
Still the trail-breaker, still the rolling
river.
Ode to Walt Whitman. IV
Far north, far north are the sources of
the great river,
The headwaters, the cold lakes,
By the little sweet-tasting brooks of the
blond country,
The country of snow and wheat,
Or west among the black mountains, the
glacial springs.
Far North and West they lie and few
come to them.
Ibid.
Rolling, rolling from Arkansas, Kansas,
Iowa,
Rolling from Ohio, Wisconsin, Illinois,
Rolling and shouting:
Till, at last, it is Mississippi,
The Father of Waters; the matchless;
the great flood

Dyed with the earth of States; with the
dust and the sun and the seed of
half the States.
Ode to Walt Whitman. IV
I have fallen in love with American
names,
The sharp names that never get fat,
The snakeskin-titles of mining-claims,
The plumed war-bonnet of Medicine
Hat,
Tucson and Deadwood and Lost Mule
Flat.
American Names
Did they never watch for Nantucket
Light?
Ibid.
I shall not rest quiet in Montparnasse.
I shall not lie easy at Winchelsea.
You may bury my body in Sussex grass,
You may bury my tongue at Champ-
médy.
I shall not be there. I shall rise and
pass.
Bury my heart at Wounded Knee.
Ibid.
Now grimy April comes again,
Maketh bloom the fire-escapes,
Maketh silvers in the rain,
Maketh winter coats and capes
Suddenly all worn and shabby
Like the fur of winter bears,
Maketh kittens, maketh baby,
Maketh kissing on the stairs.
Maketh bug crawl out of crack,
Maketh ticklings down the back
As if sunlight stroked the spine
To a hurdy-gurdy's whine
And the shower ran white wine.
For City Spring
April hieth, April spieth
Everywhere a lover lieth,
Bringeth sweetness, bringeth fever,
Will not stop at "I would liever,"
Will not heed, "Now God a mercy!"
Turneth Moral topsy-versy,
Bringeth he and she to bed,
Bringeth ill to maidenhead,
Bringeth joyance in its stead.
Ibid.
"It is eighteen years," I cried. "You
must come no more."
"We know your names. We know that
you are the dead.

Must you march forever from France
and the last, blind war?"
"Fool! From the next!" they said.
1936

ERNEST HEMINGWAY
[1898–   ]

A growing ecstasy of ordered, formal,
passionate, increasing disregard for
death. . . .

It is impossible to believe the emotional and spiritual intensity and pure,
classic beauty that can be produced by
a man, an animal, and a piece of scarlet
serge draped over a stick.
Death in the Afternoon. Chap. 18

All modern American literature comes
from one book by Mark Twain called
Huckleberry Finn. If you read it you
must stop where the Nigger Jim is
stolen from the boys. That is the real
end. The rest is just cheating. But it's
the best book we've had. All American
writing comes from that. There was
nothing before. There has been nothing
as good since.
The Green Hills of Africa. Chap. 1

Not this August, nor this September;
you have this year to do in what you
like. Not next August, nor next September; that is still too soon; they are
still too prosperous from the way things
pick up when armament factories start
at near capacity; they never fight as
long as money can still be made without. . . . But the year after that or
the year after that they fight.
Notes on the Next War [1]

The first panacea for a mismanaged
nation is inflation of the currency; the
second is war. Both bring a temporary
prosperity; both bring a permanent
ruin. But both are the refuge of political
and economic opportunists.
Ibid.

They wrote in the old days that it
is sweet and fitting to die for one's
country. But in modern war there is
nothing sweet nor fitting in your dying.
You will die like a dog for no good
reason.
Ibid.

[1] In *Esquire, Sept., 1935.*

DONALD CULROSS PEATTIE
[1898–   ]

It is natural that women should like
the birds whose domestic affairs can be
observed under the eaves; they love the
sweetest singers, the brightest plumage,
the species not too shy to be seen at
close range. For them the waders and
swimmers, the awkward of leg, the
harsh of cry, the wild of soul, have
seldom the same appeal. But that
which flees from men, that will men
have. Women of all people ought to
understand this, but they do not, quite.
An Almanac for Moderns.
November 9

In Thomas Henry Huxley Darwinism
had a champion in invincible armor.
For sheer glitter his mind has seldom
had an equal in any land or age and
he laid waste about him with the
weapon of truth. "The cradle of every
science," he chuckled, "is surrounded
by dead theologians as that of Hercules
was with strangled serpents."
Ibid. February 13

The beauty of a butterfly's wing, the
beauty of all things, is not a slave to
purpose, a drudge sold to futurity. It
is excrescence, superabundance, random
ebullience, and sheer delightful waste
to be enjoyed in its own high right.
Ibid. March 13

Life is adventure in experience, and
when you are no longer greedy for the
last drop of it, it means no more than
that you have set your face, whether
you know it or not, to the day when you
shall depart without a backward look.
Those who look backward longingly to
the end die young, at whatever age.
Ibid. March 18

The time to hear bird music is between four and six in the morning.
Seven o'clock is not too late, but by
eight the fine rapture is over, due, I
suspect, to the contentment of the inner man that comes with breakfast; a
poet should always be hungry or have
a lost love.
Ibid. April 22

RUTH PITTER

Towns and noblemen are made
By silly fortune's dole,
But birds, and they who wield the
    spade,
They are green England's singing soul.
    The Realm. Stanza 4

When we have buried her, made her
    unseen,
    We will lie down and weep;
Our part is done; we have found her a
    green
    Quiet place wherein to sleep.
    The Burial. Stanza 1

It was the mystery and the dark way
    That made them weep so sore;
They knew not whether she were grave
    or gay
    Or peaceful, or no more.
    Ibid. Stanza 2

You are afraid. You do not dare
Up to the Lion to lift your eyes,
And unashamed his beauty share
As once in that lost Paradise.
    Caged Lion. Stanza 1

His maned neck of massy girth
    Only one Arm in love enfolds:
His beauty humbled to the earth
    Only my wrathful God beholds.
    Ibid. Stanza 3

DOROTHY E. REID

A goosegirl ermined is a goosegirl still
And geese will gabble everywhere she
    goes.
    Not in Andersen

I'll spend my time till midnight, sewing
Red flannel drawers for leprechauns!
    Concession

There was a sunrise falling like red
    blood. . . .
And men and women creeping through
    the red
Of the marvellous city, could not quite
    deny
All day the life that startled them: they
    said
Beautiful things, and wept, and won-
    dered why.
    Poem Carried as a Banner

HELENE MULLINS
[1899–   ]

The anxious and distrustful constantly
Require that their companions speak
    their praise,
Holding it as a gross discourtesy
If any disagree with them.
    Only the Self-Confident

Only the stern self-confident can hold
Their peace amidst the clamor, nor be-
    tray
Their capabilities; can sit unmoved,
With all around them trembling to have
    told
The utmost of their merits; only they
Can bear to leave their strength un-
    guessed, unproved.
    Ibid.

ELWYN BROOKS WHITE
[1899–   ]

The critic leaves at curtain fall
    To find, in starting to review it,
He scarcely saw the play at all
    For watching his reaction to it.
    Critic

All poets who, when reading from
their own works, experience a choked
feeling, are major. For that matter, all
poets who read from their own works
are major, whether they choke or not.
All women poets, dead or alive, who
smoke cigars are major. All poets who
have sold a sonnet for one hundred and
twenty-five dollars to a magazine with
a paid circulation of four hundred thousand are major. A sonnet is composed
of fourteen lines; thus the payment in
this case is eight dollars and ninety-
three cents a line, which constitutes a
poet's majority.
    How to Tell a Major Poet
    from a Minor Poet

The truth is, it is fairly easy to tell
the two types apart; it is only when
one sets about trying to decide whether
what they write is any good or not that
the thing really becomes complicated.
    Ibid.

"It's broccoli, dear."
"I say it's spinach, and I say the
hell with it."
In The New Yorker

RICHARD HUGHES
[1900–   ]

Puddings should be
Full of currants, for me:
Boiled in a pail,
Tied in the tail
Of an old bleached shirt:
So hot that they hurt.
Poets, Painters, Puddings
I saw the World's arches,
The spreading roots of light,
The high wordy pillars
That hold all upright,
The deep verbal fundament
Whereon rests sure
The world on thoughtful vaulting,
Interlocked, secure.
Ecstatic Ode on Vision

MARTHA OSTENSO
[1900–   ]

Pity the Unicorn,
Pity the Hippogriff,
Souls that were never born
Out of the land of If!
The Unicorn and the Hippogriff.
Stanza 1

THOMAS WOLFE
[1900–   ]

He awakes at morning in a foreign
land, he draws his breath in labor in
the wool-soft air of Europe: the wool-
gray air is all about him like a living
substance; it is in his heart, his stomach, and his entrails; it is in the slow
and vital movements of the people; it
soaks down from the sodden skies into
the earth, into the heavy buildings, into
the limbs and hearts and brains of living men. . . .
It was there now; it will always be
there. They had it in Merry England
and they had it in Gay Paree; and they
were seldom merry, and they were
rarely gay. The wet, woolen air is over

Munich; it is over Paris; it is over
Rouen and Madame Bovary; it soaks
into England; it gets into boiled mutton and the Brussels sprouts; it gets
into Hammersmith on Sunday; it
broods over Bloomsbury and the private
hotels and the British Museum; it soaks
into the land of Europe and keeps the
grass green.
Of Time and the River. Book VII
Where can you match the mighty
music of their names? — The Monon-
gahela, the Colorado, the Rio Grande,
the Columbia, the Tennessee, the Hudson (Sweet Thames!); the Kennebec,
the Rappahannock, the Delaware, the
Penobscot, the Wabash, the Chesapeake, the Swannanoa, the Indian
River, the Niagara (Sweet Afton!);
the Saint Lawrence, the Susquehanna,
the Tombigbee, the Nantahala, the
French Broad, the Chattahoochee, the
Arizona, and the Potomac (Father
Tiber!) — these are a few of their
princely names, these are a few of their
great, proud, glittering names, fit for the
immense and lonely land that they inhabit.
Oh, Tiber! Father Tiber! You'd only
be a suckling in that mighty land!
And as for you, sweet Thames, flow
gently till I end my song: flow gently,
gentle Thames, be well-behaved, sweet
Thames, speak softly and politely,
little Thames, flow gently till I end my
song.
Ibid.
It is Europeans, for the most part,
who have constructed these great ships,
but without America they have no
meaning. These ships are alive with the
supreme ecstasy of the modern world,
which is the voyage to America. There
is no other experience that is remotely
comparable to it, in its sense of joy,
its exultancy, its drunken and magnificent hope which, against reason and
knowledge, soars into a heaven of fabulous conviction, which believes in the
miracle and sees it invariably achieved.
In this soft, this somewhat languid
air, the ship glowed like an immense
and brilliant jewel. All of her lights

were on, they burned row by row straight across her 900 feet of length, with the small, hard twinkle of cut gems: it was as if the vast, black cliff of her hull, which strangely suggested the glittering night-time cliff of the fabulous city that was her destination, had been sown with diamonds.

Of Time and the River. Book VIII

Out of one darkness the travellers have come to be taken into another, but for a moment one sees their faces, awful and still, all uplifted towards the ship. This is all: their words have vanished, all memory of the movements they made then has also vanished: one remembers only their silence and their still faces lifted in the phantasmal light of lost time; one sees them ever, still and silent, as they slide from darkness on the river of time; one sees them waiting at the ship's great side, all silent and all damned to die, with their grave, white faces lifted in a single supplication to the ship, and towards the silent row of passengers along the deck, who for a moment return their gaze with the same grave and tranquil stare. That silent meeting is a summary of all the meetings of men's lives.

Ibid.

ALAN PORTER

Every countenance
That warms and lights the heart of the beholder
Shews, clear and true, the signature of pain.

The Signature of Pain

"Good men have bags of money
And blazoned shields.
I wonder how much money
My new play yields?"
This is what Shakespeare said,
Wagging his wicked head,
Walking from Aldermanbury
To Bunhill Fields.

The Poet's Journey

Not being versed in argument
They killed the herald heaven had sent,
Taking the trouble to invent
An instrument,

A golden mechanical hammer, such
In size, he could not suffer much.

But warned by heaven,
Hours before,
He had deposited a pamphlet under
every door.

The Transit of Joy

Let him that beds a princess fear
To show himself too free,
And ceremoniously draw near:
There should between true lovers be
An excellent immodesty.

A Plea That Shame Be Forgotten

I am not one that would be thinned
Into an immaterial wind:
I have no longing to be seen
A part of April's fledge of green,
Or burn where summer suns have been.

Death. Stanza 2

Were death forgotten, days were white
Circles of unimpaired delight.

Ibid. Stanza 4

ROY CAMPBELL
[1902–   ]

You praise the firm restraint with
which they write —
I'm with you there, of course:
They use the snaffle and the curb all
right,
But where's the bloody horse?

On Some South African Novelists

We had no time for make-believe
So early each began
To wear his liver on his sleeve,
To snarl, and be an angry man:
Far in the desert we have been
Where Nature, still to poets kind,
Admits no vegetable green
To soften the determined mind.

Poets in Africa. Stanza 2

Each like a freezing salamander
Impervious and immune,
No snivelling sentiment shall pander
To our flirtations with the moon,
And though with gay batrachian chir-
rup
Her poets thrill the swampy reach,
Not with so glutinous a syrup

As moonlight shall we grease our speech.

Poets in Africa. Stanza 4

With white tails smoking free,
Long streaming manes, and arching necks, they show
Their kinship to their sisters of the sea —
And forward hurl their thunderbolts of snow.
Still out of hardship bred,
Spirits of power and beauty and delight
Have ever on such frugal pastures fed
And loved to course with tempests through the night.

Horses on the Camargue

I love to see, when leaves depart,
The clear anatomy arrive,
Winter, the paragon of art,
That kills all forms of life and feeling
Save what is pure and will survive.

Autumn

LANGSTON HUGHES [1]
[1902–   ]

De railroad bridge's
A sad song in de air.
Ever' time de trains pass
I wants to go somewhere.

Homesick Blues. Stanza 1

A bright bowl of brass is beautiful to the Lord.
Bright polished brass like the cymbals
Of King David's dancers,
Like the wine cups of Solomon.
Hey, boy!
A clean spittoon on the altar of the Lord.
A clean bright spittoon all newly polished, —
At least I can offer that.
Com'mere, boy!

Brass Spittoons

[1] Working as a busboy in Washington, he was discovered by Vachel Lindsay, who read several of his poems to a fashionable audience in the very hotel in which Hughes carried trays of dishes. This incident attracted the attention of the press of the country, and people who never would have glanced at the poetry for its own sake became interested in the career of so strange a singer. — LOUIS UNTERMEYER: *Modern American Poetry*

CHARLES AUGUSTUS LINDBERGH
[1902–   ]

We (that's my ship and I) took off rather suddenly. We had a report somewhere around 4 o'clock in the afternoon before that the weather would be fine, so we thought we would try it.

Lindbergh's Own Story [of his non-stop flight, Long Island to Paris], in The New York Times, May 23, 1927

I saw a fleet of fishing boats. . . . I flew down almost touching the craft and yelled at them, asking if I was on the right road to Ireland.

They just stared. Maybe they didn't hear me. Maybe I didn't hear them. Or maybe they thought I was just a crazy fool. An hour later I saw land.

Ibid.

OGDEN NASH
[1902–   ]

They have such refined and delicate palates
That they can discover no one worthy of their ballots,
And then when some one terrible gets elected
They say, There, that's just what I expected!

Election Day Is a Holiday

I think that I shall never see
A billboard lovely as a tree.[1]

[1] Another parody of Kilmer's poem, often quoted in trade journals (authorship already uncertain?) runs as follows:—

I think that I shall never see
Aught lovely as a pulpwood tree.

A tree that grows through sunny noons
To furnish sporting page cartoons.

A tree whose girth will prove its age
Is ample for a want ad page.

A tree with grace toward heaven rising,
Men macerate for advertising.

A tree that lifts its arms and laughs,
To be made into paragraphs.

A tree that falls before the saw,
A five-star final in the raw.

Perhaps, unless the billboards fall,
I'll never see a tree at all.
Song of the Open Road

The season when ordinarily kind-
hearted business men fill up their
pockets with cartridges
And go prowling around the woods in
search of caribous and partridges.
Ode to the N.W. by W. Wind

In the phalanx of hy-
Phenated names!
(Have you ever observed
That the name of Smith
Is the oftenest hy-
Phenated with?)
Pride Goeth Before a Raise

They take a paper and they read the
headlines,
So they've heard of unemployment and
they've heard of breadlines,
And they philanthropically cure them
all
By getting up a costume charity ball.
Ibid.

There are some people who are very
resourceful
At being remorseful,
And who apparently feel that the best
way to make friends
Is to do something terrible and then
make amends.
Hearts of Gold

Candy is dandy
But liquor is quicker.
Reflection on Ice-Breaking

Some one invented the telephone,
And interrupted a nation's slumbers,
Ringing wrong but similar numbers.
Look What You Did, Christopher

I wonder if the citizens of New York
will ever get sufficiently wroth
To remember that Tammany cooks
spoil the broth.
Speculative Reflection

A regular poet published a book,
And an excellent book it was,
But nobody gave it a second look,
As nobody often does.
A Parable for Sports Writers. III

One would be in less danger
From the wiles of the stranger

If one's own kin and kith
Were more fun to be with.
Family Court

O money, money, money, I am not necessarily one of those who think
thee holy,
But I often stop to wonder how thou
canst go out so fast when thou
comest in so slowly.
*Hymn to the Thing That Makes
the Wolf Go*

Thanksgiving, like ambassadors, cab-
inet-officers and others smeared
with political ointment,
Depends for its existence on Presidential appointment.
A Short Outline of Thanksgiving

If you are grateful for anything on any
particular day,
By the time you wake up next morning it's probably been taken away.
Ibid.

This is the sum total of Thanksgiving
lore:
Not to be thankful until you're tired of
what you're being thankful for.
Ibid.

The old men know when an old man
dies.
Old Men

Yours be the genial holly wreaths,
The stockings and the tree;
An aged world to you bequeaths
Its own forgotten glee.
A Carol for Children. Stanza 2

God rest you, merry Innocents,
While innocence endures.
A sweeter Christmas than we to ours
May you bequeath to yours.
Ibid. Stanza 9

COUNTEE CULLEN
[1903–   ]

Not for myself I make this prayer,
But for this race of mine
That stretches forth from shadowed
places
Dark hands for bread and wine.
Pagan Prayer. Stanza 1

She thinks that even up in heaven
Her class lies late and snores,

While poor black cherubs rise at seven
To do celestial chores.
Epitaph: A Lady I Know

MERRILL MOORE
[1903–   ]

Talking about men who are richer than
    they are
And telling how things that are might
    be otherwise
And looking out of the corners of their
    eyes
Are what old men inordinately like to
    do,

Men not so old that they have lost all
    care
For matters they used to pride them-
    selves about
But certainly long since past the find-
    ing out
Of whether these matters were or were
    not true.
Old Men

WILLIAM PLOMER
[1903–   ]

We saw, heraldic in the heat,
A scorpion on a stone.
The Scorpion

MacKINLAY KANTOR
[1904–   ]

I was a dog of Gettysburg. I trotted
    near the train
And nosed among the officers who
    kicked me to my pain.
A man came by . . . I could not see.
    I howled. The light was dim,
But when I brushed against his legs, I
    liked the smell of him.
Abraham Lincoln at Gettysburg.
Stanza 9

CECIL DAY LEWIS
[1905–   ]

I've heard them lilting at loom and
    belting,
Lasses lilting before dawn of day:

But now they are silent, not gamesome
    and gallant —
The flowers of the town are rotting
    away.[1]

There was laughter and loving in the
    lanes at evening;
Handsome were the boys then, and
    girls were gay.
But lost in Flanders by medalled com-
    manders
The lads of the village are vanished
    away.
A Time to Dance

Come, live with me and be my love,[2]
And we will all the pleasures prove
Of peace and plenty, bed and board,
That chance employment may afford.

I'll handle dainties on the docks
And thou shalt read of summer frocks:
At evening by the sour canals
We'll hope to hear some madrigals.
Ibid.

Stake out your claim. Go downwards.
    Bore
Through the tough crust. Oh learn to
    feel
A way in darkness to good ore.
You are the magnet and the steel.

Out of that dark a new world flowers.
There in the womb, in the rich veins
Are tools, dynamos, bridges, towers,
Your tractors and your travelling-
    cranes.
The Magnetic Mountain. 28

Make us a wind
To shake the world out of this sleepy
    sickness
Where flesh has dwindled and bright-
    ness waned!
New life multiple in seed and cell
Mounts up to brace our slackness.

[1] I've heard them lilting at our ewe-milking,
    Lasses a-lilting before dawn o' day;
But now they are moaning on ilka green
    loaning:
    "The Flowers of the Forest are a' wede
    away."
        JANE ELLIOTT [1727–1805]:
          A Lament for Flodden
          (September 9, 1513)
See Cockburn, page 240.
  [2] See Marlowe, page 31.

Oppression's passion, a full organ swell
Through our throats welling wild
Of angers in unison arise
And hunger haunted with a million
    sighs,
Make us a wind to shake the world!
        The Magnetic Mountain. 31
Spring through death's iron guard
Her million blades shall thrust;
Love that was sleeping, not extinct,
Throw off the nightmare crust.

Eyes, though not ours, shall see
Sky-high a signal flame,
The sun returned to power above
A world, but not the same.
        Ibid. 35

    The Georgian poets, a sadly pedestrian rabble, flocked along the roads their fathers had built, pointing out to each other the beauty spots and ostentatiously drinking small-beer in a desperate effort to prove their virility. The winds blew, the floods came: for a moment a few of them showed on the crest of the seventh great wave; then they were rolled under and nothing marks their graves. One only rode the whirlwind: Wilfrid Owen, killed on the Sambre canal, spoke above the barrage and the gas-cloud, saying to us, 'The poetry is in the pity.' When it was all over, it was left to an American, T. S. Eliot, to pick up some of the fragments of civilization, place them end to end, and on that crazy pavement walk precariously through the waste land.
        A Hope for Poetry [*1934*]
    Writers of my own generation are interested in politics to an extent unequalled among English writers since the French Revolution.
        The Revolution in Literature
            [*1936*]

WYSTAN HUGH AUDEN
[1907–   ]

A host of columbines and pathics
Who show the poor by mathematics
    In their defence
That wealth and poverty are merely
Mental pictures, so that clearly

Every tramp's a landlord really
    In mind-events.

Let fever sweat them till they tremble
Cramp rack their limbs till they resemble
    Cartoons by Goya:
Their daughters sterile be in rut,
May cancer rot their herring gut,
The circular madness on them shut,
    Or paranoia.
        On This Island. XIV
    Cathedrals,
Luxury liners laden with souls,
Holding to the east their hulls of stone,
        Ibid. XVII

The poet reciting to Lady Diana
While the footmen whisper 'Have a
    banana,'
The judge enforcing the obsolete law,
The banker making the loan for the
    war,

The expert designing the long-range
    gun
To exterminate everyone under the sun,
Would like to get out but can only
    mutter; —
'What can I do? It's my bread and
    butter.'
        Ibid. XVIII

Underneath the abject willow,
    Lover, sulk no more;
Act from thought should quickly follow:
    What is thinking for?
Your unique and moping station
    Proves you cold;
    Stand up and fold
Your map of desolation.
        Ibid. XXII

O for doors to be open and an invite
    with gilded edges
To dine with Lord Lobcock and Count
    Asthma on the platinum benches,
With the somersaults and fireworks, the
    roast and the smacking kisses —
    Cried the cripples to the silent
        statue,
    The six beggared cripples.
        Ibid. XXIV

GEORGE DILLON
[1907–   ]

When love was false and I was full of
    care,
And friendship cold and I was sick with
    fear,
Music, the beautiful disturber of the
    air,
Drew near,
Saying: Come with me into my country
    of air
Out of the querulous and uncivil clay;
Fling down its aching members into a
    chair,
And come away.
The Constant One. Stanzas 1 and 2

EDWARD DORO
[1909–   ]

I was eleven, hardly more,
    When first I saw a crystal boar,
Stretched on the ground in self-admir-
    ing fettle,
With purple eyes and snout of golden
    metal —
Polished by digging roots — and bones
    of coral.
Looking, I deemed he was a thing im-
    moral,
    Something a boy should never see.
    I turned and ran, precipitously.
The Boar and Shibboleth. Stanza 1
I was thrown for ever in a riot
Of gold and purple thoughts. I wait in
    quiet.
    Sometimes I say beneath my breath
    The lovely name of Shibboleth.
Ibid. Stanza 10

STEPHEN SPENDER
[1909–   ]

Central 'I' is surrounded by 'I eating',
'I loving', 'I angry', 'I excreting',
And the 'great I' planted in him
Has nothing to do with all these,

It can never claim its true place
Resting in the forehead, and secure in
    his gaze.
The 'great I' is an unfortunate intruder

Quarrelling with 'I tiring' and 'I sleep-
    ing'
And all those other 'I's who long for
    'We dying'.
Poems. 9
I think continually of those who were
    truly great.
Who, from the womb, remembered the
    soul's history
Through corridors of light where the
    hours are suns
Endless and singing. Whose lovely am-
    bition
Was that their lips, still touched with
    fire,
Should tell of the Spirit clothed from
    head to foot in song.
Ibid. 30
After the first powerful plain manifesto
The black statement of pistons, with-
    out more fuss
But gliding like a queen, she leaves the
    station.
Without bowing and with restrained
    unconcern
She passes the houses which humbly
    crowd outside,
The gasworks and at last the heavy
    page
Of death, printed by gravestones in the
    cemetery.
Beyond the town there lies the open
    country
Where, gathering speed, she acquires
    mystery,
The luminous self-possession of ships
    on ocean.
Ibid. 34, The Express

NATHALIA CRANE
[1913–   ]

Oh, I'm in love with the janitor's boy,
    And the janitor's boy loves me;
He's going to hunt for a desert isle
    In our geography.
The Janitor's Boy. Stanza 1
I linger on the flathouse roof, the moon-
    light is divine.
But my heart is all a-flutter like the
    washing on the line.
The Flathouse Roof. Stanza 1

Once a pallid vestal
  Doubted truth in blue;
Listed red as ruin,
  Harried every hue.
          The Vestal. Stanza 1

Every gaudy color
  Is a bit of truth.
          Ibid. Stanza 5

In the darkness, who would answer for
  the color of a rose,
Or the vestments of the May moth and
  the pilgrimage it goes?
          The Blind Girl. Stanza 1

I sat down on a bumble bee,
  But I arose again;

And now I know the tenseness of
  Humiliating pain.
          Suffering. Stanza 3

The steps of the paper-box factory,
As well as the gardens of kings
Are only the blue-print devices
Of love, and the commonplace things.
          The Commonplace. Stanza 6

When the moon comes over Brooklyn
  On time with the borough clock,
'Tis the same that saw Palmyra
  And the walls of Antioch.
          The Moon of Brooklyn. Stanza 1

There is a glory
  In a great mistake.
          Imperfection

MISCELLANEOUS

WALTER DE MAP
[1140-1210]

Die I must, but let me die drinking in
  an inn!
Hold the wine-cup to my lips sparkling
  from the bin!
So, when angels flutter down to take
  me from my sin,
"Ah, God have mercy on this sot," the
  cherubs will begin.[1]

> Quoted by J. R. GREEN, in A
> Short History of the English
> People, Chap. 3, Sect. 1 (There
> is also a translation by Leigh
> Hunt: "The Jovial Priest's Con-
> fession.")

MARTHA ("MOTHER") SHIPTON
[1488-1561]

Carriages without horses shall go,
And accidents fill the world with woe.
Prophecy

Around the world thoughts shall fly
In the twinkling of an eye.
Ibid.

Under water men shall walk,
Shall ride, shall sleep, and talk;
In the air men shall be seen
In white, in black, and in green.
Ibid.

Iron in the water shall float
As easy as a wooden boat.
Ibid.

WILLIAM, PRINCE OF ORANGE
[1533-1584]

There is one certain means by which

---

[1] The Latin version concludes:
*Tunc cantabunt laetius angelorum chori
Deus sit propitius isti potatori.*

I can be sure never to see my country's
ruin, — I will die in the last ditch.[1]

> HUME: *History of England
> [1622]* and J. R. GREEN: *A
> Short History of the English
> People, Chap. 9*

ROBERT GREENE
[1560-1592]

Sweet are the thoughts that savour of
  content;
The quiet mind is richer than a
  crown. . . .
A mind content both crown and kingdom is.
Farewell to Folly

RICHARD BRATHWAITE
[1588-1673]

Hanging of his cat on Monday
For killing of a mouse on Sunday.[2]
*Drunken Barnabee's Four Journeys.
Page 5 [1805 edition]*

KING CHARLES II
[1630-1685]

Good as a play.[3]
> *Exclamation in Parliament, dur-
> ing the discussion of Lord Ross's
> Divorce Bill*

---

[1] Buckingham had urged the inevitable destruction which hung over the United Provinces, and asked the Prince whether he did not
see that the commonwealth was ruined.
[2] For killing of the Lord's own mouse
  Upon the Sabbath-day.
  ANONYMOUS: *The Cameronian Cat,*
  St. 4 (written between 1642 and 1684)
[3] The king remained in the House of Peers
while his speech was taken into consideration,
—a common practice with him; for the debates amused his sated mind, and were sometimes, he used to say, as good as a comedy. — MACAULAY: *Review of the Life and
Writings of Sir William Temple*
  Nullos his mallem ludos spectasse (No
plays would I prefer to have seen than
these). — HORACE: *Satires, II, 8, 79*

JOHN DYER
[*Floruit* 1714]

While wine and friendship crown the
board,
We'll sing the joys that both afford;
And he that won't with us comply,
Down among the dead men let him lie.
Down Among the Dead Men.
Stanza 3

LORD CHARLES HAY
[? –1760]

Gentlemen of the French guard, fire
first.[1]
At the Battle of Fontenoy [*1745*]

JOSIAH WEDGWOOD
[1730–1795]

Am I not a man and brother?
On a Medallion [2] [*1787*]

WILLIAM DRENNAN
[1754–1820]

Nor one feeling of vengeance presume
to defile
The cause, or the men, of the Emerald
Isle.[3]
Erin. Stanza 3 [*1795*]

R. S. SHARPE
[1759–1835]

In two little words all the difference lies,
I always say "come," and you always
say "go." . . .
You say "go" to your man, as you lay
in your bed,
I say, "Come, Jack, with me," and I see
the work done.
Come and Go. Stanzas 7 and 8

[1] To which the Comte d'Auteroches replied,
"Sir, we never fire first; please to fire yourselves." — EDOUARD FOURNIER [1819–1880]:
L'Esprit dans l'Histoire
[2] Representing a Negro in chains, with one
knee on the ground and both hands lifted up
to heaven. This was adopted as a seal by the
Anti-Slavery Society of London.
[3] The first known use of this appellation for
Ireland.

MASON LOCKE WEEMS
[1759–1825]

"George," said his father, "do you
know who killed that beautiful little
cherry tree yonder in the garden?" . . .
Looking at his father with the sweet
face of youth brightened with the inexpressible charm of all-conquering
truth, he bravely cried out, "I can't tell
a lie, Pa; you know I can't tell a lie. I
did cut it with my hatchet."
The Life of George Washing-
ton: With Curious Anecdotes.
Equally Honorable to Himself
and Exemplary to His Young
Countrymen

SCROPE DAVIES
[1771–1852]

Babylon in all its desolation is a sight
not so awful as that of the human mind
in ruins.
Letter to Thomas Raikes
[*May 25, 1835*]

JOHN SINCLAIR
[1791–1857]

A man, whose name was Johnny Sands,
Had married Betty Haigh,
And though she brought him gold and
lands,
She proved a terrible plague.
Johnny Sands. Stanza 1

JOHN HAMILTON REYNOLDS
("PETER CORCORAN")
[1796–1852]

Throw in his hat, and with a spring
Get gallantly within the ring.
The Fancy: Poetry of the
Pugilistic Club

HOWARD FISH

The good but pine; the order of the day
Is — prey on others, or become a
prey. . . .

With which, who will not readily comply,
But rates a vagrant, and as such may
die.
The Wrongs of Man [1] [*1819*]

ALFRED AINGER
[1837–1904]

Our English critics their dull wits keep
straining,
When — Enter Taine! [2] — and all is
entertaining.
Epigram

ELIZABETH WORDSWORTH
[1840– ?]

If all good people were clever,
And all clever people were good,
The world would be nicer than ever
We thought that it possibly could.

But somehow, 'tis seldom or never
The two hit it off as they should;
The good are so harsh to the clever,
The clever so rude to the good.
The Clever and the Good

BARTLEY CAMPBELL
[1843–1888]

Rags are royal raiment when worn
for virtue's sake. [3]
The White Slave [*1882*]

JARRETT AND PALMER
[*Flourished* 1866]

Legs are staple articles and will never
go out of fashion while the world lasts.
Of the original production [*1866*]
*of their Grand Magical Spectacu-
lar Drama, The Black Crook, by
Charles M. Barras*

[1] Painted by a vandal on Grant's Tomb,
New York, August 28, 1932.
[2] Hippolyte Taine [1828–1893], famous
French critic and historian of literature.
[3] The line is carved on Campbell's monument in St. Mary's Cemetery, Pittsburgh, Pa.

MRS. EDWARD CRASTER

The centipede was happy quite
Until a toad in fun
Said, "Pray, which leg goes after
which?"
That worked her mind to such a pitch,
She lay distracted in a ditch,
Considering how to run.
*Credited, in Cassell's Weekly, to
Pinafore Poems* [*1871*]

LORD NANCY

To have a thing is nothing, if you've not
the chance to show it,
And to know a thing is nothing, unless
others know you know it.
Source unknown

KING GEORGE V
[1865–1936]

If I may be regarded as in some true
sense the head of this great and widespread family, sharing its life and sustained by its affection, this will be a full
reward for the long and sometimes anxious labours of my reign.
*Radio greeting to the British Em-
pire* [*Christmas Day, 1934*]

THE REVEREND CORNELIUS
WHAURR

In this imperfect, gloomy scene
Of complicated ill,
How rarely is a day serene,
The throbbing bosom still!
Will not a beauteous landscape bright
Or music's soothing sound,
Console the heart, afford delight,
And throw sweet peace around?
They may; but never comfort lend
Like an Accomplished Female Friend!
*The Female Friend. Stanza 1
(Quoted by E. V. Lucas and
J. C. Squire; source unknown)*

But lasting joys the man attend
Who has a Polished Female Friend!
Ibid. Stanza 3

BURTON J. HENDRICK
[1871–   ]

It is now a commonplace that the dissenting opinions of one generation become the prevailing interpretation of the next.

Bulwark of the Republic, Page 417

RUSSELL HILLARD LOINES
[1874–1922]

"Scorn not the sonnet," though its
  strength be sapped,
  Nor say malignant its inventor blundered:
The corpse that here in fourteen lines is
  wrapped
  Had otherwise been covered with a
  hundred.

On a Magazine Sonnet

FRANK ALOYSIUS ROBERT TINNEY
[1878–   ]

I ain't going to have more than three children, I read in an almanac that every fourth person born into the world is a Chinaman.

Vaudeville quip

BRUCE BAIRNSFATHER
[1887–   ]

If you know a better 'ole, go to it.
*Caption of famous cartoon
during the Great War*

ROBERT LEROY RIPLEY
[1893–   ]

Believe it or not.
*Title of syndicated
newspaper feature*

KING GEORGE VI
[1895–   ]

The highest of distinctions is service to others.
*Broadcast greeting to his em-
pire after his coronation, May
12, 1937*

In the years yet to come, some of you will travel from one part of the commonwealth to another and, moving thus within the family circle, will meet many whose thoughts are colored by the same memories, whose hearts unite in devotion to our common heritage.

Ibid.

G. L. HEMMINGER
Tobacco is a dirty weed. I like it.
It satisfies no normal need. I like it.
It makes you thin, it makes you lean,
It takes the hair right off your bean.
It's the worst darn stuff I've ever seen.
  I like it.
*First published in Penn State
Froth, November, 1915*

All the brothers were valiant,[1] and all the sisters virtuous.
*From the inscription on the tomb of
the Duchess of Newcastle in Westminster Abbey*

Art and part.

A Scottish law phrase, an accessory before and after the fact. A man is said to be *art and part* of a crime when he contrives the manner of the deed, and concurs with and encourages those who commit the crime, although he does not put his own hand to the actual execution of it. — SCOTT: *Tales of a Grandfather, Chap. 22* (Execution of Morton)

Art preservative of all arts.

From the inscription upon the façade of the house in Haarlem, Holland, formerly occupied by Laurens Koster (or Coster), who is credited, among others, with the invention of printing with movable types, about 1440 or 1446. Mention is first made of this inscription about 1628:

MEMORIAE SACRUM
TYPOGRAPHIA
ARS ARTIUM OMNIUM
CONSERVATRIX.
HIC PRIMUM INVENTA
CIRCUM ANNUM MCCCCXL.[2]

---

[1] Title of a novel [1919] by Ben Ames Williams.

[2] Compare inscription on the "Printer's Sun-Dial" at the Country Life Press (Doubleday, Doran and Company), Garden City,

Begging the question.

This is a common logical fallacy, *petitio principii;* and the first explanation of the phrase is to be found in Aristotle's *Topica, VIII, 13,* where the five ways of begging the question are set forth. The earliest English work in which the expression is found is *The Arte of Logike plainlie set forth in our English Tongue, &c.* [1584].

Bitter end.

This phrase is somewhat ambiguous as now used. The older form, "better end," was used to designate a crisis, or a moment of extremity. When in a gale a vessel has paid out all her cable, her cable has run out to the "better end," — the end which is secured within the vessel and little used. Robinson Crusoe, in describing the terrible storm in Yarmouth Roads, says: "We rode with two anchors ahead, and the cables veered out to the better end." CHAUCER, *Canterbury Tales, The Squieres Tale, Line 224,* says: "They demen gladly to the badder ende," Skeat's glossary giving "worse" as the definition for "badder."

Cockles of the heart.

R. G. Latham [1812–1888], English philologist, wrote that the most probable explanation of the phrase lies (1) in the likeness of the heart to a cockle-shell, — the base of the former being compared to the hinge of the latter; (2) in the zoological name for the cockle and its congeners, *Cardium* (heart). A contemporary explanation [1936] is the comparison of the cockle, or fire chamber, of the furnace with the chambers (ventricles and auricles) of the heart, hence, to warm the cockles of the heart. See Cervantes, page 1039.

N. Y. Authorship uncertain, perhaps the late WALTER GILLISS:
O measure of Time! Thou merest mite
Within the endless providence of God:
May thy unerring finger ever point
To those who printed first the written word.

Consistency, thou art a jewel.

A popular saying, like "Be good, and you will be happy," or "Virtue is its own reward," that, like Topsy, just "growed." From the earliest times it has been the popular tendency to call this or that cardinal virtue, or bright and shining excellence, a jewel, by way of emphasis. For example, Iago says:

"*Good name,* in man or woman, dear my lord,
Is the immediate *jewel* of their souls.*"

Shakespeare elsewhere calls experience a "jewel." Miranda says her modesty is the "jewel" in her dower; and in *All's Well that Ends Well,* Diana terms her chastity the "jewel" of her house. — R. A. WIGHT

O discretion, thou art a jewel! —
The Skylark, a Collection of Well-chosen Songs [London, 1772]

Dead as Chelsea.

To get Chelsea, to obtain the benefit of that hospital (for old soldiers). "Dead as Chelsea, by God!" an exclamation uttered by a grenadier at Fontenoy, 1745, on having his leg carried away by a cannon-ball. — *Dictionary of the Vulgar Tongue,* quoted by BRADY in *Varieties of Literature* [1826]

Dirty work at the crossroads.

Notes and Queries (London) attributes this to WALTER MELVILLE's melodrama *The Girl Who Took the Wrong Turning, or No Wedding Bells for Him.*

Don't sell America short.

Modern Version of J. P. MORGAN's saying, "Never be a bear on the United States." See MARK SULLIVAN: *Our Times,* II, 318.

Doesn't amount to Hannah Cook.

A saying common in Maine and on Cape Cod, Massachusetts, variously explained as a character who once lived on Campobello Island; a corruption of a phrase in Indian dialect; and a comparison with the worthlessness (for navigation) of a cook on board ship.

Drive a coach and six through an Act of Parliament.

Credited to Sir Stephen Rice [1637–1715], who became Chief Baron of the Exchequer, by MACAULAY in *History of England, Chap. 12*

During good behaviour.

That after the said limitation shall take effect, . . . judge's commissions be made *quando se bene gesserit.* — *Statutes 12 and 13, William III, Chap. 2, Sect. 3*

FIFTH OF NOVEMBER
(GUY FAWKES' DAY)

Don't you remember
The fifth of November,
The Gunpowder treason and Plot?

Ballad, chanted on "Pope Day" in Boston [1774]. Quoted in *The History and Antiquities of Boston* by SAMUEL GARDNER DRAKE [1798–1875], from TUDOR's *Life of Otis.*

Free soil, free men, free speech, Frémont.

Rallying cry of the Republican Party in 1856, when John Charles Frémont [1813–1890], "the Pathfinder," was the party's candidate for the presidency.

Gentle craft.

According to John Brady [died 1814], in *Clavis Calendaria* [1812], this designation arose from the fact that in an old romance, a prince named Crispin is made to exercise, in honour of his namesake, Saint Crispin, the trade of shoemaking. There is a tradition that King Edward IV, in one of his disguises, once drank with a party of shoemakers, and pledged them. The story is alluded to in the old play of *George a-Greene* [1599]:

Marry, because you have drank with the King,
And the King hath so graciously pledged you,
You shall no more be called shoemakers;

But you and yours, to the world's end,
Shall be called the trade of the gentle craft.

The goose hangs high.

Originally, perhaps, "the goose *honks* high," — it cries and flies high. Wild geese fly higher when the weather is fine or promises to be fine. Hence, the prospects are bright; everything is favourable. — *Century Dictionary*

Another explanation is that in some parts of the country a goose is hung high to season, and denotes that a feast of roast goose will soon be ready.

The Great White Way.

Title of a play (1901) by ALBERT BIGELOW PAINE [1861–1937], which was adopted as a name for Broadway and the theatrical district of New York.

Hot afternoons have been in Montana.

Title of a prize-winning poem by ELI SIEGEL, published in *The Nation,* New York, 1925.

The man on horseback.

Applied to General Georges Ernest Jean Marie Boulanger [1837–1891].

Nisi suadeat intervallis (Unless he recommends delays).

Used by Henry De Bracton [died 1268] in Folio 1243 and Folio 420 b; Register Original, 267 a.

Nothing succeeds like success.

A French proverb, *Rien ne réussit comme le succès,* quoted by DUMAS in *Ange Pitou, Vol. I, P. 72 [1854].*

Paying through the nose.

Grimm says that Odin had a poll-tax which was called in Sweden a nose-tax; it was a penny per nose, or poll. — *Deutsche Rechts Alterthümer*

Rebellion to tyrants is obedience to God.

From an inscription on the cannon near which the ashes of President Bradshaw were lodged, on the top of a high hill near Martha Bay in Jamaica. — EZRA STILES: *History of the Three Judges of King Charles I*

This supposititious epitaph was found among the papers of Mr. Jefferson, and in his handwriting. It was supposed to be one of Dr. Franklin's spirit-stirring inspirations. — H. S. RANDALL: *Life of Jefferson, Vol. III, Page 585*

Rest and be thankful.

Inscription on a stone seat on the top of one of the Highlands in Scotland. It is the title of one of Wordsworth's poems.

Roland for an Oliver.

These were the two most famous of Charlemagne's paladins, and their exploits are rendered so ridiculously and equally extravagant by the old romancers, that from them arose the saying, to signify matching one incredible lie with another, giving tit for tat, as good as one receives. In *King Henry VI, Part I, Act I, Sc. 2, Line 30*, SHAKESPEARE says [in 1589]:
England all Olivers and Rowlands bred
During the time Edward the Third did reign.

Sister Anne, do you see any one coming?

The anxious cry of Fatima, one of the wives of Bluebeard.

The public be damned.

William H. Vanderbilt [1821–1885], reply to a newspaper reporter. There are various versions of the occasion of this remark. See MELVILLE E. STONE: *Fifty Years a Journalist, Page 116*, and GUSTAVUS MYERS: *History of the Great American Fortunes*, Modern Library Giant edition, *Page 344*.

The woods are full of them.

Alexander Wilson [1766–1813], in the Preface to his *American Ornithology* [1808], quotes these words and relates the story of a boy who had been gathering flowers. On bringing them to his mother, he said: "Look, my dear ma! What beautiful flowers I have found growing in our place! Why, all the woods are full of them!"

Wisdom of many and the wit of one.

Definition of a proverb which Lord John Russell gave one morning at breakfast at Mardock's, — "One man's wit, and all men's wisdom." — *Memoirs of Sir James Mackintosh* [1765–1832], *Vol. I, Page 473*

Wooden walls of England.

The credite of the Realme, by defending the same with our Wodden Walles, as Themistocles called the Ships of Athens. — Preface to the English translation of Linschoten (London).

Worry, the interest paid by those who borrow trouble.
　　GEORGE WASHINGTON LYON [*1879–*], *in Judge, March 1, 1924*

But me no buts.
　　FIELDING: *Rape upon Rape, Act II, Sc. 2.* AARON HILL: *Snake in the Grass, Sc. 1*

Cause me no causes.
　　MASSINGER: *A New Way to Pay Old Debts, Act I, Sc. 3*

Clerk me no clerks.
　　SCOTT: *Ivanhoe, Chap. XX*

Diamond me no diamonds! prize me no prizes!
　　TENNYSON: *Idylls of the King. Elaine, Line 402*

Dick me no Dicks.
　　F. FRANKFORT MOORE: *Nell Gwyn, in The Chap-Book, March 15, 1896*

End me no ends.
　　MASSINGER: *A New Way to Pay Old Debts, Act V, Sc. 1*

Fool me no fools.
> BULWER: *Last Days of Pompeii,*
> *Book III, Chap. VI*

Front me no fronts.
> FORD: *The Lady's Trial,*
> *Act II, Sc. 1*

Grace me no grace, nor uncle me no uncle.
> SHAKESPEARE: *Richard II,*
> *Act II, Sc. 3, Line 87*

Madam me no madam.
> DRYDEN: *The Wild Gallant,*
> *Act II, Sc. 2*

Map me no maps.
> FIELDING: *Rape upon Rape,*
> *Act I, Sc. 5*

Midas me no Midas.
> DRYDEN: *The Wild Gallant,*
> *Act II, Sc. 1*

Miracle me no Miracles.
> CERVANTES: *Don Quixote,*
> *Part II, Book III, Chap. 3*

O me no O's.
> BEN JONSON: *The Case Is*
> *Altered, Act V, sc. 1*

Parish me no parishes.
> PEELE: *The Old Wives' Tale*

Petition me no petitions.
> FIELDING: *Tom Thumb, Act I, Sc. 2*

Play me no plays.
> FOOTE: *The Knight, Act II*

Plot me no plots.
> BEAUMONT AND FLETCHER: *The*
> *Knight of the Burning Pestle,*
> *Act II, Sc. 5*

Sirrah me no sirrahs.
> LONGFELLOW: *The New England*
> *Tragedies, Act III, Sc. 1*

Thank me no thankings, nor proud me no prouds.
> SHAKESPEARE: *Romeo and Juliet,*
> *Act III, Sc. 5, Line 153*

Virgin me no virgins.
> MASSINGER: *A New Way to Pay*
> *Old Debts, Act III, Sc. 3*

Vow me no vows.
> BEAUMONT AND FLETCHER: *Wit*
> *without Money, Act IV, Sc. 4*

THE NEW ENGLAND PRIMER [1]

In Adam's fall
We sinned all.

My Book and Heart
Must never part.

Young Obadias,
David, Josias, —
All were pious.

Peter denied
His Lord, and cryed.

Young Timothy
Learnt sin to fly.

Xerxes did die,
And so must I.

Zaccheus he
Did climb the tree
Our Lord to see.

Our days begin with trouble here,
  Our life is but a span,
And cruel death is always near,
  So frail a thing is man.

Now I lay me down to take my sleep,[2]
I pray the Lord my soul to keep;
If I should die before I wake,
I pray the Lord my soul to take.

> His wife, with nine small children and one at the breast, following him to the stake.
> *Martyrdom of John Rogers,*
> *Burned at Smithfield, Febru-*
> *ary 14, 1554* [3]

[1] As early as 1691, Benjamin Harris, of Boston, advertised as in press the second impression of the *New England Primer.* The oldest copy known to be extant is dated 1737.

[2] The first record of this prayer is found in the *Enchiridion Leonis* [A. D. 1160]. In the earliest edition of the *Primer,* the prayer is given as above, which is copied from the reprint of 1777. In the edition of 1784 it is altered to read, "Now I lay me down to sleep." In the edition of 1814, the second line of the prayer reads, "I pray thee, Lord, my soul to keep."

[3] The correct date is Feb. 4, 1555.

EPITAPHS

A house she hath, 'tis made of such good
  fashion,
The tenant ne'er shall pay for repara-
  tion,
Nor will the landlord ever raise her rent
Or turn her out of doors for non-pay-
  ment;
From chimney-tax this cell is free,
To such a house who would not tenant
  be?
> *For Rebecca Bogess, Folkestone,*
> *August 22, 1688*

It is so soon that I am done for,
I wonder what I was begun for.
> *For a child aged three weeks,*
> *Cheltenham Churchyard*

She tasted of life's bitter cup,
Refused to drink the potion up;
She turned her little head aside,
Disgusted with the task and died.
> *For a child aged six months*

Here lies John Knott:
His father was Knott before him,
He lived Knott, died Knott,
Yet underneath this stone doth lie
Knott christened, Knott begot,
And here he lies and still is Knott.
> *Perthshire Churchyard*

Here lie I, Martin Elginbrodde:
Ha'e mercy o' my soul, Lord God,
As I wad do, were I Lord God
And ye were Martin Elginbrodde.
> *Aberdeen Churchyard (Quoted*
> *by* GEORGE MACDONALD *in his*
> *novel, David Elginbrod [1862],*
> *Chap. 13)*

A dying preacher I have been,
To dying hearers such as you.
Though dead, a preacher still I am
To such as come my grave to view.
Let this to you a warning be
That quickly you must follow me.
> *Elder Samuel Waldo, South*
> *Dover (Wingdale) Cemetery,*
> *Dutchess County, New York,*
> *September 10, 1798*

The Queene was brought by water to
  White-hall,
At every stroake the oares teares let
  fall:
More clung about the Barge, fish under
  water
Wept out their eyes of pearle, and
  swome blinde after.
I think the Barge-men might with eas-
  ier thighes
Have rowed her thither in her peoples
  eyes,
For how so ere, thus much my thoughts
  have scand,
She'd come by water, had she come by
  land.
> *Epitaph for Queen Elizabeth,*
> *who ended this transitory life at*
> *Richmond 24 of March, 1602,*
> *the 45 yeare of her Raigne, and*
> *seventy of her age.* WILLIAM
> CAMDEN [*1551–1623*]: *Re-*
> *maines Concerning Britaine, 5th*
> *edn.* [*1637*], *Page 393*

A zealous Lock-Smith dyed of late,
And did arrive at heaven gate,
He stood without and would not knocke,
Because he meant to picke the locke.
> *Epitaph upon a Puritanicall*
> *Lock-Smith. Ibid. Page 408*

Man is a glasse, life is as water
That's weakely wall'd about:
Sinne brings in death, death breakes the
  glasse,
So runnes the water out.
> *Mans Life. Ibid. Page 414*

Here lies Sir Jenkin Grout, who loved
his friend, and persuaded his enemy:
what his mouth ate, his hand paid for:
what his servants robbed, he restored:
if a woman gave him pleasure, he supported her in pain: he never forgot his
children: and whoso touched his finger,
drew after it his whole body.
> *Quoted by* RALPH WALDO EM-
> ERSON *in his Essay, Manners*

This is the grave of Mike O'Day
Who died maintaining his right of way.
His right was clear, his will was strong,
But he's just as dead as if he'd been
  wrong.
> *Modern*

JUNIUS

One precedent creates another. They soon accumulate and constitute law. What yesterday was fact, to-day is doctrine.

The Letters of Junius.[1] *Dedication to the English Nation*

The liberty of the press is the Palladium of all the civil, political, and religious rights of an Englishman.

Ibid.

These are the gloomy companions of a disturbed imagination; the melancholy madness of poetry, without the inspiration.[2]

Ibid. VII, To Sir William Draper [*March 3, 1769*]

There are some hereditary strokes of character by which a family may be as clearly distinguished as by the blackest features of the human face.

Ibid. XII, To the Duke of Grafton [*May 30, 1769*]

I do not give you to posterity as a pattern to imitate, but as an example to deter.

Ibid.

I believe there is yet a spirit of resistance in this country, which will not submit to be oppressed; but I am sure there is a fund of good sense in this country, which cannot be deceived.

Ibid. XVI, To the Printer of the Public Advertiser (*H. S. Woodfall*) [*July 19, 1769*]

We owe it to our ancestors to preserve entire those rights, which they have delivered to our care: we owe it to

our posterity, not to suffer their dearest inheritance to be destroyed.

The Letters of Junius. XX, To the Printer of the Public Advertiser [*August 8, 1769*]

When the constitution is openly invaded, when the first original right of the people, from which all laws derive their authority, is directly attacked, inferior grievances naturally lose their force, and are suffered to pass by without punishment or observation.

Ibid. XXX, To the Printer of the Public Advertiser [*October 17, 1769*]

There is a moment of difficulty and danger at which flattery and falsehood can no longer deceive, and simplicity itself can no longer be misled.

Ibid. XXXV,[1] *To the Printer of the Public Advertiser* [*December 19, 1769*]

They [the Americans] equally detest the pageantry of a King, and the supercilious hypocrisy of a bishop.[2]

Ibid.

The least considerable man among us has an interest equal to the proudest nobleman, in the laws and constitution of his country, and is equally called upon to make a generous contribution in support of them; — whether it be the heart to conceive, the understanding to direct, or the hand to execute.[3]

Ibid. XXXVII, To the Printer of the Public Advertiser [*March 19, 1770*]

---

[1] Attributed, among others, to Sir Philip Francis, Lord Shelburne, Lord George Sackville, and Earl Temple.

[2] See Burke, page 261.

[1] This letter is of great significance in the history of the liberty of the press. The publisher was prosecuted for seditious libel, and the jury brought in a verdict of "guilty of printing and publishing only." After a second trial, Woodfall was freed on the payment of costs.

[2] See Rufus Choate, page 393.

[3] See Gibbon, page 270.

We lament the mistakes of a good man, and do not begin to detest him until he affects to renounce his principles.

The Letters of Junius. XLI, To Lord Mansfield [November 14, 1770]

The injustice to an individual is sometimes of service to the public. Facts are apt to alarm us more than the most dangerous principles.

Ibid.

An honest man, like the true religion, appeals to the understanding, or modestly confides in the internal evidence of his conscience. The impostor employs force instead of argument, imposes silence where he cannot convince, and propagates his character by the sword.

Ibid.

Private credit is wealth; — public honour is security. —The feather that adorns the royal bird, supports his flight. Strip him of his plumage, and you fix him to the earth.

Ibid. XLII, On the Falkland Islands [January 30, 1771]

If individuals have no virtues, their vices may be of use to us.

Ibid. LIX, To the Printer of the Public Advertiser [October 5, 1771]

The temple of fame is the shortest passage to riches and preferment.

Ibid.

Love not me for comely grace,
For my pleasing eye or face,
Nor for any outward part,
No, nor for a constant heart.

Included by JOHN WILBYE *[died 1614] in Second Set of Madrigals [1608]*

The King of France went up the hill
With twenty thousand men;
The King of France came down the hill,
And ne'er went up again.

Pigges Corantoe, or Newes from the North.[1] Page 3

[1] A quarto tract printed in London in 1642. This is called "Old Tarlton's Song."

Though little, I'll work as hard as a Turk,
If you'll give me employ,
To plow and sow, and reap and mow,
And be a farmer's boy.

The Farmer's Boy. Stanza 2 [before 1689]

The United Voice of all His Majesty's free and loyal Subjects in America — Liberty and Property, and no Stamps.

Motto of various American colonial newspapers [1765–1766]

Lost is our old simplicity of times,
The world abounds with laws, and teems with crimes.

On the Proceedings Against America.[1] Stanza 1

Our cargoes of meat, drink, and cloaths beat the Dutch.

Siege of Boston [1775]

Count that day lost whose low descending sun
Views from thy hand no worthy action done.[2]

Staniford's Art of Reading. Page 27 [Third edition, Boston, 1803]

No foe dare molest, where in union are join'd
The plough, loom, and chisel, with commerce combined.

Plough, Loom, and Chisel. Stanza 1 [Ode sung at the Triennial Festival of the Massachusetts Charitable Mechanic Association, Boston, 1810]

An Austrian army, awfully array'd,
Boldly by battery besiege Belgrade;
Cossack commanders cannonading come,
Deal devastation's dire destructive doom;

[1] In *The Pennsylvania Gazette, Feb. 8, 1775,* "from a late London Magazine."
[2] In the autograph album of David Krieg, in the British Museum, with the autograph of Jacob Bobart [Dec. 8, 1697] are the lines:
Virtus sui gloria.
Think that day lost whose descending sun
Views from thy hand no noble action done.
Bobart, son of a celebrated botanist, died in 1719.

Ev'ry endeavour engineers essay,
For fame, for freedom, fight, fierce furious fray.
Gen'rals 'gainst gen'rals grapple, — gracious God!
How honors Heav'n heroic hardihood!
Infuriate, indiscriminate in ill,
Just Jesus, instant innocence instill!
Kinsmen kill kinsmen, kindred kindred kill.
Labour low levels longest, loftiest lines;
Men march 'midst mounds, moats, mountains, murd'rous mines.
Now noisy, noxious numbers notice nought,
Of outward obstacles o'ercoming ought;
Poor patriots perish, persecution's pest!
Quite quiet Quakers "Quarter, quarter" quest;
Reason returns, religion, right, redounds,
Suwarrow stop such sanguinary sounds!
Truce to thee, Turkey, terror to thy train!
Unwise, unjust, unmerciful Ukraine!
Vanish vile vengeance, vanish victory vain!
Why wish we warfare? wherefore welcome won
Xerxes, Xantippus, Xavier, Xenophon?
Yield, ye young Yaghier yeomen, yield your yell!
Zimmerman's, Zoroaster's, Zeno's zeal
Again attract; arts against arms appeal.
All, all ambitious aims, avaunt, away!
Et cætera, et cætera, et cæterā.

Alliteration, or the Siege of Belgrade: a Rondeau [1]

When shall we three meet again? [2]

Parting Friends [Dartmouth College song, 1830]

[1] These lines having been incorrectly printed in a London publication, we have been favoured by the author with an authentic copy of them. — *Wheeler's Magazine* [Winchester, England, 1828], *Vol. I, P. 244*
In *The Trifler*, 1817. The lines have been attributed to the Reverend B. Poulton, of Winchester, England, and to Alaric Alexander Watts [1797–1864]. They were included in Bentley's *Miscellany* [1838], and in *Literary Frivolities*, compiled by William Dobson [1820–1884]. There are various versions of the *Alliteration*.
[2] *Macbeth, Act I, Sc. 1, Line 1.*

The cunning seldom gain their ends;
The wise are never without friends.
The Fox and the Hen. Moral [1]

A fox went out in a hungry plight
And he begged of the moon to give him light,
For he'd many miles to go that night
Before he could reach his den-O.
The Gray Goose. Stanza 1

The nox was lit by lux of Luna,
And 'twas a nox most opportuna
To catch a possum or a coona;
For nix was scattered o'er this mundus,
A shallow nix, et non profundus.
Carmen Possum

One night when the wind it blew cold,
Blew bitter across the wild moor,
Young Mary she came with her child,
Wandering home to her own father's door.
Mary of the Wild Moor. [2] *Stanza 1*

Physicians of the highest rank
(To pay their fees, we need a bank),
Combine all wisdom, art and skill,
Science and sense, in Calomel.
Calomel. Stanza 1 [before 1853]

Howe'er their patients may complain,
Of head, or heart, or nerve, or vein,
Of fever high, or parch, or swell,
The remedy is Calomel.
Ibid. Stanza 2

The sons of the prophet are brave men and bold,
And quite unaccustomed to fear,
But the bravest by far in the ranks of the Shah
Was Abdul the Bulbul Amir.
Abdul the Bulbul Amir. Stanza 1

Now the heroes were plenty and well known to fame
In the troops that were led by the Czar,
And the bravest of these was a man by the name
Of Ivan Petruski Skavar.
Ibid. Stanza 3

Oh, were you ne'er a school-boy,
And did you never train,

[1] In John Pierpont's *Young Reader* [1843].
[2] Set to music by C. H. Keith and arranged for piano by Joseph W. Turner [1846].

And feel that swelling of the heart
    You ne'er can feel again?
        Young Soldiers.[1] *Stanza 1*

We charged upon a flock of geese
    And put them all to flight.
        Ibid. Stanza 3

Oh, the praties they are small —
    Over here, over here.
Oh, the praties they are small
When we dig 'em in the fall,
And we eat 'em, coats and all,
    Full of fear, full of fear.
        Irish Famine Song [*1846–1847*]

Oh, potatoes they grow small,
    In Kansas.
Oh, potatoes they grow small,
For they plant them in the fall,
And they eat 'em skins and all,
    In Kansas.
        Kansas version of famine song

Van Amburgh is the man who goes with
    all the shows,
He gets into the lion's cage, and tells
    you all he knows.
He puts his head in the lion's mouth,
    and keeps it there a while,
And when he takes it out again, he
    greets you with a smile.
        Menagerie, or Showman's Song [2]

Oh, ye'll tak' the high road an' I'll tak'
    the low road,
An' I'll be in Scotland before ye;
But trouble it is there an' mony hearts
    are sair,[3]
On the bonnie, bonnie banks of Loch
    Lomond.
        Scottish Ballad, Loch Lomond.[4]
        Refrain

So I said, "Old man, for whom digg'st
    thou this grave
In the heart of London town?"

And the deep-toned voice of the digger
    replied —
"We're laying a gas-pipe down!"
        From the Sublime to the
        Ridiculous.[1] *Stanza 3*

You-all means a race or section,
    Family, party, tribe, or clan;
You-all means the whole connection
    Of the individual man.
        You-All. Stanza 2 [*From The*
        Richmond (Virginia) Times-
        Dispatch]

In the singular it's never
    Used in this part of the land;
But we give up hope of ever
    Making others understand.
        Ibid. Stanza 4

The lady would remind you, please,
Her name is not Lost Angie Lees,
Nor Angie anything whatever.
She hopes her friends will be so clever
To share her fit historic pride,
The *g* shall not be jellified.
O long, *g* hard, and rhyme with "yes" —
That's all about Locé Ang-El-Ess.
        Los Angeles

Just after the death of the flowers,
    And before they are buried in snow,
There comes a festival season
    When Nature is all aglow.
        Indian Summer. Stanza 1 [*1860*]

Dreamer of dreams, we take the taunt
    with gladness,
Knowing that God beyond the years we
    see
Hath wrought the dreams that count
    with men for madness
Into the fabric of the world to be.
        On the defeat by the London
        County Council of some ed-
        ucational plans; ascribed to
        F. W. H. Myers, but not
        found in his writings

I pray the prayer the Easterners do,
May the peace of Allah abide with you;
Wherever you stay, wherever you go,
May the beautiful palms of Allah grow;
Through days of labor and nights of
    rest,

---

[1] In McGuffey's *Reader.*
[2] Popular at Eton and in American colleges
in the 1860s. There are various versions.
[3] A version more familiar than the one
given above changes the third line to
But I and my true love will never meet again.
[4] Found in *The Vocal Melodies of Scotland*
[1840] and *Christie's Traditional Ballad Airs*
[1876].

[1] Included in *Course of Composition and
Rhetoric* by GEORGE PAYN QUACKENBOS
[1826–1881].

The love of good Allah make you blest.
So I touch my heart as the Easterners
   do, —
May the peace of Allah abide with you.
Salaam Alaikum (Peace Be
with You)

Listen to the Exhortation of the Dawn!
   Look to this Day!
For it is Life, the very Life of Life.
In its brief course lie all the Verities
      and Realities of your Existence:
   The Bliss of Growth,
   The Glory of Action,
   The Splendor of Beauty.
For Yesterday is but a Dream,
And To-morrow is only a Vision;
But To-day well-lived makes every
      Yesterday a Dream of Happiness,
And every To-morrow a Vision of Hope.
Look well therefore to this Day!
Such is the Salutation of the Dawn.
The Salutation of the Dawn,
from the Sanskrit

The woman was not taken
   From Adam's head, you know,
So she must not command him,
   'Tis evidently so;
The woman was not taken
   From Adam's feet, you see,
So he must not abuse her —
   The meaning seems to be.
The woman she was taken
   From under Adam's arm,
Which shows he must protect her
   From injury and harm.
Old Scotch Nuptial Song
[before 1860]

Yestreen the Queen had four Maries,
   The night she'll hae but three;
There was Mary Seaton, and Mary
      Beaton,
   And Mary Carmichael, and me.
The Queen's Maries. Stanza 19
(Oxford Book of English Verse,
No. 375)

In the days of old Rameses
That story had paresis.
Attributed to Ben King, but a
familiar saying in the White-
chapel Club, Chicago, before he
became a member. Quoted by
Kipling in The Ship That Found
Herself.

From the halls of Montezuma,
   To the shores of Tripoli,
We fight our country's battles
   On the land as on the sea.
U. S. Marines' Song. Stanza 1

If the Army and the Navy
   Ever look on Heaven's scenes,
They will find the streets are guarded
      by
   The United States Marines.
Ibid. Stanza 4

The beauty of the house is order;
The blessing of the house is content-
   ment;
The glory of the house is hospitality;
The crown of the house is godliness.
Fireplace Motto

Men are only boys grown tall;
Hearts don't change much after all.
Katie Lee and Willie Gray.
Stanza 6

May I carry, if I will,
All your burdens up the hill?
And she answered with a laugh,
No, but you may carry half.
Ibid. Stanza 8

"I drink to one," he said,
"Whose image never may depart,
Deep graven on this grateful heart,
Till memory be dead.
To one whose love for me shall last
When lighter passions long have passed,
So holy 'tis, and true."
The Knight's Toast (to his
Mother). Stanzas 7 and 8

Mr. Finney had a turnip,
   And it grew behind the barn,
And it grew, and it grew,
   And the turnip did no harm.
Mr. Finney's Turnip.[1] *Stanza 1*

Of all the funny things that live, in
      woodland, marsh, or bog,
That creep the ground or fly the air, the
      funniest thing's a frog.
The Scientific Frog. Stanza 1
[1860s]

[1] Persistently attributed to H. W. Longfellow, who denied the authorship in a letter
to George Anderson, July 11, 1881.

I belong to that highly respectable tribe
Which is known as the Shabby Gen-
teel . . .
Too proud to beg, too honest to steal.
> *The Shabby Genteel. Stanza 1
> (Sung by Sol Smith Russell
> [1848–1901] in A Poor Rela-
> tion)*

Hands off! Stand back! Leave us alone!
You shall not rob us of our own;
We will be free! We will be free!
God and Right our standard be.
> *War-Song of the Boers.
> Stanza 1 [1881]*

I'm Terence O'Reilly, I'm a man of re-
nown . . .
If they'd let me be, I'd have Ireland
free,
On the railroads you'd not pay any fare,
I'd have the United States under my
thumb,
And I'd sleep in the President's chair.
> *Is That Mr. Reilly?* [1]
> *Stanza 1 [1882]*

Sow a Thought, and you reap an Act;
Sow an Act, and you reap a Habit;
Sow a Habit, and you reap a Character;
Sow a Character, and you reap a Des-
tiny.
> *Quoted by* SAMUEL SMILES
> *[1812–1904] in Life and La-
> bour [1887]*

The Monkey married the Baboon's sister,
Smacked his lips and then he kissed her.
> *The Monkey's Wedding. Stanza 1
> (Regimental March of the Ninth
> U. S. Cavalry)*

Three thousand miles of borderline, —
nor fort nor armèd host
On all this frontier neighbor-ground
from east to western coast;
A spectacle to conjure with — a thought
to stir the blood!
A living proof to all the world of faith
in brotherhood.
> *Our Borderline. Stanza 1*

God speed that surely dawning day,
that coming hour divine,

---

[1] Assumed to be the origin of the phrase,
"the life of Reilly."

When all the nations of the earth shall
boast such borderline.
> *Our Borderline. Stanza 3*

King Arthur had three sons — that he
had;
He had three sons of yore,
And he kicked them out the door
Because they could not sing — that he
did.
> *King Arthur: English Folksong* [1]

In good old Colony times
When we lived under the King,
Three roguish chaps
Fell into mishaps
Because they could not sing.
> *Another version, once popular
> as an American college song, In
> Good Old Colony Times*

Reuben, I have long been thinking
What a good world this would be,
If the men were all transported
On this side the Northern Sea.
> *Reuben and Rachel.* [2] *Stanza 1*

Mankind looks forth with careful
glance,
Time steady plies the oar,
While old age calmly waits to hear
The keel upon the shore.
> *Life Voyage (on an engraving
> by F. T. Stuart from a painting
> by Clarence M. Dobell)*

There is never a daughter of earth but
once, ere the tale of her days is
done,
She will know the scent of the Eden
rose, just once beneath the sun!
And whatever else she may win or lose,
endure, or do, or dare,
She will never forget the enchantment
it gave to the common air;
For the world may give her content or
joy, fame, sorrow, or sacrifice,
But the hour that brought the scent of
the rose, she lived it in Paradise.
> *The Rose of Eden: Arabic
> Legend.* [3] *Stanza 3*

---

[1] From *English County Songs*, collected
[1893] by LUCY E. BROADWOOD and J. A.
FULLER MAITLAND.

[2] An adaptation of this old song, entitled
"Reuben and Cynthia," was sung in Charles
Hoyt's play, *A Trip to Chinatown* [1890].

[3] Published in *All the Year Round*, a periodical edited by Charles Dickens and contin-

I loathe, abhor, despise,
Abominate dried apple pies.
I like good bread, I like good meat,
Or anything that's fit to eat,
But of all poor grub beneath the skies,
The poorest is dried apple pies.
Give me the toothache or sore eyes
In preference to such kind of pies.

Dried Apple Pies

Tread on my corns, or tell me lies,
But don't pass me dried apple pies!

Ibid.

If I had but a thousand a year, Gaffer
Green,
If I had but a thousand a year,
What a man I would be, and what
sights I would see.

Robin Ruff.[1] *Stanza 1*

There's a place that is better than this,
Robin Ruff,
And I hope in my heart you'll go
there,
Where the poor man's as great though
he hath no estate,
Aye, as if he'd a thousand a year.

Ibid. Stanza 6

It's the 'ammer, 'ammer, 'ammer
along the 'ard 'igh road.

*Under a drawing by John Leech
[1817–1874] in London Punch,
— a veterinary and horseman
discussing a horse's legs*

If any lift of mine may ease
The burden of another,
God give me love and care and strength
To help my ailing brother.

*If Any Little Word of Mine.
Stanza 2 [1880]*

There is a mystery in human hearts,
And though we be encircled by a host
Of those who love us well and are be-
loved,

To every one of us, from time to time,
There comes a sense of utter loneliness.

A Solitary Way. Stanza 1 [1885]

And those who walk with Him from day
to day
Can never have a solitary way.

Ibid. Stanza 3

In the first person, simply *shall* fore-
tells,
In *will* a threat or else a promise dwells;
Shall in the second and third does
threat,
Will then simply foretells a future feat.

Grammar, Irish National Schools

Much that well may be thought cannot
wisely be said.

*The Priest and the Mulberry-
Tree. Stanza 5 (In Epes Sar-
gent's Standard Fourth Reader)*

Try what you will, there's nothing like
leather.

Nothing Like Leather

The sweetest lives are those to duty
wed,
Whose deeds, both great and small,
Are close-knit strands of an unbroken
thread,
Where love ennobles all.
The world may sound no trumpet, ring
no bells;
The book of life the shining record tells.

*Attributed to Elizabeth Barrett
Browning, but not found in her
writings*

The little cares that fretted me,
I lost them yesterday,
Among the fields above the sea,
Among the winds at play,
Among the lowing of the herds,
The rustling of the trees,
Among the singing of the birds,
The humming of the bees.
The foolish fears of what might pass
I cast them all away
Among the clover-scented grass,
Among the new-mown hay,
Among the hushing of the corn
Where drowsy poppies nod,

---

ued by his son, Charles, after the death of the
elder Dickens in 1870. The poem appeared in
The St. Louis Globe-Democrat, July 13, 1878.
Rudyard Kipling quotes from this poem in
"Mrs. Hauksbee Sits Out," in *Under the De-
odars.*

[1] Set to music by Henry Russell [1812–
1900].

Where ill thoughts die and good are born —
Out in the fields with God.
Out in the Fields (Anonymous, in St. Paul's Magazine, August 20, 1898, page 307. Reprinted in The Boston Globe, April 30, 1899) [1]

Monday's child is fair of face,
Tuesday's child is full of grace,
Wednesday's child is loving and giving,
Thursday's child works hard for a living.
Friday's child is full of woe,
Saturday's child has far to go,
But the child that is born on the Sabbath-day
Is brave and bonny, and good and gay.
Birthdays (Quoted in Miser Farebrother by B. L. Farjeon, Harper's Weekly, September 17, 1887)

Cut your nails on Monday, cut them for wealth,
Cut them on Tuesday, cut them for health,
Cut them on Wednesday, cut them for news,
Cut them on Thursday, a new pair of shoes.
Cut them on Friday, cut them for sorrow,
Cut them on Saturday, see sweetheart to-morrow.
Cut them on Sunday, cut them for evil,
The whole of the week you'll be ruled by the devil.
Quoted as above

Something old, something new,
Something borrowed, something blue.
Wedding Rhyme

The Pyramids first, which in Egypt were laid;
Next Babylon's Garden, for Amytis made;
Then Mausolos' Tomb of affection and guilt;
Fourth, the Temple of Dian in Ephesus built;

The Colossus of Rhodes, cast in brass, to the Sun;
Sixth, Jupiter's Statue, by Phidias done;
The Pharos of Egypt comes last, we are told,
Or the Palace of Cyrus, cemented with gold.
Seven Wonders of the Ancient World

When every pool in Eden was a mirror
That unto Eve her dainty charms proclaimed,
She went undraped without a single fear, or
Thought that she had need to be ashamed.
Needed Apples. Stanza 1 (Printed in Philip Hale's column, As the World Wags, Boston Herald, June 30, 1924)

'Twas only when she'd eaten of the apple
That she became inclined to be a prude. . . .
The snake should pass the apples 'round again.
Ibid. Stanzas 3 and 4

Every time I come to town
The boys keep kicking my dawg around;
Makes no difference if he is a hound,
They've got to quit kicking my dawg around.
Champ Clark campaign song [1912]

My granddad, viewing earth's worn cogs,
Said things were going to the dogs;
His granddad in his house of logs,
Said things were going to the dogs;
His granddad in the Flemish bogs
Said things were going to the dogs;
His granddad in his old skin togs,
Said things were going to the dogs;
There's one thing that I have to state —
The dogs have had a good long wait.
Perennial Journeys

[1] Also attributed to Mrs. Browning and to Louise Imogen Guiney. There is no convincing proof of either authorship.

Lord, through this hour
  Be Thou our Guide,
So by Thy power
  No foot shall slide.
          Westminster Chimes

Climb high
Climb far
Your goal the sky
Your aim the star.
          Inscription on Hopkins Memo-
          rial Steps, Williams College,
          Williamstown, Massachusetts

Mother, may I go out to swim?
Yes, my darling daughter:
Hang your clothes on a hickory limb
And don't go near the water.
          Origin dubious.

See the happy moron,
  He doesn't give a damn.
I wish I were a moron —
  My God, perhaps I am!
          Incorrectly attributed to Dorothy
          Parker

Lizzie Borden took an axe
And gave her mother forty whacks;

When she saw what she had done
She gave her father forty-one.
          Ballad current after the Borden
          murder, Fall River, Massachu-
          setts [August 4, 1892] [1]

Work and pray, live on hay,
You'll get pie, in the sky,
When you die —
It's a lie!
          Song of the I.W.W. (Industrial
          Workers of the World)

  Once aboard the lugger and the girl
is mine.
          Quotation from (or parody of)
          some Victorian melodrama? First
          four words used as title of novel
          by A. S. M. Hutchinson

Nunc scripsi totum: pro Christo da
mihi potum.
          Monkish inscription at the end of
          medieval manuscripts

---

[1] EDMUND PEARSON, *The Trial of Lizzie Borden*, says the verse was frequently sung to the tune of *Ta-ra-ra-boom-de-ay*.

TRANSLATIONS

ANCIENT EGYPT

To resist him that is set in authority is evil.

> *The Instruction of Ptahhotep* [1]
> [Circa *2675 B.C.*]

There it o'ertook me that I fell down for thirst, I was parched, my throat burned, and I said: "This is the taste of death."

> *The Story of Sinuke* [1]
> [Circa *2000 B.C.*]

There is none that hath turned his shaft, there is none that hath bent his bow.

> *Ibid.*

Then the ship perished, and of them that were in it not one survived. And I was cast on to an island by a wave of the sea.

> *The Story of the Shipwrecked Sailor* [1] [Circa *1700 B.C.?*]

Everywhere he feels his Heart because its vessels run to all his limbs.

> *The Beginning of the Secret Book of the Physician* [2] [Circa *1550 B.C.*]

Go not in and out in the court of justice, that thy name may not stink.

> *The Wisdom of Anii* [1]
> [Circa *900 B.C.*]

HAMMURABI
[*Circa 1955–1913 B.C.*] [3]

[*From* ROBERT FRANCIS HARPER'S *The Code of Hammurabi King of Babylon about 2250 B.C., second edition*]

I established law and justice in the land.

> *Page 9 (Prologue)*

If a man owe a debt and Adad [1] inundate his field and carry away the produce, or, through lack of water, grain have not grown in the field, in that year he shall not make any return of grain to the creditor, he shall alter his contract-tablet and he shall not pay the interest for that year.

> *Page 27 (Sect. 48)*

If a man destroy the eye of another man, they shall destroy his eye.

> *Page 73 (Sect. 196)*

HOMER [2]
[*Circa 850 B.C.*]

These things surely lie on the knees of the gods.

> *Odyssey.* [3] *Book I, Line 267*

HESIOD
[*Circa 720 B.C.?*]

Translation by J. BANKS, M.A., *with a few alterations. Bohn Classical Library*

We know to tell many fictions like to truths, and we know, when we will, to speak what is true.

> *The Theogony. Line 27*

On the tongue of such an one they shed a honeyed dew, [4] and from his lips drop gentle words.

> *Ibid. Line 82*

Night, having Sleep, the brother of Death. [5]

> *Ibid. Line 754*

---

[1] From ADOLF ERMAN [1854–]: *The Literature of the Ancient Egyptians*, translated [1927] by AYLWARD M. BLACKMAN.

[2] In *The Papyrus Ebers*, translated [1931] from the German version by CYRIL P. BRYAN.

[3] According to *Webster's New International Dictionary*, 2d ed. Authorities disagree on the probable dates.

[1] The storm god.

[2] For quotations from the *Iliad* and *Odyssey*, see Alexander Pope and William Cullen Bryant.

[3] Translated [1879] by BUTCHER AND LANG.

[4] He on honey-dew hath fed. — COLERIDGE: *Kubla Khan*

[5] Death and his brother Sleep. — SHELLEY: *Queen Mab, I*

From whose eyelids also as they gazed dropped love.

The Theogony. Line 910

Both potter is jealous of potter and craftsman of craftsman; and poor man has a grudge against poor man, and poet against poet.[1]

Works and Days. Line 25

Fools! they know not how much half exceeds the whole.[2]

Ibid. Line 40

For full indeed is earth of woes, and full the sea; and in the day as well as night diseases unbidden haunt mankind, silently bearing ills to men, for all-wise Zeus hath taken from them their voice. So utterly impossible is it to escape the will of Zeus.

Ibid. Line 101

Oft hath even a whole city reaped the evil fruit of a bad man.[3]

Ibid. Line 240

For himself doth a man work evil in working evils for another.

Ibid. Line 265

Badness, look you, you may choose easily in a heap: level is the path, and right near it dwells. But before Virtue the immortal gods have put the sweat of man's brow; and long and steep is the way to it, and rugged at the first.

Ibid. Line 287

Let it please thee to keep in order a moderate-sized farm, that so thy garners may be full of fruits in their season.

Ibid. Line 304

Invite the man that loves thee to a feast, but let alone thine enemy.

Ibid. Line 342

A bad neighbour is as great a misfortune as a good one is a great blessing.

Ibid. Line 346

Gain not base gains; base gains are the same as losses.

Ibid. Line 353

[1] See Gay, page 206.
[2] Pittacus said that half was more than the whole. — DIOGENES LAERTIUS: *Pittacus, II*
[3] One man's wickedness may easily become all men's curse. — PUBLILIUS SYRUS: *Maxim 463*

If thou shouldst lay up even a little upon a little, and shouldst do this often, soon would even this become great.

Works and Days. Line 360

At the beginning of the cask and at the end take thy fill, but be saving in the middle; for at the bottom saving comes too late. Let the price fixed with a friend be sufficient, and even dealing with a brother call in witnesses, but laughingly.

Ibid. Line 366

The morn, look you, furthers a man on his road, and furthers him too in his work.

Ibid. Line 579

Observe moderation. In all, the fitting season is best.

Ibid. Line 694

Neither make thy friend equal to a brother; but if thou shalt have made him so, be not the first to do him wrong.

Ibid. Line 707

MIMNERMUS
[*Floruit* 630–600 B. C.]

We are all clever enough at envying a famous man while he is yet alive, and at praising him when he is dead.

Fragment 1

STESICHORUS
[630–550 B. C.]
Loeb Classical Library, Lyra Graeca, Vol. 2

'Tis a vain and impotent thing to bewail the dead.

STOBAEUS: *Anthology*[1]

When a man dies, all his glory among men dies also.

Ibid.

ALCAEUS
[611–580 B. C.]
Translation by J. M. Edmonds. Loeb Classical Library, Lyra Graeca, Vol. 1

Not houses finely roofed or the stones of walls well-builded, nay nor canals

[1] Translated by J. M. EDMONDS.

and dockyards, make the city, but men able to use their opportunity.

ARISTIDES: *Rhodian Oration*

Painting a lion from the claw.

PLUTARCH: *On the Cessation of Oracles*

'Tis said that wrath is the last thing in a man to grow old.

Scholiast on Sophocles

One that hath wine as a chain about his wits, such an one lives no life at all.

DEMETRIUS: *On Poems. Papyrus of the First Century B.C. found at Herculaneum*

In fleeing the ashes he's fallen into the coals.

APOSTOLIUS: *Proverbs*

SAPPHO OF LESBOS [1]
[*Circa* 610 B. C.]

Art thou the topmost apple
The gatherers could not reach,
Reddening on the bough?

To Atthis, paraphrase by
BLISS CARMAN

I loved thee, Atthis, once — long, long ago;
Long, long ago — the memory still is dear.
Stand face to face, friend, and unveil thine eyes,
Look deep in mine and keep the dead past clear
Of all regret.

To Atthis, paraphrase by
ANNE BUNNER

For to whomsoever I do good they harm me most.

Fragment 11 [2]

Evening, thou that bringest all, whatever the light-giving dawn scattered; thou bringest the sheep, thou bringest the goat, thou bringest the child to its mother.

Fragment 93 [2]

[1] Some say the Muses are nine but how carelessly! Look at the tenth, Sappho from Lesbos. — PLATO (Loeb Classical Library, *Greek Anthology, Vol. 3, P. 281*)
[2] Translated by MARY MILLS PATRICK.

THEOGNIS
[570?–490? B. C.]

Wine is wont to show the mind of man.[1]

Maxims. Line 500

No one goes to Hades with all his immense wealth.[2]

Ibid. Line 725

ANACREON
[563–478 B. C.]

*Translation by J. M. Edmonds.
Loeb Classical Library, Lyra
Graeca, Vol. 2*

Nor in those days did Persuasion shine all silver.

Scholiast on Pindar

Doorkeepers that fight are a mischief.

Etymologicum Magnum

Shining with desire and gleaming with unguents.

PLUTARCH: *Amatorius*

SIMONIDES OF CEOS
[556–469 B. C.]

In silence also there's a worth that brings no risk.

PLUTARCH: *Sayings of Emperors.
Augustus Caesar*

There's no joy even in beautiful Wisdom, unless one have holy Health.

SEXTUS EMPIRICUS: *Against the Mathematicians*

Whereas gold is the kindest of all hosts when it shines in the sky,
It comes an evil guest unto those that receive it in their hand.

PLUTARCH: *The Malignity of Herodotus*

He that would live completely happy must before all things belong to a country that is of fair report.

AMMIANUS MARCELLINUS: *History*

The city is the teacher of the man.

PLUTARCH: *Should Old Men Govern?*

[1] In wine there is truth. — PLINY: *Natural History, Book XIV, Sect. 141.*
[2] For when he dieth he shall carry nothing away: his glory shall not descend after him. — *Psalm XLIX, 17*

Go tell the Spartans, thou that passeth
    by,
That here, obedient to their laws, we
    lie.[1]

> *Thermopylae* [2]

AESOP
[*Floruit* 550 B.C.]

Any excuse will serve a tyrant.
> *The Wolf and the Lamb*

Beware lest you lose the substance
by grasping at the shadow.
> *The Dog and the Shadow*

You may share the labours of the
great, but you will not share the spoil.
> *The Lion's Share*

You have put your head inside a
wolf's mouth and taken it out again in
safety. That ought to be reward enough
for you.
> *The Wolf and the Crane*

Better beans and bacon in peace than
cakes and ale in fear.
> *The Town Mouse and the Country Mouse*

Only cowards insult dying majesty.
> *The Sick Lion*

Little friends may prove great
friends.
> *The Lion and the Mouse*

Better no rule than cruel rule.
> *The Frogs Desiring a King*

A huge gap appeared in the side of
the mountains. At last a tiny mouse
poked its little head out of the gap.[3]
> *The Mountains in Labour*

---

[1] Ruskin said of this epitaph that it was the
noblest group of words ever uttered by man.
In Luderitzbucht Cemetery, German South-
west Africa, the lines, adapted to read:
Tell England, ye who pass this monument,
    That we who rest here, die content,
mark the grave of Rex and Wilfred Wilmslow,
who fell in the battle of Stetting [Nov., 1914].
In Southport, England, the War Memorial
bears another adaptation of the epitaph:
Tell Britain, ye who mark this monument,
    Faithful to her we fell, and rest content.
[2] Translated by WILLIAM LISLE BOWLES
[1762–1850].
[3] A mountain was in labour, sending forth
dreadful groans, and there was in the region
the highest expectation. After all, it brought
forth a mouse. — PHAEDRUS: *Fable 22, 1*

The mountains are in labour, and a ridicu-

Much outcry, little outcome.
> *The Mountains in Labour*

There is always someone worse off
than yourself.
> *The Hares and the Frogs*

It is easy to be brave from a safe
distance.
> *The Wolf and the Kid*

You will only injure yourself if you
take notice of despicable enemies.
> *The Bald Man and the Fly*

Outside show is a poor substitute for
inner worth.
> *The Fox and the Mask*

Borrowed plumes.
> *The Jay and the Peacock*

It is not only fine feathers that make
fine birds.
> *Ibid.*

Self-conceit may lead to self-destruc-
tion.
> *The Frog and the Ox*

Gratitude is the sign of noble souls.
> *Androcles*

We often despise what is most useful to us.
> *The Hart and the Hunter*

They found that even the Belly, in
its dull quiet way, was doing necessary
work for the Body, and that all must
work together or the Body will go to
pieces.
> *The Belly and the Members*

I am sure the grapes are sour.[1]
> *The Fox and the Grapes*

It is easy to despise what you cannot
get.
> *Ibid.*

Be content with your lot; one cannot be first in everything.
> *The Peacock and Juno*

Familiarity breeds contempt.[2]
> *The Fox and the Lion*

---

lous mouse will be born. — HORACE: *The Art
of Poetry, L. 139*
[1] See George Herbert, page 137. See also
La Fontaine, page 1045.
[2] This is Maxim 640 of Publilius Syrus.
Upon familiarity will grow more contempt.
    SHAKESPEARE: *The Merry Wives of
        Windsor, Act I, Sc. 1, L. 258*
See Cervantes, page 1035.

We can easily represent things as we wish them to be.

The Lion and the Statue

Then the Grasshopper knew it is best to prepare for the days of necessity.

The Ant and the Grasshopper

The little Reed, bending to the force of the wind, soon stood upright again when the storm had passed over.

The Tree and the Reed

Obscurity often brings safety.

Ibid.

The Lamb that belonged to the Sheep, whose skin the Wolf was wearing, began to follow the Wolf in the Sheep's clothing.

The Wolf in Sheep's Clothing

Appearances are deceptive.

Ibid.

The Dog barked at the Ox and attempted to bite it when it approached the manger in the hope of getting at the straw.

The Dog in the Manger [1]

People often grudge others what they cannot enjoy themselves.

Ibid.

The boy called out "Wolf, Wolf!" and the villagers came out to help him. A few days afterward he tried the same trick, and again they came to his help. Shortly after this a Wolf actually came, but this time the villagers thought the boy was deceiving them again and nobody came to his help.

The Shepherd's Boy

A liar will not be believed, even when he speaks the truth.

Ibid.

Never soar aloft on an enemy's pinions.

The Tortoise and the Birds

Do but set the example yourself, and I will follow you. Example is the best precept.[2]

The Two Crabs

Never trust a friend who deserts you at a pinch.

The Two Fellows and the Bear

[1] See Burton, page 123.
[2] Example is always more efficacious than precept. — JOHNSON: *Rasselas, Chap. 30*

United we stand, divided we fall.[1]

The Four Oxen and the Lion

A little thing in hand is worth more than a great thing in prospect.[2]

The Fisher and the Little Fish

Little by little does the trick.

The Crow and the Pitcher

I will have nought to do with a man who can blow hot and cold with the same breath.

The Man and the Satyr

Thinking to get at once all the gold the Goose could give, he killed it and opened it only to find, — nothing.

The Goose with the Golden Eggs

Put your shoulder to the wheel.

Hercules and the Waggoner

The gods help them that help themselves.

Ibid.

Please all, and you will please none.

The Man, the Boy, and the Donkey

Who is to bell the Cat? It is easy to propose impossible remedies.

Belling the Cat

When the Hare awoke from his nap, he saw the Tortoise just near the winning post. Plodding wins the race.

The Hare and the Tortoise

We would often be sorry if our wishes were gratified.[3]

The Old Man and Death

Union gives strength.

The Bundle of Sticks

While I see many hoof-marks going in, I see none coming out. It is easier to get into the enemy's toils than out again.

The Lion, the Fox, and the Beasts

The haft of the arrow had been feathered with one of the eagle's own plumes. We often give our enemies the means of our own destruction.[4]

The Eagle and the Arrow

[1] See George Pope Morris, page 404.
[2] Better one byrde in hande than ten in the wood. — HEYWOOD [1546]
[3] See Lowell, page 528.
[4] Viewed his own feather on the fatal dart.
    BYRON: *English Bards and Scotch Reviewers, L. 828*
See Waller, page 145, and Aeschylus, page 964.

Nature will out.
> *The Cat-Maiden*

Do not count your chickens before they are hatched.[1]
> *The Milkmaid and Her Pail*

Men often applaud an imitation, and hiss the real thing.
> *The Buffoon and the Countryman*

Never trust the advice of a man in difficulties.
> *The Fox and the Goat*

IBYCUS

[*Floruit circa* 550 B. C.]

Translation by J. M. EDMONDS. *Loeb Classical Library, Lyra Graeca*

You cannot find a medicine for life when once a man is dead.
> CHRYSIPPUS: *Negatives*

Every reef may be safely let out so long as the sail clears the top of the wave.
> *Scholiast on the Iliad*

Contests allow no excuses, no more do friendships.
> ZENOBIUS: *Proverbs*

The cranes of Ibycus.[2]

AESCHYLUS

[525–456 B. C.]

I would far rather be ignorant than wise in the foreboding of evil.[3]
> *Suppliants.*[4] *Nauck's Edition, No. 453*

"Honour thy father and thy mother" stands written among the three laws of most revered righteousness.[5]
> *Ibid. No. 707*

---

[1] See Samuel Butler, page 143.
[2] According to legend, Ibycus was murdered at sea, and his murderers were discovered through cranes that followed the ship. Hence, the "cranes of Ibycus" became a proverb for the agency of the gods in revealing crime.
[3] See Thomas Gray, page 243.
[4] Translated by MORRIS HICKEY MORGAN.
[5] The three great laws ascribed to Triptolemus are referred to, — namely, to honour parents; to worship the gods with the fruits of the earth; to hurt no living creature. The first two laws are also ascribed to the centaur Cheiron.

Words are the physicians of a mind diseased.[1]
> *Prometheus.*[2] *Nauck's Edition, No. 378*

Time as he grows old teaches many lessons.
> *Ibid. No. 981*

God's mouth knows not to utter falsehood, but he will perform each word.[3]
> *Ibid. No. 1032*

Too lightly opened are a woman's ears;
Her fence downtrod by many trespassers.
> *Agamemnon.*[4] *Line 486*

I think the slain
Care little if they sleep or rise again;
And we, the living, wherefore should we ache
With counting all our lost ones?
> *Ibid. Line 595*

Sweet is a grief well ended.
> *Ibid. Line 805*

For not many men, the proverb saith,
Can love a friend whom fortune prospereth
Unenvying.
> *Ibid. Line 832*

I know how men in exile feed on dreams.
> *Ibid. Line 1668*

Him who pitieth suffering men
Zeus pitieth, and his ways are sweet on earth.
> *The Eumenides.*[4] *Line 91*

Fortune is a god and rules men's life.[5]
> *The Choëphoroe.*[4] *Line 59*

Destiny
Waiteth alike for them that men call free,
And them by others mastered.
> *Ibid. Line 101*

Pleasantest
Of all ties is the tie of host and guest.
> *Ibid. Line 699*

---

[1] Apt words have power to suage
The tumours of a troubl'd mind.
> MILTON: *Samson Agonistes*
[2] Translated by MORRIS HICKEY MORGAN.
[3] God is not a man that he should lie; . . . hath he said, and shall he not do it? — *Numbers, XXIII, 19.*
[4] Translated by SIR GILBERT MURRAY.
[5] Fortune commands men, and not men fortune. — HERODOTUS: *Book VII, Polymnia, Chap. 49*

So in the Libyan fable it is told
That once an eagle, stricken with a dart,
Said, when he saw the fashion of the
    shaft,
"With our own feathers, not by others'
    hands,
Are we now smitten." [1]

Fragment 135 [2]

O Death the Healer, scorn thou not, I
    pray,
To come to me: of cureless ills thou art
The one physician. Pain lays not its
    touch
Upon a corpse.

Fragment 250 [2]

A prosperous fool is a grievous burden.

Fragment 383

Bronze is the mirror of the form; wine,
    of the heart.

Fragment 384

It is not the oath that makes us believe
    the man, but the man the oath.

Fragment 385

PINDAR
[518–438 B. C.]

Translation by Sir J. E. SANDYS.
Loeb Classical Library

The best of healers is good cheer.

Nemean Ode 4

Longer than deeds liveth the word.

Ibid.

It is the natal star that ruleth over
    every deed.

Nemean Ode 5

For whatsoever one hath well said goeth forth with a voice that never dieth.

Isthmian Ode 4

Refrain from peering too far.

Olympian Ode 1

The word that is overbearing is a
spur unto strife.

Fragment from Hymns

To foolish men belongeth a love for
things afar.

Paean 4

[1] See Waller, page 145, and Aesop, page 962.
[2] Translated by PLUMPTRE.

Every noble deed dieth, if suppressed in silence.

*Eulogy on Alexander, Son of
Amyntas*

Whether the race of men on earth
mounteth a loftier tower by justice, or
by crooked wiles, my mind is divided
in telling clearly.

Fragment

SOPHOCLES
[496–406 B. C.]

The ship of state — the gods once more,
After much rocking on a stormy surge,
Set her on even keel.

Antigone [1]

That pilot of the state
Who sets no hand to the best policy,
But remains tongue-tied through some
    terror, seems
Vilest of men.

Ibid.

None love the messenger who brings
bad news. [2]

Ibid.

For money you would sell your soul.

Ibid.

A man of worth
In his own household will appear up-
    right
In the state also.

Ibid.

There lives no greater fiend than An-
    archy;
She ruins states, turns houses out of
    doors,
Breaks up in rout the embattled sol-
    diery.

Ibid.

Do not persist, then, to retain at heart
One sole idea, that the thing is right
Which your mouth utters, and nought
    else beside.

Ibid.

[1] Translated by SIR GEORGE YOUNG [1837–
1930].
[2] The first bringer of unwelcome news
Hath but a losing office.
SHAKESPEARE: *King Henry IV, Part II,
Act I, Sc. 1, L. 100*

Though a man be wise,
It is no shame for him to live and
learn.[1]
Antigone

To err
From the right path is common to man-
kind.[2]
Ibid.

A day can prostrate and upraise again
All that is human.
Ajax [3]

To behold harms of our own hands'
doing,
Where none beside us wrought, causes
sharp ruing.
Ibid.

A woman should be seen, not heard.
Ibid.

I would not take the fellow at a gift
Who warms himself with unsubstantial
hopes;
But bravely to live on, or bravely end,[4]
Is due to gentle breeding.
Ibid.

In the ills of men
There is none sorer than Necessity.
Ibid.

Some mindfulness
A man should surely keep, of any thing
That pleased him once.
Ibid.

The happiest life consists in ignorance,
Before you learn to grieve and to re-
joice.
Ibid.

Sleep, the universal vanquisher.
Ibid.

I for my own part, having learnt of
late
Those hateful to us we are not to hate
As though they might not soon be
friends again,
Intend to measure, now, the services
I render to my friend, as if not so

To abide for ever; for of mortals most
Find friendship an unstable anchorage.[1]
Ajax

'Tis a long road knows no turning.
Ibid.

Men of perverse opinion do not know
The excellence of what is in their hands
Till some one dash it from them.
Ibid.

Death is not the worst; rather, in vain
To wish for death, and not to com-
pass it.
Electra

The flower
Of our young manhood.[3]
Oedipus Tyrannus [2]

Towers and ships are nothingness,
Void of our fellow men to inhabit them.
Ibid.

This dim-seen track-mark of an ancient
crime.
Ibid.

The Sphinx
With her enigma.
Ibid.

I benefit myself in aiding him.
Ibid.

Now am I hail-fellow-well-met with
all.[4]
Ibid.

Pride, when puffed up, vainly, with
many things

---

[1] I know, of late experience taught, that him
Who is my foe I must but hate as one
Whom I may yet call friend: and him who
loves me
Will I but serve and cherish as a man
Whose love is not abiding. Few be they
Who reaching friendship's port have there
found rest.
The Death of Ajax, translated by CHARLES
STUART CALVERLEY [1831–1884]

Long since I knew to treat my foe like one
Whom I hereafter as a friend might love
If he deserved it, and to love my friend
As if he still might one day be my foe:
For little is the trust we can repose
In human friendships.
Translator unknown

Love him so, as if you were one day to hate
him and hate him so, as you were one day to
love him. — Attributed to CHILO [flourished
556 B.C.] in MONTAIGNE's essay, *Of Friendship.*
[2] Translated by SIR GEORGE YOUNG.
[3] See Terence, page 979.
[4] See Swift, page 191.

---

[1] See Browning, page 493.
[2] To err is human. — POPE: *Essay on Criticism, Part II, L. 325*
[3] Translated by SIR GEORGE YOUNG.
[4] Where life is more terrible than death, it
is then the truest valour to dare to live. —
SIR THOMAS BROWNE [1605–1682]: *Religio
Medici* (Everyman ed), *P. 40*

Unseasonable, unfitting, mounts the
    wall,
Only to hurry to that fatal fall.[1]
                Oedipus Tyrannus

That kindred only should behold and
    hear
The griefs of kin, fits best with decency.
                        Ibid.

Of no mortal say
"That man is happy," till
Vexed by no grievous ill
He pass Life's goal.[2]
         Ibid. Closing lines

To know that all is well, even if late
We come to know it, is at least some
    gain.
                  Trachiniae [3]

There is occasion for the vigilant
To fear for one who prospers, lest he
    fall.
                        Ibid.

One must learn
By doing the thing; for though you
    think you know it
You have no certainty, until you try.
                        Ibid.

    If any
Count on two days, or any more, to
    come,
He is a fool; for a man has no morrow,
Till with good luck he has got through
    to-day.
                        Ibid.

War never slays a bad man in its course,
But the good always!
                  Philoctetes [3]

Winds are fair always, when you fly
    from harm.
                        Ibid.

---

[1] See Heywood, page 14, and Chapman,
page 29.
[2] Call no man happy till you know the nature of his death. — HERODOTUS: *Clio, Book
I, 32*

  'Tis an old well-known proverb of mankind,
"You cannot tell men's fortunes till they die,
In any case, if they be good or bad."
        SOPHOCLES: *Trachiniae*

  'Tis never seemly to felicitate
The fortunes of a man, as prosperous,
Before his life shall have been lived by him
Completely through.
        SOPHOCLES: *Tyndareus, Fragment 572*
[3] Translated by SIR GEORGE YOUNG.

Who does not befriend himself
By doing good?
             Oedipus Coloneus [1]

    To the gods alone
Belongs it never to be old or die,
But all things else melt with all-power-
    ful Time.
                        Ibid.

    If a man to you
Refused a favour, when you begged
    for it,
And would give nothing, and then
    afterwards,
When you were satisfied of your desire,
And all the grace was graceless, prof-
    fered it,
Would not the pleasure so received be
    vain? [2]
                        Ibid.

Never to have been born is much the
    best;
  And the next best, by far,
To return thence, by the way speediest,
    Where our beginnings are.
                        Ibid.

This is our portion at the close of life,
  Strengthless — companionless.
                        Ibid.

It is the merit of a general
To impart good news, and to conceal
    the bad.
                        Ibid.

The very hair on my head
Stands up for dread.[3]
                        Ibid.

A remedy too strong for the disease.
        Tereus. Fragment 514 [4]

Truly, to tell lies is not honourable;
But when the truth entails tremendous
    ruin,
To speak dishonourably is pardonable.
        Creusa. Fragment 323

Sons are the anchors of a mother's life.
        Phaedra. Fragment 612

---

[1] Translated by SIR GEORGE YOUNG.
[2] See Samuel Johnson, page 233, and Dobson, page 649.
[3] The hair of all stood up for fear. — Later
in same drama
[4] The fragments are from pages 311–377
of the Everyman Edition of *The Dramas of
Sophocles*.

To him who is in fear everything rustles.

Acrisius. Fragment 58

No falsehood lingers on into old age.

Ibid. Fragment 59

Lady, cheer up; most of our ills, blowing loudly
In dreams by night, grow milder when 'tis day.

Ibid. Fragment 63

No man loves life like him that's growing old.

Ibid. Fragment 64

War loves to prey upon the young.[1]

Scyrian Women. Fragment 498

A wise gamester ought to take the dice
Even as they fall, and pay down quietly,
Rather than grumble at his luck.

Unknown Dramas. Fragment 686

Truth ever has most strength of what men say.

Ibid. Fragment 691

A woman's vows I write upon the wave.

Ibid. Fragment 694

The friends of the unlucky are far away.

Ibid. Fragment 773

If I am Sophocles, I am not mad; and if I am mad, I am not Sophocles.

Vit. Anon.[2], P. 64

EURIPIDES [3]
[484–406 B. C.]

Old men's prayers for death are lying prayers, in which they abuse old age and long extent of life. But when death draws near, not one is willing to die, and age no longer is a burden to them.

Alcestis.[4] Line 669

---

[1] In peace, children inter their parents; war violates the order of nature, and causes parents to inter their children. — HERODOTUS: *Book I, Clio, Chap. 87*
[2] Translated by PLUMPTRE.
[3] Our Euripides, the human,
  With his droppings of warm tears,
  And his touches of things common
  Till they rose to touch the spheres.
    MRS. BROWNING: *Wine of Cyprus*
[4] Translated by MORRIS HICKEY MORGAN.

I care for riches, to make gifts
To friends, or lead a sick man back to health
With ease and plenty. Else small aid is wealth
For daily gladness; once a man be done
With hunger, rich and poor are all as one.

Electra.[1] Line 539

A hundred little things make likenesses
In brethren born, and show the father's blood.

Ibid. Line 642

Danger gleams
Like sunshine to a brave man's eyes.

Iphigenia in Tauris.[1] Line 115

How oft the darkest hour of ill
Breaks brightest into dawn.[2]

Ibid. Line 723

I think that Fortune watcheth o'er our lives,
Surer than we. But well said: he who strives
Will find his gods strive for him equally.[3]

Ibid. Line 910

The night
Is the safe time for robbers, as the light
For just men.

Ibid. Line 1024

Put not thy faith in any Greek.[4]

Ibid. Line 1205

The gifts of a bad man bring no good with them.

Medea.[5] Line 618

Moderation, the noblest gift of Heaven.

Ibid. Line 636

I know, indeed, the evil of that I purpose; but my inclination gets the better of my judgment.[6]

Ibid. Line 1078

---

[1] Translated by SIR GILBERT MURRAY.
[2] The darkest hour is that before the dawn. — HAZLITT: *English Proverbs*
[3] See George Herbert, page 137.
[4] See Virgil, page 982.
[5] Translated by MORRIS HICKEY MORGAN.
[6] See Sir Samuel Garth, page 187, Ovid, page 986, and *Romans, VII, 19.*
I find my growing judgment daily instruct me how to be better, but my untamed affections and confirmed vitiosity makes me daily

Slowly but surely withal moveth the might of the gods.[1]

Bacchae.[2] *Line 882*

Slight not what's near through aiming at what's far.

Rhesus.[2] *Line 482*

Thou didst bring me forth for all the Greeks in common, not for thyself alone.

Iphigenia in Aulis.[2] *Line 1386*

The company of just and righteous men is better than wealth and a rich estate.

Aegeus.[2] *Fragment 7*

A bad beginning makes a bad ending.

Aeolus.[2] *Fragment 32*

Time will explain it all. He is a talker, and needs no questioning before he speaks.

Ibid. Fragment 38

Waste not fresh tears over old griefs.

Alexander.[2] *Fragment 44*

The nobly born must nobly meet his fate.[3]

Alcymene.[2] *Fragment 100*

Woman is woman's natural ally.

Alope.[2] *Fragment 109*

Man's best possession is a sympathetic wife.

Antigone.[2] *Fragment 164*

Try first thyself, and after call in God; For to the worker God himself lends aid.[4]

Hippolytus. Fragment 435

Second thoughts are ever wiser.[5]

Ibid. Fragment 436

Toil, says the proverb, is the sire of fame.

Licymnius.[2] *Fragment 477*

Cowards do not count in battle; they are there, but not in it.

Meleager.[2] *Fragment 523*

A woman should be good for everything at home, but abroad good for nothing.

Meleager. Fragment 525

Silver and gold are not the only coin; virtue too passes current all over the world.

Oedipus.[1] *Fragment 546*

Where two discourse, if the one's anger rise,
The man who lets the contest fall is wise.

Protesilaus.[1] *Fragment 656*

When good men die their goodness does not perish,
But lives though they are gone. As for the bad,
All that was theirs dies and is buried with them.

Temenidae.[1] *Fragment 734*

Every man is like the company he is wont to keep.

Phoenix.[1] *Fragment 809*

Who knows but life be that which men call death,
And death what men call life?

Phrixus.[1] *Fragment 830*

Whoso neglects learning in his youth, loses the past and is dead for the future.

Ibid. Fragment 927

The gods visit the sins of the fathers upon the children.

Ibid. Fragment 970

In a case of dissension, never dare to judge till you've heard the other side.

Heracleidae.[1] (*Quoted by* ARISTOPHANES *in The Wasps*)

Leave no stone unturned.[2]

Ibid. 1002

Those whom God wishes to destroy, he first deprives of their senses.[3]

Fragment, Greek Iambic

---

do worse. — SIR THOMAS BROWNE: *Religio Medici* (Everyman ed.), *P. 47*
We naturally know what is good, but naturally pursue what is evil. — *Ibid., P. 61*
[1] See George Herbert, page 138.
[2] Translated by MORRIS HICKEY MORGAN.
[3] Noblesse oblige (Nobility has its obligation). — BOHN: *Foreign Proverbs*
[4] See George Herbert, page 137.
[5] See Tennyson, page 465.

[1] Translated by MORRIS HICKEY MORGAN.
[2] This may be traced to a response of the Delphic oracle given to Polycrates, as the best means of finding a treasure buried by Xerxes' general, Mardonius, on the field of Plataea. The oracle replied, "Turn every stone." — LEUTSCH AND SCHNEIDEWIN: *Corpus Paraemiographorum Graecorum, Vol. I, P. 146*
[3] See Dryden, page 175.
Quos deus vult perdere, prius dementat.
In Boswell's *Life of Dr. Johnson* (Everyman ed.), *Vol. 2, Pp. 442–443*, this is quoted

These men won eight victories over the Syracusans when the favor of the gods was equal for both sides.

Epitaph for the Athenians Slain in Sicily

HERODOTUS
[484–424 B. C.]

Translation by William Beloe
[1756–1817]

Call no man happy till you know the nature of his death; he is at best but fortunate.[1]

Book I, Clio. Chap. 32

They [the Persians] are accustomed to deliberate on matters of the highest moment when warm with wine; but whatever they in this situation may determine is again proposed to them on the morrow, in their cooler moments, by the person in whose house they had before assembled. If at this time also it meet their approbation, it is executed; otherwise it is rejected. Whatever also they discuss when sober, is always a second time examined after they have been drinking.[2]

Ibid. Chap. 133

They joined battle, and the Phocaeans won, yet it was but a Cadmean victory.[3]

Ibid. Chap. 166

The art of medicine in Egypt is thus exercised: one physician is confined to the study and management of one disease; there are of course a great number who practice this art; some attend to the disorders of the eyes, others to those of the head, some take care of the teeth, others are conversant with all diseases of the bowels; whilst many attend to the cure of maladies which are less conspicuous.

Book II, Euterpe. Chap. 84

They who mutually injure the state, mutually support each other.

Book III, Thalia. Chap. 82

You may have observed how the thunderbolt of Heaven chastises the insolence of the more enormous animals, whilst it passes over without injury the weak and insignificant: before these weapons of the gods you must have seen how the proudest palaces and the loftiest trees fall and perish.[1]

Book VII, Polymnia. Chap. 10

Every measure undertaken with temerity is liable to be perplexed with error, and punished by misfortune.

Ibid.

The Persian messengers travel with a velocity which nothing human can equal. . . . Neither snow, nor rain, nor heat, nor darkness, are permitted to obstruct their speed.[2]

Book VIII, Urania. Chap. 98

Nothing in human life is more to be lamented, than that a wise man should have so little influence.

Book IX, Calliope. Chap. 16

THUCYDIDES
[471–401 B. C.]

Translation [1629] by Thomas Hobbes [1588–1679]

Because in the administration it hath respect not to the few but to the mul-

---

as a saying which everybody repeats, but nobody knows where to find.

[1] See Sophocles, page 966.

[2] The ancient Goths of Germany . . . had all of them a wise custom of debating every thing of importance to their state, twice; that is, — once drunk, and once sober: — Drunk — that their councils might not want vigour; and sober — that they might not want discretion. — STERNE: *Tristram Shandy, Book V, Chap. 17*

Appeal from Philip drunk to Philip sober. — VALERIUS MAXIMUS: *Book VI, Chap. 2*

[3] A Cadmean (or a Pyrrhic) victory was one in which the victors suffered as much as their enemies. "One more such victory," said Pyrrhus, "and I am lost."

[1] It is the lofty pine that by the storm
Is oftener tossed; towers fall with heavier crash
Which higher soar.

HORACE: *Odes, Book II, X, To Licinius, L. 9*

The bigger they come, the harder they fall. — ROBERT FITZSIMMONS [1862–1917], pugilist, before his fight with James J. Jeffries, a heavier man, in San Francisco [July 25, 1902]

[2] Not snow, nor rain, nor heat, nor gloom of night stays these couriers from the swift completion of their appointed rounds. — Inscription on the Main Post Office, New York City

titude, our form of government is called a democracy. Wherein there is not only an equality amongst all men in point of law for their private controversies, but in election to public offices we consider neither class nor rank, but each man is preferred according to his virtue or to the esteem in which he is held for some special excellence: nor is any one put back even through poverty, because of the obscurity of his person, so long as he can do good service to the commonwealth.

> *History. Book II, Chap. 37, Pericles' Funeral Oration over the Athenians who fell in the first year of the Peloponnesian War*

And when Athens shall appear great to you, consider then that her glories were purchased by valiant men, and by men that learned their duty; by men that were sensible of dishonour when they came to act; by such men as, though they failed in their attempt, yet would not be wanting to the city with their virtue, but made unto it a most honourable contribution.

> *Ibid.*

To famous men all the earth is a sepulchre.

> *Ibid.*

Their virtues shall be testified not only by the inscription on stone at home but in all lands wheresoever in the unwritten record of the mind, which far beyond any monument will remain with all men everlastingly.

> *Ibid.*

SIMPLICIUS

They [atoms] move in the void and catching each other up jostle together, and some recoil in any direction that may chance, and others become entangled with one another in various degrees according to the symmetry of their shapes and sizes and positions and order, and they remain together and thus the coming into being of composite things is effected.

> *De Caelo. 242, 15* [1]

SOCRATES
[470–399 B. C.]
Translation by BENJAMIN JOWETT

Either death is a state of nothingness and utter unconsciousness, or, as men say, there is a change and migration of the soul from this world to another.

> *Apology*

No evil can happen to a good man, either in life or after death.

> *Ibid.*

Man is a prisoner who has no right to open the door of his prison and run away. . . . A man should wait, and not take his own life until God summons him.

> *Dialogues of* PLATO. *Phaedo*

The partisan, when he is engaged in a dispute, cares nothing about the rights of the question, but is anxious only to convince his hearers of his own assertions.

> *Ibid.*

False words are not only evil in themselves, but they infect the soul with evil.

> *Ibid.*

The soul takes nothing with her to the other world but her education and culture; and these, it is said, are of the greatest service or of the greatest injury to the dead man, at the very beginning of his journey thither.

> *Ibid.*

I think that I had better bathe before I drink the poison, and not give the women the trouble of washing my dead body.

> *Ibid.*

I owe a cock to Asclepius; do not forget to pay it.

> *Ibid.* (*The last words of Socrates*)

[1] Quoted by CYRIL BAILEY: *The Greek Atomists and Epicurus.*

HIPPOCRATES
[460–377 B. C.]

Translation by WILLIAM HENRY
RICH JONES [*1817–1885*]

I swear by Apollo Physician, by
Asclepius, by Health, by Panacea, and
by all the gods and goddesses, making
them my witnesses, that I will carry
out, according to my ability and judgment, this oath and this indenture. To
hold my teacher in this art equal to my
own parents; to make him partner in
my livelihood; when he is in need of
money to share mine with him; to consider his family as my own brothers,
and to teach them this art, if they want
to learn it, without fee or indenture. I
will use treatment to help the sick according to my ability and judgment,
but never with a view to injury and
wrong doing. I will keep pure and holy
both my life and my art. In whatsoever houses I enter, I will enter to help
the sick, and I will abstain from all in-
tentional wrong-doing and harm. And
whatsoever I shall see or hear in the
course of my profession in my intercourse with men, if it be what should
not be published abroad, I will never
divulge, holding such things to be holy
secrets. Now if I carry out this oath,
and break it not, may I gain forever
reputation among all men for my life
and for my art; but if I transgress it
and forswear myself, may the opposite
befall me.

The Physician's Oath

Healing is a matter of time, but it is
sometimes also a matter of opportunity.
Precepts. Chap. 1

Sometimes give your services for
nothing, calling to mind a previous
benefaction or present satisfaction. And
if there be an opportunity of serving
one who is a stranger in financial straits,
give full assistance to all such. For
where there is love of man, there is also
love of the art. For some patients,
though conscious that their condition
is perilous, recover their health simply
through their contentment with the
goodness of the physician. And it is well
to superintend the sick to make them
well, to care for the healthy to keep
them well, but also to care for one's
own self, so as to observe what is
seemly.

Precepts. Chap. 6

In all abundance there is lack.
Ibid. Chap. 8

If for the sake of a crowded audience
you do wish to hold a lecture, your ambition is no laudable one, and at least
avoid all citations from the poets, for
to quote them argues feeble industry.
Ibid. Chap. 12

Life is short and the art long.[1]
Aphorisms. Sect. I, 1

Extreme remedies are very appropriate for extreme diseases.[2]
Ibid. 6

ARISTOPHANES
[446–380 B. C.]

What heaps of things have bitten me
to the heart!
A small few pleased me, very few, just
four;
But those that vexed were sand-dune-
hundredfold.
The Acharnians [3]

If a word
Our orators let fall, save what pertains
To peace, I'll raise a storm of words,
and rain
A very tempest of abuse upon them!
Ibid.[4]

He works and blows the coals
And has plenty of other irons in the
fire.[5]
Ibid.

[1] Life is short, art is long. — SENECA: *On the
Shortness of Life, I, 1*
   The lyf so short, the craft so long to lerne.
— CHAUCER: *The Parlement of Foules, Proem,
L. 1*
[2] See Shakespeare, page 96.
   For a desperate disease a desperate cure. —
MONTAIGNE: *The Custom of the Isle of Cea,
Chap. 3*
[3] Translated by B. B. ROGERS.
[4] Translated by JOHN HOOKHAM FRERE
[1769–1846].
[5] See Francis Beaumont, page 129.

Master, shall I begin with the usual
  jokes
That the audience always laugh at?
              The Frogs [1]

Lodgings, — free from bugs and fleas,
  if possible,
If you know any such.
                    Ibid.

Brekeke-kesh, koash, koash. [2]
                    Ibid.

The men that stood for office, noted for
  acknowledged worth,
And for manly deeds of honour, and
  for honourable birth;
Train'd in exercise and art, in sacred
  dances and in song,
All are ousted and supplanted by a base
  ignoble throng.
                    Ibid.

He collected audiences about him,
And flourish'd, and exhibited, and ha-
  rangued.
                    Ibid.

A vast expenditure of human voice.
                    Ibid.

Exalted ideas of fancy require
To be clothed in a suitable vesture of
  phrase.
                    Ibid.

I laugh'd till I cried.
                    Ibid.

If we withdraw the confidence we
  placed
In these our present statesmen, and
  transfer it
To those whom we mistrusted heretofore,
This seems I think our fairest chance
  for safety:
If with our present counsellors we fail,
Then with their opposites we might
  succeed.
                    Ibid.

Shame is the apprehension of a vision
Reflected from the surface of opinion —
The opinion of the public.
                    Ibid.

[1] Translated by JOHN HOOKHAM FRERE
[1769–1846].
[2] Adapted in college cheer: Brekeke-kex,
koax, koax.

Perhaps death is life, and life is death,
And victuals and drink an illusion of
  the senses;
For what is Death but an eternal sleep?
And does not Life consist in sleeping
  and eating?
              The Frogs

Happy is the man possessing
The superior holy blessing
Of a judgment and a taste
Accurate, refined and chaste.
                    Ibid.

I commend the old proverb, "For we
must look about under every stone, lest
an orator bite us."
      The Trial of Euripides [1]

When shall I see those halcyon days? [2]
              The Clouds [3]

If you strike
Upon a thought that baffles you, break
  off
From that entanglement and try another.
So shall your wits be fresh to start
  again.
                    Ibid.

Old age is but a second childhood.
                    Ibid.

Throw fear to the wind.
              The Wasps [4]

Rais'd and swell'd with honours great
  (such on bard yet never sate)
With meekness and modesty he bore
  him;
And while his laurels grew, he kept ever
  in his view
The heights yet unconquer'd before
  him.
                    Ibid.

[1] Translated by WILLIAM JAMES HICKIE.
[2] Halcyon days. — SHAKESPEARE: *King
Henry VI, Part I, Act I, Sc. 1, L. 131*
  The appellation of Halcyon-days, which
was applied to a rare and bloodless week of
repose. — GIBBON: *Decline and Fall of the
Roman Empire, Chap. 48*
[3] Translated by THOMAS MITCHELL [1783–
1845].
[4] Translated by RICHARD CUMBERLAND
[1732–1811].

O the days that are gone by, O the days
　　that are no more,[1]
When my eye was bold and fearless,
　　and my hand was on the oar.
The Wasps
Bitt'rest stroke of all we feel it, that an
　　idle brood be fed
At our cost, who never handled oar or
　　jav'lin, never bled,
Nor so much as rais'd a blister in their
　　suff'ring country's stead.
Ibid.

DIONYSIUS THE ELDER
[430–367 B. C.]

Let thy speech be better than silence,
or be silent.
Fragment 6

PLATO
[427–347 B. C.]

Translation by BENJAMIN JOWETT.
Oxford University Press

He who is of a calm and happy nature
will hardly feel the pressure of age, but
to him who is of an opposite disposition
youth and age are equally a burden.
The Republic. Book I, 329-D

No physician, in so far as he is a
physician, considers his own good in
what he prescribes, but the good of his
patient; for the true physician is also a
ruler having the human body as a subject, and is not a mere money-maker.
Ibid. 342-D

When there is an income-tax, the just
man will pay more and the unjust less
on the same amount of income.
Ibid. 343-D

Mankind censure injustice, fearing
that they may be the victims of it and
not because they shrink from commit-
ting it.
Ibid. 344-C

---

[1] The golden olden glory of the days gone
by. — J. W. RILEY: *The Days Gone By*

The days that are no more.
TENNYSON: *The Princess. Tears, Idle Tears*

The beginning is the most important
part of the work.
The Republic. Book II, 377-B

A fit of laughter which has been in-
dulged to excess almost always produces
a violent reaction.
Ibid. Book III, 388-E

Beauty of style and harmony and
grace and good rhythm depend on simplicity.
Ibid. 400-D

Musical training is a more potent instrument than any other, because
rhythm and harmony find their way
into the inward places of the soul.
Ibid. 401-D

Gymnastic as well as music should
begin in early years.
Ibid. 403-C

They do certainly give very strange
and new-fangled names to diseases.
Ibid. 405-C

The judge should not be young; he
should have learned to know evil, not
from his own soul, but from late and
long observation of the nature of evil
in others: knowledge should be his
guide, not personal experience.
Ibid. 409-B

Everything that deceives may be said
to enchant.
Ibid. 413-C

Under the influence either of poverty
or of wealth, workmen and their work
are equally liable to degenerate.
Ibid. Book IV, 421-E

Wealth is the parent of luxury and indolence, and poverty of meanness and
viciousness, and both of discontent.
Ibid. 422

The direction in which education
starts a man will determine his future
life.
Ibid. 425-B

What is the prime of life? May it not
be defined as a period of about twenty
years in a woman's life, and thirty in a
man's?
Ibid. Book V, 460-E

Let there be one man who has a city
obedient to his will, and he might bring

into existence the ideal polity about which the world is so incredulous.

The Republic. Book V, 502-B

Astronomy compels the soul to look upwards and leads us from this world to another.

Ibid. Book VII, 529

I have hardly ever known a mathematician who was capable of reasoning.

Ibid. 531-E

Solon was under a delusion when he said that a man when he grows old may learn many things — for he can no more learn much than he can run much; youth is the time for any extraordinary toil.

Ibid. 536-D

Bodily exercise, when compulsory, does no harm to the body; but knowledge which is acquired under compulsion obtains no hold on the mind.

Ibid. 536-E

Let early education be a sort of amusement; you will then be better able to find out the natural bent.

Ibid. 537

The character of the son begins to develop when he hears his mother complaining that her husband has no place in the government, of which the consequence is that she has no precedence among other women.

Ibid. Book VIII, 549-C

Oligarchy: A government resting on a valuation of property, in which the rich have power and the poor man is deprived of it.

Ibid. 550-C

Democracy, which is a charming form of government, full of variety and disorder, and dispensing a sort of equality to equals and unequals alike.[1]

Ibid. 558-C

The people have always some champion whom they set over them and nurse into greatness. . . . This and no other is the root from which a tyrant springs; when he first appears he is a protector.

Ibid. 565-C

[1] See Aristotle, page 975.

In the early days of his power, he is full of smiles, and he salutes every one whom he meets.

The Republic. Book VIII, 566-D

When the tyrant has disposed of foreign enemies by conquest or treaty, and there is nothing to fear from them, then he is always stirring up some war or other, in order that the people may require a leader.

Ibid. 566-E

Has he not also another object which is that they may be impoverished by payment of taxes, and thus compelled to devote themselves to their daily wants and therefore less likely to conspire against him?

Ibid. 567

What a poor appearance the tales of poets make when stripped of the colours which music puts upon them, and recited in simple prose.

Ibid. Book X, 601-B

There are three arts which are concerned with all things: one which uses, another which makes, a third which imitates them.

Ibid. 601-D

No human thing is of serious importance.

Ibid.

The soul of man is immortal and imperishable.

Ibid. 608-D

These are the Fates, daughters of Necessity . . . Lachesis singing of the past, Clotho of the present, Atropos of the future.

Ibid. 617-C

You are young, my son, and, as the years go by, time will change and even reverse many of your present opinions. Refrain therefore awhile from setting yourself up as a judge of the highest matters.[1]

Laws. 888

[1] I could never divide myself from any man upon the difference of an opinion, or be angry with his judgment for not agreeing with me in that from which perhaps within a few days I should dissent myself. — Sir Thomas Browne: *Religio Medici* (Everyman ed.). P. 7

And this which you deem of no moment is the very highest of all: that is whether you have a right idea of the gods, whereby you may live your life well or ill.

Laws. 888

Not one of them who took up in his youth with this opinion that there are no gods, ever continued until old age faithful to his conviction.

Ibid.

ZEUXIS
[*Circa* 400 B.C.]

Criticism comes easier than craftsmanship.

Quoted by PLINY *in Natural History*

ARISTOTLE
[384–322 B.C.]

Poverty is the parent of revolution and crime.

Politics.[1] Book II

Even when laws have been written down, they ought not always to remain unaltered.

Ibid.

The law has no power to command obedience except that of habit, which can only be given by time, so that a readiness to change from old to new laws enfeebles the power of the law.

Ibid.

That judges of important causes should hold office for life is not a good thing, for the mind grows old as well as the body.

Ibid.

If liberty and equality, as is thought by some, are chiefly to be found in democracy, they will be best attained when all persons alike share in the government to the utmost.[2]

Ibid. Book IV

The best political community is formed by citizens of the middle class. Those States are likely to be well administered in which the middle class is large, and larger if possible than both

the other classes, or at any rate than either singly; for the addition of the middle class turns the scale and prevents either of the extremes from being dominant.

Politics. Book IV

Inferiors revolt in order that they may be equal, and equals that they may be superior. Such is the state of mind which creates revolutions.

Ibid. Book V

Revolutions break out when opposite parties, the rich and the poor, are equally balanced, and there is little or nothing between them; for, if either party were manifestly superior, the other would not risk an attack upon them.

Ibid.

All admit that in a certain sense the several kinds of character are bestowed by nature. Justice, a tendency to Temperance, Courage, and the other types of character are exhibited from the moment of birth.

Nicomachean Ethics. VI, 13, 1

In practical matters the end is not mere speculative knowledge of what is to be done, but rather the doing of it. It is not enough to know about Virtue, then, but we must endeavour to possess it, and to use it, or to take any other steps that may make us good.

Ibid. X, 9, 1

The generality of men are naturally apt to be swayed by fear rather than by reverence, and to refrain from evil rather because of the punishment that it brings, than because of its own foulness.

Ibid.

What makes men good is held by some to be nature, by others habit or training, by others instruction. As for the goodness that comes by nature, this is plainly not within our control, but is bestowed by some divine agency on certain people who truly deserve to be called fortunate.

Ibid. 9, 6

[1] Translated by BENJAMIN JOWETT.
[2] See Plato, page 974.

DEMOSTHENES
[384–322 B. C.]

I do not purchase regret at such a price.

Reply to Laïs

Though a man escape every other danger, he can never wholly escape those who do not want such a person as he is to exist.

De Falsa Legatione.[1] *228*

Every advantage in the past is judged in the light of the final issue.

First Olynthiac.[1] *11*

Like the diet prescribed by doctors, which neither restores the strength of the patient nor allows him to succumb, so these doles that you are now distributing neither suffice to ensure your safety nor allow you to renounce them and try something else.

Third Olynthiac.[1] *33*

To remind the man of the good turns you have done him is very much like a reproach.

De Corona.[1] *269*

MENANDER
[343–292 B. C.]

Translation by FRANCIS G. ALLINSON, *Loeb Classical Library*

You knew not how to live in clover.

The Girl from Samos. Act 2, Sc. 4

The man who first invented the art of supporting beggars made many wretched.

The Fishermen. Fragment

We live, not as we wish to, but as we can.

The Lady of Andros. Fragment

In many ways the saying "Know thyself" is not well said. It were more practical to say "Know other people."[2]

Thrasyleon. Fragment

I call a fig a fig, a spade a spade.[3]

Unidentified minor fragment

[1] Translation by C. A. AND J. H. VINCE, *Loeb Classical Library.*

[2] See Chaucer, page 6.

[3] Call a spade a spade. — PLUTARCH: *Philip*
A similar saying is credited to Aristophanes by LUCIAN, *Quom. Hist. sit conscrib., 41*
Brought up like a rude Macedon, and taught

A woman is necessarily an evil, but he that gets the most tolerable one is lucky.[1]

Unidentified minor fragment

Manner, not gold, is woman's best adornment.

Fragment. Quoted in The Spectator, January 3, 1712

PILPAY OR BIDPAI[2]
[*Circa* 326 B. C.?]

We ought to do our neighbour all the good we can. If you do good, good will be done to you; but if you do evil, the same will be measured back to you again.[3]

Chap. 1. Dabschelim and Pilpay

It has been the providence of Nature to give this creature [the cat] nine lives instead of one.[4]

Ibid. Fable 3, The Greedy and Ambitious Cat

There is no gathering the rose without being pricked by the thorns.[5]

Chap. 2. Fable 6, The Two Travellers

Wise men say that there are three sorts of persons who are wholly deprived of judgment, — they who are ambitious of preferments in the courts of princes; they who make use of poison

to call a spade a spade. — STEPHEN GOSSON [1554–1624]: *Ephemerides of Phialo* [1579].

I think it good plain English, without fraud,
To call a spade a spade, a bawd a bawd.
JOHN TAYLOR, the "Water Poet"
[1580–1653]

[1] Marriage is an evil that most men welcome. — MENANDER: *Fragment, Monost. 102.* Motto of *The Spectator*, December 29, 1711

[2] Theodor Benfey [1809–1881], German Orientalist, in tracing the name Pilpay or Bidpai, found that it was an appellative applied to the chief pandit or court scholar of an Indian prince. The *Fables of Pilpay*, or *Kalilah and Dimnah,* are the Arabic translation of the Pahlavi translation of the Sanskrit original of the *Panchatantra.* The first English translation appeared in 1570.

[3] And with what measure ye mete, it shall be measured to you again. — *Matthew, VII, 2*

[4] Nine lives like a cat. — HEYWOOD: *Proverbes, Part II, Chap. 4*

[5] Ne'er the rose without the thorn. — HERRICK: *The Rose*

to show their skill in curing it; and they who intrust women with their secrets.

> *Chap. 2. Fable 6, The Two Travellers*

Men are used as they use others.

> *Ibid. Fable 9, The King Who Became Just*

What is bred in the bone will never come out of the flesh.[1]

> *Ibid. Fable 14, The Two Fishermen*

Guilty consciences always make people cowards.[2]

> *Chap. 3. Fable 3, The Prince and His Minister*

Whoever . . . prefers the service of princes before his duty to his Creator, will be sure, early or late, to repent in vain.

> *Ibid.*

There are some who bear a grudge even to those that do them good.

> *Ibid. Fable 6, A Religious Doctor*

There was once, in a remote part of the East, a man who was altogether void of knowledge and experience, yet presumed to call himself a physician.

> *Ibid. Fable 8, The Ignorant Physician*

He that plants thorns must never expect to gather roses.[3]

> *Ibid.*

Honest men esteem and value nothing so much in this world as a real friend. Such a one is as it were another self, to whom we impart our most secret thoughts, who partakes of our joy, and comforts us in our affliction; add to this, that his company is an everlasting pleasure to us.

> *Chap. 4. Choice of Friends*

[1] It will not out of the flesh that is bred in the bone. — HEYWOOD: *Proverbes, Part II, Chap. 8*

[2] Conscience does make cowards of us all.
SHAKESPEARE: *Hamlet, Act III, Sc. 1, L. 83*

[3] Whatsoever a man soweth, that shall he also reap. — *Galatians, VI, 7*

As you sow, ye are like to reap.
BUTLER: *Hudibras, II, ii, 504*

That possession was the strongest tenure of the law.[1]

> *Chap. 5. Fable 4, The Cat and the Two Birds*

Wild elephants are caught by tame;
With money it is just the same.

> *The Panchatantra. Book I (Translation adapted from ARTHUR W. RYDER)*

EUCLID
[*Circa* 300 B. C.]

Pons asinorum (the bridge of asses).[2]

> *Elements. Book I, Proposition 5*

There is no royal road to geometry.[3]

> *Quoted by* PROCLUS: *Commentaria in Euclidem. Book 2, Chap. 4*

THEOCRITUS
[THIRD CENTURY B. C.]

Translation by J. M. EDMONDS, Loeb Classical Library

'Tis peace of mind, lad, we must find,
   and have a beldame nigh
To sit for us and spit for us and bid all
   ill go by.

> *The Harvest-Home. Line 126*

O cricket is to cricket dear, and ant for
   ant doth long,
The hawk's the darling of his fere, and
   o' me the Muse and her song.

> *The Third Country Singing-Match. Line 31*

O to be a frog, my lads, and live aloof
   from care.

> *The Reapers. Line 52*

Thou 'lt cut thy finger, niggard, a splitting caraway.

> *Ibid. Line 55*

A great love goes here with a little gift.

> *The Distaff. Line 24*

[1] Possession is eleven points in the law. — COLLEY CIBBER: *Woman's Wit, Act I*

[2] Too difficult for asses, or stupid boys, to get over.

[3] Ptolemy I, King of Egypt, wished to study geometry, without going over the thirteen parts of Euclid's *Elements*. He said that a short-cut would be agreeable, whereupon Euclid answered that there was no royal road to geometry. Often misquoted as "no royal road to learning."

PLAUTUS
[254–184 B. C.]

Translation by HENRY THOMAS
RILEY [1816–1878]. *The references are to the text of Ritschl's
second edition, Bohn Classical
Library*

What is yours is mine, and all mine
is yours.[1]
Trinummus. Act II, Sc. 2, Line 48
(329)

Not by years but by disposition is
wisdom acquired.
Ibid. Line 88 (367)

He whom the gods favour dies in
youth.[2]
Bacchides. Act IV, Sc. 7, Line 18
(816)

You are seeking a knot in a bulrush.[3]
Menaechmi. Act II, Sc. 1, Line 22
(247)

In the one hand he is carrying a stone,
while he shows the bread in the other.[4]
Aulularia. Act II, Sc. 2, Line 18
(195)

It was not for nothing that the raven
was just now croaking on my left hand.[5]
Ibid. Act IV, Sc. 3, Line 1 (624)

There are occasions when it is undoubtedly better to incur loss than to
make gain.
Captivi. Act II, Sc. 2, Line 77
(327)

Patience is the best remedy for every
trouble.[6]
Rudens. Act II, Sc. 5, Line 71

---

[1] See Shakespeare, page 37.
[2] The good die first.
WORDSWORTH: *The Excursion, Book I*
[3] A proverbial expression implying a desire
to create doubts and difficulties where there
really are none. It occurs in TERENCE: *Andria, Act V, Sc. 4, L. 38;* also in ENNIUS:
Saturae, 46.
[4] What man is there of you, whom if his
son ask bread, will he give him a stone? —
Matthew, VII, 9
[5] See John Gay, page 206.
[6] Patience is a remedy for every sorrow.—
PUBLILIUS SYRUS: *Maxim 170*

Consider the little mouse, how sagacious an animal it is which never entrusts its life to one hole only.[1]
Truculentus. Act IV, Sc. 4, Line 15
(868)

Nothing is there more friendly to a
man than a friend in need.[2]
Epidicus. Act III, Sc. 3, Line 44
(425)

Things which you do not hope happen more frequently than things which
you do hope.[3]
Mostellaria. Act I, Sc. 3, Line 40
(197)

To blow and swallow at the same
moment is not easy.
Ibid. Act III, Sc. 2, Line 104 (791)

QUINTUS ENNIUS
[239–169 B. C.]

No sooner said than done — so acts
your man of worth.
Annals. Book 9 (Quoted by
PRISCIANUS)

I never indulge in poetics
Unless I am down with rheumatics.
Fragment of a Satire (Quoted by
PRISCIANUS)

Let no one pay me honor with tears,
nor celebrate my funeral with mourning.[4]
Quoted by CICERO *in
De Senectute, XX*

CAECILIUS STATIUS
[220–168 B. C.]

Let him draw out his old age to dot-
age drop by drop.
Hymnis (Quoted by FESTUS)
The facts will promptly blunt his
ardor.
The Changeling (Quoted by
CHARISIUS)

---

[1] See Chaucer, page 7.
[2] A friend in need is a friend indeed. — HAZ-
LITT: *English Proverbs*
[3] The unexpected always happens. — *A common saying*
[4] No funeral gloom, my dears, when I am
gone,
Corpse-gazings, tears, black raiment, graveyard grimness.
WILLIAM ALLINGHAM [1828–1889]: *Diary*

He plants trees to benefit another generation.

Synephebi (Quoted by CICERO *in De Senectute, VII)*

TERENCE
[185–159 B. C.]

Translation by HENRY THOMAS RILEY [*1816–1878*]. *The references are to the text of the Bohn Classical Library.*

Of surpassing beauty and in the bloom of youth.

Andria. Act I, Sc. 1, Line 45 (72)

Hence these tears.

Ibid. Line 99 (126)

That is a true proverb which is wont to be commonly quoted, that "all had rather it were well for themselves than for another."

Ibid. Act II, Sc. 5, Line 15 (426)

The quarrels of lovers are the renewal of love.[1]

Ibid. Act III, Sc. 3, Line 23 (555)

Look you, I am the most concerned in my own interests.[2]

Ibid. Act IV, Sc. 1, Line 12 (636)

In fine, nothing is said now that has not been said before.[3]

Eunuchus. The Prologue, Line 41

Immortal gods! how much does one man excel another! What a difference there is between a wise person and a fool!

Ibid. Act II, Sc. 2, Line 1 (232)

I have everything, yet have nothing; and although I possess nothing, still of nothing am I in want.[4]

Ibid. Line 12 (243)

There are vicissitudes in all things.

Ibid. Line 45 (276)

The very flower of youth.[5]

Ibid. Sc. 3, Line 27 (319)

I did not care one straw.

Eunuchus. Act III, Sc. 1, Line 21 (411)

Jupiter, now assuredly is the time when I could readily consent to be slain, lest life should sully this ecstasy with some disaster.[1]

Ibid. Sc. 5, Line 2 (550)

This and a great deal more like it I have had to put up with.

Ibid. Act IV, Sc. 6, Line 8 (746)

Take care and say this with presence of mind.[2]

Ibid. Line 31 (769)

It behooves a prudent person to make trial of everything before arms.

Ibid. Sc. 7, Line 19 (789)

I know the disposition of women: when you will, they won't; when you won't, they set their hearts upon you of their own inclination.

Ibid. Line 42 (812)

I took to my heels as fast as I could.

Ibid. Act V, Sc. 2, Line 5 (844)

Many a time, . . . from a bad beginning great friendships have sprung up.   *Ibid. Line 34 (873)*

I only wish I may see your head stroked down with a slipper.[3]

Ibid. Sc. 8, Line 1 (1028)

I am a man, and nothing that concerns a man do I deem a matter of indifference to me.[4]

Heauton Timoroumenos. Act I, Sc. 1, Line 25 (77)

This is a wise maxim, "to take warning from others of what may be to your own advantage."

Ibid. Sc. 2, Line 36 (210)

That saying which I hear commonly repeated, — that time assuages sorrow.

Ibid. Act III, Sc. 1, Line 12 (421)

---

[1] See Richard Edwards, page 19.
[2] Charity begins at home, is the voice of the World. — SIR THOMAS BROWNE: *Religio Medici* (Everyman ed.), P. 72
[3] See *Ecclesiastes, I, 10* on page 1109
[4] See Wotton, page 114.
[5] See Sophocles, page 965.

[1]   If it were now to die,
'Twere now to be most happy.
SHAKESPEARE: *Othello, Act. II, Sc. 1, L. 192*
[2] Literally, "with a present mind," — equivalent to CAESAR'S *praesentia animi (De Bello Gallico, V, 43, 4)*.
[3] According to LUCIAN, there was a story that Omphale used to beat Hercules with her slipper or sandal.
[4] Quoted by CICERO in *De Officiis, I, 30*. In the Latin, Homo sum: humani nihil a me alienum puto.

Really, you have seen the old age of an eagle,[1] as the saying is.

> *Heauton Timoroumenos. Act III, Sc. 2, Line 9 (520)*

Many a time a man cannot be such as he would be, if circumstances do not admit of it.

> *Ibid. Act IV, Sc. 1, Line 53 (666)*

Nothing is so difficult but that it may be found out by seeking.

> *Ibid. Sc. 2, Line 7 (675)*

What now if the sky were to fall?[2]

> *Ibid. Line 41 (719)*

Rigorous law is often rigorous injustice.[3]

> *Ibid. Sc. 4, Line 48 (796)*

There is nothing so easy but that it becomes difficult when you do it with reluctance.

> *Ibid. Sc. 5, Line 1 (805)*

Fortune helps the brave.[4]

> *Phormio. Act I, Sc. 4, Line 26 (203)*

It is the duty of all persons, when affairs are the most prosperous,[5] then in especial to reflect within themselves in what way they are to endure adversity.

> *Ibid. Act II, Sc. 1, Line 11 (241)*

As many men, so many minds;[6] every one his own way.

> *Ibid. Sc. 4, Line 14 (454)*

As the saying is, I have got a wolf by the ears.[1]

> *Phormio. Act III, Sc. 2, Line 21 (506)*

I bid him look into the lives of men as though into a mirror, and from others to take an example for himself.

> *Adelphoe. Act III, Sc. 3, Line 61 (415)*

According as the man is, so must you humour him.

> *Ibid. Line 77 (431)*

It is a maxim of old that among themselves all things are common to friends.[2]

> *Ibid. Act V, Sc. 3, Line 18 (803)*

It is the common vice of all, in old age, to be too intent upon our interests.[3]

> *Ibid. Sc. 8, Line 30 (953)*

MARCUS TULLIUS CICERO
[106–43 B. C.]

For as lack of adornment is said to become some women, so this subtle oration, though without embellishment, gives delight.[4]

> *De Oratore. 78*

Thus in the beginning the world was so made that certain signs come before certain events.[5]

> *De Divinatione. I, 118*

He is never less at leisure than when at leisure.[6]

> *De Officiis. IX, 10*

What a time! What a civilization![7]

> *Catiline. I, 1*

For how many things, which for our own sake we should never do, do we perform for the sake of our friends.

> *De Amicitia.[8] XVI*

---

[1] This was a proverbial expression, signifying a hale and vigorous old age.

[2] See Heywood, page 12.
Some ambassadors from the Celtae, being asked by Alexander what in the world they dreaded most, answered, that they feared lest the sky should fall upon them. — ARRIANUS: *Book I, 4*

[3] Extreme law, extreme injustice, is now become a stale proverb in discourse. — CICERO: *De Officiis, I, 33*
Une extrême justice est souvent une injure (Extreme justice is often injustice). — RACINE: *Frères Ennemies, Act IV, Sc. 3*
Mais l'extrême justice est une extrême injure. — VOLTAIRE: *Oedipus, Act III, Sc. 3*

[4] PLINY THE YOUNGER says (*Book 6, Letter 16*) that PLINY THE ELDER said this during the eruption of Vesuvius: "Fortune favours the brave."

[5] CICERO: *Tusculan Questions, Book 3, 30*

[6] Quot homines, tot sententiae.

---

[1] A proverbial expression, which, according to SUETONIUS, was frequently in the mouth of Tiberius Caesar.

[2] All things are in common among friends. — DIOGENES LAERTIUS: *Diogenes, VI*

[3] CICERO quotes this in *Tusculan Questions, Book 3*. The maxim was a favorite one with the Stoic philosophers.

[4] See Thomson, page 224.

[5] See Coleridge, page 318.

[6] See Samuel Rogers, page 289.

[7] O tempora! O mores!

[8] Translated by CYRUS R. EDMONDS.

Nothing can be more disgraceful than to be at war with him with whom you have lived on terms of friendship.

De Amicitia. XXI

He removes the greatest ornament of friendship, who takes away from it respect.

Ibid. XXII

There is no greater bane to friendship than adulation, fawning, and flattery.

Ibid. XXV

Crimes are not to be measured by the issue of events, but from the bad intentions of men.

Paradox III

There is no place more delightful than home.

Epistolae. IV, 8

While the sick man has life there is hope.[1]

Ibid. IX, 10

For as I like a young man in whom there is something of the old, so I like an old man in whom there is something of the young; and he who follows this maxim, in body will possibly be an old man, but he will never be an old man in mind.

De Senectute.[2] XI

Old age is by nature rather talkative.

Ibid. XVI

Old age, especially an honored old age, has so great authority, that this is of more value than all the pleasures of youth.

Ibid. XVII

Intelligence, and reflection, and judgment, reside in old men, and if there had been none of them, no states could exist at all.

Ibid. XIX

The short period of life is long enough for living well and honourably.[3]

Ibid.

The harvest of old age is the recollection and abundance of blessings previously secured.

De Senectute. XIX

Nor, in truth, would the honours of illustrious men continue after death, if their own spirits did not make us preserve a longer remembrance of them.

Ibid. XXII

Old age is the consummation of life, just as of a play.

Ibid. XXIII

LUCRETIUS
[95–55 B. C.]

Continual dropping wears away a stone.[1]

De Rerum Natura. I, 313

The swift runners who hand over the lamp of life.

Ibid. II, 279

What is food to one man may be fierce poison to others.[2]

Ibid. IV, 637

In the midst of the fountain of wit there arises something bitter, which stings in the very flowers.[3]

Ibid. 1133

SALLUST
[86–34 B. C.]
Translation by J. C. ROLFE

Experience has shown that to be true which Appius [4] says in his verses, that every man is the architect of his own fortune; [5] and this proverb is especially true of you, who have excelled others to such a degree that men are sooner wearied in singing the praises of your deeds than you in doing deeds worthy of praise.

Speech on the State, Addressed to Caesar in His Later Years. Chap. I, Sentence 2

---

[1] While there is life, there's hope. — JOHN GAY: *The Sick Man and the Angel*
[2] Translated by CYRUS R. EDMONDS.
[3] Life is amply long for him who orders it properly. — SENECA: *On the Shortness of Life,* I, 4

[1] See Lyly, page 23.
[2] See Beaumont and Fletcher, page 132.
[3] See Byron, page 352.
[4] Appius Claudius Caecus, consul in 307 B. C.
[5] See Bacon, page 111, and Publilius, Maxim 283.

CORNELIUS NEPOS
[*Floruit* 75 B.C.]

More brawn than brain.
> *Epaminondas. Chap. V, Line 21*

VIRGIL
[70–19 B.C.]

Age carries all things, even the mind, away.
> *Bucolics. IX, Line 51*

We have now made you for a time out of marble.
> *Eclogues. VII, Line 35*

Love conquers all.[1]
> *Ibid. X, Line 69*

Be favourable to bold beginnings.[2]
> *Georgics. I, Line 40*

Practice, by taking thought, might little by little hammer out divers arts.
> *Ibid. Line 133*

Let the fields and the gliding streams in the valleys delight me. Inglorious, let me court the rivers and forests.[3]
> *Ibid. II, Line 485*

Some trouble the dangerous seas with oars, others rush to arms.
> *Ibid. Line 503*

Happy they whose walls already rise.
> *Aeneid. Book I, Line 437*

While rivers run into the sea, while on the mountains shadows move over the slopes, while heaven feeds the stars, ever shall thy honour, thy name, and thy praises endure.
> *Ibid. Line 607*

I fear the Greeks, even when bringing gifts.[4]
> *Ibid. Book II, Line 49*

Do not commit your poems to pages alone. Sing them, I pray you.
> *Ibid. Book VI, Line 74*

Easy is the descent to Avernus.
> *Aeneid. Book VI, Line 126*

Fortunate isle, the abode of the blest.
> *Ibid. Line 639*

Faith in the tale is old, but its fame is everlasting.
> *Ibid. Book IX, Line 79*

It is enough to have perished once.
> *Ibid. Line 140*

I could not bear a mother's tears.
> *Ibid. Line 289*

Steep thyself in a bowl of summertime.
> *Minor Poems. Copa: Syrisca, a Dancing Girl,[1] Line 29*

Here's Death, twitching my ear: "Live," says he, "for I'm coming."[2]
> *Ibid. Line 38*

These lines made I, another steals my honors;
So you for others, oxen, bear the yoke;
So you for others, bees, store up your honey;
So you for others, sheep, put on your fleece;
So you for others, birds, construct your nests.[3]

HORACE
[65–8 B.C.]

Everyman Edition

But if by thee place 'mid the bards I'm given,

---

[1] See Chaucer, page 5.

[2] For the reverse side of the Great Seal of the United States (first used on the silver dollar certificates, series of 1935) this line of Virgil has been adapted, changed from the imperative mood, *Audacibus annue coeptis*, to the indicative mood, *Annuit coeptis*, He smiles on our beginnings.

[3] These lines preface PHILIP FRENEAU'S poem, *The Indian Student*.

[4] See Euripides, page 967.

[1] Attributed to Virgil by CHARISIUS, the Grammarian, and by SUETONIUS, though modern scholars question the authenticity of all the minor poems.

[2] Quoted by Justice Oliver Wendell Holmes in a radio address on his ninetieth birthday [March 8, 1931].

[3] Virgil wrote a distich, praising Caesar, and Bathyllus claimed the lines. To expose him, Virgil wrote beneath the distich the following incomplete verses, and Caesar asked Bathyllus to finish the lines. He could not, and Virgil then supplied the missing words (italicized below):

> Hos ego versiculos feci, tulit alter honores;
> Sic vos non vobis, *fertis aratra boves;*
> Sic vos non vobis, *mellificatis apes;*
> Sic vos non vobis, *vellera fertis oves;*
> Sic vos non vobis, *nidificatis aves.*

With soaring head I'll strike the stars of heaven.

> *Odes, Book I.*[1] *I, To Maecenas,*
> *Line 35*

No task's too steep for human wit.

> *Ibid. III, To a Ship Bearing Virgil*
> *Over Seas, Line 37*

With equal foot Pluto knocks at hovels of the poor,
And at the tyrant's towers.

> *Ibid. IV, Spring, Line 13*

To-night with wine drown care.

> *Ibid. VII, To Plancus, Line 30*

Melt me this cold, freely the firelogs throwing
  On hearth, my Thaliarchus! And from crock
  Two-eared, of Sabine make, unlock
Wine, with four years a-glowing! [2]

> *Ibid. IX, To Thaliarchus, Line 5*

What next morn's sun may bring, forebear to ask;
But count each day that comes by gift of chance
So much to the good.

> *Ibid. Line 13*

Seize now and here the hour that is, nor trust some later day! [3]

> *Ibid. XI, Leuconoé, Last line*

Daughter, than lovely mother lovelier still.[4]

> *Ibid. XVI, A Palinode or Song*
> *of Apology, To a Beloved Girl,*
> *Line 1*

Ills which Fate forbids to heal,
Are by endurance lighter made.

> *Ibid. XXIV, Quintilius, Line 19*

One night waits all; Death's road we all must go.

> *Ibid. XXVIII, Archytas, Line 16*

Grant that in age I may not drift
Long years, my lyre forgot! [5]

> *Ibid. XXXI, To Apollo, Line 19*

---

[1] Translated by Dr. JOHN MARSHALL.
[2] Dissolve frigus, ligna super foco
  Large reponens, atque benignius
  Deprome quadrimum Sabina,
  O Thaliarche, merum diota.
    Inscription over the fireplace of the
        Harvard Club of Boston
[3] Carpe diem, quam minimum credula postero.
[4] O matre pulchra filia pulchrior.
[5] See Austin Dobson, page 649.

Brace thee, my friend, when times are hard, to show
A mind unmoved; nor less, when fair thy state,
A sober joy.

> *Odes, Book II.*[1] *III, To Dellius,*
> *Line 1*

It is the lofty pine that by the storm
Is oftener tossed; towers fall with heavier crash
Which higher soar.[2]

> *Ibid. X, To Licinius, Line 9*

Spring's flowers, howe'er they bloom, must fade again.

> *Ibid. XI, To Hirpinus Quinctius,*
> *Line 9*

And Sisyphus who bears the ban
Of labour without end.[3]

> *Ibid. XIV, To Postumus, Line 19*

Death's boatman takes no bribe, nor brings
Ev'n skilled Prometheus back from Hades' shore.

> *Ibid. XVIII, To a Miser, Line 35*

Good 'tis and fine, for fatherland to die! [4]

> *Ibid. Book III.*[5] *II, Of Roman*
> *Virtue, Line 13*

Our fathers' age, than their sires' not so good,
Bred us ev'n worse than they; a brood
We'll leave that's viler still.[6]

> *Ibid. VI, Of Rome's Degeneracy,*
> *Line 46*

Bandusia's fount, more bright than crystal.

> *Ibid. XIII, Bandusia's Fountain,*
> *Line 1*

Years with their whitening locks subdue the heart

---

[1] Translated by Dr. JOHN MARSHALL.
[2] See Herodotus, page 969.
[3] Sisyphus, by fate doomed to uplift from ground,
  And uphill thrust the stone.
    HORACE: *Epodes, XVII, Horace and*
    Canidia, L. 68 (translated by Dr. JOHN
    MARSHALL)
[4] Dulce et decorum est pro patria mori.
[5] Translated by Dr. JOHN MARSHALL.
[6] Few sons are like their father, many are worse,
  Few, indeed, are better than the father.
    HOMER: *Odyssey, Book II*

Once keen for lawsuits and the reckless
   fray;
I had not taken thus the peaceful part
   In Plancus' day.[1]
   Odes, Book III. XIV, Triumphal
      Ode to Augustus, Line 25
As riches grow, care follows, and a
   thirst
For more and more.
   Ibid. XVI, Of Riches and
      Contentment, Line 17
Learn calm to face what's pressing.
   Ibid. XXIX, To Maecenas,
      Line 33
This day I've lived.
   Ibid. Line 43
I shall not wholly die. What's best of
   me
Shall 'scape the tomb.[2]
   Ibid. XXX, To Melpomene,
      A Closing Song to His Muse,
      Line 6
Ev'n though the Golden Age upon the
   earth
Once more may live.[3]
   Ibid. Book IV.[4] *II, To Iulus An-*
      tonius, a Brother Poet, Line 39
Summer treads
On heels of Spring.
   Ibid. VII, To Torquatus, Line 9
Brave men were living before Agamem-
   non.
   Ibid. IX, To Lollius, Line 25
At the fit hour 'tis sweet to unbend.
   Ibid. XII, To Virgil, Line 28
But now Lyciscus' beauty rules the
   roast.[5]
   Epodes.[4] *XI, To Pettius, Line 23*
The laugh will then be mine.
   Ibid. XV, To Neaera, Line 24
To bronze Jove changed Earth's golden
   time;

With bronze, then iron, stamped the
   age.
   Epodes. XVI, Iron and Golden
      Age, Line 64
Then, gods, to reverent youth grant
   purity,
Grant, gods, to quiet age a peaceful
   end.
   Saecular Hymn.[1] *Line 45*
The mountains are in labour, and a
ridiculous mouse will be born.[2]
   The Art of Poetry.[3] *Line 139*
In long works sleep will sometimes
surprise, Homer himself hath been ob-
serv'd to nod.[4]
   Ibid. Line 359
No one lives content with his condition, whether reason gave it him, or
chance threw it in his way.
   Satires, Book I.[5] *I, Line 1*
We rarely find a man who can say
he has lived happy, and content with
his life can retire from the world like
a satisfied guest.
   Ibid. Line 117
This is a fault common to all singers,
that among their friends they never are
inclined to sing when they are asked,
unasked they never desist.
   Ibid. III, Line 1
There are many who recite their
writings in the middle of the forum;
and who do it while bathing: the closeness of the place gives melody to the
voice.
   Ibid. IV, Line 74
Ridicule often decides matters of importance more effectually, and in a better manner, than severity.
   Ibid. X, Line 14
Carrying timber into a wood.[6]
   Ibid. Line 34

---

[1] See Byron, page 358.
[2] I shall have more to say when I am dead.
   EDWIN ARLINGTON ROBINSON [1869–
      1935]: *John Brown, last line*
[3] See Spenser, page 25.

The golden age, which a blind tradition has
hitherto placed in the past, is before us.—
C. A. SAINT-SIMON [1675–1755], quoted by
CARLYLE in *Sartor Resartus, Book 3, Chap. 5*
[4] Translated by DR. JOHN MARSHALL.
[5] See John Skelton, page 9.

---

[1] Translated by DR. JOHN MARSHALL.
[2] See Aesop, page 961.
[3] For other passages from *The Art of Poetry*,
see the Earl of Roscommon, page 180.
[4] Indignor quandoque bonus dormitat Homerus (I feel aggrieved whenever good Homer
nods). Generally translated as, "Even the
worthy Homer sometimes nods."
[5] Translated by CHRISTOPHER SMART [1722–
1770].
[6] Or, "Carrying coals to Newcastle." See
Diogenes Laertius, page 1014.

You that intend to write what is worthy to be read more than once, blot frequently: and take no pains to make the multitude admire you, content with a few judicious readers.

Satires, Book I. X, Line 72

Now learn what and how great benefits a temperate diet will bring along with it. In the first place you will enjoy good health.

Ibid. Book II.[1] II, Line 70

Provident for the future, like a wise man in time of peace, shall make the necessary preparations for war.

Ibid. Line 110

Live undaunted; and oppose gallant breasts against the strokes of adversity.[2]

Ibid. Line 135

At Rome, you long for the country; when you are in the country, fickle, you extol the absent city to the skies.

Ibid. VII, Line 28

He has half the deed done, who has made a beginning.

Epistles, Book I.[1] II, To Lollius, Line 40

The covetous man is ever in want.

Ibid. Line 56

Sicilian tyrants never invented a greater torment than envy.

Ibid. Line 58

In the midst of hope and care, in the midst of fears and disquietudes, think every day that shines upon you is the last. Thus the hour, which shall not be expected, will come upon you an agreeable addition.

Ibid. IV, To Albius Tibullus, Line 12

When you have a mind to laugh, you shall see me, fat and sleek with good keeping, a hog of Epicurus' herd.

Ibid. Line 15

As soon as a man perceives how much the things he has discarded excel those which he pursues, let him return

in time, and resume those which he relinquished.

Epistles, Book I. VII, To Maecenas, Line 96

You may drive out nature with a fork, yet still she will return.

Ibid. X, To Aristius Fuscus, Line 24

Whatever prosperous hour Providence bestows upon you, receive it with a thankful hand: and defer not the enjoyment of the comforts of life.

Ibid. XI, To Bullatius, Line 22

They change their climate, not their disposition, who run beyond the sea.

Ibid. Line 27

That man is by no means poor, who has the use of everything he wants. If it is well with your belly, your back, and your feet, regal wealth can add nothing greater.

Ibid. XII, To Iccius, Line 4

Joys are not the property of the rich alone: nor has he lived ill, who at his birth and at his death has passed unnoticed.

Ibid. XVII, To Scaeva, Line 9

To have been acceptable to the great is not the last of praises. It is not every man's lot to gain Corinth.[1]

Ibid. Line 35

The man who makes the experiment deservedly claims the honour and the reward.

Ibid. Line 42

A word, once sent abroad, flies irrevocably.[2]

Ibid. XVIII, To Lollius, Line 70

PROPERTIUS
[54 B. C.–A. D. 2]

Never change when love has found its home.

Book I. Elegy 1, Line 36

Let each man pass his days in that wherein his skill is greatest.

Book II. Elegy 1, Line 46

---

[1] Translated by CHRISTOPHER SMART.
[2] The company is Spartan; see how all their wounds are in front. — BASSUS: *The Greek Anthology, Book 9, Epigram 279*

[1] See Walter Pater, page 646.
[2] Words once spoke can never be recall'd.
— HORACE: *De Arte Poetica, L. 390*

Scandal has ever been the doom of beauty.

> *Book II. Elegy 32, Line 26*

OVID

[43 B. C.–A. D. 18]

They come to see; they come that they themselves may be seen.[1]

> *The Art of Love. I, 99*

Nothing is stronger than custom.

> *Ibid. II, 345*

Then the omnipotent Father with his thunder made Olympus tremble, and from Ossa hurled Pelion.[2]

> *Metamorphoses. I, 154*

What you desire is not mortal.

> *Ibid. II, 55*

---

[1] See Chaucer, page 7, and Pope, page 217.
[2]   They were setting
Ossa upon Olympus, and upon
Steep Ossa leafy Pelius.
> CHAPMAN: *Homer's Odyssey,*
> *Book XI, 426*
Heav'd on Olympus tott'ring Ossa stood;
On Ossa Pelion nods with all his wood.
> POPE: *Odyssey, Book XI, 387*
Ossa on Olympus heave, on Ossa roll
Pelion with all his woods; so scale the
starry pole.
> SOTHEBY: *Odyssey, Book XI, 315*
To the Olympian summit they essay'd
To heave up Ossa, and to Ossa's crown
Branch-waving Pelion.
> COWPER: *Odyssey, Book XI, 379*
They on Olympus Ossa fain would roll;
On Ossa Pelion's leaf-quivering hill.
> WORSLEY: *Odyssey, Book XI, 414*
>   To fling
Ossa upon Olympus, and to pile
Pelion with all its growth of leafy woods
On Ossa.
> BRYANT: *Odyssey, Book XI, 390*
Ossa they pressed down with Pelion's
weight,
And on them both impos'd Olympus' hill.
> FITZ-GEFFREY: *The Life and Death of*
> *Sir Francis Drake, St. 99* [1596]
Ter sunt conati imponere Pelio Ossam.
> — VIRGIL: *Georgics, I, 281*
I would have you call to mind the strength
of the ancient giants, that undertook to lay
the high mountain Pelion on the top of Ossa,
and set among those the shady Olympus. —
RABELAIS: *Works, Book IV, Chap. 38*

I see the right, and I approve it, too,
Condemn the wrong and yet the wrong pursue.[1]

> *Metamorphoses. VII, 17*

Poetry comes fine spun from a mind at peace.

> *Tristia. Book I, Chap. 1, Line 39*

While fortune smiles you'll have a host of friends,
But they'll desert you when the storm descends.

> *Ibid. Chap. 9, Line 5*

Grateful must we be that the heart may go whithersoever it will.

> *Epistolae ex Ponto. Book III,*
> *Chap. 5, Line 48*

How little you know about the age you live in if you fancy that honey is sweeter than cash in hand.

> *Fasti. Book I, Line 191*

Janus: I bar the doors in time of peace, lest peace depart.

> *Ibid. Line 279*

The mind, conscious of rectitude, laughed to scorn the falsehood of report.[2]

> *Ibid. Book IV, Line 311*

PUBLILIUS SYRUS [3]

[*Circa* 42 B. C.]

Translation by DARIUS LYMAN.
The numbers are those of the translator.

As men, we are all equal in the presence of death.

> *Maxim 1*

To do two things at once is to do neither.

> *Maxim 7*

We are interested in others when they are interested in us.[4]

> *Maxim 16*

---

[1] The better I see and approve, the worse I follow. — SPINOZA's translation in *Ethics, Part IV*
See Euripides, page 967.
[2] The mind conscious of virtue may bring to thee suitable rewards. — VIRGIL: *Aeneid, Book I, L. 603*
[3] Commonly called Publius, but spelled Publilius by PLINY in his *Natural History, 35, Sect. 199.*
[4] We always like those who admire us. — ROCHEFOUCAULD: *Maxim 294*

Every one excels in something in which another fails.

Maxim 17

The anger of lovers renews the strength of love.[1]

Maxim 24

A god could hardly love and be wise.[2]

Maxim 25

The loss which is unknown is no loss at all.[3]

Maxim 38

He sleeps well who knows not that he sleeps ill.

Maxim 77

A good reputation is more valuable than money.[4]

Maxim 108

It is well to moor your bark with two anchors.

Maxim 119

Learn to see in another's calamity the ills which you should avoid.[5]

Maxim 120

An agreeable companion on a journey is as good as a carriage.

Maxim 143

Society in shipwreck is a comfort to all.[6]

Maxim 144

Many receive advice, few profit by it.

Maxim 149

Patience is a remedy for every sorrow.[7]

Maxim 170

While we stop to think, we often miss our opportunity.

Maxim 185

Whatever you can lose, you should reckon of no account.

Maxim 191

Even a single hair casts its shadow.

Maxim 228

It is sometimes expedient to forget who we are.

Maxim 233

We may with advantage at times forget what we know.

Maxim 234

The end justifies the means.[1]

Maxim 244

You should hammer your iron when it is glowing hot.[2]

Maxim 262

What is left when honour is lost?

Maxim 265

A fair exterior is a silent recommendation.

Maxim 267

Fortune is not satisfied with inflicting one calamity.

Maxim 274

When Fortune is on our side, popular favour bears her company.

Maxim 275

When Fortune flatters, she does it to betray.

Maxim 277

Fortune is like glass, — the brighter the glitter, the more easily broken.

Maxim 280

It is more easy to get a favour from fortune than to keep it.

Maxim 282

His own character is the arbiter of every one's fortune.[3]

Maxim 283

There are some remedies worse than the disease.[4]

Maxim 301

Powerful indeed is the empire of habit.[5]

Maxim 305

---

[1] See Richard Edwards, page 19.
[2] It is impossible to love and be wise. — BACON: *Of Love*
[3] Let him not know 't and he's not robb'd at all.
SHAKESPEARE: *Othello, Act III, Sc. 3, L. 344*
[4] A good name is better than riches. — CERVANTES: *Don Quixote, Part II, Book II, Chap. 33*
[5] The best plan is, as the common proverb has it, to profit by the folly of others. — PLINY: *Natural History, 18, Sect. 31*
[6] See *Maxim 995.*
[7] See Plautus, page 978.

---

[1] A very free translation of Honesta turpitudo est pro causa bona (Crime is honest for a good cause).

The end must justify the means.
MATTHEW PRIOR: *Hans Carvel*
[2] See Heywood, page 12.
[3] See Bacon, page 111, and Sallust, page 981.
[4] See Bacon, page 110.
Marius said, "I see the cure is not worth the pain." — PLUTARCH: *Lives, Caius Marius*
[5] Habit is second nature. — MONTAIGNE: *Essays, Book III, Chap. 10*

Amid a multitude of projects, no plan is devised.[1]

Maxim 319

It is easy for men to talk one thing and think another.

Maxim 322

When two do the same thing, it is not the same thing after all.

Maxim 338

A cock has great influence on his own dunghill.[2]

Maxim 357

Any one can hold the helm when the sea is calm.[3]

Maxim 358

No tears are shed when an enemy dies.

Maxim 376

The bow too tensely strung is easily broken.

Maxim 388

Treat your friend as if he might become an enemy.

Maxim 402

No pleasure endures unseasoned by variety.[4]

Maxim 406

The judge is condemned when the criminal is absolved.[5]

Maxim 407

Practice is the best of all instructors.[6]

Maxim 439

He who is bent on doing evil can never want occasion.

Maxim 459

One man's wickedness may easily become all men's curse.

Maxim 463

Never find your delight in another's misfortune.

Maxim 467

It is a bad plan that admits of no modification.

Maxim 469

It is better to have a little than nothing.

Maxim 484

It is an unhappy lot which finds no enemies.

Maxim 499

The fear of death is more to be dreaded than death itself.[1]

Maxim 511

A rolling stone gathers no moss.[2]

Maxim 524

Never promise more than you can perform.

Maxim 528

A wise man never refuses anything to necessity.[3]

Maxim 540

No one should be judge in his own cause.[4]

Maxim 545

Necessity knows no law except to conquer.[5]

Maxim 553

Nothing can be done at once hastily and prudently.[6]

Maxim 557

We desire nothing so much as what we ought not to have.

Maxim 559

It is only the ignorant who despise education.

Maxim 571

Do not turn back when you are just at the goal.[7]

Maxim 580

---

[1] He that hath many irons in the fire, some of them will cool. — HAZLITT: *English Proverbs*

[2] See Heywood, page 14.

[3]   The sea being smooth, How many shallow bauble boats dare sail Upon her patient breast.
SHAKESPEARE: *Troilus and Cressida, Act I, Sc. 3, L. 34*

[4] See Cowper, page 265.

[5] Judex damnatur cum nocens absolvitur, — the motto adopted for the *Edinburgh Review.*

[6] Practice makes perfect. — *Proverb*

[1] The sense of death is most in apprehension.
SHAKESPEARE: *Measure for Measure, Act III, Sc. 1, L. 76*

[2] See Heywood, page 14.

[3] Yet do I hold that mortal foolish who strives against the stress of necessity. — EURIPIDES: *Hercules Furens, L. 281*

[4] It is not permitted to the most equitable of men to be a judge in his own cause. — PASCAL: *Thoughts, Chap. 4, 1*

[5] See Milton, page 152.

[6] See Chaucer, page 7.

[7] When men are arrived at the goal, they should not turn back. — PLUTARCH: *Of the Training of Children*

It is not every question that deserves an answer.

Maxim 581

No man is happy who does not think himself so.[1]

Maxim 584

Never thrust your own sickle into another's corn.[2]

Maxim 593

You cannot put the same shoe on every foot.

Maxim 596

He bids fair to grow wise who has discovered that he is not so.

Maxim 598

A guilty conscience never feels secure.[3]

Maxim 617

Every day should be passed as if it were to be our last.[4]

Maxim 633

Familiarity breeds contempt.[5]

Maxim 640

Money alone sets all the world in motion.

Maxim 656

He who has plenty of pepper will pepper his cabbage.

Maxim 673

You should go to a pear-tree for pears, not to an elm.[6]

Maxim 674

It is a very hard undertaking to seek to please everybody.

Maxim 675

[1] No man can enjoy happiness without thinking that he enjoys it. — JOHNSON: *The Rambler, P. 150*

[2] Did thrust as now in others' corn his sickle. — DU BARTAS: *Divine Weekes and Workes, Part II, Second Weeke*

Not presuming to put my sickle in another man's corn. — NICHOLAS YONGE [died 1619]: *Musica Transalpini, Epistle Dedicatory* [1588]

[3] Conscience does make cowards of us all. SHAKESPEARE: *Hamlet, Act III, Sc. 1, L. 83*

[4] Thou wilt find rest from vain fancies if thou doest every act in life as though it were thy last. — MARCUS AURELIUS: *Meditations, II, 5*

[5] See Shakespeare, page 34.

[6] You may as well expect pears from an elm. — CERVANTES: *Don Quixote, Part II, Book II, Chap. 40*

We should provide in peace what we need in war.[1]

Maxim 709

Look for a tough wedge for a tough log.

Maxim 723

How happy the life unembarrassed by the cares of business!

Maxim 725

They who plough the sea do not carry the winds in their hands.[2]

Maxim 759

He gets through too late who goes too fast.

Maxim 767

In every enterprise consider where you would come out.[3]

Maxim 777

It takes a long time to bring excellence to maturity.

Maxim 780

The highest condition takes rise in the lowest.

Maxim 781

It matters not what you are thought to be, but what you are.

Maxim 785

No one knows what he can do till he tries.

Maxim 786

The next day is never so good as the day before.

Maxim 815

He is truly wise who gains wisdom from another's mishap.

Maxim 825

Good health and good sense are two of life's greatest blessings.

Maxim 827

It matters not how long you live, but how well.

Maxim 829

It is vain to look for a defence against lightning.

Maxim 835

[1] See Washington, page 268.

[2] The pilot cannot mitigate the billows or calm the winds. — PLUTARCH: *Of the Tranquillity of the Mind*

[3] In every affair, consider what precedes and what follows, and then undertake it. — EPICTETUS: *That Everything is to be Undertaken with Circumspection, Chap. 15*

No good man ever grew rich all at once.[1]

Maxim 837

Everything is worth what its purchaser will pay for it.[2]

Maxim 847

It is better to learn late than never.[3]

Maxim 864

Better be ignorant of a matter than half know it.[4]

Maxim 865

Better use medicines at the outset than at the last moment.

Maxim 866

Prosperity makes friends, adversity tries them.

Maxim 872

Whom Fortune wishes to destroy she first makes mad.[5]

Maxim 911

Let a fool hold his tongue and he will pass for a sage.

Maxim 914

He knows not when to be silent who knows not when to speak.

Maxim 930

You need not hang up the ivy-branch over the wine that will sell.[6]

Maxim 968

It is a consolation to the wretched to have companions in misery.[7]

Maxim 995

Unless degree is preserved, the first place is safe for no one.[8]

Maxim 1042

Confession of our faults is the next thing to innocency.

Maxim 1060

[1] No just man ever became rich all at once. — MENANDER: *Fragment*
[2]   What is worth in anything
But so much money as 'twill bring?
BUTLER: *Hudibras, Part I, Canto I, L. 465*
[3] See Shakespeare, page 46.
[4] See Bacon, page 110.
[5] See Dryden, page 175.
[6] Good wine needs no bush. — SHAKESPEARE: *As You Like It, Epilogue, L. 4*
[7] See *Maxim 144.*
See Cervantes, page 1036.
It is a comfort to the unhappy to have companions in misery. — SPINOZA: *Ethics, Part 4, Proposition 57, Note*
[8] See Shakespeare, page 75.

I have often regretted my speech, never my silence.[1]

Maxim 1070

Keep the golden mean [2] between saying too much and too little.

Maxim 1072

Speech is a mirror of the soul: as a man speaks, so is he.

Maxim 1073

SENECA
[8 B. C.–A. D. 65]

Translation by W. H. D. ROUSE,
Loeb Classical Library

What fools these mortals be.[3]

Epistles. 1, 3

It is not the man who has too little, but the man who craves more, that is poor.

Ibid. 2, 2

Love of bustle is not industry.

Ibid. 3, 5

Live among men as if God beheld you; speak to God as if men were listening.

Ibid. 10, 5

The best ideas are common property.

Ibid. 12, 11

Men do not care how nobly they live, but only how long, although it is within the reach of every man to live nobly, but within no man's power to live long.

Ibid. 22, 17

A great pilot can sail even when his canvas is rent.

Ibid. 30, 3

Man is a reasoning animal.

Ibid. 41, 8

That most knowing of persons, — gossip.

Ibid. 43, 1

[1] Simonides said "that he never repented that he held his tongue, but often that he had spoken." — PLUTARCH: *Rules for the Preservation of Health*
[2] The golden mean. — COWPER: *Translation of Horace's Odes, Book II, Ode 10, To Licinius, St. 2*
[3] Lord, what fools these mortals be. — SHAKESPEARE: *A Midsummer-Night's Dream, Act III, Sc. 2, L. 115*

It is quality rather than quantity that matters.

Epistles. 45, 1

You can tell the character of every man when you see how he receives praise.

Ibid. 52, 12

Not lost, but gone before.[1]

Ibid. 63, 16

All art is but imitation of nature.

Ibid. 65, 3

It is a rough road that leads to the heights of greatness.

Ibid. 84, 13

I was shipwrecked before I got aboard.

Ibid. 87, 1

It is better, of course, to know useless things than to know nothing.

Ibid. 88, 45

Do not ask for what you will wish you had not got.

Ibid. 95, 1

We are mad, not only individually, but nationally. We check manslaughter and isolated murders; but what of war and the much vaunted crime of slaughtering whole peoples?

Ibid. 95, 30

A great step towards independence is a good-humored stomach.

Ibid. 123, 3

Fire is the test of gold; adversity, of strong men.[2]

Moral Essays. On Providence, 5, 9

Whom they have injured they also hate.[3]

Ibid. On Anger, 2, 33

I do not distinguish by the eye, but by the mind, which is the proper judge of the man.

Ibid. On the Happy Life, 2, 2

There is no great genius without some touch of madness.[1]

Moral Essays. On Tranquillity of the Mind, 17, 10

A great fortune is a great slavery.

Ibid. To Polybius on Consolation, 6, 5

Wherever the Roman conquers, there he dwells.

Ibid. To Helvia on Consolation, 7, 7

He who receives a benefit with gratitude, repays the first instalment on his debt.

On Benefits. Book 2, 22, 1

You roll my log, and I will roll yours.

Apocolocyntosis. Chap. 9

Do you seek Alcides' equal? None is, except himself.[2]

Hercules Furens. 1, 1, 84

Successful and fortunate crime is called virtue.[3]

Ibid. 255

A good mind possesses a kingdom.[4]

Thyestes. 380

PHAEDRUS
[*Circa* A. D. 8]

Translation by HENRY THOMAS RILEY [*1816–1878*]. *Bohn Classical Library*

Submit to the present evil, lest a greater one befall you.

Book I. Fable 2, 31

He who covets what belongs to another deservedly loses his own.

Ibid. Fable 4, 1

That it is unwise to be heedless ourselves while we are giving advice to others, I will show in a few lines.

Ibid. Fable 9, 1

Whoever has even once become notorious by base fraud, even if he speaks the truth, gains no belief.

Ibid. Fable 10, 1

[1] Non amittuntur, sed praemittuntur. See Samuel Rogers, page 289.
[2] See Beaumont and Fletcher, page 131.
[3] See Dryden, page 178.

[1] An ancient commonplace, which Seneca says he quotes from ARISTOTLE: *Problemata, 30, 1.* It is also in PLATO: *Phaedrus, 245 A.* See Dryden, page 173, and Lombroso, page 1077.
[2] See Theobald, page 221.
[3] See Harrington, page 29.
[4] See Dyer, page 20.

By this story [The Fox and the Raven] it is shown how much ingenuity avails, and how wisdom is always an overmatch for strength.

Book I. Fable 13, 13

No one returns with good-will to the place which has done him a mischief.

Ibid. Fable 18, 1

It has been related that dogs drink at the river Nile running along, that they may not be seized by the crocodiles.[1]

Ibid. Fable 25, 3

Every one is bound to bear patiently the results of his own example.

Ibid. Fable 26, 12

Come of it what may, as Sinon said.

Book III. The Prologue, 27

Things are not always what they seem.[2]

Book IV. Fable 2, 5

Jupiter has loaded us with a couple of wallets: the one, filled with our own vices, he has placed at our backs; the other, heavy with those of others, he has hung before.[3]

Ibid. Fable 10, 1

A mountain was in labour, sending forth dreadful groans, and there was in the region the highest expectation. After all, it brought forth a mouse.[4]

Ibid. Fable 22, 1

A fly bit the bare pate of a bald man, who in endeavouring to crush it gave himself a hard slap. Then said the fly jeeringly, "You wanted to revenge the

---

[1] PLINY, in his *Natural History, Book 8, Sect. 148*, and AELIAN, in his *Various Histories*, relate the same fact as to the dogs drinking from the Nile. "To treat a thing as the dogs do the Nile" was a common proverb with the ancients, signifying to do it superficially.

[2] Non semper ea sunt quae videntur.
See Longfellow, page 433.

[3] Everybody has his own delusion assigned to him: but we do not see that part of the bag which hangs on our back. — CATULLUS: *Poem 22, L. 20*

Whosoever shall call me madman, shall hear as much from me, and shall learn to look back upon the bag that hangs behind me. — HORACE: *Satires, Book II, III*

All watch the wallet on the back that walks before. — PERSIUS: *4, 24*

[4] See Aesop, page 961, and Horace, page 984.

sting of a tiny insect with death; what will you do to yourself, who have added insult to injury?"[1]

Book V. Fable 3, 1

"I knew that before you were born." Let him who would instruct a wiser man consider this as said to himself.

Ibid. Fable 9, 4

PLINY THE ELDER

[A. D. 23–79]

With some alterations, from translations by JOHN BOSTOCK, M.D. [1773–1846] *and* HENRY THOMAS RILEY [1816–1878]. *Bohn Classical Library*

In comparing various authors with one another, I have discovered that some of the gravest and latest writers have transcribed, word for word, from former works, without making acknowledgment.

Natural History. Book I, Dedication, Sect. 22

The world, and whatever that be which we call the heavens, by the vault of which all things are enclosed, we must conceive to be a deity, to be eternal, without bounds, neither created nor subject at any time to destruction. To inquire what is beyond it is no concern of man; nor can the human mind form any conjecture concerning it.

Ibid. Book II, Sect. 1

It is ridiculous to suppose that the great head of things, whatever it be, pays any regard to human affairs.

Ibid. Sect. 20

Everything is soothed by oil, and this is the reason why divers send out small quantities of it from their mouths, because it smooths every part which is rough.[2]

Ibid. Sect. 234

---

[1] See Aesop, page 961.

[2] Why does pouring oil on the sea make it clear and calm? Is it for that the winds, slipping the smooth oil, have no force, nor cause any waves? — PLUTARCH: *Natural Questions, IX*

Bishop Adain [A. D. 651] gave to a company about to take a journey by sea "some holy oil,

It is far from easy to determine whether she [Nature] has proved to him a kind parent or a merciless step-mother.[1]

Natural History. Book VII, Sect. 1

Man alone at the very moment of his birth, cast naked upon the naked earth, does she abandon to cries and lamentations.[2]

Ibid. Sect. 2

To laugh, if but for an instant only, has never been granted to man before the fortieth day from his birth, and then it is looked upon as a miracle of precocity.[3]

Ibid.

Man is the only one that knows nothing, that can learn nothing without being taught. He can neither speak nor walk nor eat, and in short he can do nothing at the prompting of nature only, but weep.[4]

Ibid. Sect. 4

saying, 'I know that when you go abroad you will meet with a storm and contrary wind; but do you remember to cast this oil I give you into the sea, and the wind shall cease immediately.' " — BEDE: *Ecclesiastical History, Book III, Chap. 14*

In JARED SPARKS' edition of BENJAMIN FRANKLIN'S *Works, Vol. VI, P. 354*, there are letters between Franklin, Brownrigg, and Parish on the stilling of waves by means of oil.

[1] To man the earth seems altogether
No more a mother, but a step-dame rather.
GUILLAUME DE SALLUSTE DU BARTAS [1544–1590]: *Divine Weekes and Workes, First Weeke, Third Day*

[2] He is born naked, and falls a-whining at the first. — BURTON: *Anatomy of Melancholy, Part I, Sect. 2, Memb. 3, Subsect. 10*
And when I was born, I drew in the common air, and fell upon the earth, which is of like nature; and the first voice which I uttered was crying, as all others do. — *The Wisdom of Solomon, VII, 3*
It was the custom among the ancients to place the new-born child upon the ground immediately after its birth.

[3] This term of forty days is mentioned by ARISTOTLE in his *Natural History*, as also by some modern physiologists.

[4] No language but a cry. — TENNYSON: *In Memoriam, LIV, 5*

With man, most of his misfortunes are occasioned by man.[1]

Natural History. Book VII, Sect. 5

Indeed, what is there that does not appear marvellous when it comes to our knowledge for the first time?[2] How many things, too, are looked upon as quite impossible until they have been actually effected?

Ibid. Sect. 6

The human features and countenance, although composed of but some ten parts or little more, are so fashioned that among so many thousands of men there are no two in existence who cannot be distinguished from one another.[3]

Ibid. Sect. 8

All men possess in their bodies a poison which acts upon serpents; and the human saliva, it is said, makes them take to flight, as though they had been touched with boiling water. The same substance, it is said, destroys them the moment it enters their throat.[4]

Ibid. Sect. 15

It has been observed that the height of a man from the crown of the head to the sole of the foot is equal to the distance between the tips of the middle fingers of the two hands when extended in a straight line.

Ibid. Sect. 77

When a building is about to fall down, all the mice desert it.[5]

Ibid. Book VIII, Sect. 103

[1] Man's inhumanity to man. — BURNS: *Man Was Made to Mourn*

[2] Omne ignotum pro magnifico (Everything that is unknown is taken to be grand). — TACITUS: *Agricola, 30*

[3] See Sir Thomas Browne, page 144.

[4] Madame d'Abrantes relates that when Bonaparte was in Cairo he sent for a serpent-detecter (Psylli) to remove two serpents that had been seen in his house. He having enticed one of them from his hiding-place, caught it in one hand, just below the jaw-bone, in such a manner as to oblige the mouth to open, when spitting into it, the effect was like magic: the reptile appeared struck with instant death. — *Memoirs, Vol. I, Chap. 59*

[5] This is alluded to by CICERO in his letters to Atticus, and is mentioned by AELIAN (*Animated Nature, Book VI, Chap. 41*). Compare the modern proverb, "Rats desert a sinking ship."

Bears when first born are shapeless masses of white flesh a little larger than mice, their claws alone being prominent. The mother then licks them gradually into proper shape.[1]

Natural History. Book VIII, Sect. 126

It has become quite a common proverb that in wine there is truth.

Ibid. Book XIV, Sect. 141

Cincinnatus was ploughing his four jugera of land upon the Vaticanian Hill, — the same that are still known as the Quintian Meadows, — when the messenger brought him the dictatorship, finding him, the tradition says, stripped to the work.

Ibid. Book XVIII, Sect. 20

The agricultural population, says Cato, produces the bravest men, the most valiant soldiers, and a class of citizens the least given of all to evil designs.

Ibid. Sect. 26

Why is it that we entertain the belief that for every purpose odd numbers are the most effectual?[2]

Ibid. Book XXVIII, Sect. 23

It was a custom with Apelles, to which he most tenaciously adhered, never to let any day pass, however busy he might be, without exercising himself by tracing some outline or other, — a practice which has now passed into a proverb.[3] It was also a practice with him, when he had completed a work, to exhibit it to the view of the passers-by in his studio, while he himself, con-

[1] See Burton, page 122, and Montaigne, page 1029.

Not unlike the bear which bringeth forth
In the end of thirty dayes a shapeless birth;
But after licking, it in shape she drawes,
And by degrees she fashions out the pawes,
The head, and neck, and finally doth bring
To a perfect beast that first deformed thing.
Du Bartas: *Divine Weekes and Workes, First Weeke, First Day*

[2] See Shakespeare, page 35, and Samuel Lover, page 389.
Numero deus impare gaudet (The god delights in an odd number). — Virgil: *Eclogues, 8, 75*

[3] Nulla dies abeat, quin linea ducta supersit. — Erasmus. Generally quoted, Nulla dies sine linea (No day without a line).

cealed behind the picture, would listen to the criticisms. . . . Under these circumstances, they say that he was censured by a shoemaker for having represented the shoes with one latchet too few. The next day, the shoemaker, quite proud at seeing the former error corrected, thanks to his advice, began to criticize the leg; upon which Apelles, full of indignation, popped his head out and reminded him that a shoemaker should give no opinion beyond the shoes,[1] — a piece of advice which has equally passed into a proverbial saying.

Natural History. Book XXXV, Sect. 84

LUCAN
[A. D. 39–65]

Translation by J. D. Duff. *Loeb Classical Library*

Poverty, the mother of manhood.

The Civil War. Book I, Line 165

Delay is ever fatal to those who are prepared.

Ibid. Line 281

When the whole world is nodding to its fall, happy the man who has been able to learn already the lowly place appointed for him.

Ibid. Book IV, Line 393

Boldness is a mask for fear, however great.

Ibid. Line 702

Yonder trouble concerns the sky and sea, but not our bark; for Caesar treads the deck.[2]

Ibid. Book V, Line 584

DIO CHRYSOSTOM
[A. D. 40–120]

Translation by J. W. Cohoon. *Loeb Classical Library*

Diogenes: The man I know not, for I am not acquainted with his mind.

Fourth Discourse on Kingship. Chap. 17

[1] Ne supra crepidam sutor judicaret (Let not a shoemaker judge above his shoe), or, Let the cobbler stick to his last.
[2] See Plutarch, page 1000.

Idleness and lack of occupation are the best things in the world to ruin the foolish.

Tenth Discourse, On Servants.
Chap. 7

Like men with sore eyes: they find the light painful, while the darkness, which permits them to see nothing, is restful and agreeable.

Eleventh, or Trojan, Discourse.
Chap. 2

Most men are so completely corrupted by opinion that they would rather be notorious for the greatest calamities than suffer no ill and be unknown.

Ibid. Chap. 6

Generally speaking, men are too cowardly to be willing to undergo severe suffering, since they fear death and pain, but they highly prize being mentioned as having suffered.

Ibid. Chap. 10

MARTIAL
[A. D. 40–102]

To yield to the stronger is valor's second prize.

On the Spectacles. Epigram 32

I do not love thee, Sabidius, nor can I say why; this only I can say, I do not love thee.[1]

Epigrams. Book I, 32

I write long epigrams, you yourself write nothing. Yours are shorter.[2]

Ibid. 110

Nothing is more confident than a bad poet.[3]

Ibid. Book II, 63

He does not write at all whose poems no man reads.

Ibid. Book III, 9

The flaw which is hidden is deemed greater than it is.

Ibid. 52

The bee enclosed and through the amber shown

Seems buried in the juice which was his own.[1]

Epigrams. Book IV, 32

What is the use of brevity if it constitute a book?

Ibid. Book VIII, 29

The good man prolongs his life; to be able to enjoy one's past life is to live twice.[2]

Ibid. Book X, 23

Neither fear, nor wish for, your last day.[3]

Ibid. 47

There is no glory in outstripping donkeys.

Ibid. Book XII, 36

QUINTILIAN
[A. D. 42–118]

We give to necessity the praise of virtue.[4]

Institutiones Oratoriae.
Book I, 8, 14

A liar should have a good memory.[5]

Ibid. Book IV, 2, 91

Vain hopes are often like the dreams of those who wake.

Ibid. Book VI, 2, 30

Those who wish to appear wise among fools, among the wise seem foolish.[6]

Ibid. Book X, 7, 21

PLUTARCH
[A. D. 46–120]

Translation by JOHN DRYDEN, *revised by* ARTHUR HUGH CLOUGH. *Modern Library Giant Edition*

As geographers, Sosius, crowd into the edges of their maps parts of the world which they do not know about, adding notes in the margin to the effect that beyond this lies nothing but sandy

---

[1] See Tom Brown, page 188.
[2] An epigram of two lines has every merit, and if you exceed three lines it is rhapsody. — CYRILLUS: *The Greek Anthology, Book 9, Epigram 369*
[3] Quoted by MONTAIGNE in *Of Presumption.*

[1] See Bacon, page 111.
[2] See Alexander Pope, page 217.
[3] See Milton, page 155.
[4] See Chaucer, page 4.
[5] See Algernon Sidney, page 169.
[6] See Pope, page 215.

deserts full of wild beasts, and unapproachable bogs.[1]

Lives. *Theseus, Page 3*

From Theseus began the saying, "He is a second Hercules."

Ibid. Page 19

The most perfect soul, says Heraclitus, is a dry light, which flies out of the body as lightning breaks from a cloud.

Ibid. Romulus, Page 45

Anacharsis, coming to Athens, knocked at Solon's door, and told him that he, being a stranger, was come to be his guest, and contract a friendship with him; and Solon replying, "It is better to make friends at home," Anacharsis replied, "Then you that are at home make friendship with me."

Ibid. Solon, Page 99

Themistocles said that he certainly could not make use of any stringed instrument; could only, were a small and obscure city put into his hands, make it great and glorious.

Ibid. Themistocles, Page 134

Eurybiades lifting up his staff as if he were going to strike, Themistocles said, "Strike, if you will, but hear." [2]

Ibid. Page 141

Themistocles said to Antiphates, . . . "Time, young man, has taught us both a lesson."

Ibid. Page 145

"You speak truth," said Themistocles; "I should never have been famous if I had been of Seriphus; [3] nor you, had you been of Athens."

Ibid.

Laughing at his own son, who got his mother, and, by his mother's means, his father also, to indulge him, he told him that he had the most power of any one in Greece: "For the Athenians command the rest of Greece, I command the Athenians, your mother commands me, and you command your mother." [4]

Ibid.

Of two who made love to his daughter, he preferred the man of worth to the one who was rich, saying he desired a man without riches, rather than riches without a man.

Lives. Themistocles, Page 145

Themistocles replied that a man's discourse was like to a rich Persian carpet, the beautiful figures and patterns of which can be shown only by spreading and extending it out; when it is contracted and folded up, they are obscure and lost.[1]

Ibid. Page 152

Moderation is best, and to avoid all extremes.

Ibid. Camillus, Page 159

Caesar once, seeing some wealthy strangers at Rome, carrying up and down with them in their arms and bosoms young puppy-dogs and monkeys, embracing and making much of them, took occasion not unnaturally to ask whether the women in their country were not used to bear children.

Ibid. Pericles, Page 182

He who busies himself in mean occupations produces, in the very pains he takes about things of little or no use, an evidence against himself of his negligence and indisposition to what is really good.

Ibid. Page 183

---

[1] See Jonathan Swift, page 190.
[2] "Strike," said he, "but hear me." — *Apophthegms of Kings and Great Commanders, Themistocles*
[3] An obscure island.
[4] "Men," said Marcus Cato, "usually command women; but we command all men, and

the women command us." But this, indeed, is borrowed from the sayings of Themistocles. — *Lives, Marcus Cato, P. 416*

Diophantus, the young son of Themistocles, made his boast often and in many companies, that whatsoever pleased him pleased also all Athens; for whatever he liked, his mother liked; and whatever his mother liked, Themistocles liked; and whatever Themistocles liked, all the Athenians liked. — *Of the Training of Children*

When the son of Themistocles was a little saucy toward his mother, he said that this boy had more power than all the Grecians; for the Athenians governed Greece, he the Athenians, his wife him, and his son his wife. — *Apophthegms of Kings and Great Commanders, Themistocles*

[1] Themistocles said speech was like to tapestry; and like it, when it was spread it showed its figures, but when it was folded up, hid and spoiled them. — *Apophthegms of Kings and Great Commanders, Themistocles*

So very difficult a matter is it to trace and find out the truth of anything by history.

Lives. Pericles, Page 194

Like a skilful physician, who, in a complicated and chronic disease, as he sees occasion, at one while allows his patient the moderate use of such things as please him, at another while gives him keen pains and drugs to work the cure.

Ibid. Page 195

Be ruled by time, the wisest counsellor of all.

Ibid. Page 198

Old women should not seek to be perfumed.

Ibid. Page 203

Trees, when they are lopped and cut, grow up again in a short time,[1] but men, being once lost, cannot easily be recovered.

Ibid. Page 207

To be turned from one's course by men's opinions, by blame, and by misrepresentation, shows a man unfit to hold an office.

Ibid. Fabius, Page 216

You know, Hannibal, how to gain a victory, but not how to use it.

Ibid. Page 224

One colour, indeed, they say the chameleon cannot assume: it cannot itself appear white; but Alcibiades, whether with good men or bad, could adapt himself to his company.

Ibid. Alcibiades, Page 249

Menenius Agrippa concluded, at length, with the celebrated fable: "It once happened that all the other members of a man mutinied against the stomach, which they accused as the only idle, uncontributing part in the whole body, while the rest were put to hardships and the expense of much labour to supply and minister to its appetites."[2]

Ibid. Coriolanus, Page 266

Men are usually more stung and galled by reproachful words than hostile actions.

Lives. Timoleon, Page 316

A Roman divorced from his wife, being highly blamed by his friends, who demanded, "Was she not chaste? Was she not fair? Was she not fruitful?" holding out his shoe, asked them whether it was not new and well made. "Yet," added he, "none of you can tell where it pinches me."[1]

Ibid. Aemilius Paulus, Page 322

Petty repeated annoyances, arising from unpleasantness or incongruity of character, have been the occasion of such estrangement as to make it impossible for man and wife to live together with any content.

Ibid.

A man without one scar to show on his skin, that is smooth and sleek with ease and home-keeping habits, will undertake to define the office and duties of a general.

Ibid. Page 340

The saying of old Antigonus, who when he was to fight at Andros, and one told him, "The enemy's ships are more than ours," replied, "For how many then wilt thou reckon me?"

Ibid. Pelopidas, Page 348

Archimedes had stated, that given the force, any given weight might be moved; and even boasted . . . that if there were another earth, by going into it he could remove this.

Ibid. Marcellus, Page 367

They named it Ovation, from the Latin *ovis* (a sheep).

Ibid. Page 382

Asking him if Aristides had ever done him any injury, "None at all," said he, "neither know I the man; but I am tired of hearing him everywhere called the Just."

Ibid. Aristides, Page 396

Nor are we to use living creatures like old shoes or dishes and throw them

---

[1] The lopped tree in time may grow again,
 Most naked plants renew both fruit and
  flower.
  ROBERT SOUTHWELL: *Times Go by Turns*
[2] See Aesop, page 961.

[1] See Herbert, page 137.
 I can tell where my own shoe pinches me.
 — CERVANTES: *Don Quixote, Part I, Book IV, Chap. 5*

away when they are worn out or broken with service.

Lives. Marcus Cato, Page 415

It is a difficult task, O citizens, to make speeches to the belly, which has no ears.[1]

Ibid. Page 416

Cato used to assert that wise men profited more by fools, than fools by wise men; for that wise men avoided the faults of fools, but that fools would not imitate the good examples of wise men.

Ibid. Page 417

He said that in his whole life he most repented of three things: one was that he had trusted a secret to a woman; another, that he went by water when he might have gone by land; the third, that he had remained one whole day without doing any business of moment.

Ibid. Page 418

It was hard for him who had lived with one generation of men, to plead now before another.

Ibid. Page 422

Carthage, methinks, ought utterly to be destroyed.

Ibid. Page 431

Marius said, "I see the cure is not worth the pain."[2]

Ibid. Caius Marius, Page 496

Extraordinary rains pretty generally fall after great battles.

Ibid. Page 507

Marius said that the law spoke too softly to be heard in such a noise of war.

Ibid. Page 511

Lycurgus . . . used to say that long hair made good-looking men more beautiful, and ill-looking men more terrible.

Ibid. Lysander, Page 525

Where the lion's skin will not reach, you must patch it out with the fox's.[1]

Lives. Lysander, Page 529

Moral habits, induced by public practices, are far quicker in making their way into men's private lives, than the failings and faults of individuals are in infecting the city at large.

Ibid. Page 535

As it is in the proverb, played Cretan against Cretan.[2]

Ibid. Page 537

Did you not know, then, that to-day Lucullus dines with Lucullus?

Ibid. Lucullus, Page 622

Lucullus' furnishing a library, however, deserves praise and record, for he collected very many choice manuscripts; and the use they were put to was even more magnificent than the purchase, the library being always open, and the walks and reading-rooms about it free to all Greeks.

Ibid. Page 623

Economy, which in things inanimate is but money-making, when exercised over men becomes policy.

Ibid. Crassus, Page 651

Whoever tries for great objects must suffer something.

Ibid. Page 669

It is no great wonder if in long process of time, while fortune takes her course hither and thither, numerous coincidences should spontaneously occur. If the number and variety of subjects to be wrought upon be infinite, it is all the more easy for fortune, with such an abundance of material, to effect this similarity of results.[3]

Ibid. Sertorius, Page 678

---

[1] The belly has no ears, nor is it to be filled with fair words. — RABELAIS: *Book IV, Chap. 67*

[2] See Bacon, page 110.

In treating wounds, the cure for pain is pain.
CATO THE CENSOR [234–149 B.C.],
Book IV, Distich 40

[1] The prince must be a lion, but he must also know how to play the fox. — NICOLO MACHIAVELLI: *The Prince*

[2] He only played the Cretan with the Cretans. — PLUTARCH: *Lives, Aemilius Paulus, P. 335*

Cheat against cheat. The Cretans were notorious as liars.

[3] History repeats itself. — *Proverb*

'Tis one and the same Nature that rolls on her course, and whoever has sufficiently considered the present state of things might certainly conclude as to both the future and

Perseverance is more prevailing than violence; and many things which cannot be overcome when they are together, yield themselves up when taken little by little.

Lives. Sertorius, Page 688

Good fortune will elevate even petty minds, and give them the appearance of a certain greatness and stateliness, as from their high place they look down upon the world; but the truly noble and resolved spirit raises itself, and becomes more conspicuous in times of disaster and ill fortune.

Ibid. Eumenes, Page 703

Agesilaus being invited once to hear a man who admirably imitated the nightingale, he declined, saying he had heard the nightingale itself.[1]

Ibid. Agesilaus, Page 726

If all the world were just, there would be no need of valour.

Ibid. Page 727

It is circumstance and proper measure that give an action its character, and make it either good or bad.

Ibid. Page 736

The old proverb was now made good, "the mountain had brought forth a mouse."[2]

Ibid.

No man ever asked a favour with less offence, or conferred one with a better grace. When he gave, it was without assumption; when he received, it was with dignity and honour.

Ibid. Pompey, Page 740

Pompey bade Sylla recollect that more worshipped the rising than the setting sun.[1]

Lives. Pompey, Page 749

A dead man cannot bite.

Ibid. Page 795

Whenever Alexander heard Philip had taken any town of importance, or won any signal victory, instead of rejoicing at it altogether, he would tell his companions that his father would anticipate everything, and leave him and them no opportunities of performing great and illustrious actions.[2]

Ibid. Alexander, Page 804

When Alexander asked Diogenes whether he wanted anything, "Yes," said he, "I would have you stand from between me and the sun."

Ibid. Page 810

Alexander finding himself unable to untie the Gordium knot, the ends of which were secretly twisted round and folded up within it, cut it asunder with his sword.

Ibid. Page 813

When asked why he parted with his wife, Caesar replied, "I wished my wife to be not so much as suspected."[3]

Ibid. Caesar, Page 860

For my part, I had rather be the first man among these fellows, than the second man in Rome.[4]

Ibid. Page 861

He who reflects on another man's want of breeding, shows he wants it as much himself.

Ibid. Page 865

Using the proverb frequently in their mouths who enter upon dangerous and

---

the past. — MONTAIGNE: *Essays, Book II, Chap. 12, Apology for Raimond Sebond*

I shall be content if those shall pronounce my History useful who desire to give a view of events as they did really happen, and as they are very likely, in accordance with human nature, to repeat themselves at some future time, — if not exactly the same, yet very similar. — THUCYDIDES: *History, I, 2, 2*

What is this day supported by precedents will hereafter become a precedent. — THUCYDIDES: *Annals, XI, 24*

[1] Agesilaus being exhorted to hear one that imitated the voice of a nightingale, "I have often," said he, "heard nightingales themselves." — *Apophthegms of Kings and Great Commanders, Agesilaus*

[2] See Aesop, page 961, and Horace, page 984.

[1] See David Garrick, page 242.

He [Tiberius] upbraided Macro in no obscure and indirect terms "with forsaking the setting sun and turning to the rising." — TACITUS: *Annals, Book IV, Chap. 47, 20*

[2] While Alexander was a boy, Philip had great success in his affairs, at which he did not rejoice, but told the children that were brought up with him, "My father will leave me nothing to do." — *Apophthegms of Kings and Great Commanders, Alexander*

[3] Caesar's wife ought to be above suspicion. — *Roman Apophthegms, Caesar*

[4] I had rather be the first in this town than second in Rome. — *Ibid.*

bold attempts, "The die is cast," he took the river.[1]

Lives. Caesar, Page 874

"And this," said Caesar, "you know, young man, is more disagreeable for me to say than to do." [2]

Ibid. Page 876

Go on, my friend, and fear nothing; you carry Caesar and his fortune in your boat.[3]

Ibid. Page 877

[Cleopatra] was at a loss how to get in undiscovered, till she thought of putting herself into the coverlet of a bed and lying at length, whilst Apollodorus tied up the bedding and carried it on his back through the gates to Caesar's apartment.

Ibid. Page 883

Caesar's barber, a busy listening fellow.

Ibid.

Caesar said to the soothsayer, "The ides of March are come"; who answered him calmly, "Yes, they are come, but they are not past." [4]

Ibid. Page 890

Phocion's oratory, like small coin of great value, was to be estimated, not by its bulk, but its intrinsic worth.

Ibid. Phocion, Page 898

Even a nod from a person who is esteemed is of more force than a thousand arguments or studied sentences from others.

Ibid.

Demosthenes told Phocion, "The Athenians will kill you some day when they once are in a rage." "And you,"

---

[1] He passed the river Rubicon, saying, "Let every die be thrown." — *Ibid.*

[Caesar] merely uttered to those near him in Greek the words "Anerriphtho kubos" (let the die be cast), and led his army through the Rubicon. — *Lives, Pompey, P. 783*

[2] Caesar said to Metellus, "This, young man, is harder for me to say than do." — *Roman Apophthegms, Caesar*

[3] Trust Fortune, and know that you carry Caesar. — *Ibid.*

See Lucan, page 994.

[4] See Shakespeare, page 81.

---

said he, "if they once are in their senses." [1]

Lives. Phocion, Page 901

Men, steered by popular applause, though they bear the name of governors, are in reality the mere underlings of the multitude. The man who is completely wise and virtuous has no need at all of glory, except so far as it disposes and eases his way of action by the greater trust that it procures him.

Ibid. Agis, Page 960

Pytheas once, scoffing at Demosthenes, said that his arguments smelt of the lamp.

Ibid. Demosthenes, Page 1026

Demosthenes overcame and rendered more distinct his inarticulate and stammering pronunciation by speaking with pebbles in his mouth.

Ibid. Page 1028

In his house he had a large looking-glass, before which he would stand and go through his exercises.

Ibid.

Cicero called Aristotle a river of flowing gold, and said of Plato's Dialogues, that if Jupiter were to speak, it would be in language like theirs.

Ibid. Cicero, Page 1054

Medicine, to produce health, has to examine disease, and music, to create harmony, must investigate discord.

Ibid. Demetrius, Page 1073

Once Antigonus was told his son was ill, and went to see him. At the door he met some young beauty. Going in, he sat down by the bed and took his pulse. "The fever," said Demetrius, "has just left me." "Oh, yes," replied the father, "I met it going out at the door."

Ibid. Page 1083

"It is not," said Caesar, "these well-fed, long-haired men that I fear, but the

---

[1] Demosthenes the orator told Phocion, "If the Athenians should be mad, they would kill you." "Like enough," said he, — "me if they were mad, but you if they were wise." — *Apophthegms of Kings and Great Commanders, Phocion*

pale and the hungry-looking"; meaning Brutus and Cassius, by whose conspiracy he afterwards fell.[1]

Lives. Antony, Page 1111

There was no man of his time like Antony for addressing a multitude, or for carrying soldiers with him by the force of words.

Ibid. Page 1127

From PLUTARCH'S *Morals, by various translators; revised by* WILLIAM WATSON GOODWIN [*1831–1912*]

For water continually dropping will wear hard rocks hollow.[2]

Of the Training of Children

It is a true proverb, that if you live with a lame man you will learn to halt.

Ibid.

The very spring and root of honesty and virtue lie in the felicity of lighting on good education.

Ibid.

It is indeed a desirable thing to be well descended, but the glory belongs to our ancestors.

Ibid.

Nothing made the horse so fat as the king's eye.

Ibid.

Democritus said, words are but the shadows of actions.

Ibid.

It is a point of wisdom to be silent when occasion requires, and better than to speak, though never so well.[3]

Ibid.

Abstain from beans; that is, keep out of public offices, for anciently the choice of the officers of state was made by beans.

Ibid.

[1] See Shakespeare, page 81.
This passage is repeated in *Marcus Brutus*, P. 1190.
[2] See Lyly, page 23.
[3] Closed lips hurt no one, speaking may. — CATO THE CENSOR, *Book I, Distich 12*

The whole life of man is but a point of time; let us enjoy it, therefore, while it lasts, and not spend it to no purpose.

Of the Training of Children

An old doting fool, with one foot already in the grave.[1]

Ibid.

Xenophanes said, "I confess myself the greatest coward in the world, for I dare not do an ill thing."

Of Bashfulness

One made the observation of the people of Asia that they were all slaves to one man, merely because they could not pronounce that syllable No.[2]

Ibid.

Euripides was wont to say, "Silence is an answer to a wise man."

Ibid.

Zeno first started that doctrine that knavery is the best defence against a knave.[3]

Ibid.

Alexander wept when he heard from Anaxarchus that there was an infinite number of worlds; and his friends asking him if any accident had befallen him, he returns this answer: "Do you not think it a matter worthy of lamentation that when there is such a vast multitude of them, we have not yet conquered one?"

On the Tranquillity of the Mind

Like the man who threw a stone at a bitch, but hit his step-mother, on which he exclaimed, "Not so bad!"

Ibid.

Pittacus said, "Every one of you hath his particular plague, and my wife is mine; and he is very happy who hath this only."

Ibid.

He was a man, which, as Plato saith, is a very inconstant creature.[4]

Ibid.

[1] See Beaumont and Fletcher, page 131.
[2] See S. T. Coleridge, page 318.
[3] Set a thief to catch a thief. — BOHN'S *Handbook of Proverbs*
[4] Man in sooth is a marvellous vain, fickle, and unstable subject. — MONTAIGNE: *Works, Book I, Chap. 1, That Men by Various Ways Arrive at the Same End*

The pilot cannot mitigate the billows or calm the winds.[1]

On the Tranquillity of the Mind

All men whilst they are awake are in one common world; but each of them, when he is asleep, is in a world of his own.[2]

Of Superstition

I, for my own part, had much rather people should say of me that there neither is nor ever was such a man as Plutarch, than that they should say, "Plutarch is an unsteady, fickle, froward, vindictive, and touchy fellow."

Ibid.

Scilurus on his death-bed, being about to leave four-score sons surviving, offered a bundle of darts to each of them, and bade them break them. When all refused, drawing out one by one, he easily broke them, — thus teaching them that if they held together, they would continue strong; but if they fell out and were divided, they would become weak.[3]

Apophthegms of Kings and Great Commanders.[4] Scilurus

Dionysius the Elder, being asked whether he was at leisure, he replied, "God forbid that it should ever befall me!"

Ibid. Dionysius

A prating barber asked Archelaus how he would be trimmed. He answered, "In silence."

Ibid. Archelaus

When Philip had news brought him of divers and eminent successes in one day, "O Fortune!" said he, "for all these so great kindnesses do me some small mischief."

Ibid. Philip

There were two brothers called Both and Either; perceiving Either was a good, understanding, busy fellow, and Both a silly fellow and good for little,

Philip said, "Either is both, and Both is neither."

Apophthegms of Kings and Great Commanders. Philip

Philip being arbitrator betwixt two wicked persons, he commanded one to fly out of Macedonia and the other to pursue him.

Ibid.

Being about to pitch his camp in a likely place, and hearing there was no hay to be had for the cattle, "What a life," said he, "is ours, since we must live according to the convenience of asses!"

Ibid.

"These Macedonians," said he, "are a rude and clownish people, that call a spade a spade." [1]

Ibid.

He made one of Antipater's recommendation a judge; and perceiving afterwards that his hair and beard were dyed, he removed him, saying, "I could not think one that was faithless in his hair could be trusty in his deeds."

Ibid.

Being nimble and light-footed, his father encouraged him to run in the Olympic race. "Yes," said he, "if there were any kings there to run with me."

Ibid. Alexander

Pyrrhus said, "If I should overcome the Romans in another fight, I were undone."

Ibid. Pyrrhus

Themistocles being asked whether he would rather be Achilles or Homer, said, "Which would you rather be, — a conqueror in the Olympic games, or the crier that proclaims who are conquerors?"

Ibid. Themistocles

Alcibiades had a very handsome dog, that cost him seven thousand drachmas; and he cut off his tail, "that," said he, "the Athenians may have this story to tell of me, and may concern themselves no further with me."

Ibid. Alcibiades

---

[1] See Publilius Syrus, *Maxim 759.*
[2] A saying attributed to HERACLITUS. Quoted by ADDISON in *The Spectator, No. 487, Sept. 18, 1712.*
[3] AESOP'S fable, *The Bundle of Sticks,* has this theme.
[4] Rejected by some critics as not a genuine work of Plutarch.

[1] See Menander, page 976.

To Harmodius, descended from the ancient Harmodius, when he reviled Iphicrates [a shoemaker's son] for his mean birth, "My nobility," said he, "begins with me, but yours ends in you." [1]

Apophthegms of Kings and Great Commanders. Iphicrates

Once when Phocion had delivered an opinion which pleased the people, . . . he turned to his friend and said, "Have I not unawares spoken some mischievous thing or other?" [2]

Ibid. Phocion

Phocion compared the speeches of Leosthenes to cypress-trees. "They are tall," said he, "and comely, but bear no fruit."

Ibid.

King Agis said, "The Lacedaemonians are not wont to ask how many, but where the enemy are."

Ibid. Agis

To one that promised to give him hardy cocks that would die fighting, "Prithee," said Cleomenes, "give me cocks that will kill fighting."

Ibid. Cleomenes

A soldier told Pelopidas, "We are fallen among the enemies." Said he, "How are we fallen among them more than they among us?"

Ibid. Pelopidas

Cato the Elder wondered how that city was preserved wherein a fish was sold for more than an ox.

Roman Apophthegms. Cato the Elder

Cato instigated the magistrates to punish all offenders, saying that they that did not prevent crimes when they might, encouraged them.[3] Of young men, he liked them that blushed better than those who looked pale.

Ibid.

Cato requested old men not to add the disgrace of wickedness to old age,

which was accompanied with many other evils.

Roman Apophthegms. Cato the Elder

He said they that were serious in ridiculous matters would be ridiculous in serious affairs.

Ibid.

Cicero said loud-bawling orators were driven by their weakness to noise, as lame men to take horse.

Ibid. Cicero

After he routed Pharnaces Ponticus at the first assault, he wrote thus to his friends: "I came, I saw, I conquered." [1]

Ibid. Caesar

As Caesar was at supper the discourse was of death, — which sort was the best. "That," said he, "which is unexpected."

Ibid.

As Athenodorus was taking his leave of Caesar, "Remember," said he, "Caesar, whenever you are angry, to say or do nothing before you have repeated the four-and-twenty letters to yourself."

Ibid. Caesar Augustus

"Young men," said Caesar, "hear an old man to whom old men hearkened when he was young."

Ibid.

Custom is almost a second nature.

Rules for the Preservation of Health. 18

Epaminondas is reported wittily to have said of a good man that died about the time of the battle of Leuctra, "How came he to have so much leisure as to die, when there was so much stirring?"

Ibid. 25

Socrates thought that if all our misfortunes were laid in one common heap, whence every one must take an equal

---

[1] I am my own ancestor. — JUNOT, DUC D'ABRANTES [1771–1813], when asked about his ancestry.

[2] See Diogenes Laertius, page 1015.

[3] Pardon one offence, and you encourage the commission of many. — PUBLILIUS SYRUS: *Maxim 750*

[1] Veni, vidi, vici.

A severe critic might curtail that famous brevity of Caesar's by two thirds, drawing his pen through the supererogatory *veni* and *vidi*. — J. R. LOWELL: *The Biglow Papers, Series I, No. 7*

portion, most persons would be contented to take their own and depart.[1]

Consolation to Apollonius

Diogenes the Cynic, when a little before his death he fell into a slumber, and his physician rousing him out of it asked him whether anything ailed him, wisely answered, "Nothing, sir; only one brother anticipates another, — Sleep before Death."

Ibid.

About Pontus there are some creatures of such an extempore being that the whole term of their life is confined within the space of a day; for they are brought forth in the morning, are in the prime of their existence at noon, grow old at night, and then die.

Ibid.

There are two sentences inscribed upon the Delphic oracle, hugely accommodated to the usages of man's life: "Know thyself,"[2] and "Nothing too much"; and upon these all other precepts depend.

Ibid.

Agesilaus was very fond of his children; and it is reported that once toying with them he got astride upon a reed as upon a horse, and rode about the room; and being seen by one of his friends, he desired him not to speak of it till he had children of his own.

Laconic Apophthegms. Of Agesilaus the Great

Lysander, when Dionysius sent him two gowns, and bade him choose which he would carry to his daughter, said, "She can choose best," and so took both away with him.

Ibid. Of Lysander

[1] ADDISON's paper, *The Spectator, No. 558, June 23, 1714,* is on this theme.
The translation is somewhat ambiguous. Socrates meant that we would all prefer to bear our own lot rather than take the risk of an equal share in the world's total of grievances.
[2] See Alexander Pope, page 207. Plutarch ascribes this saying to Plato. It is also ascribed to Pythagoras, Chilo, Thales, Cleobulus, Bias, and Socrates; also to Phemonë, a mythical Greek poetess of the ante-Homeric period. JUVENAL (*Satire XI, 27*) says that this precept descended from heaven.

And when the physician said, "Sir, you are an old man," "That happens," replied Pausanias, "because you never were my doctor."

Laconic Apophthegms. Of Pausanias

When one told Plistarchus that a notorious railer spoke well of him, "I'll lay my life," said he, "somebody hath told him I am dead, for he can speak well of no man living."

Ibid. Of Plistarchus

Said Periander, "Hesiod might as well have kept his breath to cool his pottage."[1]

The Banquet of the Seven Wise Men. 14

Socrates said, "Bad men live that they may eat and drink, whereas good men eat and drink that they may live."[2]

How a Young Man Ought to Hear Poems. 4

Archimedes, as he was washing, thought of a manner of computing the proportion of gold in King Hiero's crown by seeing the water flowing over the bathing-stool. He leaped up as one possessed or inspired, crying, "I have found it! Eureka!"

Pleasure Not Attainable, According to Epicurus. 11

That proverbial saying, "Ill news goes quick and far."

Of Inquisitiveness

Spintharus, speaking in commendation of Epaminondas, says he scarce ever met with any man who knew more and spoke less.

Of Hearing. 6

It is a thing of no great difficulty to raise objections against another man's oration, — nay, it is a very easy matter; but to produce a better in its place is a work extremely troublesome.

Ibid.

Antiphanes said merrily, that in a certain city the cold was so intense that

[1] Spare your breath to cool your porridge. — RABELAIS: *Works, Book V, Chap. 28*
[2] See Fielding, page 229.
He used to say that other men lived to eat, but that he ate to live. — DIOGENES LAERTIUS: *Socrates, 14*

words were congealed as soon as spoken, but that after some time they thawed and became audible; so that the words spoken in winter were articulated next summer.[1]

Of Man's Progress in Virtue

As those persons who despair of ever being rich make little account of small expenses, thinking that little added to a little will never make any great sum.

Ibid.

What is bigger than an elephant? But this also is become man's plaything, and a spectacle at public solemnities; and it learns to skip, dance, and kneel.

Of Fortune

No man ever wetted clay and then left it, as if there would be bricks by chance and fortune.

Ibid.

Alexander was wont to say, "Were I not Alexander, I would be Diogenes."

Of the Fortune or Virtue of Alexander the Great

When the candles are out all women are fair.[2]

Conjugal Precepts

Like watermen, who look astern while they row the boat ahead.[3]

Whether 'Twas Rightfully Said, Live Concealed

Socrates said he was not an Athenian or a Greek, but a citizen of the world.[4]

Of Banishment

Anaximander says that men were first produced in fishes, and when they were grown up and able to help themselves were thrown up, and so lived upon the land.

Symposiacs. Book VIII, Question 8

Athenodorus says hydrophobia, or water-dread, was first discovered in the time of Asclepiades.

Ibid. Question 9

The great god Pan is dead.[1]

Why the Oracles Cease to Give Answers

I am whatever was, or is, or will be; and my veil no mortal ever took up.[2]

Of Isis and Osiris

When Hermodotus in his poems described Antigonus as the son of Helios, "My valet-de-chambre," said he, "is not aware of this." [3]

Ibid.

He is a fool who lets slip a bird in the hand for a bird in the bush.[4]

Of Garrulity

We are more sensible of what is done against custom than against Nature.

Of Eating of Flesh. Tract I

When Demosthenes was asked what was the first part of oratory, he answered, "Action"; and which was the second, he replied, "Action"; and which was the third, he still answered, "Action."

Lives of the Ten Orators

Xenophon says that there is no sound more pleasing than one's own praises.

Whether an Aged Man Ought to Meddle in State Affairs

---

[1] Rabelais gives a somewhat similar account, referring to Antiphanes, in *Book IV, Chaps. 55 and 56.*

See Raspe (Baron Munchausen), page 1056.

[2] When all candles be out, all cats be gray. — HEYWOOD: *Proverbes, Part I, Chap. 5*

[3] See Burton, page 122.

[4] See Boswell, page 272, and W. L. Garrison, page 424.

---

[1] Great Pan is dead. — MRS. BROWNING: *The Dead Pan, St. 26*

Plutarch relates (*Isis and Osiris*) that a ship well laden with passengers drove with the tide near the Isles of Paxi, when a loud voice was heard by most of the passengers calling unto one Thanus. The voice then said aloud to him, "When you are arrived at Palodes, take care to make it known that the great god Pan is dead."

[2] I am the things that are, and those that are to be, and those that have been. No one ever lifted my skirts; the fruit which I bore was the sun. — PROCLUS: *On Plato's Timaeus, P. 30, D.* (Inscription in the temple of Neith at Sais, in Egypt.)

[3] No man is a hero to his valet-de-chambre. — MARSHAL CATINAT [1637–1712]

Few men have been admired by their domestics. — MONTAIGNE: *Essays, Book III, Chap. 2*

This phrase, "No man is a hero to his valet," is commonly attributed to Madame de Sévigné, but on the authority of Madame Aïssé (*Letters,* edited by Jules Ravenal, 1853) it really belongs to Madame Cornuel.

[4] See Heywood, page 15, and Herbert, page 137.

Statesmen are not only liable to give an account of what they say or do in public, but there is a busy inquiry made into their very meals, beds, marriages, and every other sportive or serious action.

Political Precepts

Leo Byzantius said, "What would you do, if you saw my wife, who scarce reaches up to my knees? . . . Yet," went he on, "as little as we are, when we fall out with each other, the city of Byzantium is not big enough to hold us."

Ibid.

Cato said, "I had rather men should ask why my statue is not set up, than why it is."

Ibid.

It was the saying of Bion, that though the boys throw stones at frogs in sport, yet the frogs do not die in sport but in earnest.

Which Are the Most Crafty,
Water or Land Animals? 7

Both Empedocles and Heraclitus held it for a truth that man could not be altogether cleared from injustice in dealing with beasts as he now does.

Ibid.

For to err in opinion, though it be not the part of wise men, is at least human.[1]

Against Colotes

Simonides calls painting silent poetry, and poetry, speaking painting.

Whether the Athenians Were
More Warlike or Learned. 3

As Menander says, "For our mind is God"; and as Heraclitus, "Man's genius is a deity."

Platonic Questions

Pythagoras, when he was asked what time was, answered that it was the soul of this world.

Ibid.

JUVENAL
[A. D. 47–138]

Honesty is praised and starves.[2]

Satire I. Line 74

[1] See Pope, page 211.
[2] A favorite quotation of Linnaeus, Swedish botanist and naturalist.

No man ever became extremely wicked all at once.[1]

Satire II. Line 83

Grammarian, orator, geometrician; painter, gymnastic teacher; fortune-teller, rope-dancer, physician, conjuror, — he knew everything.[2]

Satire III. Line 76

We all live in a state of ambitious poverty.

Ibid. Line 182

ONASANDER
[*Floruit* A. D. 49]

Translation by Illinois Greek Club.
Loeb Classical Library

Vigor is found in the man who has not yet grown old, and discretion in the man who is not too young.

The General. Chap. I, Sect. 10

Envy is a pain of mind that successful men cause their neighbours.

Ibid. Chap. 42, Paragraph 25

TACITUS
[A. D. 54–119]

The Oxford Translation. Bohn
Classical Library

The images of twenty of the most illustrious families — the Manlii, the Quinctii, and other names of equal splendour — were carried before it [the bier of Junia]. Those of Brutus and Cassius were not displayed; but for that very reason they shone with pre-eminent lustre.[3]

Annals. III, 76, 11

He had talents equal to business, and aspired no higher.

Ibid. VI, 39, 17

[1] Nemo repente fit turpissimus. See Beaumont and Fletcher, page 131.
[2] See Dryden, page 174.
[3] Lord John Russell, alluding to an expression used by him ("Conspicuous by his absence") in his address to the electors of the city of London, said, "It is not an original expression of mine, but is taken from one of the greatest historians of antiquity."

Some might consider him as too fond of fame; for the desire of glory clings even to the best men longer than any other passion.[1]

History. IV, 6, 36

They make desolation, which they call peace.[2]

Agricola. 30

EPICTETUS
[Circa A. D. 60]

Translation [1865] *by* THOMAS WENTWORTH HIGGINSON [1823–1911], *based on that* [1758] *of* ELIZABETH CARTER [1717–1806]

To a reasonable creature, that alone is insupportable which is unreasonable; but everything reasonable may be supported.

Discourses. Chap. 2

When you have shut your doors, and darkened your room, remember never to say that you are alone, for you are not alone;[3] but God is within, and your genius is within, — and what need have they of light to see what you are doing?

Ibid. Chap. 14

No great thing is created suddenly, any more than a bunch of grapes or a fig. If you tell me that you desire a fig, I answer you that there must be time. Let it first blossom, then bear fruit, then ripen.

Ibid. Chap. 15

Any one thing in the creation is sufficient to demonstrate a Providence to an humble and grateful mind.

Ibid. Chap. 16

Were I a nightingale, I would act the part of a nightingale; were I a swan, the part of a swan.

Ibid.

Since it is Reason which shapes and regulates all other things, it ought not itself to be left in disorder.

Ibid. Chap. 17

Practise yourself, for heaven's sake, in little things; and thence proceed to greater.

Discourses. Chap. 18

Why, then, do you walk as if you had swallowed a ramrod?

Ibid. Chap. 21

Difficulties are things that show what men are.

Ibid. Chap. 24

If we are not stupid or insincere when we say that the good or ill of man lies within his own will, and that all beside is nothing to us, why are we still troubled?

Ibid. Chap. 25

In theory there is nothing to hinder our following what we are taught; but in life there are many things to draw us aside.

Ibid. Chap. 26

Appearances to the mind are of four kinds. Things either are what they appear to be; or they neither are, nor appear to be; or they are, and do not appear to be; or they are not, and yet appear to be. Rightly to aim in all these cases is the wise man's task.

Ibid. Chap. 27

The appearance of things to the mind is the standard of every action to man.

That We Ought Not to Be Angry with Mankind. 27

For what constitutes a child? — Ignorance. What constitutes a child? — Want of instruction; for they are our equals so far as their degree of knowledge permits.

That Courage Is Not Inconsistent with Caution. Book II, 1

The materials of action are variable, but the use we make of them should be constant.

How Nobleness of Mind May Be Consistent with Prudence. 5

Shall I show you the muscular training of a philosopher? "What muscles are those?" — A will undisappointed; evils avoided; powers daily exercised; careful resolutions; unerring decisions.

Wherein Consists the Essence of Good. 8

---

[1] See Milton, page 159.
[2] See Byron, page 356.
[3] Though in a wilderness, a man is never alone. — SIR THOMAS BROWNE: *Religio Medici* (Everyman ed.), *P. 82*

What is the first business of one who studies philosophy? To part with self-conceit. For it is impossible for any one to begin to learn what he thinks that he already knows.

How to Apply General Principles to Particular Cases. 17

Every habit and faculty is preserved and increased by correspondent actions, — as the habit of walking, by walking; or running, by running.

How the Semblances of Things Are to Be Combated. 18

Whatever you would make habitual, practise it; and if you would not make a thing habitual, do not practise it, but habituate yourself to something else.

Ibid.

Reckon the days in which you have not been angry. I used to be angry every day; now every other day; then every third and fourth day; and if you miss it so long as thirty days, offer a sacrifice of thanksgiving to God.

Ibid.

Be not hurried away by excitement, but say, "Semblance, wait for me a little. Let me see what you are and what you represent. Let me try you."

Ibid.

There are some things which men confess with ease, and others with difficulty.

Of Inconsistency. 21

Who is there whom bright and agreeable children do not attract to play and creep and prattle with them?

Concerning a Person Whom He Treated with Disregard. 24

Two rules we should always have ready, — that there is nothing good or evil save in the will; and that we are not to lead events, but to follow them.

In What Manner We Ought to Bear Sickness. Book III, 10

In every affair consider what precedes and what follows, and then undertake it.[1]

That Everything Is to Be Undertaken with Circumspection. 15

[1] See Publilius Syrus, *Maxim 777.*

First say to yourself what you would be; and then do what you have to do.

Concerning Such as Read and Dispute Ostentatiously. 23

Let not another's disobedience to Nature become an ill to you; for you were not born to be depressed and unhappy with others, but to be happy with them. And if any is unhappy, remember that he is so for himself; for God made all men to enjoy felicity and peace.

That We Ought Not to Be Affected by Things Not in Our Own Power. 24

Everything has two handles, — one by which it may be borne; another by which it cannot.[1]

Enchiridion. 43

PLINY THE YOUNGER
[A. D. 61–105]

Translation [1746] by William Melmoth [1710–1799]. *Bohn Classical Library*

Modestus said of Regulus that he was "the biggest rascal that walks upon two legs."

Letters.[2] Book I, Letter 5, 14

There is nothing to write about, you say. Well, then, write and let me know just this, — that there *is* nothing to write about; or tell me in the good old style if you are well. That's right. I am quite well.[3]

Ibid. Letter 11, 1

An object in possession seldom retains the same charm that it had in pursuit.[4]

Ibid. Book II, Letter 15, 1

[1] See Raspe, page 1056.
[2] Book VI, Letter 16 contains the description of the eruption of Vesuvius, A. D. 79, as witnessed by Pliny the Elder.
[3] This comes to inform you that I am in a perfect state of health, hoping you are in the same. Ay, that's the old beginning. — George Colman the Younger [1762–1836]: *The Heir at Law* [1797], Act III, Sc. 2
[4] See Goldsmith, page 254.

He [Pliny the Elder] used to say that "no book was so bad but some good might be got out of it." [1]

Letters. Book III, Letter 5, 10

This expression of ours, "Father of a family."

Ibid. Book V, Letter 19, 2

That indolent but agreeable condition of doing nothing.[2]

Ibid. Book VIII, Letter 9, 3

Objects which are usually the motives of our travels by land and by sea are often overlooked and neglected if they lie under our eye. . . . We put off from time to time going and seeing what we know we have an opportunity of seeing when we please.

Ibid. Letter 20, 1

His only fault is that he has no fault.[3]

Ibid. Book IX, Letter 26, 1

EMPEROR HADRIAN
[A. D. 76–138]

Dear fleeting, sweeting, little soul,
My body's comrade and its guest,
What region now must be thy goal,
Poor little wan, numb, naked soul,
Unable, as of old, to jest? [4]

Dying Farewell to His Soul, to Honor the Tomb of His Friend, Voconius

I've no mind to be a Florus,
Strolling round among the drink-shops,
Skulking round among the cook-shops,
Victim of fat-gorged mosquitoes.

Retort to Florus [5]

---

[1] "There is no book so bad," said the bachelor, "but something good may be found in it." — CERVANTES: *Don Quixote, Part II, Chap. 3*

[2] Dolce far niente (Sweet doing-nothing). — *Italian proverb*

[3] See Thomas Carlyle, page 380.

[4] Animula, vagula, blandula
Hospes comesque corporis,
Quae nunc abibis in loca,
Pallidula, frigida, nudula,
Nec, ut soles, dabis joca.

[5] Florus, born in Africa [A. D. 74], Hadrian's friend, had addressed these lines to him. The third line has been lost.

I've no mind to be a Caesar,
Strolling round among the Britons

Victim of the Scythian hoar-frosts.

MARCUS AURELIUS ANTONINUS
[A. D. 121–180]

Translation by MORRIS HICKEY MORGAN [*1859–1910*]

This Being of mine, whatever it really is, consists of a little flesh, a little breath, and the part which governs.

Meditations. II, 2

The ways of the gods are full of providence.

Ibid. 3

Thou wilt find rest from vain fancies if thou doest every act in life as though it were thy last.[1]

Ibid. 5

Find time still to be learning somewhat good, and give up being desultory.

Ibid. 7

No state sorrier than that of the man who keeps up a continual round, and pries into "the secrets of the nether world," as saith the poet, and is curious in conjecture of what is in his neighbour's heart.

Ibid. 13

Though thou be destined to live three thousand years and as many myriads besides, yet remember that no man loseth other life than that which he liveth, nor liveth other than that which he loseth.

Ibid. 14

For a man can lose neither the past nor the future; for how can one take from him that which is not his? So remember these two points: first, that each thing is of like form from everlasting and comes round again in its cycle, and that it signifies not whether a man shall look upon the same things for a hundred years or two hundred, or for an infinity of time; second, that the longest lived and the shortest lived man, when they come to die, lose one and the same thing.

Ibid.

---

[1] See Publilius Syrus, *Maxim 633.*

As for life, it is a battle and a sojourning in a strange land; but the fame that comes after is oblivion.

Meditations. II, 17

Waste not the remnant of thy life in those imaginations touching other folk, whereby thou contributest not to the common weal.

Ibid. III, 4

A man should *be* upright, not be *kept* upright.

Ibid. 5

Never esteem anything as of advantage to thee that shall make thee break thy word or lose thy self-respect.

Ibid. 7

Let no act be done at haphazard, nor otherwise than according to the finished rules that govern its kind.

Ibid. IV, 2

By a tranquil mind I mean nothing else than a mind well ordered.

Ibid. 3

Think on this doctrine, — that reasoning beings were created for one another's sake; that to be patient is a branch of justice, and that men sin without intending it.

Ibid.

The universe is change; our life is what our thoughts make it.

Ibid.

Nothing can come out of nothing,[1] any more than a thing can go back to nothing.

Ibid. 4

Death, like generation, is a secret of Nature.

Ibid. 5

That which makes the man no worse than he was makes his life no worse: it has no power to harm, without or within.

Ibid. 8

Whatever happens at all happens as it should; thou wilt find this true, if thou shouldst watch narrowly.

Ibid. 10

How much time he gains who does not look to see what his neighbour says

---

[1] See Diogenes Laertius, page 1016.

or does or thinks, but only at what he does himself, to make it just and holy.

Meditations. IV, 18

Whatever is in any way beautiful hath its source of beauty in itself, and is complete in itself; praise forms no part of it. So it is none the worse nor the better for being praised.

Ibid. 20

All that is harmony for thee, O Universe, is in harmony with me as well. Nothing that comes at the right time for thee is too early or too late for me. Everything is fruit to me that thy seasons bring, O Nature. All things come of thee, have their being in thee, and return to thee.

Ibid. 23

"Let thine occupations be few," saith the sage,[1] "if thou wouldst lead a tranquil life."

Ibid. 24

Love the little trade which thou hast learned, and be content therewith.

Ibid. 31

Remember this, — that there is a proper dignity and proportion to be observed in the performance of every act of life.

Ibid. 32

All is ephemeral, — fame and the famous as well.

Ibid. 35

Observe always that everything is the result of a change, and get used to thinking that there is nothing Nature loves so well as to change existing forms and to make new ones like them.

Ibid. 36

Search men's governing principles, and consider the wise, what they shun and what they cleave to.

Ibid. 38

Time is a sort of river of passing events, and strong is its current; no sooner is a thing brought to sight than it is swept by and another takes its place, and this too will be swept away.

Ibid. 43

---

[1] DEMOCRITUS apud Senecam: *De Ira, III, 6; De Animi Tranquillitate, 13*

All that happens is as usual and familiar as the rose in spring and the crop in summer.

Meditations. IV, 44

That which comes after ever conforms to that which has gone before.

Ibid. 45

Mark how fleeting and paltry is the estate of man, — yesterday in embryo, to-morrow a mummy or ashes. So for the hair's-breadth of time assigned to thee live rationally, and part with life cheerfully, as drops the ripe olive, extolling the season that bore it and the tree that matured it.

Ibid. 48

Deem not life a thing of consequence. For look at the yawning void of the future, and at that other limitless space, the past.

Ibid. 50

Always take the short cut; and that is the rational one. Therefore say and do everything according to soundest reason.

Ibid. 51

In the morning, when thou art sluggish at rousing thee, let this thought be present; "I am rising to a man's work."

Ibid. V, 1

A man makes no noise over a good deed, but passes on to another as a vine to bear grapes again in season.

Ibid. 6

Nothing happens to anybody which he is not fitted by nature to bear.

Ibid. 18

Live with the gods.

Ibid. 27

Look beneath the surface; let not the several quality of a thing nor its worth escape thee.

Ibid. VI, 3

The controlling Intelligence understands its own nature, and what it does, and whereon it works.

Ibid. 5

Do not think that what is hard for thee to master is impossible for man; but if a thing is possible and proper to man, deem it attainable by thee.

Ibid. 19

If any man can convince me and bring home to me that I do not think or act aright, gladly will I change; for I search after truth, by which man never yet was harmed.

Meditations. VI, 21

What is not good for the swarm is not good for the bee.

Ibid. 54

How many, once lauded in song, are given over to the forgotten; and how many who sung their praises are clean gone long ago!

Ibid. VII, 6

One Universe made up of all that is; and one God in it all, and one principle of Being, and one Law, the Reason, shared by all thinking creatures, and one Truth.

Ibid. 9

Let not thy mind run on what thou lackest as much as on what thou hast already.

Ibid. 27

Just as the sand-dunes, heaped one upon another, hide each the first, so in life the former deeds are quickly hidden by those that follow after.

Ibid. 34

The art of living is more like wrestling than dancing, in so far as it stands ready against the accidental and the unforeseen, and is not apt to fall.

Ibid. 61

Remember this, — that very little is needed to make a happy life.

Ibid. 67

Remember that to change thy mind and to follow him that sets thee right, is to be none the less the free agent that thou wast before.

Ibid. VIII, 16

Look to the essence of a thing, whether it be a point of doctrine, of practice, or of interpretation.

Ibid. 22

Be not careless in deeds, nor confused in words, nor rambling in thought.

Ibid. 51

Think not disdainfully of death, but look on it with favour; for even death is one of the things that Nature wills.

Ibid. IX, 3

A wrong-doer is often a man that has left something undone, not always he that has done something.

Meditations. IX, 5

Blot out vain pomp; check impulse; quench appetite; keep reason under its own control.

Ibid. 7

Things that have a common quality ever quickly seek their kind.

Ibid. 9

All things are the same, — familiar in enterprise, momentary in endurance, coarse in substance. All things now are as they were in the day of those whom we have buried.

Ibid. 14

Everything is in a state of metamorphosis. Thou thyself art in everlasting change and in corruption to correspond; so is the whole universe.

Ibid. 19

Forward, as occasion offers. Never look round to see whether any shall note it. . . . Be satisfied with success in even the smallest matter, and think that even such a result is no trifle.

Ibid. 29

Whatever may befall thee, it was preordained for thee from everlasting.

Ibid. X, 5

"The earth loveth the shower," and "the holy ether knoweth what love is." [1] The Universe, too, loves to create whatsoever is destined to be made.

Ibid. 21

TERTULLIAN
[A. D. 160–240]

See how these Christians love one another.

Apologeticus. 39

Blood of the martyrs is the seed of the Church.

Ibid. 50

It is certain because it is impossible. [2]

De Carne Christi. 5

---

[1] *Fragmenta Euripidis,* apud Aristotelem, *N. A. VIII, 1, 6*
[2] *Certum est, quia impossibile est.* This is usually misquoted, "Credo quia impossibile"

He who flees will fight again. [1]

De Fuga in Persecutione. 10

ATHENAEUS
[*Circa* A. D. 200]

Translation by CHARLES DUKE YONGE [*1812–1891*]

It was a saying of Demetrius Phalereus, that "Men having often abandoned what was visible for the sake of what was uncertain, have not got what they expected, and have lost what they had, — being unfortunate by an enigmatical sort of calamity."

The Deipnosophists. VI, 23

Every investigation which is guided by principles of Nature fixes its ultimate aim entirely on gratifying the stomach. [2]

Ibid. VII, 11

Dorion, ridiculing the description of a tempest in the "Nautilus" of Timotheus, said that he had seen a more formidable storm in a boiling saucepan. [3]

Ibid. VIII, 19

On one occasion some one put a very little wine into a wine-cooler, and said that it was sixteen years old. "It is very small for its age," said Gnathaena.

Ibid. XIII, 47

DIOGENES LAERTIUS [4]
[*Circa* A. D. 200]

From The Lives and Opinions of Eminent Philosophers, translated by CHARLES DUKE YONGE [*1812– 1891*]. *Bohn Classical Library*

When Thales was asked what was difficult, he said, "To know one's self."

(I believe it because it is impossible). Also attributed to St. Augustine in the form "Credo quia absurdum."
[1] See Butler, page 143.
[2] See Dr. Johnson, page 234.
[3] A tempest in a teapot. — *Proverb*
[4] There is scarce any Philosopher but dies twice or thrice in Laertius; nor almost any life without two or three deaths in Plutarch. — SIR THOMAS BROWNE: *Urn-Burial, Chap. 3*

And what was easy, "To advise another."

Thales. 9

The apophthegm "Know thyself" is his.[1]

Ibid. 13

Writers differ with respect to the apophthegms of the Seven Sages, attributing the same one to various authors.

Ibid. 14

Solon used to say that speech was the image of actions; . . . that laws were like cobwebs, — for that if any trifling or powerless thing fell into them, they held it fast; while if it were something weightier, it broke through them and was off.

Solon. 10

Solon gave the following advice: "Consider your honour, as a gentleman, of more weight than an oath."

Ibid. 12

As some say, Solon was the author of the apophthegm, "Nothing in excess."

Ibid. 16

Chilo advised, "not to speak evil of the dead." [2]

Chilo. 2

Pittacus said that half was more than the whole.[3]

Pittacus. 2

Heraclitus says that Pittacus, when he had got Alcaeus into his power, released him, saying, "Forgiveness is better than revenge." [4]

Ibid. 3

One of his sayings was, "Even the gods cannot strive against necessity." [1]

Pittacus. 4

Another was, "Watch your opportunity." [2]

Ibid. 7

Bias used to say that men ought to calculate life both as if they were fated to live a long and a short time, and that they ought to love one another as if at a future time they would come to hate one another; for that most men were bad.

Bias. 5

Ignorance plays the chief part among men, and the multitude of words.[3]

Cleobulus. 4

The saying, "Practice is everything," is Periander's.[4]

Periander. 6

Anarcharsis, on learning that the sides of a ship were four fingers thick, said that "the passengers were just that distance from death." [5]

Anarcharsis. 5

It was a common saying of Myson that men ought not to investigate things from words, but words from things; for that things are not made for the sake of words, but words for things.

Myson. 3

Epimenides was sent by his father into the field to look for a sheep, turned out of the road at mid-day and lay down in a certain cave and fell asleep, and slept there fifty-seven years; and after that, when awake, he went on looking for the sheep, thinking that he had been taking a short nap.[6]

Epimenides. 2

---

[1] See Pope, page 207, and Plutarch, page 1004.
'Tis said that Attic Solon wrote at Delphi: "Gnothi seauton," which in our tongue is "Know thyself." Many think this to be by Chilon the Laconian. — AUSONIUS DECIMUS MAGNUS [A. D. 310–394]: *The Masque of the Seven Sages, Poem 3, Chorus*
[2] De mortuis nil nisi bonum (Of the dead be nothing said but what is good).
[3] See Hesiod, page 959.
[4] Forgiveness is better than punishment; for the one is proof of a gentle, the other of a savage nature. — Quoted by EPICTETUS, *Fragment 62*

[1] Nature must obey necessity. — SHAKESPEARE: *Julius Caesar, Act IV, Sc. 3, L. 226*
[2] Observe the opportunity. — *Apocrypha: Ecclesiasticus, IV, 20*
[3] In the multitude of words there wanteth not sin. — *Proverbs, X, 19*
[4] See Publilius Syrus, *Maxim 439.*
[5] "How thick do you judge the planks of our ship to be?" "Some two good inches and upward," returned the pilot. "It seems, then, we are within two fingers' breadth of damnation." — RABELAIS: *Book IV, Chap. 23*
[6] The theme of IRVING's story of Rip Van Winkle.

Anaximander used to assert that the primary cause of all things was the Infinite, — not defining exactly whether he meant air or water or anything else.

Anaximander. 2

Anaxagoras said to a man who was grieving because he was dying in a foreign land, "The descent to Hades is the same from every place."

Anaxagoras. 6

Aristophanes turns Socrates into ridicule in his comedies, as making the worse appear the better reason.[1]

Socrates. 5

Often when he was looking on at auctions he would say, "How many things there are which I do not need!"[2]

Ibid. 10

Socrates said, "Those who want fewest things are nearest to the gods."

Ibid. 11

He said that there was one only good, namely, knowledge; and one only evil, namely, ignorance.

Ibid. 14

He declared that he knew nothing, except the fact of his ignorance.

Ibid. 16

Being asked whether it was better to marry or not, he replied, "Whichever you do, you will repent it."

Ibid.

Aristippus being asked what were the most necessary things for well-born boys to learn, said, "Those things which they will put in practice when they become men."

Aristippus. 4

Like sending owls to Athens, as the proverb goes.[3]

Plato. 32

---

[1] See Milton, page 149.
[2] Socrates once, it is said, was persuaded to go to a fair:
In his one poor cloak, in his wonted way, he stood musing there,
Stood long till a friend inquired what his thoughts might be about —
"How many things there are here that I could do better without."
    EDITH M. THOMAS [1854–1925]:
        The Burden of Possessions. St. 1
[3] See Horace, page 984.

Plato affirmed that the soul was immortal and clothed in many bodies successively.[1]

Plato. 40

Time is the image of eternity.

Ibid. 41

There is a written and an unwritten law. The one by which we regulate our constitutions in our cities is the written law; that which arises from custom is the unwritten law.

Ibid. 51

Plato was continually saying to Xenocrates, "Sacrifice to the Graces."[2]

Xenocrates. 3

Arcesilaus had a peculiar habit while conversing of using the expression, "My opinion is," and "So and so will not agree to this."

Arcesilaus. 12

Of a rich man who was niggardly he said, "That man does not own his estate, but his estate owns him."

Bion. 3

Very late in life, when he was studying geometry, some one said to Lacydes, "Is it then a time for you to be learning now?" "If it is not," he replied, "when will it be?"

Lacydes. 5

Aristotle was once asked what those who tell lies gain by it. Said he, "That when they speak truth they are not believed."

Aristotle. 11

The question was put to him, what hope is; and his answer was, "The dream of a waking man."

Ibid.

He used to say that personal beauty was a better introduction than any letter; but others say that it was Diogenes who gave this description of it, while Aristotle called beauty "the gift of God"; that Socrates called it "a short-lived tyranny"; Theophrastus, "a silent deceit"; Theocritus, "an ivory mischief."

Ibid.

---

[1] See Plato, page 974.
[2] See Chesterfield, page 222.

On one occasion Aristotle was asked how much educated men were superior to those uneducated: "As much," said he, "as the living are to the dead." [1]

Aristotle. 11

It was a saying of his that education was an ornament in prosperity and a refuge in adversity.

Ibid.

He was once asked what a friend is, and his answer was, "One soul abiding in two bodies." [2]

Ibid.

Asked what he gained from philosophy, he answered, "To do without being commanded what others do from fear of the laws."

Ibid.

The question was once put to him, how we ought to behave to our friends; and the answer he gave was, "As we should wish our friends to behave to us."

Ibid.

He used to define justice as "a virtue of the soul distributing that which each person deserved."

Ibid.

Another of his sayings was, that education was the best viaticum of old age.

Ibid.

It was a favourite expression of Theophrastus that time was the most valuable thing that a man could spend. [3]

Theophrastus. 10

Antisthenes used to say that envious people were devoured by their own disposition, just as iron is by rust.

Antisthenes. 4

When he was praised by some wicked men, he said, "I am sadly afraid that I must have done some wicked thing." [4]

Ibid.

When asked what learning was the most necessary, he said, "Not to unlearn what you have learned."

Antisthenes. 4

Diogenes would frequently praise those who were about to marry, and yet did not marry.

Diogenes. 4

"Bury me on my face," said Diogenes; and when he was asked why, he replied, "Because in a little while everything will be turned upside down."

Ibid. 6

All things are in common among friends.

Ibid.

Plato having defined man to be a two-legged animal without feathers, Diogenes plucked a cock and brought it into the Academy, and said, "This is Plato's man." On which account this addition was made to the definition, — "With broad flat nails."

Ibid.

A man once asked Diogenes what was the proper time for supper, and he made answer, "If you are a rich man, whenever you please; and if you are a poor man, whenever you can." [1]

Ibid.

Diogenes lighted a candle in the daytime, and went round saying, "I am looking for a man." [2]

Ibid.

When asked what he would take to let a man give him a blow on the head, he said, "A helmet."

Ibid.

Once he saw a youth blushing, and addressed him, "Courage, my boy! that is the complexion of virtue." [3]

Ibid.

When asked what wine he liked to drink, he replied, "That which belongs to another."

Ibid.

---

[1] Quoted with great warmth by Dr. Johnson (Boswell). — BENNET LANGTON [1737–1801]: *Collectanea*

[2] See Pope, page 219.

[3] Remember that time is money. — BENJAMIN FRANKLIN: *Advice to a Young Tradesman* [1748]

[4] See Plutarch, page 1003.

---

[1] The rich when he is hungry, the poor when he has anything to eat. — RABELAIS: *Book IV, Chap. 64*

[2] Told also of Aesop.

[3] See Mathew Henry, page 188.

Asked from what country he came, he replied, "I am a citizen of the world." [1]

Diogenes. 6

When a man reproached him for going into unclean places, he said, "The sun too penetrates into privies, but is not polluted by them." [2]

Ibid.

Diogenes said once to a person who was showing him a dial, "It is a very useful thing to save a man from being too late for supper."

Menedemus. 3

When Zeno was asked what a friend was, he replied, "Another I." [3]

Zeno. 19

They say that the first inclination which an animal has is to protect itself.

Ibid. 52

He calls drunkenness an expression identical with ruin. [4]

Pythagoras. 6

Among what he called his precepts were such as these: Do not stir the fire with a sword. Do not sit down on a bushel. Do not devour thy heart. [5]

Ib'd. 17

In the time of Pythagoras that proverbial phrase "Ipse dixit" [6] was introduced into ordinary life.

Ibid. 25

It takes a wise man to discover a wise man.

Xenophanes. 3

Protagoras asserted that there were two sides to every question, exactly opposite to each other.

Protagoras. 3

Nothing can be produced out of nothing. [7]

Diogenes of Apollonia. 2

The chief good is the suspension of the judgment, which tranquillity of mind follows, like its shadow.

Pyrrho. 11

[1] See Garrison, page 424.
[2] See Bacon, page 112.
[3] See page 1015.
[4] See Robert Hall, page 290.
[5] See Spenser, page 26.
[6] He, the master himself, said it, — an authoritative assertion.
[7] See Marcus Aurelius, page 1010.

Epicurus laid down the doctrine that pleasure was the chief good.

Epicurus. 6

ST. JEROME
[A. D. 345–420]

Translation by F. A. Wright

Avoid, as you would the plague, a clergyman who is also a man of business.

Letter 52, To Nepotian

A fat paunch never breeds fine thoughts.

Ibid.

The best almoner is he who keeps back nothing for himself.

Ibid.

It is no fault of Christianity if a hypocrite falls into sin.

Letter 125, To Rusticus

Preferring to store her money in the stomachs of the needy rather than hide it in a purse.

Letter 127, To Principia

ST. AUGUSTINE
[A. D. 354–430]

When I am here, I do not fast on Saturday; when at Rome, I do fast on Saturday. [1]

Epistle 36, To Casulanus

The spiritual virtue of a sacrament is like light, — although it passes among the impure, it is not polluted. [2]

Tract on St. John. Chap. 5, 15

ST. BENEDICT [3]
[A. D. 480–543]

We are therefore about to establish a school of the Lord's service in which we hope to introduce nothing harsh or burdensome.

Rule of St. Benedict. Prologue

[1] See Burton, page 126.
[2] See Bacon, page 112, and Diogenes Laertius, page 1016.
[3] Founder of Western monasticism.

LONGUS
[Fifth Century]

There was never any yet that wholly could escape love, and never shall there be any, never so long as beauty shall be, never so long as eyes can see.
Daphnis and Chloe.[1] *Proem, Chap. 2*

He is so poor that he could not keep a dog.
Ibid. Chap. 15

ALI BEN ABOU TALEB[2]
[? –660]

Believe me, a thousand friends suffice thee not;
In a single enemy thou hast more than enough.[3]

MEIR BEN ISAAC NEHERAI
[*Circa* 1050]

Could we with ink the ocean fill,
Were every blade of grass a quill,
Were the world of parchment made,
And every man a scribe by trade,
    To write the love
    Of God above
Would drain the ocean dry;
    Nor would the scroll
    Contain the whole,
Though stretched from sky to sky.
A Book of Jewish Thoughts Selected for the Sailors and Soldiers of England

[1] The only known Greek prose romance (pastoral).

[2] Ali Ben Abou Taleb, son-in-law of Mahomet, and fourth caliph, who was for his courage called "The Lion of God," was murdered A. D. 660. He was the author of *A Hundred Sayings.*

[3] Translated by RALPH WALDO EMERSON, and wrongly called by him a translation from Omar Khayyám.
Found in DR. HERMANN TOLOWIEZ'S *Polyglotte der Orientalischen Poesie.*
Translated by JAMES RUSSELL LOWELL thus: —
He who has a thousand friends has not a
    friend to spare,
And he who has one enemy will meet him
    everywhere.

ABU MOHAMMED KASIM BEN ALI HARIRI
[1054–1122]

We praise Thee, O God,
For whatever perspicuity of language
    Thou hast taught us
And whatever eloquence Thou hast inspired us with.
Makamat. Prayer

And we beg Thee freely to bestow
Propitious succor to lead us aright
And a heart turning in unison with truth,
And a language adorned with veracity,
And style supported by conclusiveness,
And accuracy that may exclude incorrectness,
And firmness of purpose that may overcome caprice,
And sagacity whereby we may attain discrimination.
Ibid.

Guard us from error in narration,
And keep us from folly even in pleasantry,
So that we may be safe from the censure of sarcastic tongues.
Ibid.

BERNARD OF CLUNY
[Twelfth Century]

Brief life is here our portion,
    Brief sorrow, short-lived care;
The life that knows no ending,
    The tearless life, is there.
The Celestial Country[1]

For thee, O dear, dear country,
    Mine eyes their vigils keep.
Ibid.

Jerusalem, the Golden,
    With milk and honey blest.
Ibid.

[1] Translated by JOHN MASON NEALE [1818–1866]. See Neale, page 518.

OMAR KHAYYÁM
[1070–1123]

Translation by EDWARD FITZGER-
ALD [*1809–1883*]

Come, fill the Cup, and in the fire of
    Spring
Your Winter-garment of Repentance
    fling:
  The Bird of Time has but a little way
To flutter — and the Bird is on the
    Wing.
             Rubáiyát.[1] *Stanza 7*

The Leaves of Life keep falling one by
    one.
                Ibid. Stanza 8

Each Morn a thousand Roses brings,
    you say:
Yes, but where leaves the Rose of Yes-
    terday?
                Ibid. Stanza 9

The strip of Herbage strown
That just divides the desert from the
    sown.
               Ibid. Stanza 11

A Book of Verses underneath the
    Bough,
A Jug of Wine, a Loaf of Bread — and
    Thou
  Beside me singing in the Wilder-
    ness —
Oh, Wilderness were Paradise enow!
              Ibid. Stanza 12

Ah, take the Cash, and let the Credit go,
Nor heed the rumble of a distant Drum!
              Ibid. Stanza 13

The Worldly Hope men set their Hearts
    upon
Turns Ashes — or it prospers; and
    anon,
  Like Snow upon the Desert's dusty
    Face,
Lighting a little hour or two — is gone.
             Ibid. Stanza 16

This batter'd Caravanserai
Whose Portals are alternate Night and
    Day.
              Ibid. Stanza 17

I sometimes think that never blows so
    red

---

[1] Fifth edition [1889].

The Rose as where some buried Caesar
    bled;
  That every Hyacinth the Garden
    wears
Dropt in her Lap from some once lovely
    Head.
            Rubáiyát. Stanza 19

Ah, my Belovèd, fill the Cup that clears
To-DAY of past Regrets and future
    Fears:
  To-morrow! — Why, To-morrow I
    may be
Myself with Yesterday's Sev'n thou-
    sand Years.
             Ibid. Stanza 21

Myself when young did eagerly fre-
    quent
Doctor and Saint, and heard great argu-
    ment
  About it and about: but evermore
Came out by the same door where in I
    went.
             Ibid. Stanza 27

There was the Door to which I found no
    Key;
There was the Veil through which I
    might not see.
             Ibid. Stanza 32

    "While you live,
Drink! — for, once dead, you never
    shall return."
             Ibid. Stanza 35

To-morrow's tangle to the winds resign.
             Ibid. Stanza 41

So when that Angel of the darker Drink
At last shall find you by the river-brink,
  And, offering his Cup, invite your
    Soul
Forth to your Lips to quaff — you shall
    not shrink.
             Ibid. Stanza 43

And fear not lest Existence closing your
Account, and mine, should know the
    like no more;
  The Eternal Sákí from that Bowl
    has pour'd
Millions of Bubbles like us, and will
    pour.
             Ibid. Stanza 46

A Moment's Halt — a momentary taste
Of BEING from the Well amid the
    Waste —

And, Lo! — the phantom Caravan has reach'd
The NOTHING it set out from — Oh, make haste!

Rubáiyát. Stanza 48

A Hair perhaps divides the False and True.

Ibid. Stanza 49

Waste not your Hour, nor in the vain pursuit
Of This and That endeavour and dispute.

Ibid. Stanza 54

Striking from the Calendar
Unborn To-morrow and dead Yesterday.

Ibid. Stanza 57

The Grape that can with Logic absolute
The Two-and-Seventy jarring Sects confute.

Ibid. Stanza 59

The Flower that once has blown for ever dies.

Ibid. Stanza 63

Strange, is it not? that of the myriads who
Before us pass'd the door of Darkness through,
    Not one returns to tell us of the Road,
Which to discover we must travel too.

Ibid. Stanza 64

I sent my Soul through the Invisible,
Some letter of that After-life to spell:
    And by and by my Soul return'd to me,
And answer'd "I Myself am Heav'n and Hell."

Ibid. Stanza 66

Heav'n but the Vision of fulfill'd Desire,
And Hell the Shadow from a Soul on fire.

Ibid. Stanza 67

We are no other than a moving row
Of Magic Shadow-shapes that come and go.

Ibid. Stanza 68

This Chequer-board of Nights and Days.

Ibid. Stanza 69

The Moving Finger writes; and, having writ,
Moves on: nor all your Piety nor Wit
    Shall lure it back to cancel half a Line,
Nor all your Tears wash out a Word of it.

Rubáiyát. Stanza 71

That inverted Bowl they call the Sky,
Whereunder crawling coop'd we live and die.

Ibid. Stanza 72

And this I know: whether the one True Light
Kindle to Love, or Wrath-consume me quite,
    One Flash of It within the Tavern caught
Better than in the Temple lost outright.

Ibid. Stanza 77

"And He that with his hand the Vessel made
Will surely not in after Wrath destroy."

Ibid. Stanza 85

"Some there are who tell
Of one who threatens he will toss to Hell
    The luckless Pots he marr'd in making — Pish!
He's a Good Fellow, and 'twill all be well."

Ibid. Stanza 88

Fill me with the old familiar Juice.

Ibid. Stanza 89

Indeed the Idols I have loved so long
Have done my credit in this World much wrong:
    Have drown'd my Glory in a shallow Cup,
And sold my Reputation for a Song.

Ibid. Stanza 93

I wonder often what the Vintners buy
One half so precious as the stuff they sell.

Ibid. Stanza 95

Yet Ah, that Spring should vanish with the Rose!
That Youth's sweet-scented manuscript should close!

Ibid. Stanza 96

Ah Love! could you and I with Him conspire

To grasp this Sorry Scheme of Things
    entire,
    Would not we shatter it to bits —
    and then
Re-mould it nearer to the Heart's De-
    sire!
                    Rubáiyát. Stanza 99
Yon rising Moon that looks for us
    again —
How oft hereafter will she wax and
    wane;
    How oft hereafter rising look for us
Through this same Garden — and for
    one in vain!
                    Ibid. Stanza 100
And when like her, O Sákí, you shall
    pass
Among the Guests Star-scatter'd on the
    Grass,
    And in your joyous errand reach the
    spot
Where I made One — turn down an
    empty Glass!
                    Ibid. Stanza 101

MOSES BEN MAIMON (MAIMONIDES)
[1135–1204]

Anticipate charity by preventing
poverty; assist the reduced fellowman,
either by a considerable gift, or a sum
of money, or by teaching him a trade,
or by putting him in the way of business, so that he may earn an honest
livelihood, and not be forced to the
dreadful alternative of holding out his
hand for charity. This is the highest
step and the summit of charity's golden
ladder.
                    Charity's Eight Degrees [1]

ALPHONSO THE LEARNED
[1221–1284]

Had I been present at the creation,
I would have given some useful hints
for the better ordering of the universe.[2]

[1] *New York Sun, Jan. 6, 1933.*
[2] CARLYLE says, in his *History of Frederick
the Great, Book II, Chap. 7*, that this saying
of Alphonso about Ptolemy's astronomy,
"that it seemed a crank machine; that it was

DANTE ALIGHIERI
[1265–1321]

Translation by HENRY FRANCIS
CARY [1772–1844]

All hope abandon, ye who enter here.
                    Hell. Canto III, Line 9
The wretched souls of those who lived
Without or praise or blame.
                    Ibid. Line 34
And to a part I come, where no light
    shines.
                    Ibid. Canto IV, Line 148
Avarice, envy, pride,
Three fatal sparks.
                    Ibid. Canto V, Line 74
No greater grief than to remember days
Of joy, when misery is at hand.[1]
                    Ibid. Line 118
But to the pleasant world when thou
    returnest,
Of me make mention, I entreat thee,
    there.
                    Ibid. Canto VI, Line 90
"If thou," he answered, "follow but thy
    star,
Thou canst not miss at last a glorious
    haven."
                    Ibid. Canto XV, Line 55
Do Fortune as she list, I stand pre-
    pared.
                    Ibid. Line 94
He listens to good purpose who takes
    note.
                    Ibid. Line 100
Think within thyself, so God
Fruit of thy reading give thee.
                    Ibid. Canto XX, Line 18
To fair request
Silent performance maketh best return.
                    Ibid. Canto XXIV, Line 75
Though somewhat tardy I perchance
    arrive.
                    Ibid. Canto XXVII, Line 19

pity the Creator had not taken advice," is still
remembered by mankind, — this and no other
of his many sayings.
[1]   It is the worst of woes
    That in them men look back with stream-
        ing eyes
    On bygone joy.
        Translation by JOHN JAY CHAPMAN
                            [1862–1933]
    See Longfellow, page 440.

The light bark of my genius lifts the sail.
Purgatory. Canto I, Line 2

O clear conscience, and upright!
How doth a little failing wound thee sore.
Ibid. Canto III, Line 8

Who knows most, him loss of time most grieves.
Ibid. Line 77

So wide arms
Hath goodness infinite, that it receives
All who turn to it.
Ibid. Line 118

If prayer do not aid me first,
That riseth up from heart which lives in grace,
What other kind avails, not heard in heaven?
Ibid. Canto IV, Line 129

Be as a tower, that, firmly set,
Shakes not its top for any blast that blows.
Ibid. Canto V, Line 14

I am Virgil; for no sin
Deprived of heaven, except for lack of faith.
Ibid. Canto VII, Line 6

Now was the hour that wakens fond desire
In men at sea, and melts their thoughtful heart
Who in the morn have bid sweet friends farewell.
Ibid. Canto VIII, Line 1

Grant us, this day,
Our daily manna.
Ibid. Canto XI,[1] Line 13

The noise
Of worldly fame is but a blast of wind,
That blows from diverse points, and shifts its name,
Shifting the point it blows from.
Ibid. Line 97

Consider that this day ne'er dawns again.
Ibid. Canto XII, Line 78

God be with you.
I bear you company no more.
Ibid. Canto XVI, Line 145

[1] Lines 1–24 of this canto give a paraphrase of the Lord's Prayer.

Mine eye
Was closed, and meditation changed to dream.
Purgatory. Canto XVIII, Line 142

The woes
Of Midas, which his greedy wish ensued,
Marked for derision to all future times.
Ibid. Canto XX, Line 104

Let its pure flame
From virtue flow, and love can never fail
To warm another's bosom, so the light
Shine manifestly forth.
Ibid. Canto XXII, Line 9

If too secure, I loose
The rein with a friend's license, as a friend
Forgive me, and speak now as with a friend.
Ibid. Line 19

Woman, the creature of an hour.
Ibid. Canto XXIX, Line 25

Between two kinds of food, both equally
Remote and tempting, first a man might die
Of hunger, ere he one could freely choose.
Paradise. Canto IV, Line 1

Nature, that is the seal to mortal wax.
Ibid. Canto VIII, Line 133

Whose affirmation, or denial, is
Without distinction.
Ibid. Canto XIII, Line 111

How salt the savor is of other's bread;
How hard the passage to descend and climb
By other's stairs.
Ibid. Canto XVII, Line 58

As for the leaves, that in the garden bloom,
My love for them is great, as is the good
Dealt by the eternal hand, that tends them all.
Ibid. Canto XXVI, Line 62

As one, who from a dream awaken'd, straight,
All he hath seen forgets; yet still retains
Impression of the feeling in his dream;

E'en such am I: for all the vision dies,
As 'twere, away.
Paradise. Canto XXXIII, Line 55

JEAN FROISSART
[1337–1410]

Above all flowers, I find the Daisy dear.
Above All Flowers [1]

FRANÇOIS VILLON
[1430–1484]

Where are the snows of yester-year? [2]
The Greater Testament.[3] *Ballad
of Old-Time Ladies*

All must come to the self-same bay;
Sons and servants, their days are told:
The wind carries their like away.
*Ibid. Ballad of Old-Time Lords,
No. 2*

Blonde or brunette, this rhyme applies,
Happy is he who knows them not.
*Ibid. Double Ballad to the Like
Purport*

O Virgin clean,
To whom all sinners lift their hands on
high,
Made whole in faith through Thee their
go-between.
In this belief I will to live and die.
*Ibid. Ballad of Homage to Our
Lady*

My heart shall not dissever aye from
thee
Nor thine from me, if it aright I read:
And to this end we twain together be.
*Ibid. Ballad to a Newly Married
Gentleman*

There's no right speech out of Paris
town.
*Ibid. Ballad of the Women of
Paris*

If you have money, it doth not stay,
But this way and that it wastes amain:
What does it profit you, anyway?
Ill-gotten good is nobody's gain.
*Ibid. Seemly Lesson to the Good-
for-Noughts*

[1] Translated by GRACE WARRACK.
[2] See J. H. McCarthy, page 759.
But where is last year's snow? This was the
greatest care that Villon, the Parisian poet,
took. — RABELAIS: *Book II, Chap. 14.*
[3] Translation by D. G. ROSSETTI.

I know all save myself alone.
*Ballad of Things Known and
Unknown*

For he deserves not any fortune fair
Who would wish ill unto the realm of
France.
*Ballad Against Those Who Missay
of France*

These traitorous thieves, accursèd and
unfair,
The vintners that put water in our wine.
A Merry Ballad of Vintners

In the amorous war
The wealthy gallant always gains the
day.
Ballad of Ladies' Love, No. 1

ALDUS (MANUTIUS)
[1450–1515]

Talk of nothing but business, and
despatch that business quickly.
*Placard on the door of the Aldine
Press, Venice, established about
1490* [1]

LEONARDO DA VINCI
[1452–1519]

*From his Note-Books, translated by
EDWARD McCURDY*

In rivers, the water that you touch
is the last of what has passed and the
first of that which comes: so with time
present.

Whoever in discussion adduces authority uses not intellect but memory.

No counsel is more trustworthy than
that which is given upon ships that are
in peril.

Intellectual passion drives out sensu-
ality.

Let the street be as wide as the height
of the houses.

No member needs so great a number
of muscles as the tongue; this exceeds
all the rest in the number of its movements.

[1] Quoted by Thomas Frognall Dibdin
[1776–1847] in *Introduction to the Knowledge of Rare and Valuable Editions of the
Greek and Latin Classics* [1802], *Vol. I,
P. 436.*

It is of no small benefit on finding oneself in bed in the dark to go over again in the imagination the main outlines of the forms previously studied, or of other noteworthy things conceived by ingenious speculation.

As a well-spent day brings happy sleep, so life well used brings happy death.

DESIDERIUS ERASMUS
[1465–1536]

No one is injured save by himself.[1]
Adages

I know how busy you are in your library, which is your Paradise.[2]
Letter to Bishop Fisher [1524]

NICOLÒ MACHIAVELLI [3]
[1469–1527]

There is nothing more difficult to take in hand, more perilous to conduct, or more uncertain in its success, than to take the lead in the introduction of a new order of things.
The Prince.[4] Chap. 6

The chief foundations of all states, new as well as old or composite, are good laws and good arms; and as there cannot be good laws where the state is not well armed, it follows that where they are well armed they have good laws.
Ibid. Chap. 12

Among other evils which being unarmed brings you, it causes you to be despised.
Ibid. Chap. 14

When neither their property nor their honour is touched, the majority of men live content.
Ibid. Chap. 19

---

[1] No one can harm the man who does himself no wrong. — SAINT CHRYSOSTOM [327–407]: *Letter to Olympia*

[2] Nec me fugit quam assiduus sis in bibliotheca, quae tibi Paradisi loco est. P. S. ALLEN: *Selections from Erasmus, P. 128*

[3] Every Country hath its Machiavel. — SIR THOMAS BROWNE: *Religio Medici* (Everyman ed.), *P. 24*

[4] *Translation by* W. K. MARRIOTT

There are three classes of intellects: one which comprehends by itself; another which appreciates what others comprehend; and a third which neither comprehends by itself nor by the showing of others; the first is the most excellent, the second is good, the third is useless.
The Prince. Chap. 22

Where the willingness is great, the difficulties cannot be great.
Ibid. Chap. 26

God is not willing to do everything, and thus take away our free will and that share of glory which belongs to us.
Ibid.

MICHELANGELO
[1474–1564]

The more the marble wastes,
The more the statue grows.
Sonnet

If it be true that any beauteous thing
Raises the pure and just desire of man
From earth to God, the eternal fount of all,
Such I believe my love.
Sonnet

The might of one fair face sublimes my love,
For it hath weaned my heart from low desires.
Sonnet

I live and love in God's peculiar light.
Ibid.

MARTIN LUTHER
[1483–1546]

A mighty fortress is our God,
A bulwark never failing;
Our helper He amid the flood
Of mortal ills prevailing.[1]
Psalm, Ein' Feste Burg [2]

---

[1] Great God! there is no safety here below; Thou art my fortress, thou that seem'st my foe.
FRANCIS QUARLES [1592–1644]: *Divine Poems*

[2] Translated by FREDERIC H. HEDGE.

Tell your master that if there were as many devils at Worms as tiles on its roofs, I would enter.[1]

On approaching Worms

Here I stand; I can do no otherwise. God help me. Amen![2]

Speech at the Diet of Worms

For where God built a church, there the Devil would also build a chapel.[3]

Table Talk. 67

A faithful and good servant is a real godsend; but truly 'tis a rare bird in the land.

Ibid. 156

It makes a difference whose ox is gored.[4]

Works [1854 edition]. Vol. 62, Page 449

ST. IGNATIUS LOYOLA [5]
[1491-1556]

Teach us, good Lord, to serve Thee as Thou deservest:
To give and not to count the cost;
To fight and not to heed the wounds;
To toil and not to seek for rest;
To labour and not ask for any reward

---

[1] On the 16th of April, 1521, Luther entered the imperial city [of Worms]. . . . On his approach . . . the Elector's chancellor entreated him, in the name of his master, not to enter a town where his death was decided. The answer which Luther returned was simply this. — BARON VON BUNSEN [1791-1860]: *Life of Luther*
I will go, though as many devils aim at me as there are tiles on the roofs of the houses. — LEOPOLD VON RANKE [1795-1886]: *History of the Reformation, Vol. I, P. 533,* translated by SARAH TAYLOR AUSTIN [1793-1867].
Luther it was who, when advised not to trust himself in Worms, declared, "Although there be as many devils in Worms as there are tiles on the house-tops, I will go." — ALEXANDER SMITH: *Dreamthorp, A Shelf in My Bookcase*
[2] [Luther] it was who, when brought to bay in the splendid assemblage, said, "It is neither safe nor prudent to do aught against conscience. Here stand I — I cannot do otherwise. God help me. Amen." — *Ibid.*
[3] See Burton, page 126.
[4] This is the moral of the fable of the lawyer, the farmer, and the farmer's ox, which was included in NOAH WEBSTER'S *American Spelling Book* [1802], entitled *The Partial Judge.*
[5] Founder of the Society of Jesus.

Save that of knowing that we do Thy will.

Prayer for Generosity

FRANCIS I
[1494-1547]

All is lost save honour and my life.[1]

Letter to his mother

FRANÇOIS RABELAIS
[1495-1553]

I am just going to leap into the dark.[2]

PETER ANTHONY MOTTEUX: *Life of Rabelais*

Let down the curtain: the farce is done.

Ibid.

He left a paper sealed up, wherein were found three articles as his last will: "I owe much; I have nothing; I give the rest to the poor."

Ibid.

One inch of joy surmounts of grief a span,
Because to laugh is proper to the man.

Works. To the Readers

To return to our wethers.[3]

Ibid. Book I, Chap. 1

I drink no more than a sponge.

Ibid. Chap. 5

---

[1] From the imperial camp near Pavia, Italy, after the battle of February 24, 1525, Francis I wrote to his mother: "Madame, pour vous faire savoir comme se porte le reste de mon infortune, de toutes choses ne m'est demeuré que l'honneur et la vie qui est sauvé." — HENRI MARTIN: *History of France, Vol. 8*
SISMONDI [1773-1842], *Vol. 16, Pp. 241, 242,* corrected the expression which had become altered to "Tout est perdu fors l'honneur."
The letter itself is printed entire in *Histoire Civile, Physique et Morale de Paris* by JACQUES ANTOINE DULAURE [1755-1835]: "Pour vous avertir comment se porte le ressort de mon infortune, de toutes choses ne m'est demeuré que l'honneur et la vie, — qui est sauvé."
All gone but faith in God. — BISHOP JOHN McKIM [1852-1936]: Cabled message to the New York headquarters of the Episcopal Church after the destruction of the mission by the Japanese earthquake [1923].
[2] Je m'en vay chercher un grand Peut-estre (I am going to seek a great Perhaps).
[3] Revenons à nos moutons. — A proverb taken from the farce, *L'Avocat Pierre Patelin,* by BLANCHET [1459-1519], *P. 90* [1762 ed.].

Appetite comes with eating, says Angeston.[1]

Works. Book I, Chap. 5

Thought the moon was made of green cheese.[2]

Ibid. Chap. 11

He always looked a given horse in the mouth.[3]

Ibid.

By robbing Peter he paid Paul,[4] . . . and hoped to catch larks if ever the heavens should fall.[5]

Ibid.

He laid him squat as a flounder.

Ibid. Chap. 27

Send them home as merry as crickets.

Ibid. Chap. 29

War begun without good provision of money beforehand for going through with it is but as a breathing of strength and blast that will quickly pass away. Coin is the sinews of war.[6]

Ibid. Chap. 46

How shall I be able to rule over others, that have not full power and command of myself?

Ibid. Chap. 52

Subject to a kind of disease, which at that time they called lack of money.[7]

Ibid. Book II, Chap. 16

[1] My appetite comes to me while eating. — MONTAIGNE: *Book III, Chap. 9, Of Vanity*

[2] See Heywood, page 17.

[3] See *Ibid.*, page 13, Butler, page 142, and Cervantes, page 1042.

[4] See Heywood, page 14.

[5] See *Ibid.*, page 12.

[6] AESCHINES [389–314 B. C.] ascribes to Demosthenes the expression, "The sinews of affairs are cut" (*Adv. Ctesiphon, Chap. 53*). DIOGENES LAERTIUS, in his *Life of Bion, Book IV, Chap. 7, Sect. 3*, represents Bion as saying, "Riches were the sinews of business," or, as the phrase may mean, "of the state." Referring perhaps to this maxim of the philosopher Bion, PLUTARCH says in his *Life of Cleomenes*, "He that first said that money was the sinews of affairs, seems especially in that saying to refer to war" (Modern Library Giant ed., *P. 986*). Accordingly we find money called expressly "the sinews of war" in LIBANIUS, *Oration 46*, and by the scholiast on PINDAR, *Olymp., I, 4*, and in CICERO, *Philipp., V, 2*, "nervos belli, infinitam pecuniam."

[7] Or that eternal want of pence,
    Which vexes public men.

TENNYSON:
Will Waterproof's Lyrical Monologue, St. 6

He did not care a button for it.

Works. Book II, Chap. 16

How well I feathered my nest.[1]

Ibid. Chap. 17

So much is a man worth as he esteems himself.

Ibid. Chap. 29

A good crier of green sauce.

Ibid. Chap. 31

Then I began to think that it is very true which is commonly said, that the one half of the world knoweth not how the other half liveth.

Ibid. Chap. 32

This flea which I have in mine ear.

Ibid. Book III, Chap. 31

You have there hit the nail on the head.[2]

Ibid. Chap. 34

Above the pitch, out of tune, and off the hinges.

Ibid. Book IV, Chap. 19

I'll go his halves.

Ibid. Chap. 23

The Devil was sick, — the Devil a
    monk would be;
The Devil was well, — the Devil a
    monk was he.[3]

Ibid. Chap. 24

Do not believe what I tell you here any more than if it were some tale of a tub.[4]

Ibid. Chap. 38

I would have you call to mind the strength of the ancient giants, that undertook to lay the high mountain Pelion on the top of Ossa, and set among those the shady Olympus.[5]

Ibid.

Which was performed to a T.[6]

Ibid. Chap. 41

He that has patience may compass anything.

Ibid. Chap. 48

[1] See Pepys, page 181.

[2] See Heywood, page 18.

[3] Quoted by SIR WALTER SCOTT in *The Black Dwarf, Chap. 6*.

[4] Title of a religious satire by JONATHAN SWIFT.

[5] See Ovid, page 986.

[6] See Johnson, page 238.

We will take the good will for the deed.[1]

> *Works. Book IV, Chap. 49*

You are Christians of the best edition, all picked and culled.

> *Ibid. Chap. 50*

Would you damn your precious soul?

> *Ibid. Chap. 54*

Let us fly and save our bacon.

> *Ibid. Chap. 55*

Needs must when the Devil drives.[2]

> *Ibid. Chap. 57*

Scampering as if the Devil drove them.

> *Ibid. Chap. 62*

He freshly and cheerfully asked him how a man should kill time.

> *Ibid.*

The belly has no ears, nor is it to be filled with fair words.[3]

> *Ibid.*

Whose cockloft is unfurnished.[4]

> *Ibid. Book V, Author's Prologue*

Speak the truth and shame the Devil.[5]

> *Ibid.*

Plain as a nose in a man's face.[6]

> *Ibid.*

Like hearts of oak.[7]

> *Ibid.*

You shall never want rope enough.

> *Ibid.*

Looking as like . . . as one pea does like another.[8]

> *Ibid. Chap. 2*

And thereby hangs a tale.[9]

> *Ibid. Chap. 4*

Nothing is so dear and precious as time.[10]

> *Ibid. Chap. 5*

It is meat, drink,[1] and cloth to us.

> *Works. Book V, Chap. 7*

And so on to the end of the chapter.

> *Ibid. Chap. 10*

What is got over the Devil's back is spent under the belly.[2]

> *Ibid. Chap. 11*

We have here other fish to fry.[3]

> *Ibid. Chap. 12*

What cannot be cured must be endured.[4]

> *Ibid. Chap. 15*

Thought I to myself, we shall never come off scot-free.

> *Ibid.*

It is enough to fright you out of your seven senses.[5]

> *Ibid.*

Necessity has no law.[6]

> *Ibid.*

Panurge had no sooner heard this, but he was upon the high-rope.

> *Ibid. Chap. 18*

We saw a knot of others, about a baker's dozen.

> *Ibid. Chap. 23*

Others made a virtue of necessity.[7]

> *Ibid.*

Spare your breath to cool your porridge.[8]

> *Ibid. Chap. 28*

I believe he would make three bites of a cherry.

> *Ibid.*

KENKO [9]
[FOURTEENTH CENTURY]

Too much furniture in one's living-room.

---

[1] See Swift, page 192.
[2] See Heywood, page 17.
[3] See Plutarch, page 998.
[4] See Bacon, page 113.
[5] See Shakespeare, page 62, and Johnson, page 235.
[6] See Shakespeare, page 33, and Cervantes, page 1034.
[7] See Garrick, page 242.
[8] See Lyly, page 23, Shakespeare, page 56, and Cervantes, page 1040.
[9] See Shakespeare, page 34, and Cervantes, page 1042.
[10] See Diogenes Laertius, page 1015.

[1] See Shakespeare, page 51.
[2] Isocrates was in the right to insinuate that what is got over the Devil's back is spent under his belly. — LE SAGE: *Gil Blas, Book 8, Chap. 9*
[3] I have other fish to fry. — CERVANTES: *Don Quixote, Part II, Chap. 35*
[4] See Burton, page 124.
[5] See Scott, page 310.
[6] See Diogenes Laertius, page 1013.
[7] See Chaucer, page 4, and Burton, page 125.
[8] See Plutarch, page 1004.
[9] A Japanese Buddhist.

Too many pens in a stand.
Too many Buddhas in a private shrine.
Too many rocks, trees, and herbs in a garden.
Too many children in a house.
Too many words when men meet.
Too many books in a bookcase there can never be,
Nor too much litter in a dust heap.

Fragment

GEORGIUS FABRICIUS
[1516–1571]

He doth raise his country's fame with his own
And in the mouths of nations yet unborn
His praises shall be sung; Death comes to all
But great achievements raise a monument
Which shall endure until the sun grows cold.

In Praise of Georgius Agricola [1494–1555]. Quoted by HERBERT CLARK HOOVER *and* LOU HENRY HOOVER *in their translation of Agricola's De Re Metallica, Page XXIV*

PIERRE DE RONSARD
[1524–1585]

When you are old, and in the candle light
Sit spinning by the fire at close of day,
You'll sing my songs in praise of you, and say:
"Thus Ronsard sang, whilst still my eyes were bright." [1]

Sonnet XLII, [2] *To Helen* [3]

---

[1] Compare WILLIAM BUTLER YEATS's adaptation: "When you are old and gray and full of sleep," page 790.
[2] Translated by WILLIAM A. DRAKE.
[3] Madame de Suggères.

MICHEL DE MONTAIGNE
[1533–1592]
Translation by CHARLES COTTON *[1630–1687], revised by* HAZLITT *and* WIGHT

Man in sooth is a marvellous vain, fickle, and unstable subject. [1]

Works. [2] *Book I, Chap. 1, That Men by Various Ways Arrive at the Same End*

All passions that suffer themselves to be relished and digested are but moderate. [3]

Ibid. Chap. 2, Of Sorrow

It is not without good reason said, that he who has not a good memory should never take upon him the trade of lying. [4]

Ibid. Chap. 9, Of Liars

He who should teach men to die would at the same time teach them to live. [5]

Ibid. Chap. 19, That to Study Philosophy Is to Learn to Die

The laws of conscience, which we pretend to be derived from nature, proceed from custom.

Ibid. Chap. 22, Of Custom

Accustom him to everything, that he may not be a Sir Paris, a carpet-knight, [6] but a sinewy, hardy, and vigorous young man.

Ibid. Chap. 25, On the Education of Children

It can be of no importance to me of what religion my physician or my lawyer is; this consideration has nothing in

---

[1] See Plutarch, page 1001.
[2] This book of Montaigne the world has indorsed by translating it into all tongues. — EMERSON: *Representative Men, Montaigne*
[3] See Raleigh, page 21.
Curae leves loquuntur ingentes stupent (Light griefs are loquacious, but the great are dumb). — SENECA: *Hippolytus, II, 3, 607.*
[4] See Sidney, page 169.
Mendacem memorem esse oportere (To be a liar, memory is necessary). — QUINTILIAN: *IV, 2, 91*
[5] See Tickell, page 205.
[6] See Burton, page 123, and Cervantes, page 1035.

common with the offices of friendship which they owe me.

Works. Book I, Chap. 27, Of Friendship

We were halves throughout, and to that degree that methinks, by outliving him, I defraud him of his part.

Ibid.

There are some defeats more triumphant than victories.[1]

Ibid. Chap. 30, Of Cannibals

Nothing is so firmly believed as what we least know.

Ibid. Chap. 31, Of Divine Ordinances

A wise man never loses anything if he have himself.

Ibid. Chap. 38, Of Solitude

Even opinion is of force enough to make itself to be espoused at the expense of life.

Ibid. Chap. 40, Of Good and Evil

Plato says, " 'Tis to no purpose for a sober man to knock at the door of the Muses"; and Aristotle says "that no excellent soul is exempt from a mixture of folly."[2]

Ibid. Book II, Chap. 2, Of Drunkenness

For a desperate disease a desperate cure.[3]

Ibid. Chap. 3, The Custom of the Isle of Cea

And not to serve for a table-talk.[4]

Ibid.

To which we may add this other Aristotelian consideration, that he who confers a benefit on any one loves him better than he is beloved by him again.[5]

Ibid. Chap. 8, Of the Affection of Fathers

The middle sort of historians (of which the most part are) spoil all; they will chew our meat for us.

Ibid. Chap. 10, Of Books

The only good histories are those that have been written by the persons themselves who commanded in the affairs whereof they write.

Works. Book II, Chap. 10, Of Books

She [virtue] requires a rough and stormy passage; she will have either outward difficulties to wrestle with, or internal difficulties.[1]

Ibid. Chap. 11, Of Cruelty

There is, nevertheless, a certain respect, and a general duty of humanity, that ties us, not only to beasts that have life and sense, but even to trees and plants.

Ibid.

Some impose upon the world that they believe that which they do not; others, more in number, make themselves believe that they believe, not being able to penetrate into what it is to believe.

Ibid. Chap. 12, Apology for Raimond Sebond[2]

When I play with my cat, who knows whether I do not make her more sport than she makes me?

Ibid.

'Tis one and the same Nature that rolls on her course, and whoever has sufficiently considered the present state of things might certainly conclude as to both the future and the past.[3]

Ibid.

The souls of emperors and cobblers are cast in the same mould. . . . The same reason that makes us wrangle with a neighbour causes a war betwixt princes.

Ibid.

Man is certainly stark mad; he cannot make a worm, and yet he will be making gods by dozens.

Ibid.

Why may not a goose say thus: "All the parts of the universe I have an in-

---

[1] See Bacon, page 113.
[2] See Dryden, page 173.
[3] See Shakespeare, page 96, and Dryden, page 175.
[4] Let it serve for table-talk. — SHAKE-SPEARE: *The Merchant of Venice, Act III, Sc. 5, L. 95*
[5] ARISTOTLE: *Ethics, 9, 7*

[1] Let Truth and Falsehood grapple. — MILTON: *Areopagitica*
[2] Raimond Sebond, born at Barcelona in the 14th century, died in 1432, at Toulouse, where he had lived as professor of medicine and theology.
[3] See Plutarch, page 998.

terest in: the earth serves me to walk upon, the sun to light me; the stars have their influence upon me; I have such an advantage by the winds and such by the waters; there is nothing that yon heavenly roof looks upon so favourably as me. I am the darling of Nature! Is it not man that keeps, lodges, and serves me?"

Works. Book II, Chap. 12,
Apology for Raimond Sebond

Arts and sciences are not cast in a mould, but are formed and perfected by degrees, by often handling and polishing, as bears leisurely lick their cubs into form.[1]

Ibid.

He that I am reading seems always to have the most force.

Ibid.

Apollo said that every one's true worship was that which he found in use in the place where he chanced to be.[2]

Ibid.

The mariner of old said thus to Neptune in a great tempest, "O God! thou mayest save me if thou wilt, and if thou wilt, thou mayest destroy me; but whether or no, I will steer my rudder true."[3]

Ibid. Chap. 16, Of Glory

How many worthy men have we known to survive their own reputation![4]

Ibid.

There is another sort of glory, which is the having too good an opinion of our own worth.

Ibid. Chap. 17, Of Presumption

One may be humble out of pride.

Ibid.

Nature has presented us with a large faculty of entertaining ourselves alone; and often calls us to it, to teach us that

we owe ourselves partly to society, but chiefly and mostly to ourselves.

Works. Book II, Chap. 18,
On Giving the Lie

I find that the best virtue I have has in it some tincture of vice.

Ibid. Chap. 20, That We Taste
Nothing Pure

Saying is one thing, and doing is another.

Ibid. Chap. 31, Of Anger

Is it not a noble farce, wherein kings, republics, and emperors have for so many ages played their parts, and to which the whole vast universe serves for a theatre?[1]

Ibid. Chap. 36, Of the Most
Excellent Men

Nature forms us for ourselves, not for others; to be, not to seem.

Ibid. Chap. 37, Of the Resemblance of Children to Their
Brothers

There never was in the world two opinions alike, no more than two hairs or two grains; the most universal quality is diversity.[2]

Ibid. Of the Resemblance of Children to Their Fathers

The public weal requires that men should betray, and lie, and massacre.

Ibid. Book III, Chap. 1, Of
Profit and Honesty

I will follow the right side even to the fire, but excluding the fire if I can.

Ibid.

Does not he to whom you betray another, to whom you were as welcome as to himself, know that you will at another time do as much for him?

Ibid.

Like rowers, who advance backward.[3]

Ibid.

I speak truth, not so much as I would, but as much as I dare; and I dare a little the more, as I grow older.

Ibid. Chap. 2, Of Repentance

---

[1] See Burton, page 122, and Pliny, page 994.
[2] XENOPHON: *Mem. Socratis, I, 3, 1*
[3] The pilot . . . who has been able to say, "Neptune, you shall never sink this ship except on an even keel," has fulfilled the requirements of his art. — SENECA: *Epistle 85*
[4] See Bentley, page 187.

[1] See Shakespeare, page 49.
[2] See Browne, page 144, and Plato, page 974.
[3] See Burton, page 122.

Few men have been admired by their own domestics.[1]

Works. Book III, Chap. 2,
Of Repentance

It happens as with cages: the birds without despair to get in, and those within despair of getting out.[2]

Ibid. Chap. 5, Upon Some Verses
of Virgil

And to bring in a new word by the head and shoulders, they leave out the old one.

Ibid.

All the world knows me in my book, and my book in me.

Ibid.

'Tis so much to be a king, that he only is so by being so. The strange lustre that surrounds him conceals and shrouds him from us; our sight is there broken and dissipated, being stopped and filled by the prevailing light.[3]

Ibid. Chap. 7, Of the Inconven-
ience of Greatness

We are born to inquire after truth; it belongs to a greater power to possess it. It is not, as Democritus said, hid in the bottom of the deeps, but rather elevated to an infinite height in the divine knowledge.[4]

Ibid. Chap. 8, Of the Art of
Conversation

I moreover affirm that our wisdom itself, and wisest consultations, for the most part commit themselves to the conduct of chance.[5]

Ibid.

What if he has borrowed the matter and spoiled the form, as it oft falls out?[6]

Ibid.

---

[1] See Plutarch, page 1005.
[2] See Davies, page 115.
[3] That fierce light which beats upon a throne.
   TENNYSON: *Idylls of the King, Dedication*
[4] LACTANTIUS [early 4th century]: *Divin. Inst., 3, 28*
[5] Although men flatter themselves with their great actions, they are not so often the result of great design as of chance. — ROCHE-FOUCAULD: *Maxim 57*
[6] Defacing first, then claiming as his own. CHARLES CHURCHILL: *The Apology,* L. 235

The oldest and best known evil was ever more supportable than one that was new and untried.[1]

Works. Book III, Chap. 9,
Of Vanity

Not because Socrates said so, . . . I look upon all men as my compatriots.

Ibid.

My appetite comes to me while eating.[2]

Ibid.

There is no man so good, who, were he to submit all his thoughts and actions to the laws, would not deserve hanging ten times in his life.

Ibid.

Saturninus said, "Comrades, you have lost a good captain to make him an ill general."

Ibid.

A little folly is desirable in him that will not be guilty of stupidity.[3]

Ibid.

Habit is a second nature.[4]

Ibid. Chap. 10

We seek and offer ourselves to be gulled.

Ibid. Chap. 11, Of Cripples

I have never seen a greater monster or miracle in the world than myself.

Ibid.

Men are most apt to believe what they least understand.

Ibid.

I have here only made a nosegay of culled flowers, and have brought nothing of my own but the thread that ties them together.

Ibid. Chap. 12, Of Physiognomy

Amongst so many borrowed things, I am glad if I can steal one, disguising and altering it for some new service.

Ibid.

I am further of opinion that it would be better for us to have [no laws] at

---

[1] LIVY: *23, 3*
[2] See Rabelais, page 1025.
[3] See Walpole, page 246.
[4] See Plutarch, page 1003.

all than to have them in so prodigious
numbers as we have.
Works. Book III, Chap. 13,
Of Experience

There is more ado to interpret inter-
pretations than to interpret the things,
and more books upon books than upon
all other subjects; we do nothing but
comment upon one another.
Ibid.

What can we do with those people
who will not believe anything unless it
is in print? . . . I would as soon quote
one of my friends as I would Aulus Gel-
lius or Macrobius.
Ibid.

For truth itself has not the privilege
to be spoken at all times and in all sorts.
Ibid.

The diversity of physical arguments
and opinions embraces all sorts of
methods.
Ibid.

Let us a little permit Nature to take
her own way; she better understands
her own affairs than we.
Ibid.

I have ever loved to repose myself,
whether sitting or lying, with my heels
as high or higher than my head.
Ibid.

I, who have so much and so universally adored this "excellent mediocrity"
of ancient times, and who have concluded the most moderate measure the
most perfect, shall I pretend to an unreasonable and prodigious old age?
Ibid.

Que scais-je [1] (What do I know)?
Motto on his seal

I do not understand; I pause; I examine.
Inscription for his library [2]

[1] "Que scais-je?" was the motto of Montaigne.
BYRON: *Don Juan, Canto IX, St. 17*
[2] Quoted by ALEXANDER SMITH: *Dreamthorp, On the Writing of Essays*

JAN ZAMOYSKI
[1541–1605]

The king reigns, but does not govern.[1]
Speech in the Polish Parliament
[1605], referring to King Sig-
ismund III

GUILLAUME DE SALLUSTE,
SEIGNEUR DU BARTAS
[1544–1590]

From Divine Weekes and Workes,
translated [1606] by J. SYLVESTER
[1563–1618]

The world's a stage,[2] where God's om-
nipotence,
His justice, knowledge, love, and prov-
idence
Do act the parts.
First Week. First Day

And reads, though running,[3] all these
needful motions.
Ibid.

Mercy and justice, marching cheek by
joule.
Ibid.

Not unlike the bear which bringeth
forth
In the end of thirty dayes a shapeless
birth;
But after licking, it in shape she drawes,
And by degrees she fashions out the
pawes,
The head, and neck, and finally doth
bring
To a perfect beast that first deformed
thing.[4]
Ibid.

What is well done is done soon enough.
Ibid.

And swans seem whiter if swart crowes
be by.
Ibid.

[1] Louis Adolphe Thiers adopted the epigram as the motto for his journal, the *Na-*
tionale, which he established with Mignet and
Carrel in 1830.
[2] See Shakespeare, page 49, and Du Bartas,
page 1033.
[3] See Cowper, page 266.
[4] See Montaigne, page 994.

Night's black mantle covers all alike.[1]
> *First Week. First Day*

Hot and cold, and moist and dry.[2]
> *Ibid. Second Day*

Much like the French (or like ourselves,
their apes),
Who with strange habit do disguise
their shapes;
Who loving novels, full of affectation,
Receive the manners of each other nation.[3]
> *Ibid.*

With tooth and nail.
> *Ibid.*

From the foure corners of the worlde
doe haste.[4]
> *Ibid.*

Oft seen in forehead of the frowning
skies.[5]
> *Ibid.*

Bright-flaming, heat-full fire,
The source of motion.[6]
> *Ibid.*

To man the earth seems altogether
No more a mother, but a step-dame
rather.[7]
> *Ibid. Third Day*

For where's the state beneath the firmament
That doth excel the bees for government? [8]
> *Ibid. Fifth Day, Part 1*

---

[1] Night . . . with thy black mantle.
   SHAKESPEARE: *Romeo and Juliet,*
      Act III, Sc. 2, L. 10 and 15
[2] Hot, cold, moist, and dry, four champions
   fierce.
   MILTON: *Paradise Lost, Book 2, L. 898*
[3] Report of fashions in proud Italy,
   Whose manners still our tardy apish nation
   Limps after in base imitation.
   SHAKESPEARE: *King Richard II,*
      Act II, Sc. 1, L. 21
[4] Come the three corners of the world in
   arms.
   SHAKESPEARE: *King John,*
      Act V, Sc. 7, L. 116
[5] The forehead of the morning sky.
   MILTON: *Lycidas, L. 171*
[6] *Heat Considered as a Mode of Motion,*
title of a treatise [1863] by JOHN TYNDALL
[1820-1893].
[7] See Pliny, page 993.
[8]   So work the honey-bees,
   Creatures that by a rule in Nature teach

These lovely lamps, these windows of
the soul.[1]
> *First Week. Sixth Day*

Or almost like a spider, who, confin'd
In her web's centre, shakt with every
winde,
Moves in an instant if the buzzing flie
Stir but a string of her lawn canapie.[2]
> *Ibid.*

Even as a surgeon, minding off to cut
Some cureless limb, — before in ure he
put
His violent engins on the vicious member,
Bringeth his patient in a senseless
slumber,
And grief-less then (guided by use and
art),
To save the whole, sawes off th' infested
part.
> *Ibid.*

Two souls in one, two hearts into one
heart.[3]
> *Ibid.*

Which serves for cynosure [4]
To all that sail upon the sea obscure.
> *Ibid. Seventh Day*

Living from hand to mouth.
> *Second Week. First Day, Part 4*

In the jaws of death.[5]
> *Ibid.*

Will change the pebbles of our puddly
thought
To orient pearls.[6]
> *Ibid. Third Day, Part 1*

Soft carpet-knights,[7] all scenting musk
and amber.
> *Ibid.*

The act of order to a peopled kingdom.
   SHAKESPEARE: *King Henry V,*
      Act I, Sc. 2, L. 187
[1] The windows of mine eyes.
   SHAKESPEARE: *King Richard III,*
      Act V, Sc. 3, L. 117
[2] See Davies, page 115.
[3] See Pope, page 219.
[4] The cynosure of neighbouring eyes.
      MILTON: *L'Allegro, L. 80*
[5] See Shakespeare, page 56, and Tennyson,
page 467.
[6] Sow'd the earth with orient pearl.
   MILTON: *Paradise Lost, Book 5, L. 2*
Orient pearls. — SHAKESPEARE: *A Midsummer-Night's Dream, Act IV, Sc. 1, L. 60*
[7] See Burton, page 123, and Montaigne,
page 1027.

The will for deed I doe accept.[1]

Second Week. Third Day, Part 2

Only that he may conform
To tyrant custom.[2]

Ibid.

Who breaks his faith, no faith is held
with him.

Ibid. Fourth Day, Book 2

Who well lives, long lives; for this age
of ours
Should not be numbered by years, daies,
and hours.

Ibid.

My lovely living boy,
My hope, my hap, my love, my life, my
joy.[3]

Ibid.

Out of the book of Natur's learned
brest.[4]

Ibid.

Flesh of thy flesh, nor yet bone of thy
bone.

Ibid.

Through thick and thin, both over hill
and plain.[5]

Ibid. Book 4

Weakened and wasted to skin and
bone.[6]

Ibid.

I take the world to be but as a stage,
Where net-maskt men do play their
personage.[7]

*Dialogue Between Heraclitus and
Democritus*

Made no more bones.

The Maiden Blush

---

[1] See Swift, page 192.
[2] The tyrant custom.
SHAKESPEARE: *Othello, Act I, Sc. 3, L. 230*
[3] My fair son!
My life, my joy, my food, my all the
world.
SHAKESPEARE: *King John,
Act III, Sc. 4, L. 103*
[4] The book of Nature is that which the
physician must read; and to do so he must
walk over the leaves. — PARACELSUS [1493–
1541]. Quoted in *Encyclopaedia Britannica*
(9th ed.), *Vol. 18, P. 234*
[5] See Chaucer, page 6.
[6] See John Byrom, page 221.
[7] See Shakespeare, page 49, and Du Bartas,
page 1031.

MIGUEL DE CERVANTES
[1547–1616]

From Don Quixote, translated by
PETER ANTHONY MOTTEUX [*died
1718*]. *The page numbers are those
of the Modern Library Giant edition.*

You are a King by your own Fireside, as much as any Monarch in his
Throne.

The Author's Preface. Page XIX

I was so free with him as not to mince
the matter.[1]

Ibid. Page XX

They can expect nothing but their
labour for their pains.[2]

Ibid. Page XXIII

Time out of mind.[3]

Part I. Book I, Chap. 1, Page 4

As ill-luck would have it.[4]

Ibid. Chap. 2, Page 12

The brave man carves out his fortune, and every man is the son of his
own works.[5]

Ibid. Chap. 4, Page 22

Which I have earned with the sweat
of my brows.

Ibid.

By a small sample we may judge of
the whole piece.

Ibid. Page 25

Put you in this pickle.

Ibid. Chap. 5, Page 30

Can we ever have too much of a good
thing?[6]

Ibid. Chap. 6, Page 37

Fortune may have yet a better success in reserve for you, and they who
lose to-day may win to-morrow.

Ibid. Chap. 7, Page 39

The charging of his enemy was but
the work of a moment.

Ibid. Chap. 8, Page 50

---

[1] You mince matters. — MOLIÈRE: *Tartuffe,
Act I, Sc. 1*
[2] See Shakespeare, page 74.
[3] Time out o' mind. — SHAKESPEARE: *Romeo and Juliet, Act I, Sc. 4, L. 70*
[4] As good luck would have it. — SHAKE-
SPEARE: *The Merry Wives of Windsor, Act III,
Sc. 5, L. 86*
[5] See Bacon, page 111.
[6] See Shakespeare, page 51.

I don't know that ever I saw one in my born days.[1]

Part I. Book II, Chap. 2, Page 57

Those two fatal words, Mine and Thine.[2]

Ibid. Chap. 3, Page 63

The eyes those silent tongues of Love.

Ibid. Page 65

Ambrose and his friends will carry the day.

Ibid. Chap. 4, Page 67

As good-natured a soul as e'er trod on shoe of leather.

Ibid. Page 69

And had a face like a blessing.[3]

Ibid.

He's a good man, I'll say that for him, and a true Christian every inch of him.

Ibid. Page 70

There's not the least thing can be said or done, but people will talk and find fault.[4]

Ibid.

Without a wink of sleep.[5]

Ibid. Page 72

One swallow never makes a summer.[6]

Ibid. Page 77

Everything disturbs an absent lover.

Ibid. Page 84

It is a true saying, that a man must eat a peck of salt with his friend, before he knows him.

Ibid. Book III, Chap. 1, Page 92

---

[1] Many of the phrases and proverbs are repeated elsewhere in *Don Quixote*. Only the first appearance is given here.

[2] See Boileau, page 1050.

[3] He had a face like a benediction. — JARVIS's translation

[4] See Samuel Dodge, page 474.

Take wife, or cowl; ride you, or walk:
Doubt not but tongues will have their
  talk.
        JEAN DE LA FONTAINE: *The Miller,
          His Son, and the Donkey*

Do you think you could keep people from talking? — MOLIÈRE: *Tartuffe, Act I, Sc. 1*

[5] I have not slept one wink. — SHAKESPEARE: *Cymbeline, Act III, Sc. 4, L. 103*

[6] See Heywood, page 16.

Fortune leaves always some door open to come at a remedy.

Part I. Book III, Chap. 1, Page 94

Thank you for nothing.

Ibid.

Fair and softly goes far.

Ibid. Chap. 2, Page 97

May Old Nick [1] rock my cradle.

Ibid. Chap. 3, Page 103

No limits but the sky.[2]

Ibid. Page 110

To give the devil his due.[3]

Ibid. Page 111

Plain as the nose on a man's face.[4]

Ibid. Chap. 4, Page 112

A peck of troubles.

Ibid.

The short and long is.

Ibid.

Lest we leap out of the frying-pan into the fire; [5] or, out of God's blessing into the warm sun.[5]

Ibid.

You're leaping over the hedge before you come to the stile.

Ibid. Page 117

You're taking the wrong sow by the ear.[6]

Ibid.

Paid him in his own coin.

Ibid. Page 119

Bell, book, and candle.

Ibid. Page 120

Every tooth in a man's head is more valuable than a diamond.

Ibid. Page 121

The famous Don Quixote de la Mancha, otherwise called The Knight of the Woeful Figure.[7]

Ibid. Chap. 5, Page 126

---

[1] Nick Machiavel had ne'er a trick,
  Though he gave his name to our Old Nick.
        BUTLER: *Hudibras, Part 3,
          Canto 1, L. 1313*

[2] Modern saying: The sky's the limit.

[3] See Shakespeare, page 61.

[4] See *Ibid.*, page 33.

[5] See Heywood, page 16.

[6] See *Ibid.*, page 17.

[7] Elsewhere translated as Rueful Countenance.

Let the worst come to the worst.[1]
Part I. Book III, Chap. 5, Page 127

You are come off now with a whole skin.
Ibid.

Get out of harm's way.
Ibid. Chap. 6, Page 130

Fear is sharp-sighted, and can see things under ground, and much more in the skies.
Ibid. Page 131

One of those carpet-knights[2] that abandon themselves to sleep and lazy ease.
Ibid.

A finger in every pie.[3]
Ibid. Page 133

No better than she should be.
Ibid.

Every dog has his day.
Ibid.

That's the nature of women, . . . not to love when we love them, and to love when we love them not.
Ibid.

You may go whistle for the rest.
Ibid. Page 134

Ill-luck, you know, seldom comes alone.[4]
Ibid. Page 135

Why do you lead me a wild-goose chase?
Ibid. Page 136

I find my familiarity with thee has bred contempt.[5]
Ibid.

Experience, the universal Mother of Sciences.
Ibid. Chap. 7, Page 140

I tell thee, that's Mambrino's helmet.[1]
Part I. Book III, Chap. 7, Page 141

I give up the ghost.
Ibid. Page 143

Give me but that, and let the world rub, there I'll stick.
Ibid. Page 148

Ne'er cringe nor creep, for what you by force may reap.
Ibid. Page 149

'Tis an office of more trust to shave a man's beard than to saddle a horse.
Ibid. Page 151

Sing away sorrow, cast away care.
Ibid. Chap. 8, Page 153

After meat comes mustard; or, like money to a starving man at sea, when there are no victuals to be bought with it.
Ibid.

Of good natural parts, and of a liberal education.
Ibid. Page 154

A medley of kindred, that 'twould puzzle a convocation of casuists to resolve their degrees of consanguinity.
Ibid. Page 155

I know it all by heart.
Ibid. Page 157

Let every man mind his own business.
Ibid.

Murder will out.[2]
Ibid.

Those who'll play with cats must expect to be scratched.
Ibid. Page 159

The main chance.[3]
Ibid.

Raise a hue and cry.
Ibid.

Return to our flesh-pots of Egypt.
Ibid. Page 160

Nor do they care a straw.[4]
Ibid. Chap. 9, Page 161

---

[1] See Middleton, page 116.
[2] See Burton, page 123, and Montaigne, page 1027.
[3] No pie was baked at Castlewood but her little finger was in it. — THACKERAY: *The Virginians, Chap. 5*
[4] One woe doth tread upon another's heel.
SHAKESPEARE: *Hamlet, Act IV, Sc. 7, L. 164*
[5] See Shakespeare, page 34, and Aesop, page 961.

---

[1] Mambrino, a Saracen of great valour, who had a golden helmet, which Rinaldo took from him. — ARIOSTO [1474–1533]: *Orlando Furioso, Canto I*
[2] See Chaucer, page 6.
[3] See Lyly, page 23.
[4] See Terence, page 979.

'Tis the part of a wise man to keep himself to-day for to-morrow, and not venture all his eggs in one basket.

Part I. Book III, Chap. 9, Page 162

I know what's what.

Ibid.

The ease of my burdens, the staff of my life.

Ibid. Page 163

I'm almost frighted out of my seven senses.[1]

Ibid. Page 168

Within a stone's throw of it.

Ibid. Page 170

'Tis the only comfort of the miserable to have partners in their woes.[2]

Ibid. Chap. 10, Page 173

The very remembrance of my former misfortune proves a new one to me.

Ibid. Page 174

Absence, that common cure of love.

Ibid. Page 177

Lovers are commonly industrious to make themselves uneasy.

Ibid. Page 179

From pro's and con's they fell to a warmer way of disputing.

Ibid. Page 181

Make hay while the sun shines.[3]

Ibid. Chap. 11, Page 182

I never thrust my nose into other men's porridge. It is no bread and butter of mine; every man for himself, and God for us all.[4]

Ibid. Page 183

Naked came I into the world, and naked must I go out.

Ibid.

Little said is soon amended.[5]

Ibid. Page 184

A close mouth catches no flies.

Ibid.

She may guess what I should perform in the wet, if I do so much in the dry.[1]

Part I. Book III, Chap. 11, Page 186

Mere flim-flam stories,[2] and nothing but shams and lies.

Ibid. Page 187

To tell you the truth.

Ibid. Page 190

Thou hast seen nothing yet.

Ibid.

For goodness-sake.

Ibid.

Between jest and earnest.

Ibid.

Cutting the air as swift as a witch upon a broomstick.

Ibid. Page 191

My love and hers have always been purely Platonick.

Ibid. Page 192

'Tis ten to one.

Ibid. Page 193

As sure as I'm alive.

Ibid.

There's no need to make an enquiry about a woman's pedigree, as there is of us men, when some badge of honour is bestowed on us.

Ibid. Page 194

There are but two things that chiefly excite us to love a woman, an attractive beauty, and unspotted fame.

Ibid. Page 195

'Tis ill talking of halters in the house of a man that was hanged.

Ibid.

My memory is so bad, that many times I forget my own name!

Ibid.

You're a devil at everything; and there's no kind of thing in the versal world but what you can turn your hand to.

Ibid. Page 196

'Twill grieve me so to the heart, that I shall cry my eyes out.

Ibid. Page 197

---

[1] See Scott, page 310.
[2] See Publilius Syrus, *Maxim 995*, and Spinoza, page 1049.
[3] See Heywood, page 12.
[4] See *Ibid.*, page 18.
[5] Little said is soonest mended. GEORGE WITHER: *The Shepherd's Hunting*

[1] An allusion to *Luke, XXIII, 31*, — For if they do these things in a green tree, what shall be done in the dry?
[2] You must not think to put us off with a flim-flam story. — *Don Quixote, P. 203*

Without knowing why or wherefore.
Part I. Book III, Chap. 11, Page 197
Ready to split his sides with laughing.
Ibid. Chap. 13, Page 208
As much a fool as he was, he loved money, and knew how to keep it when he had it, and was wise enough to keep his own counsel.
Ibid.
What man has assurance enough to pretend to know thoroughly the riddle of a woman's mind, and who could ever hope to fix her mutable nature? [1]
Ibid. Page 216
Demonstrations of love are never altogether displeasing to women, and the most disdainful, in spite of all their coyness, reserve a little complaisance in their hearts for their admirers.
Ibid. Book IV, Chap. 1, Page 226
My honour is dearer to me than my life.
Ibid. Page 228
On the word of a gentleman, and a Christian.
Ibid. Chap. 2, Page 236
Delay always breeds danger. [2]
Ibid. Page 240
Higgledy-piggledy.
Ibid. Page 241
Let things go at sixes and sevens. [3]
Ibid. Chap. 3, Page 250
Think before thou speakest.
Ibid. Page 252
Let us forget and forgive injuries.
Ibid. Page 254
I must speak the truth, and nothing but the truth.
Ibid. Page 255
They must needs go whom the Devil drives. [4]
Ibid. Chap. 4, Page 259
A bird in hand is worth two in the bush. [5]
Ibid.

[1] A fickle and changeful thing is woman ever. — VIRGIL: *Aeneid, Book 4, L. 569*
[2] See Shakespeare, page 68.
[3] See W. S. Gilbert, page 623.
[4] See Heywood, page 17.
[5] See *Ibid.*, page 15, and Plutarch, page 1005.

More knave than fool. [1]
Part I. Book IV, Chap. 4, Page 261
Mind your own business.
Ibid. Page 263
A fig for your great captain.
Ibid. Chap. 5, Page 267
I can tell where my own shoe pinches me; [2] and you must not think, sir, to catch old birds with chaff.
Ibid.
Within the bounds of possibility.
Ibid. Chap. 6, Page 283
The ornament of her sex. [3]
Ibid. Chap. 7, Page 287
He that gives quickly gives twice. [4]
Ibid. Page 291
Thank your stars.
Ibid. Page 292
Required in every good lover . . . the whole alphabet . . . Agreeable, Bountiful, Constant, Dutiful, Easy, Faithful, Gallant, Honourable, Ingenious, Kind, Loyal, Mild, Noble, Officious, Prudent, Quiet, Rich, Secret, True, Valiant, Wise . . . Young and Zealous.
Ibid.
Harp so on the same string.
Ibid. Chap. 8, Page 305
At his wit's end. [5]
Ibid. Page 306
She made a virtue of necessity. [6]
Ibid. Chap. 9, Page 313
Virtue is the truest nobility.
Ibid. Page 314
Here's the devil-and-all to pay.
Ibid. Chap. 10, Page 319
I begin to smell a rat. [7]
Ibid.
I'll take my corporal oath on 't.
Ibid. Page 321
The proof of the pudding is in the eating.
Ibid. Page 322

[1] More knave than fool. — CHRISTOPHER MARLOWE: *The Jew of Malta, Act 2*
[2] See Plutarch, page 997.
[3] She's the ornament of her sex. — DICKENS: *The Old Curiosity Shop, Chap. 5*
[4] Bis dat qui cito dat. — *Latin proverb*
[5] See Heywood, page 13.
[6] See Chaucer, page 4.
[7] See Middleton, page 116.

Let none presume to tell me that the pen is preferable to the sword.[1]

Part I. Book IV, Chap. 10, Page 325

By hook or by crook.[2]

Ibid. Page 328

It is past all controversy, that what costs dearest, is, and ought most to be valued.

Ibid. Chap. 11, Page 328

It seldom happens that any felicity comes so pure as not to be tempered and allayed by some mixture of sorrow.

Ibid. Chap. 14, Page 359

Stopped them in the nick.[3]

Ibid. Chap. 17, Page 383

There's no striving against the stream; and the weakest still goes to the wall.

Ibid. Chap. 20, Page 404

The bow cannot always stand bent, nor can human frailty subsist without some lawful recreation.

Ibid. Chap. 21, Page 412

Give them the slip.[4]

Ibid. Chap. 22, Page 415

Faith without good works is dead.

Ibid. Chap. 23, Page 423

I would have nobody to control me, I would be absolute; and who but I? Now, he that is absolute can do what he likes; he that can do what he likes, can take his pleasure; he that can take his pleasure, can be content; and he that can be content, has no more to desire. So the matter's over; and come what will come, I am satisfied.[5]

Ibid.

---

[1] See Edward Bulwer Lytton, page 425.
Scholars' pens carry farther, and give a louder report than thunder. — Sir Thomas Browne: *Religio Medici* (Everyman ed.), P. 70
[2] See Skelton, page 10.
[3] Nick of time. — Suckling: *The Goblins*, Act 5
[4] Judas had given them the slip. — Mathew Henry: *Commentaries, Matthew XXII*
[5] I would do what I pleased; and doing what I pleased, I should have my will; and having my will, I should be contented; and when one is contented, there is no more to be desired; and when there is no more to be desired, there is an end of it. — Jarvis's translation

Even a worm when trod upon, will turn again.[1]

Part II. Book III, Author's Preface, Page 440

It is not the hand, but the understanding of a man, that may be said to write.[2]

Ibid. Page 441

Had only now and then lucid intervals.[3]

Ibid. Chap. 1, Page 448

How blind must he be that can't see through a sieve.

Ibid. Page 450

Keep within bounds.

Ibid. Chap. 2, Page 455

When the head aches, all the members partake of the pains.[4]

Ibid.

While there's life there's hope.[5]

Ibid. Chap. 3, Page 463

Miracle me no miracles.

Ibid. Page 464

He has done like Orbaneja, the painter of Ubeda; who, being asked what he painted, answered, "As it may hit;" and when he had scrawled out a misshapen cock, was forced to write underneath in Gothic letters, "This is a cock."[6]

Ibid.

Youngsters read it, grown men understand it, and old people applaud it.

Ibid.

The most artful part in a play is the fool's.

Ibid. Page 465

---

[1] The smallest worm will turn, being trodden on.
Shakespeare: *King Henry VI, Part III, Act II, Sc. 2, L. 17*
[2] Cervantes' left hand was maimed for life by gunshot wounds in the battle of Lepanto.
[3] See Robert South, page 183.
[4] For let our finger ache, and it indues
Our other healthful members even to that sense
Of pain.
Shakespeare: *Othello, Act III, Sc. 4, L. 145*
[5] See Gay, page 206.
[6] The painter Orbaneja of Ubeda, if he chanced to draw a cock, he wrote under it, "This is a cock," lest the people should take it for a fox. — Jarvis's translation

There are men that will make you books, and turn 'em loose into the world, with as much dispatch as they would do a dish of fritters.

Part II. Book III, Chap. 3, Page 465

"There is no book so bad," said the bachelor, "but something good may be found in it." [1]

Ibid.

He that publishes a book runs a very great hazard, since nothing can be more impossible than to compose one that may secure the approbation of every reader.

Ibid. Page 466

Ready cash.

Ibid. Chap. 4, Page 468

Every man is as Heaven made him, and sometimes a great deal worse.

Ibid.

Rejoices the cockles of my heart. [2]

Ibid. Chap. 5, Page 472

There's no sauce in the world like hunger.

Ibid. Page 473

Birds of a feather flock together.

Ibid. Page 474

He casts a sheep's eye at the wench.

Ibid.

I ever loved to see everything upon the square.

Ibid. Page 475

Neither will I make myself anybody's laughing-stock.

Ibid.

That feather in their caps.

Ibid. Page 476

Stand in thy own light.

Ibid.

In the twinkling of an eye. [3]

Ibid.

Journey over all the universe in a map, without the expense and fatigue of travelling, without suffering the inconveniences of heat, cold, hunger, and thirst.

Ibid. Chap. 6, Page 479

Presume to put in her oar.

Ibid. Page 480

[1] See Pliny the Younger, page 1009.
[2] See Miscellaneous, page 944.
[3] See Shakespeare, page 45.

The fair sex. [1]

Part II. Book III, Chap. 6, Page 480

A little in one's own pocket is better than much in another man's purse. 'Tis good to keep a nest-egg. Every little makes a mickle.

Ibid. Chap. 7, Page 486

That's neither here nor there.

Ibid. Chap. 9, Page 498

Remember the old saying, "Faint heart ne'er won fair lady." [2]

Ibid. Chap. 10, Page 501

Fore-warned fore-armed.

Ibid. Page 502

As well look for a needle in a bottle of hay. [3]

Ibid.

Sleeveless errants. [4]

Ibid.

Are we to mark this day with a white or a black stone?

Ibid. Page 503

Spare your breath to cool your porridge. [5]

Ibid. Page 505

A great cry, but little wool. [6]

Ibid. Chap. 13, Page 520

The very pink of courtesy. [7]

Ibid. Page 521

Neither fish, flesh, nor good red-herring. [8]

Ibid.

I'll turn over a new leaf. [9]

Ibid. Page 524

Let every man look before he leaps. [10]

Ibid. Chap. 14, Page 528

[1] See Addison, page 198.
[2] SPENSER: *Britain's Ida, Canto V, St. 1.* ELLERTON: *George-a-Greene* (a ballad). WHETSTONE: *Rocke of Regard.* BURNS: *To Dr. Blacklock.* COLMAN: *Love Laughs at Locksmiths, Act I.* GILBERT: *Iolanthe, Act II*
[3] Needle in a bottle of hay. — NATHANIEL FIELD: *A Woman's a Weathercock* [1612]
[4] See Heywood, page 13.
[5] See Plutarch, page 1004.
[6] See John Fortescue, page 9.
[7] I am the very pink of courtesy.
   SHAKESPEARE: *Romeo and Juliet, Act II, Sc. 4, L. 63*
[8] See Heywood, page 13.
[9] See Middleton, page 117.
[10] See Heywood, page 11.

As one egg is like another.[1]

Part II. Book III, Chap. 14, Page 530

The pen is the tongue of the mind.

Ibid. Chap. 16, Page 543

Modesty is a virtue not often found among poets, for almost every one of them thinks himself the greatest in the world.

Ibid. Chap. 18, Page 555

Sings like a lark.

Ibid. Chap. 19, Page 564

Marriage is a noose.

Ibid.

She'll give Camacho the bag to hold.

Ibid. Page 565

There were but two families in the world, Have-much and Have-little.

Ibid. Chap. 20, Page 574

He preaches well that lives well, quoth Sancho, that's all the divinity I understand.

Ibid. Page 575

Love and War are the same thing, and stratagems and policy are as allowable in the one as in the other.

Ibid. Chap. 21, Page 580

A private sin is not so prejudicial in this world as a public indecency.

Ibid. Chap. 22, Page 582

He has an oar in every man's boat, and a finger in every pie.[2]

Ibid. Page 583

There is no love lost, sir.[3]

Ibid.

Come back sound, wind and limb.

Ibid. Page 587

Patience, and shuffle the cards.[4]

Ibid. Chap. 23, Page 592

Comparisons are odious.[5]

Ibid. Page 593

Tell me thy company, and I'll tell thee what thou art.[6]

Ibid. Page 594

---

[1] See Shakespeare, page 56, and Rabelais, page 1026.
[2] See Cervantes, page 1035.
[3] See Jonson, page 118.
[4] See Sir Walter Scott, page 311.
[5] See Fortescue, page 9.
[6] Show me your garden and I shall tell you what you are. — ALFRED AUSTIN: *The Garden That I Love* [1905], *P. 98*
Tell me what you eat, and I will tell you

Returning the compliment.

Part II. Book III, Chap. 25, Page 606

To-morrow will be a new day.

Ibid. Chap. 26, Page 618

Like a man of mettle.[1]

Ibid. Chap. 27, Page 625

You can see farther into a millstone than he.[2]

Ibid. Chap. 28, Page 628

I can see with half an eye.

Ibid. Chap. 29, Page 632

Scum of the world.[3]

Ibid. Page 635

The apples of his eyes.[4]

Ibid. Chap. 30, Page 637

Old . . . that's an affront no woman can well bear.

Ibid. Chap. 31, Page 644

One of the most considerable advantages the great have over their inferiors, is to have servants as good as themselves.

Ibid. Page 645

Speak the truth and shame the devil.[5]

Ibid. Page 647

"Sit there, clod-pate!" cried he; "for let me sit wherever I will, that will still be the upper end, and the place of worship to thee."[6]

Ibid. Page 648

Building castles in the air.[7]

Ibid.

Upon second thoughts.[8]

Ibid. Chap. 32, Page 653

Made 'em pay dear for their frolic.

Ibid. Page 655

---

what you are. — ANTHELME BRILLAT-SAVARIN: *Physiologie du Goût, Aphorism 4*
[1] A lad of mettle. — SHAKESPEARE: *King Henry IV, Part I, Act II, Sc. 4, L. 13*
A man of mettle. — AARON HILL: *Verses Written on a Window in Scotland*
[2] See Heywood, page 14.
[3] See R. H. Schauffler, page 860.
[4] The apple of his eye. — *Deuteronomy, XXXII, 10*
The apple of the eye. — *Psalm XVII, 8*
[5] See Shakespeare, page 62.
[6] Sit thee down, chaff-threshing churl! for let me sit where I will, that is the upper end to thee. — JARVIS's translation
See Emerson, page 414.
[7] See Burton, page 122.
[8] See Dryden, page 179

'Tis good to live and learn.
Part II. Book III, Chap. 32, Page 655
Great persons are able to do great kindnesses.
Ibid. Page 662
He's as mad as a March hare.[1]
Ibid. Chap. 33, Page 664
In the night all cats are gray.[2]
Ibid. Page 665
All is not gold that glisters.[3]
Ibid. Page 666
Honesty's the best policy.[4]
Ibid.
A good name is better than riches.[5]
Ibid. Page 668
An honest man's word is as good as his bond.
Ibid. Book IV, Chap. 34, Page 674
Heaven's help is better than early rising.
Ibid.
He would not budge an inch.[6]
Ibid. Page 677
A blot in thy scutcheon to all futurity.
Ibid. Chap. 35, Page 681
This is no time for me to mind niceties, and spelling of letters. I have other fish to fry.[7]
Ibid. Page 682
There's a time for some things, and a time for all things; a time for great things, and a time for small things.[8]
Ibid.
The worst is still behind.[9]
Ibid. Page 683
'Twill do you a world of good.
Ibid.

[1] See Heywood, page 17.
[2] See *Ibid.*, page 13.
[3] See Chaucer, page 8.
[4] I hold the maxim no less applicable to public than to private affairs, that honesty is always the best policy. — GEORGE WASHINGTON: *Farewell Address* [1796]
[5] See Publilius Syrus, *Maxim 108*, and Old Testament, page 1109.
[6] See Shakespeare, page 51.
[7] See Rabelais, page 1026.
[8] To everything there is a season, and a time to every purpose. — *Ecclesiastes, III, 1*
[9] Aun le falta la cola por desollar (The tail still remains to be flayed). — Spanish proverb

But all in good time.
Part II. Book IV, Chap. 36, Page 686
With a grain of salt.
Ibid. Chap. 37, Page 690
They had best not stir the rice, though it sticks to the pot.
Ibid. Page 691
They cover a dunghill with a piece of tapestry when a procession goes by.
Ibid.
Good wits jump; [1] a word to the wise is enough.
Ibid. Page 692
My understanding has forsook me, and is gone a wool-gathering.[2]
Ibid. Chap. 38, Page 692
You may as well expect pears from an elm.[3]
Ibid. Chap. 40, Page 704
Make it thy business to know thyself, which is the most difficult lesson in the world.[4]
Ibid. Chap. 42, Page 719
You cannot eat your cake and have your cake; [5] and store's no sore.[6]
Ibid. Chap. 43, Page 723
Diligence is the mother of good fortune.
Ibid. Page 724
What a man has, so much he's sure of.
Ibid. Page 725
When a man says, "Get out of my house! what would you have with my wife?" there's no answer to be made.
Ibid. Page 726
The pot calls the kettle black.
Ibid. Page 727
Mum's the word.[7]
Ibid. Chap. 44, Page 729
Walls have ears.[8]
Ibid. Chap. 48, Page 763
Set a beggar on horseback.[9]
Ibid. Chap. 50, Page 782

[1] See Laurence Sterne, page 241.
[2] My thoughts ran a wool-gathering; and I did like the countryman, who looked for his ass while he was mounted on his back. — *Don Quixote, P. 827*
[3] See Publilius Syrus, *Maxim 674.*
[4] See Burton, page 544.
[5] See Heywood, page 18.
[6] See *Ibid.*, page 12.
[7] See Shakespeare, page 35.
[8] See Chaucer, page 6.
[9] See Burton, page 124.

I may at last hit the nail o' the head.[1]
Part II. Book IV, Chap. 51, Page 785
When thou art at Rome, do as they do at Rome.[2]
Ibid. Chap. 54, Page 806
Man appoints, and God disappoints.[3]
Ibid. Chap. 55, Page 816
Many count their chickens before they are hatched; and where they expect bacon meet with broken bones.
Ibid.
As they use to say, spick and span new.[4]
Ibid. Chap. 58, Page 829
I think it a very happy accident.[5]
Ibid. Page 831
He that proclaims the kindnesses he has received, shows his disposition to repay 'em if he could.
Ibid. Page 835
He that errs in so considerable a passage, may well be suspected to have committed many gross errors through the whole history.
Ibid. Chap. 59, Page 843
A gift-horse should not be looked in the mouth.[6]
Ibid. Chap. 62, Page 861
I shall be as secret as the grave.
Ibid. Page 862
Now blessings light on him that first invented this same sleep! It covers a man all over, thoughts and all, like a cloak; 'tis meat for the hungry, drink for the thirsty, heat for the cold, and cold for the hot. 'Tis the current coin that purchases all the pleasures of the world cheap; and the balance that sets the king and the shepherd, the fool and the wise man even.[7]
Ibid. Chap. 68, Page 898

All the fat shall be in the fire.[1]
Part II. Book IV, Chap. 69, Page 906
There is a thing called poetical license.
Ibid. Chap. 70, Page 913
Rome was not built in a day.[2]
Ibid. Chap. 71, Page 917
The ass will carry his load, but not a double load; ride not a free horse to death.
Ibid.
I thought it working for a dead horse, because I am paid beforehand.[3]
Ibid.
Nothing like striking while the iron is hot.[4]
Ibid. Page 919
Thereby hangs a tale.[5]
Ibid. Chap. 72, Page 923
He . . . got the better of himself, and that's the best kind of victory one can wish for.
Ibid. Page 924
Every man was not born with a silver spoon in his mouth.
Ibid. Chap. 73, Page 926
Die merely of the mulligrubs.
Ibid. Chap. 74, Page 932
Get out of your doleful dumps.[6]
Ibid.
Ne'er look for birds of this year in the nests of the last.[7]
Ibid. Page 933
There is a strange charm in the thoughts of a good legacy, or the hopes of an estate, which wondrously allevi-

---

[1] See Heywood, page 18, Fletcher, page 127, and Rabelais, page 1025.
[2] See Burton, page 126.
[3] See Thomas à Kempis, page 8.
[4] See Middleton, page 116.
[5] See *Ibid.*, page 117.
[6] See Heywood, page 13, Butler, page 142, and Rabelais, page 1025.
[7] Blessing on him who invented sleep, — the mantle that covers all human thoughts, the food that appeases hunger, the drink that quenches thirst, the fire that warms cold, the cold that moderates heat, and, lastly, the gen-

eral coin that purchases all things, the balance and weight that equals the shepherd with the king, and the simple with the wise. — JARvis's translation
[1] See Heywood, page 12.
[2] See *Ibid.*, page 15.
[3] It is a heart-rending delusion and a cruel snare to be paid for your work before you accomplish it. As soon as once your work is finished you ought to be promptly paid; but to receive your lucre one minute before it is due, is to tempt Providence to make a Micawber of you. — EDMUND GOSSE: *Gossip in a Library, Beau Nash* [1891], P. 230
[4] See Heywood, page 12.
[5] See Shakespeare, page 34, and Rabelais, page 1026.
[6] See Shakespeare, page 77.
[7] See Longfellow, page 434.

ates the sorrow that men would otherwise feel for the death of friends.
> *Part II. Book IV, Chap. 74, Page 934*

For if he like a madman lived,
At least he like a wise one died.
> *Ibid. Page 935 (Don Quixote's*
> *Epitaph)*

Don't put too fine a point to your wit
for fear it should get blunted.
> *The Little Gypsy*
> *(La Gitanilla)*

My heart is wax moulded as she
pleases, but enduring as marble to retain.[1]
> *Ibid.*

BARTHOLOMEW SCHIDONI
[1560–1616]

I, too, was born in Arcadia.[2]
> *Adopted by* Goethe *as the*
> *motto for his Travels in Italy*
> *[1816]*

PIERRE CORNEILLE
[1606–1684]

We easily believe that which we wish.
> *Le Baron. Act I, Sc. 3*

Do your duty, and leave the rest to
heaven.
> *Horace [1640]. Act II, Sc. 8*

Who is all-powerful should fear everything.
> *Cinna [1640]. Act IV, Sc. 2*

The manner of giving is worth more
than the gift.
> *Le Menteur [1642]. Act I, Sc. 1*

A kindness loses its grace by being
noised abroad,
Who desires it to be remembered should
forget it.
> *Théodore. Act I, Sc. 2*

A service beyond all recompense
Weighs so heavy that it almost gives
offence.
> *Suréna [1674]. Act III, Sc. 1*

---

[1] Wax to receive, and marble to retain.
> Byron: *Beppo, St. 34*

[2] Et ego in Arcadia vixi [I, too, have lived
in Arcadia], motto used by Nicolas Poussin
(1594–1665) for his famous painting *Les
Bergers d'Arcadie*.

ISAAC DE BENSERADE
[1612–1691]

In bed we laugh, in bed we cry;
And, born in bed, in bed we die.
The near approach a bed may show
Of human bliss to human woe.
> *Translated by* Dr. Samuel
> Johnson

FRANÇOIS, DUC DE LA
ROCHEFOUCAULD
[1613–1680]

Reflections, or Sentences and Moral
Maxims

Our virtues are most frequently but
vices disguised.[1]

We have all sufficient strength to endure the misfortunes of others.
> *Maxim 19*

Philosophy triumphs easily over past
evils and future evils; but present evils
triumph over it.[2]
> *Maxim 22*

We need greater virtues to sustain
good than evil fortune.
> *Maxim 25*

Neither the sun nor death can be
looked at with a steady eye.
> *Maxim 26*

If we were without faults, we should
not take so much pleasure in remarking
them in others.
> *Maxim 31*

Interest speaks all sorts of tongues,
and plays all sorts of parts, even that
of disinterestedness.
> *Maxim 39*

We are never so happy nor so unhappy as we imagine.
> *Maxim 49*

---

[1] This epigraph, which is the key to the
system of La Rochefoucauld, is found in another form as No. 179 of the Maxims of the
first edition, 1665; it is omitted from the second and third, and reappears for the first time
in the fourth edition at the head of the Reflections. — Aime Martin

[2] See Goldsmith, page 253.

There are few people who would not be ashamed of being loved when they love no longer.

Maxim 71

True love is like ghosts, which everybody talks about and few have seen.

Maxim 76

The love of justice is simply, in the majority of men, the fear of suffering injustice.

Maxim 78

Silence is the best resolve for him who distrusts himself.

Maxim 79

Friendship is only a reciprocal conciliation of interests, and an exchange of good offices; it is a species of commerce out of which self-love always expects to gain something.

Maxim 83

Everyone complains of his memory, and no one complains of his judgment.

Maxim 89

A man who is ungrateful is often less to blame than his benefactor.

Maxim 96

The understanding is always the dupe of the heart.

Maxim 102

Nothing is given so profusely as advice.

Maxim 110

The true way to be deceived is to think oneself more knowing than others.

Maxim 127

Usually we praise only to be praised.

Maxim 146

Our repentance is not so much regret for the ill we have done as fear of the ill that may happen to us in consequence.

Maxim 180

Most people judge men only by success or by fortune.

Maxim 212

Hypocrisy is a homage vice pays to virtue.

Maxim 218

Too great haste to repay an obligation is a kind of ingratitude.

Maxim 226

There is great ability in knowing how to conceal one's ability.

Maxim 245

The pleasure of love is in loving. We are happier in the passion we feel than in that we inspire.[1]

Maxim 259

We always like those who admire us; we do not always like those whom we admire.

Maxim 294

The gratitude of most men is but a secret desire of receiving greater benefits.[2]

Maxim 298

Lovers are never tired of each other, though they always speak of themselves.

Maxim 312

We pardon in the degree that we love.

Maxim 330

We hardly find any persons of good sense save those who agree with us.[3]

Maxim 347

The greatest fault of a penetrating wit is to go beyond the mark.

Maxim 377

We may give advice, but we cannot inspire the conduct.

Maxim 378

The veracity which increases with old age is not far from folly.

Maxim 416

Nothing prevents our being natural so much as the desire to appear so.

Maxim 431

In their first passion women love their lovers, in all the others they love love.[4]

Maxim 471

Quarrels would not last long if the fault was only on one side.

Maxim 496

[1] See Shelley, page 367.
[2] See Walpole, page 200.
[3] "That was excellently observed," say I when I read a passage in another where his opinion agrees with mine. When we differ, then I pronounce him to be mistaken. — SWIFT: *Thoughts on Various Subjects*
[4] See Byron, page 359.

In the adversity of our best friends we often find something that is not exactly displeasing.[1]

To win that wonder of the world,
A smile from her bright eyes,
I fought my King, and would have hurled
The gods out of their skies.[2]

To Madame de Longueville

HANS JAKOB CHRISTOFFEL VON GRIMMELSHAUSEN
[*Circa* 1620–1676]

For gluttony and drunkenness, hunger and thirst, wenching and dicing and playing, riot and roaring, murdering and being murdered, slaying and being slain, torturing and being tortured, hunting and being hunted, harrying and being harried, robbing and being robbed, frighting and being frighted, causing trouble and suffering trouble, beating and being beaten: in a word, hurting and harming, and in turn being hurt and harmed — this was their[3] whole life. And in this career they let nothing hinder them: neither winter nor summer, snow nor ice, heat nor cold, rain nor wind, hill nor dale, wet nor dry; ditches, mountain-passes, ramparts and walls, fire and water, were all the same to them. Father nor mother, sister nor brother, no, nor the danger to their own bodies, souls, and consciences, nor even loss of life and of heaven itself, or aught else that can be named, will ever stand in their way, for ever they toil and moil at their own strange work, till at last, little by little, in battles, sieges, attacks, campaigns,

yea, and in their winter-quarters too (which are the soldiers' earthly paradise, if they can but happen upon fat peasants) they perish, they die, they rot and consume away, save but a few, who in their old age, unless they have been right thrifty reivers and robbers, do furnish us with the best of all beggars and vagabonds.

The Adventurous Simplicissimus.[1]
Book I, Chap. XVI

JEAN DE LA FONTAINE
[1621–1695]

The opinion of the strongest is always the best.

Book I. Fable 10, The Wolf
and the Lamb

By the work one knows the workman.

Ibid. Fable 21, The Hornets
and the Bees

It is a double pleasure to deceive the deceiver.

Book II. Fable 15, The Cock
and the Fox

It is impossible to please all the world and one's father.

Book III. Fable 1, The Man,
the Boy, and the Donkey

In everything one must consider the end.[2]

Ibid. Fable 5, The Fox
and the Gnat

"They are too green," he said, "and only good for fools."[3]

Ibid. Fable 11, The Fox
and the Grapes

Help thyself, and God will help thee.[4]

Book VI. Fable 18, Hercules
and the Waggoner

The sign brings customers.

Book VII. Fable 15, The
Fortune-Tellers

---

[1] This reflection, No. 99 in the edition of 1665, the author suppressed in the third edition.
In all distresses of our friends
We first consult our private ends;
While Nature, kindly bent to ease us,
Points out some circumstance to please us.
DEAN SWIFT: *A Paraphrase of*
Rochefoucauld's Maxim
[2] Quoted by EDMUND GOSSE in *Gossip in a Library, Pharamond* [1891].
[3] The *Landsknechte*, mercenary foot soldiers, of the Thirty Years' War.

[1] Translated by A. T. S. G.; published [1912] by Heinemann, London.
[2] Remember the end, and thou shalt never do amiss. — Apocrypha, *Ecclesiasticus III, 36.*
[3] Sour grapes. See George Herbert, page 137, and Aesop, page 961.
[4] See Herbert, page 137.

Let ignorance talk as it will, learning has its value.

> Book VIII. Fable 19, The
> Use of Knowledge

People who make no noise are dangerous.[1]

> Ibid. Fable 23, The Current
> and the Stream

No path of flowers leads to glory.

> Book X. Fable 14

JEAN BAPTISTE MOLIÈRE [2]
[1622–1673]

The world, dear Agnes, is a strange affair.

> L'École des Femmes [1662].
> Act II, Sc. 6

There are fagots and fagots.

> Le Médecin Malgré Lui
> [1666]. Act I, Sc. 6

We have changed all that.

> Ibid. Act II, Sc. 6

He's a wonderful talker, who has the art of telling you nothing in a great harangue.

> Le Misanthrope [1666].
> Act II, Sc. 5

He makes his cook his merit, and the world visits his dinners and not him.

> Ibid.

You see him in travail to produce bons mots.

> Ibid.

The more we love our friends, the less we flatter them; it is by excusing nothing that pure love shows itself.

> Ibid.

Doubts are more cruel than the worst of truths.

> Ibid. Act III, Sc. 7

Anyone may be an honourable man, and yet write verse badly.

> Ibid. Act IV, Sc. 1

[1] See Raleigh, page 21, and Lyly, page 24.
[2] Of all dramatists, ancient and modern, Molière is perhaps that one who has borne most constantly in mind the theory that the stage is a lay pulpit, and that its end is not merely amusement, but the reformation of manners by means of amusing spectacles. — GEORGE SAINTSBURY: *A Short History of French Literature* [1882], P. 311

If everyone were clothed with integrity, if every heart were just, frank, kindly, the other virtues would be well-nigh useless, since their chief purpose is to make us bear with patience the injustice of our fellows.

> Le Misanthrope [1666].
> Act V, Sc. 1

It is a wonderful seasoning of all enjoyments to think of those we love.

> Ibid. Sc. 4

There is no rampart that will hold out against malice.

> Tartuffe [1667]. Act I, Sc. 1

Those whose conduct gives room for talk are always the first to attack their neighbours.

> Ibid.

She is laughing in her sleeve at you.

> Ibid. Sc. 6

A woman always has her revenge ready.

> Ibid. Act II, Sc. 2

A heart that forgets us puts us on our mettle to forget just as quickly, and, if we don't succeed, at least we make believe to have succeeded.

> Ibid. Sc. 4

Although I am a pious man, I am not the less a man.

> Ibid. Act III, Sc. 3

The real Amphitryon is the Amphitryon who gives dinners.[1]

> Amphitryon [1668]. Act III, Sc. 5

Ah that I — You would have it so, you would have it so; George Dandin, you would have it so! [2] This suits you very nicely, and you are served right; you have precisely what you deserve.

> Georges Dandin [1668]. Act I, Sc. 9

Tell me to whom you are addressing yourself when you say that.

I am addressing myself — I am addressing myself to my cap.

> L'Avare [1668]. Act I, Sc. 3

The beautiful eyes of my cash-box.

> Ibid. Act V, Sc. 3

You are speaking before a man to whom all Naples is known.

> Ibid. Sc. 5

[1] See Dryden, page 179.
[2] Vous l'avez voulu, Georges Dandin.

My fair one, let us swear an eternal friendship.[1]

> *Le Bourgeois Gentilhomme*
> [*1670*]. *Act IV, Sc. 1*

I will maintain it before the whole world.

> *Ibid. Sc. 5*

What the devil did he want in that galley?[2]

> *Les Fourberies de Scapin*
> [*1671*]. *Act II, Sc. 11*

Grammar, which knows how to control even kings.[3]

> *Les Femmes Savantes* [*1672*].
> *Act II, Sc. 6*

It is seasoned throughout with Attic salt.

> *Ibid. Act III, Sc. 2*

Ah, there are no longer any children!

> *Le Malade Imaginaire* [*1673*].
> *Act II, Sc. 11*

Nearly all men die of their remedies, and not of their illnesses.

> *Ibid. Act III, Sc. 3*

BLAISE PASCAL
[1623–1662]
Translation by O. W. WIGHT

Man is but a reed, the weakest in nature, but he is a thinking reed.

> *Thoughts. Chap. 2, 10*

---

[1] See Sydney Smith, page 313.
[2] What the deuce did he want on board a Turk's galley? — CYRANO DE BERGERAC: *Le Pédant Joué, Act II, Sc. 4* [1654]
The saying of Molière came into his head: "But what the devil was he doing in that galley?" and he laughed at himself. — LYOF TOLSTOI: *War and Peace, Part IV, Chap. 6*
Often misquoted, "in that gallery," as in DICKENS's *A Tale of Two Cities, Book I, Chap. 5*: "What the devil do you do in that gallery there!"
[3] Sigismund [1361–1437], Emperor of the Holy Roman Empire, at the Council of Constance [1414], said to a prelate who had objected to his Majesty's grammar: "Ego sum rex Romanus, et supra grammaticam" (I am the Roman emperor, and am above grammar).

It is not permitted to the most equitable of men to be a judge in his own cause.

> *Thoughts. Chap. 4, 1*

Montaigne[1] is wrong in declaring that custom ought to be followed simply because it is custom, and not because it is reasonable or just.

> *Ibid. 6*

Thus we never live, but we hope to live; and always disposing ourselves to be happy, it is inevitable that we never become so.[2]

> *Ibid. Chap. 5, 2*

If the nose of Cleopatra had been shorter, the whole face of the earth would have been changed.

> *Ibid. Chap. 8, 29*

The last thing that we find in making a book is to know what we must put first.

> *Ibid. Chap. 9, 30*

Rivers are highways that move on, and bear us whither we wish to go.

> *Ibid. 38*

What a chimera, then, is man! what a novelty, what a monster, what a chaos, what a subject of contradiction, what a prodigy! A judge of all things, feeble worm of the earth, depositary of the truth, cloaca of uncertainty and error, the glory and the shame of the universe![3]

> *Ibid. Chap. 10, 1*

We know the truth, not only by the reason, but also by the heart.

> *Ibid.*

For as old age is that period of life most remote from infancy, who does not see that old age in this universal man ought not to be sought in the times nearest his birth, but in those most remote from it?[4]

> *Preface to the Treatise on Vacuum*

---

[1] Montaigne, Book I, Chap. 22.
[2] Man never is, but always to be, blest.
POPE: *Essay on Man, Epistle I, L. 96*
[3] See Pope, page 207.
[4] See Bacon, page 112.

JACQUES BÉNIGNE BOSSUET
[1627–1704]

Perfidious England.[1]
First Sermon on the Circumcision [2]

BENEDICT (BARUCH) SPINOZA [3]
[1632–1677]

Nature abhors a vacuum.
Ethics.[4] *Part I, Prop. XV, Note*

God and all the attributes of God are eternal.
Ibid. Prop. XIX

Nothing exists from whose nature some effect does not follow.
Ibid. Prop. XXXVI

He who would distinguish the true from the false must have an adequate idea of what is true and false.
Ibid. Part II, Prop. XLII, Proof

Will and Intellect are one and the same thing.
Ibid. Prop. XLIX, Corollary

He that can carp in the most eloquent or acute manner at the weakness of the human mind is held by his fellows as almost divine.
Ibid. Part III, Preface

Surely human affairs would be far happier if the power in men to be silent were the same as that to speak. But experience more than sufficiently teaches

that men govern nothing with more difficulty than their tongues.
Ethics. Part III, Prop. II, Note

Pride is therefore pleasure arising from a man's thinking too highly of himself.
Ibid. Prop. XXVI, Note

It may easily come to pass that a vain man may become proud and imagine himself pleasing to all when he is in reality a universal nuisance.
Ibid. Prop. XXX, Note

Sadness diminishes or hinders a man's power of action.
Ibid. Prop. XXXVII, Proof

Self-complacency is pleasure accompanied by the idea of oneself as cause.
Ibid. Prop. LI, Note

It therefore comes to pass that every one is fond of relating his own exploits and displaying the strength both of his body and his mind, and that men are on this account a nuisance one to the other.
Ibid. Prop. LIV, Note

I refer those actions which work out the good of the agent to courage, and those which work out the good of others to nobility. Therefore temperance, sobriety, and presence of mind in danger, etc., are species of courage; but modesty, clemency, etc., are species of nobility.
Ibid. Prop. LIX, Note

Fear cannot be without hope nor hope without fear.
Ibid. Definition XIII, Explanation

So long as a man imagines that he cannot do this or that, so long is he determined not to do it: and consequently, so long it is impossible to him that he should do it.
Ibid. Definition XXVIII, Explanation

Those who are believed to be most abject and humble are usually most ambitious and envious.
Ibid. Definition XXIX, Explanation

One and the same thing can at the same time be good, bad, and indifferent, e. g., music is good to the melancholy,

---

[1] Napoleon I in 1803 used the phrase, "perfidious Albion," which was taken up by the French press and pamphleteers, after the rupture of the Peace of Amiens.

[2] Edition Lefèvre, Paris [1836], *Vol. III,* P. 687.

[3] Ein Gottbetrunkener Mensch (A God-intoxicated man). — NOVALIS (FRIEDRICH VON HARDENBERG) [1772–1801]

The Lord blot out his name under heaven. The Lord set him apart for destruction from all the tribes of Israel, with all the curses of the firmament which are written in the Book of the Law. . . . There shall no man speak to him, no man write to him, no man show him any kindness, no man stay under the same roof with him, no man come nigh him. — Amsterdam Synagogue's curse on Spinoza [1656]

[4] Everyman edition, translated by ANDREW BOYLE, M.A.

bad to those who mourn, and neither good nor bad to the deaf.

> *Ethics. Part IV, Preface*

Those who commit suicide are powerless souls, and allow themselves to be conquered by external causes repugnant to their nature.

> *Ibid. Prop. XVIII, Note*

Man is a social animal.

> *Ibid. Prop. XXXV, Note*

Men will find that they can prepare with mutual aid far more easily what they need, and avoid far more easily the perils which beset them on all sides, by united forces.

> *Ibid.*

Avarice, ambition, lust, etc., are nothing but species of madness, although not enumerated among diseases.[1]

> *Ibid. Prop. XLIV, Note*

It is the part of a wise man to feed himself with moderate pleasant food and drink, and to take pleasure with perfumes, with the beauty of growing plants, dress, music, sports, and theatres, and other places of this kind which man may use without any hurt to his fellows.

> *Ibid. Prop. XLV, Note 2*

It is a comfort to the unhappy to have companions in misery.[2]

> *Ibid. Prop. LVII, Note*

He whose honour depends on the opinion of the mob must day by day strive with the greatest anxiety, act and scheme in order to retain his reputation. For the mob is varied and inconstant, and therefore if a reputation is not carefully preserved it dies quickly.

> *Ibid. Prop. LVIII, Note*

In refusing benefits caution must be used lest we seem to despise or to refuse them for fear of having to repay them in kind.

> *Ibid. Prop. LXX, Note*

[1] To me, avarice seems not so much a vice, as a deplorable piece of madness. — SIR THOMAS BROWNE: *Religio Medici* (Everyman ed.), *P. 86*

[2] See Publilius Syrus, *Maxim 995,* and Cervantes, page 1036.

To give aid to every poor man is far beyond the reach and power of every man. . . . Care of the poor is incumbent on society as a whole.

> *Ethics. Part IV, Appendix, XVII*

None are more taken in by flattery than the proud, who wish to be the first and are not.

> *Ibid. XXI*

Those are most desirous of honour and glory who cry out the loudest of its abuse and the vanity of the world.

> *Ibid. Part V, Prop. X, Note*

We feel and know that we are eternal.

> *Ibid. Prop. XXIII, Note*

All excellent things are as difficult as they are rare.

> *Ibid. Prop. XLII, Note*

The things which . . . are esteemed as the greatest good of all, . . . can be reduced to these three headings: to wit, Riches, Fame, and Pleasure. With these three the mind is so engrossed that it cannot scarcely think of any other good.

> *Tractatus de Intellectus*
> *Emendatione. I, 3*

Fame has also this great drawback, that if we pursue it we must direct our lives in such a way as to please the fancy of men, avoiding what they dislike and seeking what is pleasing to them.

> *Ibid. 5*

The more intelligible a thing is, the more easily it is retained in the memory, and contrariwise, the less intelligible it is, the more easily we forget it.

> *Ibid. XI, 81*

NICHOLAS BOILEAU-DESPRÉAUX
[1636–1711]

Happy who in his verse can gently steer
From grave to light, from pleasant to severe.[1]

> *The Art of Poetry. Canto I,*
> *Line 75*

Every age has its pleasures, its style of wit, and its own ways.

> *Ibid. Canto III, Line 374*

[1] See Dryden, page 177.

Plague on the fool who taught us to
    confine
The swelling thought within a measured
    line;
Who first in narrow thraldom fancy
    pent,
And chained in rhyme each pinioned
    sentiment.
Satire 2. Line 55

He [Molière] pleases all the world,
but cannot please himself.
Ibid. Line 94

In spite of every sage whom Greece can
    show,
Unerring wisdom never dwelt below;
Folly in all of every age we see,
The only difference lies in the degree.
Satire 4. Line 37

Greatest fools are oft most satisfied.
Ibid. Line 128

If your descent is from heroic sires,
Show in your life a remnant of their
    fires.
Satire 5. Line 43

Of all the creatures that creep, swim, or
    fly,
Peopling the earth, the waters, and the
    sky,
From Rome to Iceland, Paris to Japan,
I really think the greatest fool is man.
Satire 8. Line 1

Follows his wife like fringe upon her
    gown.
Ibid. Line 47

A hero may be dragged in a romance
Through ten long volumes [1] by the
    laws of France.
Hence every year our books in torrents
    run,
And Paris counts an author in each son.
Satire 9. Line 103

But satire, ever moral, ever new,
Delights the reader and instructs him,
    too.
She, if good sense refine her sterling
    page,
Oft shakes some rooted folly of the age.
Ibid. Line 257

[1] Three-volume novels, those signs-manual
of our British dulness and crafty disdain for
literature. — EDMUND GOSSE: *Gossip in a Library, The Shaving of Shagpat*

Now two punctilious envoys, Thine and
    Mine,[1]
Embroil the earth about a fancied line;
And, dwelling much on right and much
    on wrong,
Prove how the right is chiefly with the
    strong.
Satire 11. Line 141

All Europe by conflicting Faiths was
    rent,
And e'en the Orthodox on carnage
    bent;
The blind avengers of Religion's cause
Forgot each precept of her peaceful
    laws.
Satire 12. Line 169

The terrible burden of having nothing
to do.
Epistle XI

JEAN BAPTISTE RACINE
[1639–1699]

Crime like virtue has its degrees;
And timid innocence was never known
To blossom suddenly into extreme li-
    cense.
Phèdre [1677]. Act IV, Sc. 2

According to ancient, sacred custom.
Athalie [1691]. Act I, Sc. 1

To repair the irreparable ravages of
time.
Ibid. Act II, Sc. 5

JEAN DE LA BRUYERE
[1645–1696]

Liberality consists less in giving a
great deal than in gifts well-timed.
Les Caractères. Du Cœur

To laugh at men of sense is the privilege of fools.
Ibid. De la Société

Everything has been said.
Ibid. Des Ouvrages de l'Esprit

Most men make use of the first part
of their life to render the other part
wretched.
Ibid. De l'Homme

If women were by nature what they
make themselves by artifice, if their
faces suddenly became as bright or as

[1] See Cervantes, page 1034.

leaden as they make them with paint and powder, they would be inconsolable.

Les Caractères. Des Femmes

JEANNE GUYON
[1648–1717]

A little bird I am,
Shut from the fields of air;
And in my cage I sit and sing
To Him who placed me there;
Well pleased a prisoner to be,
Because, my God, it pleases Thee.
A Prisoner's Song, Castle of Vincennes, France. Stanza 1

But though my wing is closely bound,
My heart's at liberty;
My prison walls cannot control
The flight, the freedom of the soul.[1]
Ibid. Stanza 4

FRANÇOIS DE SALIGNAC DE LA MOTHE FÉNELON
[1651–1715]

That weary listlessness, which renders life unsupportable to the voluptuous and the indolent, is unknown to those who can employ themselves by reading.
Telemachus. Book II

Commerce is a kind of spring, which, diverted from its natural channel, ceases to flow. There are but two things which invite foreigners — profit and convenience. If you render commerce less convenient, or less gainful, they will insensibly forsake you.
Ibid. Book III

There were some who said that a man at the point of death was more free than all others, because death breaks every bond, and over the dead the united world has no power.
Ibid. Book V

Love is conquered only by flight. Against such an enemy, true courage consists in fear and retreat, in retreat without deliberation, and without looking back.
Ibid. Book VI

[1] See Lovelace, page 168.

By labor Wisdom gives poignancy to pleasure, and by pleasure she restores vigor to labor.
Telemachus. Book VII

Do not men die fast enough without being destroyed by each other? Can any man be insensible of the brevity of life? and can he who knows it, think life too long!
Ibid.

They that defy the tempest to gratify avarice and luxury, deserve shipwreck.
Ibid.

A kingdom is best fortified by justice, moderation, and good faith, by which neighbouring States are convinced that their territories will never be usurped.
Ibid. Book IX

Courage is a virtue only in proportion as it is directed by prudence.
Ibid. Book X

No distinction so little excites envy as that which is derived from ancestors by a long descent.
Ibid.

The art of cookery is the art of poisoning mankind, by rendering the appetite still importunate, when the wants of nature are supplied.
Ibid.

To be always ready for war, said Mentor, is the surest way to avoid it.
Ibid.

Some of the most dreadful mischiefs that afflict mankind proceed from wine; it is the cause of disease, quarrels, sedition, idleness, aversion to labour, and every species of domestic disorder.
Ibid.

The blood of a nation ought never to be shed except for its own preservation in the utmost extremity.
Ibid. Book XIII

The number of diseases is a disgrace to mankind.
Ibid.

Mankind, by the perverse depravity of their nature, esteem that which they have most desired as of no value the moment it is possessed, and torment themselves with fruitless wishes for that which is beyond their reach.

Telemachus. Book XVIII

ALAIN RENÉ LE SAGE
[1668-1747]

It may be said that his wit shines at the expense of his memory.[1]

Gil Blas. Book 3, Chap. 11

I wish you all sorts of prosperity with a little more taste.

Ibid. Book 7, Chap. 4

Isocrates was in the right to insinuate, in his elegant Greek expression, that what is got over the Devil's back is spent under his belly.[2]

Ibid. Book 8, Chap. 9

Facts are stubborn things.[3]

Ibid. Book 10, Chap. 1

Plain as a pike-staff.[4]

Ibid. Book 12, Chap. 8

BENJAMIN SCHMOLKE
[1672-1737]

The heavier cross, the heartier prayer;
The bruisèd herbs most fragrant are;
If wind and sky were always fair
The sailor would not watch the star,
And David's Psalms had ne'er been sung
If grief his heart had never wrung.

Bearing the Burden. Stanza 4

FRANÇOIS M. A. VOLTAIRE [5]
[1694-1778]

If there were no God, it would be necessary to invent him.[6]

Épître à l'Auteur du Livre des Trois Imposteurs. CXI

A witty saying proves nothing.

Le Dîner du Comte de Boulainvilliers

The king [Frederick the Great] has sent me some of his dirty linen to wash; I will wash yours another time.[1]

Reply to General Manstein

In this best of all possible worlds, the Baron's castle was the most magnificent of castles, and his lady the best of all possible Baronesses.

Candide [2] [1759]. Chap. 1

They who assert that all is well have said a foolish thing, they should have said all is for the best.

Ibid.

If this is best of possible worlds,[3] what then are the others?

Ibid. Chap. 6

Optimism is the madness of maintaining that everything is right when it is wrong.

Ibid. Chap. 19

For what end, then, has this world been formed? . . . To plague us to death.

Ibid. Chap. 21

In this country [England] it is found good, from time to time, to kill one Admiral to encourage the others.

Ibid. Chap. 23

This is the happiest of mortals, for he is above everything he possesses.

Ibid. Chap. 26

Labour preserves us from three great evils — weariness, vice, and want.

Ibid. Chap. 30

Let us work without disputing; it is the only way to render life tolerable.

Ibid.

Let us cultivate our garden.

Ibid.

Men use thought only as authority for their injustice, and employ speech only to conceal their thoughts.[4]

Dialogue 14, Le Chapon et la Poularde [1763]

---

[1] See Sheridan, page 279.
[2] See Rabelais, page 1026.
[3] See Smollett, page 248, and Lowell, page 527.
[4] See Middleton, page 116.
[5] Perhaps the only famous writer whose heart is preserved in a library — at the Bibliothèque Nationale in Paris.
[6] See Tillotson, page 172.

---

[1] Voilà le roi qui m'envoie son linge à blanchir. — VOLTAIRE: *Letter* to his niece, Mme. Denis [July 24, 1752]
See Bonaparte, page 1060.
[2] Modern Library ed.
[3] Referring to the philosophy of Leibnitz and his contemporaries.
[4] See Robert South, page 183.

History is little else than a picture of human crimes and misfortunes.[1]

> *L'Ingénu* [*1767*]. *Chap. 10*

The embarrassment of riches.[2]

> *Le Droit du Seigneur. Act II, Sc. 6*

The first who was king was a fortunate soldier:

Who serves his country well has no need of ancestors.[3]

> *Mérope. Act I, Sc. 3*

It is better to risk saving a guilty person than to condemn an innocent one.

> *Zadig. Chap. 6*

The superfluous, a very necessary thing.

> *Le Mondain. Line 21*

Love truth, but pardon error.

> *Discours sur l'Homme. Discours 3*

Crush the infamous thing [superstition].

> *Letter to d'Alembert* > *[June 23, 1760]*

In the case of news, we should always wait for the sacrament of confirmation.

> *Letter to Count d'Argental* > *[August 28, 1760]*

The first among languages is that which possesses the largest number of excellent works.

> *Letter to Deodati de Tovazzi* > *[January 24, 1761]*

There are truths which are not for all men, nor for all times.

> *Letter to Cardinal de Bernis* > *[April 23, 1761]*

The proper mean.[4]

> *Letter to Count d'Argental* > *[November 28, 1765]*

It is said that God is always on the side of the heaviest battalions.[5]

> *Letter to M. le Riche* > *[February 6, 1770]*

[1] See Gibbon, page 270.
[2] Title of a comedy by SOULAS D'ALLAINVAL, produced in 1725.
[3] See Scott, page 311.
Borrowed from LEFRANC DE POMPIGNAN's *Didon*.
[4] See Publilius Syrus, *Maxim 1072*.
[5] See Gibbon, page 271.
Napoleon said, "Providence is always on the side of the last reserve."
BUSSY RABUTIN: *Lettres, IV, 91;* SÉVIGNÉ: *Lettre à sa Fille, P. 202;* TACITUS: *Historia, LV, 17;* TERENCE: *Phormio, I, 4, 26*

It seems clear to me that God designed us to live in society — just as He has given the bees the honey; and as our social system could not subsist without the sense of justice and injustice, He has given us the power to acquire that sense.

> *Letter to Frederick the Great.*[1]

I advise you to go on living solely to enrage those who are paying your annuities. It is the only pleasure I have left.

> *Letter to Madame du Deffand* [1]

I disapprove of what you say, but I will defend to the death your right to say it.[2]

> *To Helvetius* [3]

Liberty of thought is the life of the soul.

> *Essay on Epic Poetry* > *(written in English)*

Whoe'er thou art, behold thy master, He is, or was, or is to be.

> *On a Statuette of Cupid in the* > *Cirey Gardens*

MADAME DU DEFFAND
[1697–1784]

He [Voltaire] has invented history.

> *Quoted by* FOURNIER, *L'Esprit* > *dans l'Histoire, Page 191*

It is only the first step which costs.[4]

> *In reply to Cardinal de Polignac*

[1] S. G. TALLENTYRE: *Voltaire in His Letters* [1919]
[2] I do not agree with a word that you say, but I will defend to the death your right to say it. — Variation given by WILL DURANT: *The Story of Philosophy, P. 271*
This quotation is not found *verbatim* in Voltaire's works. It seems to originate in S. G. TALLENTYRE (E. Beatrice Hall): *The Friends of Voltaire* [1907], where she employed it as a paraphrase of Voltaire's words in the *Essay on Tolerance:* "Think for yourselves and let others enjoy the privilege to do so too." The editors are under obligation to Mr. Harry Weinberger for establishing this point.
[3] S. G. TALLENTYRE: *The Friends of Voltaire, P. 199.*
[4] Voltaire wrote to Madame du Deffand [Jan., 1764] that one of her bon-mots was quoted in the notes of *La Pucelle, Canto I:* "Il n'y a que le premier pas qui coûte."

CARL LINNAEUS
[1707–1778]

To live by medicine is to live horribly.

Diaeta Naturalis. Introduction

Mingle your joys sometimes with your earnest occupation.

Quoted in biography of Linnaeus by BENJAMIN DAYDON JONES, *Chap. 9*

A professor can never better distinguish himself in his work than by encouraging a clever pupil, for the true discoverers are among them, as comets amongst the stars.

Ibid.

Live innocently; God is here.

Ibid. Chap. 15 (Inscribed over the door of Linnaeus's bedchamber)

If a tree dies, plant another in its place.

Ibid.

JEAN JACQUES ROUSSEAU
[1712–1778]

Man is born free, and everywhere he is in irons.

The Social Contract [1] [1762]. *Book I, Chap. 1*

The strongest is never strong enough to be always the master, unless he transforms strength into right, and obedience into duty.

Ibid. Chap. 3

The right of conquest has no foundation other than the right of the strongest.

Ibid. Chap. 4

As soon as public service ceases to be the chief business of the citizens, and they would rather serve with their money than with their persons, the State is not far from its fall.

Ibid. Book III, Chap. 15

Good laws lead to the making of better ones; bad ones bring about worse. As soon as any man says of the affairs

of the State, "What does it matter to me?" the State may be given up for lost.

The Social Contract [1762]. *Book III, Chap. 15*

Never exceed your rights, and they will soon become unlimited.

A Discourse on Political Economy

Money is the seed of money, and the first guinea is sometimes more difficult to acquire than the second million.

Ibid.

God makes all things good; man meddles with them and they become evil.

Émile, or Education [1] [1762]. *Book I*

Medicine is all the fashion in these days, and very naturally. It is the amusement of the idle and unemployed, who do not know what to do with their time in taking care of themselves. If by ill-luck they had happened to be born immortal, they would have been the most miserable of men; a life they could not lose would be of no value to them. Such men must have doctors to threaten and flatter them, to give them the only pleasure they can enjoy, the pleasure of not being dead.

Ibid.

Hygiene is the only useful part of medicine, and hygiene is rather a virtue than a science. Temperance and industry are man's true remedies; work sharpens his appetite and temperance teaches him to control it.

Ibid.

What wisdom can you find that is greater than kindness?

Ibid. Book II

The happiest is he who suffers least; the most miserable is he who enjoys least. Ever more sorrow than joy,— this is the lot of all of us.

Ibid.

Provided a man is not mad, he can be cured of every folly but vanity.

Ibid. Book IV

---

[1] Everyman ed., translated by G. D. H. COLE.

[1] Everyman ed., translated by BARBARA FOXLEY.

I shall always maintain that whoso says in his heart, "There is no God," while he takes the name of God upon his lips, is either a liar or a madman.
Émile, or Education [*1762*].
Book I

People who know little are usually great talkers, while men who know much say little.
Ibid.

A man says what he knows, a woman says what will please.
Ibid. Book V

Where is the man who owes nothing to the land in which he lives? Whatever that land may be, he owes to it the most precious thing possessed by man, the morality of his actions and the love of virtue.
Ibid.

I have entered on a performance which is without precedent, and will have no imitator. I propose to show my fellow-mortals a man in all the integrity of nature; and this man shall be myself.
Confessions [*1782*].
Opening words

Hatred, as well as love, renders its votaries credulous.
Ibid. Book V

My third child was carried to the foundling hospital as well as the two former, and the next two were disposed of in the same manner, for I have had five children in all.
Ibid. Book VIII

The thirst after happiness is never extinguished in the heart of man.
Ibid. Book IX

To appear the friend of a man, when in reality we are no longer so, is to reserve to ourselves the means of doing him an injury by surprising honest men into an error.
Ibid. Book X

He thinks like a philosopher, and acts like a king.
Ibid. Book XII

Salaam aliakum, i. e., Peace be with you, the common Turkish salutation.
Ibid.

MICHEL JEAN SEDAINE
[*1717–1797*]

O Richard! O my king!
The universe forsakes thee!
Sung at the Dinner given to the French Soldiers in the Opera Salon at Versailles [*October 1, 1789*]

MADAME JEANNE DE POMPADOUR
[*1721–1764*]

After us the deluge.[1]
Reply to Louis XV [*November 5, 1757*] *after the defeat of the French and Austrian armies by Frederick the Great in the battle of Rossbach. Quoted by* MADAME DE HAUSSET *in Memoirs, Page 19*

PIERRE DE BEAUMARCHAIS
[*1732–1799*]

If you assure me that your intentions are honourable.
Le Barbier de Séville [*1775*].
Act IV, Sc. 6

CHARLES JOSEPH, PRINCE DE LIGNE
[*1735–1814*]

The congress of Vienna does not walk, but it dances.[2]

RUDOLF ERICH RASPE
[*1737–1794*]

What in the dark I had taken to be a stump of a little tree appearing above the snow, to which I had tied my horse, proved to have been the weathercock of the church steeple.
Travels of Baron Munchausen [*1785*]. *Chap. 2*

[1] LAROUSE, in *Fleurs Historiques*, credits the saying to Louis XV.
[2] One of the Prince de Ligne's speeches that will last forever. — *Edinburgh Review, July, 1890, P. 244*

We all did our duty, which, in the patriot's, soldier's, and gentleman's language, is a very comprehensive word, of great honour, meaning, and import.

> *Travels of Baron Munchausen*
> *[1785]. Chap. 5*

The sprigs took root in my horse's body, grew up, and formed a bower over me.

> *Ibid.*

His tunes were frozen up in the horn, and came out now by thawing.[1]

> *Ibid. Chap. 6*

If any of the company entertain a doubt of my veracity, I shall only say to such, I pity their want of faith.

> *Ibid.*

I had the very sling in my pocket which assisted David in slaying Goliath.

> *Ibid. Chap. 10*

Upon this island of cheese grows great plenty of corn, the ears of which produce loaves of bread, ready made.

> *Ibid. Chap. 20*

I have ever confined myself to facts.

> *Ibid.*

A traveller has a right to relate and embellish his adventures as he pleases, and it is very unpolite to refuse that deference and applause they deserve.

> *Ibid. Chap. 21*

There is a right and wrong handle to everything.[2]

> *Ibid. Chap. 30*

JACQUES DELILLE
[1738–1813]

Fate makes our relatives, choice makes our friends.[3]

> *La Pitié [1803]. Canto I*

LOUIS SÉBASTIEN MERCIER
[1740–1814]

Extremes meet.

> *Tableaux de Paris [1782].*
> *Vol. IV, Chap. 348, Title*

---

[1] See Plutarch, page 1004.
[2] See Epictetus, page 1008.
[3] Friends, those relatives we make for ourselves. — ÉMILE DESCHAMPS [1791–1871]: *Epigram*

SÉBASTIEN R. N. CHAMFORT
[1741–1794]

The most useless day of all is that in which we have not laughed.

> *Maxims and Thoughts. 1*

Chance is a sobriquet for Providence.

> *Ibid. 62*

JOHANN KASPAR LAVATER
[1741–1801]

From the Aphorisms on Man [London, 1788] much admired and privately annotated by WILLIAM BLAKE. *See the one-volume edition of* BLAKE'S *Poetry and Prose, edited by* GEOFFREY KEYNES.

If you mean to know yourself, interline such of these aphorisms as affect you agreeably in reading, and set a mark to such as left a sense of uneasiness with you; and then shew your copy to whom you please.

Who has many wishes has generally but little will. Who has energy of will has few diverging wishes. Whose will is bent with energy on *one, must* renounce the wishes for *many* things.

Say not you know another entirely, till you have divided an inheritance with him.

He who, when called upon to speak a disagreeable truth, tells it boldly and has done is both bolder and milder than he who nibbles in a low voice and never ceases nibbling.[1]

The public seldom forgive twice.

Venerate four characters: the sanguine, who has checked volatility and the rage for pleasure; the choleric who has subdued passion and pride; the phlegmatic emerged from indolence; and the melancholy who has dismissed avarice, suspicion and asperity.

Trust not him with your secrets, who, when left alone in your room, turns over your papers.

---

[1] Blake's marginal comment on this was "Damn such!"

GABRIEL ROMANOVITCH DERZHAVIN
[1743–1816]

O Thou eternal One, whose presence bright
    All space doth occupy, all motion guide;
Unchanged through time's all-devastating flight,
    Thou only God, there is no God beside.
              Ode to God.[1] *Stanza 1*

Thou from primeval nothingness didst call
    First chaos, then existence.
              Ibid. Stanza 3

JOHANN WOLFGANG VON GOETHE
[1749–1832]

If you inquire what the people are like here, I must answer, "The same as everywhere!"
        The Sorrows of Werther.
              May 17th

The history of science is science itself; the history of the individual, the individual.
        Mineralogy and Geology

Three things are to be looked to in a building: that it stand on the right spot; that it be securely founded; that it be successfully executed.
    Elective Affinities.[2] *Book I, Chap. 9*

The sum which two married people owe to one another defies calculation. It is an infinite debt, which can only be discharged through all eternity.
                Ibid.

A pretty foot is a great gift of nature.
            Ibid. Chap. 11

One is never satisfied with a portrait of a person that one knows.
        Ibid. Book II, Chap. 2

[1] Translated by Sir John Bowring [1792–1872].
[2] Translated by James Anthony Froude [1818–1894]

The fate of the architect is the strangest of all. How often he expends his whole soul, his whole heart and passion, to produce buildings into which he himself may never enter.
    Elective Affinities. Book II, Chap. 3

Let us live in as small a circle as we will, we are either debtors or creditors before we have had time to look round.
            Ibid. Chap. 4

Mediocrity has no greater consolation than in the thought that genius is not immortal.
            Ibid. Chap. 5

A teacher who can arouse a feeling for one single good action, for one single good poem, accomplishes more than he who fills our memory with rows on rows of natural objects, classified with name and form.
            Ibid. Chap. 7

No one feels himself easy in a garden which does not look like the open country.
            Ibid. Chap. 8

We lay aside letters never to read them again, and at last we destroy them out of discretion, and so disappears the most beautiful, the most immediate breath of life, irrecoverably for ourselves and for others.
            Ibid. Chap. 9

Who never ate his bread in sorrow,
    Who never spent the darksome hours
Weeping, and watching for the morrow, —
    He knows you not, ye heavenly Powers.
    Wilhelm Meister's Apprenticeship.
            Book II, Chap. 13

Who longs in solitude to live,
    Ah! soon his wish will gain:
Men hope and love, men get and give,
    And leave him to his pain.
        Ibid. Book III, Chap. 1

Know'st thou the land where the lemon-trees bloom,

Where the gold orange glows in the deep
    thicket's gloom,
Where a wind ever soft from the blue
    heaven blows,
And the groves are of laurel and myrtle
    and rose? [1]
    Wilhelm Meister's Apprenticeship.
        Book III, Chap. 1

One ought, every day at least, to hear
a little song, read a good poem, see a
fine picture, and, if it were possible, to
speak a few reasonable words. [2]
    Ibid. Book V, Chap. 1

To know of some one here and there
whom we accord with, who is living on
with us, even in silence, — this makes
our earthly ball a peopled garden.
    Ibid. Book VII, Chap. 5

Art is long, life short; [3] judgment difficult, opportunity transient.
    Ibid. Chap. 9

The sagacious reader who is capable
of reading between these lines what
does not stand written in them, but is
nevertheless implied, will be able to
form some conception.
    Autobiography. Book XVIII,
        Truth and Beauty

Know'st thou yesterday, its aim and
    reason?
Work'st thou well to-day for worthier
    things?
Then calmly wait the morrow's hidden
    season,
And fear thou not what hap soe'er it
    brings.
    Zahme Xenien. Book IV [1821]

Without haste! without rest!
Bind the motto to thy breast!
Bear it with thee as a spell;
Storm or sunshine, guard it well.
    Haste Not, Rest Not. Stanza 1

To-morrow sees undone, what happens
    not to-day;
Still forward press, nor ever tire!
The possible, with steadfast trust,
Resolve should by the forelock grasp;

[1] See Byron, page 355.
[2] See Charles Eliot Norton, page 572.
[3] See Chaucer, page 3.

Then she will ne'er let go her clasp,
And labors on, because she must. [1]
    Faust.[2] Prologue for the Theatre

A king there was once reigning,
    Who had a goodly flea,
Him loved he without feigning,
    As his own son were he!
    Ibid. Mephistopheles' Song
        of the Flea

The Eternal Feminine draws us on. [3]
    Ibid. (closing line)

Light, — more light!
    Last words

JOHANN HEINRICH VOSS
[1751–1826]

Who does not love wine, women, and
    song
Remains a fool his whole life long.
    Attributed to Voss by REDLICH
    in Die poetischen Beiträge zum
    Waudsbecker Bothen [Ham-
    burg, 1871], Page 67. The cou-
    plet has also been attributed to
    Luther.

MADAME ROLAND
[1754–1793]

O Liberty! Liberty! how many
crimes are committed in thy name!
    Quoted by MACAULAY *in his*
        Essay on Mirabeau

[1] Lose this day loitering, 'twill be the same
    story
  To-morrow, and the next more dilatory;
  Each indecision brings its own delays,
  And days are lost lamenting o'er lost days.
  Are you in earnest? Seize this very minute!
  Boldness has genius, power, and magic in
    it.
  Only engage, and then the mind grows
    heated.
  Begin, and then the work will be com-
    pleted.
    JOHN ANSTER [1793–1867]: *Faust,*
      Prologue for the Theatre, Manager's
      Speech
[2] Translated by ANNA SWANWICK [1813–
1899].
[3] Das Ewig-Weibliche zieht uns hinan.

CHARLES MAURICE DE TALLEYRAND-PÉRIGORD
[1754–1838]

Black as the devil,
Hot as hell,
Pure as an angel,
Sweet as love.[1]
Recipe for Coffee
Beginning of the end.[2]

BERTRAND BARÈRE
[1755–1841]

The tree of liberty only grows when
watered by the blood of tyrants.
*Speech in the National
Convention [1792]*
It is only the dead who do not return.
Speech [1794]

ANTHELME BRILLAT-SAVARIN
[1755–1826]

Tell me what you eat, and I will tell
you what you are.[3]
Physiologie du Goût. Aphorism 4
We become cooks, but a roast cook is
born.
Ibid. Aphorism 15

GEORGES JACQUES DANTON
[1759–1794]

Boldness, again boldness, and ever
boldness.[4]
*Speech in the Legislative
Assembly [1792]*

[1] Noir comme le diable,
  Chaud comme l'enfer,
  Pur comme un ange,
  Doux comme l'amour.
This appears as an inscription on many old
coffee-pots.
[2] Fournier asserts, on the written authority
of Talleyrand's brother, that the only breviary
used by the ex-bishop was *L'Improvisateur
Français,* a compilation of anecdotes and *bon-
mots,* in twenty-one duodecimo volumes.
Whenever a good thing was wandering about
in search of a parent, he adopted it; amongst
others, "C'est le commencement de la fin."

See Shakespeare, page 43.
[3] See Cervantes, page 1040.
[4] De l'audace, encore de l'audace, et toujours
de l'audace.

JOHANN CHRISTOPH FRIEDRICH VON SCHILLER
[1759–1805]

There are three lessons I would write,
  Three words as with a burning pen,
In tracings of eternal light,
  Upon the hearts of men.
Hope, Faith, and Love. Stanza 1
Thus grave these lessons on thy soul, —
  Hope, faith, and love; and thou shalt
  find
Strength when life's surges rudest roll,
  Light when thou else wert blind!
Ibid. Stanza 5
Against stupidity the very gods
Themselves contend in vain.[1]
The Maid of Orleans. Act III, Sc. 6
The richest monarch in the Christian
  world;
The sun in my own dominions never
  sets.[2]
Don Carlos. Act I, Sc. 6
When the wine goes in, strange things
  come out.
The Piccolomini. Act II, Sc. 12
This feat of Tell, the archer, will be told
While yonder mountains stand upon
  their base.
By Heaven! the apple's cleft right
  through the core.
William Tell. Act III, Sc. 3

JOSEPH ROUGET DE LISLE
[1760–1836]

Ye sons of France, awake to glory!
  Hark! hark! what myriads bid you
  rise!
Your children, wives, and grandsires
  hoary,
  Behold their tears and hear their
  cries!
The Marseillaise.[3]

See Spenser, page 25, and Longfellow, page
438.
[1] Against boredom even the gods themselves
struggle in vain. — NIETZSCHE: *The Antichrist,*
48
[2] See Scott, page 311, and Bonaparte, page
1061.
[3] Composed in 1792 in the garrison at Stras-
bourg, and originally called *Chant de guerre
de l'armée du Rhin.* First made known in Paris

To arms! to arms! ye brave!
The avenging sword unsheathe!
March on! march on! all hearts re-
solved
On victory or death!
The Marseillaise.

AUGUST FRIEDRICH FERDINAND VON KOTZEBUE
[1761–1819]

There is another and a better world.
The Stranger. Act I, Sc. 1

CHARLES LOUIS ÉTIENNE, CHEVALIER DE PANAT
[1762–1834]

No one is right; no one could forget
anything, nor learn anything.[1]
Letter to Jacques Mallet du Pan
[*January, 1796*]

JOSEPH FOUCHÉ
[1763–1820]

"It is more than a crime; it is a political fault," [2] — words which I record,
because they have been repeated and
attributed to others.
Memoirs

Death is an eternal sleep.
*Inscription placed by his orders
on the gates of the cemeteries*
[*1794*]

MADAME DE STAËL
[1766–1817]

The sight of such a monument is like
a continuous and stationary music.[3]
Corinne [*1807*]. *Book IV, Chap. 3*

To understand all makes us very in-
dulgent.[1]
Corinne [*1807*]. *Book XVIII, Chap. 5*

ERNST F. MÜNSTER [2]
[1766–1839]

Absolutism tempered by assassina-
tion.
*Description of the Russian
Constitution*

HENRI BENJAMIN CONSTANT
[1767–1830]

I am not the rose, but I have lived
with her.[3]

NAPOLEON BONAPARTE
[1769–1821]

Soldiers, from the summit of yonder
pyramids, forty centuries look down
upon you.
In Egypt [*July 21, 1798*]

Go, sir, gallop, and don't forget that
the world was made in six days. You
can ask me for anything you like, except time.
To one of his aides [*1803*]. *Quoted
in* R. M. JOHNSTON: *The Corsican*

What is the throne? — a bit of wood
gilded and covered with velvet. I am the
state [4] — I alone am here the representative of the people. Even if I had done
wrong you should not have reproached
me in public — people wash their dirty
linen at home. France has more need of
me than I of France.
To the Senate [*1814*]

France is invaded; I go to put myself
at the head of my troops, and, with

---

by patriots from Marseilles, it took the name
from their enthusiasm.

[1] They have learned nothing and forgotten
nothing. — Attributed to Talleyrand, describing the Bourbon dynasty.

[2] Commonly quoted, "It is worse than a
crime, — it is a blunder," and attributed to
Talleyrand.

[3] Since it [architecture] is music in space, as
it were a frozen music. . . . If architecture
in general is frozen music. — FRIEDRICH VON
SCHELLING [1775–1854]: *Philosophie der
Kunst, Pp. 576, 593*

[1] See Henrietta A. Huxley, page 563.

[2] Hanoverian envoy at St. Petersburg.

[3] This saying, "Je ne suis pas la rose, mais
j'ai vécu avec elle," is attributed to Constant
by ABRAHAM HAYWARD [1801–1884] in his
Introduction to the *Autobiography and Letters* [1861] of MRS. PIOZZI.

[4] DULAURE, in *History of Paris* [1863],
P. 387, asserts that Louis XIV interrupted a
judge who used the expression, "the king and
the state," by saying, "I am the state."

God's help and their valour, I hope soon to drive the enemy beyond the frontier.

At Paris [January 23, 1814]

The bullet that will kill me is not yet cast.

At Montereau [February 17, 1814]

The Allied Powers having proclaimed that the Emperor Napoleon is the sole obstacle to the re-establishment of peace in Europe, he, faithful to his oath, declares that he is ready to descend from the throne, to quit France, and even to relinquish life, for the good of his country.

Act of Abdication [April 4, 1814]

Unite for the public safety, if you would remain an independent nation.

Proclamation to the French People
[June 22, 1815]

Wherever wood can swim, there I am sure to find this flag of England.[1]

At Rochefort [July, 1815]

Whatever shall we do in that remote spot? Well, we will write our Memoirs. Work is the scythe of time.

On board H. M. S. Bellerophon
[August, 1815]

I generally had to give in [speaking of his relations with the Empress Josephine].

On St. Helena [May 19, 1816]

My maxim was, *la carrière est ouverte aux talents,* without distinction of birth or fortune.[2]

On St. Helena [March 3, 1817]

No physicking. We are a machine made to live; we are organized for that purpose, and such is our nature; do not counteract the living principle — let it alone — leave it the liberty of self-defence — it will do better than your drugs. Our body is a watch, intended to go for a given time. The watchmaker cannot open it, and must work at random. For once that he relieves or assists it by his crooked instruments, he injures it ten times, and at last destroys it.

To Dr. Antommarchi
[October 14, 1820]

[1] See Scott, page 311, and Schiller, page 1059.
[2] See Thomas Carlyle, page 377.

Our hour is marked, and no one can claim a moment of life beyond what fate has predestined.

To Dr. Arnott [April, 1821]

I am neither an atheist nor a rationalist; I believe in God, and am of the religion of my father. I was born a Catholic, and will fulfil all the duties of that church, and receive the assistance which she administers.

On St. Helena [April 18, 1821]

I could not unbend the bow; and France has been deprived of the liberal institutions I intended to give her.

BOURRIENNE: *Memoirs, Vol. 10,*
Page 425 [May 3, 1821]

All was not lost until the moment when all had succeeded.

Ibid., Page 39. On anniversary
of Battle of Waterloo

Madame Montholon having inquired what troops he considered the best, "Those which are victorious, Madame," replied the Emperor.

Ibid. Page 399

Tête d'armée (Head of the army).

Last words [May 5, 1821]

MADEMOISELLE BERTIN
[1744–1813]

There is nothing new except what is forgotten.[1]

PIERRE JACQUES ÉTIENNE, COUNT CAMBRONNE
[1770–1842]

The guard dies, but never surrenders.[2]

Inscribed upon the monument
erected to him at Nantes

[1] Attributed to Mademoiselle Bertin, milliner to Marie Antoinette.
There is nothing new except that which has become antiquated. — Motto of the *Revue Rétrospective*
A New Thinker is only one who does not know what the old thinkers have thought. — FRANK MOORE COLBY [1865–1925].
[2] This phrase, attributed to Cambronne, who was made prisoner at Waterloo, was vehemently denied by him. It was invented by Rougemont, a prolific author of *mots,* two days after the battle, in the "Indépendant." — FOURNIER: *L'Esprit dans l'Histoire*

GEORG WILHELM FRIEDRICH HEGEL
[1770–1831]

Peoples and governments never have learned anything from history, or acted on principles deduced from it.
Philosophy of History.[1]
Introduction

Amid the pressure of great events, a general principle gives no help.
Ibid.

To him who looks upon the world rationally, the world in its turn presents a rational aspect. The relation is mutual.
Ibid.

The history of the world is none other than the progress of the consciousness of Freedom.
Ibid.

We may affirm absolutely that nothing great in the world has been accomplished without passion.
Ibid.

It is easier to discover a deficiency in individuals, in states, and in Providence, than to see their real import and value.
Ibid.

Life has a value only when it has something valuable as its object.
Ibid.

Serious occupation is labor that has reference to some want.
Ibid. Part I, Sect. 2, Chap. 1

It is a matter of perfect indifference where a thing originated; the only question is: "Is it true in and for itself?"
Ibid. Part III, Sect. 3, Chap. 2

When liberty is mentioned, we must always be careful to observe whether it is not really the assertion of private interests which is thereby designated.
Ibid. Part IV, Sect. 3, Chap. 2

The Few assume to be the *deputies*, but they are often only the *despoilers* of the Many.
Ibid. Chap. 3

[1] Translated by J. SIBREE.

ANDOCHE JUNOT, DUC D'ABRANTES
[1771–1813]

I know nothing about it; I am my own ancestor.[1]
When asked about his ancestry

MARC ANTOINE DÉSAUGIERS
[1772–1827]

When we are dead, it's for a long time.
Song, Le Délire Bacchique

FRANÇOIS HORACE BASTIEN SÉBASTIANI
[1772–1851]

Order reigns in Warsaw.[2]
Announcement of the fall of Warsaw

ÉTIENNE DE GRELLET [3] (DE MABILLIER)
[1773–1855]

I shall pass through this world but once.[4] If, therefore, there be any kindness I can show, or any good thing I can do, let me do it now; let me not defer it

[1] See Plutarch, page 1003.
Curtius Rufus seems to me to be descended from himself [a saying of Tiberius]. — TACITUS: *Annals, Book XI, Chap. 21, 16*
[2] Des lettres que je reçois de Pologne m'annoncent que la tranquillité règne à Varsovie. — DUMAS [1802–1870]: *Mémoires, Second Series, Vol. IV, Chap. 3*
[3] De Grellet was born in Limoges, France, came to America as Stephen Grellet, became a Quaker, and travelled as a missionary in the United States, Canada, and Europe. He died in Burlington, New Jersey. The saying persistently attributed to him is not found in his existing writings.
[4] If I can any way contribute to the Diversion or Improvement of the Country in which I live, I shall leave it, when I am summoned out of it, with the secret Satisfaction of thinking that I have not lived in vain. — JOSEPH ADDISON: *The Spectator, Vol. I, No. 1, March 1, 1711*
See Underwood, page 682, and Foss, page 732.

or neglect it, for I shall not pass this way again.

Attributed

BARON DE LA MOTTE FOUQUÉ
[1777–1843]

Death comes to set thee free;
Oh, meet him cheerily
  As thy true friend,
And all thy fears shall cease,
And in eternal peace
  Thy penance end.

Sintram and His Companions.[1]
Pilgrim Song, Stanza 3

HENRI BEYLE
(DE STENDHAL)
[1783–1842]

One can acquire everything in solitude — except character.

Fragments. I

Prudery is a kind of avarice, the worst of all.

Ibid. V

In matters of sentiment, the public has very crude ideas; and the most shocking fault of women is that they make the public the supreme judge of their lives.

Ibid. IX

A wise woman never yields by appointment. It should always be an unforeseen happiness.

De l'Amour. Chap. 60

The Baron could not produce epigrams; he required at least four sentences of six lines each to be brilliant.

The Red and the Black.[2] *Chap. 34*

I see but one rule: *to be clear.* If I am not clear, all *my world* crumbles to nothing.

Reply to Balzac. Oct. 30, 1840 [3]

Wit lasts no more than two centuries.

Ibid.

[1] Translated by THOMAS TRACY.
[2] Translated by C. K. SCOTT-MONCRIEFF (Modern Library ed.).
[3] In *The Charterhouse of Parma* (Modern Library ed.).

JOHANN LUDWIG UHLAND
[1787–1862]

I always have loved thee, I love thee today,
And I swear I will love thee, for ever and aye!

The Landlady's Daughter

Take, O boatman, thrice thy fee, —
Take, I give it willingly;
For, invisible to thee,
Spirits twain have crossed with me.

The Passage

ARTHUR SCHOPENHAUER [1]
[1788–1860]

A certain amount of care or pain or trouble is necessary for every man at all times. A ship without ballast is unstable and will not go straight.

Studies in Pessimism.[2] *On the Sufferings of the World*

Suicide thwarts the attainment of the highest moral aim by the fact that, for a real release from this world of misery, it substitutes one that is merely apparent.

Ibid. On Suicide

Hatred comes from the heart; contempt from the head; and neither feeling is quite within our control.

Ibid. Psychological Observations

If a man sets out to hate all the miserable creatures he meets, he will not have much energy left for anything else; whereas he can despise them, one and all, with the greatest ease.

Ibid.

Every man takes the limits of his own field of vision for the limits of the world.

Ibid.

[1] Schopenhauer was furious and refused to pay his debts to any one who spelled his name with a double "p". — CESARE LOMBROSO: *The Man of Genius, Part 1, Chap. 2*
[2] Translated by T. BAILEY SAUNDERS. Modern Library ed.
Schopenhauer wrote at an epoch in which pessimism was beginning to be fashionable, together with mysticism, and fused the whole into one philosophic system. — LOMBROSO: *Ibid., Part III, Chap. 4*

Not to go to the theatre is like making one's toilet without a mirror.

Studies in Pessimism. Psychological Observations

Every parting gives a foretaste of death; every coming together again a foretaste of the resurrection.

Ibid.

There is no absurdity so palpable but that it may be firmly planted in the human head if you only begin to inculcate it before the age of five, by constantly repeating it with an air of great solemnity.

Ibid.

Opinion is like a pendulum and obeys the same law. If it goes past the centre of gravity on one side, it must go a like distance on the other; and it is only after a certain time that it finds the true point at which it can remain at rest.

Ibid.

It is a curious fact that in bad days we can very vividly recall the good time that is now no more; but that in good days we have only a very cold and imperfect memory of the bad.

Ibid.

The fundamental fault of the female character is that it has no sense of justice.

Ibid. On Women

Dissimulation is innate in woman, and almost as much a quality of the stupid as of the clever.

Ibid.

Noise is the most impertinent of all forms of interruption. It is not only an interruption, but also a disruption of thought.

Ibid. On Noise

The most general survey shows us that the two foes of human happiness are pain and boredom.

Essays. Personality, or What a Man Is

A man who has no mental needs, because his intellect is of the narrow and normal amount, is, in the strict sense of the word, what is called a *philistine*.

Ibid.

Fame and honor are twins; and twins, too, like Castor and Pollux, of

whom one was mortal and the other was not. Fame is the undying brother of ephemeral honor.

Essays. Fame

Pride is an established conviction of one's own paramount worth in some particular respect; while vanity is the desire of rousing such a conviction in others. Pride works from within; it is the direct appreciation of oneself. Vanity is the desire to arrive at this appreciation indirectly, from without.

Ibid. Pride

Ignorance is degrading only when found in company with riches.

Ibid. On Books and Reading

Intellect is invisible to the man who has none.

Ibid. Our Relation to Others, Sect. 23

There is no more mistaken path to happiness than worldliness, revelry, high life.

Ibid. Our Relation to Ourselves, Sect. 24

To be alone is the fate of all great minds — a fate deplored at times, but still always chosen as the less grievous of two evils.

Ibid.

Rascals are always sociable, and the chief sign that a man has any nobility in his character is the little pleasure he takes in others' company.

Counsels and Maxims. Chap. 2

Do not shorten the morning by getting up late; look upon it as the quintessence of life, as to a certain extent sacred.

Ibid.

Speak without emphasizing your words. Leave other people to discover what it is that you have said; and as their minds are slow, you can make your escape in time.

Ibid. Chap. 3

ALPHONSE M. L. LAMARTINE
[1790–1869]

What is our life but a succession of preludes to that unknown song whose first solemn note is sounded by Death?

Love is the enchanted dawn of every heart, but what mortal is there over whose first joys and happiness does not break some storm, dispelling with its icy breath his fanciful illusions, and shattering his altar? What soul, thus cruelly wounded, does not at times try to dream away the recollection of such storms in the solitude of country life? And yet, man, it seems, is not able to bear the languid rest on Nature's bosom, and when the trumpet sounds the signal of danger, he hastens to join his comrades, no matter what the cause that calls him to arms. He rushes into the thickest of the fight and amid the uproar of the battle regains confidence in himself and his powers.[1]

Méditations Poétiques [1820].
Second Series, XV

NARCISSE ACHILLE, COMTE DE SALVANDY
[1795–1856]

We are dancing on a volcano.
At a fête given by the Duc d'Orléans to the King of Naples [1830]

HEINRICH HEINE [2]
[1797–1856]

Translations by LOUIS UNTER-
MEYER

"Oh, 'tis Love that makes us grateful,
Oh, 'tis Love that makes us rich!"
So sings man, and every fateful
Echo bears his amorous speech.
O, die Liebe macht uns selig.
Stanza 1

Toward France there journeyed two grenadiers
Who had been captured in Russia;
And they hung their heads and their eyes had tears

---

[1] Heading for the score of Franz Liszt's Symphonic Poem No. 3, *Les Préludes.*
[2] Therefore a secret unrest
Tortured thee, brilliant and bold.
MATTHEW ARNOLD: *Heine's Grave*

As they came to the border of Prussia.
Nach Frankreich zogen zwei Grenadier'. Stanza 1

Upon the wings of Song, love,
I would bear thee far, and go
Where the Ganges ripples along, love —
There is a place I know.
Auf Flügeln des Gesanges.
Stanza 1

A pine tree stands so lonely
In the North where the high winds blow,
He sleeps; and the whitest blanket
Wraps him in ice and snow.
Ein Fichtenbaum steht einsam.
Stanza 1

From grief too great to banish
Come songs, my lyric minions.[1]
Aus meinen grossen Schmerzen.
Stanza 1

When two who love are parted,
They talk, as friend to friend,
Clasp hands and weep a little,
And sigh without an end.
Wenn zwei von einander scheiden.
Stanza 1

I do not know why this confronts me,
This sadness, this echo of pain;
A curious legend still haunts me,
Still haunts and obsesses my brain.
*Ich weiss nicht, was soll es be-
deuten (The Lorelei). Stanza 1*

The years keep coming and going,
Men will arise and depart;
Only one thing is immortal:
The love that is in my heart.
Die Jahre kommen und gehen.
Stanza 1

Child, you are like a flower,
So sweet and pure and fair.
Du bist wie eine Blume. Stanza 1

---

[1] Out of my own great woe
I make my little songs.
Translated by MRS. BROWNING
When other men can only curse
The poet puts his woes in verse.
CHRISTOPHER MORLEY: Translation
from the Chinese of No SHO

He who, for the first time, loves,
Even vainly, is a God.
But the man who loves again,
And still vainly, is a fool.
Wer zum erstenmale liebt.
Stanza 1

Oh what lies there are in kisses!
In den Küssen, welche Lüge.
Stanza 1

Death — it is but the long, cool night;
And Life is but a sultry day.
Der Tod, das ist die kühle Nacht.
Stanza 1

The sea has its pearls,
The heaven its stars, —
But my heart, my heart,
My heart has its love.
Das Meer hat seine Perlen.
Stanza 1

Thalatta! Thalatta!
Hail to thee, oh Sea, ageless and eternal!
Thalatta! Thalatta! Stanza 1

The deep, blue eyes of Springtime
Peer from the grass beneath;
They are the tender violets
That I will twine in a wreath.
Die blauen Frühlingsaugen.
Stanza 1

Your eyes' blue depths are lifted,
With love and friendship stirred.
They smile; and, lost in dreaming,
I cannot speak a word.
Mit deinen blauen Augen.
Stanza 1

Good-Fortune is a giddy maid,
Fickle and restless as a fawn;
She smooths your hair; and then the jade
Kisses you quickly, and is gone.
Das Glück ist eine leichte Dirne.[1]
Stanza 1

But Madam Sorrow scorns all this,
She shows no eagerness for flitting;
But with a long and fervent kiss
Sits by your bed — and brings her knitting.
Ibid. Stanza 2

This is America!
This is the new world!

[1] Quoted by GEORGE ELIOT in *Daniel Deronda*. See John Hay, page 639.

Not the present European
Wasted and withering sphere.
Vitzliputzli. Prelude, Dieses ist
Amerika! Stanza 1

For Sleep is good, but Death is better still —
The best is never to be born at all.
Gross ist die Ähnlichkeit der
beiden schönen

If one has no heart, one cannot write for the masses.
Letter to Julius Campe
[March 18, 1840]

Ordinarily he is insane, but he has lucid moments [1] when he is only stupid.
Of Savoye, appointed ambassa-
dor to Frankfurt by Lamartine
[1848]

To publish even one line of an author which he himself has not intended for the public at large — especially letters which are addressed to private persons — is to commit a despicable act of felony.
Quoted by A. C. SWINBURNE *as*
heading for In Sepulcretis

AUGUST HEINRICH HOFFMANN [2]
[1798–1874]

Pauline now no more was there;
She burnt from pantalette to hair,
But in the place where she had been
A heap of ashes could be seen.
Pauline and the Matches. Stanza 6

Anything to me is sweeter
Than to see Shock-headed Peter.
Struwwelpeter

HONORÉ DE BALZAC
[1799–1850]

In the matter of commerce, encouragement does not mean protection. A nation's true policy is to relieve itself of paying tribute to other nations, but

[1] See South, page 183.
[2] Dr. Hoffmann, a physician in Frankfurt-am-Main, wrote the famous *Slovenly Peter* verses [1845] to amuse children who had to wait in his office. A free translation was done in 1891 by MARK TWAIN, then living in Berlin, for his daughters.

to do so without the humiliating assistance of custom houses and prohibitory laws. Manufacturing industry depends solely on itself, competition is its life. Protect it, and it goes to sleep; it dies from monopoly as well as from the tariff. The nation that succeeds in making all other nations its vassals will be the one which first proclaims commercial liberty; it will have enough manufacturing power to supply its productions at a cheaper price than those of its rivals.

> *The Country Doctor.*[1] *Chap. 1*

I believe in the incomprehensibility of God.

> *Letter to Madame de Hanska*
> [*1837*]

ALEXANDRE DUMAS
THE ELDER
[1802–1870]

All for one, one for all, that is our device.[2]

> *The Three Musketeers. Chap. 9*

There are virtues which become crimes by exaggeration.

> *The Count of Monte Cristo.*
> *Chap. 90*

Great is truth. Fire cannot burn, nor water drown it.

> *Ibid. Chap. 113*

All human wisdom is summed up in two words, — wait and hope.

> *Ibid. Chap. 117*

Nothing succeeds like success.[3]

> *Ange Pitou* [*1854*].
> *Vol. I, Page 72*

Look for the woman.[4]

> *The Mohicans of Paris. Vol. III,*
> *Chaps. 10 and 11*

VICTOR HUGO
[1802–1885]

The three problems of the age — the degradation of man by poverty, the

ruin of woman by starvation, and the dwarfing of childhood by physical and spiritual night.

> *Les Misérables.*[1] *Preface*

Far be it from me to insult the pun! I honour it in proportion to its merits — no more.

> *Ibid. Fantine, Book III, Chap. 7*

Indigestion is charged by God with enforcing morality on the stomach.

> *Ibid.*

Mothers' arms are made of tenderness, and sweet sleep blesses the child who lies therein.

> *Ibid. Book IV, Chap. 1*

The supreme happiness of life is the conviction that we are loved.

> *Ibid. Book V, Chap. 4*

For prying into any human affairs, none are equal to those whom it does not concern.

> *Ibid. Chap. 8*

The malicious have a dark happiness.

> *Ibid. Chap. 9*

Great grief is a divine and terrible radiance which transfigures the wretched.

> *Ibid. Chap. 13*

No human feeling can ever be so appalling as joy.

> *Ibid. Book VIII, Chap. 3*

Death has its own way of embittering victory, and it causes glory to be followed by pestilence. Typhus is the successor of triumph.

> *Ibid. Cosette, Book I, Chap. 2*

Napoleon . . . mighty somnambulist of a vanished dream.

> *Ibid. Chap. 13*

An effluence from the divine afflatus.

> *Ibid. Chap. 15*

Thank heaven, nations are great aside from the dismal chances of the sword.

> *Ibid. Chap. 16*

Waterloo is a battle of the first rank won by a captain of the second.

> *Ibid.*

---

[1] Translated by KATHERINE PRESCOTT WORMELEY.

[2] See Shakespeare, page 106.

[3] Rien ne réussit comme le succès. — French proverb

[4] Cherchez la femme.

[1] Translated by CHARLES E. WILBOUR, Modern Library Giant.

Would you realize what Revolution is, call it Progress; and would you realize what Progress is, call it To-morrow.

Les Misérables. Cosette,
Book I, Chap. 17

What is that to the Infinite?

Ibid. Chap. 18

The doll is one of the most imperious necessities, and at the same time one of the most charming instincts of female childhood.

Ibid. Book III, Chap. 8

Great blunders are often made, like large ropes, of a multitude of fibres.

Ibid. Book V, Chap. 10

Upon the first goblet he read this inscription: Monkey wine; upon the second: lion wine; upon the third: sheep wine; upon the fourth: swine wine. These four inscriptions expressed the four descending degrees of drunkenness: the first, that which enlivens; the second, that which irritates; the third, that which stupefies; finally the last, that which brutalizes.

Ibid. Book VI, Chap. 9

Philosophy should be an energy; it should find its aim and its effect in the amelioration of mankind.

Ibid. Book VII, Chap. 6

A man is not idle because he is absorbed in thought. There is a visible labour and there is an invisible labour.

Ibid. Chap. 8

To be buried in Père Lachaise is like having mahogany furniture.

Ibid. Book VIII, Chap. 5

No one ever keeps a secret so well as a child.

Ibid. Chap. 8

The peculiarity of prudery is to multiply sentinels, in proportion as the fortress is less threatened.[1]

Ibid. Marius, Book II, Chap. 8

Nothing will mix and amalgamate more easily than an old priest and an old soldier. In reality, they are the same

---

[1] That is the refuge of all old coquettes; it is hard for them to be deserted by the gallants, and from such a desertion, in their spite, they take refuge in the trade of a prude. — MOLIÈRE: *Tartuffe, Act I, Sc. 1*

kind of man. One has devoted himself to his country upon earth, the other to his country in heaven; there is no other difference.

Les Misérables. Marius,
Book III, Chap. 2

To err is human.[1]

Ibid.

He declared that man is a magnet, like the needle, and in his room he placed his bed with the head to the south and the foot to the north, so that at night the circulation of the blood should not be interfered with by the grand magnetic current of the globe.

Ibid.

He had the appearance of a caryatid in vacation; he was supporting nothing but his reverie.

Ibid. Book IV, Chap. 2

Peace is happiness digesting.

Ibid. Chap. 4

Life, misfortunes, isolation, abandonment, poverty, are battlefields which have their heroes; obscure heroes, sometimes greater than the illustrious heroes.

Ibid. Book V, Chap. 1

A creditor is worse than a master; for a master owns only your person, a creditor owns your dignity, and can belabour that.

Ibid. Chap. 2

Seeing that Mother Plutarch had a gloomy and thoughtful air, he tapped her on the shoulder and said with a smile: "We have the indigo."

Ibid. Chap. 4

Social prosperity means man happy, the citizen free, the nation great.

Ibid. Saint Denis, Book I, Chap. 4

Nothing is more dangerous than discontinued labour; it is habit lost. A habit easy to abandon, difficult to resume.

Ibid. Book II, Chap. 1

Thought is the labour of the intellect, reverie is its pleasure.

Ibid.

---

[1] See Pope, page 211.

Where the telescope ends, the microscope begins. Which of the two has the grander view?

> *Les Misérables. Saint Denis,*
> *Book III, Chap. 3*

A compliment is something like a kiss through a veil.

> *Ibid. Book VIII, Chap. 1*

Situated in the moon, kingdom of dream, province of illusion, capital Soap-Bubble.

> *Ibid. Chap. 3*

Great perils have this beauty, that they bring to light the fraternity of strangers.

> *Ibid. Book XII, Chap. 4*

Philosophy is the microscope of thought.

> *Ibid. Jean Valjean,*
> *Book II, Chap. 2*

When grace is joined with wrinkles, it is adorable. There is an unspeakable dawn in happy old age.

> *Ibid. Book V, Chap. 2*

Angel is the only word in the language which cannot be worn out. No other word would resist the pitiless use which lovers make of it.

> *Ibid. Chap. 4*

Let us, while waiting for new monuments, preserve the ancient monuments.

> *Note added to the Definitive*
> *Edition of Notre Dame de Paris*
> *[1832]*

The sea never tells what it means to do. There is everything in this abyss, even chicanery. One might almost say that the sea had designs; it advances and retreats, it proposes and retracts, it prepares a squall and then gives up its plan, it promises destruction and does not keep its word. It threatens the North, and strikes the South.

> *Ninety-Three. Part I,*
> *Book II, Chap. 7*

Nothing is more gentle than smoke, nothing more frightful. There is the smoke of peace, and the smoke of villainy. Smoke, the density and colour of smoke, makes all the difference between peace and war, between brotherhood and hatred, between hospitality and the grave, between life and death. Smoke rising through the trees may signify the most charming thing in the world, the hearth; or the most terrible, a conflagration.

> *Ninety-Three. Part I,*
> *Book IV, Chap. 7*

There is a sacred horror about everything grand. It is easy to admire mediocrity and hills; but whatever is too lofty, a genius as well as a mountain, an assembly as well as a masterpiece, seen too near, is appalling. . . . Hence, there is more dismay than admiration.

> *Ibid. Part II, Book III, Chap. 1*

The sublimest song to be heard on earth is the lisping of the human soul on the lips of children.

> *Ibid. Part III, Book III, Chap. 1*

Nothing is so like a soul as a bee. It goes from flower to flower as a soul from star to star, and it gathers honey as a soul gathers light.

> *Ibid. Chap. 3*

Popularity? It is glory's small change.

> *Ruy Blas. Act III, Sc. 5*

Each has his share of a mother's love, and all have it all.

> *Feuilles d'Automne*

To rise at six, to dine at ten,
To sup at six, to sleep at ten,
Makes a man live for ten times ten.

> *Inscription over the door of*
> *Hugo's study*

I represent a party which does not yet exist:
the party of revolution, civilization.
This party will make the twentieth century.
There will issue from it first
the United States of Europe, then
the United States of the World.

> *Prophecy in autograph on the*
> *wall of the room in which Hugo*
> *died, Place des Vosges, Paris*

CHARLES-AUGUSTIN SAINTE-BEUVE
[1804–1869]

Hugo, strong partisan
. . . fought in armor,

And held high his banner in the midst
of the tumult:
He still holds it; and Vigny, more discreet,
As if in his tower of ivory,[1] retreated
before noontime.
> *To M. Villemain. Pensées d'Août,*
> *Stanza 3 [October, 1837]*

ALEXIS CHARLES HENRI CLÉREL DE TOCQUEVILLE
[1805–1859]

The profession of law is the only aristocratic element which can be amalga-
mated without violence with the natural
elements of democracy, and which can
be advantageously and permanently
combined with them.
> *Democracy in America.*
> *Vol. I, Chap. 16*

I cannot believe that a republic could
subsist at the present time if the influence of lawyers in public business did
not increase in proportion to the power
of the people.
> *Ibid.*

Connecticut, the little yellow spot
[on the map] that makes the clock-
peddler, the schoolmaster, and the senator. The first, gives you time; the second, tells you what to do with it; and
the third makes your law and your civilization.
> *Address at an American Fourth*
> *of July celebration in Paris, soon*
> *after the publication of Democ-*
> *racy in America*

VON MÜNCH BELLINGHAUSEN
[1806–1871]

Two souls with but a single thought,
Two hearts that beat as one.[2]
> *Ingomar the Barbarian.[3] Act II*

---

[1] See Lindsay, page 858.
[2] Zwei Seelen und ein Gedanke,
Zwei Herzen und ein Schlag.
See Pope, page 219, and Motherwell, page
389.
[3] Translated by MARIA ANNE LOVELL [1803–
1877]. The play was first produced at Drury
Lane Theatre, London, in 1851.

HERMAN NEUMAN
[1806–1875]

Two chambers has the heart,
Wherein dwell Joy and Sorrow;
When Joy awakes in one,
Then slumbers Sorrow in the other.
O Joy, take care!
Speak softly,
Lest you awaken Sorrow.
> *The Heart*

MARSHAL MAURICE DE MacMAHON
[1808–1893]

I am here: I shall remain here.
> *Reply to the Commander-in-*
> *Chief, from the trenches before*
> *the Malakoff, in the siege of*
> *Sebastopol [September, 1855],*
> *when warned to beware of an ex-*
> *plosion which might follow the*
> *retreat of the Russians*

GENERAL PIERRE BOSQUET
[1810–1861]

It is magnificent, but it is not war.
> *Said of the charge of the Light*
> *Brigade at the battle of Bala-*
> *klava [October 25, 1854]*

FERDINAND FREILIGRATH
[1810–1876]

O love, while still 'tis yours to love!
O love, while love you still may keep!
The hour will come, the hour will come,
When you shall stand by graves and
weep!
> *Liebestraum*

ALFRED DE MUSSET
[1810–1857]

How glorious it is — and also how
painful — to be an exception.
> *The White Blackbird. I*

Things they don't understand always
cause a sensation among the English.
> *Ibid. VIII*

Never were there so many sleepless
nights as in the time of this man [Na-

poleon]. Never did one see so many anguished mothers gaze from the ramparts of the towns. Never was there such silence when one spoke of death. And yet there was never so much joy, life, warlike music, in all hearts. There was never such pure sunshine as that which dried all this blood. People said that God made it for this man; they called it Austerlitz weather. But he made it himself with his incessant gunfire, and the only clouds were on the morrow of his battles.

> *Confession of a Child of His Century. Chap. 2*

POPE LEO XIII (GIACCHINO PECCI)
[1810–1903]

Every man has by nature the right to possess property as his own.

> *Encyclical Letter on the Condition of Labour [May 15, 1891]*

It is impossible to reduce human society to one level.

> *Ibid.*

It is one thing to have a right to the possession of money, and another to have a right to use money as one pleases.

> *Ibid.*

When a society is perishing, the true advice to give to those who would restore it is to recall it to the principles from which it sprung.

> *Ibid.*

Among the purposes of a society should be to try to arrange for a continuous supply of work at all times and seasons.

> *Ibid.*

THÉOPHILE GAUTIER
[1811–1872]

All things return to dust
  Save beauty fashioned well;
The bust
  Outlasts the citadel.[1]

> *L'Art*

[1] Tout passe. L'art robuste
    Seul a l'éternité;
  Le buste
    Survit à la cité.
See Austin Dobson, page 648.

I am the spectre of the rose
You wore but last night at the ball.

> *The Spectre of the Rose. Stanza 1*

JULIUS KARL REINHOLD STURM
[1816–1896]

Pain's furnace heat within me quivers,
  God's breath upon the flame doth blow,
And all my heart in anguish shivers
  And trembles at the fiery glow,
And yet I whisper — as God will!
And in His hottest fire — hold still.

> *God's Anvil.[1] Stanza 1*

KARL MARX
[1818–1883]

From each according to his abilities, to each according to his needs.

> *The German Ideology [2]*
> *[1845–1846]*

Nothing can have value without being an object of utility. If it be useless, the labor contained in it is useless, cannot be reckoned as labor, and cannot therefore create value.

> *Capital.[3] Part II, Chap. 3, Page 33*

The capitalist himself is a practical man, who, it is true, does not always reflect on what he says outside his office, but who always knows what he does inside the latter.

> *Ibid. Chap. 5, Page 43*

Constant labor of one uniform kind destroys the intensity and flow of a man's animal spirits, which find recreation and delight in mere change of activity.

> *Ibid. Chap. 9, Page 74*

[1] Translated by Bishop G. W. Doane.
[2] Translated by Max Eastman.
[3] Abridged edition prepared by Julian Borchardt. Translated by Stephen L. Trask. Modern Library edition.

The intellectual desolation, artificially produced by converting immature human beings into mere machines.

Capital. Part II, Chap. 10, Page 102

Where is the medal without its reverse?

Ibid. Page 137

The battle of competition is fought by cheapening of commodities.

Ibid. Chap. 13, Page 168

The only part of the so-called national wealth that actually enters into the collective possessions of modern peoples is their national debt.

Ibid. Chap. 14, Page 199

Capitalist production begets, with the inexorability of a law of nature, its own negation.

Ibid. Chap. 15, Page 204

When commercial capital occupies a position of unquestioned ascendancy, it everywhere constitutes a system of plunder.

Ibid. Chap. 21, Page 262

The history of all hitherto existing society is the history of class struggles.

Manifesto of the Communist Party [1] *[1848]. I*

Of all the classes that stand face to face with the bourgeoisie to-day the proletariat alone is a really revolutionary class. The other classes decay and finally disappear in the race of modern industry; the proletariat is its special and essential product.[2]

Ibid.

Pauperism develops more rapidly than population and wealth.

Ibid.

In proportion as the antagonism between classes within the nation vanishes, the hostility of one nation to another will come to an end.

Manifesto of the Communist Party [1848]. *II*

The ruling ideas of each age have ever been the ideas of its ruling class.

Ibid.

Christian Socialism is but the holy water with which the priest consecrates the heartburnings of the aristocrat.

Ibid. III

The proletarians have nothing to lose but their chains. They have a world to win. Workers of the world, unite!

Ibid. IV

IVAN SERGEYEVICH TURGENIEV
[1818–1883]

That air of superiority to the rest of the world which usually disappears when once the twenties have been passed.

Fathers and Sons. [1] *Chap. 4*

That awkwardness which overtakes a young man when, just ceased to be a boy, he returns to the spot where hitherto he has ranked as a mere child.

Ibid.

That dim, murky period when regrets come to resemble hopes, and hopes are beginning to resemble regrets.

Ibid. Chap. 7

I agree with no man's opinions. I have some of my own.

Ibid. Chap. 13

The temerity to believe in nothing.

Ibid. Chap. 14

A picture may instantly present what a book could set forth only in a hundred pages.

Ibid. Chap. 16

The sensuous joy of magnanimity.

Ibid. Chap. 17

Whatever a man prays for, he prays for a miracle. Every prayer reduces itself to this: "Great God, grant that twice two be not four."

Prayer

---

[1] Written in collaboration with FRIEDRICH ENGELS. Translated by SAMUEL MOORE.

[2] By bourgeoisie is meant the class of modern capitalists, owners of the means of social production and employers of wage-labor. By proletariat, the class of modern wage-laborers who, having no means of production of their own, are reduced to selling their labor-power in order to live. — FRIEDRICH ENGELS: [1820–1895]: *Footnote to Manifesto of the Communist Party, Part I, Bourgeois and Proletarians*

---

[1] Translated by C. J. HOGARTH.

Don't forget me, but do not call me to mind either, in the midst of daily cares, pleasures and needs. . . . I do not want to disturb your life, I do not want to impede its quiet course.

Literary Remains [published in 1930]. When I Shall Be No More

MAX SCHNECKENBURGER
[1819–1849]

So long as blood shall warm our veins,
While for the sword one hand remains,
One arm to bear a gun, — no more
Shall foot of foeman tread thy shore!
Dear Fatherland, no fear be thine,
Firm stands thy guard along the Rhine.

The Watch on the Rhine.[1]
Stanza 4

GUSTAVE NADAUD
[1820–1893]

I'm growing old, I've sixty years;
  I've labored all my life in vain.
In all that time of hopes and fears,
  I've failed my dearest wish to gain.
I see full well that here below
  Bliss unalloyed there is for none,
My prayer would else fulfilment
  know —
Never have I seen Carcassonne![2]

Carcassonne.[3] *Stanza 1*

They tell me every day is there
  Not more nor less than Sunday gay;

---

[1] Written in 1840, when France was threatening the left bank of the Rhine. Set to music by Carl Wilhelm [1815–1873] in 1854.

[2] Those towers gold as ripened grain
  Perchance we may not gaze upon,
And yet, through sunshine, wind and
  rain,
We're on our way to Carcassonne.
    BERTON BRALEY: *Carcassonne*
For the sake
Of the old man who longed to hie
Him forth when autumn's work was done,
I thank the Fates that let him die
Before he looked on Carcassonne.
    GRACE NOLL CROWELL: *Carcassonne
               Attained*

[3] Translated by JOHN R. THOMPSON [1823–1873].

In shining robes and garments fair
  The people walk upon their way.
One gazes there on castle walls
  As grand as those of Babylon,
A bishop and two generals!
  What joy to be in Carcassonne!
Ah! might I but see Carcassonne!

Carcassonne. Stanza 3

Thy pardon, Father, I beseech,
  In this my prayer if I offend;
One something sees beyond his reach
  From childhood to his journey's end.
My wife, our little boy Aignan,
  Have travelled even to Narbonne;
My grandchild has seen Perpignan;
  And I — have not seen Carcassonne.

Ibid. Stanza 5

HENRI-FRÉDÉRIC AMIEL
[1821–1881]

Truth is the secret of eloquence and of virtue, the basis of moral authority; it is the highest summit of art and of life.

Journal

Life is the apprenticeship to progressive renunciation, to the steady diminution of our claims, of our hopes, of our powers, of our liberty.

Ibid.

Doing easily what others find difficult is talent; doing what is impossible for talent is genius.

Ibid.

A man without passion is only a latent force, only a possibility, like a stone waiting for the blow from the iron to give forth sparks.

Ibid.

If ignorance and passion are the foes of popular morality, it must be confessed that moral indifference is the malady of the cultivated classes.

Ibid.

Pure truth cannot be assimilated by the crowd; it must be communicated by contagion.

Ibid.

FYODOR DOSTOYEVSKY
[1821–1881]

Man is a pliable animal, a being who gets accustomed to everything!

The House of the Dead (Prison Life in Siberia).[1] *Part I, Chap. 2*

With ready-made opinions one cannot judge of crime. Its philosophy is a little more complicated than people think. It is acknowledged that neither convict prisons, nor the hulks, nor any system of hard labour ever cured a criminal.

Ibid.

Humane treatment may raise up one in whom the divine image has long been obscured. It is with the unfortunate, above all, that humane conduct is necessary.

Ibid. Chap. 9

Tyranny is a habit capable of being developed, and at last becomes a disease. . . . The man and the citizen disappear for ever in the tyrant.

Ibid. Part II, Chap. 3

Consolation is not what you need. Weep and be not consoled, but weep. Only every time that you weep be sure to remember that your little son is one of the angels of God, and rejoices at your tears, and points at them to the Lord God; and a long while yet will you keep that great mother's grief. But it will turn in the end to quiet joy, and your bitter tears will be only tears of tender sorrow that purifies the heart.

The Brothers Karamazov.[2] *Part I, Book II, Chap. 3*

Even those who have renounced Christianity and attack it, in their inmost being still follow the Christian ideal, for hitherto neither their subtlety nor the ardour of their hearts has been able to create a higher ideal of man and of virtue than the ideal given by Christ of old. When it has been attempted, the result has been only grotesque.

Ibid. Part II, Book IV, Chap. 1

[1] Everyman edition.
[2] Translated by CONSTANCE GARNETT. Modern Library edition.

Until you have become really, in actual fact, a brother to every one, brotherhood will not come to pass. No sort of scientific teaching, no kind of common interest, will ever teach men to share property and privileges with equal consideration for all. Every one will think his share too small and they will be always envying, complaining and attacking one another.

The Brothers Karamazov.
Part II, Book VI, Chap. 2

The true security is to be found in social solidarity rather than in isolated individual effort.

Ibid.

Be not forgetful of prayer. Every time you pray, if your prayer is sincere, there will be new feeling and new meaning in it, which will give you fresh courage, and you will understand that prayer is an education.

Ibid. Chap. 3

Love all God's creation,[1] the whole and every grain of sand in it. Love every leaf, every ray of God's light. Love the animals, love the plants, love everything. If you love everything, you will perceive the divine mystery in things. Once you perceive it, you will begin to comprehend it better every day. And you will come at last to love the whole world with an all-embracing love.

Ibid.

Much on earth is hidden from us, but to make up for that we have been given a precious mystic sense of our living bond with the other world, with the higher heavenly world, and the roots of our thoughts and feelings are not here but in other worlds. That is why the philosophers say that we cannot comprehend the reality of things on earth.

Ibid.

Men reject their prophets and slay them, but they love their martyrs and honour those whom they have slain.

Ibid.

[1] See *Book of Common Prayer*, page 1128.

ALEXANDRE DUMAS THE YOUNGER
[1824–1895]

Business? It's quite simple. It's other people's money.
> *La Question d'Argent* [*1857*].
> *Act II, Sc. 7*

GESTA ROMANORUM [1]

We read of a certain Roman emperor who built a magnificent palace. In digging the foundation, the workmen discovered a golden sarcophagus ornamented with three circlets, on which were inscribed, "I have expended; I have given; I have kept; I have possessed; I do possess; I have lost; I am punished. What I formerly expended, I have; what I gave away, I have." [2]
> *Tale 16*

See how the world rewards its votaries. [3]
> *Tale 36*

If the end be well, all is well. [4]
> *Tale 67*

---

[1] A collection of 181 stories, first printed about 1473. The first English version appeared in 1824, translated by the Reverend C. SWAN (Bohn Standard Library).

[2] RICHARD GOUGH [1735–1809] in *Sepulchral Monuments of Great Britain*, gives this epitaph of Robert Byrkes, which is to be found in Doncaster Church, "new cut" upon his tomb in Roman capitals: —
> Howe: Howe: who is heare:
> I, Robin of Doncaster, and Margaret my feare.
> That I spent, that I had;
> That I gave, that I have;
> That I left, that I lost.
> A.D. 1579.

The following is the epitaph of Edward Courtenay, Earl of Devonshire, according to CLEAVELAND's *Genealogical History of the Family of Courtenay, P. 142*, and quoted by GIBBON: *Decline and Fall of the Roman Empire*, Chap. 61: —
> What we gave, we have;
> What we spent, we had;
> What we left, we lost.

[3] Ecce quomodo mundus suis servitoribus reddit mercedem (See how the world its veterans rewards). — POPE: *Moral Essays, Epistle 2, L. 243*

[4] Si finis bonus est, totum bonum erit. — Probably the origin of the proverb, "All's well that ends well."

Whatever you do, do wisely, and think of the consequences.
> *Tale 103*

HENRIK IBSEN
[1828–1906]

A community is like a ship; every one ought to be prepared to take the helm.
> *An Enemy of the People. Act I*

The most crying need in the humbler ranks of life is that they should be allowed some part in the direction of public affairs. That is what will develop their faculties and intelligence and self-respect.
> *Ibid. Act II*

The public doesn't require any new ideas. The public is best served by the good, old-fashioned ideas it already has.
> *Ibid.*

An editor cannot always act as he would prefer. He is often obliged to bow to the wishes of the public in unimportant matters. Politics are the most important thing in life — for a newspaper.
> *Ibid. Act III*

The most dangerous enemy to truth and freedom amongst us is the compact majority.
> *Ibid. Act IV*

You should never wear your best trousers when you go out to fight for freedom and truth.
> *Ibid. Act V*

To crave for happiness in this world is simply to be possessed by a spirit of revolt. What right have we to happiness?
> *Ghosts. Act I*

It is not only what we have inherited from our fathers that exists again in us, but all sorts of old dead ideas and all kinds of old dead beliefs and things of that kind. They are not actually alive in us; but there they are dormant, all the same, and we can never be rid of them. Whenever I take up a newspaper and read it, I fancy I see ghosts creeping between the lines. There must be ghosts all over the world.
> *Ibid. Act II*

There can be no freedom or beauty
• about a home life that depends on borrowing and debt.

A Doll's House. Act I

A barrister's profession is such an
uncertain thing, especially if he won't
undertake unsavoury cases.

Ibid.

There are some people one loves best,
and others whom one would almost always rather have as companions.

Ibid. Act II

Marriage is a thing you've got to
give your whole mind to.

The League of Youth. Act IV

These heroes of finance are like beads
on a string — when one slips off, all the
rest follow.

Ibid.

He has the luck to be unhampered by
either character, or conviction, or social position; so that Liberalism is the
easiest thing in the world for him.

Ibid. Act V

Rob the average man of his life-
illusion, and you rob him of his happiness at the same stroke.

The Wild Duck. Act V

Look into any man's heart you please,
and you will always find, in every one,
at least one black spot which he has to
keep concealed.

Pillars of Society. Act III

The spirit of truth and the spirit of
freedom — they are the pillars of society.

Ibid. Act IV

A lie, turned topsy-turvy, can be
prinked and tinselled out, decked in
plumage new and fine, till none knows
its lean old carcass.

Peer Gynt. Act I

For fortune such as I've enjoyed I
have to thank America. My amply-
furnished library I owe to Germany's
later schools. From France, again, I get
my waistcoats, my manners, and my
spice of wit, — from England an industrious hand, and keen sense for my own
advantage. The Jew has taught me how
to wait. Some taste for *dolce far niente*
I have received from Italy, — and one

time, in a perilous pass, to eke the
measure of my days, I had recourse to
Swedish steel.

Peer Gynt. Act IV

I ho'd that man is in the right who
is most closely in league with the future.

Letter to Georg Brandes
[January 3, 1882]

COUNT LYOF NIKOLAYE-
VITCH TOLSTOI
[1828–1910]

The Frenchman is conceited from
supposing himself mentally and physically to be inordinately fascinating
both to men and to women. An Englishman is conceited on the ground of being a citizen of the best-constituted
state in the world, and also because he
as an Englishman always knows what
is the correct thing to do, and knows
that everything that he, as an Englishman, does do is indisputably the best
thing. An Italian is conceited from being
excitable and easily forgetting himself
and other people. A Russian is conceited precisely because he knows nothing and cares to know nothing, since
he does not believe it possible to know
anything fully. A conceited German is
the worst of them all, and the most
hardened of all, and the most repulsive
of all; for he imagines that he possesses
the truth in a science of his own invention, which is to him absolute truth.

War and Peace.[1] Part IX, Chap. 11

The subject of history is the life of
peoples and of humanity. To catch and
pin down in words — that is, to describe directly the life, not only of humanity, but even of a single people, appears to be impossible.

Ibid. Epilogue, Part II, Chap. 1

If the will of man were free, that is,
if every man could act as he chose, the
whole of history would be a tissue of
disconnected accidents.

Ibid. Chap. 8

---

[1] Translated by Constance Garnett. Modern Library Giant.

The most powerful weapon of ignorance — the diffusion of printed matter.

War and Peace. Epilogue, Part II,
Chap. 8

Time is infinite movement without one moment of rest.

Ibid. Chap. 10

All happy families resemble one another; every unhappy family is unhappy in its own fashion.

Anna Karénina.[1] *Part I, Chap. 1*

War on the one hand is such a terrible, such an atrocious, thing, that no man, especially no Christian man, has the right to assume the responsibility of beginning it.

Ibid. Part VIII, Chap. 15

The whole trade in the luxuries of life is brought into existence and supported by the requirements of women.

The Kreutzer Sonata. Chap. 9

His face was of that insipidly pleasing kind which women call "not bad-looking."   *Ibid. Chap. 19*

Error is the force that welds men together; truth is communicated to men only by deeds of truth.

My Religion. Chap. 12

The happiness of men consists in life. And life is in labor.

What Is to Be Done? Chap. 38

The vocation of every man and woman is to serve other people.

Ibid. Chap. 40, Note

The only significance of life consists in helping to establish the kingdom of God; and this can be done only by means of the acknowledgment and profession of the truth by each one of us.

The Kingdom of God. Chap. 12

Art is a human activity having for its purpose the transmission to others of the highest and best feelings to which men have risen.

What Is Art? Chap. 8

The more is given the less the people will work for themselves, and the less

they work the more their poverty will increase.[1]

Help for the Starving. Part III
[January, 1892]

WILHELM BUSCH [2]
[1832–1908]

Youth should heed the older-witted
  When they say, don't go too far —
Now their sins are all committed,
  Lord, how virtuous they are!

Pious Helen (Die fromme
Helene)

CESARE LOMBROSO
[1836–1909]

Not only is fame (and until recent years even liberty), denied to men of genius during their lives, but even the means of subsistence. After death they receive monuments and rhetoric by way of compensation.

The Man of Genius. Preface

Good sense travels on the well-worn paths; genius, never. And that is why the crowd, not altogether without reason, is so ready to treat great men as lunatics.[3]

Ibid.

A patient one day presented himself to Abernethy; after careful examination the celebrated practitioner said, "You need amusement; go and hear Grimaldi; he will make you laugh, and that will be better for you than any drugs." "My God," exclaimed the invalid, "but I *am* Grimaldi!" [4]

Ibid. Part I, Chap. 2

Klopstock was questioned regarding the meaning of a passage in his poem. He replied, "God and I both knew what it meant once; now God alone knows." [5]

Ibid.

---

[1] Translated by NATHAN HASKELL DOLE [1852–1935].

[1] If you stop supporting that crowd, it will support itself. — SENECA: *Epistle 20, 7*

[2] Famous artist and cartoonist, author of the German classic for children, *Max and Moritz* [1865].

[3] See Seneca, page 991.

[4] See Thackeray, page 484.

[5] Also attributed to Browning, apropos of his *Sordello*.

The appearance of a single great genius is more than equivalent to the birth of a hundred mediocrities.
The Man of Genius. Part II, Chap. 2

The strange insane poet, John Clare, who believed himself a spectator of the Battle of the Nile, and the death of Nelson; and was firmly convinced that he had been present at the death of Charles I.
Ibid. Part III, Chap. 2

"Lawsuit mania" . . . a continual craving to go to law against others, while considering themselves the injured party.
Ibid. Chap. 3

The ignorant man always adores what he cannot understand.
Ibid.

Men in general, but more particularly the insane, love to speak of themselves, and on this theme they even become eloquent.
Ibid. Part IV, Chap. 1

HENRI CAZALIS
(JEAN LAHORS)
[1840–1909]

Click, click, click . . . Death is prancing;
Death, at midnight, goes a-dancing,
Tapping on a tomb with talon thin,
Click, click, click, goes the grisly violin.
    ". . . Equality, Fraternity." [1]
         Stanza 1

ANATOLE FRANCE
[1844–1924]

I do not know any reading more easy, more fascinating, more delightful than a catalogue.
The Crime of Sylvestre Bonnard. [2]
The Log, December 24, 1849

All the historical books which contain no lies are extremely tedious.
Ibid.

[1] Translated by BERTRAM GALBRAITH. This poem inspired Camille Saint-Saëns' *Danse Macabre*, Opus 40.
[2] Translated by LAFCADIO HEARN. Modern Library edition.

Lovers who love truly do not write down their happiness.
The Crime of Sylvestre Bonnard.
The Log, November 30, 1859

The time God allots to each one of us is like a precious tissue which we embroider as we best know how.
Ibid. The Daughter of Clémentine.
Chap. 2

To know is nothing at all; to imagine is everything.
Ibid. Part II, Chap. 2

The domestic hearth. There only is real happiness.
Ibid. Chap. 3

He flattered himself on being a man without any prejudices; and this pretension itself is a very great prejudice.
Ibid. Chap. 4

Those who have given themselves the most concern about the happiness of peoples have made their neighbours very miserable.
Ibid.

Man is so made that he can only find relaxation from one kind of labor by taking up another.
Ibid.

People who have no weaknesses are terrible; there is no way of taking advantage of them.
Ibid.

The whole art of teaching is only the art of awakening the natural curiosity of young minds for the purpose of satisfying it afterwards.
Ibid.

The faculty of doubting is rare among men. A few choice spirits carry the germs of it in them, but these do not develop without training.
Penguin Island. Book VI, Chap. 2

We have medicines to make women speak; we have none to make them keep silence.
The Man Who Married a Dumb Wife. [1] *Act II, Sc. 4*

They saw Barnaby before the altar of the Blessed Virgin, head downwards, with his feet in the air, and he was juggling six balls of copper and a dozen knives. In honor of the Holy Mother of

[1] Translated by CURTIS HIDDEN PAGE.

God he was performing those feats, which aforetime had won him most renown.

Our Lady's Juggler [1]

The good critic is he who narrates the adventures of his soul among masterpieces.

La Vie Littéraire. Preface

We reproach people for talking about themselves; but it is the subject they treat best.

Ibid. Journal des Goncourt

FRIEDRICH WILHELM NIETZSCHE

[1844–1900]

Our destiny exercises its influence over us even when, as yet, we have not learned its nature: it is our future that lays down the law of our to-day.

Human, All Too Human. [2] *7*

Much more happiness is to be found in the world than gloomy eyes discover.

Ibid. 49

One must have a good memory to be able to keep the promises one makes.

Ibid. 59

One will rarely err if extreme actions be ascribed to vanity, ordinary actions to habit, and mean actions to fear.

Ibid. 74

How poor the human mind would be without vanity! It resembles a well stocked and ever renewed ware-emporium that attracts buyers of every class: they can find almost everything, have almost everything, provided they bring with them the right kind of money — admiration.

Ibid.

Every man who has declared that some other man is an ass or a scoundrel, gets angry when the other man conclusively shows that the assertion was erroneous.

Ibid. 90

Every tradition grows ever more venerable — the more remote is its origin, the more confused that origin is. The reverence due to it increases from generation to generation. The tradition finally becomes holy and inspires awe.

Human, All Too Human. 96

I teach you the Superman. Man is something that is to be surpassed.

Thus Spake Zarathustra. [1] *Prologue, Chap. 3*

Man is a rope stretched between the animal and the Superman — a rope over an abyss.

Ibid. Chap. 4

I want to teach men the sense of their existence, which is the Superman, the lightning out of the dark cloud man.

Ibid. Chap. 7

No small art is it to sleep: it is necessary for that purpose to keep awake all day.

Ibid. Part I, Chap. 2

This is hardest of all: to close the open hand out of love, and keep modest as a giver.

Ibid. Part II, Chap. 23

Beggars, however, one should entirely do away with! Verily, it annoyeth one to give unto them, and it annoyeth one not to give unto them. [2]

Ibid. Chap. 25

The sting of conscience teacheth one to sting.

Ibid.

Distrust all in whom the impulse to punish is powerful.

Ibid. Chap. 29

Ah, there are so many things betwixt heaven and earth of which only the poets have dreamed!

Ibid. Chap. 39

Believe me, friend Hollaballoo! The greatest events are not our noisiest, but our stillest hours.

Ibid. Chap. 40

Thoughts that come with doves' footsteps guide the world.

Ibid. Chap. 44

---

[1] Translated by FREDERIC CHAPMAN.
[2] Translated by ALEXANDER HARVEY.

[1] Translated by THOMAS COMMON.
[2] There is surely a Physiognomy, which those experienced and Master Mendicants observe, whereby they instantly discover a merciful aspect, and will single out a face wherein they spy the signatures and marks of Mercy. — SIR THOMAS BROWNE: *Religio Medici* (Everyman ed.), *P. 66*

Winter, a bad guest, sitteth with me at home; blue are my hands with his friendly handshaking.
Thus Spake Zarathustra.
Part III, Chap. 50

Better know nothing than half-know many things.[1]
Ibid. Part IV, Chap. 64

We ought to learn from the kine one thing: ruminating.
Ibid. Chap. 68

Then learnedst thou how much harder it is to give properly than to take properly, and that bestowing well is an art — the last, subtlest master-art of kindness.[2]
Ibid.

If ye would go up high, then use your own legs! Do not get yourselves *carried* aloft; do not seat yourselves on other people's backs and heads!
Ibid. Chap. 73, Sect. 10

From people who merely pray we must become people who bless.
Notes on Thus Spake Zarathustra. 82

It is certainly not the least charm of a theory that it is refutable.
Beyond Good and Evil.[3] I, 18

No one is such a liar as the indignant man.
Ibid. II, 26

Books for the general reader are always ill-smelling books, the odour of paltry people clings to them.
Ibid. 29

It is not the strength but the duration of great sentiments that makes great men.
Ibid. IV, 72

Woman learns how to hate in proportion as she forgets how to charm.
Ibid. 84

[1] See H. W. Shaw, page 518.
[2] Some is for gift sae lang required,
  While that the craver be so tired,
  That ere the gift deliver'ed be,
  The thank is frustrate and expired;
  In Giving sould Discretion be.
    WILLIAM DUNBAR [1460–1530]·
    Discretion in Giving
  In Taking sould Discretion be
    WILLIAM DUNBAR: *Discretion in Taking*
[3] Translated by HELEN ZIMMERN.

Our vanity is most difficult to wound just when our pride has been wounded.
Beyond Good and Evil. IV. 111

Where there is neither love nor hatred in the game, woman's play is mediocre.
Ibid. 115

In revenge and in love woman is more barbarous than man.
Ibid. 139

The thought of suicide is a great consolation:[1] by means of it one gets successfully through many a bad night.
Ibid. 157

There are few pains so grievous as to have seen, divined, or experienced how an exceptional man has missed his way and deteriorated.
Ibid. V, 203

Blessed are the forgetful: for they get the better even of their blunders.
Ibid. VII, 217

Is not life a hundred times too short for us to bore ourselves?
Ibid. 227

One does not know — cannot know — the best that is in one.
Ibid. VIII, 249

The melancholia of everything completed!
Ibid. IX, 277

The "masters" have been done away with; the morality of the vulgar man has triumphed.
Genealogy of Morals.[2] First Essay, Aphorism 9

The broad effects which can be obtained by punishment in man and beast, are the increase of fear, the sharpening of the sense of cunning, the mastery of the desires; so it is that punishment tames man, but does not make him "better."
Ibid. Second Essay, Aphorism 15

A married philosopher belongs to comedy.
Ibid. Third Essay, Aphorism 7

[1] We are in the power of no calamity while death is in our own. — SIR THOMAS BROWNE: *Religio Medici* (Everyman ed.), P. 50
[2] Translated by HORACE B. SAMUEL.

Every tiny step forward in the world was formerly made at the cost of mental and physical torture.

Genealogy of Morals. Third Essay,
Aphorism 9

The sick are the greatest danger for the healthy; it is not from the strongest that harm comes to the strong, but from the weakest.

Ibid. Aphorism 14

A strong and well-constituted man digests his experiences (deeds and misdeeds all included) just as he digests his meats, even when he has some tough morsels to swallow.

Ibid. Aphorism 16

Nothing ever succeeds which exuberant spirits have not helped to produce.

The Twilight of the Idols.[1]
Preface

Contentment preserves one even from catching cold. Has a woman who knew that she was well dressed ever caught cold? — No, not even when she had scarcely a rag to her back.

Ibid. Maxims and Missiles, 25

Without music life would be a mistake.

Ibid. 33

He who laughs best to-day, will also laugh last.[2]

Ibid. 43

That which needs to be proved cannot be worth much.

Ibid. The Problem of Socrates, 5

History is nothing more than the belief in the senses, the belief in falsehood.[3]

Ibid. "Reason" in Philosophy, 1

Unconscious gratitude for a good digestion (sometimes called "brotherly love").

Ibid. Morality as the Enemy
of Nature, 3

[1] Translated by ANTHONY M. LUDOVICI.
[2] Better the last smile than the first laughter. — JOHN RAY: *Compleat Collection of English Proverbs* [1742]. This is a variant of the familiar saying, "He laughs best who laughs last," known in all languages.
[3] See Matthew Arnold, page 548.

Two great European narcotics, alcohol and Christianity.

The Twilight of the Idols.
Things the Germans Lack, 2

Dancing in all its forms cannot be excluded from the curriculum of all noble education: dancing with the feet, with ideas, with words, and, need I add that one must also be able to dance with the pen?

Ibid. 7

In the architectural structure, man's pride, man's triumph over gravitation, man's will to power, assume a visible form. Architecture is a sort of oratory of power by means of forms.

Ibid. Skirmishes in a War
with the Age, 11

If a man have a strong faith he can indulge in the luxury of scepticism.

Ibid. 12

The sick man is a parasite of society. In certain cases it is indecent to go on living. To continue to vegetate in a state of cowardly dependence upon doctors and special treatments, once the meaning of life, the right to life, has been lost, ought to be regarded with the greatest contempt by society.

Ibid. 36

Liberal institutions straightway cease from being liberal the moment they are soundly established: once this is attained no more grievous and more thorough enemies of freedom exist than liberal institutions.

Ibid. 38

It is my ambition to say in ten sentences what everyone else says in a whole book, — what everyone else does *not* say in a whole book.

Ibid. 51

Love is the state in which man sees things most widely different from what they are. The force of illusion reaches its zenith here, as likewise the sweetening and transfiguring power. When a man is in love he endures more than at other times; he submits to everything.

The Antichrist.[1] *Aphorism 23*

[1] Translated by ANTHONY M. LUDOVICI.

Our statesmen — a body of men who are otherwise so unembarrassed, and such thorough anti-Christians in deed — still declare themselves Christians and still flock to communion.[1]

The Antichrist. Aphorism 39

God created woman. And boredom did indeed cease from that moment — but many other things ceased as well! Woman was God's *second* mistake.

Ibid. Aphorism 48

Life always gets harder toward the summit — the cold increases, responsibility increases.

Ibid. Aphorism 57

I call Christianity the one great curse, the one enormous and innermost perversion, the one great instinct of revenge, for which no means are too venomous, too underhand, too underground and too petty, — I call it the one immortal blemish of mankind.

Ibid. Aphorism 62

My doctrine is: Live that thou mayest desire to live again, — that is thy duty, — for in any case thou wilt live again!

Eternal Recurrence.[2] 27

Even a thought, even a possibility, can shatter us and transform us.

Ibid. 30

Let us stamp the impress of eternity upon our lives!

Ibid. 35

Nothing on earth consumes a man more quickly than the passion of resentment.

Ecce Homo [2]

Where one despises, one cannot wage war. Where one commands, where one sees something beneath one, one ought not to wage war.

Ibid.

I believe only in French culture, and regard everything else in Europe which calls itself "culture" as a misunderstanding. I do not even take the German kind into consideration.

Ibid.

Wherever Germany extends her sway, she ruins culture.

Ecce Homo

As an artist, a man has no home in Europe save in Paris.

Ibid.

Simply by being compelled to keep constantly on his guard, a man may grow so weak as to be unable any longer to defend himself.

Ibid.

Pathetic attitudes are not in keeping with greatness.

Ibid.

My time has not yet come either; some are born posthumously.

Ibid.

No one can draw more out of things, books included, than he already knows. A man has no ears for that to which experience has given him no access.

Ibid.

I am not successful at being pompous, the most I can do is to appear embarrassed.

Ibid.

The Germans are like women, you can scarcely ever fathom their depths — they haven't any.[1]

Ibid.

After coming in contact with a religious man, I always feel that I must wash my hands.

Ibid.

All prejudices may be traced back to the intestines. A sedentary life is the real sin against the Holy Ghost.[2]

Ibid.

One must separate from anything that forces one to repeat No again and again.

Ibid. P. 41

---

[1] The reference is to Bismarck, a sincere Christian and forger of the Ems telegram which precipitated the war of 1870.
[2] Translated by ANTHONY M. LUDOVICI.

[1] Man thinks woman profound — why? Because he can never fathom her depths. Woman is not even shallow. — *The Twilight of the Idols, Maxims and Missiles, 27*
[2] Translated by CLIFTON P. FADIMAN. Modern Library edition, P. 27.

HENRYK SIENKIEWICZ
[1846–1916]

The greater philosopher a man is, the more difficult it is for him to answer the foolish questions of common people.

Quo Vadis.[1] *Chap. 19*

A man who leaves memoirs, whether well or badly written, provided they be sincere, renders a service to future psychologists and writers.

Without Dogma.[2] *Page 1*

JORIS KARL HUYSMANS
[1848–1907]

The pleasure of travel, which only exists as a matter of fact in retrospect and seldom in the present, at the instant when it is being experienced.

Against the Grain[3] *[1884].*
Chap. 3

One could revel, for instance, in long explorations while near one's own fireside, stimulating the restive or sluggish mind, if need be, by reading some narrative of travel in distant lands.

Ibid.

Is there a woman, whose form is more dazzling, more splendid than the two locomotives that pass over the Northern Railroad lines?

Ibid.

The diamond has become notoriously common since every tradesman has taken to wearing it on his little finger.

Ibid. Chap. 5

The loveliest tune imaginable becomes vulgar and insupportable as soon as the public begins to hum it and the hurdy-gurdies make it their own.

Ibid. Chap. 9

Perfumes, in fact, rarely come from the flowers whose names they bear . . . with the exception of the inimitable jasmine which it is impossible to counterfeit.

Ibid. Chap. 10

[1] Translated by JEREMIAH CURTIN [1838–1906].
[2] Translated by IZA YOUNG.
[3] Translated by JOHN HOWARD.

Art is the only clean thing on earth, except holiness.

Les Foules de Lourdes [1906]

BARONESS BERTHA VON SUTTNER
[1848–1914]

After the verb "To Love," "To Help" is the most beautiful verb in the world!

Epigram

FRIEDRICH A. J. VON BERNHARDI
[1849–1930]

Political morality differs from individual morality, because there is no power above the State.

Quoted as the theme of The Searchlights by ALFRED NOYES

MARSHAL FERDINAND FOCH
[1852–1929]

A guest at a dinner given in honor of Marshal Foch in Denver, Colorado, said that there was nothing but wind in French politeness. Marshal Foch retorted: "Neither is there anything but wind in a pneumatic tire, yet it eases wonderfully the jolts along life's highway."

My center is giving way, my right is pushed back — excellent! I'll attack.

*Said at the Battle of the Marne,
1918.*[1]

MUTSUHITO, EMPEROR OF JAPAN
[1852–1912]

Be ever careful in your choice of
  friends,
And let your special love be given to
  those
Whose strength of character may prove
  the whip

[1] "*Mon centre cède, ma droite recule, situation excellente, j'attaque.*" Quoted by B. H. LIDDELL HART, *Reputations Ten Years After* [1928].

That drives you ever to fair Wisdom's
goal.
Wisdom's Goal [1] [*1904*]

ARTHUR RIMBAUD
[1854–1891]

A, black; E, white; I, red; O, blue;
U, green.

Sonnet, Vowels

REMY DE GOURMONT
[1858–1915]

Aesthetic emotion puts man in a state
favourable to the reception of erotic
emotion. Art is the accomplice of love.
Take love away and there is no longer
art.

Decadence [2]

I do not believe it useful to generalize
opinions, to teach admirations. It is for
each man to procure himself the emotion he needs, and the morality which
suits him.

Ibid.

It is because peoples do not know
each other that they hate each other so
little.

Ibid.

There are too few obscure writers in
French. We accustom ourselves like
cowards to love only writing that is
easy and that will soon be elementary.

Ibid.

RABINDRANATH TAGORE
[1861–   ]

Peace, my heart, let the time for parting be sweet.
Let it not be a death but completeness.
Let love melt into memory and pain
into songs.

Peace

When one knows thee, then alien
there is none, then no door is shut. Oh,
grant me my prayer that I may never
lose the touch of the one in the play of
the many.

Gitanjali

[1] Translated by ARTHUR LLOYD.
[2] Translated by W. A. BRADLEY.

Things that I longed for in vain and
things that I got — let them pass. Let
me but truly possess the things I
spurned and overlooked.

Gitanjali

Come out of thyself,
    Stand in the open;
Within thy heart wilt thou hear
    The response of all the world.

Sheaves. The Invitation

When I bring you coloured toys, my
chi'd, I understand why there is such
a play of colours on clouds, on water,
and why flowers are painted in tints.

*The Crescent Moon. When and
Why*

I do not love him because he is good,
but because he is my little child.

Ibid. The Judge

I alone have a right to blame and
punish, for he only may chastise who
loves.

Ibid.

Years mature into fruit
So that some small seeds of moments
May outlive them.

On Visiting Yale University
[*1932*]

MAURICE MAETERLINCK
[1864–   ]

The future is a world limited by ourselves; in it we discover only what concerns us and, sometimes, by chance,
what interests those whom we love the
most.

Joyzelle. Act I

Men's weaknesses are often necessary
to the purposes of life.

Ibid. Act II

All our knowledge merely helps us to
die a more painful death than the animals that know nothing. A day will
come when science will turn upon its
error and no longer hesitate to shorten
our woes. A day will come when it will
dare and act with certainty; when life,
grown wiser, will depart silently at its
hour, knowing that it has reached its
term.

Our Eternity

I have never for one instant seen clearly within myself; how then would you have me judge the deeds of others? [1]

Pelleas and Melisande.
Act I, Sc. 3

Activity and duty are not to be found by the roadside. One must await them on the threshold, ready to bid them enter at the moment of passing, and they pass every day.

Ibid. Act II, Sc. 4

Each young and beautiful being shapes around it events that are themselves young, beautiful, and happy.

Ibid. Act IV, Sc. 2

Old men have need to touch sometimes with their lips the brow of a woman or the cheek of a child, that they may believe again in the freshness of life.

Ibid.

JOSÉ ASUNCIÓN SILVA
[1865–1896]

Verse is a chalice; place within it only
    A stainless thought;
From out whose deeps the smouldering
    radiance sparkles
    Like bubbles in a golden vintage
        caught.

Art.[2] Stanza 1

EDMOND ROSTAND
[1868–1918]

A great nose indicates a great man —
Genial, courteous, intellectual,
Virile, courageous.

Cyrano de Bergerac[3] [1897].
Act I

Lightly I toss my hat away,
    Languidly over my arm let fall
The cloak that covers my bright array —

Then out swords, and to work withal!

Cyrano de Bergerac [1897]. Act I.
Ballade of the Duel,[1] Stanza 1

Free fighters, free lovers, free spenders —
The Cadets of Gascoyne — the defenders
Of old homes, old names, and old splendors.[1]

Ibid. Act II

What would you have me do?
Seek for the patronage of some great man,
And like a creeping vine on a tall tree
Crawl upward, where I cannot stand alone?
No, thank you.

Ibid.

There comes one moment, once — and God help those
Who pass that moment by! — when Beauty stands
Looking into the soul with grave, sweet eyes
That sicken at pretty words.

Ibid. Act III

And what is a kiss, when all is done?
A promise given under seal — a vow
Taken before the shrine of memory —
A signature acknowledged — a rosy dot
Over the i of Loving.

Ibid.

In the volume whose sublime
Chapters are headed with proud capitals
You are the titles and you catch the eye.

L'Aiglon[2] [1900]. Act II

How do you know I am a diplomat?
By the skilful way you hide your claws.

Ibid. Act IV

My splendid cradle, Prudhon's masterpiece!
Amidst its gold and mother-o'-pearl I slept,
A babe, whose christening was a coronation.

Ibid. Act VI

---

[1] No man can justly censure or condemn another, because indeed no man truly knows another. . . . Further, no man can judge another, because no man knows himself. — SIR THOMAS BROWNE: *Religio Medici* (Everyman ed.), *P. 72*

[2] Translated from the Spanish by THOMAS WALSH [1875–1928].

[3] Translated by BRIAN HOOKER.

[1] See Edward A. Church, page 671.

[2] Translated by LOUIS N. PARKER.

I fall back dazzled at beholding myself
all rosy red,
At having, I myself, caused the sun to
rise.
    Chantecler [1907]. Act II, Sc. 3
And sounding in advance its victory,
My song jets forth so clear, so proud,
so peremptory,
That the horizon, seized with a rosy
trembling,
Obeys me.
                     Ibid.

ANDRÉ PAUL GUILLAUME GIDE
[1869–   ]

What another would have done as
well as you, do not do it. What another
would have said as well as you, do not
say it; written as well, do not write it.
Be faithful to that which exists nowhere but in yourself — and thus make
yourself indispensable.
    Les Nourritures Terrestres. Envoi

A unanimous chorus of praise is not
an assurance of survival; authors who
please everyone at once are quickly exhausted. I would prefer to think that a
hundred years hence people will say we
did not properly understand him [Ana-
tole France].
                 Pretexts

NIKOLAI LENIN
[1870–1924]

Political institutions are a super-
structure resting on an economic foundation.
    *The Three Sources and Three
    Constituent Parts of Marxism* [1]
    [1913]

Capital, created by the labour of the
worker, oppresses the worker by under-
mining the small proprietor and creating an army of the unemployed.
                     Ibid.

Capital has conquered throughout
the world, but its victory is only an

[1] Translated by MAX EASTMAN.

earnest of the victory of labour over
capital.
    *The Three Sources and Three
    Constituent Parts of Marxism*
    [1913]

People always have been and they always will be stupid victims of deceit
and self-deception in politics, until
they learn behind every kind of moral,
religious, political, social phrase, declaration and promise to seek out the interests of this or that class or classes.
                     Ibid.

It is true that liberty is precious —
so precious that it must be rationed.
    Quoted by SIDNEY AND BEA-
    TRICE WEBB *in Soviet Commu-
    nism: a New Civilization? Page
    1035*

Uneven economic and political development is an absolute law of capitalism. Hence, the victory of socialism is
possible, first in a few or even one single
capitalist country taken separately.
    *Collected Works. Vol. XVIII,
    Page 272*

MARCEL PROUST
[1871–1922]

(*From À la Recherche du temps
perdu, translated* [1] *as Remembrance
of Things Past, Random House edition*)

In his younger days a man dreams of
possessing the heart of the woman whom
he loves; later, the feeling that he possesses the heart of a woman may be
enough to make him fall in love with
her.
          Swann's Way. Page 253

What artists call posterity is the posterity of the work of art.
    *Within a Budding Grove. Part I,
    Page 147*

The time which we have at our dis-
posal every day is elastic; the passions
that we feel expand it, those that we in-

[1] By C. K. SCOTT MONCRIEFF, except the last
section, *The Past Recaptured*, which was
translated by FREDERICK A. BLOSSOM.

spire contract it; and habit fills up what remains.

Within a Budding Grove. Part I,
Page 264

Untruthfulness and dishonesty were with me, as with most people, called into being in so immediate, so contingent a fashion, and in self-defence, by some particular interest, that my mind, fixed on some lofty ideal, allowed my character, in the darkness below, to set about those urgent, sordid tasks, and did not look down to observe them.

The Guermantes Way. Part I,
Page 82

Like everybody who is not in love, he imagined that one chose the person whom one loved after endless deliberations and on the strength of various qualities and advantages.

Cities of the Plain. Part I,
Page 132

We passionately long that there may be another life in which we shall be similar to what we are here below. But we do not pause to reflect that, even without waiting for that other life, in this life, after a few years we are unfaithful to what we have been, to what we wished to remain immortally.

Ibid. Part II, Page 8

It is often simply from want of the creative spirit that we do not go to the full extent of suffering. And the most terrible reality brings us, with our suffering, the joy of a great discovery, because it merely gives a new and clear form to what we have long been ruminating without suspecting it.

Ibid. Page 363

The almost sacred character of all flesh upon which the sufferings that we have endured on its account have come in time to confer a sort of spiritual grace.

The Captive. Page 2

I thought how markedly . . . these works [Richard Wagner's music dramas] participate in that quality of being — albeit marvellously — always incomplete, which is the peculiarity of all the great works of the nineteenth century, with which the greatest writers of that century have stamped their books, but, watching themselves at work as though they were at once author and critic, have derived from this self-contemplation a novel beauty, exterior and superior to the work itself, imposing upon it retrospectively a unity, a greatness which it does not possess.

The Captive. Page 211

The bonds that unite another person to ourself exist only in our mind. Memory as it grows fainter relaxes them, and notwithstanding the illusion by which we would fain be cheated and with which, out of love, friendship, politeness, deference, duty, we cheat other people, we exist alone. Man is the creature that cannot emerge from himself, that knows his fellows only in himself; when he asserts the contrary, he is lying.

The Sweet Cheat Gone. Page 47

We believe that according to our desire we are able to change the things round about us, we believe this because otherwise we can see no favourable solution. We forget the solution that generally comes to pass and is also favourable: we do not succeed in changing things according to our desire, but gradually our desire changes. The situation that we hoped to change because it was intolerable becomes unimportant. We have not managed to surmount the obstacle, as we were absolutely determined to do, but life has taken us round it, led us past it, and then if we turn round to gaze at the remote past, we can barely catch sight of it, so imperceptible has it become.

Ibid. Page 48

There is not a woman in the world the possession of whom is as precious as that of the truths which she reveals to us by causing us to suffer.

Ibid. Page 111

We are healed of a suffering only by experiencing it to the full.

Ibid. Page 165

Happiness is beneficial for the body but it is grief that develops the powers of the mind.

The Past Recaptured. Page 237

As for happiness, it has hardly more than one useful quality, namely to make unhappiness possible. In our happiness, we should form very sweet bonds, full of confidence and attachment, in order that the sundering of them may cause us that priceless rending of the heart which is called unhappiness.

The Past Recaptured. Page 238

PAUL VALÉRY
[1871–   ]

[Of Anatole France.] A dreamy laziness, a laziness of enormous reading difficult to distinguish from study, a laziness like the repose of a fluid over-rich with substance and which in its stillness begets crystals of perfect form.

Discours de Réception, at the French Academy [1927], where he succeeded to the chair of Anatole France

The folly of mistaking a paradox for a discovery, a metaphor for a proof, a torrent of verbiage for a spring of capital truths, and oneself for an oracle, is inborn in us.

Introduction to the Method of Leonardo da Vinci [1]

Collect all the facts that can be collected about the life of Racine and you will never learn from them the art of his verse. All criticism is dominated by the outworn theory that the man is the cause of the work as in the eyes of the law the criminal is the cause of the crime. Far rather are they both the effects.

Ibid.

PAUL RICHARD
[1874–   ]

The vagabond, when rich, is called a tourist.

The Scourge of Christ [1929]. Page 40

When the rich assemble to concern themselves with the business of the poor it is called charity. When the poor

assemble to concern themselves with the business of the rich it is called anarchy.

The Scourge of Christ [1929]. Page 63

Hunting — the least honourable form of war on the weak.

Ibid. Page 142

THOMAS MANN
[1875–   ]

Space, like time, engenders forgetfulness; but it does so by setting us bodily free from our surroundings and giving us back our primitive, unattached state. . . . Time, we say, is Lethe; but change of air is a similar draught, and, if it works less thoroughly, does so more quickly.

The Magic Mountain. [1] *Chap. 1*

A man lives not only his personal life, as an individual, but also, consciously or unconsciously, the life of his epoch and his contemporaries.

Ibid. Chap. 2

It gives me a most peculiar feeling, when somebody is so stupid, and then ill into the bargain. It must be the most melancholy thing in life. . . . One always has the idea of a stupid man as perfectly healthy and ordinary, and of illness as making one refined and clever and unusual.

Ibid. Chap. 4

The solemn, discreet, almost over-awed bearing which the young German's respect for authority leads him to assume in the presence of pens, ink, and paper, or anything else which bears to his mind an official stamp.

Ibid.

I have the feeling that once I am at home again I shall need to sleep three weeks on end to get rested from the rest I've had!

Ibid.

The only religious way to think of death is as part and parcel of life; to regard it, with the understanding and

---

[1] Translated by Thomas McGreevy.

[1] Translated by H. T. Lowe-Porter. Modern Library edition.

the emotions, as the inviolable condition of life.

The Magic Mountain. Chap. 5

Time has no divisions to mark its passage, there is never a thunder-storm or blare of trumpets to announce the beginning of a new month or year. Even when a new century begins it is only we mortals who ring bells and fire off pistols.

Ibid.

Order and simplification are the first steps toward the mastery of a subject — the actual enemy is the unknown.

Ibid.

The proud embarrassment of the artist, tasting the enjoyment of looking on his own works with the eyes of strangers.

Ibid.

Human reason needs only to will more strongly than fate, and she *is* fate.

Ibid. Chap. 6

Opinions cannot survive if one has no chance to fight for them.

Ibid.

Chop-fallen funeral processions, with their dignity curtailed by present-day traffic conditions.

Ibid.

One quickly gets readiness in an art where strong desire comes in play.

Ibid.

All interest in disease and death is only another expression of interest in life, as is proven by the humanistic faculty of medicine, that addresses life and its ails always so politely in Latin, and is only a division of the great and pressing concern which, in all sympathy, I now name by its name: the human being, the delicate child of life, man.

Ibid.

What perp'exes the world is the disparity between the swiftness of the spirit, and the immense unwieldiness, sluggishness, inertia, permanence of matter.

Ibid.

The invention of printing and the Reformation are and remain the two outstanding services of central Europe to the cause of humanity.

The Magic Mountain. Chap. 6

Speech is civilization itself. The word, even the most contradictory word, preserves contact — it is silence which isolates.

Ibid.

A man's dying is more the survivors' affair than his own.

Ibid.

What we call mourning for our dead is perhaps not so much grief at not being able to call them back as it is grief at not being able to want to do so.

Ibid. Chap. 7

Time cools, time clarifies; no mood can be maintained quite unaltered through the course of hours.

Ibid.

Seven is a good handy figure in its way, picturesque, with a savour of the mythical; one might say that it is more filling to the spirit than a dull academic half-dozen.

Ibid.

RAINER MARIA RILKE
[1875–1926]

Her smile was not meant to be seen by anyone and served its whole purpose in being smiled.

The Journal of My Other Self [1]

He was a poet and hated the approximate.

Ibid.

Is it possible that nothing real or important has yet been seen or known or said? Is it possible that mankind has had thousands of years in which to observe, reflect, and record, and has allowed these millennia to slip past, like a recess interval at school in which one eats one's sandwich and an apple?

Yes, it is possible.

Is it possible that every individual has had to be reminded that he is indeed sprung from all those who have gone before, that he has known this and

[1] Translated [1930] by JOHN LINTON.

ought not to have been persuaded dif-
ferently by others?

Yes, it is possible.

The Journal of My Other Self

Love consists in this, that two solitudes protect and touch and greet each
other.

Letters to a Young Poet [1]

The future enters into us, in order to
transform itself in us, long before it
happens.

Ibid.

ALEXANDER BISSON
[*Floruit* 1900]

Our life is like some vast lake that is
slowly filling with the stream of our
years. As the waters creep surely upward the landmarks of the past are one
by one submerged. But there shall always be memory to lift its head above
the tide until the lake is overflowing.

Madame X [2]

BENITO MUSSOLINI
[1883–   ]

Italians, love bread, heart of the home,
    savor of the repast, joy of health;
Respect bread, sweat of the brow, pride
    of labor, poem of sacrifice;
Honor bread, glory of the fields, fra-
    grance of the earth, feast of life;
Do not waste bread, richness of the
    fatherland, sweetest gift of God,
    most holy reward of human toil.

Proclamation [*April 14–15, 1928*]

Speeches made to the people are essential to the arousing of enthusiasm
for a war.

Quoted by EMIL LUDWIG *in Talks
with Mussolini* [*1932*]

Ludwig. How do you find it possible
to put up with the multitude of faces
you have to look at here day after day?

Mussolini. I merely see in them what
they say to me. I do not let them come
into contact with my inmost being. I
am no more moved by them than by

this table and these papers. I preserve
my loneliness untouched.

*Quoted by Emil Ludwig in Talks
with Mussolini* [*1932*]

War alone brings up to its highest
tension all human energy and puts the
stamp of nobility upon the peoples who
have the courage to face it.

*Written for The Italian
Encyclopedia* [1]

Three cheers for war in general!

Speech [1]

Fortunately the Italian people is not
yet accustomed to eating several times
per day.

Speech [*December, 1930*] [1]

We have buried the putrid corpse of
liberty.

Speech [2]

FRANZ KAFKA
[1884–1924]

The true way goes over a rope which
is not stretched at any great height but
just above the ground. It seems more
designed to make people stumble than
to be walked upon.

The Great Wall of China.[3]
Reflections

You do not need to leave your room.
Remain sitting at your table and listen.
Do not even listen, simply wait. Do not
even wait, be quite still and solitary.
The world will freely offer itself to you
to be unmasked, it has no choice, it will
roll in ecstasy at your feet.

Ibid.

ADOLF HITLER
[1889–   ]

Then will come a National-Socialist
State tribunal; then will November,
1918, be expiated; then heads will roll!

*Spoken in testimony at a trial of
German army officers, in Leipzig*
[*1930*] [4]

[1] Quoted in GEORGE SELDES: *Sawdust
Caesar.*

[2] Quoted in MAURICE PARMELEE: *Bolshe-
vism, Fascism and the Liberal-Democratic
State.*

[3] Translated by MR. and MRS. EDWIN
MUIR.

[4] Quoted in KONRAD HEIDEN: *Hitler, A Biography* [1936].

[1] Translated [1934] by M. D. HERTER NOR-
TON.

[2] Translated by J. W. MCCONAUGHY.

BARON EHRENFRIED GUNTHER VON HUENEFELD
[1893–1929]

To-morrow, we shall start on our great journey. After a trying period of expectancy, we have entered upon the stage of certainty. Now the last word lies with the God of weathers and to confide in Him is the duty of every sincere sportsman.

Interview, before his transatlantic air flight in the Bremen [April 12–13, 1928]

Silent I ponder. Ended is the flight,
And He whose hands upheld us in the air,
Whose grace has calmed the snowstorm and the night,
Is now with me and folds my hands in prayer.

Song of Thanks in the Lighthouse at Greenly, after the safe landing of the Bremen

He who has glimpsed the awful face of Death
Can but confess Thy mercy and Thy might;
Who never bowed his heart before Thy cross,
He never saw the unadulterate Light.

Ibid.

MISCELLANEOUS TRANSLATIONS

Arbor viva, tacui; mortua, cano
(When I was part of a living tree, I was
silent; now dead, I sing).
> *Inscription found on an old violin* [1]

A shipwrecked sailor, buried on this
    coast,
  Bids thee take sail —
Full many a gallant ship, when we were
    lost,
  Weathered the gale.[2]
> *Palatine Anthology. VII, 283,*
> *Theodoridas* [3]

Dansons la Carmagnole,
Vive le son du canon!
> *La Carmagnole* [*France, 1792*]

Dead on the field of honour.
> *From the death of Latour d'Au-*
> *vergne at Oberhausen, Bavaria*
> [*June 27, 1800*] *until 1814, his*
> *name was retained on the roll of*
> *his company of grenadiers, as a*
> *mark of honour. At each roll-*
> *call the color-sergeant made this*
> *response.*

Death is never at a loss for occasions.
> *Greek Anthology. Book IX, 488,*
> *Trypho*

Dum tacent, clamant (Though silent,
they cry aloud).
> *Inscription on a monument,*
> *Union Soldiers' Cemetery, Chal-*
> *mette, near New Orleans, Lou-*
> *isiana*

Ea discamus in terris quorum scientia
perseveret in caelis (Let us learn on
earth those things whose knowledge
might continue in heaven).
> *Motto of Saint Paul's School,*
> *Concord, New Hampshire*

Laissez faire, laissez aller (Let it be,
let it go; viz., let nature take its course).
> *Attributed to* BOISGUILBERT
> [*1646–1714*], *also to* GOURNAY,
> *Minister of Commerce at Paris*
> [*1751*], *and to* QUESNAY, *writer*
> *on political economy. Quoted by*
> ADAM SMITH *in The Wealth of*
> *Nations*

Mater ait natae, dic natae, natam
Ut moneat natae, plangere filiolam.
(The mother says to her daughter:
"Tell your daughter that she advise her
    daughter
That her daughter is crying.")
> *A distich, according to Zwingler,*
> *on a lady of the Dalburg family*
> *who saw her descendants to the*
> *sixth generation*

Medicine for the soul.
> *Inscription over the door of the*
> *Library at Thebes. —* DIODORUS
> SICULUS [*second half of first*
> *century*]: *I, 49, 3*

Never believe the impossible,
Never regret the past,
Do not long for the unattainable.
> *Aucassin and Nicolette* [*13th cen-*
> *tury*]. *Le Lai de l'Oiselet*

  Nothing is changed in France; there
is only one Frenchman more.
> *According to the Contemporary*
> *Review* [*February, 1854*] *this*
> *sentence formed the opening of*
> *an address written in the name*
> *of the Comte d'Artois by Count*
> *Beugnot, and published in the*
> *Moniteur* [*April 12, 1814*]

Terrible he rode alone,
  With his Yemen sword for aid;

---

[1] Oh all you safe and smooth of heart
  Listen to song from me,
Whose wooden throat was once a part
  Of the north side of a tree!
      WINIFRED WELLES: *The Violin*

[2] Tomb of a shipwrecked seafarer am I;
  But thou, sail on!
For homeward safe did other vessels fly,
  Though we were gone.
    ANDREW LANG [*1844–1912*]: *The*
    Sailor's Grave (from the Greek)

[3] Translated by HENRY WELLESLEY [*1791–*
1866].

Ornament it carried none
But the notches on the blade.

> *The Death Feud, an Arab War
> Song, of an age earlier than that
> of Mahomet. Anonymous trans-
> lation from Tait's Magazine
> [July, 1850]*

The world is merely a bridge; ye are to pass over it, and not to build your dwellings upon it.

> *Inscription on the Victory
> Gate, Fathepur, India. From
> Agrapha, Unwritten Sayings
> of Jesus*

Thou who passest on this path,
If hap'y thou dost mark this monu-
  ment,
Laugh not, I pray thee, though it is a
  dog's grave.
Tears fell for me, and the dust was
  heaped above me
By a master's hand.

> *Greek Anthology. Epitaph (of un-
> known authorship)*

Whatever kind of word thou speakest the like shalt thou hear.

> *Ibid. Book IX, 382
> A Homeric Cento*

When I am dead let fire destroy the world;
It matters not to me, for I am safe.

> *Ibid. Fragment 430 (of unknown
> authorship)*

Toil does not come to help the idle.

> *Greek Anthology. Fragment 440
> (of unknown authorship)*

Nothing equals the joy of the drinker, except the joy of the wine in being drunk.

> *Anonymous. Quoted by* Mau-
> rice des Ombiaux: *Nouveau
> Manuel de l'Amateur de Bour-
> goyne [1921]*

In the U.S.S.R. work is the duty of every able-bodied citizen, according to the principle: "He who does not work, neither shall he eat."

In the U.S.S.R. the principle of socialism is realised: "From each according to his ability, to each according to his work." [1]

> *Constitution of the Union
> of Soviet Socialist Republics
> [1936]. Article 12*

Citizens of the U.S.S.R. have the right to work.

> *Ibid. Article 118*

Citizens of the U.S.S.R. have the right to rest.

> *Ibid. Article 119*

Citizens of the U.S.S.R. have the right to maintenance in old age.

> *Ibid. Article 120*

Citizens of the U.S.S.R. have the right to education.

> *Ibid. Article 121*

---

[1] See Karl Marx, page 1071.

THOMAS RUSSELL

The great Jehovah speaks to us
In Genesis and Exodus;
Leviticus and Numbers see,
Followed by Deuteronomy.
Joshua and Judges sway the land,
Ruth gleans a sheaf with trembling hand,
Samuel and numerous Kings appear,
Whose Chronicles we wondering hear;
Ezra and Nehemiah now
Esther, the beauteous mourner, show;
Job speaks in sighs, David in Psalms,
The Proverbs teach to scatter alms.
Ecclesiastes then comes on
And the sweet Song of Solomon.
Isaiah, Jeremiah then,
With Lamentations takes his pen.
Ezekiel, Daniel, Hosea's lyres
Swell Joel, Amos, Obadiah's.
Next Jonah, Micah, Nahum come,
And lofty Habakkuk finds room.
While Zephaniah, Haggai call,
Rapt Zechariah builds his wall,
And Malachi with garments rent,
Concludes the ancient Testament.
        *Old Testament. (American Tract
                Society, 1852)*

Matthew and Mark, and Luke and John,
The Holy Gospels wrote,
Describing how the Saviour died —
His life — and all He taught;
Acts prove how God the Apostles owned
With signs in every place;
St. Paul, in Romans, teaches us
How man is saved by grace;
The Apostle, in Corinthians,
Instructs, exhorts, reproves;
Galatians shows that faith in Christ

Alone the Father loves.
Ephesians and Philippians tell
What Christians ought to be;
Colossians bids us live to God
And for eternity.
In Thessalonians we are taught
The Lord will come from Heaven;
In Timothy and Titus
A bishop's rule is given.
Philemon marks a Christian's love,
Which only Christians know;
Hebrews reveals the Gospel
Prefigured by the law;
James teaches without holiness
Faith is but vain and dead;
St. Peter points the narrow way
In which the saints are led;
John, in his three Epistles,
On love delights to dwell;
St. Jude gives awful warning
Of judgment, wrath, and hell;
The Revelation prophesies
Of that tremendous day
When Christ, and Christ alone, shall be
The trembling sinner's stay.
        *New Testament. (American Tract
                Society, 1852)*

These are the twelve Apostles' names:
Peter and Andrew, John and James,
Two pair of brothers who lived by the sea,
When Jesus said to them, "Follow me."
Then James the Less and Jude were called,
        too,
Philip, and also Bartholomew,
Matthew, and Thomas who doubted His word,
Simon, and Judas who sold his Lord.
        ANONYMOUS: *The Apostles*

THE KING JAMES BIBLE [1]

OLD TESTAMENT

And God said, Let there be light: and there was light.

Genesis. I, 3

It is not good that the man should be alone.

Ibid. II, 18

Bone of my bones, and flesh of my flesh.

Ibid. 23

They sewed fig-leaves together, and made themselves aprons.

Ibid. III, 7

In the sweat of thy face shalt thou eat bread.

Ibid. 19

For dust thou art, and unto dust shalt thou return.

Ibid.

The mother of all living.

Ibid. 20

Am I my brother's keeper?

Ibid. IV, 9

My punishment is greater than I can bear.

Ibid. 13

And the Lord set a mark upon Cain.

Ibid. 15

Jubal: he was the father of all such as handle the harp and organ.

Ibid. 21

And all the days of Methuselah were nine hundred and sixty years.

Ibid. V, 27

There were giants in the earth in those days.

Ibid. VI, 4

[1] Among all our joys, there was no one that more filled our hearts, than the blessed continuance of the preaching of God's sacred Word among us; which is that inestimable treasure, which excelleth all the riches of the earth; because the fruit thereof extendeth itself, not only to the time spent in this transitory world, but directeth and disposeth men unto that eternal happiness which is above in heaven. — THE TRANSLATORS

And the rain was upon the earth forty days and forty nights.

Genesis. VII, 12

The dove found no rest for the sole of her foot.

Ibid. VIII, 9

In her mouth was an olive leaf.

Ibid. 11

While the earth remaineth, seedtime and harvest, and cold and heat, and summer and winter, and day and night shall not cease.

Ibid. 22

Whoso sheddeth man's blood, by man shall his blood be shed.

Ibid. IX, 6

I do set my bow in the cloud.

Ibid. 13

Nimrod the mighty hunter.

Ibid. X, 9

Babel; because the Lord did there confound the language of all the earth.

Ibid. XI, 9

Let there be no strife, I pray thee, between me and thee.

Ibid. XIII, 8

In a good old age.

Ibid. XV, 15

His [Ishmael's] hand will be against every man, and every man's hand against him.

Ibid. XVI, 12

Old and well stricken in age.

Ibid. XVIII, 11

His [Lot's] wife looked back from behind him, and she became a pillar of salt.[1]

Ibid. XIX, 26

The voice is Jacob's voice, but the hands are the hands of Esau.

Ibid. XXVII, 22

[1] Of all Metamorphoses or transmigrations. I believe only one, that is of Lot's wife. — SIR THOMAS BROWNE: *Religio Medici* (Everyman ed.), *P. 42*

He [Jacob] dreamed, and behold a ladder set up on the earth, and the top of it reached to heaven: and behold the angels of the Lord ascending and descending it.

Genesis. XXVIII, 22

Jacob served seven years for Rachel.

Ibid. XXIX, 20

Mizpah . . . The Lord watch between me and thee, when we are absent one from another.

Ibid. XXXI, 49

I will not let thee go, except thou bless me.

Ibid. XXXII, 26

They stript Joseph out of his coat, his coat of many colours.

Ibid. XXXVII, 23

He left his garment in her hand, and fled.

Ibid. XXXIX, 12

There come seven years of great plenty throughout all the land of Egypt: And there shall arise after them seven years of famine.

Ibid. XLI, 29, 30

Bring down my gray hairs with sorrow to the grave.

Ibid. XLII, 38, and XLIV, 29

His life is bound up in the lad's life.

Ibid. XLIV, 30

Unstable as water, thou shalt not excel.

Ibid. XLIX, 4

I have been a stranger in a strange land.

Exodus. II, 22

Put off thy shoes from off thy feet, for the place whereon thou standest is holy ground.

Ibid. III, 5

A land flowing with milk and honey.[1]

Ibid. 8, and XXXIII, 3

I am slow of speech, and of a slow tongue.

Ibid. IV, 10

Ye shall no more give the people straw to make brick.

Ibid. V, 7

Darkness which may be felt.

Ibid. X, 21

[1] Also in *Jeremiah, XI, 5,* and *XXXIII, 22.*

This day [passover] shall be unto you for a memorial; and ye shall keep it a feast to the Lord throughout your generations.

Exodus. XII, 14

There was not a house where there was not one dead.[1]

Ibid. 30

The Lord went before them by day in a pillar of a cloud, to lead them the way; and by night in a pillar of fire.

Ibid. XIII, 21

They could not drink of the waters of Marah, for they were bitter.

Ibid. XV, 23

When we sat by the fleshpots.

Ibid. XVI, 3

It is manna.

Ibid. 15

Honour thy father and thy mother.[2]

Ibid. XX, 12

Eye for eye, tooth for tooth, hand for hand, foot for foot.[3]

Ibid. XXI, 24

I send an Angel before thee, to keep thee in the way.[4]

Ibid. XXIII, 20

He wrote upon the tables the words of the covenant, the ten commandments.

Ibid. XXXIV, 28

The swine . . . is unclean to you. Of their flesh shall ye not eat.

Leviticus. XI, 7, 8

[1] See John Hay, page 639.
[2] Also in *Apocrypha, Ecclesiasticus, III, 8.*

Have no other gods but me;
Unto no image bow the knee;
Take not the name of God in vain;
Do not the Sabbath day profane;
Honour thy father and thy mother too;
And see that thou no murder do;
From vile adultery keep thou clean;
And steal not, though thy state be mean;
Bear not false witness — shun that blot;
What is thy neighbour's covet not.
The Decalogue. Found in Parish Register, Lancaster, Nottinghamshire, England, 1689.
[3] Also in *Deuteronomy, XIX, 21.*
[4] I could easily believe that not only whole countries, but particular persons, have their Tutelary and Guardian Angels. — Sir Thomas Browne: *Religio Medici* (Everyman ed.), *P. 36*

Love thy neighbour as thyself.
Leviticus. XIX, 18

The Lord bless thee, and keep thee: The Lord make his face shine upon thee, and be gracious unto thee: The Lord lift up his countenance upon thee,[1] and give thee peace.
Numbers. VI, 24, 25, 26

The Lord opened the mouth of the ass, and she said unto Balaam, What have I done unto thee, that thou hast smitten me these three times?
Ibid. XXII, 28

Let me die the death of the righteous, and let my last end be like his!
Ibid. XXIII, 10

How goodly are thy tents, O Jacob, and thy tabernacles, O Israel!
Ibid. XXIV, 5

Man doth not live by bread only.[2]
Deuteronomy. VIII, 3

The wife of thy bosom.
Ibid. XIII, 6

The poor shall never cease out of the land.
Ibid. XV, 11

In the morning thou shalt say, Would God it were even! and at even thou shalt say, Would God it were morning![3]
Ibid. XXVIII, 67

Be strong and of a good courage.[4]
Ibid. XXXI, 6, 7, 23

He kept him as the apple of his eye.[5]
Ibid. XXXII, 10

Jeshurun waxed fat, and kicked.
Ibid. 15

As thy days, so shall thy strength be.
Ibid. XXXIII, 25

Underneath are the everlasting arms.
Ibid. 27

The wall of the city shall fall down flat.
Joshua. VI, 5

His fame was noised throughout all the country.
Ibid. 27

The sun stood still, and the moon stayed.
Joshua. X, 13

I am going the way of all the earth.
Ibid. XXIII, 14

I arose a mother in Israel.
Judges. V, 7

The stars in their courses fought against Sisera.
Ibid. 20

At her feet he bowed, he fell, he lay down: at her feet he bowed, he fell: where he bowed, there he fell down dead.[1]
Ibid. 27

Why tarry the wheels of his chariots?
Ibid. 28

Is not the gleaning of the grapes of Ephraim better than the vintage of Abiezer?
Ibid. VIII, 2

There was a swarm of bees and honey in the carcase of the lion.
Ibid. XIV, 8

He smote them hip and thigh.
Ibid. XV, 8

With the jaw of an ass have I slain a thousand men.
Ibid. 16

And Delilah said to Samson, Tell me, I pray thee, wherein thy great strength lieth.
Ibid. XVI, 6

The Philistines be upon thee, Samson.
Ibid. 9

So the dead which he slew at his death were more than they which he slew in his life.
Ibid. 30

From Dan even to Beer-sheba.
Ibid. XX, 1

The people arose as one man.
Ibid. 8

Whither thou goest, I will go; and where thou lodgest, I will lodge: thy people shall be my people, and thy God my God.
Ruth. I, 16

---

[1] Lift thou up the light of thy countenance upon us. — *Psalm IV, 6*
[2] Also in *Matthew, IV, 4.*
[3] See Swinburne, page 632.
[4] Also in *Joshua, I, 6* and *X, 25.*
[5] See Cervantes, page 1040. See page 1103.

[1] Such repetitions [in this verse from the Song of Deborah] I admit to be a beauty of the highest kind. — COLERIDGE: *Biographia Literaria, Chap. 17*

Let me glean and gather after the reapers among the sheaves.

Ruth. II, 7

Go not empty unto thy mother in law.

Ibid. III, 17

The Lord called Samuel; and he answered, Here am I.

1 Samuel. III, 4

Speak, Lord; for thy servant heareth.

Ibid. 9

Quit yourselves like men.

Ibid. IV, 9

The glory is departed from Israel.

Ibid. 21

Is Saul also among the prophets?

Ibid. X, 11

And all the people shouted, and said, God save the king.

Ibid. 24

A man after his own heart.

Ibid. XIII, 14

Now there was no smith found throughout all the land of Israel.

Ibid. 19

So David prevailed over the Philistine with a sling and with a stone.[1]

Ibid. XVII, 50

Saul hath slain his thousands, and David his ten thousands.

Ibid. XVIII, 7; XXI, 11; XXIX, 5

For he loved him as he loved his own soul.

Ibid. XX, 17

David therefore departed thence, and escaped to the cave Adullam.

Ibid. XXII, 1

And every one that was in distress, and every one that was in debt, and every one that was discontented, gathered themselves unto him; and he became a captain over them.

Ibid. 2

Tell it not in Gath, publish it not in the streets of Askelon.

2 Samuel. I, 20

Saul and Jonathan were lovely and pleasant in their lives, and in their death they were not divided.

2 Samuel. I, 23

How are the mighty fallen!

Ibid. 25, 27

Thy love to me was wonderful, passing the love of women.

Ibid. 26

Abner . . . smote him under the fifth rib.

Ibid. II, 23

Know ye not that there is a prince and a great man fallen this day in Israel?

Ibid. III, 38

Tarry at Jericho until your beards be grown.[1]

Ibid. X, 5

Set ye Uriah in the forefront of the hottest battle.

Ibid. XI, 15

Thou art the man.

Ibid. XII, 7

I shall go to him, but he shall not return to me.[2]

Ibid. 23

As water spilt on the ground, which cannot be gathered up again.

Ibid. XIV, 14

Would God I had died for thee, O Absalom, my son, my son!

Ibid. XVIII, 33

They were wont to speak in old time saying, They shall surely ask counsel at Abel: and so they ended the matter.

Ibid. XX, 18

The Lord is my rock, and my fortress, and my deliverer.

Ibid. XXII, 2

The sweet psalmist of Israel.

Ibid. XXIII, 1

Oh, that one would give me to drink of the water of the well of Beth-lehem which is by the gate!

Ibid. 15

A wise and an understanding heart.

1 Kings. III, 12

[1] A boy with the heart of a king
  Fitted the stone to his shepherd sling,
  And a giant fell, and a royal race was free.
  EDWARD ROWLAND SILL: *Field Notes, VII*

[1] Also in *1 Chronicles, XIX, 5.*
[2] With a change of pronouns, Lord Byron asked to have this line inscribed on the gravestone of his daughter, Allegra. — In a letter to Murray [May 26, 1822].

Many as the sand which is by the sea in multitude.

1 Kings. IV, 20

He [Solomon] spake three thousand proverbs: and his songs were a thousand and five.

Ibid. 32

So that there was neither hammer nor axe nor any tool of iron heard in the house, while it was in building.[1]

Ibid. VI, 7

A proverb and a byword.[2]

Ibid. IX, 7

The half was not told me.

Ibid. X, 7

Once in three years came the navy of Tharshish, bringing gold and silver, ivory, and apes, and peacocks.[3]

Ibid. 22

King Solomon loved many strange women.[4]

Ibid. XI, 1

I have commanded a widow woman there to sustain thee.

Ibid. XVII, 9

An handful of meal in a barrel, and a little oil in a cruse.

Ibid. 12

And the barrel of meal wasted not, neither did the cruse of oil fail.

Ibid. 16

How long halt ye between two opinions?

Ibid. XVIII, 21

There ariseth a little cloud out of the sea, like a man's hand.

Ibid. 44

A still, small voice.

Ibid. XIX, 12

Let not him that girdeth on his harness boast himself as he that putteth it off.

Ibid. XX, 11

Busy here and there.

Ibid. 40

Hast thou found me, O mine enemy?

Ibid. XXI, 20

Is it well with the child?

2 Kings. IV, 26

Death in the pot.

2 Kings. IV, 40

Are not Abana and Pharpar, rivers of Damascus, better than all the waters of Israel?

Ibid. V, 12

Is not the sound of his master's feet behind him?

Ibid. VI, 32

Is thy servant a dog, that he should do this great thing?

Ibid. VIII, 13

Like the driving of Jehu, the son of Nimshi; for he driveth furiously.

Ibid. IX, 20

Jezebel heard of it; and she painted her face, and tired her head, and looked out at a window.

Ibid. 30

A land of corn and wine.

Ibid. XVIII, 32

Set thine house in order.

Ibid. XX, 1

Our days on the earth are as a shadow.[1]

1 Chronicles. XXIX, 15

The man whom the king delighteth to honour.

Esther. VI, 6

One that feared God, and eschewed evil.

Job. I, 1

Satan came also.

Ibid. 6

The Lord gave, and the Lord hath taken away; blessed be the name of the Lord.

Ibid. 21

All that a man hath, will he give for his life.[2]

Ibid. II, 4

There the wicked cease from troubling, and there the weary be at rest.

Ibid. III, 17

Night, when deep sleep falleth on men.

Ibid. IV, 13; XXXIII, 15

---

[1] See Cowper, page 266.
[2] Also in *2 Chronicles, VII, 20.*
[3] See Masefield, page 832.
[4] See Naylor, page 754.

[1] Also in *Job, VIII, 9.*
[2] Satan's old saw being apt here — skin for skin,
All a man hath that will he give for life.
ROBERT BROWNING: *The Ring and the Book, Book I*

Man is born unto trouble, as the sparks fly upward.

Job. V, 7

He taketh the wise in their own craftiness.

Ibid. 13

Thou shalt come to thy grave in a full age, like as a shock of corn cometh in in his season.

Ibid. 26

How forcible are right words!

Ibid. VI, 25

My days are swifter than a weaver's shuttle.

Ibid. VII, 6

He shall return no more to his house, neither shall his place know him any more.[1]

Ibid. 10

I would not live alway.

Ibid. 16

The land of darkness and the shadow of death.

Ibid. X, 21

Canst thou by searching find out God?

Ibid. XI, 7

Clearer than the noonday.

Ibid. 17

No doubt but ye are the people.[2]

Ibid. XII, 2

Wisdom shall die with you.

Ibid.

Speak to the earth, and it shall teach thee.

Ibid. 8

Man that is born of a woman is of few days, and full of trouble.

Ibid. XIV, 1

If a man die, shall he live again?

Ibid. 14

Miserable comforters are ye all.

Ibid. XVI, 2

The king of terrors.

Ibid. XVIII, 14

---

[1] When a few years are come, then I shall go the way whence I shall not return. — *Job, XVI, 22*
The place thereof shall know it no more. — *Psalm CIII, 16*
[2] No doubt but ye are the People — your throne is above the King's.
KIPLING: *The Islanders*

I am escaped with the skin of my teeth.

Job. XIX, 20

Oh that my words were now written! oh that they were printed in a book!

Ibid. 23

Seeing the root of the matter is found in me.

Ibid. 28

Though wickedness be sweet in his mouth, though he hide it under his tongue.

Ibid. XX, 12

The land of the living.

Ibid. XXVIII, 13

The price of wisdom is above rubies.

Ibid. 18

When the ear heard me, then it blessed me; and when the eye saw me, it gave witness to me.

Ibid. XXIX, 11

I caused the widow's heart to sing for joy.

Ibid. 13

I was eyes to the blind, and feet was I to the lame.

Ibid. 15

The house appointed for all living.

Ibid. XXX, 23

Companion to owls.

Ibid. 29

My desire is . . . that mine adversary had written a book.

Ibid. XXXI, 35

Great men are not always wise.

Ibid. XXXII, 9

He multiplieth words without knowledge.

Ibid. XXXV, 16

Fair weather cometh out of the north.

Ibid. XXXVII, 22

Who is this that darkeneth counsel by words without knowledge?

Ibid. XXXVIII, 2

The morning stars sang together, and all the sons of God shouted for joy.

Ibid. 7

Hitherto shalt thou come, but no further; and here shall thy proud waves be stayed.

Ibid. 11

Canst thou bind the sweet influences of Pleiades, or loose the bands of Orion?
Job. XXXVII, 31

Canst thou guide Arcturus with his sons?
Ibid. 32

He smelleth the battle afar off.
Ibid. XXXIX, 25

Hard as a piece of the nether mill-stone.
Ibid. XLI, 24

He maketh the deep to boil like a pot.
Ibid. 31

I have heard of thee by the hearing of the ear; but now mine eye seeth thee.
Ibid. XLII, 5

His leaf also shall not wither.
Psalms. I, 3

I will both lay me down in peace, and sleep.[1]
Ibid. IV, 8

Out of the mouth of babes and suck-lings.
Ibid. VIII, 2

When I consider thy heavens.
Ibid. 3

What is man, that thou art mindful of him.
Ibid. 4

Thou hast made him a little lower than the angels.
Ibid. 5

Flee as a bird to your mountain.
Ibid. XI, 1

The fool hath said in his heart, There is no God.
Ibid. XIV, 1; LIII, 1

He that sweareth to his own hurt, and changeth not.
Ibid. XV, 4

The lines are fallen unto me in pleasant places; [2] yea, I have a goodly heritage.
Ibid. XVI, 6

Keep me as the apple of the eye, hide me under the shadow of thy wings.
Ibid. XVII, 8

The sorrows of death compassed me.
Ibid. XVIII, 4

[1] I will lay me down in peace, and take my rest. — *Book of Common Prayer*
[2] The lot is fallen unto me in a fair ground. — *Ibid.*

He rode upon a cherub, and did fly: yea, he did fly upon the wings of the wind.
Psalms. XVIII, 10

The heavens declare the glory of God; and the firmament showeth his handiwork.
Ibid. XIX, 1

Day unto day uttereth speech, and night unto night showeth knowledge.
Ibid. 2

And there is nothing hid from the heat thereof.
Ibid. 6

More to be desired are they than gold.
Ibid. 10

Sweeter also than honey and the honeycomb.
Ibid.

Cleanse thou me from secret faults.
Ibid. 12

Let the words of my mouth, and the meditation of my heart, be acceptable in thy sight.
Ibid. 14

I may tell all my bones.
Ibid. XXII, 17

He maketh me to lie down in green pastures: he leadeth me beside the still waters.
Ibid. XXIII, 2

The valley of the shadow of death.
Ibid. 4

Thy rod and thy staff they comfort me.
Ibid.

My cup runneth over.
Ibid. 5

Weeping may endure for a night, but joy cometh in the morning.
Ibid. XXX, 5

My times are in thy hand.
Ibid. XXXI, 15

From the strife of tongues.
Ibid. 20

He fashioneth their hearts alike.
Ibid. XXXIII, 15

Keep thy tongue from evil, and thy lips from speaking guile.
Ibid. XXXIV, 13

I have been young, and now am old;
yet have I not seen the righteous forsaken, nor his seed begging bread.

Psalms. XXXVII, 25

Spreading [1] himself like a green bay-
tree.

Ibid. 35

Mark the perfect man, and behold
the upright.

Ibid. 37

While I was musing the fire burned.

Ibid. XXXIX, 3

Lord, make me to know mine end,
and the measure of my days, what it
is; that I may know how frail I am.

Ibid. 4

Every man at his best state is altogether vanity.

Ibid. 5

He heapeth up riches, and knoweth
not who shall gather them.

Ibid. 6

Blessed is he that considereth the
poor.

Ibid. XLI, 1

As the hart panteth after the waterbrooks.

Ibid. XLII, 1

Deep calleth unto deep.

Ibid. 7

My tongue is the pen of a ready
writer.

Ibid. XLV, 1

God is our refuge and strength, a
very present help in trouble.

Ibid. XLVI, 1

Beautiful for situation, the joy of the
whole earth, is Mount Zion, . . . the
city of the great King.

Ibid. XLVIII, 2

Man being in honour abideth not; he
is like the beasts that perish.

Ibid. XLIX, 12, 20

The cattle upon a thousand hills.

Ibid. L, 10

Wash me, and I shall be whiter than
snow.

Ibid. LI, 7

Create in me a clean heart, O God;
and renew a right spirit within me.

Ibid. 10

A broken and a contrite heart.

Psalms. LI, 17

Oh that I had wings like a dove!

Ibid. LV, 6

But it was thou, a man mine equal,
my guide, and mine acquaintance.[1]

Ibid. 13

We took sweet counsel together.

Ibid. 14

The words of his mouth were
smoother than butter, but war was in
his heart.[2]

Ibid. 21

They are like the deaf adder that
stoppeth her ear; which will not
hearken to the voice of charmers,
charming never so wisely.[3]

Ibid. LVIII, 4, 5

Vain is the help of man.

Ibid. LX, 11; CVIII, 12

Lead me to the rock that is higher
than I.

Ibid. LXI, 2

Surely men of low degree are vanity,
and men of high degree are a lie: to be
laid in the balance, they are altogether
lighter than vanity.

Ibid. LXII, 9

Thou renderest to every man according to his work.

Ibid. 12

Thou crownest the year with thy
goodness.

Ibid. LXV, 11

We went through fire and through
water.

Ibid. LXVI, 12

God setteth the solitary in families.

Ibid. LXVIII, 6

He shall come down like rain upon
the mown grass.

Ibid. LXXII, 6

His enemies shall lick the dust.

Ibid. 9

---

[1] Flourishing. — *Book of Common Prayer*

[1] But it was even thou, my companion, my
guide, and mine own familiar friend. — *Book
of Common Prayer*. See note, page 1128.
Mine own familiar friend. — *Psalm XLI, 9*
[2] The words of his mouth were softer than
butter, having war in his heart. — *Book of
Common Prayer*
[3] Like the deaf adder, that stoppeth her
ears; which refuseth to hear the voice of the
charmer, charm he never so wisely. — *Ibid.*

As a dream when one awaketh.
Psalms. LXXIII, 20

Promotion cométh neither from the east, nor from the west, nor from the south.
Ibid. LXXV, 6

He putteth down one and setteth up another.
Ibid. 7

They go from strength to strength.
Ibid. LXXXIV, 7

A day in thy courts is better than a thousand. I had rather be a door-keeper in the house of my God, than to dwell in the tents of wickedness.
Ibid. 10

Mercy and truth are met together: righteousness and peace have kissed each other.
Ibid. LXXXV, 10

A thousand years in thy sight are but as yesterday when it is past, and as a watch in the night.
Ibid. XC, 4

We spend our years as a tale that is told.[1]
Ibid. 9

The days of our years are threescore years and ten; and if by reason of strength they be fourscore years, yet is their strength labour and sorrow; for it is soon cut off, and we fly away.[2]
Ibid. 10

So teach us to number our days, that we may apply our hearts unto wisdom.
Ibid. 12

Establish thou the work of our hands upon us; yea, the work of our hands establish thou it.
Ibid. 17

I will say of the Lord, He is my refuge and my fortress: my God; in him will I trust.
Ibid. XCI, 2

Nor for the pestilence that walketh in darkness; nor for the destruction that wasteth at noonday.
Psalms. XCI, 6

He shall give his angels charge over thee, to keep thee in all thy ways.
Ibid. 11

The righteous shall flourish like the palm-tree: he shall grow like a cedar in Lebanon.
Ibid. XCII, 12

The noise of many waters.
Ibid. XCIII, 4

The Lord reigneth; let the earth rejoice.
Ibid. XCVII, 1

As for man, his days are as grass: as a flower of the field, so he flourisheth.
Ibid. CIII, 15

The wind passeth over it, and it is gone; and the place thereof shall know it no more.[1]
Ibid. 16

Wine that maketh glad the heart of man.
Ibid. CIV, 15

Man goeth forth unto his work and to his labour until the evening.
Ibid. 23

They that go down to the sea in ships, that do business in great waters.
Ibid. CVII, 23

At their wits' end.
Ibid. 27

Thy people shall be willing in the day of thy power, in the beauties of holiness from the womb of the morning: thou hast the dew of thy youth.
Ibid. CX, 3

From the rising of the sun unto the going down of the same.
Ibid. CXIII, 3

I said in my haste, All men are liars.
Ibid. CXVI, 11

Precious in the sight of the Lord is the death of his saints. *Ibid. 15*

---

[1] We bring our years to an end, as it were a tale that is told. — *Book of Common Prayer*

[2] The days of our age are threescore and ten; and though men be so strong that they come to fourscore years, yet is their strength then but labour and sorrow; so soon passeth it away, and we are gone. — *Ibid.*

[1] *Gone with the Wind*, novel by MARGARET MITCHELL [1936]. The title is from *Non Sum Qualis Eram* ("Cynara") by ERNEST DOWSON: —
I have forgot much, Cynara! gone with the wind,
Flung roses, roses riotously with the throng.

The stone which the builders refused is become the head stone of the corner.[1]

Psalms. CXVIII, 22

This is the day which the Lord hath made.

Ibid. 24

I have more understanding than all my teachers: for thy testimonies are my meditations.

Ibid. CXIX, 99

A lamp unto my feet, and a light unto my path.

Ibid. 105

The sun shall not smite thee by day, nor the moon by night.

Ibid. CXXI, 6

Peace be within thy walls, and prosperity within thy palaces.

Ibid. CXXII, 7

They that sow in tears shall reap in joy.

Ibid. CXXVI, 5

Except the Lord build the house, they labour in vain that build it.

Ibid. CXXVII, 1

He giveth his beloved sleep.[2]

Ibid. 2

Happy is the man that hath his quiver full of them.

Ibid. 5

Thy children like olive plants [3] round about thy table.

Ibid. CXXVIII, 3

I will not give sleep to mine eyes, or slumber to mine eyelids.[4]

Ibid. CXXXII, 4

Behold how good and how pleasant it is for brethren to dwell together in unity.

Ibid. CXXXIII, 1

By the rivers of Babylon, there we sat down, yea, we wept, when we remembered Zion.[5]

Ibid. CXXXVII, 1

We hanged our harps upon the willows.

Psalms. CXXXVII, 2

If I forget thee, O Jerusalem, let my right hand forget her cunning.

Ibid. 5

If I take the wings of the morning, and dwell in the uttermost parts of the sea.

Ibid. CXXXIX, 9

I am fearfully and wonderfully made.

Ibid. 14

That our sons may be as plants grown up in their youth; that our daughters may be as corner stones.

Ibid. CXLIV, 12

Put not your trust in princes.

Ibid. CXLVI, 3

My son, if sinners entice thee, consent thou not.

Proverbs. I, 10

Wisdom crieth without; she uttereth her voice in the streets.

Ibid. 20

Length of days is in her right hand; and in her left hand riches and honour.

Ibid. III, 16

Her ways are ways of pleasantness, and all her paths are peace.

Ibid. 17

Wisdom is the principal thing; therefore get wisdom; and with all thy getting get understanding.

Ibid. IV, 7

The path of the just is as the shining light, that shineth more and more unto the perfect day.

Ibid. 18

Keep thy heart with all diligence; for out of it are the issues of life.

Ibid. 23

Go to the ant, thou sluggard; consider her ways, and be wise.

Ibid. VI, 6

Yet a little sleep, a little slumber, a little folding of the hands to sleep.

Ibid. 10; XXIV, 33

Can a man take fire in his bosom, and his clothes not be burned?

Ibid. VI, 27

As an ox goeth to the slaughter.[1]

Ibid. VII, 22

---

[1] Also in *Matthew, XXI, 42.*
[2] See Mrs. Browning, page 427.
[3] Like the olive branches. — *Book of Common Prayer*
[4] Also in *Proverbs, VI, 4.*
[5] By the waters of Babylon we sat down and wept, when we remembered thee, O Sion. — *Book of Common Prayer*

[1] Also in *Jeremiah, XI, 19.*

Wisdom is better than rubies.
Proverbs. VIII, 11

I love them that love me; and those that seek me early shall find me.
Ibid. 17

Stolen waters are sweet, and bread eaten in secret is pleasant.
Ibid. IX, 17

A wise son maketh a glad father.
Ibid. X, 1

The memory of the just is blessed.
Ibid. 7

In the multitude of counsellors there is safety.
Ibid. XI, 14; XXIV, 6

He that is surety for a stranger shall smart for it.
Ibid. 15

As a jewel of gold in a swine's snout, so is a fair woman which is without discretion.
Ibid. 22

Hope deferred maketh the heart sick.
Ibid. XIII, 12

The way of transgressors is hard.
Ibid. 15

He that spareth his rod hateth his son.
Ibid. 24

Fools make a mock at sin.
Ibid. XIV, 9

The heart knoweth his own bitterness; and a stranger doth not intermeddle with his joy.
Ibid. 10

The prudent man looketh well to his going.
Ibid. 15

The talk of the lips tendeth only to penury.
Ibid. 23

Righteousness exalteth a nation.
Ibid. 34

A soft answer turneth away wrath.
Ibid. XV, 1

A merry heart maketh a cheerful countenance.
Ibid. 13

He that is of a merry heart hath a continual feast.
Ibid. 15

Better is a dinner of herbs where love is, than a stalled ox and hatred therewith.
Proverbs. XV, 17

A word spoken in due season, how good is it!
Ibid. 23

A man's heart deviseth his way; but the Lord directeth his steps.
Ibid. XVI, 9

Pride goeth before destruction, and an haughty spirit before a fall.
Ibid. 18

The hoary head is a crown of glory.
Ibid. 31

He that is slow to anger is better than the mighty; and he that ruleth his spirit than he that taketh a city.
Ibid. 32

A gift is as a precious stone in the eyes of him that hath it.
Ibid. XVII, 8

He that repeateth a matter separateth very friends.
Ibid. 9

A merry heart doeth good like a medicine.
Ibid. 22

Even a fool, when he holdeth his peace, is counted wise.
Ibid. 28

Whoso findeth a wife findeth a good thing.
Ibid. XVIII, 22

A man that hath friends must show himself friendly; and there is a friend that sticketh closer than a brother.
Ibid. 24

Wealth maketh many friends.
Ibid. XIX, 4

He that hath pity upon the poor lendeth unto the Lord.[1]
Ibid. 17

Wine is a mocker, strong drink is raging.
Ibid. XX, 1

Every fool will be meddling.
Ibid. 3

[1] There is more Rhetorick in that one sentence, than in a Library of Sermons. — SIR THOMAS BROWNE: *Religio Medici* (Everyman ed.), *P. 87*

The hearing ear and the seeing eye.
Proverbs. XX, 12
It is naught, it is naught, saith the buyer; but when he is gone his way, then he boasteth.
Ibid. 14
Meddle not with him that flattereth with his lips.
Ibid. 19
The beauty of old men is the grey head.
Ibid. 29
It is better to dwell in a corner of the housetop, than with a brawling woman in a wide house.
Ibid. XXI, 9; XXV, 24
A good name is rather to be chosen than great riches.[1]
Ibid. XXII, 1
Train up a child in the way he should go: and when he is old he will not depart from it.
Ibid. 6
The borrower is servant to the lender.
Ibid. 7
Remove not the ancient landmark.
Ibid. 28
Seest thou a man diligent in his business? He shall stand before kings.
Ibid. 29
Put a knife to thy throat, if thou be a man given to appetite.
Ibid. XXIII, 2
Riches certainly make themselves wings.[2]
Ibid. 5
As he thinketh in his heart, so is he.
Ibid. 7
Drowsiness shall clothe a man with rags.
Ibid. 21
Despise not thy mother when she is old.
Ibid. 22
Look not thou upon the wine when it is red, when it giveth his colour in the cup; . . . at the last it biteth like a serpent, and stingeth like an adder.
Ibid. 31, 32

[1] See Cervantes, page 1041.
[2] See Cowper, page 265.

A wise man is strong; yea, a man of knowledge increaseth strength.
Proverbs. XXIV, 5
If thou faint in the day of adversity thy strength is small.
Ibid. 10
A word fitly spoken is like apples of gold in pictures of silver.
Ibid. XXV, 11
Heap coals of fire upon his head.
Ibid. 22
As cold waters to a thirsty soul, so is good news from a far country.
Ibid. 25
Answer a fool according to his folly.
Ibid. XXVI, 5
Seest thou a man wise in his own conceit? There is more hope of a fool than of him.
Ibid. 12
There is a lion in the way; a lion is in the streets.
Ibid. 13
Wiser in his own conceit than seven men that can render a reason.
Ibid. 16
Whoso diggeth a pit shall fall therein.
Ibid. 27
Boast not thyself of to-morrow; for thou knowest not what a day may bring forth.
Ibid. XXVII, 1
Open rebuke is better than secret love.
Ibid. 5
Faithful are the wounds of a friend.
Ibid. 6
Better is a neighbour that is near than a brother far off.
Ibid. 10
A continual dropping in a very rainy day and a contentious woman are alike.
Ibid. 15
Iron sharpeneth iron; so a man sharpeneth the countenance of his friend.
Ibid. 17
The wicked flee when no man pursueth; but the righteous are bold as a lion.
Ibid. XXVIII, 1
He that maketh haste to be rich shall not be innocent.
Ibid. 20

He that giveth unto the poor shall not lack.

Proverbs. XXVIII, 27

Where there is no vision, the people perish.

Ibid. XXIX, 18

The horseleach hath two daughters, crying, Give, give.

Ibid. XXX, 15

The way of an eagle in the air; the way of a serpent upon a rock; the way of a ship in the midst of the sea; and the way of a man with a maid.[1]

Ibid. 19

In her tongue is the law of kindness.

Ibid. XXXI, 26

She looketh well to the ways of her household, and eateth not the bread of idleness.

Ibid. 27

Her children arise up, and call her blessed.

Ibid. 28

Many daughters have done virtuously, but thou excellest them all.

Ibid. 29

Vanity of vanities, . . . all is vanity.

Ecclesiastes. I, 2; XII, 8

One generation passeth away, and another generation cometh.

Ibid. I, 4

The eye is not satisfied with seeing.

Ibid. 8

There is no new thing under the sun.

Ibid. 9

Is there anything whereof it may be said, See, this is new? It hath been already of old time, which was before us.[2]

Ibid. 10

All is vanity and vexation of spirit.

Ibid. 14

He that increaseth knowledge increaseth sorrow.

Ibid. 18

One event happeneth to them all.

Ibid. II, 14

---

[1] There be triple ways to take, of the eagle or the snake,
Or the way of a man with a maid.
KIPLING: *The Long Trail*

[2] See Terence, page 979.

To every thing there is a season, and a time to every purpose under the heaven.

Ecclesiastes. III, 1

A time to keep silence, and a time to speak.

Ibid. 7

A threefold cord is not quickly broken.

Ibid. IV, 12

Let thy words be few.

Ibid. V, 2

Better is it that thou shouldest not vow, than that thou shouldest vow and not pay.

Ibid. 5

The sleep of a labouring man is sweet.

Ibid. 12

A good name is better than precious ointment.

Ibid. VII, 1

It is better to go to the house of mourning than to go to the house of feasting.

Ibid. 2

As the crackling of thorns under a pot, so is the laughter of the fool.

Ibid. 6

In the day of prosperity be joyful, but in the day of adversity consider.

Ibid. 14

Be not righteous overmuch.

Ibid. 16

One man among a thousand have I found; but a woman among all those have I not found.

Ibid. 28

God hath made man upright; but they have sought out many inventions.

Ibid. 29

There is no discharge in that war.[1]

Ibid. VIII, 8

To eat, and to drink, and to be merry.[2]

Ibid. 15

All things come alike to all.

Ibid. IX, 2

A living dog is better than a dead lion.

Ibid. 4

---

[1] There's no discharge in the war. — KIPLING: *Boots*

[2] Also in *Luke, XII, 19.*

Whatsoever thy hand findeth to do, do it with thy might.

Ecclesiastes. IX, 10

The race is not to the swift, nor the battle to the strong.[1]

Ibid. 11

A bird of the air shall carry the voice, and that which hath wings shall tell the matter.

Ibid. X, 20

Cast thy bread upon the waters: for thou shalt find it after many days.

Ibid. XI, 1

He that observeth the wind shall not sow; and he that regardeth the clouds shall not reap.

Ibid. 4

In the morning sow thy seed, and in the evening withhold not thine hand.

Ibid. 6

Rejoice, O young man, in thy youth.

Ibid. 9

Remember now thy Creator in the days of thy youth.

Ibid. XII, 1

The grinders cease because they are few.

Ibid. 3

He shall rise up at the voice of the bird.

Ibid. 4

The grasshopper shall be a burden, and desire shall fail; because man goeth to his long home, and the mourners go about the streets.

Ibid. 5

Or ever the silver cord be loosed, or the golden bowl be broken, or the pitcher be broken at the fountain, or the wheel broken at the cistern.

Ibid. 6

Then shall the dust return to the earth as it was; and the spirit shall return unto God who gave it.

Ibid. 7

The words of the wise are as goads, and as nails fastened by the masters of assemblies.

Ibid. 11

Of making many books there is no end; and much study is a weariness of the flesh.

Ecclesiastes. XII, 12

Let us hear the conclusion of the whole matter: Fear God, and keep his commandments; for this is the whole duty of man.

Ibid. 13

I am the rose of Sharon, and the lily of the valleys.

The Song of Solomon. II, 1

For, lo! the winter is past, the rain is over and gone; the flowers appear on the earth; the time of the singing of birds is come, and the voice of the turtle is heard in our land.

Ibid. 11, 12

The little foxes, that spoil the vines.

Ibid. 15

Until the day break, and the shadows flee away.

Ibid. 17; IV, 6

Terrible as an army with banners.

Ibid. VI, 4, 10

Thy neck is as a tower of ivory.

Ibid. VII, 4

Like the best wine, . . . that goeth down sweetly, causing the lips of those that are asleep to speak.

Ibid. 9

Set me as a seal upon thine heart.

Ibid. VIII, 6

Love is strong as death; jealousy is cruel as the grave.

Ibid.

Many waters cannot quench love, neither can the floods drown it.

Ibid. 7

The ox knoweth his owner, and the ass his master's crib.

Isaiah. I, 3

The whole head is sick, and the whole heart faint.

Ibid. 5

As a lodge in a garden of cucumbers.[1]

Ibid. 8

Bring no more vain oblations.

Ibid. 13

Come now, and let us reason together.

Ibid. 18

---

[1] See Henry van Dyke, page 710.

[1] See Rossiter Johnson, page 652.

Though your sins be as scarlet, they shall be white as snow.

Isaiah. I, 18

They shall beat their swords into plowshares, and their spears into pruning-hooks; nation shall not lift up sword against nation, neither shall they learn war any more.[1]

Ibid. II, 4

In that day a man shall cast his idols . . . to the moles and to the bats.

Ibid. 20

Grind the faces of the poor.

Ibid. III, 15

Walk with stretched-forth necks and wanton eyes, walking and mincing as they go.

Ibid. 16

In that day seven women shall take hold of one man.

Ibid. IV, 1

Woe unto them that call evil good, and good evil.

Ibid. V, 20

I saw also the Lord sitting upon a throne, high and lifted up, and his train filled the temple.

Ibid. VI, 1

Holy, holy, holy, is the Lord of hosts: the whole earth is full of his glory.

Ibid. 3

Shall call his name Immanuel.

Ibid. VII, 14

A stone of stumbling.

Ibid. VIII, 14

His name shall be called Wonderful, Counsellor, The mighty God, The everlasting Father, The Prince of Peace.

Ibid. IX, 6

The ancient and honourable.

Ibid. 15

The wolf also shall dwell with the lamb, and the leopard shall lie down with the kid.

Ibid. XI, 6

How art thou fallen from heaven, O Lucifer, son of the morning!

Ibid. XIV, 12

Is this the man that made the earth to tremble, that did shake kingdoms?

Ibid. 16

[1] Also in *Joel, III, 10* and *Micah, IV, 3*.

Like the rushing of mighty waters.

Isaiah. XVII, 12

Babylon is fallen, is fallen.

Ibid. XXI, 9

Watchman, what of the night?

Ibid. 11

Let us eat and drink; for to-morrow we shall die.

Ibid. XXII, 13

Fasten him as a nail in a sure place.

Ibid. 23

Whose merchants are princes.

Ibid. XXIII, 8

A feast of fat things.

Ibid. XXV, 6

He will swallow up death in victory; and the Lord God will wipe away tears from off all faces.

Ibid. 8

Hide thyself as it were for a little moment, until the indignation be overpast.

Ibid. XXVI, 20

Leviathan, that crooked serpent . . . the dragon that is in the sea.

Ibid. XXVII, 1

For precept must be upon precept, precept upon precept; line upon line, line upon line; here a little, and there a little.

Ibid. XXVIII, 10, 13

We have made a covenant with death, and with hell are we at agreement.

Ibid. 15

It shall be a vexation only to understand the report.

Ibid. 19

Their strength is to sit still.

Ibid. XXX, 7

Now go, write it before them in a table, and note it in a book.

Ibid. 8

As the shadow of a great rock in a weary land.

Ibid. XXXII, 2

The desert shall rejoice, and blossom as the rose.

Ibid. XXXV, 1

Thou trustest in the staff of this broken reed.

Ibid. XXXVI, 6

Set thine house in order.[1]
> *Isaiah. XXXVIII, 1*

I shall go softly all my years.[2]
> *Ibid. 15*

Comfort ye my people.
> *Ibid. XL, 1*

All flesh is grass.
> *Ibid. 6*

The nations are as a drop of a bucket.
> *Ibid. 15*

They that wait upon the Lord shall renew their strength; they shall mount up with wings as eagles; they shall run, and not be weary; and they shall walk, and not faint.
> *Ibid. 31*

They helped every one his neighbour: and every one said to his brother, Be of good courage.
> *Ibid. XLI, 6*

A bruised reed shall he not break, and the smoking flax shall he not quench.
> *Ibid. XLII, 3*

The astrologers, the stargazers, the monthly prognosticators.
> *Ibid. XLVII, 13*

There is no peace, saith the Lord, unto the wicked.
> *Ibid. XLVIII, 22*

How beautiful upon the mountains are the feet of him that bringeth good tidings, that publisheth peace.
> *Ibid. LII, 7*

They shall see eye to eye.
> *Ibid. 8*

A man of sorrows, and acquainted with grief.
> *Ibid. LIII, 3*

All we like sheep have gone astray.
> *Ibid. 6*

He is brought as a lamb to the slaughter.[3]
> *Ibid. 7*

Ho, everyone that thirsteth, come ye to the waters.
> *Ibid. LV, 1*

---

[1] Also in *2 Esdras, XIV, 13.*
[2] He hoped now to walk softly all his days
In soberness of spirit.
> Robert Browning: *The Ring and the Book, II, Half-Rome*

Walk softly — and carry a big stick. — Theodore Roosevelt
[3] Also in *Jeremiah, LI, 40.*

Let the wicked forsake his way, and the unrighteous man his thoughts.
> *Isaiah. LV, 7*

A little one shall become a thousand, and a small one a strong nation.
> *Ibid. LX, 22*

Give unto them beauty for ashes, the oil of joy for mourning, the garment of praise for the spirit of heaviness.
> *Ibid. LXI, 3*

I have trodden the wine-press alone.
> *Ibid. LXIII, 3*

We all do fade as a leaf.
> *Ibid. LXIV, 6*

I am holier than thou.
> *Ibid. LXV, 5*

Peace, peace; when there is no peace.
> *Jeremiah. VI, 14; VIII, 11*

Stand ye in the ways, and see, and ask for the old paths, where is the good way, and walk therein.[1]
> *Ibid. VI, 16*

Amend your ways and your doings.
> *Ibid. VII, 3; XXVI, 13*

Is there no balm in Gilead?[2] Is there no physician there?
> *Ibid. VIII, 22*

Oh that I had in the wilderness a lodging-place of wayfaring men!
> *Ibid. IX, 2*

I will feed them . . . with wormwood, and give them water of gall to drink.
> *Ibid. 15; XXIII, 15*

Can the Ethiopian change his skin, or the leopard his spots?
> *Ibid. XIII, 23*

Her sun is gone down while it was yet day.
> *Ibid. XV, 9*

A man of strife and a man of contention.
> *Ibid. 10*

Written with a pen of iron, and with the point of a diamond.
> *Ibid. XVII, 1*

He shall be as a tree planted by the waters, and that spreadeth out her roots by the river.
> *Ibid. 8*

---

[1] Stare super vias antiquas. — *The Vulgate.*
[2] *Is* there balm in Gilead?
> Poe: *The Raven*

He shall be buried with the burial of an ass.

Jeremiah. XXII, 19

Rahel [Rachel] weeping for her children, refused to be comforted.[1]

Ibid. XXXI, 15

The fathers have eaten a sour grape, and the children's teeth are set on edge.[2]

Ibid. 29

With my whole heart and with my whole soul.

Ibid. XXXII, 41

Is it nothing to you, all ye that pass by? behold, and see if there be any sorrow like unto my sorrow.

Lamentations. I, 12

A wheel in the middle of a wheel.

Ezekiel. I, 16; X, 10

I will cause you to pass under the rod.[3]

Ibid. XX, 37

Stood at the parting of the way.

Ibid. XXI, 21

His feet part of iron and part of clay.

Daniel. II, 33

Shadrach, Meshach, and Abed-nego fell down bound into the midst of the burning fiery furnace.[4]

Ibid. III, 23

Nebuchadnezzar . . . was driven from men, and did eat grass as oxen.

Ibid. IV, 33

Belshazzar the king made a great feast to a thousand of his lords.

Ibid. V, 1

Thou art weighed in the balances, and art found wanting.

Ibid. 27

His windows being open in his chamber toward Jerusalem.

Ibid. VI, 10

According to the law of the Medes and Persians.

Ibid. 12

They brought Daniel, and cast him into the den of lions.

Ibid. 16

The Ancient of days.

Daniel. VII, 13

Many shall run to and fro, and knowledge shall be increased.

Ibid. XII; 4

They have sown the wind, and they shall reap the whirlwind.

Hosea. VIII, 7

I have multiplied visions, and used similitudes.

Ibid. XII, 10

Your old men shall dream dreams, your young men shall see visions.

Joel. II, 28

Multitudes in the valley of decision.

Ibid. III, 14

Can two walk together, except they be agreed?

Amos. III, 3

And Jonah was in the belly of the fish three days and three nights.[1]

Jonah. I, 17

They shall sit every man under his vine and under his fig-tree.[2]

Micah. IV, 4

What doth the Lord require of thee, but to do justly, and to love mercy, and to walk humbly with thy God?

Ibid. VI, 8

Write the vision, and make it plain upon tables, that he may run that readeth it.

Habakkuk. II, 2

The Lord is in his holy temple: let all the earth keep silence before him.

Ibid. 20

Your fathers, where are they? And the prophets, do they live forever?

Zechariah. I, 5

Comfortable words.

Ibid. 13

The four winds of the heaven.

Ibid. II, 6

Not by might, nor by power, but by my spirit, saith the Lord of hosts.

Ibid. IV, 6

---

[1] Also in *Matthew, II, 18*.
[2] Also in *Ezekiel, XVIII, 2*.
[3] See Mrs. Dana, page 474.
[4] See Bert Leston Taylor, page 795.

[1] There are in Scripture stories that do exceed the fables of poets. — SIR THOMAS BROWNE: *Religio Medici* (Everyman ed.), P. 25
[2] See *1 Maccabees XIV, 12* on page 1125.

For who hath despised the day of small things? [1]

Zechariah. IV, 10

Prisoners of hope.

Ibid. IX, 12

I was wounded in the house of my friends.[2]

Ibid. XIII, 6

Have we not all one father? hath not one God created us?

Malachi. II, 10

But unto you that fear my name shall the Sun of righteousness arise with healing in his wings.

Ibid. IV, 2

He shall turn the heart of the fathers to the children, and the heart of the children to their fathers.

Ibid. 6

NEW TESTAMENT

Ye are the salt of the earth: but if the salt have lost his savour, wherewith shall it be salted?

Matthew. V, 13

Ye are the light of the world. A city that is set on an hill cannot be hid.

Ibid. 14

Take heed that ye do not your alms before men, to be seen of them.

Ibid. VI, 1

When thou doest alms, let not thy left hand know what thy right hand doeth.

Ibid. 3

They think that they shall be heard for their much speaking.

Ibid. 7

Give us this day our daily bread.

Ibid. 11

Lay up for yourselves treasures in heaven.

Ibid. 20

---

[1] Hereby I learned have, not to despise
What ever thing seemes small in common eyes.
    SPENSER: *Visions of the Worlds Vanitie,
        Sonnet 5*
[2] From the house of friends comes the death stab.
    WALT WHITMAN: *Wounded in the House
        of Friends, St. 1*

Where your treasure is, there will your heart be also.

Matthew. VI, 21

The light of the body is the eye.

Ibid. 22

No man can serve two masters. . . . Ye cannot serve God and Mammon.

Ibid. 24

Take no thought for your life, what ye shall eat, or what ye shall drink.

Ibid. 25

Consider the lilies of the field, how they grow; they toil not, neither do they spin.

Ibid. 28

Take therefore no thought for the morrow; for the morrow shall take thought for the things of itself. Sufficient unto the day is the evil thereof.

Ibid. 34

Neither cast ye your pearls before swine.

Ibid. VII, 6

Ask, and it shall be given you; seek, and ye shall find; knock, and it shall be opened unto you.

Ibid. 7

Every one that asketh receiveth; and he that seeketh findeth.

Ibid. 8

Or what man is there of you, whom if his son ask bread, will he give him a stone?

Ibid. 9

Therefore all things whatsoever ye would that men should do to you, do ye even so to them: for this is the law and the prophets.

Ibid. 12

Wide is the gate, and broad is the way, that leadeth to destruction.

Ibid. 13

Strait is the gate, and narrow is the way.

Ibid. 14

By their fruits ye shall know them.

Ibid. 20

It was founded upon a rock.

Ibid. 25

The foxes have holes, and the birds of the air have nests; but the Son of Man hath not where to lay his head.

Ibid. VIII, 20

The harvest truly is plenteous, but the labourers are few.

Matthew. IX, 37

Be ye therefore wise as serpents, and harmless as doves.

Ibid. X, 16

The very hairs of your head are all numbered.

Ibid. 30

Wisdom is justified of her children.[1]

Ibid. XI, 19

The tree is known by his fruit.

Ibid. XII, 33

Out of the abundance of the heart the mouth speaketh.

Ibid. 34

Pearl of great price.[2]

Ibid. XIII, 46

A prophet is not without honour, save in his own country, and in his own house.[3]

Ibid. 57

Be of good cheer: it is I; be not afraid.

Ibid. XIV, 27

If the blind lead the blind, both shall fall into the ditch.[4]

Ibid. XV, 14

The dogs eat of the crumbs which fall from their masters' table.

Ibid. 27

When it is evening, ye say it will be fair weather: for the sky is red.[5]

Ibid. XVI, 2

The signs of the times.

Ibid. 3

Thou art Peter, and upon this rock I will build my church.

Ibid. 18

I will give unto thee the keys of heaven.

Ibid. 19

---

[1] Also in *Luke, VII, 35.*
[2] See Hawthorne, page 422.
[3] Prophets have honour all over the Earth, Except in the village where they were born.
    KIPLING: *Prophets at Home, St. 1*
See Oxyrhynchus Logia, page 1126.
[4] Quoted by CERVANTES: *Don Quixote, Part II, Book III, Chap. 13.*
[5] Red sky at night, sailors' delight,
    Red sky at morning, sailors take warning.
        Old weather rhyme

Get thee behind me, Satan.[1]

Matthew. XVI, 23

What is a man profited, if he shall gain the whole world, and lose his own soul?[2]

Ibid. 26

It is good for us to be here.

Ibid. XVII, 4

The ninety and nine.

Ibid. XVIII, 12, 13

Where two or three are gathered together in my name, there am I in the midst of them.

Ibid. 20

What therefore God hath joined together, let not man put asunder.

Ibid. XIX, 6

Love thy neighbour as thyself.

Ibid. 19

It is easier for a camel to go through the eye of a needle, than for a rich man to enter into the kingdom of God.

Ibid. 24

Borne the burden and heat of the day.

Ibid. XX, 12

Is it not lawful for me to do what I will with mine own?

Ibid. 15

They made light of it.

Ibid. XXII, 5

For many are called, but few are chosen.

Ibid. 14

Render therefore unto Caesar the things which are Caesar's.[3]

Ibid. 21

Whosoever shall exalt himself shall be abased; and he that shall humble himself shall be exalted.

Ibid. XXIII, 12

Woe unto you, . . . for ye pay tithe of mint and anise and cummin.

Ibid. 23

Blind guides, which strain at a gnat, and swallow a camel.

Ibid. 24

---

[1] Also in *Luke, IV, 8.*
[2] Also in *Mark, VIII, 36.*
[3] Also in *Mark, XII, 17.*

Whited sepulchres, which indeed appear beautiful outward, but are within full of dead men's bones.

         Matthew. XXIII, 27

As a hen gathereth her chickens under her wings.

         Ibid. 37

Wars and rumours of wars.[1]

         Ibid. XXIV, 6

The end is not yet.

         Ibid.

Abomination of desolation.[2]

         Ibid. 15

False prophets.

         Ibid. 24

Wheresoever the carcass is, there will the eagles be gathered together.

         Ibid. 28

Heaven and earth shall pass away, but my words shall not pass away.

         Ibid. 35

Well done, thou good and faithful servant.

         Ibid. XXV, 21

Unto every one that hath shall be given, and he shall have abundance; but from him that hath not shall be taken away even that which he hath.

         Ibid. 29

Inasmuch as ye have done it unto one of the least of these my brethren, ye have done it unto me.

         Ibid. 40

An alabaster box of very precious ointment.

         Ibid. XXVI, 7

Thirty pieces of silver.

         Ibid. 15

The spirit indeed is willing, but the flesh is weak.

         Ibid. 41

All they that take the sword shall perish with the sword.

         Ibid. 52

The potter's field, to bury strangers in.

         Ibid. XXVII, 7

Go ye therefore, and teach all nations.

         Ibid. XXVIII, 19

---

[1] Also in *Mark, XIII*, 7.
[2] Also in *Mark, XIII*, 14.

Lo, I am with you alway, even unto the end of the world.

         Matthew. XXVIII, 20

The voice of one crying in the wilderness.

         Mark. I, 3

The latchet of whose shoes I am not worthy to stoop down and unloose.

         Ibid. 7

I came not to call the righteous, but sinners to repentance.

         Ibid. II, 17

New wine into old bottles.

         Ibid. 22

The Sabbath was made for man, and not man for the Sabbath.

         Ibid. 27

If a house be divided against itself, that house cannot stand.

         Ibid. III, 25

He that hath ears to hear, let him hear.

         Ibid. IV, 9

First the blade, then the ear, after that the full corn in the ear.

         Ibid. 28

Peace, be still.

         Ibid. 39

My name is Legion.

         Ibid. V, 9

Clothed, and in his right mind.[1]

         Ibid. 15

My little daughter lieth at the point of death.

         Ibid. 23

I see men as trees, walking.

         Ibid. VIII, 24

Overthrew the tables of the moneychangers.

         Ibid. XI, 15

He [Judas] goeth straightway to him, and saith, Master, master; and kissed him.

         Ibid. XIV, 45

There was no room for them in the inn.[2]

         Luke. II, 7

Glory to God in the highest, and on earth peace, good will toward men.

         Ibid. 14

---

[1] Also in *Luke, VIII*, 35.
[2] See B. Y. Williams, page 904.

Lord, now lettest thou thy servant depart in peace.
Luke. II, 29

A light to lighten the Gentiles.
Ibid. 32

Wist ye not that I must be about my Father's business?
Ibid. 49

His mother kept all these sayings in her heart.
Ibid. 51

The axe is laid unto the root of the trees.
Ibid. III, 9

Physician, heal thyself.
Ibid. IV, 23

Woe unto you, when all men shall speak well of you!
Ibid. VI, 26

Nothing is secret which shall not be made manifest.
Ibid. VIII, 17

No man, having put his hand to the plough, and looking back, is fit for the kingdom of God.
Ibid. IX, 62

Peace be to this house.
Ibid. X, 5

The labourer is worthy of his hire.[1]
Ibid. 7

A certain man went down from Jerusalem to Jericho, and fell among thieves.
Ibid. 30

He passed by on the other side.
Ibid. 31

A certain Samaritan . . . had compassion on him.
Ibid. 33

Go, and do thou likewise.
Ibid. 37

But one thing is needful; and Mary hath chosen that good part which shall not be taken away from her.
Ibid. 42

He that is not with me is against me.
Ibid. XI, 23

[1] Also in *1 Timothy, V, 18.*

Soul, thou hast much goods laid up for many years; take thine ease, eat, drink, and be merry.[1]
Luke. XII, 19

This night thy soul shall be required of thee.
Ibid. 20

Let your loins be girded about, and your lights burning.
Ibid. 35

Which of you, intending to build a tower, sitteth not down first, and counteth the cost, whether he have sufficient to finish it.
Ibid. XIV, 28

Wasted his substance with riotous living.
Ibid. XV, 13

Bring hither the fatted calf.
Ibid. 23

The children of this world are in their generation wiser than the children of light.
Ibid. XVI, 8

He that is faithful in that which is least is faithful also in much; and he that is unjust in the least is unjust also in much.
Ibid. 10

It were better for him that a millstone were hanged about his neck, and he cast into the sea.
Ibid. XVII, 2

Out of thine own mouth will I judge thee.
Ibid. XIX, 22

This do in remembrance of me.[2]
Ibid. XXII, 19

He was a good man, and a just.
Ibid. XXIII, 50

Did not our heart burn within us while he talked with us?
Ibid. XXIV, 32

There was a man sent from God, whose name was John.[3]
John. I, 6

[1] To eat, drink, and be merry, because tomorrow we die.
G. J. WHYTE-MELVILLE [1821–1878]:
The Object of a Life
[2] Also in *1 Corinthians, XI, 24.*
[3] Inscription on the tomb of Don John of Austria [1547–1578], in the Escorial, Spain.

The true light, which lighteth every man that cometh into the world.

John. I, 9

Can there any good thing come out of Nazareth?

Ibid. 46

Make not my Father's house an house of merchandise.

Ibid. II, 16

The wind bloweth where it listeth.

Ibid. III, 8

For God so loved the world, that he gave his only begotten Son, that whosoever believeth in him should not perish, but have everlasting life.

Ibid. 16

He was a burning and a shining light.

Ibid. V, 35

Gather up the fragments that remain, that nothing be lost.

Ibid. VI, 12

I am the bread of life.

Ibid. 35

Judge not according to the appearance.

Ibid. VII, 24

He that is without sin among you, let him first cast a stone at her.

Ibid. VIII, 7

Neither do I condemn thee: go, and sin no more.

Ibid. 11

I am the light of the world: he that followeth me shall not walk in darkness, but shall have the light of life.

Ibid. 12

The truth shall make you free.

Ibid. 32

There is no truth in him.

Ibid. 44

The night cometh, when no man can work.

Ibid. IX, 4

I am come that they might have life, and that they might have it more abundantly.

Ibid. X, 10

I am the resurrection and the life.

Ibid. XI, 25

The poor always ye have with you.

Ibid. XII, 8

Walk while ye have the light, lest darkness come upon you.

John. XII, 35

A new commandment I give unto you, That ye love one another.

Ibid. XIII, 24

Let not your heart be troubled.

Ibid. XIV, 1

In my Father's house are many mansions.

Ibid. 2

I will not leave you comfortless.

Ibid. 18

Peace I leave with you.

Ibid. 27

Greater love hath no man than this, that a man lay down his life for his friends.

Ibid. XV, 13

Be of good cheer; I have overcome the world.

Ibid. XVI, 33

Now Barabbas was a robber.

Ibid. XVIII, 40

Thy money perish with thee.

Acts. VIII, 20

It is hard for thee to kick against the pricks.

Ibid. IX, 5

Now there was at Joppa a certain disciple named Tabitha, which by interpretation is called Dorcas: this woman was full of good works and almsdeeds which she did.

Ibid. 36

Come over into Macedonia, and help us.

Ibid. XVI, 9

Lewd fellows of the baser sort.

Ibid. XVII, 5

I found an altar with this inscription, To the Unknown God.[1]

Ibid. 23

Great is Diana of the Ephesians.

Ibid. XIX, 28

---

[1] The inscription did not run "To the unknown God," but "To the Gods of Asia and Africa, to the unknown and foreign Gods." — JEROME: *Commentar. in Epist. ad Titum I, verses 10* and *11*, in FATHER LARGENT: *St. Jerome* [1913], *P. 31*, translated by HESTER DAVENPORT.

It is more blessed to give than to receive.
Acts. XX, 35

Brought up in this city at the feet of Gamaliel.
Ibid. XXII, 3

When I have a convenient season, I will call for thee.
Ibid. XXIV, 25

I appeal unto Caesar.
Ibid. XXV, 11

Much learning doth make thee mad.
Ibid. XXVI, 24

Words of truth and soberness.
Ibid. 25

For this thing was not done in a corner.
Ibid. 26

Almost thou persuadest me to be a Christian.
Ibid. 28

Wherein thou judgest another, thou condemnest thyself.
Romans. II, 1

There is no respect of persons with God.
Ibid. 11

God forbid.
Ibid. III, 31

Who against hope believed in hope.
Ibid. IV, 18

Death hath no more dominion over him.
Ibid. VI, 9

Speak after the manner of men.
Ibid. 19

The wages of sin is death.
Ibid. 23

For the good that I would I do not; but the evil which I would not, that I do.[1]
Ibid. VII, 19

Heirs of God, and joint-heirs with Christ.
Ibid. VIII, 17

For we know that the whole creation groaneth and travaileth in pain together until now.
Ibid. 22

[1] See Euripides, page 967.

All things work together for good to them that love God.
Romans. VIII, 28

If God be for us, who can be against us.
Ibid. 31

Neither death, nor life . . . shall be able to separate us from the love of God.
Ibid. 38, 39

Hath not the potter power over the clay, of the same lump to make one vessel unto honour, and another unto dishonour?
Ibid. IX, 21

Given to hospitality.
Ibid. XII, 13

Be not wise in your own conceits.
Ibid. 16

Recompense to no man evil for evil.
Ibid. 17

If it be possible, as much as lieth in you, live peaceably with all men.
Ibid. 18

Vengeance is mine; I will repay, saith the Lord.
Ibid. 19

If thine enemy hunger, feed him; if he thirst, give him drink: for in so doing thou shalt heap coals of fire on his head.
Ibid. 20

Be not overcome of evil, but overcome evil with good.
Ibid. 21

The powers that be are ordained of God.
Ibid. XIII, 1

Render therefore to all their dues.
Ibid. 7

Owe no man anything, but to love one another.
Ibid. 8

Love is the fulfilling of the law.
Ibid. 10

Let every man be fully persuaded in his own mind.
Ibid. XIV, 5

None of us liveth to himself.
Ibid. 7

Let us therefore follow after the things which make for peace.
Ibid. 19

God hath chosen the foolish things of the world to confound the wise; and God hath chosen the weak things of the world to confound the things which are mighty.

1 Corinthians. I, 27

I have planted, Apollos watered; but God gave the increase.

Ibid. III, 6

Every man's work shall be made manifest.

Ibid. 13

Not to think of men above that which is written.[1]

Ibid. IV, 6

We are made a spectacle unto the world, and to angels, and to men.

Ibid. 9

Absent in body, but present in spirit.

Ibid. V, 3

A little leaven leaveneth the whole lump.[2]

Ibid. 6

The fashion of this world passeth away.

Ibid. VII, 31

I am made all things to all men.

Ibid. IX, 22

Let him that thinketh he standeth take heed lest he fall.

Ibid. X, 12

If a woman have long hair, it is a glory to her.

Ibid. XI, 15

Though I speak with the tongues of men and of angels, and have not charity,[3] I am become as sounding brass, or a tinkling cymbal.

Ibid. XIII, 1

Though I have all faith, so that I could remove mountains, and have not charity, I am nothing.

Ibid. 2

Charity suffereth long and is kind; charity envieth not; charity vaunteth not itself, is not puffed up.

Ibid. 4

We know in part, and we prophesy in part.

1 Corinthians. XIII, 9

When I was a child, I spake as a child. . . . When I became a man, I put away childish things.

Ibid. 11

Now we see through a glass, darkly.

Ibid. 12

And now abideth faith, hope, charity, these three; but the greatest of these is charity.

Ibid. 13

If the trumpet give an uncertain sound.

Ibid. XIV, 8

Let all things be done decently and in order.

Ibid. 40

Evil communications corrupt good manners.[1]

Ibid. XV, 33

One star differeth from another star in glory.

Ibid. 41

The first man is of the earth, earthy.

Ibid. 47

In the twinkling of an eye.[2]

Ibid. 52

O death, where is thy sting? O grave, where is thy victory? [3]

Ibid. 55

Quit you like men, be strong.

Ibid. XVI, 13

Not of the letter, but of the spirit; for the letter killeth, but the spirit giveth life.

2 Corinthians. III, 6

We have such hope, we use great plainness of speech.

Ibid. 12

The things which are seen are temporal; but the things which are not seen are eternal.

Ibid. IV, 18

We walk by faith, not by sight.

Ibid. V, 7

---

[1] Usually misquoted, "To be wise above that which is written."
[2] Also in *Galatians, V, 9*.
[3] In the Revised Version, the word "love" is substituted for "charity" throughout the chapter.

[1] Communion with the bad corrupts good character. — MENANDER: *Thais* (Loeb Classical Library, page 357)
[2] See Shakespeare, page 45.
[3] See William Watson, page 736.

Now is the accepted time.
> *2 Corinthians. VI, 2*

By evil report and good report.
> *Ibid. 8*

As having nothing, and yet possessing all things.
> *Ibid. 10*

God loveth a cheerful giver.
> *Ibid. IX, 7*

Though I be rude in speech.
> *Ibid. XI, 6*

For ye suffer fools gladly, seeing ye yourselves are wise.
> *Ibid. 19*

Forty stripes save one.
> *Ibid. 24*

A thorn in the flesh.
> *Ibid. XII, 7*

Strength is made perfect in weakness.
> *Ibid. 9*

The grace of the Lord Jesus Christ, and the love of God, and the communion of the Holy Ghost, be with you all.
> *Ibid. XIII, 14*

The right hands of fellowship.
> *Galatians. II, 9*

Weak and beggarly elements.
> *Ibid. IV, 9*

It is good to be zealously affected always in a good thing.
> *Ibid. 18*

Ye are fallen from grace.
> *Ibid. V, 4*

Every man shall bear his own burden.
> *Ibid. VI, 5*

Whatsoever a man soweth, that shall he also reap.
> *Ibid. 7*

Let us not be weary in well doing.
> *Ibid. 9*

God forbid that I should glory, save in the cross of our Lord Jesus Christ.
> *Ibid. 14*

Carried about with every wind of doctrine.
> *Ephesians. IV, 14*

Be ye angry, and sin not: let not the sun go down upon your wrath.
> *Ibid. 26*

To live is Christ, and to die is gain.
> *Philippians. I, 21*

Work out your own salvation.
> *Philippians. II, 12*

I press toward the mark for the prize of the high calling of God in Christ Jesus.
> *Ibid. III, 14*

Whose God is their belly, and whose glory is in their shame.
> *Ibid. 19*

The peace of God, which passeth all understanding.
> *Ibid. IV, 7*

Whatsoever things are true, whatsoever things are honest, whatsoever things are just, whatsoever things are pure, whatsoever things are lovely, whatsoever things are of good report; if there be any virtue, and if there be any praise, think on these things.
> *Ibid. 8*

I have learned, in whatsoever state I am, therewith to be content.
> *Ibid. 11*

Touch not; taste not; handle not.
> *Colossians. II, 21*

Set your affections on things above, not on things on the earth.
> *Ibid. III, 2*

Let your speech be alway with grace, seasoned with salt.
> *Ibid. IV, 6*

Luke, the beloved physician.
> *Ibid. 14*

Labour of love.
> *1 Thessalonians. I, 3*

Study to be quiet.
> *Ibid. IV, 11*

Putting on the breastplate of faith and love; and for an helmet, the hope of salvation.
> *Ibid. V, 8*

Prove all things; hold fast that which is good.
> *Ibid. 21*

The law is good, if a man use it lawfully.
> *1 Timothy. I, 8*

Not greedy of filthy lucre.
> *Ibid. III, 3*

Drink no longer water, but use a little wine for thy stomach's sake.
> *Ibid. V, 23*

We brought nothing into this world, and it is certain we can carry nothing out.

1 Timothy. VI, 7

The love of money is the root of all evil.

Ibid. 10

Fight the good fight.

Ibid. 12

Rich in good works.

Ibid. 18

Science falsely so called.

Ibid. 20

A workman that needeth not to be ashamed.

2 Timothy. II, 15

I have fought a good fight, I have finished my course, I have kept the faith.

Ibid. IV, 7

Alexander the coppersmith did me much evil: the Lord reward him according to his works.

Ibid. 14

Unto the pure all things are pure.

Titus. I, 15

Making mention of thee always in my prayers.

Philemon. I, 4

Such as have need of milk, and not of strong meat.

Hebrews. V, 12

Strong meat belongeth to them that are of full age.

Ibid. 14

Faith is the substance of things hoped for, the evidence of things not seen.

Ibid. XI, 1

A cloud of witnesses.

Ibid. XII, 1

The author and finisher of our faith.

Ibid. 2

Whom the Lord loveth he chasteneth.

Ibid. 6

The spirits of just men made perfect.

Ibid. 23

Be not forgetful to entertain strangers, for thereby some have entertained angels unawares.

Ibid. XIII, 2

Yesterday, and to-day, and forever.

Hebrews. XIII, 8

For here we have no continuing city, but we seek one to come.

Ibid. 14

Let patience have her perfect work.

James. I, 4

Blessed is the man that endureth temptation; for when he is tried, he shall receive the crown of life.

Ibid. 12

Every good gift and every perfect gift is from above.

Ibid. 17

No variableness, neither shadow of turning.

Ibid.

Be swift to hear, slow to speak, slow to wrath.

Ibid. 19

Unspotted from the world.

Ibid. 27

Faith without works is dead.

Ibid. II, 26

How great a matter a little fire kindleth!

Ibid. III, 5

The tongue can no man tame; it is an unruly evil.[1]

Ibid. 8

Resist the Devil, and he will flee from you.

Ibid. IV, 7

The effectual fervent prayer of a righteous man availeth much.

Ibid. V, 16

Hope to the end.

1 Peter. I, 13

Fear God. Honour the king.

Ibid. II, 17

Ornament of a meek and quiet spirit.

Ibid. III, 4

Giving honour unto the wife, as unto the weaker vessel.

Ibid. 7

Charity shall cover the multitude of sins.

Ibid. IV, 8

A crown of glory that fadeth not away.

Ibid. V, 4

[1] Usually misquoted, "The tongue is an unruly member."

Be sober, be vigilant; because your adversary, the Devil, as a roaring lion, walketh about, seeking whom he may devour.

> *I Peter. V, 8*

And the day star arise in your hearts.

> *2 Peter. I, 19*

The dog is turned to his own vomit again.

> *Ibid. II, 22*

Bowels of compassion.

> *I John. III, 17*

God is love.

> *Ibid. IV, 8*

There is no fear in love; but perfect love casteth out fear.

> *Ibid. 18*

Be thou faithful unto death.

> *Revelation. II, 10*

He shall rule them with a rod of iron.

> *Ibid. 27*

Behold, I stand at the door and knock.

> *Ibid. III, 20*

A pale horse: and his name that sat on him was Death.[1]

> *Ibid. VI, 8*

All nations, and kindreds, and people, and tongues.

> *Ibid. VII, 9*

As the voice of many waters.[2]

> *Ibid. XIV, 2*

They may rest from their labours; and their works do follow them.

> *Ibid. 13*

And he gathered them together into a place called in the Hebrew tongue Armageddon.

> *Ibid. XVI, 16*

Another book was opened, which is the book of life.

> *Ibid. XX, 12*

I saw a new heaven and a new earth.

> *Ibid. XXI, 1*

The holy city, new Jerusalem.

> *Ibid. 2*

I am Alpha and Omega, the beginning and the end, the first and the last.

> *Ibid. 6*

There shall be no night there.

> *Revelation. XXII, 5*

Without are dogs.[1]

> *Ibid. 15*

THE APOCRYPHA [2]

How exceeding strong is wine! it causeth all men to err who drink it.

> *1 Esdras. III, 18*

Ye must know that women have dominion over you: do ye not labour and toil, and give and bring all to the woman?

> *Ibid. IV, 22*

Great is truth, and mighty above all things.[3]

> *Ibid. 41*

Do right to the widow, judge for the fatherless, give to the poor, defend the orphan, clothe the naked.

> *2 Esdras. II, 20*

What is past I know, but what is for to come I know not.

> *Ibid. IV, 46*

Unto you is paradise opened.

> *Ibid. VIII, 52*

Now therefore keep thy sorrow to thyself, and bear with a good courage that which hath befallen thee.

> *Ibid. X, 15*

I shall light a candle of understanding in thine heart, which shall not be put out.[4]

> *Ibid. XIV, 25*

If thou hast abundance, give alms accordingly: if thou have but a little, be not afraid to give according to that little.

> *Tobit. IV, 8*

God, which dwelleth in heaven, prosper your journey, and the angel of God

---

[1] See John Hay, page 639.
[2] The noise of many waters. — *Psalm XCIII, 4*

[1] See E. A. Church, page 671.
[2] These books form part of the sacred literature of the Alexandrian Jews, and with the exception of *2 Esdras* are found interspersed with the Hebrew Scriptures in the ancient copies of the Septuagint, or Greek Version of the Old Testament. — *The Apocrypha According to the Authorized Version, Preface* (Oxford University Press)
[3] Magna est veritas et praevalet. — *The Vulgate, Book III* (uncanonical)
[4] See Hugh Latimer, page 10.

keep you company. So they [Azarias and Tobias] went forth both, and the young man's dog went with them.
Tobit. V, 16

Honour thy father and thy mother in law, which are now thy parents.
Ibid. X, 12

So they went their way, and the dog went after them.
Ibid. XI, 4

Ye cannot find the depth of the heart of man, neither can ye perceive the things that he thinketh: then how can ye search out God, that hath made all these things, and know his mind, or comprehend his purpose?
Judith. VIII, 14

Put on her garments of gladness.
Ibid. X, 3

Ye shall therefore among your solemn feasts keep it an high day for all feasting.[1]
Esther. XVI, 22

Our time is a very shadow that passeth away.
Wisdom of Solomon. II, 5

Let us crown ourselves with rosebuds before they be withered.
Ibid. 8

The souls of the righteous are in the hand of God, and there shall no torment touch them. In the sight of the unwise they seemed to die: and their departure is taken for misery, and their going from us to be utter destruction: but they are in peace.
Ibid. III, 1-3

They that put their trust in him shall understand the truth.
Ibid. 9

Wisdom is the gray hair unto men, and an unspotted life is old age.
Ibid. IV, 9

When I was born, I drew in the common air, and fell upon the earth, which is of like nature, and the first voice

which I uttered was crying, as all others do.[1]
Wisdom of Solomon. VII, 3

All men have one entrance into life, and the like going out.
Ibid. 6

Who can number the sand of the sea, and the drops of rain, and the days of eternity?
Ecclesiasticus. I, 2

Honour thy father and mother [2] both in word and deed, that a blessing may come upon thee from them.
Ibid. III, 8

If his understanding fail, have patience with him.
Ibid. 13

Observe the opportunity.
Ibid. IV, 20

Let not thine hand be stretched out to receive, and shut when thou shouldest repay.
Ibid. 31

A faithful friend is a strong defence: and he that hath found such an one hath found a treasure.
Ibid. VI, 14

Be not slow to visit the sick.
Ibid. VII, 35

Whatsoever thou takest in hand, remember the end, and thou shalt never do amiss.
Ibid. 36

Rejoice not over thy greatest enemy being dead, but remember that we die all.
Ibid. VIII, 7

Miss not the discourse of the elders.
Ibid. 9

Forsake not an old friend, for the new is not comparable to him. A new friend is as new wine: when it is old, thou shalt drink it with pleasure.
Ibid. IX, 10

In the day of prosperity there is a forgetfulness of affliction: and in the day of affliction there is no more remembrance of prosperity.
Ibid. XI, 25

---

[1] The Feast of Purim, celebrating the deliverance of the Jews from the persecution of Haman through the influence of Esther, Mordecai's queen.

[1] See Pliny the Elder, page 993.
[2] *Exodus, XX, 12*

He that toucheth pitch shall be de-
filed therewith.
Ecclesiasticus. XIII, 1
He will laugh thee to scorn.
Ibid. 7
A rich man beginning to fall is held
up of his friends: but a poor man being
down is thrust also away by his friends.
Ibid. 21
The heart of a man changeth his
countenance, whether it be for good or
evil: and a merry heart maketh a cheer-
ful countenance.
Ibid. 25
Wine and women will make men of
understanding to fall away.
Ibid. XIX, 2
Whether it be to friend or foe, talk
not of other men's lives.
Ibid. 8
If she go not as thou wouldst have
her, cut her off from thy flesh, and give
her a bill of divorce, and let her go.
Ibid. XXV, 26
Gladness of the heart is the life of
man, and the joyfulness of a man pro-
longeth his days.
Ibid. XXX, 22
Consider that I laboured not for my-
self only, but for all them that seek
learning.
Ibid. XXXIII, 17
Honour a physician with the honour
due unto him.
Ibid. XXXVIII, 1
When the dead is at rest, let his re-
membrance rest; and be comforted for
him, when his spirit is departed from
him.
Ibid. 23
Whose talk is of bullocks.[1]
Ibid. 25
Look upon the rainbow, and praise
him that made it.
Ibid. XLIII, 11
Let us now praise famous men.[2]
Ibid. XLIV, 1

[1] Quoted by Dr. Samuel Johnson. — Boswell's *Life of Dr. Johnson* (Everyman ed.),
Vol. II, P. 133
[2] "Let us now praise famous men." — Kipling: *A School Song*

These were honoured in their generations, and were the glory of their
times.
Ecclesiasticus. XLIV, 7
There be of them that have left a
name behind them.
Ibid. 8
His word burned like a lamp.
Ibid. XLVIII, 1
A scarecrow in a garden of cucumbers
keepeth nothing.
Baruch. VI, 70
Was not Abraham found faithful in
temptation, and it was imputed unto
him for righteousness?
1 Maccabees. II, 52
With the God of heaven it is all one,
to deliver with a great multitude, or a
small company: For the victory of
battle standeth not in the multitude of
an host; but strength cometh from
heaven.
Ibid. III, 18, 19
The noble acts which he did, and his
greatness, they are not written: for they
were very many.
Ibid. IX, 22
Ask and learn.
Ibid. X, 72
Every man sat under his vine and
his fig tree.[1]
Ibid. XIV, 12
We have been careful that they that
will read may have delight, and that
they that are desirous to commit to
memory might have ease, and that all
into whose hands it comes might have
profit.
2 Maccabees. II, 25
It is a foolish thing to make a long
prologue, and to be short in the story
itself.
Ibid. 32
Leaving his death for an example of
a noble courage, and a memorial of
virtue, not only unto young men, but
unto all his nation.
Ibid. VI, 31
Nicanor lay dead in his harness.
Ibid. XV, 28

[1] See *Micah, IV, 4* on page 1113.

If I have done well, and as is fitting,
. . . it is that which I desired; but if
slenderly and meanly, it is that which
I could attain unto.

> *2 Maccabees. XV, 38*

Speech finely framed delighteth the
ears.

> *Ibid. 39*

OXYRHYNCHUS LOGIA (AGRAPHA) [1]

Wherever there are two, they are not
without God; and wherever there is one
alone, I say I am with him. Raise the
stone, and there thou shalt find me;
cleave the wood, and there am I.[2]

> *Fifth Logion*

A prophet is not acceptable in his
own country,[3] neither doth a physician
work cures upon them that know him.

> *Sixth Logion*

A city built upon the top of a hill and
stablished can neither fall nor be hid.[4]

> *Seventh Logion*

DOUAY BIBLE [5]
[1609]

I am the angel Raphael, one of the
seven, who stand before the Lord.

> *Tobias. XII, 15*

Now Susanna was exceeding delicate,
and beautiful to behold.

> *Daniel. XIII, 31*

---

[1] In the rubbish heaps of the ancient city
of Oxyrhynchus, near the River Nile, a party
of English explorers, in the winter of 1897,
discovered a fragment of a papyrus book,
written in the second or third century, and
hitherto unknown. This single leaf contained
parts of seven short sentences of Christ, each
introduced by the words, "Jesus says." —
HENRY VAN DYKE: *The Toiling of Felix,
Preface*

[2] See van Dyke, page 709.
Raise thou the stone and find Me there,
Cleave thou the wood and there am I.
> SIR WILLIAM WATSON:
> *The Unknown God*

[3] See *Matthew, XIII, 57* on page 1115.
[4] See *Matthew, V, 14* on page 1114.
[5] The English version of the Bible for Roman Catholics was first printed in Douay,
France.

He hath sold the just man for silver,
and the poor man for a pair of shoes.

> *Amos. II, 6*

Houses of ivory shall perish.

> *Ibid. III, 15*

The faces of them all are as the
blackness of a kettle.

> *Nahum. II, 10*

You have sowed much, and brought
in little.

> *Aggeus. I, 6*

He that hath earned wages put them
into a bag with holes.

> *Ibid.*

THE KORAN
Translated [1734] by GEORGE SALE
[1697–1736]

Turn, therefore, thy face towards the
holy temple of Mecca; and wherever ye
be, turn your faces towards that place.

> *Chap. 2*

Wherever ye be, God will bring you
all back at the resurrection.

> *Ibid.*

As for him who voluntarily performeth a good work, verily God is grateful
and knowing.

> *Ibid.*

Your God is one God; there is no
God but He, the most merciful.

> *Ibid.*

O true believers, take your necessary
precautions against your enemies, and
either go forth to war in separate parties, or go forth all together in a body.

> *Chap. 4*

Fight for the religion of God.

> *Ibid.*

O men, respect women who have
borne you.

> *Ibid.*

Wheresoever ye be, death will overtake you, although ye be in lofty towers.

> *Ibid.*

Whosoever flieth from his country
for the sake of God's true religion, shall
find in the earth many forced to do the
same, and plenty of provisions.

> *Ibid.*

God loveth not the speaking ill of any one in public.

Chap. 4

Let not thy hand be tied up to thy neck; neither open it with an unbounded expansion, lest thou become worthy of reprehension, and be reduced to poverty.

Chap. 17

Of his mercy he hath made for you the night and the day, that ye may rest in the one, and may seek to obtain provision for yourself of his abundance, by your industry, in the other.

Chap. 28

If God should punish men according to what they deserve, he would not leave on the back of the earth so much as a beast.

Chap. 35

God obligeth no man to more than he hath given him ability to perform.

Chap. 65

Woe be unto those who pray, and who are negligent at their prayer: who play the hypocrites, and deny necessaries to the needy.

Chap. 107

O unbelievers, I will not worship that which ye worship; nor will ye worship that which I worship. . . . Ye have your religion, and I my religion.

Chap. 109

BOOK OF COMMON PRAYER [1]

We have left undone those things which we ought to have done; and we have done those things which we ought not to have done.

Morning Prayer

The noble army of Martyrs.

Ibid. Te Deum

Make them to be numbered [2] with thy Saints, in glory everlasting.

Ibid.

Whose service is perfect freedom.

Ibid. A Collect for Peace

---

[1] American Revision [1928].
[2] In the Latin, this word is *munerari* (rewarded), and was mistaken, perhaps, by an early copyist, for *numerari* (numbered).

Afflicted, or distressed, in mind, body, or estate.

Morning Prayer. A Prayer for All Conditions of Men

Grant us grace fearlessly to contend against evil, and to make no peace with oppression; and, that we may reverently use our freedom, help us to employ it in the maintenance of justice among men and nations.

Prayers and Thanksgivings. A Prayer for Social Justice

Deliver us, we beseech thee, in our several callings, from the service of mammon, that we may do the work which thou givest us to do, in truth, in beauty, and in righteousness, with singleness of heart as thy servants, and to the benefit of our fellow men.

Ibid. A Prayer for Every Man in His Work

From envy, hatred, and malice, and all uncharitableness.

The Litany

The world, the flesh, and the devil.

Ibid.

Give to all nations unity, peace, and concord.[1]

Ibid.

The kindly fruits of the earth.

Ibid.

Miserable sinners.[2]

Holy Communion. Exhortation

Read, mark, learn, and inwardly digest.

Collect for the Second Sunday in Advent

Renounce the devil and all his works.

Holy Baptism. Of Children

The pomps and vanity of this wicked world.

Offices of Instruction (Catechism)

---

[1] The desire for unity, the wish for peace, the longing for concord, deeply implanted in the human heart, have stirred the most powerful emotions of the race, and have been responsible for some of its noblest actions. — SIR WILLIAM OSLER: *Aequanimitas* (2d ed.), *XXI, Unity, Peace and Concord.*

[2] The invocation, "Have mercy upon us miserable sinners," was included in the Litany prior to the Revision of 1928. "Miserable offenders" appears in *Morning Prayer, A General Confession.*

To keep my hands from picking and stealing.

Offices of Instruction (Catechism)

To do my duty in that state of life unto which it shall please God to call me.

Ibid.

An outward and visible sign of an inward and spiritual grace.[1]

Ibid.

Let him now speak, or else hereafter for ever hold his peace.

Solemnization of Matrimony

To have and to hold from this day forward, for better for worse, for richer for poorer, in sickness and in health, to love and to cherish, till death us do part.

Ibid.

With this Ring I thee wed.

Ibid.

In the midst of life we are in death.[2]

Burial of the Dead. At the Grave

Earth to earth, ashes to ashes, dust to dust; in sure and certain hope of the Resurrection unto eternal life.

Ibid.

Show thy servant the light of thy countenance.

The Psalter. Psalms, XXXI, 18

But it was even thou, my companion, my guide, and mine own[3] familiar friend.

Ibid. LV, 14

God that maketh men to be of one mind in an house.

Ibid. LXVIII, 6

[1] The Sacrament.
[2] This is derived from a Latin antiphon, said to have been composed by Notker, a monk of St. Gall, in 911, while watching some workmen building a bridge at Martinsbrücke, in peril of their lives. It forms the groundwork of Luther's antiphon *De Morte*.
[3] Through a typographical error, the word "own" was changed to "old" in the first printing of the Revision of 1928.

The iron entered into his soul.

The Psalter. Psalms, CV, 18

God, in whom we live and move and have our being.

Family Prayer. Morning

O Lord, support us all the day long, until the shadows lengthen and the evening comes, and the busy world is hushed, and the fever of life is over, and our work is done. Then in thy mercy grant us a safe lodging, and a holy rest, and peace at the last.[1]

Ibid. At Night

O God of peace, who hast taught us that in returning and rest we shall be saved, in quietness and in confidence shall be our strength; By the might of thy Spirit lift us, we pray thee, to thy presence, where we may be still and know that thou art God.

Ibid. For Quiet Confidence [2]

O Heavenly Father, who hast filled the world with beauty; open, we beseech thee, our eyes to behold thy gracious hand in all thy works; that rejoicing in thy whole creation, we may learn to serve thee with gladness.[3]

Ibid. For Joy in God's Creation [4]

BOOK OF COMMON PRAYER, ENGLISH

Grant that the old Adam in these persons may be so buried, that the new man may be raised up in them.

Holy Baptism. Of Those of Riper Years

With all my worldly goods I thee endow.

Solemnization of Matrimony

[1] By Cardinal Newman.
[2] Added in the Revision of 1928.
[3] See Dostoyevsky, page 1074.
[4] Added in the Revision of 1928.

INDEX

In such indexes, although small pricks
To their subsequent volumes, there is seen
The baby figure of the giant mass
Of things to come at large.
  SHAKESPEARE: *Troilus and Cressida, Act I, Sc. 3, Line 343*

INDEX